Annual Abstract of Statistics

No 151

2015 Edition

Compiled by: Dandy Booksellers

Contacts

For information about the content of this publication, contact
Dandy Booksellers: Tel 020 7624 2993
Email: dandybooksellers@btconnect.com

Publications orders
To obtain the print version of this publication, please contact
Dandy Booksellers
Tel: 0207 624 2993
Email: dandybooksellers@btconnect.com
Fax: 0207 624 5049
Post: Unit 3&4, 31-33 Priory Park Road, London, NW6 7UP
Web: www.dandybooksellers.com

Contents

5: Social Protection

6: External trade and investment

7: Research and development

8: Personal income, expenditure & wealth

9: Lifestyles

10: Environment

11: Housing

12: Banking and Finance

12: Banking and Finance

13: Service industry

14: Defence

15: Population and vital statistics

16: Health

17: Prices

18: Production

19: National Accounts

20: Education

20: Education

21: Crime and Justice

22: Transport

22: Transport

23:Government Finance

24:Agriculture

Units of measurement

Length

1 millimetre (mm)	= 0.03937 inch	
1 centimetre (cm)	= 10 millimetres	= 0.3937 inch
1 metre (m)	= 1,000 millimetres	= 1.094 yards
1 kilometre (km)	= 1,000 metres	= 0.6214 mile
1 inch (in.)		= 25.40 millimetres or 2.540 centimetres
1 foot (ft.)	= 12 inches	= 0.3048 metre
1 yard (yd.)	= 3 feet	= 0.9144 metre
1 mile	= 1,760 yards	= 1.609 kilometres

Area

1 square millimetre (mm2)		= 0.001550 square inch
1 square metre (m2)	= one million square millimetres	= 1.196 square yards
1 hectare (ha)	= 10,000 square metres	= 2.471 acres
1 square kilometre (km2)	= one million square metres	= 247.1 acres
1 square inch (sq. in.)		= 645.2 square millimetres or 6.452 square centimetres
1 square foot (sq. ft.)	= 144 square inches	= 0.09290 square metre or 929.0 square centimetres
1 square yard (sq. yd.)	= 9 square feet	= 0.8361 square metre
1 acre	= 4,840 square yards	= 4,046 square metres or 0.4047 hectare
1 square mile (sq. mile)	= 640 acres	= 2.590 square kilometres or 259.0 hectares

Volume

1 cubic centimetre (cm3)		= 0.06102 cubic inch
1 cubic decimetre (dm3)	= 1,000 cubic centimetres	= 0.03531 cubic foot
1 cubic metre (m3)	= one million cubic centimetres	= 1.308 cubic yards
1 cubic inch (cu.in.)		=16.39 cubic centimetres
1 cubic foot (cu. ft.)	= 1,728 cubic inches	= 0.02832 cubic metre or 28.32 cubic decimetres
1 cubic yard (cu. yd.)	= 27 cubic feet	= 0.7646 cubic metre

Capacity

1 litre (l)	= 1 cubic decimetre	= 0.2200 gallon
1 hectolitre (hl)	= 100 litres	= 22.00 gallons
1 pint		= 0.5682 litre
1 quart	= 2 pints	= 1.137 litres
1 gallon	= 8 pints	= 4.546 litres
1 bulk barrel	= 36 gallons (gal.)	= 1.637 hectolitres

Weight

1 gram (g)		= 0.03527 ounce avoirdupois
1 hectogram (hg)	= 100 grams	= 3.527 ounces or 0.2205 pound
1 kilogram (kg)	= 1,000 grams or 10 hectograms	= 2.205 pounds
1 tonne (t)	= 1,000 kilograms	= 1.102 short tons or 0.9842 long ton
1 ounce avoirdupois (oz.)	= 437.5 grains	= 28.35 grams
1 pound avoirdupois (lb.)	= 16 ounces	= 0.4536 kilogram
1 hundredweight (cwt.)	= 112 pounds	= 50.80 kilograms
1 short ton	= 2,000 pounds	= 907.2 kilograms or 0.9072 tonne
1 long ton (referred to as ton)	= 2,240 pounds	= 1,016 kilograms or 1.016 tonnes
1 ounce troy	= 480 grains	= 31.10 grams

Energy

British thermal unit (Btu)	= 0.2520 kilocalorie (kcal) = 1.055 kilojoule (kj)
Therm	= 105 British thermal units = 25,200 kcal = 105,506 kj
Megawatt hour (MWh)	= 106 watt hours (Wh)
Gigawatt hour (GWh)	= 106 kilowatt hours = 34,121 therms

Food and drink

Butter	23,310 litres milk	= 1 tonne butter (average)
Cheese	10,070 litres milk	= 1 tonne cheese
Condensed milk	2,550 litres milk	= 1 tonne full cream condensed milk
	2,953 litres skimmed milk	= 1 tonne skimmed condensed milk
Milk	1 million litres	= 1,030 tonnes
Milk powder	8,054 litres milk	= 1 tonne full cream milk powder
	10,740 litres skimmed milk	= 1 tonne skimmed milk powder
Eggs	17,126 eggs	= 1 tonne (approximate)
Sugar	100 tonnes sugar beet	= 92 tonnes refined sugar
	100 tonnes cane sugar	= 96 tonnes refined sugar

Shipping

Gross tonnage — = The total volume of all the enclosed spaces of a vessel, the unit of measurement being a 'ton' of 100 cubic feet.

Deadweight tonnage — = Deadweight tonnage is the total weight in tons of 2,240 lb. that a ship can legally carry, that is the total weight of cargo, bunkers, stores and crew.

Introduction

Welcome to the 2015 edition of the Annual Abstract of Statistics. This compendium draws together statistics from a wide range of official and other authoritative sources.

Dandy Booksellers have sourced and formatted these tables under instruction from various government departments/ organisations

Current data for many of the series appearing in this Annual Abstract are contained in other ONS publications, such as Economic & Labour Market Review, Population Trends, Health Statistics Quarterly and Financial Statistics. These titles can be purchased through Dandy Booksellers.

The name (and telephone number, where this is available) of the organisation providing the statistics are shown under each table. In addition, a list of Sources is given at the back of the book, which sets out the official publications or other sources to which further reference can be made.

Identification codes

The four-letter identification code at the top of each data column, or at the side of each row is the ONS reference for this series of data on their database. Please quote the relevant code if you contact them requiring any further information about the data. On some tables it is not possible to include these codes, so please quote the table number in these cases.

Definitions and classification

Time series
So far as possible annual totals are given throughout, but quarterly or monthly figures are given where these are more suitable to the type of series.

Standard Industrial Classification

A Standard Industrial Classification (SIC) was first introduced into the UK in 1948 for use in classifying business establishments and other statistical units by the type of economic activity in which they are engaged. The classification provides a framework for the collection, tabulation, presentation and analysis of data about economic activities. Its use promotes uniformity of data collected by various government departments and agencies.

Since 1948 the classification has been revised in 1958, 1968, 1980, 1992, 2003 and 2007. One of the principal objectives of the 1980 revision was to eliminate differences from the activity classification issued by the Statistical Office of the European Communities (Eurostat) and entitled 'Nomenclature générale des activités économiques dans les Communautés Européennes', usually abbreviated to NACE.

In 1990 the European Communities introduced a new statistical classification of economic activities (NACE Rev 1) by regulation. The regulation made it obligatory for the UK to introduce a new Standard Industrial Classification SIC(92), based on NACE Rev 1. UK SIC(92) was based exactly on NACE Rev 1 but, where it was thought necessary or helpful, a fifth digit was added to form subclasses of the NACE 1 four digit system. Classification systems need to be revised periodically because, over time, new products, processes and industries emerge. In January 2003 a minor revision of NACE Rev 1, known as NACE Rev 1.1, was published in the Official Journal of the European Communities.

Consequently, the UK was obliged to introduce a new Standard Industrial Classification, SIC(2003) consistent with NACE Rev 1.1. The UK took the opportunity of the 2003 revision also to update the national Subclasses. Full details are available in UK Standard Industrial Classification of Economic Activities 2003 and the Indexes to the UK Standard Industrial Classification of Economic Activities 2003. These are the most recent that are currently used. The most up to date version is the UK Standard Industrial Classification of Economic activities 2007 (SIC2007). It will be implemented in five stages and came into effect on 1 January 2008.

- For reference year 2008, the Annual Business Inquiry (parts 1 & 2) will be based on SIC 2007

- PRODCOM will also be based on SIC 2007 from reference year 2008

- Other annual outputs will be based on SIC 2007 from reference year 2009, unless otherwise determined by regulation

- Quarterly and monthly surveys will be based on SIC 2007 from the first reference period in 2010, unless otherwise determined by regulation

- National Accounts will move to SIC 2007 in September 2011

Symbols and conventions used

Change of basis
Where consecutive figures have been compiled on different bases and are not strictly comparable, a footnote is added indicating the nature of the difference.

Geographic coverage
Statistics relate mainly to the UK. Where figures relate to other areas, this is indicated on the table.

Units of measurement
The various units of measurement used are listed after the Contents.

Rounding of figures
In tables where figures have been rounded to the nearest final digit, the constituent items may not add up exactly to the total.

Symbols
The following symbols have been used throughout:

.. = not available or not applicable (also information supressed to avoid disclosure)

- = nil or less than half the final digit shown

Office for National Statistics online:
www.ons.gov.uk
Web-based access to time series, cross-sectional data and metadata from across the Government Statistical Service (GSS), is available using the site search function from the homepage. Download many datasets, in whole or in part, or consult directory information for all GSS statistical resources, including censuses, surveys, periodicals and enquiry services. Information is posted as PDF electronic documents or in XLS and CSV formats, compatible with most spreadsheet packages.

Contact point
Dandy Booksellers welcomes any feedback on the content of the Annual Abstract, including comments on the format of the data and the selection of topics. Comments and requests for general information should be addressed to:

Dandy Booksellers
Unit 3&4
31-33 Priory Park Road
London
NW6 7UP
or
enquiries@dandybooksellers.com

this page is intentionally blank

Area

Chapter 1

Area

The United Kingdom (UK) comprises Great Britain and Northern Ireland. Great Britain comprises England, Wales and Scotland.

Physical Features

The United Kingdom (UK) constitutes the greater part of the British Isles. The largest of the islands is Great Britain. The next largest comprises Northern Ireland and the Irish Republic. Western Scotland is fringed by the large island chain known as the Hebrides, and to the north east of the Scottish mainland are the Orkney and Shetland Islands. All these, along with the Isle of Wight, Anglesey and the Isles of Scilly, form part of the UK, but the Isle of Man, in the Irish Sea and the Channel Islands, between Great Britain and France are largely self-governing and are not part of the UK. The UK is currently one of the 28 member states of the European Union. With an area of about 243 000 sq km (about 94 000 sq miles), the UK is just under 1 000 km (about 600 miles) from the south coast to the extreme north of Scotland and just under 500 km (around 300 miles) across at the widest point.

- Highest mountain: Ben Nevis, in the highlands of Scotland, at 1 343 m (4 406 ft)
- Longest river: the Severn, 354 km (220 miles) long, which rises in central Wales and flows through Shrewsbury, Worcester and Gloucester in England to the Bristol Channel
- Largest lake: Lough Neagh, Northern Ireland, at 396 sq km (153 sq miles)
- Deepest lake: Loch Morar in the Highlands of Scotland, 310 m (1 017 ft) deep
- Highest waterfall: Eas a'Chual Aluinn, from Glas Bheinn, in the highlands of Scotland, with a drop of 200 m (660 ft)
- Deepest cave: Ogof Ffynnon Ddu, Wales, at 308 m (1 010 ft) deep
- Most northerly point on the British mainland: Dunnet Head, north-east Scotland
- Most southerly point on the British mainland: Lizard Point, Cornwall
- Closest point to mainland continental Europe: Dover, Kent. The Channel Tunnel, which links England and France, is a little over 50 km (31 miles) long, of which nearly 38 km (24 miles) are actually under the Channel

Area Measurements

I'd like to get area figures for all the local authorities in the UK. Where do I look?

UK Standard Area Measurements (SAM) are now available to download free of charge from the Open Geography portal in both MS Excel and CSV formats for a variety of administrative areas (countries, counties, local authority districts, electoral wards/divisions, regions, output areas, super output areas and workplace zones). The two questions below show some statistics taken from SAM 2014 (Extent of the Realm figures).

Which is the largest local authority in the UK?

- The largest anywhere in the UK is Highland (Scotland), at 2,648,436.54 hectares (ha).
- The largest in England is Northumberland, at 507,835.00 ha.
- The largest in Wales is Powys, at 519,545.63 ha.
- The largest in Northern Ireland is Fermanagh, at 187,125.95 ha.

Which is the smallest local authority in the UK?

- The smallest anywhere in the UK is the City of London, at 314.94 ha.
- The smallest in Scotland is Dundee City, at 6,222.59 ha.
- The smallest in Wales is Blaenau Gwent, at 10,872.80 ha
- The smallest in Northern Ireland is North Down, at 8,150.19 ha.

UK Standard Area Measurements (SAM)

About UK Standard Area Measurements (SAM)

The SAM product provides a definitive list of measurements for administrative, health, Census, electoral and other geographic areas in the UK. SAM will change annually for some geographies, but for others it will be 'frozen' for several years.

The land measurement figures provided are defined by topographic boundaries (coastline and inland water), where available.

Measurements are reviewed annually and include information up to the end of December.

The measurements have been produced in conjunction with the following UK government statistical organisations and independent mapping agencies: National Records of Scotland (NRS), Northern Ireland Statistics and Research Agency (NISRA), Ordnance Survey®(OS) and Land & Property Services (LPS).

The SAM User Guide explains differences in methodology and base mapping between these agencies.

Product details

If you have any queries about this dataset, please contact:

ONS Geography Customer Services
Office for National Statistics
Segensworth Road
Titchfield
Fareham
Hampshire
PO15 5RR

Tel: 01329 444 971
Email: ons.geography@ons.gov.uk

1.1 Standard Area Measurement for UK Local Authority Districts as at 31/12/2014

Local authority name as at December 2014	Code as at December 2014	Extent of the realm (Km^2)	Area to mean high water (Km^2)	Inland water (Km^2)	Land only (Km^2)
United Kingdom	K02000001	**248540**	**244181**	**1666**	242516
Great Britain	K03000001	**234410**	**230052**	**1098**	228953
England	**E92000001**	**132948**	**130459**	**152**	130308
Hartlepool	E06000001	**98**	**94**	**0**	94
Middlesbrough	E06000002	**55**	**54**	**0**	54
Redcar and Cleveland	E06000003	**254**	**245**	**0**	245
Stockton-on-Tees	E06000004	**210**	**205**	**0**	205
Darlington	E06000005	**197**	**197**	**0**	197
Halton	E06000006	**90**	**79**	**0**	79
Warrington	E06000007	**182**	**181**	**0**	181
Blackburn with Darwen	E06000008	**137**	**137**	**0**	137
Blackpool	E06000009	**43**	**35**	**0**	35
Kingston upon Hull, City of	E06000010	**81**	**71**	**0**	71
East Riding of Yorkshire	E06000011	**2495**	**2406**	**1**	2405
North East Lincolnshire	E06000012	**204**	**192**	**0**	192
North Lincolnshire	E06000013	**876**	**846**	**0**	846
York	E06000014	**272**	**272**	**0**	272
Derby	E06000015	**78**	**78**	**0**	78
Leicester	E06000016	**73**	**73**	**0**	73
Rutland	E06000017	**394**	**394**	**12**	382
Nottingham	E06000018	**75**	**75**	**0**	75
Herefordshire, County of	E06000019	**2180**	**2180**	**0**	2180
Telford and Wrekin	E06000020	**290**	**290**	**0**	290
Stoke-on-Trent	E06000021	**93**	**93**	**0**	93
Bath and North East Somerset	E06000022	**351**	**351**	**5**	346
Bristol, City of	E06000023	**235**	**110**	**0**	110
North Somerset	E06000024	**391**	**375**	**1**	374
South Gloucestershire	E06000025	**537**	**497**	**0**	497
Plymouth	E06000026	**84**	**80**	**0**	80
Torbay	E06000027	**119**	**63**	**0**	63
Bournemouth	E06000028	**47**	**46**	**0**	46
Poole	E06000029	**75**	**65**	**0**	65
Swindon	E06000030	**230**	**230**	**0**	230
Peterborough	E06000031	**343**	**343**	**0**	343
Luton	E06000032	**43**	**43**	**0**	43
Southend-on-Sea	E06000033	**68**	**42**	**0**	42
Thurrock	E06000034	**184**	**163**	**0**	163
Medway	E06000035	**269**	**194**	**0**	194
Bracknell Forest	E06000036	**109**	**109**	**0**	109
West Berkshire	E06000037	**704**	**704**	**0**	704
Reading	E06000038	**40**	**40**	**0**	40
Slough	E06000039	**33**	**33**	**0**	33
Windsor and Maidenhead	E06000040	**198**	**198**	**2**	197
Wokingham	E06000041	**179**	**179**	**0**	179
Milton Keynes	E06000042	**309**	**309**	**0**	309
Brighton and Hove	E06000043	**85**	**83**	**0**	83
Portsmouth	E06000044	**60**	**40**	**0**	40
Southampton	E06000045	**56**	**50**	**0**	50
Isle of Wight	E06000046	**395**	**380**	**0**	380
County Durham	E06000047	**2233**	**2232**	**6**	2226
Cheshire East	E06000049	**1166**	**1166**	**0**	1166
Cheshire West and Chester	E06000050	**941**	**917**	**0**	917
Shropshire	E06000051	**3197**	**3197**	**0**	3197
Cornwall	E06000052	**3613**	**3550**	**4**	3546
Isles of Scilly	E06000053	**23**	**16**	**0**	16
Wiltshire	E06000054	**3255**	**3255**	**0**	3255
Bedford	E06000055	**476**	**476**	**0**	476
Central Bedfordshire	E06000056	**716**	**716**	**0**	716
Northumberland	E06000057	**5078**	**5026**	**12**	5014

1.1 Standard Area Measurement for UK Local Authority Districts as at 31/12/2014

Local authority name as at December 2014	Code as at December 2014	Extent of the realm (Km^2)	Area to mean high water (Km^2)	Inland water (Km^2)	Land only (Km^2)
Aylesbury Vale	E07000004	903	903	0	903
Chiltern	E07000005	196	196	0	196
South Bucks	E07000006	141	141	0	141
Wycombe	E07000007	325	325	0	325
Cambridge	E07000008	41	41	0	41
East Cambridgeshire	E07000009	652	651	0	651
Fenland	E07000010	547	546	0	546
Huntingdonshire	E07000011	913	912	6	906
South Cambridgeshire	E07000012	902	902	0	902
Allerdale	E07000026	1321	1258	16	1242
Barrow-in-Furness	E07000027	132	78	0	78
Carlisle	E07000028	1054	1039	0	1039
Copeland	E07000029	776	738	6	732
Eden	E07000030	2156	2156	14	2142
South Lakeland	E07000031	1743	1553	19	1534
Amber Valley	E07000032	265	265	0	265
Bolsover	E07000033	160	160	0	160
Chesterfield	E07000034	66	66	0	66
Derbyshire Dales	E07000035	795	795	3	792
Erewash	E07000036	110	110	0	110
High Peak	E07000037	540	540	1	539
North East Derbyshire	E07000038	276	276	0	276
South Derbyshire	E07000039	338	338	0	338
East Devon	E07000040	824	814	0	814
Exeter	E07000041	48	47	0	47
Mid Devon	E07000042	913	913	0	913
North Devon	E07000043	1105	1086	0	1086
South Hams	E07000044	905	886	0	886
Teignbridge	E07000045	681	674	0	674
Torridge	E07000046	996	985	1	984
West Devon	E07000047	1165	1161	1	1160
Christchurch	E07000048	52	50	0	50
East Dorset	E07000049	354	354	0	354
North Dorset	E07000050	609	609	0	609
Purbeck	E07000051	428	404	0	404
West Dorset	E07000052	1087	1081	0	1081
Weymouth and Portland	E07000053	43	42	0	42
Eastbourne	E07000061	46	44	0	44
Hastings	E07000062	31	30	0	30
Lewes	E07000063	294	292	0	292
Rother	E07000064	518	512	2	509
Wealden	E07000065	836	835	2	833
Basildon	E07000066	110	110	0	110
Braintree	E07000067	612	612	0	612
Brentwood	E07000068	153	153	0	153
Castle Point	E07000069	64	45	0	45
Chelmsford	E07000070	343	342	3	339
Colchester	E07000071	347	333	4	329
Epping Forest	E07000072	339	339	0	339
Harlow	E07000073	31	31	0	31
Maldon	E07000074	427	359	0	359
Rochford	E07000075	263	169	0	169
Tendring	E07000076	366	338	0	338
Uttlesford	E07000077	641	641	0	641
Cheltenham	E07000078	47	47	0	47
Cotswold	E07000079	1165	1165	0	1165
Forest of Dean	E07000080	561	526	0	526
Gloucester	E07000081	41	41	0	41
Stroud	E07000082	476	461	0	461
Tewkesbury	E07000083	415	414	0	414
Basingstoke and Deane	E07000084	634	634	0	634
East Hampshire	E07000085	514	514	0	514
Eastleigh	E07000086	85	80	0	80
Fareham	E07000087	78	74	0	74

1.1 Standard Area Measurement for UK Local Authority Districts as at 31/12/2014

Local authority name as at December 2014	Code as at December 2014	Extent of the realm (Km²)	Area to mean high water (Km²)	Inland water (Km²)	Land only (Km²)
Gosport	E07000088	28	25	0	25
Hart	E07000089	215	215	0	215
Havant	E07000090	79	55	0	55
New Forest	E07000091	777	753	0	753
Rushmoor	E07000092	39	39	0	39
Test Valley	E07000093	628	628	0	628
Winchester	E07000094	661	661	0	661
Broxbourne	E07000095	51	51	0	51
Dacorum	E07000096	212	212	0	212
Hertsmere	E07000098	101	101	0	101
North Hertfordshire	E07000099	375	375	0	375
Three Rivers	E07000102	89	89	0	89
Watford	E07000103	21	21	0	21
Ashford	E07000105	581	581	0	581
Canterbury	E07000106	321	309	0	309
Dartford	E07000107	76	73	0	73
Dover	E07000108	321	315	0	315
Gravesham	E07000109	105	99	0	99
Maidstone	E07000110	393	393	0	393
Sevenoaks	E07000111	370	370	1	369
Shepway	E07000112	365	357	0	357
Swale	E07000113	422	374	0	374
Thanet	E07000114	112	103	0	103
Tonbridge and Malling	E07000115	241	240	0	240
Tunbridge Wells	E07000116	331	331	0	331
Burnley	E07000117	111	111	0	111
Chorley	E07000118	203	203	0	203
Fylde	E07000119	183	166	0	166
Hyndburn	E07000120	73	73	0	73
Lancaster	E07000121	654	576	0	576
Pendle	E07000122	169	169	0	169
Preston	E07000123	143	142	0	142
Ribble Valley	E07000124	584	584	1	583
Rossendale	E07000125	138	138	0	138
South Ribble	E07000126	115	113	0	113
West Lancashire	E07000127	381	347	0	347
Wyre	E07000128	329	283	0	283
Blaby	E07000129	130	130	0	130
Charnwood	E07000130	279	279	0	279
Harborough	E07000131	593	593	1	592
Hinckley and Bosworth	E07000132	297	297	0	297
Melton	E07000133	481	481	0	481
North West Leicestershire	E07000134	279	279	0	279
Oadby and Wigston	E07000135	24	24	0	24
Boston	E07000136	398	365	0	365
East Lindsey	E07000137	1831	1765	0	1765
Lincoln	E07000138	36	36	0	36
North Kesteven	E07000139	922	922	0	922
South Holland	E07000140	816	751	0	751
South Kesteven	E07000141	943	943	0	943
West Lindsey	E07000142	1158	1156	0	1156
Breckland	E07000143	1305	1305	0	1305
Broadland	E07000144	553	552	0	552
Great Yarmouth	E07000145	182	174	0	174
King's Lynn and West Norfolk	E07000146	1528	1438	0	1438
North Norfolk	E07000147	991	965	2	963
Norwich	E07000148	41	39	0	39
South Norfolk	E07000149	909	908	0	908
Corby	E07000150	80	80	0	80
Daventry	E07000151	666	666	3	663
East Northamptonshire	E07000152	510	510	0	510
Kettering	E07000153	233	233	0	233
Northampton	E07000154	81	81	0	81
South Northamptonshire	E07000155	634	634	0	634

1.1 Standard Area Measurement for UK Local Authority Districts as at 31/12/2014

Local authority name as at December 2014	Code as at December 2014	Extent of the realm (Km^2)	Area to mean high water (Km^2)	Inland water (Km^2)	Land only (Km^2)
Wellingborough	E07000156	163	163	0	163
Craven	E07000163	1179	1179	1	1177
Hambleton	E07000164	1311	1311	0	1311
Harrogate	E07000165	1309	1309	1	1308
Richmondshire	E07000166	1319	1319	0	1319
Ryedale	E07000167	1507	1507	0	1507
Scarborough	E07000168	827	817	0	817
Selby	E07000169	602	599	0	599
Ashfield	E07000170	110	110	0	110
Bassetlaw	E07000171	639	638	0	638
Broxtowe	E07000172	80	80	0	80
Gedling	E07000173	120	120	0	120
Mansfield	E07000174	77	77	0	77
Newark and Sherwood	E07000175	652	651	0	651
Rushcliffe	E07000176	409	409	0	409
Cherwell	E07000177	589	589	0	589
Oxford	E07000178	46	46	0	46
South Oxfordshire	E07000179	679	679	0	679
Vale of White Horse	E07000180	579	579	1	578
West Oxfordshire	E07000181	714	714	0	714
Mendip	E07000187	739	739	0	739
Sedgemoor	E07000188	606	564	0	564
South Somerset	E07000189	959	959	0	959
Taunton Deane	E07000190	463	462	0	462
West Somerset	E07000191	747	727	1	725
Cannock Chase	E07000192	79	79	0	79
East Staffordshire	E07000193	390	390	3	387
Lichfield	E07000194	331	331	0	331
Newcastle-under-Lyme	E07000195	211	211	0	211
South Staffordshire	E07000196	407	407	0	407
Stafford	E07000197	598	598	0	598
Staffordshire Moorlands	E07000198	576	576	0	576
Tamworth	E07000199	31	31	0	31
Babergh	E07000200	612	595	1	594
Forest Heath	E07000201	378	378	0	378
Ipswich	E07000202	40	39	0	39
Mid Suffolk	E07000203	871	871	0	871
St Edmundsbury	E07000204	657	657	0	657
Suffolk Coastal	E07000205	921	892	0	892
Waveney	E07000206	375	370	0	370
Elmbridge	E07000207	96	96	1	95
Epsom and Ewell	E07000208	34	34	0	34
Guildford	E07000209	271	271	0	271
Mole Valley	E07000210	258	258	0	258
Reigate and Banstead	E07000211	129	129	0	129
Runnymede	E07000212	78	78	0	78
Spelthorne	E07000213	51	51	6	45
Surrey Heath	E07000214	95	95	0	95
Tandridge	E07000215	248	248	0	248
Waverley	E07000216	345	345	0	345
Woking	E07000217	64	64	0	64
North Warwickshire	E07000218	284	284	0	284
Nuneaton and Bedworth	E07000219	79	79	0	79
Rugby	E07000220	354	354	2	351
Stratford-on-Avon	E07000221	978	978	0	978
Warwick	E07000222	283	283	0	283
Adur	E07000223	44	42	0	42
Arun	E07000224	224	221	0	221
Chichester	E07000225	812	786	0	786
Crawley	E07000226	45	45	0	45
Horsham	E07000227	531	530	0	530
Mid Sussex	E07000228	334	334	0	334
Worthing	E07000229	34	32	0	32
Bromsgrove	E07000234	217	217	0	217

1.1 Standard Area Measurement for UK Local Authority Districts as at 31/12/2014

Local authority name as at December 2014	Code as at December 2014	Extent of the realm (Km^2)	Area to mean high water (Km^2)	Inland water (Km^2)	Land only (Km^2)
Malvern Hills	E07000235	577	577	0	577
Redditch	E07000236	54	54	0	54
Worcester	E07000237	33	33	0	33
Wychavon	E07000238	664	664	0	664
Wyre Forest	E07000239	195	195	0	195
St Albans	E07000240	161	161	0	161
Welwyn Hatfield	E07000241	130	130	0	130
East Hertfordshire	E07000242	476	476	0	476
Stevenage	E07000243	26	26	0	26
Bolton	E08000001	140	140	0	140
Bury	E08000002	99	99	0	99
Manchester	E08000003	116	116	0	116
Oldham	E08000004	142	142	0	142
Rochdale	E08000005	158	158	0	158
Salford	E08000006	97	97	0	97
Stockport	E08000007	126	126	0	126
Tameside	E08000008	103	103	0	103
Trafford	E08000009	106	106	0	106
Wigan	E08000010	188	188	0	188
Knowsley	E08000011	87	87	0	87
Liverpool	E08000012	134	112	0	112
St. Helens	E08000013	136	136	0	136
Sefton	E08000014	205	153	0	153
Wirral	E08000015	256	157	0	157
Barnsley	E08000016	329	329	0	329
Doncaster	E08000017	569	568	0	568
Rotherham	E08000018	287	287	0	287
Sheffield	E08000019	368	368	0	368
Newcastle upon Tyne	E08000021	115	113	0	113
North Tyneside	E08000022	85	82	0	82
South Tyneside	E08000023	67	64	0	64
Sunderland	E08000024	140	137	0	137
Birmingham	E08000025	268	268	0	268
Coventry	E08000026	99	99	0	99
Dudley	E08000027	98	98	0	98
Sandwell	E08000028	86	86	0	86
Solihull	E08000029	178	178	0	178
Walsall	E08000030	104	104	0	104
Wolverhampton	E08000031	69	69	0	69
Bradford	E08000032	366	366	0	366
Calderdale	E08000033	364	364	0	364
Kirklees	E08000034	409	409	0	409
Leeds	E08000035	552	552	0	552
Wakefield	E08000036	339	339	0	339
Gateshead	E08000037	144	142	0	142
City of London	E09000001	3	3	0	3
Barking and Dagenham	E09000002	38	36	0	36
Barnet	E09000003	87	87	0	87
Bexley	E09000004	64	61	0	61
Brent	E09000005	43	43	0	43
Bromley	E09000006	150	150	0	150
Camden	E09000007	22	22	0	22
Croydon	E09000008	86	86	0	86
Ealing	E09000009	56	56	0	56
Enfield	E09000010	82	82	1	81
Greenwich	E09000011	50	47	0	47
Hackney	E09000012	19	19	0	19
Hammersmith and Fulham	E09000013	17	16	0	16
Haringey	E09000014	30	30	0	30
Harrow	E09000015	50	50	0	50
Havering	E09000016	114	112	0	112
Hillingdon	E09000017	116	116	0	116
Hounslow	E09000018	57	56	0	56
Islington	E09000019	15	15	0	15

1.1 Standard Area Measurement for UK Local Authority Districts as at 31/12/2014

Local authority name as at December 2014	Code as at December 2014	Extent of the realm (Km²)	Area to mean high water (Km²)	Inland water (Km²)	Land only (Km²)
Kensington and Chelsea	E09000020	12	12	0	12
Kingston upon Thames	E09000021	37	37	0	37
Lambeth	E09000022	27	27	0	27
Lewisham	E09000023	35	35	0	35
Merton	E09000024	38	38	0	38
Newham	E09000025	39	36	0	36
Redbridge	E09000026	56	56	0	56
Richmond upon Thames	E09000027	59	57	0	57
Southwark	E09000028	30	29	0	29
Sutton	E09000029	44	44	0	44
Tower Hamlets	E09000030	22	20	0	20
Waltham Forest	E09000031	39	39	0	39
Wandsworth	E09000032	35	34	0	34
Westminster	E09000033	22	21	0	21
Scotland	**S92000003**	**80238**	**78810**	**900**	**77910**
Clackmannanshire	S12000005	164	159	0	159
Dumfries and Galloway	S12000006	6676	6438	11	6427
East Ayrshire	S12000008	1270	1270	8	1262
East Lothian	S12000010	701	679	0	679
East Renfrewshire	S12000011	174	174	0	174
Eilean Siar	S12000013	3269	3101	41	3060
Falkirk	S12000014	315	297	0	297
Fife	S12000015	1374	1325	0	1325
Highland	S12000017	26484	26162	506	25657
Inverclyde	S12000018	174	162	2	160
Midlothian	S12000019	355	355	2	354
Moray	S12000020	2257	2238	0	2238
North Ayrshire	S12000021	904	885	0	885
Orkney Islands	S12000023	1086	1013	25	989
Perth and Kinross	S12000024	5419	5384	98	5286
Scottish Borders	S12000026	4743	4739	7	4732
Shetland Islands	S12000027	1657	1468	1	1467
South Ayrshire	S12000028	1235	1224	2	1222
South Lanarkshire	S12000029	1774	1774	2	1772
Stirling	S12000030	2255	2253	66	2187
Aberdeen City	S12000033	206	186	0	186
Aberdeenshire	S12000034	6338	6318	5	6313
Argyll and Bute	S12000035	7164	7008	99	6909
City of Edinburgh	S12000036	273	263	0	263
Renfrewshire	S12000038	269	261	0	261
West Dunbartonshire	S12000039	183	177	19	159
West Lothian	S12000040	432	429	1	428
Angus	S12000041	2203	2185	4	2182
Dundee City	S12000042	62	60	0	60
North Lanarkshire	S12000044	472	472	2	470
East Dunbartonshire	S12000045	174	174	0	174
Glasgow City	S12000046	176	175	0	175

1.1 Standard Area Measurement for UK Local Authority Districts as at 31/12/2014

Local authority name as at December 2014	Code as at December 2014	Extent of the realm (Km^2)	Area to mean high water (Km^2)	Inland water (Km^2)	Land only (Km^2)
Wales	**W92000004**	**21224**	**20782**	**46**	20736
Isle of Anglesey	W06000001	**749**	**714**	**3**	711
Gwynedd	W06000002	**2622**	**2548**	**13**	2535
Conwy	W06000003	**1153**	**1130**	**4**	1126
Denbighshire	W06000004	**846**	**839**	**2**	837
Flintshire	W06000005	**489**	**437**	**0**	437
Wrexham	W06000006	**504**	**504**	**0**	504
Ceredigion	W06000008	**1806**	**1789**	**3**	1786
Pembrokeshire	W06000009	**1650**	**1619**	**0**	1619
Carmarthenshire	W06000010	**2439**	**2371**	**1**	2370
Swansea	W06000011	**421**	**380**	**0**	380
Neath Port Talbot	W06000012	**452**	**442**	**1**	441
Bridgend	W06000013	**255**	**251**	**0**	251
Vale of Glamorgan	W06000014	**340**	**331**	**0**	331
Cardiff	W06000015	**150**	**142**	**1**	141
Rhondda Cynon Taf	W06000016	**424**	**424**	**0**	424
Caerphilly	W06000018	**277**	**277**	**0**	277
Blaenau Gwent	W06000019	**109**	**109**	**0**	109
Torfaen	W06000020	**126**	**126**	**1**	126
Monmouthshire	W06000021	**886**	**850**	**1**	849
Newport	W06000022	**218**	**191**	**0**	191
Powys	W06000023	**5195**	**5195**	**15**	5181
Merthyr Tydfil	W06000024	**112**	**112**	**1**	111
Northern Ireland	**N92000002**	**14130**	**14130**	**568**	13562
Derry	95A	**380**	**380**	**0**	379
Limavady	95B	**586**	**586**	**0**	585
Coleraine	95C	**484**	**484**	**1**	483
Ballymoney	95D	**418**	**418**	**0**	418
Moyle	95E	**494**	**494**	**0**	494
Larne	95F	**336**	**336**	**1**	335
Ballymena	95G	**632**	**632**	**2**	630
Magherafelt	95H	**573**	**573**	**9**	563
Cookstown	95I	**622**	**622**	**109**	513
Strabane	95J	**859**	**859**	**1**	858
Omagh	95K	**1130**	**1130**	**1**	1129
Fermanagh	95L	**1871**	**1871**	**154**	1718
Dungannon	95M	**784**	**784**	**12**	771
Craigavon	95N	**378**	**378**	**100**	279
Armagh	95O	**671**	**671**	**2**	668
Newry and Mourne	95P	**901**	**901**	**4**	897
Banbridge	95Q	**453**	**453**	**1**	452
Down	95R	**648**	**648**	**4**	644
Lisburn	95S	**447**	**447**	**5**	442
Antrim	95T	**577**	**577**	**156**	421
Newtownabbey	95U	**151**	**151**	**0**	150
Carrickfergus	95V	**82**	**82**	**1**	81
North Down	95W	**82**	**82**	**1**	81
Ards	95X	**378**	**378**	**1**	377
Castlereagh	95Y	**85**	**85**	**0**	85
Belfast	95Z	**110**	**110**	**1**	109

Source: ONS Geography Codes
Standard Area Measurement for Local Authority Districts as at 31/12/2014

Parliamentary elections

Chapter 2

Parliamentary elections

This chapter covers parliamentary elections, by-elections and devolved assembly elections in the UK, Wales, Scotland and Northern Ireland.

Parliamentary elections (Table 2.1)

Information is supplied on the total electorate, average electorate and valid votes as a percentage of electorate. The number of seats by party is also listed.

Parliamentary by-elections (Table 2.2)

Information can be found on the votes recorded for each party and General Elections and subsequent by-elections between General Elections.

Devolved assembly elections (Tables 2.3 and 2.4)

Table 2.3 provides information on the devolved assembly elections in Wales and Scotland, listing information on the total electorate, average electorate and valid votes as a percentage of electorate. The number of seats by party is also listed. Table 2.4 provides information on the devolved assembly elections in Northern Ireland, listing information on the total electorate, average electorate and valid votes as a percentage of electorate. The number of seats by party is also listed.

2.1 Parliamentary elections[1]

United Kingdom

Thousands and percentages

		31-Mar 1966	18-Jun 1970[1]	28-Feb 1974		10-Oct 1974	03-May 1979	09-Jun 1983	11-Jun 1987	09-Apr 1992	01-May 1997	07-Jun 2001	05-May 2005	06-May 2010	07-May 2015
United Kingdom															
Electorate	DZ5P	35957	39615	40256	DZ6V	40256	41573	42704	43666	43719	43846	44403	44246	45597	46354
Average-electors per seat	DZ5T	57.1	62.9	63.4	DZ6R	63.4	65.5	66.7	67.2	67.2	66.5	67.4	68.5	70.1	71.3
Valid votes counted	DZ5X	27265	28345	31340	DZ6N	29189	31221	30671	32530	33614	31286	26367	27149	29688	30697.5
As percentage of electorate	DZ63	75.8	71.5	77.9	DZ6J	72.5	75.1	71.8	74.5	76.7	71.4	59.4	61.4	65.1	66.2
England and Wales															
Electorate	DZ5Q	31695	34931	35509	DZ6W	35509	36695	37708	38568	38648	38719	39228	39266	40565	40968
Average-electors per seat	DZ5U	57.9	63.9	64.3	DZ6S	64.3	66.5	67.2	68.8	68.8	68	68.9	69	70.8	71.6
Valid votes counted	DZ5Y	24116	24877	27735	DZ6O	25729	27609	27082	28832	29897	27679	23243	24097	26548	27034
As percentage of electorate	DZ64	76.1	71.2	78.1	DZ6K	72.5	75.2	71.8	74.8	77.5	71.5	59.3	61.4	65.4	66.0
Scotland															
Electorate	DZ5R	3360	3659	3705	DZ6X	3705	3837	3934	3995	3929	3949	3984	3840	3863	4100
Average-electors per seat	DZ5V	47.3	51.5	52.2	DZ6T	52.2	54	54.6	55.5	54.6	54.8	55.3	65.1	65.5	69.4963
Valid votes counted	DZ5Z	2553	2688	2887	DZ6P	2758	2917	2825	2968	2931	2817	2313	2334	2466	2910
As percentage of electorate	DZ65	76	73.5	77.9	DZ6L	74.5	76	71.8	74.3	74.2	71.3	58.1	60.8	63.8	71.0
Northern Ireland															
Electorate	DZ5S	902	1025	1027	DZ6Y	1037	1028	1050	1090	1141	1178	1191	1140	1169	1237
Average-electors per seat	DZ5W	75.2	85.4	85.6	DZ6U	86.4	85.6	61.8	64.1	67.1	65.4	66.2	63.3	65.0	68.7
Valid votes counted	DZ62	596	779	718	DZ6Q	702	696	765	730	785	791	810	718	674	718
As percentage of electorate	DZ66	66.1	76	69.9	DZ6M	67.7	67.7	72.9	67	68.8	67.1	68	62.9	57.6	58.1
Members of Parliament elected: (numbers)	DZV7	630	630	635	DZV8	635	635	650	650	651	659	659	646	650	650
Conservative	DZ67	253	330	296	DZ6D	276	339	396	375	336	165	166	198	306	331
Labour	DZ68	363	287	301	DZ6E	319	268	209	229	271	418	412	355	258	232
Liberal Democrat[2]	DZ69	12	6	14	DZ6F	13	11	23	22	20	46	52	62	57	8
Scottish National Party	DZ6A	–	1	7	DZ6G	11	2	2	3	3	6	5	6	6	56
Plaid Cymru	DZ6B	–	–	2	DZ6H	3	2	2	3	4	4	4	3	3	3
Other[3]	DZ6C	2	6	15	DZ6I	13	13	18	18	17	20	20	22	20	20

1 The Representation of the People Act 1969 lowered the minimum voting age from 21 to 18 years with effect from 16 February 1970.

2 Liberal before 1992. The figures for 1983 and 1987 include six and five MPs respectively who were elected for the Social Democratic Party.

3 Including the Speaker.

Source: British Electoral Facts 1832-2012
Plymouth University for the Electoral Commission: 01752 233207

13

2.2a Parliamentary by-elections

United Kingdom

	May 1997 - June 2001	General[1,2] Election May 1997	June 2001 - November 2004	General[1] Election June 2001	May 2005 - November 2009	General[1] Election May 2005	May 2010- November 2014	General[1] Election May 2010
Numbers of by-elections	17		6		14		21	
Votes recorded								
By party (percentages)								
Conservative	27.0	25.1	17.7	21.2	27.7	25.7	17.3	27.8
Labour	29.7	40.1	40.8	58.3	29.3	35.7	36.0	36.4
Liberal Democrat	22.1	14.4	31.3	13.7	20.0	20.6	8.3	18.8
Scottish National Party	6.0	4.1	-	-	9.5	6.2	1.5	0.7
Plaid Cymru	2.5	2.3	2.7	2.1	0.4	0.1	0.3	0.2
UKIP[3]							17.3	2.1
Other	12.7	14.1	7.4	4.7	13.0	11.7	19.3	13.9
Total votes recorded (percentages)	100	100	100	100	100	100	100	100
(thousands)	435	723	140	205	436	586	605	909

Source: Plymouth University for the Electoral Commission: 01752 233207

1 Votes recorded in the same seats in the previous General Election.
2 Proportions of 'other' votes inflated by the fact that votes were cast for the retiring Speaker as 'The Speaker seeking re-election' and not as a party
3 Figures for UKIP only recorded for by-elections since 2010

The Bradford West by-election of 29th March 2012 was won by the Respect candidate whose votes are included under "Other".
Similarly all votes cast in Northern Ireland by-elections have been included under "Other".

This table is no longer updated

2.2b Summary of parliamentary by-elections in Great Britain (excluding Northern Ireland), 1945-2016

	Number of by-elections	Net Seat Gains and Losses						Average change in share of vote since previous election					Average turnout
		CON	LAB	LD	SNP/PC	Other	No change	CON	LAB	LD	SNP/PC	Other	
1945-50	50	+4	-1	...	...	-3	45	3.7%	-2.3%	-1.1%	1.4%	-1.0%	67.3%
1950-51	14	...	...	...	...	...	14	+6.8%	-2.0%	-4.6%		-0.2%	68.8%
1951-55	44	+1	-1	...	...	...	43	-0.6%	+0.3%	-0.6%	+0.6%	+0.3%	58.6%
1955-59	49	-2	+4	...	...	-2	34	-8.7%	+1.3%	+6.2%	+0.3%	+0.9%	63.5%
1959-64	61	-5	+4	+1	...	...	54	-14.1%	-2.1%	+13.7%	+1.2%	+1.5%	62.9%
1964-66	13	...	-1	+1	...	...	11	+1.3%	-1.8%	+0.5%	+0.3%	+0.4%	58.2%
1966-70	37	+11	-15	+1	+2	+1	22	+6.8%	-17.3%	+3.3%	+5.5%	+1.7%	62.1%
1970-74	30	-5	...	+5	+1	-1	20	-10.7%	-4.2%	+9.0%	+4.0%	+1.9%	56.5%
1974	1	...	...	...	...	...	1	-1.1%	-3.4%	-2.3%	...	+6.8%	25.9%
1974-79	30	+6	-6	+1	...	-1	23	+9.9%	-9.3%	-4.9%	-0.3%	+4.6%	57.5%
1979-83	17	-3	+1	+4	...	-2	11	-11.4%	-10.2%	+18.6%	+1.6%	+1.4%	56.7%
1983-87	16	-4	...	+4	...	...	11	-14.0%	+0.4%	+12.3%	+0.1%	+1.2%	63.5%
1987-92	23	-7	+3	+3	+1	...	15	-11.0%	-0.8%	-0.6%	+5.7%	+6.6%	57.4%
1992-97	17	-8	+3	+4	+1	...	9	-19.9%	+7.4%	+5.2%	+2.4%	+4.9%	52.7%
1997-2001	15	-2	+1	+2	...	-1	14	-0.6%	-11.1%	+5.0%	+3.1%	+3.6%	42.4%
2001-05	6	...	-2	+2	...	...	4	-4.2%	-19.8%	+15.8%	+1.1%	+7.0%	39.3%
2005-10	14	...	-1	+1	...	...	9	+2.6%	-10.4%	+2.0%	+4.3%	+5.3%	48.8%
2010-15	19	-3	...	...	...	+3	13	-6.4%	+5.4%	-7.6%	+1.1%	+17.9%	39.6%
2015-	3	...	...	...	...	...	3	-2.5%	+2.9%	-7.8%	+5.6%	+0.9%	36.7%

Sources:

Updated on 1 June 2016

1. F.W.S. Craig, Chronology of British Parliamentary By-elections 1833-1987
2. Colin Rallings and Michael Thrasher, British Electoral Facts 1832-2006
3. House of Commons Library, RP10/50 By-election results 2005-10; SN05833 By-elections since 2010 General Election

2.2c Parliamentary by-elections in Northern Ireland, 1974-2015[5]

Date	Constituency	Result	Change in share of the vote since previous election:					Turnout
			DUP	UUP	SF	SDLP	Other	
GENERAL ELECTION 1974 (FEB)								
None								
GENERAL ELECTION 1974 (OCT)								
None								
GENERAL ELECTION 1979								
09/04/1981	Fermanagh and South Tyrone	Anti-H Block gain from Ind Rep	...	+41.0%	...	...	+51.2%	82.4%
20/08/1981	Fermanagh and South Tyrone	Anti-H Block hold	...	-3.2%	...	...	+3.2%	87.5%
04/03/1982	Belfast South	UUP hold	+22.6%	-22.4%	...	+0.9%	+29.3%	65.7%
GENERAL ELECTION 1983[6]								
23/01/1986	East Antrim	UUP hold	...	+47.5%	...	...	-4.8%	58.9%
23/01/1986	North Antrim	DUP hold	+43.2%	...	...	...	...	53.5%
23/01/1986	South Antrim	UUP hold	...	+48.5%	...	...	...	52.2%
23/01/1986	Belfast East	DUP hold	+35.6%	...	...	...	-6.1%	63.6%
23/01/1986	Belfast North	UUP hold	...	+35.3%	...	...	+13.7%	54.7%
23/01/1986	Belfast South	UUP hold	...	+21.4%	...	...	+2.4%	56.6%
23/01/1986	North Down	UPU hold	...	...	...	...	+21.9%	60.5%
23/01/1986	South Down	UUP hold	...	+8.1%	-2.2%	+5.6%	-0.6%	73.8%
23/01/1986	Fermanagh and South Tyrone	UUP hold	...	+2.1%	-7.6%	+5.0%	+0.5%	80.4%
23/01/1986	Lagan Valley	UUP hold	...	+31.5%	...	...	+7.3%	81.4%
23/01/1986	East Londonderry	UUP hold	...	+56.0%	...	...	...	47.0%
23/01/1986	Mid Ulster	DUP hold	+16.1%	...	-2.6%	+3.0%	-0.1%	77.0%
23/01/1986	Newry and Armagh	SDLP gain from UUP	...	+0.2%	-7.7%	+8.7%	-1.2%	76.6%
23/01/1986	Strangford	UUP hold	...	+45.4%	...	...	...	55.1%
23/01/1986	Upper Bann	UUP hold	...	+23.9%	...	...	+13.8%	57.2%
GENERAL ELECTION 1987								
17/05/1990	Upper Bann	UUP hold	...	-3.5%	-1.7%	-1.6%	-4.8%	53.4%
GENERAL ELECTION 1992								
15/06/1995	North Down	UKU gain from UPU	...	...	...	...	-19.3%	38.6%
GENERAL ELECTION 1997								
21/09/2000	South Antrim	DUP gain from UUP	...	-22.2%	+3.0%	-4.7%	-5.0%	43.0%
GENERAL ELECTION 2001								
None								
GENERAL ELECTION 2005								
None								
GENERAL ELECTION 2010 (up to July 2011)								
09/06/2011	Belfast West	SF hold	-1.5%	-1.4%	-0.4%	-2.9%	+6.3%	37.4%
07/03/2013	Mid Ulster	SF hold	...	...	-5.1%	+3.1%	+1.9%	55.4%
GENERAL ELECTION 2015 (up to December 2015)								
None								

Notes for table 2.2c

1. The formation of new parties in the early 1970s altered the pattern of party competition at Westminster elections. The SDLP (formed 1970) and the DUP (formed 1971) are included in Table 14b (1974-2012). Ulster Unionists are listed as Conservatives up to 1972 when they stopped taking the Conservative whip.

2. Irish Nationalist/Anti-Partitionist

3. Sinn Féin (SF) candidate T.J. Mitchell was elected as MP for Mid-Ulster at the 1955 General Election, but was in prison at the time of election and hence was disqualified from being an MP. No petition was lodged but a by-election writ was subsequently issued; in the 31 August 1955 by-election Mitchell again stood for Sinn Féin and topped the poll (therefore the by-election is here recorded as a Sinn Féin hold). However on this occasion a petition was lodged and since Mitchell was disqualified, the Conservative candidate was elected instead.

4. Prior to the by-election the seat was held by a Conservative (see footnote 1). Changes in vote share are as compared to the 1955 General Election.

* Constituency returned two MPs at previous general election. Change in vote share between general election and by-election is calculating using the total vote received by a party's candidate in the previous general election. However some electors will only voted for one candidate in the general election and of those who cast two votes, some will have voted for candidates from different parties. Additionally some parties will only have stood one candidate in a multimember seat.

5. The formation of new parties in the early 1970s altered the pattern of party competition at Westminster elections. The SDLP (formed 1970) and the DUP (formed 1971) are included in this table but not in Table 14a. The Ulster Unionist Party (UUP) took the Conservative whip at Westminster until 1972 and so in Table 14a are listed under Conservatives.

6. Multiple by-elections were held in January 1986 after fifteen unionist Members resigned their seats in protest at the Anglo-Irish Agreement.

Party descriptions:

DUP - Democratic Unionist Party	SDLP - Social Democratic and Labour Party
UUP - Ulster Unionist Party	UPU - Ulster Popular Unionist Party
SF - Sinn Fein	UKU - United Kingdom Unionist

Sources for table 2.2c

1. F.W.S. Craig, British Parliamentary Election Results 1918-1949
2. F.W.S. Craig, British Parliamentary Election Results 1950-1973
3. F.W.S. Craig, British Parliamentary Election Results 1974-1983
4. Colin Rallings and Michael Thrasher, British Parliamentary Election Results 1983-1997
5. House of Commons Library RP01/36, By-election results 1997-2000; RP05/34, By-election results 2001-05;
6. RP10/50, By-election results 2005-10; SN05833, By-elections since 2010 General Election

2.3a Devolved assembly elections

Wales and Scotland

Thousands and percentages

		06-May 1999	01-May 2003	03-May 2007	05-May 2011
Welsh Assembly					
Electorate	E28K	2205	2230	2248	2290
Average-electors per seat[1]	E28N	55.1	55.7	56.2	57.2
Valid votes counted	E28Q	1023	850	978	949
As percentage of electorate	E28T	46.4	38.1	43.5	41.5
Members elected:[2] (numbers)	E2XI	60	60	60	60
Conservative	E2WG	9	11	12	14
Labour	E2WU	28	30	26	30
Liberal Democrat	E2WW	6	6	6	5
Plaid Cymru	E2X3	17	12	15	11
Other	E2WY	–	1	1	-
Scottish Parliament					
Electorate	E28L	4024	3879	3899	3951
Average-electors per seat[1]	E28O	55.1	53.1	53.4	54.1
Valid votes counted	E28R	2342	1916	2017	1989
As percentage of electorate	E28U	58.2	49.4	51.7	50.3
Members elected:[3] (numbers)	E2XJ	129	129	129	129
Conservative	E2WH	18	18	17	15
Labour	E2WV	56	50	46	37
Liberal Democrat	E2WX	17	17	16	5
Scottish National Party	E2X4	35	27	47	69
Other	E2WZ	3	17	3	3

1 This is the average in each first-past-the-post constituency. Additional members are then elected on the basis of a regional 'list' vote.
2 Comprising 40 from constituencies and 20 from the regional 'list'.
3 Comprising 73 from constituencies and 56 from the regional 'list'.

This table is no longer updated

Sources: British Electoral Facts 1832-2012;
Plymouth University for the Electoral Commission: 01752 233207

2.3b National Assembly for Wales elections, 1999-2016

	Number of Votes					% share				
	1999	2003	2007	2011	2016	1999	2003	2007	2011	2016
Constituency votes										
LAB	384,671	340,515	314,925	401,677	353,865	37.6%	40.0%	32.2%	42.3%	34.7%
PC	290,565	180,185	219,121	182,907	209,374	28.4%	21.2%	22.4%	19.3%	20.5%
CON	162,133	169,832	218,730	237,389	215,597	15.8%	20.0%	22.4%	25.0%	21.1%
UKIP		19,795	18,047		127,038		2.3%	1.8%		12.5%
LD	137,657	120,250	144,410	100,259	78,165	13.5%	14.1%	14.8%	10.6%	7.7%
Others	47,992	20,266	62,859	27,021	35,341	4.7%	2.4%	6.4%	2.8%	3.5%
Total	1,023,018	850,843	978,092	949,253	1,019,380	100%	100%	100%	100%	100%
Constituency seats										
LAB	27	30	24	28	27	67.5%	75.0%	60.0%	70.0%	67.5%
PC	9	5	7	5	6	22.5%	12.5%	17.5%	12.5%	15.0%
CON	1	1	5	6	6	2.5%	2.5%	12.5%	15.0%	15.0%
UKIP	0	0	0	0	0	0.0%	0.0%	0.0%	0.0%	0.0%
LD	3	3	3	1	1	7.5%	7.5%	7.5%	2.5%	2.5%
Others	0	1	1	0	0	0.0%	2.5%	2.5%	0.0%	0.0%
Total:	**40**	**40**	**40**	**40**	**40**	**100%**	**100%**	**100%**	**100%**	**100%**
Regional votes										
LAB	361,657	310,658	288,955	349,935	319,196	35.4%	36.6%	29.6%	36.9%	31.5%
PC	312,048	167,653	204,757	169,799	211,548	30.5%	19.7%	21.0%	17.9%	20.8%
CON	168,206	162,725	209,154	213,773	190,846	16.5%	19.2%	21.5%	22.5%	18.8%
UKIP		29,427	38,349	43,256	132,138		3.5%	3.9%	4.6%	13.0%
LD	128,008	108,013	114,500	76,349	65,504	12.5%	12.7%	11.7%	8.0%	6.5%
Others	51,938	71,076	119,071	95,776	95,511	5.1%	8.4%	12.2%	10.1%	9.4%
Total	1,021,857	849,552	974,786	948,888	1,014,743	100%	100%	100%	100%	100%
Regional seats										
LAB	1	0	2	2	2	5.0%	0.0%	10.0%	10.0%	10.0%
PC	8	7	8	6	6	40.0%	35.0%	40.0%	30.0%	30.0%
CON	8	10	7	8	5	40.0%	50.0%	35.0%	40.0%	25.0%
UKIP	0	0	0	0	7	0.0%	0.0%	0.0%	0.0%	35.0%
LD	3	3	3	4	0	15.0%	15.0%	15.0%	20.0%	0.0%
Others	0	0	0	0	0	0.0%	0.0%	0.0%	0.0%	0.0%
Total:	**20**	**20**	**20**	**20**	**20**	**100%**	**100%**	**100%**	**100%**	**100%**
Total seats										
LAB	28	30	26	30	29	46.7%	50.0%	43.3%	50.0%	48.3%
PC	17	12	15	11	12	28.3%	20.0%	25.0%	18.3%	20.0%
CON	9	11	12	14	11	15.0%	18.3%	20.0%	23.3%	18.3%
UKIP	0	0	0	0	7	0.0%	0.0%	0.0%	0.0%	11.7%
LD	6	6	6	5	1	10.0%	10.0%	10.0%	8.3%	1.7%
Others	0	1	1	0	0	0.0%	1.7%	1.7%	0.0%	0.0%
Total:	**60**	**60**	**60**	**60**	**60**	**100%**	**100%**	**100%**	**100%**	**100%**
Constituency turnout										
	46.4%	38.2%	43.5%	41.5%	45.5%					
Regional turnout										
	46.3%	38.1%	43.4%	41.4%	45.3%					

Source: House of Commons Library Briefing Paper CBP7594, National Assembly for Wales Elections: 2016

2.3c Scottish Parliament elections, 1999-2016

	Number of votes and seats					% Share				
	1999	2003	2007	2011	2016	1999	2003	2007	2011	2016
Constituency votes										
SNP	672,768	455,742	664,227	902,915	1,059,898	28.7%	23.8%	32.9%	45.4%	46.5%
CON	364,425	318,279	334,742	276,652	501,844	15.6%	16.6%	16.6%	13.9%	22.0%
LAB	908,346	663,585	648,374	630,461	514,261	38.8%	34.6%	32.1%	31.7%	22.6%
LD	333,179	294,347	326,232	157,714	178,238	14.2%	15.4%	16.2%	7.9%	7.8%
GRN			2,971		13,172			0.1%		0.6%
Other	63,770	184,641	43,402	21,534	11,741	2.7%	9.6%	2.2%	1.1%	0.5%
Total	**2,342,488**	**1,916,594**	**2,016,977**	**1,989,276**	**2,279,154**	**100%**	**100%**	**100%**	**100%**	**100.0%**
Constituency seats										
SNP	7	9	21	53	59	9.6%	12.3%	28.8%	72.6%	80.8%
CON	0	3	4	3	7	0.0%	4.1%	5.5%	4.1%	9.6%
LAB	53	46	37	15	3	72.6%	63.0%	50.7%	20.5%	4.1%
LD	12	13	11	2	4	16.4%	17.8%	15.1%	2.7%	5.5%
GRN										
Other	1	2	0	0	0	1.4%	2.7%	0.0%	0.0%	0.0%
Total	**73**	**73**	**73**	**73**	**73**	**100%**	**100%**	**100%**	**100%**	**100%**
Regional votes										
SNP	638,644	399,659	633,401	876,421	953,587	27.3%	20.9%	31.0%	44.0%	41.7%
CON	359,109	296,929	284,005	245,967	524,220	15.4%	15.5%	13.9%	12.4%	22.9%
LAB	786,818	561,375	595,415	523,469	435,919	33.6%	29.3%	29.2%	26.3%	19.1%
LD	290,760	225,774	230,671	103,472	119,284	12.4%	11.8%	11.3%	5.2%	5.2%
GRN	84,023	132,138	82,584	86,939	150,426	3.6%	6.9%	4.0%	4.4%	6.6%
Other	179,560	299,976	215,973	154,568	102,315	7.7%	15.7%	10.6%	7.8%	4.5%
Total	**2,338,914**	**1,915,851**	**2,042,049**	**1,990,836**	**2,285,751**	**100%**	**100%**	**100%**	**100%**	**100%**
Regional Seats										
SNP	28	18	26	16	4	50.0%	32.1%	46.4%	28.6%	7.1%
CON	18	15	13	12	24	32.1%	26.8%	23.2%	21.4%	42.9%
LAB	3	4	9	22	21	5.4%	7.1%	16.1%	39.3%	37.5%
LD	5	4	5	3	1	8.9%	7.1%	8.9%	5.4%	1.8%
GRN	1	7	2	2	6	1.8%	12.5%	3.6%	3.6%	10.7%
Other	1	8	1	1	0	1.8%	14.3%	1.8%	1.8%	0.0%
Total	**56**	**56**	**56**	**56**	**56**	**100%**	**100%**	**100%**	**100%**	**100%**
Total seats										
SNP	35	27	47	69	63	62.5%	48.2%	83.9%	123.2%	112.5%
CON	18	18	17	15	31	32.1%	32.1%	30.4%	26.8%	55.4%
LAB	56	50	46	37	24	100.0%	89.3%	82.1%	66.1%	42.9%
LD	17	17	16	5	5	30.4%	30.4%	28.6%	8.9%	8.9%
GRN	1	7	2	2	6	1.8%	12.5%	3.6%	3.6%	10.7%
Other	2	10	1	1		3.6%	17.9%	1.8%	1.8%	0.0%
Total	**129**	**129**	**129**	**129**	**129**	**100%**	**100%**	**100%**	**100%**	**100%**
Constituency Turnout										
	58.8%	49.4%	51.7%	50.4%	55.6%					
Regional Turnout										
	58.7%	49.4%	52.4%	50.4%	55.7%					

Sources:

1. Colin Rallings and Michael Thrasher, British Electoral Facts 1832-2006
2. Electoral Commission, Report on the Scottish Parliament election on 5 May 2016
3. House of Commons Library Briefing Paper CBP7599, Scottish Parliament Elections: 2016
4. House of Commons Library Research Paper RP07/46, Scottish Parliament Elections: 3 May 2007
5. House of Commons Library Research Paper RP11/41, Scottish Parliament Elections: 2011
6. House of Commons Library Briefing Paper CBP-7529, Scottish Parliament Elections: 2016

2.4a Devolved assembly elections

Northern Ireland

Thousands and percentages

		25-Jun 1998	26-Nov 2003	08-Mar 2007	05-May 2011
Electorate	E28M	1179	1098	1108	1210
Average-electors per seat[1]	E28P	65.5	61	61.6	67.2
Valid votes counted	E28S	810	692	692	662
As percentage of electorate	E28V	68.7	63	63	55.7
Members elected: (numbers)	E2XK	108	108	108	108
Alliance Party	E2X5	6	6	7	8
SDLP	E2X6	24	18	16	14
Sinn Fein	E2X7	18	24	28	29
Democratic Unionist Party	E2X8	20	30	36	38
UK Unionist Party	E2X9	5	1	–	-
Ulster Unionist Party	E2XA	28	27	18	16
Other	E2X2	7	2	3	3

1 This is the average in each Westminster constituency. Six members are
elected by single transferable vote (STV) in each constituency.

This table is no longer updated

Sources: British Electoral Facts 1832-2012;
Plymouth University for the Electoral Commission: 01752233207

2.4b Northern Ireland Assembly elections: 1998-2016

	Votes and seats won					% of votes and seats won				
	1998	2003	2007	2011	2016	1998	2003	2007	2011	2016
Votes										
DUP	146,917	177,944	207,721	198,436	202,567	18.1%	25.3%	30.1%	30.0%	29.2%
Sinn Féin	142,858	162,758	180,573	178,222	166,785	17.6%	23.2%	26.2%	26.9%	24.0%
UUP	172,225	156,931	103,145	87,531	87,302	21.3%	22.3%	14.9%	13.2%	12.6%
SDLP	177,963	117,547	105,164	94,286	83,364	22.0%	16.7%	15.2%	14.2%	12.0%
Alliance	52,636	25,372	36,139	50,875	48,447	6.5%	3.6%	5.2%	7.7%	7.0%
UK Unionists	36,541	5,700	10,452	…	…	4.5%	0.8%	1.5%		
PUP	20,634	8,032	3,822	1,493	5,955	2.5%	1.1%	0.6%	0.2%	0.9%
People before Profit Alliance		…	774	5,438	13,761			0.1%	0.8%	2.0%
TUV	…	…	…	16,480	23,776				2.5%	3.4%
UKIP	…	…	…	4,152	10,109				0.6%	1.5%
Green Party	510	2,688	11,985	6,031	18,718	0.1%	0.4%	1.7%	0.9%	2.7%
Others	59,961	45,277	30,538	18,790	33,526	7.4%	6.4%	4.4%	2.8%	4.8%
Total	**810,245**	**702,249**	**690,313**	**661,734**	**694,310**	**100.0%**	**100.0%**	**100.0%**	**100.0%**	**100.0%**
Seats von										
DUP	20	30	36	38	38	18.5%	27.8%	33.3%	35.2%	35.2%
Sinn Féin	18	24	28	29	28	16.7%	22.2%	25.9%	26.9%	25.9%
UUP	28	27	18	16	16	25.9%	25.0%	16.7%	14.8%	14.8%
SDLP	24	18	16	14	12	22.2%	16.7%	14.8%	13.0%	11.1%
Alliance	6	6	7	8	8	5.6%	5.6%	6.5%	7.4%	7.4%
UK Unionists	5	1	0	…	…	4.6%	0.9%	0.0%		
PUP	2	1	1	0	0	1.9%	0.9%	0.9%	0.0%	0.0%
People before Profit Allianc	…	…	0	0	2			0.0%	0.0%	1.9%
TUV	…	…	…	1	1				0.9%	0.9%
UKIP	…	…	…	0	0				0.0%	0.0%
Green Party	0	0	1	1	2	0.0%	0.0%	0.9%	0.9%	1.9%
Others	5	1	1	1	1	4.6%	0.9%	0.9%	0.9%	0.9%
Total	**108**	**108**	**108**	**108**	**108**	**100.0%**	**100.0%**	**100.0%**	**100.0%**	**100.0%**
Turnout	**70.0%**	**64.0%**	**62.3%**	**54.7%**	**54.2%**					

Sources:
1. Colin Rallings and Michael Thrasher, British Electoral Facts 1832-2006
2. Electoral Office for Northern Ireland, www.eoni.org.uk

International development

Chapter 3

International development

Overseas development assistance

The Department for International Development (DFID) is the UK Government Department with lead responsibility for overseas development. DFID's aim is to eliminate poverty in poorer countries through achievement of the Millennium Development Goals (MDG'. Statistics relating to international development are published on a financial year basis and on a calendar year basis. Statistics on a calendar year basis allow comparisons of aid expenditure with other donor countries. Aid flows can be measured before (gross) or after (net) deductions of repayments of principal on past loans. These tables show only the gross figures.

Aid is provided in two main ways: Bilateral funding is provided directly to partner countries while multilateral funding is provided through international organisations.

Funds can only be classified as multilateral if they are channelled through an organisation on a list in the OECD –

Development Assistance Committee (DAC) Statistical Reporting Directives – which identifies all multilateral organisations. This list also highlights some bodies that might appear to be multilateral but are actually bilateral (in particular this latter category includes some international non-governmental organisations such as the International Committee of the Red Cross and some Public-Private Partnerships). The DAC list of multilaterals is updated annually based on members nominations; organisations must be engaged in development work to be classified as multilateral aid channels although money may be classified as bilateral while a case is being made for a new multilateral organisation to be recognised.

While core funding to multilateral organisations is always classified as multilateral expenditure, additional funding channelled through multilaterals is often classified as bilateral expenditure. This would be the case in circumstances where a DFID country office transfers some money to a multilateral organisation (for example UN agency) for a particular programme in that country (or region). That is where DFID has control over what the money is being spent on and/or where it is being spent. Likewise, if DFID responds to an emergency appeal from an agency for a particular country or area, the funds will be allocated as bilateral spend to that country or region. As a result, some organisations, such as UN agencies have some of their DFID funding classified as bilateral and some as multilateral.

Bilateral assistance takes various forms:

Financial Aid – Poverty Reduction Budget Support (PRBS) – Funds provided to developing countries for them to spend in support of their expenditure programmes whose long-term objective is to reduce poverty; funds are spent using the overseas governments' own financial management, procurement and accountability systems to increase ownership and long term sustainability. PRBS can take the form of a general contribution to the overall budget – general budget support – or support with a more restricted focus which is earmarked for a specific sector – sector budget support.

Other Financial Aid – Funding of projects and programmes such as Sector Wide Programmes not classified as PRBS. Financial aid in its broader sense covers all bilateral aid expenditure other than technical cooperation and administrative costs but in SID we separately categorise this further.

Technical Co-operation – Activities designed to enhance the knowledge, intellectual skills, technical expertise or the productive capability of people in recipient countries. It also covers funding of services which contribute to the design or implementation of development projects and programmes.

This assistance is mainly delivered through research and development, the use of consultants, training (generally overseas partners visiting the UK or elsewhere for a training programme) and employment of 'other Personnel' (non-DFID experts on fixed term contracts). This latter category is growing less significant over time as existing contracted staff reach the end of their assignments.

Bilateral Aid Delivered Through a Multilateral Organisation – This category covers funding that is channelled through a multilateral organisation and DFID has control over the country, sector or theme that the funds will be spent on. For example, where a DFID country office transfers money to a multilateral organisation for a particular piece of work in that country. This also includes aid delivered through multi donor funds such as the United Nations Central Emergency Response Fund (CERF).

Bilateral Aid Delivered Through a Non-Governmental Organisation (NGO) – This category covers support to the international development work of UK and international not for profit organisations such as NGOs or Civil Society Organisations. This covers Partnership Programme Arrangements (PPAs), the Civil Society Challenge Fund and other grants.

Other Bilateral Aid – This category includes any aid not elsewhere classified such as funding to other donors for shared development purposes. More information on all of the above aid types is provided in the Glossary.

Humanitarian Assistance – Provides food, aid and other humanitarian assistance including shelter, medical care and advice in emergency situations and their aftermath. Work of the conflict pools is also included.

DFID Debt Relief – This includes sums for debt relief on DFID aid loans and cancellation of debt under the Commonwealth Debt Initiative (CDI). The non-CDI DFID debt relief is reported on the basis of the 'benefit to the recipient country'. This means that figures shown represent the money available to the country in the year in question that would otherwise have been spent on debt servicing. The CDI debt cancellation is reported on a 'lump sum' basis where all outstanding amounts on a loan are shown at the time the agreement to cancel is made.

CDC Gross Investments – CDC Group PLC is wholly government owned. Its investments must have a clear development objective. The net amount (that is equity purchase less equity sales) of

CDC investments in official development assistance (ODA)-eligible countries is reported as ODA and the gross amount (that is equity purchase only) is reported in GPEX.

Non-DFID Debt Relief – Comprises CDC Debt and ECGD Debt. CDC has a portfolio of loans to governments which can become eligible for debt relief under the Heavily Indebted Poor Countries (HIPC) or other debt relief deals. In 2005/06 £90 million of debts owed to CDC were reorganised. Export Credit Guarantee Department (ECGD) is the UK's official export credit agency providing insurance for exporters against the main risks in selling overseas and guarantees to banks providing export finance. It also negotiates debt relief arrangements on commercial debt.

The Foreign and Commonwealth Office (FCO) contributes to UK GPEX in a number of ways:

The FCO Strategic Programme Fund supports a range of the UK government's international goals. Where the programme funds projects which meet the required OECD definition these projects are included in UK GPEX statistics.

The FCO supports the British Council through grant-in-aid funding. This funding goes to support a range of initiatives including building the capacity and quality of English language teaching; supporting education systems; and using cultural exchange to improve economic welfare. UK GPEX statistics include the proportion of this work which is clearly focussed on delivering economic welfare and development in ODA eligible countries.

The British Council also manages, on behalf of the FCO, the Chevening Scholarships programme, which provides funding for postgraduate students or researchers from developing countries to study in UK universities. Funding from this scheme to students from ODA eligible countries are included in UK ODA and GPEX statistics.

The FCO makes annual contributions to UN and Commonwealth organisations. A proportion of these contributions are allowed to score as ODA in line with Annex 2 of the DAC Statistical Reporting Directives.

In addition to contributing directly to the Conflict Pool (see below) the FCO is also responsible for the UK contribution to the UN Department for Peacekeeping Operations (UNDPKO). In line with DAC rules 6 per cent of donor funding to UNDPKO is allowed to score as ODA. FCO also funds other bilateral peacekeeping missions including the Organisation for Security and Cooperation in Europe (OSCE) and the European Security and Defence Policy (ESDP) civilian missions; a proportion of which is reported as bilateral GPEX.

The Conflict Pool (CP) –is governed and jointly managed by DFID, the FCO and the Ministry of Defence (MoD) to bring together the UK government's development, diplomatic and defence interest and expertise to ensure a coherent response to conflict prevention. Some of the CP's expenditure is ODA eligible. All CP funds disbursed through DFID are included in GPEX and appear in these statistics as part of DFID expenditure. The remaining figures comprise the aggregate of FCO and MOD spending. Data on the ODA eligible CP funds disbursed by the FCO and MOD are collected by DFID in liaison with programme officers in the relevant departments.

Other –includes contributions from other government departments including: Department of Energy and Climate Change; Department of Health; Department for Environment, Food & Rural

Affairs; Department for Culture, Media and Sport; Scottish Government; and the Welsh Assembly Government. It also includes estimates of the UK Border Agency's costs of supporting refugees in the UK; as well as estimates of gift aid to NGOs and other official funding to NGOs.

Comparisons are available in the OECD Development Assistance Committee's annual report.

3.1 DFID Gross Public Expenditure 2009/10 - 2013/14

£ thousands

	2009/10	2010/11	2011/12	2012/13	2013/14
DFID Bilateral Programme[1]					
Poverty Reduction Budget Support	634,101	643,671	536,662	410,133	567,073
of which					
General Budget Support	*383,150*	*360,467*	*242,290*	*167,343*	*106,600*
Sector Budget Support	*250,951*	*283,204*	*294,372*	*242,790*	*460,474*
Other Financial Aid	518,817	550,728	544,778	685,571	601,174
Technical Co-operation	419,911	467,939	527,907	638,258	901,383
Bilateral Aid Delivered through a Multilateral Organisation[2]	1,264,716	1,465,789	1,404,592	1,074,957	1,436,580
Bilateral Aid Delivered through a NGO	599,434	626,752	739,558	747,302	999,809
of which:					
Partnership Programme Agreements	*127,728*	*119,097*	*119,625*	*110,347*	*124,309*
Other CSO's	*471,706*	*507,655*	*619,933*	*636,955*	*875,500*
Other Bilateral Aid[3]	34,668	76,009	81,372	119,120	142,378
Humanitarian Assistance	434,556	350,669	354,293	476,878	866,485
DFID Debt Relief	52,061	66,460	14,954	17,169	9,172
Total DFID Bilateral Programme	**3,958,263**	**4,248,018**	**4,204,114**	**4,169,389**	**5,524,054**
DFID Multilateral Programme					
European Commission	1,186,303	1,268,563	1,220,076	1,085,769	1,095,770
World Bank	559,785	926,713	1,038,568	1,025,431	1,206,227
UN Agencies	216,315	355,337	376,708	360,304	441,269
Other Multilateral	473,934	671,061	622,373	809,804	1,563,745
Total DFID Multilateral Programme	**2,436,338**	**3,221,673**	**3,257,724**	**3,281,308**	**4,307,012**
Total DFID Programme (excl. Total Operating Costs)	**6,394,601**	**7,475,391**	**7,461,839**	**7,450,696**	**9,831,066**
DFID Total Operating Costs[4]	234,398	219,457	220,352	220,220	226,743
Total DFID Programme	**6,628,999**	**7,689,149**	**7,682,191**	**7,670,916**	**10,057,810**

Source: Department for International Development (DFID)

1. Descriptions of aid types given in Technical Note 1.

2. This covers earmarked funding provided through multilateral organisations where the recipient country, region, sector, theme or specific project are known. This figure does not include all bilateral aid spent through a multilateral organisation – other types of aid such as humanitarian assistance or debt relief also include aid spent through a multilateral organisation. In total in 2013/14 £2,015 million of bilateral aid was spent through multilateral organisations.

3. Other Bilateral Aid covers bilateral aid that does not fit into any other category.

4. Includes Front Line Delivery costs and Administration spend.

3.2 DFID Bilateral Gross Public Expenditure by Region and Country Groupings 2009/10 - 2013/14[1]

£ thousands

		Financial Aid			Technical Co-operation	Bilateral aid delivered through a Multilateral	Bilateral aid Delivered through an NGO	Other Bilateral Aid[2]	Humanitarian Assistance	DFID Debt Relief	Total DFID Bilateral Programme[5]
		General Poverty Reduction Budget Support	Sector Poverty Reduction Budget Support	Other Financial Aid[4]							
TOTAL ALL COUNTRIES	2009/10	383,150	250,951	518,817	419,911	1,264,716	599,434	34,668	434,556	52,061	3,958,263
	2010/11	360,467	283,204	550,728	467,939	1,465,789	626,752	76,009	350,669	66,460	4,248,018
	2011/12	242,290	294,372	544,778	527,907	1,404,592	739,558	81,372	354,293	14,954	4,204,115
	2012/13	167,343	242,790	685,571	638,258	1,074,957	747,302	119,120	476,878	17,169	4,169,389
	2013/14	106,600	460,474	601,174	901,383	1,436,580	999,809	142,378	866,485	9,172	5,524,054
Africa	2009/10	333,150	158,163	151,865	199,273	332,740	149,203	20,688	293,593	8,807	1,647,482
	2010/11	310,467	185,454	211,960	248,588	437,496	158,238	47,869	211,732	55,358	1,867,162
	2011/12	222,290	242,372	222,158	298,059	386,727	213,000	45,046	260,329	1,713	1,891,694
	2012/13	167,343	213,090	297,050	368,762	316,222	207,660	76,600	317,865	1,124	1,965,716
	2013/14	106,600	301,524	255,996	491,619	419,387	308,233	48,176	379,607	-	2,311,141
of which: Africa: South of Sahara	2009/10	333,150	158,163	146,365	192,648	276,347	125,616	13,213	291,836	2,022	1,539,360
	2010/11	310,467	185,454	205,460	242,213	393,112	135,751	47,445	184,984	55,358	1,760,245
	2011/12	222,290	242,372	222,158	285,327	356,386	190,709	38,047	248,159	1,713	1,807,161
	2012/13	167,343	213,090	297,050	340,240	265,232	180,258	70,965	266,401	1,124	1,801,704
	2013/14	106,600	301,524	255,996	461,636	369,362	274,171	45,601	328,780	-	2,143,668
Americas	2009/10	-	-	25,444	5,903	16,248	2,209	995	13,844	47	64,690
	2010/11	-	-	20,103	3,170	29,618	1,624	3,170	7,442	1,706	66,833
	2011/12	-	-	26,576	3,932	14,004	2,215	526	2,537	-	49,789
	2012/13	-	-	30,440	2,552	11,979	1,947	364	6,383	-	53,665
	2013/14	-	-	26,857	1,028	8,503	1,522	154	7,273	3,535	48,872
Asia	2009/10	50,000	89,289	338,246	130,317	225,697	133,166	11,691	103,187	7,553	1,089,144
	2010/11	50,000	95,250	313,750	135,553	257,527	110,479	13,349	109,028	8,508	1,093,443
	2011/12	20,000	52,000	293,140	142,103	413,386	130,578	15,342	88,841	9,218	1,164,608
	2012/13	-	29,700	349,146	158,565	230,559	154,291	17,503	147,882	9,781	1,097,428
	2013/14	-	158,950	308,699	207,705	357,438	180,964	54,985	439,868	-	1,708,610

3.2 DFID Bilateral Gross Public Expenditure by Region and Country Groupings 2009/10 - 2013/14

£ thousands

		Financial Aid			Technical Co-operation	Bilateral aid delivered through a Multilateral	Bilateral aid Delivered through an NGO	Other Bilateral Aid[2]	Humanitarian Assistance	DFID Debt Relief	Total DFID Bilateral Programme[5]
		General Poverty Reduction Budget Support	Sector Poverty Reduction Budget Support	Other Financial Aid[4]							
Europe	2009/10	-	3,500	1,076	7,522	5,949	1,346	2	1,161	297	20,853
	2010/11	-	2,500	2,239	7,030	4,703	937	68	26	365	17,868
	2011/12	-	-	-	3,230	244	344	-14	425	378	4,607
	2012/13	-	-	6,746	2,305	782	193	12	7	-	10,046
	2013/14	-	-	6,340	25	66	-	12	129	-	6,573
Pacific	2009/10	-	-	1,745	3	-	139	-	100	155	2,142
	2010/11	-	-	2,235	212	-	-	-	-	191	2,638
	2011/12	-	-	2,738	36	-	-	-	-	212	2,986
	2012/13	-	-	2,883	11	-	-	-	150	166	3,210
	2013/14	-	-	2,839	-	-	-	-	-	44	2,883
Non Region Specific	2009/10	-	-	442	76,892	684,081	313,371	1,293	22,671	35,203	1,133,952
	2010/11	-	-	442	73,386	736,445	355,473	11,553	22,442	332	1,200,074
	2011/12	-	-	167	80,546	590,230	393,421	20,473	2,161	3,433	1,090,431
	2012/13	-	-	-695	106,063	515,415	383,211	24,640	4,591	6,097	1,039,323
	2013/14	-	-	441	201,007	651,186	509,090	39,051	39,608	5,593	1,445,976
Total Developing Countries[3]	2009/10	383,150	250,951	514,817	419,384	1,263,457	599,192	34,668	434,386	52,061	3,952,066
	2010/11	360,467	283,204	550,728	467,358	1,464,655	626,506	76,009	349,290	66,460	4,244,679
	2011/12	242,290	294,372	541,881	525,763	1,404,592	739,319	81,372	354,131	14,954	4,198,672
	2012/13	167,343	242,790	685,571	638,258	1,074,957	747,302	119,120	476,878	17,169	4,169,389
	2013/14	106,600	460,474	601,174	901,264	1,436,580	999,557	171,970	866,485	9,172	5,553,275
Least Developed Countries	2009/10	285,150	139,191	240,570	137,112	240,247	163,571	20,634	279,621	3,636	1,509,732
	2010/11	274,467	167,454	248,317	165,797	396,371	164,974	36,065	199,400	19,896	1,672,742
	2011/12	210,000	210,372	196,839	160,589	408,071	221,335	36,995	147,398	4,612	1,596,211
	2012/13	153,235	203,090	329,843	220,994	273,248	232,812	66,016	282,805	4,857	1,766,900
	2013/14	93,668	299,024	302,854	295,780	426,444	298,523	59,634	344,688	44	2,120,659

3.2 DFID Bilateral Gross Public Expenditure by Region and Country Groupings 2009/10 - 2013/14[1]

£ thousands

		Financial Aid									
		General Poverty Reduction Budget Support	Sector Poverty Reduction Budget Support	Other Financial Aid[4]	Technical Co-operation	Bilateral aid delivered through a Multilateral	Bilateral aid Delivered through an NGO	Other Bilateral Aid[2]	Humanitarian Assistance	DFID Debt Relief	Total DFID Bilateral Programme[5]
Commonwealth	2009/10	330,150	133,084	341,646	207,327	144,154	152,690	7,766	77,445	1,740	**1,396,002**
	2010/11	340,467	169,254	362,725	250,728	247,917	139,987	35,191	96,664	1,111	**1,644,044**
	2011/12	222,290	147,539	441,137	278,081	305,734	191,852	30,273	94,825	1,135	**1,712,866**
	2012/13	167,343	114,290	487,666	329,497	204,792	208,203	52,367	80,472	1,291	**1,645,921**
	2013/14	-	-	-	1,546	-	252	117,901	-	-	**119,699**
of which	**2009/10**	-	-	**45,921**	**3,719**	-	**139**	-	**170**	-	**49,948**
Overseas Territories	**2010/11**	-	-	**45,882**	**7,142**	-	**242**	-	-	-	**53,267**
	2011/12	-	-	**88,269**	**4,232**	-	**90**	-	-	-	**92,591**
	2012/13	-	-	**130,123**	**3,581**	-	**201**	-	-	-	**133,905**
	2013/14	-	-	**117,901**	**1,546**	-	**252**	-	-	-	**119,699**
HIPC Countries[6]	2009/10	333,150	158,163	189,869	82,710	190,877	83,056	11,350	262,912	-478	**1,311,608**
	2010/11	310,467	185,454	193,421	115,476	318,635	88,733	26,442	184,608	55,564	**1,478,800**
	2011/12	222,290	242,372	154,929	114,231	290,711	122,120	29,698	132,324	-	**1,308,676**
	2012/13	167,343	213,090	171,428	303,951	190,153	122,886	59,125	245,884	-	**1,473,861**
	2013/14	106,600	301,524	254,558	234,391	266,066	187,735	39,630	302,209	-	**1,692,713**

Source: Department for International Development

1. Descriptions of aid types given in Technical Note 1.
2. Other Bilateral Aid covers bilateral aid not elsewhere classified
3. Developing Countries are those countries and regions in the DAC List of Recipients of Official Development Assistance. Since the 2008 edition of SID, Turks and Caicos,Barbados and Trinidad & Tobago and Saudi Arabia have been removed from the DAC list.
4. Pension payments have been reclassified from "Other Financial Aid" to "Aid from other UK Official Sources". This is consistent with the classification of spending under Department Expenditure Limits (DEL) agreed with Treasury.
5. Includes Non Region Specific
6. Highly Indebted Poor Countries

3.3: DFID Bilateral Expenditure by Input Sector Code 2009/10 to 2013/14

£ thousand

Input Sector Code	2009/10	2010/11	2011/12	2012/13	2013/14
Education:					
11010 Education Poverty Reduction Budget Support	155,629	152,581	90,301	135,395	181,996
11020 Education Unallocable/Unspecified	1,489	8,718	51,403	6,399	15,311
11110 Education Policy and Administrative Management	53,549	68,527	122,537	63,369	116,728
11120 Facilities and Training Education	34,929	31,044	44,756	25,531	8,609
11130 Teacher Training	14,135	17,775	15,879	24,181	24,727
11220 Primary Education	111,045	210,797	231,124	143,204	242,755
11230 Basic Life Skills for Youth and Adults Education	3,749	10,933	11,426	25,215	29,378
11240 Pre-School	4,717	4,337	3,717	2,123	849
11320 Secondary Education	8,040	27,059	28,089	58,090	119,432
11330 Vocational Training	4,820	8,588	6,609	7,028	7,241
11420 Higher Education	2,677	20,237	19,267	21,146	26,990
11430 Advanced Technical and Managerial Training	269	312	281	562	738
Education Total	**395,049**	**560,907**	**625,389**	**512,243**	**774,754**
Health:					
12010 Health Poverty Reduction Budget Support	111,811	100,327	57,306	48,440	46,270
12020 Health Unallocable/Unspecified	2,585	3,712	13,504	8,346	12,944
12110 Health Policy and Administrative Management	46,829	58,667	43,590	56,090	79,308
12220 Basic Health Care	91,566	74,650	105,712	144,027	151,359
12240 Basic Nutrition	19,365	23,715	37,505	49,433	64,363
12250 Infectious Disease Control	61,487	73,853	146,612	105,375	187,174
12261 Health Education	19,919	26,392	31,717	34,434	39,817
12262 Malaria Control	42,295	101,393	86,181	111,521	166,897
12263 Tuberculosis Control	13,577	44,187	10,051	12,735	12,455
12281 Health Personnel Development	10,368	7,773	12,295	12,611	19,825
13010 Population Policy and Administrative Management	2,949	7,092	6,063	5,463	11,535
13021 Reproductive Health Care	43,196	47,962	108,852	36,746	49,428
13022 Maternal and Neonatal Health	49,376	49,987	121,362	125,862	163,402
13030 Family Planning	15,252	31,082	43,767	109,727	127,019
13041 HIV/AIDS including STD Prevention	122,036	119,094	69,002	50,271	37,459
13042 HIV/AIDS including STD Treatment and Care	24,002	52,717	27,331	40,160	10,942
13081 Personnel Development for Population and Reproductive Health	6,676	7,506	8,332	7,543	9,274
Health Total	**683,289**	**830,109**	**929,182**	**958,785**	**1,189,468**
Social Infrastructure and Services:					
16011 Social Protection	156,911	186,531	103,647	104,931	138,082
16012 Social Other	27,923	48,714	83,879	53,237	88,583
16020 Employment Policy & Admin Management	623	2,956	2,924	4,271	7,459
16030 Housing Policy and Admin Management	623	73	594	566	943
16040 Low-cost Housing	2,226	1,706	5,693	7,867	3,403
16070 Poverty Reduction Budget Support-Social infrastructure and services	23,319	18,273	12,940	7,078	12,392
52010 Food Aid and Food Security Programmes	26,468	52,145	50,622	47,148	54,806
Social Infrastructure and Services Total	**238,093**	**310,396**	**260,300**	**225,098**	**305,667**
Water Supply and Sanitation:					
14010 Water Resources Policy and Administrative Management	20,611	14,317	20,655	14,926	29,139
14015 Water Resources Protection	1,323	2,335	5,216	5,192	6,541
14020 Water Supply and Sanitation Large Systems	3,081	4,869	9,175	10,934	13,458
14021 Water Supply – Large Systems	54	4,039	5,100	-	-730
14030 Basic Drinking Water	55,820	63,219	73,031	55,664	400
14031 Basic drinking water supply	72	964	891	2,581	51,941
14032 Basic sanitation	88	1,466	7,605	17,237	3,084
14040 River Development	5,439	3,688	1,360	29	25,430
14050 Waste Management and Disposal	2,900	2,669	2,519	3,737	3,328
14060 Water Poverty Reduction Budget Support	15,556	13,271	8,255	9,134	10,539
14070 Water Unallocable/Unspecified	718	868	6,976	9,623	14,315
14081 Education and Training	250	354	1,408	962	5,651
Water Supply and Sanitation Total	**105,912**	**112,061**	**142,191**	**130,020**	**163,096**
Government and Civil Society:					
15010 Government Poverty Reduction Budget Support	137,078	115,004	58,494	37,665	25,034
15020 Government Unallocated/ Unspecified	26,082	52,166	37,876	42,945	57,967
15110 Economic and Development Policy/Planning	114,791	121,076	90,314	86,146	111,772
15121 Public Sector Financial Management	113,514	105,996	132,449	126,422	83,940
15122 Corruption - Public Sector Financial Management	13,182	17,719	18,010	16,677	24,254
15130 Legal and Judicial Development	18,469	17,351	18,158	15,623	23,218

3.3: DFID Bilateral Expenditure by Input Sector Code 2009/10 to 2013/14

£ thousand

Input Sector Code	2009/10	2010/11	2011/12	2012/13	2013/14
15141 National Government Administration	16,791	30,876	33,736	49,375	43,878
15142 Local Government Administration	42,417	36,266	57,607	53,882	28,903
15150 Strengthening Civil Society	89,251	116,792	121,683	102,697	111,472
15161 Elections	18,539	33,880	28,920	1,877	33,212
15162 Human Rights	9,084	10,688	10,284	27,490	12,991
15163 Free Flow of Information	7,419	9,997	10,144	9,369	17,971
15164 Women's Equality Organisations and Institutions	6,138	12,306	11,742	13,170	21,999
15171 Culture and Recreation	143	82		-	
15172 Statistical Capacity Building	27,935	40,395	31,102	15,752	37,682
15173 Narcotics Control	46	53	24	21,880	63
15210 Security System Management and Reform	13,338	19,285	27,065	34,429	29,462
15220 Civilian Peace-Building, Conflict Prevention and Resolution	39,409	20,497	21,597	38,480	49,842
15230 Post-Conflict Peace-Building (UN)	5,689	6,520	5,719	9,257	9,130
15240 Reintegration and SALW Control	6,377	4,683	754	269	696
15250 Land Mine Clearance	9,907	9,902	11,720	10,586	8,955
15261 Child Soldiers (Prevention and Demobilisation)	261	141	159	14	
Government and Civil Society Total	**715,860**	**781,674**	**727,557**	**714,004**	**736,329**
Economic:					
Economic Infrastructure					
21010 Transport Policy and Administrative Management	39,007	65,697	42,208	53,921	52,833
21021 Road Transport: Excluding Rural Feeder Roads	36,405	37,096	26,548	24,630	31,739
21022 Road Transport: Rural Feeder Roads	8,745	15,224	17,222	9,427	26,326
21031 Other Transport	12,832	5,755	22,965	45,652	50,437
22010 Communications Policy and Administrative Management	8,150	6,065	1,680	1,649	1,998
22020 Telecommunications	9,439	8,596	8,892	1,444	364
22030 Radio/Television/Print Media: Communications	1,872	64	38	1	-
22040 Information and Communication Technology (ICT)	519	2,055	655	135	407
23010 Energy Policy and Administrative Management	23,993	35,208	12,887	14,973	26,779
23020 Power Generation/Non-Renewable Sources: Energy	7,439	11,809	9,760	3,628	5,924
23030 Power Generation/Renewable Sources: Energy	23,513	30,633	3,956	13,090	22,751
23040 Energy Access for Households, Enterprises and Communities: Energy (Wealth Creation)					17
24010 Financial Policy and Administrative Management	24,223	26,098	27,913	26,940	38,290
24020 Monetary Institutions	205,870	1,319	3,111	1,409	634
24030 Formal Sector Financial Intermediaries	6,239	10,968	12,825	14,092	48,896
24040 Informal/Semi-Formal Financial Intermediaries	6,250	7,449	6,764	10,277	26,203
24081 Education/Training in Banking and Financial Services	2,382	2,471	4,877	3,518	5,868
25010 Business Support Services and Institutions	16,947	29,087	25,071	29,458	45,966
25020 Privatisation	5,765	7,896	5,479	4,626	4,853
Production Sectors					
31110 Agriculture Policy and Administrative Management	43,937	38,879	34,080	19,891	35,408
31120 Agricultural Development	26,089	18,023	37,625	18,877	39,261
31130 Agricultural Land Resources	7,555	11,033	4,115	3,639	5,972
31163 Livestock: Agriculture	3,231	2,281	2,895	5,133	5,967
31191 Agricultural Services	1,287	865	2,766	4,617	10,101
31210 Forestry Policy and Administrative Management	16,583	30,650	4,910	15,936	14,683
31220 Forestry Development	15,320	28,989	4,351	865	419
31310 Fishing Policy and Administrative Management	2,368	3,046	1,838	1,496	1,469
31320 Fishery Development	201	265	0	9	99
32110 Industrial Policy and Administrative Management	548	1,068	1,632	2,054	1,223
32120 Industrial Development	934	2,034	2,816	1,901	4,458
32130 Small and Medium-Sized Enterprises (SME): Development	24,765	30,011	25,575	20,686	36,225
32210 Mineral/Mining Policy and Administrative Management	679	369	8,663	5,287	3,229
32310 Construction Policy and Administrative Management	105	939	2,503	1,430	1,228
32350 Production Poverty Reduction Budget Support	34,237	30,984	18,803	15,905	7,718
33110 Trade Policy and Administrative Management	34,430	30,713	19,204	18,423	19,172
33120 Trade Facilitation	29,745	40,024	11,613	16,343	22,318
33130 Regional Trade Agreements (RTAs)	3,685	6,792	4,191	6,031	13,192
33140 Multilateral Trade Negotiations	741	120	273	1,742	3,676
33181 Trade Education/Training	360	613	838	400	676
33210 Tourism Policy and Administrative Management	829	1,272	2,215	1,345	429
43050 Non-Agricultural Alternative Development	550	818	1,692	2,132	2,283
Development Planning					
43020 Poverty Reduction Budget Support for Econ. Infrastructure & Dev. Planning	108,985	67,825	42,162	26,009	42,885
43030 Urban Development and Management	16,626	30,362	19,907	28,356	26,378
43040 Rural Development	51,502	68,083	55,302	53,854	91,862
Economic Total	**865,063**	**749,546**	**542,821**	**531,231**	**780,618**

3.3: DFID Bilateral Expenditure by Input Sector Code 2009/10 to 2013/14

£ thousand

Input Sector Code	2009/10	2010/11	2011/12	2012/13	2013/14
Environment Protection:					
41010 Environmental Policy and Administrative Management	15,071	16,512	9,506	7,029	8,402
41031 Bio-Diversity	1,869	198	3,264	963	1,245
41032 Climate Change	54,926	2,191	30,997	59,724	113,595
41033 Desertification	624	101,790		1,711	
41040 Site Preservation	15	242			
41050 Flood Prevention/Control	188	22	898		6,113
41060 Environment: Poverty Reduction Budget Support	3,359	377	1,418	627	210
41070 Environment Unallocable/Unspecified	38	1,846	3,104	6,011	7,864
41081 Environmental Education/ Training	1,804	1,905	2,591	2,302	2,213
41090 Climate Change - Low Carbon Emissions			55,772	12,688	16,858
41092 Climate Change - Cross Cutting			2,811	4,319	51
41093 Climate Change - Adaptation			99,048	141,088	63,644
74010 Disaster Prevention and Preparedness	21,450	10,142	7,896	1,784	35,024
Environment Protection Total	**99,344**	**135,226**	**217,304**	**238,246**	**220,196**
Research:					
80010 Economic Research	9,784	12,651	16,350	20,533	30,275
80011 Education Research	3,076	1,775	2,884	5,121	15,597
80012 Health Research	66,816	46,997	49,312	49,412	58,734
80013 Water Supply and Sanitation Research	908	2,064	1,502	1,748	2,600
80014 Governance Research	9,923	6,825	11,836	9,781	11,054
80015 Social Research	11,529	12,257	8,327	11,248	12,850
80016 Humanitarian Research	939	1,185	1,163	1,486	6,354
80017 Renewable Natural Resources Research	20,000	7,603	6,139	1,596	1,246
80018 Environment Research	5,044	6,883	8,968	11,375	13,483
80019 Energy Research	17	817	1,037	2,553	6,346
80020 Agricultural Research	11,397	19,624	22,073	33,287	37,356
80021 Forestry Research	403	269	54		
80022 Fishery Research	70	169			23
80023 Technological Research and Development	2,436	1,541	1,210	1,670	4,486
80024 Unspecified/Unallocated Research	3,983	7,442	9,253	17,182	31,160
Research Total	**146,325**	**128,103**	**140,109**	**166,994**	**231,566**
Humanitarian Assistance:					
72010 Material Relief Assistance and Services	232,635	198,368	157,678	243,333	407,196
72040 Emergency Food Aid	96,986	68,862	106,548	145,762	259,547
72050 Relief Coordination, Protection and Support Services	56,769	61,763	38,336	69,742	128,549
73010 Reconstruction Relief and Rehabilitation	50,861	27,996	47,043	14,345	36,124
Humanitarian Assistance Total	**437,250**	**356,989**	**349,604**	**473,182**	**866,440**
Non Sector Allocable:					
Core Contributions to Multilateral Institutions - Global Partnerships					200
Core Contributions to Multilateral Institutions - Governance & Security					3,214
Core Contributions to Multilateral Institutions - MDG Humanitarian					10,014
Core Contributions to Multilateral Institutions - MDG Other Health					1,875
Core Contributions to Multilateral Institutions - MDG Water & Sanitation					2,700
88889 Multilateral Capacity Building and Administration	27,836	17,850	42,463	2,675	2,940
88890 Multilateral Institutions: Secondees to & Staffing of	1,163	1,838	4,673	5,264	4,794
60010 Action Relating to Debt	50,992	66,483	15,110	17,440	9,172
90010 Programme Partnership Agreements	129,557	116,100	91,508	124,808	124,401
91010 Administrative Costs of Donors	559	1,236			
92000 Support to Non-Governmental Organisations (NGOs)	36,422	50,815	101,785	62,436	136,946
93020 Aid to Refugees in Recipient Countries	2,349	9,164	2,344	2,882	3,035
88888 Multilateral Core Contribution				-14,249	10,797
99820 Promotion of Development Awareness	28,372	19,300	11,775	16,008	9,352
Others				-684	-63,516
Non Sector Allocable Total	**277,249**	**283,006**	**269,658**	**219,589**	**255,922**

Source: Department for International Development (DFID)

1. '-' means nil
   '0' means less than half the final digit shown
   '..' means not available
   'n/a' means not applicable
2. Figures are rounded to the nearest unit, therefore they may not add exactly to the rounded totals.
3. Negative amounts reflect accounting adjustments.

Labour market

Chapter 4

Labour Market

Labour Force Survey

Background

The Labour Force Survey (LFS) is the largest regular household survey in the UK. LFS interviews are conducted continuously throughout the year. In any three-month period, nationally representative samples of approximately 110,000 people aged 16 and over in around 50,000 households are interviewed. Each household is interviewed five times, at three-monthly intervals. The initial interview is done face-to-face by an interviewer visiting the address, except for residents north of the Caledonian Canal in Scotland. The other interviews are done by telephone wherever possible. The survey asks a series of questions about respondents' personal circumstances and their labour market activity. Most questions refer to activity in the week before the interview.

The LFS collects information on a sample of the population. To convert this information to give estimates for the population, the data must be grossed. This is achieved by calculating weighting factors (often referred to simply as weights) which can be applied to each sampled individual in such a way that the weighted-up results match estimates or projections of the total population in terms of age distribution, sex, and region of residence. There is a considerable amount of ongoing research to improve methodologies. Whenever methodologies are implemented the estimates may be revised.

The concepts and definitions used in the LFS are agreed by the International Labour Organisation (ILO) – an agency of the United Nations. The definitions are used by European Union member countries and members of the Organisation for Economic Co-operation and Development (OECD). The LFS was carried out every two years from 1973 to 1983. The ILO definition was first used in 1984. This was also the first year in which the survey was conducted on an annual basis with results available for every spring quarter (representing an average of the period from March to May). The survey moved to a continuous basis in spring 1992 in Great Britain and in winter 1994/95 in Northern Ireland, with average quarterly results published four times a year for seasonal quarters: spring (March to May), summer (June to August), autumn (September to November) and winter (December to February). From April 1998, results are published 12 times a year for the average of three consecutive months.

Strengths and limitations of the LFS

The LFS produces coherent labour market information on the basis of internationally standard concepts and definitions. It is a rich source of data on a wide variety of labour market and personal characteristics. It is the most suitable source for making comparisons between countries. The LFS is designed so that households interviewed in each three month period constitute a representative sample of UK households. The survey covers those living in private households and nurses in

National Health Service accommodation. Students living in halls of residence have been included since 1992, as information about them is collected at their parents' address.

However the LFS has its limitations. It is a sample survey and is therefore subject to sampling variability. The survey does not include people living in institutions such as hostels, hotels, boarding houses, mobile home sites or residential homes. 'Proxy' reporting (when members of the household are not present at the interview, another member of the household answers the questions on their behalf) can affect the quality of information on topics such as earnings, hours worked, benefit receipt and qualifications. Around a third of interviews are conducted 'by proxy', usually by a spouse or partner but sometimes by a parent or other near relation. LFS estimates are also potentially affected by non-response.

Sampling Variability

Survey estimates are prone to sampling variability. The easiest way to explain this concept is by example. In the September to November 1997 period, ILO unemployment in Great Britain (seasonally adjusted) stood at 1,847,000. If we drew another sample for the same period we could get a different result, perhaps 1,900,000 or 1,820,000.

In theory, we could draw many samples, and each would give a different result. This is because each sample would be made up of different people who would give different answers to the questions. The spread of these results is the sampling variability. Sampling variability is determined by a number of factors including the sample size, the variability of the population from which the sample is drawn and the sample design. Once we know the sampling variability we can calculate a range of values about the sample estimate that represents the expected variation with a given level of assurance. This is called a confidence interval. For a 95 per cent confidence interval we expect that in 95 per cent of the samples (19 times out of 20) the confidence interval will contain the true value that would be obtained by surveying the entire population. For the example given above, we can be 95 per cent confident that the true value was in the range 1,791,000 to 1,903,000.

Unreliable estimates

Estimates of small numbers have relatively wide confidence intervals making them unreliable. For this reason, the Office for National Statistics (ONS) does not currently publish LFS estimates below 10,000.

Non-response

All surveys are subject to non-response – that is respondents in the sample who either refuse to take part in the survey or who cannot be contacted. Non-response can introduce bias to a survey, particularly if the people not responding have characteristics that are different from those who do respond.

The LFS has a response rate of around 65 per cent to the first interview, and over 90 per cent of those who are interviewed once go on to complete all five interviews. These are relatively high levels for a household survey.

Any bias from non-response is minimised by weighting the results. Weighting (or grossing) converts sample data to represent the full population. In the LFS, the data are weighted separately by age, sex and area of residence to population estimates based on the census. Weighting also adjusts for people not in the survey and thus minimises non-response bias.

LFS concepts and definitions

Discouraged worker - A sub-group of the economically inactive population who said although they would like a job their main reason for not seeking work was because they believed there were no jobs available.

Economically active – People aged 16 and over who are either in employment or unemployed.

Economic activity rate – The number of people who are in employment or unemployed expressed as a percentage of the relevant population.

Economically inactive – People who are neither in employment nor unemployed. These include those who want a job but have not been seeking work in the last four weeks, those who want a job and are seeking work but not available to start, and those who do not want a job.

Employment – People aged 16 and over who did at least one hour of paid work in the reference week (as an employee or self-employed), those who had a job that they were temporarily away from, those on government-supported training and employment programmes, and those doing unpaid family work.

Employees – The division between employees and self employed is based on survey respondents' own assessment of their employment status.

Full Time – The classification of employees, self-employed and unpaid family workers in their main job as full-time or part-time is on the basis of self-assessment. However, people on government supported employment and training programmes that are at college in the reference week are classified, by convention, as part-time.

Government -supported training and employment programmes – Comprise all people aged 16 and over participating in one of the government's employment and training programmes (Youth Training, Training for Work and Community Action), together with those on similar programmes administered by Training and Enterprise Councils in England and Wales, or Local Enterprise Companies in Scotland.

Hours worked – Respondents to the LFS are asked a series of questions enabling the identification of both their usual hours and their actual hours. Total hours include overtime (paid and unpaid) and exclude lunch breaks.

Actual Hours Worked – Actual hours worked statistics measure how many hours were actually worked. These statistics are directly affected by changes in the number of people in employment and in the number of hours that individual works.

Usual Hours Worked – Usual hours worked statistics measure how many hours people usually work per week. Compared with actual hours worked, they are not affected by absences and so can provide a better measure of normal working patterns.

Unemployment – The number of unemployed people in the UK is measured through the LFS following the internationally agreed definition recommended by the International Labour Organisation (ILO), an agency of the United Nations.

Unemployed people are:

Without a job, have actively sought work in the last four weeks and are available to start work in the next two weeks, or

Out of work, have found a job and are waiting to start in the next two weeks

Unemployment (rate) – The number of unemployed people expressed as a percentage of the relevant economically active population.

Unemployment (duration) – The duration of respondents unemployment is defined as the shorter of the following two periods:

Duration of active search for work

Length of time since employment

Part-time – see full-time.

Second jobs – Jobs which LFS respondents hold in addition to a main full-time or part-time job.

Self-employment – See Employees.

Temporary employees – In the LFS these are defined as those employees who say that their main job is non permanent in one of the following ways: fixed period contract, agency temping, casual work, seasonal work or other temporary work.

Unpaid family workers – Persons doing unpaid work for a business they own or for a business that a relative owns.

International Employment Comparisons

All employment rates for European Union (EU) countries published by Eurostat (including the rate for the UK) are based on the population aged 15–64. The rates for Canada and Japan are also based on the population aged 15–64, but the rate for the US is for those aged 16–64. The employment rate for the UK published by ONS is based on the working age population aged 16–64 (men) and 16–59 (women) and therefore takes into account both the current school leaving age and state pension ages.

The unemployment rate published by Eurostat for most EU countries (but not for the UK), are calculated by extrapolating from the most recent LFS data using monthly registered unemployment data. A standard population basis (15–74) is used by Eurostat except for Spain and the UK (16–74). The unemployment rate for the US is based on those aged 16 and over, but the rates for Canada and Japan are for those aged 15 and over. All unemployment rates are seasonally adjusted.

The unemployment rate for the UK published by Eurostat is based on the population aged 16–74 while the unemployment rate for the UK published by ONS is based on those aged 16 and over. There are other minor definitional differences.

Jobseekers allowance claimant count

This is a count of all those people who are claiming Jobseeker's Allowance (JSA) at Jobcentre Plus local offices. People claiming JSA must declare that they are:

- out of work
- capable of work
- available for work
- actively seeking work

during the week in which the claim is made.
All people claiming JSA on the day of the monthly count are included in the claimant count, irrespective of whether they are actually receiving benefits. Also see table 5.6 in Social protection chapter.

Annual Survey of Hours and Earnings

The Annual Survey of Hours and Earnings (ASHE) is based on a one per cent sample of employee jobs taken from HM Revenue & Customs (HMRC) PAYE records. Information on earnings and paid hours worked is obtained from employers and treated confidentially. ASHE does not cover the self-employed nor does it cover employees not paid during the reference period.

The headline statistics for ASHE are based on the median rather than the mean. The median is the value below which 50 per cent of employees fall. It is ONS's preferred measure of average earnings as it is less affected by a relatively small number of very high earners and the skewed distribution of earnings. It therefore gives a better indication of typical pay than the mean.

The earnings information presented relates to gross pay before tax, National Insurance or other deductions, and excludes payments in kind. With the exception of annual earnings, the results are restricted to earnings relating to the survey pay period and so exclude payments of arrears from another period made during the survey period; any payments due as a result of a pay settlement but not yet paid at the time of the survey will also be excluded.

Average Weekly Earnings

The Average Weekly Earnings (AWE) indicator measures changes in the level of earnings in Great Britain. Average earnings are calculated as the total wages and salaries paid by firms, divided by the number of employees paid. It is given as a level, in pounds per employee per week. Annual growth rates are derived from the level of average weekly earnings.

The AWE data are now published on a SIC 2007 basis, and the historic time series have been re-estimated as a result.

AWE is based on the Monthly wages and Salaries Survey (MWSS). As such, it is a timely indicator of changes in the level of earnings. The survey does not cover businesses with fewer than 20 employees; an adjustment is made to AWE to reflect these businesses. Note that the survey does not include Northern Ireland.

Unlike the previous measure of average earnings (the Average Earnings Index), changes in the composition of the workforce have an impact on AWE. If a high-paying sector of the economy employs more people, other things staying the same, average earnings will increase.

Average Weekly Earnings, like AEI before it, is a measure based on earnings per employee. If the number of paid hours worked per employee change, average earnings will also change.

Trade unions

The statistics relate to all organisations of workers known to the Certification Officer with head offices in Great Britain that fall within the appropriate definition of a trade union in the Trade Union and Labour Relations (Consolidation) Act 1992. Included in the data are home and overseas membership figures of contributory and non-contributory members. Employment status of members is not provided and the figures may therefore include some people who are self-employed, unemployed or retired.

4.1 Labour Force Summary by Sex: United Kingdom

		LFS household population[1]		Headline indicators					
				Employment		Unemployment		Inactivity	
				Level	Rate[2]	Level	Rate[3]	Level	Rate[4]
		All aged 16 & over	All aged 16 to 64	All aged 16 & over	All aged 16 to 64	All aged 16 & over	All aged 16 & over	All aged 16 to 64	All aged 16 to 64
People		**MGSL**	**LF2O**	**MGRZ**	**LF24**	**MGSC**	**MGSX**	**LF2M**	**LF2S**
	Aug-Oct 2012	51,045	40,508	29,740	71.0	2,539	7.9	9,215	22.7
	Aug-Oct 2013	51,378	40,564	30,208	71.8	2,412	7.4	9,047	22.3
	Nov-Jan 2014	51,465	40,585	30,322	72.1	2,335	7.2	9,012	22.2
	Feb-Apr 2014	51,550	40,605	30,629	72.7	2,162	6.6	8,956	22.1
	May-Jul 2014	51,635	40,625	30,682	72.8	2,021	6.2	9,058	22.3
	Aug-Oct 2014	**51,718**	**40,649**	**30,796**	**73.0**	**1,958**	**6.0**	**9,056**	**22.3**
	Change on quarter	*83*	*24*	*115*	*0.2*	*-63*	*-0.2*	*-2*	*0.0*
	Change %	*0.2*	*0.1*	*0.4*		*-3.1*		*0.0*	
	Change on year	*340*	*85*	*588*	*1.1*	*-455*	*-1.4*	*9*	*0.0*
	Change %	*0.7*	*0.2*	*1.9*		*-18.8*		*0.1*	
Men		**MGSM**	**YBTG**	**MGSA**	**MGSV**	**MGSD**	**MGSY**	**YBSO**	**YBTM**
	Aug-Oct 2012	24,849	20,082	15,904	76.2	1,436	8.3	3,352	16.7
	Aug-Oct 2013	25,039	20,122	16,095	76.8	1,355	7.8	3,335	16.6
	Nov-Jan 2014	25,087	20,136	16,177	77.1	1,288	7.4	3,333	16.6
	Feb-Apr 2014	25,134	20,149	16,324	77.7	1,202	6.9	3,314	16.4
	May-Jul 2014	25,182	20,162	16,318	77.7	1,124	6.4	3,386	16.8
	Aug-Oct 2014	**25,228**	**20,178**	**16,384**	**77.9**	**1,092**	**6.2**	**3,391**	**16.8**
	Change on quarter	*46*	*15*	*66*	*0.1*	*-32*	*-0.2*	*4*	*0.0*
	Change %	*0.2*	*0.1*	*0.4*		*-2.8*		*0.1*	
	Change on year	*190*	*55*	*289*	*1.1*	*-263*	*-1.5*	*55*	*0.2*
	Change %	*0.8*	*0.3*	*1.8*		*-19.4*		*1.7*	
Women		**MGSN**	**LF2P**	**MGSB**	**LF25**	**MGSE**	**MGSZ**	**LF2N**	**LF2T**
	Aug-Oct 2012	26,196	20,426	13,836	65.9	1,103	7.4	5,863	28.7
	Aug-Oct 2013	26,340	20,441	14,113	66.9	1,058	7.0	5,712	27.9
	Nov-Jan 2014	26,378	20,449	14,145	67.2	1,047	6.9	5,679	27.8
	Feb-Apr 2014	26,416	20,456	14,305	67.8	960	6.3	5,642	27.6
	May-Jul 2014	26,454	20,463	14,364	67.9	897	5.9	5,672	27.7
	Aug-Oct 2014	**26,490**	**20,471**	**14,412**	**68.1**	**866**	**5.7**	**5,666**	**27.7**
	Change on quarter	*36*	*8*	*48*	*0.2*	*-31*	*-0.2*	*-6*	*0.0*
	Change %	*0.1*	*0.0*	*0.3*		*-3.5*		*-0.1*	
	Change on year	*150*	*30*	*299*	*1.2*	*-192*	*-1.3*	*-46*	*-0.3*
	Change %	*0.6*	*0.1*	*2.1*		*-18.1*		*-0.8*	

Source: Labour Force Survey
Labour market statistics enquiries: labour.market@ons.gsi.gov.uk

1. The Labour Force Survey (LFS) is a survey of the population of private households, student halls of residence and NHS accommodation.
2. The headline employment rate is the number of people aged 16 to 64 in employment divided by the population aged 16 to 64.
3. The headline unemployment rate is the number of unemployed people (aged 16+) divided by the economically active population (aged 16+). The economically active population is defined as those in employment plus those who are unemployed.
4. The headline inactivity rate is the number of economically inactive people aged 16 to 64 divided by the population aged 16 to 64.

Note on headline employment, unemployment and inactivity rates
The headline employment and inactivity rates are based on the population aged 16 to 64 but the headline unemployment rate is based on the economically active population aged 16 and over. The employment and inactivity rates for those aged 16 and over are affected by the inclusion of the retired population in the denominators and are therefore less meaningful than the rates for those aged from 16 to 64. However, for the unemployment rate for those aged 16 and over, no such effect occurs as the denominator for the unemployment rate is the economically active population which only includes people in work or actively seeking and able to work.

Note on headline employment, unemployment and inactivity levels
The headline employment and unemployment levels are for those aged 16 and over; they measure all people in work or actively seeking and able to work. However, the headline inactivity level is for those aged 16 to 64. The inactivity level for those aged 16 and over is less meaningful as it includes elderly people who have retired from the labour force.

4.2 Full-time, part-time and temporary workers

United Kingdom (thousands) seasonally adjusted

	All in employment					Full-time and part-time workers[1]						
	Total	Employees	Self employed	Unpaid family workers	Government supported training & employment programmes[2]	Total people working full-time	Total people working part-time	Employees working full-time	Employees working part-time	Self-employed people working full-time	Self-employed people working part-time	Total workers with second jobs
People (16+)	MGRZ	MGRN	MGRQ	MGRT	MGRW	YCBE	YCBH	YCBK	YCBN	YCBQ	YCBT	YCBW
Nov-Jan 2005	28,726	24,903	3,603	98	123	21,430	7,296	18,571	6,332	2,783	819	1,067
Dec-Feb 2005	28,794	24,944	3,619	105	126	21,510	7,284	18,633	6,312	2,799	820	1,065
Jan-Mar 2005	28,789	24,949	3,608	105	127	21,509	7,280	18,630	6,319	2,798	810	1,061
Feb-Apr 2005	28,759	24,926	3,609	103	121	21,472	7,287	18,595	6,331	2,797	812	1,067
Mar-May 2005	28,780	24,926	3,637	102	114	21,452	7,327	18,551	6,375	2,820	817	1,084
Apr-Jun 2005	28,802	24,974	3,617	99	112	21,469	7,333	18,581	6,393	2,807	810	1,078
May-Jul 2005	28,855	25,023	3,626	95	111	21,520	7,335	18,625	6,398	2,818	809	1,071
Jun-Aug 2005	28,906	25,077	3,638	85	107	21,595	7,311	18,715	6,362	2,810	827	1,066
Jul-Sep 2005	28,928	25,066	3,666	90	106	21,625	7,303	18,722	6,345	2,831	835	1,071
Aug-Oct 2005	28,913	25,073	3,646	92	102	21,625	7,288	18,742	6,331	2,813	833	1,062
Sep-Nov 2005	28,880	25,006	3,680	92	102	21,604	7,276	18,701	6,305	2,831	849	1,036
Oct-Dec 2005	28,880	24,999	3,683	90	108	21,623	7,257	18,719	6,280	2,833	850	1,032
Nov-Jan 2006	28,934	25,046	3,692	92	104	21,660	7,274	18,746	6,300	2,842	851	1,038
Dec-Feb 2006	28,988	25,092	3,714	88	94	21,678	7,309	18,761	6,331	2,851	863	1,047
Jan-Mar 2006	29,048	25,143	3,724	89	93	21,704	7,344	18,774	6,369	2,865	859	1,029
Feb-Apr 2006	29,085	25,170	3,738	85	92	21,757	7,328	18,818	6,352	2,874	865	1,035
Mar-May 2006	29,063	25,179	3,703	86	95	21,745	7,319	18,833	6,347	2,852	850	1,025
Apr-Jun 2006	29,106	25,210	3,711	91	94	21,745	7,360	18,831	6,379	2,853	858	1,048
May-Jul 2006	29,140	25,226	3,726	99	90	21,769	7,371	18,847	6,379	2,858	869	1,053
Jun-Aug 2006	29,224	25,283	3,749	105	87	21,821	7,402	18,875	6,408	2,880	869	1,060
Jul-Sep 2006	29,183	25,211	3,771	104	98	21,763	7,421	18,817	6,394	2,877	895	1,068
Aug-Oct 2006	29,189	25,195	3,795	98	101	21,709	7,480	18,755	6,440	2,888	908	1,067
Sep-Nov 2006	29,204	25,200	3,788	101	115	21,745	7,459	18,779	6,421	2,895	893	1,059
Oct-Dec 2006	29,214	25,217	3,789	102	106	21,749	7,466	18,787	6,431	2,896	893	1,081
Nov-Jan 2007	29,202	25,186	3,809	100	107	21,753	7,449	18,762	6,424	2,924	885	1,072
Dec-Feb 2007	29,175	25,155	3,816	99	105	21,748	7,427	18,760	6,394	2,922	894	1,076
Jan-Mar 2007	29,194	25,169	3,821	103	100	21,756	7,438	18,782	6,387	2,908	914	1,074
Feb-Apr 2007	29,232	25,211	3,821	101	100	21,797	7,435	18,829	6,382	2,905	915	1,095
Mar-May 2007	29,314	25,310	3,801	99	104	21,896	7,419	18,926	6,384	2,907	894	1,100
Apr-Jun 2007	29,322	25,310	3,803	98	111	21,902	7,420	18,935	6,375	2,907	896	1,107
May-Jul 2007	29,352	25,319	3,811	104	118	21,921	7,431	18,965	6,355	2,897	914	1,118
Jun-Aug 2007	29,376	25,330	3,830	102	113	21,947	7,428	18,983	6,347	2,904	926	1,117
Jul-Sep 2007	29,420	25,380	3,832	97	111	21,989	7,431	19,026	6,354	2,902	930	1,103
Aug-Oct 2007	29,470	25,422	3,841	97	111	22,038	7,433	19,067	6,355	2,911	930	1,115
Sep-Nov 2007	29,527	25,471	3,843	103	110	22,054	7,472	19,086	6,385	2,901	942	1,116
Oct-Dec 2007	29,576	25,521	3,834	106	114	22,075	7,501	19,104	6,417	2,899	936	1,126
Nov-Jan 2008	29,614	25,546	3,847	109	112	22,083	7,531	19,108	6,438	2,901	947	1,112
Dec-Feb 2008	29,676	25,557	3,892	110	117	22,130	7,546	19,100	6,457	2,955	937	1,125
Jan-Mar 2008	29,684	25,582	3,878	109	115	22,134	7,549	19,123	6,459	2,946	932	1,103
Feb-Apr 2008	29,706	25,623	3,851	115	117	22,160	7,546	19,150	6,473	2,939	911	1,121
Mar-May 2008	29,749	25,657	3,856	116	119	22,227	7,522	19,216	6,441	2,941	915	1,116
Apr-Jun 2008	29,722	25,641	3,859	111	110	22,189	7,533	19,176	6,465	2,947	912	1,130
May-Jul 2008	29,696	25,629	3,854	101	112	22,170	7,526	19,166	6,463	2,942	912	1,131
Jun-Aug 2008	29,612	25,591	3,826	90	105	22,081	7,531	19,117	6,473	2,913	913	1,120
Jul-Sep 2008	29,580	25,566	3,818	90	107	22,061	7,519	19,097	6,469	2,915	903	1,126
Aug-Oct 2008	29,535	25,545	3,794	91	105	22,010	7,525	19,075	6,469	2,886	908	1,127
Sep-Nov 2008	29,556	25,532	3,830	91	103	21,959	7,597	19,016	6,516	2,900	930	1,145
Oct-Dec 2008	29,528	25,507	3,828	94	100	21,951	7,578	19,007	6,499	2,898	930	1,142
Nov-Jan 2009	29,539	25,508	3,845	88	99	21,952	7,587	18,994	6,514	2,918	927	1,152
Dec-Feb 2009	29,429	25,416	3,826	85	102	21,843	7,586	18,867	6,549	2,919	907	1,155
Jan-Mar 2009	29,366	25,335	3,844	87	101	21,768	7,598	18,794	6,540	2,918	926	1,161
Feb-Apr 2009	29,272	25,220	3,860	88	103	21,715	7,557	18,747	6,474	2,911	949	1,156
Mar-May 2009	29,155	25,096	3,856	101	102	21,585	7,570	18,641	6,455	2,892	964	1,143
Apr-Jun 2009	29,087	25,043	3,843	98	104	21,479	7,609	18,553	6,490	2,869	974	1,126
May-Jul 2009	29,018	24,962	3,858	91	107	21,412	7,606	18,462	6,500	2,895	963	1,121
Jun-Aug 2009	29,076	24,987	3,894	84	110	21,446	7,630	18,466	6,521	2,923	971	1,139
Jul-Sep 2009	29,069	25,002	3,881	78	109	21,388	7,681	18,434	6,568	2,903	978	1,143
Aug-Oct 2009	29,084	25,019	3,881	83	102	21,349	7,734	18,392	6,627	2,909	971	1,146
Sep-Nov 2009	29,092	25,013	3,896	76	107	21,344	7,748	18,401	6,611	2,898	998	1,129
Oct-Dec 2009	29,102	24,988	3,912	87	115	21,349	7,753	18,382	6,606	2,917	995	1,129
Nov-Jan 2010	29,057	24,947	3,906	86	119	21,291	7,766	18,335	6,612	2,906	999	1,094
Dec-Feb 2010	29,024	24,902	3,909	92	122	21,281	7,743	18,320	6,583	2,913	996	1,081
Jan-Mar 2010	29,013	24,844	3,954	90	124	21,234	7,778	18,247	6,598	2,940	1,014	1,067
Feb-Apr 2010	29,048	24,857	3,973	91	126	21,221	7,827	18,221	6,635	2,949	1,024	1,097
Mar-May 2010	29,144	24,960	3,959	93	131	21,265	7,878	18,278	6,683	2,932	1,027	1,134
Apr-Jun 2010	29,192	25,019	3,949	90	133	21,301	7,891	18,315	6,704	2,928	1,021	1,136
May-Jul 2010	29,325	25,094	3,989	103	139	21,335	7,991	18,323	6,771	2,949	1,040	1,134
Jun-Aug 2010	29,339	25,105	3,993	109	132	21,314	8,025	18,291	6,814	2,962	1,031	1,121
Jul-Sep 2010	29,385	25,106	4,046	105	129	21,341	8,044	18,294	6,812	2,990	1,055	1,121
Aug-Oct 2010	29,308	25,101	3,980	99	127	21,289	8,019	18,306	6,795	2,932	1,048	1,114
Sep-Nov 2010	29,284	25,056	4,003	94	131	21,282	8,001	18,285	6,771	2,944	1,059	1,114
Oct-Dec 2010	29,324	25,098	4,009	93	125	21,326	7,999	18,337	6,761	2,938	1,071	1,121
Nov-Jan 2011	29,391	25,138	4,025	100	129	21,387	8,004	18,406	6,732	2,929	1,096	1,151
Dec-Feb 2011	29,442	25,192	4,026	98	126	21,433	8,009	18,472	6,720	2,916	1,109	1,174
Jan-Mar 2011	29,441	25,235	3,983	98	125	21,437	8,005	18,507	6,728	2,883	1,100	1,166
Feb-Apr 2011	29,436	25,217	4,009	93	117	21,414	8,021	18,474	6,743	2,893	1,116	1,153
Mar-May 2011	29,466	25,249	4,022	91	104	21,451	8,016	18,519	6,731	2,891	1,131	1,151

4.2 Full-time, part-time and temporary workers

United Kingdom (thousands) seasonally adjusted

	All in employment					Full-time and part-time workers[1]						
People (16+)	Total	Employees	Self employed	Unpaid family workers	Government supported training & employment programmes[2]	Total people working full-time	Total people working part-time	Employees working full-time	Employees working part-time	Self-employed people working full-time	Self-employed people working part-time	Total workers with second jobs
	MGRZ	MGRN	MGRQ	MGRT	MGRW	YCBE	YCBH	YCBK	YCBN	YCBQ	YCBT	YCBW
Apr-Jun 2011	29,447	25,247	4,008	96	96	21,476	7,971	18,527	6,720	2,906	1,102	1,136
May-Jul 2011	29,345	25,162	4,001	94	88	21,452	7,893	18,502	6,660	2,915	1,086	1,142
Jun-Aug 2011	29,299	25,066	4,051	100	81	21,441	7,858	18,451	6,615	2,952	1,099	1,123
Jul-Sep 2011	29,277	24,967	4,122	105	84	21,406	7,871	18,384	6,583	2,980	1,142	1,142
Aug-Oct 2011	29,297	24,944	4,156	110	88	21,397	7,900	18,323	6,622	3,022	1,133	1,141
Sep-Nov 2011	29,324	24,967	4,148	112	96	21,376	7,947	18,308	6,659	3,006	1,142	1,145
Oct-Dec 2011	29,340	25,019	4,114	110	97	21,364	7,976	18,320	6,698	2,989	1,126	1,127
Nov-Jan 2012	29,351	25,009	4,125	111	105	21,366	7,985	18,321	6,689	2,992	1,133	1,118
Dec-Feb 2012	29,386	25,014	4,152	100	120	21,346	8,041	18,303	6,712	2,987	1,165	1,147
Jan-Mar 2012	29,460	25,049	4,186	97	128	21,374	8,085	18,322	6,728	2,992	1,193	1,152
Feb-Apr 2012	29,495	25,068	4,194	99	133	21,415	8,079	18,344	6,724	3,010	1,184	1,149
Mar-May 2012	29,559	25,113	4,187	111	149	21,477	8,083	18,380	6,733	3,021	1,166	1,141
Apr-Jun 2012	29,663	25,180	4,225	112	147	21,521	8,142	18,405	6,775	3,035	1,189	1,124
May-Jul 2012	29,746	25,218	4,255	119	154	21,537	8,209	18,405	6,813	3,039	1,217	1,126
Jun-Aug 2012	29,780	25,278	4,235	112	156	21,565	8,216	18,460	6,818	3,014	1,220	1,117
Jul-Sep 2012	29,753	25,248	4,233	110	162	21,561	8,192	18,448	6,800	3,017	1,216	1,110
Aug-Oct 2012	29,740	25,240	4,225	108	166	21,554	8,186	18,435	6,805	3,025	1,201	1,121
Sep-Nov 2012	29,846	25,341	4,231	111	163	21,659	8,188	18,537	6,805	3,029	1,202	1,122
Oct-Dec 2012	29,910	25,380	4,251	112	166	21,738	8,171	18,601	6,779	3,042	1,209	1,147
Nov-Jan 2013	29,895	25,425	4,202	106	163	21,755	8,140	18,651	6,773	3,004	1,198	1,142
Dec-Feb 2013	29,827	25,355	4,215	102	154	21,703	8,124	18,599	6,756	3,006	1,209	1,121
Jan-Mar 2013	29,851	25,411	4,182	104	153	21,740	8,110	18,630	6,781	3,017	1,165	1,109
Feb-Apr 2013	29,889	25,408	4,214	106	161	21,734	8,155	18,623	6,785	3,026	1,188	1,098
Mar-May 2013	29,856	25,403	4,187	104	163	21,730	8,126	18,639	6,764	3,015	1,172	1,121
Apr-Jun 2013	29,935	25,454	4,201	115	165	21,786	8,149	18,682	6,773	3,020	1,181	1,124
May-Jul 2013	29,999	25,516	4,207	111	165	21,865	8,134	18,740	6,777	3,035	1,171	1,133
Jun-Aug 2013	30,028	25,502	4,244	116	165	21,891	8,137	18,727	6,775	3,068	1,176	1,158
Jul-Sep 2013	30,098	25,572	4,241	113	172	21,933	8,165	18,777	6,796	3,063	1,178	1,162
Aug-Oct 2013	30,208	25,629	4,296	117	167	21,982	8,226	18,802	6,827	3,093	1,203	1,165
Sep-Nov 2013	30,288	25,633	4,397	112	146	22,096	8,192	18,853	6,780	3,165	1,232	1,183
Oct-Dec 2013	30,288	25,627	4,413	107	141	22,137	8,151	18,873	6,754	3,182	1,230	1,177
Nov-Jan 2014	30,322	25,589	4,493	110	131	22,159	8,162	18,840	6,749	3,240	1,253	1,180
Dec-Feb 2014	30,491	25,719	4,524	116	132	22,240	8,252	18,894	6,825	3,260	1,265	1,156
Jan-Mar 2014	30,534	25,715	4,572	126	122	22,281	8,253	18,926	6,788	3,269	1,303	1,176
Feb-Apr 2014	30,629	25,817	4,564	127	121	22,382	8,247	19,029	6,788	3,264	1,300	1,179
Mar-May 2014	30,717	25,879	4,599	119	121	22,446	8,271	19,093	6,786	3,271	1,328	1,187
Apr-Jun 2014	30,680	25,831	4,608	115	127	22,413	8,268	19,062	6,769	3,269	1,339	1,210
May-Jul 2014	30,682	25,864	4,564	120	133	22,376	8,305	19,048	6,816	3,248	1,316	1,201
Jun-Aug 2014	30,763	25,986	4,523	126	128	22,483	8,281	19,149	6,837	3,255	1,268	1,223
Jul-Sep 2014	30,793	26,027	4,520	123	123	22,523	8,270	19,203	6,824	3,250	1,271	1,208
Aug-Oct 2014	30,796	26,029	4,535	115	117	22,542	8,254	19,223	6,807	3,253	1,282	1,204
Sep-Nov 2014	30,801	26,066	4,520	102	112	22,524	8,277	19,239	6,827	3,220	1,300	1,198
Oct-Dec 2014	30,896	26,181	4,501	102	113	22,597	8,299	19,337	6,843	3,197	1,304	1,197

Source: Labour Force Survey
Inquiries: Email: labour.market@ons.gsi.gov.uk
Tel: 01633 455 400

4.2 Full-time, part-time and temporary workers

	Temporary employees (reasons for temporary working)							Part-time workers (reasons for working part-time)[3]					
	Total	Total as % of all employees	Could not find permanent job	% that could not find permanent job	Did not want permanent job	Had a contract with period of training	Some other reason	Total[4]	Could not find full-time job	% that could not find full-time job	Did not want full-time job	Ill or disabled	Student or at school
People (16+)	YCBZ	YCCC	YCCF	YCCI	YCCL	YCCO	YCCR	YCCU	YCCX	YCDA	YCDD	YCDG	YCDJ
Nov-Jan 2005	1,499	6.0	357	23.8	426	113	603	7,152	539	7.5	5,248	167	1,170
Dec-Feb 2005	1,502	6.0	357	23.8	417	114	614	7,132	549	7.7	5,237	166	1,148
Jan-Mar 2005	1,466	5.9	357	24.4	403	102	603	7,129	568	8.0	5,220	166	1,141
Feb-Apr 2005	1,444	5.8	356	24.7	383	104	600	7,143	563	7.9	5,236	176	1,133
Mar-May 2005	1,445	5.8	357	24.7	380	105	603	7,193	585	8.1	5,271	168	1,138
Apr-Jun 2005	1,450	5.8	356	24.6	385	99	610	7,202	588	8.2	5,255	165	1,160
May-Jul 2005	1,473	5.9	355	24.1	401	107	609	7,207	592	8.2	5,246	162	1,173
Jun-Aug 2005	1,471	5.9	378	25.7	396	100	597	7,189	589	8.2	5,247	167	1,149
Jul-Sep 2005	1,481	5.9	393	26.5	394	104	590	7,181	598	8.3	5,248	169	1,139
Aug-Oct 2005	1,434	5.7	387	27.0	387	100	559	7,165	594	8.3	5,241	170	1,129
Sep-Nov 2005	1,421	5.7	371	26.1	378	102	569	7,154	614	8.6	5,227	168	1,112
Oct-Dec 2005	1,390	5.6	347	25.0	377	94	571	7,129	606	8.5	5,221	169	1,099
Nov-Jan 2006	1,432	5.7	364	25.4	388	105	575	7,150	612	8.6	5,226	169	1,107
Dec-Feb 2006	1,451	5.8	364	25.1	401	102	584	7,194	620	8.6	5,233	177	1,125
Jan-Mar 2006	1,486	5.9	374	25.2	410	114	588	7,227	620	8.6	5,256	175	1,133
Feb-Apr 2006	1,484	5.9	369	24.9	416	115	584	7,216	618	8.6	5,245	172	1,142
Mar-May 2006	1,478	5.9	369	25.0	412	115	582	7,197	610	8.5	5,228	171	1,147
Apr-Jun 2006	1,462	5.8	370	25.3	417	110	565	7,237	623	8.6	5,243	170	1,163
May-Jul 2006	1,439	5.7	359	24.9	414	99	566	7,247	632	8.7	5,233	176	1,170
Jun-Aug 2006	1,469	5.8	363	24.7	432	96	577	7,277	644	8.9	5,236	186	1,183
Jul-Sep 2006	1,466	5.8	367	25.0	433	94	573	7,290	646	8.9	5,228	186	1,197
Aug-Oct 2006	1,479	5.9	385	26.1	428	88	577	7,349	660	9.0	5,259	188	1,203
Sep-Nov 2006	1,495	5.9	391	26.2	437	94	573	7,313	662	9.1	5,240	190	1,177
Oct-Dec 2006	1,512	6.0	392	25.9	450	92	579	7,322	664	9.1	5,242	194	1,179
Nov-Jan 2007	1,529	6.1	399	26.1	442	105	583	7,309	668	9.1	5,235	198	1,166
Dec-Feb 2007	1,522	6.0	397	26.1	440	105	579	7,288	646	8.9	5,255	192	1,158
Jan-Mar 2007	1,534	6.1	405	26.4	435	112	583	7,300	660	9.0	5,257	189	1,162
Feb-Apr 2007	1,514	6.0	403	26.6	426	104	581	7,297	671	9.2	5,264	178	1,152
Mar-May 2007	1,513	6.0	407	26.9	422	101	584	7,278	685	9.4	5,246	176	1,140
Apr-Jun 2007	1,507	6.0	417	27.7	409	97	583	7,271	682	9.4	5,251	174	1,131
May-Jul 2007	1,501	5.9	411	27.4	412	92	586	7,270	697	9.6	5,228	181	1,131
Jun-Aug 2007	1,491	5.9	406	27.2	417	87	582	7,274	698	9.6	5,248	165	1,128
Jul-Sep 2007	1,485	5.9	393	26.4	421	84	587	7,285	694	9.5	5,259	169	1,127
Aug-Oct 2007	1,462	5.8	385	26.3	422	84	571	7,286	701	9.6	5,257	168	1,123
Sep-Nov 2007	1,478	5.8	380	25.7	432	83	583	7,326	698	9.5	5,286	173	1,136
Oct-Dec 2007	1,495	5.9	380	25.4	449	81	585	7,351	729	9.9	5,260	170	1,152
Nov-Jan 2008	1,473	5.8	367	24.9	440	78	588	7,385	739	10.0	5,273	174	1,160
Dec-Feb 2008	1,445	5.7	363	25.1	428	83	572	7,394	728	9.8	5,276	177	1,170
Jan-Mar 2008	1,430	5.6	363	25.4	426	83	558	7,391	705	9.5	5,290	184	1,168
Feb-Apr 2008	1,439	5.6	358	24.9	431	86	564	7,385	696	9.4	5,275	187	1,183
Mar-May 2008	1,420	5.5	357	25.1	404	85	574	7,356	671	9.1	5,281	193	1,165
Apr-Jun 2008	1,396	5.4	348	24.9	404	85	560	7,376	679	9.2	5,283	203	1,168
May-Jul 2008	1,385	5.4	351	25.3	391	88	555	7,376	689	9.3	5,268	215	1,162
Jun-Aug 2008	1,383	5.4	353	25.5	404	83	543	7,387	702	9.5	5,293	216	1,138
Jul-Sep 2008	1,390	5.4	360	25.9	402	88	540	7,373	715	9.7	5,280	207	1,130
Aug-Oct 2008	1,370	5.4	351	25.6	407	83	530	7,378	732	9.9	5,280	197	1,127
Sep-Nov 2008	1,403	5.5	364	26.0	399	84	555	7,446	753	10.1	5,312	199	1,138
Oct-Dec 2008	1,411	5.5	380	26.9	392	86	554	7,426	770	10.4	5,280	198	1,133
Nov-Jan 2009	1,425	5.6	397	27.8	390	91	546	7,441	815	11.0	5,256	191	1,133
Dec-Feb 2009	1,427	5.6	420	29.5	386	84	537	7,457	850	11.4	5,258	183	1,123
Jan-Mar 2009	1,428	5.6	426	29.8	386	81	536	7,466	875	11.7	5,257	184	1,111
Feb-Apr 2009	1,417	5.6	419	29.6	381	87	530	7,423	902	12.1	5,199	190	1,090
Mar-May 2009	1,404	5.6	417	29.7	384	92	512	7,419	936	12.6	5,163	191	1,087
Apr-Jun 2009	1,430	5.7	431	30.2	386	89	524	7,464	963	12.9	5,166	189	1,094
May-Jul 2009	1,429	5.7	443	31.0	371	84	531	7,465	972	13.0	5,176	181	1,086
Jun-Aug 2009	1,435	5.7	446	31.1	376	89	524	7,492	981	13.1	5,177	184	1,099
Jul-Sep 2009	1,450	5.8	464	32.0	377	85	525	7,547	1,002	13.3	5,196	189	1,115
Aug-Oct 2009	1,438	5.7	468	32.5	369	86	516	7,599	1,018	13.4	5,200	190	1,148
Sep-Nov 2009	1,437	5.7	490	34.1	365	76	506	7,608	1,038	13.6	5,198	183	1,144
Oct-Dec 2009	1,445	5.8	497	34.4	362	78	508	7,598	1,037	13.7	5,194	187	1,138
Nov-Jan 2010	1,451	5.8	499	34.4	370	77	505	7,611	1,045	13.7	5,197	185	1,141
Dec-Feb 2010	1,481	5.9	513	34.6	366	83	519	7,578	1,051	13.9	5,160	179	1,148
Jan-Mar 2010	1,482	6.0	513	34.6	366	79	524	7,612	1,071	14.1	5,187	168	1,140
Feb-Apr 2010	1,501	6.0	539	35.9	361	82	519	7,660	1,090	14.2	5,221	172	1,134
Mar-May 2010	1,541	6.2	554	36.0	375	80	532	7,710	1,073	13.9	5,280	167	1,148
Apr-Jun 2010	1,578	6.3	573	36.3	380	82	543	7,725	1,077	13.9	5,303	172	1,134
May-Jul 2010	1,577	6.3	571	36.2	383	80	543	7,814	1,115	14.3	5,313	171	1,175
Jun-Aug 2010	1,578	6.3	591	37.5	369	86	532	7,846	1,139	14.5	5,302	170	1,188
Jul-Sep 2010	1,588	6.3	600	37.8	370	87	531	7,868	1,153	14.7	5,311	165	1,190
Aug-Oct 2010	1,598	6.4	592	37.0	374	92	540	7,844	1,174	15.0	5,311	164	1,142
Sep-Nov 2010	1,575	6.3	589	37.4	354	94	538	7,828	1,178	15.0	5,341	172	1,085
Oct-Dec 2010	1,546	6.2	577	37.3	340	95	534	7,829	1,192	15.2	5,318	164	1,102
Nov-Jan 2011	1,567	6.2	579	37.0	341	93	553	7,828	1,180	15.1	5,349	164	1,080
Dec-Feb 2011	1,577	6.3	573	36.3	352	95	557	7,830	1,180	15.1	5,355	172	1,065
Jan-Mar 2011	1,595	6.3	579	36.3	357	100	558	7,828	1,188	15.2	5,338	182	1,063
Feb-Apr 2011	1,601	6.3	583	36.4	356	94	568	7,860	1,230	15.6	5,322	185	1,069
Mar-May 2011	1,605	6.4	582	36.3	363	92	568	7,862	1,259	16.0	5,312	180	1,056
Apr-Jun 2011	1,616	6.4	609	37.7	361	88	558	7,823	1,270	16.2	5,268	180	1,047
May-Jul 2011	1,568	6.2	578	36.9	354	85	551	7,749	1,288	16.6	5,188	182	1,033

4.2 Full-time, part-time and temporary workers

United Kingdom (thousands) seasonally adjusted

	Temporary employees (reasons for temporary working)							Part-time workers (reasons for working part-time)[3]					
	Total	Total as % of all employees	Could not find permanent job	% that could not find permanent job	Did not want permanent job	Had a contract with period of training	Some other reason	Total[4]	Could not find full-time job	% that could not find full-time job	Did not want full-time job	Ill or disabled	Student or at school
People (16+)	YCBZ	YCCC	YCCF	YCCI	YCCL	YCCO	YCCR	YCCU	YCCX	YCDA	YCDD	YCDG	YCDJ
Jun-Aug 2011	1,533	6.1	584	38.1	317	81	551	7,714	1,279	16.6	5,176	181	1,026
Jul-Sep 2011	1,525	6.1	582	38.2	330	85	528	7,726	1,275	16.5	5,177	189	1,033
Aug-Oct 2011	1,538	6.2	605	39.3	331	84	517	7,755	1,286	16.6	5,199	184	1,040
Sep-Nov 2011	1,553	6.2	594	38.2	354	89	516	7,799	1,331	17.1	5,191	184	1,049
Oct-Dec 2011	1,545	6.2	602	39.0	346	91	506	7,821	1,361	17.4	5,186	189	1,043
Nov-Jan 2012	1,559	6.2	610	39.1	342	98	509	7,822	1,397	17.9	5,164	189	1,028
Dec-Feb 2012	1,587	6.3	630	39.7	350	96	512	7,877	1,406	17.9	5,194	181	1,050
Jan-Mar 2012	1,570	6.3	618	39.4	337	90	524	7,921	1,414	17.9	5,217	191	1,048
Feb-Apr 2012	1,558	6.2	609	39.1	329	96	524	7,909	1,412	17.9	5,211	191	1,043
Mar-May 2012	1,578	6.3	638	40.4	319	95	526	7,899	1,396	17.7	5,216	191	1,044
Apr-Jun 2012	1,613	6.4	644	39.9	327	103	539	7,965	1,427	17.9	5,237	183	1,068
May-Jul 2012	1,655	6.6	661	40.0	347	100	546	8,032	1,431	17.8	5,306	181	1,066
Jun-Aug 2012	1,641	6.5	651	39.7	342	99	548	8,038	1,420	17.7	5,313	182	1,074
Jul-Sep 2012	1,628	6.4	656	40.3	336	92	542	8,016	1,414	17.6	5,317	181	1,053
Aug-Oct 2012	1,631	6.5	655	40.2	332	92	552	8,005	1,406	17.6	5,323	184	1,037
Sep-Nov 2012	1,649	6.5	655	39.7	344	90	560	8,004	1,404	17.5	5,334	182	1,024
Oct-Dec 2012	1,655	6.5	659	39.8	341	96	559	7,986	1,390	17.4	5,333	185	1,014
Nov-Jan 2013	1,640	6.5	655	40.0	334	96	555	7,972	1,407	17.7	5,323	186	996
Dec-Feb 2013	1,602	6.3	644	40.2	332	100	526	7,966	1,422	17.9	5,304	184	999
Jan-Mar 2013	1,615	6.4	651	40.3	331	104	528	7,947	1,419	17.9	5,278	178	1,016
Feb-Apr 2013	1,595	6.3	631	39.6	337	100	526	7,974	1,441	18.1	5,261	181	1,034
Mar-May 2013	1,589	6.3	625	39.3	328	103	534	7,936	1,463	18.4	5,212	180	1,017
Apr-Jun 2013	1,568	6.2	605	38.6	324	107	531	7,955	1,453	18.3	5,245	187	1,007
May-Jul 2013	1,571	6.2	607	38.7	314	112	537	7,951	1,464	18.4	5,228	187	1,009
Jun-Aug 2013	1,582	6.2	609	38.5	300	123	550	7,951	1,464	18.4	5,260	192	973
Jul-Sep 2013	1,606	6.3	603	37.5	319	126	559	7,973	1,464	18.4	5,257	193	993
Aug-Oct 2013	1,594	6.2	593	37.2	327	124	550	8,029	1,467	18.3	5,307	194	1,001
Sep-Nov 2013	1,602	6.2	583	36.4	329	130	559	8,010	1,444	18.0	5,298	191	1,026
Oct-Dec 2013	1,621	6.3	600	37.0	337	117	567	7,983	1,428	17.9	5,280	191	1,033
Nov-Jan 2014	1,621	6.3	593	36.6	347	116	566	8,002	1,437	18.0	5,282	194	1,038
Dec-Feb 2014	1,630	6.3	587	36.0	358	113	573	8,090	1,419	17.5	5,393	194	1,038
Jan-Mar 2014	1,655	6.4	593	35.9	357	117	589	8,092	1,419	17.5	5,415	191	1,024
Feb-Apr 2014	1,683	6.5	601	35.7	369	118	594	8,088	1,399	17.3	5,425	185	1,038
Mar-May 2014	1,684	6.5	602	35.7	370	121	591	8,114	1,361	16.8	5,490	192	1,032
Apr-Jun 2014	1,651	6.4	604	36.6	370	117	560	8,109	1,342	16.6	5,522	192	1,010
May-Jul 2014	1,676	6.5	613	36.6	373	121	568	8,135	1,340	16.5	5,560	182	1,011
Jun-Aug 2014	1,696	6.5	617	36.4	388	119	571	8,105	1,351	16.7	5,516	172	1,022
Jul-Sep 2014	1,701	6.5	597	35.1	420	122	563	8,095	1,340	16.5	5,522	174	1,017
Aug-Oct 2014	1,688	6.5	575	34.0	428	120	566	8,088	1,319	16.3	5,556	173	995
Sep-Nov 2014	1,679	6.4	578	34.4	416	121	564	8,127	1,319	16.2	5,570	186	1,010
Oct-Dec 2014	1,704	6.5	581	34.1	412	114	598	8,148	1,312	16.1	5,565	189	1,033

Source: Labour Force Survey
Inquiries: Email: labour.market@ons.gsi.gov.uk
Tel: 01633 455 400

4.2 Full-time, part-time and temporary workers

United Kingdom (thousands) seasonally adjusted

	All in employment					Full-time and part-time workers[1]						
	Total	Employees	Self employed	Unpaid family workers	Government supported training & employment programmes[2]	Total people working full-time	Total people working part-time	Employees working full-time	Employees working part-time	Self-employed people working full-time	Self-employed people working part-time	Total workers with second jobs
Men (16+)	MGSA	MGRO	MGRR	MGRU	MGRX	YCBF	YCBI	YCBL	YCBO	YCBR	YCBU	YCBX
Nov-Jan 2005	15,504	12,740	2,652	40	72	13,865	1,639	11,501	1,239	2,316	336	455
Dec-Feb 2005	15,515	12,751	2,650	42	71	13,877	1,638	11,518	1,234	2,313	338	449
Jan-Mar 2005	15,530	12,769	2,650	42	69	13,887	1,643	11,529	1,240	2,310	340	454
Feb-Apr 2005	15,517	12,749	2,658	42	69	13,870	1,647	11,502	1,247	2,319	339	456
Mar-May 2005	15,508	12,726	2,675	39	68	13,868	1,640	11,478	1,248	2,339	336	467
Apr-Jun 2005	15,527	12,762	2,658	37	70	13,894	1,633	11,509	1,253	2,332	326	463
May-Jul 2005	15,539	12,776	2,659	35	69	13,909	1,630	11,527	1,249	2,331	327	464
Jun-Aug 2005	15,553	12,798	2,658	33	64	13,929	1,624	11,570	1,227	2,313	346	464
Jul-Sep 2005	15,571	12,799	2,678	31	62	13,945	1,626	11,570	1,229	2,330	348	459
Aug-Oct 2005	15,571	12,809	2,672	32	58	13,942	1,629	11,582	1,227	2,320	352	451
Sep-Nov 2005	15,570	12,788	2,694	30	58	13,932	1,638	11,552	1,236	2,338	356	434
Oct-Dec 2005	15,573	12,777	2,706	29	60	13,927	1,646	11,542	1,235	2,343	363	445
Nov-Jan 2006	15,604	12,797	2,717	31	58	13,961	1,642	11,564	1,233	2,354	363	455
Dec-Feb 2006	15,614	12,809	2,717	29	59	13,960	1,654	11,566	1,244	2,351	365	457
Jan-Mar 2006	15,609	12,820	2,700	31	58	13,966	1,642	11,579	1,241	2,345	355	440
Feb-Apr 2006	15,656	12,859	2,710	30	57	14,015	1,641	11,612	1,247	2,362	348	442
Mar-May 2006	15,639	12,853	2,696	33	56	13,991	1,648	11,597	1,256	2,356	340	434
Apr-Jun 2006	15,652	12,864	2,697	36	54	13,993	1,659	11,601	1,263	2,355	343	449
May-Jul 2006	15,683	12,894	2,698	38	53	14,013	1,670	11,626	1,268	2,346	352	452
Jun-Aug 2006	15,722	12,922	2,711	42	48	14,057	1,665	11,657	1,265	2,360	351	449
Jul-Sep 2006	15,740	12,909	2,731	42	58	14,040	1,700	11,629	1,280	2,366	365	455
Aug-Oct 2006	15,738	12,894	2,743	42	59	14,007	1,731	11,591	1,303	2,372	371	456
Sep-Nov 2006	15,744	12,880	2,756	40	68	14,035	1,709	11,602	1,279	2,389	367	450
Oct-Dec 2006	15,751	12,902	2,747	41	60	14,048	1,703	11,621	1,281	2,386	362	462
Nov-Jan 2007	15,760	12,886	2,773	39	63	14,064	1,696	11,606	1,280	2,416	356	447
Dec-Feb 2007	15,752	12,885	2,768	40	58	14,052	1,700	11,609	1,276	2,403	366	461
Jan-Mar 2007	15,758	12,885	2,775	43	56	14,034	1,724	11,597	1,288	2,399	376	463
Feb-Apr 2007	15,782	12,913	2,772	40	57	14,064	1,718	11,635	1,278	2,392	380	461
Mar-May 2007	15,846	12,979	2,771	38	59	14,134	1,712	11,703	1,275	2,393	377	457
Apr-Jun 2007	15,839	12,965	2,775	36	62	14,126	1,713	11,696	1,269	2,393	382	456
May-Jul 2007	15,846	12,969	2,771	37	68	14,120	1,726	11,705	1,264	2,378	393	460
Jun-Aug 2007	15,861	12,991	2,771	38	61	14,137	1,724	11,714	1,278	2,388	383	456
Jul-Sep 2007	15,884	13,027	2,760	37	60	14,141	1,742	11,733	1,294	2,374	386	450
Aug-Oct 2007	15,903	13,036	2,774	37	56	14,176	1,726	11,754	1,282	2,390	384	458
Sep-Nov 2007	15,942	13,061	2,783	37	61	14,181	1,762	11,755	1,306	2,385	398	454
Oct-Dec 2007	15,947	13,057	2,787	39	63	14,182	1,766	11,741	1,317	2,395	392	450
Nov-Jan 2008	15,968	13,074	2,789	39	66	14,180	1,788	11,733	1,341	2,398	391	453
Dec-Feb 2008	15,993	13,054	2,825	40	74	14,197	1,796	11,714	1,340	2,435	390	461
Jan-Mar 2008	16,005	13,070	2,822	40	73	14,209	1,796	11,739	1,331	2,427	395	451
Feb-Apr 2008	16,024	13,106	2,805	42	70	14,229	1,795	11,769	1,337	2,415	391	458
Mar-May 2008	16,019	13,101	2,809	40	68	14,254	1,764	11,792	1,309	2,419	390	461
Apr-Jun 2008	16,011	13,097	2,810	40	64	14,221	1,790	11,758	1,340	2,423	387	461
May-Jul 2008	15,987	13,089	2,798	36	64	14,178	1,809	11,726	1,363	2,415	383	451
Jun-Aug 2008	15,927	13,059	2,775	30	64	14,105	1,822	11,685	1,374	2,389	386	451
Jul-Sep 2008	15,910	13,049	2,769	28	64	14,081	1,829	11,664	1,385	2,387	382	456
Aug-Oct 2008	15,864	13,029	2,736	33	67	14,024	1,840	11,639	1,390	2,355	381	452
Sep-Nov 2008	15,885	13,017	2,766	37	65	14,045	1,840	11,634	1,383	2,381	385	471
Oct-Dec 2008	15,870	12,991	2,774	41	64	14,012	1,858	11,598	1,393	2,386	388	473
Nov-Jan 2009	15,859	12,977	2,784	38	61	13,995	1,865	11,572	1,405	2,399	385	479
Dec-Feb 2009	15,786	12,921	2,771	33	61	13,935	1,851	11,504	1,417	2,399	372	483
Jan-Mar 2009	15,739	12,876	2,773	32	58	13,900	1,839	11,475	1,402	2,394	379	492
Feb-Apr 2009	15,678	12,807	2,779	33	59	13,841	1,836	11,417	1,391	2,391	388	500
Mar-May 2009	15,577	12,711	2,774	36	56	13,718	1,859	11,318	1,393	2,369	405	489
Apr-Jun 2009	15,513	12,658	2,756	40	59	13,646	1,866	11,268	1,390	2,341	415	480
May-Jul 2009	15,465	12,607	2,761	36	61	13,618	1,847	11,229	1,379	2,356	405	480
Jun-Aug 2009	15,471	12,608	2,770	33	61	13,616	1,856	11,206	1,402	2,375	395	491
Jul-Sep 2009	15,447	12,608	2,749	29	61	13,606	1,841	11,215	1,392	2,359	390	489
Aug-Oct 2009	15,448	12,588	2,769	33	58	13,591	1,857	11,189	1,400	2,373	396	494
Sep-Nov 2009	15,438	12,593	2,757	32	56	13,568	1,870	11,188	1,405	2,354	403	483
Oct-Dec 2009	15,436	12,570	2,770	37	60	13,558	1,879	11,168	1,402	2,363	407	485
Nov-Jan 2010	15,407	12,538	2,773	36	60	13,514	1,893	11,127	1,411	2,360	413	467
Dec-Feb 2010	15,404	12,539	2,763	41	63	13,511	1,893	11,129	1,409	2,354	408	457
Jan-Mar 2010	15,397	12,516	2,775	41	66	13,486	1,911	11,096	1,420	2,363	411	434
Feb-Apr 2010	15,417	12,527	2,780	42	69	13,501	1,917	11,103	1,425	2,368	412	452
Mar-May 2010	15,499	12,593	2,787	42	77	13,551	1,948	11,152	1,441	2,365	422	476
Apr-Jun 2010	15,539	12,633	2,788	41	77	13,567	1,972	11,165	1,468	2,368	420	472
May-Jul 2010	15,634	12,684	2,820	43	87	13,622	2,012	11,206	1,478	2,379	441	467
Jun-Aug 2010	15,654	12,690	2,839	42	83	13,617	2,036	11,182	1,508	2,396	442	458
Jul-Sep 2010	15,696	12,706	2,864	43	83	13,635	2,061	11,183	1,523	2,414	450	465
Aug-Oct 2010	15,658	12,726	2,808	43	81	13,590	2,068	11,202	1,524	2,357	451	459
Sep-Nov 2010	15,644	12,704	2,825	33	82	13,587	2,057	11,189	1,514	2,367	458	462
Oct-Dec 2010	15,679	12,736	2,834	34	75	13,623	2,057	11,217	1,519	2,375	459	469
Nov-Jan 2011	15,711	12,774	2,823	35	80	13,672	2,039	11,281	1,493	2,363	460	488
Dec-Feb 2011	15,717	12,786	2,820	33	77	13,695	2,022	11,322	1,464	2,350	470	509
Jan-Mar 2011	15,692	12,791	2,795	31	76	13,670	2,022	11,326	1,465	2,323	472	496
Feb-Apr 2011	15,742	12,817	2,827	28	70	13,689	2,053	11,323	1,494	2,345	481	488
Mar-May 2011	15,739	12,816	2,832	31	60	13,690	2,049	11,335	1,480	2,336	495	490

4.2 Full-time, part-time and temporary workers

United Kingdom (thousands) seasonally adjusted

	All in employment					Full-time and part-time workers[1]						
	Total	Employees	Self employed	Unpaid family workers	Government supported training & employment programmes[2]	Total people working full-time	Total people working part-time	Employees working full-time	Employees working part-time	Self-employed people working full-time	Self-employed people working part-time	Total workers with second jobs
Men (16+)	MGSA	MGRO	MGRR	MGRU	MGRX	YCBF	YCBI	YCBL	YCBO	YCBR	YCBU	YCBX
Apr-Jun 2011	15,728	12,795	2,838	38	56	13,687	2,041	11,316	1,479	2,350	488	488
May-Jul 2011	15,655	12,731	2,836	38	49	13,628	2,027	11,257	1,474	2,353	483	498
Jun-Aug 2011	15,620	12,685	2,849	40	46	13,647	1,973	11,253	1,432	2,373	476	476
Jul-Sep 2011	15,588	12,608	2,897	42	42	13,617	1,971	11,196	1,412	2,401	496	487
Aug-Oct 2011	15,607	12,604	2,919	41	43	13,616	1,991	11,155	1,449	2,434	485	492
Sep-Nov 2011	15,620	12,610	2,916	43	51	13,593	2,027	11,137	1,472	2,423	493	491
Oct-Dec 2011	15,632	12,652	2,886	41	53	13,597	2,035	11,164	1,488	2,403	483	479
Nov-Jan 2012	15,638	12,647	2,890	42	58	13,601	2,037	11,166	1,481	2,406	484	463
Dec-Feb 2012	15,690	12,684	2,902	38	66	13,592	2,098	11,153	1,531	2,404	497	488
Jan-Mar 2012	15,725	12,693	2,915	44	73	13,601	2,124	11,158	1,535	2,404	511	488
Feb-Apr 2012	15,757	12,704	2,929	45	79	13,624	2,133	11,161	1,543	2,423	506	489
Mar-May 2012	15,800	12,710	2,947	46	97	13,664	2,136	11,163	1,547	2,449	497	487
Apr-Jun 2012	15,862	12,754	2,973	42	92	13,706	2,156	11,186	1,568	2,468	505	487
May-Jul 2012	15,872	12,748	2,981	43	99	13,722	2,151	11,182	1,566	2,475	507	477
Jun-Aug 2012	15,900	12,779	2,973	46	103	13,741	2,159	11,222	1,557	2,454	519	470
Jul-Sep 2012	15,892	12,761	2,973	49	109	13,749	2,144	11,223	1,538	2,454	519	462
Aug-Oct 2012	15,904	12,769	2,972	47	115	13,774	2,130	11,244	1,525	2,457	516	460
Sep-Nov 2012	15,933	12,834	2,942	46	110	13,808	2,124	11,300	1,534	2,441	501	452
Oct-Dec 2012	15,950	12,847	2,948	45	110	13,833	2,117	11,323	1,524	2,444	504	453
Nov-Jan 2013	15,932	12,859	2,917	43	112	13,814	2,118	11,334	1,526	2,414	504	442
Dec-Feb 2013	15,882	12,805	2,932	39	107	13,783	2,100	11,306	1,498	2,410	522	438
Jan-Mar 2013	15,884	12,820	2,918	38	108	13,797	2,087	11,317	1,502	2,414	504	434
Feb-Apr 2013	15,902	12,823	2,933	37	109	13,761	2,142	11,294	1,529	2,413	520	449
Mar-May 2013	15,889	12,831	2,921	31	106	13,768	2,121	11,316	1,515	2,409	512	455
Apr-Jun 2013	15,932	12,855	2,927	43	107	13,797	2,135	11,345	1,510	2,405	522	459
May-Jul 2013	15,969	12,894	2,932	39	102	13,838	2,131	11,379	1,515	2,417	515	470
Jun-Aug 2013	15,995	12,897	2,951	45	102	13,850	2,145	11,371	1,526	2,435	516	488
Jul-Sep 2013	16,052	12,963	2,945	40	103	13,881	2,170	11,408	1,555	2,430	515	491
Aug-Oct 2013	16,095	12,969	2,977	43	106	13,911	2,184	11,414	1,555	2,452	525	490
Sep-Nov 2013	16,149	12,978	3,033	44	94	13,966	2,183	11,430	1,548	2,490	543	500
Oct-Dec 2013	16,138	12,966	3,039	45	88	13,962	2,176	11,415	1,550	2,498	541	508
Nov-Jan 2014	16,177	12,951	3,103	46	78	14,003	2,174	11,400	1,551	2,555	548	514
Dec-Feb 2014	16,257	13,008	3,122	46	82	14,075	2,182	11,441	1,567	2,578	544	516
Jan-Mar 2014	16,279	13,008	3,139	58	74	14,090	2,189	11,438	1,570	2,596	543	517
Feb-Apr 2014	16,324	13,060	3,128	63	73	14,167	2,156	11,512	1,547	2,593	535	510
Mar-May 2014	16,353	13,086	3,140	59	68	14,200	2,153	11,544	1,542	2,598	542	508
Apr-Jun 2014	16,326	13,053	3,143	56	74	14,206	2,119	11,556	1,497	2,591	552	510
May-Jul 2014	16,318	13,057	3,123	55	83	14,171	2,146	11,538	1,518	2,572	552	493
Jun-Aug 2014	16,362	13,119	3,114	54	75	14,211	2,151	11,573	1,546	2,580	533	517
Jul-Sep 2014	16,388	13,153	3,113	53	70	14,240	2,149	11,605	1,548	2,586	526	508
Aug-Oct 2014	16,384	13,168	3,099	52	65	14,240	2,144	11,623	1,545	2,576	523	512
Sep-Nov 2014	16,375	13,189	3,070	49	66	14,208	2,167	11,627	1,562	2,539	531	496
Oct-Dec 2014	16,427	13,262	3,051	48	66	14,273	2,154	11,713	1,550	2,525	526	489

Source: Labour Force Survey
Inquiries: Email: labour.market@ons.gsi.gov.uk
Tel: 01633 455 400

4.2 Full-time, part-time and temporary workers

United Kingdom (thousands) seasonally adjusted

	Temporary employees (reasons for temporary working)							Part-time workers (reasons for working part-time)[3]					
	Total	Total as % of all employees	Could not find permanent job	% that could not find permanent job	Did not want permanent job	Had a contract with period of training	Some other reason	Total[4]	Could not find full-time job	% that could not find full-time job	Did not want full-time job	Ill or disabled	Student or at school
Men (16+)	YCCA	YCCD	YCCG	YCCJ	YCCM	YCCP	YCCS	YCCV	YCCY	YCDB	YCDE	YCDH	YCDK
Nov-Jan 2005	706	5.5	203	28.7	185	54	264	1,575	228	14.5	755	66	517
Dec-Feb 2005	703	5.5	202	28.7	175	52	274	1,571	225	14.3	769	66	500
Jan-Mar 2005	693	5.4	202	29.1	173	51	267	1,580	231	14.6	769	69	498
Feb-Apr 2005	689	5.4	205	29.7	168	52	264	1,586	229	14.4	773	76	494
Mar-May 2005	687	5.4	210	30.6	159	57	262	1,584	235	14.8	766	72	497
Apr-Jun 2005	692	5.4	210	30.3	166	56	259	1,579	235	14.9	755	72	499
May-Jul 2005	691	5.4	207	30.0	172	60	252	1,576	241	15.3	748	73	500
Jun-Aug 2005	678	5.3	212	31.2	173	57	236	1,573	227	14.5	758	75	499
Jul-Sep 2005	680	5.3	212	31.2	167	59	242	1,577	228	14.4	771	76	494
Aug-Oct 2005	668	5.2	206	30.9	169	55	237	1,579	233	14.8	774	77	484
Sep-Nov 2005	660	5.2	202	30.6	166	51	242	1,592	248	15.6	779	76	478
Oct-Dec 2005	651	5.1	195	30.0	165	43	248	1,598	246	15.4	786	77	477
Nov-Jan 2006	652	5.1	195	30.0	163	50	244	1,596	245	15.3	786	76	476
Dec-Feb 2006	660	5.2	191	28.9	168	55	247	1,609	250	15.5	786	76	484
Jan-Mar 2006	666	5.2	192	28.8	168	60	247	1,596	247	15.4	778	76	482
Feb-Apr 2006	669	5.2	194	29.0	175	55	245	1,595	247	15.5	775	72	489
Mar-May 2006	666	5.2	187	28.1	173	55	251	1,596	248	15.5	774	73	490
Apr-Jun 2006	654	5.1	187	28.7	173	53	241	1,606	252	15.7	770	70	504
May-Jul 2006	643	5.0	179	27.9	168	48	248	1,620	256	15.8	772	75	509
Jun-Aug 2006	663	5.1	186	28.1	172	47	258	1,616	263	16.3	760	77	507
Jul-Sep 2006	667	5.2	193	28.9	173	47	254	1,645	270	16.4	769	74	519
Aug-Oct 2006	687	5.3	206	30.0	176	46	259	1,674	279	16.7	789	75	518
Sep-Nov 2006	700	5.4	211	30.1	182	49	258	1,646	280	17.0	780	76	498
Oct-Dec 2006	707	5.5	214	30.2	185	48	259	1,643	278	16.9	785	78	492
Nov-Jan 2007	712	5.5	209	29.3	187	56	260	1,636	281	17.2	770	83	491
Dec-Feb 2007	703	5.5	212	30.2	185	51	255	1,642	267	16.2	787	82	495
Jan-Mar 2007	713	5.5	215	30.1	183	53	261	1,664	274	16.5	798	81	500
Feb-Apr 2007	696	5.4	211	30.3	177	48	260	1,658	273	16.5	799	80	497
Mar-May 2007	696	5.4	219	31.4	174	43	261	1,653	277	16.8	804	76	487
Apr-Jun 2007	693	5.3	223	32.2	172	40	258	1,652	275	16.7	821	75	469
May-Jul 2007	689	5.3	219	31.8	177	39	255	1,658	281	17.0	832	79	453
Jun-Aug 2007	694	5.3	218	31.4	185	38	252	1,661	290	17.5	828	70	460
Jul-Sep 2007	682	5.2	206	30.2	189	37	249	1,680	293	17.4	831	72	471
Aug-Oct 2007	668	5.1	202	30.3	187	38	241	1,666	292	17.5	817	71	474
Sep-Nov 2007	684	5.2	203	29.6	192	42	247	1,704	288	16.9	834	72	498
Oct-Dec 2007	696	5.3	200	28.8	193	45	258	1,709	291	17.0	836	71	498
Nov-Jan 2008	685	5.2	188	27.4	189	43	265	1,731	292	16.9	857	69	500
Dec-Feb 2008	663	5.1	181	27.4	181	43	258	1,730	292	16.9	857	69	498
Jan-Mar 2008	657	5.0	185	28.1	182	39	251	1,726	289	16.7	860	69	494
Feb-Apr 2008	656	5.0	179	27.3	183	42	252	1,727	287	16.6	860	73	492
Mar-May 2008	648	4.9	178	27.5	165	45	259	1,699	268	15.8	859	76	479
Apr-Jun 2008	628	4.8	176	28.1	159	46	247	1,727	271	15.7	864	78	499
May-Jul 2008	611	4.7	182	29.7	143	47	239	1,747	290	16.6	858	82	503
Jun-Aug 2008	615	4.7	180	29.2	154	44	238	1,760	303	17.2	858	83	504
Jul-Sep 2008	633	4.8	184	29.1	158	46	244	1,766	315	17.8	860	81	497
Aug-Oct 2008	627	4.8	177	28.2	170	42	239	1,772	322	18.2	857	80	498
Sep-Nov 2008	635	4.9	186	29.4	155	42	251	1,767	333	18.8	847	79	492
Oct-Dec 2008	639	4.9	195	30.5	152	42	250	1,780	353	19.9	840	80	490
Nov-Jan 2009	659	5.1	215	32.6	153	47	243	1,789	379	21.2	832	77	485
Dec-Feb 2009	662	5.1	225	34.1	158	38	240	1,789	385	21.5	830	78	481
Jan-Mar 2009	664	5.2	232	35.0	155	37	239	1,781	394	22.1	821	77	474
Feb-Apr 2009	662	5.2	228	34.4	155	40	238	1,779	405	22.8	812	79	464
Mar-May 2009	649	5.1	219	33.7	153	48	229	1,798	425	23.6	806	80	467
Apr-Jun 2009	676	5.3	231	34.1	156	47	243	1,805	438	24.3	793	79	472
May-Jul 2009	680	5.4	231	34.0	151	45	253	1,784	438	24.6	789	73	466
Jun-Aug 2009	679	5.4	235	34.7	151	47	246	1,797	432	24.0	802	70	472
Jul-Sep 2009	671	5.3	240	35.8	146	44	241	1,783	433	24.3	785	79	468
Aug-Oct 2009	672	5.3	245	36.5	140	49	237	1,796	435	24.2	778	79	486
Sep-Nov 2009	685	5.4	262	38.2	145	43	235	1,807	449	24.8	787	76	478
Oct-Dec 2009	690	5.5	268	38.8	146	42	235	1,809	447	24.7	799	77	471
Nov-Jan 2010	683	5.4	259	37.9	147	41	236	1,823	449	24.6	811	75	470
Dec-Feb 2010	709	5.7	273	38.5	149	46	241	1,817	457	25.2	800	72	474
Jan-Mar 2010	707	5.6	268	37.9	151	43	245	1,832	463	25.3	808	69	479
Feb-Apr 2010	715	5.7	283	39.6	151	42	239	1,836	463	25.2	807	68	487
Mar-May 2010	733	5.8	291	39.7	158	41	244	1,863	459	24.6	834	63	497
Apr-Jun 2010	760	6.0	304	40.0	163	40	253	1,889	468	24.8	847	70	492
May-Jul 2010	753	5.9	300	39.8	160	40	253	1,920	480	25.0	848	70	509
Jun-Aug 2010	760	6.0	314	41.3	157	43	246	1,950	492	25.2	851	77	515
Jul-Sep 2010	756	5.9	319	42.2	150	44	243	1,973	501	25.4	859	72	525
Aug-Oct 2010	761	6.0	314	41.3	156	48	242	1,975	522	26.4	867	72	500
Sep-Nov 2010	744	5.9	303	40.7	151	52	238	1,972	520	26.4	878	78	482
Oct-Dec 2010	718	5.6	289	40.3	147	53	228	1,978	519	26.3	882	73	488
Nov-Jan 2011	738	5.8	299	40.5	145	51	244	1,952	511	26.2	880	73	471
Dec-Feb 2011	741	5.8	296	40.0	145	51	249	1,935	513	26.5	872	76	454
Jan-Mar 2011	752	5.9	300	40.0	146	56	250	1,937	523	27.0	869	81	441
Feb-Apr 2011	769	6.0	314	40.8	145	51	259	1,975	540	27.3	880	83	452
Mar-May 2011	771	6.0	311	40.4	149	49	262	1,976	554	28.0	889	74	438
Apr-Jun 2011	792	6.2	329	41.6	151	46	265	1,967	564	28.7	877	71	437
May-Jul 2011	760	6.0	304	40.0	154	45	257	1,959	579	29.5	865	71	423

4.2 Full-time, part-time and temporary workers

United Kingdom (thousands) seasonally adjusted

	Temporary employees (reasons for temporary working)							Part-time workers (reasons for working part-time)[3]					
	Total	Total as % of all employees	Could not find permanent job	% that could not find permanent job	Did not want permanent job	Had a contract with period of training	Some other reason	Total[4]	Could not find full-time job	% that could not find full-time job	Did not want full-time job	Ill or disabled	Student or at school
Men (16+)	YCCA	YCCD	YCCG	YCCJ	YCCM	YCCP	YCCS	YCCV	YCCY	YCDB	YCDE	YCDH	YCDK
Jun-Aug 2011	747	5.9	309	41.4	134	42	261	1,907	569	29.8	841	66	415
Jul-Sep 2011	735	5.8	302	41.1	141	43	249	1,908	555	29.1	850	66	419
Aug-Oct 2011	736	5.8	311	42.3	138	41	246	1,934	563	29.1	852	68	432
Sep-Nov 2011	733	5.8	302	41.2	152	41	238	1,964	579	29.5	857	69	441
Oct-Dec 2011	727	5.7	308	42.4	142	41	235	1,971	593	30.1	854	70	438
Nov-Jan 2012	732	5.8	313	42.7	140	45	234	1,965	604	30.7	846	73	430
Dec-Feb 2012	739	5.8	327	44.2	135	45	232	2,029	625	30.8	862	73	455
Jan-Mar 2012	742	5.8	319	43.0	139	44	240	2,046	635	31.0	868	74	457
Feb-Apr 2012	740	5.8	311	42.0	137	47	246	2,049	639	31.2	867	75	452
Mar-May 2012	738	5.8	323	43.8	134	46	235	2,045	633	31.0	866	76	453
Apr-Jun 2012	751	5.9	326	43.4	134	50	241	2,073	650	31.4	871	73	459
May-Jul 2012	761	6.0	335	44.0	135	50	241	2,074	644	31.0	881	71	458
Jun-Aug 2012	757	5.9	327	43.2	134	49	247	2,076	633	30.5	888	74	458
Jul-Sep 2012	760	6.0	335	44.0	129	45	251	2,057	632	30.7	886	70	447
Aug-Oct 2012	766	6.0	340	44.3	127	46	254	2,041	632	31.0	892	69	425
Sep-Nov 2012	778	6.1	347	44.5	135	40	256	2,034	635	31.2	896	62	413
Oct-Dec 2012	785	6.1	357	45.5	136	42	250	2,028	639	31.5	889	66	404
Nov-Jan 2013	777	6.0	350	45.1	137	42	248	2,029	640	31.6	897	64	399
Dec-Feb 2013	769	6.0	343	44.6	140	45	241	2,021	641	31.7	895	63	400
Jan-Mar 2013	755	5.9	338	44.8	138	42	236	2,006	639	31.8	878	61	406
Feb-Apr 2013	749	5.8	330	44.1	145	36	238	2,049	661	32.2	878	63	421
Mar-May 2013	753	5.9	324	43.1	140	43	246	2,027	665	32.8	863	64	408
Apr-Jun 2013	736	5.7	315	42.8	139	40	242	2,032	657	32.3	877	67	407
May-Jul 2013	743	5.8	315	42.4	133	49	246	2,032	660	32.5	878	65	407
Jun-Aug 2013	741	5.7	310	41.9	131	60	240	2,042	665	32.6	892	66	398
Jul-Sep 2013	756	5.8	306	40.5	137	67	246	2,071	668	32.3	902	72	404
Aug-Oct 2013	742	5.7	300	40.4	139	62	241	2,080	664	31.9	909	74	411
Sep-Nov 2013	756	5.8	297	39.3	136	63	259	2,089	658	31.5	909	76	430
Oct-Dec 2013	769	5.9	299	38.9	143	62	265	2,091	639	30.5	917	77	439
Nov-Jan 2014	770	5.9	299	38.9	146	59	265	2,098	652	31.1	908	79	440
Dec-Feb 2014	771	5.9	297	38.5	152	56	267	2,111	639	30.3	935	79	437
Jan-Mar 2014	783	6.0	303	38.7	144	59	278	2,114	642	30.4	947	80	425
Feb-Apr 2014	782	6.0	307	39.2	144	61	270	2,082	604	29.0	952	80	428
Mar-May 2014	777	5.9	309	39.8	143	62	264	2,085	599	28.7	959	88	419
Apr-Jun 2014	766	5.9	316	41.2	137	58	255	2,050	585	28.5	956	83	407
May-Jul 2014	778	6.0	322	41.4	140	63	253	2,071	588	28.4	973	86	405
Jun-Aug 2014	805	6.1	329	40.9	154	57	264	2,080	593	28.5	971	78	417
Jul-Sep 2014	801	6.1	308	38.5	177	62	253	2,074	586	28.3	975	79	415
Aug-Oct 2014	806	6.1	293	36.4	190	64	259	2,067	574	27.8	987	76	411
Sep-Nov 2014	793	6.0	301	37.9	179	64	249	2,092	576	27.5	992	84	423
Oct-Dec 2014	812	6.1	308	37.9	171	59	274	2,076	565	27.2	994	84	414

Source: Labour Force Survey
Inquiries: Email: labour.market@ons.gsi.gov.uk
Tel: 01633 455 400

4.2 Full-time, part-time and temporary workers

	All in employment					Full-time and part-time workers[1]						
	Total	Employees	Self employed	Unpaid family workers	Government supported training & employment programmes[2]	Total people working full-time	Total people working part-time	Employees working full-time	Employees working part-time	Self-employed people working full-time	Self-employed people working part-time	Total workers with second jobs
Women (16+)	MGSB	MGRP	MGRS	MGRV	MGRY	YCBG	YCBJ	YCBM	YCBP	YCBS	YCBV	YCBY
Nov-Jan 2005	13,222	12,163	951	58	51	7,565	5,657	7,070	5,093	467	484	611
Dec-Feb 2005	13,279	12,193	969	63	55	7,633	5,646	7,115	5,078	486	483	617
Jan-Mar 2005	13,258	12,180	958	62	57	7,622	5,636	7,101	5,079	488	470	608
Feb-Apr 2005	13,242	12,177	952	61	52	7,602	5,640	7,093	5,084	478	473	611
Mar-May 2005	13,272	12,200	963	63	46	7,585	5,687	7,073	5,127	482	481	617
Apr-Jun 2005	13,276	12,212	958	63	43	7,575	5,700	7,072	5,140	474	484	615
May-Jul 2005	13,316	12,247	968	60	42	7,611	5,705	7,097	5,149	486	481	607
Jun-Aug 2005	13,353	12,280	979	52	42	7,666	5,687	7,145	5,134	497	482	602
Jul-Sep 2005	13,357	12,267	988	58	44	7,680	5,677	7,151	5,116	501	487	612
Aug-Oct 2005	13,342	12,264	974	60	43	7,683	5,659	7,160	5,104	493	481	611
Sep-Nov 2005	13,311	12,219	986	62	44	7,672	5,639	7,149	5,069	492	493	602
Oct-Dec 2005	13,307	12,221	977	61	48	7,696	5,611	7,177	5,044	490	487	587
Nov-Jan 2006	13,330	12,249	975	60	46	7,699	5,632	7,182	5,067	488	488	583
Dec-Feb 2006	13,374	12,282	998	58	35	7,718	5,656	7,195	5,087	500	498	589
Jan-Mar 2006	13,439	12,322	1,024	58	35	7,738	5,701	7,195	5,128	520	504	589
Feb-Apr 2006	13,429	12,311	1,029	55	35	7,742	5,686	7,206	5,105	512	517	592
Mar-May 2006	13,424	12,326	1,006	53	39	7,754	5,671	7,236	5,090	496	510	591
Apr-Jun 2006	13,454	12,346	1,013	55	39	7,753	5,701	7,230	5,116	499	515	599
May-Jul 2006	13,457	12,331	1,029	60	37	7,757	5,701	7,221	5,110	512	517	601
Jun-Aug 2006	13,502	12,361	1,038	64	39	7,764	5,738	7,219	5,143	520	518	611
Jul-Sep 2006	13,443	12,301	1,040	62	39	7,722	5,721	7,188	5,114	511	529	613
Aug-Oct 2006	13,451	12,302	1,052	56	42	7,702	5,749	7,164	5,137	516	536	612
Sep-Nov 2006	13,459	12,319	1,032	60	47	7,710	5,749	7,177	5,142	507	525	609
Oct-Dec 2006	13,463	12,315	1,042	60	46	7,701	5,763	7,166	5,149	511	531	619
Nov-Jan 2007	13,441	12,299	1,036	62	44	7,689	5,752	7,155	5,144	507	529	625
Dec-Feb 2007	13,423	12,269	1,048	59	47	7,696	5,727	7,151	5,118	520	528	616
Jan-Mar 2007	13,436	12,284	1,047	61	44	7,721	5,715	7,186	5,099	509	538	611
Feb-Apr 2007	13,450	12,298	1,048	61	43	7,734	5,717	7,194	5,104	513	535	634
Mar-May 2007	13,468	12,331	1,030	61	45	7,762	5,706	7,223	5,109	513	517	643
Apr-Jun 2007	13,483	12,344	1,027	62	49	7,776	5,706	7,239	5,106	514	514	651
May-Jul 2007	13,506	12,350	1,040	66	50	7,801	5,705	7,260	5,090	519	521	658
Jun-Aug 2007	13,514	12,339	1,060	64	52	7,810	5,704	7,269	5,070	516	544	661
Jul-Sep 2007	13,536	12,353	1,072	59	52	7,847	5,689	7,293	5,061	529	543	653
Aug-Oct 2007	13,568	12,386	1,066	60	56	7,861	5,706	7,313	5,073	520	546	657
Sep-Nov 2007	13,584	12,410	1,060	66	49	7,874	5,711	7,331	5,079	516	543	661
Oct-Dec 2007	13,628	12,464	1,047	67	51	7,893	5,735	7,364	5,100	503	544	676
Nov-Jan 2008	13,646	12,472	1,058	70	45	7,903	5,743	7,375	5,097	503	556	659
Dec-Feb 2008	13,683	12,503	1,067	70	43	7,932	5,751	7,386	5,117	520	547	665
Jan-Mar 2008	13,678	12,511	1,056	69	42	7,925	5,753	7,384	5,128	519	537	652
Feb-Apr 2008	13,682	12,517	1,045	73	47	7,931	5,751	7,381	5,136	524	521	663
Mar-May 2008	13,730	12,556	1,047	76	51	7,972	5,758	7,424	5,132	523	524	658
Apr-Jun 2008	13,710	12,544	1,048	72	47	7,968	5,742	7,418	5,125	524	524	669
May-Jul 2008	13,709	12,540	1,056	65	48	7,993	5,716	7,441	5,100	527	529	680
Jun-Aug 2008	13,684	12,532	1,052	60	41	7,976	5,709	7,433	5,099	525	527	670
Jul-Sep 2008	13,670	12,518	1,049	61	43	7,980	5,690	7,434	5,084	528	521	670
Aug-Oct 2008	13,671	12,515	1,058	58	38	7,986	5,685	7,437	5,079	532	527	675
Sep-Nov 2008	13,672	12,516	1,064	54	37	7,914	5,758	7,382	5,134	519	545	673
Oct-Dec 2008	13,659	12,515	1,054	53	36	7,939	5,720	7,409	5,106	511	542	670
Nov-Jan 2009	13,680	12,530	1,061	50	39	7,957	5,722	7,421	5,109	519	542	673
Dec-Feb 2009	13,643	12,495	1,055	52	41	7,908	5,735	7,363	5,133	520	535	671
Jan-Mar 2009	13,627	12,458	1,071	55	43	7,868	5,759	7,320	5,139	524	547	669
Feb-Apr 2009	13,594	12,413	1,081	56	45	7,874	5,721	7,330	5,083	520	561	656
Mar-May 2009	13,578	12,386	1,082	64	46	7,867	5,711	7,324	5,062	523	559	655
Apr-Jun 2009	13,575	12,385	1,087	58	46	7,832	5,742	7,285	5,100	527	559	646
May-Jul 2009	13,553	12,355	1,097	55	46	7,793	5,759	7,234	5,121	539	559	641
Jun-Aug 2009	13,604	12,379	1,124	51	50	7,830	5,774	7,260	5,119	548	576	648
Jul-Sep 2009	13,622	12,394	1,132	48	48	7,782	5,840	7,218	5,176	544	588	654
Aug-Oct 2009	13,636	12,430	1,111	50	44	7,759	5,877	7,203	5,227	536	575	652
Sep-Nov 2009	13,654	12,420	1,139	43	52	7,777	5,877	7,213	5,207	544	595	647
Oct-Dec 2009	13,665	12,418	1,142	50	55	7,791	5,874	7,214	5,204	555	588	644
Nov-Jan 2010	13,650	12,409	1,133	50	59	7,777	5,873	7,207	5,201	546	587	627
Dec-Feb 2010	13,620	12,364	1,146	51	59	7,770	5,850	7,190	5,174	559	587	624
Jan-Mar 2010	13,616	12,329	1,180	50	58	7,749	5,867	7,151	5,177	577	603	633
Feb-Apr 2010	13,630	12,329	1,194	50	58	7,720	5,910	7,119	5,211	581	613	645
Mar-May 2010	13,645	12,367	1,172	51	54	7,715	5,930	7,125	5,242	567	605	658
Apr-Jun 2010	13,653	12,387	1,161	49	56	7,734	5,919	7,151	5,236	560	601	664
May-Jul 2010	13,691	12,410	1,169	60	52	7,712	5,979	7,117	5,293	570	599	667
Jun-Aug 2010	13,686	12,415	1,154	67	49	7,697	5,989	7,109	5,306	566	589	662
Jul-Sep 2010	13,689	12,400	1,181	62	46	7,706	5,983	7,111	5,289	576	606	656
Aug-Oct 2010	13,650	12,375	1,172	57	46	7,699	5,950	7,104	5,271	575	597	655
Sep-Nov 2010	13,640	12,352	1,177	61	49	7,695	5,945	7,095	5,257	577	600	652
Oct-Dec 2010	13,645	12,362	1,174	59	50	7,703	5,942	7,120	5,242	562	612	653
Nov-Jan 2011	13,680	12,364	1,202	65	49	7,715	5,965	7,126	5,238	565	636	663
Dec-Feb 2011	13,725	12,406	1,205	65	49	7,739	5,987	7,150	5,256	566	639	666
Jan-Mar 2011	13,749	12,444	1,189	66	50	7,767	5,982	7,181	5,263	561	628	670
Feb-Apr 2011	13,694	12,400	1,182	65	46	7,726	5,968	7,151	5,249	548	634	665
Mar-May 2011	13,728	12,434	1,191	60	43	7,761	5,967	7,183	5,251	555	636	661

4.2 Full-time, part-time and temporary workers

United Kingdom (thousands) seasonally adjusted

	All in employment					Full-time and part-time workers[1]						
	Total	Employees	Self employed	Unpaid family workers	Government supported training & employment programmes[2]	Total people working full-time	Total people working part-time	Employees working full-time	Employees working part-time	Self-employed people working full-time	Self-employed people working part-time	Total workers with second jobs
Women (16+)	MGSB	MGRP	MGRS	MGRV	MGRY	YCBG	YCBJ	YCBM	YCBP	YCBS	YCBV	YCBY
Apr-Jun 2011	13,719	12,452	1,171	58	39	7,789	5,930	7,211	5,241	556	615	648
May-Jul 2011	13,690	12,431	1,164	56	39	7,824	5,866	7,245	5,186	562	603	644
Jun-Aug 2011	13,679	12,381	1,202	60	35	7,794	5,884	7,198	5,184	579	623	647
Jul-Sep 2011	13,689	12,359	1,225	63	42	7,789	5,900	7,188	5,172	579	646	656
Aug-Oct 2011	13,690	12,340	1,236	69	44	7,781	5,909	7,167	5,173	588	648	649
Sep-Nov 2011	13,704	12,357	1,232	69	46	7,783	5,920	7,171	5,187	583	649	654
Oct-Dec 2011	13,707	12,367	1,228	69	44	7,766	5,941	7,156	5,210	586	642	648
Nov-Jan 2012	13,713	12,362	1,235	69	47	7,764	5,948	7,155	5,208	586	649	655
Dec-Feb 2012	13,696	12,330	1,250	62	54	7,754	5,942	7,150	5,181	582	668	658
Jan-Mar 2012	13,735	12,356	1,270	53	55	7,774	5,961	7,164	5,192	588	682	664
Feb-Apr 2012	13,738	12,364	1,265	54	55	7,792	5,946	7,182	5,182	587	678	659
Mar-May 2012	13,759	12,403	1,240	65	52	7,812	5,947	7,217	5,186	572	668	654
Apr-Jun 2012	13,801	12,426	1,251	70	55	7,815	5,987	7,218	5,207	567	684	637
May-Jul 2012	13,874	12,469	1,274	76	55	7,815	6,059	7,223	5,246	564	710	649
Jun-Aug 2012	13,880	12,498	1,262	66	53	7,824	6,056	7,238	5,260	560	702	647
Jul-Sep 2012	13,861	12,487	1,260	61	53	7,813	6,048	7,225	5,262	563	697	648
Aug-Oct 2012	13,836	12,471	1,253	61	51	7,780	6,056	7,191	5,280	568	685	661
Sep-Nov 2012	13,914	12,507	1,289	65	53	7,851	6,063	7,237	5,271	588	701	670
Oct-Dec 2012	13,959	12,533	1,303	68	56	7,905	6,054	7,278	5,255	598	705	694
Nov-Jan 2013	13,963	12,565	1,285	63	51	7,941	6,022	7,318	5,248	590	695	700
Dec-Feb 2013	13,945	12,551	1,283	64	46	7,920	6,024	7,293	5,258	596	687	684
Jan-Mar 2013	13,967	12,591	1,264	66	45	7,943	6,024	7,313	5,279	602	662	675
Feb-Apr 2013	13,987	12,585	1,281	69	52	7,973	6,013	7,329	5,256	613	668	649
Mar-May 2013	13,967	12,572	1,266	72	57	7,962	6,006	7,323	5,249	606	660	666
Apr-Jun 2013	14,004	12,599	1,274	72	58	7,989	6,014	7,337	5,262	615	660	665
May-Jul 2013	14,030	12,622	1,274	71	63	8,027	6,003	7,361	5,261	618	656	662
Jun-Aug 2013	14,033	12,605	1,293	72	63	8,041	5,993	7,356	5,249	633	660	669
Jul-Sep 2013	14,047	12,609	1,296	73	69	8,052	5,995	7,369	5,240	633	662	671
Aug-Oct 2013	14,113	12,660	1,318	74	61	8,071	6,042	7,388	5,272	641	677	675
Sep-Nov 2013	14,139	12,655	1,364	68	52	8,131	6,009	7,423	5,232	675	689	683
Oct-Dec 2013	14,150	12,661	1,373	62	53	8,175	5,974	7,457	5,204	684	689	669
Nov-Jan 2014	14,145	12,638	1,390	64	53	8,156	5,988	7,440	5,198	685	706	666
Dec-Feb 2014	14,234	12,711	1,402	70	51	8,164	6,070	7,452	5,258	681	721	640
Jan-Mar 2014	14,255	12,707	1,433	67	47	8,191	6,064	7,489	5,218	673	760	659
Feb-Apr 2014	14,305	12,757	1,435	64	48	8,215	6,090	7,517	5,240	670	765	669
Mar-May 2014	14,365	12,793	1,459	60	53	8,246	6,118	7,549	5,244	673	786	680
Apr-Jun 2014	14,355	12,778	1,465	59	52	8,206	6,149	7,506	5,272	678	787	699
May-Jul 2014	14,364	12,808	1,441	65	50	8,205	6,159	7,510	5,298	676	765	708
Jun-Aug 2014	14,401	12,866	1,410	72	53	8,271	6,130	7,576	5,291	674	735	706
Jul-Sep 2014	14,404	12,874	1,408	70	53	8,283	6,121	7,598	5,276	663	744	700
Aug-Oct 2014	14,412	12,861	1,437	63	51	8,302	6,110	7,599	5,262	678	759	691
Sep-Nov 2014	14,426	12,877	1,450	53	46	8,316	6,110	7,612	5,265	680	770	702
Oct-Dec 2014	14,469	12,918	1,450	54	47	8,325	6,145	7,625	5,294	672	778	708

Source: Labour Force Survey
Inquiries: Email: labour.market@ons.gsi.gov.uk
Tel: 01633 455 400

4.2 Full-time, part-time and temporary workers

	Temporary employees (reasons for temporary working)							Part-time workers (reasons for working part-time)[3]					
	Total	Total as % of all employees	Could not find permanent job	% that could not find permanent job	Did not want permanent job	Had a contract with period of training	Some other reason	Total[4]	Could not find full-time job	% that could not find full-time job	Did not want full-time job	Ill or disabled	Student or at school
Women (16+)	YCCB	YCCE	YCCH	YCCK	YCCN	YCCQ	YCCT	YCCW	YCCZ	YCDC	YCDF	YCDI	YCDL
Nov-Jan 2005	794	6.5	155	19.5	240	59	340	5,577	311	5.6	4,493	101	653
Dec-Feb 2005	799	6.6	156	19.5	242	62	340	5,561	324	5.8	4,469	100	648
Jan-Mar 2005	773	6.3	156	20.2	230	51	336	5,549	337	6.1	4,452	97	642
Feb-Apr 2005	755	6.2	152	20.1	215	52	337	5,557	335	6.0	4,463	100	640
Mar-May 2005	758	6.2	147	19.4	221	49	341	5,608	351	6.3	4,505	96	641
Apr-Jun 2005	759	6.2	147	19.3	219	43	350	5,623	353	6.3	4,500	92	661
May-Jul 2005	781	6.4	148	19.0	229	47	357	5,631	351	6.2	4,498	88	673
Jun-Aug 2005	793	6.5	166	21.0	223	43	361	5,616	362	6.4	4,490	91	650
Jul-Sep 2005	801	6.5	181	22.6	226	45	348	5,604	370	6.6	4,477	93	645
Aug-Oct 2005	766	6.2	181	23.6	218	45	322	5,586	361	6.5	4,467	93	645
Sep-Nov 2005	760	6.2	169	22.2	213	51	328	5,563	366	6.6	4,448	92	635
Oct-Dec 2005	739	6.1	152	20.6	213	51	324	5,531	359	6.5	4,435	92	623
Nov-Jan 2006	780	6.4	169	21.7	225	55	331	5,555	368	6.6	4,440	93	631
Dec-Feb 2006	791	6.4	173	21.9	233	48	337	5,585	370	6.6	4,447	101	642
Jan-Mar 2006	820	6.7	182	22.2	242	54	341	5,631	373	6.6	4,478	98	651
Feb-Apr 2006	816	6.6	175	21.5	242	60	339	5,621	371	6.6	4,470	100	653
Mar-May 2006	812	6.6	181	22.4	239	60	331	5,601	363	6.5	4,454	97	657
Apr-Jun 2006	808	6.5	182	22.6	245	57	324	5,631	370	6.6	4,473	101	659
May-Jul 2006	795	6.5	179	22.5	247	51	318	5,627	376	6.7	4,461	102	661
Jun-Aug 2006	806	6.5	177	22.0	260	49	319	5,660	381	6.7	4,476	109	676
Jul-Sep 2006	799	6.5	174	21.7	260	47	318	5,644	376	6.7	4,459	112	677
Aug-Oct 2006	792	6.4	180	22.7	252	42	317	5,675	381	6.7	4,470	113	685
Sep-Nov 2006	795	6.5	181	22.7	255	45	315	5,667	382	6.7	4,459	114	679
Oct-Dec 2006	805	6.5	178	22.1	265	43	319	5,679	386	6.8	4,458	116	688
Nov-Jan 2007	817	6.6	190	23.2	256	49	322	5,673	388	6.8	4,465	115	675
Dec-Feb 2007	818	6.7	185	22.6	254	55	324	5,646	380	6.7	4,468	110	663
Jan-Mar 2007	821	6.7	190	23.1	251	58	321	5,636	386	6.9	4,459	107	662
Feb-Apr 2007	817	6.6	192	23.5	249	56	320	5,639	399	7.1	4,465	98	655
Mar-May 2007	817	6.6	189	23.1	248	58	323	5,626	408	7.3	4,443	101	653
Apr-Jun 2007	814	6.6	194	23.9	237	57	326	5,619	406	7.2	4,429	99	662
May-Jul 2007	812	6.6	192	23.6	235	54	331	5,612	415	7.4	4,397	102	678
Jun-Aug 2007	798	6.5	188	23.5	232	49	329	5,613	407	7.3	4,420	95	668
Jul-Sep 2007	803	6.5	186	23.2	232	47	337	5,605	401	7.2	4,428	97	656
Aug-Oct 2007	794	6.4	182	23.0	235	46	330	5,620	409	7.3	4,440	97	650
Sep-Nov 2007	794	6.4	177	22.3	240	41	336	5,622	409	7.3	4,453	102	638
Oct-Dec 2007	799	6.4	179	22.4	256	36	327	5,642	438	7.8	4,424	99	654
Nov-Jan 2008	788	6.3	179	22.7	250	35	324	5,653	447	7.9	4,416	105	660
Dec-Feb 2008	782	6.3	181	23.2	247	40	314	5,664	437	7.7	4,419	108	671
Jan-Mar 2008	773	6.2	178	23.1	244	44	307	5,665	416	7.3	4,431	115	674
Feb-Apr 2008	783	6.3	179	22.8	248	44	312	5,657	409	7.2	4,415	114	691
Mar-May 2008	772	6.1	179	23.1	239	39	316	5,657	402	7.1	4,422	117	686
Apr-Jun 2008	767	6.1	171	22.3	245	38	313	5,649	408	7.2	4,419	126	669
May-Jul 2008	774	6.2	169	21.9	248	40	316	5,629	399	7.1	4,410	134	659
Jun-Aug 2008	768	6.1	173	22.6	251	39	305	5,627	399	7.1	4,435	133	634
Jul-Sep 2008	757	6.0	176	23.2	244	42	295	5,606	399	7.1	4,420	126	633
Aug-Oct 2008	743	5.9	174	23.4	237	41	291	5,606	409	7.3	4,423	117	629
Sep-Nov 2008	768	6.1	178	23.1	244	42	304	5,678	420	7.4	4,465	120	646
Oct-Dec 2008	772	6.2	185	24.0	240	44	303	5,646	417	7.4	4,439	118	643
Nov-Jan 2009	766	6.1	182	23.7	237	44	303	5,651	437	7.7	4,424	114	648
Dec-Feb 2009	765	6.1	195	25.5	227	46	297	5,668	465	8.2	4,428	105	643
Jan-Mar 2009	764	6.1	193	25.3	230	44	297	5,685	481	8.5	4,436	107	638
Feb-Apr 2009	755	6.1	191	25.3	226	47	292	5,644	497	8.8	4,387	112	626
Mar-May 2009	755	6.1	198	26.2	231	44	282	5,621	511	9.1	4,357	111	620
Apr-Jun 2009	754	6.1	200	26.6	230	42	282	5,660	525	9.3	4,373	110	622
May-Jul 2009	750	6.1	212	28.3	220	39	279	5,681	534	9.4	4,387	108	620
Jun-Aug 2009	756	6.1	211	27.9	225	42	279	5,695	549	9.6	4,375	114	627
Jul-Sep 2009	779	6.3	223	28.7	230	41	284	5,765	569	9.9	4,411	110	648
Aug-Oct 2009	767	6.2	223	29.0	228	36	279	5,803	583	10.0	4,422	112	662
Sep-Nov 2009	752	6.1	228	30.3	220	34	271	5,801	589	10.2	4,411	107	666
Oct-Dec 2009	755	6.1	229	30.4	216	36	273	5,789	591	10.2	4,395	110	666
Nov-Jan 2010	768	6.2	240	31.2	223	36	269	5,789	596	10.3	4,386	109	671
Dec-Feb 2010	772	6.2	240	31.1	217	37	278	5,761	594	10.3	4,360	107	674
Jan-Mar 2010	775	6.3	245	31.6	215	37	278	5,780	608	10.5	4,379	99	661
Feb-Apr 2010	786	6.4	256	32.6	210	40	280	5,824	627	10.8	4,413	104	647
Mar-May 2010	808	6.5	263	32.6	217	39	289	5,847	613	10.5	4,446	104	651
Apr-Jun 2010	818	6.6	269	32.9	217	42	290	5,837	608	10.4	4,456	102	642
May-Jul 2010	824	6.6	272	33.0	222	40	289	5,894	635	10.8	4,465	101	666
Jun-Aug 2010	818	6.6	277	33.9	211	43	286	5,896	646	11.0	4,451	93	673
Jul-Sep 2010	832	6.7	281	33.8	220	42	288	5,895	652	11.1	4,452	93	665
Aug-Oct 2010	836	6.8	277	33.2	217	44	297	5,868	652	11.1	4,444	92	642
Sep-Nov 2010	831	6.7	286	34.4	203	42	300	5,857	657	11.2	4,464	94	603
Oct-Dec 2010	828	6.7	287	34.7	193	42	306	5,851	672	11.5	4,437	91	614
Nov-Jan 2011	829	6.7	281	33.9	196	43	309	5,875	669	11.4	4,469	91	609
Dec-Feb 2011	836	6.7	277	33.1	208	44	308	5,895	668	11.3	4,483	96	611
Jan-Mar 2011	843	6.8	279	33.1	211	45	308	5,891	665	11.3	4,468	100	622
Feb-Apr 2011	831	6.7	269	32.4	210	43	309	5,885	689	11.7	4,441	102	617
Mar-May 2011	834	6.7	271	32.5	214	43	306	5,886	705	12.0	4,423	106	617
Apr-Jun 2011	824	6.6	280	34.0	210	41	293	5,856	707	12.1	4,391	109	611
May-Jul 2011	807	6.5	274	34.0	200	40	293	5,790	709	12.2	4,322	111	610

4.2 Full-time, part-time and temporary workers

United Kingdom (thousands) seasonally adjusted

	Temporary employees (reasons for temporary working)							Part-time workers (reasons for working part-time)[3]					
	Total	Total as % of all employees	Could not find permanent job	% that could not find permanent job	Did not want permanent job	Had a contract with period of training	Some other reason	Total[4]	Could not find full-time job	% that could not find full-time job	Did not want full-time job	Ill or disabled	Student or at school
Women (16+)	YCCB	YCCE	YCCH	YCCK	YCCN	YCCQ	YCCT	YCCW	YCCZ	YCDC	YCDF	YCDI	YCDL
Jun-Aug 2011	786	6.3	275	35.0	182	39	290	5,807	711	12.2	4,336	115	611
Jul-Sep 2011	790	6.4	280	35.4	189	42	279	5,818	720	12.4	4,326	123	614
Aug-Oct 2011	802	6.5	294	36.6	194	43	272	5,821	723	12.4	4,346	116	608
Sep-Nov 2011	820	6.6	292	35.6	202	48	278	5,835	753	12.9	4,334	115	608
Oct-Dec 2011	818	6.6	294	35.9	204	50	271	5,850	768	13.1	4,332	119	605
Nov-Jan 2012	827	6.7	297	35.9	203	52	275	5,857	794	13.6	4,319	116	599
Dec-Feb 2012	848	6.9	303	35.7	215	51	280	5,849	781	13.4	4,332	108	594
Jan-Mar 2012	828	6.7	300	36.2	198	46	284	5,875	779	13.3	4,349	117	590
Feb-Apr 2012	818	6.6	298	36.4	193	49	278	5,860	773	13.2	4,344	116	591
Mar-May 2012	840	6.8	315	37.5	185	50	291	5,854	763	13.0	4,350	116	591
Apr-Jun 2012	862	6.9	318	36.9	194	53	297	5,892	777	13.2	4,366	110	609
May-Jul 2012	893	7.2	327	36.6	211	51	305	5,958	787	13.2	4,425	110	608
Jun-Aug 2012	884	7.1	324	36.7	209	50	301	5,962	787	13.2	4,425	108	615
Jul-Sep 2012	867	6.9	322	37.1	207	47	291	5,959	782	13.1	4,431	111	607
Aug-Oct 2012	865	6.9	316	36.5	204	46	299	5,965	774	13.0	4,430	116	612
Sep-Nov 2012	871	7.0	309	35.4	209	49	304	5,970	769	12.9	4,438	120	610
Oct-Dec 2012	870	6.9	302	34.7	205	54	310	5,959	752	12.6	4,444	118	610
Nov-Jan 2013	864	6.9	306	35.4	196	54	307	5,943	767	12.9	4,425	122	597
Dec-Feb 2013	833	6.6	301	36.1	192	55	285	5,945	781	13.1	4,410	121	599
Jan-Mar 2013	859	6.8	313	36.4	193	62	292	5,940	781	13.1	4,399	117	610
Feb-Apr 2013	846	6.7	301	35.6	192	65	288	5,925	780	13.2	4,383	118	613
Mar-May 2013	837	6.7	301	36.0	188	60	288	5,908	798	13.5	4,349	116	609
Apr-Jun 2013	831	6.6	290	34.9	185	67	289	5,922	796	13.4	4,368	120	600
May-Jul 2013	827	6.6	292	35.3	181	63	292	5,919	804	13.6	4,350	122	602
Jun-Aug 2013	840	6.7	298	35.5	169	63	310	5,909	799	13.5	4,369	126	575
Jul-Sep 2013	850	6.7	296	34.9	182	59	313	5,903	796	13.5	4,355	122	590
Aug-Oct 2013	852	6.7	293	34.4	188	62	309	5,949	803	13.5	4,399	120	590
Sep-Nov 2013	846	6.7	286	33.8	193	67	301	5,921	786	13.3	4,389	116	596
Oct-Dec 2013	852	6.7	301	35.4	194	56	301	5,892	790	13.4	4,363	114	594
Nov-Jan 2014	852	6.7	293	34.4	201	57	300	5,903	785	13.3	4,374	115	599
Dec-Feb 2014	859	6.8	290	33.8	206	57	306	5,979	780	13.0	4,457	115	602
Jan-Mar 2014	872	6.9	291	33.3	213	58	311	5,979	776	13.0	4,468	111	599
Feb-Apr 2014	901	7.1	295	32.7	225	57	324	6,006	794	13.2	4,473	105	610
Mar-May 2014	907	7.1	293	32.3	228	59	327	6,029	762	12.6	4,531	104	613
Apr-Jun 2014	885	6.9	288	32.6	233	59	305	6,059	758	12.5	4,566	109	603
May-Jul 2014	897	7.0	291	32.4	233	58	315	6,064	752	12.4	4,587	96	606
Jun-Aug 2014	892	6.9	288	32.3	235	62	308	6,026	758	12.6	4,544	95	606
Jul-Sep 2014	901	7.0	289	32.1	243	60	310	6,020	753	12.5	4,547	95	602
Aug-Oct 2014	882	6.9	281	31.9	238	56	307	6,021	745	12.4	4,569	97	583
Sep-Nov 2014	886	6.9	278	31.3	237	57	315	6,035	743	12.3	4,578	102	587
Oct-Dec 2014	892	6.9	273	30.7	240	54	324	6,072	746	12.3	4,571	105	619

Source: Labour Force Survey
Inquiries: Email: labour.market@ons.gsi.gov.uk
Tel: 01633 455 400

Note: When comparing quarterly changes ONS recommends comparing with the previous non-overlapping 3-month average time period (eg, compare Apr-Jun with Jan-Mar, not with Mar-May).

1. The split between full-time and part-time employment is based on respondents' self-classification.

2. This series does not include all people on these programmes; it only includes those engaging in any form of work, work experience or work-related training.

3. These series cover Employees and Self-employed only. These series include some temporary employees.

4. The total includes those who did not give a reason for working part-time and it therefore does not equal the sum of the other columns in this section of the table.

4.3 Employment: by sex and age: United Kingdom

United Kingdom (thousands) seasonally adjusted

| | | Aged 16 and over | | | | | | Aged 16-64 | | | | |
| | | Employment | | Unemployment | | Inactivity | | Employment | | Unemployment | | Inactivity | |
		Level	Rate	Level	Rate	Level	Rate	Level	Rate	Level	Rate	Level	Rate
People		MGRZ	MGSR	MGSC	MGSX	MGSI	YBTC	LF2G	LF24	LF2I	LF2Q	LF2M	LF2S
	Oct-Dec 2012	29,910	58.5	2,529	7.8	18,662	36.5	28,927	71.4	2,507	8.0	9,082	22.4
	Oct-Dec 2013	30,288	58.9	2,348	7.2	18,800	36.6	29,213	72.0	2,318	7.4	9,047	22.3
	Jan-Mar 2014	30,534	59.3	2,212	6.8	18,775	36.4	29,434	72.5	2,186	6.9	8,979	22.1
	Apr-Jun 2014	30,680	59.5	2,074	6.3	18,853	36.5	29,580	72.8	2,047	6.5	8,992	22.1
	Jul-Sep 2014	30,793	59.6	1,959	6.0	18,939	36.6	29,674	73.0	1,937	6.1	9,030	22.2
	Oct-Dec 2014	**30,896**	**59.7**	**1,862**	**5.7**	**19,016**	**36.7**	**29,769**	**73.2**	**1,844**	**5.8**	**9,052**	**22.3**
	Change on quarter	*103*	*0.1*	*-97*	*-0.3*	*77*	*0.1*	*95*	*0.2*	*-93*	*-0.3*	*22*	*0.0*
	Change %	*0.3*		*-5.0*		*0.4*		*0.3*		*-4.8*		*0.2*	
	Change on year	*608*	*0.8*	*-486*	*-1.5*	*216*	*0.2*	*556*	*1.2*	*-474*	*-1.5*	*6*	*0.0*
	Change %	*2.0*		*-20.7*		*1.1*		*1.9*		*-20.4*		*0.1*	
Men		MGSA	MGSS	MGSD	MGSY	MGSJ	YBTD	YBSF	MGSV	YBSI	YBTJ	YBSO	YBTM
	Oct-Dec 2012	15,950	64.1	1,419	8.2	7,512	30.2	15,347	76.4	1,400	8.4	3,340	16.6
	Oct-Dec 2013	16,138	64.4	1,321	7.6	7,612	30.4	15,490	76.9	1,303	7.8	3,338	16.6
	Jan-Mar 2014	16,279	64.8	1,231	7.0	7,608	30.3	15,610	77.5	1,213	7.2	3,322	16.5
	Apr-Jun 2014	16,326	64.9	1,144	6.5	7,697	30.6	15,680	77.8	1,125	6.7	3,353	16.6
	Jul-Sep 2014	16,388	65.0	1,087	6.2	7,738	30.7	15,730	78.0	1,071	6.4	3,371	16.7
	Oct-Dec 2014	**16,427**	**65.0**	**1,039**	**6.0**	**7,793**	**30.9**	**15,745**	**78.0**	**1,025**	**6.1**	**3,418**	**16.9**
	Change on quarter	*38*	*0.0*	*-47*	*-0.3*	*55*	*0.2*	*14*	*0.0*	*-46*	*-0.3*	*47*	*0.2*
	Change %	*0.2*		*-4.3*		*0.7*		*0.1*		*-4.3*		*1.4*	
	Change on year	*288*	*0.7*	*-281*	*-1.6*	*181*	*0.5*	*254*	*1.0*	*-278*	*-1.6*	*80*	*0.3*
	Change %	*1.8*		*-21.3*		*2.4*		*1.6*		*-21.3*		*2.4*	
Women		MGSB	MGST	MGSE	MGSZ	MGSK	YBTE	LF2H	LF25	LF2J	LF2R	LF2N	LF2T
	Oct-Dec 2012	13,959	53.2	1,110	7.4	11,150	42.5	13,580	66.5	1,106	7.5	5,742	28.1
	Oct-Dec 2013	14,150	53.7	1,027	6.8	11,188	42.4	13,723	67.1	1,015	6.9	5,709	27.9
	Jan-Mar 2014	14,255	54.0	981	6.4	11,167	42.3	13,824	67.6	973	6.6	5,656	27.7
	Apr-Jun 2014	14,355	54.3	930	6.1	11,156	42.2	13,900	67.9	922	6.2	5,639	27.6
	Jul-Sep 2014	14,404	54.4	872	5.7	11,201	42.3	13,943	68.1	866	5.8	5,659	27.6
	Oct-Dec 2014	**14,469**	**54.6**	**822**	**5.4**	**11,223**	**42.3**	**14,024**	**68.5**	**819**	**5.5**	**5,635**	**27.5**
	Change on quarter	*65*	*0.2*	*-50*	*-0.3*	*22*	*0.0*	*81*	*0.4*	*-47*	*-0.3*	*-25*	*-0.1*
	Change %	*0.5*		*-5.7*		*0.2*		*0.6*		*-5.5*		*-0.4*	
	Change on year	*320*	*0.9*	*-205*	*-1.4*	*35*	*-0.1*	*301*	*1.4*	*-196*	*-1.4*	*-74*	*-0.4*
	Change %	*2.3*		*-20.0*		*0.3*		*2.2*		*-19.3*		*-1.3*	

| | | Aged 16-17 | | | | | | Aged 18-24 | | | | |
| | | Employment | | Unemployment | | Inactivity | | Employment | | Unemployment | | Inactivity | |
		Level	Rate	Level	Rate	Level	Rate	Level	Rate	Level	Rate	Level	Rate
People		YBTO	YBUA	YBVH	YBVK	YCAS	LWEX	YBTR	YBUD	YBVN	YBVQ	YCAV	LWFA
	Oct-Dec 2012	334	22.1	201	37.6	976	64.6	3,402	58.2	787	18.8	1,652	28.3
	Oct-Dec 2013	328	21.7	188	36.4	993	65.8	3,402	58.4	740	17.9	1,680	28.9
	Jan-Mar 2014	326	21.7	182	35.8	997	66.3	3,430	59.0	694	16.8	1,695	29.1
	Apr-Jun 2014	319	21.2	166	34.3	1,017	67.7	3,497	60.1	610	14.9	1,707	29.4
	Jul-Sep 2014	320	21.4	157	32.9	1,019	68.1	3,499	60.3	580	14.2	1,728	29.8
	Oct-Dec 2014	**346**	**23.2**	**157**	**31.2**	**986**	**66.3**	**3,494**	**60.2**	**583**	**14.3**	**1,722**	**29.7**
	Change on quarter	*26*	*1.8*	*0*	*-1.7*	*-32*	*-1.9*	*-5*	*0.0*	*3*	*0.1*	*-6*	*-0.1*
	Change %	*8.0*		*-0.1*		*-3.2*		*-0.1*		*0.6*		*-0.3*	
	Change on year	*18*	*1.5*	*-31*	*-5.2*	*-7*	*0.4*	*92*	*1.8*	*-157*	*-3.6*	*42*	*0.8*
	Change %	*5.5*		*-16.5*		*-0.7*		*2.7*		*-21.2*		*2.5*	
Men		YBTP	YBUB	YBVI	YBVL	YCAT	LWEY	YBTS	YBUE	YBVO	YBVR	YCAW	LWFB
	Oct-Dec 2012	145	18.7	110	43.2	521	67.2	1,742	59.1	463	21.0	742	25.2
	Oct-Dec 2013	148	19.1	98	39.9	528	68.2	1,743	59.1	444	20.3	761	25.8
	Jan-Mar 2014	145	18.8	93	39.1	533	69.2	1,769	60.0	416	19.0	762	25.9
	Apr-Jun 2014	139	18.0	80	36.5	550	71.6	1,791	60.8	375	17.3	782	26.5
	Jul-Sep 2014	132	17.3	75	36.3	557	72.8	1,793	60.9	356	16.6	796	27.0
	Oct-Dec 2014	**150**	**19.7**	**82**	**35.4**	**529**	**69.5**	**1,811**	**61.6**	**340**	**15.8**	**791**	**26.9**
	Change on quarter	*18*	*2.4*	*7*	*-0.9*	*-28*	*-3.4*	*18*	*0.7*	*-17*	*-0.8*	*-6*	*-0.2*
	Change %	*13.4*		*9.0*		*-5.0*		*1.0*		*-4.6*		*-0.7*	
	Change on year	*3*	*0.6*	*-16*	*-4.5*	*2*	*1.3*	*68*	*2.5*	*-104*	*-4.5*	*30*	*1.1*
	Change %	*1.8*		*-16.2*		*0.3*		*3.9*		*-23.5*		*3.9*	
Women		YBTQ	YBUC	YBVJ	YBVM	YCAU	LWEZ	YBTT	YBUF	YBVP	YBVS	YCAX	LWFC
	Oct-Dec 2012	189	25.7	91	32.5	455	61.9	1,660	57.4	324	16.3	910	31.4
	Oct-Dec 2013	180	24.5	90	33.3	466	63.3	1,659	57.7	296	15.2	919	32.0
	Jan-Mar 2014	181	24.7	89	33.0	464	63.2	1,661	57.9	277	14.3	932	32.5
	Apr-Jun 2014	180	24.5	86	32.4	467	63.7	1,706	59.5	235	12.1	925	32.3
	Jul-Sep 2014	188	25.7	82	30.3	461	63.2	1,706	59.6	224	11.6	932	32.6
	Oct-Dec 2014	**195**	**26.9**	**75**	**27.6**	**457**	**62.9**	**1,683**	**58.9**	**244**	**12.6**	**932**	**32.6**
	Change on quarter	*8*	*1.2*	*-7*	*-2.7*	*-4*	*-0.3*	*-24*	*-0.7*	*20*	*1.0*	*0*	*0.0*
	Change %	*4.2*		*-8.5*		*-0.9*		*-1.4*		*8.8*		*0.0*	
	Change on year	*15*	*2.4*	*-15*	*-5.7*	*-9*	*-0.5*	*24*	*1.2*	*-53*	*-2.5*	*12*	*0.6*
	Change %	*8.5*		*-17.0*		*-1.9*		*1.4*		*-17.8*		*1.3*	

Source: Labour Force Survey

Labour market statistics enquiries: labour.market@ons.gsi.gov.uk

4.3 Employment: by sex and age: United Kingdom

United Kingdom (thousands) seasonally adjusted

	Aged 25-34						Aged 35-49					
	Employment		Unemployment		Inactivity		Employment		Unemployment		Inactivity	
	Level	Rate	Level	Rate	Level	Rate	Level	Rate	Level	Rate	Level	Rate
People	YBTU	YBUG	YCGM	YCGP	YCAY	LWFD	YBTX	YBUJ	YCGS	YCGV	YCBB	LWFG
Oct-Dec 2012	6,723	78.8	531	7.3	1,274	14.9	10,771	82.0	607	5.3	1,755	13.4
Oct-Dec 2013	6,884	79.7	492	6.7	1,260	14.6	10,663	82.1	529	4.7	1,803	13.9
Jan-Mar 2014	6,960	80.4	458	6.2	1,238	14.3	10,731	82.8	496	4.4	1,739	13.4
Apr-Jun 2014	6,989	80.6	439	5.9	1,246	14.4	10,771	83.3	484	4.3	1,682	13.0
Jul-Sep 2014	7,004	80.6	405	5.5	1,281	14.7	10,773	83.4	467	4.2	1,673	13.0
Oct-Dec 2014	**7,006**	**80.5**	**390**	**5.3**	**1,308**	**15.0**	**10,794**	**83.7**	**414**	**3.7**	**1,685**	**13.1**
Change on quarter	*2*	*-0.1*	*-16*	*-0.2*	*27*	*0.3*	*21*	*0.3*	*-54*	*-0.5*	*12*	*0.1*
Change %	*0.0*		*-3.8*		*2.1*		*0.2*		*-11.5*		*0.7*	
Change on year	*122*	*0.8*	*-102*	*-1.4*	*48*	*0.4*	*131*	*1.7*	*-116*	*-1.0*	*-117*	*-0.8*
Change %	*1.8*		*-20.7*		*3.8*		*1.2*		*-21.9*		*-6.5*	
Men	YBTV	YBUH	YCGN	YCGQ	YCAZ	LWFE	YBTY	YBUK	YCGT	YCGW	YCBC	LWFH
Oct-Dec 2012	3,655	86.5	281	7.1	290	6.9	5,698	88.0	296	4.9	484	7.5
Oct-Dec 2013	3,726	86.9	280	7.0	280	6.5	5,636	87.9	264	4.5	510	8.0
Jan-Mar 2014	3,770	87.7	244	6.1	285	6.6	5,670	88.6	252	4.3	474	7.4
Apr-Jun 2014	3,804	88.3	224	5.6	282	6.5	5,683	89.0	243	4.1	458	7.2
Jul-Sep 2014	3,800	87.9	217	5.4	305	7.0	5,695	89.4	227	3.8	450	7.1
Oct-Dec 2014	**3,785**	**87.3**	**207**	**5.2**	**341**	**7.9**	**5,685**	**89.4**	**214**	**3.6**	**462**	**7.3**
Change on quarter	*-16*	*-0.6*	*-9*	*-0.2*	*36*	*0.8*	*-9*	*0.0*	*-13*	*-0.2*	*12*	*0.2*
Change %	*-0.4*		*-4.4*		*11.9*		*-0.2*		*-5.8*		*2.6*	
Change on year	*59*	*0.4*	*-73*	*-1.8*	*61*	*1.3*	*49*	*1.5*	*-50*	*-0.8*	*-48*	*-0.7*
Change %	*1.6*		*-26.1*		*21.6*		*0.9*		*-19.0*		*-9.5*	
Women	YBTW	YBUI	YCGO	YCGR	YCBA	LWFF	YBTZ	YBUL	YCGU	YCGX	YCBD	LWFI
Oct-Dec 2012	3,069	71.3	250	7.5	984	22.9	5,073	76.2	311	5.8	1,272	19.1
Oct-Dec 2013	3,158	72.6	211	6.3	980	22.5	5,027	76.3	266	5.0	1,292	19.6
Jan-Mar 2014	3,190	73.2	214	6.3	953	21.9	5,061	77.0	244	4.6	1,264	19.2
Apr-Jun 2014	3,185	73.0	215	6.3	964	22.1	5,088	77.6	241	4.5	1,225	18.7
Jul-Sep 2014	3,204	73.3	189	5.6	976	22.3	5,079	77.6	241	4.5	1,223	18.7
Oct-Dec 2014	**3,222**	**73.7**	**183**	**5.4**	**968**	**22.1**	**5,109**	**78.2**	**200**	**3.8**	**1,223**	**18.7**
Change on quarter	*18*	*0.4*	*-6*	*-0.2*	*-9*	*-0.2*	*30*	*0.6*	*-41*	*-0.8*	*0*	*0.0*
Change %	*0.6*		*-3.2*		*-0.9*		*0.6*		*-16.9*		*0.0*	
Change on year	*64*	*1.1*	*-28*	*-0.9*	*-13*	*-0.4*	*82*	*1.9*	*-66*	*-1.3*	*-69*	*-0.9*
Change %	*2.0*		*-13.5*		*-1.3*		*1.6*		*-24.7*		*-5.4*	

	Aged 50-64						Age 65+					
	Employment		Unemployment		Inactivity		Employment		Unemployment		Inactivity	
	Level	Rate	Level	Rate	Level	Rate	Level	Rate	Level	Rate	Level	Rate
People	LF26	LF2U	LF28	LF2E	LF2A	LF2W	LFK4	LFK6	K5HU	K5HW	LFL4	LFL6
Oct-Dec 2012	7,697	66.9	381	4.7	3,425	29.8	983	9.3	22	2.2	9,580	90.5
Oct-Dec 2013	7,937	68.3	369	4.4	3,310	28.5	1,075	9.9	30	2.7	9,753	89.8
Jan-Mar 2014	7,987	68.5	356	4.3	3,310	28.4	1,100	10.1	27	2.4	9,797	89.7
Apr-Jun 2014	8,004	68.5	347	4.2	3,340	28.6	1,101	10.0	27	2.4	9,861	89.7
Jul-Sep 2014	8,077	68.8	328	3.9	3,329	28.4	1,119	10.1	22	1.9	9,909	89.7
Oct-Dec 2014	**8,129**	**69.0**	**301**	**3.6**	**3,350**	**28.4**	**1,127**	**10.1**	**18**	**1.5**	**9,963**	**89.7**
Change on quarter	*52*	*0.2*	*-27*	*-0.3*	*21*	*0.1*	*8*	*0.0*	*-4*	*-0.4*	*54*	*0.0*
Change %	*0.6*		*-8.3*		*0.6*		*0.7*		*-18.2*		*0.5*	
Change on year	*192*	*0.7*	*-68*	*-0.9*	*41*	*-0.1*	*53*	*0.3*	*-12*	*-1.2*	*210*	*-0.1*
Change %	*2.4*		*-18.5*		*1.2*		*4.9*		*-40.8*		*2.2*	
Men	MGUX	YBUN	MGVM	MGXF	MGWB	LWFK	MGVA	YBUQ	MGVP	MGXI	MGWE	LWFN
Oct-Dec 2012	4,108	72.6	250	5.7	1,303	23.0	603	12.6	19	3.0	4,171	87.0
Oct-Dec 2013	4,238	74.2	217	4.9	1,259	22.0	648	13.1	17	2.6	4,274	86.5
Jan-Mar 2014	4,256	74.3	208	4.7	1,268	22.1	670	13.5	18	2.7	4,286	86.2
Apr-Jun 2014	4,264	74.2	203	4.6	1,281	22.3	645	12.9	19	2.8	4,344	86.7
Jul-Sep 2014	4,310	74.7	196	4.4	1,262	21.9	658	13.1	16	2.3	4,367	86.6
Oct-Dec 2014	**4,313**	**74.5**	**183**	**4.1**	**1,295**	**22.4**	**682**	**13.4**	**14**	**2.0**	**4,375**	**86.3**
Change on quarter	*3*	*-0.2*	*-14*	*-0.3*	*32*	*0.5*	*24*	*0.4*	*-1*	*-0.3*	*8*	*-0.4*
Change %	*0.1*		*-6.9*		*2.6*		*3.7*		*-8.7*		*0.2*	
Change on year	*76*	*0.3*	*-35*	*-0.8*	*36*	*0.3*	*34*	*0.3*	*-3*	*-0.6*	*101*	*-0.3*
Change %	*1.8*		*-15.9*		*2.9*		*5.3*		*-18.5*		*2.4*	
Women	LF27	LF2V	LF29	LF2F	LF2B	LF2X	LFK5	LFK7	K5HV	K5HX	LFL5	LFL7
Oct-Dec 2012	3,589	61.4	131	3.5	2,121	36.3	380	6.6	*	*	5,408	93.4
Oct-Dec 2013	3,699	62.7	152	3.9	2,051	34.8	427	7.2	13	2.9	5,479	92.6
Jan-Mar 2014	3,731	63.0	148	3.8	2,043	34.5	430	7.2	*	*	5,511	92.6
Apr-Jun 2014	3,740	62.9	144	3.7	2,058	34.6	455	7.6	*	*	5,517	92.2
Jul-Sep 2014	3,767	63.1	132	3.4	2,067	34.6	461	7.7	*	*	5,542	92.2
Oct-Dec 2014	**3,815**	**63.7**	**118**	**3.0**	**2,056**	**34.3**	**445**	**7.4**	*	*	**5,588**	**92.6**
Change on quarter	*49*	*0.6*	*-14*	*-0.4*	*-11*	*-0.3*	*-16*	*-0.3*	*	*	*46*	*0.3*
Change %	*1.3*		*-10.3*		*-0.5*		*-3.4*		*		*0.8*	
Change on year	*117*	*1.0*	*-34*	*-0.9*	*5*	*-0.4*	*18*	*0.2*	*	*	*109*	*0.0*
Change %	*3.2*		*-22.3*		*0.2*		*4.3*		*		*2.0*	

Source: Labour Force Survey

Labour market statistics enquiries: labour.market@ons.gsi.gov.uk

4.4: All in employment by industry sector

United Kingdom (thousands) not seasonally adjusted

Standard Industrial Classification (SIC) 2007[1]

People

Period	All in employment[2]	Public sector[3]	Private sector	A Agriculture, forestry & fishing	B,D,E Mining, energy and water supply	C Manufacturing	F Construction	G Wholesale, retail & repair of motor vehicles	H Transport & storage	I Accommod-ation and food services	J Information & communication	K Financial & insurance activities	L Real estate activities	M Professional, scientific & technical activities	N Administra-tive & support services	O Public admin & defence; social security	P Education	Q Human health & social work activities	R,S,T Other services
Jan-Mar 2005	28,705	6,957	21,599	288	401	3,306	2,397	4,253	1,535	1,302	1,026	1,219	224	1,735	1,350	1,953	2,733	3,469	1,413
Apr-Jun 2005	28,735	6,920	21,695	284	398	3,336	2,384	4,213	1,558	1,317	1,013	1,210	240	1,755	1,338	1,938	2,768	3,479	1,431
Jul-Sep 2005	29,035	7,021	21,900	283	406	3,317	2,458	4,239	1,576	1,281	1,024	1,287	248	1,783	1,325	1,983	2,718	3,571	1,450
Oct-Dec 2005	28,938	7,039	21,782	288	415	3,260	2,410	4,202	1,593	1,267	1,022	1,279	257	1,818	1,299	1,967	2,755	3,559	1,448
Jan-Mar 2006	28,966	7,130	21,735	273	404	3,242	2,431	4,163	1,564	1,286	1,014	1,270	252	1,835	1,276	2,020	2,836	3,576	1,426
Apr-Jun 2006	29,032	7,096	21,824	268	414	3,285	2,460	4,117	1,555	1,340	1,024	1,259	263	1,806	1,280	1,990	2,849	3,579	1,446
Jul-Sep 2006	29,289	7,018	22,165	293	424	3,280	2,510	4,154	1,574	1,382	1,045	1,252	248	1,824	1,323	1,970	2,758	3,630	1,528
Oct-Dec 2006	29,276	6,940	22,216	302	436	3,234	2,542	4,198	1,585	1,329	1,057	1,270	248	1,825	1,328	1,962	2,813	3,522	1,508
Jan-Mar 2007	29,108	6,954	22,040	288	450	3,216	2,527	4,120	1,566	1,324	1,056	1,263	257	1,874	1,304	1,980	2,798	3,500	1,473
Apr-Jun 2007	29,242	6,987	22,131	294	464	3,281	2,544	4,034	1,559	1,371	1,051	1,272	245	1,883	1,347	1,985	2,823	3,461	1,513
Jul-Sep 2007	29,525	6,919	22,466	297	469	3,269	2,558	4,090	1,556	1,406	1,062	1,304	266	1,912	1,432	1,990	2,782	3,505	1,512
Oct-Dec 2007	29,640	7,018	22,479	307	461	3,216	2,537	4,187	1,576	1,395	1,019	1,312	279	1,952	1,399	1,996	2,840	3,531	1,517
Jan-Mar 2008	29,596	7,047	22,404	334	452	3,148	2,535	4,184	1,605	1,382	1,024	1,288	263	1,939	1,398	2,011	2,847	3,566	1,509
Apr-Jun 2008	29,637	7,101	22,383	321	446	3,087	2,512	4,195	1,590	1,355	1,033	1,287	253	1,969	1,417	2,035	2,865	3,642	1,519
Jul-Sep 2008	29,685	7,039	22,508	313	463	3,068	2,583	4,248	1,606	1,355	1,063	1,272	259	1,919	1,404	2,033	2,805	3,648	1,533
Oct-Dec 2008	29,593	7,167	22,289	306	507	2,981	2,564	4,221	1,626	1,335	1,036	1,244	252	1,849	1,347	2,037	2,848	3,748	1,584
Jan-Mar 2009	29,277	7,224	21,913	322	489	2,857	2,482	4,107	1,571	1,324	1,035	1,227	273	1,842	1,309	2,009	2,919	3,772	1,579
Apr-Jun 2009	29,003	7,238	21,624	311	483	2,777	2,385	3,989	1,510	1,360	1,015	1,235	268	1,882	1,301	1,967	2,929	3,739	1,583
Jul-Sep 2009	29,170	7,278	21,745	329	491	2,813	2,311	4,031	1,463	1,428	1,020	1,246	265	1,890	1,301	1,977	2,960	3,778	1,599
Oct-Dec 2009	29,167	7,324	21,691	323	482	2,799	2,311	4,017	1,455	1,406	1,014	1,223	254	1,886	1,328	1,944	3,045	3,846	1,579
Jan-Mar 2010	28,924	7,255	21,488	336	472	2,815	2,208	3,943	1,462	1,388	1,011	1,210	263	1,882	1,319	1,930	3,062	3,824	1,549
Apr-Jun 2010	29,110	7,325	21,586	341	463	2,875	2,207	4,004	1,443	1,461	979	1,175	262	1,893	1,326	1,925	3,129	3,848	1,532
Jul-Sep 2010	29,484	7,298	21,973	369	474	2,888	2,234	4,112	1,483	1,503	1,045	1,165	301	1,852	1,341	1,925	3,120	3,821	1,594
Oct-Dec 2010	29,390	7,278	21,929	366	489	2,902	2,238	4,082	1,436	1,427	1,030	1,171	300	1,882	1,379	1,867	3,120	3,884	1,555
Jan-Mar 2011	29,350	7,315	21,842	357	497	2,860	2,212	4,034	1,451	1,417	1,059	1,179	299	1,857	1,299	1,875	3,121	3,967	1,544
Apr-Jun 2011	29,367	7,183	22,021	342	521	2,868	2,198	4,051	1,445	1,458	1,073	1,173	308	1,851	1,321	1,844	3,129	3,931	1,587
Jul-Sep 2011	29,376	7,009	22,216	370	519	2,842	2,237	4,078	1,428	1,498	1,061	1,192	300	1,888	1,339	1,852	2,986	3,981	1,639
Oct-Dec 2011	29,405	6,970	22,276	356	527	2,884	2,172	4,079	1,432	1,499	1,083	1,215	293	1,898	1,353	1,864	3,021	3,927	1,583
Jan-Mar 2012	29,365	6,952	22,208	374	534	2,850	2,148	4,018	1,430	1,438	1,124	1,199	333	1,903	1,369	1,847	3,088	3,865	1,554
Apr-Jun 2012	29,587	6,847	22,517	353	532	2,920	2,171	4,103	1,416	1,496	1,098	1,229	328	1,945	1,357	1,803	3,078	3,871	1,574
Jul-Sep 2012	29,851	6,883	22,722	356	547	2,934	2,175	4,129	1,457	1,524	1,112	1,216	329	1,983	1,372	1,827	3,021	3,947	1,607
Oct-Dec 2012	29,976	6,984	22,753	316	518	2,911	2,150	4,106	1,482	1,527	1,146	1,192	346	1,967	1,376	1,824	3,140	3,992	1,592
Oct-Dec 2013	30,355	6,901	23,221	322	512	2,958	2,201	4,100	1,542	1,556	1,197	1,169	340	2,095	1,437	1,816	3,092	4,065	1,638
Jan-Mar 2014	30,432	6,930	23,301	379	508	2,945	2,229	4,064	1,488	1,580	1,149	1,168	369	2,167	1,387	1,851	3,104	4,071	1,663
Apr-Jun 2014	30,608	6,931	23,481	395	511	2,997	2,216	3,995	1,465	1,633	1,172	1,155	358	2,139	1,439	1,806	3,214	4,100	1,692
Jul-Sep 2014	30,886	6,906	23,782	386	543	3,019	2,241	3,976	1,467	1,665	1,235	1,205	340	2,135	1,485	1,852	3,192	4,056	1,780
Oct-Dec 2014	**30,966**	**6,889**	**23,874**	**376**	**536**	**3,077**	**2,266**	**4,120**	**1,477**	**1,593**	**1,247**	**1,177**	**338**	**2,129**	**1,448**	**1,795**	**3,226**	**4,134**	**1,749**
Change on year	*611*	*-12*	*653*	*54*	*24*	*119*	*65*	*20*	*-65*	*37*	*51*	*8*	*-2*	*34*	*11*	*-21*	*134*	*69*	*110*
Change %	*2.0*	*-0.2*	*2.8*	*16.8*	*4.8*	*4.0*	*2.9*	*0.5*	*-4.2*	*2.4*	*4.2*	*0.7*	*-0.6*	*1.6*	*0.7*	*-1.2*	*4.3*	*1.7*	*6.7*

4.4: All in employment by industry sector

United Kingdom (thousands) not seasonally adjusted

Standard Industrial Classification (SIC) 2007 [1]

Men

	All in employment [2]	Public sector [3]	Private sector	Agriculture, forestry & fishing A	Mining, energy and water supply B, D, E	Manufacturing C	Construction F	Wholesale, retail & repair of motor vehicles G	Transport & storage H	Accommodation and food services I	Information & communication J	Financial & insurance activities K	Real estate activities L	Professional, scientific & technical activities M	Administrative & support services N	Public admin & defence; social security O	Education P	Human health & social work activities Q	Other services R, S, T
Jan-Mar 2005	15,461	2,486	12,892	210	317	2,529	2,080	2,124	1,241	589	715	608	117	986	736	998	755	757	638
Apr-Jun 2005	15,480	2,473	12,938	200	320	2,548	2,066	2,128	1,254	596	714	609	127	997	742	976	766	755	638
Jul-Sep 2005	15,653	2,537	13,046	201	325	2,538	2,136	2,137	1,279	564	723	635	127	993	754	1,013	770	750	649
Oct-Dec 2005	15,610	2,532	13,008	214	338	2,496	2,101	2,109	1,297	580	718	636	132	1,024	736	998	785	740	644
Jan-Mar 2006	15,541	2,563	12,912	199	322	2,491	2,105	2,077	1,261	584	723	637	134	1,023	714	1,015	809	754	629
Apr-Jun 2006	15,603	2,531	13,007	201	322	2,507	2,127	2,082	1,264	603	727	639	144	998	706	994	817	750	663
Jul-Sep 2006	15,821	2,513	13,244	218	328	2,493	2,183	2,142	1,266	629	742	628	124	1,028	712	996	785	777	711
Oct-Dec 2006	15,790	2,449	13,276	221	338	2,463	2,212	2,157	1,262	580	751	646	131	1,024	733	989	795	731	688
Jan-Mar 2007	15,691	2,436	13,197	204	346	2,452	2,210	2,135	1,242	587	758	662	125	1,024	735	1,001	770	717	661
Apr-Jun 2007	15,789	2,459	13,259	208	359	2,506	2,216	2,084	1,244	618	749	658	116	1,024	771	991	788	709	684
Jul-Sep 2007	15,964	2,423	13,465	214	363	2,464	2,244	2,103	1,245	647	754	681	126	1,052	827	1,005	784	703	686
Oct-Dec 2007	15,987	2,444	13,467	210	358	2,429	2,225	2,131	1,268	648	713	703	133	1,064	823	1,021	799	720	678
Jan-Mar 2008	15,938	2,483	13,374	223	352	2,379	2,204	2,132	1,293	631	722	692	130	1,060	804	1,039	786	756	664
Apr-Jun 2008	15,961	2,509	13,371	222	349	2,354	2,181	2,144	1,274	633	730	675	131	1,082	823	1,053	780	800	659
Jul-Sep 2008	15,990	2,488	13,422	218	370	2,316	2,249	2,177	1,275	620	752	648	143	1,066	802	1,037	741	805	704
Oct-Dec 2008	15,909	2,538	13,293	219	409	2,252	2,233	2,161	1,292	616	744	629	137	1,022	774	1,028	777	830	717
Jan-Mar 2009	15,670	2,572	13,020	247	390	2,144	2,213	2,103	1,255	604	722	624	132	1,069	715	1,003	803	828	722
Apr-Jun 2009	15,464	2,558	12,828	240	383	2,102	2,127	2,056	1,208	620	717	635	124	1,105	710	985	791	812	710
Jul-Sep 2009	15,526	2,572	12,867	252	389	2,128	2,065	2,089	1,171	645	725	642	122	1,094	695	996	831	805	726
Oct-Dec 2009	15,477	2,581	12,814	246	384	2,122	2,070	2,069	1,173	633	722	637	115	1,064	706	995	868	820	719
Jan-Mar 2010	15,326	2,533	12,694	252	380	2,154	1,971	2,037	1,181	643	710	628	118	1,089	707	984	857	792	693
Apr-Jun 2010	15,493	2,576	12,807	264	373	2,207	1,961	2,094	1,160	681	692	622	113	1,092	725	1,003	864	810	697
Jul-Sep 2010	15,773	2,601	13,047	284	381	2,213	1,992	2,159	1,173	684	748	624	132	1,070	760	994	872	804	735
Oct-Dec 2010	15,720	2,582	13,035	283	394	2,214	1,991	2,147	1,133	668	748	640	130	1,097	788	949	843	852	702
Jan-Mar 2011	15,620	2,582	12,930	270	413	2,179	1,955	2,115	1,167	643	756	647	133	1,091	724	963	848	855	697
Apr-Jun 2011	15,685	2,547	13,050	262	428	2,170	1,940	2,112	1,172	651	766	644	144	1,100	752	913	887	863	725
Jul-Sep 2011	15,666	2,453	13,136	271	422	2,167	2,005	2,082	1,149	678	752	650	154	1,105	741	904	842	851	758
Oct-Dec 2011	15,672	2,436	13,158	261	424	2,196	1,939	2,124	1,154	710	788	654	151	1,104	732	922	838	843	714
Jan-Mar 2012	15,649	2,426	13,113	270	434	2,152	1,910	2,093	1,158	678	812	635	177	1,116	741	912	867	823	696
Apr-Jun 2012	15,821	2,359	13,329	257	436	2,203	1,928	2,155	1,140	674	802	660	162	1,146	745	889	867	836	735
Jul-Sep 2012	15,969	2,385	13,424	256	440	2,220	1,942	2,159	1,173	681	803	671	156	1,151	754	922	850	841	746
Oct-Dec 2012	15,988	2,404	13,433	236	404	2,199	1,917	2,161	1,190	678	814	641	164	1,138	765	952	897	853	724
Oct-Dec 2013	16,176	2,322	13,726	233	410	2,227	1,937	2,128	1,249	733	841	652	144	1,242	804	918	846	859	763
Jan-Mar 2014	16,199	2,344	13,743	271	415	2,200	1,948	2,133	1,206	756	818	664	161	1,269	768	928	842	871	767
Apr-Jun 2014	16,288	2,357	13,820	286	415	2,241	1,946	2,067	1,170	764	848	656	152	1,261	815	923	885	889	781
Jul-Sep 2014	16,465	2,373	13,972	292	438	2,257	1,968	2,069	1,150	787	890	676	162	1,253	817	947	900	872	823
Oct-Dec 2014	**16,464**	**2,380**	**13,965**	**280**	**421**	**2,309**	**2,002**	**2,138**	**1,139**	**729**	**891**	**655**	**168**	**1,250**	**790**	**923**	**926**	**888**	**792**
Change on year	*287*	*58*	*239*	*46*	*12*	*82*	*65*	*10*	*-111*	*-5*	*49*	*2*	*24*	*8*	*-15*	*5*	*80*	*29*	*29*
Change %	*1.8*	*2.5*	*1.7*	*19.9*	*2.8*	*3.7*	*3.3*	*0.5*	*-8.9*	*-0.6*	*5.9*	*0.4*	*16.3*	*0.6*	*-1.8*	*0.5*	*9.4*	*3.3*	*3.8*

4.4: All in employment by industry sector

United Kingdom (thousands) not seasonally adjusted

Standard Industrial Classification (SIC) 2007 [1]

Women

	All in employment [2]	Public sector [3]	Private sector	Agriculture, forestry & fishing (A)	Mining, energy and water supply (B, D, E)	Manufacturing (C)	Construction (F)	Wholesale, retail & repair of motor vehicles (G)	Transport & storage (H)	Accommodation and food services (I)	Information & communication (J)	Financial & insurance activities (K)	Real estate activities (L)	Professional, scientific & technical activities (M)	Administrative & support services (N)	Public admin & defence; social security (O)	Education (P)	Human health & social work activities (Q)	Other services (R, S, T)
Jan-Mar 2005	13,244	4,470	8,707	79	83	777	317	2,129	294	713	311	610	108	748	614	955	1,978	2,712	775
Apr-Jun 2005	13,255	4,447	8,757	83	78	788	317	2,085	304	722	300	600	113	758	595	962	2,002	2,723	794
Jul-Sep 2005	13,382	4,484	8,854	82	81	779	321	2,102	298	717	301	652	122	789	571	970	1,948	2,821	800
Oct-Dec 2005	13,327	4,507	8,775	74	76	764	308	2,092	296	687	304	643	125	794	563	969	1,971	2,819	803
Jan-Mar 2006	13,424	4,566	8,823	75	82	752	326	2,086	303	703	291	632	119	812	562	1,006	2,026	2,822	797
Apr-Jun 2006	13,428	4,565	8,817	67	92	778	333	2,035	292	737	296	620	119	808	573	996	2,032	2,829	783
Jul-Sep 2006	13,468	4,505	8,922	75	96	787	327	2,012	308	753	303	624	123	796	611	975	1,973	2,853	817
Oct-Dec 2006	13,486	4,491	8,939	81	99	771	331	2,040	322	749	306	624	117	801	596	973	2,018	2,790	820
Jan-Mar 2007	13,417	4,519	8,842	85	104	764	317	1,985	324	737	298	601	131	851	569	979	2,029	2,783	812
Apr-Jun 2007	13,453	4,528	8,872	87	105	775	328	1,950	315	753	301	614	129	858	576	993	2,035	2,752	830
Jul-Sep 2007	13,561	4,496	9,001	83	105	805	314	1,986	311	759	308	623	139	860	604	986	1,998	2,802	826
Oct-Dec 2007	13,653	4,574	9,012	98	103	787	312	2,056	308	747	306	609	145	888	576	975	2,041	2,811	839
Jan-Mar 2008	13,658	4,563	9,030	112	100	769	331	2,052	311	751	302	595	133	879	594	972	2,061	2,810	845
Apr-Jun 2008	13,677	4,593	9,011	99	97	733	331	2,051	316	722	302	612	122	887	594	982	2,081	2,842	860
Jul-Sep 2008	13,695	4,551	9,086	95	93	753	334	2,071	332	734	310	624	117	853	602	996	2,065	2,843	828
Oct-Dec 2008	13,683	4,629	8,996	88	98	728	331	2,060	334	719	292	614	115	827	574	1,009	2,071	2,917	866
Jan-Mar 2009	13,606	4,652	8,894	75	99	713	270	2,004	316	719	313	603	142	773	594	1,006	2,116	2,944	857
Apr-Jun 2009	13,539	4,680	8,796	71	100	674	258	1,933	302	740	298	600	145	778	591	982	2,138	2,927	872
Jul-Sep 2009	13,644	4,705	8,878	77	102	686	246	1,942	291	783	295	605	143	796	606	981	2,130	2,973	873
Oct-Dec 2009	13,690	4,743	8,877	77	98	677	241	1,948	282	773	292	586	139	822	622	950	2,177	3,026	860
Jan-Mar 2010	13,597	4,721	8,794	84	92	661	237	1,906	281	745	301	583	144	793	613	946	2,206	3,032	856
Apr-Jun 2010	13,616	4,748	8,780	78	89	668	246	1,910	283	780	287	553	149	801	601	923	2,266	3,039	835
Jul-Sep 2010	13,710	4,697	8,926	86	93	676	241	1,953	309	819	297	542	169	782	581	931	2,247	3,017	859
Oct-Dec 2010	13,670	4,696	8,894	84	95	688	247	1,935	303	759	281	531	171	785	592	918	2,277	3,032	853
Jan-Mar 2011	13,730	4,732	8,912	87	85	681	257	1,919	285	774	303	532	167	766	575	913	2,273	3,112	847
Apr-Jun 2011	13,682	4,636	8,972	80	93	698	258	1,939	273	807	307	529	164	751	569	932	2,242	3,068	862
Jul-Sep 2011	13,710	4,556	9,080	98	96	675	232	1,937	279	820	308	542	147	783	598	948	2,144	3,130	881
Oct-Dec 2011	13,733	4,534	9,118	95	103	688	234	1,954	278	789	295	561	143	794	621	942	2,183	3,084	869
Jan-Mar 2012	13,716	4,526	9,095	104	100	698	237	1,924	272	760	312	564	156	787	628	935	2,221	3,042	858
Apr-Jun 2012	13,766	4,488	9,188	96	97	718	243	1,948	275	823	297	569	166	799	611	914	2,211	3,035	839
Jul-Sep 2012	13,882	4,498	9,297	100	107	714	233	1,970	284	846	310	545	173	832	619	905	2,171	3,107	860
Oct-Dec 2012	13,987	4,580	9,320	80	114	712	233	1,945	291	846	332	527	182	829	611	872	2,243	3,138	867
Oct-Dec 2013	14,179	4,578	9,496	88	102	731	264	1,972	292	822	356	517	196	853	633	898	2,246	3,206	875
Jan-Mar 2014	14,233	4,586	9,558	108	94	745	280	1,931	283	824	331	504	208	898	619	923	2,262	3,200	895
Apr-Jun 2014	14,320	4,574	9,662	109	96	756	269	1,928	295	869	324	499	206	878	625	883	2,329	3,212	912
Jul-Sep 2014	14,421	4,533	9,810	94	106	763	273	1,907	317	878	345	529	177	882	668	905	2,291	3,184	956
Oct-Dec 2014	**14,502**	**4,509**	**9,910**	**96**	**115**	**768**	**264**	**1,982**	**338**	**864**	**357**	**522**	**170**	**880**	**658**	**872**	**2,299**	**3,246**	**957**
Change on year	*324*	*-70*	*414*	*8*	*13*	*37*	*0*	*10*	*46*	*42*	*1*	*6*	*-26*	*26*	*26*	*-26*	*54*	*40*	*81*
Change %	*2.3*	*-1.5*	*4.4*	*8.7*	*12.6*	*5.0*	*-0.1*	*0.5*	*15.7*	*5.1*	*0.3*	*1.1*	*-13.1*	*3.1*	*4.0*	*-2.9*	*2.4*	*1.2*	*9.3*

Source: Labour Force Survey

1 The breakdown by industry sector for Q1 2009 onwards is not entirely consistent with those of previous quarters. This is because:

(a) LFS data on industrial activity were coded directly to SIC 1992 for all quarters up to and including Q4 2008 and then mapped to the new industrial classification, SIC 2007, according to the assumed relationship between the two classifications;

(b) data for Q1 2009 onwards have been coded directly to SIC 2007; and

(c) a new, automatic coding tool was introduced in January 2009.

The effect of these changes on the time series was significant for some of the industry sectors shown. **Consequently some adjustments have been made to the pre-2009 estimates to account for the estimated combined effects of the new classification and the new coding tool.** This also means that the pre-2009 estimates in this table are not the same as those obtained from LFS microdata.

More information and analysis of these effects are available in the Labour Force Survey User Guide (Volume 1) and from Labour Force Assessment Branch (tel 01633 455839 or email labour.market.assessment@ons.gov.uk).

2 Includes people with workplace outside UK and those who did not state their industry.

3 In the LFS the distinction between public and private sector is based on respondents' views about the organisation for which they work. The public sector estimates provided here do not correspond to the official Public Sector Employment estimates which are based on National Accounts definitions.

4.5a: International comparisons of employment and unemployment

		Latest period	Employment rate (%)[1,2]	Change on year %			Latest Period	Unemployment rate (%)[3]	Change on period %[6]	Change on year %
Employment rates as published by EUROSTAT: (not seasonally adjusted)					**Unemployment rates as published by EUROSTAT on 30 January 2015 (seasonally adjusted)**					
European Union (EU)					**European Union (EU)**					
Austria	YXSN	Jul-Sep 14	73.4	0.1	Austria	ZXDS	Dec 14	4.9	0.0	-0.1
Belgium	YXSO	Jul-Sep 14	62.0	-0.3	Belgium	ZXDI	Dec 14	8.4	-0.1	0.0
Bulgaria	A495	Jul-Sep 14	62.8	1.7	Bulgaria	A492	Dec 14	10.8	-0.2	-2.0
Croatia	GUMI	Jul-Sep 14	56.9	3.2	Croatia	GUMJ	Dec 14	16.4	-0.2	-0.7
Cyprus	A4AC	Jul-Sep 14	62.6	0.8	Cyprus	A4AN	Dec 14	16.4	-0.2	-0.1
Czech Republic	A4AD	Jul-Sep 14	69.3	1.3	Czech Republic	A4AO	Dec 14	5.8	0.0	-0.9
Denmark	YXSP	Jul-Sep 14	73.7	0.7	Denmark	ZXDJ	Dec 14	6.4	0.0	-0.8
Estonia	A4AE	Jul-Sep 14	70.3	1.5	Estonia	A4AP	Nov 14	6.6	-0.3	-2.4
Finland	YXSQ	Jul-Sep 14	69.8	-0.1	Finland	ZXDU	Dec 14	8.9	0.0	0.6
France	YXSR	Jul-Sep 14	64.5	-0.1	France	ZXDN	Dec 14	10.3	0.0	0.1
Germany	YXSS	Jul-Sep 14	74.2	0.4	Germany	ZXDK	Dec 14	4.8	-0.1	-0.3
Greece	YXST	Jul-Sep 14	50.2	1.1	Greece	ZXDL	Oct 14	25.8	-0.2	-2.0
Hungary	A4AF	Jul-Sep 14	62.8	3.6	Hungary	A4AQ	Nov 14	7.3	0.0	-2.0
Ireland	YXSU	Jul-Sep 14	62.2	1.1	Ireland	ZXDO	Dec 14	10.5	-0.2	-1.6
Italy	YXSV	Jul-Sep 14	56.0	0.4	Italy	ZXDP	Dec 14	12.9	-0.4	0.3
Latvia	A4AG	Jul-Sep 14	66.3	0.3	Latvia	A4AR	Q3 2014	10.7	-0.1	-1.0
Lithuania	A4AH	Jul-Sep 14	67.2	2.7	Lithuania	A4AS	Dec 14	9.4	0.0	-1.9
Luxembourg	YXSW	Jul-Sep 14	66.0	0.0	Luxembourg	ZXDQ	Dec 14	5.9	0.0	-0.1
Malta	A4AI	Jul-Sep 14	63.5	2.1	Malta	A4AT	Dec 14	5.8	0.0	-0.7
Netherlands	YXSX	Jul-Sep 14	74.2	-0.2	Netherlands	ZXDR	Dec 14	6.7	0.2	-0.3
Poland	A4AJ	Jul-Sep 14	62.5	1.8	Poland	A4AU	Dec 14	8.0	-0.2	-2.0
Portugal	YXSY	Jul-Sep 14	63.4	2.2	Portugal	ZXDT	Dec 14	13.4	-0.1	-1.8
Romania	A494	Jul-Sep 14	62.6	1.6	Romania	A48Z	Dec 14	6.4	-0.1	-0.6
Slovak Republic	A4AK	Jul-Sep 14	61.3	1.3	Slovak Republic	A4AV	Dec 14	12.5	-0.1	-1.5
Slovenia	A4AL	Jul-Sep 14	64.6	0.1	Slovenia	A4AW	Dec 14	9.7	0.0	-0.2
Spain	YXSZ	Jul-Sep 14	56.5	1.3	Spain	ZXDM	Dec 14	23.7	-0.1	-1.9
Sweden	YXTA	Jul-Sep 14	76.5	0.7	Sweden[7]	ZXDV	Dec 14	7.6	-0.2	-0.5
United Kingdom	ANZ6	Jul-Sep 14	72.2	1.4	United Kingdom[4]	ZXDW	Oct 14	5.9	0.0	-1.2
Total EU[5]	**A496**	**Jul-Sep 14**	**65.5**	**1.0**	**Total EU[5]**	**A493**	**Dec 14**	**9.9**	**-0.1**	**-0.7**
Eurozone[5]	YXTC	Jul-Sep 14	64.4	0.6	Eurozone[5]	ZXDH	Dec 14	11.4	-0.1	-0.4
Employment rates published by the Office for National Statistics					**Unemployment rate published by Office for National Statistics (seasonally adjusted)**					
United Kingdom (NSA)	LF9D	Oct-Dec 14	73.4	1.2	United Kingdom[4]	MGSX	Oct-Dec 14	5.7	-0.3	-1.5
United Kingdom (SA)	LF24	Oct-Dec 14	73.2	1.2						
Employment rates published by the OECD (seasonally adjusted)					**Unemployment rates as published by national statistical offices (seasonally adjusted)**					
Canada	A48O	Oct-Dec 14	72.6	0.3	Canada	ZXDZ	Jan 15	6.6	-0.1	-0.4
Japan	A48P	Oct-Dec 14	73.0	0.9	Japan	ZXDY	Dec 14	3.4	-0.1	-0.3
United States	A48Q	Oct-Dec 14	68.5	1.1	United States	ZXDX	Jan 15	5.7	0.1	-0.9

Sources: Eurostat, OECD, national statistical offices. Labour market statistics enquiries: labour.market@ons.gsi.gov.uk

1. All employment rates shown in this table are for those aged from 15 to 64 except for the employment rates for the UK published by the Office for National Statistics and the rate for the United States published by OECD which are for those aged from 16 to 64.

2. The employment rates for the EU are published by Eurostat (the EU's statistical office) and are not seasonally adjusted. Eurostat do not publish seasonally adjusted employment rates. The employment rates for Canada, Japan and the United States are published by the Organisation for Economic Cooperation & Development (OECD) and are seasonally adjusted.

3. Unemployment rates published by EUROSTAT for most EU countries (but not for the UK), are calculated by extrapolating from the most recent LFS data using monthly registered unemployment data. A standard population basis (15-74) is used by EUROSTAT except for Spain, Italy and the UK (16-74). The unemployment rate for the US is based on those aged 16 and over, but the rates for Canada and Japan are for those aged 15 and over. All unemployment rates are seasonally adjusted.

4. The unemployment rate for the UK published by EUROSTAT is based on the population aged 16-74 but the unemployment rate for the UK published by the Office for National Statistics is based on those aged 16 and over. There are other minor definitional differences.

5. The "Total EU" series consist of all 28 EU countries. The Eurozone figures consist of the following EU countries: Austria, Belgium, Cyprus, Estonia, Finland, France, Germany, Greece, Ireland, Italy, Latvia Luxembourg, Malta, Netherlands, Portugal, Slovak Republic, Slovenia and Spain. Lithuania joined the Eurozone on 1 January 2015 and it will be included in the Eurozone figures published in this table from the March 2015 edition of this Statistical Bulletin (when figures for January 2015 will be shown in this table).

6. Change on previous month except "Latvia" and "United Kingdom as published by Office for National Statistics" (change on previous quarter).

7. The EU unemployment rates are as published on the Eurostat database. For Sweden the rates on the database differ from those shown in the Eurostat News Release published on 30 January 2015. This is because the figures for Sweden on the Eurostat database are seasonally adjusted estimates but the figures for Sweden shown in the Eurostat News Release are the trend component.

4.5b Labour disputes

United Kingdom, not seasonally adjusted

		Working days lost (thousands)[1,2]	Working days lost in the Public Sector (thousands)[1,2]	Working days lost in the Private Sector (thousands)[1,2]	Number of stoppages[3,4]	Number of stoppages in the Public Sector[4]	Number of stoppages in the Private Sector[4]	Workers involved (thousands)[1,3]
		1	2	3	4	5	6	7
		BBFW	F8XZ	F8Y2	BLUU	F8Y3	F8Y4	BLUT
2012 Dec		4	1	3	16	7	9	3
2013 Dec		38	6	32	8	4	4	55
2014 Jan		8	1	7	15	5	10	25
Feb		32	9	23	16	5	11	27
Mar		109	104	5	15	7	8	119
Apr		11	9	2	9	3	6	7
May		16	14	2	18	10	8	9
Jun		36	29	8	26	12	14	29
Jul		386	378	9	20	10	10	427
Aug		27	25	2	18	8	10	26
Sep		3	0	3	15	6	9	1
Oct		101	96	5	27	9	18	109
Nov		44	40	5	17	7	10	27
Dec	(p)	13	11	3	15	7	8	11
Cumulative totals 12 months to:								
Dec 13		444	363	82	114	50	64	396
Dec 14	(p)	788	716	73	155	67	88	733

Relationship between columns 1=2+3; 4=5+6

Source: ONS Labour Disputes Inquiry. Labour disputes enquiries 01633 456724

1. Estimates of working days lost and workers involved are shown to the nearest thousand. Unrounded estimates of less than 500 therefore round to zero.

2. Due to rounding the working days lost for the public and private sectors may not add up to the total working days lost.

3. The latest 12 month cumulative totals for the figures in these columns will not necessarily equal the sum of the 12 months as some disputes continue for over one month. These disputes appear in each month's data, but only once in the total.

4. These series exclude disputes which do not result in a stoppage of work, those involving fewer than ten workers or lasting less than one day unless the total number of working days lost in the dispute is 100 or more.

4.6 Civil Service employment; regional distribution by government department[12]

All employees

	North West	North East	Yorkshire and the Humber	West Midlands	East Midlands	East of England	London	South East	South West	Scotland	Wales	Northern Ireland	Overseas	Not reported
31 March 2014														
Attorney General's Departments														
Attorney General's Office	0	0	0	0	0	0	40	0	0	0	0	0	0	0
Crown Prosecution Service	970	350	860	620	400	490	1,580	720	300	0	360	0	20	0
Crown Prosecution Service Inspectorate	0	0	10	0	0	0	20	0	0	0	0	0	0	0
Serious Fraud Office	0	0	0	0	0	0	320	0	0	0	0	0	0	0
Treasury Solicitor	0	0	10	0	0	0	1,240	0	10	0	0	0	0	0
Business, Innovation and Skills														
Business, Innovation and Skills (excl. agencies)	60	30	270	50	30	30	2,520	10	20	20	50	0	0	0
Advisory Conciliation and Arbitration Service	110	70	60	60	60	50	230	10	50	70	50	0	0	0
Companies House	0	0	0	0	0	0	10	0	0	30	890	20	0	0
Insolvency Service	200	50	140	430	80	180	390	120	120	40	70	0	0	0
Land Registry	610	410	240	420	580	240	270	0	1,190	0	440	0	0	0
Met Office	30	..	20	10	50	40	40	80	1,580	110	20	10	30	0
National Measurement Office	0	0	0	0	0	0	80	0	0	0	0	0	0	0
Office of Fair Trading	0	0	0	0	0	0	510	0	0	..	0	0	0	0
Ordnance Survey	30	10	20	20	20	20	20	960	20	30	20	0	0	0
Skills Funding Agency	120	80	100	520	50	50	160	120	70	0	0	0	0	0
UK Intellectual Property Office	0	0	0	0	0	0	50	0	0	0	940	0	0	0
UK Space Agency	0	0	0	0	0	0	..	0	50	0	0	0	0	0
Cabinet Office														
Cabinet Office (excl. agencies)	0	..	30	0	..	60	1,910	30	..	0	0	0	0	0
Other Cabinet Office agencies														
Government in Parliament	0	0	0	0	0	0	100	0	0	0	0	0	0	0
Government Procurement Service	250	0	..	..	..	110	50	..	0	..	60	0	0	0
Chancellor's other departments														
Government Actuary's Department	0	0	0	0	0	0	160	0	0	0	0	0	0	0
National Savings and Investments	..	..	0	0	0	0	160	0	0	10	0	0	0	0
Charity Commission														
Charity Commission	150	0	0	0	0	0	70	0	100	0	10	0	0	0
Communities and Local Government														
Department for Communities and Local Government (excl. agencies)	70	40	50	70	30	90	1,230	20	90	0	0	0	0	0
Planning Inspectorate	0	0	0	0	0	0	0	0	750	0	40	0	0	0
Queen Elizabeth II Conference Centre	0	0	0	0	0	0	50	0	0	0	0	0	0	0
Culture, Media and Sport														
Department for Culture Media and Sport	0	0	0	0	0	0	390	0	0	0	0	0	0	0
Royal Parks	0	0	0	0	0	0	110	0	0	0	0	0	0	0
Defence														
Ministry of Defence[3]	1,790	310	2,830	2,900	1,660	3,940	3,640	9,040	14,230	3,970	900	1,480	1,620	230
Defence Science and Technology Laboratory	0	0	0	..	..	10	..	2,010	1,800	0	0	0	0	0
Defence Support Group	0	0	90	970	..	90	10	90	650	80	350	10	100	0
Royal Fleet Auxiliary[3]	0	0	0	0	0	0	0	0	0	0	0	0	0	1,810
UK Hydrographic Office	0	0	0	0	0	0	0	0	1,070	..	0	0	..	0
Education														
Department for Education	230	340	380	80	40	0	1,230	0	0	0	0	0	0	0
Education Funding Agency	70	80	90	170	30	20	240	40	30	0	0	0	0	0
Standards and Testing Agency	..	0	..	60	..	0	30	0	0	0	0	0	0	0
The National College for Teaching and Leadership	100	..	10	60	140	0	30	0	0	0	0	0	0	0
Energy and Climate Change														
Department of Energy and Climate Change	0	0	0	0	0	0	1,470	0	0	100	0	0	0	0
Environment, Food and Rural Affairs														
Department for Environment Food and Rural Affairs (excl. agencies)	30	30	240	20	20	20	1,540	30	140	0	0	0	0	0
Animal Health and Veterinary Laboratories Agency	170	50	100	340	110	100	40	700	290	130	190	0	0	0
Centre for Environment Fisheries and Aquaculture Science	..	0	..	0	0	410	..	0	140	0	0	0	0	0
Food and Environment Research Agency	10	..	680	30	..	40	30	20	20	0	10	0	..	0
Office of Water Services	0	0	0	170	0	0	30	0	0	0	0	0	0	0
Rural Payments Agency	730	290	230	40	20	30	10	440	320	0	..	..	0	0
Veterinary Medicines Directorate	0	0	0	0	0	0	0	160	0	0	0	0	0	0
ESTYN														
ESTYN	0	0	0	0	0	0	0	0	0	0	110	0	0	0
Food Standards Agency														
Food Standards Agency	90	20	200	90	70	130	220	80	90	160	90	40	0	0

4.6 Civil Service employment; regional distribution by government department[12]

All employees

Headcount

	North West	North East	Yorkshire and the Humber	West Midlands	East Midlands	East of England	London	South East	South West	Scotland	Wales	Northern Ireland	Overseas	Not reported
31 March 2014														
Foreign and Commonwealth Office														
Foreign and Commonwealth Office (excl. agencies)	0	0	0	0	0	0	2,510	320	0	0	0	0	1,780	0
FCO Services	0	0	0	0	0	0	190	660	0	0	0	0	120	0
Wilton Park Executive Agency	0	0	0	0	0	0	0	70	0	0	0	0	0	0
Health														
Department of Health (excl. agencies)	50	..	640	0	0	0	1,160	20	0	0	0	0	0	50
Medicines and Healthcare Products Regulatory Agency	0	0	20	0	0	340	860	0	0	0	0	0	0	0
Public Health England	440	160	300	380	110	280	1,950	600	1,180	20	..	0	0	0
HM Revenue and Customs														
HM Revenue and Customs	12,310	11,690	4,580	3,970	3,540	3,770	7,980	4,380	2,650	8,960	3,630	1,850	0	..
Valuation Office	420	240	430	310	230	260	730	440	390	60	260	0	0	0
HM Treasury														
Debt Management Office	0	0	0	0	0	0	110	0	0	0	0	0	0	0
HM Treasury	0	0	0	0	0	30	1,190	0	0	0	0	0	..	0
Office for Budget Responsibility	0	0	0	0	0	0	20	0	0	0	0	0	0	0
Home Office[3]														
Her Majesty's Passport Office	1,200	770	20	10	10	560	570	30	20	180	180	230	0	..
Home Office (excl. agencies)	2,620	270	2,370	780	190	1,250	11,270	3,040	280	510	260	160	150	360
National Fraud Authority	0	0	0	0	0	0	10	0	0	0	0	0	0	0
International Development														
Department for International Development	0	0	0	0	0	0	790	0	0	580	0	0	530	0
Justice														
Ministry of Justice (excl. agencies)	240	40	100	190	70	30	2,390	60	50	340	730	..	0	0
Her Majesty's Courts and Tribunals Service	2,660	930	1,760	1,890	1,630	1,270	4,360	1,770	1,180	290	1,070	0	0	0
Legal Aid Agency	310	270	50	70	180	20	420	30	90	0	60	0	0	0
National Archives	0	0	0	0	0	..	620	0	0	0	0	0	0	0
National Offender Management Service	4,770	2,440	4,580	3,180	3,800	3,970	4,610	6,060	2,960	0	860	0	0	0
Office of the Public Guardian	0	0	0	440	150	0	30	0	0	0	0	0	0	0
National Crime Agency														
National Crime Agency	590	70	180	310	120	210	1,430	610	240	40	50	70	140	120
Northern Ireland Office														
Northern Ireland Office	0	0	0	0	0	0	50	0	0	0	0	50	0	0
Office for Standards in														
Office for Standards in Education, Children's Services and Skills	400	0	90	70	130	60	340	0	180	0	0	0	0	0
Office of Gas and Electricity Markets														
Office of Gas and Electricity Markets	0	0	0	0	0	0	750	0	0	90	..	0	0	0
Office of Qualifications and Examinations Regulation														
Ofqual	0	0	0	190	0	0	0	0	0	0	0	..	0	0
Scottish Government														
Scottish Government (excl. agencies)	0	0	0	0	0	0	0	0	0	5,280	0	0	10	0
Crown Office and Procurator Fiscal Service	0	0	0	0	0	0	0	0	0	1,700	0	0	0	0
Disclosure Scotland	0	0	0	0	0	0	0	0	0	210	0	0	0	0
Education Scotland	0	0	0	0	0	0	0	0	0	260	0	0	0	0
Historic Scotland	0	0	0	0	0	0	0	0	0	1,040	0	0	0	0
National Records of Scotland	0	0	0	0	0	0	0	0	0	390	0	0	0	0
Office of Accountant in Bankruptcy	0	0	0	0	0	0	0	0	0	140	0	0	0	0
Office of the Scottish Charity Regulator	0	0	0	0	0	0	0	0	0	50	0	0	0	0
Registers of Scotland	0	0	0	0	0	0	0	0	0	930	0	0	0	0
Scottish Court Service	0	0	0	0	0	0	0	0	0	1,490	0	0	0	0
Scottish Housing Regulator	0	0	0	0	0	0	0	0	0	50	0	0	0	0
Scottish Prison Service	0	0	0	0	0	0	0	0	0	4,500	0	0	0	0
Scottish Public Pensions Agency	0	0	0	0	0	0	0	0	0	280	0	0	0	0
Student Awards Agency	0	0	0	0	0	0	0	0	0	220	0	0	0	0
Transport Scotland	0	0	0	0	0	0	0	0	0	400	0	0	0	0
Scotland Office														
Scotland Office (incl. Office of the Advocate General for Scotland)	0	0	0	0	0	0	30	0	0	80	0	0	0	0
Security and Intelligence Services														
Security and Intelligence Services	0	0	0	0	0	0	0	0	5,670	0	0	0	0	0

4.6 Civil Service employment; regional distribution by government department[12]

All employees

	North West	North East	Yorkshire and the Humber	West Midlands	East Midlands	East of England	London	South East	South West	Scotland	Wales	Northern Ireland	Overseas	Not reported
31 March 2014														
Transport														
Department for Transport (excl. agencies)	0	10	10	..	20	0	1,620	190	10	0	..	0	..	0
Driver and Vehicle Licensing Agency	10	..	..	..	..	10	10	..	10	10	5,520	0	0	0
Driving Standards Agency	200	280	150	180	360	190	270	230	140	160	110	0	0	0
Highways Agency	490	20	450	910	120	440	40	640	370	0	0	0	0	0
Maritime and Coastguard Agency	40	20	50	0	..	30	20	460	140	140	130	40	0	0
Office of Rail Regulation	20	..	10	10	..	..	200	10	10	10	..	0	0	0
Vehicle and Operator Services Agency	230	70	260	180	130	200	130	220	380	160	310	0	0	0
Vehicle Certification Agency	0	0	0	0	50	..	0	..	100	0	0	0	10	0
United Kingdom Statistics Authority														
United Kingdom Statistics Authority	0	0	0	0	0	0	40	1,860	..	0	1,760	0	0	0
UK Export Finance														
UK Export Finance	..	..	0	..	..	10	210	0	..	..	..	0	0	0
UK Supreme Court														
UK Supreme Court	0	0	0	0	0	0	50	0	0	0	0	0	0	0
Wales Office														
Wales Office	0	0	0	0	0	0	20	0	0	0	20	0	0	0
Welsh Government														
Welsh Government	0	0	0	0	0	0	10	0	0	0	5,670	0	20	0
Work and Pensions														
Department for Work and Pensions[4]	18,650	9,840	9,860	8,890	5,510	4,840	9,460	6,500	5,720	10,700	5,780	0	0	190
The Health and Safety Executive	1,330	70	340	120	500	140	210	120	130	240	100	0	0	0
Total employment	52,820	29,360	32,910	29,200	20,230	24,040	76,840	42,970	44,990	44,250	31,060	3,970	4,540	2,760

Source: Annual Civil Service Employment Survey

1 Numbers are rounded to the nearest ten, and cells containing between one and five employees are represented by "..".
2 Workplace postcode data are used to derive geographical information.
3 Core Home Office estimates for 31 March 2014 include staff paid via the Foreign and Commonwealth Office employee records system (PRISM)

4.7: Unemployment by age and duration

United Kingdom (thousands) seasonally adjusted

| | All aged 16 & over | | | | | | | All aged 16 - 64 | | | | | | |
	All	Rate (%)[1]	Up to 6 months	Over 6 and up to 12 months	All over 12 months	% over 12 months	All over 24 months	All	Rate (%)[1]	Up to 6 months	Over 6 and up to 12 months	All over 12 months	% over 12 months	All over 24 months
	1	2	3	4	5	6	7	8	9	10	11	12	13	14
People	MGSC	MGSX	YBWF	YBWG	YBWH	YBWI	YBWL	LF2I	LF2Q	LF2Y	LF32	LF34	LF36	LF38
Nov-Jan 2006	1,551	5.1	966	258	327	21.1	163	1,534	5.1	956	254	324	21.1	159
Dec-Feb 2006	1,584	5.2	981	271	332	21.0	161	1,570	5.2	974	268	328	20.9	157
Jan-Mar 2006	1,604	5.2	985	280	339	21.1	164	1,590	5.3	978	278	334	21.0	159
Feb-Apr 2006	1,633	5.3	1,008	279	347	21.2	162	1,619	5.4	1,004	276	339	20.9	157
Mar-May 2006	1,664	5.4	1,014	295	355	21.3	171	1,651	5.5	1,009	293	348	21.1	167
Apr-Jun 2006	1,685	5.5	1,023	300	361	21.4	169	1,670	5.5	1,014	297	360	21.5	166
May-Jul 2006	1,698	5.5	1,021	304	373	22.0	174	1,681	5.6	1,010	301	369	22.0	171
Jun-Aug 2006	1,690	5.5	1,023	301	367	21.7	165	1,675	5.5	1,014	297	364	21.7	163
Jul-Sep 2006	1,693	5.5	1,015	288	390	23.0	181	1,678	5.6	1,009	285	383	22.9	178
Aug-Oct 2006	1,691	5.5	1,010	293	388	22.9	182	1,680	5.6	1,006	291	382	22.8	178
Sep-Nov 2006	1,674	5.4	1,000	283	391	23.3	184	1,661	5.5	996	282	383	23.1	181
Oct-Dec 2006	1,701	5.5	1,018	285	397	23.3	189	1,690	5.6	1,012	285	394	23.3	186
Nov-Jan 2007	1,703	5.5	1,026	276	400	23.5	185	1,691	5.6	1,019	275	398	23.5	183
Dec-Feb 2007	1,708	5.5	1,041	269	398	23.3	180	1,696	5.6	1,033	266	397	23.4	178
Jan-Mar 2007	1,704	5.5	1,033	277	393	23.1	179	1,689	5.6	1,026	275	388	23.0	175
Feb-Apr 2007	1,692	5.5	1,012	278	402	23.7	177	1,677	5.5	1,006	277	393	23.5	173
Mar-May 2007	1,670	5.4	999	271	399	23.9	181	1,655	5.5	993	270	392	23.7	177
Apr-Jun 2007	1,658	5.4	999	263	396	23.9	175	1,640	5.4	988	261	391	23.9	172
May-Jul 2007	1,645	5.3	988	262	394	24.0	179	1,629	5.4	981	261	388	23.8	176
Jun-Aug 2007	1,645	5.3	986	267	392	23.8	175	1,631	5.4	980	265	386	23.7	172
Jul-Sep 2007	1,650	5.3	991	268	391	23.7	176	1,638	5.4	985	267	386	23.6	173
Aug-Oct 2007	1,629	5.2	985	261	384	23.6	177	1,617	5.3	978	261	379	23.4	174
Sep-Nov 2007	1,633	5.2	984	257	391	24.0	176	1,621	5.3	979	257	385	23.8	173
Oct-Dec 2007	1,608	5.2	969	256	384	23.9	170	1,600	5.2	964	254	382	23.9	167
Nov-Jan 2008	1,617	5.2	974	262	381	23.6	180	1,606	5.3	967	259	381	23.7	177
Dec-Feb 2008	1,622	5.2	960	273	389	24.0	190	1,609	5.3	953	269	387	24.1	187
Jan-Mar 2008	1,622	5.2	958	267	398	24.5	198	1,610	5.3	952	264	394	24.5	196
Feb-Apr 2008	1,667	5.3	989	268	410	24.6	197	1,651	5.4	982	264	404	24.5	195
Mar-May 2008	1,625	5.2	954	265	406	25.0	191	1,610	5.2	947	262	401	24.9	190
Apr-Jun 2008	1,680	5.4	989	275	416	24.8	192	1,666	5.4	980	271	415	24.9	190
May-Jul 2008	1,724	5.5	1,011	278	435	25.2	206	1,711	5.6	1,005	274	432	25.2	203
Jun-Aug 2008	1,793	5.7	1,075	277	442	24.6	207	1,777	5.8	1,067	272	438	24.6	205
Jul-Sep 2008	1,840	5.9	1,112	284	444	24.1	204	1,822	5.9	1,104	279	438	24.0	203
Aug-Oct 2008	1,875	6.0	1,146	289	440	23.5	202	1,855	6.0	1,134	287	433	23.4	200
Sep-Nov 2008	1,941	6.2	1,189	313	440	22.7	199	1,922	6.2	1,177	310	434	22.6	197
Oct-Dec 2008	2,003	6.4	1,225	324	454	22.7	211	1,987	6.4	1,214	320	453	22.8	209
Nov-Jan 2009	2,057	6.5	1,250	347	460	22.4	209	2,042	6.6	1,240	342	459	22.5	206
Dec-Feb 2009	2,128	6.7	1,290	355	483	22.7	224	2,110	6.8	1,280	351	479	22.7	220
Jan-Mar 2009	2,235	7.1	1,345	381	508	22.8	232	2,215	7.2	1,335	378	502	22.7	229
Feb-Apr 2009	2,296	7.3	1,365	408	523	22.8	236	2,278	7.4	1,356	405	517	22.7	233
Mar-May 2009	2,395	7.6	1,417	442	536	22.4	237	2,376	7.7	1,407	439	531	22.3	234
Apr-Jun 2009	2,448	7.8	1,413	483	552	22.6	240	2,427	7.9	1,400	479	549	22.6	236
May-Jul 2009	2,478	7.9	1,403	495	581	23.4	246	2,455	8.0	1,390	491	574	23.4	241
Jun-Aug 2009	2,484	7.9	1,357	516	611	24.6	252	2,464	8.0	1,349	515	600	24.4	246
Jul-Sep 2009	2,475	7.8	1,306	539	631	25.5	236	2,451	8.0	1,298	534	619	25.3	229
Aug-Oct 2009	2,484	7.9	1,293	567	624	25.1	237	2,457	8.0	1,283	562	612	24.9	231
Sep-Nov 2009	2,455	7.8	1,250	568	637	25.9	236	2,428	7.9	1,239	560	629	25.9	232
Oct-Dec 2009	2,453	7.8	1,251	539	663	27.0	247	2,430	7.9	1,239	532	659	27.1	242
Nov-Jan 2010	2,434	7.7	1,199	550	685	28.1	246	2,409	7.8	1,187	542	680	28.2	242
Dec-Feb 2010	2,496	7.9	1,209	556	731	29.3	272	2,472	8.0	1,199	550	723	29.3	265
Jan-Mar 2010	2,526	8.0	1,213	546	768	30.4	283	2,501	8.1	1,203	541	756	30.2	277
Feb-Apr 2010	2,510	8.0	1,191	531	788	31.4	294	2,487	8.1	1,184	526	776	31.2	287
Mar-May 2010	2,508	7.9	1,185	521	801	32.0	303	2,486	8.1	1,178	518	790	31.8	297
Apr-Jun 2010	2,488	7.9	1,173	512	803	32.3	314	2,468	8.0	1,164	507	797	32.3	308
May-Jul 2010	2,488	7.8	1,198	486	803	32.3	322	2,469	8.0	1,189	483	797	32.3	315
Jun-Aug 2010	2,476	7.8	1,181	472	823	33.2	334	2,456	7.9	1,174	469	812	33.1	328
Jul-Sep 2010	2,470	7.8	1,197	450	823	33.3	330	2,451	7.9	1,193	447	811	33.1	325
Aug-Oct 2010	2,513	7.9	1,204	468	842	33.5	335	2,495	8.1	1,201	465	828	33.2	330
Sep-Nov 2010	2,502	7.9	1,214	452	837	33.4	337	2,481	8.0	1,206	448	827	33.3	330
Oct-Dec 2010	2,503	7.9	1,209	456	838	33.5	342	2,482	8.0	1,199	452	831	33.5	335
Nov-Jan 2011	2,524	7.9	1,220	452	852	33.8	349	2,503	8.1	1,212	449	843	33.7	342
Dec-Feb 2011	2,492	7.8	1,194	444	853	34.2	372	2,474	8.0	1,188	442	845	34.1	366
Jan-Mar 2011	2,483	7.8	1,182	443	859	34.6	389	2,466	8.0	1,177	441	848	34.4	384
Feb-Apr 2011	2,462	7.7	1,185	436	840	34.1	389	2,444	7.9	1,178	434	832	34.1	384
Mar-May 2011	2,500	7.8	1,234	447	820	32.8	388	2,482	8.0	1,228	447	807	32.5	382
Apr-Jun 2011	2,540	7.9	1,259	434	846	33.3	411	2,522	8.1	1,250	433	839	33.3	407
May-Jul 2011	2,556	8.0	1,254	442	860	33.6	420	2,535	8.2	1,243	440	851	33.6	415

4.7: Unemployment by age and duration

United Kingdom (thousands) seasonally adjusted

	All aged 16 & over							All aged 16 - 64						
	All	Rate (%)[1]	Up to 6 months	Over 6 and up to 12 months	All over 12 months	% over 12 months	All over 24 months	All	Rate (%)[1]	Up to 6 months	Over 6 and up to 12 months	All over 12 months	% over 12 months	All over 24 months
	1	2	3	4	5	6	7	8	9	10	11	12	13	14
People	MGSC	MGSX	YBWF	YBWG	YBWH	YBWI	YBWL	LF2I	LF2Q	LF2Y	LF32	LF34	LF36	LF38
Jun-Aug 2011	2,612	8.2	1,261	475	876	33.6	426	2,589	8.3	1,254	470	864	33.4	421
Jul-Sep 2011	2,664	8.3	1,283	503	878	33.0	425	2,637	8.5	1,273	498	866	32.9	420
Aug-Oct 2011	2,680	8.4	1,297	505	878	32.7	434	2,648	8.5	1,285	501	862	32.6	428
Sep-Nov 2011	2,708	8.5	1,316	527	865	31.9	427	2,680	8.6	1,299	522	859	32.0	423
Oct-Dec 2011	2,684	8.4	1,301	516	867	32.3	427	2,657	8.5	1,285	510	862	32.4	422
Nov-Jan 2012	2,670	8.3	1,298	512	859	32.2	409	2,646	8.5	1,285	506	855	32.3	403
Dec-Feb 2012	2,653	8.3	1,255	510	887	33.5	424	2,628	8.4	1,242	507	879	33.4	417
Jan-Mar 2012	2,633	8.2	1,225	521	887	33.7	429	2,604	8.4	1,212	517	874	33.6	422
Feb-Apr 2012	2,624	8.2	1,203	530	890	33.9	436	2,597	8.3	1,190	525	882	34.0	431
Mar-May 2012	2,605	8.1	1,199	515	890	34.2	444	2,581	8.3	1,188	509	884	34.2	440
Apr-Jun 2012	2,582	8.0	1,192	502	888	34.4	424	2,562	8.2	1,183	496	883	34.5	419
May-Jul 2012	2,607	8.1	1,202	497	909	34.8	444	2,584	8.2	1,193	491	900	34.8	436
Jun-Aug 2012	2,553	7.9	1,184	466	903	35.4	442	2,532	8.1	1,182	463	887	35.0	435
Jul-Sep 2012	2,542	7.9	1,193	447	902	35.5	440	2,522	8.1	1,191	444	888	35.2	433
Aug-Oct 2012	2,539	7.9	1,183	444	912	35.9	449	2,518	8.0	1,179	442	897	35.6	445
Sep-Nov 2012	2,526	7.8	1,192	435	899	35.6	437	2,503	8.0	1,183	432	888	35.5	431
Oct-Dec 2012	2,529	7.8	1,201	443	885	35.0	443	2,507	8.0	1,190	439	877	35.0	437
Nov-Jan 2013	2,533	7.8	1,194	447	892	35.2	452	2,516	8.0	1,186	444	886	35.2	447
Dec-Feb 2013	2,582	8.0	1,211	465	906	35.1	465	2,566	8.2	1,205	462	899	35.0	459
Jan-Mar 2013	2,541	7.8	1,198	435	908	35.7	467	2,523	8.0	1,192	433	898	35.6	462
Feb-Apr 2013	2,527	7.8	1,206	419	902	35.7	460	2,506	8.0	1,195	417	894	35.7	453
Mar-May 2013	2,524	7.8	1,182	421	921	36.5	476	2,502	8.0	1,169	419	914	36.5	469
Apr-Jun 2013	2,527	7.8	1,181	430	916	36.2	477	2,501	8.0	1,165	428	908	36.3	468
May-Jul 2013	2,506	7.7	1,157	446	902	36.0	472	2,480	7.9	1,139	445	897	36.2	465
Jun-Aug 2013	2,510	7.7	1,157	448	905	36.1	469	2,483	7.9	1,144	446	893	36.0	464
Jul-Sep 2013	2,488	7.6	1,168	427	894	35.9	460	2,467	7.8	1,158	424	884	35.8	458
Aug-Oct 2013	2,412	7.4	1,133	405	875	36.3	446	2,388	7.6	1,124	402	861	36.1	444
Sep-Nov 2013	2,332	7.1	1,094	396	842	36.1	450	2,309	7.3	1,080	393	836	36.2	448
Oct-Dec 2013	2,348	7.2	1,104	396	848	36.1	454	2,318	7.4	1,086	392	840	36.2	450
Nov-Jan 2014	2,335	7.2	1,118	387	831	35.6	452	2,305	7.3	1,102	382	821	35.6	448
Dec-Feb 2014	2,254	6.9	1,072	371	811	36.0	433	2,223	7.0	1,057	366	800	36.0	429
Jan-Mar 2014	2,212	6.8	1,046	350	816	36.9	447	2,186	6.9	1,036	346	804	36.8	442
Feb-Apr 2014	2,162	6.6	1,026	343	793	36.7	433	2,133	6.7	1,011	339	782	36.7	428
Mar-May 2014	2,126	6.5	1,022	349	754	35.5	418	2,096	6.6	1,008	346	742	35.4	411
Apr-Jun 2014	2,074	6.3	999	333	741	35.7	408	2,047	6.5	984	330	732	35.8	403
May-Jul 2014	2,021	6.2	978	319	724	35.8	399	1,999	6.3	965	316	719	35.9	393
Jun-Aug 2014	1,972	6.0	944	317	711	36.1	388	1,952	6.2	938	315	699	35.8	383
Jul-Sep 2014	1,959	6.0	950	321	688	35.1	376	1,937	6.1	944	319	674	34.8	370
Aug-Oct 2014	1,958	6.0	938	335	684	34.9	376	1,938	6.1	935	334	669	34.5	370
Oct-Dec 2014	**1,862**	**5.7**	**923**	**300**	**638**	**34.3**	**339**	**1,844**	**5.8**	**916**	**296**	**632**	**34.3**	**333**
Change on qtr	*-97*	*-0.3*	*-27*	*-20*	*-50*	*-0.8*	*-37*	*-93*	*-0.3*	*-28*	*-23*	*-42*	*-0.5*	*-37*
Change %	*-5.0*		*-2.8*	*-6.4*	*-7.2*		*-9.8*	*-4.8*		*-3.0*	*-7.2*	*-6.2*		*-10.0*
Change on year	*-486*	*-1.5*	*-180*	*-96*	*-210*	*-1.8*	*-114*	*-474*	*-1.5*	*-170*	*-96*	*-208*	*-1.9*	*-116*
Change %	*-20.7*		*-16.3*	*-24.2*	*-24.8*		*-25.2*	*-20.4*		*-15.7*	*-24.5*	*-24.7*		*-25.9*
Men	MGSD	MGSY	MGYK	MGYM	MGYO	YBWJ	YBWM	YBSI	YBTJ	YBWP	YBWS	YBWV	YBWY	YBXB
Nov-Jan 2006	890	5.4	504	156	230	25.8	118	878	5.4	500	154	224	25.5	114
Dec-Feb 2006	911	5.5	520	162	230	25.2	115	901	5.6	517	159	225	25.0	111
Jan-Mar 2006	930	5.6	527	166	236	25.4	119	920	5.7	524	165	231	25.1	115
Feb-Apr 2006	945	5.7	542	158	245	25.9	119	935	5.8	540	156	239	25.6	115
Mar-May 2006	966	5.8	538	171	258	26.7	129	956	5.9	533	169	255	26.6	126
Apr-Jun 2006	969	5.8	536	174	259	26.7	125	959	5.9	531	172	256	26.7	122
May-Jul 2006	973	5.8	533	178	261	26.8	127	961	5.9	526	176	259	26.9	125
Jun-Aug 2006	964	5.8	539	178	247	25.6	116	954	5.9	534	175	245	25.7	113
Jul-Sep 2006	975	5.8	537	171	267	27.3	131	962	5.9	532	168	262	27.3	128
Aug-Oct 2006	975	5.8	533	175	266	27.3	132	965	5.9	529	174	261	27.1	129
Sep-Nov 2006	951	5.7	524	168	259	27.2	129	940	5.8	520	166	254	27.0	130
Oct-Dec 2006	969	5.8	534	168	267	27.6	132	962	5.9	530	168	264	27.4	130
Nov-Jan 2007	967	5.8	530	162	274	28.4	129	958	5.9	527	161	270	28.2	128
Dec-Feb 2007	974	5.8	541	155	278	28.6	128	966	5.9	537	153	276	28.5	126
Jan-Mar 2007	970	5.8	535	163	272	28.1	127	960	5.9	531	161	268	27.9	124
Feb-Apr 2007	968	5.8	528	163	277	28.6	126	956	5.9	524	161	271	28.4	123
Mar-May 2007	953	5.7	518	161	274	28.7	131	942	5.7	513	160	269	28.5	128
Apr-Jun 2007	941	5.6	518	152	271	28.8	124	928	5.7	512	151	264	28.5	121

4.7: Unemployment by age and duration

United Kingdom (thousands) seasonally adjusted

	All aged 16 & over							All aged 16 - 64						
	All	Rate (%)[1]	Up to 6 months	Over 6 and up to 12 months	All over 12 months	% over 12 months	All over 24 months	All	Rate (%)[1]	Up to 6 months	Over 6 and up to 12 months	All over 12 months	% over 12 months	All over 24 months
	1	2	3	4	5	6	7	8	9	10	11	12	13	14
Men	MGSD	MGSY	MGYK	MGYM	MGYO	YBWJ	YBWM	YBSI	YBTJ	YBWP	YBWS	YBWV	YBWY	YBXB
May-Jul 2007	935	5.6	516	152	267	28.5	126	924	5.6	512	151	261	28.3	123
Jun-Aug 2007	933	5.6	514	153	267	28.6	123	923	5.6	509	152	262	28.4	120
Jul-Sep 2007	935	5.6	516	155	263	28.2	125	927	5.7	511	155	261	28.1	124
Aug-Oct 2007	918	5.5	505	154	259	28.2	130	909	5.5	499	154	255	28.1	127
Sep-Nov 2007	923	5.5	506	151	266	28.8	129	914	5.6	502	150	262	28.7	127
Oct-Dec 2007	909	5.4	499	151	259	28.5	122	903	5.5	497	149	256	28.4	120
Nov-Jan 2008	926	5.5	513	152	261	28.2	130	918	5.6	511	150	258	28.1	128
Dec-Feb 2008	933	5.5	506	162	265	28.4	140	924	5.6	503	159	263	28.4	138
Jan-Mar 2008	935	5.5	507	155	272	29.1	146	925	5.6	503	154	269	29.0	144
Feb-Apr 2008	945	5.6	513	155	277	29.3	142	933	5.7	507	153	273	29.3	141
Mar-May 2008	936	5.5	508	152	276	29.5	139	925	5.6	502	149	273	29.5	137
Apr-Jun 2008	978	5.8	529	159	290	29.7	142	968	5.9	524	157	287	29.7	140
May-Jul 2008	1,008	5.9	541	163	304	30.1	150	998	6.0	537	160	301	30.1	149
Jun-Aug 2008	1,048	6.2	575	162	311	29.7	150	1,036	6.3	568	158	309	29.8	149
Jul-Sep 2008	1,075	6.3	605	162	308	28.6	147	1,061	6.4	597	158	305	28.8	146
Aug-Oct 2008	1,100	6.5	638	161	300	27.3	144	1,084	6.6	628	159	297	27.4	143
Sep-Nov 2008	1,147	6.7	670	180	297	25.9	140	1,132	6.8	660	178	294	25.9	138
Oct-Dec 2008	1,191	7.0	693	190	309	25.9	151	1,180	7.1	686	187	307	26.1	150
Nov-Jan 2009	1,225	7.2	708	204	313	25.6	149	1,214	7.3	703	201	309	25.5	147
Dec-Feb 2009	1,272	7.5	739	208	325	25.6	158	1,260	7.6	733	205	321	25.5	156
Jan-Mar 2009	1,338	7.8	776	224	338	25.2	161	1,323	8.0	769	220	334	25.2	160
Feb-Apr 2009	1,383	8.1	795	247	341	24.6	164	1,370	8.2	789	244	338	24.7	162
Mar-May 2009	1,450	8.5	834	272	345	23.8	166	1,439	8.7	827	269	343	23.8	164
Apr-Jun 2009	1,490	8.8	829	305	355	23.8	164	1,475	8.9	822	303	351	23.8	161
May-Jul 2009	1,521	9.0	821	318	382	25.1	172	1,504	9.1	812	315	377	25.1	169
Jun-Aug 2009	1,531	9.0	782	341	407	26.6	179	1,515	9.2	775	340	400	26.4	175
Jul-Sep 2009	1,522	9.0	740	362	419	27.5	167	1,504	9.1	733	358	412	27.4	162
Aug-Oct 2009	1,523	9.0	728	381	414	27.2	166	1,503	9.1	719	377	407	27.1	161
Sep-Nov 2009	1,496	8.8	711	370	415	27.7	162	1,475	9.0	703	364	409	27.7	158
Oct-Dec 2009	1,485	8.8	703	344	438	29.5	169	1,469	8.9	696	340	433	29.5	167
Nov-Jan 2010	1,490	8.8	681	351	458	30.7	172	1,473	9.0	675	346	452	30.7	170
Dec-Feb 2010	1,518	9.0	669	353	496	32.7	191	1,501	9.1	663	348	489	32.6	187
Jan-Mar 2010	1,542	9.1	671	350	522	33.8	203	1,523	9.3	663	345	515	33.8	199
Feb-Apr 2010	1,524	9.0	650	336	537	35.3	211	1,507	9.2	645	332	530	35.2	207
Mar-May 2010	1,500	8.8	635	321	543	36.2	216	1,483	9.0	629	317	536	36.1	211
Apr-Jun 2010	1,476	8.7	618	309	548	37.1	223	1,461	8.8	614	306	542	37.1	218
May-Jul 2010	1,454	8.5	624	283	547	37.7	226	1,441	8.7	618	280	542	37.6	221
Jun-Aug 2010	1,439	8.4	613	269	557	38.7	234	1,425	8.6	607	266	551	38.7	230
Jul-Sep 2010	1,432	8.4	627	252	553	38.6	236	1,417	8.5	623	248	547	38.6	232
Aug-Oct 2010	1,455	8.5	637	258	560	38.5	239	1,440	8.7	632	255	554	38.4	236
Sep-Nov 2010	1,470	8.6	650	255	564	38.4	236	1,453	8.8	646	251	557	38.3	230
Oct-Dec 2010	1,457	8.5	638	258	561	38.5	237	1,442	8.7	634	255	553	38.4	232
Nov-Jan 2011	1,468	8.5	640	260	568	38.7	241	1,453	8.7	638	258	557	38.3	236
Dec-Feb 2011	1,445	8.4	626	252	568	39.3	263	1,433	8.6	623	249	560	39.1	258
Jan-Mar 2011	1,436	8.4	614	251	571	39.8	273	1,424	8.6	610	250	564	39.6	269
Feb-Apr 2011	1,428	8.3	622	247	559	39.1	279	1,415	8.5	618	245	552	39.0	275
Mar-May 2011	1,443	8.4	638	261	544	37.7	281	1,429	8.6	634	261	534	37.3	277
Apr-Jun 2011	1,461	8.5	658	245	558	38.2	290	1,450	8.7	655	244	551	38.0	288
May-Jul 2011	1,465	8.6	655	253	557	38.0	297	1,451	8.8	650	252	549	37.9	295
Jun-Aug 2011	1,508	8.8	672	270	566	37.5	302	1,495	9.0	669	266	560	37.5	299
Jul-Sep 2011	1,545	9.0	694	286	565	36.6	303	1,530	9.2	689	282	559	36.5	300
Aug-Oct 2011	1,546	9.0	699	283	564	36.5	307	1,529	9.2	692	280	556	36.4	302
Sep-Nov 2011	1,560	9.1	707	295	558	35.8	296	1,543	9.3	699	292	552	35.8	292
Oct-Dec 2011	1,543	9.0	696	290	557	36.1	292	1,526	9.2	689	287	550	36.0	288
Nov-Jan 2012	1,527	8.9	700	283	544	35.6	271	1,512	9.1	696	279	537	35.5	266
Dec-Feb 2012	1,508	8.8	669	285	554	36.7	286	1,492	9.0	662	283	546	36.6	280
Jan-Mar 2012	1,500	8.7	652	295	553	36.9	292	1,480	8.9	643	292	545	36.8	287
Feb-Apr 2012	1,492	8.6	632	300	559	37.5	299	1,474	8.8	624	297	552	37.5	295
Mar-May 2012	1,482	8.6	642	285	555	37.5	298	1,468	8.8	635	281	551	37.5	295
Apr-Jun 2012	1,465	8.5	628	278	558	38.1	286	1,453	8.7	625	275	553	38.0	282
May-Jul 2012	1,483	8.5	631	283	569	38.4	300	1,468	8.8	627	279	562	38.3	294
Jun-Aug 2012	1,446	8.3	622	264	560	38.7	300	1,432	8.5	618	261	552	38.6	294
Jul-Sep 2012	1,432	8.3	618	264	550	38.4	297	1,418	8.5	613	261	544	38.4	293
Aug-Oct 2012	1,436	8.3	613	260	562	39.2	310	1,418	8.5	606	257	555	39.1	306
Sep-Nov 2012	1,419	8.2	611	249	559	39.4	303	1,400	8.4	604	246	550	39.3	298
Oct-Dec 2012	1,419	8.2	619	243	557	39.3	304	1,400	8.4	613	241	547	39.1	298
Nov-Jan 2013	1,434	8.3	623	247	564	39.4	307	1,420	8.5	619	244	558	39.3	303

4.7: Unemployment by age and duration

	All aged 16 & over							All aged 16 - 64						
	All	Rate (%)[1]	Up to 6 months	Over 6 and up to 12 months	All over 12 months	% over 12 months	All over 24 months	All	Rate (%)[1]	Up to 6 months	Over 6 and up to 12 months	All over 12 months	% over 12 months	All over 24 months
	1	2	3	4	5	6	7	8	9	10	11	12	13	14
Men	MGSD	MGSY	MGYK	MGYM	MGYO	YBWJ	YBWM	YBSI	YBTJ	YBWP	YBWS	YBWV	YBWY	YBXB
Dec-Feb 2013	1,447	8.3	633	253	561	38.7	305	1,435	8.6	629	251	554	38.6	302
Jan-Mar 2013	1,438	8.3	637	234	566	39.4	306	1,424	8.5	632	232	560	39.3	302
Feb-Apr 2013	1,422	8.2	641	220	561	39.4	302	1,406	8.4	634	219	553	39.3	297
Mar-May 2013	1,434	8.3	629	231	574	40.0	313	1,417	8.5	619	230	567	40.1	308
Apr-Jun 2013	1,442	8.3	633	239	571	39.6	314	1,421	8.5	620	238	562	39.6	307
May-Jul 2013	1,430	8.2	617	249	565	39.5	313	1,412	8.4	605	248	559	39.6	307
Jun-Aug 2013	1,421	8.2	612	250	559	39.3	311	1,401	8.4	600	249	552	39.4	306
Jul-Sep 2013	1,390	8.0	604	233	554	39.8	307	1,375	8.2	595	230	549	40.0	304
Aug-Oct 2013	1,355	7.8	600	220	534	39.5	292	1,337	8.0	590	218	529	39.6	290
Sep-Nov 2013	1,313	7.5	579	217	516	39.3	300	1,298	7.7	570	216	512	39.4	298
Oct-Dec 2013	1,321	7.6	574	226	521	39.4	307	1,303	7.8	563	224	516	39.6	305
Nov-Jan 2014	1,288	7.4	552	223	513	39.8	303	1,269	7.6	541	221	506	39.9	301
Dec-Feb 2014	1,260	7.2	536	214	510	40.4	289	1,241	7.4	525	212	503	40.6	286
Jan-Mar 2014	1,231	7.0	516	199	516	41.9	299	1,213	7.2	508	197	508	41.9	295
Feb-Apr 2014	1,202	6.9	509	189	505	42.0	291	1,182	7.0	499	187	496	42.0	286
Mar-May 2014	1,164	6.6	496	185	483	41.5	284	1,142	6.8	487	183	472	41.4	278
Apr-Jun 2014	1,144	6.5	495	181	468	40.9	267	1,125	6.7	487	179	459	40.8	263
May-Jul 2014	1,124	6.4	497	166	461	41.0	267	1,109	6.6	489	164	455	41.0	262
Jun-Aug 2014	1,095	6.3	482	166	447	40.9	251	1,082	6.4	477	164	441	40.7	247
Jul-Sep 2014	1,087	6.2	492	168	427	39.3	233	1,071	6.4	486	166	420	39.2	228
Aug-Oct 2014	1,092	6.2	490	180	422	38.6	233	1,077	6.4	485	177	415	38.5	228
Sep-Nov 2014	1,069	6.1	489	171	409	38.3	225	1,054	6.3	484	169	401	38.1	221
Oct-Dec 2014	**1,039**	**6.0**	**474**	**164**	**402**	**38.6**	**220**	**1,025**	**6.1**	**471**	**161**	**393**	**38.3**	**216**
Change on qtr	-47	-0.3	-18	-4	-25	-0.6	-12	-46	-0.3	-14	-5	-27	-0.9	-12
Change %	-4.3		-3.7	-2.4	-5.9		-5.2	-4.3		-2.9	-2.9	-6.4		-5.5
Change on year	-281	-1.6	-100	-62	-119	-0.8	-87	-278	-1.6	-92	-63	-123	-1.2	-89
Change %	-21.3		-17.4	-27.5	-22.8		-28.2	-21.3		-16.3	-28.3	-23.8		-29.2
Women	MGSE	MGSZ	MGYL	MGYN	MGYP	YBWK	YBWN	LF2J	LF2R	LF2Z	LF33	LF35	LF37	LF39
Nov-Jan 2006	661	4.7	462	102	97	14.7	45	657	4.8	456	101	100	15.2	45
Dec-Feb 2006	673	4.8	461	110	102	15.2	46	669	4.8	457	109	103	15.4	46
Jan-Mar 2006	674	4.8	458	114	103	15.2	45	670	4.8	454	113	103	15.3	45
Feb-Apr 2006	688	4.9	465	121	102	14.8	42	684	4.9	464	120	100	14.6	42
Mar-May 2006	698	4.9	476	125	97	13.9	42	695	5.0	476	125	94	13.5	41
Apr-Jun 2006	716	5.1	487	126	103	14.3	44	712	5.1	483	125	104	14.6	44
May-Jul 2006	725	5.1	488	126	112	15.4	47	720	5.2	484	125	110	15.3	47
Jun-Aug 2006	726	5.1	484	123	119	16.4	50	721	5.2	480	122	119	16.4	50
Jul-Sep 2006	719	5.1	478	117	124	17.2	50	716	5.1	477	117	121	16.9	50
Aug-Oct 2006	717	5.1	477	118	122	17.0	50	715	5.1	476	118	121	16.9	50
Sep-Nov 2006	723	5.1	475	116	132	18.2	56	721	5.2	476	116	129	17.9	55
Oct-Dec 2006	731	5.2	484	117	130	17.7	57	729	5.2	482	117	130	17.9	56
Nov-Jan 2007	736	5.2	496	114	126	17.1	56	733	5.3	492	113	128	17.5	55
Dec-Feb 2007	734	5.2	500	114	120	16.3	52	731	5.2	496	113	121	16.6	52
Jan-Mar 2007	733	5.2	498	114	121	16.5	52	729	5.2	495	114	120	16.5	51
Feb-Apr 2007	725	5.1	484	115	125	17.2	51	721	5.2	483	116	122	16.9	51
Mar-May 2007	717	5.1	482	110	126	17.5	50	712	5.1	480	110	123	17.3	49
Apr-Jun 2007	717	5.0	481	111	125	17.4	51	713	5.1	476	109	127	17.8	51
May-Jul 2007	710	5.0	472	110	128	18.0	53	705	5.0	469	109	127	18.0	52
Jun-Aug 2007	712	5.0	472	114	126	17.7	52	708	5.1	471	113	124	17.5	51
Jul-Sep 2007	715	5.0	474	113	128	17.9	50	712	5.1	474	113	125	17.6	50
Aug-Oct 2007	712	5.0	480	107	125	17.6	47	709	5.0	479	107	123	17.4	47
Sep-Nov 2007	710	5.0	478	106	126	17.7	47	707	5.0	477	106	123	17.4	47
Oct-Dec 2007	699	4.9	470	105	125	17.9	47	696	4.9	467	105	125	18.0	47
Nov-Jan 2008	691	4.8	461	110	120	17.4	49	689	4.9	456	109	123	17.9	49
Dec-Feb 2008	689	4.8	454	111	124	17.9	50	685	4.9	450	110	125	18.2	49
Jan-Mar 2008	688	4.8	451	111	126	18.3	53	684	4.8	450	110	125	18.3	52
Feb-Apr 2008	722	5.0	476	113	133	18.5	55	718	5.1	475	112	131	18.2	55
Mar-May 2008	689	4.8	446	113	130	18.8	52	685	4.8	445	112	128	18.7	52
Apr-Jun 2008	702	4.9	461	116	126	17.9	50	698	4.9	456	114	128	18.3	50
May-Jul 2008	716	5.0	470	115	131	18.4	55	713	5.0	468	114	131	18.4	54
Jun-Aug 2008	745	5.2	500	114	131	17.6	57	741	5.2	499	113	129	17.4	56
Jul-Sep 2008	765	5.3	507	122	136	17.8	57	761	5.4	507	121	133	17.4	56
Aug-Oct 2008	775	5.4	508	128	140	18.0	58	770	5.4	507	128	136	17.6	57
Sep-Nov 2008	794	5.5	519	132	143	18.0	59	789	5.6	517	132	140	17.8	59

4.7: Unemployment by age and duration

United Kingdom (thousands) seasonally adjusted

	All aged 16 & over							All aged 16 - 64						
	All	Rate (%)[1]	Up to 6 months	Over 6 and up to 12 months	All over 12 months	% over 12 months	All over 24 months	All	Rate (%)[1]	Up to 6 months	Over 6 and up to 12 months	All over 12 months	% over 12 months	All over 24 months
	1	2	3	4	5	6	7	8	9	10	11	12	13	14
Women	MGSE	MGSZ	MGYL	MGYN	MGYP	YBWK	YBWN	LF2J	LF2R	LF2Z	LF33	LF35	LF37	LF39
Oct-Dec 2008	812	5.6	532	134	145	17.9	60	807	5.7	528	133	146	18.1	59
Nov-Jan 2009	833	5.7	543	143	147	17.7	60	828	5.8	537	141	150	18.1	59
Dec-Feb 2009	856	5.9	551	147	158	18.5	66	851	6.0	546	146	158	18.6	63
Jan-Mar 2009	897	6.2	569	158	171	19.1	72	892	6.3	566	158	168	18.8	70
Feb-Apr 2009	914	6.3	570	161	182	20.0	72	909	6.4	567	162	180	19.8	71
Mar-May 2009	944	6.5	583	170	191	20.2	71	938	6.6	580	170	188	20.0	70
Apr-Jun 2009	958	6.6	584	177	197	20.6	76	952	6.7	578	176	198	20.8	75
May-Jul 2009	957	6.6	582	177	198	20.7	74	951	6.7	578	176	197	20.7	72
Jun-Aug 2009	953	6.5	574	175	204	21.4	73	949	6.7	574	175	200	21.1	71
Jul-Sep 2009	954	6.5	566	176	211	22.2	69	947	6.6	565	175	207	21.8	68
Aug-Oct 2009	961	6.6	565	186	210	21.8	71	955	6.7	564	186	205	21.5	70
Sep-Nov 2009	959	6.6	540	198	222	23.1	75	953	6.7	536	196	221	23.1	74
Oct-Dec 2009	968	6.6	548	195	225	23.3	77	961	6.7	543	192	226	23.5	75
Nov-Jan 2010	944	6.5	518	199	226	24.0	74	936	6.6	512	196	228	24.4	72
Dec-Feb 2010	978	6.7	540	203	235	24.0	80	971	6.8	536	202	234	24.0	78
Jan-Mar 2010	984	6.7	542	196	246	25.0	81	977	6.8	541	196	241	24.6	78
Feb-Apr 2010	986	6.7	541	194	250	25.4	83	980	6.9	540	194	246	25.1	81
Mar-May 2010	1,008	6.9	549	201	258	25.6	87	1,003	7.0	549	200	254	25.3	85
Apr-Jun 2010	1,012	6.9	554	203	255	25.2	92	1,007	7.0	550	201	255	25.3	90
May-Jul 2010	1,034	7.0	575	203	256	24.7	96	1,028	7.2	571	203	255	24.8	94
Jun-Aug 2010	1,037	7.0	569	203	266	25.6	100	1,032	7.2	568	203	261	25.3	98
Jul-Sep 2010	1,038	7.1	570	199	270	26.0	94	1,034	7.2	571	199	264	25.6	92
Aug-Oct 2010	1,058	7.2	567	210	281	26.6	96	1,054	7.3	569	211	275	26.0	94
Sep-Nov 2010	1,032	7.0	563	197	272	26.4	101	1,028	7.2	560	197	271	26.3	100
Oct-Dec 2010	1,046	7.1	571	198	277	26.4	104	1,040	7.3	565	198	277	26.7	103
Nov-Jan 2011	1,056	7.2	580	192	284	26.9	108	1,050	7.3	574	191	285	27.2	106
Dec-Feb 2011	1,046	7.1	569	192	286	27.3	110	1,041	7.2	565	192	284	27.3	108
Jan-Mar 2011	1,047	7.1	568	191	288	27.5	116	1,042	7.2	567	192	284	27.2	115
Feb-Apr 2011	1,034	7.0	563	189	281	27.2	110	1,029	7.2	560	189	280	27.2	109
Mar-May 2011	1,058	7.2	596	186	276	26.1	107	1,053	7.3	594	186	273	25.9	105
Apr-Jun 2011	1,078	7.3	601	190	288	26.7	120	1,072	7.4	596	188	288	26.8	119
May-Jul 2011	1,091	7.4	599	189	303	27.8	122	1,084	7.5	593	188	302	27.9	121
Jun-Aug 2011	1,104	7.5	589	205	310	28.1	125	1,094	7.6	586	205	304	27.8	123
Jul-Sep 2011	1,119	7.6	589	217	313	28.0	122	1,107	7.7	584	216	307	27.8	120
Aug-Oct 2011	1,134	7.6	598	222	314	27.7	127	1,119	7.7	592	221	306	27.3	125
Sep-Nov 2011	1,149	7.7	609	232	307	26.7	131	1,137	7.8	600	230	307	27.0	131
Oct-Dec 2011	1,141	7.7	605	226	310	27.2	135	1,131	7.8	596	223	312	27.6	135
Nov-Jan 2012	1,143	7.7	598	229	315	27.6	138	1,134	7.8	589	227	318	28.0	138
Dec-Feb 2012	1,144	7.7	587	224	333	29.1	138	1,136	7.9	580	224	333	29.3	137
Jan-Mar 2012	1,133	7.6	573	226	334	29.5	137	1,123	7.7	569	225	329	29.3	135
Feb-Apr 2012	1,132	7.6	571	230	332	29.3	137	1,123	7.7	566	228	329	29.3	136
Mar-May 2012	1,123	7.5	557	230	335	29.9	146	1,113	7.7	553	228	333	29.9	145
Apr-Jun 2012	1,118	7.5	564	224	330	29.5	138	1,110	7.6	558	222	330	29.8	138
May-Jul 2012	1,124	7.5	571	214	339	30.2	144	1,116	7.6	566	212	338	30.3	142
Jun-Aug 2012	1,107	7.4	563	201	343	31.0	142	1,100	7.5	564	201	335	30.5	141
Jul-Sep 2012	1,110	7.4	575	183	351	31.7	143	1,104	7.6	577	183	343	31.1	140
Aug-Oct 2012	1,103	7.4	570	183	350	31.7	139	1,100	7.6	573	184	342	31.1	138
Sep-Nov 2012	1,107	7.4	581	185	340	30.7	134	1,103	7.5	579	185	338	30.7	133
Oct-Dec 2012	1,110	7.4	582	199	328	29.6	139	1,106	7.5	578	198	330	29.9	139
Nov-Jan 2013	1,099	7.3	571	201	327	29.8	145	1,096	7.5	567	200	328	30.0	144
Dec-Feb 2013	1,136	7.5	578	212	346	30.4	160	1,132	7.7	576	211	345	30.5	158
Jan-Mar 2013	1,103	7.3	561	201	342	31.0	161	1,099	7.5	560	201	338	30.7	160
Feb-Apr 2013	1,105	7.3	565	198	342	30.9	158	1,100	7.5	561	198	341	31.0	157
Mar-May 2013	1,090	7.2	553	189	347	31.8	163	1,085	7.4	550	189	346	31.9	161
Apr-Jun 2013	1,084	7.2	548	191	345	31.8	163	1,080	7.4	545	190	346	32.0	161
May-Jul 2013	1,076	7.1	541	198	337	31.4	159	1,068	7.3	534	197	338	31.6	158
Jun-Aug 2013	1,089	7.2	545	197	346	31.8	159	1,082	7.4	544	197	341	31.5	158
Jul-Sep 2013	1,098	7.3	564	194	340	31.0	153	1,092	7.4	563	194	335	30.6	153
Aug-Oct 2013	1,058	7.0	532	185	340	32.2	154	1,050	7.1	534	184	333	31.7	154
Sep-Nov 2013	1,020	6.7	515	178	326	32.0	150	1,011	6.9	511	177	324	32.0	149
Oct-Dec 2013	1,027	6.8	529	170	328	31.9	146	1,015	6.9	523	168	324	31.9	145
Nov-Jan 2014	1,047	6.9	566	164	318	30.3	149	1,036	7.0	560	161	315	30.4	148
Dec-Feb 2014	993	6.5	536	157	301	30.3	144	982	6.6	531	154	297	30.2	143
Jan-Mar 2014	981	6.4	530	152	300	30.6	148	973	6.6	528	150	296	30.4	147
Feb-Apr 2014	960	6.3	518	154	288	30.0	143	951	6.4	512	153	286	30.1	142
Mar-May 2014	961	6.3	526	164	272	28.3	135	953	6.4	520	163	270	28.3	133
Apr-Jun 2014	930	6.1	505	152	273	29.4	141	922	6.2	498	151	273	29.6	140

4.7: Unemployment by age and duration

United Kingdom (thousands) seasonally adjusted

| | All aged 16 & over | | | | | | | All aged 16 - 64 | | | | | | |
	All	Rate (%)[1]	Up to 6 months	Over 6 and up to 12 months	All over 12 months	% over 12 months	All over 24 months	All	Rate (%)[1]	Up to 6 months	Over 6 and up to 12 months	All over 12 months	% over 12 months	All over 24 months
	1	2	3	4	5	6	7	8	9	10	11	12	13	14
Women	MGSE	MGSZ	MGYL	MGYN	MGYP	YBWK	YBWN	LF2J	LF2R	LF2Z	LF33	LF35	LF37	LF39
May-Jul 2014	897	5.9	481	152	263	29.4	133	891	6.0	475	151	264	29.6	132
Jun-Aug 2014	876	5.7	462	151	263	30.1	137	870	5.9	460	152	258	29.6	136
Jul-Sep 2014	872	5.7	458	153	261	30.0	144	866	5.8	458	153	255	29.4	142
Aug-Oct 2014	866	5.7	448	155	262	30.3	143	860	5.8	450	157	254	29.5	142
Sep-Nov 2014	845	5.5	452	144	249	29.4	130	841	5.7	449	144	248	29.5	129
Oct-Dec 2014	**822**	**5.4**	**449**	**137**	**237**	**28.8**	**119**	**819**	**5.5**	**444**	**135**	**239**	**29.2**	**118**
Change on qtr	*-50*	*-0.3*	*-9*	*-17*	*-25*	*-1.2*	*-25*	*-47*	*-0.3*	*-14*	*-18*	*-15*	*-0.2*	*-25*
Change %	*-5.7*		*-1.9*	*-10.8*	*-9.5*		*-17.3*	*-5.5*		*-3.1*	*-11.8*	*-6.0*		*-17.3*
Change on year	*-205*	*-1.4*	*-80*	*-34*	*-91*	*-3.1*	*-28*	*-196*	*-1.4*	*-79*	*-33*	*-85*	*-2.7*	*-28*
Change %	*-20.0*		*-15.2*	*-19.8*	*-27.8*		*-18.8*	*-19.3*		*-15.0*	*-19.4*	*-26.2*		*-19.0*

| | 16-17 | | | | | | | 18-24 | | | | | | |
	All	Rate (%)[1]	Up to 6 months	Over 6 and up to 12 months	All over 12 months	% over 12 months	All over 24 months	All	Rate (%)[1]	Up to 6 months	Over 6 and up to 12 months	All over 12 months	% over 12 months	All over 24 months
	15	16	17	18	19	20	21	22	23	24	25	26	27	28
People	YBVH	YBVK	YBXD	YBXG	YBXJ	YBXM	YBXP	YBVN	YBVQ	YBXS	YBXV	YBXY	YBYB	YBYE
Nov-Jan 2006	186	25.5	143	30	12	6.7	*	456	11.5	302	86	69	15.1	36
Dec-Feb 2006	186	25.4	143	32	11	5.9	*	464	11.5	315	81	68	14.6	30
Jan-Mar 2006	179	24.7	133	32	13	7.2	*	472	11.7	321	80	71	14.9	32
Feb-Apr 2006	181	24.6	132	35	14	7.6	*	484	11.9	341	72	71	14.7	28
Mar-May 2006	179	24.6	130	38	12	6.4	*	499	12.3	340	80	79	15.9	34
Apr-Jun 2006	175	24.1	127	34	14	7.9	*	513	12.5	350	84	79	15.4	32
May-Jul 2006	171	23.8	125	31	16	9.1	*	527	12.8	351	88	88	16.7	35
Jun-Aug 2006	168	23.5	125	25	18	10.8	*	516	12.5	345	92	80	15.5	29
Jul-Sep 2006	180	25.0	139	25	16	8.8	*	513	12.4	335	92	85	16.7	32
Aug-Oct 2006	181	25.1	142	23	15	8.6	*	501	12.2	323	99	79	15.8	31
Sep-Nov 2006	184	25.1	140	27	17	9.1	*	482	11.8	327	84	71	14.7	29
Oct-Dec 2006	184	24.9	141	27	16	8.6	*	502	12.2	351	79	73	14.4	28
Nov-Jan 2007	185	25.3	144	27	14	7.6	*	505	12.3	357	72	76	15.1	29
Dec-Feb 2007	189	26.2	146	28	15	7.7	*	512	12.5	356	69	87	16.9	31
Jan-Mar 2007	188	26.3	147	27	14	7.4	*	514	12.5	349	78	88	17.1	31
Feb-Apr 2007	187	26.2	145	27	15	8.1	*	519	12.6	342	86	91	17.5	28
Mar-May 2007	188	26.5	147	26	15	8.1	*	523	12.7	347	87	88	16.9	29
Apr-Jun 2007	193	27.5	150	28	14	7.4	*	515	12.5	339	85	91	17.7	30
May-Jul 2007	206	28.4	156	30	20	9.7	*	496	12.1	330	79	87	17.6	31
Jun-Aug 2007	205	28.3	151	35	19	9.1	*	500	12.2	333	73	93	18.7	35
Jul-Sep 2007	212	29.1	154	37	21	9.8	*	488	11.9	328	71	89	18.3	33
Aug-Oct 2007	201	27.6	147	40	14	7.0	*	485	11.8	325	67	93	19.1	35
Sep-Nov 2007	192	26.1	141	36	15	7.6	*	490	11.9	325	70	94	19.2	32
Oct-Dec 2007	185	25.0	136	33	16	8.5	*	488	11.9	322	70	96	19.7	36
Nov-Jan 2008	176	24.1	131	31	14	7.7	*	497	12.0	332	70	95	19.2	40
Dec-Feb 2008	174	24.2	129	33	13	7.3	*	496	12.0	332	73	91	18.4	39
Jan-Mar 2008	172	24.2	127	33	12	7.0	*	505	12.2	338	72	96	19.0	42
Feb-Apr 2008	184	25.3	136	35	14	7.3	*	510	12.4	340	65	105	20.7	40
Mar-May 2008	182	25.3	134	36	13	7.1	*	497	12.0	325	66	105	21.2	39
Apr-Jun 2008	186	26.1	143	32	11	5.9	*	519	12.6	341	74	104	20.0	36
May-Jul 2008	186	26.0	142	32	12	6.6	*	530	12.8	349	78	102	19.3	38
Jun-Aug 2008	192	26.9	153	28	11	5.9	*	545	13.3	355	81	109	20.1	39
Jul-Sep 2008	187	26.5	147	29	12	6.1	*	566	13.7	377	81	108	19.0	39
Aug-Oct 2008	190	27.2	153	24	12	6.5	*	577	14.0	390	91	96	16.7	35
Sep-Nov 2008	193	27.8	147	29	16	8.3	*	597	14.4	398	99	99	16.7	36
Oct-Dec 2008	191	28.2	144	32	16	8.2	*	606	14.6	401	103	103	17.0	37
Nov-Jan 2009	198	28.5	143	38	16	8.1	*	614	14.8	402	110	102	16.6	38
Dec-Feb 2009	187	27.6	135	35	17	9.0	*	624	15.2	408	110	106	17.0	40
Jan-Mar 2009	196	29.2	143	32	22	11.0	*	668	16.3	429	123	116	17.4	45
Feb-Apr 2009	192	29.7	136	34	22	11.6	*	692	16.9	432	130	131	18.9	51
Mar-May 2009	200	31.0	144	35	21	10.5	*	722	17.6	454	135	134	18.5	49
Apr-Jun 2009	206	32.3	144	40	22	10.7	*	710	17.4	427	143	140	19.7	50
May-Jul 2009	221	35.1	156	44	21	9.5	*	711	17.5	412	148	151	21.2	54
Jun-Aug 2009	214	34.5	144	47	24	11.1	*	719	17.6	409	154	156	21.7	55

4.7: Unemployment by age and duration

United Kingdom (thousands) seasonally adjusted

	16-17							18-24						
	All	Rate (%)[1]	Up to 6 months	Over 6 and up to 12 months	All over 12 months	% over 12 months	All over 24 months	All	Rate (%)[1]	Up to 6 months	Over 6 and up to 12 months	All over 12 months	% over 12 months	All over 24 months
	15	16	17	18	19	20	21	22	23	24	25	26	27	28
People	YBVH	YBVK	YBXD	YBXG	YBXJ	YBXM	YBXP	YBVN	YBVQ	YBXS	YBXV	YBXY	YBYB	YBYE
Jul-Sep 2009	206	33.7	137	42	26	12.7	*	728	18.0	407	153	168	23.1	54
Aug-Oct 2009	198	32.6	130	40	28	14.3	*	734	18.3	424	150	159	21.7	50
Sep-Nov 2009	200	32.9	128	42	29	14.5	*	704	17.6	405	145	154	21.8	50
Oct-Dec 2009	196	33.0	130	38	29	14.6	*	704	17.5	409	140	156	22.1	51
Nov-Jan 2010	199	33.7	134	38	27	13.5	*	700	17.5	390	145	165	23.6	49
Dec-Feb 2010	199	34.1	134	35	30	15.1	*	715	17.8	388	156	171	23.9	57
Jan-Mar 2010	205	34.8	136	43	26	12.4	*	732	18.1	385	161	187	25.5	64
Feb-Apr 2010	217	36.5	143	49	25	11.6	*	721	17.8	376	154	191	26.5	71
Mar-May 2010	220	36.1	143	54	23	10.7	*	719	17.7	378	149	192	26.8	70
Apr-Jun 2010	199	33.7	132	45	22	11.2	*	728	17.9	403	141	184	25.3	72
May-Jul 2010	194	33.2	131	40	23	11.7	*	726	17.7	409	128	190	26.1	70
Jun-Aug 2010	189	32.7	128	36	25	13.3	*	741	18.0	410	126	205	27.7	70
Jul-Sep 2010	196	34.0	130	37	28	14.4	*	711	17.3	402	120	190	26.7	65
Aug-Oct 2010	213	36.2	143	41	30	14.0	*	735	17.9	405	132	198	26.9	68
Sep-Nov 2010	208	36.9	147	36	25	12.1	*	738	18.2	400	135	203	27.5	71
Oct-Dec 2010	215	37.5	154	35	26	12.0	*	745	18.2	395	141	209	28.1	76
Nov-Jan 2011	217	37.2	152	36	29	13.4	*	751	18.3	409	142	200	26.6	69
Dec-Feb 2011	220	37.4	153	39	27	12.3	*	740	18.0	406	136	198	26.8	75
Jan-Mar 2011	215	37.2	150	38	26	12.1	*	728	17.9	393	137	199	27.3	82
Feb-Apr 2011	210	36.5	144	41	26	12.2	*	702	17.3	391	124	187	26.6	84
Mar-May 2011	207	36.4	138	43	25	12.3	*	728	17.8	413	133	182	25.0	79
Apr-Jun 2011	211	37.0	145	40	26	12.2	*	756	18.4	423	129	204	27.0	94
May-Jul 2011	211	37.5	141	41	29	13.9	*	782	19.0	428	136	219	28.0	91
Jun-Aug 2011	220	38.8	143	44	33	14.9	*	803	19.5	427	147	229	28.5	96
Jul-Sep 2011	226	40.1	142	47	37	16.4	*	809	19.8	427	159	224	27.6	88
Aug-Oct 2011	217	39.5	139	46	32	14.9	*	830	20.2	441	162	228	27.4	98
Sep-Nov 2011	218	38.5	135	46	37	16.9	*	834	20.3	456	166	211	25.3	92
Oct-Dec 2011	213	37.5	134	46	33	15.6	*	826	20.1	445	168	212	25.7	94
Nov-Jan 2012	221	38.9	138	45	38	17.3	*	818	20.0	435	166	216	26.4	88
Dec-Feb 2012	219	38.0	138	46	34	15.5	*	813	19.8	415	171	227	27.9	96
Jan-Mar 2012	210	37.2	133	45	33	15.7	*	818	19.9	415	172	231	28.2	99
Feb-Apr 2012	209	37.1	137	42	30	14.2	*	814	19.9	407	184	224	27.5	99
Mar-May 2012	203	36.3	135	40	29	14.4	*	828	20.0	404	183	241	29.1	111
Apr-Jun 2012	205	36.4	137	40	29	14.2	*	819	19.6	403	177	239	29.1	99
May-Jul 2012	206	36.9	137	40	29	14.0	*	825	19.6	407	168	250	30.4	103
Jun-Aug 2012	201	36.3	132	38	32	15.8	*	780	18.7	395	141	244	31.3	104
Jul-Sep 2012	195	34.8	125	35	35	18.2	*	784	19.0	406	141	236	30.1	102
Aug-Oct 2012	203	36.9	132	35	36	17.7	*	761	18.4	392	134	234	30.8	102
Sep-Nov 2012	201	37.0	132	35	34	16.7	*	777	18.6	407	134	237	30.4	92
Oct-Dec 2012	201	37.6	136	36	30	14.7	*	787	18.8	404	133	251	31.9	103
Nov-Jan 2013	197	37.4	131	38	28	14.2	*	807	19.3	418	127	261	32.4	108
Dec-Feb 2013	198	38.1	136	36	27	13.4	*	794	19.1	405	133	255	32.2	109
Jan-Mar 2013	194	37.3	132	34	28	14.5	*	779	18.7	405	126	248	31.8	101
Feb-Apr 2013	190	36.6	131	30	29	15.3	*	771	18.6	408	126	237	30.7	96
Mar-May 2013	199	37.8	134	35	29	14.8	*	774	18.8	401	120	253	32.7	107
Apr-Jun 2013	201	38.0	140	37	24	11.8	*	795	19.4	409	130	256	32.2	112
May-Jul 2013	204	38.3	143	39	22	11.0	*	784	19.1	391	132	261	33.3	118
Jun-Aug 2013	194	36.8	135	33	26	13.4	*	793	19.3	393	149	251	31.7	115
Jul-Sep 2013	187	36.1	131	29	27	14.2	*	794	19.2	396	139	259	32.6	114
Aug-Oct 2013	189	36.0	128	33	28	14.6	*	773	18.8	390	140	244	31.5	106
Sep-Nov 2013	192	36.1	131	36	24	12.6	*	743	18.0	374	135	235	31.6	107
Oct-Dec 2013	188	36.4	126	38	24	12.7	*	740	17.9	374	130	236	31.9	115
Nov-Jan 2014	191	37.0	137	32	22	11.4	*	732	17.7	376	129	227	31.0	105
Dec-Feb 2014	181	35.9	127	31	23	12.8	*	712	17.1	366	121	225	31.6	105
Jan-Mar 2014	182	35.8	129	29	25	13.5	*	694	16.8	354	114	225	32.5	105
Feb-Apr 2014	180	35.7	123	31	27	15.0	*	675	16.3	353	107	215	31.8	103
Mar-May 2014	173	34.7	124	25	25	14.2	*	649	15.7	351	106	192	29.7	90
Apr-Jun 2014	166	34.3	120	21	25	15.3	*	610	14.9	325	104	181	29.6	85
May-Jul 2014	164	34.0	117	23	24	14.9	*	592	14.5	312	101	179	30.2	84
Jun-Aug 2014	162	33.6	110	30	21	13.1	*	572	13.9	291	93	188	32.9	88
Jul-Sep 2014	157	32.9	110	31	16	10.1	*	580	14.2	299	89	191	33.0	87
Aug-Oct 2014	154	32.5	106	32	15	10.0	*	600	14.7	307	90	203	33.8	95
Sep-Nov 2014	152	32.1	103	31	18	12.1	*	611	15.1	328	95	188	30.7	84
Oct-Dec 2014	**157**	**31.2**	**108**	**31**	**18**	**11.5**	*	**583**	**14.3**	**318**	**82**	**183**	**31.4**	**85**
Change on qtr	0	-1.7	-2	0	2	1.4	*	3	0.1	19	-7	-8	-1.6	-2
Change %	-0.1		-2.2	0.1	13.9		*	0.6		6.4	-8.4	-4.4		-2.3

4.7: Unemployment by age and duration

United Kingdom (thousands) seasonally adjusted

	16-17							18-24						
	All	Rate (%)[1]	Up to 6 months	Over 6 and up to 12 months	All over 12 months	% over 12 months	All over 24 months	All	Rate (%)[1]	Up to 6 months	Over 6 and up to 12 months	All over 12 months	% over 12 months	All over 24 months
	15	16	17	18	19	20	21	22	23	24	25	26	27	28
People	YBVH	YBVK	YBXD	YBXG	YBXJ	YBXM	YBXP	YBVN	YBVQ	YBXS	YBXV	YBXY	YBYB	YBYE
Change on year	-31	-5.2	-18	-8	-6	-1.2	*	-157	-3.6	-56	-48	-53	-0.6	-30
Change %	-16.5		-14.0	-20.3	-24.1		*	-21.2		-14.9	-36.9	-22.6		-26.3
Men	YBVI	YBVL	YBXE	YBXH	YBXK	YBXN	YBXQ	YBVO	YBVR	YBXT	YBXW	YBXZ	YBYC	YBYF
Nov-Jan 2006	101	28.6	73	19	8	8.2	*	267	12.7	166	52	49	18.4	28
Dec-Feb 2006	107	29.9	80	19	8	7.3	*	277	13.0	177	52	48	17.4	24
Jan-Mar 2006	108	30.6	79	21	9	8.2	*	281	13.1	178	50	54	19.0	27
Feb-Apr 2006	109	29.9	77	22	10	9.6	*	295	13.7	199	41	54	18.4	25
Mar-May 2006	108	30.0	75	25	9	8.0	*	296	13.8	190	46	60	20.4	29
Apr-Jun 2006	101	28.3	71	21	10	9.5	*	304	14.2	193	51	61	20.0	28
May-Jul 2006	98	27.5	69	19	10	10.5	*	307	14.2	185	55	68	22.0	31
Jun-Aug 2006	93	26.4	65	16	11	12.3	*	300	13.8	184	56	59	19.8	26
Jul-Sep 2006	102	28.6	74	18	10	10.2	*	303	13.8	181	59	63	20.8	29
Aug-Oct 2006	101	28.6	75	16	10	10.3	*	299	13.7	180	62	57	19.1	27
Sep-Nov 2006	105	29.2	77	18	10	9.6	*	285	13.2	182	53	50	17.4	23
Oct-Dec 2006	105	29.0	78	18	9	9.0	*	296	13.6	195	49	52	17.7	22
Nov-Jan 2007	105	29.6	79	17	9	8.8	*	297	13.6	195	46	57	19.2	22
Dec-Feb 2007	105	29.5	77	17	10	9.8	*	301	13.8	195	43	63	20.9	23
Jan-Mar 2007	104	29.1	78	17	9	9.0	*	300	13.7	190	49	61	20.4	23
Feb-Apr 2007	101	28.4	76	14	10	10.0	*	308	14.0	187	56	65	21.0	21
Mar-May 2007	105	29.6	79	15	11	10.1	*	307	14.0	188	56	63	20.5	23
Apr-Jun 2007	106	31.0	81	15	10	9.7	*	306	14.0	186	53	67	21.8	23
May-Jul 2007	114	32.2	85	18	12	10.5	*	290	13.5	180	48	61	21.2	25
Jun-Aug 2007	114	31.5	82	21	11	9.6	*	296	13.7	182	47	67	22.7	28
Jul-Sep 2007	114	31.4	78	22	13	11.3	*	292	13.5	185	44	64	21.7	26
Aug-Oct 2007	113	30.7	80	25	8	6.9	*	287	13.3	181	40	66	22.8	28
Sep-Nov 2007	108	28.7	77	21	10	9.2	*	289	13.3	181	43	65	22.6	27
Oct-Dec 2007	108	28.7	78	20	11	10.1	*	288	13.3	176	44	67	23.4	31
Nov-Jan 2008	101	27.0	71	19	11	11.0	*	296	13.6	182	45	69	23.3	35
Dec-Feb 2008	100	27.3	69	22	9	8.8	*	303	13.9	189	45	69	22.8	35
Jan-Mar 2008	97	26.7	68	21	8	8.3	*	310	14.2	194	44	72	23.3	38
Feb-Apr 2008	103	28.7	74	20	9	9.0	*	307	14.1	192	40	74	24.2	34
Mar-May 2008	100	28.4	74	17	9	9.1	*	299	13.7	183	42	73	24.4	31
Apr-Jun 2008	99	28.1	75	16	8	8.4	*	320	14.7	197	48	75	23.3	28
May-Jul 2008	100	28.1	76	17	8	7.6	*	333	15.3	209	51	74	22.2	29
Jun-Aug 2008	101	28.3	80	15	6	6.1	*	342	15.6	212	51	78	22.9	29
Jul-Sep 2008	101	28.0	83	12	5	5.4	*	350	15.9	220	52	78	22.2	28
Aug-Oct 2008	100	28.3	85	9	5	5.5	*	354	16.2	223	60	71	20.1	25
Sep-Nov 2008	104	29.6	80	16	8	7.8	*	365	16.7	228	64	73	20.0	25
Oct-Dec 2008	102	29.6	75	19	8	7.9	*	373	16.9	231	66	75	20.2	26
Nov-Jan 2009	104	30.2	74	21	9	9.0	*	380	17.3	233	72	76	19.9	28
Dec-Feb 2009	102	30.0	73	17	11	11.3	*	386	17.8	239	74	73	19.0	29
Jan-Mar 2009	106	31.9	78	14	14	13.4	*	406	18.8	247	80	79	19.4	33
Feb-Apr 2009	103	32.2	71	19	13	12.9	*	418	19.4	251	84	84	20.0	37
Mar-May 2009	108	34.1	75	20	14	12.5	*	437	20.2	264	88	85	19.5	37
Apr-Jun 2009	116	36.8	76	24	15	12.9	*	436	20.2	251	94	91	20.9	37
May-Jul 2009	122	39.4	79	27	15	12.7	*	450	20.8	245	99	106	23.5	42
Jun-Aug 2009	120	39.5	78	27	15	12.6	*	448	20.8	229	107	112	25.0	43
Jul-Sep 2009	109	37.7	69	26	14	12.6	*	449	21.1	224	107	118	26.3	40
Aug-Oct 2009	106	37.1	67	24	15	14.3	*	449	21.2	233	108	109	24.3	35
Sep-Nov 2009	108	39.1	69	26	14	12.6	*	426	20.3	223	95	108	25.4	39
Oct-Dec 2009	107	38.9	69	23	14	13.3	*	424	20.2	220	90	114	27.0	38
Nov-Jan 2010	108	39.8	72	23	13	12.1	*	422	20.2	208	89	125	29.6	40
Dec-Feb 2010	109	40.0	72	21	16	14.3	*	429	20.4	206	98	125	29.1	44
Jan-Mar 2010	115	41.6	74	28	13	11.4	*	444	21.0	207	102	136	30.6	50
Feb-Apr 2010	122	42.6	77	32	12	10.3	*	438	20.5	201	97	139	31.7	54
Mar-May 2010	123	41.7	76	34	13	10.8	*	429	20.1	197	91	141	32.9	55
Apr-Jun 2010	107	37.3	67	26	14	12.8	*	429	20.1	207	88	135	31.4	55
May-Jul 2010	105	37.0	69	22	14	13.4	*	424	19.6	208	79	136	32.2	53
Jun-Aug 2010	101	36.0	67	18	15	15.2	*	431	19.9	216	71	144	33.4	53
Jul-Sep 2010	105	37.4	68	21	17	15.8	*	407	18.6	214	65	128	31.5	47
Aug-Oct 2010	107	38.6	70	22	16	14.6	*	424	19.4	220	72	132	31.1	48
Sep-Nov 2010	109	39.5	74	20	15	13.4	*	432	19.9	217	79	137	31.6	46
Oct-Dec 2010	112	40.5	79	19	14	12.7	*	435	19.9	214	80	141	32.4	47
Nov-Jan 2011	118	40.7	79	21	19	16.0	*	431	19.8	216	84	131	30.4	43
Dec-Feb 2011	115	41.4	79	21	14	12.6	*	429	19.7	218	82	129	30.0	47

4.7: Unemployment by age and duration

United Kingdom (thousands) seasonally adjusted

	16-17							18-24						
	All	Rate (%)[1]	Up to 6 months	Over 6 and up to 12 months	All over 12 months	% over 12 months	All over 24 months	All	Rate (%)[1]	Up to 6 months	Over 6 and up to 12 months	All over 12 months	% over 12 months	All over 24 months
	15	16	17	18	19	20	21	22	23	24	25	26	27	28
Men	YBVI	YBVL	YBXE	YBXH	YBXK	YBXN	YBXQ	YBVO	YBVR	YBXT	YBXW	YBXZ	YBYC	YBYF
Jan-Mar 2011	110	40.5	77	19	14	13.0	*	431	19.9	212	87	132	30.7	53
Feb-Apr 2011	110	40.6	74	21	16	14.1	*	429	19.7	220	80	129	30.0	59
Mar-May 2011	109	40.3	68	25	16	14.6	*	436	20.0	228	86	122	28.0	56
Apr-Jun 2011	113	41.6	71	24	18	15.7	*	446	20.4	235	78	133	29.9	64
May-Jul 2011	112	42.5	68	24	20	18.0	*	459	21.2	232	85	142	31.0	65
Jun-Aug 2011	119	43.7	72	25	22	18.8	*	479	22.0	238	89	153	31.9	70
Jul-Sep 2011	125	45.5	77	26	23	18.3	*	488	22.6	244	97	147	30.0	66
Aug-Oct 2011	118	44.0	73	25	20	16.9	*	504	23.3	254	98	151	30.0	73
Sep-Nov 2011	113	41.3	65	24	24	21.5	*	509	23.5	269	101	138	27.2	66
Oct-Dec 2011	108	39.5	65	22	21	19.0	*	513	23.6	261	106	146	28.4	70
Nov-Jan 2012	118	43.2	72	23	24	20.0	*	514	23.6	262	103	148	28.9	63
Dec-Feb 2012	114	40.7	72	22	20	17.3	*	511	23.4	247	110	154	30.1	72
Jan-Mar 2012	108	39.1	68	22	18	16.6	*	508	23.2	242	110	156	30.7	73
Feb-Apr 2012	105	38.2	70	20	16	14.8	*	507	23.2	234	118	154	30.5	73
Mar-May 2012	107	38.7	75	17	15	13.9	*	512	23.2	228	117	167	32.6	79
Apr-Jun 2012	105	38.8	74	16	15	14.0	*	505	22.7	229	113	164	32.4	70
May-Jul 2012	102	38.1	72	18	11	10.8	*	508	22.8	229	111	169	33.2	73
Jun-Aug 2012	101	38.8	66	20	15	14.8	*	474	21.5	222	89	163	34.5	71
Jul-Sep 2012	96	37.0	61	20	15	15.8	*	474	21.6	225	89	160	33.7	70
Aug-Oct 2012	105	40.1	67	20	18	17.0	*	458	20.8	215	84	159	34.7	70
Sep-Nov 2012	106	41.5	69	19	17	15.8	*	464	21.0	215	83	166	35.7	66
Oct-Dec 2012	110	43.2	72	20	18	16.2	*	463	21.0	213	79	172	37.1	71
Nov-Jan 2013	105	41.5	67	22	16	15.4	*	478	21.7	226	79	174	36.3	72
Dec-Feb 2013	101	41.0	68	19	14	14.1	*	458	21.0	219	74	165	36.0	72
Jan-Mar 2013	102	41.3	69	19	15	14.3	*	451	20.7	220	66	166	36.7	68
Feb-Apr 2013	100	41.0	65	18	17	16.6	*	446	20.5	218	64	163	36.6	68
Mar-May 2013	105	42.4	68	23	15	14.2	*	454	21.0	220	66	168	37.0	72
Apr-Jun 2013	107	42.2	73	24	10	9.6	*	472	21.9	231	73	169	35.8	75
May-Jul 2013	115	43.8	79	25	11	9.5	*	466	21.4	221	75	169	36.4	81
Jun-Aug 2013	104	40.8	73	21	11	10.2	*	471	21.7	216	90	165	35.1	83
Jul-Sep 2013	97	39.4	68	17	11	11.9	*	469	21.5	217	85	168	35.8	81
Aug-Oct 2013	100	39.8	68	20	12	12.2	*	463	21.3	221	86	157	33.8	73
Sep-Nov 2013	105	41.1	71	21	12	11.4	*	441	20.2	207	82	153	34.6	78
Oct-Dec 2013	98	39.9	66	21	11	11.5	*	444	20.3	204	81	159	35.8	85
Nov-Jan 2014	95	39.0	67	17	11	11.6	*	433	19.8	199	82	152	35.1	75
Dec-Feb 2014	92	39.1	60	18	14	14.9	*	428	19.5	200	79	150	35.0	75
Jan-Mar 2014	93	39.1	60	17	16	16.8	*	416	19.0	191	74	151	36.3	77
Feb-Apr 2014	96	41.1	60	18	18	18.5	*	409	18.6	193	67	149	36.5	78
Mar-May 2014	87	37.9	57	13	17	19.5	*	394	18.0	192	63	139	35.3	70
Apr-Jun 2014	80	36.5	51	11	17	21.6	*	375	17.3	184	66	125	33.2	63
May-Jul 2014	79	36.7	55	10	15	19.1	*	367	17.1	183	64	120	32.7	60
Jun-Aug 2014	77	36.2	52	12	13	17.0	*	353	16.4	169	58	125	35.5	62
Jul-Sep 2014	75	36.3	54	11	11	14.0	*	356	16.6	166	60	130	36.5	59
Aug-Oct 2014	73	34.4	49	15	9	12.5	*	359	16.6	164	59	135	37.7	63
Sep-Nov 2014	76	35.3	50	17	9	12.4	*	353	16.4	172	57	124	35.2	55
Oct-Dec 2014	**82**	**35.4**	**58**	**16**	**9**	**10.4**	*	**340**	**15.8**	**172**	**44**	**124**	**36.5**	**57**
Change on qtr	*7*	*-0.9*	*4*	*5*	*-2*	*-3.6*	*	*-17*	*-0.8*	*5*	*-16*	*-6*	*0.1*	*-1*
Change %	*9.0*		*6.8*	*46.8*	*-18.8*		*	*-4.6*		*3.2*	*-27.0*	*-4.4*		*-2.1*
Change on year	*-16*	*-4.5*	*-8*	*-5*	*-3*	*-1.0*	*	*-104*	*-4.5*	*-32*	*-38*	*-35*	*0.8*	*-28*
Change %	*-16.2*		*-12.6*	*-23.2*	*-23.8*		*	*-23.5*		*-15.7*	*-46.3*	*-21.8*		*-32.6*
Women	YBVJ	YBVM	YBXF	YBXI	YBXL	YBXO	YBXR	YBVP	YBVS	YBXU	YBXX	YBYA	YBYD	YBYG
Nov-Jan 2006	85	22.7	70	10	*	4.9	*	189	10.1	136	34	20	10.5	8
Dec-Feb 2006	79	21.0	63	13	*	4.2	*	187	9.9	139	28	20	10.5	6
Jan-Mar 2006	70	19.0	54	12	*	5.6	*	191	10.0	144	31	17	8.9	5
Feb-Apr 2006	71	19.3	55	13	*	4.6	*	189	9.9	142	31	17	8.9	4
Mar-May 2006	71	19.3	54	14	*	4.1	*	203	10.5	150	34	19	9.2	5
Apr-Jun 2006	74	20.1	56	13	*	5.7	*	208	10.8	157	34	18	8.6	5
May-Jul 2006	73	20.1	56	12	5	7.3	*	220	11.4	167	33	20	9.2	4
Jun-Aug 2006	75	20.6	60	9	7	9.1	*	216	11.1	160	35	20	9.5	3
Jul-Sep 2006	78	21.4	65	7	6	7.1	*	210	10.9	154	33	22	10.6	3
Aug-Oct 2006	79	21.8	67	7	5	6.3	*	203	10.5	144	37	22	11.1	4
Sep-Nov 2006	79	21.2	63	9	7	8.5	*	197	10.2	145	31	21	10.9	5
Oct-Dec 2006	79	21.0	64	9	6	8.0	*	207	10.7	156	31	20	9.8	6
Nov-Jan 2007	80	21.3	65	10	5	6.1	*	208	10.8	162	27	19	9.2	7

4.7: Unemployment by age and duration

	16-17							18-24						
	All	Rate (%)[1]	Up to 6 months	Over 6 and up to 12 months	All over 12 months	% over 12 months	All over 24 months	All	Rate (%)[1]	Up to 6 months	Over 6 and up to 12 months	All over 12 months	% over 12 months	All over 24 months
	15	16	17	18	19	20	21	22	23	24	25	26	27	28
Women	YBVJ	YBVM	YBXF	YBXI	YBXL	YBXO	YBXR	YBVP	YBVS	YBXU	YBXX	YBYA	YBYD	YBYG
Dec-Feb 2007	84	23.0	69	11	*	5.2	*	211	11.0	161	26	24	11.2	8
Jan-Mar 2007	84	23.4	70	10	5	5.5	*	214	11.1	159	28	27	12.4	9
Feb-Apr 2007	86	24.0	68	12	5	6.0	*	211	11.0	156	30	26	12.3	7
Mar-May 2007	83	23.5	68	11	5	5.5	*	215	11.2	159	31	25	11.8	7
Apr-Jun 2007	86	24.1	70	13	*	4.7	*	209	10.8	153	31	24	11.7	7
May-Jul 2007	92	24.8	72	13	8	8.6	*	206	10.6	150	30	26	12.5	7
Jun-Aug 2007	92	25.0	69	15	8	8.5	*	204	10.5	151	26	26	12.9	8
Jul-Sep 2007	98	27.0	76	14	8	8.1	*	195	10.1	143	27	26	13.1	7
Aug-Oct 2007	88	24.4	67	15	6	7.0	*	198	10.1	144	27	27	13.7	7
Sep-Nov 2007	84	23.4	64	15	5	5.6	*	200	10.3	144	28	29	14.3	5
Oct-Dec 2007	77	21.2	59	13	5	6.2	*	200	10.3	145	26	28	14.2	5
Nov-Jan 2008	74	21.1	60	12	*	3.3	*	201	10.3	150	25	26	13.1	6
Dec-Feb 2008	75	21.1	59	11	*	5.3	*	193	9.9	143	27	22	11.6	4
Jan-Mar 2008	75	21.6	60	11	*	5.3	*	194	10.0	144	27	24	12.2	5
Feb-Apr 2008	81	22.0	62	15	*	5.3	*	204	10.5	148	25	31	15.3	6
Mar-May 2008	82	22.4	60	18	*	4.7	*	198	10.1	142	24	32	16.3	8
Apr-Jun 2008	88	24.1	69	16	*	3.1	*	198	10.2	144	25	29	14.6	8
May-Jul 2008	86	24.0	66	15	5	5.4	*	197	10.1	141	27	29	14.6	9
Jun-Aug 2008	91	25.4	73	13	5	5.7	*	204	10.6	143	30	31	15.3	10
Jul-Sep 2008	86	24.9	64	17	6	7.0	*	216	11.1	157	29	30	13.9	11
Aug-Oct 2008	90	26.0	68	15	7	7.5	*	223	11.5	167	31	25	11.3	10
Sep-Nov 2008	89	25.9	67	14	8	9.0	*	231	11.8	170	35	26	11.4	11
Oct-Dec 2008	89	26.7	69	13	8	8.5	*	234	12.0	170	37	27	11.7	11
Nov-Jan 2009	94	26.9	69	18	7	7.2	*	234	12.0	169	38	26	11.3	10
Dec-Feb 2009	85	25.2	62	18	5	6.3	*	238	12.3	170	36	33	13.7	11
Jan-Mar 2009	90	26.5	65	18	7	8.2	*	262	13.5	182	43	37	14.2	12
Feb-Apr 2009	89	27.3	65	14	9	10.1	*	274	14.1	181	46	47	17.2	14
Mar-May 2009	92	28.1	69	15	7	8.1	*	285	14.7	190	48	48	16.9	13
Apr-Jun 2009	90	27.9	68	16	7	7.8	*	274	14.2	176	49	49	17.9	13
May-Jul 2009	99	30.9	76	17	6	5.7	*	261	13.8	168	48	45	17.3	12
Jun-Aug 2009	94	29.7	66	19	9	9.3	*	271	14.1	180	47	44	16.3	12
Jul-Sep 2009	97	30.0	68	16	12	12.8	*	279	14.5	183	46	50	17.9	14
Aug-Oct 2009	92	28.7	63	16	13	14.2	*	284	14.9	192	43	50	17.6	15
Sep-Nov 2009	92	27.7	60	16	15	16.8	*	278	14.6	183	50	46	16.4	12
Oct-Dec 2009	90	27.9	61	15	14	16.0	*	280	14.6	189	50	41	14.8	13
Nov-Jan 2010	91	28.6	62	15	14	15.1	*	278	14.5	181	57	40	14.5	9
Dec-Feb 2010	90	29.0	62	14	15	16.1	*	286	14.9	182	58	46	16.0	13
Jan-Mar 2010	90	28.8	62	15	12	13.8	*	288	15.0	178	59	51	17.7	14
Feb-Apr 2010	96	30.8	66	17	13	13.3	*	284	14.7	175	56	52	18.5	17
Mar-May 2010	97	30.9	67	20	10	10.4	*	289	15.0	181	58	51	17.6	15
Apr-Jun 2010	92	30.3	65	19	9	9.4	*	299	15.4	196	53	50	16.6	16
May-Jul 2010	89	29.5	62	18	9	9.7	*	303	15.5	201	49	53	17.6	17
Jun-Aug 2010	88	29.5	61	17	10	11.0	*	310	15.9	194	55	61	19.8	17
Jul-Sep 2010	91	30.8	63	16	12	12.9	*	304	15.7	188	55	61	20.2	17
Aug-Oct 2010	106	34.0	73	18	14	13.4	*	312	16.2	185	60	66	21.2	20
Sep-Nov 2010	100	34.4	73	16	11	10.6	*	306	16.3	183	56	66	21.7	25
Oct-Dec 2010	102	34.7	75	16	11	11.2	*	310	16.3	181	61	68	22.0	29
Nov-Jan 2011	100	33.8	73	16	10	10.3	*	320	16.6	194	58	69	21.6	27
Dec-Feb 2011	105	33.9	74	18	13	12.0	*	310	16.2	188	54	69	22.3	28
Jan-Mar 2011	105	34.3	74	19	12	11.2	*	297	15.5	181	50	66	22.3	28
Feb-Apr 2011	100	32.9	70	20	10	10.1	*	273	14.5	171	43	58	21.3	26
Mar-May 2011	98	32.9	70	18	10	9.8	*	292	15.2	185	47	60	20.4	23
Apr-Jun 2011	98	32.9	74	16	8	8.1	*	310	16.0	188	51	71	22.8	31
May-Jul 2011	99	33.1	73	17	9	9.2	*	323	16.7	196	50	76	23.7	27
Jun-Aug 2011	100	34.2	71	20	10	10.2	*	324	16.8	189	59	76	23.5	26
Jul-Sep 2011	100	34.8	65	21	14	13.9	*	322	16.7	182	62	77	23.9	22
Aug-Oct 2011	99	35.2	66	20	12	12.5	*	327	16.8	186	64	76	23.4	24
Sep-Nov 2011	105	35.8	70	22	12	11.9	*	325	16.7	187	65	72	22.2	26
Oct-Dec 2011	105	35.6	69	23	13	12.2	*·	313	16.2	184	62	67	21.3	24
Nov-Jan 2012	103	35.0	66	22	15	14.2	*	304	15.9	173	63	68	22.4	25
Dec-Feb 2012	105	35.5	66	24	14	13.5	*	303	15.8	168	61	73	24.3	24
Jan-Mar 2012	102	35.3	64	23	15	14.6	*	310	16.1	173	61	75	24.2	26
Feb-Apr 2012	104	36.1	67	22	14	13.6	*	308	16.0	172	66	69	22.6	26
Mar-May 2012	96	33.9	59	23	14	15.0	*	317	16.4	176	66	74	23.4	32
Apr-Jun 2012	100	34.3	62	23	15	14.5	*	314	16.1	174	65	75	23.8	28
May-Jul 2012	104	35.7	65	22	18	17.1	*	317	16.1	178	57	82	25.8	29
Jun-Aug 2012	100	34.1	65	18	17	16.8	*	306	15.7	173	52	81	26.4	33

4.7: Unemployment by age and duration

United Kingdom (thousands) seasonally adjusted

Women

	16-17							18-24						
	All	Rate (%)[1]	Up to 6 months	Over 6 and up to 12 months	All over 12 months	% over 12 months	All over 24 months	All	Rate (%)[1]	Up to 6 months	Over 6 and up to 12 months	All over 12 months	% over 12 months	All over 24 months
	15	16	17	18	19	20	21	22	23	24	25	26	27	28
	YBVJ	YBVM	YBXF	YBXI	YBXL	YBXO	YBXR	YBVP	YBVS	YBXU	YBXX	YBYA	YBYD	YBYG
Jul-Sep 2012	99	32.9	64	15	20	20.5	*	310	16.1	182	52	76	24.6	33
Aug-Oct 2012	98	33.9	65	15	18	18.5	*	302	15.7	177	50	75	24.9	32
Sep-Nov 2012	95	33.1	63	15	17	17.7	*	313	16.0	191	51	71	22.7	26
Oct-Dec 2012	91	32.5	64	16	12	12.9	*	324	16.3	191	54	79	24.4	32
Nov-Jan 2013	92	33.6	64	16	12	12.8	*	329	16.6	192	49	88	26.6	35
Dec-Feb 2013	97	35.5	68	17	12	12.6	*	335	17.0	187	58	90	26.9	37
Jan-Mar 2013	91	33.7	63	15	14	14.8	*	327	16.6	185	60	82	25.0	33
Feb-Apr 2013	90	32.8	65	12	13	13.9	*	326	16.5	190	62	74	22.7	29
Mar-May 2013	93	33.6	66	13	15	15.6	*	320	16.4	181	54	85	26.5	35
Apr-Jun 2013	94	34.1	67	13	14	14.4	*	322	16.6	178	58	87	26.9	37
May-Jul 2013	89	33.0	64	14	12	12.9	*	318	16.5	170	57	91	28.7	36
Jun-Aug 2013	89	33.1	62	12	15	17.2	*	321	16.6	177	59	86	26.7	32
Jul-Sep 2013	90	33.1	63	12	15	16.8	*	324	16.6	179	54	91	28.0	33
Aug-Oct 2013	89	32.6	60	14	16	17.4	*	310	15.9	170	54	87	28.0	33
Sep-Nov 2013	87	31.5	60	15	12	14.0	*	302	15.5	167	53	82	27.3	30
Oct-Dec 2013	90	33.3	60	17	13	14.0	*	296	15.2	170	48	78	26.2	30
Nov-Jan 2014	96	35.3	70	15	11	11.2	*	299	15.3	177	46	76	25.2	30
Dec-Feb 2014	88	33.2	66	13	9	10.6	*	284	14.5	166	42	75	26.5	30
Jan-Mar 2014	89	33.0	69	11	9	10.0	*	277	14.3	163	41	74	26.6	28
Feb-Apr 2014	84	31.0	63	12	9	10.8	*	266	13.7	160	40	66	24.7	26
Mar-May 2014	86	32.1	66	12	8	8.9	*	255	13.1	159	43	53	20.9	20
Apr-Jun 2014	86	32.4	68	10	8	9.5	*	235	12.1	141	38	56	23.9	22
May-Jul 2014	84	31.8	62	13	9	11.1	*	225	11.6	130	37	59	26.0	24
Jun-Aug 2014	84	31.6	58	18	8	9.6	*	219	11.2	121	35	63	28.7	26
Jul-Sep 2014	82	30.3	57	20	5	6.5	*	224	11.6	133	29	61	27.5	28
Aug-Oct 2014	81	30.9	57	18	6	7.8	*	242	12.6	143	31	67	27.9	31
Sep-Nov 2014	76	29.4	53	14	9	11.8	*	259	13.5	156	39	64	24.6	29
Oct-Dec 2014	**75**	**27.6**	**51**	**14**	**10**	**12.8**	*	**244**	**12.6**	**147**	**38**	**59**	**24.1**	**27**
Change on qtr	-7	-2.7	-6	-5	4	6.2	*	20	1.0	14	9	-3	-3.3	-1
Change %	-8.5		-10.7	-26.1	79.0		*	8.8		10.3	29.7	-4.3		-2.8
Change on year	-15	-5.7	-9	-3	-3	-1.3	*	-53	-2.5	-24	-10	-19	-2.0	-3
Change %	-17.0		-15.5	-16.8	-24.4		*	-17.8		-14.0	-21.1	-24.2		-8.4

People

	25-49							50 and over						
	All	Rate (%)[1]	Up to 6 months	Over 6 and up to 12 months	All over 12 months	% over 12 months	All over 24 months	All	Rate (%)[1]	Up to 6 months	Over 6 and up to 12 months	All over 12 months	% over 12 months	All over 24 months
	29	30	31	32	33	34	35	36	37	38	39	40	41	42
	MGVI	MGXB	YBYH	YBYK	YBYN	YBYQ	YBYT	YBVT	YBVW	YBYW	YBYZ	YBZC	YBZF	YBZI
Nov-Jan 2006	683	3.8	416	106	161	23.6	72	226	2.9	105	37	84	37.3	55
Dec-Feb 2006	713	4.0	420	122	170	23.9	77	221	2.8	102	36	83	37.4	53
Jan-Mar 2006	727	4.0	429	130	168	23.2	76	226	2.9	102	37	87	38.5	56
Feb-Apr 2006	737	4.1	425	137	175	23.8	79	231	3.0	110	34	87	37.6	53
Mar-May 2006	749	4.1	424	140	185	24.7	88	238	3.0	121	37	79	33.4	48
Apr-Jun 2006	761	4.2	426	141	194	25.5	91	236	3.0	120	41	75	31.6	45
May-Jul 2006	761	4.2	428	142	191	25.1	91	239	3.0	117	44	78	32.7	48
Jun-Aug 2006	760	4.2	431	143	186	24.5	85	246	3.1	122	42	82	33.4	50
Jul-Sep 2006	751	4.1	422	130	200	26.6	93	250	3.2	120	41	89	35.7	56
Aug-Oct 2006	765	4.2	428	134	204	26.6	92	243	3.1	117	37	89	36.6	57
Sep-Nov 2006	774	4.3	430	136	208	26.9	94	234	3.0	102	37	95	40.6	62
Oct-Dec 2006	780	4.3	416	146	219	28.1	103	234	3.0	111	34	90	38.3	58
Nov-Jan 2007	774	4.3	410	142	221	28.6	103	239	3.0	115	35	89	37.2	54
Dec-Feb 2007	765	4.2	414	132	218	28.6	102	241	3.1	124	39	78	32.5	47
Jan-Mar 2007	755	4.2	416	129	211	27.9	101	246	3.1	122	44	81	32.7	46
Feb-Apr 2007	735	4.0	399	124	212	28.8	100	252	3.2	126	42	84	33.4	48
Mar-May 2007	710	3.9	389	118	203	28.6	102	249	3.1	116	41	93	37.3	49
Apr-Jun 2007	700	3.8	393	108	199	28.4	96	251	3.1	117	42	92	36.6	48
May-Jul 2007	694	3.8	389	110	196	28.2	97	248	3.1	114	44	91	36.7	49
Jun-Aug 2007	697	3.8	386	119	192	27.5	90	243	3.0	116	39	88	36.3	48
Jul-Sep 2007	705	3.9	391	125	188	26.7	89	246	3.1	117	36	93	37.9	51
Aug-Oct 2007	703	3.9	398	118	187	26.7	92	241	3.0	115	36	90	37.4	50
Sep-Nov 2007	710	3.9	401	116	193	27.1	92	241	3.0	116	35	90	37.4	52

4.7: Unemployment by age and duration

United Kingdom (thousands) seasonally adjusted

	25-49							50 and over						
	All	Rate (%)[1]	Up to 6 months	Over 6 and up to 12 months	All over 12 months	% over 12 months	All over 24 months	All	Rate (%)[1]	Up to 6 months	Over 6 and up to 12 months	All over 12 months	% over 12 months	All over 24 months
	29	30	31	32	33	34	35	36	37	38	39	40	41	42
People	MGVI	MGXB	YBYH	YBYK	YBYN	YBYQ	YBYT	YBVT	YBVW	YBYW	YBYZ	YBZC	YBZF	YBZI
Oct-Dec 2007	701	3.8	397	114	190	27.0	91	234	2.9	113	38	82	35.3	43
Nov-Jan 2008	714	3.9	399	124	190	26.6	97	230	2.8	111	37	82	35.8	43
Dec-Feb 2008	716	3.9	391	128	198	27.6	103	235	2.9	108	40	87	37.0	48
Jan-Mar 2008	714	3.9	387	126	202	28.3	103	231	2.8	106	37	88	38.1	53
Feb-Apr 2008	733	4.0	404	127	203	27.6	102	240	2.9	109	42	89	37.1	52
Mar-May 2008	715	3.9	388	124	203	28.4	100	230	2.8	107	39	85	36.8	51
Apr-Jun 2008	735	4.0	394	130	210	28.6	103	240	2.9	110	39	91	38.0	53
May-Jul 2008	760	4.1	409	128	223	29.3	109	248	3.0	111	39	97	39.3	58
Jun-Aug 2008	793	4.3	446	122	225	28.3	111	263	3.2	120	46	96	36.7	56
Jul-Sep 2008	813	4.4	456	126	231	28.4	113	273	3.3	131	48	94	34.4	53
Aug-Oct 2008	824	4.5	459	129	236	28.7	112	283	3.4	144	45	95	33.5	55
Sep-Nov 2008	855	4.7	487	141	227	26.5	110	297	3.6	156	43	97	32.8	53
Oct-Dec 2008	894	4.9	518	142	233	26.1	114	311	3.8	162	47	102	32.8	60
Nov-Jan 2009	932	5.0	542	147	243	26.1	116	314	3.8	163	51	99	31.6	56
Dec-Feb 2009	982	5.3	576	152	255	25.9	120	335	4.0	171	59	106	31.5	65
Jan-Mar 2009	1,024	5.5	595	166	263	25.7	124	347	4.2	178	61	108	31.1	62
Feb-Apr 2009	1,052	5.7	615	183	254	24.1	118	360	4.3	182	62	116	32.2	65
Mar-May 2009	1,110	6.0	635	203	272	24.5	127	362	4.3	184	68	109	30.2	59
Apr-Jun 2009	1,158	6.3	655	227	277	23.9	130	374	4.5	188	73	113	30.3	59
May-Jul 2009	1,170	6.3	643	230	297	25.4	135	376	4.5	191	73	112	29.6	56
Jun-Aug 2009	1,172	6.4	621	237	314	26.8	139	378	4.5	183	79	116	30.8	57
Jul-Sep 2009	1,165	6.3	593	255	317	27.2	126	377	4.5	169	88	120	31.8	57
Aug-Oct 2009	1,166	6.3	577	274	316	27.1	127	386	4.6	162	103	120	31.2	59
Sep-Nov 2009	1,158	6.3	552	277	329	28.4	123	393	4.7	164	103	125	31.9	62
Oct-Dec 2009	1,155	6.2	542	267	346	30.0	131	397	4.7	171	94	132	33.4	65
Nov-Jan 2010	1,142	6.2	516	270	355	31.1	132	393	4.7	159	96	137	34.9	67
Dec-Feb 2010	1,191	6.5	530	272	389	32.6	152	391	4.6	157	93	141	36.1	63
Jan-Mar 2010	1,200	6.5	542	251	408	34.0	155	388	4.6	150	91	147	37.9	64
Feb-Apr 2010	1,196	6.5	534	248	414	34.6	156	375	4.4	138	80	157	41.9	67
Mar-May 2010	1,179	6.4	520	243	415	35.2	158	390	4.6	144	76	170	43.7	74
Apr-Jun 2010	1,166	6.3	492	249	424	36.4	169	394	4.6	145	77	172	43.6	72
May-Jul 2010	1,170	6.3	504	245	421	36.0	172	398	4.6	154	74	170	42.7	77
Jun-Aug 2010	1,153	6.2	488	238	427	37.0	178	393	4.6	155	72	166	42.2	84
Jul-Sep 2010	1,164	6.3	507	227	430	37.0	185	399	4.6	158	66	175	43.8	80
Aug-Oct 2010	1,166	6.3	502	225	439	37.6	188	399	4.6	154	69	175	43.9	77
Sep-Nov 2010	1,166	6.3	514	211	441	37.8	187	390	4.5	153	69	168	43.0	76
Oct-Dec 2010	1,152	6.2	509	206	438	38.0	186	391	4.5	150	75	165	42.2	78
Nov-Jan 2011	1,165	6.3	511	201	453	38.9	198	391	4.5	148	72	171	43.6	79
Dec-Feb 2011	1,143	6.2	496	197	450	39.4	212	389	4.5	139	72	178	45.7	83
Jan-Mar 2011	1,142	6.2	490	202	451	39.5	212	398	4.6	149	66	183	46.0	92
Feb-Apr 2011	1,152	6.2	498	204	450	39.0	206	397	4.6	151	67	178	44.9	96
Mar-May 2011	1,169	6.3	524	204	441	37.7	207	397	4.5	159	67	171	43.1	99
Apr-Jun 2011	1,184	6.4	530	200	453	38.3	212	389	4.5	161	65	163	42.0	99
May-Jul 2011	1,176	6.3	524	200	453	38.5	221	386	4.5	162	66	159	41.1	102
Jun-Aug 2011	1,199	6.5	532	210	457	38.1	224	390	4.5	159	73	158	40.5	101
Jul-Sep 2011	1,208	6.5	541	221	446	36.9	229	421	4.8	174	76	172	40.8	106
Aug-Oct 2011	1,212	6.5	546	223	443	36.5	233	420	4.8	171	74	175	41.7	100
Sep-Nov 2011	1,215	6.6	549	234	432	35.6	224	442	5.0	176	81	185	41.9	107
Oct-Dec 2011	1,208	6.5	554	228	426	35.3	218	437	5.0	168	75	195	44.5	113
Nov-Jan 2012	1,198	6.5	553	227	418	34.9	206	433	4.9	172	73	187	43.1	113
Dec-Feb 2012	1,187	6.4	528	227	432	36.4	208	434	4.9	174	65	194	44.8	120
Jan-Mar 2012	1,180	6.4	516	233	430	36.4	209	425	4.8	161	71	193	45.5	120
Feb-Apr 2012	1,175	6.3	504	230	442	37.6	214	426	4.8	156	75	195	45.8	123
Mar-May 2012	1,161	6.2	498	220	443	38.1	221	412	4.6	162	72	178	43.1	110
Apr-Jun 2012	1,155	6.2	496	219	439	38.1	218	403	4.5	156	67	181	44.9	105
May-Jul 2012	1,161	6.2	509	215	437	37.7	222	415	4.6	149	74	192	46.2	115
Jun-Aug 2012	1,159	6.2	512	215	431	37.2	219	413	4.6	146	71	195	47.3	116
Jul-Sep 2012	1,157	6.2	519	202	436	37.7	220	407	4.5	143	69	194	47.7	116
Aug-Oct 2012	1,168	6.3	515	209	445	38.0	232	407	4.5	143	66	198	48.5	113
Sep-Nov 2012	1,141	6.1	506	197	438	38.4	231	407	4.5	147	69	191	46.9	110
Oct-Dec 2012	1,138	6.1	509	207	422	37.1	232	403	4.4	152	67	184	45.6	106
Nov-Jan 2013	1,133	6.1	492	217	424	37.4	235	396	4.4	153	65	179	45.1	107
Dec-Feb 2013	1,183	6.3	523	222	439	37.1	238	407	4.5	148	74	186	45.6	116
Jan-Mar 2013	1,155	6.2	503	208	444	38.5	249	413	4.5	158	67	188	45.5	115
Feb-Apr 2013	1,142	6.1	507	194	441	38.6	244	424	4.6	160	68	196	46.2	117
Mar-May 2013	1,125	6.1	485	197	443	39.4	249	426	4.7	162	68	196	46.0	116
Apr-Jun 2013	1,106	5.9	472	195	439	39.7	242	426	4.6	161	67	198	46.4	118

4.7: Unemployment by age and duration

United Kingdom (thousands) seasonally adjusted

	25-49							50 and over						
	All	Rate (%)[1]	Up to 6 months	Over 6 and up to 12 months	All over 12 months	% over 12 months	All over 24 months	All	Rate (%)[1]	Up to 6 months	Over 6 and up to 12 months	All over 12 months	% over 12 months	All over 24 months
	29	30	31	32	33	34	35	36	37	38	39	40	41	42
People	MGVI	MGXB	YBYH	YBYK	YBYN	YBYQ	YBYT	YBVT	YBVW	YBYW	YBYZ	YBZC	YBZF	YBZI
May-Jul 2013	1,098	5.9	465	208	425	38.7	234	420	4.5	159	67	194	46.2	116
Jun-Aug 2013	1,105	5.9	470	202	433	39.2	238	418	4.5	160	63	195	46.5	112
Jul-Sep 2013	1,088	5.8	473	200	415	38.2	234	419	4.5	168	58	193	46.1	109
Aug-Oct 2013	1,039	5.6	454	173	412	39.6	231	410	4.4	160	59	192	46.7	107
Sep-Nov 2013	1,006	5.4	436	165	405	40.3	234	391	4.2	154	59	178	45.5	107
Oct-Dec 2013	1,021	5.5	446	167	408	39.9	232	399	4.2	158	60	180	45.2	105
Nov-Jan 2014	1,015	5.5	445	166	404	39.8	241	397	4.2	160	60	178	44.8	104
Dec-Feb 2014	968	5.2	420	161	388	40.0	226	393	4.2	160	59	175	44.5	101
Jan-Mar 2014	954	5.1	413	152	390	40.9	233	383	4.0	151	56	177	46.1	108
Feb-Apr 2014	933	5.0	406	156	371	39.8	222	373	3.9	145	50	179	48.0	108
Mar-May 2014	922	4.9	401	166	355	38.5	212	382	4.0	147	52	182	47.8	115
Apr-Jun 2014	923	4.9	403	162	358	38.8	207	374	3.9	152	46	176	47.1	112
May-Jul 2014	906	4.9	403	154	349	38.5	198	359	3.8	147	41	172	47.9	113
Jun-Aug 2014	888	4.8	398	151	338	38.1	190	351	3.7	145	42	164	46.7	107
Jul-Sep 2014	873	4.7	387	158	327	37.5	183	350	3.7	153	43	153	43.9	102
Aug-Oct 2014	866	4.6	381	167	317	36.7	174	338	3.5	144	46	148	43.9	103
Sep-Nov 2014	825	4.4	376	143	306	37.1	167	325	3.4	134	46	145	44.6	99
Oct-Dec 2014	**803**	**4.3**	**374**	**143**	**287**	**35.7**	**155**	**319**	**3.3**	**123**	**45**	**150**	**47.2**	**100**
Change on qtr	*-69*	*-0.4*	*-13*	*-15*	*-41*	*-1.8*	*-28*	*-31*	*-0.3*	*-30*	*2*	*-3*	*3.3*	*-2*
Change %	*-7.9*		*-3.5*	*-9.5*	*-12.4*		*-15.2*	*-8.9*		*-19.6*	*4.6*	*-2.0*		*-1.9*
Change on year	*-217*	*-1.2*	*-72*	*-24*	*-121*	*-4.3*	*-77*	*-81*	*-0.9*	*-35*	*-16*	*-30*	*2.1*	*-5*
Change %	*-21.3*		*-16.2*	*-14.6*	*-29.7*		*-33.1*	*-20.2*		*-22.2*	*-26.0*	*-16.6*		*-5.0*
Men	MGVJ	MGXC	YBYI	YBYL	YBYO	YBYR	YBYU	YBVU	YBVX	YBYX	YBZA	YBZD	YBZG	YBZJ
Nov-Jan 2006	374	3.9	207	59	108	29.0	49	148	3.4	58	26	64	43.1	41
Dec-Feb 2006	384	4.0	206	67	111	29.0	52	143	3.3	57	23	63	43.8	39
Jan-Mar 2006	399	4.1	218	72	108	27.1	49	141	3.3	52	24	66	46.3	43
Feb-Apr 2006	402	4.1	214	74	115	28.5	51	139	3.2	53	21	66	47.2	43
Mar-May 2006	416	4.3	211	76	129	31.1	61	146	3.3	62	24	60	40.7	39
Apr-Jun 2006	417	4.3	208	76	132	31.7	62	146	3.3	64	26	56	38.3	35
May-Jul 2006	418	4.3	212	78	129	30.8	62	149	3.4	67	27	54	36.6	34
Jun-Aug 2006	416	4.3	218	79	119	28.6	54	156	3.5	71	26	58	37.2	35
Jul-Sep 2006	409	4.2	212	68	129	31.6	62	161	3.7	71	27	64	39.5	40
Aug-Oct 2006	415	4.2	211	72	132	31.8	62	159	3.6	68	25	67	41.7	43
Sep-Nov 2006	414	4.2	211	72	130	31.5	59	147	3.3	54	24	69	46.9	46
Oct-Dec 2006	421	4.3	203	79	140	33.2	67	147	3.3	59	22	66	44.6	42
Nov-Jan 2007	414	4.2	196	77	141	34.1	66	150	3.4	61	22	67	44.5	41
Dec-Feb 2007	416	4.3	198	71	147	35.3	70	152	3.4	70	24	58	38.1	35
Jan-Mar 2007	408	4.2	197	69	142	34.9	68	159	3.6	71	28	59	37.4	36
Feb-Apr 2007	395	4.0	188	66	141	35.8	68	165	3.7	77	27	61	37.2	36
Mar-May 2007	381	3.9	182	67	133	34.8	71	159	3.6	69	23	67	42.3	37
Apr-Jun 2007	366	3.7	180	59	126	34.5	65	163	3.6	71	25	68	41.5	36
May-Jul 2007	371	3.8	185	59	127	34.4	65	160	3.6	67	27	66	41.1	36
Jun-Aug 2007	368	3.8	181	60	127	34.5	60	155	3.5	69	25	62	39.7	34
Jul-Sep 2007	370	3.8	185	64	121	32.8	61	158	3.5	67	26	66	41.3	37
Aug-Oct 2007	365	3.7	182	63	121	33.1	65	152	3.4	62	25	65	42.5	36
Sep-Nov 2007	369	3.8	185	61	123	33.2	62	157	3.5	64	26	68	43.1	39
Oct-Dec 2007	363	3.7	185	59	119	32.8	59	150	3.3	61	28	61	40.8	32
Nov-Jan 2008	375	3.8	196	61	119	31.6	63	153	3.4	63	27	62	40.8	32
Dec-Feb 2008	376	3.8	185	66	124	33.1	67	154	3.4	62	29	63	40.9	37
Jan-Mar 2008	378	3.8	184	65	129	34.1	67	149	3.3	62	25	63	42.1	41
Feb-Apr 2008	384	3.9	186	68	130	33.8	66	151	3.3	60	27	64	42.3	41
Mar-May 2008	384	3.9	189	65	130	33.7	67	153	3.3	62	26	65	42.2	40
Apr-Jun 2008	400	4.1	196	69	134	33.6	72	159	3.5	60	26	73	45.8	42
May-Jul 2008	408	4.1	195	71	142	34.8	73	166	3.6	62	24	80	48.2	48
Jun-Aug 2008	433	4.4	216	67	151	34.8	75	171	3.7	66	30	75	44.0	46
Jul-Sep 2008	447	4.5	226	68	153	34.2	77	178	3.9	76	30	72	40.5	42
Aug-Oct 2008	459	4.7	242	65	152	33.0	77	186	4.0	87	27	72	38.6	42
Sep-Nov 2008	479	4.9	259	76	144	30.0	76	199	4.3	102	25	72	36.2	38
Oct-Dec 2008	503	5.1	279	74	150	29.9	80	214	4.6	108	30	75	35.1	45
Nov-Jan 2009	528	5.3	295	76	157	29.7	80	212	4.6	106	35	71	33.5	41
Dec-Feb 2009	556	5.6	316	75	164	29.5	81	228	4.9	111	41	76	33.5	48
Jan-Mar 2009	584	5.9	334	86	164	28.1	81	242	5.2	117	44	80	33.2	46
Feb-Apr 2009	607	6.1	349	100	158	26.1	78	254	5.4	125	44	85	33.6	49
Mar-May 2009	646	6.5	369	114	164	25.4	84	258	5.5	126	51	82	31.6	45

4.7: Unemployment by age and duration

	25-49							50 and over						
	All	Rate (%)[1]	Up to 6 months	Over 6 and up to 12 months	All over 12 months	% over 12 months	All over 24 months	All	Rate (%)[1]	Up to 6 months	Over 6 and up to 12 months	All over 12 months	% over 12 months	All over 24 months
	29	30	31	32	33	34	35	36	37	38	39	40	41	42
Men	MGVJ	MGXC	YBYI	YBYL	YBYO	YBYR	YBYU	YBVU	YBVX	YBYX	YBZA	YBZD	YBZG	YBZJ
Apr-Jun 2009	672	6.8	375	134	163	24.3	82	267	5.7	127	53	86	32.3	45
May-Jul 2009	683	6.9	370	136	177	25.8	86	266	5.7	126	56	85	31.7	44
Jun-Aug 2009	690	7.0	350	151	189	27.4	89	273	5.8	126	56	91	33.3	47
Jul-Sep 2009	694	7.0	334	163	197	28.3	83	270	5.8	113	66	91	33.6	44
Aug-Oct 2009	689	7.0	317	174	198	28.7	85	278	5.9	111	75	91	32.9	46
Sep-Nov 2009	684	6.9	309	173	201	29.5	78	278	5.9	110	76	92	33.0	45
Oct-Dec 2009	677	6.9	300	164	212	31.4	84	277	5.9	113	67	97	34.8	47
Nov-Jan 2010	681	6.9	292	170	219	32.1	85	279	5.9	108	70	101	36.3	48
Dec-Feb 2010	704	7.2	286	167	251	35.6	100	276	5.9	105	66	104	37.9	48
Jan-Mar 2010	707	7.2	288	156	263	37.2	103	275	5.8	102	64	109	39.8	49
Feb-Apr 2010	698	7.1	278	150	270	38.6	105	266	5.7	94	57	116	43.6	51
Mar-May 2010	676	6.9	265	142	269	39.8	107	271	5.8	97	54	120	44.2	54
Apr-Jun 2010	667	6.8	249	140	278	41.6	114	272	5.8	95	55	122	45.0	52
May-Jul 2010	652	6.6	245	132	275	42.2	116	273	5.7	101	51	122	44.6	56
Jun-Aug 2010	645	6.5	234	133	278	43.1	119	262	5.5	95	46	120	45.9	61
Jul-Sep 2010	649	6.6	247	123	279	43.0	128	271	5.7	99	42	130	47.8	60
Aug-Oct 2010	655	6.6	252	118	285	43.6	134	269	5.7	95	46	128	47.5	56
Sep-Nov 2010	660	6.7	262	111	287	43.5	130	269	5.6	97	46	126	47.0	58
Oct-Dec 2010	646	6.5	253	108	285	44.2	130	264	5.5	92	51	121	45.9	59
Nov-Jan 2011	653	6.6	253	107	293	44.9	138	266	5.5	93	48	125	47.0	59
Dec-Feb 2011	635	6.4	240	100	295	46.4	153	266	5.5	89	48	129	48.7	61
Jan-Mar 2011	623	6.3	231	101	291	46.8	151	272	5.7	95	44	133	48.9	67
Feb-Apr 2011	620	6.2	235	100	285	46.0	147	269	5.6	94	46	129	48.1	71
Mar-May 2011	628	6.3	248	104	277	44.1	148	269	5.6	95	45	129	47.9	75
Apr-Jun 2011	640	6.5	254	99	287	44.8	149	262	5.4	99	43	120	45.9	74
May-Jul 2011	635	6.4	255	101	279	43.9	153	259	5.4	100	43	115	44.5	76
Jun-Aug 2011	653	6.6	264	108	281	43.0	155	257	5.4	98	48	110	43.0	73
Jul-Sep 2011	654	6.6	270	111	273	41.7	158	278	5.8	103	52	123	44.1	77
Aug-Oct 2011	651	6.6	271	112	268	41.2	159	273	5.7	101	48	124	45.4	72
Sep-Nov 2011	652	6.6	270	119	263	40.4	150	286	5.9	103	51	132	46.2	77
Oct-Dec 2011	645	6.5	276	116	253	39.2	139	278	5.8	94	46	137	49.5	80
Nov-Jan 2012	623	6.3	266	113	244	39.2	128	272	5.7	100	44	128	47.1	77
Dec-Feb 2012	611	6.2	252	114	245	40.0	128	272	5.7	97	39	136	49.8	87
Jan-Mar 2012	608	6.1	247	117	244	40.2	131	275	5.7	95	46	135	49.0	88
Feb-Apr 2012	609	6.1	240	114	254	41.8	134	271	5.6	88	49	134	49.6	91
Mar-May 2012	603	6.1	244	104	256	42.3	141	260	5.3	95	47	118	45.5	76
Apr-Jun 2012	599	6.0	236	107	255	42.6	140	255	5.2	88	42	125	48.9	75
May-Jul 2012	607	6.1	244	106	257	42.4	144	266	5.4	85	49	132	49.6	83
Jun-Aug 2012	599	6.0	247	106	247	41.2	142	271	5.5	87	50	135	49.6	87
Jul-Sep 2012	594	6.0	248	103	242	40.8	140	269	5.5	84	51	133	49.5	88
Aug-Oct 2012	600	6.0	244	109	247	41.1	151	272	5.5	86	48	139	50.9	88
Sep-Nov 2012	578	5.8	239	98	240	41.6	151	272	5.5	87	48	136	50.2	83
Oct-Dec 2012	577	5.8	243	96	238	41.3	155	268	5.4	91	48	129	48.0	75
Nov-Jan 2013	585	5.9	237	101	247	42.3	156	265	5.3	93	45	127	48.0	78
Dec-Feb 2013	631	6.4	259	111	262	41.5	156	256	5.1	88	49	119	46.6	76
Jan-Mar 2013	626	6.3	254	105	267	42.6	162	258	5.2	94	45	119	46.2	74
Feb-Apr 2013	614	6.2	261	94	258	42.1	154	262	5.2	96	44	123	46.9	77
Mar-May 2013	607	6.1	241	100	266	43.8	160	268	5.4	100	43	125	46.7	78
Apr-Jun 2013	595	6.0	231	100	263	44.2	154	268	5.3	98	42	128	47.8	82
May-Jul 2013	593	6.0	229	107	257	43.4	147	257	5.1	88	42	128	49.6	82
Jun-Aug 2013	589	5.9	234	101	255	43.2	146	256	5.1	90	39	128	49.9	80
Jul-Sep 2013	576	5.8	231	95	250	43.3	149	248	4.9	88	35	125	50.3	74
Aug-Oct 2013	548	5.5	221	81	245	44.8	147	243	4.8	90	33	120	49.4	70
Sep-Nov 2013	537	5.4	214	80	243	45.2	151	230	4.5	87	34	109	47.6	69
Oct-Dec 2013	544	5.5	212	91	241	44.3	151	235	4.6	92	33	110	46.7	69
Nov-Jan 2014	527	5.3	200	88	240	45.5	161	233	4.6	87	35	111	47.5	66
Dec-Feb 2014	508	5.1	191	86	231	45.6	147	232	4.5	85	32	115	49.5	67
Jan-Mar 2014	496	5.0	187	76	233	47.0	149	226	4.4	78	31	116	51.4	73
Feb-Apr 2014	481	4.8	181	76	223	46.5	141	217	4.2	74	28	114	52.7	71
Mar-May 2014	461	4.6	174	78	209	45.4	134	223	4.3	74	31	117	52.7	77
Apr-Jun 2014	467	4.7	184	74	209	44.8	125	222	4.3	76	30	117	52.5	76
May-Jul 2014	456	4.6	180	67	208	45.7	126	222	4.3	80	25	117	52.8	79
Jun-Aug 2014	453	4.6	181	70	202	44.5	118	212	4.1	80	25	107	50.7	71
Jul-Sep 2014	443	4.5	181	74	188	42.5	107	212	4.1	91	22	98	46.2	64
Aug-Oct 2014	451	4.5	188	83	179	39.8	98	210	4.0	88	23	98	46.9	69
Sep-Nov 2014	432	4.4	183	72	178	41.1	98	207	4.0	84	26	98	47.1	68
Oct-Dec 2014	**421**	**4.3**	**174**	**77**	**169**	**40.2**	**97**	**197**	**3.8**	**70**	**26**	**100**	**50.7**	**66**

4.7: Unemployment by age and duration

United Kingdom (thousands) seasonally adjusted

	25-49							50 and over						
	All	Rate (%)[1]	Up to 6 months	Over 6 and up to 12 months	All over 12 months	% over 12 months	All over 24 months	All	Rate (%)[1]	Up to 6 months	Over 6 and up to 12 months	All over 12 months	% over 12 months	All over 24 months
	29	30	31	32	33	34	35	36	37	38	39	40	41	42
Men	MGVJ	MGXC	YBYI	YBYL	YBYO	YBYR	YBYU	YBVU	YBVX	YBYX	YBZA	YBZD	YBZG	YBZJ
Change on qtr	-23	-0.2	-6	3	-19	-2.3	-10	-15	-0.3	-21	4	2	4.5	2
Change %	-5.1		-3.5	4.1	-10.3		-9.6	-7.0		-23.0	18.1	2.1		2.4
Change on year	-123	-1.2	-38	-13	-72	-4.1	-55	-38	-0.8	-22	-6	-10	4.0	-3
Change %	-22.7		-17.9	-14.7	-29.8		-36.2	-16.1		-23.7	-18.9	-8.8		-3.7
Women	MGVK	MGXD	YBYJ	YBYM	YBYP	YBYS	YBYV	YBVV	YBVY	YBYY	YBZB	YBZE	YBZH	YBZK
Nov-Jan 2006	309	3.7	209	47	53	17.1	23	78	2.3	47	11	20	26.2	15
Dec-Feb 2006	329	3.9	215	55	59	18.0	26	78	2.3	45	13	20	25.7	14
Jan-Mar 2006	328	3.9	210	58	60	18.3	27	85	2.5	50	13	22	25.6	13
Feb-Apr 2006	335	4.0	211	64	61	18.1	28	92	2.7	57	13	21	23.0	10
Mar-May 2006	333	4.0	213	65	56	16.7	28	91	2.7	59	13	20	21.6	9
Apr-Jun 2006	344	4.1	218	64	62	17.9	29	90	2.6	56	15	19	20.7	10
May-Jul 2006	342	4.1	216	64	63	18.3	29	91	2.6	50	17	24	26.3	14
Jun-Aug 2006	344	4.1	213	64	68	19.7	30	90	2.6	51	15	24	26.9	15
Jul-Sep 2006	343	4.1	210	62	71	20.6	31	88	2.5	49	14	25	28.8	15
Aug-Oct 2006	350	4.2	216	62	72	20.5	30	84	2.4	49	12	22	26.8	14
Sep-Nov 2006	361	4.3	219	64	78	21.5	35	87	2.5	48	13	26	29.8	15
Oct-Dec 2006	359	4.3	213	66	79	22.1	35	87	2.5	51	11	24	27.7	15
Nov-Jan 2007	359	4.3	214	65	80	22.3	37	89	2.5	54	13	22	24.9	13
Dec-Feb 2007	348	4.2	216	61	71	20.5	32	90	2.6	54	15	21	22.9	12
Jan-Mar 2007	348	4.2	219	60	69	19.7	33	87	2.5	50	16	21	24.2	11
Feb-Apr 2007	340	4.1	211	59	70	20.7	32	87	2.5	49	15	23	26.3	11
Mar-May 2007	329	3.9	208	51	70	21.4	31	90	2.6	47	17	25	28.3	12
Apr-Jun 2007	334	4.0	213	49	72	21.7	31	88	2.5	46	17	24	27.6	12
May-Jul 2007	323	3.9	204	51	68	21.1	32	89	2.5	47	16	26	28.9	13
Jun-Aug 2007	329	3.9	205	59	65	19.8	30	87	2.5	47	14	26	30.3	14
Jul-Sep 2007	334	4.0	206	61	67	20.0	28	87	2.5	50	10	28	31.6	15
Aug-Oct 2007	338	4.0	216	55	67	19.7	27	88	2.5	53	10	25	28.5	14
Sep-Nov 2007	341	4.0	217	55	70	20.5	30	84	2.4	53	9	23	26.8	13
Oct-Dec 2007	338	4.0	213	55	70	20.8	32	84	2.4	53	10	21	25.5	11
Nov-Jan 2008	338	4.0	204	63	71	21.1	34	77	2.2	47	10	20	25.9	11
Dec-Feb 2008	340	4.0	205	61	73	21.6	36	81	2.3	46	11	24	29.4	11
Jan-Mar 2008	336	4.0	203	61	73	21.7	36	82	2.3	45	12	25	30.7	12
Feb-Apr 2008	349	4.1	218	59	73	20.9	36	88	2.5	49	14	25	28.2	11
Mar-May 2008	331	3.9	199	59	73	22.2	33	77	2.2	45	12	20	25.9	11
Apr-Jun 2008	335	3.9	198	61	76	22.6	31	81	2.3	50	13	18	22.5	10
May-Jul 2008	352	4.1	214	57	81	23.0	36	82	2.3	49	15	17	21.1	10
Jun-Aug 2008	360	4.2	231	55	74	20.6	36	91	2.5	54	16	21	22.8	11
Jul-Sep 2008	366	4.3	230	58	78	21.3	36	96	2.6	56	18	22	23.2	11
Aug-Oct 2008	365	4.3	217	64	85	23.2	35	97	2.7	56	18	23	23.6	13
Sep-Nov 2008	376	4.4	228	65	83	22.1	34	98	2.7	54	19	25	25.8	15
Oct-Dec 2008	391	4.6	240	68	83	21.3	34	98	2.7	54	17	27	27.8	16
Nov-Jan 2009	404	4.7	247	71	86	21.3	36	101	2.8	58	16	28	27.7	16
Dec-Feb 2009	427	5.0	260	76	91	21.3	39	107	2.9	60	18	29	27.2	16
Jan-Mar 2009	440	5.1	261	80	99	22.5	42	105	2.9	61	17	27	26.0	16
Feb-Apr 2009	445	5.2	266	83	96	21.5	40	106	2.9	58	18	31	28.9	16
Mar-May 2009	463	5.4	266	90	108	23.2	43	103	2.8	58	18	28	26.6	14
Apr-Jun 2009	487	5.7	280	93	114	23.4	48	107	2.9	61	19	27	25.2	13
May-Jul 2009	486	5.7	273	93	120	24.7	49	110	3.0	65	18	27	24.5	12
Jun-Aug 2009	482	5.6	271	86	126	26.1	49	105	2.8	57	23	25	24.1	10
Jul-Sep 2009	471	5.5	259	92	120	25.5	43	107	2.9	56	22	29	27.3	13
Aug-Oct 2009	477	5.5	260	99	118	24.7	42	108	2.9	51	28	29	26.8	14
Sep-Nov 2009	475	5.5	243	104	127	26.8	45	114	3.1	54	27	33	29.2	16
Oct-Dec 2009	478	5.5	241	103	134	28.0	47	120	3.2	57	27	36	29.9	18
Nov-Jan 2010	461	5.3	224	100	137	29.7	47	114	3.0	52	26	36	31.5	19
Dec-Feb 2010	487	5.7	244	105	138	28.3	52	115	3.1	52	26	37	31.8	16
Jan-Mar 2010	493	5.7	253	95	145	29.4	52	113	3.0	49	27	38	33.4	15
Feb-Apr 2010	498	5.8	255	98	144	29.0	51	109	2.9	45	23	41	37.7	15
Mar-May 2010	503	5.8	256	101	146	29.1	51	119	3.1	47	22	51	42.5	21
Apr-Jun 2010	499	5.8	243	109	147	29.5	54	122	3.2	51	22	50	40.6	20
May-Jul 2010	517	6.0	259	113	145	28.1	56	125	3.3	53	23	48	38.6	21
Jun-Aug 2010	508	5.9	254	105	149	29.4	60	131	3.4	60	26	46	34.8	22
Jul-Sep 2010	516	6.0	260	103	152	29.4	57	128	3.3	59	24	45	35.2	20
Aug-Oct 2010	511	5.9	250	108	154	30.0	54	130	3.4	59	23	48	36.6	21
Sep-Nov 2010	506	5.8	252	100	154	30.4	57	121	3.1	56	24	41	34.3	18

4.7: Unemployment by age and duration

	25-49						50 and over						
All	Rate (%)[1]	Up to 6 months	Over 6 and up to 12 months	All over 12 months	% over 12 months	All over 24 months	All	Rate (%)[1]	Up to 6 months	Over 6 and up to 12 months	All over 12 months	% over 12 months	All over 24 months
29	30	31	32	33	34	35	36	37	38	39	40	41	42
Women													
MGVK	MGXD	YBYJ	YBYM	YBYP	YBYS	YBYV	YBVV	YBVY	YBYY	YBZB	YBZE	YBZH	YBZK
Oct-Dec 2010	507	5.9	256	98	153	30.2	55	127	3.3	58	24	44	34.7	19
Nov-Jan 2011	512	5.9	258	94	160	31.2	60	125	3.2	55	24	45	36.4	20
Dec-Feb 2011	508	5.9	256	97	155	30.6	59	123	3.2	50	24	48	39.3	22
Jan-Mar 2011	519	6.0	259	101	159	30.7	61	127	3.2	55	22	50	39.9	25
Feb-Apr 2011	533	6.2	264	105	164	30.8	59	128	3.3	58	21	49	38.2	25
Mar-May 2011	540	6.2	277	100	164	30.4	60	128	3.3	63	22	42	33.1	23
Apr-Jun 2011	543	6.3	277	101	166	30.5	63	127	3.3	62	22	43	34.0	25
May-Jul 2011	541	6.3	269	99	174	32.1	68	128	3.3	61	23	44	34.2	26
Jun-Aug 2011	546	6.3	268	102	176	32.3	69	133	3.4	61	25	48	35.6	28
Jul-Sep 2011	555	6.4	271	110	173	31.3	71	143	3.6	70	23	49	34.3	30
Aug-Oct 2011	562	6.5	276	112	174	31.0	74	147	3.7	70	25	51	34.8	29
Sep-Nov 2011	563	6.5	279	115	169	30.0	74	156	3.9	73	30	53	34.2	30
Oct-Dec 2011	563	6.5	278	112	173	30.8	78	160	4.0	74	29	57	35.9	34
Nov-Jan 2012	575	6.6	287	115	174	30.3	77	160	4.0	72	30	58	36.4	35
Dec-Feb 2012	576	6.7	275	113	187	32.5	81	162	4.1	77	26	59	36.3	33
Jan-Mar 2012	571	6.6	269	116	186	32.5	78	150	3.7	66	25	59	39.1	32
Feb-Apr 2012	567	6.5	263	116	188	33.1	80	154	3.8	68	26	60	39.1	32
Mar-May 2012	557	6.4	254	116	187	33.6	80	152	3.8	67	26	59	39.0	33
Apr-Jun 2012	556	6.4	260	112	184	33.2	78	148	3.7	68	24	56	38.0	29
May-Jul 2012	554	6.4	264	109	180	32.5	78	149	3.7	64	25	60	40.1	32
Jun-Aug 2012	559	6.4	265	110	185	33.0	77	142	3.5	59	22	61	42.9	29
Jul-Sep 2012	563	6.5	271	98	194	34.5	80	138	3.4	59	18	61	44.1	28
Aug-Oct 2012	568	6.5	271	100	198	34.8	81	135	3.3	57	19	59	43.6	26
Sep-Nov 2012	563	6.5	267	98	198	35.1	79	135	3.3	60	21	55	40.4	28
Oct-Dec 2012	560	6.4	266	111	183	32.7	76	134	3.3	61	19	55	40.8	31
Nov-Jan 2013	548	6.3	254	117	177	32.2	79	131	3.2	60	19	51	39.3	29
Dec-Feb 2013	552	6.3	264	111	177	32.0	82	151	3.7	60	25	66	43.9	40
Jan-Mar 2013	529	6.1	248	103	178	33.6	87	156	3.8	64	23	69	44.3	41
Feb-Apr 2013	528	6.1	246	100	182	34.5	90	162	3.9	64	24	73	45.1	40
Mar-May 2013	518	6.0	244	97	177	34.1	89	158	3.8	62	25	71	44.7	38
Apr-Jun 2013	511	5.9	241	95	176	34.4	88	158	3.8	63	25	69	44.1	36
May-Jul 2013	506	5.8	237	101	168	33.2	87	163	3.9	71	26	67	40.9	34
Jun-Aug 2013	516	5.9	236	102	178	34.6	92	162	3.8	71	24	67	41.2	32
Jul-Sep 2013	512	5.9	242	105	166	32.4	85	171	4.0	80	23	68	39.9	35
Aug-Oct 2013	491	5.7	233	91	167	33.9	84	167	3.9	70	26	72	42.8	37
Sep-Nov 2013	469	5.4	222	85	163	34.7	83	161	3.8	67	26	69	42.6	38
Oct-Dec 2013	477	5.5	233	77	167	35.0	81	165	3.8	66	28	71	43.0	37
Nov-Jan 2014	487	5.6	245	78	164	33.7	80	164	3.8	73	24	67	40.9	38
Dec-Feb 2014	460	5.3	229	75	156	33.9	79	161	3.7	75	27	60	37.3	34
Jan-Mar 2014	458	5.3	226	75	157	34.3	85	157	3.6	72	24	60	38.5	35
Feb-Apr 2014	453	5.2	225	80	148	32.7	81	157	3.6	70	22	65	41.4	37
Mar-May 2014	461	5.3	227	88	146	31.7	78	159	3.6	73	21	65	40.8	37
Apr-Jun 2014	456	5.2	219	88	149	32.7	81	152	3.5	76	16	60	39.2	36
May-Jul 2014	450	5.2	223	87	140	31.2	72	138	3.2	67	16	55	39.9	33
Jun-Aug 2014	435	5.0	217	81	136	31.4	72	139	3.2	65	17	56	40.7	36
Jul-Sep 2014	429	4.9	206	84	139	32.4	76	138	3.2	62	20	56	40.4	38
Aug-Oct 2014	415	4.8	192	84	138	33.3	76	128	2.9	56	22	50	39.0	35
Sep-Nov 2014	393	4.5	193	72	129	32.7	69	117	2.7	50	20	47	40.3	31
Oct-Dec 2014	**383**	**4.4**	**199**	**66**	**118**	**30.7**	**59**	**122**	**2.8**	**53**	**18**	**51**	**41.6**	**34**
Change on qtr	*-47*	*-0.5*	*-7*	*-18*	*-21*	*-1.6*	*-18*	*-16*	*-0.4*	*-9*	*-2*	*-5*	*1.2*	*-3*
Change %	*-10.9*		*-3.5*	*-21.5*	*-15.4*		*-23.0*	*-11.7*		*-14.6*	*-10.3*	*-9.0*		*-9.1*
Change on year	*-94*	*-1.1*	*-34*	*-11*	*-49*	*-4.2*	*-22*	*-43*	*-1.1*	*-13*	*-9*	*-20*	*-1.4*	*-3*
Change %	*-19.7*		*-14.6*	*-14.4*	*-29.5*		*-27.4*	*-26.1*		*-20.0*	*-34.2*	*-28.5*		*-7.4*

Relationship between columns: 1=3+4+5; 8=10+11+12.

Source: Labour Force Survey

Labour market statistics enquiries: labour.market@ons.gsi.gov.uk

[1] Denominator = economically active for that age group.

* Sample size too small for reliable estimate.

Further information

The Labour Force Survey is a survey of the population of private households, student halls of residence and NHS accommodation

4.8 Regional labour market summary (employment, unemployment, economic activity, inactivity)

Thousands, seasonally adjusted

Headline estimates for October to December 2014

	Economically active		Employment		Unemployment		Economically inactive	
	Aged 16+	Aged 16-64	Aged 16+	Aged 16-64	Aged 16+	Aged 16+	Aged 16-64	Aged 16-64
	Level	Rate (%)[2]	Level	Rate (%)[2]	Level	Rate (%)[3]	Level	Rate (%)[2]
	1	2	3	4	5	6	7	8
North East	1,288	76.2	1,185	70.0	103	8.0	393	23.8
North West	3,532	76.0	3,303	70.9	229	6.5	1,080	24.0
Yorkshire and The Humber	2,681	77.5	2,517	72.7	164	6.1	759	22.5
East Midlands	2,364	78.4	2,249	74.5	115	4.9	623	21.6
West Midlands	2,771	76.0	2,602	71.2	169	6.1	848	24.0
East of England	3,096	80.5	2,940	76.3	156	5.0	720	19.5
London	4,577	76.9	4,282	71.9	295	6.4	1,334	23.1
South East	4,604	80.3	4,392	76.5	212	4.6	1,078	19.7
South West	2,731	79.5	2,609	75.9	122	4.5	672	20.5
England	**27,643**	**78.0**	**26,079**	**73.5**	**1,564**	**5.7**	**7,508**	**22.0**
Wales	1,477	74.3	1,378	69.2	99	6.7	491	25.7
Scotland	2,773	78.7	2,625	74.4	149	5.4	727	21.3
Great Britain	**31,893**	**77.9**	**30,081**	**73.4**	**1,812**	**5.7**	**8,727**	**22.1**
Northern Ireland	864	72.0	815	67.8	50	5.7	326	28.0
United Kingdom	**32,758**	**77.7**	**30,896**	**73.2**	**1,862**	**5.7**	**9,052**	**22.3**

Change on quarter (change since July to September 2014)[4]

	Economically active		Employment		Unemployment		Economically inactive	
	Aged 16+	Aged 16-64	Aged 16+	Aged 16-64	Aged 16+	Aged 16+	Aged 16-64	Aged 16-64
	Level	Rate (%)[2]	Level	Rate (%)[2]	Level	Rate (%)[3]	Level	Rate (%)[2]
North East	5	0.1	20	1.1	-15	-1.2	-2	-0.1
North West	41	0.6	30	0.3	11	0.2	-26	-0.6
Yorkshire and The Humber	-20	-0.4	9	0.5	-29	-1.0	15	0.4
East Midlands	19	-0.2	37	0.5	-17	-0.8	7	0.2
West Midlands	8	0.6	39	1.4	-32	-1.2	-20	-0.6
East of England	-13	-0.1	-15	-0.2	2	0.1	4	0.1
London	-13	-0.3	-20	-0.5	7	0.2	18	0.3
South East	-7	0.0	-6	0.0	0	0.0	1	0.0
South West	-13	-0.6	-6	-0.4	-7	-0.2	21	0.6
England	**6**	**0.0**	**87**	**0.2**	**-81**	**-0.3**	**18**	**0.0**
Wales	5	0.1	3	0.1	2	0.1	-2	-0.1
Scotland	5	0.1	20	0.6	-15	-0.6	-5	-0.1
Great Britain	**15**	**0.0**	**110**	**0.2**	**-94**	**-0.3**	**11**	**0.0**
Northern Ireland	-9	-1.0	-6	-0.7	-3	-0.3	11	1.0
United Kingdom	**6**	**0.0**	**103**	**0.2**	**-97**	**-0.3**	**22**	**0.0**

Change on year (change since October to December 2013)

	Economically active		Employment		Unemployment		Economically inactive	
	Aged 16+	Aged 16-64	Aged 16+	Aged 16-64	Aged 16+	Aged 16+	Aged 16-64	Aged 16-64
	Level	Rate (%)[2]	Level	Rate (%)[2]	Level	Rate (%)[3]	Level	Rate (%)[2]
North East	20	1.1	43	2.5	-23	-1.9	-18	-1.1
North West	69	1.1	117	2.2	-48	-1.5	-48	-1.1
Yorkshire and The Humber	-16	-0.3	50	1.6	-66	-2.4	13	0.3
East Midlands	37	0.5	82	2.1	-45	-2.0	-14	-0.5
West Midlands	-10	0.4	53	2.1	-63	-2.2	-13	-0.4
East of England	3	0.3	26	0.8	-22	-0.7	-7	-0.3
London	40	-0.2	118	1.2	-78	-1.8	19	0.2
South East	0	-0.4	23	0.0	-23	-0.5	22	0.4
South West	1	-0.4	50	1.1	-50	-1.8	14	0.4
England	**144**	**0.2**	**561**	**1.3**	**-417**	**-1.5**	**-33**	**-0.2**
Wales	-31	-1.9	-24	-1.5	-7	-0.3	36	1.9
Scotland	15	0.2	63	1.7	-48	-1.8	-9	-0.2
Great Britain	**128**	**0.1**	**600**	**1.2**	**-472**	**-1.5**	**-6**	**-0.1**
Northern Ireland	-6	-0.9	8	0.3	-14	-1.6	12	0.9
United Kingdom	**122**	**0.0**	**608**	**1.2**	**-486**	**-1.5**	**6**	**0.0**

Relationship between columns: 1=3+5

Source: Labour Force Survey

1. Labour Force Survey is tabulated by region of residence.

Labour market statistics enquiries: labour.market@ons.gsi.gov.uk

2. Denominator = all persons aged 16 to 64.

3. Denominator = Total economically active.

4. Quarter on quarter changes at regional level are particularly subject to sampling variability and should be interpreted in the context of changes over several quarters rather than in isolation.

4.9 claimant count rates: by region

ONS Crown Copyright Reserved [from Nomis on 2 June 2016]

Sex: Total
Rate: Workplace-based estimates

Area		January 2003 - December 2003 (inclusive)		January 2004 - December 2004 (inclusive)		January 2005 - December 2005 (inclusive)		January 2006 - December 2006 (inclusive)	
		number	rate	number	rate	number	rate	number	rate
England	E92000001	754,375	2.8	690,317	2.6	706,092	2.6	785,550	2.9
United Kingdom	K02000001	933,050	3.0	853,342	2.7	861,775	2.7	944,967	2.9
North East	E12000001	52,808	4.5	46,275	3.9	45,942	3.8	50,233	4.0
North West	E12000002	111,650	3.2	99,200	2.8	101,242	2.9	115,550	3.3
Yorkshire and The Humber	E12000003	83,708	3.3	73,400	2.8	76,017	2.9	87,358	3.3
East Midlands	E12000004	58,875	2.8	52,483	2.5	54,083	2.5	61,975	2.8
West Midlands	E12000005	94,675	3.5	88,258	3.2	93,958	3.4	108,325	3.8
East	E12000006	58,067	2.1	55,408	2.0	58,100	2.1	65,583	2.2
London	E12000007	170,692	3.6	162,750	3.4	162,950	3.4	166,833	3.4
South East	E12000008	75,558	1.7	70,675	1.6	71,625	1.6	81,675	1.8
South West	E12000009	48,342	1.8	41,867	1.6	42,175	1.6	48,017	1.8
Wales	W92000004	44,600	3.3	40,208	3.0	41,200	2.9	44,217	3.1
Scotland	S92000003	99,500	3.7	92,000	3.4	85,892	3.1	87,258	3.1
Northern Ireland	N92000002	34,575	4.1	30,817	3.6	28,592	3.3	27,875	3.2

Area		January 2007 - December 2007 (inclusive)		January 2008 - December 2008 (inclusive)		January 2009 - December 2009 (inclusive)		January 2010 - December 2010 (inclusive)	
		number	rate	number	rate	number	rate	number	rate
England	E92000001	723,100	2.6	754,108	2.7	1,275,583	4.6	1,230,708	4.4
United Kingdom	K02000001	864,467	2.6	906,083	2.7	1,527,683	4.6	1,496,358	4.6
North East	E12000001	49,275	4.0	53,717	4.3	83,775	6.7	81,417	6.5
North West	E12000002	110,092	3.1	119,708	3.4	191,708	5.3	184,017	5.2
Yorkshire and The Humber	E12000003	81,158	3.1	88,033	3.3	149,817	5.6	148,008	5.6
East Midlands	E12000004	58,483	2.6	61,408	2.7	108,300	4.8	101,492	4.5
West Midlands	E12000005	102,525	3.7	106,167	3.8	173,775	6.2	163,667	5.9
East	E12000006	61,225	2.1	63,625	2.2	115,992	3.9	111,067	3.8
London	E12000007	145,450	3.0	137,658	2.7	211,150	4.2	217,283	4.3
South East	E12000008	71,950	1.6	76,942	1.7	149,225	3.3	139,858	3.1
South West	E12000009	42,942	1.6	46,850	1.7	91,842	3.3	83,900	3.0
Wales	W92000004	40,692	2.8	45,517	3.2	77,133	5.3	73,192	5.1
Scotland	S92000003	76,300	2.7	78,633	2.8	125,958	4.5	135,733	5.0
Northern Ireland	N92000002	24,375	2.8	27,825	3.1	49,008	5.5	56,725	6.2

Area		January 2011 - December 2011 (inclusive)		January 2012 - December 2012 (inclusive)		January 2013 - December 2013 (inclusive)		January 2014 - December 2014 (inclusive)	
		number	rate	number	rate	number	rate	number	rate
England	E92000001	1,258,225	4.5	1,301,583	4.6	1,158,275	4.1	829,547	2.8
United Kingdom	K02000001	1,534,408	4.7	1,585,575	4.7	1,421,837	4.2	1,037,108	3.0
North East	E12000001	85,367	7.0	93,425	7.7	84,517	7.0	61,884	5.1
North West	E12000002	190,200	5.4	200,275	5.6	179,157	5.0	128,716	3.4
Yorkshire and The Humber	E12000003	153,267	5.8	164,075	6.2	149,918	5.6	110,590	4.2
East Midlands	E12000004	103,142	4.5	108,842	4.7	95,550	4.2	67,834	3.0
West Midlands	E12000005	164,025	6.0	164,983	5.9	149,201	5.3	109,502	3.8
East	E12000006	111,800	3.9	115,075	3.8	101,742	3.4	68,704	2.3
London	E12000007	228,000	4.5	226,708	4.3	202,074	3.7	148,173	2.6
South East	E12000008	137,242	3.0	139,333	3.0	119,517	2.6	81,511	1.7
South West	E12000009	85,183	3.1	88,867	3.2	76,600	2.7	52,632	1.8
Wales	W92000004	74,850	5.2	79,600	5.6	72,925	5.1	56,889	3.9
Scotland	S92000003	141,508	5.1	141,433	5.1	128,070	4.6	96,647	3.4
Northern Ireland	N92000002	59,825	6.6	62,958	7.1	62,567	7.0	54,025	6.0

Seasonally adjusted

Source: Office for National Statistics

From May 2013 onwards these figures are not designated as National Statistics.
From May 2013 onwards these figures are considered Experimental Statistics.
Rate figures for dates from 2014 onwards are calculated using mid-2014 workforce estimates.

4.10 Claimant count by sex and Unitary and Local Authority

from Nomis on 7 October 2016

Age 16+

not seasonally adjusted

| | Claimant Count December 2014 | | | | | | Change on Year | | | | | |
| | Levels | | | Percentage of Pop | | | Levels | | | Perentage of Pop | | |
	Total	Male	Female	Total	Male	Female	Total	Male	Female	Total	Male	Female
UNITED KINGDOM	839,195	539,975	299,220	2.0	2.6	1.5	-364,680	-240,840	-123,840	-0.9	-1.2	-0.6
GREAT BRITAIN	790,135	505,420	284,710	2.0	2.5	1.4	-355,640	-234,560	-121,085	-0.9	-1.2	-0.6
ENGLAND AND WALES	710,050	450,205	259,845	2.0	2.5	1.4	-327,415	-215,225	-112,185	-0.9	-1.2	-0.6
ENGLAND	662,745	419,125	243,620	1.9	2.4	1.4	-311,185	-204,030	-107,155	-0.9	-1.2	-0.6
NORTH EAST	50,810	34,195	16,615	3.1	4.2	2.0	-21,680	-14,040	-7,640	-1.2	-1.6	-0.9
Darlington	1,970	1,315	660	3.0	4.1	2.0	-865	-565	-295	-1.3	-1.7	-0.9
County Durham	7,675	5,075	2,595	2.3	3.1	1.6	-4,210	-2,830	-1,380	-1.3	-1.8	-0.8
Hartlepool	2,530	1,695	835	4.4	6.0	2.8	-1,405	-935	-470	-2.4	-3.2	-1.6
Middlesbrough	4,140	2,925	1,215	4.7	6.6	2.7	-2,010	-1,315	-695	-2.2	-3.0	-1.6
Northumberland	4,840	3,210	1,635	2.5	3.4	1.7	-1,725	-1,085	-630	-0.9	-1.1	-0.6
Redcar and Cleveland	3,350	2,260	1,090	4.1	5.7	2.6	-1,105	-775	-330	-1.3	-1.8	-0.7
Stockton-on-Tees	4,185	2,900	1,285	3.4	4.8	2.1	-1,675	-1,080	-595	-1.4	-1.7	-0.9
Tyne and Wear (Met County)	22,115	14,815	7,305	3.0	4.1	2.0	-8,685	-5,450	-3,230	-1.2	-1.5	-0.9
Gateshead	3,740	2,520	1,225	2.9	4.0	1.9	-1,250	-780	-465	-1.0	-1.2	-0.7
Newcastle upon Tyne	5,440	3,615	1,825	2.7	3.6	1.9	-2,520	-1,730	-790	-1.3	-1.7	-0.8
North Tyneside	3,275	2,270	1,005	2.6	3.6	1.5	-1,355	-835	-520	-1.0	-1.3	-0.8
South Tyneside	4,140	2,765	1,375	4.4	6.0	2.9	-1,490	-895	-595	-1.6	-1.9	-1.2
Sunderland	5,520	3,645	1,875	3.1	4.2	2.1	-2,070	-1,210	-860	-1.2	-1.3	-0.9
NORTH WEST	102,235	66,425	35,805	2.3	3.0	1.6	-49,840	-34,100	-15,750	-1.1	-1.5	-0.7
Blackburn with Darwen	2,335	1,535	800	2.5	3.3	1.7	-1,030	-695	-335	-1.1	-1.5	-0.8
Blackpool	3,590	2,415	1,175	4.1	5.6	2.7	-1,330	-925	-405	-1.5	-2.0	-0.9
Cheshire East	2,615	1,700	915	1.1	1.5	0.8	-1,700	-1,140	-560	-0.8	-1.0	-0.5
Cheshire West and Chester	2,745	1,765	980	1.3	1.7	0.9	-1,865	-1,270	-600	-0.9	-1.3	-0.6
Halton	2,125	1,310	810	2.6	3.3	2.0	-1,130	-815	-320	-1.4	-2.1	-0.8
Warrington	2,460	1,585	875	1.9	2.4	1.3	-1,150	-825	-325	-0.9	-1.3	-0.5
Cumbria	4,835	3,165	1,670	1.6	2.1	1.1	-1,530	-1,120	-405	-0.5	-0.7	-0.3
Allerdale	1,180	750	430	2.0	2.6	1.5	-330	-255	-75	-0.6	-0.8	-0.2
Barrow-in-Furness	1,235	840	395	3.0	4.0	1.9	-200	-165	-35	-0.4	-0.8	-0.1
Carlisle	885	550	335	1.3	1.6	1.0	-495	-340	-160	-0.7	-1.0	-0.4
Copeland	920	625	295	2.1	2.8	1.4	-235	-170	-65	-0.5	-0.8	-0.3
Eden	215	135	75	0.7	0.9	0.5	-100	-75	-25	-0.3	-0.4	-0.1
South Lakeland	395	260	135	0.7	0.9	0.4	-170	-120	-55	-0.2	-0.4	-0.2
Greater Manchester (Met County)	42,205	27,325	14,880	2.4	3.1	1.7	-22,815	-15,425	-7,390	-1.3	-1.8	-0.8
Bolton	5,060	3,295	1,765	2.9	3.8	2.0	-2,190	-1,420	-770	-1.2	-1.6	-0.9
Bury	2,505	1,615	890	2.1	2.8	1.5	-1,250	-845	-405	-1.1	-1.5	-0.7
Manchester	10,230	6,595	3,635	2.8	3.5	2.0	-5,655	-3,855	-1,800	-1.6	-2.1	-1.1
Oldham	3,675	2,260	1,410	2.6	3.2	2.0	-2,000	-1,310	-695	-1.4	-1.9	-1.0
Rochdale	2,980	1,815	1,160	2.2	2.7	1.7	-2,090	-1,405	-685	-1.6	-2.2	-1.0
Salford	3,970	2,625	1,350	2.5	3.2	1.7	-2,400	-1,685	-705	-1.5	-2.2	-1.0
Stockport	3,270	2,190	1,080	1.8	2.5	1.2	-1,560	-1,085	-470	-0.9	-1.3	-0.5
Tameside	3,485	2,285	1,200	2.5	3.3	1.7	-1,845	-1,155	-690	-1.3	-1.6	-1.0
Trafford	2,225	1,495	735	1.5	2.1	1.0	-1,180	-800	-370	-0.9	-1.1	-0.5
Wigan	4,810	3,155	1,650	2.4	3.1	1.6	-2,650	-1,860	-795	-1.3	-1.8	-0.8
Lancashire	12,070	7,895	4,175	1.6	2.2	1.1	-5,750	-3,930	-1,815	-0.8	-1.0	-0.5
Burnley	1,420	885	530	2.6	3.3	1.9	-635	-420	-220	-1.2	-1.5	-0.8
Chorley	840	555	285	1.2	1.6	0.8	-480	-305	-175	-0.7	-0.8	-0.5
Fylde	600	375	225	1.3	1.7	1.0	-360	-280	-80	-0.8	-1.2	-0.4
Hyndburn	935	605	335	1.9	2.4	1.3	-475	-330	-145	-0.9	-1.3	-0.6
Lancaster	1,660	1,125	530	1.8	2.5	1.2	-690	-495	-200	-0.8	-1.1	-0.4
Pendle	980	625	355	1.8	2.3	1.3	-530	-355	-175	-0.9	-1.2	-0.6
Preston	1,890	1,250	640	2.0	2.6	1.4	-740	-515	-220	-0.8	-1.1	-0.5
Ribble Valley	230	145	85	0.7	0.9	0.5	-125	-85	-40	-0.3	-0.4	-0.2
Rossendale	815	510	310	1.9	2.4	1.4	-255	-210	-40	-0.5	-0.9	-0.2
South Ribble	745	475	270	1.1	1.4	0.8	-365	-215	-145	-0.5	-0.7	-0.4
West Lancashire	985	680	305	1.4	2.0	0.9	-750	-500	-250	-1.1	-1.5	-0.7
Wyre	965	665	305	1.5	2.1	1.0	-355	-220	-125	-0.6	-0.8	-0.4
Merseyside (Met County)	27,255	17,725	9,530	3.1	4.1	2.1	-11,545	-7,955	-3,590	-1.3	-1.8	-0.8
Knowsley	3,170	1,925	1,240	3.4	4.3	2.5	-1,415	-965	-455	-1.5	-2.2	-0.9
Liverpool	11,625	7,575	4,050	3.6	4.7	2.5	-5,370	-3,620	-1,745	-1.6	-2.2	-1.1
Sefton	4,525	2,995	1,530	2.7	3.7	1.8	-1,895	-1,305	-590	-1.2	-1.6	-0.7
St. Helens	3,300	2,110	1,190	3.0	3.9	2.1	-1,120	-780	-340	-1.0	-1.4	-0.7
Wirral	4,635	3,120	1,515	2.4	3.3	1.5	-1,750	-1,280	-470	-0.9	-1.3	-0.5
YORKSHIRE AND THE HUMBER	90,335	59,125	31,210	2.7	3.5	1.8	-37,660	-25,220	-12,440	-1.1	-1.5	-0.8
East Riding of Yorkshire	3,620	2,380	1,245	1.8	2.4	1.2	-1,670	-1,140	-520	-0.8	-1.1	-0.5
Kingston upon Hull, City of	8,295	5,520	2,775	4.9	6.4	3.3	-3,530	-2,475	-1,050	-2.0	-2.8	-1.3
North East Lincolnshire	3,880	2,600	1,280	3.9	5.3	2.6	-1,315	-850	-465	-1.3	-1.7	-0.9
North Lincolnshire	2,635	1,705	930	2.5	3.3	1.8	-1,035	-670	-360	-1.0	-1.2	-0.7
York	1,170	785	385	0.9	1.2	0.6	-960	-635	-325	-0.7	-0.9	-0.5
North Yorkshire	4,210	2,780	1,430	1.2	1.5	0.8	-2,290	-1,425	-865	-0.6	-0.8	-0.5
Craven	325	210	115	1.0	1.3	0.7	-160	-115	-45	-0.5	-0.7	-0.3
Hambleton	440	270	170	0.8	1.0	0.6	-225	-130	-100	-0.4	-0.5	-0.4
Harrogate	635	430	210	0.7	0.9	0.4	-360	-230	-120	-0.3	-0.5	-0.3
Richmondshire	170	110	60	0.5	0.6	0.4	-245	-130	-115	-0.7	-0.6	-0.8
Ryedale	325	220	105	1.1	1.4	0.7	-190	-105	-85	-0.6	-0.7	-0.5
Scarborough	1,555	1,055	500	2.4	3.4	1.5	-815	-565	-245	-1.3	-1.7	-0.8
Selby	760	485	275	1.4	1.8	1.0	-300	-145	-155	-0.6	-0.6	-0.6
South Yorkshire (Met County)	24,935	16,350	8,585	2.9	3.7	2.0	-9,785	-6,580	-3,205	-1.1	-1.6	-0.7
Barnsley	3,755	2,385	1,370	2.5	3.2	1.8	-1,945	-1,300	-645	-1.3	-1.7	-0.9
Doncaster	5,850	3,685	2,165	3.1	3.8	2.3	-2,205	-1,465	-745	-1.1	-1.5	-0.8
Rotherham	5,060	3,365	1,700	3.1	4.2	2.1	-1,965	-1,280	-680	-1.3	-1.6	-0.8
Sheffield	10,270	6,920	3,350	2.8	3.7	1.8	-3,665	-2,525	-1,140	-1.0	-1.4	-0.7

4.10 Claimant count by sex and Unitary and Local Authority

from Nomis on 7 October 2016

Age 16+

not seasonally adjusted

	Claimant Count December 2014						Change on Year					
	Levels			Percentage of Pop			Levels			Perentage of Pop		
	Total	Male	Female	Total	Male	Female	Total	Male	Female	Total	Male	Female
West Yorkshire (Met County)	41,590	27,005	14,580	2.9	3.8	2.0	-17,085	-11,450	-5,640	-1.2	-1.5	-0.8
Bradford	12,220	7,720	4,500	3.7	4.7	2.7	-4,715	-3,040	-1,675	-1.4	-1.9	-1.0
Calderdale	3,275	2,195	1,080	2.5	3.4	1.7	-1,860	-1,175	-685	-1.4	-1.8	-1.0
Kirklees	6,885	4,470	2,415	2.5	3.3	1.8	-3,025	-2,070	-960	-1.1	-1.5	-0.7
Leeds	14,535	9,655	4,885	2.9	3.9	1.9	-5,235	-3,610	-1,620	-1.0	-1.4	-0.7
Wakefield	4,670	2,975	1,700	2.2	2.9	1.6	-2,250	-1,545	-700	-1.1	-1.4	-0.7
EAST MIDLANDS	52,645	33,350	19,295	1.8	2.3	1.3	-25,695	-16,945	-8,750	-0.9	-1.2	-0.6
Derby	3,065	1,885	1,180	1.9	2.3	1.5	-2,150	-1,440	-710	-1.4	-1.8	-0.9
Leicester	6,235	3,735	2,505	2.8	3.3	2.2	-3,400	-2,190	-1,205	-1.5	-2.0	-1.1
Nottingham	8,390	5,465	2,925	3.8	4.9	2.7	-2,870	-1,975	-895	-1.4	-1.8	-0.9
Rutland	155	105	50	0.7	0.9	0.5	-35	-15	-20	-0.1	-0.1	-0.2
Derbyshire	6,920	4,400	2,520	1.4	1.8	1.0	-3,365	-2,230	-1,135	-0.7	-0.9	-0.5
Amber Valley	980	600	380	1.3	1.6	1.0	-405	-270	-135	-0.5	-0.7	-0.3
Bolsover	765	470	290	1.6	1.9	1.2	-470	-310	-165	-1.0	-1.3	-0.7
Chesterfield	1,385	930	455	2.1	2.8	1.4	-515	-355	-160	-0.8	-1.1	-0.5
Derbyshire Dales	265	170	100	0.6	0.8	0.5	-170	-90	-75	-0.4	-0.4	-0.3
Erewash	1,325	850	475	1.9	2.4	1.3	-575	-395	-185	-0.8	-1.1	-0.5
High Peak	790	515	275	1.4	1.8	0.9	-450	-300	-150	-0.7	-1.0	-0.6
North East Derbyshire	910	560	350	1.5	1.9	1.1	-430	-315	-115	-0.7	-1.0	-0.4
South Derbyshire	505	300	200	0.8	1.0	0.6	-345	-195	-155	-0.6	-0.6	-0.5
Leicestershire	3,935	2,475	1,460	0.9	1.2	0.7	-2,490	-1,590	-895	-0.6	-0.7	-0.4
Blaby	530	330	205	0.9	1.1	0.7	-285	-170	-110	-0.5	-0.6	-0.4
Charnwood	1,000	635	370	0.9	1.1	0.7	-595	-370	-215	-0.5	-0.7	-0.4
Harborough	285	190	100	0.5	0.7	0.4	-155	-85	-65	-0.3	-0.3	-0.2
Hinckley and Bosworth	655	420	235	1.0	1.3	0.7	-535	-330	-205	-0.8	-1.0	-0.6
Melton	285	165	120	0.9	1.1	0.8	-170	-120	-50	-0.5	-0.7	-0.3
North West Leicestershire	715	460	255	1.2	1.5	0.9	-465	-315	-150	-0.8	-1.1	-0.5
Oadby and Wigston	460	285	175	1.3	1.7	1.0	-290	-195	-95	-0.9	-1.1	-0.5
Lincolnshire	8,545	5,615	2,930	1.9	2.6	1.3	-3,625	-2,390	-1,235	-0.9	-1.1	-0.6
Boston	735	480	255	1.8	2.4	1.2	-220	-150	-70	-0.6	-0.7	-0.4
East Lindsey	2,165	1,410	755	2.8	3.7	1.9	-740	-500	-240	-0.9	-1.3	-0.6
Lincoln	1,810	1,240	570	2.7	3.8	1.7	-845	-565	-280	-1.3	-1.8	-0.9
North Kesteven	665	455	210	1.0	1.4	0.6	-385	-230	-155	-0.6	-0.7	-0.5
South Holland	720	440	280	1.3	1.7	1.0	-395	-235	-160	-0.8	-0.9	-0.6
South Kesteven	1,060	680	375	1.3	1.7	0.9	-605	-410	-200	-0.7	-1.0	-0.4
West Lindsey	1,385	905	485	2.5	3.4	1.7	-440	-305	-130	-0.8	-1.1	-0.5
Northamptonshire	6,730	4,070	2,660	1.5	1.8	1.2	-3,985	-2,655	-1,330	-0.9	-1.2	-0.6
Corby	715	430	285	1.7	2.1	1.3	-540	-350	-190	-1.3	-1.7	-1.0
Daventry	410	235	175	0.8	1.0	0.7	-380	-275	-105	-0.8	-1.1	-0.5
East Northamptonshire	565	325	240	1.0	1.2	0.9	-430	-300	-130	-0.8	-1.1	-0.5
Kettering	1,000	645	360	1.7	2.2	1.2	-635	-400	-230	-1.0	-1.3	-0.8
Northampton	2,825	1,700	1,125	2.0	2.4	1.6	-1,275	-910	-365	-0.9	-1.3	-0.5
South Northamptonshire	290	175	115	0.5	0.7	0.4	-195	-125	-65	-0.4	-0.4	-0.3
Wellingborough	925	560	365	2.0	2.4	1.5	-530	-295	-235	-1.1	-1.3	-1.0
Nottinghamshire	8,670	5,605	3,065	1.7	2.3	1.2	-3,775	-2,445	-1,325	-0.8	-0.9	-0.6
Ashfield	1,705	1,065	640	2.2	2.8	1.6	-640	-420	-220	-0.9	-1.1	-0.6
Bassetlaw	1,330	865	465	1.9	2.4	1.3	-615	-370	-245	-0.8	-1.1	-0.7
Broxtowe	1,000	630	370	1.4	1.8	1.1	-540	-345	-195	-0.8	-1.0	-0.5
Gedling	1,275	845	430	1.8	2.4	1.2	-475	-330	-145	-0.6	-0.9	-0.4
Mansfield	1,645	1,075	565	2.4	3.2	1.7	-690	-465	-235	-1.1	-1.4	-0.7
Newark and Sherwood	1,025	650	380	1.4	1.8	1.0	-495	-310	-175	-0.7	-0.9	-0.5
Rushcliffe	690	470	220	1.0	1.3	0.6	-320	-210	-110	-0.4	-0.7	-0.3
WEST MIDLANDS	85,160	53,810	31,345	2.4	3.0	1.8	-42,135	-27,825	-14,310	-1.2	-1.6	-0.8
Herefordshire, County of	1,015	655	360	0.9	1.2	0.6	-815	-490	-325	-0.7	-0.8	-0.6
Shropshire	2,410	1,560	850	1.3	1.6	0.9	-1,260	-830	-430	-0.7	-0.9	-0.5
Stoke-on-Trent	3,545	2,270	1,275	2.2	2.8	1.6	-2,725	-1,745	-980	-1.7	-2.2	-1.3
Telford and Wrekin	1,920	1,220	705	1.8	2.2	1.3	-1,380	-865	-510	-1.3	-1.6	-1.0
Staffordshire	5,075	3,150	1,925	0.9	1.2	0.7	-4,270	-2,665	-1,605	-0.8	-1.0	-0.6
Cannock Chase	770	485	290	1.2	1.5	0.9	-660	-430	-225	-1.1	-1.4	-0.7
East Staffordshire	755	440	315	1.0	1.2	0.9	-390	-240	-150	-0.6	-0.7	-0.4
Lichfield	400	265	140	0.7	0.9	0.5	-420	-230	-185	-0.6	-0.7	-0.6
Newcastle-under-Lyme	905	570	335	1.1	1.4	0.8	-890	-575	-315	-1.1	-1.4	-0.8
South Staffordshire	825	505	315	1.2	1.5	0.9	-390	-235	-160	-0.6	-0.6	-0.5
Stafford	660	420	240	0.8	1.0	0.6	-540	-370	-170	-0.7	-0.9	-0.4
Staffordshire Moorlands	475	300	175	0.8	1.0	0.6	-415	-265	-145	-0.7	-0.9	-0.5
Tamworth	285	175	115	0.6	0.7	0.5	-570	-305	-255	-1.1	-1.3	-1.0
Warwickshire	3,645	2,270	1,375	1.1	1.3	0.8	-2,245	-1,465	-780	-0.6	-0.9	-0.5
North Warwickshire	365	225	140	0.9	1.2	0.7	-255	-165	-90	-0.7	-0.8	-0.5
Nuneaton and Bedworth	1,580	975	610	2.0	2.5	1.5	-895	-610	-275	-1.1	-1.5	-0.7
Rugby	720	430	290	1.1	1.4	0.9	-320	-195	-125	-0.6	-0.6	-0.4
Stratford-on-Avon	355	225	130	0.5	0.6	0.4	-225	-145	-80	-0.3	-0.5	-0.2
Warwick	625	415	210	0.7	0.9	0.5	-550	-350	-200	-0.6	-0.8	-0.4
West Midlands (Met County)	62,800	39,605	23,195	3.5	4.5	2.6	-26,575	-17,860	-8,715	-1.6	-2.1	-1.0
Birmingham	30,645	19,685	10,960	4.3	5.6	3.1	-10,630	-7,175	-3,460	-1.6	-2.1	-1.0
Coventry	4,700	2,950	1,750	2.1	2.6	1.6	-3,120	-2,110	-1,010	-1.5	-2.0	-1.0
Dudley	5,800	3,685	2,115	3.0	3.8	2.2	-2,200	-1,625	-575	-1.1	-1.7	-0.6
Sandwell	7,440	4,575	2,865	3.7	4.6	2.9	-3,380	-2,255	-1,125	-1.8	-2.3	-1.1
Solihull	2,185	1,385	800	1.7	2.2	1.2	-1,020	-655	-365	-0.8	-1.1	-0.6
Walsall	4,965	2,970	1,995	3.0	3.6	2.4	-3,050	-1,970	-1,080	-1.8	-2.3	-1.3
Wolverhampton	7,065	4,355	2,710	4.4	5.5	3.4	-3,175	-2,075	-1,100	-2.0	-2.6	-1.4
Worcestershire	4,745	3,085	1,665	1.3	1.8	0.9	-2,865	-1,895	-965	-0.9	-1.0	-0.6
Bromsgrove	605	380	225	1.0	1.3	0.8	-350	-250	-100	-0.7	-0.9	-0.3
Malvern Hills	485	310	175	1.1	1.5	0.8	-235	-170	-65	-0.6	-0.7	-0.3
Redditch	810	535	275	1.5	2.0	1.0	-570	-305	-265	-1.0	-1.1	-1.0
Worcester	1,180	795	385	1.8	2.4	1.2	-555	-375	-180	-0.8	-1.2	-0.5

4.10 Claimant count by sex and Unitary and Local Authority

from Nomis on 7 October 2016
Age 16+

not seasonally adjusted

| | Claimant Count December 2014 | | | | | | Change on Year | | | | | |
| | Levels | | | Percentage of Pop | | | Levels | | | Perentage of Pop | | |
	Total	Male	Female	Total	Male	Female	Total	Male	Female	Total	Male	Female
Wychavon	735	465	270	1.0	1.3	0.8	-345	-215	-130	-0.5	-0.6	-0.3
Wyre Forest	925	595	330	1.6	2.0	1.1	-815	-580	-235	-1.3	-2.0	-0.8
EAST OF ENGLAND	**52,405**	**32,550**	**19,855**	**1.4**	**1.8**	**1.1**	**-30,465**	**-19,480**	**-10,985**	**-0.8**	**-1.0**	**-0.6**
Bedford	2,185	1,355	830	2.1	2.7	1.6	-885	-570	-310	-0.9	-1.1	-0.6
Central Bedfordshire	1,520	915	605	0.9	1.1	0.7	-1,145	-680	-465	-0.7	-0.8	-0.6
Luton	2,790	1,615	1,175	2.0	2.3	1.8	-1,395	-830	-565	-1.1	-1.3	-0.8
Peterborough	2,240	1,285	955	1.8	2.1	1.6	-1,860	-1,135	-725	-1.6	-1.9	-1.2
Southend-on-Sea	2,480	1,565	915	2.2	2.8	1.6	-1,430	-975	-455	-1.4	-1.8	-0.9
Thurrock	2,165	1,245	920	2.1	2.4	1.7	-1,075	-635	-440	-1.0	-1.2	-0.9
Cambridgeshire	3,140	1,975	1,165	0.8	1.0	0.6	-2,585	-1,625	-960	-0.6	-0.7	-0.5
Cambridge	705	475	230	0.8	1.0	0.5	-500	-315	-180	-0.5	-0.6	-0.4
East Cambridgeshire	410	245	160	0.8	0.9	0.6	-365	-220	-150	-0.7	-0.9	-0.6
Fenland	730	435	300	1.2	1.5	1.0	-680	-415	-260	-1.2	-1.4	-0.9
Huntingdonshire	805	515	290	0.7	0.9	0.5	-690	-460	-235	-0.7	-0.9	-0.5
South Cambridgeshire	490	305	185	0.5	0.7	0.4	-350	-220	-135	-0.4	-0.4	-0.3
Essex	12,980	7,905	5,080	1.5	1.8	1.1	-7,060	-4,495	-2,560	-0.8	-1.1	-0.6
Basildon	2,200	1,300	900	1.9	2.3	1.6	-1,360	-845	-510	-1.3	-1.6	-0.9
Braintree	1,205	715	490	1.3	1.6	1.0	-610	-385	-225	-0.7	-0.8	-0.5
Brentwood	415	260	155	0.9	1.1	0.7	-220	-125	-95	-0.5	-0.6	-0.4
Castle Point	725	450	270	1.4	1.7	1.0	-405	-230	-180	-0.7	-0.9	-0.7
Chelmsford	1,370	835	540	1.3	1.5	1.0	-600	-375	-220	-0.5	-0.8	-0.4
Colchester	1,410	895	515	1.2	1.5	0.9	-955	-640	-315	-0.9	-1.2	-0.5
Epping Forest	1,060	580	475	1.3	1.5	1.2	-640	-420	-225	-0.8	-1.1	-0.5
Harlow	1,190	700	490	2.2	2.7	1.8	-785	-520	-265	-1.5	-2.0	-1.0
Maldon	395	240	155	1.0	1.3	0.8	-270	-190	-80	-0.8	-1.0	-0.4
Rochford	510	310	200	1.0	1.2	0.8	-300	-175	-125	-0.6	-0.7	-0.5
Tendring	2,170	1,420	750	2.8	3.8	1.9	-730	-465	-270	-1.0	-1.3	-0.7
Uttlesford	335	200	135	0.7	0.8	0.5	-175	-115	-60	-0.3	-0.5	-0.3
Hertfordshire	8,790	5,375	3,415	1.2	1.5	0.9	-3,985	-2,525	-1,460	-0.6	-0.7	-0.4
Broxbourne	870	485	385	1.5	1.7	1.3	-520	-275	-245	-0.8	-0.9	-0.8
Dacorum	1,205	735	470	1.3	1.6	1.0	-360	-225	-135	-0.4	-0.4	-0.3
East Hertfordshire	760	485	275	0.8	1.1	0.6	-435	-275	-160	-0.5	-0.6	-0.4
Hertsmere	820	470	345	1.3	1.5	1.1	-290	-200	-100	-0.5	-0.7	-0.3
North Hertfordshire	1,000	610	390	1.2	1.5	1.0	-475	-320	-150	-0.6	-0.8	-0.3
St Albans	705	440	260	0.8	1.0	0.6	-335	-215	-120	-0.4	-0.5	-0.2
Stevenage	1,125	700	420	2.0	2.5	1.5	-545	-355	-195	-1.0	-1.3	-0.7
Three Rivers	520	325	195	0.9	1.2	0.7	-210	-140	-70	-0.4	-0.5	-0.2
Watford	905	570	340	1.4	1.8	1.1	-355	-225	-125	-0.6	-0.8	-0.4
Welwyn Hatfield	885	555	325	1.2	1.5	0.9	-450	-285	-170	-0.6	-0.7	-0.4
Norfolk	8,180	5,385	2,795	1.6	2.1	1.1	-5,475	-3,725	-1,750	-1.0	-1.4	-0.6
Breckland	965	600	370	1.2	1.5	0.9	-705	-480	-220	-0.9	-1.2	-0.6
Broadland	575	350	225	0.8	1.0	0.6	-450	-315	-130	-0.6	-0.8	-0.3
Great Yarmouth	2,050	1,395	655	3.5	4.8	2.2	-1,090	-765	-325	-1.9	-2.6	-1.1
King`s Lynn and West Norfolk	1,190	760	430	1.4	1.8	1.0	-1,155	-770	-385	-1.3	-1.7	-0.8
North Norfolk	655	425	230	1.2	1.5	0.8	-475	-295	-180	-0.8	-1.1	-0.6
Norwich	2,030	1,395	640	2.2	2.9	1.4	-1,175	-810	-360	-1.2	-1.8	-0.6
South Norfolk	715	465	250	0.9	1.3	0.6	-435	-285	-150	-0.6	-0.7	-0.4
Suffolk	5,930	3,925	2,005	1.3	1.8	0.9	-3,575	-2,290	-1,285	-0.8	-1.0	-0.6
Babergh	475	305	170	0.9	1.2	0.6	-390	-220	-175	-0.8	-0.9	-0.7
Forest Heath	335	200	135	0.8	1.0	0.7	-270	-195	-70	-0.8	-1.0	-0.4
Ipswich	2,030	1,385	645	2.3	3.2	1.5	-1,040	-670	-370	-1.2	-1.5	-0.8
Mid Suffolk	525	315	210	0.9	1.1	0.7	-285	-175	-110	-0.5	-0.6	-0.4
St Edmundsbury	730	470	265	1.1	1.3	0.8	-380	-240	-135	-0.5	-0.7	-0.4
Suffolk Coastal	515	350	160	0.7	1.0	0.5	-300	-195	-110	-0.4	-0.5	-0.2
Waveney	1,320	900	425	2.0	2.8	1.3	-915	-600	-310	-1.4	-1.8	-0.9
LONDON	**122,875**	**72,000**	**50,875**	**2.1**	**2.5**	**1.7**	**-46,815**	**-28,280**	**-18,530**	**-0.8**	**-1.0**	**-0.7**
Inner London	59,480	35,275	24,210	2.4	2.8	2.0	-21,690	-13,075	-8,605	-1.0	-1.2	-0.7
Camden	2,865	1,710	1,155	1.7	2.0	1.4	-990	-620	-370	-0.6	-0.8	-0.5
City of London	70	45	20	1.2	1.4	0.9	-20	-10	-10	-0.3	-0.4	-0.4
Hackney	5,735	3,485	2,250	3.0	3.7	2.4	-2,080	-1,150	-935	-1.2	-1.3	-1.0
Hammersmith and Fulham	3,150	1,885	1,270	2.4	3.0	1.9	-910	-515	-390	-0.7	-0.7	-0.6
Haringey	5,625	3,380	2,245	3.0	3.5	2.4	-2,065	-1,280	-785	-1.1	-1.4	-0.9
Islington	3,960	2,390	1,570	2.4	2.9	1.9	-1,385	-810	-575	-0.9	-1.1	-0.7
Kensington and Chelsea	1,820	1,050	770	1.7	1.9	1.4	-520	-330	-190	-0.4	-0.6	-0.3
Lambeth	6,705	4,045	2,655	2.8	3.4	2.3	-2,590	-1,490	-1,105	-1.2	-1.3	-0.9
Lewisham	5,790	3,400	2,390	2.8	3.4	2.3	-1,905	-1,170	-735	-1.1	-1.2	-0.8
Newham	5,805	3,315	2,490	2.6	2.7	2.3	-2,410	-1,485	-925	-1.1	-1.4	-1.0
Southwark	6,145	3,630	2,510	2.8	3.3	2.3	-2,190	-1,300	-895	-1.0	-1.2	-0.8
Tower Hamlets	5,480	3,275	2,205	2.6	3.0	2.2	-2,320	-1,450	-870	-1.3	-1.5	-1.0
Wandsworth	3,610	2,085	1,520	1.6	1.9	1.3	-1,375	-875	-500	-0.6	-0.8	-0.4
Westminster	2,730	1,570	1,155	1.6	1.8	1.4	-915	-595	-325	-0.6	-0.7	-0.5
Outer London	63,395	36,725	26,670	1.9	2.2	1.6	-25,125	-15,205	-9,920	-0.7	-0.9	-0.6
Barking and Dagenham	3,595	2,005	1,590	2.9	3.3	2.5	-1,560	-955	-605	-1.3	-1.7	-1.0
Barnet	3,860	2,245	1,615	1.6	1.9	1.3	-1,350	-845	-505	-0.6	-0.7	-0.4
Bexley	2,210	1,185	1,030	1.5	1.6	1.3	-1,010	-600	-405	-0.7	-0.9	-0.4
Brent	5,880	3,600	2,280	2.7	3.2	2.1	-1,845	-1,125	-720	-0.8	-1.1	-0.7
Bromley	2,615	1,520	1,095	1.3	1.6	1.1	-1,420	-900	-520	-0.7	-0.9	-0.5
Croydon	4,815	2,845	1,970	2.0	2.4	1.6	-2,405	-1,385	-1,015	-1.0	-1.2	-0.8
Ealing	5,155	3,075	2,080	2.2	2.6	1.8	-1,995	-1,185	-810	-0.9	-1.0	-0.7
Enfield	5,335	2,915	2,420	2.5	2.9	2.2	-2,355	-1,345	-1,010	-1.2	-1.3	-1.0
Greenwich	4,285	2,470	1,815	2.4	2.7	2.0	-1,680	-1,065	-610	-0.9	-1.2	-0.7
Harrow	2,210	1,260	950	1.4	1.6	1.2	-710	-475	-240	-0.4	-0.6	-0.3
Havering	2,640	1,535	1,105	1.7	2.1	1.4	-1,075	-665	-410	-0.8	-0.9	-0.6
Hillingdon	2,700	1,565	1,130	1.4	1.6	1.2	-1,220	-685	-540	-0.7	-0.8	-0.6
Hounslow	3,130	1,850	1,280	1.7	2.0	1.5	-795	-495	-300	-0.5	-0.6	-0.3

4.10 Claimant count by sex and Unitary and Local Authority

from Nomis on 7 October 2016

Age 16+

not seasonally adjusted

	Claimant Count December 2014						Change on Year					
	Levels			Percentage of Pop			Levels			Perentage of Pop		
	Total	Male	Female	Total	Male	Female	Total	Male	Female	Total	Male	Female
Kingston upon Thames	1,200	685	520	1.1	1.2	0.9	-345	-170	-170	-0.3	-0.3	-0.3
Merton	2,310	1,345	965	1.7	2.0	1.4	-685	-435	-250	-0.5	-0.6	-0.3
Redbridge	3,300	1,875	1,425	1.7	2.0	1.5	-1,430	-860	-570	-0.8	-0.9	-0.6
Richmond upon Thames	1,310	750	560	1.0	1.2	0.9	-360	-240	-120	-0.3	-0.4	-0.2
Sutton	1,700	985	720	1.3	1.6	1.1	-775	-450	-315	-0.7	-0.7	-0.5
Waltham Forest	5,150	3,025	2,125	2.8	3.3	2.3	-2,110	-1,305	-805	-1.2	-1.5	-1.0
SOUTH EAST	**65,100**	**41,040**	**24,060**	**1.2**	**1.5**	**0.9**	**-33,360**	**-22,120**	**-11,240**	**-0.6**	**-0.8**	**-0.4**
Bracknell Forest	665	405	260	0.9	1.0	0.7	-430	-265	-170	-0.5	-0.7	-0.4
Brighton and Hove	3,450	2,205	1,245	1.7	2.2	1.3	-1,270	-895	-380	-0.7	-0.9	-0.4
Isle of Wight	1,970	1,300	670	2.4	3.3	1.7	-1,110	-755	-355	-1.4	-1.8	-0.8
Medway	3,780	2,350	1,430	2.1	2.6	1.6	-1,425	-945	-480	-0.9	-1.1	-0.6
Milton Keynes	2,530	1,545	985	1.5	1.8	1.2	-1,100	-640	-460	-0.7	-1.0	-0.5
Portsmouth	2,660	1,735	930	1.9	2.4	1.4	-1,185	-780	-400	-0.8	-1.1	-0.6
Reading	1,540	985	560	1.4	1.8	1.0	-795	-505	-285	-0.7	-0.9	-0.6
Slough	1,565	920	640	1.7	1.9	1.4	-1,120	-690	-440	-1.1	-1.5	-0.9
Southampton	2,495	1,630	865	1.5	1.9	1.1	-1,500	-975	-525	-0.9	-1.1	-0.6
West Berkshire	640	405	240	0.7	0.8	0.5	-375	-260	-110	-0.3	-0.6	-0.2
Windsor and Maidenhead	740	450	290	0.8	1.0	0.6	-470	-320	-150	-0.5	-0.7	-0.4
Wokingham	545	335	210	0.5	0.7	0.4	-310	-215	-100	-0.4	-0.4	-0.2
Buckinghamshire	2,785	1,735	1,050	0.9	1.1	0.6	-1,535	-995	-540	-0.5	-0.6	-0.4
Aylesbury Vale	845	530	310	0.7	0.9	0.5	-555	-360	-200	-0.5	-0.6	-0.4
Chiltern	380	230	145	0.7	0.9	0.5	-285	-210	-85	-0.5	-0.7	-0.3
South Bucks	270	160	110	0.7	0.8	0.5	-170	-90	-80	-0.4	-0.4	-0.4
Wycombe	1,295	815	480	1.2	1.5	0.9	-520	-340	-175	-0.5	-0.6	-0.3
East Sussex	5,250	3,390	1,865	1.7	2.2	1.2	-2,125	-1,455	-665	-0.7	-1.0	-0.4
Eastbourne	1,295	850	445	2.2	2.9	1.5	-495	-345	-150	-0.8	-1.2	-0.5
Hastings	1,760	1,145	615	3.1	4.1	2.1	-735	-555	-180	-1.3	-1.9	-0.6
Lewes	810	525	290	1.4	1.8	1.0	-265	-165	-95	-0.4	-0.6	-0.3
Rother	750	480	270	1.5	2.0	1.1	-335	-195	-140	-0.7	-0.8	-0.5
Wealden	640	395	245	0.7	0.9	0.5	-295	-190	-105	-0.4	-0.5	-0.3
Hampshire	6,870	4,360	2,510	0.8	1.1	0.6	-4,260	-2,745	-1,515	-0.6	-0.6	-0.4
Basingstoke and Deane	820	505	315	0.7	0.9	0.6	-620	-385	-235	-0.6	-0.7	-0.4
East Hampshire	445	275	170	0.6	0.8	0.5	-310	-180	-125	-0.5	-0.5	-0.3
Eastleigh	610	410	195	0.8	1.0	0.5	-350	-225	-130	-0.4	-0.6	-0.3
Fareham	490	325	165	0.7	0.9	0.5	-265	-155	-105	-0.4	-0.5	-0.3
Gosport	735	455	280	1.4	1.7	1.1	-340	-270	-70	-0.7	-1.1	-0.2
Hart	280	175	100	0.5	0.6	0.4	-165	-105	-65	-0.3	-0.4	-0.2
Havant	1,275	810	465	1.8	2.3	1.3	-580	-395	-185	-0.8	-1.1	-0.5
New Forest	815	530	280	0.8	1.1	0.5	-555	-355	-205	-0.5	-0.7	-0.4
Rushmoor	570	355	220	0.9	1.1	0.7	-430	-260	-165	-0.7	-0.8	-0.5
Test Valley	460	265	195	0.6	0.7	0.5	-355	-215	-140	-0.5	-0.6	-0.4
Winchester	380	250	125	0.5	0.7	0.3	-280	-200	-85	-0.4	-0.6	-0.3
Kent	14,835	9,315	5,525	1.6	2.0	1.2	-7,105	-4,890	-2,215	-0.8	-1.1	-0.5
Ashford	980	605	375	1.3	1.7	1.0	-515	-345	-165	-0.7	-0.9	-0.4
Canterbury	1,095	725	370	1.1	1.5	0.7	-685	-475	-210	-0.7	-1.0	-0.4
Dartford	795	400	395	1.2	1.2	1.2	-515	-395	-120	-0.8	-1.2	-0.4
Dover	1,510	1,015	495	2.2	3.0	1.5	-590	-400	-190	-0.9	-1.2	-0.5
Gravesham	1,305	815	495	2.0	2.5	1.5	-600	-325	-270	-0.9	-1.0	-0.8
Maidstone	1,160	685	480	1.2	1.4	0.9	-610	-420	-180	-0.6	-0.8	-0.4
Sevenoaks	595	370	225	0.8	1.1	0.6	-250	-185	-70	-0.4	-0.5	-0.2
Shepway	1,550	1,010	540	2.4	3.1	1.7	-575	-395	-180	-0.9	-1.2	-0.5
Swale	1,765	1,115	650	2.0	2.6	1.5	-960	-640	-320	-1.2	-1.5	-0.7
Thanet	2,870	1,860	1,010	3.5	4.7	2.4	-1,305	-935	-375	-1.7	-2.5	-0.9
Tonbridge and Malling	730	435	300	1.0	1.2	0.8	-310	-220	-85	-0.4	-0.6	-0.2
Tunbridge Wells	475	285	195	0.7	0.8	0.5	-200	-150	-45	-0.2	-0.4	-0.2
Oxfordshire	2,870	1,810	1,060	0.7	0.8	0.5	-1,830	-1,200	-630	-0.4	-0.6	-0.3
Cherwell	570	350	220	0.6	0.8	0.5	-295	-180	-115	-0.3	-0.4	-0.2
Oxford	975	675	300	0.9	1.2	0.5	-770	-510	-260	-0.7	-0.9	-0.5
South Oxfordshire	445	260	190	0.5	0.6	0.5	-260	-155	-100	-0.3	-0.4	-0.2
Vale of White Horse	435	275	165	0.6	0.7	0.4	-310	-205	-95	-0.4	-0.5	-0.3
West Oxfordshire	445	255	185	0.7	0.8	0.6	-195	-140	-60	-0.3	-0.4	-0.1
Surrey	4,880	2,965	1,915	0.7	0.8	0.5	-2,955	-1,935	-1,020	-0.4	-0.6	-0.3
Elmbridge	415	260	155	0.5	0.7	0.4	-335	-195	-140	-0.4	-0.5	-0.3
Epsom and Ewell	315	200	115	0.6	0.8	0.5	-225	-140	-85	-0.5	-0.6	-0.3
Guildford	645	390	255	0.7	0.8	0.6	-260	-195	-60	-0.3	-0.5	-0.1
Mole Valley	305	200	105	0.6	0.8	0.4	-185	-115	-70	-0.4	-0.4	-0.3
Reigate and Banstead	730	420	305	0.8	1.0	0.7	-430	-275	-155	-0.5	-0.6	-0.3
Runnymede	310	180	135	0.6	0.7	0.5	-255	-170	-80	-0.4	-0.6	-0.3
Spelthorne	535	315	220	0.9	1.0	0.7	-280	-190	-90	-0.4	-0.6	-0.3
Surrey Heath	320	200	115	0.6	0.7	0.4	-310	-190	-125	-0.6	-0.7	-0.5
Tandridge	425	240	190	0.8	0.9	0.7	-190	-135	-45	-0.4	-0.6	-0.2
Waverley	425	275	155	0.6	0.8	0.4	-190	-125	-60	-0.2	-0.3	-0.2
Woking	455	290	165	0.7	0.9	0.5	-300	-195	-100	-0.5	-0.6	-0.3
West Sussex	5,025	3,210	1,815	1.0	1.3	0.7	-2,455	-1,655	-800	-0.5	-0.7	-0.3
Adur	455	290	165	1.2	1.6	0.9	-215	-145	-70	-0.6	-0.8	-0.3
Arun	1,130	715	410	1.3	1.7	0.9	-465	-350	-120	-0.5	-0.8	-0.3
Chichester	710	460	250	1.1	1.4	0.7	-295	-160	-135	-0.4	-0.5	-0.4
Crawley	920	540	385	1.3	1.5	1.1	-525	-345	-175	-0.7	-1.0	-0.5
Horsham	565	385	185	0.7	1.0	0.4	-295	-215	-75	-0.4	-0.5	-0.2
Mid Sussex	440	275	165	0.5	0.6	0.4	-265	-185	-80	-0.3	-0.5	-0.2
Worthing	810	550	260	1.3	1.7	0.8	-390	-245	-145	-0.6	-0.8	-0.4
SOUTH WEST	**41,180**	**26,620**	**14,560**	**1.2**	**1.6**	**0.9**	**-23,540**	**-16,030**	**-7,510**	**-0.7**	**-1.0**	**-0.4**
Bath and North East Somerset	1,200	790	410	1.0	1.4	0.7	-575	-355	-220	-0.5	-0.6	-0.4
Bournemouth	2,000	1,345	660	1.6	2.1	1.1	-1,025	-700	-320	-1.0	-1.4	-0.5
Bristol, City of	5,930	3,875	2,055	2.0	2.5	1.4	-3,020	-2,055	-965	-1.0	-1.4	-0.7

4.10 Claimant count by sex and Unitary and Local Authority
from Nomis on 7 October 2016

Age 16+

not seasonally adjusted

	Claimant Count December 2014						Change on Year					
	Levels			Percentage of Pop			Levels			Perentage of Pop		
	Total	Male	Female	Total	Male	Female	Total	Male	Female	Total	Male	Female
Cornwall	4,655	3,015	1,640	1.4	1.9	1.0	-2,480	-1,655	-825	-0.8	-1.0	-0.5
Isles of Scilly	10	5	5	0.7	0.6	0.7	0	0	0	0.0	-0.1	0.0
North Somerset	1,425	915	510	1.2	1.5	0.8	-900	-590	-310	-0.7	-1.0	-0.5
Plymouth	3,055	2,075	980	1.8	2.4	1.2	-1,270	-910	-360	-0.8	-1.1	-0.4
Poole	985	630	355	1.1	1.4	0.8	-505	-330	-180	-0.5	-0.7	-0.4
South Gloucestershire	1,645	980	665	1.0	1.1	0.8	-805	-555	-245	-0.4	-0.7	-0.3
Swindon	1,870	1,090	780	1.3	1.5	1.1	-1,475	-970	-500	-1.1	-1.4	-0.8
Torbay	1,715	1,150	565	2.2	3.0	1.4	-920	-640	-280	-1.2	-1.7	-0.7
Wiltshire	2,555	1,610	940	0.9	1.1	0.6	-1,715	-1,200	-520	-0.5	-0.8	-0.4
Devon	4,000	2,545	1,455	0.9	1.1	0.6	-2,665	-1,860	-805	-0.6	-0.9	-0.4
East Devon	575	360	220	0.8	1.0	0.6	-315	-225	-85	-0.4	-0.6	-0.2
Exeter	755	500	250	0.9	1.2	0.6	-635	-420	-220	-0.8	-1.0	-0.5
Mid Devon	385	235	150	0.8	1.0	0.6	-240	-170	-70	-0.5	-0.8	-0.3
North Devon	555	355	200	1.0	1.3	0.7	-325	-270	-55	-0.6	-1.0	-0.2
South Hams	295	170	125	0.6	0.7	0.5	-245	-155	-90	-0.5	-0.7	-0.4
Teignbridge	645	390	255	0.9	1.1	0.7	-455	-325	-130	-0.6	-0.9	-0.3
Torridge	590	395	195	1.5	2.1	1.0	-280	-210	-70	-0.8	-1.1	-0.4
West Devon	205	140	65	0.6	0.9	0.4	-165	-85	-75	-0.6	-0.6	-0.5
Dorset	2,120	1,370	750	0.9	1.2	0.6	-1,065	-700	-360	-0.4	-0.6	-0.3
Christchurch	255	175	80	1.0	1.4	0.6	-160	-105	-55	-0.6	-0.8	-0.4
East Dorset	295	175	120	0.6	0.7	0.5	-195	-130	-65	-0.4	-0.6	-0.2
North Dorset	235	150	85	0.6	0.7	0.4	-150	-85	-65	-0.3	-0.4	-0.4
Purbeck	235	155	80	0.9	1.2	0.6	-85	-45	-40	-0.3	-0.3	-0.3
West Dorset	350	215	135	0.6	0.8	0.5	-185	-125	-65	-0.4	-0.4	-0.2
Weymouth and Portland	745	500	245	1.9	2.5	1.3	-285	-210	-80	-0.7	-1.0	-0.4
Gloucestershire	4,615	3,035	1,585	1.2	1.6	0.8	-3,015	-2,025	-985	-0.8	-1.1	-0.6
Cheltenham	925	625	300	1.2	1.7	0.8	-745	-505	-240	-1.0	-1.3	-0.6
Cotswold	315	210	105	0.6	0.9	0.4	-255	-170	-90	-0.5	-0.6	-0.4
Forest of Dean	600	390	210	1.2	1.6	0.8	-435	-305	-130	-0.8	-1.2	-0.5
Gloucester	1,640	1,095	545	2.0	2.7	1.3	-790	-480	-305	-1.0	-1.2	-0.8
Stroud	590	375	215	0.8	1.1	0.6	-450	-325	-125	-0.7	-0.9	-0.4
Tewkesbury	545	335	210	1.1	1.3	0.8	-340	-245	-95	-0.6	-1.0	-0.4
Somerset	3,395	2,190	1,205	1.1	1.4	0.7	-2,110	-1,475	-635	-0.6	-0.9	-0.4
Mendip	610	405	205	0.9	1.2	0.6	-315	-225	-90	-0.5	-0.7	-0.3
Sedgemoor	1,160	725	435	1.6	2.1	1.2	-650	-435	-210	-0.9	-1.2	-0.6
South Somerset	675	410	265	0.7	0.8	0.5	-545	-405	-135	-0.6	-0.9	-0.3
Taunton Deane	770	530	235	1.1	1.6	0.7	-430	-305	-130	-0.7	-0.9	-0.4
West Somerset	185	120	60	1.0	1.3	0.6	-170	-100	-70	-0.9	-1.1	-0.8
WALES	**47,305**	**31,085**	**16,220**	**2.5**	**3.2**	**1.7**	**-16,230**	**-11,195**	**-5,035**	**-0.8**	**-1.2**	**-0.5**
Anglesey	1,250	850	400	3.0	4.1	1.9	-455	-305	-150	-1.1	-1.5	-0.8
Gwynedd	1,655	1,100	555	2.2	2.9	1.5	-570	-420	-150	-0.8	-1.2	-0.4
Conwy	1,660	1,125	540	2.5	3.4	1.6	-685	-470	-205	-1.0	-1.4	-0.6
Denbighshire	1,425	960	465	2.5	3.5	1.6	-590	-395	-200	-1.1	-1.4	-0.7
Flintshire	1,765	1,130	635	1.9	2.4	1.3	-755	-465	-290	-0.7	-1.0	-0.6
Wrexham	2,055	1,330	725	2.4	3.1	1.7	-920	-630	-290	-1.1	-1.5	-0.7
Powys	960	630	330	1.2	1.6	0.9	-375	-250	-125	-0.5	-0.7	-0.3
Ceredigion	565	390	180	1.2	1.6	0.8	-235	-170	-65	-0.5	-0.7	-0.2
Pembrokeshire	1,840	1,290	550	2.5	3.6	1.5	-360	-200	-160	-0.5	-0.5	-0.4
Carmarthenshire	1,985	1,310	680	1.8	2.4	1.2	-850	-605	-235	-0.7	-1.1	-0.4
Swansea	3,265	2,245	1,020	2.1	2.9	1.4	-930	-635	-295	-0.6	-0.8	-0.3
Neath Port Talbot	1,940	1,240	700	2.2	2.8	1.6	-725	-545	-180	-0.8	-1.3	-0.4
Bridgend	1,870	1,180	690	2.1	2.7	1.6	-695	-520	-175	-0.8	-1.1	-0.4
The Vale of Glamorgan	1,570	1,060	510	2.0	2.7	1.3	-510	-370	-140	-0.7	-1.0	-0.3
Cardiff	6,700	4,515	2,185	2.8	3.8	1.8	-1,850	-1,245	-605	-0.8	-1.0	-0.5
Rhondda, Cynon, Taff	3,945	2,495	1,450	2.6	3.4	1.9	-1,575	-1,125	-450	-1.1	-1.5	-0.6
Merthyr Tydfil	1,135	730	410	3.0	4.0	2.1	-660	-430	-220	-1.8	-2.3	-1.2
Caerphilly	3,815	2,390	1,425	3.4	4.3	2.5	-1,050	-770	-280	-0.9	-1.4	-0.5
Blaenau Gwent	1,880	1,195	685	4.3	5.5	3.1	-780	-515	-265	-1.7	-2.3	-1.2
Torfaen	1,660	1,115	550	2.9	4.0	1.9	-630	-425	-195	-1.1	-1.5	-0.7
Monmouthshire	745	470	275	1.3	1.7	1.0	-275	-200	-75	-0.5	-0.7	-0.3
Newport	3,610	2,335	1,270	3.9	5.1	2.7	-770	-505	-270	-0.9	-1.1	-0.6
SCOTLAND	**80,080**	**55,215**	**24,865**	**2.3**	**3.2**	**1.4**	**-28,235**	**-19,335**	**-8,900**	**-0.8**	**-1.2**	**-0.5**
Aberdeen City	1,525	1,070	450	0.9	1.3	0.6	-745	-480	-275	-0.5	-0.6	-0.3
Aberdeenshire	960	650	310	0.6	0.8	0.4	-380	-245	-135	-0.2	-0.3	-0.1
Angus	1,290	870	420	1.8	2.5	1.2	-255	-185	-70	-0.4	-0.5	-0.2
Argyll and Bute	980	705	275	1.9	2.6	1.1	-500	-345	-155	-0.9	-1.3	-0.5
Clackmannanshire	1,030	675	355	3.1	4.1	2.2	-435	-335	-105	-1.3	-2.0	-0.6
Dumfries and Galloway	1,690	1,140	550	1.9	2.6	1.2	-875	-575	-305	-0.9	-1.3	-0.6
Dundee City	3,395	2,435	965	3.4	5.1	1.9	-990	-710	-275	-1.0	-1.4	-0.5
East Ayrshire	2,790	1,940	850	3.6	5.1	2.1	-1,065	-740	-325	-1.3	-1.9	-0.8
East Dunbartonshire	855	600	255	1.3	1.9	0.8	-215	-140	-75	-0.3	-0.4	-0.2
East Lothian	1,175	780	390	1.8	2.6	1.2	-470	-335	-140	-0.8	-1.0	-0.4
East Renfrewshire	695	490	210	1.2	1.8	0.7	-215	-140	-65	-0.4	-0.5	-0.3
Edinburgh, City of	6,070	4,155	1,910	1.8	2.4	1.1	-2,750	-1,910	-845	-0.8	-1.2	-0.5
Eilean Siar	350	265	85	2.1	3.2	1.0	-125	-75	-45	-0.7	-0.9	-0.6
Falkirk	2,535	1,680	850	2.5	3.4	1.7	-1,205	-905	-300	-1.2	-1.8	-0.5
Fife	5,885	4,015	1,870	2.5	3.6	1.6	-2,055	-1,300	-755	-0.9	-1.1	-0.6
Glasgow City	15,070	10,450	4,620	3.6	5.1	2.2	-3,235	-2,405	-830	-0.8	-1.2	-0.4
Highland	2,410	1,665	740	1.7	2.3	1.0	-650	-410	-245	-0.4	-0.6	-0.3
Inverclyde	1,430	1,045	380	2.8	4.2	1.5	-270	-180	-95	-0.5	-0.7	-0.3
Midlothian	975	680	295	1.8	2.6	1.1	-625	-415	-210	-1.2	-1.6	-0.7
Moray	760	505	255	1.3	1.7	0.9	-215	-140	-75	-0.3	-0.5	-0.2
North Ayrshire	3,470	2,385	1,090	4.1	5.9	2.5	-1,110	-700	-405	-1.3	-1.6	-0.9
North Lanarkshire	6,715	4,555	2,155	3.1	4.3	1.9	-2,345	-1,515	-835	-1.0	-1.3	-0.8
Orkney Islands	110	80	30	0.8	1.2	0.4	-25	-15	-10	-0.2	-0.2	-0.2

4.10 Claimant count by sex and Unitary and Local Authority

from Nomis on 7 October 2016

Age 16+

not seasonally adjusted

| | Claimant Count December 2014 | | | | | | Change on Year | | | | | |
| | Levels | | | Percentage of Pop | | | Levels | | | Perentage of Pop | | |
	Total	Male	Female	Total	Male	Female	Total	Male	Female	Total	Male	Female
Perth and Kinross	1,125	775	345	1.2	1.7	0.7	-540	-370	-175	-0.6	-0.8	-0.4
Renfrewshire	3,025	2,150	875	2.7	3.9	1.5	-1,365	-950	-420	-1.2	-1.7	-0.7
Scottish Borders	1,140	775	360	1.7	2.3	1.0	-565	-390	-180	-0.8	-1.1	-0.5
Shetland Islands	75	55	20	0.5	0.7	0.3	-65	-45	-20	-0.4	-0.6	-0.2
South Ayrshire	1,985	1,355	635	2.9	4.1	1.8	-640	-450	-185	-0.9	-1.4	-0.5
South Lanarkshire	5,250	3,590	1,660	2.6	3.6	1.6	-1,800	-1,240	-560	-0.9	-1.3	-0.5
Stirling	1,010	660	350	1.7	2.3	1.1	-500	-350	-150	-0.9	-1.2	-0.5
West Dunbartonshire	2,305	1,665	640	4.0	5.9	2.1	-805	-525	-285	-1.3	-1.9	-0.9
West Lothian	2,015	1,340	670	1.8	2.4	1.2	-1,170	-830	-345	-1.0	-1.4	-0.5
NORTHERN IRELAND	**49,065**	**34,555**	**14,510**	**4.2**	**6.0**	**2.5**	**-9,035**	**-6,280**	**-2,755**	**-0.8**	**-1.1**	**-0.4**
Antrim and Newtownabbey	2,530	1,795	735	2.9	4.2	1.6	-660	-450	-205	-0.7	-1.0	-0.5
Ards and North Down	3,300	2,330	965	3.4	4.9	1.9	-435	-295	-145	-0.4	-0.6	-0.3
Armagh City, Banbridge and Craigavon	4,520	3,100	1,420	3.5	4.8	2.2	-1,145	-815	-330	-0.9	-1.3	-0.5
Belfast	12,580	9,250	3,330	5.7	8.6	2.9	-1,920	-1,285	-635	-0.9	-1.2	-0.6
Causeway Coast and Glens	3,875	2,750	1,125	4.3	6.1	2.5	-840	-560	-280	-0.9	-1.2	-0.6
Derry City and Strabane	7,235	5,015	2,220	7.5	10.6	4.5	-555	-390	-165	-0.6	-0.9	-0.4
Fermanagh and Omagh	2,885	1,965	920	4.0	5.4	2.6	-605	-445	-160	-0.8	-1.2	-0.4
Lisburn and Castlereagh	2,145	1,485	660	2.4	3.4	1.5	-430	-300	-125	-0.6	-0.8	-0.3
Mid and East Antrim	2,815	1,930	885	3.3	4.5	2.0	-550	-390	-160	-0.4	-0.6	-0.3
Mid Ulster	2,635	1,685	950	2.9	3.7	2.1	-955	-645	-310	-1.3	-1.8	-0.8
Newry, Mourne and Down	4,550	3,250	1,300	4.1	5.9	2.3	-940	-705	-235	-0.9	-1.2	-0.5

Source: ONS Labour Market Statistics; Nomisweb

- These figures are missing.

All data are rounded to the nearest 5 and may not precisely add to the sum of the number of people claiming JSA, published on Nomis, and the number of people claiming Universal Credit required to seek work, published by DWP, due to independent rounding.

Rates for regions and countries from 2014 onwards are calculated using the mid-2014 resident population aged 16-64

The major towns and cities geography has been released as 'experimental'. This mechanism allows time for ONS to assess the response from the user community, both about its usefulness for analysis and its definitional accuracy.

4.11a Weekly pay - Gross (£) - For all employee jobs[a] by Industry: United Kingdom, 2014

Description	Code	Number of jobs[b] (thousand)	Median	Annual % change	Mean	Annual % change	Percentiles 10	20	25	30	40	60	70	75	80	90
ALL EMPLOYEES		25,036	417.9	0.6	501.5	0.0	125.5	210.9	252.0	286.7	349.2	493.7	586.6	644.2	709.1	913.6
All Industries and Services		25,026	417.9	0.6	501.6	0.0	125.5	211.0	252.1	286.8	349.3	493.9	586.7	644.3	709.2	913.7
All Index of Production Industries		2,788	526.5	0.9	599.3	-0.2	278.0	343.0	371.9	400.1	460.0	597.9	685.3	734.0	793.8	990.9
All Manufacturing		2,436	515.2	0.9	585.2	0.2	273.5	336.9	364.9	392.9	451.6	585.3	670.8	720.6	776.3	961.1
All Service Industries		21,268	396.4	0.5	486.0	0.2	113.6	191.6	230.7	266.4	329.5	473.9	568.4	624.6	689.9	899.0
AGRICULTURE, FORESTRY AND FISHING	A	134	357.9	0.5	381.2	-2.8	121.0	190.5	231.7	266.2	306.3	399.6	458.8	495.8	535.5	645.7
Crop and animal production, hunting and related service activities	1	121	349.9	1.4	370.5	-3.2	116.1	183.0	224.2	255.3	300.0	392.7	446.7	480.2	517.4	625.1
Forestry and logging	2	9	461.8	-3.9	492.4	-3.9	x	286.7	305.3	330.5	389.3	524.6	574.8	x	x	x
Fishing and aquaculture	3	x	361.7		460.9	5.7	x	x	x	297.1	321.6	x	x	x	x	x
MINING AND QUARRYING	B	44	697.5	-3.4	854.0	-5.6	392.8	492.3	517.5	552.2	617.1	804.0	919.1	1,022.6	1,164.5	x
Mining of coal and lignite	5	x	868.7	-0.2	936.2	2.4	x	x	x	640.4	744.9	x	x	x	x	x
Extraction of crude petroleum and natural gas	6	7	1,023.1	-16.3	1,212.0	-6.7	x	657.7	678.8	723.4	883.5	1,261.8	x	x	x	x
Mining of metal ores	7	:														
Other mining and quarrying	8	15	566.9	0.1	633.0	-15.0	357.3	440.1	463.8	483.1	509.6	600.8	680.8	714.7	x	x
Mining support service activities	9	18	747.4	2.9	886.8	0.4	374.9	504.4	540.9	573.7	637.8	858.1	x	x	x	x
MANUFACTURING	C	2,436	515.2	0.9	585.2	0.2	273.5	336.9	364.9	392.9	451.6	585.3	670.8	720.6	776.3	961.1
Manufacture of food products	10	357	400.0	1.8	477.6	-1.0	236.6	282.4	300.5	317.9	356.7	456.6	527.5	572.0	624.1	794.7
Manufacture of beverages	11	43	629.6	5.5	697.7	2.5	287.8	412.1	452.2	489.4	553.5	704.9	811.4	861.8	897.8	x
Manufacture of tobacco products	12	x	782.3	-12.0	765.4	-24.0	x	x	x	x	x	x	x	x	x	x
Manufacture of textiles	13	40	369.4	0.1	455.5	2.1	213.4	260.3	279.7	299.4	338.9	405.8	467.2	521.0	573.4	x
Manufacture of wearing apparel	14	21	295.3	4.0	345.8	-0.4	117.5	153.3	189.3	201.8	249.5	345.0	394.9	435.6	x	x
Manufacture of leather and related products	15	9	342.2	-1.0	365.7	-14.8	x	262.3	278.4	285.7	310.1	378.5	424.3	x	x	x
Manufacture of wood and of products of wood and cork, except furniture; manufacture of articles of straw and plaiting materials	16	51	413.9	-1.3	472.3	1.1	241.2	292.5	312.0	337.1	368.7	459.3	530.1	556.1	591.2	x
Manufacture of paper and paper products	17	59	506.0	3.8	562.8	2.3	278.0	347.0	377.2	408.8	454.3	564.2	632.9	673.3	724.0	x
Printing and reproduction of recorded media	18	97	452.3	0.2	517.3	2.1	235.6	313.8	336.6	363.5	410.5	518.3	581.2	613.3	664.5	x
Manufacture of coke and refined petroleum products	19	8	924.0	3.0	980.1	-2.9	x	580.4	645.9	704.2	835.6	976.5	x	x	x	x
Manufacture of chemicals and chemical products	20	99	575.2	3.1	652.0	3.1	297.8	372.5	404.9	434.4	505.7	648.9	736.0	793.0	870.9	1,108.6
Manufacture of basic pharmaceutical products and pharmaceutical preparations	21	63	677.6	0.6	785.6	2.9	366.8	470.7	506.8	551.1	614.9	782.6	887.6	962.1	1,036.4	x
Manufacture of rubber and plastic products	22	156	444.6	3.0	528.4	2.6	270.4	315.1	332.4	356.1	398.4	494.8	556.5	588.4	645.5	818.3
Manufacture of other non-metallic mineral products	23	82	513.0	-1.7	560.3	0.3	279.0	343.9	373.1	397.0	454.6	575.4	637.8	676.8	719.7	x
Manufacture of basic metals	24	92	628.7	2.7	659.6	2.7	374.6	446.7	480.8	515.2	576.0	681.2	757.4	804.4	847.6	979.5
Manufacture of fabricated metal products, except machinery and equipment	25	273	487.4	0.0	535.8	0.8	268.3	335.5	360.0	384.4	435.2	552.6	615.4	652.6	710.8	838.4
Manufacture of computer, electronic and optical products	26	129	592.2	1.2	646.2	-2.8	306.2	371.6	407.5	426.5	488.7	674.4	769.7	805.6	863.9	1,035.9
Manufacture of electrical equipment	27	101	490.4	2.9	573.1	1.7	276.9	331.9	353.8	378.0	423.0	546.5	646.2	691.8	753.4	958.2
Manufacture of machinery and equipment n.e.c.	28	206	562.1	0.3	629.2	0.3	324.0	388.2	412.7	444.7	502.4	634.4	708.5	751.4	800.4	968.2
Manufacture of motor vehicles, trailers and semi-trailers	29	166	608.1	1.1	674.2	-1.2	350.1	421.6	453.4	487.8	552.4	690.1	767.4	807.4	875.3	1,055.4
Manufacture of other transport equipment	30	175	703.7	2.1	759.5	3.6	439.3	521.9	564.4	583.7	649.8	765.0	826.1	873.2	920.2	1,117.5
Manufacture of furniture	31	62	389.0	-1.6	456.1	-1.1	238.9	276.4	297.1	316.4	358.0	440.8	501.3	541.9	594.5	x
Other manufacturing	32	67	438.6	2.9	484.3	-0.1	224.8	288.2	316.1	331.4	381.3	479.1	541.4	574.9	625.4	x
Repair and installation of machinery and equipment	33	79	594.1	-4.5	684.5	-2.3	292.8	387.6	431.3	469.2	520.2	681.0	780.8	828.8	914.9	x
ELECTRICITY, GAS, STEAM AND AIR CONDITIONING SUPPLY	D	166	663.8	-3.2	747.5	-1.8	342.0	413.2	460.0	507.3	594.9	756.1	867.9	944.2	1,023.8	1,245.2
Electricity, gas, steam and air conditioning supply	35	166	663.8	-3.2	747.5	-1.8	342.0	413.2	460.0	507.3	594.9	756.1	867.9	944.2	1,023.8	1,245.2
WATER SUPPLY; SEWERAGE, WASTE MANAGEMENT AND REMEDIATION ACTIVITIES	E	142	528.2	0.3	590.3	-0.9	287.2	352.6	383.3	413.1	477.0	585.1	662.2	711.0	755.2	948.9
Water collection, treatment and supply	36	41	586.0	-0.3	642.1	2.9	367.0	448.2	470.0	496.4	533.1	632.0	712.7	735.9	772.0	x
Sewerage	37	13	589.4	15.0	633.7	6.6	319.7	419.7	466.3	488.9	535.7	621.4	721.9	784.1	841.1	x
Waste collection, treatment and disposal activities; materials recovery	38	87	489.4	-0.1	562.6	-3.3	268.5	321.7	348.3	376.4	425.0	544.0	619.8	672.5	726.9	x
Remediation activities and other waste management services	39	x	x		x		x	x	x	x	x	x	x	x	x	x
CONSTRUCTION	F	837	523.2	0.7	591.6	-0.9	224.0	343.8	375.8	410.5	472.0	590.2	676.2	728.3	790.8	1,008.2
Construction of buildings	41	232	523.2	-1.0	628.7	-2.0	240.0	350.5	382.5	421.6	479.1	598.0	705.3	769.9	852.2	1,146.8

4.11a Weekly pay - Gross (£) - For all employee jobs[a] by Industry: United Kingdom, 2014

Description	Code	Number of jobs[b] (thousand)	Median	Annual % change	Mean	Annual % change	Percentiles									
							10	20	25	30	40	60	70	75	80	90
Civil engineering	42	187	589.3	4.0	659.1	0.5	300.0	396.0	431.4	465.3	517.5	673.4	772.4	813.7	878.6	1,098.3
Specialised construction activities	43	418	500.0	0.0	540.9	-0.1	192.0	317.5	352.0	383.3	443.6	559.9	624.5	670.8	715.1	884.9
WHOLESALE AND RETAIL TRADE; REPAIR OF MOTOR VEHICLES AND MOTORCYCLES	G	3,636	311.4	1.2	389.4	0.5	99.7	146.7	172.5	202.1	263.3	364.1	437.7	480.0	536.6	731.9
Wholesale and retail trade and repair of motor vehicles and motorcycles	45	417	405.3	1.8	459.9	0.7	177.7	269.0	291.2	313.2	358.8	452.5	508.9	538.0	580.2	728.5
Wholesale trade, except of motor vehicles and motorcycles	46	991	451.8	1.9	558.5	0.4	224.3	298.3	325.2	345.4	393.3	514.8	597.5	657.0	736.8	998.6
Retail trade, except of motor vehicles and motorcycles	47	2,227	237.8	1.8	301.0	0.3	80.5	114.0	131.3	149.5	189.2	282.5	332.3	364.1	408.8	566.4
TRANSPORTATION AND STORAGE	H	1,047	501.5	1.6	565.9	0.1	268.2	350.0	379.5	405.9	448.5	560.7	631.2	677.9	737.2	925.4
Land transport and transport via pipelines	49	461	505.3	0.5	540.9	0.3	249.1	352.0	380.0	404.4	450.9	558.7	621.7	664.1	716.6	881.6
Water transport	50	12	505.9	-0.1	577.9	-3.8	x	349.9	354.4	384.1	458.8	547.5	585.6	x	x	x
Air transport	51	66	648.2	3.1	768.4	-6.4	298.0	388.9	431.8	465.5	551.5	721.9	835.5	914.7	1,021.2	x
Warehousing and support activities for transportation	52	302	525.4	1.4	612.5	0.5	287.5	351.8	379.0	403.7	465.0	603.2	689.0	748.1	826.8	1,043.2
Postal and courier activities	53	205	451.4	3.0	487.0	3.1	261.5	337.6	368.4	402.2	421.3	491.1	537.0	569.5	599.9	709.9
ACCOMMODATION AND FOOD SERVICE ACTIVITIES	I	1,290	210.0	3.0	248.8	1.6	56.8	94.7	108.6	127.0	164.1	255.5	299.1	325.8	356.5	459.9
Accommodation	55	291	268.3	3.7	300.1	1.2	78.5	132.6	157.8	186.7	230.3	300.1	340.0	365.8	399.6	532.6
Food and beverage service activities	56	999	190.1	2.5	233.8	1.9	51.3	88.3	101.0	116.1	151.4	236.9	283.9	310.2	342.6	438.0
INFORMATION AND COMMUNICATION	J	977	625.7	0.4	726.8	0.2	263.5	379.2	421.6	467.3	544.6	719.4	836.8	900.8	985.4	1,266.5
Publishing activities	58	151	517.5	3.8	654.3	8.2	x	307.4	354.6	383.3	451.2	594.2	689.2	761.3	817.0	1,059.0
Motion picture, video and television programme production, sound recording and music publishing activities	59	53	485.6	12.4	557.7	-4.0	112.0	191.8	234.7	306.2	383.3	574.9	698.7	766.4	796.6	x
Programming and broadcasting activities	60	43	720.1	2.6	797.1	0.4	396.3	479.1	524.3	571.4	660.5	791.4	878.1	919.9	974.0	x
Telecommunications	61	209	619.7	1.9	714.1	1.0	309.3	421.6	459.3	495.5	554.5	688.3	799.7	862.4	938.4	1,183.9
Computer programming, consultancy and related activities	62	456	666.3	-1.5	765.1	-1.3	287.5	392.9	443.9	492.4	574.9	774.1	900.3	968.0	1,066.0	1,356.5
Information service activities	63	65	674.9	-4.8	757.7	-4.6	299.0	390.7	433.8	492.1	603.6	776.6	910.1	984.1	1,073.2	x
FINANCIAL AND INSURANCE ACTIVITIES	K	981	624.6	3.7	892.1	3.9	287.0	355.7	388.0	430.7	517.2	766.6	955.0	1,085.6	1,245.7	1,775.5
Financial service activities, except insurance and pension funding	64	530	650.0	7.9	936.3	7.2	288.2	359.7	392.9	434.3	519.3	804.9	1,006.2	1,149.9	1,309.1	1,845.2
Insurance, reinsurance and pension funding, except compulsory social security	65	109	596.1	3.7	770.1	0.1	306.6	361.9	400.4	439.8	520.4	689.6	814.7	896.9	1,051.6	1,448.1
Activities auxiliary to financial services and insurance activities	66	342	613.3	0.2	862.5	-0.7	273.1	346.3	381.0	421.6	507.9	747.4	923.9	1,044.2	1,189.3	1,784.9
REAL ESTATE ACTIVITIES	L	328	442.0	2.2	511.3	2.9	159.4	269.5	305.9	331.8	385.1	498.3	571.5	605.0	662.6	903.4
Real estate activities	68	328	442.0	2.2	511.3	2.9	159.4	269.5	305.9	331.8	385.1	498.3	571.5	605.0	662.6	903.4
PROFESSIONAL, SCIENTIFIC AND TECHNICAL ACTIVITIES	M	1,583	550.6	0.8	660.6	-2.0	182.8	297.1	345.0	383.3	469.5	640.3	749.7	821.1	908.4	1,230.2
Legal and accounting activities	69	486	501.7	-3.0	637.0	-2.8	191.5	285.5	319.1	354.6	424.8	600.4	718.7	795.3	872.9	1,245.4
Activities of head offices; management consultancy activities	70	326	527.9	-2.9	677.7	-7.6	151.5	236.6	287.5	345.0	431.5	632.4	766.6	839.9	942.9	1,380.4
Architectural and engineering activities; technical testing and analysis	71	396	612.6	2.0	709.3	1.7	270.7	383.3	431.2	470.5	536.6	689.9	797.0	862.7	957.3	1,206.9
Scientific research and development	72	110	687.6	0.1	791.8	-1.4	345.3	474.7	511.8	552.4	621.5	755.1	873.4	936.2	1,046.9	1,280.5
Advertising and market research	73	121	535.1	8.4	629.1	-2.3	146.7	304.1	360.8	402.5	478.3	623.8	741.2	785.8	860.2	1,119.3
Other professional, scientific and technical activities	74	101	437.9	3.5	513.2	3.6	129.8	191.7	231.0	270.5	364.2	517.8	609.4	669.6	726.5	963.6
Veterinary activities	75	43	362.8	1.9	449.8	5.3	148.9	201.2	239.2	272.9	318.6	412.2	527.9	611.0	670.6	x
ADMINISTRATIVE AND SUPPORT SERVICE ACTIVITIES	N	1,647	323.4	1.1	389.3	0.7	87.6	149.7	188.7	227.2	276.2	379.2	450.6	493.9	547.3	728.1
Rental and leasing activities	77	120	455.4	2.1	512.5	-0.3	203.4	306.6	332.9	356.4	403.6	504.1	569.9	611.3	674.9	848.2
Employment activities	78	595	304.4	1.8	364.8	0.3	107.2	182.1	208.9	234.6	265.0	348.5	413.4	451.8	498.3	643.9
Travel agency, tour operator and other reservation service and related activities	79	76	421.6	-1.3	512.8	-8.8	176.1	241.2	269.9	296.4	348.3	488.9	568.9	613.3	665.9	x
Security and investigation activities	80	127	385.5	-1.3	403.3	2.5	134.8	249.7	285.2	307.0	350.1	422.7	463.2	491.4	527.6	633.1
Services to buildings and landscape activities	81	409	196.5	-1.8	280.9	0.5	61.1	79.0	93.5	105.0	141.0	275.8	339.8	380.2	430.6	618.6
Office administrative, office support and other business support activities	82	320	383.3	-4.6	491.9	-4.4	138.0	230.3	263.7	286.7	328.7	458.9	549.8	607.8	683.3	942.7
PUBLIC ADMINISTRATION AND DEFENCE; COMPULSORY SOCIAL SECURITY	O	1,289	549.9	0.7	575.1	0.3	256.2	355.6	385.5	418.8	480.2	607.3	679.1	723.1	766.1	900.3
Public administration and defence; compulsory social security	84	1,289	549.9	0.7	575.1	0.3	256.2	355.6	385.5	418.8	480.2	607.3	679.1	723.1	766.1	900.3
EDUCATION	P	3,758	417.9	1.3	464.5	1.8	105.1	191.0	229.3	265.3	343.5	501.8	602.2	659.8	710.7	856.6

4.11a   Weekly pay - Gross (£) - For all employee jobs[a] by Industry: United Kingdom, 2014

Description	Code	Number of jobs[b] (thousand)	Median	Annual % change	Mean	Annual % change	Percentiles 10	20	25	30	40	60	70	75	80	90
Education	85	3,758	417.9	1.3	464.5	1.8	105.1	191.0	229.3	265.3	343.5	501.8	602.2	659.8	710.7	856.6
HUMAN HEALTH AND SOCIAL WORK ACTIVITIES	Q	3,747	372.5	-0.6	459.2	-0.5	138.7	205.4	235.8	264.0	318.0	440.4	533.1	580.8	642.0	808.6
Human health activities	86	2,410	445.2	-1.2	537.3	-0.7	177.2	260.6	295.4	325.9	379.7	529.4	611.8	661.8	723.9	909.3
Residential care activities	87	667	271.2	0.4	318.2	2.4	116.6	167.8	185.8	204.4	239.6	310.6	357.5	391.0	430.9	565.8
Social work activities without accommodation	88	670	275.4	-2.4	318.8	-1.9	90.2	140.0	165.6	189.4	236.1	319.8	383.4	423.6	465.4	599.9
ARTS, ENTERTAINMENT AND RECREATION	R	504	280.3	-0.8	354.5	-2.3	38.0	87.9	114.7	144.4	209.3	334.9	402.5	445.7	499.0	667.7
Creative, arts and entertainment activities	90	45	447.3	9.1	511.3	3.8	103.6	183.9	230.0	316.2	383.3	530.4	612.4	644.6	686.2	x
Libraries, archives, museums and other cultural activities	91	54	408.8	4.1	420.6	1.0	x	164.6	221.9	263.0	342.9	464.2	516.9	564.9	603.7	x
Gambling and betting activities	92	104	301.4	1.5	342.6	-5.8	116.7	174.0	199.4	215.2	262.9	330.8	371.7	403.8	437.4	x
Sports activities and amusement and recreation activities	93	301	213.0	-5.1	323.5	-1.9	27.6	53.4	75.2	95.3	147.0	287.5	352.5	394.8	447.2	624.6
OTHER SERVICE ACTIVITIES	S	422	337.2	-2.5	402.2	-1.2	84.5	138.8	167.7	199.9	268.3	407.6	479.1	525.1	589.9	782.0
Activities of membership organisations	94	200	399.1	2.2	437.4	-2.3	64.2	144.1	187.8	229.9	322.0	449.3	527.1	587.7	654.1	839.7
Repair of computers and personal and household goods	95	38	506.0	2.3	607.7	4.7	256.7	323.3	359.0	384.3	457.3	571.8	660.6	732.3	828.2	x
Other personal service activities	96	183	254.8	-3.4	320.8	-0.8	93.2	121.8	139.8	154.7	205.6	306.2	380.6	406.3	459.9	607.5
ACTIVITIES OF HOUSEHOLDS AS EMPLOYERS; UNDIFFERENTIATED GOODS-AND SERVICES-PRODUCING ACTIVITIES OF HOUSEHOLDS FOR OWN USE	T	59	129.9	-14.7	185.0	-11.1	26.5	46.3	57.2	67.9	93.2	173.1	212.4	246.7	304.2	x
Activities of households as employers of domestic personnel	97	59	129.9	-14.7	185.0	-11.1	26.5	46.3	57.2	67.9	93.2	173.1	212.4	246.7	304.2	x
Undifferentiated goods- and services-producing activities of private households for own use	98	:														
ACTIVITIES OF EXTRATERRITORIAL ORGANISATIONS AND BODIES	U	x	x		x		x	x	x	x	x	x	x	x	x	x
Activities of extraterritorial organisations and bodies	99	x	x		x		x	x	x	x	x	x	x	x	x	x
NOT CLASSIFIED	10	x	x		266.0	4.5	x	x	x	x	x	286.6	345.7	x	x	x

a Employees on adult rates whose pay for the survey pay-period was not affected by absence.

b Figures for Number of Jobs are for indicative purposes only and should not be considered an accurate estimate of employee job counts.

KEY - The colour coding indicates the quality of each estimate; jobs, median, mean and percentiles but not the annual percentage change.

The quality of an estimate is measured by its coefficient of variation (CV), which is the ratio of the standard error of an estimate to the estimate.

Key	Statistical robustness
CV <= 5%	Estimates are considered precise
CV > 5% and <= 10%	Estimates are considered reasonably precise
CV > 10% and <= 20%	Estimates are considered acceptable
x = CV > 20%	Estimates are considered unreliable for practical purposes
.. = disclosive	
: = not applicable	
- = nil or negligible	

Source: Annual Survey of Hours and Earnings, Office for National Statistics.

Table 4.11b   Hourly pay - Gross (£) - For all employee jobs[a] by industry: United Kingdom, 2014

Description	Code	Number of jobs[b] (thousand)	Median	Annual % change	Mean	Annual % change	Percentiles 10	20	25	30	40	60	70	75	80	90
ALL EMPLOYEES		25,036	11.61	0.2	15.12	-0.1	6.66	7.62	8.15	8.75	10.01	13.63	16.17	17.72	19.60	25.45
All Industries and Services		25,026	11.62	0.2	15.12	-0.1	6.66	7.62	8.15	8.75	10.01	13.64	16.17	17.72	19.60	25.46
All Index of Production Industries		2,788	12.94	0.2	15.24	-0.4	7.50	8.84	9.44	10.05	11.45	14.79	17.14	18.50	20.12	25.59
All Manufacturing		2,436	12.65	0.6	14.86	0.0	7.40	8.63	9.24	9.87	11.20	14.39	16.73	18.01	19.64	24.79
All Service Industries		21,268	11.35	0.2	15.15	0.0	6.57	7.49	7.99	8.51	9.81	13.43	16.06	17.66	19.59	25.52
AGRICULTURE, FORESTRY AND FISHING	A	134	8.87	0.5	10.21	-1.9	6.44	7.00	7.22	7.50	8.03	9.72	10.79	11.50	12.39	16.47
Crop and animal production, hunting and related service activities	1	121	8.65	0.6	9.92	-2.0	6.40	7.00	7.17	7.38	8.00	9.50	10.42	11.12	11.98	15.24
Forestry and logging	2	9	11.93	-3.6	13.30	-3.6	x	8.07	8.68	9.84	10.86	12.93	14.63	16.77	x	x
Fishing and aquaculture	3	x	9.20	1.5	11.95	-1.5	x	x	x	7.87	8.77	x	x	x	x	x
MINING AND QUARRYING	B	44	17.02	-4.6	20.86	-5.2	9.70	11.50	12.46	13.08	14.98	20.08	23.28	25.07	x	x
Mining of coal and lignite	5	x	16.77	-4.7	19.28	-1.7	x	x	13.26	13.65	14.87	18.60	x	x	x	x
Extraction of crude petroleum and natural gas	6	7	26.52	-20.1	33.11	-7.4	x	18.37	19.51	20.53	23.92	x	x	x	x	x
Mining of metal ores	7	:														
Other mining and quarrying	8	15	12.80	4.3	14.72	-13.8	8.66	9.64	9.85	10.34	12.00	13.94	15.56	16.33	x	x
Mining support service activities	9	18	19.45	0.5	22.66	1.1	10.44	13.14	13.69	14.78	17.00	21.61	24.91	x	x	x
MANUFACTURING	C	2,436	12.65	0.6	14.86	0.0	7.40	8.63	9.24	9.87	11.20	14.39	16.73	18.01	19.64	24.79
Manufacture of food products	10	357	9.58	1.2	11.97	-1.5	6.64	7.26	7.55	7.95	8.62	10.83	12.41	13.60	15.14	19.81
Manufacture of beverages	11	43	15.44	-1.1	18.48	4.0	8.50	10.97	11.70	12.16	13.55	17.86	20.66	22.28	24.29	x
Manufacture of tobacco products	12	x	21.39	-8.9	21.01	-22.9	x	x	x	x	x	22.92	x	x	x	x
Manufacture of textiles	13	40	9.19	-0.5	11.64	-1.2	6.51	6.96	7.29	7.56	8.34	9.73	11.67	12.54	13.81	x
Manufacture of wearing apparel	14	21	8.74	10.8	10.50	-1.8	6.31	6.50	6.75	7.12	8.00	9.58	10.51	11.26	x	x
Manufacture of leather and related products	15	9	8.89	2.8	10.05	-12.9	x	7.42	7.53	7.87	8.52	9.41	10.91	x	x	x
Manufacture of wood and of products of wood and cork, except furniture; manufacture of articles of straw and plaiting materials	16	51	10.05	0.8	11.74	2.4	6.88	7.76	8.14	8.50	9.02	10.90	12.05	12.55	13.39	x
Manufacture of paper and paper products	17	59	12.70	4.5	14.44	1.9	7.53	8.83	9.40	10.22	11.56	14.02	15.93	17.08	18.68	x
Printing and reproduction of recorded media	18	97	11.76	1.1	13.75	3.1	7.56	8.62	9.10	9.50	10.47	13.00	14.37	15.28	16.64	x
Manufacture of coke and refined petroleum products	19	8	24.58	7.2	25.81	1.2	x	16.14	17.34	20.24	21.46	25.59	x	x	x	x
Manufacture of chemicals and chemical products	20	99	14.81	3.5	17.03	3.2	8.05	9.87	10.61	11.27	12.89	16.61	18.91	20.21	21.78	29.35
Manufacture of basic pharmaceutical products and pharmaceutical preparations	21	63	18.06	2.5	20.87	3.7	10.11	12.44	13.34	14.35	16.36	20.38	22.71	25.27	27.62	x
Manufacture of rubber and plastic products	22	156	10.67	0.5	13.29	2.3	7.18	8.09	8.49	8.89	9.75	12.08	13.71	14.98	15.95	20.42
Manufacture of other non-metallic mineral products	23	82	11.98	0.6	14.04	2.1	7.43	8.85	9.37	9.85	10.90	13.70	15.79	17.01	18.04	x
Manufacture of basic metals	24	92	15.39	1.3	16.52	2.3	9.24	11.26	12.04	12.78	14.10	17.01	18.71	20.06	21.88	25.62
Manufacture of fabricated metal products, except machinery and equipment	25	273	11.77	0.6	13.15	-0.3	7.50	8.68	9.21	9.65	10.72	12.98	14.41	15.41	16.62	20.49
Manufacture of computer, electronic and optical products	26	129	15.39	0.4	17.01	-3.1	8.16	9.81	10.52	11.10	12.96	17.64	19.81	21.00	22.76	27.65
Manufacture of electrical equipment	27	101	12.41	3.4	14.99	2.5	7.75	8.78	9.28	10.01	10.98	14.06	16.67	18.03	19.49	25.60
Manufacture of machinery and equipment n.e.c.	28	206	13.80	0.8	15.84	0.7	8.44	9.97	10.59	11.18	12.47	15.39	17.42	18.72	20.28	25.19
Manufacture of motor vehicles, trailers and semi-trailers	29	166	15.25	0.2	16.62	-2.2	8.66	10.34	11.07	11.97	13.43	17.36	19.29	20.63	21.98	25.94
Manufacture of other transport equipment	30	175	17.84	1.3	19.26	2.5	11.30	13.14	14.03	14.75	16.36	19.37	21.52	22.52	24.03	29.75
Manufacture of furniture	31	62	9.53	-0.3	11.35	-1.9	6.55	7.27	7.60	7.97	8.70	10.59	11.77	12.55	13.41	x
Other manufacturing	32	67	11.45	4.4	13.35	2.2	7.30	8.11	8.63	9.13	10.18	12.55	13.90	15.18	16.94	x
Repair and installation of machinery and equipment	33	79	14.41	-3.7	16.81	-3.1	8.09	10.11	10.91	11.55	12.71	15.95	18.64	19.82	21.45	x
ELECTRICITY, GAS, STEAM AND AIR CONDITIONING SUPPLY	D	166	17.77	-1.1	20.21	-1.2	9.95	11.60	12.75	13.81	16.01	19.76	22.31	24.16	26.79	32.71
Electricity, gas, steam and air conditioning supply	35	166	17.77	-1.1	20.21	-1.2	9.95	11.60	12.75	13.81	16.01	19.76	22.31	24.16	26.79	32.71
WATER SUPPLY; SEWERAGE, WASTE MANAGEMENT AND REMEDIATION ACTIVITIES	E	142	12.54	-0.9	14.55	-1.3	7.65	8.95	9.42	9.94	11.15	13.97	15.63	16.98	18.42	23.91
Water collection, treatment and supply	36	41	14.89	2.1	16.89	2.7	10.15	11.75	12.30	12.94	14.02	16.24	17.93	18.69	19.66	x
Sewerage	37	13	13.55	2.8	15.80	7.2	8.67	10.20	11.07	11.74	12.87	15.15	18.93	x	x	x
Waste collection, treatment and disposal activities; materials recovery	38	87	10.65	-5.3	13.42	-3.7	7.20	8.04	8.55	9.01	9.77	12.20	13.93	15.05	16.96	x
Remediation activities and other waste management services	39	x	9.48		x		x	x	x	x	x	x	x	x	x	x
CONSTRUCTION	F	837	12.84	1.3	14.98	-0.9	7.95	9.25	9.89	10.46	11.63	14.20	16.01	17.19	18.75	24.06
Construction of buildings	41	232	13.16	-0.9	16.40	-2.9	8.15	9.58	10.14	10.83	11.98	14.78	17.40	19.04	20.95	28.51

Table 4.11b Hourly pay - Gross (£) - For all employee jobs[a] by industry: United Kingdom, 2014

Description	Code	Number of jobs[b] (thousand)	Median	Annual % change	Mean	Annual % change	Percentiles 10	20	25	30	40	60	70	75	80	90
Civil engineering	42	187	13.48	3.1	15.64	-1.0	8.27	9.67	10.27	11.00	12.16	15.16	17.35	18.74	20.06	25.54
Specialised construction activities	43	418	12.40	1.2	13.89	1.5	7.57	8.97	9.50	10.00	11.24	13.63	15.00	15.91	17.04	21.08
WHOLESALE AND RETAIL TRADE; REPAIR OF MOTOR VEHICLES AND MOTORCYCLES	G	3,636	8.62	1.5	12.08	0.7	6.36	6.78	6.96	7.17	7.79	9.63	11.17	12.25	13.58	19.16
Wholesale and retail trade and repair of motor vehicles and motorcycles	45	417	9.88	1.5	11.84	0.8	6.44	7.14	7.56	8.00	8.95	10.88	12.11	12.97	13.90	17.87
Wholesale trade, except of motor vehicles and motorcycles	46	991	11.38	1.3	14.85	1.0	7.00	8.03	8.51	9.00	10.06	12.93	15.33	16.86	19.13	26.60
Retail trade, except of motor vehicles and motorcycles	47	2,227	7.65	2.0	10.52	0.3	6.31	6.57	6.74	6.87	7.17	8.37	9.27	9.98	10.92	14.82
TRANSPORTATION AND STORAGE	H	1,047	11.80	0.8	14.21	0.1	7.82	9.00	9.53	10.10	10.76	13.18	15.19	16.33	18.06	24.51
Land transport and transport via pipelines	49	461	11.19	0.4	13.05	0.4	7.56	8.58	9.03	9.41	10.30	12.29	14.14	15.49	16.73	23.09
Water transport	50	12	13.80	2.4	16.14	2.5	8.12	9.27	9.75	10.57	12.37	14.43	17.43	x	x	x
Air transport	51	66	18.86	-4.6	22.66	-7.7	9.34	12.09	13.29	14.49	15.96	21.66	25.22	27.90	30.63	x
Warehousing and support activities for transportation	52	302	12.75	1.8	15.42	0.3	7.92	8.94	9.47	10.06	11.24	14.71	16.90	18.19	20.56	27.23
Postal and courier activities	53	205	11.22	4.3	12.65	3.9	8.22	10.18	10.67	10.71	10.71	12.12	12.95	13.51	14.43	17.14
ACCOMMODATION AND FOOD SERVICE ACTIVITIES	I	1,290	6.80	2.7	8.60	0.4	5.64	x	6.31	6.31	6.50	7.25	7.87	8.31	8.94	11.22
Accommodation	55	291	7.25	2.1	9.25	-0.8	x	6.31	6.36	6.50	6.82	7.78	8.65	9.37	10.00	13.33
Food and beverage service activities	56	999	6.67	2.6	8.38	0.9	5.50	x	x	6.31	6.44	7.07	7.66	8.00	8.55	10.68
INFORMATION AND COMMUNICATION	J	977	16.99	1.0	20.42	0.4	8.62	10.94	11.98	13.03	14.82	19.31	22.36	24.02	26.53	34.13
Publishing activities	58	151	15.03	3.8	20.63	8.7	7.91	9.87	10.68	11.50	13.10	17.22	19.75	21.03	22.98	30.50
Motion picture, video and television programme production, sound recording and music publishing activities	59	53	13.28	10.2	16.75	-6.8	6.36	7.25	8.11	8.91	11.02	15.31	18.29	20.40	21.90	x
Programming and broadcasting activities	60	43	19.45	0.0	22.15	0.2	10.83	13.46	14.37	15.85	17.81	21.82	23.81	25.03	27.34	x
Telecommunications	61	209	15.82	0.0	18.84	0.6	8.74	11.24	12.15	13.24	14.29	17.68	20.12	21.76	23.79	30.67
Computer programming, consultancy and related activities	62	456	18.16	-1.0	21.30	-0.4	9.24	11.50	12.75	13.75	15.83	20.86	24.03	26.27	28.79	36.77
Information service activities	63	65	18.21	-4.5	20.90	-4.8	8.81	11.17	12.20	13.51	15.81	20.46	24.14	26.09	28.37	x
FINANCIAL AND INSURANCE ACTIVITIES	K	981	17.88	3.7	25.99	3.4	9.10	10.64	11.52	12.58	14.85	21.80	27.14	30.58	35.05	49.59
Financial service activities, except insurance and pension funding	64	530	18.66	7.3	27.53	6.3	9.33	10.82	11.74	12.79	15.03	22.95	28.75	32.73	37.27	51.99
Insurance, reinsurance and pension funding, except compulsory social security	65	109	16.77	1.8	22.15	-0.3	8.94	10.70	11.65	12.55	14.73	19.63	23.38	25.69	29.88	41.21
Activities auxiliary to financial services and insurance activities	66	342	17.53	0.9	24.87	-0.5	8.75	10.34	11.21	12.18	14.51	21.19	25.90	29.27	33.44	49.28
REAL ESTATE ACTIVITIES	L	328	12.33	2.9	15.11	3.5	7.50	8.65	9.20	9.81	11.01	13.77	15.69	16.84	18.17	24.83
Real estate activities	68	328	12.33	2.9	15.11	3.5	7.50	8.65	9.20	9.81	11.01	13.77	15.69	16.84	18.17	24.83
PROFESSIONAL, SCIENTIFIC AND TECHNICAL ACTIVITIES	M	1,583	15.45	0.8	19.43	-1.8	7.84	9.71	10.49	11.49	13.31	17.89	20.75	22.72	24.95	33.73
Legal and accounting activities	69	486	15.05	-2.0	19.45	-3.0	7.70	9.40	10.13	10.94	12.80	17.80	20.84	22.77	25.02	35.53
Activities of head offices; management consultancy activities	70	326	15.00	-2.2	20.27	-5.3	7.17	9.16	9.96	10.63	12.79	17.59	20.79	23.00	25.64	37.72
Architectural and engineering activities; technical testing and analysis	71	396	16.21	1.5	19.47	2.0	8.97	11.03	11.92	12.77	14.39	18.62	21.20	23.15	25.17	31.85
Scientific research and development	72	110	18.60	-0.3	22.18	0.0	10.79	13.18	14.01	15.28	17.06	20.64	24.02	25.56	28.05	35.05
Advertising and market research	73	121	14.95	5.3	18.98	-5.3	8.00	9.81	10.74	11.60	12.91	17.53	20.25	21.46	23.98	31.88
Other professional, scientific and technical activities	74	101	12.88	3.1	15.91	1.6	6.95	8.21	9.09	9.81	10.79	14.50	17.04	18.62	20.34	26.68
Veterinary activities	75	43	10.33	-0.2	14.00	7.0	7.06	7.78	8.15	8.60	9.48	12.00	15.86	17.28	19.35	x
ADMINISTRATIVE AND SUPPORT SERVICE ACTIVITIES	N	1,647	8.86	0.3	11.80	-0.4	6.31	6.61	6.95	7.21	7.93	10.00	11.75	12.85	14.37	19.35
Rental and leasing activities	77	120	11.02	5.2	12.84	2.2	6.89	7.87	8.39	8.87	9.93	11.94	13.51	14.54	15.87	20.82
Employment activities	78	595	8.60	-3.6	10.94	-2.0	6.31	6.50	6.79	7.07	7.74	9.68	11.36	12.44	13.70	18.20
Travel agency, tour operator and other reservation service and related activities	79	76	11.56	-3.7	14.84	-4.9	6.81	7.70	8.18	8.58	9.60	13.38	15.14	16.29	18.23	x
Security and investigation activities	80	127	8.71	3.5	9.85	3.4	6.59	7.07	7.32	7.61	8.04	9.43	10.22	10.88	11.33	14.10
Services to buildings and landscape activities	81	409	7.34	-0.3	10.40	0.8	6.31	6.31	6.38	6.50	6.88	8.00	9.24	10.00	11.02	15.46
Office administrative, office support and other business support activities	82	320	10.85	-2.0	14.55	-3.4	6.73	7.52	7.96	8.36	9.47	12.61	15.21	16.51	18.63	25.52
PUBLIC ADMINISTRATION AND DEFENCE; COMPULSORY SOCIAL SECURITY	O	1,289	14.70	1.2	16.16	1.0	9.39	10.50	11.31	12.08	13.43	16.18	17.96	18.83	19.89	23.49
Public administration and defence; compulsory social security	84	1,289	14.70	1.2	16.16	1.0	9.39	10.50	11.31	12.08	13.43	16.18	17.96	18.83	19.89	23.49
EDUCATION	P	3,758	13.81	1.5	16.37	1.3	7.43	8.44	9.02	9.82	11.54	16.45	19.23	20.91	22.53	27.23

Table 4.11b Hourly pay - Gross (£) - For all employee jobs[a] by industry: United Kingdom, 2014

Description	Code	Number of jobs[b] (thousand)	Median	Annual % change	Mean	Annual % change	Percentiles 10	20	25	30	40	60	70	75	80	90
Education	85	3,758	13.81	1.5	16.37	1.3	7.43	8.44	9.02	9.82	11.54	16.45	19.23	20.91	22.53	27.23
HUMAN HEALTH AND SOCIAL WORK ACTIVITIES	Q	3,747	11.70	-0.8	14.56	-0.8	6.93	7.88	8.38	8.91	10.08	13.72	15.89	17.31	18.48	22.86
Human health activities	86	2,410	14.27	0.0	16.80	-1.2	8.30	9.48	10.00	10.87	12.31	16.01	17.86	19.16	20.73	25.25
Residential care activities	87	667	7.90	1.2	9.81	2.1	6.35	6.56	6.74	6.94	7.38	8.66	9.90	10.84	12.02	14.76
Social work activities without accommodation	88	670	8.90	-1.3	10.95	-2.0	6.50	7.00	7.25	7.51	8.09	10.01	11.57	12.50	13.75	17.54
ARTS, ENTERTAINMENT AND RECREATION	R	504	8.83	0.4	12.84	-0.1	6.31	6.65	7.00	7.33	8.08	10.00	11.79	13.05	14.86	19.56
Creative, arts and entertainment activities	90	45	12.78	6.1	15.91	2.9	6.94	8.22	8.89	9.37	10.86	14.68	16.42	17.32	19.03	x
Libraries, archives, museums and other cultural activities	91	54	11.51	1.6	13.92	2.1	6.75	7.93	8.46	8.92	10.45	13.07	15.29	16.71	17.61	x
Gambling and betting activities	92	104	8.10	2.0	10.19	-4.3	6.40	6.61	6.81	7.04	7.63	8.63	9.44	10.00	10.79	x
Sports activities and amusement and recreation activities	93	301	8.51	-0.6	13.26	-0.5	6.31	6.50	6.75	7.07	7.76	9.60	11.21	12.50	14.18	19.40
OTHER SERVICE ACTIVITIES	S	422	10.18	-0.4	13.42	-0.1	6.31	7.00	7.40	7.86	8.88	11.67	13.60	14.98	16.66	22.41
Activities of membership organisations	94	200	11.78	-0.1	15.28	-1.6	6.87	8.00	8.57	9.14	10.49	13.54	15.94	17.52	19.53	24.11
Repair of computers and personal and household goods	95	38	13.09	2.2	16.06	3.7	7.41	8.82	9.96	10.32	11.87	15.06	17.00	18.55	21.31	x
Other personal service activities	96	183	8.15	-1.1	10.77	1.1	6.31	6.35	6.53	6.80	7.40	9.19	10.49	11.37	12.36	16.10
ACTIVITIES OF HOUSEHOLDS AS EMPLOYERS; UNDIFFERENTIATED GOODS-AND SERVICES-PRODUCING ACTIVITIES OF HOUSEHOLDS FOR OWN USE	T	59	9.00	3.0	9.76	0.8	7.00	7.53	7.96	8.00	8.50	9.38	10.00	10.50	11.00	x
Activities of households as employers of domestic personnel	97	59	9.00	3.0	9.76	0.8	7.00	7.53	7.96	8.00	8.50	9.38	10.00	10.50	11.00	x
Undifferentiated goods- and services-producing activities of private households for own use	98	:														
ACTIVITIES OF EXTRATERRITORIAL ORGANISATIONS AND BODIES	U	x	x		15.27	-3.6	x	x	x	x	x	x	x	x	x	x
Activities of extraterritorial organisations and bodies	99	x	x		15.27	-3.6	x	x	x	x	x	x	x	x	x	x
NOT CLASSIFIED		10	7.88	-2.0	9.37	1.2	6.31	6.52	6.67	6.82	7.39	9.26	x	x	x	x

a Employees on adult rates whose pay for the survey pay-period was not affected by absence.

b Figures for Number of Jobs are for indicative purposes only and should not be considered an accurate estimate of employee job counts.

KEY - The colour coding indicates the quality of each estimate; jobs, median, mean and percentiles but not the annual percentage change.

The quality of an estimate is measured by its coefficient of variation (CV), which is the ratio of the standard error of an estimate to the estimate.

Source: Annual Survey of Hours and Earnings, Office for National Statistics.

Key	Statistical robustness
CV <= 5%	Estimates are considered precise
CV > 5% and <= 10%	Estimates are considered reasonably precise
CV > 10% and <= 20%	Estimates are considered acceptable
x = CV > 20%	Estimates are considered unreliable for practical purposes
.. = disclosive	
: = not applicable	
- = nil or negligible	

4.12a Weekly pay - Gross (£) - For all employee jobs[a]: United Kingdom, 2014

Description	Number of jobs[b] (thousand)	Median	Annual % change	Mean	Annual % change	Percentiles									
						10	20	25	30	40	60	70	75	80	90
All Employees	25,036	417.9	0.6	501.5	0.0	125.5	210.9	252.0	286.7	349.2	493.7	586.6	644.2	709.1	913.6
Male	12,632	507.4	-0.1	606.1	-0.9	196.2	300.7	336.2	370.0	436.6	586.5	684.6	746.1	816.7	1,064.8
Female	12,404	330.4	1.0	395.0	1.3	98.2	155.7	185.7	215.4	272.9	393.8	475.3	525.2	583.9	752.0
Full-Time	17,877	518.3	0.2	620.8	0.1	287.9	344.6	369.9	397.9	455.0	591.1	679.7	733.8	797.8	1,025.3
Part-Time	7,159	161.0	0.8	203.5	0.9	50.0	84.4	100.3	112.0	138.7	188.7	223.4	246.4	278.1	396.6
Male Full-Time	10,821	558.6	0.4	674.0	-0.4	306.6	369.5	400.0	428.7	490.4	634.0	730.5	788.5	862.4	1,125.6
Male Part-Time	1,811	151.4	1.4	200.5	-0.6	43.8	75.6	90.3	102.4	129.2	176.4	206.7	230.0	259.9	384.7
Female Full-Time	7,056	461.5	0.6	539.3	1.2	268.3	315.1	336.7	358.9	407.8	528.3	607.3	656.5	707.5	863.4
Female Part-Time	5,348	166.0	1.2	204.5	1.4	52.1	88.3	102.1	115.0	142.0	192.4	228.7	252.3	284.5	397.4

a Employees on adult rates whose pay for the survey pay-period was not affected by absence.

b Figures for Number of Jobs are for indicative purposes only and should not be considered an accurate estimate of employee job counts.

KEY - The colour coding indicates the quality of each estimate; jobs, median, mean and percentiles but not the annual percentage change.

The quality of an estimate is measured by its coefficient of variation (CV), which is the ratio of the standard error of an estimate to the estimate.

Source: Annual Survey of Hours and Earnings, Office for National Statistics

4.12b Hourly pay - Excluding overtime (£) - For all employee jobs[a]: United Kingdom, 2014

Description	Code	Number of jobs[b] (thousand)	Median	Annual % change	Mean	Annual % change	Percentiles 10	20	25	30	40	60	70	75	80	90
ALL EMPLOYEES		25,036	11.55	0.1	15.17	-0.1	6.64	7.59	8.10	8.69	10.00	13.57	16.11	17.66	19.53	25.42
All Industries and Services		25,026	11.55	0.1	15.17	-0.1	6.65	7.59	8.11	8.69	10.00	13.57	16.12	17.66	19.53	25.43
All Index of Production Industries		2,788	12.75	0.1	15.20	-0.3	7.40	8.64	9.25	9.93	11.25	14.56	16.91	18.33	20.00	25.56
All Manufacturing		2,436	12.43	0.4	14.82	0.1	7.27	8.48	9.08	9.71	11.02	14.17	16.48	17.86	19.48	24.78
All Service Industries		21,268	11.30	0.1	15.21	0.1	6.57	7.47	7.96	8.50	9.78	13.42	16.03	17.66	19.54	25.51
AGRICULTURE, FORESTRY AND FISHING	A	134	8.55	-0.2	10.09	-2.1	6.31	7.00	7.10	7.36	7.99	9.27	10.50	11.32	12.31	16.49
Crop and animal production, hunting and related service activities	1	121	8.43	1.1	9.78	-2.4	6.31	6.96	7.03	7.25	7.85	9.00	10.00	10.89	11.76	15.29
Forestry and logging	2	9	11.93	-3.2	13.28	-3.8	x	8.07	8.68	9.84	10.86	12.42	14.63	17.16	x	x
Fishing and aquaculture	3	x	9.20	2.1	11.94	-0.6	x	x	x	7.83	8.71	x	x	x	x	x
MINING AND QUARRYING	B	44	16.84	-3.1	20.99	-6.2	9.36	11.23	12.28	12.98	14.65	20.14	23.36	24.86	27.04	x
Mining of coal and lignite	5	x	15.30	-12.6	19.00	-3.2	x	x	12.07	12.45	12.98	17.86	x	x	x	x
Extraction of crude petroleum and natural gas	6	7	25.66	-22.7	33.14	-7.4	x	18.37	19.51	20.53	23.92	x	x	x	x	x
Mining of metal ores	7	:														
Other mining and quarrying	8	15	12.80	5.2	14.61	-15.9	8.52	9.19	9.68	10.03	11.77	13.76	15.37	16.05	x	x
Mining support service activities	9	18	19.45	2.5	22.76	1.4	10.27	13.26	13.72	14.73	16.77	21.77	x	x	x	x
MANUFACTURING	C	2,436	12.43	0.4	14.82	0.1	7.27	8.48	9.08	9.71	11.02	14.17	16.48	17.86	19.48	24.78
Manufacture of food products	10	357	9.43	1.5	11.95	-1.5	6.55	7.07	7.41	7.74	8.45	10.71	12.31	13.51	14.98	19.73
Manufacture of beverages	11	43	15.10	-3.7	18.46	3.6	8.44	10.84	11.57	12.16	13.23	17.84	20.45	22.15	24.04	x
Manufacture of tobacco products	12	x	21.23	-8.5	20.48	-24.1	x	x	x	x	x	x	x	x	x	x
Manufacture of textiles	13	40	9.12	-0.9	11.59	-1.0	6.49	6.84	7.18	7.51	8.26	9.69	11.46	12.33	13.41	x
Manufacture of wearing apparel	14	21	8.83	12.7	10.46	-2.0	6.31	6.50	6.75	7.07	7.93	9.50	10.39	11.26	x	x
Manufacture of leather and related products	15	9	8.87	2.5	9.97	-13.7	x	7.42	7.48	7.70	8.30	9.41	10.91	x	x	x
Manufacture of wood and of products of wood and cork, except furniture; manufacture of articles of straw and plaiting materials	16	51	9.73	0.4	11.69	2.3	6.75	7.57	8.00	8.29	8.95	10.76	11.70	12.38	13.15	x
Manufacture of paper and paper products	17	59	12.48	3.3	14.39	2.0	7.20	8.73	9.32	10.08	11.30	13.93	15.50	16.89	18.66	x
Printing and reproduction of recorded media	18	97	11.70	1.2	13.72	3.2	7.50	8.56	8.99	9.43	10.35	12.78	14.31	15.24	16.51	x
Manufacture of coke and refined petroleum products	19	8	24.05	4.9	25.87	1.9	x	16.14	17.34	20.24	21.46	25.59	x	x	x	x
Manufacture of chemicals and chemical products	20	99	14.63	3.3	16.97	2.8	7.87	9.83	10.50	11.16	12.59	16.37	18.49	20.03	21.64	29.35
Manufacture of basic pharmaceutical products and pharmaceutical preparations	21	63	17.94	2.7	20.85	3.7	9.95	12.43	13.28	14.08	16.36	19.98	22.60	25.24	27.62	x
Manufacture of rubber and plastic products	22	156	10.60	1.4	13.29	2.6	7.12	7.96	8.36	8.75	9.58	11.89	13.54	14.69	15.84	20.34
Manufacture of other non-metallic mineral products	23	82	11.90	2.0	14.09	3.0	7.20	8.53	9.17	9.55	10.67	13.78	15.40	16.94	18.05	x
Manufacture of basic metals	24	92	15.15	1.0	16.51	2.1	9.08	11.17	11.80	12.50	13.96	16.70	18.62	20.04	21.88	25.62
Manufacture of fabricated metal products, except machinery and equipment	25	273	11.46	0.4	13.04	0.0	7.39	8.50	9.00	9.43	10.50	12.54	14.08	15.23	16.41	20.21
Manufacture of computer, electronic and optical products	26	129	15.21	0.6	16.98	-3.2	7.99	9.65	10.39	11.00	12.79	17.41	19.70	20.95	22.63	27.67
Manufacture of electrical equipment	27	101	12.20	2.4	14.95	2.3	7.58	8.66	9.20	9.84	10.94	13.82	16.30	17.96	19.39	25.60
Manufacture of machinery and equipment n.e.c.	28	206	13.50	1.5	15.75	0.7	8.27	9.81	10.39	10.90	12.14	15.04	17.26	18.60	20.08	25.15
Manufacture of motor vehicles, trailers and semi-trailers	29	166	15.14	1.3	16.51	-2.1	8.46	10.12	11.00	11.80	13.22	17.07	18.95	20.57	21.77	26.02
Manufacture of other transport equipment	30	175	17.65	1.8	19.35	3.0	10.93	12.84	13.64	14.51	16.05	19.27	21.49	22.50	24.07	29.83
Manufacture of furniture	31	62	9.42	-1.0	11.24	-2.3	6.53	7.22	7.50	7.85	8.66	10.31	11.40	12.03	13.12	x
Other manufacturing	32	67	11.32	3.6	13.32	2.1	7.29	8.09	8.55	9.04	10.12	12.44	13.90	15.05	16.82	x
Repair and installation of machinery and equipment	33	79	14.00	-4.3	16.57	-3.5	8.02	10.00	10.70	11.24	12.52	15.44	18.13	19.24	21.17	x
ELECTRICITY, GAS, STEAM AND AIR CONDITIONING SUPPLY	D	166	17.56	0.7	20.06	-0.8	9.92	11.56	12.65	13.75	16.00	19.55	22.13	24.10	26.40	32.56
Electricity, gas, steam and air conditioning supply	35	166	17.56	0.7	20.06	-0.8	9.92	11.56	12.65	13.75	16.00	19.55	22.13	24.10	26.40	32.56
WATER SUPPLY; SEWERAGE, WASTE MANAGEMENT AND REMEDIATION ACTIVITIES	E	142	12.30	-2.4	14.47	-1.6	7.50	8.74	9.15	9.75	10.85	13.82	15.56	16.67	18.30	23.91
Water collection, treatment and supply	36	41	14.82	3.3	16.85	2.7	10.11	11.55	12.16	12.67	13.83	15.89	17.65	18.46	19.53	x
Sewerage	37	13	13.55	2.8	15.98	7.3	8.36	10.20	10.79	11.17	12.56	15.03	18.93	x	x	x
Waste collection, treatment and disposal activities; materials recovery	38	87	10.48	-5.3	13.26	-4.2	7.07	8.00	8.36	8.83	9.59	12.00	13.63	14.97	16.54	x
Remediation activities and other waste management services	39	x	9.48		x		x	x	x	x	x	x	x	x	x	x
CONSTRUCTION	F	837	12.65	1.2	14.92	-0.9	7.90	9.17	9.80	10.35	11.50	14.00	15.82	17.01	18.62	24.10
Construction of buildings	41	232	13.11	-0.8	16.41	-3.0	8.13	9.57	10.02	10.67	11.95	14.55	17.18	18.94	20.94	28.61
Civil engineering	42	187	13.33	2.4	15.61	-1.1	8.12	9.50	10.13	10.89	12.00	14.97	17.17	18.56	20.04	25.55

4.12b Hourly pay - Excluding overtime (£) - For all employee jobs[a]: United Kingdom, 2014

Description	Code	Number of jobs[b] (thousand)	Median	Annual % change	Mean	Annual % change	Percentiles 10	20	25	30	40	60	70	75	80	90
Specialised construction activities	43	418	12.24	1.4	13.76	1.7	7.50	8.89	9.41	10.00	11.09	13.37	14.82	15.71	16.83	20.88
WHOLESALE AND RETAIL TRADE; REPAIR OF MOTOR VEHICLES AND MOTORCYCLES	G	3,636	8.54	0.9	12.15	0.6	6.35	6.77	6.95	7.15	7.74	9.56	11.05	12.15	13.53	19.16
Wholesale and retail trade and repair of motor vehicles and motorcycles	45	417	9.83	2.0	11.83	1.0	6.41	7.09	7.52	7.98	8.86	10.76	12.00	12.82	13.77	17.86
Wholesale trade, except of motor vehicles and motorcycles	46	991	11.30	1.9	14.90	1.1	6.98	7.99	8.43	8.94	10.00	12.87	15.29	16.83	19.07	26.63
Retail trade, except of motor vehicles and motorcycles	47	2,227	7.61	1.5	10.59	0.0	6.31	6.57	6.73	6.87	7.15	8.29	9.18	9.85	10.80	14.81
TRANSPORTATION AND STORAGE	H	1,047	11.75	0.6	14.27	-0.1	7.75	8.90	9.42	10.00	10.71	13.17	15.14	16.31	18.04	24.35
Land transport and transport via pipelines	49	461	11.11	0.0	13.02	0.3	7.50	8.47	8.95	9.32	10.23	12.21	14.06	15.39	16.66	23.01
Water transport	50	12	13.80	2.5	16.11	1.4	8.10	9.16	9.74	10.48	12.22	14.43	17.43	x	x	x
Air transport	51	66	18.74	-5.0	22.74	-8.0	9.48	12.18	13.40	14.44	15.90	21.66	25.12	27.88	30.63	x
Warehousing and support activities for transportation	52	302	12.72	1.7	15.50	0.2	7.82	8.87	9.37	9.92	11.19	14.70	16.73	18.28	20.56	27.11
Postal and courier activities	53	205	11.16	3.9	12.74	3.9	8.22	10.12	10.71	10.71	10.71	12.23	12.97	13.60	14.59	17.17
ACCOMMODATION AND FOOD SERVICE ACTIVITIES	I	1,290	6.80	2.7	8.61	0.3	5.64	x	6.31	6.31	6.50	7.25	7.87	8.31	8.94	11.20
Accommodation	55	291	7.23	1.7	9.26	-1.0	x	6.31	6.35	6.50	6.81	7.78	8.65	9.36	10.00	13.30
Food and beverage service activities	56	999	6.67	2.6	8.38	0.8	5.50	x	x	6.31	6.43	7.07	7.65	8.00	8.56	10.65
INFORMATION AND COMMUNICATION	J	977	16.95	1.1	20.45	0.6	8.62	10.91	11.98	12.98	14.72	19.24	22.30	24.02	26.51	34.12
Publishing activities	58	151	14.99	3.4	20.64	8.7	7.91	9.84	10.67	11.49	13.08	17.19	19.80	21.03	22.98	30.50
Motion picture, video and television programme production, sound recording and music publishing activities	59	53	13.11	9.3	16.77	-6.5	6.36	7.25	8.11	8.96	11.02	15.31	18.29	20.40	21.90	x
Programming and broadcasting activities	60	43	19.70	1.5	22.15	0.2	10.83	13.46	14.37	15.85	17.77	21.72	23.81	25.07	27.34	x
Telecommunications	61	209	15.70	0.1	18.83	0.9	8.70	11.17	12.00	13.21	14.06	17.52	19.89	21.75	23.75	30.67
Computer programming, consultancy and related activities	62	456	18.06	-1.3	21.34	-0.2	9.21	11.54	12.73	13.69	15.81	20.84	24.02	26.15	28.75	36.77
Information service activities	63	65	18.06	-5.3	20.90	-4.8	8.81	11.17	12.11	13.51	15.76	20.46	24.14	26.09	28.37	x
FINANCIAL AND INSURANCE ACTIVITIES	K	981	17.84	3.6	26.07	3.4	9.05	10.59	11.49	12.51	14.82	21.78	27.05	30.49	35.02	49.59
Financial service activities, except insurance and pension funding	64	530	18.61	7.1	27.63	6.3	9.31	10.78	11.68	12.75	15.01	22.94	28.62	32.73	37.26	51.99
Insurance, reinsurance and pension funding, except compulsory social security	65	109	16.73	1.8	22.15	-0.6	8.90	10.61	11.64	12.54	14.55	19.63	23.38	25.69	29.61	41.21
Activities auxiliary to financial services and insurance activities	66	342	17.51	0.8	24.94	-0.6	8.75	10.28	11.04	12.12	14.49	21.11	25.77	29.15	33.33	49.28
REAL ESTATE ACTIVITIES	L	328	12.32	2.8	15.16	3.8	7.50	8.65	9.20	9.76	11.01	13.75	15.66	16.77	18.15	25.00
Real estate activities	68	328	12.32	2.8	15.16	3.8	7.50	8.65	9.20	9.76	11.01	13.75	15.66	16.77	18.15	25.00
PROFESSIONAL, SCIENTIFIC AND TECHNICAL ACTIVITIES	M	1,583	15.37	0.2	19.46	-1.9	7.79	9.66	10.46	11.42	13.29	17.88	20.68	22.63	24.92	33.73
Legal and accounting activities	69	486	15.05	-1.9	19.48	-3.0	7.67	9.40	10.13	10.94	12.77	17.78	20.80	22.76	25.00	35.53
Activities of head offices; management consultancy activities	70	326	14.90	-2.0	20.32	-5.4	7.15	9.12	9.91	10.57	12.78	17.53	20.79	22.99	25.66	37.72
Architectural and engineering activities; technical testing and analysis	71	396	16.18	1.9	19.46	2.0	8.94	11.00	11.84	12.69	14.37	18.45	21.19	23.09	25.04	31.82
Scientific research and development	72	110	18.60	-0.2	22.19	-0.4	10.73	13.12	13.91	15.17	16.94	20.59	24.01	25.55	28.05	35.05
Advertising and market research	73	121	14.94	5.5	19.00	-5.3	8.00	9.81	10.73	11.60	12.86	17.53	20.25	21.46	23.98	31.88
Other professional, scientific and technical activities	74	101	12.88	3.1	15.95	1.7	6.95	8.14	9.06	9.81	10.73	14.50	17.04	18.62	20.34	26.68
Veterinary activities	75	43	10.27	-0.4	14.05	7.0	7.05	7.76	8.15	8.58	9.48	12.00	15.90	17.34	19.31	x
ADMINISTRATIVE AND SUPPORT SERVICE ACTIVITIES	N	1,647	8.80	0.3	11.79	-0.4	6.31	6.59	6.92	7.19	7.89	10.00	11.71	12.78	14.32	19.31
Rental and leasing activities	77	120	10.82	4.5	12.82	2.0	6.87	7.79	8.32	8.80	9.83	11.80	13.47	14.35	15.86	20.82
Employment activities	78	595	8.52	-3.7	10.92	-2.0	6.31	6.50	6.75	7.01	7.69	9.64	11.29	12.39	13.69	18.15
Travel agency, tour operator and other reservation service and related activities	79	76	11.48	-3.9	14.87	-5.1	6.81	7.70	8.16	8.53	9.60	13.32	15.22	16.29	18.11	x
Security and investigation activities	80	127	8.73	3.6	9.81	3.5	6.60	7.07	7.35	7.60	8.05	9.43	10.18	10.85	11.32	14.05
Services to buildings and landscape activities	81	409	7.31	-0.5	10.34	0.7	x	6.31	6.38	6.50	6.86	8.00	9.14	9.90	10.99	15.37
Office administrative, office support and other business support activities	82	320	10.84	-1.5	14.57	-3.5	6.72	7.50	7.91	8.32	9.44	12.58	15.08	16.43	18.60	25.51
PUBLIC ADMINISTRATION AND DEFENCE; COMPULSORY SOCIAL SECURITY	O	1,289	14.70	1.2	16.14	0.9	9.36	10.47	11.28	12.08	13.43	16.17	17.96	18.73	19.77	23.38
Public administration and defence; compulsory social security	84	1,289	14.70	1.2	16.14	0.9	9.36	10.47	11.28	12.08	13.43	16.17	17.96	18.73	19.77	23.38
EDUCATION	P	3,758	13.76	1.5	16.42	1.3	7.43	8.44	9.00	9.81	11.51	16.43	19.21	20.90	22.53	27.23
Education	85	3,758	13.76	1.5	16.42	1.3	7.43	8.44	9.00	9.81	11.51	16.43	19.21	20.90	22.53	27.23

4.12b Hourly pay - Excluding overtime (£) - For all employee jobs[a]: United Kingdom, 2014

Description	Code	Number of jobs[b] (thousand)	Median	Annual % change	Mean	Annual % change	Percentiles 10	20	25	30	40	60	70	75	80	90
HUMAN HEALTH AND SOCIAL WORK ACTIVITIES	Q	3,747	11.71	-0.8	14.59	-0.6	6.93	7.88	8.39	8.91	10.11	13.78	15.89	17.31	18.47	22.80
Human health activities	86	2,410	14.27	0.0	16.81	-0.9	8.31	9.50	10.03	10.92	12.38	16.02	17.84	19.13	20.72	25.16
Residential care activities	87	667	7.90	1.3	9.88	2.5	6.35	6.56	6.75	6.94	7.36	8.69	9.97	10.91	12.08	14.85
Social work activities without accommodation	88	670	8.91	-1.3	10.99	-2.2	6.50	7.00	7.25	7.51	8.10	10.01	11.58	12.56	13.75	17.51
ARTS, ENTERTAINMENT AND RECREATION	R	504	8.80	0.7	12.96	0.0	6.31	6.61	7.00	7.31	8.06	10.00	11.73	13.03	14.79	19.47
Creative, arts and entertainment activities	90	45	12.78	7.3	15.92	3.1	6.92	8.20	8.64	9.37	10.69	14.61	16.34	17.39	18.88	x
Libraries, archives, museums and other cultural activities	91	54	11.51	3.8	13.96	2.4	6.74	7.93	8.47	8.87	10.45	13.13	15.29	16.71	17.61	x
Gambling and betting activities	92	104	8.10	2.5	10.37	-4.3	6.39	6.57	6.76	7.04	7.70	8.61	9.45	9.97	10.78	x
Sports activities and amusement and recreation activities	93	301	8.50	-0.5	13.32	-0.4	6.31	6.50	6.73	7.03	7.74	9.58	11.21	12.50	14.15	19.31
OTHER SERVICE ACTIVITIES	S	422	10.13	-0.6	13.41	-0.3	6.31	7.00	7.38	7.85	8.87	11.62	13.54	14.95	16.62	22.41
Activities of membership organisations	94	200	11.76	-0.3	15.29	-1.6	6.87	8.00	8.55	9.14	10.48	13.51	15.94	17.50	19.53	24.11
Repair of computers and personal and household goods	95	38	12.98	3.9	15.87	2.7	7.39	8.81	9.68	10.25	11.71	15.02	16.94	18.54	20.95	x
Other personal service activities	96	183	8.15	-1.1	10.76	1.0	6.31	6.35	6.52	6.79	7.37	9.19	10.41	11.29	12.32	16.01
ACTIVITIES OF HOUSEHOLDS AS EMPLOYERS; UNDIFFERENTIATED GOODS-AND SERVICES-PRODUCING ACTIVITIES OF HOUSEHOLDS FOR OWN USE	T	59	8.96	3.0	9.74	0.7	7.00	7.53	7.96	8.00	8.50	9.33	10.00	10.45	10.98	x
Activities of households as employers of domestic personnel	97	59	8.96	3.0	9.74	0.7	7.00	7.53	7.96	8.00	8.50	9.33	10.00	10.45	10.98	x
Undifferentiated goods- and services-producing activities of private households for own use	98	:														
ACTIVITIES OF EXTRATERRITORIAL ORGANISATIONS AND BODIES	U	x	x		15.27	-3.6	x	x	x	x	x	x	x	x	x	x
Activities of extraterritorial organisations and bodies	99	x	x		15.27	-3.6	x	x	x	x	x	x	x	x	x	x
NOT CLASSIFIED		10	7.89	-1.8	9.39	2.0	6.31	6.52	6.67	6.82	7.39	9.26	x	x	x	x

a Employees on adult rates whose pay for the survey pay-period was not affected by absence.

b Figures for Number of Jobs are for indicative purposes only and should not be considered an accurate estimate of employee job counts.

KEY - The colour coding indicates the quality of each estimate; jobs, median, mean and percentiles but not the annual percentage change.

The quality of an estimate is measured by its coefficient of variation (CV), which is the ratio of the standard error of an estimate to the estimate.

Source: Annual Survey of Hours and Earnings, Office for National Statistics.

Key	Statistical robustness
CV <= 5%	Estimates are considered precise
CV > 5% and <= 10%	Estimates are considered reasonably precise
CV > 10% and <= 20%	Estimates are considered acceptable
x = CV > 20%	Estimates are considered unreliable for practical purposes
.. = disclosive	
: = not applicable	
- = nil or negligible	

4.13 Average weekly earnings: main industrial sectors Great Britain

Great Britain
Standard Industrial Classification 2007

	Whole economy		Manufacturing		Construction		Services		Distribution Hotels and Restuarants	
	Actual	Seasonally adjusted	Actual	Seasonally adjusted	Actual	Seasonally adjusted	Actual	Seasonally adjusted	Actual	Seasonally adjusted
	KA46	KAB9	K55I	K5CA	K55L	K5CD	K55O	K5BZ	K55R	K5CG
2000	318	317	369	369	378	377	303	303	215	215
2001	335	334	383	383	407	407	320	320	223	223
2002	345	345	397	397	418	417	331	330	232	232
2003	356	356	412	411	436	436	342	341	237	237
2004	372	371	431	431	448	448	358	357	245	245
2005	389	388	447	447	461	461	375	375	254	254
2006	407	407	464	464	490	490	393	393	263	263
2007	427	427	483	483	522	522	413	412	279	279
2008	443	442	498	497	531	531	429	428	286	286
2009	442	441	503	503	536	536	427	427	290	290
2010	452	451	525	523	536	535	437	437	297	296
2011	463	462	532	531	544	544	449	449	300	300
2012	469	468	541	541	547	548	455	454	307	307
2013	474	474	554	554	547	549	460	460	316	315
2014	481	480	566	565	556	556	466	465	320	320

	Finance and Business Industries		Private Sector		Public Sector		Private Sector Excl Financial Services	
	Actual	Seasonally adjusted	Actual	Seasonally adjusted	Actual	Seasonally adjusted	Actual	Seasonally adjusted
	K55U	K5C4	KA4O	KAC4	KA4R	KAC7	KA4U	KAD8
2000	389	390	319	318	314	313	314	314
2001	417	418	335	335	331	330	331	329
2002	423	424	345	345	344	343	344	342
2003	434	434	355	355	360	359	360	358
2004	458	458	371	370	376	374	375	374
2005	485	486	387	387	396	394	395	394
2006	519	519	406	406	410	408	410	408
2007	546	545	428	427	424	422	424	421
2008	573	570	443	442	439	436	438	436
2009	552	553	439	438	452	451	450	448
2010	579	579	448	447	467	466	459	459
2011	611	610	458	458	479	479	468	467
2012	612	611	464	464	487	487	476	475
2013	613	612	470	470	490	490	480	480
2014	615	614	478	477	493	492	487	486

Source: Office for National Statistics: 01633 456780

4.14a Average Weekly Earnings by Industry (Not Seasonally Adjusted)

All figures are in pounds (£)

	Agriculture, Forestry and (A)			Mining and Quarrying (B)			Manufacturing - Food Products, (C1)			Manufacturing - Textiles, (C2)		
	Average Weekly Earnings	of which		Average Weekly Earnings	Of which		Average Weekly Earnings	Of which		Average Weekly Earnings	Of which	
		Bonuses	Arrears		Bonuses	Arrears		Bonuses	Arrears		Bonuses	Arrears
CDID	K57A	K57B	K57C	K57D	K57E	K57F	K57G	K57H	K57I	K57J	K57K	K57L
2010 Jan	343	4	0	1021	112	0	487	9	0	367	20	0
2010 Feb	358	26	0	1092	152	1	471	14	0	357	18	1
2010 Mar	360	17	0	1583	639	0	581	106	0	400	39	15
2010 Apr	340	7	0	1001	72	0	487	24	0	362	12	0
2010 May	322	2	0	966	51	0	462	8	0	360	12	0
2010 Jun	328	2	0	968	48	1	473	12	1	359	8	0
2010 Jul	336	4	0	970	36	3	464	12	0	368	14	0
2010 Aug	330	12	0	979	45	1	461	6	1	366	10	0
2010 Sep	327	4	0	975	59	0	482	32	0	361	6	0
2010 Oct	370	28	0	965	43	0	463	8	0	366	12	0
2010 Nov	362	8	0	973	53	2	461	7	1	363	9	0
2010 Dec	403	53	0	1027	114	0	509	47	1	369	20	0
2011 Jan	329	5	0	1049	110	0	465	6	3	364	13	0
2011 Feb	322	4	0	1091	173	1	463	11	0	360	15	0
2011 Mar	358	15	0	1583	659	1	549	86	0	385	38	1
2011 Apr	334	2	0	1062	133	0	501	30	0	360	12	0
2011 May	317	2	0	1023	66	1	464	6	0	361	8	0
2011 Jun	307	1	0	1011	56	0	471	14	0	365	10	0
2011 Jul	335	24	0	1057	97	1	457	5	0	362	8	0
2011 Aug	328	11	0	994	36	0	462	5	0	358	6	0
2011 Sep	312	2	0	1007	48	0	498	34	1	364	9	0
2011 Oct	331	10	0	1004	34	0	462	5	0	366	8	0
2011 Nov	325	6	0	1021	40	1	470	4	0	369	10	0
2011 Dec	371	38	0	1067	97	1	509	32	0	378	22	0
2012 Jan	323	3	0	1250	261	6	462	8	0	355	8	0
2012 Feb	327	6	0	1141	161	0	465	10	0	369	18	0
2012 Mar	339	17	0	1538	551	2	513	47	0	367	20	0
2012 Apr	313	3	0	1135	137	0	475	15	1	359	10	0
2012 May	313	5	0	1071	60	0	472	12	1	367	10	0
2012 Jun	323	3	0	1034	54	0	479	12	0	370	16	0
2012 Jul	343	14	0	1038	57	0	468	8	0	381	14	0
2012 Aug	337	8	0	1023	36	0	468	4	0	375	9	0
2012 Sep	335	6	0	1027	36	1	492	23	0	382	11	0
2012 Oct	328	4	1	1040	42	3	474	11	0	380	10	0
2012 Nov	334	5	0	1071	59	5	467	4	0	389	17	0
2012 Dec	359	28	2	1075	83	4	504	27	0	396	29	0
2013 Jan	340	6	0	1210	227	0	473	7	8	377	10	0
2013 Feb	345	5	0	1200	199	3	489	16	0	381	12	0
2013 Mar	342	3	0	1538	541	3	540	46	2	397	26	0
2013 Apr	352	4	0	1269	272	1	497	14	0	387	14	0
2013 May	347	3	0	1186	166	0	490	5	1	383	10	0
2013 Jun	335	3	0	1091	57	2	496	9	1	386	10	0
2013 Jul	337	2	0	1087	40	0	485	7	1	385	8	0
2013 Aug	335	3	0	1102	45	6	481	5	0	385	13	0
2013 Sep	342	3	0	1132	51	1	500	18	0	397	15	0
2013 Oct	346	2	0	1139	52	3	491	10	0	388	10	1
2013 Nov	335	3	0	1118	49	1	492	4	0	394	10	0
2013 Dec	390	53	0	1150	85	0	535	44	0	401	34	0
2014 Jan	339	3	0	1189	115	2	498	6	0	379	8	0
2014 Feb	350	5	0	1209	143	8	510	20	1	378	9	0
2014 Mar	352	2	1	1629	580	3	524	53	0	383	15	0
2014 Apr	345	3	0	1308	237	0	490	9	0	376	11	0
2014 May	334	3	0	1277	178	1	485	5	1	369	6	0
2014 Jun	336	5	0	1148	78	0	493	16	0	374	7	0
2014 Jul	347	13	0	1130	60	1	484	8	0	372	8	0
2014 Aug	331	2	0	1119	45	3	481	4	0	368	6	0
2014 Sep	337	5	0	1133	54	0	498	19	0	375	8	0
2014 Oct	345	3	0	1142	63	0	480	6	0	378	10	0
2014 Nov	342	3	0	1111	46	0	498	23	0	384	8	0
2014 Dec	394	43	1	1152	93	1	521	43	0	399	23	0
2015 Jan	352	13	0	1139	105	0	485	10	0	385	12	0
2015 Feb	353	4	0	1178	130	0	495	18	0	385	10	0
2015 Mar	370	7	0	1534	488	0	521	52	0	401	26	0
2015 Apr	374	4	0	1235	173	1	487	14	0	389	20	1
2015 May	362	5	0	1153	93	0	481	10	1	378	11	0
2015 Jun	357	8	0	1147	73	0	476	9	0	381	7	0
2015 Jul	374	18	0	1101	37	1	474	7	0	387	12	0
2015 Aug	374	10	0	1113	39	0	470	2	1	382	5	0
2015 Sep	372	7	0	1132	60	0	492	18	0	388	10	0
2015 Oct	370	7	0	1122	50	1	485	9	0	389	10	0
2015 Nov	388	3	0	1119	63	0	488	10	1	390	11	0
2015 Dec	396	17	0	1135	72	0	525	37	3	410	32	0
2016 Jan	396	20	0	1199	134	0	488	10	1	389	9	0
2016 Feb (r)	393	5	0	1365	312	2	499	18	1	378	8	0
2016 Mar (p)	406	6	0	1626	570	2	562	77	1	395	30	0

p = Provisional

r = Revised

Source: Monthly wages and salaries survey

Inquiries: Email: ster@ons.gsi.gov.uk

Tel: 01633 456773

4.14a Average Weekly Earnings by Industry (Not Seasonally Adjusted)

All figures are in pounds (£)

CDID	Manufacturing - Chemicals and (C3) Average Weekly Earnings	Of which Bonuses	Of which Arrears	Manufacturing - Basic Metals (C4) Average Weekly Earnings	Of which Bonuses	Of which Arrears	Manufacturing - Engineering (C5) Average Weekly Earnings	Of which Bonuses	Of which Arrears	Other Manufacturing (C6) Average Weekly Earnings	Of which Bonuses	Of which Arrears
	K57M	K57N	K57O	K57P	K57Q	K57R	K57S	K57T	K57U	K57V	K57W	K57X
2010 Jan	639	26	0	502	19	0	557	12	0	469	10	0
2010 Feb	673	62	1	529	24	2	577	31	1	477	20	0
2010 Mar	823	207	0	591	89	1	627	70	1	505	45	0
2010 Apr	670	61	1	528	25	0	582	24	1	470	11	0
2010 May	634	21	0	524	19	0	572	15	1	467	9	0
2010 Jun	635	15	1	523	21	1	569	11	1	472	11	0
2010 Jul	637	14	1	531	22	1	568	13	1	476	16	0
2010 Aug	622	11	0	514	10	0	568	10	0	469	9	0
2010 Sep	623	11	1	521	8	4	568	7	0	471	10	0
2010 Oct	650	18	1	524	20	0	571	11	0	476	13	1
2010 Nov	657	15	1	518	9	0	575	11	1	476	13	0
2010 Dec	681	35	0	512	14	0	593	29	1	485	26	0
2011 Jan	661	28	0	524	21	2	593	28	0	467	11	0
2011 Feb	660	27	0	516	15	1	590	31	1	478	21	0
2011 Mar	958	324	1	564	54	0	638	70	3	502	42	1
2011 Apr	698	67	1	527	22	0	595	30	1	471	15	0
2011 May	664	16	1	534	23	0	580	17	2	468	9	1
2011 Jun	663	18	1	532	14	0	591	24	1	472	14	0
2011 Jul	678	29	1	544	24	1	581	15	1	476	15	1
2011 Aug	660	11	1	520	7	1	571	9	1	470	9	0
2011 Sep	665	22	2	523	7	0	576	10	1	472	8	0
2011 Oct	655	14	1	534	16	1	582	9	5	474	12	0
2011 Nov	661	12	3	527	13	1	593	13	4	480	15	0
2011 Dec	687	36	4	529	29	1	595	24	2	491	26	0
2012 Jan	676	25	10	533	20	0	593	19	1	474	14	0
2012 Feb	666	25	2	528	16	0	612	42	1	479	17	0
2012 Mar	906	266	0	557	39	0	643	66	1	516	46	1
2012 Apr	734	85	1	558	37	1	608	27	2	489	20	0
2012 May	674	19	1	545	24	1	600	18	1	483	13	0
2012 Jun	682	24	1	534	21	0	613	28	1	483	13	1
2012 Jul	681	21	4	541	21	0	602	17	0	480	12	0
2012 Aug	676	19	1	518	8	0	596	13	1	481	10	0
2012 Sep	666	13	1	520	9	0	591	7	4	483	10	0
2012 Oct	671	17	0	523	12	0	596	8	1	484	13	0
2012 Nov	687	17	2	530	14	2	599	15	1	490	15	0
2012 Dec	720	36	1	538	24	4	610	27	0	497	23	0
2013 Jan	701	21	6	532	13	6	605	20	0	484	12	0
2013 Feb	705	31	0	527	17	4	616	28	0	491	16	0
2013 Mar	952	271	0	556	42	1	668	78	1	524	46	0
2013 Apr	818	150	1	542	25	0	634	36	1	504	26	1
2013 May	695	22	2	534	21	0	615	16	1	491	13	0
2013 Jun	698	15	0	533	21	0	644	42	1	489	11	0
2013 Jul	694	12	0	527	17	0	626	22	2	490	13	0
2013 Aug	700	17	0	511	6	0	613	15	1	488	9	1
2013 Sep	690	21	1	526	11	0	602	6	0	490	11	1
2013 Oct	689	16	1	536	12	0	611	11	1	493	10	1
2013 Nov	691	16	0	543	17	0	621	14	1	498	16	2
2013 Dec	709	28	1	561	33	9	627	23	1	512	26	0
2014 Jan	675	21	0	537	15	0	642	30	3	498	14	1
2014 Feb	687	23	0	543	20	0	642	25	2	501	18	1
2014 Mar	1024	352	1	560	34	0	693	76	1	538	53	1
2014 Apr	785	115	1	542	18	0	653	32	1	517	28	1
2014 May	696	14	1	545	17	1	637	20	1	507	15	1
2014 Jun	694	15	1	552	22	0	668	46	3	506	13	0
2014 Jul	709	34	1	549	18	0	639	23	0	500	13	1
2014 Aug	704	28	0	528	6	2	621	8	1	500	12	0
2014 Sep	700	24	1	547	12	4	622	9	0	503	13	1
2014 Oct	691	16	1	553	14	0	627	9	0	502	11	0
2014 Nov	673	13	0	555	16	0	631	10	1	504	13	0
2014 Dec	689	31	0	572	39	1	663	41	2	518	31	0
2015 Jan	682	25	0	550	17	0	642	16	2	502	19	0
2015 Feb	716	38	1	543	13	6	645	18	1	503	17	0
2015 Mar	1033	347	1	580	45	6	714	82	2	555	70	0
2015 Apr	797	118	1	562	22	0	670	30	2	522	32	0
2015 May	708	13	0	549	12	1	652	17	1	505	14	0
2015 Jun	710	17	0	563	19	0	693	56	1	514	19	0
2015 Jul	734	44	2	567	17	3	647	17	1	519	22	1
2015 Aug	710	15	1	548	6	1	631	9	1	515	17	0
2015 Sep	722	19	4	561	11	1	630	7	0	506	11	0
2015 Oct	721	25	1	564	13	1	634	9	0	509	13	1
2015 Nov	706	15	0	566	16	0	638	10	0	517	14	0
2015 Dec	738	42	1	583	37	0	656	25	0	536	35	0
2016 Jan	705	14	2	558	10	0	654	18	1	517	18	0
2016 Feb (r)	714	22	0	566	19	1	651	18	1	517	20	0
2016 Mar (p)	1130	429	1	582	37	0	706	72	1	552	50	1

p = Provisional

r = Revised

Source: Monthly wages and salaries survey

Inquiries: Email: ster@ons.gsi.gov.uk

Tel: 01633 456773

4.14a Average Weekly Earnings by Industry (Not Seasonally Adjusted)

All figures are in pounds (£)

CDID	Electricity, Gas and Water (D, E) Average Weekly Earnings	Of which Bonuses	Of which Arrears	Construction (F) Average Weekly Earnings	Of which Bonuses	Of which Arrears	Wholesale Trade (G46) Average Weekly Earnings	Of which Bonuses	Of which Arrears	Retail Trade and Repairs (G45 & G47) Average Weekly Earnings	Of which Bonuses	Of which Arrears
	K57Y	K57Z	K582	K583	K584	K585	K586	K587	K588	K589	K58A	K58B
2010 Jan	595	20	1	540	15	0	512	42	1	258	13	0
2010 Feb	601	22	1	537	14	0	523	58	0	266	22	0
2010 Mar	670	83	2	592	67	0	610	136	2	294	46	0
2010 Apr	608	31	1	535	12	1	503	34	0	270	23	0
2010 May	595	21	0	527	12	0	496	29	0	261	14	0
2010 Jun	661	81	3	531	14	0	497	32	0	267	16	0
2010 Jul	621	29	4	526	14	0	501	34	0	265	15	0
2010 Aug	599	22	2	515	9	0	489	27	0	261	11	0
2010 Sep	599	21	3	532	19	0	489	25	0	260	8	0
2010 Oct	606	21	1	527	8	0	490	29	0	257	12	0
2010 Nov	612	26	1	532	15	0	490	29	0	258	12	0
2010 Dec	621	36	1	533	25	0	516	58	0	256	12	0
2011 Jan	607	27	1	540	14	0	510	43	0	263	12	0
2011 Feb	604	24	3	547	21	1	504	45	0	265	19	0
2011 Mar	644	81	1	585	56	0	566	99	0	285	38	0
2011 Apr	615	42	1	532	14	0	503	37	0	272	18	0
2011 May	582	17	5	532	11	0	501	30	1	270	16	0
2011 Jun	653	89	3	546	18	0	522	53	1	272	20	0
2011 Jul	637	69	0	537	12	0	519	48	1	267	16	0
2011 Aug	592	31	1	530	9	0	507	38	0	262	10	0
2011 Sep	592	19	2	545	20	0	501	30	0	260	9	0
2011 Oct	597	18	1	537	12	0	511	34	0	264	13	0
2011 Nov	607	21	6	548	21	0	504	27	1	261	11	0
2011 Dec	611	25	3	548	27	0	540	61	0	258	10	0
2012 Jan	602	24	0	542	13	0	538	56	0	266	12	0
2012 Feb	603	31	1	543	15	0	533	54	0	270	18	0
2012 Mar	659	86	1	592	51	3	584	103	1	289	34	0
2012 Apr	618	36	0	547	16	0	527	42	0	275	18	1
2012 May	595	17	2	551	13	0	526	39	1	275	16	0
2012 Jun	660	80	1	557	22	0	542	54	0	277	16	0
2012 Jul	640	59	2	547	16	0	533	43	1	273	15	0
2012 Aug	593	15	1	528	8	0	532	43	0	271	15	0
2012 Sep	598	17	2	540	18	0	523	34	0	268	11	0
2012 Oct	611	19	5	538	15	0	535	38	1	272	15	0
2012 Nov	618	24	2	543	17	0	528	31	1	268	14	0
2012 Dec	613	22	1	541	25	0	542	49	1	266	14	0
2013 Jan	601	20	0	528	12	1	557	58	0	270	13	0
2013 Feb	612	26	4	539	13	1	559	63	0	271	19	0
2013 Mar	655	72	0	559	29	1	585	82	2	292	35	0
2013 Apr	640	47	1	567	29	1	593	83	0	280	21	1
2013 May	611	23	0	547	14	1	550	42	1	283	23	0
2013 Jun	667	70	1	551	20	1	564	53	0	280	16	0
2013 Jul	642	54	0	544	16	1	571	60	1	283	18	0
2013 Aug	615	23	1	538	11	1	559	50	0	285	21	0
2013 Sep	601	11	2	554	24	1	547	39	0	276	11	0
2013 Oct	612	18	2	537	13	1	554	38	0	282	18	0
2013 Nov	617	14	7	546	17	1	544	43	0	276	13	0
2013 Dec	620	20	3	552	25	1	574	65	0	275	13	0
2014 Jan	623	19	1	559	16	1	592	60	1	282	14	0
2014 Feb	624	18	1	546	15	0	551	49	0	279	14	0
2014 Mar	694	81	5	568	40	0	613	110	1	305	38	0
2014 Apr	666	48	12	544	19	0	564	62	1	296	25	0
2014 May	629	23	2	539	13	0	534	31	0	298	25	0
2014 Jun	676	72	1	555	22	0	555	54	0	288	14	0
2014 Jul	663	56	3	566	28	0	547	49	1	288	16	0
2014 Aug	638	26	2	545	14	1	534	42	1	288	14	0
2014 Sep	622	17	1	566	29	1	540	38	0	289	11	0
2014 Oct	622	13	2	551	14	0	541	39	0	294	18	0
2014 Nov	637	18	8	562	22	0	536	39	0	290	16	0
2014 Dec	624	13	1	571	34	1	565	66	1	288	13	0
2015 Jan	626	21	1	548	16	0	564	60	0	304	18	0
2015 Feb	645	36	6	553	13	0	563	65	0	300	15	0
2015 Mar	695	87	1	600	46	0	677	172	1	328	40	0
2015 Apr	669	56	4	562	21	0	559	57	0	319	26	0
2015 May	641	23	2	572	30	0	549	39	0	318	26	0
2015 Jun	692	70	2	567	20	0	559	52	0	309	18	0
2015 Jul	661	51	1	605	31	0	567	58	0	310	20	0
2015 Aug	642	30	1	582	14	0	552	40	0	305	17	0
2015 Sep	621	15	3	595	28	0	536	36	0	304	15	0
2015 Oct	619	11	1	590	17	1	536	36	0	307	19	0
2015 Nov	626	17	2	598	21	1	542	41	1	303	16	0
2015 Dec	627	13	3	603	35	0	583	72	1	303	16	0
2016 Jan	622	16	1	602	22	1	563	51	0	308	18	0
2016 Feb (r)	653	32	4	602	20	0	594	72	0	307	17	0
2016 Mar (p)	703	85	1	634	50	1	651	123	1	330	37	0

p = Provisional
r = Revised

Source: Monthly wages and salaries survey
Inquiries: Email: ster@ons.gsi.gov.uk
Tel: 01633 456773

4.14a Average Weekly Earnings by Industry (Not Seasonally Adjusted)

All figures are in pounds (£)

CDID	Transport and Storage (H) Average Weekly Earnings	Of which Bonuses	Of which Arrears	Accommodation and Food (I) Average Weekly Earnings	Of which Bonuses	Of which Arrears	Information and (J) Average Weekly Earnings	Of which Bonuses	Of which Arrears	Financial & Insurance (K) Average Weekly Earnings	Of which Bonuses	Of which Arrears
	K58F	K58G	K58H	K58C	K58D	K58E	K5E9	K5EA	K5EB	K58I	K58J	K58K
2010 Jan	488	5	0	213	4	0	713	59	1	984	283	1
2010 Feb	491	8	2	222	8	0	746	95	1	1694	975	10
2010 Mar	517	29	1	221	7	0	827	169	1	1438	714	2
2010 Apr	497	9	2	217	4	0	704	46	2	789	71	1
2010 May	496	8	1	221	8	0	725	59	1	887	162	2
2010 Jun	521	32	1	215	3	0	782	114	1	975	239	5
2010 Jul	500	6	1	215	4	0	727	55	0	804	60	2
2010 Aug	498	4	0	223	3	0	734	58	6	780	47	1
2010 Sep	500	3	0	221	3	0	726	53	2	839	112	1
2010 Oct	502	6	0	226	4	0	719	45	1	793	57	1
2010 Nov	505	6	1	219	7	0	726	48	1	787	54	1
2010 Dec	513	10	1	222	7	0	740	65	0	878	138	0
2011 Jan	505	7	0	218	5	0	753	72	2	1235	473	0
2011 Feb	504	7	0	225	9	0	765	83	1	1662	901	1
2011 Mar	524	31	1	224	8	0	858	178	1	1541	783	2
2011 Apr	514	14	1	222	5	0	736	55	1	850	86	0
2011 May	512	10	1	225	8	0	747	61	1	892	121	1
2011 Jun	515	14	3	223	3	1	808	128	1	1064	296	1
2011 Jul	520	18	2	224	6	1	744	62	1	878	114	1
2011 Aug	509	6	1	222	3	0	782	96	1	814	50	2
2011 Sep	509	5	2	221	4	0	738	51	1	871	105	1
2011 Oct	508	5	1	222	5	1	745	65	1	830	51	1
2011 Nov	519	6	7	226	9	1	745	57	0	825	47	0
2011 Dec	523	10	2	228	8	0	746	64	1	903	121	0
2012 Jan	514	7	0	230	6	0	761	82	1	1091	323	0
2012 Feb	525	17	0	234	11	0	781	97	1	1486	712	2
2012 Mar	535	26	0	227	7	0	857	168	2	1504	728	3
2012 Apr	534	17	1	227	5	1	756	70	1	896	117	0
2012 May	529	9	1	231	8	0	768	80	2	874	95	1
2012 Jun	549	26	2	229	4	0	816	136	2	999	225	3
2012 Jul	530	6	1	231	5	0	769	80	1	860	88	0
2012 Aug	544	18	1	232	4	0	779	81	1	841	67	1
2012 Sep	534	12	0	229	3	0	768	71	3	855	85	1
2012 Oct	534	13	1	226	5	0	747	51	1	819	47	1
2012 Nov	529	7	2	230	6	0	766	65	1	819	41	1
2012 Dec	551	23	2	234	8	1	757	56	1	898	114	0
2013 Jan	526	7	0	222	5	1	779	78	2	1130	351	1
2013 Feb	529	15	0	226	8	0	809	104	2	1532	746	1
2013 Mar	546	26	1	227	7	0	837	138	1	1551	763	0
2013 Apr	549	21	5	230	8	0	811	100	2	1063	267	1
2013 May	541	9	1	234	9	0	776	62	2	968	170	0
2013 Jun	565	34	1	228	4	0	830	111	5	1049	258	0
2013 Jul	538	10	1	231	5	0	778	64	2	865	75	1
2013 Aug	539	13	1	231	4	0	789	70	2	852	64	0
2013 Sep	533	4	1	230	4	0	780	66	1	875	87	0
2013 Oct	537	7	2	229	3	0	770	54	2	839	51	1
2013 Nov	542	7	5	232	6	0	762	49	1	841	53	1
2013 Dec	573	35	1	237	8	1	773	54	1	939	142	0
2014 Jan	534	7	1	232	7	1	793	76	3	1138	351	0
2014 Feb	634	38	68	234	8	0	817	98	2	1659	856	3
2014 Mar	556	29	1	232	7	0	851	141	2	1643	826	3
2014 Apr	556	20	1	232	7	0	825	107	2	941	131	1
2014 May	551	13	1	238	11	0	783	70	1	961	155	1
2014 Jun	568	33	2	232	8	0	838	114	2	991	187	1
2014 Jul	559	23	0	232	6	0	773	49	3	865	60	2
2014 Aug	540	5	0	232	4	0	799	75	2	903	66	2
2014 Sep	539	5	1	228	5	1	761	39	2	933	91	1
2014 Oct	548	13	1	231	4	1	786	58	1	897	53	3
2014 Nov	548	7	1	234	8	1	786	59	2	898	54	0
2014 Dec	579	31	0	242	12	1	815	64	2	1056	202	2
2015 Jan	547	9	3	237	5	1	825	85	4	1190	339	1
2015 Feb	553	18	0	242	10	1	856	107	3	1592	732	5
2015 Mar	554	19	1	243	10	1	921	170	1	1816	958	1
2015 Apr	562	20	4	240	8	1	830	80	1	1062	189	2
2015 May	555	13	0	248	11	1	828	80	2	1025	155	1
2015 Jun	577	38	1	240	5	1	857	107	1	1002	126	7
2015 Jul	549	10	1	244	5	1	834	82	0	967	94	3
2015 Aug	555	10	2	242	4	0	843	99	1	963	91	1
2015 Sep	552	8	1	240	5	0	793	51	2	963	91	1
2015 Oct	550	6	0	244	5	0	822	79	1	936	63	1
2015 Nov	552	10	1	246	8	0	804	61	2	927	49	1
2015 Dec	578	32	0	251	12	0	824	76	3	1097	208	2
2016 Jan	555	8	2	243	6	0	845	99	1	1267	382	0
2016 Feb (r)	561	19	1	246	9	0	830	94	1	1460	567	5
2016 Mar (p)	575	33	0	246	10	0	890	151	1	1984	1090	3

p = Provisional

r = Revised

Source: Monthly wages and salaries survey
Inquiries: Email: ster@ons.gsi.gov.uk
Tel: 01633 456773

4.14a Average Weekly Earnings by Industry (Not Seasonally Adjusted)

All figures are in pounds (£)

CDID	Real Estate Activities (L) Average Weekly Earnings	Of which Bonuses	Of which Arrears	Professional, Scientific & (M) Average Weekly Earnings	Of which Bonuses	Of which Arrears	Administrative and Support (N) Average Weekly Earnings	Of which Bonuses	Of which Arrears	Public Administration (O) Average Weekly Earnings	Of which Bonuses	Of which Arrears
	K58L	K58M	K58N	K5EC	K5ED	K5EE	K5EF	K5EG	K5EH	K58O	K58P	K58Q
2010 Jan	456	28	0	637	23	1	343	11	0	521	1	1
2010 Feb	456	15	1	652	37	1	333	13	0	521	1	1
2010 Mar	521	83	0	719	96	3	353	23	0	521	2	1
2010 Apr	451	15	0	648	28	0	342	12	0	522	1	0
2010 May	454	14	0	635	18	0	341	9	0	522	2	0
2010 Jun	463	24	0	641	22	1	334	8	0	524	3	1
2010 Jul	481	34	3	634	31	1	339	15	0	532	3	1
2010 Aug	465	27	0	635	20	1	331	10	0	535	11	0
2010 Sep	466	27	1	636	18	1	330	9	0	528	1	1
2010 Oct	471	30	0	646	28	1	334	11	0	529	1	0
2010 Nov	472	30	0	656	31	1	329	9	0	533	3	1
2010 Dec	481	34	0	687	56	1	331	14	0	537	8	0
2011 Jan	489	33	1	660	29	0	338	13	0	536	1	0
2011 Feb	480	26	1	673	35	1	329	12	0	534	2	0
2011 Mar	529	69	1	780	144	1	351	33	0	537	4	0
2011 Apr	495	34	0	670	28	0	326	13	0	537	2	0
2011 May	484	27	0	674	32	0	330	8	0	537	2	0
2011 Jun	506	48	0	672	33	0	340	14	0	542	6	0
2011 Jul	501	41	1	699	56	0	344	16	0	539	5	0
2011 Aug	486	35	0	660	21	1	340	13	0	545	11	0
2011 Sep	479	27	0	663	18	0	332	9	0	545	1	0
2011 Oct	488	35	0	679	29	0	338	11	0	538	1	0
2011 Nov	501	43	3	684	36	1	335	9	0	537	2	0
2011 Dec	511	48	1	711	59	0	355	24	0	540	6	0
2012 Jan	487	30	0	684	38	1	351	12	0	535	1	0
2012 Feb	498	38	0	698	50	1	353	13	0	538	1	0
2012 Mar	605	140	0	789	136	1	381	38	0	541	2	0
2012 Apr	499	33	0	694	41	0	351	13	0	545	0	0
2012 May	488	32	0	683	31	0	350	10	0	543	1	0
2012 Jun	511	51	0	687	29	0	347	10	0	550	5	0
2012 Jul	513	55	0	711	61	1	351	12	0	551	5	0
2012 Aug	481	29	0	677	27	1	352	9	0	547	3	0
2012 Sep	494	37	1	669	24	1	346	9	0	554	7	1
2012 Oct	497	41	0	664	24	1	348	10	0	547	2	1
2012 Nov	493	37	0	671	29	1	346	8	0	544	2	0
2012 Dec	506	53	0	711	72	1	358	21	0	543	2	2
2013 Jan	498	49	2	658	23	0	348	11	0	546	1	1
2013 Feb	477	33	1	682	36	1	350	13	0	535	0	0
2013 Mar	533	85	1	740	89	2	371	36	0	536	3	0
2013 Apr	533	83	0	706	56	2	357	20	0	537	1	0
2013 May	501	47	0	672	33	1	357	15	0	537	0	0
2013 Jun	504	48	0	676	39	1	345	9	0	540	3	0
2013 Jul	522	68	0	691	48	2	355	15	0	543	6	0
2013 Aug	501	46	1	661	24	0	351	9	0	540	1	4
2013 Sep	493	46	0	669	29	1	344	9	0	547	7	0
2013 Oct	500	51	0	669	24	1	344	10	0	537	1	0
2013 Nov	485	43	0	666	22	1	343	8	0	537	1	0
2013 Dec	512	52	0	713	67	0	364	26	0	540	2	1
2014 Jan	488	41	0	666	22	1	359	19	1	545	1	1
2014 Feb	480	34	0	674	34	0	349	16	0	541	1	1
2014 Mar	562	106	1	749	103	1	370	34	0	548	2	4
2014 Apr	525	68	2	693	46	1	352	17	0	553	7	3
2014 May	509	53	0	683	43	1	355	12	0	547	1	1
2014 Jun	516	52	2	697	57	1	356	13	0	549	3	0
2014 Jul	538	80	1	689	47	1	362	13	0	549	4	3
2014 Aug	496	40	0	669	27	1	365	10	0	547	3	1
2014 Sep	496	31	1	670	27	1	367	10	0	555	7	0
2014 Oct	508	42	1	679	26	1	375	13	0	552	1	1
2014 Nov	499	36	0	674	25	1	364	10	0	549	1	1
2014 Dec	540	70	1	736	85	1	378	27	0	554	1	1
2015 Jan	505	36	0	671	21	1	370	14	0	551	0	1
2015 Feb	502	40	1	708	54	0	381	23	1	551	2	1
2015 Mar	625	162	1	783	124	1	398	35	0	548	2	0
2015 Apr	504	41	1	698	46	1	388	18	0	552	1	1
2015 May	522	64	0	684	36	1	392	14	1	552	1	0
2015 Jun	530	64	3	696	46	1	389	13	1	551	2	0
2015 Jul	569	97	1	693	50	1	383	13	0	554	4	0
2015 Aug	506	35	1	674	34	2	383	11	0	552	2	1
2015 Sep	506	32	0	662	20	0	377	11	0	561	8	1
2015 Oct	510	38	1	669	29	1	384	12	0	556	2	1
2015 Nov	499	29	0	667	23	1	381	11	0	553	1	1
2015 Dec	520	45	0	731	78	1	394	22	0	550	1	0
2016 Jan	509	33	0	678	25	1	395	17	1	556	0	1
2016 Feb (r)	517	38	0	703	56	1	405	22	0	555	1	0
2016 Mar (p)	692	207	1	765	119	2	415	34	0	553	2	0

p = Provisional

r = Revised

Source: Monthly wages and salaries survey
Inquiries: Email: ster@ons.gsi.gov.uk
Tel: 01633 456773

4.14a Average Weekly Earnings by Industry (Not Seasonally Adjusted)

All figures are in pounds (£)

CDID	Education (P) Average Weekly Earnings	Of which Bonuses	Of which Arrears	Health and Social Work (Q) Average Weekly Earnings	Of which Bonuses	Of which Arrears	Arts, Entertainment and (R) Average Weekly Earnings	Of which Bonuses	Of which Arrears	Other Service Activities (S) Average Weekly Earnings	Of which Bonuses	Of which Arrears
	K58R	K58S	K58T	K58U	K58V	K58W	K5EI	K5EJ	K5EK	K58X	K58Y	K58Z
2010 Jan	393	1	1	388	1	0	322	17	0	401	16	0
2010 Feb	392	1	0	392	1	0	307	9	0	368	14	0
2010 Mar	393	2	0	390	1	0	333	35	0	411	63	1
2010 Apr	395	1	0	397	0	0	302	8	0	365	15	0
2010 May	394	1	0	398	0	0	304	8	0	353	11	0
2010 Jun	394	1	0	399	0	0	309	11	1	360	8	1
2010 Jul	397	2	0	396	0	0	319	10	1	356	7	0
2010 Aug	398	1	0	395	0	0	325	10	0	359	11	0
2010 Sep	404	1	1	397	0	0	323	6	0	352	8	0
2010 Oct	400	1	1	396	0	0	315	5	0	345	8	0
2010 Nov	400	1	1	398	0	0	317	8	0	354	13	0
2010 Dec	401	1	0	398	1	0	328	15	0	353	10	0
2011 Jan	397	0	0	398	0	0	329	13	0	350	14	1
2011 Feb	398	0	1	398	1	1	319	15	1	361	17	1
2011 Mar	401	2	0	398	1	0	331	23	0	400	50	1
2011 Apr	403	1	0	400	1	0	314	9	0	363	12	0
2011 May	400	1	0	401	0	0	311	10	2	355	10	1
2011 Jun	401	1	0	401	0	0	312	9	0	358	8	1
2011 Jul	402	1	0	399	1	0	320	13	0	362	11	1
2011 Aug	407	1	0	397	0	0	327	17	0	357	8	1
2011 Sep	409	1	0	400	1	0	323	12	0	355	8	0
2011 Oct	404	1	0	399	1	0	313	5	0	357	7	0
2011 Nov	401	1	0	401	0	0	323	9	0	364	13	1
2011 Dec	401	2	0	402	1	0	339	14	0	365	14	0
2012 Jan	395	0	0	402	0	0	342	16	0	352	14	1
2012 Feb	396	1	0	403	1	0	331	7	0	350	19	0
2012 Mar	398	1	0	403	2	0	340	26	0	348	22	0
2012 Apr	400	1	0	404	0	0	331	10	1	343	12	0
2012 May	399	1	0	407	0	0	334	11	0	341	12	0
2012 Jun	402	1	0	404	0	0	361	24	0	346	15	0
2012 Jul	402	1	0	405	1	0	346	11	1	342	13	0
2012 Aug	409	1	0	404	1	0	358	10	0	344	12	0
2012 Sep	411	1	0	403	1	0	361	13	0	332	7	0
2012 Oct	407	0	0	404	1	0	349	6	0	329	8	0
2012 Nov	406	0	0	406	0	0	355	13	0	337	13	0
2012 Dec	407	1	1	407	1	0	371	14	0	341	14	0
2013 Jan	402	1	1	409	0	0	363	16	0	342	11	0
2013 Feb	399	0	0	402	1	0	354	5	0	338	11	0
2013 Mar	400	2	0	404	2	0	356	19	0	344	20	0
2013 Apr	403	0	0	410	1	0	361	18	0	346	13	0
2013 May	404	1	0	408	1	0	364	19	0	346	9	0
2013 Jun	404	1	0	406	1	0	372	18	0	349	7	0
2013 Jul	406	1	0	406	1	0	362	10	0	347	10	0
2013 Aug	411	1	1	401	0	0	365	12	0	348	9	0
2013 Sep	414	0	0	404	1	0	364	19	0	341	6	0
2013 Oct	413	1	1	403	1	0	348	4	0	353	6	5
2013 Nov	411	1	1	404	1	0	350	13	0	356	9	1
2013 Dec	415	1	1	406	1	0	346	14	0	360	10	0
2014 Jan	408	0	0	408	1	0	364	12	1	362	13	1
2014 Feb	409	0	0	404	1	0	335	6	0	437	79	0
2014 Mar	410	3	0	403	1	0	330	13	0	390	30	2
2014 Apr	412	1	1	407	1	0	353	14	0	369	15	0
2014 May	413	1	2	408	1	0	346	13	0	368	11	1
2014 Jun	412	1	0	408	1	0	357	15	0	364	8	0
2014 Jul	414	1	0	405	0	0	353	7	0	369	12	0
2014 Aug	421	1	0	402	1	0	342	6	1	373	12	0
2014 Sep	424	1	0	408	1	0	348	16	0	373	7	1
2014 Oct	421	1	0	406	0	0	338	9	1	372	9	0
2014 Nov	418	1	0	408	1	0	341	8	1	356	10	0
2014 Dec	425	2	2	408	1	0	347	19	1	364	15	0
2015 Jan	419	1	0	410	1	0	357	15	1	360	16	0
2015 Feb	417	0	0	407	0	0	337	11	0	362	17	0
2015 Mar	419	3	0	408	1	0	348	22	0	381	34	0
2015 Apr	419	1	0	412	1	0	355	25	0	369	19	0
2015 May	418	0	0	414	1	0	343	11	0	366	13	0
2015 Jun	421	2	0	414	0	0	375	19	0	369	12	0
2015 Jul	422	1	0	411	0	0	381	17	1	370	16	0
2015 Aug	427	2	0	407	0	0	374	20	0	367	15	0
2015 Sep	430	1	0	412	2	0	390	30	0	358	10	0
2015 Oct	426	1	0	408	0	0	356	11	0	359	10	0
2015 Nov	426	1	2	410	1	0	354	7	0	361	10	0
2015 Dec	428	1	1	411	1	0	367	15	3	367	17	0
2016 Jan	424	2	1	412	1	0	375	10	0	386	24	1
2016 Feb (r)	423	1	0	412	0	1	366	11	0	383	21	0
2016 Mar (p)	423	1	0	411	1	1	370	15	0	395	31	0

p = Provisional

r = Revised

Source: Monthly wages and salaries survey

Inquiries: Email: ster@ons.gsi.gov.uk

Tel: 01633 456773

4.14b Average Weekly Earnings - Regular Pay

Great Britain, seasonally adjusted

	Whole Economy			Private sector [3 4 5]			Public sector [3 4 5]		
	Weekly Earnings (£)	% changes year on year		Weekly Earnings (£)	% changes year on year		Weekly Earnings (£)	% changes year on year	
		Single month	3 month average [2]		Single month	3 month average [2]		Single month	3 month average [2]
	KAI7	KAI8	KAI9	KAJ2	KAJ3	KAJ4	KAJ5	KAJ6	KAJ7
Jan 03	334	3.4	3.1	330	3.2	2.8	348	4.1	4.2
Feb 03	335	2.9	3.1	331	2.5	2.7	350	4.4	4.3
Mar 03	335	2.9	3.1	331	2.4	2.7	351	4.3	4.3
Apr 03	336	3.0	3.0	332	2.6	2.5	352	4.5	4.4
May 03	337	3.3	3.1	333	3.0	2.7	353	4.3	4.4
Jun 03	338	2.9	3.1	334	2.3	2.6	355	4.4	4.4
Jul 03	339	2.9	3.0	334	2.4	2.6	359	4.8	4.5
Aug 03	340	3.6	3.1	334	2.7	2.5	362	6.3	5.2
Sep 03	341	3.6	3.4	336	3.0	2.7	361	5.6	5.6
Oct 03	342	3.7	3.6	337	3.2	3.0	361	4.9	5.6
Nov 03	344	3.8	3.7	338	3.4	3.2	363	4.9	5.2
Dec 03	345	4.3	3.9	340	4.1	3.6	363	4.6	4.8
Jan 04	345	3.4	3.8	340	3.1	3.5	364	4.5	4.7
Feb 04	346	3.3	3.7	340	2.8	3.3	365	4.1	4.4
Mar 04	347	3.4	3.4	341	3.1	3.0	366	4.3	4.3
Apr 04	348	3.5	3.4	343	3.2	3.0	369	4.7	4.4
May 04	350	3.6	3.5	344	3.2	3.2	370	4.9	4.6
Jun 04	351	3.7	3.6	345	3.4	3.3	371	4.5	4.7
Jul 04	352	3.8	3.7	346	3.7	3.4	373	4.0	4.5
Aug 04	353	3.9	3.8	348	4.0	3.7	375	3.5	4.0
Sep 04	354	3.7	3.8	348	3.5	3.7	376	4.2	3.9
Oct 04	356	3.9	3.8	350	3.7	3.7	378	4.7	4.1
Nov 04	356	3.7	3.8	350	3.5	3.6	379	4.3	4.4
Dec 04	359	4.1	3.9	354	4.1	3.8	378	4.1	4.4
Jan 05	360	4.2	4.0	353	3.9	3.8	382	4.9	4.4
Feb 05	360	4.2	4.1	354	4.2	4.0	383	4.9	4.7
Mar 05	362	4.4	4.3	356	4.2	4.1	386	5.4	5.1
Apr 05	363	4.3	4.3	357	4.0	4.1	389	5.4	5.3
May 05	364	4.2	4.3	357	3.7	4.0	391	5.5	5.4
Jun 05	365	4.2	4.2	358	3.9	3.9	391	5.3	5.4
Jul 05	367	4.4	4.3	361	4.2	3.9	392	5.1	5.3
Aug 05	369	4.4	4.3	362	4.1	4.1	394	5.0	5.1
Sep 05	370	4.6	4.5	363	4.4	4.2	396	5.2	5.1
Oct 05	371	4.2	4.4	363	4.0	4.2	397	5.1	5.1
Nov 05	371	4.2	4.3	364	4.0	4.1	398	5.2	5.2
Dec 05	372	3.7	4.0	365	3.3	3.8	400	5.7	5.3
Jan 06	374	4.1	4.0	367	4.0	3.8	400	4.8	5.2
Feb 06	375	4.2	4.0	369	4.0	3.7	403	5.2	5.2
Mar 06	376	3.8	4.1	370	4.0	4.0	400	3.6	4.5
Apr 06	377	3.7	3.9	371	4.0	4.0	401	3.1	3.9
May 06	379	4.0	3.8	373	4.5	4.1	401	2.6	3.1
Jun 06	381	4.2	4.0	374	4.5	4.3	405	3.4	3.0
Jul 06	381	3.6	3.9	374	3.7	4.2	405	3.3	3.1
Aug 06	381	3.4	3.7	375	3.6	3.9	405	3.0	3.3
Sep 06	383	3.5	3.5	377	3.9	3.7	406	2.6	3.0
Oct 06	386	4.0	3.7	379	4.4	4.0	409	2.9	2.9
Nov 06	386	4.0	3.8	380	4.4	4.2	409	2.7	2.8
Dec 06	388	4.1	4.0	382	4.5	4.4	412	3.0	2.9
Jan 07	388	3.7	3.9	381	3.8	4.2	414	3.4	3.0
Feb 07	390	3.8	3.9	384	4.2	4.1	413	2.7	3.0
Mar 07	392	4.2	3.9	386	4.3	4.1	415	3.6	3.3
Apr 07	392	4.0	4.0	386	4.2	4.2	414	3.3	3.2
May 07	395	4.2	4.1	389	4.4	4.3	416	3.7	3.6
Jun 07	397	4.2	4.1	391	4.5	4.3	417	3.1	3.4
Jul 07	398	4.6	4.3	393	5.1	4.7	417	3.0	3.3
Aug 07	400	4.9	4.6	395	5.2	4.9	419	3.4	3.2
Sep 07	400	4.5	4.7	395	4.8	5.1	420	3.4	3.3
Oct 07	401	3.9	4.4	395	4.1	4.7	421	2.9	3.2
Nov 07	403	4.2	4.2	397	4.5	4.5	423	3.3	3.2
Dec 07	403	4.0	4.0	397	4.1	4.3	425	3.2	3.1
Jan 08	404	4.1	4.1	398	4.5	4.4	426	3.0	3.1
Feb 08	406	4.2	4.1	401	4.4	4.3	429	3.7	3.3
Mar 08	408	4.1	4.1	402	4.1	4.3	430	3.8	3.5
Apr 08	411	4.8	4.4	405	4.8	4.4	433	4.4	4.0
May 08	409	3.8	4.2	404	3.7	4.2	431	3.6	4.0
Jun 08	411	3.5	4.0	405	3.7	4.1	430	3.0	3.7
Jul 08	412	3.4	3.6	406	3.2	3.5	433	3.9	3.5
Aug 08	413	3.3	3.4	407	3.1	3.3	435	3.7	3.5
Sep 08	414	3.3	3.3	408	3.1	3.2	436	3.8	3.8
Oct 08	415	3.6	3.4	409	3.6	3.3	436	3.6	3.7

4.14b Average Weekly Earnings - Regular Pay

Great Britain, seasonally adjusted

Standard Industrial Classification (2007)

	Whole Economy				Private sector [3][4][5]				Public sector [3][4][5]		
	Weekly Earnings (£)	% changes year on year		Weekly Earnings (£)	% changes year on year		Weekly Earnings (£)	% changes year on year	
		Single month	3 month average [2]		Single month	3 month average [2]		Single month	3 month average [2]
	KAI7	KAI8	KAI9	KAJ2	KAJ3	KAJ4	KAJ5	KAJ6	KAJ7
Nov 08	416	3.2	3.4	410	3.1	3.3	437	3.5	3.6
Dec 08	416	3.1	3.3	410	3.1	3.2	438	3.1	3.4
Jan 09	416	2.8	3.1	410	2.8	3.0	439	3.0	3.2
Feb 09	417	2.6	2.9	410	2.4	2.8	442	3.0	3.0
Mar 09	417	2.1	2.5	410	2.2	2.5	440	2.3	2.7
Apr 09	418	1.8	2.2	411	1.5	2.0	444	2.6	2.6
May 09	419	2.2	2.1	411	1.9	1.9	446	3.5	2.8
Jun 09	419	2.0	2.0	411	1.4	1.6	448	4.3	3.5
Jul 09	418	1.4	1.9	408	0.6	1.3	450	3.7	3.9
Aug 09	418	1.3	1.6	409	0.4	0.8	451	3.7	3.9
Sep 09	419	1.4	1.4	410	0.5	0.5	452	3.8	3.7
Oct 09	419	1.0	1.2	410	0.1	0.3	452	3.7	3.7
Nov 09	420	1.0	1.1	410	0.0	0.2	455	3.9	3.8
Dec 09	421	1.3	1.1	411	0.4	0.2	455	4.0	3.9
Jan 10	423	1.8	1.4	414	1.0	0.5	457	4.2	4.0
Feb 10	423	1.5	1.6	413	0.6	0.7	459	3.8	4.0
Mar 10	425	2.1	1.8	416	1.3	1.0	457	3.8	4.0
Apr 10	424	1.4	1.7	414	0.6	0.9	460	3.6	3.7
May 10	424	1.2	1.6	413	0.4	0.8	461	3.2	3.5
Jun 10	425	1.4	1.3	414	0.8	0.6	460	2.6	3.1
Jul 10	427	2.2	1.6	416	1.9	1.0	462	2.7	2.8
Aug 10	428	2.3	2.0	417	2.2	1.6	463	2.5	2.6
Sep 10	428	2.2	2.2	417	1.8	2.0	464	2.7	2.6
Oct 10	429	2.2	2.2	418	2.0	2.0	466	3.1	2.8
Nov 10	430	2.4	2.3	418	2.2	2.0	467	2.8	2.8
Dec 10	429	1.9	2.2	418	1.5	1.9	468	2.8	2.9
Jan 11	433	2.2	2.2	422	1.9	1.9	470	2.7	2.8
Feb 11	432	2.1	2.1	420	1.9	1.8	471	2.6	2.7
Mar 11	432	1.7	2.0	420	1.1	1.6	472	3.2	2.9
Apr 11	433	2.1	1.9	421	1.8	1.6	471	2.6	2.8
May 11	433	2.3	2.0	422	2.3	1.8	472	2.4	2.7
Jun 11	433	2.0	2.1	422	1.9	2.0	471	2.5	2.5
Jul 11	434	1.6	2.0	423	1.7	2.0	471	2.1	2.3
Aug 11	434	1.5	1.7	423	1.4	1.7	472	2.1	2.2
Sep 11	436	1.7	1.6	425	1.7	1.6	474	2.1	2.1
Oct 11	437	1.8	1.7	426	1.9	1.7	475	1.9	2.0
Nov 11	438	1.8	1.8	427	2.0	1.9	476	1.8	1.9
Dec 11	438	1.9	1.9	427	2.2	2.0	475	1.3	1.7
Jan 12	437	1.0	1.6	427	1.2	1.8	474	1.0	1.4
Feb 12	439	1.7	1.5	429	2.0	1.8	476	1.2	1.2
Mar 12	441	1.9	1.5	430	2.2	1.8	477	1.2	1.1
Apr 12	440	1.7	1.8	429	2.0	2.1	478	1.4	1.3
May 12	441	1.7	1.8	430	1.9	2.0	479	1.4	1.3
Jun 12	442	2.0	1.8	431	2.2	2.0	482	2.3	1.7
Jul 12	442	1.9	1.9	431	1.9	2.0	484	2.7	2.2
Aug 12	444	2.1	2.0	432	2.1	2.0	487	3.1	2.7
Sep 12	442	1.5	1.9	431	1.6	1.8	484	2.2	2.7
Oct 12	442	1.3	1.6	431	1.3	1.7	484	1.9	2.4
Nov 12	444	1.4	1.4	433	1.5	1.5	484	1.8	2.0
Dec 12	443	1.2	1.3	432	1.3	1.4	483	1.8	1.8
Jan 13	442	1.1	1.2	431	1.0	1.2	483	1.9	1.8
Feb 13	443	0.7	1.0	432	0.8	1.0	482	1.1	1.6
Mar 13	443	0.6	0.8	432	0.6	0.8	483	1.3	1.4
Apr 13	446	1.4	0.9	436	1.5	1.0	485	1.4	1.3
May 13	446	1.1	1.0	435	1.1	1.0	485	1.4	1.4
Jun 13	446	0.9	1.1	436	1.1	1.2	485	0.5	1.1
Jul 13	446	1.0	1.0	436	1.3	1.1	485	0.2	0.7
Aug 13	446	0.6	0.8	436	1.0	1.1	483	-0.7	0.0
Sep 13	446	0.8	0.8	436	1.0	1.1	485	0.1	-0.1
Oct 13	447	1.0	0.8	437	1.3	1.1	487	0.6	0.0
Nov 13	447	0.7	0.8	437	1.0	1.1	486	0.3	0.4
Dec 13	449	1.3	1.0	439	1.6	1.3	488	1.0	0.6
Jan 14	450	1.7	1.2	440	2.2	1.6	488	0.9	0.7
Feb 14	448	1.2	1.4	438	1.4	1.7	487	1.2	1.0
Mar 14	447	1.0	1.3	437	1.1	1.6	489	1.2	1.1
Apr 14	448	0.5	0.9	439	0.7	1.1	487	0.5	0.9
May 14	449	0.7	0.7	440	1.1	1.0	487	0.3	0.7
Jun 14	449	0.8	0.7	440	1.1	1.0	488	0.7	0.5
Jul 14	450	0.8	0.8	441	1.0	1.1	488	0.8	0.6
Aug 14	451	1.1	0.9	443	1.4	1.2	489	1.3	0.9

4.14b Average Weekly Earnings - Regular Pay

Great Britain, seasonally adjusted

Standard Industrial Classification (2007)

	Whole Economy				Private sector [345]				Public sector [345]		
	Weekly Earnings (£)	% changes year on year		Weekly Earnings (£)	% changes year on year			Weekly Earnings (£)	% changes year on year	
		Single month	3 month average [2]		Single month	3 month average [2]			Single month	3 month average [2]
	KAI7	KAI8	KAI9	KAJ2	KAJ3	KAJ4		KAJ5	KAJ6	KAJ7
Sep 14	454	1.8	1.2	446	2.3	1.6		489	0.9	1.0
Oct 14	456	2.0	1.7	448	2.5	2.1		490	0.5	0.9
Nov 14	455	1.8	1.9	447	2.1	2.3		489	0.8	0.7
Dec 14	456	1.7	1.8	448	2.0	2.2		491	0.6	0.6
Jan 15	457	1.6	1.7	449	1.9	2.0		491	0.7	0.7

Source: Monthly Wages & Salaries Survey

Inquiries Email: labour.market@ons.gsi.gov.uk

Tel: 01633 455400

Earnings enquiries: 01633 456773

1. Estimates of regular pay exclude bonuses and arrears of pay.

2. The three month average figures are the changes in the average seasonally adjusted values for the three months ending with the relevant month compared with the same period a year earlier.

3. From July 2009 Royal Bank of Scotland Group plc is classified to the public sector; for earlier time periods it is classified to the private sector. Between July 2009 and March 2014 Lloyds Banking Group plc is classified to the public sector; it is classified to the private sector for earlier and later time periods.

4. Between June 2010 and May 2012 English Further Education Corporations and Sixth Form College Corporations are classified to the public sector. Before June 2010 and after May 2012 they are classified to the private sector.

5. From October 2013 Royal Mail plc is classified to the private sector; previously it is in the public sector.

4.14b Average Weekly Earnings - Regular Pay

Great Britain, seasonally adjusted

	Services, SIC 2007 sections G-S			Finance and business services, SIC 2007 sections K-N			Public sector excluding financial services [4][5]		
	Weekly Earnings (£)	% changes year on year		Weekly Earnings (£)	% changes year on year		Weekly Earnings (£)	% changes year on year	
		Single month	3 month average [2]		Single month	3 month average [2]		Single month	3 month average [2]
	K5DL	K5DM	K5DN	K5DO	K5DP	K5DQ	KAK6	KAK7	KAK8
Jan 03	319	3.7	3.3	390	3.4	2.4	348	4.2	4.3
Feb 03	320	3.1	3.3	392	2.9	2.5	350	4.3	4.3
Mar 03	321	2.9	3.3	392	2.9	3.1	351	4.3	4.3
Apr 03	322	3.3	3.1	393	3.0	2.9	352	4.6	4.4
May 03	323	3.5	3.3	395	3.9	3.3	352	4.1	4.3
Jun 03	324	2.9	3.2	393	2.7	3.2	355	4.6	4.4
Jul 03	324	3.2	3.2	393	2.7	3.1	359	4.7	4.4
Aug 03	326	4.0	3.4	393	2.8	2.7	362	6.4	5.2
Sep 03	327	3.9	3.7	395	2.8	2.8	361	5.6	5.6
Oct 03	328	4.0	4.0	398	3.3	3.0	361	5.0	5.7
Nov 03	329	4.0	4.0	398	3.0	3.0	362	4.8	5.2
Dec 03	330	4.6	4.2	399	4.4	3.6	364	4.7	4.9
Jan 04	331	3.5	4.0	399	2.5	3.3	363	4.3	4.6
Feb 04	331	3.3	3.8	398	1.7	2.8	366	4.7	4.6
Mar 04	331	3.3	3.4	400	2.1	2.1	367	4.5	4.5
Apr 04	333	3.6	3.4	402	2.1	2.0	369	4.6	4.6
May 04	334	3.7	3.5	405	2.6	2.3	370	5.0	4.7
Jun 04	336	3.8	3.7	404	2.6	2.5	371	4.5	4.7
Jul 04	337	3.9	3.8	405	3.0	2.8	372	3.9	4.4
Aug 04	338	3.9	3.8	407	3.6	3.1	375	3.6	4.0
Sep 04	339	3.8	3.9	409	3.4	3.3	376	4.1	3.9
Oct 04	341	4.2	4.0	410	3.1	3.4	378	4.6	4.1
Nov 04	341	3.9	4.0	411	3.2	3.2	379	4.5	4.4
Dec 04	345	4.5	4.2	415	4.1	3.5	379	4.0	4.4
Jan 05	345	4.4	4.2	416	4.2	3.8	382	5.0	4.5
Feb 05	346	4.7	4.5	420	5.5	4.6	382	4.3	4.5
Mar 05	348	5.1	4.7	422	5.4	5.0	386	5.3	4.9
Apr 05	349	4.8	4.8	423	5.2	5.4	388	5.4	5.0
May 05	350	4.7	4.8	423	4.5	5.0	391	5.7	5.4
Jun 05	351	4.7	4.7	423	4.7	4.8	390	5.2	5.4
Jul 05	354	5.0	4.8	429	5.9	5.0	392	5.2	5.4
Aug 05	355	4.8	4.8	429	5.3	5.3	394	5.1	5.1
Sep 05	356	5.0	4.9	430	5.3	5.5	396	5.2	5.1
Oct 05	356	4.4	4.7	430	4.9	5.1	397	5.1	5.1
Nov 05	357	4.5	4.6	431	4.7	5.0	398	5.2	5.2
Dec 05	358	3.8	4.2	430	3.6	4.4	399	5.5	5.3
Jan 06	360	4.4	4.2	435	4.5	4.3	400	4.7	5.1
Feb 06	360	4.1	4.1	433	3.1	3.7	402	5.4	5.2
Mar 06	361	3.8	4.1	439	4.0	3.8	400	3.6	4.5
Apr 06	362	3.6	3.9	439	3.9	3.7	400	3.1	4.0
May 06	363	3.7	3.7	440	4.0	4.0	401	2.6	3.1
Jun 06	366	4.1	3.8	443	4.9	4.3	404	3.4	3.0
Jul 06	366	3.4	3.7	443	3.3	4.0	405	3.5	3.2
Aug 06	366	3.3	3.6	445	3.8	4.0	405	2.9	3.3
Sep 06	368	3.4	3.3	446	3.6	3.6	406	2.7	3.0
Oct 06	370	4.0	3.5	447	4.0	3.8	408	2.8	2.8
Nov 06	371	4.0	3.8	448	3.9	3.8	409	2.8	2.8
Dec 06	373	4.2	4.1	452	5.0	4.3	411	3.0	2.9
Jan 07	372	3.5	3.9	444	2.2	3.7	414	3.7	3.1
Feb 07	375	4.1	3.9	450	4.0	3.7	413	2.7	3.1
Mar 07	376	4.1	3.9	452	3.1	3.1	414	3.7	3.4
Apr 07	377	4.2	4.1	455	3.7	3.6	413	3.3	3.2
May 07	380	4.6	4.3	459	4.2	3.6	415	3.6	3.5
Jun 07	381	4.3	4.4	461	4.0	3.9	416	3.1	3.3
Jul 07	382	4.5	4.5	463	4.5	4.2	417	2.8	3.1
Aug 07	384	4.8	4.6	464	4.1	4.2	419	3.5	3.1
Sep 07	385	4.6	4.6	467	4.8	4.5	420	3.3	3.2
Oct 07	385	3.9	4.4	468	4.6	4.5	421	3.1	3.3
Nov 07	387	4.3	4.3	471	5.3	4.9	422	3.1	3.2
Dec 07	388	4.0	4.1	473	4.7	4.8	425	3.4	3.2
Jan 08	389	4.3	4.2	470	5.8	5.2	426	2.8	3.1
Feb 08	390	4.1	4.1	475	5.5	5.3	428	3.6	3.3
Mar 08	393	4.3	4.2	476	5.2	5.5	430	3.8	3.4
Apr 08	395	4.9	4.4	479	5.2	5.3	431	4.4	3.9
May 08	394	3.7	4.3	477	4.0	4.8	431	3.7	4.0
Jun 08	395	3.5	4.0	483	4.7	4.6	428	2.9	3.7
Jul 08	396	3.7	3.6	486	5.1	4.6	433	4.0	3.6
Aug 08	398	3.6	3.6	489	5.4	5.1	434	3.6	3.5
Sep 08	399	3.6	3.7	489	4.7	5.1	435	3.8	3.8
Oct 08	400	3.9	3.7	490	4.7	4.9	436	3.5	3.6

4.14b Average Weekly Earnings - Regular Pay

Great Britain, seasonally adjusted

	Services, SIC 2007 sections G-S			Finance and business services, SIC 2007 sections K-N			Public sector excluding financial services [4][5]		
	Weekly Earnings (£)	% changes year on year		Weekly Earnings (£)	% changes year on year		Weekly Earnings (£)	% changes year on year	
		Single month	3 month average [2]		Single month	3 month average [2]		Single month	3 month average [2]
	K5DL	K5DM	K5DN	K5DO	K5DP	K5DQ	KAK6	KAK7	KAK8
Nov 08	400	3.3	3.6	490	4.0	4.5	437	3.6	3.6
Dec 08	400	3.3	3.5	488	3.3	4.0	438	3.0	3.4
Jan 09	400	3.0	3.2	490	4.4	3.9	439	3.0	3.2
Feb 09	402	3.1	3.1	491	3.4	3.7	441	3.1	3.1
Mar 09	402	2.3	2.8	493	3.6	3.8	439	2.0	2.7
Apr 09	403	2.0	2.5	494	3.1	3.4	443	2.8	2.7
May 09	404	2.6	2.3	494	3.6	3.4	445	3.3	2.7
Jun 09	404	2.4	2.3	494	2.5	3.1	447	4.3	3.5
Jul 09	404	1.8	2.3	494	1.6	2.5	446	2.8	3.5
Aug 09	403	1.4	1.9	495	1.2	1.7	448	3.1	3.4
Sep 09	404	1.5	1.6	495	1.2	1.3	448	2.8	2.9
Oct 09	404	1.1	1.3	495	1.0	1.1	448	2.9	2.9
Nov 09	404	1.1	1.2	498	1.6	1.3	450	2.8	2.8
Dec 09	405	1.2	1.1	498	2.0	1.5	451	2.8	2.8
Jan 10	408	1.8	1.4	502	2.3	1.9	452	2.9	2.9
Feb 10	407	1.2	1.4	498	1.3	1.8	453	2.7	2.8
Mar 10	409	1.8	1.6	506	2.7	2.1	452	3.1	2.9
Apr 10	408	1.2	1.4	503	1.9	2.0	455	2.5	2.8
May 10	408	1.1	1.4	504	2.0	2.2	456	2.4	2.6
Jun 10	409	1.2	1.2	504	1.9	1.9	453	1.5	2.1
Jul 10	412	2.1	1.5	511	3.5	2.4	457	2.5	2.1
Aug 10	413	2.3	1.9	513	3.7	3.0	457	2.0	2.0
Sep 10	414	2.3	2.2	515	4.2	3.8	459	2.7	2.4
Oct 10	414	2.3	2.3	518	4.6	4.2	460	2.6	2.4
Nov 10	415	2.6	2.4	519	4.3	4.4	462	2.7	2.7
Dec 10	415	2.4	2.5	523	5.0	4.6	463	2.8	2.7
Jan 11	418	2.6	2.5	530	5.6	5.0	464	2.8	2.8
Feb 11	418	2.5	2.5	526	5.6	5.4	465	2.5	2.7
Mar 11	418	2.0	2.4	525	3.8	5.0	466	3.1	2.8
Apr 11	418	2.5	2.4	527	4.8	4.7	465	2.3	2.6
May 11	419	2.7	2.4	531	5.4	4.7	465	2.0	2.5
Jun 11	419	2.3	2.5	531	5.4	5.2	465	2.5	2.3
Jul 11	419	1.8	2.3	531	3.9	4.9	464	1.6	2.1
Aug 11	419	1.6	1.9	529	3.1	4.1	466	2.1	2.1
Sep 11	421	1.7	1.7	533	3.4	3.4	467	1.6	1.8
Oct 11	422	2.1	1.8	537	3.8	3.4	467	1.5	1.8
Nov 11	423	1.9	1.9	537	3.4	3.5	467	1.1	1.4
Dec 11	423	2.0	2.0	541	3.4	3.5	467	0.8	1.1
Jan 12	422	1.0	1.7	537	1.4	2.8	466	0.4	0.7
Feb 12	425	1.7	1.6	540	2.8	2.6	469	0.9	0.7
Mar 12	425	1.9	1.6	543	3.3	2.5	470	0.8	0.7
Apr 12	425	1.6	1.7	541	2.6	2.9	470	1.1	0.9
May 12	426	1.5	1.7	540	1.7	2.6	470	1.2	1.0
Jun 12	427	1.9	1.7	542	2.2	2.2	474	2.1	1.4
Jul 12	427	1.8	1.8	540	1.7	1.9	476	2.6	2.0
Aug 12	429	2.3	2.0	542	2.5	2.1	479	2.7	2.5
Sep 12	428	1.6	1.9	540	1.5	1.9	477	2.1	2.5
Oct 12	428	1.3	1.7	538	0.1	1.4	477	2.0	2.3
Nov 12	429	1.5	1.5	540	0.5	0.7	477	2.1	2.1
Dec 12	429	1.3	1.4	538	-0.5	0.1	475	1.9	2.0
Jan 13	427	1.2	1.3	537	0.0	0.0	476	2.0	2.0
Feb 13	427	0.6	1.0	539	-0.3	-0.3	474	1.0	1.7
Mar 13	428	0.5	0.7	538	-0.8	-0.4	475	1.1	1.4
Apr 13	430	1.2	0.7	540	-0.1	-0.4	477	1.5	1.2
May 13	430	1.0	0.9	539	-0.3	-0.4	478	1.6	1.4
Jun 13	430	0.8	1.0	536	-1.1	-0.5	477	0.6	1.2
Jul 13	431	1.0	0.9	538	-0.4	-0.6	478	0.4	0.8
Aug 13	431	0.4	0.8	536	-1.0	-0.9	477	-0.3	0.2
Sep 13	431	0.7	0.7	535	-1.1	-0.8	478	0.4	0.2
Oct 13	432	0.9	0.7	534	-0.7	-0.9	481	0.9	0.3
Nov 13	431	0.5	0.7	534	-1.0	-0.9	480	0.8	0.7
Dec 13	434	1.1	0.8	539	0.2	-0.5	481	1.2	0.9
Jan 14	433	1.3	1.0	536	-0.2	-0.4	482	1.4	1.1
Feb 14	431	1.0	1.1	533	-1.2	-0.4	482	1.8	1.5
Mar 14	432	1.0	1.1	538	-0.1	-0.5	482	1.4	1.5
Apr 14	432	0.5	0.8	535	-1.0	-0.8	482	1.2	1.4
May 14	433	0.6	0.7	535	-0.7	-0.6	483	1.2	1.2
Jun 14	434	0.8	0.6	536	0.1	-0.5	484	1.4	1.2
Jul 14	434	0.6	0.7	538	0.0	-0.2	484	1.2	1.3
Aug 14	436	1.1	0.8	543	1.3	0.5	484	1.4	1.3

4.14b Average Weekly Earnings - Regular Pay

Great Britain, seasonally adjusted

Standard Industrial Classification (2007)

	Services, SIC 2007 sections G-S			Finance and business services, SIC 2007 sections K-N			Public sector excluding financial services [4][5]		
	Weekly Earnings (£)	% changes year on year		Weekly Earnings (£)	% changes year on year		Weekly Earnings (£)	% changes year on year	
		Single month	3 month average [2]		Single month	3 month average [2]		Single month	3 month average [2]
	K5DL	K5DM	K5DN	K5DO	K5DP	K5DQ	KAK6	KAK7	KAK8
Sep 14	439	1.9	1.2	548	2.5	1.3	485	1.4	1.4
Oct 14	440	2.0	1.7	552	3.4	2.4	486	1.0	1.3
Nov 14	439	1.8	1.9	548	2.6	2.8	486	1.1	1.2
Dec 14	441	1.7	1.9	548	1.6	2.5	488	1.5	1.2
Jan 15	442	2.1	1.9	550	2.6	2.2	488	1.1	1.2

Source: Monthly Wages & Salaries Survey

Inquiries Email: labour.market@ons.gsi.gov.uk

Tel: 01633 455400

Earnings enquiries: 01633 456773

1. Estimates of regular pay exclude bonuses and arrears of pay.

2. The three month average figures are the changes in the average seasonally adjusted values for the three months ending with the relevant month compared with the same period a year earlier.

3. From July 2009 Royal Bank of Scotland Group plc is classified to the public sector; for earlier time periods it is classified to the private sector. Between July 2009 and March 2014 Lloyds Banking Group plc is classified to the public sector; it is classified to the private sector for earlier and later time periods.

4. Between June 2010 and May 2012 English Further Education Corporations and Sixth Form College Corporations are classified to the public sector. Before June 2010 and after May 2012 they are classified to the private sector.

5. From October 2013 Royal Mail plc is classified to the private sector; previously it is in the public sector.

4.14b Average Weekly Earnings - Regular Pay

Great Britain, seasonally adjusted

	Manufacturing, SIC 2007 section C			Construction, SIC 2007 section F			Wholesaling, retailing, hotels & restaurants, SIC 2007 sections G & I		
	Weekly Earnings (£)	% changes year on year		Weekly Earnings (£)	% changes year on year		Weekly Earnings (£)	% changes year on year	
		Single month	3 month average [2]		Single month	3 month average [2]		Single month	3 month average [2]
	K5DU	K5DV	K5DW	K5DX	K5DY	K5DZ	K5E2	K5E3	K5E4
Jan 03	389	3.1	3.2	407	4.5	2.9	223	5.4	4.5
Feb 03	390	2.9	3.2	411	3.1	3.1	221	4.1	4.5
Mar 03	389	2.9	3.0	412	3.7	3.8	221	3.2	4.2
Apr 03	392	2.9	2.9	414	5.0	3.9	222	3.4	3.6
May 03	394	2.8	2.9	412	3.3	4.0	223	3.5	3.4
Jun 03	396	3.0	2.9	418	5.0	4.4	223	1.6	2.8
Jul 03	397	2.9	2.9	414	3.6	4.0	222	1.5	2.2
Aug 03	398	3.2	3.1	415	4.1	4.2	223	1.6	1.6
Sep 03	401	4.0	3.4	420	4.8	4.2	224	2.1	1.8
Oct 03	401	3.6	3.6	421	5.3	4.7	223	1.8	1.9
Nov 03	402	4.3	4.0	421	3.9	4.7	224	2.1	2.0
Dec 03	405	4.1	4.0	427	5.9	5.0	226	3.2	2.4
Jan 04	406	4.4	4.2	426	4.6	4.8	226	1.7	2.3
Feb 04	407	4.5	4.3	427	3.9	4.8	227	2.6	2.5
Mar 04	410	5.2	4.7	431	4.8	4.4	227	2.8	2.4
Apr 04	409	4.4	4.7	432	4.3	4.3	229	3.3	2.9
May 04	412	4.6	4.8	431	4.6	4.6	230	3.1	3.1
Jun 04	414	4.6	4.5	426	1.9	3.6	231	3.7	3.4
Jul 04	416	4.9	4.7	427	3.2	3.2	232	4.2	3.7
Aug 04	417	4.7	4.7	433	4.4	3.2	232	4.1	4.0
Sep 04	418	4.4	4.7	426	1.5	3.0	232	3.8	4.0
Oct 04	421	5.0	4.7	424	0.6	2.2	234	4.7	4.2
Nov 04	422	4.8	4.7	426	1.2	1.1	234	4.2	4.2
Dec 04	421	4.0	4.6	428	0.4	0.7	236	4.5	4.5
Jan 05	422	4.0	4.2	439	3.0	1.5	237	4.5	4.4
Feb 05	423	3.9	3.9	425	-0.4	1.0	237	4.5	4.5
Mar 05	426	3.9	3.9	430	-0.4	0.7	238	4.6	4.5
Apr 05	427	4.5	4.1	429	-0.8	-0.5	239	4.1	4.4
May 05	427	3.7	4.0	432	0.3	-0.3	237	2.9	3.9
Jun 05	428	3.6	3.9	433	1.6	0.4	239	3.3	3.5
Jul 05	430	3.4	3.5	435	1.7	1.2	240	3.6	3.3
Aug 05	432	3.7	3.6	443	2.3	1.9	242	4.6	3.8
Sep 05	434	3.7	3.6	443	4.0	2.7	241	4.0	4.1
Oct 05	434	3.2	3.5	447	5.4	3.9	244	4.3	4.3
Nov 05	435	3.1	3.3	449	5.5	5.0	244	4.6	4.3
Dec 05	437	3.7	3.3	446	4.1	5.0	244	3.4	4.1
Jan 06	436	3.3	3.4	452	3.0	4.2	245	3.7	3.9
Feb 06	442	4.5	3.8	456	7.3	4.8	246	3.5	3.5
Mar 06	441	3.5	3.8	454	5.7	5.3	245	3.1	3.4
Apr 06	443	3.7	3.9	460	7.3	6.8	245	2.6	3.1
May 06	446	4.3	3.8	466	7.9	7.0	248	4.5	3.4
Jun 06	444	3.6	3.9	467	8.0	7.7	248	3.8	3.7
Jul 06	442	2.7	3.5	472	8.6	8.2	248	3.5	3.9
Aug 06	446	3.2	3.2	468	5.6	7.4	248	2.3	3.2
Sep 06	448	3.4	3.1	472	6.5	6.9	250	3.7	3.2
Oct 06	450	3.7	3.4	474	6.2	6.1	253	3.6	3.2
Nov 06	451	3.7	3.6	474	5.4	6.0	255	4.3	3.9
Dec 06	450	3.0	3.5	476	6.8	6.1	256	4.8	4.2
Jan 07	456	4.6	3.8	476	5.3	5.8	254	3.5	4.2
Feb 07	457	3.4	3.7	471	3.4	5.1	257	4.7	4.3
Mar 07	460	4.5	4.2	480	5.6	4.7	258	5.2	4.5
Apr 07	457	3.3	3.7	479	4.1	4.4	260	5.9	5.3
May 07	459	2.9	3.6	480	3.1	4.3	260	4.8	5.3
Jun 07	461	3.7	3.3	485	3.8	3.7	261	5.3	5.3
Jul 07	462	4.7	3.8	505	7.0	4.7	262	5.6	5.2
Aug 07	462	3.6	4.0	507	8.5	6.5	263	6.2	5.7
Sep 07	463	3.2	3.8	509	7.8	7.8	263	5.0	5.6
Oct 07	464	3.2	3.3	501	5.7	7.3	264	4.4	5.2
Nov 07	464	3.0	3.1	504	6.5	6.6	264	3.6	4.3
Dec 07	465	3.3	3.2	504	5.8	6.0	263	2.8	3.6
Jan 08	469	2.8	3.0	493	3.7	5.3	265	4.4	3.6
Feb 08	472	3.3	3.1	502	6.5	5.3	265	3.0	3.4
Mar 08	472	2.5	2.8	500	4.3	4.8	268	3.7	3.7
Apr 08	474	3.6	3.1	504	5.2	5.3	271	4.2	3.6
May 08	474	3.3	3.2	506	5.4	4.9	269	3.5	3.8
Jun 08	475	3.1	3.3	509	4.9	5.2	268	2.9	3.6
Jul 08	476	3.0	3.2	509	0.8	3.7	267	2.0	2.8
Aug 08	476	2.9	3.0	503	-0.9	1.6	269	2.1	2.3
Sep 08	476	2.9	2.9	511	0.3	0.1	270	2.9	2.3
Oct 08	477	2.8	2.9	515	2.6	0.7	269	2.2	2.4

4.14b Average Weekly Earnings - Regular Pay

Great Britain, seasonally adjusted

	Manufacturing, SIC 2007 section C			Construction, SIC 2007 section F			Wholesaling, retailing, hotels & restaurants, SIC 2007 sections G & I		
	Weekly Earnings (£)	% changes year on year		Weekly Earnings (£)	% changes year on year		Weekly Earnings (£)	% changes year on year	
		Single month	3 month average [2]		Single month	3 month average [2]		Single month	3 month average [2]
	K5DU	K5DV	K5DW	K5DX	K5DY	K5DZ	K5E2	K5E3	K5E4
Nov 08	481	3.5	3.1	514	1.8	1.6	268	1.5	2.2
Dec 08	480	3.2	3.2	513	1.9	2.1	271	2.9	2.2
Jan 09	479	2.1	2.9	516	4.6	2.8	271	2.2	2.2
Feb 09	478	1.2	2.2	514	2.3	2.9	274	3.5	2.8
Mar 09	478	1.2	1.5	515	2.9	3.3	272	1.7	2.5
Apr 09	480	1.3	1.2	516	2.5	2.6	271	0.1	1.7
May 09	481	1.6	1.4	514	1.6	2.3	272	1.1	1.0
Jun 09	484	2.0	1.6	506	-0.7	1.1	272	1.3	0.8
Jul 09	480	0.8	1.4	513	0.7	0.6	273	2.0	1.4
Aug 09	484	1.7	1.5	517	2.9	1.0	272	1.3	1.5
Sep 09	486	2.1	1.5	516	1.1	1.6	274	1.2	1.5
Oct 09	488	2.2	2.0	521	1.2	1.7	274	1.8	1.4
Nov 09	489	1.7	2.0	521	1.3	1.2	274	2.2	1.8
Dec 09	499	4.0	2.6	524	2.0	1.5	276	1.9	2.0
Jan 10	499	4.2	3.3	522	1.3	1.6	275	1.7	1.9
Feb 10	500	4.8	4.3	523	1.8	1.7	277	1.2	1.6
Mar 10	504	5.4	4.8	520	1.1	1.4	279	2.4	1.7
Apr 10	501	4.5	4.9	522	1.1	1.3	277	2.1	1.9
May 10	501	4.1	4.7	516	0.4	0.9	276	1.4	2.0
Jun 10	502	3.7	4.1	514	1.7	1.1	278	2.2	1.9
Jul 10	501	4.4	4.1	512	-0.2	0.6	278	2.0	1.9
Aug 10	504	4.3	4.1	512	-1.1	0.1	279	2.6	2.3
Sep 10	504	3.7	4.1	514	-0.4	-0.6	279	2.0	2.2
Oct 10	504	3.3	3.7	518	-0.6	-0.7	278	1.2	2.0
Nov 10	504	3.2	3.4	516	-0.8	-0.6	278	1.5	1.6
Dec 10	505	1.2	2.5	512	-2.3	-1.2	277	0.4	1.0
Jan 11	506	1.5	2.0	523	0.2	-1.0	279	1.3	1.0
Feb 11	505	0.9	1.2	526	0.5	-0.5	278	0.4	0.7
Mar 11	506	0.6	1.0	523	0.6	0.4	278	-0.2	0.5
Apr 11	506	0.9	0.8	518	-0.9	0.1	281	1.5	0.5
May 11	507	1.1	0.9	521	1.0	0.2	281	2.1	1.1
Jun 11	508	1.1	1.0	524	1.9	0.7	280	0.9	1.5
Jul 11	510	1.6	1.3	524	2.4	1.8	280	0.7	1.2
Aug 11	511	1.3	1.3	527	2.9	2.4	281	0.6	0.7
Sep 11	513	1.8	1.6	526	2.3	2.6	281	0.5	0.6
Oct 11	512	1.5	1.5	525	1.4	2.2	282	1.6	0.9
Nov 11	514	1.9	1.7	526	2.0	1.9	284	2.2	1.4
Dec 11	513	1.6	1.7	525	2.6	2.0	284	2.5	2.1
Jan 12	513	1.2	1.6	526	0.5	1.7	285	2.2	2.3
Feb 12	514	1.7	1.5	528	0.4	1.2	286	3.0	2.5
Mar 12	516	1.8	1.6	532	1.7	0.9	286	2.7	2.6
Apr 12	517	2.2	1.9	531	2.6	1.6	286	1.9	2.5
May 12	519	2.4	2.2	538	3.3	2.5	287	2.0	2.2
Jun 12	519	2.2	2.3	532	1.5	2.5	289	3.2	2.4
Jul 12	521	2.2	2.3	531	1.2	2.0	289	3.0	2.7
Aug 12	522	2.3	2.2	524	-0.5	0.8	288	2.7	3.0
Sep 12	522	1.8	2.1	523	-0.6	0.0	288	2.7	2.8
Oct 12	522	2.1	2.1	524	-0.2	-0.4	289	2.3	2.5
Nov 12	522	1.5	1.8	525	-0.2	-0.3	291	2.4	2.5
Dec 12	525	2.2	1.9	520	-0.8	-0.4	290	2.0	2.2
Jan 13	523	2.0	1.9	513	-2.5	-1.2	287	0.7	1.7
Feb 13	527	2.6	2.3	525	-0.6	-1.3	287	0.3	1.0
Mar 13	529	2.6	2.4	528	-0.9	-1.3	290	1.3	0.7
Apr 13	530	2.5	2.6	534	0.6	-0.3	291	1.9	1.1
May 13	530	2.2	2.4	534	-0.9	-0.4	291	1.5	1.6
Jun 13	531	2.4	2.4	528	-0.8	-0.4	294	1.8	1.7
Jul 13	532	2.1	2.2	526	-0.9	-0.9	296	2.7	2.0
Aug 13	532	1.8	2.1	530	1.2	-0.2	296	2.8	2.4
Sep 13	532	1.9	1.9	530	1.3	0.5	296	2.8	2.8
Oct 13	534	2.2	2.0	525	0.2	0.9	298	3.1	2.9
Nov 13	537	2.9	2.3	527	0.4	0.6	297	2.1	2.6
Dec 13	538	2.4	2.5	531	2.0	0.9	298	2.9	2.7
Jan 14	540	3.2	2.9	541	5.4	2.6	301	4.8	3.3
Feb 14	543	3.0	2.9	531	1.1	2.8	297	3.4	3.7
Mar 14	537	1.6	2.6	521	-1.3	1.7	296	2.3	3.5
Apr 14	540	1.8	2.1	527	-1.4	-0.5	297	1.9	2.5
May 14	540	1.9	1.8	528	-1.1	-1.2	298	2.3	2.2
Jun 14	541	1.8	1.8	531	0.6	-0.6	297	0.9	1.7
Jul 14	540	1.5	1.7	535	1.8	0.4	297	0.0	1.1
Aug 14	541	1.7	1.7	533	0.5	1.0	298	0.5	0.5

4.14b Average Weekly Earnings - Regular Pay

Great Britain, seasonally adjusted

	Manufacturing, SIC 2007 section C			Construction, SIC 2007 section F			Wholesaling, retailing, hotels & restaurants, SIC 2007 sections G & I		
	Weekly Earnings (£)	% changes year on year		Weekly Earnings (£)	% changes year on year		Weekly Earnings (£)	% changes year on year	
		Single month	3 month average [2]		Single month	3 month average [2]		Single month	3 month average [2]
	K5DU	K5DV	K5DW	K5DX	K5DY	K5DZ	K5E2	K5E3	K5E4
Sep 14	542	2.0	1.7	536	1.3	1.2	301	1.5	0.7
Oct 14	543	1.8	1.8	538	2.5	1.4	302	1.3	1.1
Nov 14	542	1.0	1.6	538	2.0	1.9	302	1.7	1.5
Dec 14	542	0.8	1.2	541	2.0	2.2	303	1.7	1.6
Jan 15	542	0.5	0.8	531	-1.8	0.7	306	1.9	1.8

Source: Monthly Wages & Salaries Survey

Inquiries Email: labour.market@ons.gsi.gov.uk

Tel: 01633 455400

Earnings enquiries: 01633 456773

1. Estimates of regular pay exclude bonuses and arrears of pay.

2. The three month average figures are the changes in the average seasonally adjusted values for the three months ending with the relevant month compared with the same period a year earlier.

3. From July 2009 Royal Bank of Scotland Group plc is classified to the public sector; for earlier time periods it is classified to the private sector. Between July 2009 and March 2014 Lloyds Banking Group plc is classified to the public sector; it is classified to the private sector for earlier and later time periods.

4. Between June 2010 and May 2012 English Further Education Corporations and Sixth Form College Corporations are classified to the public sector. Before June 2010 and after May 2012 they are classified to the private sector.

5. From October 2013 Royal Mail plc is classified to the private sector; previously it is in the public sector.

4.14c Average Weekly Earnings - Bonus Pay

Great Britain, seasonally adjusted

Standard Industrial Classification (2007)

	Whole Economy			Private sector [2][3][4]			Public sector [2][3][4]		
	Weekly Earnings (£)	% changes year on year		Weekly Earnings (£)	% changes year on year		Weekly Earnings (£)	% changes year on year	
		Single month	3 month average [1]		Single month	3 month average [1]		Single month	3 month average [1]
	KAF4	KAF5	KAF6	KAF7	KAF8	KAF9	KAG2	KAG3	KAG4
Jan 03	16	-13.7	-6.9	16	-18.2	-7.0	3	-12.5	35.1
Feb 03	17	-3.3	-7.0	19	-3.2	-7.9	3	-20.9	10.0
Mar 03	20	18.7	0.1	24	20.8	-0.4	3	-11.0	-15.0
Apr 03	16	-10.9	1.2	20	-5.6	3.7	3	-19.8	-17.4
May 03	17	-9.1	-0.8	19	-6.2	2.6	3	-28.5	-20.1
Jun 03	17	-3.7	-7.9	20	-4.3	-5.4	4	38.3	-5.8
Jul 03	18	-2.3	-5.1	22	2.0	-2.8	3	-9.6	-2.2
Aug 03	17	-7.2	-4.4	20	-6.0	-2.8	3	27.7	17.1
Sep 03	18	0.7	-3.0	22	3.6	-0.2	3	-8.6	0.5
Oct 03	20	15.2	2.7	24	18.1	5.0	3	-8.5	1.0
Nov 03	18	0.8	5.5	22	6.5	9.3	2	-28.7	-15.2
Dec 03	18	-0.7	5.0	21	4.7	9.7	3	3.4	-11.6
Jan 04	20	27.1	8.5	30	83.2	27.5	3	16.5	-4.0
Feb 04	17	-1.9	7.7	21	7.4	28.4	3	3.1	7.5
Mar 04	21	3.1	8.7	25	5.4	27.5	3	14.8	11.5
Apr 04	21	33.2	10.5	24	21.7	11.1	3	6.8	8.3
May 04	20	21.0	17.9	26	31.9	18.7	3	11.0	10.9
Jun 04	20	13.9	22.5	24	20.8	24.7	3	-20.8	-4.0
Jul 04	20	10.8	15.1	23	5.7	18.9	3	-4.4	-7.2
Aug 04	20	21.0	15.1	23	15.1	13.6	3	9.1	-7.2
Sep 04	22	21.3	17.7	26	17.9	12.8	3	-2.4	0.7
Oct 04	24	18.6	20.2	27	11.6	14.7	3	2.8	3.2
Nov 04	22	25.2	21.6	26	15.1	14.7	3	38.7	10.9
Dec 04	22	24.1	22.4	24	12.7	13.1	3	10.1	15.4
Jan 05	23	11.1	19.7	31	3.7	9.8	3	-2.4	13.0
Feb 05	21	23.0	18.9	25	20.2	11.1	3	7.4	4.9
Mar 05	21	2.5	11.5	25	2.3	7.8	3	-9.1	-1.8
Apr 05	22	4.6	9.1	26	8.1	9.7	4	18.8	5.1
May 05	22	11.2	6.0	26	1.0	3.8	4	21.6	9.5
Jun 05	21	9.0	8.2	26	8.3	5.7	4	10.2	16.6
Jul 05	22	13.2	11.1	26	14.0	7.5	4	38.0	22.6
Aug 05	26	26.1	16.2	30	26.8	16.3	4	32.5	26.4
Sep 05	24	8.9	16.0	28	9.2	16.4	5	55.3	41.6
Oct 05	24	-0.4	10.9	28	2.6	12.3	5	53.5	46.7
Nov 05	25	13.0	7.0	30	16.0	9.2	4	23.2	43.5
Dec 05	25	15.0	8.9	29	18.7	12.2	5	34.1	36.6
Jan 06	23	1.6	9.8	30	-4.9	8.8	6	69.9	42.2
Feb 06	25	21.0	12.3	30	18.7	9.6	5	54.3	52.3
Mar 06	27	25.7	15.8	32	24.6	11.5	5	51.8	58.8
Apr 06	26	17.2	21.3	31	18.4	20.6	5	36.7	47.1
May 06	26	17.7	20.1	30	17.0	20.0	5	37.4	41.5
Jun 06	29	34.0	22.8	34	32.4	22.6	5	28.0	34.0
Jul 06	29	28.4	26.6	34	29.2	26.2	5	19.4	27.9
Aug 06	28	8.6	22.8	32	9.7	23.1	5	7.9	17.9
Sep 06	25	5.7	13.8	29	5.3	14.3	4	-18.5	2.1
Oct 06	27	11.6	8.6	32	15.3	10.1	6	21.1	3.6
Nov 06	28	8.7	8.7	33	11.6	10.7	3	-20.3	-5.0
Dec 06	32	26.8	15.7	38	32.2	19.6	5	7.5	4.0
Jan 07	31	35.7	23.3	39	32.6	25.3	4	-22.8	-12.1
Feb 07	33	30.1	30.7	38	29.0	31.3	4	-29.3	-15.6
Mar 07	30	10.4	24.8	34	8.0	22.9	5	9.6	-14.8
Apr 07	29	11.2	17.0	34	12.1	16.1	5	4.2	-5.3
May 07	29	10.4	10.7	35	14.5	11.5	5	8.6	7.4
Jun 07	30	4.9	8.7	35	4.7	10.2	6	23.5	11.9
Jul 07	31	6.7	7.2	36	8.0	8.8	5	3.7	11.8
Aug 07	31	10.4	7.3	37	13.0	8.5	5	3.9	10.3
Sep 07	34	34.8	16.6	40	35.3	18.1	5	27.3	10.4
Oct 07	30	14.0	19.3	37	16.2	21.1	3	-49.4	-11.4
Nov 07	32	16.5	21.5	40	18.2	22.8	5	55.5	-0.2
Dec 07	29	-8.6	6.5	36	-6.3	8.6	5	-6.9	-10.1
Jan 08	31	0.2	2.1	40	2.3	4.1	4	-7.1	9.0
Feb 08	35	6.4	-0.6	40	4.9	0.3	5	42.7	6.7
Mar 08	32	10.0	5.5	36	6.2	4.4	4	-30.1	-3.0
Apr 08	31	8.1	8.1	38	10.5	7.1	4	-24.1	-9.6
May 08	33	12.6	10.2	41	17.9	11.6	5	-7.8	-20.5
Jun 08	30	0.6	7.0	37	3.5	10.6	5	-10.6	-14.0
Jul 08	30	-0.6	4.1	37	0.4	7.1	6	21.1	0.0
Aug 08	29	-4.5	-1.5	36	-1.8	0.6	6	19.7	8.8
Sep 08	29	-13.1	-6.3	34	-13.5	-5.2	6	16.0	19.0
Oct 08	30	-0.2	-6.2	37	-0.5	-5.5	5	78.8	31.9

4.14c Average Weekly Earnings - Bonus Pay

Great Britain, seasonally adjusted

Standard Industrial Classification (2007)

	Whole Economy			Private sector [2][3][4]			Public sector [2][3][4]		
	Weekly Earnings (£)	% changes year on year		Weekly Earnings (£)	% changes year on year		Weekly Earnings (£)	% changes year on year	
		Single month	3 month average [1]		Single month	3 month average [1]		Single month	3 month average [1]
	KAF4	KAF5	KAF6	KAF7	KAF8	KAF9	KAG2	KAG3	KAG4
Nov 08	26	-18.1	-10.7	32	-18.1	-10.9	6	22.6	33.0
Dec 08	27	-7.0	-8.6	34	-4.6	-8.0	6	20.9	34.9
Jan 09	27	-12.5	-12.7	25	-37.2	-20.6	5	35.3	25.7
Feb 09	18	-48.5	-24.0	21	-47.3	-30.7	5	0.7	17.6
Mar 09	19	-42.2	-35.0	26	-27.4	-37.6	6	68.9	31.4
Apr 09	30	-5.4	-32.7	37	-1.8	-25.8	6	39.7	32.7
May 09	26	-21.5	-23.2	30	-25.9	-18.4	4	-10.5	28.3
Jun 09	21	-29.6	-18.7	32	-11.6	-13.4	4	-22.2	-0.9
Jul 09	25	-19.0	-23.3	30	-17.6	-18.6	4	-37.9	-24.5
Aug 09	25	-14.1	-21.0	31	-14.1	-14.4	4	-38.7	-33.4
Sep 09	24	-17.2	-16.8	31	-11.1	-14.3	6	6.3	-24.1
Oct 09	25	-17.7	-16.4	31	-15.6	-13.6	5	-5.0	-13.1
Nov 09	27	1.1	-11.8	33	2.6	-8.4	5	-21.6	-7.3
Dec 09	28	3.5	-4.9	34	-0.2	-4.8	4	-31.4	-19.8
Jan 10	23	-17.5	-4.4	23	-7.7	-1.3	6	5.0	-16.5
Feb 10	27	53.7	8.0	33	56.7	12.4	5	5.6	-7.6
Mar 10	27	42.2	19.9	36	34.8	26.4	4	-29.6	-7.7
Apr 10	23	-21.8	16.6	30	-20.1	16.1	5	-4.6	-10.8
May 10	26	-0.2	1.9	34	13.6	6.1	5	21.0	-7.1
Jun 10	24	12.9	-4.9	28	-13.1	-7.7	5	23.9	11.8
Jul 10	22	-9.2	0.6	28	-6.9	-2.4	5	30.1	24.8
Aug 10	23	-7.8	-2.1	28	-8.4	-9.6	5	40.6	31.2
Sep 10	25	4.5	-4.2	32	3.7	-3.9	5	-23.1	9.2
Oct 10	25	2.2	-0.4	31	1.3	-1.1	6	19.9	7.4
Nov 10	26	-3.6	0.9	32	-4.7	0.0	6	22.6	4.4
Dec 10	26	-7.6	-3.2	32	-6.1	-3.3	5	28.2	23.2
Jan 11	30	35.0	6.3	35	49.3	8.7	5	-18.7	7.9
Feb 11	27	0.2	7.5	33	0.6	10.6	6	10.3	4.0
Mar 11	28	5.0	12.1	36	0.6	12.9	6	44.5	9.4
Apr 11	25	5.8	3.6	32	6.4	2.4	5	0.0	16.6
May 11	26	0.9	3.9	34	-1.1	1.7	5	-6.2	10.6
Jun 11	30	23.4	9.9	36	26.4	9.7	6	20.2	4.4
Jul 11	31	37.6	19.8	36	26.6	16.0	20	305.7	101.9
Aug 11	28	18.1	26.1	34	18.5	23.8	6	9.7	109.8
Sep 11	26	3.4	19.0	32	0.5	14.6	5	18.3	112.4
Oct 11	27	7.8	9.5	34	7.0	8.3	4	-29.7	-2.8
Nov 11	27	6.9	6.0	33	5.6	4.3	5	-7.2	-8.2
Dec 11	27	2.9	5.9	32	1.5	4.7	5	-4.4	-14.3
Jan 12	27	-12.4	-1.6	32	-9.1	-0.9	6	35.6	6.4
Feb 12	26	-5.1	-5.3	32	-4.7	-4.3	4	-30.5	-2.5
Mar 12	27	-4.9	-7.6	33	-7.2	-7.0	5	-22.6	-9.5
Apr 12	27	8.2	-1.0	34	7.0	-1.9	4	-18.4	-24.0
May 12	26	0.4	0.9	33	-3.1	-1.4	5	7.6	-12.1
Jun 12	28	-6.9	0.1	34	-5.8	-0.9	6	-9.0	-6.9
Jul 12	29	-6.1	-4.4	35	-0.9	-3.2	5	-72.5	-46.9
Aug 12	29	5.7	-2.7	34	0.6	-2.1	10	77.4	-33.8
Sep 12	28	6.9	1.8	33	4.6	1.4	6	10.0	-31.1
Oct 12	27	-0.2	4.1	32	-3.6	0.5	9	118.1	64.6
Nov 12	28	1.2	2.6	33	-0.6	0.0	6	16.8	42.5
Dec 12	27	0.7	0.6	32	-1.8	-2.0	7	44.3	55.2
Jan 13	27	2.3	1.4	33	4.3	0.6	5	-16.8	12.1
Feb 13	27	3.2	2.1	33	3.1	1.8	3	-31.1	-1.4
Mar 13	25	-7.3	-0.6	30	-9.9	-1.0	5	-6.5	-17.4
Apr 13	41	53.1	16.4	52	51.7	15.5	4	-3.7	-13.2
May 13	31	18.4	21.4	39	17.5	20.1	5	-14.5	-8.7
Jun 13	29	4.0	24.9	35	5.2	25.0	6	-0.8	-6.5
Jul 13	28	-3.4	5.9	34	-3.8	6.1	4	-32.2	-15.8
Aug 13	29	-0.4	0.0	35	4.1	1.8	5	-52.5	-33.4
Sep 13	29	4.7	0.3	35	5.4	1.8	5	-19.6	-38.1
Oct 13	28	2.2	2.1	33	2.9	4.1	3	-63.7	-48.7
Nov 13	27	-1.0	2.0	33	-0.7	2.6	4	-42.6	-45.2
Dec 13	29	7.7	2.9	34	7.9	3.3	2	-70.1	-59.6
Jan 14	28	3.4	3.3	34	3.8	3.6	4	-16.1	-45.4
Feb 14	29	7.7	6.2	35	8.3	6.6	4	48.4	-28.8
Mar 14	27	9.4	6.7	32	6.2	6.1	5	2.5	5.2
Apr 14	30	-26.5	-6.9	36	-29.7	-9.4	5	23.7	21.3
May 14	30	-3.8	-10.0	36	-6.3	-13.2	3	-45.3	-7.6
Jun 14	28	-1.7	-12.4	39	9.5	-11.5	3	-53.9	-28.6
Jul 14	27	-2.9	-2.8	31	-9.1	-2.0	5	39.1	-26.1
Aug 14	27	-7.7	-4.1	32	-8.3	-2.6	2	-53.7	-28.9

4.14c Average Weekly Earnings - Bonus Pay

Great Britain, seasonally adjusted

Standard Industrial Classification (2007)

	Whole Economy			Private sector [2][3][4]			Public sector [2][3][4]		
	Weekly Earnings (£)	% changes year on year		Weekly Earnings (£)	% changes year on year		Weekly Earnings (£)	% changes year on year	
		Single month	3 month average [1]		Single month	3 month average [1]		Single month	3 month average [1]
	KAF4	KAF5	KAF6	KAF7	KAF8	KAF9	KAG2	KAG3	KAG4
Sep 14	28	-5.2	-5.3	33	-5.9	-7.8	3	-45.5	-24.5
Oct 14	29	4.7	-2.8	34	3.0	-3.9	3	-16.5	-41.0
Nov 14	30	9.1	2.7	36	8.6	1.7	3	-29.7	-32.4
Dec 14	32	10.3	8.0	38	11.5	7.7	4	101.3	5.1
Jan 15	28	-1.3	6.0	33	-3.5	5.5	1	-71.7	-21.0

Source: Monthly Wages & Salaries Survey

Inquiries Email: labour.market@ons.gsi.gov.uk

Tel: 01633 455400

Earnings enquiries: 01633 456773

1. The three month average figures are the changes in the average seasonally adjusted values for the three months ending with the relevant month compared with the same period a year earlier.

2. From July 2009 Royal Bank of Scotland Group plc is classified to the public sector; for earlier time periods it is classified to the private sector. Between July 2009 and March 2014 Lloyds Banking Group plc is classified to the public sector; it is classified to the private sector for earlier and later time periods.

3. Between June 2010 and May 2012 English Further Education Corporations and Sixth Form College Corporations are classified to the public sector. Before June 2010 and after May 2012 they are classified to the private sector.

4. From October 2013 Royal Mail plc is classified to the private sector; previously it is in the public sector.

4.14c Average Weekly Earnings - Bonus Pay
Great Britain, seasonally adjusted

	Services, SIC 2007 sections G-S			Finance and business services, SIC 2007 sections K-N			Public sector excluding financial services [3][4]		
	Weekly Earnings (£)	% changes year on year		Weekly Earnings (£)	% changes year on year		Weekly Earnings (£)	% changes year on year	
		Single month	3 month average [1]		Single month	3 month average [1]		Single month	3 month average [1]
	K5CS	K5CT	K5CU	K5CV	K5CW	K5CX	KAH3	KAH4	KAH5
Jan 03	16	-18.0	-8.5	31	-24.8	-12.2	2	-14.5	33.3
Feb 03	17	-6.5	-10.0	41	-2.4	-12.2	2	-9.1	15.6
Mar 03	18	15.2	-4.2	42	14.5	-5.1	2	-13.8	-12.5
Apr 03	17	-11.3	-1.7	38	-3.7	2.4	2	-24.4	-16.1
May 03	17	-9.7	-2.9	39	-3.1	2.2	2	-29.4	-22.9
Jun 03	18	-5.1	-8.7	37	-9.0	-5.3	3	36.6	-8.3
Jul 03	18	-4.1	-6.3	40	-10.1	-7.5	2	-12.5	-4.0
Aug 03	17	-10.6	-6.6	38	-7.7	-9.0	2	24.3	14.4
Sep 03	18	-4.1	-6.3	38	-12.5	-10.1	2	-10.3	-2.1
Oct 03	20	12.7	-0.9	47	14.3	-2.2	2	-9.8	-0.9
Nov 03	18	-2.6	1.9	42	2.6	1.1	2	-30.8	-16.9
Dec 03	18	-2.0	2.6	31	-18.9	-0.3	2	1.2	-13.5
Jan 04	21	29.4	7.3	49	56.9	10.5	2	14.6	-6.3
Feb 04	17	-1.6	7.9	38	-7.0	6.9	2	-0.5	4.9
Mar 04	21	10.9	12.4	50	20.9	20.7	2	11.1	8.3
Apr 04	23	36.9	15.0	54	44.1	18.6	2	6.5	5.7
May 04	20	16.2	21.0	54	39.6	34.5	2	9.5	9.1
Jun 04	20	14.1	22.2	47	27.6	37.2	2	-21.7	-5.0
Jul 04	20	9.9	13.4	50	26.0	31.1	2	-5.3	-8.3
Aug 04	21	19.8	14.5	38	0.4	18.1	2	7.6	-8.3
Sep 04	22	23.4	17.6	47	22.0	16.3	2	-4.9	-0.9
Oct 04	24	20.7	21.3	65	38.9	21.8	2	-0.2	0.8
Nov 04	23	25.9	23.2	51	22.8	28.5	2	34.4	7.6
Dec 04	23	26.9	24.3	53	70.4	41.5	2	8.3	12.4
Jan 05	23	11.3	20.9	55	11.0	30.2	2	-3.6	10.8
Feb 05	21	22.3	19.7	51	32.9	33.7	2	4.2	2.9
Mar 05	21	3.3	11.7	52	4.4	14.7	2	-5.1	-1.7
Apr 05	23	0.1	7.4	54	0.0	10.4	2	12.0	3.4
May 05	23	13.6	5.4	51	-6.6	-0.9	2	14.8	6.9
Jun 05	22	9.3	7.3	60	27.4	6.0	2	4.4	10.2
Jul 05	23	12.6	11.8	54	7.7	8.7	3	32.9	16.7
Aug 05	26	28.4	16.8	67	76.8	33.9	3	27.4	21.0
Sep 05	24	9.6	16.7	64	37.4	37.4	3	50.8	36.7
Oct 05	24	-1.9	11.1	60	-8.1	27.6	3	53.0	43.2
Nov 05	26	14.6	7.2	67	31.7	17.5	3	19.3	40.7
Dec 05	26	15.9	9.2	62	16.6	11.7	3	30.3	33.9
Jan 06	23	1.5	10.6	57	4.5	17.3	4	71.9	40.1
Feb 06	25	21.2	12.6	65	28.0	16.1	4	74.4	57.9
Mar 06	28	30.0	17.1	71	35.8	22.5	3	50.4	65.6
Apr 06	27	16.0	22.2	70	28.7	30.8	3	36.2	53.2
May 06	27	19.8	21.7	71	38.9	34.4	3	35.4	40.4
Jun 06	30	35.8	23.7	96	60.4	43.4	3	25.7	32.3
Jul 06	30	32.4	29.3	82	51.5	50.9	3	17.4	25.8
Aug 06	29	8.6	24.6	77	15.5	41.2	3	6.7	16.0
Sep 06	25	4.0	14.4	61	-4.4	19.1	2	-21.5	0.0
Oct 06	27	10.6	7.8	73	23.0	11.2	4	17.8	1.2
Nov 06	29	11.3	8.7	81	20.3	12.9	2	-21.5	-7.2
Dec 06	37	40.1	20.9	107	72.8	38.4	3	4.5	1.8
Jan 07	32	38.4	29.6	81	42.8	44.6	3	-25.4	-14.5
Feb 07	33	29.9	36.1	84	28.1	47.7	3	-24.6	-16.4
Mar 07	30	8.6	24.8	75	4.7	23.8	3	-0.8	-17.7
Apr 07	30	12.3	16.7	77	10.4	14.0	3	-3.2	-10.4
May 07	30	9.9	10.3	75	5.5	6.9	3	5.8	0.6
Jun 07	30	1.8	7.8	75	-22.0	-4.2	4	19.6	7.3
Jul 07	31	4.6	5.3	77	-5.2	-8.6	3	0.6	8.6
Aug 07	32	10.4	5.6	80	4.0	-8.7	3	1.4	7.1
Sep 07	35	39.4	17.1	92	49.3	13.2	3	24.3	7.5
Oct 07	31	18.6	22.2	74	1.2	16.2	2	-50.8	-14.0
Nov 07	33	14.8	23.7	80	-1.0	14.0	3	54.1	-3.1
Dec 07	31	-14.9	4.1	75	-29.8	-12.2	3	-9.7	-12.7
Jan 08	32	0.4	-1.0	80	-1.4	-12.6	2	-8.6	6.8
Feb 08	35	6.7	-3.1	87	4.5	-10.7	2	-13.9	-10.7
Mar 08	33	9.6	5.5	83	11.5	4.7	2	-40.4	-21.9
Apr 08	33	8.7	8.3	79	1.8	5.9	3	2.9	-17.6
May 08	33	11.0	9.8	91	22.6	11.9	3	-9.5	-15.8
Jun 08	31	2.8	7.5	92	22.8	15.6	3	-14.8	-7.7
Jul 08	31	-0.6	4.3	79	2.0	15.6	4	19.8	-2.4
Aug 08	31	-3.0	-0.3	73	-8.6	5.1	4	18.6	6.7
Sep 08	30	-13.8	-6.1	82	-10.0	-5.8	3	15.6	18.0
Oct 08	32	1.8	-5.3	88	18.7	-0.9	3	79.5	31.7

4.14c Average Weekly Earnings - Bonus Pay

Great Britain, seasonally adjusted

	Services, SIC 2007 sections G-S			Finance and business services, SIC 2007 sections K-N			Public sector excluding financial services [3][4]		
	Weekly Earnings (£)	% changes year on year		Weekly Earnings (£)	% changes year on year		Weekly Earnings (£)	% changes year on year	
		Single month	3 month average [1]		Single month	3 month average [1]		Single month	3 month average [1]
	K5CS	K5CT	K5CU	K5CV	K5CW	K5CX	KAH3	KAH4	KAH5
Nov 08	28	-16.1	-9.7	65	-19.4	-4.4	4	27.7	35.3
Dec 08	30	-2.1	-5.7	81	7.2	1.6	3	16.0	35.6
Jan 09	29	-8.7	-9.1	77	-3.6	-5.5	2	-6.0	13.8
Feb 09	18	-50.2	-21.5	44	-49.3	-16.7	4	60.5	22.7
Mar 09	18	-43.8	-34.8	47	-43.1	-32.6	4	96.2	45.9
Apr 09	31	-4.9	-33.5	85	8.5	-29.0	5	55.2	67.3
May 09	26	-20.5	-23.1	53	-42.4	-26.8	3	-12.6	39.1
Jun 09	22	-30.6	-18.5	55	-40.8	-26.6	2	-26.3	5.6
Jul 09	26	-17.3	-22.8	63	-20.9	-35.4	2	-46.4	-29.7
Aug 09	26	-14.9	-21.0	68	-7.7	-24.5	2	-55.0	-43.5
Sep 09	26	-15.7	-16.0	60	-27.2	-19.0	3	-10.9	-38.1
Oct 09	25	-20.5	-17.1	64	-27.5	-21.5	2	-39.8	-35.7
Nov 09	27	-2.3	-13.2	69	6.7	-18.0	2	-53.3	-35.5
Dec 09	30	0.1	-7.9	84	4.3	-7.0	2	-43.4	-46.0
Jan 10	24	-18.1	-6.8	63	-19.3	-3.2	2	-6.6	-38.5
Feb 10	27	55.4	5.7	75	70.2	9.7	2	-54.4	-38.8
Mar 10	26	42.0	18.5	66	38.8	20.4	4	18.0	-16.1
Apr 10	24	-22.3	15.8	63	-26.8	15.0	1	-69.9	-38.9
May 10	26	-1.5	0.6	77	46.7	10.8	2	-26.0	-30.5
Jun 10	25	16.2	-4.8	68	23.9	7.7	2	-14.5	-45.0
Jul 10	24	-7.9	1.5	57	-8.2	19.2	2	-22.9	-21.3
Aug 10	24	-8.9	-1.2	66	-2.8	3.3	2	1.7	-12.8
Sep 10	26	1.7	-5.1	73	22.1	3.3	2	-49.4	-28.8
Oct 10	26	0.5	-2.3	72	12.8	10.2	2	-0.5	-22.2
Nov 10	26	-3.2	-0.4	73	5.3	13.0	2	-3.6	-23.0
Dec 10	27	-12.8	-5.6	69	-18.0	-1.5	2	-10.0	-4.6
Jan 11	33	36.9	5.0	99	57.8	11.5	1	-36.6	-17.9
Feb 11	27	0.2	6.2	76	0.2	9.5	2	15.8	-12.2
Mar 11	29	9.4	14.7	78	18.4	23.7	2	-57.0	-36.2
Apr 11	25	3.0	4.2	68	8.0	8.5	2	48.4	-19.8
May 11	26	0.2	4.2	72	-7.2	5.6	2	-18.9	-27.7
Jun 11	31	23.1	8.8	87	28.9	9.2	1	-42.2	-9.1
Jul 11	33	39.9	20.5	86	50.4	21.2	4	128.7	14.7
Aug 11	28	19.2	27.3	71	7.3	27.9	2	10.2	25.9
Sep 11	26	1.8	19.7	72	-2.3	16.3	2	4.3	46.7
Oct 11	28	10.3	10.2	73	1.4	1.9	1	-26.8	-5.6
Nov 11	28	4.8	5.6	76	5.0	1.3	2	4.4	-7.3
Dec 11	27	1.7	5.5	71	2.8	3.1	2	-6.6	-10.4
Jan 12	28	-15.9	-4.1	73	-26.3	-8.5	2	49.7	13.5
Feb 12	26	-4.9	-7.1	67	-11.6	-13.5	2	-25.2	1.3
Mar 12	28	-1.9	-8.0	74	-4.4	-15.2	2	-14.5	-1.8
Apr 12	28	11.4	1.2	75	11.4	-2.0	1	-31.7	-24.2
May 12	26	-1.4	2.4	59	-18.3	-4.1	2	7.8	-14.8
Jun 12	28	-9.3	-0.5	67	-22.8	-11.2	2	57.2	1.7
Jul 12	30	-8.3	-6.7	78	-10.3	-17.1	2	-50.7	-16.4
Aug 12	30	5.8	-4.3	76	7.6	-9.6	2	24.8	-10.6
Sep 12	29	10.1	1.7	69	-4.0	-2.8	2	33.7	-11.3
Oct 12	28	-2.1	4.5	67	-7.4	-1.4	4	188.3	76.0
Nov 12	28	1.4	3.0	68	-11.4	-7.7	2	18.4	73.7
Dec 12	27	1.0	0.1	71	0.1	-6.4	3	73.9	86.9
Jan 13	28	0.7	1.0	74	1.5	-3.5	2	-18.7	20.4
Feb 13	27	4.1	1.9	69	4.0	1.8	1	-35.4	4.7
Mar 13	26	-6.0	-0.5	68	-8.2	-1.1	2	11.5	-14.3
Apr 13	44	57.8	18.8	128	69.8	22.7	2	33.3	2.9
May 13	31	20.8	24.1	82	39.3	33.4	2	11.0	18.0
Jun 13	29	4.1	27.6	76	12.3	41.7	2	27.1	23.3
Jul 13	29	-4.5	6.1	70	-10.2	11.5	2	-7.4	10.3
Aug 13	29	-1.9	-0.9	71	-6.1	-1.9	2	-33.6	-7.4
Sep 13	30	4.1	-0.9	74	8.1	-3.1	2	-23.8	-22.9
Oct 13	28	2.7	1.6	71	5.9	2.3	1	-74.5	-50.9
Nov 13	28	0.6	2.5	70	3.4	5.8	1	-55.8	-56.9
Dec 13	29	7.0	3.4	74	4.3	4.5	1	-70.4	-68.8
Jan 14	28	1.5	3.0	72	-1.8	1.9	1	-27.0	-54.5
Feb 14	30	10.0	6.1	75	8.4	3.5	1	-6.5	-45.3
Mar 14	28	7.5	6.3	70	3.2	3.2	1	-28.2	-22.9
Apr 14	32	-27.7	-7.6	72	-43.9	-18.1	5	159.3	54.2
May 14	30	-3.5	-11.0	76	-7.2	-21.5	1	-34.8	34.7
Jun 14	28	-2.5	-13.4	69	-8.1	-23.9	1	-44.5	24.0
Jul 14	26	-9.0	-5.0	65	-6.8	-7.4	3	65.6	-10.5
Aug 14	27	-8.6	-6.7	71	-0.1	-5.1	1	-52.9	-14.0

4.14c Average Weekly Earnings - Bonus Pay

Great Britain, seasonally adjusted

	Services, SIC 2007 sections G-S			Finance and business services, SIC 2007 sections K-N			Public sector excluding financial services [3][4]		
	Weekly Earnings (£)	% changes year on year		Weekly Earnings (£)	% changes year on year		Weekly Earnings (£)	% changes year on year	
		Single month	3 month average [1]		Single month	3 month average [1]		Single month	3 month average [1]
	K5CS	K5CT	K5CU	K5CV	K5CW	K5CX	KAH3	KAH4	KAH5
Sep 14	28	-9.0	-8.8	71	-4.0	-3.6	1	-18.1	-1.1
Oct 14	30	4.9	-4.4	72	0.5	-1.3	1	36.5	-17.0
Nov 14	30	7.6	0.9	74	5.3	0.5	1	41.8	13.6
Dec 14	32	10.4	7.6	80	8.0	4.6	2	99.7	56.4
Jan 15	28	-1.2	5.6	67	-8.0	1.8	1	-53.2	18.6

Source: Monthly Wages & Salaries Survey

Inquiries Email: labour.market@ons.gsi.gov.uk

Tel: 01633 455400

Earnings enquiries: 01633 456773

1. The three month average figures are the changes in the average seasonally adjusted values for the three months ending with the relevant month compared with the same period a year earlier.

2. From July 2009 Royal Bank of Scotland Group plc is classified to the public sector; for earlier time periods it is classified to the private sector. Between July 2009 and March 2014 Lloyds Banking Group plc is classified to the public sector; it is classified to the private sector for earlier and later time periods.

3. Between June 2010 and May 2012 English Further Education Corporations and Sixth Form College Corporations are classified to the public sector. Before June 2010 and after May 2012 they are classified to the private sector.

4. From October 2013 Royal Mail plc is classified to the private sector; previously it is in the public sector.

4.14c Average Weekly Earnings - Bonus Pay

Great Britain, seasonally adjusted

Standard Industrial Classification (2007)

	Manufacturing, SIC 2007 section C			Construction, SIC 2007 section F			Wholesaling, retailing, hotels & restaurants, SIC 2007 sections G & I		
	Weekly Earnings (£)	% changes year on year		Weekly Earnings (£)	% changes year on year		Weekly Earnings (£)	% changes year on year	
		Single month	3 month average [1]		Single month	3 month average [1]		Single month	3 month average [1]
	K5D3	K5D4	K5D5	K5D6	K5D7	K5D8	K5D9	K5DA	K5DB
Jan 03	16	16.9	8.0	22	36.2	-1.0	16	-0.4	-1.4
Feb 03	17	25.9	15.6	20	2.4	10.9	15	2.9	-0.1
Mar 03	16	5.6	15.8	24	18.6	17.9	14	-5.0	-0.9
Apr 03	13	-11.3	6.4	20	-27.3	-4.9	12	-20.2	-7.7
May 03	16	14.8	2.9	17	-11.0	-8.8	13	-19.7	-15.1
Jun 03	13	-16.8	-5.1	18	-10.9	-17.7	14	-16.6	-18.8
Jul 03	17	16.5	4.0	19	-9.2	-10.4	14	2.9	-11.7
Aug 03	17	24.9	7.1	20	-13.4	-11.3	13	-15.1	-10.1
Sep 03	16	11.0	17.4	22	9.2	-4.9	14	-9.2	-7.5
Oct 03	16	11.3	15.7	24	40.2	9.3	15	-5.8	-10.0
Nov 03	19	31.0	18.0	22	29.8	25.3	13	-16.7	-10.6
Dec 03	15	-3.7	12.7	21	8.8	25.6	18	20.7	-1.1
Jan 04	17	8.5	11.7	21	-3.5	10.3	14	-12.2	-3.2
Feb 04	14	-18.1	-5.0	20	1.9	2.1	15	0.4	2.7
Mar 04	16	-0.3	-3.8	23	-2.5	-1.5	13	-4.4	-5.5
Apr 04	16	23.8	-0.3	21	4.9	1.2	15	24.3	5.8
May 04	19	19.8	13.7	25	52.0	15.0	14	9.2	9.0
Jun 04	16	24.6	22.5	20	7.0	19.8	14	6.3	12.9
Jul 04	17	3.1	15.1	22	12.6	22.8	15	1.3	5.4
Aug 04	18	6.8	10.5	18	-10.7	2.7	15	14.5	7.1
Sep 04	20	27.7	12.2	15	-33.3	-11.6	16	17.6	10.9
Oct 04	19	16.3	16.6	18	-23.5	-22.9	14	-1.5	9.9
Nov 04	17	-12.0	9.0	26	21.4	-12.4	15	11.1	8.8
Dec 04	22	45.1	13.8	20	-1.7	-2.1	15	-14.0	-2.8
Jan 05	18	7.7	11.1	24	14.6	11.6	16	13.5	1.8
Feb 05	17	19.9	23.6	23	14.2	9.0	16	4.5	0.0
Mar 05	17	5.7	10.7	26	10.7	13.1	13	-4.8	4.5
Apr 05	18	16.1	13.6	24	14.3	13.0	15	-1.0	-0.3
May 05	17	-11.6	2.5	26	4.3	9.4	15	8.1	0.8
Jun 05	16	-0.5	0.5	23	16.6	11.1	14	-2.3	1.5
Jul 05	18	6.8	-2.1	24	9.4	9.6	14	-4.0	0.5
Aug 05	19	1.5	2.6	20	10.9	12.3	14	-5.3	-3.9
Sep 05	17	-16.7	-3.4	21	41.3	18.6	15	-9.4	-6.3
Oct 05	18	-4.5	-6.8	25	34.6	28.3	15	2.4	-4.4
Nov 05	19	13.6	-3.3	26	-0.8	20.7	15	-0.2	-2.7
Dec 05	19	-11.3	-1.6	25	21.5	16.2	16	4.7	2.3
Jan 06	19	6.8	2.0	26	7.6	8.5	15	-5.8	-0.4
Feb 06	21	22.6	4.7	27	17.7	15.3	13	-15.6	-5.6
Mar 06	19	13.0	14.0	23	-8.0	5.3	15	13.7	-3.6
Apr 06	20	10.8	15.4	24	0.7	3.1	14	-3.8	-2.9
May 06	19	14.5	12.7	25	-6.2	-4.6	14	-7.1	0.3
Jun 06	20	20.1	14.9	27	15.9	3.0	15	5.3	-2.0
Jul 06	19	2.8	12.1	27	15.3	7.7	17	19.1	5.5
Aug 06	18	-1.9	6.4	27	38.0	22.3	15	4.2	9.5
Sep 06	21	24.9	8.0	21	-1.3	16.9	15	-1.3	7.2
Oct 06	24	36.6	19.4	25	2.7	12.1	15	0.5	1.1
Nov 06	20	1.0	20.1	23	-11.8	-3.7	15	1.2	0.1
Dec 06	20	2.7	12.8	25	1.4	-2.7	15	-4.6	-1.0
Jan 07	21	9.7	4.5	25	-1.9	-4.2	16	9.1	1.7
Feb 07	22	4.5	5.6	46	68.5	24.0	17	26.6	9.3
Mar 07	21	8.0	7.3	26	10.1	27.0	19	28.2	21.1
Apr 07	21	1.4	4.5	29	20.0	34.7	18	25.1	26.6
May 07	22	17.6	8.8	31	24.8	18.4	19	37.5	30.2
Jun 07	24	21.3	13.2	35	32.8	26.1	20	37.6	33.4
Jul 07	23	24.7	21.2	28	4.3	20.4	20	20.9	31.4
Aug 07	23	23.3	23.0	27	0.4	12.3	18	21.0	26.3
Sep 07	23	10.9	19.3	32	55.8	17.0	21	40.8	27.2
Oct 07	23	-5.5	8.2	29	15.0	21.0	21	42.5	34.8
Nov 07	24	24.1	8.8	33	45.3	37.3	19	30.0	37.8
Dec 07	24	23.2	12.5	35	37.9	32.3	19	22.0	31.4
Jan 08	22	2.9	16.4	32	28.7	37.0	17	7.4	19.5
Feb 08	23	3.7	9.5	32	-31.3	2.4	18	8.9	12.6
Mar 08	19	-6.1	0.2	28	8.7	-5.1	20	5.7	7.3
Apr 08	24	13.9	3.8	26	-11.0	-15.2	19	8.6	7.7
May 08	35	54.0	21.5	27	-11.6	-5.3	20	5.1	6.4
Jun 08	24	1.9	23.1	23	-35.4	-20.3	18	-9.9	0.8
Jul 08	27	16.3	23.6	23	-18.9	-22.7	19	-8.3	-4.6
Aug 08	22	-3.5	5.0	26	-6.6	-21.6	17	-2.1	-7.0
Sep 08	22	-5.2	2.7	28	-14.6	-13.5	16	-21.4	-11.0
Oct 08	24	5.4	-1.1	22	-23.2	-14.9	16	-26.4	-17.4

4.14c Average Weekly Earnings - Bonus Pay

Great Britain, seasonally adjusted

	Manufacturing, SIC 2007 section C			Construction, SIC 2007 section F			Wholesaling, retailing, hotels & restaurants, SIC 2007 sections G & I		
	Weekly Earnings (£)	% changes year on year		Weekly Earnings (£)	% changes year on year		Weekly Earnings (£)	% changes year on year	
		Single month	3 month average [1]		Single month	3 month average [1]		Single month	3 month average [1]
	K5D3	K5D4	K5D5	K5D6	K5D7	K5D8	K5D9	K5DA	K5DB
Nov 08	19	-20.3	-7.0	22	-33.5	-23.9	18	-6.7	-18.5
Dec 08	21	-11.9	-9.3	21	-39.8	-32.7	16	-13.5	-15.9
Jan 09	21	-3.8	-12.3	18	-42.8	-38.7	18	5.8	-5.1
Feb 09	19	-18.5	-11.5	21	-33.8	-38.9	18	-2.4	-3.7
Mar 09	22	10.4	-4.7	24	-13.8	-30.9	16	-19.6	-6.1
Apr 09	25	5.0	-1.5	24	-4.9	-18.6	17	-13.5	-12.1
May 09	20	-40.9	-14.1	18	-34.4	-17.9	18	-12.6	-15.2
Jun 09	19	-22.2	-22.2	19	-15.7	-18.7	17	-8.8	-11.7
Jul 09	18	-33.9	-33.4	19	-19.2	-23.8	16	-11.5	-11.0
Aug 09	19	-13.5	-23.9	19	-24.5	-20.0	18	4.5	-5.5
Sep 09	20	-9.7	-20.1	18	-36.3	-27.2	17	4.9	-1.1
Oct 09	18	-25.7	-16.6	20	-9.2	-24.3	17	9.7	6.3
Nov 09	21	7.1	-10.6	22	0.1	-16.7	17	-5.5	2.6
Dec 09	21	-3.7	-8.6	21	-1.2	-3.5	16	-1.0	0.7
Jan 10	20	-3.2	-0.1	22	18.9	5.3	18	-0.7	-2.4
Feb 10	22	18.1	3.1	21	0.2	5.4	19	7.6	2.0
Mar 10	22	4.2	5.9	24	-0.2	5.5	24	53.0	18.7
Apr 10	19	-22.9	-2.2	16	-35.1	-12.3	17	2.6	20.3
May 10	20	-0.7	-7.4	18	0.8	-12.7	16	-10.3	14.0
Jun 10	15	-19.3	-14.8	15	-24.8	-21.4	16	-4.0	-4.0
Jul 10	22	22.9	0.6	17	-7.3	-10.8	16	0.2	-4.8
Aug 10	22	18.6	7.2	17	-10.3	-14.2	16	-14.9	-6.5
Sep 10	22	11.6	17.5	17	-4.3	-7.4	17	-1.2	-5.6
Oct 10	26	43.0	23.9	14	-30.3	-15.6	17	-1.4	-6.0
Nov 10	20	-2.5	16.2	16	-29.1	-22.3	19	9.9	2.4
Dec 10	23	10.0	15.5	18	-13.0	-24.2	20	24.4	10.7
Jan 11	24	16.6	7.9	19	-12.3	-18.2	17	-5.1	9.1
Feb 11	21	-2.9	7.6	25	18.6	-2.3	18	-4.0	4.2
Mar 11	22	0.2	4.3	21	-13.5	-3.0	19	-20.4	-10.8
Apr 11	22	15.0	3.6	18	10.9	3.9	16	-10.1	-12.3
May 11	21	2.2	5.4	17	-6.8	-4.8	17	8.8	-9.3
Jun 11	20	30.5	14.5	19	33.7	11.1	23	40.7	12.6
Jul 11	22	0.3	8.9	15	-13.6	2.7	20	23.5	24.4
Aug 11	20	-12.5	3.2	17	-2.6	4.3	18	14.2	26.3
Sep 11	24	11.3	-0.4	17	3.9	-4.1	19	10.4	16.0
Oct 11	21	-18.8	-7.3	21	47.5	14.4	19	11.5	12.0
Nov 11	22	6.0	-1.6	22	39.5	29.1	18	-4.3	5.5
Dec 11	21	-5.2	-7.0	19	7.2	29.7	19	-2.9	1.0
Jan 12	22	-8.8	-3.1	18	-5.6	12.1	20	14.4	2.0
Feb 12	24	13.7	-0.5	18	-27.3	-10.6	19	6.9	5.7
Mar 12	19	-14.7	-3.7	20	-5.1	-13.8	18	-4.9	5.1
Apr 12	23	2.7	0.3	20	13.3	-8.7	16	2.5	1.3
May 12	25	21.2	2.6	19	14.6	6.7	19	9.2	2.0
Jun 12	21	8.6	10.7	23	19.5	16.0	20	-10.5	-0.7
Jul 12	21	-4.3	8.2	18	21.4	18.5	18	-10.9	-5.0
Aug 12	25	27.8	10.0	16	-3.6	12.4	23	28.5	0.8
Sep 12	21	-14.9	1.2	16	-9.0	2.1	21	11.4	8.8
Oct 12	22	6.7	4.9	24	16.5	2.3	21	10.2	16.5
Nov 12	23	7.1	-1.1	17	-20.3	-4.3	20	11.3	11.0
Dec 12	20	-5.0	2.9	18	-9.0	-4.4	19	0.2	7.1
Jan 13	19	-11.4	-3.1	17	-7.3	-12.7	20	2.7	4.6
Feb 13	21	-11.4	-9.3	17	-4.6	-7.0	21	6.9	3.3
Mar 13	21	7.7	-5.8	12	-41.4	-18.5	17	-8.0	0.7
Apr 13	28	22.2	5.7	34	73.3	9.5	25	54.9	16.0
May 13	23	-10.2	5.9	19	1.2	11.2	23	22.9	21.8
Jun 13	23	8.4	6.2	21	-8.4	20.7	20	0.4	23.9
Jul 13	22	1.8	-0.6	17	-4.4	-4.1	23	29.7	17.0
Aug 13	25	-0.2	3.2	21	30.1	3.8	28	23.5	17.7
Sep 13	21	1.1	0.8	21	32.1	18.3	23	9.6	20.7
Oct 13	23	2.8	1.2	21	-15.8	10.8	22	6.8	13.6
Nov 13	23	-1.4	0.8	17	-2.1	1.5	22	10.5	9.0
Dec 13	23	12.8	4.4	18	0.6	-6.9	22	11.3	9.5
Jan 14	25	29.5	12.7	21	26.8	8.2	21	6.4	9.4
Feb 14	22	2.3	14.4	20	13.3	13.4	17	-19.8	-1.0
Mar 14	23	10.5	13.6	17	46.6	26.7	20	17.9	0.4
Apr 14	23	-16.3	-2.6	22	-36.2	-7.5	22	-9.1	-5.3
May 14	23	4.1	-2.0	17	-10.8	-14.0	22	-6.2	-1.0
Jun 14	25	8.4	-2.2	23	7.2	-17.4	21	3.3	-4.4
Jul 14	24	11.8	8.1	29	66.7	18.9	20	-13.9	-6.0
Aug 14	22	-10.0	2.9	27	26.7	31.3	21	-26.2	-13.9

4.14c Average Weekly Earnings - Bonus Pay

Great Britain, seasonally adjusted

Standard Industrial Classification (2007)

	Manufacturing, SIC 2007 section C			Construction, SIC 2007 section F			Wholesaling, retailing, hotels & restaurants, SIC 2007 sections G & I		
	Weekly Earnings (£)	% changes year on year		Weekly Earnings (£)	% changes year on year		Weekly Earnings (£)	% changes year on year	
		Single month	3 month average [1]		Single month	3 month average [1]		Single month	3 month average [1]
	K5D3	K5D4	K5D5	K5D6	K5D7	K5D8	K5D9	K5DA	K5DB
Sep 14	25	19.4	6.2	26	24.0	37.4	22	-3.1	-15.3
Oct 14	21	-6.4	0.2	22	8.5	19.8	22	1.0	-10.8
Nov 14	25	8.0	6.7	24	39.2	23.0	23	4.8	0.8
Dec 14	28	20.2	7.3	24	36.3	26.8	22	3.0	2.9
Jan 15	23	-5.5	7.2	21	-4.1	21.8	23	7.4	5.0

Source: Monthly Wages & Salaries Survey

Inquiries Email: labour.market@ons.gsi.gov.uk

Tel: 01633 455400

Earnings enquiries: 01633 456773

1. The three month average figures are the changes in the average seasonally adjusted values for the three months ending with the relevant month compared with the same period a year earlier.

2. From July 2009 Royal Bank of Scotland Group plc is classified to the public sector; for earlier time periods it is classified to the private sector. Between July 2009 and March 2014 Lloyds Banking Group plc is classified to the public sector; it is classified to the private sector for earlier and later time periods.

3. Between June 2010 and May 2012 English Further Education Corporations and Sixth Form College Corporations are classified to the public sector. Before June 2010 and after May 2012 they are classified to the private sector.

4. From October 2013 Royal Mail plc is classified to the private sector; previously it is in the public sector.

4.14d Average Weekly Earnings in the public sector for selected activities (Not Seasonally Adjusted)

CDID	Public Administration (Public Sector) (O)			Education (Public Sector) (P)			Health and Social Work (Public Sector) (Q)			Arts, Entertainment and Recreation (Public Sector) (R)		
	Average Weekly Earnings	Of which Bonuses	Arrears	Average Weekly Earnings	Of which Bonuses	Arrears	Average Weekly Earnings	Of which Bonuses	Arrears	Average Weekly Earnings	Of which Bonuses	Arrears
	K5BE	K5BF	K5BG	K5BH	K5BI	K5BJ	K5BK	K5BL	K5BM	K5BN	K5BO	K5BP
2010 Jan	520	1	1	369	0	0	505	0	0	415	0	4
2010 Feb	520	1	1	371	0	0	509	0	0	412	0	0
2010 Mar	521	2	1	371	1	0	502	0	0	409	1	0
2010 Apr	522	1	0	374	1	0	516	0	0	413	1	0
2010 May	521	2	0	372	0	0	522	0	0	418	9	0
2010 Jun	524	3	1	371	0	0	524	0	0	420	11	0
2010 Jul	530	3	1	373	1	0	521	0	0	412	6	2
2010 Aug	535	11	0	374	1	0	514	0	0	414	1	0
2010 Sep	528	1	1	380	1	1	520	0	0	416	0	0
2010 Oct	529	1	0	378	0	1	520	0	0	418	0	0
2010 Nov	534	3	1	379	0	1	522	0	0	420	2	2
2010 Dec	538	8	0	381	1	0	525	0	0	424	2	0
2011 Jan	537	1	0	377	0	0	527	0	0	427	2	0
2011 Feb	535	2	0	378	0	0	527	0	0	423	0	0
2011 Mar	534	1	0	381	0	0	527	0	0	430	0	0
2011 Apr	537	1	0	384	0	1	530	0	1	433	5	0
2011 May	538	1	0	378	0	0	532	0	0	458	29	1
2011 Jun	542	6	0	379	0	0	534	0	0	428	3	0
2011 Jul	539	5	0	380	1	0	528	0	0	421	0	0
2011 Aug	545	11	0	383	0	0	524	0	0	424	4	0
2011 Sep	545	1	0	384	0	0	528	0	0	418	0	0
2011 Oct	538	1	0	381	1	0	529	0	0	419	0	0
2011 Nov	537	2	0	380	0	1	533	0	0	423	1	1
2011 Dec	540	6	0	379	0	0	533	0	0	427	0	0
2012 Jan	535	1	0	375	0	0	534	0	0	435	1	0
2012 Feb	538	1	0	377	0	0	537	0	0	463	0	0
2012 Mar	541	2	0	377	0	0	536	0	0	462	0	0
2012 Apr	545	0	0	381	0	0	540	0	0	463	1	1
2012 May	543	1	0	379	0	0	543	0	0	501	44	0
2012 Jun	550	5	0	381	0	0	541	0	0	463	5	0
2012 Jul	551	5	0	382	1	0	542	0	0	461	0	2
2012 Aug	547	3	0	387	0	0	536	0	0	455	0	0
2012 Sep	554	7	1	388	0	0	537	0	0	437	3	1
2012 Oct	547	2	1	385	0	0	536	0	0	462	41	0
2012 Nov	544	2	0	385	0	0	538	0	0	442	1	2
2012 Dec	543	2	2	385	0	0	537	0	0	444	5	0
2013 Jan	546	1	1	381	0	0	540	0	0	442	0	2
2013 Feb	535	0	0	380	0	0	538	0	0	441	0	0
2013 Mar	536	3	0	379	0	0	538	0	0	451	0	0
2013 Apr	537	1	0	384	0	0	547	0	0	450	3	0
2013 May	537	0	0	383	0	0	546	0	0	447	5	0
2013 Jun	540	3	0	382	0	0	545	0	0	449	4	1
2013 Jul	543	6	0	384	1	0	546	0	0	449	4	3
2013 Aug	540	1	4	386	0	1	536	0	0	442	1	1
2013 Sep	547	7	0	390	0	1	541	0	0	439	1	0
2013 Oct	537	1	0	390	0	1	543	0	0	441	1	1
2013 Nov	537	1	0	387	0	1	543	0	0	450	1	0
2013 Dec	540	2	1	391	0	1	543	0	0	444	0	0
2014 Jan	545	1	1	386	0	0	545	0	0	447	0	3
2014 Feb	541	1	1	388	0	0	544	0	1	450	0	0
2014 Mar	548	2	4	387	0	0	539	0	0	448	0	0
2014 Apr	553	7	3	392	0	2	547	0	0	454	1	0
2014 May	547	1	1	392	0	3	550	0	1	454	2	0
2014 Jun	549	3	0	390	0	0	549	0	0	453	5	0
2014 Jul	549	4	3	391	0	0	547	0	0	451	5	1
2014 Aug	547	3	1	393	1	0	538	0	0	448	6	0
2014 Sep	555	7	0	397	0	0	545	0	0	451	0	0
2014 Oct (r)	552	1	1	395	0	0	540	0	0	448	1	3
2014 Nov (p)	549	1	1	395	0	0	542	0	0	447	2	0

Source: Monthly Wages & Salaries Survey

p = Provisional

r = Revised

All figures are in pounds (£)

4.15a Weekly pay - Gross (£) - For all employee jobs[a] by age group and occupation:United Kingdom, 2014

Description	Code	Number of jobs[b] (thousand)	Median	Annual % change	Mean	Annual % change	Percentiles 10	20	25	30	40	60	70	75	80	90
All employees		25,036	417.9	0.6	501.5	0.0	125.5	210.9	252.0	286.7	349.2	493.7	586.6	644.2	709.1	913.6
18-21		1,265	193.6	13.1	204.3	5.3	44.2	76.1	91.5	107.1	145.9	235.3	270.2	288.0	308.7	370.7
22-29		4,329	371.5	1.4	402.6	0.3	136.0	225.9	257.6	283.2	325.8	421.6	479.1	514.0	553.5	668.0
30-39		5,726	484.4	0.3	550.4	-0.3	162.8	269.2	308.7	344.9	414.9	565.1	652.1	702.6	763.1	952.5
40-49		6,453	480.7	0.8	582.0	1.0	154.0	248.0	289.3	328.8	402.5	573.7	677.2	736.4	805.9	1,057.3
50-59		5,176	446.7	0.5	550.8	0.0	150.0	235.1	274.8	309.2	375.0	534.5	638.1	699.0	772.1	1,003.3
60+		1,866	332.2	1.0	418.1	-0.4	86.4	139.7	165.8	198.9	264.5	400.1	485.1	537.3	601.0	816.7
18-21 ALL OCCUPATIONS		1,265	193.6	13.1	204.3	5.3	44.2	76.1	91.5	107.1	145.9	235.3	270.2	288.0	308.7	370.7
18-21 Managers, directors and senior officials	1	17	374.2	19.9	388.8	-4.0	x	284.6	297.8	315.1	336.3	394.5	428.4	435.6	455.5	x
18-21 Corporate managers and directors	11	12	325.7	15.2	375.3	8.5	x	273.1	x	285.1	313.2	377.5	411.7	x	x	x
18-21 Other managers and proprietors	12	x	396.5		424.4		x	x	x	x	x	x	x	x	x	x
18-21 Professional occupations	2	27	348.2	-3.6	343.7	-7.8	x	249.1	268.3	284.1	307.2	364.3	417.1	421.5	440.8	513.9
18-21 Science, research, engineering and technology professionals	21	9	364.1	0.4	382.3	-2.6	x	x	x	342.9	358.7	365.2	414.6	x	x	x
18-21 Health professionals	22	6	397.8		336.3	10.7	x	x	x	x	x	410.6	431.4	x	x	x
18-21 Teaching and educational professionals	23	x	x		248.2	-27.7	x	x	x	x	x	x	x	x	x	x
18-21 Business, media and public service professionals	24	x	320.5	-10.9	372.2	-7.0	x	x	x	286.9	306.6	x	x	x	x	x
18-21 Associate professional and technical occupations	3	107	303.4	10.6	294.5	9.0	x	120.7	167.7	226.9	267.9	326.0	363.4	392.7	422.3	482.7
18-21 Science, engineering and technology associate professionals	31	27	326.5	4.0	351.7	9.0	212.5	248.8	263.7	277.9	301.7	364.7	422.5	439.9	464.9	x
18-21 Health and social care associate professionals	32	8	x		192.3		x	x	x	x	x	x	x	x	x	x
18-21 Protective service occupations	33	x	414.9	-3.3	369.8	-21.7	x	x	x	x	x	x	x	x	x	x
18-21 Culture, media and sports occupations	34	20	x		232.0	78.5	x	x	x	x	x	x	x	x	x	x
18-21 Business and public service associate professionals	35	48	315.0	-1.3	300.8	-9.5	x	x	217.7	248.4	287.5	337.3	363.0	389.7	417.8	x
18-21 Administrative and secretarial occupations	4	126	252.5	-2.0	244.5	2.2	70.7	126.2	149.5	184.5	224.5	276.3	301.8	311.7	325.8	383.2
18-21 Administrative occupations	41	105	258.5	-0.5	248.9	2.7	76.7	130.6	154.0	186.2	230.0	282.5	305.0	312.7	327.8	383.3
18-21 Secretarial and related occupations	42	21	230.6	-7.1	222.2	-1.3	x	x	126.0	149.7	204.0	255.5	274.9	288.0	311.0	x
18-21 Skilled trades occupations	5	77	298.4	-0.5	311.9	-3.1	151.1	216.9	232.5	250.2	276.7	322.5	356.5	377.9	399.7	485.4
18-21 Skilled agricultural and related trades	51	x	282.2	7.0	267.1	10.9	x	x	x	x	x	299.0	x	x	x	x
18-21 Skilled metal, electrical and electronic trades	52	39	319.0	-3.6	344.7	-8.7	202.9	242.9	254.4	271.1	290.7	353.0	391.0	404.9	434.8	530.0
18-21 Skilled construction and building trades	53	11	315.9	4.0	350.7	4.3	x	226.8	248.1	256.1	297.4	348.7	386.7	433.9	x	x
18-21 Textiles, printing and other skilled trades	54	23	266.4	5.0	247.9	-2.4	x	x	160.3	208.1	228.9	282.5	310.8	321.2	329.5	x
18-21 Caring, leisure and other service occupations	6	181	207.3	0.9	199.5	0.4	46.9	94.2	112.0	135.4	174.8	233.9	258.3	271.3	286.4	325.4
18-21 Caring personal service occupations	61	136	219.2	3.5	208.5	2.4	56.0	103.8	127.4	150.6	192.1	244.4	266.5	278.9	290.3	333.3
18-21 Leisure, travel and related personal service occupations	62	45	166.4	-11.0	172.2	-6.6	37.3	66.5	87.5	102.8	127.9	203.1	230.3	242.9	254.7	x
18-21 Sales and customer service occupations	7	293	123.2	4.4	150.7	5.0	42.6	62.8	74.2	81.6	100.9	153.4	192.3	217.7	243.1	291.1
18-21 Sales occupations	71	248	113.8	2.5	142.8	5.6	40.2	59.0	67.7	77.0	94.7	143.9	182.3	202.0	229.4	277.9
18-21 Customer service occupations	72	45	173.9	-9.3	194.5	-2.0	79.9	100.4	104.3	112.5	134.9	233.2	268.4	280.6	293.3	327.7
18-21 Process, plant and machine operatives	8	35	286.2	0.5	294.9	0.2	108.5	198.4	213.0	233.0	259.3	311.8	344.8	356.6	387.4	458.9
18-21 Process, plant and machine operatives	81	28	291.6	-0.3	307.5	0.0	151.4	211.9	229.7	246.1	266.0	312.4	346.0	370.8	390.4	465.9
18-21 Transport and mobile machine drivers and operatives	82	7	245.6	20.2	247.6	7.1	x	87.8	x	x	x	299.6	325.0	333.7	x	x
18-21 Elementary occupations	9	402	139.7	10.1	163.4	6.5	35.0	59.3	71.0	82.4	108.6	178.4	220.0	241.8	262.5	315.4
18-21 Elementary trades and related occupations	91	30	271.9	1.0	269.7	0.8	93.6	157.8	198.8	224.9	251.4	291.2	316.4	329.9	353.8	x
18-21 Elementary administration and service occupations	92	373	131.7	9.1	155.0	7.3	32.7	55.7	67.6	78.4	101.7	165.1	208.1	228.6	249.2	302.9
22-29 ALL OCCUPATIONS		4,329	371.5	1.4	402.6	0.3	136.0	225.9	257.6	283.2	325.8	421.6	479.1	514.0	553.5	668.0
22-29 Managers, directors and senior officials	1	192	479.1	3.7	575.9	4.3	285.6	347.6	368.0	391.5	431.2	543.9	615.6	670.8	749.1	973.9
22-29 Corporate managers and directors	11	149	510.0	4.3	613.3	3.6	303.8	364.1	385.7	404.7	454.2	574.9	664.7	721.6	785.3	1,039.4
22-29 Other managers and proprietors	12	44	411.6	4.3	448.6	3.6	252.7	306.1	325.7	345.1	382.3	460.0	500.0	535.9	573.9	x
22-29 Professional occupations	2	849	536.6	-0.2	565.5	0.4	344.8	417.9	440.8	460.0	499.1	579.9	629.1	659.8	698.4	831.0
22-29 Science, research, engineering and technology professionals	21	206	557.6	0.0	586.3	-0.9	372.0	427.4	459.0	479.1	516.1	602.3	646.6	670.8	725.5	851.5
22-29 Health professionals	22	206	546.9	-1.2	571.6	-0.1	331.6	432.7	456.6	477.6	514.0	586.4	636.6	664.2	726.3	862.5
22-29 Teaching and educational professionals	23	199	487.2	1.0	481.0	-0.1	243.3	396.6	x	418.0	450.9	524.9	566.0	582.3	608.7	668.6
22-29 Business, media and public service professionals	24	238	570.4	0.9	612.9	1.1	357.2	421.6	451.6	479.1	517.5	614.8	689.9	726.7	766.6	900.8
22-29 Associate professional and technical occupations	3	679	471.8	1.8	504.2	-0.6	282.8	345.4	371.7	392.9	430.5	509.7	561.3	583.9	621.0	728.3

4.15a Weekly pay - Gross (£) - For all employee jobs[a] by age group and occupation: United Kingdom, 2014

Description	Code	Number of jobs[b] (thousand)	Median	Annual % change	Mean	Annual % change	Percentiles 10	20	25	30	40	60	70	75	80	90
22-29 Science, engineering and technology associate professionals	31	128	445.4	3.1	468.5	2.3	304.8	350.8	368.3	384.5	416.8	479.1	517.8	547.2	572.0	671.2
22-29 Health and social care associate professionals	32	50	396.6	0.0	378.8	-0.5	x	235.0	278.4	320.5	360.9	428.8	456.6	480.0	497.9	x
22-29 Protective service occupations	33	47	580.4	-0.7	556.7	-3.3	392.2	450.4	470.9	503.3	551.8	600.6	624.1	638.4	658.7	x
22-29 Culture, media and sports occupations	34	60	380.9	-2.7	x		77.3	167.3	230.9	284.3	332.7	423.4	466.4	496.7	532.1	x
22-29 Business and public service associate professionals	35	395	488.7	2.0	523.5	-0.5	307.2	366.0	388.6	410.7	450.4	532.0	576.9	613.3	655.7	766.6
22-29 Administrative and secretarial occupations	4	508	345.0	0.3	352.5	0.2	159.2	247.8	269.1	288.0	318.2	373.7	409.3	431.2	455.3	527.0
22-29 Administrative occupations	41	423	350.6	0.9	362.4	0.6	175.0	262.1	287.5	301.4	325.8	382.4	417.4	437.6	460.0	533.8
22-29 Secretarial and related occupations	42	85	291.9	-2.3	303.2	-1.5	118.6	170.2	197.0	232.3	268.3	330.6	371.4	394.9	415.8	502.5
22-29 Skilled trades occupations	5	365	419.3	2.9	447.4	2.2	256.5	305.6	325.8	344.2	383.6	457.4	500.0	528.4	564.4	676.9
22-29 Skilled agricultural and related trades	51	21	325.1	2.5	323.9	-0.7	x	255.7	281.4	292.3	311.3	342.7	358.4	390.2	401.4	x
22-29 Skilled metal, electrical and electronic trades	52	172	491.1	3.6	522.5	3.4	314.5	374.8	396.1	418.2	457.4	530.2	574.9	601.6	636.6	741.3
22-29 Skilled construction and building trades	53	66	446.7	0.2	479.9	2.1	290.0	360.0	380.2	397.8	424.6	483.4	524.3	551.5	585.1	x
22-29 Textiles, printing and other skilled trades	54	106	327.8	2.7	329.5	1.7	189.9	251.3	268.8	280.9	306.0	346.7	383.2	394.7	409.3	450.2
22-29 Caring, leisure and other service occupations	6	453	257.0	0.2	256.8	0.0	96.8	142.0	171.4	192.6	228.9	284.8	315.7	331.4	348.8	407.1
22-29 Caring personal service occupations	61	365	257.3	0.7	255.7	0.3	99.2	150.8	174.4	194.9	229.9	284.0	315.1	330.3	346.8	400.0
22-29 Leisure, travel and related personal service occupations	62	88	253.8	-3.2	261.5	-1.2	92.8	126.0	141.4	179.0	224.2	287.5	316.5	338.2	359.2	431.7
22-29 Sales and customer service occupations	7	521	257.0	3.2	254.2	1.7	92.9	127.4	147.1	167.7	213.6	287.5	314.9	331.3	351.1	412.0
22-29 Sales occupations	71	380	229.9	3.5	234.4	3.6	84.8	116.6	131.9	149.1	186.4	265.6	296.3	311.7	327.9	383.3
22-29 Customer service occupations	72	142	306.5	-3.1	307.3	-3.7	126.3	189.1	221.4	251.9	284.1	331.9	363.5	383.3	401.3	458.4
22-29 Process, plant and machine operatives	8	188	361.8	1.5	393.0	1.1	225.6	268.3	282.5	301.9	333.8	399.0	450.8	479.1	512.7	607.1
22-29 Process, plant and machine operatives	81	130	359.9	3.4	393.3	3.1	246.1	273.2	289.5	303.7	333.4	392.6	445.8	470.7	505.0	605.1
22-29 Transport and mobile machine drivers and operatives	82	59	370.5	-3.4	392.3	-3.5	171.0	246.1	268.9	292.0	338.0	417.9	461.1	493.1	528.9	607.7
22-29 Elementary occupations	9	573	252.4	2.6	251.8	2.9	77.9	121.5	145.9	168.8	214.9	282.4	312.4	332.4	356.2	420.7
22-29 Elementary trades and related occupations	91	79	331.2	3.3	344.4	5.7	199.5	255.1	266.8	282.8	304.6	360.0	385.0	407.0	426.4	502.7
22-29 Elementary administration and service occupations	92	494	236.5	1.9	237.0	2.0	69.9	110.3	130.4	151.4	197.4	267.4	299.0	315.3	337.6	402.6
30-39 ALL OCCUPATIONS		5,726	484.4	0.3	550.4	-0.3	162.8	269.2	308.7	344.9	414.9	565.1	652.1	702.6	763.1	952.5
30-39 Managers, directors and senior officials	1	562	721.7	1.1	874.2	-0.3	328.2	436.9	479.1	518.6	613.3	838.3	996.6	1,103.1	1,231.0	1,596.5
30-39 Corporate managers and directors	11	472	781.4	1.0	930.5	-0.6	336.0	462.0	506.6	557.9	670.4	902.4	1,077.3	1,188.2	1,287.9	1,673.2
30-39 Other managers and proprietors	12	90	525.5	5.1	579.1	-0.6	298.2	367.6	382.7	414.4	466.3	584.5	649.9	697.8	737.9	889.1
30-39 Professional occupations	2	1,492	671.2	1.1	714.5	0.9	348.3	467.4	512.7	551.3	614.9	735.3	804.9	850.9	901.0	1,097.9
30-39 Science, research, engineering and technology professionals	21	367	740.7	1.6	792.3	1.2	467.2	561.7	598.9	632.4	683.0	804.9	883.2	923.9	987.8	1,149.9
30-39 Health professionals	22	354	600.2	-0.3	667.6	1.3	288.3	395.3	438.5	476.4	544.3	661.8	747.5	794.0	870.5	1,125.8
30-39 Teaching and educational professionals	23	371	661.6	1.0	626.7	0.9	267.4	403.8	451.6	507.1	600.4	710.7	766.5	790.4	825.3	906.6
30-39 Business, media and public service professionals	24	401	687.5	1.7	765.8	-0.4	406.7	507.3	545.7	576.6	634.2	752.4	830.5	881.5	958.2	1,206.8
30-39 Associate professional and technical occupations	3	1,008	580.6	0.2	636.2	-0.4	320.5	413.5	443.9	476.7	527.6	636.3	704.3	747.4	798.7	969.0
30-39 Science, engineering and technology associate professionals	31	167	537.1	0.1	577.9	-0.1	345.0	410.3	440.8	463.5	498.3	588.4	636.2	670.0	701.4	842.8
30-39 Health and social care associate professionals	32	86	437.2	-2.8	432.3	-0.7	176.8	262.5	312.4	350.0	402.6	479.3	522.6	539.1	567.4	664.7
30-39 Protective service occupations	33	138	663.1	-0.4	671.5	-0.1	472.8	557.4	572.0	590.0	633.0	702.5	741.2	767.3	799.8	860.6
30-39 Culture, media and sports occupations	34	65	479.5	-1.8	493.9	2.6	138.2	258.8	304.9	352.5	428.1	536.6	575.0	613.3	651.6	x
30-39 Business and public service associate professionals	35	551	607.1	1.2	693.5	-0.3	342.9	426.8	460.0	490.6	548.1	670.8	761.1	813.8	877.9	1,120.6
30-39 Administrative and secretarial occupations	4	595	366.0	1.4	386.3	0.8	150.9	211.0	246.5	278.3	326.1	408.0	454.6	485.5	522.8	633.4
30-39 Administrative occupations	41	501	372.4	1.2	395.8	0.3	158.9	230.0	263.8	293.3	335.6	416.4	460.0	493.3	528.9	641.2
30-39 Secretarial and related occupations	42	94	306.6	0.9	335.7	2.0	118.3	160.3	184.2	202.3	252.9	361.7	421.6	447.9	484.0	595.1
30-39 Skilled trades occupations	5	451	467.8	2.8	494.4	0.9	266.7	329.0	354.3	380.1	427.0	512.2	564.0	595.8	637.4	765.1
30-39 Skilled agricultural and related trades	51	24	353.6	-0.8	370.2	2.1	265.7	287.1	301.6	317.5	337.2	375.0	416.5	425.3	449.0	x
30-39 Skilled metal, electrical and electronic trades	52	224	541.5	-1.4	577.7	-0.4	345.0	419.5	437.4	459.5	502.9	593.2	652.6	686.3	728.2	842.7
30-39 Skilled construction and building trades	53	74	487.3	4.4	505.2	1.4	320.0	379.7	400.5	425.2	457.7	514.2	546.6	567.7	596.0	x
30-39 Textiles, printing and other skilled trades	54	129	354.0	2.7	366.8	5.2	161.1	246.9	278.0	294.2	324.7	388.3	428.0	447.3	473.8	552.4

4.15a Weekly pay - Gross (£) - For all employee jobs[a] by age group and occupation: United Kingdom, 2014

Description	Code	Number of jobs[b] (thousand)	Median	Annual % change	Mean	Annual % change	Percentiles 10	20	25	30	40	60	70	75	80	90
30-39 Caring, leisure and other service occupations	6	460	252.5	0.1	267.0	-2.0	100.6	142.0	159.2	179.9	213.8	287.5	328.8	351.5	379.1	451.2
30-39 Caring personal service occupations	61	388	248.9	0.9	258.5	-1.2	97.8	140.2	158.7	178.6	211.8	280.4	319.7	342.2	369.3	434.9
30-39 Leisure, travel and related personal service occupations	62	72	289.4	-7.0	312.4	-5.5	110.0	148.6	165.6	187.8	238.4	329.7	377.1	417.8	453.8	559.9
30-39 Sales and customer service occupations	7	354	274.8	0.9	292.5	-0.6	102.9	139.9	156.5	178.2	226.5	312.5	357.8	384.8	417.4	507.5
30-39 Sales occupations	71	236	236.1	2.5	259.5	0.9	95.2	124.0	138.8	151.4	189.3	277.7	315.5	341.2	370.3	452.2
30-39 Customer service occupations	72	118	344.7	-2.2	358.6	-3.5	149.3	203.0	233.8	265.6	307.7	383.0	424.6	451.2	485.1	573.5
30-39 Process, plant and machine operatives	8	287	425.9	1.7	462.8	3.1	251.8	305.4	326.1	345.3	385.3	480.9	534.4	564.7	600.3	713.8
30-39 Process, plant and machine operatives	81	158	408.6	1.8	454.0	3.3	255.6	299.3	314.4	330.0	367.1	459.0	524.0	559.2	593.0	710.6
30-39 Transport and mobile machine drivers and operatives	82	129	444.6	0.9	473.6	2.9	240.5	322.4	346.1	370.0	402.7	499.3	542.1	571.0	614.5	721.1
30-39 Elementary occupations	9	517	264.6	0.1	272.9	0.7	63.9	107.2	128.1	152.4	217.3	303.4	348.2	375.3	408.3	490.4
30-39 Elementary trades and related occupations	91	64	331.9	-2.0	348.1	0.5	167.7	252.2	259.6	273.1	300.0	366.0	399.5	421.6	449.9	529.4
30-39 Elementary administration and service occupations	92	453	251.0	0.8	262.3	0.9	60.1	101.0	118.3	139.8	194.0	291.2	336.2	364.0	399.0	483.8
40-49 ALL OCCUPATIONS		6,453	480.7	0.8	582.0	1.0	154.0	248.0	289.3	328.8	402.5	573.7	677.2	736.4	805.9	1,057.3
40-49 Managers, directors and senior officials	1	758	812.1	0.9	1,014.0	1.0	322.0	473.0	535.8	588.2	697.6	958.2	1,140.3	1,237.3	1,379.9	1,867.2
40-49 Corporate managers and directors	11	650	869.1	1.1	1,067.9	0.9	330.5	505.3	568.1	625.1	740.1	1,019.0	1,195.6	1,300.2	1,470.3	1,916.5
40-49 Other managers and proprietors	12	109	595.6	3.5	691.3	0.5	277.7	377.8	416.8	459.8	533.2	671.0	770.2	820.3	871.0	1,162.1
40-49 Professional occupations	2	1,467	703.1	1.4	765.2	1.3	322.8	456.3	508.6	555.3	634.9	775.9	863.4	913.6	982.1	1,226.6
40-49 Science, research, engineering and technology professionals	21	332	817.7	2.1	869.1	1.2	493.1	600.2	642.2	677.5	744.3	881.4	961.5	1,024.8	1,087.6	1,284.6
40-49 Health professionals	22	410	614.2	0.6	714.6	-0.2	274.3	389.9	434.9	476.1	547.5	671.0	753.9	790.0	862.4	1,305.6
40-49 Teaching and educational professionals	23	380	692.5	0.9	672.5	1.2	244.8	397.0	445.1	501.5	623.5	750.9	822.8	863.4	906.1	1,051.2
40-49 Business, media and public service professionals	24	344	724.3	4.1	827.6	2.9	379.0	492.0	542.3	584.2	653.5	804.9	916.3	977.4	1,055.0	1,350.1
40-49 Associate professional and technical occupations	3	989	613.3	2.0	691.7	2.0	307.1	415.0	452.2	482.7	551.3	688.7	765.5	809.8	876.1	1,106.9
40-49 Science, engineering and technology associate professionals	31	160	571.1	6.4	597.1	4.1	314.4	393.9	432.5	463.4	513.2	613.3	673.7	707.6	746.5	888.3
40-49 Health and social care associate professionals	32	95	444.4	0.0	452.1	-1.9	176.7	263.5	318.7	357.2	397.3	491.5	535.1	570.3	607.9	707.2
40-49 Protective service occupations	33	144	732.9	-0.2	745.0	1.1	528.5	578.3	614.0	649.6	706.9	779.8	817.8	847.1	877.2	987.8
40-49 Culture, media and sports occupations	34	47	466.6	10.7	479.9	3.7	x	x	196.1	239.1	381.5	534.9	620.5	674.0	736.4	x
40-49 Business and public service associate professionals	35	543	636.6	0.7	765.8	0.9	344.8	435.4	468.8	498.3	566.2	720.5	823.4	897.9	988.7	1,340.3
40-49 Administrative and secretarial occupations	4	749	352.6	3.0	380.6	2.0	147.2	196.9	228.5	258.7	309.9	395.0	449.8	479.5	518.9	642.2
40-49 Administrative occupations	41	590	365.4	3.3	393.1	2.1	150.9	213.4	246.0	277.9	322.8	406.6	460.0	491.1	529.4	657.5
40-49 Secretarial and related occupations	42	160	298.1	0.7	334.8	0.8	129.2	172.5	188.9	208.8	250.9	349.7	402.5	430.2	477.1	584.5
40-49 Skilled trades occupations	5	487	489.2	0.2	524.3	-0.1	232.0	334.9	372.5	394.9	439.8	541.1	605.4	639.4	685.4	827.7
40-49 Skilled agricultural and related trades	51	25	379.4	1.1	408.4	-0.5	253.5	292.3	304.3	323.7	351.6	411.2	444.1	455.8	493.9	x
40-49 Skilled metal, electrical and electronic trades	52	261	569.3	1.5	613.5	0.7	370.9	424.0	449.8	474.2	519.1	619.8	680.9	721.5	771.5	920.2
40-49 Skilled construction and building trades	53	79	506.8	1.0	545.6	0.8	342.7	402.7	424.4	438.7	477.3	542.8	595.6	616.8	664.5	x
40-49 Textiles, printing and other skilled trades	54	122	320.2	-4.2	343.7	-4.1	134.1	188.4	210.2	233.4	282.0	377.0	406.5	431.1	469.5	573.2
40-49 Caring, leisure and other service occupations	6	636	257.9	0.7	279.7	0.4	104.9	155.7	175.7	194.0	226.1	295.4	333.9	359.9	384.7	462.9
40-49 Caring personal service occupations	61	541	252.9	1.8	268.7	1.1	107.7	158.6	175.8	192.9	223.0	287.5	324.1	348.9	372.6	441.0
40-49 Leisure, travel and related personal service occupations	62	95	299.0	-4.1	342.8	-3.3	98.9	144.9	175.1	200.4	249.9	344.1	414.6	458.3	500.8	652.2
40-49 Sales and customer service occupations	7	339	246.9	1.7	283.2	0.5	101.8	131.1	149.9	166.4	203.4	288.4	335.4	362.3	396.4	511.3
40-49 Sales occupations	71	239	215.6	1.5	246.0	-0.4	96.6	120.1	133.0	149.9	181.4	252.5	290.3	314.0	343.4	437.1
40-49 Customer service occupations	72	100	343.3	-1.4	371.9	-1.1	134.2	186.8	214.3	247.0	300.0	375.9	431.8	467.3	507.8	639.2
40-49 Process, plant and machine operatives	8	414	455.0	0.0	486.5	0.2	261.2	320.2	341.8	362.0	403.7	506.7	562.5	593.0	633.2	755.9
40-49 Process, plant and machine operatives	81	190	426.0	-1.0	471.9	0.5	253.0	301.5	320.0	335.4	379.7	480.5	543.6	578.2	629.0	741.2
40-49 Transport and mobile machine drivers and operatives	82	224	475.4	0.8	498.9	0.0	277.5	342.8	362.0	381.3	427.0	525.0	575.4	599.2	635.9	767.7
40-49 Elementary occupations	9	615	246.7	1.9	267.6	2.2	59.5	100.5	117.3	139.6	187.7	294.5	351.8	379.7	415.4	502.1
40-49 Elementary trades and related occupations	91	72[b]	360.7	-0.8	385.1	0.0	182.6	254.3	280.0	293.5	327.6	391.7	438.9	469.5	502.2	617.0
40-49 Elementary administration and service occupations	92	544	221.8	2.6	252.1	2.8	56.4	91.5	108.8	127.0	167.1	274.9	331.9	363.5	400.0	487.4
50-59 ALL OCCUPATIONS		5,176	446.7	0.5	550.8	0.0	150.0	235.1	274.8	309.2	375.0	534.5	638.1	699.0	772.1	1,003.3

4.15a Weekly pay - Gross (£) - For all employee jobs[a] by age group and occupation: United Kingdom, 2014

Description	Code	Number of jobs[b] (thousand)	Median	Annual % change	Mean	Annual % change	Percentiles 10	20	25	30	40	60	70	75	80	90
50-59 Managers, directors and senior officials	1	574	775.1	0.7	976.6	-0.9	294.1	443.3	501.0	562.7	667.8	919.9	1,089.9	1,207.7	1,351.9	1,782.2
50-59 Corporate managers and directors	11	482	829.4	1.1	1,031.0	-1.6	295.0	460.0	536.6	593.5	710.7	987.3	1,167.4	1,299.3	1,437.4	1,870.7
50-59 Other managers and proprietors	12	92	592.4	1.1	690.9	1.6	292.3	392.7	430.2	467.0	523.6	660.7	748.8	835.0	902.3	1,090.9
50-59 Professional occupations	2	1,124	695.0	0.5	751.5	-0.1	288.7	426.9	479.7	535.0	623.8	771.3	847.9	901.0	966.3	1,192.0
50-59 Science, research, engineering and technology professionals	21	218	795.8	0.2	862.1	0.0	477.0	603.0	639.4	675.5	739.5	881.5	965.5	1,018.4	1,090.6	1,282.0
50-59 Health professionals	22	340	601.9	0.0	708.3	-1.7	242.2	356.5	399.3	440.6	529.4	668.0	755.5	785.1	842.9	1,119.4
50-59 Teaching and educational professionals	23	315	711.5	1.0	707.6	1.5	221.5	400.3	457.4	526.4	648.8	782.7	853.2	889.4	939.6	1,106.3
50-59 Business, media and public service professionals	24	252	689.9	0.7	769.0	0.1	341.6	460.0	507.9	556.1	629.6	770.0	862.4	921.6	991.8	1,245.7
50-59 Associate professional and technical occupations	3	634	580.7	3.3	662.7	5.1	285.0	391.6	426.3	461.5	523.6	655.5	741.3	789.4	848.1	1,078.8
50-59 Science, engineering and technology associate professionals	31	121	565.4	1.2	594.5	2.4	306.6	387.0	425.6	457.5	518.1	608.0	676.9	720.3	758.1	909.0
50-59 Health and social care associate professionals	32	79	442.3	2.8	444.6	0.6	196.4	269.1	306.6	343.4	395.1	483.9	527.7	547.1	583.6	685.7
50-59 Protective service occupations	33	60	718.4	1.7	716.7	2.3	416.2	514.7	555.0	570.6	653.4	766.4	809.0	851.0	878.2	974.1
50-59 Culture, media and sports occupations	34	25	414.9	-1.9	501.9	-7.1	x	x	x	x	307.4	485.9	548.2	602.5	x	x
50-59 Business and public service associate professionals	35	349	629.6	5.9	738.0	6.4	327.8	423.1	462.1	488.7	554.3	709.1	800.1	862.4	959.0	1,257.9
50-59 Administrative and secretarial occupations	4	736	345.0	1.2	371.0	1.3	145.2	195.2	224.5	254.7	306.8	383.3	429.3	458.9	498.3	611.8
50-59 Administrative occupations	41	554	362.2	1.9	388.0	1.8	151.8	215.8	247.6	278.7	324.9	398.6	445.6	476.5	512.5	626.7
50-59 Secretarial and related occupations	42	182	295.7	1.0	319.3	-0.2	117.7	161.0	180.1	197.5	246.9	333.0	374.9	405.2	431.1	534.7
50-59 Skilled trades occupations	5	393	500.0	0.0	526.4	0.6	242.7	332.5	363.7	395.8	448.2	550.6	613.2	650.7	689.2	827.9
50-59 Skilled agricultural and related trades	51	24	348.2	-2.3	369.7	0.3	233.0	283.5	288.7	305.0	331.5	370.3	396.3	416.5	430.1	x
50-59 Skilled metal, electrical and electronic trades	52	222	574.7	0.2	611.6	1.9	371.6	437.9	463.4	486.4	529.1	617.8	677.8	713.4	758.5	891.9
50-59 Skilled construction and building trades	53	57	507.9	-1.6	553.1	-0.7	323.9	407.4	426.8	441.9	475.1	550.3	605.2	646.2	679.0	x
50-59 Textiles, printing and other skilled trades	54	90	307.6	-3.2	340.6	0.2	139.5	183.6	209.8	234.0	277.5	348.7	394.0	417.3	454.5	569.1
50-59 Caring, leisure and other service occupations	6	503	269.8	0.2	288.4	0.5	112.7	164.1	181.9	200.3	235.5	305.5	349.8	374.1	399.5	470.6
50-59 Caring personal service occupations	61	426	267.2	0.5	281.5	0.8	113.0	164.9	181.8	200.2	234.5	302.7	343.7	369.3	391.3	454.4
50-59 Leisure, travel and related personal service occupations	62	77	288.8	-3.7	326.1	-0.7	110.3	158.5	182.0	201.8	244.5	332.2	380.8	416.9	455.1	604.1
50-59 Sales and customer service occupations	7	307	230.0	-0.6	268.3	0.6	101.6	133.1	147.3	161.9	193.9	268.0	313.0	339.4	366.9	482.5
50-59 Sales occupations	71	223	204.5	1.7	235.1	0.4	98.3	125.5	137.7	149.5	174.9	239.3	275.3	296.3	322.0	402.3
50-59 Customer service occupations	72	83	326.8	-2.1	357.3	-1.3	127.5	181.2	205.6	229.6	273.4	360.6	421.4	451.0	489.2	605.4
50-59 Process, plant and machine operatives	8	371	437.0	1.0	467.0	1.9	237.3	300.4	321.9	347.4	386.7	490.8	547.5	585.4	621.0	737.3
50-59 Process, plant and machine operatives	81	170	416.5	1.0	455.3	1.4	243.2	290.8	308.2	327.6	367.9	474.4	536.3	572.3	618.9	720.0
50-59 Transport and mobile machine drivers and operatives	82	201	447.8	-0.2	476.9	2.3	231.2	314.3	340.0	364.1	407.1	498.4	557.8	589.5	623.1	749.8
50-59 Elementary occupations	9	534	260.0	0.5	271.9	-0.1	63.7	104.7	126.2	148.7	204.7	305.5	354.3	378.3	416.4	496.3
50-59 Elementary trades and related occupations	91	64	356.8	-1.7	370.1	-4.0	191.3	254.7	272.7	290.3	323.1	386.9	417.6	446.4	480.8	556.3
50-59 Elementary administration and service occupations	92	470	241.0	1.4	258.4	0.9	61.9	97.1	114.3	134.1	183.7	289.6	337.1	365.3	401.3	483.9
60+ ALL OCCUPATIONS		1,866	332.2	1.0	418.1	-0.4	86.4	139.7	165.8	198.9	264.5	400.1	485.1	537.3	601.0	816.7
60+ Managers, directors and senior officials	1	191	594.0	0.1	763.7	-3.3	154.3	251.4	304.6	357.6	479.1	718.9	881.6	962.6	1,103.7	1,506.8
60+ Corporate managers and directors	11	158	632.6	0.5	806.4	-4.0	155.2	248.6	306.4	367.1	500.2	753.5	930.0	1,041.9	1,172.9	1,610.0
60+ Other managers and proprietors	12	34	487.5	-2.1	565.2	-4.3	153.2	271.6	297.4	334.3	428.4	584.7	668.4	728.3	777.3	x
60+ Professional occupations	2	322	540.1	0.6	618.9	0.1	132.4	256.0	308.0	345.0	437.8	645.9	747.5	803.1	869.8	1,127.6
60+ Science, research, engineering and technology professionals	21	58	745.7	2.3	754.6	2.1	320.1	460.4	518.1	565.4	659.1	821.0	893.7	928.6	1,017.1	x
60+ Health professionals	22	77	458.9	1.9	605.0	-2.5	152.7	261.9	288.4	321.4	381.8	531.6	606.1	672.1	747.4	x
60+ Teaching and educational professionals	23	107	450.2	1.6	546.1	1.2	87.6	150.1	200.1	256.7	339.4	604.3	713.6	786.0	863.4	1,061.9
60+ Business, media and public service professionals	24	80	574.8	-1.6	631.3	-2.5	150.2	314.8	341.2	388.7	468.3	640.8	733.5	767.7	860.1	x
60+ Associate professional and technical occupations	3	179	464.6	0.7	510.1	2.2	134.8	248.0	297.4	338.5	400.1	521.2	599.6	647.4	706.9	892.7
60+ Science, engineering and technology associate professionals	31	39	493.9	0.8	528.0	2.0	243.2	345.9	361.3	390.9	456.7	536.2	599.4	645.4	701.6	x
60+ Health and social care associate professionals	32	21	339.9	10.9	330.8	1.9	x	158.9	176.6	200.9	251.3	389.0	424.1	458.1	489.3	x
60+ Protective service occupations	33	10	468.1	5.3	480.5	1.1	x	x	346.9	370.4	420.9	526.8	572.8	591.0	x	x
60+ Culture, media and sports occupations	34	11	x		306.3	-1.4	x	x	x	x	x	x	x	x	x	x
60+ Business and public service associate professionals	35	97	494.9	1.0	568.6	2.7	153.4	288.8	327.9	359.3	428.0	581.9	656.6	716.6	802.0	989.9

4.15a   Weekly pay - Gross (£) - For all employee jobs[a] by age group and occupation: United Kingdom, 2014

Description	Code	Number of jobs[b] (thousand)	Median	Annual % change	Mean	Annual % change	Percentiles 10	20	25	30	40	60	70	75	80	90
60+ Administrative and secretarial occupations	4	294	261.6	2.4	293.0	2.1	73.8	130.0	149.0	170.6	217.7	315.1	366.3	398.8	428.3	527.7
60+ Administrative occupations	41	210	281.1	4.5	302.4	2.9	70.0	134.4	153.3	180.0	230.0	333.6	376.7	410.0	440.8	536.7
60+ Secretarial and related occupations	42	85	232.3	0.7	269.8	-0.1	78.0	118.4	136.8	151.9	191.6	269.9	324.2	360.0	396.7	509.5
60+ Skilled trades occupations	5	154	452.5	1.2	465.2	0.2	182.4	286.7	318.5	347.5	409.4	499.3	552.5	584.7	618.0	736.3
60+ Skilled agricultural and related trades	51	12	295.0	2.6	293.3	1.4	x	148.1	x	203.7	260.2	322.1	353.2	370.4	x	x
60+ Skilled metal, electrical and electronic trades	52	85	523.6	0.5	543.7	0.0	313.1	390.8	417.6	439.1	483.7	562.9	610.0	649.9	672.8	769.6
60+ Skilled construction and building trades	53	24	473.7	2.1	507.5	0.3	266.1	374.9	404.7	419.6	445.5	500.3	551.9	598.9	634.5	x
60+ Textiles, printing and other skilled trades	54	34	298.0	4.1	300.5	1.9	115.4	149.3	168.3	182.6	226.9	330.4	367.6	397.0	413.8	x
60+ Caring, leisure and other service occupations	6	175	214.8	-1.0	233.2	-1.0	60.1	104.0	122.4	141.0	180.0	255.8	299.0	325.5	357.1	421.6
60+ Caring personal service occupations	61	135	215.6	-1.1	233.0	0.4	63.7	110.3	129.3	145.8	184.4	253.7	295.9	322.7	350.4	413.4
60+ Leisure, travel and related personal service occupations	62	39	206.2	-2.1	234.1	-4.8	46.0	79.8	100.3	114.9	158.9	266.1	310.8	332.9	373.5	x
60+ Sales and customer service occupations	7	132	156.5	0.1	193.2	-3.3	71.7	95.9	104.0	113.7	133.4	186.4	223.5	250.7	272.4	358.0
60+ Sales occupations	71	108	147.7	-2.7	179.8	-2.3	68.5	94.2	102.7	111.2	128.8	171.5	208.2	224.1	251.1	322.7
60+ Customer service occupations	72	24	228.3	1.2	254.5	-5.2	81.2	104.6	124.7	145.5	182.0	271.5	336.5	350.0	370.5	x
60+ Process, plant and machine operatives	8	173	355.3	1.0	374.8	2.7	123.2	188.7	221.2	251.5	300.2	404.7	458.9	491.9	530.0	642.8
60+ Process, plant and machine operatives	81	59	362.1	2.9	392.6	4.6	159.1	227.4	253.8	268.5	312.0	406.8	472.4	490.7	533.6	x
60+ Transport and mobile machine drivers and operatives	82	114	353.4	0.6	365.7	1.7	105.5	170.0	196.3	228.6	298.2	403.2	451.9	491.9	524.2	635.7
60+ Elementary occupations	9	247	177.1	4.9	222.8	4.6	50.5	75.3	87.6	101.1	134.9	244.2	299.8	329.9	362.5	444.4
60+ Elementary trades and related occupations	91	27	324.0	0.7	339.3	1.9	121.4	206.3	252.9	266.7	296.8	360.8	393.4	415.4	451.0	x
60+ Elementary administration and service occupations	92	219	157.6	4.3	208.2	4.4	47.8	70.0	81.5	94.7	122.6	214.3	276.1	309.8	346.8	429.0
Not Classified		:														

Source: Annual Survey of Hours and Earnings, Office for National Statistics.

a Employees on adult rates whose pay for the survey pay-period was not affected by absence.

b Figures for Number of Jobs are for indicative purposes only and should not be considered an accurate estimate of employee job counts.

KEY - The colour coding indicates the quality of each estimate; jobs, median, mean and percentiles but not the annual percentage change.

The quality of an estimate is measured by its coefficient of variation (CV), which is the ratio of the standard error of an estimate to the estimate.

Key	Statistical robustness
CV <= 5%	Estimates are considered precise
CV > 5% and <= 10%	Estimates are considered reasonably precise
CV > 10% and <= 20%	Estimates are considered acceptable
x = CV > 20%	Estimates are considered unreliable for practical purposes
.. = disclosive	
: = not applicable	
- = nil or negligible	

4.15b Hourly pay - Gross (£) - For all employee jobs[a] by age group and occupation: United Kingdom, 2014

Description	Code	Number of jobs[b] (thousand)	Annual Median	% change	Annual Mean	% change	Percentiles 10	20	25	30	40	60	70	75	80	90
All employees		25,036	11.61	0.2	15.12	-0.1	6.66	7.62	8.15	8.75	10.01	13.63	16.17	17.72	19.60	25.45
18-21		1,265	6.92	3.0	7.68	0.8	5.25	6.30	6.31	6.34	6.57	7.28	7.85	8.18	8.62	10.26
22-29		4,329	9.90	0.8	11.66	0.7	6.50	7.18	7.54	7.97	8.84	11.21	12.85	13.80	14.88	18.04
30-39		5,726	13.29	-0.3	15.96	-0.4	7.11	8.42	9.11	9.86	11.47	15.36	17.88	19.29	20.95	26.48
40-49		6,453	13.29	0.8	17.13	0.9	7.12	8.40	9.04	9.78	11.33	15.67	18.53	20.24	22.13	29.02
50-59		5,176	12.51	0.1	16.40	-0.2	7.06	8.20	8.82	9.41	10.79	14.67	17.63	19.21	21.21	27.82
60+		1,866	10.75	0.8	14.51	-0.6	6.75	7.56	8.00	8.50	9.57	12.40	14.76	16.44	18.32	24.92
18-21 ALL OCCUPATIONS		1,265	6.92	3.0	7.68	0.8	5.25	6.30	6.31	6.34	6.57	7.28	7.85	8.18	8.62	10.26
18-21 Managers, directors and senior officials	1	17	8.00	4.1	9.16	-17.3	x	7.18	7.29	7.44	7.63	8.31	9.78	10.35	11.13	x
18-21 Corporate managers and directors	11	12	8.00	6.1	9.18	0.6	x	6.82	x	7.19	7.43	8.17	x	x	x	x
18-21 Other managers and proprietors	12	x	8.47		9.10		x	x	x	x	x	x	x	x	x	x
18-21 Professional occupations	2	27	10.34	-6.0	10.90	-3.0	7.56	7.93	8.24	8.60	9.32	11.82	12.85	13.52	14.29	
18-21 Science, research, engineering and technology professionals	21	9	9.93	-0.1	11.13	1.7	x	x	x	8.90	9.36	11.44	x	x	x	x
18-21 Health professionals	22	6	10.94	32.0	10.17	0.1	x	x	x	x	10.21	11.49	11.98	x	x	x
18-21 Teaching and educational professionals	23	x	13.68	1.4	13.96	-4.4	x	x	x	x	12.52	x	x	x	x	x
18-21 Business, media and public service professionals	24	x	8.41	-12.9	10.16	-8.4	x	x	x	8.02	8.24	8.88	x	x	x	x
18-21 Associate professional and technical occupations	3	107	8.79	1.2	9.69	0.2	6.37	7.10	7.50	7.78	8.18	9.58	10.40	11.10	11.90	14.34
18-21 Science, engineering and technology associate professionals	31	27	8.77	3.2	9.53	5.0	6.44	7.27	7.54	7.75	8.06	9.78	10.56	11.30	11.83	x
18-21 Health and social care associate professionals	32	8	8.67	4.6	8.55	-10.8	x	x	x	7.92	8.22	8.95	x	x	x	x
18-21 Protective service occupations	33	x	10.35	0.1	10.25	-7.6	x	x	x	x	x	x	x	x	x	x
18-21 Culture, media and sports occupations	34	20	9.70	20.3	12.18	34.5	6.25	7.10	7.19	8.04	8.56	11.19	x	x	x	x
18-21 Business and public service associate professionals	35	48	8.54	-2.1	9.28	-7.4	6.25	6.75	7.36	7.67	8.11	9.18	9.86	10.26	10.60	x
18-21 Administrative and secretarial occupations	4	126	7.69	-1.2	8.13	0.3	6.00	6.39	6.51	6.77	7.23	8.18	8.68	9.01	9.44	10.99
18-21 Administrative occupations	41	105	7.85	-1.0	8.18	0.0	5.98	6.38	6.57	6.81	7.38	8.23	8.75	9.16	9.56	11.31
18-21 Secretarial and related occupations	42	21	7.15	-0.6	7.85	1.3	6.00	6.35	6.47	6.60	6.92	7.51	8.01	8.50	8.94	x
18-21 Skilled trades occupations	5	77	7.29	1.2	8.07	-2.3	5.54	6.31	6.40	6.50	6.99	7.71	8.44	8.89	9.58	11.24
18-21 Skilled agricultural and related trades	51	x	7.11	5.3	7.42	4.1	x	x	x	6.64	7.00	7.33	x	x	x	x
18-21 Skilled metal, electrical and electronic trades	52	39	7.80	-2.5	8.52	-7.2	5.50	6.35	6.55	6.92	7.39	8.43	9.29	9.82	10.46	x
18-21 Skilled construction and building trades	53	11	7.66	2.0	8.54	2.9	x	6.03	6.29	6.32	6.92	8.47	10.00	10.15	x	x
18-21 Textiles, printing and other skilled trades	54	23	6.81	3.1	7.08	0.9	5.79	6.31	6.34	6.39	6.50	7.00	7.27	7.49	7.67	x
18-21 Caring, leisure and other service occupations	6	181	7.00	0.4	7.17	-1.8	5.37	6.31	6.33	6.41	6.63	7.33	7.85	8.07	8.38	9.51
18-21 Caring personal service occupations	61	136	7.05	0.9	7.21	-1.4	5.50	6.31	6.38	6.48	6.73	7.44	7.96	8.19	8.50	9.82
18-21 Leisure, travel and related personal service occupations	62	45	6.61	-2.2	7.04	-3.4	5.08	6.00	x	6.31	6.42	7.04	7.42	7.82	7.91	x
18-21 Sales and customer service occupations	7	293	6.80	2.3	7.18	2.3	5.21	6.30	6.31	6.35	6.57	7.02	7.29	7.50	7.81	9.02
18-21 Sales occupations	71	248	6.75	2.2	7.13	3.4	5.13	6.24	6.31	6.31	6.50	7.00	7.24	7.44	7.75	9.03
18-21 Customer service occupations	72	45	6.97	-2.4	7.37	-2.6	6.18	6.43	6.57	6.62	6.87	7.20	7.50	7.75	8.13	8.94
18-21 Process, plant and machine operatives	8	35	7.18	-3.7	8.05	-2.1	5.66	x	6.31	6.45	6.85	7.80	8.55	8.82	9.26	10.28
18-21 Process, plant and machine operatives	81	28	7.18	-3.8	8.14	-1.0	5.61	x	6.31	6.43	6.86	7.88	8.58	8.91	9.33	10.88
18-21 Transport and mobile machine drivers and operatives	82	7	7.13	-0.6	7.63	-6.6	x	6.31	6.31	6.45	6.75	7.68	8.18	8.52	x	x
18-21 Elementary occupations	9	402	6.40	2.8	6.84	1.6	5.05	5.64	6.05	x	6.31	6.63	7.00	7.14	7.45	8.35
18-21 Elementary trades and related occupations	91	30	7.00	1.4	7.34	-2.7	5.97	x	6.31	6.32	6.57	7.25	7.65	8.00	8.06	x
18-21 Elementary administration and service occupations	92	373	6.38	2.9	6.77	2.2	5.05	5.63	6.00	6.29	6.31	6.57	6.92	7.08	7.36	8.30
22-29 ALL OCCUPATIONS		4,329	9.90	0.8	11.66	0.7	6.50	7.18	7.54	7.97	8.84	11.21	12.85	13.80	14.88	18.04
22-29 Managers, directors and senior officials	1	192	12.25	4.4	15.07	5.9	7.84	8.88	9.32	9.82	10.99	13.87	16.15	17.43	19.20	26.55
22-29 Corporate managers and directors	11	149	13.03	4.2	16.13	4.7	8.11	9.27	9.80	10.42	11.50	15.02	17.39	19.17	21.23	29.00
22-29 Other managers and proprietors	12	44	10.10	4.2	11.55	6.5	7.51	8.06	8.42	8.68	9.30	11.26	12.73	13.35	13.99	x
22-29 Professional occupations	2	849	15.30	0.1	16.09	-0.1	10.40	12.01	12.73	13.19	14.24	16.42	17.88	18.87	20.12	23.01
22-29 Science, research, engineering and technology professionals	21	206	14.69	1.3	15.49	0.0	10.05	11.40	12.02	12.70	13.69	15.85	17.10	17.89	19.03	21.93
22-29 Health professionals	22	206	14.62	-2.3	15.56	-0.4	10.94	12.17	12.71	13.17	13.92	15.53	16.77	17.63	18.96	21.75
22-29 Teaching and educational professionals	23	199	16.45	-0.9	16.61	-0.3	11.80	13.04	13.87	14.32	15.34	17.47	18.82	19.60	20.67	23.29
22-29 Business, media and public service professionals	24	238	15.46	0.8	16.73	0.6	9.63	11.50	12.12	12.79	14.17	16.74	18.65	19.72	21.03	24.79
22-29 Associate professional and technical occupations	3	679	12.59	1.0	13.90	0.1	8.43	9.62	10.19	10.69	11.60	13.68	14.88	15.50	16.42	19.39
22-29 Science, engineering and technology associate professionals	31	128	11.62	2.8	12.34	2.2	8.34	9.25	9.70	10.20	10.95	12.39	13.36	14.08	14.80	17.21

4.15b Hourly pay - Gross (£) - For all employee jobs[a] by age group and occupation: United Kingdom, 2014

Description	Code	Number of jobs[b] (thousand)	Median	Annual % change	Mean	Annual % change	Percentiles 10	20	25	30	40	60	70	75	80	90
22-29 Health and social care associate professionals	32	50	11.26	1.0	11.94	0.7	7.98	8.96	9.49	9.88	10.29	12.11	12.95	13.18	13.94	x
22-29 Protective service occupations	33	47	14.41	-1.6	14.19	-3.1	10.66	12.51	12.89	13.39	13.86	14.88	15.42	15.71	16.34	x
22-29 Culture, media and sports occupations	34	60	11.80	0.0	x		7.30	8.62	9.00	9.52	10.69	12.50	13.95	14.54	15.33	x
22-29 Business and public service associate professionals	35	395	13.08	2.3	14.24	0.2	8.62	9.95	10.48	10.99	11.98	14.24	15.61	16.40	17.57	21.07
22-29 Administrative and secretarial occupations	4	508	9.50	1.1	10.32	0.8	7.00	7.67	8.01	8.30	8.92	10.16	11.03	11.60	12.26	14.37
22-29 Administrative occupations	41	423	9.64	0.7	10.48	0.9	7.15	7.93	8.21	8.53	9.07	10.33	11.24	11.75	12.38	14.45
22-29 Secretarial and related occupations	42	85	8.50	0.2	9.49	0.6	6.55	7.00	7.16	7.41	7.94	9.21	10.12	10.66	11.37	13.69
22-29 Skilled trades occupations	5	365	10.00	1.4	10.89	1.9	6.93	7.56	7.99	8.26	9.05	10.95	12.08	12.88	13.66	15.87
22-29 Skilled agricultural and related trades	51	21	8.00	1.2	8.50	1.2	6.58	7.11	7.42	7.49	7.68	8.69	9.07	9.48	10.23	x
22-29 Skilled metal, electrical and electronic trades	52	172	11.83	2.2	12.42	3.1	8.00	8.99	9.38	9.91	10.85	12.90	13.89	14.53	15.32	17.33
22-29 Skilled construction and building trades	53	66	11.00	3.8	11.58	3.3	7.91	8.86	9.17	9.55	10.41	11.76	12.60	13.12	13.97	x
22-29 Textiles, printing and other skilled trades	54	106	7.69	-0.7	8.26	-0.3	6.39	6.78	7.00	7.13	7.50	8.11	8.59	9.00	9.44	10.43
22-29 Caring, leisure and other service occupations	6	453	7.86	1.0	8.41	0.3	6.39	6.67	6.86	7.03	7.46	8.30	8.95	9.33	9.85	11.35
22-29 Caring personal service occupations	61	365	7.87	1.2	8.35	0.0	6.41	6.70	6.90	7.06	7.49	8.34	8.97	9.32	9.81	11.23
22-29 Leisure, travel and related personal service occupations	62	88	7.79	0.3	8.70	1.7	6.31	6.53	6.72	6.96	7.31	8.23	8.80	9.39	9.99	11.85
22-29 Sales and customer service occupations	7	521	7.55	2.0	8.47	1.9	6.31	6.53	6.69	6.87	7.16	8.03	8.74	9.13	9.58	11.06
22-29 Sales occupations	71	380	7.30	3.4	8.15	3.4	6.31	6.45	6.56	6.73	7.00	7.71	8.26	8.63	9.07	10.35
22-29 Customer service occupations	72	142	8.48	-2.9	9.19	-1.6	6.52	6.90	7.17	7.46	7.92	9.12	9.83	10.21	10.76	12.16
22-29 Process, plant and machine operatives	8	188	8.79	2.4	9.70	2.1	6.44	6.97	7.24	7.48	8.17	9.50	10.31	11.00	11.50	13.93
22-29 Process, plant and machine operatives	81	130	8.79	3.9	9.75	3.3	6.47	6.91	7.19	7.46	8.16	9.56	10.37	11.25	11.84	14.26
22-29 Transport and mobile machine drivers and operatives	82	59	8.76	0.0	9.60	-0.7	6.34	7.02	7.26	7.50	8.22	9.39	10.21	10.68	11.01	x
22-29 Elementary occupations	9	573	7.10	1.4	7.96	1.7	6.31	6.31	6.38	6.50	6.78	7.52	8.07	8.45	8.84	10.20
22-29 Elementary trades and related occupations	91	79	7.80	1.2	8.43	2.6	6.31	6.50	6.77	7.00	7.37	8.34	8.77	9.24	9.74	10.70
22-29 Elementary administration and service occupations	92	494	7.00	1.4	7.85	1.5	x	6.31	6.35	6.46	6.70	7.44	7.96	8.29	8.70	10.02
30-39 ALL OCCUPATIONS		5,726	13.29	-0.3	15.96	-0.4	7.11	8.42	9.11	9.86	11.47	15.36	17.88	19.29	20.95	26.48
30-39 Managers, directors and senior officials	1	562	19.17	1.5	23.45	0.8	9.00	11.51	12.68	13.81	16.33	22.29	26.58	29.72	33.28	44.12
30-39 Corporate managers and directors	11	472	20.89	1.8	25.17	0.8	9.50	12.49	13.70	15.08	17.85	24.07	28.80	32.06	35.13	46.24
30-39 Other managers and proprietors	12	90	13.10	2.9	14.92	-1.5	8.01	9.43	10.00	10.59	11.76	14.77	16.75	17.81	19.24	23.62
30-39 Professional occupations	2	1,492	19.70	0.7	21.22	0.5	12.78	14.93	15.84	16.70	18.23	21.30	23.36	24.62	26.23	31.24
30-39 Science, research, engineering and technology professionals	21	367	19.81	1.9	21.14	1.0	12.77	15.04	16.09	16.88	18.34	21.21	23.35	24.54	26.09	30.40
30-39 Health professionals	22	354	17.87	0.2	20.26	0.7	12.33	14.26	14.71	15.33	16.68	19.29	21.15	22.43	24.43	31.94
30-39 Teaching and educational professionals	23	371	21.82	0.8	21.91	0.2	13.92	17.15	18.33	19.08	20.40	23.29	24.91	25.88	26.90	30.47
30-39 Business, media and public service professionals	24	401	19.15	1.3	21.59	0.0	12.52	14.67	15.45	16.29	17.73	20.83	22.99	24.24	26.33	32.95
30-39 Associate professional and technical occupations	3	1,008	15.48	-0.2	17.54	-0.2	10.10	11.74	12.41	13.04	14.31	16.90	18.61	19.69	20.91	26.24
30-39 Science, engineering and technology associate professionals	31	167	14.19	0.8	15.33	-0.1	9.55	11.00	11.54	12.19	13.02	15.38	16.73	17.49	18.42	21.76
30-39 Health and social care associate professionals	32	86	12.75	-0.8	13.55	-1.3	9.05	10.27	10.76	11.25	11.87	13.75	14.58	14.99	15.66	18.02
30-39 Protective service occupations	33	138	16.50	0.6	16.74	0.5	13.13	14.12	14.56	15.00	15.83	17.42	18.23	18.63	19.18	20.74
30-39 Culture, media and sports occupations	34	65	13.97	2.4	15.43	4.4	9.01	10.91	11.56	11.99	12.78	15.05	16.17	17.15	18.88	x
30-39 Business and public service associate professionals	35	551	16.50	0.8	19.24	-0.3	10.22	12.01	12.75	13.51	14.95	18.33	20.54	21.97	23.80	30.66
30-39 Administrative and secretarial occupations	4	595	10.65	1.1	12.02	0.2	7.46	8.44	8.82	9.16	9.86	11.54	12.77	13.54	14.51	17.56
30-39 Administrative occupations	41	501	10.77	1.2	12.12	-0.1	7.58	8.59	8.95	9.32	9.99	11.72	12.91	13.70	14.62	17.64
30-39 Secretarial and related occupations	42	94	9.90	0.5	11.42	1.0	7.01	7.69	8.00	8.44	9.07	10.95	12.00	12.61	13.45	17.20
30-39 Skilled trades occupations	5	451	11.18	0.8	12.13	0.1	7.30	8.37	8.85	9.26	10.20	12.17	13.42	14.11	14.89	17.59
30-39 Skilled agricultural and related trades	51	24	9.09	0.0	9.41	-0.6	6.90	7.48	7.64	7.98	8.45	9.62	10.01	10.38	11.22	x
30-39 Skilled metal, electrical and electronic trades	52	224	12.92	0.1	13.75	0.1	8.75	10.00	10.56	11.05	12.08	14.00	15.25	15.94	17.09	19.43
30-39 Skilled construction and building trades	53	74[b]	11.58	3.3	12.07	1.3	8.43	9.30	9.61	10.00	10.84	12.34	13.16	13.74	14.16	x
30-39 Textiles, printing and other skilled trades	54	129	8.66	2.2	9.58	1.7	6.50	7.01	7.37	7.50	8.07	9.28	10.21	10.68	11.17	13.01
30-39 Caring, leisure and other service occupations	6	460	8.44	-1.8	9.29	-1.8	6.52	7.01	7.23	7.48	7.95	9.09	9.91	10.43	11.03	12.89

4.15b Hourly pay - Gross (£) - For all employee jobs[a] by age group and occupation: United Kingdom, 2014

Description	Code	Number of jobs[b] (thousand)	Median	Annual % change	Mean	Annual % change	Percentiles 10	20	25	30	40	60	70	75	80	90
30-39 Caring personal service occupations	61	388	8.40	-1.1	9.10	-1.2	6.56	7.02	7.25	7.48	7.92	9.01	9.81	10.24	10.85	12.32
30-39 Leisure, travel and related personal service occupations	62	72	8.80	-4.7	10.29	-4.7	6.45	6.93	7.12	7.49	8.09	9.46	10.86	11.61	12.82	15.04
30-39 Sales and customer service occupations	7	354	8.19	0.4	9.65	-0.3	6.33	6.66	6.90	7.08	7.60	8.98	10.00	10.53	11.30	13.54
30-39 Sales occupations	71	236	7.58	1.1	8.95	0.8	6.31	6.50	6.65	6.87	7.14	8.10	8.86	9.39	10.02	12.17
30-39 Customer service occupations	72	118	9.94	-2.2	10.90	-2.3	6.70	7.67	7.99	8.46	9.22	10.72	11.74	12.28	13.03	15.38
30-39 Process, plant and machine operatives	8	287	9.90	2.2	10.88	1.9	6.81	7.57	7.99	8.31	9.03	10.77	11.80	12.44	13.24	15.66
30-39 Process, plant and machine operatives	81	158	9.80	2.6	10.93	1.9	6.76	7.50	7.83	8.15	8.92	10.74	11.95	12.85	13.89	16.40
30-39 Transport and mobile machine drivers and operatives	82	129	10.00	1.7	10.82	2.0	6.95	7.74	8.13	8.50	9.16	10.78	11.62	12.17	12.80	14.86
30-39 Elementary occupations	9	517	7.58	-0.2	8.78	0.6	6.31	6.42	6.54	6.74	7.11	8.14	8.97	9.47	10.12	11.89
30-39 Elementary trades and related occupations	91	64	8.02	-0.8	8.85	0.0	6.31	6.55	6.74	7.00	7.48	8.75	9.50	10.00	10.57	11.93
30-39 Elementary administration and service occupations	92	453	7.52	0.3	8.77	0.7	6.31	6.41	6.51	6.70	7.08	8.08	8.85	9.38	10.02	11.86
40-49 ALL OCCUPATIONS		6,453	13.29	0.8	17.13	0.9	7.12	8.40	9.04	9.78	11.33	15.67	18.53	20.24	22.13	29.02
40-49 Managers, directors and senior officials	1	758	21.45	1.0	27.45	2.1	9.66	13.00	14.39	15.81	18.52	25.45	30.19	33.40	37.48	50.39
40-49 Corporate managers and directors	11	650	23.15	2.7	28.97	2.0	10.13	13.85	15.41	16.71	19.69	27.11	32.01	35.21	39.42	52.35
40-49 Other managers and proprietors	12	109	15.55	2.7	18.49	1.3	8.62	10.08	11.11	12.13	13.83	17.62	20.36	21.65	23.43	30.91
40-49 Professional occupations	2	1,467	20.74	0.5	23.16	1.1	13.10	15.54	16.54	17.47	19.01	22.60	24.92	26.52	28.55	35.01
40-49 Science, research, engineering and technology professionals	21	332	21.77	1.5	23.41	0.9	13.76	16.43	17.40	18.21	19.86	23.74	25.97	27.43	29.08	34.01
40-49 Health professionals	22	410	18.29	-0.7	22.13	-0.7	12.84	14.41	15.14	15.89	17.30	20.12	21.49	22.94	24.47	36.36
40-49 Teaching and educational professionals	23	380	22.75	-0.4	23.62	0.8	14.20	17.76	18.79	19.57	21.42	24.41	26.36	27.88	29.35	34.40
40-49 Business, media and public service professionals	24	344	20.31	3.4	23.62	3.2	12.04	15.08	16.09	16.90	18.41	22.47	25.31	27.10	28.92	36.95
40-49 Associate professional and technical occupations	3	989	16.42	1.5	19.13	1.6	10.16	12.04	12.80	13.46	14.92	18.10	20.10	21.10	22.69	29.16
40-49 Science, engineering and technology associate professionals	31	160	14.73	4.0	15.88	3.0	9.25	10.91	11.62	12.30	13.43	16.00	17.61	18.13	19.01	22.59
40-49 Health and social care associate professionals	32	95	12.93	-0.4	14.08	-0.1	9.11	10.41	10.76	11.14	11.91	13.90	15.29	16.26	17.21	19.32
40-49 Protective service occupations	33	144	18.30	0.8	18.36	1.8	13.42	14.69	15.47	16.10	17.61	19.24	20.15	20.52	21.11	22.55
40-49 Culture, media and sports occupations	34	47	14.89	-0.8	16.74	-1.7	8.97	10.66	11.47	12.42	13.66	16.48	18.65	20.00	20.86	x
40-49 Business and public service associate professionals	35	543	17.21	0.5	21.32	0.7	10.46	12.41	13.08	13.98	15.50	19.61	22.44	24.28	26.87	36.40
40-49 Administrative and secretarial occupations	4	749	10.69	2.0	12.28	1.5	7.61	8.48	8.88	9.20	9.89	11.61	12.86	13.58	14.53	17.89
40-49 Administrative occupations	41	590	10.89	1.9	12.45	1.2	7.78	8.65	9.00	9.39	10.01	11.90	13.05	13.72	14.79	18.06
40-49 Secretarial and related occupations	42	160	9.87	0.5	11.59	2.4	7.25	7.96	8.23	8.59	9.20	11.00	11.76	12.57	13.75	17.02
40-49 Skilled trades occupations	5	487	11.96	-0.1	13.07	0.4	7.37	8.77	9.32	9.82	10.84	13.00	14.18	15.01	16.03	19.09
40-49 Skilled agricultural and related trades	51	25	9.82	3.5	10.65	2.5	7.00	7.50	7.91	8.51	9.20	10.40	10.94	11.50	12.59	x
40-49 Skilled metal, electrical and electronic trades	52	261	13.43	0.9	14.48	0.8	9.32	10.50	11.05	11.61	12.50	14.41	15.81	16.79	17.68	20.62
40-49 Skilled construction and building trades	53	79	12.38	-1.0	13.26	0.6	8.99	9.85	10.31	10.77	11.64	13.21	14.00	14.55	15.41	x
40-49 Textiles, printing and other skilled trades	54	122	8.52	-0.2	9.81	-2.7	6.44	6.86	7.18	7.41	8.00	9.23	10.11	10.67	11.29	13.51
40-49 Caring, leisure and other service occupations	6	636	8.64	-0.1	9.64	-0.6	6.64	7.19	7.43	7.65	8.12	9.30	10.05	10.58	11.21	13.05
40-49 Caring personal service occupations	61	541	8.59	0.0	9.28	-0.5	6.67	7.19	7.42	7.63	8.09	9.19	9.98	10.40	10.96	12.45
40-49 Leisure, travel and related personal service occupations	62	95	8.97	-0.3	11.63	-0.8	6.49	7.19	7.45	7.86	8.38	10.00	11.49	12.53	14.08	20.19
40-49 Sales and customer service occupations	7	339	7.88	1.0	9.67	0.5	6.35	6.62	6.81	6.96	7.31	8.65	9.60	10.15	10.94	13.60
40-49 Sales occupations	71	239	7.38	1.3	8.73	-0.5	6.31	6.52	6.69	6.82	7.05	7.88	8.59	9.04	9.56	11.50
40-49 Customer service occupations	72	100	9.96	-1.0	11.63	0.5	6.57	7.30	7.81	8.22	9.07	10.83	12.06	12.80	13.68	16.84
40-49 Process, plant and machine operatives	8	414	10.20	0.6	11.35	0.5	7.00	8.00	8.37	8.73	9.50	11.09	12.13	12.92	13.80	16.67
40-49 Process, plant and machine operatives	81	190	10.22	-0.1	11.61	1.5	6.80	7.67	8.13	8.48	9.37	11.28	12.71	13.64	14.89	18.00
40-49 Transport and mobile machine drivers and operatives	82	224	10.18	1.1	11.15	-0.2	7.25	8.20	8.62	8.96	9.54	10.92	11.81	12.36	13.17	15.58
40-49b Elementary occupations	9	615	7.68	1.1	9.06	1.3	6.31	6.46	6.58	6.80	7.21	8.33	9.16	9.70	10.44	12.10
40-49 Elementary trades and related occupations	91	72	8.67	-3.7	9.64	0.0	6.40	6.82	7.06	7.26	7.83	9.37	10.26	10.72	11.41	13.43
40-49 Elementary administration and service occupations	92	544	7.64	2.0	8.95	1.6	6.31	6.44	6.54	6.74	7.13	8.21	8.97	9.50	10.23	11.90
50-59 ALL OCCUPATIONS		5,176	12.51	0.1	16.40	-0.2	7.06	8.20	8.82	9.41	10.79	14.67	17.63	19.21	21.21	27.82
50-59 Managers, directors and senior officials	1	574	20.92	0.9	26.74	-0.4	9.42	12.58	14.01	15.30	17.79	24.45	29.17	32.36	36.65	48.57

4.15b Hourly pay - Gross (£) - For all employee jobs[a] by age group and occupation: United Kingdom, 2014

Description	Code	Number of jobs[b] (thousand)	Median	Annual % change	Mean	Annual % change	Percentiles 10	20	25	30	40	60	70	75	80	90
50-59 Corporate managers and directors	11	482	22.33	1.3	28.28	-0.9	9.69	13.22	14.78	16.33	19.11	26.20	31.16	34.68	38.69	50.82
50-59 Other managers and proprietors	12	92	15.76	-0.7	18.73	0.8	8.47	10.80	11.75	12.55	14.15	17.55	20.31	21.80	23.92	29.12
50-59 Professional occupations	2	1,124	20.73	-0.1	23.09	-0.4	12.80	15.33	16.39	17.33	18.93	22.47	24.97	26.31	28.43	34.83
50-59 Science, research, engineering and technology professionals	21	218	21.24	-0.2	23.15	-0.2	13.69	16.31	17.32	18.01	19.64	23.64	25.82	27.14	28.88	34.21
50-59 Health professionals	22	340	18.27	-0.9	22.43	-1.4	12.58	14.27	14.93	15.80	17.44	20.13	21.35	22.68	24.31	34.68
50-59 Teaching and educational professionals	23	315	23.74	0.5	24.91	0.7	14.52	18.23	19.10	20.29	21.94	25.57	27.66	28.94	30.47	35.67
50-59 Business, media and public service professionals	24	252	19.42	2.1	21.98	0.0	11.35	14.32	15.48	16.35	17.72	21.26	23.25	25.00	26.77	34.59
50-59 Associate professional and technical occupations	3	634	15.81	4.0	18.57	4.6	9.85	11.54	12.37	12.99	14.32	17.61	19.56	20.87	22.41	29.24
50-59 Science, engineering and technology associate professionals	31	121	14.87	2.5	15.81	2.3	9.00	10.52	11.46	12.17	13.49	15.98	17.66	18.47	19.61	23.15
50-59 Health and social care associate professionals	32	79	12.97	2.7	13.82	0.7	9.04	10.15	10.70	11.18	12.07	13.65	14.64	15.60	16.47	18.68
50-59 Protective service occupations	33	60	18.14	1.8	18.15	1.5	11.97	13.75	14.50	14.80	16.34	19.23	20.32	21.18	21.87	x
50-59 Culture, media and sports occupations	34	25	14.30	-4.7	19.04	-7.1	8.59	10.68	11.26	12.00	13.26	16.19	18.20	19.66	21.14	x
50-59 Business and public service associate professionals	35	349	16.99	5.3	20.60	6.1	10.43	12.36	12.82	13.67	15.29	19.03	21.61	23.27	25.85	34.48
50-59 Administrative and secretarial occupations	4	736	10.42	1.5	12.02	1.6	7.61	8.50	8.86	9.07	9.82	11.26	12.33	13.04	13.90	17.12
50-59 Administrative occupations	41	554	10.61	0.5	12.25	1.4	7.81	8.74	8.98	9.35	9.96	11.51	12.65	13.42	14.26	17.41
50-59 Secretarial and related occupations	42	182	9.75	1.5	11.21	2.6	7.29	7.95	8.22	8.50	9.02	10.45	11.26	11.94	12.73	15.52
50-59 Skilled trades occupations	5	393	12.24	-0.3	13.33	0.8	7.53	8.75	9.32	10.00	11.15	13.40	14.59	15.34	16.62	19.46
50-59 Skilled agricultural and related trades	51	24	9.23	-2.2	9.92	-2.4	6.91	7.34	7.78	8.12	8.64	9.81	10.45	10.92	11.36	x
50-59 Skilled metal, electrical and electronic trades	52	222	13.90	1.7	14.78	2.3	9.40	10.93	11.39	11.92	12.94	14.81	16.28	17.10	17.96	20.90
50-59 Skilled construction and building trades	53	57	12.59	-0.2	13.31	-0.4	8.59	10.18	10.65	11.10	11.73	13.24	14.28	14.78	15.46	18.21
50-59 Textiles, printing and other skilled trades	54	90	8.49	-2.7	9.97	-0.6	6.61	7.09	7.37	7.56	8.01	9.00	9.90	10.48	11.43	13.76
50-59 Caring, leisure and other service occupations	6	503	8.89	0.1	9.72	-0.5	6.74	7.25	7.54	7.76	8.32	9.57	10.27	10.84	11.33	13.08
50-59 Caring personal service occupations	61	426	8.89	0.0	9.53	-0.4	6.75	7.26	7.55	7.77	8.33	9.56	10.26	10.79	11.26	12.80
50-59 Leisure, travel and related personal service occupations	62	77	8.83	0.0	10.69	-0.8	6.68	7.22	7.50	7.71	8.22	9.64	10.54	11.29	12.23	16.03
50-59 Sales and customer service occupations	7	307	7.64	1.9	9.27	0.5	6.35	6.58	6.76	6.89	7.17	8.24	9.08	9.65	10.35	13.06
50-59 Sales occupations	71	223	7.27	1.7	8.41	0.2	6.31	6.53	6.65	6.80	6.98	7.69	8.25	8.64	9.04	10.83
50-59 Customer service occupations	72	83	9.68	-1.3	11.29	0.0	6.57	7.14	7.57	8.00	8.91	10.58	11.76	12.52	13.44	16.78
50-59 Process, plant and machine operatives	8	371	10.15	1.9	11.19	1.8	6.90	7.70	8.10	8.53	9.27	11.00	12.08	12.75	13.81	16.56
50-59 Process, plant and machine operatives	81	170	10.27	2.4	11.41	0.9	6.74	7.50	7.90	8.36	9.21	11.32	12.75	13.77	14.73	17.35
50-59 Transport and mobile machine drivers and operatives	82	201	10.08	1.7	11.03	2.6	7.03	7.86	8.29	8.62	9.30	10.77	11.66	12.23	12.90	15.55
50-59 Elementary occupations	9	534	7.76	0.6	9.02	-0.1	6.31	6.53	6.71	6.92	7.33	8.38	9.17	9.75	10.46	12.09
50-59 Elementary trades and related occupations	91	64	8.63	0.0	9.44	-1.1	6.34	6.90	7.12	7.42	7.99	9.32	10.13	10.61	11.10	13.07
50-59 Elementary administration and service occupations	92	470	7.68	0.9	8.94	0.2	6.31	6.50	6.67	6.87	7.26	8.26	9.02	9.60	10.30	12.00
60+ ALL OCCUPATIONS		1,866	10.75	0.8	14.51	-0.6	6.75	7.56	8.00	8.50	9.57	12.40	14.76	16.44	18.32	24.92
60+ Managers, directors and senior officials	1	191	17.37	0.6	23.30	-0.4	8.23	10.02	11.11	12.40	14.99	20.69	25.09	28.55	31.95	43.05
60+ Corporate managers and directors	11	158	18.70	2.3	24.81	-0.8	8.33	10.34	11.41	13.02	15.73	22.12	27.43	30.17	34.13	46.43
60+ Other managers and proprietors	12	34	13.93	-1.3	16.60	-2.9	7.87	9.06	9.80	11.03	12.26	16.39	18.09	19.46	21.60	x
60+ Professional occupations	2	322	20.28	-0.8	22.91	-0.9	12.11	14.62	15.84	16.90	18.20	22.35	24.84	26.75	28.79	35.21
60+ Science, research, engineering and technology professionals	21	58	20.37	0.6	21.80	2.0	12.46	14.98	15.78	16.83	18.68	22.49	24.43	26.17	27.68	x
60+ Health professionals	22	77	17.69	-0.6	23.28	-2.6	12.53	14.25	14.41	15.28	17.15	19.48	21.25	22.65	24.72	x
60+ Teaching and educational professionals	23	107	23.72	0.0	25.40	-1.8	14.41	17.52	18.73	19.96	21.91	25.52	28.49	29.36	30.95	37.10
60+ Business, media and public service professionals	24	80	17.88	-1.1	21.14	0.1	10.00	12.32	13.86	14.86	16.82	19.75	21.84	23.72	26.19	x
60+ Associate professional and technical occupations	3	179	13.97	-0.8	16.42	2.2	8.88	10.22	10.93	11.40	12.65	15.42	17.54	18.88	20.54	26.24
60+ Science, engineering and technology associate professionals	31	39	13.35	-2.1	14.92	2.7	9.14	10.21	10.58	11.13	12.31	14.81	16.56	17.46	18.02	x
60+ Health and social care associate professionals	32	21	12.17	-1.0	13.05	1.6	8.61	9.55	9.99	10.30	11.26	12.90	13.86	14.16	15.14	x
60+ Protective service occupations	33	10	14.46	2.3	15.15	7.3	9.40	10.92	12.17	12.52	13.48	16.19	x	x	x	x
60+ Culture, media and sports occupations	34	11	13.17	-3.7	15.62	-5.7	8.61	9.68	10.00	10.36	11.43	15.19	17.09	x	x	x
60+ Business and public service associate professionals	35	97	14.82	-0.4	17.87	2.2	8.90	10.61	11.27	11.98	13.25	16.84	19.12	20.69	22.56	x
60+ Administrative and secretarial occupations	4	294	10.00	0.3	11.49	0.3	7.48	8.18	8.55	8.91	9.54	10.85	11.93	12.60	13.44	16.27

4.15b Hourly pay - Gross (£) - For all employee jobs[a] by age group and occupation: United Kingdom, 2014

Description	Code	Number of jobs[b] (thousand)	Median	Annual % change	Mean	Annual % change	Percentiles 10	20	25	30	40	60	70	75	80	90
60+ Administrative occupations	41	210	10.17	1.7	11.61	0.8	7.50	8.28	8.70	9.00	9.73	11.02	12.02	12.80	13.66	16.38
60+ Secretarial and related occupations	42	85	9.76	-0.7	11.16	-1.1	7.33	7.91	8.27	8.60	9.10	10.42	11.26	12.12	12.99	15.79
60+ Skilled trades occupations	5	154	11.50	1.1	12.49	0.6	7.38	8.49	9.00	9.55	10.61	12.51	13.57	14.40	15.32	17.71
60+ Skilled agricultural and related trades	51	12	8.20	-1.2	9.42	2.7	6.49	6.77	6.98	7.22	7.75	8.77	9.59	x	x	x
60+ Skilled metal, electrical and electronic trades	52	85	13.05	1.5	13.71	1.6	8.94	10.40	10.95	11.33	12.19	13.86	15.11	15.77	16.32	18.65
60+ Skilled construction and building trades	53	24	11.77	-0.4	12.74	-1.5	9.49	10.00	10.38	10.68	11.09	12.52	13.41	13.80	15.26	x
60+ Textiles, printing and other skilled trades	54	34	8.56	2.6	9.52	-0.6	6.53	7.16	7.47	7.67	8.07	8.98	9.59	9.99	10.30	x
60+ Caring, leisure and other service occupations	6	175	8.75	2.1	9.33	-0.4	6.69	7.20	7.48	7.71	8.21	9.25	10.00	10.47	10.91	12.51
60+ Caring personal service occupations	61	135	8.87	1.4	9.31	0.4	6.70	7.24	7.51	7.76	8.34	9.39	10.10	10.58	11.06	12.61
60+ Leisure, travel and related personal service occupations	62	39	8.26	-0.5	9.42	-2.5	6.50	7.00	7.26	7.54	7.98	8.82	9.62	10.06	10.45	x
60+ Sales and customer service occupations	7	132	7.28	1.5	8.35	-2.3	6.32	6.52	6.64	6.77	6.97	7.64	8.26	8.63	9.14	10.70
60+ Sales occupations	71	108	7.10	1.0	8.01	-1.0	6.31	6.50	6.58	6.70	6.92	7.41	7.89	8.24	8.69	9.87
60+ Customer service occupations	72	24	8.38	-1.5	9.68	-6.0	6.57	6.87	7.11	7.36	7.96	9.12	9.95	10.56	11.12	x
60+ Process, plant and machine operatives	8	173	9.11	1.6	10.31	2.9	6.44	7.05	7.35	7.67	8.34	9.95	10.82	11.46	12.13	14.06
60+ Process, plant and machine operatives	81	59	9.39	1.0	10.86	4.3	6.64	7.20	7.50	7.79	8.68	10.58	11.87	12.44	13.09	15.53
60+ Transport and mobile machine drivers and operatives	82	114	9.00	2.2	10.04	2.2	6.38	7.00	7.23	7.60	8.29	9.67	10.47	10.89	11.51	13.38
60+ Elementary occupations	9	247	7.51	2.9	8.67	2.0	6.31	6.48	6.60	6.76	7.10	7.98	8.70	9.17	9.80	11.52
60+ Elementary trades and related occupations	91	27	8.36	-0.7	9.22	-0.2	6.41	6.87	7.03	7.32	7.83	9.16	9.91	10.49	11.00	x
60+ Elementary administration and service occupations	92	219	7.43	3.3	8.57	2.3	6.31	6.45	6.55	6.71	7.05	7.86	8.50	9.00	9.58	11.26
Not Classified		:														

Source: Annual Survey of Hours and Earnings, Office for National Statistics.

a Employees on adult rates whose pay for the survey pay-period was not affected by absence.
b Figures for Number of Jobs are for indicative purposes only and should not be considered an accurate estimate of employee job counts.
KEY - The colour coding indicates the quality of each estimate; jobs, median, mean and percentiles but not the annual percentage change.
The quality of an estimate is measured by its coefficient of variation (CV), which is the ratio of the standard error of an estimate to the estimate.

Key	Statistical robustness
CV <= 5%	Estimates are considered precise
CV > 5% and <= 10%	Estimates are considered reasonably precise
CV > 10% and <= 20%	Estimates are considered acceptable
x = CV > 20%	Estimates are considered unreliable for practical purposes
.. = disclosive	
: = not applicable	
- = nil or negligible	

4.16 Median[1] weekly and hourly earnings of full-time employees[2] by age group: United Kingdom April 2006 to 2014

	18-21	22-29	30-39	40-49	50-59	60+
Median gross weekly earnings						
All	**JRG9**	**JRH2**	**JRH3**	**JRH4**	**JEH5**	**JRH6**
2006	250.6	376.5	496.1	502.5	465.4	400.0
2007	265.5	387.8	509.0	517.3	479.1	418.7
2008	271.6	400.0	532.7	539.9	504.1	437.5
2009	277.5	407.1	541.8	550.5	514.0	446.3
2010	277.4	411.2	547.8	559.6	528.2	457.3
2011	277.8	406.6	553.7	564.7	531.8	466.1
2012	279.7	412.0	557.7	573.1	535.9	476.1
2013	287.5	420.6	562.9	579.9	551.0	490.4
2014	290.0	424.8	566.0	588.2	556.1	491.3
Men	**JRH8**	**JRH9**	**JRI2**	**JRI3**	**JRI4**	**JRI5**
2006	261.5	390.6	525.0	558.7	516.0	421.6
2007	275.9	402.5	539.0	574.9	534.4	440.9
2008	280.0	416.7	566.3	599.1	563.6	462.6
2009	285.7	421.6	571.1	605.2	569.7	469.0
2010	285.9	421.2	573.7	613.7	582.7	483.0
2011	288.2	413.7	574.9	618.9	586.7	496.3
2012	295.4	420.6	574.9	622.9	598.2	508.3
2013	299.0	430.6	579.6	637.8	613.3	527.5
2014	301.7	435.6	578.6	641.3	621.1	528.0
Women	**JRI7**	**JRI8**	**JRI9**	**JRJ2**	**JRJ3**	**JRJ4**
2006	240.4	362.7	444.0	410.2	385.0	343.7
2007	254.3	374.1	460.6	420.3	395.6	356.1
2008	258.8	384.7	480.9	437.3	419.7	376.4
2009	268.3	392.9	497.9	457.7	432.8	382.1
2010	268.3	401.3	507.9	472.2	440.9	389.0
2011	264.7	398.5	519.4	477.1	449.1	399.6
2012	266.3	402.5	527.0	484.4	446.0	407.4
2013	276.2	405.7	533.8	494.1	463.5	416.1
2014	279.2	414.0	537.3	507.3	465.4	412.0

4.16 Median[1] weekly and hourly earnings of full-time employees[2] by age group: United Kingdom April 2006 to 2013

	18-21	22-29	30-39	40-49	50-59	60+
Median hourly earnings (excluding overtime)						
All	JRJ6	JRJ7	JRJ8	JRJ9	JRK2	JRK3
2006	6.31	9.50	12.43	12.49	11.50	9.72
2007	6.60	9.80	12.77	12.77	11.87	10.09
2008	6.75	10.12	13.34	13.31	12.53	10.57
2009	7.00	10.43	13.82	13.83	12.95	10.97
2010	7.00	10.34	13.91	14.01	13.19	11.18
2011	6.97	10.23	14.07	14.16	13.34	11.46
2012	7.00	10.34	14.23	14.37	13.55	11.83
2013	7.20	10.60	14.37	14.63	13.89	12.13
2014	7.25	10.76	14.37	14.82	14.00	12.22
Men	JRK5	JRK6	JRK7	JRK8	JRK9	JRL2
2006	6.37	9.51	12.78	13.46	12.28	9.96
2007	6.65	9.80	13.10	13.77	12.79	10.31
2008	6.85	10.13	13.70	14.37	13.52	10.89
2009	7.09	10.45	14.15	14.95	13.91	11.25
2010	7.05	10.26	14.07	14.95	14.25	11.50
2011	7.07	10.08	14.14	15.14	14.31	11.84
2012	7.24	10.22	14.28	15.27	14.68	12.15
2013	7.27	10.57	14.43	15.62	15.00	12.61
2014	7.42	10.73	14.35	15.69	15.13	12.78
Women	JRL4	JRL5	JRL6	JRL7	JRL8	JRL9
2006	6.24	9.48	11.87	10.95	10.24	9.17
2007	6.55	9.79	12.28	11.14	10.54	9.48
2008	6.64	10.12	12.78	11.57	11.10	9.82
2009	6.93	10.40	13.29	12.21	11.52	10.23
2010	6.90	10.48	13.66	12.54	11.84	10.40
2011	6.76	10.45	13.99	12.77	12.02	10.64
2012	6.82	10.53	14.18	12.93	11.99	10.99
2013	7.15	10.64	14.28	13.18	12.38	11.10
2014	7.06	10.81	14.37	13.53	12.41	10.99

1. Median values are less affected by extremes of earnings at either ends of the scale with half the employees earning above the stated amount and half below.
2. Data relate to full-time employees on adult rates whose pay for the survey pay-period was not affected by absence.

Source: Annual Survey of Hours and Earnings: 01633 456 120

4.17: Trade Unions 2014-15

Trade unions: distribution by size

Number of Members	Number of Unions	Membership	Number of Unions		Membership of all Unions	
			Per cent	Cumulative Per cent	Per cent	Cumulative Per cent
Under 100	31	1,164	19.4	19.4	0.0	0.0
100-499	22	6,367	13.8	33.1	0.1	0.1
500-999	17	12,578	10.6	43.8	0.2	0.3
1,000-2,499	24	39,477	15.0	58.8	0.6	0.9
2,500-4,999	12	43,360	7.5	66.3	0.6	1.5
5,000-9,999	12	88,089	7.5	73.8	1.3	2.7
10,000-14,999	2	23,265	1.3	75.0	0.3	3.1
15,000-24,999	12	247,692	7.5	82.5	3.5	6.6
25,000-49,999	11	371,602	6.9	89.4	5.3	11.9
50,000-99,999	4	274,024	2.5	91.9	3.9	15.8
100,000-249,999	6	1,022,421	3.8	95.6	14.6	30.4
250,000 and over	7	4,880,488	4.4	100.0	69.6	100.0
Total	160	7,010,527	100	100	100	100

The trade union membership of 7,010,527 recorded in this annual report compares to 7,086,116 reported in the previous annual report. This indicates a decrease of 75,589 members or 1.07%. The total recorded membership of around 7.0 million compares with a peak of 13.2 million in 1979, a fall of about 47%.

The following table shows the four trade unions whose membership has most increased or decreased since the previous reporting period.

Trade Union: Changes in Membership

	Total Membership		
	2013-2014	2012-2013	% changes
Increases			
Union of Construction, Allied Trades and Technicians	86,983	84,377	3.1
Union of Shop Distributive and Allied Workers	433,402	425,652	1.8
Royal College of Nursing of the United Kingdom	421,558	415,843	1.4
GMB	617,064	613,384	0.6
Decreases			
Public and Commercial Service Union	247,345	262,819	-5.9
Association of Teachers and Lecturers	198,102	208,844	-5.1
UNISON	1,282,560	1,301,500	-1.5
Unite the Union	1,405,071	1,424,303	-1.4

The annual returns submitted by unions to the Certification Officer require each union to provide figures for both total membership and members who pay contributions. There can be significant differences between these figures. This is usually the result of total membership figures including retired and unemployed members, members on long term sick and maternity/child care leave and those on career breaks. The returns submitted by unions during this reporting period show that the total number of contributing members was around 92.1% of the total number of members. This compared to 90.9% in the preceding year.

Source: Certification Officer Annual Report 2014/15

Social protection

Chapter 5

Social Protection

(Tables 5.2 to 5.11, 5.13 and 5.15 to 5.19)

Tables 5.2 to 5.6, 5.9 to 5.11 and 5.13 to 5.19 give details of contributors and beneficiaries under the National Insurance and Industrial Injury Acts, supplementary benefits and war pensions.

There are five classes of National Insurance Contributions (NICs):

Class 1 Earnings-related contributions paid on earnings from employment. Employees pay primary Class 1 contributions and employers pay secondary Class 1 contributions. Payment of Class 1 contributions builds up entitlement to contributory benefits which include Basic State Pension; Additional State Pension (State Earnings Related Pension Scheme SERPS and from April 2002, State Second Pension, S2P); Contribution Based Jobseeker's Allowance; Bereavement Benefits; Incapacity Benefit; and the new Employment and Support Allowance.

Primary class 1 contributions stop at State Pension age, but not Class 1 secondary contributions paid by employers. There are reduced contribution rates where the employee contracts out of S2P (previously SERPS). They still receive a Basic State Pension but an Occupational or Personal Pension instead of the Additional State Second Pension.

Class 2 Flat rate contributions paid by the self-employed whose profits are above the small earnings exception. Payment of Class 2 contributions builds up entitlement to the contributory benefits which include Basic State Pension; Bereavement Benefits; Maternity Allowance; Incapacity Benefit; and the Employment and Support Allowance, but not Additional State Second Pension or Contribution Based Jobseeker's Allowance (JSA).

Class 2 contributions stop at State Pension age.

Class 3 Flat rate voluntary contributions, which can be paid by someone whose contribution record is insufficient. Payment of Class 3 contributions builds up entitlement to contributory benefits which include Basic State Pension and Bereavement Benefits. (Tables 5.2 to 5.11, 5.13 and 5.15 to 5.19) Tables 5.2 to 5.6, 5.9 to 5.11 and 5.13 to 5.19 give details of contributors and beneficiaries under the National Insurance and Industrial Injury Acts, supplementary benefits and war pensions.

Class 3A - A new type of voluntary contribution, has been available from October 2015 for those who will have reached state pension age by 6 April 2016. Unlike normal NICs, these are made in a one-off lump-sum payment. Making them allows you to boost your state pension- by up to a maximum extra of £25 per week. The idea is to bring the state pension you receive into line with the new single-tier state pension which begins on 6 April 2016 for people who reach state pension age after that date.

Class 4 Profit-related contributions paid by the self employed in addition to Class 2 contributions. Class 4 contributions stop at State Pension age. Under some circumstances people who are not in employment do not have to make voluntary contributions to accrue a qualifying year for Basic State Pension.

Home Responsibilities Protection

Home Responsibilities Protection (HRP) was introduced to help to protect the basic State Pension of those precluded from regular employment because they are caring for children or a sick or disabled person at home. To be entitled to HRP, a person must have been precluded from regular employment for a full tax year. HRP reduces the amount of qualifying years a person would otherwise need for a Basic State Pension. The scheme ceased on the 6th April 2010 and has been replaced by new weekly credits which can be claimed if qualifying criteria are met.

National Insurance Credits

In addition to paying, or being treated as having paid contributions, a person can be credited with National Insurance contributions (NIC) credits. Contribution credits help to protect people's rights to State Retirement Pension and other Social Security Benefits.

A person is likely to be entitled to contributions credits if they are: a student in full time education or training, in receipt of Jobseeker's Allowance, unable to work due to sickness or disability, entitled to Statutory Maternity Pay or Statutory Adoption Pay, or they have received Carer's Allowance.

Credits are automatically awarded for men aged 60 to 65 provided they are not liable to pay Class 1 or 2 NICs, and to young people for the tax years containing their 16th, 17th and 18th birthdays.

Jobseeker's Allowance (Table 5.6)

Jobseeker's Allowance (JSA) replaced Unemployment Benefit and Income Support for unemployed claimants on 7 October 1996. It is a unified benefit with two routes of entry: contribution-based, which depends mainly upon National Insurance contributions, and income-based, which depends mainly upon a means test. Some claimants can qualify by either route. In practice they receive income-based JSA but have an underlying entitlement to the contribution based element.

Employment and Support Allowance, Invalidity Benefit and Incapacity Benefit (Table 5.7)

Incapacity Benefit replaced Sickness Benefit and Invalidity Benefit from 13 April 1995. The first condition for entitlement to these contributory benefits is that the claimants are incapable of work because of illness or disablement. The second is that they satisfy the contribution conditions, which depend on contributions paid as an employed (Class 1) or self-employed person (Class 2). Under Sickness and Invalidity Benefits the contribution conditions were automatically treated as satisfied if a person was incapable of work because of an industrial accident or prescribed disease. Under Incapacity Benefit those who do not satisfy the contribution conditions do not have them treated as satisfied. Class 1A contributions paid by employers are in respect of the benefit of cars provided for the private use of employees, and the free fuel provided for private use. These contributions do not provide any type of benefit cover.

Since 6 April 1983, most people working for an employer and paying National Insurance contributions as employed persons receive Statutory Sick Pay (SSP) from their employer when they are off work sick. Until 5 April 1986 SSP was payable for a maximum of eight weeks, since this date SSP has been payable for 28 weeks. People who do not work for an employer, and employees who are excluded from the SSP scheme, or those who have run out of SSP before reaching the maximum of 28 weeks and are still sick, can claim benefit. Any period of SSP is excluded from the tables.

Spells of incapacity of three days or less do not count as periods of interruption of employment and are excluded from the tables. Exceptions are where people are receiving regular weekly treatment by dialysis or treatment by radiotherapy, chemotherapy or plasmapheresis where two days in any six consecutive days make up a period of interruption of employment, and those whose incapacity for work ends within three days of the end of SSP entitlement.

At the beginning of a period of incapacity, benefit is subject to three waiting days, except where there was an earlier spell of incapacity of more than three days in the previous eight weeks. Employees entitled to SSP for less than 28 weeks and who are still sick can get Sickness Benefit or Incapacity Benefit Short Term (Low) until they reach a total of 28 weeks provided they satisfy the conditions.

After 28 weeks of SSP and/or Sickness Benefit (SB), Invalidity Benefit (IVB) was payable up to pension age for as long as the incapacity lasted. From pension age, IVB was paid at the person's State Pension rate, until entitlement ceased when SP was paid, or until deemed pension age (70 for a man, 65 for a woman). People who were on Sickness or Invalidity Benefit on 12 April 1995 were automatically transferred to Incapacity Benefit, payable on the same basis as before.

For people on Incapacity Benefit under State Pension age there are two short-term rates: the lower rate is paid for the first 28 weeks of sickness and the higher rate for weeks 29 to 52. From week 53 the Long Term rate Incapacity Benefit is payable. The Short Term rate Incapacity Benefit is based on State Pension entitlement for people over State Pension age and is paid for up to a year if incapacity began before pension age.

The long-term rate of Incapacity Benefit applies to people under State Pension age who have been sick for more than a year. People with a terminal illness, or who are receiving the higher rate care component of Disability Living Allowance, will get the Long Term rate. The Long Term rate is not paid for people over pension age.

Under Incapacity Benefit, for the first 28 weeks of incapacity, people previously in work will be assessed on the 'own occupation' test – the claimant's ability to do their own job. Otherwise, incapacity will be based on a personal capability assessment, which will assess ability to carry out a range of work-related activities. The test will apply after 28 weeks of incapacity or from the start of the claim for people who did not previously have a job. Certain people will be exempted from this test.

The tables exclude all men aged over 65 and women aged over 60 who are in receipt of State Pension, and all people over deemed pension age (70 for a man and 65 for a woman), members of the armed forces, mariners while at sea, and married women and certain widows who have chosen not to be insured for sickness benefit. The tables include a number of individuals who were unemployed prior to incapacity.

The Short Term (Higher) and Long Term rates of Incapacity Benefit are treated as taxable income. There were transitional provisions for people who were on Sickness or Invalidity Benefit on 12 April 1995. They were automatically transferred to Incapacity Benefit, payable on the same basis as before. Former IVB recipients continue to get Additional Pension entitlement, but frozen at 1994 levels. Also their IVB is not subject to tax. If they were over State Pension age on 12 April 1995 they may get Incapacity Benefit for up to five years beyond pension age.

Employment and Support Allowance (ESA) replaced Incapacity Benefit and Income Support paid on the grounds of incapacity for new claims from 27 October 2008. ESA consists of two phases. The first, the assessment phase rate, is paid for the first 13 weeks of the claim whilst a decision is made on the claimants capability through the 'Work Capability Asessment'. The second, or main phase begins after 14 weeks, but only if the 'Work Capability Asessment' has deemed the claimants illness or disability as a limitation on their ability to work.

Within the main phase there are two groups, 'The Work Related Activity Group' and 'The Support Group'. If a claimant is placed in the first, they are expected to take part in work focused interviews with a personal advisor. They will be given support to help them prepare for work and on gaining work will receive a work related activity component in addition to their basic rate. If the claimant is placed in the second group due to their illness or disability having a severe effect upon their ability to work, the claimant will not be expected to work at all, but can do so on a voluntary basis. These claimants will receive a support component in addition to their basic rate.

Child Benefits (Table 5.9a and 5.9b)

You get child ebenfit if you are responsible for a child under 16 (or under 20 if they stay in approved education or training.
Approved education
Education must be full-time (more than an average of 12 hours a week supervised study or course-related work experience) and can include:
A levels or similar - eg Pre-U, International Baccalaureate
Scottish Highers
NVQs and other vocational qualifications up to level 3
home education - if started before your child turned 16
traineeships in England
Courses are not approved if paid for by an employer or 'advanced', eg a university degree or BTEC Higher National Certificate.

Approved training
Approved training should be unpaid and can include:
Access to Apprenticeships in England
Foundation Apprenticeships or Traineeships in Wales
Employability Fund programmes or Get Ready for Work (if started before 1 April 2013) in Scotland
Training for Success, Pathways to Success or Collaboration and Innovation Programme in Northern Ireland
Courses that are part of a job contract are not approved.

Guardian's Allowance is an additional allowance for people bringing up a child because one or both of their parents has died. They must be getting Child Benefit (CB) for the child. The table shows the number of families in the UK in receipt of CB. The numbers shown in the table are estimates based on a random 5 per cent sample of awards current at 31 August, and are therefore subject to sampling error. The figures take no account of new claims, or revisions to claims that were received or processed after 31 August, even if they are backdated to start before 31 August.

Child and Working Tax Credits (New Tax Credits) (Table 5.10 and 5.11)

Child and Working Tax Credits (CTC and WTC) replaced Working Families' Tax Credit (WFTC) from 6th April 2003. CTC and WTC are claimed by individuals, or jointly by couples, whether or not they have children.

CTC provides support to families for the children (up to the 31 August after their 16th birthday) and the 'qualifying' young people (in full-time non-advanced education until their 20th birthday) for which they are responsible. It is paid in addition to CB.

WTC tops up the earnings of families on low or moderate incomes. People working for at least 16 hours a week can claim it if they: (a) are responsible for at least one child or qualifying young person, (b) have a disability which puts them at a disadvantage in getting a job or, (c) in the first year of work, having returned to work aged at least 50 after a period of at least six months receiving out-of-work benefits. Other adults also qualify if they are aged at least 25 and work for at least 30 hours a week.

Widow's Allowance and Bereavement Benefit (Table 5.12 and 5.13)

Widow's Allowance is payable to women widowed on or after 11 April 1988 and up to and including 8 April 2001. There are three types of Widow's Benefits: Widow's Payment, Widowed Mother's Allowance and Widow's Pension. Women widowed before 11 April 1988 continue to receive Widow's Benefit based on the rules that existed before that date. Bereavement Benefit was introduced on 9 April 2001 as a replacement for Widow's Benefit, payable to both men and women widowed on or after 9 April 2001. There are three types of Bereavement Benefits available: Bereavement Payment, Widowed Parent's Allowance and Bereavement Allowance.

5.1 National Insurance Fund (Great Britain)

For the year ended 31 March

£ 000

	2011	2012	2013	2014
Receipts				
Opening balance	48,786,585 [3]	43,163,939	38,593,953	29,082,990
National Insurance Contributions	74,181,834	78,423,776	79,119,934	82,236,514
Compensation for statutory pay recoveries	2,100,796	3,008,707	2,559,760	2,319,000
Income from Investment Account	204,124	188,825	161,550	125,749
State Scheme Premiums [2]	47,299	36,733	30,861	56,408
Other receipts	46,657	46,401	36,164	29,586
Redundancy receipts	49,281	49,274	38,320	56,408
Total Receipts	**76,629,991**	**81,753,716**	**81,946,589**	**84,807,252**
Less				
Payments				
Benefit payments	77,799,137	82,357,733	87,464,810	88,933,118
of which				
State Pension	*69,346,701*	*74,110,982*	*80,008,745*	*82,522,101*
Incapacity Benefit	*5,598,835*	*4,981,255*	*3,355,345*	*1,213,380*
Employment and Support Alllowance	*958,990*	*1,410,890*	*2,312,374*	*3,554,301*
Jobseeker's Allowance (Contributory)	*811,621*	*757,582*	*669,184*	*533,630*
Bereavement Benefits	*615,455*	*605,011*	*598,431*	*587,821*
Maternity Allowance	*343,412*	*366,968*	*395,522*	*397,608*
Christmas Bonus	*122,215*	*123,203*	*123,308*	*122,356*
Guardian's Allowance and Child's Special Allowance	*1,908*	*1,842*	*1,901*	*1,921*
Personal Pensions [1]	2,313,669	2,139,042	2,124,560	15,913
Administrative costs	1,419,801	1,125,019	916,875	903,502
Redundancy payments	445,623	406,631	453,577	356,069
Transfers to Northern Ireland NIF	125,000	145,000	334,000	315,000
Other payments	149,407	150,277	163,730	170,778
Total Payments	**82,252,637**	**86,323,702**	**91,457,552**	**90,694,380**
Excess of payments over receipts	(5,622,646)	(4,569,986)	(9,510,963)	(5,887,128)
Opening balance	48,786,585	43,163,939	38,593,953	29,082,990
Less excess of payments over receipts	(5,622,646)	(4,569,986)	(9,510,963)	(5,887,128)
Closing balance	**43,163,939**	**38,593,953**	**29,082,990**	**23,195,862**

Source: HM Revenue and Customs, Department for Work and Pensions

1. On 5 April 2012 the abolition of contracting-out on a defined contribution basis took place resulting in these contributions no longer being received. As the payments were made a year in arrears, from April 2013, the number of transactions has greatly reduced as only late payments and recoveries are being dealt with.

2. State Scheme Premiums are payable to the Fund in respect of employed persons' who cease to be covered, in certain specified circumstances, by a contracted-out pension scheme.

3. Opening balance has been restated based on analysis of prior year data as better management information has become available.

5.2 National Insurance Contributions

For the year ended 31 March	Notes	2012	2013	2014	2015
Class 1 (employed earner)	i	75,528,875	75,873,021	79,067,796	80,814,248
Class 1A and 1B	ii	987,226	1,047,965	1,118,263	1,078,274
Class 2 (Self-employed flat rate)	iii	229,516	341,361	327,180	353,608
Class 3 (Voluntary contributions)	iv	48,876	40,274	31,627	23,129
Class 4 (Self-employed earnings related)	v	1,629,283	1,817,313	1,689,648	1,842,303
		78,423,776	79,119,934	82,236,514	84,112,562

Source: HMRC National Insurance Fund Account Great Britain

Notes

i. Class 1 contributions comprise two parts: primary contributions payable by employees and secondary contributions payable by employers.

ii. Class 1A contributions are paid by employers on most benefits provided to employees.
Class 1B contributions are payable by employers where they have entered into a PAYE settlement agreement for tax enabling them to settle their National Insurance and income tax liability in a lump sum after the end of the tax year. The figures for Class IA and Class 1B have been combined.

iii. Class 2 self-employed persons pay flat rate weekly contributions.

iv. Class 3 voluntary flat rate contributions are paid to maintain contributors' National Insurance record for certain benefit and/or pension purposes.

v. Class 4 self employed persons pay earnings related contributions.

5.3 Main Features of National Insurance contributions (NCIS) 1999-2000 to 2015-2016

	Rate in 1999-2000	Rate in 2000-2001	Rate in 2001-2002	Rate in 2002-2003	Rate in 2003-2004	Rate in 2004-2005	Rate in 2005-2006	Rate in 2006-2007	Rate in 2007-2008	Rate in 2008-2009
Class 1										
Lower earnings limit (LEL) – a week	£66	£67	£72	£75	£77	£79	£82	£84	£87	£90
Primary threshold (PT) – a week	-	-	£87	£89	£89	£91	£94	£97	£100	£105
Secondary threshold (ST) – a week	£83	£84	£87	£89	£89	£91	£94	£97	£100	£105
Upper accruals Point (UAP) – a week (1)	-	-	-	-	-	-	-	-	-	-
Upper earnings limit (UEL) – a week (2)	£500	£535	£575	£585	£595	£610	£630	£645	£670	£770
Primary contributions (employee)										
Main contribution rate (PT to UEL) (3)	10.0%	10.0%	10.0%	10.0%	11.0%	11.0%	11.0%	11.0%	11.0%	11.0%
Additional contribution rate (above UEL)	-	-	-	-	1.0%	1.0%	1.0%	1.0%	1.0%	1.0%
Contracted out rebate (LEL to UAP/UEL) (4) (5)	1.6%	1.6%	1.6%	1.6%	1.6%	1.6%	1.6%	1.6%	1.6%	1.6%
Reduced rate for married women and widow optants (6)	3.85%	3.85%	3.85%	3.85%	4.85%	4.85%	4.85%	4.85%	4.85%	4.85%
Secondary contributions (employer)										
Contribution rate (above ST)	12.2%	12.2%	11.9%	11.8%	12.8%	12.8%	12.8%	12.8%	12.8%	12.8%
Contracted out rebate (LEL to UAP/UEL) (5)										
- COSRS	3.0%	3.0%	3.0%	3.5%	3.5%	3.5%	3.5%	3.5%	3.7%	3.7%
- COMPS (7)	0.6%	0.6%	0.6%	1.0%	1.0%	1.0%	1.0%	1.0%	1.4%	1.4%
Class 1A and 1B										
Contribution rate (8)	12.2%	12.2%	11.9%	11.8%	12.8%	12.8%	12.8%	12.8%	12.8%	12.8%
Class 2										
Flat-rate contribution – a week	£6.55	£2.00	£2.00	£2.00	£2.00	£2.05	£2.10	£2.10	£2.20	£2.30
Small earnings exception / Small Profits Threshold – a year (11)	£3,770	£3,825	£3,955	£4,025	£4,095	£4,215	£4,345	£4,465	£4,635	£4,825
Class 3										
Flat-rate contribution – a week (9)	£6.45	£6.55	£6.75	£6.85	£6.95	£7.15	£7.35	£7.55	£7.80	£8.10
Class 4										
Lower profits limit (LPL) – a year	£7,530	£4,385	£4,535	£4,615	£4,615	£4,745	£4,895	£5,035	£5,225	£5,435
Upper profits limit (UPL) – a year (2)	£26,000	£27,820	£29,900	£30,420	£30,940	£31,720	£32,760	£33,540	£34,840	£40,040
Main contribution rate (LPL to UPL)	6%	7%	7%	7%	8%	8%	8%	8%	8%	8%
Additional contribution rate (above UPL)	-	-	-	-	1%	1%	1%	1%	1%	1%

Source: HM Revenue & Customs

5.3 Main Features of National Insurance contributions (NCIS) 1999-2000 to 2015-2016

	Rate in 2009-2010	Rate in 2010-11	Rate in 2011-12	Rate in 2012-13 (10)	Rate in 2013-14 (10)	Rate in 2014-15 (10)	Rate in 2015-16 (10)
Class 1							
Lower earnings limit (LEL) – a week	£95	£97	£102	£107	£109	£111	£112
Primary threshold (PT) – a week	£110	£110	£139	£146	£149	£153	£155
Secondary threshold (ST) – a week	£110	£110	£136	£144	£148	£153	£156
Upper accruals Point (UAP) – a week (1)	£770	£770	£770	£770	£770	£770	£770
Upper earnings limit (UEL) – a week (2)	£844	£844	£817	£817	£797	£805	£815
Primary contributions (employee)							
Main contribution rate (PT to UEL) (3)	11.0%	11.0%	12.0%	12.0%	12.0%	12.0%	12.0%
Additional contribution rate (above UEL)	1.0%	1.0%	2.0%	2.0%	2.0%	2.0%	2.0%
Contracted out rebate (LEL to UAP/UEL) (4) (5)	1.6%	1.6%	1.6%	1.4%	1.4%	1.4%	1.4%
Reduced rate for married women and widow optants (6)	4.85%	4.85%	5.85%	5.85%	5.85%	5.85%	5.85%
Secondary contributions (employer)							
Contribution rate (above ST)	12.8%	12.8%	13.8%	13.8%	13.8%	13.8%	13.8%
Contracted out rebate (LEL to UAP/UEL) (5)							
- COSRS	3.7%	3.7%	3.7%	3.4%	3.4%	3.4%	3.4%
- COMPS (7)	1.4%	1.4%	1.4%	-	-	-	-
Class 1A and 1B							
Contribution rate (8)	12.8%	12.8%	13.8%	13.8%	13.8%	13.8%	13.8%
Class 2							
Flat-rate contribution – a week	£2.40	£2.40	£2.50	£2.65	£2.70	£2.75	£2.80
Small earnings exception / Small Profits Threshold – a year (11)	£5,075	£5,075	£5,315	£5,595	£5,725	£5,885	£5,965
Class 3							
Flat-rate contribution – a week (9)	£12.05	£12.05	£12.60	£13.25	£13.55	£13.90	£14.10
Class 4							
Lower profits limit (LPL) – a year	£5,715	£5,715	£7,225	£7,605	£7,755	£7,956	£8,060
Upper profits limit (UPL) – a year (2)	£43,875	£43,875	£42,475	£42,475	£41,450	£41,865	£42,385
Main contribution rate (LPL to UPL)	8%	8%	9%	9%	9%	9%	9%
Additional contribution rate (above UPL)	1%	1%	2%	2%	2%	2%	2%

Source: HM Revenue & Customs

5.3 Main Features of National Insurance contributions (NCIS) 1999-2000 to 2015-2016

(1) The upper accruals point was introduced in April 2009 until April 2015-16. It is no longer needed after the contracting out rebates are abolished from 2016-17 onwards.

(2) From April 2009 the upper earnings limit and upper profits limit were aligned to the income tax higher rate threshold.

(3) Between LEL and UEL for 1999-2000.

(4) For Appropriate Personal Pension Schemes (APPS) both employer and employee pay NICs at the full contracted-out rate and in the following tax year on submission of the end-of-year returns HMRC pay an age related rebate direct to the schemes. The employee's share of this rebate is 1.6%.

(5) Up to and including 2008-09, the rebate applies between the LEL and the UEL. From 2009-10 onwards the rebate applies between the LEL and UAP.
The rebates are abolished from 2016-17 onwards.

(6) Married women opting to pay contributions at the reduced rate earn no entitlement to contributory National Insurance benefits as a result of these contributions.
No women have been allowed to exercise this option since 1977.

(7) For employers operating a COMPS, in addition to the reduction shown in secondary Class 1 contributions, in the following tax year on submission of end-of-year returns, HMRC pay an additional "top-up" rebate direct to the scheme. As with APPS, this rebate is age related. COMPs are abolished from 2012-13 onwards.

(8) From April 2000 the Class 1A liability for employers was extended from company cars and fuel to include other taxable benefits not already attracting a Class 1 liability.
Class 1A and Class 1B contributions are paid in the year following accrual.

(9) Class 3 contribution rules changed in 2009-10 to allow those reaching state pension age before April 2015 with 20 qualifying years to purchase up to 6 additional years.

(10) From 2012-13 the default indexation assumption for NICs is CPI (excluding the secondary threshold up until 2016-17).

(11) The Small Profits Threshold replaced the Small Earnings Exception on 6 April 2015.

Notes:

Class 1 National Insurance Contributions (NICs)

Class 1 NICs are earnings related contributions paid by employed earners who are below State Pension age and their employers. The contributions are paid at either the contracted-out rate or the not contracted-out rate. The contracted-out rate is payable only where the employee is a member of a contracted-out occupational scheme in place of State Second Pension (formerly SERPS). Class 1 NICs are collected by HMRC along with income tax under the Pay As You Earn (PAYE) scheme.

Class 1A National Insurance Contributions (NICs)

Class 1A NICs are paid only by employers on the value of most taxable benefits-in-kind provided to employees, such as private use of company cars and fuel, private medical insurance, accommodation and loan benefits. They do not give any benefit rights.

Class 1B National Insurance Contributions (NICs)

Class 1B NICs were introduced on 6 April 1999. Like Class 1A they are also paid only by employers and cover PAYE Settlement Agreements (PSA) under which employers agree to meet the income tax liability arising on a restricted range of benefits. Class 1B is payable on the value of the items included in the PSA that would otherwise attract a Class 1 or Class 1A liability and the value of the income tax met by the employer. They do not give any benefit rights.

Class 2 National Insurance Contributions (NICs)

Class 2 contributions are a flat rate weekly liability payable by all self-employed people over 16 (up to State Pension age) unless they have applied for and been granted a "small earnings exception" (SEE) because their earnings from self-employment are expected to be low, although they may still pay if they choose to. Class 2 NICs can be paid up to six years after the tax year in which they are due. Class 4 NICS may also have to be paid if their profits for the year are over the lower profits limit (see below).

Class 3 National Insurance Contributions (NICs)

Class 3 NICs may be paid voluntarily by people aged 16 and over (but below State Pension age) to help them qualify for State Pension and Bereavement Benefits if their contribution record would not otherwise be sufficient. Contributions are flat rate and can be paid up to six years after the year in which they are due.

Class 4 National Insurance Contributions (NICs)

Class 4 NICS are paid by the self-employed whose profits are above the lower profits limit. They are profit related and do not count for any benefits themselves.

5.4 Proposed benefit and pension rates 2014 to 2015

Proposed benefit and pension rates 2014 to 2015 (Weekly rates unless otherwise shown)	RATES 2013	RATES 2014
ATTENDANCE ALLOWANCE		
higher rate	79.15	81.30
lower rate	53.00	54.45
BEREAVEMENT BENEFIT		
Bereavement payment (lump sum)	2000.00	2000.00
Widowed parent's allowance	108.30	111.20
Bereavement Allowance		
standard rate	108.30	111.20
age-related		
age 54	100.72	103.42
53	93.14	95.63
52	85.56	87.85
51	77.98	80.06
50	70.40	72.28
49	62.81	64.50
48	55.23	56.71
47	47.65	48.93
46	40.07	41.14
45	32.49	33.36
BENEFIT CAP		
In Housing Benefit (weekly rate)		
Couples and lone parents	500.00	500.00
Single persons without children	350.00	350.00
In Universal Credit (monthly rate)		
Joint claimants and single claimants with children	2167.00	2167.00
Joint claimants and single claimants without children	1517.00	1517.00
CAPITAL LIMITS - rules common to Income Support, income based Jobseeker's Allowance,		
income-related Employment and Support Allowance, Pension Credit, and		
Housing Benefit, and Universal Credit		
unless stated otherwise		
upper limit	16000.00	16000.00
upper limit - Pension Credit and those getting Housing Benefit and Pension Credit Guarantee Credit	No limit	No limit
Amount disregarded - all benefits except Pension Credit and Housing Benefit for those above the qualifying age for Guarantee Credit	6000.00	6000.00
Amount disregarded - Pension Credit and Housing Benefit for those above the qualifying age for Pension Credit	10000.00	10000.00
child disregard (not Pension Credit or Employment and Support Allowance)	3000.00	3000.00
amt disregarded (living in RC/NH)	10000.00	10000.00

5.4 Proposed benefit and pension rates 2014 to 2015

Proposed benefit and pension rates 2014 to 2015 (Weekly rates unless otherwise shown)	RATES 2013	RATES 2014

Tariff income
    £1 for every £250, or part thereof, between the amount of
    capital disregarded and the capital upper limit		

Tariff income - Pension Credit and Housing Benefit where clmt/ptner is over
Guarantee Credit qualifying age
    £1 for every £500, or part thereof, between the amount of
    capital disregarded and capital upper limit		

CARER'S ALLOWANCE	59.75	61.35
DEDUCTIONS - rules common to Income Support, Jobseeker's Allowance, Employment and Support Allowance, Pension Credit and Housing Benefit unless stated otherwise		
Non-dependant deductions from housing benefit and from IS, JSA(IB), ESA(IR) and Pension Credit		
aged 25 and over in receipt of IS and JSA(IB), in receipt of main phase ESA(IR), aged 18 or over, not in remunerative work	13.60	14.15
aged 18 or over and in remunerative work		
- gross income: less than £128	13.60	14.15
- gross income: £128 to £187.99	31.25	32.45
- gross income: £188 to £244.99	42.90	44.55
- gross income: £245 to £325.99	70.20	72.95
- gross income: £326 to £405.99	79.95	83.05
- gross income: £406 and above	87.75	91.15
Deductions from housing benefit		
Service charges for fuel		
heating	25.60	27.55
hot water	2.95	3.20
lighting	2.05	2.20
cooking	2.95	3.20
Amount ineligible for meals		
three or more meals a day		
single claimant	25.85	26.55
each person in family aged 16 or over	25.85	26.55
each child under 16	13.10	13.45
less than three meals a day		
single claimant	17.20	17.65
each person in family aged 16 or over	17.20	17.65
each child under 16	8.65	8.90
breakfast only - claimant and each member of the family	3.15	3.25
Amount for personal expenses (not HB)	23.50	23.75

5.4 Proposed benefit and pension rates 2014 to 2015

Proposed benefit and pension rates 2014 to 2015 (Weekly rates unless otherwise shown)	RATES 2013	RATES 2014
Third party deductions from IS, JSA(IB), ESA(IR) and Pension Credit for;		
arrears of housing, fuel and water costs	3.60	3.65
council tax etc. and deductions for ELDS and ILS.		
child support, contribution towards maintenance (CTM)		
standard deduction	7.20	7.30
lower deduction	3.60	3.65
arrears of Community Charge		
court order against claimant	3.60	3.65
court order against couple	5.65	5.70
fine or compensation order		
standard rate	5.00	5.00
lower rate	3.60	3.65
Maximum deduction rates for recovery of overpayments (not /JSA(C)/ESA(C))		
ordinary overpayments	10.80	10.95
where claimant convicted of fraud	18.00	18.25
Deductions from JSA(C) and ESA (C)		
Arrears of Comm. Charge & overpayment recovery		
Age 16 - 24	18.93	19.11
Age 25 +	23.90	24.13
Arrears of Council Tax & Fines		
Age 16 - 24	22.72	22.94
Age 25 +	28.68	28.96
Max. dedn for arrears of Child Maintenance		
Age 16 - 24	18.93	19.11
Age 25 +	23.90	24.13

DEPENDENCY INCREASES

Adult dependency increases for spouse or person looking after children - payable with;		
State Pension on own insurance (Cat A or B)	63.20	64.90
long term Incapacity Benefit	58.85	60.45
Severe Disablement Allowance	35.35	36.30
Carers Allowance	35.15	36.10
short-term Incapacity Benefit (over state pension age)	56.65	58.20
short-term Incapacity Benefit (under State Pension age)	45.85	47.10
Child Dependency Increases - payable with;		
State Pension; Widowed Mothers/Parents Allowance;	11.35	11.35
short-term Incapacity benefit - higher rate or over state pension age;		

5.4 Proposed benefit and pension rates 2014 to 2015

Proposed benefit and pension rates 2014 to 2015 (Weekly rates unless otherwise shown)	RATES 2013	RATES 2014
long-term Incapacity Benefit; Carer's Allowance; Severe Disablement Allowance; Industrial Death Benefit (higher rate);		
NB - The rate of child dependency increase is adjusted where it is payable for the eldest child for whom child benefit is also paid. The weekly rate in such cases is reduced by the difference (less £3.65) between the ChB rates for the eldest and subsequent children.	8.10	8.05

DISABILITY LIVING ALLOWANCE

	RATES 2013	RATES 2014
Care Component		
Highest	79.15	81.30
Middle	53.00	54.45
Lowest	21.00	21.55
Mobility Component		
Higher	55.25	56.75
Lower	21.00	21.55

DISREGARDS

	RATES 2013	RATES 2014
Housing Benefit		
Earnings disregards		
standard (single claimant)	5.00	5.00
couple	10.00	10.00
higher (special occupations/circumstances)	20.00	20.00
lone parent	25.00	25.00
childcare charges	175.00	175.00
childcare charges (2 or more children)	300.00	300.00
permitted work higher	99.50	101.00
permitted work lower	20.00	20.00
Other Income disregards		
adult maintenance disregard	15.00	15.00
war disablement pension and war widows pension	10.00	10.00
widowed mothers/parents allowance	15.00	15.00
Armed Forces Compensation Scheme	10.00	10.00
student loan	10.00	10.00
student's covenanted income	5.00	5.00
income from boarders (plus 50% of the balance)	20.00	20.00
additional earnings disregard	17.10	17.10
income from subtenants (£20 fixed from April 08)	20.00	20.00

**Income Support, income-based Jobseeker's Allowance,
Income-related Employment and Support Allowance (ESA(IR)) and Pension
Credit**

	RATES 2013	RATES 2014
Earnings disregards		
standard (single claimant) (not ESA(IR))	5.00	5.00
couple (not ESA(IR))	10.00	10.00
higher (special occupations/circumstances)	20.00	20.00
partner of claimant (ESA(IR))	20.00 (maximum)	20.00 (maximum)
Other Income disregards		

5.4 Proposed benefit and pension rates 2014 to 2015

Proposed benefit and pension rates 2014 to 2015	RATES	RATES
(Weekly rates unless otherwise shown)	2013	2014
war disablement pension and war widows pension	10.00	10.00
widowed mothers/parents allowance	10.00	10.00
Armed Forces Compensation Scheme	10.00	10.00
student loan (not Pension Credit)	10.00	10.00
student's covenanted income (not Pension Credit)	5.00	5.00
income from boarders (plus 50% of the balance)	20.00	20.00
income from subtenants (£20 fixed from April 08)	20.00	20.00

EARNINGS RULES

Carers Allowance	100.00	100.00
Limit of earnings from councillor's allowance	99.50	101.00
Permitted work earnings limit - higher	99.50	101.00
- lower	20.00	20.00
Industrial injuries unemployability supplement permitted earnings level (annual amount)	5174.00	5252.00

Earnings level at which adult dependency (ADI) increases are affected with:

short-term incapacity benefit where claimant is		
(a) under state pension age	45.85	47.10
(b) over state pension age	56.65	58.20
state pension, long term incapacity benefit, severe disablement allowance, unemployability supplement - payable when dependant		
(a) is living with claimant	71.70	72.40
(b) still qualifies for the tapered earnings rule	45.09	45.09
Earnings level at which ADI is affected when dependant is not living with claimant;		
state pension,	63.20	64.90
long-term incapacity benefit,	58.85	60.45
unemployability supplement,	59.75	61.35
severe disablement allowance	35.35	36.30
Carers allowance	35.15	36.10
Earnings level at which child dependency increases are affected		
for first child	220.00	225.00
additional amount for each subsequent child	29.00	30.00
Pension income threshold for incapacity benefit	85.00	85.00
Pension income threshold for contributory Employment Support Allowance	85.00	85.00

5.4 Proposed benefit and pension rates 2014 to 2015

Proposed benefit and pension rates 2014 to 2015 (Weekly rates unless otherwise shown)	RATES 2013	RATES 2014
EMPLOYMENT AND SUPPORT ALLOWANCE		
Personal Allowances		
Single		
under 25	56.80	57.35
25 or over	71.70	72.40
lone parent		
under 18	56.80	57.35
18 or over	71.70	72.40
couple		
both under 18	56.80	57.35
both under 18 with child	85.80	86.65
both under 18 (main phase)	71.70	72.40
both under 18 with child (main phase)	112.55	113.70
one 18 or over, one under 18 (certain conditions apply)	112.55	113.70
both over 18	112.55	113.70
claimant under 25, partner under 18	56.80	57.35
claimant 25 or over, partner under 18	71.70	72.40
claimant (main phase), partner under 18	71.70	72.40
Premiums		
enhanced disability		
single	15.15	15.55
couple	21.75	22.35
severe disability		
single	59.50	61.10
couple (lower rate)	59.50	61.10
couple (higher rate)	119.00	122.20
carer	33.30	34.20
pensioner		
single with WRAC	45.25	47.20
single with support component	38.90	40.20
single with no component	73.70	75.95
couple with WRAC	81.05	84.05
couple with support component	74.70	77.05
couple with no component	109.50	112.80
Components		
Work-related Activity	28.45	28.75
Support	34.80	35.75
HOUSING BENEFIT		
Personal allowances		

5.4 Proposed benefit and pension rates 2014 to 2015

Proposed benefit and pension rates 2014 to 2015	RATES	RATES
(Weekly rates unless otherwise shown)	2013	2014
single		
under 25	56.80	57.35
25 or over	71.70	72.40
entitled to main phase ESA	71.70	72.40
lone parent		
under 18	56.80	57.35
18 or over	71.70	72.40
entitled to main phase ESA	71.70	72.40
couple		
both under 18	85.80	86.65
one or both 18 or over	112.55	113.70
claimant entitled to main phase ESA	112.55	113.70
dependent children	65.62	66.33
pensioner		
single/lone parent has attained the qualifying age for Pension Credit but under 65.	145.40	148.35
couple – one or both has attained the qualifying age for Pension Credit but both under 65	222.05	226.50
single / lone parent - 65 and over	163.50	165.15
couple - one or both 65 and over	244.95	247.20
Premiums		
family	17.40	17.45
family (lone parent rate)	22.20	22.20
disability		
single	31.00	31.85
couple	44.20	45.40
enhanced disability		
single	15.15	15.55
disabled child	23.45	24.08
couple	21.75	22.35
severe disability		
single	59.50	61.10
couple (lower rate)	59.50	61.10
couple (higher rate)	119.00	122.20
disabled child	57.89	59.50
carer	33.30	34.20
ESA components		
work-related activity	28.45	28.75
support	34.80	35.75

5.4 Proposed benefit and pension rates 2014 to 2015

Proposed benefit and pension rates 2014 to 2015 (Weekly rates unless otherwise shown)	RATES 2013	RATES 2014
INCAPACITY BENEFIT		
Long-term Incapacity Benefit	101.35	104.10
Short-term Incapacity Benefit (under state pension age)		
lower rate	76.45	78.50
higher rate	90.50	92.95
Short-term Incapacity Benefit (over state pension age)		
lower rate	97.25	99.90
higher rate	101.35	104.10
Increase of Long-term Incapacity Benefit for age		
higher rate	10.70	11.00
lower rate	6.00	6.15
Invalidity Allowance (Transitional)		
higher rate	10.70	11.00
middle rate	6.00	6.15
lower rate	6.00	6.15
INCOME SUPPORT		
Personal Allowances		
single		
under 25	56.80	57.35
25 or over	71.70	72.40
lone parent		
under 18	56.80	57.35
18 or over	71.70	72.40
couple		
both under 18	56.80	57.35
both under 18 - higher rate	85.80	86.65
one under 18, one under 25	56.80	57.35
one under 18, one 25 and over	71.70	72.40
both 18 or over	112.55	113.70
dependent children	65.62	66.33
Premiums		
family / lone parent	17.40	17.45
pensioner (applies to couples only)	109.50	112.80
disability		
single	31.00	31.85
couple	44.20	45.40
enhanced disability		

5.4 Proposed benefit and pension rates 2014 to 2015

Proposed benefit and pension rates 2014 to 2015 (Weekly rates unless otherwise shown)		RATES 2013	RATES 2014
single		15.15	15.55
disabled child		23.45	24.08
	couple	21.75	22.35
severe disability			
single		59.50	61.10
couple (lower rate)		59.50	61.10
couple (higher rate)		119.00	122.20
disabled child		57.89	59.50
carer		33.30	34.20
Relevant sum for strikers		39.00	40.00
INDUSTRIAL DEATH BENEFIT			
Widow's pension			
higher rate		110.15	113.10
lower rate		33.05	33.93
Widower's pension		110.15	113.10
INDUSTRIAL INJURIES DISABLEMENT BENEFIT			
Standard rate			
100%		161.60	166.00
90%		145.44	149.40
80%		129.28	132.80
70%		113.12	116.20
60%		96.96	99.60
50%		80.80	83.00
40%		64.64	66.40
30%		48.48	49.80
20%		32.32	33.20
Maximum life gratuity (lump sum)		10730.00	11020.00
Unemployability Supplement		99.90	102.60
increase for early incapacity			
higher rate		20.70	21.25
middle rate		13.30	13.70
lower rate		6.65	6.85
Maximum reduced earnings allowance		64.64	66.40
Maximum retirement allowance		16.16	16.60
Constant attendance allowance			
exceptional rate		129.40	132.80
intermediate rate		97.05	99.60
normal maximum rate		64.70	66.40

5.4 Proposed benefit and pension rates 2014 to 2015

Proposed benefit and pension rates 2014 to 2015 (Weekly rates unless otherwise shown)	RATES 2013	RATES 2014
part-time rate	32.35	33.20
Exceptionally severe disablement allowance	64.70	66.40
JOBSEEKER'S ALLOWANCE		
Contribution based JSA - Personal rates		
under 25	56.80	57.35
25 or over	71.70	72.40
Income-based JSA - personal allowances		
under 25	56.80	57.35
25 or over	71.70	72.40
lone parent		
under 18	56.80	57.35
18 or over	71.70	72.40
couple		
both under 18	56.80	57.35
both under 18 - higher rate	85.80	86.65
one under 18, one under 25	56.80	57.35
one under 18, one 25 and over	71.70	72.40
both 18 or over	112.55	113.70
dependent children	65.62	66.33
Premiums		
family / lone parent	17.40	17.45
pensioner		
single	73.70	75.95
couple	109.50	112.80
disability		
single	31.00	31.85
couple	44.20	45.40
enhanced disability		
single	15.15	15.55
disabled child	23.45	24.08
couple	21.75	22.35
severe disability		
single	59.50	61.10
couple (lower rate)	59.50	61.10
couple (higher rate)	119.00	122.20
disabled child	57.89	59.50
carer	33.30	34.20

5.4 Proposed benefit and pension rates 2014 to 2015

Proposed benefit and pension rates 2014 to 2015 (Weekly rates unless otherwise shown)	RATES 2013	RATES 2014
Prescribed sum for strikers	39.00	40.00
MATERNITY ALLOWANCE		
Standard rate	136.78	138.18
MA threshold	30.00	30.00
PENSION CREDIT		
Standard minimum guarantee		
single	145.40	148.35
couple	222.05	226.50
Additional amount for severe disability		
single	59.50	61.10
couple (one qualifies)	59.50	61.10
couple (both qualify)	119.00	122.20
Additional amount for carers	33.30	34.20
Savings credit		
threshold - single	115.30	120.35
threshold - couple	183.90	192.00
maximum - single	18.06	16.80
maximum - couple	22.89	20.70
Amount for claimant and first spouse in polygamous marriage	222.05	226.50
Additional amount for additional spouse	76.65	78.15
Non-State Pensions (for Pension Credit purposes)		
Statutory minimum increase to non-state pensions	2.20%	2.70%
PERSONAL INDEPENDENCE PAYMENT		
Daily living component		
Enhanced	79.15	81.30
Standard	53.00	54.45
Mobility component		
Enhanced	55.25	56.75
Standard	21.00	21.55
SEVERE DISABLEMENT ALLOWANCE		
Basic rate	71.80	73.75
Age-related addition (from Dec 90)		
Higher rate	10.70	11.00
Middle rate	6.00	6.15
Lower rate	6.00	6.15

5.4 Proposed benefit and pension rates 2014 to 2015

Proposed benefit and pension rates 2014 to 2015 (Weekly rates unless otherwise shown)	RATES 2013	RATES 2014
STATE PENSION		
Category A or B	110.15	113.10
Category B(lower) - spouse or civil partner's insurance	66.00	67.80
Category C or D - non-contributory	66.00	67.80
Additional pension	2.20%	2.70%
Increments to:-		
Basic pension	2.20%	2.70%
Additional pension	2.20%	2.70%
Graduated Retirement Benefit (GRB)	2.20%	2.70%
Inheritable lump sum	2.20%	2.70%
Contracted-out Deduction from AP in respect of pre-April 1988 contracted-out earnings	Nil	Nil
Contracted-out Deduction from AP in respect of contracted-out earnings from April 1988 to 1997	2.20%	2.70%
Graduated Retirement Benefit (unit)	0.1279	0.1314
Increase of long term incapacity for age	2.20%	2.70%
Addition at age 80	0.25	0.25
Increase of Long-term incapacity for age		
higher rate	20.70	21.25
lower rate	10.35	10.65
Invalidity Allowance (Transitional) for State Pension recipients		
higher rate	20.70	21.25
middle rate	13.30	13.70
lower rate	6.65	6.85
STATUTORY ADOPTION PAY		
Earnings threshold	109.00	111.00
Standard Rate	136.78	138.18
STATUTORY MATERNITY PAY		
Earnings threshold	109.00	111.00
Standard rate	136.78	138.18
STATUTORY PATERNITY PAY		
Earnings threshold	109.00	111.00
Standard Rate	136.78	138.18
Additional statutory paternity pay	136.78	138.18

5.4 Proposed benefit and pension rates 2014 to 2015

Proposed benefit and pension rates 2014 to 2015 (Weekly rates unless otherwise shown)	RATES 2013	RATES 2014
STATUTORY SICK PAY		
Earnings threshold	109.00	111.00
Standard rate	86.70	87.55
UNIVERSAL CREDIT (monthly rates)		
Universal Credit Minimum Amount	0.01	0.01
Universal Credit Amounts		
Standard allowance		
Single		
Single under 25	246.81	249.28
Single 25 or over	311.55	314.67
Couple		
Joint claimants both under 25	387.42	391.29
Joint claimants, one or both 25 or over	489.06	493.95
Child element		
First child	272.08	274.58
Second/ subsequent child	226.67	229.17
Disabled child additions		
Lower rate addition	123.62	124.86
Higher rate addition	352.92	362.92
Limited Capability for Work element	123.62	124.86
Limited Capability for Work and Work-Related Activity element	303.66	311.86
Carer element	144.70	148.61
Childcare element		
Maximum for one child	532.29	532.29
Maximum for two or more children	912.50	912.50
Non-dependants' housing cost contributions	68.00	68.68
Work allowances		
Higher work allowance (no housing element)		
Single		
Single claimant, no dependent children	111.00	111.00
Single claimant, one or more children	734.00	734.00
Single claimant, limited capability for work	647.00	647.00
Joint claimants		
Joint claimant, no dependent children	111.00	111.00
Joint claimant, one or more children	536.00	536.00
Joint claimant, limited capability for work	647.00	647.00
Lower work allowance		
Single		
Single claimant, no dependent children	111.00	111.00
Single claimant, one or more children	263.00	263.00
Single claimant, limited capability for work	192.00	192.00
Joint claimants		
Joint claimant, no dependent children	111.00	111.00
Joint claimant, one or more children	222.00	222.00

5.4 Proposed benefit and pension rates 2014 to 2015

Proposed benefit and pension rates 2014 to 2015 (Weekly rates unless otherwise shown)	RATES 2013	RATES 2014
Joint claimant, limited capability for work	192.00	192.00
Assumed income from capital	4.35	4.35
Third Party Deductions at 5% of UC Standard Allowance for:		
Single		
Single under 25	12.34	12.46
Single 25 or over	15.58	15.73
Couple		
Joint claimants both under 25	19.37	19.56
Joint claimants, one or both 25 or over	24.45	24.70
Maximum deductions for Fines	108.35	108.35
Overall Maximum Deduction Rate at 40% of UC Standard Allowance:		
Single		
Single under 25	98.72	99.71
Single 25 or over	124.62	125.87
Couple		
Joint claimants both under 25	154.97	156.52
Joint claimants, one or both 25 or over	195.62	197.58
Fraud Overpayments, Recoverable Hardship Payments and Administrative Penalties at 40% of UC Standard Allowance		
Single		
Single under 25	98.72	99.71
Single 25 or over	124.62	125.87
Couple		
Joint claimants both under 25	154.97	156.52
Joint claimants, one or both 25 or over	195.62	197.58
Normal Overpayments and Civil Penalties at 15% of UC Standard Allowance		
Single		
Single under 25	37.02	37.39
Single 25 or over	46.73	47.20
Couple		
Joint claimants both under 25	58.11	58.69
Joint claimants, one or both 25 or over	73.36	74.09
Normal Overpayments and Civil Penalties at 25% of UC Standard Allowance if claimant's and/or partner's earnings are over the Work Allowance		

5.4 Proposed benefit and pension rates 2014 to 2015

Proposed benefit and pension rates 2014 to 2015 (Weekly rates unless otherwise shown)	RATES 2013	RATES 2014
Single		
Single under 25	61.70	62.32
Single 25 or over	77.89	78.67
Couple		
Joint claimants both under 25	96.86	97.82
Joint claimants, one or both 25 or over	122.27	123.49
WIDOW'S BENEFIT		
Widowed mother's allowance	108.30	111.20
Widow's pension		
standard rate	108.30	111.20
age-related		
age 54 (49)	100.72	103.42
53 (48)	93.14	95.63
52 (47)	85.56	87.85
51 (46)	77.98	80.06
50 (45)	70.40	72.28
49 (44)	62.81	64.50
48 (43)	55.23	56.71
47 (42)	47.65	48.93
46 (41)	40.07	41.14
45 (40)	32.49	33.36

Note: For deaths occurring before 11 April 1988
refer to age-points shown in brackets.

Source: Department for Work and Pensions

5.5 Number of Persons claiming benefits: Caseloads by age group, thousands

	2003/04 Outturn	2004/05 Outturn	2005/06 Outturn	2006/07 Outturn	2007/08 Outturn	2008/09 Outturn	2009/10 Outturn	2010/11 Outturn	2011/12 Outturn	2012/13 Outturn	2013/14 Outturn
Benefits directed at Children											
Attendance Allowance (in payment)	-	-	-	-	-	-	-	-	-	-	-
Child Benefit & One Parent Benefit	-	-	-	-	-	-	-	-	-	-	-
number of children covered	-	-	-	-	-	-	-	-	-	-	-
Disability Living Allowance	270	279	286	292	300	310	322	331	339	350	362
of which in payment	270	279	286	292	300	310	322	331	339	350	362
of which entitlement without payment	-	-	-	-	-	-	-	-	-	-	-
Mobility Allowance	-	-	-	-	-	-	-	-	-	-	-
Benefits Directed at People of Working Age											
Armed Forces Independence Payment											1
Attendance Allowance (in payment)	-	-	-	-	-	-	-	-	-	-	-
Bereavement Benefits	203	180	163	147	129	117	108	101	95	91	95
Carer's Allowance	455	467	475	485	496	519	550	584	615	650	685
of which in payment	386	407	422	432	442	462	491	523	558	595	633
of which entitlement without payment	69	60	53	52	54	57	59	61	57	55	51
Christmas Bonus - non-contributory	1,854	1,921	1,912	1,920	2,003	3,164	3,246	3,227	3,212	3,240	3,215
Council Tax Benefit	2,358	2,473	2,603	2,570	2,533	2,566	2,940	3,172	3,254	3,368	-
Disability Living Allowance	1,553	1,596	1,627	1,657	1,692	1,733	1,780	1,819	1,847	1,877	1,866
of which in payment	1,539	1,582	1,612	1,641	1,676	1,715	1,761	1,800	1,828	1,858	1,846
of which entitlement without payment	14	14	15	16	16	17	19	19	20	20	20
Disability Working Allowance	-	-	-	-	-	-	-	-	-	-	-
Employment and Support Allowance	-	-	-	-	-	136	391	579	811	1,365	1,921
of which contributory	-	-	-	-	-	59	145	199	262	364	493
of which contributory and income-based	-	-	-	-	-	6	22	38	59	103	180
of which income-based	-	-	-	-	-	56	168	275	424	784	1,117
of which credits only	-	-	-	-	-	16	56	67	65	114	131
Family Credit	-	-	-	-	-	-	-	-	-	-	-
Housing Benefit	2,267	2,387	2,495	2,518	2,527	2,625	2,981	3,224	3,356	3,502	3,520
Incapacity Benefit, Invalidity Benefit & Sickness Benefit	2,504	2,510	2,475	2,443	2,415	2,332	2,031	1,827	1,577	965	366
of which in payment	1,570	1,543	1,500	1,456	1,413	1,346	1,177	1,054	909	566	192
of which credits only	934	967	975	987	1,002	986	854	773	668	399	174
Income Support	2,218	2,187	2,142	2,135	2,117	2,087	1,935	1,803	1,619	1,254	939
Industrial Injuries benefits	192	187	182	176	170	164	157	152	146	137	137
Jobseeker's Allowance	898	819	870	927	818	1,025	1,538	1,415	1,515	1,507	1,273
of which contributory	185	158	165	157	142	244	321	234	212	178	145
of which contributory and income-based	18	14	15	15	13	21	30	22	19	18	15
of which income-based	631	588	632	691	609	695	1,072	1,069	1,208	1,242	1,045
of which credits only	64	59	58	64	54	66	114	91	77	69	68
Maternity Allowance	22	26	29	27	44	54	56	54	57	60	58
Mobility Allowance	-	-	-	-	-	-	-	-	-	-	-
Personal Independence Payment	-	-	-	-	-	-	-	-	-	-	12
of which in payment	-	-	-	-	-	-	-	-	-	-	12
of which entitlement without payment	-	-	-	-	-	-	-	-	-	-	-
Severe Disablement Allowance	274	260	246	234	221	210	200	191	184	177	167
Statutory Maternity Pay	104	137	154	154	197	248	253	274	273	276	272
Unemployment Benefit	-	-	-	-	-	-	-	-	-	-	-
Benefits Directed at Pensioners											
Attendance Allowance	1,547	1,589	1,629	1,666	1,700	1,737	1,776	1,782	1,756	1,710	1,641
of which in payment	1,343	1,400	1,445	1,489	1,528	1,568	1,607	1,619	1,597	1,553	1,490
of which entitlement without payment	204	189	184	177	172	169	169	163	160	158	151
Bereavement Benefits	27	26	23	21	19	14	11	10	11	11	3
Carer's Allowance	178	235	279	319	356	388	411	420	417	405	387
of which in payment	20	22	24	26	28	30	31	30	26	22	20
of which entitlement without payment	158	213	255	292	327	357	381	390	391	383	367
Christmas Bonus - contributory	12,232	12,302	12,387	12,586	12,728	11,754	12,123	12,239	12,335	12,346	12,253
Council Tax Benefit	2,335	2,442	2,426	2,510	2,535	2,592	2,631	2,633	2,620	2,544	-
Disability Living Allowance	784	826	864	903	949	991	1,031	1,055	1,066	1,079	1,079
of which in payment	779	821	859	897	942	984	1,023	1,046	1,057	1,070	1,069
of which entitlement without payment	5	5	5	6	6	7	8	9	9	9	10
Housing Benefit	1,546	1,554	1,491	1,503	1,509	1,541	1,566	1,574	1,576	1,551	1,505
Incapacity Benefit, Invalidity Benefit & Sickness Benefit	-	-	-	-	-	-	-	-	-	-	-
of which in payment	-	-	-	-	-	-	-	-	-	-	-
of which credits only	-	-	-	-	-	-	-	-	-	-	-
Industrial Injuries benefits	150	153	156	159	171	172	176	182	185	187	189

5.5 Number of Persons claiming benefits: Caseloads by age group, thousands

	2003/04 Outturn	2004/05 Outturn	2005/06 Outturn	2006/07 Outturn	2007/08 Outturn	2008/09 Outturn	2009/10 Outturn	2010/11 Outturn	2011/12 Outturn	2012/13 Outturn	2013/14 Outturn
Income Support	-	-	-	-	-	-	-	-	-	-	-
Mobility Allowance	-	-	-	-	-	-	-	-	-	-	-
Over-75 TV Licence	3,839	3,892	3,965	3,982	3,993	4,079	4,206	4,236	4,277	4,316	4,414
Pension Credit	1,979	2,594	2,700	2,729	2,732	2,724	2,736	2,718	2,649	2,505	2,380
Personal Independence Payment	-	-	-	-	-	-	-	-	-	-	1
of which in payment	-	-	-	-	-	-	-	-	-	-	1
of which entitlement without payment	-	-	-	-	-	-	-	-	-	-	-
State Pension	11,320	11,477	11,585	11,715	11,938	12,160	12,410	12,566	12,667	12,810	12,888
of which contributory	11,297	11,454	11,562	11,692	11,913	12,134	12,382	12,537	12,634	12,775	12,846
of which basic element	11,231	11,384	11,492	11,617	11,837	12,053	12,285	12,460	12,556	12,737	12,814
of which earnings-related element ("Additional Pension", "SERPS" or "S2P")	7,122	7,425	7,700	7,963	8,324	8,673	9,052	9,320	9,549	9,848	10,021
of which Graduated Retirement Benefit	9,117	9,296	9,439	9,594	9,842	10,087	10,358	10,563	10,702	10,874	10,984
of which lump sums (covering all contributory elements)	-	-	-	8	24	46	58	66	59	56	56
of which new State Pension (excluding protected payments)											
of which new State Pension Protected Payments (including inherited elements)											
of which non-contributory ("Category D")	23	23	23	23	25	26	28	29	33	35	42
Severe Disablement Allowance	41	42	42	42	42	41	40	39	36	34	31
Winter Fuel Payments	11,486	11,430	11,555	11,750	12,123	12,421	12,681	12,783	12,686	12,683	12,585

Source: Department for Work and Pensions (DWP)

5.6 Jobseeker's Allowance[1,2,3] claimants: by benefit entitlement Great Britain

As at May

Thousands

		2003	2004	2005	2006	2007	2008	2009	2010	2011	2012	2013 *	2014 *
All Persons													
All with benefit - total	KXDX	797.9	699.6	728.3	812	730.8	718	1316.4	1237.3	1298.3	1377	1433	1035.3
Contribution-based JSA only	KXDY	160.4	131	139.5	134.6	113.6	127.8	341.8	205.3	182.7	159.5	142.4	97.3
Contribution based JSA & income-based JSA	KXDZ	18.1	13.5	13.5	13	11.9	12.8	34.6	21.1	19.9	16.8	14.9	10.9
Income-based JSA only payment	KXEA	619.4	555.1	575.3	664.5	605.3	577.4	940	1010.9	1096	1201	1156	842.4
No benefit in payment	KXEB	87.9	77.8	72.4	83.9	76.4	69.9	126.6	117.3	105.8	107.2	119.4	84.7
Males													
All with benefit - total	KXED	605.6	527.2	545.3	606.8	537.8	529.9	978.9	890.9	879.8	930	938.4	665.7
Contribution-based JSA only	KXEE	114.1	93.8	99.5	95.8	79.6	90.6	248.7	143.4	118.9	103.5	94.1	62
Contribution based JSA & income-based JSA	KXEF	15.9	12.3	12.6	12	10.7	11.7	31.2	18.1	16.9	13.7	12.6	8.9
Income-based JSA only payment	KXEG	475.6	421.1	433.2	498.9	447.5	427.6	698.9	729.5	744	812.8	753	539.1
No benefit in payment	KXEH	60.3	52.7	49.8	56.6	51.7	46.7	88.8	82.2	69.3	71.6	78.7	55.8
Females													
All with benefit - total	KXEJ	192.3	172.4	182.9	205.3	193	188.1	337.6	346.4	418.4	447	494.3	369.5
Contribution-based JSA only	KXEK	46.3	37.2	40	38.7	34	37.2	93.1	61.9	63.7	56	48.3	35.3
Contribution based JSA & income-based JSA	KXEL	2.2	1.2	0.8	1	1.2	1.2	3.4	3.0	3	3.1	2.3	2
Income-based JSA only payment	KXEM	143.8	134	142.1	165.5	157.8	149.8	241.1	281.4	351.7	387.9	403	303.3
No benefit in payment	KXEN	27.6	25	22.6	27.2	24.8	23.2	37.7	35.1	36.5	35.5	40.7	28.9

Sources: Department for Work and Pensions

1. Jobseeker's Allowance (JSA) has two routes of entry: contrbution-based which depends mainly upon national insurance contributions and income-based which depends mainly on a means test. Some claimants can qualify by either route. In practice they receive income-based JSA but have an under lying entitlement to the contribution-based element.

2 Figures are given at May each year and have been derived by applying 5% proportions to 100% totals taken from the DWP 100% Work and Pensions Longitudinal Study (WPLS).

3 Figures are rounded to the nearest hundred and quoted in thousands. They may not sum due to rounding.

* 5% sample data - DWP recommends that, where the detail is only available on the 5% sample data, the proportions derived should be applied to the overall 100% total for the benefit.

5.7 Employment and Support Allowance and Incapacity Benefit[1,2,3] claimants:
by sex, age and duration of spell
Great Britain and Overseas (excluding Northern Ireland).

Thousands

At end of May

		2002	2003	2004	2005	2006	2007	2008[4]	2009	2010	2011	2012	2013	2014
Males														
All durations: All ages	KJJA	1526.17	1525.02	1517.62	1492.38	1455.52	1428.65	1399.58	1419.43	1409.10	1358.24	1,312.25	1,252.36	1,250.99
Under 20	KJJB	21.79	21.81	22.04	21.45	19.95	18.66	17.25	18.09	17.33	15.6	15.66	15.90	21.33
20-29	KJJC	133.83	138.54	142.68	143.24	141.8	146.07	149.47	159.1	160.91	156.22	156.71	159.44	180.29
30-39	KJJD	250.79	254.3	253.32	245.61	233.7	224.29	215.51	215.95	213.57	201.58	195.39	189.43	208.79
40-49	KJJE	304.47	311.85	318.04	320.77	319.77	320.24	319.22	330.96	335.93	328.57	319.31	304.49	309.69
50-59	KJJF	478.01	472.03	463.37	451.93	439.54	418.26	404.76	405.59	403.61	391.96	384.28	369.52	376.74
60-64	KJJG	337.22	326.45	318.12	309.36	300.73	301.1	293.33	289.57	277.30	263.8	240.26	212.72	153.15
65 and over	KJJH	0.05	0.05	0.05	0.04	0.02	0.03	0.04	0.17	0.46	0.48	0.60	0.82	0.98
Unknown											0.04	0.03	0.03	0.02
Over six months: All ages	KJJI	1346.8	1359.53	1359.08	1347.43	1323.2	1291.32	1266.8	1253.91	1251.24	1213.77	1,050.73	950.15	1021.05
Under 20	KJJJ	6.91	13.4	13.78	13.51	12.85	11.7	10.9	10.42	10.50	9.29	9.46	9.50	14.30
20-29	KJJK	96.61	105.72	110.85	114.57	115.21	117.83	121.9	124.5	128.76	125.36	115.47	114.37	137.80
30-39	KJJL	213.19	217.05	217.81	213.91	205.36	195.22	188.25	182.41	180.52	170.92	145.09	139.67	165.79
40-49	KJJM	271.25	278.53	285.9	290.72	291.36	289.94	289.72	293.13	298.29	294.15	249.83	230.62	256.27
50-59	KJJN	438.55	434.04	427.06	418.6	409.46	387.76	374.75	368.48	367.26	360.03	311.58	278.75	317.56
60-64	KJJO	320.26	310.75	303.64	296.1	288.93	288.85	281.25	274.93	265.52	253.54	218.74	176.44	128.44
65 and over	KJJP	0.03	0.03	0.04	0.02	0.02	0.03	0.03	0.05	0.39	0.43	0.53	0.76	0.86
Unknown											0.04	0.03	0.03	0.02
Females														
All durations: All ages	KJJQ	944.44	969.44	990.84	998.2	994.33	988.93	982.33	998.74	1007.13	1026.38	1,037.34	1,033.19	1067.92
Under 20	KJJR	21.51	21.49	21.48	20.51	18.92	17.86	16.79	15.68	14.54	13.05	13.01	13.26	18.74
20-29	KJJS	96.66	100.78	105.02	108.61	109.73	114.42	117.91	121.5	122.82	121.54	121.56	123.93	140.27
30-39	KJJT	175.37	177.7	177.91	173.45	167.36	162.39	156.95	156.85	157.74	157.34	155.59	156.43	173.84
40-49	KJJU	252.82	262.2	270.9	276.62	279.32	283.45	285.84	296.87	305.06	305.31	299.72	287.89	301.47
50-59	KJJV	398.06	407.24	415.52	418.99	418.99	410.8	404.82	407.82	406.97	401.12	397.31	381.70	355.49
60 and over	KJJW	0.03	0.03	0.02	0.02	0.02	0.02	0.02	0.02	0.01	27.98	50.13	69.96	78.09
Unknown											0.03	0.02	0.02	0.02
Over six months: All ages	KJJX	825.25	858.03	880.52	894.57	896.33	885.69	881.41	882.94	888.73	905.11	817.68	787.01	881.84
Under 20	KJJY	7.41	12.35	12.4	12.1	11.13	10.2	9.55	8.75	8.15	7.16	7.31	7.46	12.15
20-29	KJJZ	72.32	79.63	84.02	88.98	90.99	93.6	97.24	99.15	100.81	99.22	90.34	89.68	107.74
30-39	KJKA	151.59	154.19	154.95	152.48	148	142.28	137.59	134.9	134.29	131.11	116.57	116.53	140.24
40-49	KJKB	225.65	234.71	243.52	250.11	253.5	255.99	258.74	263.7	269.48	269.38	234.09	222.46	253.55
50-59	KJKC	368.25	377.12	385.61	390.88	392.69	383.6	378.27	376.43	375.99	371.76	322.89	293.82	301.40
60 and over	KJKD	0.03	0.03	0.02	0.02	0.02	0.02	0.02	0.02	0.02	26.45	46.46	57.03	66.75
Unknown											0.03	0.02	0.02	0.01
Unknown Gender														
All durations	EW44	0.54	0.44	0.31	0.26	0.15	0.13	0.11	0.23	3.86	-	-	-	-
Over 6 months	EW45	0.29	0.21	0.16	0.13	0.1	0.09	0.09	0.1	3.67	-	-	-	-

Source: Department for Work and Pensions Work and Pensions Longitudinal Study 100% data

Definitions and conventions. Caseload figures are rounded to the nearest ten and displayed in thousands. Totals may not sum due to rounding.

1 Figures are given at May each year.

2 Table includes Employment and Support Allowance and Incapacity Benefit ONLY claimants and not those claiming Severe Disablement Allowance (SDA).

3 From 27th October 2008, new claims to Incapacity Benefit can also be allocated, on incapacity grounds, to the newly introduced Employment and Support Allowance (ESA).

4 Due to rounding errors several figures have been revised for May 2008.

5 2011 figures provided by IGS in relation to FOI 2013-2248 therefore 'Unknown' categories are different to previous years but match IGS published information on IB and ESA

5.8 Attendance allowance - cases in payment[1]: Age and gender of claimant Great Britain

At May each year   Thousands

		2005	2006	2007	2008	2009	2010	2011	2012	2013	2014
Males: All ages	JT9Z	436.9	459.5	478.4	497.2	516.5	531.5	530.00	526.1	504.92	493.89
Unknown age	JTA2	–	–	–	–	–	–	0.02	0.02	0.02	0.02
65 - 69	JTA3	22	22.3	22.8	23.5	24.4	24.8	23.8	23.3	21.2	20.66
70 - 74	JTA4	61.6	64.2	66.8	70.2	73.7	74.9	71.9	68.8	63.6	59.93
75 - 79	JTA5	104.2	104.8	106.3	109.1	112.4	114.9	113.7	112.3	107.3	104.10
80 - 84	JTA6	125.3	130.4	133.1	135.4	137.8	139.9	137.6	135.3	130.0	125.69
85 - 89	JTA7	78.7	89.4	98.5	107.7	116	118.1	118.00	117.0	112.7	111.21
90 and over	JTA8	45.1	48.4	50.8	51.2	52.2	58.9	65.00	69.4	70.1	72.29
Females: All ages	JTA9	982.6	1006.2	1029.1	1049.5	1069.3	1082.8	1069.1	1047.5	997.9	963.27
Unknown age	JTB2	–	–	–	–	–	–	0.03	0.03	0.03	0.03
65 - 69	JTB3	27.7	28.3	28.4	29.1	30	30.3	28.7	27.2	23.8	22.52
70 - 74	JTB4	92	93.6	96.4	99.6	103.5	104.5	99.7	93.9	85.3	78.52
75 - 79	JTB5	189.1	186.8	185.8	186.7	188.4	188.4	182.2	176.5	166.3	158.57
80 - 84	JTB6	282	279.4	278.3	277.7	277.7	277.0	269.2	259.8	244.9	231.85
85 - 89	JTB7	221.4	241.6	259.3	276.7	290.9	286.6	279.8	271.7	258.8	250.12
90 and over	JTB8	170.4	176.4	180.9	179.6	178.8	196.0	209.6	218.5	218.7	221.66

1 Totals show the number of people in receipt of allowance, and exclude people
with entitlement where the payment has been suspended, for example if they are in hospital.

Sources: DWP Information, Governance and Security,
Work and Pensions Longitudinal Study

Caseload figures are rounded to the nearest ten

5.9a: Families and children receiving Child Benefit, in each country and English Region, 2003 to 2014

Thousands

Time Series	United Kingdom [1]	Great Britain	England and Wales	England	North East	North West	Yorkshire and the Humber	East Midlands	West Midlands	East	London	South East	South West	Wales	Scotland	Northern Ireland	Foreign and not known [1]
Area Codes [2]	K02000001	K03000001	K04000001	E92000001	E12000001	E12000002	E12000003	E12000004	E12000005	E12000006	E12000007	E12000008	E12000009	W92000004	S92000003	N92000002	n/a
Number of families																	
August 2003	7,246,335	7,000,770	6,394,870	6,037,500	318,470	861,775	619,630	517,590	663,400	653,695	876,120	956,080	570,735	357,370	605,900	225,885	19,675
August 2004	7,296,495	7,055,160	6,448,355	6,087,500	317,515	863,070	622,065	520,870	667,175	660,390	894,090	965,480	576,845	360,855	606,805	226,850	14,485
August 2005	7,315,165	7,074,665	6,470,575	6,110,190	315,855	860,660	622,475	522,195	667,565	664,155	909,045	970,225	578,015	360,385	604,085	226,800	13,705
August 2006	7,413,475	7,129,720	6,528,205	6,168,010	316,665	864,650	626,740	527,105	672,220	671,850	926,055	981,015	581,705	360,195	601,515	230,140	53,615
August 2007	7,475,035	7,212,565	6,605,270	6,241,895	318,020	869,475	631,995	535,775	678,300	683,780	937,480	995,990	591,085	363,375	607,290	230,825	31,650
August 2008	7,582,990	7,320,990	6,708,080	6,341,345	319,815	876,795	640,670	543,350	686,910	696,485	964,180	1,013,595	599,550	366,735	612,910	233,830	28,165
August 2009	7,769,880	7,485,730	6,864,935	6,492,290	324,525	892,240	653,645	554,925	701,070	713,455	1,002,815	1,038,010	611,600	372,650	620,795	238,605	45,545
August 2010	7,841,675	7,557,305	6,935,695	6,562,705	324,265	894,940	657,700	559,645	705,640	723,030	1,028,265	1,051,885	617,340	372,985	621,615	240,985	43,385
August 2011	7,884,760	7,600,115	6,979,465	6,606,285	323,155	895,670	659,240	561,885	708,325	730,180	1,044,355	1,061,870	621,605	373,180	620,650	242,310	42,335
August 2012	7,920,495	7,641,575	7,022,780	6,650,070	321,310	895,845	661,370	564,385	711,110	737,485	1,061,620	1,071,795	625,145	372,705	618,795	243,185	35,735
August 2013	7,550,265	7,279,100	6,691,985	6,328,460	311,725	868,775	643,560	545,720	692,110	690,410	996,490	979,075	600,590	363,525	587,115	239,125	32,040
August 2014	7,461,675	7,195,865	6,619,190	6,259,275	307,860	862,015	640,080	542,575	688,340	681,035	982,060	959,600	595,710	359,910	576,675	237,865	27,945
Number of children																	
August 2003	13,138,075	12,670,975	11,625,050	10,983,290	552,970	1,549,900	1,116,630	934,450	1,219,985	1,200,175	1,613,235	1,754,585	1,041,360	641,755	1,045,925	439,870	27,230
August 2004	13,096,760	12,635,505	11,600,380	10,960,280	544,840	1,534,595	1,109,155	930,920	1,214,695	1,200,175	1,632,425	1,752,995	1,040,475	640,100	1,035,125	435,690	25,565
August 2005	13,111,665	12,654,135	11,626,490	10,988,765	540,940	1,528,255	1,109,150	932,310	1,215,315	1,204,750	1,658,755	1,758,520	1,040,780	637,725	1,027,640	431,995	25,535
August 2006	13,233,320	12,706,365	11,685,995	11,050,975	540,980	1,529,585	1,113,190	936,980	1,219,915	1,212,530	1,686,375	1,768,965	1,042,445	635,020	1,020,370	435,485	91,475
August 2007	13,267,355	12,778,460	11,754,415	11,117,770	540,610	1,529,060	1,117,760	946,090	1,225,025	1,225,485	1,699,215	1,782,530	1,052,000	636,645	1,024,045	433,370	55,525
August 2008	13,340,565	12,857,555	11,831,255	11,194,420	539,840	1,528,890	1,124,420	951,000	1,231,190	1,235,400	1,732,120	1,795,225	1,056,340	636,835	1,026,300	434,390	48,625
August 2009	13,604,375	13,088,240	12,054,140	11,409,950	546,125	1,549,625	1,143,245	967,010	1,251,900	1,258,520	1,794,220	1,827,530	1,071,775	644,190	1,034,095	440,570	75,565
August 2010	13,685,250	13,170,155	12,138,365	11,495,395	544,775	1,551,080	1,147,440	971,690	1,257,180	1,269,870	1,831,965	1,843,465	1,077,930	642,965	1,031,795	443,110	71,985
August 2011	13,721,160	13,207,465	12,179,715	11,537,505	542,680	1,549,475	1,148,450	973,310	1,259,770	1,276,525	1,853,670	1,852,950	1,080,680	642,210	1,027,750	444,285	69,410
August 2012	13,771,635	13,267,355	12,243,960	11,602,370	540,060	1,550,880	1,153,480	976,870	1,265,765	1,284,980	1,880,560	1,865,335	1,084,435	641,590	1,023,390	445,220	59,055
August 2013	13,107,460	12,618,675	11,651,810	11,026,465	525,215	1,505,780	1,124,295	943,980	1,233,780	1,198,215	1,763,895	1,693,670	1,037,630	625,345	966,865	437,440	51,345
August 2014	12,962,175	12,482,260	11,532,980	10,913,100	520,170	1,497,345	1,121,595	938,835	1,229,210	1,181,620	1,738,575	1,656,975	1,028,775	619,885	949,280	435,055	44,860

Source: HM Revenue and Customs

Footnotes
1 Includes Foreign and not known
2 Area codes implemented from 1 January 2011; in line with the new GSS Coding and Naming policy.

5.9b: Families receiving Child Benefit nationally, in each country and English Region, August 2014

Area names	Area Codes [1]	Number of families, by size						Number of children in these families, by age				
		Total	One child	Two children	Three children	Four children	Five or more children	Total	Under 5	5-10	11-15	16 and over
United Kingdom [2]	K02000001	7,461,675	3,576,725	2,718,895	844,435	234,340	87,280	12,962,175	3,599,460	4,225,520	3,260,025	1,877,165
Great Britain	K03000001	7,195,865	3,456,870	2,623,025	807,645	224,100	84,230	12,482,260	3,468,420	4,072,980	3,141,000	1,799,855
England and Wales	K04000001	6,619,190	3,158,745	2,417,050	751,500	211,325	80,565	11,532,980	3,208,140	3,757,380	2,889,870	1,677,590
England	E92000001	6,259,275	2,984,820	2,285,595	711,145	200,820	76,900	10,913,100	3,041,065	3,558,755	2,731,765	1,581,515
North East	E12000001	307,860	155,130	109,280	31,885	8,470	3,100	520,170	143,045	168,145	130,830	78,145
North West	E12000002	862,015	419,470	305,735	97,315	28,260	11,235	1,497,345	413,840	486,885	374,740	221,885
Yorkshire and the Humber	E12000003	640,080	305,235	230,990	73,075	22,260	8,520	1,121,595	314,740	366,005	279,185	161,660
East Midlands	E12000004	542,575	259,320	201,440	59,405	16,250	6,160	938,835	260,295	304,340	237,180	137,025
West Midlands	E12000005	688,340	322,325	245,445	82,995	26,210	11,365	1,229,210	342,220	400,000	308,300	178,695
East	E12000006	681,035	318,400	259,590	76,980	19,720	6,340	1,181,620	327,935	383,840	297,915	171,930
London	E12000007	982,060	475,500	335,145	118,900	36,210	16,305	1,738,575	495,700	581,600	423,540	237,730
South East	E12000008	959,600	450,380	368,120	105,700	26,965	8,430	1,656,975	459,065	539,250	418,635	240,025
South West	E12000009	595,710	279,065	229,845	64,890	16,470	5,440	1,028,775	284,225	328,690	261,440	154,420
Wales	W92000004	359,910	173,925	131,455	40,355	10,510	3,670	619,885	167,075	198,625	158,105	96,075
Scotland	S92000003	576,675	298,120	205,975	56,145	12,775	3,660	949,280	260,280	315,600	251,130	122,265
Northern Ireland	N92000002	237,865	104,320	86,455	34,450	9,725	2,915	435,055	118,420	137,795	108,250	70,595
Foreign and not known	N/A	27,945	15,535	9,415	2,345	515	135	44,860	12,620	14,745	10,775	6,715

Source: HM Revenue and Customs

Footnotes
1 Area codes implemented from 1 January 2011; in line with the new GSS Coding and Naming policy.
2 Includes Foreign and not known.

5.10 Child Tax Credit or Working Tax Credit elements and thresholds

Annual rate (£), except where specified

	2003-04	2004-05	2005-06	2006-07	2007-08	2008-09	2009-10	2010-11	2011-12	2012-13	2013-14	2014-15
Child Tax Credit												
Family element	545	545	545	545	545	545	545	545	545	545	545	545
Family element, baby addition[1]	545	545	545	545	545	545	545	545	-	-	-	-
Child element[2]	1,445	1,625	1,690	1,765	1,845	2,085	2,235	2,300	2,555	2,690	2,720	2,750
Disabled child additional element[3]	2,155	2,215	2,285	2,350	2,440	2,540	2,670	2,715	2,800	2,950	3,015	3,100
Severely disabled child additional element[4]	865	890	920	945	980	1,020	1,075	1,095	1,130	1,190	1,220	1,255
Working Tax Credit												
Basic element	1,525	1,570	1,620	1,665	1,730	1,800	1,890	1,920	1,920	1,920	1,920	1,940
Couples and lone parent element	1,500	1,545	1,595	1,640	1,700	1,770	1,860	1,890	1,950	1,950	1,970	1,990
30 hour element[5]	620	640	660	680	705	735	775	790	790	790	790	800
Disabled worker element	2,040	2,100	2,165	2,225	2,310	2,405	2,530	2,570	2,650	2,790	2,855	2,935
Severely disabled adult element	865	890	920	945	980	1,020	1,075	1,095	1,130	1,190	1,220	1,255
50+ return to work payment[6]												
16 but less than 30 hours per week	1,045	1,075	1,110	1,140	1,185	1,235	1,300	1,320	1,365	-	-	-
at least 30 hours per week	1,565	1,610	1,660	1,705	1,770	1,840	1,935	1,965	2,030	-	-	-
Childcare element												
Maximum eligible costs allowed (£ per week)												
Eligible costs incurred for 1 child	135	135	175	175	175	175	175	175	175	175	175	175
Eligible costs incurred for 2+ children	200	200	300	300	300	300	300	300	300	300	300	300
Percentage of eligible costs covered	*70%*	*70%*	*70%*	*80%*	*80%*	*80%*	*80%*	*80%*	*70%*	*70%*	*70%*	*70%*
Common features												
First income threshold[7]	5,060	5,060	5,220	5,220	5,220	6,420	6,420	6,420	6,420	6,420	6,420	6,420
First withdrawal rate	*37%*	*37%*	*37%*	*37%*	*37%*	*39%*	*39%*	*39%*	*41%*	*41%*	*41%*	*41%*
Second income threshold[8]	50,000	50,000	50,000	50,000	50,000	50,000	50,000	50,000	40,000	-	-	-
Second withdrawal rate	*1 in 15*	*1 in 15*	*1 in 15*	*1 in 15*	*1 in 15*	*1 in 15*	*1 in 15*	*1 in 15*	*41%*	-	-	-
First income threshold for those entitled to Child Tax Credit only[9]	13,230	13,480	13,910	14,155	14,495	15,575	16,040	16,190	15,860	15,860	15,910	16,010
Income increase disregard	2,500	2,500	2,500	25,000	25,000	25,000	25,000	25,000	10,000	10,000	5,000	5,000
Income fall disregard[10]										2,500	2,500	2,500
Minimum award payable	26	26	26	26	26	26	26	26	26	26	26	26

Source: HM Revenue and Customs

[1] Payable to families for any period during which they have one or more children aged under 1. Abolished 6 April 2011.

[2] Payable for each child up to 31 August after their 16th birthday, and for each young person for any period in which they are aged under 20 (under 19 to 2005-06) and in full-time non-advanced education, or under 19 and in their first 20 weeks of registration with the Careers service or Connexions.

[3] Payable in addition to the child element for each disabled child.

[4] Payable in addition to the disabled child element for each severely disabled child.

[5] Payable for any period during which normal hours worked (for a couple, summed over the two partners) is at least 30 per week.

[6] Payable for each qualifying adult for the first 12 months following a return to work.Abolished 6 April 2012.

[7] Income is net of pension contributions, and excludes Child Benefit, Housing benefit, Council tax benefit, maintenance and the first £300 of family income other than from work or benefits. The award is reduced by the excess of income over the first threshold, multiplied by the first withdrawal rate.

[8] For those entitled to the Child Tax Credit, the award is reduced only down to the family element, plus the baby addition where relevant, less the excess of income over the second threshold multiplied by the second withdrawal rate. Abolished 6 April 2012.

[9] Those also receiving Income Support, income-based Jobseeker's Allowance or Pension Credit are passported to maximum CTC with no tapering.

[10] Introduced from 6 April 2012, this drop in income is disregarded in the calculation of Tax Credit awards.

5.11: Number of families and children with Child Tax Credit or Working Tax Credit, by level of award [3] 2014-15

Thousands

| | New Area Codes [1] | In-work families | | | | | | Number of children in recipient families | | |
| | | With children | | | Of which, lone parents | With no children | Total in receipt (out-of-work and in-work families) | | In-work families | |
		Total out-of-work families	Receiving WTC and CTC	Receiving CTC only		Receiving WTC only		Total out-of-work families	Receiving WTC and CTC	Receiving CTC only
United Kingdom [2]	K02000001	**1,311**	**1,785**	**825**	**1,151**	**508**	**4,429**	**2,506**	**3,263**	**1,691**
Great Britain	K03000001	**1,251**	**1,723**	**794**	**1,111**	**487**	**4,255**	**2,393**	**3,151**	**1,623**
England and Wales	K04000001	**1,151**	**1,594**	**733**	**1,012**	**438**	**3,915**	**2,216**	**2,940**	**1,502**
England	E92000001	**1,080**	**1,506**	**689**	**954**	**408**	**3,683**	**2,083**	**2,784**	**1,414**
North East	E12000001	64	77	33	52	30	204	119	134	65
North West	E12000002	163	230	94	148	75	562	312	422	189
Yorkshire and the Humber	E12000003	117	171	76	100	53	416	229	320	154
East Midlands	E12000004	86	131	69	82	40	326	168	237	141
West Midlands	E12000005	131	176	82	102	47	435	263	338	168
East	E12000006	101	143	78	94	33	354	193	258	162
London	E12000007	205	257	81	159	46	589	391	502	164
South East	E12000008	131	188	100	129	43	462	251	338	209
South West	E12000009	83	132	78	86	42	335	157	235	162
Wales	W92000004	71	88	43	58	30	232	134	155	88
Scotland	S92000003	101	129	61	99	49	339	177	212	121
Northern Ireland	N92000002	51	58	29	39	20	158	96	104	64
Foreign and not known [4]	n/a	7	1	1	1	1	10	14	2	3

Source: HM Revenue and Customs

Tax Credit Finalised Awards 2014-15: Geographical Analysis

Footnotes

[1] Area codes implemented from 1 January 2011 in line with the new GSS Coding and Naming policy.

[2] Includes Foreign and not known

[3] All figures are rounded to the nearest integer therefore not all totals may exactly equal the sums of their respective components.

[4] "Foreign and not known" consists of a small proportion of recipient families and children who do not live within England, Scotland, Northern Island or Wales. They may for instance be a Crown servant posted overseas, or living in a British Crown Dependency. Due to the small size of this population we combine them into one group which also consists of those whom, at the time of publication, either have a UK postcode that does not match to a geographical office region code, or do not have a postcode in the available data.

5.12 Widows' Allowance (excluding bereavement payment[1,2,3]): by type of benefit Great Britain

Number in receipt of widows benefit as at May each year

Thousands

		2006	2007	2008	2009	2010	2011	2012	2013	2014
All Widows' Benefit (excluding bereavement allowance)										
All ages	KJGA	117.7	96.89	77.9	62.14	50.75	44	38	33	28.52
Unknown Age	EW4O	–	0.02	–	–	–	–	–	–	–
18 - 24	EW4P	–	–	–	–	–	–	–	–	–
25 - 29	EW4Q	0.1	0.04	0.02	0.01	–	–	–	–	–
30 - 34	EW4R	0.5	0.32	0.2	0.13	0.08	0.05	0.02	0.01	–
35 - 39	EW4S	2.1	1.53	1.08	0.74	0.50	0.34	0.22	0.14	0.09
40 - 44	EW4T	4.9	3.93	3.04	2.31	1.72	1.22	0.84	0.59	0.38
45 - 49	EW4U	9.1	7.58	6.26	5.14	4.20	3.38	2.71	2.07	1.52
50 - 54	EW4V	21.8	17.69	14.42	11.72	9.76	8.09	6.77	5.60	4.63
55 - 59	EW4W	57.3	45.78	36.86	30.37	24.62	20.00	16.31	13.26	10.80
60 - 64	EW4X	21.8	20.01	16.01	11.71	9.86	10.93	11.13	11.24	11.10
Widowed parents' allowance - with dependant children										
All ages	KJGG	19	15.6	12.6	9.98	7.91	6.11	4.61	3.35	2.34
Unknown Age	EW4Y	–	–	–	–	–	–	–	–	–
18 - 24	EW4Z	–	–	–	–	–	–	–	–	–
25 - 29	EW52	0.1	0.03	0.02	0.01	–	–	–	–	–
30 - 34	EW53	0.5	0.31	0.19	0.12	0.07	0.04	0.02	0.01	–
35 - 39	EW54	2.1	1.49	1.05	0.72	0.49	0.32	0.21	0.13	0.08
40 - 44	EW55	4.6	3.75	2.92	2.23	1.65	1.18	0.80	0.57	0.36
45 - 49	EW56	5.6	4.71	3.87	3.13	2.61	2.04	1.56	1.12	0.78
50 - 54	EW57	4.1	3.58	3.1	2.53	2.08	1.68	1.32	1.00	0.72
55 - 59	EW58	1.8	1.57	1.33	1.13	0.92	0.75	0.62	0.45	0.34
60 - 64	EW59	0.2	0.17	0.13	0.1	0.09	0.09	0.08	0.07	0.06
Widowed parents' allowance - without dependant children										
All ages	KJGM	0.8	0.69	0.54	0.46	0.39	0.28	0.22	0.17	0.12
Unknown Age	EW5A	–	–	–	–	–	–	–	–	–
18 - 24	EW5B	–	–	–	–	–	–	–	–	–
25 - 29	EW5C	–	–	–	–	–	–	–	–	–
30 - 34	EW5D	–	0.01	0.01	0.01	0.01	–	–	–	–
35 - 39	EW5E	0.1	0.04	0.03	0.02	0.02	0.01	0.01	0.01	0.01
40 - 44	EW5F	0.2	0.13	0.09	0.07	0.06	0.04	0.03	0.02	0.01
45 - 49	EW5G	0.2	0.21	0.17	0.15	0.12	0.09	0.07	0.05	0.03
50 - 54	EW5H	0.2	0.17	0.13	0.13	0.12	0.08	0.06	0.05	0.04
55 - 59	EW5I	0.1	0.11	0.1	0.07	0.06	0.04	0.04	0.02	0.02
60 - 64	EW5J	–	0.02	0.01	0.01	0.01	0.01	0.01	0.01	0.01
Age-related bereavement allowance										
All ages	KJGS	84	70.13	57.37	46.58	38.55	34.2	30.16	26.7	23.73
Unknown Age	EW5K	–	0.01	–	–	–	–	–	–	–
18 - 24	EW5L	–	–	–	–	–	–	–	–	–
25 - 29	EW5M	–	–	–	–	–	–	–	–	–
30 - 34	EW5N	–	–	–	–	–	–	–	–	–
35 - 39	EW5O	–	–	–	–	–	–	–	–	–
40 - 44	EW5P	0.1	0.06	0.03	0.01	–	–	–	–	–
45 - 49	EW5Q	3.3	2.66	2.23	1.86	1.47	1.24	1.08	0.90	0.72
50 - 54	EW5R	17.2	13.75	11.08	9.01	7.55	6.32	5.39	4.55	3.87
55 - 59	EW5S	50.9	40.57	32.61	26.83	21.74	17.71	14.44	11.80	9.68
60 - 64	EW5T	12.5	13.08	11.42	8.87	7.78	6.92	9.25	9.47	9.46
Bereavement allowance (Not age related)										
All ages	KJGW	13.9	10.47	7.39	5.12	3.90	3.41	3.02	2.67	2.33
Unknown Age	EW5U	–	–	–	–	–	–	–	–	–
18 - 24	EW5V	–	–	–	–	–	–	–	–	–
25 - 29	EW5W	–	–	–	–	–	–	–	–	–
30 - 34	EW5X	–	–	–	–	–	–	–	–	–
35 - 39	EW5Y	–	–	–	–	–	–	–	–	–
40 - 44	EW5Z	–	–	–	–	–	–	–	–	–
45 - 49	EW62	–	–	–	–	–	–	–	–	–
50 - 54	EW63	0.3	0.2	0.11	0.05	0.01	0.01	–	–	–
55 - 59	EW64	4.4	3.53	2.82	2.33	1.90	1.5	1.22	0.99	0.76
60 - 64	EW65	9.1	6.74	4.45	2.74	1.98	1.91	1.79	1.69	1.57

Sources: DWP Information, Governance and Security, Work and Pensions Longitudinal Study.

1 "-" Nil or Negligible; "." Not applicable; Caseload figures are rounded to the nearest ten; Some additional disclosure control has also been applied. Average amounts are shown as pounds per week and rounded to the nearest penny. Totals may not sum due to rounding.
2 Caseload (Thousands) All Claimants of Widows Benefit are female. No new claims for WA have been accepted since April 2001 when it was replaced by Bereavement Allowance
3 Figures include overseas cases.

STATE PENSION AGE:

The age at which men and women reach State Pension age is gradually increasing. Under current legislation, State Pension age for women will equalise with State Pension age for men at 65 in 2018. Both men's and women's State Pension age will increase from 65 to 66 between December 2018 and October 2020. The Pensions Bill 2013-14 contains provision for a State Pension age of 67 to be reached by 2028. For more information see https://www.gov.uk/government/uploads/system/uploads/attachment_data/file/207966/espa.pdf.

5.13 Bereavement Allowance[1,2] (excluding bereavement payment): by sex, type of benefit and age of widow/er Great Britain.

Thousands

		Males						Females				
		2010	2011	2012	2013	2014		2010	2011	2012	2013	2014
All Bereavement Benefit (excluding bereavement allowance)												
All ages	WLSX	18.67	18.59	18.78	18.76	18.56	WLTC	44.64	46.18	47.40	48.79	49.66
18 - 24	EVW9	-	-	.	.	.	EVY2	0.04	0.05	0.05	0.04	0.03
25 - 29	EVX2	0.05	0.06	0.05	0.04	0.05	EVY3	0.52	0.48	0.47	0.48	0.40
30 - 34	EVX3	0.26	0.24	0.25	0.26	0.26	EVY4	1.71	1.67	1.69	1.78	1.76
35 - 39	EVX4	0.99	0.88	0.84	0.79	0.75	EVY5	4.27	4.01	3.86	3.82	3.75
40 - 44	EVX5	2.32	2.13	2.15	2.10	1.94	EVY6	7.74	7.77	7.76	7.67	7.44
45 - 49	EVX6	3.98	4.00	3.92	3.81	3.75	EVY7	10.78	11.09	11.30	11.17	11.30
50 - 54	EVX7	3.77	3.82	3.97	4.10	4.16	EVY8	10.3	10.58	10.76	10.94	11.14
55 - 59	EVX8	3.42	3.41	3.53	3.57	3.59	EVY9	9.18	9.38	9.51	9.79	9.65
60 - 64	EVX9	3.87	4.05	4.08	4.08	4.05	EVZ2	0.11	1.15	1.99	3.11	4.18
Widowed parents' allowance - with dependant children												
All ages	WLUD	11.78	11.58	11.68	11.64	11.46	WLUH	32.47	33.27	33.90	34.30	34.46
18 - 24	EVZ3	-	-	.	.	.	EW24	0.04	0.05	0.05	0.04	0.03
25 - 29	EVZ4	0.05	0.06	0.05	0.04	0.05	EW25	0.52	0.48	0.46	0.47	0.40
30 - 34	EVZ5	0.26	0.24	0.25	0.26	0.26	EW26	1.7	1.66	1.68	1.76	1.76
35 - 39	EVZ6	0.99	0.88	0.84	0.79	0.75	EW27	4.24	3.98	3.85	3.81	3.74
40 - 44	EVZ7	2.31	2.12	2.15	2.09	1.94	EW28	7.69	0.73	7.73	7.64	7.41
45 - 49	EVZ8	3.47	3.51	3.41	3.33	3.25	EW29	9.22	9.56	9.81	9.81	9.93
50 - 54	EVZ9	2.67	2.7	2.86	2.97	3.03	EW2A	6.58	6.97	7.12	7.31	7.56
55 - 59	EW22	1.42	1.45	1.46	1.49	1.55	EW2B	2.47	2.69	2.93	3.09	3.16
60 - 64	EW23	0.61	0.63	0.66	0.65	0.63	EW2C	0.01	0.14	0.25	0.37	0.45
Widowed parents' allowance - without dependant children												
All ages	WLVK	0.04	0.03	0.03	0.02	0.02	WMMR	0.25	0.21	0.18	0.16	0.13
18 - 24	EW2D	-	-	.	.	.	EW2M	-	-	.	.	.
25 - 29	EW2E	-	-	.	.	.	EW2N	-	-	.	.	.
30 - 34	EW2F	-	-	.	.	.	EW2O	0.01	0.01	0.01	0.01	.
35 - 39	EW2G	-	-	.	.	.	EW2P	0.03	0.02	0.01	0.01	0.01
40 - 44	EW2H	0.01	0.01	0.01	0.01	-	EW2Q	0.05	0.04	0.04	0.03	0.02
45 - 49	EW2I	0.01	0.01	0.01	0.01	0.01	EW2R	0.07	0.06	0.06	0.05	0.04
50 - 54	EW2J	0.01	0.01	.	.	0.01	EW2S	0.04	0.05	0.04	0.04	0.04
55 - 59	EW2K	0.01	0.01	.	.	-	EW2T	0.03	0.02	0.01	0.01	0.01
60 - 64	EW2L	-	-	.	.	.	EW2U	-	-	.	.	.
Age-related bereavement allowance												
All ages	WMOB	1.76	1.75	1.75	1.75	1.78	WMOC	5.63	5.51	5.53	5.38	5.37
18 - 24	EW2V	-	-	.	.	.	EW36	-	-	.	.	.
25 - 29	EW2W	-	-	.	.	.	EW37	-	-	.	.	.
30 - 34	EW2X	-	-	.	.	.	EW38	-	-	.	.	.
35 - 39	EW2Y	-	-	.	.	.	EW39	-	-	.	.	.
40 - 44	EW2Z	-	-	.	.	.	EW3A	-	-	.	.	.
45 - 49	EW32	0.5	0.49	0.49	0.47	0.49	EW3B	1.48	1.46	1.43	1.32	1.34
50 - 54	EW33	1.1	1.11	0.11	0.12	1.13	EW3C	3.67	3.56	3.60	3.59	3.53
55 - 59	EW34	0.16	0.15	0.15	0.15	0.16	EW3D	0.47	0.49	0.51	0.48	0.50
60 - 64	EW35	-	-	.	.	.	EW3E	-	-	.	.	.
Bereavement allowance (not age related)												
All ages	WMOX	5.09	5.22	5.33	5.35	5.30	WMOY	6.3	7.19	7.80	8.94	9.69
18 - 24	EW3F	-	-	.	.	.	EW3O	-	-	.	.	.
25 - 29	EW3G	-	-	.	.	.	EW3P	-	-	.	.	.
30 - 34	EW3H	-	-	.	.	.	EW3Q	-	-	.	.	.
35 - 39	EW3I	-	-	.	.	.	EW3R	-	-	.	.	.
40 - 44	EW3J	-	-	.	.	.	EW3S	-	-	.	.	.
45 - 49	EW3K	-	-	.	.	.	EW3T	-	-	.	.	.
50 - 54	EW3L	-	-	.	.	.	EW3U	-	-	.	.	.
55 - 59	EW3M	1.83	1.8	1.91	1.91	1.88	EW3V	6.2	6.18	6.06	6.21	5.97
60 - 64	EW3N	3.26	3.42	3.42	3.43	3.42	EW3W	0.1	1.00	1.73	2.74	3.72

Sources: DWP Information, Governance and Security, Work and Pensions Longitudinal Study

1 Figures include overseas cases.

2 Figures are given at May each year and are taken from the DWP 100%   Work and Pensions Longitudinal Study (WPLS).

"-" Nil or Negligible; "." Not applicable; Caseload figures are rounded to the nearest ten; Some additional disclosure control has also been applied. Average amounts are shown as pounds per week and rounded to the nearest penny. Totals may not sum due to rounding.

Notes:

Type of BA The category 'WPA with dependants' will include clients getting paid at the personal rate only due to the introduction of of Child Tax Credits in April 2003. To obtain figures for those who still receive Child Dependancy Increases, under the transitional protection arrangements, use the 'type of dependant' option.

STATE PENSION AGE: The age at which men and women reach State Pension age is gradually increasing. Under current legislation, State Pension age for women will equalise with State Pension age for men at 65 in 2018. Both men's and women's State Pension age will increase from 65 to 66 between December 2018 and October 2020. The Pensions Bill 2013-14 contains provision for a State Pension age of 67 to be reached by 2028. For more information see https://www.gov.uk/government/uploads/system/uploads/attachment_data/file/207966/espa.pdf.

5.14 Contributory and non-contributory retirement pensions:[1,2] by sex and age of claimant Great Britain and Overseas.

At May each year.

Thousands and percentages

		2005	2006	2007	2008	2009	2010	2011	2012	2013	2014
Men:											
Age-groups:											
65-69	KJSB	1364.1	1341.5	1332.77	1350.61	1389.85	1,441.17	1,498.78	1,629.37	1705.34	1740.27
Percentage	KJSC	31.4	30.6	30.03	29.84	29.99	30.28	30.77	32.14	32.59	32.35
70-74	KJSD	1150	1160.1	1177.96	1205.7	1232.97	1,252.63	1249.42	1,256.65	1286.51	1330.41
Percentage	KJSE	26.5	26.5	26.54	26.63	26.61	26.32	25.65	24.79	24.58	24.73
75-79	KJSF	887.1	903	918.47	932.17	942.03	958.54	975.17	996.90	1025.20	1054.99
Percentage	KJSG	20.4	20.6	20.7	20.59	20.33	20.14	20.02	19.67	19.59	19.61
80-84	KJSH	593.3	596.9	604.74	614.77	627.28	644.94	663.35	680.67	695.95	710.47
Percentage	KJSI	13.7	13.6	13.63	13.58	13.54	13.55	13.62	13.43	13.30	13.21
85-89	KJSJ	246.4	273.1	296.36	317.9	335.49	340.87	348.51	357.78	365.24	378.93
Percentage	KJSK	5.7	6.2	6.68	7.02	7.24	7.16	7.16	7.06	6.98	7.04
90 and over	KJSL	100.2	103.6	106.13	105.33	105.62	120.82	135.62	147.15	154.43	164.14
Percentage	KJSM	2.3	2.4	2.39	2.33	2.28	2.54	2.79	2.90	2.95	3.05
Unknown age	EW3Y	1.1	1.2	1.45	0.19	0.24	0.23	0.27	0.27	0.29	0.29
Percentage	EW3Z	–	–	–	–	–	–	–	–	–	–
Total all ages	KJSA	4342.2	4379.5	4437.99	4526.79	4633.62	4,759.36	4871.26	5068.96	5233.15	5379.68
Women:											
Age-groups:											
60-64	KJSO	1498.7	1524	1628.19	1695.88	1734.92	1,747.21	1621.44	1391.16	1178.35	990.34
Percentage	KJSP	20.8	21	21.98	22.47	22.62	22.45	20.94	18.07	15.45	13.08
65-69	KJSQ	1464.2	1453.1	1456.08	1484.8	1527.47	1,576.10	1632.12	1768.96	1847.19	1883.33
Percentage	KJSR	20.3	20	19.65	19.67	19.91	20.25	21.1	22.98	24.22	24.87
70-74	KJSS	1314.5	1312.7	1322.14	1343.22	1366.91	1,382.42	1377.54	1385.36	1415.89	1459.75
Percentage	KJST	18.2	18.1	17.85	17.8	17.82	17.77	17.79	18.00	18.56	19.28
75-79	KJSU	1158.6	1165.5	1168.86	1170.01	1166.2	1,168.83	1172.33	1185.64	1207.02	1232.19
Percentage	KJSV	16.1	16	15.78	15.5	15.2	15.02	15.14	15.40	15.82	16.27
80-84	KJSW	951.6	933.3	923.7	919.11	921.01	931.08	942.31	950.53	955.31	957.64
Percentage	KJSX	13.2	12.9	12.47	12.18	12.01	11.97	12.17	12.35	12.52	12.65
85-89	KJSY	511	552.7	587.91	621.15	643.5	634.29	628.71	626.68	625.48	634.32
Percentage	KJSZ	7.1	7.6	7.94	8.23	8.39	8.15	8.12	8.14	8.20	8.38
90 and over	KJTA	314.9	319.4	319.9	313.66	310.07	341.10	370.18	389.38	398.29	413.80
Percentage	KJTB	4.4	4.4	4.32	4.16	4.04	4.38	4.78	5.06	5.22	5.47
Unknown age	EW42	1.3	1.5	1.67	0.37	0.38	0.35	0.35	0.35	0.43	0.44
Percentage	EW43	–	–	–	–	–	–	–	–	–	–
Total all ages	KJSN	7214.7	7262.3	7408.44	7548.2	7670.44	7,781.39	7744.98	7698.12	7627.94	7571.82

Source: DWP Information, Governance and Security, Work and Pensions Longitudinal Study.

1 See chapter text.

2 Caseloads include both contributory and non-contributory state pensioners.

"-" Nil or Negligible; "." Not applicable; Caseload figures are rounded to the nearest ten; Some additional disclosure control has also been applied. Average amounts are shown as pounds per week and rounded to the nearest penny. Totals may not sum due to rounding.

STATE PENSION AGE: *The age at which men and women reach State Pension age is gradually increasing. Under current legislation, State Pension age for women will equalise with State Pension age for men at 65 in 2018. Both men's and women's State Pension age will increase from 65 to 66 between December 2018 and October 2020. The Pensions Bill 2013-14 contains provision for a State Pension age of 67 to be reached by 2028. For more information see https://www.gov.uk/government/uploads/system/uploads/attachment_data/file/207966/espa.pdf.*

5.15a War pensions: estimated number of pensioners[1] Great Britain

At 31 March each year

Thousands

		2003	2004	2005	'2006[2]	2007	2008	2009	2010	2011	2012	2013	2014
Disablement	KADH	212.18	201.55	191.75	182.8	173.85	165.17	157.13	148.95	141.72	134.43	127.60	121.90
Widows and dependants	KADI	48.61	46.04	43.55	41.05	38.69	36.1	33.62	31.45	29.20	27.11	25.10	23.11
Total	KADG	260.79	247.59	235.3	223.85	212.54	201.27	190.75	180.40	170.92	161.54	152.70	145.01

Source: Ministry of Defence/DASA

1 See chapter text. From 1914 war, 1939 war and later service.

2 The discontinuity between 2005 and 2006 is due to improvements in data processing.

5.15b War Pensions in payment by type of pension, gender and financial year end, 31 March 2010 to 31 March 2014, numbers

	Awards in payment at:				
	31-Mar-10	31-Mar-11	31-Mar-12	Mar-2013	Mar-2014
ALL IN PAYMENT	**180,400**	**170,910**	**161,535**	**152,695**	**145,005**
Men	**142,770**	**135,740**	**128,720**	**122,105**	**116,610**
Women	**37,630**	**35,175**	**32,820**	**30,590**	**28,395**
Disablement Pensioners	**148,945**	**141,715**	**134,430**	**127,590**	**121,900**
Men	142,135	135,120	128,130	121,530	116,055
Women	6,810	6,595	6,305	6,060	5,845
War Widow(er)s	**30,655**	**28,425**	**26,375**	**24,415**	**22,445**
Men	75	75	80	85	80
Women	30,580	28,350	26,295	24,330	22,365
Other Pensioners	**795**	**770**	**730**	**690**	**660**
Men	555	540	510	490	470
Women	240	230	220	200	185

Source: Ministry of Defence/DASA

5.16 Income support[1],[2] by statistical group[3]: number of claimants receiving weekly payment

Great Britain   Thousands[4]

		2006	2007	2008	2009	2010	2011	2012	2013	2014
All income support claimants (including MIG from 2003)[5]	F8YY	2125.1	2128.4	2102.3	1990.0	1852.3	1703.2	1417.1	1021.9	840.8
Incapacity Benefits	F8YZ	1191.7	1193.5	1191.4	1097.0	996.6	924.9	654.13	328.09	167.64
Lone Parent	F8Z2	774.9	765.6	738.6	720.5	679.2	595.4	577.08	499.73	474.73
Carer	F8Z3	81.7	84.3	87.3	93.8	103.9	115.7	129.75	145.84	156.50
Others on Income Related Benefits	F8Z4	76.8	84.9	85.0	78.9	72.7	67.2	56.1	48.2	41.9

Sources: DWP Information, Governance and Security, Work and Pensions Longitudinal Study

1 Figures are given at May each year and are taken from the DWP 100% Work and Pensions Longitudinal Study (WPLS).

2 From 27th October 2008, new claims to Income Support can also be allocated, on incapacity grounds, to the newly introduced Employment and Support Allowance (ESA).

3 Statistical Group is a hierarchical variable. A person who fits into more than one category will only appear in the top-most one for which they are eligible. These statistical groups differ from the groups shown in the 5% sample tables. Lone Parents are defined as claimants on Income Support with child under 16 and no partner. Lone Parent Obligations were introduced from 24th November 2008 affecting the eligibility criteria based on the age of the youngest child. For more information see http://83.244.183.180/100pc/is/tabtool_is.html.

4 Figures are rounded to the nearest hundred and quoted in thousands.

5 Totals may not sum due to rounding.

"-" Nil or Negligible; "." Not applicable; Caseload figures are rounded to the nearest ten; Some additional disclosure control has also been applied.

STATE PENSION AGE: The age at which men and women reach State Pension age is gradually increasing. Under current legislation, State Pension age for women will equalise with State Pension age for men at 65 in 2018. Both men's and women's State Pension age will increase from 65 to 66 between December 2018 and October 2020. The Pensions Bill 2013-14 contains provision for a State Pension age of 67 to be reached by 2028. For more information see https://www.gov.uk/government/uploads/system/uploads/attachment_data/file/207966/espa.pdf.

Time Series Universal Credit: Universal Credit (UC) is a new benefit that was introduced in April 2013 and will replace six existing benefits and tax credits with a single monthly payment. UC will eventually replace: Income-based Jobseeker's Allowance, Income-related Employment and Support Allowance, Income Support, Working Tax Credit, Child Tax Credit and Housing Benefit. Further information and statistics relating to UC can be found at: https://www.gov.uk/government/collections/universal-credit-statistics.html After August 2003 there was a sharp decline in the number of claimants aged 60 or over. This is due to the migration of most existing Minimum Income Guarantee claimants (1.8 million) to Pension Credit, which was introduced in October 2003. Some residual cases remain.

5.17 Pension Credit[1]: number of claimants

Great Britain
End of May

Thousands[2]

		2006	2007	2008	2009	2010	2011	2012	2013	2014
All Pension Credit	**F8Z5**	2717.4	2733.5	2719.1	2730.6	2734.2	2674.7	2541.5	2413.9	2270.3
Guarantee Credit Only	**F8Z6**	775.6	805.7	882.1	925.7	954.4	937	1015.9	968.4	950.2
Guarantee Credit and Savings Credit	**F8Z7**	1343.2	1330.1	1246.2	1205.2	1202.4	1148.1	964.3	906.6	824.3
Savings Credit	**F8Z8**	598.6	597.7	590.8	599.6	577.4	589.6	561.4	538.8	495.8

1 Source: DWP 100% Work and Pensions Longitudinal study (WPLS).

Caseload figures are rounded to the nearest ten. Totals may not sum due to rounding.

Source: DWP Information, Governance and Security, Work and Pensions Longitudinal Study.

Caseload - number of claimants (Thousands) - Pension Credit was introduced on 6 October 2003 and replaced Minimum Income Guarantee (Income Support for people aged 60 or over). The vast majority of people who were previously in receipt of the Minimum Income Guarantee transferred to Pension Credit in October 2003. These Pension Credit statistics are produced on a different basis to the Early Estimates. The latter are more timely but operational processing times mean that a number of claim commencements and terminations are not reflected in them. Cases receiving a zero payment amount are recorded in the unknown payment category.

Type of Pension Credit - Certain aspects of the April 2012 uprating for Pension Credit were applied to the administrative computer system in advance, before the February 2012 statistics were extracted. Hence, the statistics in February 2012 show the Pension Credit type based on 2012/13 rates. However, the amounts in payment had not been adjusted and claimants were still being paid the correct rate of benefit, based on 2011/12 rates.

Time Series Includes Minimum Income Guarantee (MIG) cases: households on Income Support where the claimant and/or partner are aged 60 or over. About 1.8 million MIG cases transferred to Pension Credit on 6th October 2003.

STATE PENSION AGE: The age at which women reach State Pension age is gradually increasing from 60 to 65 between April 2010 and April 2016 to November 2018. Under current legislation, State Pension age for men and women is planned to increase to: 66 between November 2018 and October 2020; 67 between 2034 and 2036; 68 between 2044 and 2046. This will introduce a small increase to the number of working age benefit recipients and a small reduction to the number of pension age recipients. Figures from May 2010 onwards reflect this change. For more information see http://statistics.dwp.gov.uk/asd/espa.pdf.

5.18 Income support: average weekly amounts of benefit[1,2,3]

Great Britain
As at May

£ per week

		2005	2006	2007	2008	2009	2010	2011	2012	2013	2014
All income support claimants	**F8ZF**	85.89	83.54	82.45	82.55	85.17	85.01	84.88	83.93	76.42	71.69
Incapacity benefits[4]	**F8ZG**	77.12	78.35	80.04	81.85	89.22	91.81	93.66	93.69	82.12	67.46
Lone Parent[4]	**F8ZH**	102.85	94.88	89.70	87.37	82.79	79.02	75.94	76.54	74.09	72.75
Carer[4]	**F8ZI**	73.03	71.13	70.82	70.21	71.85	70.90	69.94	72.23	72.32	72.16
Others on income related benefits[4]	**F8ZJ**	62.81	62.78	62.47	63.02	66.35	67.87	68.82	73.19	74.11	74.88

1 Figures are given at May each year and are taken from the DWP 100% Work and Pensions Longitudinal Study (WPLS).

Source: DWP Information, Governance and Security, Work and Pensions Longitudinal Study.

2 The amount of Income Support is affected by the introduction in April 2003 of Child Tax Credit. From that date there were no new child dependency increases awarded to IS claimants, although existing CDIs were transitionally protected.

3 Average amounts are shown as pounds per week and rounded to the nearest penny.

4 Statistical Group is a hierarchical variable. A person who fits into more than one category will only appear in the top-most one for which they are eligible. These statistical groups differ from the groups shown in the 5% sample tables. Lone Parents are defined as claimants on Income Support with child under 16 and no partner. Lone Parent Obligations were introduced from 24th November 2008 affecting the eligibility criteria based on the age of the youngest child. For more information see http://83.244.183.180/100pc/is/tabtool_is.html.

5.19 Pension Credit: average weekly amounts of benefit[1]

Great Britain

As at May										£ per week[2]
		2006	2007	2008	2009	2010	2011	2012	2013	2014
All Pension Credit	**F8ZA**	46.75	50.04	52.69	55.56	57.39	57.74	57.60	57.12	56.31
Guarantee Credit Only	**F8ZB**	79.56	83.74	85.07	88.86	90.73	92.51	90.12	90.06	88.33
Guarantee Credit and Savings Credit	**F8ZC**	43.11	46.11	48.29	50.81	51.75	52.04	52.26	49.41	47.38
Savings Credit only	**F8ZD**	12.39	13.36	13.62	13.71	14.01	13.57	11.36	10.87	9.80

1 Figures are given in each May and are taken from the DWP 100% Work and Pensions Longitudinal Study (WPLS).

2 Average amounts are shown as pounds per week and rounded to the nearest penny.

Source: DWP Information, Governance and Security, Work and Pensions Longitudinal Study.

Certain aspects of the April 2012 uprating for Pension Credit were applied to the administrative computer system in advance, before the February 2012 statistics were extracted. Hence, the statistics in February 2012 show the Pension Credit type based on 2012/13 rates. However, the amounts in payment had not been adjusted and claimants were still being paid the correct rate of benefit, based on 2011/12 rates.

Average weekly amount of benefit Average amounts are calculated for claimants included in the table. Use the "Subset" option to select the claimants you wish to analyse. The averages include a small number of cases recorded as getting zero amounts of benefit. DWP analysts are currently investigating an increase in the number of cases recorded as getting zero amounts of benefit in May 2014.

STATE PENSION AGE: The age at which women reach State Pension age is gradually increasing from 60 to 65 between April 2010 and April 2016 to November 2018. Under current legislation, State Pension age for men and women is planned to increase to: 66 between November 2018 and October 2020; 67 between 2034 and 2036; 68 between 2044 and 2046. This will introduce a small increase to the number of working age benefit recipients and a small reduction to the number of pension age recipients. Figures from May 2010 onwards reflect this change. For more information see http://statistics.dwp.gov.uk/asd/espa.pdf.

External trade and investment

Chapter 6

External trade and investment

External trade (Table 6.1 and 6.3 to 6.6)

The statistics in this section are on the basis of Balance of Payments (BoP). They are compiled from information provided to HM Revenue and Customs (HMRC) by importers and exporters on the basis of Overseas Trade Statistics (OTS) which values exports 'f.o.b.' (free on board) and imports 'c.i.f.' (including insurance and freight). In addition to deducting these freight costs and insurance premiums from the OTS figures, coverage adjustments are made to convert the OTS data to a BoP basis. Adjustments are also made to the level of all exports and European Union (EU) imports to take account of estimated under-recording. The adjustments are set out and described in the annual United Kingdom *Balance of Payments Pink Book* (Office for National Statistics (ONS)). These adjustments are made to conform to the definitions in the 5th edition of the IMF Balance of Payments Manual.

Aggregate estimates of trade in goods, seasonally adjusted and on a BoP basis, are published monthly in the ONS statistical bulletin UK Trade.

Overseas Trade Statistics

HMRC provide accurate and up to date information via the website: www.uktradeinfo.com
They also produce publications entitled 'Overseas Trade Statistics'.

Import penetration and export sales ratios (Table 6.2)

The ratios were first introduced in the August 1977 edition of *Economic Trends* in an article entitled 'The Home and Export Performance of United Kingdom Industries'. The article described the conceptual and methodological problems involved in measuring such variables as import penetration.

The industries are grouped according to the 2007 Standard Industrial Classification at 2-digit level.

Table 6.3 to 6.6

The series are now available as datasets in the UK Trade release, which is updated monthly

International trade in services (Tables 6.7 and 6.8)

These data relate to overseas trade in services and cover both production and non-production industries (excluding the public sector). In terms of the types of services traded these include royalties, various forms of consultancy, computing and telecommunications services, advertising and market research and other business services. A separate inquiry covers the film and television industries. The surveys cover receipts from the provision of services to residents of other countries (exports) and payments to residents of other countries for services rendered (imports).

Sources of data

The International Trade in Services (ITIS) surveys (which consist of a quarterly component addressed to the largest businesses and an annual component for the remainder) are based on a sample of companies derived from the Inter-departmental Business Register in addition to a reference list and from 2007 onwards a sample of approximately 5000 contributors from the Annual Business Inquiry (ABI). The companies are asked to show the amounts for their imports and exports against the geographical area to which they were paid or from which they were received, irrespective of where they were first earned.

The purpose of the ITIS survey is to record international transactions which impact on the UK's BoP. Exports and imports of goods are generally excluded, as they will have been counted in the estimate for trade in goods. However earnings from third country trade – that is, from arranging the sale of goods between two countries other than the UK and where the goods never physically enter the UK (known as merchanting) – are included. Earnings from commodity trading are also included. Together, these two comprise trade related services.

Royalties are a large part of the total trade in services collected in the ITIS survey. These cover transactions for items such as printed matter, sound recordings, performing rights, patents, licences, trademarks, designs, copyrights, manufacturing rights, the use of technical know-how and technical assistance.

Balance of Payments (Tables 6.9 to 6.12)

Tables 6.9 to 6.12 are derived from *United Kingdom Balance of Payments: The Pink Book* 2014 edition. The following general notes to the tables provide brief definitions and explanations of the figures and terms used. Further notes are included in the Pink Book.

Summary of Balance of Payments

The BoP consists of the current account, the capital account, the financial account and the International Investment Position (IIP). The current account consists of trade in goods and services, income, and current transfers. Income consists of investment income and compensation of employees. The capital account mainly consists of capital transfers and the financial account covers financial transactions. The IIP covers balance sheet levels of UK external assets and liabilities. Every credit entry in the balance of payments accounts should, in theory, be matched by a corresponding debit entry so that total current, capital and financial account credits should be equal to, and therefore offset by, total debits. In practice there is a discrepancy termed net errors and omissions.

Current account

Trade in goods

The goods account covers exports and imports of goods. Imports of motor cars from Japan, for example, are recorded as debits in the trade in goods account, whereas exports of vehicles manufactured in the UK are recorded as credits. Trade in goods forms a component of the expenditure measure of gross domestic product (GDP).

Trade in services

The services account covers exports and imports of services, for example civil aviation. Passenger tickets for travel on UK aircraft sold abroad, for example, are recorded as credits in the services account, whereas the purchases of airline tickets from foreign airlines by UK passengers are recorded as debits. Trade in services, along with trade in goods, forms a component of the expenditure measure of GDP.

Income

The income account consists of compensation of employees and investment income and is dominated by the latter. Compensation of employees covers employment income from cross-border and seasonal workers which is less significant in the UK than in other countries. Investment income covers earnings (for example, profits, dividends and interest payments and receipts) arising from cross-border investment in financial assets and liabilities. For example, earnings on foreign bonds and shares held by financial institutions based in the UK are recorded as credits in the investment income account, whereas earnings on UK company securities held abroad are recorded as investment income debits. Investment income forms a component of gross national income (GNI) but not GDP.

Current transfers

Current transfers are composed of central government transfers (for example, taxes and payments to and receipts from, the EU) and other transfers (for example gifts in cash or kind received by private individuals from abroad or receipts from the EU where the UK government acts as an agent for the ultimate beneficiary of the transfer). Current transfers do not form a component either of GDP or of GNI. For example, payments to the UK farming industry under the EU Agricultural Guarantee Fund are recorded as credits in the current transfers account, while payments of EU agricultural levies by the UK farming industry are recorded as debits in the current transfers account.

Capital account

Capital account transactions involve transfers of ownership of fixed assets, transfers of funds associated with acquisition or disposal of fixed assets and cancellation of liabilities by creditors without any counterparts being received in return. The main components are migrants transfers, EU transfers relating to fixed capital formation (regional development fund and agricultural guidance fund) and debt forgiveness. Funds brought into the UK by new immigrants would, for example, be recorded as credits in the capital account, while funds sent abroad by UK residents emigrating to other countries would be recorded as debits in the capital account. The size of capital account transactions are quite minor compared with the current and financial accounts.

Financial account

While investment income covers earnings arising from cross-border investments in financial assets and liabilities, the financial account of the balance of payments covers the flows of such investments. Earnings on foreign bonds and shares held by financial institutions based in the UK are, for example, recorded as credits in the investment income account, but the acquisition of such foreign securities by UK-based financial institutions are recorded as net debits in the financial account or portfolio investment abroad. Similarly, the acquisitions of UK company securities held by foreign residents are recorded in the financial account as net credits or portfolio investment in the UK.

International Investment Position

While the financial account covers the flows of foreign investments and financial assets and liabilities, the IIP records the levels of external assets and liabilities. While the acquisition of foreign securities by UK-based financial institutions are recorded in the financial account as net debits, the total holdings of foreign securities by UK-based financial institutions are recorded as levels of UK external assets. Similarly, the holdings of UK company securities held by foreign residents are recorded as levels of UK liabilities.

Foreign direct investment (Tables 6.13 to 6.18)

Direct investment refers to investment that adds to, deducts from, or acquires a lasting interest in an enterprise operating in an economy other than that of the investor – the investor's purpose being to have an effective voice in the management of the enterprise. (For the purposes of the statistical inquiry, an effective voice is taken as equivalent to a holding of 10 per cent or more in the foreign enterprise.) Other investments in which the investor does not have an effective voice in the management of the enterprise are mainly portfolio investments and these are not covered here.

Direct investment is a financial concept and is not the same as capital expenditure on fixed assets. It covers only the money invested in a related concern by the parent company and the concern will then decide how to use the money. A related concern may also raise money locally without reference to the parent company.

The investment figures are published on a net basis; that is they consist of investments net of disinvestments by a company into its foreign subsidiaries, associate companies and branches.

Definitional changes from 1997

The new European System of Accounts (ESA(95)) definitions were introduced from the 1997 estimates. The changes were as follows:

i.   Previously, for the measurement of direct investment, an effective voice in the management of an enterprise was taken as the equivalent of a 20 per cent shareholding. This is now 10 per cent

ii.   The Channel Islands and the Isle of Man have been excluded from the definition of the economic territory of the UK. Prior to 1987 these islands were considered to be part of the UK

iii.   Interest received or paid was replaced by interest accrued in the figures on earnings from direct investment. There is deemed to be little or no impact arising from this definitional change on the estimates

A further change caused by the move to ESA(95) is that withholding taxes payable on direct investment earnings are now measured. Earnings were shown gross of these taxes in the Balance of Payments 2005 Pink Book. However, for the purposes of this business monitor earnings are calculated net of tax, as before.

New register sources available from 1998 have led to revisions of the figures from that year onwards. These sources gave an improved estimate of the population satisfying the criteria for foreign direct investment.

From the 2005 surveys new data sources have allowed the inclusion of data for the previously excluded Private Property (outward & inward surveys) and Public Corporations (outward surveys) sectors. From the 2006 surveys the tax data previously excluded from the FDI surveys are now also included in the final earnings figures for both the outward & inward surveys. This now means that there are no coherence issues between the FDI annual surveys and the quarterly Balance of Payments figures as published in the latest Balance of Payments Pink Book.

Definitional changes have been introduced from 1997 and the register changes from 1998. Data prior to these years have not been reworked in Tables 6.13 to 6.18. For clarity, the Offshore Islands are identified separately on the tables. Breaks in the series for the other definitional changes are not quantified but are relatively small. More detailed information on the effect of these changes appears in the business monitor MA4 – Foreign Direct Investment 2002, which was published in February 2003 and is available from the ONS website.

Sources of data

The figures in Tables 6.13 to 6.18 are based on annual inquiries into foreign direct investment for 2014. These were sample surveys which involved sending approximately 1530 forms to UK businesses investing abroad, and 2370 forms to UK businesses in which foreign parents and associates had invested. The tables also contain some revisions as a result of new information coming to light in the course of the latest surveys. Further details from the latest annual surveys, including analyses by industry and by components of direct investment, are available in business monitor MA4.

Country allocation

The analysis of inward investment is based on the country of ownership of the immediate parent company. Thus, inward investment in a UK company may be attributed to the country of the intervening overseas subsidiary, rather than the country of the ultimate parent. Similarly, the country analysis of outward investment is based on the country of ownership of the immediate subsidiary; for example, to the extent that overseas investment in the UK is channelled through holding companies in the Netherlands, the underlying flow of investment from this country is overstated and the inflow from originating countries is understated.

Further information

More detailed statistics on foreign direct investment are available on request from Michael Hardie, Office for National Statistics, Telephone: +44 (0)1633 455923, email fdi@ons.gsi.gov.uk

6.1 Trade in goods[1]
United Kingdom
Balance of payments basis

£million and Indices 2013=100

		2002	2003	2004	2005	2006	2007	2008	2009	2010	2011	2012	2013	2014
Value (£ million)														
Exports of goods	BOKG	186776	188546	191608	212053	243957	222964	254577	229107	270196	308171	304302	306226	293739
Imports of goods	BOKH	235729	239505	253549	282213	322920	313504	349603	315731	367580	403126	412528	423811	415469
Balance on trade in goods	BOKI	-48953	-50959	-61941	-70160	-78963	-90540	-95026	-86624	-97384	-94955	-110907	-120664	-122575
Price index numbers														
Exports of goods	BQKR	68.4	69.7	70.3	72.8	74	73.6	83.7	84.5	90.3	97.4	97.3	100	94.2
Imports of goods	BQKS	73.1	73	72.5	75.7	78.1	78.2	89.2	90.2	94.5	102.5	102.7	100	98.6
Terms of trade[2]	BQKT	93.6	95.5	97	96.2	94.8	94.1	93.8	93.7	95.6	95	94.7	100	95.5
Volume index numbers														
Exports of goods	BQKU	83.9	83.2	84.5	91.3	103.6	95.3	96.7	86.4	96.2	102.7	101	100	101.6
Imports of goods	BQKV	75.1	76.7	82.1	88.1	98.1	95.2	93.7	84.4	94.1	95.6	98	100	103.3

Source: Office for National Statistics: 01633 456294

1 See chapter text. Statistics of trade in goods on a balance of payments basis are obtained by making certain adjustments in respect of valuation and coverage to the statistics recorded in the Overseas Trade Statistics. These adjustments are described in detail in The Pink Book.
2 Export price index as a percentage of the import price index.

Table 6.1 may show revisions to data going back over time. This is mainly to reflect revised data from HMRC and other data suppliers, later survey data and a re-assessment of seasonal factors.

6.2 Sales of products manufactured in the United Kingdom by Industry Division

S - Suppressed as disclosive

£ Thousands

Industry	SIC(07) Division	2010	2011	2012	2013
Other mining and quarrying	8	2,289,614	2,255,125	S	2,299,263
Manufacture of food products	10	58,468,601	60,663,124	62,897,838	66,030,444
Manufacture of beverages	11	12,397,869	12,875,926	12,375,786	12,386,202
Manufacture of tobacco products	12	1,625,505	1,672,839	1,793,420	1,723,231
Manufacture of textiles	13	3,887,733	4,047,168	4,134,488	S
Manufacture of wearing apparel	14	1,568,459	1,490,960	1,634,262	1,634,497
Manufacture of leather and related products	15	S	618,239	646,669	726,732
Manufacture of wood and of products of wood and cork, except furniture; manufacture of articles of straw and plaiting materials	16	S	5,577,606	5,739,940	6,096,793
Manufacture of paper and paper products	17	9,689,632	S	10,018,458	S
Printing and reproduction of recorded media	18	8,715,583	8,927,210	8,672,310	8,054,509
Manufacture of coke and refined petroleum products	19	S	S	S	S
Manufacture of chemicals and chemical products	20	23,074,946	S	S	S
Manufacture of basic pharmaceutical products and pharmaceutical preparations	21	14,723,163	13,901,544	12,288,627	12,047,139
Manufacture of rubber and plastic products	22	S	S	S	S
Manufacture of other non-metallic mineral products	23	9,733,216	10,249,359	10,167,511	10,358,525
Manufacture of basic metals	24	7,391,321	8,500,016	7,422,006	6,825,251
Manufacture of fabricated metal products, except machinery and equipment	25	S	S	S	24,266,120
Manufacture of computer, electronic and optical products	26	13,458,189	12,857,258	S	12,558,623
Manufacture of electrical equipment	27	10,963,840	11,864,709	S	S
Manufacture of machinery and equipment n.e.c.	28	22,769,955	S	26,920,747	S
Manufacture of motor vehicles, trailers and semi-trailers	29	S	38,446,099	39,296,813	S
Manufacture of other transport equipment	30	20,531,722	21,392,793	23,839,850	26,471,305
Manufacture of furniture	31	5,643,486	S	6,098,141	6,305,793
Other manufacturing	32	4,541,098	S	S	S
Repair and installation of machinery and equipment	33	11,809,272	12,589,466	S	13,987,075
Total		324,799,390	341,030,726	341,984,772	354,721,188

Source: Office for National Statistics (ONS)

Note: Information in this table relates to products corresponding to a division irrespective of which division the business making the product is classified to.

6.3 United Kingdom exports: by commodity[1,2]

Seasonally adjusted

£ million

		2004	2005	2006	2007	2008	2009	2010	2011	2012	2013	2014
0. Food and live animals	BOGG	6711	6932	6872	7774	9082	9482	11623	14142	12103	12983	12134
01. Meat and meat preparations	BOGS	662	717	724	789	1086	1166	1311	1569	1455	1691	1675
02. Dairy products and eggs	BQMS	790	723	718	808	887	836	1037	1248	1167	1378	1501
04 & 08. Cereals and animal feeding stuffs	BQMT	1568	1554	1575	1781	2291	2371	2586	2746	2776	2830	2862
05. Vegetables and fruit	BQMU	506	514	588	608	695	761	814	882	855	783	618
1. Beverages and tobacco	BQMZ	4145	4111	4182	4386	5030	5353	5950	6962	6935	7265	6878
11. Beverages	BQNB	3386	3497	3717	4085	4582	4951	5626	6819	6861	6999	6616
12. Tobacco	BQOW	759	614	465	301	448	402	324	143	74	266	262
2. Crude materials	BQOX	3438	3610	4615	5167	6247	4795	6915	8551	7984	7154	6528
of which:												
24. Wood, lumber and cork	BQOY	116	131	145	143	125	83	111	113	107	154	162
25. Pulp and waste paper	BQOZ	243	282	338	415	478	354	542	623	544	503	483
26. Textile fibres	BQPA	508	497	545	497	540	573	674	782	821	764	692
28. Metal ores	BQPB	1558	1642	2415	2877	3659	2512	4114	5074	4517	4059	3675
3. Fuels	BOPN	17808	21464	24757	24369	35428	26970	35115	42713	43714	42878	36078
33. Petroleum and petroleum products	ELBL	16092	19741	22594	22397	31857	24568	31288	37966	39516	39292	32899
32, 34 & 35. Coal, gas and electricity	BOQI	1716	1723	2163	1972	3571	2402	3827	4747	4198	3586	3179
4. Animal and vegetable oils and fats	BQPI	198	235	273	326	360	375	421	440	480	492	460
5. Chemicals	ENDG	31831	33115	37128	38814	43792	46927	50821	53065	52953	48992	47851
of which:												
51. Organic chemicals	BQPJ	6001	6676	7987	7567	8376	9071	8838	9163	9013	7688	6601
52. Inorganic chemicals	BQPK	1555	1564	2145	2819	2978	2834	3481	3018	2885	2564	1809
53. Colouring materials	CSCE	1606	1605	1600	1669	1844	1693	1951	2165	1995	2033	2045
54. Medicinal products	BQPL	12265	12203	13773	14555	17301	20457	22319	22823	23467	20532	21089
55. Toilet preparations	CSCF	3108	3208	3444	3677	3940	4128	4292	4843	4843	5313	5207
57 & 58. Plastics	BQQA	3791	4220	4438	4593	4847	4389	5310	5854	5627	5546	5637
6. Manufactures classified chiefly by material	BQQB	24511	26492	27632	29246	32293	24452	29140	34767	32273	31817	28916
of which:												
63. Wood and cork manufactures	BQQC	289	249	276	273	243	220	224	253	265	247	257
64. Paper and paperboard manufactures	BQQD	2010	2053	2015	2112	2338	2281	2338	2376	2289	2281	2200
65. Textile manufactures	BQQE	2833	2632	2687	2582	2593	2371	2596	2791	2735	2805	2816
67. Iron and steel	BQQF	4230	5148	5121	5995	6841	4572	5032	6027	5754	6096	6085
68. Non-ferrous metals	BQQG	3249	3882	4828	5762	6843	3965	5832	8574	6824	7160	6772
69. Metal manufactures	BQQH	3848	4037	4489	4616	4983	4190	4437	4761	4823	4782	5337
7. Machinery and transport equipment	BQQI	77969	88923	110094	82200	88724	79169	92411	103106	104227	109703	108774
71-716, 72, 73 & 74. Mechanical machinery	BQQK	23716	25609	28104	28850	32178	29265	32786	38493	39355	41662	39923
716, 75, 76 & 77. Electrical machinery	BQQL	28519	37093	55168	23917	24966	23919	25587	25962	24009	24034	24495
78. Road vehicles	BQQM	18220	19158	19335	21035	22433	17006	23322	27366	28948	31511	32164
79. Other transport equipment	BQQN	7514	7063	7487	8398	9147	8979	10716	11285	11915	12496	12192
8. Miscellaneous manufactures	BQQO	22850	25049	25928	26630	28431	27686	31249	33534	35696	36964	38482
of which:												
84. Clothing	CSCN	2702	2694	2860	3085	3300	3423	3659	4208	4448	5158	5518
85. Footwear	CSCP	417	469	523	543	622	723	852	932	1035	1245	1279
87 & 88. Scientific and photographic	BQQQ	7016	7228	7347	7035	8038	8281	9275	10177	10373	11132	11127
9. Other commodities and transactions	BOQL	1949	2810	3367	3550	5578	5537	7171	11904	8777	8517	6103
Total United Kingdom exports	BOKG	191410	212741	244848	222462	254965	230746	270816	309184	305142	306765	292204

Source: Office for National Statistics: 01633 456294

1 See chapter text. The numbers on the left hand side of the table refer to the code numbers of the Standard International Trade Classification, Revision

3, which was introduced in January 1988.

2 Balance of payments consistent basis.

6.4 United Kingdom imports: by commodity [1,2]

Seasonally adjusted

		2004	2005	2006	2007	2008	2009	2010	2011	2012	2013	2014
0. Food and live animals	BQQR	17223	18625	19762	21303	25290	26328	27147	29387	30033	31250	31194
of which:												
01. Meat and meat preparations	BQQS	3470	3659	3788	3980	4607	4910	5006	5607	5599	5745	6164
02. Dairy products and eggs	BQQT	1631	1724	1802	1836	2289	2321	2429	2535	2616	2898	2844
04 & 08. Cereals and animal feeding stuffs	BQQU	2324	2383	2482	2911	3812	3923	3973	4137	4604	5543	5179
05. Vegetables and fruit	BQQV	4832	5360	5769	6207	7050	7039	7431	7890	7966	7278	7097
1. Beverages and tobacco	BQQW	5303	5383	5548	5760	6290	6498	6801	7025	6991	7505	7493
11. Beverages	EGAT	3828	3938	4159	4412	4812	5081	5318	5589	5703	5954	5903
12. Tobacco	EMAI	1475	1445	1389	1348	1478	1417	1483	1436	1288	1551	1590
2. Crude materials	ENVB	5722	6151	7089	8630	9583	6542	9119	10391	9227	11043	10525
of which:												
24. Wood, lumber and cork	ENVC	1350	1376	1452	1801	1408	1169	1465	1426	1458	2328	2635
25. Pulp and waste paper	EQAH	480	474	533	516	612	452	596	629	517	519	524
26. Textile fibres	EQAP	323	303	299	322	338	290	355	455	379	403	415
28. Metalores	EHAA	1652	2008	2649	3760	4646	2257	3887	4741	3930	4753	4100
3. Fuels	BQAT	17938	26361	31326	32205	48894	35410	44803	61630	65167	61495	52951
33. Petroleum and petroleum products	ENXO	15725	22405	26447	27127	38393	28025	36013	49395	53804	49145	42958
32, 34 & 35. Coal, gas and electricity	BPBI	2213	3956	4879	5078	10501	7385	8790	12235	11363	12350	9993
4. Animal and vegetable oils and fats	EHAB	625	646	778	897	1397	1052	1128	1493	1413	1385	1199
5. Chemicals	ENGA	30006	31201	33216	36743	40423	41665	47175	50899	53156	51134	52504
of which:												
51. Organic chemicals	EHAC	6876	7324	7698	8644	8454	8277	9390	10078	10076	8115	6854
52. Inorganic chemicals	EHAE	1388	1534	2130	2694	2763	2745	2952	3606	3195	2548	2276
53. Colouring materials	CSCR	1063	1078	1084	1157	1227	1144	1253	1325	1360	1382	1390
54. Medicinal products	EHAF	10274	10233	10728	12045	13533	15888	17671	18442	21507	21168	23843
55. Toilet preparations	CSCS	2914	3071	3325	3438	3926	4158	4416	4653	4736	5054	5171
57 & 58. Plastics	EHAG	4774	5073	5354	5687	6221	5556	6848	7720	7505	7934	8007
6. Manufactures classified chiefly by material	EHAH	32057	33283	37632	39725	41895	35887	43542	49047	49759	46442	43634
of which:												
63. Wood and cork manufactures	EHAI	1614	1533	1581	1738	1729	1477	1664	1690	1660	1800	1974
64. Paper and paperboard manufactures	EHAJ	4875	4842	5023	5235	5482	5501	5885	6017	5680	5855	5956
65. Textile manufactures	EHAK	3941	3664	3996	4083	4082	3823	4290	4591	4520	4727	4893
67. Iron and steel	EHAL	4120	4348	5071	5927	6556	3850	5162	6476	6163	5323	5804
68. Non-ferrous metals	EHAM	3626	3938	6177	6231	6434	6355	8669	10119	12555	9561	7963
69. Metal manufactures	EHAN	4961	5355	5843	6543	6970	5957	6865	7532	7576	8023	8273
7. Machinery and transport equipment	EHAO	103988	117180	139454	117427	120769	107225	129108	128563	130919	139972	146846
71 - 716, 72, 73 & 74. Mechanical machinery	EHAQ	19607	21892	22309	25500	29065	24407	28743	32735	34252	35834	36798
716, 75, 76 & 77. Electrical machinery	EHAR	45602	55446	75108	46009	47199	44528	50947	51090	50549	52449	51780
78. Road vehicles	EHAS	30739	31476	32560	36532	33886	26160	33653	36650	36532	40861	45673
79. Other transport equipment	EHAT	8040	8366	9477	9386	10619	12130	15765	8088	9586	10828	12595
8. Miscellaneous manufactures	EHAU	38710	41104	44801	47940	51042	50063	54714	58544	59504	60687	63242
of which:												
84. Clothing	CSDR	9583	10210	11956	12364	13196	13840	14822	16129	15793	16496	17414
85. Footwear	CSDS	2475	2605	2713	2681	2843	3100	3606	3684	3852	4014	4335
87 & 88. Scientific and photographic	EHAW	7290	7482	7614	7531	8447	8495	9113	9558	10068	10727	10866
9. Other commodities and transactions	BQAW	1977	2279	3314	2874	4020	5061	4043	4734	4631	10544	7294
Total United Kingdom imports	BOKH	253549	282213	322920	313504	349603	315731	367580	401713	410800	421457	416882

Source: Office for National Statistics: 01633 456294

1 See chapter text. The numbers on the left hand side of the table refer to the code numbers of the Standard International Trade Classification, Revision 3, which was introduced in January 1988.

2 Balance of payments consistent basis.

6.5 Trade in goods - Exports
Seasonally adjusted

£ million

		2005	2006	2007	2008	2009	2010	2011	2012	2013	2014
Exports (Credits)											
Europe											
European Union (EU)											
Austria	QBRY	1344	1674	1376	1480	1294	1485	1733	1553	1675	1669
Belgium	QDOH	11269	13009	11823	13417	10870	13478	16248	14212	13828	11856
Bulgaria	QAMF	220	226	202	258	201	257	335	311	394	453
Croatia	QAMM	113	144	159	217	212	175	152	145	108	150
Cyprus	QDNZ	360	1042	414	539	625	569	708	443	452	493
Czech Republic	QDLF	1091	1569	1400	1556	1446	1843	1967	1827	1929	2007
Denmark	QBSE	2337	3835	2181	2603	2484	2783	3077	2687	2878	2954
Estonia	QAMN	115	469	228	224	140	197	288	288	331	283
Finland	QBSH	1532	1810	1959	1916	1330	1516	1694	1548	1559	1635
France	QDJA	20133	28904	18137	18151	17255	19441	22475	20886	20977	19046
Germany	QDJD	23491	27135	25045	28308	24562	28788	34870	32544	29796	30664
Greece	QDJG	1383	1463	1354	1665	1630	1398	1234	909	943	1041
Hungary	QDLI	844	836	863	1012	855	1190	1216	1092	1234	1327
Ireland	QDJJ	16458	17131	17800	19176	15959	17085	18223	17234	18592	18104
Italy	QDJM	8876	9434	9206	9442	8385	8957	10248	8046	8513	8794
Latvia	QAMO	101	585	145	172	109	172	246	257	380	336
Lithuania	QAMP	166	236	311	285	176	234	280	376	326	297
Luxembourg	QDOK	212	1622	272	210	198	254	283	227	239	223
Malta	QDOC	240	318	362	449	402	399	460	393	446	365
Netherlands	QDJP	12897	16576	15193	20071	18299	22174	24992	25033	25424	22299
Poland	QDLL	1671	2774	2375	3024	2803	3840	4411	3417	3841	3885
Portugal	QDJT	1716	2325	1484	1648	1545	1857	1794	1371	1358	1350
Romania	QAMQ	658	605	664	758	687	793	793	978	940	935
Slovak Republic	QAMR	260	275	380	455	378	472	567	528	471	447
Slovenia	QAMS	167	194	204	230	179	227	252	219	209	242
Spain	QDJW	10782	12484	10062	10309	9249	10051	9952	8478	8663	9276
Sweden	QDJZ	4633	5151	4908	5236	4228	5628	6402	5721	5760	5341
European Central Bank	QARP	-	-	-	-	-	-	-	-	-	-
EU Institutions	EOAY	-	-	-	-	-	-	-	-	-	-
Total EU28	L87R	123069	151826	128507	142811	125501	145173	165085	150685	151256	145472
European Free Trade Association (EFTA)											
Iceland	QDKW	176	190	202	188	128	132	148	190	172	138
Liechtenstein	EPOW	2	22	3	9	5	25	13	9	4	14
Norway	QDKZ	2213	2168	2723	2832	2725	3105	3379	3564	3463	3758
Switzerland	QDLC	5046	4315	3942	4816	3993	5499	6307	7067	6140	10285
Total EFTA	EPOT	7437	6695	6870	7845	6851	8761	9847	10830	9779	14195
Other Europe											
Albania	QAMC	16	17	19	16	18	21	19	22	21	22
Belarus	QAME	56	64	69	90	81	121	132	129	99	90
Russia	QDLO	1867	2069	2851	4334	2457	3679	5217	5668	5278	4149
Turkey	QDLR	2169	2489	2348	2605	2368	3256	3937	3695	4085	3598
Ukraine	QAMT	268	341	443	613	588	473	567	600	599	442
Serbia and Montenegro	QAMW	57	89	107	130	103	98	121	132	149	118
of which: Serbia	KN2P	57	89	99	120	99	94	113	122	134	114
Montenegro	KN2M	-	-	8	10	4	4	8	10	15	4
Other	BOQE	251	340	294	563	505	809	973	1053	1127	829
Total Europe	EPLM	135190	163930	141508	159007	138472	162391	185898	172814	172393	168915
Americas											
Argentina	QAOM	156	217	225	319	255	358	414	388	376	234
Brazil	QDLU	830	920	1070	1691	1793	2224	2470	2667	2716	1923
Canada	QATH	3205	3884	3276	3245	3334	4134	4754	4164	4002	3228
Chile	QAMG	148	188	183	267	514	632	799	682	1155	1028
Colombia	QAML	113	135	139	161	172	230	314	330	368	366
Mexico	QDLX	620	743	763	905	752	954	1007	1135	1175	896
United States of America	J8V9	30422	32179	32113	35278	34048	38139	40120	41261	39611	37116
Uruguay	QAMU	37	42	36	65	60	79	122	115	174	108
Venezuela	QAMV	225	235	250	282	300	273	327	410	313	141
Other Central American Countries	BOQQ	651	759	767	943	704	849	899	951	886	805
Other	BOQT	152	173	183	248	234	394	477	657	607	430
Total Americas	EPLO	36559	39475	39005	43404	42166	48266	51703	52760	51383	46275
Asia											
China	QDMA	2894	3495	4494	5798	5564	8131	10274	11338	13466	15520
Hong Kong	QDMD	3035	2875	2651	3665	3741	4468	5385	5394	5640	6344
India	QDMG	2855	2942	3770	4957	3088	4519	6660	5445	6426	6343
Indonesia	QDMJ	368	319	294	394	365	462	672	655	704	499
Iran	QAON	453	434	399	442	406	307	190	109	84	87
Israel	QDMM	1327	1318	1238	1339	1148	1391	1654	1548	1421	1133
Japan	QAMJ	3844	4135	3861	3916	3572	4348	4730	4932	4813	4264
Malaysia	QDMP	1071	887	953	1134	1052	1276	1486	1540	1649	1477
Pakistan	QDMS	452	496	428	479	477	462	534	563	490	620
Philippines	QDMV	267	240	249	243	268	284	293	331	382	301
Saudi Arabia	QDMY	1572	1698	1919	2284	2375	2533	2774	3156	3468	3840
Singapore	QDNB	2044	2329	2440	2814	2933	3416	3743	4403	4228	3412
South Korea	QDNE	1652	1754	1861	2560	2172	2350	2689	4943	5189	5605
Taiwan	QDNH	928	915	935	887	797	1118	1388	1155	1239	1289

6.5 Trade in goods - Exports

Seasonally adjusted

£ million

		2005	2006	2007	2008	2009	2010	2011	2012	2013	2014
Thailand	QDNK	623	572	599	758	916	1139	1418	2003	1965	1463
Residual Gulf Arabian Countries	BOQW	6951	5200	4514	6040	5783	6607	7479	8542	9546	9298
Other Near & Middle Eastern Countries	QARJ	714	978	745	1031	1099	1319	1370	1346	1277	1332
Other	BORB	558	673	1587	843	982	1216	1362	1333	1473	1341
Total Asia	EPLP	31608	31260	32937	39584	36738	45346	54101	58736	63460	64168
Australasia & Oceania											
Australia	QDNN	2544	2498	2582	3103	2962	3368	4396	4749	4311	3676
New Zealand	QDNQ	406	377	359	388	350	414	543	619	650	591
Other	EGIZ	81	75	66	102	92	82	68	86	61	56
Total Australasia & Oceania	EPLQ	3031	2950	3007	3593	3404	3864	5007	5454	5022	4323
Africa											
Egypt	QDNT	536	588	689	945	1009	1200	1104	963	974	998
Morocco	QAOO	248	306	313	517	311	567	567	649	476	529
South Africa	QDNW	2039	2190	2155	2648	2257	2895	3466	3219	2572	2177
Other North Africa	BORU	472	501	507	811	959	909	639	740	939	862
Other	BOQH	2370	2757	2843	4068	3791	4758	5686	6286	5928	4647
Total Africa	EPLN	5665	6342	6507	8989	8327	10329	11462	11857	10889	9213
International Organisations	EPLR	-	-	-	-	-	-	-	-	-	-
World total	LQAD	212053	243957	222964	254577	229107	270196	308171	301621	303147	292894

Source: Office for National Statistics

Note: On the advice of ONS, we have replaced table 6.5 with a new table. The new format contains different ONS 4 digit codes, many contain the letter Q at the beginning which means the figures have been seasonally adjusted.

6.6 Trade in goods - Imports
Seasonally adjusted

£ million

		2005	2006	2007	2008	2009	2010	2011	2012	2013	2014
Imports (Debits)											
Europe											
European Union (EU)											
Austria	QBRZ	2521	2789	2525	2388	2319	2670	2979	2633	2885	2973
Belgium	QDOI	14428	15391	15225	16705	15292	17348	19340	18501	20449	20982
Bulgaria	QAMZ	174	198	241	215	183	233	289	285	418	365
Croatia	QANC	50	67	74	88	78	98	106	78	127	57
Cyprus	QDOA	281	1718	196	156	123	106	142	168	135	125
Czech Republic	QDLG	1923	2961	3027	3658	3398	4050	4290	4544	4698	4739
Denmark	QBSF	4512	6539	3492	3998	3910	4180	6151	5929	5871	4628
Estonia	QAND	374	2110	240	151	129	167	225	238	193	154
Finland	QBTG	2481	3086	2655	2834	2147	2183	2464	2187	2515	2552
France	QDJB	22535	26854	22256	23657	20829	21913	23305	22865	24425	25165
Germany	QDJE	40073	42242	45268	45623	40936	47160	51071	53408	56808	60561
Greece	QDJH	740	815	657	676	570	716	676	695	762	724
Hungary	QDLJ	1909	2370	2408	2578	2585	3299	3120	2677	2665	2525
Ireland	QDJK	10645	10799	11494	12477	12659	13067	13200	13044	12537	11855
Italy	QDJN	12976	12973	13512	14427	12583	14162	14242	14491	15285	16508
Latvia	QANE	736	806	638	423	341	443	448	412	600	435
Lithuania	QANF	285	282	313	361	377	562	613	842	907	1056
Luxembourg	QDOL	942	2727	707	846	628	956	937	685	368	436
Malta	QDOD	182	164	183	138	106	171	169	128	105	119
Netherlands	QDJQ	20935	22601	23520	26387	22367	26865	28875	31750	35227	33017
Poland	QDLM	2369	3686	3749	4396	4759	6206	7157	7522	7956	7774
Portugal	QDJU	2070	3192	1534	1781	1455	1780	1826	1769	1980	2268
Romania	QANG	824	835	960	822	803	1265	1302	1294	1507	1522
Slovak Republic	QANH	382	850	1296	1665	1636	1648	1534	1607	1864	2010
Slovenia	QANI	206	749	320	325	258	363	366	348	328	296
Spain	QDJX	11778	12078	10643	10982	9756	10545	11931	11728	12436	13754
Sweden	QDKA	5590	6223	5381	6994	5835	6916	7797	9211	7613	8134
European Central Bank	QARQ	-	-	-	-	-	-	-	-	-	-
EU Institutions	EOBS	-	-	-	-	-	-	-	-	-	-
Total EU28	L87T	161921	185105	172514	184751	166062	189072	204555	209039	220664	224734
European Free Trade Association (EFTA)											
Iceland	QDKX	348	406	414	467	489	433	418	393	379	429
Liechtenstein	EPOX	16	39	38	34	21	10	7	2	3	4
Norway	QDLA	12217	14777	14563	21945	16200	21022	26493	24764	20437	18527
Switzerland	QDLD	3813	4421	4817	5363	5393	7460	7622	9047	8182	7790
Total EFTA	EPOU	16394	19643	19832	27809	22103	28925	34540	34206	29001	26750
Other Europe											
Albania	QAMX	-	-	-	-	-	-	1	-	8	7
Belarus	QAMY	271	730	594	105	20	37	48	90	76	56
Russia	QDLP	4969	5808	5428	6971	4638	5243	7440	8443	7116	6252
Turkey	QDLS	3496	3983	4679	4951	4659	5341	5549	5750	6178	6404
Ukraine	QANJ	80	120	118	147	145	282	355	296	394	442
Serbia and Montenegro	QANM	43	65	74	90	74	93	97	83	114	83
of which: Serbia	KN2Q	43	65	74	88	74	92	96	80	113	83
Montenegro	KN2N	-	-	-	2	-	1	1	3	1	-
Other	BOQF	204	183	194	212	255	242	286	345	340	369
Total Europe	EPMM	187378	215637	203433	225036	197956	229235	252871	258252	263891	265097
Americas											
Argentina	QAOP	271	348	417	569	668	664	618	642	656	647
Brazil	QDLV	1738	1940	2060	2654	2564	3109	2721	2446	2553	2634
Canada	QATI	4073	4933	5783	5716	4461	5762	6131	5532	5728	7181
Chile	QANA	484	527	495	587	600	582	619	593	646	601
Colombia	QANB	298	304	367	699	582	675	921	938	827	655
Mexico	QDLY	426	429	553	780	756	1033	1083	719	757	786
United States of America	J8VA	21674	25504	25560	25508	24198	26946	28694	29837	27560	28099
Uruguay	QANK	58	66	71	116	113	101	116	119	97	89
Venezuela	QANL	384	607	487	615	426	421	407	472	258	184
Other Central American											
Countries	BOQR	1168	1387	1150	1368	1247	1141	1048	833	1091	1099
Other	BOQU	224	301	251	367	352	363	460	501	497	557
Total Americas	EPMO	30798	36346	37194	38979	35967	40797	42818	42632	40670	42532
Asia											
China	QDMB	13175	16059	19038	23744	25255	30898	31847	31694	35921	36885
Hong Kong	QDME	6572	7473	6976	8161	7752	8164	7613	7389	7363	7421
India	QDMH	2927	3705	3971	4920	5408	5406	6190	6521	9673	7737
Indonesia	QDMK	897	1034	1003	1217	1239	1391	1347	1275	1251	1052
Iran	QAOQ	25	60	55	69	211	206	376	121	35	21
Israel	QDMN	983	961	1043	1172	1098	1562	2264	2410	1906	945
Japan	QAMK	8461	7860	7893	8534	6664	8093	8852	8523	7604	7242
Malaysia	QDMQ	1799	1923	1704	1893	1666	1835	1776	1716	1680	1739
Pakistan	QDMT	475	508	494	635	701	808	886	842	956	940
Philippines	QDMW	711	749	720	635	396	525	479	454	403	331
Saudi Arabia	QDMZ	1824	1334	909	720	672	792	1098	1719	2837	2718
Singapore	QDNC	3804	3800	4077	4040	3586	4136	3872	3729	2704	3080
South Korea	QDNF	2984	3069	2984	3508	2859	2561	2612	3241	3394	3186
Taiwan	QDNI	2224	2388	2415	2628	2265	3110	3483	3963	3621	3511
Thailand	QDNL	1717	1966	2016	2448	2320	2680	2588	2617	2724	2434

6.6 Trade in goods - Imports

Seasonally adjusted

£ million

		2005	2006	2007	2008	2009	2010	2011	2012	2013	2014
Residual Gulf Arabian Countries	BOQX	1978	2245	2132	2395	2817	5381	8836	7218	7378	5329
Other Near & Middle Eastern Countries	QARK	200	753	376	435	343	298	445	825	348	449
Other	BORD	2021	2469	2638	3152	3622	3901	4959	6482	7152	5929
Total Asia	EPMP	52777	58356	60444	70306	68874	82531	89927	90739	96950	90949
Australasia & Oceania											
Australia	QDNO	2028	2087	2186	2379	2222	2306	2433	2419	2221	1735
New Zealand	QDNR	575	603	657	751	819	842	871	893	890	716
Other	HFKF	131	130	117	169	168	107	197	164	185	155
Total Australasia & Oceania	EPMQ	2734	2820	2960	3299	3209	3255	3501	3476	3296	2606
Africa											
Egypt	QDNU	333	665	534	648	687	656	827	648	809	710
Morocco	QAOR	407	365	422	439	335	343	416	476	530	566
South Africa	QDNX	3931	3965	3138	4780	3851	4417	2948	3303	2135	2678
Other North Africa	BORW	995	1733	1703	2368	1843	2849	2245	4244	5248	3771
Other	BOQJ	2860	3033	3676	3748	3009	3497	7573	8758	10282	6560
Total Africa	EPMN	8526	9761	9473	11983	9725	11762	14009	17429	19004	14285
International Organisations	EPMR	-	-	-	-	-	-	-	-	-	
World total	LQBL	282213	322920	313504	349603	315731	367580	403126	412528	423811	415469

Source: Office for National Statistics

Note: On the advice of ONS, we have replaced table 6.6 with a new table. The new format contains different ONS 4 digit codes, many contain the letter Q at the beginning which means the figures have been seasonally adjusted.

6.7 Total International Trade in Services all industries (excluding travel, transport and banking) analysed by product 2013-2014

£ million

	Exports		Imports		Balance	
	2013	2014	2013	2014	2013	2014
Agricultural and Mining Services						
Agricultural, forestry and fishing	15	55	25	116	-10	-61
Mining and oil and gas extraction services	1,180	1,459	145	70	1,035	1,390
Total Agricultural and Mining services	**1,196**	**1,515**	**170**	**186**	**1,025**	**1,329**
Manufacturing, Maintenance and On-site Processing Services						
Waste treatment and depolution services	34	128	44	150	-10	-21
Manufacturing services on goods owned by others	2,555	2,103	760	581	1,795	1,521
Maintenance and repair services	1,366	2,012	463	440	903	1,572
Total Manufacturing, Maintenance and On-site Processing services	**3,956**	**4,243**	**1,267**	**1,171**	**2,688**	**3,072**
Business and Professional Services						
Accountancy, auditing, bookkeeping and tax consulting services	1,680	1,898	806	818	874	1,080
Advertising, market research and public opinion polling services	4,337	4,971	2,911	2,692	1,426	2,279
Business management and management consulting services	6,302	7,279	3,129	2,938	3,173	4,342
Public relations services	428	392	132	125	296	267
Recruitment services	1,412	1,359	763	428	649	931
Legal services	4,074	4,577	845	934	3,229	3,643
Operating leasing services	483	452	942	1,416	-459	-964
Procurement services	100	76	267	254	-167	-178
Property management services	371	583	134	167	238	415
Other business and professional services	4,480	3,867	2,539	2,197	1,942	1,670
Services between related enterprises	11,662	11,407	8,424	8,622	3,239	2,785
Total Business and Professional Services	**35,330**	**36,861**	**20,891**	**20,590**	**14,439**	**16,271**
Research and Development Services						
Provision of R&D services	5,141	5,086	3,828	3,750	1,313	1,336
Provision of product development and testing activities	784	975	256	307	528	668
Total Research and Development Services	**5,925**	**6,061**	**4,084**	**4,057**	**1,841**	**2,004**
Intellectual Property						
Trade marks, franchises, brands or design rights						
Outright sales and purchases	668	287	660	744	8	-457
Charges or payments for the use of	4,388	5,453	2,894	3,150	1,494	2,303
Copyrighted literary works, sound recordings, films, television prgrammes and databases						
Outright sales and purchases	720	300	510	142	210	158
Charges or payments for the use of	4,390	4,734	2,663	3,247	1,727	1,487
Patents and other intellectual property that are the end result of research and development						
Outright sales and purchases	119	65	70	31	49	34
Charges or payments for the use of	1,446	1,561	669	586	776	975
Total intellectual property	**11,730**	**12,400**	**7,466**	**7,901**	**4,265**	**4,499**
Telecommunication, Computer and Information Services						
Postal and courier	1,056	1,112	629	622	427	490
Telecommunications	5,978	7,256	3,616	4,640	2,362	2,616
Computer Services	6,696	7,739	4,689	4,635	2,008	3,104
Publishing Services	740	1,014	90	189	651	825
News agency Services	459	463	97	68	361	394
Information Services	1,422	1,700	501	559	921	1,141
Total Telecommunication, Computer and Information Services	**16,352**	**19,285**	**9,622**	**10,714**	**6,730**	**8,572**
Construction Services						
Construction in the UK	147	209	889	1,011	-742	-802
Construction outside the UK	2,101	2,522	567	947	1,534	1,575
Total Construction Services	**2,248**	**2,732**	**1,456**	**1,958**	**792**	**773**

6.7 Total International Trade in Services all industries (excluding travel, transport and banking) analysed by product 2013-2014

£ million

	Exports		Imports		Balance	
	2013	2014	2013	2014	2013	2014
Financial Services						
Financial	14,909	13,585	2,935	2,356	11,974	11,229
Insurance and Pension Services						
Insurance and Pension Services Claims	3,435	3,084			3,435	3,084
Insurance and Pension Services Premiums			742	596	-742	-596
Merchanting and Other Trade related Services						
Merchanting	3,585	1,395	437	1,099	3,147	296
Other trade - related services	1,516	1,788	629	634	887	1,154
Total Merchanting and Other Trade related Services	**5,101**	**3,183**	**1,067**	**1,733**	**4,034**	**1,451**
Personal, Cultural and Recreational Services						
Audio- Visual and related services	1,307	1,319	580	537	726	782
Medical Services	57	34	18	14	39	20
Training and educational services	265	317	119	47	146	269
Heritage and recreational services	349	208	31	42	319	165
Social, domestic and other personal services	36	70	17	36	18	34
Total Personal, Cultural and Recreational Services	**2,014**	**1,947**	**765**	**676**	**1,248**	**1,272**
Technical and Scientific Services						
Architectural services	483	451	111	120	372	330
Engineering Services	7,068	7,031	1,241	1,116	5,827	5,915
Scientific and other techinical services inc surveying	1,845	1,672	487	416	1,358	1,256
Total Technical Services	**9,395**	**9,153**	**1,839**	**1,652**	**7,556**	**7,501**
Other Trade in Services						
Other trade in services	5,603	5,654	1,083	866	4,520	4,789
Total International Trade in Services	**117,193**	**119,703**	**53,387**	**54,455**	**63,806**	**65,248**

Source: Office for National Statistics

- Denotes nil or less than £500,000
.. Denotes disclosive data

The sum of constituent items may not always agree exactly with the totals shown due to rounding

Data from 2013 has been collected in accordance with BPM6 regulations

6.8 Total International Trade in Services (excluding travel, transport and banking) analysed by continents and countries 2012 - 2014

£ million

	Exports			Imports			Balances		
	2012	2013	2014	2012	2013	2014	2012	2013	2014
Europe									
European Union (EU)									
Austria	340	365	373	158	245	380	183	120	-6
Belgium	1,596	2,064	1,730	1,007	1,199	1,010	589	865	720
Bulgaria	77	93	96	37	87	57	40	6	39
Croatia		45	55		25	16		20	40
Cyprus	301	456	230	110	285	141	191	171	89
Czech Republic	313	351	332	144	243	178	168	108	155
Denmark	1,237	1,539	1,514	441	563	713	796	976	801
Estonia	38	30	46	15	29	25	22	1	22
Finland	719	624	791	211	229	216	508	395	574
France	4,547	4,798	4,650	3,518	3,274	3,586	1,029	1,524	1,064
Germany	6,018	7,490	7,171	4,102	4,736	5,287	1,915	2,754	1,883
Greece	434	438	398	122	152	111	312	286	287
Hungary	342	248	280	238	196	178	104	52	102
Irish Republic	6,346	6,697	6,598	2,597	4,084	3,335	3,748	2,613	3,263
Italy	1,928	2,411	2,292	1,415	1,324	1,542	513	1,087	750
Latvia	32	46	35	9	25	15	24	21	20
Lithuania	29	61	49	20	24	26	9	37	23
Luxembourg	1,683	2,090	2,255	1,182	1,404	1,693	501	686	562
Malta	183	265	207	37	65	55	146	200	152
Netherlands	5,373	5,584	7,580	1,657	2,727	2,393	3,717	2,857	5,187
Poland	636	679	818	407	521	506	229	158	312
Portugal	289	474	455	156	195	277	133	279	178
Romania	211	242	223	94	125	153	117	117	69
Slovakia	199	205	133	48	83	82	151	122	51
Slovenia	..	..	..	..	..	..	..	30	50
Spain	1,791	1,863	2,070	1,056	1,305	1,392	735	558	679
Sweden	1,686	1,930	2,009	1,381	1,183	1,167	305	747	841
EU Institutions	..	..	..	..	..	..	..	16	18
Total European Union (EU)	**36,497**	**41,148**	**42,475**	**20,281**	**24,342**	**24,554**	**16,217**	**16,806**	**17,921**
European Free Trade Association (EFTA)									
Iceland	84	74	96	14	9	24	69	65	72
Liechtenstein	55	32	36	3	3	2	52	29	34
Norway	1,723	2,194	2,212	441	459	466	1,282	1,735	1,746
Switzerland	6,248	7,712	7,204	1,307	2,179	1,791	4,941	5,533	5,413
Total EFTA	**8,109**	**10,012**	**9,548**	**1,765**	**2,650**	**2,283**	**6,344**	**7,362**	**7,265**
Other Europe									
Russia	754	944	1,133	210	390	288	544	554	845
Channel Islands	2,073	1,843	1,550	255	232	291	1,818	1,611	1,259
Isle of Man	68	93	435	12	13	14	56	80	421
Turkey	549	564	582	121	188	127	429	376	454
Rest of Europe	900	622	800	223	241	201	677	381	599
Europe Unallocated	3,013	1,924	2,188	1,326	1,303	1,326	1,687	621	862
Total Europe	**51,963**	**57,150**	**58,711**	**24,192**	**29,359**	**29,085**	**27,771**	**27,791**	**29,626**
America									
Brazil	743	819	797	183	140	149	560	679	648
Canada	1,368	1,815	1,414	583	760	791	785	1,055	623
Mexico	171	224	261	59	43	40	112	181	222
USA	22,759	26,504	27,821	10,654	11,642	12,945	12,104	14,862	14,875
Rest of America	3,184	3,182	2,806	599	697	861	2,585	2,485	1,945
America Unallocated	580	371	425	114	54	76	466	317	349
Total America	**28,805**	**32,915**	**33,523**	**12,193**	**13,336**	**14,863**	**16,612**	**19,579**	**18,661**

6.8 Total International Trade in Services (excluding travel, transport and banking) analysed by continents and countries 2012 - 2014

£ million

	Exports			Imports			Balances		
	2012	2013	2014	2012	2013	2014	2012	2013	2014
Asia									
China	1,183	1,180	1,058	427	591	521	757	589	537
Hong Kong	757	895	1,006	637	638	666	120	257	341
India	717	863	975	1,241	1,355	1,519	-524	-492	-544
Indonesia	141	167	171	25	43	55	116	124	115
Israel	433	329	351	333	363	241	100	-34	109
Japan	1,995	2,140	2,456	1,579	1,238	1,410	417	902	1,046
Malaysia	413	498	438	88	60	191	325	438	247
Pakistan	103	104	181	40	106	93	63	-2	88
Philippines	84	92	90	124	121	127	-40	-29	-37
Saudi Arabia	3,483	5,315	4,289	322	113	71	3,162	5,202	4,218
Singapore	1,346	1,411	2,077	1,070	1,192	1,507	275	219	570
South Korea	626	700	800	201	203	205	425	497	595
Taiwan	387	366	317	72	87	100	316	279	217
Thailand	213	294	286	56	57	172	157	237	114
Rest of Asia	3,616	4,580	4,485	1,005	1,452	946	2,611	3,128	3,539
Asia Unallocated	786	726	714	588	418	424	198	308	290
Total Asia	**16,284**	**19,660**	**19,703**	**7,807**	**8,037**	**8,248**	**8,477**	**11,623**	**11,454**
Australasia and Oceania									
Australia	1,785	..	1,863	855	..	873	931	1,101	990
New Zealand	154	219	220	46	75	39	109	144	181
Rest of Australia and Oceania	224	..	..	13	..	..	211	152	74
Oceania Unallocated	21	-	..	5	-	..	16	-	1
Total Australasia and Oceania	**2,185**	**2,365**	**2,175**	**918**	**968**	**929**	**1,266**	**1,397**	**1,246**
Africa									
Nigeria	507	562	493	140	297	75	367	265	418
South Africa	1,127	968	1,167	307	332	325	820	636	842
Rest of Africa	2,453	2,793	3,160	371	637	574	2,082	2,156	2,585
Africa Unallocated	326	233	261	279	239	186	47	-6	75
Total Africa	**4,412**	**4,556**	**5,081**	**1,097**	**1,505**	**1,160**	**3,316**	**3,051**	**3,921**
Total Unallocated	180	547	..	192	182	..	-12	365	340
International Organisations	-	-	..	-	-	..	-	-	1
TOTAL INTERNATIONAL TRADE IN SERVICES	**103,828**	**117,193**	**119,703**	**46,399**	**53,387**	**54,455**	**57,430**	**63,806**	**65,248**

Source: Office for National Statistics

- Denotes nil or less than £500,000
.. Denotes disclosive data

The sum of constituent items may not always agree exactly with the totals shown due to rounding

Data from 2013 has been collected in accordance with BPM6 regulation

See background notes for geographical groupings

Excludes the activities of banking and travel industries

Estimates for Croatia have been published for the first time in 2013. Previously this was included in the Rest of Europe.

6.9 Summary of balance of payments in 2013

£ million

	Credits	Debits
1. Current account		
A. Goods and services	511 275	543 375
1. Goods	306 810	417 006
2. Services	204 465	126 369
2.1. Manufacturing physical inputs owned by others	2 937	680
2.2. Maintenance and repair	911	345
2.3. Transport	24 215	22 489
2.4. Travel	26 244	33 741
2.5. Construction	3 110	1 572
2.6. Insurance and pension services	21 784	1 422
2.7. Financial	46 725	8 598
2.8. Intellectual property	8 246	5 451
2.9. Telecommunications, computer and information services	13 093	7 887
2.10. Other business	49 949	36 806
2.11. Personal, cultural and recreational services	4 539	3 308
2.12. Government	2 712	4 070
B. Primary income	161 756	174 890
1. Compensation of employees	1 097	1 422
2. Investment income	158 204	170 541
2.1. Direct investment	84 516	59 237
2.2. Portfolio investment	47 608	74 916
2.3. Other investment	25 431	36 388
2.4. Reserve assets	649	
3. Other primary income	2 455	2 926
C. Secondary income	17 621	44 783
1. General government	4 259	27 336
2. Other sectors	13 362	17 447
Total current account	**690 652**	**763 047**
2. Capital account		
1. Capital transfers	917	399
2. Acquisition/disposal of non-produced, non-financial assets	878	866
Total capital account	1 795	1 265

	Net acquisition of financial assets	Net incurrence of liabilities
3. Financial account		
1. Direct investment	−12 700	27 378
Abroad	−12 700	
1.1. Equity capital other than reinvestment of earnings	−19 206	
1.2. Reinvestment of earnings	8 440	
1.3. Debt instruments[1]	−1 934	
In United Kingdom		27 378
1.1. Equity capital other than reinvestment of earnings		23 880
1.2. Reinvestment of earnings		9 120
1.3. Debt instruments[2]		−5 622
2. Portfolio investment	1 198	30 694
Assets	1 198	
2.1. Equity and investment fund shares	−15 866	
2.2. Debt securities	17 064	
Liabilities		30 694
2.1. Equity and investment fund shares		18 254
2.2. Debt securities		12 440
3. Financial derivatives and employee stock options (net)	13 968	
4. Other investment	−210 460	−198 513
Assets	−210 460	
4.1. Other equity	123	
4.2. Currency and deposits	−194 269	
4.3. Loans	−14 897	
4.4. Trade credit and advances	−1 160	
4.5. Other accounts receivable	257	
Liabilities		−198 513
4.1. Currency and deposits		−278 105
4.2. Loans		78 668
4.3. Insurance, pensions and standardised guarantee schemes		−248
4.4. Trade credit and advances		−
4.5. Other accounts payable		1 172
4.6. Special drawing rights		−
5. Reserve assets	4 961	
5.1. Monetary gold	−	
5.2. Special drawing rights	43	
5.3. Reserve position in the IMF	−84	
5.4. Other reserve assets	5 002	
Total financial account	**−203 033**	**−140 441**

1 Debt instrument transactions on direct investment abroad represents claims on affiliated enterprises plus claims on direct investors.

2 Debt instrument transactions on direct investment in the United Kingdom represents liabilities to direct investors plus liabilities to affiliated enterprises

Source: Office for National Statistics

6.10 Summary of Balance of payments: Balances (net credits less net debits)

£ million

			Current account										
	Trade in goods	Trade in services	Total goods and services	Compensat-ion of employees	Investment income	Other primary income	Total primary income	Secondary income	Current balance	Current balance as % of GDP[1]	Capital account	Financial account	Net errors & omissions
	LQCT	KTMS	KTMY	KTMP	HMBM	MT5W	HMBP	KTNF	HBOG	AA6H	FKMJ	-HBNT	HHDH
1946	−101	−274	−375	−20	76	−	56	166	−153	..	−21	−181	−7
1947	−358	−197	−555	−19	140	−	121	123	−311	..	−21	−552	−220
1948	−152	−64	−216	−20	223	−	203	96	83	0.7	−17	58	−8
1949	−138	−43	−181	−20	206	−	186	29	34	0.3	−12	103	80
1950	−55	−4	−59	−21	378	−	357	39	337	2.6	−10	447	119
1951	−693	32	−661	−21	322	−	301	29	−331	−2.3	−15	−426	−81
1952	−274	123	−151	−22	231	−	209	169	227	1.4	−15	229	15
1953	−246	123	−123	−25	207	−	182	143	202	1.2	−13	177	−14
1954	−213	115	−98	−27	227	−	200	55	157	0.9	−13	174	27
1955	−319	42	−277	−27	149	−	122	43	−112	−0.6	−15	−34	89
1956	44	26	70	−30	203	−	173	2	245	1.2	−13	250	12
1957	−39	121	82	−32	223	−	191	−5	268	1.2	−13	313	48
1958	22	119	141	−34	261	−	227	4	372	1.6	−10	411	37
1959	−128	118	−10	−37	233	−	196	−	186	0.8	−5	68	−125
1960	−417	39	−378	−35	201	−	166	−6	−218	−0.8	−6	7	218
1961	−160	51	−109	−35	223	−	188	−9	70	0.3	−12	−23	−97
1962	−120	50	−70	−37	301	−	264	−14	180	0.6	−12	195	11
1963	−143	4	−139	−38	364	−	326	−37	150	0.5	−16	30	−124
1964	−574	−34	−608	−33	365	−	332	−74	−350	−1.1	−17	−392	−48
1965	−288	−66	−354	−34	405	−	371	−75	−58	−0.2	−18	−49	2
1966	−144	44	−100	−39	358	−	319	−91	128	0.3	−19	−22	−164
1967	−647	157	−490	−39	354	−	315	−118	−293	−0.7	−25	−179	93
1968	−770	341	−429	−48	303	−	255	−119	−293	−0.7	−26	−688	−431
1969	−283	392	109	−47	468	−	421	−109	421	0.9	−23	794	327
1970	−94	455	361	−56	527	−	471	−89	743	1.4	−22	818	21
1971	121	617	738	−63	454	−	391	−90	1 039	1.8	−23	1 330	230
1972	−828	722	−106	−52	350	−	298	−142	50	0.1	−35	−477	−584
1973	−2 676	907	−1 769	−68	970	−	902	−336	−1 203	−1.6	−39	−1 031	108
1974	−5 357	1 292	−4 065	−92	1 010	−	918	−302	−3 449	−4.1	−34	−3 185	182
1975	−3 379	1 708	−1 671	−102	257	−	155	−313	−1 829	−1.7	−36	−1 569	162
1976	−4 080	2 872	−1 208	−140	760	−	620	−534	−1 122	−0.9	−12	−507	477
1977	−2 440	3 704	1 264	−152	−678	−	−830	−889	−455	−0.3	11	3 286	3 561
1978	−1 711	4 215	2 504	−140	−300	−	−440	−1 420	644	0.4	−79	2 655	1 913
1979	−3 514	4 573	1 059	−130	−342	−	−472	−1 777	−1 190	−0.6	−103	−864	241
1980	1 124	4 414	5 538	−82	−2 268	−	−2 350	−1 653	1 535	0.7	−4	2 157	421
1981	2 986	4 776	7 762	−66	−1 883	−	−1 949	−1 219	4 594	1.8	−79	5 312	545
1982	1 614	4 261	5 875	−95	−2 336	−	−2 431	−1 476	1 968	0.7	6	1 233	−1 006
1983	−1 893	5 406	3 513	−89	−1 050	−	−1 139	−1 391	983	0.3	75	3 287	1 954
1984	−5 736	6 101	365	−94	−326	−	−420	−1 566	−1 621	−0.5	107	7 130	8 317
1985	−3 754	8 499	4 745	−120	−2 609	−	−2 729	−2 924	−908	−0.3	185	1 657	2 042
1986	−9 968	8 182	−1 786	−156	71	−	−85	−2 094	−3 965	−1.0	135	122	3 601
1987	−12 093	9 163	−2 930	−174	−855	−	−1 029	−3 437	−7 396	−1.7	333	−10 606	−3 938
1988	−22 028	7 506	−14 522	−64	−1 438	−	−1 502	−3 293	−19 317	−4.0	235	−16 989	1 618
1989	−25 214	7 543	−17 671	−138	−2 683	−	−2 821	−4 228	−24 720	−4.7	270	−13 614	10 346
1990	−19 279	8 879	−10 400	−110	−5 085	−	−5 195	−4 802	−20 397	−3.6	497	−22 272	−2 944
1991	−10 918	9 106	−1 812	−63	−6 266	−	−6 329	−999	−9 140	−1.5	290	−7 855	300
1992	−13 787	9 706	−4 081	−49	−1 786	−	−1 835	−5 228	−11 144	−1.8	421	−16 311	−6 325
1993	−13 881	12 086	−1 795	35	−3 420	−	−3 385	−5 056	−10 236	−1.6	309	−22 278	−13 166
1994	−11 973	12 632	659	−170	523	−	353	−5 187	−4 175	−0.6	33	3 240	6 535
1995	−12 985	16 195	3 210	−296	−1 669	−	−1 965	−7 363	−6 118	−0.8	533	1 717	6 340
1996	−14 736	17 249	2 513	93	−3 494	−	−3 401	−4 539	−5 427	−0.7	1 260	940	4 093
1997	−12 696	17 487	4 791	83	−657	686	112	−6 211	−1 308	−0.1	796	6 346	6 858
1998	−22 200	15 436	−6 764	−10	11 397	819	12 206	−8 990	−3 548	−0.4	53	−879	2 616
1999	−29 357	14 157	−15 200	201	−2 822	711	−1 910	−8 033	−25 143	−2.6	122	−21 026	3 995
2000	−34 072	13 934	−20 138	150	5 281	441	5 872	−10 216	−24 482	−2.4	793	−13 779	9 910
2001	−41 538	16 640	−24 898	66	9 051	579	9 696	−6 971	−22 173	−2.1	351	−30 096	−8 274
2002	−47 038	16 999	−30 039	67	16 210	968	17 245	−9 427	−22 221	−2.0	−311	−25 163	−2 631
2003	−48 838	21 604	−27 234	59	17 548	1 272	18 879	−10 841	−19 196	−1.6	62	−12 334	6 800
2004	−62 950	27 564	−35 386	−493	20 909	1 279	21 695	−11 096	−24 787	−2.0	281	−15 256	9 250
2005	−69 634	34 991	−34 643	−609	30 150	1 147	30 688	−12 893	−16 848	−1.3	−437	−18 024	−739
2006	−77 421	44 202	−33 219	−956	14 566	892	14 500	−12 680	−31 397	−2.2	−1 081	−32 307	171
2007	−93 296	52 602	−40 694	−733	14 258	540	14 065	−13 996	−40 625	−2.7	310	−35 592	4 723
2008	−96 415	51 514	−44 901	−713	2 874	415	2 576	−14 112	−56 437	−3.7	785	−45 865	9 787
2009	−83 591	55 476	−28 115	−258	2 030	766	2 538	−15 826	−41 403	−2.8	915	−31 435	9 053
2010	−97 410	60 352	−37 058	−388	17 444	114	17 170	−20 696	−40 584	−2.6	910	−28 735	10 939
2011	−96 515	72 690	−23 825	−171	18 671	229	18 729	−21 937	−27 033	−1.7	837	−14 697	11 499
2012	−108 972	74 503	−34 469	−147	−4 841	−273	−5 261	−22 195	−61 925	−3.7	835	−49 129	11 961
2013	−110 196	78 096	−32 100	−325	−12 337	−471	−13 134	−27 162	−72 395	−4.2	530	−62 592	9 273

1 Using series YBHA: GDP at current market prices.

Source: Office for National Statistics

6.11 Balance of payments: current account

£ million

		1992	1993	1994	1995	1996	1997	1998	1999	2000	2001	2002
Credits												
Exports of goods and services												
Exports of goods	LQAD	107 863	122 229	135 143	153 577	167 196	172 637	164 183	166 717	187 932	189 746	187 792
Exports of services	KTMQ	41 271	47 868	52 944	59 051	64 934	67 019	70 029	75 597	81 358	88 067	92 892
Total exports of goods and services	KTMW	149 134	170 097	188 087	212 628	232 130	239 656	234 212	242 314	269 290	277 813	280 684
Primary income												
Compensation of employees	KTMN	551	595	681	887	911	1 007	840	961	1 034	1 089	1 123
Investment income	HMBN	65 168	70 944	72 585	85 490	89 794	96 040	105 785	103 272	134 317	139 686	124 002
Other primary income	MT5S	–	–	–	–	–	3 068	2 937	2 781	2 571	2 679	2 912
Total primary income	HMBQ	65 719	71 539	73 266	86 377	90 705	100 115	109 562	107 014	137 922	143 454	128 037
Secondary income												
General government	FJUM	2 180	2 826	2 138	1 730	2 828	2 393	1 767	3 542	2 465	4 991	3 663
Other sectors	FJUN	9 945	9 085	8 918	10 213	11 372	8 503	8 439	6 215	6 280	6 020	7 695
Total secondary income	KTND	12 125	11 911	11 056	11 943	14 200	10 896	10 206	9 757	8 745	11 011	11 358
Total	HBOE	**226 978**	**253 547**	**272 409**	**310 948**	**337 035**	**350 667**	**353 980**	**359 085**	**415 957**	**432 278**	**420 079**
Debits												
Imports of goods and services												
Imports of goods	LQBL	121 650	136 110	147 116	166 562	181 932	185 333	186 383	196 074	222 004	231 284	234 830
Imports of services	KTMR	31 565	35 782	40 312	42 856	47 685	49 532	54 593	61 440	67 424	71 427	75 893
Total imports of goods and services	KTMX	153 215	171 892	187 428	209 418	229 617	234 865	240 976	257 514	289 428	302 711	310 723
Primary income												
Compensation of employees	KTMO	600	560	851	1 183	818	924	850	760	884	1 023	1 056
Investment income	HMBO	66 954	74 364	72 062	87 159	93 288	96 697	94 388	106 094	129 036	130 635	107 792
Other primary income	MT5U	–	–	–	–	–	2 382	2 118	2 070	2 130	2 100	1 944
Total primary income	HMBR	67 554	74 924	72 913	88 342	94 106	100 003	97 356	108 924	132 050	133 758	110 792
Secondary income												
General government	FJUO	3 506	4 156	4 795	4 811	5 081	8 484	10 813	11 082	11 982	11 134	12 013
Other sectors	FJUP	13 847	12 811	11 448	14 495	13 658	8 623	8 383	6 708	6 979	6 848	8 772
Total secondary income	KTNE	17 353	16 967	16 243	19 306	18 739	17 107	19 196	17 790	18 961	17 982	20 785
Total	HBOF	**238 122**	**263 783**	**276 584**	**317 066**	**342 462**	**351 975**	**357 528**	**384 228**	**440 439**	**454 451**	**442 300**
Balances												
Trade in goods and services												
Trade in goods	LQCT	–13 787	–13 881	–11 973	–12 985	–14 736	–12 696	–22 200	–29 357	–34 072	–41 538	–47 038
Trade in services	KTMS	9 706	12 086	12 632	16 195	17 249	17 487	15 436	14 157	13 934	16 640	16 999
Total trade in goods and services	KTMY	–4 081	–1 795	659	3 210	2 513	4 791	–6 764	–15 200	–20 138	–24 898	–30 039
Primary income												
Compensation of employees	KTMP	–49	35	–170	–296	93	83	–10	201	150	66	67
Investment income	HMBM	–1 786	–3 420	523	–1 669	–3 494	–657	11 397	–2 822	5 281	9 051	16 210
Other primary income	MT5W	–	–	–	–	–	686	819	711	441	579	968
Total primary income	HMBP	–1 835	–3 385	353	–1 965	–3 401	112	12 206	–1 910	5 872	9 696	17 245
Secondary income												
General government	FJUQ	–1 326	–1 330	–2 657	–3 081	–2 253	–6 091	–9 046	–7 540	–9 517	–6 143	–8 350
Other sectors	FJUR	–3 902	–3 726	–2 530	–4 282	–2 286	–120	56	–493	–699	–828	–1 077
Total secondary income	KTNF	–5 228	–5 056	–5 187	–7 363	–4 539	–6 211	–8 990	–8 033	–10 216	–6 971	–9 427
Total (Current balance)	HBOG	**–11 144**	**–10 236**	**–4 175**	**–6 118**	**–5 427**	**–1 308**	**–3 548**	**–25 143**	**–24 482**	**–22 173**	**–22 221**

6.11 Balance of payments: current account

£ million

		2003	2004	2005	2006	2007	2008	2009	2010	2011	2012	2013
Credits												
Exports of goods and services												
Exports of goods	LQAD	189 489	191 410	212 741	244 848	222 462	254 965	230 746	270 816	309 184	305 142	306 810
Exports of services	KTMQ	104 271	114 358	128 949	145 546	157 306	165 935	169 514	176 241	190 268	195 593	204 465
Total exports of goods and services	KTMW	293 760	305 768	341 690	390 394	379 768	420 900	400 260	447 057	499 452	500 735	511 275
Primary income												
Compensation of employees	KTMN	1 118	934	977	942	987	1 050	1 179	1 100	1 124	1 127	1 097
Investment income	HMBN	124 710	140 745	192 849	249 122	307 686	287 572	174 559	173 484	199 905	168 708	158 204
Other primary income	MT5S	3 227	3 449	3 408	3 221	2 952	3 051	3 411	3 059	3 166	2 625	2 455
Total primary income	HMBQ	129 055	145 128	197 234	253 283	311 625	291 673	179 149	177 643	204 195	172 460	161 756
Secondary income												
General government	FJUM	3 968	4 299	4 385	4 471	4 408	5 720	6 271	3 842	3 536	3 707	4 259
Other sectors	FJUN	8 148	8 563	10 665	15 806	9 416	14 568	11 498	10 919	9 943	12 121	13 362
Total secondary income	KTND	12 116	12 862	15 050	20 277	13 824	20 288	17 769	14 761	13 479	15 828	17 621
Total	HBOE	**434 931**	**463 758**	**553 974**	**663 954**	**705 217**	**732 861**	**597 178**	**639 461**	**717 126**	**689 023**	**690 652**
Debits												
Imports of goods and services												
Imports of goods	LQBL	238 327	254 360	282 375	322 269	315 758	351 380	314 337	368 226	405 699	414 114	417 006
Imports of services	KTMR	82 667	86 794	93 958	101 344	104 704	114 421	114 038	115 889	117 578	121 090	126 369
Total imports of goods and services	KTMX	320 994	341 154	376 333	423 613	420 462	465 801	428 375	484 115	523 277	535 204	543 375
Primary income												
Compensation of employees	KTMO	1 059	1 427	1 586	1 898	1 720	1 763	1 437	1 488	1 295	1 274	1 422
Investment income	HMBO	107 162	119 836	162 699	234 556	293 428	284 698	172 529	156 040	181 234	173 549	170 541
Other primary income	MT5U	1 955	2 170	2 261	2 329	2 412	2 636	2 645	2 945	2 937	2 898	2 926
Total primary income	HMBR	110 176	123 433	166 546	238 783	297 560	289 097	176 611	160 473	185 466	177 721	174 890
Secondary income												
General government	FJUO	13 667	13 809	15 624	16 041	16 401	16 984	19 258	20 933	21 980	22 251	27 336
Other sectors	FJUP	9 290	10 149	12 319	16 916	11 419	17 416	14 337	14 524	13 436	15 772	17 447
Total secondary income	KTNE	22 957	23 958	27 943	32 957	27 820	34 400	33 595	35 457	35 416	38 023	44 783
Total	HBOF	**454 127**	**488 545**	**570 822**	**695 353**	**745 842**	**789 298**	**638 581**	**680 045**	**744 159**	**750 948**	**763 047**
Balances												
Trade in goods and services												
Trade in goods	LQCT	−48 838	−62 950	−69 634	−77 421	−93 296	−96 415	−83 591	−97 410	−96 515	−108 972	−110 196
Trade in services	KTMS	21 604	27 564	34 991	44 202	52 602	51 514	55 476	60 352	72 690	74 503	78 096
Total trade in goods and services	KTMY	−27 234	−35 386	−34 643	−33 219	−40 694	−44 901	−28 115	−37 058	−23 825	−34 469	−32 100
Primary income												
Compensation of employees	KTMP	59	−493	−609	−956	−733	−713	−258	−388	−171	−147	−325
Investment income	HMBM	17 548	20 909	30 150	14 566	14 258	2 874	2 030	17 444	18 671	−4 841	−12 337
Other primary income	MT5W	1 272	1 279	1 147	892	540	415	766	114	229	−273	−471
Total primary income	HMBP	18 879	21 695	30 688	14 500	14 065	2 576	2 538	17 170	18 729	−5 261	−13 134
Secondary income												
General government	FJUQ	−9 699	−9 510	−11 239	−11 570	−11 993	−11 264	−12 987	−17 091	−18 444	−18 544	−23 077
Other sectors	FJUR	−1 142	−1 586	−1 654	−1 110	−2 003	−2 848	−2 839	−3 605	−3 493	−3 651	−4 085
Total secondary income	KTNF	−10 841	−11 096	−12 893	−12 680	−13 996	−14 112	−15 826	−20 696	−21 937	−22 195	−27 162
Total (Current balance)	HBOG	**−19 196**	**−24 787**	**−16 848**	**−31 397**	**−40 625**	**−56 437**	**−41 403**	**−40 584**	**−27 033**	**−61 925**	**−72 395**

Source: Office for National Statistics

6.12 Balance of payments: Summary of international investment position, financial account and investment income

£ billion

		2003	2004	2005	2006	2007	2008	2009	2010	2011	2012	2013
Investment abroad												
International investment position												
Direct investment	N2V3	861.3	864.0	941.1	981.2	1 126.5	1 390.8	1 224.6	1 310.7	1 343.9	1 398.0	1 228.2
Portfolio investment	HHZZ	958.0	1 120.0	1 383.1	1 556.2	1 722.8	1 696.8	1 923.3	2 144.2	2 138.5	2 356.3	2 506.8
Financial derivatives	JX96		709.4	820.1	853.7	1 378.2	4 040.2	2 176.4	2 962.9	3 617.8	3 060.1	2 424.4
Other investment	HLXV	1 825.0	2 136.4	2 735.4	2 934.7	3 703.2	4 168.5	3 476.6	3 762.9	4 050.9	3 719.6	3 487.4
Reserve assets	LTEB	23.8	23.2	24.7	22.9	26.7	36.3	40.1	49.7	56.8	61.7	61.4
Total	HBQA	3 668.2	4 853.1	5 904.4	6 348.8	7 957.4	11 332.6	8 841.0	10 230.4	11 207.9	10 595.8	9 708.3
Financial account transactions[1]												
Direct investment	-N2SV	53.1	68.9	82.2	74.1	175.8	195.1	−38.2	34.8	57.6	31.5	−12.7
Portfolio investment	-HHZC	36.3	146.7	160.5	144.8	100.5	−113.0	179.8	100.8	12.5	131.8	1.2
Financial derivatives (net)	-ZPNN	5.4	6.8	−5.8	−20.6	27.0	121.7	−29.1	−25.5	3.1	−30.0	14.0
Other investment	-XBMM	263.7	330.6	498.7	395.2	660.9	−651.3	−349.3	239.8	104.4	−230.4	−210.5
Reserve assets	-LTCV	−1.6	0.2	0.7	−0.4	1.2	−1.3	5.8	6.1	4.9	7.6	5.0
Total	-HBNR	357.0	553.2	736.3	593.1	965.4	−448.8	−231.0	356.0	182.5	−89.4	−203.0
Investment income												
Direct investment	N2QP	57.4	65.8	83.3	91.5	100.9	86.3	73.8	92.4	104.2	85.2	84.5
Portfolio investment	HLYX	33.5	38.0	46.9	57.0	68.8	69.7	56.1	50.0	54.4	50.8	47.6
Other investment	AIOP	33.0	36.2	61.9	99.9	137.4	130.8	43.9	30.3	40.5	32.0	25.4
Reserve assets	HHCB	0.8	0.7	0.7	0.6	0.6	0.8	0.8	0.7	0.8	0.7	0.6
Total	HMBN	124.7	140.7	192.8	249.1	307.7	287.6	174.6	173.5	199.9	168.7	158.2
Investment in the UK												
International investment position												
Direct investment	N2UG	505.5	538.2	703.4	787.4	805.2	959.5	897.1	965.2	1 010.9	1 204.4	1 261.7
Portfolio investment	HLXW	1 096.8	1 259.0	1 499.1	1 744.2	2 023.7	2 040.0	2 437.5	2 565.9	2 515.7	2 533.1	2 490.3
Financial derivatives	JX97		715.0	831.1	890.5	1 392.2	3 915.3	2 096.8	2 895.0	3 554.9	3 032.2	2 376.7
Other investment	HLYD	2 127.6	2 483.9	2 975.5	3 110.3	3 903.3	4 328.9	3 608.5	3 898.3	4 197.9	4 073.1	3 846.1
Total	HBQB	3 729.9	4 996.1	6 009.1	6 532.4	8 124.5	11 243.7	9 040.0	10 324.4	11 279.5	10 842.8	9 974.8
Financial account transactions												
Direct investment	N2SA	22.3	47.9	140.2	113.7	107.0	143.1	6.8	42.8	16.4	50.8	27.4
Portfolio investment	HHZF	132.2	145.8	206.6	199.8	208.7	134.1	211.1	87.3	5.6	−77.6	30.7
Other investment	XBMN	214.8	374.7	407.5	311.9	685.3	−680.2	−417.4	254.6	175.2	−13.5	−198.5
Total	HBNS	369.3	568.4	754.3	625.5	1 001.0	−403.0	−199.6	384.7	197.2	−40.3	−140.4
Investment income												
Direct investment	N2Q4	24.8	28.6	33.9	53.8	63.8	62.9	52.9	47.6	53.7	52.7	59.2
Portfolio investment	HLZC	34.3	39.9	49.5	62.7	71.7	77.5	61.4	63.8	73.1	74.0	74.9
Other investment	HLZN	48.0	51.4	79.3	118.1	157.9	144.3	58.2	44.6	54.4	46.9	36.4
Total	HMBO	107.2	119.8	162.7	234.6	293.4	284.7	172.5	156.0	181.2	173.5	170.5
Net investment												
International investment position												
Direct investment	MU7O	355.8	325.9	237.7	193.8	321.3	431.3	327.5	345.5	333.0	193.6	−33.4
Portfolio investment	CGNH	−138.8	−139.0	−116.0	−188.0	−300.9	−343.2	−514.1	−421.6	−377.2	−176.7	16.6
Financial derivatives	JX98		−5.6	−11.0	−36.8	−14.1	124.9	79.6	67.8	62.9	27.9	47.7
Other investment	CGNG	−302.6	−347.5	−240.1	−175.5	−200.1	−160.4	−131.9	−135.5	−147.0	−353.4	−358.6
Reserve assets	LTEB	23.8	23.2	24.7	22.9	26.7	36.3	40.1	49.7	56.8	61.7	61.4
Net investment position	HBQC	−61.7	−143.1	−104.7	−183.6	−167.1	88.9	−198.9	−94.0	−71.6	−247.0	−266.5
Financial account transactions[1]												
Direct investment	-MU7M	30.9	21.0	−58.0	−39.6	68.8	52.0	−45.0	−8.0	41.2	−19.3	−40.1
Portfolio investment	-HHZD	−95.9	0.9	−46.1	−55.0	−108.2	−247.1	−31.3	13.5	6.9	209.4	−29.5
Financial derivatives	-ZPNN	5.4	6.8	−5.8	−20.6	27.0	121.7	−29.1	−25.5	3.1	−30.0	14.0
Other investment	-HHYR	48.9	−44.1	91.2	83.3	−24.4	28.9	68.1	−14.9	−70.8	−216.9	−11.9
Reserve assets	-LTCV	−1.6	0.2	0.7	−0.4	1.2	−1.3	5.8	6.1	4.9	7.6	5.0
Net transactions	-HBNT	−12.3	−15.3	−18.0	−32.3	−35.6	−45.9	−31.4	−28.7	−14.7	−49.1	−62.6
Investment income												
Direct investment	MU7E	32.6	37.2	49.5	37.7	37.1	23.4	20.9	44.8	50.5	32.5	25.3
Portfolio investment	HLZX	−0.8	−1.8	−2.6	−5.7	−3.0	−7.8	−5.4	−13.8	−18.7	−23.2	−27.3
Other investment	CGNA	−15.1	−15.2	−17.4	−18.1	−20.4	−13.5	−14.3	−14.3	−13.8	−14.9	−11.0
Reserve assets	HHCB	0.8	0.7	0.7	0.6	0.6	0.8	0.8	0.7	0.8	0.7	0.6
Net earnings	HMBM	17.5	20.9	30.1	14.6	14.3	2.9	2.0	17.4	18.7	−4.8	−12.3

1 When downloading data from the Pink Book dataset users should reverse the sign of series that have an identifier that is prefixed with a minus sign.

Source: Office for National Statistics

6.13 Net foreign direct investment flows abroad analysed by area and main country, 2005 to 2014 (Directional)

£ million

	2005	2006	2007	2008	2009	2010	2011	2012	2013	2014
EUROPE	**12,105**	**16,899**	**90,683**	**50,863**	**15,690**	**11,374**	**27,312**	**2,008**	**-18,311**	**-98,329**
EU	13,337	4,038	69,836	47,298	-7,047	9,761	15,856	-2,262	-9,987	-74,560
AUSTRIA	-301	-94	110	-159	-154	2,389	-16	-576	83	-123
BELGIUM	970	-4,356	1,037	1,656	-1,307	7,594	5,575	1,359	-4,057	374
BULGARIA	11	-5	..	43	11	-80	-1	-6	6	15
CROATIA	..	..	..	..	..	..	..	12	11	15
CYPRUS	69	98	365	294	63	-290	-184	-19	35	-30
CZECH REPUBLIC	24	-160	59	371	-105	-182	-80	829	259	0
DENMARK	391	1,529	539	2,774	-2,170	511	-240	96	-122	0
ESTONIA	2	3	-3	-20	38	9	0	6	15	11
FINLAND	707	106	268	63	-95	-41	-393	3	2	-47
FRANCE	3,138	1,175	4,536	5,979	-1,248	3,382	1,823	8,100	-8,838	511
GERMANY	-479	3,186	2,260	2,268	3,186	-1,644	444	-1,209	833	4,569
GREECE	63	15	286	362	-366	33	-230	-105	34	97
HUNGARY	1,821	39	88	164	76	85	50	59	30	-89
IRISH REPUBLIC	-1,181	5,161	3,995	-2,098	3,530	-7,731	3,260	5,431	-1,323	1,015
ITALY	191	-397	2,904	463	-3,801	362	-92	-718	-403	2,185
LATVIA	-1	4	65	142	-51	-19	-24	37	50	-5
LITHUANIA	-4	1	..	..	..	3	6	3	23	-2
LUXEMBOURG	-1,213	-14,131	25,453	6,094	4,874	5,820	7,947	-4,350	-6,265	-77,532
MALTA	142	891	-1,952	..	..	..	..	-230	289	1,044
NETHERLANDS	4,821	1,350	22,176	11,056	-14,072	-638	-1,194	-10,609	7,924	-7,854
POLAND	150	397	-500	-128	1,261	73	134	208	881	234
PORTUGAL	603	314	278	341	277	576	104	115	197	43
ROMANIA	101	40	117	211	27	22	61	-3	188	10
SLOVAKIA	21	18	90	104	-29	-17	23	34	-25	-95
SLOVENIA	-5	14	9	12	9	..	..	-56	6	-2
SPAIN	564	2,177	4,155	12,974	1,628	2,148	-566	122	-832	1,873
SWEDEN	2,732	6,669	3,501	3,155	1,314	-2,025	-454	-781	1,013	-778
EFTA	547	6,926	3,620	2,476	4,550	1,468	1,834	4,600	3,317	2,241
of which										
NORWAY	-831	3	1,060	1,556	1,693	-759	1,045	322	-703	78
SWITZERLAND	1,330	6,948	2,653	1,054	2,956	2,221	791	4,291	4,010	2,162
OTHER EUROPEAN COUNTRIES	-1,779	5,935	17,227	1,088	18,188	145	9,621	-331	-11,642	-26,010
of which										
RUSSIA	349	-13	1,334	3,919	-353	-1,859	467	-2,662	..	4,178
UK OFFSHORE ISLANDS	-2,341	5,023	14,752	-4,278	17,848	1,036	8,468	1,720	-2,389	-26,565
THE AMERICAS	**20,689**	**19,100**	**53,837**	**33,574**	**-2,218**	**-13,814**	**14,675**	**15,791**	**41,580**	**8,741**
of which										
BERMUDA	653	908	2,082	3,913	-2,160	-479	-1,238	494	1,722	1,371
BRAZIL	48	354	791	832	525	1,605	1,723	521	68	1,719
CANADA	3,372	8,130	15,468	-1,075	-2,732	-8,528	1,372	5,408	660	266
CHILE	790	25	110	-315	59	204	469	14	110	185
COLOMBIA	-687	315	126	157	311	402	-769	..	116	-10
MEXICO	168	334	128	409	57	503	1,015	541	781	578
PANAMA	27	7	-18	-4	60	40	36	25	59	-32
USA	15,041	-1,803	30,820	27,568	7,851	-9,025	12,055	9,321	36,423	2,848
ASIA	**5,399**	**7,992**	**7,734**	**6,364**	**8,575**	**8,401**	**20,526**	**-3,099**	**-6,525**	**9,900**
NEAR & MIDDLE EAST COUNTRIES	398	1,219	2,044	2,884	1,330	-1,136	4,754	-7,356	-9,116	1,719
of which										
GULF ARABIAN COUNTRIES	577	329	482	544	1,424	830	167	-294	938	-1,529
OTHER ASIAN COUNTRIES	5,001	6,773	5,689	3,480	7,245	9,538	15,772	4,257	2,592	8,181
of which										
CHINA	598	374	1,138	290	343	797	1,311	506	633	446
HONG KONG	1,547	1,674	1,503	305	1,798	2,180	3,475	3,760	3,732	1,683
INDIA	616	104	650	437	695	1,856	7,090	-228	664	336
INDONESIA	-116	196	-140	-68	594	1,021	3,308	1,190	426	173
JAPAN	247	440	1,141	-140	923	-568	1,996	499	-1,477	-57
MALAYSIA	244	241	216	321	337	603	585	84	318	1,529
SINGAPORE	-508	2,621	-1,265	183	-582	392	-4,733	-1,698	-946	1,827

6.13 Net foreign direct investment flows abroad analysed by area and main country, 2005 to 2014 (Directional)

£ million

	2005	2006	2007	2008	2009	2010	2011	2012	2013	2014
SOUTH KOREA	2,247	679	488	810	566	833	411	528	380	401
THAILAND	228	536	3	192	331	154	178	158	238	212
AUSTRALASIA & OCEANIA	**423**	**3,132**	**2,149**	**7,662**	**-3,543**	**11,704**	**803**	**1,139**	**8,414**	**-2,956**
of which										
AUSTRALIA	444	2,743	2,012	6,590	-4,625	11,487	338	983	8,206	-3,235
NEW ZEALAND	-56	405	125	126	1,078	156	373	140	141	134
AFRICA	**5,843**	**-235**	**4,726**	**881**	**6,590**	**7,822**	**-3,186**	**11,554**	**3,265**	**2,708**
of which										
KENYA	73	62	97	67	115	195	63	-35	109	93
NIGERIA	-108	44	56	273	763	228	354	76	-875	-212
SOUTH AFRICA	4,368	1,466	1,734	1,317	994	2,459	1,814	5,163	1,614	942
ZIMBABWE	18	8	4	-6	1	12	25	18	8	-9
WORLD TOTAL	**44,458**	**46,887**	**159,129**	**99,322**	**25,094**	**25,486**	**60,130**	**27,392**	**28,424**	**-79,936**
OECD	35,305	21,276	125,975	83,393	1,164	7,674	36,119	20,257	38,137	-72,261
CENTRAL & EASTERN EUROPE	158	76	0	53	40	-26	-3	10	65	42

The sum of constituent items may not always agree exactly with the totals shown due to rounding.

A negative sign before values indicates a net disinvestment abroad.

.. Indicates data are disclosive

- Indicates nil data

Source: Office for National Statistics

6.14 FDI International investment positions abroad analysed by area and main country, 2005 to 2014 (Directional)

£ million

	2005	2006	2007	2008	2009	2010	2011	2012	2013	2014
EUROPE	**387,324**	**402,593**	**527,997**	**600,375**	**552,235**	**612,848**	**614,775**	**572,301**	**493,043**	**474,523**
EU	339,691	314,481	412,024	513,506	477,747	539,683	533,266	495,633	407,257	404,168
AUSTRIA	4,005	2,402	2,579	2,707	3,746	1,054	999	347	931	980
BELGIUM	13,492	4,380	6,887	11,207	14,615	41,128	38,027	16,702	12,541	10,922
BULGARIA	53	46	46	143	117	104	88	55	117	135
CROATIA	..	..	..	..	..	..	..	185	249	224
CYPRUS	59	561	683	363	498	560	643	1,260	714	527
CZECH REPUBLIC	823	523	632	1,011	510	533	438	1,347	1,750	1,675
DENMARK	5,090	7,782	6,220	10,809	6,995	7,940	7,152	24,496	7,472	7,019
ESTONIA	7	-1	7	25	33	62	86	63	110	120
FINLAND	2,465	1,287	2,329	609	396	1,190	1,533	193	722	1,050
FRANCE	47,348	36,327	39,598	42,111	39,944	54,841	53,459	66,165	37,661	38,236
GERMANY	20,753	17,602	19,766	30,550	26,896	22,476	20,482	15,586	20,749	23,763
GREECE	625	562	864	1,047	910	2,028	1,417	1,308	1,622	1,557
HUNGARY	2,491	1,795	1,870	2,136	697	635	1,007	1,039	673	895
IRISH REPUBLIC	26,824	26,432	25,362	30,529	34,859	40,927	44,844	44,380	31,875	33,774
ITALY	10,872	7,924	12,786	10,734	11,689	11,971	11,708	10,585	10,689	9,937
LATVIA	22	27	..	95	1	-26	48	71	143	105
LITHUANIA	16	6	11	..	25	..	41	45	49	62
LUXEMBOURG	97,260	62,355	95,915	137,065	124,582	140,457	137,410	122,127	104,676	108,090
MALTA	-459	2,399	3,263	..	1,467	824	333	1,766	254	..
NETHERLANDS	64,511	92,783	138,769	160,172	146,027	145,279	144,966	129,036	132,026	118,779
POLAND	1,974	2,519	2,078	2,914	3,723	3,647	3,796	4,056	4,880	4,992
PORTUGAL	2,702	3,167	3,366	3,528	3,311	3,665	3,014	2,853	1,543	2,530
ROMANIA	356	247	402	675	558	549	530	591	822	844
SLOVAKIA	93	136	184	392	253	262	275	203	268	235
SLOVENIA	3	53	..	52	52	..	320	262	101	..
SPAIN	25,604	25,233	30,879	37,105	32,552	35,836	37,343	31,528	14,062	16,265
SWEDEN	12,702	17,935	17,388	26,069	23,289	23,305	23,309	19,570	20,557	18,033
EFTA	12,933	12,637	17,745	20,119	25,927	26,373	23,761	25,206	28,618	17,392
of which										
NORWAY	4,498	2,116	2,370	3,927	5,310	5,532	4,664	4,782	3,795	2,659
SWITZERLAND	7,979	10,239	15,124	15,790	20,202	20,813	19,071	20,404	24,820	14,711
OTHER EUROPEAN COUNTRIES	34,700	75,475	98,228	66,750	48,561	46,792	57,747	51,462	57,168	52,963
of which										
RUSSIA	1,814	6,054	7,182	10,380	10,042	10,019	7,863	5,688	13,899	13,700
UK OFFSHORE ISLANDS	29,954	65,814	86,482	49,921	31,225	29,483	41,723	35,263	33,499	32,138
THE AMERICAS	**216,343**	**256,423**	**292,687**	**354,745**	**300,175**	**265,351**	**286,481**	**283,762**	**319,441**	**355,968**
of which										
BERMUDA	10,604	13,889	13,839	24,027	15,707	16,123	15,625	15,349	15,908	26,459
BRAZIL	3,220	2,824	3,717	6,502	4,602	6,442	14,113	14,079	11,863	14,700
CANADA	12,812	19,188	28,980	29,216	28,879	32,546	27,602	30,936	28,088	28,822
CHILE	2,814	563	439	320	226	506	744	721	879	1,333
COLOMBIA	1,132	985	1,109	1,520	1,975	2,553	439	-117	673	604
MEXICO	2,860	2,337	3,791	3,548	2,489	3,088	5,007	4,076	5,906	6,471
PANAMA	166	..	..	168	182	183	297	..	..	..
USA	164,405	180,629	202,117	246,063	224,957	184,788	205,481	190,418	226,026	239,805
ASIA	**54,919**	**54,377**	**60,887**	**77,412**	**80,647**	**105,706**	**121,635**	**101,521**	**125,055**	**121,007**
NEAR & MIDDLE EAST COUNTRIES	3,733	6,874	9,984	14,690	18,514	24,084	28,544	13,064	28,709	13,730
of which										
GULF ARABIAN COUNTRIES	3,013	4,756	6,320	8,926	12,800	16,153	20,598	10,194	23,903	6,817
OTHER ASIAN COUNTRIES	51,187	47,503	50,903	62,723	62,133	81,622	93,091	88,456	96,346	107,277
of which										
CHINA	2,685	2,228	2,719	4,571	4,446	5,760	6,337	6,509	6,527	7,445
HONG KONG	20,432	22,256	25,517	28,666	24,342	27,675	31,015	36,701	48,891	52,328
INDIA	2,126	1,977	2,942	3,475	9,287	10,890	13,618	5,090	3,755	3,143
INDONESIA	1,168	982	825	1,035	1,848	2,651	5,457	4,091	3,640	4,529
JAPAN	6,076	2,485	592	1,901	2,943	2,588	5,833	6,306	4,810	4,101
MALAYSIA	1,455	1,174	1,233	891	884	1,364	1,736	1,912	4,023	3,256
SINGAPORE	7,144	6,684	6,220	10,479	6,284	7,969	9,538	9,046	11,742	16,740
SOUTH KOREA	4,586	3,763	4,457	3,048	3,243	4,160	4,403	4,470	4,283	4,774
THAILAND	1,281	1,407	1,456	1,708	1,201	1,288	1,363	1,492	2,084	2,738
AUSTRALASIA & OCEANIA	**16,694**	**12,665**	**16,173**	**19,930**	**18,893**	**32,051**	**37,161**	**43,532**	**50,611**	**21,357**
of which										
AUSTRALIA	14,627	11,571	15,391	18,024	16,091	31,490	36,201	42,430	49,399	19,902
NEW ZEALAND	1,176	923	682	580	1,509	457	641	665	694	845

6.14 FDI International investment positions abroad analysed by area and main country, 2005 to 2014 (Directional)

£ million

	2005	2006	2007	2008	2009	2010	2011	2012	2013	2014
AFRICA	**20,834**	**15,105**	**18,516**	**21,104**	**29,548**	**30,143**	**30,848**	**42,292**	**36,425**	**42,495**
of which										
KENYA	281	313	331	372	396	474	579	479	490	531
NIGERIA	924	1,011	744	1,349	2,071	1,858	2,175	1,743	1,171	1,484
SOUTH AFRICA	13,733	8,255	9,533	10,994	14,404	10,245	10,609	13,015	10,515	12,669
ZIMBABWE	50	58	32	35	29	15	14	32	63	83
WORLD TOTAL	**696,113**	**741,163**	**916,261**	**1,073,613**	**981,481**	**1,046,098**	**1,090,900**	**1,043,408**	**1,024,575**	**1,015,351**
OECD	561,694	547,303	684,619	837,804	785,854	827,827	845,859	803,561	757,976	726,579
CENTRAL & EASTERN EUROPE	640	515	65	275	312	239	245	-7	123	202

The sum of constituent items may not always agree exactly with the totals shown due to rounding.
A negative sign before values indicates a net disinvestment abroad.

.. Indicates data are disclosive
- Indicates nil data

Source: Office for National Statistics

6.15 Earnings from foreign direct investment abroad analysed by area and main country, 2005 to 2014 (Directional)

£ million

	2005	2006	2007	2008	2009	2010	2011	2012	2013	2014
EUROPE	**32,186**	**38,957**	**44,062**	**43,598**	**34,944**	**30,867**	**45,661**	**27,436**	**30,866**	**20,545**
EU	23,904	28,337	34,284	37,521	28,673	20,889	35,899	22,165	24,022	15,763
AUSTRIA	301	186	247	169	259	139	0	-149	-1	-9
BELGIUM	818	875	1,312	1,568	1,443	1,171	1,853	1,357	545	462
BULGARIA	9	3	-9	-3	5	0	8	0	21	20
CROATIA	..	..	..	..	..	..	..	-3	11	27
CYPRUS	37	171	366	92	57	-8	-58	138	33	-19
CZECH REPUBLIC	108	-64	72	-134	-127	-70	42	212	180	174
DENMARK	387	411	580	530	216	628	586	474	407	360
ESTONIA	..	11	5	6	26	17	23	14	6	17
FINLAND	103	69	281	131	120	184	218	56	63	205
FRANCE	2,957	3,344	3,007	1,769	1,437	3,419	3,531	2,661	2,108	544
GERMANY	2,685	2,189	2,890	3,116	2,732	1,492	1,649	52	1,512	129
GREECE	160	151	223	102	208	-51	19	-39	46	70
HUNGARY	295	83	96	77	32	22	94	114	72	-4
IRISH REPUBLIC	2,835	2,525	3,049	1,879	-2,747	-10,064	-756	1,207	2,459	1,227
ITALY	732	696	837	311	32	630	251	349	357	677
LATVIA	..	5	4	-18	-26	..	..	33	28	-5
LITHUANIA	-	-	2	-	0	2	4	4	2	5
LUXEMBOURG	4,006	7,626	8,030	13,185	11,547	10,357	12,002	7,329	4,049	2,179
MALTA	31	-185	-56	50	334	27	-21	69	..	526
NETHERLANDS	5,344	7,251	9,725	9,460	8,210	9,743	12,658	4,593	8,496	5,460
POLAND	293	373	256	414	693	363	486	543	598	623
PORTUGAL	297	234	264	271	155	292	38	278	39	149
ROMANIA	26	43	76	111	92	12	66	76	..	102
SLOVAKIA	34	24	103	20	22	37	42	29	36	51
SLOVENIA	17	5	11	14	5	..	..	-38	15	13
SPAIN	1,023	918	1,021	1,083	764	-53	463	-531	912	1,000
SWEDEN	1,395	1,395	1,896	3,325	3,187	2,475	2,715	3,333	2,357	1,779
EFTA	3,334	3,759	4,987	4,765	3,311	5,577	5,183	3,361	4,221	1,687
of which										
NORWAY	937	345	296	578	577	537	515	-420	300	526
SWITZERLAND	2,396	3,411	4,377	3,872	2,460	4,849	4,667	3,788	3,921	1,159
OTHER EUROPEAN COUNTRIES	4,948	6,861	4,791	1,312	2,959	4,401	4,578	1,911	2,622	3,094
of which										
RUSSIA	1,681	1,715	1,180	1,811	1,492	1,584	2,996	311	1,795	1,292
UK OFFSHORE ISLANDS	3,017	4,580	3,138	-993	707	2,401	1,058	1,090	476	1,475
THE AMERICAS	**26,585**	**26,461**	**28,527**	**9,871**	**13,450**	**21,476**	**26,635**	**24,058**	**24,230**	**22,714**
of which										
BERMUDA	1,561	..	1,557	1,558	1,178	2,338	1,450	2,159	2,612	2,447
BRAZIL	866	577	712	725	1,225	1,063	1,303	1,059	329	1,260
CANADA	1,895	1,769	1,653	-2,501	-477	468	-42	417	364	232
CHILE	1,164	771	777	678	531	125	322	89	91	94
COLOMBIA	414	274	190	320	137	280	..	-441	36	13
MEXICO	536	531	563	293	260	545	1,364	756	753	713
PANAMA	50	23	42	..	65	53	83	61	76	..
USA	18,244	17,112	19,110	6,034	8,865	14,634	20,127	17,758	17,614	15,739
ASIA	**10,975**	**11,621**	**11,389**	**9,129**	**11,917**	**15,901**	**18,952**	**17,030**	**14,851**	**15,653**
NEAR & MIDDLE EAST COUNTRIES	1,053	1,430	2,563	2,341	1,744	2,049	2,704	862	3,172	2,477
of which										
GULF ARABIAN COUNTRIES	688	717	983	405	868	773	975	722	1,929	1,142
OTHER ASIAN COUNTRIES	9,922	10,191	8,826	6,788	10,173	13,852	16,248	16,168	11,679	13,176
of which										
CHINA	580	445	504	265	579	815	821	1,291	625	504
HONG KONG	3,553	3,786	4,163	1,448	1,316	3,119	4,362	4,846	5,207	4,756
INDIA	626	715	798	690	1,046	1,647	1,794	1,459	1,552	1,365
INDONESIA	226	336	153	105	420	562	1,091	1,094	709	786
JAPAN	482	388	145	304	344	284	366	213	447	394
MALAYSIA	508	494	595	526	731	810	592	571	614	966
SINGAPORE	2,510	2,285	478	1,663	2,553	2,469	3,267	2,963	-296	1,669
SOUTH KOREA	683	532	519	536	568	907	609	763	648	563
THAILAND	171	-121	23	-132	199	221	222	246	304	302
AUSTRALASIA & OCEANIA	**3,157**	**3,065**	**3,716**	**3,134**	**4,323**	**6,007**	**2,359**	**3,809**	**3,644**	**2,900**
of which										
AUSTRALIA	2,681	2,665	3,294	2,734	3,843	5,545	2,044	3,512	3,356	2,615
NEW ZEALAND	359	388	379	329	402	371	209	236	209	164

6.15 Earnings from foreign direct investment abroad analysed by area and main country, 2005 to 2014 (Directional)

£ million

	2005	2006	2007	2008	2009	2010	2011	2012	2013	2014
AFRICA	**5,764**	**3,488**	**4,548**	**3,765**	**3,298**	**6,084**	**6,355**	**7,535**	**5,113**	**3,750**
of which										
KENYA	70	88	89	100	141	174	144	8	112	82
NIGERIA	197	133	78	212	108	660	1,045	1,263	376	680
SOUTH AFRICA	3,768	1,620	2,236	1,143	1,199	2,588	2,596	3,192	2,227	1,551
ZIMBABWE	16	10	6	-5	-4	5	23	23	12	12
WORLD TOTAL	**78,667**	**83,591**	**92,242**	**69,500**	**67,942**	**80,334**	**99,962**	**79,869**	**78,704**	**65,563**
OECD	52,138	55,675	64,794	50,006	45,802	49,160	66,062	49,223	52,184	37,484
CENTRAL & EASTERN EUROPE	76	62	-11	25	28	-3	0	-3	3	-7

The sum of constituent items may not always agree exactly with the totals shown due to rounding.
A negative sign before values indicates a net disinvestment abroad.

.. Indicates data are disclosive
- Indicates nil data

Source: Office for National Statistics

6.16 Net foreign direct investment flows into the United Kingdom analysed by area and main country, 2005 to 2014 (Directional)

£ million

	2005	2006	2007	2008	2009	2010	2011	2012	2013	2014
EUROPE	**80,087**	**53,837**	**49,752**	**25,258**	**32,075**	**355**	**12,736**	**23,032**	**9,452**	**3,979**
EU	71,034	47,698	39,348	24,122	25,739	-6,574	17,688	15,052	-469	5,268
AUSTRIA	..	..	..	..	..	84	..	-126	21	17
BELGIUM	23	670	317	-547	367	146	9,057	2,018	724	-771
BULGARIA	..	..	1	..	..	..	..	-2	0	-1
CROATIA	..	..	..	..	..	..	..	..	..	..
CYPRUS	7	18	75	30	19	47	97	-206	265	193
CZECH REPUBLIC	..	..	..	..	..	0	..	9	..	0
DENMARK	-1,246	13	-18	1,577	-414	-209	79	408	-1,291	187
ESTONIA	-	-	-	..	-	..	..	..	..	..
FINLAND	238	44	21	-25	131	64	63	-10	139	48
FRANCE	..	..	..	..	..	-4,523	..	6,933	-5,116	4,565
GERMANY	7,279	5,566	16,616	4,454	5,473	2,711	-4,171	2,886	2,789	1,951
GREECE	14	17	17	11	74	197	99	59	-10	5
HUNGARY	1	3	1	-	0	0	1	..	-20	..
IRISH REPUBLIC	..	..	..	..	..	1,238	..	717	98	108
ITALY	-42	282	288	-282	-655	146	399	750	775	233
LATVIA	..	..	0	..	-	-	-	..	..	..
LITHUANIA	0	0	-	-	-	-	-	..	..	..
LUXEMBOURG	..	..	..	..	..	-3,490	..	4,648	-1,040	1,498
MALTA	1	2	6	1	-14	4	27	-58	19	170
NETHERLANDS	50,366	13,715	2,471	17,668	-9,977	-4,216	12,068	-2,602	1,251	-3,907
POLAND	1	50	-29	7	0	2	4	-7	11	8
PORTUGAL	..	..	..	..	..	44	..	-1	-18	14
ROMANIA	..	..	4	-	..	..	1	-9	0	0
SLOVAKIA	..	..	1	..	..	..	..	0	..	-1
SLOVENIA	..	..	3	-	..	..	0	0	..	-1
SPAIN	..	..	..	..	..	889	..	-378	977	571
SWEDEN	393	508	-117	575	56	294	803	172	-25	622
EFTA	9,050	5,321	8,793	-4,082	1,973	2,567	-2,396	6,432	8,277	2,907
of which										
NORWAY	..	..	..	..	..	216	..	-495	483	1,167
SWITZERLAND	7,405	4,786	8,159	-3,094	1,839	1,876	-2,000	6,904	7,959	1,775
OTHER EUROPEAN COUNTRIES	3	817	1,611	5,219	4,363	4,362	-2,555	1,548	1,644	-4,196
of which										
RUSSIA	..	..	..	..	..	..	..	-87	-19	-118
UK OFFSHORE ISLANDS	-60	733	1,248	4,208	4,255	3,984	-2,717	-772	1,662	-4,048
THE AMERICAS	**17,422**	**17,242**	**32,460**	**18,614**	**16,774**	**28,636**	**11,621**	**8,129**	**17,859**	**16,796**
of which										
BRAZIL	6	..	2	1	..	..	1	-7	-4	-4
CANADA	1,632	3,509	799	343	-1,265	3,680	-231	1,700	1,277	2,036
USA	15,589	12,313	27,975	18,135	15,175	22,829	12,268	6,013	16,545	15,178
ASIA	**-4,168**	**11,806**	**9,938**	**4,026**	**-2,330**	**5,324**	**2,842**	**3,735**	**4,570**	**6,283**
NEAR & MIDDLE EAST COUNTRIES	736	5,034	-979	-635	274	335	-895	464	542	325
OTHER ASIAN COUNTRIES	-4,904	6,772	10,919	4,662	-2,604	4,988	3,738	3,271	4,029	5,958
of which										
CHINA	13	12	16	-20	123	9	..	809	..	584
HONG KONG	315	92	-1,919	737	-152	2,995	2,004	596	1,009	280
INDIA	138	265	151	2,638	20	48	563	-15	-158	121
JAPAN	..	..	..	..	..	-90	..	859	2,238	2,210
SINGAPORE	46	..	6,749	268	136	1	-467	20	-28	2,346
SOUTH KOREA	175	-85	5	247	11	..	38	106	-18	90
AUSTRALASIA & OCEANIA	**..**	**..**	**..**	**..**	**..**	**-2,388**	**..**	**10,020**	**921**	**298**
of which										
AUSTRALIA	3,396	1,479	588	-66	2,471	-2,392	1,597	10,020	..	422
NEW ZEALAND	-	54	-48	-20	-20	4	9	-11	..	24

6.16 Net foreign direct investment flows into the United Kingdom analysed by area and main country, 2005 to 2014 (Directional)

£ million

	2005	2006	2007	2008	2009	2010	2011	2012	2013	2014
AFRICA	**66**	**131**	**459**	**1,083**	**18**	**181**	**75**	**-319**	**214**	**445**
of which										
SOUTH AFRICA	25	101	438	..	31	35	81	-359	214	423
WORLD TOTAL	**96,803**	**84,885**	**93,148**	**48,875**	**48,986**	**32,106**	**28,883**	**44,596**	**33,016**	**27,801**
OECD	95,187	73,961	83,165	39,384	41,296	21,921	30,096	40,447	28,459	27,814
CENTRAL & EASTERN EUROPE	..	..	..	..	..	..	..	..	..	..

The sum of constituent items may not always agree exactly with the totals shown due to rounding.
A negative sign before values indicates a net disinvestment in the UK.

.. Indicates data are disclosive
- Indicates nil data

Source: Office for National Statistics

205

6.17 FDI International investment positions in the United Kingdom analysed by area and main country, 2005 to 2014 (Directional)

£ million

	2005	2006	2007	2008	2009	2010	2011	2012	2013	2014
EUROPE	277,027	332,077	354,382	389,925	416,484	417,201	447,608	553,813	553,889	608,736
EU	244,392	299,906	308,996	335,526	362,673	353,741	371,932	464,790	458,244	495,798
AUSTRIA	561	848	1,030	840	935	1,076	2,435	5,296	2,565	2,316
BELGIUM	4,481	5,609	4,545	4,121	4,341	7,846	16,177	10,787	24,841	25,603
BULGARIA	..	..	..	..	..	..	..	..	7	6
CROATIA	..	..	..	..	..	..	..	..	..	..
CYPRUS	100	162	437	494	316	2,307	2,536	4,090	3,605	3,715
CZECH REPUBLIC	3	..	8	18	1	7	26	103	26	10
DENMARK	1,404	4,344	5,530	8,706	5,357	3,140	3,710	6,020	8,861	6,746
ESTONIA	-	-	..	..	-	..	..	..	..	..
FINLAND	756	817	708	736	753	780	875	2,178	1,474	1,492
FRANCE	56,309	59,998	54,303	51,838	73,534	67,241	61,236	78,547	64,727	76,048
GERMANY	51,469	54,382	64,558	71,755	67,784	51,677	50,046	66,966	47,241	50,089
GREECE	103	121	174	221	456	668	805	325	511	194
HUNGARY	9	12	12	20	5	10	14	86	..	-10
IRISH REPUBLIC	7,146	8,186	8,839	10,204	10,886	9,524	11,013	9,314	11,911	13,733
ITALY	6,122	4,482	4,901	6,258	4,854	753	2,106	9,147	13,481	4,440
LATVIA	..	..	..	..	..	-	-	..	..	..
LITHUANIA	-	-	-	-	-	-	-	..	..	..
LUXEMBOURG	7,880	16,021	20,399	26,833	48,756	58,233	47,941	57,046	71,455	78,852
MALTA	12	12	62	69	48	172	292	974	969	633
NETHERLANDS	95,579	119,843	110,903	137,248	110,878	112,291	126,715	148,987	147,586	175,997
POLAND	21	96	75	76	16	26	98	198	209	109
PORTUGAL	111	122	222	308	600	892	302	571	515	471
ROMANIA	..	..	..	..	..	..	11	76	9	9
SLOVAKIA	-	..	..	..	..	..	..	..	6	4
SLOVENIA	..	..	9	13	..	7	0	..	7	9
SPAIN	8,782	20,658	27,876	11,178	26,781	33,344	40,447	56,300	49,470	45,690
SWEDEN	3,467	4,113	4,312	4,453	6,265	3,680	5,141	7,716	8,479	9,605
EFTA	25,033	22,358	32,570	29,931	29,654	35,771	41,470	35,521	45,986	48,078
of which										
NORWAY	1,085	969	1,522	1,789	1,776	1,723	2,400	4,913	3,861	5,390
SWITZERLAND	21,624	19,033	28,936	26,783	26,885	33,043	36,140	29,722	39,289	39,850
OTHER EUROPEAN COUNTRIES	7,602	9,813	12,816	24,468	24,158	27,689	34,205	53,502	49,659	64,860
of which										
RUSSIA	..	..	179	1,581	743	1,200	1,343	912	1,647	..
UK OFFSHORE ISLANDS	7,059	9,111	11,963	22,026	23,025	26,120	32,183	45,100	46,562	61,810
THE AMERICAS	174,037	200,709	202,062	209,792	208,475	242,270	263,464	305,076	277,561	336,772
of which										
BRAZIL	77	134	21	9	..	..	17	-10	121	15
CANADA	15,587	19,369	20,835	21,333	19,535	19,259	18,028	14,637	19,656	22,199
USA	149,759	170,880	167,008	168,689	170,206	198,163	219,181	260,518	215,899	252,975
ASIA	24,101	39,436	53,166	50,419	42,521	54,791	66,426	67,698	72,532	73,628
NEAR & MIDDLE EAST COUNTRIES	2,970	10,160	6,449	5,389	3,780	4,498	5,137	3,772	4,900	6,346
OTHER ASIAN COUNTRIES	21,131	29,275	46,717	45,030	38,741	50,293	61,289	63,926	67,632	67,282
of which										
CHINA	111	99	202	427	618	378	780	1,151	..	1,148
HONG KONG	..	..	..	..	6,641	9,579	20,504	10,322	11,622	12,750
INDIA	518	798	1,376	3,591	1,900	2,846	2,921	2,072	1,676	2,130
JAPAN	10,513	14,766	25,479	30,643	24,646	27,638	31,512	40,667	34,145	38,237
SINGAPORE	1,034	4,046	12,197	1,555	3,526	6,115	3,829	4,125	3,655	8,653
SOUTH KOREA	638	798	779	914	703	2,867	953	2,516	2,389	2,271
AUSTRALASIA & OCEANIA	12,537	7,623	9,412	8,122	12,705	9,721	12,941	32,074	3,953	12,190
of which										
AUSTRALIA	12,313	7,093	8,974	7,842	12,466	9,478	11,926	31,478	..	11,473
NEW ZEALAND	224	428	430	279	239	239	289	579	..	352

6.17 FDI International investment positions in the United Kingdom analysed by area and main country, 2005 to 2014 (Directional)

£ million

	2005	2006	2007	2008	2009	2010	2011	2012	2013	2014
AFRICA	**510**	**469**	**1,397**	**2,115**	**1,088**	**1,574**	**2,220**	**1,430**	**2,345**	**3,008**
of which										
SOUTH AFRICA	186	130	900	1,600	501	570	1,124	353	1,274	2,221
WORLD TOTAL	**488,212**	**580,313**	**620,419**	**660,373**	**681,273**	**725,557**	**792,660**	**960,091**	**910,280**	**1,034,335**
OECD	458,185	535,218	564,201	594,466	619,512	644,444	690,293	845,903	773,602	865,309
CENTRAL & EASTERN EUROPE	..	..	6	..	..	..	..	..	..	..

The sum of constituent items may not always agree exactly with the totals shown due to rounding.
A negative sign before values indicates a net disinvestment in the UK.

.. Indicates data are disclosive
- Indicates nil data

Source: Office for National Statistics

6.18 Earnings from foreign direct investment in the United Kingdom analysed by area and main country, 2005 to 2014 (Directional)

£ million

	2005	2006	2007	2008	2009	2010	2011	2012	2013	2014
EUROPE	**17,592**	**27,447**	**26,174**	**-17,381**	**9,438**	**20,481**	**21,139**	**24,000**	**27,239**	**27,225**
EU	15,278	22,919	24,144	-3,729	9,817	15,301	17,607	22,510	24,990	23,797
AUSTRIA	60	207	211	-45	85	112	171	207	141	169
BELGIUM	367	646	577	286	-218	488	1,020	950	1,962	1,674
BULGARIA	-	-	..	..	..	..	..	0	1	0
CROATIA	..	..	..	..	..	..	..	..	..	..
CYPRUS	24	44	66	57	33	147	124	198	235	309
CZECH REPUBLIC	0	..	1	1	..	0	18	..	6	1
DENMARK	326	204	-70	-175	-257	91	-91	175	421	163
ESTONIA	-	-	..	..	-	..	..	..	..	..
FINLAND	61	93	181	50	96	98	76	198	145	140
FRANCE	5,121	5,329	3,489	1,351	9,249	4,670	5,119	2,850	2,326	3,236
GERMANY	4,037	4,541	5,789	-823	-1,902	4,945	3,778	6,275	6,490	5,662
GREECE	49	70	104	212	193	338	67	124	121	68
HUNGARY	1	3	1	..	..	1	1	1	15	2
IRISH REPUBLIC	724	1,012	1,202	-132	-1,785	-2,598	333	521	491	440
ITALY	483	477	577	466	430	269	174	1,147	1,221	552
LATVIA	..	..	..	..	-	-	-	..	0	..
LITHUANIA	1	1	-	-	-	-	-	..	..	..
LUXEMBOURG	214	79	463	619	937	1,500	699	2,084	1,853	1,525
MALTA	0	3	7	28	22	46	47	92	71	160
NETHERLANDS	2,800	7,283	8,393	-7,297	-464	2,962	4,180	4,343	6,065	5,463
POLAND	1	8	6	3	1	2	4	5	6	8
PORTUGAL	30	48	54	50	42	52	-66	68	37	156
ROMANIA	..	..	..	..	..	..	1	0	1	1
SLOVAKIA	5	5	3	..	..	..	..	0	..	..
SLOVENIA	..	..	..	..	..	0	1	-1	1	0
SPAIN	773	2,536	2,696	1,255	3,023	1,636	1,359	2,697	2,686	3,177
SWEDEN	182	316	386	368	337	541	592	575	697	890
EFTA	1,495	3,366	264	-16,382	-2,352	1,029	1,419	-559	363	1,809
of which										
NORWAY	82	169	194	262	15	29	215	399	685	757
SWITZERLAND	1,320	2,933	-286	-15,112	-2,411	528	821	-941	-488	755
OTHER EUROPEAN COUNTRIES	819	1,162	1,767	2,731	1,975	4,152	2,113	2,050	1,886	1,618
of which										
RUSSIA	..	..	7	-77	-14	40	101	-47	129	-38
UK OFFSHORE ISLANDS	757	1,107	1,752	2,891	1,939	4,090	2,001	1,878	1,661	1,576
THE AMERICAS	**16,460**	**20,154**	**17,158**	**21,033**	**18,584**	**17,333**	**20,121**	**21,109**	**20,822**	**19,522**
of which										
BRAZIL	-4	-4	6	-6	..	32	9	12	17	3
CANADA	1,348	1,458	-250	-2,856	350	912	453	790	1,963	1,836
USA	14,156	16,828	15,060	22,518	16,931	14,993	17,920	19,165	17,588	14,039
ASIA	**937**	**2,710**	**447**	**-1,316**	**-3,631**	**-202**	**2,835**	**3,871**	**2,431**	**5,448**
NEAR & MIDDLE EAST COUNTRIES	354	564	237	216	101	135	483	468	646	532
OTHER ASIAN COUNTRIES	583	2,145	210	-1,533	-3,731	-337	2,352	3,403	1,784	4,916
of which										
CHINA	-63	-35	17	-38	34	25	31	121	201	204
HONG KONG	..	-597	..	-337	-89	549	55	591	1,179	952
INDIA	65	132	140	261	89	161	700	118	59	175
JAPAN	1,089	1,956	-216	-2,000	-3,979	-1,646	394	2,062	627	2,045
SINGAPORE	85	259	609	166	-213	-64	821	231	-220	1,492
SOUTH KOREA	72	104	125	134	59	116	49	100	136	-96
AUSTRALASIA & OCEANIA	**535**	**1,259**	**1,222**	**613**	**2,143**	**-30**	**140**	**224**	**264**	**162**
of which										
AUSTRALIA	521	876	1,196	629	2,152	-47	154	195	220	380
NEW ZEALAND	13	46	25	-13	-4	18	6	20	181	35

6.18 Earnings from foreign direct investment in the United Kingdom analysed by area and main country, 2005 to 2014 (Directional)

£ million

	2005	2006	2007	2008	2009	2010	2011	2012	2013	2014
AFRICA	**65**	**80**	**137**	**166**	**47**	**51**	**152**	**-322**	**84**	**-43**
of which										
SOUTH AFRICA	25	31	82	126	67	23	82	-364	17	-98
WORLD TOTAL	**35,588**	**51,650**	**45,138**	**3,113**	**26,581**	**37,631**	**44,388**	**48,882**	**50,839**	**52,315**
OECD	33,927	47,476	40,242	-1,792	22,914	30,470	37,463	44,024	45,699	43,169
CENTRAL & EASTERN EUROPE	..	..	1	..	..	0	..	..	..	..

The sum of constituent items may not always agree exactly with the totals shown due to rounding.
A negative sign before values indicates a net disinvestment in the UK.

.. Indicates data are disclosive
- Indicates nil data

Source: Office for National Statistics

209

this page is intentionally blank

Research and development

Chapter 7

Research and development

(Tables 7.1 to 7.5)

Research and experimental development (R&D) is defined for statistical purposes as 'creative work undertaken on a systematic basis in order to increase the stock of knowledge, including knowledge of man, culture and society, and the use of this stock of knowledge to devise new applications'.

R&D is financed and carried out mainly by businesses, the Government, and institutions of higher education. A small amount is performed by non-profit-making bodies. Gross Expenditure on R&D (GERD) is an indicator of the total amount of R&D performed within the UK: it has been approximately 2 per cent of GDP in recent years. Detailed figures are reported each year in a statistical bulletin published in March. Table 7.1 shows the main components of GERD.

ONS conducts an annual survey of expenditure and employment on R&D performed by government, and of government funding of R&D. The survey collects data for the reference period along with future estimates. Until 1993 the detailed results were reported in the *Annual Review of Government Funded R&D*. From 1997 the results have appeared in the Science, Engineering and Technology (SET) Statistics published by the Department for Business, Innovation and Skills (BIS). Table 7.2 gives some broad totals for gross expenditure by government (expenditure before deducting funds received by government for R&D). Table 7.3 gives a breakdown of net expenditure (receipts are deducted).

The ONS conducts an annual survey of R&D in business. Tables 7.4 and 7.5 give a summary of the main trends up to 2014.

Statistics on expenditure and employment on R&D in higher education institutions (HEIs) are based on information collected by Higher Education Funding Councils and the Higher Education Statistics Agency (HESA). In 1994 a new methodology was introduced to estimate expenditure on R&D in HEIs. This is based on the allocation of various Funding Council Grants. Full details of the new methodology are contained in science, engineering and technology (SET) Statistics available on the BIS website at: https://www.gov.uk/government/collections/science-engineering-and-technology-statistics

The most comprehensive international comparisons of resources devoted to R&D appear in Main Science and Technology Indicators published by the Organisation for Economic Co-operation and Development (OECD). The Statistical Office of the European Union and the United Nations also compile R&D statistics based on figures supplied by member states.

To make international comparisons more reliable the OECD have published a series of manuals giving guidance on how to measure various components of R&D inputs and outputs. The most important of these is the Frascati Manual, which defines R&D and recommends how resources for R&D should be measured. The UK follows the Frascati Manual as far as possible.

For information on available aggregated data on Research and Development please call Office for National Statistics on 01633 456728.

7.1a Expenditure on R & D in the UK by performing and funding sectors, 2013

Current prices		Sector performing the R&D						£ million
	Government	Research Councils	Higher Education	Business Enterprise	Private Non-Profit[1]	Total	Overseas
Sector providing the funds							
Government	1,050	77	380	1,646	61	**3,214**	547
Research Councils	60	600	2,121	3	115	**2,899**	200
Higher Education Funding Councils	-	-	2,297	-	-	**2,297**	-
Higher Education	1	13	300	-	54	**368**	-
Business Enterprise	239	25	313	12,750	16	**13,343**	3,305
Private Non-Profit	5	48	1,051	74	185	**1,362**	-
Overseas	112	51	1,167	3,975	87	**5,393**	-
TOTAL	**1,467**	**813**	**7,628**	**18,448**	**518**	**28,875**	-
of which:							
Civil	1,303	813	7,592	16,734	516	**26,959**	-
Defence[1]	164	-	37	1,713	2	**1,916**	-

Source: Office for National Statistics

1. Private Non-Profit defence has been estimated using the 2012 data, as no survey data available for 2013.

- denotes nil, figures unavailable or too small to display.

7.1b Expenditure on research and development in the UK by sector of performance: 2005 to 2013

		2005	2006	2007	2008	2009	2010	2011	2012	£ million 2013
Sector performing the R&D										
Current prices										
TOTAL	**GLBA**	**22,106**	**22,993**	**24,696**	**25,345**	**25,632**	**26,173**	**27,452** [†]	**26,988**	**28,875**
Government	**GLBK**	1,238	1,252	1,320	1,348	1,406	1,372	1,321	1,332 [†]	1,467
Research Councils	**DMRS**	1,051	1,061	1,034	1,041	1,097	1,141	1,035 [†]	804	813
Business Enterprise	**GLBL**	13,734	14,144	15,676	15,814	15,532	16,045	17,452 [†]	17,144	18,448
Higher Education	**GLBM**	5,580	6,022	6,119	6,545	6,931	6,963	7,117 [†]	7,163	7,628
Private Non-Profit	**GLBN**	502	513	546	595	666	652	526 [†]	545	518
As % of GDP		1.64	1.61	1.65	1.69	1.71	1.66	1.69	1.62	1.67

	2005	2006	2007	2008	2009	2010	2011	2012	2013
Sector performing the R&D									
Constant prices (2013)[1]									
TOTAL	**26,677**	**27,015**	**28,191**	**28,224**	**27,824**	**27,646**	**28,487**	**27,561**	**28,875**
Government	1,494	1,471	1,507	1,501	1,526	1,449	1,371	1,360	1,467
Research Councils	1,268	1,247	1,180	1,159	1,191	1,205	1,074	821	813
Business Enterprise	16,574	16,618	17,895	17,610	16,860	16,948	18,110	17,508	18,448
Higher Education	6,734	7,075	6,985	7,288	7,524	7,355	7,385	7,315	7,628
Private Non-Profit	606	603	623	663	723	689	546	557	518

Source: Office for National Statistics

1. Please note that the latest deflators have been applied to the business research and development estimates in this bulletin which has resulted in small differences being observed between the BERD and GERD publications.

[†] crosses denote earliest data revision.

7.2 Gross central government expenditure on research and development

United Kingdom

£ million

	2007/08		2008/09		2009/10		2010/11		2011/12r		2012/13r	
	Intra-mural[2]	Extra-mural	Intra-mural	Extra-mural	Intra-mural	Extra-mural	Intra-mural	Extra-mural	Intra-mural	Extra-mural	Intra-mural	Extra-mural
Defence	279	1941	262	1812	288	1551	226	1556	158	1190	150	1353
Research councils	1034	2005	1041	2297	1097	2434	1141	2414	1035	2440	804	2487
Higher education institutes	-	2234	-	2227	-	2395	-	2303	-	2257	-	2185
Other programmes	410	1019	419	1064	421	1276	400	1236	418	1411	444	1443
Total (excluding NHS)	1723	7199	1722	7400	1806	7656	1767	7509	1611	7298	1398	7468

Source: Office for National Statistics 01633 456763

1. Extramural Includes work performed overseas
2. From 2007/08 expenditure data no longer includes VAT.
r - revised data

7.2 Expenditure on R&D in the UK by Performing and Funding Sectors, 2014

Current prices	Sector performing the R&D						£ million
	Government	Research Councils	Higher Education	Business Enterprise	Private Non-Profit[1]	Total	Overseas
Sector providing the funds							
Government	944	83	436	1,856	75	**3,394**	617
Research Councils	62	599	2,143	2	138	**2,944**	208
Higher Education Funding Councils	-	-	2,341	-	-	**2,341**	-
Higher Education	4	12	307	-	56	**379**	-
Business Enterprise	237	29	336	14,083	17	**14,701**	5,632
Private Non-Profit	10	39	1,097	136	190	**1,473**	-
Overseas	144	58	1,228	3,859	78	**5,367**	-
Total	**1,401**	**821**	**7,889**	**19,935**	**554**	**30,600**	-
of which:							
Civil	1,244	821	7,849	18,381	552	**28,846**	-
Defence	158	-	40	1,554	2	**1,754**	-

Source: Office for National Statistics

1. Private Non-Profit totals have been estimated using the 2013 data, as no survey data available for 2014
- denotes nil, figures unavailable or too small to display

Please note - Differences may occur between totals and the sum of their independently rounded components

7.3 UK government net expenditure on R&D by socio-economic objective, percentage share: 2007 to 2014

Current prices

£ million

	2007	2008	2009	2010	2011	2012	2013	2014
TOTAL	8,825	9,107	9,371	9,260	8,995	8,990 †	9,883	10,063

	2007	2008	2009	2010	2011	2012	2013	2014
Per cent								
TOTAL	100	100	100	100	100	100	100	100
Agriculture	3	3	4	3	4	4	4	3
Industrial production and technology	-	1	2	1	2	1	2	2
Energy	1	1	1	1	2	2	2	3
Transport, telecommunication, other infrastructure	1	1	1	1	3	3	3	4
Environment	2	3	3	3	3	3	3	2
Health	17	18	19	21	22	22	23 †	22
Education	1	1	1	1	-	-	-	-
Exploration and exploitation of the earth	3	3	3	3	3	3	3	4
General advancement of knowledge: R&D financed from General University Funds	25	24	26	25	25	24	23	23
Exploration and exploitation of space	2	2	2	2	3	3 †	4	3
Defence	24	22	19	18	15	16	15 †	17
Culture, recreation, religion and mass media	2	2	2	2	2	1 †	1	1
Political and social systems, structures and processes	1	2	2	2	1	3 †	3	3
General advancement of knowledge: R&D financed from other sources	18	18	17	18	13	13	13	12

Source: Office for National Statistics

- denotes nil, figures unavailable or too small to display.

† denotes earliest data revision.

7.4 Expenditure on Civil and Defence R&D performed in UK businesses: Broad product groups, 2011-2014

£ million

		Civil					Defence			
		2011	2012	2013	2014		2011	2012	2013	2014
CURRENT PRICES										
TOTAL	DLBV	15,667	15,808 †	17,145	18,381	DLBW	1,785	1,601 †	1,654	1,554
Manufacturing	DLEP	10,815	10,868 †	11,404	11,952	DLEX	1,647	1,515 †	1,491	1,375
Chemicals	DLEQ	..	..	..	..	DLEY	..	..	..	..
Mechanical engineering	DLER	520	575 †	615	660	DLEZ	572	526	522 †	443
Electrical machinery	DLES	847	1,069	1,194 †	1,308	DLFA	353	270	199 †	189
Transport equipment	DLET	..	..	..	..	DLFB	..	..	..	..
Aerospace	DLEU	1,036	1,162 †	1,229	1,339	DLFC	402	349 †	410	357
Other manufacturing	DLEV	1,398	1,388 †	1,481	1,670	DLFD	98	130 †	116	113
Services	DLEW	4,425	..	5,095 †	..	DLFE	138	..	163	..
Other: Total	LDIL	426	..	646	..	LDJJ	-	..	-	..
Agriculture, hunting & forestry; Fishing	LDIN	133	132	121 †	119	LDJL	-	-	-	-
Extractive industries	LDIS	195	172 †	294	315	LDKF	-	-	-	-
Electricity, gas & water supply; Waste management	LDJB	68	..	140	144	LDKG	-	-	-	-
Construction	LDJG	31	..	91	..	LDKS	-	..	-	..

£ million

		2011	2012	2013	2014		2011	2012	2013	2014
CONSTANT PRICES (2014)										
TOTAL	DLBA	16,523	16,372	17,390	18,381	DLBB	1,883	1,658	1,678	1,554
Manufacturing	DLBD	11,406	11,256	11,567	11,952	DLBL	1,737	1,569	1,512	1,375
Chemicals	DLBE	..	..	..	..	DLBM	..	..	..	..
Mechanical engineering	DLBF	548	596	624	660	DLBN	603	545	529	443
Electrical machinery	DLBG	893	1,107	1,211	1,308	DLBO	372	280	202	189
Transport equipment	DLBH	..	..	..	..	DLBP	..	..	..	..
Aerospace	DLBI	1,093	1,203	1,247	1,339	DLBQ	424	361	416	357
Other manufacturing	DLBJ	1,474	1,438	1,502	1,670	DLBR	103	135	118	113
Services	DLBK	4,667	..	5,168	..	DLBS	146	..	165	..
Other: Total	C3ZE	449	..	655	..	C3ZJ	-	..	-	..
Agriculture, hunting & forestry; Fishing	C3ZF	140	137	123	119	C3ZK	-	-	-	-
Extractive industries	C3ZG	206	178	298	315	C3ZL	-	-	-	-
Electricity, gas & water supply; Waste management	C3ZH	72	122	142	144	C3ZM	-	-	-	-
Construction	C3ZI	33	..	92	..	C3ZN	-	..	-	..

Source: Office for National Statistics

	2011	2012	2013	2014		2011	2012	2013	2014
GDP deflator used to convert current prices to constant prices	94.818	96.555	98.589	100		94.818	96.555	98.589	100

1. - denotes nil, figures unavailable or too small to display.
2. .. denotes disclosive figures.
3. † crosses denote earliest data revision.
4. Differences may occur between totals and the sum of their independently rounded components.

7.5a Sources of funds for R&D performed in UK businesses: 2011 to 2014

CURRENT PRICES

		2011	2012	2013	2014
£ Million					
TOTAL	**DLBX**	**17,452**	**17,409** [†]	**18,799**	**19,935**
UK Government	DLDO	1,513	1,430 [†]	1,802	1,857
Overseas total of which:	DLHK	3,939	3,850 [†]	3,848	3,843
European Commission grants	DLDQ	55	55 [†]	61	61
Other Overseas	DLDS	3,884	3,796 [†]	3,787	3,782
Other UK Business	DLDU	595	344 [†]	351	376
Own funds	DLDW	11,283	11,696 [†]	12,691	13,707
Other	DLDY	122	88 [†]	106	152

	2011	2012	2013	2014
Per cent				
TOTAL	**100**	**100**	**100**	**100**
UK Government	9	8	10 [†]	9
Overseas total of which:	23	22 [†]	20	19
European Commission grants	-	-	-	-
Other Overseas	22	22 [†]	20	19
Other UK Business	3	2	2	2
Own funds	65	67 [†]	68	69
Other	1	1 [†]	1	1

Source: Office for National Statistics

1. - denotes nil, figures unavailable or too small to display.
2. [†] crosses denote earliest data revision.
3. Differences may occur between totals and the sum of their independently rounded components.
4. The sum of percentages may be more or less than 100 due to rounding.
5. 'Other' includes funds from UK Private Non-Profit organisations and
   Higher Education establishments, and from 2011, international organisations.

7.5b Sources of funds for R&D performed in UK businesses: Civil and Defence, 2011 to 2014

CURRENT PRICES
£ million

		Civil					Defence			
		2011	2012	2013	2014		2011	2012	2013	2014
UK Government	DLFG	394	366 †	719	796	DLFN	1,119	1,064 †	1,083	1,061
Overseas total of which:	DLHS	3,788	3,691 †	3,688	3,696	DLIF	151	159 †	160	148
European Commission grants	DLFH	53	52 †	60	60	DLFO	3	2	1 †	1
Other Overseas	DLFI	3,735	3,639 †	3,628	3,636	DLFP	149	157 †	158	147
Other UK Business	DLFJ	485	277 †	..	323	DLFQ	109	68 †	..	53
Own	DLFK	10,922	11,392 †	12,380	13,426	DLFR	361	304	312 †	281
Other	DLFL	78	82 †	..	141	DLFS	44	6	..	11
TOTAL	**DLBV**	**15,667**	**15,808** †	**17,145**	**18,381**	**DLBW**	**1,785**	**1,601** †	**1,654**	**1,554**

Source: Office for National Statistics

1. - denotes nil, figures unavailable or too small to display.
2. .. denotes disclosive figures.
3. † crosses denote earliest data revision.
4. Differences may occur between totals and the sum of their independently rounded components.
5. 'Other' includes funds from UK Private Non-Profit organisations and Higher Education establishments, and from 2011, international organisations.

Income and wealth

Chapter 8

Personal income, expenditure and wealth

Distribution of total incomes (Table 8.1)

The information shown in Table 8.1 comes from the Survey of Personal Incomes. This is an annual survey covering approximately 600,000 individuals across the whole of the UK. It is based on administrative data held by HM Revenue & Customs (HMRC) on individuals who could be liable for tax.

The table relates only to those individuals who are taxpayers. The distributions only cover incomes as computed for tax purposes, and above a level which for each year corresponds approximately to the single person's allowance. Incomes below these levels are not shown because the information about them is incomplete.

Some components of investment income (for example interest and dividends), from which tax has been deducted at source, are not always held on HMRC business systems. Estimates of missing bank and building society interest and dividends from UK companies are included in these tables. The missing investment income is distributed to cases, so that the population as a whole has amounts consistent with evidence from other sources. For example, amounts of tax accounted for by deposit takers and the tendency to hold interest-bearing accounts as indicated by household surveys.

Superannuation contributions are estimated and included in total income. They have been distributed among earners in the Survey of Personal Incomes sample, by a method consistent with information about the number of employees who are contracted in or out of the State Earnings Related Pension Scheme (SERPS) and the proportion of their earnings contributed.

When comparing results of these surveys across years, it should be noted that the Survey of Personal Incomes is not a longitudinal survey. However, sample sizes have increased in recent years to increase precision.

Effects of taxes and benefits, by household type (Table 8.2)

Original income is the total income in cash of all the members of the household before receipt of state benefits or the deduction of taxes. It includes income from employment, self-employment, investment income and occupational pensions. Gross income is original income plus cash benefits received from government (retirement pensions, child benefit, and so on). Disposal income is the income available for consumption; it is equal to gross income less direct taxes (which include income tax, national insurance contributions, and council tax). By further allowing for taxes paid on goods and services purchased, such as VAT, an estimate of post-tax income is derived. These income figures are derived from estimates made by the Office for National Statistics (ONS) based largely on information from the Living Costs and Food Survey (LFC) and published each year on the ONS website.

In Table 8.2, a retired household is defined as one where the combined income of retired members amounts to at least half the total gross income of the household; where a retired person is defined as anyone who describes themselves as retired, or anyone over the minimum National Insurance (NI) pension age describing themselves as 'unoccupied' or 'sick or injured but not intending to seek work.

Children are defined as persons aged under 16 or between 16 and 18, unmarried and receiving full-time non-advanced further education.

Living Costs and Food Survey (Tables 8.3–8.5)

The Living Costs and Food Survey (LCF) is a sample survey of private households in the UK. The LCF sample is representative of all regions of the UK and of different types of households. The survey is continuous, with interviews spread evenly over the year to ensure that estimates are not biased by seasonal variation. The survey results show how households spend their money; how much goes on food, clothing and so on, how spending patterns vary depending upon income, household composition, and regional location of households. From January 2006 the survey has been conducted on a calendar-year basis, therefore the latest results refer to the January to December 2014 period.

One of the main purposes of the LCF is to define the 'basket of goods' for the Retail Prices Index (RPI) and the Consumer Prices Index (CPI). The RPI has a vital role in the up rating of state pensions and welfare benefits, while the CPI is a key instrument of the Government's monetary policy. Information from the survey is also a major source for estimates of household expenditure in the UK National Accounts. In addition, many other government departments use LCF data as a basis for policy making, for example in the areas of housing and transport. The Department for Environment, Food and Rural Affairs (Defra) uses LCF data to report on trends in food consumption and nutrient intake within the UK. Users of the LCF outside government include independent research institutes, academic researchers and business and market researchers. Like all surveys based on a sample of the population, its results are subject to sampling variability and potentially to some bias due to non-response. The results of the survey are published in an annual report the latest being The Family Spending 2015 edition. The report includes a list of definitions used in the survey, items on which information is collected, and a brief account of the fieldwork procedure.

8.1 Distribution of total income before and after tax by gender, 2012-13

Taxpayers only

Numbers: thousands; Amounts: £ million

Total

Range of total income (lower limit) £	Before tax, by range of total income before tax				After tax, by range of total income after tax			
	No. of taxpayers	Total income before tax	Total tax	Total income after tax	No. of taxpayers	Total income before tax	Total tax	Total income after tax
8,105 [a]	1,960	17,600	337	17,300	2,390	22,000	513	21,500
10,000	2,640	29,200	1,130	28,100	3,240	37,600	1,750	35,900
12,000	4,050	54,500	3,570	50,900	4,850	70,600	5,350	65,300
15,000	5,700	99,200	9,450	89,700	6,260	121,000	12,800	108,000
20,000	7,210	177,000	21,900	155,000	7,100	199,000	26,500	173,000
30,000	6,080	231,000	34,000	197,000	5,030	226,000	37,200	188,000
50,000	1,500	87,000	17,700	69,300	948	72,800	17,800	55,000
70,000	746	61,600	15,500	46,100	458	52,900	15,800	37,100
100,000	394	47,200	14,300	32,900	193	34,700	11,800	22,800
150,000	135	23,000	7,710	15,300	54	14,800	5,570	9,240
200,000	88	21,100	7,800	13,300	36	14,500	5,780	8,680
300,000	46	17,500	6,980	10,500	20	12,900	5,370	7,530
500,000	24	16,300	6,900	9,430	10	11,600	5,000	6,590
1,000,000	11	22,800	9,910	12,900	4	13,900	5,830	8,040
All ranges	30,600	904,000	157,000	747,000	30,600	904,000	157,000	747,000

Male

Range of total income (lower limit) £	Before tax, by range of total income before tax				After tax, by range of total income after tax			
	No. of taxpayers	Total income before tax	Total tax	Total income after tax	No. of taxpayers	Total income before tax	Total tax	Total income after tax
8,105 [a]	823	7,360	147	7,210	996	9,130	222	8,910
10,000	1,110	12,300	468	11,800	1,390	16,200	744	15,500
12,000	1,900	25,600	1,650	24,000	2,360	34,400	2,590	31,800
15,000	3,000	52,200	4,930	47,300	3,450	67,000	7,030	60,000
20,000	4,290	105,000	13,100	92,300	4,380	124,000	16,500	107,000
30,000	3,960	151,000	22,400	129,000	3,390	154,000	25,700	128,000
50,000	1,090	63,300	12,900	50,300	709	54,600	13,400	41,200
70,000	563	46,500	11,800	34,800	358	41,500	12,500	29,000
100,000	312	37,400	11,400	26,000	157	28,400	9,730	18,700
150,000	111	18,900	6,340	12,600	46	12,700	4,790	7,900
200,000	74	17,700	6,570	11,200	31	12,600	5,070	7,560
300,000	40	15,300	6,130	9,170	18	11,500	4,780	6,680
500,000	21	14,500	6,140	8,400	9	10,600	4,600	6,030
1,000,000	10	20,900	9,070	11,800	3	12,700	5,310	7,340
All ranges	17,300	589,000	113,000	476,000	17,300	589,000	113,000	476,000

8.1 Distribution of total income before and after tax by gender, 2012-13

Taxpayers only   Numbers: thousands; Amounts: £ million

Range of total income (lower limit) £	Female							
	Before tax, by range of total income before tax				After tax, by range of total income after tax			
	No. of taxpayers	Total income before tax	Total tax	Total income after tax	No. of taxpayers	Total income before tax	Total tax	Total income after tax
8,105 [a]	1,140	10,200	190	10,100	1,390	12,800	291	12,600
10,000	1,530	16,900	666	16,200	1,850	21,400	1,010	20,400
12,000	2,150	28,900	1,920	26,900	2,490	36,200	2,770	33,500
15,000	2,700	46,900	4,530	42,400	2,810	54,200	5,770	48,500
20,000	2,920	71,100	8,780	62,300	2,710	75,800	10,000	65,800
30,000	2,120	79,700	11,600	68,100	1,630	71,900	11,500	60,300
50,000	412	23,800	4,730	19,000	239	18,200	4,350	13,800
70,000	183	15,100	3,740	11,300	100	11,400	3,310	8,080
100,000	83	9,850	2,940	6,910	35	6,280	2,100	4,170
150,000	24	4,140	1,370	2,770	8	2,120	779	1,340
200,000	14	3,380	1,240	2,140	5	1,830	711	1,120
300,000	6	2,150	852	1,300	2	1,450	599	849
500,000	3	1,790	754	1,040	1	958	401	557
1,000,000	1	1,920	836	1,090	-	1,230	524	701
All ranges	13,300	316,000	44,100	272,000	13,300	316,000	44,100	272,000

Source: Survey of Personal Incomes 2012-13

Footnote

(a) Can include some taxpayers who are not entitled to a Personal Allowance whose total income can be less than the Personal Allowance of £8,105 for 2012-13 (see Annex B for details).

Notes on the Table

1. This table only covers individuals with some liability to tax.

2. It should be noted that individuals may not necessarily fall into the same total income range for before and after tax breakdowns. Total income before tax is used to assign people to an income range for columns 2 to 5, whereas total income after the deduction of tax is used to assign individuals to an income band for columns 6 to 9.

3. For more information about the SPI and symbols used in this table, please refer to Personal Income Statistics release:
https://www.gov.uk/government/collections/personal-incomes-statistics

8.2 Summary of the effects of taxes and benefits, by household type,[1] 2013/14

	Retired households					Non-Retired households		
	1 adult Men	1 adult Women	All 1 adult	2 or more adults		1 adult Men[2]	1 adult Women[2]	All 1 adult[2]
Average per household (£ per year)								
Original income	8 080	6 484	6 977	17 056		23 356	18 344	21 233
plus Cash benefits	9 024	9 223	9 162	12 707		2 648	3 008	2 800
Gross income	17 104	15 706	16 138	29 762		26 004	21 352	24 033
less Direct taxes and employees' NIC	1 832	1 576	1 655	3 869		5 662	4 317	5 092
Disposable income	15 273	14 131	14 483	25 893		20 342	17 035	18 941
Equivalised[3] disposable income	*22 867*	*21 184*	*21 704*	*25 130*		*30 514*	*25 553*	*28 412*
less Indirect taxes	2 781	2 314	2 458	5 916		3 834	3 588	3 730
Post-tax income	12 491	11 817	12 025	19 977		16 508	13 447	15 211
plus Benefits in kind	4 602	5 044	4 907	7 564		1 467	1 565	1 509
Final income	17 094	16 860	16 932	27 541		17 975	15 012	16 720

	Non-Retired households							
	2 adults[2]	3 or more adults[2]	1 adult with children[3]	2 adults with 1 child	2 adults with 2 children	2 adults with 3 or more children	3 or more adults with children	All house- holds
Average per household (£ per year)								
Original income	46 499	55 499	13 208	45 992	55 043	40 190	49 361	33 155
plus Cash benefits	2 859	3 930	10 114	3 787	3 948	9 912	7 271	6 045
Gross income	49 358	59 429	23 322	49 779	58 990	50 103	56 631	39 200
less Direct taxes and employees' NIC	10 464	11 466	2 306	10 138	13 186	9 041	10 111	7 415
Disposable income	38 894	47 963	21 016	39 641	45 804	41 062	46 521	31 786
Equivalised[4] disposable income	*38 894*	*32 350*	*20 269*	*32 107*	*31 722*	*23 912*	*25 661*	*29 477*
less Indirect taxes	7 064	9 681	4 217	6 681	7 628	7 589	9 633	5 987
Post-tax income	31 830	38 282	16 799	32 960	38 176	33 473	36 888	25 799
plus Benefits in kind	3 277	6 167	11 345	8 525	13 686	20 760	15 322	6 894
Final income	35 107	44 450	28 145	41 485	51 861	54 233	52 209	32 692

Source: Office for National Statistics

Notes:

1 See Methodology and Coherence section for definitions of retired households, adults and children.

2 Without children.

3 Children are defined as people aged under 16 or aged between 16 and 19, not married nor in a Civil Partnership, nor living with a partner; and living with parent(s)/guardian(s); and and receiving non-advanced further education or in unwaged-government training.

4 Using the modified-OECD scale.

8.3 Income and sources of income, 1970 to 2014

United Kingdom

	Weighted number of house-holds	Number of house-holds in the sample	Weekly household income[1]				Source of income					
			Current prices		Constant prices[2]		Wages and salaries	Self employ-ment	Invest-ments	Annuities and pensions[3]	Social security benefits[4]	Other sources
			Dispo-sable	Gross	Dispo-sable	Gross						
	(000s)	Number	£	£	£	£	Percentage of gross weekly household income					
1970		6,390	28	34	294	354	77	7	4	3	9	1
1980		6,940	115	140	351	429	75	6	3	3	13	1
1990		7,050	258	317	462	568	67	10	6	5	11	1
1995-96		6,800	307	381	454	563	64	9	5	7	14	2
1996-97		6,420	325	397	470	574	65	9	4	7	14	1
1997-98		6,410	343	421	488	599	67	8	4	7	13	1
1998-99[5]	24,660	6,630	371	457	519	640	68	8	4	7	12	1
1999-2000	25,340	7,100	391	480	541	664	66	10	5	7	12	1
2000-01	25,030	6,640	409	503	562	690	67	9	4	7	12	1
2001-02[6]	24,450	7,470	447	547	604	740	68	8	4	7	12	1
2002-03	24,350	6,930	453	552	606	739	68	8	3	7	12	1
2003-04	24,670	7,050	464	570	613	753	67	9	3	7	13	1
2004-05	24,430	6,800	489	601	636	781	68	8	3	7	13	1
2005-06	24,800	6,790	500	616	637	785	67	8	3	7	13	1
2006[7]	24,790	6,650	521	642	652	803	67	9	3	7	12	1
2006[8]	25,440	6,650	515	635	645	794	67	9	3	7	13	1
2007	25,350	6,140	534	659	653	806	67	8	4	7	13	1
2008	25,690	5,850	582	713	686	841	67	9	4	7	12	1
2009	25,980	5,830	558	683	645	788	66	8	3	8	14	1
2010	26,320	5,260	578	700	647	783	65	10	2	8	14	1
2011	26,110	5,690	587	713	628	763	66	7	2	9	14	1
2012	26,410	5,600	597	720	621	749	65	8	3	9	14	1
2013[9]	26,840	5,140	614	739	624	750	65	7	3	9	14	1
2014	26,600	5,130	653	780	653	780	65	7	4	9	14	2

Please see background notes for symbols and conventions used in this report.

1 Does not include imputed income from owner-occupied and rent-free households.

2 Constant prices have been deflated using the CPI All Items Index for years from 1998. Before 1988, the index is based on modelled or indicative data.

3 Other than social security benefits.

4 Excluding housing benefit and council tax benefit (rates rebate in Northern Ireland) and their predecessors in earlier years - see survey methodology.

5 Based on weighted data from 1998-99 onwards.

6 From 2001-02 onwards, weighting is based on the population estimates from the 2001 Census.

7 From 1998-99 to this version of 2006, figures shown are based on weighted data using non-response weights based on the 1991 Census and population figures from the 1991 and 2001 Censuses.

8 From this version of 2006 until 2012, figures shown are based on weighted data using non-response weights and population figures based on the 2001 Census.

9 From 2013, figures are based on weighted data using non-response weights based on the 2001 Census and population estimates based on the 2011 Census.

ONS, Family Spending 2014, © Crown copyright 2015

8.4 Household expenditure at 2014 prices[1]

UK, survey year ending March 2002 to 2014

	2001-02	2002-03	2003-04	2004-05	2005-06	2006[2]	2006[3]	2007	2008	2009	2010	2011	2012	2013[4]	2014
Weighted number of households (thousands)	24,450	24,350	24,670	24,430	24,800	24,790	25,440	25,350	25,690	25,980	26,320	26,110	26,410	26,840	26,600
Total number of households in sample	7,470	6,930	7,050	6,800	6,790	6,650	6,650	6,140	5,850	5,830	5,260	5,690	5,600	5,140	5,130
Total number of persons in sample	18,120	16,590	16,970	16,260	16,090	15,850	15,850	14,650	13,830	13,740	12,180	13,430	13,180	12,120	12,120
Total number of adults in sample	13,450	12,450	12,620	12,260	12,170	12,000	12,000	11,220	10,640	10,650	9,430	10,330	10,200	9,350	9,440
Weighted average number of persons per household	2.4	2.4	2.4	2.4	2.4	2.4	2.3	2.4	2.4	2.3	2.3	2.4	2.3	2.4	2.4

Commodity or service	Average weekly household expenditure (£)														
1 Food and non-alcoholic drinks	62.00	63.50	63.50	65.10	65.00	65.70	64.90	64.50	62.30	60.80	60.00	58.60	58.80	58.70	58.80
2 Alcoholic drinks, tobacco and narcotics	19.10	18.70	18.90	17.90	16.70	16.90	16.80	16.40	15.20	15.10	15.10	14.10	13.90	12.60	12.30
3 Clothing and footwear	15.50	16.20	17.10	18.90	19.00	20.00	19.70	19.60	20.60	21.70	24.40	22.20	23.70	22.70	23.70
4 Housing (net)[5], fuel and power	63.50	63.80	66.10	65.60	67.30	67.40	67.30	69.90	65.90	68.30	71.70	71.20	72.90	76.60	72.70
5 Household goods and services	36.30	36.10	37.50	37.90	36.10	36.60	36.20	36.50	35.10	31.50	34.40	28.50	29.00	33.40	35.40
6 Health	6.50	6.70	6.80	6.60	7.10	7.40	7.30	7.00	6.10	6.10	5.60	7.20	6.70	6.40	7.10
7 Transport	88.20	88.80	88.50	83.90	83.40	82.30	80.70	79.50	77.30	70.70	72.40	68.10	65.00	70.60	74.80
8 Communication	11.50	11.60	12.30	13.00	13.40	13.20	13.10	13.90	14.30	13.80	14.70	14.40	14.40	14.60	15.50
9 Recreation and culture	54.20	55.80	57.50	59.90	59.20	60.70	59.70	60.10	63.30	60.20	59.30	65.20	62.70	64.40	68.80
10 Education	15.60	13.70	13.00	15.40	14.80	15.30	14.80	12.70	10.40	10.80	14.80	9.90	8.70	9.70	9.80
11 Restaurants and hotels	49.70	51.00	48.80	49.00	48.20	48.60	48.20	46.10	45.00	44.70	44.40	43.00	42.60	41.40	42.50
12 Miscellaneous goods and services	41.50	43.70	43.20	43.40	41.30	41.70	41.30	40.00	39.50	38.00	38.00	39.90	38.80	39.10	40.00
1-12 All expenditure groups	463.60	469.70	473.20	476.60	471.40	475.70	470.10	466.20	455.00	441.70	455.00	442.30	437.10	450.30	461.20
13 Other expenditure items[6]	78.90	76.40	77.40	77.70	80.70	79.00	76.90	72.50	76.00	78.90	72.50	73.20	70.30	73.60	70.10
Total expenditure	**542.50**	**546.20**	**550.60**	**554.30**	**552.10**	**554.70**	**547.00**	**538.70**	**530.90**	**520.70**	**527.50**	**515.40**	**507.40**	**523.90**	**531.30**

Average weekly expenditure per person (£)															
Total expenditure	228.30	229.30	233.60	232.20	234.20	234.60	234.00	228.60	225.20	222.50	226.20	218.90	216.60	222.20	221.80

Average weekly household income (£)															
Gross income (£)	740	739	753	781	785	803	794	806	841	788	783	763	749	750	780
Disposable income (£)	604	606	613	636	637	652	645	653	686	645	647	628	621	624	653

Note: The commodity and service categories are not comparable to those in publications before 2001-02.

1 Figures have been deflated to 2014 prices using deflators specific to the COICOP category.

2 From 2001-02 to this version of 2006, figures shown are based on weighted data using non-response weights based on the 1991 Census and population figures from the 1991 and 2001 Censuses.

3 From this version of 2006 until 2012, figures shown are based on weighted data using non-response weights and population figures based on the 2001 Census

4 From 2013, figures are based on weighted data using non-response weights based on the 2001 Census and population estimates based on the 2011 Census

5 Excluding mortgage interest payments, council tax and Northern Ireland rates.

6 An improvement to the imputation of mortgage interest payments has been implemented for 2006 data onwards. This means there is a slight discontinuity between 2006 and earlier years.

ONS, Family Spending 2014, © Crown copyright 2015

8.5 Percentage of households with durable goods
United Kingdom, 1998/99 to 2014

	Car/ van	Central heating[1]	Washing machine	Tumble dryer	Dish- washer	Micro- wave	Tele- phone	Mobile phone	DVD Player	Home computer	Internet connection
1998-99 [2]	72	89	92	51	23	79	95	27	--	33	10
1999-2000	71	90	91	52	23	80	95	44	--	38	19
2000-01	72	91	93	53	25	84	93	47	--	44	32
2001-02 [3]	74	92	93	54	27	86	94	64	--	49	39
2002-03	74	93	94	56	29	87	94	70	31	55	45
2003-04	75	94	94	57	31	89	92	76	50	58	49
2004-05	75	95	95	58	33	90	93	78	67	62	53
2005-06	74	94	95	58	35	91	92	79	79	65	55
2006 [4]	76	95	96	59	38	91	91	80	83	67	59
2006 [5]	74	95	96	59	37	91	91	79	83	67	58
2007	75	95	96	57	37	91	89	78	86	70	61
2008	74	95	96	59	37	92	90	79	88	72	66
2009	76	95	96	58	39	93	88	81	90	75	71
2010	75	96	96	57	40	92	87	80	88	77	73
2011	75	96	97	56	41	92	88	87	88	79	77
2012	75	96	97	56	42	93	88	87	87	81	79
2013	76	96	97	56	42	92	89	92	85	83	82
2014	76	96	97	56	44	92	88	94	83	85	84

-- Data not available.

1 Full or partial.

2 From this version of 1998-99, figures shown are based on weighted data and including children's expenditure.

3 From 2001-02 onwards, weighting is based on the population figures from the 2001 census.

4 From 1998-99 to this version of 2006, figures shown are based on weighted data using non-response weights based on the 1991 Census and population figures from the 1991 and 2001 Census.

5 From this version of 2006, figures shown are based on weighted data using updated weights, with non-response weights and population figures based on the 2001 Census.

ONS, Family Spending 2014, © Crown copyright 2015

this page is intentionally blank

Lifestyles

Chapter 9

Lifestyles

Expenditure by the Department for Culture, Media and Sport (Table 9.1)
The figures in this table are taken from the department's Annual Report and are outturn figures for each of the headings shown (later figures are the estimated outturn). The department's planned expenditure for future years is also shown.

International tourism and holidays abroad (Tables 9.8 and 9.9)
The figures in these tables are compiled using data from the International Passenger Survey (IPS).   A holiday abroad is a visit made for holiday purposes. Business trips and visits to friends and relatives are excluded.

Domestic tourism (Table 9.10)
The figures in this table are compiled using data from the Visit England. Data includes total number of trips taken as well as number of bednights and expenditure, as well as average trip totals.

Gambling (Table 9.12)
The National Lottery figures in this table are the latest figures released by The National Lottery Commission at the time of going to press. They represent ticket sales (money staked1) for each of the games which comprise the lottery. The figures have been adjusted to real terms using the Retail Prices Index (RPI).
The National Lottery started on the 19 November 1994 with the first instant ticket being sold in March 1995. The sum of the individual games may not agree exactly with the figures for total sales which also include the Easy Play games which started in 1998 but were dropped in 1999. The other gambling figures in this table are obtained from the Gambling Commission (formerly the Gaming Board) and HM Revenue & Customs (HMRC). The figures have been adjusted to real terms using the Retail Prices Index (RPI).

9.1 Expenditure by the Department for Culture, Media and Sport

Resource DEL (£'000s)	2007-08 Outturn	2008-09 Outturn	2009-10 Outturn	2010-11 Outturn	2011-12 Outturn	2012-13 Outturn	2013-14 Outturn	2014-15 Outturn	2015-16 Plans
Support for the Museums and Galleries sector	12,619	4,230	4,170	3,831	13,336	12,664	16,267	16,003	17,167
Museums and Galleries sponsored ALBs (net)	334,044	278,988	357,425	361,853	306,816	359,754	354,959	329,932	375,872
Libraries sponsored ALBs (net)	99,452	104,277	103,587	106,243	113,172	110,753	101,374	98,369	109,040
Museums, libraries and archives council (net)	59,804	61,838	58,376	64,474	43,741	8,632	-	-	-
Support for the Arts sector	3,088	(1,273)	(3,821)	(1,737)	2,373	(53,218)	(67,219)	(58,465)	(78,678)
Arts and culture ALBs (net)	402,293	413,791	420,612	420,204	380,835	446,545	442,838	433,475	442,554
Support for the Sports sector	8,525	2,203	8,801	1,098	5,394	6,847	21,147	18,075	7,432
Sport sponsored ALBs (net)	141,744	161,154	151,945	148,362	136,077	144,942	114,967	113,206	116,512
Ceremonial and support for the Heritage sector	19,064	20,633	18,555	22,200	13,946	22,161	16,690	29,456	39,778
Heritage sponsored ALBs (net)	141,608	151,149	151,825	144,270	130,737	97,567	92,975	112,768	91,482
The Royal Parks	18,999	20,092	18,487	15,759	17,162	16,955	13,637	14,600	13,687
Support for the Tourism sector	1,985	2,230	127	2,362	16	70	10	(200)	-
Tourism sponsored ALBs (net)	53,848	52,985	50,450	39,479	45,494	47,824	48,200	46,502	33,902
Support for the Broadcasting and Media sector	4,417	2,722	2,624	1,561	3,218	15,161	12,063	34,551	7,118
Broadcasting and Media sponsored ALBs (net)	118,109	129,542	136,260	138,139	170,893	183,597	96,731	84,181	114,211
Administration and Research	53,309	56,476	56,448	53,406	58,429	51,679	34,863	39,211	48,026
Support for Horseracing and the Gambling sector	(11,518)	(5,121)	(3,732)	(4,020)	2,700	(1,560)	(1,603)	(843)	(1,817)
Gambling Commission(net)	16,610	7,927	5,801	4,107	4,722	1,959	3,097	1,449	3,617
Olympics - legacy programmes	459	(67)	524	13,022	65,868	501,628	(18,083)	(33,823)	13,186
London 2012(net)	24,130	(2,703)	(35,363)	(18,700)	45,399	1,575,240	(29,477)	55,715	-
Government Equalities Office	5,969	10,333	13,998	11,611	7,080	15,283	7,298	12,059	11,531
Equalitiy and Human Rights Commission (net)	74,129	59,395	55,700	52,800	42,982	26,683	19,230	19,388	22,109
Spectrum Management Receipts	-	-	-	-	-	(60,142)	(54,535)	(52,594)	(61,800)
Total resource DEL	**1,582,687**	**1,530,801**	**1,572,799**	**1,580,324**	**1,610,390**	**3,531,024**	**1,225,429**	**1,323,015**	**1,324,929**

Resource DEL (£'000s)	2007-08 Outturn	2008-09 Outturn	2009-10 Outturn	2010-11 Outturn	2011-12 Outturn	2012-13 Outturn	2013-14 Outturn	2014-15 Outturn	2015-16 Plans
Total resource DEL (brought forward)	1,582,687	1,530,801	1,572,799	1,580,324	1,610,390	3,531,024	1,225,429	1,323,015	1,324,929
Of which:									
Staff costs	632,674	585,335	604,087	606,177	648,611	593,804	631,494	559,636	222,207
Purchase of goods and services	817,214	852,475	795,638	745,002	931,655	849,574	1,088,665	917,056	530,085
Income from sales of goods and services	(400,225)	(435,149)	(371,751)	(364,397)	(402,992)	(273,532)	(474,637)	(105,758)	(24,500)
Current grants to local government (net)	48,672	91,378	38,415	57,507	(26,931)	10,603	(7,008)	27,794	-
Current grants to persons and non-profit bodies (net)	575,071	580,437	649,477	606,302	585,540	786,028	502,356	541,107	533,585
Current grants abroad (net)	(12,410)	906	493	823	136	-	(1,528)	13,269	-
Subsidies to private sector companies	-	-	-	-	-	-	157	-	-
Subsidies to public corporations	-	-	-	82,590	74,880	522,976	10,026	54,411	(10)
Rentals	-	-	-	800	6,346	3,545	33,199	24,410	-
Depreciation [1]	107,081	28,571	115,617	109,300	114,120	1,443,884	157,153	104,391	185,328
Change in pension scheme liabilities[2]	-	-	-	100	471	12	(44)	-	-
Other resource	(185,390)	(173,152)	(259,177)	(263,880)	(321,446)	(405,870)	(714,404)	(813,301)	(121,766)

Resource AME (£'000s)	2007-08 Outturn	2008-09 Outturn	2009-10 Outturn	2010-11 Outturn	2011-12 Outturn	2012-13 Outturn	2013-14 Outturn	2014-15 Outturn	2015-16 Plans
British Broadcasting Corporation(net)	2,962,800	2,868,987	3,020,000	3,121,360	2,608,460	3,224,802	3,050,735	3,386,240	3,398,064
Provisions, Impairments and other AME spend	6,786	(276)	13,027	96,255	35,957	19,449	16,854	(27,281)	44,067
Lottery Grants	882,351	1,010,728	1,000,814	994,845	1,334,509	1,450,239	1,352,673	1,594,409	1,261,800
London 2012(net)	(507)	13,667	26,057	156,592	(155,839)	(30,996)	102,138	-	-
Gambling levy bodies	-	-	-	-	(30,535)	(10,268)	(2,721)	4,021	-
Total resource AME	**3,851,430**	**3,893,106**	**4,059,898**	**4,369,052**	**3,792,552**	**4,653,226**	**4,519,679**	**4,957,389**	**4,703,931**

9.1 Expenditure by the Department for Culture, Media and Sport

Resource AME (£'000s)	2007-08 Outturn	2008-09 Outturn	2009-10 Outturn	2010-11 Outturn	2011-12 Outturn	2012-13 Outturn	2013-14 Outturn	2014-15 Outturn	2015-16 Plans
Total resource AME	3,851,430	3,893,106	4,059,898	4,369,052	3,792,552	4,653,226	4,519,679	4,957,389	4,703,931
Of which:									
Staff costs	1,097,800	974,130	1,248,000	1,053,000	1,199,758	921,649	929,732	1,041,638	1,419,824
Purchase of goods and services	2,375,000	2,410,870	2,279,000	2,630,510	1,973,067	2,812,655	2,470,057	2,695,639	2,484,206
Income from sales of goods and services	-	-	-	-	-	(328,808)	-	-	(180,902)
Current grants to local government (net)	43,953	102,440	79,898	73,666	57,497	20,812	34,896	32,218	65,754
Current grants to persons and non-profit bodies (net)	729,672	784,288	784,245	761,179	961,726	557,133	1,245,777	1,470,874	1,196,046
Subsidies to public corporations	-	-	-	-	-	-	24	4,823	-
Rentals	-	-	-	-	-	80,775	104,496	106,848	-
Depreciation [1]	35,000	84,787	93,000	69,585	124,644	237,372	278,390	211,087	181,861
Take up of provisions	12,911	17,283	41,771	292,898	(96,968)	592,197	29,422	21,713	1,033
Release of provision	(6,632)	(3,892)	(2,687)	(6,041)	(16,345)	(40,604)	(11,576)	(15,813)	-
Change in pension scheme liabilities[2]	-	-	-	-	-	162,422	178,831	192,115	-
Unwinding of the discount rate on pension scheme liabilities[2]	-	-	-	-	560,222	730,035	82,412	70,459	10,298
Release of provisions covering payments of pension benefits	-	-	-	-	-	(234)	(14,336)	(11,769)	-
Other resource	(436,274)	(476,800)	(463,329)	(505,745)	(971,049)	(1,092,178)	(808,446)	862,443	(474,189)
Total resource budget	5,434,117	5,423,907	5,632,697	5,949,376	5,402,942	8,184,250	5,745,108	6,280,404	6,028,860
Of which: Depreciation[1]	142,081	113,358	208,617	178,885	238,764	1,681,256	435,543	315,478	367,189

Source: Department for Culture, Media and Sport

1 Depreciation includes impairment

2 Pension schemes report under IAS19 Employee Benefits accounting requirements. These figures, therefore, include cash payments made and contributions received, as well as certain non-cash items.

9.2 Estimates of Average Issue Readership of National Daily Newspapers
rolling 12 months' periods ending

000's

		2011 Mar	2011 Jun	2011 Sept	2011 Dec	2012 Mar	2012 Jun	2012 Sep	2012 Dec	2013 Mar	2013 Jun	2013 Sep	2013 Dec	2014 Mar	2014 Jun	2014 Sep	2014 Dec	2015 Mar
The Sun	WSDV	7,722	7,683	7,652	7,480	7,331	7,244	7,084	7,007	6,707	6,435	6,123	5,841	5,685	5,508	5,421	5,347	5,178
Daily Mail	WSEI	4,775	4,622	4,561	4,455	4,426	4,385	4,320	4,258	4,245	4,298	4,269	4,215	4,074	3,866	3,833	3,745	3,704
Daily Mirror/Daily Record	WSEH	4,026	3,997	4,114	4,053	4,046	3,995	3,849	3,773	3,614	3,512	3,357	3,167	2,975	2,893	2,908	2,881	2,796
Daily Mirror	WSEM	3,163	3,163	3,251	3,200	3,196	3,178	3,062	2,995	2,856	2,775	2,639	2,456	2,309	2,230	2,251	2,281	2,211
The Daily Telegraph	WSEN	1,693	1,688	1,584	1,562	1,468	1,387	1,394	1,346	1,352	1,348	1,312	1,318	1,313	1,261	1,237	1,192	1,119
The Times	WSES	1,552	1,486	1,435	1,385	1,359	1,302	1,310	1,311	1,300	1,261	1,240	1,147	1,155	1,110	1,047	1,062	995
Daily Express	WSEP	1,504	1,457	1,439	1,417	1,329	1,304	1,265	1,192	1,157	1,123	1,114	1,095	1,114	1,097	1,079	1,079	993
Daily Star	WSEQ	1,488	1,498	1,506	1,452	1,409	1,439	1,421	1,358	1,279	1,211	1,158	1,113	1,090	1,039	978	1,010	943
The Guardian	WSET	1,154	1,143	1,119	1,120	1,058	1,081	1,062	1,050	1,027	935	890	843	793	748	744	748	761
i		-	-	-	-	-	564	561	612	579	545	568	559	563	584	573	579	549
The Independent	WSEU	562	535	541	530	533	537	506	490	443	397	393	348	309	261	264	262	272
Financial Times[1]	WSEY	367	344	325	317	301	300	285	319	312	305	296	235	-	-	-	-	-
Any national morning	WSEZ	19,751	19,481	19,391	19,124	18,679	18,466	18,069	17,825	17,403	20,852	20,181	19,347	19,092	18,384	18,106	17,929	17,331

Source: National Readership Surveys Ltd.

1. NRS ceased to publish estimates for Financial Times as of 2014 data, so data cannot be provided for March 2014 onwards.

9.3 Jobs in the Creative Economy in 2013, by gender

	Male	Female	% Female
Advertising and marketing	271,000	212,000	43.9%
Architecture	99,000	37,000	27.4%
Crafts	75,000	21,000	21.9%
Design: product, graphic and fashion design	95,000	82,000	46.4%
Film, TV, video, radio and photography	166,000	93,000	36.1%
IT, software and computer services	673,000	152,000	18.4%
Museums, galleries and libraries	33,000	76,000	69.5%
Music, performing and visual arts	151,000	148,000	49.5%
Publishing	116,000	115,000	49.8%
Creative Economy Total	1,678,000	937,000	35.8%

Source: Department for Culture, Media and Sport

9.4 Selected activities performed in free time, by age, 2014/15 England

	Age					All aged 16+
	16 -24	**25-44**	**45-64**	**65-74**	**75+**	
	%	%	%	%	%	%
Watching TV	89.2	89.1	91.6	93.8	94.3	90.9
Spending time with friends/family	93.6	90.3	87.6	89.2	83.1	89.1
Listening to music	90.0	79.5	78.3	73.5	66.7	78.7
Shopping	76.2	75.6	77.5	79.9	77.0	76.9
Eating out at restaurants	76.1	76.6	75.2	74.8	63.3	74.6
Internet/emailing	88.2	83.0	72.7	56.0	29.0	72.1
Reading	58.8	63.8	71.2	79.4	74.0	68.2
Days out or visits to places	66.9	73.3	68.8	70.7	53.0	68.7
Sport/exercise	64.5	63.2	56.7	53.9	35.5	57.6
Going to the cinema	75.2	58.6	48.6	38.8	20.6	51.9
Going to pubs/bars/clubs	62.2	53.2	53.3	43.8	27.9	50.9
Gardening	13.1	43.3	62.8	72.5	59.1	50.0
Theatre/music concerts	44.3	41.5	50.9	51.0	32.3	45.1
DIY	23.3	44.6	49.1	45.0	26.3	41.2
Visiting historic sites	25.5	41.0	48.8	51.7	29.2	41.3
Visiting museums/galleries	27.1	38.1	43.3	45.7	26.8	37.9
Playing computer games	57.3	37.3	20.6	14.0	5.6	29.2
Arts and crafts	21.0	24.9	22.8	28.1	19.2	23.5
Playing a musical instrument	16.4	10.7	9.5	8.3	4.8	10.3

Source: Taking Part 2014/15. Department for Culture, Media and Sport

9.5 Films

United Kingdom

Numbers and £ million

	Production of UK films[1,4]		Expenditure on feature films			
	Films produced in the UK (numbers)	Production costs (current prices)	UK box office	Video [2] rental	Video[2] retail[3]	Video on Demand
	KWGD	KWGE	KWHU	KWHV	KWHW	
1998	83	389	547	437	453	33
1999	92	507	563	408	451	40
2000	80	578	583	444	601	50
2001	74	379	645	494	821	65
2002	119	551	755	494	1,175	63
2003	198	1,119	742	462	1,392	68
2004	173	875	770	476	1,557	73
2005	174	582	770	389	1,399	74
2006	139	826	762	327	1,302	67
2007	136	836	821	280	1,440	75
2008	143	721.6 [4]	850	265	1,454	101
2009	163	1123.0 [4]	944	263	1,311	120
2010	141	1292.8 [4]	988	253	1,267	130
2011	166	1274.0 [4]	1,040	246	1,165	150
2012	173	994 [4]	1,099	229	968	236
2013	169	1172.0	1,083	149	940	323

Source: BFI Statistical Yearbooks 2014-2016

1 Includes films with a production budget of £500,000 or more.

2 Video includes only rental and retail of physical discs, and does not include downloads.

3 In 2005 the British Video Association changed its methodology for producing market value which has necessitated a change to historical figures quoted.

4. Prior to 2010, the Research and Statistics Unit tracked all features shooting in the UK with a minimum budget of £500,000. However, evidence from a variety of sources (data on British film certification and the 2008 UK Film Council report Low and Micro-Budget Film Production in the UK) revealed a substantial number of films produced below this budget level. In order to broaden the evidence base, production tracking was extended to include feature films with budgets under £500,000 and data was collected from 2008 onwards.

Figures not adjusted for inflation

9.6 Box office top 20 films released in the UK and Republic of Ireland, 2013

	Title	Country of origin	Box office gross (£ million)	Number of opening weekend cinemas	Opening weekend gross (£ million)	Distributor
1	Despicable Me 2*	USA	47.5	534	14.8	Universal
2	The Hobbit: The Desolation of Smaug*	USA/NZ	42.9	585	9.3	Warner Bros
3	Les Misérables	UK/USA	40.8	590	8.1	Universal
4	Frozen*	USA	38.6	507	4.7	Walt Disney
5	Iron Man 3	USA/China	37	555	13.7	Walt Disney
6	The Hunger Games: Catching Fire*	USA	34.1	555	12.2	Lionsgate
7	Gravity*	UK/USA	31.1	540	6.2	Warner Bros
8	Monsters University*	USA	30.7	525	3.5	Walt Disney
9	Man of Steel	USA/Can	30	573	11.2	Warner Bros
10	The Croods*	USA	26.8	524	5.4	20th Century Fox
11	Star Trek Into Darkness	USA	25.8	556	8.4	Paramount
12	Fast & Furious 6	UK/USA	25.3	462	8.7	Universal
13	Wreck-It Ralph	USA	23.8	501	4.5	Walt Disney
14	Thor: The Dark World*	UK/USA	20.1	522	8.7	Walt Disney
15	The Hangover Part III	USA	19.3	473	6	Warner Bros
16	Captain Phillips*	UK/USA	16.1	536	3.5	Sony Pictures
17	Django Unchained	USA	15.7	445	2.8	Sony Pictures
18	The Great Gatsby	Aus/USA	15.7	524	4.1	Warner Bros
19	Oz: The Great and Powerful	USA	15.3	530	3.7	Walt Disney
20	World War Z	UK/USA	14.6	488	4.5	Paramount

Source: Rentrak, BFI RSU analysis

Notes:

Box office gross = cumulative total up to 23 February 2014.

* Film still on release on 23 February 2014.

9.7 Full year accommodation usage figures by visitors from overseas for 2004-2014 (Excluding 2013)

Data	Accommodation	2004	2005	2006	2007	2008	2009	2010	2011	2012	2014
Total Visits (000s)	All staying visits	25,677	28,038	30,654	30,871	30,142	28,208	28,300	29,197	29,282	32,613
	Bed & Breakfast	1,177	1,221	1,242	1,174	1,118	1,065	1,083	996	1,003	1,043
	Camping/mobile home	295	381	425	394	298	333	312	302	284	335
	Free guest with relatives or friends	10,174	11,144	12,081	11,944	12,056	11,165	10,570	10,646	10,811	11,120
	Holiday village/Centre	37	60	44	67	59	77	41	49	59	170
	Hostel/university/school	949	1,096	1,167	1,203	1,138	1,218	1,102	1,180	1,174	1,144
	Hotel/guest house	11,451	12,465	13,939	14,156	13,472	13,001	13,841	14,446	14,406	16,383
	Other	1,815	1,855	2,143	2,073	1,930	1,470	1,518	1,360	1,439	1,971
	Own home	413	412	466	446	418	385	358	392	364	382
	Paying guest family or friends house	610	616	595	567	650	461	465	577	537	583
	Rented house	740	806	832	836	868	934	882	958	1,002	1,361
Total Nights (000s)	All staying visits	227,406	249,181	273,417	251,522	245,775	229,391	227,960	234,363	230,149	264,366
	Bed & Breakfast	8,576	7,840	7,411	7,078	6,500	5,804	6,341	5,639	5,307	5,809
	Camping/mobile home	3,015	4,705	4,350	4,182	2,988	3,296	2,904	3,229	2,757	3,047
	Free guest with relatives or friends	113,736	121,487	133,209	121,272	122,898	111,947	107,642	108,703	107,575	111,173
	Holiday village/Centre	222	346	336	576	329	448	321	321	393	1,522
	Hostel/university/school	16,757	17,863	21,103	15,680	15,443	16,775	16,305	18,670	18,236	18,543
	Hotel/guest house	45,291	51,069	57,540	57,174	55,133	54,246	58,741	60,365	60,081	72,640
	Other	5,546	7,078	6,930	6,452	6,597	4,397	4,982	4,990	4,635	10,428
	Own home	4,638	5,507	7,895	5,169	5,110	4,524	5,068	5,625	4,895	5,412
	Paying guest family or friends house	8,807	8,716	9,692	8,240	7,961	5,423	5,148	6,574	7,433	7,060
	Rented house	20,818	24,570	24,950	25,695	22,817	22,362	20,482	20,237	18,838	28,731
Total Spend (£m)	All staying visits	12,798	14,011	15,759	15,699	16,058	16,354	16,649	17,666	18,245	21,578
	Bed & Breakfast	481	511	512	488	470	459	522	470	457	562
	Camping/mobile home	97	112	142	146	111	144	129	128	111	134
	Free guest with relatives or friends	3,822	3,972	4,498	4,207	4,501	4,425	4,254	4,371	4,515	4,593
	Holiday village/Centre	9	12	17	27	22	27	23	23	27	84
	Hostel/university/school	739	848	937	829	813	1,055	1,004	1,122	1,083	1,350
	Hotel/guest house	5,826	6,547	7,580	7,916	7,914	7,773	8,577	9,138	9,626	11,254
	Other	263	308	245	328	337	328	272	307	265	529
	Own home	354	357	412	402	429	531	354	377	505	515
	Paying guest family or friends house	345	393	439	385	379	364	340	426	475	445
	Rented house	861	951	977	971	1,084	1,245	1,172	1,305	1,181	2,111
Sample	All staying visits	37,321	39,977	40,410	36,432	31,854	41,952	41,948	38,144	37,666	37,359
	Bed & Breakfast	1,570	1,617	1,471	1,266	1,137	1,469	1,518	1,252	1,224	1,129
	Camping/mobile home	250	322	339	320	298	363	378	379	325	360
	Free guest with relatives or friends	15,167	16,363	16,256	14,386	12,831	16,976	16,003	14,233	14,207	13,133
	Holiday village/Centre	45	64	53	59	46	99	49	55	82	177
	Hostel/university/school	1,232	1,372	1,348	1,261	1,153	1,616	1,510	1,382	1,381	1,158
	Hotel/guest house	18,716	19,971	20,585	18,560	15,641	20,885	21,998	19,765	19,458	19,842
	Other	965	893	910	864	873	1,008	1,033	1,136	1,174	1,314
	Own home	730	744	740	645	522	656	637	545	594	528
	Paying guest family or friends house	562	599	527	487	507	529	538	637	548	558
	Rented house	1,101	1,161	1,164	1,034	973	1,457	1,397	1,291	1,334	1,607

Source: International Passenger Survey, Office for National Statistics

Please note: For 2013 the accommodation categories were reduced therefore we have included the analysis separately. ONS reverted to the full accommodation options for 2014 data, so this has been shown next to the 2012 data.

9.7 Full year accommodation usage figures by visitors from overseas 2013

		Year
Data	Accommodation	**2013**
Total Visits (000s)	All staying visits	31,064
	Own Home	366
	Hotels or similar	16,852
	Camp/caravan sites	480
	Other Short Term Rented	2,100
	Friends or Relatives	10,569
	Other (Non Rented or Long Term Rented)	2,299
Total Nights (000s)	All staying visits	245,412
	Own Home	5,453
	Hotels or similar	77,553
	Camp/caravan sites	3,980
	Other Short Term Rented	34,680
	Friends or Relatives	105,763
	Other (Non Rented or Long Term Rented)	17,983
Total Spend (£m)	All staying visits	20,938
	Own Home	531
	Hotels or similar	11,956
	Camp/caravan sites	225
	Other Short Term Rented	2,514
	Friends or Relatives	4,656
	Other (Non Rented or Long Term Rented)	1,056
Sample	All staying visits	39,416
	Own Home	566
	Hotels or similar	22,514
	Camp/caravan sites	602
	Other Short Term Rented	2,561
	Friends or Relatives	13,609
	Other (Non Rented or Long Term Rented)	1,910

Source: International Passenger Survey, Office for National Statistics

Please note: For 2013 the accommodation categories were reduced therefore the analysis has been shown separately. ONS reverted to the full accommodation options for 2014 data which is shown in the previous table.

9.8 International tourism[1]

Thousands and £ million

	Visits to the UK by overseas residents (thousands)	Spending in the UK by overseas residents		Visits overseas by UK residents (thousands)	Spending overseas by UK residents	
		Current prices	Constant 1995 prices		Current prices	Constant 1995 prices
2000	25,209	12,805	11,102	56,837	24,251	27,281
2001	22,835	11,306	9,528	58,281	25,332	27,710
2002	24,180	11,737	9,641	59,377	26,962	29,311
2003	24,715	11,855	9,451	61,424	28,550	28,677
2004	27,755	13,047	10,146	64,194	30,285	30,444
2005	29,970	14,248	10,714	66,441	32,154	30,954
2006	32,713	16,002	11,641	69,536	34,411	30,904
2007	32,778	15,960	11,389	69,450	35,013	32,477
2008	31,888	16,323	11,276	69,011	36,838	28,657
2009	29,889	16,592	11,032	58,614	31,694	22,673
2010	29,803	16,899	10,644	55,562	31,820	22,116
2011	30,798	17,998	10,870	56,836	31,701	20,569
2012	31,084	18,640	10,842	56,538	32,450	22,024
2013	32,692	21,258	11,740	57,792	34,510	23,613
2014	34,377	21,849	11,874	60,082	35,537	23,800

1 See chapter text

Sources: International Passenger Survey
Office for National Statistics;
01633 456032

9.9 Holidays abroad:[1] by destination

Percentages

		2002	2003	2004	2005	2006	2007	2008	2009	2010	2011	2012	2013	2014
Spain	JTKC	28.5	29.8	28.4	27.2	27.8	26.5	26.6	26.5	25.9	25.8	27.0	27.5	28.2
France	JTKD	19	18.1	17.3	16.6	15.9	16.7	16.7	18.6	18.3	17.4	17.2	16.4	15.5
Greece	JTKF	7	6.6	5.7	5.1	5.0	5.0	4.2	4.4	4.8	4.8	4.5	4.4	4.5
USA	JTKE	5.4	5.5	6.1	6.0	5.1	5.2	5.4	5.4	4.9	5.2	5.2	5.0	5.4
Italy	JTKG	4.6	5	5	5.4	5.4	5.6	5.2	4.7	4.6	4.5	5.0	5.3	5.3
Irish Republic	JTKI	4.1	3.7	3.8	3.8	4.0	3.3	3.2	3.2	2.5	2.9	2.3	2.2	2.6
Portugal	JTKH	4	4	3.5	3.6	3.7	4.1	4.8	4.1	4.4	4.5	4.5	4.8	4.7
Cyprus	JTKL	3	2.7	2.6	2.8	2.4	2.4	2.4	2.1	2.1	2.2	2.0	1.5	1.3
Netherlands	JTKK	2.8	2.6	2.6	2.5	2.7	2.4	2.1	2.2	2.2	2.6	2.6	2.7	3.1
Turkey	JTKJ	2.2	2.3	2.3	2.7	2.7	2.8	3.7	3.5	4.7	3.7	3.3	2.8	2.9
Belgium	JTKM	2	2.2	1.8	1.9	2.0	2.2	2.0	1.9	1.7	2	2.5	2.3	2.5
Germany	JTKN	1.5	1.2	1.6	1.7	1.7	2.0	1.9	1.7	1.7	2.2	2.0	2.3	2.1
Austria	JTKP	1.4	1.1	1.4	1.3	1.2	1.2	1.4	1.4	1.5	1	1.1	1.2	1.0
Malta	JTKO	1	1	1	1.1	1.0	0.9	0.9	0.8	1.0	1	1.0	1.2	1.1
Other countries	JTKQ	13.6	14.2	16.8	18.4	20	19.6	19.5	19.5	19.6	20.2	13.3	13.4	13.3

1 See chapter text.

Sources: International Passenger Survey, Office for National Statistics;
01633 456032

9.10 All Tourism

	2009	2010	2011	2012	2013	2014	2015
TRIPS (millions)	122.537	115.711	126.635	126.019	122.905	114.242	124.426
BEDNIGHTS (millions)	387.448	361.398	387.329	388.24	373.607	349.546	377.101
EXPENDITURE (£ millions)	£20,971	£19,797	£22,666	£23,976	£23,294	£22,692	£24,825
Av. Trip Length	3.16	3.12	3.06	3.08	3.04	3.06	3.03
Av. £ / Night	£54	£55	£59	£62	£62	£65	£66
Av. £ / Trip	£171	£171	£179	£190	£190	£199	£200

Source: Visit England

Please note that the latest 2015 results are provisional and subject to minor changes in subsequent months due to the inclusion of trip-takers returning from late trips.

All expenditure figures are in historic prices

9.11 All tourism in Great Britain

	GB	England	Scotland	Wales	GB	England	Scotland	Wales	GB	England	Scotland	Wales
	Millions				Millions				£millions			
All tourism – 2013	122.91	101.76	12.12	9.93	373.6	297.2	42.7	33.7	£23,294	£18,710	£2,889	£1,696
All tourism – 2014	114.24	92.61	12.52	10.00	349.5	272.9	41.6	35.1	£22,692	£18,085	£2,871	£1,735
Purpose												
Leisure	95.44	76.65	10.34	9.20	303.1	234.7	35.6	32.7	£18,055	£14,110	£2,360	£1,585
Total holiday	**79.21**	**63.00**	**8.87**	**7.97**	**264.4**	**203.1**	**31.6**	**29.8**	**£16,286**	**£12,690**	**£2,124**	**£1,472**
Holiday	52.90	40.74	6.30	6.36	184.8	137.3	23.1	24.3	£13,065	£10,046	£1,732	£1,287
VFR-holiday	26.31	22.26	2.57	1.61	79.6	65.8	8.4	5.4	£3,221	£2,644	£392	£184
VFR-other	16.23	13.65	1.47	1.22	38.6	31.6	4.1	3.0	£1,769	£1,419	£236	£114
VFR	42.53	35.91	4.04	2.84	118.3	97.4	12.5	8.4	£4,990	£4,064	£628	£298
Total business	**15.89**	**13.55**	**1.92**	**0.57**	**37.5**	**31.0**	**5.1**	**1.4**	**£4,101**	**£3,499**	**£465**	**£137**
Business travel	15.89	13.55	1.92	0.57	37.5	31.0	5.1	1.4	£4,101	£3,499	£465	£137
To attend a conference	1.05	0.86	0.13	0.06	2.1	1.7	0.2	0.2	£207	£174	£20	£12

Source: The GB Tourist 2014

British residents made an estimated 114 million trips in Great Britain in 2013, representing 350 million bed nights and £23 billion in spending.

Total holidays (including visiting friends and relatives) are the main purpose of trips taken, accounting for two thirds (69%) of trips taken and are even more important in terms of nights (76%) and spending (72%). Visits to friends and relatives (VFR) for mainly holiday purposes account for one in four trips and nights away (23%) but are less significant in terms of spending (14%). Business and work is the main purpose for around one in seven trips (14%) accounting for one in nine nights (11%). These are higher spending trips, accounting for just under a fifth (18%) of all tourism spending.

Friends' and relatives' homes (including owned second homes) are a widely used type of accommodation accounting for almost four in ten of all trips (36%). This reflects not only visits to friends and relatives as such, but also holidays spent staying with friends and relatives. With no real accommodation costs, trips staying at friends' and relatives' homes account for only 17% of spending on all tourism trips.

Commercial accommodation is used on just over half of trips (55%), but these trips represent a much higher share of spending (79%). Commercial accommodation is mainly serviced (42% of trips) where trips tend to be shorter in duration (31% of nights) but higher spending (55%). Hotels and motels account for 35% of trips and 47% of spend; guest houses and B&Bs account for 6% of trips and 8% of spend. Self-catering rented accommodation is used on a lower volume of trips (21%), but these trips are longer (26% of nights) and therefore slightly above average in terms of spending (23%).

The car is the dominant form of transport with three quarters (75%) of trips using a private car for the longest part of the journey from home to the destination

Firm bookings are made before more than half of all trips (56%), but it would be higher were it not for the high level of staying at friends and relatives' homes and using personal transport, where advance booking is less relevant

Large cities/large towns (41%) are the major destinations of tourism trips, followed by small towns (23%), the seaside (20%) and countryside/villages (19%)

9.12 Gambling

United Kingdom

£ million[1] and numbers

		2001 /02	2002 /03	2003 /04	2004 /05	2005 /06	2006 /07	2007 /08	2008 /09	2009 /10	2010 /11	2011 /12	2012 /13	2013 /14
Money staked on gambling														
National Lottery -Total	C229	5,029	4,670	4,614	4,757	5,000	4,911	4,966	5,149	5,477	5,825	6,503	6,977	6,736
Lotto including on-line	C3PU	4,038	3,479	3,225	3,225	3,021	2,858	2,752	2,698	2,661	2,667	2,475	2,345	2,475
Lotto Plus 5 [6]		-	-	-	-	-	-	-	-	-	-	101.7	78.7	36.4
Instants[2] (Scratchcards)	C3PV	606	592	641	729	804	943	1,109	1,221	1,340	1,436	1,726	2,062	2,141
Thunderball	C3PW	254	287	351	343	355	329	309	297	286	356	331	341	295
Lottery Extra[3]	C3PX	131	90	78	77	57	12	0	-	-	-	-	-	-
HotPicks	C3PY	..	222	244	219	228	222	210	211	210	206	200	193	179
Euromillions	C3Q2	..	..	15	104	427	464	476	618	881	1,056	1,666	1,984	1,609
Daily Play	C3Q3	..	..	45	59	54	49	50	50	49	46	4.3	-	-
Dream number[4]		..	..	..	..	..	59	59	54	50	39	-	-	-
Number operating in GB:														
Casinos	JE55	122	126	131	138	140	138	144	145	141	149	146	144	147
betting shops[5]	JE5B	..	..	..	..	..	..	8,800	8,862	8,822	9,067	9128	9,076	9,118

Sources: National Lottery Commission;

Gambling Commission: 0121 230 6666;

1 Adjusted to real terms using the Retail Prices Index.

2 From 2003/04 includes Inter-active Instant Win Games

3 Discontinued games

4 Started July 2006 and discontinued February 2011. Replaced by Lotto Plus 5

5 The Gambling Commission started regulating the betting industry from 1 September 2007, the number of betting shops is an ABB estimate.

6 launched in February 2011 and discontinued September 2013

9.12 Gambling

Remote Data - turnover and gross gambling yield

	General Remote Data (£m) - turnover						
	Apr 2008 Mar 2009	Apr 2009 Mar 2010	Apr 2010 Mar 2011	Apr 2011 Mar 2012	Apr 2012 Mar 2013	Apr 2013 Mar 2014	Apr 2014 Oct 2014
Betting	10,263.69	10,825.64	12,999.82	14,098.91	19,529.33	25,398.18	18,217.08
Betting Exchange	n/a	n/a	n/a	n/a	n/a	n/a	n/a
Bingo	3.94	20.44	26.24	28.17	33.78	44.40	58.72
Casino	950.07	684.71	340.55	512.25	877.51	678.80	423.72
Pool Betting	n/a	n/a	n/a	154.11	184.74	207.48	115.08
Total	11,217.70	11,530.79	13,366.61	14,793.44	20,625.36	26,328.86	18,814.61
Percentage change		3%	16%	11%	39%	28%	-29%

	General Remote Data (£m) - gross gambling yield						
	Apr 2008 Mar 2009	Apr 2009 Mar 2010	Apr 2010 Mar 2011	Apr 2011 Mar 2012	Apr 2012 Mar 2013	Apr 2013 Mar 2014	Apr 2014 Oct 2014
Betting	640.77	460.85	492.25	563.96	751.70	979.83	653.61
Betting Exchange	142.54	146.91	145.93	46.04	32.51	29.80	13.63
Bingo	0.47	1.51	2.19	2.03	2.46	4.32	5.25
Casino	33.08	22.95	12.69	20.24	42.49	27.49	15.59
Pool betting	n/a	n/a	n/a	77.92	103.45	93.22	65.45
Total	816.86	632.22	653.06	710.19	932.61	1,134.66	753.53
Percentage change		-23%	3%	9%	31%	22%	-34%

	Betting Data (£m) - turnover						
	Apr 2008 Mar 2009	Apr 2009 Mar 2010	Apr 2010 Mar 2011	Apr 2011 Mar 2012	Apr 2012 Mar 2013	Apr 2013 Mar 2014	Apr 2014 Oct 2014
Cricket	n/a	n/a	n/a	320.77	333.44	490.29	246.96
Dogs	n/a	83.79	71.50	59.33	90.93	127.65	80.68
Financials	n/a	n/a	n/a	205.41	314.47	341.75	230.27
Football	n/a	4,130.06	5,402.97	5,396.85	7,770.87	10,183.82	8,867.68
Golf	n/a	n/a	n/a	52.25	60.18	103.46	50.24
Horses	n/a	2,402.45	2,441.95	1,956.56	1,881.32	1,985.53	1,360.88
Tennis	n/a	n/a	n/a	2,071.02	3,948.78	5,155.91	3,466.69
Other	n/a	4,209.34	5,083.39	4,190.83	5,314.06	7,217.24	4,028.78
Total	10,263.69	10,825.64	12,999.81	14,253.02	19,714.05	25,605.65	18,332.17
Percentage change		5%	20%	10%	38%	30%	-28%

	Betting Data (£m) - gross gambling yield						
	Apr 2008 Mar 2009	Apr 2009 Mar 2010	Apr 2010 Mar 2011	Apr 2011 Mar 2012	Apr 2012 Mar 2013	Apr 2013 Mar 2014	Apr 2014 Oct 2014
Cricket	n/a	n/a	n/a	6.16	9.23	6.36	4.79
Dogs	n/a	11.06	9.44	5.83	8.05	9.89	5.58
Financials	n/a	n/a	n/a	2.73	8.96	8.65	4.06
Football	n/a	172.19	271.19	281.23	377.22	488.25	394.56
Golf	n/a	n/a	n/a	2.50	1.17	2.93	-1.34
Horses	n/a	201.29	105.97	92.21	111.99	114.00	51.76
Tennis	n/a	n/a	n/a	68.81	121.61	166.15	116.25
Other	n/a	223.22	251.59	228.44	249.42	306.63	157.02
Total	640.77	607.76	638.19	687.91	887.65	1,102.86	732.69
Percentage change		-5%	5%	8%	29%	24%	-34%

	Casino Data (£m) - turnover						
	Apr 2008 Mar 2009	Apr 2009 Mar 2010	Apr 2010 Mar 2011	Apr 2011 Mar 2012	Apr 2012 Mar 2013	Apr 2013 Mar 2014	Apr 2014 Oct 2014
Card Game	n/a	48.90	43.71	27.84	56.26	45.08	43.57
Peer to Peer	n/a	n/a	n/a	n/a	n/a	n/a	n/a
Slots	n/a	86.08	102.18	200.50	405.95	366.13	245.35
Table Game	n/a	508.21	144.16	238.00	399.44	264.37	114.33
Other	n/a	41.52	50.50	45.89	15.87	3.23	20.46
Total	950.07	684.71	340.55	512.23	877.51	678.81	423.72
Percentage change		-28%	-50%	50%	71%	-23%	-38%

	Casino Data (£m) - gross gambling yield						
	Apr 2008 Mar 2009	Apr 2009 Mar 2010	Apr 2010 Mar 2011	Apr 2011 Mar 2012	Apr 2012 Mar 2013	Apr 2013 Mar 2014	Apr 2014 Oct 2014
Card Game	n/a	1.47	1.59	1.10	2.55	1.69	1.22
Peer to Peer	n/a	0.78	0.01	0.02	0.00	0.00	0.03
Slots	n/a	5.11	6.24	12.44	25.52	22.08	12.57
Table Game	n/a	13.41	3.24	4.95	10.32	3.61	1.28
Other	n/a	2.18	1.61	1.73	4.10	0.11	0.49
Total	33.08	22.95	12.69	20.24	42.49	27.49	15.59
Percentage change		-31%	-45%	59%	110%	-35%	-43%

9.12 Gambling
Remote Data - turnover and gross gambling yield

	Gambling Software Income (£m)						
	2008/09	2009/10	2010/11	2011/12	2012/13	2013/14	2014/15
Game Sales	n/a	n/a	n/a	3.85	3.68	13.35	16.61
Game Shared Income	n/a	n/a	n/a	14.88	15.21	17.85	15.07
Game Total Revenue	n/a	n/a	n/a	18.73	18.89	31.20	31.68
Game % change					1%	65%	2%
Platform Sales	n/a	n/a	n/a	65.18	62.91	70.98	31.63
Platform Shared Income	n/a	n/a	n/a	20.85	19.59	24.58	19.96
Platform Total Revenue	n/a	n/a	n/a	86.03	82.50	95.56	51.59
Platform % change					-4%	16%	-46%
Other Sales	n/a	n/a	n/a	1.72	0.65	9.72	4.76
Other Shared Income	n/a	n/a	n/a	0.73	2.32	4.41	4.75
Other Total Revenue	n/a	n/a	n/a	2.45	2.97	14.13	9.51
Other % change					21%	376%	-33%

	Number of employees						
	at 31 Mar 2009	at 31 Mar 2010	at 31 Mar 2011	at 31 Mar 2012	at 31 Mar 2013	at 31 Mar 2014	at 30 Sep 2014
Number of employees	n/a	7,496	6,438	5,832	4,725	5,835	6,285

	Accounts						
	Apr 2008 Mar 2009	Apr 2009 Mar 2010	Apr 2010 Mar 2011	Apr 2011 Mar 2012	Apr 2012 Mar 2013	Apr 2013 Mar 2014	Oct 2013 Sep 2014
Customer accounts	16.14	16.57	14.92	15.18	16.53	16.99	18.14
Active customer accounts	4.92	4.19	3.50	3.99	4.66	4.88	5.59
New player registrations	4.22	3.95	3.31	3.83	4.62	5.68	6.24
Funds held in customer accounts (£m)	281.02	256.76	265.95	147.13	185.09	205.15	228.29

	Social responsibility data						
	Apr 2008 Mar 2009	Apr 2009 Mar 2010	Apr 2010 Mar 2011	Apr 2011 Mar 2012	Apr 2012 Mar 2013	Apr 2013 Mar 2014	Apr 2014 Oct 2014
Self-exclusions	46,359	40,358	33,953	34,321	37,746	69,413	94,326
Known breaches of self-exclusion	7,198	7,480	2,533	2,317	2,031	2,126	1,189
Number of individuals who cancelled their self-exclusion after minimum period	1,540	1,525	1,581	1,508	1,984	3,800	2,296
Challenged when attempting to gamble but unable to prove age	159	109	74				
Challenged having gambled but unable to prove age				188	432	493	404

Notes on the data in this section:

1. All years above refer to the period April-March unless otherwise stated.
2. The betting exchange sector saw a large decrease from April 2009-March 2010 to April 2011-March 2012. This is a result of Betfair moving its' previously Commission regulated business offshore during quarter 1 of 2011/12.
3. In 2008/09, betting data was not collected on individual sports. It wasn't until 2011/12 when the Commission collected data on the full list of sports in the table above. Between 2009/10 and 2010/11 data on cricket, financials, golf and tennis were captured under under 'Other'. Similarly, casino data was not collected on individual games in 2008/09.
4. Customers will often have accounts with more than one operator and therefore the data in the accounts table above relates to accounts rather than the individuals holding those accounts.
6. The number of people who have self excluded and the number of people who have cancelled their self exclusion may be lower than these figures as individuals may have self excluded from more than one site or operator and therefore been counted more than once. The number of breaches represents the number of separate incidents, rather than the number of individuals. The majority of the figures in the 'known breaches / attempted breaches of self exclusion' field are incidents where a customer has attempted to breach their self exclusion but has been successfully detected and prevented from gambling by the operator.
7. The increase in self-exclusions is attributable to the introduction of automated self-exclusion process by an operator.
8. As of October 2011, the question 'challenged when attempting to gamble but unable to prove age' and the guidance issued in association with this question changed to 'challenged having gambled and unable to prove age'.
9. The Commission began collecting data on gambling software licence holders in 2011.
10. Shared Income includes income generated from gambling software provided to organisations for which royalties are received.
11. The above data only relates to operators licensed by the Commission.
12. Following a consultation the Commission revised the way it collects data on gambling software and no longer collects income by software type. The figures presented therefore cover the period from April 2014 to December 2014 only.

9.12 Gambling - Remote: Gambling (Licensing and Advertising) Act Data

All data 1st November 2014 to 31st March 2015

GB only remote data

Turnover	Proprietary	Revenue Share	Total
Betting	5,308.21	-	5,308.21
Bingo	302.43	-	302.43
Casino	8,164.88	-	8,164.88
Pool Betting	25.03	-	25.03
Total	**13,800.55**	**-**	**13,800.55**

GGY	Proprietary	Revenue Share	Total
Betting	317.83	154.91	472.74
Betting Exchange	55.66	-	55.66
Bingo	38.36	44.26	82.62
Casino	359.88	474.37	834.25
Pool Betting	6.26	-	6.26
Total	**777.98**	**673.54**	**1,451.51**

Betting Turnover	Proprietary	Revenue Share	Total
Cricket	236.78	-	236.78
Dogs	85.87	-	85.87
Financials	56.50	-	56.50
Football	2,113.48	-	2,113.48
Golf	34.11	-	34.11
Horses	1,624.03	-	1,624.03
Tennis	441.74	-	441.74
Other	740.73	-	740.73
Total	**5,333.24**	**-**	**5,333.24**

Betting GGY	Proprietary	Revenue Share	Total
Cricket	4.79	-	4.79
Dogs	9.26	-	9.26
Financials	3.10	-	3.10
Football	168.44	-	168.44
Golf	3.63	-	3.63
Horses	127.86	-	127.86
Tennis	25.31	-	25.31
Other	37.35	-	37.35
Unallocated rev share	-	154.91	154.91
Total	**379.74**	**154.91**	**534.65**

Casino Turnover	Proprietary	Revenue Share	Total
Card Game	815.54	-	815.54
Slots	5,477.10	-	5,477.10
Table Game	1,592.33	-	1,592.33
Other	279.91	-	279.91
Total	**8,164.88**	**-**	**8,164.88**

Casino GGY	Proprietary	RevenueShare	Total
Card Game	20.52	47.18	67.70
Peer to Peer	30.50	6.17	36.67
Slots	253.93	278.60	532.54
Table Game	46.45	93.88	140.34
Other	8.47	48.53	57.01
Total	**359.88**	**474.37**	**834.25**

Social responsibility data

Self-exclusions	185,459
Known breaches of self-exclusion	13,096
Number of individuals who cancelled their self-exclusion after minimum period	16,884
Challenged having gambled but unable to prove age	16,162

Accounts

Funds held in customer accounts	463.36
Active Number accounts GC Licensed Facilities	15.62

Headcount

GB workforce	7,136

Total remote data

Turnover	Proprietary	Revenue Share	Total
Betting	5,705.68	-	5,705.68
Bingo	307.69	-	307.69
Casino	11,494.36	-	11,494.36
Pool Betting	88.02	-	88.02
Total	**17,595.75**	**-**	**17,595.75**

GGY	Proprietary	Revenue Share	Total
Betting	371.95	157.17	529.13
Betting Exchange	60.34	-	60.34
Bingo	38.89	41.56	80.45
Casino	484.67	557.11	1,041.78
Pool Betting	33.66	-	33.66
Total	**989.51**	**755.84**	**1,745.35**

Betting Turnover	Proprietary	Revenue Share	Total
Cricket	237.63	-	237.63
Dogs	96.78	-	96.78
Financials	61.77	-	61.77
Football	2,232.28	-	2,232.28
Golf	35.61	-	35.61
Horses	1,676.84	-	1,676.84
Tennis	469.17	-	469.17
Other	983.64	-	983.64
Total	**5,793.70**	**-**	**5,793.70**

Betting GGY	Proprietary	Revenue Share	Total
Cricket	5.32	-	5.32
Dogs	11.50	-	11.50
Financials	3.42	-	3.42
Football	194.43	-	194.43
Golf	3.75	-	3.75
Horses	142.22	-	142.22
Tennis	28.57	-	28.57
Other	76.74	-	76.74
Unallocated rev share	-	157.17	157.17
Total	**465.95**	**157.17**	**623.12**

Casino Turnover	Proprietary	Revenue Share	Total
Card Game	867.25	-	867.25
Slots	6,553.88	-	6,553.88
Table Game	1,848.08	-	1,848.08
Other	2,225.15	-	2,225.15
Total	**11,494.36**	**-**	**11,494.36**

Casino GGY	Proprietary	RevenueShare	Total
Card Game	22.37	48.68	71.05
Peer to Peer	39.03	8.59	47.62
Slots	298.21	280.51	578.72
Table Game	52.91	91.41	144.33
Other	72.14	127.91	200.06
Total	**484.67**	**557.11**	**1041.78**

Accounts

Funds held in customer accounts	648.19
Active Number accounts GC Licensed Facilities	18.34

Structure of the remote gambling industry.

Since 1st November 2014 the Commission has been collecting GGY derived from revenue share agreements between licensed operators.

To mitigate against the risk of double counting this revenue, the Commission requires operators to report only their relevant portion of the revenue share. Business to business operators are not required to submit the wagered or payout amount of a product meaning this information is only reported to the Commission once, by the business to customer operators. Further details of this arrangement can be seen in the remote regulatory returns consultation responses document, especially Annex A.

Due to the complex nature of large remote businesses the Commission is working with operators to ensure the reported data are consistent with the requirements set out in the regulatory returns.

The dataset does not breakdown the revenue share for betting operators into individual sports, instead is recorded against "Revenue share".

9.13 Most Popular Boy and Girl Baby Names in England and Wales, 2013

Rank	Boys Name	Rank	Boys Name	Rank	Girls Name	Rank	Girls Name
1	OLIVER	51	RYAN	1	AMELIA	51	MAYA *
2	JACK	52	TOMMY *	2	OLIVIA	52	AMELIE *
3	HARRY	53	MICHAEL	3	EMILY	53	LACEY *
4	JACOB	54	REUBEN *	4	AVA *	54	WILLOW *
5	CHARLIE	55	NATHAN	5	ISLA *	55	EMMA
6	THOMAS	56	BLAKE *	6	JESSICA	56	BELLA *
7	OSCAR	57	MOHAMMAD	7	POPPY	57	ELEANOR
8	WILLIAM	58	JENSON *	8	ISABELLA	58	ESME *
9	JAMES	59	BOBBY *	9	SOPHIE	59	ELIZA *
10	GEORGE	60	LUCA	10	MIA	59	GEORGIA
11	ALFIE	61	CHARLES	11	RUBY	61	HARRIET
12	JOSHUA	62	FRANKIE *	12	LILY	62	GRACIE *
13	NOAH	63	DEXTER *	13	GRACE	63	ANNABELLE *
14	ETHAN	64	KAI	14	EVIE	64	EMILIA *
15	MUHAMMAD	65	ALEX	15	SOPHIA	65	AMBER
16	ARCHIE	66	CONNOR	16	ELLA	66	IVY *
17	LEO	67	LIAM	17	SCARLETT *	67	BROOKE
18	HENRY	68	JAMIE	18	CHLOE	68	ROSE *
19	JOSEPH	69	ELIJAH *	19	ISABELLE	69	ANNA
19	SAMUEL	70	STANLEY *	20	FREYA	70	ZARA
21	RILEY *	71	LOUIE *	21	CHARLOTTE	71	LEAH
22	DANIEL	72	JUDE	22	SIENNA *	72	MOLLIE
23	MOHAMMED	73	CALLUM	23	DAISY	73	MARTHA *
24	ALEXANDER	74	HUGO *	24	PHOEBE	74	FAITH
25	MAX	74	LEON	25	MILLIE	75	HOLLIE
26	LUCAS	76	ELLIOT	26	EVA *	76	AMY
27	MASON	77	LOUIS	27	ALICE	77	BETHANY
28	LOGAN	78	THEODORE *	28	LUCY	78	VIOLET *
29	ISAAC	79	GABRIEL *	29	FLORENCE *	79	KATIE
30	BENJAMIN	80	OLLIE *	30	SOFIA *	80	MARYAM *
31	DYLAN	81	AARON	31	LAYLA *	81	FRANCESCA
32	JAKE	82	FREDERICK *	32	LOLA *	82	JULIA *
33	EDWARD	83	EVAN *	33	HOLLY	83	MARIA *
34	FINLEY	84	ELLIOTT *	34	IMOGEN	84	DARCEY *
35	FREDDIE *	85	OWEN	35	MOLLY	85	ISABEL
36	HARRISON	86	TEDDY *	36	MATILDA *	86	TILLY *
37	TYLER	87	FINLAY	37	LILLY *	87	MADDISON *
38	SEBASTIAN	88	CALEB *	38	ROSIE	88	VICTORIA
39	ZACHARY *	89	IBRAHIM *	39	ELIZABETH	89	ISOBEL
40	ADAM	90	RONNIE *	40	ERIN	90	NIAMH
41	THEO *	91	FELIX *	41	MAISIE	91	SKYE *
42	JAYDEN *	92	AIDEN *	42	LEXI *	92	MADISON
43	ARTHUR *	93	CAMERON	43	ELLIE	93	DARCY
44	TOBY	94	AUSTIN *	44	HANNAH	93	AISHA *
45	LUKE	95	KIAN	45	EVELYN *	95	BEATRICE *
46	LEWIS	96	RORY *	46	ABIGAIL	96	SARAH
47	MATTHEW	97	SETH *	47	ELSIE *	97	ZOE
48	HARVEY	98	ROBERT	48	SUMMER	98	PAIGE
49	HARLEY *	99	ALBERT *	49	MEGAN	99	HEIDI *
50	DAVID	100	SONNY *	50	JASMINE	100=	LYDIA
						100=	SARA *

Source: Office for National Statistics (ONS)

Notes:

These rankings have been produced using the exact spelling of the name given at birth registration. Similar names with different spellings have been counted separately. Births where the name was not stated have been excluded from these figures. Of the 358,383 baby boys in the 2013 dataset, 12 were excluded for this reason.

* denotes new entry to top 100

9.14a Libraries overview
Great Britain

Percentages

	2005/06	2006/07	2007/08	2008/09	2009/10	2010/11	2011/12	2012/13	2013/14
	%	%	%	%	%	% (1)	% (1)	% (1)	% (1)
Has visited a public library in the last year (2)	48.2	46.1	45.0	41.1	39.4	**39.7**	**38.8**	**37.0**	**35.4**
Frequency of attendance (2)									
1-2 times a year	10.4	10.3	10.5	8.9	7.9	**8.9**	**8.4**	**8.7**	**8.5**
3-4 times a year	13.4	12.9	13.0	11.4	10.9	**11.6**	**12.2**	**10.8**	**9.9**
At least once a month	16.4	15.7	14.9	13.3	12.8	**13.4**	**12.4**	**12.4**	**12.2**
At least once a week	7.9	7.2	6.7	5.9	5.4	**5.8**	**5.7**	**5.0**	**4.9**
Has not visited	51.8	53.9	55.0	60.5	63.0	**60.3**	**61.2**	**63.0**	**64.6**

Notes
(1) Figures in bold indicate a significant change from 2005/06.
(2) Figures exclude people who have visited a library for the purposes of paid work or academic study except in 2008/09 and 2009/10

Source: DCMS Taking Part Survey 2013/14 Q4
https://www.gov.uk/government/statistics/taking-part-201314-quarter-4-statistical-release

9.14b Proportion who have visited a public library in the last year - area-level breakdown

percentages

	2005/06	2006/07	2007/08	2008/09	2009/10	2010/11	2011/12	2012/13	2013/14
	%	%	%	%	%	% (1)	% (1)	% (1)	% (1)
Index of deprivation									
1- Most deprived	N/A	N/A	N/A	N/A	37.6	39.8	37.3	40.1	40.4
2	N/A	N/A	N/A	N/A	32.8	38.2	37.0	35.7	35.3
3	N/A	N/A	N/A	N/A	38.3	39.2	39.2	33.5	33.4
4	N/A	N/A	N/A	N/A	36.1	41.2	39.1	35.0	33.3
5	N/A	N/A	N/A	N/A	42.1	38.4	40.6	35.3	35.7
6	N/A	N/A	N/A	N/A	38.7	36.4	38.3	37.5	36.1
7	N/A	N/A	N/A	N/A	39.9	40.7	40.4	34.8	33.3
8	N/A	N/A	N/A	N/A	34.6	40.1	33.8	37.1	32.7
9	N/A	N/A	N/A	N/A	45.4	**38.7**	42.2	41.8	**37.1**
10- Least deprived	N/A	N/A	N/A	N/A	46.3	43.5	39.8	**38.4**	**36.8**
Region									
North East	44.9	43.9	**40.1**	**37.1**	**42.9**	**38.8**	**36.3**	**38.2**	**34.1**
North West	46.9	46.2	45.0	**42.1**	**41.4**	**43.0**	**37.5**	**37.8**	**35.4**
Yorkshire and Humberside	42.1	40.5	**36.6**	**33.7**	**30.0**	**33.6**	**33.4**	**34.9**	**33.1**
East Midlands	44.7	42.9	44.3	**38.8**	**42.7**	**35.8**	**37.7**	**34.9**	**32.3**
West Midlands	47.6	47.1	**43.5**	**39.3**	**38.0**	**36.6**	**40.1**	**35.5**	**34.8**
East of England	50.5	47.5	45.5	**42.9**	**39.5**	**42.4**	**41.2**	**37.5**	**37.0**
London	52.6	**49.2**	49.5	**43.6**	**38.1**	**43.1**	**43.1**	**41.9**	**40.9**
South East	51.0	48.3	48.5	**44.5**	**43.5**	**40.5**	**37.4**	**34.6**	**34.0**
South West	47.9	45.1	45.5	**41.8**	**38.8**	**38.8**	**40.0**	**36.3**	**33.6**
Urban	48.5	**46.5**	**45.6**	**41.6**	40.1	40.0	39.2	**37.8**	36.4
Rural	47.1	44.7	**42.8**	**38.9**	36.5	**38.2**	36.9	33.7	31.4
ACORN									
Wealthy Achievers	50.9	48.9	**47.4**	**42.1**	**39.9**	**40.7**	**40.6**	**38.4**	33.8
Urban Prosperity	57.3	51.0	**52.0**	**41.8**	**42.6**	**43.9**	**41.9**	**39.2**	38.3
Comfortably Off	48.5	**46.4**	**44.2**	**41.9**	**41.9**	**38.2**	**37.9**	**35.4**	35.0
Moderate Means	45.3	45.0	**42.4**	**41.5**	**37.7**	**41.3**	**38.9**	**36.9**	35.7
Hard-pressed	40.9	39.8	41.0	**37.5**	**33.9**	**36.9**	**35.8**	**36.4**	35.9
Unclassified	61.7	50.0	**62.7**	**46.9**	*	*	*	*	40.3
All	48.2	**46.1**	**45.0**	**41.1**	**39.4**	**39.7**	**38.8**	**37.0**	**35.4**

Notes
(1) Figures in bold indicate a significant change from 2005/06.
(2) Index of deprivation data not available pre-2009/10. For Index of Deprivation data, figures in bold indicate a significant change from 2009/10.
(3) *= N too small to report

Source: DCMS Taking Part Survey 2013/14 Q4
https://www.gov.uk/government/statistics/taking-part-201314-quarter-4-statistical-release

9.14c Proportion who have visited a public library in the last year - demographic breakdown

Percentages

	2005/06	2006/07	2007/08	2008/09	2009/10	2010/11	2011/12	2012/13	2013/14
						%	%	%	%
	%	%	%	%	%	(1)	(1)	(1)	(1)
Age									
16-24	51.0	**47.1**	**45.4**	**42.8**	**40.0**	**34.4**	**34.5**	**32.3**	**33.4**
25-44	51.2	50.2	49.5	**43.7**	**40.9**	**44.6**	**44.0**	**42.2**	**40.4**
45-64	45.7	44.3	**42.1**	**38.8**	**39.5**	**36.0**	**36.1**	**33.1**	**30.9**
65-74	46.7	44.4	44.7	42.0	**39.3**	44.3	**35.8**	**38.6**	**37.1**
75+	42.3	**37.1**	**37.6**	**35.0**	**32.9**	37.1	38.9	36.5	33.3
Sex									
Male	43.8	**42.1**	**40.2**	**35.3**	**35.5**	**34.3**	**33.6**	**31.4**	**29.7**
Female	52.3	**49.9**	**49.6**	**46.5**	**43.2**	**44.8**	**43.8**	**42.3**	**40.8**
NS-SEC									
Upper socio-economic group	52.1	**50.2**	**48.0**	**43.3**	**43.1**	**43.9**	**42.3**	**39.7**	**36.7**
Lower socio-economic group	40.1	**38.1**	38.7	**35.1**	**32.3**	**33.6**	**33.5**	**33.0**	**32.4**
Employment status									
Not working	49.7	**46.7**	**46.6**	**44.0**	**42.4**	**42.9**	**41.7**	**41.0**	**38.3**
Working	47.2	**45.7**	**44.0**	**39.0**	**37.4**	**37.5**	**36.8**	**34.3**	**33.4**
Tenure									
Owners	48.7	**46.4**	**44.8**	**41.1**	**39.8**	**40.1**	**39.2**	**37.0**	**34.9**
Social rented sector	41.9	40.5	42.2	39.0	36.8	37.0	37.2	38.6	38.1
Private rented sector	53.3	51.0	**49.2**	**43.0**	**39.8**	**40.2**	**38.7**	**35.8**	**35.0**
Ethnicity									
White	47.2	**44.9**	43.6	**40.1**	**37.9**	**38.3**	**37.8**	**35.9**	**33.8**
Black or ethnic minority	57.5	56.7	57.9	**50.2**	**50.6**	**50.0**	**46.5**	**45.1**	**47.8**
Religion									
No religion	46.8	45.5	45.3	40.1	35.2	37.8	36.8	33.2	34.4
Christian	47.3	**44.8**	**43.7**	**40.3**	**39.7**	**39.2**	**38.8**	**37.7**	**34.3**
Other religion	58.2	58.9	57.1	52.7	53.0	**48.2**	**44.4**	**46.9**	**48.3**
Long-standing illness or disability									
No	50.0	**48.0**	**46.0**	**42.1**	**40.4**	**40.1**	**39.2**	**36.9**	**36.0**
Yes	43.8	**41.5**	42.4	**38.4**	**36.8**	**38.5**	**37.9**	**37.3**	**34.2**
All	48.2	**46.1**	**45.0**	**41.1**	**39.4**	**39.7**	**38.8**	**37.0**	**35.4**

Source: DCMS Taking part Survey 2013/14 Q4
https://www.gov.uk/government/statistics/taking-part-201314-quarter-4-statistical-release

Notes
(1) Figures in bold indicate a significant change from 2005/06.

9.15 Museums and Galleries Overview (adults)

Percentages

	2006/07	2007/08	2008/09	2009/10	2010/11	2011/12	2012/13	2013/14
					%	%	%	%
	%	%	%	%	(1)	(1)	(1)	(1)
Has visited a museum or gallery in the last year [2]	41.5	**43.5**	43.4	**46.0**	**46.3**	**48.9**	**52.8**	**52.8**
Frequency of attendance [2]								
1-2 times a year	25.3	26.3	26.1	**27.9**	**27.4**	**29.6**	**31.3**	**31.3**
3-4 times a year	12.9	13.8	13.9	14.1	**14.7**	**15.3**	**17.2**	**17.2**
At least once a month	2.8	3.2	2.9	3.6	**3.6**	3.4	3.5	3.5
At least once a week	**0.4**	0.3	0.4	0.4	**0.5**	**0.5**	**0.6**	0.6
Has not visited	58.5	**56.5**	56.7	**54.0**	**53.7**	**51.1**	**47.2**	**47.2**

Notes
(1) Figures in bold indicate a significant change from 2005/06. For purpose of visit data, figures in bold indicate a significant change from 2008/09.
(2) Figures exclude people who have visited a museum or gallery for the purposes of paid work or academic study

Source: DCMS Taking Part Survey 2013/14 Q4
https://www.gov.uk/government/statistics/taking-part-201314-quarter-4-statistical-release

9.16 Participation in voluntary activities, 2003 to 2014/15
England

Percentages

| | At least once a month | | | | | | | | |
	2003	2005	2007/08	2008/09	2009/10	2010/11	2012/13	2013/14	2014/15
Informal volunteering[1]	37	37	35	35	29	29	36	35	34
Formal volunteering [2]	28	29	27	26	25	25	29	27	27
Any volunteering [3]	**50**	**50**	**48**	**47**	**42**	**41**	**49**	48	47
	At least once in last year								
Informal volunteering	63	68	64	62	54	55	62	64	59
Formal volunteering	42	44	43	41	40	39	44	41	42
Any volunteering	**73**	**76**	**73**	**71**	**66**	**65**	**72**	**72**	**69**

Source: Community Life Survey 2014/15

1 *Informal volunteering: Giving unpaid help as an individual to people who are not relatives.*

2 *Formal volunteering: Giving unpaid help through groups, clubs or organisations to benefit other people or the environment.*

3 *Participated in either formal or informal volunteering.*

9.17 UK residents' visits to friends and relatives[1] abroad: by destination

United Kingdom

Percentages[2]

	2003	2006	2009	2011	2012	2013	2014
Irish Republic	16	15	14	13	10	10	11
France	13	11	11	10	10	10	11
Poland	1	6	9	9	9	9	9
Spain	9	9	8	7	8	8	8
Germany	6	6	5	5	5	5	5
USA	7	6	5	5	4	4	4
India	3	3	4	4	4	4	4
Italy	4	4	4	3	4	4	4
Netherlands	4	3	3	3	3	3	3
Pakistan	3	3	3	3	3	3	3
Other countries	34	35	36	39	39	39	37
All destinations (=100%) (millions)	8.5	12.0	11.6	11.6	11.8	12.3	13.3

Source: International Passenger Survey,
Office for National Statistics

1 As a proportion of all visits to friends and relatives taken abroad by residents of the UK.
Excludes business trips and other miscellaneous visits.

2 Percentages may not add up to 100 per cent due to rounding.

9.18 The Internet

Internet activities by age group and sex, 2014
Within the last 3 months %

	Age group						Sex		
	16-24	25-34	35-44	45-54	55-64	65+	Men	Women	All
Sending/receiving emails	80	86	86	83	75	49	75	75	**75**
Finding information about goods and services	71	84	87	84	75	44	74	72	**73**
Reading or downloading online news, newspapers or magazines	65	73	69	60	48	24	60	50	**55**
Social networking (eg Facebook or Twitter)	91	80	68	54	37	13	53	56	**54**
Using services related to travel or travel related accommodation	38	53	52	54	44	22	46	40	**43**
Internet banking	56	71	66	62	47	23	54	52	**53**
Selling goods or services over the Internet	24	36	35	26	15	8	25	22	**23**
Playing or downloading games, images, films or music	68	61	58	42	29	14	48	40	**44**
Creating websites or blogs	10	11	8	6	4	2	8	5	**6**
Making an appointment with a doctor or other health practitioner	8	8	11	13	15	5	9	11	**10**

Base: Adults (aged 16+) in Great Britain.

Percentages sum to more than 100 because respondents can give more than one answer.

Source: Office for National Statistics

Purchases made over the Internet, by age group and sex, 2014
Bought within the last 12 months %

	Age group						Sex		
	16-24	25-34	35-44	45-54	55-64	65+	Men	Women	All
Clothes, sports goods	63	64	63	52	42	19	46	52	**49**
Household goods (eg furniture, toys etc)	28	59	55	49	40	21	42	42	**42**
Travel arrangements (eg transport tickets, car hire)	32	44	47	46	38	16	38	36	**37**
Holiday accomodation	27	42	47	49	40	16	37	36	**36**
Tickets for events	43	44	43	43	32	11	35	35	**35**
Books, magazines, newspapers	27	38	37	39	33	17	29	33	**31**
Films, music, including downloads	45	51	38	33	19	7	35	27	**31**
Electronic equipment (inlcuding cameras)	28	38	33	29	17	8	32	18	**25**
Food or groceries	18	38	34	27	17	7	20	26	**23**
Share purchases, insurance policies etc	13	28	29	28	21	9	25	18	**21**
Telecommunication services	13	26	22	21	15	6	21	13	**17**
Other computer software and upgrades	15	21	22	21	12	6	23	9	**16**
Video games software and upgrades	24	24	20	16	5	3	20	10	**15**
Computer hardware	11	21	18	19	11	5	20	8	**14**
Medicine	5	12	11	10	13	5	10	9	**9**
E-learning material	10	10	10	9	6	2	8	7	**8**

Base: Adults (aged 16+) in Great Britain.

Source: Office for National Statistics

Households with Internet access, 2005 to 2014
%

Year	
GB 2005	55
2006	57
2007	61
2008	65
2009	70
2010	73
2011	77
2012	80
2013	83
2014	84

Source: Office for National Statistics

Notes:

GB estimates from 2005 to 2014.

Source: Opinions and Lifestyle Survey, formerly known as the Opinions/Omnibus Survey from 2005.

All estimates relate to January to March for each year, except 2005 which relates to May.

During 2005, estimates were published at irregular intervals as Topic Based Summaries. These are no longer available on the ONS website.

9.19 Radio Listening

	Adult (15+) Population '000	Weekly Reach '000's	Weekly Reach %	Average Hours Per Head	Average Hours Per Listener	Total Hours ('000's)	Share of Listening %
Quarterly Summary of Radio Listening - Survey period ending June 2015							
All Radio	53,575	48,184	90	19.5	21.7	1,045,885	100.0
All BBC Radio	53,575	35,016	65	10.4	15.8	554,759	53.0
BBC Local Radio	53,575	8,837	16	1.5	8.9	78,823	7.5
All Commercial Radio	53,575	34,628	65	8.7	13.4	464,053	44.4
All National Commercial	53,575	17,944	33	2.8	8.5	151,871	14.5
All Local Commercial (National TSA)	53,575	27,466	51	5.8	11.4	312,183	29.8
All BBC Network Radio	53,575	31,926	60	8.9	14.9	475,936	45.5
BBC Radio 1	53,575	10,436	19	1.3	6.5	67,378	6.4
BBC Radio 2	53,575	15,141	28	3.4	12.2	184,016	17.6
BBC Radio 3	53,575	1,894	4	0.2	6.9	13,101	1.3
BBC Radio 4	53,575	10,574	20	2.3	11.5	121,872	11.7
BBC Radio 4 (including 4 Extra)	53,575	10,965	20	2.5	12.2	133,949	12.8
BBC Radio 4 Extra	53,575	1,954	4	0.2	6.2	12,077	1.2
BBC Radio 5 live	53,575	5,322	10	0.7	6.8	36,436	3.5
BBC Radio 5 live (inc. sports extra)	53,575	5,836	11	0.8	7.3	42,591	4.1
BBC Radio 5 live sports extra	53,575	1,625	3	0.1	3.8	6,155	0.6
BBC 6 Music	53,575	2,055	4	0.4	9.1	18,771	1.8
1Xtra from the BBC	53,575	958	2	0.1	5.5	5,281	0.5
BBC Asian Network UK	53,575	607	1	0.1	6.4	3,866	0.4
BBC World Service	53,575	1,548	3	0.1	4.6	7,179	0.7

STATION SUMMARY ANALYSIS - RAJAR REPORTING PERIOD 2015 Q1
(Report 1690) All Radio, Adults Only
Quarterly Weighted Data

		Age Group of Respondent					
	Total	15-24	25-34	35-44	45-54	55-64	65+
Unw. Sample	23,876	2,771	2,860	3,575	4,287	4,155	6,228
Est. Pop'n	53,502	8,237	8,888	8,428	9,149	7,355	11,446
ALL RADIO							
Weekly Reach 000s	47,799	6,869	7,637	7,668	8,571	6,797	10,257
Weekly Reach %	89.3	83.4	85.9	91	93.7	92.4	89.6
Total Hours	1,017,509	103,003	135,741	156,029	198,749	170,004	253,983
Average Hours Per Head	19	12.5	15.3	18.5	21.7	23.1	22.2
Average Hours Per Listener	21.3	15	17.8	20.3	23.2	25	24.8

Source: RAJAR

Environment

Chapter 10

Environment

Air emissions (Table 10.2 to 10.8)

Emissions of air pollutants arise from a wide variety of sources. The National Atmospheric Emissions Inventory (NAEI) is prepared annually for the Government and the devolved administrations by AEA Energy and Environment, with the work being co-ordinated by the Department of Energy and Climate Change (DECC). Information is available for a range of point sources including the most significant polluters. However, a different approach has to be taken for diffuse sources such as transport and domestic emissions, where this type of information is not available. Estimates for these are derived from statistical information and from research on emission factors for stationary and mobile sources. Although for any given year considerable uncertainties surround the emission estimates for each pollutant, trends over time are likely to be more reliable.

UK national emission estimates are updated annually and any developments in methodology are applied retrospectively to earlier years. Adjustments in the methodology are made to accommodate new technical information and to improve international comparability.

Three different classification systems are used in the tables presented here; a National Accounts basis (Table 10.2), the format required by the Inter-governmental Panel on Climate Change (IPCC) (Table 10.3) and the National Communications (NC) categories (Tables 10.5-10.7).

The NC source categories are detailed below together with details of the main sources of these emissions:

Energy supply total: Power stations, refineries, manufacture of solid fuels and other energy industries, solid fuel transformation, exploration, production and transport of oils, offshore oil and gas – venting and flaring, power stations - FGD, coal mining and handling, and exploration, production and transport of gas.

Business total: Iron and steel – combustion, other industrial combustion, miscellaneous industrial and commercial combustion, energy recovery from waste fuels, refrigeration and air conditioning, foams, fire fighting, solvents, one components foams, and electronics, electrical insulation and sporting goods.

Transport total: Civil aviation (domestic, landing and take off, and cruise), passenger cars, light duty vehicles, buses, HGVs, mopeds & motorcycles, LPG emissions (all vehicles), other road vehicle engines, railways, railways – stationary combustion, national navigation, fishing vessels, military aircraft and shipping, and aircraft – support vehicles.

Residential total: Residential combustion, use of non aerosol consumer products, accidental vehicle fires, and aerosols and metered dose inhalers.

Agriculture total: Stationary and mobile combustion, breakdown of pesticides, enteric fermentation (cattle, sheep, goats, horses, pigs, and deer), wastes (cattle, sheep, goats, horses, pigs, poultry, and deer), manure liquid systems, manure solid storage and dry lot, other manure management, direct soil emission, and field burning of agricultural wastes.

Industrial process total: Sinter production, cement production, lime production, limestone and dolomite use, soda ash production and use, fletton bricks, ammonia production, iron and steel, nitric acid production, adipic acid production, other – chemical industry, halocarbon production, and magnesiun cover gas.

Land-use change: Forest land remaining forest land, forest land biomass burning, land converted *to forest land, direct N2O emissions from N fertilisation of forest land, cropland liming, cropland* *remaining cropland, cropland biomass burning, land converted to cropland, N2O emissions from* *disturbance associated with land-use conversion to cropland, grassland biomass burning,* *grassland liming, grassland remaining grassland, land converted to grassland, wetlands remaining* *wetland, Non-CO2 emissions from drainage of soils and wetlands, settlements biomass burning,* *land converted to settlements, and harvested wood.*

Waste management total: Landfill, waste-water handling, and waste incineration.

Atmospheric emissions on a National Accounts basis (Table 10.1)

The air and energy accounts are produced for ONS by AEA Technology plc based on data compiled for the National Atmospheric Emissions Inventory (NAEI)7 and UK Greenhouse Gas Inventory (GHGI)8. Every year a programme of development work is undertaken to optimise the methodologies employed in compiling the accounts. Assessments in previous years have indicated that a number of splits used to apportion road transport source data to more than one industry should be reviewed. The results of this review have been implemented in the 2011 UK Environmental Accounts for reference period 2009 and years back to 1990.

The industry breakdown used in the accounts has moved to using the Standard Industrial Classification 2007 (SIC 2007). Historically, the accounts were based on Environmental Accounts codes (EAcodes) based on SIC 2003. This change will allow the accounts which are broken down by industry to be more readily compared with other economic statistics. A methodology article that outlines this change in more detail was published on the ONS website in May 2011: http//www.statistics.gov.uk/cci/article.asp?id=2694. As a result while names given to the breakdown maybe similar they are not necessarily the same.

The National Accounts figures in Table 10.2 differ from those on an IPCC basis, in that they include estimated emissions from fuels purchased by UK resident households and companies either at home or abroad (including emissions from UK international shipping and aircraft operators), and exclude emissions in the UK resulting from the activities of non-residents. This allows for a more consistent comparison with key National Accounts indicators such as Gross Domestic Product (GDP).

Greenhouse gases include carbon dioxide, methane, nitrous oxide, hydro-fluorocarbons, perfluorocarbons and sulphur hexafluoride which are expressed in thousand tonnes of carbon dioxide equivalent.

Acid rain precursors include sulphur dioxide, nitrogen oxides and ammonia which are expressed as thousand tonnes of sulphur dioxide equivalent.

Road Transport Emissions (Table 10.2)

Various pollutants are emitted from road transport into the atmosphere. Table 10.2 shows emissions by pollutant generated from combustion by road vehicles.

Greenhouse gas emissions related to road transport generally increased from the early 1990s until 2007. However, since 2008 emissions have declined, which in part reflects both the economic downturn and the continuation of the trend toward more energy efficient vehicles.

Estimated total emissions of greenhouse gases on an IPCC basis (Table 10.3)

The IPCC classification is used to report greenhouse gas emissions under the UN Framework Convention on Climate Change (UNFCCC) and includes Land Use Change and all emissions from Domestic aviation and shipping, but excludes International aviation and shipping bunkers. Estimates of the relative contribution to global warming of the main greenhouse gases, or classes of gases, are presented weighted by their global warming potential.

Greenhouse gas emissions bridging table (Table 10.4)
National Accounts measure to UNFCCC measure

The air and energy accounts are produced for ONS by AEA Technology plc based on data compiled for the National Atmospheric Emissions Inventory (NAEI)7 and UK Greenhouse Gas Inventory (GHGI)8. Every year a programme of development work is undertaken to optimise the methodologies employed in compiling the accounts. Assessments in previous years have indicated that a number of splits used to apportion road transport source data to more than one industry should be reviewed. The results of this review have been implemented in the 2011 UK Environmental Accounts for reference period 2009 and years back to 1990. There are a number of formats for the reporting and recording of atmospheric emissions data, including those used by the Department of Energy and Climate Change (DECC) for reporting greenhouse gases under UNFCCC and the Kyoto Protocol, and for reporting air pollutant emissions to the UN Economic Commission for Europe (UNECE), which differ from the National Accounts consistent measure published by the Office for National Statistics (ONS).

Differences between the National Accounts measure and those for reporting under UNFCCC and the Kyoto Protocol, following the guidance of the IPCC, are shown in Table 10.4.

Emissions of carbon dioxide (Table 10.5)

Carbon dioxide is the main man-made contributor to global warming. Emissions of greenhouse gases on a UK residency basis were estimated to be 643.1 million tonnes carbon dioxide equivalent (Mt CO2e) in 2013. This was 2.0% lower than the 2012 figure of 656.5 Mt CO2e, and 23.6% lower than the 1990 figure of 842.0 Mt CO2e.

Carbon dioxide was the dominant greenhouse gas, accounting for 84.4% of total emissions in 2013 Over the period 1990 to 2013, carbon dioxide emissions decreased by 14.1%

Emissions of methane (Table 10.6)

Weighted by global warming potential, methane accounted for about 8.7 per cent of the UK's greenhouse gas emissions in 2013. One of the main drivers behind the fall in methane emissions was the "energy supply, water and waste" sector. Between 1990 and 2013, there was a reduction of 67.9% in the emissions of methane from this sector, driven largely by a fall in emissions from landfill.

Emissions of nitrous oxide (Table 10.7)

Weighted by global warming potential, nitrous oxide emissions accounted for about 4.2 per cent of the UK's man-made greenhouse gas emissions in 2013. The fall in emissions of nitrous oxide is due in large part to a 97.8% fall in emissions from the manufacturing sector. A major factor here was the fitting of abatement equipment in the UK's only adipic acid factory in 1998, followed by its closure and the termination of industrial adipic acid production in the UK in 2009.

Material Flow Account (Table 10.8)

Economy-wide material flow accounts estimate the physical flow of materials through our economy. As well as providing an aggregate overview of the annual extraction of raw materials, they also measure the physical amounts of imports and exports. This information is important in attempting to understand resource productivity. For example, they shed light on the depletion of natural resources and seek to promote a sustainable and more resource-efficient economy.

Annual rainfall (Table 10.9)

Regional rainfall is derived by the Met Office's National Climate Information Centre for the National Hydrological Monitoring Programme at the Centre for Ecology and Hydrology. These monthly area rainfalls are based initially on a subset of rain gauges (circa 350) but are updated after four to five months with figures using the majority of the UK's rain gauge network.

The regions of England shown in this table correspond to the original nine English regions of the National Rivers Authority (NRA). The NRA became part of the Environment Agency on its creation in April 1996. The figures in this table relate to the country of Wales, not the Environment Agency Welsh Region.

UK weather summary (Table 10.10)

Table 10.10 represents an initial assessment of the weather that was experienced across the UK and how it compares with the 1961 to 1990 average.

Final averages use quality controlled data from the UK climate network of observing stations. They show the Met Office's best assessment of the weather that was experienced across the UK during the years and how it compares with the 1961 to 1990 average. The columns headed 'Anom' (anomaly) show the difference from, or percentage of, the 1961 to 1990 long-term average.

Biological and chemical quality of rivers and canals (Table 10.11)

Table 10.11 shows a Summary of River Basin District Ecological and Chemical Status from 2009-2014. It looks at each river basin district in terms of Percent of surface water bodies that are at good chemical status or better and also Percent of surface water bodies are at good ecological status/potential or better. Improvements are measured in terms of the number of water bodies meeting good status

Status of Rivers and Canals in Scotland (Table 10.12)

Looks at the overall status of rivers & canals in Scotland, including water quality.

Reservoir stocks in England and Wales (Table 10.13)

Data are collected for a network of major reservoirs (or reservoir groups) in England and Wales for the National Hydrological Monitoring Programme at the Centre for Ecology and Hydrology. Figures of usable capacity are supplied by the Water PLCs and the Environment Agency at the start of each month and are aggregated to provide an index of the total reservoir stocks for England and Wales.

Water industry expenditure (Table 10.14)

The data is taken from the annual regulatory accounts (and the June return submission to Ofwat) of water and sewerage companies and water companies of England and Wales.

Operating expenditure includes: employment costs, power, Environment Agency charges, bulk supply imports, general overheads, customer services, scientific services, local authority rates, local authority sewerage agencies, materials and consumables, charge for bad and doubtful debts, current cost depreciation and the infrastructure renewals charge.

Capital expenditure figures represent all capital additions (both maintenance and enhancement) but exclude infrastructure renewals expenditure. Figures quoted are before deducting grants and contributions, typically received from developers. Adopted assets at nil cost are not included.

Water pollution incidents (Table 10.15)

The Environment Agency responds to complaints and reported incidents of pollution in England and Wales. Each incident is then logged and categorised according to its severity. The category describes the impact of each incident on water, land and air. The impact of an incident on each medium is considered and reported separately. If no impact has occurred for a particular medium, the incident is reported as a category 4. Before 1999, the reporting system was used only for water pollution incidents; thus the total number of substantiated incidents was lower, as it did not include incidents not relating to the water environment.

Bathing waters (Table 10.16)

Under the EC Bathing Water Directive 76/160/EEC, 11 physical, chemical and microbiological parameters are measured including total and faecal coliforms which are generally considered to be the most important indicators of the extent to which water is contaminated by sewage. The mandatory value for total coliforms is 10,000 per 100 ml, and for faecal coliforms 2,000 per 100 ml. For a bathing water to comply with the coliform standards, the Directive requires that at least 95 per cent of samples taken for each of these parameters over the bathing season are less than or equal to the mandatory values. In the UK a minimum of 20 samples are normally taken at each site. In practice this means that where 20 samples are taken, a maximum of only one sample may exceed the mandatory value for the bathing water to comply, and where less than 20 samples are taken none may exceed the mandatory value for the bathing water to comply.

The bathing water season is from mid-May to end-September in England and Wales, but shorter in Scotland and Northern Ireland. Bathing waters which are closed for the season are excluded for that year.

The table shows Environment Agency regions for England and Wales, the boundaries of which are based on river catchment areas and not county borders. In particular, the figures shown for Wales are the Environment Agency Welsh Region, the boundary of which does not coincide with the boundary of Wales.

Surface and groundwater abstractions (Table 10.17)

Significant changes in the way data is collected and/or reported were made in 1991 (due to the Water Resources Act 1991) and 1999 (commission of National Abstraction Licensing Database). Figures are therefore not strictly comparable with those in previous/intervening years. From 1999, data have been stored and retrieved from one system nationally and are therefore more accurate and reliable. Some regions report licensed and actual abstracts for financial rather than calendar years. As figures represent an average for the whole year expressed as daily amounts, differences between amounts reported for financial and calendar years are small.

Under the Water Act 2003, abstraction of less than 20 m3/day became exempt from the requirement to hold a licence as of 1 April 2005. As a result over 22,000 licences were deregulated, mainly for agricultural or private water supply purposes. However, due to the small volumes involved, this has had a minimal affect on the estimated licensed and actual abstraction totals.

The following changes have occurred in the classification of individual sources:
• Spray irrigation: this category includes small amounts of non-agricultural spray irrigation
• Mineral washing: from 1999 this was not reported as a separate category; licences for 'Mineral washing' are now contained in 'Other industry'
• Private water supply: this was shown as separate category from 1992 and includes private abstractions for domestic use and individual households
• Fish farming, cress growing, amenity ponds: includes amenity ponds, but excludes miscellaneous from 1991

Estimates of remaining recoverable oil and gas reserves (Table 10.18)

Only a small proportion of the estimated remaining recoverable reserves of oil and gas are known with any degree of certainty. The latest oil and gas data for 2013 shows that the upper range of total UK oil reserves was estimated to be around 2.4 billion tonnes, while UK gas reserves were around 1647 billion cubic metres. Of these, proven reserves of oil were 0.4 billion tonnes and proven reserves of gas were 241 billion cubic metres.

Local authority collected (Table 10.19)

Local authority collected includes household and non-household waste that is collected and disposed of by local authorities. It includes regular household collections, specific recycling collections, and special collections of bulky items, waste received at civic amenity sites, and waste collected from non-household sources that come under the control of local authorities.

Waste arisings from households (Table 10.20)

The 'waste from households' calculation was first published by Defra in May 2014. It was introduced for statistical purposes to provide a harmonised UK indicator with a comparable calculation in each of the four UK countries and to provide a consistent approach to report recycling rates at UK level on a calendar year basis under the Waste Framework Directive (2008/98/EC). The waste from household measure is a narrower measure than the 'household waste' measure which was previously used and excludes waste not considered to have come directly from households, such as recycling from street bins, parks and grounds.

Chartered Institute of Environmental Health Survey of Local Authority Noise Enforcement Activity (Table 10.21)

Every year the CIEH collects data on noise complaints made to local authorities and on the enforcement actions consequently taken by them. The data helps to inform policy and practice in environmental protection and public health and, in particular, the survey results provide the source of data for the Public Health England Outcome Indicator on noise. This, part of the Public Health Outcomes Framework, provides recognition of noise as one of the wider determinants of health.

Government revenue from environmental taxes (Table 10.22)

Environmental taxes data are based on the definition outlined in Regulation (EU) No 691/2011 on European environmental economic accounts. The European Statistical Office (Eurostat) define an environmental tax as a tax whose base is a physical unit (for example, a litre of petrol or a passenger flight) that has a proven negative impact on the environment. These taxes are designed to promote environmentally positive behaviour, reduce damaging effects on the environment and generate revenue that can potentially be used to promote further environmental protection.

In 2014, revenue from environmentally related taxes stood at £44.6 billion. This corresponded to 2.5% of the UK's gross domestic product (GDP). Looking over the time series as a whole, environmental taxes as a share of GDP has remained at a broadly consistent level of between 2% and 3%

10.1 Atmospheric emissions[1]
2013

	Total greenhouse gas emissions	Carbon Dioxide (CO2)	Methane (CH4)	Nitrous Oxide (N2O)	Hydrofluoro-carbons (HFCs)	Perfluoro-carbons (PFCs)	Sulphur hexafluoride (SF6)
Thousand tonnes CO2 equivalent							
Agriculture, forestry and fishing	55777	7037	26930	21767	43	–	–
Mining and quarrying	20023	16655	3062	296	10	–	–
Manufacturing	91926	89427	243	539	1251	249	218
Electricity, gas, steam and air conditioning supply; water supply sewerage, waste management activities and remediation services	189755	161973	24512	2769	240	4	258
Construction	11213	10512	19	311	370	–	–
Wholesale and retail trade; repair of motor vehicles and motorcycles	19685	14005	22	138	5520	–	–
Transport and storage; information and communication	82005	80189	161	788	868	–	–
Accommodation and food services	4319	3615	9	16	678	–	–
Financial and insurance activities	211	90	–	9	112	–	–
Real estate activities; professional scientific and technical activities; administration and support service activities	6462	5499	8	32	916	–	7
Public administration and defence; compulsory social security	6010	5605	7	46	233	–	118
Education	3834	3514	7	14	299	–	–
Human health and social work activities	5234	4754	10	7	461	–	1
Arts, entertainment and recreation; other service activities	3233	2964	5	13	250	–	–
Activities of households as employers; undifferentiated goods and services-producing activities of households for own use	232	231	1	1	–	–	–
Consumer expenditure	143169	136755	957	568	4890	–	–
Total	643087	542825	55954	27314	16139	253	602
Of which: emissions from road transport[2]	112337	111331	47	960	–	–	–

	Total acid rain precursors	Sulphur Dioxide (SO2)	Nitrogen Oxides (NOx)	Ammonia (NH3)
Thousand tonnes SO2 equivalent				
Agriculture, forestry and fishing	449	–	19	429
Mining and quarrying	53	9	43	–
Manufacturing	308	185	115	8
Electricity, gas, steam and air conditioning supply; water supply, sewerage, waste management activities and remediation services	378	158	198	22
Construction	30	–	30	–
Wholesale and retail trade; repair of motor vehicles and motorcycles	28	–	27	–
Transport and storage; information and communication	379	91	288	1
Accommodation and food services	3	–	3	–
Financial and insurance activities	–	–	–	–
Real estate activities; professional scientific and technical activities; administrative and support service activities	10	–	9	1
Public administration and defence; compulsory social security	28	4	18	6
Education	6	2	–	–
Human health and social work activities	4	–	4	–
Arts, entertainment and recreation; other service activities	12	–	4	8
Activities of households as employers; undifferentiated goods and services-producing activities of households for own use	–	–	–	–
Consumer expenditure	200	27	132	41
Total (excluding natural world)	1889	479	893	516
Of which: emissions from road transport[2]	242	–	228	14

	Thousand tonnes						Tonnes		
	PM10[3]	PM2.5[3]	CO	NMVOC[4]	Benzene	Butadiene	Lead	Cadmium	Mercury
Agriculture, forestry and fishing	32.01	13	76.92	173.58	0.11	0.04	0.4	0.04	0.02
Mining and quarrying	7.46	1.84	27.62	89.45	0.33	–	0.34	0.03	0.02
Manufacturing	22.8	16.25	600.18	262.69	1.93	0.22	48.23	1.28	3.05
Electricity, gas, steam and air conditioning supply; water supply, sewerage, waste management activities and remediation services	7.82	4.83	89.63	36.88	1.27	0.01	4.61	0.15	1.99
Construction	3.96	2.84	172.69	46.47	0.47	0.14	0.3	0.04	0.02
Wholesale and retail trade; repair of motor vehicles and motorcycles	2.55	1.8	16.87	36.43	0.09	0.04	1.52	0.04	0.02
Transport and storage; information and communication	25.86	23.47	82.6	24.6	1.71	0.22	2.39	0.91	0.11
Accommodation and food services	0.2	0.18	2.07	0.57	0.02	–	0.02	–	–
Financial and insurance activities	0.06	0.05	0.39	0.13	–	–	0.01	–	–
Real estate activities; professional scientific and technical activities; administration and support service activities	0.75	0.58	18.4	1.39	0.05	0.02	0.05	0.01	–
Public administration and defence: compulsory social security	0.9	0.8	19.54	2.05	0.14	0.02	0.13	0.02	0.01
Education	0.49	0.45	2.36	0.25	0.01	–	0.73	0.01	0.07
Human health and social work activities	0.18	0.16	2.27	1.02	0.02	–	0.01	–	–
Arts, entertainment and recreation; other service activities	0.34	0.28	4.75	1.91	0.02	–	0.09	0.01	0.56
Activities of households as employers; undifferentiated goods and services-producing activities of households for own use	–	–	49.11	1.7	0.12	0.02	–	–	–
Consumer expenditure	37.22	31.92	848.22	202.49	2.49	0.43	5.54	0.42	0.32
Total (excluding natural world)	142.6	98.46	2013.63	881.6	8.78	1.18	64.37	2.96	6.17
Of which: emissions from road transport[2]	21.64	15.08	564.04	34.33	1.32	0.53	1.61	0.35	0.22

Source: Ricardo Energy & Environment, ONS

1. Components may not sum to totals due to rounding.

2. Includes emissions from fuel sources which are used by road vehicles (eg HGVs, LGVs, cars and motorcycles) across all industries.

3. PM10 is particulate matter arising from various sources including fuel combustion, quarrying and construction, and formation of 'secondary' particles in the atmosphere from reactions involving other pollutants - sulphur dioxide, nitrogen oxides, ammonia and NMVOCs.

4. Non-methane Volatile Compounds, including benzene and 1,3-butadiene.

10.2 Road Transport[1] Emissions by Pollutant, 2000 to 2013

UK resident basis

All weights in thousand tonnes

Greenhouse gases are comprised of carbon dioxide, methane and nitrous oxide. Weight in carbon dioxide equivalent

Acid rain precursors are comprised of sulphur dioxide, nitrogen oxides and ammonia. Weight in sulphur dioxide equivalent

Pollutant	2000	2001	2002	2003	2004	2005	2006	2007	2008	2009	2010	2011	2012	2013
Greenhouse gases	118,482.2	118,203.0	120,513.4	120,112.3	120,833.8	121,574.9	121,924.5	123,554.2	119,509.4	115,731.8	114,981.3	113,333.9	112,756.3	112,337.5
of which	0.0	0.0	0.0	0.0	0.0	0.0	0.0	0.0	0.0	0.0	0.0	0.0	0.0	0.0
Carbon dioxide	116,754.6	116,609.6	118,991.6	118,698.3	119,491.3	120,295.9	120,710.1	122,375.0	118,516.6	114,825.2	114,071.1	112,397.9	111,786.4	111,330.9
Methane	300.5	259.1	233.9	206.3	184.9	169.3	152.0	137.5	118.2	84.5	72.1	62.9	54.7	46.8
Nitrous oxide	1,427.1	1,334.2	1,287.9	1,207.7	1,157.6	1,109.7	1,062.5	1,041.7	874.6	822.1	838.1	873.0	915.2	959.7
Acid rain precursors	561.0	531.4	500.9	471.4	448.8	425.8	409.1	389.5	362.5	299.8	283.6	267.4	253.1	242.0
of which	0.0	0.0	0.0	0.0	0.0	0.0	0.0	0.0	0.0	0.0	0.0	0.0	0.0	0.0
Sulphur dioxide	5.9	3.4	3.0	3.0	2.7	2.4	2.1	1.7	1.0	0.5	0.5	0.5	0.5	0.4
Nitrogen Oxides as NO2	510.9	486.9	459.4	433.2	413.3	393.3	378.9	362.1	338.7	277.6	263.8	249.8	237.4	227.9
Ammonia	44.2	41.1	38.5	35.1	32.8	30.2	28.1	25.7	22.8	21.8	19.3	17.2	15.2	13.6
PM$_{10}$	35.0	34.4	33.3	32.5	31.8	30.9	30.1	29.2	27.8	26.4	25.7	23.9	22.8	21.6
PM$_{2.5}$	27.8	27.2	26.0	25.2	24.5	23.7	22.8	21.9	20.7	19.5	18.8	17.2	16.2	15.1
Carbon monoxide	3,852.6	3,465.0	3,089.9	2,757.0	2,457.8	2,141.0	1,883.7	1,602.3	1,432.1	1,071.9	904.4	739.5	653.6	564.0
Non Methane VOC	405.5	362.6	306.3	255.5	213.0	177.6	151.0	126.2	108.4	71.5	58.8	47.6	40.7	34.3
Benzene	12.2	12.2	11.5	10.7	9.7	8.5	7.4	6.0	5.2	3.7	2.8	2.2	1.7	1.3
1,3-Butadiene	5.9	5.0	4.3	3.6	3.1	2.7	2.4	2.0	1.8	1.1	0.9	0.8	0.6	0.5
Cadmium	0.4	0.4	0.4	0.4	0.4	0.4	0.4	0.4	0.4	0.4	0.4	0.4	0.4	0.4
Lead	2.2	2.0	2.0	2.0	2.0	2.1	2.1	1.8	1.7	1.6	1.6	1.6	1.6	1.6
Mercury	0.3	0.3	0.3	0.3	0.3	0.3	0.3	0.3	0.2	0.2	0.2	0.2	0.2	0.2

Source: Ricardo-AEA, ONS

[1] Emissions from fuel sources which are used by road vehicles across industry groups.

For any further information about road transport and associated emissions please contact us at environment.accounts@ons.gsi.gov.uk

10.3 UK Greenhouse Gas Emissions headline results

UK and Crown Dependencies 1999-2013, MtCO₂e

Mt CO_2e

	1999	2000	2001	2002	2003	2004	2005	2006	2007	2008	2009	2010	2011	2012	2013
Net CO_2 emissions (emissions minus removals)	553.0	559.5	568.0	550.4	561.3	561.5	557.8	555.6	546.7	532.9	482.2	500.8	457.5	476.3	467.5
Methane (CH_4)	118.8	113.9	109.3	107.1	102.1	97.3	92.1	88.2	84.2	78.3	71.9	67.0	64.0	61.2	56.2
Nitrous Oxide (N_2O)	37.1	36.6	34.7	32.9	32.7	33.3	32.2	31.2	30.9	30.2	28.5	28.9	27.7	27.7	27.6
Hydrofluorocarbons (HFC)	11.9	10.5	11.4	11.8	13.1	12.2	13.1	13.9	14.2	14.8	15.2	15.7	16.0	16.2	16.2
Perfluorocarbons (PFC)	0.5	0.6	0.5	0.4	0.4	0.4	0.4	0.4	0.3	0.3	0.2	0.3	0.4	0.3	0.3
Sulphur hexafluoride (SF_6)	1.5	1.8	1.5	1.5	1.3	1.1	1.1	0.8	0.8	0.7	0.7	0.7	0.6	0.6	0.6
Nitrogen Trifluoride (NF_3)	0.0	0.0	0.0	0.0	0.0	0.0	0.0	0.0	0.0	0.0	0.0	0.0	0.0	0.0	0.0
Total greenhouse gas emissions	722.9	722.8	725.4	704.2	710.9	705.8	696.6	690.1	677.2	657.1	598.6	613.3	566.2	582.2	568.3

Notes:

1. The entire time series is revised each year to take account of methodological improvements.

2. Nitrogen trifluoride emissions are being reported for the first time this year, following the introduction of updated guidelines for emissions reporting.

Uncertainty in estimates and Global Warming Potential[1] (GWP) of UK Greenhouse Gas emissions: 1990/2013

UK, Crown Dependencies and Overseas Territories 1990/2013

Pollutant		GWP[1]	1990 emissions[2] (thousand tonnes CO_2 equivalent)	2013 emissions[2] (thousand tonnes CO_2 equivalent)	Uncertainty[3] in 2013 emissions	Range of uncertainty in 2013 emissions 2.5 percentile	Range of uncertainty in 2013 emissions 97.5 percentile	Percentage change between 2013 and 1990	Range of likely % change 'between 2013 and 1990[4] 2.5 percentile	Range of likely % change 'between 2013 and 1990[4] 97.5 percentile
Carbon dioxide[5]	CO_2	1	599,341	469,209	2%	459,112	479,454	-22%	-23%	-20%
Methane	CH_4	25	137,343	56,456	19%	46,864	68,331	-58%	-68%	-47%
Nitrous Oxide	N_2O	298	57,054	27,781	58%	17,597	49,566	-51%	-67%	-35%
Hydrofluorocarbons	HFC	12 - 14,800	14,553	16,263	9%	14,876	17,664	12%	-5%	34%
Perfluorocarbons	PFC	7,390 - 17,340	1,652	254	25%	196	321	-85%	-88%	-80%
Sulphur hexafluoride	SF_6	22,800	1,279	602	10%	539	663	-53%	-59%	-45%
Nitrogen trifluoride	NF_3	17,200	0	0	47%	0	1	-13%	-55%	74%
All greenhouse gases weighted by GWP			811,222	570,565	4%	551,861	596,613	-30%	-33%	-27%

Source: Department of Energy and Climate Change

Notes:

1. The GWP (Global Warming Potential) of a greenhouse gas measures its effectiveness in global warming over 100 years relative to carbon dioxide.

2. 1990 and 2013 estimates, and the percentage change, are presented as the central estimate from the model. These differ from the actual emissions estimates.

3. Expressed as a percentage relative to the mean value 2013 emissions. Calculated as 0.5*R/E where R is the difference between 2.5 and 97.5 percentiles and E is the mean.

4. Equivalent to a 95 per cent probability that the percentage change between 1990 and 2013 is between the two values shown. Values include uncertainties for overseas territories data.

5. CO_2 emissions are net emissions. Total emissions minus removals.

6. Figures include emissions for the UK, Crown Dependencies and the Overseas Territories. Uncertainties are not calculated for different geographical coverages but would be expected to be similar.

10.4 Summary Greenhouse Gas Emissions Bridging Table showing relationship of Environmental Accounts measure to UNFCCC[1] measure

UK [5][6][9]   Thousand tonnes CO_2 equivalent

	1990	1995	2000	2005	2010	2012	2013
Greenhouse gases[2] - CO_2, CH_4, N_2O, HFCs, PFCs SF_6 and NF_3							
Environmental Account	841,966	799,824	777,951	774,946	687,085	656,541	643,087
less							
Bunker emissions[3]	24,195	28,251	36,917	42,814	40,874	40,988	40,546
CO2 biomass[4]	2,545	4,327	5,087	8,749	16,062	17,081	20,414
Cross-boundary[5]	11,663	11,949	16,026	25,628	14,350	13,119	10,317
plus							
Crown Dependencies[6]	1,861	2,015	2,041	1,754	1,815	1,813	1,785
Land-Use, Land-Use Change and Forestry (LULUCF)[7]	3,989	3,298	865	-2,909	-4,279	-4,956	-5,249
DECC reported (Excluding Overseas Territories)[8][9]	809,413	760,609	722,827	696,599	613,334	582,209	568,347
plus							
Overseas Territories (including net emissions from land use change/forestry)	1,793	1,764	1,853	2,119	2,170	2,056	2,105
UNFCCC reported in the UK Greenhouse Gas Inventory[8]	811,206	762,373	724,680	698,719	615,504	584,265	570,452
Kyoto greenhouse gas basket (baseline taken from the Assigned Amount Report)[8][9]	*782,211*	*731,138*	*702,892*	*686,279*	*610,300*	*583,126*	*-*

Source: Ricardo-AEA, DECC, ONS

1 United Nations Framework Convention on Climate Change http://unfccc.int/2860.php
2 Carbon dioxide, methane, nitrous oxide, hydrofluorocarbons, perfluorocarbons, sulphur hexafluoride and nitrogen trifluoride expressed as thousand tonnes of carbon dioxide equivalent
3 Bunker emissions include IPCC memo items International Aviation and International Shipping
4 Emissions arising from wood, straw, biogases and poultry litter combustion for energy production
5 Emissions generated by UK households and business transport and travel abroad, net of emissions generated by non-residents travel and transport in the UK
6 Emissions of Crown dependancies; Guernsey, Jersey, Isle of Man.
7 Emissions from deforestation, soils and changes in forest and other woody biomass.
8 https://www.gov.uk/government/statistics/final-uk-emissions-estimates
9 This is the UK total for the sum of the 7 pollutants and differs slightly from the Kyoto greenhouse gas basket totals which uses a narrower definition of Land Use, Land Use Change and Forestry and includes emissions from UK Overseas Territories (Gibraltar, the Falkland Islands, the Cayman Islands, Montserrat, Bermuda)

10.5 Estimated emissions of carbon dioxide (CO_2) by source, 1998-2013

UK and Crown Dependencies

Units: Million Tonnes

NC Category	1998	1999	2000	2001	2002	2003	2004	2005	2006	2007	2008	2009	2010	2011	2012	2013
Energy Supply	203.4	193.1	203.6	214.0	212.0	219.4	217.4	218.7	224.4	219.3	213.0	190.0	196.4	182.3	193.3	180.8
Business	108.0	110.3	109.7	107.5	96.5	99.1	98.3	97.1	94.1	92.3	89.5	76.3	79.3	73.4	72.9	75.5
Transport	124.9	126.0	124.9	125.1	127.6	127.2	128.5	129.3	129.9	131.3	125.7	120.9	119.3	117.5	116.9	115.7
Public	12.9	12.8	12.0	12.2	10.3	10.2	11.2	11.1	10.1	9.4	10.7	9.2	9.7	9.3	9.3	9.5
Residential	86.0	85.8	86.1	88.4	85.0	85.8	87.2	83.0	80.3	76.8	78.6	75.3	84.9	64.9	74.4	74.7
Agriculture	6.3	6.2	5.8	5.8	5.8	5.9	5.7	5.6	5.4	5.4	4.9	5.2	5.2	5.4	5.1	4.9
Industrial Process	17.5	17.6	17.1	15.7	14.8	15.6	16.0	16.4	15.5	16.8	15.1	10.0	10.6	10.1	9.9	12.2
Land Use Change	0.9	0.8	-0.2	-1.1	-2.1	-2.5	-3.3	-3.8	-4.4	-4.8	-4.9	-4.9	-5.1	-5.6	-5.8	-6.0
Waste Management	0.5	0.5	0.5	0.5	0.5	0.5	0.4	0.4	0.3	0.3	0.3	0.3	0.3	0.3	0.2	0.3
Grand Total	560.6	553.0	559.5	568.0	550.4	561.3	561.5	557.8	555.6	546.7	532.9	482.2	500.8	457.5	476.3	467.5

Source: Department of Energy and Climate Change

Notes:
1. The entire time series is revised each year to take account of methodological improvements.

10.6 Estimated emissions of methane (CH$_4$) by source, 2001-2013

UK and Crown Dependencies, thousand tonnes

Thousand tonnes

NC Category	2001	2002	2003	2004	2005	2006	2007	2008	2009	2010	2011	2012	2013
Energy Supply	606.7	584.2	522.3	510.9	443.9	411.3	392.9	375.4	372.2	361.0	352.3	349.3	303.6
Business	5.0	4.9	5.4	4.8	4.7	4.5	4.5	4.7	4.0	4.3	4.3	4.2	4.4
Transport	12.7	11.5	10.2	9.2	8.5	7.7	7.0	6.1	4.5	3.9	3.4	3.0	2.6
Public	1.1	0.9	0.9	1.0	1.0	0.9	0.8	0.9	0.8	0.8	0.8	0.8	0.8
Residential	28.6	23.6	21.9	20.8	18.7	19.4	21.1	22.4	21.6	24.6	21.8	23.3	23.4
Agriculture	1172.6	1149.8	1157.9	1166.4	1151.2	1143.8	1130.4	1104.9	1088.6	1094.3	1089.2	1085.2	1080.9
Industrial Process	5.9	6.0	6.7	5.9	5.1	5.1	5.6	4.3	4.7	4.8	4.3	4.7	5.1
Land Use Change	1.8	1.8	3.0	1.9	2.2	1.8	2.3	1.8	2.0	1.9	1.6	2.7	1.4
Waste Management	2536.2	2502.5	2354.0	2173.1	2048.2	1932.1	1804.9	1613.1	1376.8	1184.4	1080.3	974.9	825.2
Grand Total	**4,370.7**	**4,285.1**	**4,082.3**	**3,893.9**	**3,683.4**	**3,526.6**	**3,369.4**	**3,133.6**	**2,875.2**	**2,680.1**	**2,558.0**	**2,448.2**	**2,247.4**

Source: Department of Energy and Climate Change

Notes:

1. The entire time series is revised each year to take account of methodological improvements.

10.7 Estimated emissions of nitrous oxide (N$_2$O) by source, 1999-2013

UK and Crown Dependencies 1999-2013, Mt CO$_2$e

Mt CO$_2$e

NC Category	1999	2000	2001	2002	2003	2004	2005	2006	2007	2008	2009	2010	2011	2012	2013
Energy Supply	1.3	1.4	1.5	1.5	1.6	1.5	1.5	1.6	1.5	1.4	1.2	1.2	1.3	1.5	1.4
Business	1.1	1.1	1.1	1.1	1.1	1.2	1.2	1.2	1.2	1.1	0.9	0.9	0.8	0.9	0.8
Transport	1.5	1.5	1.4	1.3	1.3	1.2	1.2	1.1	1.1	1.0	0.9	0.9	0.9	1.0	1.0
Public	0.0	0.0	0.0	0.0	0.0	0.0	0.0	0.0	0.0	0.0	0.0	0.0	0.0	0.0	0.0
Residential	0.2	0.2	0.2	0.1	0.1	0.1	0.1	0.1	0.1	0.1	0.1	0.1	0.1	0.1	0.1
Agriculture	25.4	24.6	23.5	23.7	23.5	23.3	22.9	22.5	22.0	21.8	21.7	22.0	21.9	21.7	21.8
Industrial Process	5.2	5.4	4.7	2.7	2.9	3.7	2.9	2.3	2.7	2.5	1.2	1.3	0.2	0.1	0.1
Land Use Change	1.0	1.0	1.0	0.9	0.9	0.9	0.9	0.8	0.8	0.8	0.8	0.7	0.7	0.7	0.7
Waste Management	1.3	1.3	1.3	1.3	1.3	1.4	1.4	1.4	1.5	1.5	1.6	1.6	1.6	1.7	1.7
Grand Total	**37.1**	**36.6**	**34.7**	**32.9**	**32.7**	**33.3**	**32.2**	**31.2**	**30.9**	**30.2**	**28.5**	**28.9**	**27.7**	**27.7**	**27.6**

Source: Department of Energy and Climate Change

Notes:

1. The entire time series is revised each year to take account of methodological improvements.

10.8 Material flow account for the United Kingdom 2001 to 2013

1,000 Metric tonnes

Domestic extraction	2001	2002	2003	2004	2005	2006	2007	2008	2009	2010	2011	2012	2013
Biomass	**145,579**	**153,941**	**149,492**	**150,388**	**144,780**	**146,656**	**145,895**	**153,050**	**153,220**	**152,112**	**158,878**	**149,838**	**162,571**
Crops	39,352	44,746	42,341	42,746	41,649	39,698	37,157	43,711	42,359	39,777	42,745	37,350	40,163
Crop residues (used), fodder crops and grazed biomass	100,614	103,670	101,552	101,864	97,249	101,199	102,633	103,606	104,999	105,791	109,428	105,690	115,233
Wood	4,672	4,617	4,775	4,915	5,039	4,963	5,311	4,958	5,092	5,730	5,907	5,963	6,348
Wild fish catch and aquatic plants/animals	940	908	826	862	843	796	794	775	770	814	799	835	827
Metal ores (gross ores)	**7**	**6**	**6**	**5**	**4**	**4**	**3**	**3**	**4**	**4**	**4**	**1**	**1**
Iron	1	0	1	1	0	0	0	0	0	0	0	0	0
Non-ferrous metal	7	6	6	4	3	3	3	3	4	4	4	1	1
Non-metallic minerals	**310,881**	**293,164**	**287,885**	**300,018**	**290,601**	**291,300**	**295,217**	**261,116**	**210,290**	**204,761**	**207,706**	**191,875**	**195,866**
Limestone and gypsum	89,938	82,388	80,635	83,334	79,296	81,928	85,191	75,345	61,311	58,185	59,300	56,000	58,100
Clays and kaolin	14,140	13,925	14,224	14,504	14,221	13,437	13,135	11,014	7,226	8,084	8,536	7,491	8,419
Sand and gravel	176,727	167,856	164,899	174,227	170,603	169,275	173,861	155,996	126,935	122,202	123,756	112,228	113,938
Other	30,076	28,995	28,127	27,953	26,481	26,660	23,030	18,762	14,818	16,290	16,114	16,156	15,409
Fossil energy materials/carriers	**254,457**	**248,955**	**237,442**	**216,568**	**193,416**	**175,259**	**165,428**	**159,059**	**145,689**	**138,580**	**115,916**	**100,450**	**90,286**
Coal and other solid energy materials/carriers	33,296	30,722	29,791	26,046	21,631	19,717	17,673	18,626	18,542	19,172	19,248	17,475	13,792
Crude oil, condensate and natural gas liquids	116,678	115,944	106,073	95,374	84,721	76,579	76,575	71,665	68,198	62,962	51,972	44,560	40,646
Natural gas	104,483	102,289	101,578	95,148	87,063	78,964	71,179	68,767	58,950	56,446	44,696	38,415	35,848
Total domestic extraction	**710,924**	**696,066**	**674,825**	**666,979**	**628,800**	**613,219**	**606,543**	**573,228**	**509,203**	**495,457**	**482,504**	**442,164**	**448,724**

1.Totals may not sum due to rounding.

Sources: Department for Environment, Food and Rural Affairs; Food and Agriculture Organization of the United Nations; Eurostat; European Forest Institute; Kentish Cobnuts Association; British Geological Survey

The symbol ':' denotes that the data are not available

The symbol ' —' denotes that the data are not applicable (or zero)

1,000 Metric tonnes

Imports	2001	2002	2003	2004	2005	2006	2007	2008	2009	2010	2011	2012	2013
Biomass and biomass products	49,668	50,184	52,631	53,671	53,935	53,710	53,867	52,312	49,423	51,425	50,468	52,387	58,501
Metal ores and concentrates, raw and processed	42,167	41,035	42,348	45,964	43,623	45,291	47,862	42,605	26,955	32,936	33,522	33,855	37,972
Non-metallic minerals, raw and processed	14,845	17,013	16,240	16,989	16,752	16,454	17,160	16,337	12,684	15,078	15,904	13,904	14,505
Fossil energy materials/carriers, raw and processed	109,127	105,309	113,301	138,367	148,165	159,123	159,103	152,461	148,598	148,014	160,229	171,578	166,562
Other products	16,832	15,170	15,793	18,258	16,915	17,167	17,038	16,469	14,858	16,541	15,611	15,102	15,951
Waste imported for final treatment and disposal	1	4	2	1	1	15	10	13	19	22	5	5	30
Total imports	**232,640**	**228,715**	**240,314**	**273,252**	**279,392**	**291,759**	**295,039**	**280,197**	**252,537**	**264,016**	**275,740**	**286,830**	**293,521**

1,000 Metric tonnes

Exports	2001	2002	2003	2004	2005	2006	2007	2008	2009	2010	2011	2012	2013
Biomass and biomass products	13,850	15,686	20,289	19,118	20,005	20,704	21,374	21,543	20,159	22,413	21,950	22,103	21,239
Metal ores and concentrates, raw and processed	21,870	22,155	24,952	26,677	26,355	27,216	27,335	27,176	20,709	23,502	24,502	23,991	25,316
Non-metallic minerals, raw and processed	21,867	20,445	20,312	21,928	22,634	23,591	22,840	21,170	17,094	16,681	17,034	14,444	15,119
Fossil energy materials/carriers, raw and processed	127,540	129,791	114,128	108,739	98,716	93,760	90,402	89,444	87,836	95,693	92,063	88,728	84,759
Other products	8,832	8,596	8,934	8,685	9,423	8,504	9,539	8,754	7,721	7,716	7,739	7,705	7,693
Waste exported for final treatment and disposal	0	5	2	4	2	3	0	1	3	3	4	5	124
Total exports	**193,959**	**196,678**	**188,616**	**185,150**	**177,134**	**173,778**	**171,491**	**168,087**	**153,523**	**166,008**	**163,291**	**156,976**	**154,250**

Source: HM Revenue & Customs

1.Totals may not sum due to rounding.

10.8 Material flow account for the United Kingdom 2001 to 2013

1,000 Metric tonnes

Indicators	2001	2002	2003	2004	2005	2006	2007	2008	2009	2010	2011	2012	2013
Domestic Material Consumption (Domestic extraction + Imports - Exports)	749,605	728,102	726,523	755,080	731,058	731,200	730,091	685,338	608,217	593,465	594,953	572,018	587,994
Biomass	181,397	188,439	181,835	184,941	178,710	179,662	178,387	183,819	182,484	181,124	187,396	180,122	199,832
Metal ores	20,305	18,886	17,403	19,293	17,271	18,079	20,530	15,433	6,250	9,438	9,025	9,866	12,657
Non-metallic minerals	303,860	289,732	283,813	295,080	284,720	284,162	289,537	256,283	205,879	203,157	206,577	191,335	195,252
Fossil fuels	236,044	224,473	236,615	246,197	242,865	240,623	234,128	222,076	206,452	190,901	184,082	183,300	172,090
Physical Trade Balance (Imports-Exports)	38,681	32,037	51,698	88,101	102,258	117,981	123,548	112,109	99,014	98,009	112,449	129,854	139,271
Direct Material Input (Domestic extraction + Imports)	943,564	924,780	915,139	940,230	908,192	904,978	901,582	853,425	761,740	759,473	758,243	728,994	742,245

1. Indicators were calculated using unrounded data.

Sources: Office for National Statistics

2. Estimates for indirect flows and raw material consumption are currently under development.

Metric tonnes

Per capita (person)	2001	2002	2003	2004	2005	2006	2007	2008	2009	2010	2011	2012	2013
Mid-year population estimates (persons)[1]	59,113,000	59,365,700	59,636,700	59,950,400	60,413,300	60,827,100	61,319,100	61,823,800	62,260,500	62,759,500	63,285,100	63,705,000	64,105,700
Domestic extraction	12.0	11.7	11.3	11.1	10.4	10.1	9.9	9.3	8.2	7.9	7.6	6.9	7.0
Total imports	3.9	3.9	4.0	4.6	4.6	4.8	4.8	4.5	4.1	4.2	4.4	4.5	4.6
Total exports	3.3	3.3	3.2	3.1	2.9	2.9	2.8	2.7	2.5	2.6	2.6	2.5	2.4
Domestic Material Consumption (DMC)	12.7	12.3	12.2	12.6	12.1	12.0	11.9	11.1	9.8	9.5	9.4	9.0	9.2
Direct Material Input (DMI)	16.0	15.6	15.3	15.7	15.0	14.9	14.7	13.8	12.2	12.1	12.0	11.4	11.6

1. Available here: http://www.ons.gov.uk/ons/rel/pop-estimate/population-estimates-for-uk--england-and-wales--scotland-and-northern-ireland/mid-2014/index.html

The symbol '..' denotes that the data are not available

10.9 Annual rainfall: by region

United Kingdom

Millimetres and percentages

Region		1971 - 2000[2] rainfall average (= 100%) millimetres	2000	2001	2002	2003	2004	2005	2006	2007	2008	2009	2010	2011	2012	2013	2014
United Kingdom	JSJB	1084	123	97	118	83	112	100	109	111	120	112	88	108	123	101	120
North West	JSJC	1177	132	94	121	85	116	96	114	110	126	113	84	116	136	97	111
Northumbria	JSJD	831	132	106	124	80	120	111	101	105	135	116	105	104	144	106	110
Severn Trent[1]	JSJE	759	132	104	119	81	110	92	103	123	121	103	84	74	139	100	121
Yorkshire	JSJF	814	136	100	126	82	114	96	110	115	130	105	91	89	143	91	114
Anglian	JSJG	603	129	124	118	86	115	89	102	118	116	99	97	73	138	93	122
Thames	JSLK	700	137	116	128	81	103	79	106	118	115	104	87	79	134	101	130
Southern	JSLL	782	148	114	129	85	97	79	101	106	108	109	94	81	130	107	137
Wessex	JSLM	866	136	100	132	83	98	89	100	113	116	107	80	84	140	101	128
South West	JSLN	1208	128	92	121	78	99	90	92	110	112	110	83	86	133	103	115
England	JSLO	819	133	105	123	83	109	91	103	114	120	107	89	87	137	99	120
Wales	JSLP	1373	133	98	119	83	108	95	107	108	121	109	82	94	124	98	113
Scotland	JSLQ	1440	113	91	112	84	117	110	114	109	120	117	87	131	112	102	122
Northern Ireland	JSLR	1111	110	81	127	84	98	96	104	99	114	114	94	115	107	103	117

Sources: Met Office; National Hydrological Monitoring Programme, Centre for Ecology and Hydrology

1. The regions of England shown in this table correspond to the original nine English regions of the National Rivers Authority (NRA); the NRA became part of the Environment Agency upon its creation in April 1996. The exception to this is the Severn Trent region, part of which (the upper Severn) lies in Wales.

2. 1971-2000 averages have been derived using arithmetic averages of Met Office areal rainfall.

10.10 UK Annual Weather Summary

	Max Temp		Min Temp		Mean Temp		Sunshine		Rainfall	
	Actual (degrees celsius)	Anomaly (degrees celsius)	Actual (degrees celsius)	Anomaly (degrees celsius)	Actual (degrees celsius)	Anomaly (degrees celsius)	Actual (hours/ day)	Anomaly (%)	Actual (mm)	Anomaly (%)
	WLRL	WLRM	WLRO	WLRP	WLRR	WLRS	WLRX	WLRY	WLSH	WLSI
1990	13.1	1.2	5.8	0.9	9.4	1.1	1490.7	111.4	1172.8	106.7
1991	12.1	0.3	5.1	0.2	8.6	0.3	1302.0	97.3	998.2	90.8
1992	12.3	0.4	5.2	0.4	8.7	0.4	1290.8	96.5	1186.8	107.9
1993	11.8	-0.1	5.0	0.1	8.4	0.0	1218.6	91.1	1121.1	102.0
1994	12.4	0.5	5.5	0.6	8.9	0.6	1366.9	102.2	1184.7	107.7
1995	13.0	1.1	5.4	0.6	9.2	0.9	1588.5	118.7	1023.7	93.1
1996	11.7	-0.1	4.7	-0.1	8.2	-0.2	1403.5	104.9	916.6	83.4
1997	13.1	1.3	5.8	1.0	9.4	1.1	1430.3	106.9	1024.0	93.1
1998	12.6	0.8	5.8	1.0	9.1	0.8	1268.4	94.8	1265.1	115.1
1999	13.0	1.1	5.9	1.0	9.4	1.1	1419.4	106.1	1239.1	112.5
2000	12.7	0.8	5.6	0.8	9.1	0.8	1367.5	102.2	1337.3	121.5
2001	12.4	0.6	5.3	0.5	8.8	0.5	1411.9	105.5	1052.8	95.5
2002	13.0	1.1	6.0	1.2	9.5	1.2	1304.0	97.5	1283.7	116.5
2003	13.5	1.6	5.6	0.7	9.5	1.2	1587.4	118.7	904.2	82.0
2004	13.0	1.2	6.0	1.2	9.5	1.2	1361.4	101.8	1210.1	110.1
2005	13.1	1.2	5.9	1.1	9.5	1.1	1399.2	104.6	1083.0	98.4
2006	13.4	1.5	6.1	1.3	9.7	1.4	1495.9	111.8	1175.9	106.8
2007	13.3	1.4	6.0	1.1	9.6	1.3	1450.7	108.4	1197.1	108.8
2008	12.7	0.8	5.5	0.6	9.1	0.7	1388.8	103.8	1295.0	117.7
2009	12.8	1.0	5.6	0.7	9.2	0.9	1467.4	109.7	1213.3	110.2
2010	11.7	-0.1	4.2	-0.6	8.0	-0.4	1456.0	108.8	950.5	86.4
2011	13.5	1.5	6.0	1.2	9.6	1.3	1406.2	105.0	1172.5	107
2012	12.4	0.5	5.2	0.4	8.8	0.4	1340.5	100	1334.8	121
2013	12.4	0.5	5.2	0.4	8.8	0.5	1421.1	106	1091	99
2014	13.5	1.7	6.3	1.5	9.9	1.6	1426.6	107	1300.5	118

Source: Met Office

10.11 Summary of River Basin District Ecological and Chemical Status 2009-2014

River Basin District	Percent of surface water bodies are at good chemical status or better					
	2009	2010	2011	2012	2013	2014
Solway Tweed	50	89	89	88	91	91
Northumbria	50	68	72	68	70	75
Humber	77	79	83	77	76	77
Anglian	85	89	92	87	84	83
Thames	75	76	79	74	72	70
South East	88	91	93	88	88	87
South West	77	80	83	84	79	79
Severn	78	83	88	82	82	83
Dee	75	92	92	87	82	67
North West	70	75	72	71	74	76

River Basin District	Percent of surface water bodies are at good ecological status/potential or better					
	2009	2010	2011	2012	2013	2014
Solway Tweed	44	43	45	48	41	41
Northumbria	43	41	43	40	42	38
Humber	18	16	17	18	17	16
Anglian	18	19	18	18	17	13
Thames	23	22	22	18	19	14
South East	19	15	16	15	15	13
South West	33	31	34	32	31	27
Severn	29	30	30	30	29	26
Dee	28	26	30	30	25	15
North West	30	31	30	29	30	28

Source: Environment Agency

% of English water bodies only

Improvements measured in terms of the number of water bodies meeting good status

10.12 Overall status of rivers & canals in Scotland, 2013

	High	Max EP	Good	Good EP	Moderate	Moderate EP	Poor	Poor Ep	Bad	Bad EP
No. of river water bodies	154	0	1022	145	493	122	295	83	55	36
Length of river water bodies (km)	1293	0	10007	1339	6182	1214	3155	948	629	346
% of length of river water bodies	5.1%	0.0%	39.8%	5.3%	24.6%	4.8%	12.6%	3.8%	2.5%	1.4%

Water Quality 2013

	High	Good	Moderate	Poor	bad
No. of river water bodies	873	1100	377	43	12
Length of river water bodies (km)	8764.8	11561	4223.9	427.5	135.2
% of length of river water bodies	34.9%	46.0%	16.8%	1.7%	0.5%

Source: Scottish Environment Protection Agency

10.13 Monthly reservoir stocks for England & Wales[1]

Percentages

		2002	2003	2004	2005	2006	2007	2008	2009	2010	2011	2012	2013	2014
January	JTAS	93.7	95.0	93.8	92.3	88.7	93.7	95.7	95.3	92.4	89.8	90.4	96.7	98.2
February	JTAT	95.5	92.1	92.1	92.1	91.2	96.7	95.6	93.4	91.8	93.7	92.0	93.8	98.1
March	JTAU	94.5	92.3	94.4	93.6	96.2	95.2	97.3	94.5	94.1	92.2	89.2	92.0	96.4
April	JTAV	91.9	88.6	94.7	95.0	93.4	91.9	95.1	92.0	91.9	88.9	94.0	94.5	95.4
May	JTAW	97.0	93.1	90.5	93.0	94.4	91.1	92.6	93.3	86.2	87.4	93.6	94.5	96.1
June	JTAX	94.9	87.0	84.8	85.6	88.4	94.4	90.6	88.6	79.0	86.7	97.8	90.8	91.3
July	JTAY	91.1	81.1	78.5	77.9	77.2	93.5	92.0	91.1	77.3	84.7	96.8	83.7	82.9
August	JTAZ	85.9	69.9	82.4	71.5	70.7	88.3	92.5	89.7	75.5	79.9	96.0	82.2	81.5
September	JTBA	77.3	60.4	84.2	67.4	67.8	86.1	90.9	84.0	81.1	81.0	95.3	77.7	73.6
October	JTBB	82.9	53.0	87.5	77.2	80.0	81.2	93.8	82.3	82.0	80.0	94.3	87.6	79.8
November	JTBC	91.8	60.9	86.2	83.8	89.8	82.4	93.1	93.0	86.9	79.7	95.8	88.3	83.6
December	JTBD	95.1	79.9	91.2	85.9	92.2	89.8	92.4	90.6	84.3	88.6	97.6	95.4	92.0

1 Reservoir stocks are the percentage of useable capacity based on a representative selection of reservoirs; the percentages relate to the end of each month.

Sources: Water PLCs;

Environment Agency;

National Hydrological Monitoring Programme, Centre for Ecology and Hydrology: 01491 838800

10.14a Current cost profit and loss account for the 12 months ended 31 March 2015 (appointed business only)

Columns are grouped: **WaSC** (Anglian … Yorkshire), **WoC** (Affinity … Sutton and East Surrey) and **Total only** (Northern Ireland, Scottish).

Water

Description	Anglian	Welsh	Northumbrian	Severn Trent	Southern	South West	Thames	United Utilities	Wessex	Yorkshire	Affinity	Bournemouth	Bristol	Dee Valley	Portsmouth	South East	South Staffs / Cambridge	Sutton and East Surrey	Northern Ireland	Scottish
Turnover																				
Unmeasured - household	113.854	163.100	220.500	350.900	30.800	58.300	508.900	373.300	69.500	208.200	127.900	11.025	59.600	8.634	21.018	69.650	58.700	29.643		
Unmeasured - non-household	0.538	2.500	2.600	2.800	1.200	1.400	7.600	4.400	2.500	1.200	2.592	0.454	1.200	0.111	0.304	1.605	1.393	0.252		
Measured - household	250.634	63.800	126.000	208.500	119.200	114.000	218.300	186.500	68.100	133.700	102.336	18.229	38.700	8.106	6.331	93.328	35.030	19.607		
Measured - non-household	86.271	71.600	66.900	137.500	30.900	48.600	178.700	137.400	43.000	84.000	56.552	9.426	23.500	7.518	8.820	40.462	25.468	8.898		
Trade effluent	0.000	0.000	0.000	0.000	0.000	0.000	0.000	0.000	0.000	0.000	0.000	0.000	0.000	0.000	0.000	0.000	0.000	0.000		
Bulk supplies/inter company payments	6.499	9.800	0.800	5.300	2.600	8.100	3.400	0.700	0.400	0.400	3.040	0.010	0.600	0.004	0.226	0.003	0.461	0.038		
Other third party services (incl non-potable water)	12.562	21.800	9.300	37.300	6.600	5.200	2.700	6.200	0.100	0.200	1.104	0.197	1.200	0.096	1.407	0.000	0.808	1.123		
Other sources	36.608	8.400	28.400	1.700	7.400	0.000	42.900	59.800	15.100	36.700	0.000	5.507	6.200	0.000	0.095	4.918	0.513	1.240		
Total turnover	506.966	341.100	454.500	744.000	198.700	235.600	962.500	768.300	198.700	464.400	293.524	44.848	131.000	24.469	38.201	209.966	122.373	60.801		
Current cost operating costs - wholesale	-329.232	-233.100	-276.000	-486.700	-147.600	-127.900	-610.900	-448.500	-124.100	-287.800	-184.015	-29.021	-95.000	-16.430	-28.096	-127.929	-76.853	-40.321		
Current cost operating costs - retail	-37.948	-31.700	-43.500	-65.200	-30.400	-17.800	-111.800	-84.000	-15.700	-29.300	-36.295	-4.698	-11.300	-4.069	-5.255	-18.224	-18.308	-6.635		
Operating income	-0.154	0.000	-0.200	1.700	-2.400	0.500	8.000	-1.200	-0.200	1.100	-0.979	0.000	-0.200	0.000	0.003	-0.001	0.224	13.845		
Working capital adjustment	-0.299	0.000	-0.200	-0.200	0.100	-0.100	1.200	0.000	-0.100	0.400	0.192	-0.032	0.100	0.015	0.046	0.076	0.114	0.056		
Current cost operating profit	139.333	76.300	134.600	193.600	18.400	90.300	249.000	234.600	58.600	148.800	72.427	11.097	24.600	3.985	4.899	63.888	27.551	13.901		
Other income	0.000	0.000	0.000	0.000	0.000	0.000	0.900	0.000	0.000	0.000	0.000	0.115	0.300	0.054	0.000	0.658	0.000	0.892		
Net Interest	0.000	-75.900	0.000	0.000	0.000	0.000	0.000	0.000	0.000	0.000	-35.664	-4.970	-11.600	-2.557	-2.809	-47.997	-11.498	-9.873		
Financing adjustment	0.000	6.200	0.000	0.000	0.000	0.000	0.000	0.000	0.000	0.000	7.714	0.781	1.900	-0.029	0.021	6.759	0.097	0.265		
Current cost profit before taxation	139.333	6.600	134.600	193.600	18.400	90.300	249.900	234.600	58.600	148.800	44.477	7.023	15.200	1.453	2.111	23.308	16.150	5.185		
Net revenue movement out of tariff basket	0.698	0.200	0.200	-0.200	0.000	-0.400	1.200	0.500	0.100	0.100	-0.160	0.028	-0.100	0.000	-0.002	0.147	0.412	0.002		
Back-billing amount identified	0.000	0.000	0.000	0.000	0.000	0.000	4.100	0.000	0.000	0.200	3.540	0.000	0.000	0.000	0.000	0.000	0.127	0.000		

Sewerage

Description	Anglian	Welsh	Northumbrian	Severn Trent	Southern	South West	Thames	United Utilities	Wessex	Yorkshire	Affinity	Bournemouth	Bristol	Dee Valley	Portsmouth	South East	South Staffs / Cambridge	Sutton and East Surrey	Northern Ireland	Scottish
Turnover																				
Unmeasured - household	185.523	226.000	161.100	375.900	174.400	70.400	523.900	408.400	136.600	249.300	0.000	0.000	0.000	0.000	0.000	0.000	0.000	0.000		
Unmeasured - non-household	1.279	3.200	4.100	8.200	5.600	2.200	4.100	6.300	3.200	2.300	0.000	0.000	0.000	0.000	0.000	0.000	0.000	0.000		
Measured - household	405.678	99.100	59.700	195.700	332.200	147.700	295.800	217.000	122.600	164.800	0.000	0.000	0.000	0.000	0.000	0.000	0.000	0.000		
Measured - non-household	82.924	60.700	61.000	181.500	81.000	44.700	150.300	252.800	52.300	78.100	0.000	0.000	0.000	0.000	0.000	0.000	0.000	0.000		
Trade effluent	8.184	9.700	3.000	13.200	7.700	4.400	8.200	22.400	4.300	11.900	0.000	0.000	0.000	0.000	0.000	0.000	0.000	0.000		
Bulk supplies/inter company payments	1.817	10.000	0.000	0.000	0.000	9.600	0.000	0.100	0.100	0.000	0.000	0.000	0.000	0.000	0.000	0.000	0.000	0.000		
Other third party services (incl non-potable water)	0.000	1.100	0.200	37.700	3.300	3.200	2.000	0.900	1.300	0.900	0.000	0.000	0.000	0.000	0.000	0.000	0.000	0.000		
Other sources	34.475	0.000	17.300	4.700	19.000	0.000	47.800	50.700	13.800	33.100	0.000	0.000	0.000	0.000	0.000	0.000	0.000	0.000		
Total turnover	719.880	409.800	307.000	816.900	623.200	282.200	1 036.100	957.300	334.200	540.400	0.000	0.000	0.000	0.000	0.000	0.000	0.000	0.000		
Current cost operating costs - wholesale	-475.520	-224.500	-183.200	-480.100	-365.600	-174.400	-652.900	-535.400	-175.300	-365.000	0.000	0.000	0.000	0.000	0.000	0.000	0.000	0.000		
Current cost operating costs - retail	-46.042	38.100	-17.100	-64.400	-54.200	-18.000	-84.100	-93.900	-16.300	-34.100	0.000	0.000	0.000	0.000	0.000	0.000	0.000	0.000		
Operating income	-0.126	0.000	0.700	1.700	-4.200	0.800	8.600	-4.800	-0.700	0.700	0.000	0.000	0.000	0.000	0.000	0.000	0.000	0.000		
Working capital adjustment	-0.299	0.100	-0.100	-0.200	0.500	-0.100	1.300	0.000	-0.400	0.500	0.000	0.000	0.000	0.000	0.000	0.000	0.000	0.000		
Current cost operating profit	197.893	147.300	107.300	273.900	199.700	90.500	309.000	323.200	141.500	142.500	0.000	0.000	0.000	0.000	0.000	0.000	0.000	0.000		
Other income	0.000	0.000	0.000	0.000	0.000	0.000	1.200	0.000	0.000	0.000	0.000	0.000	0.000	0.000	0.000	0.000	0.000	0.000		
Net Interest	0.000	-75.300	0.000	0.000	0.000	0.000	0.000	0.000	0.000	0.000	0.000	0.000	0.000	0.000	0.000	0.000	0.000	0.000		
Financing adjustment	0.000	6.200	0.000	0.000	0.000	0.000	0.000	0.000	0.000	0.000	0.000	0.000	0.000	0.000	0.000	0.000	0.000	0.000		
Current cost profit before taxation	197.893	78.200	107.300	273.900	199.700	90.500	310.200	323.200	141.500	142.500	0.000	0.000	0.000	0.000	0.000	0.000	0.000	0.000		
Net revenue movement out of tariff basket	0.743	0.000	0.200	-0.300	-1.000	-0.200	2.300	-0.300	0.000	-0.600	0.000	0.000	0.000	0.000	0.000	0.000	0.000	0.000		
Back-billing amount identified	0.000	0.000	0.000	0.000	0.000	0.000	2.900	0.000	0.000	0.200	0.000	0.000	0.000	0.000	0.000	0.000	0.000	0.000		

Total

Description	Anglian	Welsh	Northumbrian	Severn Trent	Southern	South West	Thames	United Utilities	Wessex	Yorkshire	Affinity	Bournemouth	Bristol	Dee Valley	Portsmouth	South East	South Staffs / Cambridge	Sutton and East Surrey	Northern Ireland	Scottish
Turnover																				
Unmeasured - household	299.377	389.100	382.200	726.800	205.200	128.700	1 032.800	781.300	206.100	457.500	127.900	11.025	59.600	8.634	21.018	69.650	58.700	29.643		
Unmeasured - non-household	1.817	5.700	6.700	11.000	6.800	3.600	15.700	10.700	5.700	3.500	2.592	0.454	1.200	0.111	0.304	1.605	1.393	0.252		
Measured - household	656.312	162.900	185.700	404.200	451.400	261.700	514.100	403.500	190.700	298.500	102.336	18.229	38.700	8.106	6.331	93.328	35.030	19.607		
Measured - non-household	169.195	132.300	127.900	319.000	111.900	93.300	329.000	390.200	95.300	162.100	56.552	9.426	23.500	7.518	8.820	40.462	25.468	8.898		
Trade effluent	8.184	9.700	3.000	13.200	7.700	4.400	8.200	22.400	4.300	11.900	0.000	0.000	0.000	0.000	0.000	0.000	0.000	0.000		
Bulk supplies/inter company payments	8.316	19.800	0.800	5.300	2.600	17.700	3.400	0.800	0.500	0.400	3.040	0.010	0.600	0.004	0.226	0.003	0.461	0.038		
Other third party services (incl non-potable water)	12.562	22.900	9.500	75.000	9.900	8.400	4.700	7.100	1.400	1.100	1.104	0.197	1.200	0.096	1.407	0.000	0.808	1.123		
Other sources	71.083	8.400	45.700	6.400	26.400	0.000	90.700	110.500	28.900	69.800	0.000	5.507	6.200	0.000	0.095	4.918	0.513	1.240		

10.14a Current cost profit and loss account for the 12 months ended 31 March 2015 (appointed business only)

Description	WaSC										WoC									
	Anglian	Welsh	Northumbrian	Severn Trent	Southern	South West	Thames	United Utilities	Wessex	Yorkshire	Affinity	Bournemouth	Bristol	Dee Valley	Portsmouth	South East	South Staffs / Cambridge	Sutton and East Surrey	Northern Ireland (Total only)	Scottish
Total turnover	1,226.846	750.900	761.500	1,560.900	821.900	517.800	1,998.600	1,725.600	532.900	1,004.800	293.524	44.848	131.000	24.469	38.201	209.966	122.373	60.801	364.407	
Current cost operating costs - wholesale	-804.752	-457.600	-459.200	-966.800	-513.200	-302.300	-1,263.800	-983.900	-299.400	-652.800	-184.015	-29.021	-95.000	-16.430	-28.096	-127.929	-76.853	-40.321	0.000	
Current cost operating costs - retail	-83.991	-69.800	-60.600	-129.600	-84.600	-35.800	-195.900	-177.900	-32.000	-63.400	-36.295	-4.698	-11.300	-4.069	-5.255	-18.224	-18.308	-6.635	0.000	
Current cost operating costs - total																			-306.136	
Operating income	-0.280	0.000	0.500	3.400	-6.600	1.300	16.600	-6.000	-0.900	1.800	-0.979	0.000	-0.200	0.000	0.003	-0.001	0.224	13.845	0.000	
Working capital adjustment	-0.598	0.100	-0.300	-0.400	0.600	-0.200	2.500	0.000	-0.500	0.900	0.192	-0.032	0.100	0.015	0.046	0.076	0.114	0.056	0.840	
Current cost operating profit	337.226	223.600	241.900	467.500	218.100	180.800	558.000	557.800	200.100	291.300	72.427	11.097	24.600	3.985	4.899	63.888	27.551	13.901	59.111	
Exceptional item	0.000	0.000	0.100	1.200	2.600	11.800	2.100	1.000	0.400	2.000	0.000	0.115	0.300	0.054	0.000	0.658	0.000	0.892	0.000	
Other income	-101.561	-151.200	-123.300	-366.100	-125.700	-53.200	-365.300	-350.400	-79.000	-214.400	-35.664	-4.970	-11.600	-2.557	-2.809	-47.997	-11.498	-9.873	-51.957	
Net Interest	7.225	12.400	17.100	31.400	28.800	15.700	18.500	29.200	10.400	6.800	7.714	0.781	1.900	-0.029	0.021	6.759	0.097	0.265	9.183	
Financing adjustment						0.400														
Current cost profit before taxation	242.890	84.800	135.800	134.000	123.800	155.500	213.300	237.600	131.900	85.700	44.477	7.023	15.200	1.453	2.111	23.308	16.150	5.185	16.337	
Net revenue movement out of tariff basket	1.441	0.200	0.200	-0.500	-1.000	-0.600	3.500	0.200	0.100	-0.500	-0.160	0.028	-0.100	0.000	-0.002	0.147	0.412	0.002	0.000	
Back-billing amount identified	0.000	0.000	0.000	0.000	0.000	0.000	7.000	0.000	0.000	0.400	3.540	0.000	0.000	0.000	0.000	0.000	0.127	0.000	0.000	

10.14b Water Industry Regulatory Capital Values

RCV roll forward for indexation (£ million)	
RCV at 31 March 2016 as published in April 2015[1]	64,688
Indexation	1,006
RCV at 31 March 2016 in March 2016 prices[2]	65,695

Wholesale water RCV (£ million)	2015-16	2016-17	2017-18	2018-19	2019-20
Opening RCV	27,443	27,886	28,483	28,995	29,318
RCV additions (from totex)	1,604	1,772	1,679	1,514	1,300
Less RCV run-off and depreciation	-1,161	-1,173	-1,165	-1,188	-1,213
Other adjustments[3]	0	-2	-2	-2	-1
Closing RCV	27,886	28,483	28,995	29,318	29,404
Average RCV (year average)	27,488	28,004	28,555	28,970	29,174

Wholesale water RCV breakdown (£ million)	2015-16	2016-17	2017-18	2018-19	2019-20
2015 RCV	26,314	25,243	24,250	23,301	22,388
Totex RCV	1,571	3,240	4,744	6,017	7,016
Total	27,886	28,483	28,995	29,318	29,404

Wholesale wastewater RCV (£ million)	2015-16	2016-17	2017-18	2018-19	2019-20
Opening RCV	37,268	37,809	38,438	39,075	39,587
RCV additions (from totex)	2,186	2,280	2,291	2,177	1,804
Less RCV run-off and depreciation	-1,646	-1,651	-1,654	-1,665	-1,657
Other adjustments[3]	0	0	0	0	0
Closing RCV	37,809	38,438	39,075	39,587	39,734
Average RCV (year average)	37,299	37,880	38,509	39,080	39,408

Wholesale wastewater RCV breakdown (£ million)	2015-16	2016-17	2017-18	2018-19	2019-20
2015 RCV	35,661	34,129	32,678	31,300	30,005
Totex RCV	2,148	4,309	6,397	8,287	9,730
Total	37,809	38,438	39,075	39,587	39,734

Source: OFWAT

Notes

1 Presented in March 2015 prices

2 Does not include the impact of the Competition and Markets Authority's (CMA) final determination for Bristol Water

3 Impact of the reduction in allowed totex and the associated RCV run-off as included in the CMA's final determination for Bristol Water

10.15 Summary of pollution incidents by area and incident category, England 2014

	Water						Land						Air					
	Cat 1	Cat 2	Cat 3	Cat 4	Total	Cat 1 and 2 Total	Cat 1	Cat 2	Cat 3	Cat 4	Total	Cat 1 and 2 Total	Cat 1	Cat 2	Cat 3	Cat 4	Total	Cat 1 and 2 Total
North and East																		
Northumberland, Durham and Tees	8	15	0	8	31	23	0	5	7	19	31	5	0	4	3	24	31	4
Cumbria and Lancashire	4	25	3	14	46	29	0	7	4	35	46	7	1	12	4	29	46	13
Yorkshire	6	36	4	23	69	42	1	9	6	53	69	10	1	24	4	40	69	25
Derbyshire, Nottinghamshire and Leicestershire	1	14	1	26	42	15	0	10	12	20	42	10	0	19	3	20	42	19
Lincolnshire and Northamptonshire	2	15	1	2	20	17	0	1	1	18	20	1	0	2	0	18	20	2
West																		
Greater Manchester, Merseyside and Cheshire	1	11	1	12	25	12	0	7	2	16	25	7	0	10	0	15	25	10
Staffordshire, Warwickshire and West Midlands	2	16	2	22	42	18	0	3	5	34	42	3	0	22	3	17	42	22
Shropshire, Herefordshire, Worcestershire and Gloucestershire	4	17	4	17	42	21	0	7	2	33	42	7	0	15	3	24	42	15
Wessex	2	32	3	13	50	34	0	7	9	34	50	7	0	12	8	30	50	12
Devon and Cornwall	4	13	0	7	24	17	0	3	3	18	24	3	0	6	1	17	24	6
South East																		
Cambridgeshire and Bedfordshire	3	15	0	14	32	18	0	5	3	24	32	5	1	9	0	22	32	10
Essex, Norfolk and Suffolk	4	16	2	18	40	20	0	5	0	35	40	5	1	17	1	21	40	18
Hertfordshire and North London	1	20	6	30	57	21	0	8	3	46	57	8	0	29	6	22	57	29
West Thames	5	27	0	7	39	32	1	0	6	32	39	1	3	4	4	28	39	7
Solent and South Downs	1	14	1	0	16	15	0	1	1	14	16	1	0	0	1	15	16	0
Kent and South London	5	18	5	6	34	23	0	8	2	24	34	8	0	5	1	28	34	5
Total	53	304	33	219	609	357	2	86	66	455	609	88	7	190	42	370	609	197

Source: Environment Agency

Data does not include incidents relating to:

Fisheries incidents – for incidents involving illegal fishing and illegal fish movements, fish disease, fishery management activities and fish kills from non-pollution causes, including low flows and low dissolved oxygen.

Water Resources incidents – for incidents involving the quantity of a water resource.

Waterways incidents – for incidents on a waterway where the Environment Agency are the competent authority for navigation.
Flood and Coastal Risk Management incidents – for incidents which involve actual or potential flooding and land drainage works on main river or where regional bylaws apply.

Only incidents where investigations and response have been completed are included. Some incidents may take an extended period of months, or exceptionally years, to be completed.

The dataset only includes substantiated incidents and their environmental impact. These are where the Environment Agency have confirmation that the incident took place either by a visit, or it is corroborated by other information.

10.16a 2014 mandatory compliance[1] results for bathing waters in the UK

Coastal Bathing Waters (results for 2013 are in brackets)

Region *	Mandatory Pass	Fail	Total	Compliance%
North East	53 (54)	1 (0)	54 (54)	98.1 (100)
Anglian	40 (40)	0 (0)	40 (40)	100 (100)
South East	91 (90)	0 (0)	91 (90)	100 (100)
South West	192 (191)	1 (1)	193 (192)	99.5 (99.5)
North West	27 (25)	0 (4)	27 (29)	100 (86.2)
England	**403 (400)**	**2 (5)**	**405 (405)**	**99.5 (98.8)**
Wales	**101 (99)**	**0 (1)**	**101 (100)**	**100 (99.0)**
Scotland	**79 (80)**	**2 (0)**	**81 (80)**	**97.5 (100)**
Northern Ireland	**22 (23)**	**1 (0)**	**23 (23)**	**95.7 (100)**
UK COASTAL WATERS	**605 (602)**	**5 (6)**	**610 (608)**	**99.2 (99.0)**

Inland Bathing Waters (results for 2013 are in brackets)

Region*	Mandatory Pass	Fail	Total	Compliance %
Midland	1 (1)	0 (0)	1 (1)	100 (100)
South East	6 (6)	0 (0)	6 (6)	100 (100)
South West	1 (-)	0 (-)	1 (0)	100 (-)
North West	3 (3)	0 (0)	3 (3)	100 (100)
England	**11 (10)**	**0 (0)**	**11 (10)**	**100 (100)**
Wales	**1 (-)**	**0 (-)**	**1 (0)**	**100 (-)**
Scotland	**3 (3)**	**0 (0)**	**3 (3)**	**100 (100)**
UK INLAND WATERS	**15 (13)**	**0 (0)**	**15 (13)**	**100 (100)**

[1] Figures shown are for compliance with the mandatory microbiological standards set by the EC Bathing Water Directive (76/160/EEC)

* Environment Agency operational region. The inland bathing water in South West region has been designated in 2014.

Source: Department for Environment, Food and Rural Affairs

10.16b 2014 guideline[2] compliance results for bathing waters in the UK

Coastal Bathing Waters (results for 2013 are in brackets)

Region *	Guideline Pass	Fail	Total	Compliance %
North East	45 (46)	9 (8)	54 (54)	83.3 (85.2)
Anglian	36 (34)	4 (6)	40 (40)	90.0 (85.0)
South East	73 (78)	18 (12)	91 (90)	80.2 (86.7)
South West	163 (174)	30 (18)	193 (192)	84.5 (90.6)
North West	10 (6)	17 (23)	27 (29)	37.0 (20.7)
England	**327 (338)**	**78 (67)**	**405 (405)**	**80.7 (83.5)**
Wales	**89 (89)**	**12 (11)**	**101 (100)**	**88.1 (89.0)**
Scotland	**45 (47)**	**36 (33)**	**81 (80)**	**55.6 (58.8)**
Northern Ireland	**16 (20)**	**7 (3)**	**23 (23)**	**69.6 (87.0)**
UK COASTAL WATERS	**477 (494)**	**133 (114)**	**610 (608)**	**78.2 (81.3)**

Inland Bathing Waters (Results for 2013 are in brackets)

Region *	Guideline Pass	Fail	Total	Compliance %
Midlands	0 (1)	1 (0)	0 (1)	0 (100)
South East	1 (1)	5 (5)	6 (6)	16.7 (16.7)
South West	0 (-)	1 (-)	1 (0)	0 (-)
North West	3 (2)	0 (1)	3 (3)	100 (66.7)
England	**4 (4)**	**7 (6)**	**11(10)**	**36.4 (40.0)**
Wales	**1 (-)**	**0 (-)**	**1 (0)**	**100 (-)**
Scotland	**1 (0)**	**2 (3)**	**3 (3)**	**33.3 (0)**
UK INLAND WATERS	**6 (4)**	**9 (9)**	**15 (13)**	**40.0 (30.8)**

[2] These figures show compliance with the equivalent single standard that is being used during the transitional period from 2012 - 2014 as the revised Directive (2006/7/EC) is implemented.

* Environment Agency operational regions. The inland bathing water in South West region has been designated in 2014

Source: Department for Environment, Food and Rural Affairs

10.17 Estimated abstractions from all surface and groundwater sources: by purpose[1]

England and Wales

million cubic metres

		2002	2003	2004	2005	2006	2007	2008	2009	2010	2011	2012	2013	2014
Public water supply	JZLA	6,183	6,036	6,298	6,342	6,207	5,979	5,944	5,768	5,977	5,829	5,844	5,879	5,777
Spray irrigation [(a)]	JZLB	91	116	83	81	101	58	58	86	106	117	49	100	90
Agriculture (excl spray irrigation)	JZLC	44	49	44	22	18	26	14	17	24	26	25	26	27
Electricity supply industry[2 (b)]	JZLD	12,938	11,555	11,189	10,956	11,737	11,856	12,128	10,977	10,868	10,716	13,309	13,343	6,669
Other industry[3]	JZLE	1,784	2,160	2,409	2,314	2,379	1,886	1,814	2,065	1,815	1,737	2,011	1,728	2,838
Fish farming, cress growing, amenity ponds	JYXG	1,173	1,241	1,490	1,334	1,322	1,245	1,043	953	1,059	848	974	947	962
Private water supply	JZLG	20	15	10	9	14	11	9	9	8	9	10	9	10
Other	JZLH	28	27	28	22	32	41	27	28	22	22	27	33	28
Total	JZLI	22,259	21,199	21,552	21,080	21,809	21,105	21,036	19,899	19,875	19,304	22,251	22,065	19,828

1 See chapter text.

Source: Environment Agency

2 Increased electricity supply abstraction from 2002 due to issue of 2 new abstraction licences

3 Three abstraction licences in 2003 re-assigned to "other industry" from "electricty supply"

(a) Includes small amounts of non-agricultural spray irrigation

(b) The Electricity Supply Industry category includes hydropower licences.

10.18 Estimates of remaining recoverable oil & gas reserves and resources, 2003-2013

		2002	2003	2004	2005	2006	2007	2008	2009	2010	2011	2012	2013
OIL (million tonnes)													
Annual production		116	106	95	85	77	77	72	68	63	52	45	41
Discovered reserves													
Proven	JKOV	595	571	533	516	479	452	408	378	374	413	405	404
Probable	JKOW	325	286	283	300	298	328	361	390	377	374	405	342
Proven + Probable	JKOX	920	857	816	816	776	780	770	769	751	788	811	746
Possible	JKOY	425	410	512	451	478	399	360	343	342	319	253	338
Maximum	JKOZ	1,345	1,267	1,328	1,267	1,254	1,179	1,130	1,112	1,093	1,106	1,064	1,084
Range of undiscovered resources													
Lower	JKNY	272	323	396	346	438	379	454	397	475	422	455	453
Upper	JKNZ	1,770	1,826	1,830	1,581	1,637	1,577	1,561	1,477	1,374	1,321	1344	1331
Range of total reserves and resources													
Lower[1]	JKOA	867	894	929	862	917	831	862	775	849	835	860	857
Upper[2]	JKOB	3,115	3,093	3,158	2,848	2,891	2,756	2,691	2,589	2,467	2,427	2,408	2,415
Expected level of reserves[3]													
Opening stocks	JKOC	955	920	857	816	816	776	780	770	769	751	788	811
Extraction[4]	JKOD	-116	-106	-95	-85	-77	-77	-72	-68	-63	-52	-45	-41
Other volume changes	JKOE	81	43	54	85	37	81	62	67	45	89	68	106
Closing stocks	JKOF	920	857	816	816	776	780	770	769	751	788	811	746
GAS (billion cubic metres)		**2002**	**2003**	**2004**	**2005**	**2006**	**2007**	**2008**	**2009**	**2010**	**2011**	**2012**	**2013**
Annual production		102	102	95	86	78	70	68	57	55	43	37	34
Discovered reserves													
Proven	JKOH	630	590	531	481	412	343	292	256	253	246	244	241
Probable	JKOI	370	315	296	247	272	304	309	308	267	246	217	211
Proven plus Probable	JKOJ	1,000	905	826	728	684	647	601	564	520	493	461	452
Possible	JKOK	330	336	343	278	283	293	306	276	261	216	238	198
Maximum	JKOL	1,330	1,241	1,169	1,006	967	940	907	840	781	709	699	650
Range of undiscovered resources													
Lower	JKOM	238	279	293	226	301	280	319	300	363	353	370	357
Upper	JKON	1,386	1,259	1,245	1,035	1,049	1,039	1,043	949	1,021	977	1011	997
Range of total reserves and resources													
Lower[1]	JKOO	868	869	824	707	713	623	611	556	616	599	614	598
Upper[2]	JKOP	2,716	2,500	2,414	2,041	2,016	1,979	1,950	1,789	1,802	1,686	1,710	1,647
Expected Level of Reserves[3]													
Opening stocks	JKOQ	1,100	1,000	905	826	728	684	647	601	564	520	493	461
Extraction[4]	JKOR	-102	-102	-95	-86	-78	-70	-68	-57	-55	-43	-37	-34
Other volume changes	JKOS	2	7	16	-12	34	33	22	20	10	16	5	25
Closing stocks	JKOT	1,000	905	826	728	684	647	601	564	520	493	461	452

Sources: Office for National Statistics, Department of Energy and Climate Change

All data refer to end of year.
Components may not sum to totals due to rounding.
1. The lower end of the range of total reserves and resources has been calculated as the sum of proven reserves and the lower end of the range of undiscovered resources.
2. The upper end of the range of total reserves and resources is the sum of proven, probable and possible reserves and the upper end of the range of undiscovered resources.
3. Expected reserves are the sum of proven and probable reserves.
4. The negative of extraction is shown here for the purposes of the calculation only. Of itself, extraction should be considered as a positive value.

10.19a Local Authority Collected Waste Generation from 2001/02 to 2013/14

England

Thousand tonnes

Household waste from:	2001/02	2002/03	2003/04	2004/05	2005/06	2006/07r	2007/08	2008/09r	2009/10	2010/11	2011/12	2012/13	2013/14
Regular household collection	16,683	16,528	16,066	15,470	14,616	14,050	13,046	12,076	11,432	11,048	10,586	10,317	10,308
Other household sources	1,277	1,351	1,244	1,205	1,314	1,173	1,073	1,026	1,070	1,047	997	1,027	1,099
Civic amenity sites	4,367	4,213	3,616	3,198	2,726	2,576	2,434	2,086	1,765	1,635	1,470	1,477	1,568
Household recycling	3,197	3,740	4,521	5,785	6,796	7,976	8,735	9,146	9,398	9,724	9,846	9,759	9,980
Total household	25,524	25,832	25,448	25,658	25,454	25,775	25,287	24,334	23,666	23,454	22,899	22,580	22,967
Non household sources (excl. recycling)	2,656	2,730	2,650	2,795	2,289	2,408	2,250	2,063	1,999	1,882	1,654	1,558	1,600
Non household recycling	724	832	1,016	1,167	1,003	961	969	936	877	864	866	817	950
Total LA collected waste	28,905	29,394	29,114	29,619	28,745	29,144	28,506	27,334	26,541	26,200	25,419	24,955	25,518

There has been a revision to 2008/09 to include asbestos in "Other household sources" instead of "Non household sources".
2010/11 data has been revised slightly due to data issues.

Source: Department for Environment, Food & Rural Affairs

10.19b Waste managed (tonnes) by management method and year 2012-13 onwards

	2012-13	2013-14	2014-15
Total Municipal Waste Collected/Generated	1553511.534	1557229	1543357.32
Total Waste Reused/Recycled/Composted (Statutory Target) (1)	811865.985	846091	868079.46
Total Waste Reused/Recycled/Composted (Statutory Target) (1)			
Household Waste Reused/Recycled (2)	499946.4776	429863	430264.88
Household Waste Composted (3)	265133.1467	274265	281762.43
Non-Household Waste Reused/Recycled (4)	28622.11644	128310	141705.77
Non-Household Waste Composted (5)	18164.2443	13653	14346.36
Waste sent for other recovery (6)	1801.856	4532	4923.87
Other recovery: Recycling (7)	-	-	1488
Other recovery: Composting (8)	-	-	3436
Waste Incinerated with Energy Recovery	71887.638	89907	182961.26
Waste Incinerated without Energy Recovery	363.827	341	245.08
Waste Landfilled	640904.458	587390	453497.37
Percentage of Waste Reused/Recycled/Composted (Statutory Target) (9)	52.26005519	54.33310793	56.24617506
Percentage of Waste Reused/Recycled/Composted (Statutory Target) (9)			
Percentage of Household Waste Reused/Recycled (10)	32.18170362	27.60425396	27.87850062
Percentage of Household Waste Composted (11)	17.0666996	17.61241588	18.25646118
Percentage of Non-Household Waste Reused/Recycled (12)	1.842414157	8.239625335	9.18165665
Percentage of Non-Household Waste Composted (13)	1.169237814	0.876876969	0.929555315

Source: WasteDataFlow, Natural Resources Wales

1. Total waste reused/recycled/composted as defined by the Statutory Local Authority Recovery Target (LART)

2. Household waste sent to be reused/recycled as defined by the Statutory Local Authority Recovery Target (LART)

3. Household waste sent to be composted as defined by the Statutory Local Authority Recovery Target (LART)

4. Non-Household waste sent to be reused/recycled as defined by the Statutory Local Authority Recovery Target (LART)

5. Non-Household waste sent to be composted as defined by the Statutory Local Authority Recovery Target (LART)

6. Other waste sent for recycling and/or composting that is not included in the statutory target definition

7. Other waste sent for recycling that is not included in the statutory target definition

8. Other waste sent for composting that is not included in the statutory target definition

9. Total waste reused/recycled/composted (as defined by the Statutory Local Authority Recovery Target, LART), as a percentage of total municipal waste collected/generated

10. Household waste sent to be reused/recycled (as defined by the Statutory Local Authority Recovery Target, LART), as a percentage of total municipal waste collected/generated

11. Household waste sent to be composted (as defined by the Statutory Local Authority Recovery Target, LART), as a percentage of total municipal waste collected/generated

12. Non-Household waste sent to be reused/recycled (as defined by the Statutory Local Authority Recovery Target, LART), as a percentage of total municipal waste collected/generated

13. Non-Household waste sent to be composted (as defined by the Statutory Local Authority Recovery Target, LART), as a percentage of total municipal waste collected/generated

. The data item is not applicable.

From 1 April 2012, there have been changes in definitions relating to local authority municipal waste. These changes affect the total amount of local authority municipal waste generated and the percentage reused, recycled or composted in Wales. A detailed description of these definition changes and their impacts can be found in the Statistical article Local Authority Municipal Waste Management

10.19c Household waste - Summary data 2014, Scotland

Local Authority	Generated (tonnes)	Recycled (tonnes)	Percentage Recycled (%)	Other diversion from landfill (tonnes)	Percentage Other diversion from Landfill (%)	Landfilled (tonnes)	Percentage Landfilled (%)	Recycled - OLD METHOD* (Tonnes)	Percentage Recycled - OLD METHOD*(%)	Other diversion - OLD METHOD (tonnes)	Percentage Other diversion - OLD METHOD* (%)
Aberdeen City	96,130	36,742	38.2	354	0.4	59,034	61.4	36,742	38.2	354	0.4
Aberdeenshire	131,390	52,479	39.9	177	0.1	78,734	59.9	52,479	39.9	177	0.1
Angus	58,892	30,879	52.4	13,050	22.2	14,963	25.4	30,879	52.4	13,050	22.2
Argyll & Bute	52,359	15,655	29.9	9,511	18.2	27,192	51.9	18,456	35.2	6,710	12.8
Clackmannanshire	26,786	14,929	55.7	1,085	4.1	10,772	40.2	14,929	55.7	1,085	4.1
Dumfries & Galloway	76,454	15,940	20.8	34,701	45.4	25,813	33.8	17,139	22.4	33,502	43.8
Dundee City	63,738	20,290	31.8	39,054	61.3	4,394	6.9	20,290	31.8	39,054	61.3
East Ayrshire	56,392	28,381	50.3	8,614	15.3	19,407	34.4	28,381	50.3	8,614	15.3
East Dunbartonshire	52,897	23,533	44.5	6,272	11.9	23,093	43.7	26,677	50.4	3,127	5.9
East Lothian	52,660	22,523	42.8	4,008	7.6	26,123	49.6	22,523	42.8	4,008	7.6
East Renfrewshire	46,224	25,950	56.1	335	0.7	19,939	43.1	25,950	56.1	335	0.7
Edinburgh, City of	189,525	70,451	37.2	11,160	5.9	107,914	56.9	76,073	40.1	5,539	2.9
Eilean Siar	13,479	2,914	21.6	1,910	14.2	8,655	64.2	4,817	35.7	8	0.1
Falkirk	73,620	39,980	54.3	121	0.2	33,519	45.5	39,980	54.3	121	0.2
Fife	188,213	101,060	53.7	4,485	2.4	82,667	43.9	101,060	53.7	4,485	2.4
Glasgow City	224,488	57,839	25.8	1,838	0.8	164,811	73.4	57,839	25.8	1,838	0.8
Highland	131,228	60,471	46.1	1,754	1.3	69,015	52.6	61,625	47.0	600	0.5
Inverclyde	28,458	16,171	56.8	142	0.5	12,144	42.7	16,171	56.8	142	0.5
Midlothian	40,726	19,111	46.9	27	0.1	21,588	53.0	19,111	46.9	27	0.1
Moray	50,902	27,681	54.4	0	0.0	23,221	45.6	27,681	54.4	0	0.0
North Ayrshire	65,064	36,743	56.5	613	0.9	27,708	42.6	36,773	56.5	583	0.9
North Lanarkshire	150,309	62,528	41.6	5,980	4.0	81,801	54.4	62,689	41.7	5,818	3.9
Orkney Islands	10,568	1,831	17.3	5,070	48.0	3,011	28.5	2,583	24.4	4,318	40.9
Perth & Kinross	74,949	42,372	56.5	1,860	2.5	30,715	41.0	42,890	57.2	1,342	1.8
Renfrewshire	80,858	37,658	46.6	17,709	21.9	25,493	31.5	37,658	46.6	17,709	21.9
Scottish Borders	49,952	18,345	36.7	940	1.9	30,666	61.4	18,345	36.7	940	1.9
Shetland Islands	9,942	899	9.0	6,900	69.4	2,143	21.6	899	9.0	6,900	69.4
South Ayrshire	55,477	27,751	50.0	8,622	15.5	19,105	34.4	28,852	52.0	7,521	13.6
South Lanarkshire	153,492	69,000	45.0	960	0.6	83,531	54.4	69,960	45.6	0	0.0
Stirling	40,565	21,551	53.1	1,811	4.5	17,192	42.4	21,551	53.1	1,811	4.5
West Dunbartonshire	40,338	17,876	44.3	2,421	6.0	20,041	49.7	17,876	44.3	2,421	6.0
West Lothian	73,485	33,715	45.9	1,708	2.3	38,009	51.7	34,083	46.4	1,340	1.8
Total Scotland	**2,459,559**	**1,053,249**	**42.8**	**193,190**	**7.9**	**1,212,411**	**49.3**	**1,072,961**	**43.6**	**173,477**	**7.1**

Source: Scottish Environment Protection Agency

*Including composted wastes that do not reach the quality standards set by PAS 100/110 in the recycled figures.

10.19d LAC municipal waste sent for recycling & composting, KPI(e), and landfilled, KPI(f), for Northern Ireland, 2013/14

Unit: Tonnes, Percentages

Area	KPI(i) LAC municipal waste arisings (tonnes)	LAC municipal dry recycling (tonnes)	LAC municipal composting (tonnes)	Total LAC municipal dry recycling & composting (tonnes)	LAC municipal dry recycling rate	LAC municipal composting rate	KPI(e) LAC municipal waste sent for recycling (inc composting) as a % of LAC municipal waste arisings	LAC municipal waste landfilled (tonnes)	KPI(f) LAC municipal waste landfilled as a % of total LAC municipal waste arisings	LAC municipal waste energy recovery (mixed residual LACMW) (tonnes)	LAC municipal waste energy recovery (specific streams e.g. wood) (tonnes)	LAC municipal waste preparing for reuse (tonnes)	LAC municipal waste unclassified (tonnes)
arc21													
Antrim	34,381	10,452	8,886	19,337	30.4%	25.8%	56.2%	11,990	34.9%	787	2,010	71	186
Ards	41,575	6,305	8,116	14,421	15.2%	19.5%	34.7%	25,652	61.7%	194	1,297	10	0
Ballymena	30,924	7,624	7,787	15,411	24.7%	25.2%	49.8%	14,701	47.5%	289	518	5	0
Belfast	146,216	34,498	17,983	52,481	23.6%	12.3%	35.9%	62,594	42.8%	26,844	689	46	3,562
Carrickfergus	19,723	4,221	3,739	7,960	21.4%	19.0%	40.4%	11,516	58.4%	56	171	0	20
Castlereagh	30,222	5,875	6,716	12,591	19.4%	22.2%	41.7%	16,982	56.2%	81	336	35	196
Down	35,020	5,564	4,491	10,055	15.9%	12.8%	28.7%	23,644	67.5%	613	709	0	0
Larne	20,402	6,093	4,127	10,221	29.9%	20.2%	50.1%	9,643	47.3%	151	323	7	58
Lisburn	57,236	11,759	11,986	23,745	20.5%	20.9%	41.5%	30,037	52.5%	1,925	1,266	31	232
Newtownabbey	44,277	10,214	10,307	20,521	23.1%	23.3%	46.3%	21,132	47.7%	878	1,467	0	277
North Down	49,937	11,986	9,806	21,792	24.0%	19.6%	43.6%	25,728	51.5%	217	2,067	135	0
All arc21	**509,911**	**114,590**	**93,943**	**208,534**	**22.5%**	**18.4%**	**40.9%**	**253,618**	**49.7%**	**32,036**	**10,855**	**341**	**4,531**
NWRWMG													
Ballymoney	14,645	2,817	2,076	4,893	19.2%	14.2%	33.4%	8,994	61.4%	460	298	0	0
Coleraine	33,448	7,381	4,649	12,029	22.1%	13.9%	36.0%	16,034	47.9%	4,085	1,300	0	0
Derry	53,977	16,835	2,210	19,044	31.2%	4.1%	35.3%	21,246	39.4%	11,070	2,296	148	172
Limavady	17,901	5,713	2,029	7,742	31.9%	11.3%	43.2%	8,469	47.3%	1,082	506	103	0
Magherafelt	23,727	6,314	6,293	12,607	26.6%	26.5%	53.1%	6,664	28.1%	3,659	798	0	0
Moyle	9,325	2,703	1,238	3,940	29.0%	13.3%	42.3%	3,857	41.4%	1,201	327	0	0
Strabane	17,786	4,170	978	5,148	23.4%	5.5%	28.9%	11,085	62.3%	806	497	0	250
All NWRWMG	**170,810**	**45,931**	**19,473**	**65,404**	**26.9%**	**11.4%**	**38.3%**	**76,351**	**44.7%**	**22,363**	**6,020**	**251**	**422**
SWaMP2008													
Armagh	26,864	5,805	5,293	11,098	21.6%	19.7%	41.3%	11,169	41.6%	3,954	423	73	148
Banbridge	25,184	6,208	8,395	14,603	24.7%	33.3%	58.0%	7,587	30.1%	2,689	232	0	73
Cookstown	19,571	4,774	3,520	8,294	24.4%	18.0%	42.4%	10,158	51.9%	853	227	0	39
Craigavon	46,694	11,507	8,531	20,038	24.6%	18.3%	42.9%	17,144	36.7%	8,492	794	0	225
Dungannon	29,201	6,224	5,435	11,659	21.3%	18.6%	39.9%	15,145	51.9%	1,512	861	1	23
Fermanagh	27,342	8,120	2,454	10,574	29.7%	9.0%	38.7%	16,243	59.4%	130	189	115	91
Newry & Mourne	44,995	9,594	5,592	15,186	21.3%	12.4%	33.7%	28,692	63.8%	655	387	0	75
Omagh	23,841	6,062	4,230	10,293	25.4%	17.7%	43.2%	12,885	54.0%	80	629	0	46
All SWaMP2008	**243,691**	**58,293**	**43,451**	**101,744**	**23.9%**	**17.8%**	**41.8%**	**119,023**	**48.8%**	**18,365**	**3,743**	**189**	**629**
Northern Ireland	**924,412**	**218,815**	**156,867**	**375,681**	**23.7%**	**17.0%**	**40.6%**	**448,991**	**48.6%**	**72,764**	**20,618**	**780**	**5,581**

Source: NIEA

Note: Rates calculated by dividing total tonnage of LAC municipal waste sent for recycling, composting and landfill by total LAC municipal waste arisings.

Note: Unclassified waste is calculated as a residual amount of municipal waste after municipal waste sent to landfill, sent for recycling (including composting), sent for energy recovery and preparing for reuse have been accounted for, instead of being extracted directly from the WasteDataFlow system. The majority of the total unclassified tonnage can be attributed to moisture and/or gaseous losses.

Note: The sum of the tonnages for recycling and composting, landfill, energy recovery, preparing for reuse and unclassified may not equal waste arisings due to rounding.

Note: Small negative tonnages can arise in the unclassified column if more waste is sent for treatment in the year than was actually collected as is more likely at Councils operating Transfer Stations

KPI (a)

10.19d Household waste sent for recycling and composting, KPI(a), for Northern Ireland, 2013/14

Area	Household waste arisings (tonnes)	Household dry recycling (tonnes)	Household composting (tonnes)	Total household dry recyling & composting (tonnes)	Household dry recycling rate	Household composting rate	Household waste sent for recycling (inc composting) as a % of household waste arisings
arc21							
Antrim	28,956	6,142	8,886	15,028	21.2%	30.7%	51.9%
Ards	38,582	6,062	8,116	14,179	15.7%	21.0%	36.7%
Ballymena	28,235	6,141	7,787	13,928	21.8%	27.6%	49.3%
Belfast	122,339	31,619	17,414	49,034	25.8%	14.2%	40.1%
Carrickfergus	17,370	3,301	3,739	7,040	19.0%	21.5%	40.5%
Castlereagh	28,077	4,878	6,714	11,592	17.4%	23.9%	41.3%
Down	30,328	5,408	4,416	9,824	17.8%	14.6%	32.4%
Larne	16,821	3,799	4,127	7,926	22.6%	24.5%	47.1%
Lisburn	51,186	9,085	11,986	21,071	17.7%	23.4%	41.2%
Newtownabbey	40,706	8,465	10,164	18,629	20.8%	25.0%	45.8%
North Down	40,258	7,451	9,558	17,010	18.5%	23.7%	42.3%
All arc21	**442,858**	**92,352**	**92,908**	**185,260**	**20.9%**	**21.0%**	**41.8%**
NWRWMG							
Ballymoney	13,240	2,517	2,076	4,592	19.0%	15.7%	34.7%
Coleraine	29,743	6,815	4,649	11,464	22.9%	15.6%	38.5%
Derry	46,107	13,855	2,102	15,956	30.0%	4.6%	34.6%
Limavady	15,807	4,078	2,029	6,108	25.8%	12.8%	38.6%
Magherafelt	20,666	4,921	6,293	11,215	23.8%	30.5%	54.3%
Moyle	8,890	2,628	1,238	3,865	29.6%	13.9%	43.5%
Strabane	16,391	4,010	978	4,989	24.5%	6.0%	30.4%
All NWRWMG	**150,844**	**38,825**	**19,365**	**58,190**	**25.7%**	**12.8%**	**38.6%**
SWaMP2008							
Armagh	24,664	4,833	5,067	9,900	19.6%	20.5%	40.1%
Banbridge	23,501	5,114	8,075	13,189	21.8%	34.4%	56.1%
Cookstown	17,055	3,724	3,520	7,244	21.8%	20.6%	42.5%
Craigavon	41,938	9,537	8,446	17,984	22.7%	20.1%	42.9%
Dungannon	27,401	5,946	5,435	11,380	21.7%	19.8%	41.5%
Fermanagh	24,486	6,391	2,454	8,845	26.1%	10.0%	36.1%
Newry & Mourne	39,937	9,433	5,592	15,025	23.6%	14.0%	37.6%
Omagh	22,080	5,344	4,230	9,575	24.2%	19.2%	43.4%
All SWaMP2008	**221,062**	**50,322**	**42,820**	**93,142**	**22.8%**	**19.4%**	**42.1%**
Northern Ireland	**814,764**	**181,499**	**155,092**	**336,591**	**22.3%**	**19.0%**	**41.3%**

Source: NIEA

Note: Rates calculated by dividing total tonnage of household waste sent for recycling and composting by total household waste arisings.

Note: The tonnages of recycled (including composted) and landfilled waste may not always equal the waste arisings because the recycling measures were defined to capture outputs from recovery processes which excludes reuse.

Note: The percentage of recycled (including composted) and landfilled waste may not always equal 100% because the recycling measures were defined to capture outputs from recovery processes which excludes reuse.

10.19d Household waste landfilled, KPI(b), and generated per household, KPI(h), and per capita, KPI(p), in Northern Ireland, 2013/14

Unit: Tonnes, Percentages

Area	Household waste landfilled (tonnes)	KPI (b) Household waste landfilled as a % of household waste arisings	Estimated households (March 2014)	KPI(h) Annual household waste collected per household (tonnes)	Population (2013)	KPI(p) Annual household waste collected per capita (kilogrammes)
arc21						
Antrim	10,953	37.8%	20,555	1.409	53,978	536
Ards	22,968	59.5%	32,063	1.203	78,549	491
Ballymena	13,546	48.0%	25,335	1.114	64,762	436
Belfast	49,079	40.1%	121,775	1.005	281,735	434
Carrickfergus	10,093	58.1%	16,326	1.064	39,015	445
Castlereagh	15,855	56.5%	28,210	0.995	67,883	414
Down	19,269	63.5%	26,639	1.138	70,825	428
Larne	8,417	50.0%	13,532	1.243	32,220	522
Lisburn	26,887	52.5%	47,047	1.088	121,990	420
Newtownabbey	19,580	48.1%	34,630	1.175	85,558	476
North Down	20,907	51.9%	33,830	1.190	79,424	507
All arc21	**217,555**	**49.1%**	**399,942**	**1.107**	**975,939**	**454**
NWRWMG						
Ballymoney	7,939	60.0%	11,672	1.134	31,659	418
Coleraine	13,538	45.5%	23,987	1.240	59,043	504
Derry	18,438	40.0%	41,511	1.111	108,610	425
Limavady	8,098	51.2%	12,328	1.282	33,886	466
Magherafelt	5,599	27.1%	15,580	1.326	45,826	451
Moyle	3,531	39.7%	6,807	1.306	17,111	520
Strabane	9,961	60.8%	15,016	1.092	40,022	410
All NWRWMG	**67,104**	**44.5%**	**126,901**	**1.189**	**336,157**	**449**
SWaMP2008						
Armagh	10,438	42.3%	22,263	1.108	60,423	408
Banbridge	7,398	31.5%	18,790	1.251	48,905	481
Cookstown	8,819	51.7%	13,281	1.284	37,552	454
Craigavon	15,388	36.7%	36,696	1.143	95,474	439
Dungannon	13,781	50.3%	21,151	1.296	59,298	462
Fermanagh	15,170	62.0%	23,912	1.024	62,527	392
Newry & Mourne	23,920	59.9%	36,183	1.104	101,612	393
Omagh	11,844	53.6%	18,814	1.174	51,838	426
All SWaMP2008	**106,756**	**48.3%**	**191,090**	**1.157**	**517,629**	**427**
Northern Ireland	**391,415**	**48.0%**	**717,933**	**1.135**	**1,829,725**	**445**

Source: NIEA, NISRA, DSD

Note: Rates calculated by dividing total tonnage of household waste sent to landfill by total household waste arisings.

10.20a Waste arisings from households (Million tonnes) and household expenditure (2014 prices) UK, 2010 - 2014

Waste from Households arisings (million tonnes)	2010	2011	2012	2013	2014
UK	27.0	26.8	26.4	25.9	26.8
England	22.1	22.2	22.0	21.6	22.4
Scotland	2.6	2.5	2.4	2.3	2.3
Wales	1.3	1.3	1.3	1.3	1.3
Northern Ireland	0.8	0.8	0.8	0.8	0.8
UK total household annual expenditure £th (2014 prices)	27.4	26.8	26.4	27.2	27.6

10.20b Waste from households, England, 2010 – 2014 *(Waste Prevention Metric)*

	2010	2011	2012	2013	2014
Total waste generated from households (000 tonnes)	22,131	22,170	21,956	21,564	22,355
Waste generated (kg per person)	425	419	411	403	413

Notes: Waste from households' includes waste from: Regular household collection, Civic amenity sites, 'Bulky waste' 'Other household waste'. It does not include street cleaning/sweeping, gully emptying, separately collected healthcare waste, asbestos waste. 'Waste from households' is a narrower measure than 'municipal waste' and 'council collected waste'.

- The 'waste from households' calculation was first published by Defra in May 2014. It was introduced for statistical purposes to provide a harmonised UK indicator with a comparable calculation in each of the four UK countries and to provide a consistent approach to report recycling rates at UK level on a calendar year basis under the Waste Framework Directive (2008/98/EC).
- The waste from household measure is a narrower measure than the 'household waste' measure which was previously used and excludes waste not considered to have come directly from households, such as recycling from street bins, parks and grounds.
- Waste arising from households in the UK increased by 3.3 per cent between 2013 and 2014. The 2014 tonnage is a decrease of 0.6 per cent since 2010.
- The total weekly average household expenditure in the UK increased by over 1 per cent in 2014 compared to 2013.

Source: Department for Environment, Food & Rural Affairs; Office for National Statistics

10.20c: Waste from Households, UK and country split, 2010-14

Year	Measure	UK	England	NI	Scotland	Wales
2010	Arisings ('000 tonnes)	26,954	22,131	829	2,649	1,344
	Recycled ('000 tonnes)	10,879	9,112	315	861	591
	Recycling rate	40.4%	41.2%	38.0%	32.5%	44.0%
2011	Arisings ('000 tonnes)	26,793	22,170	810	2,484	1,329
	Recycled ('000 tonnes)	11,496	9,596	327	922	651
	Recycling rate	42.9%	43.3%	40.4%	37.1%	49.0%
2012	Arisings ('000 tonnes)	26,428	21,956	783	2,383	1,306
	Recycled ('000 tonnes)	11,603	9,684	326	912	681
	Recycling rate	43.9%	44.1%	41.7%	38.3%	52.1%
2013	Arisings ('000 tonnes)	25,929	21,564	781	2,311	1,274
	Recycled ('000 tonnes)	11,445	9,523	335	916	671
	Recycling rate	44.1%	44.2%	42.9%	39.6%	52.6%
2014	Arisings ('000 tonnes)	26,797	22,355	808	2,349	1,285
	Recycled ('000 tonnes)	12,044	10,025	352	962	705
	Recycling rate	44.9%	44.8%	43.6%	41.0%	54.8%

Recycling rate = Recycled ('000 tonnes) as a percentage of Arisings ('000 tonnes)

This update includes minor revisions to England figures 2010-12 and Wales figures 2012

Source: Waste Data Flow

Notes for users:

1) UK estimates for 'Waste from households' have been calculated in accordance with the Waste Framework Directive.

2) 'Waste from households' includes waste from: Regular household collection, Civic amenity sites, 'Bulky waste' 'Other household waste'

3) 'Waste from households' excludes waste from: Street cleaning/sweeping, Gully emptying, Separately collected healthcare waste, Asbestos waste

4) Whilst the general approach is consistent across UK countries, aggregation method and the wording of some questions completed by Local Authorities varies.

5) Users should be aware that individual UK countries other than England publish household recycling estimates using alternative measures and as such may differ from the estimates published here.

6) Local Authorities in England may also use an alternative measure.

10.20d Packaging waste and recycling / recovery, split by material, UK

	Packaging waste arising (thousand tonnes)		Total recovered / recycled (thousand tonnes)		Achieved recovery / recycling rate (%)		EU target recovery / recycling rate (%)	
	2012	2013	2012	2013	2012	2013	2012	2013
Metal	808	806	421	462	52.1%	57.4%	50.0%	50.0%
of which: Aluminium	162	164	62	71	38.5%	43.4%	n/a	n/a
of which: Steel	646	642	358	391	55.5%	60.9%	n/a	n/a
Paper	3,848	3,868	3,328	3,459	86.5%	89.4%	60.0%	60.0%
Glass	2,399	2,399	1,627	1,639	67.8%	68.3%	60.0%	60.0%
Plastic	2,554	2,260	644	714	25.2%	31.6%	22.5%	22.5%
Wood	1,024	1,029	525	436	51.3%	42.3%	15.0%	15.0%
Other materials	23	23	0	0	0.0%	0.0%	n/a	n/a
Total (for recycling)	10,655	10,384	6,544	6,710	61.4%	64.6%	55.0%	55.0%
Total (for recovery)	10,655	10,384	821	838	7.7%	8.1%	n/a	n/a
Total (for recycling and recovery)	10,655	10,384	7,365	7,548	69.1%	72.7%	60.0%	60.0%

Source: Defra

Notes for users:

1) Theses statistics have been calculated to fulfil a reporting requirement to Eurostat at UK level in relation to the EC Packaging and Packaging Waste Directive (94/62/EC). The 2013 figures were submitted to Eurostat in June 2015. The 2012 figures were submitted to Eurostat in June 2014.

2) Figures are compiled from the National Packaging Waste Database (NPWD) and industry reports.

3) 'Recovery' refer specifically to waste used for energy recovery.

4) The recovery figure includes waste sent to facilities that did not meet the R1 recovery energy efficiency thresholds, but were considered eligible based on the Packaging Directive, which states "'energy recovery' shall mean the use of combustible packaging waste as a means to generate energy through direct incineration with or without other waste but with recovery of the heat".

10.21 CIEH Survey of Local Authority Noise Enforcement Activity 2013-14

England and Wales Data represents 150 (43%) of 348 local authorities

	INDUSTRY		COMMERCE / LEISURE			RESIDENTIAL			CONSTRUCTION ETC	VME's	TOTAL'S	
	Agricultural Premises	Industrial / Warehousing / Distribution Premises	"On"-licensed Premises e.g. Pubs, Clubs, Restaurants	Commercial Premises e.g. Offices, Shops, Public transport	Leisure Premises e.g. Sports Facilities, Funfairs	Single Family House / Bungalow	Flats / Maisonettes	Other Residential e.g. Hostels, HMOs, Boarding Schools	Construction / Demolition Sites	Vehicles, Machinery and Equipment in Streets	SUM OF COLUMNS[4]	TOTAL OF ALL COMPLAINTS[5]
COMPLAINTS												
Number of Noise Complaints Received in Year	975	2,286	10,442	7,290	2,355	71,031	19,832	2,244	6,209	3,717	126,381	145,514
Number of Noise Complaints Resolved in Year	867	2,012	8,522	6,360	2,079	63,686	17,188	2,156	4,653	3,317	110,840	120,950
Number of Noise Incidents Complained-of	836	1,685	7,636	5,828	1,820	58,885	13,490	1,829	4,703	2,914	99,626	116,390
Number of Noise Incidents Per Million Population	57	88	376	296	95	3,008	766	117	234	149	5,186	5,626
Incidents Confirmed as Potentially Actionable [1,2]	249	611	3,071	2,807	636	19,550	6,499	789	1,748	1,145	37,105	
STATUTORY NUISANCES REMEDIED WITHOUT A NOTICE [3,6]												
Nuisance Ceased and Not Likely to Recur	62	102	496	440	100	4,822	1,378	171	337	250	8,158	
Referred to Other Services	20	25	69	88	29	942	239	16	135	61	1,624	
Resolved Informally	52	239	1,022	800	214	5,395	1,177	133	607	398	10,037	
No Action Possible	28	103	320	289	92	2,918	809	50	157	146	4,912	
NOTICES SERVED [6]												
S.80 EPA 1990 Abatement Notice	12	26	209	89	23	1,005	330	37	17	41	1,789	2,251
S.60 & S.61 CoPA 1974 Control of Construction Noise									633	1	634	650
Noise Act 1996 Warning Notice			76	50		990	56	1			1,173	1,458
Noise Act 1996 Fixed Penalty						4	1				5	
S.80(4A) EPA 1990 Fixed Penalty (Lond)						5	1				6	
APPEALS AGAINST NOTICES [6]												
Number of Appeals Allowed in Whole or in Part	1		1	1		4	1				8	
PROSECUTIONS BEGUN [6]												
Breach of Abatement Notice		2	31	6	1	142	36	4	12	10	244	318
Breach of Restriction on, or Prior Consent for, Construction Noise									10		10	14
Noise Act 1996												
Convictions Gained			2		1	39	11				53	
OTHER REMEDIES [6]												
Nuisance Remedied by the LA in Default			3	8		76	20	3		6	116	121
Number of Seizures				2		55	17	1		3	78	

[1] Incidents Confirmed as Potentially Actionable includes all those 'triggers' giving rise to formal enforcement power (described previously as "incidents confirmed as statutory nuisances etc")

[2] The sum of actions taken to resolve nuisances may exceed the Incidents Confirmed as Potentially Actionable figure because not all local authorities could provide data on incidents and more than one formal action may be taken to resolve a nuisance

[3] "Nuisances" here means statutory nuisances

[4] The sum of columns value is calculated, information provided by local authorities providing sub-total data only is not included here

[5] The Total of all Complaints column includes noise activity unaccounted for in previous columns

[6] Figures reported from 2005-06 may seem lower than previous years as they have not been subject to a 'grossing' calculation. Before 2005-06, where responding authorities were not able to provide data on the questions concerning outcome of noise incidents, estimates were made by pro-rating on number of noise incidents complained of

Source: Chartered Institute of Environmental Health.

Website: http://www.cieh.org

10.22 Government revenue from environmental taxes in the UK, 2003 to 2014

£ million

Environmental tax	2003	2004	2005	2006	2007	2008	2009	2010	2011	2012	2013	2014
Energy taxes	**23,730**	**24,685**	**24,666**	**24,859**	**26,035**	**26,503**	**27,728**	**29,118**	**29,339**	**29,995**	**31,120**	**32,499**
Tax on Hydrocarbon oils [2,3]	22,476	23,412	23,346	23,448	24,512	24,790	25,894	27,013	26,923	26,703	26,697	27,094
Climate Change Levy[4]	828	756	747	711	690	717	693	666	675	624	1,098	1,500
Fossil Fuel Levy	:	:	:	:	:	:	:	:	:	:	:	:
Gas Levy	:	:	:	:	:	:	:	:	:	:	:	:
Hydro-Benefit	44	40	10	:	:	:	:	:	:	:	:	:
Renewable Energy Obligations	382	477	563	700	833	996	1,099	1,243	1,423	2,046	2,388	2,931
Emmisions Trading Scheme (EU-ETS)	:	:	:	:	:	:	42	196	318	278	330	356
Carbon Reduction Commitment	:	:	:	:	:	:	:	:	:	344	607	618
Transport taxes	**5,662**	**5,824**	**5,756**	**6,096**	**7,526**	**7,704**	**7,944**	**8,742**	**9,434**	**9,930**	**10,352**	**10,574**
Air Passenger Duty	781	856	896	961	1,883	1,876	1,800	2,094	2,605	2,766	2,960	3,154
Rail Franchise Premia	161	205	98	125	244	285	496	792	993	1,275	1,275	1,417
Northern Ireland Driver Vehicle Agency	:	:	:	:	15	19	18	16	16	16	16	16
Motor vehicle duties paid by businesses	797	808	809	865	878	885	908	937	931	940	977	958
Motor vehicle duty paid by households	3,923	3,955	3,953	4,145	4,506	4,639	4,722	4,903	4,889	4,933	5,124	5,029
Boat Licenses	:	:	:	:	:	:	:	:	:	:	:	:
Pollution/Resources taxes	**964**	**1,019**	**1,080**	**1,145**	**1,236**	**1,308**	**1,137**	**1,375**	**1,403**	**1,379**	**1,494**	**1,512**
Landfill Tax	607	672	733	804	877	954	842	1,065	1,090	1,094	1,191	1,146
Fishing Licenses	17	19	20	20	20	20	20	20	23	21	21	21
Aggregates levy	340	328	327	321	339	334	275	290	290	264	282	345
Total environmental taxes	**30,356**	**31,528**	**31,502**	**32,100**	**34,797**	**35,515**	**36,809**	**39,235**	**40,176**	**41,304**	**42,966**	**44,585**
Total taxes and social contributions	395,024	422,753	451,695	487,685	509,434	521,177	484,379	520,583	549,889	554,884	576,538	595,224
As a percentage of total taxes and social contributions (%)	**7.7**	**7.5**	**7.0**	**6.6**	**6.8**	**6.8**	**7.6**	**7.5**	**7.3**	**7.4**	**7.5**	**7.5**
Gross Domestic Product (GDP)	1,190,525	1,255,191	1,326,660	1,403,726	1,480,956	1,518,675	1,482,144	1,558,365	1,617,677	1,655,384	1,713,122	1,791,490
As a percentage of GDP (%)	**2.5**	**2.5**	**2.4**	**2.3**	**2.3**	**2.3**	**2.5**	**2.5**	**2.5**	**2.5**	**2.5**	**2.5**

Source: Office for National Statistics

1 All data are presented in current prices i.e. not adjusted for inflation

2 Includes unleaded petrol (including super unleaded), leaded petrol, lead replacement petrol, ultra low suplhur petrol, diesel and ultra low sulphur diesel

3 Duty incentives have concentrated production on ultra low sulphur varieties.

4 Includes Carbon Price Floor from 2013.

The symbol ':' denotes 'not applicable'.

Housing

Chapter 11

Housing

Permanent dwellings (Table 11.1, 11.3)

Local housing authorities include: the Commission for the New Towns and New Towns Development Corporations; Communities Scotland; and the Northern Ireland Housing Executive. The figures shown for housing associations include dwellings provided by housing associations other than the Communities Scotland and the Northern Ireland Housing Executive and include those provided or authorised by government departments for the families of police, prison staff, the Armed Forces and certain other services.

Mortgage possession actions by region (Table 11.6)

The table shows mortgage possession actions in the county courts of England and Wales and excludes a small number of mortgage actions in the High Court.

A claimant begins an action for an order for possession of a property by issuing a claim in the county court, either by using the Possession Claim Online system or locally through a county court. In mortgage possession cases, the usual procedure is for the claim being issued to be given a hearing date before a district judge. The court, following a judicial hearing, may grant an order for possession immediately. This entitles the claimants to apply for a warrant to have the defendant evicted. However, even where a warrant for possession is issued, the parties can still negotiate a compromise to prevent eviction.

Frequently the court grants the claimant possession but suspends the operation of the order. Provided the defendant complies with the terms of suspension, which usually require the defendant to pay the current mortgage instalments plus some of the accrued arrears, the possession order cannot be enforced.

The mortgage possession figures do not indicate how many houses have actually been repossessed through the courts. Repossessions can occur without a court order being made while not all court orders result in repossession.

A new mortgage pre-action protocol (MPAP), approved by the Master of the Rolls, was introduced for possession claims in the County Courts with effect from 19 November 2008. The MPAP gives clear guidance on what the courts expect lenders and borrowers to have done prior to a claim being issued.

Evidence from administrative records from Qtr4 2008 suggests that this date coincided with a fall of around 50% in the daily and weekly numbers of new mortgage repossession claims being issued in the courts.

It therefore seems highly likely that the launch of the MPAP has led to a fall in the number of new claims being issued since introduction of MPAP (19th November to 31st December 2008).

Mortgage possession orders are typically made (where necessary) around 8 weeks after the corresponding claims are issued.

Households in Temporary Accommodation under homelessness provisions (Tables 11.7, 11.8, 11.9)

Comprises households in accommodation arranged by local authorities pending enquiries or after being accepted as owed a main homeless duty under the 1996 Act (includes residual cases awaiting re-housing under the 1985 Act). Excludes "homeless at home" cases. The data shown for Wales includes "homeless at home" cases.

11.1a Dwelling stock: by tenure[1], England

Thousands of dwellings

	Owner Occupied	Rented Privately or with a job or business	Rented from Private Registered Providers	Rented from Local Authorities	Other public sector dwellings	All Dwellings
2000	14,600	2,089	1,273	3,012	101	21,075
2001	14,735	2,133	1,424	2,812	103	21,207
2002	14,846	2,197	1,492	2,706	112	21,354
2003 [4]	14,752	2,549	1,651	2,457	104	21,513
2004 [4]	14,986	2,578	1,702	2,335	83	21,684
2005 [4]	15,100	2,720	1,802	2,166	82	21,870
2006 [4]	15,052	2,987	1,865	2,087	82	22,073
2007 [4]	15,093	3,182	1,951	1,987	75	22,288
2008 [4]	15,067	3,443	2,056	1,870	74	22,511
2009 [4]	14,968	3,705	2,128	1,820	74	22,694
2010 [4]	14,895	3,912	2,180	1,786	66	22,839
2011 [4]	14,827	4,105	2,255	1,726	63	22,976
2012 [4] [P]	14,754	4,286	2,304	1,693	75	23,111
2013 [4] [P]	14,685	4,465	2,331	1,682	73	23,236
2014 [4] [P R]	14,674	4,623	2,343	1,669	64	23,372

Source: Department for Communities and Local Government

Contact: 0303 44 41864

E-Mail: housing.statistics@communities.gsi.gov.uk

1. For detailed definitions of all tenures, see Definitions of housing terms in Housing Statistics home page.

2. Figures for census years are based on census output.

3. Series from 1992 to 2001 for England has been adjusted so that the 2001 total dwelling estimate matches the 2001 Census.
   Series from 2002 to 2011 for England has been adjusted so that the 2011 total dwelling estimate matches the 2011 Census.
   Estimates from 2002 are based on local authority and Private Registered Provider (housing association) dwelling counts,
   the Labour Force Survey and, from 2003, the English Housing Survey. Estimates may not be strictly comparable between periods.

4. From 2003 the figures for owner-occupied and the private rental sector for England have been produced using a new
   improved methodology as detailed in the dwelling stock release. Previous to this vacancy was not accounted for.

R- Revised from previous publication

P - Provisional

Data for earlier years are less reliable and definitions may not be consistent throughout the series

Stock estimates are expressed to the nearest thousand but should not be regarded as accurate to the last digit

Components may not sum to totals due to rounding

11.1b Dwelling stock: by tenure[1,2], Wales

Thousands of dwellings

	Owner Occupied	Rented Privately or with a job or business	Rented from Housing Associations	Rented from Local Authorities	All Dwellings
2001 [5]	941	90	55	188	1,275
2002 [5]	957	89	57	183	1,285
2003 [5]	966	97	57	176	1,296
2004 [5]	979	104	64	160	1,307
2005 [5]	989	109	65	156	1,319
2006 [5]	997	113	66	154	1,331
2007 [5]	1,002	122	67	153	1,343
2008 [5]	1,001	135	89	130	1,355
2009 [5]	989	157	107	113	1,366
2010 [5]	984	170	110	111	1,375
2011 [5]	981	180	134	89	1,384
2012 [5]	977	189	135	88	1,389
2013 [5]	983	188	135	88	1,394
2014 [5]	981	196	135	88	1,400

Source: Welsh Assembly Government

Contact: 0303 44 41864

E-Mail: housing.statistics@communities.gsi.gov.uk

1. For detailed definitions of all tenures, see Definitions of housing terms in Housing Statistics home page.

2. Owner-occupied tenure includes owner-occupied, intermediate and other.

3. April data for census years are based on census output.

4. Data for years 1969 to 1990 sourced from Department of Environment publications:
   Housing and Construction Statistics, 1967-1979, 1977-1987,1980-1990 and 1990-1997.

5. The tenure split between owner-occupied and privately rented dwellings has been calculated from 1997 onwards using
   information from the Labour Force Survey. These figures were revised in January 2011 following a re-weighting of the
   Labour Force Survey data.

R - Revised

P - Provisional

These data are produced and published separately by the Welsh Assembly Government, and although the figures in this table are correct at the time of its latest update they may be superseded before the next update.

Data for earlier years are less reliable and definitions may not be consistent throughout the series.

Stock estimates are expressed to the nearest thousand but should not be regarded as accurate to the last digit.

Components may not sum to totals due to rounding.

11.1c Dwelling stock: by tenure[1,2,3,4,5], Scotland

Thousands of dwellings

	Owner Occupied	Rented Privately or with a job or business	Rented from Housing Associations	Rented from Local Authorities	All Dwellings
31 December[4]					
1999	1,435	155	131	583	**2,303**
2000	1,472	155	137	557	**2,322**
31 March[4]					
2001	1,439	181	139	553	**2,312**
2002	1,477	179	143	531	**2,329**
2003	1,505	188	238	416	**2,347**
2004	1,513	213	251	389	**2,367**
2005	1,536	225	251	374	**2,387**
2006	1,559	234	251	362	**2,406**
2007	1,562	259	261	346	**2,428**
2008	1,592	259	269	330	**2,451**
2009	1,590	285	268	326	**2,469**
2010	1,584	303	272	323	**2,482**
2011	1,580	320	275	320	**2,495**
2012	1,545	366	277	319	**2,508**
2013	1,537	389	277	318	**2,521**
2014	1,544	394	277	318	**2,534**

Source: Scottish Government

Contact: 0303 44 41864

E-Mail: housing.statistics@communities.gsi.gov.uk

1. For detailed definitions of all tenures, see Definitions of housing terms in Housing Statistics home page

2. April data for census years are based on census output

3. Data for years 1969 to 1989 sourced from Department of Environment publications:

   Housing and Construction Statistics, 1967-1979, 1977-1987,1980-1990 and 1990-1997.

4. Estimates from 1990 onwards are based on the Census (1991, 2001, 2011), council tax records and exemptions,

   social sector stock counts, and private tenure splits from the Scottish Household Survey and are not strictly comparable with earlier figures. These are not all collected for the same timescales and may not be exact counts, even rounded to the nearest thousand.

5. In order to include vacant private sector dwellings in table 107, estimates for vacant private sector stock in the Scottish

   statistics have been apportioned according to the % of occupied dwellings for the private sector tenures.

R- Revised from previous publication

P- Provisional

These data are produced and published separately by the Scottish Government, and although the figures in this table are correct at the time of its latest update they may be superseded before the next update.

Data for earlier years are less reliable and definitions may not be consistent throughout the series.

Stock estimates are expressed to the nearest thousand but should not be regarded as accurate to the last digit.

Components may not sum to totals due to rounding.

11.1d Household Tenure 2008-09 to 2014-15[1,2,3,4,5] Northern Ireland

All households

Percentages

Tenure	2008-09	2009-10	2010-11	2011-12	2012-13	2013-14	2014-15
Owned outright	36	36	35	35	36	38	37
Owned with mortgage[2]	33	34	33	31	30	29	31
Rented- NIHE[3]	14	13	12	14	12	12	11
Rented other[4]	16	16	19	19	20	19	20
rented from housing association	..	..	..	..	*4*	*3*	*4*
rented privately	..	..	..	..	*16*	*16*	*16*
Rent free[5]	1	2	1	1	1	1	1
Bases=100%	2,474	2,761	2,718	2,778	2,710	2,736	2,521

SOURCE: Continuous Household Survey

1. See Appendix 1: Data Source - Supply here: https://www.communities-ni.gov.uk/sites/default/files/publications/dsd/ni-housing-stats-1415.pdf
2. Includes properties being purchased through the co-ownership scheme.
3. NIHE - Northern Ireland Housing Executive
4. Includes properties which are rented from a housing association, rented privately.
5. Includes squatting and rent free

11.2 Dwelling stock: by tenure[1], Great Britain

Thousands of dwellings

	Owner Occupied	Rented Privately or with a job	Rented from Housing Associations	Rented from Local Authorities	Other public sector dwellings	All Dwellings
31 December [3]						
1981	11,936	2,288	468	6,388	..	**21,077**
1982	12,357	2,201	480	6,196	..	**21,233**
1983	12,740	2,121	497	6,060	..	**21,419**
1984	13,099	2,040	516	5,959	..	**21,615**
1985	13,440	1,963	537	5,863	..	**21,803**
1986	13,790	1,885	551	5,776	..	**22,002**
1987	13,968	2,139	586	5,599	..	**22,293**
1988	14,424	2,077	614	5,412	..	**22,527**
1989	14,832	2,069	652	5,190	..	**22,743**
1990	15,099	2,123	702	5,015	..	**22,940**
31 March [3,4]						
1991	15,155	1,990	701	4,966	167	**22,979**
1992	15,367	2,058	733	4,879	151	**23,190**
1993	15,523	2,120	811	4,759	153	**23,366**
1994	15,695	2,184	884	4,634	150	**23,546**
1995	15,869	2,255	976	4,496	145	**23,739**
1996	16,013	2,332	1,078	4,369	141	**23,931**
1997	16,215	2,361	1,132	4,273	132	**24,113**
1998	16,461	2,367	1,205	4,140	121	**24,296**
1999	16,734	2,324	1,319	3,983	110	**24,469**
2000	16,949	2,350	1,458	3,788	101	**24,645**
2001 R	17,115	2,404	1,618	3,553	103	**24,794**
2002 R	17,280	2,465	1,692	3,420	112	**24,968**
2003 [5]	17,223	2,834	1,946	3,049	104	**25,156**
2004 [5] R	17,478	2,895	2,017	2,884	83	**25,358**
2005 [5] R	17,625	3,054	2,118	2,696	82	**25,576**
2006 [5] R	17,608	3,334	2,182	2,603	82	**25,810**
2007 [5] R	17,657	3,563	2,279	2,486	75	**26,059**
2008 [5] R	17,660	3,837	2,414	2,330	74	**26,317**
2009 [5] R	17,547	4,147	2,503	2,259	74	**26,529**
2010 [5] R	17,463	4,385	2,562	2,220	66	**26,696**
2011 [5] R	17,388	4,605	2,664	2,135	63	**26,855**
2012 R	17,276	4,841	2,716	2,100	75	**27,008**
2013 P R	17,205	5,042	2,743	2,088	73	**27,151**

1. For detailed definitions of all tenures, see Definitions of housing terms in Housing Statistics home page. 'Other public sector dwellings' figures
are currently only available for England.

2. Figures for census years are based on census output

3. Data for years 1969 to 1990 sourced from Department of Environment publications:
   Housing and Construction Statistics, 1967-1979, 1977-1987, 1980-1990 and 1990-1997.
   Great Britain totals from 2002 are derived by summing country totals at 31st March.
   For 1991 to 2001 Scotland stock levels from the year before is added into the UK total.

4. Series from 1992 to 2011 for England has been adjusted so that the 2001 and 2011 total dwelling estimate matches the 2001 and 2011 Census.
   Estimates from 2002 are based on local authority and housing association dwelling counts,
   the Labour Force Survey and, from 2003, the English Housing Survey. Estimates may not be strictly comparable between periods.

5. From 2003 the figures for owner-occupied and the private rental sector for England have been produced using a new improved
   methodology as detailed in the dwelling stock release. Previous to this vacancy was not accounted for.

R- Revised from previous publication
P- Provisional

Data for earlier years are less reliable and definitions may not be consistent throughout the series

Stock estimates are expressed to the nearest thousand but should not be regarded as accurate to the last digit

Components may not sum to totals due to rounding

Contact: 0303 44 41864
E-Mail: housing.statistics@Communities.gsi.gov.uk

Source:
Department for Communities and Local Government
Welsh Assembly Government
Scottish Government
Department for Social Development (Northern Ireland)

11.3 House building: permanent dwellings completed, by tenure[1] and country[2]

Number of dwellings

	Financial Year		United Kingdom	England	Wales	Scotland	Northern Ireland
All Dwellings	1993-94		186,850	147,710	9,870	22,110	7,160
	1994-95		195,580	157,970	9,070	21,810	6,730
	1995-96		197,710	154,600	9,170	24,690	9,250
	1996-97		185,940	146,250	10,090	20,700	8,910
	1997-98		190,760	149,560	8,430	22,590	10,180
	1998-99		178,290	140,260	7,740	20,660	9,640
	1999-00		184,010	141,800	8,710	23,110	10,400
	2000-01		175,370	133,260	8,330	22,110	11,670
	2001-02	R	174,200	129,870	8,270	22,570	13,490
	2002-03		183,210	137,740	8,310	22,750	14,420
	2003-04		190,590	143,960	8,300	23,820	14,510
	2004-05	R	205,390	155,890	8,490	26,470	14,540
	2005-06 [3]	R	210,310	163,400	8,250	24,950	13,710
	2006-07 [3]	R	215,210	167,680	9,330	24,270	13,930
	2007-08	R	215,860	170,610	8,660	25,790	10,800
	2008-09	R	178,550	140,990	7,120	21,010	9,430
	2009-10	R	151,220	119,910	6,170	17,110	8,020
	2010-11	R	136,010	107,870	5,510	16,420	6,210
	2011-12	R	145,780	118,510	5,580	15,980	5,720
	2012-13	R	133,000	107,980	5,450	14,050	5,530
	2013-14	R	138,350	112,330	5,840	14,870	5,320
Private Enterprise	1993-94		146,750	116,050	6,650	18,310	5,730
	1994-95		155,290	125,740	6,300	17,890	5,350
	1995-96		156,540	123,620	6,880	19,200	6,850
	1996-97		153,450	121,170	7,520	17,490	7,270
	1997-98		160,680	127,840	6,490	17,980	8,370
	1998-99		154,560	121,190	6,440	18,780	8,140
	1999-00		160,520	124,470	7,860	19,070	9,120
	2000-01		152,740	116,640	7,390	18,200	10,510
	2001-02	R	153,580	115,700	7,490	18,310	12,070
	2002-03		164,300	124,460	7,520	18,940	13,390
	2003-04		172,360	130,100	7,860	20,450	13,950
	2004-05	R	183,710	139,130	7,990	22,440	14,150
	2005-06 [3]	R	185,830	144,940	7,880	20,260	12,760
	2006-07 [3]	R	188,560	145,680	8,990	21,040	12,850
	2007-08	R	187,280	147,170	8,320	21,660	10,140
	2008-09	R	145,290	113,800	6,430	16,100	8,960
	2009-10	R	116,410	93,030	5,290	11,120	6,960
	2010-11	R	103,870	83,180	4,510	10,690	5,480
	2011-12	R	108,780	89,120	4,750	10,090	4,830
	2012-13	R	103,180	84,550	4,710	9,840	4,070
	2013-14	R	109,820	89,630	5,160	10,820	4,200
Housing Associations	1993-94		36,580	30,210	3,010	2,820	550
	1994-95		37,240	31,380	2,570	2,790	500
	1995-96		38,170	30,230	2,130	4,780	1,040
	1996-97		30,950	24,630	2,550	2,960	810
	1997-98		28,550	21,400	1,940	4,490	730
	1998-99		22,870	18,890	1,270	1,750	960
	1999-00		23,170	17,270	850	3,960	1,090
	2000-01		22,250	16,430	900	3,800	1,110
	2001-02	R	20,400	14,100	710	4,200	1,390
	2002-03		18,610	13,080	780	3,720	1,030

11.3 House building: permanent dwellings completed, by tenure[1] and country[2]

Number of dwellings

	Financial Year		United Kingdom	England	Wales	Scotland	Northern Ireland
	2003-04		18,020	13,670	420	3,370	560
	2004-05	R	21,550	16,660	480	4,020	390
	2005-06 [3]	R	24,160	18,160	350	4,700	950
	2006-07 [3]	R	26,400	21,750	350	3,230	1,080
	2007-08	R	28,330	23,220	340	4,100	660
	2008-09	R	32,430	26,690	690	4,580	470
	2009-10	R	34,030	26,520	880	5,580	1,060
	2010-11	R	30,380	23,550	990	5,110	740
	2011-12	R	33,950	27,460	830	4,780	890
	2012-13	R	27,500	22,060	740	3,240	1,450
	2013-14	R	26,480	21,790	670	2,910	1,110
Local Authorities	1993-94		3,530	1,450	210	980	890
	1994-95		3,060	850	200	1,130	880
	1995-96		3,010	760	160	720	1,360
	1996-97		1,540	450	20	240	820
	1997-98		1,520	320	-	110	1,080
	1998-99		870	180	30	120	540
	1999-00		320	60	-	70	190
	2000-01		380	180	50	110	50
	2001-02	R	230	60	70	70	30
	2002-03		300	200	10	90	-
	2003-04		210	190	20	-	-
	2004-05	R	130	100	30	-	-
	2005-06 [3]	R	320	300	20	-	-
	2006-07 [3]	R	260	250	-	10	-
	2007-08	R	250	220	10	30	-
	2008-09	R	830	490	-	340	-
	2009-10	R	780	370	-	410	-
	2010-11	R	1,760	1,140	-	610	-
	2011-12	R	3,080	1,960	-	1,110	-
	2012-13	R	2,330	1,360	-	960	-
	2013-14	R	2,060	910	10	1,140	-

1. For detailed definitions of all tenures see definitions of housing terms on Housing Statistics home page

2. Northern Ireland data prior to 2005 is sourced from the Department of Communities, which use different definitions and adjust their data. Further information can be viewed at:

https://www.communities-ni.gov.uk/publications/review-new-dwelling-starts-and-completions

3. Figures from October 2005 to March 2007 in England are missing a small number of starts and completions that were inspected by independent approved inspectors. These data are included from 'June 2007

Totals may not equal the sum of component parts due to rounding to the nearest 10

- Less than 5 dwellings

P Figure provisional and subject to revision

R Revised from previous release

.. Not available

Contact:
Telephone: 0303 444 1864
Email: housing.statistics@communities.gsi.gov.uk

Source:
P2 returns from local authorities
National House-Building Council (NHBC)
Approved inspector data returns
Welsh Assembly Government
Scottish Government
Department of Finance and Personnel (DFPNI)
District Council Building Control (NI)

11.4a Housebuilding: permanent dwellings completed, by house and flat, number of bedroom and tenure[1], ENGLAND

Percentage of all dwellings

Financial Year		2001 /02 [2]	2002 /03 [2]	2003 /04 [2]	2004 /05 [2]	2005 /06 [2]	2006 /07 [2]	2007 /08 [2]	2008 /09 [2]	2009 /10 [2]	2010 /11 [2]	2011 /12 [2]	2012 /13 [2]	2013 /14 [2]
Private Enterprise														
Houses	1 bedroom	0	0	0	0	0		0	0	1	1	1	1	1
	2 bedrooms	9	9	8	7	6	6	7	8	8	9	10	10	9
	3 bedrooms	30	29	28	28	26	27	26	25	28	33	32	33	33
	4 or more bedrooms	39	36	31	25	22	22	21	21	24	27	26	28	31
	All	78	74	67	60	55	56	55	54	60	70	69	71	74
Flats	1 bedroom	6	5	7	9	9	9	9	12	11	6	8	7	7
	2 bedrooms	15	19	24	30	35	34	35	33	28	23	22	20	19
	3 bedrooms	1	1	1	1	1	1	1	1	1	1	1	1	1
	4 or more bedrooms	0	0	0	0	0	0	0	0	0	0	0	0	0
	All	22	26	33	40	45	44	45	46	40	30	31	29	26
Houses and flats	1 bedroom	6	6	8	9	9	9	10	12	11	7	8	8	7
	2 bedrooms	24	28	32	37	41	40	41	41	35	33	32	30	28
	3 bedrooms	31	30	29	29	28	28	27	26	29	34	33	34	34
	4 or more bedrooms	39	36	32	25	22	22	22	21	25	27	27	28	31
	All	100	100	100	100	100	100	100	100	100	100	100	100	100
Housing Associations														
Houses	1 bedroom	2	2	1	1	1	0	0	0	1	1	0	1	1
	2 bedrooms	29	24	23	19	18	15	15	17	16	19	21	22	26
	3 bedrooms	28	27	24	22	19	16	15	17	19	23	24	25	28
	4 or more bedrooms	5	8	6	5	4	3	3	3	5	6	5	5	5
	All	64	62	54	47	42	34	34	37	40	50	51	53	60
Flats	1 bedroom	15	14	13	17	18	23	18	17	17	13	11	12	10
	2 bedrooms	20	22	31	34	38	41	45	44	38	34	33	31	27
	3 bedrooms	1	2	1	2	2	1	2	2	3	3	4	4	3
	4 or more bedrooms	0	1	1	0	0	0	1	0	1	1	1	1	0
	All	36	39	46	53	58	66	66	63	60	50	49	47	40
Houses and flats	1 bedroom	17	17	14	18	19	24	18	17	18	14	12	13	11
	2 bedrooms	49	45	54	52	56	56	60	61	54	54	54	53	53
	3 bedrooms	28	29	25	24	21	17	18	18	22	26	28	29	30
	4 or more bedrooms	5	9	7	5	4	3	4	4	6	7	6	6	6
	All	100	100	100	100	100	100	100	100	100	100	100	100	100
All tenures														
Houses	1 bedroom	0	1	0	0	0		0	0	1	1	1	1	1
	2 bedrooms	11	10	9	8	8	8	8	10	10	12	13	12	13
	3 bedrooms	28	29	28	27	26	25	25	23	25	30	30	31	32
	4 or more bedrooms	37	34	30	23	20	20	19	16	19	22	21	23	26
	All	77	73	66	59	54	53	52	50	55	65	64	67	71
Flats	1 bedroom	6	6	8	10	10	11	11	13	12	8	9	8	7
	2 bedrooms	15	19	24	30	35	35	36	36	31	26	25	22	20
	3 bedrooms	1	1	1	1	1	1	1	1	1	1	2	2	1
	4 or more bedrooms	0	0	0	0	0	0	0	0	0	0	0	0	0
	All	23	27	34	41	46	47	48	50	45	35	36	33	29
Houses and flats	1 bedroom	7	6	8	10	10	11	11	13	13	8	9	9	8
	2 bedrooms	25	29	33	38	42	42	44	46	40	38	38	35	33
	3 bedrooms	31	30	29	28	27	27	26	24	27	32	32	33	33
	4 or more bedrooms	37	34	30	23	21	20	19	17	20	22	21	23	26
	All	100	100	100	100	100	100	100	100	100	100	100	100	100

Source: Department for Communities and Local Government

1. For detailed definitions of all tenures, see Definitions of housing terms in Housing Statistics home page
2. Figures for 2001/02 onwards are based on NHBC data only, so there is some degree of variability owing to partial coverage.
3. The England worksheet and charts have been corrected following initial publication.

Contact:
Telephone: 0303 444 8279
E-Mail: housing.statistics@communities.gsi.gov.uk

11.4b Housebuilding completions: by number of bedrooms , Wales

Percentages

		2000 /01	2001 /02	2002 /03	2003 /04	2004 /05	2005 /06	2006 /07	2007 /08	2008 /09	2009 /10	2010 /11	2011 /12	2012 /13	2013 /14
Wales[1]															
1 bedroom	**JUWO**	5	4	6	6	7	9	11	10	16	11	10	11	7	11
2 bedrooms	**JUWP**	18	19	18	20	21	27	28	30	33	33	29	28	24	24
3 bedrooms	**JUWQ**	42	39	35	37	35	35	33	33	30	36	39	36	39	37
4 or more bedrooms	**JUWR**	34	38	41	37	37	30	28	27	22	20	22	25	29	28
All houses and flats	**JUWS**	100	100	100	100	100	100	100	100	100	100	100	100	100	100

Sources: Welsh Government

1 Figures for all years for Wales are based on the reports of local authority building inspectors and the National House Building Council (NHBC). It does not include information from other private approved inspector.

11.5 Mortgage possession workload in the county courts of England and Wales, 2003 - 2014

Year	Quarter	Claims Issued	Orders			Warrants	Repossessions by county court bailiffs	Properties taken into possession[2] in UK
			Outright	Suspended	Total			
2003		65,373	16,495	24,547	41,042	31,481	6,692	8,500
2004		76,993	20,048	26,639	46,687	33,042	7,074	8,200
2005		114,733	32,757	38,211	70,968	48,513	12,794	14,500
2006		131,248	46,288	44,895	91,183	66,060	20,960	21,000
2007		137,725	58,250	49,259	107,509	73,890	23,831	25,900
2008		142,741	70,804	61,994	132,798	89,748	35,792	40,000
2009		93,533	44,856	38,039	82,895	77,461	32,457	48,300
2010		75,431	32,940	29,235	62,175	63,532	23,612	38,100
2011		73,181	30,190	29,697	59,887	65,371	25,463	37,100
2012		59,877	24,129	23,935	48,064	59,040	19,728	34,000
2013		53,659	20,718	19,585	40,303	52,305	15,692	28,900
2014 (p)		40,303	15,822	13,227	29,049	41,891	11,976	
2010	Q1	18,805	8,322	7,225	15,547	16,397	6,889	10,800
	Q2	18,395	7,959	6,804	14,763	16,071	5,927	9,800
	Q3	20,384	8,849	7,799	16,648	16,690	5,898	9,300
	Q4	17,847	7,810	7,407	15,217	14,374	4,898	8,200
2011	Q1	19,608	8,122	7,732	15,854	17,330	6,538	9,600
	Q2	18,339	7,388	7,336	14,724	16,403	6,170	9,300
	Q3	18,763	7,790	7,762	15,552	16,409	7,274	9,500
	Q4	16,471	6,890	6,867	13,757	15,229	5,481	8,700
2012	Q1	16,963	6,763	7,116	13,879	16,136	6,072	9,600
	Q2	14,615	6,032	6,152	12,184	14,373	4,825	8,500
	Q3	14,168	5,556	5,437	10,993	14,557	4,676	8,200
	Q4	14,131	5,778	5,230	11,008	13,974	4,155	7,700
2013	Q1	14,375	5,674	5,260	10,934	13,580	4,474	8,000
	Q2	12,881	5,187	5,059	10,246	13,529	4,087	7,600
	Q3	14,256	4974	4,723	9,697	13,039	3,733	7,200
	Q4	12,147	4,883	4,543	9,426	12,157	3,398	6,100
2014	Q1	12,706	4,648	4,277	8,925	12,391	3,709	6,400
	Q2	10,773	4,400	3,539	7,939	11,121	3,028	5,400
	Q3 (r)	9,731	3,940	3,201	7,141	10,067	2,805	5,000
	Q4 (p)	7,093	2,834	2,210	5,044	8,312	2,434	..

Source: HM Courts and Tribunals Service CaseMan, Possession Claim On-Line (PCOL) and Council of Mortgage Lenders (CML)

Notes:

[1] Data relating to 1999 onwards are sourced from county court administrative systems and exclude duplicate observations. Data prior to 1999 are sourced from manual counts made by court staff.

[2] Council of Mortgage Lenders (CML) statistics for the latest quarter are unavailable prior to this bulletin being published as the MOJ does not have pre-release access to them. Please also note this figure relates to repossessions made in the United Kingdom whereas all other statistics in this bulletin relate to England and Wales. It should also be noted that these figures are rounded by the CML to the nearest hundred. Please see the CML website http://www.cml.org.uk/cml/statistics for more information about these statistics.

.. = data not available

(p) = provisional

(r)= revised

11.6 Mortgage arrears and repossessions

Year	2003	2004	2005	2006	2007	2008	2009	2010	2011	2012	2013	2014
Number of mortgages at year end (000s)	11,452	11,515	11,608	11,746	11,852	11,667	11,504	11,478	11,384	11,284	11,186	11,076
Repossessions during year	8,500	8,200	14,500	21,000	25,900	40,000	48,900	38,500	37,300	33,900	28,900	21,000
Cases in mortgage arrears												
12+ months arrears	12,600	11,000	15,000	15,700	15,300	29,500	69,500	63,700	54,400	48,500	41,100	31,400
6 - 12 months arrears	31,000	29,900	38,600	34,900	40,500	72,000	93,900	80,500	72,200	69,900	60,700	46,200
3 - 6 months arrears	55,800	60,500	69,400	64,900	71,700	117,400	112,400	103,300	99,000	97,200	86,600	70,100
3 - 5 months arrears	–	–	–	–	–	–	–	–	–	–	–	–

Sources: Compendium of Housing Finance Statistics & Housing Finance, Council of Mortgage Lenders, Janet Ford, Roof (3-5 months arrears).

Notes: Properties taken into possession include those voluntarily surrendered. The CML 3-6, 6-12 & 12+ months arrears figures are for the end of the year. Changes in the mortgage rate have the effect of changing monthly mortgage repayments and hence the number of months in arrears which a given amount

The Janet Ford figures for 3-5 months arrears are for the March of the year; her survey of mortgage arrears was discontinued from following the introduction of the CML 3-6 months arrears series.

11.7 Households in temporary accommodation[1] by type of accommodation, at the end of each quarter, England, 2001 - 2014

		Total in TA[1] (Temporary Accommodation)				Bed and breakfast hotels (including shared annexes)[2]							Hostels (including women's refuges)		
		Total	% change on same quarter in previous year	of which: with children[4,7]	Total number of children[5,7]	Total	% of Total TA	of which: with children[4,7]	with children and resident more than 6 weeks	of which: pending review /appeal	of which: headed by a 16/17 year old	of which: resident more than 6 weeks	Total	% of Total TA	of which: with children[4]
Number and percentage of total households in TA (%)															
2001 Q1		75,200	15%	..	..	10,860	14%	..	..	..	..	..	10,610	14%	..
Q2		75,920	12%	..	..	11,390	15%	..	..	..	..	..	10,320	14%	..
Q3		77,800	8%	..	..	12,220	16%	..	..	..	..	..	11,270	14%	..
Q4		77,510	6%	..	..	11,860	15%	..	..	..	..	..	10,680	14%	..
2002 Q1		80,200	7%	54,660	..	12,710	16%	6,960	..	..	..	..	9,570	12%	5,540
Q2		81,660	8%	58,870	..	12,720	16%	6,830	..	..	..	..	9,770	12%	6,030
Q3		85,010	9%	61,740	..	13,950	16%	6,970	..	..	..	..	9,720	11%	6,280
Q4		85,140	10%	60,310	..	13,240	16%	5,870	3,050	..	..	..	9,650	11%	5,770
2003 Q1		89,040	11%	61,510	..	12,440	14%	5,230	2,910	..	..	..	10,050	11%	6,040
Q2		91,870	13%	65,040	..	11,380	12%	3,940	2,120	..	..	..	10,420	11%	6,360
Q3		94,440	11%	67,260	..	10,310	11%	3,200	1,590	..	..	..	10,800	11%	6,450
Q4		94,610	11%	67,540	..	8,420	9%	1,730	940	..	..	..	10,370	11%	6,060
2004 Q1		97,680	10%	70,580	..	7,090	7%	820	30	..	..	..	10,790	11%	6,280
Q2		99,530	8%	71,640	121,590	7,240	7%	1,100	60	..	..	..	10,570	11%	6,090
Q3		101,300	7%	72,510	122,530	7,450	7%	1,420	180	..	..	..	10,380	10%	5,960
Q4		101,030	7%	72,800	124,630	6,450	6%	820	100	..	..	..	10,070	10%	5,650
2005 Q1		101,070	3%	72,670	125,860	6,780	7%	1,180	110	..	..	..	10,280	10%	5,830
Q2		100,970	1%	72,810	124,900	6,290	6%	1,300	130	50	..	..	9,870	10%	5,440
Q3		101,020	0%	74,180	127,990	6,100	6%	1,470	150	40	..	..	10,020	10%	5,410
Q4		98,730	-2%	72,920	127,620	4,950	5%	820	140	30	..	..	9,230	9%	4,990
2006 Q1		96,370	-5%	71,560	127,650	5,150	5%	1,020	110	30	..	..	9,010	9%	4,960
Q2		93,910	-7%	69,790	130,470	4,890	5%	1,050	100	50	..	..	8,940	10%	4,820
Q3		93,090	-8%	69,500	129,340	4,900	5%	1,100	120	40	..	..	8,460	9%	4,460
Q4		89,510	-9%	65,770	122,080	4,210	5%	650	110	40	..	..	7,850	9%	3,950
2007 Q1		87,120	-10%	65,210	125,430	4,310	5%	980	80	30	..	..	7,640	9%	4,030
Q2		84,900	-10%	64,020	117,340	4,070	5%	940	100	30	670	300	7,230	9%	3,890
Q3		82,750	-11%	62,830	117,090	4,090	5%	900	130	30	690	300	7,180	9%	3,850
Q4		79,500	-11%	59,990	112,260	3,530	4%	700	120	20	550	270	6,620	8%	3,490
2008 Q1		77,510	-11%	59,230	110,360	3,840	5%	1,030	160	30	560	250	6,450	8%	3,580
Q2		74,690	-12%	57,210	107,050	3,440	5%	1,030	180	30	420	160	6,020	8%	3,350
Q3		72,130	-13%	55,850	104,640	3,230	4%	940	160	30	400	150	5,800	8%	3,190
Q4		67,480	-15%	52,290	98,880	2,560	4%	520	100	20	330	150	5,250	8%	2,830
2009 Q1		64,000	-17%	49,030	92,590	2,450	4%	470	70	10	340	120	5,170	8%	2,740
Q2		60,230	-19%	45,940	87,030	2,150	4%	510	80	20	310	130	4,710	8%	2,430
Q3		56,920	-21%	43,400	82,780	2,050	4%	510	130	20	230	100	4,480	8%	2,330
Q4		53,370	-21%	40,560	77,990	1,880	4%	400	120	10	170	70	4,150	8%	2,150
2010 Q1		51,310	-20%	39,200	74,610	2,050	4%	630	100	10	180	60	4,240	8%	2,270
Q2		50,400	-16%	37,940	72,590	2,410	5%	740	160	10	190	70	4,320	9%	2,380
Q3		49,680	-13%	37,620	71,460	2,660	5%	930	140	10	210	80	4,360	9%	2,440
Q4		48,010	-10%	36,230	69,050	2,310	5%	660	150	10	140	50	4,160	9%	2,270
2011 Q1		48,240	-6%	36,640	69,660	2,750	6%	1,030	200	10	160	50	4,250	9%	2,330
Q2		48,330	-4%	35,950	68,770	3,120	6%	1,210	240	20	150	40	4,370	9%	2,340
Q3		49,100	-1%	36,680	69,850	3,370	7%	1,340	310	40	140	50	4,380	9%	2,370
Q4		48,920	2%	36,600	69,460	3,170	6%	1,310	450	60	100	30	4,310	9%	2,380
2012 Q1		50,430	5%	37,190	70,090	3,960	8%	1,660	480	60	150	50	4,360	9%	2,350
Q2		51,630	7%	39,470	73,890	4,230	8%	1,900	680	70	140	50	4,350	8%	2,610
Q3		52,960	8%	40,090	75,460	4,120	8%	1,920	870	100	120	50	4,390	8%	2,690
Q4		53,140	9%	40,830	76,740	3,820	7%	1,600	770	100	80	50	4,280	8%	2,610
2013 Q1		55,320	10%	40,450	76,040	4,510	8%	1,970	760	50	100	40	4,480	8%	2,710
Q2		55,840	8%	42,800	79,030	4,350	8%	2,090	740	70	80	20	4,590	8%	2,890
Q3		57,410	8%	42,210	78,770	4,610	8%	2,110	800	80	70	20	4,700	8%	2,960
Q4		56,940	7%	43,750	80,970	3,920	7%	1,560	500	60	70	20	4,710	8%	2,950
2014 Q1		58,410	6%	43,410	80,660	4,370	7%	1,900	440	40	60	20	4,880	8%	3,010
Q2		59,570	7%	44,390	84,750	4,590	8%	2,130	610	50	70	20	4,980	8%	3,100
Q3		60,900	6%	45,590	87,410	4,680	8%	2,060	470	60	70	20	5,010	8%	3,030
Q4		61,930	9%	46,690	90,400	4,540	7%	2,040	780	60	40	20	5,090	8%	3,200

11.7 Households in temporary accommodation[1] by type of accommodation, at the end of each quarter, England, 2001 - 2014

		Local Authority or Housing Association (LA/HA) stock[6]			Leased from the Private Sector by an LA or HA[6]			Other Private Sector accommodation[2] (including private landlord)			Of which: in TA in another local authority district	Duty owed, no accommodation secured[3]					
		Total	% of Total TA	of which: with children[4,7]	Total	% of Total TA	of which: with children[4,7]	Total	% of Total TA	of which: with children[4,7]		a main duty accepted	% change from previous quarter	of which: with children[4]	All including decision pending	% change from previous quarter	Total with children[4], including decision pending
Number and percentage of total households in TA (%)																	
2001	Q1	25,480	34%	..	21,900	29%	..	6,350	8%	..	6,150	8,420	11%	..	12,730	4.1%	..
	Q2	25,450	34%	..	21,970	29%	..	6,790	9%	..	7,440	8,870	5%	..	13,240	4.0%	..
	Q3	25,930	33%	..	20,050	26%	..	8,320	11%	..	8,240	8,090	-9%	..	11,820	-10.7%	..
	Q4	26,580	34%	..	20,600	27%	..	7,800	10%	..	8,460	8,600	6%	..	12,000	1.5%	..
2002	Q1	27,760	35%	19,160	20,660	26%	17,070	9,500	12%	5,930	9,670	8,620	0%	..	11,990	-0.1%	3,320
	Q2	28,470	35%	21,360	22,610	28%	18,570	8,090	10%	6,090	8,190	8,890	3%	..	12,440	3.8%	4,450
	Q3	28,870	34%	21,130	23,850	28%	20,600	8,620	10%	6,760	11,550	10,390	17%	..	14,440	16.1%	6,760
	Q4	27,580	32%	20,380	25,940	30%	21,630	8,740	10%	6,660	12,310	9,760	-6%	..	14,800	2.5%	5,830
2003	Q1	28,250	32%	19,690	28,370	32%	23,240	9,920	11%	7,310	11,470	10,580	8%	..	16,280	10.0%	7,550
	Q2	27,590	30%	19,900	31,460	34%	26,630	11,020	12%	8,220	10,880	13,310	26%	..	19,380	19.0%	9,410
	Q3	27,560	29%	19,650	35,140	37%	29,950	10,640	11%	8,020	9,880	15,370	15%	..	23,060	19.0%	10,140
	Q4	27,480	29%	19,450	38,730	41%	33,340	9,620	10%	6,960	10,440	17,500	14%	..	23,070	0.0%	10,990
2004	Q1	27,890	29%	20,120	42,390	43%	36,390	9,530	10%	6,970	9,850	15,870	-9%	..	21,940	-4.9%	11,610
	Q2	27,960	28%	20,070	42,630	43%	35,900	11,130	11%	8,480	9,480	17,030	7%	..	23,000	4.9%	13,230
	Q3	28,220	28%	20,070	43,720	43%	36,650	11,530	11%	8,420	10,030	17,100	0%	..	23,200	0.9%	13,400
	Q4	27,730	27%	19,730	46,140	46%	38,750	10,640	11%	7,840	8,610	16,100	-6%	..	20,930	-9.8%	11,880
2005	Q1	26,630	26%	18,610	46,530	46%	39,170	10,860	11%	7,880	11,660	15,290	-5%		20,910	-0.1%	12,850
	Q2	27,430	27%	19,070	46,990	47%	39,600	10,390	10%	7,390	11,790	16,020	5%	10,470	..	..	..
	Q3	25,030	25%	17,620	48,860	48%	41,500	11,020	11%	8,190	13,430	15,140	-6%	10,270	..	..	..
	Q4	24,220	25%	17,110	49,910	51%	42,310	10,420	11%	7,700	10,700	11,570	-24%	7,840	..	..	..
2006	Q1	22,350	23%	16,080	49,660	52%	41,960	10,200	11%	7,550	11,080	11,010	-5%	7,210	..	..	..
	Q2	20,790	22%	14,880	49,320	53%	41,740	9,970	11%	7,290	11,590	10,210	-7%	6,920	..	..	..
	Q3	20,180	22%	14,830	49,700	53%	41,980	9,850	11%	7,140	11,620	9,720	-5%	6,550	..	..	..
	Q4	18,840	21%	13,930	48,850	55%	40,130	9,770	11%	7,120	9,950	8,470	-13%	5,740	..	..	..
2007	Q1	18,040	21%	13,510	45,600	52%	38,600	11,540	13%	8,090	10,130	8,780	4%	5,910	..	..	..
	Q2	17,240	20%	12,970	44,610	53%	37,920	11,750	14%	8,290	10,490	9,150	4%	6,280	..	..	..
	Q3	16,490	20%	12,410	43,430	52%	37,100	11,570	14%	8,580	11,130	9,540	4%	6,300	..	..	..
	Q4	15,910	20%	11,780	41,730	52%	35,380	11,710	15%	8,640	10,820	8,080	-15%	5,510	..	..	..
2008	Q1	14,740	19%	11,080	40,480	52%	34,610	12,000	15%	8,930	10,200	7,470	-8%	5,180	..	..	..
	Q2	14,030	19%	10,660	41,130	55%	34,900	10,070	13%	7,270	8,720	7,890	6%	5,630	..	..	..
	Q3	13,420	19%	10,240	39,990	55%	34,390	9,710	13%	7,090	7,620	6,740	-15%	4,520	..	..	..
	Q4	11,930	18%	8,990	38,790	57%	33,560	8,950	13%	6,400	7,360	6,070	-10%	4,030	..	..	..
2009	Q1	10,480	16%	7,800	37,450	59%	32,050	8,460	13%	5,970	7,960	5,560	-9%	3,740	..	..	..
	Q2	9,520	16%	6,970	35,920	60%	30,620	7,930	13%	5,410	7,880	4,560	-18%	2,940	..	..	..
	Q3	8,780	15%	6,390	34,130	60%	29,090	7,490	13%	5,080	6,550	4,350	-5%	2,770	..	..	..
	Q4	8,180	15%	5,950	32,430	61%	27,540	6,730	13%	4,520	5,780	4,150	-5%	2,540	..	..	..
2010	Q1	7,790	15%	5,790	30,920	60%	26,310	6,320	12%	4,210	5,430	3,710	-11%	2,320	..	..	..
	Q2	7,650	15%	5,570	29,820	59%	25,210	6,200	12%	4,040	5,630	3,780	2%	2,510	..	..	..
	Q3	7,610	15%	5,480	28,740	58%	24,570	6,320	13%	4,200	5,880	4,100	8%	2,700	..	..	..
	Q4	7,430	15%	5,440	27,730	58%	23,620	6,380	13%	4,250	5,810	4,410	8%	2,970	..	..	..
2011	Q1	7,490	16%	5,500	26,960	56%	23,170	6,790	14%	4,620	6,300	4,770	8%	3,270	..	..	..
	Q2	7,570	16%	5,460	26,240	54%	22,170	7,050	15%	4,780	6,290	4,770	0%	3,420	..	..	..
	Q3	7,890	16%	5,810	26,380	54%	22,250	7,090	14%	4,910	6,850	5,110	7%	3,590	..	..	..
	Q4	7,990	16%	5,840	26,080	53%	21,800	7,370	15%	5,280	7,350	5,490	8%	3,550	..	..	..
2012	Q1	8,270	16%	6,000	26,040	52%	21,490	7,810	15%	5,690	7,870	5,400	-2%	3,860	..	..	..
	Q2	8,600	17%	6,470	25,960	50%	22,240	8,500	16%	6,250	8,170	5,500	2%	3,830	..	..	..
	Q3	8,930	17%	6,730	26,290	50%	21,880	9,230	17%	6,860	8,520	5,560	1%	4,080	..	..	..
	Q4	9,090	17%	6,830	26,310	50%	22,490	9,630	18%	7,300	9,270	5,690	2%	3,950	..	..	..
2013	Q1	9,270	17%	7,020	26,260	47%	21,020	10,810	20%	7,730	9,130	5,930	4%	4,270	..	..	..
	Q2	10,060	18%	7,860	24,780	44%	21,210	12,070	22%	8,750	11,280	5,510	-7%	3,870	..	..	..
	Q3	9,810	17%	7,290	25,660	45%	21,460	12,630	22%	8,390	11,860	5,010	-9%	3,520	..	..	..
	Q4	9,560	17%	7,280	25,460	45%	21,450	13,280	23%	10,520	12,190	4,930	-2%	3,460	..	..	..
2014	Q1	9,880	17%	7,530	25,270	43%	20,250	14,010	24%	10,720	12,910	5,620	14%	3,960	..	..	..
	Q2	10,120	17%	7,760	24,800	42%	19,770	15,090	25%	11,630	14,130	5,310	-5%	3,880	..	..	..
	Q3	10,070	17%	7,770	23,290	38%	18,560	17,850	29%	14,170	15,460	6,120	15%	4,420	..	..	..
	Q4	10,530	17%	8,070	23,460	38%	18,940	18,320	30%	14,440	15,990	5,820	-5%	4,290	..	..	..

Notes

1. Households in accommodation arranged by local authorities pending enquiries or after being accepted as homeless under the 1996 Act (includes residual cases awaiting re-housing under the 1985 Act).

2. Other private sector accommodation includes accommodation that has been leased directly by the household from a private landlord where this arrangement is temporary, supported lodgings, and mobile homes such as caravans. From 2002 Q1, some self-contained accommodation in Annex-style units previously recorded under B&B is now more appropriately attributed to Private Sector Accommodation. The Homelessness (Suitability of Accommodation) (England) Order 2003 came into force on 1 April 2004. This prohibits the use of B&B accommodation for families except in an emergency and even then for no longer than six weeks.

3. "Duty owed, but no accommodation has been secured" are households accepted as owed a main duty but able to remain in their existing accommodation for the immediate future. Cases in the final two columns include those households awaiting a decision on their application. Since Q2 2005, this can only apply once an appeal has been accepted as owed a main duty.

4. Includes expectant mothers with no other dependent children.

5. Includes expected children.

6. Housing Association (HA) - this was previously known as "Registered Social Landlord".

7. Includes revised figures from Newham for 2015 Q2, which were previously imputed.

.. Data not collected.

. Not calculated.

P Provisional data

R Revised data

Totals may not equal the sum of components because of rounding.

Totals include estimated data to account for non-response.

Source: Department for Communities and Local Government
DCLG P1E Homelessness returns (quarterly)

11.8 Homeless Households in temporary accomodation at the end of the period - as at 31 March each year, Wales

		2004-05 Annual	2005-06 Annual	2006-07 Annual	2007-08 Annual	2008-09 Annual	2009-10 Annual	2010-11 Annual	2011-12 Annual	2012-13 Annual	2013-14 Annual
Total accommodated at the end of quarter		3350	3440	3150	2880	2815	2490	2640	2770	2525	2295
Total accommodated at the end of quarter	Private sector accommodation (1)	415	505	710	900	1070	1050	1080	1065	1010	910
	Public sector accommodation (2)	460	615	575	445	415	390	435	380	380	440
	Hostels and women's refuges	310	450	405	475	510	400	415	485	505	510
	Bed and breakfast	760	595	380	280	255	235	240	310	300	185
	Other	170	300	230	190	105	*	*	5	10	*
	Homeless at home	1230	980	855	585	465	415	470	525	320	245
	Accommodation type unknown	.	.	.	.	.	.	.	.	.	.

Source: Welsh Government, Homelessness data collection

Contact: stats.housing@wales.gsi.gov.uk

1. Private sector accommodation includes private sector accommodation leased by the local authority, RSLs and directly with a private sector landlord

2. Public sector accommodation includes within local authority stock and RSL stock on assured shorthold tenancies

. The data item is not applicable.

* The data item is disclosive or not sufficiently robust for publication

11.9 Households in temporary accommodation by accommodation type, Scotland

All households		Social sector accommodation[1]		Hostel		Bed & Breakfast		Other[2]		Total	
		Number	%	Number	%	Number	%	Number	%	Number	%
2004	as at 31 March	3,537	55	1,586	25	1,190	18	132	2	6,445	100
	as at 30 June	3,754	56	1,514	23	1,273	19	105	2	6,646	100
	as at 30 September	3,894	56	1,590	23	1,331	19	110	2	6,925	100
	as at 31 December	4,071	59	1,521	22	1,243	18	117	2	6,952	100
2005	as at 31 March	4,136	57	1,490	20	1,516	21	159	2	7,301	100
	as at 30 June	4,324	59	1,340	18	1,413	19	264	4	7,341	100
	as at 30 September	4,606	60	1,320	17	1,424	19	333	4	7,683	100
	as at 31 December	4,525	60	1,295	17	1,323	18	356	5	7,499	100
2006	as at 31 March	4,747	59	1,328	17	1,494	19	416	5	7,985	100
	as at 30 June	4,732	60	1,342	17	1,362	17	452	6	7,888	100
	as at 30 September	4,880	60	1,301	16	1,491	18	439	5	8,111	100
	as at 31 December	4,981	62	1,235	15	1,391	17	482	6	8,089	100
2007	as at 31 March	5,164	60	1,242	14	1,528	18	643	7	8,577	100
	as at 30 June	5,075	60	1,170	14	1,588	19	690	8	8,523	100
	as at 30 September	5,104	61	1,134	13	1,492	18	671	8	8,401	100
	as at 31 December	5,460	63	1,104	13	1,348	16	721	8	8,633	100
2008	as at 31 March[3]	6,134	64	1,079	11	1,609	17	713	7	9,535	100
	as at 30 June	6,079	62	1,064	11	1,791	18	815	8	9,749	100
	as at 30 September	6,131	62	1,058	11	1,780	18	848	9	9,817	100
	as at 31 December	5,931	62	1,019	11	1,662	17	924	10	9,536	100
2009	as at 31 March	6,355	63	994	10	1,748	17	956	10	10,053	100
	as at 30 June	6,294	62	1,186	12	1,654	16	1,072	11	10,206	100
	as at 30 September	6,438	62	1,221	12	1,584	15	1,100	11	10,343	100
	as at 31 December	6,378	62	1,234	12	1,515	15	1,151	11	10,278	100
2010	as at 31 March	6,775	63	1,217	11	1,765	16	972	9	10,729	100
	as at 30 June	6,938	62	1,267	11	1,940	17	958	9	11,103	100
	as at 30 September	7,124	63	1,369	12	1,673	15	1,098	10	11,264	100
	as at 31 December	7,272	66	1,339	12	1,418	13	1,066	10	11,095	100
2011	as at 31 March	7,215	64	1,371	12	1,544	14	1,124	10	11,254	100
	as at 30 June	7,443	67	1,349	12	1,414	13	953	9	11,159	100
	as at 30 September	7,382	67	1,329	12	1,433	13	916	8	11,060	100
	as at 31 December	7,102	66	1,310	12	1,232	12	1,041	10	10,685	100
2012	as at 31 March	7,093	66	1,333	12	1,281	12	1,043	10	10,750	100
	as at 30 June	7,106	68	1,190	11	1,205	12	965	9	10,466	100
	as at 30 September	7,146	68	1,333	13	1,090	10	977	9	10,546	100
	as at 31 December	6,920	67	1,292	13	1,063	10	977	10	10,252	100
2013	as at 31 March	7,061	67	1,290	12	1,170	11	950	9	10,471	100
	as at 30 June	6,965	66	1,451	14	1,104	11	972	9	10,492	100
	as at 30 September	6,877	67	1,503	15	1,001	10	887	9	10,268	100
	as at 31 December	6,687	67	1,496	15	932	9	848	9	9,963	100
2014	as at 31 March	6,405	62	1,813	18	1,125	11	938	9	10,281	100
	as at 30 June	6,310	62	1,830	18	1,073	11	981	10	10,194	100
	as at 30 September	6,509	63	1,714	17	1,070	10	1,035	10	10,328	100
	as at 31 December	6,365	62	1,766	17	1,030	10	1,057	10	10,218	100

Source: Scottish Government

1. Includes Glasgow Housing Association stock from 2003, and all other housing associations from June 2005 onward.

2. The category 'other' includes mainly private landlords. Prior to June 1999 the figures may also include an unknown number of local authority-owned chalets or mobile homes.

3. From 31 March 2008 there is a break in comparability in numbers in temporary accommodation in Glasgow-see below

Background to discontinuity in Glasgow data from 31 March 2008
From 31 March 2008 there is a break in comparability in the information on numbers of homeless applicants in temporary accommodation
in Glasgow. The number of homeless households in temporary accommodation in Glasgow includes asylum applications given indefinite
leave to remain in the United Kingdom and who are in temporary accommodation. From 31 March 2008 there was an significant increase in such households
as a consequence of the 'legacy' case reviews undertaken by the Home Office. This introduces a discontinuity in the statistics for both Glasgow and for
Scotland in the totals for all households and households with children. To bridge the discontinuity Glasgow have provided figures on the numbers
of such households included at the end of each quarter from 31 March 2008.

this page is intentionally blank

Banking, insurance

Chapter 12

Banking, insurance

Industrial analysis of monetary financial institutions deposits and lending
(Tables 12.4 and 12.5)

These data collate information from UK MFIs on deposits from and lending to UK residents other than MFIs and are separated into 18 broad industrial categories, based upon the SIC classification system. Until Q3 2007, the analysis of lending covered loans, advances (including under reverse repos), finance leasing, acceptances and facilities (all in sterling and other currencies) provided by reporting MFIs to their UK resident non-MFI customers, as well as MFI holdings of sterling and euro commercial paper issued by these resident customers. Following a review of statistical data collected, acceptances and holdings of sterling and euro commercial paper are no longer collected at the industry level detail with effect from Q4 2007 data. Total lending therefore reflects loans and advances (including under reverse repos) only, from Q4 2007 data.

Consumer credit (Excluding Student Loans)
(Table 12.12)

Following an ONS review in August 1997, data for 'other specialist lenders' were improved and revised back to January 1995. Total outstanding consumer credit was revised upwards by £2.6bn. Flows were break adjusted. Monthly data are available for lending by retailers from January 1997 but are not available for lending by insurance companies. The missing monthly data have been interpolated from quarterly data.

Within total consumer credit (excluding student loans) outstanding, credit card lending had been underestimated and 'other' consumer credit overestimated prior to January 1999 as a result of a longstanding inconsistency. The credit card element had previously covered sterling credit card lending to the UK household sector by only UK banks and building societies. Credit card lending by other specialist lenders and retailers (where they finance lending themselves) could not be separately identified and so was included within the 'other' consumer credit component.

From January 1999 onwards this inconsistency has been corrected, as credit card lending by other specialist lenders can be separately identified. As a result, data from January 1999 onwards for credit card lending and for 'other' consumer credit are not directly comparable with those for earlier periods. The change affects all three measures of credit card lending (gross, net and amounts outstanding), with an equal offsetting change to 'other' consumer credit. In non-seasonally adjusted terms, gross credit card lending was on average around £800 million per month higher since January 1999, whilst the amount outstanding of credit card debt was boosted by £4.8 billion in January 1999. The changes to net credit card lending are much smaller in absolute terms, with no discernible change to trend.

From November 2006, the Bank of England ceased to update the separate data on consumer credit provided by other specialist lenders, retailers, and insurance companies, previously contained in Table A5.6 of Monetary and Financial Statistics. The final month for which separate data are available on the Bank's Statistical Interactive Database is November 2006. The three categories have been merged into "other consumer credit lenders".

Prior to January 2008, building societies' lending was unsecured lending to individuals including sterling bridging loans (prior to October 1998 this was class 3 lending to individuals). Building societies gross lending through overdrafts is no longer included from January 2008.

http://www.bankofengland.co.uk/boeapps/iadb/newintermed.asp

12.1a Central bank's balance sheet - Bank of England 'Bank return'

£ millions   Not seasonally adjusted

Amounts outstanding of consolidated Issue and Banking department liabilities

	Sterling notes in circulation total	Sterling reserve balance liabilities	Sterling short-term open market operations with Bank of England counterparties	of which: one week sterling	of which: fine-tuning sterling	of which: other maturity within maintenance period sterling	Foreign currency public securities issued total	Sterling cash ratio deposits from monetary financial institutions	Other liabilities total	Total liabilities
	RPWB55A [a] [b]	RPWB56A [a]	RPWB9R6	RPWB9R8	RPWB58A [a]	RPWBV79	RPWB59A [a]	RPWB62A [c] [d]	RPWB63A [c] [d]	RPWB75A [c] [d]
02-Jul-14	61,641	303,764	-	-	-	-	3,501	4,128	31,554	404,588
09-Jul-14	61,644	303,718	-	-	-	-	3,504	4,128	31,970	404,964
16-Jul-14	61,685	303,931	-	-	-	-	3,504	4,128	31,558	404,806
23-Jul-14	61,770	303,509	-	-	-	-	3,526	4,128	32,047	404,980
30-Jul-14	62,163	303,183	-	-	-	-	3,550	4,128	31,946	404,971
06-Aug-14	62,150	304,120	-	-	-	-	3,571	4,128	31,202	405,170
13-Aug-14	62,080	303,843	-	-	-	-	3,602	4,128	31,304	404,956
20-Aug-14	62,109	303,539	-	-	-	-	3,611	4,128	31,557	404,945
27-Aug-14	62,512	302,778	-	-	-	-	3,623	4,128	32,144	405,184
03-Sep-14	62,365	301,950	-	-	-	-	3,651	4,128	33,360	405,455
10-Sep-14	62,341	288,265	-	-	-	-	3,717	4,128	46,502	404,953
17-Sep-14	62,391	289,724	-	-	-	-	3,678	4,128	44,378	404,299
24-Sep-14	62,598	289,788	-	-	-	-	3,672	4,128	44,947	405,132
01-Oct-14	62,704	293,613	-	-	-	-	3,708	n/a	n/a	n/a
08-Oct-14	62,617	299,079	-	-	-	-	3,739	n/a	n/a	n/a
15-Oct-14	62,607	300,727	-	-	-	-	3,792	n/a	n/a	n/a
22-Oct-14	62,562	304,393	-	-	-	-	3,750	n/a	n/a	n/a
29-Oct-14	63,059	302,106	-	-	-	-	3,725	n/a	n/a	n/a
05-Nov-14	63,060	304,766	-	-	-	-	3,761	n/a	n/a	n/a
12-Nov-14	63,108	304,993	-	-	-	-	3,796	n/a	n/a	n/a
19-Nov-14	63,128	304,297	-	-	-	-	3,835	n/a	n/a	n/a
26-Nov-14	63,672	303,509	-	-	-	-	3,805	n/a	n/a	n/a
03-Dec-14	64,298	303,668	-	-	-	-	3,824	n/a	n/a	n/a
10-Dec-14	64,724	300,956	-	-	-	-	3,827	n/a	n/a	n/a
17-Dec-14	65,253	300,352	-	-	-	-	3,839	n/a	n/a	n/a
24-Dec-14	66,876	299,414	-	-	-	-	3,861	n/a	n/a	n/a
31-Dec-14	66,038	298,544	-	-	-	-	3,851	n/a	n/a	n/a
07-Jan-15	64,454	301,237	-	-	-	-	3,980	n/a	n/a	n/a
14-Jan-15	63,275	303,304	-	-	-	-	3,954	n/a	n/a	n/a
21-Jan-15	62,905	304,769	-	-	-	-	3,981	n/a	n/a	n/a
28-Jan-15	62,941	304,983	-	-	-	-	3,961	n/a	n/a	n/a
04-Feb-15	63,282	306,174	-	-	-	-	3,951	n/a	n/a	n/a
11-Feb-15	63,284	306,302	-	-	-	-	3,933	n/a	n/a	n/a
18-Feb-15	63,008	307,311	-	-	-	-	3,891	n/a	n/a	n/a
25-Feb-15	63,309	307,017	-	-	-	-	3,875	n/a	n/a	n/a
04-Mar-15	63,584	306,862	-	-	-	-	3,935	n/a	n/a	n/a
11-Mar-15	63,691	303,217	-	-	-	-	4,004	n/a	n/a	n/a
18-Mar-15	63,715	304,713	-	-	-	-	4,020	n/a	n/a	n/a
25-Mar-15	64,104	305,656	-	-	-	-	4,020	n/a	n/a	n/a
01-Apr-15	65,030	304,265	-	-	-	-	4,068	n/a	n/a	n/a
08-Apr-15	65,256	304,285	-	-	-	-	4,042	n/a	n/a	n/a
15-Apr-15	64,494	309,000	-	-	-	-	4,069	n/a	n/a	n/a
22-Apr-15	64,364	309,803	-	-	-	-	4,009	n/a	n/a	n/a
29-Apr-15	64,809	312,707	-	-	-	-	3,897	n/a	n/a	n/a
06-May-15	65,415	312,342	-	-	-	-	3,948	n/a	n/a	n/a
13-May-15	64,529	313,855	-	-	-	-	3,831	n/a	n/a	n/a
20-May-15	64,675	318,172	-	-	-	-	3,878	n/a	n/a	n/a
27-May-15	65,316	317,155	-	-	-	-	3,926	n/a	n/a	n/a
03-Jun-15	65,197	316,634	-	-	-	-	3,925	n/a	n/a	n/a
10-Jun-15	65,167	314,440	-	-	-	-	3,868	n/a	n/a	n/a
17-Jun-15	65,054	315,355	-	-	-	-	3,827	n/a	n/a	n/a
24-Jun-15	65,184	315,669	-	-	-	-	3,828	n/a	n/a	n/a

© Bank of England.

Notes to table

[a] This series formed part of the Bank Return, which was published between 24 May 2006 and 29 September 2014, and now forms part of the Weekly Report. More information on changes made to the Bank's monetary policy operations and their impact on published data can be found in `The implications of money market reform for data published in Monetary and Financial Statistics' in the June 2006 issue of Bank of England: Monetary and Financial Statistics.

[b] This series increased by around £1.5bn on 25 November 2009 as a result of the additional backing by Bank of England notes for commercial banknote issue in Scotland and Northern Ireland. For details, see the October 2009 article in Monetary and Financial Statistics at; http://www.bankofengland.co.uk/statistics/pages/ms/articles.aspx (25 Nov 2009)

[c] Following Bank of England money market reform on 18 May 2006 the Bank of England 'Bank Return' was changed. This series forms part of the new Bank Return, with data starting on 24 May 2006. More information on changes made to the Bank's monetary policy operations and their impact on published data can be found in `The implications of money market reform for data published in Monetary and Financial Statistics' in the June 2006 issue of Bank of England: Monetary and Financial Statistics.

[d] This series was discontinued in September 2014. For more information, please see www.bankofengland.co.uk/publications/Pages/news/2014/095.aspx.

12.1b Central bank's balance sheet - Bank of England 'Bank return'

£ millions Not seasonally adjusted

Amounts outstanding of consolidated Issue and Banking Department assets

		Weekly amounts outstanding							
		of which:			Sterling long-term operations with Bank of England counterparties	Sterling Ways and Means advances to HM government	Bonds and other securities acquired via market transactions	Other assets	Total assets
	Short-term open market operations with Bank of England counterparties	One week sterling reverse repos with Bank of England counterparties	Sterling fine-tuning reverse repos with Bank of England counterparties	Sterling other maturity within maintenance period reverse repos with Bank of England counterparties					
	RPWB66A	RPWB67A	RPWB68A	RPWBL59	RPWB69A	RPWB72A	RPWB73A	RPWB74A	RPWB75A
	[a]	[a]	[a]		[a]	[b] [c]	[d] [c] [e]	[c] [e]	[c] [e]
02-Jul-14	-	-	-	-	1,908	370	16,345	385,964	404,588
09-Jul-14	-	-	-	-	1,908	370	16,418	386,268	404,964
16-Jul-14	-	-	-	-	2,127	370	16,117	386,191	404,806
23-Jul-14	-	-	-	-	2,127	370	16,314	386,169	404,980
30-Jul-14	-	-	-	-	2,127	370	15,991	386,483	404,971
06-Aug-14	-	-	-	-	2,127	370	16,246	386,427	405,170
13-Aug-14	-	-	-	-	2,127	370	16,508	385,951	404,956
20-Aug-14	-	-	-	-	1,562	370	16,842	386,171	404,945
27-Aug-14	-	-	-	-	1,562	370	17,207	386,045	405,184
03-Sep-14	-	-	-	-	1,562	370	17,532	385,991	405,455
10-Sep-14	-	-	-	-	1,562	370	16,942	386,079	404,953
17-Sep-14	-	-	-	-	1,658	370	16,640	385,631	404,299
24-Sep-14	-	-	-	-	1,658	370	16,628	386,476	405,132
01-Oct-14	-	-	-	-	1,658	370	n/a	n/a	n/a
08-Oct-14	-	-	-	-	1,658	370	n/a	n/a	n/a
15-Oct-14	-	-	-	-	1,746	370	n/a	n/a	n/a
22-Oct-14	-	-	-	-	1,746	370	n/a	n/a	n/a
29-Oct-14	-	-	-	-	1,746	370	n/a	n/a	n/a
05-Nov-14	-	-	-	-	1,746	370	n/a	n/a	n/a
12-Nov-14	-	-	-	-	1,746	370	n/a	n/a	n/a
19-Nov-14	-	-	-	-	1,903	370	n/a	n/a	n/a
26-Nov-14	-	-	-	-	1,903	370	n/a	n/a	n/a
03-Dec-14	-	-	-	-	1,903	370	n/a	n/a	n/a
10-Dec-14	-	-	-	-	1,903	370	n/a	n/a	n/a
17-Dec-14	-	-	-	-	2,298	370	n/a	n/a	n/a
24-Dec-14	-	-	-	-	2,298	370	n/a	n/a	n/a
31-Dec-14	-	-	-	-	2,298	370	n/a	n/a	n/a
07-Jan-15	-	-	-	-	2,298	370	n/a	n/a	n/a
14-Jan-15	-	-	-	-	2,339	370	n/a	n/a	n/a
21-Jan-15	-	-	-	-	2,339	370	n/a	n/a	n/a
28-Jan-15	-	-	-	-	2,339	370	n/a	n/a	n/a
04-Feb-15	-	-	-	-	2,339	370	n/a	n/a	n/a
11-Feb-15	-	-	-	-	2,339	370	n/a	n/a	n/a
18-Feb-15	-	-	-	-	2,994	370	n/a	n/a	n/a
25-Feb-15	-	-	-	-	2,994	370	n/a	n/a	n/a
04-Mar-15	-	-	-	-	2,994	370	n/a	n/a	n/a
11-Mar-15	-	-	-	-	2,994	370	n/a	n/a	n/a
18-Mar-15	-	-	-	-	5,180	370	n/a	n/a	n/a
25-Mar-15	-	-	-	-	5,180	370	n/a	n/a	n/a
01-Apr-15	-	-	-	-	5,180	370	n/a	n/a	n/a
08-Apr-15	-	-	-	-	5,180	370	n/a	n/a	n/a
15-Apr-15	-	-	-	-	8,412	370	n/a	n/a	n/a
22-Apr-15	-	-	-	-	8,412	370	n/a	n/a	n/a
29-Apr-15	-	-	-	-	8,412	370	n/a	n/a	n/a
06-May-15	-	-	-	-	8,412	370	n/a	n/a	n/a
13-May-15	-	-	-	-	8,412	370	n/a	n/a	n/a
20-May-15	-	-	-	-	12,565	370	n/a	n/a	n/a
27-May-15	-	-	-	-	12,565	370	n/a	n/a	n/a
03-Jun-15	-	-	-	-	12,565	370	n/a	n/a	n/a
10-Jun-15	-	-	-	-	12,565	370	n/a	n/a	n/a
17-Jun-15	-	-	-	-	13,372	370	n/a	n/a	n/a
24-Jun-15	-	-	-	-	13,372	370	n/a	n/a	n/a

© Bank of England.

Notes to table

[a] This series formed part of the Bank Return, which was published between 24 May 2006 and 29 September 2014, and now forms part of the Weekly Report. More information on changes made to the Bank's monetary policy operations and their impact on published data can be found in 'The implications of money market reform for data published in Monetary and Financial Statistics' in the June 2006 issue of Bank of England: Monetary and Financial Statistics.

[b] The Debt Management Office announced on 24 January 2008 that HM Treasury had instructed an initial part repayment of the Ways and Means balance, with a payment to the Bank of England of £4.0bn, which is first shown in this table on 30 January 2008. The Ways and Means facility is the central government's overdraft facility at the Bank of England.

[c] Following Bank of England money market reform on 18 May 2006 the Bank of England 'Bank Return' was changed. This series forms part of the new Bank Return, with data starting on 24 May 2006. More information on changes made to the Bank's monetary policy operations and their impact on published data can be found in 'The implications of money market reform for data published in Monetary and Financial Statistics' in the June 2006 issue of Bank of England: Monetary and Financial Statistics.

[d] As part of the Bank of England's reformed framework for implementing monetary policy, the Bank announced in May 2006 its intention to conduct open market operations to make outright purchases of gilts and high-quality foreign currency government bonds. The first of these gilt-purchase open market operations took place in January 2008.

[e] This series was discontinued in September 2014. For more information, please see www.bankofengland.co.uk/publications/Pages/news/2014/095.aspx.

12.1c Central bank's balance sheet - Bank of England 'Bank return'

£ millions   Not seasonally adjusted

Amounts outstanding of Issue Department liabilities

	Weekly amounts outstanding of Bank of England Issue Department		
	Sterling notes in circulation total	Sterling notes in Bank of England Banking Department	Total liabilities
	RPWAEFA	**RPWAEFB**	**RPWBL37**
	[a] [b]	[c] [a] [b]	[a] [b]
09-Oct-13	59,759	-	59,759
16-Oct-13	59,737	-	59,737
23-Oct-13	59,809	-	59,809
30-Oct-13	60,226	-	60,226
06-Nov-13	60,224	-	60,224
13-Nov-13	60,092	-	60,092
20-Nov-13	60,273	-	60,273
27-Nov-13	60,617	-	60,617
04-Dec-13	61,171	-	61,171
11-Dec-13	61,489	-	61,489
18-Dec-13	62,117	-	62,117
25-Dec-13	63,425	-	63,425
01-Jan-14	62,470	-	62,470
08-Jan-14	60,517	-	60,517
15-Jan-14	59,688	-	59,688
22-Jan-14	59,438	-	59,438
29-Jan-14	59,478	-	59,478
05-Feb-14	59,528	-	59,528
12-Feb-14	59,444	-	59,444
19-Feb-14	59,391	-	59,391
26-Feb-14	59,610	-	59,610
05-Mar-14	59,721	-	59,721
12-Mar-14	59,758	-	59,758
19-Mar-14	59,820	-	59,820
26-Mar-14	60,104	-	60,104
02-Apr-14	60,447	-	60,447
09-Apr-14	60,479	-	60,479
16-Apr-14	61,421	-	61,421
23-Apr-14	61,661	-	61,661
30-Apr-14	61,255	-	61,255
07-May-14	61,436	-	61,436
14-May-14	60,778	-	60,778
21-May-14	60,993	-	60,993
28-May-14	61,436	-	61,436
04-Jun-14	61,175	-	61,175
11-Jun-14	61,157	-	61,157
18-Jun-14	61,164	-	61,164
25-Jun-14	61,410	-	61,410
02-Jul-14	61,641	-	61,641
09-Jul-14	61,644	-	61,644
16-Jul-14	61,685	-	61,685
23-Jul-14	61,770	-	61,770
30-Jul-14	62,163	-	62,163
06-Aug-14	62,150	-	62,150
13-Aug-14	62,080	-	62,080
20-Aug-14	62,109	-	62,109
27-Aug-14	62,512	-	62,512
03-Sep-14	62,365	-	62,365
10-Sep-14	62,341	-	62,341
17-Sep-14	62,391	-	62,391
24-Sep-14	62,598	-	62,598

Notes to table   Source: Bank of England

[a] Following Bank of England money market reform on 18 May 2006 the Bank of England 'Bank Return' was changed. This series forms part of the new Bank Return, with data starting on 24 May 2006. More information on changes made to the Bank's monetary policy operations and their impact on published data can be found in `The implications of money market reform for data published in Monetary and Financial Statistics' in the June 2006 issue of Bank of England: Monetary and Financial Statistics.

[b] This series was discontinued in September 2014. For more information, please see www.bankofengland.co.uk/publications/Pages/news/2014/095.aspx.

[c] On 1 August 2006, the Bank ceased using 'Notes in Banking Department' in the Issue Department balance sheet as a balancing item to ensure that the total liabilities of Issue Department were rounded-up to the nearest £10 million. Consequently, the total liabilities of Issue Department are now equal to 'Notes in circulation', which are notes that have been issued and paid for. The entry for `Notes in Banking Department' does not reflect the value of physical notes held on Bank premises.

© **Bank of England.**

12.1d Central bank's balance sheet - Bank of England 'Bank return'

£ millions   Not seasonally adjusted

Amounts outstanding of Issue Department assets

	Weekly amounts outstanding of Bank of England Issue Department							
		of which:		Sterling longer-term reverse repos with Bank of England counterparties	Sterling Ways and Means advances to HM government	Bonds and other securities acquired via market transactions	Other assets total	**Total assets**
	Sterling short-term open market operations with Bank of England counterparties	one week sterling reverse repos with Bank of England counterparties	Sterling fine-tuning reverse repos with Bank of England counterparties					
	RPWBL29	RPWBL32	RPWBL33	RPWBL34	RPWB54A	RPWBL35	RPWBL36	RPWBL37
	[b] [c]	[b] [c]	[b] [c]	[b] [c]	[a] [b] [c]	[d] [b] [c]	[b] [b] [c]	[b] [c]
02-Oct-13	-	-	-	45	370	4,279	55,159	59,853
09-Oct-13	-	-	-	45	370	4,279	55,065	59,759
16-Oct-13	-	-	-	5	370	4,279	55,083	59,737
23-Oct-13	-	-	-	5	370	4,279	55,156	59,809
30-Oct-13	-	-	-	5	370	4,279	55,572	60,226
06-Nov-13	-	-	-	5	370	4,279	55,570	60,224
13-Nov-13	-	-	-	5	370	4,279	55,438	60,092
20-Nov-13	-	-	-	5	370	4,279	55,619	60,273
27-Nov-13	-	-	-	5	370	4,279	55,963	60,617
04-Dec-13	-	-	-	5	370	4,247	56,549	61,171
11-Dec-13	-	-	-	5	370	4,247	56,866	61,489
18-Dec-13	-	-	-	55	370	4,247	57,444	62,117
25-Dec-13	-	-	-	55	370	4,247	58,752	63,425
01-Jan-14	-	-	-	55	370	4,247	57,797	62,470
08-Jan-14	-	-	-	55	370	4,247	55,845	60,517
15-Jan-14	-	-	-	255	370	4,247	54,815	59,688
22-Jan-14	-	-	-	255	370	4,247	54,565	59,438
29-Jan-14	-	-	-	255	370	4,247	54,606	59,478
05-Feb-14	-	-	-	255	370	4,247	54,656	59,528
12-Feb-14	-	-	-	255	370	4,247	54,572	59,444
19-Feb-14	-	-	-	495	370	4,247	54,279	59,391
26-Feb-14	-	-	-	495	370	4,247	54,498	59,610
05-Mar-14	-	-	-	495	370	4,224	54,633	59,721
12-Mar-14	-	-	-	495	370	4,224	54,669	59,758
19-Mar-14	-	-	-	588	370	4,224	54,639	59,820
26-Mar-14	-	-	-	588	370	4,224	54,922	60,104
02-Apr-14	-	-	-	588	370	4,224	55,265	60,447
09-Apr-14	-	-	-	588	370	4,224	55,297	60,479
16-Apr-14	-	-	-	513	370	4,224	56,314	61,421
23-Apr-14	-	-	-	513	370	4,224	56,555	61,661
30-Apr-14	-	-	-	513	370	4,224	56,148	61,255
07-May-14	-	-	-	513	370	4,224	56,330	61,436
14-May-14	-	-	-	513	370	4,224	55,672	60,778
21-May-14	-	-	-	623	370	4,224	55,776	60,993
28-May-14	-	-	-	623	370	4,224	56,219	61,436
04-Jun-14	-	-	-	623	370	4,217	55,965	61,175
11-Jun-14	-	-	-	623	370	4,217	55,947	61,157
18-Jun-14	-	-	-	763	370	4,217	55,815	61,164
25-Jun-14	-	-	-	763	370	4,217	56,060	61,410
02-Jul-14	-	-	-	763	370	4,217	56,291	61,641
09-Jul-14	-	-	-	763	370	4,217	56,294	61,644
16-Jul-14	-	-	-	897	370	4,217	56,201	61,685
23-Jul-14	-	-	-	897	370	4,217	56,287	61,770
30-Jul-14	-	-	-	897	370	4,217	56,679	62,163
06-Aug-14	-	-	-	897	370	4,217	56,666	62,150
13-Aug-14	-	-	-	897	370	4,217	56,596	62,080
20-Aug-14	-	-	-	897	370	4,217	56,626	62,109
27-Aug-14	-	-	-	897	370	4,217	57,028	62,512
03-Sep-14	-	-	-	897	370	4,235	56,864	62,365
10-Sep-14	-	-	-	897	370	4,018	57,056	62,341
17-Sep-14	-	-	-	994	370	4,018	57,009	62,391
24-Sep-14	-	-	-	994	370	4,018	57,216	62,598

Source: Bank of England

Notes:

[a] The Debt Management Office announced on 24 January 2008 that HM Treasury had instructed an initial part repayment of the Ways and Means balance, with a payment to the Bank of England of £4.0bn, which is first shown in this table on 30 January 2008. The Ways and Means facility is the central government's overdraft facility at the Bank of England.

[b] Following Bank of England money market reform on 18 May 2006 the Bank of England 'Bank Return' was changed. This series forms part of the new Bank Return, with data starting on 24 May 2006. More information on changes made to the Bank's monetary policy operations and their impact on published data can be found in `The implications of money market reform for data published in Monetary and Financial Statistics' in the June 2006 issue of Bank of England: Monetary and Financial Statistics.

[c] This series was discontinued in September 2014. For more information, please see www.bankofengland.co.uk/publications/Pages/news/2014/095.aspx.

[d] As part of the Bank of England's reformed framework for implementing monetary policy, the Bank announced in May 2006 its intention to conduct open market operations to make outright purchases of gilts and high-quality foreign currency government bonds. The first of these gilt-purchase open market operations took place in January 2008.

12.1e Central bank's balance sheet - Bank of England 'Bank return'

£ millions   Not seasonally adjusted

Amounts outstanding of Banking Department liabilities

Weekly amounts outstanding of Bank of England Banking Department

	Sterling reserve balance liabilities	Short-term open market operations	of which: one week sterling	of which: fine-tuning sterling	of which: other maturity within maintenance period sterling	Foreign currency public securities issued	Cash ratio deposits from monetary financial institutions	Other liabilities	Total liabilities
	RPWBL38 [b] [a]	RPWB9R5 [a]	RPWB9R7 [a]	RPWBL42 [b] [a]	RPWBV78 [a]	RPWBL43 [b] [a]	RPWBL44 [b] [a]	RPWBL45 [b] [a]	RPWBL56 [b] [a]
02-Oct-13	298,608	-	-	-	-	3,710	4,013	91,251	397,582
09-Oct-13	299,406	-	-	-	-	3,777	4,013	91,357	398,552
16-Oct-13	299,272	-	-	-	-	3,778	4,013	91,499	398,562
23-Oct-13	298,058	-	-	-	-	3,726	4,013	92,500	398,296
30-Oct-13	302,460	-	-	-	-	3,747	4,013	88,418	398,637
06-Nov-13	302,399	-	-	-	-	3,744	4,013	89,530	399,687
13-Nov-13	303,169	-	-	-	-	3,763	4,013	89,268	400,214
20-Nov-13	302,828	-	-	-	-	3,723	4,013	89,054	399,618
27-Nov-13	300,503	-	-	-	-	3,698	4,013	90,562	398,777
04-Dec-13	301,488	-	-	-	-	3,683	4,078	88,101	397,351
11-Dec-13	298,923	-	-	-	-	3,676	4,078	90,089	396,766
18-Dec-13	297,716	-	-	-	-	3,669	4,078	91,344	396,807
25-Dec-13	297,183	-	-	-	-	3,670	4,078	92,125	397,056
01-Jan-14	297,036	-	-	-	-	3,634	4,078	91,840	396,588
08-Jan-14	299,413	-	-	-	-	3,647	4,078	89,662	396,800
15-Jan-14	300,820	-	-	-	-	3,674	4,078	88,177	396,750
22-Jan-14	300,583	-	-	-	-	3,624	4,078	88,710	396,995
29-Jan-14	302,310	-	-	-	-	3,632	4,078	87,387	397,407
05-Feb-14	302,188	-	-	-	-	3,687	4,078	87,988	397,942
12-Feb-14	303,994	-	-	-	-	3,624	4,078	85,593	397,290
19-Feb-14	305,951	-	-	-	-	3,597	4,078	84,351	397,977
26-Feb-14	305,743	-	-	-	-	3,612	4,078	85,071	398,505
05-Mar-14	306,104	-	-	-	-	3,592	4,078	84,846	398,620
12-Mar-14	295,540	-	-	-	-	3,620	4,073	96,991	400,223
19-Mar-14	299,620	-	-	-	-	3,616	4,073	91,814	399,122
26-Mar-14	300,100	-	-	-	-	3,624	4,073	90,807	398,604
02-Apr-14	299,696	-	-	-	-	3,608	4,073	91,467	398,844
09-Apr-14	300,649	-	-	-	-	3,587	4,073	90,397	398,706
16-Apr-14	299,695	-	-	-	-	3,580	4,078	91,262	398,616
23-Apr-14	303,399	-	-	-	-	3,581	4,078	87,170	398,228
30-Apr-14	303,808	-	-	-	-	3,560	4,078	87,061	398,506
07-May-14	304,262	-	-	-	-	3,544	4,078	86,419	398,303
14-May-14	304,876	-	-	-	-	3,589	4,078	85,136	397,680
21-May-14	304,879	-	-	-	-	3,567	4,078	85,433	397,958
28-May-14	305,548	-	-	-	-	3,605	4,078	84,977	398,208
04-Jun-14	305,980	-	-	-	-	3,590	4,128	84,271	397,969
11-Jun-14	303,405	-	-	-	-	3,581	4,128	87,048	398,162
18-Jun-14	303,435	-	-	-	-	3,547	4,128	87,820	398,930
25-Jun-14	303,599	-	-	-	-	3,540	4,128	88,180	399,447
02-Jul-14	303,764	-	-	-	-	3,501	4,128	87,845	399,238
09-Jul-14	303,718	-	-	-	-	3,504	4,128	88,264	399,614
16-Jul-14	303,931	-	-	-	-	3,504	4,128	87,759	399,322
23-Jul-14	303,509	-	-	-	-	3,526	4,128	88,333	399,496
30-Jul-14	303,183	-	-	-	-	3,550	4,128	88,626	399,487
06-Aug-14	304,120	-	-	-	-	3,571	4,128	87,868	399,687
13-Aug-14	303,843	-	-	-	-	3,602	4,128	87,900	399,473
20-Aug-14	303,539	-	-	-	-	3,611	4,128	88,183	399,461
27-Aug-14	302,778	-	-	-	-	3,623	4,128	89,172	399,700
03-Sep-14	301,950	-	-	-	-	3,651	4,128	90,224	399,953
10-Sep-14	288,265	-	-	-	-	3,717	4,128	103,558	399,668
17-Sep-14	289,724	-	-	-	-	3,678	4,128	101,387	398,916
24-Sep-14	289,788	-	-	-	-	3,672	4,128	102,163	399,750

Notes to table

Source: Bank of England

Notes:
[a] This series was discontinued in September 2014. For more information, please see www.bankofengland.co.uk/publications/Pages/news/2014/095.aspx.

[b] Following Bank of England money market reform on 18 May 2006 the Bank of England 'Bank Return' was changed. This series forms part of the new Bank Return, with data starting on 24 May 2006. More information on changes made to the Bank's monetary policy operations and their impact on published data can be found in 'The implications of money market reform for data published in Monetary and Financial Statistics' in the June 2006 issue of Bank of England: Monetary and Financial Statistics.

12.1f Central bank's balance sheet - Bank of England 'Bank return'

£ millions   Not seasonally adjusted

Amounts outstanding of Banking Department assets

	Weekly amounts outstanding of Bank of England Banking Department								
			of which:						
	Sterling Short-term open market operations with Bank of England counterparties	one week sterling reverse repos with Bank of England counterparties	Sterling fine-tuning reverse repos with Bank of England counterparties	Other maturity reverse repos with Bank of England counterparties	Longer-term reverse repos with Bank of England counterparties	Bonds and other securities acquired via market transactions	Sterling notes issued by Bank of England Issue Department	Other assets total	Total assets
	RPWBL48	RPWBL49	RPWBL52	RPWBL98	RPWB3J2	RPWBL53	RPWBL54	RPWBL55	RPWBL56
	[b] [a]	[b] [a]	[b] [a]	[a]	[a]	[b] [a]	[c] [b] [a]	[b] [a]	[b] [a]
02-Oct-13	-	-	-	-	170	12,430	-	384,982	397,582
09-Oct-13	-	-	-	-	170	12,717	-	385,665	398,552
16-Oct-13	-	-	-	-	150	12,785	-	385,627	398,562
23-Oct-13	-	-	-	-	150	12,993	-	385,153	398,296
30-Oct-13	-	-	-	-	150	13,183	-	385,304	398,637
06-Nov-13	-	-	-	-	150	12,919	-	386,617	399,687
13-Nov-13	-	-	-	-	150	13,015	-	387,049	400,214
20-Nov-13	-	-	-	-	100	12,835	-	386,683	399,618
27-Nov-13	-	-	-	-	100	12,688	-	385,989	398,777
04-Dec-13	-	-	-	-	100	12,163	-	385,088	397,351
11-Dec-13	-	-	-	-	100	12,141	-	384,525	396,766
18-Dec-13	-	-	-	-	70	12,245	-	384,492	396,807
25-Dec-13	-	-	-	-	70	12,191	-	384,796	397,056
01-Jan-14	-	-	-	-	70	12,153	-	384,366	396,588
08-Jan-14	-	-	-	-	70	11,894	-	384,836	396,800
15-Jan-14	-	-	-	-	70	11,992	-	384,687	396,750
22-Jan-14	-	-	-	-	70	11,909	-	385,015	396,995
29-Jan-14	-	-	-	-	70	11,918	-	385,420	397,407
05-Feb-14	-	-	-	-	70	12,165	-	385,706	397,942
12-Feb-14	-	-	-	-	70	11,915	-	385,305	397,290
19-Feb-14	-	-	-	-	670	12,065	-	385,242	397,977
26-Feb-14	-	-	-	-	670	12,342	-	385,493	398,505
05-Mar-14	-	-	-	-	670	11,647	-	386,303	398,620
12-Mar-14	-	-	-	-	670	12,963	-	386,590	400,223
19-Mar-14	-	-	-	-	725	13,018	-	385,379	399,122
26-Mar-14	-	-	-	-	725	13,013	-	384,866	398,604
02-Apr-14	-	-	-	-	725	12,937	-	385,182	398,844
09-Apr-14	-	-	-	-	725	12,945	-	385,036	398,706
16-Apr-14	-	-	-	-	800	12,966	-	384,850	398,616
23-Apr-14	-	-	-	-	800	12,965	-	384,463	398,228
30-Apr-14	-	-	-	-	800	12,680	-	385,026	398,506
07-May-14	-	-	-	-	800	12,671	-	384,832	398,303
14-May-14	-	-	-	-	800	12,703	-	384,176	397,680
21-May-14	-	-	-	-	850	12,634	-	384,473	397,958
28-May-14	-	-	-	-	850	12,710	-	384,649	398,208
04-Jun-14	-	-	-	-	850	12,343	-	384,776	397,969
11-Jun-14	-	-	-	-	850	12,552	-	384,760	398,162
18-Jun-14	-	-	-	-	1,145	12,398	-	385,387	398,930
25-Jun-14	-	-	-	-	1,145	12,457	-	385,845	399,447
02-Jul-14	-	-	-	-	1,145	12,129	-	385,964	399,238
09-Jul-14	-	-	-	-	1,145	12,201	-	386,268	399,614
16-Jul-14	-	-	-	-	1,230	11,901	-	386,191	399,322
23-Jul-14	-	-	-	-	1,230	12,097	-	386,169	399,496
30-Jul-14	-	-	-	-	1,230	11,774	-	386,483	399,487
06-Aug-14	-	-	-	-	1,230	12,030	-	386,427	399,687
13-Aug-14	-	-	-	-	1,230	12,292	-	385,951	399,473
20-Aug-14	-	-	-	-	665	12,625	-	386,171	399,461
27-Aug-14	-	-	-	-	665	12,991	-	386,045	399,700
03-Sep-14	-	-	-	-	665	13,297	-	385,991	399,953
10-Sep-14	-	-	-	-	665	12,924	-	386,079	399,668
17-Sep-14	-	-	-	-	664	12,621	-	385,631	398,916
24-Sep-14	-	-	-	-	664	12,610	-	386,476	399,750

Source: Bank of England

Notes to table

[a] This series was discontinued in September 2014. For more information, please see www.bankofengland.co.uk/publications/Pages/news/2014/095.aspx.

[b] Following Bank of England money market reform on 18 May 2006 the Bank of England 'Bank Return' was changed. This series forms part of the new Bank Return, with data starting on 24 May 2006. More information on changes made to the Bank's monetary policy operations and their impact on published data can be found in `The implications of money market reform for data published in Monetary and Financial Statistics' in the June 2006 issue of Bank of England: Monetary and Financial Statistics.

[c] On 1 August 2006, the Bank ceased using 'Notes in Banking Department' in the Issue Department balance sheet as a balancing item to ensure that the total liabilities of Issue Department were rounded-up to the nearest £10 million. Consequently, the total liabilities of Issue Department are now equal to 'Notes in circulation', which are notes that have been issued and paid for. The entry for `Notes in Banking Department' does not reflect the value of physical notes held on Bank premises.

12.1g Bank of England consolidated balance sheet, Quarterly

£ millions   Not seasonally adjusted

Amounts outstanding

| | Reserves balances | Short-term open market operations | | | | Notes in circulation | Cash ratio deposits | Other sterling liabilities | Capital and reserves (equity) | Foreign currency public securities issued | Other foreign currency liabilities | Total liabilities |
| | | fine-tuning | one-week | other maturity within-maintenance period | Total | | | | | | | |
RPQ	B56A (a) #	B58A (a) #	B9R8 (a) #	BV79 (a) #	B9R6 (a) #	B55A (a) #	B62A (a) #	Z6MO (a) #	Z6MS (a) #	B59A (a) #	Z6MT (a) #	B75A (a) #
2013 Q2	294,746	-	-	-	-	60,335	4,013	26,276	3,214	3,717	9,704	402,005
Q3	297,036	-	-	-	-	62,470	4,078	22,100	3,129	3,634	8,734	401,181
Q4	297,848	-	-	-	-	60,659	4,078	24,141	3,034	3,601	10,203	403,564
2014 Q1	302,868	-	-	-	-	61,761	4,128	18,912	3,032	3,517	9,835	404,053
Q2	291,312	-	-	-	-	62,713	4,128	30,605	3,127	3,703	9,477	405,065
Q3	298,544	-	-	-	-	66,038	4,098	21,385	3,328	3,851	9,338	406,582
Q4	304,207	-	-	-	-	64,639	4,098	21,674	3,457	4,060	8,640	410,775
2015 Q1	313,598	-	-	-	-	65,561	4,075	18,755	3,327	3,829	7,728	416,873

Source: Bank of Engand

Notes to table

(a) This series is a component of the Bank of England consolidated balance sheet which is published as a complement to the Bank of England Weekly Report published in Table B1.1.2.

Explanatory notes to this table are available on the Bank of England website: http://www.bankofengland.co.uk/statistics/Pages/iadb/notesiadb/weeklyreport.aspx

12.1h Bank of England consolidated balance sheet, Quarterly

£ millions   Not seasonally adjusted

Amounts outstanding

	Short-term open market operations				Long-term operations			Sterling denominated bond holdings	Loan to Asset Purchase Facility	Ways and means advance to the National Loans Fund	Other sterling assets	Foreign currency reserve assets	Other foreign currency assets	Total assets
	fine-tuning	one-week	other maturity within-maintenance period	Total	indexed long-term repo	contingent term repo facility	Total							
RPQ	B68A (b)	B67A (b)	BL59 (b)	B66A (b)	Z4TJ (b)	Z4TK (b)	B69A (b)	Z4TL (b)	Z4TM (b)	B72A (b)	Z6MW (b)	Z4TN (b)	Z6MX (b)	B75A (b)
	#	#	#	#	#	#	#	#	#	#	#	#	#	#
2013 Q2	-	-	-	-	-	-	-							
Q3	-	-	-	-	215	-	215	10,055	375,000	370	734	3,718	11,913	402,005
Q4	-	-	-	-	125	-	125	9,978	375,000	370	708	3,648	11,352	401,181
2014 Q1	-	-	-	-	1,313	-	1,313	10,174	375,000	370	807	3,588	12,312	403,564
Q2	-	-	-	-	1,908	-	1,908	10,264	375,000	370	612	3,508	12,391	404,053
Q3	-	-	-	-	1,658	-	1,658	10,245	375,000	370	805	3,686	13,301	405,065
Q4	-	-	-	-	2,298	-	2,298	10,709	375,000	370	801	3,843	13,561	406,582
2015 Q1	-	-	-	-	5,180	-	5,180	10,842	375,000	370	841	4,047	14,495	410,775
Q2	-	-	-	-	13,372	-	13,372	10,657	375,000	370	725	3,826	12,924	416,873

Notes to table

(b)This series is a component of the Bank of England consolidated balance sheet which is published as a complement to the Bank of England Weekly Report

Explanatory notes to this table can be found on the Bank of england webiste: http://www.bankofengland.co.uk/statistics/Pages/iadb/notesiadb/weeklyreport.aspx

12.2a Annual clearing volumes and values

Clearing volumes thousands

	Annual volumes		
	2014	**2015**	**Change 2015 on 2014 %**
Bacs			
Standing orders	18,678	19,471	4%
Direct Credits	2,150,557	2,152,226	-
Direct Debits	3,671,997	3,908,346	6%
Total BACS	**5,841,232**	**6,080,043**	**4%**
CHAPS Clearing Company			
Retail and Commercial (MT 103)	28,689	29,336	2%
Wholesale Financial (MT202)	7,833	8,212	5%
Total CHAPS	**36,521**	**37,548**	**3%**
Faster Payments			
Standing Order Payments	329,858	343,642	4%
Single Immediate Payments	609,879	730,675	20%
Forward Dated Payments	159,153	170,339	7%
Return Payments	2,040	2,378	17%
Total Faster Payments	**1,100,930**	**1,247,035**	**13%**
Cheque and Credit Clearing Company			
Cheques	464,191	404,134	-13%
Credits	34,962	28,049	-20%
Euro debits	108	89	-18%
Total Cheque & Credit	**499,262**	**432,273**	**-13%**
Currency Clearing: US Dollar	21.6	17.1	-21%
Total all Clearing Companies	**7,477,967**	**7,796,915**	**4%**

Clearing values £ millions

	Annual values		
	2014	**2015**	**Change 2015 on 2014 %**
Bacs			
Standing orders and Bacs Direct Credits	3,253,279	3,374,815	4%
Direct Debits	1,167,266	1,215,396	4%
Total BACS	4,420,546	**4,590,211**	**4%**
CHAPS Clearing Company			
Retail and Commercial (MT 103)	14,886,852	16,730,137	12%
Wholesale Financial (MT202)	53,072,638	51,681,041	-3%
Total CHAPS	67,959,491	**68,411,178**	**1%**
Faster Payments			
Standing Order Payments	97,121	107,202	10%
Single Immediate Payments	517,641	619,301	20%
Forward Dated Payments	288,034	313,099	9%
Return Payments	999	1,114	12%
Total Faster Payments	903,794	**1,040,717**	**15%**
Cheque and Credit Clearing Company			
Cheques	498,729	454,838	-9%
Credits	19,659	17,216	-12%
Euro debits	1,289	1,208	-6%
Total	519,677	473,261	-9%
Currency Clearing: US Dollar	249	**273**	**10%**
Total all Clearing Companies	73,803,757	**74,515,641**	**1%**

Source: UK Payments Administration Ltd

(a) Totals, averages and percentages are calculated using unrounded data. The values of all euro and US Dollar clearings are shown as £ sterling equivalent.

(b) 253 clearing days were used to calculate the average daily statistics for both 2015 and 2014. In terms of Faster Payments, 253 clearing days were used for Standing Orders and 365 days for other payment types.

(c) A description of the United Kingdom payment clearings together with more comprehensive statistics over a longer period is available from the Information Management team. These data are published annually in UK Payment Statistics

12.2b Bacs volumes and values

Annual volumes thousands

	Standing orders		Bacs Direct Credits		Bacs Euro Credits		Direct Debits		Total volumes	
	Number	% Change	Number	% Change	Number	% Change	Number	% Change	Number	% Change
2003	288,443	5.6	1,341,945	14.4	54	45.0	2,429,915	6.2	4,060,357	8.7
2004	301,879	4.7	1,710,673	27.5	84	55.5	2,589,934	6.6	4,602,570	13.4
2005	318,022	5.3	2,093,859	22.4	12	48.6	2,722,245	5.1	5,134,250	11.6
2006	332,245	4.5	2,171,586	3.7	157	25.9	2,857,761	5.0	5,361,749	4.4
2007	347,347	4.5	2,233,106	2.8	181	15.8	2,296,474	3.7	5,544,109	3.4
2008	323,843	-6.8	2,254,875	1.0	176	-3.2	3,076,857	3.8	5,655,751	2.0
2009	199,759	-38.3	2,289,813	1.5	193	10.0	3,149,153	2.3	5,638,919	-0.3
2010	150,307	-24.8	2,292,942	0.1	143	26.0	3,229,338	2.5	5,672,730	0.6
2011	123,652	-17.7	2,270,987	-1.0			3,322,360	2.9	5,716,999	0.8
2012	17,074	-86.2	2,182,667	-3.9			3,416,651	2.8	5,616,392	-1.8
2013	18,405	8%	2,151,718	-1.0			3,524,905	3.0	5,695,028	1.0
2014	18,678	1%	2,150,557	-			3,671,997	4.0	5,841,232	3.0
2015	19,471	4%	2,152,226	-			3,908,346	6.0	6,080,043	4.0

Average values £ millions

	Bacs Direct Credits [a]		Bacs Euro Credits		Direct Debits		Total volumes	
	Number	% Change	Number	% Change	Number	% Change	Number	% Change
2003	1,910,251	8.3	1,924	53.9	662,192	7.3	2,574,367	8.1
2004	2,131,031	11.6	2,040	6.0	750,381	13.3	2,883,452	12.0
2005	2,350,644	10.3	2,524	23.7	797,039	6.2	3,150,207	9.3
2006	2,581,682	9.8	2,819	11.7	844,832	6.0	3,429,333	8.9
2007	2,808,349	8.8	3,965	40.6	883,592	4.6	3,695,906	7.8
2008	3,006,159	7.0	4,806	21.2	935,356	5.9	3,946,321	6.8
2009	2,969,711	-1.2	5,255	9.3	885,708	-5.3	3,860,674	-2.2
2010	3,111,218	4.8	3,033	-42.3	948,137	7.0	4,062,388	5.2
2011	3,318,536	6.7			1,044,677	10.2	4,363,214	7.4
2012	3,036,714	-8.5			1,075,507	3.0	4,112,222	-5.8
2013	3,103,579	2.0			1,115,065	4.0	4,218,644	3.0
2014	3,253,279	5.0			1,167,266	5.0	4,420,546	5.0
2015	3,374,815	4.0			1,215,396	4.0	4,590,211	4.0

Source: UK Payments Administration Ltd

(a) Values represent standing orders and Bacs Direct Credits combined

Bacs has 16 members and is responsible for the processing of bulk payments through its two principle payment schemes; Direct Debit and Bacs Direct Credit.

The Euro Debit Credit Service ceased operation on 29 October 2010

12.2c CHAPS volumes and values

Annual volumes thousands

	CHAPS Sterling [a]		CHAPS Euro						Total volumes [a]	
			Domestic (a)		Target					
					Transmitted to		Received from			
	Number	% Change	Number	% Change	Number	% Change	Number	% Change	Number	% Change
2003	27,215	6.5	1,399	13.1	2,904	19.2	1,685	4.7	33,202	7.6
2004	28,322	4.1	1,378	-1.5	3,314	14.1	1,849	9.7	34,862	5.0
2005	29,686	4.8	1,484	7.7	3,597	8.6	1,988	7.5	36,756	5.4
2006	33,030	11.3	1,461	-1.6	4,115	14.4	2,080	4.6	40,686	10.7
2007	35,588	7.7	1,455	-0.3	4,263	3.6	2,229	7.1	43,535	7.0
2008	34,606	-2.8	220	-84.9	379	-91.1	593	-73.4	35,797	-17.8
2009	31,926	-7.7							31,926	-10.8
2010	32,169	0.8							32,169	0.8
2011	34,024	5.8							34,024	5.8
2012	33,936	-0.3							33,936	-0.3
2013	34,976	3.0							34,976	3.0
2014	36,521	4.0							36,521	4.0
2015	37,548	3.0							36,521	3.0

Annual Values £ millions

	CHAPS Sterling [a]		CHAPS Euro (sterling equivalent)						Total values [a]	
			Domestic (a)		Target					
					Transmitted to		Received from			
	Number	% Change	Number	% Change	Number	% Change	Number	% Change	Number	% Change
2003	51,613,456	-0.5	5,114,198	22.7	15,924,879	21.5	15,923,974	21.5	88,576,506	7.7
2004	52,347,525	1.4	4,509,924	-11.8	17,238,602	8.2	17,238,737	8.3	91,334,788	3.1
2005	52,671,592	0.6	6,069,146	34.6	19,180,194	11.3	19,179,273	11.3	97,100,206	6.3
2006	59,437,370	12.8	7,365,558	21.4	21,415,027	11.7	21,419,195	11.7	109,637,149	12.9
2007	69,352,322	16.7	6,781,942	-7.9	25,266,729	18.0	25,268,856	18.0	126,669,848	15.5
2008	73,625,908	6.2	574,610	-91.5	4,413,570	-82.5	4,403,022	-82.6	83,017,110	-34.5
2009	64,616,956	-12.2							64,616,956	-22.2
2010	61,587,609	-4.7							61,587,609	-4.7
2011	63,876,772	3.7							63,876,772	3.7
2012	71,716,857	12.3							71,716,857	12.3
2013	70,138,927	-2.0							70,138,927	-2.0
2014	67,959,491	-3.0							67,959,491	-3.0
2015	68,411,178	1.0							68,411,178	1.0

Source: UK Payments Administration Ltd

(a) NewCHAPS was launched on 27 August 2001 and since this date CHAPS Sterling and CHAPS Euro Domestic figures include all CHAPS traffic

The CHAPS Scheme enables same-day bank-to-bank payments in sterling and has 23 direct participants

12.2d Faster Payments volumes and values

Annual volumes thousands

	Standing Order Payments		Single Immediate Payments		Forward Dated Payments		Return Payments		Total volumes[a]	
	Number	% Change	Number	% Change	Number	% Change	Number	% Change	Number	% Change
2003										
2004										
2005										
2006										
2007										
2008	37,574	*	36,325	*	8,708	*	182	*	82,789	*
2009	156,865	*	109,337	*	27,912	*	673	*	294,787	*
2010	203,055	29.4	181,195	65.7	40,632	45.6	880	30.6	425,761	44.4
2011	235,654	16.1	237,718	31.2	50,861	25.2	1,092	24.2	525,325	23.4
2012	299,630	27.1	379,844	59.8	129,829	155.3	1,788	63.6	811,090	54.4
2013	312,995	4.0	502,025	32.0	150,381	16.0	2,228	25.0	967,629	19.0
2014	329,858	5.0	609,879	21.0	159,153	6.0	2,040	- 8.0	1,100,930	14.0
2015	343,642	4.0	730,675	20.0	170,339	7.0	2,378	17.0	1,247,035	13.0

Annual values £ millions

	Standing Order Payments		Single Immediate Payments		Forward Dated Payments		Return Payments		Total values[a]	
	Value	% Change	Value	% Change	Value	% Change	Value	% Change	Value	% Change
2003										
2004										
2005										
2006										
2007										
2008	3,341	*	22,015	*	7,473	*	42	*	32,871	*
2009	26,527	*	59,015	*	20,544	*	136	*	106,223	*
2010	38,963	46.9	92,847	57.3	32,193	56.7	208	52.9	164,211	54.6
2011	50,206	28.9	135,101	45.5	49,429	53.5	308	47.9	235,044	43.1
2012	80,009	59.4	328,685	143.3	208,252	321.3	965	213.0	617,911	162.9
2013	88,885	11.0	423,571	29.0	257,794	24.0	1,111	15.0	771,361	25.0
2014	97,121	9.0	517,641	22.0	288,034	12.0	999	-10.0	903,794	17.0
2015	107,202	10.0	619,301	20.0	313,099	9.0	1,114	12.0	1,040,717	15.0

Source: UK Payments Administration Ltd

[a] The UK Faster Payments Service was launched on 27 May 2008.

The Faster Payments Service enables internet, mobile and telephone banking payments, as well as standing orders, to be processed almost instantaneously, 24 hours a day, 7 days a week. 10 banks and building societies operated in the service in 2015.

12.2e Inter-bank cheque volumes and values

Annual volumes thousands

	Exchanged in Great Britain					Total volumes	
	Cheques			Euro debits			
	Number	% Change		Number	% Change	Number	% Change
2003	1,519,117	-6.3		759	3.6	1,519,876	-6.3
2004	1,423,742	-6.3		724	-4.6	1,424,465	-6.3
2005	1,325,762	-6.9		637	-12.0	1,326,399	-6.9
2006	1,237,401	-6.7		586	-7.9	1,237,987	-6.7
2007	1,124,869	-9.1		531	-9.5	1,125,400	-9.1
2008	1,007,379	-10.4		445	-16.1	1,007,824	-10.4
2009	875,533	-13.1		351	-21.2	875,884	-13.1
2010	775,643	-11.4		279	-20.5	775,922	-11.4
2011	682,082	-12.1		223	-20.1	682,305	-12.1
2012	597,076	-12.5		165	-25.7	597,241	-12.5
2013	525,295	-12.0		131	-21.0	525,426	-12.0
2014	464,191	-12.0		108	-17.0	464,299	-12.0
2015	404,134	-13.0		89	-18.0	404,223	-13.0

Annual values £ millions

	Exchanged in Great Britain					Total values	
	Cheques			Euro debits			
	Value	% Change		Value	% Change	Value	% Change
2003	1,240,685	-3.2		3,898	13.8	1,244,583	-3.1
2004	1,210,057	-2.5		3,456	-11.4	1,213,513	-2.5
2005	1,152,256	-4.8		3,206	-7.2	1,155,462	-4.8
2006	1,171,062	1.6		3,111	-3.0	1,174,174	1.6
2007	1,156,684	-1.2		2,970	-4.6	1,159,653	-1.2
2008	1,075,694	-7.0		2,980	0.4	1,078,674	-7.0
2009	870,591	-19.1		2,993	0.4	873,584	-19.0
2010	761,081	-12.6		1,767	-41.0	762,848	-12.7
2011	675,706	-11.2		1,559	-11.8	677,266	-11.2
2012	601,256	-11.0		1,188	-23.9	602,444	-11.0
2013	535,513	-11.0		1,166	-2.0	536,679	-11.0
2014	498,729	- 7.0		1,289	11.0	500,018	- 7.0
2015	454,838	- 9.0		1,208	-6.0	456,046	- 8.8

Source: UK Payments Administration Ltd

The Cheque & Credit Clearing Company was established in 1985 and took over responsibility for managing the operation of the two bulk paper clearings for England and Wales.

From December 1996 the Cheque and Credit Clearing Company also took over responsibility for managing the operation of the inter-bank clearings in Scotland. The clearing of cheque and credit payments in Northern Ireland is managed by the Belfast Bankers' Clearing Company Limited (BBCCL)

12.2f Inter-bank credit volumes and values

Annual volumes thousands

	Exchanged in Great Britain		Total volumes	
	Number	% Change	Number	% Change
2003	140,792	-6.4	140,792	-6.4
2004	132,899	-5.6	132,899	-5.6
2005	123,280	-7.2	123,280	-7.2
2006	108,309	-12.1	108,309	-12.1
2007	96,290	-11.1	96,290	-11.1
2008	86,442	-10.2	86,442	-10.2
2009	73,686	-14.8	73,686	-14.8
2010	61,662	-16.3	61,662	-16.3
2011	53,934	-12.5	53,934	-12.5
2012	46,927	-12.9	46,927	-12.9
2013	40,569	-14.0	40,569	-14.0
2014	34,962	-14.0	34,962	-14.0
2015	28,049	-20.0	28,049	20.0

Annual values £ millions

	Exchanged in Great Britain		Total values	
	Value	% Change	Value	% Change
2003	74,366	-7.6	74,366	-7.6
2004	68,261	-8.2	68,261	-8.2
2005	61,844	-9.4	61,844	-9.4
2006	59,309	-4.1	59,309	-4.1
2007	57,347	-3.3	57,347	-3.3
2008	51,641	-9.9	51,641	-9.9
2009	41,624	-19.4	41,624	-19.4
2010	32,312	-22.4	32,312	-22.4
2011	27,990	-13.4	27,990	-13.4
2012	23,802	-15.0	23,802	-15.0
2013	21,109	-11.0	21,109	-11.0
2014	19,659	-7.0	19,659	- 7.0
2015	17,216	-12.0	17,216	- 12.0

Source: UK Payments Administration Ltd

The Cheque & Credit Clearing Company was established in 1985 and took over responsibility for managing the operation of the two bulk paper clearings for England and Wales.

From December 1996 the Cheque and Credit Clearing Company also took over responsibility for managing the operation of the inter-bank clearings in Scotland. The clearing of cheque and credit payments in Northern Ireland is managed by the Belfast Bankers' Clearing Company Limited (BBCCL)

12.3a Monetary financial institutions' (excluding central bank) balance sheet

£ millions   Not seasonally adjusted

Amounts outstanding of sterling liabilities

	Notes outstanding and cash loaded cards	Sight deposits UK MFIs	of which intragroup banks	UK public sector	Other UK residents	Non-residents	Time deposits UK MFIs	of which intragroup banks	UK public sector	Other UK residents	of which SAYE	of which cash ISAs	Non-residents
RPM	**B3LM**	**B3GL**	**B8ZC**	**B3MM**	**B3NM**	**B3OM**	**B3HL**	**B8ZE**	**B3PM**	**B3QM**	**B3RM**	**B3SM**	**B3TM**
2014 May	6,713	106,531	90,274	15,336	1,099,700	141,090	138,836	131,530	19,914	761,630	1,096	230,987	194,642
Jun	6,720	105,876	89,695	14,575	1,117,183	144,330	139,657	132,963	20,289	755,540	1,211	230,752	190,299
Jul	6,732	94,126	79,727	15,164	1,105,619	145,022	136,755	129,078	21,055	759,777	1,225	238,593	186,191
Aug	6,801	95,817	81,188	14,227	1,112,259	140,505	135,735	128,223	20,807	759,558	1,236	241,719	189,966
Sep	6,764	98,245	83,644	13,938	1,126,047	146,254	137,628	130,140	20,154	755,280	1,108	243,485	185,874
Oct	6,803	96,691	82,111	14,560	1,123,571	144,177	138,696	131,345	20,013	742,033	1,154	244,899	183,831
Nov	6,836	100,007	85,192	13,940	1,135,457	145,187	146,538	140,001	19,311	735,392	1,202	245,850	182,894
Dec	7,095	107,959	93,751	14,227	1,147,349	150,731	141,205	135,640	17,791	737,138	1,289	246,432	191,528
2015 Jan	6,824	119,954	102,936	15,486	1,145,124	146,519	140,913	135,129	17,783	710,232	1,209	246,481	187,361
Feb	6,769	116,303	100,489	14,678	1,144,217	142,548	133,404	127,645	17,958	705,186	1,100	246,540	182,676
Mar	6,820	125,471	108,555	13,851	1,174,246	158,621	137,003	131,363	17,009	704,161	1,112	249,513	183,740
Apr	6,811	126,482	110,219	15,305	1,163,124	143,921	131,869	126,537	18,372	709,044	1,094	256,526	195,141
May	6,857	122,076	106,802	14,627	1,168,681	144,400	133,173	127,343	18,935	712,114	1,094	258,427	189,658
Jun	6,897	124,515	110,150	14,111	1,187,258 (a)	149,164	131,622	126,169	18,631	700,730 (b)	1,193	259,279	191,776
Jul	6,782	122,708	105,865	15,519	1,189,927	146,148	133,656	128,130	19,643	700,924	1,142	259,784	190,227
Aug	6,920	114,575	96,536	15,292	1,180,716	150,071	137,550	132,179	19,624	694,980	1,187	260,670	191,724
Sep	7,003	114,839	97,975	15,160	1,198,656	158,909	131,347	126,145	19,546	683,894	1,169	261,334	202,359
Oct	7,018	118,714	102,816	15,570	1,204,978	143,841	141,442	135,968	19,566	686,144	1,192	261,875	193,505
Nov	7,108	122,413	105,979	15,351	1,215,760	150,548	143,778	137,477	19,339	682,340	1,166	262,321	193,282
Dec	7,232	120,345	106,354	15,880	1,219,920	158,148	146,287	140,366	18,741	682,826	1,120	262,591	208,259
2016 Jan	6,997	116,615	101,441	16,617	1,218,570	158,484	138,517	132,667	18,463	674,235	1,119	262,923	200,850
Feb	6,966	116,650	100,824	16,012	1,237,202	158,086	138,712	132,503	17,581	670,527	972	263,504	176,619
Mar	7,065	106,174	89,056	15,189	1,264,267	166,282	142,403	136,776	15,435	654,894 (c)	975	265,493	178,697
Apr	7,065	101,302	85,421	16,396	1,248,936	161,536	143,052	135,024	16,577	662,510	999	270,865	185,569

Source: Bank of England

319

12.3a Monetary financial institutions' (excluding central bank) balance sheet

£ millions   Not seasonally adjusted

Amounts outstanding of sterling liabilities

RPM	UK MFIs	Sale and repurchase agreements — of which intragroup banks	UK public sector	Other UK residents	Non-residents	Acceptances granted	CDs and other paper issued — CDs and Commercial paper	Bonds with maturity of up to and incl. 5 years	Bonds with maturity of greater than 5 years	Total	Total sterling deposits	Sterling items in suspense and transmission	Net derivatives	Accrued amounts payable	Sterling capital and other internal funds	Total sterling liabilities
	B3IL	B8ZA	B3UM	B3VM	B3WM	B3XM	B2TL	B6OI	B2TM	B3YM	B3ZM	B3GN	B3HN	B3IN	B3JN	B3KN
2014 May	83,097	53,532	1,557	122,157	72,957	154	82,240	22,975	42,091	147,306	2,904,905	40,498	-14,765	24,954	455,739	3,418,043
Jun	84,149	55,113	1,279	117,067	75,286	124	80,517	21,533	41,585	143,634	2,909,286	40,747	-21,088	22,849	445,697	3,404,212
Jul	74,417	44,245	4,282	119,798	76,224	150	82,355	22,319	42,705	147,380	2,885,961	47,185	-22,785	23,681	422,472 (d)(e)	3,363,246 (d)(e)
Aug	74,076	47,099	7,518	125,388	70,518	152	81,730	22,030	41,626	145,386	2,891,911	42,174	-9,817	23,937	426,393 (f)	3,381,400 (f)
Sep	56,811	36,268	796	103,057	68,517	162	81,884	23,103	41,203	146,190	2,858,953	49,388	-14,052	26,884	405,101	3,333,038
Oct	59,600	37,737	4,440	116,195	66,614	173	81,953	22,994	41,674	146,621	2,857,214	38,432	-12,151	23,829	431,090	3,345,216
Nov	60,997	38,054	5,372	115,389	63,626	169	80,333	23,459	39,942	143,734	2,868,012	39,932	-1,693	24,095	430,707	3,367,888
Dec	64,292	36,212	1,351	97,280	69,829	167	85,318	23,143	39,128	147,589	2,888,436	19,975	7	25,080	435,056	3,375,648
2015 Jan	75,875	46,874	2,822	103,421	70,008	159	86,166	23,279	39,572	149,016	2,884,674	44,328	-4,499	25,759	452,653	3,409,739
Feb	74,528	45,580	3,224	105,481	66,160	162	87,650	23,833	38,815	150,297	2,856,821	46,097	-26,705	27,881	452,042	3,362,904
Mar	72,399	46,430	2,872	94,351	67,154	171	94,278	23,959	37,596	155,834	2,906,882	42,791	-1,434	24,463	421,774	3,401,295
Apr	72,532	42,171	6,081	99,656	72,625	182	97,466	24,909	38,897	161,272	2,915,606	42,945	-26,399	22,126	412,800	3,373,889
May	70,533	36,324	5,321	103,772	71,496	186	97,475	24,757	39,113	161,346	2,916,319	43,635	-28,569	23,535	425,786	3,387,563
Jun	73,899	41,645	6,319	88,013	73,064	191	94,811	23,795	39,429	158,035	2,917,327	42,858	-42,943	22,364	412,889	3,359,393
Jul	71,766	41,013	7,518	98,846	72,931	201	94,683	23,966	38,619	157,269	2,927,283	45,045	-33,575	22,172	419,573	3,387,280
Aug	76,837	43,273	9,014	100,388	62,624	207	98,382	24,606	37,515	160,502	2,914,104	40,934	-32,257	22,037	443,887	3,395,625
Sep	76,057	44,758	100	76,264	62,230	206	94,308	26,069	37,478	157,854	2,897,419	33,900	-49,440	20,775	470,328	3,379,984
Oct	54,981	24,988	1,779	80,450	64,883	203	94,050	25,411	37,324	156,785	2,882,841	40,003	-39,511	20,288	441,532	3,352,172
Nov	48,202	21,953	1,998	85,158	67,449	193	93,462	24,799	36,056	154,317	2,900,129	39,850	-40,962	21,010	439,618	3,366,752
Dec	48,670	21,220	1,852	73,380	61,785	192	97,325	25,743	35,743	158,811	2,915,095	20,822	-54,546	21,136	446,084	3,355,823
2016 Jan	46,043	18,401	1,774	75,871	68,286	185	96,077	26,313	35,670	158,060	2,892,570	54,025	-28,529	22,582	434,102	3,381,747
Feb	48,599	19,209	1,609	78,575	58,133	169	97,325	27,341	35,693	160,359	2,878,833	40,442	1,782	23,742	409,127	3,360,891
Mar	54,471	18,309	310	70,684	68,543	157	101,297	26,186	35,841	163,325	2,900,830 (c)	36,852	-56,499	21,772	411,753 (c)	3,321,772 (c)
Apr	58,112	18,056	5,861	73,908	69,809	161	101,954	27,012	36,191	165,156	2,908,886	41,635	-61,064	20,792	401,842 (g)	3,319,155 (g)

Source: Bank of England

Notes to table

Movements in amounts outstanding can reflect breaks in data series as well as underlying flows. For changes data, users are recommended to refer directly to the appropriate series or data tables. Further explanation can be found at: www.bankofengland.co.uk/statistics/Pages/iadb/notesiadb/Changes_flows_growth_rates.aspx.

(a) Due to improvements in reporting at one institution, the amounts outstanding increased by £8bn. This effect has been adjusted out of the flows for June 2015.
(b) Due to improvements in reporting at one institution, the amounts outstanding decreased by £8bn. This effect has been adjusted out of the flows for June 2015.
(c) Due to changes in reporting at one institution, the amounts outstanding decreased by £5bn. This effect has been adjusted out of the flows for March 2016.
(d) Due to improvements in reporting at one institution, the amounts outstanding decreased by £36bn. This effect has been adjusted out of the flows for July 2014.
(e) Due to improvements in reporting at one institution, the amounts outstanding decreased by £16bn. This effect has been adjusted out of the flows for July 2014.
(f) Due to improvements in reporting at one institution, the amounts outstanding increased by £9bn. This effect has been adjusted out of the flows for August 2014.
(g) Due to a loan transfer by one reporting institution, the amounts outstanding increased by £7bn. This effect has been adjusted out of the flows for April 2016.

12.3b Monetary financial institutions' (excluding central bank) balance sheet

£ millions   Not seasonally adjusted

Amounts outstanding of foreign currency liabilities (including euro)

RPM	Sight and time deposits					Acceptances granted	Sale and repurchase agreements				
	UK MFIs	of which intragroup banks	UK public sector	Other UK residents	Non-residents		UK MFIs	of which intragroup banks	UK public sector	Other UK residents	Non-residents
	B3JL	B8ZM	B2UP	B2UV	B3NN	B3KQ	B3KL	B8ZK	B3PN	B3QN	B3RN
2014 May	193,570	139,619	1,555	249,499	1,736,770	2,285	101,284	58,080	1,716	123,036	501,404
Jun	204,656	150,075	1,464	235,829	1,709,038	2,462	104,550	60,802	1,491	115,245	470,177
Jul	197,948	142,469	1,456	234,164	1,722,367	2,574	105,105	55,762	1,350	108,622	490,589
Aug	206,478	148,312	1,755	226,024	1,740,391	2,817	112,483	64,716	1,577	123,065	496,824
Sep	205,454	148,000	1,723	225,875	1,753,569	2,804	103,744	61,778	2,126	122,692	481,528
Oct	199,117	142,011	2,654	224,023	1,756,418	2,388	101,776	57,460	3,101	115,803	476,922
Nov	201,799	142,001	2,662	235,710	1,836,005	2,169	94,381	52,292	1,916	121,063	485,537
Dec	209,411	147,159	2,193	235,409	1,783,641	1,961	93,547	56,835	1,400	104,348	461,559
2015 Jan	217,970	147,456	2,258	237,714	1,863,441	1,951	99,949	60,721	1,138	111,073	478,307
Feb	221,894	157,382	2,504	235,331	1,784,462	1,851	97,880	59,716	461	115,421	503,543
Mar	226,012	156,438	2,006	242,036	1,800,011	2,016	99,099	61,519	2,226	113,025	480,280
Apr	231,024	160,571	1,987	241,405	1,781,449	1,910	102,996	61,829	529	108,737	492,743
May	226,957	157,390	2,151	239,188	1,698,733	1,771	100,491	60,398	1,387	106,635	483,520
Jun	204,555	139,633	1,944	236,303 (h)	1,616,357	2,186	95,799	60,418	1,217	101,341	459,339
Jul	202,152	136,511	2,035	242,928	1,593,452	2,079	93,164	57,607	1,645	99,608	465,403
Aug	214,788	143,310	2,210	257,472	1,645,700	2,591	92,212	55,587	883	103,610	482,597
Sep	213,562	145,493	2,197	257,835	1,634,396	2,661	89,565	55,966	466	106,396	476,000
Oct	207,649	143,258	2,259	255,116	1,590,307	2,672	86,375	52,933	634	101,705	480,363
Nov	205,433	144,698	2,288	255,561	1,616,872 (i)	2,498	90,517	56,718	522	104,582	489,453
Dec	207,571	148,067	2,194	255,042	1,631,182	2,767	84,360	51,732	1,531	104,574	457,350
2016 Jan	208,903	145,866	2,353	274,162	1,692,801	2,405	79,019	49,908	1,414	112,701	510,595
Feb	220,714	153,042	2,575	280,680	1,734,659	2,085	78,876	48,844	1,268	116,940	500,825
Mar	209,638	147,854	2,341	282,593	1,696,210	2,380	72,791	43,819	112	116,514	485,146
Apr	218,782	157,918	2,484	279,697	1,648,171	2,499	75,776	44,160	1,293	118,167	494,227

Source: Bank of England

12.3b Monetary financial institutions' (excluding central bank) balance sheet

£ millions   Not seasonally adjusted

Amounts outstanding of foreign currency liabilities (including euro)

	CDs and Commercial paper	CDs and other paper Issued: Bonds with maturity of up to and incl. 5 years	Bonds with maturity of greater than 5 years	Total	Total foreign currency deposits	Items in suspense and transmission	Net derivatives	Accrued amounts payable	Capital and other internal funds	Total foreign currency liabilities	Total liabilities
RPM	B2TP	B6OK	B2TQ	B3SN	B3TN	B3UN	B3VN	B3WN	B3XN	B3YN	B3ZN
2014 May	113,578	191,126	207,292	511,996	3,423,115	209,818	3,692	16,342	169,863	3,822,831	7,240,874
Jun	107,965	183,283	205,036	496,284	3,341,194	183,283	3,922	17,071	182,680	3,728,150	7,132,362
Jul	118,126	179,131	204,005	501,261	3,365,436	191,464	5,355	16,812	159,989	3,739,055 (j)	7,102,301 (j)(k)(l)
Aug	123,456	181,437	206,418	511,312	3,422,726	185,709	-3,981	17,243	148,878	3,770,575	7,151,974 (m)
Sep	116,281	180,418	206,296	502,995	3,402,510	182,229	-989	14,952	181,703	3,780,404	7,113,442
Oct	118,712	178,367	207,615	504,694	3,386,895	171,240	2,617	17,049	149,259	3,727,060	7,072,276
Nov	122,348	180,831	214,203	517,382	3,498,623	164,318	-11,132	17,269	158,138	3,827,216	7,195,104
Dec	111,607	176,874	209,595	498,077	3,391,546	80,066	-8,637	16,047	149,644	3,628,667	7,004,315
2015 Jan	119,053	175,093	210,608	504,754	3,518,555	202,607	1,264	15,629	138,348	3,876,403	7,286,141
Feb	119,327	174,127	202,690	496,144	3,459,491	190,632	21,248	13,330	139,779	3,824,481	7,187,385
Mar	110,783	176,422	219,472	506,677	3,473,389	171,267	2,564	15,178	163,695	3,826,094	7,227,389
Apr	116,472	168,700	221,153	506,326	3,469,105	195,148	24,846	14,707	176,172	3,879,979	7,253,868
May	119,244	172,061	223,984	515,289	3,376,121	188,336	17,581	13,353	159,571	3,754,962	7,142,526
Jun	105,961	170,613	215,308	491,882	3,210,923	150,709	23,241	14,181	165,262	3,564,315	6,923,708
Jul	112,496	167,072	213,860	493,428	3,195,894	154,392	17,794	13,101	146,864	3,528,044	6,915,324
Aug	120,184	177,053	210,055	507,292	3,309,353	131,345	14,041	14,519	131,383	3,600,641	6,996,265
Sep	109,758	172,859	215,890	498,507	3,281,585	142,124	15,285	14,440	112,295	3,565,730	6,945,714
Oct	105,051	170,570	216,084	491,704	3,218,784	176,321	7,407	13,786	124,784	3,541,082	6,893,254
Nov	101,608	171,133	214,350	487,091	3,254,818 (i)	165,454	8,540	14,782	138,760	3,582,354 (i)	6,949,106 (i)
Dec	98,101	172,035	218,066	488,202	3,234,772	84,019	21,951	14,273	151,705	3,506,720	6,862,543
2016 Jan	104,410	174,158	223,095	501,663	3,386,015	187,523	-13,622	12,320	166,672	3,738,908	7,120,654
Feb	110,507	178,379	230,433	519,319	3,457,942	186,073	-38,983	12,265	190,236	3,807,533	7,168,425
Mar	108,703	172,030	229,819	510,552	3,378,278	175,831	16,255	12,075	179,607	3,762,046	7,083,818 (n)
Apr	108,345	174,537	231,395	514,277	3,355,373	205,251	19,926	11,980	192,849	3,785,380	7,104,535 (o)

Source: Bank of England

Notes to table

Movements in amounts outstanding can reflect breaks in data series as well as underlying flows. For changes data, users are recommended to refer directly to the appropriate series or data tables. Further explanation can be found at: www.bankofengland.co.uk/statistics/Pages/iadb/notesiadb/Changes_flows_growth_rates.aspx.

(h) Due to improvements in reporting at one institution, the amounts outstanding increased/decreased by £8bn. This effect has been adjusted out of the flows for June 2015.
(i) Due to changes in reporting at one institution, the amounts outstanding decreased by £18bn. This effect has been adjusted out of the flows for November 2015.
(j) Due to improvements in reporting at one institution, the amounts outstanding decreased by £11bn. This effect has been adjusted out of the flows for July 2014.
(k) Due to improvements in reporting at one institution, the amounts outstanding decreased by £36bn. This effect has been adjusted out of the flows for July 2014.
(l) Due to improvements in reporting at one institution, the amounts outstanding decreased by £16bn. This effect has been adjusted out of the flows for July 2014.
(m) Due to improvements in reporting at one institution, the amounts outstanding increased by £9bn. This effect has been adjusted out of the flows for August 2014.
(n) Due to changes in reporting at one institution, the amounts outstanding decreased by £5bn. This effect has been adjusted out of the flows for March 2016.
(o) Due to a loan transfer by one reporting institution, the amounts outstanding increased by £7bn. This effect has been adjusted out of the flows for April 2016.

Copyright guidance and the related UK Open Government Licence can be viewed here: www.bankofengland.co.uk/Pages/disclaimer.aspx.

12.3c Monetary financial institutions' (excluding central bank) balance sheet

£ millions   Not seasonally adjusted

Amounts outstanding of sterling assets

| | Notes coin | With UK central bank | | UK MFIs | of which intragroup banks | Loans | | | Acceptances granted | | | |
| | | Cash ratio deposits | Other | | | UK MFIs CDs | UK MFIs commercial paper | Non-residents | UK MFIs | UK public sector | Other UK residents | Non-residents |
RPM	B3UO	B3VO	B3WO	B3NL	B8ZI	B3OL	B3PL	B3XO	B3QL	B3YO	B3ZO	B3GP
2014 May	9,281	4,078	298,596	245,988	225,310	5,166	52	107,620	43	-	101	10
Jun	8,690	4,127	299,827	247,712	226,742	5,445	60	100,024	23	-	91	10
Jul	9,180	4,127	298,395	231,463	213,018	5,469	122	97,504	23	-	111	16
Aug	9,017	4,125	301,141	229,165	209,737	5,228	75	105,395	24	-	108	20
Sep	9,031	4,128	290,686	232,962	213,844	4,490	128	104,679	24	-	114	24
Oct	9,215	4,128	304,927	231,977	213,071	4,167	149	104,136	24	-	121	28
Nov	8,859	4,139	305,128	245,351	225,188	3,753	176	103,269	23	-	117	29
Dec	11,188	4,098	302,085	249,808	229,734	3,397	236	102,010	24	-	117	26
2015 Jan	9,504	4,098	306,099	260,440	237,180	3,948	240	103,150	15	-	115	29
Feb	9,158	4,098	309,879	248,555	227,787	4,038	225	100,478	15	-	119	28
Mar	9,587	4,098	306,342	261,000	239,841	4,251	246	110,471	15	-	127	30
Apr	9,727	4,097	311,963	258,160	236,587	4,517	186	109,260	14	-	137	30
May	9,315	4,099	315,603	252,979	233,605	4,774	222	108,333	14	-	138	34
Jun	9,522	4,075	307,854	254,850	236,018	4,309	169	113,390	14	-	143	33
Jul	9,589	4,075	315,240	254,144	234,141	3,880	165	111,067	14	-	151	35
Aug	9,335	4,075	312,599	249,423	229,078	3,977	246	111,015	15	-	156	36
Sep	9,530	4,075	294,725	244,999	224,354	3,703	123	123,614	15	-	157	34
Oct	9,559	4,075	304,625	257,960	238,638	3,912	143	112,837	15	-	156	33
Nov	9,373	4,079	305,635	264,325	243,833	3,850	171	110,479	-	-	159	34
Dec	10,943	4,136	302,471	263,449	246,696	3,478	164	117,292	-	-	157	35
2016 Jan	9,460	4,136	304,721	251,630	234,082	3,875	183	116,236	-	-	152	33
Feb	9,309	4,136	305,759	253,020	233,981	3,798	85	111,677	-	-	136	33
Mar	10,730	4,136	301,075	247,944	225,945	3,638	44	120,187	-	-	126	31
Apr	9,901	4,136	310,636	243,055	220,723	3,485	44	122,173	-	-	126	36

Source: Bank of England

12.3c Monetary financial institutions' (excluding central bank) balance sheet

£ millions   Not seasonally adjusted

Amounts outstanding of sterling assets

RPM	Treasury bills	UK MFIs bills	Bills Other UK residents	Bills Non-residents	Sales and repurchase agreements UK MFIs	of which intragroup banks	UK public sector	Other UK residents	Non-residents	Advances UK public sector	Other UK residents	Non-residents
	B3HP	B3RL	B3IP	B3JP	B3SL	B8ZG	B3KP	B3LP	B3MP	B2UK	B3OP	B3PP
2014 May	6,597	32	292	3,777	82,614	53,198	93	124,533	50,560	8,089	1,808,240	83,643
Jun	4,761	40	290	3,848	82,643	54,745	1	129,020	54,689	8,275	1,810,555	84,939
Jul	3,337	33	368	3,894	72,182	43,851	102	127,944	54,209	8,158	1,814,737	76,129
Aug	5,994	43	259	4,382	72,109	46,723	1,203	124,285	58,319	8,176	1,822,335	83,199
Sep	5,164	34	246	3,818	54,452	35,881	90	128,371	52,615	8,177	1,817,448	84,880
Oct	6,693	42	288	1,524	57,224	37,302	-	128,247	54,276	8,673	1,813,994	83,745
Nov	7,651	53	332	1,474	58,367	37,728	190	129,720	53,843	8,935	1,806,975	83,704
Dec	6,680	54	303	1,480	61,623	35,787	25	121,142	57,003	8,754	1,798,499	80,859
2015 Jan	5,718	50	242	1,316	73,896	46,785	20	126,102	55,403	8,859	1,800,763	85,309
Feb	6,716	63	166	1,211	70,499	45,531	8	125,695	56,254	8,837	1,803,833	87,509
Mar	5,336	51	146	1,106	66,008	46,473	5	132,857	53,351	8,981	1,812,720	84,331
Apr	5,099	48	192	1,389	62,904	42,203	8	131,907	58,330	8,952	1,810,306	82,118
May	6,757	60	158	1,266	58,045	36,781	-	136,579	56,850	8,589	1,809,611	84,033
Jun	7,027	64	146	1,020	61,169	42,060	65	129,625	53,909	8,551	1,804,213	87,657
Jul	7,970	53	119	857	56,635	41,323	26	130,026	49,391	8,306	1,827,304	90,862
Aug	9,797	77	113	850	60,692	43,733	849	136,738	47,191	8,695	1,826,000	91,434
Sep	9,317	82	160	834	60,889	45,190	2	131,829	51,411	8,536	1,830,196	89,657
Oct	9,605	86	110	826	41,334	25,599	-	123,011	49,596	8,333	1,834,682	89,228
Nov	9,027	85	104	822	35,069	22,762	31	129,523	52,029	8,694	1,833,644	89,243
Dec	8,393	162	111	825	33,023	21,350	9	126,685	49,812	8,483	1,839,562	89,712
2016 Jan	9,489	231	152	749	30,696	18,831	75	123,963	52,458	8,577	1,849,610	90,255
Feb	9,504	213	19	663	33,874	19,491	102	129,285	46,728	8,607	1,861,142	88,432
Mar	7,582	210	78	670	35,338	18,457	35	131,574	48,390	8,565	1,866,642	88,688
Apr	7,024	242	78	774	38,494	18,203	29	130,032	52,214	8,634	1,860,023 (s)	90,104

Source: Bank of England

12.3c Monetary financial institutions' (excluding central bank) balance sheet

£ millions   Not seasonally adjusted

Amounts outstanding of sterling assets

| RPM | UK government bonds | Investments | | Other UK residents | Non-residents | Items in suspense and collection | Accrued amounts receivable | Other assets | Total sterling assets |
		Other UK public sector	UK MFIs						
	B3QP	B3RP	B3TL	B3SP	B3TP	B3UP	B3VP	B3WP	B3XP
2014 May	122,499	201	86,039	238,537	46,186	41,518	15,098	26,075	3,415,559
Jun	123,688	199	86,760	233,839	45,956	40,418	15,041	26,086	3,417,056
Jul	126,566	205	38,582 (t)(u)	238,782	46,608	46,040	14,128	25,980	3,344,394 (t)(u)
Aug	126,529	217	43,743 (v)	236,781	45,501	43,960	15,907	26,126	3,375,369 (v)
Sep	123,706	219	43,970	231,766	47,492	53,289	14,376	25,803	3,342,179
Oct	131,934	231	44,757	224,241	48,516	40,880	14,104	26,392	3,344,635
Nov	139,662	255	45,421	227,568	46,956	41,775	15,671	26,555	3,365,952
Dec	139,126	279	46,359	239,634	50,066	21,706	13,931	26,670	3,347,185
2015 Jan	138,473	240	48,234	218,879	50,496	44,489	13,794	26,816	3,386,738
Feb	126,965	211	49,198	216,637	51,006	43,074	14,458	26,635	3,365,566
Mar	124,935	219	49,728	209,666	52,157	41,866	13,639	27,328	3,380,595
Apr	125,411	219	50,362	211,490	51,384	40,846	13,302	27,728	3,380,088
May	128,585	227	50,304	214,319	52,464	42,337	13,899	27,807	3,387,400
Jun	129,657	222	50,885	212,627	51,191	41,457	14,971	27,888	3,376,701
Jul	137,671	187	49,354	209,284	52,342	41,725	13,242	28,224	3,401,937
Aug	144,085	201	49,466	196,262	50,932	38,926	14,932	28,043	3,396,160
Sep	139,145	214	48,573	195,280	49,538	32,249	14,121	28,529	3,371,536
Oct	139,788	192	48,896	198,504	49,279	35,990	14,593	28,809	3,366,177
Nov	144,760	182	49,788	201,057	48,211	38,742	14,992	28,933	3,383,039
Dec	136,527	178	53,257	203,648	46,118	18,684	14,377	28,537	3,360,227
2016 Jan	138,282	235	52,931	197,906	47,819	52,625	14,729	28,597	3,389,805
Feb	141,249	260	50,889	193,750	50,205	39,343	15,445	28,808	3,386,472
Mar	141,039	236	50,165	195,393	50,315	36,483	14,641	29,468	3,393,422
Apr	143,359	230	50,343	195,492	47,349	43,055	14,463	29,430	3,404,959 (s)

Source: Bank of England

Notes to table

Movements in amounts outstanding can reflect breaks in data series as well as underlying flows. For changes data, users are recommended to refer directly to the appropriate series or data tables. Further explanation can be found at: www.bankofengland.co.uk/statistics/Pages/iadb/notesiadb/Changes_flows_growth_rates.aspx.

(s) Due to a loan transfer by one reporting institution, the amounts outstanding increased by £7bn. This effect has been adjusted out of the flows for April 2016.
(t) Due to improvements in reporting at one institution, the amounts outstanding decreased by £36bn. This effect has been adjusted out of the flows for July 2014.
(u) Due to improvements in reporting at one institution, the amounts outstanding decreased by £13bn. This effect has been adjusted out of the flows for July 2014.
(v) Due to improvements in reporting at one institution, the amounts outstanding increased by £9bn. This effect has been adjusted out of the flows for August 2014.

Copyright guidance and the related UK Open Government Licence can be viewed here: www.bankofengland.co.uk/Pages/disclaimer.aspx.

12.3d Monetary financial institutions' (excluding central bank) balance sheet

£ millions   Not seasonally adjusted

Amounts outstanding of foreign currency assets (including euro)

| | | Loans and advances | | | | | Sale and repurchase agreements | | | | | Acceptances granted | Total bills |
| | UK MFIs | of which intragroup banks | UK MFIs' CDs etc. | UK public sector | Other UK residents | Non-residents | UK MFIs | of which intragroup banks | UK public sector | Other UK residents | Non-residents | | |
RPM	B3UL	B8ZQ	B3VL	B2UN	B3ZP	B2UH	B3WL	B8ZO	B3HQ	B3IQ	B3JQ	B3KQ	B3LQ
2014 May	186,365	137,825	3,347	54	228,571	1,683,591	97,773	58,108	3,107	144,070	590,748	2,285	36,925
Jun	196,879	147,834	2,755	65	212,933	1,639,465	100,343	60,804	2,415	135,671	571,748	2,462	36,317
Jul	191,969	140,652	2,157	41	211,486	1,676,714	100,454	55,783	2,431	133,684	587,685	2,574	33,928
Aug	200,703	147,139	1,475	49	208,141	1,693,374	106,152	64,718	1,926	136,353	592,816	2,817	33,685
Sep	199,429	146,564	1,577	42	213,823	1,698,627	98,237	61,777	2,088	137,525	583,745	2,804	37,113
Oct	191,757	139,844	1,068	1,305	206,028	1,691,640	95,534	57,520	2,697	137,185	567,618	2,388	35,141
Nov	196,125	139,248	1,320	1,347	213,604	1,753,273	89,130	52,056	2,241	139,241	567,119	2,169	36,973
Dec	200,371	144,776	1,275	1,202	215,359	1,726,750	84,071	56,836	1,351	120,142	561,947	1,961	37,343
2015 Jan	209,112	145,054	1,691	1,053	224,363	1,777,517	91,468	60,315	1,534	124,786	572,817	1,951	37,171
Feb	217,181	155,262	1,939	950	219,089	1,705,007	91,593	59,540	1,074	129,494	583,235	1,851	36,808
Mar	222,139	155,703	2,394	935	224,909	1,742,021	93,788	61,503	2,677	127,585	568,692	2,016	38,352
Apr	228,375	159,950	2,689	830	227,302	1,753,335	96,605	61,796	1,252	132,339	561,711	1,910	39,649
May	225,239	157,280	2,661	671	215,144	1,706,250	92,097	60,715	1,840	120,577	541,389	1,771	36,398
Jun	197,757	139,490	2,851	656	221,602	1,616,720	91,008	60,619	1,356	114,705	523,995	2,186	36,078
Jul	194,989	135,983	2,294	487	218,372	1,626,042	87,980	57,810	1,901	109,136	511,280	2,079	34,410
Aug	209,801	144,212	2,362	493	224,429	1,677,387	88,542	55,763	614	111,866	527,482	2,591	36,064
Sep	200,903	145,590	2,191	528	227,153	1,650,999	86,526	55,905	1,209	112,038	541,150	2,661	38,204
Oct	196,990	143,371	1,815	483	227,366	1,604,135	81,502	52,913	1,542	105,680	514,778	2,672	37,991
Nov	197,812	145,797	1,465	446	223,831	1,636,970	85,340	56,703	872	105,282	517,221	2,498	41,643
Dec	197,651	148,459	1,110	494	220,646	1,691,114	77,282	51,805	1,417	100,525	516,203	2,767	44,279
2016 Jan	195,957	146,249	1,052	568	232,201	1,786,536	76,412	49,968	1,600	111,056	543,274	2,405	42,382
Feb	207,542	153,751	1,218	656	247,067	1,771,320	76,697	49,377	1,163	122,409	561,171	2,085	45,599
Mar	199,497	148,544	1,310	624	233,809	1,731,322	69,105	44,479	275	114,579	564,808	2,380	45,031
Apr	209,621	158,630	1,303	579	236,650	1,680,870	72,927	44,765	1,326	120,129	565,392	2,499	42,010

Source: Bank of England

12.3d Monetary financial institutions' (excluding central bank) balance sheet

£ millions

Amounts outstanding of foreign currency assets (including euro)

RPM	UK government bonds	Investments Other UK public sector	Investments UK MFIs	Other UK residents	Non-residents	Items in suspense and collection	Accrued amounts receivable	Other assets	Total foreign currency assets	Total assets	Holdings of own sterling acceptances	Holdings of own foreign currency acceptances
	B3MQ	B3NQ	B3XL	B3OQ	B3PQ	B3QQ	B3RQ	B3SQ	B3TQ	B3UQ	B3IM	B3JM
2014 May	78	-8	21,175	45,683	491,554	222,981	15,965	51,050	3,825,315	7,240,874	121	1,512
Jun	66	-28	20,400	44,811	487,834	194,192	16,133	50,843	3,715,306	7,132,362	111	1,393
Jul	53	39	28,313	41,071	474,490 (w)	206,307	15,803	48,708	3,757,908 (w)	7,102,301 (w)(x)(y)	106	1,360
Aug	36	30	20,266	41,128	481,040	190,776	16,214	49,626	3,776,605	7,151,974 (z)	114	1,244
Sep	19	34	18,778	41,373	485,276	187,535	16,095	47,143	3,771,263	7,113,442	136	1,320
Oct	184	21	17,937	40,647	497,865	177,854	15,674	45,101	3,727,641	7,072,276	132	1,286
Nov	265	-	19,018	41,665	530,258	174,271	14,985	46,149	3,829,152	7,195,104	149	1,306
Dec	275	-	16,486	28,978	513,703	87,167	13,344	45,404	3,657,130	7,004,315	148	1,321
2015 Jan	233	-	15,695	28,228	536,802	214,400	12,172	48,410	3,899,403	7,286,141	114	1,427
Feb	188	1	15,048	26,824	531,444	201,607	12,910	45,578	3,821,819	7,187,385	113	1,349
Mar	279	1	14,754	27,169	535,321	183,839	13,115	46,809	3,846,794	7,227,389	121	1,550
Apr	271	1	14,881	26,276	520,498	208,651	13,466	43,738	3,873,780	7,253,868	122	1,279
May	249	1	14,619	25,607	511,639	199,845	13,890	45,239	3,755,125	7,142,526	120	1,280
Jun	282	1	13,605	23,303	475,800	168,789	12,516	43,796	3,547,007	6,923,708	103	1,326
Jul	424	-	12,495	22,926	470,897	165,081	11,188	41,403	3,513,387	6,915,324	104	1,154
Aug	463	-	13,310	22,406	479,567	147,106	11,788	43,831	3,600,105	6,996,265	126	1,276
Sep	428	-	12,482	22,558	468,933	150,192	11,326	44,698	3,574,178	6,945,714	184	1,252
Oct	420	-	12,382	20,605	482,378	182,474	11,025	42,841	3,527,078	6,893,254	194	1,248
Nov	422	-	14,847	19,681	491,695	173,396	11,385	41,261	3,566,067	6,949,106	187	1,264
Dec	471	-	14,218	19,525	475,134	89,329	10,761	39,389	3,502,316	6,862,543	189	1,173
2016 Jan	473	-	14,898	19,107	475,717	197,818	11,153	38,239	3,730,849	7,120,654	176	1,123
Feb	504	1	14,918	19,378	459,136	197,071	10,893	43,124	3,781,952	7,168,425	156	1,028
Mar	569	2	14,124	19,651	446,141	192,914	11,202	43,053	3,690,396	7,083,818	118	1,017
Apr	660	1	15,568	17,823	457,046	222,109	10,039	43,022	3,699,575	7,104,535	119	856

Source: Bank of England

Notes to table

Movements in amounts outstanding can reflect breaks in data series as well as underlying flows. For changes data, users are recommended to refer directly to the appropriate series or data tables. Further explanation can be found at: www.bankofengland.co.uk/statistics/iadb/Pages/iadb/notesiadb/Changes_flows_growth_rates.aspx.

(w) Due to improvements in reporting at one institution, the amounts outstanding decreased by £11bn. This effect has been adjusted out of the flows for July 2014.
(x) Due to improvements in reporting at one institution, the amounts outstanding decreased by £36bn. This effect has been adjusted out of the flows for July 2014.
(y) Due to improvements in reporting at one institution, the amounts outstanding decreased by £13bn. This effect has been adjusted out of the flows for July 2014.
(z) Due to improvements in reporting at one institution, the amounts outstanding increased by £9bn. This effect has been adjusted out of the flows for August 2014.

12.3e Monetary financial institutions' (excluding central bank) balance sheet

£ millions   Not seasonally adjusted

Changes in sterling liabilities

| RPM | Notes outstanding & cash loaded cards | Sight deposits | | | | | Time deposits | | | | | | |
| | | UK MFIs | of which intragroup banks | UK public sector | Other UK residents | Non-residents | UK MFIs | of which intragroup banks | UK public sector | Other UK residents | of which SAYE | of which cash ISAs | Non-residents |
	B4IJ	B4GA	B8ZD	B4CF	B4BH	B4DD	B4HA	B8ZF	B4DF	B4CH	B4FH	B4DH	B4ED
2014 May	68	7,801	6,852	-1,390	12,677	9,967	-4,286	-3,181	1,055	-12,280	-92	1,091	-1,505
Jun	7	-655	-579	-732	17,453	1,340	821	1,433	375	-6,118	115	-235	-4,360
Jul	12	-11,750	-9,967	639	-12,470	77	-2,901	-3,885	778	2,725	14	7,841	-4,108
Aug	69	1,691	1,461	-937	5,796	-4,536	-1,021	-854	-248	-219	11	3,125	3,775
Sep	-37	2,427	2,456	-289	13,547	5,730	1,893	1,917	-699	-4,231	-128	1,766	-4,092
Oct	38	-1,519	-1,532	-300	-1,589	-2,078	1,068	1,205	-141	-13,878	46	1,414	-2,043
Nov	33	3,422	3,080	-620	12,838	1,230	7,842	8,656	-651	-6,409	48	926	-936
Dec	259	7,952	8,559	287	11,892	5,543	-4,931	-4,361	-1,520	1,344	87	582	8,634
2015 Jan	-270	11,995	9,185	1,259	-3,480	-4,211	-291	-511	-7	-24,336	-80	50	-3,367
Feb	-56	-3,651	-2,448	-808	-855	-3,972	-7,509	-7,484	174	-6,151	-109	59	-4,685
Mar	51	9,168	8,067	-809	27,208	15,294	3,599	3,718	-949	201	12	2,973	829
Apr	-8	1,011	1,664	1,454	-7,128	-14,699	-5,134	-4,826	1,363	4,846	-18	7,013	11,402
May	46	-4,405	-3,417	-678	5,594	246	1,304	806	563	-262	-	1,901	-5,677
Jun	40	2,439	3,348	-516	10,995	4,765	-1,551	-1,174	-304	-3,802	98	852	2,117
Jul	-116	-1,808	-4,285	1,313	2,567	-3,016	2,034	1,961	1,013	194	-51	505	-1,524
Aug	138	-8,087	-9,329	-244	-8,522	5,453	4,089	4,049	-19	-6,617	44	885	-8
Sep	83	263	1,438	-132	17,255	7,510	-6,203	-6,034	-78	-11,151	-18	664	12,099
Oct	16	3,875	4,841	410	6,322	-15,068	1,085	813	20	2,754	24	541	-9,167
Nov	89	4,066	3,164	-219	10,855	6,717	2,336	1,509	-227	-3,054	-26	446	-223
Dec	125	-2,068	374	528	4,170	7,175	2,510	2,889	-598	-275	-47	270	14,976
2016 Jan	-236	-3,677	-4,910	737	-1,586	264	-7,735	-7,698	-278	-8,443	-1	267	-7,442
Feb	-31	35	-617	-612	18,511	-432	195	-165	-892	-3,516	16	581	-24,251
Mar	99	-10,476	-11,768	-809	27,036	8,195	3,699	4,281	-2,146	-10,425	3	1,989	2,078
Apr	-	-4,693	-3,635	1,229	-16,319	-4,483	456	-1,752	1,120	6,801	23	5,372	6,542

Source: Bank of England

12.3e Monetary financial institutions' (excluding central bank) balance sheet

£ millions Not seasonally adjusted

Changes in sterling liabilities

	UK MFIs	of which intragroup banks	Liabilities under sale and repurchase agreements			Acceptances granted	CDs and other paper issued				Total sterling deposits	Sterling items in suspense and transmission	Net derivatives	Accrued amounts payable	Sterling capital and other internal funds	Total sterling liabilities
			UK public sector	Other UK residents	Non-residents		CDs and Commercial paper	Bonds with maturity of up to and incl. 5 years	Bonds with maturity of greater than 5 years	Total						
RPM	B4IA	B8ZB	B4EF	B4EH	B4FD	B4BK	B2SU	B6OH	B2TK	B4EJ	B4FJ	B4AK	B4GJ	B4CJ	B4DJ	B4JJ
2014 May	7,306	7,564	-685	461	-874	-5	872	-445	-384	43	18,285	-11,115	8,874	1,023	5,970	23,103
Jun	1,052	1,581	-278	-5,090	2,329	-30	-1,723	-1,443	-603	-3,769	2,339	249	-6,193	-2,107	-3,164	-8,868
Jul	-9,732	-10,868	3,003	2,731	939	25	1,838	787	1,120	3,745	-26,296	6,438	-1,697	837	25,933	5,228
Aug	-341	2,854	3,235	5,589	-5,706	2	-625	-289	-1,080	-1,994	5,087	-5,011	12,968	256	-7,756	5,613
Sep	-17,264	-10,831	-6,722	-23,782	-550	10	153	1,073	-422	804	-33,217	7,215	-4,236	2,947	-15,520	-42,848
Oct	2,789	1,469	3,645	13,138	-1,903	11	69	-109	471	431	-2,369	-10,956	1,901	-2,426	23,791	9,979
Nov	1,396	317	932	-806	-2,988	-4	-1,620	465	-1,732	-2,887	12,359	1,500	10,458	266	-11,312	13,304
Dec	3,296	-1,842	-4,021	-18,109	6,204	-2	4,985	-316	-814	3,855	20,425	-19,957	1,730	1,028	9,608	13,093
2015 Jan	11,582	10,663	1,471	6,140	179	-7	848	-664	444	628	-2,447	24,352	-4,506	679	11,171	28,979
Feb	-1,347	-1,295	401	2,061	-3,848	2	1,484	1	-204	1,281	-28,906	1,769	-22,206	2,123	9,159	-38,117
Mar	-2,128	851	-352	-11,780	1,644	10	3,724	127	-1,355	2,495	44,429	-3,306	20,886	-3,282	-23,153	35,625
Apr	133	-4,259	3,209	5,305	5,472	11	3,188	949	1,301	5,438	12,680	155	-24,965	-2,337	4,408	-10,068
May	-1,999	-5,847	-759	4,090	-1,103	4	10	-151	516	374	-2,708	690	-2,170	1,628	14,650	12,135
Jun	3,366	5,321	998	-15,759	1,568	4	-2,665	-962	316	-3,311	1,008	-777	-14,374	-1,171	-3,627	-18,900
Jul	-2,133	-632	1,199	10,833	-133	10	-127	171	-810	-766	9,784	2,186	9,368	-191	6,095	27,126
Aug	4,831	2,260	1,496	2,433	-8,648	6	3,698	-209	-256	3,233	-10,603	-4,111	1,318	-135	30,246	16,852
Sep	-780	1,485	-8,914	-24,124	-395	-1	-4,074	1,463	-37	-2,648	-17,298	-7,034	-15,616	-1,266	25,369	-15,762
Oct	-21,076	-19,770	1,679	4,186	2,653	-3	-258	-658	-153	-1,069	-23,398	6,103	9,929	-485	-27,710	-35,546
Nov	-6,779	-3,035	220	4,708	2,566	-10	-588	-612	-1,268	-2,468	18,488	-153	-1,451	722	-7,657	10,038
Dec	218	-982	-147	-12,053	-5,140	-1	3,863	944	-314	4,494	13,790	-19,028	-12,298	99	2,827	-14,486
2016 Jan	-2,627	-2,819	-78	2,491	6,501	-7	-1,249	570	-72	-752	-22,631	33,204	26,017	1,450	-14,215	23,589
Feb	2,556	809	-165	2,704	-10,152	-16	1,249	1,028	22	2,299	-13,737	-13,422	30,311	625	-24,087	-20,340
Mar	5,872	-900	-1,298	-7,892	10,409	-12	3,972	-1,155	148	2,966	27,199	-3,590	-58,281	-1,970	-3,387	-39,929
Apr	3,641	-253	5,550	3,294	1,267	4	657	748	12	1,416	5,825	5,024	-5,134	-1,039	-13,992	-9,316

Source: Bank of England

Notes to table

Full explanatory notes to this table can be found on the Bank of England website: http://www.bankofengland.co.uk/mfsd/iadb/notesiadb/MFIs_exICB.htm

Copyright guidance and the related UK Open Government Licence can be viewed here: www.bankofengland.co.uk/Pages/disclaimer.aspx.

12.3f Monetary financial institutions' (excluding central bank) balance sheet

£ millions   Not seasonally adjusted

Changes in foreign currency liabilities (including euro)

RPM	Sight and time deposits					Acceptances granted	Sale and repurchase agreements				
	UK MFIs	of which intragroup banks	UK public sector	Other UK residents	Non-residents		UK MFIs	of which intragroup banks	UK public sector	Other UK residents	Non-residents
	B4GB	B8ZN	B2VP	B2VV	B2VJ	B4HM	B4HB	B8ZL	B4GG	B4GI	B4HE
2014 May	-13,676	-10,656	-74	708	23,675	-58	-10,293	-8,371	-26	1,428	9,133
Jun	13,848	12,626	-68	-9,704	-4,122	208	3,330	3,668	-200	-4,217	-22,975
Jul	-6,572	-7,513	-19	-3,017	6,684	103	709	-4,949	-133	-6,386	19,110
Aug	7,257	4,836	281	-10,326	3,694	216	6,676	8,560	222	13,763	1,617
Sep	-941	-317	-57	-1,674	7,890	-35	-8,507	-2,871	584	218	-17,754
Oct	-7,719	-7,069	159	-3,086	-11,383	-442	-2,731	-4,802	984	-7,747	-8,763
Nov	512	-2,304	-36	9,904	50,972	-257	-8,925	-6,088	-1,187	3,676	1,377
Dec	9,753	6,747	-450	894	-39,871	-202	628	5,184	-499	-15,572	-21,765
2015 Jan	9,218	674	57	-1,387	66,339	-80	7,082	4,395	-270	6,424	10,048
Feb	10,640	15,079	309	3,980	-25,547	-47	1,062	866	-653	8,107	40,296
Mar	1,310	-3,191	-546	334	-21,113	117	-87	1,097	1,761	-4,212	-35,263
Apr	6,860	5,608	3	4,121	8,822	-69	4,789	894	-1,695	-3,124	21,818
May	-2,222	-2,226	168	-171	-77,376	-142	-1,823	-1,068	860	-1,520	-7,434
Jun	-18,785	-15,054	-168	2,623	-47,739	456	-2,797	1,223	-155	-3,180	-13,441
Jul	-2,798	-3,421	85	5,608	-28,154	-112	-2,875	-2,967	428	-1,954	4,148
Aug	8,097	3,562	133	9,975	17,491	474	-3,204	-3,371	-793	442	5,101
Sep	-3,214	720	-34	-3,244	-30,236	50	-3,505	-207	-421	1,569	-12,568
Oct	-1,102	1,317	109	2,912	-8,475	55	-926	-1,639	184	-2,006	15,177
Nov	-1,082	1,632	16	-1,972	37,026	-197	4,275	3,890	-101	2,990	4,192
Dec	-3,072	-1,355	-151	-5,363	-28,787	216	-8,386	-7,011	975	-2,520	-39,373
2016 Jan	-5,606	-7,719	81	9,258	-1,288	-444	-8,501	-3,767	-173	3,989	34,433
Feb	7,619	3,999	176	829	5,211	-358	-1,777	-2,047	-174	1,249	-20,970
Mar	-9,991	-4,290	-286	6,191	-19,595	328	-6,044	-5,074	-1,155	-237	-7,846
Apr	10,875	11,837	179	3,072	-16,828	154	3,585	989	1,198	3,446	16,159

Source: Bank of England

Notes to table

Explananatory notes to this table can be found on the Bank of England website: http://www.bankofengland.co.uk/mfsd/iadb/notesiadb/MFIs_exICB.htm

Copyright guidance and the related UK Open Government Licence can be viewed here: www.bankofengland.co.uk/Pages/disclaimer.aspx.

12.3f Monetary financial institutions' (excluding central bank) balance sheet

£ millions   Not seasonally adjusted

Changes in foreign currency liabilities (including euro)

RPM	CDs and Commercial paper	CDs and other paper Issued — Bonds with maturity of up to and incl. 5 years	Bonds with maturity of greater than 5 years	Total	Total foreign currency deposits	Items in suspense and transmission	Net derivatives	Accrued amounts payable	Capital and other internal funds	Total foreign currency liabilities	Total liabilities
	B2TN	B6OJ	B2TO	B4CM	B4DM	B4GM	B4EM	B4AM	B4BM	B4FM	B4JM
2014 May	4,760	-2,108	4,317	6,970	17,787	-32,772	6,619	791	-19,878	-27,453	-4,349
Jun	-3,722	-4,915	1,656	-6,980	-30,880	-24,741	3,086	860	15,245	-36,429	-45,297
Jul	9,926	-3,974	-384	5,568	16,048	9,119	984	-170	-22,020	3,961	9,189
Aug	4,249	1,072	1,283	6,604	30,004	-5,915	-9,306	424	-12,760	2,447	8,060
Sep	-6,848	-646	1,075	-6,419	-26,695	-2,333	3,022	-2,164	34,349	6,179	-36,669
Oct	1,330	-3,318	27	-1,961	-42,690	-11,439	3,440	2,067	-35,148	-83,769	-73,791
Nov	1,411	13	3,660	5,083	61,117	-10,108	-13,845	98	1,739	39,001	52,305
Dec	-9,822	-2,329	-2,017	-14,168	-81,252	-83,241	2,642	-1,077	-6,749	-169,678	-156,585
2015 Jan	6,962	-6,361	1,863	2,464	99,895	124,826	11,562	-193	-36,692	199,398	228,377
Feb	3,941	-985	4,091	7,047	45,194	-8,686	22,309	-2,092	7,174	63,899	25,782
Mar	-11,660	-1,130	6,647	-6,143	-63,842	-19,566	-18,463	1,988	18,685	-81,198	-45,573
Apr	7,261	-5,296	3,373	5,338	46,863	23,220	22,379	-512	14,263	106,214	96,146
May	3,144	4,190	4,529	11,863	-77,797	-6,142	-7,040	-1,271	-9,871	-102,120	-89,984
Jun	-10,793	2,056	-4,615	-13,352	-96,538	-36,585	5,683	908	25,263	-101,268	-120,168
Jul	6,190	-3,947	-3,158	-915	-26,539	3,674	-5,468	-1,102	-23,270	-52,704	-25,577
Aug	4,943	-616	-2,528	1,799	39,514	-25,204	-3,925	1,237	-10,584	1,037	17,890
Sep	-11,646	-6,106	2,755	-14,996	-66,601	10,197	482	-132	-14,829	-70,883	-86,645
Oct	-2,055	1,767	5,702	5,413	11,343	36,709	-7,667	-480	11,728	51,633	16,088
Nov	-3,739	-199	-2,471	-6,409	38,738	-9,495	1,740	1,111	8,770	40,864	50,902
Dec	-6,584	-3,740	-3,710	-14,034	-100,494	-84,569	7,656	143	16,623	-160,642	-175,127
2016 Jan	2,358	-4,401	-3,155	-5,198	26,550	101,753	-36,162	-2,113	10,284	100,311	123,900
Feb	3,798	-113	2,141	5,826	-2,370	-3,510	-26,192	190	9,838	-22,044	-42,384
Mar	-854	-4,838	-414	-6,106	-44,741	-11,346	55,926	-270	-12,269	-12,700	-52,629
Apr	1,383	822	8,136	10,341	32,180	30,967	3,950	-276	12,214	79,035	69,719

Source: Bank of England

Notes to table
Explananatory notes to this table can be found on the Bank of England website: http://www.bankofengland.co.uk/mfsd/iadb/notesiadb/MFIs_exICB.htm
Copyright guidance and the related UK Open Government Licence can be viewed here: www.bankofengland.co.uk/Pages/disclaimer.aspx.

12.3g Monetary financial institutions' (excluding central bank) balance sheet

£ millions   Not seasonally adjusted

Changes in sterling assets

RPM	Notes and coin	With UK central bank		Loans					Acceptances granted			
		Cash ratio deposits	Other	UK MFIs	of which intragroup banks	UK MFIs' CDs etc	UK MFIs commercial paper	Non-residents	UK MFIs	UK public sector	Other UK residents	Non-residents
	B4II	B3YR	B3ZR	B4DC	B8ZJ	B4JB	B4BC	B4BD	B4EC	B4FF	B3TR	B4GD
2014 May	-294	3	-3,724	3,440	3,463	-97	9	6,512	-	-	-1	-3
Jun	-591	49	1,231	1,718	1,432	278	8	-7,596	-20	-	-10	-
Jul	491	-	-1,432	-16,234	-13,725	24	62	-2,520	-	-	20	6
Aug	-163	-2	2,746	1,208	225	-241	-46	7,891	-	-	-3	5
Sep	13	2	-10,455	3,799	4,107	-738	53	-716	-	-	7	4
Oct	185	1	14,241	-542	-773	-323	21	-543	1	-	7	4
Nov	-356	10	201	13,374	12,117	-415	27	-866	-1	-	-4	1
Dec	2,329	-41	-3,043	4,460	4,548	-355	60	-1,227	-	-	-	-2
2015 Jan	-1,684	-	4,014	10,631	7,446	551	4	1,140	-8	-	-1	2
Feb	-346	-	3,780	-11,900	-9,393	90	-16	-2,673	-	-	3	-1
Mar	429	-	-3,537	12,516	12,054	213	-42	9,993	-	-	8	2
Apr	140	-	5,621	-2,839	-3,254	266	-60	-1,210	-	-	10	-
May	-412	2	3,639	-5,181	-2,982	256	36	-928	-	-	-	4
Jun	207	-24	-7,749	1,871	2,412	-465	-52	5,058	-	-	5	-1
Jul	66	-	7,386	-695	-1,872	-429	-5	-2,309	-	-	8	1
Aug	-254	-	-2,641	-4,721	-5,063	97	82	-52	-	-	4	1
Sep	195	-	-17,874	-4,438	-4,724	-238	-14	12,502	-	-	2	-3
Oct	29	-	9,900	3,965	5,274	209	20	-10,777	-	-	-2	-1
Nov	-186	4	1,035	6,366	5,195	-63	28	-2,358	-14	-	3	1
Dec	1,558	57	-3,164	753	2,863	-371	-7	6,813	-	-	-2	1
2016 Jan	-1,483	-	2,250	-11,778	-12,612	397	19	-1,056	-	-	-5	-2
Feb	-151	-	1,038	1,390	-101	-77	-98	-4,559	-	-	-17	-
Mar	1,420	-	-4,684	-5,013	-7,976	-160	-41	8,482	-	-	-10	-2
Apr	-829	-	9,561	-4,882	-5,221	-153	1	1,997	-	-	-1	5

Source: Bank of England

12.3g Monetary financial institutions' (excluding central bank) balance sheet

£ millions   Not seasonally adjusted

Changes in sterling assets

| RPM | Bills | | | | UK MFIs | Claims under sale and repurchase agreements | | | | | Advances | | |
| | Treasury bills | UK MFIs bills | Other UK | Non-residents | | of which intragroup banks | UK public sector | Other UK residents | Non-residents | UK public sector | Other UK residents | Non-residents |
	B4BA	B4IB	B4HG	B4IC	B4FA	B8ZH	B4BF	B4AH	B4CD	B2VK	B2VQ	B4HC
2014 May	-1,245	7	-15	261	7,881	7,642	82	4,612	-965	-197	-4,853	6,491
Jun	-1,836	8	-2	70	29	1,547	-91	4,487	4,129	186	1,212	1,277
Jul	-1,424	-7	78	46	-10,461	-10,894	101	-1,076	-480	-86	4,439	-9,201
Aug	2,658	10	-110	488	-73	2,872	1,101	-3,659	4,110	18	4,593	7,073
Sep	-831	-9	-12	-564	-17,656	-10,843	-1,114	2,894	-4,513	1	-4,185	1,481
Oct	1,530	8	41	-2,294	2,772	1,422	-90	-123	1,662	-158	-4,318	-1,089
Nov	958	11	44	-50	1,143	426	190	1,473	-433	262	-5,777	109
Dec	-972	1	-29	6	3,256	-1,941	-165	-8,578	3,160	-181	-5,208	-1,018
2015 Jan	-962	-4	-61	-164	12,273	10,998	-5	4,960	-1,600	105	5,212	4,461
Feb	818	13	-76	-105	-3,397	-1,254	-12	-407	850	-22	3,490	2,212
Mar	-1,380	-12	-20	-105	-4,491	942	-3	5,135	-2,903	145	7,823	-3,198
Apr	-238	-3	46	283	-3,104	-4,270	3	-951	4,979	-29	2,394	-2,204
May	1,659	12	-34	-123	-4,859	-5,422	-8	4,670	-1,477	-319	554	1,899
Jun	-957	4	-12	-246	3,123	5,279	65	-6,955	-2,941	-38	-3,881	3,632
Jul	943	-11	-27	-163	-4,533	-737	-39	401	-4,518	-365	23,254	3,221
Aug	1,826	25	-6	-7	4,057	2,410	823	6,712	-654	390	-143	711
Sep	-494	5	47	-17	196	1,457	-847	-4,909	4,220	-159	4,913	-1,106
Oct	288	3	-50	-8	-19,554	-19,591	-2	-8,817	-1,815	-203	5,039	-409
Nov	-626	-	-6	-4	-6,266	-2,837	31	6,512	2,433	361	-528	38
Dec	-634	77	7	3	-2,046	-1,412	-22	-2,838	-2,217	-211	2,416	489
2016 Jan	821	68	40	-76	-2,327	-2,519	66	-2,722	2,647	93	9,586	566
Feb	-660	-17	-133	-86	3,178	661	26	5,321	-5,730	30	12,404	-2,539
Mar	-1,777	-3	59	7	1,464	-1,035	-67	2,289	1,662	-42	5,862	272
Apr	-558	32	-	104	3,348	-253	-6	-1,734	3,824	67	-13,432	537

Source: Bank of England

12.3g Monetary financial institutions' (excluding central bank) balance sheet

£ millions Not seasonally adjusted

Changes in sterling assets

RPM	UK government bonds	Other UK public sector	Investments UK MFIs	Other UK residents	Non-residents	Items in suspense and collection	Accrued amounts receivable	Other assets	Total sterling assets
	B4CA	B4IE	B4CC	B4IG	B4JC	B4BJ	B4HI	B4JI	B4AJ
2014 May	691	16	-105	2,330	1,932	-9,032	1,110	-757	14,092
Jun	1,836	-2	918	-95	413	-1,099	-57	11	6,460
Jul	1,930	7	1,437	1,580	609	5,622	-906	-105	-27,480
Aug	-1,080	12	-4,057	-2,824	-2,460	-2,080	1,780	146	17,042
Sep	-4,038	2	322	-824	1,928	9,329	-1,532	-323	-27,678
Oct	6,588	13	776	-6,164	173	-12,409	-293	582	257
Nov	4,431	24	539	-2,688	-2,828	895	1,567	163	12,006
Dec	-3,025	23	971	16,100	1,580	-20,069	-1,732	115	-13,583
2015 Jan	-6,643	-39	1,666	-20,226	-2,035	22,783	-72	145	34,442
Feb	-4,657	-29	1,076	-2,583	2,370	-1,416	664	-182	-12,454
Mar	-2,683	8	390	-4,058	-466	-1,208	-820	391	12,128
Apr	3,111	1	707	-271	1,176	-1,020	-336	399	6,870
May	3,354	8	-83	-417	1,398	1,491	597	36	5,774
Jun	4,532	-5	874	936	1,318	-880	1,072	81	-1,428
Jul	5,130	-35	-1,556	-681	486	268	-1,729	336	24,408
Aug	7,155	14	334	-9,045	-1,699	-2,800	1,691	-181	1,720
Sep	-6,710	13	-802	-296	-2,015	-6,677	-972	470	-25,008
Oct	2,297	-21	346	1,418	369	3,741	472	280	-13,283
Nov	4,507	-10	777	-958	-2,032	2,752	399	124	12,320
Dec	-6,764	-4	1,755	2,130	-2,886	-20,058	-805	-398	-26,368
2016 Jan	-2,527	57	-107	-1,468	-448	33,993	380	61	27,045
Feb	2,730	25	-1,759	-39	-742	-13,282	891	36	-2,817
Mar	591	-24	-920	-485	555	-2,859	-804	366	6,137
Apr	3,272	-7	-19	-509	-2,340	6,572	-166	-40	4,644

Notes to table
Explanatory notes to this table can be found on the Bank of England website: http://www.bankofengland.co.uk/mfsd/iadb/notesiadb/MFIs_exICB.htm
Copyright guidance and the related UK Open Government Licence can be viewed here: www.bankofengland.co.uk/Pages/disclaimer.aspx.

Source: Bank of England

12.3h Monetary financial institutions' (excluding central bank) balance sheet

£ millions Not seasonally adjusted

Changes in foreign currency assets (including euro)

| RPM | Loans and advances | | | | | | Claims under sale and repurchase agreements | | | | | Acceptances granted | Total Bills |
| | UK MFIs | of which intragroup banks | UK MFIs' CDs etc. | UK public sector | Other UK residents | Non-residents | UK MFIs | of which intragroup banks | UK public sector | Other UK residents | Non-residents | | |
	B4EB	B8ZR	B4AF	B2VN	B2VT	B2VH	B4FB	B8ZP	B4EG	B4EI	B4FE	B4HM	B4GL
2014 May	-13,642	-10,478	-296	-	-160	27,812	-8,176	-8,320	1,038	-2,240	100	-58	-179
Jun	13,212	12,184	-543	12	-12,465	-17,305	4,295	3,645	-646	-6,242	-9,277	208	-25
Jul	-4,806	-7,072	-589	-24	-3,048	30,962	229	-4,928	29	-1,517	14,431	103	-2,375
Aug	7,505	5,516	-696	7	-5,345	2,092	5,003	8,541	-515	1,932	-345	216	-502
Sep	-1,187	-510	108	-6	4,774	-309	-7,764	-2,864	165	1,974	-11,290	-35	3,411
Oct	-8,864	-7,734	-525	-20	-8,329	-20,486	-3,450	-4,746	600	-1,231	-20,824	-442	-2,280
Nov	1,602	-2,765	233	21	4,620	34,832	-7,870	-6,396	-499	126	-7,926	-257	1,267
Dec	6,247	7,120	-30	-119	3,023	-13,039	-2,859	5,421	-866	-17,598	-3,609	-202	644
2015 Jan	9,455	924	436	-111	6,340	27,365	7,929	4,043	206	5,081	1,474	-80	-558
Feb	13,810	14,543	301	-70	1,495	-20,677	2,934	1,041	-423	8,896	28,398	-47	782
Mar	2,213	-1,685	-165	-13	917	67	961	1,327	1,594	-4,004	-29,229	117	743
Apr	8,147	5,654	298	-110	5,916	39,258	3,691	802	-1,420	5,818	4,271	-69	1,979
May	-1,862	-1,702	-6	-149	-9,129	-41,967	-3,912	-702	599	-12,185	-17,081	-142	-2,959
Jun	-23,945	-15,132	228	-5	11,127	-53,787	685	1,053	-463	-3,678	-5,129	456	376
Jul	-3,148	-3,789	-558	-194	-4,103	4,856	-3,259	-2,952	545	-5,820	-15,031	-112	-1,741
Aug	10,481	4,999	12	-9	1,484	18,270	-1,571	-3,381	-1,306	-133	3,404	474	770
Sep	-10,223	-52	-37	30	-86	-41,653	-2,910	-414	586	-1,066	6,855	50	1,641
Oct	526	1,277	-325	-31	5,334	-9,905	-2,916	-1,640	354	-3,645	-14,655	55	678
Nov	1,814	2,684	-330	-29	-3,941	43,141	3,983	3,944	-680	-212	-3,604	-197	3,390
Dec	-5,076	-1,651	-408	28	-8,924	9,129	-10,693	-6,829	524	-8,080	-6,826	216	1,395
2016 Jan	-8,136	-7,722	-96	56	3,210	10,029	-3,780	-3,778	131	6,624	5,939	-444	-3,606
Feb	7,196	4,306	142	75	10,003	-33,227	-1,247	-1,582	-467	8,394	4,895	-358	843
Mar	-7,077	-4,472	82	-41	-9,638	-22,724	-7,491	-4,943	-880	-7,366	13,870	328	84
Apr	13,121	12,418	8	-38	6,095	-20,793	4,943	946	1,067	6,803	8,161	154	-2,636

Source: Bank of England

12.3h Monetary financial institutions' (excluding central bank) balance sheet

£ millions Not seasonally adjusted

Changes in foreign currency assets (including euro)

RPM	UK government bonds	Other UK public sector	Investments UK MFIs	Other UK residents	Non-residents	Items in suspense and collection	Accrued amounts receivable	Other assets	Total foreign currency assets	Total assets	Holdings of own sterling acceptances	Holdings of own foreign currency acceptances
	B4EA	B4CG	B4AG	B4CI	B4DE	B4JL	B4FL	B4HL	B4IL	B4IM	B3VR	B3XR
2014 May	-	-21	1,355	6	15,486	-38,260	162	-1,387	-18,461	-4,369	-	28
Jun	-11	-21	-479	462	1,886	-25,684	425	439	-51,759	-45,299	-10	-94
Jul	-14	67	-474	-168	-5,840	12,488	-381	-2,405	36,669	9,189	-5	-47
Aug	-18	-8	1,673	-293	-3,706	-16,720	258	453	-9,009	8,032	8	-135
Sep	-17	4	-1,385	-9	8,264	-2,639	-200	-2,829	-8,974	-36,652	22	51
Oct	56	-13	-961	-1,204	6,586	-11,037	-522	-1,118	-74,063	-73,806	-4	-50
Nov	78	-21	826	-106	19,496	-5,970	-848	678	40,279	52,285	17	-4
Dec	13	-	-2,324	-9,974	-13,933	-86,076	-1,547	-755	-143,002	-156,585	-2	11
2015 Jan	-41	-	-676	-1,187	10,452	127,535	-1,283	1,561	193,896	228,338	-34	57
Feb	-39	-	-211	-151	10,538	-6,792	1,073	-1,568	38,248	25,794	-1	-40
Mar	88	-	-720	-684	-8,573	-21,106	222	-142	-57,712	-45,584	8	149
Apr	-5	-	206	-236	-3,780	26,685	626	-1,984	89,293	96,164	-	-228
May	-20	-	-155	-818	-314	-7,662	432	1,577	-95,753	-89,979	-2	-7
Jun	38	-	-796	412	-14,872	-27,764	-1,072	-520	-118,709	-120,137	-17	82
Jul	142	-1	-1,133	-2,166	-10,173	-4,144	-1,394	-2,561	-49,995	-25,587	1	-182
Aug	33	-	529	-1,395	4,390	-21,284	361	1,675	16,183	17,904	22	102
Sep	-40	-	-940	184	-14,684	1,549	-588	-300	-61,631	-86,639	58	-39
Oct	-	-	180	-1,491	19,934	36,233	-59	-1,104	29,163	15,880	11	19
Nov	-3	-	869	-1,297	6,717	-9,107	269	-2,192	38,591	50,911	-7	-12
Dec	1	-	-1,078	-974	-27,029	-88,388	10	-2,609	-148,781	-175,149	2	-109
2016 Jan	-15	-	220	-569	-14,734	104,504	6	-2,526	96,813	123,858	-13	-96
Feb	22	1	-278	113	-33,657	-4,884	-484	3,312	-39,606	-42,423	-20	-114
Mar	77	1	-826	250	-15,822	-2,972	430	940	-58,774	-52,637	-38	20
Apr	119	-1	543	-1,295	17,007	31,941	-690	576	65,085	69,729	1	-147

Source: Bank of England

Notes to table

Explanatory notes to this table can be found on the Bank of England website: http://www.bankofengland.co.uk/mfsd/iadb/notesiadb/MFIs_exlCB.htm

Copyright guidance and the related UK Open Government Licence can be viewed here: www.bankofengland.co.uk/Pages/disclaimer.aspx.

12.4a Industrial analysis of monetary financial institutions' lending to UK residents

£ millions Not seasonally adjusted

Amounts outstanding of lending in sterling

RPM	Agriculture, hunting and forestry	Fishing	Mining and quarrying	Food, beverages and tobacco	Textiles, wearing apparel and leather	Pulp, paper, and printing	Chemicals, pharmaceuticals, rubber and plastics	Manufacturing Non-metallic mineral products and metals	Machinery, equipment and transport equipment	Electrical, medical and optical equipment	Other manufacturing	Total	Electricity, gas steam and air conditioning	Electricity, gas and water supply Water collection and sewerage	Waste management related services and remediation activities	Total
	TBUC	TBUD	TBUE	TBUG	TBUH	TBUI	TBUJ	TBUK	TBUL	TBUM	TBUN	TBUF	TBUO	TBUP	B3F9	B3FN
2014 May	15,124	244	2,594	3,853	537	1,993	2,473	3,470	5,218	1,839	2,432	21,815	7,846	2,660	2,011	12,517
Jun	15,376	252	2,553	3,897	567	2,012	2,719	3,420	4,861	1,836	2,398	21,711	8,018	2,603	1,991	12,612
Jul	15,571	258	2,594	3,967	584	1,841	2,728	3,475	5,185	1,965	2,433	22,178	8,057	2,625	1,936	12,618
Aug	15,692	255	2,607	4,323	576	1,937	2,721	3,492	5,328	1,833	2,443	22,651	7,823	2,672	1,972	12,467
Sep	15,812	254	2,682	4,420	562	1,995	2,768	3,771	5,649	1,875	2,411	23,451	7,857	2,685	1,944	12,486
Oct	16,055	255	2,763	4,461	553	1,982	2,845	3,722	5,887	1,907	2,409	23,767	8,075	2,700	1,973	12,748
Nov	16,212	253	2,704	5,250	540	1,993	2,841	3,532	5,621	1,926	2,478	24,182	7,848	2,606	1,967	12,421
Dec	15,684	244	2,553	4,962	591	2,031	2,811	3,405	5,001	1,774	2,463	23,038	8,767	2,581	1,844	13,192
2015 Jan	15,761	238	2,646	4,533	600	2,070	2,822	3,419	5,116	1,878	2,449	22,888	8,775	2,715	1,908	13,399
Feb	15,884	238	2,609	4,927	616	2,039	2,806	3,514	5,119	1,845	2,522	23,388	8,442	2,886	1,921	13,249
Mar	16,121	240	2,474	4,521	663	1,999	2,848	3,573	5,293	1,869	2,606	23,372	8,576	3,232	2,022	13,831
Apr	16,241	230	2,539	4,704	682	2,038	2,949	3,459	5,136	1,909	2,561	23,440	8,537	2,732	2,041	13,310
May	16,433	235	2,746	4,467	737	2,105	2,895	3,292	5,530	1,960	2,633	23,619	8,521	2,663	2,009	13,193
Jun	16,711	235	1,990	4,498	747	1,995	2,845	3,208	5,362	2,027	2,656	23,339	8,544	2,630	1,996	13,170
Jul	16,938	241	1,942	4,448	720	1,988	2,879	3,206	5,456	2,043	2,697	23,437	8,544	2,649	1,986	13,180
Aug	17,020	243	1,982	4,499	735	2,020	3,039	3,318	5,652	1,965	2,717	23,946	8,002	2,617	2,031	12,650
Sep	17,291	242	1,966	4,502	772	2,023	3,064	3,219	5,743	2,067	2,740	24,130	8,047	2,566	1,988	12,601
Oct	17,519	244	1,921	4,339	766	1,816	3,045	3,335	5,919	2,254	2,834	24,308	8,464	2,504	2,042	13,010
Nov	17,623	239	1,794	4,382	744	1,887	3,230	3,291	5,756	2,261	2,798	24,349	8,369	2,639	2,071	13,080
Dec	17,539	228	1,761	4,429	747	1,816	3,114	3,054	5,600	2,002	2,766	23,529	8,584	2,869	2,051	13,504
2016 Jan	17,435	234	1,840	4,419	729	1,883	3,355	3,062	5,773	1,855	2,640	23,715	8,572	2,969	2,086	13,627
Feb	17,370	229	1,820	4,344	690	1,847	3,242	3,100	5,946	1,872	2,632	23,672	8,930	2,958	2,144	14,032
Mar	17,456	229	1,770	4,382	700	1,844	3,491	3,024	5,807	1,739	2,605	23,592	8,988	3,211	2,093	14,292
Apr	17,446	226	1,711	4,735	700	1,822	3,457	3,083	5,363	1,837	2,589	23,585	9,125	3,359	2,125	14,609

Source: Bank of England

12.4a Industrial analysis of monetary financial institutions' lending to UK residents

£ millions Not seasonally adjusted

Amounts outstanding of lending in sterling

RPM	Development of buildings	Construction					Wholesale and retail trade				Accommodation and food service activities	Transport, storage and communication		
		Construction of commercial buildings	Construction of domestic buildings	Civil Engineering	Other construction activities	Total	Wholesale and retail trade and repair of motor vehicles and motorcycles	Wholesale trade, excluding motor vehicles and motor cycles	Retail trade excluding motor vehicles and motor cycles	Total		Transportation and storage	Information and communication	Total
	B7EB	B3I6	B3LX	B4PK	B4PX	TBUQ	TBUS	TBUT	TBUU	TBUR	TBUV	B5PK	B5PR	TBUW
2014 May	32,036	5,217	4,385	3,074	5,938	50,650	9,556	10,402	16,566	36,523	23,473	12,353	9,356	21,709
Jun	31,861	4,948	3,988	2,548	5,943	49,287	9,749	10,333	16,932	37,015	23,436	12,364	8,713	21,077
Jul	31,490	5,073	4,015	2,835	5,991	49,405	10,087	10,444	16,658	37,189	23,664	12,062	8,438	20,500
Aug	31,392	5,019	4,048	2,997	6,042	49,499	10,576	10,406	17,000 (d)	37,982 (d)	23,377	11,719	8,355	20,074
Sep	31,012	5,067	4,100	2,999	6,011	49,188	9,655	10,094	17,112	36,861	22,871	11,944	8,432	20,377
Oct	30,538	5,072	4,241	3,100	5,896	48,846	9,009	10,436	17,348	36,792	22,903	11,923	8,452	20,374
Nov	30,126	5,106	4,185	2,603	5,579	47,598	9,465	10,568	17,047	37,081	22,189	11,551	8,548	20,099
Dec	28,946	4,614	3,689	2,161	5,443	44,852	9,841	10,005	17,510	37,356	22,196	11,988	8,745	20,733
2015 Jan	19,780 (a)	4,713	4,031	2,376	5,477	36,377 (a)	10,128	10,043	17,869	38,039	22,414	12,063	8,364	20,427
Feb	19,270	4,763	4,158	2,294	5,550	36,035	11,424	10,258	17,128	38,809	22,262	12,263	8,513	20,776
Mar	18,801	4,849	4,320	2,571	5,503	36,044	10,605	10,200	18,336	39,141	21,993	12,503	9,187	21,691
Apr	18,748	4,885	4,440	2,564	5,691	36,328	10,307	10,087	14,632 (e)	35,026 (e)	22,662	12,305	8,922	21,228
May	18,626	4,820	4,554	2,623	5,771	36,395	10,494	10,271	14,531	35,297	22,680	12,120	9,032	21,152
Jun	17,670	4,383	3,992	2,506	5,707	34,258	10,752	10,194	14,574	35,520	21,996	11,959	9,270	21,228
Jul	17,408	4,469	4,225	2,653	5,858	34,612	11,151	10,167	14,657	35,975	22,500	12,188	9,301	21,489
Aug	16,938	4,568	4,387	2,757	5,859	34,509	11,575	10,547	14,509	36,631	22,362	11,946	9,186	21,133
Sep	16,639	4,595	4,468	2,860	5,800	34,363	11,222	10,422	15,011	36,655	21,875	11,701	9,659	21,360
Oct	16,300	4,890	4,412	2,949	5,562	34,113	11,426	10,601	15,322	37,350	21,890	11,895	9,980	21,875
Nov	16,146	5,063	4,677	2,971	5,560	34,417	11,591	10,604	15,256	37,451	22,032	12,028	9,655	21,684
Dec	15,970	4,555	3,935	2,350	5,457	32,269	11,572	10,146	15,021	36,739	22,142	12,142	9,781	21,924
2016 Jan	15,971	4,757	4,221	2,887	5,645	33,481	12,205	10,939	15,176	38,319	22,453	12,351	12,472	24,823
Feb	16,742 (b)	4,454	4,573	3,280	5,555	34,603 (b)	13,360	10,857	15,754	39,971	22,479	12,612	11,339	23,952
Mar	14,967 (c)	4,282	4,655	3,175	5,477	32,556 (c)	12,637	10,518	16,191	39,345	22,600	11,928	8,968	20,896
Apr	14,856	4,322	4,557	3,193	5,503	32,430	12,158	10,571	16,273	39,003	22,803	12,001	8,371	20,373

Source: Bank of England

12.4a Industrial analysis of monetary financial institutions' lending to UK residents

£ millions Not seasonally adjusted

Amounts outstanding of lending in sterling

RPM	Real estate, professional services and support activities				Public administration and defence	Education	Human health and social work	Recreational, personal and community service activities			Financial intermediation (excluding insurance and pension funds)				
	Buying, selling and renting of real estate	Professional, scientific and technical activities	Administrative and support services	Total				Recreational, cultural and sporting activities	Personal and community service activities	Total	Financial leasing corporations	Non-bank credit grantors excluding credit unions and SPVs	Credit unions	Factoring corporations	Mortgage and housing credit corporations excluding SPVs
	TBUY	B6PD	B6PQ	TBUX	TBVD	TBVE	TBVF	TBVH	TBVG	B6PT	TBVJ	TBVK	TBVL	TBVM	TBVN
2014 May	138,201	14,276	19,538	172,015	7,919	10,845	20,133	5,819	3,343	9,162	24,034	12,110	-	4,573	48,960
Jun	137,261	15,502 (k)	19,633	172,397 (k)	7,861	10,865	20,341	5,481	3,355	8,835	24,300	12,260	-	4,733	49,165
Jul	136,158	16,542	19,805	172,505	7,874	10,998	20,289	5,459	3,316	8,775	24,359	12,506	-	4,720	49,997
Aug	135,893	16,902	20,027	172,821	8,979	11,014	20,199	5,436	3,338	8,774	24,207	17,337 (l)	1	4,814	49,136
Sep	134,157	16,437	19,908	170,503	8,031	10,861	19,788	5,423	3,270	8,694	24,281	17,409	1	4,998	48,658
Oct	131,737	16,125	20,118	167,980	8,440	10,918	19,685	5,410	3,223	8,632	24,284	15,655	-	4,820	48,391
Nov	130,514	16,446	20,784	167,744	8,689	10,849	19,736	5,461	3,329	8,790	24,323	15,744	1	5,058	47,938
Dec	128,986 (f)	15,911	19,990	164,887 (f)	8,487	10,966	19,676	5,426	3,245	8,671	24,915	15,479	1	4,864	48,052
2015 Jan	137,300 (g)	16,819	19,953	174,071 (g)	8,588	10,777	19,681	5,298	3,237	8,535	24,877	15,381	1	4,459	48,351
Feb	137,055	17,270	20,019	174,343	8,525	10,857	19,672	5,237	3,271	8,507	25,095	17,021	1	4,710	48,646
Mar	135,998	17,476	19,610	173,084	8,594	10,944	19,818	5,183	3,243	8,426	24,643	17,066	1	4,459	49,340
Apr	136,646 (h)	17,227	19,188	173,061 (h)	8,595	11,027	19,824	5,264	3,246	8,510	24,358	17,194	1	4,465	49,783
May	135,761	16,942	19,226	171,928	8,171	11,014	20,056	5,195	3,255	8,451	24,371	17,319	1	4,858	48,527
Jun	135,118	14,480	18,711	168,309	8,182	11,010	19,921	5,158	3,316	8,473	24,720	18,324	1	4,854	49,489
Jul	134,788	15,353	19,095	169,235	7,928	11,127	19,799	5,058	3,321	8,379	24,908	18,715	1	5,033	50,201
Aug	134,616	15,695	19,474	169,784	8,818	11,156	20,187	4,924	3,306	8,230	24,587	18,696	1	5,425	49,734
Sep	134,284	15,742	19,381	169,408	7,903	10,838	19,981	4,932	3,267	8,199	24,777	19,591	1	5,061	48,669
Oct	133,757	15,696	19,910	169,362	7,917	10,863	19,783	5,165	3,287	8,452	24,861	19,312	1	4,759	49,285
Nov	133,011	15,558	20,364	168,933	7,982	10,785	20,097	5,171	3,323	8,494	24,801	19,245	1	4,882	49,074
Dec	133,825	14,971	20,448	169,244	8,107	10,756	19,851	5,069	3,240	8,309	24,528	19,347	1	4,624	52,488 (n)
2016 Jan	133,281	15,977	20,032	169,289	7,946	10,671	20,211	5,034	3,233	8,267	23,603	18,341 (m)	1	4,559	53,410
Feb	132,844 (i)	16,013	20,651	169,508 (i)	7,973	10,722	20,237	4,982	3,308	8,290	23,477	18,678	1	4,534	53,822
Mar	136,335 (j)	15,789	21,018	173,142 (j)	7,769	10,730	20,229	5,126	3,286	8,412	23,953	19,066	2	5,288	54,677
Apr	135,422	15,500	21,456	172,377	8,088	10,661	19,974	4,998	3,341	8,340	24,145	19,624	1	5,377	49,008

Source: Bank of England

12.4a Industrial analysis of monetary financial institutions' lending to UK residents

£ millions Not seasonally adjusted

Amounts outstanding of lending in sterling

	Investment and unit trusts excluding money market mutual funds	Money market mutual funds	Bank holding companies	Securities dealers	SPVs related to securitisation	Other financial intermediaries	of which intragroup activity	Total	Insurance companies	Pension funds	Total	Fund management activities	Central clearing counterparties	Other auxiliary activities	Total	Total
					Financial intermediation (excluding insurance and pension funds)				Insurance companies & pension funds				Activities auxiliary to financial intermediation — Other			
RPM	TBVO	TBVP	TBVQ	TBVR	B6PY	TBVS	B3U8	TBVI	B3V6	B3W4	TBVT	TBVU	B7FX	B8FD	TBVV	B8FJ
2014 May	4,513	76	34,033	25,930	14,606	72,669	64,987	241,501	8,767	7,251	16,018	52,051	62,578	2,878	65,456	117,507
Jun	4,243	73	32,931	29,491	14,581	68,951	61,265	240,730	7,894	8,499	16,392	56,788	62,981	2,973	65,954	122,742
Jul	4,182	31	32,949	27,450	13,965	69,735	62,493	239,894	7,806	7,981	15,787	58,266	61,572	2,823	64,395	122,661
Aug	4,359	18	32,759	28,141	15,142	68,756	61,153	244,668 (l)	8,862	7,686	16,548	57,475	57,214	2,964	60,178	117,653
Sep	4,561	17	29,461	25,372	15,234	66,238	58,478	236,231	9,932	9,221	19,153	54,436 (s)	64,111	2,935	67,046	121,482 (s)
Oct	4,766	18	30,443	23,684	14,345	62,550	54,966	228,957	9,298	9,849	19,147	55,572	64,097	2,922	67,019	122,591
Nov	4,729	18	19,442	23,179	14,458	63,759	56,133	218,649	9,576	8,735	18,310	59,069	65,451	2,930	68,381	127,450
Dec	4,741	18	18,069	22,498	16,457	59,905	52,339	215,000	9,396	9,473	18,870	61,003	52,526	2,977	55,503	116,506
2015 Jan	3,711	19	18,099	22,508	14,843	60,187	51,496	212,434	11,569	9,693	21,262	64,034	56,724	3,196	59,920	123,954
Feb	3,845	27	18,035	25,378	14,643	59,098	50,735	216,499	10,236	8,894	19,130	61,968	56,939	3,128	60,067	122,035
Mar	4,240	27	18,830	22,876	14,315	66,274	57,814	222,072	11,285	10,477	21,762	68,163 (t)	55,549	3,138	58,687	126,850 (t)
Apr	4,268	38	19,749	22,909	14,420	64,021	55,678	221,206	11,819	9,612	21,431	67,905	55,544	3,297	58,841	126,746
May	4,203	59	19,792	20,906	14,478	64,723	56,029	219,236	11,694	8,298	19,993	69,251	59,484	3,663	63,148	132,399
Jun	4,598	42	19,021	22,669	13,710	62,732	54,510	220,160	9,472	8,735	18,207	69,115	50,974	3,011	53,984	123,099
Jul	4,488	26	25,895	26,934	15,607	63,647	54,823	235,456	9,984	9,104	19,089	69,194	50,367	2,901	53,268	122,462
Aug	5,326	26	18,536	25,606	16,616	63,916	55,150	228,467	9,003	9,374	18,378	68,094	59,759	2,685	62,444	130,538
Sep	6,138	28	18,527	28,584	18,410	61,027	52,346	230,813	6,541	9,960	16,501	72,955	50,434	2,598	53,032	125,987
Oct	6,000	26	19,953 (o)	24,207	18,971	59,410 (r)	50,955	226,786 (o)(r)	5,172	10,952	16,123	70,853 (u)	46,081 (w)	2,810	48,891 (w)	119,744 (u)(w)
Nov	6,401	38	19,901	24,213	17,874	53,157	44,805	219,587	6,987	11,002	17,989	72,481	50,259	2,670	52,929	125,409
Dec	7,152	46	19,360	25,202	19,220 (p)	50,907	43,000	222,874 (n)(p)	5,672	10,463	16,135	74,221	45,326	2,645	47,971	122,191
2016 Jan	8,510	49	19,531	25,197	19,787 (q)	46,637	39,732	219,627 (m)(q)	6,054	11,108	17,162	80,338 (v)	39,274 (x)	2,814	42,088 (v)(x)	122,426 (v)(x)
Feb	8,678	53	20,071	26,491	19,708	47,131	40,218	222,644	6,971	13,158	20,129	89,728	36,301	2,920	39,221	128,948
Mar	9,683	97	19,984	27,885	19,702	43,234	36,330	223,571	7,553	13,120	20,673	92,832	33,196	2,871	36,067	128,899
Apr	9,800	78	20,187	30,378	16,068	40,727	34,171	215,392	6,538	11,321	17,859	90,036	33,343 (y)	3,227	36,569 (y)	126,605 (y)

Source: Bank of England

12.4a Industrial analysis of monetary financial institutions' lending to UK residents

£ millions

Amounts outstanding of lending in sterling

RPM	Total financial and non-financial businesses Z949	Individuals and individual trusts — Lending secured on dwellings inc. bridging finance TBVX	Other loans and advances TBVY	Total TBVW	Total UK residents TBUA
2014 May	779,751	1,052,455	108,749	1,161,203	1,940,954
Jun	783,480 (k)	1,054,852	109,519	1,164,371	1,947,851 (k)
Jul	782,761	1,058,195	109,985	1,168,180	1,950,941
Aug	785,260 (d)(l)	1,060,446	110,293	1,170,739	1,955,999 (d)(l)
Sep	778,725 (s)	1,062,676	112,685 (ad)	1,175,360 (ag)	1,954,085 (s)(ag)
Oct	770,853	1,065,274	114,788 (ae)	1,180,061 (ae)	1,950,915 (ae)
Nov	762,957	1,067,277	115,586	1,182,863	1,945,820
Dec	742,911 (f)	1,068,894	116,615	1,185,509	1,928,420 (f)
2015 Jan	751,491	1,068,314 (z)	115,939	1,184,253 (z)	1,935,745 (z)
Feb	752,828	1,070,289 (aa)	115,256 (af)	1,185,545	1,938,373
Mar	766,457 (t)	1,071,350	116,757	1,188,107	1,954,564 (t)
Apr	761,405 (e)	1,072,741	117,028	1,189,769	1,951,173 (e)
May	762,996	1,074,583	117,200	1,191,783	1,954,779
Jun	745,809	1,078,371	118,274	1,196,644	1,942,453
Jul	763,788	1,082,965	118,908	1,201,873	1,965,661
Aug	766,034	1,086,800	119,447	1,206,247	1,972,281
Sep	760,113	1,090,374	120,075	1,210,449	1,970,562
Oct	751,259 (o)(r)(u)(w)	1,094,581	120,186	1,214,767	1,966,026 (o)(r)(u)(w)
Nov	751,945	1,098,575	121,372	1,219,947	1,971,892
Dec	747,102 (n)(p)	1,105,445 (ab)	122,193	1,227,638 (ab)	1,974,740 (n)(p)(ab)
2016 Jan	751,525 (m)(q)(v)(x)	1,108,163	122,216	1,230,379	1,981,904 (m)(q)(v)(x)
Feb	766,580 (b)(i)	1,109,821	122,735	1,232,556	1,999,136 (b)(i)
Mar	766,163	1,116,906	123,746	1,240,652	2,006,815
Apr	751,483 (y)	1,123,505 (ac)	123,730	1,247,235 (ac)	1,998,717 (y)(ac)

Source: Bank of England

Notes to table

Movements in amounts outstanding can reflect breaks in data series as well as underlying flows. For changes data, users are recommended to refer directly to the appropriate series or data tables.
www.bankofengland.co.uk/statistics/Pages/iadb/notesiadb/Changes_flows_growth_rates.aspx.

(a) Due to improvements in reporting at one institution the amounts outstanding decreased by £9bn. This effect has been adjusted out of the flows for January 2015.
(b) Due to improvements in reporting at one institution, the amounts outstanding increased by £1bn. This effect has been adjusted out of the flows for February 2016.
(c) Due to improvements in reporting at one institution, th   mounts outstanding increased by £1bn. This effect has been adjusted out of the flows for March 2016.
(d) Due to a change in treatment at one institution, the amounts outstanding decreased by £1bn. This effect has been adjusted out of the flows for August 2014.
(e) Due to a change in treatment at one institution, the amounts outstanding decreased by £4bn. This effect has been adjusted out of the flows for April 2015.
(f) Due to a loan transfer by one reporting institution, the amounts outstanding decreased by £1bn. This effect has been adjusted out of the flows for December 2014.
(g) Due to improvements in reporting at one institution the amounts outstanding increased by £9bn. This effect has been adjusted out of the flows for January 2015.
(h) Due to a change in the reporting population, the amounts outstanding increased by £1bn. This effect has been adjusted out of the flows for April 2015.
(i) Due to improvements in reporting at one institution, the amounts outstanding decreased by £1bn. This effect has been adjusted out of the flows for February 2016.
(j) Due to improvements in reporting at one institution, the amounts outstanding increased by £1bn. This effect has been adjusted out of the flows for March 2016.
(k) Due to a change in accounting treatment at one reporting institution, the amounts outstanding increased by £2bn. This effect has been adjusted out of the flows for June 2014.
(l) Due to improvements in reporting at one institution, the amounts outstanding increased by £4bn. This effect has been adjusted out of the flows for August 2014.
(m) Due to improvements in reporting at one reporting institution, the amounts outstanding decreased by £1bn. This effect has been adjusted out of the flows for January 2016.
(n) Due to a restructuring at one reporting institution, the amounts outstanding increased by £4bn. This effect has been adjusted out of the flows for December 2015.
(o) Due to improvements in reporting at one institution, the amounts outstanding increased by £1bn. This effect has been adjusted out of the flows for October 2015.
(p) Due to a restructuring at one reporting institution, the amounts outstanding decreased by £4bn. This effect has been adjusted out of the flows for December 2015.
(q) Due to improvements in reporting at one institution, the amounts outstanding increased by £1bn. This effect has been adjusted out of the flows for January 2016.
(r) Due to improvements in reporting at one institution, the amounts outstanding decreased by £1bn. This effect has been adjusted out of the flows for October 2015.
(s) Due to improvements in reporting at one institution, the amounts outstanding increased by £1bn. This effect has been adjusted out of the flows for September 2014.
(t) Due to improvements in reporting at one institution, the amounts outstanding increased by £2bn. This effect has been adjusted out of the flows for March 2015.
(u) Due to a change in the reporting population, the amounts outstanding decreased by £2bn. This effect has been adjusted out of the flows for October 2015.
(v) Due to a change in the reporting population, the amounts outstanding increased by £3bn. This effect has been adjusted out of the flows for January 2016.
(w) Due to a change in the reporting population, the amounts outstanding increased by £3bn. This effect has been adjusted out of the flows for October 2015.
(x) Due to a change in the reporting population, the amounts outstanding decreased by £4bn. This effect has been adjusted out of the flows for January 2016.
(y) Due to improvements in reporting at one institution, the amounts outstanding increased by £2bn. This effect has been adjusted out of the flows for April 2016.
(z) Due to a loan transfer by one reporting institution, the amounts outstanding decreased by £2bn. This effect has been adjusted out of the flows for January 2015.
(aa) Due to improvements in reporting at one institution, the amounts outstanding increased by £1bn. This effect has been adjusted out of the flows for February 2015.
(ab) Due to a loan transfer by one reporting institution, the amounts outstanding increased by £3bn. This effect has been adjusted out of the flows for December 2015.
(ac) Due to a loan transfer by one reporting institution, the amounts outstanding increased by £7bn. This effect has been adjusted out of the flows for April 2016.
(ad) Due to a change in the reporting population, the amounts outstanding increased by £2bn. This effect has been adjusted out of the flows for September 2014.
(ae) Due to a loan transfer by one reporting institution, the amounts outstanding increased by £2bn. This effect has been adjusted out of the flows for October 2014.
(af) Due to improvements in reporting at one institution, the amounts outstanding increased by £1bn. This effect has been adjusted out of the flows for February 2015.
(ag) Due to a change in the reporting population, the amounts outstanding increased by £2bn. This effect has been adjusted out of the flows for September 2014.

12.4b Industrial analysis of monetary financial institutions' lending to UK residents

£ millions   Not seasonally adjusted

Amounts outstanding of lending in all currencies

RPM	Agriculture, hunting and forestry	Fishing	Mining and quarrying	Manufacturing									Electricity, gas and water supply			
				Food, beverages and tobacco	Textiles, wearing apparel and leather	Pulp, paper and printing	Chemicals, pharmaceuticals, rubber and plastics	Non-metallic mineral products and metals	Machinery, equipment and transport equipment	Electrical, medical and optical equipment	Other manufacturing	Total	Electricity, gas steam and air conditioning	Water collection and sewerage	Waste management related services and remediation activities	Total
	TBSC	TBSD	TBSE	TBSG	TBSH	TBSI	TBSJ	TBSK	TBSL	TBSM	TBSN	TBSF	TBSO	TBSP	B3FA	B3FO
2014 May	15,386	248	5,366	4,758	881	2,599	5,281	4,878	7,633	2,837	3,685	32,552	8,620	2,679	2,084	13,383
Jun	15,625	256	5,512	4,783	909	2,626	5,445	4,812	7,401	2,944	3,512	32,432	8,693	2,622	2,012	13,327
Jul	15,779	262	5,403	4,978	985	2,681	5,432	4,841	7,620	2,976	3,560	33,073	8,818	2,643	1,971	13,432
Aug	15,901	258	5,286	5,216	981	2,771	5,475	4,911	7,587	2,850	3,576	33,367	8,556	2,690	2,034	13,280
Sep	16,028	257	5,832	5,505	997	2,704	5,720	5,245	8,564	2,876	3,428	35,038	8,496	2,702	1,984	13,183
Oct	16,289	258	5,980	5,593	994	2,502	5,691	5,325	8,599	2,884	3,435	35,024	8,617	2,718	2,000	13,334
Nov	16,467	257	6,008	6,446	976	2,697	5,730	5,369	8,254	2,879	3,419	35,767	8,434	2,623	2,026	13,084
Dec	15,909	247	5,877	6,439	995	2,776	5,641	5,266	7,768	2,760	3,404	35,049	9,304	2,595	1,855	13,754
2015 Jan	15,997	242	6,338	5,813	1,039	2,813	5,593	5,191	8,026	2,879	3,541	34,894	9,289	2,717	2,036	14,042
Feb	16,117	242	6,314	6,290	1,044	2,763	5,767	5,291	7,935	2,787	3,553	35,430	8,935	2,887	1,974	13,796
Mar	16,408	244	6,910	5,796	1,124	2,672	5,822	5,368	8,261	2,840	3,668	35,550	9,143	3,234	2,063	14,439
Apr	16,548	234	6,713	5,702	1,069	2,566	5,838	5,157	7,931	2,834	3,543	34,640	9,082	2,734	2,124	13,940
May	16,723	239	7,064	5,389	1,115	2,802	5,898	5,260	8,249	2,918	3,675	35,306	8,984	2,664	2,094	13,743
Jun	16,886	239	6,718	7,688	1,114	2,770	5,897	5,019	8,219	3,004	3,542	37,253	8,980	2,631	2,075	13,685
Jul	17,116	244	6,355	6,050	1,129	2,829	5,854	4,984	8,200	2,960	3,640	35,646	8,997	2,650	2,007	13,654
Aug	17,227	246	6,579	6,173	1,163	2,859	6,222	5,165	8,621	2,974	3,675	36,853	8,525	2,617	2,074	13,216
Sep	17,486	246	6,982	6,249	1,214	2,549	5,855	5,067	8,926	3,115	3,525	36,499	8,539	2,567	2,021	13,127
Oct	17,709	248	6,859	5,650	1,204	2,197	5,803	5,127	9,089	3,356	3,678	36,104	9,019	2,504	2,093	13,615
Nov	17,812	243	6,362	5,790	1,154	2,331	6,021	4,940	9,270	3,469	3,633	36,607	9,020	2,639	2,146	13,805
Dec	17,752	232	6,416	5,974	1,140	2,321	5,783	4,714	8,715	3,053	3,489	35,189	9,213	2,869	2,125	14,207
2016 Jan	17,653	259	6,229	5,941	1,167	2,421	5,874	4,746	8,849	2,881	3,635	35,513	9,499	2,969	2,192	14,660
Feb	17,558	253	6,512	5,973	1,105	2,421	6,241	4,937	8,778	2,972	3,746	36,172	9,922	2,960	2,247	15,129
Mar	17,657	254	6,465	5,877	1,152	2,388	6,539	4,878	8,563	2,731	3,966	36,095	9,898	3,211	2,326	15,436
Apr	17,647	248	6,213	6,489	1,113	2,275	6,594	4,867	7,986	2,896	4,028	36,246	9,991	3,359	2,319	15,669

Source: Bank of England

12.4b Industrial analysis of monetary financial institutions' lending to UK residents

£ millions   Not seasonally adjusted

Amounts outstanding of lending in all currencies

| | Development of buildings | Construction | | | | | Wholesale and retail trade | | | | Accommodation and food service activities | Transport, storage and communication | | |
| | | Construction of commercial buildings | Construction of domestic buildings | Civil Engineering | Other construction activities | Total | Wholesale and retail trade and repair of motor vehicles and motorcycles | Wholesale trade, excluding motor vehicles and motor cycles | Retail trade excluding motor vehicles and motor cycles | Total | | Transportation and storage | Information and communication | Total |
RPM	B7EC	B3I7	B3LY	B4PL	B4PY	TBSQ	TBSS	TBST	TBSU	TBSR	TBSV	B5PL	B5PS	TBSW
2014 May	32,335	5,281	4,385	3,239	6,082	51,322	10,162	13,682	17,960	41,803	23,796	15,733	12,219	27,951
Jun	32,139	5,011	3,988	2,715	6,086	49,940	10,256	13,637	18,351	42,244	23,850	15,412	11,017	26,429
Jul	31,763	5,136	4,015	3,137	6,116	50,167	10,531	13,784	18,182	42,497	24,156	15,159	11,249	26,408
Aug	31,688	5,083	4,049	3,286	6,175	50,280	10,991	14,164	18,431 (au)	43,586 (au)	23,951	14,946	11,220	26,166
Sep	31,309	5,126	4,100	3,267	6,136	49,940	10,056	14,327	18,554	42,936	23,459	15,040	11,595	26,635
Oct	30,852	5,133	4,241	3,271	6,020	49,517	9,431	14,759	18,948	43,138	23,413	15,175	12,101	27,276
Nov	30,427	5,169	4,185	2,929	5,701	48,411	9,914	15,177	18,580	43,671	22,728	14,814	12,374	27,187
Dec	29,130	4,669	3,689	2,456	5,599	45,543	10,426	14,398	19,119	43,942	22,751	15,223	12,587	27,810
2015 Jan	19,957 (ar)	4,779	4,032	2,667	5,642	37,076 (ar)	10,663	14,006	19,160	43,829	23,007	15,486	12,527	28,013
Feb	19,440	4,827	4,159	2,588	5,665	36,678	11,909	13,982	18,431	44,322	22,835	15,439	12,635	28,074
Mar	18,965	4,906	4,320	2,876	5,615	36,683	11,121	14,456	19,862	45,439	22,547	15,309	13,365	28,673
Apr	18,908	4,954	4,440	2,863	5,821	36,985	10,923	14,385	15,907 (av)	41,215 (av)	23,246	15,172	13,672	28,844
May	18,783	4,895	4,554	2,920	5,893	37,045	11,088	14,546	15,888	41,522	23,114	14,950	13,536	28,486
Jun	17,817	4,440	3,996	2,943	5,791	34,987	11,250	14,488	15,918	41,656	22,386	14,526	13,394	27,920
Jul	17,554	4,532	4,229	3,101	5,939	35,355	11,628	14,091	16,031	41,750	22,820	14,738	13,930	28,669
Aug	17,088	4,635	4,434	3,093	5,946	35,196	12,187	14,553	15,896	42,636	22,784	14,731	13,821	28,552
Sep	16,811	4,662	4,476	3,326	5,910	35,184	11,899	14,312	16,422	42,633	22,316	14,327	13,898	28,225
Oct	16,453	4,956	4,415	3,272	5,677	34,774	12,009	14,771	16,614	43,394	22,331	14,512	14,293	28,805
Nov	16,321	5,130	4,681	3,296	5,677	35,105	12,172	14,589	16,584	43,344	22,487	14,416	13,709	28,125
Dec	16,154	4,629	3,939	2,683	5,570	32,974	12,138	14,515	16,381	43,034	22,539	14,903	14,142	29,044
2016 Jan	16,164	4,838	4,225	3,230	5,764	34,222	12,828	15,019	16,666	44,513	22,798	15,412	17,197	32,610
Feb	16,909 (as)	4,549	4,578	3,627	5,681	35,344 (as)	13,995	15,145	17,537	46,678	22,832	16,400	15,812	32,212
Mar	15,097 (at)	4,382	4,660	3,537	5,600	33,276 (at)	13,288	14,741	18,145	46,173	22,986	15,414	13,418	28,832
Apr	14,986	4,426	4,561	3,567	5,625	33,166	12,911	14,622	18,469	46,001	23,148	15,457	12,105	27,562

Source: Bank of England

12.4b Industrial analysis of monetary financial institutions' lending to UK residents

£ millions   Not seasonally adjusted

Amounts outstanding of lending in all currencies

	Buying, selling and renting of real estate	Real estate, professional services and support activities			Public administration and defence	Education	Human health and social work	Recreational, personal and community service activities			Financial intermediation (excluding insurance and pension funds)				
		Professional, scientific and technical activities	Administrative and support services	Total				Recreational, cultural and sporting activities	Personal and community service activities	Total	Financial leasing corporations	Non-bank credit grantors excluding credit unions and SPVs	Credit unions	Factoring corporations	Mortgage and housing credit corporations excluding SPVs
RPM	TBSY	B6PE	B6PP	TBSX	TBTD	TBTE	TBTF	TBTH	TBTG	B6H5	TBTJ	TBTK	TBTL	TBTM	TBTN
2014 May	139,304	16,764	23,218	179,287	11,035	10,890	20,273	6,205	3,435	9,640	28,077	12,261	1	4,934	49,340
Jun	138,325	18,452 (bb)	23,302	180,078 (bb)	10,288	10,917	20,486	5,818	3,442	9,261	27,880	12,450	1	5,208	49,542
Jul	137,224	19,991	23,651	180,865	10,322	11,045	20,438	5,793	3,417	9,210	28,043	12,687	1	5,100	50,364
Aug	137,112	20,320	23,862	181,294	10,930	11,058	20,366	5,567	3,439	9,006	28,461	17,528 (bc)	1	5,210	49,493
Sep	135,341	19,432	23,803	178,577	10,143	10,904	19,998	5,547	3,371	8,918	28,607	17,636	1	5,454	49,073
Oct	132,950	19,146	23,495	175,590	12,406	10,962	19,894	5,541	3,343	8,883	28,591	15,889	1	5,234	48,824
Nov	131,562	20,158	24,187	175,907	12,271	10,892	19,942	5,595	3,482	9,076	28,716	15,979	1	5,557	48,287
Dec	129,844 (aw)	19,991	23,316	173,150 (aw)	11,033	11,017	19,873	5,551	3,369	8,919	28,830	15,768	1	5,299	48,251
2015 Jan	138,200 (ax)	20,794	23,278	182,272 (ax)	11,184	10,816	19,886	5,439	3,363	8,802	28,773	15,675	1	4,881	48,549
Feb	138,004	21,226	23,199	182,429	10,553	10,892	19,853	5,376	3,389	8,765	28,960	17,350	1	5,112	48,845
Mar	137,008	21,819	22,625	181,451	12,191	10,988	20,018	5,563	3,328	8,891	28,431	17,375	1	4,879	50,134
Apr	137,738 (ay)	21,526	22,011	181,275 (ay)	10,687	11,075	20,029	5,628	3,333	8,961	27,933	17,601	1	4,841	50,567
May	136,865	21,244	22,301	180,410	10,692	11,063	20,255	5,610	3,338	8,947	27,891	17,572	1	5,242	49,283
Jun	136,192	17,696	21,810	175,697	10,207	11,062	20,118	5,511	3,433	8,944	28,206	18,554	1	5,466	50,242
Jul	135,886	18,619	22,396	176,902	10,314	11,167	19,996	5,394	3,427	8,821	28,535	18,936	1	5,490	51,018
Aug	135,766	19,009	22,744	177,518	9,900	11,194	20,398	5,255	3,408	8,664	28,390	19,026	1	5,850	50,537
Sep	135,552	19,184	23,071	177,807	9,633	10,867	20,196	5,368	3,346	8,714	28,519	19,910	1	5,557	49,448
Oct	135,765	19,151	23,378	178,294	9,934	10,880	19,975	5,614	3,365	8,979	29,340	19,619	1	5,214	50,029
Nov	134,877	18,914	23,970	177,761	9,299	10,802	20,265	5,657	3,395	9,052	29,368	19,536	1	5,330	49,862
Dec	135,684	18,446	23,821	177,951	9,986	10,773	19,960	5,612	3,314	8,926	29,233	19,556	1	5,063	53,415 (be)
2016 Jan	135,168	19,565	23,494	178,226	10,125	10,689	20,330	5,598	3,309	8,907	28,376	18,651 (bd)	1	5,020	54,374
Feb	134,299 (az)	19,426	24,520	178,245 (az)	9,781	10,742	20,363	5,577	3,391	8,969	28,563	18,999	1	4,956	54,865
Mar	137,403 (ba)	19,353	25,134	181,891 (ba)	8,657	10,754	20,391	5,695	3,382	9,077	28,875	19,347	4	5,784	55,731
Apr	136,234	19,020	25,694	180,949	9,943	10,699	20,127	5,494	3,426	8,920	28,994	19,921	1	5,852	49,990

Source: Bank of England

12.4b Industrial analysis of monetary financial institutions' lending to UK residents

£ millions   Not seasonally adjusted

Amounts outstanding of lending in all currencies

	Financial intermediation (excluding insurance and pension funds)								Insurance companies & pension funds		
	Investment and unit trusts excluding money market mutual funds	Money market mutual funds	Bank holding companies	Securities dealers	SPVs related to securitisation	Other financial intermediaries	of which intragroup activity	Total	Insurance companies	Pension funds	Total
RPM	TBTO	TBTP	TBTQ	TBTR	B6PZ	TBTS	B3U9	TBTI	B3V7	B3W5	TBTT
2014 May	9,679	118	44,296	142,793	16,036	121,703	106,404	429,239	11,121	7,679	18,800
Jun	7,939	111	42,616	147,038	15,992	106,993	91,051	415,770	10,301	8,997	19,297
Jul	8,116	37	41,687	142,748	14,894	107,756	92,213	411,434	10,363	8,675	19,038
Aug	7,771	22	41,749	133,473	16,088	107,181	91,251	406,977 (bc)	11,986	8,468	20,454
Sep	8,735	17	38,283	134,047	17,308	104,498	88,807	403,658	12,900	10,540	23,439
Oct	9,071	18	39,448	132,475	15,735	101,792	86,211	397,077	12,495	10,723	23,218
Nov	9,375	18	28,023	134,762	15,860	102,115	87,474	388,694	13,339	9,728	23,067
Dec	9,735	18	27,156	128,568	17,793	98,143	83,678	379,561	13,154	10,484	23,638
2015 Jan	7,379 (bf)	58	27,285	136,980	16,106	97,343	81,328	383,030 (bf)	15,961	11,085	27,046
Feb	8,057	77	26,675	140,078	15,846	96,202	80,766	387,203	15,140	10,431	25,571
Mar	8,445	98	26,914	142,655	15,562	100,021	84,832	394,515	16,460	11,681	28,141
Apr	9,074	186	30,910	142,526	15,627	97,880	82,724	397,144	18,312	10,935	29,247
May	8,658	114	27,669 (bg)	126,953	15,719	97,135	81,741	376,239 (bg)	17,608	9,458	27,065
Jun	8,694	43	27,177	125,496	14,761	95,899	80,218	374,538	14,996	9,833	24,829
Jul	7,901	26	35,757	122,847	16,693	96,224	80,541	383,427	15,659	9,942	25,601
Aug	9,527	26	27,010	122,309	17,806	97,621	82,050	378,104	14,672	10,184	24,857
Sep	10,166	29	26,778	132,118	19,687	96,227	79,333	388,440	12,880	10,808	23,688
Oct	9,811	28	28,399 (bh)	118,976	20,124	93,884 (bk)	78,081	375,425 (bh)(bk)	11,084	12,621	23,705
Nov	10,326	38	28,831	115,982	19,028	87,677	72,354	365,979	12,704	12,399	25,103
Dec	11,602	70	29,608	112,357	21,295 (bi)	85,901	70,198	368,101 (be)(bi)	10,973	11,734	22,706
2016 Jan	13,530	76	30,252	117,325	20,453 (bj)	83,373	67,685	371,432 (bd)(bj)	11,857	12,158	24,015
Feb	13,320	77	31,706	125,172	20,443	85,483	69,860	383,585	14,298	14,388	28,686
Mar	14,226	163	31,074	117,994	20,470	78,936	63,819	372,604	14,930	14,144	29,074
Apr	14,322	130	30,849	129,734	16,850	82,810 (bl)(bm)	67,757 (bl)(bm)	379,452 (bl)(bm)	13,589	12,146	25,735

Source: Bank of England

12.4b Industrial analysis of monetary financial institutions' lending to UK residents

£ millions   Not seasonally adjusted

Amounts outstanding of lending in all currencies

RPM	Fund management activities	Activities auxiliary to financial intermediation				Total financial and non-financial businesses	Individuals and individual trusts			Total UK residents
		Central clearing counterparties	Other				Lending secured on dwellings inc. bridging finance	Other loans and advances	Total	
			Other auxiliary activities	Total	Total					
	TBTU	B3X2	B8FE	TBTV	B5H8	Z92T	TBTX	TBTY	TBTW	TBSA
2014 May	107,870	145,466	9,393	154,859	262,729	1,153,700	1,052,982	110,074	1,163,057	2,316,757
Jun	110,012	137,408	9,575	146,983	256,995	1,132,706 (bb)	1,055,361	110,868	1,166,230	2,298,935 (bb)
Jul	108,181	136,692	10,170	146,862	255,042	1,128,572	1,058,682	111,329	1,170,010	2,298,583
Aug	113,319	133,848	10,567	144,415	257,734	1,129,894 (au)(bc)	1,060,928	111,646	1,172,574	2,302,468 (au)(bc)
Sep	111,979 (bn)	138,614	10,801	149,415	261,394 (bn)	1,130,339 (bn)	1,063,163	114,061 (cd)	1,177,224 (cg)	2,307,563 (bn)(cg)
Oct	102,795	140,126	10,982	151,107	253,902	1,116,160	1,065,770	116,199 (ce)	1,181,969 (ce)	2,298,129 (ce)
Nov	111,306	140,795	11,912	152,707	264,013	1,117,443	1,067,783	117,026	1,184,809	2,302,252
Dec	110,496	118,290	12,202	130,493	240,989	1,079,062 (aw)	1,069,391	118,020	1,187,412	2,266,473 (aw)
2015 Jan	115,774 (bo)	126,346	12,758	139,104	254,878 (bo)	1,101,351	1,068,790 (bz)	117,340	1,186,130 (bz)	2,287,481 (bz)
Feb	113,350	127,000	12,455	139,456	252,805	1,101,880	1,070,509 (ca)	116,590 (cf)	1,187,098	2,288,979
Mar	125,233 (bp)	120,069	12,600	132,669	257,902 (bp)	1,120,991 (bp)	1,071,564	118,147	1,189,710	2,310,702 (bp)
Apr	124,784	123,550	12,442	135,992	260,776	1,121,558 (av)	1,072,934	118,405	1,191,339	2,312,896 (av)
May	124,129 (bq)	124,244	13,151	137,395	261,525 (bq)	1,099,437 (bg)(bq)	1,074,775	118,563	1,193,338	2,292,775 (bg)(bq)
Jun	139,591	102,980	12,919	115,899	255,490	1,082,616	1,078,553	119,604	1,198,157	2,280,773
Jul	139,889	100,968	13,494	114,462	254,351	1,092,189	1,083,143	120,226	1,203,369	2,295,558
Aug	140,596	113,627	13,774	127,401	267,997	1,101,921	1,086,972	120,792	1,207,764	2,309,685
Sep	143,201	101,707	12,556	114,263	257,465	1,099,510	1,090,549	121,431	1,211,980	2,311,489
Oct	146,772 (br)	94,626 (bt)	12,406	107,032 (bt)	253,804 (br)(bt)	1,084,837 (bh)(bk)(br)(bt)	1,094,753	121,507	1,216,260	2,301,097 (bh)(bk)(br)(bt)
Nov	143,672	99,859 (bu)	15,195 (bw)	115,054	258,726	1,080,877	1,098,747	122,698	1,221,445	2,302,322
Dec	138,054	95,503	15,511	111,014	249,068	1,068,859 (be)(bi)	1,105,593 (cb)	123,616	1,229,210 (cb)	2,298,068 (be)(bi)(cb)
2016 Jan	152,697 (bs)	94,171 (bv)	16,875	111,046 (bv)	263,743 (bs)(bv)	1,095,922 (bd)(bj)(bs)(bv)	1,108,314	122,974	1,231,288	2,327,210 (bd)(bj)(bs)(bv)
Feb	167,129	99,320	17,398	116,718	283,847	1,136,906 (as)(az)	1,109,972	123,552	1,233,524	2,370,430 (as)(az)
Mar	167,690	90,045	17,072	107,117	274,806	1,114,426	1,117,055	124,621	1,241,676	2,356,102
Apr	165,186	90,561 (bm)	11,682 (bx)(by)	102,243 (bm)(bx)(by)	267,429 (bx)(by)	1,109,154 (bl)(bm)(bx)(by)	1,123,648 (cc)	124,599	1,248,247 (cc)	2,357,401 (bl)(bm)(bx)(by)(cc)

Source: Bank of England

12.4b Industrial analysis of monetary financial institutions' lending to UK residents

£ millions   Not seasonally adjusted

Notes to table

Movements in amounts outstanding can reflect breaks in data series as well as underlying flows. For changes data, users are recommended to refer directly to the appropriate series or data tables. Further explanation can be found at: www.bankofengland.co.uk/statistics/Pages/iadb/notesiadb/Changes_flows_growth_rates.aspx.

(ar) Due to improvements in reporting at one institution the amounts outstanding decreased by £9bn. This effect has been adjusted out of the flows for January 2015.

(as) Due to improvements in reporting at one institution, the amounts outstanding increased by £1bn. This effect has been adjusted out of the flows for February 2016.

(at) Due to improvements in reporting at one institution, the amounts outstanding decreased by £1bn. This effect has been adjusted out of the flows for March 2016.

(au) Due to a change in treatment at one institution, the amounts outstanding increased by £1bn. This effect has been adjusted out of the flows for August 2014.

(av) Due to a change in treatment at one institution, the amounts outstanding decreased by £4bn. This effect has been adjusted out of the flows for April 2015.

(aw) Due to a loan transfer by one reporting institution, the amounts outstanding decreased by £1bn. This effect has been adjusted out of the flows for December 2014.

(ax) Due to improvements in reporting at one institution the amounts outstanding increased by £9bn. This effect has been adjusted out of the flows for January 2015.

(ay) Due to a change in the reporting population, the amounts outstanding increased by £1bn. This effect has been adjusted out of the flows for April 2015.

(az) Due to improvements in reporting at one institution, the amounts outstanding decreased by £1bn. This effect has been adjusted out of the flows for February 2016.

(ba) Due to improvements in reporting at one institution, the amounts outstanding increased by £1bn. This effect has been adjusted out of the flows for March 2016.

(bb) Due to a change in accounting treatment at one reporting institution, the amounts outstanding increased by £2bn. This effect has been adjusted out of the flows for June 2014.

(bc) Due to improvements in reporting at one institution, the amounts outstanding increased by £4bn. This effect has been adjusted out of the flows for August 2014.

(bd) Due to improvements in reporting at one institution, the amounts outstanding decreased by £1bn. This effect has been adjusted out of the flows for January 2016.

(be) Due to a restructuring at one reporting institution, the amounts outstanding increased by £4bn. This effect has been adjusted out of the flows for December 2015.

(bf) Due to improvements in reporting at one reporting institution, the amounts outstanding decreased by £2bn. This effect has been adjusted out of the flows for January 2015.

(bg) Due to improvements in reporting at one institution, the amounts outstanding decreased by £2bn. This effect has been adjusted out of the flows for May 2015.

(bh) Due to improvements in reporting at one institution, the amounts outstanding increased by £1bn. This effect has been adjusted out of the flows for October 2015.

(bi) Due to a restructuring at one reporting institution, the amounts outstanding decreased by £4bn. This effect has been adjusted out of the flows for December 2015.

(bj) Due to improvements in reporting at one institution, the amounts outstanding increased by £1bn. This effect has been adjusted out of the flows for January 2016.

(bk) Due to improvements in reporting at one institution, the amounts outstanding decreased by £1bn. This effect has been adjusted out of the flows for October 2015.

(bl) Due to improvements in reporting at one institution, the amounts outstanding increased by £4bn. This effect has been adjusted out of the flows for April 2016.

(bm) Due to improvements in reporting at one institution, the amounts outstanding increased by £1bn. This effect has been adjusted out of the flows for April 2016.

(bn) Due to improvements in reporting at one institution, the amounts outstanding increased by £1bn. This effect has been adjusted out of the flows for September 2014.

(bo) Due to improvements in reporting at one reporting institution, the amounts outstanding increased by £2bn. This effect has been adjusted out of the flows for January 2015.

(bp) Due to improvements in reporting at one institution, the amounts outstanding increased by £2bn. This effect has been adjusted out of the flows for March 2015.

(bq) Due to improvements in reporting at one institution, the amounts outstanding increased by £2bn. This effect has been adjusted out of the flows for May 2015.

(br) Due to a change in the reporting population, the amounts outstanding decreased by £2bn. This effect has been adjusted out of the flows for October 2015.

(bs) Due to a change in the reporting population, the amounts outstanding increased by £3bn. This effect has been adjusted out of the flows for January 2016.

(bt) Due to a change in the reporting population, the amounts outstanding increased by £3bn. This effect has been adjusted out of the flows for October 2015.

(bu) Due to changes in reporting at one institution, the amounts outstanding decreased by £2bn. This effect has been adjusted out of the flows for November 2015.

(bv) Due to a change in the reporting population, the amounts outstanding decreased by £4bn. This effect has been adjusted out of the flows for January 2016.

(bw) Due to changes in reporting at one institution, the amounts outstanding increased by £2bn. This effect has been adjusted out of the flows for November 2015.

(bx) Due to improvements in reporting at one institution, the amounts outstanding decreased by £1bn. This effect has been adjusted out of the flows for April 2016.

(by) Due to improvements in reporting at one institution, the amounts outstanding decreased by £4bn. This effect has been adjusted out of the flows for April 2016.

(bz) Due to a loan transfer by one reporting institution, the amounts outstanding decreased by £2bn. This effect has been adjusted out of the flows for January 2015.

(ca) Due to improvements in reporting at one institution, the amounts outstanding increased by £1bn. This effect has been adjusted out of the flows for February 2015.

(cb) Due to a loan transfer by one reporting institution, the amounts outstanding increased by £3bn. This effect has been adjusted out of the flows for December 2015.

(cc) Due to a loan transfer by one reporting institution, the amounts outstanding increased by £7bn. This effect has been adjusted out of the flows for April 2016.

(cd) Due to a change in the reporting population, the amounts outstanding increased by £2bn. This effect has been adjusted out of the flows for September 2014.

(ce) Due to a loan transfer by one reporting institution, the amounts outstanding increased by £2bn. This effect has been adjusted out of the flows for October 2014.

(cf) Due to improvements in reporting at one institution, the amounts outstanding decreased by £1bn. This effect has been adjusted out of the flows for February 2015.

(cg) Due to a change in the reporting population, the amounts outstanding increased by £2bn. This effect has been adjusted out of the flows for September 2014.

12.4c Industrial analysis of monetary financial institutions' lending to UK residents

£ millions   Not seasonally adjusted

Amounts outstanding of facilities granted in sterling

| RPM | Agriculture, hunting and forestry | Fishing | Mining and quarrying | Manufacturing | | | | | | | | Total | Electricity, gas and water supply | | | Total |
| | | | | Food, beverages and tobacco | Textiles, wearing apparel and leather | Pulp, paper, and printing | Chemicals, pharmaceuticals, rubber and plastics | Non-metallic mineral products and metals | Machinery, equipment and transport equipment | Electrical, medical and optical equipment | Other manufacturing | | Electricity, gas steam and air conditioning | Water collection and sewerage | Waste management related services and remediation activities | |
	TCCC	TCCD	TCCE	TCCG	TCCH	TCCI	TCCJ	TCCK	TCCL	TCCM	TCCN	TCCF	TCCO	TCCP	B3FE	B3FS
2014 May	18,031	287	3,822	6,957	793	2,656	6,650	5,131	9,334	3,026	3,542	38,088	12,362	5,615	2,872	20,850
Jun	18,356	280	3,813	7,485	842	2,677	6,947	5,190	8,990	3,096	3,583	38,811	13,326	5,865	2,838	22,029
Jul	18,287	293	3,690	7,752	857	2,396	7,077	5,195	9,270	3,192	3,695	39,434	13,304	5,927	2,676	21,907
Aug	18,541	291	3,687	7,824	854	2,466	7,025	5,339	9,436	3,063	3,744	39,752	13,136	5,940	2,666	21,742
Sep	18,537	289	3,706	7,850	875	2,670	7,132	5,625	9,865	3,059	3,747	40,824	13,339	5,841	2,665	21,845
Oct	18,736	291	3,847	7,902	828	2,832	7,207	5,742	10,131	3,027	3,634	41,303	13,436	5,968	2,692	22,096
Nov	18,890	288	3,783	8,640	824	2,731	7,254	5,530	9,853	3,040	3,759	41,630	13,099	5,778	2,716	21,594
Dec	18,900	284	3,722	8,336	882	2,737	7,242	5,347	9,568	3,001	3,839	40,951	13,755	6,078	2,681	22,515
2015 Jan	18,880	279	3,766	8,021	896	2,757	7,243	5,255	9,561	2,998	3,810	40,542	13,610	5,996	2,630	22,236
Feb	18,921	277	3,786	8,233	905	2,724	7,036	5,407	9,650	2,954	3,888	40,797	13,646	6,234	2,662	22,542
Mar	18,988	280	3,606	8,064	990	2,800	7,197	5,497	9,709	3,040	3,930	41,228	13,735	6,502	2,775	23,013
Apr	22,662 (ch)	285	3,706	8,823	1,047	3,094	7,444	5,639	10,196	3,113	3,925	43,282	13,914	6,484	2,911	23,308
May	22,853	284	8,077	8,748	1,106	3,004	7,361	5,282	10,799	3,219	3,910	43,429	13,962	6,393	2,790	23,146
Jun	23,108	303	7,240	8,771	1,122	2,896	6,836	5,262	10,524	3,352	3,950	42,714	13,982	6,242	2,815	23,040
Jul	23,391	307	7,162	8,656	1,061	2,743	6,941	5,281	10,898	3,340	4,078	42,998	13,894	6,332	2,791	23,017
Aug	23,535	310	7,195	8,693	1,085	2,721	7,093	5,422	10,922	3,160	4,076	43,173	13,328	6,334	2,858	22,520
Sep	23,839	296	7,387	8,893	1,141	2,853	7,140	5,398	11,097	3,316	4,205	44,044	14,232	6,390	2,829	23,451
Oct	24,029	291	7,464	8,664	1,156	2,706	6,840	5,468	11,115	3,391	4,369	43,708	14,899	6,361	2,955	24,215
Nov	24,080	288	7,273	8,584	1,131	2,740	7,196	5,390	10,870	3,384	4,319	43,614	14,761	6,669	2,976	24,406
Dec	24,136	277	7,237	8,796	1,147	2,585	7,143	5,246	11,120	3,102	4,343	43,483	15,496	7,130	2,951	25,577
2016 Jan	24,105	282	7,454	8,717	1,130	2,612	7,428	5,191	11,193	3,040	4,168	43,477	15,563	7,212	2,893	25,669
Feb	24,070	281	2,939	8,573	1,101	2,612	7,554	5,187	11,398	3,058	4,147	43,629	16,184	7,208	2,956	26,347
Mar	24,202	282	2,856	8,790	1,100	2,613	7,471	5,149	11,306	3,048	4,111	43,589	15,978	7,313	2,889	26,180
Apr	24,156	276	2,868	9,236	1,090	2,723	7,594	5,182	11,025	3,052	4,073	43,974	16,359	7,336	2,889	26,585

Source: Bank of England

12.4c Industrial analysis of monetary financial institutions' lending to UK residents

£ millions Not seasonally adjusted

Amounts outstanding of facilities granted in sterling

	Development of buildings	Construction of commercial buildings	Construction of domestic buildings	Civil Engineering	Other construction activities	Total	Wholesale and retail trade and repair of motor vehicles and motorcycles	Wholesale trade, excluding motor vehicles and motor cycles	Retail trade excluding motor vehicles and motor cycles	Total	Accommodation and food service activities	Transportation and storage	Information and communication	Total
RPM	B7EG	B3ID	B4PC	B4PP	B5QH	TCCQ	TCCS	TCCT	TCCU	TCCR	TCCV	B5PP	B5PW	TCCW
2014 May	37,885	6,626	7,673	4,800	7,677	64,660	11,561	15,492	24,254	51,306	26,794	20,361	13,495	33,856
Jun	38,028	6,728	7,664	4,517	7,664	64,601	11,885	15,650	24,468	52,003	26,441	21,184 (cs)	13,125 (cs)	34,309 (cs)
Jul	37,439	6,751	7,674	4,763	7,646	64,274	12,049	15,724	24,367	52,141	26,847	20,842	13,056	33,898
Aug	37,127	6,660	7,698	4,855	7,722	64,062	12,704	15,734	24,896	53,334 (cq)	26,589	20,820	12,790	33,609
Sep	36,865	6,674	7,732	4,608	7,752	63,630	11,722	15,922	26,092	53,736	26,394	21,142	13,340	34,482
Oct	36,598	6,579	7,683	4,671	7,677	63,208	11,143	16,084	26,684	53,912	26,146	21,149	13,631	34,780
Nov	36,235	6,569	7,463	4,571	7,313	62,150	11,442	15,938	26,632	54,012	25,616	20,297	13,281	33,578
Dec	34,700	6,217	7,422	4,534	7,221	60,094	11,816	15,603	27,224	54,644	25,566	20,416	13,662	34,078
2015 Jan	23,294 (ci)	6,141	7,153	4,563	7,162	48,314 (ci)	12,197	15,285	27,295	54,778	25,556	20,523	13,580	34,104
Feb	23,017	6,123	7,100	4,366	7,176	47,782	13,569	15,517	26,821	55,908	25,382	20,506	13,720	34,226
Mar	22,628	6,134	7,151	4,575	7,105	47,591	12,761	15,557	27,666	55,985	25,361	20,790	15,792	36,581
Apr	23,116	6,222	7,408	4,559	7,625	48,930	12,978	17,172 (cn)	25,544 (co)(cp)	55,694 (cn)(co)(cp)	27,295 (cr)	20,583	15,774	36,357
May	23,137	6,196	7,571	4,464	7,775	49,143	13,148	17,355	25,423	55,926	27,427	20,556	16,062	36,618
Jun	22,169	5,911	7,498	4,501	7,703	47,782	13,406	17,846	25,810	57,062	26,715	20,523	16,494	37,017
Jul	21,491	5,948	7,907	4,786	7,914	48,047	13,882	17,508	25,950	57,339	27,092	20,545	18,432	38,976
Aug	21,082	6,174	7,945	4,960	7,936	48,097	14,307	18,032	25,993	58,332	26,835	20,313	18,108	38,421
Sep	20,599	6,216	7,947	4,948	8,058	47,768	14,049	19,258	26,388	59,696	27,031	20,429	19,048	39,478
Oct	20,302	6,479	7,991	5,045	7,817	47,633	14,164	18,947	26,480	59,591	27,032	20,465	20,008	40,473
Nov	20,292	6,636	8,169	5,085	7,773	47,955	14,324	19,130	26,613	60,067	26,978	20,510	19,925	40,435
Dec	20,045	6,274	7,891	4,784	7,718	46,712	14,372	18,588	26,704	59,664	26,900	20,722	20,154	40,876
2016 Jan	19,971	6,347	8,066	5,032	7,836	47,252	14,888	19,597	27,007	61,493	27,305	20,760	20,405	41,164
Feb	21,587 (cj)	5,405 (cj)	9,065	5,316	7,694	49,067 (cj)(cl)	16,285	20,068	27,332	63,685	27,204	20,835	19,216	40,051
Mar	19,015 (ck)	5,188	9,252	5,175	7,625	46,255 (ck)	15,719	19,948	27,445	63,112	27,478	20,218	17,654	37,871
Apr	19,153	5,283	9,218	5,176	7,713	46,542	16,463 (cm)	19,401	27,687	63,550 (cm)	27,618	20,364	16,291	36,655

Source: Bank of England

12.4c Industrial analysis of monetary financial institutions' lending to UK residents

£ millions   Not seasonally adjusted

Amounts outstanding of facilities granted in sterling

RPM	Real estate, professional services and support activities				Public administration and defence	Education	Human health and social work	Recreational, personal and community service activities			Financial intermediation (excluding insurance and pension funds)				
	Buying, selling and renting of real estate	Professional, scientific and technical activities	Administrative and support services	Total				Recreational, cultural and sporting activities	Personal and community service activities	Total	Financial leasing corporations	Non-bank credit grantors excluding credit unions and SPVs	Credit unions	Factoring corporations	Mortgage and housing credit corporations excluding SPVs
	TCCY	B6PH	B3S2	TCCX	TCDD	TCDE	TCDF	TCDH	TCDG	B3SR	TCDJ	TCDK	TCDL	TCDM	TCDN
2014 May	158,236	20,877	25,692	204,805	9,226	12,953	22,393	7,457	3,889	11,346	26,077	13,680	1	4,818	49,893
Jun	157,178	22,255 (db)	26,010	205,443 (db)	9,457	12,939	22,505	6,927	3,895	10,822	26,250	13,813	1	4,960	50,088
Jul	156,235	22,819	26,082	205,136	9,564	13,117	22,582	6,892	3,891	10,784	26,345	14,009	1	4,955	51,265
Aug	156,298	23,111	26,592	206,002	10,513	13,135	22,655	7,002	3,885	10,887	26,679	18,647 (dg)	2	5,059	50,202
Sep	153,985	22,558	26,388	202,931	9,526	13,117	22,018	6,896	3,802	10,698	26,182	18,620	2	5,254	49,669
Oct	152,721	22,450	27,039	202,209	9,944	13,058	21,855	6,853	3,821	10,674	26,341	17,429	2	5,094	49,357
Nov	151,198	22,795	27,257	201,250	10,393	13,008	21,786	6,786	3,883	10,669	26,358	17,437	2	5,320	48,990
Dec	149,533 (ct)	22,166	26,725	198,423 (ct)	10,223	13,126	21,750	6,868	3,894	10,762	26,934	17,040	2	5,126	49,081
2015 Jan	159,766 (cu)	22,795	26,861	209,421 (cu)	10,427	12,909	21,864	6,667	3,803	10,470	26,880	17,019	2	4,789	49,365
Feb	159,239	23,018	26,359	208,616	10,427	13,023	21,866	6,655	3,824	10,479	27,201	18,693	2	4,961	49,453
Mar	158,912	23,363	25,930	208,205	10,808	13,189	22,046	6,689	3,788	10,477	26,746	18,366	2	4,745	50,252
Apr	163,724 (cv)(cw)	24,210 (dc)	26,865 (dd)	214,799 (cv)(cw)(dc)(dd)	11,057	13,847	23,175 (de)	7,019	4,163	11,182	28,868 (df)	23,282 (dh)	2	4,967	50,678
May	162,958	23,992	26,496	213,446	10,294	13,838	23,475	6,927	4,148	11,075	28,740	23,337	2	5,341	49,554
Jun	162,894	21,409	26,127	210,430	10,283	13,942	23,418	6,917	4,245	11,163	29,014	24,480	2	5,365	50,480
Jul	162,203	22,488	26,353	211,044	10,178	13,989	23,230	6,880	4,265	11,146	29,236	24,972	2	5,554	51,230
Aug	162,211	22,521	26,826	211,558	11,030	13,944	23,526	6,717	4,242	10,959	29,086	25,039	2	5,969	50,741
Sep	161,568	22,851	27,374	211,793	10,114	13,719	23,301	6,669	4,225	10,894	29,321	25,160	2	5,696	49,572
Oct	160,923	23,049	28,099	212,070	10,047	13,744	23,095	7,125	4,247	11,373	29,364	24,988	2	4,978	50,082
Nov	160,937	23,212	28,345	212,495	10,052	13,599	23,333	7,295	4,325	11,620	29,265	24,780	2	5,106	49,999
Dec	161,978 (cx)	22,614	28,912	213,504 (cx)	10,331	13,310	23,098	7,038	4,161	11,198	28,950	24,862	2	4,847	53,335 (dj)
2016 Jan	161,868	23,371	28,560	213,799	9,956	13,224	23,447	7,083	4,161	11,244	27,974	23,879 (di)	2	4,812	54,251
Feb	161,364 (cy)(cz)	23,014	28,891	213,269 (cy)(cz)	10,157	13,328	23,470	7,249	4,248	11,497	27,853	24,117	2	4,725	54,663
Mar	165,871 (da)	23,190	29,167	218,228 (da)	10,043	13,294	23,389	7,378	4,230	11,608	28,282	20,249	3	5,404	54,975
Apr	165,830	23,005	29,645	218,480	10,267	13,205	23,280	7,352	4,299	11,651	28,208	20,869	1	5,578	49,298

Source: Bank of England

12.4c Industrial analysis of monetary financial institutions' lending to UK residents

£ millions   Not seasonally adjusted

Amounts outstanding of facilities granted in sterling

RPM	Financial intermediation (excluding insurance and pension funds)								Insurance companies & pension funds		
	Investment and unit trusts excluding money market mutual funds	Money market mutual funds	Bank holding companies	Securities dealers	SPVs related to securitisation	Other financial intermediaries	of which intragroup activity	Total	Insurance companies	Pension funds	Total
	TCDO	TCDP	TCDQ	TCDR	B8EX	TCDS	B7FF	TCDI	B7FK	B3W9	TCDT
2014 May	6,468	130	34,041	26,532	15,520	76,252	65,263	253,413	12,910	7,807	20,717
Jun	6,321	128	32,978	31,112 (cs)	15,460	72,777	61,778	253,888 (cs)	12,708	9,056	21,764
Jul	6,278	85	32,959	28,931	14,846	73,300	63,006	252,974	12,590	8,527	21,117
Aug	6,397	72	32,867	29,646	16,021	72,275	61,751	257,868 (dg)	13,531	8,141	21,672
Sep	5,707	71	29,571	25,860	17,163	70,165	58,996	248,263	14,589	9,633	24,222
Oct	5,983	21	30,594	24,224	16,070	67,046	55,555	242,162	14,050	10,263	24,313
Nov	6,067	21	19,643	23,661	16,156	67,683	56,719	231,339	14,364	9,156	23,521
Dec	6,019	21	18,125	22,986	18,251	64,165	52,974	227,749	14,414	9,895	24,310
2015 Jan	4,961	28	18,142	23,144	17,094	64,279	52,132	225,704	16,618	10,108	26,726
Feb	5,275	36	18,039	25,987	16,510	63,024	51,367	229,181	15,564	9,306	24,870
Mar	5,510	36	18,833	23,528	16,247	70,268	58,447	234,534	16,567	10,944	27,512
Apr	5,717	45	19,780	23,576	16,227	68,035	56,318	241,176 (df)(dh)	17,023	10,247	27,270
May	5,702	65	19,807	21,663	16,184	68,713	56,666	239,108	16,806	8,933	25,739
Jun	5,912	48	19,052	23,501	15,837	67,125	55,147	240,817	14,583	9,361	23,945
Jul	5,844	30	26,148	27,714	18,143	67,581	55,203	256,455	15,067	9,730	24,797
Aug	6,652	30	18,772	26,305	19,315	67,827	55,442	249,739	13,846	10,025	23,870
Sep	7,944	33	18,878	29,254	21,563	64,615	52,410	252,038	11,586	10,614	22,201
Oct	8,019	32	20,229 (dk)	24,948	21,528	63,226 (dn)	51,021	247,395 (dk)(dn)	10,188	11,611	21,799
Nov	8,555	43	20,197	24,924	22,378	57,289	44,898	242,537	11,962	11,617	23,579
Dec	9,178	51	19,660	25,867	21,810 (dl)	54,578	43,066	243,139 (dj)(dl)	10,526	11,079	21,605
2016 Jan	10,438	54	19,862	26,007	23,708 (dm)	50,008	39,746	240,997 (dj)(dm)	11,263	11,721	22,984
Feb	10,626	58	20,396	27,313	23,237	50,378	40,882	243,368	11,920	13,836	25,756
Mar	11,458	104	20,308	28,872	23,485	46,862	36,995	240,001	12,486	13,783	26,269
Apr	11,979	87	20,595	31,221	19,976	44,679	34,835	232,494	11,380	11,985	23,365

Source: Bank of England

12.4c Industrial analysis of monetary financial institutions' lending to UK residents

£ millions   Not seasonally adjusted

Amounts outstanding of facilities granted in sterling

| RPM | Fund management activities | Activities auxiliary to financial intermediation – Other | | | Total | Total financial and non-financial businesses | Individuals and individual trusts | | | Total UK residents |
| | | Central clearing counterparties | Other auxiliary activities | Total | | | Lending secured on dwellings inc. bridging finance | Other loans and advances | Total | |
	TCDU	B3X6	B3Y4	TCDV	B8FO	Z94D	TCDX	TCDY	TCDW	TCCA
2014 May	53,213	62,579	4,061	66,639	119,852	912,401	1,112,799	165,978	1,278,777	2,191,177
Jun	57,654	63,097	4,220	67,317	124,971	922,435 (db)(du)	1,115,321	166,843	1,282,164	2,204,599 (db)(du)
Jul	59,178	61,647	4,160	65,807	124,985	921,031	1,120,432	167,052	1,287,484	2,208,515
Aug	58,284	57,282	4,259	61,540	119,825	924,164 (cq)(dg)	1,121,704	167,309	1,289,012	2,213,177 (cq)(dg)
Sep	55,130 (do)	64,229	4,352	68,581	123,711 (do)	917,930 (do)	1,122,302	170,098 (eb)	1,292,400 (eb)	2,210,329 (do)(eb)
Oct	56,474	64,215	4,388	68,603	125,077	913,610	1,124,991	181,071 (ec)	1,306,063 (ec)	2,219,673 (ec)
Nov	59,908	65,573	4,424	69,997	129,906	903,412	1,126,436	182,214	1,308,650	2,212,062
Dec	62,179	52,542	4,244	56,786	118,965	886,063 (ct)	1,126,593	183,173	1,309,765	2,195,828 (ct)
2015 Jan	65,442	56,735	4,242	60,978	126,420	892,395	1,123,698 (dv)	182,864	1,306,561 (dv)	2,198,956 (dv)
Feb	63,294	56,947	4,277	61,224	124,519	892,602	1,125,080 (dw)	181,847 (ed)	1,306,928	2,199,529
Mar	69,449 (dp)	55,563	4,164	59,727	129,175 (dp)	908,580 (dp)	1,128,080	183,213	1,311,292	2,219,872 (dp)
Apr	69,254	55,600	4,345	59,945	129,199	933,226 (ch)(cn)(co)(cv)(df)(dh)	1,127,233 (dx)	190,912 (ee)	1,318,146 (dx)(ee)	2,251,371 (ch)(cn)(co)(cv)(df)(dh)(dx)(ee)
May	70,561	59,514	4,742	64,256	134,817	938,694	1,126,681	191,348	1,318,029	2,256,724
Jun	70,378	51,009	4,076	55,084	125,462	924,440	1,131,704	192,355	1,324,059	2,248,499
Jul	70,745	50,396	3,910	54,306	125,051	944,218	1,135,074	193,616	1,328,690	2,272,908
Aug	69,574	59,779	3,797	63,576	133,151	946,196	1,136,217	198,003	1,334,220	2,280,415
Sep	74,461	50,443	4,016	54,459	128,920	945,970	1,140,079	199,088	1,339,166	2,285,136
Oct	72,242 (dq)	46,122 (ds)	4,151	50,273 (ds)	122,516 (dq)(ds)	936,476 (dk)(dn)(dq)(ds)	1,144,725	199,885	1,344,610	2,281,086 (dk)(dn)(dq)(ds)
Nov	73,904	50,360	4,123	54,482	128,386	940,699	1,149,226	200,713	1,349,939	2,290,638
Dec	76,208	45,522	3,925	49,446	125,654	936,701 (cx)(dj)(dl)	1,159,523 (dy)(dz)	198,236 (ef)	1,357,759 (dy)(dz)(ef)	2,294,461 (cx)(dj)(dl)(dy)(dz)(ef)
2016 Jan	81,983 (dr)	39,532 (dt)	4,078	43,611 (dt)	125,594 (dr)(dt)	939,446 (di)(dm)(dr)(dt)	1,160,485	199,024	1,359,508	2,298,954 (di)(dm)(dr)(dt)
Feb	91,390	36,539	3,930	40,468	131,859	949,978 (cj)(cl)(cy)(cz)	1,163,166	200,123	1,363,289	2,313,266 (cj)(cl)(cy)(cz)
Mar	94,585	33,517	3,890	37,407	131,992	946,650	1,169,905	201,195	1,371,100	2,317,751
Apr	91,853	33,518 (cm)	4,233	37,752 (cm)	129,605 (cm)	934,570 (cm)	1,178,777 (ea)	201,862	1,380,639	2,315,210 (cm)(ea)

Source: Bank of England

12.4c Industrial analysis of monetary financial institutions' lending to UK residents

£ millions   Not seasonally adjusted

Notes to table

Movements in amounts outstanding can reflect breaks in data series as well as underlying flows. For changes data, users are recommended to refer directly to the appropriate series or data tables. Further explanation can be found at: www.bankofengland.co.uk/statistics/Pages/iadb/notesiadb/Changes_flows_growth_rates.aspx.

(ch) Due to improvements in reporting at one institution, the amounts outstanding increased by £3bn. This effect has been adjusted out of the flows for April 2015.

(ci) Due to improvements in reporting at one institution the amounts outstanding decreased by £11bn. This effect has been adjusted out of the flows for January 2015.

(cj) Due to improvements in reporting at one institution, the amounts outstanding increased by £1bn. This effect has been adjusted out of the flows for February 2016.

(ck) Due to improvements in reporting at one institution, the amounts outstanding increased by £2bn. This effect has been adjusted out of the flows for March 2016.

(cl) Due to improvements in reporting at one institution, the amounts outstanding decreased by £1bn. This effect has been adjusted out of the flows for February 2016.

(cm) Due to improvements in reporting at one institution, the amounts outstanding increased by £1bn. This effect has been adjusted out of the flows for April 2016.

(cn) Due to improvements in reporting at one institution, the amounts outstanding increased by £2bn. This effect has been adjusted out of the flows for April 2015.

(co) Due to a change in treatment at one institution, the amounts outstanding decreased by £4bn. This has been adjusted out of the flows for April 2015,

(cp) Due to improvements in reporting at one institution, the amounts outstanding increased by £1bn. This effect has been adjusted out of the flows for April 2015.

(cq) Due to a change in treatment at one institution, the amounts outstanding increased by £1bn. This effect has been adjusted out of the flows for August 2014.

(cr) Due to improvements in reporting at one institution, the amounts outstanding increased by £1bn. This effect has been adjusted out of the flows for April 2015.

(cs) Due to improvements in reporting at one institution, the amounts outstanding increased by £1bn. This effect has been adjusted out of the flows for June 2014.

(ct) Due to a loan transfer by one reporting institution, the amounts outstanding decreased by £1bn. This effect has been adjusted out of the flows for December 2014.

(cu) Due to improvements in reporting at one institution the amounts outstanding increased by £11bn. This effect has been adjusted out of the flows for January 2015.

(cv) Due to improvements in reporting at one institution, the amounts outstanding increased by £3bn. This effect has been adjusted out of the flows for April 2015.

(cw) Due to a change in the reporting population, the amounts outstanding increased by £1bn. This effect has been adjusted out of the flows for April 2015.

(cx) Due to a change in the reporting population, the amounts outstanding increased by £1bn. This effect has been adjusted out of the flows for December 2015.

(cy) Due to improvements in reporting at one institution the amounts outstanding decreased by £1bn. This effect has been adjusted out of the flows for February 2016.

(cz) Due to improvements in reporting at one institution, the amounts outstanding decreased by £1bn. This effect has been adjusted out of the flows for February 2016.

(da) Due to improvements in reporting at one institution, the amounts outstanding increased by £2bn. This effect has been adjusted out of the flows for March 2016.

(db) Due to a change in accounting treatment at one reporting institution, the amounts outstanding increased by £2bn. This effect has been adjusted out of the flows for June 2014.

(dc) Due to improvements in reporting at one institution, the amounts outstanding increased by £1bn. This effect has been adjusted out of the flows for April 2015.

(dd) Due to improvements in reporting at one institution, the amounts outstanding increased by £1bn. This effect has been adjusted out of the flows for April 2015.

(de) Due to improvements in reporting at one institution, the amounts outstanding increased by £1bn. This effect has been adjusted out of the flows for April 2015.

(df) Due to improvements in reporting at one institution, the amounts outstanding increased by £2bn. This effect has been adjusted out of the flows for April 2015.

(dg) Due to improvements in reporting at one institution, the amounts outstanding increased by £4bn. This effect has been adjusted out of the flows for August 2014.

(dh) Due to improvements in reporting at one institution, the amounts outstanding increased by £5bn. This effect has been adjusted out of the flows for April 2015.

(di) Due to improvements in reporting at one institution, the amounts outstanding decreased by £1bn. This effect has been adjusted out of the flows for January 2016.

(dj) Due to a restructuring at one reporting institution, the amounts outstanding increased by £4bn. This effect has been adjusted out of the flows for December 2015.

(dk) Due to improvements in reporting at one institution, the amounts outstanding increased by £1bn. This effect has been adjusted out of the flows for October 2015.

(dl) Due to a restructuring at one reporting institution, the amounts outstanding decreased by £4bn. This effect has been adjusted out of the flows for December 2015.

(dm) Due to improvements in reporting at one institution, the amounts outstanding increased by £1bn. This effect has been adjusted out of the flows for January 2016.

(dn) Due to improvements in reporting at one institution, the amounts outstanding decreased by £1bn. This effect has been adjusted out of the flows for October 2015.

(do) Due to improvements in reporting at one institution, the amounts outstanding increased by £1bn. This effect has been adjusted out of the flows for September 2014.

(dp) Due to improvements in reporting at one institution, the amounts outstanding increased by £2bn. This effect has been adjusted out of the flows for March 2015.

(dq) Due to a change in the reporting population, the amounts outstanding increased by £2bn. This effect has been adjusted out of the flows for October 2015.

(dr) Due to a change in the reporting population, the amounts outstanding increased by £3bn. This effect has been adjusted out of the flows for January 2016.

(ds) Due to a change in the reporting population, the amounts outstanding increased by £3bn. This effect has been adjusted out of the flows for October 2015.

(dt) Due to a change in the reporting population, the amounts outstanding decreased by £4bn. This effect has been adjusted out of the flows for January 2016.

(du) Due to improvements in reporting at one institution, the amounts outstanding increased by £2bn. This effect has been adjusted out of the flows for June 2014.

(dv) Due to a loan transfer by one reporting institution, the amounts outstanding decreased by £2bn. This effect has been adjusted out of the flows for January 2015.

(dw) Due to a loan transfer by one reporting institution, the amounts outstanding increased by £1bn. This effect has been adjusted out of the flows for February 2015.

(dx) Due to improvements in reporting at one institution, the amounts outstanding decreased by £4bn. This effect has been adjusted out of the flows for April 2015.

(dy) Due to a loan transfer by one reporting institution, the amounts outstanding increased by £3bn. This effect has been adjusted out of the flows for December 2015.

(dz) Due to improvements in reporting at one institution, the amounts outstanding increased by £5bn. This effect has been adjusted out of the flows for December 2015.

(ea) Due to a loan transfer by one reporting institution, the amounts outstanding increased by £7bn. This effect has been adjusted out of the flows for April 2015.

(eb) Due to a change in the reporting population, the amounts outstanding increased by £2bn. This effect has been adjusted out of the flows for September 2014.

(ec) Due to a loan transfer by one reporting institution, the amounts outstanding increased by £2bn. This effect has been adjusted out of the flows for October 2014.

(ed) Due to improvements in reporting at one institution, the amounts outstanding increased by £10bn. This effect has been adjusted out of the flows for February 2015.

(ee) Due to improvements in reporting at one institution, the amounts outstanding increased by £1bn. This effect has been adjusted out of the flows for April 2015.

(ef) Due to improvements in reporting at one institution, the amounts outstanding increased by £7bn. This effect has been adjusted out of the flows for April 2015.

(ef) Due to improvements in reporting at one institution, the amounts outstanding decreased by £3bn. This effect has been adjusted out of the flows for December 2015.

Copyright guidance and the related UK Open Government Licence can be viewed here: www.bankofengland.co.uk/Pages/disclaimer.aspx.

12.4d Industrial analysis of monetary financial institutions' lending to UK residents

£ millions   Not seasonally adjusted

Amounts outstanding of facilities granted in all currencies

	Agriculture, hunting and forestry	Fishing	Mining and quarrying	Manufacturing									Electricity, gas and water supply			
				Food, beverages and tobacco	Textiles, wearing apparel and leather	Pulp, paper, and printing	Chemicals, pharmaceuticals, rubber and plastics	Non-metallic mineral products and metals	Machinery, equipment and transport equipment	Electrical, medical and optical equipment	Other manufacturing	Total	Electricity, gas steam and air conditioning	Water collection and sewerage	Waste management related services and remediation activities	Total
RPM	TCAC	TCAD	TCAE	TCAG	TCAH	TCAI	TCAJ	TCAK	TCAL	TCAM	TCAN	TCAF	TCAO	TCAP	B3FF	B3FT
2014 May	18,378	291	22,980	14,689	1,381	4,110	15,425	8,379	14,362	4,864	5,451	68,661	19,055	6,067	3,224	28,346
Jun	18,703	290	23,597	15,635	1,430	4,162	15,599	8,853	14,489	5,192	5,407	70,768	20,268	6,321	3,142	29,731
Jul	18,634	301	24,128	19,123	1,537	3,923	15,838	8,468	15,041	5,110	5,543	74,583	20,051	6,384	2,968	29,404
Aug	18,898	300	24,439	18,993	1,549	3,748	15,913	8,884	14,987	4,990	5,555	74,619	20,494	6,393	2,986	29,874
Sep	18,901	297	25,350	20,118	1,583	3,856	16,139	9,205	15,498	4,925	5,588	76,912	20,864	6,293	2,971	30,128
Oct	19,117	299	25,649	20,987	1,550	3,999	16,204	9,499	15,590	4,847	5,448	78,124	20,961	6,457	2,979	30,397
Nov	19,272	292	25,956	21,971	1,535	3,930	16,675	9,562	15,318	4,909	5,368	79,267	20,890	6,327	3,054	30,270
Dec	19,285	288	26,174	21,735	1,594	3,988	16,349	9,337	15,263	4,991	5,539	78,797	21,230	6,532	2,967	30,730
2015 Jan	19,304	283	27,080	21,588	1,635	3,980	17,082	9,002	15,339	4,935	5,665	79,227	21,333	6,424	3,036	30,793
Feb	19,355	286	26,666	21,272	1,596	4,028	16,253	9,218	15,391	4,795	5,627	78,179	21,656	6,616	2,986	31,258
Mar	19,436	284	27,846	22,795	1,731	4,088	16,741	9,288	15,601	4,926	5,768	80,938	21,587	6,994	3,071	31,652
Apr	23,141 (eg)	289	30,810	23,265	1,750	4,269	16,185	9,278	16,050	4,936	5,586	81,320	21,811	7,093	3,270	32,175
May	23,317	288	32,432	23,229	1,860	4,245	15,734	9,002	16,627	5,100	5,670	81,466	21,188	7,006	3,153	31,347
Jun	23,379	306	32,542	21,172	1,821	4,286	15,753	8,915	16,685	5,413	5,561	79,606	22,036	6,992	3,169	32,197
Jul	23,656	310	32,770	19,662	1,746	4,139	15,693	8,741	16,925	5,225	5,793	77,924	22,380	7,056	3,064	32,500
Aug	23,837	314	33,606	19,513	1,761	4,158	16,205	8,965	17,497	5,099	5,807	79,006	21,904	7,022	3,166	32,091
Sep	24,123	319	31,810	19,036	1,799	3,965	16,083	8,972	17,641	5,313	5,760	78,570	22,492	7,077	3,072	32,642
Oct	24,311	295	31,355	18,021	1,832	3,710	15,630	9,121	17,644	5,367	5,950	77,276	22,449	7,048	3,176	32,674
Nov	24,365	293	31,575	17,830	1,786	3,805	16,490	8,851	17,838	5,510	5,944	78,055	22,557	7,381	3,225	33,162
Dec	24,446	286	32,380 (eh)	17,783	1,791	3,702	16,636	8,871	18,321	5,219	5,858	78,181	23,611	7,842	3,206	34,659
2016 Jan	24,431	312	32,661	17,856	1,814	3,745	16,689	8,723	18,416	5,090	5,867	78,200	23,900	7,891	3,244	35,035
Feb	24,380	311	28,697	18,202	1,746	3,726	17,900	8,879	18,507	5,177	5,973	80,109	24,155	7,899	3,207	35,260
Mar	24,508	315	28,223	18,150	1,778	3,708	17,690	8,833	18,330	5,161	6,241	79,893	23,830	7,938	3,290	35,058
Apr	24,463	307	25,894	19,127	1,715	3,823	17,188	8,785	18,051	5,152	6,318	80,158	22,808	7,939	3,237	33,984

Source: Bank of England

12.4d Industrial analysis of monetary financial institutions' lending to UK residents

£ millions Not seasonally adjusted

Amounts outstanding of facilities granted in all currencies

| | | Construction | | | | | Wholesale and retail trade | | | | Accommodation and food service activities | Transport, storage and communication | | |
	Development of buildings	Construction of commercial buildings	Construction of domestic buildings	Civil Engineering	Other construction activities	Total	Wholesale and retail trade and repair of motor vehicles and motorcycles	Wholesale trade, excluding motor vehicles and motor cycles	Retail trade excluding motor vehicles and motor cycles	Total		Transportation and storage	Information and communication	Total
RPM	B7EH	B3IE	B4PD	B3KK	B5PC	TCAQ	TCAS	TCAT	TCAU	TCAR	TCAV	B3NF	B5PX	TCAW
2014 May	38,942	7,475	7,827	5,546	7,948	67,738	12,656	22,237	30,172	65,066	28,463	26,337	24,303	50,640
Jun	39,000	7,553	7,862	5,444	7,924	67,784	12,910	23,148	30,424	66,482	28,120	26,700 (es)	23,946	50,646 (es)
Jul	38,348	7,473	7,841	5,597	7,897	67,156	13,163	23,337	30,078	66,578	28,279	26,405	28,276	54,681
Aug	38,041	7,387	7,865	5,647	7,983	66,924	13,929	23,520	30,692	68,141 (eq)	28,149	26,614	26,275	52,889
Sep	37,803	7,267	7,887	5,409	8,011	66,378	12,974	24,457	32,689	70,120	28,006	26,703	26,415	53,118
Oct	37,575	7,175	7,825	5,307	7,941	65,824	12,585	24,946	34,209	71,740	27,721	27,386	27,367	54,752
Nov	37,243	7,109	7,609	5,464	7,549	64,974	12,744	25,415	32,907	71,067	27,243	26,258	26,383	52,640
Dec	35,652	6,854	7,631	5,384	7,468	62,989	13,062	24,383	34,258	71,703	27,123	26,280	26,664	52,944
2015 Jan	23,794 (ei)	6,809	7,342	5,345	7,394	50,684 (ei)	13,259	23,543	33,688	70,490	27,062	26,578	26,787	53,365
Feb	23,496	6,783	7,270	5,116	7,357	50,022	14,573	23,344	33,228	71,145	26,838	26,445	26,672	53,118
Mar	23,104	6,718	7,300	5,304	7,286	49,713	13,808	24,308	34,132	72,248	27,135	26,560	28,342	54,901
Apr	23,557	6,819	7,542	5,224	7,826	50,968	14,343	25,803 (en)	31,970 (eo)(ep)	72,117 (en)(eo)(ep)	28,953 (er)	26,461	28,656	55,117
May	23,574	6,789	7,698	5,118	7,991	51,170	14,396	25,929	31,972	72,297	29,171	27,128	28,905	56,034
Jun	22,638	6,622	7,691	5,333	7,888	50,171	14,577	25,769	32,203	72,549	28,493	26,523	29,043	55,565
Jul	21,942	6,598	8,053	5,648	8,098	50,339	15,017	25,254	32,410	72,681	28,792	26,323	31,226	57,550
Aug	21,558	6,727	8,120	5,886	8,118	50,409	15,572	26,403	32,652	74,628	28,656	26,551	31,077	57,628
Sep	21,081	6,722	8,086	5,818	8,254	49,960	15,381	27,183	32,658	75,222	28,927	26,991	32,469	59,460
Oct	20,740	6,993	8,141	5,772	8,009	49,655	15,413	26,878	32,666	74,957	28,950	26,713	33,203	59,916
Nov	20,787	7,122	8,330	5,984	7,968	50,191	15,460	26,781	32,964	75,205	28,930	26,605	33,831	60,436
Dec	20,550	6,974	8,089	5,618	7,940	49,171	15,563	26,802	33,151	75,516	28,780	27,537	35,472	63,009
2016 Jan	20,494	6,926	8,260	5,800	8,048	49,528	16,077	27,660	33,424	77,161	29,171	27,803	36,467	64,270
Feb	22,155 (ei)	5,876 (el)	9,317	6,013	7,909	51,269 (ei)(el)	17,479	28,770	33,950	80,199	29,078	28,266	35,473	63,739
Mar	19,550 (ek)	5,703	9,494	6,031	7,830	48,607 (ek)	16,954	28,603	34,151	79,708	29,417	27,530	33,719	61,249
Apr	19,681	5,762	9,482	5,970	7,912	48,807	17,929 (em)	27,983	34,540	80,452 (em)	29,484	27,674	31,589	59,263

Source: Bank of England

12.4d Industrial analysis of monetary financial institutions' lending to UK residents

£ millions   Not seasonally adjusted

Amounts outstanding of facilities granted in all currencies

| | Real estate, professional services and support activities | | | | | | | Recreational, personal and community service activities | | | Financial intermediation (excluding insurance and pension funds) | | | | |
| | Buying, selling and renting of real estate | Professional, scientific and technical activities | Administrative and support services | Total | Public administration and defence | Education | Human health and social work | Recreational, cultural and sporting activities | Personal and community service activities | Total | Financial leasing corporations | Non-bank credit grantors excluding credit unions and SPVs | Credit unions | Factoring corporations | Mortgage and housing credit corporations excluding SPVs |
RPM	TCAY	B3QF	B3S3	TCAX	TCBD	TCBE	TCBF	TCBH	TCBG	B3T2	TCBJ	TCBK	TCBL	TCBM	TCBN
2014 May	161,345	27,050	33,022	221,417	12,367	13,016	22,717	8,656	4,151	12,807	30,141	14,454	2	5,271	50,427
Jun	160,191 (fa)	29,088 (fa)	33,416	222,694 (fa)	11,908	13,007	22,836	7,924	4,143	12,067	29,850	14,574	2	5,499	50,620
Jul	159,218	30,411	33,477	223,106	12,036	13,177	22,913	7,901	4,164	12,065	30,049	14,803	2	5,392	51,787
Aug	159,284	30,609	33,682	223,575	12,489	13,193	23,009	8,078	4,168	12,246	30,953	19,316 (ff)	2	5,540	50,733
Sep	156,989	29,335	33,499	219,824	11,649	13,172	22,415	7,783	4,084	11,867	30,529	19,437	3	5,783	50,241
Oct	155,963	29,480	33,468	218,911	13,921	13,117	22,231	7,796	4,121	11,917	30,674	18,255	3	5,527	49,943
Nov	154,405	30,497	33,606	218,508	13,997	13,067	22,167	7,641	4,217	11,858	30,791	18,310	3	5,887	49,528
Dec	152,503 (et)	30,433	33,018	215,954 (et)	12,791	13,203	22,162	7,723	4,204	11,928	30,875	17,968	2	5,623	49,476
2015 Jan	163,164 (eu)	31,085	33,176	227,425 (eu)	13,055	12,967	22,267	7,586	4,110	11,695	30,804	17,919	2	5,283	49,759
Feb	162,449	31,238	32,486	226,174	12,493	13,064	22,241	7,565	4,127	11,692	31,094	19,676	2	5,441	49,849
Mar	162,037	31,975	32,139	226,152	14,457	13,246	22,452	8,098	4,149	12,247	30,652	19,368	2	5,247	51,230
Apr	166,778 (ev)(ew)	32,964 (fb)	32,952 (fc)	232,694 (ev)(ew)(fb)(fc)	13,199	13,908	23,566 (fd)	8,292	4,573	12,865	32,472 (fe)	24,267 (fg)	2	5,432	51,650
May	166,015	32,445	33,114	231,574	12,861	13,899	23,876	8,220	4,546	12,766	32,288	24,190	2	5,789	50,498
Jun	165,865	28,560	33,179	227,604	12,357	14,012	23,837	8,080	4,719	12,799	32,528	25,276	3	6,040	51,419
Jul	165,424	29,615	33,345	228,385	12,614	14,045	23,655	7,977	4,737	12,714	32,890	25,730	3	6,077	52,235
Aug	165,427	29,484	33,735	228,647	12,153	14,003	23,972	7,916	4,719	12,635	32,988	25,980	3	6,460	51,724
Sep	165,307	30,108	34,597	230,012	11,869	13,769	23,744	7,898	4,591	12,489	33,471	26,103	2	6,262	50,530
Oct	165,386	30,058	34,803	230,246	12,094	13,781	23,482	8,483	4,622	13,105	33,870	25,900	2	5,484	51,014
Nov	165,117	30,490	35,332	230,939	11,391	13,643	23,735	8,597	4,690	13,287	33,860	25,558	2	5,609	50,964
Dec	166,285 (eh)	30,149	35,789	232,223 (eh)	12,239	13,353	23,411	8,398	4,530	12,928	33,663	25,619	3	5,347	54,440 (fi)
2016 Jan	166,283	30,937	35,302	232,521	12,154	13,271	23,761	8,431	4,543	12,974	32,754	24,803 (fh)	3	5,311	55,390
Feb	165,258 (ex)(ey)	30,620	36,443	232,322 (ex)(ey)	11,977	13,375	23,823	8,608	4,625	13,232	32,947	25,158	2	5,183	55,881
Mar	169,322 (ez)	30,361	36,850	236,533 (ez)	10,942	13,333	23,782	8,727	4,662	13,389	33,216	21,265	5	5,932	56,203
Apr	169,000	30,076	37,493	236,570	12,133	13,256	23,605	8,615	4,626	13,241	33,073	21,861	2	6,102	50,453

Source: Bank of England

12.4d Industrial analysis of monetary financial institutions' lending to UK residents

£ millions Not seasonally adjusted

Amounts outstanding of facilities granted in all currencies

| | Financial intermediation (excluding insurance and pension funds) | | | | | | | | Insurance companies & pension funds | | |
| | Investment and unit trusts excluding money market mutual funds | Money market mutual funds | Bank holding companies | Securities dealers | SPVs related to securitisation | Other financial intermediaries | of which intragroup activity | Total | Insurance companies | Pension funds | Total |
RPM	TCBO	TCBP	TCBQ	TCBR	B7FB	TCBS	B7FG	TCBI	B7FL	B7FQ	TCBT
2014 May	13,305	173	44,320	144,437	17,186	135,778	106,713	455,493	18,120	8,328	26,449
Jun	11,784	168	42,869	149,855 (es)	17,105	120,935	91,596	443,259 (es)	17,894	9,648	27,542
Jul	11,755	93	41,828	145,665	16,010	121,103	92,766	438,487	18,148	9,314	27,462
Aug	11,715	76	41,937	136,279	17,205	120,580	91,883	434,337 (ff)	20,058	8,956	29,014
Sep	11,792	71	38,403	135,919	19,552	118,468	89,372	430,195	20,966	10,984	31,950
Oct	12,127	21	39,610	134,039	17,779	116,332	86,831	424,309	20,652	11,169	31,821
Nov	12,583	21	28,242	136,295	17,808	116,354	88,078	415,822	21,708	10,182	31,891
Dec	12,767	21	27,230	130,710	20,045	113,402	84,351	408,120	21,567	10,939	32,506
2015 Jan	10,419 (fj)	67	27,349	138,799	18,615	112,220	84,620	411,237 (fj)	24,614	11,532	36,146
Feb	11,028	86	26,730	141,823	17,965	110,858	83,949	414,551	24,030	10,875	34,906
Mar	11,347	106	26,937	144,825	17,543	115,365	88,094	422,623	25,204	12,182	37,386
Apr	12,402	192	31,157	144,661	17,639	113,030	85,940	432,906 (fe)(fg)	26,876	11,603	38,480
May	12,491	121	27,902 (fk)	129,138	17,612	111,934	84,831	411,965 (fk)	26,218	10,131	36,349
Jun	12,299	48	27,416	127,892	17,145	111,610	83,764	411,675	23,542	10,461	34,003
Jul	12,244	30	36,224	125,118	19,630	110,792	83,408	420,975	24,159	10,569	34,728
Aug	13,922	31	27,475	124,397	20,891	112,390	84,863	416,262	22,994	10,837	33,831
Sep	15,301	34	27,152	134,202	23,232	110,544	81,924	426,834	21,553	11,464	33,017
Oct	15,805	34	28,721 (fl)	121,427 (fm)	23,041	108,576 (fq)	80,646	413,875 (fl)(fm)(fq)	19,728	13,282	33,009
Nov	16,742	44	29,173	118,394	23,997	103,125	74,984	407,468	21,077	13,016	34,092
Dec	16,775	125	29,953	114,898	24,325 (fo)	101,502	72,770	406,650 (fi)(fo)	19,314	12,352	31,666
2016 Jan	18,638	135	30,632	119,914	24,811 (fp)	98,803	70,293	411,194 (fh)(fp)	20,723	12,773	33,495
Feb	18,795	122	32,149	127,765	24,531	100,748	72,518	423,281	22,962	15,067	38,029
Mar	19,481	193	31,501	120,520	24,747	95,167	68,437	408,232	23,498	14,808	38,307
Apr	20,000	164	31,368	137,570 (fn)	21,370	99,035 (em)(fr)	71,926 (em)(fr)	420,996 (em)(fn)(fr)	21,912	12,812	34,724

Source: Bank of England

12.4d Industrial analysis of monetary financial institutions' lending to UK residents

£ millions Not seasonally adjusted

Amounts outstanding of facilities granted in all currencies

RPM	Fund management activities	Activities auxiliary to financial intermediation			Total	Total financial and non-financial businesses	Individuals and individual trusts			Total UK residents
		Central clearing counterparties	Other auxiliary activities	Total			Lending secured on dwellings inc. bridging finance	Other loans and advances	Total	
	TCBU	B3X7	B3Y5	TCBV	B322	Z94H	TCBX	TCBY	TCBW	TCAA
2014 May	110,475	145,703	11,295	156,998	267,473	1,382,302	1,113,334	167,335	1,280,669	2,662,971
Jun	112,174	137,885	11,548	149,433	261,607	1,371,038 (fa)(ge)	1,115,846	168,293	1,284,138	2,655,176 (fa)(ge)
Jul	110,348	137,139	12,352	149,491	259,839	1,372,831	1,120,933	168,493	1,289,426	2,662,257
Aug	115,239	134,280	12,561	146,841	262,080	1,374,175 (eq)(ff)	1,122,193	168,704	1,290,898	2,665,073 (eq)(ff)
Sep	113,728 (fs)	139,131	12,932	152,064	265,792 (fs)	1,376,075 (fs)	1,122,802	171,538 (gl)	1,294,340 (gl)	2,670,415 (fs)(gl)
Oct	104,994	140,635	13,157	153,792	258,786	1,368,638	1,125,495	182,553 (gm)	1,308,048 (gm)	2,676,686 (gm)
Nov	113,550	141,302	14,033	155,336	268,886	1,367,175	1,126,946	183,724	1,310,669	2,677,844
Dec	112,857	118,491	14,204	132,695	245,553	1,332,249 (et)	1,127,095	184,615	1,311,710	2,643,959 (et)
2015 Jan	118,490 (ft)	126,501	14,516	141,016	259,507 (ft)	1,352,587	1,124,178 (gf)	184,303	1,308,481 (gf)	2,661,068 (gf)
Feb	116,050	127,173	14,185	141,358	257,407	1,349,395	1,125,302 (gg)	183,245 (gn)	1,308,547	2,657,943
Mar	128,021 (fu)	120,155	14,309	134,464	262,485 (fu)	1,375,201 (fu)	1,128,296	184,659	1,312,955	2,688,156 (fu)
Apr	127,787	123,679	14,172	137,851	265,638	1,408,142 (eg)(en)(eo)(ev)(fe)(fg)	1,127,429 (gh)	192,345 (go)	1,319,774 (gh)(go)	2,727,916 (eg)(en)(eo)(ev)(fe)(fg)(gh)(go)
May	126,950 (fv)	124,354	14,960	139,314	266,264 (fv)	1,387,076 (fk)(fv)	1,126,876	192,763	1,319,639	2,706,714 (fk)(fv)
Jun	142,060	103,093	14,654	117,747	259,807	1,370,902	1,131,888	193,738	1,325,626	2,696,528
Jul	142,492	101,078	15,216	116,293	258,785	1,382,424	1,135,255	194,977	1,330,231	2,712,655
Aug	143,270	113,740	15,640	129,380	272,650	1,394,327	1,136,392	199,398	1,335,790	2,730,117
Sep	146,117	101,803	14,748	116,551	262,667	1,395,435	1,140,256	200,581	1,340,837	2,736,272
Oct	149,530 (fw)	94,755 (fy)	14,593	109,349 (fy)	258,879 (fw)(fy)	1,377,861 (fl)(fm)(fq)(fw)(fy)	1,144,899	201,346	1,346,245	2,724,106 (fl)(fm)(fq)(fw)(fy)
Nov	146,842	100,031 (fz)	17,655 (gb)	117,686	264,528	1,381,296	1,149,399	202,269	1,351,668	2,732,963 (gq)
Dec	141,519	95,700	17,692	113,392	254,911	1,373,810 (eh)(fi)(fo)	1,159,673 (gi)(gj)	199,775 (gp)	1,359,448 (gi)(gj)(gp)	2,733,259 (eh)(fi)(fo)(gi)(gj)(gp)
2016 Jan	155,912 (fx)	94,430 (ga)	19,004	113,434 (ga)	269,346 (fx)(ga)	1,399,484 (fh)(fp)(fx)(ga)	1,160,637	199,838	1,360,475	2,759,959 (fh)(fp)(fx)(ga)
Feb	170,698	99,558	19,284	118,842	289,539	1,438,622 (ej)(el)(ex)(ey)	1,163,318	200,997	1,364,315	2,802,938 (ej)(el)(ex)(ey)
Mar	171,096	90,367	18,932	109,299	280,395	1,411,890	1,170,055	202,130	1,372,185	2,784,075
Apr	168,797	90,736 (em)	13,522 (gc)(gd)	104,258 (gc)(gd)	273,055 (em)(gc)(gd)	1,410,391 (em)(em)(fn)(fr)(gc)(gd)	1,178,920 (gk)	202,788	1,381,709 (gk)	2,792,099 (em)(em)(fn)(fr)(gc)(gd)

Source: Bank of England

12.4d Industrial analysis of monetary financial institutions' lending to UK residents

£ millions Not seasonally adjusted

Notes to table

Movements in amounts outstanding can reflect breaks in data series as well as underlying flows. For changes data, users are recommended to refer directly to the appropriate series or data tables.

Further explanation can be found at: www.bankofengland.co.uk/statistics/Pages/iadb/notesiadb/Changes_flows_growth_rates.aspx.

(eg) Due to improvements in reporting at one institution, the amounts outstanding increased by £3bn. This effect has been adjusted out of the flows for April 2015.

(eh) Due to a change in the reporting population, the amounts outstanding increased by £1bn. This effect has been adjusted out of the flows for December 2015.

(ei) Due to improvements in reporting at one institution the amounts outstanding decreased by £11bn. This effect has been adjusted out of the flows for January 2015.

(ej) Due to improvements in reporting at one institution, the amounts outstanding increased by £1bn. This effect has been adjusted out of the flows for February 2016.

(ek) Due to improvements in reporting at one institution, the amounts outstanding decreased by £2bn. This effect has been adjusted out of the flows for March 2016.

(el) Due to improvements in reporting at one institution, the amounts outstanding decreased by £1bn. This effect has been adjusted out of the flows for February 2016.

(em) Due to improvements in reporting at one institution, the amounts outstanding increased by £1bn. This effect has been adjusted out of the flows for April 2016.

(en) Due to improvements in reporting at one institution, the amounts outstanding increased by £2bn. This effect has been adjusted out of the flows for April 2015.

(eo) Due to a change in treatment at one institution, the amounts outstanding decreased by £4bn. This effect has been adjusted out of the flows for April 2015.

(ep) Due to improvements in reporting at one institution, the amounts outstanding increased by £1bn. This effect has been adjusted out of the flows for April 2015.

(eq) Due to a change in treatment at one institution, the amounts outstanding increased by £1bn. This effect has been adjusted out of the flows for August 2014.

(er) Due to improvements in reporting at one institution, the amounts outstanding increased by £1bn. This effect has been adjusted out of the flows for April 2015.

(es) Due to improvements in reporting at one institution, the amounts outstanding increased by £1bn. This effect has been adjusted out of the flows for June 2014.

(et) Due to a loan transfer by one reporting institution, the amounts outstanding decreased by £1bn. This effect has been adjusted out of the flows for December 2014.

(eu) Due to improvements in reporting at one institution, the amounts outstanding increased by £11bn. This effect has been adjusted out of the flows for January 2015.

(ev) Due to improvements in reporting at one institution, the amounts outstanding increased by £3bn. This effect has been adjusted out of the flows for April 2015.

(ew) Due to a change in the reporting population, the amounts outstanding increased by £1bn. This effect has been adjusted out of the flows for April 2015.

(ex) Due to improvements in reporting at one institution, the amounts outstanding decreased by £1bn. This effect has been adjusted out of the flows for February 2016.

(ey) Due to improvements in reporting at one institution, the amounts outstanding decreased by £1bn. This effect has been adjusted out of the flows for February 2016.

(ez) Due to improvements in reporting at one institution, the amounts outstanding increased by £2bn. This effect has been adjusted out of the flows for March 2016.

(fa) Due to a change in accounting treatment at one reporting institution, the amounts outstanding increased by £2bn. This effect has been adjusted out of the flows for June 2014.

(fb) Due to improvements in reporting at one institution, the amounts outstanding increased by £1bn. This effect has been adjusted out of the flows for April 2015.

(fc) Due to improvements in reporting at one institution, the amounts outstanding increased by £1bn. This effect has been adjusted out of the flows for April 2015.

(fd) Due to improvements in reporting at one institution, the amounts outstanding increased by £1bn. This effect has been adjusted out of the flows for April 2015.

(fe) Due to improvements in reporting at one institution, the amounts outstanding increased by £2bn. This effect has been adjusted out of the flows for April 2015.

(ff) Due to improvements in reporting at one institution, the amounts outstanding increased by £4bn. This effect has been adjusted out of the flows for August 2014.

(fg) Due to improvements in reporting at one institution, the amounts outstanding increased by £5bn. This effect has been adjusted out of the flows for April 2015.

(fh) Due to improvements in reporting at one institution, the amounts outstanding decreased by £1bn. This effect has been adjusted out of the flows for January 2016.

(fi) Due to a restructuring at one reporting institution, the amounts outstanding increased by £4bn. This effect has been adjusted out of the flows for December 2015.

(fj) Due to improvements in reporting at one reporting institution, the amounts outstanding decreased by £2bn. This effect has been adjusted out of the flows for January 2015.

(fk) Due to improvements in reporting at one institution, the amounts outstanding decreased by £2bn. This effect has been adjusted out of the flows for May 2015.

(fl) Due to improvements in reporting at one institution, the amounts outstanding increased by £1bn. This effect has been adjusted out of the flows for October 2015.

(fm) Due to a change in the reporting population, the amounts outstanding decreased by £1bn. This effect has been adjusted out of the flows for October 2015.

(fn) Due to improvements in reporting at one institution, the amounts outstanding increased by £5bn. This effect has been adjusted out of the flows for April 2016.

(fo) Due to a restructuring at one reporting institution, the amounts outstanding decreased by £4bn. This effect has been adjusted out of the flows for December 2015.

(fp) Due to improvements in reporting at one institution, the amounts outstanding increased by £1bn. This effect has been adjusted out of the flows for January 2016.

(fq) Due to improvements in reporting at one institution, the amounts outstanding decreased by £1bn. This effect has been adjusted out of the flows for October 2015.

(fr) Due to improvements in reporting at one institution, the amounts outstanding increased by £4bn. This effect has been adjusted out of the flows for April 2016.

(fs) Due to improvements in reporting at one institution, the amounts outstanding increased by £1bn. This effect has been adjusted out of the flows for September 2014.

(ft) Due to a loan transfer by one reporting institution, the amounts outstanding increased by £2bn. This effect has been adjusted out of the flows for January 2015.

(fu) Due to improvements in reporting at one institution, the amounts outstanding increased by £2bn. This effect has been adjusted out of the flows for April 2015.

(fv) Due to improvements in reporting at one institution, the amounts outstanding increased by £2bn. This effect has been adjusted out of the flows for March 2015.

(fw) Due to a change in the reporting population, the amounts outstanding decreased by £2bn. This effect has been adjusted out of the flows for October 2015.

(fx) Due to a change in the reporting population, the amounts outstanding increased by £3bn. This effect has been adjusted out of the flows for January 2016.

(fy) Due to a change in the reporting population, the amounts outstanding increased by £3bn. This effect has been adjusted out of the flows for October 2015.

(fz) Due to changes in reporting at one institution, the amounts outstanding decreased by £2bn. This effect has been adjusted out of the flows for November 2015.

(ga) Due to a change in the reporting population, the amounts outstanding decreased by £4bn. This effect has been adjusted out of the flows for January 2016.

(gb) Due to changes in reporting at one institution, the amounts outstanding increased by £2bn. This effect has been adjusted out of the flows for November 2015.

(gc) Due to improvements in reporting at one institution, the amounts outstanding decreased by £4bn. This effect has been adjusted out of the flows for April 2016.

(gd) Due to improvements in reporting at one institution, the amounts outstanding decreased by £1bn. This effect has been adjusted out of the flows for April 2016.

(ge) Due to improvements in reporting at one institution, the amounts outstanding increased by £2bn. This effect has been adjusted out of the flows for June 2014.

(gf) Due to a loan transfer by one reporting institution, the amounts outstanding decreased by £2bn. This effect has been adjusted out of the flows for January 2015.

(gg) Due to improvements in reporting at one institution, the amounts outstanding increased by £1bn. This effect has been adjusted out of the flows for February 2015.

(gh) Due to improvements in reporting at one institution, the amounts outstanding decreased by £4bn. This effect has been adjusted out of the flows for April 2015.

(gi) Due to a loan transfer by one reporting institution, the amounts outstanding increased by £3bn. This effect has been adjusted out of the flows for December 2015.

(gj) Due to improvements in reporting at one institution, the amounts outstanding increased by £2bn. This effect has been adjusted out of the flows for March 2015.

(gk) Due to a loan transfer by one reporting institution, the amounts outstanding increased by £5bn. This effect has been adjusted out of the flows for December 2015.

(gl) Due to a change in the reporting population, the amounts outstanding increased by £7bn. This effect has been adjusted out of the flows for September 2014.

(gm) Due to a loan transfer by one reporting institution, the amounts outstanding increased by £10bn. This effect has been adjusted out of the flows for October 2014.

(gn) Due to improvements in reporting at one institution, the amounts outstanding decreased by £1bn. This effect has been adjusted out of the flows for February 2015.

(go) Due to improvements in reporting at one institution, the amounts outstanding decreased by £7bn. This effect has been adjusted out of the flows for April 2015.

(gp) Due to improvements in reporting at one institution, the amounts outstanding decreased by £3bn. This effect has been adjusted out of the flows for December 2015.

(gq) Due to changes in reporting at one institution, the amounts outstanding increased by £7bn. This effect has been adjusted out of the flows for November 2015.

12.5a Industrial analysis of monetary financial institutions' deposits from UK residents

£ millions Not seasonally adjusted

Amounts outstanding of deposit liabilities (including under repo) in sterling

RPM	Agriculture, hunting and forestry	Fishing	Mining and quarrying	Food, beverages and tobacco	Textiles, wearing apparel and leather	Pulp, paper, and printing	Chemicals, pharmaceuticals, rubber and plastics	Manufacturing Non-metallic mineral products and metals	Machinery, equipment and transport equipment	Electrical, medical and optical equipment	Other manufacturing	Total	Electricity, gas steam and air conditioning	Electricity, gas and water supply Water collection and sewerage	Waste management related services and remediation activities	Total
	TDCB	TDCC	TDCD	TDCF	TDCG	TDCH	TDCI	TDCJ	TDCK	TDCL	TDCM	TDCE	TDCN	TDCO	BE2M	B3FI
2014 May	5,683	291	4,816	3,383	957	1,338	4,376	4,878	8,176	4,193	3,812	31,114	4,308	2,551	1,331	8,191
Jun	5,673	289	5,222	3,277	951	1,321	4,473	5,002	7,819	4,300	3,582	30,725	4,020	2,629	1,361	8,010
Jul	5,542	259	4,500	3,361	955	1,272	4,478	5,032	8,152	3,995	3,721	30,965	3,942	2,661	1,305	7,908
Aug	5,518	227	4,914	3,309	967	1,249	4,562	5,007	7,433	4,115	3,693	30,335	4,270	2,608	1,360	8,238
Sep	5,552	229	4,674	3,450	988	1,247	5,011	5,316	7,343	4,140	4,097	31,592	3,968	2,801	1,398	8,167
Oct	5,585	232	4,607	3,317	1,019	1,257	4,542	5,431	7,962	4,136	4,211	31,873	3,993	2,876	1,331	8,200
Nov	5,589	269	5,468	3,456	1,064	1,363	4,414	5,472	7,942	4,219	4,365	32,294	4,056	2,859	1,404	8,318
Dec	6,485	258	5,803	3,739	1,067	1,405	4,852	5,377	8,735	4,285	4,164	33,626	4,768	2,853	1,416	9,036
2015 Jan	6,266	252	4,832	3,295	1,042	1,368	4,215	5,215	8,322	4,244	4,084	31,785	4,308	2,809	1,405	8,523
Feb	6,183	260	5,025	2,945	988	1,318	4,691	5,172	8,345	4,293	3,835	31,587	4,767	2,432	1,363	8,563
Mar	6,070	258	5,820	3,095	1,088	1,425	4,645	5,338	8,326	4,437	4,039	32,393	5,603	2,546	1,426	9,575
Apr	5,931	240	5,790	2,907	1,083	1,419	4,649	5,326	8,730	4,358	4,221	32,693	5,489	2,281	1,431	9,200
May	5,873	238	6,300	2,774	1,103	1,423	4,804	5,295	8,449	4,437	4,106	32,391	5,881	2,534	1,444	9,859
Jun	5,791	251	6,176	3,336	1,127	1,442	5,064	5,289	9,145	4,619	4,226	34,247	6,080	2,665	1,542	10,286
Jul	5,782	238	6,793	3,582	1,146	1,421	4,628	5,600	9,138	4,521	4,141	34,177	5,558	2,648	1,444	9,650
Aug	5,815	236	6,872 (a)	3,740	1,131	1,343	5,120	5,543	8,642	4,595	4,135	34,250	5,721	2,589	1,532	9,842
Sep	5,862	243	8,991	3,954	1,265	1,332	5,520	5,805	8,652	4,656	4,386	35,569	5,749	2,407	1,625	9,781
Oct	5,795	234	9,642	4,275	1,264	1,369	5,242	5,822	9,203	4,783	4,337	36,296	5,251	2,358	1,550	9,159
Nov	5,840	245	11,127	4,428	1,296	1,466	5,424	5,970	8,694	4,764	4,476	36,518	5,708	2,373	1,560	9,641
Dec	6,083	250	9,573	4,154	1,360	1,551	5,399	6,214	10,708	4,738	4,631	38,756	6,335	2,294	1,578	10,207
2016 Jan	6,225	239	10,389	4,081	1,355	1,667	5,370	5,826	9,906	4,721	4,466	37,392	5,122	2,205	1,509	8,836
Feb	6,201	260	3,508	3,688	1,353	1,640	5,466	5,731	9,960	4,724	4,505	37,068	5,638	2,310	1,502	9,450
Mar	6,160	267	3,208	3,828	1,335	1,668	5,361	5,801	10,056	4,523	4,718	37,290	6,436	2,286	1,733	10,455
Apr	6,160	259	2,918	3,787	1,315	1,650	4,913	5,813	9,527	4,571	4,668	36,244	6,137	2,150	1,521	9,809

Source: Bank of England

12.5a Industrial analysis of monetary financial institutions' deposits from UK residents

£ millions   Not seasonally adjusted

Amounts outstanding of deposit liabilities (including under repo) in sterling

| | Development of buildings | Construction | | | | | Wholesale and retail trade | | | | Accommodation and food service activities | Transport, storage and communication | | |
| | | Construction of commercial buildings | Construction of domestic buildings | Civil Engineering | Other construction activities | Total | Wholesale and retail trade and repair of motor vehicles and motorcycles | Wholesale trade, excluding motor vehicles and motor cycles | Retail trade excluding motor vehicles and motor cycles | Total | | Transportation and storage | Information and communication | Total |
RPM	B3FW	B7EK	B3LS	B3JO	B4PS	TDCP	TDCR	TDCS	TDCT	TDCQ	TDCU	B5PF	B3NI	TDCV
2014 May	6,491	3,528	3,060	4,359	8,945	26,383	4,560	12,759	14,317	31,635	7,355	12,287	21,036	33,322
Jun	7,517	3,711	3,648	4,660	9,034	28,570	4,896	13,035	14,164	32,095	7,612	12,058	20,415 (d)	32,472 (d)
Jul	6,951	3,719	3,155	4,352	9,295	27,471	4,876	12,935	14,138	31,949	8,408	13,222	20,385	33,607
Aug	6,788	3,664	3,225	4,489	9,374	27,540	5,064	13,020	15,496 (b)	33,580 (b)	8,145	12,864	19,294	32,159
Sep	7,081	3,813	2,821	4,391	9,574	27,680	5,053	13,115	15,180	33,348	8,338	12,360	20,901	33,261
Oct	7,054	3,634	3,223	4,434	9,874	28,220	5,123	13,798	15,212	34,133	7,534	12,933	21,011	33,944
Nov	6,891	3,678	3,345	4,599	10,120	28,632	5,268	13,842	16,051	35,161	7,380	13,521	20,288	33,810
Dec	6,885	3,895	3,783	5,132	10,390	30,086	4,769	14,647	20,978	40,393	7,443	13,983	21,192	35,175
2015 Jan	6,882	3,692	3,195	4,675	9,947	28,392	4,582	14,209	19,423	38,213	7,066	12,643	23,036	35,679
Feb	6,970	3,708	3,222	4,722	9,865	28,487	4,873	13,841	18,649	37,363	6,877	12,588	22,671	35,260
Mar	7,221	3,862	3,342	5,353	10,208	29,985	5,089	14,326	18,990	38,405	7,013	13,194	22,649	35,843
Apr	7,187	3,824	3,344	4,872	10,220	29,448	5,174	13,946	14,743 (c)	33,863 (c)	7,513	13,317	23,228	36,545
May	7,458	3,794	3,070	4,908	10,142	29,371	5,014	14,300	14,520	33,834	7,641	13,365	23,571	36,936
Jun	7,668	3,651	3,779	5,143	10,452	30,692	4,990	14,501	15,107	34,598	7,531	12,486	22,577	35,063
Jul	7,505	3,711	3,522	4,945	10,702	30,385	5,096	14,723	14,772	34,590	7,866	12,717	22,497	35,214
Aug	7,464	3,790	3,682	5,145	10,768	30,850	5,191	14,274	14,855	34,321	7,968	12,742	21,892	34,633
Sep	7,585	3,772	3,408	5,137	10,888	30,789	5,363	14,590	14,975	34,928	8,431	13,257	21,954	35,211
Oct	7,576	3,733	3,619	5,257	11,305	31,490	5,067	14,849	16,992	36,908	8,408	14,413	22,180	36,594
Nov	7,637	3,820	3,751	5,464	11,487	32,159	5,111	15,218	16,908	37,237	8,409	13,586	23,195	36,782
Dec	7,941	4,049	4,184	5,762	11,735	33,671	5,040	15,554	19,592	40,186	8,416	12,538	23,719	36,257
2016 Jan	7,781	3,795	3,607	5,192	11,214	31,590	5,086	15,314	15,493	35,892	7,881	13,720	22,843	36,563
Feb	7,774	3,860	3,650	5,260	11,037	31,580	5,529	15,277	16,483	37,288	7,945	13,848	25,630	39,478
Mar	8,118	4,046	3,647	5,714	11,181	32,705	5,427	15,344	16,015	36,786	8,325	14,049	25,820	39,868
Apr	7,952	4,043	3,608	5,436	11,382	32,422	5,543	14,660	16,160	36,363	7,914	13,430	24,406	37,837

Source: Bank of England

12.5a Industrial analysis of monetary financial institutions' deposits from UK residents

£ millions   Not seasonally adjusted

Amounts outstanding of deposit liabilities (including under repo) in sterling

RPM	Real estate, professional services and support activities				Public administration and defence	Education	Human health and social work	Recreational, personal and community service activities			Financial intermediation (excluding insurance and pension funds)						
	Buying, selling and renting of real estate	Professional, scientific and technical activities	Administrative and support services	Total				Recreational, cultural and sporting activities	Personal and community service activities	Total	Financial leasing corporations	Non-bank credit grantors excluding credit unions and SPVs	Credit unions	Factoring corporations	Mortgage and housing credit corporations excluding SPVs	Investment and unit trusts excluding money market mutual funds	Money market mutual funds
	TDCX	B3ON	B6PK	TDCW	TDDB	TDDC	TDDD	TDDF	TDDE	B3S6	TDDH	TDDI	TDDJ	TDDK	TDDL	TDDM	TDDN
2014 May	34,017	64,824	19,853	118,694	31,796	19,645	16,537	11,740	17,279	29,020	9,916	2,314	994	909	14,314	23,931	625
Jun	36,277	67,319	20,505	124,101	31,450	19,062	16,845	10,220 (f)	17,318	27,537 (f)	9,778	2,374	985	958	14,401	22,983	386
Jul	34,659	68,719	21,635	125,013	34,991	18,048	16,920	10,325	17,213	27,538	9,744	2,362	954	945	14,646	20,876	787
Aug	34,403	66,758	20,854	122,014	37,323	17,742	17,480	10,658	17,136	27,793	9,695	2,451	944	1,080	14,210	20,888	1,285
Sep	37,325	66,608	20,841	124,774	29,811	18,812	18,074	10,412	17,608	28,020	9,655	2,537	974	998	14,483	19,953	746
Oct	36,374	66,458	20,926	123,758	33,767	19,161	18,590	10,248	17,655	27,903	9,589	2,874	969	992	13,799	18,815	840
Nov	36,100	67,925	20,949	124,974	33,571	18,457	18,611	10,080	17,576	27,657	10,766 (g)	2,836	962	922	13,161	19,646	933
Dec	38,515	63,723	20,878	123,116	28,673	17,851	18,666	10,037	17,504	27,541	11,263	2,429	949	848	13,219	18,722	1,007
2015 Jan	36,697	65,128	20,483	122,308	31,007	18,731	18,579	10,244	17,735	27,979	11,725	2,619	975	950	13,145	18,220	924
Feb	36,538	64,656	22,057	123,251	30,979	18,844	18,456	10,290	17,601	27,891	11,709	2,690	967	889	11,134 (h)	18,334	734
Mar	39,300	68,817	23,477 (e)	131,593 (e)	29,261	17,925	18,694	10,533	17,637	28,170	11,235	2,799	981	913	10,500	18,211	772
Apr	38,266	68,042	22,381	128,689	34,892	18,829	18,699	10,543	17,706	28,250	10,876	2,721	989	929	10,500	18,604	754
May	37,675	68,457	22,986	129,118	34,007	20,617	18,938	10,672	17,788	28,460	10,813	2,959	995	976	10,412	19,087	917
Jun	40,171	70,299	23,698	134,168	34,344	19,923	19,222	10,728	17,905	28,633	10,777	2,789	1,016	861	9,766	19,278	829
Jul	39,743	72,512	23,706	135,962	37,486	19,096	19,138	11,127	17,843	28,970	10,721	2,933	1,029	1,146	10,128	18,139	602
Aug	39,295	71,390	23,247	133,932	38,481	18,835	19,008	11,272	17,673	28,945	10,715	3,196	1,046	1,130	9,646	17,365	710
Sep	42,641	72,227	23,404	138,272	29,504	19,677	18,981	10,998	17,886	28,884	10,838	3,460	1,058	873	9,428	17,668	756
Oct	41,652	72,358	22,753	136,763	30,092	20,533	19,270	10,793	17,931	28,723	11,062	3,484	1,102	899	9,440	18,151	592
Nov	41,106	76,425	22,851	140,383	31,109	19,388	19,521	10,604	17,874	28,478	10,456	3,770	1,041	949	9,569	17,938	770
Dec	42,913	72,009	22,705	137,628	31,112	18,507	19,538	10,635	17,858	28,493	9,825	3,749	1,049	948	9,309	18,725	547
2016 Jan	41,705	72,505	22,315	136,526	30,361	19,768	19,216	11,138	18,041	29,179	8,967	3,323	1,059	960	9,336	18,644	1,022
Feb	40,940	73,319	23,015	137,273	28,983	20,180	19,466	11,181	18,246	29,426	9,026	3,562	1,089	861	9,285	19,842	910
Mar	44,000	79,880	24,136	148,016	25,512	18,926	19,470	11,104	18,142	29,246	8,987	3,581	1,103	981	8,823	19,704	939
Apr	42,148	71,647	23,886	137,682	33,478	20,075	19,623	10,992	18,244	29,236	9,062	3,759	1,104	1,052	8,949	17,985	606

Source: Bank of England

12.5a Industrial analysis of monetary financial institutions' deposits from UK residents

£ millions   Not seasonally adjusted

Amounts outstanding of deposit liabilities (including under repo) in sterling

RPM	Financial intermediation (excluding insurance and pension funds)						Insurance companies & pension funds			Fund management activities	Activities auxiliary to financial intermediation			Total	Total financial and non-financial businesses	Individuals and individual trusts	Total UK residents
	Bank holding companies	Securities dealers	SPVs related to securitisation	Other financial intermediaries	of which intragroup activity	Total	Insurance companies	Pension funds	Total		Central clearing counterparties	Other auxiliary activities	Total				
	TDDO	TDDP	B3T5	TDDQ	B3U3	TDDG	B7FI	B3VH	TDDR	TDDS	B7FT	B7FY	TDDT	B3Y8	Z945	TDDU	TDCA
2014 May	23,151	35,812	159,562	78,450	51,289	349,976	25,129	25,417	50,546	67,768	86,634	13,294	99,928	167,696	932,700	1,087,593	2,020,293
Jun	22,661	40,473	161,946	76,451	49,033	353,395	24,087	26,224	50,311	69,396	81,451	13,860	95,311	164,707	938,077	1,087,856	2,025,932
Jul	22,573	39,975	159,566 (j)	75,663	48,660	348,090 (j)	23,177	25,289	48,466	66,793	88,068	13,722	101,791	168,584	938,261 (j)	1,087,435	2,025,696 (j)
Aug	22,123	39,890	160,646	71,228 (q)	47,488	344,440 (q)	23,404	25,430	48,834	71,645 (v)	92,719	14,449	107,168	178,813 (v)	945,094 (b)	1,094,664	2,039,757 (b)
Sep	25,035	35,718 (i)	161,388	71,472	45,860	342,958 (i)	24,369	27,164	51,532	74,244 (w)(x)	67,418	14,649	82,067	156,311 (w)(x)	923,134 (w)	1,096,138	2,019,272 (w)
Oct	24,013	32,746	146,377	69,775	46,156	320,791	22,538	25,837	48,374	72,995	83,649	14,032	97,681	170,675	917,346	1,103,466	2,020,812
Nov	15,785	34,240	147,288	70,096 (r)	44,778 (r)	316,636	22,750	26,164	48,914	68,523	88,016	14,476	102,491	171,014	916,756	1,108,105	2,024,860
Dec	11,507	32,184	152,567	72,975	46,331	317,671	23,455	25,171	48,626	67,071	71,857	14,019	85,876	152,947	903,396	1,111,740	2,015,136
2015 Jan	11,878	32,500	130,266	70,949	44,333	294,151	29,111	24,690	53,802	71,770	77,358	13,778	91,136	162,906	890,470	1,104,399	1,994,868
Feb	11,945	31,359	125,633 (k)	69,288	43,581	284,682	26,592	25,184	51,776	75,217	77,901	13,723	91,624	166,841	882,322	1,108,421	1,990,744
Mar	17,842	31,444	124,201	72,273	45,449	291,171	28,740	25,725	54,466	73,303	71,134	14,942	86,076	159,379	896,023 (e)	1,110,467	2,006,490 (e)
Apr	18,249	32,227	119,499	69,860	43,729	285,209	29,171	25,962	55,133	73,667	74,226	15,411	89,637	163,304	894,228 (c)	1,117,355 (aa)	2,011,582 (c)
May	18,960	30,340	121,271 (l)	70,723	44,492	287,452 (l)	26,659	25,092	51,751	74,111	79,197	15,303	94,500	168,610	901,395 (l)	1,121,912	2,023,307 (l)
Jun	17,391	30,903	122,102	70,264	43,707	285,976	26,835	23,981	50,816	71,082	68,852	15,317	84,169	155,251	892,968	1,122,093	2,015,062
Jul	17,741	29,589	118,886	72,259	45,401	283,172	24,684	23,683	48,367	75,493	80,121	15,308	95,430	170,923	907,809	1,124,569	2,032,378
Aug	17,167	30,473	108,882	66,060 (s)	44,688	266,390 (s)	23,269	23,413	46,681	72,622 (y)	85,089	15,205	100,294	172,917 (y)	889,976 (a)	1,130,038	2,020,013 (a)
Sep	10,288	29,099	110,781	66,275	43,927	260,523	22,838	24,103	46,942	76,067	58,326	15,603	73,929	149,997	862,584	1,131,035	1,993,619
Oct	9,345	27,574	110,153 (m)	65,644	43,513	257,447 (m)	22,324	23,177	45,501	75,889	64,657	15,199	79,856	155,745	868,599 (m)	1,139,888	2,008,487 (m)
Nov	9,928	28,535	107,148	64,673	43,024	254,777	22,742	22,971	45,714	74,900	69,361	15,899	85,260	160,159	877,488	1,142,458	2,019,946
Dec	10,105	26,853	107,854	67,101	44,576	256,066	21,628	23,332	44,960	66,949	58,570	15,945	74,514	141,464	861,167	1,151,799	2,012,966
2016 Jan	10,293	28,556	99,845	65,344	42,707	247,348	21,519	25,317	46,835	72,871	60,589	16,514	77,103	149,974	854,213	1,151,007	2,005,221
Feb	11,512	28,374	100,449 (n)(o)	63,546	41,805	248,455 (n)(o)	21,478	25,279	46,757	77,978	65,712	17,512	83,224	161,202	864,521	1,156,985 (ab)(ac)	2,021,506
Mar	10,565	28,342	98,834	63,699 (t)	42,579	245,557 (t)	23,321	20,627 (u)	43,948 (u)	76,955 (z)	51,431	18,302	69,732	146,687 (z)	852,426 (u)	1,168,353	2,020,779 (u)
Apr	10,130	27,188	97,640 (p)	61,364	41,065	238,839 (p)	20,962	21,673	42,635	76,947	54,877	17,657	72,534	149,481	840,973 (p)	1,183,216	2,024,189 (p)

Source: Bank of England

12.5a Industrial analysis of monetary financial institutions' deposits from UK residents

£ millions   Not seasonally adjusted

Notes to table

Movements in amounts outstanding can reflect breaks in data series as well as underlying flows. For changes data, users are recommended to refer directly to the appropriate series or data tables. www.bankofengland.co.uk/statistics/Pages/iadb/notesiadb/Changes_flows_growth_rates.aspx.

(a) Due to improvements in reporting at one institution, the amounts outstanding decreased by £1bn. This effect has been adjusted out of the flows for August 2015.

(b) Due to a change in treatment at one institution, the amounts outstanding increased by £1bn. This effect has been adjusted out of the flows for August 2014.

(c) Due to a change in treatment at one institution, the amounts outstanding decreased by £4bn. This effect has been adjusted out of the flows for April 2015.

(d) Due to improvements in reporting at one institution, the amounts outstanding increased by £1bn. This effect has been adjusted out of the flows for June 2014.

(e) Due to improvements in reporting at one institution, the amounts outstanding increased by £1bn. This effect has been adjusted out of the flows for March 2015.

(f) Due to improvements in reporting at one institution, the amounts outstanding decreased by £1bn. This effect has been adjusted out of the flows for June 2014.

(g) Due to improvements in reporting at one institution, the amounts outstanding increased by £1bn. This effect has been adjusted out of the flows for November 2014.

(h) Due to improvements in reporting at one institution, the amounts outstanding decreased by £1bn. This effect has been adjusted out of the flows for February 2015.

(i) Due to improvements in reporting at one institution, the amounts outstanding decreased by £1bn. This effect has been adjusted out of the flows for September 2014.

(j) Due to improvements in reporting at one institution, the amounts outstanding increased by £2bn. This effect has been adjusted out of the flows for July 2014.

(k) Due to improvements in reporting at one institution, the amounts outstanding increased by £1bn. This effect has been adjusted out of the flows for February 2015.

(l) Due to improvements in reporting at one institution, the amounts outstanding increased by £3bn. This effect has been adjusted out of the flows for May 2015.

(m) Due to additional information provided by one reporting institution, this series has been revised upwards by £1bn for October 2015.

(n) Due to improvements in reporting at one institution, the amounts outstanding decreased by £1bn. This effect has been adjusted out of the flows for March 2016.

(o) Due to improvements in reporting at one institution, this series has been revised downwards by £1bn.

(p) Due to a loan transfer by one reporting institution, the amounts outstanding increased by £1bn. This effect has been adjusted out of the flows for April 2016.

(q) Due to improvements in reporting at one institution, the amounts outstanding decreased by £1bn. This effect has been adjusted out of the flows for August 2014.

(r) Due to improvements in reporting at one institution, the amounts outstanding decreased by £1bn. This effect has been adjusted out of the flows for November 2014.

(s) Due to improvements in reporting at one institution, the amounts outstanding decreased by £4bn. This effect has been adjusted out of the flows for August 2015.

(t) Due to improvements in reporting at one institution, the amounts outstanding decreased by £2bn. This effect has been adjusted out of the flows for March 2016.

(u) Due to changes in reporting at one institution, the amounts outstanding decreased by £5bn. This effect has been adjusted out of the flows for March 2016.

(v) Due to improvements in reporting at one institution, the amounts outstanding increased by £1bn. This effect has been adjusted out of the flows for August 2014.

(w) Due to improvements in reporting at one institution, the amounts outstanding increased by £1bn. This effect has been adjusted out of the flows for September 2014.

(x) Due to improvements in reporting at one institution, the amounts outstanding increased by £1bn. This effect has been adjusted out of the flows for September 2014.

(y) Due to improvements in reporting at one institution, the amounts outstanding increased by £5bn. This effect has been adjusted out of the flows for August 2015.

(z) Due to improvements in reporting at one institution, the amounts outstanding increased by £2bn. This effect has been adjusted out of the flows for March 2016.

(aa) Due to a change in the reporting population, the amounts outstanding increased by £1bn. This effect has been adjusted out of the flows for April 2015.

(ab) Due to improvements in reporting at one institution, the amounts outstanding increased by £1bn. This effect has been adjusted out of the flows for March 2016.

(ac) Due to improvements in reporting at one institution, this series has been revised upwards by £1bn.

Copyright guidance and the related UK Open Government Licence can be viewed here: www.bankofengland.co.uk/Pages/disclaimer.aspx.

12.5b Industrial analysis of monetary financial institutions' deposits from UK residents

£ millions Not seasonally adjusted

Amounts outstanding of deposit liabilities (including under repo) in all currencies

| | Agriculture, hunting and forestry | Fishing | Mining and quarrying | Manufacturing | | | | | | | | | Electricity, gas and water supply | | | Total |
| | | | | Food, beverages and tobacco | Textiles, wearing apparel and leather | Pulp, paper, and printing | Chemicals, pharmaceuticals, rubber and plastics | Non-metallic mineral products and metals | Machinery, equipment and transport equipment | Electrical, medical and optical equipment | Other manufacturing | Total | Electricity, gas steam and air conditioning | Water collection and sewerage | Waste management related services and remediation activities | |
RPM	TDAB	TDAC	TDAD	TDAF	TDAG	TDAH	TDAI	TDAJ	TDAK	TDAL	TDAM	TDAE	TDAN	TDAO	BE2N	B3FJ
2014 May	5,838	304	15,542	4,480	1,344	1,881	7,313	6,326	10,731	6,308	4,595	42,976	5,105	2,584	1,478	9,167
Jun	5,829	304	15,864	4,333	1,280	2,042	7,534	6,233	11,301	6,596	4,301	43,620	4,809	2,666	1,501	8,975
Jul	5,710	272	14,909	5,312	1,267	1,954	7,848	6,284	11,031	6,011	4,401	44,107	4,971	2,696	1,452	9,119
Aug	5,666	240	15,739	4,984	1,326	1,953	7,954	6,322	10,427	6,230	4,444	43,641	5,028	2,637	1,487	9,152
Sep	5,815	238	15,672	5,352	1,349	1,840	8,762	6,449	10,159	6,376	4,801	45,090	4,842	2,831	1,530	9,203
Oct	5,756	241	13,555	4,531	1,338	1,840	8,298	6,461	10,980	6,239	4,883	44,571	4,846	2,911	1,466	9,223
Nov	5,721	292	19,023	4,534	1,394	2,005	8,879	6,565	10,540	6,331	5,013	45,261	4,888	2,887	1,522	9,296
Dec	6,674	284	16,533	4,810	1,416	2,248	9,493	6,826	12,189	6,555	5,035	48,571	5,765	2,881	1,577	10,222
2015 Jan	6,431	274	17,353	4,045	1,384	2,151	8,571	6,791	11,009	6,397	4,826	45,173	5,432	2,836	1,577	9,845
Feb	6,325	288	18,510	3,715	1,317	2,052	9,037	6,803	10,895	6,324	4,654	44,797	5,698	2,459	1,536	9,693
Mar	6,205	287	16,210	4,176	1,456	2,002	10,108	6,642	10,920	7,208	4,820	47,331	6,588	2,581	1,650	10,819
Apr	6,075	265	16,211	3,747	1,450	2,010	9,189	6,411	11,217	6,999	4,900	45,923	6,436	2,305	1,619	10,360
May	6,008	273	19,221	3,598	1,458	2,004	9,753	6,425	11,281	7,117	4,968	46,603	6,871	2,560	1,643	11,073
Jun	5,925	281	17,303	4,141	1,493	2,033	10,038	6,365	12,276	7,074	4,936	48,354	6,800	2,691	1,747	11,238
Jul	5,911	267	18,123	5,010	1,522	2,040	10,016	6,638	11,832	6,701	4,867	48,625	6,396	2,668	1,621	10,685
Aug	5,951	263	21,726	5,142	1,507	1,922	11,104	6,700	11,454	6,788	4,971	49,588	7,030	2,611	1,703	11,344
Sep	5,991	266	21,526	6,177	1,637	1,775	11,085	6,840	11,633	6,815	5,180	51,141	6,883	2,427	1,771	11,082
Oct	5,926	258	21,062	5,338	1,619	1,820	10,621	6,938	12,123	6,975	5,097	50,531	6,412	2,384	1,679	10,475
Nov	5,985	279	24,371	5,321	1,648	1,909	11,086	7,104	11,546	6,904	5,207	50,726	6,954	2,394	1,692	11,040
Dec	6,235	265	22,570	4,790	1,704	2,052	10,875	7,391	14,795	7,041	5,382	54,031	7,509	2,320	1,685	11,515
2016 Jan	6,384	256	21,783	5,110	1,686	2,153	10,716	7,107	13,086	7,421	5,473	52,751	6,057	2,231	1,627	9,915
Feb	6,368	284	11,922	4,645	1,602	2,163	11,163	7,113	13,769	7,193	5,769	53,417	6,695	2,334	1,656	10,685
Mar	6,320	289	12,480	4,812	1,602	2,064	10,990	6,990	14,004	6,979	5,916	53,356	7,363	2,304	1,909	11,576
Apr	6,343	285	11,706	4,768	1,577	2,111	10,421	6,968	13,204	6,693	6,059	51,801	7,101	2,170	1,690	10,961

Source: Bank of England

12.5b Industrial analysis of monetary financial institutions' deposits from UK residents

£ millions Not seasonally adjusted

Amounts outstanding of deposit liabilities (including under repo) in all currencies

| | Development of buildings | Construction | | | | | Wholesale and retail trade | | | | Accommodation and food service activities | Transport, storage and communication | | |
| | | Construction of commercial buildings | Construction of domestic buildings | Civil Engineering | Other construction activities | Total | Wholesale and retail trade and repair of motor vehicles and motorcycles | Wholesale trade, excluding motor vehicles and motor cycles | Retail trade excluding motor vehicles and motor cycles | Total | | Transportation and storage | Information and communication | Total |
RPM	B3FX	B7EL	B3LT	B4PG	B4PT	TDAP	TDAR	TDAS	TDAT	TDAQ	TDAU	B5PG	B3NJ	TDAV
2014 May	6,511	3,631	3,068	4,527	9,117	26,854	4,868	17,648	15,778	38,293	8,129	15,473	25,124	40,597
Jun	7,536	3,795	3,656	4,883	9,201	29,070	5,227	17,645	15,837	38,708	8,326	15,028	25,021 (ak)	40,049 (ak)
Jul	6,973	3,796	3,165	4,587	9,447	27,967	5,178	18,128	15,373	38,679	9,060	16,208	24,489	40,698
Aug	6,812	3,733	3,236	4,703	9,566	28,050	5,338	17,663	16,645 (ai)	39,646 (ai)	8,730	15,752	23,323	39,075
Sep	7,106	3,874	2,832	4,617	9,777	28,207	5,395	17,824	16,551	39,769	8,943	15,449	25,346	40,795
Oct	7,079	3,722	3,234	4,628	10,062	28,726	5,426	18,956	16,659	41,041	8,088	16,064	25,480	41,544
Nov	6,914	3,737	3,355	4,923	10,329	29,258	5,613	18,295	17,632	41,540	7,963	16,799	24,175	40,974
Dec	6,911	3,918	3,794	5,529	10,529	30,680	5,078	19,600	22,456	47,135	8,026	17,728	25,407	43,135
2015 Jan	6,909	3,710	3,207	5,045	10,099	28,969	4,906	19,013	20,892	44,811	7,579	15,580	27,579	43,159
Feb	6,997	3,737	3,231	5,071	10,012	29,049	5,168	18,567	20,123	43,858	7,562	15,317	27,426	42,742
Mar	7,246	3,901	3,353	5,709	10,343	30,553	5,431	18,970	20,414	44,815	7,770	16,209	27,699	43,907
Apr	7,213	3,856	3,354	5,230	10,365	30,019	5,696	18,978	16,216 (ai)	40,889 (ai)	8,168	16,121	28,083	44,204
May	7,493	3,830	3,079	5,269	10,294	29,965	5,469	19,210	15,937	40,616	8,370	17,384	28,106	45,490
Jun	7,703	3,725	3,790	5,526	10,618	31,361	5,387	19,102	16,584	41,073	8,325	15,660	28,161	43,821
Jul	7,543	3,746	3,534	5,265	10,871	30,960	5,438	19,758	16,226	41,422	8,485	16,203	27,147	43,350
Aug	7,503	3,833	3,697	5,446	10,941	31,419	5,556	19,578	16,306	41,440	8,523	15,951	26,537	42,489
Sep	7,621	3,801	3,419	5,499	11,044	31,385	5,724	19,764	16,487	41,975	8,973	16,310	26,754	43,064
Oct	7,621	3,763	3,631	5,640	11,469	32,125	5,388	20,283	18,524	44,195	8,946	17,210	26,442	43,652
Nov	7,685	3,856	3,763	5,876	11,662	32,841	5,541	20,849	18,426	44,816	8,951	16,722	27,589	44,310
Dec	7,992	4,105	4,198	6,178	11,915	34,389	5,325	20,498	21,306	47,129	8,876	15,679	28,705	44,384
2016 Jan	7,834	3,846	3,617	5,688	11,403	32,388	5,444	20,135	17,257	42,836	8,364	17,166	27,846	45,012
Feb	7,833	3,916	3,661	5,822	11,238	32,471	5,961	20,605	18,297	44,864	8,454	17,254	31,332	48,586
Mar	8,179	4,121	3,659	6,215	11,388	33,562	5,845	20,514	17,861	44,220	8,797	17,120	32,020	49,140
Apr	8,010	4,084	3,619	5,832	11,544	33,089	5,893	19,899	17,981	43,773	8,392	16,273	29,763	46,037

Source: Bank of England

12.5b Industrial analysis of monetary financial institutions' deposits from UK residents

£ millions Not seasonally adjusted

Amounts outstanding of deposit liabilities (including under repo) in all currencies

	Real estate, professional services and support activities				Public administration and defence	Education	Human health and social work	Recreational, personal and community service activities			Financial intermediation (excluding insurance and pension funds)							
	Buying, selling and renting of real estate	Professional, scientific and technical activities	Administrative and support services	Total				Recreational, cultural and sporting activities	Personal and community service activities	Total	Financial leasing corporations	Non-bank credit grantors excluding credit unions and SPVs	Credit unions	Factoring corporations	Mortgage and housing credit corporations excluding SPVs	Investment and unit trusts excluding money market mutual funds	Money market mutual funds	Bank holding companies
RPM	TDAX	B3TK	B6PL	TDAW	TDBB	TDBC	TDBD	TDBF	TDBE	B3S7	TDBH	TDBI	TDBJ	TDBK	TDBL	TDBM	TDBN	TDBO
2014 May	34,649	72,220	23,641	130,511	35,024	20,399	17,305	13,047	18,069	31,116	10,368	2,856	994	961	15,177	31,710	804	45,423
Jun	36,950	74,391	24,486	135,827	34,355	19,790	17,596	11,488 (am)	18,164 (am)	29,652 (am)	10,186	2,784	986	1,016	15,244	29,242	603	44,391
Jul	35,378	75,494	25,948	136,820	37,733	18,749	17,683	11,637	18,043	29,680	10,160	2,827	954	1,022	15,301	27,387	887	43,222
Aug	35,184	73,726	24,833	133,744	40,515	18,411	18,267	11,867	17,965	29,832	10,182	2,925	945	1,128	14,901	26,900	1,536	44,282
Sep	38,074	72,888	24,837	135,799	33,495	19,554	18,872	11,576	18,560	30,136	10,137	2,994	974	1,065	15,188	26,071	982	46,514
Oct	37,214	72,814	24,502	134,530	39,361	19,865	19,405	11,365	18,431	29,795	10,082	3,298	976	1,073	13,953	25,320	926	47,015
Nov	36,961	74,234	24,674	135,869	37,965	19,179	19,441	11,195	18,367	29,562	11,209 (an)	3,329	965	1,019	13,287	26,391	1,123	43,997
Dec	39,318	70,117	24,603	134,038	32,075	18,626	19,580	11,152	18,455	29,607	11,740	2,868	950	936	13,338	25,316	1,155	36,947
2015 Jan	37,495	71,519	24,535	133,550	34,212	19,501	19,500	11,341	18,578	29,919	12,223	3,048	976	1,011	13,244	24,050	1,003	36,628
Feb	37,344	71,133	25,970	134,446	33,780	19,603	19,363	11,392	18,489	29,881	12,242	3,107	968	975	11,220 (ao)	24,128	853	35,921
Mar	40,192	75,807	27,468 (al)	143,467 (al)	33,362	18,630	19,642	11,683	18,636	30,319	11,708	3,290	982	1,012	10,599	24,105	962	43,453
Apr	39,007	74,763	26,286	140,056	37,269	19,545	19,501	11,613	18,679	30,292	11,306	3,230	990	1,063	10,578	25,223	899	45,125
May	38,512	76,124	27,211	141,848	37,405	21,335	19,746	11,839	18,734	30,574	11,278	3,470	996	1,067	10,476	25,568	1,057	42,150 (ap)
Jun	40,941	77,732	27,796	146,468	37,384	20,652	20,002	12,101	18,812	30,913	11,139	3,258	1,017	944	9,838	25,523	973	42,947
Jul	40,553	79,431	27,785	147,769	41,027	19,786	19,908	12,673	18,662	31,335	11,110	3,444	1,029	1,216	10,189	24,401	728	43,849
Aug	40,073	78,416	27,936	146,425	41,418	19,583	19,786	12,690	18,532	31,222	11,092	3,750	1,047	1,211	9,721	23,966	879	46,268
Sep	43,570	79,328	28,317	151,214	32,012	20,474	19,782	12,491	18,667	31,158	11,239	3,964	1,058	935	9,523	23,849	923	37,965
Oct	42,486	78,834	27,371	148,691	32,867	21,339	20,076	12,262	18,672	30,934	11,556	3,992	1,102	965	9,522	24,510	861	36,234
Nov	41,955	83,050	26,929	151,934	33,819	20,149	20,326	12,138	18,606	30,744	11,257	4,261	1,042	1,029	9,631	25,051	1,007	37,209
Dec	43,804	79,167	26,788	149,758	34,745	19,327	20,371	12,110	18,781	30,891	10,530	4,010	1,049	1,083	9,400	25,261	727	42,879
2016 Jan	42,621	79,936	26,592	149,148	34,061	20,554	20,053	12,618	18,917	31,536	9,585	3,616	1,060	1,031	9,458	25,802	1,184	49,779
Feb	41,771	80,519	27,701	149,992	32,719	20,964	20,250	12,724	19,240	31,964	9,753	3,872	1,090	942	9,437	27,185	972	51,441
Mar	44,780	87,206	29,485	161,471	27,841	19,742	20,279	12,888	19,049	31,937	9,678	3,886	1,104	1,055	8,969	26,194	1,069	61,005
Apr	42,991	78,583	29,100	150,673	37,151	20,837	20,437	12,739	19,187	31,926	9,752	4,258	1,105	1,143	9,093	25,560	773	54,952

Source: Bank of England

12.5b Industrial analysis of monetary financial institutions' deposits from UK residents

£ millions Not seasonally adjusted

Amounts outstanding of deposit liabilities (including under repo) in all currencies

	Securities dealers	Financial intermediation (excluding insurance and pension funds)				Insurance companies	Pension funds	Total	Fund management activities	Activities auxiliary to financial intermediation			Total	Total financial and non-financial businesses	Individuals and individuals trusts	Total UK residents
		SPVs related to securitisation	Other financial intermediaries	of which intragroup activity	Total					Central clearing counterparties	Other auxiliary activities	Total				
											Other					
RPM	TDBP	B3T6	TDBQ	B3U4	TDBG	B3V2	B7FO	TDBR	TDBS	B7FU	B7FZ	TDBT	BSH5	Z6ZX	TDBU	TDAA
2014 May	117,741	160,958	123,157	86,373	510,148	33,344	29,120	62,464	139,066	150,750	18,777	169,527	308,594	1,303,260	1,092,840	2,396,100
Jun	114,540	162,955	110,473	74,060	492,422	31,548	29,790	61,338	140,326	145,581 (bk)	19,263	164,844 (bk)	305,170 (bk)	1,286,898 (bk)	1,093,063	2,379,961 (bk)
Jul	110,575	160,246 (as)	109,951	73,963	482,531 (as)	30,062	28,876	58,938	140,071	146,139	19,757	165,896	305,967	1,278,624 (as)	1,092,663	2,371,287 (as)
Aug	100,667	161,320	106,066 (az)	73,682	470,852 (az)	30,186	29,219	59,405	152,776 (bf)	157,085	21,636	178,721	331,497 (bf)	1,292,463 (ai)	1,099,715	2,392,178 (ai)
Sep	99,340 (aq)	162,024	106,746	72,156	472,033 (aq)	31,114	31,113	62,227	153,489 (bg)(bh)	129,916	21,281	151,197	304,685 (bg)(bh)	1,270,533 (bg)	1,101,154	2,371,687 (bg)
Oct	90,671	147,074	104,956	72,920	445,346	30,037	29,370	59,407	150,518	146,295	20,708	167,002	317,521	1,257,976	1,108,417	2,366,392
Nov	93,653	147,918	106,855 (ba)	72,804 (ba)	449,746	29,908	30,309	60,217	147,811	153,498	20,940	174,438	322,249	1,273,556	1,112,655	2,386,211
Dec	94,607	153,201	107,893	73,203	448,950	30,461	28,809	59,271	134,620	132,940	21,081	154,020	288,641	1,242,048	1,116,438	2,358,486
2015 Jan	98,505	130,847	107,007	72,244	428,542	36,849	28,707	65,556	144,357	138,046	21,146	159,192	303,549	1,237,925	1,109,126	2,347,051
Feb	97,206	126,087 (at)	106,833	73,094	419,540	34,109	29,280	63,389	147,005	140,706	20,703	161,409	308,414	1,231,240	1,113,220	2,344,460
Mar	99,098	124,751	107,702	73,564	427,660	35,935	29,371	65,306	147,861	133,648	22,035	155,683	303,543	1,249,826 (al)	1,115,958	2,365,784 (al)
Apr	96,007	120,033	105,578	71,577	420,032	35,620	30,078	65,698	145,113	138,623	22,972	161,595	306,709	1,241,216 (aj)	1,123,024 (bl)	2,364,240 (aj)
May	92,005	121,798 (au)	105,693	71,047	415,558 (ap)(au)	33,421	29,204	62,624	146,090	137,460	23,468	160,928	307,019	1,243,730 (ap)(au)	1,127,801	2,371,531 (ap)(au)
Jun	89,683	122,450	103,282	69,160	411,054	32,933	28,353	61,286	141,725	126,984	23,680	150,664	292,389	1,227,829	1,128,038	2,355,868
Jul	90,780	119,401	106,007	71,584	412,154	31,244	28,611	59,855	147,767	136,370	24,094	160,464	308,231	1,247,895	1,130,699	2,378,594
Aug	95,240	110,307	100,251 (bb)	71,616	403,730 (bb)	29,685	27,954	57,640	147,689 (bi)	144,440	23,257	167,698	315,387 (bi)	1,247,936	1,136,252	2,384,187
Sep	92,822	112,134	101,810	71,141	396,221	29,109	28,205	57,314	156,076	119,320	24,325	143,646	299,722	1,223,300	1,137,214	2,360,514
Oct	89,530	112,272 (av)	99,835	70,368	390,381 (av)	28,829	27,484	56,313	161,118	119,659	23,705	143,365	304,483 (av)	1,222,255 (av)	1,145,947	2,368,201 (av)
Nov	89,715	109,480	100,124	70,437	389,805	30,006	27,007	57,013	154,119	127,764	25,204	152,968	307,087	1,234,196	1,148,704	2,382,900
Dec	83,844	109,943	102,697	72,446	391,424	28,902	27,445	56,347	139,452	121,444	25,003	146,448	285,900	1,218,155	1,158,155	2,376,310
2016 Jan	93,021	102,005	102,266	71,114	398,806	29,208	29,451	58,659	153,437	127,205	26,213	153,418	306,855	1,239,361	1,157,062	2,396,423
Feb	93,430	102,719 (aw)(ax)	101,482	71,948	402,325 (aw)(ax)	28,925	30,066	58,991	162,933	135,008	27,851	162,860	325,792	1,260,047	1,162,923 (bm)(bn)	2,422,970
Mar	90,293	100,951	99,342 (bc)	70,926	403,546 (bc)	30,218	24,482 (be)	54,700 (be)	159,546 (bj)	120,337	28,874	149,210	308,756 (bj)	1,248,013 (be)	1,174,327	2,422,340 (be)
Apr	93,037 (ar)	99,750 (ay)	95,835	67,894 (bd)	395,258 (ay)(bd)	28,025	26,550	54,575	162,745	122,658	27,837	150,495	313,241	1,236,482 (ar)(ay)(bd)	1,189,348	2,425,830 (ar)(ay)(bd)

Source: Bank of England

12.5b Industrial analysis of monetary financial institutions' deposits from UK residents

£ millions Not seasonally adjusted

Notes to table

Movements in amounts outstanding can reflect breaks in data series as well as underlying flows. For changes data, users are recommended to refer directly to the appropriate series or data tables. www.bankofengland.co.uk/statistics/Pages/iadb/notesiadb/Changes_flows_growth_rates.aspx.

(ai) Due to a change in treatment at one institution, the amounts outstanding increased by £1bn. This effect has been adjusted out of the flows for August 2014.

(aj) Due to a change in treatment at one institution, the amounts outstanding decreased by £4bn. This effect has been adjusted out of the flows for April 2015.

(ak) Due to improvements in reporting at one institution, the amounts outstanding increased by £1bn. This effect has been adjusted out of the flows for June 2014.

(al) Due to improvements in reporting at one institution, the amounts outstanding increased by £1bn. This effect has been adjusted out of the flows for March 2015.

(am) Due to improvements in reporting at one institution, the amounts outstanding decreased by £1bn. This effect has been adjusted out of the flows for June 2014.

(an) Due to improvements in reporting at one institution, the amounts outstanding increased by £1bn. This effect has been adjusted out of the flows for November 2014.

(ao) Due to improvements in reporting at one institution, the amounts outstanding decreased by £1bn. This effect has been adjusted out of the flows for February 2015.

(ap) Due to improvements in reporting at one institution, the amounts outstanding decreased by £2bn. This effect has been adjusted out of the flows for May 2015.

(aq) Due to improvements in reporting at one institution, the amounts outstanding decreased by £1bn. This effect has been adjusted out of the flows for September 2014.

(ar) Due to improvements in reporting at one institution, the amounts outstanding decreased by £1bn. This effect has been adjusted out of the flows for April 2016.

(as) Due to improvements in reporting at one institution, the amounts outstanding increased by £2bn. This effect has been adjusted out of the flows for July 2014.

(at) Due to improvements in reporting at one institution, the amounts outstanding increased by £1bn. This effect has been adjusted out of the flows for February 2015.

(au) Due to improvements in reporting at one institution, the amounts outstanding increased by £3bn. This effect has been adjusted out of the flows for May 2015.

(av) Due to additional information provided by one reporting institution, this series has been revised upwards by £1bn for October 2015.

(aw) Due to improvements in reporting at one institution, the amounts outstanding decreased by £1bn. This effect has been adjusted out of the flows for March 2016.

(ax) Due to improvements in reporting at one institution, this series has been revised downwards by £1bn.

(ay) Due to a loan transfer by one reporting institution, the amounts outstanding increased by £1bn. This effect has been adjusted out of the flows for April 2016.

(az) Due to improvements in reporting at one institution, the amounts outstanding decreased by £1bn. This effect has been adjusted out of the flows for August 2014.

(ba) Due to improvements in reporting at one institution, the amounts outstanding decreased by £1bn. This effect has been adjusted out of the flows for November 2014.

(bb) Due to improvements in reporting at one institution, the amounts outstanding decreased by £4bn. This effect has been adjusted out of the flows for August 2015.

(bc) Due to improvements in reporting at one institution, the amounts outstanding decreased by £2bn. This effect has been adjusted out of the flows for March 2016.

(bd) Due to improvements in reporting at one institution, the amounts outstanding decreased by £2bn. This effect has been adjusted out of the flows for April 2016.

(be) Due to changes in reporting at one institution, the amounts outstanding decreased by £5bn. This effect has been adjusted out of the flows for March 2016.

(bf) Due to improvements in reporting at one institution, the amounts outstanding increased by £1bn. This effect has been adjusted out of the flows for August 2014.

(bg) Due to improvements in reporting at one institution, the amounts outstanding increased by £1bn. This effect has been adjusted out of the flows for September 2014.

(bh) Due to improvements in reporting at one institution, the amounts outstanding increased by £1bn. This effect has been adjusted out of the flows for September 2014.

(bi) Due to improvements in reporting at one institution, the amounts outstanding increased by £5bn. This effect has been adjusted out of the flows for August 2015.

(bj) Due to improvements in reporting at one institution, the amounts outstanding increased by £2bn. This effect has been adjusted out of the flows for March 2016.

(bk) Due to improvements in reporting at one institution, the amounts outstanding decreased by £2bn. This effect has been adjusted out of the flows for June 2014.

(bl) Due to a change in the reporting population, the amounts outstanding increased by £1bn. This effect has been adjusted out of the flows for April 2015.

(bm) Due to improvements in reporting at one institution, the amounts outstanding increased by £1bn. This effect has been adjusted out of the flows for March 2016.

(bn) Due to improvements in reporting at one institution, this series has been revised upwards by £1bn.

Copyright guidance and the related UK Open Government Licence can be viewed here: www.bankofengland.co.uk/Pages/disclaimer.aspx.

12.6a Components of M4

£ millions   Seasonally adjusted

Amounts outstanding

| LPM | Retail deposits and cash in M4 | | | Wholesale deposits in M4 | | M4 | M3 |
| | Deposits | Notes and coin | Total | Deposits | of which repos | | (estimate of EMU aggregate for the UK) |
	B3SF	VQJO	VQWK (a)	VRGP	VZZQ	AUYN	VWYZ (b)
2014 May	1,392,694	60,479	1,453,173	646,100	118,973	2,094,578	2,363,587
Jun	1,399,283	60,918	1,460,201	648,802 (f)	121,506	2,104,968 (f)	2,361,481 (f)
Jul	1,404,874	61,470	1,466,344	643,591	114,526	2,109,641	2,358,726
Aug	1,411,764	61,619	1,473,383	641,932	119,512	2,120,243	2,376,145
Sep	1,415,406	62,299	1,477,705	627,248	104,096	2,108,230	2,369,469
Oct	1,422,367	62,408	1,484,775	615,897 (g)	110,440	2,101,401 (g)	2,360,012
Nov	1,425,631	62,838	1,488,469	608,562	110,500	2,103,094	2,365,776
Dec	1,431,732	62,925	1,494,657	607,578	110,897	2,105,101	2,366,386
2015 Jan	1,438,914	63,137	1,502,051	590,426	101,434	2,092,655	2,356,160
Feb	1,441,788	63,321	1,505,109	582,658	100,745	2,088,804	2,347,635
Mar	1,446,789	64,164	1,510,954	594,021	104,128	2,096,659	2,369,364
Apr	1,449,048 (c)	64,199	1,513,247 (c)	595,308	98,673	2,102,184 (c)	2,370,133
May	1,453,770	64,232	1,518,002	600,905 (h)	102,677	2,115,560 (h)	2,364,114
Jun	1,472,428 (d)	64,788	1,537,216 (d)	571,629 (i)	93,668	2,105,391	2,352,120
Jul	1,479,539	64,764	1,544,303	582,856	94,673	2,127,075	2,374,205
Aug	1,483,162	65,992	1,549,154	562,931	94,829	2,117,022	2,379,868
Sep	1,491,474	65,783	1,557,257	538,324	79,015	2,097,292	2,376,093
Oct	1,502,578	65,966	1,568,544	541,497	75,856	2,110,552	2,383,319
Nov	1,506,938	66,434	1,573,373	539,222	80,471	2,119,752	2,381,142
Dec	1,515,765	66,963	1,582,728	532,927	79,726	2,116,780	2,401,269
2016 Jan	1,521,537	67,371	1,588,908	531,707	76,718	2,119,395	2,419,584
Feb	1,531,464	68,176	1,599,640	535,801	75,638	2,139,614	2,439,614
Mar	1,487,294 (e)	68,565	1,555,859 (e)	577,706 (j)(k)	75,404	2,125,401 (k)	2,446,197
Apr	1,494,451	69,221	1,563,672	568,906	72,866	2,125,366	2,441,014

Notes to table   Source: Bank of England

Movements in amounts outstanding can reflect breaks in data series as well as underlying flows. For changes and growth rates data, users are recommended to refer directly to the appropriate series or data tables. Further details can be found at www.bankofengland.co.uk/statistics/Pages/iadb/notesiadb/Changes_flows_growth_rates.aspx

(a) A minor change was made to the definition of Retail M4 in October 2007. From October data onwards, non-interest-bearing bank deposits are only included in Retail M4 when reporters identify them explicitly as being taken from retail sources. There was also a change to the reporting population in October 2007. Together these led to a break in the amount outstanding of Retail M4 in October 2007. The effect of this has been removed from the flows data.

(b) Due to corrections to data calculations, this series has been revised from January 2008 to March 2015.

(c) Due to a change in treatment at one institution, the amounts outstanding decreased by £4bn. This effect has been adjusted out of the flows for April 2015.

(d) Due to improvements in reporting at one institution, the amounts outstanding increased by £15bn. This effect has been adjusted out of the flows for June 2015.

(e) Due to improvements in reporting at one institution, the amounts outstanding decreased by £52bn. This effect has been adjusted out of the flows for March 2016.

(f) Due to improvements in reporting at one institution, the amounts outstanding increased by £3bn. This effect has been adjusted out of the flows for June 2014.

(g) Due to a classification change, the amounts outstanding decreased by £5bn. This effect has been adjusted out of the flows for October 2014.

(h) Due to improvements in reporting at one institution, the amounts outstanding increased by £3bn. This effect has been adjusted out of the flows for May 2015.

(i) Due to improvements in reporting at one institution, the amounts outstanding decreased by £15bn. This effect has been adjusted out of the flows for June 2015.

(j) Due to improvements in reporting at one institution, the amounts outstanding increased by £52bn. This effect has been adjusted out of the flows for March 2016.

(k) Due to changes in reporting at one institution, the amounts outstanding decreased by £5bn. This effect has been adjusted out of the flows for March 2016.

Copyright guidance and the related UK Open Government Licence can be viewed here: www.bankofengland.co.uk/Pages/disclaimer.aspx.

12.6b Components of M4

£ millions   Not seasonally adjusted

Changes

	Retail deposits and cash in M4					Wholesale deposits in M4		M4	M3
		Deposits		Notes and	Total	Deposits	of which		(estimate of
	Total	of which:		coin			repos		EMU aggregate
		Private	Household						for the UK)
		non-financial	sector						
		corporations							
LPM	**VRLW**	**Z599**	**Z59A**	**VQLU**	**VQZA**	**VRLR**	**VWDN**	**AUZI**	**VWXK**
2014 May	8,061	1,831	6,100	1,025	9,087	-9,773	461	-687	6,382
Jun	8,774	7,736	3,625	232	9,006	-3,218	-5,090	5,788	-5,242
Jul	-2,294	-576	-1,663	190	-2,104	-2,553	2,731	-4,657	-11,672
Aug	6,143	-326	6,043	913	7,056	3,464	5,589	10,521	14,422
Sep	7,501	4,426	10,413	-463	7,038	-21,724	-23,782	-14,686	-13,163
Oct	4,649	839	6,422	968	5,616	-5,996	13,138	-380	-10,601
Nov	6,595	2,073	4,687	1,504	8,099	-1,256	-806	6,842	20,405
Dec	11,349	6,301	3,933	-352	10,997	-13,961	-18,109	-2,964	-21,185
2015 Jan	-11,277	-4,901	-6,404	-1,110	-12,387	-9,732	6,140	-22,119	-13,083
Feb	4,675	-602	4,421	465	5,140	-6,681	2,061	-1,541	7,331
Mar	19,730	11,239	494	428	20,158	-2,379	-11,780	17,778	12,664
Apr	2,758	-1,992	6,100	364	3,122	3,707	5,305	6,829	8,843
May	6,238	576	4,499	1,045	7,283	3,179	4,090	10,462	10,030
Jun	6,112	7,265	254	-585	5,527	-15,793	-15,759	-10,266	-11,551
Jul	-1,198	404	1,465	980	-218	15,738	10,833	15,520	20,153
Aug	2,813	-1,746	4,783	645	3,458	-14,627	2,433	-11,168	-794
Sep	11,979	6,492	1,726	-837	11,142	-31,155	-24,124	-20,013	-19,725
Oct	8,748	677	9,125	1,204	9,952	5,716	4,186	15,667	16,048
Nov	6,782	3,797	1,978	837	7,620	3,361	4,708	10,981	14,833
Dec	14,750	4,095	8,768	766	15,516	-19,412	-12,053	-3,896	-15,450
2016 Jan	-10,121	-7,372	-1,399	-710	-10,831	577	2,491	-10,253	5,011
Feb	11,877	528	4,150	481	12,358	7,858	2,704	20,216	21,380
Mar	22,444	7,658	11,079	820	23,265	-12,482	-7,892	10,783	14,632
Apr	3,761	-8,072	15,245	1,479	5,240	-9,276	3,294	-4,035	3,518

Notes to table   Source: Bank of England

Explanatory notes to the table can be found on the Bank of England website: http://www.bankofengland.co.uk/statistics/Pages/iadb/notesiadb/m4.aspx

Copyright guidance and the related UK Open Government Licence can be viewed here: www.bankofengland.co.uk/Pages/disclaimer.aspx.

12.7 Counterparts to changes in M4: alternative presentation

£ millions Not seasonally adjusted

Changes

| | Public sector net cash requirement (PSNCR) | M4 private sector net purchases (-) of Central Government debt | | | | | | M4 private sector net purchases of other public sector debt | | | |
| | | Gilts | Sterling treasury bills | Tax instruments | National Savings | Other | Total | Local government debt (-) | Public corporation debt (-) | Other public sector purchases of M4 private sector debt (+) | Total |
LPM	ABEN (e)	AVBY	VQLK	VQLG	VQLJ	VQLI	RCMD	VQLL	VQLO	VQLQ	AVBV
2014 May	11,922	5,306	1,630	-276	-261	-9,680	**-3,282**	-177	-	260	**83**
Jun	19,459	-16,092	-2,068	-4	-1,507	-2,053	**-21,723**	-289	-	40	**-249**
Jul	-4,359	-12,448	-395	-40	-744	15,760	**2,134**	-368	-	30	**-338**
Aug	4,515	-11,846	1,637	20	-702	5,254	**-5,637**	-8	-	178	**170**
Sep	23,063	11,069	-11,293	-77	-714	-29,618	**-30,633**	-91	-	-446	**-537**
Oct	-3,461	-3,244	5,871	-30	-685	12,935	**14,847**	64	-	-281	**-217**
Nov	8,310	-2,010	-2,820	-5	-543	1,469	**-3,909**	208	-	-429	**-221**
Dec	26,599	-4,427	-4,870	-57	-423	-9,734	**-19,511**	76	-	-350	**-274**
2015 Jan	-16,991	-1,114	553	-5	-6,893	2,388	**-5,070**	-199	-	782	**583**
Feb	1,325	-1,896	1,548	126	-3,275	345	**-3,151**	164	-	362	**526**
Mar	22,980	2,966	-5,641	105	-2,085	-6,049	**-10,705**	149	-	-481	**-332**
Apr	-6,699	-1,369	3,508	6	-2,125	12,467	**12,486**	-1,406	-	2,119	**713**
May	11,376	3,873	-1,290	-	-1,826	278	**1,035**	-368	-	-127	**-495**
Jun	18,158	-11,675	-4,259	7	-1,489	2,612	**-14,804**	220	-	-170	**50**
Jul	-5,159	5,666	5,226	-5	-1,046	10,242	**20,084**	-346	-	943	**597**
Aug	1,110	-3,165	-1,024	-20	-728	6,358	**1,422**	-191	-	194	**3**
Sep	20,377	5,744	-2,712	36	-662	-23,537	**-21,131**	111	-	-121	**-10**
Oct	-2,650	6,097	3,571	-20	-940	12,612	**21,319**	99	-	430	**529**
Nov	10,938	11,094	-4,631	-5	-655	-1,620	**4,183**	-53	-	-578	**-631**
Dec	13,262	-13,523	-6,912	-61	-710	2,639	**-18,567**	218	-	-546	**-328**
2016 Jan	-22,859	7,293	2,708	-17	107	-1,039	**9,054**	56	-	948	**1,004**
Feb	2,499	-6,793	2,375	241	-690	3,156	**-1,711**	290	-	-1,027	**-737**
Mar	22,436	380	-3,377	19	-571	-4,699	**-8,249**	499	-	-1,861	**-1,362**
Apr	-1,654	-11,840	5,281	-47	-978	2,073	**-5,511**	-466	-	3,049	**2,583**

£ millions Not seasonally adjusted

Changes

| | Purchases of public sector net debt (-) | External and foreign currency finance of public sector | | | | Public sector contribution | M4 lending | | | |
| | | Non-residents' purchases of gilts (-) | Non-residents' purchases of £TBs (-) | Other | Total | | Loans | of which reverse repos | Investments | Total |
LPM	VQLN	VQCZ	VRME	VQOC	VQDC	VWZL (f)	Z5MB	VWDP	VYAP	BF37 (g)
2014 May	**-3,200**	-9,606	84	1,093	**-8,429**	**293**	930	4,612	2,330	**3,259**
Jun	**-21,972**	3,986	-268	90	**3,808**	**1,295**	5,274	4,487	-95	**5,178**
Jul	**1,796**	-2,153	127	159	**-1,866**	**-4,430**	2,283	-1,076	1,580	**3,864**
Aug	**-5,467**	848	-55	948	**1,741**	**789**	1,918	-3,659	-2,824	**-906**
Sep	**-31,169**	3,344	-1,284	-880	**1,179**	**-6,927**	-732	2,894	-824	**-1,555**
Oct	**14,630**	347	1,279	1,557	**3,183**	**14,352**	-4,834	-123	-6,164	**-10,998**
Nov	**-4,130**	-16	-615	2,066	**1,435**	**5,615**	-4,035	1,473	-2,688	**-6,723**
Dec	**-19,785**	-6,151	25	-508	**-6,635**	**180**	-12,992	-8,578	16,100	**3,108**
2015 Jan	**-4,487**	6,044	693	4,320	**11,056**	**-10,422**	9,378	4,960	-20,226	**-10,848**
Feb	**-2,625**	-5,837	825	4,193	**-819**	**-2,119**	1,389	-407	-2,583	**-1,194**
Mar	**-11,036**	-14,772	-2,069	4,029	**-12,812**	**-868**	13,380	5,135	-4,058	**9,322**
Apr	**13,199**	-6,201	-211	-1,526	**-7,939**	**-1,438**	584	-951	-271	**312**
May	**540**	-8,476	-1,126	2,907	**-6,695**	**5,221**	5,155	4,670	-417	**4,738**
Jun	**-14,753**	4,317	-1,154	-3,033	**130**	**3,535**	-10,779	-6,955	936	**-9,843**
Jul	**20,680**	-13,320	-1,077	3,876	**-10,520**	**5,002**	22,891	401	-681	**22,210**
Aug	**1,425**	4,136	-612	1,081	**4,605**	**7,140**	6,649	6,712	-9,045	**-2,396**
Sep	**-21,142**	3,169	43	-3,947	**-735**	**-1,499**	374	-4,909	-296	**79**
Oct	**21,847**	-18,252	-396	2,488	**-16,161**	**3,037**	-5,001	-8,817	1,418	**-3,583**
Nov	**3,552**	-12,986	-1,702	2,301	**-12,387**	**2,104**	7,221	6,512	-958	**6,263**
Dec	**-18,896**	1,688	-318	-1,479	**-109**	**-5,742**	-1,437	-2,838	2,130	**693**
2016 Jan	**10,057**	6,273	-750	1,348	**6,871**	**-5,930**	8,092	-2,722	-1,468	**6,624**
Feb	**-2,448**	3,029	1,320	3,426	**7,776**	**7,827**	17,447	5,321	-39	**17,408**
Mar	**-9,611**	-7,811	189	-2,032	**-9,654**	**3,170**	8,566	2,289	-485	**8,081**
Apr	**-2,928**	-214	-63	-989	**-1,266**	**-5,848**	-14,841	-1,734	-509	**-15,349**

12.7 Counterparts to changes in M4: alternative presentation

£ millions Not seasonally adjusted

Changes

LPM	External and foreign currency flows			Total external counterparts	Net non-deposit £ liabilities (-)	M4
	Net sterling deposits from non-residents (-)	Net foreign currency liabilities (-)	Total			
	B69P	**B72P**	**AVBW**	**VQLP**	**VWZV**	**AUZI**
2014 May	1,055	9,392	**10,446**	2,017	-14,685	**-687**
Jun	3,770	-14,898	**-11,128**	-7,320	10,443	**5,788**
Jul	-11,530	32,996	**21,466**	19,600	-25,557	**-4,657**
Aug	27,597	-11,218	**16,378**	18,120	-5,741	**10,521**
Sep	-4,641	-14,402	**-19,044**	-17,864	12,840	**-14,686**
Oct	4,802	9,839	**14,641**	17,824	-18,374	**-380**
Nov	1,732	1,370	**3,102**	4,537	4,848	**6,842**
Dec	-18,468	26,890	**8,422**	1,788	-14,673	**-2,964**
2015 Jan	7,742	-4,531	**3,211**	14,267	-4,060	**-22,119**
Feb	14,961	-25,252	**-10,291**	-11,110	12,063	**-1,541**
Mar	-18,425	23,782	**5,357**	-7,456	3,967	**17,778**
Apr	-758	-16,974	**-17,732**	-25,670	25,687	**6,829**
May	7,861	6,128	**13,989**	7,294	-13,486	**10,462**
Jun	-3,825	-17,821	**-21,646**	-21,516	17,688	**-10,266**
Jul	3,433	3,019	**6,452**	-4,068	-18,144	**15,520**
Aug	-2,468	15,368	**12,900**	17,505	-28,813	**-11,168**
Sep	-16,803	9,218	**-7,585**	-8,320	-11,008	**-20,013**
Oct	16,692	-22,518	**-5,826**	-21,987	22,040	**15,667**
Nov	-6,144	-2,276	**-8,421**	-20,808	11,035	**10,981**
Dec	-18,236	12,049	**-6,187**	-6,296	7,341	**-3,896**
2016 Jan	3,609	-3,236	**373**	7,244	-11,320	**-10,253**
Feb	20,343	-17,344	**2,998**	10,774	-8,017	**20,216**
Mar	-13,064	-45,943	**-59,007**	-68,662	58,538	**10,783**
Apr	7,565	-13,880	**-6,315**	-7,581	23,477	**-4,035**

Source: Bank of England

Notes to table

(e) This estimate of the Public Sector Net Cash Requirement may differ from the headline measure published by the Office for National Statistics (ONS). The Bank of England's measure is maintained to ensure the 'Alternative Counterparts' analysis continues to balance. More details on this can be found in article www.bankofengland.co.uk/statistics/Documents/ms/articles/art2may09.pdf.

(f) Net sterling lending to the public sector includes holdings of coin. Coin is a liability of Central Government and therefore outside of the MFIs' consolidated balance sheet. Holdings of coin are a component of M4 and are therefore included here in order to reconcile the counterparts.

(g) Please note that the compilation and descriptions of some credit series have changed from publication of April 2015 data, as described in Bankstats, April 2015, 'Changes to the treatment of loan transfers and lending to housing associations', available at www.bankofengland.co.uk/statistics/Documents/ms/articles/art1apr15.pdf.

12.8 Selected retail banks' base rate

Daily average of 4 UK Banks' base rates

Date of change	New rate	Date of change	New rate	Date of change	New rate
09-Jan-86	12.5	17-Sep-92	10.5	05-Jul-07	5.75
19-Mar-86	11.5	18-Sep-92	10	06-Dec-07	5.5
08-Apr-86	11.13	22-Sep-92	9	07-Feb-08	5.25
09-Apr-86	11	16-Oct-92	8.25	10-Apr-08	5
21-Apr-86	10.5	19-Oct-92	8	08-Oct-08	4.5
23-May-86	10.25	13-Nov-92	7	06-Nov-08	3
27-May-86	10	26-Jan-93	6	04-Dec-08	2
14-Oct-86	10.5	23-Nov-93	5.5	08-Jan-09	1.5
15-Oct-86	11	08-Feb-94	5.25	05-Feb-09	1
10-Mar-87	10.5	12-Sep-94	5.75	05-Mar-09	0.5
18-Mar-87	10.25	07-Dec-94	6.25	04-Jan-10	0.5
19-Mar-87	10	02-Feb-95	6.63	31-Dec-10	0.5
28-Apr-87	9.88	03-Feb-95	6.75	04-Jan-11	0.5
29-Apr-87	9.5	13-Dec-95	6.5	30-Dec-11	0.5
11-May-87	9	18-Jan-96	6.25	03-Jan-12	0.5
06-Aug-87	9.25	08-Mar-96	6	31-Dec-12	0.5
07-Aug-87	10	06-Jun-96	5.75	02-Jan-13	0.5
23-Oct-87	9.88	30-Oct-96	5.94	31-Dec-13	0.5
26-Oct-87	9.5	31-Oct-96	6	31-Jan-14	0.5
04-Nov-87	9.38	06-May-97	6.25	31-Dec-14	0.5
05-Nov-87	9	06-Jun-97	6.44		
04-Dec-87	8.5	09-Jun-97	6.5		
02-Feb-88	9	10-Jul-97	6.75		
17-Mar-88	8.63	07-Aug-97	7		
18-Mar-88	8.5	06-Nov-97	7.25		
11-Apr-88	8	04-Jun-98	7.5		
17-May-88	7.88	08-Oct-98	7.25		
18-May-88	7.5	06-Nov-98	6.75		
02-Jun-88	7.75	10-Dec-98	6.25		
03-Jun-88	8	07-Jan-99	6		
06-Jun-88	8.25	04-Feb-99	5.5		
07-Jun-88	8.5	08-Apr-99	5.25		
22-Jun-88	8.88	10-Jun-99	5		
23-Jun-88	9	08-Sep-99	5.19		
28-Jun-88	9.25	10-Sep-99	5.25		
29-Jun-88	9.5	04-Nov-99	5.5		
04-Jul-88	9.88	14-Jan-00	5.75		
05-Jul-88	10	10-Feb-00	6		
18-Jul-88	10.38	08-Feb-01	5.75		
19-Jul-88	10.5	05-Apr-01	5.5		
08-Aug-88	10.88	10-May-01	5.25		
09-Aug-88	11	02-Aug-01	5		
25-Aug-88	11.75	18-Sep-01	4.75		
26-Aug-88	12	04-Oct-01	4.5		
25-Nov-88	13	08-Nov-01	4		
24-May-89	14	07-Feb-03	3.75		
05-Oct-89	15	11-Jul-03	3.5		
08-Oct-90	14	06-Nov-03	3.75		
13-Feb-91	13.5	05-Feb-04	4		
27-Feb-91	13	07-May-04	4.25		
22-Mar-91	12.5	10-Jun-04	4.5		
12-Apr-91	12	05-Aug-04	4.75		
24-May-91	11.5	04-Aug-05	4.5		
12-Jul-91	11	03-Aug-06	4.75		
04-Sep-91	10.5	09-Nov-06	5		
05-May-92	10	11-Jan-07	5.25		
16-Sep-92	12	10-May-07	5.5		

1 Data obtained from Barclays Bank, Lloyds/TSB Bank, HSBC Bank and National Westminster Bank whose rates are used to compile this series.

2 Where all the rates did not change on the same day a spread is shown.

Source: Bank of England: 020 7601 3644

12.9 Average three month sterling money market rates

Monthly average rate of discount, 3 month Treasury bills, Sterling IUMAAJNB		Monthly average of Eligible bills discount rate, 3 month (a) IUMAAJND		Monthly average Sterling 3 month mean interbank lending rate IUMAAMIJ		Monthly average of Sterling certificates of deposit interest rate, 3 months, mean offer/bid IUMAVCDA	
31-Jan-99	5.2781	31-Jan-99	5.63	31-Jan-99	5.7985	31-Jan-99	5.74
28-Feb-99	5.0407	28-Feb-99	5.28	28-Feb-99	5.4328	28-Feb-99	5.38
31-Mar-99	4.9192	31-Mar-99	5.11	31-Mar-99	5.303	31-Mar-99	5.26
30-Apr-99	4.9003	30-Apr-99	5.02	30-Apr-99	5.2313	30-Apr-99	5.19
31-May-99	4.9302	31-May-99	5.08	31-May-99	5.2482	31-May-99	5.22
30-Jun-99	4.7598	30-Jun-99	4.94	30-Jun-99	5.1234	30-Jun-99	5.09
31-Jul-99	4.7596	31-Jul-99	4.89	31-Jul-99	5.0657	31-Jul-99	5.03
31-Aug-99	4.8495	31-Aug-99	4.94	31-Aug-99	5.1795	31-Aug-99	5.14
30-Sep-99	5.1223	30-Sep-99	5.16	30-Sep-99	5.3168	30-Sep-99	5.28
31-Oct-99	5.2315	31-Oct-99	5.42	31-Oct-99	5.9388	31-Oct-99	5.86
30-Nov-99	5.2018	30-Nov-99	5.43	30-Nov-99	5.7824	30-Nov-99	5.72
31-Dec-99	5.4637	31-Dec-99	5.59	31-Dec-99	5.9656	31-Dec-99	5.89
31-Jan-00	5.7218	31-Jan-00	5.9	31-Jan-00	6.0578	31-Jan-00	6.02
29-Feb-00	5.8346	29-Feb-00	6.01	29-Feb-00	6.1492	29-Feb-00	6.1
31-Mar-00	5.8582	31-Mar-00	5.98	31-Mar-00	6.1458	31-Mar-00	6.09
30-Apr-00	5.9178	30-Apr-00	6.05	30-Apr-00	6.2129	30-Apr-00	6.17
31-May-00	5.9501	31-May-00	6.09	31-May-00	6.2289	31-May-00	6.19
30-Jun-00	5.8535	30-Jun-00	6.03	30-Jun-00	6.1423	30-Jun-00	6.1
31-Jul-00	5.8333	31-Jul-00	5.97	31-Jul-00	6.1146	31-Jul-00	6.08
31-Aug-00	5.8103	31-Aug-00	5.97	31-Aug-00	6.1365	31-Aug-00	6.09
30-Sep-00	5.7798	30-Sep-00	5.95	30-Sep-00	6.1191	30-Sep-00	6.08
31-Oct-00	5.7482	31-Oct-00	5.92	31-Oct-00	6.081	31-Oct-00	6.05
30-Nov-00	5.6833	30-Nov-00	5.88	30-Nov-00	6.0007	30-Nov-00	5.98
31-Dec-00	5.6229	31-Dec-00	5.78	31-Dec-00	5.8882	31-Dec-00	5.85
31-Jan-01	5.4852	31-Jan-01	5.64	31-Jan-01	5.7642	31-Jan-01	5.73
28-Feb-01	5.4582	28-Feb-01	5.56	28-Feb-01	5.6854	28-Feb-01	5.66
31-Mar-01	5.2286	31-Mar-01	5.37	31-Mar-01	5.473	31-Mar-01	5.44
30-Apr-01	5.1158	30-Apr-01	5.21	30-Apr-01	5.3323	30-Apr-01	5.3
31-May-01	4.9765	31-May-01	5.06	31-May-01	5.1727	31-May-01	5.15
30-Jun-01	4.991	30-Jun-01	5.08	30-Jun-01	5.189	30-Jun-01	5.16
31-Jul-01	5.0052	31-Jul-01	5.07	31-Jul-01	5.1917	31-Jul-01	5.17
31-Aug-01	4.7198	31-Aug-01	4.82	31-Aug-01	4.9269	31-Aug-01	4.9
30-Sep-01	4.4297	30-Sep-01	4.57	30-Sep-01	4.6485	30-Sep-01	4.62
31-Oct-01	4.1567	31-Oct-01	4.26	31-Oct-01	4.3594	31-Oct-01	4.33
30-Nov-01	3.7799	30-Nov-01	3.85	30-Nov-01	3.9326	30-Nov-01	3.91
31-Dec-01	3.8296	31-Dec-01	3.88	31-Dec-01	3.9852	31-Dec-01	3.96
31-Jan-02	3.8321	31-Jan-02	3.91	31-Jan-02	3.978	31-Jan-02	3.96
28-Feb-02	3.868	28-Feb-02	3.92	28-Feb-02	3.9805	28-Feb-02	3.96
31-Mar-02	3.9672	31-Mar-02	3.99	31-Mar-02	4.0609	31-Mar-02	4.04
30-Apr-02	3.9693	30-Apr-02	4.04	30-Apr-02	4.1086	30-Apr-02	4.08
31-May-02	3.9525	31-May-02	4.01	31-May-02	4.0795	31-May-02	4.06
30-Jun-02	3.9767	30-Jun-02	4.04	30-Jun-02	4.112	30-Jun-02	4.09
31-Jul-02	3.8408	31-Jul-02	3.94	31-Jul-02	3.9925	31-Jul-02	3.97
31-Aug-02	3.7663	31-Aug-02	3.86	31-Aug-02	3.9174	31-Aug-02	3.9
30-Sep-02	3.7861	30-Sep-02	3.86	30-Sep-02	3.9315	30-Sep-02	3.91
31-Oct-02	3.7509	31-Oct-02	3.82	31-Oct-02	3.9015	31-Oct-02	3.88
30-Nov-02	3.8033	30-Nov-02	3.84	30-Nov-02	3.9091	30-Nov-02	3.89
31-Dec-02	3.8418	31-Dec-02	3.71	31-Dec-02	3.9488	31-Dec-02	3.93
31-Jan-03	3.7993	31-Jan-03	3.87	31-Jan-03	3.9132	31-Jan-03	3.9
28-Feb-03	3.4993	28-Feb-03	3.65	28-Feb-03	3.6888	28-Feb-03	3.68
31-Mar-03	3.4721	31-Mar-03	3.54	31-Mar-03	3.5838	31-Mar-03	3.57
30-Apr-03	3.4537	30-Apr-03	3.52	30-Apr-03	3.576	30-Apr-03	3.57
31-May-03	3.4366	31-May-03	3.52	31-May-03	3.5665	31-May-03	3.56
30-Jun-03	3.4724	30-Jun-03	3.45	30-Jun-03	3.5702	30-Jun-03	3.56

12.9 Average three month sterling money market rates

Monthly average rate of discount, 3 month Treasury bills, Sterling IUMAAJNB		Monthly average of Eligible bills discount rate, 3 month (a) IUMAAJND		Monthly average Sterling 3 month mean interbank lending rate IUMAAMIJ		Monthly average of Sterling certificates of deposit interest rate, 3 months, mean offer/bid IUMAVCDA	
31-Jul-03	3.3119	31-Jul-03	3.39	31-Jul-03	3.42	31-Jul-03	3.41
31-Aug-03	3.3998	31-Aug-03	3.42	31-Aug-03	3.4518	31-Aug-03	3.44
30-Sep-03	3.5239	30-Sep-03	3.59	30-Sep-03	3.6311	30-Sep-03	3.62
31-Oct-03	3.6514	31-Oct-03	3.69	31-Oct-03	3.727	31-Oct-03	3.72
30-Nov-03	3.808	30-Nov-03	3.88	30-Nov-03	3.9085	30-Nov-03	3.9
31-Dec-03	3.8298	31-Dec-03	3.9	31-Dec-03	3.949	31-Dec-03	3.94
31-Jan-04	3.8983	31-Jan-04	3.94	31-Jan-04	3.986	31-Jan-04	3.98
29-Feb-04	3.9788	29-Feb-04	4.06	29-Feb-04	4.101	29-Feb-04	4.09
31-Mar-04	4.1025	31-Mar-04	4.19	31-Mar-04	4.2328	31-Mar-04	4.22
30-Apr-04	4.1862	30-Apr-04	4.28	30-Apr-04	4.3288	30-Apr-04	4.32
31-May-04	4.34	31-May-04	4.42	31-May-04	4.4555	31-May-04	4.45
30-Jun-04	4.5793	30-Jun-04	4.68	30-Jun-04	4.7305	30-Jun-04	4.72
31-Jul-04	4.6424	31-Jul-04	4.75	31-Jul-04	4.7859	31-Jul-04	4.79
31-Aug-04	4.7218	31-Aug-04	4.85	31-Aug-04	4.8938	31-Aug-04	4.89
30-Sep-04	4.6937	30-Sep-04	4.83	30-Sep-04	4.8743	30-Sep-04	4.87
31-Oct-04	4.679	31-Oct-04	4.79	31-Oct-04	4.8336	31-Oct-04	4.83
30-Nov-04	4.6578	30-Nov-04	4.78	30-Nov-04	4.8159	30-Nov-04	4.81
31-Dec-04	4.677	31-Dec-04	4.77	31-Dec-04	4.8057	31-Dec-04	4.8
31-Jan-05	4.6568	31-Jan-05	4.75	31-Jan-05	4.8045	31-Jan-05	4.8
28-Feb-05	4.6858	28-Feb-05	4.78	28-Feb-05	4.822	28-Feb-05	4.82
31-Mar-05	4.7691	31-Mar-05	4.88	31-Mar-05	4.9186	31-Mar-05	4.91
30-Apr-05	4.7047	30-Apr-05	4.84	30-Apr-05	4.8756	30-Apr-05	4.86
31-May-05	4.6618	31-May-05	4.8	31-May-05	4.8253	31-May-05	4.82
30-Jun-05	4.6175	30-Jun-05	4.76	30-Jun-05	4.7777	30-Jun-05	4.78
31-Jul-05	4.4609	31-Jul-05	4.57	31-Jul-05	4.5948	31-Jul-05	4.6
31-Aug-05	4.4057	31-Aug-05	4.51	31-Aug-05	4.533	31-Aug-05	4.53
30-Sep-05	4.4037	30-Sep-05	-	30-Sep-05	4.5359	30-Sep-05	4.54
31-Oct-05	4.402	31-Oct-05	-	31-Oct-05	4.525	31-Oct-05	4.52
30-Nov-05	4.4169	30-Nov-05	-	30-Nov-05	4.5614	30-Nov-05	4.56
31-Dec-05	4.4287	31-Dec-05	-	31-Dec-05	4.587	31-Dec-05	4.58
31-Jan-06	4.3906	31-Jan-06	-	31-Jan-06	4.5369	31-Jan-06	4.54
28-Feb-06	4.3839	28-Feb-06	-	28-Feb-06	4.5203	28-Feb-06	4.52
31-Mar-06	4.3956	31-Mar-06	-	31-Mar-06	4.5263	31-Mar-06	4.53
30-Apr-06	4.4196	30-Apr-06	-	30-Apr-06	4.5725	30-Apr-06	4.57
31-May-06	4.5012	31-May-06	-	31-May-06	4.6519	31-May-06	4.65
30-Jun-06	4.5414	30-Jun-06	-	30-Jun-06	4.6927	30-Jun-06	4.69
31-Jul-06	4.534	31-Jul-06	-	31-Jul-06	4.6838	31-Jul-06	4.68
31-Aug-06	4.7544	31-Aug-06	-	31-Aug-06	4.8968	31-Aug-06	4.89
30-Sep-06	4.8359	30-Sep-06	-	30-Sep-06	4.9819	30-Sep-06	4.98
31-Oct-06	4.9357	31-Oct-06	-	31-Oct-06	5.0909	31-Oct-06	5.09
30-Nov-06	5.0095	30-Nov-06	-	30-Nov-06	5.1791	30-Nov-06	5.18
31-Dec-06	5.0759	31-Dec-06	-	31-Dec-06	5.2453	31-Dec-06	5.24
31-Jan-07	5.304	31-Jan-07	-	31-Jan-07	5.4545	31-Jan-07	5.45
28-Feb-07	5.3393	28-Feb-07	-	28-Feb-07	5.5248	28-Feb-07	5.51
31-Mar-07	5.3274	31-Mar-07	-	31-Mar-07	5.5041	31-Mar-07	5.52
30-Apr-07	5.4329	30-Apr-07	-	30-Apr-07	5.6058	30-Apr-07	5.69
31-May-07	5.5516	31-May-07	-	31-May-07	5.7221	31-May-07	5.84
30-Jun-07	5.6702	30-Jun-07	-	30-Jun-07	5.8348	30-Jun-07	5.94
31-Jul-07	5.7742	31-Jul-07	-	31-Jul-07	5.9789	31-Jul-07	6.11
31-Aug-07	5.7943	31-Aug-07	-	31-Aug-07	6.3389	31-Aug-07	6.35
30-Sep-07	5.6896	30-Sep-07	-	30-Sep-07	6.5813	30-Sep-07	6.54
31-Oct-07	5.6058	31-Oct-07	-	31-Oct-07	6.2122	31-Oct-07	6.21
30-Nov-07	5.4986	30-Nov-07	-	30-Nov-07	6.3564	30-Nov-07	6.34
31-Dec-07	5.3034	31-Dec-07	-	31-Dec-07	6.3542	31-Dec-07	6.35

12.9 Average three month sterling money market rates

Monthly average rate of discount, 3 month Treasury bills, Sterling IUMAAJNB		Monthly average of Eligible bills discount rate, 3 month (a) IUMAAJND		Monthly average Sterling 3 month mean interbank lending rate IUMAAMIJ		Monthly average of Sterling certificates of deposit interest rate, 3 months, mean offer/bid IUMAVCDA	
31-Jan-08	5.1215	31-Jan-08	-	31-Jan-08	5.6071	31-Jan-08	5.61
29-Feb-08	5.0178	29-Feb-08	-	29-Feb-08	5.6083	29-Feb-08	5.6
31-Mar-08	4.8835	31-Mar-08	-	31-Mar-08	5.8555	31-Mar-08	5.85
30-Apr-08	4.8258	30-Apr-08	-	30-Apr-08	5.8961	30-Apr-08	5.89
31-May-08	4.9496	31-May-08	-	31-May-08	5.7933	31-May-08	5.79
30-Jun-08	5.1138	30-Jun-08	-	30-Jun-08	5.9002	30-Jun-08	5.89
31-Jul-08	5.0843	31-Jul-08	-	31-Jul-08	5.803	31-Jul-08	5.8
31-Aug-08	4.9539	31-Aug-08	-	31-Aug-08	5.7588	31-Aug-08	5.75
30-Sep-08	4.7425	30-Sep-08	-	30-Sep-08	5.8698	30-Sep-08	5.86
31-Oct-08	3.6788	31-Oct-08	-	31-Oct-08	6.1772	31-Oct-08	6.16
30-Nov-08	1.9948	30-Nov-08	-	30-Nov-08	4.3955	30-Nov-08	4.4
31-Dec-08	1.2875	31-Dec-08	-	31-Dec-08	3.2143	31-Dec-08	3.21
31-Jan-09	0.8945	31-Jan-09	-	31-Jan-09	2.28	31-Jan-09	2.29
28-Feb-09	0.7177	28-Feb-09	-	28-Feb-09	2.0758	28-Feb-09	2.06
31-Mar-09	0.6035	31-Mar-09	-	31-Mar-09	1.8273	31-Mar-09	1.79
30-Apr-09	0.625	30-Apr-09	-	30-Apr-09	1.4838	30-Apr-09	1.43
31-May-09	0.5271	31-May-09	-	31-May-09	1.3026	31-May-09	1.27
30-Jun-09	0.5037	30-Jun-09	-	30-Jun-09	1.2057	30-Jun-09	1.14
31-Jul-09	0.4397	31-Jul-09	-	31-Jul-09	1.0293	31-Jul-09	0.92
31-Aug-09	0.3946	31-Aug-09	-	31-Aug-09	0.7963	31-Aug-09	0.69
30-Sep-09	0.3761	30-Sep-09	-	30-Sep-09	0.617	30-Sep-09	0.51
31-Oct-09	0.4315	31-Oct-09	-	31-Oct-09	0.5636	31-Oct-09	0.5
30-Nov-09	0.4459	30-Nov-09	-	30-Nov-09	0.5976	30-Nov-09	0.58
31-Dec-09	0.3587	31-Dec-09	-	31-Dec-09	0.6071	31-Dec-09	0.58
31-Jan-10	0.4874	31-Jan-10	-	31-Jan-10	0.6013	31-Jan-10	0.58
28-Feb-10	0.4878	28-Feb-10	-	28-Feb-10	0.5995	28-Feb-10	0.58
31-Mar-10	0.5109	31-Mar-10	-	31-Mar-10	0.6002	31-Mar-10	0.6
30-Apr-10	0.5083	30-Apr-10	-	30-Apr-10	0.6	30-Apr-10	0.63
31-May-10	0.4976	31-May-10	-	31-May-10	0.6645	31-May-10	0.68
30-Jun-10	0.4839	30-Jun-10	-	30-Jun-10	0.7045	30-Jun-10	0.77
31-Jul-10	0.498	31-Jul-10	-	31-Jul-10	0.75	31-Jul-10	0.78
31-Aug-10	0.4945	31-Aug-10	-	31-Aug-10	0.75	31-Aug-10	0.7655
30-Sep-10	0.4966	30-Sep-10	-	30-Sep-10	0.7545	30-Sep-10	0.725
31-Oct-10	0.5061	31-Oct-10	-	31-Oct-10	0.75	31-Oct-10	0.725
30-Nov-10	0.4935	30-Nov-10	-	30-Nov-10	0.75	30-Nov-10	0.725
31-Dec-10	0.4913	31-Dec-10	-	31-Dec-10	0.755	31-Dec-10	0.7655
31-Jan-11	0.5055	31-Jan-11	-	31-Jan-11	0.7785	31-Jan-11	0.825
28-Feb-11	0.5363	28-Feb-11	-	28-Feb-11	0.775	28-Feb-11	0.825
31-Mar-11	0.5603	31-Mar-11	-	31-Mar-11	0.7811	31-Mar-11	0.8315
30-Apr-11	0.5676	30-Apr-11	-	30-Apr-11	0.8	30-Apr-11	0.875
31-May-11	0.5265	31-May-11	-	31-May-11	0.8	31-May-11	0.875
30-Jun-11	0.5174	30-Jun-11	-	30-Jun-11	0.8464	30-Jun-11	0.875
31-Jul-11	0.4996	31-Jul-11	-	31-Jul-11	0.86	31-Jul-11	0.875
31-Aug-11	0.4531	31-Aug-11	-	31-Aug-11	0.8873	31-Aug-11	0.9114
30-Sep-11	0.4649	30-Sep-11	-	30-Sep-11	0.9664	30-Sep-11	1.0077
31-Oct-11	0.4608	31-Oct-11	-	31-Oct-11	1.0179	31-Oct-11	1.0593
30-Nov-11	0.4387	30-Nov-11	-	30-Nov-11	1.0511	30-Nov-11	1.0968
31-Dec-11	0.2996	31-Dec-11	-	31-Dec-11	1.0878	31-Dec-11	1.15
31-Jan-12	0.3239	31-Jan-12	-	31-Jan-12	1.1086	31-Jan-12	1.175
29-Feb-12	0.3912	29-Feb-12	-	29-Feb-12	1.0971	29-Feb-12	1.156
31-Mar-12	0.4248	31-Mar-12	-	31-Mar-12	1.0752	31-Mar-12	1.1164
30-Apr-12	0.4236	30-Apr-12	-	30-Apr-12	1.0558	30-Apr-12	1.0992
31-May-12	0.3561	31-May-12	-	31-May-12	1.0143	31-May-12	1.0891
30-Jun-12	0.3422	30-Jun-12	-	30-Jun-12	0.9658	30-Jun-12	1.0376

12.9 Average three month sterling money market rates

Monthly average rate of discount, 3 month Treasury bills, Sterling IUMAAJNB		Monthly average of Eligible bills discount rate, 3 month (a) IUMAAJND		Monthly average Sterling 3 month mean interbank lending rate IUMAAMIJ		Monthly average of Sterling certificates of deposit interest rate, 3 months, mean offer/bid IUMAVCDA	
31-Jul-12	0.2943	31-Jul-12	-	31-Jul-12	0.8627	31-Jul-12	0.8691
31-Aug-12	0.2398	31-Aug-12	-	31-Aug-12	0.7048	31-Aug-12	0.7405
30-Sep-12	0.2478	30-Sep-12	-	30-Sep-12	0.6418	30-Sep-12	0.6825
31-Oct-12	0.2368	31-Oct-12	-	31-Oct-12	0.535	31-Oct-12	0.575
30-Nov-12	0.2243	30-Nov-12	-	30-Nov-12	0.5034	30-Nov-12	0.575
31-Dec-12	0.249	31-Dec-12	-	31-Dec-12	0.5	31-Dec-12	0.575
31-Jan-13	0.2677	31-Jan-13	-	31-Jan-13	0.4927	31-Jan-13	0.575
28-Feb-13	0.3147	28-Feb-13	-	28-Feb-13	0.49	28-Feb-13	0.575
31-Mar-13	0.3391	31-Mar-13	-	31-Mar-13	0.4865	31-Mar-13	0.5655
30-Apr-13	0.3447	30-Apr-13	-	30-Apr-13	0.485	30-Apr-13	0.5731
31-May-13	0.3065	31-May-13	-	31-May-13	0.485	31-May-13	0.5512
30-Jun-13	0.3066	30-Jun-13	-	30-Jun-13	0.485	30-Jun-13	0.525
31-Jul-13	0.3124	31-Jul-13	-	31-Jul-13	0.4839	31-Jul-13	0.525
31-Aug-13	0.2812	31-Aug-13	-	31-Aug-13	0.485	31-Aug-13	0.525
30-Sep-13	0.289	30-Sep-13	-	30-Sep-13	0.4931	30-Sep-13	0.525
31-Oct-13	0.3141	31-Oct-13	-	31-Oct-13	0.495	31-Oct-13	0.525
30-Nov-13	0.2865	30-Nov-13	-	30-Nov-13	0.5017	30-Nov-13	0.5512
31-Dec-13	0.2555	31-Dec-13	-	31-Dec-13	0.5335	31-Dec-13	0.575
31-Jan-14	0.3211	31-Jan-14	-	31-Jan-14	0.5318	31-Jan-14	0.575
28-Feb-14	0.3624	28-Feb-14	-	28-Feb-14	0.5288	28-Feb-14	0.575
31-Mar-14	0.3882	31-Mar-14	-	31-Mar-14	0.53	31-Mar-14	0.575
30-Apr-14	0.3688	30-Apr-14	-	30-Apr-14	0.532	30-Apr-14	0.575
31-May-14	0.284	31-May-14	-	31-May-14	0.55	31-May-14	0.575
30-Jun-14	0.3586	30-Jun-14	-	30-Jun-14	0.55	30-Jun-14	0.575
31-Jul-14	0.4271	31-Jul-14	-	31-Jul-14	0.5487	31-Jul-14	0.575
31-Aug-14	0.3978	31-Aug-14	-	31-Aug-14	0.545	31-Aug-14	0.575
30-Sep-14	0.4351	30-Sep-14	-	30-Sep-14	0.5505	30-Sep-14	0.567
31-Oct-14	0.3964	31-Oct-14	-	31-Oct-14	0.5426	31-Oct-14	0.5511
30-Nov-14	0.4114	30-Nov-14	-	30-Nov-14	0.53	30-Nov-14	0.5538
31-Dec-14	0.4101	31-Dec-14	-	31-Dec-14	0.53	31-Dec-14	0.5524
31-Jan-15	0.377	31-Jan-15	-	31-Jan-15	0.53	31-Jan-15	0.5512
28-Feb-15	0.338	28-Feb-15	-	28-Feb-15	0.53	28-Feb-15	0.55
31-Mar-15	0.4295	31-Mar-15	-	31-Mar-15	0.53	31-Mar-15	0.5511
30-Apr-15	0.4322	30-Apr-15	-	30-Apr-15	0.533	30-Apr-15	0.55
31-May-15	0.4511	31-May-15	-	31-May-15	0.54	31-May-15	0.5532
30-Jun-15	0.467	30-Jun-15	-	30-Jun-15	0.5505	30-Jun-15	0.55
31-Jul-15	0.4895	31-Jul-15	-	31-Jul-15	0.567	31-Jul-15	0.55
31-Aug-15	0.4643	31-Aug-15	-	31-Aug-15	0.57	31-Aug-15	0.55
30-Sep-15	0.4532	30-Sep-15	-	30-Sep-15	0.57	30-Sep-15	0.55
31-Oct-15	0.48	31-Oct-15	-	31-Oct-15	0.57	31-Oct-15	0.55
30-Nov-15	0.4806	30-Nov-15	-	30-Nov-15	0.57	30-Nov-15	0.55
31-Dec-15	0.4551	31-Dec-15	-	31-Dec-15	0.57	31-Dec-15	0.5786

Source: Bank of England

Notes:

Data provided is for general reference purposes. Every effort is made to ensure that it is up to date and accurate.

The Bank of England does not warrant, or accept responsibility/liability for, the accuracy/completeness of content, or loss/damage, whether direct, indirect or consequential, which may arise from reliance on said data. We reserve the right to change information published, including timing and methods used. We give no assurance that data currently published will be in the future.

(a) This series discontinued at end of August 2005

12.10 Average Foreign Exchange rates

Monthly average Old IMF-based Effective exchange rate index, Sterling (a) (1990 average = 100) XUMAGBG		Monthly average Effective exchange rate index, Sterling (Jan 2005 = 100) XUMABK67		Monthly average Spot exchange rate, US$ into Sterling XUMAUSS		Monthly average Spot exchange rate, Euro into Sterling XUMAERS	
31-Jan-99	99.57	31-Jan-99	96.0553	31-Jan-99	1.6509	31-Jan-99	1.4236
28-Feb-99	100.84	28-Feb-99	96.8798	28-Feb-99	1.6276	28-Feb-99	1.4534
31-Mar-99	102.84	31-Mar-99	98.5188	31-Mar-99	1.622	31-Mar-99	1.4902
30-Apr-99	103.36	30-Apr-99	98.5421	30-Apr-99	1.6105	30-Apr-99	1.5051
31-May-99	104.25	31-May-99	99.3295	31-May-99	1.6154	31-May-99	1.5185
30-Jun-99	104.71	30-Jun-99	99.3021	30-Jun-99	1.595	30-Jun-99	1.5374
31-Jul-99	103.45	31-Jul-99	98.1193	31-Jul-99	1.5747	31-Jul-99	1.5204
31-Aug-99	103.34	31-Aug-99	98.3593	31-Aug-99	1.6073	31-Aug-99	1.5146
30-Sep-99	104.7	30-Sep-99	99.5328	30-Sep-99	1.6243	30-Sep-99	1.5458
31-Oct-99	105.37	31-Oct-99	100.3902	31-Oct-99	1.6572	31-Oct-99	1.5491
30-Nov-99	105.74	30-Nov-99	100.3017	30-Nov-99	1.6214	30-Nov-99	1.5706
31-Dec-99	106.68	31-Dec-99	100.9186	31-Dec-99	1.6132	31-Dec-99	1.5953
31-Jan-00	108.55	31-Jan-00	102.5157	31-Jan-00	1.6402	31-Jan-00	1.6201
29-Feb-00	108.44	29-Feb-00	102.1472	29-Feb-00	1.5998	29-Feb-00	1.6266
31-Mar-00	108.41	31-Mar-00	101.9453	31-Mar-00	1.5802	31-Mar-00	1.6377
30-Apr-00	110.06	30-Apr-00	103.2995	30-Apr-00	1.5837	30-Apr-00	1.673
31-May-00	108.52	31-May-00	101.3365	31-May-00	1.5075	31-May-00	1.6655
30-Jun-00	104.64	30-Jun-00	98.3073	30-Jun-00	1.5089	30-Jun-00	1.5882
31-Jul-00	105.63	31-Jul-00	99.0756	31-Jul-00	1.5088	31-Jul-00	1.6052
31-Aug-00	107.38	31-Aug-00	100.1868	31-Aug-00	1.491	31-Aug-00	1.6478
30-Sep-00	106.21	30-Sep-00	98.7449	30-Sep-00	1.4355	30-Sep-00	1.6471
31-Oct-00	109.19	31-Oct-00	101.3373	31-Oct-00	1.4511	31-Oct-00	1.6994
30-Nov-00	107.27	30-Nov-00	99.6607	30-Nov-00	1.4256	30-Nov-00	1.6664
31-Dec-00	106.39	31-Dec-00	99.4105	31-Dec-00	1.4625	31-Dec-00	1.6302
31-Jan-01	104.43	31-Jan-01	98.2353	31-Jan-01	1.4769	31-Jan-01	1.5753
28-Feb-01	104.14	28-Feb-01	97.7169	28-Feb-01	1.4529	28-Feb-01	1.5786
31-Mar-01	105.02	31-Mar-01	98.4519	31-Mar-01	1.4454	31-Mar-01	1.5901
30-Apr-01	105.85	30-Apr-01	99.0724	30-Apr-01	1.435	30-Apr-01	1.6084
31-May-01	106.56	31-May-01	99.3896	31-May-01	1.4259	31-May-01	1.6304
30-Jun-01	106.77	30-Jun-01	99.216	30-Jun-01	1.4014	30-Jun-01	1.6434
31-Jul-01	107.18	31-Jul-01	99.7541	31-Jul-01	1.4139	31-Jul-01	1.6433
31-Aug-01	105.09	31-Aug-01	98.4273	31-Aug-01	1.4365	31-Aug-01	1.5955
30-Sep-01	106.08	30-Sep-01	99.5939	30-Sep-01	1.4635	30-Sep-01	1.606
31-Oct-01	105.78	31-Oct-01	99.3526	31-Oct-01	1.4517	31-Oct-01	1.6024
30-Nov-01	106.14	30-Nov-01	99.4494	30-Nov-01	1.4358	30-Nov-01	1.6166
31-Dec-01	106.49	31-Dec-01	100.0888	31-Dec-01	1.4409	31-Dec-01	1.6151
31-Jan-02	106.9	31-Jan-02	100.2589	31-Jan-02	1.4323	31-Jan-02	1.6222
28-Feb-02	107.36	28-Feb-02	100.4827	28-Feb-02	1.4231	28-Feb-02	1.6348
31-Mar-02	106.48	31-Mar-02	99.7934	31-Mar-02	1.4225	31-Mar-02	1.6224
30-Apr-02	107.13	30-Apr-02	100.5207	30-Apr-02	1.4434	30-Apr-02	1.6282
31-May-02	105.32	31-May-02	99.1543	31-May-02	1.4593	31-May-02	1.5914
30-Jun-02	103.58	30-Jun-02	98.0048	30-Jun-02	1.4863	30-Jun-02	1.5515
31-Jul-02	105.29	31-Jul-02	100.1553	31-Jul-02	1.5546	31-Jul-02	1.5665
31-Aug-02	105.38	31-Aug-02	100.0897	31-Aug-02	1.5377	31-Aug-02	1.5723
30-Sep-02	106.46	30-Sep-02	101.2319	30-Sep-02	1.5561	30-Sep-02	1.5861
31-Oct-02	106.67	31-Oct-02	101.4439	31-Oct-02	1.5574	31-Oct-02	1.5868
30-Nov-02	105.87	30-Nov-02	100.8848	30-Nov-02	1.5723	30-Nov-02	1.5694
31-Dec-02	105.48	31-Dec-02	100.6644	31-Dec-02	1.5863	31-Dec-02	1.5566
31-Jan-03	104.04	31-Jan-03	99.896	31-Jan-03	1.6169	31-Jan-03	1.5222
28-Feb-03	102.42	28-Feb-03	98.4721	28-Feb-03	1.6085	28-Feb-03	1.4924
31-Mar-03	100.6	31-Mar-03	96.8015	31-Mar-03	1.5836	31-Mar-03	1.4649
30-Apr-03	99.8	30-Apr-03	95.9552	30-Apr-03	1.5747	30-Apr-03	1.4505
31-May-03	97.9	31-May-03	94.886	31-May-03	1.623	31-May-03	1.403
30-Jun-03	99.64	30-Jun-03	96.6134	30-Jun-03	1.6606	30-Jun-03	1.4234
31-Jul-03	99.4	31-Jul-03	95.9153	31-Jul-03	1.6242	31-Jul-03	1.4277

12.10 Average Foreign Exchange rates

Monthly average Old IMF-based Effective exchange rate index, Sterling (a) (1990 average = 100) XUMAGBG		Monthly average Effective exchange rate index, Sterling (Jan 2005 = 100) XUMABK67		Monthly average Spot exchange rate, US$ into Sterling XUMAUSS		Monthly average Spot exchange rate, Euro into Sterling XUMAERS	
31-Aug-03	99.01	31-Aug-03	95.2458	31-Aug-03	1.595	31-Aug-03	1.4286
30-Sep-03	99.24	30-Sep-03	95.5646	30-Sep-03	1.6131	30-Sep-03	1.4338
31-Oct-03	99.82	31-Oct-03	96.7181	31-Oct-03	1.6787	31-Oct-03	1.4334
30-Nov-03	100.42	30-Nov-03	97.3166	30-Nov-03	1.6901	30-Nov-03	1.4426
31-Dec-03	100.29	31-Dec-03	97.8696	31-Dec-03	1.7507	31-Dec-03	1.4246
31-Jan-04	102.38	31-Jan-04	100.1608	31-Jan-04	1.8234	31-Jan-04	1.4447
29-Feb-04	104.84	29-Feb-04	102.5025	29-Feb-04	1.8673	29-Feb-04	1.4774
31-Mar-04	104.99	31-Mar-04	102.1883	31-Mar-04	1.8267	31-Mar-04	1.489
30-Apr-04	105.18	30-Apr-04	102.1368	30-Apr-04	1.8005	30-Apr-04	1.5022
31-May-04	104.63	31-May-04	101.7869	31-May-04	1.7876	31-May-04	1.4894
30-Jun-04	105.8	30-Jun-04	103.0588	30-Jun-04	1.8275	30-Jun-04	1.505
31-Jul-04	105.89	31-Jul-04	103.166	31-Jul-04	1.8429	31-Jul-04	1.5023
31-Aug-04	105.16	31-Aug-04	102.4288	31-Aug-04	1.8216	31-Aug-04	1.4933
30-Sep-04	103.32	30-Sep-04	100.7155	30-Sep-04	1.7922	30-Sep-04	1.4676
31-Oct-04	102.17	31-Oct-04	99.8302	31-Oct-04	1.8065	31-Oct-04	1.4455
30-Nov-04	101.73	30-Nov-04	99.7586	30-Nov-04	1.8603	30-Nov-04	1.4311
31-Dec-04	103.15	31-Dec-04	101.2975	31-Dec-04	1.9275	31-Dec-04	1.4401
31-Jan-05	102.1	31-Jan-05	100	31-Jan-05	1.8764	31-Jan-05	1.4331
28-Feb-05	103.29	28-Feb-05	100.9793	28-Feb-05	1.8871	28-Feb-05	1.4499
31-Mar-05	103.21	31-Mar-05	101.0494	31-Mar-05	1.9078	31-Mar-05	1.444
30-Apr-05	104.38	30-Apr-05	102.0108	30-Apr-05	1.896	30-Apr-05	1.4652
31-May-05	103.55	31-May-05	100.9896	31-May-05	1.8538	31-May-05	1.4611
30-Jun-05	104.92	30-Jun-05	101.7514	30-Jun-05	1.8179	30-Jun-05	1.4952
31-Jul-05	102.14	31-Jul-05	98.8169	31-Jul-05	1.7509	31-Jul-05	1.4547
31-Aug-05	102.85	31-Aug-05	99.701	31-Aug-05	1.7943	31-Aug-05	1.4592
30-Sep-05	103.91	30-Sep-05	100.6456	30-Sep-05	1.8081	30-Sep-05	1.4761
31-Oct-05	103.09	31-Oct-05	99.6485	31-Oct-05	1.764	31-Oct-05	1.4674
30-Nov-05	103.16	30-Nov-05	99.4194	30-Nov-05	1.7341	30-Nov-05	1.4719
31-Dec-05	103.32	31-Dec-05	99.501	31-Dec-05	1.7462	31-Dec-05	1.4725
31-Jan-06	102.67	31-Jan-06	99.0364	31-Jan-06	1.7678	31-Jan-06	1.4582
28-Feb-06	102.83	28-Feb-06	98.9166	28-Feb-06	1.747	28-Feb-06	1.4637
31-Mar-06	102.09	31-Mar-06	98.3581	31-Mar-06	1.7435	31-Mar-06	1.45
30-Apr-06	101.87	30-Apr-06	98.3685	30-Apr-06	1.7685	30-Apr-06	1.4402
31-May-06	104.14	31-May-06	101.2653	31-May-06	1.8702	31-May-06	1.4637
30-Jun-06	-	30-Jun-06	100.9566	30-Jun-06	1.8428	30-Jun-06	1.456
31-Jul-06	-	31-Jul-06	100.9426	31-Jul-06	1.8447	31-Jul-06	1.454
31-Aug-06	-	31-Aug-06	102.9586	31-Aug-06	1.8944	31-Aug-06	1.4785
30-Sep-06	-	30-Sep-06	103.0143	30-Sep-06	1.8847	30-Sep-06	1.4811
31-Oct-06	-	31-Oct-06	103.1454	31-Oct-06	1.8755	31-Oct-06	1.4869
30-Nov-06	-	30-Nov-06	103.4688	30-Nov-06	1.9119	30-Nov-06	1.4834
31-Dec-06	-	31-Dec-06	104.5336	31-Dec-06	1.9633	31-Dec-06	1.486
31-Jan-07	-	31-Jan-07	105.5737	31-Jan-07	1.9587	31-Jan-07	1.5079
28-Feb-07	-	28-Feb-07	105.0315	28-Feb-07	1.9581	28-Feb-07	1.4969
31-Mar-07	-	31-Mar-07	103.5673	31-Mar-07	1.9471	31-Mar-07	1.4703
30-Apr-07	-	30-Apr-07	104.2683	30-Apr-07	1.9909	30-Apr-07	1.4713
31-May-07	-	31-May-07	103.9117	31-May-07	1.9836	31-May-07	1.4677
30-Jun-07	-	30-Jun-07	104.5062	30-Jun-07	1.9864	30-Jun-07	1.4805
31-Jul-07	-	31-Jul-07	105.2356	31-Jul-07	2.0338	31-Jul-07	1.4821
31-Aug-07	-	31-Aug-07	104.5357	31-Aug-07	2.0111	31-Aug-07	1.4762
30-Sep-07	-	30-Sep-07	103.3042	30-Sep-07	2.0185	30-Sep-07	1.4515
31-Oct-07	-	31-Oct-07	102.8112	31-Oct-07	2.0446	31-Oct-07	1.437
30-Nov-07	-	30-Nov-07	101.8977	30-Nov-07	2.0701	30-Nov-07	1.4106
31-Dec-07	-	31-Dec-07	99.9273	31-Dec-07	2.0185	31-Dec-07	1.3863
31-Jan-08	-	31-Jan-08	96.6593	31-Jan-08	1.9698	31-Jan-08	1.3383
29-Feb-08	-	29-Feb-08	96.1702	29-Feb-08	1.9638	29-Feb-08	1.3316

12.10 Average Foreign Exchange rates

Monthly average Old IMF-based Effective exchange rate index, Sterling (a) (1990 average = 100) XUMAGBG		Monthly average Effective exchange rate index, Sterling (Jan 2005 = 100) XUMABK67		Monthly average Spot exchange rate, US$ into Sterling XUMAUSS		Monthly average Spot exchange rate, Euro into Sterling XUMAERS	
31-Mar-08	-	31-Mar-08	94.7859	31-Mar-08	2.0032	31-Mar-08	1.2897
30-Apr-08	-	30-Apr-08	93.0097	30-Apr-08	1.9817	30-Apr-08	1.258
31-May-08	-	31-May-08	93.0104	31-May-08	1.9641	31-May-08	1.2633
30-Jun-08	-	30-Jun-08	93.1297	30-Jun-08	1.9658	30-Jun-08	1.2636
31-Jul-08	-	31-Jul-08	93.2514	31-Jul-08	1.988	31-Jul-08	1.2615
31-Aug-08	-	31-Aug-08	91.6751	31-Aug-08	1.8889	31-Aug-08	1.2614
30-Sep-08	-	30-Sep-08	90.0269	30-Sep-08	1.7986	30-Sep-08	1.2531
31-Oct-08	-	31-Oct-08	89.6315	31-Oct-08	1.69	31-Oct-08	1.2718
30-Nov-08	-	30-Nov-08	83.8153	30-Nov-08	1.5338	30-Nov-08	1.2041
31-Dec-08	-	31-Dec-08	78.4564	31-Dec-08	1.4859	31-Dec-08	1.1043
31-Jan-09	-	31-Jan-09	77.2817	31-Jan-09	1.4452	31-Jan-09	1.0919
28-Feb-09	-	28-Feb-09	79.1628	28-Feb-09	1.4411	28-Feb-09	1.1264
31-Mar-09	-	31-Mar-09	77.2397	31-Mar-09	1.4174	31-Mar-09	1.0867
30-Apr-09	-	30-Apr-09	79.1164	30-Apr-09	1.4715	30-Apr-09	1.1157
31-May-09	-	31-May-09	80.6493	31-May-09	1.5429	31-May-09	1.1295
30-Jun-09	-	30-Jun-09	84.1926	30-Jun-09	1.6366	30-Jun-09	1.1682
31-Jul-09	-	31-Jul-09	83.7762	31-Jul-09	1.6366	31-Jul-09	1.1622
31-Aug-09	-	31-Aug-09	83.6592	31-Aug-09	1.6539	31-Aug-09	1.1597
30-Sep-09	-	30-Sep-09	81.3416	30-Sep-09	1.6328	30-Sep-09	1.1212
31-Oct-09	-	31-Oct-09	79.5593	31-Oct-09	1.6199	31-Oct-09	1.0928
30-Nov-09	-	30-Nov-09	81.1204	30-Nov-09	1.6597	30-Nov-09	1.1126
31-Dec-09	-	31-Dec-09	80.4824	31-Dec-09	1.6239	31-Dec-09	1.1127
31-Jan-10	-	31-Jan-10	81.0251	31-Jan-10	1.6162	31-Jan-10	1.1327
28-Feb-10	-	28-Feb-10	80.3045	28-Feb-10	1.5615	28-Feb-10	1.1415
31-Mar-10	-	31-Mar-10	77.5255	31-Mar-10	1.5053	31-Mar-10	1.1092
30-Apr-10	-	30-Apr-10	79.3959	30-Apr-10	1.534	30-Apr-10	1.1436
31-May-10	-	31-May-10	79.2555	31-May-10	1.4627	31-May-10	1.1685
30-Jun-10	-	30-Jun-10	81.0388	30-Jun-10	1.4761	30-Jun-10	1.2082
31-Jul-10	-	31-Jul-10	81.428	31-Jul-10	1.5299	31-Jul-10	1.1959
31-Aug-10	-	31-Aug-10	82.6428	31-Aug-10	1.566	31-Aug-10	1.2132
30-Sep-10	-	30-Sep-10	81.2188	30-Sep-10	1.5578	30-Sep-10	1.1901
31-Oct-10	-	31-Oct-10	79.5097	31-Oct-10	1.5862	31-Oct-10	1.1412
30-Nov-10	-	30-Nov-10	80.9626	30-Nov-10	1.5961	30-Nov-10	1.1701
31-Dec-10	-	31-Dec-10	80.4149	31-Dec-10	1.5603	31-Dec-10	1.1802
31-Jan-11	-	31-Jan-11	80.7151	31-Jan-11	1.5795	31-Jan-11	1.1817
28-Feb-11	-	28-Feb-11	81.4931	28-Feb-11	1.613	28-Feb-11	1.1815
31-Mar-11	-	31-Mar-11	80.2528	31-Mar-11	1.6159	31-Mar-11	1.1527
30-Apr-11	-	30-Apr-11	79.6699	30-Apr-11	1.6345	30-Apr-11	1.1331
31-May-11	-	31-May-11	79.7758	31-May-11	1.6312	31-May-11	1.1403
30-Jun-11	-	30-Jun-11	78.8778	30-Jun-11	1.6214	30-Jun-11	1.1261
31-Jul-11	-	31-Jul-11	78.7605	31-Jul-11	1.6145	31-Jul-11	1.1308
31-Aug-11	-	31-Aug-11	79.6347	31-Aug-11	1.6348	31-Aug-11	1.1422
30-Sep-11	-	30-Sep-11	79.2592	30-Sep-11	1.5783	30-Sep-11	1.147
31-Oct-11	-	31-Oct-11	79.5319	31-Oct-11	1.576	31-Oct-11	1.1487
30-Nov-11	-	30-Nov-11	80.4719	30-Nov-11	1.5804	30-Nov-11	1.1659
31-Dec-11	-	31-Dec-11	80.9048	31-Dec-11	1.5585	31-Dec-11	1.1843
31-Jan-12	-	31-Jan-12	81.1111	31-Jan-12	1.551	31-Jan-12	1.2034
29-Feb-12	-	29-Feb-12	80.9898	29-Feb-12	1.5802	29-Feb-12	1.1941
31-Mar-12	-	31-Mar-12	81.4138	31-Mar-12	1.5823	31-Mar-12	1.1981
30-Apr-12	-	30-Apr-12	82.5582	30-Apr-12	1.6014	30-Apr-12	1.2161
31-May-12	-	31-May-12	83.8035	31-May-12	1.5905	31-May-12	1.244
30-Jun-12	-	30-Jun-12	83.0865	30-Jun-12	1.5571	30-Jun-12	1.2416
31-Jul-12	-	31-Jul-12	83.9961	31-Jul-12	1.5589	31-Jul-12	1.2688
31-Aug-12	-	31-Aug-12	84.0119	31-Aug-12	1.5719	31-Aug-12	1.2676
30-Sep-12	-	30-Sep-12	84.2241	30-Sep-12	1.6116	30-Sep-12	1.2524

12.10 Average Foreign Exchange rates

Monthly average Old IMF-based Effective exchange rate index, Sterling (a) (1990 average = 100) XUMAGBG		Monthly average Effective exchange rate index, Sterling (Jan 2005 = 100) XUMABK67		Monthly average Spot exchange rate, US$ into Sterling XUMAUSS		Monthly average Spot exchange rate, Euro into Sterling XUMAERS	
31-Oct-12	-	31-Oct-12	83.6177	31-Oct-12	1.6079	31-Oct-12	1.2393
30-Nov-12	-	30-Nov-12	83.6784	30-Nov-12	1.5961	30-Nov-12	1.244
31-Dec-12	-	31-Dec-12	83.5782	31-Dec-12	1.6144	31-Dec-12	1.231
31-Jan-13	-	31-Jan-13	82.1828	31-Jan-13	1.5957	31-Jan-13	1.2
28-Feb-13	-	28-Feb-13	79.7012	28-Feb-13	1.5478	28-Feb-13	1.1594
31-Mar-13	-	31-Mar-13	79.0971	31-Mar-13	1.5076	31-Mar-13	1.1634
30-Apr-13	-	30-Apr-13	80.1276	30-Apr-13	1.5316	30-Apr-13	1.175
31-May-13	-	31-May-13	80.4243	31-May-13	1.5285	31-May-13	1.1777
30-Jun-13	-	30-Jun-13	80.9967	30-Jun-13	1.5478	30-Jun-13	1.174
31-Jul-13	-	31-Jul-13	79.9687	31-Jul-13	1.5172	31-Jul-13	1.16
31-Aug-13	-	31-Aug-13	80.9916	31-Aug-13	1.5507	31-Aug-13	1.1649
30-Sep-13	-	30-Sep-13	82.7421	30-Sep-13	1.5865	30-Sep-13	1.1883
31-Oct-13	-	31-Oct-13	82.6728	31-Oct-13	1.6094	31-Oct-13	1.1797
30-Nov-13	-	30-Nov-13	83.5664	30-Nov-13	1.6104	30-Nov-13	1.1938
31-Dec-13	-	31-Dec-13	84.4287	31-Dec-13	1.6375	31-Dec-13	1.1947
31-Jan-14	-	31-Jan-14	85.4342	31-Jan-14	1.647	31-Jan-14	1.2097
28-Feb-14	-	28-Feb-14	85.7492	28-Feb-14	1.6567	28-Feb-14	1.2122
31-Mar-14	-	31-Mar-14	85.5427	31-Mar-14	1.6622	31-Mar-14	1.2021
30-Apr-14	-	30-Apr-14	86.1889	30-Apr-14	1.6743	30-Apr-14	1.2125
31-May-14	-	31-May-14	86.8518	31-May-14	1.6844	31-May-14	1.2267
30-Jun-14	-	30-Jun-14	87.6907	30-Jun-14	1.6906	30-Jun-14	1.2436
31-Jul-14	-	31-Jul-14	88.7494	31-Jul-14	1.7069	31-Jul-14	1.2611
31-Aug-14	-	31-Aug-14	87.7731	31-Aug-14	1.6709	31-Aug-14	1.2542
30-Sep-14	-	30-Sep-14	87.5078	30-Sep-14	1.6305	30-Sep-14	1.2639
31-Oct-14	-	31-Oct-14	87.3544	31-Oct-14	1.6068	31-Oct-14	1.2678
30-Nov-14	-	30-Nov-14	86.9791	30-Nov-14	1.578	30-Nov-14	1.2646
31-Dec-14	-	31-Dec-14	87.5065	31-Dec-14	1.564	31-Dec-14	1.2686
31-Jan-15	-	31-Jan-15	87.752	31-Jan-15	1.5143	31-Jan-15	1.3045
28-Feb-15	-	28-Feb-15	90.0559	28-Feb-15	1.5334	28-Feb-15	1.3503
31-Mar-15	-	31-Mar-15	90.4062	31-Mar-15	1.4957	31-Mar-15	1.3825
30-Apr-15	-	30-Apr-15	90.1613	30-Apr-15	1.4967	30-Apr-15	1.3856
31-May-15	-	31-May-15	91.327	31-May-15	1.547	31-May-15	1.3852
30-Jun-15	-	30-Jun-15	92.1117	30-Jun-15	1.5568	30-Jun-15	1.3879
31-Jul-15	-	31-Jul-15	93.3044	31-Jul-15	1.556	31-Jul-15	1.4139
31-Aug-15	-	31-Aug-15	93.45	31-Aug-15	1.5583	31-Aug-15	1.4004
30-Sep-15	-	30-Sep-15	91.8039	30-Sep-15	1.5326	30-Sep-15	1.3665
31-Oct-15	-	31-Oct-15	91.5676	31-Oct-15	1.5339	31-Oct-15	1.3657
30-Nov-15	-	30-Nov-15	93.362	30-Nov-15	1.519	30-Nov-15	1.4168
31-Dec-15	-	31-Dec-15	91.5147	31-Dec-15	1.4983	31-Dec-15	1.3769

(a) This series was discontinued in May 2006

Source: Bank of England

12.11 Average zero coupon yields

End month level of yield from British Government Securities, 5 year Nominal Zero Coupon IUMSNZC [b]		End month level of yield from British Government Securities, 10 year Nominal Zero Coupon IUMMNZC [b]		End month level of yield from British Government Securities, 20 year Nominal Zero Coupon IUMLNZC [b]		Monthly average yield from British Government Securities, 10 year Real Zero Coupon IUMAMRZC [a]		Monthly average yield from British Government Securities, 20 year Real Zero Coupon IUMALRZC [a]	
31-Jan-00	6.2861	31-Jan-00	5.6139	31-Jan-00	4.479	31-Jan-00	2.1092	31-Jan-00	2.0073
29-Feb-00	6.0103	29-Feb-00	5.335	29-Feb-00	4.3632	29-Feb-00	2.1685	29-Feb-00	1.9533
31-Mar-00	5.8575	31-Mar-00	5.1478	31-Mar-00	4.3495	31-Mar-00	2.0489	31-Mar-00	1.7809
30-Apr-00	5.7047	30-Apr-00	5.0977	30-Apr-00	4.2623	30-Apr-00	2.0737	30-Apr-00	1.8364
31-May-00	5.6958	31-May-00	5.0513	31-May-00	4.3045	31-May-00	2.1386	31-May-00	1.9033
30-Jun-00	5.595	30-Jun-00	5.0731	30-Jun-00	4.3797	30-Jun-00	2.1202	30-Jun-00	1.8707
31-Jul-00	5.6384	31-Jul-00	5.1357	31-Jul-00	4.4363	31-Jul-00	2.1409	31-Jul-00	1.8992
31-Aug-00	5.6807	31-Aug-00	5.2491	31-Aug-00	4.5683	31-Aug-00	2.2278	31-Aug-00	1.9479
30-Sep-00	5.5287	30-Sep-00	5.1367	30-Sep-00	4.6199	30-Sep-00	2.2736	30-Sep-00	1.9532
31-Oct-00	5.4743	31-Oct-00	5.0874	31-Oct-00	4.5168	31-Oct-00	2.3268	31-Oct-00	1.9916
30-Nov-00	5.1547	30-Nov-00	4.7891	30-Nov-00	4.2618	30-Nov-00	2.3179	30-Nov-00	1.9296
31-Dec-00	5.083	31-Dec-00	4.7809	31-Dec-00	4.291	31-Dec-00	2.2104	31-Dec-00	1.8589
31-Jan-01	4.978	31-Jan-01	4.6718	31-Jan-01	4.3694	31-Jan-01	2.2154	31-Jan-01	1.8684
28-Feb-01	4.9824	28-Feb-01	4.7079	28-Feb-01	4.378	28-Feb-01	2.2144	28-Feb-01	1.8523
31-Mar-01	4.8425	31-Mar-01	4.7218	31-Mar-01	4.5984	31-Mar-01	2.2702	31-Mar-01	1.9601
30-Apr-01	5.126	30-Apr-01	5.065	30-Apr-01	4.8872	30-Apr-01	2.5368	30-Apr-01	2.2434
31-May-01	5.2777	31-May-01	5.1627	31-May-01	5.0197	31-May-01	2.5735	31-May-01	2.3112
30-Jun-01	5.4376	30-Jun-01	5.2329	30-Jun-01	5.0078	30-Jun-01	2.5725	30-Jun-01	2.2817
31-Jul-01	5.1702	31-Jul-01	5.0002	31-Jul-01	4.7653	31-Jul-01	2.5826	31-Jul-01	2.2629
31-Aug-01	4.9746	31-Aug-01	4.8652	31-Aug-01	4.682	31-Aug-01	2.3919	31-Aug-01	2.1494
30-Sep-01	4.8735	30-Sep-01	4.9172	30-Sep-01	4.8559	30-Sep-01	2.4992	30-Sep-01	2.3047
31-Oct-01	4.5126	31-Oct-01	4.5368	31-Oct-01	4.4576	31-Oct-01	2.5713	31-Oct-01	2.3376
30-Nov-01	4.6523	30-Nov-01	4.6479	30-Nov-01	4.5089	30-Nov-01	2.3844	30-Nov-01	2.1178
31-Dec-01	5.0788	31-Dec-01	5.0326	31-Dec-01	4.782	31-Dec-01	2.5171	31-Dec-01	2.2145
31-Jan-02	4.9044	31-Jan-02	4.8138	31-Jan-02	4.6689	31-Jan-02	2.4923	31-Jan-02	2.2395
28-Feb-02	4.9428	28-Feb-02	4.923	28-Feb-02	4.7928	28-Feb-02	2.4722	28-Feb-02	2.2767
31-Mar-02	5.3046	31-Mar-02	5.2456	31-Mar-02	5.0823	31-Mar-02	2.5074	31-Mar-02	2.3014
30-Apr-02	5.1522	30-Apr-02	5.1553	30-Apr-02	5.0257	30-Apr-02	2.4157	30-Apr-02	2.2401
31-May-02	5.2156	31-May-02	5.2282	31-May-02	5.1364	31-May-02	2.4142	31-May-02	2.2421
30-Jun-02	5.0148	30-Jun-02	4.9715	30-Jun-02	4.8164	30-Jun-02	2.3162	30-Jun-02	2.1556
31-Jul-02	4.7231	31-Jul-02	4.9201	31-Jul-02	4.8015	31-Jul-02	2.409	31-Jul-02	2.2475
31-Aug-02	4.4976	31-Aug-02	4.6394	31-Aug-02	4.4857	31-Aug-02	2.3109	31-Aug-02	2.1482
30-Sep-02	4.1825	30-Sep-02	4.412	30-Sep-02	4.3797	30-Sep-02	2.1834	30-Sep-02	2.0609
31-Oct-02	4.3315	31-Oct-02	4.5992	31-Oct-02	4.5466	31-Oct-02	2.3919	31-Oct-02	2.236
30-Nov-02	4.5062	30-Nov-02	4.6898	30-Nov-02	4.6549	30-Nov-02	2.3853	30-Nov-02	2.2838
31-Dec-02	4.1583	31-Dec-02	4.3967	31-Dec-02	4.4607	31-Dec-02	2.3083	31-Dec-02	2.2482
31-Jan-03	4.0136	31-Jan-03	4.2807	31-Jan-03	4.374	31-Jan-03	2.0797	31-Jan-03	2.0936
28-Feb-03	3.7987	28-Feb-03	4.227	28-Feb-03	4.4687	28-Feb-03	1.787	28-Feb-03	1.979
31-Mar-03	3.9584	31-Mar-03	4.3549	31-Mar-03	4.5931	31-Mar-03	1.8418	31-Mar-03	2.0679
30-Apr-03	4.0086	30-Apr-03	4.4202	30-Apr-03	4.6491	30-Apr-03	1.9411	30-Apr-03	2.1236
31-May-03	3.7737	31-May-03	4.1579	31-May-03	4.4323	31-May-03	1.7954	31-May-03	2.0315
30-Jun-03	3.8401	30-Jun-03	4.2698	30-Jun-03	4.6015	30-Jun-03	1.6503	30-Jun-03	1.9703
31-Jul-03	4.2291	31-Jul-03	4.6075	31-Jul-03	4.8344	31-Jul-03	1.8311	31-Jul-03	2.1601
31-Aug-03	4.4574	31-Aug-03	4.6562	31-Aug-03	4.6988	31-Aug-03	1.9459	31-Aug-03	2.141
30-Sep-03	4.3404	30-Sep-03	4.5844	30-Sep-03	4.6736	30-Sep-03	2.0465	30-Sep-03	2.1819
31-Oct-03	4.9274	31-Oct-03	5.0093	31-Oct-03	4.859	31-Oct-03	2.1484	31-Oct-03	2.2234
30-Nov-03	4.911	30-Nov-03	5.0473	30-Nov-03	4.8909	30-Nov-03	2.2143	30-Nov-03	2.2058
31-Dec-03	4.612	31-Dec-03	4.7733	31-Dec-03	4.7034	31-Dec-03	2.034	31-Dec-03	2.0784
31-Jan-04	4.7324	31-Jan-04	4.8572	31-Jan-04	4.7485	31-Jan-04	1.9359	31-Jan-04	1.9606
29-Feb-04	4.5996	29-Feb-04	4.735	29-Feb-04	4.7232	29-Feb-04	1.959	29-Feb-04	1.901
31-Mar-04	4.6154	31-Mar-04	4.7184	31-Mar-04	4.6453	31-Mar-04	1.8077	31-Mar-04	1.7684
30-Apr-04	4.8491	30-Apr-04	4.9564	30-Apr-04	4.839	30-Apr-04	1.9295	30-Apr-04	1.848
31-May-04	5.1163	31-May-04	5.1062	31-May-04	4.8917	31-May-04	2.0517	31-May-04	1.8784
30-Jun-04	5.039	30-Jun-04	5.0587	30-Jun-04	4.84	30-Jun-04	2.1008	30-Jun-04	1.8799
31-Jul-04	5.0958	31-Jul-04	5.0518	31-Jul-04	4.7933	31-Jul-04	2.0733	31-Jul-04	1.8713
31-Aug-04	4.8585	31-Aug-04	4.881	31-Aug-04	4.6547	31-Aug-04	2.0347	31-Aug-04	1.8228
30-Sep-04	4.7433	30-Sep-04	4.7878	30-Sep-04	4.6312	30-Sep-04	1.9736	30-Sep-04	1.798
31-Oct-04	4.6267	31-Oct-04	4.7002	31-Oct-04	4.5693	31-Oct-04	1.8877	31-Oct-04	1.7646
30-Nov-04	4.473	30-Nov-04	4.5606	30-Nov-04	4.4453	30-Nov-04	1.8755	30-Nov-04	1.7059
31-Dec-04	4.4287	31-Dec-04	4.4872	31-Dec-04	4.4097	31-Dec-04	1.7552	31-Dec-04	1.5992
31-Jan-05	4.4769	31-Jan-05	4.5419	31-Jan-05	4.4811	31-Jan-05	1.7474	31-Jan-05	1.5862
28-Feb-05	4.6761	28-Feb-05	4.6514	28-Feb-05	4.5249	28-Feb-05	1.77	28-Feb-05	1.5918
31-Mar-05	4.6106	31-Mar-05	4.6357	31-Mar-05	4.5618	31-Mar-05	1.874	31-Mar-05	1.7246
30-Apr-05	4.444	30-Apr-05	4.4735	30-Apr-05	4.4264	30-Apr-05	1.7638	30-Apr-05	1.6408
31-May-05	4.2051	31-May-05	4.2823	31-May-05	4.3326	31-May-05	1.6959	31-May-05	1.5704

12.11 Average zero coupon yields

End month level of yield from British Government Securities, 5 year Nominal Zero Coupon IUMSNZC [b]		End month level of yield from British Government Securities, 10 year Nominal Zero Coupon IUMMNZC [b]		End month level of yield from British Government Securities, 20 year Nominal Zero Coupon IUMLNZC [b]		Monthly average yield from British Government Securities, 10 year Real Zero Coupon IUMAMRZC [a]		Monthly average yield from British Government Securities, 20 year Real Zero Coupon IUMALRZC [a]	
30-Jun-05	4.0387	30-Jun-05	4.1519	30-Jun-05	4.2073	30-Jun-05	1.6498	30-Jun-05	1.5324
31-Jul-05	4.2154	31-Jul-05	4.2892	31-Jul-05	4.3179	31-Jul-05	1.6469	31-Jul-05	1.5442
31-Aug-05	4.0641	31-Aug-05	4.1248	31-Aug-05	4.1705	31-Aug-05	1.6095	31-Aug-05	1.4945
30-Sep-05	4.1884	30-Sep-05	4.2489	30-Sep-05	4.2336	30-Sep-05	1.5097	30-Sep-05	1.4043
31-Oct-05	4.2874	31-Oct-05	4.2833	31-Oct-05	4.238	31-Oct-05	1.5665	31-Oct-05	1.3974
30-Nov-05	4.2061	30-Nov-05	4.1685	30-Nov-05	4.0854	30-Nov-05	1.541	30-Nov-05	1.2925
31-Dec-05	4.1019	31-Dec-05	4.0505	31-Dec-05	3.9626	31-Dec-05	1.4668	31-Dec-05	1.2015
31-Jan-06	4.172	31-Jan-06	4.0817	31-Jan-06	3.8631	31-Jan-06	1.2921	31-Jan-06	0.9687
28-Feb-06	4.2134	28-Feb-06	4.1211	28-Feb-06	3.9088	28-Feb-06	1.3237	28-Feb-06	0.9897
31-Mar-06	4.3946	31-Mar-06	4.3444	31-Mar-06	4.1388	31-Mar-06	1.4135	31-Mar-06	1.1011
30-Apr-06	4.6102	30-Apr-06	4.5855	30-Apr-06	4.3286	30-Apr-06	1.542	30-Apr-06	1.2818
31-May-06	4.6302	31-May-06	4.5395	31-May-06	4.2978	31-May-06	1.6291	31-May-06	1.3321
30-Jun-06	4.7356	30-Jun-06	4.6536	30-Jun-06	4.4151	30-Jun-06	1.6832	30-Jun-06	1.3862
31-Jul-06	4.6631	31-Jul-06	4.5482	31-Jul-06	4.2984	31-Jul-06	1.6457	31-Jul-06	1.3078
31-Aug-06	4.6343	31-Aug-06	4.4391	31-Aug-06	4.163	31-Aug-06	1.5515	31-Aug-06	1.2077
30-Sep-06	4.6412	30-Sep-06	4.4471	30-Sep-06	4.1548	30-Sep-06	1.4912	30-Sep-06	1.1173
31-Oct-06	4.6979	31-Oct-06	4.4201	31-Oct-06	4.0629	31-Oct-06	1.5738	31-Oct-06	1.1275
30-Nov-06	4.6926	30-Nov-06	4.4113	30-Nov-06	4.0858	30-Nov-06	1.4736	30-Nov-06	1.0294
31-Dec-06	4.9131	31-Dec-06	4.6318	31-Dec-06	4.2526	31-Dec-06	1.5561	31-Dec-06	1.1073
31-Jan-07	5.1482	31-Jan-07	4.855	31-Jan-07	4.4219	31-Jan-07	1.7849	31-Jan-07	1.2302
28-Feb-07	4.9735	28-Feb-07	4.6791	28-Feb-07	4.3078	28-Feb-07	1.7983	28-Feb-07	1.2474
31-Mar-07	5.1338	31-Mar-07	4.8548	31-Mar-07	4.4697	31-Mar-07	1.7002	31-Mar-07	1.1947
30-Apr-07	5.194	30-Apr-07	4.9284	30-Apr-07	4.5536	30-Apr-07	1.9068	30-Apr-07	1.3595
31-May-07	5.448	31-May-07	5.1283	31-May-07	4.6951	31-May-07	2.0466	31-May-07	1.4583
30-Jun-07	5.6348	30-Jun-07	5.3604	30-Jun-07	4.8891	30-Jun-07	2.2101	30-Jun-07	1.5415
31-Jul-07	5.3529	31-Jul-07	5.1173	31-Jul-07	4.6572	31-Jul-07	2.1934	31-Jul-07	1.5156
31-Aug-07	5.1209	31-Aug-07	4.9347	31-Aug-07	4.5484	31-Aug-07	1.9666	31-Aug-07	1.3126
30-Sep-07	4.9798	30-Sep-07	4.9495	30-Sep-07	4.6447	30-Sep-07	1.7894	30-Sep-07	1.2421
31-Oct-07	4.9395	31-Oct-07	4.8667	31-Oct-07	4.5916	31-Oct-07	1.7455	31-Oct-07	1.2495
30-Nov-07	4.5718	30-Nov-07	4.6361	30-Nov-07	4.5157	30-Nov-07	1.4823	30-Nov-07	1.095
31-Dec-07	4.4137	31-Dec-07	4.5151	31-Dec-07	4.3859	31-Dec-07	1.4983	31-Dec-07	1.0845
31-Jan-08	4.2964	31-Jan-08	4.4877	31-Jan-08	4.4193	31-Jan-08	1.3032	31-Jan-08	0.9192
29-Feb-08	4.1991	29-Feb-08	4.5274	29-Feb-08	4.503	29-Feb-08	1.3276	29-Feb-08	1.0259
31-Mar-08	3.9541	31-Mar-08	4.424	31-Mar-08	4.6048	31-Mar-08	1.0236	31-Mar-08	0.8844
30-Apr-08	4.4429	30-Apr-08	4.733	30-Apr-08	4.7139	30-Apr-08	1.2032	30-Apr-08	1.0184
31-May-08	4.94	31-May-08	4.9984	31-May-08	4.8293	31-May-08	1.3612	31-May-08	0.9959
30-Jun-08	5.1659	30-Jun-08	5.1663	30-Jun-08	4.8995	30-Jun-08	1.3581	30-Jun-08	0.8405
31-Jul-08	4.7675	31-Jul-08	4.8448	31-Jul-08	4.7434	31-Jul-08	1.2887	31-Jul-08	0.8261
31-Aug-08	4.4108	31-Aug-08	4.5222	31-Aug-08	4.5953	31-Aug-08	1.1652	31-Aug-08	0.6719
30-Sep-08	4.208	30-Sep-08	4.5137	30-Sep-08	4.6924	30-Sep-08	1.2511	30-Sep-08	0.7995
31-Oct-08	3.9697	31-Oct-08	4.713	31-Oct-08	4.9258	31-Oct-08	2.0565	31-Oct-08	1.3285
30-Nov-08	3.3664	30-Nov-08	4.0317	30-Nov-08	4.5731	30-Nov-08	2.58	30-Nov-08	1.3657
31-Dec-08	2.708	31-Dec-08	3.4126	31-Dec-08	4.066	31-Dec-08	2.1901	31-Dec-08	1.2361
31-Jan-09	2.8834	31-Jan-09	4.0861	31-Jan-09	4.7012	31-Jan-09	1.5257	31-Jan-09	1.052
28-Feb-09	2.6227	28-Feb-09	3.8159	28-Feb-09	4.7151	28-Feb-09	1.2501	28-Feb-09	1.1934
31-Mar-09	2.4459	31-Mar-09	3.311	31-Mar-09	4.2558	31-Mar-09	1.1902	31-Mar-09	1.1852
30-Apr-09	2.594	30-Apr-09	3.6361	30-Apr-09	4.5822	30-Apr-09	1.0832	30-Apr-09	1.1448
31-May-09	2.7154	31-May-09	3.8141	31-May-09	4.7127	31-May-09	1.0904	31-May-09	1.0545
30-Jun-09	2.9717	30-Jun-09	3.703	30-Jun-09	4.5708	30-Jun-09	1.0821	30-Jun-09	1.0074
31-Jul-09	3.083	31-Jul-09	3.9125	31-Jul-09	4.7431	31-Jul-09	1.2285	31-Jul-09	0.9964
31-Aug-09	2.6877	31-Aug-09	3.6313	31-Aug-09	4.1118	31-Aug-09	1.1562	31-Aug-09	0.8698
30-Sep-09	2.6807	30-Sep-09	3.7123	30-Sep-09	4.1499	30-Sep-09	1.0559	30-Sep-09	0.8862
31-Oct-09	2.7662	31-Oct-09	3.7684	31-Oct-09	4.2789	31-Oct-09	0.703	31-Oct-09	0.7436
30-Nov-09	2.6607	30-Nov-09	3.6987	30-Nov-09	4.2359	30-Nov-09	0.774	30-Nov-09	0.7106
31-Dec-09	2.9821	31-Dec-09	4.203	31-Dec-09	4.5939	31-Dec-09	0.8046	31-Dec-09	0.7645
31-Jan-10	2.9411	31-Jan-10	4.1135	31-Jan-10	4.5279	31-Jan-10	0.8237	31-Jan-10	0.8421
28-Feb-10	2.7834	28-Feb-10	4.2373	28-Feb-10	4.7692	28-Feb-10	0.9608	28-Feb-10	1.0657
31-Mar-10	2.7852	31-Mar-10	4.1764	31-Mar-10	4.6577	31-Mar-10	0.8276	31-Mar-10	0.9801
30-Apr-10	2.7534	30-Apr-10	4.1034	30-Apr-10	4.6279	30-Apr-10	0.7118	30-Apr-10	0.9024
31-May-10	2.4101	31-May-10	3.7919	31-May-10	4.4818	31-May-10	0.7264	31-May-10	0.9331
30-Jun-10	2.2133	30-Jun-10	3.5853	30-Jun-10	4.3767	30-Jun-10	0.7631	30-Jun-10	0.9715
31-Jul-10	2.2281	31-Jul-10	3.5691	31-Jul-10	4.4956	31-Jul-10	0.8433	31-Jul-10	1.0381
31-Aug-10	1.7575	31-Aug-10	3.0217	31-Aug-10	3.9415	31-Aug-10	0.6535	31-Aug-10	0.9004
30-Sep-10	1.813	30-Sep-10	3.1512	30-Sep-10	4.0071	30-Sep-10	0.4628	30-Sep-10	0.7343
31-Oct-10	1.878	31-Oct-10	3.3042	31-Oct-10	4.3031	31-Oct-10	0.3775	31-Oct-10	0.7099

12.11 Average zero coupon yields

End month level of yield from British Government Securities, 5 year Nominal Zero Coupon IUMSNZC [b]		End month level of yield from British Government Securities, 10 year Nominal Zero Coupon IUMMNZC [b]		End month level of yield from British Government Securities, 20 year Nominal Zero Coupon IUMLNZC [b]		Monthly average yield from British Government Securities, 10 year Real Zero Coupon IUMAMRZC [a]		Monthly average yield from British Government Securities, 20 year Real Zero Coupon IUMALRZC [a]	
30-Nov-10	2.0313	30-Nov-10	3.4591	30-Nov-10	4.4002	30-Nov-10	0.4815	30-Nov-10	0.8143
31-Dec-10	2.314	31-Dec-10	3.6174	31-Dec-10	4.3314	31-Dec-10	0.6754	31-Dec-10	0.8243
31-Jan-11	2.5858	31-Jan-11	3.8827	31-Jan-11	4.5822	31-Jan-11	0.6353	31-Jan-11	0.8637
28-Feb-11	2.6508	28-Feb-11	3.8872	28-Feb-11	4.5184	28-Feb-11	0.7203	28-Feb-11	0.8809
31-Mar-11	2.6575	31-Mar-11	3.8974	31-Mar-11	4.5078	31-Mar-11	0.5424	31-Mar-11	0.8003
30-Apr-11	2.4534	30-Apr-11	3.7116	30-Apr-11	4.3435	30-Apr-11	0.5699	30-Apr-11	0.8156
31-May-11	2.2507	31-May-11	3.5655	31-May-11	4.3125	31-May-11	0.4104	31-May-11	0.793
30-Jun-11	2.2036	30-Jun-11	3.6665	30-Jun-11	4.4964	30-Jun-11	0.2576	30-Jun-11	0.6595
31-Jul-11	1.7512	31-Jul-11	3.1755	31-Jul-11	4.2227	31-Jul-11	0.1927	31-Jul-11	0.5845
31-Aug-11	1.6065	31-Aug-11	2.9038	31-Aug-11	4.0173	31-Aug-11	-0.1442	31-Aug-11	0.4083
30-Sep-11	1.4048	30-Sep-11	2.5096	30-Sep-11	3.5397	30-Sep-11	-0.2071	30-Sep-11	0.3008
31-Oct-11	1.3719	31-Oct-11	2.5642	31-Oct-11	3.4276	31-Oct-11	-0.1245	31-Oct-11	0.337
30-Nov-11	1.2752	30-Nov-11	2.4275	30-Nov-11	3.1294	30-Nov-11	-0.3177	30-Nov-11	0.1173
31-Dec-11	1.001	31-Dec-11	2.105	31-Dec-11	3.0454	31-Dec-11	-0.475	31-Dec-11	-0.0286
31-Jan-12	0.9544	31-Jan-12	2.0983	31-Jan-12	3.0189	31-Jan-12	-0.5915	31-Jan-12	-0.1548
29-Feb-12	1.001	29-Feb-12	2.2582	29-Feb-12	3.2967	29-Feb-12	-0.5785	29-Feb-12	-0.0236
31-Mar-12	1.0698	31-Mar-12	2.3289	31-Mar-12	3.447	31-Mar-12	-0.5281	31-Mar-12	0.0341
30-Apr-12	1.1164	30-Apr-12	2.2516	30-Apr-12	3.3938	30-Apr-12	-0.5759	30-Apr-12	-0.0135
31-May-12	0.6748	31-May-12	1.673	31-May-12	2.8994	31-May-12	-0.6844	31-May-12	-0.0644
30-Jun-12	0.8284	30-Jun-12	1.8661	30-Jun-12	2.9815	30-Jun-12	-0.5935	30-Jun-12	-0.0546
31-Jul-12	0.566	31-Jul-12	1.6099	31-Jul-12	2.7932	31-Jul-12	-0.6427	31-Jul-12	-0.0304
31-Aug-12	0.5849	31-Aug-12	1.6346	31-Aug-12	2.8217	31-Aug-12	-0.6944	31-Aug-12	-0.023
30-Sep-12	0.6798	30-Sep-12	1.6958	30-Sep-12	2.9454	30-Sep-12	-0.6639	30-Sep-12	0.0775
31-Oct-12	0.8255	31-Oct-12	1.879	31-Oct-12	3.0256	31-Oct-12	-0.5872	31-Oct-12	0.1513
30-Nov-12	0.8264	30-Nov-12	1.794	30-Nov-12	2.9544	30-Nov-12	-0.6283	30-Nov-12	0.0967
31-Dec-12	0.8853	31-Dec-12	1.8782	31-Dec-12	3.023	31-Dec-12	-0.7274	31-Dec-12	-0.011
31-Jan-13	1.098	31-Jan-13	2.2055	31-Jan-13	3.3222	31-Jan-13	-0.825	31-Jan-13	-0.0952
28-Feb-13	0.9145	28-Feb-13	2.1054	28-Feb-13	3.2498	28-Feb-13	-1.01	28-Feb-13	-0.1883
31-Mar-13	0.7439	31-Mar-13	1.8933	31-Mar-13	3.0961	31-Mar-13	-1.2531	31-Mar-13	-0.3
30-Apr-13	0.73	30-Apr-13	1.7929	30-Apr-13	2.9541	30-Apr-13	-1.3223	30-Apr-13	-0.4891
31-May-13	1.02	31-May-13	2.1641	31-May-13	3.2631	31-May-13	-1.0738	31-May-13	-0.3514
30-Jun-13	1.3933	30-Jun-13	2.618	30-Jun-13	3.5337	30-Jun-13	-0.6377	30-Jun-13	-0.1279
31-Jul-13	1.2511	31-Jul-13	2.5513	31-Jul-13	3.5392	31-Jul-13	-0.5794	31-Jul-13	-0.0071
31-Aug-13	1.5644	31-Aug-13	2.8265	31-Aug-13	3.6373	31-Aug-13	-0.3798	31-Aug-13	0.0923
30-Sep-13	1.5498	30-Sep-13	2.7601	30-Sep-13	3.5437	30-Sep-13	-0.2206	30-Sep-13	0.1506
31-Oct-13	1.5122	31-Oct-13	2.7053	31-Oct-13	3.4942	31-Oct-13	-0.3819	31-Oct-13	0.0185
30-Nov-13	1.6323	30-Nov-13	2.8783	30-Nov-13	3.6515	30-Nov-13	-0.2983	30-Nov-13	0.0607
31-Dec-13	1.9931	31-Dec-13	3.1577	31-Dec-13	3.7316	31-Dec-13	-0.1979	31-Dec-13	0.1006
31-Jan-14	1.7819	31-Jan-14	2.8386	31-Jan-14	3.5521	31-Jan-14	-0.1654	31-Jan-14	0.127
28-Feb-14	1.798	28-Feb-14	2.8582	28-Feb-14	3.5484	28-Feb-14	-0.1897	28-Feb-14	0.1043
31-Mar-14	1.8714	31-Mar-14	2.8707	31-Mar-14	3.5515	31-Mar-14	-0.3044	31-Mar-14	0.0121
30-Apr-14	1.857	30-Apr-14	2.8105	30-Apr-14	3.4992	30-Apr-14	-0.353	30-Apr-14	-0.0318
31-May-14	1.7997	31-May-14	2.7043	31-May-14	3.412	31-May-14	-0.389	31-May-14	-0.0859
30-Jun-14	1.9945	30-Jun-14	2.8146	30-Jun-14	3.4523	30-Jun-14	-0.296	30-Jun-14	-0.0483
31-Jul-14	1.9847	31-Jul-14	2.7619	31-Jul-14	3.3233	31-Jul-14	-0.3139	31-Jul-14	-0.0823
31-Aug-14	1.6987	31-Aug-14	2.3948	31-Aug-14	2.9663	31-Aug-14	-0.4716	31-Aug-14	-0.2406
30-Sep-14	1.781	30-Sep-14	2.4682	30-Sep-14	3.0612	30-Sep-14	-0.5363	30-Sep-14	-0.2837
31-Oct-14	1.5647	31-Oct-14	2.3054	31-Oct-14	2.9766	31-Oct-14	-0.6198	31-Oct-14	-0.4459
30-Nov-14	1.3003	30-Nov-14	1.9853	30-Nov-14	2.6605	30-Nov-14	-0.7384	30-Nov-14	-0.5418
31-Dec-14	1.1987	31-Dec-14	1.8196	31-Dec-14	2.4808	31-Dec-14	-0.9321	31-Dec-14	-0.7607
31-Jan-15	0.9086	31-Jan-15	1.3867	31-Jan-15	2.0083	31-Jan-15	-1.0627	31-Jan-15	-0.9397
28-Feb-15	1.2811	28-Feb-15	1.8567	28-Feb-15	2.4648	28-Feb-15	-0.889	28-Feb-15	-0.7763
31-Mar-15	1.0851	31-Mar-15	1.6605	31-Mar-15	2.2909	31-Mar-15	-0.9312	31-Mar-15	-0.7988
30-Apr-15	1.3017	30-Apr-15	1.9447	30-Apr-15	2.5347	30-Apr-15	-1.0478	30-Apr-15	-0.9476
31-May-15	1.263	31-May-15	1.9178	31-May-15	2.5294	31-May-15	-0.8922	31-May-15	-0.8103
30-Jun-15	1.4567	30-Jun-15	2.1552	30-Jun-15	2.7485	30-Jun-15	-0.7817	30-Jun-15	-0.7055
31-Jul-15	1.3892	31-Jul-15	2.0074	31-Jul-15	2.5863	31-Jul-15	-0.7795	31-Jul-15	-0.738
31-Aug-15	1.3454	31-Aug-15	1.9669	31-Aug-15	2.5998	31-Aug-15	-0.8518	31-Aug-15	-0.8919
30-Sep-15	1.184	30-Sep-15	1.7919	30-Sep-15	2.5118	30-Sep-15	-0.8676	30-Sep-15	-0.8608
31-Oct-15	1.2853	31-Oct-15	1.9457	31-Oct-15	2.6502	31-Oct-15	-0.845	31-Oct-15	-0.8112
30-Nov-15	1.2399	30-Nov-15	1.8741	30-Nov-15	2.5946	30-Nov-15	-0.7842	30-Nov-15	-0.7553
31-Dec-15	1.3752	31-Dec-15	2.0097	31-Dec-15	2.7092	31-Dec-15	-0.7589	31-Dec-15	-0.7717

Notes:

Source: Bank of England

[a] Calculated using the Variable Roughness Penalty (VRP) model.

[b] Calculated by the Bank of England using the Variable Roughness Penalty (VRP) model

12.12 Consumer credit excluding student loans

£ millions   Not seasonally adjusted

Net lending - monthly changes

	MFIs sterling net unsecured lending for individuals	of which: mutuals	Other consumer credit lenders (excluding Student Loans Company) sterling net unsecured lending for individuals	Total (excluding Student Loans Company) sterling net unsecured lending for individuals	of which: credit card lending to individuals	other consumer credit lending to individuals
	LPMVVXP	LPMB3VC	LPMB4TH	LPMB3PT	LPMVZQS	LPMB4TV
	[a] [b] [c] [d] [e] [f]	[a] [g]	[a]			
31-Jan-11	-961	46	-576	-1537	-896	-641
28-Feb-11	-419	11	-375	-794	-201	-593
31-Mar-11	-230	43	187	-43	-326	283
30-Apr-11	317	33	-26	291	773	-481
31-May-11	21	51	-236	-215	55	-270
30-Jun-11	328	46	-7	321	246	75
31-Jul-11	-208	89	-115	-322	141	-463
31-Aug-11	488	89	-191	298	262	36
30-Sep-11	-193	11	432	239	236	3
31-Oct-11	-125	27	-25	-150	-154	4
30-Nov-11	225	34	167	392	376	17
31-Dec-11	-326	40	231	-94	718	-812
31-Jan-12	-881	10	-203	-1084	-969	-116
29-Feb-12	-973	5	-245	-1219	-518	-701
31-Mar-12	-192	23	755	563	-22	585
30-Apr-12	-19	55	41	22	192	-169
31-May-12	-178	48	180	2	-19	21
30-Jun-12	193	10	407	600	568	33
31-Jul-12	-25	74	70	45	-218	263
31-Aug-12	-337	46	-66	-404	227	-630
30-Sep-12	635	27	830	1465	424	1040
31-Oct-12	-442	24	136	-306	-354	48
30-Nov-12	-1	27	352	352	680	-328
31-Dec-12	1688	61	432	2121	1158	963
31-Jan-13	-534	-6	-277	-811	-1052	241
28-Feb-13	244	75	-447	-202	-22	-180
31-Mar-13	-46	38	901	855	-40	895
30-Apr-13	729	45	93	822	374	448
31-May-13	250	7	171	421	268	153
30-Jun-13	314	13	289	603	522	81
31-Jul-13	718	14	123	841	-43	884
31-Aug-13	584	-1	53	637	544	93
30-Sep-13	941	-9	961	1902	276	1627
31-Oct-13	-327	-27	316	-11	-151	140
30-Nov-13	269	-35	511	780	999	-219
31-Dec-13	1259	-	582	1840	917	924
31-Jan-14	-762	-	-17	-780	-825	46
28-Feb-14	4	-	-160	-155	-90	-66
31-Mar-14	787	-	1012	1799	-276	2075
30-Apr-14	528	-	-18	510	602	-92
31-May-14	501	-	230	731	210	521
30-Jun-14	840	-	143	983	352	630
31-Jul-14	751	-	346	1097	166	931
31-Aug-14	480	-	216	696	542	154
30-Sep-14	1021	-	1125	2146	143	2003
31-Oct-14	59	-	316	375	92	283
30-Nov-14	862	-	522	1384	851	533
31-Dec-14	1115	-	496	1611	1150	461

Source: Bank of England

Notes:

MFIs - Monetary Financial Institutions

[a] These series may be affected by securitisations and loan transfers up to December 2009.

[b] Please note that the compilation and descriptions of some credit series have changed from publication of April 2015 data, as described in Bankstats, April 2015, 'Changes to the treatment of loan transfers and lending to housing associations', available at www.bankofengland.co.uk/statistics/Documents/ms/articles/art1apr15.pdf.

[c] From December 1995 to August 1997, subsidiaries set up to take deposits in the Channel Islands & Isle of Man were classified as "building societies"; their balance sheets were consolidated with those of their parents and included in these data. From Sept 1997 the Channel Islands & Isle of Man were reclassified as non-residents, the balance sheets of these subsidiaries have been deconsolidated from those of their parents and are excluded from these data. See explanatory notes for further details. (30 Sep 1997)

[d] The timing of self-assessment income tax payments may have boosted M4 lending to households and reduced its M4 holdings in January, which was reversed in February. (31 Jan 2000 - 29 Feb 2000)

[e] Following the transition of building societies' statistical reporting from the FSA to the Bank of England on 1 January 2008, some minor changes to the building societies' contribution to the calculation of the Monthly Sectoral Analysis of M4 and M4 Lending have been implemented. The effects of these have been removed from the flows data, and are small in terms of the amounts outstanding (31 Jan 2008)

[f] Separate data for banks and building societies have been discontinued from January 2010 onwards. For details, see the Monetary and Financial Statistics article http://www.bankofengland.co.uk/statistics/documents/ms/articles/artjan10.pdf. (31 Jan 2010)

[g] This series will be discontinued with effect from December 2013 data. Further information can be found in Bankstats, December 2013, `Changes to publication of data for mutually owned monetary financial institutions', available at www.bankofengland.co.uk/statistics/Documents/ms/articles/art1dec13.pdf.

12.13a INVESTMENT TRUSTS' ASSETS AND LIABILITIES AT MARKET VALUES

£ million at end of year

		2003	2004	2005	2006	2007	2008	2009	2010	2011	2012	2013
ASSETS												
UK government securities denominated in sterling	RLLT	302	466	768	533	715	628	585	466	681	857	487
Index-linked	AFIS	0	0	0	0	0	0	0	8	95	c	45
Other[1]	K5HJ	302	466	768	533	715	628	585	458	586	c	442
UK government securities denominated in foreign currency	CBPP	0	0	0	0	0	0	0	0	0	0	0
UK local authority investments[2]	AHBR	0	0	0	0	0	0	0	0	0	0	0
Other UK public sector investments[3]	AHBS	5	0	0	0	0	0	0	0	0	0	0
UK ordinary shares Quoted[4]	AHBM	22,403	22,598	24,021	21,843	21,848	13,428	16,297	17,547	17,329	18,655	18,907
Unquoted	AHBQ	889	1,343	1,016	1,027	1,186	938	1,349	1,336	1,437	1,363	1,323
Overseas ordinary shares	AHCC	20,294	18,967	23,065	21,659	25,795	18,385	23,865	29,341	29,083	30,758	31,859
Other corporate securities[5] UK	CBGZ	1,079	1,270	673	1,071	1,259	813	665	560	529	470	498
Overseas	CBHA	603	682	937	741	1,038	623	939	1,304	1,344	1,129	1,217
UK authorised unit trust units	AHBT	79	149	140	24	0	28	33	42	76	53	86
Overseas government, provincial and municipal securities	AHBY	122	33	168	4	151	410	256	410	254	251	118
UK existing buildings, property, land and new construction work	CBHB	498	39	117	252	154	142	141	197	1,522	1,538	158
Other longer-term assets not elsewhere classified[6]	AMSE	1,760	1,665	2,359	2,898	3,462	3,684	3,824	4,618	5,439	5,744	6,240
LONGER-TERM ASSETS	**AHBD**	**48,034**	**47,212**	**53,264**	**50,052**	**55,608**	**39,079**	**47,954**	**55,821**	**57,694**	**60,818**	**60,893**
Short-term assets	CBGX	2,535	3,100	3,032	2,138	3,303	3,397	2,522	2,174	2,893	3,015	2,848
TOTAL ASSETS	**CBGW**	**50,569**	**50,312**	**56,296**	**52,190**	**58,911**	**42,476**	**50,476**	**57,995**	**60,587**	**63,833**	**63,741**
LIABILITIES												
Borrowing from UK and overseas	CBHD	3,207	2,797	2,771	2,900	2,708	2,553	2,216	2,359	2,897	2,845	3,652
Other UK borrowing[8]	CBHG	1,189	843	670	952	988	1,012	1,062	1,123	914	865	989
Other overseas borrowing[9]	CBHI	0	0	0	2	0	225	185	186	126	117	11
Issued share and loan capital[10]	CBHK	9,873	8,210	7,155	5,492	5,659	3,834	3,627	3,361	4,395	4,345	3,741
TOTAL LIABILITIES	**CBHO**	**14,269**	**11,850**	**10,596**	**9,346**	**9,355**	**7,624**	**7,090**	**7,029**	**8,332**	**8,172**	**8,393**
NET ASSETS	**CBHM**	**36,300**	**38,462**	**45,700**	**42,844**	**49,556**	**34,852**	**43,386**	**50,966**	**52,255**	**55,661**	**55,348**

Source: Office for National Statistics

c Suppressed to avoid the disclosure of confidential data.

1 Includes securities of: 0 up to 15 years maturity; over 15 years maturity and undated maturity. Excludes treasury bills and index-linked securities.
2 Includes local authority securities; negotiable bonds; loans and mortgages.
3 Includes public corporation loans and mortgages and other public sector investments not elsewhere classified.
4 Includes investment trust securities.
5 Includes corporate bonds and preference shares.
6 Includes UK unauthorised unit trust units; UK open-ended investment companies; overseas mutual fund investments; other UK fixed assets; overseas fixed assets; overseas direct investment and other UK and overseas assets not elsewhere classified.
7 Sterling and foreign currency. Includes foreign currency liabilities on back-to-back loans and overdrafts.
8 Includes sterling and foreign currency borrowing from building societies; issue of securities (other than ordinary shares); issue of sterling commercial paper and other borrowing not elsewhere classified (such as borrowing from parent, subsidiary and associate companies and other related concerns).
9 Includes borrowing from related companies and other borrowing not elsewhere classified.
10 Quoted and unquoted. Includes ordinary shares; preference shares; deferred stocks; bonds; debentures and loan stocks.

12.13b UNIT TRUSTS AND PROPERTY UNIT TRUSTS' BALANCE SHEET ASSETS AND LIABILITIES AT MARKET VALUES

£ million at end of year

		2003	2004	2005	2006	2007	2008	2009	2010	2011	2012	2013
ASSETS												
UK government securities denominated in sterling[1]	CBHT	9,125	9,768	25,181	31,603	32,120	33,466	29,331	33,306	37,116	36,033	37,275
Ordinary shares[2]												
UK	RLIB	116,407	130,230	157,149	185,637	195,009	143,550	167,401	204,616	179,940	201,822	234,866
Overseas	RLIC	75,074	81,034	105,443	127,409	142,211	113,667	150,863	200,028	187,714	215,705	265,209
Other corporate securities[3]												
UK	CBHU	23,972	22,467	29,293	29,876	30,626	30,174	36,646	52,786	52,735	63,546	60,803
Overseas	CBHV	9,840	13,142	16,057	25,617	30,029	30,442	43,301	49,098	48,388	62,870	67,946
Overseas government, provincial and municipal securities	CBHW	2,267	2,347	3,412	3,532	3,880	5,754	5,810	9,251	14,797	19,604	19,698
UK existing buildings, property, land and new construction work	RLIE	5,125	5,909	9,623	12,781	12,480	8,518	7,248	9,484	13,220	13,498	13,576
Other longer-term assets not elsewhere classified[4]	CBHX	10,940	14,261	22,327	29,765	38,707	42,670	49,417	60,029	66,640	81,849	105,015
Short-term assets	CBHS	12,090	11,497	16,417	20,653	27,969	35,224	37,263	48,382	45,001	53,734	62,021
of which: Derivative contracts with UK and overseas counterparties which have a positive (asset) value[5]	KUU5	4,028	2,099	4,745	4,552	7,271	13,151	17,132	25,944	18,168	25,644	27,923
TOTAL ASSETS	**CBHR**	**264,840**	**290,655**	**384,902**	**466,873**	**513,031**	**443,465**	**527,280**	**666,980**	**645,551**	**748,661**	**866,409**
LIABILITIES												
Borrowing from UK and overseas banks[6]	RLLF	425	413	1,456	2,544	2,603	3,486	1,541	991	1,992	3,430	3,154
Other UK borrowing[7]	RLLH	85	27	130	16	36	80	26	74	350	83	34
Other overseas borrowing[8]	RLLI	26	1	1	0	0	0	54	0	0	0	0
Derivative contracts with UK and overseas counterparties which have a negative (liability) value[5]	KUU6	2,169	1,611	2,814	3,701	6,382	11,890	15,294	23,676	17,464	22,832	26,255
Other creditors, provisions and liabilities not elsewhere classified	KUU7	1,289	1,835	2,425	3,370	2,562	3,442	5,524	7,228	14,087	5,460	1,740
Liability attributable to unit and share holders	RLLG	260,846	286,768	378,076	457,242	501,448	424,567	504,841	635,011	611,658	716,856	835,226
TOTAL LIABILITIES	**RLLE**	**264,840**	**290,655**	**384,902**	**466,873**	**513,031**	**443,465**	**527,280**	**666,980**	**645,551**	**748,661**	**866,409**

c Suppressed to avoid the disclosure of confidential data.

Source: Office for National Statistics

1 Includes securities of: 0 up to 15 years maturity; over 15 years maturity; undated maturity and index-linked. Excludes treasury bills.
2 UK and overseas. Quoted and unquoted. Includes investment trust securities.
3 Includes corporate bonds and preference shares.
4 UK and overseas. Includes UK government securities denominated in foreign currency; local authority and public corporation securities; mutual fund investments; other UK fixed assets; overseas fixed assets; direct investment and other assets not elsewhere classified.
5 Includes credit default products; employee stock options; other options; other swaps; futures; forwards and other derivative contracts not elsewhere classified.
6 Sterling and foreign currency. Includes foreign currency liabilities on back-to-back loans and
7 Includes sterling and foreign currency borrowing from building societies; issue of securities (other than ordinary shares); issue of sterling commercial paper and other borrowing not elsewhere classified (such as borrowing from parent, subsidiary and associate companies and other related concerns).
8 Includes borrowing from related companies and other borrowing not elsewhere classified.

12.14 SELF-ADMINISTERED PENSION FUNDS[1] BALANCE SHEET ASSETS AND LIABILITIES AT MARKET VALUES

£ million at end of year

		2003	2004	2005	2006	2007	2008	2009	2010	2011	2012	2013
ASSETS												
UK government securities denominated in sterling	AHVK	88,803	87,579	94,325	104,910	113,617	98,577	108,871	122,007	167,372	199,400	227,528
Index-linked	AHWC	52,041	46,333	48,821	53,858	64,797	58,564	70,317	83,016	110,808	142,565	159,843
Other[2]	J8Y5	36,762	41,246	45,504	51,052	48,820	40,013	38,554	38,991	56,564	56,835	67,685
UK government securities denominated in foreign currency	RYEX	0	44	45	27	42	4	126	89	1,287	5,695	275
UK local authority investments[3]	AHVO	8	4	4	2	5	0	2	274	113	263	291
Other UK public sector investments[4]	JE5J	639	656	846	1,118	1,351	1,259	2,347	2,911	1,703	1,611	3,862
UK PUBLIC SECTOR SECURITIES	**RYHC**	**89,450**	**88,283**	**95,220**	**106,057**	**115,015**	**99,840**	**111,346**	**125,281**	**170,475**	**206,969**	**231,956**
UK corporate bonds[5]	JX62	36,918	42,871	47,912	54,626	57,306	55,741	64,351	59,469	61,586	64,508	64,581
Sterling	GQFT	36,415	42,151	47,061	53,190	55,550	53,765	62,073	57,086	59,322	61,896	61,938
Foreign currency	GQFU	503	720	851	1,436	1,756	1,976	2,278	2,383	2,264	2,612	2,643
UK ordinary shares[6]	AHVP	186,426	180,561	199,199	208,473	152,048	110,571	116,710	121,882	108,631	111,913	109,777
UK preference shares[6]	J8YF	164	156	153	276	235	775	833	16	11	29	51
Overseas corporate securities	JRS8	138,215	156,278	203,562	224,514	215,068	175,747	214,230	222,751	211,562	226,274	232,277
Bonds	RLPF	12,301	15,794	19,891	30,867	44,387	47,612	57,920	60,826	61,129	60,424	61,655
Ordinary shares	AHVR	125,740	140,282	183,060	192,978	169,598	127,525	155,577	161,043	149,638	165,141	170,007
Preference shares	RLPC	174	202	611	669	1,083	610	733	882	795	709	615
Mutual fund investments	JRS9	117,834	144,265	192,033	215,218	254,936	211,724	286,493	369,955	385,337	448,583	476,623
UK	J8Y7	97,218	115,622	150,316	168,635	194,833	148,798	203,523	266,058	264,652	293,071	302,024
Unit trust units[7]	JX63	77,468	86,005	105,429	115,872	147,536	110,558	148,642	178,027	172,120	208,155	212,566
Other[8]	JX64	19,750	29,617	44,887	52,763	47,297	38,240	54,881	88,031	92,532	84,916	89,458
Overseas	JE4P	20,616	28,643	41,717	46,583	60,103	62,926	82,970	103,897	120,685	155,512	174,599
CORPORATE SECURITIES	**RYHN**	**479,557**	**524,131**	**642,859**	**703,107**	**679,593**	**554,558**	**682,617**	**774,073**	**767,127**	**851,307**	**883,309**
Overseas government, provincial and municipal securities	AHVT	16,340	15,075	19,037	21,776	22,434	21,527	16,900	17,335	21,424	23,768	23,462
Loans	JRT4	35	44	9	42	417	518	1,768	2,343	1,656	1,313	324
UK[9]	JE5E	35	44	6	6	12	0	116	81	77	170	c
Overseas[10]	AHVZ	0	0	3	36	405	518	1,652	2,262	1,579	1,143	c
Fixed assets[11]	JRT5	30,775	30,676	31,742	34,608	30,466	22,892	24,957	30,159	32,991	30,705	33,695
UK	JE5F	30,621	30,554	31,616	34,435	30,306	22,818	24,718	28,991	32,178	30,372	33,064
Overseas	GOLB	154	122	126	173	160	74	239	1,168	813	333	631
Investment in insurance managed funds, insurance policies and annuities	RYHS	43,063	67,936	86,336	92,387	103,610	86,541	70,318	80,613	93,823	99,896	110,723
Other longer-term assets not elsewhere classified[12]	J8YA	14,327	17,071	21,423	31,234	41,455	45,301	51,100	69,419	81,562	90,893	109,368
OTHER LONGER-TERM ASSETS	**RYHW**	**104,540**	**130,802**	**158,547**	**180,047**	**198,382**	**176,779**	**165,043**	**199,869**	**231,456**	**246,575**	**277,572**
LONGER-TERM ASSETS	**RYHX**	**673,547**	**743,216**	**896,626**	**989,211**	**992,990**	**831,177**	**959,006**	**1,099,223**	**1,169,058**	**1,304,851**	**1,392,837**

Source: Office for National Statistics

c Suppressed to avoid the disclosure of confidential data.

1 Combined public and private sector. Data from the pension funds surveys are of lower quality than equivalent data from other institutional groups because of the difficulties in constructing a suitable sampling frame of pension funds.
2 Includes securities of: 0 up to 15 years maturity; over 15 years maturity and undated maturity. Excludes treasury bills and index-linked securities.
3 Includes local authority securities; negotiable bonds; loans and mortgages.
4 Includes public corporation loans and mortgages and other public sector investments not elsewhere classified.
5 Issued by: banks; building societies and other corporates.
6 Quoted and unquoted.
7 Authorised and unauthorised.
8 Includes property unit trusts; investment trust securities; open-ended investment companies; hedge funds and other mutual fund investments not elsewhere
9 Includes sterling asset backed loans; loans to individuals secured on dwellings; other loans to individuals (including policy loans); loans to businesses and other loans not elsewhere classified. Excludes loans to UK associate companies; bank term deposits and building society investments.
10 Includes loans to parent companies; subsidiaries; associates and other loans not elsewhere classified. Excludes loans categorised as direct investment; loans covered by Export Credit Guarantee Department (ECGD), specific bank guarantees or ECGD buyer credit guarantees.
11 UK and overseas. Includes existing buildings; property; land; new construction work; vehicles; machinery and equipment; valuables and intangibles. Includes the capital value of assets bought on hire purchase or acquired (as lessee) under a finance leasing arrangement and assets acquired for hiring, renting and operating leasing purposes. Excludes the capital value of assets acquired but leased out to others under finance leasing arrangements.
12 UK and overseas. Includes certificates of tax deposit; insurance policies; annuities and loans covered by Export Credit Guarantee Department (ECGD), specific bank guarantees or ECGD buyer credit guarantees. Excludes pre-payments and debtors.

12.14 SELF-ADMINISTERED PENSION FUNDS[1] BALANCE SHEET ASSETS AND LIABILITIES AT MARKET VALUES

continued

£ million at end of year

ASSETS		2003	2004	2005	2006	2007	2008	2009	2010	2011	2012	2013
Cash	GNOR	0	0	0	0	0	0	0	0	0	0	0
Balances with banks and building societies in the UK	JX5Q	16,103	16,216	17,789	22,823	25,974	20,133	23,054	23,736	23,854	22,929	22,701
Sterling	JX5S	14,349	14,064	15,510	20,211	22,615	16,802	19,099	20,043	20,159	18,901	18,193
Foreign currency	JX5U	1,754	2,152	2,279	2,612	3,359	3,331	3,955	3,693	3,695	4,028	4,508
Balances with overseas banks	GNOW	249	287	361	525	807	351	134	197	72	157	349
Other liquid deposits[13]	GNOX	1,883	1,782	3,010	3,891	5,392	4,300	12,431	9,631	11,956	15,265	20,505
Certificates of deposit issued by banks and building societies in the UK[14]	IX8H	2,063	1,678	2,649	4,932	8,156	6,480	2,269	2,472	6,498	2,069	1,288
Money market instruments issued by HM Treasury[15]	IX9J	206	69	89	22	304	548	1,709	1,109	1,734	4,116	1,167
UK local authority debt	AHVF	276	337	270	221	205	323	210	116	157	232	130
Commercial paper issued by UK companies[16]	GQFR	197	175	476	401	857	367	664	1,135	993	1,254	334
Other UK money market instruments[17]	GOZR	497	1,428	883	1,174	1,893	1,959	2,822	3,416	3,936	2,716	4,655
Money market instruments issued by non-resident businesses	GOZS	441	413	384	449	1,279	911	963	2,067	3,709	2,752	2,752
Other short-term assets not elsewhere classified[18]	JX5W	721	1,365	1,854	1,898	1,304	3,474	3,113	3,644	2,311	1,904	1,788
Balances outstanding from stockbrokers and securities dealers[19]	RYIL	5,383	8,939	18,879	24,812	28,297	30,536	11,281	7,145	8,241	6,213	5,989
Income accrued on investments and rents	RYIM	2,256	1,921	1,970	2,303	2,744	2,576	2,714	2,761	2,930	2,872	3,169
Amounts outstanding from HM Revenue and Customs[19]	RYIN	22	28	29	16	15	23	32	37	53	67	54
Other debtors and assets not elsewhere classified	RYIO	15,794	22,838	25,006	35,224	22,454	24,565	21,464	13,159	8,902	11,387	7,543
Derivative contracts with UK counterparties which have a positive (asset) value[20]	JRO3	3,089	10,235	22,157	24,357	29,789	35,194	61,862	99,420	170,170	186,184	191,511
Derivative contracts with overseas counterparties which have a positive (asset) value[20]	GOJU	561	2,962	2,668	5,995	8,652	5,835	20,534	19,803	29,445	38,324	49,910
TOTAL ASSETS	**RYIR**	**723,288**	**813,889**	**995,100**	**1,118,254**	**1,131,112**	**968,752**	**1,124,262**	**1,289,071**	**1,444,019**	**1,603,292**	**1,706,682**
LIABILITIES												
Borrowing[21]	GQED	5,216	8,133	11,678	14,661	16,180	4,461	3,859	2,830	3,361	10,603	16,050
Balances owed to stockbrokers and securities dealers[19]	RYIS	5,472	9,248	18,722	25,954	33,965	37,912	13,707	7,312	9,688	7,816	8,267
Pensions due but not paid[22]	RYIT	248	138	86	285	220	167	280	271	300	5,152	2,672
Derivative contracts with UK counterparties which have a negative (liability) value[20]	JRP9	1,817	7,873	16,818	17,231	26,187	27,533	37,689	78,322	147,217	149,493	161,962
Derivative contracts with overseas counterparties which have a negative (liability) value[20]	GKGR	437	3,082	2,785	7,036	11,275	6,335	41,110	37,345	42,712	60,725	73,848
Other creditors, provisions and liabilities not elsewhere classified	RYIU	16,008	22,107	24,834	36,208	18,327	20,577	21,603	18,889	9,905	9,011	13,236
Market value of pension funds[23]	AHVA	694,090	763,308	920,177	1,016,879	1,024,958	871,767	1,006,014	1,144,102	1,230,836	1,360,492	1,430,647
TOTAL LIABILITIES	**RYIR**	**723,288**	**813,889**	**995,100**	**1,118,254**	**1,131,112**	**968,752**	**1,124,262**	**1,289,071**	**1,444,019**	**1,603,292**	**1,706,682**

Source: Office for National Statistics

c Suppressed to avoid the disclosure of confidential data.

1 Combined public and private sector. Data from the pension funds surveys are of lower quality than equivalent data from other institutional groups because of the difficulties in constructing a suitable sampling frame of pension funds.
13 Includes money market funds; liquidity funds and cash liquidity funds.
14 Sterling and foreign currency.
15 Includes treasury bills. Excludes UK government securities.
16 Sterling and foreign currency commercial paper issued by: banks; building societies; other financial institutions and other issuing companies.
17 Includes floating rate notes maturing within one year of issue.
18 UK and overseas. Excludes derivative contracts.
19 Gross value.
20 Includes credit default products; employee stock options; other options; other swaps; futures; forwards and other derivative contracts not elsewhere classified.
21 UK and overseas. Includes from a UK perspective: sterling and foreign currency borrowing from UK banks and building societies; borrowing arising from the issue of floating rate notes and preference shares; foreign currency liabilities on back-to-back loans; overdrafts and other borrowing not elsewhere classified. Includes from an overseas perspective: borrowing from banks and other borrowing not elsewhere classified.
22 Excludes any estimated future liabilities.
23 Net value as found in statement of net assets.

12.15a INSURANCE COMPANIES' BALANCE SHEET: LONG-TERM BUSINESS ASSETS AND LIABILITIES AT MARKET VALUES

£ million at end of year

		2003	2004	2005	2006	2007	2008	2009	2010	2011	2012	2013
ASSETS												
UK government securities denominated in sterling	AHNJ	142,920	157,019	161,906	161,641	158,694	166,879	167,247	182,506	205,223	187,145	170,950
Index-linked	AHQI	23,186	28,673	33,722	41,104	45,902	54,387	57,157	66,115	78,354	72,499	71,234
Other[1]	J5HZ	119,734	128,346	128,184	120,537	112,792	112,492	110,090	116,391	126,869	114,646	99,716
UK government securities denominated in foreign currency	RGBV	56	0	206	12	0	0	0	0	0	0	0
UK local authority investments[2]	AHNN	1,547	2,044	1,840	1,614	998	776	655	768	813	770	3,168
Other UK public sector investments[3]	RGCS	613	254	801	651	634	872	1,461	2,189	2,207	2,197	3,684
UK PUBLIC SECTOR SECURITIES	**RYEK**	**145,136**	**159,317**	**164,753**	**163,918**	**160,326**	**168,527**	**169,363**	**185,463**	**208,243**	**190,112**	**177,802**
UK corporate bonds[4]	IFLF	151,703	150,884	165,918	159,073	159,273	159,789	160,532	158,987	163,348	178,627	167,021
Sterling	IFLG	146,410	144,280	158,995	150,907	153,694	154,525	155,184	156,477	160,842	174,682	165,453
Foreign currency	IFLH	5,293	6,604	6,923	8,166	5,579	5,264	5,348	2,510	2,506	3,945	1,568
UK ordinary shares[5]	IFLI	235,601	237,610	273,679	299,717	293,655	188,430	209,992	207,971	177,480	162,949	170,841
UK preference shares[5]	RLOL	1,126	1,198	1,228	1,231	983	724	624	648	536	375	340
Overseas corporate securities	IFLJ	110,193	130,098	165,452	194,997	234,388	219,957	266,280	278,930	262,823	303,565	315,453
Bonds	RLOP	32,507	40,281	45,970	57,774	69,696	85,077	111,866	112,338	115,744	127,629	119,631
Ordinary shares	AHNQ	77,501	89,654	119,207	136,652	163,249	134,211	153,500	165,216	145,932	173,982	194,250
Preference shares	RLOM	185	163	275	571	1,443	669	914	1,376	1,147	1,954	1,572
Mutual fund investments[6]	IFLK	89,523	108,019	168,896	192,516	222,081	186,950	230,247	259,457	265,750	328,657	360,502
CORPORATE SECURITIES	**RYEO**	**588,146**	**627,809**	**775,173**	**847,534**	**910,380**	**755,850**	**867,675**	**905,993**	**869,937**	**974,173**	**1,014,157**
Overseas government, provincial and municipal securities	AHNS	20,561	20,161	16,065	21,078	25,787	29,053	24,601	25,363	23,727	26,928	30,013
Other longer-term assets not elsewhere classified[7]	JX8D	77,739	89,063	83,665	92,326	99,316	76,139	67,531	74,900	81,916	81,039	74,737
OTHER LONGER-TERM ASSETS	**RYER**	**98,300**	**109,224**	**99,730**	**113,404**	**125,103**	**105,192**	**92,132**	**100,263**	**105,643**	**107,967**	**104,750**
LONGER-TERM ASSETS	**RYES**	**831,582**	**896,350**	**1,039,656**	**1,124,856**	**1,195,809**	**1,029,569**	**1,129,170**	**1,191,719**	**1,183,823**	**1,272,252**	**1,296,709**

Source: Office for National Statistics

c Suppressed to avoid the disclosure of confidential data.

1 Includes securities of: 0 up to 15 years maturity; over 15 years maturity and undated maturity. Excludes treasury bills and index-linked securities.
2 Includes local authority securities; negotiable bonds; loans and mortgages.
3 Includes public corporation loans and mortgages and other public sector investments not elsewhere classified.
4 Issued by: banks; building societies and other corporates.
5 Quoted and unquoted.
6 UK and overseas. Includes authorised and unauthorised unit trust units; investment trust securities; open-ended investment companies; hedge funds and other mutual fund investments not elsewhere classified.
7 UK and overseas. Includes loans; fixed assets and other longer-term assets not elsewhere classified.

12.15a INSURANCE COMPANIES' BALANCE SHEET: LONG-TERM BUSINESS ASSETS AND LIABILITIES AT MARKET VALUES

continued

£ million at end of year

		2003	2004	2005	2006	2007	2008	2009	2010	2011	2012	2013
ASSETS												
Cash	HLGW	29	15	29	0	0	0	0	0	0	0	0
Balances with banks and building societies in the UK	JX2C	26,527	28,018	31,606	34,454	48,619	51,139	44,483	34,026	34,998	35,424	26,785
Sterling	JX3R	24,928	26,116	30,221	32,653	45,948	47,456	42,097	32,387	32,698	33,805	24,616
Foreign currency	JX3T	1,599	1,902	1,385	1,801	2,671	3,683	2,386	1,639	2,300	1,619	2,169
Balances with overseas banks	HLHB	1,067	1,086	1,454	1,022	1,484	2,816	3,758	2,766	1,726	1,381	3,143
Other liquid deposits [8]	HLHC	787	1,522	1,215	333	678	1,638	12,385	14,076	15,891	17,257	38,843
Certificates of deposit issued by banks and building societies in the UK [9]	AHND	19,344	18,733	14,200	17,256	15,177	11,401	8,177	8,622	6,158	5,769	5,318
Money market instruments issued by HM Treasury [10]	RGBM	334	534	537	685	785	179	1,344	509	1,392	1,081	2,688
UK local authority debt	AHNF	0	0	0	0	0	0	0	0	0	0	1
Commercial paper issued by UK	JF77	3,512	2,884	5,130	2,714	2,723	2,268	1,806	646	891	496	648
Other UK money market instruments [12]	HLHL	1,562	1,997	2,670	3,538	3,071	3,159	2,959	3,208	5,501	3,540	2,055
Money market instruments issued by non-resident businesses	HLHM	1,990	952	1,681	405	859	689	1,755	2,956	1,530	2,068	907
Other short-term assets not elsewhere classified [13]	JX2E	1,525	2,615	10,432	10,749	20,965	19,555	10,076	5,232	6,159	6,008	5,582
Balances due from stockbrokers and securities dealers [14]	RGBU	176	-228	-1,052	-345	140	-399	-1,159	-834	-1,245	-1,145	-1,228
SHORT-TERM ASSETS (excluding derivatives)	**RYEW**	**56,853**	**58,128**	**67,902**	**70,811**	**94,501**	**92,445**	**85,584**	**71,207**	**73,001**	**71,879**	**84,742**
Derivative contracts with UK and overseas counterparties which have a positive (asset) value [15]	IFKX	4,545	3,743	5,739	5,937	5,205	17,892	10,317	12,399	24,060	20,805	18,144
Agents' balances and outstanding premiums in respect of direct insurance and facultative reinsurance contracts [16]												
UK	RYPA	635	269	500	669	738	535	467	515	554	620	769
Overseas	RYPB	73	106	-103	-136	-177	0	1	3	3	0	0
Reinsurance, coinsurance and treaty balances [17]												
UK	RYPC	3,187	2,965	2,607	3,462	-413	-1,000	3,817	-838	-1,147	-1,778	2,109
Overseas	RYPD	825	415	929	1,105	836	-7,355	-8,232	-6,020	-6,035	-6,425	-5,590
Outstanding interest, dividends and rents [18]	RYPH	6,866	7,476	7,897	7,330	8,690	9,256	9,158	8,591	8,511	8,716	7,762
Other debtors and assets not elsewhere classified [19]	RYPF	28,548	23,028	19,694	44,923	51,373	37,342	33,162	30,366	28,806	27,717	28,595
Direct investment for non-insurance subsidiary and associate companies in the UK [20]	RYET	4,191	3,971	8,390	13,016	9,186	11,484	10,129	5,097	7,249	8,880	8,125
Direct investment for UK insurance subsidiary, associate and holding companies [20]	RYEU	5,054	3,473	2,528	6,114	7,578	7,890	7,234	6,720	7,152	4,275	3,865
Direct investment for overseas subsidiaries, associates, branches and agencies [20]	RYEV	6,330	2,181	4,455	3,341	3,832	5,011	4,141	4,131	3,340	3,470	4,296
TOTAL ASSETS	**RKBI**	**948,689**	**1,002,105**	**1,160,194**	**1,281,428**	**1,377,158**	**1,203,069**	**1,284,948**	**1,323,890**	**1,329,317**	**1,410,411**	**1,449,526**

Source: Office for National Statistics

c Suppressed to avoid the disclosure of confidential data.

8 Includes money market funds; liquidity funds and cash liquidity funds.
9 Sterling and foreign currency.
10 Includes treasury bills. Excludes UK government securities.
11 Sterling and foreign currency commercial paper issued by: banks; building societies; other financial institutions and other issuing companies.
12 Includes floating rate notes maturing within one year of issue.
13 UK and overseas. Excludes derivative contracts.
14 Net of balances owed. Includes amounts due on securities bought and sold for future settlement.
15 Includes credit default products; employee stock options; other options; other swaps; futures; forwards and other derivative contracts not elsewhere classified.
16 Net of insurance liabilities.
17 Net of reinsurance bought and sold.
18 Net value.
19 Includes deferred acquisition costs.
20 Net asset value of attributable companies.

12.15a INSURANCE COMPANIES' BALANCE SHEET: LONG-TERM BUSINESS ASSETS AND LIABILITIES AT MARKET VALUES

continued

£ million at end of year

		2003	2004	2005	2006	2007	2008	2009	2010	2011	2012	2013
LIABILITIES												
Borrowing	AHNI	15,617	14,536	15,224	14,369	12,426	12,467	10,866	12,542	12,084	10,660	10,112
Banks and building societies in the UK[9]	JX2G	4,164	5,362	5,043	2,867	3,801	5,089	3,305	2,099	1,980	961	1,011
Other UK[21]	ICXU	10,923	8,381	9,030	9,537	6,699	4,832	5,460	8,112	8,730	9,075	8,368
Overseas[22]	RGDD	530	793	1,151	1,965	1,926	2,546	2,101	2,331	1,374	624	733
Long-term business insurance and investment contract liabilities[23]	RKDC	824,766	873,071	1,037,658	1,125,221	1,205,183	1,069,993	1,153,944	1,178,823	1,171,844	1,241,671	1,277,415
Claims admitted but not paid[23]	RKBM	3,699	3,579	3,481	3,513	3,848	3,426	4,637	2,946	3,072	3,387	3,608
Provisions for taxation and dividends payable[24]	KVE9	4,084	4,961	8,245	8,120	7,489	60	1,781	2,973	1,993	2,400	2,919
Other creditors, provisions and liabilities not elsewhere classified[25]	RYPL	15,870	16,738	16,907	33,192	39,527	52,849	47,803	53,826	66,466	69,971	68,289
Excess of total assets over liabilities in respect of: long-term business; minority interests in UK subsidiary companies; shareholders' capital and reserves and any other reserves[26]	A4YP	84,653	89,220	78,679	97,013	108,685	64,274	65,917	72,780	73,858	82,322	87,183
TOTAL LIABILITIES	RKBI	948,689	1,002,105	1,160,194	1,281,428	1,377,158	1,203,069	1,284,948	1,323,890	1,329,317	1,410,411	1,449,526

Source: Office for National Statistics

c Suppressed to avoid the disclosure of confidential data.

9 Sterling and foreign currency.
21 Includes issue of securities (other than ordinary shares); issue of sterling commercial paper and other borrowing not elsewhere classified.
22 Includes borrowing from banks; related companies and other borrowing not elsewhere classified.
23 Net of reinsurers share.
24 UK and overseas. Includes deferred tax net of amounts receivable.
25 UK and overseas. Includes derivative contracts which have a negative (liability) value.
26 Includes unallocated divisible surplus and the 'net worth' of UK branches of overseas companies, including profit and loss account balances.

12.15b INSURANCE COMPANIES' BALANCE SHEET: GENERAL BUSINESS ASSETS AND LIABILITIES AT MARKET VALUES

£ million at end of year

		2003	2004	2005	2006	2007	2008	2009	2010	2011	2012	2013
ASSETS												
UK government securities denominated in sterling	AHMJ	19,645	19,662	19,818	19,296	16,026	18,441	16,969	13,631	13,384	11,774	12,855
Index-linked	AHMZ	453	345	538	603	297	1,622	1,991	1,731	1,724	2,150	2,355
Other[1]	J8EX	19,192	19,317	19,280	18,693	15,729	16,819	14,978	11,900	11,660	9,624	10,500
UK government securities denominated in foreign currency	RYMQ	0	35	12	72	69	3	0	0	c	13	18
UK local authority investments[2]	AHMN	10	49	44	0	3	0	0	0	c	0	0
Other UK public sector investments[3]	RYMU	3	54	6	0	10	0	65	249	c	252	209
UK PUBLIC SECTOR SECURITIES	**RYMV**	**19,658**	**19,800**	**19,880**	**19,368**	**16,108**	**18,444**	**17,034**	**13,880**	**13,907**	**12,039**	**13,082**
UK corporate bonds[4]	IFVV	7,233	9,826	10,815	11,797	13,397	12,060	13,550	10,487	10,817	12,127	12,355
Sterling	IFVW	7,067	9,637	9,932	11,057	12,647	11,009	12,288	9,544	10,217	11,264	11,610
Foreign currency	IFVX	166	189	883	740	750	1,051	1,262	943	600	863	745
UK ordinary shares[5]	IFVY	6,548	8,724	9,864	10,138	9,006	10,501	9,963	9,525	8,435	8,732	7,846
UK preference shares[5]	RLOT	143	54	40	9	44	29	26	26	25	21	21
Overseas corporate securities	IFVZ	7,124	11,520	12,645	18,636	14,773	20,258	23,002	17,594	18,636	24,380	24,638
Bonds	RLOX	5,473	9,762	10,866	16,128	12,872	18,081	21,017	15,847	16,939	21,872	21,834
Ordinary shares	AHMQ	1,638	1,758	1,779	2,507	1,901	2,175	1,976	1,741	1,692	2,501	c
Preference shares	RLOU	13	0	0	1	0	2	9	6	5	7	c
Mutual fund investments[6]	IFWA	1,563	2,470	1,270	1,256	1,780	1,911	3,498	4,878	5,802	4,236	4,686
CORPORATE SECURITIES	**RYNF**	**22,611**	**32,594**	**34,634**	**41,836**	**39,000**	**44,759**	**50,039**	**42,510**	**43,715**	**49,496**	**49,546**
Overseas government, provincial and municipal securities	AHMS	5,720	6,662	7,341	8,035	4,869	8,505	7,204	5,126	5,524	9,355	9,584
Other longer-term assets not elsewhere classified[7]	JX8E	3,335	4,451	6,362	6,746	7,059	8,269	7,338	9,158	9,938	10,148	9,606
OTHER LONGER-TERM ASSETS	**RYNO**	**9,055**	**11,113**	**13,703**	**14,781**	**11,928**	**16,774**	**14,542**	**14,284**	**15,462**	**19,503**	**19,190**
LONGER-TERM ASSETS	**RYNP**	**51,324**	**63,507**	**68,217**	**75,985**	**67,036**	**79,977**	**81,615**	**70,674**	**73,084**	**81,038**	**81,818**

Source: Office for National Statistics

c Suppressed to avoid the disclosure of confidential data.

1 Includes securities of: 0 up to 15 years maturity; over 15 years maturity and undated maturity. Excludes treasury bills and index-linked securities.
2 Includes local authority securities; negotiable bonds; loans and mortgages.
3 Includes public corporation loans and mortgages and other public sector investments not elsewhere classified.
4 Issued by: banks; building societies and other corporates.
5 Quoted and unquoted.
6 UK and overseas. Includes authorised and unauthorised unit trust units; investment trust securities; open-ended investment companies; hedge funds and other mutual fund investments not elsewhere classified.
7 UK and overseas. Includes loans; fixed assets and other longer-term assets not elsewhere classified.

12.15b INSURANCE COMPANIES' BALANCE SHEET: GENERAL BUSINESS ASSETS AND LIABILITIES AT MARKET VALUES

continued

£ million at end of year

		2003	2004	2005	2006	2007	2008	2009	2010	2011	2012	2013
ASSETS												
Cash	HLMN	12	23	63	0	0	0	0	0	0	0	0
Balances with banks and building societies in the UK	JX3H	12,683	18,051	9,116	9,327	8,949	9,871	10,227	7,961	7,619	7,032	6,970
Sterling	JX43	11,257	16,485	7,952	6,501	6,907	8,170	8,763	6,730	6,532	5,988	5,583
Foreign currency	JX45	1,426	1,566	1,164	2,826	2,042	1,701	1,464	1,231	1,087	1,044	1,387
Balances with overseas banks	HLMS	700	1,523	1,116	1,031	1,015	1,250	1,138	981	1,150	1,841	1,369
Other liquid deposits[8]	HLMT	103	204	70	396	375	869	2,476	3,326	2,916	3,753	3,021
Certificates of deposit issued by banks and building societies in the UK[9]	IX8K	3,486	6,808	8,402	7,708	8,264	7,775	2,002	558	843	1,223	1,403
Money market instruments issued by HM Treasury[10]	ICWI	20	444	1,670	379	342	708	979	327	237	1,675	1,214
UK local authority debt	AHMF	3	0	0	0	0	0	0	0	0	0	0
Commercial paper issued by UK companies[11]	JF75	607	441	610	732	2,682	1,640	1,630	275	281	509	461
Other UK money market instruments[12]	HLNC	1,209	160	139	68	90	278	346	359	360	253	340
Money market instruments issued by non-resident businesses	HLND	1,239	1,619	2,429	3,516	3,261	2,277	2,321	545	745	449	1,120
Other short-term assets not elsewhere classified[13]	JX2I	171	138	2,992	1,733	612	1,576	718	725	933	1,064	781
Balances due from stockbrokers and securities dealers[14]	RYMA	-160	-61	3	-66	25	891	52	90	26	-1	37
SHORT-TERM ASSETS (excluding derivatives)	**RYME**	**20,073**	**29,350**	**26,610**	**24,824**	**25,615**	**27,135**	**21,889**	**15,147**	**15,110**	**17,798**	**16,716**
Derivative contracts with UK and overseas counterparties which have a positive (asset) value[15]	IFVJ	104	122	44	45	208	685	455	906	629	3,032	4,099
Agents' balances and outstanding premiums in respect of direct insurance and facultative reinsurance contracts[16]												
UK	RYMF	8,390	8,450	7,991	9,060	8,216	9,022	8,171	8,470	8,222	9,584	9,089
Overseas	RYMG	816	1,385	572	480	575	55	73	-15	-200	711	868
Reinsurance, coinsurance and treaty balances[17]												
UK	RYMH	698	942	934	1,290	1,164	1,092	1,730	-165	-258	-182	-233
Overseas	RYMI	-14	-919	-1,501	-48	-23	537	491	375	921	-4	217
Outstanding interest, dividends and rents[18]	RYPN	982	1,156	905	1,067	1,255	1,108	958	765	726	724	881
Other debtors and assets not elsewhere classified[19]	RKAC	12,273	11,462	12,405	15,814	19,096	17,189	10,785	11,064	10,683	14,281	12,905
Direct investment for non-insurance subsidiary and associate companies in the UK[20]	RYNR	13,408	19,028	20,530	20,111	21,954	21,259	21,181	18,206	18,627	19,876	20,510
Direct investment for UK insurance subsidiary, associate and holding companies[20]	RYNS	2,918	2,280	6,071	4,745	6,936	7,669	7,159	6,252	6,795	6,365	6,886
Direct investment for overseas subsidiaries, associates, branches and agencies[20]	RYNT	5,718	5,507	6,446	9,657	9,445	10,815	12,124	9,868	9,073	8,004	7,147
TOTAL ASSETS	**RKBY**	**116,690**	**142,270**	**149,224**	**163,030**	**161,477**	**176,543**	**166,631**	**141,547**	**143,412**	**161,227**	**160,903**

Source: *Office for National Statistics*

c Suppressed to avoid the disclosure of confidential data.

8 Includes money market funds; liquidity funds and cash liquidity funds.
9 Sterling and foreign currency.
10 Includes treasury bills. Excludes UK government securities.
11 Sterling and foreign currency commercial paper issued by: banks; building societies; other financial institutions and other issuing companies.
12 Includes floating rate notes maturing within one year of issue.
13 UK and overseas. Excludes derivative contracts.
14 Net of balances owed. Includes amounts due on securities bought and sold for future settlement.
15 Includes credit default products; employee stock options; other options; other swaps; futures; forwards and other derivative contracts not elsewhere classified.
16 Net of insurance liabilities.
17 Net of reinsurance bought and sold.
18 Net value.
19 Includes deferred acquisition costs.
20 Net asset value of attributable companies.

12.15b INSURANCE COMPANIES' BALANCE SHEET: GENERAL BUSINESS ASSETS AND LIABILITIES AT MARKET VALUES

continued

£ million at end of year

		2003	2004	2005	2006	2007	2008	2009	2010	2011	2012	2013
LIABILITIES												
Borrowing	AHMI	14,306	17,256	14,790	19,052	18,597	20,214	15,602	14,431	14,281	12,460	12,133
Banks and building societies in the UK[9]	JX3J	2,046	4,519	893	3,148	675	343	744	621	606	819	794
Other UK[21]	IFHX	9,342	10,261	11,080	10,445	10,885	13,179	9,965	9,835	8,991	8,401	8,792
Overseas[22]	RYMD	2,918	2,476	2,817	5,459	7,037	6,692	4,893	3,975	4,684	3,240	2,547
General business technical reserves [23]	RKCT	63,463	67,241	71,710	77,221	71,146	76,980	70,947	58,484	57,539	61,771	59,738
Provisions for taxation and dividends payable[24]	KVF2	2,000	2,429	1,806	2,656	2,486	858	345	40	7	240	424
Other creditors, provisions and liabilities not elsewhere classified [25]	RYPR	9,567	10,817	10,718	16,226	22,069	21,149	19,976	18,367	19,362	25,757	24,989
Excess of total assets over liabilities in respect of minority interests in UK subsidiary companies, shareholders' capital and reserves and any other reserves[26]	A8SI	27,354	44,527	50,200	47,875	47,179	57,342	59,761	50,225	52,223	60,999	63,619
TOTAL LIABILITIES	**RKBY**	**116,690**	**142,270**	**149,224**	**163,030**	**161,477**	**176,543**	**166,631**	**141,547**	**143,412**	**161,227**	**160,903**

Source: Office for National Statistics

c Suppressed to avoid the disclosure of confidential data.

9 Sterling and foreign currency.
21 Includes issue of securities (other than ordinary shares); issue of sterling commercial paper and other borrowing not elsewhere classified.
22 Includes borrowing from banks; related companies and other borrowing not elsewhere classified.
23 Net of reinsurers share.
24 UK and overseas. Includes deferred tax net of amounts receivable.
25 UK and overseas. Includes derivative contracts which have a negative (liability) value.
26 Includes the 'net worth' of UK branches of overseas companies, including profit and loss account balances.

12.16a Individual insolvencies

England and Wales, not seasonally adjusted

	Total individual insolvencies	Bankruptcies[1]	Debt relief orders[2]	Individual voluntary arrangements[3]
2006	107,288	62,956	z	44,332
2007	106,645	64,480	z	42,165
2008	106,544	67,428	z	39,116
2009	134,142	74,670	11,831	47,641
2010	135,045	59,173	25,179	50,693
2011	119,943	41,876	29,009	49,058
2012	109,640	31,787	31,179	46,674
2013	100,998	24,571	27,546	48,881
2014	99,223	20,345	26,688	52,190

Source: The Insolvency Service

[1] Figures from 2011 Q2 onwards based on the date the bankruptcy order was granted by the court.

[2] Debt Relief Orders (DROs) came into effect on 6 April 2009 as an alternative route into individual insolvency. In April 2011 a change was introduced to the legislation to allow those who have built up value in a pension scheme to apply for debt relief under these provisions.

[3] Includes Deeds of Arrangement.

12.16b Individual insolvencies

Scotland, not seasonally adjusted

	Total individual insolvencies	Sequestrations (of which LILA/MAP)[1,2]		Protected trust deeds
2006	13,789	5,566	z	8,223
2007	13,924	6,331	z	7,593
2008	19,991	12,449	(7,133)	7,542
2009	23,541	14,415	(8,774)	9,126
2010	20,344	11,906	(6,801)	8,438
2011	19,650	11,128	(4,812)	8,522
2012	18,402	9,630	(3,886)	8,772
2013	14,250	7,189	(2,728)	7,061
2014	11,622	6,747	(2,533)	4,875

Source: Accountant in Bankruptcy.

[1] On 1 April 2008, Part 1 of the Bankruptcy and Diligence etc. (Scotland) Act 2007 came into force making significant changes to some aspects of sequestration (bankruptcy), debt relief and debt enforcement in Scotland. This included the introduction of the new route into bankruptcy for people with low income and low assets (LILA). Of the number or sequestrations, individuals who meet LILA criteria are shown in brackets.

[2] On 1 April 2015, part of the Bankruptcy and Debt Advice (Scotland) Act came into force making significant changes to some aspects of sequestration (bankruptcy). This included the introduction of the Minimal Asset Process (MAP), which replaced the LILA route into sequestration; mandatory debt advice for people seeking statutory debt relief; a new online process for applying for sequestration; and an additional year for people to make contributions to repaying their debts (increasing from three years to four, in line with protected trust deeds).

12.16c Individual insolvencies

Northern Ireland, not seasonally adjusted

	Total individual insolvencies	Bankruptcies	Debt relief orders[1]	Individual voluntary arrangements
2006	1,809	1,035	z	774
2007	1,338	898	z	440
2008	1,638	1,079	z	559
2009	1,958	1,236	z	722
2010	2,323	1,321	z	1,002
2011	2,839	1,615	112	1,112
2012	3,189	1,452	506	1,231
2013	3,373	1,347	593	1,433
2014	3,395	1,367	536	1,492

Source: Department for Enterprise, Trade and Investment, Northern Ireland.

[1] Debt relief orders came into effect on 30 June 2011.

12.17a Company insolvencies[1,2]

England and Wales, not seasonally adjusted

	Total new company insolvencies[2,3]	Compulsory liquidations[3,4]	New creditors' voluntary liquidations[3]	Administrations[5,6,7]	Company voluntary arrangements[8]	Receivership appointments[9]
2006	17,588 r	5,418	7,921 r	3,447 r	483 r	206 r
2007	15,866	5,165	7,625	2,531	417	128
2008	21,072	5,494	9,995	4,808	586	189
2009	24,011	5,643	13,509	4,019	723	117
2010	19,796	4,792	11,507	2,682	766	49
2011	20,285	5,003	11,947	2,539	748	48
2012	19,349	4,261	11,906	2,334	816	32
2013	17,682 r	3,632	11,453	2,009	571 r	17
2014	16,317	3,755	10,401	1,587	552	22

Sources: Insolvency Service (compulsory liquidations only); Companies House (all other insolvency types).

[1] Data from 2000Q1 are not consistent with earlier data because of a change to the methodology. This does not affect compulsory liquidations.

[2] Excludes creditors' voluntary liquidations following administration (See Table 2).

[3] Includes partnership winding-up orders.

[4] Figures from 2011 Q2 onwards based on the date the winding-up order was granted by the court.

[5] Releases prior to 2012 Q4 showed administrations separately as "Administrator Appointments" and "In Administration - Enterprise Act".

[6] The figure for Q4 2006 includes 844 separate, limited companies created and managed by "Safe Solutions Accountancy Limited" for which Grant Thornton was appointed administrator.

[7] The figure for Q3 2008 includes 728 separate managed service companies.

[8] The figure for Q2 2012 includes 104 new CVAs recorded under "Health and Social Work" in June reflecting the fact that on 20 June 2012 156 companies in the Southern Cross Healthcare Group had CVAs approved.

[9] Data before 2000 Q1 include Law of Property Act and fixed charge receiverships, which are not insolvencies but which cannot be identified separately to insolvent receiverships under the previous methodology.

12.17b Company insolvencies[2]
Scotland, not seasonally adjusted

	Total new company insolvencies[2]	Compulsory liquidations[3]	New creditors' voluntary liquidations[2]	Administrations	Company voluntary arrangements	Receivership appointments
2006	563 r	268 r	170 r	85 r	6 r	34
2007	640	400	122	64	7	47
2008	893	561	104	190	4	34
2009	1,027	556	171	259	8	33
2010	1,302	780	252	212	7	51
2011	1,453	923	269	211	13	37
2012	1,377	921	232	169	24	31
2013	897	484	258	122	16	17
2014	963	650	207	87	14	5

Source: Companies House.

[1] Data from 2000Q1 are not consistent with earlier data because of a change to the methodology.

[2] Data before 2000Q1 includes creditors' voluntary liquidations following administration as under the previous methodology it is not possible to separate these CVLs out.

[3] Includes provisional liquidations.

12.17c Company insolvencies[1,2]
Northern Ireland, not seasonally adjusted

	Total new company insolvencies[4]	Compulsory liquidations[3]	New creditors' voluntary liquidations[4,5]	Administrations[4]	Company voluntary arrangements[4]	Administrative receiverships[4]
2006	:	78	50	:	:	:
2007	:	122	42	:	:	:
2008	:	158	51	:	:	:
2009	:	164	86	:	:	:
2010	494	250	116	78	42	8
2011	437	208	116	68	26	19
2012	526	252	136	83	41	14
2013	357	178	98	47	33	1
2014	380	221	90	29	37	3

Sources: Department for Enterprise, Trade and Investment, Northern Ireland.; Companies House

[1] Includes partnerships.

[2] Data from 2009Q4 are not consistent with earlier data because of a change to the methodology. This does not affect compulsory liquidations. Data for Northern Ireland prior to 2010 are not available under the new methodology.

[3] Source: Department for Enterprise, Trade and Investment, Northern Ireland.

[4] Source: Companies House.

[5] Data before 2009Q4 includes creditors' voluntary liquidations following administration as under the previous methodology it is not possible to separate these CVLs out.

12.18a Monetary financial institutions' consolidated balance sheet

£ millions   Not seasonally adjusted

Amounts outstanding of liabilities

	Currency, deposits and money market instruments						Financial derivatives (net)		Other securities issued		Other liabilities		Total liabilities/ assets
	Private sector		Public sector		Non-residents								
	Sterling	Foreign currency	Sterling	Foreign currency	Sterling	Foreign currency	Sterling	Foreign currency	Sterling	Foreign currency	Sterling	Foreign currency	
LPM	VYAX	VYAY	VYAZ	VYBA	VYBB	VYBC	VWKM	VWKN	VWKO	VWKP	VWKQ	VWKR	VYBF
2014 Jun	2,104,817	412,112	43,653	3,365	453,403	2,406,602	-21,592	3,877	41,585	205,036	471,795	199,789	6,324,439
Jul	2,102,569	402,085	48,678	3,300	453,679	2,445,407	-20,437	5,077	42,705	204,005	449,121 (s)(t)	176,847 (w)	6,313,035 (s)(t)(w)
Aug	2,115,059	412,185	50,543	3,772	443,672	2,481,708	4,302	-4,382	41,626	206,418	453,506 (u)	166,168	6,374,577 (u)
Sep	2,102,082	410,491	43,306	4,098	444,407	2,472,673	-2,215	-1,604	41,203	206,296	435,114	196,696	6,352,547
Oct	2,097,776	402,136	49,545	5,858	437,580	2,471,766	472	1,955	41,674	207,615	458,178	166,353	6,340,908
Nov	2,103,303	418,423	50,026	4,995	431,768	2,562,399	22,255	-11,655	39,942	214,203	458,182	175,453	6,469,295
Dec	2,100,406	402,438	45,247	3,756	453,082	2,477,018	30,436	-9,357	39,128	209,595	463,456	165,745	6,380,952
2015 Jan	2,077,449	410,779	47,889	3,569	446,343	2,577,407	41,088	4	39,572	210,608	481,919	154,036	6,490,661
Feb	2,077,481	410,801	46,499	3,128	433,929	2,521,992	2,309	20,044	38,815	202,690	483,332	153,166	6,394,185
Mar	2,099,436	414,287	43,341	4,444	456,694	2,507,151	34,967	1,482	37,596	219,472	449,452	178,921	6,447,244
Apr	2,102,399	406,861	47,769	2,732	460,255	2,500,784	-2,240	24,340	38,897	221,153	438,037	190,929	6,431,916
May	2,116,173	404,672	47,185	3,974	453,648	2,414,093	-3,044	16,953	39,113	223,984	452,517	172,962	6,342,230
Jun	2,106,004	394,423	47,390	3,379	464,438	2,291,417	-24,075	22,662	39,429	215,308	438,619	179,470	6,178,464
Jul	2,121,569	401,210	48,058	3,889	457,683	2,282,627	-9,634	17,183	38,619	213,860	446,052	159,985	6,181,101
Aug	2,110,501	421,135	51,197	3,337	456,768	2,363,067	-7,316	13,914	37,515	210,055	469,229	145,922	6,275,324
Sep	2,091,326	426,145	42,431	2,929	487,155	2,337,968	-19,802	15,023	37,478	215,890	494,349	126,742	6,257,633
Oct	2,106,479	418,221	43,322	3,134	458,012	2,294,800	-16,499	6,889	37,324	216,084	465,060	138,585	6,171,410
Nov	2,116,357	420,329	45,688	3,187	462,180	2,325,240 (r)	-14,733	7,684	36,056	214,350	463,862	153,565	6,233,766 (r)
Dec	2,114,150	421,919	43,402	4,027	482,408	2,307,176	-32,442	21,615	35,743	218,066	470,386	165,995	6,252,446
2016 Jan	2,103,977	448,854	43,559	4,165	480,944	2,426,080	5,172	-13,794	35,670	223,095	460,059	179,012	6,396,792
Feb	2,124,161	461,032	42,173	4,372	446,937	2,466,834	41,133	-39,043	35,693	230,433	436,441	203,328	6,453,495
Mar	2,129,637 (q)	458,844	37,571	2,787	471,090	2,403,993	-18,147	16,777	35,841	229,819	437,540	191,691	6,397,443 (q)
Apr	2,127,300	458,250	46,358	4,105	467,482	2,367,934	-31,331	20,265	36,191	231,395	426,646 (v)	204,842	6,359,437 (v)
May	2,148,889	458,893	46,795	3,585	457,028	2,371,286	-32,035	23,567	35,886	226,790	437,777	187,267	6,365,728

Source: Bank of England

Notes to table

Movements in amounts outstanding can reflect breaks in data series as well as underlying flows. For changes data, users are recommended to refer directly to the appropriate series or data tables. Further explanation can be found at: www.bankofengland.co.uk/statistics/Pages/iadb/notesiadb/Changes_flows_growth_rates.aspx.

(q) Due to changes in reporting at one institution, the amounts outstanding decreased by £5bn. This effect has been adjusted out of the flows for March 2016.
(r) Due to changes in reporting at one institution, the amounts outstanding decreased by £18bn. This effect has been adjusted out of the flows for November 2015.
(s) Due to improvements in reporting at one institution, the amounts outstanding decreased by £36bn. This effect has been adjusted out of the flows for July 2014.
(t) Due to improvements in reporting at one institution, the amounts outstanding decreased by £16bn. This effect has been adjusted out of the flows for July 2014.
(u) Due to improvements in reporting at one institution, the amounts outstanding increased by £9bn. This effect has been adjusted out of the flows for August 2014.
(v) Due to a loan transfer by one reporting institution, the amounts outstanding decreased by £7bn. This effect has been adjusted out of the flows for April 2016.
(w) Due to improvements in reporting at one institution, the amounts outstanding decreased by £11bn. This effect has been adjusted out of the flows for July 2014.

Copyright guidance and the related UK Open Government Licence can be viewed here: www.bankofengland.co.uk/Pages/disclaimer.aspx.

12.18b Monetary financial institutions' consolidated balance sheet

£ millions   Not seasonally adjusted

Amounts outstanding of assets

	Loans						Securities (other than financial derivatives)						Other assets	
	Private sector		Public sector		Non-residents		Private sector		Public sector		Non-residents			
	Sterling	Foreign currency	Sterling	Foreign currency	Sterling	Foreign currency	Sterling	Foreign currency	Sterling	Foreign currency	Sterling	Foreign currency	Sterling	Foreign currency
LPM	VYBG	VYBH	VYBI	VYBJ	VYBK	VYBL	VYBM	VYBN	VYBO	VYBP	VYBQ	VYBR	VYBS	VYBT
2014 Jun	1,940,974 (x)	349,241	13,431	2,480	243,867	2,282,857	233,839	44,811	505,652	38	46,286	492,948	119,915	48,100
Jul	1,942,994	347,104	12,049	2,472	231,777	2,332,008	238,782	41,071	511,671	91	46,937	479,295 (z)	70,428 (aa)(ab)	56,356
Aug	1,946,690	344,722	15,790	2,005	250,786	2,351,854	236,781	41,128	525,572	66	45,825	485,931	78,200 (ac)	49,227
Sep	1,946,448	351,903	13,853	2,160	245,441	2,350,666	231,766	41,373	508,206	53	47,814	489,867	75,712	47,284
Oct	1,942,335	343,140	15,767	4,044	243,101	2,323,809	224,241	40,647	529,575	205	48,819	502,371	76,892	45,961
Nov	1,937,096	354,438	17,381	3,600	241,979	2,389,274	227,568	41,665	549,076	265	47,258	534,803	79,201	45,691
Dec	1,920,959	334,285	15,870	2,565	241,383	2,355,617	239,634	28,977	552,494	275	50,371	518,324	78,389	41,809
2015 Jan	1,927,390	349,029	14,990	2,599	245,134	2,421,735	218,879	28,228	569,064	233	50,772	541,304	79,909	41,394
Feb	1,928,364	350,701	15,942	2,036	245,165	2,358,610	216,637	26,824	540,779	188	51,280	534,827	81,323	41,510
Mar	1,944,811	355,220	14,701	3,612	248,837	2,384,629	209,666	27,169	542,815	279	52,430	539,712	81,707	41,656
Apr	1,940,587	363,034	14,440	2,082	250,425	2,388,843	211,490	26,276	535,024	272	51,655	524,550	81,910	41,329
May	1,944,495	337,889	15,711	2,510	249,910	2,318,568	214,319	25,607	539,671	250	52,716	515,649	83,057	41,879
Jun	1,932,199	338,643	16,005	2,013	255,507	2,211,602	212,627	23,303	531,409	283	51,442	479,731	84,722	38,978
Jul	1,954,923	328,693	16,658	2,388	251,704	2,204,048	209,284	22,926	544,558	424	52,591	474,899	81,782	36,221
Aug	1,960,495	339,399	19,680	1,107	249,574	2,277,746	196,262	22,406	551,938	463	51,180	483,669	83,562	37,841
Sep	1,960,156	338,891	18,222	1,737	264,683	2,264,604	195,280	22,558	548,147	428	49,786	473,485	82,500	37,154
Oct	1,954,598	332,938	18,297	2,024	251,523	2,190,161	198,504	20,605	546,048	420	49,526	486,960	83,563	36,243
Nov	1,961,428	330,069	18,102	1,317	251,696	2,227,058	201,057	19,681	554,544	422	48,457	496,268	84,758	38,908
Dec	1,962,835	321,152	17,258	1,911	256,181	2,280,659	203,648	19,525	540,558	471	46,245	479,855	85,489	36,658
2016 Jan	1,971,390	343,714	18,534	2,169	258,686	2,383,122	197,906	19,107	551,779	473	47,946	481,025	85,260	35,681

Source: Bank of England

Notes to table

Movements in amounts outstanding can reflect breaks in data series as well as underlying flows. For changes data, users are recommended to refer directly to the appropriate series or data tables. Further explanation can be found at: www.bankofengland.co.uk/statistics/Pages/iadb/notesiadb/Changes_flows_growth_rates.aspx.

(x) Due to a change in accounting treatment at one reporting institution, the amounts outstanding increased by £2bn. This effect has been adjusted out of the flows for June 2014.
(y) Due to a loan transfer by one reporting institution, the amounts outstanding increased by £7bn. This effect has been adjusted out of the flows for April 2016.
(z) Due to improvements in reporting at one institution, the amounts outstanding decreased by £11bn. This effect has been adjusted out of the flows for July 2014.
(aa) Due to improvements in reporting at one institution, the amounts outstanding decreased by £36bn. This effect has been adjusted out of the flows for July 2014.
(ab) Due to improvements in reporting at one institution, the amounts outstanding decreased by £13bn. This effect has been adjusted out of the flows for July 2014.
(ac) Due to improvements in reporting at one institution, the amounts outstanding increased by £9bn. This effect has been adjusted out of the flows for August 2014.

12.18c Monetary financial institutions' consolidated balance sheet

£ millions Not seasonally adjusted

Changes in liabilities

	Currency, deposits and money market instruments						Financial derivatives (net)		Other securities issued		Other liabilities		Total liabilities/ assets
	Private sector		Public sector		Non-residents								
	Sterling	Foreign currency	Sterling	Foreign currency	Sterling	Foreign currency	Sterling	Foreign currency	Sterling	Foreign currency	Sterling	Foreign currency	
LPM	VYAA	VYAB	VYAC	VYAD	VYAE	VYAF	VWKG	VWKH	VWKI	VWKJ	VWKK	VWKL	VYAI
2014 Jun	5,780	-15,752	-1,140	-374	-5,477	-31,777	-8,344	3,147	-603	1,656	-289	16,051	-37,121
Jul	-4,679	-11,027	5,088	-63	-342	30,856	1,155	766	1,120	-384	23,409	-21,999	23,898
Aug	10,494	6,954	1,865	448	-10,534	15,788	24,740	-9,431	-1,080	1,283	-19,270	-12,309	8,948
Sep	-14,718	-2,449	-7,283	342	2,214	-16,236	-6,518	2,833	-422	1,075	-8,342	32,597	-16,908
Oct	-437	-10,784	1,565	994	-6,888	-20,927	2,688	3,383	471	27	16,362	-33,069	-46,614
Nov	6,787	12,067	533	-913	-5,557	50,719	21,783	-13,737	-1,732	3,660	-22,621	1,717	52,705
Dec	-3,007	-13,336	-4,778	-1,197	21,253	-68,969	8,210	2,480	-814	-2,017	6,535	-7,547	-63,188
2015 Jan	-22,121	3,194	2,642	-197	-6,059	76,791	10,651	11,070	444	1,863	-5,457	-36,130	36,689
Feb	-1,541	10,216	-1,391	-347	-12,543	15,686	-38,779	22,414	-204	4,091	28,340	5,242	31,185
Mar	17,769	-5,337	-3,140	1,264	21,610	-67,120	28,272	-18,339	-1,355	6,647	-30,797	21,060	-29,466
Apr	6,828	-1,104	4,428	-1,689	3,540	32,839	-37,207	22,946	1,301	3,373	10,382	13,379	59,015
May	10,457	747	-584	1,253	-7,007	-78,784	-803	-7,142	516	4,529	14,854	-10,887	-72,852
Jun	-10,284	-1,760	205	-540	10,762	-73,266	-21,032	5,753	316	-4,615	4,841	26,200	-63,420
Jul	15,498	5,467	572	505	-6,722	-16,428	14,442	-5,501	-810	-3,158	1,596	-24,378	-18,916
Aug	-11,191	8,584	3,122	-633	526	24,027	2,318	-3,494	-256	-2,528	28,203	-9,491	39,188
Sep	-20,023	-494	-8,767	-437	30,463	-52,416	-10,919	333	-37	2,755	20,790	-14,956	-53,707
Oct	15,635	1,415	891	276	-29,463	8,352	3,303	-7,876	-153	5,702	-24,117	11,416	-14,619
Nov	10,897	-143	2,366	56	4,249	35,690	1,766	1,434	-1,268	-2,471	-10,357	10,324	52,542
Dec	-3,923	-7,289	-2,286	734	20,035	-74,178	-16,422	8,097	-314	-3,710	8,163	16,409	-54,685
2016 Jan	-10,285	10,907	157	-8	-1,565	29,496	37,614	-36,119	-72	-3,155	-26,217	8,065	8,818

Source: Bank of England

Notes to table
Explanatory notes to this table can be downloaded from the Bank of England website : http://www.bankofengland.co.uk/statistics/Pages/iadb/notesiadb/mfi_bs.aspx
Copyright guidance and the related UK Open Government Licence can be viewed here: www.bankofengland.co.uk/Pages/disclaimer.aspx.

12.18d Monetary financial institutions' consolidated balance sheet

£ millions Not seasonally adjusted

Changes in assets

	Loans						Securities (other than financial derivatives)						Other assets	
	Private sector		Public sector		Non-residents		Private sector		Public sector		Non-residents			
	Sterling	Foreign currency	Sterling	Foreign currency	Sterling	Foreign currency	Sterling	Foreign currency	Sterling	Foreign currency	Sterling	Foreign currency	Sterling	Foreign currency
LPM	VYAJ	VYAK	VYAL	VYAM	VYAN	VYAO	VYAP	VYAQ	VYAR	VYAS	VYAT	VYAU	VYAV	VYAW
2014 Jun	5,274	-18,529	-1,762	-634	-2,122	-26,111	-95	462	1,909	-31	415	2,093	1,207	804
Jul	2,283	-3,347	-1,351	5	-12,479	41,114	1,580	-167	1,987	52	607	-6,144	127	-370
Aug	1,918	-5,245	3,741	-477	19,539	-972	-2,824	-293	-1,112	-26	-2,476	-3,730	-1,351	2,257
Sep	-732	7,004	-1,937	160	-4,353	-9,180	-824	-9	-12,305	-14	1,926	8,008	-2,442	-2,209
Oct	-4,834	-10,258	1,260	593	-2,233	-45,320	-6,164	-1,204	14,600	43	148	6,449	1,147	-839
Nov	-4,035	6,299	1,614	-506	-987	30,518	-2,688	-106	4,479	56	-2,838	19,417	2,277	-793
Dec	-12,992	-17,158	-1,511	-985	1,203	-18,081	16,100	-9,974	-3,131	14	1,582	-13,821	-743	-3,690
2015 Jan	9,378	12,279	-879	93	3,764	31,759	-20,226	-1,187	-6,904	-41	-2,080	10,247	1,578	-1,092
Feb	1,389	12,687	772	-491	40	9,270	-2,583	-151	-4,282	-39	2,379	9,539	1,420	1,235
Mar	13,380	-2,857	-1,240	1,568	3,663	-27,990	-4,058	-684	-2,778	88	-476	-7,616	87	-553
Apr	584	12,746	-262	-1,530	1,596	45,343	-271	-236	3,251	-5	1,185	-4,038	163	490
May	5,155	-22,645	1,316	450	-527	-61,450	-417	-817	3,317	-20	1,380	-288	1,082	614
Jun	-10,779	7,892	-933	-468	5,607	-57,096	936	412	4,656	38	1,328	-14,778	1,814	-2,049
Jul	22,891	-11,126	533	351	-3,771	-14,595	-681	-2,166	5,020	141	482	-10,151	-2,916	-2,927
Aug	6,649	3,143	3,022	-1,315	-242	26,023	-9,045	-1,395	7,220	33	-1,705	4,454	1,456	892
Sep	374	-4,489	-1,471	616	15,682	-36,905	-296	184	-8,806	-40	-2,024	-14,271	-1,168	-1,092
Oct	-5,001	1,990	74	323	-13,138	-23,916	1,418	-1,491	3,818	-	378	20,028	1,066	-166
Nov	7,221	-3,284	-243	-709	147	40,269	-958	-1,297	4,624	-3	-2,038	6,693	1,175	944
Dec	-1,437	-18,822	-843	552	4,787	593	2,130	-974	-7,190	1	-3,011	-26,988	-1,231	-2,251
2016 Jan	8,092	10,120	1,001	187	2,520	12,714	-1,468	-475	-6,828	-15	-460	-14,322	11	-2,259

Source: Bank of England

Notes to table

Explanatory notes to this table can be found on the Bank of England website: http://www.bankofengland.co.uk/mfsd/iadb/notesiadb/mfi_bs.htm

Copyright guidance and the related UK Open Government Licence can be viewed here: www.bankofengland.co.uk/Pages/disclaimer.aspx.

12.19 Selected interest rates, exchange rates and security prices

Monthly average of 4 UK Banks' base rates IUMAAMIH [a] [b]		Monthly average rate of discount, 3 month Treasury bills, Sterling IUMAAJNB		Monthly average yield from British Government Securities, 20 year Nominal Par Yield IUMALNPY [c] [d]		Monthly average Spot exchange rate, US$ into Sterling XUMAUSS	
31-Jan-07	5.17	31-Jan-07	5.304	31-Jan-07	4.5131	31-Jan-07	1.9587
28-Feb-07	5.25	28-Feb-07	5.3393	28-Feb-07	4.5597	28-Feb-07	1.9581
31-Mar-07	5.25	31-Mar-07	5.3274	31-Mar-07	4.5195	31-Mar-07	1.9471
30-Apr-07	5.25	30-Apr-07	5.4329	30-Apr-07	4.735	30-Apr-07	1.9909
31-May-07	5.43	31-May-07	5.5516	31-May-07	4.8163	31-May-07	1.9836
30-Jun-07	5.5	30-Jun-07	5.6702	30-Jun-07	5.0696	30-Jun-07	1.9864
31-Jul-07	5.72	31-Jul-07	5.7742	31-Jul-07	5.026	31-Jul-07	2.0338
31-Aug-07	5.75	31-Aug-07	5.7943	31-Aug-07	4.8049	31-Aug-07	2.0111
30-Sep-07	5.75	30-Sep-07	5.6896	30-Sep-07	4.7407	30-Sep-07	2.0185
31-Oct-07	5.75	31-Oct-07	5.6058	31-Oct-07	4.7394	31-Oct-07	2.0446
30-Nov-07	5.75	30-Nov-07	5.4986	30-Nov-07	4.5924	30-Nov-07	2.0701
31-Dec-07	5.54	31-Dec-07	5.3034	31-Dec-07	4.5916	31-Dec-07	2.0185
31-Jan-08	5.5	31-Jan-08	5.1215	31-Jan-08	4.4578	31-Jan-08	1.9698
29-Feb-08	5.3	29-Feb-08	5.0178	29-Feb-08	4.6173	29-Feb-08	1.9638
31-Mar-08	5.25	31-Mar-08	4.8835	31-Mar-08	4.5401	31-Mar-08	2.0032
30-Apr-08	5.08	30-Apr-08	4.8258	30-Apr-08	4.7315	30-Apr-08	1.9817
31-May-08	5	31-May-08	4.9496	31-May-08	4.8539	31-May-08	1.9641
30-Jun-08	5	30-Jun-08	5.1138	30-Jun-08	5.0261	30-Jun-08	1.9658
31-Jul-08	5	31-Jul-08	5.0843	31-Jul-08	4.9391	31-Jul-08	1.988
31-Aug-08	5	31-Aug-08	4.9539	31-Aug-08	4.7438	31-Aug-08	1.8889
30-Sep-08	5	30-Sep-08	4.7425	30-Sep-08	4.6619	30-Sep-08	1.7986
31-Oct-08	4.61	31-Oct-08	3.6788	31-Oct-08	4.7579	31-Oct-08	1.69
30-Nov-08	3.23	30-Nov-08	1.9948	30-Nov-08	4.6898	30-Nov-08	1.5338
31-Dec-08	2.14	31-Dec-08	1.2875	31-Dec-08	4.1461	31-Dec-08	1.4859
31-Jan-09	1.6	31-Jan-09	0.8945	31-Jan-09	4.2758	31-Jan-09	1.4452
28-Feb-09	1.08	28-Feb-09	0.7177	28-Feb-09	4.3394	28-Feb-09	1.4411
31-Mar-09	0.57	31-Mar-09	0.6035	31-Mar-09	4.007	31-Mar-09	1.4174
30-Apr-09	0.5	30-Apr-09	0.625	30-Apr-09	4.2419	30-Apr-09	1.4715
31-May-09	0.5	31-May-09	0.5271	31-May-09	4.3752	31-May-09	1.5429
30-Jun-09	0.5	30-Jun-09	0.5037	30-Jun-09	4.471	30-Jun-09	1.6366
31-Jul-09	0.5	31-Jul-09	0.4397	31-Jul-09	4.4588	31-Jul-09	1.6366
31-Aug-09	0.5	31-Aug-09	0.3946	31-Aug-09	4.2164	31-Aug-09	1.6539
30-Sep-09	0.5	30-Sep-09	0.3761	30-Sep-09	4.0688	30-Sep-09	1.6328
31-Oct-09	0.5	31-Oct-09	0.4315	31-Oct-09	4.05	31-Oct-09	1.6199
30-Nov-09	0.5	30-Nov-09	0.4459	30-Nov-09	4.2177	30-Nov-09	1.6597
31-Dec-09	0.5	31-Dec-09	0.3587	31-Dec-09	4.3306	31-Dec-09	1.6239
31-Jan-10	0.5	31-Jan-10	0.4874	31-Jan-10	4.4161	31-Jan-10	1.6162
28-Feb-10	0.5	28-Feb-10	0.4878	28-Feb-10	4.5158	28-Feb-10	1.5615
31-Mar-10	0.5	31-Mar-10	0.5109	31-Mar-10	4.5698	31-Mar-10	1.5053
30-Apr-10	0.5	30-Apr-10	0.5083	30-Apr-10	4.558	30-Apr-10	1.534
31-May-10	0.5	31-May-10	0.4976	31-May-10	4.3143	31-May-10	1.4627
30-Jun-10	0.5	30-Jun-10	0.4839	30-Jun-10	4.2079	30-Jun-10	1.4761
31-Jul-10	0.5	31-Jul-10	0.498	31-Jul-10	4.1754	31-Jul-10	1.5299
31-Aug-10	0.5	31-Aug-10	0.4945	31-Aug-10	3.9824	31-Aug-10	1.566
30-Sep-10	0.5	30-Sep-10	0.4966	30-Sep-10	3.8954	30-Sep-10	1.5578
31-Oct-10	0.5	31-Oct-10	0.5061	31-Oct-10	3.8876	31-Oct-10	1.5862
30-Nov-10	0.5	30-Nov-10	0.4935	30-Nov-10	4.1149	30-Nov-10	1.5961
31-Dec-10	0.5	31-Dec-10	0.4913	31-Dec-10	4.2568	31-Dec-10	1.5603
31-Jan-11	0.5	31-Jan-11	0.5055	31-Jan-11	4.3204	31-Jan-11	1.5795
28-Feb-11	0.5	28-Feb-11	0.5363	28-Feb-11	4.405	28-Feb-11	1.613
31-Mar-11	0.5	31-Mar-11	0.5603	31-Mar-11	4.298	31-Mar-11	1.6159

12.19 Selected interest rates, exchange rates and security prices

Monthly average of 4 UK Banks' base rates IUMAAMIH [a] [b]		Monthly average rate of discount, 3 month Treasury bills, Sterling IUMAAJNB		Monthly average yield from British Government Securities, 20 year Nominal Par Yield IUMALNPY [c] [d]		Monthly average Spot exchange rate, US$ into Sterling XUMAUSS	
30-Apr-11	0.5	30-Apr-11	0.5676	30-Apr-11	4.2933	30-Apr-11	1.6345
31-May-11	0.5	31-May-11	0.5265	31-May-11	4.1371	31-May-11	1.6312
30-Jun-11	0.5	30-Jun-11	0.5174	30-Jun-11	4.1277	30-Jun-11	1.6214
31-Jul-11	0.5	31-Jul-11	0.4996	31-Jul-11	4.0974	31-Jul-11	1.6145
31-Aug-11	0.5	31-Aug-11	0.4531	31-Aug-11	3.7132	31-Aug-11	1.6348
30-Sep-11	0.5	30-Sep-11	0.4649	30-Sep-11	3.4205	30-Sep-11	1.5783
31-Oct-11	0.5	31-Oct-11	0.4608	31-Oct-11	3.2581	31-Oct-11	1.576
30-Nov-11	0.5	30-Nov-11	0.4387	30-Nov-11	3.0313	30-Nov-11	1.5804
31-Dec-11	0.5	31-Dec-11	0.2996	31-Dec-11	2.9803	31-Dec-11	1.5585
31-Jan-12	0.5	31-Jan-12	0.3239	31-Jan-12	2.906	31-Jan-12	1.551
29-Feb-12	0.5	29-Feb-12	0.3912	29-Feb-12	3.089	29-Feb-12	1.5802
31-Mar-12	0.5	31-Mar-12	0.4248	31-Mar-12	3.1744	31-Mar-12	1.5823
30-Apr-12	0.5	30-Apr-12	0.4236	30-Apr-12	3.1259	30-Apr-12	1.6014
31-May-12	0.5	31-May-12	0.3561	31-May-12	2.9073	31-May-12	1.5905
30-Jun-12	0.5	30-Jun-12	0.3422	30-Jun-12	2.725	30-Jun-12	1.5571
31-Jul-12	0.5	31-Jul-12	0.2943	31-Jul-12	2.6453	31-Jul-12	1.5589
31-Aug-12	0.5	31-Aug-12	0.2398	31-Aug-12	2.65	31-Aug-12	1.5719
30-Sep-12	0.5	30-Sep-12	0.2478	30-Sep-12	2.7497	30-Sep-12	1.6116
31-Oct-12	0.5	31-Oct-12	0.2368	31-Oct-12	2.7969	31-Oct-12	1.6079
30-Nov-12	0.5	30-Nov-12	0.2243	30-Nov-12	2.7846	30-Nov-12	1.5961
31-Dec-12	0.5	31-Dec-12	0.249	31-Dec-12	2.8391	31-Dec-12	1.6144
31-Jan-13	0.5	31-Jan-13	0.2677	31-Jan-13	3.0069	31-Jan-13	1.5957
28-Feb-13	0.5	28-Feb-13	0.3147	28-Feb-13	3.1035	28-Feb-13	1.5478
31-Mar-13	0.5	31-Mar-13	0.3391	31-Mar-13	2.9654	31-Mar-13	1.5076
30-Apr-13	0.5	30-Apr-13	0.3447	30-Apr-13	2.776	30-Apr-13	1.5316
31-May-13	0.5	31-May-13	0.3065	31-May-13	2.9096	31-May-13	1.5285
30-Jun-13	0.5	30-Jun-13	0.3066	30-Jun-13	3.1584	30-Jun-13	1.5478
31-Jul-13	0.5	31-Jul-13	0.3124	31-Jul-13	3.2719	31-Jul-13	1.5172
31-Aug-13	0.5	31-Aug-13	0.2812	31-Aug-13	3.4083	31-Aug-13	1.5507
30-Sep-13	0.5	30-Sep-13	0.289	30-Sep-13	3.4662	30-Sep-13	1.5865
31-Oct-13	0.5	31-Oct-13	0.3141	31-Oct-13	3.3198	31-Oct-13	1.6094
30-Nov-13	0.5	30-Nov-13	0.2865	30-Nov-13	3.3978	30-Nov-13	1.6104
31-Dec-13	0.5	31-Dec-13	0.2555	31-Dec-13	3.497	31-Dec-13	1.6375
31-Jan-14	0.5	31-Jan-14	0.3211	31-Jan-14	3.4287	31-Jan-14	1.647
28-Feb-14	0.5	28-Feb-14	0.3624	28-Feb-14	3.3668	28-Feb-14	1.6567
31-Mar-14	0.5	31-Mar-14	0.3882	31-Mar-14	3.3469	31-Mar-14	1.6622
30-Apr-14	0.5	30-Apr-14	0.3688	30-Apr-14	3.3127	30-Apr-14	1.6743
31-May-14	0.5	31-May-14	0.284	31-May-14	3.2387	31-May-14	1.6844
30-Jun-14	0.5	30-Jun-14	0.3586	30-Jun-14	3.3055	30-Jun-14	1.6906
31-Jul-14	0.5	31-Jul-14	0.4271	31-Jul-14	3.228	31-Jul-14	1.7069
31-Aug-14	0.5	31-Aug-14	0.3978	31-Aug-14	2.9986	31-Aug-14	1.6709
30-Sep-14	0.5	30-Sep-14	0.4351	30-Sep-14	2.978	30-Sep-14	1.6305
31-Oct-14	0.5	31-Oct-14	0.3964	31-Oct-14	2.7955	31-Oct-14	1.6068
30-Nov-14	0.5	30-Nov-14	0.4114	30-Nov-14	2.7235	30-Nov-14	1.578
31-Dec-14	0.5	31-Dec-14	0.4101	31-Dec-14	2.4744	31-Dec-14	1.564

Source: Bank of England

Notes:

[a] Data obtained from Barclays Bank, Lloyds Bank, HSBC, and National Westminster Bank whose rates are used to compile this series. Where all the rates did not change on the same day a spread is shown.

[b] This series will end on 31-July-2015

[c] Calculated using the Variable Roughness Penalty (VRP) model.

[d] The monthly average figure is calculated using the available daily observations within each month.

12.20 Mergers and Acquisitions in the UK by other UK Companies: Category of Expenditure

£ million

		Expenditure				Percentage of Expenditure		
		Cash						
	Total	Independent Companies	Subsidiaries	Issues of Ordinary Shares[2]	Issues of Fixed Interest Securities[2]	Cash	Issues of Ordinary Shares	Issues of Fixed Interest Securities
	DUCM	DWVW	DWVX	AIHD	AIHE	DWVY	DWVZ	DWWA
Annual								
2003	18,679	8,956	7,183	1,667	873	86	9	5
2004	31,408	12,080	7,822	10,338	1,168	63	33	4
2005	25,134	13,425	8,510	2,768	431	87	11	2
2006	28,511	..	8,131	..	335	..	..	2
2007	26,778	13,671	6,507	4,909	1,691	76	18	6
2008	36,469	31,333	2,851	1,910	375	94	5	1
2009	12,195	2,937	709	8,435	114	30	69	1
2010[1]	12,605	6,175	4,520	1,560	350	85	12	3
2011	8,089	4,432	2,667	719	271	87	10	4
2012	3,413	1,937	789	419	268	82	10	8
2013	7,665	3,690	3,475	353	147	92	6	2
2014	8,032	3,249	1,947	2,782	51	65	35	–
Quarterly								
2009 Q2	729	130	150	437	12	38	60	2
2009 Q3	1,886	1,409	214	254	9	87	13	–
2009 Q4	1,374	1,066	217	45	46	94	3	3
2010 Q1[1]	1,361	765	525	58	13	95	4	1
2010 Q2	2,032	986	714	275	57	83	14	3
2010 Q3	2,949	1,165	814	839	131	68	28	4
2010 Q4	6,263	3,259	2,467	388	149	92	6	2
2011 Q1	1,500	552	651	240	57	80	16	4
2011 Q2	3,346	2,355	704	204	83	92	6	2
2011 Q3	1,452	828	462	75	87	89	5	6
2011 Q4	1,791	697	850	200	44	87	11	2
2012 Q1	1,070	518	199	323	30	67	30	3
2012 Q2	1,041	575	269	54	143	81	5	14
2012 Q3	610	409	100	8	93	84	1	15
2012 Q4	692	435	221	34	2	95	5	–
2013 Q1	2,825	567	2,216	26	16	98	1	1
2013 Q2	2,438	1,992	316	80	50	95	3	2
2013 Q3	1,166	587	332	230	17	79	20	1
2013 Q4	1,236	544	611	17	64	94	1	5
2014 Q1	1,613	896	103	612	2	62	38	–
2014 Q2	1,625	478	1,051	50	45 [†]	94	3	3
2014 Q3	3,152	476	656	2,019	–	36	64	–
2014 Q4	1,642	1,399	137	101	4	94	6	–
2015 Q1	1,755 [†]	1,075 [†]	314 [†]	281	84	79	16	5

† indicates earliest revision, if any
– indicates data is zero or less than £0.5m
Disclosive data indicated by ..

1 The deal identification threshold has been increased from Q1 2010 from £0.1m to £1.0m and as a consequence there may be a discontinuity in the number and value of transaction reported.
2 Issued to the vendor company as payment.

Source: Mergers and Acquisitions Surveys, Office for National Statistics

Service industry

Chapter 13

Service industry

Annual Business Inquiry (Tables 13.1, 13.3 and 13.4)

The Annual Business Inquiry (ABI) estimates cover all UK businesses registered for Value Added Tax (VAT) and/or Pay As You Earn (PAYE). The businesses are classified to the 2007 Standard Industrial Classification (SIC(2007)) headings listed in the tables. The ABI obtains details on these businesses from the Office for National Statistics (ONS) Inter-Departmental Business Register (IDBR).

As with all its statistical inquiries, ONS is concerned to minimise the form-filling burden of individual contributors and as such the ABI is a sample inquiry. The sample was designed as a stratified random sample of about 66,600 businesses; the inquiry population is stratified by SIC(2007) and employment using the information from the register.

The inquiry results are grossed up to the total population so that they relate to all active UK businesses on the IDBR for the sectors covered.

The results meet a wide range of needs for government, economic analysts and the business community at large. In official statistics the inquiry is an important source for the national accounts and input-output tables, and also provides weights for the indices of production and producer prices. Additionally, inquiry results enable the UK to meet statistical requirements of the European Union.

Data from 1995 and 1996 were calculated on a different basis from those for 1997 and later years. In order to provide a link between the two data series, the 1995 and 1996 data were subsequently reworked to provide estimates on a consistent basis.

Revised ABI results down to SIC(2007) 4 digit class level for 1995–2007, giving both analysis and tabular detail, are available from the ONS website at: www.statistics.gov.uk, with further extracts and bespoke analyses available on request. This service replaces existing publications.

Retail trade: index numbers of value and volume (Table 13.2)

The main purpose of the Retail Sales Inquiry (RSI) is to provide up-to-date information on short period movements in the level of retail sales. In principle, the RSI covers the retail activity of every business classified in the retail sector (Division 52 of the 2007 Standard Industrial Classification (SIC(2007)) in Great Britain. A business will be classified to the retail sector if its main activity is one of the individual 4 digit SIC categories within Division 52. The retail activity of a business is then defined by its retail turnover, that is the sale of all retail goods (note that petrol, for example, is not a retail good).

The RSI is compiled from the information returned to the statutory inquiries into the distribution and services sector. The inquiry is addressed to a stratified sample of 5,000 businesses classified to the retail sector, the stratification being by 'type of store' (the individual 4 digit SIC categories within Division 52) and by size. The sample structure is designed to ensure that the inquiry estimates are as accurate as possible. In terms of the selection, this means that:

• each of the individual 4 digit SIC categories are represented – their coverage depending upon the relative size of the category and the variability of the data

• within each 4 digit SIC category the larger retailers tend to be fully enumerated with decreasing proportions of medium and smaller retailers

The structure of the inquiry is updated periodically by reference to the more comprehensive results of the Annual Business Inquiry (ABI). The monthly inquiry also incorporates a rotation element for the smallest retailers. This helps to spread the burden more fairly, as well as improving the representativeness between successive benchmarks.

13.1a Retail Trade, except of motor vehicles and motorcycles

Standard Industrial Classification (Revised 2007) Division Group Class	Description	Year	Number of enterprises	Total turnover	Approximate gross value added at basic prices (aGVA)	Total purchases of goods, materials and services	Total employment - point in time [1]	Total employment - average during the year [1]
			Number	£ million	£ million	£ million	Thousand	Thousand
47	Retail trade, except of motor vehicles and motorcycles	2008	194,677	311,745	65,123	246,237	3,054	3,106
		2009	187,890	319,318	69,924	249,058	3,073	3,139
		2010	187,230	332,131	71,500	261,676	3,016	3,040
		2011	189,119	342,147	70,871	271,203	3,032	3,060
		2012	187,616	349,327	73,876	275,052	3,029	3,062
		2013	189,828	359,088	81,368	278,326	3,052	3,084

Standard Industrial Classification (Revised 2007) Division Group Class	Description	Year	Total employment costs	Total net capital expenditure	Total capital expenditure- acquisitions	Total capital expenditure - disposals	Total stocks and work in progress - value at end of year	Total stocks and work in progress - value at beginning of year	Total stocks and work in progress - increase during year
			£ million	£ million	£ million	£ million	£ million	£ million	£ million
47	Retail trade, except of motor vehicles and motorcycles	2008	38,466	9,069	10,495	1,426	26,110	25,519	591
		2009	38,914	7,784	9,113	1,330	26,539	25,759	781
		2010	39,816	6,149	9,258	3,108	28,743	26,425	2,317
		2011	41,592	9,051	10,879	1,828	30,356	28,964	1,392
		2012	42,184	9,477	10,789	1,312	30,021	28,720	1,301
		2013	43,441	9,510	10,627	1,117	31,791	29,863	1,929

Source: Annual Business Survey (ABS)

The sum of constituent items in tables may not always agree exactly with the totals shown due to rounding

1. Total employment - point in time and Total employment - average during the year are from the Business Register and Employment Survey (BRES). Caution should be taken when combining financial data from the ABS with employment data from BRES due to differences in methodology.

More information can be found in the ABS Technical Report.:
http://www.ons.gov.uk/file?uri=/businessindustryandtrade/business/businessservices/methodologies/annualbusinesssurveyabs/abstechnicalreport2014tcm77368873.pdf

13.1b Retail trade, except of motor vehicles and motor-cycles

				£ million (Inclusive of VAT)	
	2009	2010	2011	2012	2013
TOTAL TURNOVER	**350,269**	**367,446**	**385,692**	**393,423**	**404,534**
RETAIL TURNOVER	**331,256**	**347,144**	**363,280**	**368,176**	**378,917**
Fruit (including fresh, chilled, dried, frozen, canned and processed)	6,469	6,821	7,662	6,846	7,132
Vegetables (including fresh, chilled, dried, frozen canned and processed)	9,949	10,533	10,677	12,380	13,219
Meat (including fresh, chilled, smoked, frozen, canned and processed)	17,855	17,909	19,541	20,254	21,230
Fish, crustaceans and molluscs (including fresh, chilled, smoked, frozen, canned and processed)	2,989	2,978	3,295	3,453	3,458
Bakery products and cereals (including rice and pasta products)	16,719	17,875	18,818	20,078	20,352
Sugar, jam, honey, chocolate and confectionery (including ice-cream)	8,618	8,844	8,688	9,162	9,829
Alcoholic drink	15,609	16,618	17,445	18,184	19,219
Non-alcoholic beverages (including tea, coffee, fruit drinks and vegetable drinks)	7,756	8,018	9,176	9,161	9,652
Tobacco (excluding smokers requisites e.g. pipes, lighters etc)	11,411	11,369	11,838	11,885	11,405
Milk, cheese and eggs (including yoghurts and cream)	11,562	10,918	11,219	11,441	11,579
Oils and fats (including butter and margarine)	1,440	1,444	1,613	1,611	1,695
Food products not elsewhere classified (including sauces, herbs spices, soups)	5,149	4,427	4,528	3,890	3,858
Pharmaceutical products	3,636	3,946	4,390	4,725	4,916
National Health Receipts	11,792	12,067	11,405	11,680	11,100
Other medical products and therapeutic appliances and equipment	3,213	4,210	3,638	4,067	3,913
Other appliances, articles and products for personal care	13,148	14,109	15,107	15,702	16,776
Other articles of clothing, accessories for making clothing	2,505	3,395	3,781	4,051	4,317
Garments	35,556	36,706	37,976	38,730	41,466
Footwear (excluding sports shoes)	7,685	7,458	7,720	8,720	8,765
Travel goods and other personal effects not elsewhere classified	1,722	2,352	2,518	2,506	3,183
Household textiles (including furnishing fabrics, curtains etc)	4,535	4,862	4,188	4,158	4,731
Household and personal appliances whether electric or not	6,736	6,917	7,278	7,367	6,768
Glassware, tableware and household utensils (including non-electric)	2,824	2,754	3,369	3,668	3,899
Furniture and furnishings	13,226	12,313	13,475	12,395	13,606
Audio and visual equipment (including radios, televisions and video recorders)	6,016	6,245	5,353	5,821	4,916
Recording material for pictures and sound (including audio and video tapes, blank and pre recorded records etc)	3,052	2,787	2,547	2,668	2,560
Information processing equipment (including printers, software, calculators and typewriters)	4,384	4,530	5,425	4,862	5,475
Decorating and DIY supplies	6,820	7,319	7,528	5,580	6,500
Tools and equipment for house and garden	2,964	3,088	3,566	3,887	4,235
Books	2,623	2,648	2,579	3,084	2,623
Newspapers and periodicals	3,405	3,947	3,675	3,410	2,906
Stationery and drawing materials and miscellaneous printed matter	4,423	4,025	4,432	4,397	4,620
Carpets and other floor coverings (excluding bathroom mats, rush and door mats)	2,840	2,824	3,159	3,144	2,806
Photographic and cinematographic equipment and optical instruments	1,854	1,625	1,643	1,298	736
Telephone and telefax equipment (including mobile phones)	3,249	3,143	3,665	4,437	4,481
Jewellery, silverware and plate; watches and clocks	5,693	6,045	6,235	6,626	6,340
Works of art and antiques (including furniture, floor coverings and jewellery)	1,347	1,756	1,493	1,254	1,807
Equipment and accessories for sport, camping, recreation and musical instruments	4,416	4,864	5,118	4,944	4,355
Spare parts and accessories for all types of vehicle and sales of bicycles	924	1,148	983	950	1,244
Games, toys, hobbies (including video game software, video game computers that plug into the tv, video-games cassettes and CD-ROM'S)	7,484	7,514	7,492	7,154	7,018
Other goods not elsewhere classified (including sale of new postage stamps and sales of liquid and solid fuels)	5,007	5,896	5,929	5,788	6,689
Non-durable household goods (including household cleaning, maintenance products) & paper products and other non-durable household goods	5,280	4,727	4,923	4,936	5,596
Natural or artificial plants and flowers	2,973	3,609	4,023	3,501	3,772
Pets and related products (including pet food)	3,884	3,896	4,166	4,154	4,664
Petrol, diesel, lubricating oil and other petroleum products	30,515	36,664	40,001	40,171	39,507

The following symbols and abbreviations are used throughout the ABS releases;

Source: Annual Business Survey (ABS)

*   Information suppressed to avoid disclosure

..   not available

-    nil or less than half the level of rounding

The sum of constituent items in tables may not always agree exactly with the totals shown due to rounding.

13.2 Retail trade: index numbers of value and volume of sales[1]

Great Britain

Non-seasonally adjusted

		Sales in 2014 £ thousand	2004	2005	2006	2007	2008	2009	2010	2011	2012	2013	2014
Value													
All retailing	J5AH	378,053,162	77.2	78.2	81.1	84.3	87.5	88.2	90.6	95.3	97.5	100	103
Large	J5AI	298,505,890	72	73.4	76.8	80.5	84.4	85.8	89.9	94.6	97.2	100	102.5
Small	J5AJ	79,547,283	97	96.5	97.7	98.9	99.6	97.4	93.4	97.9	98.7	100	104.9
All retailing excluding automotive fuel	J43S	339,724,267	78.8	79.6	81.6	84.5	87.1	88.9	91.1	94.3	96.8	100	103.8
Predominantly food stores	EAFS	154,559,455	71.7	74	76.7	79.9	84.5	89.1	90.5	94.4	97.1	100	101.1
Predominantly non-food stores	EAFT	158,583,175	90.4	90	91.3	94.1	94.5	93	95.3	96.7	98.3	100	105.4
Non specialised predominantly non-food stores	EAGE	31,776,062	77	76.7	78.9	81.9	79.7	81.1	86.8	90.2	95.7	100	105.4
Textile, clothing, footwear and leather	EAFU	46,201,355	80.4	81.1	84.8	87.2	86.9	87.9	92.7	96.2	97.7	100	103.6
Household goods stores	EAFV	31,311,220	118.5	114.6	115.4	119.4	116.8	111	106.6	104.2	103.2	100	105.6
Other specialised non-food stores	EAFW	49,294,538	90.9	91.4	90.3	92.5	97.1	94	96.1	96.8	97.3	100	107
Non-store retailing	J596	26,581,637	50.9	50.8	51.9	54	57.7	61.5	68	78.1	85.6	100	111.4
Automotive fuel	J43H	38,328,895	63.8	66	77.1	82.6	90.7	82.9	86.8	103.4	103.2	100	96.3
Volume													
All retailing	J5DD	378,053,162	92.2	93.1	95.9	98.6	98.6	99	98	98.2	98.7	100	103.7
All retailing excluding automotive fuel	J448	339,724,267	90.7	92	94.1	96.5	97	97.6	97.7	97.4	98.3	100	104
Predominantly food stores	EAGW	154,559,455	99.4	101.2	102.6	103.4	102.4	103.5	101.7	100.5	100.3	100	100.8
Predominantly non-food stores	EAGX	158,583,175	88.9	90	92.7	96.5	97.7	97.2	98.2	97.4	98.2	100	106.1
Non specialised predominantly non-food stores	EAHI	31,776,062	82.9	83.1	85.6	88.4	85.3	86	90	91.1	95.8	100	106.1
Textile, clothing, footwear and leather	EAGY	46,201,355	72.4	75.1	80.4	84.2	86.8	92.6	97.5	98.4	98.9	100	103.5
Household goods stores	EAGZ	31,311,220	118	115.9	119.4	124.7	122.4	115.7	108.5	103.8	102.2	100	106.7
Other specialised non-food stores	EAHA	49,294,538	90.7	93	92.5	95.9	100.5	97.1	97.6	96.3	96.6	100	108.4
Non-store retailing	J5CL	26,581,637	53.3	53.3	54.6	56.9	60	64.5	70	78.7	85.9	100	111.8
Automotive fuel	J43V	38,328,895	107.1	102.2	113.4	117.8	113.2	111.5	100.5	104.8	102.4	100	101.1

Weekly average (2013=100)

1 See chapter text.

Please note that the indices have been re-referenced so the value of 100 is in 2013

Source: Office for National Statistics

13.3 Wholesale and retail trade and repair of motor vehicles and motorcycles

Standard Industrial Classification (Revised 2007) Division Group Class	Description	Year	Number of enterprises	Total turnover	Approximate gross value added at basic prices (aGVA)	Total purchases of goods, materials and services	Total employment point in time [1]	Total employment average during the year [1]	Total employment costs
			Number	£ million	£ million	£ million	Thousand	Thousand	£ million
45	Wholesale and retail trade and repair of motor vehicles and motorcycles	2008	67,683	135,669	20,957	115,372	532	535	10,925
		2009	66,372	125,764	18,348	105,457	500	539	10,445
		2010	66,239	132,077	22,150	111,243	511	510	10,439
		2011	67,298	137,364	23,419	115,292	523	535	10,658
		2012	67,274	142,461	22,347	120,649	510	522	10,615
		2013	67,754	152,510	24,236	129,877	525	537	11,570

Standard Industrial Classification (Revised 2007) Division Group Class	Description	Year	Total net capital expenditure	Total capital expenditure- acquisitions	Total capital expenditure - disposals	Total stocks and work in progress - value at end of year	Total stocks and work in progress - value at beginning of year	Total stocks and work in progress - increase during year
			£ million	£ million	£ million	£ million	£ million	£ million
45	Wholesale and retail trade and repair of motor vehicles and motorcycles	2008	1,044	2,110	1,066	16,136	15,402	735
		2009	885	1,669	784	13,624	15,545	-1,921
		2010	1,035	1,747	711	15,008	13,640	1,368
		2011	1,292	2,067	775	16,451	15,107	1,344
		2012	1,174	1,927	753	17,067	16,490	577
		2013	1,530	2,296	766	18,139	16,525	1,613

Source: Annual Business Survey (ABS)

The following symbols and abbreviations are used throughout the ABS releases;
* Information suppressed to avoid disclosure
.. not available
- nil or less than half the level of rounding

The sum of constituent items in tables may not always agree exactly with the totals shown due to rounding.

Notes:

1. Total employment - point in time and Total employment - average during the year are from the Business Register and Employment Survey (BRES). Caution should be taken when combining financial data from the ABS with employment data from BRES due to differences in methodology. More information can be found in the ABS Technical Report.

13.4 Accommodation and food service activities

Standard Industrial Classification (Revised 2007) Section Division Group Class	Description	Year	Number of enterprises	Total turnover	Approximate gross value added at basic prices (aGVA)	Total purchases of goods, materials and services	Total employment - point in time [1]	Total employment - average during the year [1]	Total employment costs
			Number	£ million	£ million	£ million	Thousand	Thousand	£ million
I	Accommodation and food service activities	2008	136,504	67,674	31,620	36,047	1,971	1,967	18,737
		2009	129,112	66,195	29,375	36,745	1,919	1,812	19,012
		2010	127,844	68,346	31,435	36,883	1,869	1,855	19,074
		2011	130,336	72,322	34,826	37,563	1,937	1,869	19,987
		2012	128,831	74,355	37,764	37,272	1,970	1,910	21,132
		2013	131,322	77,033	38,357	38,625	2,029	1,970	21,611
55	Accommodation	2008	15,725	17,532	9,573	7,962	392	389	4,806
		2009	15,157	17,235	9,231	7,973	393	360	4,724
		2010	15,075	17,650	9,087	8,603	388	377	5,075
		2011	15,159	18,566	9,838	8,775	429	407	5,331
		2012	15,205	19,822	11,149	8,677	426	409	5,752
		2013	15,365	20,222	11,353	8,860	433	416	5,646
55.1	Hotels and similar accommodation	2008	10,178	13,596	7,732	5,872	328	328	4,011
		2009	9,687	13,624	7,439	6,171	325	297	3,942
		2010	9,559	13,493	7,102	6,399	321	316	4,173
		2011	9,575	14,150	7,619	6,532	358	342	4,424
		2012	9,449	15,186	8,572	6,609	351	339	4,823
		2013	9,364	15,764	8,925	6,852	356	344	4,703
55.2	Holiday and other short stay accommodation	2008	2,973	1,313	633	683	27	26	307
		2009	3,351	1,219	661	554	30	29	289
		2010	3,318	1,603	846	776	29	26	339
		2011	3,296	1,476	726	774	33	30	351
		2012	3,247	1,497	913	590	33	31	344
		2013	3,411	1,562	969	601	32	30	343
55.3	Camping grounds, recreational vehicle parks and trailer parks	2008	1,728	2,441	1,113	1,321	33	31	433
		2009	1,711	2,230	1,033	1,184	34	31	448
		2010	1,735	2,325	1,031	1,307	*	*	495
		2011	1,775	2,739	1,385	1,378	34	31	507
		2012	1,796	2,771	1,415	1,360	37	34	516
		2013	1,818	2,630	1,292	1,310	39	37	524
55.9	Other accommodation	2008	846	182	95	86	4	4	55
		2009	408	162	98	64	3	3	46
		2010	463	229	108	121	*	*	69
		2011	513	200	108	92	4	4	49
		2012	713	368	250	118	5	4	70
		2013	772	265	168	98	6	5	76
56	Food and beverage service activities	2008	120,779	50,141	22,047	28,085	1,578	1,578	13,930
		2009	113,955	48,960	20,144	28,772	1,526	1,452	14,288
		2010	112,769	50,696	22,348	28,281	1,481	1,478	13,998
		2011	115,177	53,756	24,988	28,787	1,507	1,462	14,656
		2012	113,626	54,533	26,615	28,594	1,544	1,501	15,380
		2013	115,957	56,811	27,003	29,765	1,596	1,553	15,964
56.1	Restaurants and mobile food service activities	2008	63,368	22,452	10,018	12,436	753	753	6,255
		2009	61,192	22,658	9,910	12,765	737	644	6,460
		2010	61,387	23,017	10,407	12,623	705	684	6,306
		2011	63,712	25,690	12,301	13,447	767	765	6,886
		2012	64,460	25,934	13,367	13,332	782	783	7,187
		2013	67,144	28,740	14,328	14,454	859	860	8,067
56.2	Event catering and other food service activities	2008	7,536	7,539	3,824	3,717	263	260	2,950
		2009	7,049	6,811	2,786	4,029	210	235	2,952
		2010	7,031	7,971	4,003	3,970	227	253	3,149
		2011	7,967	8,553	4,418	4,138	231	212	3,204
		2012	7,651	8,925	4,430	4,521	262	249	3,688
		2013	8,003	8,269	3,928	4,343	233	222	3,381
56.21	Event catering activities	2008	6,649	7,000	3,553	3,450	250	247	2,788
		2009	6,070	6,139	2,505	3,636	197	222	2,782
		2010	5,767	7,289	3,710	3,581	211	236	2,957
		2011	6,267	7,837	4,119	3,715	213	196	2,993
		2012	5,514	7,844	3,879	3,968	241	228	3,411
		2013	5,885	3,196	1,394	1,809	86	82	967
56.29	Other food service activities	2008	887	539	271	268	13	13	162
		2009	979	672	281	393	12	12	170
		2010	1,264	682	293	389	16	17	192
		2011	1,700	716	299	422	18	17	211
		2012	2,137	1,081	551	552	21	20	278
		2013	2,118	5,073	2,534	2,534	147	140	2,414
56.3	Beverage serving activities	2008	49,875	20,150	8,204	11,931	562	567	4,726
		2009	45,714	19,491	7,448	11,979	579	574	4,876
		2010	44,351	19,709	7,938	11,688	549	540	4,543
		2011	43,498	19,513	8,269	11,203	509	484	4,566
		2012	41,515	19,675	8,817	10,742	501	469	4,504
		2013	40,810	19,802	8,748	10,968	503	471	4,516

13.4 Accommodation and food service activities

Standard Industrial Classification (Revised 2007) Section Division Group Class	Description	Year	Total net capital expenditure	Total capital expenditure- acquisitions	Total capital expenditure - disposals	Total stocks and work in progress - value at end of year	Total stocks and work in progress - value at beginning of year	Total stocks and work in progress - increase during year
			£ million	£ million	£ million	£ million	£ million	£ million
I	Accommodation and food service activities	2008	4,132	4,634	502	1,393	1,355	37
		2009	3,443	3,803	360	1,318	1,303	15
		2010	2,807	3,804	997	1,481	1,403	79
		2011	3,311	4,339	1,028	1,484	1,368	117
		2012	3,930	4,704	774	1,716	1,713	3
		2013	3,946	4,837	891	1,544	1,523	21
55	Accommodation	2008	2,155	2,289	134	378	379	-1
		2009	1,628	1,728	100	359	391	-32
		2010	1,301	1,489	188	488	445	43
		2011	1,416	1,641	225	506	443	63
		2012	1,898	2,050	152	469	452	17
		2013	1,836	2,045	209	397	413	-16
55.1	Hotels and similar accommodation	2008	1,774	1,848	74	193	187	6
		2009	1,390	1,433	43	181	197	-15
		2010	936	1,072	136	250	231	20
		2011	946	1,137	191	201	176	25
		2012	1,282	1,397	115	185	172	13
		2013	1,173	1,335	162	207	189	18
55.2	Holiday and other short stay accommodation	2008	111	129	17	50	48	2
		2009	50	67	17	24	29	-5
		2010	186	214	28	75	66	9
		2011	169	184	15	59	45	15
		2012	254	269	16	64	58	6
		2013	195	216	21	37	34	3
55.3	Camping grounds, recreational vehicle parks and trailer parks	2008	*	277	*	133	142	-9
		2009	138	*	*	153	164	-11
		2010	160	181	21	159	145	14
		2011	238	257	18	245	222	23
		2012	258	279	21	217	219	-3
		2013	254	278	24	152	190	-38
55.9	Other accommodation	2008	*	35	*	2	2	-
		2009	50	*	*	1	1	-
		2010	19	22	4	3	3	-
		2011	62	63	1	1	1	-
		2012	104	105	1	3	3	-
		2013	214	216	2	1	-	-
56	Food and beverage service activities	2008	1,978	2,346	368	1,015	976	39
		2009	1,815	2,075	260	959	912	47
		2010	1,507	2,316	809	993	958	35
		2011	1,895	2,698	803	978	925	54
		2012	2,032	2,654	622	1,247	1,261	-13
		2013	2,110	2,792	682	1,147	1,110	37
56.1	Restaurants and mobile food service activities	2008	1,021	1,124	103	453	433	20
		2009	1,104	1,250	146	437	408	29
		2010	998	1,185	187	429	402	27
		2011	1,203	1,327	123	412	379	33
		2012	1,380	1,512	132	562	532	30
		2013	1,449	1,645	196	480	454	26
56.2	Event catering and other food service activities	2008	88	99	10	145	145	1
		2009	44	49	5	103	98	5
		2010	135	176	41	126	122	4
		2011	175	188	14	145	140	5
		2012	127	135	8	158	154	4
		2013	110	117	7	176	167	9
56.21	Event catering activities	2008	83	93	10	139	139	1
		2009	33	37	4	87	84	3
		2010	117	155	38	111	107	4
		2011	116	129	13	123	124	-1
		2012	113	120	7	133	131	2
		2013	48	52	5	77	68	9
56.29	Other food service activities	2008	5	6	-	6	6	-
		2009	11	12	1	16	14	2
		2010	18	21	2	15	15	-
		2011	59	60	1	22	16	6
		2012	14	15	1	24	23	1
		2013	62	65	3	100	99	1
56.3	Beverage serving activities	2008	868	1,123	255	416	398	18
		2009	667	776	109	419	406	13
		2010	374	955	581	438	434	5
		2011	517	1,183	666	421	405	16
		2012	524	1,007	483	527	575	-47
		2013	551	1,030	479	491	488	2

Source: Annual Business Survey (ABS)

The following symbols and abbreviations are used throughout the ABS releases;

* Information suppressed to avoid disclosure   .. not available   - nil or less than half the level of rounding

The sum of constituent items in tables may not always agree exactly with the totals shown due to rounding.

1. Total employment - point in time and Total employment - average during the year are from the Business Register and Employment Survey (BRES). Caution should be taken when combining financial data from the ABS with employment data from BRES due to differences in methodology. More information can be found in the ABS Technical Report.

Defence

Chapter 14

Defence

This section includes figures on Defence expenditure, on the size and role of the Armed Forces and on related support activities. Much of the material used in this section can be found in UK Defence Statistics

Table 14.1 United Kingdom Defence Expenditure by Commodity Block

This table shows a breakdown of Resource & Capital DEL and AME by Commodity Block. Under Clear Line of Sight (CLoS), the main MOD expenditure categories are now presented as Commodity Blocks. This provides a more meaningful description of the Department's planned and actual spend, and enables a clearer understanding of the MOD's plans and expenditure over the Spending Review period.

Please refer to the Resource Accounting & Budgeting section of UK Defence Statistics to view important information relating to the introduction of the International Financial Reporting Standard (IFRS), the implementation of the Clear Line of Sight (CLoS) Alignment project and accounting changes from 2011/12, which have led to presentational changes to the reporting of MOD accounts.

Prior to 2011/12, when Commodity Block reporting was first introduced, information contained in this table was reported in Table 1.3a of UK Defence Statistics 2012.

The data are derived directly from the MOD Departmental Resource Accounts.

Further information about the quality of data and methods used in the production of these statistics, along with details of their intended use can be found in the Background Quality Report - Departmental Resources Statistics.

Table 14.2 Intake to UK Regular Forces by Service and sex
Women accounted for 8.4 per cent of the intake to UK Regular Forces in 2012/13, which represents a gradual decline since 2006/07.

Table 14.3 provides information on the formation of the United Kingdom's Armed Forces

Table 14.3a shows the number of submarines and ships in the Royal Navy and Royal Fleet Auxiliary, Royal Marine Commando units, squadrons of helicopters and fixed-wing aircraft in the Fleet Air Arm, and Reserve Units at 1 April 2014. The figures show overall unit numbers only; they do not reflect the level of readiness at which the unit is held which changes throughout the year.

Table 14.3b shows the numbers of Regiments and Infantry battalions in the Regular Army and Army Reserves; and Corps, Divisional and Brigade headquarters. Key points - 2014 saw the first change in the number of combat arms regiments in the Army since 2008. The number of Army Reserves regiments has remained the same but the number of Regular Army combat arms regiments has decreased from 46 to 43. This is mainly due to regiment mergers.

Table 14.3c shows the number of squadrons in the Royal Air Force (RAF) and the Royal Auxiliary Air Force (RAuxAF). Key point - there has been a decrease in the number of RAF squadrons in 2014 from 9 to 7. This is due to 12 Sqn and 617 Sqn standing down on 31 March 2014.

Table 14.3d shows the number of regiments and squadrons in the Joint Units, Special Forces, Joint Helicopter Command and Joint Force Harrier.

Table 14.4 Outflow from UK Regular Forces, trained and untrained
Figures show outflow from UK Regular Forces, both trained and untrained, including personnel leaving the Services, deaths and recalled reservists on release. They do not include promotion from Ranks to Officers or flows between Services.
UK Regular Forces comprises trained and untrained Full-time personnel but does not include Gurkhas, FTRS personnel and reservists.

Table 14.5 United Kingdom Armed Forces Full-time trained strength and requirement, at 1 April each year

The Full-Time Trained Strength of the UK Armed Forces is defined as comprising of trained UK Regular Forces, trained Gurkhas and elements of the FTRS (Full Time Reserve Service) personnel. It does not include mobilised reservists.
The full-time trained strength of the UK Armed Forces was 150,890 at 1 April 2014, down 9820 since 1 April 2013 and down 39,380 since 1 April 2000.

The requirement for the UK's full-time trained Armed Forces decreased from 198,160 in 2000 to 174,840 in 2012 and 159,640 in 2014. The rate of decrease has been greatest in the RAF, followed by the Naval Service and least in the Army.

The deficit between strength and requirement of full-time trained Armed Forces has decreased from 7,880 at 1 April 2000 to 4,830 at 1 April 2012 to 8,750 in April 2014. The largest deficit as a percentage of requirement is in the Army (7.4% deficit), where the strength has fallen faster than the requirement in the last year.

Table 14.6a Civilian personnel, at 1 April each year
The Ministry of Defence civilian population (Level 0) has continued to decrease, falling from 85,850 at 1 April 2010 to 58,160 at 1 April 2015, a reduction of 27,690 (32.3 per cent). The largest fall in the population occurred when the Voluntary Early Release Scheme (VERS) was in effect between October 2011 and March 2014. The majority of reductions in the Level 0 FTE workforce were directed by policy deriving from the Strategic Defence and Security Review (SDSR) which introduced two Voluntary Early Release Schemes (VERS) covering exits in 2011-12 and 2012-14.

Between 1 April 2010 and 1 April 2015 the overall strength in Level 1 MOD personnel fell from 65,920 to 48,650, a reduction of 17,270 personnel (26.2 per cent) over the period. Across the same period the total of Permanent personnel fell by 16,650 (26.3 per cent) and Casual personnel fell by 180 (57.1 per cent). Overall MOD Main Industrial and Non-industrial personnel fell by 16,830 personnel (26.5 per cent) across the VERS period. RFA totals fell by 430 personnel (18.6 per cent) across the same period.

Table 14.6b Civilian personnel by budgetary area and grade equivalent, at 1 April each year
Civilian personnel numbers have declined by 30.1 per cent since April 2010, falling from 73,320 to 51,250 at 1 April 2015. There has been a larger proportionate reduction in Industrial personnel compared with Non Industrial personnel (34.5 percent and 24.8 per cent fall at 1 April 2015 compared with 1 April 2010). The reductions in strength are a result of the Strategic Defence and Security Review (SDSR) which introduced two Voluntary Early Release Schemes (VERS) covering exits in 2011-12 and 2012-14. Personnel reductions under the SDSR are set to continue until 2020 from the baseline start point of April 2010. It is not possible to directly compare personnel numbers in Head Office and Corporate Support (formally Centre TLB), and Joint Forces Command (formally Chief of Joint Operations) as these are new and separate organisations.

Non Industrial personnel have declined since April 2010 from 52,570 to 39,540 at 1 April 2015 a reduction of 13,030 personnel (24.8 per cent) over this period. The largest falls have been in Land Command 4,480 personnel (37.8 per cent) and Air Command 2,050 personnel (35.3 per cent) who have had consistent declines in Pay Band D and below since 2010, leading to a 37.6 per cent decrease at these grades from 2010 to 2015.

Table 14.7a Land holdings by country and whether owned, leased or with legal rights, at 1 April each year
At 1st April 2014, the MOD owned 227,300 hectares of land and foreshore (either freehold or leasehold), and held rights over a further 222,000 hectares. In total, this is about 1.8% of the UK land mass.

Since 2013, there has been a decrease in the freehold and leasehold figure by 700 hectares, or 0.3%. This decrease is in accordance with the trends in the estate over recent years as the Department seeks to divest itself of properties that are surplus to requirements.

England accounts for the largest portion of land owned or with rights held, at 259,400 hectares (or 58% of the MOD total), a decrease of 2,100 hectares, or 0.8%, since 2013

Table 14.7b Service Family Accommodation in the United Kingdom, at 31 March each year
At 31 March 2014 there were 49,400 Service Family Accommodation (SFA) properties in the UK, which is broadly unchanged over the past year.

9,300 properties are currently vacant (19% of the total), a further increase from the recent low of 6,000 properties (12%) in 2011. The increase in the vacancy rate since 2011 can be partly explained by the Armed Forces Redundancy Program, the Army Basing Strategy and development of the new MOD Footprint Strategy, which have resulted in some SFA, previously earmarked for disposal, being retained.

Table 14.8a Location of Service and civilian personnel in the United Kingdom, at 1 April each year
The strength of UK-based civilian personnel has reduced from 53,050 in 2013 to 51,610 in 2014, a decrease of 2.7 per cent. The total strength of MOD service personnel based in Northern Ireland has continued to reduce, falling from 4,030 in 2013 to 3,790 in 2014. Since 2000, the number of Service personnel stationed in Northern Ireland has been reduced from 8,390 to 2,340, whilst the civilian strength has fallen during the same period from 3,250 to 1,450. The South East Region has the largest population of UK Service personnel, with 39,300, although the South West has the largest population of civilians, with 17,040.

Table 14.8b Global locations of Service and civilian personnel, at 1 April each year
At 1 April 2014, 88% of UK Regular Armed Forces and 93% of MOD civilians excluding LEC personnel were stationed in the UK.

The strength of UK Regular Forces stationed in the UK fell by 9,120 (6.1%) between 1 April 2013 and 1 April 2014 from 150,310 to 141,180. Over the same period, the number of UK civilian personnel decreased by 1,440 (2.7%) from 53,050 to 51,610.

The strength of UK Regular Forces stationed overseas decreased from 20,060 to 18,070 (9.9%) between 1 April 2013 and 1 April 2014. Over the same period, the number of MOD civilian personnel based overseas decreased from 10,000 to 8,580 (14.1%).

The number of UK Regular Armed Forces personnel stationed in Germany continued to decrease from 14,840 to 12,960 (12.7%) between 1 April 2013 and 1 April 2014 in line with the announcement made during the Strategic Defence & Security Review (SDSR). Despite this decrease, Germany still has the second largest population of MOD personnel after the UK

Table 14.9a UK regular Armed Forces deaths by Service, Year of occurrence 2005-2014, numbers, age and gender standardised rates
In 2014, there were 68 deaths in the regular Armed Forces. Of these, 12 deaths were in the Naval Service, 40 in the Army and 16 in the RAF. In 2014 the mortality rate for the UK Armed Forces was 42 per 100,000. This was a decrease from the previous year

Table 14.10a UK & Overseas Callouts, Incidents and Persons Moved, 2005 to 2014
Table 14.10a shows the number of incidents, callouts and persons moved each year between 2005 and 2014. Between 2005 and 2009 the number of callouts increased year-on-year. Callout numbers peaked in 2009, and since then the number of callouts fell year-on-year.

14.10b Search and Rescue Helicopters - UK & Overseas Callouts and Persons Moved by Unit
This data focuses on SAR helicopter callouts, excluding Mountain Rescue Teams.
Table 14.10b presents the number of callouts by unit and number of Persons moved by Unit between 2005 and 2014. The unit with the highest number of callouts during 2014 was RAF Valley, with 329, closely followed by HMS Gannet with 299. This is the third year in a row that RAF Valley has had the highest number of callouts in a year, although it has been among the top three units with the highest number of callouts for the past six years. RAF Valley moved the highest number of persons during 2014 with 299, followed by HMS Gannet with 255. For the past five years HMS Gannet and RAF Valley have been the two units with the highest number of persons moved.
RAF Wattisham moved the lowest number of persons of the UK units during 2014, with 84.

14.10c Search and Rescue Helicopters: UK & Overseas Callouts by Assistance Type, 2005 to 2014
14.10c presents callout numbers by assistance type between 2005 and 2014. The assistance type with the largest number of callouts during 2014 was Medrescue with 823 helicopter callouts. Most of the other callout types have very low numbers. The second half of the table shows the number of persons moved by assistance type between 2005 and 2014. In 2014, most number of persons moved were for Medrescue, with a similar proportion to recent years.

14.10d Strength of United Kingdom Medical Staff
The figures shown in 14.10d are for regular personnel only and therefore do not represent the strength of either Reserve or veterinarian personnel.

14.11 Number of vessels boarded by the Royal Navy Fishery Protection Squadron within British fishing limits and convictions arising from these boardings each financial year

This table shows the activities of the Royal Navy Fishery Protection Squadron operating within British fishery limits under contract to the Marine Maritime Organisation (MMO). Boardings carried out by vessels of the Scottish Executive Environment Directorate and the Department of Agriculture and Rural Development for Northern Ireland are not included. The data in this Table are outside the scope of National Statistics since they have not been put forward for assessment by the UK Statistics Authority.

Convictions arising from Royal Navy boardings are convictions of infringements detected by the Royal Navy Fishery Protection vessels in that year operating under contract to DEFRA. Figures may change retrospectively as some cases may not be heard in court until a year or more after the initial Royal Navy boarding.

in financial year 08/09, the Marine and Fisheries Agency introduced the Fisheries Administration Penalty (FAP). This has streamlined the penalty process, and has removed the necessity for most of the crews of vessels that would previously have been sent to Court from actually having to attend Court, where they would probably have been convicted. Convictions from 2008/09 onwards are based on the number of offences addressed by the Courts that resulted in a Court conviction, not the number of fishing vessel crews that attended Court. That is, the same fishing vessel crew could be required to attend Court for one or more offences to be heard and each offence would count separately.

From April 2013, an agreement that FPS ships would no longer be exclusively tasked with Marine Enforcement came into effect, meaning there would be less less time available for boardings.

In 2013/14 575 vessels were boarded by the Royal Navy Fisheries Protection Squadron, the lowest figure in the last six years. This had resulted in 17 court convictions by the time the information was available.

14.1 Defence Expenditure by Commodity Block

Inclusive of non-recoverable VAT at Current Prices (£ million)

	Outturn 2011/12	Outturn 2012/13	Outturn 2013/14
Defence Spending	**37 169**	**34 260**	**34 559**
Departmental Expenditure Limits (DEL)	**46 994**	**43 718**	**44 020**
Cash Resource DEL	**37 980**	**35 874**	**36 448**
Personnel Costs	12 846	11 921	11 473
of which: Service Personnel Costs [2]	10 101	9 598	9 156
Civilian Personnel Costs [3]	2 745	2 323	2 318
Infrastructure Costs[4]	4 580	4 594	4 707
Inventory Consumption[5]	2 535	2 312	2 161
Equipment Support Costs[6]	6 256	5 588	6 411
Other Costs & Services[7]	1 850	1 923	2 027
Receipts & Other Income[8]	-1 327	-1 277	-1 196
Depreciation & Impairment[9]	9 825	9 458	9 462
Cash Release of Provisions[10]	348	239	178
Research & Development Costs[11]	833	944	988
Conflict Pool	46	44	50
Arm's Length Bodies[1,12]	187	127	187
Capital DEL[13]	**9 014**	**7 843**	**7 572**
Single Use Military Equipment[14]	5 284	4 768	4 528
Other (Fiscal)[15]	3 883	3 141	3 091
Asset/Estate Disposal Costs	- 150	- 64	- 44
New Loans and Loan Repayments	- 5	- 6	- 6
Arm's Length Bodies	2	3	3
Annually Managed Expenditure (AME)	**957**	**1 831**	**835**
Resource AME	**967**	**1 867**	**963**
Depreciation & Impairment	510	1 062	- 208
Provisions	- 460	318	148
Cash Release of Provisions	- 345	- 239	- 203
Movement on Fair Value of Financial Instruments	347	- 183	368
War Pensions Benefits	916	908	859
Capital AME	**- 10**	**- 35**	**- 129**
Provision Costs (Release)	- 10	- 35	- 129

Source: Defence Economics (Defence Expenditure Analysis) and Defence Resources

1. From 2014/15 a small amount of Depreciation (£16m), from the Arm's Length Bodies Resource DEL total, has been included in the calculation of Defence Spending.
2. Military officers and other ranks pay and other allowances; SCAPE; Employer's National Insurance Contributions (ERNIC).
3. Civilian pay and other allowances; pension contributions; Employer's National Insurance Contributions (ERNIC).
4. Property management; service charges; IT & communications costs; utilities costs.
5. Munitions; stores; fuel (marine & aviation); clothing; other materials consumed e.g. stationary, sundries, general stores etc.
6. Equipment support costs, including leases & hire charges for plant, machinery and transport.
7. Travel & subsistence; professional services & fees; training.
8. Receipts from various sources; costs recoveries; dividends; interest.
9. Depreciation & impairments on Non-Current Assets (Property, SUME, dual purpose).
10. Nuclear and non nuclear provisions e.g. staff redundancies, legal costs, environmental, etc.
11. Research and Development expenditure is incurred mainly for the future benefit of the Department. Such expenditure is primarily incurred on the development of new Single Use Military Equipment (SUME) and on the improvement of the effectiveness and capability of existing SUME.
12. Council of Reserve Forces and Cadet Associations; Royal Hospital Chelsea; National Army Museum; RAF Museum; National Museum of the Royal Navy; Commonwealth War Graves Commission; From 2014/15 includes the Single Source Regulations Office.
13. Expenditure on the acquisition of Non-Current Assets.
14. Single Use Military Equipment (SUME) are assets which only have a military use, such as tanks and fighter aircraft. Dual use items i.e. those that also have a civilian use are recorded under the other category.
15. Expenditure on Property, Plant and dual use military equipment that could be used by civilian organisations for the production of goods and services.

14.2 Intake[1] to UK Regular Forces [2] by sex, trained and untrained

| | Financial Year 2011/12 | Financial Year 2012/13 | 12-Months Ending: | | | | 1 Apr 2014 to 31 Dec 2014 |
			2014 31 Mar	2014 30 Jun	2014 30 Sep	2014 31 Dec	
ALL SERVICES	**14 800**	**14 370**	**11 880**	**11 720**	**12 040**	**12 340**	**8 880**
Percentage female	*8.7%*	*8.4%*	*9.6%*	*10.0%*	*10.1%*	*10.4%*	*11.0%*
Officers	**1 070**	**1 060**	**1 070**	**1 090**	**1 110**	**1 140**	**840**
of which female	180	170	160	170	170	160	130
Percentage female	*16.8%*	*16.4%*	*15.2%*	*15.3%*	*15.1%*	*14.3%*	*15.1%*
Other Ranks	**13 730**	**13 310**	**10 820**	**10 640**	**10 940**	**11 200**	**8 040**
of which female	1 110	1 030	980	1 010	1 050	1 120	850
Percentage female	*8.1%*	*7.7%*	*9.1%*	*9.5%*	*9.6%*	*10.0%*	*10.5%*
RN/RM	**2 220**	**2 770**	**3 170**	**3 080**	**2 990**	**3 060**	**2 130**
Percentage female	*8.3%*	*7.3%*	*8.0%*	*8.4%*	*9.1%*	*9.6%*	*10.2%*
Officers	**280**	**280**	**290**	**300**	**310**	**350**	**280**
of which female	40	40	40	40	30	40	40
Percentage female	*13.5%*	*12.5%*	*12.2%*	*12.1%*	*10.6%*	*11.8%*	*12.3%*
Other Ranks	**1 940**	**2 490**	**2 890**	**2 780**	**2 680**	**2 720**	**1 850**
of which female	150	170	220	220	240	250	180
Percentage female	*7.5%*	*6.7%*	*7.5%*	*8.0%*	*8.9%*	*9.4%*	*9.9%*
ARMY	**11 190**	**10 300**	**7 020**	**6 840**	**7 230**	**7 380**	**5 340**
Percentage female	*8.3%*	*8.1%*	*9.3%*	*9.6%*	*9.2%*	*9.8%*	*10.1%*
Officers	**710**	**640**	**580**	**570**	**550**	**540**	**360**
of which female	110	100	80	80	80	80	60
Percentage female	*16.0%*	*15.3%*	*13.9%*	*13.6%*	*14.7%*	*14.6%*	*15.9%*
Other Ranks	**10 480**	**9 660**	**6 440**	**6 280**	**6 680**	**6 840**	**4 980**
of which female	810	740	580	580	580	640	480
Percentage female	*7.7%*	*7.6%*	*8.9%*	*9.3%*	*8.7%*	*9.4%*	*9.7%*
ROYAL AIR FORCE	**1 390**	**1 310**	**1 690**	**1 800**	**1 830**	**1 900**	**1 410**
Percentage female	*13.1%*	*12.9%*	*13.8%*	*14.3%*	*15.4%*	*14.1%*	*15.2%*
Officers	**80**	**140**	**200**	**210**	**240**	**260**	**200**
of which female	30	40	50	50	50	40	30
Percentage female	*36.3%*	*29.7%*	*23.4%*	*24.4%*	*21.6%*	*17.3%*	*17.4%*
Other Ranks	**1 310**	**1 170**	**1 490**	**1 580**	**1 590**	**1 640**	**1 210**
of which female	150	130	190	200	230	220	180
Percentage female	*11.7%*	*10.9%*	*12.5%*	*12.9%*	*14.4%*	*13.6%*	*14.8%*

Source: Defence Statistics (Tri-Service)

1. Figures show intake to UK Regular Forces, both trained and untrained, which comprises new entrants, re-entrants, direct trained entrants (including professionally qualified Officers), intake to the Army from the Gurkhas and intake from the reserves. They exclude all movements within the Regular Forces; including flows from untrained to trained strength, transfers between Services and flows from Rank to Officer due to

2. UK Regular Forces comprises trained and untrained Full-time personnel but does not include Gurkhas, FTRS personnel and reservists.

Percentages are calculated from unrounded data.

Information showing intake to the UK Regular Forces by Service can be seen on a monthly basis in Table 3 of the UK Armed Forces Monthly Report which can be found at www.gov.uk/government/collections/uk-armed-forces-monthly-manning-statistics-index

14.3a Number of vessels in the Royal Navy and Royal Fleet Auxiliary, and squadrons in the Fleet Air Arm, at 1 April each year

These figures show overall unit numbers only; they do not reflect the level of readiness at which each unit is held, which changes throughout the year. Readiness refers to the length of time it would take for a vessel to be ready for deployment.

This table is a National Statistic.

		2000	2008	2009	2010	2011	2012	2013	2014
Royal Navy submarines	**Total**	**16**	**13**	**12**	**11**	**11**	**11**	**11**	**11**
Of which:									
Trident / Polaris	Vessels	4	4	4	4	4	4	4	4
Fleet	Vessels	12	9	8 [2]	7 [3]	7	7	7 [4,5]	7
Royal Navy ships	**Total**	**89**	**74**	**73**	**71**	**67**	**65**	**66**	**65**
Of which:									
Aircraft Carriers	Vessels	3	2	2	2	- [6,7]	-	-	-
Landing Platform Docks / Helicopter	Vessels	3	3	3	3	4 [7]	4	4	4
Destroyers	Vessels	11	8	7 [8]	6 [9]	6 [10]	5 [11]	6	6
Frigates	Vessels	21	17	17	17	15 [12]	13 [13]	13	13
Mine countermeasures vessels	Vessels	21	16	16	16	15 [14]	15	15	15
Patrol ships and craft	Vessels	23	22 [15]	22	22	22	22	22	22
Survey ships	Vessels	6	5	5	4 [16]	4	4	4	4
Ice patrol ships	Vessels	1	1	1	1 [17]	1 [17]	2 [18]	2 [18]	1 #
Royal Fleet Auxiliary Service	**Total**	**22**	**18**	**16**	**16**	**14**	**13**	**13**	**13**
Of which:									
Tankers	Vessels	9 [r]	6 [r,19]	6	6	6 [r,22]	5	5	5
Fleet Replenishment Ships	Vessels	- [r]	2	2 [r,20]	2 [r,21]	1 [r]	1 [r]	1 [r]	1
Solid Support Ships	Vessels	4	4	2 [20]	2	2	2	2	2
Primary Casualty Receiving Ship[23]	Vessels	1	1	1	1	1	1	1	1
Landing Ships	Vessels	5	4 [24,25]	4	4	3 [26]	3	3	3
Forward Repair Ships	Vessels	1	1	1	1	1	1	1	1
Roll-on Roll-off vessels[27]	Vessels	2	- [r]	- [r]	- [r]	- [r]	- [r]	- [r]	-
Royal Marines									
RM Commando	Commando	3	3	3	3	3	3	3	3
Command Support Group	Commando	1	1	1	1	1	1	1	1
Infantry Battalion	Battalion	-	1 [28]	1	1	1	1	1	- #
Logistic unit	Regiments	1	1	1	1	1	1	1	1
Artillery unit	Regiments	1	1	1	1	1	1	1	1
Engineer unit	Squadrons	1	1	1	1	1	1	1	1
Nuclear Guarding and Fleet Security	Squadrons	1	3	3	4 [29]	4	4	4	3 #
Assault (landing craft)	Squadrons	3	4	4	4	4	4	3 [30]	3
Naval Aircraft									
Fixed Wing Aircraft[32]	Squadrons	1	- [r]	- [r]	- [r]	-	-	-	1
Helicopters[33, 34]	Squadrons	10 [r]	8 [r]	8 [r]	8 [r]	8 [r]	8 [r]	8 [r]	8
Reserve Units									
Royal Navy Reserve Units	Units	..	14	14	14	14	14	14	14
Royal Marine Reserve Units	Units	..	5	5	5	5	5	5	5

Source: MOD Finance & Military Capability

Footnotes located on the next page.

14.3a Number of vessels in the Royal Navy and Royal Fleet Auxiliary, and squadrons in the Fleet Air Arm, at 1 April each year

1. HMS Sovereign was withdrawn from service during the year.
2. HMS Superb was withdrawn from service during the year.
3. HMS Trafalgar and HMS Sceptre were withdrawn from service during the year. HMS Astute undergoing sea trials.
4. HMS Turbulent was withdrawn from service in July 2012.
5. HMS Ambush undergoing sea trials.
6. HMS Ark Royal withdrawn from service.
7. HMS Illustrious converted into a Helicopter Landing Platform.
8. HMS Southampton was withdrawn from service during the year.
9. HMS Exeter and HMS Nottingham were withdrawn from service during the year. HMS Daring entered full service during 2010.
10. HMS Dauntless entered service and HMS Manchester was withdrawn from service during the year.
11. HMS Diamond entered service, HMS Gloucester and HMS Liverpool were decommissioned.
12. HMS Chatham and HMS Campbeltown were withdrawn from service during the year.
13. HMS Cumberland and HMS Cornwall were decommissioned in year.
14. HMS Walney was withdrawn from service during the year.
15. HMS Clyde entered service during the year. HMS Dumbarton Castle was withdrawn from service.
16. HMS Roebuck was withdrawn from service during the year.
17. HMS Endurance non-operational while options for her repair or replacement were considered.
18. HMS Endurance non-operational while options for her repair or replacement were considered. Replaced on an operational basis by HMS Protector.
19. RFA Brambleleaf, RFA Oakleaf and RFA Grey Rover were withdrawn from service during this period.
20. Two vessels re-categorised as Fleet Replenishment ships to reflect their primary role.
21. RFA Fort George was withdrawn from service during the year.
22. RFA Bayleaf was withdrawn from service during the year.
23. Secondary role of Aviation Training Ship.
24. RFA Lyme Bay, Cardigan Bay and Mounts Bay entered service 2005/06. RFA Largs Bay entered service 2006/07.
25. The following were withdrawn from service: RFA Sir Geraint 2002, Sir Percivale 2005, Sir Tristram & Sir Galahad 2006, Sir Bedivere 2007.
26. RFA Largs Bay was sold to Australia in January 2011 as a result of SDSR10.
27. This role ceased for the RFA in 2004 and transferred to Chartered Shipping administered by Defence Supply Chain Operational Movements (DSCOM).
28. 1 Rifles became part of 3 Commando Brigade on 1 April 2008.
29. Fleet Protection Group Royal Marines expanded by one squadron (P Sqn) during Mar-Sep 2010.
30. A Landing Craft Assault Squadron has been disestablished as a result of SDSR10.
31. HMS ENDURANCE now withdrawn from service.
32. Excludes Joint Force Harrier squadrons from 1 April 2000.
33. Excludes Joint Helicopter Command squadrons from 1 October 1999.
34. Excludes all Operational Conversion Units (OCU) / Operational Evaluation Units (OEU) from 1 April 2004. Other Training squadrons have also been excluded.
35. 1 Rifles reverted to an Army Battalion in 2013.
36. P Sqn were disbanded in 2013.

r Some of the figures in this table have been corrected following a review by the MOD Finance and Military Capability branches, due to concerns raised about previously published figures. (1) Historic figures of tankers and fleet replenishment ships have been corrected due to the addition of solid support ships. This provides a clearer picture of vessels in the RFA, as each of these types of vessel has a distinct role. (2) Previous editions of this table incorrectly stated the MOD had a number of roll-on roll-off vessels in the Fleet Air Arm. However, the ownership of these vessels transferred from the RFA in 2004 as discussed in footnote 27. (3) Corrections have been made to the number of Naval aircraft squadrons following clarification of the squadrons excluded from these historic figures (see footnotes 32-34).

14.3b Number of Regiments, Infantry Battalions and Major Headquarters in the Regular Army and Army Reserves[1], at 1 April each year

This table is a National Statistic.

		2000	2008	2009	2010	2011	2012	2013	2014
Combat arms									
Armour									
Regular Army	Regiments	10	10	10	10	10	10	10	10
Army Reserves	Regiments	4	4	4	4	4	4	4	4
Infantry									
Regular Army [2]	Battalions	40	36	36	36	36	36	36	33 [3]
Army Reserves	Battalions	15	14	14	14	14	14	14	14
Home Service Forces	Battalions	7	-	-	-	-	-	-	-
Combat support									
Artillery									
Regular Army [4]	Regiments	15	14	14	14	14	14	13	13
Army Reserves [5]	Regiments	7	7	7	7	7	7	7	7
Engineers									
Regular Army	Regiments	11	11	11	12 [6]	12	14	13 [7]	13
Army Reserves	Regiments	6	6	6	5	5	5	5	5
Signals									
Regular Army	Regiments	11	12	12	12	12	11	11	11
Army Reserves	Regiments	11	11	5 [8]	5	5	5	5	5
Combat service support									
Equipment support									
Regular Army	Battalions	7	7	7	7	7	7	6 [9]	6
Army Reserves	Battalions	4	2 #	2	2	2	2	2	2
Logistics									
Regular Army	Regiments	22	17	17	17	17	17	16 #	14 [12]
Army Reserves	Regiments	17	17	17	17	17	17	17	17 [13]
Medical Regiments / Field Hospitals									
Regular Army	Number	8	8	8	9	9	9	9	9
Army Reserves	Number	15	15	15	15	15	15	15	15
Corps, Division & Brigade HQ									
NATO Corps HQ		1	1	1	1	1	1	1	1
Division / District HQ									
Deployable		2	2	2	2	2	2	2	2
Non-deployable		4	5	5	5	5	5	4 #	4
Brigade HQ [15]									
Deployable		7	7	7	7	7	7	6 #	6
Non-deployable		15	9	9	10	10	10	10	10

Source: Army HQ Plans Directorate

1. Previously known as the Territorial Army.

2. Excludes Special Forces Support Group.

3. 1 R WELSH and 2 R WELSH merged Mar 14; 2 YORKS and 3 YORKS merged 2013; 5 SCOTS regiment reduced to a Public Duties Independent Company Mar 14.

4. Excludes 14th Regiment Royal Artillery. Also excludes 40th Regiment Royal Artillery which was disbanded due to Planning Round 2011.

5. Includes the Honourable Artillery Company.

6. 101 Engr Regt (EOD) was 'regularised' under Op ENTIRETY, in order to support ongoing operations in Afghanistan.

7. 38 Engineer Regiment were disbanded in Planning Round 2011.

8. Restructuring of Royal Electrical and Mechanical Engineers was announced in 2008.

9. 19 Combat Service Support Batallion REME disbanded in January 2013 in Planning Round 2011. 01 Bn & 104 Bn REME form a single Regular Force Support Battalion.

10. As a result of Planning Round 2009, six R Signals Regiments (V) were removed from the force structure.

11. 8 Regiment Royal Logistics Corps disbanded in Planning Round 2011.

12. 24 Regiment and 12 Logistic Support Regiment removed from ORBAT as at Mar 14.

13. 168 Pioneer Regiment Royal Logistics Corp disbanded Feb 2014, with effect post 1 Apr 2014.

14. HQ 2 DIV, HQ 4 DIV and HQ 5 DIV all disbanded in 12/13; HQ Sp Comd was established in 12/13.

15. Brigade HQ figures do not include Logistics or Specialist Brigades.

16. HQ 19 Lt Brigade were disbanded in Planning Round 2011.

14.3c Number of Squadrons in the Royal Air Force and the Royal Auxiliary Air Force, at 1 April each year

This table excludes Operational Conversion Units, which train qualified aircrew for different aircraft types.
This table is a National Statistic.

		2000	2008	2009	2010	2011	2012	2013	2014
Regular Air Force									
Multi-roled Fast Jet Squadrons [1,2]	Squadrons	17	11	11	10[3]	10[4]	8[5]	9[6]	7[20]
Maritime patrol	Squadrons	3	2	2	2	2	-[7]	-	-
ISTAR (inc Airborne Early Warning)	Squadrons	2	4	4	4	4	5[8]	6[9]	6
Air transport / Air Refuelling	Squadrons	8	8	8	8	7[10]	7	7	6[21]
Search and Rescue	Squadrons	2	2	2	2	2	2	2	2
RAF FP Wg	HQs	..	7	7	8	8	8	8	8
RAF Ground based air defence [11]	Squadrons	*	-	-	-	-	-	-	-
RAF Regiment Field [11]	Squadrons	*	7	7	8	8	8	8	8
RAF Regt (Jt CBRN) [12]	Squadrons	-	1	1	1	1	-	-	-
Defence CBRN Wing [12,25]	HQs	-	-	-	-	-	1	1	1
	Squadrons	-	-	-	-	-	2	2	2
RAF Police Force [13]	HQs	*	*	*	*	*	* ‖[13]	3	3
	Squadrons	*	*	*	*	*	* ‖	9	9
Tactical Provost Wg	HQs	-	1	1	1	1	1 ‖	*	*
	Squadrons	-	1	1	1	1	1 ‖	*	*
Specialist Policing Wg	HQs	-	1	1	1	1	1 ‖	*	*
	Squadrons	-	3	3	3	3	3 ‖	*	*
General Policing Wg	HQs	-	1	1	1	1	1 ‖	*	*
	Squadrons	-	4	4	4	4	4 ‖	*	*
Tactical Communications Wg [14]	Squadrons	*	4	4	4	4	4	4	4
Auxiliary Air Force [25]									
Air Movements	Squadrons	1	1	1	1	1	1	1	1
Aeromedical	Squadrons	2	2	2	2	2	2	2	2
Flight Operations	Squadrons	-	-	-	-	-	1	1	1
General Support	Squadrons	-	-	-	-	-	-	2[15]	3
HQ Augmentation	Squadrons	1	1	1	1	1	1	1[r]	1
Intelligence	Squadrons	2	2	2	2	2	2	2	2
Photographic Interpretation	Squadrons	1	1	1	1	1	1	1	1
Public Relations	Squadrons	1	1	1	1	1	1	1	1
RAuxAF Regt Field	Squadrons	4	3	3	3	3	3	4[16]	5[22]
FP Operations Support	Squadrons	4	4	4	4	4	4	1[17]	-[22]
RAF Police	Squadrons	-	1	1	1	1	1	2[18]	2
RAuxAF Regt CBRN [24]	Squadrons	-	1	1	1	1	1	1	1
A4 - Logs	Squadrons	-	-	-	-	-	-	2[19]	2
Reserve Aircrew - Air Mobility	Squadrons	-	-	- -	-	-	-	1	1
RAF Reserve - Sponsored Reserves									
Meteorological [23]	Units	1	1	1	1	1	1	1	1

Source: MOD Finance & Military Capability

Footnotes continued on the next page.

1. Excludes Joint Force Harrier squadrons. See Table 4.01.07 - Joint units.
2. From 2006, four Air Defence squadrons amalgamated with Strike/Attack, Offensive support and Reconnaissance squadrons to form multi-roled fast jet squadrons. One Reconnaissance squadron was re-roled ISTAR. One squadron was disbanded.
3. 43 Sqn was stood down on 1 July 2009.
4. 6 Sqn (Typhoon) stood up 6 Sep 2010. 111 Sqn (Tornado F3) stood down 22 Mar 2011.
5. 13 Sqn and 14 Sqn (both Tornado GR4) were disbanded on 1 Jun 2011. (See further footnote below on 14 Sqn)
6. 1 Sqn (Typhoon) reformed 15 Sep 2012.
7. 201 Sqn and 120 Sqn were disbanded on 26 May 2011.
8. 14 Sqn was subsequently stood up on 14 October 2011. This unit replaced the flight within 5 Sqn operating the R1 Shadow aircraft.
9. 13 Sqn (MQ9) reformed 26 Oct 2012.
10. 70 Sqn disbanded 10 Sep 2010.
11. Delivery of Ground based air defence has been vested with the Army since 2008. The remaining 2 squadrons were combined on 1 Apr 2008 to provide a 7th Field Sqn (15 Sqn RAF Regt).
12. Defence CBRN Wing was established on 14 Dec 2011 on the disbandment of the Joint CBRN Regiment.
13. RAF Police re-brigaded on 1 Apr 2012 following a Planning Round 2011 option that directed a 15% reduction in manning numbers. The previous definitions of Tactical Provost, Specialist and General Wings are no longer appropriate.
14. TCW has existed as a formed unit since 1969 and is currently subordinate to 90 Signals Unit at RAF Leeming. 90 Signals Unit comprises one HQ and 8 Sqns; 4 x TCW and 4 x Force Generation Wg (FGW); it has existed since 2006. All but 2 Sqns have some form of deployable function.
15. 611 Sqn stood up Oct 2012, 502 Sqn stood up Jan 2013
16. 501 Sqn RAuxAF Ops Spt - Regt staff regenerated into newly created 2624 RAuxAF Regt Sqn at BZN.
17. 501 and 504 RAuxAF Ops Spt Sqns transfer to A4. 603 RAuxAF Sqn transfered to RAFP.
18. Reflects the transfer of 603 Sqn to RAF Police.
19. 501 and 504 RAuxAF Logs Sqns.
20. 12 Sqn and 617 Sqn stood down on 31 March 2014.
21. Number 216 Sqn disbanded March 2014.
22. 609 Sqn now Regt Field previously reported as Operations Support.
23. Previously reported as an Royal Auxillary Air Force squadron.
24. CBRN is also known as: Chemical, Biological, Radiological and Nuclear.
25. Note that this is not a comprehensive list of Auxiliary Air Force squadrons, as for example some units that form part of the Air Combat Service Support Units are not included.

r The 2013 edition of this publication incorrectly stated that there were three HQ Augmentation Squadrons in 2013. The reason for this error is that 2 General Support Squadrons were incorrectly declared as HQ Augmentation Squadrons.

14.3d Number of Regiments and Squadrons in selected Joint Units, at 1 April each year

This table excludes Operational Conversion Units, which train qualified aircrew for different aircraft types.

This table is a National Statistic.

		2008	2009	2010	2011	2012	2013	2014
Joint Units								
Joint Nuclear Biological Chemical	Regiments	1	1	1	1	- [3]	-	-
Special Forces								
Special Air Service	Regiments	1	1	1	1	1	1	1
Special Air Service - Army Reserves	Regiments	2	2	2	2	2	2	2
Special Boat Service	Units[1]	1	1	1	1	1	1	1
Special Forces Support Group Battalion [2]	Battalions	1	1	1	1	1	1	1
Joint Helicopter Command								
Royal Navy Helicopter	Squadrons[4]	4	4	4	4	4	4	4 [14]
Army Aviation [5]	Regiments	5	5	5	5	5	5	5
Army Aviation - Army Reserves	Regiments	2	1 [7]	1	1	1	1	1
Royal Air Force Helicopter	Squadrons[4]	6 [8]	6	6	6	6	6 ͬ	6 [15]
Royal Auxiliary Air Force [9]	Squadrons[4]	1	1	1	1	1	1	1
Joint Special Forces Air Wing	Units	1	1	1	1	1	1	1
Joint Force Harrier								
Royal Navy	Squadrons[4]	2	2	1 #	- #	-	-	-
Royal Air Force	Squadrons[4]	2	2	1 #	- #	-	-	-

Source: MOD Finance & Military Capability

1. The units for the Special Boat Service have been changed from Squadrons to Units so that the same level of formation is given for all Special Forces.

2. The Special Forces Support Group was formed as a result of the Ministerial Announcement on 16 Dec 2004 as part of The Future Army Structure. It is a Tri-Service Unit based on 1 PARA, to provide specialist support to Special Forces.

3. The JNBC regiment disbanded on the formation of the Defence CBRN Wing on 14 December 2011.

4. The term "squadron" has different meanings among the three Services: see the Glossary for details.

5. These figures exclude the School of Army Aviation, 667 (D&T) Sqn and 657 Sqn and three independent Army Air Corps flights (7, 25 and 29 Flts).

6. 6 Regt AAC(V) formed on 1 April 2007.

7. 7 Regt AAC(V) was disbanded 31 March 2009.

8. Reflects the standing up of 78 Sqn RAF to accommodate the endorsed increase in Merlin Mk3 crews and aircraft.

9. No 606 (Chiltern) Squadron provides a pool of trained personnel to provide combat service support to the Support Helicopter Force in training and on operations in times of crisis and war.

10. On the reduction in the Joint Force Harrier force from 1 April 2010, the Fleet Air Arm Strike Wing was counted as 1 Sqn.

11. 800 RNAS was disbanded on 28 January 2011.

12. 20 Sqn was disbanded 31 March 2010.

13. 1 Sqn was disbanded on 28 January 2011.

14. Although Commando Helicopter Force have 4x Sqns, currently the Merlin Sqn are going through transition to Merlin based out of RAF Benson under Command of the RAF until they move to Yeovilton under RN in March 15 and March 16.

15. Merlin Sqns (2x RAF Sqn) currently going through transition to RN.

r The 2013 edition of this publication incorrectly stated that there were 7 RAF Helicopter squadrons in 2013.

14.4 Outflow[1] from UK Regular Forces[2], trained and untrained

	Financial Year 2011/12	Financial Year 2012/13	12-Months Ending: 2014 31 Mar	2014 30 Jun	2014 30 Sep	2014 31 Dec	1 Apr 2013 to 31 Dec 2013	1 Apr 2014 to 31 Dec 2014
ALL SERVICES	**21 370**	**23 520**	**23 000**	**22 350**	**21 920**	**18 820**	**18 470**	**14 290**
Trained	17 650	20 010	20 190	19 740	19 410	16 300	16 320	12 430
Untrained	3 720	3 510	2 800	2 610	2 510	2 520	2 140	1 860
Officers	**2 560**	**3 040**	**2 640**	**2 500**	**2 410**	**2 190**	**2 150**	**1 700**
Trained	2 380	2 680	2 500	2 380	2 300	2 070	2 040	1 610
Untrained	180	360	140	120	110	120	120	90
Other Ranks	**18 810**	**20 480**	**20 350**	**19 850**	**19 510**	**16 630**	**16 320**	**12 600**
Trained	15 280	17 330	17 690	17 370	17 110	14 230	14 290	10 820
Untrained	3 540	3 150	2 660	2 480	2 400	2 410	2 030	1 770
RN/RM	**4 320**	**4 350**	**3 790**	**3 680**	**3 600**	**3 510**	**2 850**	**2 580**
Trained	3 750	3 710	3 070	2 980	2 890	2 830	2 350	2 110
Untrained	570	640	710	700	710	680	500	470
Officers	**570**	**590**	**520**	**490**	**470**	**450**	**410**	**340**
Trained	510	530	460	430	420	400	360	310
Untrained	60	60	60	60	50	50	50	40
Other Ranks	**3 750**	**3 760**	**3 270**	**3 200**	**3 130**	**3 060**	**2 440**	**2 240**
Trained	3 240	3 180	2 620	2 540	2 470	2 430	1 990	1 800
Untrained	500	580	650	650	660	630	460	430
ARMY	**13 200**	**14 890**	**15 740**	**15 450**	**15 100**	**12 090**	**12 910**	**9 270**
Trained	10 310	12 370	13 800	13 690	13 470	10 440	11 380	8 030
Untrained	2 900	2 520	1 940	1 760	1 630	1 650	1 530	1 240
Officers	**1 240**	**1 460**	**1 480**	**1 430**	**1 360**	**1 150**	**1 230**	**900**
Trained	1 190	1 380	1 420	1 380	1 320	1 110	1 180	860
Untrained	60	90	60	50	40	40	50	40
Other Ranks	**11 960**	**13 430**	**14 250**	**14 020**	**13 740**	**10 940**	**11 680**	**8 370**
Trained	9 120	10 990	12 370	12 310	12 150	9 340	10 200	7 160
Untrained	2 840	2 440	1 880	1 710	1 590	1 610	1 480	1 210
ROYAL AIR FORCE	**3 850**	**4 280**	**3 480**	**3 220**	**3 220**	**3 210**	**2 700**	**2 440**
Trained	3 590	3 940	3 320	3 070	3 050	3 020	2 590	2 290
Untrained	260	350	150	140	170	190	110	150
Officers	**740**	**990**	**640**	**580**	**580**	**590**	**510**	**450**
Trained	680	780	620	560	560	560	490	440
Untrained	60	210	20	20	20	20	20	20
Other Ranks	**3 110**	**3 300**	**2 830**	**2 630**	**2 640**	**2 630**	**2 190**	**1 990**
Trained	2 910	3 160	2 700	2 510	2 490	2 460	2 100	1 860
Untrained	200	140	130	120	150	170	100	130

Source: Defence Statistics (Tri-Service)

1. Figures show outflow from UK Regular Forces, both trained and untrained, including personnel leaving the Services, deaths and recalled reservists on release. They do not include promotion from Ranks to Officers or flows between Services and are not comparable with gains to trained strength figures in Table 10 which include promotion from Ranks to Officers.

2. UK Regular Forces comprises trained and untrained Full-time personnel but does not include Gurkhas, FTRS personnel and reservists.

Information showing outflow from the UK Regular Forces by Service can be seen on a monthly basis in Table 3 of the UK Armed Forces Monthly Personnel Report which can be found at: www.gov.uk/government/collections/uk-armed-forces-monthly-manning-statistics-index

14.5 Full-Time Trained Strength[1] and Requirement, at 1 April each year

This table is a National Statistic.

Number of personnel (unless stated otherwise)

	2000	2008	2009	2010	2011	2012	2013	2014
All Services								
Requirement	198 160	179 270	178 860	178 750	179 250	174 840	162 940	159 640
Strength[2]	190 270	173 530	174 170	177 890	176 860	170 010	160 710	150 890
Surplus/Deficit	-7 880	-5 740	-4 690	- 860	-2 390	-4 830	-2 230	-8 750
Surplus/Deficit as % of requirement	-4.0	-3.2	-2.6	-0.5	-1.3	-2.8	-1.4	-5.5
By Service:								
RN/RM								
Requirement	39 860	36 260	35 760	35 790	35 700	34 800	30 530	30 340
Strength[2]	38 880	35 050	35 020	35 500	35 420	33 290	31 420	30 510
Surplus/Deficit	- 990	-1 210	- 740	- 290	- 280	-1 510	890	170
Surplus/Deficit as % of requirement	-2.5	-3.3	-2.1	-0.8	-0.8	-4.3	2.9	0.6
Army								
Requirement	106 400	101 800	101 790	102 160	102 210	101 210	96 790	94 100
Strength[2]	100 190	98 070	99 510	102 260	101 340	98 600	93 940	87 180
Surplus/Deficit	-6 210	-3 730	-2 280	100	- 870	-2 610	-2 850	-6 930
Surplus/Deficit as % of requirement	-5.8	-3.7	-2.2	0.1	-0.8	-2.6	-2.9	-7.4
Royal Air Force								
Requirement	51 900	41 210	41 310	40 800	41 340	38 830	35 620	35 200
Strength[2]	51 210	40 400	39 640	40 130	40 090	38 120	35 350	33 210
Surplus/Deficit	- 690	- 800	-1 670	- 670	-1 250	- 700	- 270	-1 990
Surplus/Deficit as % of requirement	-1.3	-1.9	-4.1	-1.7	-3.0	-1.8	-0.8	-5.7

Source: Defence Statistics (Tri-Service)

1. The Full-Time Trained Strength of the UK Armed Forces is defined as comprising of trained UK Regular Forces, trained Gurkhas and elements of the FTRS (Full Time Reserve Service) personnel. It does not include mobilised reservists.
2. From 1 April 2010 some elements of the FTRS are excluded. For a full description of FTRS please refer to the Glossary of Terms and Abbreviations at the end of the Tri-Service Personnel Bulletin (see link below).

14.6a Civilian personnel[1], at 1 April each year

FTE

	2010	2011	2012	2013	2014	2015
Civilian Level 0[1]	**85 850**	**83 060** [e]	**71 010** [e]	**65 400**	**62 500**	**58 160**
Civilian Level 1[1]	**65 920**	**63 130**	**54 510**	**49 980**	**48 400**	**48 650**
Civilian Level 1 - Permanent	**63 270**	**60 660**	**52 480**	**47 950**	**46 470**	**46 620**
Non-industrial	52 350	50 150	43 890	40 300	38 940	39 410
Industrial	10 930	10 510	8 590	7 650	7 530	7 210
Civilian Level 1 - Casual[2]	**320**	**120**	**30**	**120**	**120**	**140**
Non-industrial	230	50	20	110	100	130
Industrial	90	70	10	10	10	10
Civilian Level 1 - RFA[3]	**2 330**	**2 360**	**2 000**	**1 900**	**1 820**	**1 890**
Trading Funds[4]	**9 730**	**9 350**	**7 110**	**7 170**	**7 110**	**4 490**
Permanent	9 620	9 290	7 000	7 050	7 000	4 410
Casual[2]	110	60	110	120	110	90
Locally Engaged Civilians	**10 200**	**10 580** [e]	**9 390** [e]	**8 250**	**6 990**	**5 020**

Source: Defence Statistics (Civilian)

1. Civilian Level 0 and Level 1 are defined in the Glossary.
2. Casual staff are usually engaged for less than 12 months.
3. RFA personnel are assumed to be permanent.
4. At 1 October 2011 the Meteorological Office transferred to the Department for Business Innovation and Skills (1,800 personnel - FTE). As of 1 April 2015 DSG were privatised transferring to Babcock affecting approximately 2,400 personnel.

14.6b Civilian personnel[1] by Top Level Budget and grade equivalent [2], at 1 April each year

FTE

Grade	2010	2011	2012	2013	2014	2015
Civilian Personnel [1]	**73 320**	**70 130**	**59 630**	**55 240**	**53 690**	**51 250**
Non Industrial	**52 570**	**50 200**	**43 910**	**40 410**	**39 040**	**39 540**
of which						
Navy Command	**1 860**	**1 800**	**1 530**	**1 590**	**2 010**	**2 070**
Pay Band C and above	540	530	500	540	760	810
Pay Band D and below	1 320	1 250	1 020	1 030	1 230	1 230
Other non-industrial [3]	10	10	10	10	20	20
Land Command	**11 860**	**10 690**	**9 440**	**7 960**	**7 510**	**7 380**
Pay Band C and above	3 450	3 170	2 950	2 590	2 350	2 360
Pay Band D and below	8 270	7 530	6 490	5 360	5 150	5 020
Other non-industrial [3]	150	-	-	10	10	-
Air Command	**5 810**	**5 670**	**4 770**	**4 050**	**3 830**	**3 760**
Pay Band C and above	1 150	1 180	1 060	890	850	850
Pay Band D and below	4 660	4 480	3 710	3 160	2 980	2 910
Other non-industrial[3]	-	-	-	-	-	-
Centre TLB	**16 110**	**15 360**	..	..	..	..
Pay Band C and above	4 120	4 180	..	..	..	..
Pay Band D and below	11 890	11 180	..	..	..	..
Other non-industrial [3]	100	-	..	..	..	..
Head Office & Corporate Services	..	..	**10 970**	**7 230**	**7 230**	**7 610**
Pay Band C and above	..	..	2 680	2 510	2 700	2 860
Pay Band D and below	..	..	8 300	4 720	4 530	4 740
Other non-industrial [3]	..	..	-	-	-	10
Chief of Joint Operations	**290**	**260**	..	..	..	..
Pay Band C and above	160	150	..	..	..	..
Pay Band D and below	120	110	..	..	..	..
Other non-industrial [3]	-	-	..	..	..	..
Joint Forces Command	..	..	**2 680**	**3 570**	**5 210**	**5 510**
Pay Band C and above	..	..	1 210	1 660	2 860	3 030
Pay Band D and below	..	..	1 450	1 890	2 340	2 450
Other non-industrial[3]	..	..	20	10	10	20
Defence Equipment & Support	**13 840**	**13 570**	**12 170**	**11 000**	**8 940**	**9 130**
Pay Band C and above	8 410	8 610	7 860	7 430	6 110	6 400
Pay Band D and below	5 410	4 950	4 300	3 570	2 800	2 730
Other non-industrial [3]	20	-	10	-	20	-
Defence Infrastructure Organisation	**2 700**	**2 850**	**2 350**	**5 010**	**4 240**	**4 060**
Pay Band C and above	1 500	1 560	1 360	1 380	1 470	1 480
Pay Band D and below	1 200	1 290	990	3 630	2 770	2 570
Other non-industrial [3]	-	-	-	-	-	10
Unknown[4]	**100**	**10**	**10**	**20**	**60**	**20**
Pay Band C and above	60	-	-	10	40	10
Pay Band D and below	30	10	10	10	20	-
Other non-industrial [3]	10	-	-	-	-	-

14.6b Civilian personnel[1] by Top Level Budget and grade equivalent[2], at 1 April each year

FTE

Grade	2010	2011	2012	2013	2014	2015
Industrial	**11 020**	**10 580**	**8 600**	**7 660**	**7 540**	**7 220**
Navy Command	570	540	470	440	480	460
Land Command	4 620	4 230	3 720	3 460	3 440	3 310
Air Command	2 850	2 760	1 770	1 500	1 410	1 280
Centre TLB	540	510	-	-	-	-
Head Office & Corporate Services	-	-	80	70	70	230
Chief of Joint Operations	-	-	-	-	-	-
Joint Forces Command	-	-	380	350	360	360
Defence Equipment & Support	2 310	2 190	1 920	1 550	1 510	1 480
Defence Infrastructure Organisation	130	340	260	280	280	110
Unknown	-	-	..	..	..	..
Trading Funds	**9 730**	**9 350**	**7 110**	**7 170**	**7 110**	**4 490**
Defence Science & Technology Laboratory	3 700	3 640	3 640	3 720	3 690	3 550
Defence Support Group [5]	3 230	2 960	2 490	2 420	2 400	*
Hydrographic Office	970	960	980	1 030	1 020	940
Met Office [5]	1 840	1 800	*	*	*	*

Source: Defence Statistics (Civilian)

1. Civilian personnel is defined as personnel employed in MOD Main Core TLBs and Trading Funds. Royal Fleet Auxiliary and Locally engaged civilians are excluded from all data in this table.
2. Grade equivalent is shown in terms of the broader banding structure and is based on paid grade.
3. Includes industrial personnel on temporary promotion to non-industrial grades and personnel for whom no grade information is available.
4. Personnel for whom no Top Level Budget (TLB) information is available are included in this section of the table.
5. In October 2011 responsibility for management of the Meteorological Office personnel (1,800) transferred to Department for Business, Innovation and Skills. As of 1 April 2015 DSG were privatised transferring to Babcock affecting approximately 2,400 personnel.

14.7a Land holdings by type of use and whether owned, leased or with legal rights, at 1 April each year

This table is a National Statistic.

Thousand hectares

	2000	2008	2009 [1]	2010 [1]	2011 [2,3]	2012	2013	2014 [4]
Total land & foreshore holdings and Rights held [5]	**363.3**	**373.4**	**372.0**	**371.0 ‖**	**435.3**	**434.1**	**432.9 ‖**	**449.3**
Land and foreshore holdings	238.5	240.3	239.0	238.0 ‖	230.4	229.1	228.0	227.3
Freehold	219.9	220.0	219.0	218.0 ‖	209.8	208.8	207.7	207.0
Leasehold	18.6	20.3	20.0	20.0 ‖	20.6	20.3	20.3	20.3
Rights held [5]	124.8	133.1	133.0	133.0 ‖	204.9	204.9	204.9 ‖	222.0
Of which:								
Naval Service	**39.3**	**43.6**	**44.0**	**44.0 ‖**	**2.3**	**2.3**	**2.3**	**2.3**
Land and foreshore holdings	13.1	17.4	18.0	18.0 ‖	2.2	2.3	2.3	2.2
Freehold	10.7	14.9	15.0	15.0 ‖	2.1	2.1	2.1	2.0
Leasehold	2.4	2.5	3.0	3.0 ‖	0.1	0.2	0.2	0.2
Rights held [5]	26.2	26.2	26.0	26.0 ‖	0.1	0.1	0.1	0.1
Army	**243.9**	**245.2**	**245.0**	**245.0 ‖**	**15.1**	**15.1**	**14.7**	**14.6**
Land and foreshore holdings	155.9	157.1	157.0	157.0 ‖	14.7	14.6	14.3	14.2
Freehold	152.1	151.4	151.0	151.0 ‖	14.2	14.1	13.8	13.7
Leasehold	3.8	5.7	6.0	6.0 ‖	0.5	0.5	0.5	0.5
Rights held [5]	88.0	88.1	88.0	88.0 ‖	0.5	0.5	0.4	0.4
Royal Air Force	**48.6**	**46.6**	**46.0**	**45.0 ‖**	**21.7**	**21.7**	**21.7**	**21.4**
Land and foreshore holdings	39.3	37.3	37.0	36.0 ‖	21.7	21.6	21.6	21.4
Freehold	30.9	29.0	28.0	28.0 ‖	17.8	17.7	17.7	17.5
Leasehold	8.4	8.3	8.0	8.0 ‖	3.9	3.9	3.9	3.9
Rights held [5]	9.3	9.3	9.0	9.0 ‖	-	-	-	-
The Centre [6]	**27.4**	**34.5**	**34.0**	**34.0 ‖**	**392.8**	**391.8**	**391.1 ‖**	**406.6**
Land and foreshore holdings	26.1	25.0	25.0	25.0 ‖	188.6	187.4	186.8	185.2
Freehold	25.1	24.0	24.0	24.0 ‖	172.7	171.9	171.2	169.7
Leasehold	1.0	1.0	1.0	1.0 ‖	15.9	15.5	15.6	15.5
Rights held [5]	1.3	9.5	10.0	10.0 ‖	204.3	204.4	204.4 ‖	221.4
Other [7]	**4.1**	**3.8**	**4.0**	**4.0 ‖**	**3.3**	**3.2**	**3.1**	**4.3**
Land and foreshore holdings	4.1	3.8	4.0	4.0 ‖	3.3	3.1	3.1	4.3
Freehold	1.0	0.8	1.0	1.0 ‖	3.2	3.0	3.0	4.1
Leasehold	3.1	3.0	3.0	3.0 ‖	0.1	0.1	0.1	0.2
Rights held [5]	-	-	-	- ‖	-	-	-	-

Source: MOD Defence Infrastructure Organisation (DIO)

1. The figures presented for years 2009 and 2010 were rounded to the nearest thousand hectares.
2. Data from 2011 has been compiled using a new spatial dataset which allows for greater accuracy in the measurement of the estate. Because of this new dataset, comparable figures for earlier years are not available. Figures have been rounded to the nearest hundred hectares.
3. The large changes in the allocations to parent service areas between 2010 and 2011 reflect the outcome of the Defence Estate Training Review, with the Training Estate now transferred to the Defence Infrastructure Organisation, part of the Centre.
4. Part of the Kinlochleven Training Area in Scotland, over which MOD holds rights, is now included, having been omitted from figures previously reported. It was highlighted by data quality improvement work as a result of the introduction of the DIO's Infrastructure Management System.
5. Rights held are land and foreshore that are not owned by, or leased to MOD, but over which the Department has limited rights under grants and rights.
6. The Centre includes Defence Equipment & Support, Defence Infrastructure Organisation (including former Defence Training Estate (hence marked increase in values from 2011) and Service family quarters leased from Annington Property Ltd.) and Centre TLBs.
7. Includes Permanent Joint Headquarters and Trading Funds.

Further Information about these statistics can be found in the 2014 edition of Statistical Bulletin 6.01 Land Holdings:
https://www.gov.uk/government/collections/mod-land-holdings-bulletin-index

Further information about the quality of data and methods used in the production of these statistics, along with details of their intended use can be found in the Background Quality Report:
https://www.gov.uk/government/statistics/mod-land-holdings-bulletin-2014

14.7b Service Family Accommodation in the United Kingdom at 31 March each year

This table is a National Statistic.

Thousands of dwellings

	2000	2008	2009	2010	2011	2012	2013	2014
Permanent holdings	**64.8**	**51.2**	**49.9**	**49.1**	**49.1**	**49.0**	**49.4**	**49.4**
By country:								
England & Wales	55.9	45.2	44.9	44.1	44.2	44.0	44.5	44.5
Scotland	5.7	3.6	3.2	3.2	3.2	3.3	3.3	3.3
Northern Ireland	3.2	2.4	1.8	1.8	1.7	1.7	1.6	1.6
Vacant properties	**14.7**	**10.5**	**8.4**	**7.3**	**6.0**	**6.5**	**7.7**	**9.3**
By country:								
England & Wales	12.6	8.1	7.3	6.1	5.0	5.0	6.1	7.5
Scotland	1.7	0.9	0.6	0.6	0.5	0.7	0.7	0.8
Northern Ireland	0.4	1.5	0.5	0.6	0.5	0.8	0.9	1.0
Vacant properties as a percentage of all dwellings	*23*	*21*	*17*	*15*	*12*	*13*	*16*	*19*
By country:								
England & Wales	*23*	*18*	*16*	*14*	*11*	*11*	*14*	*17*
Scotland	*30*	*25*	*19*	*18*	*16*	*24*	*21*	*23*
Northern Ireland	*13*	*63*	*28*	*34*	*29*	*40*	*56*	*63*

Source: MOD Defence Infrastructure Organisation

14.8a Location of Service and civilian personnel[1,2] in the United Kingdom, at 1 April each year

FTE

	2000 [3]	2008	2009	2010	2011	2012	2013	2014
United Kingdom	**267 700**	**231 350**	**233 290**	**236 710**	**229 400**	**214 190**	**203 360**	**192 800**
Service	170 300	158 450	162 670	166 100	161 790	156 970	150 310	141 180
Civilian	97 410	72 900	70 620	70 610	67 610	57 220	53 050	51 610
England	**222 560**	**202 710**	**204 400**	**207 890**	**201 320**	**188 810**	**180 080**	**170 680**
Service	143 040	140 120	143 540	146 950	142 860	139 260	133 810	125 640
Civilian	79 520	62 590	60 860	60 940	58 450	49 560	46 270	45 040
Wales	**8 260**	**4 800**	**4 730**	**4 900**	**4 580**	**4 150**	**3 910**	**3 810**
Service	3 220	2 630	2 720	2 930	2 820	2 780	2 650	2 600
Civilian	5 040	2 170	2 010	1 970	1 760	1 370	1 260	1 210
Scotland	**24 680**	**17 960**	**17 880**	**17 840**	**17 630**	**15 880**	**15 340**	**14 510**
Service	15 080	11 960	12 020	12 080	12 090	11 190	11 310	10 600
Civilian	9 600	5 990	5 860	5 760	5 540	4 690	4 020	3 910
Northern Ireland	**11 640**	**5 880**	**6 280**	**6 080**	**5 870**	**5 350**	**4 030**	**3 790**
Service	8 390	3 730	4 390	4 140	4 010	3 740	2 530	2 340
Civilian	3 250	2 150	1 890	1 930	1 850	1 610	1 500	1 450

Source: Defence Statistics (Tri-Service)

Service and Civilian personnel[1,2] by Region

FTE

	Service			Civilian		
	2013	2014	% change	2013	2014	% change
United Kingdom	**150 310**	**141 180**	**-6.1**	**53 050**	**51 610**	**-2.7**
England	**133 810**	**125 640**	**-6.1**	**46 270**	**45 040**	**-2.7**
East of England	15 210	14 540	-4.4	4 110	3 890	-5.4
East Midlands	8 610	8 890	3.2	1 700	1 580	-7.2
London	5 070	4 670	-7.9	3 690	3 490	-5.5
North East	1 390	1 220	-11.6	320	290	-8.2
North West	2 110	1 560	-25.7	1 810	1 640	-9.3
South East	42 330	39 300	-7.2	11 050	10 520	-4.8
South West	37 230	36 520	-1.9	16 950	17 040	0.5
West Midlands	6 280	6 300	0.4	3 690	3 770	2.2
Yorkshire and The Humber	15 590	12 640	-18.9	2 950	2 810	-4.5
Wales	**2 650**	**2 600**	**-2.0**	**1 260**	**1 210**	**-4.0**
Scotland	**11 310**	**10 600**	**-6.3**	**4 020**	**3 910**	**-2.7**
Northern Ireland	**2 530**	**2 340**	**-7.6**	**1 500**	**1 450**	**-3.4**

Source: Defence Statistics (Tri-Service)

1. Service personnel figures are for UK Regular Forces based in the UK. They include all trained and untrained Personnel and exclude Gurkhas, Full Time Reserve Service personnel and mobilised reservists.

2. Civilian personnel includes Trading Fund staff and exclude RFAs and LECs.

3. 2000 figures are as at 1 July.

14.8b Global locations of Service[1] and civilian personnel [2,3], at 1 April each year

Number: FTE

		2000 [4]	2008	2009	2010	2011	2012	2013	2014
Global Total		**333 960**	**276 410**	**275 220**	**277 560**	**269 420**	**250 810**	**236 110**	**222 130**
	Service	213 220	186 910	188 600	191 710	186 360	179 800	170 710	159 630
	Civilian Level 0	120 740	89 500	86 620	85 850	83 060	71 010	65 400	62 500
United Kingdom Total		**267 700**	**231 350**	**233 290**	**236 710**	**229 390**	**214 190**	**203 360**	**192 800**
	Service	170 300	158 450	162 670	166 100	161 790	156 970	150 310	141 180
	Civilian	97 410	72 900	70 620	70 610	67 610	57 220	53 050	51 610
Overseas Total		**54 000**	**41 270**	**38 240**	**37 650**	**36 910**	**33 710**	**30 050**	**26 660**
	Service	37 200	27 590	25 350	25 260	24 230	22 440	20 060	18 070
	Civilian	16 800	13 680	12 890	12 400	12 680	11 270	10 000	8 580
EUROPE (exc. UK) *of which:*		..	**36 800**	**33 670**	**33 000**	**31 300**	**29 050**	**25 610**	**22 570**
Germany	Service	..	21 650	19 100	19 100	18 240	16 990	14 840	12 960
	Civilian	..	7 820	7 420	7 020	6 470	5 800	5 300	4 250
Cyprus	Service	3 510	2 780	2 910	2 880	2 830	2 590	2 400	2 340
	Civilian	..	1 850	1 640	1 610	1 570	1 670	1 380	1 330
Belgium	Service	..	390	410	410	340	330	330	320
	Civilian	..	..	..	140	100	100	40	60
Gibraltar	Service	550	280	260	270	260	230	200	180
	Civilian	..	750	730	730	750	650	530	550
Italy	Service	..	250	260	250	210	170	140	140
	Civilian	..	..	..	60	50	50	20	30
ASIA (EXC. MIDDLE EAST)		..	**1 430**	**1 600**	**1 920**	**2 080**	**2 110**	**2 020**	**1 710**
	Service	970	260	260	260	280	260	260	260
	Civilian	..	1 170	1 340	1 660	1 800	1 860	1 760	1 450
NORTH AFRICA / MIDDLE EAST		..	**960**	**730**	**460**	**500**	**430**	**420**	**440**
	Service	1 300	360	370	380	420	340	330	350
	Civilian	..	600	360	80	80	90	90	90
SUB SAHARAN AFRICA *of which:*		..	**650**	**680**	**690**	**1 540**	**890**	**730**	**670**
Kenya[6]	Service	-	30	80	90	140	180	180	200
	Civilian	..	230	320	360	1 190	640	480	420
Sierra Leone	Service	-	80	60	30	30	20	20	10
	Civilian	..	220	150	150	130	-	-	-

Continued on the next page

14.8b Global locations of Service[1] and civilian personnel [2,3], at 1 April each year

		2000 [4]	2008	2009	2010	2011	2012	2013	2014
NORTH AMERICA		..	**880**	**920**	**990**	**980**	**990**	**1 000**	**1 010**
of which:									
United States	Service	910	420	470	520	550	560	560	570
	Civilian	..	180	160	160	150	150	150	160
Canada	Service	1 610	270	270	270	270	270	280	270
	Civilian	..	10	10	50	10	10	10	10
CENTRAL AMERICA / CARIBBEAN		..	**260**	**250**	**240**	**240**	**70**	**70**	**70**
	Service	-	80	70	70	70	10	10	10
	Civilian	..	180	180	170	160	60	60	60
SOUTH AMERICA		..	**20**	**20**	**20**	**20**	**20**	**20**	**20**
	Service	-	10	10	10	10	10	10	10
	Civilian	..	10	10	10	10	10	10	10
SOUTH ATLANTIC		..	**190**	**310**	**270**	**180**	**80**	**110**	**100**
of which:									
Falkland Islands	Service	780	130	250	220	120	50	70	70
	Civilian	..	50	50	40	40	30	30	30
OCEANIA		..	**80**	**60**	**60**	**70**	**70**	**70**	**70**
	Service	20	60	50	50	50	60	60	60
	Civilian	..	20	20	10	20	10	10	10
Unallocated		-	**1 520**	**1 390**	**860**	**760**	**910**	**800**	**860**
	Service	5 720	880	580	350	340	390	350	370
	Civilian	4 080	650	800	520	420	520	450	490
Royal Fleet Auxiliaries	**Civilian**	**2 450**	**2 270**	**2 300**	**2 330**	**2 360**	**2 000**	**1 900**	**1 820**

Source: Defence Statistics (Tri-Service)

1. Service personnel figures are for UK Regular Forces. They include all trained and untrained Personnel and exclude Gurkhas, Full Time Reserve Service personnel and mobilised reservists.

2. Civilian Level 0 and Level 1 are defined in the Glossary.

3. UK civilian totals include Trading Fund personnel but exclude RFA and LEC personnel and those with an unknown location. Overseas civilian includes LEC personnel.

4. Detailed break down of LEC data for 2000 are not available. The "Overseas Total" for year 2000 subsumes the total LEC figure. 2000 figures as at 1 July.

5. The increase in civilian numbers in 2011 reflects the additional requirements for locally engaged civilian to support military exercises.

14.9a UK regular Armed Forces deaths by Service, Year of occurrence 2005-2014, numbers, age and gender standardised rates.

Year	All		Naval Service		Army		RAF	
	Number	Rate	Number	Rate	Number	Rate	Number	Rate
2005	160	82	27	70	93	91	40	72
2006	191	99	33	85	111	95	47	92
2007	204	106	27	74	145	128	32	74
2008	137	74	40	110	79	74	18	37
2009	205	107	23	58	158	133	24	55
2010	187	97	30	77	136	116	21	50
2011	132	69	19	52	98	88	15	33
2012	130	72	20	59	95	89	15	42
2013	86	50	13	42	63	65	10	23
2014	68	42	12	35	40	42	16	40

Source: Defence Statistics (Health)

Rates have been age and gender standardised to the 2014 Armed Forces population, expressed per 100,000 strength.

14.9b UK Regular Armed Forces deaths by Service, 2005-2014, numbers, Standardised Mortality Ratios (SMR) (95% confidence intervals (CI)).

Year	All			Naval Service			Army			RAF		
	Number	SMR	(95% CI)	Number	SMR	(95% CI)	Number	SMR	(95% CI)	Number	SMR	(95% CI)
2005	160	75	(64-88)	27	62	(41-91)	93	87.61153956	(71-107)	40	62.48911	(46-85)
2006	191	87	(76-101)	33	73	(52-103)	111	99.70681409	(83-120)	47	75.41417	(57-100)
2007	204	96	(84-110)	27	61	(40-89)	145	132.0440764	(112-155)	32	55.0789	(39-78)
2008	137	65	(55-76)	40	89	(65-122)	79	71.88921705	(58-90)	18	31.54793	(19-50)
2009	205	99	(86-113)	23	53	(33-79)	158	145.5606818	(125-170)	24	43.24544	(28-64)
2010	187	94	(81-108)	30	71	(50-102)	136	130.9681753	(111-155)	21	39.37523	(24-60)
2011	132	71	(60-84)	19	48	(29-76)	98	100.2919584	(82-122)	15	30.44807	(17-50)
2012	130	76	(64-90)	20	56	(34-86)	95	104.7418751	(86-128)	15	33.68819	(19-56)
2013	86	52	(42-65)	13	37	(20-63)	63	72.5911087	(57-93)	10	23.72698	(11-44)
2014	68	44	(35-56)	12	35	(18-61)	40	49.84235416	(37-68)	16	39.60561	(23-64)

Change in how UK deaths collated, prior to 2006 includes deaths occurred in year, post 2006 includes deaths registered in year. Standardised mortality ratios have been age and gender standardised.

Source: Defence Statistics (Health)

14.10a UK Military Search and Rescue - UK & Overseas Callouts, Incidents and Persons Moved, 2005 to 2014

	Incidents			Callouts			Persons Moved		
	All	UK	Overseas	All	UK	Overseas	All	UK	Overseas
2005	1,641	1,584	57	1,766	1,702	64	1,431	1,384	47
2006	1,767	1,703	64	1,948	1,875	73	1,538	1,463	75
2007	1,877	1,803	74	2,065	1,973	92	1,817	1,767	50
2008	2,025	1,941	84	2,179	2,083	96	1,763	1,607	156
2009	2,262	2,191	71	2,418	2,337	81	1,873	1,810	63
2010	1,960	1,901	59	2,050	1,983	67	1,647	1,605	42
2011	1,864	1,801	63	1,921	1,856	65	1,560	1,501	59
2012	1,774	1,733	41	1,879	1,837	42	1,550	1,522	28
2013	1,817	1,777	40	1,918	1,874	44	1,696	1,660	36
2014	1,811	1,767	44	1,906	1,862	44	1,580	1,530	50

Source: UK Defence Statistics, Ministry of Defence

14.10b UK & Overseas Callouts and Persons Moved by Unit, 2005 to 2014

UK & Overseas Callouts by Unit, 2005 to 2014

	RAF Boulmer	RAF Lossiemouth	RAF Leconfield	RAF Valley	RAF Chivenor	RAF Wattisham	RAF UK Total	RNAS Culdrose	HMS Gannet	RN Total	UK Other	UK Total	Cyprus	Falklands	Overseas Total
2005	144	200	135	218	281	131	1,109	211	267	478	5	1,592	39	24	63
2006	206	217	147	225	293	163	1,251	228	269	497	8	1,756	35	38	73
2007	170	188	222	234	256	183	1,253	231	359	590	7	1,850	53	39	92
2008	211	275	232	222	262	174	1,376	204	382	586	1	1,963	30	66	96
2009	214	236	204	322	340	162	1,478	311	447	758	1	2,237	36	45	81
2010	193	175	174	268	339	133	1,282	260	379	639	0	1,921	29	38	67
2011	181	207	168	276	267	157	1,256	244	298	542	1	1,799	24	41	65
2012	141	216	129	300	266	160	1,212	251	298	549	0	1,761	20	22	42
2013	157	231	134	335	238	121	1,216	257	329	586	0	1,802	12	32	44
2014	160	212	135	329	285	127	1,248	252	299	551	0	1,799	6	38	44

UK & Overseas Persons Moved by Unit, 2005 to 2014

	RAF Boulmer	RAF Lossiemouth	RAF Leconfield	RAF Valley	RAF Chivenor	RAF Wattisham	RAF UK Total	RNAS Culdrose	HMS Gannet	RN Total	UK Other	UK Total	Cyprus	Falklands	Overseas Total
2005	136	181	94	195	216	83	905	154	226	380	2	1,287	17	30	47
2006	132	180	125	202	213	110	962	176	303	479	6	1,447	5	70	75
2007	136	160	315	236	224	122	1,193	220	286	506	27	1,726	11	39	50
2008	185	199	163	217	211	87	1,062	169	347	516	0	1,578	5	151	156
2009	149	171	132	296	304	82	1,134	278	378	656	1	1,791	9	54	63
2010	169	156	120	263	256	83	1,047	215	324	539	0	1,586	5	37	42
2011	121	239	125	246	203	96	1,030	219	240	459	0	1,489	15	44	59
2012	129	205	97	284	187	80	982	235	285	520	0	1,502	3	25	28
2013	145	219	94	352	191	83	1,084	212	327	539	0	1,623	2	34	36
2014	115	213	86	299	225	84	1,022	221	255	476	0	1,498	2	48	50

Source: UK Defence Statistics, ARCC Database

14.10c Search and Rescue Helicopters: UK & Overseas callouts and Persons Moved by Assistance Type, 2005 to 2014

UK & Overseas Callouts by Assistance Type, 2005 to 2014

	2005	2006	2007	2008	2009	2010	2011	2012	2013	2014
Rescue	115	100	106	99	97	105	87	81	77	88
Search-Rescue[5]	0	0	30	33	75	40	30	39	56	50
Medrescue	675	751	703	744	914	839	843	808	873	823
Search-Medrescue[5]	0	0	38	55	59	61	53	46	54	57
Medtransfer	157	191	209	229	224	210	182	169	201	193
Recovery	30	33	15	29	19	13	14	21	13	16
Search-Recovery[5]	0	0	2	8	16	7	7	8	15	8
Transfer	28	24	18	16	15	12	10	9	11	5
Civil Aid	22	23	41	26	17	20	10	5	2	0
Search	246	289	284	291	297	189	202	178	137	185
Top Cover	38	28	35	15	28	22	24	19	19	8
Assist	29	33	25	27	34	31	20	35	21	36
Search-Assist[5]	0	0	37	53	49	19	27	36	28	28
Recalled	183	222	212	277	280	243	224	221	209	209
Not Required	98	83	113	80	104	88	94	97	85	82
False Alarm	10	9	25	31	36	29	10	9	12	21
Hoax	6	10	12	14 [r]	11	15	7	3	5	5
Precaution	4	8	5	1	2	9	6	5	2	4
Aborted	14	25	27	23	34	33	9	9	22	19
Search-Aborted[5]	0	0	5	8	7	3	5	5	4	6
Total Callouts	**1,655**	**1,829**	**1,942**	**2,059** [r]	**2,318**	**1,988**	**1,864**	**1,803**	**1,846**	**1,843**

UK & Overseas Persons Moved by Assistance Type, 2005 to 2014

	2005	2006	2007	2008	2009	2010	2011	2012	2013	2014
Rescue	322	407	575	383	289	290	301	287	238	272
Search-Rescue	0	0	56	70	155	82	55	100	112	90
Medrescue	791	852	839	821	1,026	917	910	860	949	869
Search-Medrescue	0	0	56	65	70	68	59	48	62	68
Medtransfer	159	192	212	243	238	227	190	185	220	215
Recovery	30	39	16	28	22	15	14	27	24	20
Search-Recovery	0	0	2	9	20	8	7	10	16	9
Transfer	32	32	20	115	34	21	12	13	38	5
Total Persons Moved	**1,334**	**1,522**	**1,776**	**1,734**	**1,854**	**1,628**	**1,548**	**1,530**	**1,659**	**1,548**

5. Here was a change in callout classification in 2007. Prior to 2007, 'Search-Rescue' was included in 'Rescue', 'Search-Medrescue' was included in 'Medrescue', 'Search-Recovery' was included in 'Recovery', 'Search-Assist' was included in 'Assist' and 'Search-Aborted' was included in 'Aborted'.

Source: UK Defence Statistics, ARCC Database

Other Search and Rescue

In addition to the RAF and Royal Navy, a number of non-military organisations provide SAR coverage throughout the UK. The activities of most of these non-military organisations are outside the scope of this report; however background information on some of the organisations involved is provided below.

Maritime and Coastguard Agency

In addition to the eight military aeronautical SAR units, additional aeronautical SAR coverage is provided by four Maritime and Coastguard Agency (MCA) helicopter units. Although these are not part of the military SAR service, the MCA helicopters are coordinated by the ARCC at Kinloss Barracks, to provide integrated coverage across the UK. A summary of callouts for this quarter is provided in this report.

In addition to its aeronautical coverage, the MCA provides maritime SAR coverage throughout the UK. Details of maritime SAR callouts are not included in this report. Further information is available at:

http://www.dft.gov.uk/mca/mcga07-home/emergencyresponse/mcga-searchandrescue.htm

RNLI

The RNLI is a charitable organisation providing 24 hour lifeboat SAR coverage around the coast of the UK and Republic of Ireland, along with a seasonal lifeguard service.

http://www.rnli.org.uk/

Mountain Rescue Teams

A number of voluntary Mountain Rescue services operate throughout the UK. These often work in conjunction with the military SAR service. Details of non-military Mountain Rescue callouts are not included in this report. Further information can be found at:

http://www.mountain.rescue.org.uk/
http://www.mrcofs.org/

Air Ambulance

Air Ambulance services operate throughout the UK, providing emergency medical assistance. Further information is available at:

http://www.associationofairambulances.co.uk/

14.10d Strength of Uniformed United Kingdom Medical Staff, 2011-2014

	2011	2012	2013	2014
Qualified Doctors	588	575	578	604
Qualified Dentists	245	244	226	207
Nursing Services	1329	1461	1286	1298
Support Staff	4038	4000	4127	4125
Total	**6200**	**6280**	**6217**	**6234**

Source: Headquarters of the Surgeon General

14.11 Number of vessels boarded by the Royal Navy Fishery Protection Squadron within British fishery limits each financial year

The data in this table are not National Statistics, and they have not been put forward to the UK Statistics Authority for assessment.

Number of vessels boarded

	2000/01	2008/09	2009/10	2010/11	2011/12	2012/13	2013/14 [1]
Vessels boarded	**1 603**	**1 102**	**1 201**	**1 399**	**1 408**	898 ||	575
By sea areas [2]:							
North Sea	627	306	338	411	417	169 ||	172
Bristol Channel, Celtic Sea, English Channel, Irish Sea, and Western Approaches	976	796	863	988	991	729 ||	403

Source: Marine Management Organisation

1. From April 2013, an agreement that FPS ships would no longer be exclusively tasked with Marine Enforcement came into effect, meaning there would be less less time available for boardings.

2. The Faroes, Rockall and West of Scotland are not covered by the Royal Navy Fishery Protection Squadron.

Convictions and Financial Administration Penalties arising from the boarding of vessels by the Royal Navy Fishery Protection Squadron within British fishery limits each financial year

The data in this Table are not National Statistics, and they have not been put forward to the UK Statistics Authority for assessment.

Number of convictions and Financial Administration Penalties

	2000/01		2008/09 [1]	2009/10	2010/11	2011/12	2012/13	2013/14
Convictions and FAPs arising from boardings	**48**	||	**30**	**10**	**29**	**17**	**13**	**17** [r]
By nationality:								
Belgium	4	||	5	3	1	2	2	1
Denmark	3	||	-	-	-	-	-	-
Eire	4	||	-	1	3	3	1	2
Faroes	3	||	-	-	-	-	-	-
France	8	||	12	1	14	6	6	4 [r]
Germany	-	||	-	-	2	-	-	-
Netherlands	6	||	2	-	3	2	2	1 [r]
Spain	-	||	3	1	1	2	-	-
United Kingdom	20	||	8	4	5	2	2	9 [r]

Source: Marine Management Organisation

1. From 2008/09, these figures include Financial Administration Penalties.

[p] The number of convictions and FAPs is provisional and may increase due to some cases being concluded a year or more after the initial boarding.

Population and vital statistics

Chapter 15

Population and Vital Statistics

This section begins with a summary of population figures for the United Kingdom and constituent countries for 1851 to 2041 and for Great Britain from 1801 (Table 15.1). Table 15.2 analyses the components of population change. Table 15.3 gives details of the national sex and age structures for years up to the present date, with projected figures up to the year 2114. Legal marital condition of the population is shown in Table 15.4. The distribution of population at regional and local levels is summarised in Table 15.5.

In the main, historical series relate to census information, while mid-year estimates, which make allowance for under-enumeration in the census, are given for the recent past and the present (from 1961 onwards).

Population
(Tables 15.1 - 15.3)

Figures shown in these tables relate to the population enumerated at successive censuses, (up to 1961), mid-year estimates (from 1973 to 2014) and population projections (up to 2041). Further information can be found on the National Statistics website www.ons.gov.uk.

Definition of resident population

The estimated resident population of an area includes all people who usually live there, whatever their nationality. Members of HM and US Armed Forces in England and Wales are included on a residential basis wherever possible. HM Forces stationed outside England and Wales are not included. Students are taken to be resident at their term time address.

The projections of the resident population of the United Kingdom and constituent countries were prepared by the National Statistics Centre for Demography within ONS, in consultation with the Registrars General, as a common framework for use in national planning in a number of different fields. New projections are made every second year on assumptions regarding future fertility, mortality and migration which seem most appropriate on the basis of the statistical evidence available at the time. The population projections in Tables 15.1 -15.3 are based on the estimates of the population of the United Kingdom at mid-2014 made by the Registrars General.

Marital condition (de jure): estimated population
(Table 15.4)

This table shows population estimates by marital status

Geographical distribution of the population
(Table 15.5)

The mid-year population estimates are provided for standard regions of the United Kingdom, for metropolitan areas, for broad groupings of local authority districts by type within England and Wales, and for some of the larger cities. Projections of future sub-national population levels are prepared from time to time by the Registrar General, but are not shown in this publication.

Migration into and out of the United Kingdom
(Tables 15.7 - 15.8)

A long-term international migrant is defined as a person who changes his or her country of usual residence for a period of at least a year,so that the country of destination effectively becomes the country of usual residence.

The main source of long-term international migration data is the International Passenger Survey (IPS). This is a continuous voluntary sample survey that provides information on passengers entering and leaving the UK by the principal air, sea and tunnel routes. Being a sample survey, the IPS is subject to some uncertainty; therefore it should be noted that long-term international migration estimates, in particular the difference between inflow and outflow, may be subject to large sampling errors. The IPS excludes routes between the Channel Islands and Isle of Man and the rest of the world.

The IPS data are supplemented with four types of additional information in order to provide a full picture of total long-term international migration, known as Long-Term International Migration or LTIM:

1. The IPS is based on intentions to migrate and intentions are liable to change. Adjustments are made for visitor switchers (those who intend to stay in the UK or abroad for less than one year but subsequently stay for longer and become migrants) and for migrant switchers (those who intend to stay in the UK or abroad for one year or more but then return earlier so are no longer migrants). These adjustments are primarily based on IPS data but for years prior to 2001, Home Office data on short-term visitors who were subsequently granted an extension of stay for a year or longer for other reasons have been incorporated.

2. Home Office data on applications for asylum and dependants of asylum seekers entering the UK are used to estimate inflows of asylum seekers and dependants not already captured by the I PS. In addition, Home Office data on removals and refusals are used to estimate outflows of failed asylum seekers not identified by the IPS.

3. Migration flows between the UK and the Irish Republic were added to the data to 2007 as the IPS did not cover this route until recently. These flows were obtained mainly from the Quarterly National Household Survey and were agreed between the Irish Central Statistics Office and ONS. From 2008 onwards, estimates of migration between the UK and Irish Republic come from the IPS.

4. Migration flows to and from Northern Ireland are added to the IPS data for Great Britain from 2008 onwards. These flows are obtained from the Irish Quarterly National Household Survey (from CSO Ireland) and health card registration data (from Northern Ireland Statistics Research Agency (NISRA)). These data are now deemed a better source for Northern Irish flows than IPS data. Prior to 2008, estimates of migration to and from Northern Ireland came from the IPS.

Grants for settlement in the United Kingdom
(Table 15.9)

This table presents in geographic regions, the statistics of individual countries of nationality, arranged alphabetically within each region. The figures are on a different basis from those derived from IPS (Tables 15.9 and 15.10) and relate only to people subject to immigration control. Persons granted settlement are allowed to stay indefinitely in the United Kingdom. They exclude temporary migrants such as students and generally relate only to non-EEA nationals. Settlement can occur several years after entry to the country.

Applications received for asylum in the United Kingdom, excluding dependants
(Table 15.10)

This table shows statistics of applications for asylum in the United Kingdom. Figures are shown for the main applicant nationalities by geographic region. The basis of assessing asylum applications, and hence of deciding whether to grant asylum in the United Kingdom, is the 1951 United Nations Convention on Refugees.

Marriages
(Table 15.11)
This table shows the number of marriages by type of ceremony and denomination.

Births
(Tables 15.14 –15.16)

For Scotland and Northern Ireland the number of births relate to those registered during the year. For England and Wales the figures up to and including 1930-32 are for those registered, while later figures relate to births occurring in each year.

All data for England and Wales and for Scotland include births occurring in those countries to mothers not usually resident in them. Data for Northern Ireland, and hence UK, prior to 1981 include births occurring in Northern Ireland to non-resident mothers; from 1981, such births are excluded.

Deaths
(Tables 15.17 - 15.18)

The figures relate to the number of deaths registered during each calendar year.

Infant and maternal mortality
(Table 15.18)

On 1 October 1992 the legal definition of a stillbirth was altered from a baby born dead after 28 completed weeks gestation or more, to one born after 24 completed weeks of gestation or more. The 258 stillbirths of 24 to 27 weeks gestation that which occurred between 1 October and 31 December 1992 are excluded from this table.

**Life tables
(Table 15.19)**

The current set of interim life tables are constructed from the estimated populations in 2012-2014 and corresponding data on births, infant deaths and deaths by individual age registered in those years.

**Adoptions
(Table 15.20)**

The figures shown within these tables relate to the date the adoption was entered in the Adopted Children Register. Figures based on the date of court order are available for England and Wales in the volumes Adoptions in England and Wales, Marriages in England and Wales and Divorces in England and Wales available on the National Statistics website www.statistics.gov.uk.

15.1 Population summary: by country and sex

Thousands

	United Kingdom			England and Wales			Wales	Scotland			Northern Ireland		
	Persons	Males	Females	Persons	Males	Females	Persons	Persons	Males	Females	Persons	Males	Females
Enumerated population: census figures													
1801	..	..	..	8,893	4,255	4,638	587	1,608	739	869	..	..	..
1851	22,259	10,855	11,404	17,928	8,781	9,146	1,163	2,889	1,376	1,513	1,442	698	745
1901	38,237	18,492	19,745	32,528	15,729	16,799	2,013	4,472	2,174	2,298	1,237	590	647
1911	42,082	20,357	21,725	36,070	17,446	18,625	2,421	4,761	2,309	2,452	1,251	603	648
1921[1]	44,027	21,033	22,994	37,887	18,075	19,811	2,656	4,882	2,348	2,535	1,258	610	648
1931[1]	46,038	22,060	23,978	39,952	19,133	20,819	2,593	4,843	2,326	2,517	1,243	601	642
1951	50,225	24,118	26,107	43,758	21,016	22,742	2,599	5,096	2,434	2,662	1,371	668	703
1961	52,709	25,481	27,228	46,105	22,304	23,801	2,644	5,179	2,483	2,697	1,425	694	731
Resident population: mid-year estimates													
	DYAY	BBAB	BBAC	BBAD	BBAE	BBAF	KGJM	BBAG	BBAH	BBAI	BBAJ	BBAK	BBAL
1973	56,223	27,332	28,891	49,459	24,061	25,399	2,773	5,234	2,515	2,719	1,530	756	774
1974	56,236	27,349	28,887	49,468	24,075	25,393	2,785	5,241	2,519	2,722	1,527	755	772
1975	56,226	27,361	28,865	49,470	24,091	25,378	2,795	5,232	2,516	2,716	1,524	753	770
1976	56,216	27,360	28,856	49,459	24,089	25,370	2,799	5,233	2,517	2,716	1,524	754	769
1977	56,190	27,345	28,845	49,440	24,076	25,364	2,801	5,226	2,515	2,711	1,523	754	769
1978	56,178	27,330	28,848	49,443	24,067	25,375	2,804	5,212	2,509	2,704	1,523	754	770
1979	56,240	27,373	28,867	49,508	24,113	25,395	2,810	5,204	2,505	2,699	1,528	755	773
1980	56,330	27,411	28,919	49,603	24,156	25,448	2,816	5,194	2,501	2,693	1,533	755	778
1981	56,357	27,412	28,946	49,634	24,160	25,474	2,813	5,180	2,495	2,685	1,543	757	786
1982	56,291	27,364	28,927	49,582	24,119	25,462	2,804	5,165	2,487	2,677	1,545	757	788
1983	56,316	27,371	28,944	49,617	24,133	25,484	2,803	5,148	2,479	2,669	1,551	759	792
1984	56,409	27,421	28,989	49,713	24,185	25,528	2,801	5,139	2,475	2,664	1,557	761	796
1985	56,554	27,489	29,065	49,861	24,254	25,606	2,803	5,128	2,470	2,658	1,565	765	800
1986	56,684	27,542	29,142	49,999	24,311	25,687	2,811	5,112	2,462	2,649	1,574	768	805
1987	56,804	27,599	29,205	50,123	24,371	25,752	2,823	5,099	2,455	2,644	1,582	773	809
1988	56,916	27,652	29,265	50,254	24,434	25,820	2,841	5,077	2,444	2,633	1,585	774	812
1989	57,076	27,729	29,348	50,408	24,510	25,898	2,855	5,078	2,443	2,635	1,590	776	814
1990	57,237	27,819	29,419	50,561	24,597	25,964	2,862	5,081	2,444	2,637	1,596	778	818
1991	57,439	27,909	29,530	50,748	24,681	26,067	2,873	5,083	2,445	2,639	1,607	783	824
1992	57,585	27,977	29,608	50,876	24,739	26,136	2,878	5,086	2,445	2,640	1,623	792	831
1993	57,714	28,039	29,675	50,986	24,793	26,193	2,884	5,092	2,448	2,644	1,636	798	837
1994	57,862	28,108	29,754	51,116	24,853	26,263	2,887	5,102	2,453	2,649	1,644	802	842
1995	58,025	28,204	29,821	51,272	24,946	26,326	2,889	5,104	2,453	2,650	1,649	804	845
1996	58,164	28,287	29,877	51,410	25,030	26,381	2,891	5,092	2,447	2,645	1,662	810	851
1997	58,314	28,371	29,943	51,560	25,113	26,446	2,895	5,083	2,442	2,641	1,671	816	856
1998	58,475	28,458	30,017	51,720	25,201	26,519	2,900	5,077	2,439	2,638	1,678	819	859
1999	58,684	28,578	30,106	51,933	25,323	26,610	2,901	5,072	2,437	2,635	1,679	818	861
2000	58,886	28,690	30,196	52,140	25,438	26,702	2,907	5,063	2,432	2,631	1,683	820	862
2001	59,113	28,832	30,281	52,360	25,574	26,786	2,910	5,064	2,434	2,630	1,689	824	865
2002	59,366	28,973	30,393	52,602	25,708	26,894	2,923	5,066	2,436	2,630	1,697	829	868
2003	59,637	29,125	30,511	52,863	25,854	27,009	2,938	5,069	2,438	2,630	1,705	833	872
2004	59,950	29,297	30,653	53,152	26,012	27,140	2,957	5,084	2,447	2,638	1,714	838	876
2005	60,413	29,541	30,872	53,575	26,234	27,341	2,969	5,110	2,461	2,649	1,728	845	882
2006	60,827	29,762	31,065	53,951	26,433	27,518	2,986	5,133	2,475	2,658	1,743	853	890
2007	61,319	30,028	31,291	54,387	26,669	27,718	3,006	5,170	2,497	2,673	1,762	862	899
2009	62,260	30,532	31,728	55,235	27,122	28,114	3,039	5,232	2,532	2,700	1,793	879	915
2010	62,759	30,805	31,954	55,692	27,373	28,320	3,050	5,262	2,548	2,714	1,805	885	920
2011	63,285	31,097	32,188	56,171	27,638	28,533	3,064	5,300	2,570	2,730	1,814	889	925
2012	63,705	31,315	32,390	56,568	27,843	28,724	3,074	5,314	2,577	2,736	1,824	895	929
2013	64,106	31,533	32,571	56,948	28,049	28,899	3,082	5,328	2,587	2,741	1,830	897	933
2014	64,597	31,794	32,803	57,409	28,295	29,114	3,092	5,347	2,597	2,751	1,840	903	938
Resident population: projections (mid-year)[2]													
	C59J	C59K	C59L	C59M	C59N	C59O	C59P	C59Q	C59R	C59S	C59T	C59U	C59V
2016	65,572	32,334	33,239	58,330	28,803	29,526	3,111	5,380	2,616	2,765	1,863	915	948
2021	67,781	33,531	34,251	60,406	29,925	30,481	3,158	5,462	2,663	2,799	1,913	943	970
2026	69,844	34,632	35,212	62,341	30,954	31,387	3,206	5,548	2,712	2,837	1,954	965	989
2031	71,707	35,622	36,086	64,098	31,885	32,213	3,245	5,624	2,754	2,870	1,986	983	1,003
2036	73,361	36,504	36,857	65,674	32,722	32,952	3,270	5,678	2,786	2,892	2,009	996	1,013
2041	74,884	37,326	37,558	67,140	33,510	33,630	3,286	5,715	2,808	2,907	2,029	1,008	1,021

1 Figures for Northern Ireland are estimated. The population at the Census of 1926 was
1,257 thousand (608 thousand males and 648 thousand females).

2 These projections are 2014-based.

Sources: Office for National Statistics: 01329 444661;
National Records of Scotland
Northern Ireland Statistics and Research Agency;

15.2a Population projections by the Office for National Statistics
United Kingdom, PERSONS, thousands

2014-based
Principal projection

Components of change (mid-year to mid-year), total fertility rate
and expectation of life at birth based on the mortality rates for the year

	2014 -2015	2015 -2016	2016 -2017	2017 -2018	2018 -2019	2019 -2020	2020 -2021	2021 -2022	2022 -2023	2023 -2024	2024 -2025	2025 -2026	2026 -2027	2027 -2028	2028 -2029	2029 -2030	2030 -2031	2031 -2032	2032 -2033	2033 -2034
Population at start	64,597	65,097	65,572	66,030	66,487	66,928	67,360	67,781	68,203	68,622	69,036	69,444	69,844	70,234	70,616	70,989	71,353	71,707	72,053	72,391
Births	776	784	791	797	802	805	808	810	812	811	809	807	804	803	801	800	799	800	800	802
Deaths	605	565	565	566	567	569	571	574	578	582	587	592	599	606	613	621	630	639	648	657
Natural change	171	219	226	231	234	236	237	236	234	229	223	214	206	197	188	179	170	161	153	145
International migration inflows	653	582	559	555	537	528	518	518	518	518	518	518	518	518	518	518	518	518	518	518
Crossborder migration inflows	-	-	-	-	-	-	-	-	-	-	-	-	-	-	-	-	-	-	-	-
International migration outflows	324	326	327	329	330	332	333	333	333	333	333	333	333	333	333	333	333	333	333	333
Crossborder migration outflows	-	-	-	-	-	-	-	-	-	-	-	-	-	-	-	-	-	-	-	-
Net international migration	329	256	232	226	206	196	185	185	185	185	185	185	185	185	185	185	185	185	185	185
Net crossborder migration	-	-	-	-	-	-	-	-	-	-	-	-	-	-	-	-	-	-	-	-
Net migration	329	256	232	226	206	196	185	185	185	185	185	185	185	185	185	185	185	185	185	185
Total change	500	475	458	457	441	432	422	421	419	414	408	399	391	382	373	364	355	346	338	330
Population at end	65,097	65,572	66,030	66,487	66,928	67,360	67,781	68,203	68,622	69,036	69,444	69,844	70,234	70,616	70,989	71,353	71,707	72,053	72,391	72,721
Annual growth rate	0.77%	0.73%	0.70%	0.69%	0.66%	0.65%	0.63%	0.62%	0.61%	0.60%	0.59%	0.58%	0.56%	0.54%	0.53%	0.51%	0.50%	0.48%	0.47%	0.46%
Total fertility rate (TFR)	1.81	1.81	1.82	1.83	1.84	1.84	1.85	1.86	1.87	1.87	1.87	1.87	1.88	1.88	1.88	1.88	1.89	1.88	1.89	1.89
EOLB Males	78.9	79.8	80.0	80.3	80.5	80.8	81.0	81.2	81.4	81.7	81.9	82.1	82.2	82.4	82.6	82.8	82.9	83.1	83.3	83.4
Females	82.5	83.4	83.5	83.7	83.9	84.1	84.3	84.5	84.6	84.8	85.0	85.1	85.3	85.5	85.6	85.8	85.9	86.0	86.2	86.3

	2034 -2035	2035 -2036	2036 -2037	2037 -2038	2038 -2039	2039 -2040	2040 -2041	2041 -2042	2042 -2043	2043 -2044	2044 -2045	2045 -2046	2046 -2047	2047 -2048	2048 -2049	2049 -2050	2050 -2051	2051 -2052	2052 -2053	2053 -2054
Population at start	72,721	73,044	73,361	73,673	73,980	74,284	74,585	74,884	75,180	75,474	75,766	76,055	76,342	76,626	76,907	77,184	77,457	77,726	77,991	78,252
Births	805	808	812	817	823	828	834	839	844	848	852	855	858	859	861	862	863	864	865	865
Deaths	667	676	685	695	704	712	720	728	735	741	747	753	759	764	769	774	779	784	788	792
Natural change	138	132	127	123	119	116	113	111	109	107	105	102	99	96	92	88	84	80	76	73
International migration inflows	518	518	518	518	518	518	518	518	518	518	518	518	518	518	518	518	518	518	518	518
Crossborder migration inflows	-	-	-	-	-	-	-	-	-	-	-	-	-	-	-	-	-	-	-	-
International migration outflows	333	333	333	333	333	333	333	333	333	333	333	333	333	333	333	333	333	333	333	333
Crossborder migration outflows	-	-	-	-	-	-	-	-	-	-	-	-	-	-	-	-	-	-	-	-
Net international migration	185	185	185	185	185	185	185	185	185	185	185	185	185	185	185	185	185	185	185	185
Net crossborder migration	-	-	-	-	-	-	-	-	-	-	-	-	-	-	-	-	-	-	-	-
Net migration	185	185	185	185	185	185	185	185	185	185	185	185	185	185	185	185	185	185	185	185
Total change	323	317	312	308	304	301	298	296	294	292	290	287	284	281	277	273	269	265	261	258
Population at end	73,044	73,361	73,673	73,980	74,284	74,585	74,884	75,180	75,474	75,766	76,055	76,342	76,626	76,907	77,184	77,457	77,726	77,991	78,252	78,510
Annual growth rate	0.44%	0.43%	0.43%	0.42%	0.41%	0.41%	0.40%	0.40%	0.39%	0.39%	0.38%	0.38%	0.37%	0.37%	0.36%	0.35%	0.35%	0.34%	0.34%	0.33%
Total fertility rate (TFR)	1.89	1.89	1.89	1.89	1.89	1.89	1.89	1.89	1.89	1.89	1.89	1.89	1.89	1.89	1.89	1.89	1.89	1.89	1.89	1.89
EOLB Males	83.5	83.7	83.8	83.9	84.1	84.2	84.3	84.4	84.6	84.7	84.8	84.9	85.1	85.2	85.3	85.4	85.6	85.7	85.8	85.9
Females	86.4	86.6	86.7	86.8	86.9	87.0	87.1	87.2	87.4	87.5	87.6	87.7	87.8	87.9	88.0	88.2	88.3	88.4	88.5	88.6

15.2a Population projections by the Office for National Statistics
United Kingdom, PERSONS, thousands

2014-based
Principal projection

Components of change (mid-year to mid-year), total fertility rate and expectation of life at birth based on the mortality rates for the year

	2054 -2055	2055 -2056	2056 -2057	2057 -2058	2058 -2059	2059 -2060	2060 -2061	2061 -2062	2062 -2063	2063 -2064	2064 -2065	2065 -2066	2066 -2067	2067 -2068	2068 -2069	2069 -2070	2070 -2071	2071 -2072	2072 -2073	2073 -2074
Population at start	78,510	78,765	79,016	79,266	79,513	79,759	80,004	80,249	80,495	80,743	80,992	81,244	81,499	81,758	82,020	82,287	82,557	82,830	83,107	83,387
Births	866	866	867	868	868	869	870	871	872	874	876	878	880	883	885	888	891	895	898	901
Deaths	796	800	803	805	807	809	810	810	810	809	808	807	806	805	804	803	803	803	803	803
Natural change	70	67	64	62	61	60	60	61	62	64	67	70	74	77	81	85	89	92	95	98
International migration inflows	518	518	518	518	518	518	518	518	518	518	518	518	518	518	518	518	518	518	518	518
Crossborder migration inflows	-	-	-	-	-	-	-	-	-	-	-	-	-	-	-	-	-	-	-	-
International migration outflows	333	333	333	333	333	333	333	333	333	333	333	333	333	333	333	333	333	333	333	333
Crossborder migration outflows	-	-	-	-	-	-	-	-	-	-	-	-	-	-	-	-	-	-	-	-
Net international migration	185	185	185	185	185	185	185	185	185	185	185	185	185	185	185	185	185	185	185	185
Net crossborder migration	-	-	-	-	-	-	-	-	-	-	-	-	-	-	-	-	-	-	-	-
Net migration	185	185	185	185	185	185	185	185	185	185	185	185	185	185	185	185	185	185	185	185
Total change	255	252	249	247	246	245	245	246	247	249	252	255	259	262	266	270	274	277	280	283
Population at end	78,765	79,016	79,266	79,513	79,759	80,004	80,249	80,495	80,743	80,992	81,244	81,499	81,758	82,020	82,287	82,557	82,830	83,107	83,387	83,670
Annual growth rate	0.32%	0.32%	0.32%	0.31%	0.31%	0.31%	0.31%	0.31%	0.31%	0.31%	0.31%	0.31%	0.32%	0.32%	0.32%	0.33%	0.33%	0.33%	0.34%	0.34%
Total fertility rate (TFR)	1.89	1.89	1.89	1.89	1.89	1.89	1.89	1.89	1.89	1.89	1.89	1.89	1.89	1.89	1.89	1.89	1.89	1.89	1.89	1.89
EOLB Males	86.1	86.2	86.3	86.4	86.5	86.7	86.8	86.9	87.0	87.1	87.3	87.4	87.5	87.6	87.8	87.9	88.0	88.1	88.2	88.4
Females	88.7	88.8	89.0	89.1	89.2	89.3	89.4	89.5	89.6	89.7	89.9	90.0	90.1	90.2	90.3	90.4	90.5	90.6	90.8	90.9

	2074 -2075	2075 -2076	2076 -2077	2077 -2078	2078 -2079	2079 -2080	2080 -2081	2081 -2082	2082 -2083	2083 -2084	2084 -2085	2085 -2086	2086 -2087	2087 -2088	2088 -2089	2089 -2090	2090 -2091	2091 -2092	2092 -2093	2093 -2094
Population at start	83,670	83,955	84,241	84,529	84,817	85,105	85,394	85,683	85,971	86,259	86,546	86,833	87,121	87,408	87,696	87,984	88,273	88,563	88,854	89,146
Births	904	907	909	912	914	916	918	920	921	923	924	925	926	927	928	930	931	932	933	935
Deaths	804	805	807	809	811	813	815	817	818	820	822	823	824	825	825	826	826	826	826	826
Natural change	100	101	102	103	104	104	104	103	103	102	102	102	102	103	103	104	105	106	107	109
International migration inflows	518	518	518	518	518	518	518	518	518	518	518	518	518	518	518	518	518	518	518	518
Crossborder migration inflows	-	-	-	-	-	-	-	-	-	-	-	-	-	-	-	-	-	-	-	-
International migration outflows	333	333	333	333	333	333	333	333	333	333	333	333	333	333	333	333	333	333	333	333
Crossborder migration outflows	-	-	-	-	-	-	-	-	-	-	-	-	-	-	-	-	-	-	-	-
Net international migration	185	185	185	185	185	185	185	185	185	185	185	185	185	185	185	185	185	185	185	185
Net crossborder migration	-	-	-	-	-	-	-	-	-	-	-	-	-	-	-	-	-	-	-	-
Net migration	185	185	185	185	185	185	185	185	185	185	185	185	185	185	185	185	185	185	185	185
Total change	285	286	287	288	289	289	289	288	288	288	287	287	287	288	288	289	290	291	292	294
Population at end	83,955	84,241	84,529	84,817	85,105	85,394	85,683	85,971	86,259	86,546	86,833	87,121	87,408	87,696	87,984	88,273	88,563	88,854	89,146	89,440
Annual growth rate	0.34%	0.34%	0.34%	0.34%	0.34%	0.34%	0.34%	0.34%	0.33%	0.33%	0.33%	0.33%	0.33%	0.33%	0.33%	0.33%	0.33%	0.33%	0.33%	0.33%
Total fertility rate (TFR)	1.89	1.89	1.89	1.89	1.89	1.89	1.89	1.89	1.89	1.89	1.89	1.89	1.89	1.89	1.89	1.89	1.89	1.89	1.89	1.89
EOLB Males	88.5	88.6	88.7	88.8	89.0	89.1	89.2	89.3	89.4	89.6	89.7	89.8	89.9	90.0	90.2	90.3	90.4	90.5	90.7	90.8
Females	91.0	91.1	91.2	91.3	91.4	91.5	91.7	91.8	91.9	92.0	92.1	92.2	92.3	92.4	92.6	92.7	92.8	92.9	93.0	93.1

15.2a Population projections by the Office for National Statistics
United Kingdom, PERSONS, thousands

2014-based
Principal projection

Components of change (mid-year to mid-year), total fertility rate and expectation of life at birth based on the mortality rates for the year

	2094 -2095	2095 -2096	2096 -2097	2097 -2098	2098 -2099	2099 -2100	2100 -2101	2101 -2102	2102 -2103	2103 -2104	2104 -2105	2105 -2106	2106 -2107	2107 -2108	2108 -2109	2109 -2110	2110 -2111	2111 -2112	2112 -2113	2113 -2114
Population at start	89,440	89,735	90,031	90,329	90,628	90,927	91,228	91,528	91,830	92,131	92,432	92,733	93,033	93,332	93,631	93,929	94,226	94,523	94,818	95,113
Births	937	938	940	942	944	947	949	951	953	956	958	960	963	965	967	969	971	973	975	976
Deaths	827	827	828	829	830	831	833	835	837	840	842	845	848	851	854	857	860	862	865	867
Natural change	110	111	113	114	115	115	116	116	116	116	116	115	115	114	113	112	111	111	110	109
International migration inflows	518	518	518	518	518	518	518	518	518	518	518	518	518	518	518	518	518	518	518	518
Crossborder migration inflows	-	-	-	-	-	-	-	-	-	-	-	-	-	-	-	-	-	-	-	-
International migration outflows	333	333	333	333	333	333	333	333	333	333	333	333	333	333	333	333	333	333	333	333
Crossborder migration outflows	-	-	-	-	-	-	-	-	-	-	-	-	-	-	-	-	-	-	-	-
Net international migration	185	185	185	185	185	185	185	185	185	185	185	185	185	185	185	185	185	185	185	185
Net crossborder migration	-	-	-	-	-	-	-	-	-	-	-	-	-	-	-	-	-	-	-	-
Net migration	185	185	185	185	185	185	185	185	185	185	185	185	185	185	185	185	185	185	185	185
Total change	295	296	298	299	300	300	301	301	301	301	301	300	300	299	298	297	296	296	295	294
Population at end	89,735	90,031	90,329	90,628	90,927	91,228	91,528	91,830	92,131	92,432	92,733	93,033	93,332	93,631	93,929	94,226	94,523	94,818	95,113	95,408
Annual growth rate	0.33%	0.33%	0.33%	0.33%	0.33%	0.33%	0.33%	0.33%	0.33%	0.33%	0.33%	0.32%	0.32%	0.32%	0.32%	0.32%	0.31%	0.31%	0.31%	0.31%
Total fertility rate (TFR)	1.89	1.89	1.89	1.89	1.89	1.89	1.89	1.89	1.89	1.89	1.89	1.89	1.89	1.89	1.89	1.89	1.89	1.89	1.89	1.89
EOLB Males	90.9	91.0	91.1	91.3	91.4	91.5	91.6	91.7	91.9	92.0	92.1	92.2	92.3	92.5	92.6	92.7	92.8	92.9	93.1	93.2
Females	93.2	93.3	93.5	93.6	93.7	93.8	93.9	94.0	94.1	94.3	94.4	94.5	94.6	94.7	94.8	94.9	95.0	95.2	95.3	95.4

Source: Office for National Statistics

Note: Figures may not add exactly due to rounding.
* Children under 16. Working age and pensionable age populations based on state pension age (SPA) for given year.
Between 2012 and 2018, SPA will change from 65 years for men and 61 years for women, to 65 years for both sexes.
Then between 2019 and 2020, SPA will change from 65 years to 66 years for both men and women.
Between 2026 and 2027 SPA will increase to 67 years and between 2044 and 2046 to 68 years for both sexes. This is based on SPA under the 2014 Pensions Act.
** This is consistent with the age-group definitions used in ONS Labour Market Statistics.

15.2b Population projections by the Office for National Statistics
England and Wales, PERSONS, thousands

2014-based
Principal projection

Components of change (mid-year to mid-year), total fertility rate
and expectation of life at birth based on the mortality rates for the year

	2014 -2015	2015 -2016	2016 -2017	2017 -2018	2018 -2019	2019 -2020	2020 -2021	2021 -2022	2022 -2023	2023 -2024	2024 -2025	2025 -2026	2026 -2027	2027 -2028	2028 -2029	2029 -2030	2030 -2031	2031 -2032	2032 -2033	2033 -2034
Population at start	57,409	57,881	58,330	58,761	59,191	59,606	60,011	60,406	60,801	61,194	61,583	61,966	62,341	62,708	63,067	63,419	63,763	64,098	64,426	64,747
Births	696	704	711	717	722	725	727	730	731	730	729	726	724	723	721	721	720	721	722	724
Deaths	531	496	496	497	498	500	502	504	507	511	516	521	527	533	540	547	554	562	571	579
Natural change	165	208	215	220	223	225	225	225	223	219	213	206	198	190	182	174	166	158	151	145
International migration inflows	602	536	513	508	490	481	472	472	472	472	472	472	472	472	472	472	472	472	472	472
Crossborder migration inflows	48	48	49	49	49	48	48	48	48	48	48	48	48	48	48	48	48	48	48	48
International migration outflows	289	291	292	293	295	296	297	297	297	297	297	297	297	297	297	297	297	297	297	297
Crossborder migration outflows	53	53	53	53	53	53	53	53	53	53	53	53	53	53	53	53	53	53	53	53
Net international migration	312	245	221	215	196	185	175	175	175	175	175	175	175	175	175	175	175	175	175	175
Net crossborder migration	-5	-5	-5	-5	-5	-5	-5	-5	-5	-5	-5	-5	-5	-5	-5	-5	-5	-5	-5	-5
Net migration	308	240	217	211	191	180	170	170	170	170	170	170	170	170	170	170	170	170	170	170
Total change	472	448	431	431	414	405	395	393	393	389	383	375	367	359	352	344	336	328	321	314
Population at end	57,881	58,330	58,761	59,191	59,606	60,011	60,406	60,801	61,194	61,583	61,966	62,341	62,708	63,067	63,419	63,763	64,098	64,426	64,747	65,062
Annual growth rate	0.82%	0.77%	0.74%	0.73%	0.70%	0.68%	0.66%	0.65%	0.65%	0.64%	0.62%	0.61%	0.59%	0.57%	0.56%	0.54%	0.53%	0.51%	0.50%	0.49%
Total fertility rate (TFR)	1.82	1.83	1.84	1.85	1.85	1.86	1.87	1.88	1.88	1.89	1.89	1.89	1.89	1.89	1.89	1.90	1.90	1.90	1.90	1.90
EOLB Males	79.2	80.0	80.3	80.5	80.8	81.0	81.2	81.4	81.7	81.9	82.1	82.3	82.5	82.6	82.8	83.0	83.1	83.3	83.5	83.6
Females	82.7	83.6	83.8	83.9	84.1	84.3	84.5	84.7	84.9	85.0	85.2	85.4	85.5	85.7	85.8	86.0	86.1	86.2	86.4	86.5

	2034 -2035	2035 -2036	2036 -2037	2037 -2038	2038 -2039	2039 -2040	2040 -2041	2041 -2042	2042 -2043	2043 -2044	2044 -2045	2045 -2046	2046 -2047	2047 -2048	2048 -2049	2049 -2050	2050 -2051	2051 -2052	2052 -2053	2053 -2054
Population at start	65,062	65,370	65,674	65,973	66,269	66,562	66,852	67,140	67,427	67,712	67,995	68,277	68,557	68,834	69,109	69,380	69,648	69,913	70,175	70,432
Births	726	730	734	739	744	749	754	759	764	768	772	775	778	780	781	783	784	785	785	786
Deaths	588	596	605	613	621	629	636	643	649	655	660	665	670	675	680	684	689	693	697	701
Natural change	139	134	129	126	123	120	119	117	115	114	112	110	108	105	102	99	95	92	88	85
International migration inflows	472	472	472	472	472	472	472	472	472	472	472	472	472	472	472	472	472	472	472	472
Crossborder migration inflows	48	48	48	48	48	48	48	48	48	48	48	48	48	48	48	48	48	48	48	48
International migration outflows	297	297	297	297	297	297	297	297	297	297	297	297	297	297	297	297	297	297	297	297
Crossborder migration outflows	53	53	53	53	53	53	53	53	53	53	53	53	53	53	53	53	53	53	53	53
Net international migration	175	175	175	175	175	175	175	175	175	175	175	175	175	175	175	175	175	175	175	175
Net crossborder migration	-5	-5	-5	-5	-5	-5	-5	-5	-5	-5	-5	-5	-5	-5	-5	-5	-5	-5	-5	-5
Net migration	170	170	170	170	170	170	170	170	170	170	170	170	170	170	170	170	170	170	170	170
Total change	309	304	299	296	293	290	288	287	285	284	282	280	277	275	271	268	265	261	258	255
Population at end	65,370	65,674	65,973	66,269	66,562	66,852	67,140	67,427	67,712	67,995	68,277	68,557	68,834	69,109	69,380	69,648	69,913	70,175	70,432	70,687
Annual growth rate	0.47%	0.46%	0.46%	0.45%	0.44%	0.44%	0.43%	0.43%	0.42%	0.42%	0.41%	0.41%	0.40%	0.40%	0.39%	0.39%	0.38%	0.37%	0.37%	0.36%
Total fertility rate (TFR)	1.90	1.90	1.90	1.90	1.90	1.90	1.90	1.90	1.90	1.90	1.90	1.90	1.90	1.90	1.90	1.90	1.90	1.90	1.90	1.90
EOLB Males	83.7	83.9	84.0	84.1	84.3	84.4	84.5	84.6	84.8	84.9	85.0	85.1	85.2	85.4	85.5	85.6	85.7	85.9	86.0	86.1
Females	86.6	86.8	86.9	87.0	87.1	87.2	87.3	87.5	87.6	87.7	87.8	87.9	88.0	88.1	88.2	88.4	88.5	88.6	88.7	88.8

**2014-based
Principal projection**

15.2b Population projections by the Office for National Statistics
England and Wales, PERSONS, thousands

Components of change (mid-year to mid-year), total fertility rate and expectation of life at birth based on the mortality rates for the year

	2054-2055	2055-2056	2056-2057	2057-2058	2058-2059	2059-2060	2060-2061	2061-2062	2062-2063	2063-2064	2064-2065	2065-2066	2066-2067	2067-2068	2068-2069	2069-2070	2070-2071	2071-2072	2072-2073	2073-2074
Population at start	70,687	70,939	71,187	71,434	71,679	71,922	72,164	72,407	72,649	72,893	73,139	73,387	73,638	73,891	74,149	74,409	74,673	74,941	75,211	75,485
Births	787	788	788	789	790	791	791	793	794	796	797	800	802	804	807	810	813	816	820	823
Deaths	705	708	711	714	716	718	719	720	720	720	719	719	718	717	716	716	716	716	716	717
Natural change	82	79	77	75	74	73	73	73	74	76	78	81	84	87	91	94	98	101	104	106
International migration inflows	472	472	472	472	472	472	472	472	472	472	472	472	472	472	472	472	472	472	472	472
Crossborder migration inflows	48	48	48	48	48	48	48	48	48	48	48	48	48	48	48	48	48	48	48	48
International migration outflows	297	297	297	297	297	297	297	297	297	297	297	297	297	297	297	297	297	297	297	297
Crossborder migration outflows	53	53	53	53	53	53	53	53	53	53	53	53	53	53	53	53	53	53	53	53
Net international migration	175	175	175	175	175	175	175	175	175	175	175	175	175	175	175	175	175	175	175	175
Net crossborder migration	-5	-5	-5	-5	-5	-5	-5	-5	-5	-5	-5	-5	-5	-5	-5	-5	-5	-5	-5	-5
Net migration	170	170	170	170	170	170	170	170	170	170	170	170	170	170	170	170	170	170	170	170
Total change	252	249	247	245	243	242	242	243	244	246	248	251	254	257	261	264	267	271	273	276
Population at end	70,939	71,187	71,434	71,679	71,922	72,164	72,407	72,649	72,893	73,139	73,387	73,638	73,891	74,149	74,409	74,673	74,941	75,211	75,485	75,761
Annual growth rate	0.36%	0.35%	0.35%	0.34%	0.34%	0.34%	0.34%	0.34%	0.34%	0.34%	0.34%	0.34%	0.34%	0.35%	0.35%	0.35%	0.36%	0.36%	0.36%	0.37%
Total fertility rate (TFR)	1.90	1.90	1.90	1.90	1.90	1.90	1.90	1.90	1.90	1.90	1.90	1.90	1.90	1.90	1.90	1.90	1.90	1.90	1.90	1.90
EOLB Males	86.2	86.3	86.5	86.6	86.7	86.8	86.9	87.1	87.2	87.3	87.4	87.5	87.7	87.8	87.9	88.0	88.1	88.3	88.4	88.5
Females	88.9	89.0	89.1	89.3	89.4	89.5	89.6	89.7	89.8	89.9	90.0	90.1	90.3	90.4	90.5	90.6	90.7	90.8	90.9	91.0

	2074-2075	2075-2076	2076-2077	2077-2078	2078-2079	2079-2080	2080-2081	2081-2082	2082-2083	2083-2084	2084-2085	2085-2086	2086-2087	2087-2088	2088-2089	2089-2090	2090-2091	2091-2092	2092-2093	2093-2094
Population at start	75,761	76,038	76,317	76,598	76,879	77,161	77,442	77,724	78,005	78,286	78,567	78,847	79,128	79,408	79,689	79,970	80,252	80,535	80,818	81,103
Births	826	828	831	834	836	838	840	842	843	844	846	847	848	849	851	852	853	854	856	857
Deaths	718	719	720	722	724	726	728	730	732	733	735	736	737	738	739	740	740	740	741	741
Natural change	108	110	111	112	112	112	112	112	111	111	111	111	111	111	112	112	113	114	115	116
International migration inflows	472	472	472	472	472	472	472	472	472	472	472	472	472	472	472	472	472	472	472	472
Crossborder migration inflows	48	48	48	48	48	48	48	48	48	48	48	48	48	48	48	48	48	48	48	48
International migration outflows	297	297	297	297	297	297	297	297	297	297	297	297	297	297	297	297	297	297	297	297
Crossborder migration outflows	53	53	53	53	53	53	53	53	53	53	53	53	53	53	53	53	53	53	53	53
Net international migration	175	175	175	175	175	175	175	175	175	175	175	175	175	175	175	175	175	175	175	175
Net crossborder migration	-5	-5	-5	-5	-5	-5	-5	-5	-5	-5	-5	-5	-5	-5	-5	-5	-5	-5	-5	-5
Net migration	170	170	170	170	170	170	170	170	170	170	170	170	170	170	170	170	170	170	170	170
Total change	278	279	280	281	282	282	282	281	281	281	281	280	280	281	281	282	283	284	285	286
Population at end	76,038	76,317	76,598	76,879	77,161	77,442	77,724	78,005	78,286	78,567	78,847	79,128	79,408	79,689	79,970	80,252	80,535	80,818	81,103	81,389
Annual growth rate	0.37%	0.37%	0.37%	0.37%	0.37%	0.37%	0.36%	0.36%	0.36%	0.36%	0.36%	0.36%	0.35%	0.35%	0.35%	0.35%	0.35%	0.35%	0.35%	0.35%
Total fertility rate (TFR)	1.90	1.90	1.90	1.90	1.90	1.90	1.90	1.90	1.90	1.90	1.90	1.90	1.90	1.90	1.90	1.90	1.90	1.90	1.90	1.90
EOLB Males	88.6	88.7	88.9	89.0	89.1	89.2	89.3	89.5	89.6	89.7	89.8	89.9	90.1	90.2	90.3	90.4	90.5	90.7	90.8	90.9
Females	91.2	91.3	91.4	91.5	91.6	91.7	91.8	91.9	92.0	92.2	92.3	92.4	92.5	92.6	92.7	92.8	92.9	93.0	93.2	93.3

15.2b Population projections by the Office for National Statistics
England and Wales, PERSONS, thousands

2014-based
Principal projection

Components of change (mid-year to mid-year), total fertility rate and expectation of life at birth based on the mortality rates for the year

	2094 -2095	2095 -2096	2096 -2097	2097 -2098	2098 -2099	2099 -2100	2100 -2101	2101 -2102	2102 -2103	2103 -2104	2104 -2105	2105 -2106	2106 -2107	2107 -2108	2108 -2109	2109 -2110	2110 -2111	2111 -2112	2112 -2113	2113 -2114
Population at start	81,389	81,676	81,964	82,253	82,543	82,834	83,125	83,417	83,709	84,001	84,293	84,584	84,875	85,166	85,455	85,744	86,032	86,320	86,606	86,892
Births	859	861	863	865	867	869	871	874	876	878	881	883	885	887	889	892	893	895	897	899
Deaths	742	742	743	744	746	747	749	751	753	756	759	761	764	767	770	773	776	778	781	783
Natural change	117	118	119	120	121	122	122	122	122	122	122	121	121	120	119	119	118	117	116	116
International migration inflows	472	472	472	472	472	472	472	472	472	472	472	472	472	472	472	472	472	472	472	472
Crossborder migration inflows	48	48	49	49	49	49	49	49	49	49	49	49	49	49	49	49	49	49	49	49
International migration outflows	297	297	297	297	297	297	297	297	297	297	297	297	297	297	297	297	297	297	297	297
Crossborder migration outflows	53	53	53	53	53	53	53	53	54	54	54	54	54	54	54	54	54	54	54	54
Net international migration	175	175	175	175	175	175	175	175	175	175	175	175	175	175	175	175	175	175	175	175
Net crossborder migration	-5	-5	-5	-5	-5	-5	-5	-5	-5	-5	-5	-5	-5	-5	-5	-5	-5	-5	-5	-5
Net migration	170	170	170	170	170	170	170	170	170	170	170	170	170	170	170	170	170	170	170	170
Total change	287	288	289	290	291	291	292	292	292	292	292	291	290	290	289	288	287	287	286	285
Population at end	81,676	81,964	82,253	82,543	82,834	83,125	83,417	83,709	84,001	84,293	84,584	84,875	85,166	85,455	85,744	86,032	86,320	86,606	86,892	87,178
Annual growth rate	0.35%	0.35%	0.35%	0.35%	0.35%	0.35%	0.35%	0.35%	0.35%	0.35%	0.35%	0.34%	0.34%	0.34%	0.34%	0.34%	0.33%	0.33%	0.33%	0.33%
Total fertility rate (TFR)	1.90	1.90	1.90	1.90	1.90	1.90	1.90	1.90	1.90	1.90	1.90	1.90	1.90	1.90	1.90	1.90	1.90	1.90	1.90	1.90
EOLB Males	91.0	91.1	91.3	91.4	91.5	91.6	91.7	91.9	92.0	92.1	92.2	92.3	92.4	92.6	92.7	92.8	92.9	93.0	93.2	93.3
Females	93.4	93.5	93.6	93.7	93.8	93.9	94.1	94.2	94.3	94.4	94.5	94.6	94.7	94.8	95.0	95.1	95.2	95.3	95.4	95.5

Note: Figures may not add exactly due to rounding.
* Children under 16. Working age and pensionable age populations based on state pension age (SPA) for given year.
Between 2012 and 2018, SPA will change from 65 years for men and 61 years for women, to 65 years for both sexes.
Then between 2019 and 2020, SPA will change from 65 years to 66 years for both men and women.
Between 2026 and 2027 SPA will increase to 67 years and between 2044 and 2046 to 68 years for both sexes. This is based on SPA under the 2014 Pensions Act.
** This is consistent with the age-group definitions used in ONS Labour Market Statistics.

Source: Office for National Statistics

2014-based Principal projection

15.2c Population projections by the Office for National Statistics
Scotland, PERSONS, thousands

Components of change (mid-year to mid-year), total fertility rate and expectation of life at birth based on the mortality rates for the year

	2014-2015	2015-2016	2016-2017	2017-2018	2018-2019	2019-2020	2020-2021	2021-2022	2022-2023	2023-2024	2024-2025	2025-2026	2026-2027	2027-2028	2028-2029	2029-2030	2030-2031	2031-2032	2032-2033	2033-2034
Population at start	5,348	5,365	5,380	5,396	5,412	5,428	5,445	5,462	5,480	5,497	5,514	5,532	5,548	5,565	5,581	5,596	5,610	5,624	5,636	5,648
Births	56	56	55	56	56	57	57	57	57	57	58	58	57	57	57	57	56	56	56	56
Deaths	58	54	54	54	54	54	54	55	55	55	55	56	56	57	57	58	58	59	60	60
Natural change	-2	2	1	2	2	2	3	3	3	2	2	2	1	1	0	-1	-2	-3	-3	-4
International migration inflows	39	33	33	33	33	33	33	33	33	33	33	33	33	33	33	33	33	33	33	33
Crossborder migration inflows	47	47	47	47	47	47	47	47	47	47	46	46	47	47	47	47	47	47	47	47
International migration outflows	25	25	25	25	24	24	24	24	24	24	24	24	24	24	24	24	24	24	24	24
Crossborder migration outflows	41	42	42	42	42	42	41	41	41	41	41	41	41	41	41	41	41	41	41	41
Net international migration	14	8	9	9	9	9	9	9	9	9	9	9	9	9	9	9	9	9	9	9
Net crossborder migration	6	5	5	5	5	5	5	5	5	5	6	6	6	6	6	6	6	6	6	6
Net migration	19	14	14	14	14	15	15	15	15	15	15	15	15	15	15	15	15	15	15	15
Total change	17	16	15	16	16	17	17	17	17	17	17	17	16	16	15	14	13	13	12	11
Population at end	5,365	5,380	5,396	5,412	5,428	5,445	5,462	5,480	5,497	5,514	5,532	5,548	5,565	5,581	5,596	5,610	5,624	5,636	5,648	5,659
Annual growth rate	0.32%	0.29%	0.29%	0.29%	0.30%	0.31%	0.32%	0.32%	0.32%	0.32%	0.31%	0.30%	0.30%	0.28%	0.27%	0.26%	0.24%	0.22%	0.21%	0.19%
Total fertility rate (TFR)	1.59	1.58	1.56	1.57	1.58	1.59	1.60	1.61	1.62	1.63	1.65	1.66	1.66	1.67	1.68	1.68	1.69	1.69	1.70	1.70
EOLB Males	76.6	77.7	77.9	78.2	78.5	78.7	78.9	79.2	79.4	79.6	79.9	80.1	80.3	80.5	80.7	80.9	81.0	81.2	81.4	81.5
Females	80.7	81.5	81.7	81.9	82.0	82.2	82.4	82.5	82.7	82.9	83.0	83.2	83.3	83.5	83.6	83.8	83.9	84.1	84.2	84.3

	2034-2035	2035-2036	2036-2037	2037-2038	2038-2039	2039-2040	2040-2041	2041-2042	2042-2043	2043-2044	2044-2045	2045-2046	2046-2047	2047-2048	2048-2049	2049-2050	2050-2051	2051-2052	2052-2053	2053-2054
Population at start	5,659	5,669	5,678	5,686	5,694	5,701	5,708	5,715	5,721	5,726	5,732	5,737	5,741	5,745	5,749	5,753	5,756	5,759	5,761	5,764
Births	56	56	56	56	56	56	56	56	56	56	56	56	56	56	56	56	56	56	56	56
Deaths	61	61	62	63	63	64	65	65	66	66	67	67	67	68	68	68	68	69	69	69
Natural change	-5	-6	-6	-7	-8	-8	-9	-9	-9	-10	-10	-11	-11	-11	-12	-12	-12	-12	-12	-12
International migration inflows	33	33	33	33	33	33	33	33	33	33	33	33	33	33	33	33	33	33	33	33
Crossborder migration inflows	46	46	46	46	46	46	46	46	46	47	47	47	47	47	47	47	47	47	47	47
International migration outflows	24	24	24	24	24	24	24	24	24	24	24	24	24	24	24	24	24	24	24	24
Crossborder migration outflows	41	41	41	41	41	41	41	41	41	41	41	41	41	41	41	41	41	41	41	41
Net international migration	9	9	9	9	9	9	9	9	9	9	9	9	9	9	9	9	9	9	9	9
Net crossborder migration	6	5	5	5	5	6	6	6	6	6	6	6	6	6	6	6	6	6	6	6
Net migration	15	15	15	15	15	15	15	15	15	15	15	15	15	15	15	15	15	15	15	15
Total change	10	9	8	8	7	7	6	6	6	5	5	5	4	4	3	3	3	3	3	3
Population at end	5,669	5,678	5,686	5,694	5,701	5,708	5,715	5,721	5,726	5,732	5,737	5,741	5,745	5,749	5,753	5,756	5,759	5,761	5,764	5,767
Annual growth rate	0.18%	0.16%	0.15%	0.14%	0.13%	0.12%	0.11%	0.11%	0.10%	0.09%	0.09%	0.08%	0.07%	0.07%	0.06%	0.06%	0.05%	0.05%	0.05%	0.04%
Total fertility rate (TFR)	1.70	1.70	1.70	1.70	1.70	1.70	1.70	1.70	1.70	1.70	1.70	1.70	1.70	1.70	1.70	1.70	1.70	1.70	1.70	1.70
EOLB Males	81.7	81.8	82.0	82.1	82.3	82.4	82.5	82.7	82.8	82.9	83.0	83.2	83.3	83.4	83.6	83.7	83.8	84.0	84.1	84.2
Females	84.5	84.6	84.7	84.8	85.0	85.1	85.2	85.3	85.4	85.5	85.7	85.8	85.9	86.0	86.1	86.3	86.4	86.5	86.6	86.7

15.2c Population projections by the Office for National Statistics
Scotland, PERSONS, thousands

2014-based
Principal projection

Components of change (mid-year to mid-year), total fertility rate and expectation of life at birth based on the mortality rates for the year

	2054-2055	2055-2056	2056-2057	2057-2058	2058-2059	2059-2060	2060-2061	2061-2062	2062-2063	2063-2064	2064-2065	2065-2066	2066-2067	2067-2068	2068-2069	2069-2070	2070-2071	2071-2072	2072-2073	2073-2074
Population at start	5,767	5,769	5,772	5,774	5,777	5,780	5,783	5,786	5,790	5,794	5,798	5,802	5,807	5,812	5,817	5,823	5,828	5,834	5,840	5,846
Births	56	56	56	56	56	56	56	56	56	56	56	56	56	56	56	56	56	56	56	56
Deaths	69	69	69	69	68	68	68	68	67	67	67	66	66	66	65	65	65	65	65	65
Natural change	-13	-12	-12	-12	-12	-12	-12	-11	-11	-11	-11	-10	-10	-10	-10	-9	-9	-9	-9	-9
International migration inflows	33	33	33	33	33	33	33	33	33	33	33	33	33	33	33	33	33	33	33	33
Crossborder migration inflows	47	47	47	47	47	46	46	46	46	46	46	46	47	47	47	47	47	47	47	47
International migration outflows	24	24	24	24	24	24	24	24	24	24	24	24	24	24	24	24	24	24	24	24
Crossborder migration outflows	41	41	41	41	41	41	41	41	41	41	41	41	41	41	41	41	41	41	41	41
Net international migration	9	9	9	9	9	9	9	9	9	9	9	9	9	9	9	9	9	9	9	9
Net crossborder migration	6	6	6	6	6	6	6	6	6	6	6	6	6	6	6	6	6	6	6	6
Net migration	15	15	15	15	15	15	15	15	15	15	15	15	15	15	15	15	15	15	15	15
Total change	3	3	3	3	3	3	3	4	4	4	4	5	5	5	5	6	6	6	6	6
Population at end	5,769	5,772	5,774	5,777	5,780	5,783	5,786	5,790	5,794	5,798	5,802	5,807	5,812	5,817	5,823	5,828	5,834	5,840	5,846	5,853
Annual growth rate	0.04%	0.05%	0.05%	0.05%	0.05%	0.05%	0.06%	0.06%	0.07%	0.07%	0.08%	0.08%	0.09%	0.09%	0.09%	0.10%	0.10%	0.11%	0.11%	0.11%
Total fertility rate (TFR)	1.70	1.70	1.70	1.70	1.70	1.70	1.70	1.70	1.70	1.70	1.70	1.70	1.70	1.70	1.70	1.70	1.70	1.70	1.70	1.70
EOLB Males	84.4	84.5	84.6	84.7	84.9	85.0	85.1	85.3	85.4	85.5	85.6	85.8	85.9	86.0	86.2	86.3	86.4	86.5	86.7	86.8
Females	86.9	87.0	87.1	87.2	87.3	87.4	87.6	87.7	87.8	87.9	88.0	88.2	88.3	88.4	88.5	88.6	88.7	88.9	89.0	89.1

	2074-2075	2075-2076	2076-2077	2077-2078	2078-2079	2079-2080	2080-2081	2081-2082	2082-2083	2083-2084	2084-2085	2085-2086	2086-2087	2087-2088	2088-2089	2089-2090	2090-2091	2091-2092	2092-2093	2093-2094
Population at start	5,853	5,859	5,865	5,871	5,877	5,884	5,890	5,896	5,902	5,908	5,913	5,919	5,925	5,931	5,937	5,943	5,950	5,956	5,963	5,970
Births	56	56	56	56	56	56	56	56	56	56	56	56	56	56	56	56	56	56	56	56
Deaths	65	65	65	65	65	65	65	65	65	65	65	65	65	65	65	65	65	64	64	64
Natural change	-9	-9	-9	-9	-9	-9	-9	-9	-9	-9	-9	-9	-9	-9	-9	-9	-9	-8	-8	-8
International migration inflows	33	33	33	33	33	33	33	33	33	33	33	33	33	33	33	33	33	33	33	33
Crossborder migration inflows	47	47	47	47	47	47	47	47	47	47	47	47	47	47	47	47	47	47	47	47
International migration outflows	24	24	24	24	24	24	24	24	24	24	24	24	24	24	24	24	24	24	24	24
Crossborder migration outflows	41	41	41	41	41	41	41	41	41	41	41	41	41	41	41	41	41	41	41	41
Net international migration	9	9	9	9	9	9	9	9	9	9	9	9	9	9	9	9	9	9	9	9
Net crossborder migration	6	6	6	6	6	6	6	6	6	6	6	6	6	6	6	6	6	6	6	6
Net migration	15	15	15	15	15	15	15	15	15	15	15	15	15	15	15	15	15	15	15	15
Total change	6	6	6	6	6	6	6	6	6	6	6	6	6	6	6	6	6	7	7	7
Population at end	5,859	5,865	5,871	5,877	5,884	5,890	5,896	5,902	5,908	5,913	5,919	5,925	5,931	5,937	5,943	5,950	5,956	5,963	5,970	5,977
Annual growth rate	0.11%	0.11%	0.11%	0.11%	0.10%	0.10%	0.10%	0.10%	0.10%	0.10%	0.10%	0.10%	0.10%	0.10%	0.10%	0.11%	0.11%	0.11%	0.11%	0.12%
Total fertility rate (TFR)	1.70	1.70	1.70	1.70	1.70	1.70	1.70	1.70	1.70	1.70	1.70	1.70	1.70	1.70	1.70	1.70	1.70	1.70	1.70	1.70
EOLB Males	86.9	87.1	87.2	87.3	87.4	87.6	87.7	87.8	87.9	88.1	88.2	88.3	88.5	88.6	88.7	88.8	89.0	89.1	89.2	89.3
Females	89.2	89.3	89.5	89.6	89.7	89.8	89.9	90.0	90.2	90.3	90.4	90.5	90.6	90.8	90.9	91.0	91.1	91.2	91.3	91.5

15.2c Population projections by the Office for National Statistics
Scotland, PERSONS, thousands

2014-based
Principal projection

Components of change (mid-year to mid-year), total fertility rate
and expectation of life at birth based on the mortality rates for the year

	2094 -2095	2095 -2096	2096 -2097	2097 -2098	2098 -2099	2099 -2100	2100 -2101	2101 -2102	2102 -2103	2103 -2104	2104 -2105	2105 -2106	2106 -2107	2107 -2108	2108 -2109	2109 -2110	2110 -2111	2111 -2112	2112 -2113	2113 -2114
Population at start	5,977	5,984	5,991	5,999	6,006	6,014	6,022	6,030	6,038	6,046	6,054	6,062	6,070	6,079	6,087	6,095	6,103	6,111	6,119	6,127
Births	56	56	56	56	56	56	56	56	56	56	56	56	56	56	56	56	56	56	56	56
Deaths	64	64	63	63	63	63	63	63	63	63	63	63	63	63	63	63	63	63	63	63
Natural change	-8	-8	-8	-7	-7	-7	-7	-7	-7	-7	-7	-7	-7	-7	-7	-7	-7	-7	-7	-7
International migration inflows	33	33	33	33	33	33	33	33	33	33	33	33	33	33	33	33	33	33	33	33
Crossborder migration inflows	47	47	47	47	47	47	47	47	47	47	47	47	47	47	47	47	47	47	47	47
International migration outflows	24	24	24	24	24	24	24	24	24	24	24	24	24	24	24	24	24	24	24	24
Crossborder migration outflows	41	41	41	41	41	41	41	41	41	41	41	41	41	41	41	41	41	42	42	42
Net international migration	9	9	9	9	9	9	9	9	9	9	9	9	9	9	9	9	9	9	9	9
Net crossborder migration	6	6	6	6	6	6	6	6	6	6	6	6	6	6	6	6	6	6	6	6
Net migration	15	15	15	15	15	15	15	15	15	15	15	15	15	15	15	15	15	15	15	15
Total change	7	7	7	8	8	8	8	8	8	8	8	8	8	8	8	8	8	8	8	8
Population at end	5,984	5,991	5,999	6,006	6,014	6,022	6,030	6,038	6,046	6,054	6,062	6,070	6,079	6,087	6,095	6,103	6,111	6,119	6,127	6,135
Annual growth rate	0.12%	0.12%	0.12%	0.13%	0.13%	0.13%	0.13%	0.13%	0.13%	0.13%	0.13%	0.13%	0.13%	0.13%	0.13%	0.13%	0.13%	0.13%	0.13%	0.13%
Total fertility rate (TFR)	1.70	1.70	1.70	1.70	1.70	1.70	1.70	1.70	1.70	1.70	1.70	1.70	1.70	1.70	1.70	1.70	1.70	1.70	1.70	1.70
EOLB Males	89.5	89.6	89.7	89.9	90.0	90.1	90.2	90.4	90.5	90.6	90.7	90.9	91.0	91.1	91.3	91.4	91.5	91.6	91.8	91.9
Females	91.6	91.7	91.8	91.9	92.1	92.2	92.3	92.4	92.5	92.6	92.8	92.9	93.0	93.1	93.2	93.4	93.5	93.6	93.7	93.8

Source: Office for National Statistics

Note: Figures may not add exactly due to rounding.
* Children under 16. Working age and pensionable age populations based on state pension age (SPA) for given year.
Between 2012 and 2018, SPA will change from 65 years for men and 61 years for women, to 65 years for both sexes.
Then between 2019 and 2020, SPA will change from 65 years to 66 years for both men and women.
Between 2026 and 2027 SPA will increase to 67 years and between 2044 and 2046 to 68 years for both sexes. This is based on SPA under the 2014 Pensions Act.
** This is consistent with the age-group definitions used in ONS Labour Market Statistics.

15.2d Population projections by the Office for National Statistics
Northern Ireland, PERSONS, thousands

2014-based
Principal projection

Components of change (mid-year to mid-year), total fertility rate
and expectation of life at birth based on the mortality rates for the year

	2014-2015	2015-2016	2016-2017	2017-2018	2018-2019	2019-2020	2020-2021	2021-2022	2022-2023	2023-2024	2024-2025	2025-2026	2026-2027	2027-2028	2028-2029	2029-2030	2030-2031	2031-2032	2032-2033	2033-2034
Population at start	1,840	1,851	1,863	1,874	1,884	1,894	1,904	1,913	1,922	1,930	1,939	1,947	1,954	1,961	1,968	1,974	1,980	1,986	1,991	1,996
Births	24	24	24	24	24	24	24	24	24	23	23	23	23	23	23	23	22	22	22	22
Deaths	16	15	15	15	15	15	15	15	15	16	16	16	16	16	17	17	17	17	18	18
Natural change	9	9	9	9	9	9	9	9	8	8	7	7	7	6	6	6	5	5	5	5
International migration inflows	13	13	13	13	13	13	13	13	13	13	13	13	13	13	13	13	13	13	13	13
Crossborder migration inflows	11	11	11	11	11	11	10	10	10	10	10	10	10	10	10	10	10	10	10	10
International migration outflows	10	10	11	11	11	12	12	12	12	12	12	12	12	12	12	12	12	12	12	12
Crossborder migration outflows	11	11	11	11	11	11	11	11	11	11	11	11	11	11	11	11	11	11	11	11
Net international migration	3	3	2	2	2	1	1	1	1	1	1	1	1	1	1	1	1	1	1	1
Net crossborder migration	-1	-1	-1	-1	-1	-1	-1	-1	-1	-1	-1	-1	-1	-1	-1	-1	-1	-1	-1	-1
Net migration	2	2	1	1	1	1	0	0	0	0	0	0	0	0	0	0	0	0	0	0
Total change	11	11	11	10	10	10	9	9	9	8	8	8	7	7	6	6	6	5	5	5
Population at end	1,851	1,863	1,874	1,884	1,894	1,904	1,913	1,922	1,930	1,939	1,947	1,954	1,961	1,968	1,974	1,980	1,986	1,991	1,996	2,000
Annual growth rate	0.58%	0.62%	0.58%	0.56%	0.54%	0.51%	0.48%	0.47%	0.45%	0.43%	0.41%	0.39%	0.36%	0.34%	0.32%	0.30%	0.28%	0.26%	0.25%	0.24%
Total fertility rate (TFR)	1.95	1.97	1.97	1.97	1.98	1.98	1.99	1.99	2.00	2.00	2.00	2.00	2.00	2.00	2.00	2.00	2.00	2.00	2.00	2.00
EOLB Males	78.2	78.9	79.1	79.4	79.7	79.9	80.2	80.4	80.6	80.8	81.0	81.2	81.4	81.6	81.8	82.0	82.2	82.3	82.5	82.6
Females	82.1	82.9	83.1	83.3	83.5	83.7	83.9	84.1	84.2	84.4	84.6	84.7	84.9	85.0	85.2	85.3	85.5	85.6	85.8	85.9

	2034-2035	2035-2036	2036-2037	2037-2038	2038-2039	2039-2040	2040-2041	2041-2042	2042-2043	2043-2044	2044-2045	2045-2046	2046-2047	2047-2048	2048-2049	2049-2050	2050-2051	2051-2052	2052-2053	2053-2054
Population at start	2,000	2,005	2,009	2,013	2,017	2,021	2,025	2,029	2,032	2,035	2,039	2,042	2,044	2,047	2,049	2,051	2,053	2,054	2,055	2,056
Births	22	23	23	23	23	23	23	23	23	23	23	23	23	23	23	23	23	23	23	23
Deaths	18	18	19	19	19	20	20	20	20	21	21	21	21	21	22	22	22	22	22	22
Natural change	4	4	4	4	4	4	3	3	3	3	3	2	2	2	2	1	1	1	1	0
International migration inflows	13	13	13	13	13	13	13	13	13	13	13	13	13	13	13	13	13	13	13	13
Crossborder migration inflows	10	10	10	10	10	10	10	10	10	10	10	10	10	10	10	10	10	10	10	10
International migration outflows	12	12	12	12	12	12	12	12	12	12	12	12	12	12	12	12	12	12	12	12
Crossborder migration outflows	11	11	11	11	11	11	11	11	11	11	11	11	11	11	11	11	11	11	11	11
Net international migration	1	1	1	1	1	1	1	1	1	1	1	1	1	1	1	1	1	1	1	1
Net crossborder migration	-1	-1	-1	-1	-1	-1	-1	-1	-1	-1	-1	-1	-1	-1	-1	-1	-1	-1	-1	-1
Net migration	0	0	0	0	0	0	0	0	0	0	0	0	0	0	0	0	0	0	0	0
Total change	5	4	4	4	4	4	4	3	3	3	3	3	2	2	2	2	1	1	1	1
Population at end	2,005	2,009	2,013	2,017	2,021	2,025	2,029	2,032	2,035	2,039	2,042	2,044	2,047	2,049	2,051	2,053	2,054	2,055	2,056	2,057
Annual growth rate	0.23%	0.21%	0.21%	0.20%	0.19%	0.19%	0.18%	0.17%	0.16%	0.15%	0.14%	0.13%	0.12%	0.11%	0.10%	0.08%	0.07%	0.06%	0.04%	0.03%
Total fertility rate (TFR)	2.00	2.00	2.00	2.00	2.00	2.00	2.00	2.00	2.00	2.00	2.00	2.00	2.00	2.00	2.00	2.00	2.00	2.00	2.00	2.00
EOLB Males	82.8	82.9	83.1	83.2	83.3	83.4	83.6	83.7	83.8	83.9	84.1	84.2	84.3	84.5	84.6	84.7	84.8	85.0	85.1	85.2
Females	86.0	86.1	86.3	86.4	86.5	86.6	86.7	86.8	86.9	87.1	87.2	87.3	87.4	87.5	87.6	87.7	87.9	88.0	88.1	88.2

2014-based Principal projection

15.2d Population projections by the Office for National Statistics
Northern Ireland, PERSONS, thousands

Components of change (mid-year to mid-year), total fertility rate and expectation of life at birth based on the mortality rates for the year

	2054–2055	2055–2056	2056–2057	2057–2058	2058–2059	2059–2060	2060–2061	2061–2062	2062–2063	2063–2064	2064–2065	2065–2066	2066–2067	2067–2068	2068–2069	2069–2070	2070–2071	2071–2072	2072–2073	2073–2074
Population at start	2,057	2,057	2,057	2,057	2,057	2,057	2,057	2,056	2,056	2,056	2,055	2,055	2,055	2,054	2,055	2,055	2,055	2,055	2,056	2,056
Births	23	23	22	22	22	22	22	22	22	22	22	22	22	22	22	22	22	22	22	22
Deaths	23	23	23	23	23	23	23	23	23	23	23	23	23	22	22	22	22	22	22	22
Natural change	0	0	0	0	0	-1	-1	-1	-1	-1	-1	0	0	0	0	0	0	0	0	0
International migration inflows	13	13	13	13	13	13	13	13	13	13	13	13	13	13	13	13	13	13	13	13
Crossborder migration inflows	10	10	10	10	10	10	10	10	10	10	10	10	10	10	10	10	10	10	10	10
International migration outflows	12	12	12	12	12	12	12	12	12	12	12	12	12	12	12	12	12	12	12	12
Crossborder migration outflows	11	11	11	11	11	11	11	11	11	11	11	11	11	11	11	11	11	11	11	11
Net international migration	1	1	1	1	1	1	1	1	1	1	1	1	1	1	1	1	1	1	1	1
Net crossborder migration	-1	-1	-1	-1	-1	-1	-1	-1	-1	-1	-1	-1	-1	-1	-1	-1	-1	-1	-1	-1
Net migration	0	0	0	0	0	0	0	0	0	0	0	0	0	0	0	0	0	0	0	0
Total change	0	0	0	0	0	0	0	0	0	0	0	0	0	0	0	0	0	0	0	1
Population at end	2,057	2,057	2,057	2,057	2,057	2,057	2,056	2,056	2,056	2,055	2,055	2,055	2,054	2,055	2,055	2,055	2,055	2,056	2,056	2,057
Annual growth rate	0.02%	0.01%	0.00%	-0.01%	-0.01%	-0.02%	-0.02%	-0.02%	-0.02%	-0.02%	-0.01%	-0.01%	-0.01%	0.00%	0.01%	0.01%	0.02%	0.02%	0.03%	0.03%
Total fertility rate (TFR)	2.00	2.00	2.00	2.00	2.00	2.00	2.00	2.00	2.00	2.00	2.00	2.00	2.00	2.00	2.00	2.00	2.00	2.00	2.00	2.00
EOLB Males	85.3	85.5	85.6	85.7	85.8	86.0	86.1	86.2	86.3	86.5	86.6	86.7	86.8	87.0	87.1	87.2	87.3	87.5	87.6	87.7
Females	88.3	88.4	88.5	88.6	88.8	88.9	89.0	89.1	89.2	89.3	89.4	89.5	89.7	89.8	89.9	90.0	90.1	90.2	90.3	90.5

	2074–2075	2075–2076	2076–2077	2077–2078	2078–2079	2079–2080	2080–2081	2081–2082	2082–2083	2083–2084	2084–2085	2085–2086	2086–2087	2087–2088	2088–2089	2089–2090	2090–2091	2091–2092	2092–2093	2093–2094
Population at start	2,057	2,058	2,059	2,059	2,060	2,061	2,062	2,063	2,064	2,065	2,066	2,067	2,067	2,068	2,069	2,070	2,071	2,072	2,073	2,074
Births	22	22	22	22	22	22	22	22	22	22	22	22	22	22	22	22	22	22	22	22
Deaths	22	22	22	22	22	22	22	22	22	22	22	22	21	21	21	21	21	21	21	21
Natural change	0	1	1	1	1	1	1	1	1	1	1	1	1	1	1	1	1	1	1	1
International migration inflows	13	13	13	13	13	13	13	13	13	13	13	13	13	13	13	13	13	13	13	13
Crossborder migration inflows	10	10	10	10	10	10	10	10	10	10	10	10	10	10	10	10	10	10	10	10
International migration outflows	12	12	12	12	12	12	12	12	12	12	12	12	12	12	12	12	12	12	12	12
Crossborder migration outflows	11	11	11	11	11	11	11	11	11	11	11	11	11	11	11	11	11	11	11	11
Net international migration	1	1	1	1	1	1	1	1	1	1	1	1	1	1	1	1	1	1	1	1
Net crossborder migration	-1	-1	-1	-1	-1	-1	-1	-1	-1	-1	-1	-1	-1	-1	-1	-1	-1	-1	-1	-1
Net migration	0	0	0	0	0	0	0	0	0	0	0	0	0	0	0	0	0	0	0	0
Total change	1	1	0	1	1	1	1	1	1	1	1	0	1	1	1	1	1	1	1	0
Population at end	2,058	2,059	2,059	2,060	2,061	2,062	2,063	2,064	2,065	2,066	2,067	2,067	2,068	2,069	2,070	2,071	2,072	2,073	2,074	2,074
Annual growth rate	0.04%	0.04%	0.04%	0.04%	0.04%	0.04%	0.04%	0.04%	0.04%	0.04%	0.04%	0.04%	0.04%	0.04%	0.04%	0.04%	0.04%	0.04%	0.04%	0.05%
Total fertility rate (TFR)	2.00	2.00	2.00	2.00	2.00	2.00	2.00	2.00	2.00	2.00	2.00	2.00	2.00	2.00	2.00	2.00	2.00	2.00	2.00	2.00
EOLB Males	87.8	88.0	88.1	88.2	88.3	88.5	88.6	88.7	88.8	88.9	89.1	89.2	89.3	89.4	89.6	89.7	89.8	89.9	90.1	90.2
Females	90.6	90.7	90.8	90.9	91.0	91.1	91.2	91.4	91.5	91.6	91.7	91.8	91.9	92.0	92.1	92.3	92.4	92.5	92.6	92.7

15.2d Population projections by the Office for National Statistics
Northern Ireland, PERSONS, thousands

2014-based
Principal projection

Components of change (mid-year to mid-year), total fertility rate
and expectation of life at birth based on the mortality rates for the year

	2094 -2095	2095 -2096	2096 -2097	2097 -2098	2098 -2099	2099 -2100	2100 -2101	2101 -2102	2102 -2103	2103 -2104	2104 -2105	2105 -2106	2106 -2107	2107 -2108	2108 -2109	2109 -2110	2110 -2111	2111 -2112	2112 -2113	2113 -2114
Population at start	2,074	2,075	2,076	2,077	2,078	2,079	2,080	2,081	2,082	2,083	2,084	2,085	2,086	2,087	2,088	2,089	2,090	2,091	2,092	2,094
Births	22	22	22	22	22	22	22	22	22	22	22	22	22	22	22	22	22	22	22	22
Deaths	21	21	21	21	21	21	21	21	21	21	21	21	21	21	21	21	21	21	21	21
Natural change	1	1	1	1	1	1	1	1	1	1	1	1	1	1	1	1	1	1	1	1
International migration inflows	13	13	13	13	13	13	13	13	13	13	13	13	13	13	13	13	13	13	13	13
Crossborder migration inflows	10	10	10	10	10	10	10	10	10	10	10	10	10	10	10	10	10	10	10	10
International migration outflows	12	12	12	12	12	12	12	12	12	12	12	12	12	12	12	12	12	12	12	12
Crossborder migration outflows	11	11	11	11	11	11	11	11	11	11	11	11	11	11	11	11	11	11	11	11
Net international migration	1	1	1	1	1	1	1	1	1	1	1	1	1	1	1	1	1	1	1	1
Net crossborder migration	-1	-1	-1	-1	-1	-1	-1	-1	-1	-1	-1	-1	-1	-1	-1	-1	-1	-1	-1	-1
Net migration	0	0	0	0	0	0	0	0	0	0	0	0	0	0	0	0	0	0	0	0
Total change	1	1	1	1	1	1	1	1	1	1	1	1	1	1	1	1	1	1	1	1
Population at end	2,075	2,076	2,077	2,078	2,079	2,080	2,081	2,082	2,083	2,084	2,085	2,086	2,087	2,088	2,089	2,090	2,091	2,092	2,093	2,095
Annual growth rate	0.05%	0.05%	0.05%	0.05%	0.05%	0.05%	0.05%	0.05%	0.05%	0.05%	0.05%	0.05%	0.05%	0.05%	0.05%	0.05%	0.04%	0.04%	0.04%	0.04%
Total fertility rate (TFR)	2.00	2.00	2.00	2.00	2.00	2.00	2.00	2.00	2.00	2.00	2.00	2.00	2.00	2.00	2.00	2.00	2.00	2.00	2.00	2.00
EOLB Males	90.3	90.4	90.6	90.7	90.8	90.9	91.0	91.2	91.3	91.4	91.5	91.7	91.8	91.9	92.0	92.2	92.3	92.4	92.5	92.6
Females	92.8	92.9	93.0	93.2	93.3	93.4	93.5	93.6	93.7	93.8	94.0	94.1	94.2	94.3	94.4	94.5	94.6	94.7	94.9	95.0

Source: Office for National Statistics

Note: Figures may not add exactly due to rounding.
* Children under 16. Working age and pensionable age populations based on state pension age (SPA) for given year.
Between 2012 and 2018, SPA will change from 65 years for men and 61 years for women, to 65 years for both sexes.
Then between 2019 and 2020, SPA will change from 65 years to 66 years for both men and women.
Between 2026 and 2027 SPA will increase to 67 years and between 2044 and 2046 to 68 years for both sexes. This is based on SPA under the 2014 Pensions Act.
** This is consistent with the age-group definitions used in ONS Labour Market Statistics.

15.3a Mid-2014 Population estimates for United Kingdom by sex and single year of age

Ages	Persons	Males	Females	Ages	Persons	Males	Females
All Ages	64,596,752	31,793,606	32,803,146	45	924,572	455,317	469,255
0	778,365	398,997	379,368	46	925,262	455,778	469,484
1	799,689	410,138	389,551	47	938,200	464,071	474,129
2	828,035	424,084	403,951	48	938,109	461,610	476,499
3	817,703	418,717	398,986	49	946,384	465,864	480,520
4	802,851	410,610	392,241	50	937,343	461,541	475,802
5	795,304	406,814	388,490	51	918,420	453,132	465,288
6	801,582	410,302	391,280	52	898,807	444,765	454,042
7	774,783	397,054	377,729	53	868,951	430,028	438,923
8	758,635	388,063	370,572	54	834,496	412,989	421,507
9	728,820	373,006	355,814	55	816,860	403,877	412,983
10	715,874	366,463	349,411	56	798,452	394,739	403,713
11	695,512	356,301	339,211	57	769,793	380,158	389,635
12	684,817	350,571	334,246	58	742,465	366,613	375,852
13	703,502	359,210	344,292	59	715,304	352,170	363,134
14	722,252	370,466	351,786	60	716,755	351,859	364,896
15	745,738	382,196	363,542	61	707,761	347,724	360,037
16	755,713	387,348	368,365	62	687,590	336,380	351,210
17	778,479	399,339	379,140	63	692,953	338,723	354,230
18	781,757	403,292	378,465	64	706,530	344,106	362,424
19	790,575	405,326	385,249	65	723,588	353,019	370,569
20	825,988	423,227	402,761	66	761,546	370,692	390,854
21	835,000	425,645	409,355	67	823,666	401,134	422,532
22	870,754	439,175	431,579	68	636,560	308,634	327,926
23	897,324	456,389	440,935	69	616,428	297,414	319,014
24	884,093	449,824	434,269	70	614,029	296,179	317,850
25	876,931	441,752	435,179	71	572,282	273,379	298,903
26	887,260	444,147	443,113	72	511,473	242,111	269,362
27	868,635	430,783	437,852	73	460,767	216,089	244,678
28	877,071	439,328	437,743	74	475,010	222,378	252,632
29	881,130	440,748	440,382	75	469,132	218,365	250,767
30	861,361	428,719	432,642	76	453,979	210,403	243,576
31	869,615	431,951	437,664	77	428,664	196,229	232,435
32	869,997	430,780	439,217	78	405,667	183,406	222,261
33	877,344	435,537	441,807	79	382,724	171,366	211,358
34	877,878	436,154	441,724	80	351,581	154,878	196,703
35	841,783	419,401	422,382	81	331,083	143,293	187,790
36	785,466	391,384	394,082	82	317,551	134,979	182,572
37	773,664	386,312	387,352	83	296,568	122,881	173,687
38	788,937	392,139	396,798	84	271,261	109,047	162,214
39	804,262	399,506	404,756	85 / 85+	240,521	94,562	145,959
40	818,572	405,724	412,848	86	211,901	81,066	130,835
41	855,331	424,493	430,838	87	189,460	70,907	118,553
42	892,858	442,516	450,342	88	167,109	60,111	106,998
43	922,327	454,033	468,294	89	143,400	49,450	93,950
44	901,418	444,445	456,973	90	550,810	157,781	393,029

Source: Office for National Statistics
Note: It is ONS policy to publish estimates to the nearest hundred persons. Rounded (and particularly unit)
estimates cannot be precisely accurate.
: Data not available

15.3b Population projections by the Office for National Statistics
United Kingdom, PERSONS, thousands

2014-based
Principal projection

Projected populations at mid-years by age last birthday

Ages	2014	2015	2016	2017	2018	2019	2020	2021	2022	2023	2024	2025	2026	2027	2028	2029	2030	2031	2032	2033
Thousands																				
0-14	11,408	11,509	11,629	11,768	11,901	12,012	12,111	12,180	12,232	12,258	12,286	12,303	12,299	12,278	12,280	12,299	12,321	12,336	12,345	12,349
15-29	12,556	12,595	12,570	12,518	12,449	12,396	12,334	12,272	12,239	12,258	12,271	12,319	12,386	12,468	12,546	12,615	12,701	12,812	12,946	13,073
30-44	12,741	12,751	12,731	12,734	12,801	12,898	13,025	13,191	13,361	13,497	13,580	13,603	13,624	13,651	13,656	13,658	13,615	13,553	13,476	13,387
45-59	12,973	13,135	13,290	13,389	13,425	13,408	13,360	13,266	13,129	12,988	12,886	12,814	12,751	12,683	12,631	12,573	12,563	12,535	12,534	12,596
60-74	9,707	9,834	10,013	10,175	10,314	10,438	10,582	10,746	10,777	10,889	11,057	11,252	11,453	11,660	11,840	12,013	12,166	12,317	12,417	12,457
75 & over	5,211	5,274	5,340	5,445	5,596	5,776	5,947	6,128	6,463	6,731	6,955	7,154	7,331	7,493	7,663	7,831	7,986	8,154	8,335	8,528
All ages	64,597	65,097	65,572	66,030	66,487	66,928	67,360	67,781	68,203	68,622	69,036	69,444	69,844	70,234	70,616	70,989	71,353	71,707	72,053	72,391
Percentages																				
0-14	17.7	17.7	17.7	17.8	17.9	17.9	18.0	18.0	17.9	17.9	17.8	17.7	17.6	17.5	17.4	17.3	17.3	17.2	17.1	17.1
15-29	19.4	19.3	19.2	19.0	18.7	18.5	18.3	18.1	17.9	17.9	17.8	17.7	17.7	17.8	17.8	17.8	17.8	17.9	18.0	18.1
30-44	19.7	19.6	19.4	19.3	19.3	19.3	19.3	19.5	19.6	19.7	19.7	19.6	19.5	19.4	19.3	19.2	19.1	18.9	18.7	18.5
45-59	20.1	20.2	20.3	20.3	20.2	20.0	19.8	19.6	19.3	18.9	18.7	18.5	18.3	18.1	17.9	17.7	17.6	17.5	17.4	17.4
60-74	15.0	15.1	15.3	15.4	15.5	15.6	15.7	15.9	15.8	15.9	16.0	16.2	16.4	16.6	16.8	16.9	17.1	17.2	17.2	17.2
75 & over	8.1	8.1	8.1	8.2	8.4	8.6	8.8	9.0	9.5	9.8	10.1	10.3	10.5	10.7	10.9	11.0	11.2	11.4	11.6	11.8
All ages	100.0	100.0	100.0	100.0	100.0	100.0	100.0	100.0	100.0	100.0	100.0	100.0	100.0	100.0	100.0	100.0	100.0	100.0	100.0	100.0
Mean age	40.3	40.4	40.5	40.6	40.8	40.9	41.0	41.2	41.3	41.4	41.6	41.7	41.9	42.0	42.1	42.3	42.4	42.6	42.7	42.8
Median age	40.0	40.0	40.0	40.0	40.1	40.2	40.3	40.5	40.6	40.7	40.9	41.0	41.1	41.3	41.4	41.6	41.7	41.9	42.0	42.2

Ages	2034	2035	2036	2037	2038	2039	2040	2041	2042	2043	2044	2045	2046	2047	2048	2049	2050	2051	2052	2053
Thousands																				
0-14	12,350	12,350	12,350	12,353	12,359	12,371	12,391	12,418	12,453	12,494	12,542	12,594	12,650	12,708	12,767	12,826	12,884	12,940	12,991	13,039
15-29	13,182	13,280	13,349	13,403	13,428	13,457	13,474	13,470	13,450	13,452	13,472	13,494	13,509	13,518	13,522	13,524	13,524	13,525	13,528	13,534
30-44	13,324	13,258	13,198	13,168	13,188	13,203	13,252	13,320	13,403	13,483	13,552	13,639	13,750	13,884	14,011	14,120	14,219	14,288	14,342	14,368
45-59	12,691	12,816	12,983	13,152	13,288	13,372	13,398	13,422	13,451	13,458	13,463	13,423	13,364	13,291	13,206	13,146	13,085	13,030	13,004	13,028
60-74	12,448	12,411	12,332	12,216	12,096	12,015	11,964	11,921	11,873	11,839	11,800	11,805	11,795	11,809	11,880	11,979	12,106	12,271	12,437	12,571
75 & over	8,726	8,928	9,148	9,382	9,621	9,866	10,108	10,333	10,550	10,748	10,937	11,101	11,274	11,416	11,520	11,588	11,639	11,672	11,689	11,712
All ages	72,721	73,044	73,361	73,673	73,980	74,284	74,585	74,884	75,180	75,474	75,766	76,055	76,342	76,626	76,907	77,184	77,457	77,726	77,991	78,252
Percentages																				
0-14	17.0	16.9	16.8	16.8	16.7	16.7	16.6	16.6	16.6	16.6	16.6	16.6	16.6	16.6	16.6	16.6	16.6	16.6	16.7	16.7
15-29	18.1	18.2	18.2	18.2	18.2	18.1	18.1	18.0	17.9	17.8	17.8	17.7	17.7	17.6	17.6	17.5	17.5	17.4	17.3	17.3
30-44	18.3	18.2	18.0	17.9	17.8	17.8	17.8	17.8	17.8	17.9	17.9	17.9	18.0	18.1	18.2	18.3	18.4	18.4	18.4	18.4
45-59	17.5	17.5	17.7	17.9	18.0	18.0	18.0	17.9	17.9	17.8	17.8	17.6	17.5	17.3	17.2	17.0	16.9	16.8	16.7	16.6
60-74	17.1	17.0	16.8	16.6	16.3	16.2	16.0	15.9	15.8	15.7	15.6	15.5	15.4	15.4	15.4	15.5	15.6	15.8	15.9	16.1
75 & over	12.0	12.2	12.5	12.7	13.0	13.3	13.6	13.8	14.0	14.2	14.4	14.6	14.8	14.9	15.0	15.0	15.0	15.0	15.0	15.0
All ages	100.0	100.0	100.0	100.0	100.0	100.0	100.0	100.0	100.0	100.0	100.0	100.0	100.0	100.0	100.0	100.0	100.0	100.0	100.0	100.0
Mean age	42.9	43.1	43.2	43.3	43.4	43.5	43.5	43.6	43.7	43.8	43.8	43.9	43.9	44.0	44.0	44.1	44.1	44.2	44.2	44.3
Median age	42.3	42.5	42.6	42.7	42.8	42.9	43.0	43.0	43.0	43.0	43.0	42.9	42.9	42.9	42.8	42.9	42.9	43.0	43.0	43.1

2014-based
Principal projection

15.3b Population projections by the Office for National Statistics
United Kingdom, PERSONS, thousands

Projected populations at mid-years by age last birthday

Ages	2054	2055	2056	2057	2058	2059	2060	2061	2062	2063	2064	2065	2066	2067	2068	2069	2070	2071	2072	2073
Thousands																				
0-14	13,082	13,120	13,153	13,182	13,206	13,227	13,244	13,259	13,273	13,286	13,299	13,313	13,327	13,344	13,362	13,382	13,405	13,431	13,458	13,489
15-29	13,547	13,566	13,594	13,629	13,670	13,718	13,770	13,826	13,885	13,944	14,004	14,061	14,117	14,169	14,217	14,260	14,298	14,331	14,360	14,384
30-44	14,398	14,416	14,413	14,394	14,397	14,417	14,441	14,456	14,466	14,471	14,473	14,474	14,476	14,480	14,487	14,500	14,520	14,549	14,584	14,627
45-59	13,046	13,098	13,169	13,254	13,336	13,407	13,495	13,607	13,740	13,867	13,977	14,076	14,147	14,202	14,230	14,262	14,282	14,282	14,266	14,272
60-74	12,658	12,690	12,721	12,756	12,769	12,779	12,747	12,698	12,634	12,560	12,511	12,462	12,420	12,407	12,441	12,470	12,530	12,608	12,700	12,788
75 & over	11,780	11,875	11,967	12,052	12,135	12,211	12,307	12,403	12,497	12,614	12,728	12,858	13,012	13,157	13,283	13,412	13,521	13,629	13,738	13,828
All ages	78,510	78,765	79,016	79,266	79,513	79,759	80,004	80,249	80,495	80,743	80,992	81,244	81,499	81,758	82,020	82,287	82,557	82,830	83,107	83,387
Percentages																				
0-14	16.7	16.7	16.6	16.6	16.6	16.6	16.6	16.5	16.5	16.5	16.4	16.4	16.4	16.3	16.3	16.3	16.2	16.2	16.2	16.2
15-29	17.3	17.2	17.2	17.2	17.2	17.2	17.2	17.2	17.2	17.3	17.3	17.3	17.3	17.3	17.3	17.3	17.3	17.3	17.3	17.3
30-44	18.3	18.3	18.2	18.2	18.1	18.1	18.0	18.0	18.0	17.9	17.9	17.8	17.8	17.7	17.7	17.6	17.6	17.6	17.5	17.5
45-59	16.6	16.6	16.7	16.7	16.8	16.8	16.9	17.0	17.1	17.2	17.3	17.3	17.4	17.4	17.3	17.3	17.3	17.2	17.2	17.1
60-74	16.1	16.1	16.1	16.1	16.1	16.0	15.9	15.8	15.7	15.6	15.4	15.3	15.2	15.2	15.2	15.2	15.2	15.2	15.3	15.3
75 & over	15.0	15.1	15.1	15.2	15.3	15.3	15.4	15.5	15.5	15.6	15.7	15.8	16.0	16.1	16.2	16.3	16.4	16.5	16.5	16.6
All ages	100.0	100.0	100.0	100.0	100.0	100.0	100.0	100.0	100.0	100.0	100.0	100.0	100.0	100.0	100.0	100.0	100.0	100.0	100.0	100.0
Mean age	44.3	44.4	44.4	44.4	44.5	44.5	44.5	44.6	44.6	44.7	44.7	44.7	44.8	44.8	44.9	44.9	45.0	45.0	45.1	45.1
Median age	43.1	43.2	43.3	43.3	43.4	43.4	43.5	43.5	43.6	43.6	43.7	43.7	43.8	43.8	43.9	44.0	44.0	44.1	44.1	44.2

Ages	2074	2075	2076	2077	2078	2079	2080	2081	2082	2083	2084	2085	2086	2087	2088	2089	2090	2091	2092	2093
Thousands																				
0-14	13,522	13,557	13,594	13,633	13,673	13,714	13,755	13,795	13,836	13,875	13,912	13,948	13,982	14,014	14,043	14,071	14,097	14,121	14,144	14,166
15-29	14,405	14,423	14,438	14,452	14,465	14,479	14,492	14,507	14,524	14,542	14,563	14,586	14,611	14,639	14,670	14,703	14,738	14,775	14,814	14,854
30-44	14,675	14,728	14,785	14,844	14,903	14,963	15,022	15,078	15,130	15,178	15,222	15,261	15,295	15,324	15,349	15,370	15,388	15,404	15,419	15,433
45-59	14,294	14,319	14,337	14,349	14,356	14,360	14,363	14,367	14,373	14,383	14,398	14,421	14,451	14,488	14,532	14,582	14,637	14,695	14,755	14,816
60-74	12,864	12,955	13,068	13,201	13,327	13,437	13,537	13,611	13,670	13,705	13,742	13,768	13,776	13,769	13,781	13,809	13,839	13,862	13,880	13,893
75 & over	13,910	13,973	14,019	14,051	14,092	14,153	14,225	14,324	14,438	14,576	14,709	14,850	15,006	15,174	15,320	15,449	15,573	15,705	15,841	15,984
All ages	83,670	83,955	84,241	84,529	84,817	85,105	85,394	85,683	85,971	86,259	86,546	86,833	87,121	87,408	87,696	87,984	88,273	88,563	88,854	89,146
Percentages																				
0-14	16.2	16.1	16.1	16.1	16.1	16.1	16.1	16.1	16.1	16.1	16.1	16.1	16.0	16.0	16.0	16.0	16.0	15.9	15.9	15.9
15-29	17.2	17.2	17.1	17.1	17.1	17.0	17.0	16.9	16.9	16.9	16.8	16.8	16.8	16.7	16.7	16.7	16.7	16.7	16.7	16.7
30-44	17.5	17.5	17.6	17.6	17.6	17.6	17.6	17.6	17.6	17.6	17.6	17.6	17.6	17.5	17.5	17.5	17.4	17.4	17.4	17.3
45-59	17.1	17.1	17.0	17.0	17.0	16.9	16.9	16.8	16.7	16.7	16.6	16.6	16.6	16.6	16.6	16.6	16.6	16.6	16.6	16.6
60-74	15.4	15.4	15.5	15.6	15.7	15.8	15.9	15.9	15.9	15.9	15.9	15.9	15.8	15.8	15.7	15.7	15.7	15.7	15.6	15.6
75 & over	16.6	16.6	16.6	16.6	16.6	16.6	16.7	16.7	16.8	16.9	17.0	17.1	17.2	17.4	17.5	17.6	17.6	17.7	17.8	17.9
All ages	100.0	100.0	100.0	100.0	100.0	100.0	100.0	100.0	100.0	100.0	100.0	100.0	100.0	100.0	100.0	100.0	100.0	100.0	100.0	100.0
Mean age	45.2	45.2	45.3	45.3	45.3	45.4	45.4	45.5	45.5	45.6	45.6	45.7	45.7	45.8	45.8	45.9	45.9	46.0	46.1	46.1
Median age	44.2	44.2	44.3	44.3	44.3	44.4	44.4	44.4	44.5	44.5	44.6	44.6	44.7	44.7	44.8	44.8	44.9	45.0	45.0	45.1

15.3b Population projections by the Office for National Statistics
United Kingdom, PERSONS, thousands

2014-based
Principal projection

Projected populations at mid-years by age last birthday

Ages	2094	2095	2096	2097	2098	2099	2100	2101	2102	2103	2104	2105	2106	2107	2108	2109	2110	2111	2112	2113	2114
Thousands																					
0-14	14,187	14,207	14,228	14,249	14,270	14,292	14,315	14,339	14,364	14,390	14,418	14,447	14,477	14,508	14,539	14,571	14,604	14,637	14,669	14,702	14,734
15-29	14,895	14,937	14,978	15,018	15,057	15,095	15,131	15,165	15,196	15,226	15,254	15,280	15,305	15,328	15,349	15,371	15,391	15,412	15,433	15,454	15,476
30-44	15,447	15,461	15,476	15,493	15,512	15,534	15,557	15,583	15,612	15,643	15,676	15,712	15,750	15,789	15,830	15,871	15,913	15,954	15,995	16,034	16,072
45-59	14,877	14,937	14,994	15,048	15,098	15,143	15,183	15,218	15,249	15,275	15,298	15,318	15,335	15,352	15,367	15,382	15,398	15,415	15,434	15,454	15,477
60-74	13,903	13,913	13,923	13,936	13,952	13,973	14,001	14,037	14,080	14,129	14,183	14,242	14,304	14,369	14,434	14,498	14,562	14,622	14,680	14,733	14,782
75 & over	16,130	16,280	16,432	16,585	16,739	16,891	17,041	17,187	17,329	17,467	17,602	17,734	17,862	17,988	18,112	18,236	18,359	18,483	18,608	18,736	18,867
All ages	89,440	89,735	90,031	90,329	90,628	90,927	91,228	91,528	91,830	92,131	92,432	92,733	93,033	93,332	93,631	93,929	94,226	94,523	94,818	95,113	95,408
Percentages																					
0-14	15.9	15.8	15.8	15.8	15.7	15.7	15.7	15.7	15.6	15.6	15.6	15.6	15.6	15.5	15.5	15.5	15.5	15.5	15.5	15.5	15.4
15-29	16.7	16.6	16.6	16.6	16.6	16.6	16.6	16.6	16.5	16.5	16.5	16.5	16.5	16.4	16.4	16.4	16.3	16.3	16.3	16.2	16.2
30-44	17.3	17.2	17.2	17.2	17.1	17.1	17.1	17.0	17.0	17.0	17.0	16.9	16.9	16.9	16.9	16.9	16.9	16.9	16.9	16.9	16.8
45-59	16.6	16.6	16.7	16.7	16.7	16.7	16.6	16.6	16.6	16.6	16.6	16.5	16.5	16.4	16.4	16.4	16.3	16.3	16.3	16.2	16.2
60-74	15.5	15.5	15.5	15.4	15.4	15.4	15.3	15.3	15.3	15.3	15.3	15.4	15.4	15.4	15.4	15.4	15.5	15.5	15.5	15.5	15.5
75 & over	18.0	18.1	18.3	18.4	18.5	18.6	18.7	18.8	18.9	19.0	19.0	19.1	19.2	19.3	19.3	19.4	19.5	19.6	19.6	19.7	19.8
All ages	100.0	100.0	100.0	100.0	100.0	100.0	100.0	100.0	100.0	100.0	100.0	100.0	100.0	100.0	100.0	100.0	100.0	100.0	100.0	100.0	100.0
Mean age	46.2	46.2	46.3	46.3	46.4	46.5	46.5	46.6	46.7	46.7	46.8	46.8	46.9	46.9	47.0	47.1	47.1	47.2	47.2	47.3	47.3
Median age	45.2	45.3	45.3	45.4	45.5	45.5	45.6	45.7	45.7	45.8	45.8	45.9	46.0	46.0	46.1	46.1	46.2	46.2	46.3	46.3	46.4

Source: Office for National Statistics

Note: Figures may not add exactly due to rounding.
* Children under 16. Working age and pensionable age populations based on state pension age (SPA) for given year.
Between 2012 and 2018, SPA will change from 65 years for men and 61 years for women, to 65 years for both sexes.
Then between 2019 and 2020, SPA will change from 65 years to 66 years for both men and women.
Between 2026 and 2027 SPA will increase to 67 years and between 2044 and 2046 to 68 years for both sexes. This is based on SPA under the 2014 Pensions Act.
** This is consistent with the age-group definitions used in ONS Labour Market Statistics.

15.3b Population projections by the Office for National Statistics
United Kingdom, MALES, thousands

2014-based
Principal projection

Projected populations at mid-years by age last birthday

Ages	2014	2015	2016	2017	2018	2019	2020	2021	2022	2023	2024	2025	2026	2027	2028	2029	2030	2031	2032	2033
Thousands																				
0-14	5,841	5,893	5,956	6,028	6,097	6,155	6,206	6,242	6,270	6,284	6,299	6,309	6,307	6,297	6,297	6,307	6,318	6,326	6,330	6,332
15-29	6,369	6,405	6,406	6,398	6,376	6,359	6,332	6,304	6,296	6,308	6,314	6,339	6,372	6,414	6,456	6,492	6,536	6,595	6,664	6,730
30-44	6,323	6,332	6,328	6,328	6,364	6,419	6,494	6,588	6,679	6,759	6,815	6,842	6,871	6,902	6,921	6,938	6,931	6,911	6,889	6,856
45-59	6,403	6,478	6,549	6,595	6,610	6,597	6,571	6,521	6,454	6,384	6,336	6,301	6,271	6,234	6,208	6,181	6,178	6,169	6,168	6,201
60-74	4,700	4,762	4,851	4,931	5,000	5,060	5,131	5,210	5,227	5,281	5,361	5,454	5,549	5,650	5,735	5,818	5,888	5,958	6,005	6,024
75 & over	2,159	2,202	2,244	2,303	2,385	2,481	2,571	2,665	2,832	2,965	3,077	3,175	3,262	3,342	3,425	3,506	3,581	3,663	3,750	3,843
All ages	31,794	32,073	32,334	32,584	32,832	33,071	33,304	33,531	33,757	33,981	34,202	34,419	34,632	34,839	35,042	35,240	35,433	35,622	35,806	35,985
Percentages																				
0-14	18.4	18.4	18.4	18.5	18.6	18.6	18.6	18.6	18.6	18.5	18.4	18.3	18.2	18.1	18.0	17.9	17.8	17.8	17.7	17.6
15-29	20.0	20.0	19.8	19.6	19.4	19.2	19.0	18.8	18.6	18.6	18.5	18.4	18.4	18.4	18.4	18.4	18.4	18.5	18.6	18.7
30-44	19.9	19.7	19.6	19.4	19.4	19.4	19.5	19.6	19.8	19.9	19.9	19.9	19.8	19.8	19.8	19.7	19.6	19.4	19.2	19.1
45-59	20.1	20.2	20.3	20.2	20.1	19.9	19.7	19.4	19.1	18.8	18.5	18.3	18.1	17.9	17.7	17.5	17.4	17.3	17.2	17.2
60-74	14.8	14.8	15.0	15.1	15.2	15.3	15.4	15.5	15.5	15.5	15.7	15.8	16.0	16.2	16.4	16.5	16.6	16.7	16.8	16.7
75 & over	6.8	6.9	6.9	7.1	7.3	7.5	7.7	7.9	8.4	8.7	9.0	9.2	9.4	9.6	9.8	9.9	10.1	10.3	10.5	10.7
All ages	100.0	100.0	100.0	100.0	100.0	100.0	100.0	100.0	100.0	100.0	100.0	100.0	100.0	100.0	100.0	100.0	100.0	100.0	100.0	100.0
Mean age	39.3	39.4	39.5	39.6	39.8	39.9	40.1	40.2	40.3	40.5	40.6	40.8	40.9	41.0	41.2	41.3	41.5	41.6	41.7	41.8
Median age	38.8	38.8	38.8	38.8	38.9	39.0	39.2	39.3	39.4	39.5	39.6	39.7	39.9	40.0	40.1	40.3	40.4	40.6	40.8	40.9

Ages	2034	2035	2036	2037	2038	2039	2040	2041	2042	2043	2044	2045	2046	2047	2048	2049	2050	2051	2052	2053
Thousands																				
0-14	6,333	6,333	6,333	6,335	6,338	6,344	6,354	6,368	6,386	6,407	6,431	6,458	6,487	6,517	6,547	6,577	6,607	6,635	6,662	6,686
15-29	6,787	6,838	6,874	6,902	6,916	6,932	6,941	6,940	6,930	6,931	6,940	6,952	6,960	6,964	6,966	6,967	6,967	6,968	6,969	6,973
30-44	6,833	6,804	6,778	6,771	6,784	6,792	6,817	6,851	6,894	6,936	6,973	7,018	7,077	7,146	7,212	7,269	7,320	7,357	7,385	7,399
45-59	6,255	6,328	6,422	6,513	6,592	6,649	6,677	6,708	6,740	6,760	6,778	6,772	6,755	6,734	6,704	6,683	6,657	6,633	6,629	6,644
60-74	6,017	5,997	5,957	5,901	5,845	5,808	5,786	5,766	5,742	5,727	5,710	5,716	5,717	5,723	5,762	5,818	5,892	5,985	6,073	6,150
75 & over	3,938	4,034	4,139	4,250	4,362	4,476	4,589	4,693	4,795	4,886	4,973	5,048	5,127	5,193	5,241	5,271	5,293	5,307	5,315	5,326
All ages	36,161	36,334	36,504	36,672	36,837	37,001	37,164	37,326	37,487	37,647	37,806	37,964	38,122	38,277	38,432	38,585	38,736	38,885	39,033	39,179
Percentages																				
0-14	17.5	17.4	17.3	17.3	17.2	17.1	17.1	17.1	17.0	17.0	17.0	17.0	17.0	17.0	17.0	17.0	17.1	17.1	17.1	17.1
15-29	18.8	18.8	18.8	18.8	18.8	18.7	18.7	18.6	18.5	18.4	18.4	18.3	18.3	18.2	18.1	18.1	18.0	17.9	17.9	17.8
30-44	18.9	18.7	18.6	18.5	18.4	18.4	18.3	18.4	18.4	18.4	18.4	18.5	18.6	18.7	18.8	18.8	18.9	18.9	18.9	18.9
45-59	17.3	17.4	17.6	17.8	17.9	18.0	18.0	18.0	18.0	18.0	17.9	17.8	17.7	17.6	17.4	17.3	17.2	17.1	17.0	17.0
60-74	16.6	16.5	16.3	16.1	15.9	15.7	15.6	15.4	15.3	15.2	15.1	15.1	15.0	15.0	15.0	15.1	15.2	15.4	15.6	15.7
75 & over	10.9	11.1	11.3	11.6	11.8	12.1	12.3	12.6	12.8	13.0	13.2	13.3	13.4	13.6	13.6	13.7	13.7	13.6	13.6	13.6
All ages	100.0	100.0	100.0	100.0	100.0	100.0	100.0	100.0	100.0	100.0	100.0	100.0	100.0	100.0	100.0	100.0	100.0	100.0	100.0	100.0
Mean age	42.0	42.1	42.2	42.3	42.4	42.5	42.6	42.6	42.7	42.8	42.8	42.9	43.0	43.0	43.1	43.1	43.2	43.2	43.3	43.3
Median age	41.1	41.2	41.3	41.4	41.5	41.6	41.6	41.7	41.7	41.6	41.6	41.6	41.6	41.6	41.6	41.7	41.8	41.8	41.9	42.0

15.3b Population projections by the Office for National Statistics
United Kingdom, MALES, thousands

2014-based
Principal projection

Projected populations at mid-years by age last birthday

Ages	2054	2055	2056	2057	2058	2059	2060	2061	2062	2063	2064	2065	2066	2067	2068	2069	2070	2071	2072	2073
Thousands																				
0-14	6,708	6,728	6,745	6,759	6,772	6,782	6,791	6,799	6,806	6,813	6,820	6,827	6,834	6,843	6,852	6,862	6,874	6,887	6,901	6,917
15-29	6,979	6,989	7,003	7,021	7,043	7,067	7,094	7,123	7,153	7,183	7,214	7,243	7,272	7,298	7,323	7,345	7,365	7,382	7,397	7,409
30-44	7,416	7,426	7,425	7,416	7,417	7,427	7,439	7,448	7,453	7,455	7,457	7,457	7,459	7,461	7,465	7,472	7,482	7,497	7,515	7,537
45-59	6,654	6,681	6,716	6,761	6,804	6,842	6,888	6,947	7,016	7,082	7,139	7,191	7,228	7,257	7,273	7,291	7,302	7,303	7,296	7,299
60-74	6,208	6,240	6,273	6,308	6,330	6,351	6,349	6,335	6,319	6,294	6,279	6,260	6,244	6,246	6,267	6,283	6,315	6,355	6,403	6,450
75 & over	5,358	5,403	5,446	5,485	5,524	5,561	5,609	5,659	5,704	5,765	5,827	5,901	5,987	6,065	6,139	6,215	6,282	6,349	6,415	6,471
All ages	39,324	39,467	39,609	39,750	39,891	40,031	40,171	40,311	40,451	40,593	40,735	40,879	41,024	41,170	41,319	41,468	41,620	41,773	41,927	42,083
Percentages																				
0-14	17.1	17.0	17.0	17.0	17.0	16.9	16.9	16.9	16.8	16.8	16.7	16.7	16.7	16.6	16.6	16.5	16.5	16.5	16.5	16.4
15-29	17.7	17.7	17.7	17.7	17.7	17.7	17.7	17.7	17.7	17.7	17.7	17.7	17.7	17.7	17.7	17.7	17.7	17.7	17.6	17.6
30-44	18.9	18.8	18.7	18.7	18.6	18.6	18.5	18.5	18.4	18.4	18.3	18.2	18.2	18.1	18.1	18.0	18.0	17.9	17.9	17.9
45-59	16.9	16.9	17.0	17.0	17.1	17.1	17.1	17.2	17.3	17.4	17.5	17.6	17.6	17.6	17.6	17.6	17.5	17.5	17.4	17.3
60-74	15.8	15.8	15.8	15.9	15.9	15.9	15.8	15.7	15.6	15.5	15.4	15.3	15.2	15.2	15.2	15.2	15.2	15.2	15.3	15.3
75 & over	13.6	13.7	13.7	13.8	13.8	13.9	14.0	14.0	14.1	14.2	14.3	14.4	14.6	14.7	14.9	15.0	15.1	15.2	15.3	15.4
All ages	100.0	100.0	100.0	100.0	100.0	100.0	100.0	100.0	100.0	100.0	100.0	100.0	100.0	100.0	100.0	100.0	100.0	100.0	100.0	100.0
Mean age	43.4	43.4	43.4	43.5	43.5	43.6	43.6	43.7	43.7	43.8	43.8	43.9	43.9	44.0	44.1	44.1	44.2	44.2	44.3	44.4
Median age	42.1	42.2	42.2	42.3	42.3	42.4	42.4	42.5	42.6	42.7	42.7	42.8	42.9	43.0	43.0	43.1	43.2	43.2	43.3	43.3

Ages	2074	2075	2076	2077	2078	2079	2080	2081	2082	2083	2084	2085	2086	2087	2088	2089	2090	2091	2092	2093
Thousands																				
0-14	6,934	6,952	6,971	6,991	7,011	7,032	7,053	7,074	7,095	7,115	7,134	7,152	7,170	7,186	7,201	7,215	7,229	7,241	7,253	7,264
15-29	7,420	7,429	7,437	7,444	7,451	7,458	7,465	7,472	7,481	7,490	7,501	7,513	7,526	7,540	7,556	7,573	7,591	7,610	7,630	7,650
30-44	7,562	7,589	7,611	7,648	7,679	7,710	7,740	7,769	7,796	7,820	7,843	7,863	7,880	7,895	7,908	7,919	7,929	7,937	7,945	7,952
45-59	7,310	7,323	7,333	7,339	7,343	7,346	7,348	7,350	7,354	7,359	7,368	7,379	7,395	7,415	7,438	7,463	7,492	7,522	7,553	7,584
60-74	6,491	6,538	6,598	6,666	6,732	6,789	6,841	6,880	6,912	6,931	6,952	6,967	6,973	6,970	6,977	6,992	7,008	7,021	7,031	7,038
75 & over	6,523	6,565	6,597	6,623	6,653	6,692	6,736	6,794	6,859	6,935	7,009	7,086	7,171	7,261	7,340	7,411	7,478	7,549	7,622	7,697
All ages	42,239	42,396	42,554	42,711	42,869	43,026	43,183	43,340	43,496	43,651	43,806	43,960	44,114	44,267	44,421	44,574	44,726	44,879	45,033	45,186
Percentages																				
0-14	16.4	16.4	16.4	16.4	16.4	16.3	16.3	16.3	16.3	16.3	16.3	16.3	16.3	16.2	16.2	16.2	16.2	16.1	16.1	16.1
15-29	17.6	17.5	17.5	17.4	17.4	17.3	17.3	17.2	17.2	17.2	17.1	17.1	17.1	17.0	17.0	17.0	17.0	17.0	16.9	16.9
30-44	17.9	17.9	17.9	17.9	17.9	17.9	17.9	17.9	17.9	17.9	17.9	17.9	17.9	17.8	17.8	17.8	17.7	17.7	17.6	17.6
45-59	17.3	17.3	17.2	17.2	17.1	17.1	17.0	17.0	16.9	16.9	16.8	16.8	16.8	16.7	16.7	16.7	16.7	16.8	16.8	16.8
60-74	15.4	15.4	15.5	15.6	15.7	15.8	15.8	15.9	15.9	15.9	15.9	15.8	15.8	15.7	15.7	15.7	15.7	15.6	15.6	15.6
75 & over	15.4	15.5	15.5	15.5	15.5	15.6	15.6	15.7	15.8	15.9	16.0	16.1	16.3	16.4	16.5	16.6	16.7	16.8	16.9	17.0
All ages	100.0	100.0	100.0	100.0	100.0	100.0	100.0	100.0	100.0	100.0	100.0	100.0	100.0	100.0	100.0	100.0	100.0	100.0	100.0	100.0
Mean age	44.4	44.5	44.5	44.6	44.7	44.7	44.8	44.8	44.9	44.9	45.0	45.1	45.1	45.2	45.2	45.3	45.4	45.4	45.5	45.5
Median age	43.4	43.4	43.5	43.5	43.6	43.6	43.7	43.7	43.8	43.8	43.9	43.9	44.0	44.1	44.1	44.2	44.3	44.3	44.4	44.5

15.3b Population projections by the Office for National Statistics
United Kingdom, MALES, thousands

2014-based
Principal projection

Projected populations at mid-years by age last birthday

Ages	2094	2095	2096	2097	2098	2099	2100	2101	2102	2103	2104	2105	2106	2107	2108	2109	2110	2111	2112	2113	2114
Thousands																					
0-14	7,275	7,285	7,296	7,307	7,317	7,329	7,340	7,353	7,366	7,379	7,393	7,408	7,423	7,439	7,455	7,472	7,489	7,505	7,522	7,539	7,555
15-29	7,671	7,693	7,714	7,734	7,754	7,774	7,792	7,810	7,826	7,841	7,856	7,869	7,881	7,893	7,904	7,915	7,926	7,937	7,947	7,958	7,970
30-44	7,959	7,967	7,975	7,984	7,993	8,004	8,016	8,030	8,045	8,061	8,078	8,096	8,116	8,136	8,157	8,178	8,199	8,221	8,242	8,262	8,282
45-59	7,616	7,647	7,676	7,704	7,730	7,753	7,774	7,792	7,808	7,822	7,834	7,844	7,854	7,862	7,871	7,879	7,887	7,896	7,906	7,917	7,929
60-74	7,044	7,050	7,057	7,064	7,073	7,085	7,100	7,119	7,142	7,168	7,196	7,227	7,259	7,293	7,327	7,360	7,393	7,425	7,455	7,482	7,508
75 & over	7,774	7,852	7,931	8,010	8,090	8,168	8,245	8,320	8,393	8,463	8,532	8,599	8,665	8,729	8,792	8,855	8,917	8,980	9,044	9,110	9,176
All ages	45,340	45,494	45,648	45,803	45,957	46,113	46,268	46,423	46,579	46,734	46,889	47,044	47,198	47,352	47,506	47,659	47,812	47,964	48,116	48,268	48,419
Percentages																					
0-14	16.0	16.0	16.0	16.0	15.9	15.9	15.9	15.8	15.8	15.8	15.8	15.7	15.7	15.7	15.7	15.7	15.7	15.6	15.6	15.6	15.6
15-29	16.9	16.9	16.9	16.9	16.9	16.9	16.8	16.8	16.8	16.8	16.8	16.7	16.7	16.7	16.6	16.6	16.6	16.5	16.5	16.5	16.5
30-44	17.6	17.5	17.5	17.4	17.4	17.4	17.3	17.3	17.3	17.2	17.2	17.2	17.2	17.2	17.2	17.2	17.1	17.1	17.1	17.1	17.1
45-59	16.8	16.8	16.8	16.8	16.8	16.8	16.8	16.8	16.8	16.7	16.7	16.7	16.6	16.6	16.6	16.5	16.5	16.5	16.4	16.4	16.4
60-74	15.5	15.5	15.5	15.4	15.4	15.4	15.3	15.3	15.3	15.3	15.3	15.4	15.4	15.4	15.4	15.4	15.5	15.5	15.5	15.5	15.5
75 & over	17.1	17.3	17.4	17.5	17.6	17.7	17.8	17.9	18.0	18.1	18.2	18.3	18.4	18.4	18.5	18.6	18.7	18.7	18.8	18.9	19.0
All ages	100.0	100.0	100.0	100.0	100.0	100.0	100.0	100.0	100.0	100.0	100.0	100.0	100.0	100.0	100.0	100.0	100.0	100.0	100.0	100.0	100.0
Mean age	45.6	45.7	45.7	45.8	45.8	45.9	46.0	46.0	46.1	46.2	46.2	46.3	46.4	46.4	46.5	46.5	46.6	46.6	46.7	46.8	46.8
Median age	44.6	44.6	44.7	44.8	44.8	44.9	45.0	45.0	45.1	45.2	45.2	45.3	45.3	45.4	45.4	45.5	45.5	45.6	45.6	45.7	45.8

Source: Office for National Statistics

Note: Figures may not add exactly due to rounding.
* Children under 16. Working age and pensionable age populations based on state pension age (SPA) for given year.
Between 2012 and 2018, SPA will change from 65 years for men and 61 years for women, to 65 years for both sexes.
Then between 2019 and 2020, SPA will change from 65 years to 66 years for both men and women.
Between 2026 and 2027 SPA will increase to 67 years and between 2044 and 2046 to 68 years for both sexes. This is based on SPA under the 2014 Pensions Act.
** This is consistent with the age-group definitions used in ONS Labour Market Statistics.

15.3b Population projections by the Office for National Statistics
United Kingdom, FEMALES, thousands

2014-based
Principal projection

Projected populations at mid-years by age last birthday

Ages	2014	2015	2016	2017	2018	2019	2020	2021	2022	2023	2024	2025	2026	2027	2028	2029	2030	2031	2032	2033
Thousands																				
0-14	5,567	5,616	5,673	5,740	5,804	5,857	5,905	5,937	5,963	5,974	5,987	5,994	5,991	5,981	5,983	5,992	6,003	6,010	6,015	6,016
15-29	6,188	6,190	6,164	6,121	6,073	6,037	6,002	5,968	5,944	5,950	5,957	5,980	6,014	6,054	6,091	6,123	6,165	6,217	6,282	6,343
30-44	6,418	6,419	6,403	6,406	6,437	6,479	6,531	6,603	6,682	6,739	6,766	6,762	6,753	6,749	6,735	6,720	6,685	6,642	6,588	6,531
45-59	6,571	6,657	6,741	6,794	6,816	6,810	6,790	6,744	6,676	6,604	6,551	6,513	6,480	6,449	6,422	6,392	6,384	6,365	6,367	6,395
60-74	5,007	5,072	5,162	5,244	5,314	5,378	5,452	5,536	5,551	5,608	5,696	5,798	5,904	6,010	6,105	6,196	6,278	6,359	6,412	6,434
75 & over	3,053	3,072	3,096	3,141	3,211	3,295	3,376	3,463	3,631	3,766	3,878	3,979	4,069	4,152	4,238	4,325	4,405	4,491	4,585	4,685
All ages	32,803	33,024	33,239	33,446	33,654	33,857	34,056	34,251	34,446	34,641	34,834	35,025	35,212	35,395	35,574	35,749	35,920	36,086	36,248	36,405
Percentages																				
0-14	17.0	17.0	17.1	17.2	17.2	17.3	17.3	17.3	17.3	17.2	17.2	17.1	17.0	16.9	16.8	16.8	16.7	16.7	16.6	16.5
15-29	18.9	18.7	18.5	18.3	18.0	17.8	17.6	17.4	17.3	17.2	17.1	17.1	17.1	17.1	17.1	17.1	17.2	17.2	17.3	17.4
30-44	19.6	19.4	19.3	19.2	19.1	19.1	19.2	19.3	19.4	19.5	19.4	19.3	19.2	19.1	18.9	18.8	18.6	18.4	18.2	17.9
45-59	20.0	20.2	20.3	20.3	20.3	20.1	19.9	19.7	19.4	19.1	18.8	18.6	18.4	18.2	18.1	17.9	17.8	17.6	17.6	17.6
60-74	15.3	15.4	15.5	15.7	15.8	15.9	16.0	16.2	16.1	16.2	16.4	16.6	16.8	17.0	17.2	17.3	17.5	17.6	17.7	17.7
75 & over	9.3	9.3	9.3	9.4	9.5	9.7	9.9	10.1	10.5	10.9	11.1	11.4	11.6	11.7	11.9	12.1	12.3	12.4	12.6	12.9
All ages	100.0	100.0	100.0	100.0	100.0	100.0	100.0	100.0	100.0	100.0	100.0	100.0	100.0	100.0	100.0	100.0	100.0	100.0	100.0	100.0
Mean age	41.3	41.3	41.5	41.6	41.7	41.8	42.0	42.1	42.2	42.4	42.5	42.7	42.8	42.9	43.1	43.2	43.4	43.5	43.6	43.8
Median age	41.1	41.1	41.2	41.3	41.3	41.4	41.5	41.6	41.8	41.9	42.1	42.2	42.4	42.5	42.7	42.9	43.0	43.2	43.3	43.5

Ages	2034	2035	2036	2037	2038	2039	2040	2041	2042	2043	2044	2045	2046	2047	2048	2049	2050	2051	2052	2053
Thousands																				
0-14	6,017	6,017	6,017	6,018	6,021	6,027	6,037	6,050	6,067	6,087	6,110	6,136	6,163	6,191	6,220	6,249	6,277	6,304	6,330	6,353
15-29	6,396	6,443	6,475	6,501	6,512	6,525	6,532	6,530	6,520	6,522	6,531	6,542	6,550	6,554	6,556	6,556	6,556	6,557	6,558	6,561
30-44	6,490	6,454	6,420	6,397	6,404	6,411	6,434	6,469	6,509	6,546	6,579	6,621	6,673	6,738	6,799	6,852	6,899	6,931	6,957	6,969
45-59	6,436	6,488	6,561	6,639	6,696	6,724	6,721	6,714	6,711	6,698	6,684	6,650	6,610	6,557	6,502	6,463	6,428	6,396	6,375	6,384
60-74	6,431	6,414	6,375	6,314	6,251	6,207	6,178	6,154	6,131	6,112	6,090	6,089	6,078	6,086	6,118	6,161	6,215	6,287	6,364	6,420
75 & over	4,789	4,894	5,009	5,132	5,259	5,389	5,519	5,640	5,755	5,862	5,964	6,052	6,147	6,223	6,279	6,317	6,346	6,365	6,374	6,387
All ages	36,559	36,710	36,857	37,001	37,143	37,283	37,421	37,558	37,693	37,827	37,960	38,091	38,221	38,349	38,475	38,599	38,721	38,841	38,958	39,074
Percentages																				
0-14	16.5	16.4	16.3	16.3	16.2	16.2	16.1	16.1	16.1	16.1	16.1	16.1	16.1	16.1	16.2	16.2	16.2	16.2	16.2	16.3
15-29	17.5	17.6	17.6	17.6	17.5	17.5	17.5	17.4	17.3	17.2	17.2	17.2	17.1	17.1	17.0	17.0	16.9	16.9	16.8	16.8
30-44	17.8	17.6	17.4	17.3	17.2	17.2	17.2	17.2	17.3	17.3	17.3	17.4	17.5	17.6	17.7	17.8	17.8	17.8	17.9	17.8
45-59	17.6	17.7	17.8	17.9	18.0	18.0	18.0	17.9	17.8	17.7	17.6	17.5	17.3	17.1	16.9	16.7	16.6	16.5	16.4	16.3
60-74	17.6	17.5	17.3	17.1	16.8	16.6	16.5	16.4	16.3	16.2	16.0	16.0	15.9	15.9	15.9	16.0	16.0	16.2	16.3	16.4
75 & over	13.1	13.3	13.6	13.9	14.2	14.5	14.7	15.0	15.3	15.5	15.7	15.9	16.1	16.2	16.3	16.4	16.4	16.4	16.4	16.3
All ages	100.0	100.0	100.0	100.0	100.0	100.0	100.0	100.0	100.0	100.0	100.0	100.0	100.0	100.0	100.0	100.0	100.0	100.0	100.0	100.0
Mean age	43.9	44.0	44.1	44.2	44.3	44.4	44.5	44.6	44.7	44.7	44.8	44.9	44.9	45.0	45.0	45.1	45.1	45.2	45.2	45.2
Median age	43.6	43.8	44.0	44.1	44.2	44.3	44.3	44.4	44.4	44.4	44.4	44.4	44.3	44.2	44.2	44.2	44.1	44.2	44.2	44.2

2014-based Principal projection

15.3b Population projections by the Office for National Statistics
United Kingdom, FEMALES, thousands

Projected populations at mid-years by age last birthday

Ages	2054	2055	2056	2057	2058	2059	2060	2061	2062	2063	2064	2065	2066	2067	2068	2069	2070	2071	2072	2073
Thousands																				
0-14	6,374	6,392	6,408	6,422	6,434	6,444	6,453	6,460	6,467	6,473	6,479	6,486	6,493	6,501	6,510	6,520	6,531	6,543	6,557	6,572
15-29	6,567	6,577	6,590	6,607	6,628	6,651	6,676	6,704	6,732	6,761	6,790	6,818	6,845	6,870	6,894	6,915	6,933	6,950	6,964	6,975
30-44	6,982	6,990	6,988	6,978	6,980	6,990	7,001	7,009	7,013	7,016	7,016	7,017	7,017	7,019	7,022	7,029	7,038	7,052	7,069	7,090
45-59	6,392	6,417	6,452	6,493	6,531	6,565	6,607	6,660	6,724	6,785	6,838	6,885	6,918	6,945	6,957	6,971	6,980	6,979	6,970	6,973
60-74	6,450	6,450	6,447	6,448	6,438	6,428	6,399	6,362	6,315	6,266	6,232	6,202	6,176	6,161	6,174	6,186	6,215	6,254	6,297	6,338
75 & over	6,422	6,472	6,521	6,567	6,611	6,651	6,698	6,744	6,793	6,849	6,902	6,958	7,025	7,091	7,144	7,197	7,239	7,280	7,323	7,357
All ages	39,187	39,298	39,408	39,516	39,622	39,728	39,833	39,939	40,044	40,150	40,257	40,365	40,475	40,588	40,702	40,818	40,937	41,057	41,180	41,305
Percentages																				
0-14	16.3	16.3	16.3	16.3	16.2	16.2	16.2	16.2	16.1	16.1	16.1	16.1	16.0	16.0	16.0	16.0	16.0	15.9	15.9	15.9
15-29	16.8	16.7	16.7	16.7	16.7	16.7	16.8	16.8	16.8	16.8	16.9	16.9	16.9	16.9	16.9	16.9	16.9	16.9	16.9	16.9
30-44	17.8	17.8	17.7	17.7	17.6	17.6	17.6	17.5	17.5	17.5	17.4	17.4	17.3	17.3	17.3	17.2	17.2	17.2	17.2	17.2
45-59	16.3	16.3	16.4	16.4	16.5	16.5	16.6	16.7	16.8	16.9	17.0	17.1	17.1	17.1	17.1	17.1	17.1	17.0	16.9	16.9
60-74	16.5	16.4	16.4	16.3	16.2	16.2	16.1	15.9	15.8	15.6	15.5	15.4	15.3	15.2	15.2	15.2	15.2	15.2	15.3	15.3
75 & over	16.4	16.5	16.5	16.6	16.7	16.7	16.8	16.9	17.0	17.1	17.1	17.2	17.4	17.5	17.6	17.6	17.7	17.7	17.8	17.8
All ages	100.0	100.0	100.0	100.0	100.0	100.0	100.0	100.0	100.0	100.0	100.0	100.0	100.0	100.0	100.0	100.0	100.0	100.0	100.0	100.0
Mean age	45.3	45.3	45.3	45.4	45.4	45.4	45.5	45.5	45.5	45.5	45.6	45.6	45.6	45.7	45.7	45.7	45.8	45.8	45.8	45.9
Median age	44.3	44.3	44.4	44.5	44.5	44.5	44.5	44.6	44.6	44.6	44.7	44.7	44.7	44.8	44.8	44.9	44.9	45.0	45.0	45.0

Ages	2074	2075	2076	2077	2078	2079	2080	2081	2082	2083	2084	2085	2086	2087	2088	2089	2090	2091	2092	2093
Thousands																				
0-14	6,588	6,605	6,623	6,642	6,661	6,681	6,701	6,721	6,741	6,760	6,778	6,796	6,812	6,828	6,842	6,856	6,868	6,880	6,891	6,902
15-29	6,985	6,994	7,002	7,008	7,015	7,021	7,028	7,035	7,043	7,052	7,062	7,073	7,086	7,099	7,114	7,130	7,147	7,165	7,184	7,204
30-44	7,113	7,139	7,166	7,195	7,224	7,253	7,282	7,309	7,334	7,358	7,379	7,398	7,414	7,428	7,441	7,451	7,460	7,467	7,474	7,481
45-59	6,984	6,996	7,004	7,009	7,012	7,014	7,015	7,017	7,019	7,024	7,031	7,041	7,055	7,073	7,095	7,119	7,145	7,173	7,202	7,232
60-74	6,373	6,417	6,470	6,534	6,595	6,648	6,696	6,730	6,758	6,774	6,790	6,801	6,803	6,798	6,804	6,817	6,831	6,842	6,849	6,855
75 & over	7,387	7,408	7,422	7,428	7,440	7,461	7,489	7,530	7,579	7,641	7,700	7,764	7,836	7,913	7,980	8,038	8,095	8,156	8,220	8,287
All ages	41,431	41,559	41,687	41,817	41,948	42,079	42,211	42,343	42,475	42,608	42,740	42,873	43,007	43,141	43,275	43,410	43,546	43,683	43,821	43,960
Percentages																				
0-14	15.9	15.9	15.9	15.9	15.9	15.9	15.9	15.9	15.9	15.9	15.9	15.9	15.8	15.8	15.8	15.8	15.8	15.7	15.7	15.7
15-29	16.9	16.8	16.8	16.8	16.7	16.7	16.6	16.6	16.6	16.6	16.5	16.5	16.5	16.5	16.4	16.4	16.4	16.4	16.4	16.4
30-44	17.2	17.2	17.2	17.2	17.2	17.2	17.3	17.3	17.3	17.3	17.3	17.3	17.2	17.2	17.2	17.2	17.1	17.1	17.1	17.0
45-59	16.9	16.8	16.8	16.8	16.7	16.7	16.6	16.6	16.5	16.5	16.4	16.4	16.4	16.4	16.4	16.4	16.4	16.4	16.4	16.5
60-74	15.4	15.4	15.5	15.6	15.7	15.8	15.9	15.9	15.9	15.9	15.9	15.9	15.8	15.8	15.7	15.7	15.7	15.7	15.6	15.6
75 & over	17.8	17.8	17.8	17.8	17.7	17.7	17.7	17.8	17.8	17.9	18.0	18.1	18.2	18.3	18.4	18.5	18.6	18.7	18.8	18.9
All ages	100.0	100.0	100.0	100.0	100.0	100.0	100.0	100.0	100.0	100.0	100.0	100.0	100.0	100.0	100.0	100.0	100.0	100.0	100.0	100.0
Mean age	45.9	45.9	46.0	46.0	46.1	46.1	46.1	46.2	46.2	46.2	46.3	46.3	46.4	46.4	46.5	46.5	46.5	46.6	46.6	46.7
Median age	45.1	45.1	45.1	45.1	45.2	45.2	45.2	45.2	45.3	45.3	45.3	45.4	45.4	45.4	45.5	45.5	45.6	45.7	45.7	45.8

15.3b Population projections by the Office for National Statistics
United Kingdom, FEMALES, thousands

2014-based
Principal projection

Projected populations at mid-years by age last birthday

Ages	2094	2095	2096	2097	2098	2099	2100	2101	2102	2103	2104	2105	2106	2107	2108	2109	2110	2111	2112	2113	2114
Thousands																					
0-14	6,912	6,922	6,932	6,942	6,953	6,963	6,974	6,986	6,998	7,011	7,025	7,039	7,053	7,068	7,084	7,099	7,115	7,131	7,147	7,163	7,179
15-29	7,224	7,244	7,264	7,284	7,303	7,321	7,338	7,355	7,371	7,385	7,399	7,411	7,423	7,434	7,445	7,455	7,465	7,475	7,486	7,496	7,507
30-44	7,487	7,494	7,502	7,510	7,519	7,529	7,541	7,553	7,567	7,582	7,598	7,616	7,634	7,653	7,673	7,693	7,713	7,733	7,753	7,772	7,791
45-59	7,261	7,290	7,318	7,344	7,368	7,390	7,409	7,426	7,441	7,453	7,464	7,473	7,482	7,489	7,496	7,504	7,511	7,519	7,528	7,538	7,548
60-74	6,859	6,863	6,867	6,872	6,879	6,888	6,901	6,918	6,938	6,961	6,987	7,015	7,045	7,076	7,107	7,138	7,168	7,198	7,225	7,250	7,274
75 & over	8,356	8,428	8,501	8,575	8,649	8,723	8,796	8,867	8,936	9,004	9,070	9,134	9,197	9,259	9,320	9,381	9,441	9,502	9,564	9,626	9,690
All ages	44,100	44,241	44,383	44,526	44,670	44,815	44,960	45,105	45,251	45,397	45,543	45,689	45,835	45,980	46,125	46,270	46,415	46,559	46,702	46,845	46,988
Percentages																					
0-14	15.7	15.6	15.6	15.6	15.6	15.5	15.5	15.5	15.5	15.4	15.4	15.4	15.4	15.4	15.4	15.3	15.3	15.3	15.3	15.3	15.3
15-29	16.4	16.4	16.4	16.4	16.3	16.3	16.3	16.3	16.3	16.3	16.2	16.2	16.2	16.2	16.1	16.1	16.1	16.1	16.0	16.0	16.0
30-44	17.0	16.9	16.9	16.9	16.8	16.8	16.8	16.7	16.7	16.7	16.7	16.7	16.7	16.6	16.6	16.6	16.6	16.6	16.6	16.6	16.6
45-59	16.5	16.5	16.5	16.5	16.5	16.5	16.5	16.5	16.4	16.4	16.4	16.4	16.3	16.3	16.3	16.2	16.2	16.1	16.1	16.1	16.1
60-74	15.6	15.5	15.5	15.4	15.4	15.4	15.4	15.3	15.3	15.3	15.3	15.4	15.4	15.4	15.4	15.4	15.4	15.5	15.5	15.5	15.5
75 & over	18.9	19.0	19.2	19.3	19.4	19.5	19.6	19.7	19.7	19.8	19.9	20.0	20.1	20.1	20.2	20.3	20.3	20.4	20.5	20.5	20.6
All ages	100.0	100.0	100.0	100.0	100.0	100.0	100.0	100.0	100.0	100.0	100.0	100.0	100.0	100.0	100.0	100.0	100.0	100.0	100.0	100.0	100.0
Mean age	46.7	46.8	46.9	46.9	47.0	47.0	47.1	47.2	47.2	47.3	47.3	47.4	47.4	47.5	47.6	47.6	47.7	47.7	47.8	47.8	47.9
Median age	45.9	45.9	46.0	46.1	46.1	46.2	46.3	46.3	46.4	46.4	46.5	46.6	46.6	46.7	46.7	46.8	46.8	46.9	46.9	47.0	47.0

Note: Figures may not add exactly due to rounding.
* Children under 16. Working age and pensionable age populations based on state pension age (SPA) for given year.
Between 2012 and 2018, SPA will change from 65 years for men and 61 years for women, to 65 years for both sexes.
Then between 2019 and 2020, SPA will change from 65 years to 66 years for both men and women.
Between 2026 and 2027 SPA will increase to 67 years and between 2044 and 2046 to 68 years for both sexes. This is based on SPA under the 2014 Pensions Act.
** This is consistent with the age-group definitions used in ONS Labour Market Statistics.

Source: Office for National Statistics

5.3c Mid-2014 Population estimates for England and Wales by sex and single year of age

Ages	Persons	Males	Females	Ages	Persons	Males	Females
All Ages	57,408,654	28,294,511	29,114,143	45	819,777	404,612	415,165
0	697,813	357,644	340,169	46	818,410	403,988	414,422
1	717,402	368,150	349,252	47	830,790	411,595	419,195
2	743,077	380,486	362,591	48	831,144	409,558	421,586
3	731,084	374,507	356,577	49	836,055	412,066	423,989
4	719,256	368,032	351,224	50	828,481	408,716	419,765
5	709,836	363,278	346,558	51	810,389	400,303	410,086
6	716,270	366,804	349,466	52	793,357	393,040	400,317
7	693,077	355,224	337,853	53	765,797	379,530	386,267
8	679,134	347,486	331,648	54	734,922	364,115	370,807
9	650,372	332,653	317,719	55	718,435	355,810	362,625
10	638,713	326,681	312,032	56	702,589	347,888	354,701
11	620,519	318,061	302,458	57	676,654	334,470	342,184
12	609,986	312,413	297,573	58	652,449	322,384	330,065
13	626,214	319,871	306,343	59	629,148	309,897	319,251
14	642,714	329,404	313,310	60	631,867	310,034	321,833
15	662,930	339,755	323,175	61	624,503	306,940	317,563
16	671,384	344,125	327,259	62	607,406	297,110	310,296
17	691,529	354,853	336,676	63	612,134	299,244	312,890
18	693,488	357,965	335,523	64	625,554	304,443	321,111
19	700,070	359,162	340,908	65	641,331	312,914	328,417
20	732,405	375,776	356,629	66	677,476	329,910	347,566
21	740,343	378,275	362,068	67	734,310	358,049	376,261
22	769,591	389,014	380,577	68	565,948	274,541	291,407
23	795,593	405,559	390,034	69	549,229	265,492	283,737
24	786,063	400,763	385,300	70	546,155	263,763	282,392
25	780,202	393,300	386,902	71	507,206	242,951	264,255
26	789,508	395,587	393,921	72	452,410	214,787	237,623
27	772,803	383,485	389,318	73	406,555	191,355	215,200
28	781,742	392,176	389,566	74	420,701	197,747	222,954
29	786,228	394,195	392,033	75	416,017	194,301	221,716
30	768,972	383,515	385,457	76	403,059	187,466	215,593
31	776,409	386,452	389,957	77	380,522	175,147	205,375
32	775,861	385,095	390,766	78	360,032	163,634	196,398
33	783,144	389,438	393,706	79	339,937	152,992	186,945
34	784,895	390,681	394,214	80	312,287	138,252	174,035
35	752,419	375,609	376,810	81	294,490	128,138	166,352
36	701,376	350,437	350,939	82	282,672	120,922	161,750
37	690,972	345,551	345,421	83	264,809	110,308	154,501
38	702,444	349,753	352,691	84	242,927	98,281	144,646
39	716,540	356,716	359,824	85 / 85+	215,312	85,165	130,147
40	729,222	361,909	367,313	86	190,230	73,233	116,997
41	761,120	378,349	382,771	87	170,093	64,114	105,979
42	793,841	394,397	399,444	88	150,189	54,423	95,766
43	819,907	404,660	415,247	89	129,328	44,771	84,557
44	799,870	395,330	404,540	90	499,230	143,536	355,694

Source: Office for National Statistics

Note: It is ONS policy to publish estimates to the nearest hundred persons. Rounded (and particularly unit) estimates cannot be precisely accurate.

: Data not available

15.3d Population projections by the Office for National Statistics
England, PERSONS, thousands

2014-based
Principal projection

Projected populations at mid-years by age last birthday

Ages	2014	2015	2016	2017	2018	2019	2020	2021	2022	2023	2024	2025	2026	2027	2028	2029	2030	2031	2032	2033
Thousands																				
0-14	9,676	9,773	9,887	10,016	10,138	10,241	10,333	10,397	10,448	10,477	10,508	10,526	10,528	10,512	10,516	10,535	10,557	10,572	10,581	10,586
15-29	10,556	10,598	10,585	10,550	10,501	10,465	10,420	10,378	10,362	10,387	10,406	10,458	10,523	10,605	10,683	10,751	10,833	10,937	11,061	11,178
30-44	10,811	10,830	10,822	10,831	10,893	10,979	11,089	11,231	11,373	11,488	11,557	11,575	11,594	11,617	11,622	11,625	11,590	11,541	11,481	11,411
45-59	10,822	10,968	11,109	11,205	11,248	11,246	11,219	11,152	11,051	10,945	10,873	10,826	10,783	10,736	10,703	10,665	10,664	10,648	10,653	10,709
60-74	8,077	8,183	8,334	8,470	8,586	8,686	8,804	8,938	8,961	9,053	9,195	9,360	9,534	9,712	9,867	10,019	10,155	10,291	10,385	10,430
75 & over	4,375	4,428	4,481	4,568	4,696	4,849	4,997	5,152	5,439	5,668	5,857	6,025	6,174	6,311	6,454	6,594	6,724	6,864	7,014	7,176
All ages	54,317	54,780	55,219	55,640	56,061	56,466	56,862	57,248	57,634	58,017	58,396	58,769	59,135	59,493	59,844	60,188	60,524	60,853	61,175	61,491
Percentages																				
0-14	17.8	17.8	17.9	18.0	18.1	18.1	18.2	18.2	18.1	18.1	18.0	17.9	17.8	17.7	17.6	17.5	17.4	17.4	17.3	17.2
15-29	19.4	19.3	19.2	19.0	18.7	18.5	18.3	18.1	18.0	17.9	17.8	17.8	17.8	17.8	17.9	17.9	17.9	18.0	18.1	18.2
30-44	19.9	19.8	19.6	19.5	19.4	19.4	19.5	19.6	19.7	19.8	19.8	19.7	19.6	19.5	19.4	19.3	19.1	19.0	18.8	18.6
45-59	19.9	20.0	20.1	20.1	20.1	19.9	19.7	19.5	19.2	18.9	18.6	18.4	18.2	18.0	17.9	17.7	17.6	17.5	17.4	17.4
60-74	14.9	14.9	15.1	15.2	15.3	15.4	15.5	15.6	15.5	15.6	15.7	15.9	16.1	16.3	16.5	16.6	16.8	16.9	17.0	17.0
75 & over	8.1	8.1	8.1	8.2	8.4	8.6	8.8	9.0	9.4	9.8	10.0	10.3	10.4	10.6	10.8	11.0	11.1	11.3	11.5	11.7
All ages	100.0	100.0	100.0	100.0	100.0	100.0	100.0	100.0	100.0	100.0	100.0	100.0	100.0	100.0	100.0	100.0	100.0	100.0	100.0	100.0
Mean age	40.2	40.2	40.4	40.5	40.6	40.7	40.9	41.0	41.1	41.3	41.4	41.5	41.7	41.8	42.0	42.1	42.2	42.4	42.5	42.6
Median age	39.7	39.7	39.8	39.8	39.8	39.9	40.1	40.2	40.3	40.5	40.6	40.7	40.9	41.0	41.1	41.3	41.4	41.6	41.8	41.9

Ages	2034	2035	2036	2037	2038	2039	2040	2041	2042	2043	2044	2045	2046	2047	2048	2049	2050	2051	2052	2053
Thousands																				
0-14	10,589	10,592	10,596	10,602	10,612	10,628	10,650	10,679	10,716	10,758	10,805	10,857	10,911	10,968	11,025	11,083	11,139	11,192	11,242	11,288
15-29	11,280	11,372	11,437	11,489	11,517	11,549	11,567	11,569	11,553	11,557	11,576	11,598	11,613	11,622	11,627	11,631	11,634	11,638	11,645	11,655
30-44	11,364	11,314	11,273	11,259	11,284	11,305	11,358	11,424	11,508	11,587	11,657	11,740	11,844	11,968	12,085	12,186	12,278	12,343	12,395	12,424
45-59	10,792	10,901	11,042	11,183	11,297	11,367	11,387	11,408	11,433	11,439	11,444	11,412	11,365	11,308	11,242	11,198	11,152	11,116	11,105	11,134
60-74	10,434	10,415	10,361	10,275	10,186	10,132	10,101	10,074	10,043	10,025	10,001	10,013	10,011	10,027	10,090	10,176	10,285	10,425	10,563	10,674
75 & over	7,341	7,510	7,695	7,892	8,094	8,301	8,506	8,700	8,886	9,055	9,219	9,362	9,514	9,640	9,736	9,802	9,854	9,891	9,915	9,945
All ages	61,800	62,104	62,404	62,700	62,992	63,282	63,569	63,854	64,138	64,421	64,702	64,981	65,259	65,534	65,806	66,076	66,342	66,605	66,864	67,120
Percentages																				
0-14	17.1	17.1	17.0	16.9	16.8	16.8	16.8	16.7	16.7	16.7	16.7	16.7	16.7	16.7	16.8	16.8	16.8	16.8	16.8	16.8
15-29	18.3	18.3	18.3	18.3	18.3	18.2	18.2	18.1	18.0	17.9	17.9	17.8	17.8	17.7	17.7	17.6	17.5	17.5	17.4	17.4
30-44	18.4	18.2	18.1	18.0	17.9	17.9	17.9	17.9	17.9	18.0	18.0	18.1	18.1	18.3	18.4	18.4	18.5	18.5	18.5	18.5
45-59	17.5	17.6	17.7	17.8	17.9	18.0	17.9	17.9	17.8	17.8	17.7	17.6	17.4	17.3	17.1	16.9	16.8	16.7	16.6	16.6
60-74	16.9	16.8	16.6	16.4	16.2	16.0	15.9	15.8	15.7	15.6	15.5	15.4	15.3	15.3	15.3	15.4	15.5	15.7	15.8	15.9
75 & over	11.9	12.1	12.3	12.6	12.8	13.1	13.4	13.6	13.9	14.1	14.2	14.4	14.6	14.7	14.8	14.8	14.9	14.8	14.8	14.8
All ages	100.0	100.0	100.0	100.0	100.0	100.0	100.0	100.0	100.0	100.0	100.0	100.0	100.0	100.0	100.0	100.0	100.0	100.0	100.0	100.0
Mean age	42.8	42.9	43.0	43.1	43.2	43.3	43.4	43.4	43.5	43.6	43.6	43.7	43.7	43.8	43.9	43.9	43.9	44.0	44.0	44.1
Median age	42.1	42.2	42.3	42.4	42.5	42.6	42.6	42.7	42.7	42.7	42.6	42.6	42.5	42.5	42.5	42.6	42.6	42.7	42.7	42.8

15.3d Population projections by the Office for National Statistics
England, PERSONS, thousands

2014-based
Principal projection

Projected populations at mid-years by age last birthday

Ages	2054	2055	2056	2057	2058	2059	2060	2061	2062	2063	2064	2065	2066	2067	2068	2069	2070	2071	2072	2073
Thousands																				
0-14	11,330	11,368	11,401	11,430	11,455	11,476	11,495	11,512	11,527	11,541	11,556	11,571	11,588	11,605	11,625	11,646	11,670	11,697	11,725	11,756
15-29	11,671	11,693	11,722	11,759	11,801	11,849	11,900	11,955	12,012	12,069	12,127	12,183	12,236	12,287	12,333	12,375	12,413	12,446	12,475	12,500
30-44	12,456	12,475	12,478	12,463	12,468	12,488	12,510	12,526	12,536	12,541	12,545	12,549	12,554	12,561	12,572	12,588	12,611	12,641	12,678	12,721
45-59	11,157	11,212	11,281	11,366	11,447	11,518	11,602	11,706	11,829	11,946	12,047	12,139	12,205	12,257	12,288	12,322	12,343	12,348	12,336	12,342
60-74	10,746	10,771	10,798	10,827	10,839	10,848	10,824	10,784	10,735	10,679	10,643	10,608	10,583	10,582	10,619	10,651	10,712	10,786	10,876	10,961
75 & over	10,012	10,102	10,189	10,268	10,346	10,418	10,506	10,594	10,678	10,782	10,882	10,996	11,129	11,252	11,361	11,472	11,565	11,659	11,753	11,832
All ages	67,373	67,622	67,869	68,113	68,356	68,597	68,837	69,077	69,317	69,558	69,801	70,046	70,293	70,544	70,797	71,054	71,314	71,577	71,843	72,112
Percentages																				
0-14	16.8	16.8	16.8	16.8	16.8	16.7	16.7	16.7	16.6	16.6	16.6	16.5	16.5	16.5	16.4	16.4	16.4	16.3	16.3	16.3
15-29	17.3	17.3	17.3	17.3	17.3	17.3	17.3	17.3	17.3	17.4	17.4	17.4	17.4	17.4	17.4	17.4	17.4	17.4	17.4	17.3
30-44	18.5	18.4	18.4	18.3	18.2	18.2	18.2	18.1	18.1	18.0	18.0	17.9	17.9	17.8	17.8	17.7	17.7	17.7	17.6	17.6
45-59	16.6	16.6	16.6	16.7	16.7	16.8	16.9	16.9	17.1	17.2	17.3	17.3	17.4	17.4	17.4	17.3	17.3	17.3	17.2	17.1
60-74	16.0	15.9	15.9	15.9	15.9	15.8	15.7	15.6	15.5	15.4	15.2	15.1	15.1	15.0	15.0	15.0	15.0	15.1	15.1	15.2
75 & over	14.9	14.9	15.0	15.1	15.1	15.2	15.3	15.3	15.4	15.5	15.6	15.7	15.8	15.9	16.0	16.1	16.2	16.3	16.4	16.4
All ages	100.0	100.0	100.0	100.0	100.0	100.0	100.0	100.0	100.0	100.0	100.0	100.0	100.0	100.0	100.0	100.0	100.0	100.0	100.0	100.0
Mean age	44.1	44.2	44.2	44.2	44.3	44.3	44.4	44.4	44.4	44.5	44.5	44.6	44.6	44.6	44.7	44.7	44.8	44.8	44.9	44.9
Median age	42.9	42.9	43.0	43.1	43.1	43.1	43.2	43.2	43.3	43.3	43.4	43.5	43.5	43.6	43.6	43.7	43.8	43.8	43.8	43.9

Ages	2074	2075	2076	2077	2078	2079	2080	2081	2082	2083	2084	2085	2086	2087	2088	2089	2090	2091	2092	2093
Thousands																				
0-14	11,789	11,824	11,861	11,900	11,940	11,980	12,020	12,060	12,100	12,138	12,176	12,211	12,245	12,276	12,306	12,334	12,361	12,385	12,409	12,431
15-29	12,521	12,540	12,557	12,572	12,587	12,602	12,617	12,633	12,651	12,671	12,693	12,717	12,743	12,772	12,803	12,836	12,871	12,908	12,947	12,987
30-44	12,769	12,821	12,876	12,933	12,992	13,049	13,106	13,160	13,210	13,257	13,300	13,338	13,371	13,401	13,426	13,448	13,467	13,484	13,500	13,515
45-59	12,364	12,388	12,405	12,416	12,424	12,429	12,435	12,441	12,451	12,463	12,481	12,506	12,538	12,576	12,620	12,669	12,723	12,779	12,837	12,897
60-74	11,036	11,121	11,226	11,348	11,463	11,564	11,656	11,724	11,780	11,815	11,853	11,879	11,891	11,886	11,898	11,924	11,952	11,974	11,990	12,002
75 & over	11,904	11,961	12,005	12,036	12,077	12,134	12,201	12,293	12,397	12,520	12,639	12,767	12,906	13,058	13,192	13,310	13,425	13,546	13,672	13,803
All ages	72,383	72,656	72,930	73,206	73,482	73,759	74,035	74,312	74,589	74,865	75,141	75,417	75,693	75,969	76,245	76,522	76,799	77,077	77,356	77,636
Percentages																				
0-14	16.3	16.3	16.3	16.3	16.2	16.2	16.2	16.2	16.2	16.2	16.2	16.2	16.2	16.2	16.1	16.1	16.1	16.1	16.0	16.0
15-29	17.3	17.3	17.2	17.2	17.1	17.1	17.0	17.0	17.0	16.9	16.9	16.9	16.8	16.8	16.8	16.8	16.8	16.7	16.7	16.7
30-44	17.6	17.6	17.7	17.7	17.7	17.7	17.7	17.7	17.7	17.7	17.7	17.7	17.7	17.6	17.6	17.6	17.5	17.5	17.5	17.4
45-59	17.1	17.0	17.0	17.0	16.9	16.9	16.8	16.7	16.7	16.6	16.6	16.6	16.6	16.6	16.6	16.6	16.6	16.6	16.6	16.6
60-74	15.2	15.3	15.4	15.5	15.6	15.7	15.7	15.8	15.8	15.8	15.8	15.8	15.7	15.6	15.6	15.6	15.6	15.5	15.5	15.5
75 & over	16.4	16.5	16.5	16.4	16.4	16.5	16.5	16.5	16.6	16.7	16.8	16.9	17.1	17.2	17.3	17.4	17.5	17.6	17.7	17.8
All ages	100.0	100.0	100.0	100.0	100.0	100.0	100.0	100.0	100.0	100.0	100.0	100.0	100.0	100.0	100.0	100.0	100.0	100.0	100.0	100.0
Mean age	45.0	45.0	45.1	45.1	45.2	45.2	45.3	45.3	45.4	45.4	45.5	45.5	45.6	45.6	45.7	45.7	45.8	45.8	45.9	45.9
Median age	43.9	44.0	44.0	44.0	44.1	44.1	44.1	44.2	44.2	44.3	44.3	44.4	44.4	44.5	44.6	44.6	44.7	44.7	44.8	44.9

15.3d Population projections by the Office for National Statistics
England, PERSONS, thousands

2014-based
Principal projection

Projected populations at mid-years by age last birthday

Ages	2094	2095	2096	2097	2098	2099	2100	2101	2102	2103	2104	2105	2106	2107	2108	2109	2110	2111	2112	2113	2114
Thousands																					
0-14	12,453	12,475	12,496	12,518	12,540	12,562	12,586	12,610	12,636	12,663	12,691	12,720	12,750	12,781	12,812	12,844	12,877	12,909	12,942	12,974	13,006
15-29	13,027	13,068	13,108	13,148	13,186	13,223	13,259	13,293	13,324	13,354	13,382	13,409	13,434	13,457	13,480	13,502	13,523	13,545	13,566	13,588	13,611
30-44	13,531	13,546	13,563	13,581	13,602	13,624	13,648	13,675	13,704	13,735	13,769	13,805	13,842	13,881	13,921	13,962	14,003	14,044	14,084	14,123	14,160
45-59	12,955	13,013	13,067	13,119	13,167	13,210	13,249	13,284	13,315	13,341	13,365	13,385	13,404	13,421	13,437	13,454	13,471	13,489	13,508	13,530	13,553
60-74	12,013	12,024	12,036	12,051	12,069	12,092	12,121	12,157	12,200	12,248	12,301	12,358	12,417	12,479	12,541	12,602	12,662	12,720	12,774	12,825	12,871
75 & over	13,937	14,074	14,211	14,350	14,489	14,626	14,760	14,891	15,018	15,142	15,262	15,380	15,495	15,609	15,720	15,831	15,942	16,054	16,167	16,283	16,401
All ages	77,917	78,199	78,482	78,766	79,051	79,337	79,623	79,910	80,197	80,484	80,770	81,056	81,342	81,627	81,912	82,195	82,478	82,760	83,041	83,322	83,602
Percentages																					
0-14	16.0	16.0	15.9	15.9	15.9	15.8	15.8	15.8	15.8	15.7	15.7	15.7	15.7	15.7	15.6	15.6	15.6	15.6	15.6	15.6	15.6
15-29	16.7	16.7	16.7	16.7	16.7	16.7	16.7	16.6	16.6	16.6	16.6	16.5	16.5	16.5	16.5	16.4	16.4	16.4	16.3	16.3	16.3
30-44	17.4	17.3	17.3	17.2	17.2	17.2	17.1	17.1	17.1	17.1	17.0	17.0	17.0	17.0	17.0	17.0	17.0	17.0	17.0	16.9	16.9
45-59	16.6	16.6	16.7	16.7	16.7	16.7	16.6	16.6	16.6	16.6	16.5	16.5	16.5	16.4	16.4	16.4	16.3	16.3	16.3	16.2	16.2
60-74	15.4	15.4	15.3	15.3	15.3	15.2	15.2	15.2	15.2	15.2	15.2	15.2	15.3	15.3	15.3	15.3	15.4	15.4	15.4	15.4	15.4
75 & over	17.9	18.0	18.1	18.2	18.3	18.4	18.5	18.6	18.7	18.8	18.9	19.0	19.0	19.1	19.2	19.3	19.3	19.4	19.5	19.5	19.6
All ages	100.0	100.0	100.0	100.0	100.0	100.0	100.0	100.0	100.0	100.0	100.0	100.0	100.0	100.0	100.0	100.0	100.0	100.0	100.0	100.0	100.0
Mean age	46.0	46.1	46.1	46.2	46.2	46.3	46.4	46.4	46.5	46.6	46.6	46.7	46.7	46.8	46.9	46.9	47.0	47.0	47.1	47.1	47.2
Median age	44.9	45.0	45.1	45.2	45.2	45.3	45.4	45.4	45.5	45.5	45.6	45.7	45.7	45.8	45.8	45.9	45.9	46.0	46.0	46.1	46.1

Source: Office for National Statistics

Note: Figures may not add exactly due to rounding.
* Children under 16. Working age and pensionable age populations based on state pension age (SPA) for given year.
Between 2012 and 2018, SPA will change from 65 years for men and 61 years for women, to 65 years for both sexes.
Then between 2019 and 2020, SPA will change from 65 years to 66 years for both men and women.
Between 2026 and 2027 SPA will increase to 67 years and between 2044 and 2046 to 68 years for both sexes. This is based on SPA under the 2014 Pensions Act.
** This is consistent with the age-group definitions used in ONS Labour Market Statistics.

15.3d Population projections by the Office for National Statistics
England, MALES, thousands

2014-based
Principal projection

Projected populations at mid-years by age last birthday

Ages	2014	2015	2016	2017	2018	2019	2020	2021	2022	2023	2024	2025	2026	2027	2028	2029	2030	2031	2032	2033
Thousands																				
0-14	4,954	5,005	5,065	5,131	5,195	5,249	5,297	5,331	5,357	5,373	5,390	5,400	5,401	5,393	5,394	5,404	5,415	5,423	5,428	5,430
15-29	5,357	5,393	5,398	5,396	5,383	5,373	5,354	5,335	5,333	5,348	5,359	5,385	5,418	5,460	5,502	5,538	5,580	5,635	5,700	5,760
30-44	5,378	5,391	5,391	5,393	5,426	5,474	5,539	5,619	5,696	5,763	5,810	5,832	5,857	5,883	5,899	5,914	5,908	5,893	5,877	5,853
45-59	5,351	5,421	5,486	5,532	5,550	5,546	5,530	5,495	5,444	5,393	5,359	5,336	5,315	5,290	5,273	5,255	5,256	5,252	5,252	5,281
60-74	3,913	3,965	4,040	4,107	4,164	4,213	4,271	4,336	4,348	4,393	4,461	4,541	4,624	4,711	4,785	4,857	4,922	4,985	5,030	5,051
75 & over	1,820	1,856	1,890	1,939	2,008	2,089	2,167	2,247	2,389	2,502	2,596	2,678	2,751	2,817	2,887	2,954	3,017	3,084	3,156	3,234
All ages	26,773	27,030	27,270	27,499	27,727	27,944	28,157	28,363	28,569	28,773	28,974	29,172	29,365	29,555	29,740	29,921	30,099	30,273	30,443	30,610
Percentages																				
0-14	18.5	18.5	18.6	18.7	18.7	18.8	18.8	18.8	18.8	18.7	18.6	18.5	18.4	18.2	18.1	18.1	18.0	17.9	17.8	17.7
15-29	20.0	20.0	19.8	19.6	19.4	19.2	19.0	18.8	18.7	18.6	18.5	18.5	18.4	18.5	18.5	18.5	18.5	18.6	18.7	18.8
30-44	20.1	19.9	19.8	19.6	19.6	19.6	19.7	19.8	19.9	20.0	20.1	20.0	19.9	19.9	19.8	19.8	19.6	19.5	19.3	19.1
45-59	20.0	20.1	20.1	20.1	20.0	19.8	19.6	19.4	19.1	18.7	18.5	18.3	18.1	17.9	17.7	17.6	17.5	17.3	17.3	17.3
60-74	14.6	14.7	14.8	14.9	15.0	15.1	15.2	15.3	15.2	15.3	15.4	15.6	15.7	15.9	16.1	16.2	16.4	16.5	16.5	16.5
75 & over	6.8	6.9	6.9	7.1	7.2	7.5	7.7	7.9	8.4	8.7	9.0	9.2	9.4	9.5	9.7	9.9	10.0	10.2	10.4	10.6
All ages	100.0	100.0	100.0	100.0	100.0	100.0	100.0	100.0	100.0	100.0	100.0	100.0	100.0	100.0	100.0	100.0	100.0	100.0	100.0	100.0
Mean age	39.2	39.3	39.4	39.5	39.6	39.8	39.9	40.0	40.2	40.3	40.5	40.6	40.7	40.9	41.0	41.1	41.3	41.4	41.5	41.7
Median age	38.6	38.6	38.6	38.6	38.7	38.8	38.9	39.1	39.2	39.3	39.4	39.5	39.6	39.8	39.9	40.0	40.2	40.4	40.5	40.7

Ages	2034	2035	2036	2037	2038	2039	2040	2041	2042	2043	2044	2045	2046	2047	2048	2049	2050	2051	2052	2053
Thousands																				
0-14	5,432	5,433	5,435	5,439	5,444	5,452	5,463	5,478	5,497	5,518	5,543	5,569	5,597	5,626	5,656	5,685	5,714	5,741	5,767	5,790
15-29	5,813	5,862	5,896	5,923	5,938	5,955	5,965	5,967	5,959	5,960	5,970	5,981	5,989	5,994	5,996	5,998	6,000	6,002	6,006	6,011
30-44	5,837	5,815	5,797	5,797	5,812	5,823	5,851	5,884	5,927	5,970	6,006	6,049	6,105	6,169	6,229	6,282	6,331	6,365	6,392	6,407
45-59	5,328	5,391	5,472	5,548	5,614	5,661	5,684	5,710	5,737	5,754	5,770	5,765	5,751	5,737	5,714	5,700	5,681	5,665	5,667	5,684
60-74	5,051	5,040	5,012	4,971	4,930	4,906	4,893	4,881	4,865	4,857	4,847	4,855	4,858	4,865	4,899	4,946	5,010	5,089	5,163	5,227
75 & over	3,313	3,394	3,482	3,575	3,670	3,767	3,861	3,951	4,038	4,117	4,193	4,259	4,329	4,388	4,432	4,461	4,484	4,500	4,511	4,525
All ages	30,774	30,935	31,094	31,252	31,408	31,563	31,717	31,871	32,023	32,176	32,328	32,479	32,629	32,778	32,926	33,073	33,218	33,362	33,504	33,645
Percentages																				
0-14	17.7	17.6	17.5	17.4	17.3	17.3	17.2	17.2	17.2	17.2	17.1	17.1	17.2	17.2	17.2	17.2	17.2	17.2	17.2	17.2
15-29	18.9	18.9	19.0	19.0	18.9	18.9	18.8	18.7	18.6	18.5	18.5	18.4	18.4	18.3	18.2	18.1	18.1	18.0	17.9	17.9
30-44	19.0	18.8	18.6	18.5	18.5	18.4	18.4	18.5	18.5	18.6	18.6	18.6	18.7	18.8	18.9	19.0	19.1	19.1	19.1	19.0
45-59	17.3	17.4	17.6	17.8	17.9	17.9	17.9	17.9	17.9	17.9	17.8	17.8	17.6	17.5	17.4	17.2	17.1	17.0	16.9	16.9
60-74	16.4	16.3	16.1	15.9	15.7	15.5	15.4	15.3	15.2	15.1	15.0	14.9	14.9	14.8	14.8	15.0	15.1	15.3	15.4	15.5
75 & over	10.8	11.0	11.2	11.4	11.7	11.9	12.2	12.4	12.6	12.8	13.0	13.1	13.3	13.4	13.5	13.5	13.5	13.5	13.5	13.5
All ages	100.0	100.0	100.0	100.0	100.0	100.0	100.0	100.0	100.0	100.0	100.0	100.0	100.0	100.0	100.0	100.0	100.0	100.0	100.0	100.0
Mean age	41.8	41.9	42.0	42.1	42.2	42.3	42.4	42.4	42.5	42.6	42.6	42.7	42.8	42.8	42.9	42.9	43.0	43.0	43.1	43.1
Median age	40.8	40.9	41.0	41.1	41.2	41.3	41.3	41.4	41.4	41.3	41.3	41.3	41.3	41.3	41.3	41.4	41.5	41.5	41.6	41.7

15.3d Population projections by the Office for National Statistics
England, MALES, thousands

2014-based
Principal projection

Projected populations at mid-years by age last birthday

Ages	2054	2055	2056	2057	2058	2059	2060	2061	2062	2063	2064	2065	2066	2067	2068	2069	2070	2071	2072	2073
Thousands																				
0-14	5,812	5,831	5,848	5,863	5,876	5,887	5,896	5,905	5,913	5,920	5,928	5,935	5,944	5,953	5,963	5,974	5,986	6,000	6,014	6,030
15-29	6,019	6,030	6,046	6,064	6,086	6,110	6,137	6,165	6,194	6,223	6,253	6,282	6,309	6,335	6,359	6,380	6,399	6,416	6,431	6,444
30-44	6,425	6,436	6,438	6,431	6,432	6,442	6,454	6,462	6,467	6,470	6,473	6,475	6,477	6,481	6,487	6,495	6,507	6,523	6,542	6,564
45-59	5,697	5,726	5,760	5,804	5,848	5,885	5,929	5,984	6,048	6,108	6,161	6,209	6,244	6,272	6,288	6,307	6,319	6,322	6,317	6,320
60-74	5,275	5,300	5,328	5,357	5,377	5,394	5,393	5,383	5,372	5,354	5,344	5,330	5,322	5,328	5,350	5,368	5,400	5,438	5,486	5,531
75 & over	4,557	4,600	4,640	4,676	4,713	4,747	4,791	4,836	4,876	4,929	4,983	5,047	5,121	5,188	5,251	5,316	5,372	5,430	5,487	5,535
All ages	33,785	33,923	34,060	34,196	34,331	34,466	34,600	34,735	34,870	35,005	35,141	35,278	35,417	35,557	35,698	35,840	35,984	36,130	36,276	36,424
Percentages																				
0-14	17.2	17.2	17.2	17.1	17.1	17.1	17.0	17.0	17.0	16.9	16.9	16.8	16.8	16.7	16.7	16.7	16.6	16.6	16.6	16.6
15-29	17.8	17.8	17.7	17.7	17.7	17.7	17.7	17.7	17.8	17.8	17.8	17.8	17.8	17.8	17.8	17.8	17.8	17.8	17.7	17.7
30-44	19.0	19.0	18.9	18.8	18.7	18.7	18.7	18.6	18.5	18.5	18.4	18.4	18.3	18.2	18.2	18.1	18.1	18.1	18.0	18.0
45-59	16.9	16.9	16.9	17.0	17.0	17.1	17.1	17.2	17.3	17.4	17.5	17.6	17.6	17.6	17.6	17.6	17.6	17.5	17.4	17.4
60-74	15.6	15.6	15.6	15.7	15.7	15.7	15.6	15.5	15.4	15.3	15.2	15.1	15.0	15.0	15.0	15.0	15.0	15.1	15.1	15.2
75 & over	13.5	13.6	13.6	13.7	13.7	13.8	13.8	13.9	14.0	14.1	14.2	14.3	14.5	14.6	14.7	14.8	14.9	15.0	15.1	15.2
All ages	100.0	100.0	100.0	100.0	100.0	100.0	100.0	100.0	100.0	100.0	100.0	100.0	100.0	100.0	100.0	100.0	100.0	100.0	100.0	100.0
Mean age	43.2	43.2	43.3	43.3	43.4	43.4	43.5	43.5	43.6	43.6	43.7	43.7	43.8	43.8	43.9	43.9	44.0	44.1	44.1	44.2
Median age	41.8	41.9	41.9	42.0	42.1	42.1	42.2	42.3	42.3	42.4	42.5	42.6	42.6	42.7	42.8	42.8	42.9	43.0	43.0	43.1

Ages	2074	2075	2076	2077	2078	2079	2080	2081	2082	2083	2084	2085	2086	2087	2088	2089	2090	2091	2092	2093
Thousands																				
0-14	6,047	6,065	6,084	6,104	6,124	6,145	6,166	6,186	6,206	6,226	6,245	6,263	6,281	6,297	6,312	6,327	6,340	6,353	6,365	6,376
15-29	6,455	6,465	6,473	6,481	6,489	6,497	6,504	6,513	6,522	6,532	6,543	6,555	6,569	6,584	6,600	6,617	6,635	6,654	6,674	6,694
30-44	6,588	6,615	6,644	6,673	6,703	6,732	6,761	6,789	6,815	6,839	6,861	6,881	6,898	6,913	6,926	6,937	6,947	6,956	6,964	6,972
45-59	6,331	6,343	6,352	6,358	6,363	6,366	6,369	6,373	6,378	6,385	6,394	6,407	6,424	6,444	6,466	6,492	6,519	6,549	6,579	6,609
60-74	5,571	5,615	5,671	5,734	5,793	5,846	5,894	5,930	5,960	5,979	6,000	6,015	6,022	6,020	6,027	6,041	6,056	6,067	6,076	6,083
75 & over	5,580	5,617	5,646	5,670	5,698	5,734	5,775	5,827	5,886	5,954	6,019	6,088	6,164	6,245	6,318	6,382	6,444	6,509	6,576	6,645
All ages	36,572	36,721	36,871	37,020	37,170	37,320	37,469	37,618	37,767	37,915	38,062	38,210	38,356	38,503	38,649	38,795	38,941	39,087	39,233	39,380
Percentages																				
0-14	16.5	16.5	16.5	16.5	16.5	16.5	16.5	16.4	16.4	16.4	16.4	16.4	16.4	16.4	16.3	16.3	16.3	16.3	16.2	16.2
15-29	17.7	17.6	17.6	17.5	17.5	17.4	17.4	17.3	17.3	17.2	17.2	17.2	17.1	17.1	17.1	17.1	17.0	17.0	17.0	17.0
30-44	18.0	18.0	18.0	18.0	18.0	18.0	18.0	18.0	18.0	18.0	18.0	18.0	18.0	18.0	17.9	17.9	17.8	17.8	17.8	17.7
45-59	17.3	17.3	17.2	17.2	17.1	17.1	17.0	16.9	16.9	16.8	16.8	16.8	16.7	16.7	16.7	16.7	16.7	16.8	16.8	16.8
60-74	15.2	15.3	15.4	15.5	15.6	15.7	15.7	15.8	15.8	15.8	15.8	15.7	15.7	15.6	15.6	15.6	15.6	15.5	15.5	15.4
75 & over	15.3	15.3	15.3	15.3	15.3	15.4	15.4	15.5	15.6	15.7	15.8	15.9	16.1	16.2	16.3	16.5	16.5	16.7	16.8	16.9
All ages	100.0	100.0	100.0	100.0	100.0	100.0	100.0	100.0	100.0	100.0	100.0	100.0	100.0	100.0	100.0	100.0	100.0	100.0	100.0	100.0
Mean age	44.2	44.3	44.4	44.4	44.5	44.5	44.6	44.7	44.7	44.8	44.8	44.9	44.9	45.0	45.1	45.1	45.2	45.2	45.3	45.4
Median age	43.1	43.2	43.2	43.3	43.3	43.3	43.4	43.4	43.5	43.5	43.6	43.7	43.7	43.8	43.9	43.9	44.0	44.1	44.2	44.2

15.3d Population projections by the Office for National Statistics
England, MALES, thousands

2014-based
Principal projection

Projected populations at mid-years by age last birthday

Ages	2094	2095	2096	2097	2098	2099	2100	2101	2102	2103	2104	2105	2106	2107	2108	2109	2110	2111	2112	2113	2114
Thousands																					
0-14	6,388	6,399	6,409	6,420	6,432	6,443	6,456	6,468	6,481	6,495	6,509	6,524	6,540	6,555	6,571	6,588	6,604	6,621	6,638	6,654	6,671
15-29	6,715	6,735	6,756	6,776	6,796	6,815	6,834	6,851	6,867	6,883	6,897	6,910	6,923	6,935	6,947	6,958	6,969	6,980	6,991	7,003	7,014
30-44	6,980	6,988	6,997	7,006	7,017	7,028	7,041	7,055	7,070	7,086	7,103	7,121	7,141	7,161	7,181	7,202	7,223	7,244	7,265	7,285	7,304
45-59	6,639	6,669	6,697	6,724	6,748	6,771	6,791	6,809	6,825	6,839	6,851	6,862	6,871	6,880	6,889	6,898	6,907	6,916	6,926	6,937	6,950
60-74	6,090	6,096	6,103	6,111	6,121	6,134	6,149	6,169	6,191	6,216	6,244	6,274	6,305	6,336	6,368	6,400	6,432	6,461	6,490	6,516	6,540
75 & over	6,715	6,786	6,857	6,929	7,000	7,071	7,139	7,206	7,271	7,334	7,396	7,456	7,514	7,572	7,628	7,685	7,741	7,798	7,855	7,914	7,974
All ages	39,526	39,673	39,820	39,967	40,114	40,262	40,410	40,557	40,705	40,853	41,000	41,147	41,293	41,440	41,586	41,731	41,876	42,021	42,165	42,309	42,453
Percentages																					
0-14	16.2	16.1	16.1	16.1	16.0	16.0	16.0	15.9	15.9	15.9	15.9	15.9	15.8	15.8	15.8	15.8	15.8	15.8	15.7	15.7	15.7
15-29	17.0	17.0	17.0	17.0	16.9	16.9	16.9	16.9	16.9	16.8	16.8	16.8	16.8	16.7	16.7	16.7	16.6	16.6	16.6	16.6	16.5
30-44	17.7	17.6	17.6	17.5	17.5	17.5	17.4	17.4	17.4	17.3	17.3	17.3	17.3	17.3	17.3	17.3	17.2	17.2	17.2	17.2	17.2
45-59	16.8	16.8	16.8	16.8	16.8	16.8	16.8	16.8	16.8	16.7	16.7	16.7	16.6	16.6	16.6	16.5	16.5	16.5	16.4	16.4	16.4
60-74	15.4	15.4	15.3	15.3	15.3	15.2	15.2	15.2	15.2	15.2	15.2	15.2	15.3	15.3	15.3	15.3	15.4	15.4	15.4	15.4	15.4
75 & over	17.0	17.1	17.2	17.3	17.5	17.6	17.7	17.8	17.9	18.0	18.0	18.1	18.2	18.3	18.3	18.4	18.5	18.6	18.6	18.7	18.8
All ages	100.0	100.0	100.0	100.0	100.0	100.0	100.0	100.0	100.0	100.0	100.0	100.0	100.0	100.0	100.0	100.0	100.0	100.0	100.0	100.0	100.0
Mean age	45.4	45.5	45.6	45.6	45.7	45.8	45.8	45.9	45.9	46.0	46.1	46.1	46.2	46.3	46.3	46.4	46.4	46.5	46.5	46.6	46.6
Median age	44.3	44.4	44.5	44.5	44.6	44.7	44.7	44.8	44.9	44.9	45.0	45.0	45.1	45.1	45.2	45.3	45.3	45.4	45.4	45.5	45.5

Source: Office for National Statistics

Note: Figures may not add exactly due to rounding.
* Children under 16. Working age and pensionable age populations based on state pension age (SPA) for given year.
Between 2012 and 2018, SPA will change from 65 years for men and 61 years for women, to 65 years for both sexes.
Then between 2019 and 2020, SPA will change from 65 years to 66 years for both men and women.
Between 2026 and 2027 SPA will increase to 67 years and between 2044 and 2046 to 68 years for both sexes. This is based on SPA under the 2014 Pensions Act.
** This is consistent with the age-group definitions used in ONS Labour Market Statistics.

15.3d Population projections by the Office for National Statistics
England, FEMALES, thousands

2014-based
Principal projection

Projected populations at mid-years by age last birthday

Ages	2014	2015	2016	2017	2018	2019	2020	2021	2022	2023	2024	2025	2026	2027	2028	2029	2030	2031	2032	2033
Thousands																				
0-14	4,722	4,768	4,822	4,884	4,943	4,992	5,036	5,066	5,091	5,104	5,118	5,126	5,127	5,119	5,122	5,131	5,142	5,149	5,153	5,156
15-29	5,198	5,205	5,187	5,154	5,118	5,092	5,066	5,043	5,029	5,039	5,048	5,072	5,105	5,144	5,181	5,213	5,253	5,302	5,362	5,418
30-44	5,433	5,439	5,432	5,438	5,467	5,505	5,550	5,612	5,677	5,725	5,747	5,743	5,737	5,734	5,722	5,710	5,682	5,647	5,603	5,558
45-59	5,471	5,547	5,623	5,674	5,697	5,700	5,689	5,657	5,606	5,552	5,515	5,490	5,467	5,446	5,430	5,410	5,408	5,397	5,401	5,428
60-74	4,164	4,218	4,294	4,364	4,422	4,473	4,533	4,602	4,613	4,660	4,734	4,819	4,910	5,001	5,083	5,162	5,233	5,306	5,355	5,379
75 & over	2,555	2,572	2,591	2,629	2,688	2,760	2,831	2,905	3,050	3,165	3,261	3,347	3,423	3,494	3,567	3,640	3,707	3,780	3,858	3,942
All ages	27,543	27,750	27,949	28,142	28,335	28,522	28,705	28,885	29,065	29,245	29,423	29,598	29,770	29,939	30,104	30,267	30,425	30,581	30,732	30,881
Percentages																				
0-14	17.1	17.2	17.3	17.4	17.4	17.5	17.5	17.5	17.5	17.5	17.4	17.3	17.2	17.1	17.0	17.0	16.9	16.8	16.8	16.7
15-29	18.9	18.8	18.6	18.3	18.1	17.9	17.6	17.5	17.3	17.2	17.2	17.1	17.1	17.2	17.2	17.2	17.3	17.3	17.4	17.5
30-44	19.7	19.6	19.4	19.3	19.3	19.3	19.3	19.4	19.5	19.6	19.5	19.4	19.3	19.2	19.0	18.9	18.7	18.5	18.2	18.0
45-59	19.9	20.0	20.1	20.2	20.1	20.0	19.8	19.6	19.3	19.0	18.7	18.5	18.4	18.2	18.0	17.9	17.8	17.6	17.6	17.6
60-74	15.1	15.2	15.4	15.5	15.6	15.7	15.8	15.9	15.9	15.9	16.1	16.3	16.5	16.7	16.9	17.1	17.2	17.4	17.4	17.4
75 & over	9.3	9.3	9.3	9.3	9.5	9.7	9.9	10.1	10.5	10.8	11.1	11.3	11.5	11.7	11.8	12.0	12.2	12.4	12.6	12.8
All ages	100.0	100.0	100.0	100.0	100.0	100.0	100.0	100.0	100.0	100.0	100.0	100.0	100.0	100.0	100.0	100.0	100.0	100.0	100.0	100.0
Mean age	41.1	41.2	41.3	41.4	41.5	41.7	41.8	41.9	42.1	42.2	42.3	42.5	42.6	42.8	42.9	43.0	43.2	43.3	43.5	43.6
Median age	40.8	40.9	40.9	41.0	41.0	41.1	41.2	41.3	41.5	41.7	41.8	42.0	42.1	42.3	42.4	42.6	42.7	42.9	43.1	43.2

Ages	2034	2035	2036	2037	2038	2039	2040	2041	2042	2043	2044	2045	2046	2047	2048	2049	2050	2051	2052	2053
Thousands																				
0-14	5,157	5,158	5,160	5,164	5,168	5,176	5,187	5,201	5,219	5,239	5,262	5,287	5,314	5,342	5,370	5,398	5,425	5,451	5,475	5,498
15-29	5,467	5,511	5,541	5,566	5,579	5,593	5,602	5,602	5,594	5,597	5,606	5,617	5,624	5,629	5,631	5,633	5,634	5,636	5,639	5,644
30-44	5,527	5,499	5,476	5,462	5,472	5,482	5,507	5,541	5,580	5,618	5,650	5,690	5,739	5,799	5,856	5,904	5,948	5,978	6,003	6,016
45-59	5,464	5,509	5,571	5,636	5,683	5,706	5,703	5,698	5,696	5,685	5,674	5,647	5,614	5,572	5,528	5,498	5,472	5,450	5,438	5,450
60-74	5,384	5,375	5,348	5,304	5,256	5,226	5,208	5,193	5,178	5,168	5,155	5,158	5,153	5,162	5,192	5,229	5,275	5,336	5,400	5,447
75 & over	4,028	4,117	4,213	4,317	4,424	4,535	4,645	4,749	4,847	4,938	5,026	5,103	5,186	5,253	5,304	5,341	5,370	5,391	5,404	5,419
All ages	31,026	31,169	31,310	31,448	31,584	31,718	31,852	31,984	32,115	32,245	32,374	32,503	32,630	32,756	32,880	33,003	33,124	33,243	33,360	33,475
Percentages																				
0-14	16.6	16.5	16.5	16.4	16.4	16.3	16.3	16.3	16.3	16.2	16.3	16.3	16.3	16.3	16.3	16.4	16.4	16.4	16.4	16.4
15-29	17.6	17.7	17.7	17.7	17.7	17.6	17.6	17.5	17.4	17.4	17.3	17.3	17.2	17.2	17.1	17.1	17.0	17.0	16.9	16.9
30-44	17.8	17.6	17.5	17.4	17.3	17.3	17.3	17.3	17.4	17.4	17.5	17.5	17.6	17.7	17.8	17.9	18.0	18.0	18.0	18.0
45-59	17.6	17.7	17.8	17.9	18.0	18.0	17.9	17.8	17.7	17.6	17.5	17.4	17.2	17.0	16.8	16.7	16.5	16.4	16.3	16.3
60-74	17.4	17.2	17.1	16.9	16.6	16.5	16.4	16.2	16.1	16.0	15.9	15.9	15.8	15.8	15.8	15.8	15.9	16.1	16.2	16.3
75 & over	13.0	13.2	13.5	13.7	14.0	14.3	14.6	14.8	15.1	15.3	15.5	15.7	15.9	16.0	16.1	16.2	16.2	16.2	16.2	16.2
All ages	100.0	100.0	100.0	100.0	100.0	100.0	100.0	100.0	100.0	100.0	100.0	100.0	100.0	100.0	100.0	100.0	100.0	100.0	100.0	100.0
Mean age	43.7	43.8	43.9	44.1	44.2	44.2	44.3	44.4	44.5	44.6	44.6	44.7	44.7	44.8	44.8	44.9	44.9	45.0	45.0	45.0
Median age	43.4	43.5	43.7	43.8	43.9	43.9	44.0	44.1	44.1	44.1	44.1	44.0	43.9	43.9	43.8	43.8	43.8	43.8	43.9	43.9

2014-based
Principal projection

15.3d Population projections by the Office for National Statistics
England, FEMALES, thousands

Projected populations at mid-years by age last birthday

Ages	2054	2055	2056	2057	2058	2059	2060	2061	2062	2063	2064	2065	2066	2067	2068	2069	2070	2071	2072	2073
Thousands																				
0-14	5,518	5,537	5,553	5,567	5,579	5,590	5,599	5,607	5,614	5,621	5,628	5,636	5,644	5,652	5,662	5,672	5,684	5,697	5,711	5,726
15-29	5,652	5,663	5,677	5,695	5,715	5,738	5,764	5,790	5,818	5,846	5,874	5,901	5,927	5,952	5,974	5,995	6,013	6,030	6,044	6,056
30-44	6,031	6,039	6,040	6,033	6,036	6,045	6,056	6,064	6,068	6,071	6,072	6,074	6,076	6,080	6,085	6,093	6,104	6,118	6,136	6,157
45-59	5,461	5,487	5,521	5,562	5,599	5,633	5,673	5,722	5,781	5,838	5,886	5,930	5,960	5,985	6,000	6,015	6,024	6,026	6,019	6,023
60-74	5,471	5,471	5,469	5,470	5,462	5,454	5,431	5,402	5,364	5,325	5,299	5,277	5,261	5,254	5,269	5,283	5,312	5,348	5,391	5,430
75 & over	5,455	5,503	5,549	5,592	5,633	5,671	5,715	5,758	5,802	5,853	5,900	5,949	6,008	6,064	6,110	6,156	6,193	6,229	6,267	6,297
All ages	33,588	33,699	33,809	33,918	34,025	34,131	34,237	34,342	34,448	34,553	34,660	34,768	34,877	34,987	35,099	35,214	35,330	35,447	35,567	35,688
Percentages																				
0-14	16.4	16.4	16.4	16.4	16.4	16.4	16.4	16.3	16.3	16.3	16.2	16.2	16.2	16.2	16.1	16.1	16.1	16.1	16.1	16.0
15-29	16.8	16.8	16.8	16.8	16.8	16.8	16.8	16.9	16.9	16.9	16.9	17.0	17.0	17.0	17.0	17.0	17.0	17.0	17.0	17.0
30-44	18.0	17.9	17.9	17.8	17.7	17.7	17.7	17.7	17.6	17.6	17.5	17.5	17.4	17.4	17.3	17.3	17.3	17.3	17.3	17.3
45-59	16.3	16.3	16.3	16.4	16.5	16.5	16.6	16.7	16.8	16.9	17.0	17.1	17.1	17.1	17.1	17.1	17.1	17.0	16.9	16.9
60-74	16.3	16.2	16.2	16.1	16.1	16.0	15.9	15.7	15.6	15.4	15.3	15.2	15.1	15.0	15.0	15.0	15.0	15.1	15.2	15.2
75 & over	16.2	16.3	16.4	16.5	16.6	16.6	16.7	16.8	16.8	16.9	17.0	17.1	17.2	17.3	17.4	17.5	17.5	17.6	17.6	17.6
All ages	100.0	100.0	100.0	100.0	100.0	100.0	100.0	100.0	100.0	100.0	100.0	100.0	100.0	100.0	100.0	100.0	100.0	100.0	100.0	100.0
Mean age	45.1	45.1	45.1	45.2	45.2	45.2	45.3	45.3	45.3	45.4	45.4	45.4	45.5	45.5	45.5	45.6	45.6	45.6	45.7	45.7
Median age	44.0	44.0	44.1	44.2	44.2	44.2	44.2	44.3	44.3	44.4	44.4	44.4	44.5	44.5	44.6	44.6	44.7	44.7	44.7	44.8

Ages	2074	2075	2076	2077	2078	2079	2080	2081	2082	2083	2084	2085	2086	2087	2088	2089	2090	2091	2092	2093
Thousands																				
0-14	5,742	5,759	5,777	5,796	5,815	5,835	5,855	5,874	5,894	5,912	5,930	5,948	5,964	5,980	5,994	6,008	6,021	6,033	6,044	6,055
15-29	6,066	6,075	6,084	6,091	6,098	6,105	6,113	6,121	6,129	6,139	6,150	6,161	6,174	6,188	6,203	6,219	6,236	6,255	6,273	6,293
30-44	6,180	6,206	6,233	6,260	6,289	6,317	6,344	6,371	6,395	6,418	6,439	6,457	6,473	6,488	6,500	6,511	6,520	6,528	6,536	6,543
45-59	6,033	6,044	6,052	6,058	6,061	6,063	6,066	6,069	6,073	6,079	6,087	6,099	6,114	6,132	6,154	6,178	6,203	6,231	6,259	6,288
60-74	5,465	5,506	5,555	5,614	5,670	5,718	5,762	5,794	5,820	5,836	5,853	5,865	5,866	5,866	5,871	5,883	5,896	5,906	5,919	5,919
75 & over	6,324	6,344	6,358	6,366	6,379	6,400	6,427	6,466	6,511	6,566	6,620	6,678	6,742	6,813	6,874	6,928	6,981	7,037	7,097	7,159
All ages	35,811	35,935	36,060	36,185	36,312	36,439	36,566	36,694	36,822	36,951	37,079	37,208	37,337	37,466	37,596	37,727	37,858	37,990	38,123	38,256
Percentages																				
0-14	16.0	16.0	16.0	16.0	16.0	16.0	16.0	16.0	16.0	16.0	16.0	16.0	16.0	16.0	15.9	15.9	15.9	15.9	15.9	15.8
15-29	16.9	16.9	16.9	16.8	16.8	16.8	16.7	16.7	16.6	16.6	16.6	16.6	16.5	16.5	16.5	16.5	16.5	16.5	16.5	16.4
30-44	17.3	17.3	17.3	17.3	17.3	17.3	17.4	17.4	17.4	17.4	17.4	17.4	17.3	17.3	17.3	17.3	17.2	17.2	17.1	17.1
45-59	16.8	16.8	16.8	16.7	16.7	16.6	16.6	16.5	16.5	16.5	16.4	16.4	16.4	16.4	16.4	16.4	16.4	16.4	16.4	16.4
60-74	15.3	15.3	15.4	15.5	15.6	15.7	15.8	15.8	15.8	15.8	15.8	15.8	15.7	15.7	15.6	15.6	15.6	15.5	15.5	15.5
75 & over	17.7	17.7	17.6	17.6	17.6	17.6	17.6	17.6	17.7	17.8	17.9	17.9	18.1	18.2	18.3	18.4	18.4	18.5	18.6	18.7
All ages	100.0	100.0	100.0	100.0	100.0	100.0	100.0	100.0	100.0	100.0	100.0	100.0	100.0	100.0	100.0	100.0	100.0	100.0	100.0	100.0
Mean age	45.7	45.8	45.8	45.8	45.9	45.9	46.0	46.0	46.0	46.1	46.1	46.2	46.2	46.2	46.3	46.3	46.4	46.4	46.5	46.5
Median age	44.8	44.8	44.8	44.9	44.9	44.9	44.9	45.0	45.0	45.0	45.1	45.1	45.1	45.2	45.2	45.3	45.4	45.4	45.5	45.5

15.3d Population projections by the Office for National Statistics
England, FEMALES, thousands

2014-based
Principal projection

Projected populations at mid-years by age last birthday

Ages	2094	2095	2096	2097	2098	2099	2100	2101	2102	2103	2104	2105	2106	2107	2108	2109	2110	2111	2112	2113	2114
Thousands																					
0-14	6,066	6,076	6,087	6,097	6,108	6,119	6,130	6,142	6,155	6,168	6,181	6,196	6,210	6,225	6,241	6,256	6,272	6,288	6,304	6,319	6,335
15-29	6,312	6,332	6,352	6,371	6,390	6,408	6,425	6,442	6,457	6,472	6,486	6,498	6,511	6,522	6,533	6,544	6,554	6,565	6,575	6,586	6,597
30-44	6,550	6,558	6,566	6,575	6,585	6,595	6,607	6,620	6,634	6,650	6,666	6,683	6,702	6,721	6,740	6,760	6,780	6,799	6,819	6,838	6,856
45-59	6,316	6,344	6,370	6,395	6,418	6,440	6,458	6,475	6,490	6,503	6,514	6,524	6,532	6,540	6,548	6,556	6,564	6,573	6,582	6,592	6,603
60-74	5,923	5,928	5,933	5,939	5,947	5,958	5,972	5,989	6,009	6,032	6,057	6,084	6,113	6,142	6,172	6,202	6,231	6,258	6,285	6,309	6,331
75 & over	7,223	7,288	7,354	7,421	7,488	7,555	7,621	7,684	7,747	7,807	7,867	7,924	7,981	8,037	8,092	8,147	8,201	8,256	8,312	8,369	8,427
All ages	38,391	38,526	38,662	38,799	38,937	39,075	39,214	39,353	39,492	39,631	39,770	39,910	40,049	40,187	40,326	40,464	40,602	40,739	40,876	41,013	41,149
Percentages																					
0-14	15.8	15.8	15.7	15.7	15.7	15.7	15.6	15.6	15.6	15.6	15.5	15.5	15.5	15.5	15.5	15.5	15.4	15.4	15.4	15.4	15.4
15-29	16.4	16.4	16.4	16.4	16.4	16.4	16.4	16.4	16.4	16.3	16.3	16.3	16.3	16.2	16.2	16.2	16.1	16.1	16.1	16.1	16.0
30-44	17.1	17.0	17.0	16.9	16.9	16.9	16.8	16.8	16.8	16.8	16.8	16.7	16.7	16.7	16.7	16.7	16.7	16.7	16.7	16.7	16.7
45-59	16.5	16.5	16.5	16.5	16.5	16.5	16.5	16.5	16.4	16.4	16.4	16.3	16.3	16.3	16.2	16.2	16.2	16.1	16.1	16.1	16.0
60-74	15.4	15.4	15.3	15.3	15.3	15.2	15.2	15.2	15.2	15.2	15.2	15.2	15.3	15.3	15.3	15.3	15.3	15.4	15.4	15.4	15.4
75 & over	18.8	18.9	19.0	19.1	19.2	19.3	19.4	19.5	19.6	19.7	19.8	19.9	19.9	20.0	20.1	20.1	20.2	20.3	20.3	20.4	20.5
All ages	100.0	100.0	100.0	100.0	100.0	100.0	100.0	100.0	100.0	100.0	100.0	100.0	100.0	100.0	100.0	100.0	100.0	100.0	100.0	100.0	100.0
Mean age	46.6	46.6	46.7	46.8	46.8	46.9	46.9	47.0	47.1	47.1	47.2	47.2	47.3	47.4	47.4	47.5	47.5	47.6	47.6	47.7	47.7
Median age	45.6	45.7	45.8	45.8	45.9	46.0	46.0	46.1	46.1	46.2	46.3	46.3	46.4	46.4	46.5	46.5	46.6	46.6	46.7	46.7	46.8

Source: Office for National Statistics

Note: Figures may not add exactly due to rounding.
* Children under 16. Working age and pensionable age populations based on state pension age (SPA) for given year.
Between 2012 and 2018, SPA will change from 65 years for men and 61 years for women, to 65 years for both sexes.
Then between 2019 and 2020, SPA will change from 65 years to 66 years for both men and women.
Between 2026 and 2027 SPA will increase to 67 years and between 2044 and 2046 to 68 years for both sexes. This is based on SPA under the 2014 Pensions Act.
** This is consistent with the age-group definitions used in ONS Labour Market Statistics.

2014-based
Principal projection

15.3d Population projections by the Office for National Statistics
Wales, PERSONS, thousands

Projected populations at mid-years by age last birthday

Ages	2014	2015	2016	2017	2018	2019	2020	2021	2022	2023	2024	2025	2026	2027	2028	2029	2030	2031	2032	2033
Thousands																				
0-14	519	520	522	525	528	531	533	534	535	535	535	535	533	533	533	534	535	535	536	536
15-29	598	599	597	594	590	585	580	574	570	568	565	564	565	565	565	565	565	567	570	573
30-44	546	542	537	534	534	538	543	551	559	567	572	574	576	579	580	582	581	579	575	571
45-59	626	630	635	636	634	629	622	612	601	590	580	572	565	557	551	543	539	533	530	531
60-74	526	531	537	542	547	551	555	561	560	561	567	573	579	585	590	596	600	605	607	605
75 & over	276	279	283	289	297	307	316	324	342	356	368	378	387	395	404	412	418	425	433	441
All ages	3,092	3,101	3,111	3,120	3,130	3,139	3,149	3,158	3,168	3,177	3,187	3,196	3,206	3,215	3,223	3,231	3,238	3,245	3,251	3,257
Percentages																				
0-14	16.8	16.8	16.8	16.8	16.9	16.9	16.9	16.9	16.9	16.8	16.8	16.7	16.6	16.6	16.5	16.5	16.5	16.5	16.5	16.5
15-29	19.3	19.3	19.2	19.0	18.8	18.6	18.4	18.2	18.0	17.9	17.7	17.7	17.6	17.6	17.5	17.5	17.9	17.8	17.7	17.6
30-44	17.7	17.5	17.3	17.1	17.1	17.1	17.3	17.5	17.6	17.8	18.0	18.0	18.0	18.0	18.0	18.0	17.9	17.8	17.7	17.5
45-59	20.3	20.3	20.4	20.4	20.3	20.0	19.7	19.4	19.0	18.6	18.2	17.9	17.6	17.3	17.1	16.8	16.6	16.4	16.3	16.3
60-74	17.0	17.1	17.3	17.4	17.5	17.5	17.6	17.8	17.7	17.7	17.8	17.9	18.1	18.2	18.3	18.4	18.5	18.7	18.7	18.6
75 & over	8.9	9.0	9.1	9.3	9.5	9.8	10.0	10.3	10.8	11.2	11.5	11.8	12.1	12.3	12.5	12.7	12.9	13.1	13.3	13.5
All ages	100.0	100.0	100.0	100.0	100.0	100.0	100.0	100.0	100.0	100.0	100.0	100.0	100.0	100.0	100.0	100.0	100.0	100.0	100.0	100.0
Mean age	41.6	41.7	41.9	42.0	42.2	42.3	42.5	42.5	42.8	42.9	43.0	43.2	43.3	43.4	43.6	43.7	43.8	43.9	44.0	44.2
Median age	42.1	42.2	42.4	42.4	42.5	42.5	42.5	42.5	42.6	42.7	42.8	42.9	43.0	43.1	43.1	43.2	43.3	43.4	43.5	43.7

Ages	2034	2035	2036	2037	2038	2039	2040	2041	2042	2043	2044	2045	2046	2047	2048	2049	2050	2051	2052	2053
Thousands																				
0-14	536	535	534	533	532	530	529	529	528	528	528	528	528	529	529	530	531	531	532	533
15-29	576	578	579	580	579	580	579	578	578	578	579	580	581	581	581	581	580	579	578	576
30-44	566	562	557	553	551	549	548	548	548	547	547	547	549	552	555	558	560	561	562	562
45-59	534	540	548	556	564	570	572	573	577	579	580	579	577	574	570	565	561	556	553	551
60-74	601	594	586	576	565	556	550	544	537	531	525	521	517	515	516	520	526	534	542	550
75 & over	449	457	466	476	485	496	505	514	522	528	535	540	546	550	552	551	549	547	543	540
All ages	3,262	3,266	3,270	3,273	3,277	3,280	3,283	3,286	3,289	3,291	3,294	3,296	3,298	3,300	3,302	3,305	3,307	3,308	3,310	3,312
Percentages																				
0-14	16.4	16.4	16.3	16.3	16.2	16.2	16.1	16.1	16.1	16.0	16.0	16.0	16.0	16.0	16.0	16.0	16.1	16.1	16.1	16.1
15-29	17.7	17.7	17.7	17.7	17.7	17.7	17.7	17.6	17.6	17.6	17.6	17.6	17.6	17.6	17.6	17.6	17.5	17.5	17.4	17.4
30-44	17.4	17.2	17.0	16.9	16.8	16.7	16.7	16.7	16.7	16.6	16.6	16.6	16.6	16.7	16.8	16.9	16.9	17.0	17.0	17.0
45-59	16.4	16.5	16.8	17.0	17.2	17.4	17.4	17.5	17.5	17.6	17.6	17.6	17.5	17.4	17.2	17.1	17.0	16.8	16.7	16.6
60-74	18.4	18.2	17.9	17.6	17.2	17.0	16.7	16.5	16.3	16.1	15.9	15.8	15.7	15.6	15.6	15.7	15.9	16.1	16.4	16.6
75 & over	13.8	14.0	14.3	14.5	14.8	15.1	15.4	15.6	15.9	16.1	16.3	16.4	16.6	16.7	16.7	16.7	16.6	16.5	16.4	16.3
All ages	100.0	100.0	100.0	100.0	100.0	100.0	100.0	100.0	100.0	100.0	100.0	100.0	100.0	100.0	100.0	100.0	100.0	100.0	100.0	100.0
Mean age	44.3	44.4	44.5	44.5	44.6	44.7	44.8	44.8	44.9	44.9	45.0	45.0	45.1	45.1	45.1	45.2	45.2	45.2	45.3	45.3
Median age	43.8	44.0	44.1	44.3	44.4	44.5	44.6	44.7	44.8	44.8	44.8	44.8	44.7	44.7	44.6	44.5	44.5	44.5	44.6	44.6

15.3d Population projections by the Office for National Statistics
Wales, PERSONS, thousands

2014-based
Principal projection

Projected populations at mid-years by age last birthday

Ages	2054	2055	2056	2057	2058	2059	2060	2061	2062	2063	2064	2065	2066	2067	2068	2069	2070	2071	2072	2073
Thousands																				
0-14	533	534	534	534	535	535	535	535	535	535	534	534	534	534	533	533	533	533	532	532
15-29	575	574	573	573	573	573	573	574	574	575	575	576	577	578	578	579	579	580	580	580
30-44	562	562	560	560	560	561	562	563	563	563	563	562	561	560	559	558	557	557	556	556
45-59	548	548	548	548	548	547	548	550	553	556	559	561	563	564	564	564	564	563	562	562
60-74	556	559	561	565	567	568	568	566	563	559	555	551	547	544	543	541	541	542	542	542
75 & over	539	540	541	541	541	541	542	543	545	548	551	556	562	568	574	581	586	590	596	600
All ages	3,314	3,316	3,318	3,321	3,323	3,325	3,327	3,330	3,332	3,335	3,338	3,341	3,344	3,348	3,351	3,355	3,360	3,364	3,368	3,373
Percentages																				
0-14	16.1	16.1	16.1	16.1	16.1	16.1	16.1	16.1	16.0	16.0	16.0	16.0	16.0	15.9	15.9	15.9	15.9	15.8	15.8	15.8
15-29	17.4	17.3	17.3	17.3	17.2	17.2	17.2	17.2	17.2	17.2	17.2	17.2	17.3	17.3	17.3	17.3	17.2	17.2	17.2	17.2
30-44	17.0	16.9	16.9	16.9	16.9	16.9	16.9	16.9	16.9	16.9	16.9	16.8	16.8	16.7	16.7	16.6	16.6	16.5	16.5	16.5
45-59	16.5	16.5	16.5	16.5	16.5	16.5	16.5	16.5	16.6	16.7	16.7	16.8	16.8	16.8	16.8	16.8	16.8	16.7	16.7	16.7
60-74	16.8	16.9	16.9	17.0	17.1	17.1	17.1	17.0	16.9	16.8	16.6	16.5	16.4	16.3	16.2	16.1	16.1	16.1	16.1	16.1
75 & over	16.3	16.3	16.3	16.3	16.3	16.3	16.3	16.3	16.3	16.4	16.5	16.6	16.8	17.0	17.1	17.3	17.4	17.5	17.7	17.8
All ages	100.0	100.0	100.0	100.0	100.0	100.0	100.0	100.0	100.0	100.0	100.0	100.0	100.0	100.0	100.0	100.0	100.0	100.0	100.0	100.0
Mean age	45.3	45.3	45.3	45.4	45.4	45.4	45.4	45.5	45.5	45.5	45.5	45.6	45.6	45.6	45.7	45.7	45.8	45.8	45.9	45.9
Median age	44.6	44.7	44.8	44.8	44.8	44.8	44.8	44.8	44.8	44.9	44.9	44.9	45.0	45.1	45.1	45.2	45.3	45.3	45.4	45.5

Ages	2074	2075	2076	2077	2078	2079	2080	2081	2082	2083	2084	2085	2086	2087	2088	2089	2090	2091	2092	2093
Thousands																				
0-14	532	532	532	533	533	533	533	534	534	534	535	535	535	536	536	536	536	536	536	536
15-29	580	580	580	580	580	580	580	579	579	579	579	578	578	578	578	578	578	578	578	579
30-44	556	556	557	557	558	558	559	560	561	561	562	562	563	563	563	563	563	563	563	563
45-59	563	565	565	566	566	566	566	565	564	563	562	561	560	560	560	560	560	561	561	562
60-74	542	543	545	549	552	555	558	560	561	561	562	562	561	561	562	563	565	566	566	567
75 & over	603	605	607	607	608	609	611	614	618	623	627	631	637	642	645	648	651	653	656	660
All ages	3,378	3,382	3,387	3,392	3,397	3,402	3,407	3,412	3,416	3,421	3,426	3,430	3,435	3,439	3,444	3,449	3,453	3,458	3,462	3,467
Percentages																				
0-14	15.8	15.7	15.7	15.7	15.7	15.7	15.7	15.6	15.6	15.6	15.6	15.6	15.6	15.6	15.6	15.5	15.5	15.5	15.5	15.5
15-29	17.2	17.2	17.1	17.1	17.1	17.0	17.0	17.0	17.0	16.9	16.9	16.9	16.8	16.8	16.8	16.8	16.7	16.7	16.7	16.7
30-44	16.5	16.4	16.4	16.4	16.4	16.4	16.4	16.4	16.4	16.4	16.4	16.4	16.4	16.4	16.4	16.3	16.3	16.3	16.3	16.2
45-59	16.7	16.7	16.7	16.7	16.7	16.6	16.6	16.6	16.5	16.5	16.4	16.4	16.3	16.3	16.3	16.2	16.2	16.2	16.2	16.2
60-74	16.1	16.1	16.1	16.2	16.3	16.3	16.4	16.4	16.4	16.4	16.4	16.4	16.3	16.3	16.3	16.3	16.4	16.4	16.4	16.4
75 & over	17.9	17.9	17.9	17.9	17.9	17.9	17.9	18.0	18.1	18.2	18.3	18.4	18.5	18.7	18.7	18.8	18.8	18.9	19.0	19.0
All ages	100.0	100.0	100.0	100.0	100.0	100.0	100.0	100.0	100.0	100.0	100.0	100.0	100.0	100.0	100.0	100.0	100.0	100.0	100.0	100.0
Mean age	46.0	46.1	46.1	46.2	46.2	46.3	46.3	46.4	46.4	46.5	46.5	46.6	46.6	46.7	46.7	46.8	46.8	46.9	46.9	47.0
Median age	45.5	45.6	45.7	45.7	45.8	45.8	45.8	45.9	45.9	46.0	46.0	46.1	46.1	46.2	46.2	46.3	46.3	46.4	46.4	46.5

15.3d Population projections by the Office for National Statistics
Wales, PERSONS, thousands

2014-based
Principal projection

Projected populations at mid-years by age last birthday

Ages	2094	2095	2096	2097	2098	2099	2100	2101	2102	2103	2104	2105	2106	2107	2108	2109	2110	2111	2112	2113	2114
Thousands																					
0-14	536	536	536	536	536	536	536	536	536	536	536	536	536	536	536	536	537	537	537	537	537
15-29	579	579	580	580	580	581	581	581	582	582	582	582	582	582	582	582	582	582	582	582	582
30-44	563	563	563	562	562	562	562	562	561	561	561	562	562	562	562	562	563	563	563	564	564
45-59	563	564	565	565	566	567	567	568	568	569	569	569	569	569	569	569	569	569	568	568	568
60-74	567	567	566	566	565	564	564	563	563	563	564	564	565	566	567	568	569	570	571	572	573
75 & over	664	668	672	677	682	687	692	697	702	706	711	715	719	723	727	731	735	739	742	746	750
All ages	3,472	3,477	3,481	3,486	3,491	3,496	3,502	3,507	3,512	3,517	3,523	3,528	3,533	3,538	3,544	3,549	3,554	3,560	3,565	3,570	3,575
Percentages																					
0-14	15.4	15.4	15.4	15.4	15.4	15.3	15.3	15.3	15.3	15.2	15.2	15.2	15.2	15.2	15.1	15.1	15.1	15.1	15.1	15.0	15.0
15-29	16.7	16.7	16.7	16.6	16.6	16.6	16.6	16.6	16.6	16.5	16.5	16.5	16.5	16.5	16.4	16.4	16.4	16.4	16.3	16.3	16.3
30-44	16.2	16.2	16.2	16.1	16.1	16.1	16.2	16.0	16.0	16.0	15.9	15.9	15.9	15.9	15.9	15.8	15.8	15.8	15.8	15.8	15.8
45-59	16.2	16.2	16.2	16.2	16.2	16.2	16.2	16.2	16.2	16.2	16.1	16.1	16.1	16.1	16.1	16.0	16.0	16.0	15.9	15.9	15.9
60-74	16.3	16.3	16.3	16.2	16.2	16.1	16.1	16.1	16.0	16.0	16.0	16.0	16.0	16.0	16.0	16.0	16.0	16.0	16.0	16.0	16.0
75 & over	19.1	19.2	19.3	19.4	19.5	19.6	19.8	19.9	20.0	20.1	20.2	20.3	20.3	20.4	20.5	20.6	20.7	20.8	20.8	20.9	21.0
All ages	100.0	100.0	100.0	100.0	100.0	100.0	100.0	100.0	100.0	100.0	100.0	100.0	100.0	100.0	100.0	100.0	100.0	100.0	100.0	100.0	100.0
Mean age	47.0	47.1	47.1	47.2	47.2	47.3	47.4	47.4	47.5	47.5	47.6	47.7	47.7	47.8	47.8	47.9	48.0	48.0	48.1	48.1	48.2
Median age	46.5	46.6	46.7	46.7	46.8	46.9	46.9	47.0	47.1	47.1	47.2	47.2	47.3	47.4	47.4	47.5	47.6	47.6	47.7	47.7	47.8

Source: Office for National Statistics

Note: Figures may not add exactly due to rounding.

* Children under 16. Working age and pensionable age populations based on state pension age (SPA) for given year.

Between 2012 and 2018, SPA will change from 65 years for men and 61 years for women, to 65 years for both sexes.

Then between 2019 and 2020, SPA will change from 65 years to 66 years for both men and women.

Between 2026 and 2027 SPA will increase to 67 years and between 2044 and 2046 to 68 years for both sexes. This is based on SPA under the 2014 Pensions Act.

** This is consistent with the age-group definitions used in ONS Labour Market Statistics.

15.3d Population projections by the Office for National Statistics
Wales, MALES, thousands

2014-based
Principal projection

Projected populations at mid-years by age last birthday

Ages	2014	2015	2016	2017	2018	2019	2020	2021	2022	2023	2024	2025	2026	2027	2028	2029	2030	2031	2032	2033
Thousands																				
0-14	266	267	267	269	270	272	273	274	274	274	274	274	273	273	273	273	274	274	274	274
15-29	307	308	308	307	306	304	301	299	297	296	294	294	294	294	294	294	294	295	297	298
30-44	270	269	267	265	266	268	271	276	280	285	288	290	292	294	296	297	297	297	296	294
45-59	307	309	311	311	310	307	304	299	294	288	283	280	276	272	269	266	264	262	260	261
60-74	256	258	261	264	266	267	269	272	272	272	274	277	280	283	285	288	290	292	293	292
75 & over	115	117	120	123	128	133	138	142	151	158	164	169	174	178	182	185	189	192	195	199
All ages	1,521	1,528	1,534	1,539	1,545	1,551	1,557	1,562	1,568	1,573	1,579	1,584	1,589	1,594	1,599	1,604	1,608	1,612	1,616	1,619
Percentages																				
0-14	17.5	17.5	17.4	17.5	17.5	17.5	17.6	17.5	17.5	17.4	17.4	17.3	17.2	17.1	17.1	17.0	17.0	17.0	17.0	17.0
15-29	20.2	20.2	20.1	20.0	19.8	19.6	19.4	19.1	19.0	18.8	18.7	18.6	18.5	18.4	18.4	18.3	18.3	18.3	18.4	18.4
30-44	17.8	17.6	17.4	17.2	17.2	17.3	17.4	17.7	17.9	18.1	18.3	18.3	18.4	18.5	18.5	18.5	18.5	18.4	18.3	18.2
45-59	20.2	20.2	20.3	20.2	20.0	19.8	19.5	19.1	18.7	18.3	17.9	17.7	17.4	17.1	16.9	16.6	16.4	16.2	16.1	16.1
60-74	16.8	16.9	17.0	17.1	17.2	17.2	17.3	17.4	17.3	17.3	17.4	17.5	17.6	17.8	17.8	18.0	18.0	18.1	18.1	18.0
75 & over	7.6	7.7	7.8	8.0	8.3	8.6	8.9	9.1	9.6	10.1	10.4	10.7	10.9	11.1	11.4	11.6	11.7	11.9	12.1	12.3
All ages	100.0	100.0	100.0	100.0	100.0	100.0	100.0	100.0	100.0	100.0	100.0	100.0	100.0	100.0	100.0	100.0	100.0	100.0	100.0	100.0
Mean age	40.5	40.6	40.8	41.0	41.1	41.3	41.4	41.6	41.7	41.8	42.0	42.1	42.2	42.4	42.5	42.6	42.7	42.9	43.0	43.1
Median age	40.8	40.8	40.8	40.8	40.8	40.8	40.9	41.0	41.1	41.2	41.2	41.3	41.3	41.4	41.5	41.6	41.7	41.8	42.0	42.1

Ages	2034	2035	2036	2037	2038	2039	2040	2041	2042	2043	2044	2045	2046	2047	2048	2049	2050	2051	2052	2053
Thousands																				
0-14	274	274	274	273	272	272	271	271	271	270	270	271	271	271	271	272	272	272	273	273
15-29	300	301	301	302	301	302	301	301	301	301	301	302	302	302	302	302	302	301	301	300
30-44	292	290	288	287	286	285	284	284	284	284	284	284	285	286	288	289	290	291	291	291
45-59	264	267	272	276	280	284	286	288	291	292	293	294	294	293	291	289	287	285	284	284
60-74	290	287	283	278	273	269	266	263	260	257	254	253	251	250	252	254	258	263	267	271
75 & over	203	206	211	215	220	224	229	233	236	239	243	245	248	249	250	250	249	247	246	244
All ages	1,622	1,625	1,628	1,630	1,633	1,635	1,637	1,639	1,642	1,644	1,646	1,648	1,650	1,652	1,654	1,656	1,658	1,660	1,661	1,663
Percentages																				
0-14	16.9	16.9	16.8	16.7	16.7	16.6	16.6	16.5	16.5	16.5	16.4	16.4	16.4	16.4	16.4	16.4	16.4	16.4	16.4	16.4
15-29	18.5	18.5	18.5	18.5	18.5	18.4	18.4	18.3	18.3	18.3	18.3	18.3	18.3	18.3	18.3	18.2	18.2	18.1	18.1	18.0
30-44	18.0	17.9	17.7	17.6	17.5	17.4	17.4	17.3	17.3	17.3	17.2	17.2	17.3	17.3	17.4	17.5	17.5	17.5	17.5	17.5
45-59	16.2	16.4	16.7	16.9	17.2	17.4	17.5	17.6	17.7	17.8	17.8	17.8	17.8	17.7	17.6	17.5	17.3	17.2	17.1	17.1
60-74	17.9	17.6	17.4	17.0	16.7	16.4	16.2	16.0	15.8	15.6	15.5	15.3	15.2	15.2	15.2	15.4	15.5	15.8	16.0	16.3
75 & over	12.5	12.7	12.9	13.2	13.5	13.7	14.0	14.2	14.4	14.6	14.7	14.9	15.0	15.1	15.1	15.1	15.0	14.9	14.8	14.7
All ages	100.0	100.0	100.0	100.0	100.0	100.0	100.0	100.0	100.0	100.0	100.0	100.0	100.0	100.0	100.0	100.0	100.0	100.0	100.0	100.0
Mean age	43.2	43.3	43.4	43.4	43.5	43.6	43.7	43.7	43.8	43.8	43.9	43.9	44.0	44.0	44.0	44.1	44.1	44.2	44.2	44.2
Median age	42.3	42.4	42.6	42.8	42.9	43.0	43.1	43.2	43.2	43.2	43.2	43.2	43.1	43.1	43.1	43.1	43.1	43.2	43.3	43.3

15.3d Population projections by the Office for National Statistics
Wales, MALES, thousands

2014-based
Principal projection

Projected populations at mid-years by age last birthday

Ages	2054	2055	2056	2057	2058	2059	2060	2061	2062	2063	2064	2065	2066	2067	2068	2069	2070	2071	2072	2073
Thousands																				
0-14	273	273	274	274	274	274	274	274	274	274	274	274	273	273	273	273	273	273	273	273
15-29	299	299	298	298	298	298	298	298	299	299	299	300	300	301	301	301	301	302	302	302
30-44	291	291	291	290	290	291	291	292	292	292	292	292	291	291	290	289	289	289	288	288
45-59	282	282	282	282	282	282	282	283	284	286	287	289	289	290	290	290	290	290	289	289
60-74	275	277	280	282	284	286	286	286	285	284	282	280	279	278	278	277	276	277	277	277
75 & over	244	245	245	245	246	246	247	248	249	251	253	256	260	263	267	271	274	277	281	284
All ages	1,665	1,667	1,669	1,671	1,674	1,676	1,678	1,680	1,683	1,685	1,687	1,690	1,693	1,695	1,698	1,701	1,704	1,707	1,710	1,713
Percentages																				
0-14	16.4	16.4	16.4	16.4	16.4	16.3	16.3	16.3	16.3	16.3	16.2	16.2	16.2	16.1	16.1	16.1	16.0	16.0	16.0	15.9
15-29	18.0	17.9	17.9	17.8	17.8	17.8	17.8	17.8	17.8	17.7	17.7	17.7	17.7	17.7	17.7	17.7	17.7	17.7	17.6	17.6
30-44	17.5	17.5	17.4	17.4	17.4	17.4	17.4	17.4	17.3	17.3	17.3	17.2	17.2	17.1	17.1	17.0	17.0	16.9	16.9	16.8
45-59	16.9	16.9	16.9	16.8	16.8	16.8	16.8	16.8	16.9	17.0	17.0	17.1	17.1	17.1	17.1	17.1	17.0	17.0	16.9	16.9
60-74	16.5	16.6	16.7	16.9	17.0	17.0	17.0	17.0	17.0	16.8	16.7	16.6	16.5	16.4	16.3	16.3	16.2	16.2	16.2	16.2
75 & over	14.7	14.7	14.7	14.7	14.7	14.7	14.7	14.7	14.8	14.9	15.0	15.2	15.4	15.5	15.7	15.9	16.1	16.3	16.4	16.5
All ages	100.0	100.0	100.0	100.0	100.0	100.0	100.0	100.0	100.0	100.0	100.0	100.0	100.0	100.0	100.0	100.0	100.0	100.0	100.0	100.0
Mean age	44.3	44.3	44.3	44.4	44.4	44.4	44.5	44.5	44.6	44.6	44.7	44.7	44.8	44.8	44.9	45.0	45.0	45.1	45.2	45.2
Median age	43.4	43.5	43.6	43.6	43.6	43.7	43.7	43.7	43.8	43.8	43.9	44.0	44.1	44.1	44.2	44.3	44.4	44.5	44.6	44.7

Ages	2074	2075	2076	2077	2078	2079	2080	2081	2082	2083	2084	2085	2086	2087	2088	2089	2090	2091	2092	2093
Thousands																				
0-14	273	273	273	273	273	273	273	273	274	274	274	274	274	274	275	275	275	275	275	275
15-29	302	302	302	302	302	302	302	301	301	301	301	301	301	301	301	301	301	301	301	301
30-44	288	288	289	289	289	290	290	290	291	291	291	292	292	292	292	292	292	292	292	292
45-59	290	291	291	291	291	291	291	291	290	290	289	289	288	288	288	288	289	289	290	290
60-74	278	278	279	281	282	284	285	286	287	287	288	288	288	288	288	289	289	290	290	291
75 & over	286	288	289	290	291	292	293	295	297	300	303	305	308	311	313	315	317	318	320	322
All ages	1,716	1,719	1,722	1,726	1,729	1,732	1,735	1,738	1,741	1,743	1,746	1,749	1,752	1,754	1,757	1,760	1,762	1,765	1,768	1,770
Percentages																				
0-14	15.9	15.9	15.8	15.8	15.8	15.8	15.8	15.7	15.7	15.7	15.7	15.7	15.7	15.6	15.6	15.6	15.6	15.6	15.5	15.5
15-29	17.6	17.6	17.5	17.5	17.5	17.4	17.4	17.3	17.3	17.3	17.2	17.2	17.2	17.1	17.1	17.1	17.1	17.1	17.0	17.0
30-44	16.8	16.8	16.8	16.7	16.7	16.7	16.7	16.7	16.7	16.7	16.7	16.7	16.7	16.6	16.6	16.6	16.6	16.6	16.5	16.5
45-59	16.9	16.9	16.9	16.9	16.9	16.8	16.8	16.7	16.7	16.6	16.6	16.5	16.5	16.4	16.4	16.4	16.4	16.4	16.4	16.4
60-74	16.2	16.2	16.2	16.3	16.3	16.4	16.5	16.5	16.5	16.5	16.5	16.5	16.4	16.4	16.4	16.4	16.4	16.4	16.4	16.4
75 & over	16.7	16.7	16.8	16.8	16.8	16.9	16.9	17.0	17.1	17.2	17.3	17.5	17.6	17.7	17.8	17.9	18.0	18.0	18.1	18.2
All ages	100.0	100.0	100.0	100.0	100.0	100.0	100.0	100.0	100.0	100.0	100.0	100.0	100.0	100.0	100.0	100.0	100.0	100.0	100.0	100.0
Mean age	45.3	45.4	45.5	45.5	45.6	45.7	45.7	45.8	45.8	45.9	46.0	46.0	46.1	46.1	46.2	46.3	46.3	46.4	46.4	46.5
Median age	44.7	44.8	44.9	45.0	45.0	45.1	45.1	45.2	45.2	45.3	45.3	45.4	45.5	45.5	45.6	45.6	45.7	45.8	45.8	45.9

15.3d Population projections by the Office for National Statistics
Wales, MALES, thousands

2014-based
Principal projection

Projected populations at mid-years by age last birthday

Ages	2094	2095	2096	2097	2098	2099	2100	2101	2102	2103	2104	2105	2106	2107	2108	2109	2110	2111	2112	2113	2114
Thousands																					
0-14	275	275	275	275	275	275	275	275	275	275	275	275	275	275	275	275	275	275	275	275	275
15-29	301	301	302	302	302	302	302	303	303	303	303	303	303	303	303	303	303	303	303	303	303
30-44	292	292	292	292	292	292	291	291	291	291	291	291	291	292	292	292	292	292	292	293	293
45-59	290	290	291	291	292	292	292	293	293	293	293	293	293	293	293	293	293	293	293	293	293
60-74	291	291	291	290	290	289	289	289	289	289	290	290	290	291	291	292	293	293	294	294	295
75 & over	324	326	329	331	334	336	339	342	344	347	349	351	353	355	358	360	362	364	366	368	370
All ages	1,773	1,776	1,778	1,781	1,784	1,786	1,789	1,792	1,795	1,798	1,800	1,803	1,806	1,809	1,812	1,815	1,817	1,820	1,823	1,826	1,829
Percentages																					
0-14	15.5	15.5	15.4	15.4	15.4	15.4	15.3	15.3	15.3	15.3	15.2	15.2	15.2	15.2	15.2	15.1	15.1	15.1	15.1	15.1	15.1
15-29	17.0	17.0	17.0	16.9	16.9	16.9	16.9	16.9	16.9	16.8	16.8	16.8	16.8	16.8	16.7	16.7	16.7	16.6	16.6	16.6	16.6
30-44	16.5	16.4	16.4	16.4	16.4	16.3	16.3	16.3	16.2	16.2	16.2	16.2	16.1	16.1	16.1	16.1	16.1	16.1	16.0	16.0	16.0
45-59	16.4	16.4	16.4	16.4	16.4	16.4	16.3	16.3	16.3	16.3	16.3	16.3	16.2	16.2	16.2	16.2	16.1	16.1	16.1	16.1	16.0
60-74	16.4	16.4	16.3	16.3	16.2	16.2	16.2	16.1	16.1	16.1	16.1	16.1	16.1	16.1	16.1	16.1	16.1	16.1	16.1	16.1	16.1
75 & over	18.3	18.4	18.5	18.6	18.7	18.8	19.0	19.1	19.2	19.3	19.4	19.5	19.6	19.7	19.7	19.8	19.9	20.0	20.1	20.1	20.2
All ages	100.0	100.0	100.0	100.0	100.0	100.0	100.0	100.0	100.0	100.0	100.0	100.0	100.0	100.0	100.0	100.0	100.0	100.0	100.0	100.0	100.0
Mean age	46.5	46.6	46.6	46.7	46.8	46.8	46.9	46.9	47.0	47.1	47.1	47.2	47.3	47.3	47.4	47.4	47.5	47.6	47.6	47.7	47.7
Median age	45.9	46.0	46.1	46.1	46.2	46.3	46.4	46.4	46.5	46.6	46.6	46.7	46.8	46.8	46.9	46.9	47.0	47.1	47.1	47.2	47.2

Source: Office for National Statistics

Note: Figures may not add exactly due to rounding.
* Children under 16. Working age and pensionable age populations based on state pension age (SPA) for given year.
Between 2012 and 2018, SPA will change from 65 years for men and 61 years for women, to 65 years for both sexes.
Then between 2019 and 2020, SPA will change from 65 years to 66 years for both men and women.
Between 2026 and 2027 SPA will increase to 67 years and between 2044 and 2046 to 68 years for both sexes. This is based on SPA under the 2014 Pensions Act.
** This is consistent with the age-group definitions used in ONS Labour Market Statistics.

15.3d Population projections by the Office for National Statistics
Wales, FEMALES, thousands

2014-based
Principal projection

Projected populations at mid-years by age last birthday

Ages	2014	2015	2016	2017	2018	2019	2020	2021	2022	2023	2024	2025	2026	2027	2028	2029	2030	2031	2032	2033
Thousands																				
0-14	253	253	254	256	258	259	260	261	261	261	261	261	260	260	260	260	261	261	261	261
15-29	291	291	289	287	284	281	279	276	273	272	270	270	271	271	271	271	271	272	274	275
30-44	276	274	270	269	268	270	272	275	279	282	284	284	284	285	285	285	283	282	279	276
45-59	319	322	324	325	324	322	318	313	308	302	297	293	289	285	281	277	275	271	270	269
60-74	270	273	276	279	281	283	286	289	289	289	292	296	299	302	305	308	310	313	314	313
75 & over	161	162	163	166	169	174	178	182	191	198	204	209	214	218	222	226	230	234	238	242
All ages	1,571	1,574	1,577	1,581	1,585	1,588	1,592	1,596	1,600	1,604	1,608	1,612	1,616	1,620	1,624	1,627	1,630	1,633	1,635	1,637
Percentages																				
0-14	16.1	16.1	16.1	16.2	16.3	16.3	16.3	16.3	16.3	16.3	16.2	16.2	16.1	16.0	16.0	16.0	16.0	16.0	16.0	16.0
15-29	18.6	18.5	18.3	18.1	17.9	17.7	17.5	17.3	17.1	16.9	16.8	16.8	16.8	16.7	16.7	16.6	16.6	16.7	16.7	16.8
30-44	17.6	17.4	17.1	17.0	16.9	17.0	17.1	17.2	17.4	17.6	17.7	17.6	17.6	17.6	17.5	17.5	17.4	17.2	17.1	16.9
45-59	20.3	20.4	20.6	20.6	20.5	20.2	20.0	19.6	19.2	18.8	18.5	18.2	17.9	17.6	17.3	17.0	16.9	16.6	16.5	16.5
60-74	17.2	17.3	17.5	17.6	17.7	17.8	18.0	18.1	18.0	18.0	18.2	18.3	18.5	18.7	18.8	18.9	19.0	19.2	19.2	19.1
75 & over	10.3	10.3	10.4	10.5	10.7	10.9	11.2	11.4	11.9	12.3	12.7	13.0	13.2	13.4	13.7	13.9	14.1	14.3	14.5	14.8
All ages	100.0	100.0	100.0	100.0	100.0	100.0	100.0	100.0	100.0	100.0	100.0	100.0	100.0	100.0	100.0	100.0	100.0	100.0	100.0	100.0
Mean age	42.7	42.8	42.9	43.0	43.2	43.3	43.5	43.6	43.8	43.9	44.1	44.2	44.3	44.5	44.6	44.7	44.9	45.0	45.1	45.2
Median age	43.4	43.5	43.7	43.9	44.0	44.1	44.2	44.2	44.2	44.3	44.4	44.5	44.6	44.7	44.8	44.9	45.0	45.1	45.2	45.3

Ages	2034	2035	2036	2037	2038	2039	2040	2041	2042	2043	2044	2045	2046	2047	2048	2049	2050	2051	2052	2053
Thousands																				
0-14	261	261	260	260	259	259	258	258	258	257	257	257	258	258	258	258	259	259	259	260
15-29	276	277	278	278	278	278	278	277	277	277	278	278	279	279	279	279	278	278	277	277
30-44	274	271	269	266	265	264	264	264	264	264	263	263	264	266	267	269	270	270	271	271
45-59	271	273	276	280	284	286	286	286	286	287	287	285	284	281	278	276	273	271	268	267
60-74	311	308	303	298	293	288	284	281	277	274	270	268	265	264	264	266	268	272	276	279
75 & over	246	251	256	261	266	271	276	281	285	289	293	295	299	301	302	302	301	299	297	296
All ages	1,639	1,641	1,642	1,643	1,644	1,645	1,646	1,646	1,647	1,647	1,648	1,648	1,648	1,649	1,649	1,649	1,649	1,649	1,649	1,649
Percentages																				
0-14	15.9	15.9	15.9	15.8	15.8	15.7	15.7	15.7	15.6	15.6	15.6	15.6	15.6	15.6	15.7	15.7	15.7	15.7	15.7	15.8
15-29	16.9	16.9	16.9	16.9	16.9	16.9	16.9	16.9	16.8	16.8	16.9	16.9	16.9	16.9	16.9	16.9	16.9	16.8	16.8	16.8
30-44	16.7	16.5	16.4	16.2	16.1	16.0	16.0	16.0	16.0	16.0	16.0	16.0	16.0	16.1	16.2	16.3	16.4	16.4	16.4	16.4
45-59	16.5	16.6	16.8	17.1	17.2	17.4	17.4	17.3	17.4	17.4	17.4	17.3	17.2	17.1	16.9	16.7	16.6	16.4	16.3	16.2
60-74	19.0	18.8	18.5	18.1	17.8	17.5	17.3	17.0	16.8	16.6	16.4	16.3	16.1	16.0	16.0	16.1	16.3	16.5	16.7	16.9
75 & over	15.0	15.3	15.6	15.9	16.2	16.5	16.8	17.1	17.3	17.5	17.8	17.9	18.1	18.2	18.3	18.3	18.2	18.1	18.0	17.9
All ages	100.0	100.0	100.0	100.0	100.0	100.0	100.0	100.0	100.0	100.0	100.0	100.0	100.0	100.0	100.0	100.0	100.0	100.0	100.0	100.0
Mean age	45.3	45.4	45.5	45.6	45.7	45.8	45.9	45.9	46.0	46.0	46.1	46.1	46.2	46.2	46.2	46.2	46.3	46.3	46.3	46.3
Median age	45.4	45.6	45.7	45.9	46.0	46.1	46.2	46.3	46.3	46.4	46.4	46.4	46.4	46.3	46.2	46.1	46.0	46.0	46.0	45.9

15.3d Population projections by the Office for National Statistics
Wales, FEMALES, thousands

2014-based
Principal projection

Projected populations at mid-years by age last birthday

Ages	2054	2055	2056	2057	2058	2059	2060	2061	2062	2063	2064	2065	2066	2067	2068	2069	2070	2071	2072	2073
Thousands																				
0-14	260	260	260	261	261	261	261	261	261	261	261	260	260	260	260	260	260	260	260	260
15-29	276	275	275	275	275	275	275	275	275	276	276	276	277	277	277	278	278	278	278	278
30-44	271	271	270	269	270	270	271	271	271	271	271	271	270	270	269	269	268	268	268	268
45-59	266	266	266	266	266	266	266	267	269	270	272	273	273	274	274	274	274	273	273	273
60-74	281	282	282	283	283	283	282	280	278	275	273	270	268	266	265	264	264	265	265	265
75 & over	295	295	295	295	295	295	295	295	296	297	298	300	303	305	308	310	311	313	315	316
All ages	1,649	1,649	1,649	1,649	1,649	1,649	1,649	1,649	1,650	1,650	1,650	1,651	1,652	1,652	1,653	1,654	1,655	1,657	1,658	1,660
Percentages																				
0-14	15.8	15.8	15.8	15.8	15.8	15.8	15.8	15.8	15.8	15.8	15.8	15.8	15.8	15.7	15.7	15.7	15.7	15.7	15.7	15.6
15-29	16.7	16.7	16.7	16.7	16.7	16.7	16.7	16.7	16.7	16.7	16.7	16.7	16.8	16.8	16.8	16.8	16.8	16.8	16.8	16.8
30-44	16.4	16.4	16.4	16.3	16.3	16.4	16.4	16.4	16.4	16.4	16.4	16.4	16.4	16.3	16.3	16.2	16.2	16.2	16.1	16.1
45-59	16.1	16.1	16.2	16.1	16.1	16.1	16.1	16.2	16.3	16.4	16.5	16.5	16.6	16.6	16.6	16.6	16.5	16.5	16.4	16.4
60-74	17.0	17.1	17.1	17.1	17.1	17.2	17.1	17.0	16.8	16.7	16.5	16.4	16.2	16.1	16.0	16.0	16.0	16.0	16.0	16.0
75 & over	17.9	17.9	17.9	17.9	17.9	17.9	17.9	17.9	17.9	18.0	18.1	18.2	18.3	18.5	18.6	18.7	18.8	18.9	19.0	19.0
All ages	100.0	100.0	100.0	100.0	100.0	100.0	100.0	100.0	100.0	100.0	100.0	100.0	100.0	100.0	100.0	100.0	100.0	100.0	100.0	100.0
Mean age	46.3	46.3	46.4	46.4	46.4	46.4	46.4	46.4	46.4	46.4	46.4	46.4	46.5	46.5	46.5	46.5	46.6	46.6	46.6	46.7
Median age	46.0	46.0	46.0	46.0	46.1	46.1	46.0	46.0	46.0	46.0	46.0	46.0	46.0	46.0	46.1	46.1	46.2	46.2	46.3	46.3

Ages	2074	2075	2076	2077	2078	2079	2080	2081	2082	2083	2084	2085	2086	2087	2088	2089	2090	2091	2092	2093
Thousands																				
0-14	260	260	260	260	260	260	260	260	260	261	261	261	261	261	261	261	261	261	261	261
15-29	278	278	278	278	278	278	278	278	278	278	278	277	277	277	277	277	277	277	277	278
30-44	268	268	268	268	268	269	269	269	270	270	270	271	272	271	271	271	271	271	271	271
45-59	274	274	274	275	275	275	274	274	274	273	272	272	272	272	272	272	272	272	272	273
60-74	265	265	266	268	270	271	272	273	274	274	274	274	274	274	274	275	275	276	276	276
75 & over	317	318	318	317	317	317	318	319	320	322	324	326	328	330	332	333	334	335	337	338
All ages	1,661	1,663	1,665	1,667	1,668	1,670	1,672	1,674	1,676	1,678	1,680	1,681	1,683	1,685	1,687	1,689	1,691	1,693	1,695	1,697
Percentages																				
0-14	15.6	15.6	15.6	15.6	15.6	15.6	15.6	15.5	15.5	15.5	15.5	15.5	15.5	15.5	15.5	15.5	15.5	15.4	15.4	15.4
15-29	16.8	16.7	16.7	16.7	16.7	16.7	16.6	16.6	16.6	16.6	16.5	16.5	16.5	16.5	16.4	16.4	16.4	16.4	16.4	16.4
30-44	16.1	16.1	16.1	16.1	16.1	16.1	16.1	16.1	16.1	16.1	16.1	16.1	16.1	16.1	16.1	16.1	16.0	16.0	16.0	16.0
45-59	16.5	16.5	16.5	16.5	16.5	16.4	16.4	16.4	16.3	16.3	16.2	16.2	16.1	16.2	16.1	16.1	16.1	16.1	16.1	16.1
60-74	15.9	16.0	16.0	16.1	16.2	16.2	16.3	16.3	16.3	16.3	16.3	16.3	16.3	16.2	16.2	16.3	16.3	16.3	16.3	16.3
75 & over	19.1	19.1	19.1	19.0	19.0	19.0	19.0	19.1	19.1	19.2	19.3	19.4	19.5	19.6	19.7	19.7	19.8	19.8	19.9	19.9
All ages	100.0	100.0	100.0	100.0	100.0	100.0	100.0	100.0	100.0	100.0	100.0	100.0	100.0	100.0	100.0	100.0	100.0	100.0	100.0	100.0
Mean age	46.7	46.7	46.8	46.8	46.9	46.9	47.0	47.0	47.0	47.1	47.1	47.2	47.2	47.3	47.3	47.3	47.4	47.4	47.5	47.5
Median age	46.4	46.4	46.5	46.5	46.5	46.6	46.6	46.6	46.7	46.7	46.7	46.8	46.8	46.8	46.9	46.9	47.0	47.0	47.1	47.1

15.3d Population projections by the Office for National Statistics
Wales, FEMALES, thousands

2014-based
Principal projection

Projected populations at mid-years by age last birthday

Ages	2094	2095	2096	2097	2098	2099	2100	2101	2102	2103	2104	2105	2106	2107	2108	2109	2110	2111	2112	2113	2114
Thousands																					
0-14	261	261	261	261	261	261	261	261	261	261	261	261	261	261	262	262	262	262	262	262	262
15-29	278	278	278	278	278	279	279	279	279	279	279	279	279	279	279	279	279	279	279	279	279
30-44	271	271	271	271	270	270	270	270	270	270	270	270	270	270	270	271	271	271	271	271	271
45-59	273	273	274	274	274	275	275	275	275	275	276	276	276	276	276	276	275	275	275	275	275
60-74	276	276	276	275	275	275	274	274	274	274	274	275	275	275	276	276	277	277	278	278	279
75 & over	340	342	344	346	348	351	353	355	357	360	362	364	366	368	369	371	373	375	377	379	381
All ages	1,699	1,701	1,703	1,706	1,708	1,710	1,712	1,715	1,717	1,720	1,722	1,725	1,727	1,729	1,732	1,734	1,737	1,739	1,742	1,744	1,747
Percentages																					
0-14	15.4	15.4	15.3	15.3	15.3	15.3	15.3	15.2	15.2	15.2	15.2	15.2	15.1	15.1	15.1	15.1	15.1	15.1	15.0	15.0	15.0
15-29	16.3	16.3	16.3	16.3	16.3	16.3	16.3	16.3	16.2	16.2	16.2	16.2	16.2	16.1	16.1	16.1	16.1	16.1	16.0	16.0	16.0
30-44	15.9	15.9	15.9	15.9	15.8	15.8	15.8	15.8	15.7	15.7	15.7	15.7	15.6	15.6	15.6	15.6	15.6	15.6	15.6	15.5	15.5
45-59	16.1	16.1	16.1	16.1	16.1	16.1	16.0	16.0	16.0	16.0	16.0	16.0	16.0	15.9	15.9	15.9	15.9	15.8	15.8	15.8	15.7
60-74	16.3	16.2	16.2	16.1	16.1	16.1	16.0	16.0	16.0	15.9	15.9	15.9	15.9	15.9	15.9	15.9	15.9	15.9	15.9	15.9	15.9
75 & over	20.0	20.1	20.2	20.3	20.4	20.5	20.6	20.7	20.8	20.9	21.0	21.1	21.2	21.3	21.3	21.4	21.5	21.6	21.6	21.7	21.8
All ages	100.0	100.0	100.0	100.0	100.0	100.0	100.0	100.0	100.0	100.0	100.0	100.0	100.0	100.0	100.0	100.0	100.0	100.0	100.0	100.0	100.0
Mean age	47.5	47.6	47.6	47.7	47.7	47.8	47.9	47.9	48.0	48.0	48.1	48.1	48.2	48.3	48.3	48.4	48.4	48.5	48.5	48.6	48.7
Median age	47.2	47.2	47.3	47.3	47.4	47.5	47.5	47.6	47.7	47.7	47.8	47.8	47.9	48.0	48.0	48.1	48.1	48.2	48.3	48.3	48.4

Source: Office for National Statistics

Note: Figures may not add exactly due to rounding.
* Children under 16. Working age and pensionable age populations based on state pension age (SPA) for given year.
Between 2012 and 2018, SPA will change from 65 years for men and 61 years for women, to 65 years for both sexes.
Then between 2019 and 2020, SPA will change from 65 years to 66 years for both men and women.
Between 2026 and 2027 SPA will increase to 67 years and between 2044 and 2046 to 68 years for both sexes. This is based on SPA under the 2014 Pensions Act.
** This is consistent with the age-group definitions used in ONS Labour Market Statistics.

15.3e Mid-2014 Population estimates for Scotland by sex and single year of age

Ages	Persons	Males	Females	Ages	Persons	Males	Females
All Ages	5,347,600	2,596,384	2,751,216	45	78,704	37,998	40,706
0	56,297	28,913	27,384	46	80,275	38,731	41,544
1	57,452	29,337	28,115	47	80,894	39,506	41,388
2	59,228	30,424	28,804	48	80,402	38,983	41,419
3	61,007	31,184	29,823	49	83,320	40,584	42,736
4	58,246	29,656	28,590	50	82,301	39,732	42,569
5	59,776	30,352	29,424	51	82,094	39,875	42,219
6	59,654	30,378	29,276	52	80,198	39,351	40,847
7	57,256	29,262	27,994	53	78,284	38,243	40,041
8	56,157	28,610	27,547	54	75,709	37,187	38,522
9	55,742	28,635	27,107	55	75,231	36,592	38,639
10	54,680	28,184	26,496	56	73,040	35,552	37,488
11	53,042	27,029	26,013	57	71,239	34,895	36,344
12	52,773	26,889	25,884	58	68,986	33,754	35,232
13	54,991	27,929	27,062	59	66,112	32,194	33,918
14	56,376	29,027	27,349	60	65,213	31,896	33,317
15	58,605	30,060	28,545	61	64,041	31,236	32,805
16	59,820	30,657	29,163	62	61,738	30,105	31,633
17	62,081	31,830	30,251	63	62,323	30,290	32,033
18	63,580	32,612	30,968	64	62,486	30,600	31,886
19	66,767	33,734	33,033	65	64,029	31,190	32,839
20	69,591	35,028	34,563	66	65,871	31,986	33,885
21	70,981	35,258	35,723	67	71,190	34,396	36,794
22	76,655	37,784	38,871	68	53,809	26,017	27,792
23	77,059	38,453	38,606	69	50,624	24,005	26,619
24	73,341	36,695	36,646	70	51,457	24,560	26,897
25	72,174	36,179	35,995	71	49,324	22,961	26,363
26	72,901	36,253	36,648	72	45,065	20,722	24,343
27	70,831	34,898	35,933	73	41,614	18,871	22,743
28	70,296	34,875	35,421	74	42,171	19,059	23,112
29	69,960	34,277	35,683	75	40,960	18,503	22,457
30	67,738	33,152	34,586	76	39,528	17,736	21,792
31	68,791	33,589	35,202	77	37,184	16,146	21,038
32	69,734	33,800	35,934	78	35,471	15,326	20,145
33	69,279	33,945	35,334	79	33,262	14,229	19,033
34	67,955	33,300	34,655	80	30,577	12,878	17,699
35	65,523	32,397	33,126	81	28,216	11,713	16,503
36	61,183	29,842	31,341	82	27,169	10,938	16,231
37	60,046	29,753	30,293	83	24,595	9,747	14,848
38	63,747	31,344	32,403	84	21,898	8,348	13,550
39	64,388	31,368	33,020	85 / 85+	19,411	7,278	12,133
40	65,328	32,149	33,179	86	16,640	6,022	10,618
41	69,348	33,967	35,381	87	14,852	5,219	9,633
42	73,800	35,725	38,075	88	13,103	4,448	8,655
43	76,644	36,863	39,781	89	10,827	3,623	7,204
44	75,798	36,585	39,213	90	39,542	10,978	28,564

Source: Office for National Statistics

Note: It is ONS policy to publish estimates to the nearest hundred persons. Rounded (and particularly unit) estimates cannot be precisely accurate.

: Data not available

15.3f Population projections by the Office for National Statistics
Scotland, PERSONS, thousands

2014-based
Principal projection

Projected populations at mid-years by age last birthday

Ages	2014	2015	2016	2017	2018	2019	2020	2021	2022	2023	2024	2025	2026	2027	2028	2029	2030	2031	2032	2033
Thousands																				
0-14	853	854	856	860	865	867	870	872	873	872	871	871	868	867	867	868	869	870	871	872
15-29	1,035	1,032	1,025	1,014	1,002	993	983	970	959	954	949	945	944	943	943	942	944	946	951	955
30-44	1,019	1,015	1,009	1,007	1,012	1,020	1,030	1,045	1,063	1,076	1,085	1,090	1,093	1,094	1,093	1,093	1,088	1,081	1,072	1,060
45-59	1,157	1,163	1,168	1,168	1,163	1,151	1,139	1,123	1,103	1,082	1,065	1,050	1,039	1,029	1,019	1,009	1,004	999	998	1,003
60-74	851	862	878	894	908	923	940	957	961	973	987	1,004	1,018	1,034	1,047	1,058	1,065	1,071	1,073	1,069
75 & over	433	438	444	452	462	474	484	495	521	540	557	572	586	599	612	626	640	656	672	689
All ages	5,348	5,365	5,380	5,396	5,412	5,428	5,445	5,462	5,480	5,497	5,514	5,532	5,548	5,565	5,581	5,596	5,610	5,624	5,636	5,648
Percentages																				
0-14	15.9	15.9	15.9	15.9	16.0	16.0	16.0	16.0	15.9	15.9	15.8	15.7	15.6	15.6	15.5	15.5	15.5	15.5	15.5	15.4
15-29	19.3	19.2	19.0	18.8	18.5	18.3	18.1	17.8	17.5	17.4	17.2	17.1	17.0	16.9	16.9	16.8	16.8	16.8	16.9	16.9
30-44	19.1	18.9	18.8	18.7	18.7	18.8	18.9	19.1	19.4	19.6	19.7	19.7	19.7	19.7	19.6	19.5	19.4	19.2	19.0	18.8
45-59	21.6	21.7	21.7	21.7	21.5	21.2	20.9	20.6	20.1	19.7	19.3	19.0	18.7	18.5	18.3	18.0	17.9	17.8	17.7	17.8
60-74	15.9	16.1	16.3	16.6	16.8	17.0	17.3	17.5	17.5	17.7	17.9	18.1	18.4	18.6	18.8	18.9	19.0	19.0	19.0	18.9
75 & over	8.1	8.2	8.3	8.4	8.5	8.7	8.9	9.1	9.5	9.8	10.1	10.3	10.6	10.8	11.0	11.2	11.4	11.7	11.9	12.2
All ages	100.0	100.0	100.0	100.0	100.0	100.0	100.0	100.0	100.0	100.0	100.0	100.0	100.0	100.0	100.0	100.0	100.0	100.0	100.0	100.0
Mean age	41.3	41.5	41.7	41.8	42.0	42.2	42.3	42.5	42.7	42.8	43.0	43.1	43.3	43.4	43.5	43.7	43.8	44.0	44.1	44.2
Median age	41.9	42.0	42.1	42.2	42.3	42.4	42.4	42.5	42.6	42.7	42.9	43.0	43.1	43.2	43.4	43.5	43.7	43.8	44.0	44.1

Ages	2034	2035	2036	2037	2038	2039	2040	2041	2042	2043	2044	2045	2046	2047	2048	2049	2050	2051	2052	2053
Thousands																				
0-14	871	871	870	868	866	865	863	862	860	859	859	858	858	858	859	859	860	860	861	862
15-29	958	960	962	963	962	961	961	958	957	958	958	959	961	962	962	962	962	960	959	957
30-44	1,051	1,042	1,030	1,019	1,015	1,010	1,006	1,006	1,005	1,004	1,004	1,005	1,007	1,012	1,016	1,019	1,022	1,024	1,025	1,024
45-59	1,012	1,022	1,037	1,056	1,069	1,078	1,084	1,086	1,088	1,088	1,088	1,083	1,077	1,067	1,056	1,048	1,039	1,027	1,016	1,012
60-74	1,059	1,048	1,035	1,017	998	984	972	963	955	947	940	937	934	935	941	950	961	976	995	1,008
75 & over	707	725	744	763	784	803	823	839	856	871	884	894	904	911	914	914	913	911	905	901
All ages	5,659	5,669	5,678	5,686	5,694	5,701	5,708	5,715	5,721	5,726	5,732	5,737	5,741	5,745	5,749	5,753	5,756	5,759	5,761	5,764
Percentages																				
0-14	15.4	15.4	15.3	15.3	15.2	15.2	15.1	15.1	15.0	15.0	15.0	15.0	14.9	14.9	14.9	14.9	14.9	14.9	14.9	14.9
15-29	16.9	16.9	16.9	16.9	16.9	16.9	16.8	16.8	16.7	16.7	16.7	16.7	16.7	16.7	16.7	16.7	16.7	16.7	16.6	16.6
30-44	18.6	18.4	18.1	17.9	17.8	17.7	17.6	17.6	17.6	17.5	17.5	17.5	17.5	17.6	17.7	17.7	17.8	17.8	17.8	17.8
45-59	17.9	18.0	18.3	18.6	18.8	18.9	19.0	19.0	19.0	19.0	19.0	18.9	18.8	18.6	18.4	18.2	18.1	18.0	17.6	17.6
60-74	18.7	18.5	18.2	17.9	17.5	17.3	17.0	16.9	16.7	16.5	16.4	16.3	16.3	16.3	16.4	16.5	16.7	17.0	17.3	17.5
75 & over	12.5	12.8	13.1	13.4	13.8	14.1	14.4	14.7	15.0	15.2	15.4	15.6	15.7	15.9	15.9	15.9	15.9	15.8	15.7	15.6
All ages	100.0	100.0	100.0	100.0	100.0	100.0	100.0	100.0	100.0	100.0	100.0	100.0	100.0	100.0	100.0	100.0	100.0	100.0	100.0	100.0
Mean age	44.4	44.5	44.6	44.7	44.8	44.9	45.0	45.1	45.2	45.3	45.3	45.4	45.5	45.5	45.6	45.6	45.7	45.7	45.7	45.8
Median age	44.3	44.5	44.7	44.9	45.1	45.2	45.3	45.4	45.5	45.6	45.7	45.7	45.7	45.7	45.6	45.6	45.5	45.5	45.5	45.6

15.3f Population projections by the Office for National Statistics
Scotland, PERSONS, thousands

2014-based
Principal projection

Projected populations at mid-years by age last birthday

Ages	2054	2055	2056	2057	2058	2059	2060	2061	2062	2063	2064	2065	2066	2067	2068	2069	2070	2071	2072	2073
Thousands																				
0-14	862	863	863	863	864	864	863	863	863	863	863	862	862	861	861	861	860	860	859	859
15-29	955	954	952	951	950	949	949	949	949	949	950	950	951	952	952	953	954	954	954	954
30-44	1,023	1,024	1,021	1,020	1,020	1,021	1,022	1,023	1,025	1,025	1,025	1,025	1,024	1,022	1,021	1,019	1,018	1,016	1,015	1,014
45-59	1,009	1,004	1,004	1,004	1,004	1,004	1,005	1,008	1,013	1,017	1,021	1,023	1,024	1,022	1,021	1,019	1,018	1,016	1,015	1,014
60-74	1,017	1,023	1,026	1,028	1,029	1,029	1,025	1,019	1,011	1,001	993	986	975	966	963	961	958	959	960	960
75 & over	900	902	905	908	911	914	918	924	930	938	947	956	969	983	993	1,003	1,013	1,021	1,029	1,035
All ages	5,767	5,769	5,772	5,774	5,777	5,780	5,783	5,786	5,790	5,794	5,798	5,802	5,807	5,812	5,817	5,823	5,828	5,834	5,840	5,846
Percentages																				
0-14	15.0	15.0	15.0	15.0	14.9	14.9	14.9	14.9	14.9	14.9	14.9	14.9	14.8	14.8	14.8	14.8	14.8	14.7	14.7	14.7
15-29	16.6	16.5	16.5	16.5	16.4	16.4	16.4	16.4	16.4	16.4	16.4	16.4	16.4	16.4	16.4	16.4	16.4	16.4	16.3	16.3
30-44	17.7	17.7	17.7	17.7	17.7	17.7	17.7	17.7	17.7	17.7	17.7	17.7	17.6	17.7	17.5	17.5	17.6	17.4	17.4	17.3
45-59	17.5	17.4	17.4	17.4	17.4	17.4	17.4	17.4	17.5	17.6	17.6	17.6	17.7	17.7	17.7	17.6	17.6	17.6	17.5	17.5
60-74	17.6	17.7	17.8	17.8	17.8	17.8	17.7	17.6	17.5	17.3	17.1	17.0	16.8	16.6	16.6	16.5	16.4	16.4	16.4	16.4
75 & over	15.6	15.6	15.7	15.7	15.8	15.8	15.9	16.0	16.1	16.2	16.3	16.5	16.7	16.9	17.1	17.2	17.4	17.5	17.6	17.7
All ages	100.0	100.0	100.0	100.0	100.0	100.0	100.0	100.0	100.0	100.0	100.0	100.0	100.0	100.0	100.0	100.0	100.0	100.0	100.0	100.0
Mean age	45.8	45.8	45.9	45.9	45.9	46.0	46.0	46.0	46.1	46.1	46.1	46.2	46.2	46.3	46.3	46.4	46.4	46.5	46.5	46.6
Median age	45.6	45.6	45.7	45.8	45.8	45.8	45.8	45.9	45.9	45.9	45.9	45.9	46.0	46.0	46.1	46.1	46.2	46.3	46.3	46.4

Ages	2074	2075	2076	2077	2078	2079	2080	2081	2082	2083	2084	2085	2086	2087	2088	2089	2090	2091	2092	2093
Thousands																				
0-14	858	858	858	857	857	857	857	858	858	858	858	858	859	859	859	859	859	859	859	859
15-29	954	954	954	954	954	954	953	953	952	952	952	951	951	950	950	949	949	949	948	948
30-44	1,013	1,013	1,013	1,013	1,014	1,014	1,015	1,016	1,017	1,017	1,018	1,019	1,019	1,019	1,020	1,020	1,020	1,020	1,020	1,019
45-59	1,025	1,026	1,028	1,029	1,030	1,030	1,030	1,029	1,028	1,027	1,025	1,024	1,023	1,022	1,021	1,021	1,021	1,021	1,021	1,022
60-74	961	964	967	971	976	980	983	986	988	988	988	989	988	988	989	991	993	995	997	998
75 & over	1,040	1,043	1,046	1,046	1,046	1,048	1,051	1,054	1,059	1,065	1,072	1,078	1,086	1,093	1,099	1,104	1,109	1,113	1,118	1,123
All ages	5,853	5,859	5,865	5,871	5,877	5,884	5,890	5,896	5,902	5,908	5,913	5,919	5,925	5,931	5,937	5,943	5,950	5,956	5,963	5,970
Percentages																				
0-14	14.7	14.6	14.6	14.6	14.6	14.6	14.6	14.5	14.5	14.5	14.5	14.5	14.5	14.5	14.5	14.5	14.4	14.4	14.4	14.4
15-29	16.3	16.3	16.3	16.2	16.2	16.2	16.2	16.2	16.1	16.1	16.1	16.1	16.0	16.0	16.0	16.0	15.9	15.9	15.9	15.9
30-44	17.3	17.3	17.3	17.3	17.2	17.2	17.2	17.2	17.2	17.2	17.2	17.2	17.2	17.2	17.2	17.2	17.1	17.1	17.1	17.1
45-59	17.5	17.5	17.5	17.5	17.5	17.5	17.5	17.5	17.4	17.4	17.3	17.3	17.3	17.2	17.2	17.2	17.2	17.1	17.1	17.1
60-74	16.4	16.4	16.5	16.5	16.6	16.7	16.7	16.7	16.7	16.7	16.7	16.7	16.7	16.7	16.7	16.7	16.7	16.7	16.7	16.7
75 & over	17.8	17.8	17.8	17.8	17.8	17.8	17.8	17.9	17.9	18.0	18.1	18.2	18.3	18.4	18.5	18.6	18.6	18.7	18.7	18.8
All ages	100.0	100.0	100.0	100.0	100.0	100.0	100.0	100.0	100.0	100.0	100.0	100.0	100.0	100.0	100.0	100.0	100.0	100.0	100.0	100.0
Mean age	46.6	46.7	46.7	46.8	46.7	46.9	46.9	47.0	47.0	47.1	47.1	47.2	47.2	47.3	47.3	47.3	47.4	47.4	47.5	47.5
Median age	46.5	46.5	46.6	46.6	46.7	46.7	46.8	46.8	46.8	46.9	46.9	46.9	47.0	47.0	47.1	47.1	47.1	47.2	47.3	47.3

15.3f Population projections by the Office for National Statistics
Scotland, PERSONS, thousands

2014-based
Principal projection

Projected populations at mid-years by age last birthday

Ages	2094	2095	2096	2097	2098	2099	2100	2101	2102	2103	2104	2105	2106	2107	2108	2109	2110	2111	2112	2113	2114
Thousands																					
0-14	859	859	859	858	858	858	858	858	857	857	857	857	857	857	857	856	856	856	856	856	857
15-29	948	948	948	949	949	949	949	950	950	950	950	950	950	950	950	950	950	950	950	949	949
30-44	1,019	1,019	1,019	1,018	1,018	1,018	1,017	1,017	1,016	1,016	1,016	1,015	1,015	1,015	1,015	1,015	1,015	1,015	1,016	1,016	1,016
45-59	1,023	1,023	1,024	1,025	1,026	1,027	1,028	1,029	1,029	1,030	1,030	1,030	1,030	1,030	1,030	1,030	1,030	1,030	1,030	1,030	1,029
60-74	999	999	999	998	997	996	995	995	994	994	994	995	996	997	998	999	1,000	1,002	1,003	1,004	1,006
75 & over	1,129	1,135	1,142	1,150	1,158	1,166	1,174	1,182	1,191	1,199	1,207	1,215	1,223	1,230	1,237	1,244	1,251	1,258	1,265	1,272	1,279
All ages	5,977	5,984	5,991	5,999	6,006	6,014	6,022	6,030	6,038	6,046	6,054	6,062	6,070	6,079	6,087	6,095	6,103	6,111	6,119	6,127	6,135
Percentages																					
0-14	14.4	14.4	14.3	14.3	14.3	14.3	14.2	14.2	14.2	14.2	14.2	14.1	14.1	14.1	14.1	14.1	14.0	14.0	14.0	14.0	14.0
15-29	15.9	15.8	15.8	15.8	15.8	15.8	15.8	15.7	15.7	15.7	15.7	15.7	15.7	15.6	15.6	15.6	15.6	15.5	15.5	15.5	15.5
30-44	17.1	17.0	17.0	17.0	16.9	16.9	16.9	16.9	16.8	16.8	16.8	16.7	16.7	16.7	16.7	16.7	16.6	16.6	16.6	16.6	16.6
45-59	17.1	17.1	17.1	17.1	17.1	17.1	17.1	17.1	17.0	17.0	17.0	17.0	17.0	16.9	16.9	16.9	16.9	16.9	16.8	16.8	16.8
60-74	16.7	16.7	16.7	16.6	16.6	16.6	16.5	16.5	16.5	16.4	16.4	16.4	16.4	16.4	16.4	16.4	16.4	16.4	16.4	16.4	16.4
75 & over	18.9	19.0	19.1	19.2	19.3	19.4	19.5	19.6	19.7	19.8	19.9	20.0	20.1	20.2	20.3	20.4	20.5	20.6	20.7	20.8	20.8
All ages	100.0	100.0	100.0	100.0	100.0	100.0	100.0	100.0	100.0	100.0	100.0	100.0	100.0	100.0	100.0	100.0	100.0	100.0	100.0	100.0	100.0
Mean age	47.6	47.6	47.7	47.7	47.8	47.9	47.9	48.0	48.0	48.1	48.2	48.2	48.3	48.3	48.4	48.5	48.5	48.6	48.6	48.7	48.8
Median age	47.4	47.4	47.5	47.5	47.6	47.7	47.7	47.8	47.8	47.9	48.0	48.0	48.1	48.2	48.2	48.3	48.4	48.4	48.5	48.5	48.6

Source: Office for National Statistics

Note: Figures may not add exactly due to rounding.

* Children under 16. Working age and pensionable age populations based on state pension age (SPA) for given year.
Between 2012 and 2018, SPA will change from 65 years for men and 61 years for women, to 65 years for both sexes.
Then between 2019 and 2020, SPA will change from 65 years to 66 years for both men and women.
Between 2026 and 2027 SPA will increase to 67 years and between 2044 and 2046 to 68 years for both sexes. This is based on SPA under the 2014 Pensions Act.
** This is consistent with the age-group definitions used in ONS Labour Market Statistics.

491

15.3f Population projections by the Office for National Statistics
Scotland, MALES, thousands

2014-based
Principal projection

Projected populations at mid-years by age last birthday

Ages	2014	2015	2016	2017	2018	2019	2020	2021	2022	2023	2024	2025	2026	2027	2028	2029	2030	2031	2032	2033
Thousands																				
0-14	436	436	438	440	442	443	444	445	446	446	445	445	444	443	444	444	444	445	446	446
15-29	519	519	515	511	505	501	497	491	486	484	481	479	478	478	477	477	478	479	481	484
30-44	498	496	494	493	496	500	506	514	523	530	535	538	541	543	544	545	543	541	537	532
45-59	563	566	567	566	563	558	551	543	533	523	515	508	503	497	492	488	486	484	484	487
60-74	408	414	422	430	437	444	453	461	463	468	475	482	489	496	502	507	510	512	512	510
75 & over	173	176	180	184	190	197	202	209	222	232	242	250	257	264	271	278	285	293	301	309
All ages	2,596	2,606	2,616	2,625	2,634	2,643	2,653	2,663	2,673	2,683	2,693	2,702	2,712	2,721	2,730	2,738	2,746	2,754	2,761	2,768
Percentages																				
0-14	16.8	16.7	16.7	16.8	16.8	16.8	16.7	16.7	16.7	16.6	16.5	16.5	16.4	16.3	16.2	16.2	16.2	16.2	16.1	16.1
15-29	20.0	19.9	19.7	19.5	19.2	19.0	18.7	18.4	18.2	18.0	17.9	17.7	17.6	17.6	17.5	17.4	17.4	17.4	17.4	17.5
30-44	19.2	19.0	18.9	18.8	18.8	18.9	19.1	19.3	19.6	19.7	19.9	19.9	19.9	19.9	19.9	19.9	19.8	19.6	19.4	19.2
45-59	21.7	21.7	21.7	21.6	21.4	21.1	20.8	20.4	20.0	19.5	19.1	18.8	18.5	18.3	18.0	17.8	17.7	17.6	17.5	17.6
60-74	15.7	15.9	16.1	16.4	16.6	16.8	17.1	17.3	17.3	17.5	17.6	17.8	18.0	18.2	18.4	18.5	18.6	18.6	18.5	18.4
75 & over	6.7	6.8	6.9	7.0	7.2	7.4	7.6	7.9	8.3	8.7	9.0	9.2	9.5	9.7	9.9	10.1	10.4	10.6	10.9	11.2
All ages	100.0	100.0	100.0	100.0	100.0	100.0	100.0	100.0	100.0	100.0	100.0	100.0	100.0	100.0	100.0	100.0	100.0	100.0	100.0	100.0
Mean age	40.2	40.4	40.6	40.8	40.9	41.1	41.3	41.5	41.6	41.8	42.0	42.1	42.3	42.4	42.6	42.7	42.9	43.0	43.1	43.3
Median age	40.7	40.7	40.8	40.9	40.9	41.0	41.1	41.2	41.3	41.5	41.6	41.7	41.8	41.9	42.1	42.2	42.4	42.6	42.7	42.9

Ages	2034	2035	2036	2037	2038	2039	2040	2041	2042	2043	2044	2045	2046	2047	2048	2049	2050	2051	2052	2053
Thousands																				
0-14	446	445	445	444	443	442	442	441	440	440	439	439	439	439	439	439	440	440	440	441
15-29	485	486	487	488	487	487	487	486	485	485	486	486	487	488	488	488	488	487	486	485
30-44	528	524	518	513	511	509	507	506	506	506	505	506	507	510	512	513	515	516	517	516
45-59	492	498	505	515	522	527	531	533	535	537	538	537	534	531	526	522	518	513	508	506
60-74	506	500	494	485	476	470	464	461	456	453	450	449	448	449	452	457	463	471	480	487
75 & over	318	327	336	346	355	364	374	381	389	396	402	406	410	413	415	415	414	413	411	409
All ages	2,774	2,780	2,786	2,791	2,795	2,800	2,804	2,808	2,812	2,816	2,819	2,823	2,826	2,829	2,832	2,834	2,837	2,840	2,842	2,845
Percentages																				
0-14	16.1	16.0	16.0	15.9	15.9	15.8	15.7	15.7	15.6	15.6	15.6	15.6	15.5	15.5	15.5	15.5	15.5	15.5	15.5	15.5
15-29	17.5	17.5	17.5	17.5	17.4	17.4	17.4	17.3	17.3	17.2	17.2	17.2	17.2	17.2	17.2	17.2	17.2	17.1	17.1	17.1
30-44	19.0	18.8	18.6	18.4	18.3	18.2	18.1	18.0	18.0	18.0	17.9	17.9	18.0	18.0	18.1	18.1	18.1	18.2	18.2	18.1
45-59	17.7	17.9	18.1	18.4	18.7	18.8	18.9	19.0	19.0	19.1	19.1	19.0	18.9	18.8	18.6	18.4	18.3	18.0	17.9	17.8
60-74	18.2	18.0	17.7	17.4	17.0	16.8	16.6	16.4	16.2	16.1	15.9	15.9	15.9	15.9	16.0	16.1	16.3	16.6	16.9	17.1
75 & over	11.5	11.8	12.1	12.4	12.7	13.0	13.3	13.6	13.8	14.1	14.2	14.4	14.5	14.6	14.7	14.6	14.6	14.5	14.5	14.4
All ages	100.0	100.0	100.0	100.0	100.0	100.0	100.0	100.0	100.0	100.0	100.0	100.0	100.0	100.0	100.0	100.0	100.0	100.0	100.0	100.0
Mean age	43.4	43.5	43.6	43.7	43.9	44.0	44.1	44.1	44.2	44.3	44.4	44.4	44.5	44.6	44.6	44.7	44.7	44.8	44.8	44.8
Median age	43.1	43.3	43.5	43.7	43.8	44.0	44.1	44.2	44.3	44.3	44.4	44.4	44.3	44.3	44.3	44.3	44.3	44.3	44.4	44.4

15.3f Population projections by the Office for National Statistics
Scotland, MALES, thousands

2014-based
Principal projection

Projected populations at mid-years by age last birthday

Ages	2054	2055	2056	2057	2058	2059	2060	2061	2062	2063	2064	2065	2066	2067	2068	2069	2070	2071	2072	2073
Thousands																				
0-14	441	441	442	442	442	442	442	442	442	441	441	441	441	441	441	440	440	440	440	439
15-29	484	484	483	482	482	481	481	481	481	481	481	482	482	483	483	483	484	484	484	484
30-44	516	516	515	514	515	515	516	516	517	517	517	517	516	516	515	514	513	513	512	512
45-59	504	502	502	502	502	502	503	504	507	509	511	512	513	514	514	514	514	513	513	513
60-74	493	497	499	502	503	505	504	502	498	494	491	488	483	479	478	477	475	476	476	477
75 & over	409	410	411	413	414	415	418	421	424	429	434	439	446	453	459	464	470	475	480	484
All ages	2,847	2,850	2,852	2,855	2,857	2,860	2,863	2,866	2,869	2,872	2,875	2,878	2,882	2,885	2,889	2,893	2,897	2,901	2,905	2,909
Percentages																				
0-14	15.5	15.5	15.5	15.5	15.5	15.4	15.4	15.4	15.4	15.4	15.3	15.3	15.3	15.3	15.2	15.2	15.2	15.2	15.1	15.1
15-29	17.0	17.0	16.9	16.9	16.9	16.8	16.8	16.8	16.8	16.8	16.7	16.7	16.7	16.7	16.7	16.7	16.7	16.7	16.7	16.6
30-44	18.1	18.1	18.1	18.0	18.0	18.0	18.0	18.0	18.0	18.0	18.0	18.0	17.9	17.9	17.8	17.8	17.7	17.7	17.6	17.6
45-59	17.7	17.6	17.6	17.6	17.6	17.5	17.6	17.6	17.7	17.7	17.8	17.8	17.8	17.8	17.8	17.8	17.8	17.7	17.7	17.6
60-74	17.3	17.4	17.5	17.6	17.6	17.6	17.6	17.5	17.4	17.2	17.1	16.9	16.8	16.6	16.5	16.5	16.4	16.4	16.4	16.4
75 & over	14.4	14.4	14.4	14.5	14.5	14.5	14.6	14.7	14.8	14.9	15.1	15.2	15.5	15.7	15.9	16.1	16.2	16.4	16.5	16.6
All ages	100.0	100.0	100.0	100.0	100.0	100.0	100.0	100.0	100.0	100.0	100.0	100.0	100.0	100.0	100.0	100.0	100.0	100.0	100.0	100.0
Mean age	44.9	44.9	45.0	45.0	45.0	45.1	45.1	45.2	45.2	45.3	45.3	45.4	45.4	45.5	45.5	45.6	45.7	45.7	45.8	45.8
Median age	44.5	44.5	44.6	44.7	44.7	44.8	44.8	44.8	44.8	44.9	44.9	45.0	45.0	45.1	45.2	45.3	45.3	45.4	45.5	45.6

Ages	2074	2075	2076	2077	2078	2079	2080	2081	2082	2083	2084	2085	2086	2087	2088	2089	2090	2091	2092	2093
Thousands																				
0-14	439	439	439	439	439	439	439	439	439	439	439	439	439	439	439	439	440	440	440	440
15-29	484	484	484	484	484	484	483	483	483	483	483	482	482	482	482	481	481	481	481	481
30-44	511	511	511	511	512	512	512	513	513	514	514	514	515	515	515	515	515	515	515	515
45-59	514	515	515	516	517	517	517	516	516	515	514	514	513	513	513	512	512	512	513	513
60-74	477	478	480	483	485	487	489	490	492	492	492	493	492	492	493	494	495	496	497	498
75 & over	487	489	491	492	492	494	496	498	501	505	508	512	516	520	523	526	529	532	534	537
All ages	2,913	2,917	2,921	2,925	2,928	2,932	2,936	2,940	2,943	2,947	2,951	2,954	2,958	2,961	2,965	2,968	2,972	2,976	2,980	2,983
Percentages																				
0-14	15.1	15.0	15.0	15.0	15.0	15.0	14.9	14.9	14.9	14.9	14.9	14.9	14.8	14.8	14.8	14.8	14.8	14.8	14.8	14.7
15-29	16.6	16.6	16.6	16.5	16.5	16.5	16.5	16.4	16.4	16.4	16.4	16.3	16.3	16.3	16.2	16.2	16.2	16.2	16.1	16.1
30-44	17.6	17.5	17.5	17.5	17.5	17.5	17.5	17.4	17.4	17.4	17.4	17.4	17.4	17.4	17.4	17.3	17.3	17.3	17.3	17.3
45-59	17.6	17.6	17.6	17.7	17.6	17.6	17.6	17.6	17.5	17.5	17.4	17.4	17.4	17.3	17.3	17.3	17.2	17.2	17.2	17.2
60-74	16.4	16.4	16.4	16.5	16.6	16.6	16.6	16.7	16.7	16.7	16.7	16.7	16.7	16.6	16.6	16.6	16.7	16.7	16.7	16.7
75 & over	16.7	16.8	16.8	16.8	16.8	16.8	16.9	16.9	17.0	17.1	17.2	17.3	17.5	17.6	17.7	17.7	17.8	17.9	17.9	18.0
All ages	100.0	100.0	100.0	100.0	100.0	100.0	100.0	100.0	100.0	100.0	100.0	100.0	100.0	100.0	100.0	100.0	100.0	100.0	100.0	100.0
Mean age	45.9	46.0	46.0	46.1	46.2	46.2	46.3	46.3	46.4	46.4	46.5	46.5	46.6	46.6	46.7	46.7	46.8	46.9	46.9	47.0
Median age	45.6	45.7	45.8	45.8	45.9	45.9	46.0	46.0	46.1	46.1	46.2	46.2	46.3	46.3	46.4	46.4	46.5	46.5	46.6	46.6

15.3f Population projections by the Office for National Statistics
Scotland, MALES, thousands

2014-based
Principal projection

Projected populations at mid-years by age last birthday

Ages	2094	2095	2096	2097	2098	2099	2100	2101	2102	2103	2104	2105	2106	2107	2108	2109	2110	2111	2112	2113	2114
Thousands																					
0-14	439	439	439	439	439	439	439	439	439	439	438	438	438	438	438	438	438	438	438	438	438
15-29	481	481	481	481	481	481	481	482	482	482	482	482	482	482	482	482	482	482	482	482	481
30-44	515	515	514	514	514	514	514	514	513	513	513	513	513	513	513	513	513	513	513	513	513
45-59	514	514	515	515	516	516	517	517	517	517	518	518	518	518	518	518	518	518	518	518	518
60-74	498	499	499	498	498	498	497	497	497	497	497	497	498	498	499	500	500	501	502	503	503
75 & over	540	544	547	551	555	560	564	568	573	577	581	585	589	593	597	600	604	607	611	614	618
All ages	2,987	2,991	2,995	2,999	3,003	3,008	3,012	3,016	3,020	3,025	3,029	3,033	3,038	3,042	3,046	3,051	3,055	3,059	3,063	3,068	3,072
Percentages																					
0-14	14.7	14.7	14.7	14.6	14.6	14.6	14.6	14.5	14.5	14.5	14.5	14.5	14.4	14.4	14.4	14.4	14.3	14.3	14.3	14.3	14.3
15-29	16.1	16.1	16.1	16.0	16.0	16.0	16.0	16.0	15.9	15.9	15.9	15.9	15.9	15.8	15.8	15.8	15.8	15.7	15.7	15.7	15.7
30-44	17.2	17.2	17.2	17.1	17.1	17.1	17.1	17.0	17.0	17.0	16.9	16.9	16.9	16.9	16.8	16.8	16.8	16.8	16.7	16.7	16.7
45-59	17.2	17.2	17.2	17.2	17.2	17.2	17.2	17.1	17.1	17.1	17.1	17.1	17.0	17.0	17.0	17.0	17.0	16.9	16.9	16.9	16.8
60-74	16.7	16.7	16.6	16.6	16.6	16.5	16.5	16.5	16.5	16.4	16.4	16.4	16.4	16.4	16.4	16.4	16.4	16.4	16.4	16.4	16.4
75 & over	18.1	18.2	18.3	18.4	18.5	18.6	18.7	18.8	19.0	19.1	19.2	19.3	19.4	19.5	19.6	19.7	19.8	19.9	19.9	20.0	20.1
All ages	100.0	100.0	100.0	100.0	100.0	100.0	100.0	100.0	100.0	100.0	100.0	100.0	100.0	100.0	100.0	100.0	100.0	100.0	100.0	100.0	100.0
Mean age	47.0	47.1	47.1	47.2	47.2	47.3	47.4	47.4	47.5	47.6	47.6	47.7	47.7	47.8	47.9	47.9	48.0	48.1	48.1	48.2	48.2
Median age	46.7	46.8	46.8	46.9	47.0	47.0	47.1	47.1	47.2	47.3	47.4	47.4	47.5	47.6	47.6	47.7	47.7	47.8	47.9	47.9	48.0

Source: Office for National Statistics

Note: Figures may not add exactly due to rounding.
* Children under 16. Working age and pensionable age populations based on state pension age (SPA) for given year.
Between 2012 and 2018, SPA will change from 65 years for men and 61 years for women, to 65 years for both sexes.
Then between 2019 and 2020, SPA will change from 65 years to 66 years for both men and women.
Between 2026 and 2027 SPA will increase to 67 years and between 2044 and 2046 to 68 years for both sexes. This is based on SPA under the 2014 Pensions Act.
** This is consistent with the age-group definitions used in ONS Labour Market Statistics.

15.3f Population projections by the Office for National Statistics
Scotland, FEMALES, thousands

2014-based
Principal projection

Projected populations at mid-years by age last birthday

Ages	2014	2015	2016	2017	2018	2019	2020	2021	2022	2023	2024	2025	2026	2027	2028	2029	2030	2031	2032	2033
Thousands																				
0-14	417	418	419	421	422	424	425	426	427	426	425	425	424	423	423	424	424	425	425	426
15-29	516	514	509	503	497	491	486	480	473	470	468	466	466	465	465	465	466	467	469	471
30-44	522	519	515	514	516	520	524	531	541	547	550	552	552	551	550	548	544	541	535	529
45-59	594	598	601	602	599	594	588	580	570	559	550	542	537	532	526	521	518	515	514	516
60-74	443	448	456	464	471	479	487	496	498	505	513	522	529	538	545	551	555	559	561	558
75 & over	260	262	264	267	272	277	281	286	298	308	316	323	329	335	342	348	355	363	371	380
All ages	2,751	2,758	2,765	2,771	2,778	2,785	2,792	2,799	2,807	2,814	2,822	2,829	2,837	2,844	2,851	2,858	2,864	2,870	2,875	2,880
Percentages																				
0-14	15.2	15.1	15.1	15.2	15.2	15.2	15.2	15.2	15.2	15.1	15.0	15.0	14.9	14.9	14.9	14.8	14.8	14.8	14.8	14.8
15-29	18.8	18.6	18.4	18.2	17.9	17.6	17.4	17.1	16.9	16.7	16.6	16.5	16.4	16.4	16.3	16.3	16.3	16.3	16.3	16.4
30-44	19.0	18.8	18.6	18.5	18.6	18.7	18.8	19.0	19.3	19.4	19.5	19.5	19.5	19.4	19.3	19.2	19.0	18.8	18.6	18.4
45-59	21.6	21.7	21.7	21.7	21.6	21.3	21.1	20.7	20.3	19.9	19.5	19.2	18.9	18.7	18.5	18.2	18.1	17.9	17.9	17.9
60-74	16.1	16.3	16.5	16.7	16.9	17.2	17.4	17.7	17.8	17.9	18.2	18.4	18.7	18.9	19.1	19.3	19.4	19.5	19.5	19.4
75 & over	9.5	9.5	9.6	9.6	9.8	9.9	10.1	10.2	10.6	10.9	11.2	11.4	11.6	11.8	12.0	12.2	12.4	12.6	12.9	13.2
All ages	100.0	100.0	100.0	100.0	100.0	100.0	100.0	100.0	100.0	100.0	100.0	100.0	100.0	100.0	100.0	100.0	100.0	100.0	100.0	100.0
Mean age	42.4	42.5	42.7	42.8	43.0	43.2	43.3	43.5	43.6	43.8	43.9	44.1	44.2	44.3	44.5	44.6	44.8	44.9	45.0	45.2
Median age	43.0	43.2	43.4	43.5	43.6	43.7	43.8	43.8	43.8	43.9	44.1	44.2	44.4	44.5	44.6	44.8	44.9	45.1	45.2	45.4

Ages	2034	2035	2036	2037	2038	2039	2040	2041	2042	2043	2044	2045	2046	2047	2048	2049	2050	2051	2052	2053
Thousands																				
0-14	426	425	425	424	423	422	422	421	420	420	419	419	419	419	419	420	420	420	421	421
15-29	473	474	475	475	475	474	474	472	472	472	473	473	474	474	474	474	474	473	473	472
30-44	524	519	512	506	503	501	499	499	499	498	498	499	500	502	504	506	507	508	509	508
45-59	520	525	532	541	547	551	553	553	552	551	550	546	542	537	531	526	521	515	514	516
60-74	553	548	541	531	522	514	507	503	499	495	490	489	486	486	489	493	498	505	514	520
75 & over	389	398	407	417	428	439	449	458	467	475	482	488	494	498	500	499	499	497	494	492
All ages	2,885	2,889	2,892	2,896	2,899	2,902	2,904	2,907	2,909	2,911	2,912	2,914	2,915	2,916	2,917	2,918	2,919	2,919	2,919	2,919
Percentages																				
0-14	14.8	14.7	14.7	14.6	14.6	14.6	14.5	14.5	14.4	14.4	14.4	14.4	14.4	14.4	14.4	14.4	14.4	14.4	14.4	14.4
15-29	16.4	16.4	16.4	16.4	16.4	16.3	16.3	16.3	16.2	16.2	16.2	16.2	16.2	16.3	16.3	16.3	16.2	16.2	16.2	16.2
30-44	18.2	18.0	17.7	17.5	17.4	17.3	17.2	17.2	17.1	17.1	17.1	17.1	17.2	17.2	17.3	17.3	17.4	17.4	17.4	17.4
45-59	18.0	18.2	18.4	18.7	18.9	19.0	19.0	19.0	19.0	18.9	18.9	18.7	18.6	18.4	18.2	18.0	17.8	17.6	17.6	17.3
60-74	19.2	19.0	18.7	18.4	18.0	17.7	17.5	17.3	17.2	17.0	16.8	16.8	16.7	16.7	16.8	16.9	17.1	17.3	17.6	17.8
75 & over	13.5	13.8	14.1	14.4	14.8	15.1	15.5	15.8	16.0	16.3	16.6	16.7	16.9	17.1	17.1	17.1	17.1	17.0	16.9	16.9
All ages	100.0	100.0	100.0	100.0	100.0	100.0	100.0	100.0	100.0	100.0	100.0	100.0	100.0	100.0	100.0	100.0	100.0	100.0	100.0	100.0
Mean age	45.3	45.4	45.5	45.6	45.7	45.8	45.9	46.0	46.1	46.2	46.3	46.3	46.4	46.4	46.5	46.5	46.6	46.6	46.7	46.7
Median age	45.5	45.7	45.9	46.1	46.3	46.4	46.6	46.7	46.8	46.9	46.9	47.0	47.0	47.0	46.9	46.9	46.8	46.8	46.7	46.7

15.3f Population projections by the Office for National Statistics
Scotland, FEMALES, thousands

2014-based
Principal projection

Projected populations at mid-years by age last birthday

Ages	2054	2055	2056	2057	2058	2059	2060	2061	2062	2063	2064	2065	2066	2067	2068	2069	2070	2071	2072	2073
Thousands																				
0-14	421	421	422	422	422	422	422	422	422	421	421	421	421	421	421	420	420	420	420	419
15-29	471	470	469	469	468	468	468	468	468	468	468	468	469	469	470	470	470	470	470	470
30-44	507	507	506	506	506	506	507	507	508	508	508	508	507	506	506	505	504	503	503	502
45-59	504	502	502	502	502	502	503	504	506	508	510	511	512	513	513	512	512	511	510	511
60-74	524	526	527	526	525	524	521	518	513	507	502	498	493	487	485	484	482	483	483	484
75 & over	491	492	494	496	497	498	501	503	506	510	513	517	523	530	534	539	543	546	549	551
All ages	2,920	2,920	2,920	2,920	2,920	2,920	2,920	2,921	2,921	2,922	2,923	2,924	2,925	2,926	2,928	2,930	2,932	2,933	2,936	2,938
Percentages																				
0-14	14.4	14.4	14.4	14.4	14.4	14.4	14.4	14.4	14.4	14.4	14.4	14.4	14.4	14.4	14.4	14.3	14.3	14.3	14.3	14.3
15-29	16.1	16.1	16.1	16.1	16.0	16.0	16.0	16.0	16.0	16.0	16.0	16.0	16.0	16.0	16.0	16.0	16.0	16.0	16.0	16.0
30-44	17.4	17.4	17.3	17.3	17.3	17.3	17.3	17.4	17.4	17.4	17.4	17.4	17.3	17.3	17.3	17.2	17.2	17.2	17.1	17.1
45-59	17.3	17.2	17.2	17.2	17.2	17.2	17.2	17.3	17.5	17.4	17.4	17.5	17.5	17.5	17.5	17.5	17.5	17.4	17.4	17.4
60-74	18.0	18.0	18.0	18.0	18.0	18.0	17.8	17.7	17.5	17.4	17.2	17.0	16.8	16.6	16.6	16.5	16.5	16.5	16.5	16.5
75 & over	16.8	16.9	16.9	17.0	17.0	17.1	17.1	17.2	17.3	17.4	17.6	17.7	17.9	18.1	18.2	18.4	18.5	18.6	18.7	18.8
All ages	100.0	100.0	100.0	100.0	100.0	100.0	100.0	100.0	100.0	100.0	100.0	100.0	100.0	100.0	100.0	100.0	100.0	100.0	100.0	100.0
Mean age	46.7	46.8	46.8	46.8	46.8	46.8	46.9	46.9	46.9	46.9	47.0	47.0	47.0	47.1	47.1	47.1	47.2	47.2	47.3	47.3
Median age	46.7	46.7	46.8	46.8	46.9	46.9	46.9	46.9	46.9	46.9	46.9	46.9	46.9	47.0	47.0	47.0	47.1	47.1	47.2	47.2

Ages	2074	2075	2076	2077	2078	2079	2080	2081	2082	2083	2084	2085	2086	2087	2088	2089	2090	2091	2092	2093
Thousands																				
0-14	419	419	419	419	419	419	419	419	419	419	419	419	419	419	419	420	420	420	420	420
15-29	470	470	470	470	470	470	470	470	469	469	469	469	469	468	468	468	468	468	467	467
30-44	502	502	502	502	502	502	503	503	503	504	504	504	505	505	505	505	505	505	505	505
45-59	511	512	512	513	513	514	513	513	512	512	511	510	509	509	508	508	508	508	508	509
60-74	484	485	486	489	491	493	494	496	497	496	496	496	496	496	496	497	498	498	499	500
75 & over	553	554	555	554	554	554	555	556	558	561	564	566	570	573	576	578	580	582	584	586
All ages	2,940	2,942	2,945	2,947	2,949	2,951	2,954	2,956	2,958	2,961	2,963	2,965	2,968	2,970	2,972	2,975	2,978	2,980	2,983	2,986
Percentages																				
0-14	14.3	14.2	14.2	14.2	14.2	14.2	14.2	14.2	14.2	14.2	14.1	14.1	14.1	14.1	14.1	14.1	14.1	14.1	14.1	14.0
15-29	16.0	16.0	16.0	16.0	15.9	15.9	15.9	15.9	15.9	15.8	15.8	15.8	15.8	15.8	15.7	15.7	15.7	15.7	15.7	15.7
30-44	17.1	17.1	17.0	17.0	17.0	17.0	17.0	17.0	17.0	17.0	17.0	17.0	17.0	17.0	17.0	17.0	17.0	16.9	16.9	16.9
45-59	17.4	17.4	17.4	17.4	17.4	17.4	17.4	17.3	17.3	17.3	17.2	17.2	17.2	17.1	17.1	17.1	17.1	17.1	17.0	17.0
60-74	16.5	16.5	16.5	16.6	16.6	16.7	16.7	16.8	16.8	16.8	16.7	16.7	16.7	16.7	16.7	16.7	16.7	16.7	16.7	16.7
75 & over	18.8	18.8	18.8	18.8	18.8	18.8	18.8	18.8	18.9	18.9	19.0	19.1	19.2	19.3	19.4	19.4	19.5	19.5	19.6	19.6
All ages	100.0	100.0	100.0	100.0	100.0	100.0	100.0	100.0	100.0	100.0	100.0	100.0	100.0	100.0	100.0	100.0	100.0	100.0	100.0	100.0
Mean age	47.3	47.4	47.4	47.5	47.5	47.6	47.6	47.6	47.7	47.7	47.8	47.8	47.8	47.9	47.9	47.9	48.0	48.0	48.1	48.1
Median age	47.3	47.3	47.4	47.4	47.5	47.5	47.5	47.6	47.6	47.6	47.6	47.7	47.7	47.7	47.8	47.8	47.8	47.9	47.9	48.0

15.3f Population projections by the Office for National Statistics
Scotland, FEMALES, thousands

2014-based
Principal projection

Projected populations at mid-years by age last birthday

Ages	2094	2095	2096	2097	2098	2099	2100	2101	2102	2103	2104	2105	2106	2107	2108	2109	2110	2111	2112	2113	2114
Thousands																					
0-14	420	419	419	419	419	419	419	419	419	419	419	418	418	418	418	418	418	418	418	418	418
15-29	467	467	468	468	468	468	468	468	468	468	468	468	468	468	468	468	468	468	468	468	468
30-44	505	504	504	504	504	504	503	503	503	503	503	502	502	502	502	502	502	502	502	503	503
45-59	509	509	510	510	511	511	512	512	512	512	512	512	512	512	512	512	512	512	512	512	512
60-74	500	500	500	500	499	499	498	498	498	497	497	498	498	498	499	499	500	500	501	502	502
75 & over	589	592	595	599	602	606	610	614	618	622	626	630	633	637	641	644	647	651	654	657	661
All ages	2,989	2,993	2,996	2,999	3,003	3,006	3,010	3,014	3,017	3,021	3,025	3,029	3,033	3,037	3,040	3,044	3,048	3,052	3,056	3,060	3,063
Percentages																					
0-14	14.0	14.0	14.0	14.0	14.0	13.9	13.9	13.9	13.9	13.9	13.8	13.8	13.8	13.8	13.8	13.7	13.7	13.7	13.7	13.7	13.7
15-29	15.6	15.6	15.6	15.6	15.6	15.6	15.5	15.5	15.5	15.5	15.5	15.5	15.4	15.4	15.4	15.4	15.4	15.3	15.3	15.3	15.3
30-44	16.9	16.9	16.8	16.8	16.8	16.8	16.7	16.7	16.7	16.6	16.6	16.6	16.6	16.6	16.5	16.5	16.5	16.6	16.4	16.4	16.4
45-59	17.0	17.0	17.0	17.0	17.0	17.0	17.0	17.0	17.0	17.0	16.9	16.9	16.9	16.9	16.9	16.8	16.8	16.8	16.8	16.7	16.7
60-74	16.7	16.7	16.7	16.7	16.6	16.6	16.6	16.5	16.5	16.5	16.4	16.4	16.4	16.4	16.4	16.4	16.4	16.4	16.4	16.4	16.4
75 & over	19.7	19.8	19.9	20.0	20.1	20.2	20.3	20.4	20.5	20.6	20.7	20.8	20.9	21.0	21.1	21.2	21.2	21.3	21.4	21.5	21.6
All ages	100.0	100.0	100.0	100.0	100.0	100.0	100.0	100.0	100.0	100.0	100.0	100.0	100.0	100.0	100.0	100.0	100.0	100.0	100.0	100.0	100.0
Mean age	48.2	48.2	48.3	48.3	48.4	48.4	48.5	48.5	48.6	48.6	48.7	48.8	48.8	48.8	48.9	49.0	49.1	49.1	49.2	49.2	49.3
Median age	48.0	48.1	48.1	48.2	48.3	48.3	48.4	48.4	48.5	48.6	48.6	48.7	48.7	48.8	48.9	48.9	49.0	49.0	49.1	49.2	49.2

Source: Office for National Statistics

Note: Figures may not add exactly due to rounding.

* Children under 16. Working age and pensionable age populations based on state pension age (SPA) for given year.

Between 2012 and 2018, SPA will change from 60 years for women, to 65 years for both sexes.

Then between 2019 and 2020, SPA will change from 65 years to 66 years for both men and women.

Between 2026 and 2027 SPA will increase to 67 years and between 2044 and 2046 to 68 years for both sexes. This is based on SPA under the 2014 Pensions Act.

** This is consistent with the age-group definitions used in ONS Labour Market Statistics.

15.3g Mid-2014 Population estimates for Northern Ireland by sex and single year of age

Ages	Persons	Males	Females	Ages	Persons	Males	Females
All Ages	1,840,498	902,711	937,787	45	26,091	12,707	13,384
0	24,255	12,440	11,815	46	26,577	13,059	13,518
1	24,835	12,651	12,184	47	26,516	12,970	13,546
2	25,730	13,174	12,556	48	26,563	13,069	13,494
3	25,612	13,026	12,586	49	27,009	13,214	13,795
4	25,349	12,922	12,427	50	26,561	13,093	13,468
5	25,692	13,184	12,508	51	25,937	12,954	12,983
6	25,658	13,120	12,538	52	25,252	12,374	12,878
7	24,450	12,568	11,882	53	24,870	12,255	12,615
8	23,344	11,967	11,377	54	23,865	11,687	12,178
9	22,706	11,718	10,988	55	23,194	11,475	11,719
10	22,481	11,598	10,883	56	22,823	11,299	11,524
11	21,951	11,211	10,740	57	21,900	10,793	11,107
12	22,058	11,269	10,789	58	21,030	10,475	10,555
13	22,297	11,410	10,887	59	20,044	10,079	9,965
14	23,162	12,035	11,127	60	19,675	9,929	9,746
15	24,203	12,381	11,822	61	19,217	9,548	9,669
16	24,509	12,566	11,943	62	18,446	9,165	9,281
17	24,869	12,656	12,213	63	18,496	9,189	9,307
18	24,689	12,715	11,974	64	18,490	9,063	9,427
19	23,738	12,430	11,308	65	18,228	8,915	9,313
20	23,992	12,423	11,569	66	18,199	8,796	9,403
21	23,676	12,112	11,564	67	18,166	8,689	9,477
22	24,508	12,377	12,131	68	16,803	8,076	8,727
23	24,672	12,377	12,295	69	16,575	7,917	8,658
24	24,689	12,366	12,323	70	16,417	7,856	8,561
25	24,555	12,273	12,282	71	15,752	7,467	8,285
26	24,851	12,307	12,544	72	13,998	6,602	7,396
27	25,001	12,400	12,601	73	12,598	5,863	6,735
28	25,033	12,277	12,756	74	12,138	5,572	6,566
29	24,942	12,276	12,666	75	12,155	5,561	6,594
30	24,651	12,052	12,599	76	11,392	5,201	6,191
31	24,415	11,910	12,505	77	10,958	4,936	6,022
32	24,402	11,885	12,517	78	10,164	4,446	5,718
33	24,921	12,154	12,767	79	9,525	4,145	5,380
34	25,028	12,173	12,855	80	8,717	3,748	4,969
35	23,841	11,395	12,446	81	8,377	3,442	4,935
36	22,907	11,105	11,802	82	7,710	3,119	4,591
37	22,646	11,008	11,638	83	7,164	2,826	4,338
38	22,746	11,042	11,704	84	6,436	2,418	4,018
39	23,334	11,422	11,912	85 / 85+	5,798	2,119	3,679
40	24,022	11,666	12,356	86	5,031	1,811	3,220
41	24,863	12,177	12,686	87	4,515	1,574	2,941
42	25,217	12,394	12,823	88	3,817	1,240	2,577
43	25,776	12,510	13,266	89	3,245	1,056	2,189
44	25,750	12,530	13,220	90	12,038	3,267	8,771

Source: Office for National Statistics

Note: It is ONS policy to publish estimates to the nearest hundred persons. Rounded (and particularly unit) estimates cannot be precisely accurate.

: Data not available

15.3h Population projections by the Office for National Statistics
Northern Ireland, PERSONS, thousands

2014-based
Principal projection

Projected populations at mid-years by age last birthday

Ages	2014	2015	2016	2017	2018	2019	2020	2021	2022	2023	2024	2025	2026	2027	2028	2029	2030	2031	2032	2033
Thousands																				
0-14	360	362	365	368	371	373	375	376	376	374	373	371	369	366	364	363	361	359	357	356
15-29	368	366	363	360	356	354	351	349	348	349	350	352	354	355	356	357	359	361	364	366
30-44	365	363	362	362	361	362	363	364	366	366	366	364	363	362	361	359	356	353	349	345
45-59	368	373	377	380	381	381	380	378	375	371	368	366	364	361	358	356	355	354	353	353
60-74	253	258	264	269	274	278	284	290	295	302	308	316	322	329	335	341	345	349	352	354
75 & over	127	129	132	135	140	146	151	156	162	168	173	178	183	188	193	198	204	209	215	222
All ages	1,840	1,851	1,863	1,874	1,884	1,894	1,904	1,913	1,922	1,930	1,939	1,947	1,954	1,961	1,968	1,974	1,980	1,986	1,991	1,996
Percentages																				
0-14	19.5	19.5	19.6	19.6	19.7	19.7	19.7	19.7	19.6	19.4	19.2	19.1	18.9	18.7	18.5	18.4	18.2	18.1	18.0	17.8
15-29	20.0	19.8	19.5	19.2	18.9	18.7	18.5	18.3	18.1	18.1	18.1	18.1	18.1	18.1	18.1	18.1	18.1	18.2	18.3	18.4
30-44	19.8	19.6	19.5	19.3	19.2	19.1	19.0	19.0	19.0	19.0	18.9	18.7	18.6	18.4	18.3	18.2	18.0	17.8	17.5	17.3
45-59	20.0	20.2	20.2	20.3	20.2	20.1	20.0	19.7	19.5	19.2	19.0	18.8	18.6	18.4	18.2	18.1	17.9	17.8	17.7	17.7
60-74	13.8	13.9	14.2	14.4	14.5	14.7	14.9	15.2	15.4	15.6	15.9	16.2	16.5	16.8	17.0	17.3	17.4	17.6	17.7	17.7
75 & over	6.9	7.0	7.1	7.2	7.5	7.7	7.9	8.2	8.4	8.7	8.9	9.2	9.4	9.6	9.8	10.0	10.3	10.5	10.8	11.1
All ages	100.0	100.0	100.0	100.0	100.0	100.0	100.0	100.0	100.0	100.0	100.0	100.0	100.0	100.0	100.0	100.0	100.0	100.0	100.0	100.0
Mean age	38.7	38.8	39.0	39.2	39.4	39.6	39.8	40.0	40.2	40.4	40.6	40.8	41.0	41.2	41.4	41.6	41.8	42.0	42.2	42.4
Median age	38.0	38.1	38.3	38.5	38.7	38.9	39.2	39.4	39.6	39.8	40.1	40.3	40.5	40.8	41.0	41.2	41.5	41.7	41.9	42.1

Ages	2034	2035	2036	2037	2038	2039	2040	2041	2042	2043	2044	2045	2046	2047	2048	2049	2050	2051	2052	2053
Thousands																				
0-14	354	352	351	350	349	349	348	349	349	349	350	351	352	353	354	355	355	356	356	356
15-29	369	370	371	371	370	368	366	364	362	360	359	357	355	353	352	350	349	347	346	346
30-44	343	340	338	337	338	339	340	342	343	344	345	347	349	352	355	357	359	360	360	358
45-59	353	354	355	357	358	358	356	354	353	352	351	348	345	341	338	335	333	331	330	331
60-74	354	353	351	349	346	343	341	340	338	336	334	334	333	332	332	333	334	336	337	338
75 & over	229	235	243	250	258	265	273	280	287	294	300	305	310	314	318	321	323	324	326	327
All ages	2,000	2,005	2,009	2,013	2,017	2,021	2,025	2,029	2,032	2,035	2,039	2,042	2,044	2,047	2,049	2,051	2,053	2,054	2,055	2,056
Percentages																				
0-14	17.7	17.6	17.5	17.4	17.3	17.2	17.2	17.2	17.2	17.2	17.2	17.2	17.2	17.2	17.3	17.3	17.3	17.3	17.3	17.3
15-29	18.4	18.5	18.5	18.4	18.3	18.2	18.1	18.0	17.8	17.7	17.6	17.5	17.4	17.3	17.2	17.1	17.0	16.9	16.9	16.8
30-44	17.1	17.0	16.8	16.7	16.7	16.8	16.8	16.8	16.9	16.9	16.9	17.0	17.1	17.2	17.3	17.4	17.5	17.5	17.5	17.4
45-59	17.6	17.6	17.7	17.7	17.7	17.7	17.6	17.5	17.4	17.3	17.2	17.1	16.9	16.7	16.5	16.3	16.2	16.1	16.0	16.1
60-74	17.7	17.6	17.5	17.3	17.1	17.0	16.9	16.8	16.6	16.5	16.4	16.3	16.3	16.2	16.2	16.2	16.3	16.3	16.4	16.5
75 & over	11.4	11.7	12.1	12.4	12.8	13.1	13.5	13.8	14.1	14.4	14.7	14.9	15.2	15.4	15.5	15.7	15.7	15.8	15.8	15.9
All ages	100.0	100.0	100.0	100.0	100.0	100.0	100.0	100.0	100.0	100.0	100.0	100.0	100.0	100.0	100.0	100.0	100.0	100.0	100.0	100.0
Mean age	42.6	42.7	42.9	43.1	43.2	43.3	43.5	43.6	43.7	43.8	43.9	44.0	44.1	44.2	44.2	44.3	44.4	44.5	44.5	44.6
Median age	42.3	42.5	42.7	42.8	42.9	43.0	43.2	43.3	43.3	43.4	43.4	43.4	43.3	43.3	43.3	43.3	43.4	43.5	43.6	43.7

15.3h Population projections by the Office for National Statistics
Northern Ireland, PERSONS, thousands

2014-based
Principal projection

Projected populations at mid-years by age last birthday

Ages	2054	2055	2056	2057	2058	2059	2060	2061	2062	2063	2064	2065	2066	2067	2068	2069	2070	2071	2072	2073
Thousands																				
0-14	356	356	355	354	353	352	351	350	348	347	346	345	344	343	343	342	342	342	342	342
15-29	345	345	346	346	347	347	348	349	350	351	352	352	353	353	353	353	352	352	351	350
30-44	357	355	353	351	349	348	346	345	343	341	340	338	337	336	335	335	335	335	336	336
45-59	332	333	335	336	337	338	340	343	346	348	350	352	353	353	352	350	349	347	345	343
60-74	339	337	336	335	334	333	331	328	325	322	319	317	315	315	316	317	319	321	323	324
75 & over	328	331	333	335	337	338	340	342	344	346	348	350	352	354	355	357	357	359	360	361
All ages	2,057	2,057	2,057	2,057	2,057	2,057	2,057	2,056	2,056	2,056	2,055	2,055	2,055	2,054	2,055	2,055	2,055	2,055	2,056	2,056
Percentages																				
0-14	17.3	17.3	17.3	17.2	17.2	17.1	17.1	17.0	16.9	16.9	16.8	16.8	16.8	16.7	16.7	16.7	16.6	16.6	16.6	16.6
15-29	16.8	16.8	16.8	16.8	16.8	16.9	16.9	17.0	17.0	17.1	17.1	17.1	17.2	17.2	17.2	17.2	17.1	17.1	17.1	17.0
30-44	17.3	17.3	17.2	17.1	17.0	16.9	16.8	16.8	16.7	16.6	16.5	16.5	16.4	16.4	16.3	16.3	16.3	16.3	16.3	16.3
45-59	16.1	16.2	16.3	16.3	16.4	16.4	16.5	16.7	16.8	16.9	17.1	17.1	17.2	17.2	17.1	17.1	17.0	16.9	16.8	16.7
60-74	16.5	16.4	16.3	16.3	16.3	16.2	16.1	15.9	15.8	15.6	15.5	15.4	15.4	15.3	15.4	15.4	15.5	15.6	15.7	15.8
75 & over	16.0	16.1	16.2	16.3	16.4	16.5	16.6	16.7	16.8	16.8	16.9	17.0	17.1	17.2	17.3	17.4	17.4	17.4	17.5	17.6
All ages	100.0	100.0	100.0	100.0	100.0	100.0	100.0	100.0	100.0	100.0	100.0	100.0	100.0	100.0	100.0	100.0	100.0	100.0	100.0	100.0
Mean age	44.6	44.7	44.8	44.8	44.9	44.9	45.0	45.0	45.1	45.1	45.2	45.2	45.2	45.3	45.3	45.4	45.4	45.5	45.5	45.6
Median age	43.8	43.9	44.0	44.1	44.1	44.2	44.3	44.4	44.4	44.5	44.6	44.6	44.7	44.8	44.8	44.9	44.9	45.0	45.0	45.0

Ages	2074	2075	2076	2077	2078	2079	2080	2081	2082	2083	2084	2085	2086	2087	2088	2089	2090	2091	2092	2093
Thousands																				
0-14	342	342	342	343	343	343	344	344	344	344	344	344	343	343	342	342	341	341	340	339
15-29	349	348	347	345	344	343	342	342	341	340	340	340	339	339	339	340	340	340	340	341
30-44	337	338	339	340	340	341	342	342	343	343	343	342	342	341	340	339	338	337	336	335
45-59	342	340	339	337	336	334	333	332	331	330	330	330	330	331	331	332	333	334	335	336
60-74	325	327	330	333	335	338	339	341	341	340	338	337	335	334	332	331	330	328	327	326
75 & over	362	363	362	362	361	361	362	363	365	368	371	374	377	381	384	387	389	392	395	398
All ages	2,057	2,058	2,059	2,059	2,060	2,061	2,062	2,063	2,064	2,065	2,066	2,067	2,067	2,068	2,069	2,070	2,071	2,072	2,073	2,074
Percentages																				
0-14	16.6	16.6	16.6	16.6	16.6	16.7	16.7	16.7	16.7	16.7	16.6	16.6	16.6	16.6	16.5	16.5	16.5	16.4	16.4	16.4
15-29	17.0	16.9	16.8	16.8	16.7	16.7	16.6	16.6	16.5	16.5	16.5	16.4	16.4	16.4	16.4	16.4	16.4	16.4	16.4	16.4
30-44	16.4	16.4	16.5	16.5	16.5	16.6	16.6	16.6	16.6	16.6	16.6	16.6	16.5	16.5	16.4	16.4	16.3	16.3	16.2	16.1
45-59	16.6	16.5	16.5	16.4	16.3	16.2	16.1	16.1	16.0	16.0	16.0	16.0	16.0	16.0	16.0	16.0	16.1	16.1	16.2	16.1
60-74	15.8	15.9	16.0	16.1	16.3	16.4	16.5	16.5	16.5	16.5	16.4	16.3	16.2	16.1	16.1	16.0	15.9	15.9	15.8	15.7
75 & over	17.6	17.6	17.6	17.6	17.5	17.5	17.5	17.6	17.7	17.8	18.0	18.1	18.3	18.4	18.6	18.7	18.8	18.9	19.0	19.2
All ages	100.0	100.0	100.0	100.0	100.0	100.0	100.0	100.0	100.0	100.0	100.0	100.0	100.0	100.0	100.0	100.0	100.0	100.0	100.0	100.0
Mean age	45.6	45.6	45.7	45.7	45.8	45.8	45.9	45.9	46.0	46.0	46.1	46.1	46.2	46.2	46.3	46.3	46.4	46.4	46.5	46.6
Median age	45.0	45.1	45.1	45.1	45.1	45.1	45.1	45.2	45.2	45.2	45.3	45.3	45.4	45.5	45.6	45.6	45.7	45.8	45.9	46.0

15.3h Population projections by the Office for National Statistics
Northern Ireland, PERSONS, thousands

2014-based
Principal projection

Projected populations at mid-years by age last birthday

Ages	2094	2095	2096	2097	2098	2099	2100	2101	2102	2103	2104	2105	2106	2107	2108	2109	2110	2111	2112	2113	2114
Thousands																					
0-14	339	338	337	337	336	336	335	335	335	335	334	334	334	334	334	334	334	334	334	334	334
15-29	341	341	341	341	342	341	341	341	341	340	340	339	338	338	337	336	336	335	335	334	334
30-44	334	333	332	331	331	330	330	330	330	330	330	330	331	331	331	331	332	332	332	332	332
45-59	337	337	338	338	338	338	338	337	337	336	335	334	333	332	331	330	329	328	327	327	326
60-74	324	323	322	322	321	321	321	322	322	323	324	325	326	327	328	329	330	331	331	331	331
75 & over	400	403	406	408	411	413	415	417	419	421	422	424	425	427	428	429	430	432	433	435	437
All ages	2,074	2,075	2,076	2,078	2,079	2,080	2,081	2,082	2,083	2,084	2,085	2,086	2,087	2,088	2,089	2,090	2,091	2,092	2,093	2,094	2,095
Percentages																					
0-14	16.3	16.3	16.2	16.2	16.2	16.1	16.1	16.1	16.1	16.1	16.0	16.0	16.0	16.0	16.0	16.0	16.1	16.0	16.0	16.0	16.0
15-29	16.4	16.4	16.4	16.4	16.4	16.4	16.4	16.4	16.4	16.3	16.3	16.3	16.2	16.2	16.1	16.1	16.1	16.0	16.0	16.0	15.9
30-44	16.1	16.0	16.0	15.9	15.9	15.9	15.9	15.8	15.8	15.8	15.8	15.8	15.8	15.9	15.8	15.8	15.9	15.9	15.9	15.8	15.8
45-59	16.2	16.3	16.3	16.3	16.3	16.3	16.2	16.2	16.2	16.1	16.1	16.0	15.9	15.9	15.7	15.7	15.7	15.8	15.8	15.8	15.6
60-74	15.6	15.6	15.5	15.5	15.5	15.4	15.4	15.4	15.5	15.5	15.5	15.6	15.6	15.7	15.7	15.7	15.8	15.8	15.8	15.8	15.8
75 & over	19.3	19.4	19.5	19.7	19.8	19.9	20.0	20.0	20.1	20.2	20.3	20.3	20.4	20.4	20.5	20.5	20.6	20.6	20.7	20.8	20.9
All ages	100.0	100.0	100.0	100.0	100.0	100.0	100.0	100.0	100.0	100.0	100.0	100.0	100.0	100.0	100.0	100.0	100.0	100.0	100.0	100.0	100.0
Mean age	46.6	46.7	46.8	46.8	46.9	47.0	47.0	47.1	47.1	47.2	47.3	47.3	47.4	47.4	47.5	47.5	47.6	47.6	47.7	47.7	47.8
Median age	46.1	46.1	46.2	46.3	46.4	46.5	46.5	46.6	46.7	46.7	46.8	46.8	46.9	46.9	46.9	47.0	47.0	47.1	47.1	47.1	47.2

Source: Office for National Statistics

Note: Figures may not add exactly due to rounding.

* Children under 16. Working age and pensionable age populations based on state pension age (SPA) for given year.
Between 2012 and 2018, SPA will change from 65 years for men and 61 years for women, to 65 years for both sexes.
Then between 2019 and 2020, SPA will change from 65 years to 66 years for both men and women.
Between 2026 and 2027 SPA will increase to 67 years and between 2044 and 2046 to 68 years for both sexes. This is based on SPA under the 2014 Pensions Act.
** This is consistent with the age-group definitions used in ONS Labour Market Statistics.

15.3h Population projections by the Office for National Statistics
Northern Ireland, MALES, thousands

2014-based
Principal projection

Projected populations at mid-years by age last birthday

Ages	2014	2015	2016	2017	2018	2019	2020	2021	2022	2023	2024	2025	2026	2027	2028	2029	2030	2031	2032	2033
Thousands																				
0-14	184	185	187	188	190	191	192	192	192	191	190	190	189	187	186	185	185	184	183	182
15-29	186	186	185	183	182	181	180	179	179	180	180	181	181	182	183	183	184	185	186	188
30-44	177	177	177	177	177	177	178	179	180	181	182	182	182	182	182	182	181	180	179	177
45-59	182	183	185	186	187	186	186	184	183	180	179	177	176	175	173	172	172	171	171	171
60-74	123	125	128	131	133	136	138	141	144	147	151	154	157	160	163	165	167	169	170	170
75 & over	51	52	54	56	59	61	64	67	70	72	75	78	81	83	86	89	91	94	97	100
All ages	903	909	915	921	927	932	938	943	948	952	957	961	965	969	973	977	980	983	986	989
Percentages																				
0-14	20.4	20.4	20.4	20.4	20.5	20.5	20.5	20.4	20.3	20.1	19.9	19.7	19.5	19.3	19.1	19.0	18.8	18.7	18.5	18.4
15-29	20.6	20.4	20.2	19.9	19.6	19.4	19.2	19.0	18.9	18.9	18.8	18.8	18.8	18.8	18.8	18.7	18.7	18.8	18.9	19.0
30-44	19.7	19.5	19.3	19.2	19.0	19.0	19.0	19.0	19.0	19.0	19.0	18.9	18.8	18.8	18.7	18.6	18.5	18.3	18.1	17.9
45-59	20.1	20.2	20.2	20.2	20.1	20.0	19.8	19.5	19.3	19.0	18.7	18.4	18.2	18.0	17.8	17.6	17.5	17.4	17.4	17.3
60-74	13.6	13.8	14.0	14.2	14.4	14.6	14.7	15.0	15.2	15.5	15.7	16.0	16.3	16.5	16.7	16.9	17.0	17.1	17.2	17.2
75 & over	5.6	5.7	5.9	6.1	6.3	6.6	6.8	7.1	7.3	7.6	7.9	8.1	8.4	8.6	8.8	9.1	9.3	9.6	9.9	10.2
All ages	100.0	100.0	100.0	100.0	100.0	100.0	100.0	100.0	100.0	100.0	100.0	100.0	100.0	100.0	100.0	100.0	100.0	100.0	100.0	100.0
Mean age	37.7	37.8	38.0	38.2	38.4	38.6	38.8	39.0	39.2	39.4	39.6	39.8	40.0	40.2	40.5	40.7	40.9	41.0	41.2	41.4
Median age	36.9	37.0	37.1	37.3	37.5	37.7	37.9	38.1	38.3	38.5	38.7	39.0	39.2	39.4	39.6	39.8	40.0	40.3	40.5	40.7

Ages	2034	2035	2036	2037	2038	2039	2040	2041	2042	2043	2044	2045	2046	2047	2048	2049	2050	2051	2052	2053
Thousands																				
0-14	181	180	179	179	178	178	178	178	178	179	179	180	180	181	181	181	182	182	182	182
15-29	189	189	190	190	189	188	187	186	185	184	183	183	182	181	180	179	178	178	177	177
30-44	176	175	175	174	175	175	176	176	177	177	178	179	180	181	183	184	185	185	185	184
45-59	172	172	174	175	176	177	177	177	177	177	177	177	175	174	173	172	171	170	170	170
60-74	170	170	169	167	166	164	163	162	161	160	159	159	159	159	159	160	161	162	163	164
75 & over	104	107	110	114	117	121	124	128	131	134	136	139	141	143	144	146	146	147	147	147
All ages	991	994	996	999	1,001	1,003	1,005	1,008	1,010	1,012	1,014	1,015	1,017	1,019	1,020	1,021	1,023	1,024	1,025	1,026
Percentages																				
0-14	18.3	18.1	18.0	17.9	17.8	17.8	17.7	17.7	17.7	17.7	17.7	17.7	17.7	17.7	17.7	17.8	17.8	17.8	17.8	17.8
15-29	19.0	19.1	19.1	19.0	18.9	18.7	18.6	18.5	18.3	18.2	18.1	18.0	17.9	17.8	17.6	17.5	17.4	17.4	17.3	17.2
30-44	17.8	17.6	17.5	17.5	17.5	17.5	17.5	17.5	17.5	17.5	17.6	17.6	17.7	17.8	17.9	18.0	18.1	18.1	18.1	18.0
45-59	17.3	17.3	17.4	17.5	17.6	17.6	17.6	17.6	17.5	17.5	17.5	17.4	17.2	17.1	16.9	16.8	16.7	16.6	16.6	16.6
60-74	17.2	17.1	16.9	16.7	16.5	16.3	16.2	16.1	16.0	15.8	15.7	15.7	15.6	15.6	15.6	15.6	15.7	15.8	15.9	16.0
75 & over	10.4	10.7	11.1	11.4	11.7	12.0	12.4	12.7	13.0	13.2	13.5	13.7	13.8	14.0	14.2	14.2	14.3	14.3	14.3	14.4
All ages	100.0	100.0	100.0	100.0	100.0	100.0	100.0	100.0	100.0	100.0	100.0	100.0	100.0	100.0	100.0	100.0	100.0	100.0	100.0	100.0
Mean age	41.6	41.8	41.9	42.1	42.2	42.4	42.5	42.6	42.7	42.8	42.9	43.0	43.1	43.2	43.2	43.3	43.4	43.4	43.5	43.6
Median age	40.9	41.0	41.2	41.4	41.5	41.6	41.7	41.8	41.9	41.9	41.9	41.9	41.9	41.9	42.0	42.1	42.2	42.3	42.4	42.5

15.3h Population projections by the Office for National Statistics
Northern Ireland, MALES, thousands

2014-based
Principal projection

Projected populations at mid-years by age last birthday

Ages	2054	2055	2056	2057	2058	2059	2060	2061	2062	2063	2064	2065	2066	2067	2068	2069	2070	2071	2072	2073
Thousands																				
0-14	182	182	182	181	181	180	179	179	178	178	177	177	176	176	175	175	175	175	175	175
15-29	177	177	177	177	177	178	178	179	179	180	180	180	181	181	181	181	180	180	180	179
30-44	183	183	182	181	180	179	178	177	177	176	175	174	174	173	173	173	173	173	173	173
45-59	171	171	172	173	173	174	175	176	177	179	180	181	181	181	181	180	179	178	177	176
60-74	165	166	166	166	166	166	166	165	164	163	162	161	161	161	161	162	163	163	164	165
75 & over	148	149	150	151	151	152	153	154	155	156	158	159	160	162	163	164	165	166	168	169
All ages	1,026	1,027	1,028	1,028	1,029	1,029	1,030	1,030	1,031	1,031	1,031	1,032	1,032	1,033	1,033	1,034	1,035	1,036	1,036	1,037
Percentages																				
0-14	17.7	17.7	17.7	17.6	17.6	17.5	17.4	17.4	17.3	17.2	17.2	17.1	17.1	17.0	17.0	16.9	16.9	16.9	16.9	16.9
15-29	17.2	17.2	17.2	17.2	17.2	17.3	17.3	17.3	17.4	17.4	17.5	17.5	17.5	17.5	17.5	17.5	17.4	17.4	17.3	17.3
30-44	17.9	17.8	17.7	17.6	17.5	17.4	17.3	17.2	17.1	17.1	17.0	16.9	16.8	16.8	16.7	16.7	16.7	16.7	16.7	16.7
45-59	16.7	16.7	16.7	16.8	16.8	16.9	17.0	17.1	17.2	17.4	17.4	17.5	17.6	17.5	17.5	17.4	17.3	17.2	17.1	17.0
60-74	16.1	16.1	16.1	16.2	16.2	16.2	16.1	16.0	15.9	15.8	15.7	15.6	15.6	15.5	15.6	15.7	15.7	15.8	15.9	15.9
75 & over	14.4	14.5	14.6	14.6	14.7	14.8	14.9	15.0	15.1	15.2	15.3	15.4	15.5	15.6	15.7	15.9	16.0	16.1	16.2	16.3
All ages	100.0	100.0	100.0	100.0	100.0	100.0	100.0	100.0	100.0	100.0	100.0	100.0	100.0	100.0	100.0	100.0	100.0	100.0	100.0	100.0
Mean age	43.6	43.7	43.8	43.8	43.9	44.0	44.0	44.1	44.1	44.2	44.2	44.3	44.4	44.5	44.5	44.6	44.7	44.7	44.8	44.8
Median age	42.7	42.8	42.9	43.0	43.1	43.2	43.3	43.4	43.4	43.5	43.6	43.7	43.8	43.9	44.0	44.0	44.1	44.1	44.2	44.2

Ages	2074	2075	2076	2077	2078	2079	2080	2081	2082	2083	2084	2085	2086	2087	2088	2089	2090	2091	2092	2093
Thousands																				
0-14	175	175	175	175	175	176	176	176	176	176	176	176	176	175	175	175	175	174	174	174
15-29	179	178	177	177	176	176	175	175	175	174	174	174	174	174	174	174	174	174	174	174
30-44	174	174	175	175	176	176	176	177	177	177	177	176	176	176	175	175	174	174	173	173
45-59	176	175	174	173	172	172	171	171	170	170	170	172	170	170	170	171	171	172	172	173
60-74	166	166	168	169	171	172	173	173	173	173	172	172	171	170	169	169	168	167	167	166
75 & over	170	171	171	171	171	172	173	173	175	177	179	180	182	184	186	187	189	190	192	193
All ages	1,038	1,039	1,040	1,041	1,042	1,043	1,044	1,044	1,045	1,046	1,047	1,048	1,048	1,049	1,050	1,050	1,051	1,052	1,052	1,053
Percentages																				
0-14	16.8	16.8	16.8	16.8	16.8	16.8	16.8	16.8	16.8	16.8	16.8	16.8	16.8	16.7	16.7	16.6	16.6	16.6	16.5	16.5
15-29	17.2	17.1	17.1	17.0	16.9	16.9	16.8	16.7	16.7	16.7	16.6	16.6	16.6	16.6	16.6	16.6	16.6	16.6	16.6	16.6
30-44	16.7	16.8	16.8	16.8	16.8	16.9	16.9	16.9	16.9	16.9	16.9	16.8	16.8	16.8	16.7	16.6	16.6	16.5	16.5	16.4
45-59	16.9	16.8	16.7	16.6	16.6	16.5	16.4	16.3	16.3	16.2	16.2	16.2	16.2	16.2	16.2	16.3	16.3	16.3	16.4	16.4
60-74	16.0	16.0	16.1	16.3	16.4	16.5	16.5	16.6	16.6	16.5	16.4	16.4	16.3	16.2	16.1	16.1	16.0	15.9	15.8	15.8
75 & over	16.4	16.4	16.4	16.4	16.4	16.5	16.5	16.6	16.7	16.9	17.1	17.2	17.4	17.6	17.7	17.8	18.0	18.1	18.2	18.4
All ages	100.0	100.0	100.0	100.0	100.0	100.0	100.0	100.0	100.0	100.0	100.0	100.0	100.0	100.0	100.0	100.0	100.0	100.0	100.0	100.0
Mean age	44.9	45.0	45.0	45.1	45.1	45.2	45.3	45.3	45.4	45.5	45.5	45.6	45.6	45.7	45.8	45.8	45.9	46.0	46.0	46.1
Median age	44.3	44.3	44.4	44.4	44.4	44.5	44.5	44.6	44.6	44.7	44.7	44.8	44.9	45.0	45.0	45.1	45.2	45.3	45.4	45.5

15.3h Population projections by the Office for National Statistics
Northern Ireland, MALES, thousands

2014-based
Principal projection

Projected populations at mid-years by age last birthday

Ages	2094	2095	2096	2097	2098	2099	2100	2101	2102	2103	2104	2105	2106	2107	2108	2109	2110	2111	2112	2113	2114
Thousands																					
0-14	173	173	172	172	172	172	171	171	171	171	171	171	171	171	171	171	171	171	171	171	171
15-29	175	175	175	175	175	175	175	175	174	174	174	174	173	173	173	172	172	172	171	171	171
30-44	172	172	171	171	171	171	170	170	170	170	170	171	171	171	171	171	171	171	171	171	171
45-59	173	173	174	174	174	174	174	174	173	173	172	172	171	171	170	170	169	169	169	168	168
60-74	165	165	164	164	164	164	164	164	165	165	165	166	167	167	168	168	169	169	169	169	169
75 & over	195	196	198	199	200	202	203	204	205	206	206	207	208	209	209	210	211	212	212	213	214
All ages	1,053	1,054	1,055	1,055	1,056	1,057	1,057	1,058	1,058	1,059	1,060	1,060	1,061	1,062	1,062	1,063	1,063	1,064	1,064	1,065	1,065
Percentages																					
0-14	16.4	16.4	16.4	16.3	16.3	16.2	16.2	16.2	16.2	16.2	16.1	16.1	16.1	16.1	16.1	16.1	16.1	16.1	16.1	16.1	16.0
15-29	16.6	16.6	16.6	16.6	16.6	16.5	16.5	16.5	16.5	16.4	16.4	16.4	16.3	16.3	16.3	16.2	16.2	16.1	16.1	16.1	16.0
30-44	16.3	16.3	16.2	16.2	16.2	16.1	16.1	16.1	16.1	16.1	16.1	16.1	16.1	16.1	16.1	16.1	16.1	16.1	16.1	16.1	16.1
45-59	16.4	16.5	16.5	16.5	16.5	16.5	16.4	16.4	16.4	16.3	16.3	16.2	16.2	16.1	16.0	16.0	15.9	15.9	15.9	15.8	15.8
60-74	15.7	15.6	15.6	15.6	15.5	15.5	15.5	15.5	15.5	15.6	15.6	15.7	15.7	15.7	15.8	15.8	15.9	15.9	15.9	15.9	15.9
75 & over	18.5	18.6	18.8	18.9	19.0	19.1	19.2	19.3	19.3	19.4	19.5	19.5	19.6	19.7	19.7	19.8	19.8	19.9	20.0	20.0	20.1
All ages	100.0	100.0	100.0	100.0	100.0	100.0	100.0	100.0	100.0	100.0	100.0	100.0	100.0	100.0	100.0	100.0	100.0	100.0	100.0	100.0	100.0
Mean age	46.2	46.3	46.3	46.4	46.5	46.5	46.6	46.7	46.7	46.8	46.8	46.9	47.0	47.0	47.1	47.1	47.2	47.2	47.3	47.3	47.4
Median age	45.6	45.7	45.7	45.8	45.9	46.0	46.0	46.1	46.2	46.2	46.3	46.3	46.4	46.4	46.5	46.5	46.6	46.6	46.6	46.7	46.7

Note: Figures may not add exactly due to rounding.
* Children under 16. Working age and pensionable age populations based on state pension age (SPA) for given year.
Between 2012 and 2018, SPA will change from 65 years for men and 61 years for women, to 65 years for both sexes.
Then between 2019 and 2020, SPA will change from 65 years to 66 years for both men and women.
Between 2026 and 2027 SPA will increase to 67 years and between 2044 and 2046 to 68 years for both sexes. This is based on SPA under the 2014 Pensions Act.
** This is consistent with the age-group definitions used in ONS Labour Market Statistics.

Source: Office for National Statistics

2014-based
Principal projection

15.3h Population projections by the Office for National Statistics
Northern Ireland, FEMALES, thousands

Projected populations at mid-years by age last birthday

Ages	2014	2015	2016	2017	2018	2019	2020	2021	2022	2023	2024	2025	2026	2027	2028	2029	2030	2031	2032	2033
Thousands																				
0-14	175	176	178	179	181	182	183	184	184	183	182	181	180	179	178	177	176	176	175	174
15-29	182	180	178	177	174	173	171	170	169	170	170	171	172	173	174	174	175	176	177	179
30-44	187	186	186	185	185	185	185	185	186	185	184	182	181	180	178	177	175	173	170	168
45-59	187	190	192	194	195	195	195	193	192	191	190	188	188	186	185	184	183	182	182	181
60-74	131	133	135	138	140	143	145	149	151	154	158	162	165	169	172	176	178	181	182	183
75 & over	76	77	78	80	82	84	87	89	92	95	98	100	103	105	107	110	112	115	118	122
All ages	938	942	948	952	957	962	966	970	974	978	982	985	989	992	995	998	1,000	1,003	1,005	1,007
Percentages																				
0-14	18.7	18.7	18.8	18.8	18.9	18.9	19.0	18.9	18.9	18.7	18.6	18.4	18.2	18.0	17.9	17.8	17.6	17.5	17.4	17.3
15-29	19.4	19.1	18.8	18.5	18.2	18.0	17.7	17.5	17.4	17.3	17.3	17.4	17.4	17.4	17.4	17.4	17.5	17.6	17.7	17.7
30-44	20.0	19.8	19.6	19.5	19.3	19.2	19.1	19.1	19.0	18.9	18.8	18.5	18.3	18.1	17.9	17.7	17.5	17.2	17.0	16.7
45-59	19.9	20.1	20.3	20.3	20.3	20.3	20.1	19.9	19.7	19.5	19.3	19.1	19.0	18.8	18.6	18.5	18.3	18.2	18.1	18.0
60-74	13.9	14.1	14.3	14.5	14.7	14.8	15.1	15.3	15.5	15.8	16.1	16.4	16.7	17.0	17.3	17.6	17.8	18.0	18.1	18.2
75 & over	8.1	8.1	8.2	8.4	8.6	8.8	9.0	9.2	9.5	9.7	10.0	10.2	10.4	10.6	10.8	11.0	11.2	11.5	11.8	12.1
All ages	100.0	100.0	100.0	100.0	100.0	100.0	100.0	100.0	100.0	100.0	100.0	100.0	100.0	100.0	100.0	100.0	100.0	100.0	100.0	100.0
Mean age	39.7	39.8	40.0	40.1	40.3	40.5	40.7	40.9	41.1	41.3	41.5	41.7	41.9	42.1	42.3	42.5	42.7	42.9	43.1	43.3
Median age	39.1	39.2	39.4	39.6	39.8	40.0	40.3	40.6	40.8	41.1	41.3	41.6	41.9	42.1	42.4	42.6	42.9	43.1	43.3	43.6

Ages	2034	2035	2036	2037	2038	2039	2040	2041	2042	2043	2044	2045	2046	2047	2048	2049	2050	2051	2052	2053
Thousands																				
0-14	173	172	171	171	171	170	170	170	170	171	171	172	172	172	173	173	174	174	174	174
15-29	180	181	181	181	181	180	179	178	177	176	175	174	173	173	172	171	170	170	169	169
30-44	166	165	163	163	163	164	165	165	166	167	167	168	169	171	172	173	174	175	175	174
45-59	181	181	182	182	182	181	179	177	176	175	174	172	169	167	165	163	162	161	160	160
60-74	184	183	183	181	180	179	178	178	177	176	175	174	174	173	173	173	173	174	174	174
75 & over	125	129	133	136	140	144	149	153	156	160	163	166	169	172	174	176	177	178	179	179
All ages	1,009	1,011	1,013	1,015	1,016	1,018	1,020	1,021	1,023	1,024	1,025	1,026	1,027	1,028	1,029	1,029	1,030	1,030	1,030	1,030
Percentages																				
0-14	17.1	17.0	16.9	16.8	16.8	16.7	16.7	16.7	16.7	16.7	16.7	16.7	16.7	16.8	16.8	16.8	16.9	16.9	16.9	16.9
15-29	17.8	17.9	17.9	17.9	17.8	17.7	17.6	17.4	17.3	17.2	17.1	17.0	16.9	16.8	16.7	16.6	16.5	16.5	16.4	16.4
30-44	16.5	16.3	16.1	16.0	16.0	16.1	16.1	16.2	16.2	16.3	16.3	16.4	16.5	16.6	16.7	16.8	16.9	17.0	17.0	16.9
45-59	17.9	17.9	17.9	17.9	17.9	17.8	17.5	17.4	17.2	17.1	16.9	16.7	16.5	16.3	16.1	15.9	15.7	15.6	15.5	15.5
60-74	18.2	18.1	18.0	17.9	17.7	17.6	17.5	17.4	17.3	17.2	17.1	17.0	16.9	16.9	16.8	16.8	16.8	16.9	16.9	16.9
75 & over	12.4	12.7	13.1	13.4	13.8	14.2	14.6	14.9	15.3	15.6	15.9	16.2	16.5	16.7	16.9	17.1	17.2	17.3	17.4	17.4
All ages	100.0	100.0	100.0	100.0	100.0	100.0	100.0	100.0	100.0	100.0	100.0	100.0	100.0	100.0	100.0	100.0	100.0	100.0	100.0	100.0
Mean age	43.5	43.7	43.9	44.0	44.2	44.3	44.4	44.6	44.7	44.8	44.9	45.0	45.1	45.2	45.3	45.3	45.4	45.5	45.5	45.6
Median age	43.8	44.0	44.2	44.3	44.5	44.6	44.6	44.7	44.8	44.9	44.9	44.9	44.9	44.8	44.8	44.7	44.7	44.7	44.8	44.9

15.3h Population projections by the Office for National Statistics
Northern Ireland, FEMALES, thousands

2014-based
Principal projection

Projected populations at mid-years by age last birthday

Ages	2054	2055	2056	2057	2058	2059	2060	2061	2062	2063	2064	2065	2066	2067	2068	2069	2070	2071	2072	2073
Thousands																				
0-14	174	174	173	173	173	172	171	171	170	170	169	169	168	168	168	167	167	167	167	167
15-29	169	169	169	169	169	170	170	170	171	171	172	172	172	172	172	172	172	172	171	171
30-44	173	172	171	170	169	169	168	167	166	165	165	164	163	163	163	162	162	162	163	163
45-59	161	162	163	163	164	164	165	167	168	169	171	172	172	172	171	171	170	169	168	167
60-74	173	171	170	169	168	167	165	163	161	159	157	156	155	154	155	155	157	157	158	159
75 & over	181	182	183	184	185	186	187	188	189	190	190	191	192	192	192	193	192	192	192	192
All ages	1,030	1,030	1,030	1,029	1,028	1,028	1,027	1,026	1,025	1,025	1,024	1,023	1,022	1,022	1,021	1,020	1,020	1,020	1,019	1,019
Percentages																				
0-14	16.9	16.9	16.8	16.8	16.8	16.7	16.7	16.6	16.6	16.6	16.5	16.5	16.5	16.4	16.4	16.4	16.4	16.4	16.4	16.4
15-29	16.4	16.4	16.4	16.4	16.5	16.5	16.6	16.6	16.7	16.7	16.8	16.8	16.8	16.9	16.9	16.9	16.9	16.8	16.8	16.8
30-44	16.8	16.7	16.6	16.5	16.5	16.4	16.3	16.3	16.2	16.1	16.1	16.0	16.0	15.9	15.9	15.9	15.9	15.9	16.0	16.0
45-59	15.6	15.7	15.8	15.9	15.9	16.0	16.1	16.3	16.4	16.5	16.7	16.8	16.8	16.9	16.8	16.7	16.7	16.6	16.5	16.4
60-74	16.8	16.6	16.5	16.4	16.3	16.2	16.1	15.9	15.7	15.5	15.4	15.2	15.1	15.1	15.2	15.2	15.3	15.4	15.5	15.6
75 & over	17.5	17.7	17.8	17.9	18.0	18.1	18.2	18.3	18.4	18.5	18.6	18.7	18.7	18.8	18.8	18.9	18.8	18.8	18.9	18.9
All ages	100.0	100.0	100.0	100.0	100.0	100.0	100.0	100.0	100.0	100.0	100.0	100.0	100.0	100.0	100.0	100.0	100.0	100.0	100.0	100.0
Mean age	45.7	45.7	45.8	45.8	45.8	45.9	45.9	46.0	46.0	46.0	46.1	46.1	46.1	46.1	46.2	46.2	46.2	46.2	46.3	46.3
Median age	44.9	45.0	45.1	45.2	45.3	45.3	45.4	45.4	45.5	45.5	45.6	45.6	45.7	45.7	45.7	45.8	45.8	45.8	45.8	45.8

Ages	2074	2075	2076	2077	2078	2079	2080	2081	2082	2083	2084	2085	2086	2087	2088	2089	2090	2091	2092	2093
Thousands																				
0-14	167	167	167	167	168	168	168	168	168	168	168	168	168	167	167	167	167	166	166	166
15-29	170	170	169	169	168	168	167	167	166	166	166	166	166	166	166	166	166	166	166	166
30-44	163	164	164	165	165	165	166	166	166	166	166	166	165	165	165	164	164	163	163	162
45-59	166	166	165	164	163	162	162	161	161	160	160	160	160	161	161	161	162	162	163	163
60-74	159	161	162	163	165	166	167	167	167	167	166	166	165	164	163	162	162	161	160	160
75 & over	193	192	191	191	190	190	189	189	190	191	193	194	195	197	198	199	200	202	203	204
All ages	1,019	1,019	1,019	1,019	1,019	1,019	1,019	1,019	1,019	1,019	1,019	1,019	1,019	1,019	1,019	1,020	1,020	1,020	1,020	1,021
Percentages																				
0-14	16.4	16.4	16.4	16.4	16.5	16.5	16.5	16.5	16.5	16.5	16.5	16.5	16.5	16.4	16.4	16.4	16.3	16.3	16.3	16.2
15-29	16.7	16.7	16.6	16.6	16.5	16.5	16.4	16.4	16.3	16.3	16.3	16.3	16.3	16.2	16.2	16.3	16.3	16.3	16.3	16.3
30-44	16.0	16.1	16.1	16.2	16.2	16.2	16.3	16.3	16.3	16.3	16.3	16.3	16.2	16.2	16.2	16.1	16.0	16.0	15.9	15.9
45-59	16.3	16.3	16.2	16.1	16.0	16.0	15.9	15.8	15.8	15.8	15.7	15.7	15.7	15.8	15.8	15.9	15.9	15.9	15.9	16.0
60-74	15.7	15.8	15.9	16.0	16.2	16.3	16.4	16.4	16.4	16.4	16.3	16.2	16.2	16.1	16.0	15.9	15.9	15.8	15.7	15.6
75 & over	18.9	18.8	18.8	18.7	18.7	18.6	18.6	18.6	18.7	18.8	18.9	19.0	19.2	19.3	19.4	19.5	19.6	19.8	19.9	20.0
All ages	100.0	100.0	100.0	100.0	100.0	100.0	100.0	100.0	100.0	100.0	100.0	100.0	100.0	100.0	100.0	100.0	100.0	100.0	100.0	100.0
Mean age	46.3	46.3	46.4	46.4	46.4	46.4	46.5	46.5	46.5	46.6	46.6	46.6	46.7	46.7	46.8	46.8	46.9	46.9	47.0	47.0
Median age	45.8	45.8	45.8	45.8	45.8	45.8	45.8	45.8	45.8	45.9	45.9	45.9	46.0	46.0	46.1	46.2	46.2	46.3	46.4	46.5

15.3h Population projections by the Office for National Statistics
Northern Ireland, FEMALES, thousands

2014-based
Principal projection

Projected populations at mid-years by age last birthday

Ages	2094	2095	2096	2097	2098	2099	2100	2101	2102	2103	2104	2105	2106	2107	2108	2109	2110	2111	2112	2113	2114
Thousands																					
0-14	165	165	165	164	164	164	164	164	164	163	163	163	163	163	163	163	163	163	163	163	163
15-29	166	166	167	167	167	167	166	166	166	166	166	165	165	165	164	164	164	164	163	163	163
30-44	162	161	161	160	160	160	160	160	160	160	160	160	160	160	160	160	160	160	161	161	161
45-59	163	164	164	164	164	164	164	164	163	163	162	162	161	161	160	161	161	162	162	162	162
60-74	159	158	158	157	157	157	157	157	158	158	158	159	159	160	160	161	161	162	162	162	162
75 & over	205	207	208	209	210	211	212	213	214	215	216	217	217	218	218	219	220	220	221	222	223
All ages	1,021	1,021	1,022	1,022	1,023	1,023	1,024	1,024	1,024	1,025	1,025	1,026	1,026	1,027	1,027	1,027	1,028	1,028	1,029	1,029	1,029
Percentages																					
0-14	16.2	16.2	16.1	16.1	16.1	16.0	16.0	16.0	16.0	15.9	15.9	15.9	15.9	15.9	15.9	15.9	15.9	15.9	15.9	15.9	15.9
15-29	16.3	16.3	16.3	16.3	16.3	16.3	16.3	16.2	16.2	16.2	16.2	16.1	16.1	16.1	16.0	16.0	15.9	15.9	15.9	15.9	15.8
30-44	15.8	15.8	15.7	15.7	15.6	15.6	15.6	15.6	15.6	15.6	15.6	15.6	15.6	15.6	15.6	15.6	15.6	15.6	15.6	15.6	15.6
45-59	16.0	16.0	16.1	16.1	16.1	16.0	16.0	16.0	15.9	15.9	15.8	15.8	15.7	15.7	15.6	15.7	15.7	15.7	15.7	15.7	15.7
60-74	15.6	15.5	15.4	15.4	15.4	15.4	15.4	15.4	15.4	15.4	15.4	15.5	15.5	15.6	15.6	15.7	15.7	15.7	15.7	15.7	15.7
75 & over	20.1	20.2	20.4	20.5	20.6	20.7	20.8	20.8	20.9	21.0	21.0	21.1	21.2	21.2	21.3	21.3	21.4	21.4	21.5	21.6	21.6
All ages	100.0	100.0	100.0	100.0	100.0	100.0	100.0	100.0	100.0	100.0	100.0	100.0	100.0	100.0	100.0	100.0	100.0	100.0	100.0	100.0	100.0
Mean age	47.1	47.2	47.2	47.3	47.3	47.4	47.5	47.5	47.6	47.7	47.7	47.8	47.8	47.9	47.9	48.0	48.0	48.1	48.1	48.2	48.2
Median age	46.6	46.7	46.7	46.8	46.9	47.0	47.0	47.1	47.2	47.2	47.3	47.3	47.4	47.4	47.4	47.5	47.5	47.5	47.6	47.6	47.7

Source: Office for National Statistics

Note: Figures may not add exactly due to rounding.
* Children under 16. Working age and pensionable age populations based on state pension age (SPA) for given year.
Between 2012 and 2018, SPA will change from 65 years for men and 61 years for women, to 65 years for both sexes.
Then between 2019 and 2020, SPA will change from 65 years to 66 years for both men and women.
Between 2026 and 2027 SPA will increase to 67 years and between 2044 and 2046 to 68 years for both sexes. This is based on SPA under the 2014 Pensions Act.
** This is consistent with the age-group definitions used in ONS Labour Market Statistics.

15.4 Families by family type and presence of children

United Kingdom, 1998-2014

thousands

Number of families	1998 Estimate	1998 CI+/-	1999 Estimate	1999 CI+/-	2000 Estimate	2000 CI+/-	2001 Estimate	2001 CI+/-	2002 Estimate	2002 CI+/-	2003 Estimate	2003 CI+/-	2004 Estimate	2004 CI+/-	2005 Estimate	2005 CI+/-	2006 Estimate	2006 CI+/-	2007 Estimate	2007 CI+/-	2008 Estimate	2008 CI+/-	2009 Estimate	2009 CI+/-	2010 Estimate	2010 CI+/-	2011 Estimate	2011 CI+/-	2012 Estimate	2012 CI+/-	2013 Estimate	2013 CI+/-	2014 Estimate	2014 CI+/-
Married couple family	12,497	70	12,417	69	12,443	69	12,280	71	12,252	72	12,219	74	12,210	77	12,278	78	12,237	80	12,246	82	12,216	83	12,267	85	12,287	88	12,208	102	12,303	102	12,376	106	12,476	104
No children	5,871	65	5,880	65	5,977	66	5,892	67	5,958	67	5,976	69	5,922	71	6,006	72	6,046	72	5,997	74	6,042	75	5,961	76	6,039	79	5,983	92	5,987	91	5,942	95	6,083	94
Dependent children	5,013	52	4,936	52	4,918	53	4,833	54	4,777	54	4,746	56	4,689	57	4,732	58	4,682	59	4,689	60	4,642	61	4,709	63	4,701	65	4,641	67	4,697	67	4,748	69	4,751	67
Non-dependent children only	1,612	45	1,601	46	1,548	43	1,555	44	1,517	44	1,497	45	1,599	47	1,539	47	1,509	47	1,560	48	1,532	49	1,597	50	1,548	51	1,584	52	1,619	53	1,686	55	1,642	54
Civil partner couple family	N/A	N/A	N/A	N/A	N/A	N/A	N/A	N/A	N/A	N/A	N/A	N/A	N/A	N/A	N/A	N/A	13	13	33	9	40	9	41	9	45	10	60	12	67	12	64	13	61	12
No children or non-dependent children only	N/A	N/A	N/A	N/A	N/A	N/A	N/A	N/A	N/A	N/A	N/A	N/A	N/A	N/A	N/A	N/A	13	13	29	8	37	9	37	9	43	10	54	12	61	12	55	13	49	11
Dependent children																			4	2	3	2	4	3	2	2	5	3	6	3	9	4	12	5
Opposite sex cohabiting couple family	1,728	52	1,855	53	1,984	52	2,129	55	2,156	55	2,242	58	2,298	60	2,392	62	2,457	63	2,549	65	2,653	67	2,689	69	2,749	71	2,863	76	2,880	75	2,826	78	2,975	78
No children	1,036	41	1,083	41	1,184	42	1,260	44	1,267	44	1,354	47	1,331	47	1,409	49	1,419	50	1,480	52	1,522	53	1,564	55	1,556	56	1,632	60	1,619	60	1,524	60	1,666	63
Dependent children	638	30	718	32	739	32	808	34	809	34	819	36	885	38	899	38	954	40	974	40	1,040	42	1,025	43	1,077	45	1,107	47	1,130	47	1,170	49	1,163	48
Non-dependent children only	54	9	54	9	61	10	61	10	79	12	68	11	81	12	85	13	85	13	96	14	92	14	101	15	116	16	123	17	130	18	133	18	146	19
Same sex cohabiting couple family	30	7	31	7	38	8	45	9	46	9	53	10	61	11	57	11	68	12	61	11	61	11	54	11	51	11	63	13	70	13	89	16	84	15
No children or non-dependent children only	29	7	30	7	37	7	44	8	45	9	52	10	60	11	54	11	65	11	58	11	58	11	51	11	48	11	61	13	64	13	84	16	75	14
Dependent children	1	1	1	1	1	1	1	1	1	1	1	1	1	1	3	2	3	2	3	2	3	2	3	2	3	2	3	2	6	3	5	3	9	4
Lone parent family	2,474	55	2,490	55	2,428	55	2,512	58	2,548	57	2,597	60	2,685	62	2,697	63	2,695	63	2,692	64	2,759	66	2,889	68	2,943	70	2,909	71	3,043	74	3,004	77	3,005	75
Dependent children	1,719	43	1,742	43	1,698	44	1,745	45	1,809	45	1,804	47	1,869	49	1,883	49	1,870	50	1,880	50	1,905	52	1,989	54	2,002	54	1,991	56	2,056	57	1,974	58	1,981	57
Non-dependent children only	755	34	748	34	731	34	767	35	740	35	793	37	817	38	814	39	825	39	812	39	854	41	901	43	942	44	918	45	986	47	1,030	50	1,024	49
Lone mother family	2,163	50	2,162	50	2,108	50	2,159	51	2,207	51	2,250	53	2,320	55	2,352	56	2,347	57	2,339	57	2,414	59	2,512	61	2,562	63	2,565	65	2,637	66	2,597	69	2,611	68
Dependent children	1,558	40	1,579	40	1,550	41	1,575	42	1,636	42	1,626	43	1,686	45	1,708	46	1,701	46	1,713	47	1,736	48	1,803	50	1,813	51	1,826	53	1,878	54	1,806	55	1,810	54
Non-dependent children only	605	30	583	29	558	29	584	30	571	30	625	32	634	33	644	34	646	34	627	33	678	35	709	37	749	39	739	39	759	40	791	43	801	43
Lone father family	311	21	328	22	320	22	353	24	342	24	347	24	366	26	345	25	347	26	353	26	345	26	377	28	381	28	344	28	405	30	408	31	395	30
Dependent children	161	15	163	16	147	15	170	16	172	17	178	17	183	17	175	18	169	18	167	18	169	18	185	19	188	20	165	19	178	20	168	20	171	20
Non-dependent children only	150	15	165	16	173	17	184	18	169	17	168	17	183	19	170	18	178	19	186	19	176	19	192	20	193	21	179	20	227	24	240	25	223	24
All families	16,729	73	16,793	71	16,893	73	16,966	61	17,002	62	17,110	65	17,254	67	17,424	67	17,470	69	17,571	71	17,729	72	17,940	73	18,075	75	18,102	90	18,362	89	18,359	94	18,601	93
No children	6,936	73	6,993	73	7,198	73	7,196	75	7,270	75	7,383	78	7,314	80	7,469	81	7,542	82	7,553	84	7,657	85	7,612	87	7,686	90	7,730	103	7,727	101	7,602	106	7,871	106
Dependent children	7,371	44	7,398	44	7,355	44	7,386	44	7,396	45	7,370	46	7,444	47	7,517	48	7,509	48	7,550	50	7,592	50	7,729	52	7,784	53	7,747	55	7,896	55	7,905	57	7,916	55
Non-dependent children only	2,421	55	2,403	56	2,339	52	2,383	53	2,336	53	2,358	54	2,497	57	2,438	57	2,420	58	2,469	59	2,480	60	2,599	62	2,605	64	2,625	65	2,739	66	2,851	69	2,813	68

Source: Labour Force Survey (LFS), Office for National Statistics
Produced by Demographic Analysis Unit, Office for National Statistics
families@ons.gsi.gov.uk

1. Totals may not sum due to rounding.
2. In the table ... indicates that the data are not sufficiently reliable to be published.
3. The robustness of an estimate is presented in two ways:

The coefficient of variation (CV) indicates the robustness

$$\frac{\text{standard error}}{\text{estimate}} \times 100,$$

where standard error is an estimate of the margin of error associated with a sample survey. The coloured shading on the table indicates the precision of each estimate as follows:

Statistical Robustness

CV ≤ 5	Estimates are considered precise
CV > 5 and ≤ 10	Estimates are considered reasonably precise
CV > 10 and ≤ 20	Estimates are considered acceptable
CV > 20	Estimates are considered unreliable for practical purposes

Confidence intervals are also presented. CI+/- is the upper(+) and lower(-) 95% confidence interval. It is defined as **1.96 x standard error**. The confidence interval provides an estimated range of values in which an actual data value is likely to fall 95% of the time. For example, there were 12,280,000 married couple families in 2001. This estimate has a confidence interval of 71,000, meaning that there is 95 per cent confidence that the true value is 12,280,000 ± 71,000 or between 12,209,000 and 12,351,000.

4. Civil partnerships were introduced in the UK in December 2005.
5. Marriages of same sex couples were introduced in England and Wales in March 2014 and in Scotland in December 2014. Estimates relating to same sex married couples are presented along with opposite sex married couples within the 'Married couple family' category.
6. Families with no children and non-dependent children only have been added together for civil partner couple families and same sex cohabiting couple families to improve the robustness of the estimates.
7. A family is a married, civil partnered or cohabiting couple with or without children, or a lone parent with at least one child. Children may be dependent or non-dependent.
8. Dependent children are those living with their parent(s) and either (a) aged under 16, or (b) aged 16 to 18 in full-time education, excluding children aged 16 to 18 who have a spouse, partner or child living in the household.
9. Non-dependent children are those living with their parent(s), and either (a) aged 19 or over, or, (b) aged 16 to 18 who are not in full-time education or who have a spouse, partner or child living in the household. Non-dependent children are sometimes called adult children.
10. Families with no children are families where there are no children currently living in the household. This does not necessarily indicate that the adult(s) in the household have never had children.

15.5 Geographical distribution of the population

All Persons

Name	Code	Mid-year population estimate		
		2012	2013	2014
UNITED KINGDOM	**K02000001**	**63,705,030**	**64,105,654**	**64,596,752**
GREAT BRITAIN	**K03000001**	**61,881,396**	**62,275,929**	**62,756,254**
ENGLAND AND WALES	K04000001	56,567,796	56,948,229	57,408,654
ENGLAND	E92000001	53,493,729	53,865,817	54,316,618
WALES	W92000004	3,074,067	3,082,412	3,092,036
SCOTLAND	S92000003	5,313,600	5,327,700	5,347,600
NORTHERN IRELAND	N92000002	1,823,634	1,829,725	1,840,498
NORTH EAST	**E12000001**	**2,602,310**	**2,610,481**	**2,618,710**
County Durham	E06000047	514,348	515,957	517,773
Darlington	E06000005	105,248	105,396	105,367
Hartlepool	E06000001	92,238	92,665	92,590
Middlesbrough	E06000002	138,744	138,939	139,119
Northumberland	E06000057	316,116	315,806	315,987
Redcar and Cleveland	E06000003	134,998	134,945	135,042
Stockton-on-Tees	E06000004	192,406	193,196	194,119
Tyne and Wear (Met County)	E11000007	1,108,212	1,113,577	1,118,713
Gateshead	E08000037	200,153	199,998	200,505
Newcastle upon Tyne	E08000021	282,442	286,821	289,835
North Tyneside	E08000022	201,446	202,152	202,744
South Tyneside	E08000023	148,428	148,526	148,740
Sunderland	E08000024	275,743	276,080	276,889
NORTH WEST	**E12000002**	**7,084,337**	**7,103,260**	**7,132,991**
Blackburn with Darwen	E06000008	147,713	147,369	146,743
Blackpool	E06000009	141,976	141,400	140,501
Cheshire East	E06000049	372,146	372,707	374,179
Cheshire West and Chester	E06000050	330,200	331,026	332,210
Halton	E06000006	125,692	125,970	126,354
Warrington	E06000007	203,652	205,109	206,428
Cumbria	E10000006	499,104	498,070	497,874
Allerdale	E07000026	96,268	96,208	96,471
Barrow-in-Furness	E07000027	68,446	67,831	67,648
Carlisle	E07000028	107,952	107,949	108,022
Copeland	E07000029	70,329	70,019	69,832
Eden	E07000030	52,656	52,607	52,630
South Lakeland	E07000031	103,453	103,456	103,271
Greater Manchester (Met County)	E11000001	2,702,209	2,714,944	2,732,854
Bolton	E08000001	278,984	280,057	280,439
Bury	E08000002	186,199	186,527	187,474
Manchester	E08000003	510,772	514,417	520,215
Oldham	E08000004	225,875	227,312	228,765
Rochdale	E08000005	212,020	212,120	212,962
Salford	E08000006	237,085	239,013	242,040
Stockport	E08000007	283,897	285,032	286,755
Tameside	E08000008	220,241	220,597	220,771
Trafford	E08000009	228,466	230,179	232,458
Wigan	E08000010	318,670	319,690	320,975
Lancashire	E10000017	1,175,979	1,180,076	1,184,735
Burnley	E07000117	87,127	86,894	87,291
Chorley	E07000118	109,077	110,505	111,607
Fylde	E07000119	76,020	76,442	77,042
Hyndburn	E07000120	80,190	80,046	80,208
Lancaster	E07000121	139,665	140,575	141,277
Pendle	E07000122	89,613	90,131	89,840
Preston	E07000123	140,540	140,418	140,452
Ribble Valley	E07000124	57,596	57,858	58,091
Rossendale	E07000125	68,366	68,744	69,168
South Ribble	E07000126	108,971	108,913	109,077
West Lancashire	E07000127	110,925	111,314	111,940
Wyre	E07000128	107,889	108,236	108,742
Merseyside (Met County)	E11000002	1,385,666	1,386,589	1,391,113
Knowsley	E08000011	145,936	146,086	146,407
Liverpool	E08000012	469,690	470,780	473,073

15.5 Geographical distribution of the population

All Persons

Name	Code	Mid-year population estimate		
		2012	2013	2014
Sefton	E08000014	273,697	273,207	273,531
St. Helens	E08000013	176,114	176,221	177,188
Wirral	E08000015	320,229	320,295	320,914
YORKSHIRE AND THE HUMBER	**E12000003**	**5,316,691**	**5,337,710**	**5,360,027**
East Riding of Yorkshire	E06000011	335,887	336,007	337,115
Kingston upon Hull, City of	E06000010	257,204	257,589	257,710
North East Lincolnshire	E06000012	159,727	159,827	159,804
North Lincolnshire	E06000013	168,372	168,760	169,247
York	E06000014	200,018	202,433	204,439
North Yorkshire	E10000023	602,628	602,749	601,536
Craven	E07000163	55,457	55,540	55,696
Hambleton	E07000164	89,748	89,913	89,828
Harrogate	E07000165	158,610	158,249	157,267
Richmondshire	E07000166	53,935	53,884	52,729
Ryedale	E07000167	52,102	52,212	52,655
Scarborough	E07000168	108,632	108,223	108,006
Selby	E07000169	84,144	84,728	85,355
South Yorkshire (Met County)	E11000003	1,352,144	1,358,153	1,365,847
Barnsley	E08000016	233,671	235,757	237,843
Doncaster	E08000017	302,739	303,622	304,185
Rotherham	E08000018	258,352	258,689	260,070
Sheffield	E08000019	557,382	560,085	563,749
West Yorkshire (Met County)	E11000006	2,240,711	2,252,192	2,264,329
Bradford	E08000032	524,619	526,369	528,155
Calderdale	E08000033	205,293	206,355	207,376
Kirklees	E08000034	425,517	428,279	431,020
Leeds	E08000035	757,655	761,481	766,399
Wakefield	E08000036	327,627	329,708	331,379
EAST MIDLANDS	**E12000004**	**4,567,731**	**4,598,729**	**4,637,413**
Derby	E06000015	250,568	251,423	252,463
Leicester	E06000016	331,606	333,812	337,653
Nottingham	E06000018	308,735	310,837	314,268
Rutland	E06000017	37,015	37,606	38,022
Derbyshire	E10000007	773,522	776,160	779,804
Amber Valley	E07000032	122,746	123,498	123,942
Bolsover	E07000033	76,447	76,729	77,155
Chesterfield	E07000034	103,782	104,030	104,288
Derbyshire Dales	E07000035	71,336	71,266	71,281
Erewash	E07000036	112,809	113,170	114,048
High Peak	E07000037	91,118	91,111	91,364
North East Derbyshire	E07000038	99,325	99,281	99,352
South Derbyshire	E07000039	95,959	97,075	98,374
Leicestershire	E10000018	656,698	661,575	667,905
Blaby	E07000129	94,593	95,092	95,851
Charnwood	E07000130	168,779	170,645	173,545
Harborough	E07000131	86,389	87,450	88,008
Hinckley and Bosworth	E07000132	106,046	106,613	107,722
Melton	E07000133	50,770	50,836	50,969
North West Leicestershire	E07000134	94,018	94,814	95,882
Oadby and Wigston	E07000135	56,103	56,125	55,928
Lincolnshire	E10000019	718,838	724,453	731,516
Boston	E07000136	64,793	65,870	66,458
East Lindsey	E07000137	136,596	136,711	137,623
Lincoln	E07000138	94,588	95,623	96,202
North Kesteven	E07000139	109,263	109,906	111,046
South Holland	E07000140	88,518	89,243	90,419
South Kesteven	E07000141	135,033	136,385	137,981
West Lindsey	E07000142	90,047	90,715	91,787
Northamptonshire	E10000021	700,576	706,647	714,392
Corby	E07000150	63,073	64,212	65,434
Daventry	E07000151	78,281	78,556	79,036
East Northamptonshire	E07000152	87,365	87,969	88,872
Kettering	E07000153	94,841	95,748	96,945

15.5 Geographical distribution of the population

All Persons

Name	Code	Mid-year population estimate		
		2012	2013	2014
Northampton	E07000154	214,566	216,739	219,495
South Northamptonshire	E07000155	86,350	87,465	88,164
Wellingborough	E07000156	76,100	75,958	76,446
Nottinghamshire	E10000024	790,173	796,216	801,390
Ashfield	E07000170	120,131	121,553	122,508
Bassetlaw	E07000171	113,178	113,654	114,143
Broxtowe	E07000172	110,716	111,243	111,780
Gedling	E07000173	114,052	114,818	115,638
Mansfield	E07000174	104,737	105,296	105,893
Newark and Sherwood	E07000175	115,761	116,817	117,758
Rushcliffe	E07000176	111,598	112,835	113,670
WEST MIDLANDS	**E12000005**	**5,642,569**	**5,674,712**	**5,713,284**
Herefordshire, County of	E06000019	184,932	186,087	187,160
Shropshire	E06000051	308,207	308,567	310,121
Stoke-on-Trent	E06000021	249,903	250,227	251,027
Telford and Wrekin	E06000020	167,682	168,452	169,440
Staffordshire	E10000028	852,123	857,007	860,165
Cannock Chase	E07000192	97,940	98,119	98,549
East Staffordshire	E07000193	114,388	114,922	115,663
Lichfield	E07000194	101,186	101,768	102,093
Newcastle-under-Lyme	E07000195	124,183	125,239	126,052
South Staffordshire	E07000196	108,441	110,295	110,692
Stafford	E07000197	131,630	132,092	132,241
Staffordshire Moorlands	E07000198	97,237	97,415	97,763
Tamworth	E07000199	77,118	77,157	77,112
Warwickshire	E10000031	547,974	548,729	551,594
North Warwickshire	E07000218	62,200	62,124	62,468
Nuneaton and Bedworth	E07000219	125,805	126,003	126,174
Rugby	E07000220	100,751	101,373	102,500
Stratford-on-Avon	E07000221	120,578	120,767	121,056
Warwick	E07000222	138,640	138,462	139,396
West Midlands (Met County)	E11000005	2,762,716	2,783,475	2,808,356
Birmingham	E08000025	1,085,417	1,092,330	1,101,360
Coventry	E08000026	323,132	329,810	337,428
Dudley	E08000027	313,589	314,427	315,799
Sandwell	E08000028	311,304	314,329	316,719
Solihull	E08000029	207,380	208,861	209,890
Walsall	E08000030	270,924	272,161	274,173
Wolverhampton	E08000031	250,970	251,557	252,987
Worcestershire	E10000034	569,032	572,168	575,421
Bromsgrove	E07000234	94,285	94,744	95,485
Malvern Hills	E07000235	74,980	75,339	75,911
Redditch	E07000236	84,419	84,521	84,471
Worcester	E07000237	99,604	100,405	100,842
Wychavon	E07000238	117,670	118,738	119,752
Wyre Forest	E07000239	98,074	98,421	98,960
EAST	**E12000006**	**5,907,348**	**5,954,169**	**6,018,383**
Bedford	E06000055	159,207	161,382	163,924
Central Bedfordshire	E06000056	259,969	264,528	269,076
Luton	E06000032	205,843	207,989	210,962
Peterborough	E06000031	186,372	188,373	190,461
Southend-on-Sea	E06000033	174,838	175,798	177,931
Thurrock	E06000034	159,533	160,849	163,270
Cambridgeshire	E10000003	628,339	632,095	639,818
Cambridge	E07000008	125,155	126,480	128,515
East Cambridgeshire	E07000009	85,097	85,398	86,685
Fenland	E07000010	95,996	96,729	97,732
Huntingdonshire	E07000011	171,023	172,056	173,605
South Cambridgeshire	E07000012	151,068	151,432	153,281
Essex	E10000012	1,406,517	1,416,405	1,431,953
Basildon	E07000066	176,474	178,362	180,521
Braintree	E07000067	148,384	149,108	149,985
Brentwood	E07000068	74,020	74,460	75,645

15.5 Geographical distribution of the population

All Persons

Name	Code	Mid-year population estimate		
		2012	2013	2014
Castle Point	E07000069	88,218	88,570	88,907
Chelmsford	E07000070	169,335	170,256	171,633
Colchester	E07000071	176,008	177,626	180,420
Epping Forest	E07000072	126,080	127,170	128,777
Harlow	E07000073	82,676	83,372	84,564
Maldon	E07000074	61,918	62,166	62,767
Rochford	E07000075	83,869	83,911	84,776
Tendring	E07000076	138,285	138,721	139,916
Uttlesford	E07000077	81,250	82,683	84,042
Hertfordshire	E10000015	1,129,096	1,140,706	1,154,766
Broxbourne	E07000095	94,497	94,985	95,748
Dacorum	E07000096	146,727	148,196	149,741
East Hertfordshire	E07000242	139,458	141,076	143,021
Hertsmere	E07000098	100,710	101,271	102,427
North Hertfordshire	E07000099	128,428	129,318	131,046
St Albans	E07000240	141,899	143,094	144,834
Stevenage	E07000243	84,798	85,474	85,997
Three Rivers	E07000102	88,801	89,495	90,423
Watford	E07000103	91,732	93,736	95,505
Welwyn Hatfield	E07000241	112,046	114,061	116,024
Norfolk	E10000020	865,302	870,146	877,710
Breckland	E07000143	131,857	132,587	133,986
Broadland	E07000144	125,215	125,499	125,961
Great Yarmouth	E07000145	97,570	97,796	98,172
King's Lynn and West Norfolk	E07000146	148,628	148,758	150,026
North Norfolk	E07000147	101,790	102,043	102,867
Norwich	E07000148	134,264	135,893	137,472
South Norfolk	E07000149	125,978	127,570	129,226
Suffolk	E10000029	732,332	735,898	738,512
Babergh	E07000200	87,917	88,289	88,845
Forest Heath	E07000201	60,735	63,264	62,812
Ipswich	E07000202	134,466	134,693	134,966
Mid Suffolk	E07000203	97,611	97,973	99,121
St Edmundsbury	E07000204	111,610	111,312	112,073
Suffolk Coastal	E07000205	124,323	124,405	124,776
Waveney	E07000206	115,670	115,962	115,919
LONDON	**E12000007**	**8,308,369**	**8,416,535**	**8,538,689**
Camden	E09000007	224,962	229,719	234,846
City of London	E09000001	7,604	7,648	8,072
Hackney	E09000012	252,119	257,379	263,150
Hammersmith and Fulham	E09000013	179,850	178,685	178,365
Haringey	E09000014	258,912	263,386	267,541
Islington	E09000019	211,047	215,667	221,030
Kensington and Chelsea	E09000020	155,930	155,594	156,190
Lambeth	E09000022	310,200	314,242	318,216
Lewisham	E09000023	281,556	286,180	291,933
Newham	E09000025	314,084	318,227	324,322
Southwark	E09000028	293,530	298,464	302,538
Tower Hamlets	E09000030	263,003	272,890	284,015
Wandsworth	E09000032	308,312	310,516	312,145
Westminster	E09000033	223,858	226,841	233,292
Barking and Dagenham	E09000002	190,560	194,352	198,294
Barnet	E09000003	363,956	369,088	374,915
Bexley	E09000004	234,271	236,687	239,865
Brent	E09000005	314,660	317,264	320,762
Bromley	E09000006	314,036	317,899	321,278
Croydon	E09000008	368,886	372,752	376,040
Ealing	E09000009	340,671	342,494	342,118
Enfield	E09000010	317,287	320,524	324,574
Greenwich	E09000011	260,068	264,008	268,678
Harrow	E09000015	242,377	243,372	246,011
Havering	E09000016	239,733	242,080	245,974
Hillingdon	E09000017	281,756	286,806	292,690

15.5 Geographical distribution of the population

All Persons

Name	Code	Mid-year population estimate		
		2012	2013	2014
Hounslow	E09000018	259,052	262,407	265,568
Kingston upon Thames	E09000021	163,906	166,793	169,958
Merton	E09000024	202,225	203,223	203,515
Redbridge	E09000026	284,617	288,272	293,055
Richmond upon Thames	E09000027	189,145	191,365	193,585
Sutton	E09000029	193,630	195,914	198,134
Waltham Forest	E09000031	262,566	265,797	268,020
SOUTH EAST	**E12000008**	**8,724,737**	**8,792,626**	**8,873,818**
Bracknell Forest	E06000036	115,058	116,567	118,025
Brighton and Hove	E06000043	275,762	278,112	281,076
Isle of Wight	E06000046	138,748	138,393	139,105
Medway	E06000035	268,218	271,105	274,015
Milton Keynes	E06000042	252,358	255,692	259,245
Portsmouth	E06000044	206,836	207,460	209,085
Reading	E06000038	157,112	159,247	160,825
Slough	E06000039	141,838	143,024	144,575
Southampton	E06000045	239,428	242,141	245,290
West Berkshire	E06000037	154,486	155,392	155,732
Windsor and Maidenhead	E06000040	145,822	146,335	147,400
Wokingham	E06000041	156,663	157,866	159,097
Buckinghamshire	E10000002	511,488	516,096	521,922
Aylesbury Vale	E07000004	177,793	181,071	184,560
Chiltern	E07000005	92,954	93,250	93,972
South Bucks	E07000006	67,435	67,941	68,512
Wycombe	E07000007	173,306	173,834	174,878
East Sussex	E10000011	531,201	534,402	539,766
Eastbourne	E07000061	100,049	100,537	101,547
Hastings	E07000062	90,345	90,754	91,093
Lewes	E07000063	98,690	99,479	100,229
Rother	E07000064	91,088	91,054	92,130
Wealden	E07000065	151,029	152,578	154,767
Hampshire	E10000014	1,330,153	1,337,730	1,346,136
Basingstoke and Deane	E07000084	170,492	171,852	172,870
East Hampshire	E07000085	116,400	117,088	117,483
Eastleigh	E07000086	126,764	127,722	128,877
Fareham	E07000087	112,802	113,614	114,331
Gosport	E07000088	83,276	83,503	84,287
Hart	E07000089	92,162	92,720	93,325
Havant	E07000090	121,271	121,562	122,210
New Forest	E07000091	177,382	178,062	178,907
Rushmoor	E07000092	94,870	94,971	95,296
Test Valley	E07000093	117,032	118,372	119,332
Winchester	E07000094	117,702	118,264	119,218
Kent	E10000016	1,480,166	1,493,512	1,510,354
Ashford	E07000105	120,116	121,723	123,285
Canterbury	E07000106	153,399	155,307	157,649
Dartford	E07000107	98,940	100,569	102,234
Dover	E07000108	111,765	112,338	113,066
Gravesham	E07000109	102,764	103,752	105,261
Maidstone	E07000110	157,297	159,325	161,819
Sevenoaks	E07000111	116,400	117,035	117,811
Shepway	E07000112	108,700	108,832	109,452
Swale	E07000113	137,670	139,171	140,836
Thanet	E07000114	135,661	136,766	138,410
Tonbridge and Malling	E07000115	121,912	123,001	124,426
Tunbridge Wells	E07000116	115,542	115,693	116,105
Oxfordshire	E10000025	660,772	666,082	672,516
Cherwell	E07000177	142,822	143,659	144,494
Oxford	E07000178	152,527	154,773	157,997
South Oxfordshire	E07000179	135,541	136,015	137,015
Vale of White Horse	E07000180	122,764	123,646	124,852
West Oxfordshire	E07000181	107,118	107,989	108,158
Surrey	E10000030	1,143,509	1,152,114	1,161,256

15.5 Geographical distribution of the population
All Persons

Name	Code	Mid-year population estimate		
		2012	2013	2014
Elmbridge	E07000207	131,512	132,179	132,769
Epsom and Ewell	E07000208	76,052	77,131	78,318
Guildford	E07000209	139,710	141,009	142,958
Mole Valley	E07000210	85,846	86,309	86,234
Reigate and Banstead	E07000211	139,888	141,073	143,094
Runnymede	E07000212	82,189	83,448	84,584
Spelthorne	E07000213	96,744	97,456	98,106
Surrey Heath	E07000214	86,614	86,904	87,533
Tandridge	E07000215	83,693	84,612	85,374
Waverley	E07000216	121,884	122,426	122,860
Woking	E07000217	99,377	99,567	99,426
West Sussex	E10000032	815,119	821,356	828,398
Adur	E07000223	61,929	62,505	63,176
Arun	E07000224	151,384	152,818	154,414
Chichester	E07000225	114,521	115,301	115,527
Crawley	E07000226	108,302	108,971	109,883
Horsham	E07000227	132,160	132,878	134,158
Mid Sussex	E07000228	141,162	142,766	144,377
Worthing	E07000229	105,661	106,117	106,863
SOUTH WEST	**E12000009**	**5,339,637**	**5,377,595**	**5,423,303**
Bath and North East Somerset	E06000022	177,643	180,097	182,021
Bournemouth	E06000028	186,744	188,733	191,390
Bristol, City of	E06000023	432,451	437,492	442,474
Cornwall	E06000052	537,914	541,319	545,335
Isles of Scilly	E06000053	2,264	2,251	2,280
North Somerset	E06000024	204,385	206,135	208,154
Plymouth	E06000026	258,026	259,175	261,546
Poole	E06000029	148,615	149,009	150,109
South Gloucestershire	E06000025	266,147	269,107	271,556
Swindon	E06000030	211,934	214,037	215,799
Torbay	E06000027	131,492	132,075	132,984
Wiltshire	E06000054	476,816	479,634	483,143
Devon	E10000008	753,157	758,052	765,302
East Devon	E07000040	134,359	134,898	136,374
Exeter	E07000041	119,397	121,800	124,328
Mid Devon	E07000042	78,335	78,670	79,198
North Devon	E07000043	93,847	93,825	94,059
South Hams	E07000044	83,597	83,850	84,108
Teignbridge	E07000045	125,020	126,001	127,357
Torridge	E07000046	64,743	65,089	65,618
West Devon	E07000047	53,859	53,919	54,260
Dorset	E10000009	414,940	416,721	418,269
Christchurch	E07000048	47,987	48,368	48,895
East Dorset	E07000049	87,755	87,899	88,186
North Dorset	E07000050	69,348	69,883	70,043
Purbeck	E07000051	45,289	45,411	45,679
West Dorset	E07000052	99,532	100,026	100,474
Weymouth and Portland	E07000053	65,029	65,134	64,992
Gloucestershire	E10000013	602,159	605,654	611,332
Cheltenham	E07000078	116,080	115,900	116,495
Cotswold	E07000079	83,562	84,079	84,637
Forest of Dean	E07000080	82,731	82,937	83,674
Gloucester	E07000081	123,439	124,562	125,649
Stroud	E07000082	113,363	113,920	115,093
Tewkesbury	E07000083	82,984	84,256	85,784
Somerset	E10000027	534,950	538,104	541,609
Mendip	E07000187	109,938	110,181	110,844
Sedgemoor	E07000188	116,071	117,544	119,057
South Somerset	E07000189	163,012	163,943	164,569
Taunton Deane	E07000190	111,370	112,116	112,817
West Somerset	E07000191	34,559	34,320	34,322

15.5 Geographical distribution of the population

All Persons

Name	Code	Mid-year population estimate		
		2012	2013	2014
WALES	**W92000004**	**3,074,067**	**3,082,412**	**3,092,036**
Isle of Anglesey	W06000001	70,049	70,091	70,169
Gwynedd	W06000002	122,142	121,911	122,273
Conwy	W06000003	115,515	115,835	116,287
Denbighshire	W06000004	94,066	94,510	94,791
Flintshire	W06000005	152,743	153,240	153,804
Wrexham	W06000006	135,919	136,399	136,714
Powys	W06000023	132,952	132,705	132,675
Ceredigion	W06000008	76,046	75,964	75,425
Pembrokeshire	W06000009	123,035	123,261	123,666
Carmarthenshire	W06000010	184,317	184,681	184,898
Swansea	W06000011	239,633	240,332	241,297
Neath Port Talbot	W06000012	140,108	139,898	140,490
Bridgend	W06000013	139,740	140,480	141,214
The Vale of Glamorgan	W06000014	126,831	127,159	127,685
Cardiff	W06000015	348,493	351,710	354,294
Rhondda Cynon Taf	W06000016	235,599	236,114	236,888
Merthyr Tydfil	W06000024	58,898	59,021	59,065
Caerphilly	W06000018	179,022	179,247	179,941
Blaenau Gwent	W06000019	69,822	69,789	69,674
Torfaen	W06000020	91,372	91,407	91,609
Monmouthshire	W06000021	91,659	92,100	92,336
Newport	W06000022	146,106	146,558	146,841
SCOTLAND	**S92000003**	**5,313,600**	**5,327,700**	**5,347,600**
Aberdeen City	S12000033	224,970	227,130	228,920
Aberdeenshire	S12000034	255,540	257,740	260,530
Angus	S12000041	116,210	116,240	116,740
Argyll and Bute	S12000035	86,900	88,050	87,650
Clackmannanshire	S12000005	51,280	51,280	492,610
Dumfries and Galloway	S12000006	150,830	150,270	51,190
Dundee City	S12000042	147,800	148,170	149,960
East Ayrshire	S12000008	122,720	122,440	148,130
East Dunbartonshire	S12000045	105,880	105,860	122,130
East Lothian	S12000010	100,850	101,360	106,710
East Renfrewshire	S12000011	91,030	91,500	102,090
City of Edinburgh	S12000036	482,640	487,500	92,410
Eilean Siar	S12000013	27,560	27,400	157,690
Falkirk	S12000014	156,800	157,140	367,250
Fife	S12000015	366,220	366,910	599,640
Glasgow City	S12000046	595,080	596,550	233,080
Highland	S12000017	232,910	232,950	79,890
Inverclyde	S12000018	80,680	80,310	86,220
Midlothian	S12000019	84,240	84,700	94,770
Moray	S12000020	92,910	94,350	27,250
North Ayrshire	S12000021	137,560	136,920	136,480
North Lanarkshire	S12000044	337,870	337,730	338,000
Orkney Islands	S12000023	21,530	21,570	21,580
Perth and Kinross	S12000024	147,740	147,750	148,930
Renfrewshire	S12000038	174,310	173,900	174,230
Scottish Borders	S12000026	113,710	113,870	114,040
Shetland Islands	S12000027	23,210	23,200	23,220
South Ayrshire	S12000028	112,910	112,850	112,530
South Lanarkshire	S12000029	314,360	314,850	315,300
Stirling	S12000030	91,020	91,260	91,520
West Dunbartonshire	S12000039	90,340	89,810	89,710
West Lothian	S12000040	175,990	176,140	177,200
Northern Ireland Districts before 1 April 2015				
NORTHERN IRELAND	**N92000002**	**1,823,634**	**1,829,725**	**1,829,725**
Antrim	95T	53,835	53,978	53,978
Ards	95X	78,550	78,549	78,549
Armagh	95O	60,147	60,423	60,423

15.5 Geographical distribution of the population
All Persons

Name	Code	Mid-year population estimate		
		2012	2013	2014
Ballymena	95G	64,551	64,762	64,762
Ballymoney	95D	31,551	31,659	31,659
Banbridge	95Q	48,730	48,905	48,905
Belfast	95Z	280,537	281,735	281,735
Carrickfergus	95V	39,096	39,015	39,015
Castlereagh	95Y	67,716	67,883	67,883
Coleraine	95C	58,993	59,043	59,043
Cookstown	95I	37,411	37,552	37,552
Craigavon	95N	94,597	95,474	95,474
Derry	95A	108,586	108,610	108,610
Down	95R	70,440	70,825	70,825
Dungannon	95M	58,813	59,298	59,298
Fermanagh	95L	62,400	62,527	62,527
Larne	95F	32,191	32,220	32,220
Limavady	95B	33,761	33,886	33,886
Lisburn	95S	121,687	121,990	121,990
Magherafelt	95H	45,450	45,826	45,826
Moyle	95E	17,129	17,111	17,111
Newry and Mourne	95P	100,858	101,612	101,612
Newtownabbey	95U	85,322	85,558	85,558
North Down	95W	79,420	79,424	79,424
Omagh	95K	51,830	51,838	51,838
Strabane	95J	40,033	40,022	40,022
Northern Ireland Districts after 1 April 2015				
NORTHERN IRELAND	**N92000002**	1,823,634	1,829,725	1,840,498
Antrim and Newtownabbey	N09000001			:
Ards and North Down	N09000011			:
Armagh City, Banbridge and Craigavon	N09000002			:
Belfast	N09000003			:
Causeway Coast and Glens	N09000004			:
Derry City and Strabane	N09000005			:
Fermanagh and Omagh	N09000006			:
Lisburn and Castlereagh	N09000007			:
Mid and East Antrim	N09000008			:
Mid Ulster	N09000009			:
Newry, Mourne and Down	N09000010			:

Source: Office for National Statistics

: Data not available

At a subnational level, the population estimates reflect boundaries in place as of the reference year; for Northern Ireland the 11 New Local Government Districts (LGD2014) introduced on 1 Apr 2015.

15.6 Overseas-born population in the United Kingdom, excluding some residents in communal establishments, by sex, by country of birth [1,2,3]

January 2012 to December 2012

United Kingdom

60 most common countries of birth

thousands

	Country	Total estimate	CI[4,5] +/-	Male estimate	CI +/-	Female estimate	CI +/-		Country	Total estimate	CI[4,5] +/-	Male estimate	CI +/-	Female estimate	CI +/-
1	India	752	38	388	27	364	26	31	Afghanistan	63	11	37	8	25	7
2	Poland	658	36	309	24	348	26	32	Slovakia	61	11	27	7	35	8
3	Pakistan	477	30	245	22	232	21	33	Bulgaria	60	11	32	8	28	7
4	Republic of Ireland	407	28	171	18	236	21	34	Netherlands	59	11	31	8	28	7
5	Germany	306	24	134	16	172	18	35	Malaysia	55	10	23	7	31	8
6	Bangladesh	246	22	129	16	118	15	36	New Zealand	54	10	26	7	28	7
7	United States of America	217	20	96	14	121	15	37	Brazil	52	10	24	7	28	7
8	South Africa	209	20	102	14	107	14	38	Cyprus (European Union)	51	10	27	7	24	7
9	China	200	20	88	13	112	15	39	Hungary	50	10	25	7	25	7
10	Nigeria	185	19	96	14	89	13	40	Czech Republic	49	10	23	7	25	7
11	Jamaica	150	17	65	11	85	13	41	Mauritius	48	10	22	7	26	7
12	Kenya	146	17	74	12	72	12	42	Russia	46	9	15	5	31	8
13	France	140	16	66	11	73	12	43	Nepal	44	9	23	7	21	6
14	Italy	135	16	73	12	62	11	44	Singapore	41	9	17	6	24	7
15	Sri Lanka	135	16	71	12	63	11	45	Thailand	41	9	8	4	33	8
16	Lithuania	132	16	61	11	71	12	46	Japan	41	9	16	5	25	7
17	Philippines	125	16	48	10	77	12	47	Taiwan	39	9	14	5	25	7
18	Zimbabwe	114	15	53	10	62	11	48	Greece	37	8	20	6	17	6
19	Australia	110	15	54	10	56	10	49	Zambia	35	8	16	6	19	6
20	Romania	106	14	50	10	56	10	50	Saudi Arabia	34	8	17	6	17	6
21	Somalia	96	14	40	9	56	10	51	Belgium	32	8	14	5	18	6
22	Portugal	93	13	45	9	48	10	52	Tanzania	32	8	17	6	15	5
23	Canada	91	13	38	9	52	10	53	Sweden	31	8	13	5	19	6
24	Turkey	84	13	45	9	39	9	54	Egypt	30	8	17	6	13	5
25	Spain	84	13	38	9	46	9	55	Malta	29	7	14	5	15	5
26	Ghana	83	13	35	8	48	10	56	Vietnam	29	7	14	5	15	5
27	Iran	74	12	42	9	32	8	57	Colombia	27	7	9	4	18	6
28	Iraq	72	12	43	9	29	7	58	Congo (Democratic Republic)	24	7	9	4	15	5
29	Latvia	70	12	30	8	40	9	59	Kosovo	24	7	14	5	9	4
30	Uganda	66	11	31	8	35	8	60	Ukraine	23	7	7	4	16	6

January 2013 to December 2013

United Kingdom

60 most common countries of birth

thousands

	Country	Total estimate	CI[4,5] +/-	Male estimate	CI +/-	Female estimate	CI +/-		Country	Total estimate	CI[4,5] +/-	Male estimate	CI +/-	Female estimate	CI +/-
1	India	760	38	387	27	372	27	31	Nepal	67	11	35	8	31	8
2	Poland	688	37	325	25	363	27	32	New Zealand	64	11	30	8	34	8
3	Pakistan	516	32	273	23	242	22	33	Afghanistan	60	11	36	8	24	7
4	Republic of Ireland	378	27	166	18	213	20	34	Malaysia	59	11	24	7	35	8
5	Germany	297	24	134	16	163	18	35	Uganda	58	11	24	7	34	8
6	Bangladesh	228	21	118	15	110	15	36	Netherlands	57	10	26	7	30	8
7	South Africa	221	21	107	14	114	15	37	Cyprus (European Union)	54	10	25	7	29	8
8	United States of America	197	20	91	13	106	14	38	Bulgaria	53	10	24	7	29	7
9	China	191	19	81	13	110	15	39	Brazil	52	10	24	7	28	7
10	Nigeria	185	19	94	13	92	13	40	Slovakia	52	10	23	7	29	8
11	Jamaica	152	17	69	12	83	13	41	Russia	49	10	18	6	31	8
12	France	150	17	64	11	86	13	42	Czech Republic	45	9	22	7	23	7
13	Kenya	147	17	73	12	74	12	43	Thailand	43	9	8	4	35	8
14	Lithuania	144	17	63	11	81	13	44	Greece	40	9	22	7	18	6
15	Italy	144	17	74	12	70	12	45	Taiwan	39	9	16	6	23	7
16	Romania	136	16	72	12	64	11	46	Mauritius	39	9	21	6	18	6
17	Sri Lanka	133	16	70	12	63	11	47	Singapore	37	9	17	6	20	6
18	Philippines	131	16	53	10	78	12	48	Japan	36	8	12	5	24	7
19	Australia	113	15	53	10	60	11	49	Egypt	33	8	17	6	17	6
20	Portugal	110	15	55	10	55	10	50	Malta	31	8	14	5	17	6
21	Zimbabwe	110	15	52	10	58	11	51	Saudi Arabia	31	8	18	6	13	5
22	Somalia	103	14	38	9	65	11	52	Colombia	30	8	11	5	19	6
23	Ghana	98	14	44	9	54	10	53	Tanzania	30	8	14	5	16	6
24	Spain	93	13	41	9	53	10	54	Zambia	30	8	16	6	14	5
25	Canada	84	13	34	8	50	10	55	Vietnam	27	7	13	5	15	5
26	Latvia	82	13	36	8	47	10	56	Sweden	27	7	9	4	18	6
27	Turkey	79	12	40	9	39	9	57	Ukraine	27	7	9	4	18	6
28	Iran	74	12	44	9	30	8	58	Belgium	27	7	14	5	13	5
29	Hungary	71	12	36	8	35	8	59	Trinidad and Tobago	25	7	10	4	15	5
30	Iraq	70	12	42	9	27	7	60	Switzerland	23	7	10	4	13	5

Source: Annual Population Survey (APS), ONS

Totals may not sum due to rounding

. = no contact c = not available due to disclosure control

: = not available 0~ = rounded to zero

1. Estimates are based on the Annual Population Survey (APS) which is made up of wave 1 and wave 5 of the Labour Force Survey (LFS) plus annual sample boosts which are included primarily to enhance the geographical coverage. As some residents of communal establishments are excluded from the coverage of this survey the estimates in this table are different from the standard ONS mid-year population estimates, which cover all usual residents. For a more comprehensive estimate of the UK population, please refer to:
http://www.ons.gov.uk/ons/rel/pop-estimate/population-estimates-for-uk--england-and-wales--scotland-and-northern-ireland/index.html
APS and LFS data were re-weighted in October 2014 and March 2015 respectively in line with the results of the 2011 Census. All Population by Country of Birth and Nationality tables have been revised in the light of the re-weighting exercise.

2. It should be noted that the LFS :-
* excludes students in halls who do not have a UK resident parent
* excludes people in most other types of communal establishments (eg hotels, boarding houses, hostels, mobile home sites, etc)
* is grossed to population estimates of those living in private households. An adjustment is made for those who live in some NHS accommodation and halls of residence whose parents live in the UK. For this reason the sum of those born in the UK and outside the UK may not agree with the published population estimate.

3. The LFS weighting does not adjust for non-response bias by the country of birth variable.
4. CI+/- is the upper(+) and lower(-) 95% confidence limits. It is defined as:
1.96 x standard error
5. If the confidence interval is higher than the estimate, it is not considered reliable for practical purposes.

15.7 Long-Term International Migration, 1991 to 2014
United Kingdom,
England and Wales

thousands

Year	All citizenships 2011 Census Revisions[1] Estimate	+/-CI	British Estimate	+/-CI	Non-British Estimate	+/-CI	European Union[2] Estimate	+/-CI	European Union EU15 Estimate	+/-CI	European Union EU8 Estimate	+/-CI	Non-European Union[3] All Estimate	+/-CI	Commonwealth[4] All[4] Estimate	+/-CI	Old Estimate	+/-CI	New[4] Estimate	+/-CI	Other Foreign[5] Estimate	+/-CI	All citizenships Original Estimates[1] Estimate	+/-CI
United Kingdom																								
Inflow																								
1991	329	23	110	17	219	16	53	11	53	11	z	z	167	12	85	9	26	7	59	5	82	9		
1992	268	20	93	16	175	13	44	9	44	9	z	z	131	9	65	6	18	4	46	5	67	7		
1993	266	19	86	13	179	13	44	7	44	7	z	z	135	11	70	8	23	6	47	4	65	8		
1994	315	23	109	17	206	15	50	9	50	9	z	z	156	12	80	7	21	4	59	5	76	10		
1995	312	22	84	14	228	17	61	11	61	11	z	z	167	13	85	8	27	6	58	5	82	10		
1996	318	25	94	17	224	18	72	13	72	13	z	z	152	12	78	9	29	7	49	5	74	9		
1997	327	27	90	15	237	23	71	18	71	18	z	z	166	13	90	11	31	6	59	9	76	8		
1998	391	27	104	16	287	22	82	15	82	15	z	z	206	16	105	13	54	8	51	10	101	8		
1999	454	31	115	18	338	25	66	16	66	16	z	z	272	19	123	14	55	9	68	11	150	13		
2000	479	31	99	17	379	26	63	14	63	14	z	z	316	22	147	18	56	15	91	9	169	13		
2001	481	30	110	18	370	25	58	16	58	16	z	z	313	19	149	14	65	10	84	10	164	12		
2002	516	32	98	19	418	26	61	16	61	16	z	z	357	20	155	13	63	8	92	10	201	16		
2003	511	33	100	18	411	27	66	18	66	18	z	z	344	20	167	14	62	8	105	11	177	15		
2004	589	40	89	14	500	38	130	22	77	15	53	16	370	30	215	20	73	12	141	16	155	23		
2005	567	37	98	18	469	33	152	23	73	14	76	18	317	24	180	16	62	10	117	13	137	17		
2006	596	39	83	17	513	35	170	26	74	13	92	22	343	24	201	19	62	10	139	16	143	16		
2007	574	40	74	14	500	37	195	29	77	17	112	24	305	23	174	17	45	7	129	15	131	16		
2008	590	39	85	16	505	36	198	28	90	19	89	19	307	22	165	16	44	9	121	13	142	15		
2009	567	30	96	14	471	26	167	19	82	13	68	13	303	18	171	13	30	6	141	12	132	12		
2010	591	31	93	15	498	27	176	21	76	13	86	16	322	17	187	12	31	6	156	11	135	12		
2011	566	28	78	12	488	25	174	18	83	12	77	12	314	18	179	13	29	6	151	12	135	12		
2012	498	27	80	12	418	25	158	18	85	12	60	13	260	17	129	12	31	7	98	10	131	12		
2013	526	29	76	12	450	27	201	20	104	13	70	12	248	18	101	10	23	5	78	8	147	15		
2014	632	36	81	14	551	34	264	25	129	17	80	15	287	22	127	14	37	7	90	13	160	17		
Outflow																								
1991	285	23	154	18	130	15	53	10	53	10	z	z	77	10	35	6	18	4	17	5	43	8		
1992	281	21	155	17	126	13	38	5	38	5	z	z	88	12	31	5	18	4	13	3	57	11		
1993	266	20	149	16	118	11	40	7	40	7	z	z	77	9	34	6	17	4	17	4	43	7		
1994	238	20	125	15	113	13	42	8	42	8	z	z	71	10	31	6	14	4	17	4	40	9		
1995	236	19	135	15	101	11	38	7	38	7	z	z	63	9	29	6	18	5	12	3	34	6		
1996	264	28	156	25	108	11	44	7	44	7	z	z	64	9	32	6	17	4	14	4	32	7		
1997	279	24	149	19	131	15	53	10	53	10	z	z	77	10	40	7	20	6	20	4	37	7		
1998	251	22	126	18	126	12	49	8	49	8	z	z	77	9	33	6	20	4	13	4	44	8		
1999	291	24	139	16	152	18	59	13	59	13	z	z	93	13	41	8	29	7	12	4	52	10		
2000	321	27	161	19	160	19	57	13	57	13	z	z	103	14	47	8	32	6	15	4	55	12		
2001	309	25	159	19	150	17	51	12	51	12	z	z	99	12	51	8	32	6	19	5	49	9		
2002	363	29	186	23	177	19	54	13	54	13	z	z	122	14	58	9	42	8	16	4	64	11		
2003	363	32	191	23	172	22	51	17	51	17	z	z	121	15	59	9	42	8	17	4	62	11		
2004	344	28	196	23	148	16	43	10	39	9	3	3	104	13	53	8	33	6	19	5	52	10		
2005	361	31	186	22	175	21	56	13	40	11	15	8	119	17	60	9	37	7	23	6	59	14		
2006	398	34	207	26	192	22	66	16	44	11	22	11	126	15	66	11	42	8	24	6	60	11		
2007	341	27	171	20	169	18	69	15	41	11	25	10	101	10	58	7	31	4	26	6	43	7		
2008	427	41	173	22	255	34	134	32	54	15	69	21	120	12	66	9	35	6	31	7	55	8		
2009	368	22	140	11	228	18	109	16	53	11	52	12	119	9	66	6	32	5	34	4	53	6		
2010	339	20	136	11	203	16	99	14	58	12	37	8	104	8	52	5	22	4	30	4	52	6		
2011	351	22	149	13	202	17	92	14	49	10	37	9	110	10	60	6	21	4	39	5	50	8		
2012	321	20	143	14	179	14	75	11	41	8	30	8	103	8	53	6	17	3	36	5	51	6		
2013	317	19	134	12	183	15	78	12	47	10	26	7	105	9	53	5	18	3	36	4	52	7		
2014	319	22	137	13	182	18	89	15	51	12	32	9	93	10	42	5	14	4	28	4	51	9		
Balance																								
1991	+ 44	33	- 44	24	+ 89	22	- 1	15	- 1	15	z	z	+ 89	16	+ 50	11	+ 8	8	+ 42	7	39	12		
1992	- 13	29	- 62	23	+ 49	18	+ 5	10	+ 5	10	z	z	+ 44	15	+ 34	8	0~	5	+ 33	6	+ 10	13		
1993	- 1	27	- 62	21	+ 62	17	+ 4	10	+ 4	10	z	z	+ 58	14	+ 36	10	+ 6	8	+ 30	6	+ 22	11		
1994	+ 77	30	- 16	23	+ 94	20	+ 9	12	+ 9	12	z	z	+ 85	16	+ 49	9	+ 7	6	+ 42	7	+ 36	14		
1995	+ 76	29	- 51	21	+ 127	20	+ 23	13	+ 23	13	z	z	+ 104	16	+ 56	10	+ 9	8	+ 46	6	+ 48	12		
1996	+ 55	37	- 62	30	+ 116	21	+ 28	15	+ 28	15	z	z	+ 88	15	+ 47	10	+ 12	8	+ 35	7	+ 41	11		
1997	+ 48	36	- 59	24	+ 107	27	+ 18	21	+ 18	21	z	z	+ 88	17	+ 50	13	+ 11	9	+ 39	10	+ 38	11		
1998	+ 140	35	- 22	24	+ 162	25	+ 33	17	+ 33	17	z	z	+ 129	18	+ 72	14	+ 34	9	+ 38	11	+ 57	11		
1999	+ 163	39	- 24	24	+ 187	31	+ 8	20	+ 8	20	z	z	+ 179	23	+ 82	16	+ 26	11	+ 56	12	+ 98	17		
2000	+ 158	41	- 62	25	+ 220	32	+ 6	19	+ 6	19	z	z	+ 214	26	+ 100	19	+ 24	16	+ 76	10	+ 114	18		
2001	+ 179	:	- 48	26	+ 220	30	+ 7	20	+ 7	20	z	z	+ 213	22	+ 98	16	+ 33	12	+ 65	11	+ 115	15	+ 171	40
2002	+ 172	:	- 88	29	+ 241	32	+ 7	21	+ 7	21	z	z	+ 234	24	+ 97	15	+ 21	11	+ 77	10	+ 137	19	+ 153	43
2003	+ 185	:	- 91	29	+ 239	35	+ 15	25	+ 15	25	z	z	+ 224	25	+ 109	17	+ 20	12	+ 88	12	+ 115	19	+ 148	46
2004	+ 268	:	- 107	27	+ 352	41	+ 87	24	+ 38	18	+ 49	17	+ 266	33	+ 162	22	+ 40	14	+ 122	17	+ 104	25	+ 245	49
2005	+ 267	:	- 88	29	+ 294	39	+ 96	27	+ 33	17	+ 61	20	+ 198	29	+ 120	19	+ 25	12	+ 94	14	+ 78	22	+ 206	49
2006	+ 265	:	- 124	31	+ 322	41	+ 104	30	+ 30	17	+ 71	24	+ 218	29	+ 135	21	+ 20	13	+ 115	17	+ 83	19	+ 198	52
2007	+ 273	:	- 97	24	+ 330	41	+ 127	33	+ 36	20	+ 87	26	+ 204	25	+ 116	18	+ 13	8	+ 103	16	+ 88	17	+ 233	48
2008	+ 229	:	- 87	28	+ 251	50	+ 63	43	+ 37	24	+ 20	28	+ 187	25	+ 100	18	+ 9	10	+ 91	15	+ 87	17	+ 163	57
2009	+ 229	:	- 44	18	+ 242	32	+ 58	25	+ 29	17	+ 16	18	+ 184	20	+ 105	15	- 2	8	+ 107	12	+ 79	13	+ 198	37
2010	+ 256	:	- 43	18	+ 294	32	+ 77	25	+ 18	17	+ 49	18	+ 217	19	+ 135	13	+ 9	7	+ 126	12	+ 83	13	+ 252	37
2011	+ 205	:	- 70	18	+ 286	31	+ 82	23	+ 34	16	+ 40	15	+ 204	20	+ 119	15	+ 8	7	+ 111	13	+ 85	14	+ 215	35
2012	+ 177	34	- 63	19	+ 239	28	+ 82	21	+ 44	14	+ 30	15	+ 157	19	+ 76	13	+ 15	7	+ 61	11	+ 81	14		
2013	+ 209	35	- 57	16	+ 267	31	+ 123	24	+ 58	16	+ 44	14	+ 143	19	+ 48	11	+ 6	6	+ 42	9	+ 95	16		
2014	+ 313	43	- 55	19	+ 368	38	+ 174	29	+ 79	21	+ 48	18	+ 194	25	+ 85	15	+ 23	8	+ 62	13	+ 109	19		

15.7 Long-Term International Migration, 1991 to 2014
United Kingdom,
England and Wales

thousands

Year	All citizenships 2011 Census Revisions[1] Estimate	+/-CI	British Estimate	+/-CI	Non-British Estimate	+/-CI	European Union[2] Estimate	+/-CI	European Union EU15 Estimate	+/-CI	European Union EU8 Estimate	+/-CI	Non-European Union[3] All Estimate	+/-CI	Commonwealth[4] All[4] Estimate	+/-CI	Old Estimate	+/-CI	New[4] Estimate	+/-CI	Other Foreign[5] Estimate	+/-CI	All citizenships Original Estimates[1] Estimate	+/-CI
England and Wales																							
Inflow																							
1991	304	22	98	15	207	16	50	11	50	11	z	z	157	12	81	9	25	7	57	5	76	8		
1992	251	20	87	16	164	12	42	9	42	9	z	z	123	8	60	6	18	4	42	4	63	6		
1993	249	18	80	12	170	13	40	6	40	6	z	z	130	11	67	7	22	6	45	4	62	8		
1994	292	21	94	15	199	15	47	9	47	9	z	z	151	12	78	6	21	4	58	5	73	10		
1995	299	22	79	14	220	17	59	11	59	11	z	z	162	13	83	8	25	6	58	5	79	10		
1996	300	23	86	15	214	17	67	13	67	13	z	z	147	12	77	9	29	7	48	5	70	8		
1997	310	26	85	15	226	22	69	18	69	18	z	z	157	12	86	10	29	5	57	8	71	7		
1998	370	26	96	15	274	21	76	15	76	15	z	z	198	15	101	13	53	8	48	10	97	8		
1999	424	29	101	16	323	24	63	16	63	16	z	z	260	18	117	13	51	8	65	11	143	13		
2000	446	28	95	16	351	23	53	12	53	12	z	z	298	20	140	17	51	14	89	9	158	11		
2001	449	29	99	17	350	24	56	16	56	16	z	z	295	18	139	13	59	9	79	10	156	12		
2002	485	31	92	18	394	25	57	16	57	16	z	z	337	19	149	12	61	8	89	9	188	14		
2003	480	31	93	17	387	26	61	18	61	18	z	z	326	19	159	13	58	8	101	11	167	14		
2004	549	38	82	13	467	36	122	21	72	14	50	16	345	29	199	19	70	12	129	15	146	22		
2005	523	36	87	17	436	32	143	22	66	13	74	18	293	22	167	15	56	9	111	13	126	16		
2006	549	36	78	16	471	33	149	23	67	12	78	19	322	23	186	18	55	9	131	15	136	15		
2007	524	38	65	13	460	35	175	28	68	16	101	23	285	21	163	15	43	7	120	14	122	15		
2008	528	36	67	13	461	34	178	27	75	17	84	19	283	21	157	15	40	8	117	13	126	15		
2009	507	28	83	13	424	25	142	18	69	12	58	13	282	17	160	12	25	5	135	11	122	11		
2010	532	29	80	14	451	26	151	20	68	12	72	15	300	16	175	12	28	5	147	11	124	11		
2011	515	26	71	12	445	24	153	17	74	12	67	12	291	17	169	12	27	5	142	11	122	12		
2012	451	26	72	11	380	23	138	16	74	11	52	11	241	16	121	11	30	7	92	9	120	12		
2013	484	28	70	11	413	26	183	19	94	12	63	12	230	17	95	9	22	5	72	8	135	14		
2014	583	34	76	14	507	31	240	25	116	16	74	15	267	19	120	12	35	7	84	10	147	14		
Outflow																							
1991	253	21	138	17	115	13	45	9	45	9	z	z	71	9	32	6	17	4	14	4	39	7		
1992	248	19	135	15	113	12	34	5	34	5	z	z	79	11	29	5	17	4	12	3	49	9		
1993	244	19	137	16	107	11	37	7	37	7	z	z	70	8	31	5	15	4	16	4	39	6		
1994	216	19	113	14	103	12	36	7	36	7	z	z	67	10	29	6	13	4	16	4	38	8		
1995	216	18	124	15	92	11	33	7	33	7	z	z	59	8	28	6	17	5	11	3	31	6		
1996	238	27	141	24	97	11	39	6	39	6	z	z	58	8	28	5	16	4	12	3	30	7		
1997	244	21	125	16	120	14	48	10	48	10	z	z	72	10	37	7	19	6	18	4	35	7		
1998	223	20	107	16	116	12	44	8	44	8	z	z	72	9	31	5	19	4	12	3	41	7		
1999	273	24	129	16	144	18	56	12	56	12	z	z	88	12	39	8	28	7	11	4	49	10		
2000	291	26	141	18	151	19	55	13	55	13	z	z	96	14	44	7	30	6	14	4	52	12		
2001	282	24	143	18	138	16	46	12	46	12	z	z	93	11	48	8	30	6	18	5	44	8		
2002	328	28	168	21	159	18	47	12	47	12	z	z	112	13	52	8	38	7	14	4	60	10		
2003	333	31	174	22	159	22	47	16	47	16	z	z	112	14	54	9	38	8	16	4	59	11		
2004	311	27	175	22	135	15	41	10	37	9	3	3	94	12	48	7	31	6	17	4	46	9		
2005	328	29	171	22	157	19	50	10	35	10	15	8	106	15	55	9	34	7	21	6	51	12		
2006	369	33	192	25	177	21	60	15	38	10	22	11	117	15	62	10	39	8	22	6	55	10		
2007	307	25	152	19	155	17	60	14	38	11	20	9	94	9	53	6	29	4	23	5	42	7		
2008	393	40	157	21	235	34	126	32	49	15	65	20	110	11	59	8	32	5	27	6	50	8		
2009	328	20	123	10	205	18	98	16	49	11	46	11	107	8	61	6	31	5	31	4	46	5		
2010	308	19	123	10	184	16	89	14	54	11	32	8	95	7	48	5	21	4	27	4	47	5		
2011	312	20	134	12	178	16	78	13	42	9	31	9	100	9	55	6	18	3	37	5	45	7		
2012	286	19	126	13	160	14	66	11	38	8	24	7	94	8	49	6	16	3	34	5	45	6		
2013	280	18	118	11	163	14	68	12	42	9	22	7	95	8	48	5	16	3	32	4	46	6		
2014	285	21	124	12	161	17	76	14	44	11	27	8	85	10	39	5	13	3	26	4	45	9		
Balance																							
1991	+ 51	31	- 40	23	+ 91	20	+ 5	14	+ 5	14	z	z	+ 86	15	+ 50	10	+ 7	8	+ 42	7	+ 37	10		
1992	+ 4	27	- 48	21	+ 51	17	+ 7	10	+ 7	10	z	z	+ 44	14	+ 30	7	+ 1	5	+ 29	5	+ 14	11		
1993	+ 5	26	- 57	20	+ 62	16	+ 3	9	+ 3	9	z	z	+ 59	14	+ 36	9	+ 7	7	+ 30	6	+ 23	10		
1994	+ 77	28	- 19	20	+ 96	19	+ 12	11	+ 12	11	z	z	+ 84	16	+ 49	9	+ 8	6	+ 42	7	+ 35	13		
1995	+ 83	28	- 45	20	+ 129	20	+ 25	13	+ 25	13	z	z	+ 103	15	+ 55	10	+ 8	8	+ 47	6	+ 48	11		
1996	+ 62	35	- 55	29	+ 117	20	+ 27	14	+ 27	14	z	z	+ 90	15	+ 49	10	+ 12	8	+ 37	6	+ 41	11		
1997	+ 66	34	- 40	22	+ 106	26	+ 21	21	+ 21	21	z	z	+ 85	15	+ 49	12	+ 10	8	+ 39	9	+ 36	10		
1998	+ 147	33	- 10	22	+ 157	24	+ 31	17	+ 31	17	z	z	+ 126	18	+ 70	14	+ 34	9	+ 36	10	+ 56	11		
1999	+ 151	38	- 28	23	+ 179	30	+ 7	20	+ 7	20	z	z	+ 171	22	+ 77	15	+ 23	10	+ 54	11	+ 94	16		
2000	+ 154	38	- 46	24	+ 200	30	- 2	17	- 2	17	z	z	+ 202	24	+ 96	18	+ 22	15	+ 74	10	+ 105	16		
2001	+ 167	38	- 45	24	+ 212	29	+ 10	20	+ 10	20	z	z	+ 202	21	+ 90	16	+ 29	11	+ 61	11	+ 112	14		
2002	+ 158	41	- 77	28	+ 234	30	+ 9	20	+ 9	20	z	z	+ 225	23	+ 97	15	+ 22	11	+ 75	10	+ 128	18		
2003	+ 147	44	- 81	28	+ 228	34	+ 14	24	+ 14	24	z	z	+ 214	24	+ 105	16	+ 21	11	+ 84	12	+ 108	18		
2004	+ 238	47	- 94	26	+ 332	39	+ 81	23	+ 35	17	+ 46	16	+ 251	31	+ 151	20	+ 38	13	+ 112	15	+ 100	24		
2005	+ 195	46	- 84	27	+ 279	37	+ 92	26	+ 31	16	+ 59	20	+ 186	27	+ 112	18	+ 22	11	+ 90	14	+ 75	20		

15.7 Long-Term International Migration, 1991 to 2014
United Kingdom,
England and Wales

thousands

Year	All citizenships 2011 Census Revisions[1] Estimate	+/-CI	British Estimate	+/-CI	Non-British Estimate	+/-CI	European Union[2] Estimate	+/-CI	European Union EU15 Estimate	+/-CI	European Union EU8 Estimate	+/-CI	Non-European Union[3] All Estimate	+/-CI	Commonwealth[4] All[4] Estimate	+/-CI	Old Estimate	+/-CI	New[4] Estimate	+/-CI	Other Foreign[5] Estimate	+/-CI	All citizenships Original Estimates[1] Estimate	+/-CI
2006	+ 180	49	- 114	30	+ 294	39	+ 89	27	+ 29	16	+ 56	22	+ 205	28	+ 124	20	+ 16	12	+ 109	16	+ 81	19		
2007	+ 217	45	- 88	23	+ 305	39	+ 115	32	+ 30	19	+ 81	25	+ 190	23	+ 110	17	+ 14	8	+ 97	15	+ 80	16		
2008	+ 135	54	- 90	25	+ 225	48	+ 52	42	+ 26	22	+ 19	28	+ 173	24	+ 97	17	+ 8	10	+ 89	14	+ 76	16		
2009	+ 179	35	- 40	17	+ 219	30	+ 44	24	+ 20	16	+ 12	17	+ 174	18	+ 99	14	- 5	7	+ 104	12	+ 76	12		
2010	+ 224	35	- 43	17	+ 267	30	+ 62	24	+ 14	17	+ 39	17	+ 205	18	+ 127	13	+ 7	6	+ 120	11	+ 78	12		
2011	+ 203	33	- 64	17	+ 267	29	+ 75	21	+ 32	15	+ 37	15	+ 192	19	+ 114	13	+ 8	6	+ 106	12	+ 77	14		
2012	+ 165	32	- 54	18	+ 219	27	+ 73	19	+ 37	13	+ 28	13	+ 147	18	+ 72	13	+ 14	7	+ 58	10	+ 75	13		
2013	+ 203	33	- 47	15	+ 250	29	+ 115	23	+ 52	15	+ 40	13	+ 136	19	+ 47	10	+ 7	6	+ 40	9	+ 89	16		
2014	+ 298	40	- 49	18	+ 347	36	+ 165	28	+ 72	20	+ 47	17	+ 182	21	+ 81	13	+ 22	8	+ 59	10	+ 102	17		

Source: Office for National Statistics (ONS), Home Office, Central Statistics Office (CSO) Ireland, Northern Ireland Statistics and Research Agency (NISRA).

Totals may not sum due to rounding.

"z" - Not applicable, ":" - Not available, "0~" - Rounds to zero. Please see the Notes worksheet for more information.

1   Net migration ("Balance") figures for the United Kingdom for 2001 to 2011 have been revised in light of the results of the 2011 Census. The original published estimates are shown to the right of the table. The revisions are not reflected in the remainder of the table. The sums of the disaggregated estimates will not therefore match the revised balances. Users should continue to use the estimates in the table to analyse detailed breakdowns of inflows and outflows of long-term international migrants but, in doing so, should bear in mind that the headline net migration estimates have been revised.

2   European Union estimates are for the EU15 (Austria, Belgium, Denmark, Finland, France, Germany, Greece, Republic of Ireland, Italy, Luxembourg, Netherlands, Portugal, Spain and Sweden) up to 2003, the EU25 (the EU15 and the EU8 groupings plus Malta and Cyprus) from 2004 to 2006, the EU27 (the EU25 plus Bulgaria and Romania) from 2007 and the EU28 (the EU27 plus Croatia) from July 2013. Estimates are also shown separately for the EU15, the EU8 (Czech Republic, Estonia, Hungary, Latvia, Lithuania, Poland, Slovakia and Slovenia) and the EU2 (Bulgaria and Romania). British citizens are excluded from all citizenship groupings and are shown separately.

3   Excludes British and other European Union citizens as defined in footnote 2.

4   From 2004 onwards, All and New Commonwealth exclude Malta and Cyprus.

5   From 2004 onwards, Other Foreign excludes the eight central and eastern European member states that joined the EU in May 2004 (the EU8). From 2007 onwards, Other Foreign excludes Bulgaria and Romania which joined the EU in January 2007. From July 2013 onwards, Other Foreign excludes Croatia which joined the EU in July 2013.

Statistically Significant Increase   Statistically Significant Decrease

The latest estimates (2014) have been compared with the corresponding estimates for the period one year earlier (2013). Where changes have been found to be statistically significant, the relevant pair of estimates have been highlighted by setting their background colour.

Highlights significant changes over the last year

15.8 Long-Term International Migration, 1991 to 2014
United Kingdom, England and Wales
Country of Last or Next Residence (old country groupings)

thousands

Year	All countries		European Union[2]		European Union EU15		European Union EU8		Non-European Union[3] All		Commonwealth[4] All[4]		Commonwealth All		Australia		Canada		New Zealand		South Africa	
	2011 Census Revisions[1] Estimate	+/-CI	Estimate	+/-CI	Estimate	+/-CI	Estimate	+/-CI	Estimate	+/-CI	Estimate	+/-CI	Estimate	+/-CI	Estimate	+/-CI	Estimate	+/-CI	Estimate	+/-CI	Estimate	+/-CI

United Kingdom

Inflow

Year	Est	CI	Est	CI	Est	CI	Est	CI	Est	CI	Est	CI	Est	CI	Est	CI	Est	CI	Est	CI	Est	CI
1991	329	23	95	17	95	17	z	z	234	16	130	12	51	9	28	6	6	2	10	4	7	4
1992	268	20	89	17	89	17	z	z	179	12	96	8	38	6	20	4	4	2	8	3	6	3
1993	266	19	75	13	75	13	z	z	191	14	103	10	42	8	22	6	5	2	6	2	9	3
1994	315	23	95	17	95	17	z	z	220	16	112	9	42	6	19	4	6	2	8	3	9	3
1995	312	22	89	15	89	15	z	z	223	16	111	10	41	7	19	4	8	4	9	4	5	2
1996	318	25	98	18	98	18	z	z	220	17	112	11	48	8	22	5	7	3	9	4	11	4
1997	327	27	100	22	100	22	z	z	226	16	121	12	53	8	22	5	9	4	10	3	13	4
1998	391	27	109	18	109	18	z	z	282	20	148	16	84	11	38	7	9	5	16	4	20	6
1999	454	31	96	20	96	20	z	z	358	23	174	17	92	12	40	7	6	3	16	5	29	7
2000	479	31	89	19	89	19	z	z	389	25	189	20	85	17	35	7	10	5	18	6	22	13
2001	481	30	84	19	84	19	z	z	397	23	199	17	99	13	52	10	7	3	17	7	23	5
2002	516	32	90	22	90	22	z	z	426	24	188	14	86	10	38	6	8	3	13	4	28	6
2003	511	33	101	23	101	23	z	z	410	23	204	16	92	11	40	7	12	4	12	4	28	6
2004	589	40	153	24	98	18	54	16	436	32	249	21	96	12	39	7	7	4	13	4	37	9
2005	567	37	186	27	107	19	76	18	381	26	219	19	90	12	39	7	7	3	15	6	29	7
2006	596	39	210	30	110	20	93	22	386	25	219	19	80	11	40	8	7	2	12	4	21	6
2007	574	40	220	31	100	19	113	24	354	25	200	18	65	9	31	6	6	3	10	3	17	5
2008	590	39	224	30	114	22	89	19	366	25	196	18	68	11	29	7	10	6	9	2	20	7
2009	567	30	198	21	114	15	67	13	368	21	204	15	56	9	29	6	8	4	8	3	11	4
2010	591	31	208	24	110	17	81	15	383	19	219	14	57	8	30	5	9	3	11	5	7	3
2011	566	28	203	20	107	15	77	12	363	19	204	14	51	8	26	5	9	5	8	3	8	3
2012	498	27	182	20	112	14	57	13	316	19	153	13	51	8	28	6	9	3	9	3	5	3
2013	526	29	220	22	125	17	70	12	306	19	133	11	46	7	29	6	7	3	5	2	5	2
2014	632	36	287	27	155	20	79	15	345	24	154	16	59	9	31	6	14	5	8	3	6	2

Outflow

Year	Est	CI	Est	CI	Est	CI	Est	CI	Est	CI	Est	CI	Est	CI	Est	CI	Est	CI	Est	CI	Est	CI
1991	285	23	95	16	95	16	z	z	189	16	101	12	68	9	38	6	15	5	9	3	7	3
1992	281	21	86	13	86	13	z	z	195	16	87	8	57	7	35	5	7	2	10	3	5	3
1993	266	20	88	14	88	14	z	z	178	14	92	10	61	8	38	6	9	4	10	3	4	2
1994	238	20	76	14	76	14	z	z	162	15	81	10	51	8	28	5	7	3	12	5	4	2
1995	236	19	76	13	76	13	z	z	161	13	81	9	58	7	33	5	7	3	12	3	6	3
1996	264	28	94	23	94	23	z	z	170	15	94	11	63	8	36	5	9	4	13	3	5	2
1997	279	24	92	18	92	18	z	z	187	17	100	11	65	9	35	6	9	4	13	4	8	4
1998	251	22	85	17	85	17	z	z	167	14	83	10	59	8	36	6	7	4	11	3	6	2
1999	291	24	103	17	103	17	z	z	188	17	101	11	80	10	53	8	8	3	12	3	7	3
2000	321	27	103	17	103	17	z	z	217	20	111	12	86	11	54	9	8	3	17	4	7	3
2001	309	25	95	19	95	19	z	z	214	17	114	12	88	11	54	7	10	5	16	4	8	3
2002	363	29	128	23	128	23	z	z	234	19	123	12	94	11	53	7	13	5	18	4	10	4
2003	363	32	123	24	123	24	z	z	240	21	131	14	104	12	62	10	7	4	21	5	14	5
2004	344	28	125	21	111	19	6	4	219	19	125	14	95	12	54	9	12	5	20	5	9	4
2005	361	31	138	23	118	21	17	9	223	21	128	14	99	12	51	8	12	5	22	5	13	4
2006	398	34	145	26	118	23	24	11	253	21	148	16	114	14	68	11	11	5	21	5	14	5
2007	341	27	131	22	98	19	25	10	210	15	127	11	94	9	58	7	8	3	17	4	11	3
2008	427	41	202	38	123	26	66	20	225	15	119	10	86	8	55	6	11	4	13	2	7	3
2009	368	22	144	18	88	14	50	11	224	12	127	9	88	7	57	6	11	3	14	3	6	2
2010	339	20	136	16	92	14	38	8	204	11	102	7	64	6	40	4	9	2	9	2	7	2
2011	351	22	124	16	80	13	36	9	226	15	124	10	74	8	48	5	8	2	14	5	3	1
2012	321	20	114	16	79	13	26	6	207	12	114	8	69	6	48	5	9	3	8	2	4	2
2013	317	19	114	15	79	13	26	7	203	12	109	8	68	7	44	6	11	3	10	3	3	1
2014	319	22	127	18	87	15	33	8	192	14	95	8	61	7	38	5	10	3	10	2	3	2

Balance

Year	Est	CI	Est	CI	Est	CI	Est	CI	Est	CI	Est	CI	Est	CI	Est	CI	Est	CI	Est	CI	Est	CI
1991	+ 44	33	0~	24	0~	24	z	z	+ 44	23	+ 29	16	- 17	12	- 10	8	- 10	6	+ 2	5	+ 1	6
1992	- 13	29	+ 3	21	+ 3	21	z	z	- 16	20	+ 9	12	- 19	9	- 15	6	- 3	3	- 2	4	+ 1	4
1993	- 1	27	- 14	19	- 14	19	z	z	+ 13	19	+ 10	14	- 18	11	- 15	9	- 5	4	- 3	4	+ 5	4
1994	+ 77	30	+ 19	22	+ 19	22	z	z	+ 58	21	+ 31	13	- 9	10	- 9	6	- 2	4	- 4	6	+ 5	4
1995	+ 76	29	+ 13	20	+ 13	20	z	z	+ 63	21	+ 30	13	- 17	10	- 13	6	0~	5	- 3	5	- 1	3
1996	+ 55	37	+ 5	30	+ 5	30	z	z	+ 50	22	+ 17	16	- 15	12	- 14	8	- 2	6	- 4	5	+ 5	5
1997	+ 48	36	+ 9	28	+ 9	28	z	z	+ 39	23	+ 21	16	- 12	12	- 13	8	0~	6	- 4	4	+ 5	6
1998	+ 140	35	+ 24	25	+ 24	25	z	z	+ 116	24	+ 65	19	+ 25	14	+ 3	9	+ 2	6	+ 5	6	+ 15	6
1999	+ 163	39	- 7	27	- 7	27	z	z	+ 170	29	+ 73	20	+ 12	15	- 13	11	- 2	5	+ 5	6	+ 22	8
2000	+ 158	41	- 14	25	- 14	25	z	z	+ 172	32	+ 78	23	- 1	20	- 18	12	+ 2	6	+ 1	7	+ 15	13
2001	+ 179	:	- 11	27	- 11	27	z	z	+ 183	29	+ 85	21	+ 11	17	- 1	12	- 3	6	+ 1	8	+ 14	6
2002	+ 172	:	- 38	31	- 38	31	z	z	+ 191	30	+ 65	19	- 8	14	- 15	10	- 5	6	- 6	6	+ 17	7
2003	+ 185	:	- 23	34	- 23	34	z	z	+ 170	31	+ 74	21	- 12	17	- 23	12	+ 5	6	- 8	6	+ 14	8
2004	+ 268	:	+ 28	32	- 14	26	+ 47	17	+ 217	37	+ 123	26	+ 2	17	- 16	11	- 4	6	- 7	7	+ 28	9
2005	+ 267	:	+ 48	35	- 11	29	+ 59	20	+ 158	34	+ 91	24	- 9	16	- 12	11	- 5	6	- 8	8	+ 15	8
2006	+ 265	:	+ 65	40	- 8	31	+ 69	25	+ 133	33	+ 72	25	- 34	18	- 28	13	- 4	5	- 9	7	+ 7	8
2007	+ 273	:	+ 88	38	+ 2	27	+ 88	26	+ 145	29	+ 73	21	- 29	13	- 27	10	- 2	4	- 7	5	+ 6	6
2008	+ 229	:	+ 21	49	- 9	34	+ 23	28	+ 142	29	+ 76	20	- 18	14	- 26	9	- 1	7	- 4	3	+ 14	7
2009	+ 229	:	+ 54	28	+ 26	21	+ 18	17	+ 144	24	+ 77	17	- 32	12	- 27	9	- 3	4	- 6	4	+ 4	5
2010	+ 256	:	+ 73	27	+ 18	22	+ 43	17	+ 179	23	+ 117	16	- 7	10	- 10	7	0~	4	+ 2	5	+ 1	4
2011	+ 205	:	+ 79	26	+ 27	19	+ 41	15	+ 137	24	+ 80	17	- 23	12	- 22	8	+ 1	6	- 6	6	+ 5	3
2012	+ 177	34	+ 67	26	+ 33	19	+ 31	14	+ 109	22	+ 39	15	- 19	10	- 20	8	+ 1	4	+ 1	4	+ 1	3
2013	+ 209	35	+ 106	26	+ 46	21	+ 44	14	+ 104	23	+ 24	14	- 21	10	- 15	8	- 3	5	- 5	3	+ 2	3
2014	+ 313	43	+ 160	33	+ 67	25	+ 47	17	+ 153	28	+ 59	17	- 2	11	- 7	8	- 4	6	- 1	4	+ 3	3

15.8 Long-Term International Migration, 1991 to 2014
United Kingdom, England and Wales
Country of Last or Next Residence (old country groupings)

thousands

Year	Commonwealth⁴ All⁴ Est	+/-CI	New Commonwealth⁴ Other African Est	+/-CI	Indian Subcontinent Est	+/-CI	Other⁴ Est	+/-CI	Non-European Union³ All⁵ Est	+/-CI	Other Foreign⁵ Remainder of Europe⁵ Est	+/-CI	United States of America Est	+/-CI	Rest of America Est	+/-CI	Middle East Est	+/-CI	Other Est	+/-CI	All countries Original Estimates¹ Est	+/-CI

United Kingdom

Inflow

Year	All⁴	+/-CI	Other African	+/-CI	Indian Subcontinent	+/-CI	Other⁴	+/-CI	All⁵	+/-CI	Rem. Europe	+/-CI	USA	+/-CI	Rest America	+/-CI	Middle East	+/-CI	Other	+/-CI	Orig. Est	+/-CI
1991	79	8	27	5	33	4	19	4	104	10	23	5	24	5	4	1	11	2	42	7		
1992	57	6	17	2	23	3	17	4	84	8	21	5	18	4	5	1	8	2	32	5		
1993	60	6	18	2	27	5	15	3	88	10	23	7	23	5	4	1	10	2	29	4		
1994	71	6	23	3	27	3	20	4	108	13	26	8	29	7	5	2	12	4	36	6		
1995	71	7	23	2	28	4	21	5	112	12	23	6	27	6	4	1	13	4	45	8		
1996	64	7	19	4	27	4	18	4	109	12	20	5	32	8	4	1	14	4	39	7		
1997	67	9	13	4	31	6	23	5	106	11	23	5	23	6	5	2	15	4	39	6		
1998	64	11	20	9	27	4	17	4	134	12	32	4	37	8	4	2	13	4	48	6		
1999	83	12	24	8	40	7	19	5	183	16	57	11	31	7	7	3	15	3	74	9		
2000	104	11	30	7	50	6	24	5	200	14	50	7	24	5	12	5	30	5	85	9		
2001	101	12	30	7	51	8	19	5	197	15	37	6	25	5	6	2	31	8	99	10		
2002	102	10	41	7	46	6	15	4	237	19	47	9	29	9	7	2	33	4	122	12		
2003	113	12	40	8	58	8	15	4	206	16	35	9	30	6	8	3	26	5	107	11		
2004	152	17	45	9	90	14	17	5	187	24	18	6	27	8	9	5	29	11	104	18		
2005	130	15	32	7	86	13	11	4	162	18	20	7	25	6	7	2	19	5	90	14		
2006	139	16	23	5	102	14	14	5	167	16	21	7	23	5	8	4	21	5	93	12		
2007	135	15	24	5	95	13	16	6	154	17	17	8	23	5	10	4	23	5	82	12		
2008	128	14	31	8	80	10	17	6	171	18	14	5	28	7	12	6	30	9	87	11		
2009	148	12	31	6	101	10	16	4	164	15	13	7	31	8	9	3	26	5	84	9		
2010	162	11	23	4	121	9	19	5	163	13	14	4	22	5	10	4	24	5	94	10		
2011	153	12	19	4	122	10	12	4	159	13	12	4	23	5	6	2	26	5	91	10		
2012	102	10	19	4	69	8	14	4	163	14	16	5	27	6	7	3	24	5	89	10		
2013	87	9	17	3	55	7	15	5	173	16	18	5	21	4	8	3	25	4	102	13		
2014	95	13	15	4	66	12	14	4	191	19	15	6	28	7	20	8	34	7	95	12		

Outflow

Year	All⁴	+/-CI	Other African	+/-CI	Indian Subcontinent	+/-CI	Other⁴	+/-CI	All⁵	+/-CI	Rem. Europe	+/-CI	USA	+/-CI	Rest America	+/-CI	Middle East	+/-CI	Other	+/-CI	Orig. Est	+/-CI
1991	33	7	9	5	10	3	14	5	88	12	12	5	35	8	5	2	14	4	23	5		
1992	29	5	8	3	8	2	14	4	108	14	20	8	40	8	5	3	15	4	28	6		
1993	31	5	8	3	9	3	14	4	86	10	12	4	36	7	5	3	11	3	22	4		
1994	30	6	7	3	7	2	16	4	81	11	18	7	27	5	6	3	13	4	18	3		
1995	23	5	5	2	6	2	12	4	80	10	12	4	30	6	3	2	10	3	25	5		
1996	31	8	9	5	6	3	15	5	76	10	16	7	26	5	3	1	8	3	23	5		
1997	35	6	7	3	9	3	18	4	88	13	21	9	28	7	2	1	13	3	22	5		
1998	24	5	5	3	7	2	11	3	84	11	17	6	27	5	4	2	9	3	27	5		
1999	21	5	3	2	5	2	14	5	87	13	16	7	33	8	4	2	10	4	24	6		
2000	26	6	7	4	8	2	10	4	106	16	22	11	33	8	6	3	15	5	30	7		
2001	26	5	5	2	11	3	10	3	100	13	24	7	28	6	4	2	9	3	34	8		
2002	29	6	5	2	11	3	13	5	112	14	28	8	37	8	3	2	12	4	31	7		
2003	27	6	6	3	11	4	10	4	109	15	35	10	27	7	6	3	7	4	34	8		
2004	31	8	6	3	9	4	15	6	93	13	13	5	25	7	7	4	11	4	37	8		
2005	29	7	6	3	16	5	7	4	95	16	17	6	24	9	8	5	11	3	34	10		
2006	33	8	7	3	17	5	10	5	106	15	17	7	29	7	6	3	16	6	38	8		
2007	33	6	5	1	18	5	9	3	83	10	15	6	18	4	7	3	11	2	31	6		
2008	34	6	8	4	17	4	9	3	105	11	15	6	23	5	10	3	21	5	36	5		
2009	39	4	8	2	23	3	8	2	97	8	11	3	27	5	5	2	15	3	39	5		
2010	38	4	8	2	21	3	8	2	102	9	15	4	25	4	5	2	15	3	43	5		
2011	50	6	7	3	29	4	13	3	103	11	17	8	24	4	4	2	17	3	41	5		
2012	45	5	8	3	26	4	10	3	93	8	9	3	20	3	5	2	14	3	45	6		
2013	41	5	7	2	24	3	11	3	94	8	12	4	24	5	4	1	14	3	41	5		
2014	34	4	6	2	20	3	9	2	97	11	13	4	17	3	4	2	19	4	44	9		

Balance

Year	All⁴	+/-CI	Other African	+/-CI	Indian Subcontinent	+/-CI	Other⁴	+/-CI	All⁵	+/-CI	Rem. Europe	+/-CI	USA	+/-CI	Rest America	+/-CI	Middle East	+/-CI	Other	+/-CI	Orig. Est	+/-CI
1991	+ 46	11	+ 18	7	+ 23	5	+ 5	7	+ 16	16	+ 11	7	- 10	9	- 1	2	- 3	4	+ 19	9		
1992	+ 28	8	+ 9	4	+ 15	4	+ 3	6	- 25	16	0~	10	- 22	9	0~	3	- 7	4	+ 4	8		
1993	+ 29	8	+ 10	4	+ 19	5	+ 1	5	+ 3	14	+ 12	8	- 13	8	- 1	3	- 1	4	+ 7	6		
1994	+ 41	8	+ 16	4	+ 20	4	+ 4	6	+ 27	17	+ 9	11	+ 2	9	- 1	3	- 1	6	+ 18	7		
1995	+ 47	8	+ 17	3	+ 22	4	+ 8	6	+ 32	16	+ 12	7	- 3	9	+ 1	2	+ 3	5	+ 20	9		
1996	+ 33	11	+ 10	6	+ 20	5	+ 2	7	+ 33	16	+ 4	8	+ 7	9	+ 1	2	+ 5	5	+ 16	9		
1997	+ 32	11	+ 6	5	+ 22	7	+ 5	7	+ 18	17	+ 2	10	- 5	9	+ 3	2	+ 2	5	+ 16	8		
1998	+ 40	12	+ 14	10	+ 20	5	+ 6	6	+ 50	16	+ 15	7	+ 10	10	0~	3	+ 4	5	+ 21	8		
1999	+ 62	13	+ 22	8	+ 35	8	+ 5	7	+ 97	21	+ 41	13	- 2	11	+ 3	4	+ 5	5	+ 50	10		
2000	+ 79	12	+ 23	8	+ 42	7	+ 14	7	+ 94	22	+ 28	13	- 10	9	+ 6	6	+ 15	7	+ 55	12		
2001	+ 74	13	+ 25	7	+ 40	8	+ 10	6	+ 98	20	+ 13	10	- 3	8	+ 2	3	+ 21	8	+ 65	13	+ 171	40
2002	+ 73	12	+ 36	7	+ 36	7	+ 2	6	+ 126	24	+ 19	12	- 9	12	+ 4	3	+ 21	6	+ 91	14	+ 153	43
2003	+ 86	14	+ 34	8	+ 47	9	+ 5	6	+ 97	22	0~	13	+ 3	9	+ 2	4	+ 19	6	+ 73	14	+ 148	46
2004	+ 122	19	+ 39	10	+ 81	14	+ 2	8	+ 94	27	+ 5	8	+ 2	10	+ 2	6	+ 18	12	+ 68	20	+ 245	49
2005	+ 101	17	+ 26	8	+ 70	14	+ 4	6	+ 67	24	+ 3	9	+ 1	11	- 1	5	+ 8	6	+ 56	17	+ 206	49
2006	+ 106	17	+ 16	6	+ 85	15	+ 4	7	+ 61	22	+ 4	10	- 6	9	+ 3	5	+ 6	8	+ 55	14	+ 198	52
2007	+ 103	17	+ 19	6	+ 77	14	+ 7	7	+ 72	20	+ 2	10	+ 4	7	+ 2	5	+ 12	6	+ 51	13	+ 233	48
2008	+ 94	15	+ 23	8	+ 63	11	+ 8	6	+ 65	21	- 2	8	+ 5	8	+ 2	7	+ 9	11	+ 51	13	+ 163	57
2009	+ 109	13	+ 23	6	+ 78	10	+ 8	5	+ 67	17	+ 2	7	+ 4	9	+ 4	4	+ 11	6	+ 46	10	+ 198	37
2010	+ 124	12	+ 15	5	+ 99	10	+ 11	6	+ 62	16	- 1	6	- 3	6	+ 5	4	+ 10	6	+ 52	12	+ 252	37
2011	+ 103	13	+ 12	5	+ 93	11	- 1	5	+ 56	17	- 5	8	- 1	6	+ 2	3	+ 9	6	+ 50	11	+ 215	35
2012	+ 58	11	+ 10	5	+ 43	9	+ 4	5	+ 70	16	+ 7	5	+ 7	7	+ 2	3	+ 10	6	+ 44	12		
2013	+ 46	10	+ 10	4	+ 31	7	+ 4	5	+ 79	18	+ 6	6	- 3	6	+ 4	3	+ 11	5	+ 61	14		
2014	+ 60	14	+ 10	5	+ 45	12	+ 5	4	+ 95	22	+ 2	8	+ 11	8	+ 16	8	+ 14	8	+ 50	15		

15.8 Long-Term International Migration, 1991 to 2014
United Kingdom, England and Wales
Country of Last or Next Residence (old country groupings)

thousands

Year	All countries Estimate	+/-CI	European Union[2] Estimate	+/-CI	European Union EU15 Estimate	+/-CI	European Union EU8 Estimate	+/-CI	Non-EU[3] All Estimate	+/-CI	Commonwealth[4] All[4] Estimate	+/-CI	Commonwealth All Estimate	+/-CI	Australia Estimate	+/-CI	Canada Estimate	+/-CI	New Zealand Estimate	+/-CI	South Africa Estimate	+/-CI
	(2011 Census Revisions[1])																					
England and Wales																						
Inflow																						
1991	304	22	89	17	89	17	z	z	215	14	120	11	44	8	25	5	5	2	10	4	4	2
1992	251	20	85	17	85	17	z	z	166	11	87	8	35	5	19	4	4	2	7	3	5	2
1993	249	18	67	11	67	11	z	z	183	14	98	10	40	8	22	6	5	2	6	2	8	3
1994	292	21	86	15	86	15	z	z	207	15	108	9	40	6	18	4	6	2	8	3	8	3
1995	299	22	85	15	85	15	z	z	214	15	107	9	37	7	18	4	6	2	9	4	4	2
1996	300	23	89	17	89	17	z	z	210	16	108	11	45	8	21	5	6	3	9	4	9	3
1997	310	26	99	22	99	22	z	z	212	15	116	11	50	7	21	5	7	3	9	2	13	4
1998	370	26	101	18	101	18	z	z	269	19	139	15	79	11	36	7	8	4	16	4	20	6
1999	424	29	92	20	92	20	z	z	332	21	162	16	83	10	37	7	6	3	13	3	27	6
2000	446	28	77	16	77	16	z	z	369	23	182	19	80	16	33	7	6	3	18	6	22	13
2001	449	29	80	19	80	19	z	z	369	22	183	16	89	12	45	8	5	2	17	7	22	4
2002	485	31	84	21	84	21	z	z	401	22	179	14	82	9	36	6	7	2	12	4	27	6
2003	480	31	93	22	93	22	z	z	387	22	192	15	83	10	37	7	9	3	11	3	27	6
2004	549	38	144	24	92	18	51	16	404	30	231	20	91	12	37	7	7	4	12	4	35	8
2005	523	36	175	26	98	19	74	18	348	24	202	18	80	10	35	6	6	2	12	4	28	7
2006	549	36	190	28	104	19	79	19	359	24	203	18	71	10	34	6	7	2	11	4	19	6
2007	524	38	195	30	86	18	102	23	330	23	187	17	60	9	29	6	6	3	10	3	15	5
2008	528	36	199	28	95	19	84	19	329	23	183	16	61	10	27	6	6	3	8	2	19	7
2009	507	28	168	20	95	14	58	13	339	20	188	14	46	7	25	5	7	3	6	2	7	3
2010	532	29	178	23	94	16	69	15	353	18	205	14	53	8	28	5	7	3	10	5	7	3
2011	515	26	179	19	95	14	68	12	336	18	191	13	46	7	24	5	8	3	7	2	7	3
2012	451	26	160	18	98	13	50	11	291	18	142	12	46	8	25	6	9	3	8	3	5	3
2013	484	28	199	21	112	16	63	12	285	19	126	11	44	7	28	6	7	3	5	2	5	2
2014	583	34	261	27	138	20	73	15	322	21	145	13	56	8	29	6	13	5	8	3	6	2
Outflow																						
1991	253	21	87	16	87	16	z	z	166	14	89	10	58	7	34	5	11	4	8	3	5	2
1992	248	19	78	13	78	13	z	z	170	14	79	8	53	6	32	5	7	2	9	3	4	2
1993	244	19	82	14	82	14	z	z	162	13	85	9	56	7	36	6	8	3	9	3	3	2
1994	216	19	67	13	67	13	z	z	149	14	72	9	44	7	24	4	7	3	9	3	4	2
1995	216	18	69	13	69	13	z	z	147	12	74	8	54	7	30	5	7	3	11	3	6	3
1996	238	27	85	23	85	23	z	z	152	14	83	10	55	7	31	5	6	3	13	3	5	2
1997	244	21	78	15	78	15	z	z	166	15	90	10	58	8	32	5	6	2	12	3	8	4
1998	223	20	74	16	74	16	z	z	148	13	70	8	49	7	30	5	4	2	9	3	6	2
1999	273	24	96	17	96	17	z	z	177	16	95	11	75	10	49	8	7	3	11	3	7	3
2000	291	26	95	17	95	17	z	z	196	19	102	12	78	10	49	9	7	3	15	4	7	3
2001	282	24	89	18	89	18	z	z	193	16	104	11	79	10	48	7	8	4	15	4	8	3
2002	328	28	113	21	113	21	z	z	214	18	110	11	85	10	49	7	11	5	16	4	10	3
2003	333	31	115	24	115	24	z	z	218	20	117	13	92	12	56	9	5	2	18	5	13	5
2004	311	27	116	20	104	19	6	4	195	18	113	13	86	11	49	8	10	5	18	5	9	4
2005	328	29	126	22	106	20	17	9	202	19	116	13	90	11	47	8	10	4	20	5	13	4
2006	369	33	137	26	111	23	24	11	232	20	137	15	105	13	62	10	10	5	19	5	14	5
2007	307	25	119	21	90	19	20	9	188	14	112	10	83	8	50	6	7	3	15	3	11	3
2008	393	40	186	37	111	25	62	20	207	14	111	9	80	7	53	6	9	3	13	2	6	2
2009	328	20	128	17	78	13	43	11	201	11	115	8	79	7	50	6	10	3	13	3	6	2
2010	308	19	122	16	84	13	33	8	186	10	94	7	59	5	36	4	8	2	9	2	6	2
2011	312	20	108	15	71	12	30	8	204	14	112	9	66	8	43	5	8	2	13	5	3	1
2012	286	19	101	16	71	12	20	5	186	11	104	8	63	6	43	5	7	2	4	2	4	2
2013	280	18	101	14	72	12	22	6	180	11	94	8	57	6	37	5	9	3	8	2	3	1
2014	285	21	111	17	77	14	28	8	173	13	87	8	55	6	34	5	9	3	9	2	2	1
Balance																						
1991	+ 51	31	+ 2	23	+ 2	23	z	z	+ 49	20	+ 32	15	- 14	11	- 9	8	- 6	4	+ 2	5	- 1	3
1992	+ 4	27	+ 8	21	+ 8	21	z	z	- 4	18	+ 8	11	- 18	8	- 13	6	- 3	3	- 2	4	+ 1	3
1993	+ 5	26	- 16	18	- 16	18	z	z	+ 21	18	+ 14	13	- 15	11	- 14	9	- 3	4	- 3	3	+ 5	4
1994	+ 77	28	+ 18	20	+ 18	20	z	z	+ 58	20	+ 36	12	- 4	9	- 6	6	- 1	4	- 2	5	+ 5	4
1995	+ 83	28	+ 16	20	+ 16	20	z	z	+ 67	20	+ 33	12	- 17	9	- 11	6	- 1	4	- 2	5	- 2	3
1996	+ 62	35	+ 4	29	+ 4	29	z	z	+ 58	21	+ 26	15	- 10	10	- 10	7	0~	4	- 4	5	+ 4	4
1997	+ 66	34	+ 21	26	+ 21	26	z	z	+ 45	21	+ 26	15	- 8	11	- 10	7	+ 1	4	- 3	4	+ 5	6
1998	+ 147	33	+ 26	24	+ 26	24	z	z	+ 120	23	+ 69	17	+ 30	13	+ 5	9	+ 3	5	+ 7	5	+ 14	6
1999	+ 151	38	- 4	26	- 4	26	z	z	+ 155	27	+ 68	19	+ 8	14	- 12	10	- 1	5	+ 2	5	+ 20	7
2000	+ 154	38	- 18	24	- 18	24	z	z	+ 172	30	+ 80	23	+ 2	19	- 16	11	0~	4	+ 3	7	+ 15	13
2001	+ 167	38	- 9	27	- 9	27	z	z	+ 176	27	+ 79	19	+ 10	15	- 3	11	- 3	5	+ 1	8	+ 14	5
2002	+ 158	41	- 29	30	- 29	30	z	z	+ 187	29	+ 69	18	- 4	14	- 13	9	- 4	5	- 4	5	+ 18	7
2003	+ 147	44	- 23	33	- 23	33	z	z	+ 169	29	+ 75	20	- 9	15	- 19	11	+ 4	4	- 8	5	+ 13	8
2004	+ 238	47	+ 28	31	- 12	26	+ 45	16	+ 210	35	+ 118	24	+ 5	16	- 12	11	- 3	6	- 6	6	+ 26	9
2005	+ 195	46	+ 49	34	- 8	27	+ 57	20	+ 146	31	+ 85	22	- 10	15	- 12	10	- 4	5	- 8	7	+ 15	8
2006	+ 180	49	+ 52	38	- 7	30	+ 55	22	+ 127	31	+ 66	24	- 34	17	- 28	12	- 4	5	- 8	6	+ 6	8
2007	+ 217	45	+ 76	37	- 4	26	+ 82	25	+ 141	27	+ 75	19	- 23	12	- 21	8	- 1	4	- 5	5	+ 13	7
2008	+ 135	54	+ 12	47	- 16	31	+ 22	27	+ 123	27	+ 71	19	- 20	12	- 25	8	- 3	4	- 4	3	+ 13	7
2009	+ 179	35	+ 41	26	+ 17	19	+ 14	17	+ 138	22	+ 73	16	- 34	10	- 25	8	- 3	4	- 7	3	+ 1	3
2010	+ 224	35	+ 57	27	+ 10	21	+ 36	17	+ 167	21	+ 111	15	- 6	10	- 8	7	- 1	3	+ 2	5	+ 1	4
2011	+ 203	33	+ 71	24	+ 24	18	+ 38	15	+ 132	23	+ 79	16	- 20	11	- 18	7	0~	4	- 6	5	+ 5	3
2012	+ 165	32	+ 59	24	+ 27	18	+ 30	12	+ 106	21	+ 38	15	- 17	10	- 18	8	0~	4	+ 1	3	0~	3
2013	+ 203	33	+ 98	25	+ 41	20	+ 41	13	+ 105	22	+ 31	13	- 13	9	- 9	7	- 3	4	- 3	3	+ 2	3
2014	+ 298	40	+ 149	32	+ 61	24	+ 45	17	+ 149	25	+ 58	15	+ 1	11	- 5	7	+ 4	6	- 1	4	+ 3	3

Source: Office for National Statistics (ONS), Home Office, Central Statistics Office (CSO) Ireland, Northern Ireland Statistics and Research Agency (NISRA)

15.8 Long-Term International Migration, 1991 to 2014
United Kingdom, England and Wales
Country of Last or Next Residence (old country groupings)

thousands

Column groupings: **Non-European Union[3]** — **Commonwealth[4]** (All[4]; New Commonwealth[4]: Other African, Indian Subcontinent, Other[4]) — **Other Foreign[5]** (All[5]; Remainder of Europe[5]; United States of America; Rest of America; Middle East; Other) — **All countries** (Original Estimates[1])

England and Wales

Inflow

Year	All[4]	+/-CI	Other African	+/-CI	Indian Subcont.	+/-CI	Other[4]	+/-CI	All[5]	+/-CI	Rem. of Europe	+/-CI	USA	+/-CI	Rest of America	+/-CI	Middle East	+/-CI	Other	+/-CI	All countries	+/-CI
1991	76	8	26	5	32	4	18	4	95	9	20	4	21	4	4	1	10	2	39	6		
1992	52	5	17	2	22	3	13	3	79	8	20	5	17	4	4	1	8	2	30	4		
1993	58	6	17	2	27	4	14	3	84	10	22	7	21	4	3	1	10	2	28	4		
1994	68	6	23	3	27	3	18	4	99	12	25	8	22	5	5	2	11	4	35	6		
1995	70	7	22	2	27	4	20	5	107	12	23	6	23	6	4	1	13	4	44	8		
1996	63	7	19	4	26	4	18	4	102	11	18	4	29	7	4	1	12	4	38	7		
1997	66	9	13	4	30	6	23	5	96	9	22	5	20	5	5	2	14	3	35	5		
1998	60	10	17	8	27	4	16	4	129	11	31	4	35	8	4	2	12	4	47	6		
1999	79	12	23	8	38	7	18	5	170	14	56	10	25	5	7	3	14	3	68	7		
2000	102	11	30	7	49	6	24	5	187	13	49	7	22	4	9	4	29	5	78	8		
2001	94	11	28	7	48	7	17	4	187	15	35	6	22	4	6	2	29	8	95	10		
2002	98	10	39	7	45	6	14	4	222	17	45	9	26	8	7	2	30	4	114	11		
2003	108	12	39	8	55	7	15	4	196	16	32	8	29	6	7	3	25	5	102	11		
2004	139	16	40	8	85	13	15	4	174	23	17	5	25	7	8	4	27	11	96	17		
2005	121	15	30	6	81	12	10	4	147	17	18	7	21	5	7	2	17	5	83	14		
2006	132	15	22	5	96	13	14	5	157	15	20	7	22	5	7	3	20	5	88	12		
2007	126	14	23	5	88	12	16	6	143	16	15	8	21	5	9	4	21	5	77	11		
2008	122	13	29	7	78	10	16	6	147	15	12	5	24	7	10	5	23	5	78	11		
2009	143	12	30	6	97	9	16	4	150	14	12	7	26	7	9	3	24	5	79	9		
2010	152	11	21	4	114	9	17	5	148	12	12	4	19	4	9	3	22	4	87	10		
2011	145	11	18	4	116	10	11	3	145	13	12	4	20	4	6	2	24	5	84	10		
2012	96	9	17	4	67	8	12	4	149	14	14	4	25	6	6	3	22	5	82	10		
2013	82	8	16	3	51	6	14	4	159	15	15	5	19	4	7	3	23	4	96	13		
2014	89	10	15	4	62	8	13	4	177	16	13	4	26	7	19	8	31	6	87	10		

Outflow

Year	All[4]	+/-CI	Other African	+/-CI	Indian Subcont.	+/-CI	Other[4]	+/-CI	All[5]	+/-CI	Rem. of Europe	+/-CI	USA	+/-CI	Rest of America	+/-CI	Middle East	+/-CI	Other	+/-CI	All countries	+/-CI
1991	30	7	8	5	9	3	13	5	78	10	10	5	29	6	5	2	13	4	21	5		
1992	27	5	7	2	7	2	12	3	91	12	17	8	31	6	5	3	13	3	25	5		
1993	29	5	7	3	8	3	13	4	77	9	10	4	31	5	5	3	10	3	21	4		
1994	28	5	7	3	6	2	15	4	77	10	16	7	26	5	6	3	12	4	17	3		
1995	20	4	5	2	5	2	11	3	73	9	11	4	28	6	3	2	9	3	22	4		
1996	27	7	8	5	5	2	14	5	70	10	14	6	25	5	3	1	7	3	21	4		
1997	32	6	7	3	9	3	16	4	76	12	20	9	23	5	2	1	11	3	19	4		
1998	21	5	4	3	7	2	10	3	78	10	14	5	25	5	4	2	8	3	27	5		
1999	20	5	3	2	5	2	12	4	82	12	16	7	31	7	4	2	10	4	22	5		
2000	24	6	6	4	8	2	10	4	95	15	21	11	29	7	5	3	12	4	28	7		
2001	25	5	5	2	11	3	9	3	89	11	23	7	26	6	4	2	9	3	27	5		
2002	24	6	5	2	10	3	10	4	104	14	27	8	34	7	3	1	11	4	30	7		
2003	24	6	5	3	10	3	9	4	101	15	33	9	25	6	5	2	5	3	33	8		
2004	27	7	6	3	9	4	12	5	82	12	12	5	22	6	7	4	8	3	33	8		
2005	26	7	6	3	14	5	7	4	86	14	16	6	19	6	6	3	10	3	33	10		
2006	32	8	6	3	16	5	10	5	95	14	16	7	25	7	5	3	15	6	33	8		
2007	29	5	5	1	16	4	8	2	77	10	15	6	16	4	7	3	10	2	28	5		
2008	31	6	8	4	15	4	8	3	95	11	15	6	20	4	9	3	19	5	31	5		
2009	36	4	7	2	22	3	7	2	86	7	11	3	22	4	5	2	14	3	34	4		
2010	35	4	8	2	20	3	8	2	92	8	14	4	23	4	5	2	13	3	38	4		
2011	46	5	7	3	27	4	12	3	92	10	15	7	22	4	4	2	15	3	36	4		
2012	41	5	8	3	24	4	9	2	82	8	8	3	18	3	5	2	11	3	39	5		
2013	38	5	6	2	21	3	10	3	85	8	11	4	20	3	3	1	13	3	38	5		
2014	32	4	5	2	19	3	8	2	86	10	11	4	16	3	4	2	17	3	39	8		

Balance

Year	All[4]	+/-CI	Other African	+/-CI	Indian Subcont.	+/-CI	Other[4]	+/-CI	All[5]	+/-CI	Rem. of Europe	+/-CI	USA	+/-CI	Rest of America	+/-CI	Middle East	+/-CI	Other	+/-CI	All countries	+/-CI
1991	+ 45	11	+ 18	7	+ 23	5	+ 5	7	+ 17	13	+ 11	6	- 7	7	- 1	2	- 2	4	+ 17	8		
1992	+ 25	7	+ 9	3	+ 15	4	+ 1	5	- 12	14	+ 3	9	- 14	7	- 1	3	- 5	4	+ 5	7		
1993	+ 29	8	+ 10	4	+ 18	5	+ 1	5	+ 7	13	+ 12	8	- 10	7	- 1	3	0~	4	+ 7	6		
1994	+ 40	8	+ 17	4	+ 20	4	+ 3	6	+ 22	16	+ 9	10	- 3	7	- 1	3	- 1	5	+ 18	6		
1995	+ 49	8	+ 18	3	+ 22	4	+ 9	6	+ 34	15	+ 13	7	- 6	8	+ 1	2	+ 3	5	+ 23	9		
1996	+ 36	10	+ 11	6	+ 21	4	+ 3	7	+ 32	15	+ 4	8	+ 4	8	+ 1	2	+ 5	4	+ 18	9		
1997	+ 34	10	+ 6	5	+ 21	6	+ 7	6	+ 20	15	+ 2	10	- 3	7	+ 2	2	+ 3	5	+ 16	6		
1998	+ 39	12	+ 13	9	+ 20	5	+ 7	5	+ 51	15	+ 17	6	+ 10	9	0~	3	+ 4	5	+ 20	8		
1999	+ 59	13	+ 21	8	+ 33	7	+ 6	7	+ 88	19	+ 40	13	- 7	9	+ 3	4	+ 4	5	+ 47	9		
2000	+ 79	12	+ 24	8	+ 41	7	+ 14	7	+ 92	20	+ 28	13	- 7	8	+ 4	5	+ 17	6	+ 50	11		
2001	+ 69	12	+ 23	7	+ 38	8	+ 8	5	+ 98	19	+ 12	10	- 4	7	+ 2	3	+ 20	8	+ 68	11		
2002	+ 73	12	+ 34	7	+ 35	7	+ 4	6	+ 118	22	+ 19	12	- 8	11	+ 4	3	+ 19	6	+ 84	13		
2003	+ 84	13	+ 34	8	+ 44	8	+ 6	6	+ 94	22	- 1	13	+ 4	9	+ 3	4	+ 19	6	+ 70	13		
2004	+ 112	17	+ 34	8	+ 76	13	+ 3	7	+ 92	26	+ 5	7	+ 3	9	+ 1	6	+ 19	12	+ 64	19		
2005	+ 95	16	+ 24	7	+ 67	13	+ 3	6	+ 61	22	+ 1	9	+ 2	8	+ 1	4	+ 7	6	+ 50	17		
2006	+ 100	17	+ 16	6	+ 80	14	+ 5	7	+ 62	21	+ 4	10	- 3	8	+ 1	4	+ 4	7	+ 55	14		
2007	+ 97	15	+ 18	5	+ 72	13	+ 8	7	+ 66	19	0~	10	+ 5	6	+ 2	5	+ 11	5	+ 49	12		
2008	+ 91	14	+ 21	8	+ 62	10	+ 8	6	+ 52	19	- 3	8	+ 3	8	0~	6	+ 4	8	+ 47	12		
2009	+ 107	13	+ 22	6	+ 76	10	+ 9	5	+ 65	16	+ 2	7	+ 4	8	+ 4	4	+ 10	5	+ 45	10		
2010	+ 117	12	+ 14	5	+ 94	9	+ 9	5	+ 56	15	- 3	6	- 4	6	+ 4	4	+ 9	5	+ 49	10		
2011	+ 99	12	+ 11	5	+ 89	11	- 1	4	+ 53	16	- 3	8	- 2	6	+ 2	3	+ 9	6	+ 47	11		
2012	+ 55	11	+ 9	5	+ 42	8	+ 3	4	+ 68	15	+ 6	5	+ 7	7	+ 2	3	+ 10	6	+ 43	11		
2013	+ 44	9	+ 10	4	+ 30	7	+ 4	5	+ 74	17	+ 4	6	- 1	5	+ 4	3	+ 10	5	+ 58	14		
2014	+ 57	11	+ 10	5	+ 43	9	+ 5	4	+ 91	19	+ 2	6	+ 10	8	+ 15	8	+ 15	7	+ 48	13		

Source: Office for National Statistics (ONS), Home Office, Central Statistics Office (CSO) Ireland, Northern Ireland Statistics and Research Agency (NISRA)

15.8 Long-Term International Migration, 1991 to 2014
United Kingdom, England and Wales
Country of Last or Next Residence (old country groupings)

thousands

Totals may not sum due to rounding.

"z" - Not applicable, ":" - Not available, "0~" - Rounds to zero.

1   Net migration ("Balance") figures for the United Kingdom for 2001 to 2011 have been revised in light of the results of the 2011 Census. The original published estimates are shown to the right of the table. The revisions are not reflected in the remainder of the table. The sums of the disaggregated estimates will not therefore match the revised balances. Users should continue to use the estimates in the table to analys detailed breakdowns of inflows and outflows of long-term international migrants but, in doing so, should bear in mind that the headline net migration estimates have been revised.

2   European Union estimates are for the EU15 (Austria, Belgium, Denmark, Finland, France, Germany, Greece, Republic of Ireland, Italy, Luxembourg, Netherlands, Portugal, Spain and Sweden) up to 2003, the EU25 (the EU15 and the EU8 groupings plus Malta and Cyprus) from 2004 to 2006, the EU27 (the EU25 plus Bulgaria and Romania) from 2007 and the EU28 (the EU27 plus Croatia) from July 2013. Estimates are also shown separately for the EU15 and the EU8 (Czech Republic, Estonia, Hungary, Latvia, Lithuania, Poland, Slovakia and Slovenia)

3. Excludes migrants to and from European Union countries as defined in footnote 2.

4   From 2004 onwards, All, New and Other Commonwealth exclude Malta and Cyprus.

5   From 2004 onwards, Other Foreign and Remainder of Europe excludes the eight central and eastern European member states that joined the EU in May 2004 (the EU8). From 2007 onwards, Other Foreign and Remainder of Europe excludes Bulgaria and Romania which joined the EU in January 2007. From July 2013 onwards, Other Foreign and Remainder of Europe excludes Croatia which joined the EU in July 2013.

Statistically Significant Increase   Statistically Significant Decrease

The latest estimates (2014) have been compared with the corresponding estimates for the period one year earlier (2013). Where changes have been found to be statistically significant, the relevant pair of estimates have been highlighted by setting their background colour.

Published on 26 November 2015 by the Office for National Statistics. Email: migstatsunit@ons.gsi.gov.uk

Highlights significant changes over the last year

15.9 Grants of settlement by country of nationality and category and in-country refusals of settlement

Year	Geographical region	Country of nationality	Total grants of settlement
2014	*Total	*Total	104,057
2014	Africa North	*Total Africa North	2,062
2014	Africa Sub-Saharan	*Total Africa Sub-Saharan	28,240
2014	America North	*Total America North	4,689
2014	America Central and South	*Total America Central and South	3,612
2014	Asia Central	*Total Asia Central	2,045
2014	Asia East	*Total Asia East	6,032
2014	Asia South	*Total Asia South	38,820
2014	Asia South East	*Total Asia South East	5,152
2014	EU 14	*Total EU 14	z
2014	EU 2	*Total EU 2	z
2014	EU 8	*Total EU 8	z
2014	EU Other	*Total EU Other	z
2014	Europe Other	*Total Europe Other	5,317
2014	Middle East	*Total Middle East	4,164
2014	Oceania	*Total Oceania	3,698
2014	Other	*Total Other	226
2014	Asia Central	Afghanistan	1,724
2014	Europe Other	Albania	281
2014	Africa North	Algeria	413
2014	Oceania	American Samoa	0
2014	Europe Other	Andorra	0
2014	Africa Sub-Saharan	Angola	106
2014	Other	Anguilla (British)	0
2014	America Central and South	Antigua and Barbuda	13
2014	America Central and South	Argentina	112
2014	Europe Other	Armenia	48
2014	America Central and South	Aruba	1
2014	Oceania	Australia	2,368
2014	EU 14	Austria	z
2014	Europe Other	Azerbaijan	119
2014	America Central and South	Bahamas, The	9
2014	Middle East	Bahrain	20
2014	Asia South	Bangladesh	3,573
2014	America Central and South	Barbados	38
2014	Europe Other	Belarus	152
2014	EU 14	Belgium	z
2014	America Central and South	Belize	11
2014	Africa Sub-Saharan	Benin	7
2014	Other	Bermuda (British)	0
2014	Asia South	Bhutan	19
2014	America Central and South	Bolivia	69
2014	America Central and South	Bonaire, Sint Eustatius and Saba	0
2014	Europe Other	Bosnia and Herzegovina	33
2014	Africa Sub-Saharan	Botswana	27
2014	America Central and South	Brazil	632
2014	Other	British overseas citizens	12
2014	Asia South East	Brunei	10
2014	EU 2	Bulgaria	z
2014	Africa Sub-Saharan	Burkina	5
2014	Asia South East	Burma	281
2014	Africa Sub-Saharan	Burundi	24
2014	Asia South East	Cambodia	18
2014	Africa Sub-Saharan	Cameroon	308
2014	America North	Canada	1,040
2014	Africa Sub-Saharan	Cape Verde	1
2014	Other	Cayman Islands (British)	0
2014	Africa Sub-Saharan	Central African Republic	1
2014	Africa Sub-Saharan	Chad	15
2014	America Central and South	Chile	57
2014	Asia East	China	4,346
2014	Oceania	Christmas Island	0
2014	Oceania	Cocos (Keeling) Islands	0
2014	America Central and South	Colombia	338
2014	Africa Sub-Saharan	Comoros	0
2014	Africa Sub-Saharan	Congo	57
2014	Africa Sub-Saharan	Congo (Democratic Republic)	797
2014	Oceania	Cook Islands	0

15.9 Grants of settlement by country of nationality and category and in-country refusals of settlement

Year	Geographical region	Country of nationality	Total grants of settlement
2014	America Central and South	Costa Rica	12
2014	EU Other	Croatia	z
2014	America Central and South	Cuba	33
2014	America Central and South	Curacao	0
2014	EU Other	Cyprus	z
2014	Europe Other	Cyprus (Northern part of)	7
2014	EU 8	Czech Republic	z
2014	EU 14	Denmark	z
2014	Africa Sub-Saharan	Djibouti	3
2014	America Central and South	Dominica	24
2014	America Central and South	Dominican Republic	15
2014	Asia South East	East Timor	0
2014	America Central and South	Ecuador	95
2014	Africa North	Egypt	594
2014	America Central and South	El Salvador	5
2014	Africa Sub-Saharan	Equatorial Guinea	0
2014	Africa Sub-Saharan	Eritrea	1,915
2014	EU 8	Estonia	z
2014	Africa Sub-Saharan	Ethiopia	374
2014	Other	Falkland Islands (British)	0
2014	Europe Other	Faroe Islands	0
2014	Oceania	Fiji	227
2014	EU 14	Finland	z
2014	Europe Other	Former Yugoslavia	12
2014	EU 14	France	z
2014	America Central and South	French Guiana	0
2014	Oceania	French Polynesia	0
2014	Africa Sub-Saharan	Gabon	4
2014	Africa Sub-Saharan	Gambia, The	364
2014	Europe Other	Georgia	89
2014	EU 14	Germany	z
2014	Africa Sub-Saharan	Ghana	1,493
2014	Other	Gibraltar (British)	0
2014	EU 14	Greece	z
2014	Europe Other	Greenland	0
2014	America Central and South	Grenada	55
2014	America Central and South	Guadeloupe	0
2014	Oceania	Guam	0
2014	America Central and South	Guatemala	14
2014	Africa Sub-Saharan	Guinea	84
2014	Africa Sub-Saharan	Guinea-Bissau	1
2014	America Central and South	Guyana	71
2014	America Central and South	Haiti	2
2014	Oceania	Heard Island and McDonald Islands	0
2014	America Central and South	Honduras	5
2014	Asia East	Hong Kong	211
2014	EU 8	Hungary	z
2014	Europe Other	Iceland	z
2014	Asia South	India	17,278
2014	Asia South East	Indonesia	149
2014	Middle East	Iran	1,686
2014	Middle East	Iraq	1,279
2014	EU 14	Ireland	z
2014	Middle East	Israel	196
2014	EU 14	Italy	z
2014	Africa Sub-Saharan	Ivory Coast	129
2014	America Central and South	Jamaica	1,213
2014	Asia East	Japan	674
2014	Middle East	Jordan	129
2014	Asia Central	Kazakhstan	119
2014	Africa Sub-Saharan	Kenya	651
2014	Oceania	Kiribati	1
2014	Asia East	Korea (North)	14
2014	Asia East	Korea (South)	526
2014	Europe Other	Kosovo	170
2014	Middle East	Kuwait	88
2014	Asia Central	Kyrgyzstan	30
2014	Asia South East	Laos	3

15.9 Grants of settlement by country of nationality and category and in-country refusals of settlement

Year	Geographical region	Country of nationality	Total grants of settlement
2014	EU 8	Latvia	z
2014	Middle East	Lebanon	173
2014	Africa Sub-Saharan	Lesotho	2
2014	Africa Sub-Saharan	Liberia	41
2014	Africa North	Libya	132
2014	Europe Other	Liechtenstein	z
2014	EU 8	Lithuania	z
2014	EU 14	Luxembourg	z
2014	Asia East	Macau	2
2014	Europe Other	Macedonia	28
2014	Africa Sub-Saharan	Madagascar	4
2014	Africa Sub-Saharan	Malawi	201
2014	Asia South East	Malaysia	829
2014	Asia South	Maldives	12
2014	Africa Sub-Saharan	Mali	5
2014	EU Other	Malta	z
2014	Oceania	Marshall Islands	0
2014	America Central and South	Martinique	0
2014	Africa North	Mauritania	4
2014	Africa Sub-Saharan	Mauritius	852
2014	Africa Sub-Saharan	Mayotte	0
2014	America Central and South	Mexico	230
2014	Oceania	Micronesia	0
2014	Europe Other	Moldova	52
2014	Europe Other	Monaco	2
2014	Asia East	Mongolia	71
2014	Europe Other	Montenegro	5
2014	Other	Montserrat (British)	0
2014	Africa North	Morocco	374
2014	Africa Sub-Saharan	Mozambique	4
2014	Africa Sub-Saharan	Namibia	45
2014	Oceania	Nauru	0
2014	Asia South	Nepal	1,839
2014	EU 14	Netherlands	z
2014	America Central and South	Netherlands Antilles	z
2014	Oceania	New Caledonia	0
2014	Oceania	New Zealand	1,099
2014	America Central and South	Nicaragua	4
2014	Africa Sub-Saharan	Niger	9
2014	Africa Sub-Saharan	Nigeria	5,389
2014	Oceania	Niue	0
2014	Oceania	Norfolk Island	0
2014	Oceania	Northern Mariana Islands	0
2014	Europe Other	Norway	z
2014	Middle East	Occupied Palestinian Territories	143
2014	Middle East	Oman	4
2014	Other	Other and unknown	19
2014	Asia South	Pakistan	13,163
2014	Oceania	Palau	0
2014	America Central and South	Panama	7
2014	Oceania	Papua New Guinea	1
2014	America Central and South	Paraguay	2
2014	America Central and South	Peru	80
2014	Asia South East	Philippines	2,506
2014	Other	Pitcairn Islands (British)	0
2014	EU 8	Poland	z
2014	EU 14	Portugal	z
2014	America North	Puerto Rico	0
2014	Middle East	Qatar	2
2014	Other	Refugee	120
2014	Africa Sub-Saharan	Reunion	0
2014	EU 2	Romania	z
2014	Europe Other	Russia	1,295
2014	Africa Sub-Saharan	Rwanda	31
2014	Oceania	Samoa	2
2014	Europe Other	San Marino	0
2014	Africa Sub-Saharan	Sao Tome and Principe	0
2014	Middle East	Saudi Arabia	66

15.9 Grants of settlement by country of nationality and category and in-country refusals of settlement

Year	Geographical region	Country of nationality	Total grants of settlement
2014	Africa Sub-Saharan	Senegal	23
2014	Europe Other	Serbia	131
2014	Europe Other	Serbia and Montenegro	z
2014	Africa Sub-Saharan	Seychelles	18
2014	Africa Sub-Saharan	Sierra Leone	274
2014	Asia South East	Singapore	186
2014	EU 8	Slovakia	z
2014	EU 8	Slovenia	z
2014	Oceania	Solomon Islands	0
2014	Africa Sub-Saharan	Somalia	2,432
2014	Africa Sub-Saharan	South Africa	3,213
2014	Other	South Georgia and South Sandwich Islands	0
2014	EU 14	Spain	z
2014	Asia South	Sri Lanka	2,936
2014	Other	St. Helena (British)	0
2014	America Central and South	St. Kitts and Nevis	3
2014	America Central and South	St. Lucia	77
2014	America Central and South	St. Maarten (Dutch Part)	0
2014	America Central and South	St. Martin (French Part)	0
2014	America Central and South	St. Pierre and Miquelon	0
2014	America Central and South	St. Vincent and the Grenadines	71
2014	Other	Stateless	75
2014	Africa North	Sudan	355
2014	Africa Sub-Saharan	Sudan (South)	1
2014	America Central and South	Surinam	3
2014	Europe Other	Svalbard and Jan Mayen	0
2014	Africa Sub-Saharan	Swaziland	14
2014	EU 14	Sweden	z
2014	Europe Other	Switzerland	z
2014	Middle East	Syria	255
2014	Asia East	Taiwan	188
2014	Asia Central	Tajikistan	13
2014	Africa Sub-Saharan	Tanzania	205
2014	Asia South East	Thailand	871
2014	Africa Sub-Saharan	Togo	16
2014	Oceania	Tokelau	0
2014	Oceania	Tonga	0
2014	America Central and South	Trinidad and Tobago	208
2014	Africa North	Tunisia	190
2014	Europe Other	Turkey	2,396
2014	Asia Central	Turkmenistan	25
2014	Other	Turks and Caicos Islands (British)	0
2014	Oceania	Tuvalu	0
2014	Africa Sub-Saharan	Uganda	365
2014	Europe Other	Ukraine	497
2014	Middle East	United Arab Emirates	9
2014	America North	United States	3,649
2014	America Central and South	Uruguay	5
2014	Asia Central	Uzbekistan	134
2014	Oceania	Vanuatu	0
2014	Europe Other	Vatican City	0
2014	America Central and South	Venezuela	98
2014	Asia South East	Vietnam	299
2014	Other	Virgin Islands (British)	0
2014	America North	Virgin Islands (US)	0
2014	Oceania	Wallis and Futuna	0
2014	Africa North	Western Sahara	0
2014	Middle East	Yemen	114
2014	Africa Sub-Saharan	Zambia	196
2014	Africa Sub-Saharan	Zimbabwe	8,534

Source: Home Office Immigration Statistics

z = Not applicable.
: = Not available.

15.10 Asylum applications and initial decisions for main applicants, by country of nationality

Year	Geographical region	Country of nationality	Total applications
2014	*Total	*Total	25,033
2014	**Africa North**	***Total Africa North**	**2,284**
2014	**Africa Sub-Saharan**	***Total Africa Sub-Saharan**	**6,585**
2014	**America North**	***Total America North**	**38**
2014	**America Central and South**	***Total America Central and South**	**291**
2014	**Asia Central**	***Total Asia Central**	**1,168**
2014	**Asia East**	***Total Asia East**	**691**
2014	**Asia South**	***Total Asia South**	**5,517**
2014	**Asia South East**	***Total Asia South East**	**634**
2014	**EU 14**	***Total EU 14**	**18**
2014	**EU 2**	***Total EU 2**	**8**
2014	**EU 8**	***Total EU 8**	**186**
2014	**EU Other**	***Total EU Other**	**1**
2014	**Europe Other**	***Total Europe Other**	**2,220**
2014	**Middle East**	***Total Middle East**	**5,039**
2014	**Oceania**	***Total Oceania**	**10**
2014	**Other**	***Total Other**	**343**
2014	Asia Central	Afghanistan	1,139
2014	Europe Other	Albania	1,576
2014	Africa North	Algeria	125
2014	Oceania	American Samoa	0
2014	Europe Other	Andorra	0
2014	Africa Sub-Saharan	Angola	39
2014	Other	Anguilla (British)	0
2014	America Central and South	Antigua and Barbuda	3
2014	America Central and South	Argentina	1
2014	Europe Other	Armenia	11
2014	America Central and South	Aruba	0
2014	Oceania	Australia	6
2014	EU 14	Austria	0
2014	Europe Other	Azerbaijan	5
2014	America Central and South	Bahamas, The	0
2014	Middle East	Bahrain	13
2014	Asia South	Bangladesh	748
2014	America Central and South	Barbados	7
2014	Europe Other	Belarus	19
2014	EU 14	Belgium	1
2014	America Central and South	Belize	1
2014	Africa Sub-Saharan	Benin	3
2014	Other	Bermuda (British)	0
2014	Asia South	Bhutan	3
2014	America Central and South	Bolivia	6
2014	America Central and South	Bonaire, Sint Eustatius and Saba	0
2014	Europe Other	Bosnia and Herzegovina	2
2014	Africa Sub-Saharan	Botswana	12
2014	America Central and South	Brazil	19
2014	Other	British overseas citizens	3
2014	Asia South East	Brunei	0
2014	EU 2	Bulgaria	1
2014	Africa Sub-Saharan	Burkina	0
2014	Asia South East	Burma	151
2014	Africa Sub-Saharan	Burundi	3
2014	Asia South East	Cambodia	0
2014	Africa Sub-Saharan	Cameroon	133
2014	America North	Canada	6
2014	Africa Sub-Saharan	Cape Verde	0
2014	Other	Cayman Islands (British)	0
2014	Africa Sub-Saharan	Central African Republic	8
2014	Africa Sub-Saharan	Chad	9
2014	America Central and South	Chile	2
2014	Asia East	China	643
2014	Oceania	Christmas Island	0
2014	Oceania	Cocos (Keeling) Islands	0
2014	America Central and South	Colombia	7
2014	Africa Sub-Saharan	Comoros	0
2014	Africa Sub-Saharan	Congo	21
2014	Africa Sub-Saharan	Congo (Democratic Republic)	211
2014	Oceania	Cook Islands	0
2014	America Central and South	Costa Rica	3
2014	EU Other	Croatia	1
2014	America Central and South	Cuba	2
2014	America Central and South	Curacao	0
2014	EU Other	Cyprus	0

15.10 Asylum applications and initial decisions for main applicants, by country of nationality

Year	Geographical region	Country of nationality	Total applications
2014	Europe Other	Cyprus (Northern part of)	1
2014	EU 8	Czech Republic	8
2014	EU 14	Denmark	0
2014	Africa Sub-Saharan	Djibouti	1
2014	America Central and South	Dominica	0
2014	America Central and South	Dominican Republic	1
2014	Asia South East	East Timor	0
2014	America Central and South	Ecuador	2
2014	Africa North	Egypt	274
2014	America Central and South	El Salvador	11
2014	Africa Sub-Saharan	Equatorial Guinea	2
2014	Africa Sub-Saharan	Eritrea	3,233
2014	EU 8	Estonia	0
2014	Africa Sub-Saharan	Ethiopia	250
2014	Other	Falkland Islands (British)	0
2014	Europe Other	Faroe Islands	0
2014	Oceania	Fiji	2
2014	EU 14	Finland	0
2014	Europe Other	Former Yugoslavia	1
2014	EU 14	France	4
2014	America Central and South	French Guiana	0
2014	Oceania	French Polynesia	0
2014	Africa Sub-Saharan	Gabon	0
2014	Africa Sub-Saharan	Gambia, The	194
2014	Europe Other	Georgia	31
2014	EU 14	Germany	3
2014	Africa Sub-Saharan	Ghana	132
2014	Other	Gibraltar (British)	0
2014	EU 14	Greece	1
2014	Europe Other	Greenland	0
2014	America Central and South	Grenada	4
2014	America Central and South	Guadeloupe	0
2014	Oceania	Guam	0
2014	America Central and South	Guatemala	1
2014	Africa Sub-Saharan	Guinea	30
2014	Africa Sub-Saharan	Guinea-Bissau	1
2014	America Central and South	Guyana	4
2014	America Central and South	Haiti	2
2014	Oceania	Heard Island and McDonald Islands	0
2014	America Central and South	Honduras	12
2014	Asia East	Hong Kong	2
2014	EU 8	Hungary	4
2014	Europe Other	Iceland	0
2014	Asia South	India	703
2014	Asia South East	Indonesia	5
2014	Middle East	Iran	2,000
2014	Middle East	Iraq	588
2014	EU 14	Ireland	1
2014	Middle East	Israel	4
2014	EU 14	Italy	0
2014	Africa Sub-Saharan	Ivory Coast	44
2014	America Central and South	Jamaica	133
2014	Asia East	Japan	2
2014	Middle East	Jordan	29
2014	Asia Central	Kazakhstan	3
2014	Africa Sub-Saharan	Kenya	64
2014	Oceania	Kiribati	0
2014	Asia East	Korea (North)	23
2014	Asia East	Korea (South)	7
2014	Europe Other	Kosovo	24
2014	Middle East	Kuwait	71
2014	Asia Central	Kyrgyzstan	5
2014	Asia South East	Laos	1
2014	EU 8	Latvia	11
2014	Middle East	Lebanon	47
2014	Africa Sub-Saharan	Lesotho	1
2014	Africa Sub-Saharan	Liberia	6
2014	Africa North	Libya	328
2014	Europe Other	Liechtenstein	0
2014	EU 8	Lithuania	20
2014	EU 14	Luxembourg	0
2014	Asia East	Macau	0
2014	Europe Other	Macedonia	3

15.10 Asylum applications and initial decisions for main applicants, by country of nationality

Year	Geographical region	Country of nationality	Total applications
2014	Africa Sub-Saharan	Madagascar	1
2014	Africa Sub-Saharan	Malawi	85
2014	Asia South East	Malaysia	52
2014	Asia South	Maldives	2
2014	Africa Sub-Saharan	Mali	15
2014	EU Other	Malta	0
2014	Oceania	Marshall Islands	0
2014	America Central and South	Martinique	0
2014	Africa North	Mauritania	3
2014	Africa Sub-Saharan	Mauritius	32
2014	Africa Sub-Saharan	Mayotte	0
2014	America Central and South	Mexico	9
2014	Oceania	Micronesia	0
2014	Europe Other	Moldova	1
2014	Europe Other	Monaco	0
2014	Asia East	Mongolia	14
2014	Europe Other	Montenegro	0
2014	Other	Montserrat (British)	0
2014	Africa North	Morocco	63
2014	Africa Sub-Saharan	Mozambique	0
2014	Africa Sub-Saharan	Namibia	23
2014	Oceania	Nauru	0
2014	Asia South	Nepal	43
2014	EU 14	Netherlands	1
2014	America Central and South	Netherlands Antilles	z
2014	Oceania	New Caledonia	0
2014	Oceania	New Zealand	1
2014	America Central and South	Nicaragua	2
2014	Africa Sub-Saharan	Niger	4
2014	Africa Sub-Saharan	Nigeria	899
2014	Oceania	Niue	0
2014	Oceania	Norfolk Island	0
2014	Oceania	Northern Mariana Islands	0
2014	Europe Other	Norway	0
2014	Middle East	Occupied Palestinian Territories	157
2014	Middle East	Oman	9
2014	Other	Other and unknown	6
2014	Asia South	Pakistan	2,726
2014	Oceania	Palau	0
2014	America Central and South	Panama	1
2014	Oceania	Papua New Guinea	0
2014	America Central and South	Paraguay	0
2014	America Central and South	Peru	0
2014	Asia South East	Philippines	29
2014	Other	Pitcairn Islands (British)	0
2014	EU 8	Poland	141
2014	EU 14	Portugal	6
2014	America North	Puerto Rico	0
2014	Middle East	Qatar	2
2014	Other	Refugee	118
2014	Africa Sub-Saharan	Reunion	0
2014	EU 2	Romania	7
2014	Europe Other	Russia	67
2014	Africa Sub-Saharan	Rwanda	15
2014	Oceania	Samoa	0
2014	Europe Other	San Marino	0
2014	Africa Sub-Saharan	Sao Tome and Principe	0
2014	Middle East	Saudi Arabia	18
2014	Africa Sub-Saharan	Senegal	23
2014	Europe Other	Serbia	0
2014	Europe Other	Serbia and Montenegro	z
2014	Africa Sub-Saharan	Seychelles	5
2014	Africa Sub-Saharan	Sierra Leone	66
2014	Asia South East	Singapore	4
2014	EU 8	Slovakia	2
2014	EU 8	Slovenia	0
2014	Oceania	Solomon Islands	0
2014	Africa Sub-Saharan	Somalia	333
2014	Africa Sub-Saharan	South Africa	59
2014	Other	South Georgia and South Sandwich Islar	0
2014	EU 14	Spain	1
2014	Asia South	Sri Lanka	1,292
2014	Other	St. Helena (British)	0

15.10 Asylum applications and initial decisions for main applicants, by country of nationality

Year	Geographical region	Country of nationality	Total applications
2014	America Central and South	St. Kitts and Nevis	2
2014	America Central and South	St. Lucia	2
2014	America Central and South	St. Maarten (Dutch Part)	0
2014	America Central and South	St. Martin (French Part)	0
2014	America Central and South	St. Pierre and Miquelon	0
2014	America Central and South	St. Vincent and the Grenadines	5
2014	Other	Stateless	216
2014	Africa North	Sudan	1,449
2014	Africa Sub-Saharan	Sudan (South)	8
2014	America Central and South	Surinam	0
2014	Europe Other	Svalbard and Jan Mayen	0
2014	Africa Sub-Saharan	Swaziland	22
2014	EU 14	Sweden	0
2014	Europe Other	Switzerland	0
2014	Middle East	Syria	2,025
2014	Asia East	Taiwan	0
2014	Asia Central	Tajikistan	1
2014	Africa Sub-Saharan	Tanzania	27
2014	Asia South East	Thailand	11
2014	Africa Sub-Saharan	Togo	1
2014	Oceania	Tokelau	0
2014	Oceania	Tonga	1
2014	America Central and South	Trinidad and Tobago	18
2014	Africa North	Tunisia	40
2014	Europe Other	Turkey	271
2014	Asia Central	Turkmenistan	5
2014	Other	Turks and Caicos Islands (British)	0
2014	Oceania	Tuvalu	0
2014	Africa Sub-Saharan	Uganda	256
2014	Europe Other	Ukraine	208
2014	Middle East	United Arab Emirates	10
2014	America North	United States	32
2014	America Central and South	Uruguay	1
2014	Asia Central	Uzbekistan	15
2014	Oceania	Vanuatu	0
2014	Europe Other	Vatican City	0
2014	America Central and South	Venezuela	30
2014	Asia South East	Vietnam	381
2014	Other	Virgin Islands (British)	0
2014	America North	Virgin Islands (US)	0
2014	Oceania	Wallis and Futuna	0
2014	Africa North	Western Sahara	2
2014	Middle East	Yemen	66
2014	Africa Sub-Saharan	Zambia	28
2014	Africa Sub-Saharan	Zimbabwe	286

Source: Home Office Immigration Statistics

z = Not applicable.

: = Not available.

Figures shown for 1989 to 1993 were rounded to the nearest 5 (- = 0, * = 1 or 2) and may not sum to the totals shown because of independent rounding. Data, after April 2000 for asylum applications and May 2000 for asylum decisions, have been taken from the Asylum Case Information Database. Prior to this date manual counts were taken.

The tables do not include grants of asylum or ELR (exceptional leave to remain) or refusals on non-compliance grounds under the backlog criteria in 1999 and 2000 which aimed to reduce the pre-1996 asylum application backlog.

Fresh claims' are when a human rights or asylum claim has been refused, withdrawn or treated as withdrawn under paragraph 333C of Immigration Rule 353 and any appeal relating to that claim is no longer pending, the decision maker will consider any further submissions and, if rejected, will then determine whether they amount to a fresh claim. The submissions will amount to a fresh claim if they are significantly different from the material that has previously been considered. The submissions will only be significantly different if the content: had not already been considered; and taken together with the previously considered material, created a realistic prospect of success, not withstanding its rejection.

'Pending' cases are those asylum applications, including fresh claims, lodged since 1 April 2006 which are still under consideration at the end of the reference period.

15.11 Number of marriages by type of ceremony and denomination, 1837 to 2013
England and Wales

Year (selected years only prior to 1962 [1])	All marriages	Marriages of opposite sex couples						
		Civil ceremonies		Religious ceremonies				
		All	Approved Premises [2]	All	Church of England and Church in Wales	Roman Catholic	Other Christian denominations [3]	Other [4]
2013	240,854	172,254	147,875	68,600	50,226	7,550	8,035	2,789
2012	263,640	184,167	156,548	79,473	58,797	8,664	9,027	2,985
2011	249,133	174,681	143,296	74,452	54,463	8,390	8,844	2,755
2010	243,808	165,680	125,612	78,128	57,607	8,622	9,032	2,867
2009	232,443	155,950	111,313	76,493	56,236	8,426	8,973	2,858
2008	235,794	157,296	106,298	78,498	57,057	8,909	9,745	2,787
2007	235,367	156,198	101,158	79,169	57,101	8,904	10,351	2,813
2006	239,454	158,350	95,763	81,104	57,963	9,263	11,249	2,629
2005	247,805	162,169	90,239	85,636	61,155	9,599	12,315	2,567
2004	273,069	184,913	85,154	88,156	62,006	9,850	13,578	2,722
2003	270,109	183,124	73,784	86,985	60,385	9,858	14,188	2,554
2002	255,596	169,210	61,749	86,386	58,980	10,044	14,844	2,518
2001	249,227	160,238	50,149	88,989	60,878	10,518	15,210	2,383
2000	267,961	170,800	45,792	97,161	65,536	11,312	17,751	2,562
1999	263,515	162,679	37,709	100,836	67,219	12,399	18,690	2,528
1998	267,303	163,072	28,879	104,231	69,494	12,615	19,746	2,376
1997	272,536	165,516	22,052	107,020	70,310	13,125	21,211	2,374
1996	278,975	164,158	15,210	114,817	75,147	13,989	23,605	2,076
1995 [2]	283,012	155,490	2,496	127,522	83,685	15,181	26,622	2,034
1994	291,069	152,113	z	138,956	90,703	16,429	29,807	2,017
1993	299,197	152,930	z	146,267	96,060	17,465	30,804	1,938
1992	311,564	156,967	z	154,597	101,883	18,795	32,006	1,913
1991	306,756	151,333	z	155,423	102,840	19,551	31,069	1,963
1990	331,150	156,875	z	174,275	115,328	22,455	34,599	1,893
1989	346,697	166,651	z	180,046	118,956	23,737	35,551	1,802
1988	348,492	168,897	z	179,595	118,423	24,372	34,975	1,825
1987	351,761	168,190	z	183,571	121,293	25,020	35,589	1,669
1986	347,924	168,255	z	179,669	117,804	24,578	35,507	1,780
1985	346,389	169,025	z	177,364	116,378	25,207	33,938	1,841
1984	349,186	170,506	z	178,680	117,506	25,609	33,866	1,699
1983	344,334	167,327	z	177,007	116,854	25,211	33,252	1,690
1982	342,166	165,089	z	177,077	116,978	24,834	33,835	1,430
1981	351,973	172,514	z	179,459	118,435	26,097	33,439	1,488
1980	370,022	183,395	z	186,627	123,400	28,553	33,164	1,510
1979	368,853	187,381	z	181,472	119,420	28,477	32,007	1,568
1978	368,258	186,239	z	182,019	119,970	28,654	31,882	1,513
1977	356,954	180,446	z	176,508	116,749	28,204	30,008	1,547
1976	358,567	179,330	z	179,237	119,569	28,714	29,462	1,492
1975	380,620	181,824	z	198,796	133,074	32,307	31,845	1,570
1974 [5]	384,389	178,710	z	205,679	137,767	33,702	34,210	
1973	400,435	184,724	z	215,711	143,853	36,267	35,591	
1972	426,241	194,134	z	232,107	155,538	39,694	36,875	
1971	404,737	167,101	z	237,636	160,165	41,399	36,072	
1970	415,487	164,119	z	251,368	170,146	43,658	37,564	
1969	396,746	143,115	z	253,631	172,067	43,441	38,123	
1968	407,822	144,572	z	263,250	178,700	44,931	39,619	
1967	386,052	131,576	z	254,476	173,278	43,305	37,893	
1966	384,497	127,502	z	256,995	175,254	43,814	37,927	
1965	371,127	118,034	z	253,093	171,848	43,192	38,053	
1964	359,307	111,053	z	248,254	167,742	42,525	37,987	
1963	351,329	107,384	z	243,945	163,837	42,272	37,836	
1962	347,732	103,102	z	244,630	164,707	42,788	37,135	
1957	346,903	97,084	z	249,819	172,010	39,960	37,849	
1952	349,308	106,777	z	242,531	173,282	33,050	36,199	
1934	342,307	97,120	z	245,187	183,123	22,323	39,741	
1929	313,316	80,475	z	232,841	176,113	18,711	38,017	
1924	296,416	70,604	z	225,812	171,480	16,286	38,046	
1919	369,411	85,330	z	284,081	220,557	19,078	44,446	
1914	294,401	70,880	z	223,521	171,700	13,729	38,092	
1913	286,583	62,328	z	224,255	172,640	13,349	38,266	
1912	283,834	58,367	z	225,467	174,357	12,715	38,395	
1911	274,943	57,435	z	217,508	167,925	12,002	37,581	
1910	267,721	54,678	z	213,043	164,945	11,312	36,786	
1909	260,544	53,505	z	207,039	159,991	10,962	36,086	
1908	264,940	54,048	z	210,892	163,086	10,940	36,866	
1907	276,421	54,026	z	222,395	172,497	11,700	38,198	
1906	270,038	50,682	z	219,356	170,579	11,455	37,322	
1905	260,742	47,768	z	212,974	165,747	10,812	36,415	
1904	257,856	46,247	z	211,609	165,519	10,450	35,640	
1903	261,103	44,520	z	216,583	170,044	10,621	35,918	
1902	261,750	42,761	z	218,989	173,011	10,606	35,372	
1901	259,400	41,067	z	218,333	172,679	10,624	35,030	
1900	257,480	39,471	z	218,009	173,060	10,267	34,682	
1899	262,334	39,403	z	222,931	177,896	10,686	34,349	
1898	255,379	37,938	z	217,441	174,826	10,164	32,451	
1897	249,145	36,626	z	212,519	170,806	10,095	31,618	
1896	242,764	35,439	z	207,325	166,871	10,042	30,412	

15.11 Number of marriages by type of ceremony and denomination, 1837 to 2013
England and Wales

Year (selected years only prior to 1962 [1])	All marriages	Civil ceremonies		Religious ceremonies				
		All	Approved Premises [2]	All	Church of England and Church in Wales	Roman Catholic	Other Christian denominations [3]	Other [4]
1895	228,204	33,749	z	194,455	156,469	9,405	28,581	
1894	226,449	33,550	z	192,899	155,352	9,453	28,094	
1893	218,689	31,379	z	187,310	151,309	9,019	26,982	
1892	227,135	31,416	z	195,719	158,632	9,133	27,954	
1891	226,526	30,809	z	195,717	158,439	9,517	27,761	
1890	223,028	30,376	z	192,652	156,371	9,596	26,685	
1889	213,865	29,779	z	184,086	149,356	8,988	25,742	
1888	203,821	27,809	z	176,012	142,863	8,632	24,517	
1887	200,518	27,335	z	173,183	140,607	8,611	23,965	
1886	196,071	25,590	z	170,481	138,571	8,220	23,690	
1885	197,745	25,851	z	171,894	139,913	8,162	23,819	
1884	204,301	26,786	z	177,515	144,344	8,783	24,388	
1883	206,384	26,547	z	179,837	147,000	8,980	23,857	
1882	204,405	25,717	z	178,688	146,102	9,235	23,351	
1881	197,290	25,055	z	172,235	140,995	8,784	22,456	
1880	191,965	24,180	z	167,785	137,661	8,210	21,914	
1879	182,082	21,769	z	160,313	131,689	7,437	21,187	
1878	190,054	22,056	z	167,998	137,969	7,980	22,049	
1877	194,352	21,269	z	173,083	142,396	8,277	22,410	
1876	201,874	21,709	z	180,165	148,910	8,577	22,678	
1875	201,212	21,002	z	180,210	149,685	8,411	22,114	
1874	202,010	21,256	z	180,754	150,819	8,179	21,756	
1873	205,615	21,178	z	184,437	154,581	8,222	21,634	
1872	201,267	19,995	z	181,272	152,364	8,427	20,481	
1871	190,112	18,378	z	171,734	144,663	7,647	19,424	
1870	181,655	17,848	z	163,807	137,986	7,391	18,430	
1869	176,970	16,745	z	160,225	135,082	7,231	17,912	
1868	176,962	15,878	z	161,084	136,038	7,517	17,529	
1867	179,154	15,058	z	164,096	138,930	7,918	17,248	
1866	187,776	15,246	z	172,530	146,040	8,911	17,579	
1865	185,474	14,792	z	170,682	145,104	8,742	16,836	
1864	180,387	14,611	z	165,776	141,083	8,659	16,034	
1863	173,510	13,589	z	159,921	136,743	8,095	15,083	
1862	164,030	12,723	z	151,307	129,733	7,345	14,229	
1861	163,706	11,725	z	151,981	130,697	7,782	13,502	
1860	170,156	11,257	z	158,899	137,370	7,800	13,729	
1859	167,723	10,844	z	156,879	136,210	7,756	12,913	
1858	156,070	9,952	z	146,118	128,082	6,643	11,393	
1857	159,097	9,642	z	149,455	131,031	7,360	11,064	
1856	159,337	8,097	z	151,240	133,619	7,527	10,094	
1855	152,113	7,441	z	144,672	127,751	7,344	9,577	
1854	159,727	7,593	z	152,134	134,109	7,813	10,212	
1853	164,520	7,598	z	156,922	138,042	8,375	10,505	
1852	158,782	7,100	z	151,682	133,882	7,479	10,321	
1851	154,206	6,813	z	147,393	130,958	6,570	9,865	
1850	152,744	6,207	z	146,537	130,959	5,623	9,955	
1849	141,883	5,558	z	136,325	123,182	4,199	8,944	
1848	138,230	4,790	z	133,440	121,469	3,658	8,313	
1847	135,845	4,258	z	131,587	120,876	2,961	7,750	
1846	145,664	4,167	z	141,497	130,509	3,027	7,961	
1845	143,743	3,977	z	139,766	129,515	2,816	7,435	
1844	132,249	3,446	z	128,803	120,009	2,280	6,514	
1843	123,818	2,817	z	121,001	113,637	7,213		151
1842	118,825	2,357	z	116,468	110,047	6,258		163
1841	122,496	2,064	z	120,432	114,371	5,948		113
1841 - Year ending 30 June	122,482	2,036	z	120,446	114,448	5,882		116
1840 - Year ending 30 June	124,329	1,938	z	122,391	117,018	5,221		152
1839 - Year ending 30 June	121,083	1,564	z	119,519	114,632	4,727		160
1838 - Year ending 30 June	111,481	1,093	z	110,388	107,201	3,052		135
1837 - 1 July 1937 to 31 December 1937	58,479	431	z	58,048	56,832	1,142		74

1 Data are not available for years not shown.

Source: Office for National Statistics

2 Approved premises are buildings such as hotels, historic buildings and stately homes licensed for civil marriages. Data on approved premises is from 1 April 1995.
3 'Other Christian denominations' include Methodist, Calvinistic Methodist, United Reform Church, Congregationalist, Baptist, Presbyterian, Society of Friends (Quakers), Salvation Army, Brethren, Mormon, Unitarian and Jehovah's Witnesses.
4 'Other' include Jews, Muslim and Sikh.
5 Prior to 1975 further information on denominations was not published.

15.12 Duration of marriage at divorce by age of wife at marriage, 1983-2013

England and Wales

Numbers

Year of divorce	Age of wife at marriage	All durations	Duration of marriage (completed years)								
			0-2 years	0 years	1 year	2 years	3 years	4 years	5-9 years	5 years	6 years
2013	All ages	114,720	6,271	79	2,055	4,137	5,647	6,272	30,996	6,449	6,410
	Under 20	8,115	185	3	62	120	184	243	1,462	304	302
	20-24	35,388	1,428	19	447	962	1,370	1,561	7,540	1,538	1,568
	25-29	33,404	1,959	19	634	1,306	1,814	1,863	8,858	1,934	1,898
	30-44	33,340	2,196	29	720	1,447	1,897	2,204	11,422	2,251	2,288
	45 and over	4,473	503	9	192	302	382	401	1,714	422	354
2012	All ages	118,140	6,268	49	2,033	4,186	5,710	6,550	33,027	6,748	6,542
	Under 20	9,195	193	3	47	143	248	326	1,790	349	316
	20-24	37,445	1,513	7	485	1,021	1,454	1,674	8,183	1,695	1,613
	25-29	34,055	1,937	19	632	1,286	1,738	1,958	9,374	2,038	1,895
	30-44	33,018	2,120	13	689	1,418	1,908	2,160	11,925	2,247	2,349
	45 and over	4,427	505	7	180	318	362	432	1,755	419	369
2011	All ages	117,558	5,803	30	1,748	4,025	5,890	6,654	32,989	6,727	7,111
	Under 20	9,727	238	1	59	178	309	329	1,915	344	400
	20-24	38,327	1,392	10	416	966	1,535	1,681	8,320	1,745	1,751
	25-29	33,379	1,783	11	544	1,228	1,734	1,986	9,406	1,949	2,001
	30-44	31,999	1,924	4	576	1,344	1,931	2,246	11,736	2,332	2,604
	45 and over	4,126	466	4	153	309	381	412	1,612	357	355
2010	All ages	119,589	6,278	17	1,897	4,364	6,109	6,936	33,700	7,418	7,652
	Under 20	10,619	255	0	85	170	332	351	2,085	450	489
	20-24	39,963	1,528	4	429	1,095	1,551	1,849	8,624	1,895	2,072
	25-29	33,309	1,874	3	583	1,288	1,795	1,947	9,609	2,072	2,123
	30-44	31,660	2,134	8	624	1,502	2,009	2,404	11,834	2,597	2,607
	45 and over	4,038	487	2	176	309	422	385	1,548	404	361
2009	All ages	113,949	6,270	21	1,951	4,298	5,884	6,947	31,290	7,561	6,864
	Under 20	10,529	267	1	60	206	293	371	1,943	478	439
	20-24	39,231	1,540	1	472	1,067	1,516	1,813	8,350	2,065	1,889
	25-29	31,400	1,808	8	572	1,228	1,715	1,986	8,994	2,106	1,898
	30-44	29,021	2,184	7	683	1,494	1,981	2,389	10,610	2,554	2,307
	45 and over	3,768	471	4	164	303	379	388	1,393	358	331
2008	All ages	121,708	6,937	27	2,103	4,807	6,776	7,929	31,803	7,369	6,714
	Under 20	11,657	319	1	78	240	365	500	1,948	478	407
	20-24	42,578	1,685	10	463	1,212	1,798	2,103	8,401	2,043	1,879
	25-29	33,050	2,044	7	621	1,416	1,875	2,148	9,287	1,985	1,863
	30-44	30,642	2,379	7	741	1,631	2,349	2,751	10,819	2,512	2,304
	45 and over	3,781	510	2	200	308	389	427	1,348	351	261
2007	All ages	128,131	8,195	38	2,558	5,599	7,206	7,574	32,419	7,164	7,046
	Under 20	13,224	411	1	120	290	417	487	2,053	430	470
	20-24	45,806	2,039	7	623	1,409	1,905	1,977	8,481	1,928	1,814
	25-29	34,564	2,234	13	668	1,553	1,990	2,115	9,987	2,099	2,106
	30-44	30,808	2,942	11	929	2,002	2,521	2,591	10,617	2,403	2,366
	45 and over	3,729	569	6	218	345	373	404	1,281	304	290
2006	All ages	132,140	8,763	37	2,793	5,933	7,226	7,376	33,736	7,398	7,310
	Under 20	14,441	503	2	157	344	376	447	2,232	474	506
	20-24	48,396	2,240	9	668	1,563	1,975	1,997	8,954	1,967	1,901
	25-29	35,054	2,381	13	796	1,572	2,052	2,172	10,416	2,182	2,181
	30-44	30,613	3,087	6	966	2,115	2,441	2,424	10,858	2,473	2,437
	45 and over	3,636	552	7	206	339	382	336	1,276	302	285
2005	All ages	141,322	9,573	49	3,181	6,343	7,520	8,175	36,064	7,920	7,697
	Under 20	16,473	537	2	148	387	515	579	2,389	576	544
	20-24	52,884	2,469	15	783	1,671	2,025	2,203	9,961	2,083	2,016
	25-29	36,992	2,545	9	845	1,691	2,081	2,507	11,296	2,367	2,431
	30-44	31,213	3,413	17	1,171	2,225	2,540	2,554	11,025	2,545	2,406
	45 and over	3,760	609	6	234	369	359	332	1,393	349	300
2004	All ages	152,923	10,101	42	3,345	6,714	8,319	8,894	39,681	8,840	8,375
	Under 20	18,655	626	3	201	422	557	662	2,626	667	581
	20-24	59,356	2,662	7	854	1,801	2,361	2,494	11,818	2,477	2,359
	25-29	39,459	2,871	8	947	1,916	2,480	2,642	12,426	2,674	2,593
	30-44	31,631	3,353	15	1,122	2,216	2,542	2,724	11,356	2,679	2,515
	45 and over	3,822	589	9	221	359	379	372	1,455	343	327

15.12 Duration of marriage at divorce by age of wife at marriage, 1983-2013

England and Wales | | | | | | | | | | **Numbers**

Year of divorce	Age of wife at marriage	Duration of marriage (completed years)								Not stated	Median duration
		7 years	8 years	9 years	10-14 years	15-19 years	20-24 years	25-29 years	30 years and over		
2013	**All ages**	**6,005**	**6,152**	**5,980**	**21,652**	**15,687**	**11,880**	**7,691**	**8,624**	0	11.7
	Under 20	258	304	294	1,125	822	883	969	2,242	0	:
	20-24	1,460	1,515	1,459	5,130	4,742	5,039	4,074	4,504	0	:
	25-29	1,719	1,691	1,616	6,792	5,316	3,772	1,762	1,268	0	:
	30-44	2,266	2,318	2,299	7,743	4,408	2,049	839	582	0	:
	45 and over	302	324	312	862	399	137	47	28	0	:
2012	**All ages**	**6,919**	**6,961**	**5,857**	**22,356**	**15,733**	**12,215**	**7,649**	**8,632**	0	11.5
	Under 20	361	406	358	1,259	795	1,056	1,088	2,440	0	:
	20-24	1,700	1,746	1,429	5,523	5,142	5,498	4,024	4,434	0	:
	25-29	1,910	1,843	1,688	7,188	5,426	3,541	1,669	1,224	0	:
	30-44	2,576	2,634	2,119	7,551	4,048	1,984	816	506	0	:
	45 and over	372	332	263	835	322	136	52	28	0	:
2011	**All ages**	**7,263**	**6,389**	**5,499**	**22,126**	**15,547**	**12,228**	**7,712**	**8,609**	0	11.5
	Under 20	487	384	300	1,276	901	1,111	1,130	2,518	0	:
	20-24	1,902	1,619	1,303	5,749	5,361	5,834	4,052	4,403	0	:
	25-29	2,042	1,756	1,658	7,097	5,198	3,370	1,644	1,161	0	:
	30-44	2,488	2,323	1,989	7,267	3,754	1,804	831	506	0	:
	45 and over	344	307	249	737	333	109	55	21	0	:
2010	**All ages**	**7,101**	**5,995**	**5,534**	**22,105**	**15,772**	**12,412**	**7,639**	**8,638**	0	11.4
	Under 20	432	381	333	1,280	1,012	1,305	1,366	2,633	0	:
	20-24	1,825	1,481	1,351	5,967	5,920	5,929	4,117	4,478	0	:
	25-29	2,018	1,690	1,706	7,163	5,134	3,369	1,351	1,067	0	:
	30-44	2,527	2,189	1,914	6,961	3,419	1,693	770	436	0	:
	45 and over	299	254	230	734	287	116	35	24	0	:
2009	**All ages**	**5,968**	**5,634**	**5,263**	**20,591**	**15,390**	**11,855**	**7,490**	**8,225**	7	11.4
	Under 20	355	357	314	1,177	1,092	1,337	1,484	2,565	0	:
	20-24	1,629	1,466	1,301	5,909	5,944	5,964	3,956	4,235	4	:
	25-29	1,679	1,648	1,663	6,704	4,926	2,983	1,299	985	0	:
	30-44	2,068	1,919	1,762	6,090	3,128	1,494	713	429	3	:
	45 and over	237	244	223	711	300	77	38	11	0	:
2008	**All ages**	**6,365**	**6,034**	**5,321**	**21,561**	**16,945**	**12,706**	**8,136**	**8,907**	8	11.5
	Under 20	358	363	342	1,174	1,274	1,526	1,749	2,800	2	:
	20-24	1,619	1,528	1,332	6,315	6,881	6,511	4,247	4,632	5	:
	25-29	1,880	1,862	1,697	7,075	5,204	2,945	1,389	1,082	1	:
	30-44	2,228	2,032	1,743	6,324	3,295	1,620	722	383	0	:
	45 and over	280	249	207	673	291	104	29	10	0	:
2007	**All ages**	**6,560**	**6,072**	**5,577**	**23,427**	**18,203**	**13,117**	**8,701**	**9,282**	7	11.7
	Under 20	423	395	335	1,240	1,542	1,929	2,099	3,045	1	:
	20-24	1,650	1,607	1,482	7,397	7,930	6,757	4,498	4,820	2	:
	25-29	2,021	1,953	1,808	7,777	5,240	2,802	1,377	1,039	3	:
	30-44	2,203	1,890	1,755	6,343	3,219	1,526	686	362	1	:
	45 and over	263	227	197	670	272	103	41	16	0	:
2006	**All ages**	**6,769**	**6,249**	**6,010**	**24,606**	**18,735**	**13,472**	**8,764**	**9,449**	13	11.6
	Under 20	490	397	365	1,491	1,831	2,191	2,241	3,128	1	:
	20-24	1,751	1,681	1,654	8,443	8,470	6,949	4,415	4,947	6	:
	25-29	2,159	2,004	1,890	7,708	5,157	2,745	1,365	1,053	5	:
	30-44	2,107	1,939	1,902	6,263	3,034	1,483	717	305	1	:
	45 and over	262	228	199	701	243	104	26	16	0	:
2005	**All ages**	**7,343**	**6,801**	**6,303**	**26,310**	**20,310**	**14,268**	**9,241**	**9,852**	9	11.6
	Under 20	478	429	362	1,722	2,299	2,605	2,571	3,255	1	:
	20-24	2,007	1,920	1,935	9,570	9,450	7,368	4,636	5,200	2	:
	25-29	2,291	2,173	2,034	8,364	5,146	2,683	1,310	1,058	2	:
	30-44	2,266	2,040	1,768	5,965	3,161	1,526	699	326	4	:
	45 and over	301	239	204	689	254	86	25	13	0	:
2004	**All ages**	**7,900**	**7,683**	**6,883**	**28,984**	**21,515**	**15,431**	**9,705**	**10,293**	0	11.5
	Under 20	498	485	395	2,133	2,737	3,103	2,804	3,407	0	:
	20-24	2,324	2,389	2,269	11,471	10,355	7,893	4,792	5,510	0	:
	25-29	2,517	2,436	2,206	8,671	5,082	2,823	1,427	1,037	0	:
	30-44	2,274	2,111	1,777	6,064	3,093	1,539	639	321	0	:
	45 and over	287	262	236	645	248	73	43	18	0	:

15.12 Duration of marriage at divorce by age of wife at marriage, 1983-2013

England and Wales   Numbers

Year of divorce	Age of wife at marriage	All durations	Duration of marriage (completed years)								
			0-2 years	0 years	1 year	2 years	3 years	4 years	5-9 years	5 years	6 years
2003	All ages	153,065	10,286	42	3,283	6,961	8,276	8,882	40,497	8,968	8,639
	Under 20	20,008	694	0	198	496	591	662	2,644	614	562
	20-24	60,883	2,735	11	825	1,899	2,352	2,587	12,944	2,636	2,564
	25-29	38,628	2,954	9	903	2,042	2,554	2,715	12,663	2,778	2,716
	30-44	29,873	3,304	10	1,131	2,163	2,444	2,554	10,865	2,600	2,468
	45 and over	3,673	599	12	226	361	335	364	1,381	340	329
2002	All ages	147,735	10,239	31	3,326	6,882	8,325	8,780	39,730	8,823	8,370
	Under 20	19,828	684	3	184	497	623	597	2,589	591	541
	20-24	60,353	2,833	6	878	1,949	2,411	2,696	13,727	2,739	2,754
	25-29	36,387	2,903	8	906	1,989	2,581	2,778	12,269	2,795	2,602
	30-44	27,803	3,250	7	1,132	2,111	2,366	2,387	9,865	2,374	2,171
	45 and over	3,364	569	7	226	336	344	322	1,280	324	302
2001	All ages	143,818	10,190	36	3,413	6,741	8,206	8,591	39,079	8,632	8,329
	Under 20	20,218	738	3	225	510	634	560	2,676	574	498
	20-24	60,211	2,809	12	870	1,927	2,472	2,711	14,418	2,900	2,938
	25-29	34,759	3,041	10	973	2,058	2,571	2,737	11,728	2,648	2,600
	30-44	25,405	3,054	6	1,116	1,932	2,177	2,246	9,059	2,202	2,028
	45 and over	3,225	548	5	229	314	352	337	1,198	308	265
2000	All ages	141,135	10,438	52	3,494	6,892	8,296	8,740	38,206	8,506	8,148
	Under 20	20,930	846	2	284	560	598	575	2,937	571	594
	20-24	59,874	2,954	8	925	2,021	2,631	2,978	14,663	3,014	3,021
	25-29	33,282	3,095	17	1,038	2,040	2,567	2,675	11,443	2,625	2,510
	30-44	23,912	2,971	14	1,012	1,945	2,159	2,179	8,082	2,032	1,779
	45 and over	3,137	572	11	235	326	341	333	1,081	264	244
1999	All ages	144,556	11,350	49	3,813	7,488	8,833	9,124	39,676	8,958	8,521
	Under 20	22,486	868	5	268	595	658	625	3,367	604	691
	20-24	62,853	3,445	15	1,125	2,305	2,965	3,366	16,221	3,440	3,404
	25-29	32,867	3,182	6	1,074	2,102	2,710	2,745	11,170	2,670	2,432
	30-44	23,270	3,197	14	1,082	2,101	2,147	2,076	7,898	1,982	1,735
	45 and over	3,080	658	9	264	385	353	312	1,020	262	259
1998	All ages	145,214	12,247	68	4,191	7,988	9,270	9,619	40,239	9,180	8,497
	Under 20	24,276	976	7	327	642	704	785	3,858	753	762
	20-24	64,453	4,000	16	1,303	2,681	3,475	3,737	17,413	3,800	3,586
	25-29	31,533	3,510	21	1,144	2,345	2,697	2,787	10,518	2,569	2,289
	30-44	22,076	3,162	18	1,140	2,004	2,062	2,027	7,478	1,801	1,631
	45 and over	2,876	599	6	277	316	332	283	972	257	229
1997	All ages	146,689	12,596	61	4,369	8,166	9,410	9,761	41,260	9,326	8,580
	Under 20	25,579	1,024	7	359	658	757	809	4,424	857	851
	20-24	66,167	4,412	10	1,449	2,953	3,773	4,114	18,226	3,917	3,736
	25-29	31,022	3,576	13	1,213	2,350	2,706	2,712	10,417	2,591	2,263
	30-44	21,017	2,958	20	1,073	1,865	1,879	1,818	7,241	1,719	1,513
	45 and over	2,904	626	11	275	340	295	308	952	242	217
1996	All ages	157,107	14,021	76	5,010	8,935	10,467	10,436	44,609	10,042	9,850
	Under 20	29,927	1,178	4	383	791	970	1,022	5,543	1,128	1,165
	20-24	71,123	5,289	20	1,744	3,525	4,236	4,392	20,221	4,408	4,417
	25-29	31,396	3,872	23	1,384	2,465	2,901	2,778	10,373	2,557	2,359
	30-44	21,640	3,018	15	1,197	1,806	2,008	1,919	7,480	1,702	1,691
	45 and over	3,021	664	14	302	348	352	325	992	247	218
1995	All ages	155,499	14,015	95	4,944	8,976	10,209	10,283	44,304	10,447	9,812
	Under 20	31,322	1,374	8	418	948	1,090	1,158	5,894	1,224	1,180
	20-24	71,360	5,634	28	1,948	3,658	4,375	4,477	20,360	4,748	4,457
	25-29	29,441	3,568	17	1,257	2,294	2,591	2,576	9,892	2,523	2,255
	30-44	20,506	2,817	26	1,034	1,757	1,842	1,792	7,208	1,684	1,707
	45 and over	2,870	622	16	287	319	311	280	950	268	213
1994	All ages	158,175	13,841	81	4,895	8,865	10,400	11,454	44,769	10,836	9,896
	Under 20	34,069	1,582	6	518	1,058	1,297	1,468	6,805	1,404	1,418
	20-24	73,291	5,689	19	1,956	3,714	4,518	5,106	21,102	4,975	4,681
	25-29	28,360	3,408	24	1,208	2,176	2,520	2,698	9,187	2,414	2,077
	30-44	19,686	2,574	17	959	1,598	1,749	1,838	6,807	1,806	1,523
	45 and over	2,769	588	15	254	319	316	344	868	237	197

15.12 Duration of marriage at divorce by age of wife at marriage, 1983-2013

England and Wales
Numbers

Year of divorce	Age of wife at marriage	Duration of marriage (completed years)								Not stated	Median duration
		7 years	8 years	9 years	10-14 years	15-19 years	20-24 years	25-29 years	30 years and over		
2003	**All ages**	**8,228**	**7,686**	**6,976**	**29,751**	**20,863**	**14,974**	**9,627**	**9,907**	**2**	**11.3**
	Under 20	551	495	422	2,613	2,911	3,559	2,985	3,349	0	:
	20-24	2,569	2,622	2,553	12,281	10,413	7,534	4,708	5,327	2	
	25-29	2,594	2,361	2,214	8,537	4,508	2,409	1,333	955	0	
	30-44	2,232	1,965	1,600	5,679	2,811	1,391	564	261	0	
	45 and over	282	243	187	641	220	81	37	15	0	
2002	**All ages**	**8,020**	**7,564**	**6,953**	**28,592**	**19,784**	**13,989**	**9,106**	**9,190**	**0**	**11.1**
	Under 20	481	517	459	2,774	3,160	3,439	2,891	3,071	0	:
	20-24	2,795	2,770	2,669	12,516	9,810	6,845	4,480	5,035	0	
	25-29	2,514	2,265	2,093	7,524	4,032	2,279	1,175	846	0	
	30-44	1,985	1,796	1,539	5,249	2,577	1,355	523	231	0	
	45 and over	245	216	193	529	205	71	37	7	0	
2001	**All ages**	**7,909**	**7,463**	**6,746**	**28,176**	**18,603**	**13,318**	**8,986**	**8,667**	**2**	**10.9**
	Under 20	524	513	567	2,999	3,309	3,607	2,830	2,865	0	:
	20-24	2,925	2,943	2,712	12,875	9,251	6,432	4,505	4,736	2	
	25-29	2,398	2,183	1,899	7,075	3,587	2,052	1,158	810	0	
	30-44	1,810	1,612	1,407	4,721	2,270	1,157	475	246	0	
	45 and over	252	212	161	506	186	70	18	10	0	
2000	**All ages**	**7,778**	**7,183**	**6,591**	**27,459**	**17,870**	**12,907**	**9,017**	**8,196**	**6**	**10.7**
	Under 20	566	604	602	3,230	3,413	3,556	3,003	2,770	2	:
	20-24	2,959	2,909	2,760	12,720	8,839	6,142	4,479	4,465	3	
	25-29	2,356	2,046	1,906	6,521	3,192	1,995	1,078	715	1	
	30-44	1,665	1,429	1,177	4,461	2,250	1,145	433	232	0	
	45 and over	232	195	146	527	176	69	24	14	0	
1999	**All ages**	**7,861**	**7,338**	**6,998**	**27,384**	**18,072**	**12,888**	**9,349**	**7,871**	**9**	**10.5**
	Under 20	620	722	730	3,532	3,886	3,874	3,040	2,633	3	:
	20-24	3,217	3,111	3,049	12,984	8,729	5,960	4,871	4,308	4	
	25-29	2,205	2,044	1,819	6,209	3,127	1,950	1,053	720	1	
	30-44	1,622	1,312	1,247	4,191	2,156	1,037	362	205	1	
	45 and over	197	149	153	468	174	67	23	5	0	
1998	**All ages**	**7,785**	**7,757**	**7,020**	**26,698**	**17,934**	**12,675**	**9,056**	**7,468**	**8**	**10.2**
	Under 20	740	823	780	3,986	4,364	4,020	3,075	2,508	0	:
	20-24	3,435	3,413	3,179	12,757	8,469	5,833	4,738	4,028	3	
	25-29	2,026	1,955	1,679	5,599	2,955	1,851	896	716	4	
	30-44	1,398	1,419	1,229	3,907	1,993	911	325	210	1	
	45 and over	186	147	153	449	153	60	22	6	0	
1997	**All ages**	**8,324**	**7,935**	**7,095**	**26,215**	**18,027**	**13,148**	**9,058**	**7,202**	**12**	**10.0**
	Under 20	923	894	899	4,197	4,648	4,284	2,957	2,476	3	:
	20-24	3,750	3,540	3,283	12,447	8,298	6,082	4,971	3,837	7	
	25-29	2,065	1,918	1,580	5,353	2,881	1,860	834	681	2	
	30-44	1,409	1,400	1,200	3,776	2,006	869	274	196	0	
	45 and over	177	183	133	442	194	53	22	12	0	
1996	**All ages**	**9,092**	**8,171**	**7,454**	**27,332**	**19,321**	**14,236**	**9,511**	**7,165**	**9**	**9.9**
	Under 20	1,120	1,116	1,014	5,084	5,507	4,867	3,294	2,461	1	:
	20-24	4,029	3,776	3,591	12,921	8,558	6,549	5,112	3,841	4	
	25-29	2,168	1,734	1,555	5,119	2,998	1,882	805	665	3	
	30-44	1,549	1,375	1,163	3,765	2,087	887	285	190	1	
	45 and over	226	170	131	443	171	51	15	8	0	
1995	**All ages**	**8,822**	**7,965**	**7,258**	**27,365**	**18,943**	**14,483**	**8,925**	**6,962**	**10**	**9.6**
	Under 20	1,161	1,176	1,153	5,768	5,604	5,009	3,072	2,350	3	:
	20-24	4,051	3,668	3,436	12,640	8,476	6,815	4,860	3,718	5	
	25-29	2,023	1,664	1,427	4,781	2,832	1,796	711	692	2	
	30-44	1,426	1,275	1,116	3,727	1,868	795	268	189	0	
	45 and over	161	182	126	449	163	68	14	13	0	
1994	**All ages**	**8,881**	**7,900**	**7,256**	**28,073**	**19,200**	**14,891**	**8,801**	**6,739**	**7**	**9.8**
	Under 20	1,403	1,327	1,253	6,458	6,077	5,101	3,050	2,230	1	14.6
	20-24	4,222	3,727	3497	12,808	8,351	7,303	4,777	3,633	4	10.1
	25-29	1,774	1,559	1,363	4,733	2,804	1,663	675	670	2	7.6
	30-44	1,315	1,144	1,019	3,693	1,785	761	278	201	0	7.1
	45 and over	167	143	124	381	183	63	21	5	0	5.5

15.12 Duration of marriage at divorce by age of wife at marriage, 1983-2013

England and Wales — Numbers

Year of divorce	Age of wife at marriage	All durations	Duration of marriage (completed years)								
			0-2 years	0 years	1 year	2 years	3 years	4 years	5-9 years	5 years	6 years
1993	All ages	165,018	14,096	74	4,708	9,314	11,357	11,799	46,536	11,137	10,352
	Under 20	38,811	1,867	9	583	1,275	1,668	1,653	8,196	1,713	1,685
	20-24	76,853	6,163	12	2,045	4,106	5,066	5,470	21,731	5,194	4,901
	25-29	27,178	3,051	27	953	2,071	2,439	2,506	8,777	2,282	1,970
	30-44	19,357	2,419	18	878	1,523	1,832	1,827	6,920	1,722	1,562
	45 and over	2,819	596	8	249	339	352	343	912	226	234
1992	All ages	160,385	14,247	62	4,630	9,555	11,299	11,352	43,745	10,417	9,459
	Under 20	39,734	1,990	3	590	1,397	1,736	1,739	8,544	1,798	1,697
	20-24	74,701	6,208	19	1,949	4,240	5,159	5,510	20,464	4,952	4,469
	25-29	25,173	2,992	11	1,010	1,971	2,241	2,213	7,759	1,952	1,796
	30-44	18,011	2,430	16	832	1,582	1,822	1,631	6,054	1,476	1,275
	45 and over	2,766	627	13	249	365	341	259	924	239	222
1991	All ages	158,745	15,332	62	5,239	10,031	11,321	11,126	42,735	10,049	9,345
	Under 20	40,594	2,387	1	780	1,606	1,894	2,014	9,143	1,857	1,805
	20-24	74,050	6,863	17	2,271	4,575	5,308	5,292	19,926	4,808	4,493
	25-29	24,025	2,942	12	1,003	1,927	2,162	2,014	7,048	1,776	1,571
	30-44	17,359	2,486	16	892	1,578	1,640	1,556	5,765	1,390	1,269
	45 and over	2,717	654	16	293	345	317	250	853	218	207
1990	All ages	153,386	15,122	64	5,142	9,916	10,863	10,314	42,061	9,883	9,025
	Under 20	41,116	2,558	6	788	1,764	1,993	1,961	9,790	2,030	1,917
	20-24	71,489	6,919	20	2,312	4,587	5,115	4,981	19,248	4,702	4,265
	25-29	21,701	2,637	11	906	1,720	1,898	1,721	6,567	1,627	1,462
	30-44	16,387	2,378	16	866	1,496	1,533	1,386	5,608	1,297	1,214
	45 and over	2,693	630	11	270	349	324	265	848	227	167
1989	All ages	150,872	15,231	56	5,420	9,755	10,372	10,116	42,108	9,569	8,928
	Under 20	42,612	2,915	11	980	1,924	2,059	2,144	10,798	2,209	2,199
	20-24	69,424	6,956	18	2,424	4,514	4,886	4,783	18,725	4,377	4,042
	25-29	20,369	2,468	8	887	1,573	1,651	1,580	6,189	1,476	1,360
	30-44	15,774	2,272	12	853	1,407	1,487	1,338	5,535	1,286	1,118
	45 and over	2,693	620	7	276	337	289	271	861	221	209
1988	All ages	152,633	15,003	88	5,403	9,512	10,213	10,376	42,617	9,730	9,080
	Under 20	44,693	3,151	7	1,055	2,089	2,296	2,472	11,676	2,374	2,424
	20-24	69,489	6,676	31	2,339	4,306	4,751	4,777	18,310	4,378	3,936
	25-29	20,267	2,298	16	854	1,428	1,525	1,543	6,167	1,464	1,331
	30-44	15,472	2,207	17	852	1,338	1,328	1,368	5,584	1,302	1,182
	45 and over	2,712	671	17	303	351	313	216	880	212	207
1987	All ages	151,007	14,549	:	:	:	10,248	10,626	43,150	10,262	9,626
	Under 20	46,097	3,387	:	:	:	2,554	2,755	12,428	2,823	2,628
	20-24	68,345	6,393	:	:	:	4,643	4,751	18,180	4,461	4,190
	25-29	19,049	2,045	:	:	:	1,449	1,449	6,088	1,420	1,353
	30-44	14,802	2,085	:	:	:	1,293	1,405	5,549	1,327	1,242
	45 and over	2,714	639	:	:	:	309	266	905	231	213
1986	All ages	153,903	14,596	:	:	:	11,683	12,358	42,187	10,656	9,329
	Under 20	48,621	3,735	:	:	:	3,239	3,618	12,978	3,204	2,863
	20-24	68,387	6,216	:	:	:	5,020	5,257	17,059	4,446	3,713
	25-29	18,990	1,955	:	:	:	1,504	1,561	5,845	1,369	1,296
	30-44	15,064	2,068	:	:	:	1,553	1,583	5,369	1,387	1,248
	45 and over	2,841	622	:	:	:	367	339	936	250	209
1985	All ages	160,300	14,662	:	:	:	16,929	14,185	41,537	10,942	9,352
	Under 20	52,858	4,034	:	:	:	5,320	4,481	13,455	3,471	3,008
	20-24	69,663	5,927	:	:	:	6,983	5,735	16,294	4,374	3,607
	25-29	18,689	1,748	:	:	:	1,894	1,720	5,620	1,408	1,269
	30-44	15,765	2,160	:	:	:	2,187	1,827	5,181	1,403	1,249
	45 and over	3,325	793	:	:	:	545	422	987	286	219
1984	All ages	144,501	1,336	:	:	:	15,296	13,868	40,866	10,434	8,830
	Under 20	49,610	304	:	:	:	5,084	4,577	13,821	3,452	2,994
	20-24	62,642	427	:	:	:	6,107	5,443	15,716	4,020	3,371
	25-29	16,811	183	:	:	:	1,707	1,737	5,477	1,329	1,118
	30-44	12,944	289	:	:	:	1,921	1,739	4,895	1,362	1,126
	45 and over	2,494	133	:	:	:	477	372	957	271	221
1983	All ages	147,479	1,528	:	:	:	15,706	13,863	42,041	10,413	8,785
	Under 20	52,547	389	:	:	:	5,529	4,866	15,084	3,693	3,129
	20-24	63,382	477	:	:	:	6,054	5,228	15,887	3,942	3,294
	25-29	16,351	196	:	:	:	1,723	1,654	5,362	1,270	1,130
	30-44	12,675	326	:	:	:	1,904	1,725	4,726	1,253	1,027
	45 and over	2,524	140	:	:	:	496	390	982	255	205

Source: Office for National Statistics

15.12 Duration of marriage at divorce by age of wife at marriage, 1983-2013

England and Wales

Numbers

Year of divorce	Age of wife at marriage	Duration of marriage (completed years)								Not stated	Median duration
		7 years	8 years	9 years	10-14 years	15-19 years	20-24 years	25-29 years	30 years and over		
1993	All ages	9,029	8,475	7,543	30,156	20,233	15,503	8,426	6,907	5	9.8
	Under 20	1,593	1,621	1,584	7,812	6,830	5,452	3,065	2,267	1	13.9
	20-24	4,311	3,892	3,433	13,538	8,796	7,909	4,434	3,743	3	10.0
	25-29	1,624	1,627	1,274	4,753	2,808	1,497	671	675	1	7.8
	30-44	1,328	1,177	1,131	3,667	1,648	588	242	214	0	7.0
	45 and over	173	158	121	386	151	57	14	8	0	5.4
1992	All ages	8,708	7,914	7,247	29,285	20,160	15,488	8,098	6,704	7	9.9
	Under 20	1,708	1,670	1,671	8,192	6,920	5,395	3,090	2,125	3	13.5
	20-24	4,090	3,694	3,259	12,837	8,721	8,038	4,067	3,694	3	10.0
	25-29	1,513	1,340	1,158	4,401	2,791	1,448	633	694	1	7.9
	30-44	1,219	1,059	1,025	3,477	1,552	570	289	186	0	6.9
	45 and over	178	151	134	378	176	37	19	5	0	5.6
1991	All ages	8,423	7,797	7,121	28,791	20,127	14,957	7,845	6,492	19	9.8
	Under 20	1,808	1,883	1,790	8,295	6,988	5,112	2,825	1,930	6	12.7
	20-24	3,902	3,506	3,217	12,304	8,775	7,924	4,066	3,581	11	9.9
	25-29	1,438	1,228	1,035	4,417	2,686	1,318	685	751	2	8.1
	30-44	1,118	1,033	955	3,355	1,521	553	261	222	0	7.0
	45 and over	157	147	124	420	157	50	8	8	0	5.7
1990	All ages	8,289	7,634	7,230	27,310	19,819	14,186	7,479	6,216	16	9.8
	Under 20	1,950	1,933	1,960	8,313	7,122	4,974	2,648	1,755	2	12.4
	20-24	3,767	3,380	3,134	11,542	8,786	7,500	3,897	3,490	11	9.8
	25-29	1,316	1,144	1,018	3,893	2,416	1,156	639	772	2	8.2
	30-44	1,101	1,016	980	3,163	1,330	514	283	191	1	7.0
	45 and over	155	161	138	399	165	42	12	8	0	6.0
1989	All ages	8,392	7,887	7,332	26,281	19,418	13,575	7,333	6,419	19	9.7
	Under 20	2,233	2,037	2,120	8,289	6,951	4,963	2,632	1,854	7	11.9
	20-24	3,698	3,538	3,070	10,775	8,890	7,051	3,758	3,590	10	9.8
	25-29	1,210	1,113	1,030	3,900	2,201	1,026	640	713	1	8.4
	30-44	1,094	1,054	983	2,885	1,226	491	286	253	1	7.0
	45 and over	157	145	129	432	150	44	17	9	0	5.8
1988	All ages	8,784	7,906	7,117	26,545	20,132	13,723	7,476	6,548	0	9.7
	Under 20	2,410	2,352	2,116	8,648	7,126	4,896	2,571	1,857	0	11.5
	20-24	3,813	3,247	2,936	10,753	9,646	7,074	3,915	3,587	0	10.1
	25-29	1,256	1,083	1,033	3,962	2,046	1,180	698	848	0	8.7
	30-44	1,137	1,069	894	2,787	1,149	527	274	248	0	7.0
	45 and over	168	155	138	395	165	46	18	8	0	5.7
1987	All ages	8,781	7,827	6,654	26,194	19,576	12,970	7,314	6,380	0	9.5
	Under 20	2,592	2,324	2,061	8,925	7,019	4,820	2,472	1,737	0	11.0
	20-24	3,652	3,212	2,665	10,656	9,671	6,602	3,861	3,588	0	10.1
	25-29	1,196	1,127	992	3,723	1,791	1,021	694	789	0	8.5
	30-44	1,163	993	824	2,475	975	488	276	256	0	6.8
	45 and over	178	171	112	415	120	39	11	10	0	5.1
1986	All ages	8,457	7,465	6,280	26,718	19,547	12,909	7,357	6,539	9	9.4
	Under 20	2,616	2,313	1,982	9,208	6,946	4,810	2,317	1,766	4	10.4
	20-24	3,410	2,981	2509	10,953	9,857	6,376	3,986	3,661	2	10.3
	25-29	1,205	1,044	931	3,679	1,688	1,145	736	874	3	8.6
	30-44	1,034	969	731	2,477	940	541	301	232	0	6.4
	45 and over	192	158	127	401	116	37	17	6	0	5.4
1985	All ages	7,932	6,884	6,427	27,087	19,460	12,463	7,388	6,576	13	8.9
	Under 20	2,553	2,262	2,161	9,658	7,125	4,645	2,347	1,789	4	9.6
	20-24	3,114	2,705	2,494	11,276	9,665	6,122	4,016	3,638	7	10.0
	25-29	1,054	981	908	3,388	1,630	1,122	700	865	2	8.3
	30-44	1,015	781	733	2,348	935	538	315	274	0	6.0
	45 and over	196	155	131	417	105	36	10	10	0	4.8
1984	All ages	7,854	7,105	6,643	27,336	19,108	12,516	7,528	6,637	10	10.1
	Under 20	2,640	2,450	2,285	9,933	7,127	4,614	2,410	1,737	3	10.4
	20-24	3,060	2,687	2,578	11,723	9,412	6,154	3,942	3,711	7	11.5
	25-29	1,048	1,034	948	3,209	1,578	1,159	827	934	0	9.3
	30-44	911	793	703	2,093	884	545	328	250	0	6.8
	45 and over	195	141	129	378	107	44	21	5	0	6.0
1983	All ages	8,072	7,662	7,109	28,432	19,103	12,579	7,529	6,661	37	10.1
	Under 20	2,867	2,752	2,643	10,412	7,596	4,599	2,331	1,728	13	10.2
	20-24	3,111	2,916	2,624	12,764	8,987	6,227	4,045	3,699	14	11.6
	25-29	1,042	997	923	2,999	1,551	1,129	786	943	8	9.2
	30-44	846	825	775	1,899	865	587	355	286	2	7.1
	45 and over	206	172	144	358	104	37	12	5	0	5.9

Source: Office for National Statistics

15.13 Duration of marriage at divorce by age of husband at marriage, 2003-2013

England and Wales

Numbers

Year of divorce	Age of husband at marriage	All durations	Duration of marriage (completed years)								
			0-2 years	0 years	1 year	2 years	3 years	4 years	5-9 years	5 years	6 years
2013	All ages	114,720	6,271	79	2,055	4,137	5,647	6,272	30,996	6,449	6,410
	Under 20	2,390	67	1	20	46	55	62	441	94	103
	20-24	25,080	852	9	273	570	830	932	4,599	946	964
	25-29	35,535	1,860	23	600	1,237	1,682	1,870	8,492	1,808	1,738
	30-44	44,049	2,725	35	887	1,803	2,497	2,762	14,505	2,946	2,967
	45 and over	7,666	767	11	275	481	583	646	2,959	655	638
2012	All ages	118,140	6,268	49	2,033	4,186	5,710	6,550	33,027	6,748	6,542
	Under 20	2,710	61	1	19	41	74	96	468	86	92
	20-24	26,783	907	4	257	646	857	1,032	5,132	1,050	985
	25-29	36,697	1,814	21	596	1,197	1,699	1,921	9,215	2,005	1,801
	30-44	44,375	2,706	16	884	1,806	2,483	2,824	15,263	2,949	3,070
	45 and over	7,575	780	7	277	496	597	677	2,949	658	594
2011	All ages	117,558	5,803	30	1,748	4,025	5,890	6,654	32,989	6,727	7,111
	Under 20	2,871	75	0	19	56	87	101	536	108	124
	20-24	27,934	813	4	213	596	910	1,034	5,343	1,092	1,135
	25-29	36,299	1,679	13	489	1,177	1,780	1,890	9,183	1,919	1,883
	30-44	43,304	2,547	6	793	1,748	2,493	2,965	15,209	3,022	3,345
	45 and over	7,150	689	7	234	448	620	664	2,718	586	624
2010	All ages	119,589	6,278	17	1,897	4,364	6,109	6,936	33,700	7,418	7,652
	Under 20	2,958	74	0	20	54	86	97	542	115	120
	20-24	29,661	909	2	251	656	951	1,145	5,437	1,240	1,247
	25-29	36,920	1,740	5	522	1,213	1,723	1,969	9,584	1,998	2,185
	30-44	43,027	2,763	8	829	1,926	2,697	3,070	15,439	3,380	3,468
	45 and over	7,023	792	2	275	515	652	655	2,698	685	632
2009	All ages	113,949	6,270	21	1,951	4,298	5,884	6,947	31,290	7,561	6,864
	Under 20	3,066	74	0	24	50	75	114	543	129	98
	20-24	29,150	883	1	246	636	894	1,193	5,281	1,305	1,221
	25-29	35,305	1,746	4	553	1,189	1,702	1,991	9,186	2,188	1,912
	30-44	39,984	2,810	9	856	1,945	2,623	3,032	13,948	3,370	3,104
	45 and over	6,444	757	7	272	478	590	617	2,332	569	529
2008	All ages	121,708	6,937	27	2,103	4,807	6,776	7,929	31,803	7,369	6,714
	Under 20	3,364	91	0	29	62	98	130	564	125	125
	20-24	32,151	1,006	4	236	766	1,090	1,319	5,161	1,281	1,132
	25-29	37,895	1,978	9	604	1,365	1,889	2,278	9,594	2,013	1,972
	30-44	41,529	3,051	9	941	2,101	3,040	3,544	14,089	3,345	2,979
	45 and over	6,769	811	5	293	513	659	658	2,395	605	506
2007	All ages	128,131	8,195	38	2,558	5,599	7,206	7,574	32,419	7,164	7,046
	Under 20	4,036	132	0	36	96	122	146	611	131	151
	20-24	35,408	1,238	4	364	870	1,214	1,275	5,430	1,198	1,153
	25-29	39,546	2,202	13	659	1,530	1,986	2,109	10,074	2,129	2,133
	30-44	42,408	3,736	12	1,171	2,553	3,279	3,351	13,960	3,163	3,085
	45 and over	6,733	887	9	328	550	605	693	2,344	543	524
2006	All ages	132,140	8,763	37	2,793	5,933	7,226	7,376	33,736	7,398	7,310
	Under 20	4,115	140	0	49	91	119	132	630	142	143
	20-24	38,096	1,400	4	411	985	1,192	1,239	5,727	1,211	1,204
	25-29	40,683	2,304	10	724	1,570	2,054	2,176	10,907	2,285	2,295
	30-44	42,417	4,002	14	1,287	2,701	3,234	3,238	14,093	3,209	3,146
	45 and over	6,829	917	9	322	586	627	591	2,379	551	522
2005	All ages	141,322	9573	49	3,181	6,343	7,520	8,175	36,064	7,920	7,697
	Under 20	4,685	175	0	53	122	159	139	634	166	134
	20-24	42,354	1,516	5	497	1,014	1,308	1,415	6,526	1,328	1,309
	25-29	43,807	2,625	18	836	1,771	2,175	2,529	11,853	2,547	2,481
	30-44	43,631	4,287	13	1,472	2,802	3,250	3,466	14,547	3,270	3,219
	45 and over	6,845	970	13	323	634	628	626	2,504	609	554
2004	All ages	152,923	10,101	42	3,345	6,714	8,319	8,894	39,681	8,840	8,375
	Under 20	5,392	178	0	52	126	146	187	680	186	136
	20-24	47,794	1,680	7	552	1,121	1,475	1,538	7,762	1,572	1,540
	25-29	48,067	2,863	7	881	1,975	2,568	2,974	13,672	2,982	2,812
	30-44	44,701	4,428	19	1,507	2,902	3,468	3,531	15,035	3,505	3,299
	45 and over	6,969	952	9	353	590	662	664	2,532	595	588
2003	All ages	153,065	10,286	42	3,283	6,961	8,276	8,882	40,497	8,968	8,639
	Under 20	5,764	191	0	58	133	157	169	690	176	148
	20-24	50,015	1,720	4	483	1,233	1,484	1,658	8,685	1,675	1,718
	25-29	47,353	3,021	5	927	2,089	2,702	2,960	13,881	3,000	2,901
	30-44	43,173	4,386	17	1,456	2,913	3,362	3,459	14,702	3,519	3,328
	45 and over	6,760	968	16	359	593	571	636	2,539	598	544

Source: Office for National Statistics

15.13 Duration of marriage at divorce by age of husband at marriage, 2003-2013

England and Wales

Numbers

Year of divorce	Age of husband at marriage	Duration of marriage (completed years)								Not stated	Median duration
		7 years	8 years	9 years	10-14 years	15-19 years	20-24 years	25-29 years	30 years and over		
2013	**All ages**	**6,005**	**6,152**	**5,980**	**21,652**	**15,687**	**11,880**	**7,691**	**8,624**	0	11.7
	Under 20	62	91	91	322	222	246	261	714	0	:
	20-24	902	916	871	3,203	2,999	3,707	3,214	4,744	0	:
	25-29	1,661	1,649	1,636	6,582	5,829	4,464	2,628	2,128	0	:
	30-44	2,818	2,924	2,850	9,981	5,925	3,173	1,489	992	0	:
	45 and over	562	572	532	1,564	712	290	99	46	0	
2012	**All ages**	**6,919**	**6,961**	**5,857**	**22,356**	**15,733**	**12,215**	**7,649**	**8,632**	0	11.5
	Under 20	99	99	92	359	243	285	296	828	0	:
	20-24	1,095	1,056	946	3,388	3,318	4,039	3,334	4,776	0	:
	25-29	1,810	1,953	1,646	7,133	5,902	4,518	2,447	2,048	0	:
	30-44	3,241	3,277	2,726	10,022	5,629	3,056	1,461	931	0	:
	45 and over	674	576	447	1,454	641	317	111	49	0	
2011	**All ages**	**7,263**	**6,389**	**5,499**	**22,126**	**15,547**	**12,228**	**7,712**	**8,609**	0	11.5
	Under 20	116	115	73	365	226	309	358	814	0	:
	20-24	1,228	1,024	864	3,599	3,622	4,365	3,444	4,804	0	:
	25-29	2,062	1,766	1,553	7,217	5,803	4,318	2,380	2,049	0	:
	30-44	3,264	2,997	2,581	9,549	5,252	2,962	1,434	893	0	:
	45 and over	593	487	428	1,396	644	274	96	49	0	
2010	**All ages**	**7,101**	**5,995**	**5,534**	**22,105**	**15,772**	**12,412**	**7,639**	**8,638**	0	11.4
	Under 20	98	123	86	345	277	323	371	843	0	:
	20-24	1,167	904	879	3,769	4,147	4,715	3,596	4,992	0	:
	25-29	2,022	1,726	1,653	7,523	5,757	4,398	2,234	1,992	0	:
	30-44	3,269	2,801	2,521	9,150	5,021	2,738	1,373	776	0	:
	45 and over	545	441	395	1,318	570	238	65	35	0	
2009	**All ages**	**5,968**	**5,634**	**5,263**	**20,591**	**15,390**	**11,855**	**7,490**	**8,225**	7	11.4
	Under 20	106	108	102	316	296	343	429	876	0	:
	20-24	1,004	912	839	3,716	4,298	4,673	3,545	4,665	2	:
	25-29	1,732	1,719	1,635	7,059	5,566	4,022	2,124	1,907	2	:
	30-44	2,690	2,458	2,326	8,270	4,620	2,617	1,306	755	3	
	45 and over	436	437	361	1,230	610	200	86	22	0	
2008	**All ages**	**6,365**	**6,034**	**5,321**	**21,561**	**16,945**	**12,706**	**8,136**	**8,907**	8	11.5
	Under 20	113	90	111	321	342	407	501	909	1	:
	20-24	987	922	839	4,134	4,924	5,257	3,993	5,265	2	:
	25-29	1,910	1,908	1,791	7,677	6,168	4,089	2,233	1,984	5	:
	30-44	2,860	2,697	2,208	8,147	4,911	2,701	1,317	729	0	
	45 and over	495	417	372	1,282	600	252	92	20	0	
2007	**All ages**	**6,560**	**6,072**	**5,577**	**23,427**	**18,203**	**13,117**	**8,701**	**9,282**	7	11.7
	Under 20	139	108	82	353	425	516	661	1,070	0	:
	20-24	1,045	1,077	957	4,993	5,878	5,654	4,230	5,494	2	:
	25-29	2,003	1,961	1,848	8,330	6,392	4,045	2,396	2,009	3	:
	30-44	2,892	2,522	2,298	8,441	4,939	2,695	1,332	673	2	
	45 and over	481	404	392	1,310	569	207	82	36	0	:
2006	**All ages**	**6,769**	**6,249**	**6,010**	**24,606**	**18,735**	**13,472**	**8,764**	**9,449**	13	11.6
	Under 20	145	106	94	370	463	569	666	1,025	1	:
	20-24	1,130	1,099	1,083	5,866	6,495	5,991	4,431	5,752	3	:
	25-29	2,199	2,085	2,043	8,483	6,388	4,053	2,268	2,044	6	:
	30-44	2,783	2,571	2,384	8,503	4,814	2,615	1,317	598	3	
	45 and over	512	388	406	1,384	575	244	82	30	0	
2005	**All ages**	**7,343**	**6,801**	**6,303**	**26,310**	**20,310**	**14,268**	**9,241**	**9,852**	9	11.6
	Under 20	116	125	93	445	575	734	761	1,062	1	:
	20-24	1,303	1,317	1,269	6,815	7,425	6,596	4,831	5,921	1	:
	25-29	2,437	2,267	2,121	9,377	6,742	4,049	2,313	2,142	2	:
	30-44	2,951	2,651	2,456	8,448	4,979	2,672	1,274	703	5	
	45 and over	536	441	364	1,225	589	217	62	24	0	:
2004	**All ages**	**7,900**	**7,683**	**6,883**	**28,984**	**21,515**	**15,431**	**9,705**	**10,293**	0	11.5
	Under 20	127	120	111	596	710	894	849	1,152	0	:
	20-24	1,543	1,585	1,522	8,361	8,403	7,232	5,081	6,262	0	:
	25-29	2,699	2,699	2,480	10,158	6,893	4,251	2,510	2,178	0	:
	30-44	3,016	2,851	2,364	8,605	4,924	2,838	1,200	672	0	
	45 and over	515	428	406	1,264	585	216	65	29	0	:
2003	**All ages**	**8,228**	**7,686**	**6,976**	**29,751**	**20,863**	**14,974**	**9,627**	**9,907**	2	11.3
	Under 20	127	122	117	705	798	1,064	902	1,087	1	:
	20-24	1,751	1,760	1,781	9,169	8,627	7,216	5,204	6,251	1	:
	25-29	2,781	2,745	2,454	10,243	6,314	3,938	2,330	1,964	0	:
	30-44	3,015	2,616	2,224	8,378	4,617	2,573	1,119	577	0	
	45 and over	554	443	400	1,256	507	183	72	28	0	:

Source: Office for National Statistics

15.14 Live births by administrative area of usual residence, numbers, sex, general fertility rates and total fertility rates, 2014

England and Wales: regions (within England), unitary authorities, counties, districts, London Boroughs, local health boards (within Wales)

	Total Live Births	Male	Female	General Fertility Rate (GFR)[2]	Total Fertility Rate (TFR)[3]
UNITED KINGDOM	776,352	398,371	377,981	61.6	1.82
ENGLAND, WALES AND ELSEWHERE	695,233	356,772	338,461	62.1	1.83
ENGLAND	661,496	339,382	322,114	62.2	1.83
NORTH EAST	28,456	14,714	13,742	57.6	1.72
County Durham UA	5,361	2,679	2,682	56.4	1.71
Darlington UA	1,226	644	582	62.5	1.92
Hartlepool UA	1,043	549	494	60.9	1.82
Middlesbrough UA	2,003	1,020	983	72.0	2.09
Northumberland UA	2,753	1,432	1,321	54.0	1.68
Redcar and Cleveland UA	1,422	754	668	60.2	1.82
Stockton-on-Tees UA	2,329	1,205	1,124	62.8	1.85
Tyne and Wear (Met County)	12,319	6,431	5,888	55.3	1.63
Gateshead	2,274	1,160	1,114	59.5	1.74
Newcastle upon Tyne	3,283	1,723	1,560	49.5	1.53
North Tyneside	2,293	1,226	1,067	60.6	1.80
South Tyneside	1,591	836	755	58.6	1.74
Sunderland	2,878	1,486	1,392	54.4	1.62
NORTH WEST	85,606	43,835	41,771	62.5	1.86
Blackburn with Darwen UA	2,212	1,120	1,092	75.8	2.25
Blackpool UA	1,819	915	904	72.5	2.17
Cheshire East UA	3,749	1,898	1,851	59.4	1.88
Cheshire West and Chester UA	3,527	1,819	1,708	58.8	1.82
Halton UA	1,556	826	730	64.4	1.94
Warrington UA	2,346	1,220	1,126	60.9	1.85
Cumbria	4,760	2,429	2,331	58.4	1.83
Allerdale	902	424	478	58.1	1.86
Barrow-in-Furness	727	368	359	61.4	1.89
Carlisle	1,261	632	629	64.2	1.94
Copeland	677	361	316	58.2	1.80
Eden	399	216	183	50.7	1.66
South Lakeland	794	428	366	52.8	1.72
Greater Manchester (Met County)	36,402	18,600	17,802	65.0	1.89
Bolton	3,758	1,926	1,832	69.5	2.08
Bury	2,329	1,237	1,092	65.9	1.98
Manchester	7,964	4,080	3,884	59.4	1.69
Oldham	3,282	1,650	1,632	73.9	2.19
Rochdale	2,844	1,470	1,374	68.0	2.02
Salford	3,512	1,814	1,698	67.7	1.89
Stockport	3,387	1,694	1,693	65.2	1.96
Tameside	2,975	1,472	1,503	70.3	2.08
Trafford	2,700	1,386	1,314	61.6	1.85
Wigan	3,651	1,871	1,780	60.7	1.83
Lancashire	13,210	6,757	6,453	60.9	1.86
Burnley	1,122	569	553	68.0	1.98
Chorley	1,231	623	608	61.2	1.88
Fylde	600	299	301	53.1	1.67
Hyndburn	1,085	545	540	71.0	2.13
Lancaster	1,497	755	742	52.5	1.70
Pendle	1,304	704	600	77.6	2.26
Preston	1,869	926	943	62.5	1.86
Ribble Valley	457	244	213	49.7	1.67
Rossendale	837	440	397	65.1	2.00
South Ribble	1,206	629	577	61.7	1.89
West Lancashire	1,011	514	497	49.8	1.68
Wyre	991	509	482	59.1	1.88
Merseyside (Met County)	16,025	8,251	7,774	59.2	1.76
Knowsley	1,892	938	954	65.4	1.93
Liverpool	5,851	3,002	2,849	54.9	1.62
Sefton	2,778	1,434	1,344	60.2	1.86
St. Helens	1,968	1,023	945	60.5	1.83
Wirral	3,536	1,854	1,682	62.7	1.92
YORKSHIRE AND THE HUMBER	64,078	32,813	31,265	61.9	1.85
East Riding of Yorkshire UA	3,009	1,580	1,429	56.6	1.87
Kingston upon Hull, City of UA	3,537	1,804	1,733	65.3	1.82
North East Lincolnshire UA	1,942	982	960	66.8	1.97
North Lincolnshire UA	1,734	888	846	58.6	1.77
York UA	2,016	1,034	982	45.3	1.45

15.14 Live births by administrative area of usual residence, numbers, sex, general fertility rates and total fertility rates, 2014

England and Wales: regions (within England), unitary authorities, counties, districts, London Boroughs, local health boards (within Wales)

	Total Live Births	Male	Female	General Fertility Rate (GFR)[2]	Total Fertility Rate (TFR)[3]
North Yorkshire	**5,626**	**2,902**	**2,724**	**59.4**	**1.90**
Craven	441	244	197	52.7	1.78
Hambleton	820	418	402	60.6	1.98
Harrogate	1,426	719	707	56.6	1.82
Richmondshire	510	277	233	63.5	2.00
Ryedale	458	230	228	59.3	1.97
Scarborough	1,035	556	479	61.4	1.90
Selby	936	458	478	62.5	1.96
South Yorkshire (Met County)	**15,997**	**8,209**	**7,788**	**59.3**	**1.76**
Barnsley	2,789	1,394	1,395	63.3	1.91
Doncaster	3,561	1,811	1,750	64.1	1.90
Rotherham	3,072	1,553	1,519	64.4	1.95
Sheffield	6,575	3,451	3,124	53.7	1.64
West Yorkshire (Met County)	**30,217**	**15,414**	**14,803**	**65.6**	**1.93**
Bradford	8,100	4,032	4,068	76.2	2.24
Calderdale	2,533	1,331	1,202	66.1	2.03
Kirklees	5,472	2,835	2,637	65.3	1.96
Leeds	10,136	5,148	4,988	59.6	1.77
Wakefield	3,976	2,068	1,908	64.1	1.91
EAST MIDLANDS	**53,170**	**27,294**	**25,876**	**60.7**	**1.84**
Derby UA	**3,512**	**1,806**	**1,706**	**68.3**	**1.99**
Leicester UA	**5,264**	**2,731**	**2,533**	**66.8**	**1.93**
Nottingham UA	**4,242**	**2,176**	**2,066**	**55.0**	**1.70**
Rutland UA	**341**	**175**	**166**	**59.8**	**2.06**
Derbyshire	**7,866**	**3,986**	**3,880**	**57.5**	**1.80**
Amber Valley	1,248	648	600	57.1	1.78
Bolsover	822	396	426	58.7	1.81
Chesterfield	1,144	575	569	60.4	1.85
Derbyshire Dales	525	272	253	51.7	1.77
Erewash	1,296	670	626	60.9	1.85
High Peak	882	431	451	55.7	1.77
North East Derbyshire	875	427	448	53.8	1.72
South Derbyshire	1,074	567	507	58.4	1.80
Leicestershire	**6,789**	**3,493**	**3,296**	**56.1**	**1.75**
Blaby	1,062	557	505	61.6	1.86
Charnwood	1,766	902	864	50.9	1.59
Harborough	817	438	379	56.9	1.88
Hinckley and Bosworth	1,091	566	525	58.1	1.78
Melton	512	252	260	59.9	1.89
North West Leicestershire	974	478	496	56.8	1.78
Oadby and Wigston	567	300	267	55.6	1.79
Lincolnshire	**7,748**	**3,990**	**3,758**	**61.1**	**1.88**
Boston	857	417	440	71.4	2.08
East Lindsey	1,202	622	580	61.1	1.95
Lincoln	1,240	633	607	54.4	1.62
North Kesteven	1,098	577	521	59.2	1.90
South Holland	959	483	476	63.0	1.97
South Kesteven	1,480	773	707	62.2	1.99
West Lindsey	912	485	427	61.7	2.01
Northamptonshire	**8,746**	**4,502**	**4,244**	**65.0**	**1.97**
Corby	913	473	440	69.4	1.98
Daventry	706	371	335	54.6	1.79
East Northamptonshire	858	412	446	55.5	1.82
Kettering	1,243	629	614	68.8	2.12
Northampton	3,236	1,681	1,555	70.0	2.00
South Northamptonshire	837	431	406	56.6	1.83
Wellingborough	953	505	448	68.0	2.12
Nottinghamshire	**8,662**	**4,435**	**4,227**	**60.4**	**1.86**
Ashfield	1,449	735	714	63.2	1.92
Bassetlaw	1,189	599	590	61.3	1.95
Broxtowe	1,206	626	580	59.0	1.76
Gedling	1,243	617	626	59.4	1.83
Mansfield	1,305	694	611	66.2	1.95
Newark and Sherwood	1,233	635	598	61.8	1.94
Rushcliffe	1,037	529	508	51.9	1.63
WEST MIDLANDS	**70,123**	**35,988**	**34,135**	**64.1**	**1.92**
Herefordshire, County of UA	**1,728**	**933**	**795**	**57.3**	**1.77**
Shropshire UA	**2,835**	**1,468**	**1,367**	**57.1**	**1.81**
Stoke-on-Trent UA	**3,641**	**1,854**	**1,787**	**73.5**	**2.12**
Telford and Wrekin UA	**2,043**	**1,017**	**1,026**	**63.2**	**1.92**

15.14 Live births by administrative area of usual residence, numbers, sex, general fertility rates and total fertility rates, 2014

England and Wales: regions (within England), unitary authorities, counties, districts, London Boroughs, local health boards (within Wales)

	Total Live Births	Male	Female	General Fertility Rate (GFR)[2]	Total Fertility Rate (TFR)[3]
Staffordshire	**8,672**	**4,465**	**4,207**	**57.7**	**1.79**
Cannock Chase	1,104	579	525	59.3	1.80
East Staffordshire	1,438	724	714	69.3	2.10
Lichfield	982	497	485	58.5	1.85
Newcastle-under-Lyme	1,291	660	631	54.1	1.68
South Staffordshire	907	455	452	51.7	1.68
Stafford	1,201	644	557	54.0	1.68
Staffordshire Moorlands	846	458	388	54.5	1.79
Tamworth	903	448	455	60.1	1.81
Warwickshire	**5,885**	**3,017**	**2,868**	**59.4**	**1.82**
North Warwickshire	568	297	271	53.3	1.69
Nuneaton and Bedworth	1,528	770	758	64.9	1.94
Rugby	1,246	629	617	66.6	2.05
Stratford-on-Avon	1,037	556	481	55.5	1.80
Warwick	1,506	765	741	54.9	1.70
West Midlands (Met County)	**39,425**	**20,232**	**19,193**	**67.7**	**1.98**
Birmingham	16,925	8,764	8,161	69.0	2.01
Coventry	4,572	2,364	2,208	61.1	1.78
Dudley	3,758	1,889	1,869	65.0	1.97
Sandwell	4,680	2,413	2,267	72.5	2.10
Solihull	2,261	1,169	1,092	61.3	1.92
Walsall	3,748	1,862	1,886	71.2	2.10
Wolverhampton	3,481	1,771	1,710	68.9	2.02
Worcestershire	**5,894**	**3,002**	**2,892**	**59.0**	**1.83**
Bromsgrove	908	455	453	57.9	1.88
Malvern Hills	598	313	285	53.5	1.79
Redditch	1,108	570	538	67.7	1.99
Worcester	1,184	620	564	55.3	1.65
Wychavon	1,052	529	523	55.8	1.80
Wyre Forest	1,044	515	529	63.6	1.99
EAST	**71,855**	**36,964**	**34,891**	**64.1**	**1.92**
Bedford UA	**2,150**	**1,102**	**1,048**	**67.8**	**2.03**
Central Bedfordshire UA	**3,246**	**1,688**	**1,558**	**64.5**	**1.92**
Luton UA	**3,481**	**1,807**	**1,674**	**76.1**	**2.12**
Peterborough UA	**3,134**	**1,650**	**1,484**	**80.8**	**2.34**
Southend-on-Sea UA	**2,212**	**1,121**	**1,091**	**65.3**	**1.97**
Thurrock UA	**2,356**	**1,179**	**1,177**	**68.7**	**2.02**
Cambridgeshire	**7,269**	**3,755**	**3,514**	**58.7**	**1.76**
Cambridge	1,421	738	683	44.1	1.40
East Cambridgeshire	1,035	533	502	65.5	1.97
Fenland	1,118	565	553	66.6	2.04
Huntingdonshire	1,966	1,031	935	62.5	1.91
South Cambridgeshire	1,729	888	841	62.8	1.90
Essex	**16,449**	**8,477**	**7,972**	**63.4**	**1.93**
Basildon	2,425	1,223	1,202	68.7	2.05
Braintree	1,644	854	790	60.6	1.86
Brentwood	874	479	395	64.0	1.94
Castle Point	861	442	419	59.2	1.88
Chelmsford	1,957	1,034	923	60.8	1.80
Colchester	2,229	1,163	1,066	61.3	1.81
Epping Forest	1,478	745	733	61.9	1.84
Harlow	1,364	697	667	79.5	2.31
Maldon	535	278	257	54.3	1.80
Rochford	794	388	406	55.5	1.83
Tendring	1,370	739	631	67.0	2.14
Uttlesford	918	435	483	63.4	2.04
Hertfordshire	**14,493**	**7,474**	**7,019**	**63.9**	**1.87**
Broxbourne	1,223	620	603	65.6	1.93
Dacorum	1,901	989	912	66.2	1.95
East Hertfordshire	1,625	836	789	60.6	1.83
Hertsmere	1,357	693	664	68.7	2.02
North Hertfordshire	1,535	820	715	62.8	1.87
St Albans	1,808	930	878	65.2	1.86
Stevenage	1,170	584	586	67.0	1.93
Three Rivers	1,024	522	502	60.9	1.83
Watford	1,484	781	703	69.3	1.86
Welwyn Hatfield	1,366	699	667	54.5	1.67
Norfolk	**9,105**	**4,635**	**4,470**	**60.3**	**1.83**
Breckland	1,432	729	703	65.5	2.02
Broadland	1,069	548	521	53.5	1.75
Great Yarmouth	1,076	570	506	65.2	1.97
King's Lynn and West Norfolk	1,650	842	808	68.0	2.09
North Norfolk	786	407	379	56.9	1.82

15.14 Live births by administrative area of usual residence, numbers, sex, general fertility rates and total fertility rates, 2014

England and Wales: regions (within England), unitary authorities, counties, districts, London Boroughs, local health boards (within Wales)

	Total Live Births	Male	Female	General Fertility Rate (GFR)[2]	Total Fertility Rate (TFR)[3]
Norwich	1,761	875	886	52.9	1.52
South Norfolk	1,331	664	667	62.6	2.01
Suffolk	**7,960**	**4,076**	**3,884**	**63.9**	**1.96**
Babergh	756	383	373	55.7	1.86
Forest Heath	1,015	514	501	82.7	2.31
Ipswich	1,866	948	918	67.8	1.94
Mid Suffolk	917	487	430	58.6	1.87
St Edmundsbury	1,155	587	568	60.9	1.86
Suffolk Coastal	1,058	549	509	58.2	1.97
Waveney	1,193	608	585	64.9	2.00
LONDON	**127,399**	**65,525**	**61,874**	**63.3**	**1.71**
Inner London	**50,574**	**25,910**	**24,664**	**56.5**	**1.51**
Camden	2,700	1,414	1,286	44.3	1.24
City of London	61	33	28	37.3	0.96
Hackney	4,377	2,271	2,106	60.1	1.66
Hammersmith and Fulham	2,440	1,225	1,215	51.5	1.37
Haringey	4,006	2,027	1,979	61.0	1.67
Islington	2,879	1,498	1,381	46.0	1.29
Kensington and Chelsea	1,821	902	919	50.9	1.31
Lambeth	4,528	2,356	2,172	52.0	1.43
Lewisham	4,759	2,393	2,366	65.8	1.79
Newham	6,023	3,104	2,919	76.6	2.05
Southwark	4,647	2,363	2,284	57.0	1.55
Tower Hamlets	4,619	2,379	2,240	56.6	1.46
Wandsworth	5,110	2,585	2,525	56.4	1.47
Westminster	2,604	1,360	1,244	46.5	1.20
Outer London	**76,825**	**39,615**	**37,210**	**68.7**	**1.92**
Barking and Dagenham	3,569	1,779	1,790	79.4	2.28
Barnet	5,244	2,704	2,540	64.1	1.75
Bexley	3,037	1,574	1,463	63.1	1.88
Brent	5,078	2,618	2,460	70.0	1.91
Bromley	4,086	2,092	1,994	64.8	1.88
Croydon	5,645	2,898	2,747	70.3	2.01
Ealing	5,474	2,834	2,640	71.5	1.94
Enfield	4,824	2,463	2,361	68.2	1.94
Greenwich	4,368	2,219	2,149	69.7	1.92
Harrow	3,525	1,822	1,703	69.7	1.92
Havering	3,150	1,609	1,541	65.9	1.93
Hillingdon	4,423	2,309	2,114	69.2	1.94
Hounslow	4,245	2,183	2,062	70.2	1.90
Kingston upon Thames	2,247	1,154	1,093	57.4	1.63
Merton	3,274	1,732	1,542	69.9	1.86
Redbridge	4,678	2,430	2,248	72.0	1.99
Richmond upon Thames	2,589	1,340	1,249	64.2	1.68
Sutton	2,751	1,431	1,320	66.9	1.93
Waltham Forest	4,618	2,424	2,194	74.2	2.03
SOUTH EAST	**102,406**	**52,430**	**49,976**	**61.4**	**1.86**
Bracknell Forest UA	**1,510**	**742**	**768**	**63.1**	**1.85**
Brighton and Hove UA	**2,987**	**1,533**	**1,454**	**44.8**	**1.39**
Isle of Wight UA	**1,316**	**663**	**653**	**62.1**	**1.99**
Medway UA	**3,531**	**1,817**	**1,714**	**63.9**	**1.89**
Milton Keynes UA	**3,667**	**1,867**	**1,800**	**68.2**	**1.98**
Portsmouth UA	**2,685**	**1,362**	**1,323**	**58.3**	**1.71**
Reading UA	**2,554**	**1,318**	**1,236**	**67.0**	**1.87**
Slough UA	**2,591**	**1,344**	**1,247**	**78.8**	**2.18**
Southampton UA	**3,306**	**1,723**	**1,583**	**57.3**	**1.67**
West Berkshire UA	**1,852**	**891**	**961**	**66.2**	**2.09**
Windsor and Maidenhead UA	**1,672**	**837**	**835**	**61.4**	**1.80**
Wokingham UA	**1,811**	**948**	**863**	**62.3**	**1.88**
Buckinghamshire	**5,989**	**3,047**	**2,942**	**63.2**	**1.93**
Aylesbury Vale	2,207	1,160	1,047	64.0	1.94
Chiltern	916	478	438	61.0	1.98
South Bucks	727	350	377	62.4	1.89
Wycombe	2,139	1,059	1,080	63.5	1.92
East Sussex	**5,152**	**2,595**	**2,557**	**59.5**	**1.89**
Eastbourne	1,110	538	572	62.2	1.89
Hastings	1,084	543	541	64.3	1.93
Lewes	897	450	447	56.9	1.82
Rother	705	374	331	57.1	1.88
Wealden	1,356	690	666	57.1	1.90
Hampshire	**14,453**	**7,484**	**6,969**	**60.9**	**1.89**
Basingstoke and Deane	2,111	1,132	979	63.5	1.89
East Hampshire	1,117	570	547	58.5	1.95

15.14 Live births by administrative area of usual residence, numbers, sex, general fertility rates and total fertility rates, 2014

England and Wales: regions (within England), unitary authorities, counties, districts, London Boroughs, local health boards (within Wales)

	Total Live Births	Male	Female	General Fertility Rate (GFR)[2]	Total Fertility Rate (TFR)[3]
Eastleigh	1,548	758	790	64.0	1.90
Fareham	1,030	520	510	54.0	1.72
Gosport	942	498	444	61.4	1.85
Hart	1,036	541	495	64.0	2.01
Havant	1,237	617	620	60.0	1.87
New Forest	1,546	810	736	57.4	1.84
Rushmoor	1,381	742	639	67.9	1.98
Test Valley	1,279	660	619	62.6	2.02
Winchester	1,226	636	590	55.6	1.85
Kent	**17,305**	**8,767**	**8,538**	**62.4**	**1.92**
Ashford	1,474	747	727	64.8	2.02
Canterbury	1,366	706	660	41.3	1.49
Dartford	1,494	742	752	70.3	2.02
Dover	1,170	580	590	62.9	1.97
Gravesham	1,454	746	708	70.6	2.10
Maidstone	1,979	1,037	942	66.1	1.98
Sevenoaks	1,298	638	660	64.3	2.01
Shepway	1,092	531	561	61.1	1.89
Swale	1,771	900	871	69.3	2.13
Thanet	1,586	806	780	66.0	2.01
Tonbridge and Malling	1,424	737	687	62.8	2.02
Tunbridge Wells	1,197	597	600	57.6	1.80
Oxfordshire	**7,775**	**4,009**	**3,766**	**58.6**	**1.75**
Cherwell	1,817	946	871	66.5	2.01
Oxford	1,845	948	897	44.3	1.41
South Oxfordshire	1,508	765	743	64.8	2.04
Vale of White Horse	1,416	748	668	65.1	1.96
West Oxfordshire	1,189	602	587	63.3	1.93
Surrey	**13,531**	**6,901**	**6,630**	**62.8**	**1.89**
Elmbridge	1,785	904	881	75.8	2.24
Epsom and Ewell	920	458	462	60.9	1.86
Guildford	1,542	817	725	52.2	1.61
Mole Valley	800	405	395	57.7	1.86
Reigate and Banstead	1,846	936	910	68.6	2.00
Runnymede	970	466	504	53.4	1.74
Spelthorne	1,260	650	610	67.7	1.97
Surrey Heath	932	490	442	60.5	1.89
Tandridge	904	462	442	60.6	1.87
Waverley	1,214	631	583	59.6	1.91
Woking	1,358	682	676	71.0	2.04
West Sussex	**8,719**	**4,582**	**4,137**	**61.2**	**1.88**
Adur	692	350	342	64.1	1.99
Arun	1,463	763	700	61.1	1.90
Chichester	1,060	560	500	59.2	1.93
Crawley	1,618	883	735	68.8	1.92
Horsham	1,229	634	595	56.1	1.81
Mid Sussex	1,521	794	727	60.0	1.84
Worthing	1,136	598	538	59.7	1.82
SOUTH WEST	**58,403**	**29,819**	**28,584**	**60.5**	**1.85**
Bath and North East Somerset UA	**1,702**	**868**	**834**	**46.5**	**1.59**
Bournemouth UA	**2,224**	**1,138**	**1,086**	**54.8**	**1.59**
Bristol, City of UA	**6,442**	**3,304**	**3,138**	**61.6**	**1.76**
Cornwall UA and Isles of Scilly UA [4]	**5,447**	**2,796**	**2,651**	**60.5**	**1.92**
North Somerset UA	**2,192**	**1,141**	**1,051**	**63.4**	**1.98**
Plymouth UA	**3,101**	**1,570**	**1,531**	**58.1**	**1.73**
Poole UA	**1,647**	**829**	**818**	**62.6**	**1.88**
South Gloucestershire UA	**3,138**	**1,560**	**1,578**	**61.9**	**1.88**
Swindon UA	**2,923**	**1,474**	**1,449**	**67.9**	**2.00**
Torbay UA	**1,443**	**725**	**718**	**68.4**	**2.12**
Wiltshire UA	**5,290**	**2,741**	**2,549**	**64.4**	**2.06**
Devon	**7,153**	**3,635**	**3,518**	**57.4**	**1.80**
East Devon	1,166	601	565	61.2	2.02
Exeter	1,346	704	642	46.1	1.46
Mid Devon	805	416	389	62.7	2.01
North Devon	933	472	461	63.3	2.00
South Hams	702	338	364	59.9	1.96
Teignbridge	1,169	589	580	60.2	1.90
Torridge	565	294	271	57.4	1.83
West Devon	467	221	246	59.8	1.91
Dorset	**3,482**	**1,770**	**1,712**	**57.7**	**1.88**
Christchurch	378	195	183	55.0	1.80
East Dorset	662	340	322	55.3	1.86
North Dorset	631	317	314	59.1	1.92
Purbeck	408	199	209	61.4	1.97

15.14 Live births by administrative area of usual residence, numbers, sex, general fertility rates and total fertility rates, 2014

England and Wales: regions (within England), unitary authorities, counties, districts, London Boroughs, local health boards (within Wales)

	Total Live Births	Male	Female	General Fertility Rate (GFR)[2]	Total Fertility Rate (TFR)[3]
West Dorset	791	403	388	56.8	1.89
Weymouth and Portland	612	316	296	59.6	1.87
Gloucestershire	**6,631**	**3,364**	**3,267**	**61.3**	**1.89**
Cheltenham	1,435	722	713	60.0	1.78
Cotswold	681	354	327	51.9	1.73
Forest of Dean	779	396	383	58.4	1.95
Gloucester	1,730	880	850	69.4	2.01
Stroud	1,014	502	512	54.8	1.80
Tewkesbury	992	510	482	69.2	2.14
Somerset	**5,588**	**2,904**	**2,684**	**63.2**	**1.99**
Mendip	1,117	595	522	60.8	2.01
Sedgemoor	1,287	682	605	65.4	2.05
South Somerset	1,675	830	845	63.6	1.99
Taunton Deane	1,241	653	588	63.3	1.96
West Somerset	268	144	124	59.3	1.84
WALES	**33,544**	**17,292**	**16,252**	**59.1**	**1.78**
Isle of Anglesey	747	404	343	67.6	2.08
Gwynedd	1,175	615	560	54.4	1.75
Conwy	1,106	559	547	62.1	1.96
Denbighshire	1,111	567	544	71.7	2.25
Flintshire	1,623	853	770	59.5	1.84
Wrexham	1,603	801	802	64.5	1.93
Powys	1,149	622	527	58.2	1.90
Ceredigion	601	279	322	44.4	1.64
Pembrokeshire	1,229	620	609	62.5	1.96
Carmarthenshire	1,809	943	866	58.5	1.79
Swansea	2,522	1,332	1,190	54.7	1.65
Neath Port Talbot	1,488	767	721	59.2	1.78
Bridgend	1,482	770	712	58.5	1.78
The Vale of Glamorgan	1,265	635	630	56.6	1.79
Cardiff	4,606	2,338	2,268	55.8	1.66
Rhondda, Cynon, Taff	2,721	1,384	1,337	59.7	1.77
Merthyr Tydfil	744	361	383	65.6	1.89
Caerphilly	2,126	1,096	1,030	62.0	1.85
Blaenau Gwent	771	410	361	58.7	1.72
Torfaen	1,006	533	473	59.8	1.78
Monmouthshire	770	395	375	54.2	1.80
Newport	1,890	1,008	882	66.1	1.94
Betsi Cadwaladr University	7,365	3,799	3,566	62.4	1.92
Powys Teaching	1,149	622	527	58.2	1.90
Hywel Dda	3,639	1,842	1,797	56.8	1.77
Abertawe Bro Morgannwg University	5,492	2,869	2,623	56.9	1.71
Cwm Taf	3,465	1,745	1,720	60.9	1.79
Aneurin Bevan	6,563	3,442	3,121	61.3	1.84
Cardiff and Vale University	5,871	2,973	2,898	55.9	1.68
Usual residence outside England and Wales where birth occurred in England and Wales	**193**	**98**	**95**	**0**	**0**

Source: Office for National Statistics

A birth to a mother whose usual residence is outside England and Wales is assigned to the country of residence. These births are included in total figures for "England, Wales and elsewhere " but are excluded from any sub-divisions of England and Wales. The England and Wales and elsewhere figures correspond to figures published at the national level for England and Wales not based on area of usual residence.

The Human Fertilisation and Embryology Act (HFEA) 2008 contained provisions enabling two females in a same-sex couple to register a birth from 1 September 2009 onwards. Due to the small numbers, births registered to a same-sex couple in a civil partnership (713 in 2014) are included with marital births while births registered to a same-sex couple outside a civil partnership (277 in 2014) are included with births outside marriage. Births registered under HFEA are reported only for England and Wales and no sub division thereof.

1 Live births per 1,000 population (all persons and all ages). This has been calculated using the mid-2014 population estimates.
2 The General Fertility Rate (GFR) is the number of live births per 1,000 women aged 15 to 44. The GFRs have been calculated using the mid-2014 population estimates.
3 The Total Fertility Rate (TFR) is the average number of live children that a group of women would bear if they experienced the age-specific fertility rates of the calendar year in question throughout their childbearing lifespan. The national TFRs have been calculated using the number of live births by single year of age and the mid-2014 population estimates. The sub-national TFRs have been calculated using the number of live births by five year age groups and the mid-2014 population estimates.

4 To preserve confidentiality, counts for City of London and Isles of Scilly have been combined with those for Hackney LB and Cornwall UA respectively
: denotes not available

15.15 Live births by age of mother and registration type[1], 1982-2013

England and Wales

Year	Type of Registration		Age of mother at birth						
		All ages	Under 20	20-24	25-29	30-34	35-39	40-44	45 and over
		Numbers of births							
2013	All	698,512	29,136	119,719	196,693	212,306	111,500	27,148	2,010
	Within Marriage/Civil Partnership[1]	367,618	1,272	25,794	102,106	144,376	76,046	16,783	1,241
	Outside Marriage/Civil Partnership[1]	330,894	27,864	93,925	94,587	67,930	35,454	10,365	769
	Joint Registrations same address	218,049	11,220	56,805	66,103	49,922	26,234	7,282	483
	Joint Registrations different address	73,546	10,628	25,440	18,908	11,195	5,499	1,736	140
	Sole Registrations	39,299	6,016	11,680	9,576	6,813	3,721	1,347	146
2012	All	729,674	33,815	132,456	202,370	216,242	114,797	28,019	1,975
	Within Marriage/Civil Partnership[1]	383,189	1,295	29,627	106,555	148,403	78,689	17,380	1,240
	Outside Marriage/Civil Partnership[1]	346,485	32,520	102,829	95,815	67,839	36,108	10,639	735
	Joint Registrations same address	227,337	13,326	62,151	67,031	50,094	26,731	7,528	476
	Joint Registrations different address	77,269	12,327	27,867	18,759	10,872	5,529	1,809	106
	Sole Registrations	41,879	6,867	12,811	10,025	6,873	3,848	1,302	153
2011	All	723,913	36,435	134,946	200,587	207,151	115,444	27,518	1,832
	Within Marriage/Civil Partnership[1]	382,574	1,410	31,785	107,383	143,519	79,951	17,388	1,138
	Outside Marriage/Civil Partnership[1]	341,339	35,025	103,161	93,204	63,632	35,493	10,130	694
	Joint Registrations same address	226,057	14,600	63,287	66,102	47,706	26,688	7,213	461
	Joint Registrations different address	73,464	12,960	26,826	17,379	9,489	5,093	1,603	114
	Sole Registrations	41,818	7,465	13,048	9,723	6,437	3,712	1,314	119
2010	All	723,165	40,591	137,312	199,233	202,457	115,841	25,973	1,758
	Within Marriage/Civil Partnership[1]	384,375	1,684	33,955	108,465	141,873	80,846	16,404	1,148
	Outside Marriage/Civil Partnership[1]	338,790	38,907	103,357	90,768	60,584	34,995	9,569	610
	Joint Registrations same address	224,001	16,401	63,816	64,656	45,498	26,453	6,769	408
	Joint Registrations different address	72,297	14,352	26,184	16,393	8,838	4,903	1,525	102
	Sole Registrations	42,492	8,154	13,357	9,719	6,248	3,639	1,275	100
2009	All	706,248	43,243	136,012	194,129	191,600	114,288	25,357	1,619
	Within Marriage/Civil Partnership[1]	380,069	2,334	35,920	108,499	135,802	80,156	16,318	1,040
	Outside Marriage/Civil Partnership[1]	326,179	40,909	100,092	85,630	55,798	34,132	9,039	579
	Joint Registrations same address	214,189	17,200	61,813	60,876	41,831	25,637	6,444	388
	Joint Registrations different address	68,251	14,778	24,376	14,811	7,991	4,790	1,420	85
	Sole Registrations	43,739	8,931	13,903	9,943	5,976	3,705	1,175	106
2008	All	708,711	44,691	135,971	192,960	192,450	116,220	24,991	1,428
	Within Marriage	387,930	2,739	38,239	110,353	138,066	81,602	15,991	940
	Outside Marriage	320,781	41,952	97,732	82,607	54,384	34,618	9,000	488
	Joint Registrations same address	210,076	17,231	59,913	59,104	41,178	26,036	6,289	325
	Joint Registrations different address	65,241	15,161	23,102	13,543	7,257	4,662	1,441	75
	Sole Registrations	45,464	9,560	14,717	9,960	5,949	3,920	1,270	88
2007	All	690,013	44,805	130,784	182,570	191,124	115,380	24,041	1,309
	Within Marriage	384,463	3,087	38,859	106,603	138,157	81,399	15,484	874
	Outside Marriage	305,550	41,718	91,925	75,967	52,967	33,981	8,557	435
	Joint Registrations same address	198,470	17,036	55,904	54,040	39,783	25,383	6,050	274
	Joint Registrations different address	61,379	14,714	21,415	12,204	7,024	4,587	1,359	76
	Sole Registrations	45,701	9,968	14,606	9,723	6,160	4,011	1,148	85
2006	All	669,601	45,509	127,828	172,642	189,407	110,509	22,512	1,194
	Within Marriage	378,225	3,199	40,126	103,348	137,996	78,269	14,511	776
	Outside Marriage	291,376	42,310	87,702	69,294	51,411	32,240	8,001	418
	Joint Registrations same address	185,461	17,061	52,162	48,474	38,133	23,897	5,469	265
	Joint Registrations different address	60,460	14,870	20,755	11,651	7,159	4,578	1,375	72
	Sole Registrations	45,455	10,379	14,785	9,169	6,119	3,765	1,157	81

15.15 Live births by age of mother and registration type[1], 1982-2013

England and Wales

Year	Type of Registration		Age of mother at birth						
		All ages	Under 20	20-24	25-29	30-34	35-39	40-44	45 and over
		Numbers of births							
2005	All	645,835	44,830	122,145	164,348	188,153	104,113	21,155	1,091
	Within Marriage	369,330	3,654	40,010	99,957	137,401	73,810	13,760	738
	Outside Marriage	276,505	41,176	82,135	64,391	50,752	30,303	7,395	353
	Joint Registrations same address	175,555	16,316	48,755	45,165	37,764	22,265	5,057	233
	Joint Registrations different address	55,780	14,108	18,909	10,320	6,801	4,289	1,287	66
	Sole Registrations	45,170	10,752	14,471	8,906	6,187	3,749	1,051	54
2004	All	639,721	45,094	121,072	159,984	190,550	102,228	19,884	909
	Within Marriage	369,997	4,063	41,285	98,539	139,838	72,555	13,098	619
	Outside Marriage	269,724	41,031	79,787	61,445	50,712	29,673	6,786	290
	Joint Registrations same address	171,498	16,262	47,793	43,038	37,820	21,758	4,648	179
	Joint Registrations different address	52,854	13,608	17,628	9,620	6,713	4,133	1,096	56
	Sole Registrations	45,372	11,161	14,366	8,787	6,179	3,782	1,042	55
2003	All	621,469	44,236	116,622	156,931	187,214	97,386	18,205	875
	Within Marriage	364,244	4,338	40,887	98,694	138,002	69,595	12,113	615
	Outside Marriage	257,225	39,898	75,735	58,237	49,212	27,791	6,092	260
	Joint Registrations same address	163,374	16,000	45,225	40,867	36,630	20,335	4,151	166
	Joint Registrations different address	48,976	12,706	16,076	8,815	6,488	3,831	1,014	46
	Sole Registrations	44,875	11,192	14,434	8,555	6,094	3,625	927	48
2002	All	596,122	43,467	110,959	153,379	180,532	90,449	16,441	895
	Within Marriage	354,090	4,582	40,712	97,583	134,093	65,369	11,110	641
	Outside Marriage	242,032	38,885	70,247	55,796	46,439	25,080	5,331	254
	Joint Registrations same address	154,086	15,824	42,315	39,554	34,326	18,236	3,656	175
	Joint Registrations different address	44,817	11,832	14,333	8,109	6,164	3,471	866	42
	Sole Registrations	43,129	11,229	13,599	8,133	5,949	3,373	809	37
2001	All	594,634	44,189	108,844	159,926	178,920	86,495	15,499	761
	Within Marriage	356,548	4,640	40,736	103,131	133,710	63,202	10,582	547
	Outside Marriage	238,086	39,549	68,108	56,795	45,210	23,293	4,917	214
	Joint Registrations same address	150,421	16,215	40,843	39,797	33,306	16,790	3,341	129
	Joint Registrations different address	43,921	11,665	13,682	8,416	6,029	3,290	800	39
	Sole Registrations	43,744	11,669	13,583	8,582	5,875	3,213	776	46
2000	All	604,441	45,846	107,741	170,701	180,113	84,974	14,403	663
	Within Marriage	365,836	4,742	40,262	111,606	136,165	62,671	9,910	480
	Outside Marriage	238,605	41,104	67,479	59,095	43,948	22,303	4,493	183
	Joint Registrations same address	149,510	17,011	40,450	41,236	31,795	15,836	3,055	127
	Joint Registrations different address	43,322	11,634	13,110	8,646	6,037	3,158	706	31
	Sole Registrations	45,773	12,459	13,919	9,213	6,116	3,309	732	25
1999	All	621,872	48,375	110,722	181,931	185,311	81,281	13,617	635
	Within Marriage	379,983	5,333	43,190	120,716	140,330	60,470	9,466	478
	Outside Marriage	241,889	43,042	67,532	61,215	44,981	20,811	4,151	157
	Joint Registrations same address	149,584	17,833	40,190	42,126	32,152	14,455	2,725	103
	Joint Registrations different address	44,102	12,015	12,865	9,153	6,214	3,135	695	25
	Sole Registrations	48,203	13,194	14,477	9,936	6,615	3,221	731	29
1998	All	635,901	48,285	113,537	193,144	188,499	78,881	12,980	575
	Within Marriage	395,290	5,278	45,724	130,747	144,599	59,320	9,189	433
	Outside Marriage	240,611	43,007	67,813	62,397	43,900	19,561	3,791	142
	Joint Registrations same address	146,521	17,589	39,818	42,212	30,938	16,410	3,118	114
	Joint Registrations different address	44,130	11,588	13,157	9,513	6,194			
	Sole Registrations	49,960	13,830	14,838	10,672	6,768	3,151	673	28

15.15 Live births by age of mother and registration type[1], 1982-2013

England and Wales

Year	Type of Registration	All ages	Under 20	20-24	25-29	30-34	35-39	40-44	45 and over
		Numbers of births							
1997	All	643,095	46,372	118,589	202,792	187,528	74,900	12,332	582
	Within Marriage	404,873	5,233	49,068	139,383	145,293	56,671	8,797	428
	Outside Marriage	238,222	41,139	69,521	63,409	42,235	18,229	3,535	154
	Joint Registrations same address	141,740	16,551	39,784	42,020	28,715	15,179	2,860	122
	Joint Registrations different address	45,900	11,365	14,147	10,374	6,523			
	Sole Registrations	50,582	13,223	15,590	11,015	6,997	3,050	675	32
1996	All	649,485	44,667	125,732	211,103	186,377	69,503	11,516	587
	Within Marriage	416,822	5,365	54,651	148,770	145,898	53,265	8,421	452
	Outside Marriage	232,663	39,302	71,081	62,333	40,479	16,238	3,095	135
	Joint Registrations same address	135,282	15,410	39,978	40,384	26,875	13,347	2,517	107
	Joint Registrations different address	46,365	10,946	14,858	10,599	6,626			
	Sole Registrations	51,016	12,946	16,245	11,350	6,978	2,891	578	28
1995	All	648,138	41,938	130,744	217,418	181,202	65,517	10,779	540
	Within Marriage	428,189	5,623	61,029	157,855	144,200	51,129	7,944	409
	Outside Marriage	219,949	36,315	69,715	59,563	37,002	14,388	2,835	131
	Joint Registrations same address	127,789	14,424	39,274	38,376	24,376	11,859	2,335	99
	Joint Registrations different address	44,244	10,011	14,815	10,323	6,141			
	Sole Registrations	47,916	11,880	15,626	10,864	6,485	2,529	500	32
1994	All	664,726	42,026	140,240	229,102	179,568	63,061	10,241	488
	Within Marriage	449,190	6,099	69,227	170,605	145,563	49,668	7,662	366
	Outside Marriage	215,536	35,927	71,013	58,497	34,005	13,393	2,579	122
	Joint Registrations same address	123,874	14,168	39,827	37,168	22,288	10,892	2,084	97
	Joint Registrations different address	42,632	9,752	14,778	9,939	5,513			
	Sole Registrations	49,030	12,007	16,408	11,390	6,204	2,501	495	25
1993	All	673,467	45,121	151,975	235,961	171,061	58,824	9,986	539
	Within Marriage	456,919	6,875	76,950	178,456	139,671	46,919	7,621	427
	Outside Marriage	216,548	38,246	75,025	57,505	31,390	11,905	2,365	112
	Joint Registrations same address	118,758	14,134	40,168	35,307	20,084	9,569	1,882	85
	Joint Registrations different address	47,548	11,577	17,381	10,780	5,339			
	Sole Registrations	50,242	12,535	17,476	11,418	5,967	2,336	483	27
1992	All	689,656	47,861	163,311	244,798	166,839	56,650	9,696	501
	Within Marriage	474,431	7,787	86,220	188,928	137,904	45,733	7,456	403
	Outside Marriage	215,225	40,074	77,091	55,870	28,935	10,917	2,240	98
	Joint Registrations same address	119,239	15,236	42,063	34,756	18,673	8,784	1,811	78
	Joint Registrations different address	44,514	11,381	16,658	9,693	4,620			
	Sole Registrations	51,472	13,457	18,370	11,421	5,642	2,133	429	20
1991	All	699,217	52,396	173,356	248,727	161,259	53,644	9,316	519
	Within Marriage	487,923	8,948	95,605	196,281	135,542	43,810	7,294	443
	Outside Marriage	211,294	43,448	77,751	52,446	25,717	9,834	2,022	76
	Joint Registrations same address	115,298	16,351	42,245	32,532	16,468	7,861	1,594	60
	Joint Registrations different address	41,865	11,848	15,835	8,518	3,851			
	Sole Registrations	54,131	15,249	19,671	11,396	5,398	1,973	428	16
1990	All	706,140	55,541	180,136	252,577	156,264	51,905	9,220	497
	Within Marriage	506,141	10,958	106,188	204,701	133,384	43,179	7,302	429
	Outside Marriage	199,999	44,583	73,948	47,876	22,880	8,726	1,918	68
	Joint Registrations same address	106,001	16,311	39,062	29,181	14,585	6,793	1,505	55
	Joint Registrations different address	39,167	12,081	14,751	7,555	3,289			
	Sole Registrations	54,831	16,191	20,135	11,140	5,006	1,933	413	13

15 Live births by age of mother and registration type[1], 1982-2013

England and Wales

Year	Type of Registration	All ages	Under 20	20-24	25-29	30-34	35-39	40-44	45 and over
		Numbers of births							
1989	All	687,725	55,543	185,239	242,822	145,320	49,465	8,845	491
	Within Marriage	501,921	12,027	114,456	200,961	125,439	41,528	7,079	431
	Outside Marriage	185,804	43,516	70,783	41,861	19,881	7,937	1,766	60
	Joint Registrations same address	95,858	15,686	36,582	24,859	12,543	6,156	1,341	49
	Joint Registrations different address	36,409	11,688	14,022	6,603	2,738			11
	Sole Registrations	53,537	16,142	20,179	10,399	4,600	1,781	425	11
1988	All	693,577	58,741	193,726	243,460	140,974	47,649	8,520	507
	Within Marriage	516,225	14,099	125,575	205,292	123,384	40,400	7,025	450
	Outside Marriage	177,352	44,642	68,151	38,168	17,590	7,249	1,495	57
	Joint Registrations same address	87,601	15,304	33,994	22,070	10,765	5,607	1,159	44
	Joint Registrations different address	35,807	12,240	13,807	5,913	2,505			
	Sole Registrations	53,944	17,098	20,350	10,185	4,320	1,642	336	13
1987	All	681,511	57,545	193,232	238,929	136,558	46,604	8,112	531
	Within Marriage	523,080	15,588	132,809	206,036	121,252	40,159	6,751	485
	Outside Marriage	158,431	41,957	60,423	32,893	15,306	6,445	1,361	46
	Joint Registrations same address	75,572	13,808	29,114	18,671	9,210	4,836	1,026	31
	Joint Registrations different address	32,385	11,362	12,365	5,313	2,221			
	Sole Registrations	50,474	16,787	18,944	8,909	3,875	1,609	335	15
1986	All	661,018	57,406	192,064	229,035	129,487	45,465	7,033	528
	Within Marriage	519,673	17,793	137,985	201,323	116,369	39,753	5,959	491
	Outside Marriage	141,345	39,613	54,079	27,712	13,118	5,712	1,074	37
	Joint Registrations same address	65,844	12,908	25,760	15,300	7,849	4,233	768	26
	Joint Registrations different address	27,679	10,326	10,397	4,166	1,790			
	Sole Registrations	47,822	16,379	17,922	8,246	3,479	1,479	306	11
1985	All	656,417	56,929	193,958	227,486	126,185	44,393	6,882	584
	Within Marriage	530,167	20,057	146,262	203,272	114,862	39,293	5,883	538
	Outside Marriage	126,250	36,872	47,696	24,214	11,323	5,100	999	46
	Joint Registrations	81,792	21,000	31,256	16,856	8,177	3,736	734	33
	Sole Registrations	44,458	15,872	16,440	7,358	3,146	1,364	265	13
1984	All	636,818	54,508	191,455	218,031	122,774	42,921	6,576	553
	Within Marriage	526,353	21,373	150,371	197,401	112,660	38,350	5,691	507
	Outside Marriage	110,465	33,135	41,084	20,630	10,114	4,571	885	46
	Joint Registrations	69,872	18,207	26,208	14,247	7,290	3,302	591	27
	Sole Registrations	40,593	14,928	14,876	6,383	2,824	1,269	294	19
1983	All	629,134	54,059	191,852	214,078	120,996	41,277	6,210	662
	Within Marriage	529,923	23,636	155,209	196,162	111,722	37,160	5,422	612
	Outside Marriage	99,211	30,423	36,643	17,916	9,274	4,117	788	50
	Joint Registrations	60,794	16,072	22,550	12,097	6,623	2,892	526	34
	Sole Registrations	38,417	14,351	14,093	5,819	2,651	1,225	262	16
1982	All	625,931	55,435	192,322	211,905	120,758	38,992	5,886	633
	Within Marriage	536,074	26,696	159,911	195,839	112,625	35,310	5,118	575
	Outside Marriage	89,857	28,739	32,411	16,066	8,133	3,682	768	58
	Joint Registrations	53,404	14,286	19,420	10,683	5,835	2,596	539	45
	Sole Registrations	36,453	14,453	12,991	5,383	2,298	1,086	229	13

1. . The Human Fertilisation and Embryology Act 2008 contained provisions enabling two females in a same-sex couple to register birth from 1 September 2009 onwards. Due to the small numbers, births registered to a same-sex couple in a civil partnership (655 in 2013) are included with marital births while births registered to a same-sex couple outside a civil partnership (259 in 2013) are included with births outside marriage.
2. . 1981 births for age-groups are based on a 10 per cent sample

Source: Office for National Statistics

15.16 Legal abortions: countries of Great Britain by (i) age, (ii) gestation weeks, (iii) procedure, (iv) parity, (v) previous abortions, (vi) grounds and (vii) principal medical condition for abortions performed under ground E, 2014

Country of abortion   numbers and percentages

	England & Wales		Scotland		Great Britain	
All legal abortions	**190,092**	*100%*	**11,475**	*100%*	**201,567**	*100%*
(i) Age						
Under 16	2,453	*1*	172	*1*	2,625	*1*
16-17	8,806	*5*	627	*5*	9,433	*5*
18-19	16,692	*9*	1,167	*10*	17,859	*9*
20-24	54,045	*28*	3,495	*30*	57,540	*29*
25-29	45,439	*24*	2,683	*23*	48,122	*24*
30-34	33,253	*17*	1,824	*16*	35,077	*17*
35+	29,404	*15*	1,507	*13*	30,911	*15*
(ii) Gestation weeks						
3 - 9	151,570	*80*	9,236	*80*	160,806	*80*
10 - 12	22,289	*12*	1,452	*13*	23,741	*12*
13 - 19	13,113	*7*	735	*6*	13,848	*7*
20 and over	3,120	*2*	52	*0*	3,172	*2*
(iii) Procedure						
Surgical	95,083	*50*	2,246	*20*	97,329	*48*
Medical	95,009	*50*	9,229	*80*	104,238	*52*
(iv) Parity (number of previous pregnancies resulting in live or stillbirth)						
0	88,230	*46*	5,529	*48*	93,759	*47*
1+	101,862	*54*	5,946	*52*	107,808	*53*
(v) Number of previous pregnancies resulting in abortion under the Act						
0	120,058	*63*	7 840	*68*	127,898	*63*
1+	70,034	*37*	3 635	*32*	73,669	*37*
(vi) Grounds						
A (alone or with B, C or D) or F or G	118	*0*	*	.	*	.
B (alone or with C or D)	146	*0*	*	.	*	.
C (alone)	185,279	*97*	11,306	*99*	196,585	*98*
D (alone or with C)	1,254	*1*	13	*0*	1,267	*1*
E (alone one with A, B, C or D)	3,295	*2*	152	*1*	3,447	*2*
(vii) Principal medical condition for abortions performed under ground E						
Total Ground E	**3,295**	*100%*	**152** [1]	*100%*	**3,447**	*100%*
The nervous system (Q00 - Q07)	743	*23*	40	*26*	783	*23*
Other congenital malformations (Q10-Q89)	782	*24*	36	*24*	818	*24*
Chromosomal abnormalities (Q90 - Q99)	1,243	*38*	66	*43*	1,309	*38*
Other	527	*16*	10	*7*	537	*16*

* Adhering to ISD Statistical Disclosure Control Protocol.   Source: ISD Scotland, Department of Health
. Not available

[1] Some notifications record more than one Statutory Ground, therefore totals may not match with the numbers released by ISD Scotland.

Note: percentages are rounded and may not add up to 100

Abortions performed under ground E - abortions were carried out under ground E (risk that the child would be born handicapped)

15.17 Death[1] rates per 1,000 population: by age and sex, 2014

England and Wales

Age	Males	Females	Age	Males	Females	Age	Males	Females
All ages	8.66	8.80						
0–4	0.94	0.81	35–39	1.13	0.67	70–74	23.69	15.76
0	4.09	3.63	35	0.99	0.55	70	18.89	12.70
1	0.36	0.22	36	0.97	0.63	71	21.22	14.04
2	0.16	0.14	37	1.04	0.65	72	24.25	15.92
3	0.14	0.12	38	1.34	0.79	73	26.69	17.80
4	0.07	0.08	39	1.33	0.74	74	29.62	19.56
5–9	0.09	0.08	40–44	1.70	1.08	75–79	39.60	27.21
5	0.09	0.07	40	1.54	0.94	75	32.34	22.01
6	0.11	0.08	41	1.66	0.97	76	35.62	24.15
7	0.08	0.09	42	1.54	1.06	77	39.12	27.21
8	0.07	0.07	43	1.77	1.19	78	44.40	29.54
9	0.11	0.07	44	1.95	1.22	79	49.09	34.44
10–14	0.11	0.08	45–49	2.50	1.57	80–84	70.20	51.20
10	0.10	0.07	45	2.26	1.41	80	56.61	39.49
11	0.09	0.04 u	46	2.34	1.45	81	62.51	44.72
12	0.11	0.05 u	47	2.45	1.54	82	70.27	50.54
13	0.11	0.10	48	2.56	1.69	83	79.78	58.11
14	0.13	0.12	49	2.89	1.76	84	88.49	66.12
15–19	0.31	0.18	50–54	3.64	2.44	85–89	124.73	95.43
15	0.14	0.14	50	2.99	2.10	85	101.81	74.41
16	0.23	0.18	51	3.42	2.24	86	112.50	85.77
17	0.28	0.15	52	3.58	2.47	87	128.57	97.41
18	0.42	0.21	53	3.95	2.60	88	143.74	108.26
19	0.45	0.20	54	4.34	2.87	89	159.70	124.16
20–24	0.49	0.22	55–59	5.80	3.80	90 and over	227.42	198.98
20	0.44	0.19	55	4.78	3.24			
21	0.48	0.22	56	5.04	3.46			
22	0.47	0.24	57	5.63	3.87			
23	0.55	0.24	58	6.53	4.04			
24	0.52	0.22	59	7.25	4.51			
25–29	0.61	0.29	60–64	9.41	6.11			
25	0.46	0.25	60	7.71	5.11			
26	0.67	0.26	61	8.42	5.60			
27	0.63	0.23	62	9.53	6.02			
28	0.61	0.34	63	10.18	6.54			
29	0.67	0.35	64	11.29	7.29			
30–34	0.79	0.44	65–69	14.21	9.18			
30	0.78	0.33	65	12.03	7.79			
31	0.71	0.41	66	12.76	8.07			
32	0.72	0.41	67	13.71	8.67			
33	0.80	0.50	68	15.86	10.73			
34	0.91	0.55	69	17.56	11.23			

Source: Office for National Statistics

Notes

The male age-specific death rate is greater than the female age-specific death rate for each age group. The overall female death rate is however higher than the male rate. This is due to the underlying age distribution of the male and female population and the female population being greater than the male population at older ages where the number of deaths are highest.

1 Death figures are based on deaths registered rather than deaths occurring in a calendar year. For information on registration delays for a range of causes, see:

www.ons.gov.uk/ons/guide-method/user-guidance/health-and-life-events/impact-of-registration-delays-on-mortality-statistics/index.html

u Denotes low reliability

15.18 Stillbirth[1,2] and infant death[3] rates: age at death, 1921 to 2014

England and Wales

Infant mortality per 1,000 live births[3] at various ages | Stillbirths[2] and infant deaths per 1,000 total births

Period	Under 1 year	Neonatal mortality Under 4 weeks	Early neonatal Under 1 week	Under 1 day	1 day and under 1 week	Late neo-natal 1 week and under 4 weeks	Postneonatal mortality 4 weeks and under 1 year	4 weeks and under 3 months	3 months and under 6 months	6 months and under 1 year	Still-births	Still-births plus deaths under 1 week	Still-births plus deaths under 4 weeks	Still-births plus deaths under 1 year
1921	82.8	35.3	22.4	10.8	11.6	12.9	47.5	14.8	14.0	18.6	:	:	:	:
1922	77.1	34.1	22.0	10.4	11.6	12.1	43.0	12.7	11.0	19.3	:	:	:	:
1923	69.4	31.9	21.1	10.2	10.9	10.8	37.5	11.3	10.0	16.1	:	:	:	:
1924	75.1	33.1	21.8	10.6	11.2	11.3	42.0	12.5	10.9	18.6	:	:	:	:
1925	75.0	32.3	21.2	10.1	11.1	11.1	42.7	12.6	11.3	18.8	:	:	:	:
1926	70.2	31.9	21.3	10.0	11.3	10.6	38.3	11.6	10.4	16.3	:	:	:	:
1927	69.7	32.3	22.2	10.6	11.6	10.1	37.4	10.7	9.7	16.9	38.8	59.6	69.3	105.3
1928	65.1	31.1	21.6	10.4	11.2	9.5	34.0	10.7	9.2	14.1	40.1	60.8	69.9	102.6
1929	74.4	32.8	22.3	10.4	11.9	10.6	41.5	11.6	10.7	19.3	40.0	61.4	71.6	111.4
1930	60.0	30.9	22.0	10.4	11.6	8.9	29.1	9.6	7.8	11.6	40.8	61.9	70.4	98.3
1931	65.7	31.5	22.1	10.4	11.7	9.5	34.2	10.8	9.2	14.2	40.9	62.1	71.2	104.5
1932	64.5	31.5	22.4	10.6	11.8	9.2	33.0	10.8	9.0	13.2	41.3	62.6	71.6	103.7
1933	62.7	32.1	22.9	11.0	11.8	9.3	30.6	9.8	8.6	12.2	41.4	63.4	72.3	102.5
1934	59.3	31.4	22.7	10.9	11.8	8.7	27.9	8.9	7.7	11.3	40.5	62.2	70.5	96.7
1935	57.0	30.4	22.0	10.7	11.3	8.4	26.6	9.1	7.7	9.8	40.7	61.9	69.9	95.4
1936	58.7	30.2	21.9	10.7	11.3	8.2	28.5	9.3	8.3	10.9	39.7	60.8	68.7	95.9
1937	57.7	29.7	22.0	10.8	11.2	7.8	28.0	9.4	8.3	10.3	39.0	60.2	67.6	94.4
1938	52.8	28.3	21.1	10.3	10.8	7.1	24.5	8.2	7.3	9.0	38.3	58.6	65.5	88.9
1939	50.6	28.3	21.2	10.3	10.9	7.1	22.2	7.9	7.0	7.3	38.1	58.5	65.3	86.9
1940	56.8	29.6	21.3	9.8	11.5	8.3	27.2	9.3	8.2	9.7	37.2	57.7	65.7	92.5
1941	60.0	29.0	20.7	10.1	10.6	8.3	31.1	11.3	9.7	10.1	34.8	54.7	62.7	92.4
1942	50.6	27.2	19.6	9.6	10.0	7.7	23.4	8.7	7.5	7.2	33.2	52.1	59.4	81.1
1943	49.1	25.2	18.3	9.1	9.2	6.9	23.9	8.8	7.8	7.3	30.1	47.9	54.6	77.5
1944	45.4	24.4	17.5	8.8	8.8	6.9	21.1	8.0	7.0	6.1	27.6	44.5	51.1	70.9
1945	46.0	24.8	18.0	9.0	9.0	6.8	21.3	8.2	7.0	6.1	27.6	45.2	51.8	73.4
1946	42.9	24.5	17.8	8.7	9.1	6.7	18.4	7.1	6.1	5.2	27.2	44.3	50.7	66.9
1947	41.4	22.7	16.5	7.8	8.7	6.2	18.6	6.9	6.0	5.7	24.1	40.3	46.4	65.0
1948	33.9	19.7	15.6	7.8	7.9	4.1	14.2	5.5	4.8	3.9	23.2	38.5	42.5	56.8
1949	32.4	19.3	15.6	7.6	8.0	3.7	13.0	4.8	4.4	3.8	22.7	38.0	41.5	54.6
1950	29.6	18.5	15.2	7.2	8.0	3.3	11.1	4.3	3.7	3.1	22.6	37.4	40.7	51.7
1951	29.7	18.8	15.5	7.5	8.0	3.3	10.9	4.1	3.6	3.2	23.0	38.2	41.5	52.2
1952	27.6	18.3	15.2	7.6	7.6	3.2	9.3	3.7	3.0	2.6	22.7	37.5	40.6	49.6
1953	26.8	17.7	14.8	7.4	7.4	2.9	9.1	3.4	3.0	2.7	22.4	36.9	39.7	48.6
1954	25.4	17.7	14.9	7.6	7.4	2.8	7.7	3.0	2.6	2.1	23.5	38.1	40.8	48.4
1955	24.9	17.3	14.6	7.6	7.0	2.6	7.6	2.9	2.6	2.1	23.2	37.4	40.0	47.5
1956	23.7	16.8	14.2	7.4	6.8	2.6	6.9	2.7	2.3	1.8	22.9	36.7	39.3	46.0
1957	23.1	16.5	14.1	7.6	6.5	2.4	6.7	2.6	2.1	1.9	22.5	36.2	38.5	45.1
1958	22.5	16.2	13.8	7.5	6.3	2.4	6.4	2.6	2.1	1.7	21.5	35.0	37.3	43.6
1959	22.2	15.9	13.6	7.6	6.0	2.3	6.3	2.4	2.1	1.8	20.8	34.1	36.3	42.6
1960	21.8	15.5	13.3	7.5	5.8	2.2	6.3	2.5	2.1	1.6	19.8	32.8	35.0	41.1
1961	21.4	15.3	13.3	7.6	5.7	2.1	6.1	2.4	2.0	1.7	19.0	32.0	34.1	40.0
1962	21.7	15.1	13.0	7.4	5.6	2.1	6.6	2.5	2.3	1.8	18.1	30.8	32.9	39.4
1963	21.1	14.3	12.3	7.2	5.1	2.0	6.9	2.7	2.4	1.8	17.2	29.3	31.3	38.0
1964	19.9	13.8	12.0	7.1	4.9	1.8	6.1	2.4	2.1	1.6	16.3	28.2	29.9	35.9
1965	19.0	13.0	11.3	6.6	4.7	1.7	6.0	2.4	2.1	1.6	15.8	26.9	28.6	34.5
1966	19.0	12.9	11.1	6.5	4.6	1.7	6.1	2.5	2.0	1.6	15.3	26.3	28.0	34.1
1967	18.3	12.5	10.7	6.3	4.4	1.8	5.8	2.4	2.0	1.4	14.8	25.4	27.2	32.9
1968	18.3	12.4	10.6	6.3	4.3	1.8	5.9	2.4	2.1	1.5	14.3	24.7	26.4	32.3
1969	18.0	12.0	10.3	6.0	4.3	1.7	6.0	2.5	2.1	1.5	13.2	23.4	25.1	31.0
1970	18.2	12.3	10.6	6.3	4.3	1.7	5.9	2.6	2.0	1.3	13.0	23.5	25.2	31.0
1971	17.5	11.6	9.9	6.0	3.9	1.7	5.9	2.6	2.0	1.3	12.5	22.3	24.0	29.8
1972	17.2	11.5	9.8	5.8	4.1	1.7	5.7	2.4	2.0	1.4	12.0	21.7	23.4	29.0
1973	16.9	11.1	9.5	5.5	4.0	1.6	5.7	2.5	1.9	1.3	11.6	21.0	22.6	28.3
1974	16.3	11.0	9.4	5.2	4.2	1.7	5.3	2.3	1.9	1.1	11.1	20.4	22.0	27.3
1975	15.7	10.7	9.1	5.0	4.1	1.7	5.0	2.2	1.7	1.1	10.3	19.3	20.9	25.9
1976	14.3	9.7	8.2	4.7	3.5	1.5	4.6	1.9	1.6	1.1	9.7	17.7	19.3	23.8
1977	13.8	9.3	7.6	4.2	3.5	1.6	4.5	1.9	1.6	1.1	9.4	17.0	18.6	23.0
1978	13.2	8.7	7.1	3.7	3.4	1.6	4.5	1.9	1.6	1.0	8.5	15.5	17.1	21.6
1979	12.8	8.2	6.8	3.7	3.0	1.5	4.6	1.9	1.7	1.0	8.0	14.7	16.1	20.7
1980	12.0	7.7	6.2	3.4	2.8	1.5	4.4	1.8	1.5	1.1	7.2	13.3	14.8	19.2
1981	11.1	6.7	5.3	2.9	2.3	1.4	4.4	1.8	1.6	1.0	6.6	11.8	13.2	17.6

5.18 Stillbirth[1,2] and infant death[3] rates: age at death, 1921 to 2014

England and Wales

Infant mortality per 1,000 live births[3] at various ages

Stillbirths[2] and infant deaths per 1,000 total births

Period	Under 1 year	Neonatal mortality					Postneonatal mortality				Still-births	Still-births plus deaths under 1 week	Still-births plus deaths under 4 weeks	Still-births plus deaths under 1 year
		Under 4 weeks	Early neonatal			Late neo-natal	4 weeks and under 1 year	4 weeks and under 3 months	3 months and under 6 months	6 months and under 1 year				
			Under 1 week	Under 1 day	1 day and under 1 week	1 week and under 4 weeks								
1982	10.8	6.3	5.0	2.8	2.2	1.2	4.6	1.9	1.6	1.1	6.3	11.3	12.5	17.0
1983	10.1	5.9	4.7	2.6	2.1	1.2	4.3	1.9	1.5	0.9	5.7	10.4	11.6	15.8
1984	9.5	5.6	4.4	2.6	1.9	1.1	3.9	1.6	1.3	0.9	5.7	10.1	11.2	15.1
1985	9.4	5.4	4.3	2.5	1.9	1.0	4.0	1.7	1.4	0.9	5.5	9.8	10.9	14.8
1986	9.6	5.3	4.3	2.4	1.8	1.0	4.3	1.8	1.5	1.0	5.3	9.6	10.6	14.8
1987	9.2	5.1	3.9	2.3	1.6	1.1	4.1	1.8	1.5	0.9	5.0	8.9	10.0	14.2
1988	9.0	4.9	3.9	2.2	1.7	1.0	4.1	1.7	1.5	0.9	4.9	8.7	9.8	13.8
1989	8.4	4.8	3.7	2.1	1.6	1.1	3.7	1.6	1.3	0.8	4.7	8.3	9.4	13.1
1990	7.9	4.6	3.5	2.0	1.5	1.0	3.3	1.3	1.2	0.7	4.6	8.1	9.1	12.4
1991	7.4	4.4	3.4	2.0	1.4	0.9	3.0	1.2	1.0	0.7	4.6	8.0	9.0	12.0
1992	6.6	4.3	3.3	2.0	1.4	1.0	2.3	1.0	0.8	0.6	4.3	7.6	8.5	10.8
1993	6.3	4.2	3.2	1.9	1.3	0.9	2.1	0.9	0.7	0.6	5.7	8.9	9.8	12.0
1994	6.2	4.1	3.2	1.9	1.4	0.9	2.1	0.8	0.7	0.6	5.7	8.9	9.8	11.9
1995	6.1	4.2	3.2	1.8	1.5	0.9	2.0	0.9	0.6	0.5	5.5	8.7	9.7	11.6
1996	6.1	4.1	3.2	1.9	1.3	0.9	2.0	0.9	0.6	0.5	5.4	8.6	9.5	11.5
1997	5.9	3.9	3.0	1.8	1.2	0.9	2.0	0.9	0.6	0.5	5.3	8.3	9.2	11.2
1998	5.7	3.8	2.9	1.7	1.2	0.9	1.9	0.9	0.6	0.4	5.3	8.2	9.1	11.0
1999	5.8	3.9	2.9	1.7	1.2	1.0	1.9	0.9	0.6	0.5	5.3	8.2	9.2	11.1
2000	5.6	3.9	2.9	1.7	1.2	1.0	1.7	0.8	0.5	0.4	5.3	8.2	9.1	10.8
2001	5.4	3.6	2.7	1.7	1.0	0.9	1.9	0.8	0.5	0.5	5.3	8.0	8.9	10.7
2002	5.2	3.6	2.7	1.7	1.0	1.0	1.7	0.8	0.0	0.0	5.6	8.0	9.0	11.0
2003	5.3	3.6	2.8	1.8	1.0	0.8	1.7	0.8	0.4	0.4	5.8	8.6	9.4	11.1
2004	5.0	3.5	2.7	1.7	1.0	0.8	1.6	0.8	0.4	0.4	5.7	8.4	9.2	10.7
2005	5.0	3.4	2.6	1.7	1.0	0.8	1.6	0.8	0.5	0.4	5.4	8.0	8.8	10.4
2006	5.0	3.5	2.6	1.7	0.9	0.9	1.5	0.7	0.4	0.3	5.4	8.0	8.8	10.3
2007	4.7	3.3	2.5	1.6	0.9	0.7	1.5	0.7	0.4	0.4	5.2	7.7	8.4	9.9
2008	4.6	3.2	2.4	1.6	0.8	0.7	1.4	0.7	0.4	0.3	5.1	7.5	8.3	9.7
2009	4.5	3.1	2.4	1.5	0.9	0.7	1.4	0.7	0.4	0.3	5.2	7.6	8.3	9.7
2010	4.3	2.9	2.3	1.5	0.8	0.6	1.3	0.7	0.3	0.3	5.1	7.4	8.0	9.3
2011	4.2	3.0	2.3	1.5	0.7	0.7	1.2	0.6	0.3	0.3	5.2	7.5	8.2	9.4
2012	4.0	2.8	2.2	1.5	0.6	0.6	1.2	0.6	0.3	0.3	4.9	7.0	7.6	8.8
2013	3.8	2.7	2.0	1.4	0.6	0.6	1.2	0.6	0.3	0.3	4.7	6.7	7.3	8.5
2014	3.6	2.5	2.0	1.3	0.6	0.6	1.1	0.5	0.3	0.2	4.7	6.6	7.2	8.3

Source: Office for National Statistics

1 Registration of stillbirths commenced on 1 July 1927. Annual figures for 1927 are estimated.
2 From 1927 to 30 September 1992 stillbirths relate to fetal deaths at or over 28 weeks gestation, and from 1 October 1992 at or over 24 weeks gestation.
3 Infant deaths are based on the live births occurring in the year, except in the years 1931-56 when they were based on related live births - that is, the combined live births of the associated and preceding years to which they relate.

15.19 Interim Life Tables
Period expectation of life based on data for the years 2011-2014

United Kingdom

Age x	Males l_x	Males e_x	Females l_x	Females e_x
0	100000.0	79.07	100000.0	82.81
5	99493.0	74.47	99584.4	78.15
10	99447.8	69.50	99546.3	73.18
15	99393.8	64.54	99506.0	68.21
20	99235.8	59.64	99425.3	63.26
25	98989.7	54.78	99317.7	58.33
30	98677.7	49.94	99173.6	53.41
35	98269.6	45.14	98953.2	48.52
40	97679.9	40.40	98621.9	43.67
45	96819.8	35.73	98097.9	38.89
50	95593.9	31.16	97307.4	34.19
55	93808.2	26.70	96066.8	29.60
60	91008.6	22.44	94135.6	25.15
65	86711.1	18.42	91213.9	20.87
70	80479.9	14.64	86864.0	16.78
75	70953.1	11.24	79927.6	13.00
80	57543.4	8.25	69130.1	9.61
85	39588.0	5.82	52643.9	6.80
90	20254.6	4.03	31508.1	4.65
95	6520.8	2.79	12442.6	3.17
100	1041.4	2.07	2590.9	2.24

England & Wales

Age x	Males l_x	Males e_x	Females l_x	Females e_x
0	100000.0	79.30	100000.0	83.01
5	99490.4	74.70	99581.0	78.35
10	99446.0	69.73	99542.4	73.38
15	99394.1	64.77	99501.7	68.41
20	99242.7	59.86	99424.6	63.46
25	99006.0	55.00	99320.3	58.53
30	98712.4	50.15	99181.4	53.61
35	98329.2	45.34	98968.2	48.71
40	97772.2	40.58	98644.6	43.87
45	96947.8	35.91	98136.5	39.08
50	95759.1	31.32	97365.5	34.37
55	94020.4	26.85	96162.3	29.76
60	91287.9	22.57	94280.8	25.30
65	87060.9	18.54	91424.8	21.01
70	80947.2	14.74	87177.2	16.91
75	71567.3	11.32	80391.0	13.11
80	58279.1	8.30	69818.7	9.69
85	40288.4	5.85	53440.8	6.84
90	20742.9	4.04	32189.2	4.67
95	6706.4	2.80	12791.1	3.19
100	1078.9	2.07	2691.4	2.25

Scotland

Age x	Males l_x	Males e_x	Females l_x	Females e_x
0	100000	77.05	100000	81.06
5	99546.5	72.39	99626.6	76.37
10	99496.0	67.43	99596.7	71.39
15	99431.6	62.47	99559.8	66.41
20	99246.1	57.58	99450.0	61.48
25	98947.9	52.75	99315.7	56.56
30	98477.4	47.99	99121.2	51.67
35	97826.1	43.29	98819.2	46.82
40	96907.3	38.68	98390.6	42.01
45	95669.1	34.14	97705.7	37.29
50	94088.2	29.67	96721.2	32.64
55	91886.7	25.32	95164.7	28.13
60	88483.3	21.19	92817.7	23.78
65	83515.7	17.29	89318.4	19.61
70	76191.7	13.70	84011.1	15.67
75	65309.8	10.54	75653.3	12.11
80	50918.1	7.79	63160.3	8.98
85	33394.6	5.53	45843.6	6.38
90	16012.2	3.93	25763.9	4.41
95	4904.0	2.67	9506.8	3.00
100	732.9	2.01	1783.0	2.11

Northern Ireland

Age x	Males l_x	Males e_x	Females l_x	Females e_x
0	100000.0	78.25	100000.0	82.28
5	99444.2	73.69	99583.6	77.62
10	99389.9	68.73	99540.2	72.66
15	99302.6	63.78	99504.6	67.68
20	99030.1	58.95	99397.1	62.75
25	98643.4	54.17	99268.7	57.83
30	98198.3	49.41	99103.8	52.92
35	97670.4	44.66	98889.1	48.03
40	96968.2	39.96	98589.8	43.17
45	96088.2	35.30	98053.7	38.39
50	94795.2	30.75	97264.5	33.68
55	92894.0	26.32	95887.7	29.12
60	90030.4	22.08	93801.6	24.71
65	85747.5	18.05	90679.8	20.47
70	79214.7	14.32	86076.6	16.43
75	69603.2	10.93	79299.0	12.60
80	55691.9	8.00	67419.0	9.36
85	37426.8	5.65	50550.7	6.59
90	18404.4	3.95	29475.9	4.49
95	5782.0	2.67	11301.3	2.95
100			2106.0	2.05

Data published to age 95 due to very low numbers of deaths and population.   Source: Office for National Statistics

l_x is the number of survivors to exact age x of 100,000 live births of the same sex who are assumed to be subject throughout their lives to the mortality rates experienced in the three year period to which the National Life Table relates.

e_x is the average period expectation of life at exact age x, that is the average number of years that those aged x exact will live thereafter based on the mortality rates experienced in the three year period to which the National Life Table relates.

15.20a Adoption Orders[1] granted by sex and age band, 2011-2014

England & Wales

Year	Total adoption orders: All Ages	adoption orders granted by Age of adopted child					
		< 1 year	1-4 yrs	5-9 yrs	10-14 yrs	15-17 yrs	Other[2]
Total							
2011	**4,709**	90	2,924	1,075	457	133	30
2012	**5,260**	121	3,286	1,238	439	158	18
2013	**6,078**	169	4,037	1,338	368	141	25
2014	**6,750**	235	4,628	1,358	345	146	38
Males							
2011	2,330	53	530	1465	216	61	5
2012	2,648	58	621	1683	205	70	11
2013	2,985	80	679	1996	173	51	6
2014	3,435	111	2428	655	165	60	16
Females							
2011	2,365	37	545	1459	241	72	11
2012	2,611	63	617	1603	234	88	6
2013	3,090	89	659	2041	195	90	16
2014	3,305	124	2200	703	180	86	12
Gender Unknown							
2011	14	0	0	0	0	0	14
2012	1	0	0	0	0	0	1
2013	3	0	0	0	0	0	3
2014	10	0	0	0	0	0	10

Source: Ministry of Justice, Family Court Statistics

Notes:

1) Figures are for adoption orders only. Figures for orders issued for related non-adoption orders are not included in this summary

2) 'Other' includes those who were aged 18 by the time the order was made, or where the age was not correctly recorded.

Note:

Prior to 2011, National Statistics on Adoptions in england and Wales were published by ONS: http://www.ons.gov.uk/ons/taxonomy/index.html?nscl=Adoptions Data in ONS publications are based on adoption data provided by the General Register Office, which maintains the Adopted Child Register using copies of adoption orders issued by courts. There are small differences between the number of adoptions as recorded by the two sets of statistics.

During the transition period over 2009/2010 when courts were starting to implement the new administrative data systems not all adoption orders made were recorded on the system, resulting in MoJ figures held for adoptions being around 15 per cent lower than those published by ONS. Since 2011 all courts dealing with family matters in England and Wales have been using the Familyman administrative system and hand-written notifications of adoptions to GRO have been phased out. This has resulted in figures for the ONS and MoJ being much closer.

Please see the joint statement produced by MoJ, ONS and GRO on the differences in these adoption statistics attached to the 2012 Q4 edition of Court Statistics Quarterly for further details.

15.20b Adoptions by age of child and relationship of the adopter(s), Scotland 2014

Age and sex of child		Total	Relationship of adopter(s)				
			Both parents	Step-parent	Grandparent(s)	Other relation(s)	No relation
All ages	**P**	**455**	**5**	**89**	**5**	**14**	**342**
	M	**227**	**3**	**47**	**2**	**9**	**166**
	F	**228**	**2**	**42**	**3**	**5**	**176**
Months							
less than 6	M	1	-	1	-	-	-
	F	4	-	4	-	-	-
6-8	M	5	1	3	-	-	1
	F	5	1	1	-	1	2
9-11	M	3	-	-	-	-	3
	F	5	-	-	-	-	5
12-17	M	16	-	-	-	1	15
	F	12	-	-	-	-	12
18-23	M	17	-	1	-	-	16
	F	17	-	-	-	-	17
Years							
2	M	28	1	1	1	2	23
	F	45	1	2	1	1	40
3-4	M	70	1	7	-	5	57
	F	54	-	5	-	1	48
5-9	M	60	-	15	-	1	44
	F	56	-	9	1	2	44
10-14	M	22	-	15	1	-	6
	F	19	-	13	1	-	5
15 and over	M	5	-	4	-	-	1
	F	11	-	8	-	-	3

.Source: GRO-Scotland

15.20c Adoptions - Northern Ireland, 2009-2013

Persons	All ages		Under 1		1-4		5-9		10-14		15-17	
Year	Numbers	Percentage	Numbers	Percentage	Numbers	Percentage	Numbers	Percentage	Numbers	Percentage	Numbers	Percentage
2009	116	100%	1	1%	43	37%	46	40%	20	17%	6	5%
2010	116	100%	3	3%	46	40%	46	40%	17	15%	4	3%
2011	104	100%	3	3%	40	38%	40	38%	13	13%	8	8%
2012	127	100%	1	1%	66	52%	39	31%	13	10%	8	6%
2013	130	100%	0	0%	67	52%	51	39%	9	7%	3	2%

Males	All ages		Under 1		1-4		5-9		10-14		15-17	
Year	Numbers	Percentage	Numbers	Percentage	Numbers	Percentage	Numbers	Percentage	Numbers	Percentage	Numbers	Percentage
2009	55	100%	0	0%	24	44%	20	36%	10	18%	1	2%
2010	56	100%	2	4%	26	46%	21	38%	6	11%	1	2%
2011	47	100%	0	0%	19	40%	18	38%	6	13%	4	9%
2012	68	100%	0	0%	33	49%	21	31%	10	15%	4	6%
2013	69	100%	0	0%	30	43%	32	46%	6	9%	1	1%

Females	All ages		Under 1		1-4		5-9		10-14		15-17	
Year	Numbers	Percentage	Numbers	Percentage	Numbers	Percentage	Numbers	Percentage	Numbers	Percentage	Numbers	Percentage
2009	61	100%	1	2%	19	31%	26	43%	10	16%	5	8%
2010	60	100%	1	2%	20	33%	25	42%	11	18%	3	5%
2011	57	100%	3	5%	21	37%	22	39%	7	12%	4	7%
2012	59	100%	1	2%	33	56%	18	31%	3	5%	4	7%
2013	61	100%	0	0%	37	61%	19	31%	3	5%	2	3%

Source: Northern Ireland Statistics and Research Agency (NISRA)

Health

Chapter 16

Health

Deaths: analysed by cause (Table 16.6)

All figures in this table for England and Wales represent the number of deaths occurring in each calendar year. All data for Scotland and Northern Ireland relate to the number of deaths registered during each calendar year. From 2001, all three constituent countries of the UK are coding their causes of death using the latest, tenth, revision of the International Statistical Classification of Diseases and Related Health Problems (ICD-10). All cause of death information from 2001 (also for 2000 for Scotland) presented in this table is based on the revised classification.

To assist users in assessing any discontinuities arising from the introduction of the revised classification, bridge-coding exercises were carried out on all deaths registered in 1999 in England and Wales and also in Scotland. For further information about ICD-10 and the bridge-coding carried out by The Office for National Statistics (ONS), see the ONS Report: Results of the ICD-10 bridge-coding study, England and Wales, Statistics Quarterly 14 (2002), pages 75–83 or log on to the Office for National Statistics (ONS) website at: www.ons.gov.uk. For information on the Scottish bridge-coding exercise, consult the Annual Report of the General Register Office for Scotland or log on to their website at: www.gro-scotland.gov.uk. No bridge-coding exercise was conducted for Northern Ireland.

Neonatal deaths and homicide and assault

For England and Wales, neonatal deaths (those at age under 28 days) are included in the number of total deaths but excluded from the cause figures. This has particular impact on the totals shown for the chapters covered by the ranges P and Q, 'Conditions originating in the perinatal period' and 'Congenital malformations, deformations and chromosomal abnormalities'. These are considerably lower than the actual number of deaths because it is not possible to assign an underlying cause of death from the neonatal death certificate used in England and Wales.

Also, for England and Wales only, the total number shown for Homicide and assault, X85–Y09, will not be a true representation because the registration of these deaths is often delayed by adjourned inquests.

Occupational ill health (Tables 16.8 and 16.9)

There are a number of sources of data on the extent of
occupational or work-related ill health in Great Britain.
For some potentially severe lung diseases caused by
exposures which are highly unlikely to be found in a
non-occupational setting, it is useful to count the number
of death certificates issued each year. This is also true
for mesothelioma, a cancer affecting the lining of the
lungs and stomach, for which the number of cases with
non-occupational causes is likely to be larger (although
still a minority). Table 16.9 shows the number of deaths
for mesothelioma and asbestosis (linked to exposure
to asbestos), pneumoconiosis (linked to coal dust or
silica), byssinosis (linked to cotton dust) and some
forms of allergic alveolitis (including farmer's lung). For
asbestos-related diseases the figures are derived
from a special register maintained by HSE.

Most conditions which can be caused or made worse
by work can also arise from other factors. The remaining
sources of data on work-related ill health rely on
attribution of individual cases of illness to work causes.
In The Health and Occupation Reporting Network
(THOR), this is done by specialist doctors – either occupational
physicians or those working in particular disease specialisms
(covering musculoskeletal, psychological, respiratory, skin, audio
logical and infectious disease). Table 16.8 presents data from
THOR for the last three years. It should be noted that not all
cases of occupational disease will be seen by participating
specialists; for example, the number of deaths due to
mesothelioma (shown in Table 16.9) is known to be greater than
the number of cases reported to THOR.

Injuries at work (Table 16.10)

The Reporting of Injuries, Diseases and Dangerous Occurrences
Regulations 1995 (RIDDOR) places a legal duty on employers
to report injuries arising from work activity to the relevant
enforcing authority, namely HSE, local authorities and the Office
of Rail Regulation (ORR). These include injuries to employees,
self-employed people and members of the public. From 12
September 2011 the reporting of all RIDDOR incidents will move
to a predominantly online system.
While the enforcing authorities are informed about almost all
relevant fatal workplace injuries, it is known that non-fatal injuries
are substantially under-reported. Currently, it is estimated that
just over half of all such injuries to employees are actually
reported, with the self-employed reporting a much smaller
proportion. These results are achieved by comparing reported
non-fatal injuries (major as well as over-3-day), with results from
the Labour Force Survey (LFS).

16.1a. NHS Hospital and Community Health Services (HCHS): Ambulance staff by type 2005-2014

England as at 30 September each year

Headcount

	2005	2006	2007	2008	2009	2010	2011	2012	2013	2014
Total ambulance staff	28,180	28,648	28,471	30,518	32,284	33,163	32,902	32,076	32,817	33,597
Qualified ambulance staff	18,117	16,176	17,028	17,451	17,922	18,450	18,687	18,645	18,734	18,673
Manager	773	614	598	685	692	696	700	657	603	618
Emergency care practitioner	..	438	646	705	750	780	770	742	722	688
Paramedic	8,311	8,222	8,241	9,203	10,089	10,678	11,368	11,954	12,556	12,757
Ambulance technician	..	6,902	7,543	6,858	6,391	6,300	5,853	5,295	4,861	4,614
Ambulance personnel (old definition)	9,033	..	..	..	..	..	..	..	..	..
Support to ambulance staff	10,063	12,472	11,443	13,067	14,362	14,738	14,238	13,451	14,112	14,946
Ambulance personnel (new definition)	..	4,630	4,537	5,438	6,347	6,444	6,398	6,290	6,673	6,905
Trainee ambulance technician	..	1,829	1,147	1,258	1,415	1,481	1,193	875	666	1,200
Trainee ambulance personnel	2,201	..	..	..	..	..	..	..	..	..
Clerical & administrative	3,286	3,247	3,340	3,882	4,161	4,384	4,303	4,382	4,948	5,573
Estates (maintenance & works)	268	205	166	220	189	226	232	237	226	187
Healthcare assistant	2,794	834	992	845	936	960	958	980	919	359
Support worker	1,514	1,727	1,261	1,424	1,314	1,254	1,162	695	692	736

Source: Health and Social Care Information Centre 2014 Non-Medical Workforce Census.

Notes:

'..' denotes not applicable

These statistics relate to the contracted positions within English NHS organisations and may include those where the person assigned to the position is temporarily absent, for example on maternity leave.

Headcount totals are unlikely to equal the sum of components.
Further information on the headcount methodology is available in the Census publication.

16.1b NHS Labour Turnover and Stability Analysis
Welsh Ambulance Trust

		Headcount
As of 31 Dec 2014	**Occupation Code**	
	Ambulance Officer	43
	Urgent Care Assistant	155
	Paramedic Practitioner	31
	Paramedic	919
	Ambulance Technician	389
	Staff Group Summary Total	1537

Source: Welsh Ambulance Service NHS Trust

16.1c Ambulance Staff by type: Scotland
As of December 2014

Whole-time equivalent (WTE)

	Total	Under 20	20 - 24	25 - 29	30 - 34	35 - 39	40 - 44	45 - 49	50 - 54	55 - 59	60 - 64	65 +
Ambulance services	**2,432.7**	**2.6**	**91.7**	**206.2**	**179.3**	**280.0**	**365.1**	**401.7**	**379.0**	**299.3**	**188.5**	**39.3**
Ambulance care assistant	818.9	-	6.7	7.0	10.2	51.2	121.7	147.0	185.0	131.3	127.2	31.7
Auxiliary	-	-	-	-	-	-	-	-	-	-	-	-
Driver	47.1	-	-	0.7	-	0.8	3.0	7.1	10.9	9.1	12.4	3.1
EMDC / control	327.3	2.6	31.0	45.5	51.5	50.7	37.5	44.7	26.6	28.2	9.0	-
Paramedic[1]	x	x	x	x	x	x	x	x	x	x	x	x
Technician	1,159.7	-	54.0	153.0	115.7	166.4	189.0	190.8	136.5	113.0	36.9	4.5
Other	79.6	-	-	-	2.0	11.0	14.0	12.0	20.0	17.6	3.0	-
Not assimilated / not known	-	-	-	-	-	-	-	-	-	-	-	-

Source: Scottish Workforce Information Standard System (SWISS)

1. From 1st April 2013 paramedics have been reclassified from ambulance services staff to allied health professions.

Whole time equivalent (WTE) adjusts headcount staff figures to take account of part time staff.

- nil

x not applicable

These figures apply to those staff assimilated to the Agenda for Change (AfC) ambulance services job family and those staff not yet assimilated but where an ambulance services staff group has been identified.
The ambulance services job family was renamed in 2011, previously it was known as emergency services.

16.1d Ambulance Staff by Type: Northern Ireland

Headcount

		2005	2006	2007	2008	2009	2010	2011	2012	2013	2014
Northern Ireland											
Total Ambulance staff	JHQ9	911	989	1,007	1,025	1,036	1026	1045	1052	1086	1060
Emergency Medical Technicians and Paramedics	JHR2	576	637	659	625	629	598	610	618	620	600
Other/Patient care services	JHR3	211	220	219	231	227	244	240	231	263	257
Control Assistants	JHR4	61	63	67	94	108	106	102	107	108	108
Ambulance Officers	JHR5	63	69	62	75	72	78	93	96	95	95

Source: Human Resource, Payroll, Travel & Subsistence System; Department of Health

16.2 Hospital and primary care services Scotland

			2000 /01	2001 /02	2002 /03	2003 /04	2004 /05	2005 /06	2006 /07
Hospital and community services In-patients:[1,2]									
Average available staffed beds	KDEA	Thousands	32.1	30.9	29.8	28.9	28.1	27.4	26.9
Average occupied beds:									
All departments	KDEB	"	25.8	25.1	24.2	23.2	22.5	22.1	21.7
Psychiatric and learning disability	KDEC	"	7.6	7.0	6.4	5.9	5.5	5.2	4.9
Discharges or deaths[3]	KDED	"	972	969	959	989	1,003	1,015	1,037
Outpatients:[2,4]									
New cases	KDEE	"	2,749	2,728	2,731	2,750	2,718	2,762	2,827
Total attendances	KDEF	"	6,382	6,254	6,193	6,147	5,981	6,060	6,048
Medical and dental staff:[5,6,22]	JYXO	Headcount	9,325	9,644	10,256	10,407	10,658	10,871	11,201
Whole-time	KDEG	"	7,216	7,530	8,115	8,349	8,612	8,796	9,201
Part-time	KDEH	"	1,648	1,681	1,697	1,636	1,630	1,670	1,607
Honorary	JYXN	"	495	468	468	437	431	418	411
Professional and technical staff:[6,7,22]									
Whole-time	KDEI	"	11,261	11,705	12,265	12,942	13,258	13,750	14,323
Part-time	KDEJ	"	5,483	5,852	6,273	6,708	6,968	7,440	7,990
Nursing and midwifery staff:[6,8,22]									
Whole-time	KDEK	"	32,401	33,334	34,294	34,939	35,338	36,093	37,104
Part-time	KDEL	"	29,131	29,004	29,015	29,354	29,484	29,688	29,995
Administrative and clerical staff:[6,9,22]									
Whole-time	KDEM	"	14,710	15,361	16,200	17,260	17,806	18,434	18,907
Part-time	KDEN	"	7,677	8,075	8,630	9,307	9,943	10,707	11,375
Domestic, transport, etc, staff:[6,10,22]									
Whole-time	KDEO	"	7,848	7,625	7,768	8,234	8,305	8,516	8,697
Part-time	KDEP	"	12 272	11 522	11 915	12 588	12 324	12 545	12 675
Primary care services									
Primary Medical services									
General medical practitioners (GPs):[11,23]	JX4B	Headcount	4,253	4,346	4,361	4,447	4,456	4,521	4,597
Performer[12,23]	KDET	"	3,710	3,761	3,770	3,805	3,782	3,763	3,770
Performer salaried[13,23]	KDEU	"	99	108	114	155	188	288	354
Performer registrar	JX4C	"	261	283	284	281	282	300	308
Performer retainee[14,23]	JX4D	"	184	196	194	209	208	176	169
Expenditure on Primary Medical Services[15,23]	KDEW	£million	405	430	468	519	628	701	700
Pharmaceutical services[16]									
Prescriptions dispensed	KDEX	Millions	63	66	70	72	75	77	80
Payments to pharmacists (gross)	KDEY	£million	737	808	887	963	984	1016	1045
Average gross cost per prescription	KDEZ	£	11.7	12.2	12.8	13.3	12.6	12.5	12.1
Dental services									
Dentists on list[17]	KDFA	Headcount	1,808	1,844	1,869	1,882	1,900	1,936	2,009
Number of courses of treatment completed	KDFB	Thousands	3,389	3,359	3,420	3,359	3,375	3,348	3,387
Payments to dentists (gross)	KDFC	£million	163	165	172	170	174	179	188
Payments by patients	KDFD	"	51	52	55	53	54	54	46
Payments out of public funds	KDFE	"	112	113	118	117	120	125	143
Average gross cost per course	KDFF	£	38	38	40	40	40	41	42
General ophthalmic services Number of Eye Exams given[18,19,20,21]	KDFG	Thousands	-	-	-	-	-	-	1,578
Number of vouchers claimed to provide pairs of glasses/ contact lenses[19,22]	KDFH	"	-	-	-	-	-	-	465
Payments out of public funds forsight testing and dispensing[21]	KDFK	£ million	..	..	..	..	..	..	66

Sources: ISD Scotland, Scottish Workforce Information Standard System (SWISS); NHS National Services Scotland

16.2 Hospital and primary care services Scotland

			2007 /08	2008 /09	2009 /10	2010 /11	2011 /12	2012 /13	2013 /14
Hospital and community services In-patients:[1,2]									
Average available staffed beds	KDEA	Thousands	26.3	25.8	24.9	23.9	23.3	22.9	22.6
Average occupied beds:									
All departments	KDEB	"	21.0	20.6	19.9	19.2	18.8	18.7	18.5
Psychiatric and learning disability	KDEC	"	4.6	4.3	4.1	3.8	3.6	3.6	3.5
Discharges or deaths[3]	KDED	"	1,066	1,091	1,090	1,096	1,114	1,140	1,232
Outpatients:[2,4]									
New cases	KDEE	"	2,894	3,003	3,026	3,042	3,013	2,995	2726
Total attendances	KDEF	"	6,093	6,271	6,208	6,203	6,222	6,163	6177
Medical and dental staff:[5,6,22]	JYXO	Headcount	11,822	12,534	12,619	12,757	13,336	13,317	13,569
Whole-time	KDEG	"	9,828	9,971	9,975	9,973	10,360	10,296	10,511
Part-time	KDEH	"	2,028	2,252	2,444	2,563	2,797	2,849	2,878
Honorary	JYXN	"	418	377	247	263	252	243	238
Professional and technical staff:[6,7,22]									
Whole-time	KDEI	"	13,642	14,567	15,403	15,590	15,021	14,866	16,403
Part-time	KDEJ	"	7,953	8,375	9,036	9,504	9,689	9,924	10,319
Nursing and midwifery staff:[6,8,22]									
Whole-time	KDEK	"	37,071	37,654	37,995	37,165	35,547	35,015	35,803
Part-time	KDEL	"	29,544	29,555	29,949	30,261	30,065	30,518	30,719
Administrative and clerical staff:[6,9,22]									
Whole-time	KDEM	"	18,181	18,158	19,007	18,686	17,639	17,147	17,370
Part-time	KDEN	"	10,836	11,231	11,679	11,703	11,345	11,140	11,242
Domestic, transport, etc, staff:[6,10,22]									
Whole-time	KDEO		10,205	10,623	11,037	10,927	10,522	10,469	9,251
Part-time	KDEP		12,819	12,874	13,138	12,576	12,042	12,051	12,001
Primary care services									
Primary Medical services									
General medical practitioners (GPs):[11,23]	JX4B	Headcount	4,686	4,890	4,907	4,905	4,888	4,856	4,881
Performer[12,23]	KDET	"	3,785	3,783	3,805	3,777	3,748	3,742	3,727
Performer salaried[13,23]	KDEU	"	418	460	487	482	523	530	543
Performer registrar	JX4C	"	325	490	465	497	478	455	488
Performer retainee[14,23]	JX4D	"	164	164	159	156	145	138	133
Expenditure on Primary Medical Services[15,23]	KDEW	£million	705	701	729	741	747	756	763
Pharmaceutical services[16]									
Prescriptions dispensed	KDEX	Millions	82	86	89	91	95	97	99
Payments to pharmacists (gross)	KDEY	£million	1067	1107	1139	1160	1177	1118	1145
Average gross cost per prescription	KDEZ	£	11.7	11.4	11.1	11.0	10.7	9.9	9.9
Dental services									
Dentists on list[17]	KDFA	Headcount	2,099	2,204	2,313	2,354	2,486	2,520	2564
Number of courses of treatment completed	KDFB	Thousands	3,401	3,548	3,686	3,830	4,100	4,289	4,418
Payments to dentists (gross)	KDFC	£million	199	220	231	243	255	260	N/A
Payments by patients	KDFD	"	47	50	52	55	59	62	N/A
Payments out of public funds	KDFE	"	152	170	180	188	196	198	N/A
Average gross cost per course	KDFF	£	43	45					
General ophthalmic services Number of Eye Exams given[18,19,20,21]	KDFG	Thousands	1,630	1,728	1,775	1,804	1,913	1,932	2,306
Number of vouchers claimed to provide pairs of glasses/ contact lenses[19,22]	KDFH	"	468	483	493	489	504	487	494
Payments out of public funds forsight testing and dispensing[21]	KDFK	£ million	79	86	91	90	96	96	N/A

Sources: ISD Scotland, Scottish Workforce Information Standard System (SWISS); NHS National Services Scotland

16.2 Hospital and primary care services Scotland

1 Excludes joint user and contractual hospitals.

2 In year to 31 March.

3 Includes transfers out and emergency inpatients treated in day bed units.

4 Including attendances at accident and emergency consultant clinics.

5 As at 30 September. Figures exclude officers holding honorary locum appointments. Part-time includes maximum part-time appointments. There is an element of double counting of "heads" in this table as doctors can hold more than one contract. For example, they may hold contracts of different type, eg part time and honorary. Doctors holding two or more contracts of the same type, eg part time, are not double counted. Doctors, whose sum of contracts amounts to whole time, are classed as such. Figures have been revised due to coding changes.

6 The change in both collection and presentation of workforce data due to changes to staff groupings under Agenda for Change has inevitably meant that the amount of historical trend analysis of data is limited, though still available for some high level groupings.

7 As at 30 September. Comprises Therapeutic, Healthcare science, Technical and Pharmacy staff.

8 As at 30 September. Includes Health Care Assistants. Figures post 2003 have been amended due to a coding error resulting in some staff previously in this group being moved to the admin and clerical group.

9 As at 30 September. Comprises Senior Management and Administrative and Clerical staff. Figures for 2003 onwards have been amended due to the inclusion of some staff previously in the nursing and midwifery staff group

10 As at 30 September. Comprises Ambulance, Works, Ancillary and Trades.

11 Contracted GP's in post in Scottish general practices, at 1 October up to 2003/04 and 30 Sept for 2004/05 onwards. Excludes GP locums and GPs working only in Out of Hours services. The total may not equal the sum of the figures for individual GP designations as some GPs hold more than one contract.

12 For 2004/05 onwards this group comprised mainly of Provider (partner) GPs. Known prior to 2004/05 as Principal GPs.

13 Up to 2003/04 this group comprises salaried GPs plus associates, assistants and 'other' GPs. Terminology changed with the introduction of the new GMS contract in April 2004. 14 Data on the number of GP retainees not available prior to 2000.

15 Total expenditure on General Medical Services/Primary Medical Services Source: NHS Scotland Costs Book "R390" tables, www.isdscotland.org/costs

Note, the contractual arrangements for payments to many general practices changed with the introduction of the new GMS contract in April 2004.

16 For prescriptions dispensed in financial year by all community pharmacists (including stock orders), dispensing doctors and appliance suppliers. Gross total excludes patient charges.

17 Comprises of non-salaried GDS principal dentists only as at 31 March.

18 As a result of a number of data quality issues, eye examination data have been revised. It is therefore strongly advised that any previously held data are discarded and the revised data reported here are used.

19 Data on eye examinations and vouchers are sourced from OPTIX, the electronic system for recording ophtalmic payment information.

20 Figures represent the total number of fully funded NHS eye examinations.

21 Fully funded NHS eye examinations were extended to all on 1st April 2006.

22 General Ophthalmic Service GOS(S)3 forms are referred to as 'vouchers' and are used to provide eye glasses/contact lenses Headcount refers to the actual number of individuals (employees) working within the NHSS. This eliminates any double counting that may exist as a result of an employee holding more than one post. Please note due to revisions in the headcount measure, it is not possible to compare data prior to 2007.

23 Figures have been revised and differ from those previously published due to improvements in source data quality.

*** Figures not yet published.

Update to Secondary Care Notes

Average available staffed beds The daily average number of beds which are staffed and are available for the reception of inpatients (borrowed and temporary beds

Average occupied beds The average of available staffed beds that were occupied by inpatients during the financial year.

16.3 Hospital and general health services
Northern Ireland

			2003	2004	2005	2006	2007	2008
Hospital services[1]								
In-patients:								
Beds available[2]	KDGA	Numbers	8,347	8,323	8,238	7,976	7,827	7,636
Average daily occupation of beds	KDGB	Percentages	84	84	84	83	83	82
Discharges or deaths[3]	KDGC	Thousands	332	337	296	295	306	311
Out-patients:[4]								
New cases	KDGD	"	1,014	1,027	1,040	1,081	1,115	1,149
Total attendances	KDGE	"	2,161	2,175	2,219	2,233	2,282	2,256
General health services								
Medical services[1]								
Doctors (principals) on the list[5,6]	KDGF	Numbers	1,076	1,078	1,084	1,100	1,127	1,148
Number of patients per doctor	KDGG	"	1,658	1,663	1,655	1,631	1,626	1,618
Gross Payments to doctors[7]	KDGH	£ thousand	96,894	..	..	..	..	..
Pharmaceutical services[8]								
Prescription forms dispensed	KDGI	Thousands	15,158	15,283	15,860	16,393	17,280	17,910
Number of prescriptions	KDGJ	"	26,656	27,401	28,417	29,599	30,864	32,107
Gross Cost[9]	KDGK	£ thousand	362,401	382,789	390,763	408,771	425,440	445,184
Charges[10]	KDGL	"	9,798	10,262	10,676	11,298	11,943	10,243
Net Cost[9]	KDGM	"	352,602	372,527	380,087	397,473	413,497	434,940
Average gross cost per prescription[9]	KDGN	£	14	14	14	14	14	14
Dental services[8,11]								
Dentists on the list[5]	KDGO	Numbers	696	720	722	751	763	795
Number of courses of paid treatment	KDGP	Thousands	1,107	1,086	1,084	1,064	1,002	1,034
Gross cost	KDGQ	£ thousand	66,910	67,294	69,480	65,172	68,775	71,401
Patients	KDGR	Thousands	919	907	910	900	859	868
Contributions (Net cost)	KDGS	£ thousand	50,282	50,498	52,308	50,068	53,301	55,801
Average gross cost per paid treatment	KDGT	£	60	62	64	61	69	69
Ophthalmic services[8]								
Number of sight tests given[12]	KDGU	Thousands	346	347	360	368	385	404
Number of optical appliances supplied[13]	KDGV	"	192	189	194	196	200	210
Cost of service (gross)[14]	KDGW	£ thousand	13,981	14,395	15,868	16,280	16,970	18,468
Health and social services[15]								
Medical and dental staff:								
Whole-time	KDGZ	Numbers	2,606	2,749	2,947	3,152	3,250	3,278
Part-time	KDHA	"	619	626	561	554	587	603
Nursing and midwifery staff:								
Whole-time	KDHB	"	10,709	11,116	11,395	11,454	11,623	11,512
Part-time	KDHC	"	8,665	8,850	9,015	9,072	9,310	9,251
Administrative and clerical staff:								
Whole-time	KDHD	"	8,188	8,676	8,878	8,938	8,683	8,255
Part-time	KDHE	"	3,579	3,828	4,160	4,221	4,226	4,196
Professional and technical staff:								
Whole-time	KDHF	"	4,155	4,518	4,685	4,758	4,936	4,619
Part-time	KDHG	"	1,605	1,724	1,822	2,021	2,076	2,347
Social services staff(excluding casual home helps):								
Whole-time	KDHH	"	3,454	3,709	3,773	3,889	4,014	4,441
Part-time	KDHI	"	1,093	1,197	1,289	1,417	2,041	2,808
Ancillary and other staff:								
Whole-time	KDHJ	"	3,413	3,469	3,722	3,833	3,857	3,831
Part-time	KDHK	"	5,410	5,580	5,486	5,892	5,667	4,794
Cost of services (gross)[14]	KDHL	£ thousand	2,113,453	..	..	..	..	..
Payments by recipients	KDHM	Thousands	87,999	..	..	..	..	..
Payments out of public funds	KDHN	£ thousand	2,025,454	..	..	..	..	..

16.3 Hospital and general health services
Northern Ireland

			2009	2010	2011	2012	2013	2014
Hospital services[1]								
In-patients:								
Beds available[2]	KDGA	Numbers	7,274	6,732	6,439	6,288	6,172	6,056
Average daily occupation of beds	KDGB	Percentages	82	83	84	84	83	83
Discharges or deaths[3]	KDGC	Thousands	300	295	295	301	304	308
Out-patients:[4]								
New cases	KDGD	"	1,150	1,148	1,123	1,124	1,144	1,146
Total attendances	KDGE	"	2,231	2,234	2,239	2,247	2,288	2,240
General health services								
Medical services[1]								
Doctors (principals) on the list[5,6]	KDGF	Numbers	1,156	1,160	1,163	1,170	1,171	1,211
Number of patients per doctor	KDGG	"	1,615	1,623	1,631	1,631	1,639	1,599
Gross Payments to doctors[7]	KDGH	£ thousand	..	..	..	..	..	..
Pharmaceutical services[8]								
Prescription forms dispensed	KDGI	Thousands	19,241	20,411	20,860	21,416	21,723	22,473
Number of prescriptions	KDGJ	"	34,263	36,298	36,916	38,614	40,019	40,377
Gross Cost[9]	KDGK	£ thousand	470,049	490,670	462,947	457,492	463,206	478,328
Charges[10]	KDGL	"	4,447	0	0	0	0	0
Net Cost[9]	KDGM	"	465,603	490,670	462,947	457,492	463,206	478,328
Average gross cost per prescription[9]	KDGN	£	14	14	13	12	12	12
Dental services[8,11]								
Dentists on the list[5]	KDGO	Numbers	816	889	1,010	1,044	1,049	1,125
Number of courses of paid treatment	KDGP	Thousands	1,051	1,172	1,231	1,283	1,335	1,336
Gross cost	KDGQ	£ thousand	73,741	81,621	84,659	90,759	92,984	94,681
Patients	KDGR	Thousands	885	1,001	1,119	1,147	1,166	1,175
Contributions (Net cost)	KDGS	£ thousand	57,897	64,280	66,533	69,960	73,520	74,640
Average gross cost per paid treatment	KDGT	£	70	70	69	71	70	71
Ophthalmic services[8]								
Number of sight tests given[12]	KDGU	Thousands	413	425	435	438	446	454
Number of optical appliances supplied[13]	KDGV	"	212	219	226	233	235	236
Cost of service (gross)[14]	KDGW	£ thousand	19,638	19,823	20,220	20,836	21,346	21,815
Health and social services[15]								
Medical and dental staff:								
Whole-time	KDGZ	Numbers	3,301	3,294	3,347	3,415	3,358	3,539
Part-time	KDHA	"	599	618	649	677	697	810
Nursing and midwifery staff:								
Whole-time	KDHB	"	11,716	11,292	11,171	11,426	11,722	11,970
Part-time	KDHC	"	9,277	9,470	9,356	9,422	9,453	9,436
Administrative and clerical staff:								
Whole-time	KDHD	"	8,197	7,880	7,795	8,106	8,201	8,237
Part-time	KDHE	"	4,286	4,280	4,304	4,447	4,498	4,512
Professional and technical staff:								
Whole-time	KDHF	"	4,704	4,748	4,807	5,069	5,233	5,340
Part-time	KDHG	"	2,423	2,533	2,639	2,725	2,859	3,005
Social services staff(excluding casual home helps):								
Whole-time	KDHH	"	4,619	4,632	4,581	4,622	4,689	4,778
Part-time	KDHI	"	2,863	2,877	2,896	2,919	2,930	2,844
Ancillary and other staff:								
Whole-time	KDHJ	"	3,816	3,855	3,814	3,740	3,726	3,731
Part-time	KDHK	"	4,904	4,805	4,582	4,598	4,636	4,338
Cost of services (gross)[14]	KDHL	£ thousand	..	..	..	..	..	..
Payments by recipients	KDHM	Thousands	..	..	..	..	..	..
Payments out of public funds	KDHN	£ thousand	..	..	..	..	..	..

Sources: Business Services Organisation (BSO) Northern Ireland: 028 9053 2975;
Dept of Health, Social Services & Public Safety Northern Ireland: 028 9052 2509;
(Figures on Hospital Services: 028 9052 2800)

16.3 Hospital and general health services

Northern Ireland

1 Financial Year.

2 Average available beds in wards open overnight during the year.

3 Includes transfers to other hospitals. This figure also excludes day case admissions.

4 Includes consultant outpatient clinics and Accident and Emergency departments.

5 At beginning of period for Dentists. Doctors numbers at 2002 (Oct), 2003 (Nov), 2004, 2005 & 2006 (Oct).

6 From 2003 onwards (UPE's).

7 These costs refer to the majority of non-cash limited services: further expenditure under GMS is allocated through HSS Boards on a cash limited basis. Change between 2002 and 2003 is due to advance payments being made in relation to the new GMS contract introduced in April 2004.

8 From 1995 onwards figures are taken from financial year.

9 Gross cost is defined as net ingredient costs plus on-cost, fees and other payments.

10 Excludes amount paid by patients for pre-payment certificates.

11 Due to changes in the Dental Contract which came into force in October 1990 dentists are paid under a combination of headings relating to Capitation and Continuing Care patients. Prior to this, payment was simply on an item of service basis.

12 Excluding sight tests given in hospitals and under the school health service and in the home.

13 Relates to the number of vouchers supplied and excludes repair/replace spectacles.

14 Figures relate to the costs of the hospital, community health and personal social services,and have been estimated from financial year data.

15 Workforce figures are headcounts at 30th September and are taken from the Human Resources Management System system. All workforce figures have been revised and now exclude Home Helps, Bank staff, staff on career breaks, Chairperson / Members of Boards and staff with a whole-time equivalent equal to or less than 0.03. The Ancillary and Other staff category includes Ancillary & General/Support Services staff, Works & Maintenance/Estates staff and Ambulance staff for all years, and from 2008 also includes Generic staff who are multidisciplinary staff. Due to Agenda for Change, new grade codes were introduced (from 2007 onwards) which resulted in some staff moving between categories. Backward comparison of the workforce is therefore not advised due to variations in definitions. 2014 figures onwards will include Northern Ireland Medical & Dental Training Agency staff and GP trainees working in Trusts.

16.4 NHS Hospital & Community Health Service (HCHS) and General Practice workforce as at 30 September each specified year
England

headcount & percentages

	2004	2005	2006	2007	2008	2009	2010[1]	2011	2012	2013	2014	Change 2013-2014	% change 2013-2014	Change 2004-2014	Average Annual % change 2004-2014
Total	1,260,860	1,298,202	1,284,261	1,272,884	1,308,774	1,365,303	1,387,191	1,361,533	1,358,295	1,364,165	1,387,692	23,527	1.7%	126,832	1.0%
Total HCHS medical and dental staff (incl HPCAs)	86,996	90,630	93,320	94,638	98,703	102,961	103,912	105,711	107,242	108,732	110,632	1,900	1.7%	23,636	2.4%
Total HCHS non-medical staff	1,030,800	1,063,121	1,038,368	1,027,299	1,060,629	1,110,138	1,109,195	1,083,637	1,075,035	1,078,425	1,098,170	19,745	1.8%	67,370	0.6%
Total GPs	34,855	35,944	36,008	36,420	37,720	40,269	39,409	39,780	40,265	40,236	40,584	348	0.9%	5,729	1.5%
Total GP Practice staff[6]	112,254	112,094	119,642	117,375	114,483	114,268	136,831	134,177	137,290	138,056	139,352	1,296	0.9%	27,098	2.2%
Professionally qualified clinical staff	622,720	643,219	643,906	645,933	661,993	683,703	687,009	686,747	687,810	692,157	701,872	9,715	1.4%	79,152	1.2%
All doctors[2]	117,806	122,987	126,251	128,210	133,662	140,897	141,326	143,836	146,075	147,807	150,273	2,466	1.7%	32,467	2.5%
Consultants (including Directors of public health)	30,650	31,993	32,874	33,674	34,910	36,950	37,752	39,088	40,394	41,220	42,733	1,513	3.7%	12,083	3.4%
Registrars	16,823	18,006	18,808	30,759	35,042	37,108	38,158	38,891	39,404	40,492	41,010	518	1.3%	24,187	9.3%
Other doctors in training and equivalents	24,874	26,305	27,461	16,024	14,136	14,394	14,034	14,018	13,952	14,118	14,106	-12	-0.1%	-10,768	-5.5%
Hospital practitioners and clinical assistants (non-dental specialties)[2]	4,045	3,587	3,077	2,848	2,761	2,333	2,148	1,782	1,547	1,254	1,013	-241	-19.2%	-3,032	-12.9%
Other medical and dental staff	10,604	10,739	11,100	11,333	11,854	12,176	12,223	12,292	12,302	11,983	12,081	98	0.8%	1,477	1.3%
GPs total	34,855	35,944	36,008	36,420	37,720	40,269	39,409	39,780	40,265	40,236	40,584	348	0.9%	5,729	1.5%
GPs (excluding retainers and registrars)	31,523	32,738	33,091	33,364	34,010	35,917	35,120	35,415	35,527	35,561	35,819	258	0.7%	4,296	1.3%
GP Providers	28,781	29,340	27,691	27,342	27,347	27,613	27,036	27,218	26,886	26,635	26,183	-452	-1.7%	-2,598	-0.9%
Other GPs	2,742	3,398	5,400	6,022	6,663	8,304	8,319	8,585	8,898	9,153	9,885	732	8.0%	7,143	13.7%
GP registrars[5,7]	2,562	2,564	2,278	2,491	3,203	3,881	3,880	4,013	4,426	4,404	4,512	108	2.5%	1,950	5.8%
GP retainers	770	642	639	565	507	471	419	365	321	284	262	-22	-7.7%	-508	-10.2%
Total qualified nursing staff[3]	358,759	367,581	366,981	363,719	368,425	375,505	375,950	372,277	369,868	371,777	377,191	5,414	1.5%	18,432	0.5%
Qualified nursing, midwifery & health visiting staff	336,615	344,677	343,184	340,859	346,377	353,570	352,104	348,693	346,410	347,944	353,359	5,415	1.6%	16,744	0.5%
GP practice nurses[6]	22,144	22,904	23,797	22,860	22,048	21,935	23,846	23,584	23,458	23,833	23,832	-1	0.0%	1,688	0.7%
Total qualified scientific, therapeutic & technical staff[8]	128,883	134,534	134,498	136,976	142,455	149,379	151,607	152,216	153,472	154,109	155,960	1,851	1.2%	27,077	1.9%
Qualified Allied Health Professions	65,515	67,841	67,483	68,687	71,301	73,953	74,374	74,647	74,902	76,163	77,947	1,784	2.3%	12,432	1.8%
Qualified Healthcare Scientists	28,242	30,046	30,453	30,158	30,925	32,161	31,972	31,481	31,173	29,617	27,368	-2,249	-7.6%	-874	-0.3%
Other qualified scientific, therapeutic & technical staff	35,126	36,647	36,562	38,131	40,229	43,265	45,337	46,167	47,490	48,429	50,728	2,299	4.7%	15,602	3.7%
Qualified ambulance staff[4]	17,272	18,117	16,176	17,028	17,451	17,922	18,450	18,687	18,645	18,734	18,673	-61	-0.3%	1,401	0.8%
Support to clinical staff	336,044	344,971	334,713	324,249	334,929	352,800	356,410	347,064	343,927	348,999	360,402	11,403	3.3%	24,358	0.7%
Support to doctors & nursing staff	271,389	279,193	267,934	259,547	266,070	278,390	279,522	271,384	269,714	274,144	281,498	7,354	2.7%	10,109	0.4%
Support to scientific, therapeutic & technical staff	55,025	55,715	54,307	53,259	55,792	60,048	62,726	62,057	61,345	61,312	64,502	3,190	5.2%	9,477	1.6%
Support to ambulance staff	9,630	10,063	12,472	11,443	13,067	14,362	14,738	14,238	13,451	14,112	14,946	834	5.9%	5,316	4.5%
NHS infrastructure support	211,489	220,387	209,387	207,778	219,064	236,103	233,342	219,624	215,071	211,185	212,123	938	0.4%	634	0.0%
Central functions	99,831	105,565	101,860	100,177	105,354	115,818	116,846	109,315	106,696	104,130	106,178	2,048	2.0%	6,347	0.6%
Hotel, property & estates	73,932	75,431	70,776	71,102	73,797	75,624	74,712	72,283	71,242	70,892	69,053	-1,839	-2.6%	-4,879	-0.7%
Manager & senior manager	37,726	39,391	36,751	36,499	39,913	44,661	41,962	38,214	37,314	36,360	37,078	718	2.0%	-648	-0.2%

16.4 NHS Hospital & Community Health Service (HCHS) and General Practice workforce as at 30 September each specified year
England

headcount & percentages

Other non-medical staff or those with unknown classification	497	435	410	409	353	364	356	266	237	220	209	-11	-5.0%	-288	-8.3%
Other GP practice staff [6]	90,110	89,190	95,845	94,515	92,436	92,333	112,985	110,593	113,832	114,223	115,520	1,297	1.1%	25,410	2.5%

Source: Health and Social Care Information Centre

Notes:

1 The new headcount methodology is not fully comparable with data for years prior to 2010, due to improvements that make it a more stringent count of absolute staff numbers
  Headcount totals are unlikely to equal the sum of components. Further information on the headcount methodology is available in the Census publication.
2 In order to avoid double counting Hosptial Practitioners & Clinical Assistants (HPCAs) are excluded from the all doctors totals, as they are predominantly GPs that work part time in hospitals (applies to headcount data only).
3 Nursing and midwifery figures exclude students on training courses leading to a first qualification as a nurse or midwife.
4 In 2006 ambulance staff were collected under new, more detailed, occupation codes. As a result, qualified totals and support to ambulance staff totals are not directly comparable with previous years.
5 GP Registrar count from 2008 onwards represents an improvement in data collection processes and comparisons with previous years should be treated with caution
6 Practice staff figures for 2010 & 2011 were revised in 2012. Further details can be found in the data quality statement/methodology. This will affect any related totals and comparisons with years prior to 2010.
7 From 2012 GP Registrars have been removed from the GP Workforce collection where a duplicate record already exists on the Electronic Staff Record. Due to a change in coding practices in some regions GP Registrars are increasingly recorded
  on the ESR system rather than the GP Exeter Payment System. All these staff are not shown in the GP Registrar totals but are included in the HCHS Medical and Dental Registrars total
8 A reclassification of healthcare scientists in 2013/14 has led to a shift in numbers within qualified scientific, therapeutic and technical staff, this affects 2014 data.

These statistics relate to the contracted positions within English NHS organisations and may include those where the person assigned to the position is temporarily absent, for example on maternity leave.
From 2011 the bank staff return was suspended (and formally ceased in 2013). All data (for all years) in these tables excludes bank staff
From April 2013 Public Health England was excluded from workforce publications.

16.5 Staffing summary
Wales

	Unit (a)	2010	2011	2012	2013	2014
Directly employed NHS staff:						
Medical and dental staff (b):						
Hospital medical staff	Fte	5,370	5,490	5,544	5,713	5,654
Of which consultants	Fte	2,045	2,128	2,180	2,230	2,221
Community/Public health medical staff	Fte	84	84	88	79	76
Hospital dental staff	Fte	168	161	161	168	164
Of which consultants	Fte	45	44	44	46	49
Community/Public health dental staff	Fte	104	109	115	114	117
Total	**Fte**	**5,725**	**5,844**	**5,909**	**6,073**	**6,011**
Nursing, midwifery and health visiting staff	Fte	28,157	27,980	28,068	28,254	28,300
of which qualified	Fte	21,831	21,748	21,823	22,005	22,053
Scientific, therapeutic and technical staff	Fte	11,507	11,472	11,549	11,616	11,671
Health care assistants and other support staff	Fte	10,033	9,718	9,793	9,699	9,650
Administration and estates staff	Fte	15,472	15,192	15,039	15,120	15,172
Ambulance staff	Fte	1,427	1,457	1,511	1,499	1,544
Other (c)	Fte	166	173	133	131	115
Total	**Fte**	**72,487**	**71,836**	**72,002**	**72,393**	**72,464**
Family Practitioners:						
General medical practitioners (d)	Number	1,991	2,009 (r)	1,997 (r)	2,026	2,006
General dental practitioners (e)	Number	1,310	1,349	1,360	1,392	1,438
Ophthalmic medical practitioners (f)	Number	16	12	14	8	7
Ophthalmic opticians (f)	Number	740	756	795	773	769

Source: Health Statistics and Analysis Unit. Welsh Government

(a)   Fte = whole-time equivalent.
(b)   Excludes locum staff.
(c)   Professional advisors and staff on general payments, eg Macmillan and Marie Curie nurses.
(d)   At 30 September. All practitioners excluding GP registrars, GP Retainers and locums
(e)   Number of dental performers who have any NHS activity recorded against them via FP17 claim forms at any time in the year ending 31 March.
(f)   At 31 December.
(r)   Revised.

16.6 Deaths[1]: underlying cause, sex and age-group, Summary

	England and Wales		2012 Age-group All ages		2013 Age-group All ages		2014 Age-group All ages
ICD-10 code	Underlying cause (excludes deaths under 28 days for individual causes)						
A00-R99, U00-Y89	All causes, all ages	M F	240,238 259,093	M F	245,585 261,205	M F	245,585 261,205
	All causes, ages under 28 days	M F	1,196 904	M F	1,084 813	M F	1,084 813
A00-R99, U00-Y89	All causes, ages 28 days and over	M F	239,042 258,189	M F	244,501 260,392	M F	244,501 260,392
A00-B99	I Certain infectious and parasitic diseases	M F	2,271 2,838	M F	2,403 2,902	M F	2,403 2,902
C00-D48	II Neoplasms	M F	76,695 68,700	M F	76,962 68,382	M F	76,962 68,382
D50-D89	III Diseases of the blood and blood-forming organs and certain disorders involving the immune mechanism	M F	422 521	M F	440 516	M F	440 516
E00-E90	IV Endocrine, nutritional and metabolic diseases	M F	3,132 3,578	M F	3,184 3,594	M F	3,184 3,594
F00-F99	V Mental and behavioural disorders	M F	11,710 24,155	M F	12,655 25,578	M F	12,655 25,578
G00-G99	VI Diseases of the nervous system	M F	9,499 11,674	M F	10,173 12,331	M F	10,173 12,331
H00-H59	VII Diseases of the eye and adnexa	M F	11 9	M F	2 10	M F	2 10
H60-H95	VIII Diseases of the ear and mastoid process	M F	14 7	M F	2 10	M F	2 10
I00-I99	IX Diseases of the circulatory system	M F	69,516 71,846	M F	70,336 69,965	M F	70,336 69,965
J00-J99	X Diseases of the respiratory system	M F	33,463 37,245	M F	35,115 39,114	M F	35,115 39,114
K00-K93	XI Diseases of the digestive system	M F	11,766 12,807	M F	11,712 12,646	M F	11,712 12,646
L00-L99	XII Diseases of the skin and subcutaneous tissue	M F	564 1,111	M F	605 1,115	M F	605 1,115
M00-M99	XIII Diseases of the musculoskeletal system and connective tissue	M F	1,397 2,933	M F	1,368 2,853	M F	1,368 2,853
N00-N99	XIV Diseases of the genitourinary system	M F	4,080 5,682	M F	4,073 5,558	M F	4,073 5,558
O00-O99	XV Pregnancy, childbirth and the puerperium	F	46	F	47	F	47
P00-P96	XVI Certain conditions originating in the perinatal period	M F	114 91	M F	111 56	M F	111 56
Q00-Q99	XVII Congenital malformations, deformations and chromosomal abnormalities	M F	595 554	M F	576 550	M F	576 550
R00-R99	XVIII Symptoms, signs and abnormal clinical and laboratory findings, not elsewhere classified	M F	2,800 7,923	M F	2,851 8,167	M F	2,851 8,167
U509, V01-Y89	XX External causes of morbidity and mortality	M F	10,993 6,469	M F	11,923 6,998	M F	11,923 6,998

Source: Office for National Statistics

1 Death figures are based on deaths registered rather than deaths occurring in a calendar year. For more infomation on registration delays see www.ons.gov.uk/ons/guide-method/user-guidance/health-and-life-events/impact-of-registration-delays-on-mortality-statistics/index.html

16.7a Notifications of infectious diseases , 2005-2014

England and Wales

Disease	2005	2006	2007	2008	2009	2010	2011	2012	2013	2014
Acute encephalitis	19	19	18	24	16	16	13	9	15	11
Acute infectious hepatitis	.	.	.	.	.	475	408	253	253	865
Acute Meningitis	1381	1494	1251	1181	1219	922	538	522	545	474
Acute poliomyelitis	.	.	.	.	1	.	1	.	.	1
Anthrax	.	1	.	1	.	5	.	2	1	.
Botulism	.	.	.	.	.	2	.	.	.	.
Brucellosis	.	.	.	.	.	.	3	3	1	4
Cholera	34	37	41	40	35	35	16	7	3	10
Diphtheria	9	10	9	6	11	9	2	4	9	14
Dysentery	1237	1122	1217	1166	1218	267	.	.	.	.
Enteric fever (typhoid or paratyphoid fever)	.	.	.	.	.	272	224	137	127	157
Food poisoning	70407	70603	72382	68962	74974	57041	24384	20680	15350	17402
Haemolytic uraemic syndrome (HUS)	.	.	.	.	.	1	5	1	4	6
Infectious bloody diarrhoea	.	.	.	.	.	386	469	418	399	511
Invasive group A streptococcal disease	.	.	.	.	.	215	186	194	223	369
Legionnaires' Disease	.	.	.	.	.	102	73	80	82	151
Leprosy	.	.	.	.	.	1	1	8	4	8
Leptospirosis	31	24	37	44	29	5	.	.	.	.
Malaria	679	613	426	386	381	327	296	267	226	201
Measles	2089	3705	3670	5088	5191	2235	2355	4211	6193	1851
Meningococcal septicaemia	721	657	673	528	495	367	261	301	300	277
Mumps	56256	12841	7196	7827	18629	10402	6888	7530	10095	8334
Ophthalmia neonatorum	87	100	83	77	90	18	.	.	.	.
Other	.	.	.	.	.	1974	2780	4751	5017	4660
Paratyphoid fever	119	185	126	170	130	33	.	.	.	.
Rabies	.	.	.	.	.	.	.	1	.	.
Rubella	1155	1221	1082	1096	1130	631	476	756	553	425
Scarlet fever	1678	2166	1948	2920	4176	2969	2719	4254	4643	15637
Tetanus	3	.	4	7	6	6	2	7	2	4
Tuberculosis	7628	7621	6989	7319	7241	8333	9227	9101	8137	7261
Typhoid fever	179	201	208	240	210	68	.	.	.	.
Typhus fever	1	6	.	4	.	2	.	4	2	1
Viral haemorrhagic fever	.	5	1	3	5	3	3	7	6	11
Viral hepatitis	4109	4007	3857	4756	4979	1043	.	.	.	.
Whooping cough	594	550	1089	1512	1155	405	911	6557	3273	2506
Yellow fever	2	.	.	.	.	.	.	.	.	.

Source: Public Health England

1. As from 6th April 2010 the following diseases are no longer notifiable but may still be reported under the Other disease category: Dysentery, Leptospirosis, Ophthalmia neonatorum, Viral hepatitis

2. As from 6th April 2010 the following diseases became notifiable: Botulism, Brucellosis, Haemolytic Uraemic Syndrome (HUS), Infectious bloody diarrhoea, Legionnaire's disease,

3. As from 6th April 2010 Typhoid and Paratyphoid fever have been grouped under Enteric fever.

4. As from week 35 of 2010 Food poisoning 'otherwise ascertained' cases are no longer collected.

5. As from 6th April 2010 the Other disease category may be used to notify any cases that may present a significant risk to human health.

6. A proportion of notified cases are shown subsequently not to be the implicated infection.

7. Any disease not mentioned on a table may be assumed Where a disease is not mentioned on a table it may be assumed that no notifications were received.

16.7b Notifications of infectious diseases, 2002-2013

Scotland

Notifiable Disease [1,2,3]	2002	2003	2004	2005	2006	2007	2008	2009	2010	2011	2012	2013
Botulism	..	..	..	..	..	..	..	..	0	3	0	..
Anthrax	0	0	0	0	1	0	0	4	39	0	4	1
Brucellosis	..	..	..	..	..	..	..	..	1	1	0	1
Cholera	2	1	1	6	3	8	3	5	3	3	1	1
Clinical Syndrome E.coli O 157 infection	..	..	..	..	..	..	..	..	33	4	17	3
Diphtheria	0	0	0	0	0	1	0	0	0	0	0	1
Haemolytic Uraemic Syndrome (HUS)	..	..	..	..	..	..	..	..	5	3	1	5
Haemophilus influenzae type b (Hib)	..	..	..	..	..	..	..	..	3	6	0	..
Measles	399	181	257	186	259	168	219	172	93	82	99	162
Meningococcal disease	175	117	147	139	140	150	120	122	93	103	89	83
Mumps	259	181	3 595	5 698	2 917	2 741	720	1129	727	607	920	503
Necrotizing fasciitis	..	..	..	..	..	..	..	..	2	12	4	7
Paratyphoid	0	0	0	0	0	1	4	2	2	1	0	..
Pertussis (Whooping cough)	99	60	87	51	67	98	134	104	45	85	2068	1 134
Poliomyelitis	0	0	0	0	0	0	0	0	0	0	0	..
Rabies	1	0	0	0	0	0	0	0	0	0	0	..
Rubella	292	130	222	141	153	146	106	93	39	21	43	22
Tetanus	1	1	1	1	0	0	0	0	0	0	0	..
Typhoid	4	2	2	1	3	3	3	1	6	3	2	8
Viral haemorrhagic fevers	0	0	0	0	0	0	0	0	0	0	1	..

.. Not available

1 Figures for all years are confirmed notifications

Source: Health Protection Scotland SIDSS2

Queries to: patriciacassels@nhs.net (tel 0141 300 1148)

2 The following diseases were also notifiable but there were no cases in 2012: Plague, Severe Acute Respiratory Syndrome (SARS), Smallpox, Tularemia, West Nile fever, Yellow fever

3 From 2010 the following diseases are no longer notifiable - Bacillary dysentery, Chickenpox, Erysipelas, Food poisoning, Legionellosis, Leptospirosis, Lyme disease, Malaria, Puerperal fever, Scarlet fever, Toxoplasmosis, Typhus fever and Viral hepatitis

16.7c Notifications of Infectious diseases
Northern Ireland

Description	2010	2011	2012	2013	2014
Acute Encephalitis/Meningitis Bacterial	49	28	37	61	57
Acute Encephalitis/Meningitis Viral	11	13	10	7	13
Anthrax	0	0	0	2	0
Chickenpox	2111	1566	2126	1574	1675
Cholera	0	0	0	0	0
Diphtheria	0	0	0	0	0
Dysentery	6	7	11	6	24
Food Poisoning	1550	1575	1777	1707	1820
Gastroenteritis (< 2years)	18089	661	799	571	447
Hepatitis A	4	0	4	4	3
Hepatitis B	90	129	130	114	102
Hepatitis Unspecified	0	0	0	0	0
Legionnaires' Disease	4	4	6	10	7
Leptospirosis	0	3	3	2	0
Malaria	6	1	5	5	6
Measles	72	27	43	57	17
Meningococcal Septicaemia	38	45	33	27	30
Mumps	212	123	298	694	126
Paratyphoid Fever	0	0	0	1	1
Plague	0	0	0	0	0
Poliomyelitis (Acute)	0	0	0	0	0
Poliomyelitis (Paralytic)	0	0	0	0	0
Rabies	0	0	0	0	0
Relapsing Fever	0	0	0	0	0
Rubella	18	18	13	17	10
Scarlet Fever	154	130	196	190	625
Smallpox	0	0	0	0	0
Tetanus	0	1	1	1	0
Tuberculosis (Non Pulmonary)	32	14	45	40	71
Tuberculosis (Pulmonary)	34	44	51	34	36
Typhoid	1	1	1	1	0
Typhus	0	0	0	0	0
Viral Haemorraghic Fever	0	0	2	1	0
Whooping Cough	18	18	394	76	39
Yellow Fever	0	0	0	0	0

Public Health Agency, Northern Ireland

16.8a Work-related and occupational respiratory disease: estimated number of cases reported by chest physicians to SWORD 2006-2013 and by occupational physicians to OPRA 2007-2010 by sex and diagnostic category

Sex		Chest physicians (SWORD)							Occupational Physicians (OPRA) (c)				
All cases (b)	Diagnostic category	2007	2008	2009	2010	2011	2012	2013r	2006	2007	2008	2009	2010
	Allergic alveolitis	19	87	39	29	25	56	53	-	-	-	13	-
	Asthma	251	307	181	205	159	189	189	145	104	55	47	65
	Bronchitis/emphysema	15	18	69	18	52	19	26	-	2	12	-	-
	Infectious diseases	28	24	25	2	60	25	14	2	36	-	24	12
	Inhalation accidents	5	38	50	3	14	3	1	4	16	1	-	50
	Lung cancer	104	91	86	71	133	16	88	2	-	-	-	-
	Malignant mesothelioma	884	611	559	522	472	577	658	16	1	14	-	-
	Benign pleural disease	1008	1114	893	790	831	711	708	12	-	-	12	1
	Pneumoconiosis	167	145	208	110	224	159	276	3	5	-	-	-
	Other	81	56	100	61	105	61	105	47	114	80	77	30
	Total diagnoses	**2562**	**2491**	**2210**	**1811**	**2075**	**1816**	**2118**	**231**	**278**	**162**	**173**	**158**
	Total cases (a)	**2534**	**2442**	**2135**	**1760**	**2009**	**1750**	**2033**	**230**	**278**	**161**	**172**	**157**

Source: Health and Safety Executive (HSE)

Notes:

(a) Individuals may have more than one diagnosis.

(b) May not equal males plus females because sex is not recorded for some cases.

(c) No OPRA data are available for the annual statistics after 2010.

(d) Some physicians report on a sample basis, for one month in each year. Estimated totals for these are calculated by multiplying the actual number of cases reported by 12.

"-" means zero.

p Provisional data.

r Revised

16.8b Work-related mental ill-health cases reported to THOR-GP by diagnosis 2012 to 2014

Mental ill-health diagnoses	*Number of cases reported to THOR-GP aggregate total 2012 to 2014	% of all diagnoses
Anxiety/depression	1008	37
Post-traumatic stress disorder (PTSD)	12	0
Other stress	1548	56
Alcohol & drug abuse	84	3
Other diagnoses	48	2
Other stress symptoms	60	2
Total diagnoses	2760	100
Total cases	2664	

Source: Health and Safety Executive (HSE)

* This estimate has an adjustment applied for sample reporting, but not an adjustment for the response rate. This is because there is no evidence indicating that non-responding GPs would report, on average, the same number of cases as those who responded.

16.8c Work-related skin disease: estimated number of cases reported by dermatologists to EPIDERM 2007 - 2013 and by occupational physicians to OPRA 2006 - 2010, by diagnostic category

Sex	Diagnostic category	Dermatologists (EPIDERM)							Occupational physicians (OPRA) (c)				
		2007	2008	2009	2010	2011	2012	2013r	2006	2007	2008	2009	2010
All cases(b)	Contact dermatitis	1386	1325	1423	1281	1208	1151	964	596	488	322	373	342
	Contact urticaria	73	43	44	55	38	31	11	26	15	13	14	13
	Folliculitis /acne	11	17	3	-	1	-	-	-	-	1	-	-
	Infective skin disease	3	2	13	14	1	-	1	-	14	36	2	12
	Mechanical skin disease	8	9	18	18	14	6	26	1	-	1	12	-
	Nail conditions	25	13	13	1	-	1	13	-	-	-	-	-
	Skin neoplasia	622	418	492	390	231	314	296	-	-	-	-	-
	Other dermatoses	35	30	72	30	72	3	28	68	40	36	40	37
	Total number of diagnoses	2163	1857	2078	1789	1565	1506	1339	691	557	409	441	404
	Total number of individuals[a]	2137	1839	2015	1745	1550	1480	1310	679	556	409	440	392

Source: Health and Safety Executive (HSE)

Notes:

(a) Individuals may have more than one diagnosis.

(b) May not equal males plus females because sex is not recorded for some cases.

(c) No OPRA data are available for the annual statistics after 2010.

(d) Some physicians report on a sample basis, for one month in each year. Estimated totals for these are calculated by multiplying the actual number of cases reported by 12.

"-" means zero.

p Provisional data.

r Revised

16.8d Work-related musculoskeletal cases reported to THOR-GP by anatomical site 2012 to 2014

Anatomical site	*Number of cases reported to THOR-GP aggregate total 2012 to 2014	% of all diagnoses
Hand/wrist/arm	792	21
Elbow	408	11
Shoulder	372	10
Neck/thoracic spine	240	6
Lumbar spine/trunk	1152	31
Hip/knee	444	12
Ankle/foot	156	4
Other	144	4
Total diagnoses	3708	100
Total cases	3480	

Source: Health and Safety Executive (HSE)

* This estimate has an adjustment applied for sample reporting, but not an adjustment for the response rate. This is because there is no evidence indicating that non-responding GPs would report, on average, the same number of cases as those who responded.

16.9 Deaths due to occupationally related lung disease in Great Britain, 2000 to 2013

Numbers

	2000	2001	2002	2003	2004	2005	2006	2007	2008	2009	2010	2011	2012	2013
Asbestosis (without Mesothelioma) [1,3]	186	233	234	236	268	303	327	320	367	412	414	429	464	477
Mesothelioma [2,4]	1633	1860	1867	1887	1978	2049	2060	2176	2265	2336	2360	2312	2549	2556
Pneumoconiosis due to dust containing silica(a)	24 (1)	19 (1)	28	13	13 (1)	10	14	7	10 (2)	18 (2)	13	16	11	18 (1)
Other non-asbestosis pneumoconiosis(b)	255	221 (1)	243 (8)	218 (1)	201 (1)	184 (1)	153	142 (1)	129 (1)	131	121	136	140	147
Byssinosis(c)	4 (2)	2 (1)	0	3 (2)	4 (3)	3 (1)	5 (3)	2 (1)	1	2 (1)	2 (2)	1 (1)	1 (1)	1 (1)
Farmer's lung and other occupational allergic alveolitis(d)	7	7 (1)	6 (2)	7 (2)	5	13	10	5 (2)	7 (2)	7 (1)	8	9 (2)	10	4
Total	**2109**	**2342**	**2378**	**2364**	**2469**	**2562**	**2569**	**2652**	**2779**	**2906**	**2918**	**2903**	**3175**	**3203**

Source: ONS, GRO(S), Health and Safety Executive

(a) ICD9 code 502; ICD10 code J62

(b) ICD9 codes 500, 503, 505; ICD10 codes J60, J63-J64

(c) ICD9 code 504; ICD10 code J66

(d) ICD9 codes 495.0, 495.3, 495.4, 495.5, 495.6, 495.8; ICD10 codes J670, J673-J676, J678

The figure is the number of deaths coded to the disease as underlying cause.

Figures in brackets show the number of females. Where no figure is given, all cases were male.

1. Some death certificates mention asbestosis with lung cancer and/or mesothelioma. In some cases - particularly where mesothelioma is mentioned - the word "asbestosis" may have been used incorrectly to indicate the role of asbestos in causing mesothelioma and/or lung cancer

2. The Office for National Statistics (ONS) discontinued medical enquiries in 1993. Therefore, for deaths registered from 1993 onwards, there is often less information available to accurately code the specific site of the mesothelioma

3. For inclusion into the Asbestosis register the cause of death on the death certificate must mention the word Asbestosis

4. Total for Great Britain may include a small number of persons with overseas addresses.

16.10 Reported injuries to employees and the self-employed in Great Britain, detailed industry and severity of injury, 2013/14r

Detailed industry +	Section	Division	Employees Number Fatal injuries	Major or specified injuries	Over-7-day injuries	Total injuries	Rate Fatal injuries	Major or specified injuries	Over-7-day injuries	Total injuries	Self-employed Number Fatal injuries	Major or specified injuries	Over-7-day injuries	Total injuries
Agriculture, Forestry and Fishing (1)	A	01-03	10	344	517	871	6.54	224.9	338.0	569.4	17	74	22	113
Crop and animal production, hunting and related service activities	A	01	9	277	411	697	6.76	208.2	308.9	523.9	17	48	13	78
Forestry and logging	A	02	1	50	65	116	7.40	370.0	481.0	858.4	-	23	8	31
Fishing and aquaculture (1)	A	03	-	17	41	58	-	265.3	639.7	905.0	-	3	1	4
Mining and Quarrying	B	05-09	3	115	248	366	2.64	101.1	218.1	321.9	-	1	1	2
Mining of coal and lignite	B	05	-	27	75	102	-	#	#	#	-	-	-	-
Extraction of crude petroleum and natural gas	B	06	1	44	99	144	6.42	282.7	636.0	925.1	-	-	1	1
Mining of metal ores	B	07	-	-	-	-	-	#	#	#	-	-	-	-
Other mining and quarrying	B	08	2	41	63	106	9.79	200.6	308.2	518.6	-	1	-	1
Mining support service activities	B	09	-	3	11	14	-	4.2	15.5	19.8	-	-	-	-
Manufacturing	C	10-33	10	3,165	10,502	13,677	0.38	120.4	399.4	520.2	5	72	58	135
Manufacture of food products	C	10	2	637	2,900	3,539	0.64	202.4	921.4	1,124.4	1	9	11	21
Manufacture of beverages	C	11	-	54	213	267	-	103.6	408.6	512.2	-	1	-	1
Manufacture of tobacco products	C	12	-	4	7	11	-	#	#	#	-	-	-	-
Manufacture of textiles	C	13	1	54	174	229	1.88	101.7	327.6	431.1	-	1	-	1
Manufacture of wearing apparel	C	14	-	3	13	16	-	9.2	39.7	48.8	-	-	-	-
Manufacture of leather and related products	C	15	-	1	12	13	-	8.7	103.9	112.5	-	-	-	-
Manufacture of wood and of products of wood and cork, except furniture; manufacture of articles of straw and plaiting materials	C	16	-	155	368	523	-	284.4	675.1	959.5	-	9	1	10
Manufacture of paper and paper products	C	17	-	85	237	322	-	152.2	424.3	576.5	-	-	-	-
Printing and reproduction of recorded media	C	18	-	76	293	369	-	68.5	264.1	332.6	1	-	-	1
Manufacture of coke and refined petroleum products	C	19	-	18	10	28	-	62.1	34.5	96.6	-	-	-	-
Manufacture of chemicals and chemical products	C	20	-	80	196	276	-	73.6	180.4	254.0	-	1	2	3
Manufacture of basic pharmaceutical products and pharmaceutical preparations	C	21	-	33	113	146	-	31.3	107.1	138.4	-	2	1	3
Manufacture of rubber and plastic products	C	22	-	169	589	758	-	121.5	423.5	545.0	-	2	-	2
Manufacture of non-metallic mineral products	C	23	1	111	327	439	1.31	145.7	429.3	576.3	-	7	2	9
Manufacture of basic metals	C	24	1	219	618	838	1.03	224.9	634.7	860.6	-	-	1	1
Manufacture of fabricated metal products, except machinery and equipment	C	25	2	322	911	1,235	0.91	146.9	415.5	563.3	1	9	5	15
Manufacture of computer, electronic and optical products	C	26	-	19	58	77	-	11.2	34.2	45.4	-	2	-	2
Manufacture of electrical equipment	C	27	1	41	124	166	1.35	55.3	167.4	224.0	-	-	-	-
Manufacture of machinery and equipment not elsewhere classified	C	28	2	150	377	529	0.84	63.1	158.5	222.4	-	5	1	6
Manufacture of motor vehicles, trailers and semi-trailers	C	29	-	167	519	686	-	97.6	303.2	400.8	-	-	4	4
Manufacture of other transport equipment	C	30	-	90	298	388	-	51.5	170.5	222.0	-	1	2	3
Manufacture of furniture	C	31	-	56	234	290	-	74.2	310.1	384.4	-	3	6	9
Other manufacturing	C	32	-	440	1,480	1,920	-	502.3	1,689.6	2,191.9	-	11	14	25
Repair and installation of machinery and equipment	C	33	-	181	431	612	-	102.7	244.5	347.2	2	9	8	19
Electricity, Gas, Steam and Air Conditioning Supply	D	35	1	91	175	267	0.58	53.2	102.2	156.0	-	8	5	13
Water Supply; Sewerage; Waste Management and Remediation Activities	E	36-39	3	579	1,829	2,411	1.47	284.0	897.1	1,182.6	2	19	10	31
Water collection, treatment and supply	E	36	-	49	116	165	-	81.7	193.4	275.2	-	5	1	6
Sewerage	E	37	1	41	130	172	12.22	500.9	1,588.1	2,101.1	-	-	3	3
Waste collection, treatment and disposal activities; materials recovery	E	38	2	478	1,543	2,023	1.75	418.5	1,350.9	1,771.2	2	13	6	21
Remediation activities and other waste management services	E	39	-	11	40	51	-	51.2	186.0	237.2	-	1	-	1
Construction	F	41-43	30	1,911	3,325	5,266	2.37	150.7	262.2	415.2	14	688	605	1,307
Construction of buildings	F	41	7	807	1,373	2,187	1.40	161.3	274.5	437.2	3	460	445	908
Civil engineering	F	42	2	265	489	756	0.81	107.0	197.5	305.3	-	33	36	69
Specialised construction activities	F	43	21	839	1,463	2,323	4.04	161.2	281.2	446.5	11	195	124	330
Total Service industries	G-U	45-99	35	12,913	42,957	55,905	0.17	62.0	206.1	268.2	6	234	205	445
Wholesale and retail trade and repair of motor vehicles and motorcycles	G	45	4	276	620	900	1.06	73.0	164.1	238.1	1	2	5	8
Wholesale trade, except of motor vehicles and motorcycles	G	46	1	335	1,160	1,496	0.16	52.9	183.1	236.2	1	4	5	10
Retail trade, except of motor vehicles and motor-cycles	G	47	3	1,599	5,647	7,249	0.12	61.5	217.2	278.8	-	9	13	22
Land transport and transport via pipelines	H	49	6	572	1,782	2,360	1.19	113.4	353.1	467.7	1	14	8	23
Water transport (2)	H	50	-	47	151	198	-	118.0	379.0	497.0	-	-	1	1
Air transport	H	51	-	81	716	797	-	149.3	1,320.1	1,469.4	-	1	1	2
Warehousing and support activities for transportation	H	52	4	1,152	4,652	5,808	1.22	350.3	1,414.4	1,765.9	-	23	31	54
Postal and courier activities	H	53	-	389	1,282	1,671	-	138.9	457.9	596.9	-	9	8	17
Accommodation	I	55	-	399	1,156	1,555	-	129.6	375.6	505.3	-	7	14	21
Food and beverage service activities	I	56	1	715	2,688	3,404	..	64.9	244.0	309.0	-	10	11	21
Publishing activities	J	58	-	5	22	27	-	3.2	13.9	17.1	-	-	-	-
Motion picture, video and television programme production, sound recording and music publishing activities	J	59	-	10	84	94	-	12.9	108.0	120.9	-	3	3	6
Programming and broadcasting activities	J	60	-	16	38	54	-	28.0	66.4	94.4	-	3	2	5
Telecommunications	J	61	1	94	251	346	0.61	57.1	152.4	210.0	-	2	2	4
Computer programming, consultancy and related activities	J	62	-	14	26	40	-	3.0	5.6	8.6	-	-	-	-
Information service activities	J	63	-	31	56	87	-	105.1	189.9	295.0	-	1	-	1
Financial service activities, except insurance and pension funding	K	64	-	113	242	355	-	22.0	47.1	69.0	-	2	1	3

16.10 Reported injuries to employees and the self-employed in Great Britain, detailed industry and severity of injury, 2013/14r

Detailed industry +	Section	Division	Employees Number				Employees Rate (per 100,000 employees)				Self-employed Number			
			Fatal injuries	Major or specified injuries	Over-7-day injuries	Total injuries	Fatal injuries	Major or specified injuries	Over-7-day injuries	Total injuries	Fatal injuries	Major or specified injuries	Over-7-day injuries	Total injuries
Insurance, reinsurance and pension funding, except compulsory social security	K	65	-	14	41	55	-	6.2	18.3	24.5	-	1	-	1
Activities auxiliary to financial services and insurance activities	K	66	-	2	30	32	-	.6	9.4	10.0	-	-	-	-
Real estate activities	L	68	-	47	160	207	-	17.4	59.3	76.7	-	-	-	-
Legal and accounting activities	M	69	-	25	38	63	-	6.7	10.2	16.9	-	-	-	-
Activities of head offices; management consultancy activities	M	70	-	23	32	55	-	7.1	9.9	17.1	-	-	2	2
Architectural and engineering activities; technical testing and analysis	M	71	-	7	11	18	-	1.7	2.7	4.4	-	-	-	-
Scientific research and development	M	72	-	16	34	50	-	17.0	36.2	53.2	-	-	-	-
Advertising and market research	M	73	-	8	14	22	-	5.5	9.6	15.2	-	-	-	-
Other professional, scientific and technical activities	M	74	-	28	57	85	-	22.5	45.8	68.3	-	1	1	2
Veterinary activities	M	75	-	46	72	118	-	90.0	140.9	231.0	-	5	-	5
Rental and leasing activities	N	77	2	84	195	281	1.87	78.6	182.5	263.0	-	3	5	8
Employment activities	N	78	2	15	32	49	1.03	7.7	16.4	25.2	-	-	-	-
Travel agency, tour operator and other reservation service and related activities	N	79	-	4	2	6	-	4.2	2.1	6.3	-	-	-	-
Security and investigation activities	N	80	1	175	496	672	0.58	101.8	288.5	390.9	-	3	1	4
Services to buildings and landscape activities	N	81	2	459	1,285	1,746	0.51	117.0	327.6	445.1	2	24	19	45
Office administrative, office support and other business support activities	N	82	-	133	271	404	-	80.6	164.3	244.9	-	8	2	10
Public administration and defence; compulsory social security	O	84	1	1,184	3,791	4,976	..	65.4	209.5	275.0	-	9	3	12
Education	P	85	1	1,706	3,086	4,793	..	57.4	103.9	161.3	-	17	6	23
Human health activities	Q	86	-	1,334	7,590	8,924	-	66.3	377.2	443.5	-	10	17	27
Residential care activities	Q	87	1	703	2,658	3,362	0.12	81.9	309.8	391.9	-	6	5	11
Social work activities without accommodation	Q	88	-	356	1,189	1,545	-	42.3	141.4	183.8	-	2	-	2
Creative, arts and entertainment activities	R	90	-	71	91	162	-	144.3	185.0	329.3	-	18	11	29
Libraries, archives, museums and other cultural activities	R	91	1	42	63	106	0.99	41.7	62.5	105.2	-	2	2	4
Gambling and betting activities	R	92	1	35	70	106	1.14	39.8	79.7	120.7	-	-	-	-
Sports activities and amusement and recreation activities	R	93	2	339	520	861	0.56	95.6	146.7	242.9	-	19	14	33
Activities of membership organisations	S	94	-	70	117	187	-	29.1	48.6	77.7	-	1	3	4
Repair of computers and personal and household goods	S	95	1	12	59	72	1.81	21.7	106.7	130.2	-	1	1	2
Other personal service activities	S	96	-	127	380	507	-	55.4	165.7	221.1	1	14	8	23
Activities of households as employers of domestic personnel	T	97	-	-	-	-	-	-	-	-	-	-	-	-
Undifferentiated goods- and services-producing activities of private households for own use	T	98	-	-	-	-	-	-	-	-	-	-	-	-
Activities of extraterritorial organisations and bodies	U	99	-	-	-	-	-	-	-	-	-	-	-	-
All industries	A-U	01-99	92	19,118	59,553	78,763	0.36	74.7	232.7	307.7	44	1,096	906	2,046

Source: RIDDOR - Reporting of Injuries, Diseases and Dangerous Occurrences Regulations (as amended)

r = Revised

Key changes to the reporting system and the legal requirements have occurred in recent years. From September 2011 the RIDDOR notification system used by employers changed, with reporting now being predominantly online, using newly designed forms and online guidance. In April 2012 there was a legislative change to RIDDOR, namely those injuries to workers which result in the person being incapacitated for more than three days, where the reporting threshold changed to over-7-days. The requirement remains for duty-holders to record over-3-day injuries, but not to report them. RIDDOR underwent a further, more extensive legislative change in October 2013. A key change at this time was the introduction of the 'specified injury' category to replace the 'major injury' category. More information on data changes affecting RIDDOR statistics is available at:
www.hse.gov.uk/statistics/riddor-notification.htm

+ HSE is now recording and publishing data in Standard Industrial Classification (SIC) 2007 format. Data from previous years which was collected in the SIC1992/2003 formats has been computer recoded to the SIC2007 coding to allow comparisons over time. For more information see:
www.hse.gov.uk/statistics/industry/sic2007.htm
(1) Excludes sea fishing.
(2) Injuries arising from shore-based services only. Excludes incidents reported under merchant shipping legislation.

Rates of injury
The Annual Population Survey (APS) is the source of employment data used as the denominator for rates of injury in this document. For more information see:
www.hse.gov.uk/statistics/sources.htm#employment

2013/14 rates have been revised (October 2015) as APS data sets have been reweighted to reflect population estimates based on the 2011 Census.
Rates of fatal injury are expressed to two decimal places.
Employment numbers are too small to provide reliable rate estimates.
.. The rate of injury is below 0.1.

this page is intentionally blank

Prices

Chapter 17

Prices

Producer price index numbers
(Tables 17.1 and 17.2)

The producer price indices (PPIs) were published for the first time in August 1983, replacing the former wholesale price indices. Full details of the differences between the two indices were given in an article published in British Business, 15 April 1983. The producer price indices are calculated using the same general methodology as that used by the wholesale price indices.

The high level index numbers in Tables 17.1 and 17.2 are constructed on a net sector basis. That is to say, they are intended to measure only transactions between the sector concerned and other sectors. Within-sector transactions are excluded. Index numbers for the whole of manufacturing are thus not weighted averages of sector index numbers.

The index numbers for selected industries in Tables 17.1 and 17.2 are constructed on a gross sector basis, that is, all transactions are included in deriving the weighting patterns, including sales within the same industry.

Producer Prices has implemented the change to the Standard Industrial Classification 2007 (SIC 2007). The most significant change to PPI output prices involves the reclassification of 'recovered secondary raw materials' and 'publishing'. These are no longer classified in the manufacturing sector, but are classified under services. In addition to this, a new SIC division, 'repair, installation and maintenance of machinery and equipment' has been created.

Fundamental changes have been made to the classification of the PPI Trade surveys, Import Price indices (IPI) and Export Price Indices (EPI). As part of the reclassification project the classification of these trade surveys have become compliant with Eurostat's Short Term Statistics Regulation. The collection of IPI and EPI will now be on an SIC basis, a switch from the Standard International Trade Classification (SITC) and Combined Nomenclature (CN) previously used. PPI input prices are heavily dependant on IPI.

Further details are available from the Office for National Statistics website: www.ons.gov.uk.

Purchasing power of the pound
(Table 17.3)

Changes in the internal purchasing power of a currency may be defined as the 'inverse' of changes in the levels of prices; when prices go up, the amount which can be purchased with a given sum of money goes down. Movements in the internal purchasing power of the pound are based on the consumers' expenditure deflator (CED) prior to 1962 and on the general index of retail prices (RPI) from January 1962 onwards. The CED shows the movement in prices implied by the national accounts estimates of consumers' expenditure valued at current and at constant prices, while the RPI is constructed directly by weighting together monthly movements in prices according to a given pattern of household expenditure derived from the Expenditure and Food Survey. If the purchasing power of the pound is taken to be 100p in a particular month (quarter, year), the comparable purchasing power in a subsequent month (quarter, year) is:

$$100 \times \frac{\text{earlier period price index}}{\text{later period price index}}$$

where the price index used is the CED for years 1946–1961

Consumer prices index
(Table 17.4)

The CPI is the main UK domestic measure of consumer price inflation for macroeconomic purposes. It forms the basis for the Government's target for inflation that the Bank of England's Monetary Policy Committee (MPC) is required to achieve. From April 2011 the CPI is also being used for the indexation of benefits, tax credits and public service pensions. The uprating is based on the 12-month change in the September CPI.

Internationally, the CPI is known as the Harmonised Index of Consumer Prices (HICP). HICPs are calculated in each Member State of the European Union, according to rules specified in a series of European regulations developed by Eurostat in conjunction with the EU Member States. HICPs are used to compare inflation rates across the European Union. Since January 1999, the HICP has also been used by the European Central Bank (ECB) as the measure of price stability across the euro area.

The official CPI series starts in 1996 but estimates for earlier periods are available back to 1988. These estimates are broadly consistent with data from 1996 but should be treated with some caution.

A full description of how the CPI is compiled is given in the Consumer Price Indices Technical Manual at: www.ons.gov.uk/ons/guide-method/user-guidance/prices/cpi-and-rpi/index.html

Retail prices index
(Table 17.5)

The all items retail prices index (RPI) is the most long-standing general purpose measure of inflation in the UK. Historically the uses of the RPI include the indexation of various prices and incomes and the uprating of pensions, state benefits and index-linked gilts, as well as the revalorisation of excise duties. Please note, though, that from April 2011 the CPI is being used to uprate benefits, tax credits and public service pensions. RPI data are available back to 1947 but have been re-referenced on several occasions since then, generally accompanied by changes to the coverage and/or structure of the detailed sub-components.

A full description of how the RPI is compiled is given in the Consumer Price Indices Technical Manual at: www.ons.gov.uk/ons/guide-method/user-guidance/prices/cpi-and-rpi/index.html

Further details are available from the Office for National Statistics website: www.ons.gov.uk/ons/taxonomy/index.html?nscl=Price+Indices+and+Inflation

Tax and price index (TPI)
(Table 17.6)

The purpose and methodology of the TPI were described in an article in the August 1979 issue (No. 310) of Economic Trends. The TPI measures the change in gross taxable income needed for taxpayers to maintain their purchasing power, allowing for changes in retail prices. The TPI thus takes account of the changes to direct taxes (and employees' National Insurance (NI) contributions) faced by a representative cross-section of taxpayers as well as changes in the retail prices index (RPI).
When direct taxation or employees' NI contributions change, the TPI will rise by less than or more than the RPI according to the type of changes made. Between Budgets, the monthly increase in the TPI is normally slightly larger than that in the RPI, since all the extra income needed to offset any rise in retail prices is fully taxed.

Index numbers of agricultural prices
(Tables 17.7 and 17.8)

The indices of producer prices of agricultural products are designed to provide short-term and medium-term indications of movements in these prices. All annual series are baseweighted Laspeyres type, using value weights derived from the Economic Accounts for Agriculture prepared for the Statistical Office of the European Union. Prices are measured exclusive of VAT. For Table 17.7, it has generally been necessary to measure the prices of materials (inputs) ex-supplier. For Table 17.8, it has generally been necessary to measure the prices received by producers (outputs) at the first marketing stage. The construction of the indices enables them to be combined with similar indices for other member countries of the EU to provide an overall indication of trends within the Union which appears in the Union's Eurostat series of publications.

Index numbers at a more detailed level and for earlier based series are available from the Department for Environment, Food and Rural Affairs, Room 309, Foss House, Kingspool 1–2 Peasholme Green, York, YO1 7PX, tel 01904 456561

17.1 Producer Price Index (2010=100, SIC2007)

Net Sector Input Price Indices of Materials & Fuel purchased

	6207000050: NSI - All Manufacturing including CCL	6207000010: NSI - All Manufacturing, materials only	6207000060: NSI - Fuel Purchased by Manufacturing Industry including CCL	6207990050: NSI - Materials & Fuels Purchased other than FBTP Industries, NSA	6207998950: NSI - All Manufacturing excl FBTP (incl CCL) - SA	6207990010: NSI - Materials Purchased other than FBTP Industries, NSA
	K646 NSA	K644 NSA	K647 NSA	K655 NSA	K658 SA	K653 NSA
2009	92.6	90.9	107.4	95.5	95.6	93.6
2010	100.0	100.0	100.0	100.0	100.0	100.0
2011	114.5	115.1	109.7	109.1	109.1	109.1
2012	116.0	115.9	117.6	108.9	108.9	107.5
2013	117.4	116.6	125.0	109.3	109.3	106.8
2014	109.7	108.3	122.4	105.3	105.0	102.4
2012 JAN	115.8	115.7	117.7	110.1	109.6	109.0
FEB	118.3	118.1	121.1	111.0	110.0	109.5
MAR	119.8	120.2	117.4	110.9	109.4	110.1
APR	118.3	118.5	117.4	110.1	109.3	109.0
MAY	115.5	115.6	115.3	108.9	108.6	107.9
JUN	113.4	113.3	114.4	108.4	108.8	107.5
JUL	113.1	113.1	113.3	107.3	108.0	106.4
AUG	115.1	115.5	112.3	107.1	108.0	106.3
SEP	115.0	115.0	116.1	107.2	108.2	105.8
OCT	115.6	115.3	119.5	108.0	108.6	106.2
NOV	116.0	115.3	122.8	108.6	108.9	106.3
DEC	116.3	115.4	124.5	108.7	108.9	106.2
2013 JAN	117.7	117.1	123.8	109.9	109.6	107.7
FEB	120.7	120.4	124.0	112.1	111.2	110.1
MAR	120.9	120.0	129.9	112.7	111.3	110.0
APR	118.6	117.6	127.3	111.1	110.4	108.6
MAY	117.1	116.6	121.9	109.3	109.2	107.2
JUN	116.8	116.4	120.4	108.4	108.9	106.4
JUL	118.4	117.9	123.5	109.5	110.1	107.2
AUG	117.2	116.6	122.7	108.6	109.5	106.4
SEP	116.1	115.5	121.5	107.6	108.5	105.3
OCT	115.6	114.4	126.5	107.8	108.2	104.8
NOV	114.9	113.5	127.9	107.5	107.7	104.2
DEC	115.3	113.5	130.8	107.2	107.2	103.4
2014 JAN	114.3	112.6	130.4	106.8	106.5	103.1
FEB	113.7	112.1	127.9	106.4	105.8	102.9
MAR	113.3	111.7	127.5	106.6	105.4	103.2
APR	112.3	111.1	122.4	105.5	105.1	102.6
MAY	112.5	111.6	120.3	105.0	105.1	102.4
JUN	111.4	110.7	117.2	104.6	104.9	102.4
JUL	109.5	108.8	114.7	103.8	104.8	102.0
AUG	108.4	107.6	115.1	104.3	105.1	102.4
SEP	107.5	106.4	117.7	104.7	105.5	102.5
OCT	106.2	104.3	122.3	105.2	105.3	102.4
NOV	105.4	103.0	127.3	105.7	105.4	102.2
DEC	101.9	99.1	126.1	104.7	104.5	101.2
2015 JAN	98.2	95.3	123.0	103.4	103.2	100.2
FEB	98.4	95.5	122.8	102.1	101.6	98.6
MAR	98.5	95.8	122.0	101.9	100.9	98.6
APR	99.8	97.7	117.2	101.5	101.0	98.8
MAY	99.1	97.1	116.4	100.8	100.8	98.2
JUN	96.9	94.7	115.4	99.9	100.2	97.3

17.1 Producer Price Index (2010=100, SIC2007)

Gross Sector Price Indices of Materials & Fuel purchased

	6107113140: GSI Sub-section - Inputs for Manuf of Textiles & Textile products	6107215000: GSI (excl. CCL) - Inputs for Manuf of Leather & Related products	6107216000: GSI (excl. CCL) - Inputs for Manuf of Wood & products of Wood/Cork	6107117180: GSI Sub-section - Inputs for Manuf of Pulp, Paper & Paper products	6107219000: GSI (excl. CCL) - Inputs for Manuf of Coke & Refined Petroleum products	6107120000: GSI Sub-section - Inputs for Manuf of Chemicals, Chemical products	6107222000: GSI (excl. CCL) - Inputs for Manufacture of Rubber/Plastic products
	MC36 NSA	MC3O NSA	MC3P NSA	MC39 NSA	MC3R NSA	MC3B NSA	MB4R NSA
2009	97.4	97.5	94.9	98.3	78.1	95.8	95.2
2010	100.0	100.0	100.0	100.0	100.0	100.0	100.0
2011	108.2	108.8	106.3	106.9	133.4	111.5	108.7
2012	110.4	110.7	108.5	107.4	136.9	111.8	108.9
2013	111.2	114.0	109.9	108.2	135.5	110.3	108.7
2014	110.5	113.2	111.9	107.6	118.3	106.3	105.9
2012 JAN	110.2	109.6	107.7	108.6	136.2	111.1	107.9
FEB	110.4	109.7	108.1	108.1	144.1	112.1	109.1
MAR	110.7	109.9	108.5	107.8	151.8	113.4	110.0
APR	109.9	111.1	108.9	107.9	146.1	113.9	110.4
MAY	109.9	111.2	108.6	107.5	136.6	113.3	110.2
JUN	109.5	110.7	108.4	107.4	123.3	111.4	108.9
JUL	110.0	110.3	108.4	107.0	127.3	109.5	107.1
AUG	110.3	110.2	108.6	106.6	137.7	110.7	108.0
SEP	110.7	110.8	108.8	106.6	137.1	111.3	108.5
OCT	111.2	111.4	108.7	106.9	136.4	111.6	108.9
NOV	111.3	111.5	108.6	107.1	134.2	111.6	109.0
DEC	110.4	111.5	108.5	107.2	132.5	111.5	109.1
2013 JAN	110.7	112.0	108.8	107.5	136.5	111.5	109.3
FEB	111.3	112.5	109.4	108.0	144.1	112.1	109.7
MAR	111.9	113.5	109.9	108.8	141.2	113.0	110.6
APR	111.4	114.1	110.0	108.4	132.9	111.6	109.6
MAY	111.3	114.1	109.4	107.9	131.7	110.2	108.5
JUN	111.1	114.3	109.4	107.8	130.0	109.7	108.3
JUL	111.5	114.9	109.8	108.2	137.8	110.0	108.2
AUG	111.3	114.8	109.9	108.1	139.0	110.2	108.5
SEP	111.0	115.0	109.8	108.0	138.0	109.8	108.1
OCT	110.7	114.8	110.6	108.4	133.0	108.9	108.0
NOV	110.7	114.4	110.6	108.5	130.1	108.0	107.5
DEC	110.9	114.1	110.8	108.5	132.1	108.0	107.5
2014 JAN	111.0	114.3	111.0	108.7	129.2	107.8	107.3
FEB	110.9	113.9	111.2	108.6	128.7	108.0	107.3
MAR	111.0	114.0	111.3	108.7	126.6	108.1	107.3
APR	110.8	114.5	112.0	108.1	125.6	107.6	106.7
MAY	110.7	114.2	112.0	107.7	126.5	107.1	106.4
JUN	110.4	113.7	112.0	107.2	127.6	106.4	105.9
JUL	110.1	113.2	111.9	106.7	123.3	105.8	105.4
AUG	110.0	112.5	112.1	106.7	120.1	105.5	105.2
SEP	110.2	111.9	112.2	106.8	116.5	105.3	105.0
OCT	110.5	111.9	112.3	107.2	107.9	105.2	105.2
NOV	110.6	112.3	112.3	107.6	101.4	104.9	105.0
DEC	110.3	111.8	112.0	107.5	85.8	103.7	104.3
2015 JAN	109.7	111.5	111.5	107.0	72.2	101.9	102.8
FEB	109.4	111.6	111.5	106.7	76.7	101.3	102.2
MAR	109.2	112.1	111.5	106.4	80.2	101.2	102.0
APR	108.9	112.7	111.3	106.0	82.0	101.2	102.0
MAY	108.7	112.0	111.2	106.0	84.2	101.9	102.6
JUN	108.5	111.6	111.1	105.5	81.2	101.3	102.4

17.1 Producer Price Index (2010=100, SIC2007)

Gross Sector Price Indices of Materials & Fuel purchased

	6107123000: GSI - Purchases of materials and fuels for Manufacture of Other Non-Metallic Mineral Products	6107124250: GSI Sub-section - Inputs of Manuf of Basic Metals & Fabricated products	6107126270: GSI Sub-section - Inputs for Manuf of Computer, Elect & Opt products	6107228000: GSI (excl. CCL) - Inputs for Manufacture of Machinery & Equipment	6107129300: GSI Sub-section - Inputs for Manufacture of Motor Vechicles	6107131330: GSI Sub-section - Inputs for Manuf of Other Manufactured Goods n.e.c
	MC3E	MC3F	MC3G	MB4U	MC3I	MC3J
		NSA	NSA	NSA	NSA	NSA
2009	98.0	92.5	97.0	96.8	97.4	96.4
2010	100.0	100.0	100.0	100.0	100.0	100.0
2011	109.1	110.1	103.3	105.3	104.1	104.5
2012	111.7	108.4	103.1	105.3	104.0	105.4
2013	111.9	107.0	103.1	105.6	104.3	106.3
2014	110.4	103.6	103.0	104.4	103.1	106.4
2012 JAN	111.9	109.4	103.3	105.6	104.2	105.3
FEB	112.7	111.2	103.7	106.2	104.8	105.8
MAR	113.1	111.6	103.9	106.3	104.9	106.0
APR	113.1	110.5	103.5	106.0	104.3	105.9
MAY	112.1	108.8	103.3	105.5	103.9	105.6
JUN	111.1	107.1	103.0	105.2	104.1	105.5
JUL	110.1	106.6	102.8	104.9	103.6	105.2
AUG	109.6	106.5	102.7	104.5	103.4	105.0
SEP	110.6	107.4	102.6	104.8	103.4	105.0
OCT	111.5	107.5	102.8	104.9	103.7	105.2
NOV	111.9	106.9	102.7	104.7	103.8	105.1
DEC	112.1	107.1	102.3	104.8	103.8	105.0
2013 JAN	112.3	108.0	102.7	105.5	104.6	105.8
FEB	113.1	109.9	103.6	106.7	105.4	106.8
MAR	114.1	110.2	104.2	107.0	105.3	107.2
APR	112.8	108.2	103.8	106.4	104.8	106.8
MAY	111.3	106.9	103.4	105.6	104.4	106.5
JUN	110.7	106.0	103.1	105.3	104.1	106.2
JUL	111.9	106.5	103.3	105.6	104.5	106.6
AUG	111.4	106.8	103.2	105.5	104.3	106.3
SEP	111.2	16.0	102.9	105.0	103.7	105.9
OCT	111.3	105.5	102.7	104.9	103.8	105.8
NOV	111.5	105.2	102.5	104.7	103.6	105.7
DEC	111.5	105.0	102.3	104.5	103.4	105.5
2014 JAN	112.1	104.8	102.8	104.6	103.3	106.3
FEB	111.9	104.6	102.7	104.4	103.3	106.4
MAR	111.9	104.7	102.8	104.7	103.5	106.5
APR	110.3	103.8	102.5	104.2	103.1	106.1
MAY	110.1	103.9	102.4	104.3	103.1	106.1
JUN	109.8	103.9	103.0	104.2	102.9	106.3
JUL	108.8	103.4	102.7	104.0	102.7	106.0
AUG	108.8	103.8	103.1	104.4	103.0	106.3
SEP	109.7	103.4	103.2	104.3	102.9	106.5
OCT	110.4	103.0	103.4	104.5	103.2	106.7
NOV	110.9	102.7	103.5	104.6	103.3	106.9
DEC	110.3	101.2	103.4	104.3	103.0	106.7
2015 JAN	110	99.2	103.3	103.7	102.5	106.5
FEB	109.7	98.5	102.8	103.3	102.0	106.6
MAR	109.9	98.3	102.8	103.1	101.8	106.7
APR	109	97.7	102.7	102.8	101.9	106.6
MAY	109.4	97.6	102.6	102.8	101.9	106.2
JUN	108.8	96.4	102.3	102.3	101.5	105.9

Source: Office for National Statistics (ONS)

Climate change Levy was introduced in April 2001

Rebasing the Producer Price Index, including trade prices (PPI) and the Services Producer Price Index (SPPI) onto 2010=100 occurred at the end of 2013.
Further information can be found at: http://www.ons.gov.uk/ons/rel/ppi2/producer-price-index/ppi-rebasing-2010---100/index.html

Accurac
Figures for the latest two months are provisional and the latest five months are subject to revisions in light of (a) late and revised respondent data and (b), for the seasonally adjusted series; revisions to seasonal adjustment factors are re-estimated every month. A routine seasonal adjustment review is normally conducted in the autumn each year.

Abreviations
NSI - Net Sector Input
FBTP - Food, Beverages and Tobacco Products
NSA - Not Seasonally Adjusted
SA - Seasonally Adjusted
GSI - Gross Sector Input
CCL - Climate Change Levy

17.2 Producer Price Index of Output (2010=100, SIC2007)

	Net Sector Output Price Indices of Materials & Fuel purchased		Gross Sector Output Price Indices of Materials & Fuel purchased (All Manufacturing & Selected Industries)				
	7200700000: Net Sector Output - Output of Manufactured products	7200799000: Net Sector Output - All Manufacturing excl Food, Beverages Tobacco	7111101280: Gross Sector Output - Food Products, Beverages & Tobacco incl duty	7112130000: Textiles	7112140000: Wearing Apparel	7112150000: Leather & related products	7112160000: Wood, Products of Wood & Cork, except Furniture; Articles of Straw
	JVZ7 NSA	K3BI NSA	K65A NSA	K37R NSA	K37S NSA	K37T NSA	K37U NSA
2008	96.9	97.1	95.7	95.6	99.6	98.7	94.8
2009	97.4	98.5	98.9	98.2	99.7	93.7	96.2
2010	100.0	100.0	100.0	100.0	100.0	100.0	100.0
2011	104.8	102.8	106.6	107.0	102.8	116.5	105.2
2012	107.0	103.9	110.9	110.6	106.1	119.0	109.0
2013	108.4	104.8	114.8	111.4	106.9	123.9	110.4
2014	108.4	105.7	113.7	112.5	110.7	124.2	113.9
2012 JAN	105.9	103.4	108.8	110.6	104.7	114.8	107.6
FEB	106.3	103.7	109.0	110.2	105.1	114.8	107.9
MAR	106.8	103.8	109.8	110.4	105.4	115.6	108.3
APR	107.2	104.0	110.4	108.8	105.7	119.4	108.9
MAY	107.0	104.0	110.8	109.1	106.5	119.6	108.9
JUN	106.6	103.9	110.9	109.2	105.9	120.1	109.1
JUL	106.8	104.0	111.0	111.2	106.7	119.6	109.4
AUG	107.2	104.0	111.3	111.4	106.6	118.9	109.4
SEP	107.5	104.1	111.7	111.9	106.7	119.7	109.6
OCT	107.6	104.1	111.8	112.1	106.7	121.2	109.5
NOV	107.4	104.1	112.5	112.3	106.4	122.2	109.4
DEC	107.2	103.9	112.7	110.5	106.5	122.3	109.6
2013 JAN	107.6	104.2	113.2	110.8	106.6	122.3	109.7
FEB	108.1	104.4	113.4	111.2	106.6	122.4	109.7
MAR	108.4	104.7	114.0	111.2	106.6	122.5	109.9
APR	108.3	104.8	114.7	111.1	106.6	123.6	110.1
MAY	108.3	104.8	115.0	111.8	107.3	124.4	109.7
JUN	108.4	104.8	115.3	111.8	107.3	124.5	109.9
JUL	108.7	104.9	115.5	111.8	107.3	124.3	110.1
AUG	108.8	104.9	115.4	111.7	106.7	124.4	110.5
SEP	108.8	104.9	115.5	111.7	106.7	124.7	110.7
OCT	108.5	104.9	115.2	111.0	106.7	124.7	111.1
NOV	108.3	104.8	115.3	111.3	107.0	124.7	111.4
DEC	108.3	104.9	114.9	111.6	107.0	124.7	111.5
2014 JAN	108.6	105.4	114.9	112.0	109.5	124.5	112.0
FEB	108.7	105.6	114.9	112.1	109.6	124.6	112.9
MAR	108.8	105.8	115.1	112.2	110.0	125.0	113.0
APR	108.9	105.8	115.2	112.6	110.2	125.8	113.2
MAY	108.8	105.8	114.7	112.7	110.2	124.7	113.6
JUN	108.7	105.8	114.0	112.7	111.3	124.3	114.0
JUL	108.6	105.7	113.9	112.7	111.3	124.5	114.4
AUG	108.5	105.8	113.2	112.3	111.4	124.1	114.8
SEP	108.3	105.7	112.8	112.7	111.4	122.9	115.0
OCT	107.7	105.5	112.0	112.7	111.4	123.8	114.8
NOV	107.6	105.7	111.7	112.7	111.1	124.4	114.7
DEC	107.1	105.7	111.8	112.7	111.1	122.2	114.9
2015 JAN	106.6	105.9	111.8	112.8	112.1	123.1	115.1
FEB	106.8	105.9	111.7	112.9	112.1	123.6	115.4
MAR	106.9	105.9	112.1	112.6	112.1	123.5	115.4
APR	107.0	105.9	112.1	112.5	112.0	123.6	115.3
MAY	107.1	105.9	111.8	112.0	112.0	122.2	115.1
JUN	107.1	105.9	111.9	111.9	112.0	122.3	115.1

17.2 Producer Price Index of Output (2010=100, SIC2007)

Gross Sector Output Price Indices of Materials & Fuel purchased (All Manufacturing & Selected Industries)

	7112170000: Paper & Paper products	7112180000: Printing & Recording Services	7112200000: Chemicals & Chemical products	7112220000: Rubber & Plastics products	7112230000: Other Non-Metallic Mineral products	7112240000: Basic Metals	7112260000: Computer, Electronic & Optical products
	K37V NSA	K37W NSA	K37Z NSA	K383 NSA	K384 NSA	K385 NSA	K387 NSA
2008	97.1	99.6	96.4	96.5	97.2	99.7	97.5
2009	97.4	100.6	98.8	97.8	99.5	90.8	98.3
2010	100.0	100.0	100.0	100.0	100.0	100.0	100.0
2011	107.7	100.4	107.8	105.4	102.7	108.8	98.2
2012	106.9	99.9	108.4	107.0	106.4	104.7	96.5
2013	106.6	99.3	106.5	108.5	107.7	102.0	96.9
2014	106.9	100.0	104.8	108.7	109.6	99.7	97.5
2012 JAN	109.3	100.4	107.7	106.2	105.0	106.1	97.2
FEB	107.6	100.4	108.6	106.1	105.9	107.6	97.2
MAR	107.5	100.1	109.6	106.5	106.3	107.5	97.2
APR	107.6	100.2	109.9	106.8	106.6	106.8	96.6
MAY	107.4	100.4	109.7	107.0	106.4	105.8	96.5
JUN	107.5	100.2	108.3	106.9	106.3	104.8	96.3
JUL	107.3	100.2	106.9	106.9	106.3	103.9	96.8
AUG	106.4	99.4	107.7	107.1	106.5	102.3	96.6
SEP	105.7	99.5	108.1	107.4	106.6	103.4	96.5
OCT	105.7	99.4	108.0	107.5	106.9	103.2	96.3
NOV	105.6	99.3	107.9	107.3	106.8	102.4	95.9
DEC	105.5	99.3	108.1	107.7	106.7	102.6	94.7
2013 JAN	105.7	99.5	108.0	108.4	107.5	103.3	94.9
FEB	105.6	99.3	107.9	108.3	107.7	104.3	95.1
MAR	106.2	99.2	108.4	108.3	107.7	104.3	95.9
APR	106.3	99.1	107.7	108.4	107.7	102.9	96.9
MAY	106.4	99.0	106.8	108.5	107.2	102.3	97.2
JUN	106.4	99.1	106.2	108.7	107.3	101.3	97.1
JUL	106.4	99.1	105.9	108.4	107.5	100.9	97.2
AUG	106.7	99.0	106.2	108.7	107.6	101.5	97.3
SEP	107.0	99.4	106.0	108.6	107.8	101.1	97.8
OCT	107.2	99.6	105.3	108.7	107.9	100.8	97.8
NOV	107.6	99.4	104.6	108.6	108.2	100.8	97.6
DEC	107.2	99.6	104.6	108.5	108.1	100.4	97.5
2014 JAN	107.4	99.7	105.1	108.6	108.8	100.5	97.4
FEB	107.6	100.5	105.6	109.1	109.5	100.3	97.3
MAR	107.7	100.1	105.7	109.2	109.8	100.6	97.4
APR	107.6	100.0	105.7	108.7	109.9	99.1	97.4
MAY	107.2	100.4	105.6	108.6	109.5	99.4	97.2
JUN	107.0	100.3	105.1	108.6	109.7	100.1	97.2
JUL	106.5	100.4	104.8	108.6	109.6	99.8	97.6
AUG	106.4	100.5	104.5	108.7	109.6	100.4	97.5
SEP	106.3	99.7	104.2	108.6	109.4	99.2	97.6
OCT	106.4	99.6	104.1	108.5	109.5	99.3	97.6
NOV	106.4	99.6	104.1	108.4	109.7	99.2	97.6
DEC	106.6	99.7	103.7	108.5	109.6	98.5	97.8
2015 JAN	106.7	99.5	102.9	108.2	110.8	96.6	98.1
FEB	106.7	99.9	102.7	108.0	111.3	95.5	98.0
MAR	106.0	99.9	102.5	107.8	111.8	95.0	97.9
APR	106.5	100.2	102.6	107.5	111.9	93.9	98.1
MAY	106.5	100.3	102.7	107.3	111.9	93.0	97.9
JUN	106.3	100.3	102.5	107.4	112.0	92.0	97.9

17.2 Producer Price Index of Output (2010=100, SIC2007)

Gross Sector Output Price Indices of Materials & Fuel purchased (All Manufacturing & Selected Industries)

	7112270000: Electrical Equipment	7112280000: Machinery & Equipment n.e.c.	7112290000: Motor Vehicles, Trailers & Semi-trailers	7112300000: Other Transport Equipment	7112310000: Furniture	7112320000: Other Manufactured Goods	Output in the Construction Industry All New Work *	Mix-adjusted house price index of new dwellings **
	K388 NSA	K389 NSA	K38A NSA	K38B NSA	K38C NSA	K38D NSA	(2013=100)	
2008	94.3	97.5	96.2	97.1	96.7	97.2	105.6	164.4
2009	96.9	98.8	99.4	99.1	98.3	98.9	103.2	150.6
2010	100.0	100.0	100.0	100.0	100.0	100.0	98.9	158.1
2011	102.9	103.3	100.9	101.3	102.7	102.0	100.0	170.5
2012	102.8	105.5	101.5	102.9	105.1	104.0	103.3	177.2
2013	103.0	108.2	102.5	105.1	105.8	105.3	100.0	180.3
2014	103.7	109.8	102.0	107.4	107.2	107.2	103.7	193.3
2012 JAN	102.1	104.4	100.9	102.0	104.2	103.5	95.5	183.1
FEB	102.5	104.4	101.2	102.0	104.4	105.3	95.8	181.4
MAR	103.0	105.1	101.2	102.1	104.3	104.1	96.0	179.0
APR	102.9	105.4	101.6	102.0	105.0	104.1	96.2	176.9
MAY	102.8	105.5	101.4	102.5	105.3	104.1	96.4	177.5
JUN	102.6	105.7	101.5	102.9	105.3	104.1	96.6	177.4
JUL	102.8	105.5	101.3	103.9	105.4	104.0	96.9	174.1
AUG	102.9	105.4	101.3	103.8	105.4	103.8	97.1	175.9
SEP	102.8	105.8	101.8	102.9	105.6	103.6	97.2	169.3
OCT	103.0	105.9	101.9	103.5	105.6	103.6	97.2	171.4
NOV	103.0	106.1	101.7	103.7	105.5	103.8	97.4	174.8
DEC	103.0	106.2	101.9	103.7	105.4	104.0	97.6	185.7
2013 JAN	103.3	106.4	102.4	103.8	105.6	104.4	98.0	183.3
FEB	103.3	107.5	102.6	104.5	105.6	104.6	98.3	180.9
MAR	103.4	107.8	102.5	104.9	105.5	104.8	98.7	180.8
APR	103.4	108.2	102.2	105.1	105.6	104.9	99.0	184.8
MAY	103.3	108.2	102.2	105.2	105.7	104.9	99.4	180.1
JUN	103.3	108.3	102.3	105.0	105.6	105.5	99.6	183.3
JUL	103.1	108.8	102.8	105.2	105.8	105.5	100.0	174.6
AUG	102.6	108.6	102.7	105.6	105.8	105.7	100.4	175.8
SEP	102.6	108.4	102.5	105.5	106.0	105.8	100.8	178.1
OCT	102.6	108.6	102.6	105.5	106.0	105.8	101.4	176.9
NOV	102.8	108.7	102.3	105.5	106.0	105.6	101.9	179.1
DEC	102.7	108.5	102.3	105.4	106.2	105.5	102.5	185.7
2014 JAN	103.1	109.1	102.4	106.3	106.8	105.9	104.2	188.0
FEB	103.3	109.3	102.5	106.4	106.8	105.9	103.5	192.1
MAR	103.3	109.5	102.6	106.7	106.9	107.1	103.2	184.7
APR	103.2	109.6	102.2	107.0	107.0	107.1	102.9	189.4
MAY	103.5	109.6	102.3	107.4	107.3	107.2	102.8	192.6
JUN	103.7	109.5	102.0	107.5	107.3	107.2	103.6	190.4
JUL	103.7	109.6	101.6	107.8	107.3	107.3	104.1	197.5
AUG	103.8	109.9	101.8	107.8	107.3	107.3	103.5	197.5
SEP	104.1	110.0	101.6	107.9	107.4	107.4	104.0	196.4
OCT	104.1	110.2	101.5	107.8	107.5	107.9	104.1	190.9
NOV	104.0	110.3	101.5	107.9	107.6	108.0	104.3	197.4
DEC	104.0	110.4	101.5	107.9	107.5	107.9	104.1	203.1
2015 JAN	104.5	110.6	101.2	108.4	107.7	108.0	104.4	199.3
FEB	104.5	111.1	100.8	109.1	107.7	108.0	104.9	197.6
MAR	104.5	110.9	100.5	108.5	107.7	107.6	106.2	209.8
APR	104.6	110.8	100.4	108.5	108.4	107.8	105.1	206.5
MAY	104.5	110.9	100.5	108.4	108.6	107.9	105.2	212.0
JUN	104.5	111.1	100.4	108.4	108.8	107.8	105.5	208.5

Climate change Levy was introduced in April 2001

Rebasing the Producer Price Index, including trade prices (PPI) and the Services Producer Price Index (SPPI) onto 2010=100 occurred at the end of 2013. Further information can be found at:
http://www.ons.gov.uk/ons/rel/ppi2/producer-price-index/ppi-rebasing-2010---100/index.html
* All New Work uses the base of 2013=100

Source: Office for National Statistics
Department for Communities and Local Government

Accuracy - Figures for the latest two months are provisional and the latest five months are subject to revisions in light of (a) late and revised respondent data and (b), for the seasonally adjusted series; revisions to seasonal adjustment factors are re-estimated every month. A routine seasonal adjustment review is normally conducted in the autumn each year.

Abreviations
NSI - Net Sector Input
FBTP - Food, Beverages and Tobacco Products
NSA - Not Seasonally Adjusted
SA - Seasonally Adjusted
GSI - Gross Sector Input
CCL - Climate Change Levy

* JYYC 'Quarterly construction output price index' was previously published in Annual Abstract of Statistics has now been replaced by Table 9a, section 'All New Work' from Output in the Construction Industry

** Mix-adjusted house price index of new dwellings was sourced from table 5 of the ONS House Price Index (HPI) monthly and quarterly tables

17.3 Internal purchasing power of the pound (based on RPI)[1,2,3,4]: 1991 to 2014

pence

	1991	1992	1993	1994	1995	1996	1997	1998	1999	2000	2001	2002	2003	2004	2005	2006	2007	2008	2009	2010	2011	2012	2013	2014
	BASX	CZVM	CBXX	DOFX	DOHR	DOLM	DTUL	CDQG	JKZZ	ZMHO	IKHI	FAUI	SEZH	C687	E9AO	GB4Y	HT4R	J5TL	JRT3	K9AD	KO2K	KVO5	MF5D	MZX3
1980	200	207	211	216	223	228	236	244	247	255	259	264	271	279	287	296	309	321	320	334	352	363	374	385
1981	179	185	188	193	199	204	211	218	221	228	232	236	242	250	257	265	276	287	286	299	315	325	334	344
1982	164	171	173	177	184	188	194	201	204	210	213	217	223	230	236	244	254	265	263	275	290	299	308	317
1983	157	163	166	170	176	180	185	192	195	200	204	207	213	220	226	233	243	253	252	263	277	286	294	303
1984	150	155	158	162	167	171	177	183	185	191	194	198	203	209	215	222	232	241	240	251	264	272	280	289
1985	141	146	149	152	158	161	166	172	175	180	183	186	192	197	203	209	218	227	226	236	249	257	264	272
1986	136	142	144	147	152	156	161	167	169	174	177	180	185	191	196	203	211	220	218	229	240	248	256	263
1987	131	136	138	141	146	150	155	160	162	167	170	173	178	183	188	194	203	211	210	219	231	238	245	253
1988	125	130	132	135	139	143	147	152	155	159	162	165	170	175	180	185	193	201	200	209	220	227	234	241
1989	116	120	122	125	129	133	137	141	144	148	150	153	157	162	167	172	179	186	185	194	204	211	217	223
1990	106	110	112	114	118	121	125	129	131	135	137	140	144	148	152	157	164	170	169	177	186	192	198	204
1991	100	104	105	108	112	114	118	122	124	128	130	132	136	140	144	148	155	161	160	167	176	182	187	193
1992	96	100	102	104	108	110	114	118	119	123	125	127	131	135	139	143	149	155	154	161	170	175	181	186
1993	95	98	100	102	106	109	112	116	118	121	123	125	129	133	136	141	147	153	152	159	167	173	178	183
1994	93	96	98	100	103	106	109	113	115	118	120	122	126	130	133	137	143	149	148	155	163	168	174	179
1995	90	93	94	97	100	102	106	109	111	114	116	118	122	125	129	133	139	144	143	150	158	163	168	173
1996	87	91	92	94	98	100	103	107	108	112	113	115	119	122	126	130	135	141	140	146	154	159	164	169
1997	85	88	89	92	95	97	100	103	105	108	110	112	115	119	122	126	131	136	136	142	149	154	159	163
1998	82	85	86	88	92	94	97	100	102	105	106	108	111	115	118	122	127	132	131	137	144	149	154	158
1999	81	84	85	87	90	92	95	98	100	103	105	107	110	113	116	120	125	130	129	135	142	147	151	156
2000	78	81	83	85	88	90	92	96	97	100	102	103	106	110	113	116	121	126	125	131	138	143	147	151
2001	77	80	81	83	86	88	91	94	95	98	100	102	105	108	111	114	119	124	123	129	136	140	144	149
2002	76	79	80	82	85	87	89	92	94	97	98	100	103	106	109	112	117	122	121	127	133	138	142	146
2003	74	76	78	79	82	84	87	90	91	94	96	97	100	103	106	109	111	115	118	123	130	134	138	142
2004	72	74	75	77	80	82	84	87	89	91	93	94	97	100	103	106	108	112	111	116	123	126	130	134
2005	70	72	73	75	78	80	82	85	86	89	90	92	94	97	100	103	108	112	111	116	123	126	130	134
2006	67	70	71	73	75	77	80	82	83	86	87	89	92	94	97	100	104	108	108	113	119	123	126	130
2007	65	67	68	70	72	74	76	79	80	82	84	85	88	90	93	96	100	104	103	108	114	117	121	125
2008	62	64	65	67	69	71	73	76	77	79	81	82	84	87	89	92	96	100	99	104	109	113	116	120
2009	62	65	66	67	70	71	74	76	77	80	81	82	85	87	90	93	92	96	96	100	105	109	112	115
2010	60	62	63	64	67	68	70	73	74	76	78	79	81	84	86	89	92	96	96	100	105	109	112	115
2011	57	59	60	61	63	65	67	69	70	72	74	75	77	79	82	84	88	91	91	95	100	103	106	109
2012	55	57	58	59	61	63	65	67	68	70	71	73	75	77	79	82	85	89	88	92	97	100	103	106
2013	53	55	56	58	60	61	63	65	66	68	69	70	72	75	77	79	83	86	85	89	94	97	100	103
2014	52	54	55	56	58	59	61	63	64	66	67	68	70	73	75	77	80	83	83	87	91	94	97	100

1. To find the purchasing power of the pound in 2001, given that it was 100 pence in 1990, select the column headed 1990 and look at the 2001 row. The result is 73 pence.

2. Changes in the internal purchasing power of a currency may be defined as the 'inverse' of changes in the levels of prices; when prices go up, the amount which can be purchased with a given sum of money goes down. The monthly figures of the all items RPI can be used to obtain estimates of the changes in prices or in purchasing power between any 2 months. To find the purchasing power of the pound in one month, given that it was 100p in a previous month the calculation is: 100p multiplied by the earlier month RPI then divided by the later month RPI Comparisons between any 2 years may be made in the same way using the annual averages of the RPI found in table 5.3. These figure are reproduced in the above table.

In accordance with the *Statistics and Registration Service Act 2007*, the Retail Prices Index and its derivatives have been assessed against the Code of Practice for Official Statistics and found not to meet the required standards for designation as National Statistics. A full report can be found at: http://www.statisticsauthority.gov.uk/

Source:

Office for National Statistics

Prices Division

2.001 Cardiff Road

Newport

South Wales

NP10 8XG

Tel: +44 (0) 1633 456900

http://www.ons.gov.uk

17.4 CPI: Detailed figures by division[1]

	Food and non-alcoholic beverages	Alcoholic beverages and tobacco	Clothing and footwear	Housing, water, electricity, gas & other fuels	Furniture, household equipment & routine maintenance	Health [2]	Transport	Communication	Recreation and culture	Education [2]	Restaurants and hotels	Miscellaneous goods and services [2]	CPI (overall index)
COICOP Division	01	02	03	04	05	06	07	08	09	10	11	12	
Weights													
	CHZR	CHZS	CHZT	CHZU	CHZV	CHZW	CHZX	CHZY	CHZZ	CJUU	CJUV	CJUW	CHZQ
2015	110	43	70	128	59	25	149	31	147	26	121	91	1 000
Monthly indices (2005=100)													
	D7BU	D7BV	D7BW	D7BX	D7BY	D7BZ	D7C2	D7C3	D7C4	D7C5	D7C6	D7C7	D7BT
2013 Jul	143.5	150.1	78.8	150.5	117.8	126.9	137.5	111.8	101.1	201.5	129.5	120.4	125.8
Aug	144.2	150.0	80.4	150.5	119.9	127.1	138.9	111.6	101.1	201.5	129.5	120.5	126.4
Sep	144.4	150.7	83.7	150.7	120.1	127.4	137.0	111.7	101.7	205.4	130.1	120.9	126.8
Oct	144.6	151.1	84.6	150.6	119.7	127.2	134.9	112.0	101.9	222.2	130.3	120.7	126.9
Nov	144.6	151.0	85.2	150.6	119.6	127.1	134.2	111.8	102.3	222.2	130.5	121.0	127.0
Dec	145.1	149.2	84.4	154.0	121.6	127.2	135.6	112.2	101.9	222.2	130.5	120.7	127.5
2014 Jan	145.4	153.8	79.9	153.8	117.9	128.0	134.7	112.8	101.4	222.2	130.3	120.4	126.7
Feb	146.1	152.4	80.8	153.9	120.8	128.6	135.1	113.0	102.2	222.2	130.8	120.7	127.4
Mar	145.4	152.8	82.2	153.7	121.1	128.8	135.1	113.3	102.6	222.2	131.4	121.1	127.7
Apr	144.7	154.1	83.0	154.6	120.1	129.8	137.7	113.2	102.5	222.2	131.6	120.6	128.1
May	143.0	156.4	83.0	154.7	120.7	129.9	136.8	112.6	102.9	222.2	132.1	120.4	128.0
Jun	143.2	156.5	83.4	154.7	120.9	130.0	137.6	112.5	102.9	222.2	132.6	120.3	128.3
Jul	143.0	155.4	78.7	155.2	119.2	130.2	139.3	112.6	102.7	222.2	133.1	119.8	127.8
Aug	142.6	156.9	80.7	155.3	120.3	130.8	140.5	112.5	102.6	222.2	132.9	120.0	128.3
Sep	142.4	158.0	83.9	155.4	121.0	130.5	137.1	112.7	102.5	226.5	133.1	120.4	128.4
Oct	142.5	159.0	84.4	155.5	119.7	130.0	135.6	112.7	102.9	244.3	133.6	120.2	128.5
Nov	142.2	157.0	85.0	155.6	119.9	129.7	133.9	112.4	102.7	244.3	133.5	120.1	128.2
Dec	142.6	156.7	84.1	155.5	121.8	129.9	133.7	113.1	102.5	244.3	133.5	120.0	128.2
2015 Jan	141.7	158.9	81.0	155.3	118.8	130.8	131.0	113.1	101.5	244.3	133.3	119.9	127.1
Feb	141.3	158.2	82.1	155.3	120.4	131.0	131.5	114.0	101.4	244.3	133.6	120.2	127.4
Mar	141.1	158.0	82.1	154.7	120.9	131.5	132.5	114.3	101.9	244.3	134.0	120.5	127.6
Apr	140.6	158.7	82.7	155.3	119.4	132.4	133.9	114.3	102.1	244.3	134.3	120.5	128.0
May	140.4	159.9	83.1	155.3	120.1	132.8	134.7	114.0	101.9	244.3	134.6	120.3	128.2
Jun	140.1	160.1	82.8	155.4	120.5	132.0	135.0	113.7	101.9	244.3	135.1	120.5	128.2
Jul	139.1	158.4	80.0	155.8	118.8	133.2	136.6	114.1	102.0	244.3	135.3	120.6	128.0
Percentage change on a year earlier													
	D7G8	D7G9	D7GA	D7GB	D7GC	D7GD	D7GE	D7GF	D7GG	D7GH	D7GI	D7GJ	D7G7
2013 Jul	3.9	6.3	2.5	4.3	0.1	2.7	1.5	2.8	0.7	19.7	2.5	1.5	2.8
Aug	4.1	6.0	1.6	4.2	1.1	2.9	1.2	2.5	0.9	19.7	2.4	1.2	2.7
Sep	4.3	5.4	1.1	4.2	0.7	2.9	1.1	2.6	0.9	21.4	2.6	0.9	2.7
Oct	3.9	5.4	1.0	4.1	1.0	2.6	−0.3	2.7	0.7	10.3	2.8	0.7	2.2
Nov	2.8	5.8	1.1	3.4	1.0	2.5	0.2	2.8	1.1	10.3	2.3	0.5	2.1
Dec	1.9	5.8	1.6	3.7	1.4	2.5	0.5	3.3	0.8	10.3	2.3	0.3	2.0
2014 Jan	2.0	4.5	1.7	3.6	0.6	2.9	0.5	2.8	0.4	10.3	2.2	0.7	1.9
Feb	1.8	4.1	0.8	3.2	1.6	3.4	−0.4	2.0	0.7	10.3	2.3	0.8	1.7
Mar	1.7	5.0	0.2	3.1	1.1	3.4	−1.0	2.3	0.6	10.3	2.6	0.9	1.6
Apr	0.5	3.5	1.2	3.0	1.5	2.9	1.6	1.9	0.5	10.3	2.3	0.3	1.8
May	−0.6	4.6	−0.1	3.2	0.9	3.1	0.4	1.0	1.1	10.3	2.3	0.3	1.5
Jun	−	5.0	2.4	3.2	1.6	3.1	0.9	0.9	1.3	10.3	2.6	−	1.9
Jul	−0.4	3.6	−0.2	3.2	1.1	2.6	1.3	0.7	1.5	10.3	2.8	−0.6	1.6
Aug	−1.1	4.6	0.4	3.2	0.4	2.9	1.2	0.8	1.4	10.3	2.6	−0.4	1.5
Sep	−1.4	4.9	0.2	3.1	0.8	2.5	0.1	0.9	0.7	10.3	2.3	−0.5	1.2
Oct	−1.4	5.2	−0.2	3.2	0.1	2.2	0.5	0.6	1.0	10.0	2.5	−0.3	1.3
Nov	−1.7	4.0	−0.2	3.3	0.3	2.0	−0.2	0.5	0.3	10.0	2.4	−0.8	1.0
Dec	−1.7	5.0	−0.3	1.0	0.2	2.1	−1.4	0.7	0.6	10.0	2.3	−0.6	0.5
2015 Jan	−2.5	3.3	1.4	1.0	0.8	2.2	−2.8	0.2	0.1	10.0	2.4	−0.4	0.3
Feb	−3.3	3.8	1.7	0.9	−0.3	1.8	−2.7	0.9	−0.8	10.0	2.2	−0.4	−
Mar	−3.0	3.4	−0.2	0.7	−0.2	2.1	−1.9	0.9	−0.7	10.0	2.0	−0.5	−
Apr	−2.8	3.0	−0.4	0.5	−0.5	2.0	−2.8	1.0	−0.4	10.0	2.0	−0.1	−0.1
May	−1.8	2.2	0.2	0.4	−0.5	2.2	−1.5	1.2	−1.0	10.0	1.9	−0.1	0.1
Jun	−2.2	2.3	−0.8	0.4	−0.3	1.6	*−1.8	1.1	−1.0	10.0	1.9	0.1	−
Jul	−2.7	1.9	1.7	0.4	−0.3	2.3	−1.9	1.3	−0.6	10.0	1.6	0.7	0.1

Key: - zero or negligible

Source: Office for National Statistics

1 More detailed CPI data are available at http://www.ons.gov.uk

2 The coverage of these categories was extended in January 2000; further extensions to coverage came into effect in January 2001 for health and miscellaneous goods and services; the coverage of miscellaneous goods and services was further extended with effect from January 2002.

17.5 Retail Prices Index[1] United Kingdom

Indices (13 January 1987=100)

	All items (RPI)	All items excluding mortgage interest payments (RPIX)	mortgage interest payments and depreci-ation	Housing	All items excluding Food	All items excluding Seasonal food[2]	Food and catering	Alcohol and tobacco	Housing and household expend-iture	Pesonal expend-iture	Travel and leisure	Consumer durables[4]	All items excluding mortgage interest payments and indirect taxes (RPIY)[3]
Weights	CZGU	CZGY	DOGZ	CZGX	CZGV	CZGW	CBVV	CBVW	CBVX	CBVY	CBVZ	CBWA	
2001	1000	954	914	795	884	982	169	97	362	96	276	125	
2002	1000	964	924	801	886	980	166	99	363	94	278	126	
2003	1000	961	919	797	891	983	160	98	365	92	285	126	
2004	1000	961	914	791	889	981	160	97	367	93	283	121	
2005	1000	950	901	776	890	981	159	96	387	89	269	122	
2006	1000	950	906	778	895	983	155	96	392	90	267	117	
2007	1000	945	895	762	895	981	152	95	408	83	262	109	
2008	1000	940	885	746	889	980	158	86	417	83	256	104	
2009	1000	959	909	764	882	979	168	90	416	80	246	106	
2010	1000	966	911	763	888	981	159	91	403	81	266	105	
2011	1000	968	914	762	882	980	165	88	408	82	257	106	
2012	1000	971	915	763	886	981	161	85	412	84	258	100	
2013	1000	971	913	746	884	980	163	91	419	83	244	96	
2014	1000	970	912	747	886	981	161	87	424	85	243	98	
2015	1000	971	898	737	891	982	156	83	432	83	246	94	
Annual averages	CHAW	CHMK	CHON	CHAZ	CHAY	CHAX	CHBS	CHBT	CHBU	CHBV	CHBW	CHBY	CBZW
2001	173.3	171.3	169.5	163.7	178.0	174.3	162.2	216.9	180.0	135.7	172.0	105.0	163.7
2002	176.2	175.1	172.5	166.0	181.1	177.2	164.8	222.3	184.6	133.2	174.2	101.9	167.5
2003	181.3	180.0	176.2	168.9	186.7	182.4	167.9	228.0	194.3	133.2	177.0	99.8	172.0
2004	186.7	184.0	179.1	170.9	192.8	187.9	170.0	233.6	207.4	131.5	178.1	97.7	175.5
2005	192.0	188.2	182.6	173.7	198.7	193.3	172.9	239.8	219.4	131.0	179.2	95.3	179.4
2006	198.1	193.7	187.8	178.3	205.2	199.5	176.9	247.1	231.8	131.7	181.1	94.0	184.8
2007	206.6	199.9	193.3	183.2	213.9	207.9	184.3	256.2	248.1	132.9	183.8	93.3	190.8
2008	214.8	208.5	201.9	191.3	221.2	216.0	198.5	266.7	258.6	132.4	189.0	91.6	199.2
2009	213.7	212.6	207.2	196.3	218.3	214.6	207.6	276.7	247.4	134.1	191.2	90.7	204.8
2010	223.6	222.7	217	206.5	228.8	224.5	214.1	289.9	253.8	138.2	207.6	94.4	211.9
2011	235.2	234.5	229.3	219.6	240.5	236.3	225.6	311.3	262.5	149.8	220.1	99.7	220.4
2012	242.7	242.0	237.0	227.4	248.2	243.9	232.9	327.1	270.9	158.2	224.1	104.1	227.7
2013	250.1	249.4	244.4	235.1	255.5	251.2	240.8	341.9	279.7	166.8	226.8	108.8	235.0
2014	256.0	255.5	249.5	240.2	262.4	257.3	242.5	354.9	288.2	175.0	228.7	113.5	241.2
Monthly figures													
2014 Aug	257.0	256.5	250.2	240.8	263.7	258.5	241.7	356.7	289.5	174.1	231.2	113.0	242.2
Sep	257.6	257.1	250.6	241.1	264.4	259.0	241.4	358.3	290.6	178.1	229.6	115.2	242.7
Oct	257.7	257.2	250.7	241.2	264.5	259.1	241.9	360.6	290.9	178.7	228.6	114.9	243.0
Nov	257.1	256.6	250.0	240.3	264.0	258.5	241.0	358.5	291.1	179.5	226.8	115.3	242.3
Dec	257.5	257.0	250.4	240.7	264.3	258.9	241.8	358.2	292.0	178.6	226.9	116.1	242.8
2015 Jan	255.4	254.8	248.1	238.0	262.0	256.8	241.0	361.1	290.5	175.4	222.5	112.2	240.1
Feb	256.7	256.2	249.4	239.6	263.5	258.0	241.0	360.6	292.0	180.0	223.1	116.3	241.4
Mar	257.1	256.6	249.9	240.2	264.2	258.5	240.6	360.9	291.8	181.6	224.5	117.7	241.9
Apr	258.0	257.5	250.7	240.7	265.2	259.4	240.3	361.8	292.5	182.9	226.1	117.2	242.6
May	258.5	258.1	251.3	241.3	265.9	260.0	241.1	363.1	292.8	183.2	227.2	117.8	243.2
June	258.9	258.5	251.6	241.6	266.4	260.4	240.0	364.0	293.4	183.0	227.9	118.4	243.6
July	258.6	258.2	251.2	241.0	266.3	260.2	238.7	361.9	293.1	180.0	229.6	115.2	243.5
Aug	259.8	259.5	252.3	242.2	267.6	261.4	239.2	364.4	294.5	181.8	230.5	117.6	244.8

1 See chapter text.

2 Seasonal food is defined as items of food the prices of which show significant seasonal variations. These are fresh fruit and vegetables, fresh fish, eggs and home-killed lamb.

3 There are no weights available for RPIY. The taxes excluded are council tax, VAT, duties, car purchase tax and vehicle excise duty, insurance premium tax and airport tax.

4 Consumer durables: Furniture, furnishings, electrical appliances and other household equipment, men's, women's and children's outerwear, footwear, audio-visual equipment, CDs and tapes, toys, photographic and sports goods.

In accordance with the *Statistics and Registration Service Act 2007*, the Retail Prices Index and its derivatives have been assessed against the Code of Practice for Official Statistics and found not to meet the required standards for designation as National Statistics. A full report can be found at:
http://www.statisticsauthority.gov.uk/

Source: Office for National Statistics: 020 7533 5874

17.6 Tax and Price Index[1] United Kingdom

Indices and percentages

Tax and Price Index: (January 1987=100)
DQAB

	2000	2001	2002	2003	2004	2005	2006	2007	2008	2009	2010	2011	2012	2013	2014	2015
January	152.7	156.7	156.5	161.4	166.9	172.1	175.9	183.3	190.7	188.6	194.7	205.5	212.8	218.8	222.7	223.9
February	153.7	157.6	157.0	162.3	167.6	172.8	176.7	184.8	192.3	189.8	196.0	207.7	214.6	220.5	224.2	225.2
March	154.6	157.8	157.7	163.0	168.4	173.7	177.4	186.1	192.9	189.7	197.4	208.8	215.6	221.6	224.8	225.6
April	155.7	156.3	158.6	164.9	168.9	174.1	178.3	186.3	192.2	188.5	199.5	209.2	215.6	219.7	224.2	225.1
May	156.3	157.4	159.1	165.2	169.7	174.5	179.5	187.1	193.4	189.7	200.3	210.0	215.5	220.2	224.4	225.5
June	156.7	157.6	159.1	165.0	170.0	174.7	180.3	188.2	195.1	190.2	200.8	210.0	214.9	219.9	224.8	225.9
July	156.1	156.5	158.8	165.0	170.0	174.7	180.3	187.0	194.8	190.2	200.3	209.5	215.2	219.9	224.5	225.6
August	156.1	157.2	159.3	165.4	170.6	175.1	181.0	188.2	195.5	191.3	201.2	210.9	216.1	221.1	225.5	226.7
September	157.3	157.8	160.6	166.3	171.3	175.6	181.9	188.9	196.7	192.2	201.9	212.7	217.2	222.0	226.1	226.6
October	157.2	157.5	160.9	166.4	171.8	175.8	182.2	189.8	196.0	192.9	202.4	212.8	218.6	222.0	226.1	226.5
November	157.7	156.8	161.2	166.5	172.2	176.1	182.8	190.6	194.3	193.4	203.4	213.2	218.6	222.2	225.6	226.7
December	157.8	156.6	161.5	167.3	173.1	176.6	184.4	191.8	191.2	194.8	204.9	214.1	219.8	223.5	226.0	227.6

Retail Prices Index: (January 1987=100)
CHAW

	2000	2001	2002	2003	2004	2005	2006	2007	2008	2009	2010	2011	2012	2013	2014	2015
January	166.6	171.1	173.3	178.4	183.1	188.9	193.4	201.6	209.8	210.1	217.9	229.0	238.0	245.8	252.6	255.4
February	167.5	172.0	173.8	179.3	183.8	189.6	194.2	203.1	211.4	211.4	219.2	231.3	239.9	247.6	254.2	256.7
March	168.4	172.2	174.5	179.9	184.6	190.5	195.0	204.4	212.1	211.3	220.7	232.5	240.8	248.7	254.8	257.1
April	170.1	173.1	175.7	181.2	185.7	191.6	196.5	205.4	214.0	211.5	222.8	234.4	242.5	249.5	255.7	258.0
May	170.7	174.2	176.2	181.5	186.5	192.0	197.7	206.2	215.1	212.8	223.6	235.2	242.4	250.0	255.9	258.5
June	171.1	174.4	176.2	181.3	186.8	192.2	198.5	207.3	216.8	213.4	224.1	235.2	241.8	249.7	256.3	258.9
July	170.5	173.3	175.9	181.3	186.8	192.2	198.5	206.1	216.5	213.4	223.6	234.7	242.1	249.7	256.0	258.6
August	170.5	174.0	176.4	181.6	187.4	192.6	199.2	207.3	217.2	214.4	224.5	236.1	243.0	251.0	257.0	259.8
September	171.7	174.6	177.6	182.5	188.1	193.1	200.1	208.0	218.4	215.3	225.3	237.9	244.2	251.9	257.6	259.6
October	171.6	174.3	177.9	182.6	188.6	193.3	200.4	208.9	217.7	216.0	225.8	238.0	245.6	251.9	257.7	259.5
November	172.1	173.6	178.2	182.7	189.0	193.6	201.1	209.7	216.0	216.6	226.8	238.5	245.6	252.1	257.1	259.8
December	172.2	173.4	178.5	183.5	189.9	194.1	202.7	210.9	212.9	218.0	228.4	239.4	246.8	253.4	257.5	260.6

Percentage changes on one year earlier[1] CZVL

Tax and Price Index[1]

	2000	2001	2002	2003	2004	2005	2006	2007	2008	2009	2010	2011	2012	2013	2014	2015
January	1.5	2.6	-0.1	3.1	3.4	3.1	2.2	4.2	4.0	-1.1	3.2	5.5	3.6	2.8	1.8	0.5
February	1.9	2.5	-0.4	3.4	3.3	3.1	2.3	4.6	4.1	-1.3	3.3	6.0	3.3	2.7	1.7	0.4
March	2.2	2.1	-0.1	3.4	3.3	3.1	2.1	4.9	3.7	-1.7	4.1	5.8	3.3	2.8	1.4	0.4
April	3.0	0.4	1.5	4.0	2.4	3.1	2.4	4.5	3.2	-1.9	5.8	4.9	3.1	1.9	2.0	0.4
May	3.0	0.7	1.1	3.8	2.7	2.8	2.9	4.2	3.4	-1.9	5.6	4.8	2.6	2.2	1.9	0.5
June	3.3	0.6	1.0	3.7	3.0	2.8	3.2	4.4	3.7	-2.5	5.6	4.6	2.3	2.3	2.2	0.5
July	3.3	0.3	1.5	3.9	3.0	2.8	3.2	3.7	4.2	-2.4	5.3	4.6	2.7	2.2	2.1	0.5
August	3.0	0.7	1.3	3.8	3.1	2.6	3.4	4.0	3.9	-2.1	5.2	4.8	2.5	2.3	2.0	0.5
September	3.3	0.3	1.8	3.5	3.0	2.5	3.6	3.8	4.1	-2.3	5.0	5.3	2.1	2.2	1.8	0.2
October	3.0	0.2	2.2	3.4	3.2	2.3	3.6	4.2	3.3	-1.6	4.9	5.1	2.7	1.6	1.8	0.2
November	3.2	-0.6	2.8	3.3	3.4	2.3	3.8	4.3	1.9	-0.5	5.2	4.8	2.5	1.6	1.5	0.5
December	2.9	-0.8	3.1	3.6	3.5	2.0	4.4	4.0	-0.3	1.9	5.2	4.5	2.7	1.7	1.1	0.7

Retail Prices Index - CZBH

	2000	2001	2002	2003	2004	2005	2006	2007	2008	2009	2010	2011	2012	2013	2014	2015
January	2.0	2.7	1.3	2.9	2.6	3.2	2.4	4.2	4.1	0.1	3.7	5.1	3.9	3.3	2.8	1.1
February	2.3	2.7	1.0	3.2	2.5	3.2	2.4	4.6	4.1	-	3.7	5.5	3.7	3.2	2.7	1.0
March	2.6	2.3	1.3	3.1	2.6	3.2	2.4	4.8	3.8	-0.4	4.4	5.3	3.6	3.3	2.5	0.9
April	3.0	1.8	1.5	3.1	2.5	3.2	2.6	4.5	4.2	-1.2	5.3	5.2	3.5	2.9	2.5	0.9
May	3.1	2.1	1.1	3.0	2.8	2.9	3.0	4.3	4.3	-1.1	5.1	5.2	3.1	3.1	2.4	1.0
June	3.3	1.9	1.0	2.9	3.0	2.9	3.3	4.4	4.6	-1.6	5.0	5.0	2.8	3.3	2.6	1.0
July	3.3	1.6	1.5	3.1	3.0	2.9	3.3	3.8	5.0	-1.4	4.8	5.0	3.2	3.1	2.5	1.0
August	3.0	2.1	1.4	2.9	3.2	2.8	3.4	4.1	4.8	-1.3	4.7	5.2	2.9	3.3	2.4	1.1
September	3.3	1.7	1.7	2.8	3.1	2.7	3.6	3.9	5.0	-1.4	4.6	5.6	2.6	3.2	2.3	0.8
October	3.1	1.6	2.1	2.6	3.3	2.5	3.7	4.2	4.2	-0.8	4.5	5.4	3.2	2.6	2.3	0.7
November	3.2	0.9	2.6	2.5	3.4	2.4	3.9	4.3	3.0	0.3	4.7	5.2	3.0	2.6	2.0	1.1
December	2.9	0.7	2.9	2.8	3.5	2.2	4.4	4.0	0.9	2.4	4.8	4.8	3.1	2.7	1.6	1.2

Source: Office for National Statistics: 020 7533 5874

Key: - zero or negligible   .. not available
1. In accordance with the *Statistics and Registration Service Act 2007*, the Retail Prices Index
and its derivatives have been assessed against the Code of Practice for Official Statistics and
found not to meet the required standards for designation as National Statistics. A full report
can be found at: http://www.statisticsauthority.gov.uk/

17.7 Index of Producer Prices of Agricultural Products, UK (2010=100)

		2005	2006	2007	2008	2009	2010	2011	2012	2013	2014
Total Inputs	a	75.3	78.1	84.8	103.2	95.9	100.0	112.2	114.0	116.9	112.1
All goods and services currently consumed in agriculture	a	73.2	76.2	83.6	105.0	95.7	100.0	113.9	116.4	119.7	112.8
Seeds	a	93.5	86.3	97.2	111.2	105.0	100.0	105.8	98.5	110.2	98.1
Energy and lubricants		67.3	75.8	78.2	107.0	88.3	100.0	118.2	122.4	123.4	119.1
Electricity		64.9	79.7	84.4	100.5	102.2	100.0	108.8	113.4	121.9	128.4
Fuels for heating		58.6	68.2	75.0	101.4	81.4	100.0	110.7	120.0	128.1	133.5
Motor fuels		69.2	75.5	76.7	109.6	85.0	100.0	122.0	125.4	123.3	114.6
Fertilisers and soil improvers		58.9	62.6	67.8	148.5	102.3	100.0	130.4	125.2	113.1	106.5
Straight fertilisers		61.3	66.0	69.8	152.9	93.7	100.0	140.7	128.2	115.2	111.2
Straight fertilisers - nitrogenous		63.7	68.8	71.6	151.8	89.1	100.0	144.5	130.7	118.0	114.9
Straight fertilisers - phosphatic		48.0	48.0	69.0	184.3	111.3	100.0	131.0	120.2	97.5	90.0
Straight fertilisers - potassic		42.1	44.8	51.3	148.2	134.6	100.0	105.2	105.5	94.7	82.2
Compound fertilisers		52.9	55.4	62.4	147.1	112.6	100.0	120.5	123.6	111.3	100.6
Other fertilisers and soil improvers		93.0	96.2	100.8	105.6	105.8	100.0	100.0	102.4	105.5	109.1
Plant protection products	a	94.9	97.3	98.8	100.9	102.8	100.0	100.7	102.0	97.7	102.6
Fungicides		96.8	98.3	99.6	101.9	103.5	100.0	110.6	109.3	99.9	103.5
Insecticides		80.6	85.7	89.6	91.4	102.2	100.0	89.5	67.3	61.0	67.5
Herbicides	a	95.2	98.4	99.8	101.9	102.3	100.0	95.1	89.1	91.6	96.7
Other plant protection products		96.4	96.5	97.8	99.5	102.7	100.0	98.6	151.3	137.3	145.2
Veterinary services	a	83.9	89.8	91.2	87.6	88.0	100.0	102.0	103.5	106.1	107.0
Animal feedingstuffs	q	63.7	66.0	80.1	103.7	95.4	100.0	120.7	128.5	139.4	120.7
Straight feedingstuffs		60.0	62.6	81.7	106.1	90.1	100.0	122.9	135.7	147.6	120.1
Cereal and milling by products		61.3	69.0	96.7	127.2	90.5	100.0	151.6	153.8	161.4	124.1
Feed wheat		57.2	65.5	91.2	123.8	91.3	100.0	143.8	144.6	157.0	124.3
Feed barley		66.5	73.5	105.1	132.5	90.0	100.0	159.9	163.7	165.8	124.4
Feed oats		68.8	74.3	90.8	111.7	80.3	100.0	184.8	198.4	180.7	111.1
Oilcakes		51.9	51.2	64.7	93.8	90.5	100.0	96.6	124.2	138.7	111.9
Soya bean meal		44.0	49.8	66.2	108.6	93.4	100.0	117.3	134.4	137.3	108.4
Sunflower seed meal		52.0	49.8	60.6	90.9	97.1	100.0	97.8	126.0	141.3	112.6
Rape seed meal		54.8	53.9	72.9	99.1	77.6	100.0	91.6	113.4	131.2	105.5
Products of animal origin (incl. white fish meal)		42.3	61.0	58.0	58.6	67.2	100.0	101.9	103.5	108.8	113.6
Other straights		68.9	68.8	84.9	96.6	90.0	100.0	120.8	128.4	142.8	125.4
Field peas		58.5	55.6	99.3	119.9	93.2	100.0	126.4	140.4	171.1	144.8
Field beans		56.4	54.8	97.7	114.9	88.8	100.0	125.3	141.1	177.4	142.3
Soya beans		56.8	60.1	59.3	67.8	81.1	100.0	103.9	110.6	122.0	122.8
Compound feedingstuffs	q	66.2	68.2	79.1	102.2	98.9	100.0	119.2	123.7	134.0	121.1
Compound feedingstuffs for cattle and calves	q	68.9	69.8	80.1	103.8	101.0	100.0	117.8	125.6	135.6	124.7
Compound feedingstuffs for pigs	q	64.6	68.1	79.3	98.6	95.3	100.0	118.7	123.5	128.6	117.4
Compound feedingstuffs for poultry	q	62.7	65.8	77.4	101.5	97.3	100.0	120.8	121.2	132.9	116.9
Compound feedingstuffs for sheep	q	72.9	72.7	81.9	103.8	103.3	100.0	119.8	127.3	142.2	130.7
Maintenance of Materials		79.0	83.5	86.6	91.6	95.8	100.0	104.9	106.5	108.3	110.3
Maintenance of Buildings		76.8	81.6	87.7	94.0	93.8	100.0	107.4	109.8	110.1	110.9
Other goods and services	a	81.1	83.6	88.3	93.0	93.3	100.0	106.0	107.2	109.6	110.2
Goods and services contributing to investment	a	86.2	87.9	90.9	94.3	96.9	100.0	103.6	101.7	102.9	108.7
Materials	a	89.4	90.0	91.8	94.3	97.3	100.0	103.0	99.1	100.4	108.5
Machinery and other equipment	a	87.5	88.5	92.1	97.4	99.7	100.0	103.8	94.3	96.8	115.9
Plant and machinery for cultivation		85.0	86.2	90.4	96.6	99.5	100.0	104.7	93.4	95.9	117.7
Farm machinery and installations	a	96.7	96.8	98.2	100.3	100.1	100.0	100.6	97.4	100.4	109.0
Transport Equipment		90.8	91.1	91.6	92.0	95.6	100.0	102.4	102.8	103.0	103.0
Tractors		86.6	87.8	89.1	91.4	95.9	100.0	103.7	104.6	105.3	105.1
Other vehicles		107.7	104.8	102.1	95.1	94.4	100.0	98.2	96.3	95.0	95.0
Buildings		79.0	83.7	89.3	95.0	95.2	100.0	105.8	107.4	107.7	108.4
Other (Engineering and soil improvement operations)		83.4	84.9	89.0	93.1	97.9	100.0	102.5	104.5	107.2	110.7

Source: Department for Environment, Food and Rural Affairs
Enquiries Defra prices team. Tel: ++44(0)20802 66247

a:- Part or all of the series is made up of annual data
q:- Part or all of the series is made up of quarterly data

17.8 Index of Producer Prices of Agricultural Products, UK (2010=100)

		2005	2006	2007	2008	2009	2010	2011	2012	2013	2014
Total Outputs	a	69.6	72.3	82.2	98.9	95.0	100.0	113.0	118.6	125.4	114.1
Crop products	a	67.4	73.2	88.0	103.6	89.1	100.0	117.8	124.1	128.6	107.8
Cereals	a	59.5	66.2	96.8	124.0	89.6	100.0	144.8	149.7	153.1	120.6
Wheat	a	57.0	64.2	93.2	121.5	90.5	100.0	141.7	144.3	151.9	121.3
Wheat - Feeding	a	56.6	65.1	92.1	120.0	89.5	100.0	141.0	143.7	152.8	120.8
Wheat - Breadmaking		58.3	60.2	95.5	124.0	95.7	100.0	138.3	141.7	141.9	122.4
Wheat - Other Milling		58.2	63.4	98.6	129.1	90.0	100.0	152.2	152.7	158.4	123.8
Barley	a	66.1	71.5	107.9	132.6	88.0	100.0	150.3	160.9	154.4	119.2
Barley - Feeding	a	65.2	71.4	103.8	126.0	86.3	100.0	155.5	159.9	158.6	120.2
Barley - Malting		67.9	71.6	117.1	147.1	91.7	100.0	138.9	163.2	145.2	117.2
Oats	a	67.6	73.6	91.9	113.1	82.7	100.0	177.8	190.1	173.7	112.6
Oats - Milling		65.6	71.6	91.1	110.0	82.6	100.0	170.4	183.2	155.8	108.4
Oats - Feeding	a	70.8	76.6	93.1	118.0	82.7	100.0	189.7	201.0	202.0	119.3
Potatoes		70.3	92.1	104.4	108.7	86.6	100.0	107.1	121.9	156.1	103.7
Potatoes - Earlies		55.5	79.3	61.7	89.4	61.4	100.0	65.9	125.2	122.6	65.0
Potatoes - Main Crop		71.6	93.6	108.6	110.9	88.5	100.0	111.1	122.2	160.7	107.3
Industrial Crops	a	62.4	64.7	73.6	112.4	93.5	100.0	132.0	130.0	121.5	101.8
Oilseed Rape (non set aside)		49.3	58.9	69.7	118.7	91.5	100.0	143.3	139.1	127.0	99.7
Sugar Beet	a	101.5	81.2	83.7	93.6	99.0	100.0	99.9	104.3	105.7	108.9
Forage plants		62.6	62.8	73.7	80.5	84.1	100.0	112.6	106.2	114.8	107.3
Hay and dried grass		53.7	54.8	69.0	65.0	69.5	100.0	136.9	100.4	86.3	84.7
Straw		54.8	51.4	63.1	70.9	80.1	100.0	113.5	100.6	104.3	99.4
Other forage plants		56.3	54.9	94.3	111.1	87.6	100.0	127.5	136.9	168.3	138.6
Fresh Vegetables		79.3	85.3	93.3	91.9	87.8	100.0	92.7	108.6	110.2	96.1
Cauliflowers		78.5	77.9	91.5	93.4	89.4	100.0	96.3	118.4	102.0	105.3
Tomatoes		73.3	80.8	82.3	87.1	75.9	100.0	78.9	90.7	88.3	90.1
Cabbages		77.2	83.1	102.5	99.2	92.0	100.0	108.4	120.3	113.4	94.9
Lettuce		74.5	82.8	78.7	91.4	79.4	100.0	85.5	110.1	104.9	100.0
Carrots		85.7	91.9	106.4	110.7	114.7	100.0	108.0	124.2	124.4	89.8
Onions		41.6	56.1	77.1	56.1	57.1	100.0	94.1	68.3	96.9	94.9
Beans (Green)		69.0	87.9	106.2	94.8	84.4	100.0	89.8	132.6	124.1	103.5
Mushrooms		109.2	100.9	95.0	79.6	86.0	100.0	87.4	104.4	117.7	144.3
Fresh Fruit		73.9	77.3	84.0	96.6	95.6	100.0	98.7	103.7	104.8	97.6
Dessert Apples		68.3	76.1	86.7	92.1	96.6	100.0	107.0	118.0	117.1	104.0
Cooking Apples		78.2	87.0	97.5	122.5	99.6	100.0	104.0	132.0	158.1	109.1
Dessert Pears		76.2	82.2	80.3	106.2	113.3	100.0	101.2	116.9	129.4	102.8
Strawberries		73.8	70.5	73.1	83.8	90.9	100.0	91.8	87.4	84.0	91.4
Raspberries		76.7	83.9	96.6	97.7	99.0	100.0	102.2	96.5	96.2	88.7
Flowers and plants	a	71.5	73.6	77.5	83.6	86.6	100.0	99.1	109.3	110.9	108.3
Other crop products	a	89.3	93.1	83.7	79.1	103.7	100.0	93.3	98.7	98.7	98.7
Seeds	a	89.3	93.1	83.7	79.1	103.7	100.0	93.3	98.7	98.7	98.7
Animals and animal products	a	71.1	71.7	78.0	95.6	99.3	100.0	109.5	114.7	123.2	118.7
Animals (for slaughter & export)		69.0	71.0	73.9	90.2	100.8	100.0	109.6	114.6	120.0	113.4
Cattle and calves		67.3	73.8	75.0	98.4	104.9	100.0	116.4	129.3	137.7	123.2
Cattle (clean)		69.5	75.2	76.3	98.4	105.0	100.0	115.1	129.0	139.0	124.5
Cows and Bulls		55.2	65.7	67.5	98.2	103.9	100.0	123.8	131.2	131.1	116.5
Calves		63.4	80.1	84.7	102.5	128.6	100.0	112.7	126.7	118.4	110.3
Pigs		73.5	74.2	76.0	89.5	103.1	100.0	102.1	106.3	116.7	111.7
Pigs (clean)		73.3	74.0	76.3	89.2	102.9	100.0	102.2	106.2	116.9	112.2
Sows and Boars		75.5	76.5	60.8	97.3	114.1	100.0	96.1	114.1	107.2	91.7
Sheep and lambs		61.8	63.4	56.7	72.1	91.1	100.0	112.3	105.1	102.0	106.1
Sheep and lambs (clean)		64.1	65.4	58.0	74.5	92.0	100.0	111.7	104.7	104.2	106.5
Ewes and Rams		45.5	48.3	47.2	54.7	84.0	100.0	116.2	108.6	85.8	103.1
All Poultry	a	73.4	70.1	81.0	89.5	99.5	100.0	102.9	105.0	109.3	106.0
Chickens	a	74.6	70.5	82.1	87.4	99.3	100.0	102.1	103.7	107.5	103.3
Turkeys		64.3	63.7	74.2	101.4	101.6	100.0	106.8	112.4	118.5	118.4
Animal products	a	74.5	72.7	84.3	104.1	96.9	100.0	109.4	114.8	128.1	126.9
Milk		74.9	72.8	84.3	105.2	96.1	100.0	111.0	113.8	128.2	127.7
Eggs	q	74.7	76.9	87.8	103.2	105.7	100.0	99.9	124.0	130.8	122.2
Intensive eggs	q	66.1	71.4	80.6	98.1	103.5	100.0	101.6	135.7	139.6	127.4
Free range eggs	q	80.5	80.7	92.6	106.6	107.2	100.0	98.7	116.2	124.9	118.7
Wool clip	a	45.6	16.6	35.4	32.4	47.1	100.0	121.6	75.5	101.0	155.9

a:- Part or all of the series is made up of annual data
q:- Part or all of the series is made up of quarterly data

Source: Department for Environment, Food and Rural Affairs
Enquiries Defra prices team. Tel: ++44(0)20802 66247
or email: prices@defra.gsi.gov.uk

17.9 Harmonised Indices of Consumer Prices (HICPs) - International Comparisons: EU Countries: 2010 to 2015 Percentage change over 12 months

per cent

	Austria	Belgium	Bulgaria	Cyprus	Czech Republic	Denmark	Estonia	Finland	France	Germany	Greece	Hungary	Ireland	Italy	Latvia
	D7SK	D7SL	GHY8	D7RO	D7RP	D7SM	D7RQ	D7SN	D7SO	D7SP	D7SQ	D7RR	D7SS	D7ST	D7RS
Annual average															
2010	1.7	2.3	3.0	2.6	1.2	2.2	2.7	1.7	1.7	1.1	4.7	4.7	-1.6	1.6	-1.2
2011	3.6	3.4	3.4	3.5	2.2	2.7	5.1	3.3	2.3	2.5	3.1	3.9	1.2	2.9	4.2
2012	2.6	2.6	2.4	3.1	3.5	2.4	4.2	3.2	2.2	2.1	1.0	5.7	1.9	3.3	2.3
2013	2.1	1.2	0.4	0.4	1.4	0.5	3.2	2.2	1.0	1.6	-0.9	1.7	0.5	1.2	-
2014	1.5	0.5	-1.6	-0.3	0.4	0.4	0.5	1.2	0.6	0.8	-1.4		0.3	0.2	0.7
Monthly															
Jul 2014	1.7	0.5	-1.1	0.9	0.5	0.5	-	1.0	0.6	0.7	-0.8	0.5	0.4	-	0.6
Aug	1.5	0.4	-1.0	0.8	0.7	0.3	-0.2	1.2	0.5	0.8	-0.2	0.3	0.6	-0.1	0.8
Sep	1.4	0.2	-1.4	-	0.8	0.3	0.2	1.5	0.4	0.8	-1.1	-0.5	0.5	-0.1	1.2
Oct	1.4	0.3	-1.5	0.3	0.8	0.2	0.5	1.2	0.5	0.8	-1.8	-0.3	0.4	0.2	0.7
Nov	1.5	0.1	-1.9	-	0.6	0.3	-	1.1	0.4	0.5	-1.2	0.1	0.2	0.3	0.9
Dec	0.8	-0.4	-2.0	-1.0	-	0.1	0.1	0.6	0.1	-	-2.5	-0.8	-0.3	-	0.3
Jan 2015	0.5	-0.6	-2.4	-0.7	-0.1	-0.3	-0.5	-0.1	-0.4	-0.4	-2.8	-1.4	-0.4	-0.5	-0.3
Feb	0.5	-0.4	-1.7	-0.8	-	-0.1	-0.2	-0.1	-0.3	-	-1.9	-0.9	-0.4	0.1	-
Mar	0.9	-0.1	-1.1	-1.4	0.1	0.3	-	-	-	0.2	-1.9	-0.5	-0.2	-	0.5
Apr	0.9	0.4	-0.9	-1.7	0.5	0.4	0.4	-0.1	0.1	0.3	-1.8	-	-0.3	-0.1	0.6
May	1.0	0.8	-0.3	-1.7	0.7	0.4	0.5	0.1	0.3	0.6	-1.4	0.6	0.2	0.2	1.2
Jun	1.0	0.9	-0.6	-2.1	0.9	0.4	0.3	0.1	0.3	0.2	-1.1	0.7	0.4	0.2	0.7

per cent

	Lithuania	Luxembourg	Malta	Netherlands	Poland	Portugal	Romania	Slovakia	Slovenia	Spain	Sweden	United Kingdom [1]	EICP [2] EU 25 average [3]	EICP [2] EU 28 average [3]	MUICP average [4]
	D7RT	D7SU	D7RU	D7SV	D7RV	D7SX	GHY7	D7RW	D7RX	D7SY	D7SZ	D7G7	D7RY	GJ2E	D7SR
Annual average															
2010	1.2	2.8	2.0	0.9	2.6	1.4	6.1	0.7	2.1	2.0	1.9	3.3	..	2.1	1.6
2011	4.1	3.7	2.5	2.5	3.9	3.6	5.8	4.1	2.1	3.0	1.4	4.5	..	3.1	2.7
2012	3.2	2.9	3.2	2.8	3.7	2.8	3.4	3.7	2.8	2.4	0.9	2.8	..	2.6	2.5
2013	1.2	1.7	1.0	2.6	0.8	0.4	3.2	1.5	1.9	1.5	0.4	2.6	..	1.5	1.4
2014	0.2	0.7	0.8	0.3	0.1	-0.2	1.4	-0.1	0.4	-0.2	0.2	1.5	..	0.5	0.4
Monthly															
Jul 2014	0.5	1.2	0.6	0.3	-	-0.7	1.5	-0.1	0.3	-0.4	0.4	1.6	..	0.5	0.4
Aug	0.3	0.7	0.8	0.4	-0.1	-0.1	1.3	-0.2	-	-0.5	0.2	1.5	..	0.5	0.4
Sep	-	0.3	0.6	0.3	-0.2	-	1.8	-0.1	-0.1	-0.3	-	1.2	..	0.4	0.3
Oct	0.3	0.4	0.7	0.4	-0.3	0.1	1.8	-	0.1	-0.2	0.3	1.3	..	0.5	0.4
Nov	0.4	0.2	0.7	0.3	-0.3	0.1	1.5	-	0.1	-0.5	0.3	1.0	..	0.3	0.3
Dec	-0.1	-0.9	0.4	-0.1	-0.7	-0.3	1.0	-0.1	-0.1	-1.1	0.3	0.5	..	-0.1	-0.2
Jan 2015	-1.4	-1.2	0.8	-0.7	-1.1	-0.4	0.5	-0.5	-0.7	-1.5	0.4	0.3	..	-0.5	-0.6
Feb	-1.5	-0.3	0.6	-0.5	-1.3	-0.1	0.4	-0.6	-0.5	-1.2	0.7	-	..	-0.3	-0.3
Mar	-1.1	0.1	0.5	-0.3	-1.2	0.4	0.8	-0.4	-0.4	-0.8	0.7	-	..	-0.1	-0.1
Apr	-0.6	-	1.4	-	-0.8	0.5	0.6	-0.1	-0.7	-0.7	0.5	-0.1	..	-	-
May	-	0.4	1.3	0.7	-0.6	1.0	1.3	-0.1	-0.8	-0.3	0.9	0.1	..	0.3	0.3
Jun	-0.2	0.5	1.1	0.5	-0.5	0.8	-0.9	-0.1	-0.9	-	0.4	-	..	0.1	0.2

Key: - zero or negligible .. Not available * Provisional

[+] Date of earliest revision ø Estimated

1. Published as the CPI in the U

2. The EICP (European Index of Consumer Prices) is the offic l EU aggregate. It covers 15 member states until April 2004, 25 member states from May 2004 to Dec 2006, and 27 member states from Jan 2007. The EU 25 annual average for 2004 is calculated from the EU 15 average from January to April and the EU 25 average from May to December.

3. The coverage of the European Union was extended to includ Cyprus, Czech Republic, Estonia, Hungary, Latvia, Lithuania, Malta, Poland, Slovakia and Slovenia with effect from 1 May 2004, and Bulgaria and Romania from 1 Jan 2007. Data for the EU 25 average is available from May 2004 and for the EU 27 average from Jan 2007.

4. The coverage of the Monetary Union Indices of Consumer Prices (MUICP) was extended to include Greece with effect from Jan 2001 and Slovakia from Jan 2009.

Source:
Office for National Statistics
Prices Division
2.001 Cardiff Road
Newport
South Wales
NP10 8XG

http://www.ons.gov.uk

Eurostat
www.ec.europa.eu/eurostat

this page is intentionally blank

Production

Chapter 18

Production

Annual Business Survey
(Table 18.1)

The Annual Business Survey (ABS) estimates cover all UK businesses registered for Value Added Tax (VAT) and/or Pay As You Earn (PAYE) classified to the 2007 Standard Industrial Classification (SIC (2007)) headings listed in the tables. The ABS obtains details on these businesses from the Office for National Statistics (ONS) Inter-Departmental Business Register (IDBR).

As with all its statistical inquiries, ONS is concerned to minimise the form-filling burden of individual contributors and as such the ABS is a sample inquiry. The sample was designed as a stratified random sample of about 66,300 businesses; the inquiry population is stratified by SIC (2007) and employment using the information from the register.

The inquiry results are grossed up to the total population so that they relate to all active UK businesses on the IDBR for the sectors covered.

The results meet a wide range of needs for government, economic analysts and the business community at large. In official statistics the inquiry is an important source for the national accounts and input-output tables, and also provides weights for the indices of production and producer prices. Inquiry results also enable the UK to meet statistical requirements of the European Union.

UK Manufacturer's Sales by Industry
(Table 18.2)

Table 18.2 lists total UK manufacturers' sales by industry.

Number of local units in manufacturing industries
(Table 18.3)

The table shows the number of local units (sites) in manufacturing by employment size band. The classification breakdown is at division level (two digit) as classified to SIC(2007) held on the Inter-Departmental Business Register (IDBR).
UK Business: Activity, Size and Location provides further details and contains detailed information regarding enterprises in the UK including size, classification, and local units in the UK including size, classification and location.

Production of primary fuels
(Table 18.4)

This table shows indigenous production of primary fuels. It includes the extraction or capture of primary commodities and the generation or manufacture of secondary commodities. Production is always gross; that is, it includes the quantities used during the extraction or manufacturing process. Primary fuels are coal, natural gas (including colliery methane), oil, primary electricity (that is, electricity generated by hydro, nuclear wind and tide stations and also electricity imported from France through the interconnector) and renewables (includes solid renewables such as wood, straw and waste and gaseous renewables such as landfill gas and sewage gas). The figures are presented on a common basis expressed in million tonnes of oil equivalent. Estimates of the gross calorific values used for converting the statistics for the various fuels to these are given in the Digest of UK Energy Statistics available on the DECC website.

Total inland energy consumption
(Table 18.5)

This table shows energy consumption by fuel and final energy consumption by fuel and class of consumer. Primary energy consumption covers consumption of all primary fuels (defined above) for energy purposes. This measure of energy consumption includes energy that is lost by converting primary fuels into secondary fuels (the energy lost burning coal to generate electricity or the energy used by refineries to separate crude oil into fractions) in addition to losses in distribution. The other common way of measuring energy consumption is to measure the energy content of the fuels supplied to consumers. This is called final energy consumption. It is net of fuel used by the energy industries, conversion, transmission and distribution losses. The figures are presented on a common basis, measured as energy supplied and expressed in million tonnes of oil equivalent. Estimates of the gross calorific values used for converting the statistics for the various fuels to these are given in the Digest of UK Energy Statistics available on the DECC website.

So far as practicable the user categories have been grouped on the basis of the SIC(2007) although the methods used by each of the supply industries to identify end users are slightly different. Chapter 1 of the Digest of UK Energy Statistics gives more information on these figures.

Coal
(Table 18.6)

Since 1995, aggregate data on coal production have been obtained from the Coal Authority. In addition, main coal producers provide data in response to an annual Department of Energy and Climate Change (DECC) inquiry which covers production (deep mined and opencast), trade, stocks and disposals. HM Revenue & Customs (HMRC) also provides trade data for solid fuels. DECC collects information on the use of coal from the UK Iron and Steel Statistics Bureau and consumption of coal for electricity generation is covered by data provided by the electricity generators.

Gas
(Table 18.7)

Production figures, covering the production of gas from the UK Continental Shelf offshore and onshore gas fields and gas obtained during the production of oil, are obtained from returns made under the DECC's Petroleum Production Reporting System. Additional information is used on imports and exports of gas and details from the operators of gas terminals in the UK to complete the picture.

It is no longer possible to present information on fuels input into the gas industry and gas output and sales in the same format as in previous editions of this table. As such, users are directed to Chapter 4 of the Digest of UK Energy Statistics, where more detailed information on gas production and consumption in the UK is available.

DECC carry out an annual survey of gas suppliers to obtain details of gas sales to the various categories of consumer. Estimates are included for the suppliers with the smallest market share, since the DECC inquiry covers only the largest suppliers (that is, those known to supply more than 1,750 GWh per year).

Electricity
(Tables 18.8–18.10)

Tables 18.8 to 18.10 cover all generators and suppliers of electricity in the UK. The relationship between generation, supply, availability and consumption is as follows:

Electricity generated

less electricity used on works

equals electricity supplied (gross)

less electricity used in pumping at pumped storage stations.

equals electricity supplied (net)

plus imports (net of exports) of electricity

equals electricity available

less losses and statistical differences

equals electricity consumed

In Table 18.8 'major power producers' are those generating companies corresponding to the old public sector supply system:
• AES Electric Ltd.
• Baglan Generation Ltd.
• Barking Power Ltd.
• British Energy plc
• Centrica Energy
• Coolkeeragh ESB Ltd.
• Corby Power Ltd.
• Coryton Energy Company Ltd.
• Derwent Cogeneration Ltd.
• Drax Power Ltd.
• EDF Energy plc
• E.ON UK plc
• Energy Power Resources Ltd.
• Gaz De France
• GDF Suez Teesside Power Ltd
• Immingham CHP
• International Power plc
• Magnox Electric Ltd.
• Premier Power Ltd.
• RGS Energy Ltd.
• Rocksavage Power Company Ltd.
• RWE Npower plc
• Scottish Power plc
• Scottish and Southern Energy plc
• Seabank Power Ltd.
• SELCHP Ltd.
• Spalding Energy Company Ltd.
• Uskmouth Power Company Ltd.
• Western Power Generation Ltd.

Additionally, from 2007, the following major wind farm companies are included as 'major power producers':

• Airtricity
• Cumbria Wind Farms
• Fred Olsen
• H G Capital
• Renewable Energy Systems
• Vattenfall Wind

In Table 18.10 all fuels are converted to the common unit of million tonnes of oil equivalent, that is, the amounts of oil which would be needed to produce the output of electricity generated from those fuels.

More detailed statistics on energy are given in the Digest of United Kingdom Energy Statistics. Readers may wish to note that the production and consumption of fuels are presented using commodity balances. A commodity balance shows the flows of an individual fuel through from production to final consumption, showing its use in transformation and energy industry own use.

Oil and oil products
(Tables 18.11–18.13)

Data on the production of crude oil, condensates and natural gases given in Table 18.11 are collected by DECC direct from the operators of production facilities and terminals situated on UK territory, either onshore or offshore, that is, on the UK Continental Shelf. Data are also collected from the companies on their trade in oil and oil products. These data are used in preference to the foreign trade as recorded by HMRC in Overseas Trade Statistics.

Data on the internal UK oil industry (that is, on the supply, refining and distribution of oil and oil products in the UK) are collected by the UK Petroleum Industry Association. These data, reported by individual refining companies and wholesalers and supplemented where necessary by data from other sources, provide the contents of Tables 18.12 and 18.13. The data are presented in terms of deliveries to the inland UK market. This is regarded as an acceptable proxy for actual consumption of products. The main shortcoming is that, while changes in stocks held by companies in central storage areas are taken into account, changes in the levels of stocks further down the retail ladder (such as stocks held on petrol station forecourts) are not. This is not thought to result in a significant degree of difference in the data.

Iron and steel
(Tables 18.14–18.16)
Iron and steel industry
The general definition of the UK iron and steel industry is based on groups 271 'ECSC iron and steel', 272 'Tubes', and 273 'Primary Transformation' of the UK SIC(92), except those parts of groups 272 and 273 which cover cast iron pipes, drawn wire, cold formed sections and Ferro alloys.

The definition excludes certain products which may be made by works within the industry, such as refined iron, finished steel castings, steel tyres, wheels, axles and rolled rings, open and closed die forgings, colliery arches and springs. Iron foundries and steel stockholders are also considered to be outside of the industry.

Statistics

The statistics for the UK iron and steel industry are compiled by the Iron and Steel Statistics Bureau (ISSB) Ltd from data collected from UK steel producing companies, with the exception of trade data which is based on HMRC data.

'Crude steel' is the total of usable ingots, usable continuously cast semi-finished products and liquid steel for castings.

'Production of finished products' is the total production at the mill of that product after deduction of any material which is immediately scrapped

'Deliveries' are based on invoiced tonnages and will include deliveries made to steel stockholders and service centres by the UK steel industry.

For more detailed information on definitions etc please contact ISSB Ltd. on 020 7343 3900.

Fertilisers
(Table 18.17)
Table 18.17 gives the quantity of the fertiliser nutrients nitrogen (N), phosphate (P2O5) and potash (K2O) used by UK farmers during the growing season, or fertiliser year, which is taken as the year ending in June.

Minerals
(Table 18.18)
Table 18.18 gives, separately for Great Britain and Northern Ireland, the production of minerals extracted from the ground. The figures for chemicals and metals are estimated from the quality of the ore which is extracted. The data come from an annual census of the quarrying industry, which, for Great Britain, is conducted by ONS for Communities and Local Government and Business, Innovation and Skills (BIS) –formally known as Business, Enterprise and Regulatory Reform (BERR)

Building materials
(Table 18.19)
Table 18.19 gives the production and deliveries of a number of building materials, including bricks, concrete blocks, sand and gravel, slate, cement, concrete roofing tiles and ready mixed cement. This data comes from the Monthly Bulletin of Building Materials and Components.

Construction
(Tables 18.20–18.21)
The value of output represents the value of construction work done during the quarter in Great Britain and is derived from returns made by private contractors and public authorities with their own direct labour forces. The series (and the accompanying index of the volume of output) include estimates of the output of small firms and self-employed workers not recorded in the regular quarterly output inquiry.

The new orders statistics are collected from private contractors and analysed by the principal types of construction work involved. The series includes speculative work for eventual sale or lease undertaken on the initiative of the respondent where no formal contract or order is involved.

Engineering turnover and orders
(Tables 18.22–18.23)
The figures represent the output of UK-based manufacturers classified to Subsections DK and DL of the SIC(2007). They are derived from the monthly production inquiry (MPI) and include estimates for non-responders and for establishments which are not sampled.

Drink and tobacco
(Tables 18.24–18.25)

Data for these tables are derived by HMRC from the systems for collecting excise duties.
Alcoholic drinks and tobacco products become liable for duty when released for consumption in the
UK. Figures for releases include both home-produced products and commercial imports. Production
figures are also available for potable spirits distilled and beer brewed in the UK.

Alcoholic drink
(Table 18.24)

The figures for imported ad other spirits released for home consumption include gin and other
UK produced spirits for which a breakdown is not available.

Since June 1993 beer duty has been charged when the beer leaves the brewery or other registered
premises. Previously duty was chargeable at an earlier stage (the worts stage) in the brewing process
and an allowance was made for wastage. Figures for years prior to 1994 include adjustments to bring
them into line with current data. The change in June 1993 also led to the availability of data on the
strength; a series in hectolitres of pure alcohol is shown from 1994.

Made wine with alcoholic strength from 1.2 per cent to 5.5 per cent is termed 'coolers'. Included in
'coolers' are alcoholic lemonade and similar products of appropriate strength. From 28 April 2002
duty on spirit-based 'coolers' (ready to drink products) is charged at the same rate as spirits per litre
of alcohol. Made wine coolers include only wine based 'coolers' from this period.

Tobacco products
(Table 18.25)

Releases of cigarettes and other tobacco products tend to be higher in the period before a Budget.
Products may then be stocked, duty paid, before being sold.

The industries are now grouped according to the 2007 Standard Industrial Classification at 2-digit level.

18.1 Production and Construction Industries

Description		Year	Number of enterprises	Total turnover	Approximate gross value added at basic prices (aGVA)	Total purchases of goods, materials and services	Total employment - point in time [1]	Total employment - average during the year [1]
Standard Industrial Classification (Revised 2007)			Number	£ million	£ million	£ million	Thousand	Thousand
B-F	Production and Construction	2011	396,645	892,105	285,411	591,094	4,202	4,245
		2012	391,516	893,690	288,924	587,760	4,156	4,161
		2013	401,360	909,589	295,200	599,281	4,125	4,129
B-E	Production industries	2011	131,430	702,639	215,261	471,926	2,851	2,854
		2012	134,410	703,277	215,117	470,931	2,855	2,865
		2013	138,848	711,301	217,593	477,694	2,827	2,835
B	Mining and quarrying	2011	1,206	53,951	28,597	26,469	65	63
		2012	1,263	51,173	24,581	27,945	76	75
		2013	1,308	49,409	22,055	28,886	66	65
05	Mining of coal and lignite	2011	21	*	*	744	6	7
		2012	*	*	*	*	7	8
		2013	20	*	*	506	5	5
06	Extraction of crude petroleum and natural gas	2011	124	42,317	24,589	18,928	13	13
		2012	151	37,430	19,720	19,167	16	15
		2013	157	34,884	17,060	19,486	15	14
07	Mining of metal ores	2011	4	*	*	4	-	-
		2012	*	*	*	*	*	*
		2013	7	*	*	2	*	*
08	Other mining and quarrying	2011	718	4,097	1,205	2,793	*	*
		2012	703	5,359	1,501	3,726	27	27
		2013	715	6,144	1,878	4,130	20	20
09	Mining support service activities	2011	339	6,358	2,367	4,001	*	*
		2012	378	7,083	2,961	4,189	*	*
		2013	409	7,566	2,807	4,761	*	*
C	Manufacturing	2011	122,591	516,408	149,313	349,623	2,495	2,510
		2012	124,514	513,437	149,498	344,634	2,482	2,500
		2013	127,900	517,798	155,099	344,303	2,466	2,483
10	Manufacture of food products	2011	6,444	73,175	19,271	54,355	377	376
		2012	6,642	76,445	18,664	57,977	363	359
		2013	6,890	77,571	20,187	57,580	373	369
11	Manufacture of beverages	2011	1,034	17,635	*	*	*	*
		2012	1,127	18,396	*	*	43	43
		2013	1,340	*	*	*	44	44
12	Manufacture of tobacco products	2011	10	10,418	*	*	*	*
		2012	11	10,990	*	*	*	*
		2013	10	*	*	*	*	*
13	Manufacture of textiles	2011	3,871	5,473	1,847	3,668	54	54
		2012	3,778	5,313	2,262	3,053	55	54
		2013	3,842	5,285	2,110	3,147	56	56
14	Manufacture of wearing apparel	2011	3,378	2,834	831	2,009	29	30
		2012	3,384	2,653	744	1,895	29	29
		2013	3,392	2,749	911	1,848	33	34
15	Manufacture of leather and related products	2011	540	976	365	642	*	*
		2012	559	970	313	647	*	*
		2013	551	975	386	602	*	*

18.1 Production and Construction Industries

	Description	Year	Number of enterprises	Total turnover	Approximate gross value added at basic prices (aGVA)	Total purchases of goods, materials and services	Total employment - point in time [1]	Total employment - average during the year [1]
16	Manufacture of wood and of products of wood and cork, except furniture; manufacture of articles of straw and plaiting materials	2011	7,321	6,806	2,454	4,363	61	58
		2012	7,105	6,752	2,673	4,136	68	66
		2013	7,327	7,156	2,582	4,566	67	64
17	Manufacture of paper and paper products	2011	1,679	11,507	4,049	7,561	56	58
		2012	1,576	10,827	3,859	6,910	56	58
		2013	1,550	10,906	3,693	7,295	53	54
18	Printing and reproduction of recorded media	2011	13,923	11,411	5,337	6,113	121	127
		2012	13,259	10,943	4,966	5,955	115	120
		2013	12,988	10,755	5,056	5,729	104	108
19	Manufacture of coke and refined petroleum products	2011	164	49,895	2,232	38,281	10	9
		2012	149	53,725	2,226	42,590	11	10
		2013	131	48,260	1,321	38,584	*	*
20	Manufacture of chemicals and chemical products	2011	2,464	38,874	8,910	30,330	114	117
		2012	2,468	31,201	8,500	22,758	109	111
		2013	2,549	31,388	8,534	22,900	104	106
21	Manufacture of basic pharmaceutical products and pharmaceutical preparations	2011	448	17,248	7,417	9,863	44	45
		2012	510	16,027	6,736	9,402	50	50
		2013	529	15,021	6,334	8,548	*	*
22	Manufacture of rubber and plastic products	2011	5,809	22,182	7,881	14,478	156	154
		2012	5,696	21,925	8,048	13,969	155	154
		2013	5,693	22,658	8,154	14,502	162	161
23	Manufacture of other non-metallic mineral products	2011	3,799	14,248	3,987	10,187	96	96
		2012	3,625	12,462	3,735	8,680	86	87
		2013	3,625	12,756	3,831	8,827	78	78
24	Manufacture basic metals	2011	1,403	19,661	4,600	15,320	75	76
		2012	1,400	17,548	3,628	13,653	71	71
		2013	1,485	18,284	4,065	14,148	70	71
25	Manufacture of fabricated metal products, except machinery and equipment	2011	24,801	31,745	13,170	18,866	305	302
		2012	24,050	33,093	14,483	18,711	292	296
		2013	24,364	33,221	14,259	19,088	297	300
26	Manufacture of computer, electronic and optical products	2011	6,117	19,592	8,560	11,289	122	128
		2012	5,874	18,358	8,025	10,403	123	128
		2013	6,009	19,642	7,808	11,683	132	138
27	Manufacture of electrical equipment	2011	2,951	14,016	4,450	9,561	97	95
		2012	2,971	14,446	4,869	9,567	87	86
		2013	3,017	13,561	4,551	9,051	86	85
28	Manufacture of machinery and equipment n.e.c	2011	8,251	37,833	13,423	24,879	201	199
		2012	7,948	37,173	14,455	22,696	208	205
		2013	7,932	34,755	13,026	21,992	202	200
29	Manufacture of motor vehicles, and semi-trailers	2011	2,703	54,375	11,253	43,546	131	129
		2012	2,614	55,353	10,856	44,758	137	135
		2013	2,672	60,654	14,592	46,142	145	143
30	Manufacture of other transport	2011	1,817	28,208	9,605	18,436	139	134
		2012	1,876	29,197	9,680	19,839	134	131
		2013	1,943	31,595	11,562	20,202	134	131
31	Manufacture of furniture	2011	6,129	6,460	2,599	3,913	75	81
		2012	6,131	6,589	2,585	4,026	79	86
		2013	6,022	7,006	2,838	4,187	77	83

18.1 Production and Construction Industries

	Description	Year	Number of enterprises	Total turnover	Approximate gross value added at basic prices (aGVA)	Total purchases of goods, materials and services	Total employment - point in time [1]	Total employment - average during the year [1]
32	Other manufacturing	2011	9,838	9,502	3,987	5,615	88	95
		2012	9,988	8,949	3,812	5,194	91	100
		2013	9,759	9,241	3,644	5,715	74	81
33	Repair and installation of machinery and equipment	2011	7,697	12,336	5,634	6,651	86	89
		2012	11,773	14,104	6,564	7,686	107	109
		2013	14,280	15,604	7,761	8,025	106	108
D	Electricity, gas, steam and air conditioning supply	2011	1,219	100,735	21,206	80,139	131	123
		2012	1,825	106,916	24,151	82,879	136	129
		2013	2,574	111,056	23,848	87,897	129	122
E	Water supply, sewerage, waste management, and remediation activities	2011	6,414	31,544	16,145	15,695	159	158
		2012	6,808	31,751	16,887	15,473	162	161
		2013	7,066	33,038	16,591	16,608	165	164
36	Water collection, treatment and	2011	119	10,246	8,024	2,485	*	*
		2012	120	11,049	9,033	2,681	*	*
		2013	107	11,859	9,483	2,912	40	40
37	Sewerage	2011	896	2,361	1,927	608	11	11
		2012	899	2,586	1,921	818	15	15
		2013	920	2,741	1,648	1,090	18	18
38	Waste collection, treatment and disposal activities; materials recovery	2011	4,940	18,789	6,098	12,546	111	110
		2012	5,186	17,804	5,734	11,851	105	104
		2013	5,343	18,066	5,286	12,402	102	102
39	Remediation activities and other waste management services	2011	459	148	96	55	*	*
		2012	603	311	199	123	*	*
		2013	696	372	173	204	4	4
F	Construction	2011	265,215	189,467	70,150	119,168	1,352	1,391
		2012	257,106	190,413	73,807	116,829	1,300	1,296
		2013	262,512	198,288	77,607	121,587	1,299	1,295
41	Construction of buildings	2011	73,696	71,561	23,440	47,483	393	403
		2012	67,554	75,292	27,312	47,548	369	376
		2013	69,672	79,069	29,152	50,411	363	371
42	Civil engineering	2011	20,093	39,332	12,446	27,322	200	202
		2012	19,682	37,025	12,485	24,794	207	205
		2013	20,285	39,756	13,687	26,346	196	194
43	Specialised construction activities	2011	171,426	78,575	34,264	44,362	759	786
		2012	169,870	78,095	34,010	44,487	725	715
		2013	172,555	79,463	34,768	44,829	740	730

18.1 Production and Construction Industries

	Description	Year	Total employment costs	Total net capital expenditure	Total capital expenditure- acquisitions	Total capital expenditure - disposals	Total stocks and work in progress - value at end of year	Total stocks and work in progress - value at beginning of year	Total stocks and work in progress - increase during year
Standard Industrial Classification (Revised 2007)			£ million	£ million	£ million	£ million	£ million	£ million	£ million
B-F	Production and Construction	2011	125,296	43,208	50,673	7,465	93,753	88,680	5,071
		2012	127,164	42,749	54,088	11,339	95,111	93,980	1,132
		2013	130,688	46,383	56,725	10,344	96,944	93,511	3,433
B-E	Production industries	2011	89,836	36,431	39,446	3,015	59,943	54,897	5,047
		2012	92,982	40,694	44,742	4,048	59,641	58,850	791
		2013	96,158	41,672	46,231	4,560	62,099	59,804	2,295
B	Mining and quarrying	2011	4,681	8,910	9,184	274	1,970	1,774	195
		2012	5,263	9,402	10,887	1,484	2,019	1,906	113
		2013	5,745	12,092	13,459	1,368	2,173	2,039	134
05	Mining of coal and lignite	2011	303	*	126	*	110	107	3
		2012	*	*	*	*	*	*	*
		2013	254	*	*	*	52	55	-3
06	Extraction of crude petroleum and natural gas	2011	2,120	*	8,445	*	1,137	953	184
		2012	2,388	8,927	10,201	1,274	1,055	979	76
		2013	2,757	*	*	*	1,239	1,097	142
07	Mining of metal ores	2011	2	3	3	-	-	-	-
		2012	*	*	*	*	*	*	*
		2013	-	1	1	-	-	-	-
08	Other mining and quarrying	2011	705	202	256	54	321	328	-7
		2012	854	160	238	78	417	418	-1
		2013	866	142	223	81	457	468	-11
09	Mining support service activities	2011	1,552	331	355	24	401	387	15
		2012	1,665	360	398	38	476	402	74
		2013	1,867	544	582	38	425	419	6
C	Manufacturing	2011	74,964	11,573	13,707	2,133	53,680	49,401	4,278
		2012	76,955	12,589	14,614	2,026	53,081	52,507	575
		2013	79,182	11,723	14,245	2,522	54,954	53,269	1,684
10	Manufacture of food products	2011	9,433	1,739	1,958	219	4,725	4,219	507
		2012	9,609	1,822	1,989	167	5,013	4,801	212
		2013	9,739	2,128	2,250	122	5,280	5,097	183
11	Manufacture of beverages	2011	1,820	659	*	*	5,406	5,047	359
		2012	1,780	714	*	*	5,729	5,392	337
		2013	1,880	666	811	146	6,267	5,722	546
12	Manufacture of tobacco products	2011	132	50	*	*	175	222	-48
		2012	135	84	*	*	177	173	4
		2013	154	47	49	1	170	179	-9
13	Manufacture of textiles	2011	1,144	137	153	16	745	696	48
		2012	1,086	131	143	12	710	703	7
		2013	1,094	95	106	11	740	744	-4
14	Manufacture of wearing apparel	2011	479	49	52	3	369	352	18
		2012	444	13	29	16	336	348	-13
		2013	522	33	39	6	310	301	9
15	Manufacture of leather and related products	2011	186	25	25	1	179	146	34
		2012	199	29	31	2	160	166	-6
		2013	187	21	22	2	160	144	16

18.1 Production and Construction Industries

	Description	Year	Total employment costs	Total net capital expenditure	Total capital expenditure- acquisitions	Total capital expenditure - disposals	Total stocks and work in progress - value at end of year	Total stocks and work in progress - value at beginning of year	Total stocks and work in progress - increase during year
16	Manufacture of wood and of products of wood and cork, except furniture; manufacture of articles of straw and plaiting materials	2011	1,398	128	192	64	608	623	-15
		2012	1,403	122	171	49	659	621	38
		2013	1,419	202	233	31	662	665	-3
17	Manufacture of paper and paper products	2011	1,889	310	354	43	920	828	91
		2012	1,794	340	379	39	831	897	-66
		2013	1,842	307	368	61	886	813	72
18	Printing and reproduction of recorded media	2011	2,842	280	420	140	498	485	13
		2012	2,811	288	458	170	428	437	-10
		2013	2,788	368	436	68	469	444	24
19	Manufacture of coke and refined petroleum products	2011	969	535	560	25	3,854	2,842	1,012
		2012	1,111	509	531	22	2,841	3,759	-919
		2013	781	506	563	57	3,045	2,893	152
20	Manufacture of chemicals and chemical products	2011	4,381	953	1,101	148	4,005	3,665	340
		2012	4,293	1,174	1,266	92	3,473	3,426	46
		2013	4,350	981	1,177	196	3,495	3,415	80
21	Manufacture of basic pharmaceutical products and pharmaceutical preparations	2011	1,847	438	465	27	1,893	1,878	14
		2012	2,478	428	453	24	2,075	1,984	90
		2013	2,457	473	475	3	1,934	2,008	-75
22	Manufacture of rubber and plastic products	2011	4,143	508	609	100	2,004	1,835	170
		2012	4,222	610	725	115	1,986	1,900	85
		2013	4,352	582	693	111	2,014	2,012	2
23	Manufacture of other non-metallic mineral products	2011	2,732	347	423	76	1,504	1,431	73
		2012	2,527	353	522	168	1,380	1,339	41
		2013	2,541	456	581	125	1,293	1,319	-25
24	Manufacture basic metals	2011	2,863	431	489	58	2,728	2,460	268
		2012	2,766	454	495	42	2,474	2,746	-272
		2013	2,780	364	373	9	2,362	2,479	-117
25	Manufacture of fabricated metal products, except machinery and equipment	2011	7,809	908	1,051	143	3,511	3,235	276
		2012	8,287	896	1,068	172	3,596	3,513	83
		2013	8,169	849	988	139	3,682	3,566	116
26	Manufacture of computer, electronic and optical products	2011	4,168	480	553	73	2,601	2,338	263
		2012	4,138	542	610	68	2,623	2,563	60
		2013	4,629	442	527	85	2,632	2,803	-172
27	Manufacture of electrical equipment	2011	2,545	158	236	78	1,743	1,730	13
		2012	2,727	190	297	107	1,729	1,722	7
		2013	2,821	312	357	45	1,767	1,748	19
28	Manufacture of machinery and equipment n.e.c	2011	7,016	471	847	376	4,409	3,927	482
		2012	6,674	853	962	109	4,054	4,082	-28
		2013	7,210	633	788	155	4,494	4,199	295
29	Manufacture of motor vehicles, and semi-trailers	2011	5,077	1,662	1,715	53	3,770	3,277	492
		2012	5,889	1,650	1,945	295	4,092	3,755	337
		2013	6,060	*	1,525	*	4,192	4,065	128
30	Manufacture of other transport	2011	5,322	709	858	149	5,109	5,305	-196
		2012	5,544	802	920	118	5,463	5,149	314
		2013	5,870	*	1,012	*	5,721	5,567	154
31	Manufacture of furniture	2011	1,663	124	168	44	587	533	54
		2012	1,613	124	137	13	680	656	24
		2013	1,664	142	160	18	587	570	17

18.1 Production and Construction Industries

	Description	Year	Total employment costs	Total net capital expenditure	Total capital expenditure- acquisitions	Total capital expenditure - disposals	Total stocks and work in progress - value at end of year	Total stocks and work in progress - value at beginning of year	Total stocks and work in progress - increase during year
32	Other manufacturing	2011	2,139	275	319	45	1,202	1,140	62
		2012	2,069	266	308	42	1,125	1,069	57
		2013	2,057	360	392	33	1,228	1,123	106
33	Repair and installation of machinery and equipment	2011	2,969	198	260	62	1,138	1,187	-50
		2012	3,356	193	298	105	1,448	1,304	144
		2013	3,817	248	317	69	1,565	1,394	170
D	Electricity, gas, steam and air conditioning supply	2011	5,765	9,801	10,256	455	3,381	2,935	446
		2012	6,028	11,961	12,357	396	3,557	3,446	111
		2013	6,215	11,189	11,634	446	4,055	3,458	598
E	Water supply, sewerage, waste management, and remediation activities	2011	4,426	6,147	6,299	152	913	786	127
		2012	4,736	6,742	6,884	142	983	991	-8
		2013	5,016	6,668	6,893	225	917	1,038	-121
36	Water collection, treatment and	2011	1,391	4,000	4,028	27	175	193	-17
		2012	1,534	4,330	4,356	26	180	175	5
		2013	1,656	4,315	4,348	33	193	183	10
37	Sewerage	2011	355	*	*	27	18	13	5
		2012	395	*	*	24	18	18	-
		2013	404	*	*	22	18	21	-3
38	Waste collection, treatment and disposal activities; materials recovery	2011	2,611	*	*	98	715	579	137
		2012	2,740	*	*	91	766	791	-24
		2013	2,893	*	*	169	691	824	-133
39	Remediation activities and other waste management services	2011	68	30	30	-	4	1	3
		2012	67	11	13	2	18	7	11
		2013	63	7	8	1	14	9	5
F	Construction	2011	35,460	6,777	11,227	4,451	33,809	33,784	25
		2012	34,182	2,055	9,346	7,291	35,471	35,130	341
		2013	34,530	4,711	10,494	5,783	34,845	33,707	1,138
41	Construction of buildings	2011	10,463	4,902	8,474	3,572	27,601	28,156	-554
		2012	9,636	165	6,675	6,510	28,637	29,005	-368
		2013	10,358	2,998	8,060	5,062	27,688	27,093	595
42	Civil engineering	2011	7,673	598	867	268	2,721	2,362	359
		2012	7,576	597	848	251	2,829	2,604	226
		2013	7,567	410	700	290	2,263	2,013	250
43	Specialised construction activities	2011	17,324	1,276	1,887	610	3,486	3,266	220
		2012	16,970	1,293	1,823	530	4,004	3,522	483
		2013	16,606	1,302	1,734	432	4,894	4,602	292

*   Information suppressed to avoid disclosure

..   not available

-   nil or less than half the level of rounding

Source: Annual Business Survey (ABS)

The sum of constituent items in tables may not always agree exactly with the totals shown due to rounding.

1. Total employment - point in time and Total employment - average during the year are from the Business Register and Employment Survey (BRES). Caution should be taken when combining financial data from the ABS with employment data from BRES due to differences in methodology. More information can be found in the ABS Technical Report.

18.2 UK Manufacturer's Sales by Industry

Industry	SIC(07)	2008	2009	2010	2011	2012	2013	2014
Other mining and quarrying								
Quarrying of ornamental and building stone, limestone, gypsum, chalk and slate	08110	12	9	S	12	383	S	S
Operation of gravel and sand pits; mining of clays and kaolin	08120	95	68	74	54	1,330	S	S
Mining of chemical and fertiliser minerals	08910	S	S	S	S	S	S	S
Extraction of salt	08930	S	S	S	S	331	S	S
Other mining and quarrying n.e.c.	08990	S	S	S	S	33	S	S
Manufacture of food products								
Processing and preserving of meat	10110	4,489	4,473	4,637	5,035	5,835	6,189	6,596
Processing and preserving of poultry meat	10120	2,618	2,682	2,732	2,894	2,947	3,402	3,712
Production of meat and poultry meat products	10130	5,084	5,222	5,383	5,318	5,593	5,266	5,476
Processing and preserving of fish, crustaceans and molluscs	10200	1,700	1,620	1,887	2,106	2,220	2,108	2,224
Processing and preserving of potatoes	10310	S	S	S	S	S	S	1,212
Manufacture of fruit and vegetable juice	10320	592	491	495	549	574	611	650
Other processing and preserving of fruit and vegetables	10390	2,580	2,720	2,841	2,910	2,900	3,030	3,165
Manufacture of oils and fats	10410	2,256	981	930	1,198	1,150	1,130	1,066
Manufacture of margarine and similar edible fats	10420	S	S	S	S	484	466	S
Operation of dairies and cheese making	10510	6,637	6,445	6,829	7,075	6,792	7,068	7,929
Manufacture of ice cream	10520	593	562	600	566	591	634	681
Manufacture of grain mill products	10610	3,583	3,506	3,410	3,770	3,736	S	S
Manufacture of starches and starch products	10620	437	374	304	S	319	385	325
Manufacture of bread; manufacture of fresh pastry goods and cakes	10710	5,581	5,282	S	S	5,752	6,023	6,281
Manufacture of rusks and biscuits; manufacture of preserved pastry goods and cakes	10720	3,229	S	3,695	S	3,958	4,434	4,307
Manufacture of macaroni, noodles, couscous and similar farinaceous products	10730	30	S	35	S	S	S	S
Manufacture of sugar	10810	1,108	1,128	1,076	S	1,183	1,210	1,049
Manufacture of cocoa, chocolate and sugar confectionery	10820	3,704	3,528	3,781	2,707	2,613	2,620	2,648
Processing of tea and coffee	10830	1,618	S	S	S	S	S	S
Manufacture of condiments and seasonings	10840	1,453	1,416	1,482	1,636	1,812	1,936	1,959
Manufacture of prepared meals and dishes	10850	1,781	2,302	2,477	2,546	S	S	3,116
Manufacture of homogenised food preparations and dietetic food	10860	S	30	29	33	30	29	18
Manufacture of other food products n.e.c.	10890	2,773	2,991	3,019	3,295	3,588	3,759	3,648
Manufacture of prepared feeds for farm animals	10910	3,173	3,002	3,278	3,811	3,787	4,329	4,113
Manufacture of prepared pet foods	10920	1,385	1,508	1,536	1,541	1,537	1,666	1,662
Manufacture of beverages								
Distilling, rectifying and blending of spirits	11010	2,662	2,502	S	S	3,723	S	S
Manufacture of wine from grape	11020	S	S	S	S	S	S	S
Manufacture of cider and other fruit wines	11030	547	641	574	760	771	921	859
Manufacture of other non-distilled fermented beverages	11040	0	0	0	0	0	0	0
Manufacture of beer	11050	3,757	4,766	3,914	4,081	3,269	3,297	3,286
Manufacture of malt	11060	S	418	S	377	S	S	S
Manufacture of soft drinks; production of mineral waters and other bottled waters	11070	S	3,538	3,963	S	S	S	S
Manufacture of tobacco products								
Manufacture of tobacco products	12000	1,735	1,912	1,626	1,673	1,793	1,723	1,614
Manufacture of textiles								
Preparation and spinning of textile fibres	13100	591	315	367	384	385	396	387
Weaving of textiles	13200	548	469	542	591	608	619	627
Finishing of textiles	13300	538	414	490	517	492	500	534
Manufacture of knitted and crocheted fabrics	13910	155	134	S	S	S	S	S
Manufacture of made-up textile articles, except apparel	13920	1,340	1,042	1,094	1,064	1,169	1,094	1,146
Manufacture of carpets and rugs	13930	735	691	675	S	700	708	737
Manufacture of cordage, rope, twine and netting	13940	88	64	46	52	56	50	59
Manufacture of non-wovens and articles made from non-wovens, except apparel	13950	S	S	S	172	S	178	174
Manufacture of other technical and industrial textiles	13960	S	S	279	309	293	315	332
Manufacture of other textiles n.e.c.	13990	129	102	108	108	106	114	130
Manufacture of wearing apparel								
Manufacture of leather clothes	14110	4	6	S	S	4	4	5
Manufacture of workwear	14120	255	214	191	171	147	107	100
Manufacture of other outerwear	14130	667	551	538	474	595	620	697

18.2 UK Manufacturer's Sales by Industry

Industry	SIC(07)	2008	2009	2010	2011	2012	2013	2014
Manufacture of underwear	14140	448	397	S	388	415	388	393
Manufacture of other wearing apparel and accessories	14190	250	242	215	198	223	258	285
Manufacture of articles of fur	14200	S	0	S	S	1	1	S
Manufacture of knitted and crocheted hosiery	14310	110	S	108	95	86	84	89
Manufacture of other knitted and crocheted apparel	14390	138	113	124	159	162	172	191
Manufacture of leather and related products								
Tanning and dressing of leather; dressing and dyeing of fur	15110	183	150	228	263	248	310	249
Manufacture of luggage, handbags and the like, saddlery and harness	15120	130	111	134	119	147	133	205
Manufacture of footwear	15200	S	S	S	236	252	284	264
Manufacture of wood and of products of wood and cork; except furniture; manufacture of articles of straw and plaiting materials								
Sawmilling and planing of wood	16100	891	797	897	968	985	1,037	1,136
Manufacture of veneer sheets and wood-based panels	16210	959	801	836	856	928	909	1,011
Manufacture of assembled parquet floors	16220	2	S	S	2	3	5	4
Manufacture of other builders' carpentry and joinery	16230	3,588	2,803	3,212	3,014	2,983	3,317	3,719
Manufacture of wooden containers	16240	463	388	434	401	513	492	568
Manufacture of other products of wood; manufacture of articles of cork, straw and plaiting materials	16290	441	334	332	336	328	337	415
Manufacture of paper and paper products								
Manufacture of pulp	17110	S	S	S	S	S	S	S
Manufacture of paper and paperboard	17120	2,664	2,309	2,437	2,507	2,481	2,384	2,357
Manufacture of corrugated paper and paperboard and of containers of paper and paperboard	17210	3,551	3,097	3,399	3,815	3,921	3,967	3,974
Manufacture of household and sanitary goods and of toilet requisites	17220	1,985	2,201	S	2,302	S	2,067	S
Manufacture of paper stationery	17230	756	641	548	548	531	419	456
Manufacture of wallpaper	17240	S	113	136	132	134	141	122
Manufacture of other articles of paper and paperboard	17290	1,296	970	962	989	945	999	1,153
Printing and reproduction of recorded media								
Printing of newspapers	18110	304	217	218	219	S	159	S
Other printing	18120	7,726	7,478	7,659	7,965	7,722	7,162	7,468
Pre-press and pre-media services	18130	837	470	455	404	387	381	392
Binding and related services	18140	320	275	271	232	238	243	216
Reproduction of recorded media	18200	214	167	111	S	S	110	98
Manufacture of coke and refined petroleum products								
Manufacture of coke oven products	19100	S	S	S	S	S	S	S
Manufacture of chemicals and chemical products								
Manufacture of industrial gases	20110	581	528	594	623	631	692	667
Manufacture of dyes and pigments	20120	1,124	930	1,001	1,066	914	932	972
Manufacture of other inorganic basic chemicals	20130	1,235	1,100	1,187	1,209	949	955	775
Manufacture of other organic basic chemicals	20140	4,529	3,111	3,579	3,597	2,940	2,792	2,641
Manufacture of fertilisers and nitrogen compounds	20150	1,362	1,118	1,294	1,550	1,603	1,647	1,477
Manufacture of plastics in primary forms	20160	3,564	3,038	3,518	3,930	3,524	3,543	3,530
Manufacture of synthetic rubber in primary forms	20170	503	298	392	S	S	303	173
Manufacture of pesticides and other agrochemical products	20200	520	624	577	582	605	622	651
Manufacture of paints, varnishes and similar coatings, printing ink and mastics	20300	2,977	2,761	2,847	3,086	2,950	3,068	3,357
Manufacture of soap and detergents, cleaning and polishing preparations	20410	1,550	1,662	1,755	1,752	1,784	1,754	1,749
Manufacture of perfumes and toilet preparations	20420	2,267	2,243	2,380	2,356	2,392	2,602	2,655
Manufacture of explosives	20510	163	186	171	159	154	S	133
Production of glues	20520	340	340	342	357	382	383	374
Manufacture of essential oils	20530	S	642	690	878	860	717	771
Manufacture of other chemical products n.e.c.	20590	2,681	2,645	2,612	2,606	2,456	2,630	2,548
Manufacture of man-made fibres	20600	287	211	208	256	300	200	167
Manufacture of basic pharmaceutical products and pharmaceutical preparations								
Manufacture of basic pharmaceutical products	21100	797	495	559	936	794	777	752
Manufacture of pharmaceutical preparations	21200	9,396	12,702	14,159	12,965	11,495	11,270	10,133

18.2 UK Manufacturer's Sales by Industry

Industry	SIC(07)	2008	2009	2010	2011	2012	2013	2014
Manufacture of rubber and plastic products								
Manufacture of rubber tyres and tubes; retreading and rebuilding of rubber tyres	22110	S	S	S	S	S	S	S
Manufacture of other rubber products	22190	1,542	1,276	1,399	1,607	1,602	1,571	1,607
Manufacture of plastic plates, sheets, tubes and profiles	22210	4,613	4,065	4,471	4,574	4,707	4,740	5,031
Manufacture of plastic packing goods	22220	2,878	2,651	2,852	3,295	3,441	3,255	3,426
Manufacture of builders ware of plastic	22230	4,104	3,634	3,795	3,478	3,368	4,108	4,333
Manufacture of other plastic products	22290	3,129	2,762	3,011	3,424	3,537	4,288	4,598
Manufacture of other non-metallic mineral products								
Manufacture of flat glass	23110	S	S	S	S	S	177	S
Shaping and processing of flat glass	23120	1,347	1,143	1,237	1,115	1,123	1,116	1,105
Manufacture of hollow glass	23130	585	635	654	694	724	726	750
Manufacture of glass fibres	23140	405	374	424	432	423	397	414
Manufacture and processing of other glass, including technical glassware	23190	153	119	125	172	174	S	137
Manufacture of refractory products	23200	247	237	234	276	259	246	238
Manufacture of ceramic tiles and flags	23310	91	88	76	74	78	90	95
Manufacture of bricks, tiles and construction products, in baked clay	23320	532	S	S	478	465	S	598
Manufacture of ceramic household and ornamental articles	23410	248	205	236	S	S	S	295
Manufacture of ceramic sanitary fixtures	23420	S	S	S	110	S	S	S
Manufacture of ceramic insulators and insulating fittings	23430	36	34	35	31	S	S	S
Manufacture of other technical ceramic products	23440	S	S	26	28	S	S	S
Manufacture of other ceramic products	23490	S	18	19	27	28	22	S
Manufacture of cement	23510	1,046	814	S	714	702	673	S
Manufacture of lime and plaster	23520	235	S	184	S	208	S	235
Manufacture of concrete products for construction purposes	23610	S	S	S	1,474	S	S	1,950
Manufacture of plaster products for construction purposes	23620	S	S	S	S	S	S	S
Manufacture of ready-mixed concrete	23630	1,384	1,208	1,095	1,127	1,088	1,180	1,299
Manufacture of mortars	23640	S	104	118	S	S	S	S
Manufacture of fibrecement	23650	89	S	S	S	76	70	81
Manufacture of other articles of concrete, plaster and cement	23690	163	134	S	146	167	S	S
Cutting, shaping and finishing of stone	23700	445	463	402	420	414	404	418
Production of abrasive products	23910	S	109	90	100	S	140	139
Manufacture of other non-metallic mineral products n.e.c.	23990	1,063	1,280	1,320	1,484	1,517	1,459	1,578
Manufacture of basic metals								
Manufacture of tubes, pipes, hollow profiles and related fittings, of steel	24200	1,603	S	1,266	1,544	1,557	1,317	1,197
Cold drawing of bars	24310	153	76	128	190	168	150	152
Cold rolling of narrow strip	24320	98	31	S	S	S	S	S
Cold forming or folding	24330	S	S	S	S	S	S	S
Cold drawing of wire	24340	S	S	S	S	157	153	140
Precious metals production	24410	504	443	643	875	481	371	260
Aluminium production	24420	2,061	1,211	1,478	1,646	1,259	1,124	1,177
Lead, zinc and tin production	24430	461	S	541	529	507	506	513
Copper production	24440	735	454	637	727	615	577	471
Other non-ferrous metal production	24450	1,317	923	1,046	1,011	1,017	970	933
Casting of iron	24510	427	256	316	421	415	411	413
Casting of steel	24520	332	299	287	388	333	351	297
Casting of light metals	24530	421	294	362	388	359	401	432
Casting of other non-ferrous metals	24540	206	157	184	224	224	188	184
Manufacture of fabricated metal products; except machinery and equipment								
Manufacture of metal structures and parts of structures	25110	6,944	5,801	5,418	5,682	5,463	5,407	6,015
Manufacture of doors and windows of metal	25120	1,597	1,278	1,235	1,217	1,286	1,375	1,516
Manufacture of central heating radiators and boilers	25210	832	S	787	798	803	870	900
Manufacture of other tanks, reservoirs and containers of metal	25290	455	379	324	395	430	429	415
Manufacture of steam generators, except central heating hot water boilers	25300	578	S	S	S	S	S	S
Manufacture of weapons and ammunition	25400	2,709	2,912	2,032	1,941	1,881	1,667	1,478
Forging, pressing, stamping and roll-forming of metal; powder metallurgy	25500	1,958	1,319	1,608	1,839	1,968	1,900	1,968
Treatment and coating of metals	25610	1,223	1,054	1,045	1,187	1,263	1,325	1,341
Machining	25620	4,098	3,383	3,629	4,243	4,559	4,825	5,068
Manufacture of cutlery	25710	S	21	20	23	25	22	24
Manufacture of locks and hinges	25720	573	491	537	561	514	498	534
Manufacture of tools	25730	857	730	796	799	825	867	959

18.2 UK Manufacturer's Sales by Industry

Industry	SIC(07)	2008	2009	2010	2011	2012	2013	2014
Manufacture of steel drums and similar containers	25910	113	96	107	112	106	S	S
Manufacture of light metal packaging	25920	1,357	S	1,533	1,499	1,395	S	S
Manufacture of wire products, chain and springs	25930	937	768	857	904	782	800	780
Manufacture of fasteners and screw machine products	25940	412	340	364	454	469	476	512
Manufacture of other fabricated metal products n.e.c.	25990	1,836	1,386	1,595	1,747	1,810	1,906	2,020
Manufacture of computer; electronic and optical products								
Manufacture of electronic components	26110	1,378	1,048	1,296	1,301	897	1,104	828
Manufacture of loaded electronic boards	26120	576	937	1,044	1,256	1,167	1,017	887
Manufacture of computers and peripheral equipment	26200	1,373	1,359	1,182	1,270	1,182	1,403	S
Manufacture of communication equipment	26300	2,085	1,754	1,736	1,691	1,460	1,362	1,269
Manufacture of consumer electronics	26400	1,382	S	S	404	383	355	405
Manufacture of instruments and appliances for measuring, testing and navigation	26510	4,838	4,817	5,112	5,544	5,658	5,668	5,895
Manufacture of watches and clocks	26520	31	S	34	30	31	24	22
Manufacture of irradiation, electromedical and electrotherapeutic equipment	26600	837	787	S	S	S	S	S
Manufacture of optical instruments and photographic equipment	26700	357	304	332	394	374	333	351
Manufacture of magnetic and optical media	26800	11	12	9	S	13	S	11
Manufacture of electrical equipment								
Manufacture of electric motors, generators and transformers	27110	2,749	2,187	2,602	3,153	3,060	2,763	2,581
Manufacture of electricity distribution and control apparatus	27120	1,664	1,465	1,891	2,086	2,173	2,288	2,352
Manufacture of batteries and accumulators	27200	S	224	247	S	259	S	274
Manufacture of fibre optic cables	27310	110	92	124	S	114	97	106
Manufacture of other electronic and electric wires and cables	27320	1,240	952	1,263	1,399	1,311	1,206	1,218
Manufacture of wiring devices	27330	656	423	576	601	S	590	560
Manufacture of electric lighting equipment	27400	1,324	1,020	1,142	1,293	1,334	1,352	1,542
Manufacture of electric domestic appliances	27510	1,424	1,272	1,277	1,268	1,156	1,186	900
Manufacture of non-electric domestic appliances	27520	S	406	427	463	346	359	S
Manufacture of other electrical equipment	27900	1,436	1,101	1,356	1,211	1,231	1,208	1,191
Manufacture of machinery and equipment n.e.c.								
Manufacture of engines and turbines, except aircraft, vehicle and cycle engines	28110	4,364	3,263	3,662	4,303	4,232	3,623	3,782
Manufacture of fluid power equipment	28120	887	606	791	977	1,037	979	1,054
Manufacture of other pumps and compressors	28130	2,282	1,984	2,175	2,447	2,215	2,167	2,014
Manufacture of other taps and valves	28140	1,141	1,063	1,103	1,303	1,400	1,729	2,435
Manufacture of bearings, gears, gearing and driving elements	28150	1,105	812	903	1,027	1,004	993	1,048
Manufacture of ovens, furnaces and furnace burners	28210	289	239	222	271	295	220	203
Manufacture of lifting and handling equipment	28220	2,684	1,965	1,842	2,132	2,326	2,365	2,549
Manufacture of office machinery and equipment (except computers and peripheral equipment)	28230	419	410	524	548	607	S	700**
Manufacture of power-driven hand tools	28240	S	70	100	S	151	166	174
Manufacture of non-domestic cooling and ventilation equipment	28250	2,717	S	2,502	2,371	2,260	2,286	2,558
Manufacture of other general-purpose machinery n.e.c.	28290	2,246	1,969	1,990	2,090	2,125	2,163	2,350
Manufacture of agricultural and forestry machinery	28300	1,378	1,177	1,275	1,483	1,767	1,618	1,592
Manufacture of metal forming machinery	28410	488	334	389	554	679	663	650
Manufacture of other machine tools	28490	300	247	280	329	351	303	324
Manufacture of machinery for metallurgy	28910	S	60	76	97	82	88	86
Manufacture of machinery for mining, quarrying and construction	28920	4,108	2,171	2,894	4,087	4,471	4,291	4,238
Manufacture of machinery for food, beverage and tobacco processing	28930	481	424	467	461	428	479	481
Manufacture of machinery for textile, apparel and leather production	28940	91	77	67	82	59	58	63
Manufacture of machinery for paper and paperboard production	28950	126	109	134	135	126	125	107
Manufacture of plastics and rubber machinery	28960	107	51	68	86	78	70	60
Manufacture of other special-purpose machinery n.e.c.	28990	1,415	972	1,181	1,252	1,227	1,051	1,197
Manufacture of motor vehicles; trailers and semi-trailers								
Manufacture of motor vehicles	29100	24,382	18,506	25,590	27,516	28,004	34,204	35,926
Manufacture of bodies (coachwork) for motor vehicles; manufacture of trailers and semi-trailers	29200	2,634	1,890	2,097	2,165	2,153	1,904	2,058
Manufacture of electrical and electronic equipment for motor vehicles	29310	666	515	S	544	346	S	258
Manufacture of other parts and accessories for motor vehicles	29320	8,970	6,345	8,301	8,222	8,794	8,618	9,100
Manufacture of other transport equipment								
Building of ships and floating structures	30110	2,171	2,456	2,756	2,903	S	3,775	S
Building of pleasure and sporting boats	30120	945	842	850	792	824	747	665

18.2 UK Manufacturer's Sales by Industry

Industry	SIC(07)	2008	2009	2010	2011	2012	2013	2014
Manufacture of railway locomotives and rolling stock	30200	S	S	S	1,366	S	S	1,083
Manufacture of air and spacecraft and related machinery	30300	14,283	15,815	15,378	15,853	17,265	20,316	20,692
Manufacturer of military fighting vehicles	30400	412	430	513	S	S	S	S
Manufacture of motorcycles	30910	S	S	S	S	S	S	S
Manufacture of bicycles and invalid carriages	30920	101	115	115	113	129	134	148
Manufacture of other transport equipment n.e.c.	30990	72	51	41	S	S	40	44
Manufacture of furniture								
Manufacture of office and shop furniture	31010	1,452	1,032	1,011	1,100	1,217	1,081	1,189
Manufacture of kitchen furniture	31020	1,098	1,016	1,036	1,055	1,094	1,356	1,349
Manufacture of mattresses	31030	536	544	587	S	579	612	694
Manufacture of other furniture	31090	3,170	2,783	2,988	3,084	3,208	3,257	3,356
Other manufacturing								
Striking of coins	32110	S	184	206	S	S	S	S
Manufacture of jewellery and related articles	32120	370	S	411	437	420	428	428
Manufacture of imitation jewellery and related articles	32130	S	44	48	45	37	36	41
Manufacture of musical instruments	32200	27	24	16	18	20	22	21
Manufacture of sports goods	32300	293	S	324	369	344	348	353
Manufacture of games and toys	32400	205	210	171	162	155	210	316
Manufacture of medical and dental instruments and supplies	32500	2,753	2,783	2,667	2,541	2,629	2,597	2,719
Manufacture of brooms and brushes	32910	112	105	105	91	85	79	100
Other manufacturing n.e.c.	32990	606	589	531	572	662	694	634
Repair and installation of machinery and equipment								
Repair of fabricated metal products	33110	666	455	800	977	1,017	1,236	1,119
Repair of machinery	33120	3,251	3,130	2,759	2,983	3,034	3,150	3,114
Repair of electronic and optical equipment	33130	S	654	618	631	598	S	772
Repair of electrical equipment	33140	619	522	439	476	528	537	492
Repair and maintenance of ships and boats	33150	378	327	338	331	404	456	459
Repair and maintenance of aircraft and spacecraft	33160	2,767	2,904	2,557	S	3,333	3,488	3,589
Repair and maintenance of other transport equipment	33170	747	S	S	S	855	1,119	S
Repair of other equipment	33190	3	S	S	S	S	S	S
Installation of industrial machinery and equipment	33200	3,307	2,914	S	3,379	3,273	3,214	3,348
Total		331,894	299,845	324,799	341,031	341,985	354,721	363,947

Source: Office for National Statistics

Note: Information in this table relate to products corresponding to an industry irrespective of which SIC the business making the product is classified.

**Note: This value has been unsuppressed and rounded to the nearest £100 million to allow it to be published

S - A volume or unit value suppressed as disclosive

Previous PRODCOM codes and the incorporation of additional back data
Following user feedback for a longer time series to aid statistical analysis of trends, 2008 and 2009 back data were included to these reference tables at provisional 2014 results, in addition to the 2010 to 2014 data. However, caution should be exercised when comparing certain values, due to the continuously evolving nature of the PRODCOM question list which is set by Eurostat, the European Union's Statistical Authority, in the face of new or changing products and industries. The changes can make backwards comparability difficult, as some codes may appear or disappear in future publications. In this publication, only products included in the most recent PRODCOM list have been included. This leads to difficulties with some aggregate figures in previous years, where the parts do not sum to the whole; this is caused by some of those parts being now-defunct product codes that are not included here, so the sum of the actual values in the table may not equal the aggregate total.

Suppression of data
Statistical disclosure control methodology is applied to PRODCOM data. This ensures that information attributable to an individual or individual organisation is not identifiable in any published outputs. The Code of Practice for Official Statistics, and specifically the Principle on Confidentiality (P.C) set out practices for how ONS protects data from being disclosed. The P.C includes the statement that ONS outputs should "ensure that official statistics do not reveal the identity of an individual or organisation, or any private information relating to them, taking into account other relevant sources of information". More information can be found in National Statistician's Guidance: Confidentiality of Official Statistics, on the statistical disclosure control methodology page of the ONS website.

18.3 United Kingdom Business Entities - Number of Local Units by 2 Digit SIC and Employment Size Band, 2014

	Local Units Employment Size Bands:							
	Total	0-4	5-9	10-19	20-49	50-99	100-249	250+
SIC07 : Total	2,721,240	1,862,395	393,555	227,675	148,470	50,435	26,900	11,810
SIC07 : 01 : Crop and animal production; hunting and related service activities	140,700	123,530	12,770	3,000	1,010	235	115	40
SIC07 : 02 : Forestry and logging	3,885	3,255	385	160	65	20	0	0
SIC07 : 03 : Fishing and aquaculture	4,015	3,585	310	95	20	5	0	0
SIC07 : 05 : Mining of coal and lignite	30	5	0	0	5	10	5	5
SIC07 : 06 : Extraction of crude petroleum and natural gas	170	75	25	10	15	10	15	20
SIC07 : 07 : Mining of metal ores	0	0	0	0	0	0	0	0
SIC07 : 08 : Other mining and quarrying	1,455	715	305	240	150	30	15	0
SIC07 : 09 : Mining support service activities	430	265	35	35	25	40	15	15
SIC07 : 10 : Manufacture of food products	8,420	3,450	1,600	1,180	930	475	420	365
SIC07 : 11 : Manufacture of beverages	1,625	980	230	165	125	45	50	30
SIC07 : 12 : Manufacture of tobacco products	10	5	5	0	0	0	0	0
SIC07 : 13 : Manufacture of textiles	4,085	2,345	740	470	330	105	80	15
SIC07 : 14 : Manufacture of wearing apparel	3,595	2,265	625	410	215	60	15	5
SIC07 : 15 : Manufacture of leather and related products	585	350	100	55	45	20	10	5
SIC07 : 16 : Manufacture of wood and of products of wood and cork; except furniture; manufacture of articles of straw and plaiting materials	7,895	5,090	1,330	805	460	150	50	10
SIC07 : 17 : Manufacture of paper and paper products	1,700	690	225	230	245	145	135	30
SIC07 : 18 : Printing and reproduction of recorded media	13,380	9,035	2,090	1,185	710	210	120	30
SIC07 : 19 : Manufacture of coke and refined petroleum products	155	60	20	20	20	15	10	10
SIC07 : 20 : Manufacture of chemicals and chemical products	3,015	1,340	440	370	425	215	160	65
SIC07 : 21 : Manufacture of basic pharmaceutical products and pharmaceutical preparations	595	345	55	35	40	35	35	50
SIC07 : 22 : Manufacture of rubber and plastic products	6,320	2,490	1,170	1,050	865	415	255	75
SIC07 : 23 : Manufacture of other non-metallic mineral products	5,000	2,730	865	635	435	190	110	35
SIC07 : 24 : Manufacture of basic metals	1,665	755	215	210	250	120	75	40
SIC07 : 25 : Manufacture of fabricated metal products; except machinery and equipment	26,480	15,340	4,505	3,290	2,265	725	295	60
SIC07 : 26 : Manufacture of computer; electronic and optical products	6,405	3,710	905	665	600	295	165	65
SIC07 : 27 : Manufacture of electrical equipment	3,265	1,480	485	455	445	215	135	50
SIC07 : 28 : Manufacture of machinery and equipment n.e.c.	8,550	4,330	1,465	1,030	950	415	260	100
SIC07 : 29 : Manufacture of motor vehicles; trailers and semi-trailers	2,945	1,545	445	300	265	170	120	100
SIC07 : 30 : Manufacture of other transport equipment	2,300	1,475	255	150	135	100	90	95
SIC07 : 31 : Manufacture of furniture	6,230	3,690	1,070	705	455	180	95	35
SIC07 : 32 : Other manufacturing	10,040	6,945	1,705	745	415	115	85	30
SIC07 : 33 : Repair and installation of machinery and equipment	13,050	10,020	1,355	830	495	185	105	60
SIC07 : 35 : Electricity; gas; steam and air conditioning supply	3,595	2,365	390	285	185	140	130	100
SIC07 : 36 : Water collection; treatment and supply	945	395	185	140	110	60	30	25
SIC07 : 37 : Sewerage	1,390	750	245	165	150	50	20	10
SIC07 : 38 : Waste collection; treatment and disposal activities; materials recovery	7,795	4,060	1,390	970	835	340	160	40
SIC07 : 39 : Remediation activities and other waste management services	785	545	125	80	30	5	0	0
SIC07 : 41 : Construction of buildings	76,630	64,225	7,060	2,935	1,450	560	320	80

18.3 United Kingdom Business Entities - Number of Local Units by 2 Digit SIC and Employment Size Band, 2014

	Total	0-4	5-9	10-19	20-49	50-99	100-249	250+
					Local Units Employment Size Bands:			
SIC07 : 42 : Civil engineering	21,870	16,085	2,690	1,405	970	400	220	100
SIC07 : 43 : Specialised construction activities	176,915	146,450	17,710	7,875	3,530	930	345	75
SIC07 : 45 : Wholesale and retail trade and repair of motor vehicles and motorcycles	78,555	52,200	14,900	6,075	4,065	1,040	245	30
SIC07 : 46 : Wholesale trade; except of motor vehicles and motorcycles	124,970	77,725	22,335	14,000	7,465	2,175	940	330
SIC07 : 47 : Retail trade; except of motor vehicles and motorcycles	287,590	164,680	65,540	33,675	16,090	3,775	2,360	1,470
SIC07 : 49 : Land transport and transport via pipelines	49,895	36,155	5,715	3,770	2,430	930	595	300
SIC07 : 50 : Water transport	1,605	1,100	225	140	90	25	20	5
SIC07 : 51 : Air transport	1,165	715	130	100	75	40	60	45
SIC07 : 52 : Warehousing and support activities for transportation	18,840	10,210	3,025	2,200	1,845	790	495	275
SIC07 : 53 : Postal and courier activities	17,570	12,630	1,710	970	1,080	705	345	130
SIC07 : 55 : Accommodation	19,960	7,800	3,595	3,375	3,180	1,255	660	95
SIC07 : 56 : Food and beverage service activities	151,850	63,885	42,500	26,880	15,570	2,300	595	120
SIC07 : 58 : Publishing activities	11,430	8,470	1,255	790	525	190	120	80
SIC07 : 59 : Motion picture; video and television programme production; sound recording and music publishing activities	21,605	19,055	1,010	665	535	235	75	30
SIC07 : 60 : Programming and broadcasting activities	2,110	1,685	165	105	90	30	20	15
SIC07 : 61 : Telecommunications	11,065	7,750	1,250	790	640	260	220	155
SIC07 : 62 : Computer programming; consultancy and related activities	133,425	119,515	6,355	3,815	2,340	795	415	190
SIC07 : 63 : Information service activities	7,790	6,240	750	405	215	80	55	45
SIC07 : 64 : Financial service activities; except insurance and pension funding	25,975	13,235	6,050	3,800	1,975	350	255	310
SIC07 : 65 : Insurance; reinsurance and pension funding; except compulsory social security	6,485	5,680	205	175	140	85	80	120
SIC07 : 66 : Activities auxiliary to financial services and insurance activities	32,120	23,100	4,255	2,150	1,370	580	415	250
SIC07 : 68 : Real estate activities	97,300	75,620	13,320	5,540	1,820	510	390	100
SIC07 : 69 : Legal and accounting activities	75,600	55,755	9,605	5,765	2,970	840	430	235
SIC07 : 70 : Activities of head offices; management consultancy activities	150,630	136,390	7,055	3,690	2,035	765	450	245
SIC07 : 71 : Architectural and engineering activities; technical testing and analysis	90,640	76,835	6,530	3,925	2,185	700	325	140
SIC07 : 72 : Scientific research and development	4,950	3,340	515	385	315	165	135	95
SIC07 : 73 : Advertising and market research	22,195	17,765	2,080	1,130	705	255	175	85
SIC07 : 74 : Other professional; scientific and technical activities	65,870	59,130	4,235	1,650	645	150	50	10
SIC07 : 75 : Veterinary activities	5,240	2,255	1,280	1,125	510	55	15	0
SIC07 : 77 : Rental and leasing activities	20,335	13,320	3,625	2,035	970	245	120	20
SIC07 : 78 : Employment activities	26,100	14,780	3,090	2,285	2,400	1,650	1,285	610
SIC07 : 79 : Travel agency; tour operator and other reservation service and related activities	10,580	6,265	2,645	965	410	175	85	35
SIC07 : 80 : Security and investigation activities	9,580	6,475	1,150	745	575	280	210	145
SIC07 : 81 : Services to buildings and landscape activities	52,060	35,825	8,005	4,215	2,305	840	520	350
SIC07 : 82 : Office administrative; office support and other business support activities	73,175	61,145	6,335	3,195	1,445	515	340	200
SIC07 : 84 : Public administration and defence; compulsory social security	25,475	9,905	3,360	3,495	3,770	2,005	1,645	1,295
SIC07 : 85 : Education	69,915	23,425	8,800	8,800	15,180	8,265	4,490	955
SIC07 : 86 : Human health activities	67,665	32,825	12,410	10,700	7,595	2,060	1,245	830
SIC07 : 87 : Residential care activities	30,515	7,970	4,505	6,025	7,900	3,345	690	80

18.3 United Kingdom Business Entities - Number of Local Units by 2 Digit SIC and Employment Size Band, 2014

				Local Units Employment Size Bands:					
	Total	0-4	5-9	10-19	20-49	50-99	100-249	250+
SIC07 : 88 : Social work activities without accommodation	60,615	23,175	13,710	11,960	8,230	2,320	995	225
SIC07 : 90 : Creative; arts and entertainment activities	28,740	26,005	1,465	640	360	165	90	15
SIC07 : 91 : Libraries; archives; museums and other cultural activities	6,150	2,890	1,385	865	655	220	95	40
SIC07 : 92 : Gambling and betting activities	11,745	4,130	6,555	395	445	120	85	15
SIC07 : 93 : Sports activities and amusement and recreation activities	32,175	18,340	5,105	4,140	2,900	1,095	480	115
SIC07 : 94 : Activities of membership organisations	25,450	16,470	4,650	2,410	1,280	365	205	70
SIC07 : 95 : Repair of computers and personal and household goods	8,515	7,020	810	395	185	60	30	15
SIC07 : 96 : Other personal service activities	68,095	46,735	14,835	4,935	1,290	195	85	20
SIC07 : 97 : Activities of households as employers of domestic personnel	0	0	0	0	0	0	0	0
SIC07 : 98 : Undifferentiated goods- and services-producing activities of private households for own use	0	0	0	0	0	0	0	0
SIC07 : 99 : Activities of extraterritorial organisations and bodies	5	5	0	0	0	0	0	0

Source: Office for National Statistics

18.4 Production of primary fuels

United Kingdom

Million tonnes of oil equivalent

	1999	2000	2001	2002	2003	2004	2005	2006	2007	2008	2009	2010	2011	2012	2013	2014
Coal	23.2	19.6	20.0	18.8	17.6	15.6	12.7	11.4	10.7	11.3	11.0	11.4r	11.5r	10.6r	8.0r	7.3
Petroleum [1]	150.2	138.3	127.8	127.0	116.2	104.5	92.9	84.0	83.9	78.7	74.7	69.0	56.9	48.8	44.5	43.7
Natural Gas [2]	99.1	108.4	105.9	103.6	103.0	96.4	88.2	80.0	72.1	69.7	59.7	57.2	45.3	38.9	36.5	36.6
Primary electricity [3]	22.9	20.2	21.2	20.6	20.4	18.7	19.0	17.9	14.9	13.0r	16.5r	15.1r	17.5r	17.5r	18.5r	17.5
Renewable energy [4]	2.3	2.3	2.5	2.8	3.0	3.1	3.7	4.0	4.3	18.0	21.9	32.4	35.1	34.9	33.9	7.9
Total Production	297.7	288.7	277.4	272.9	260.3	238.4	216.5	197.2	186.0	177.7	167.4	158.6	137.3	122.6	114.9	112.9

r - revised data

Source: Department of Energy and Climate Change

(1) Crude oil plus all condensates and petroleum gases extracted at gas separation plants.

(2) Includes colliery methane.

(3) Nuclear and natural flow hydro electricty excluding generation of pumped storage stations. From 1988 includes generation at wind stations.

(4) Includes solar and geothermal heat, solid renewable sources (wood, waste, etc), and gaseous renewable sources (landfill gas, sewage gas) from 1988.

Datasource
DUKES 1.1.2

18.5 Total inland energy consumption

United Kingdom

Million tonnes of oil equivalent

	1999	2000	2001	2002	2003	2004	2005	2006	2007	2008	2009	2010	2011	2012	2013	2014
Inland energy consumption of primary fuels and equivalents	231.3	234.8	236.9	229.6	231.9	233.6	236.3	233.1	227.5	225.6r	211.7r	219.4r	203.4r	208.0r	207.0r	193.4
Coal	36.0	38.5	40.8	37.7	40.5	39.1	39.9	43.4	41.0	38.2	31.2	32.6	32.2	40.9	39.1	31.7
Petroleum	76.4	76.7	75.9	73.5	73.0	75.1	78.2	77.4	76.3	74.4	70.9	70.2	67.8	67.0	66.1	65.8
Primary electricity	24.2	21.4	22.1	21.3	20.6	19.4	19.8	18.5	15.4	13.9r	16.7r	15.3r	18.0r	18.5r	19.7r	19.2
Natural gas	92.5	95.9	95.6	94.3	94.6	96.6	94.3	89.4	90.2	93.2	86.3	93.6	77.6	73.3	72.7	65.9
Renewables and waste	2.2	2.3	2.5	2.8	3.1	3.5	4.2	4.4	4.7	6.0	6.7	7.6	7.7	8.3	9.4	10.7
Total consumption by final users	156.5	159.4	160.9	156.5	158.1	159.9	159.7	157.0	154.3	154.5	144.0	150.6	138.4	142.4	143.3	135.3
Final energy consumption by type of fuel																
Coal (direct use)	3.5	2.7	2.7	2.2	2.1	2.0	1.7	1.6	1.8	1.8	1.7	1.9	1.8	1.7	1.9	1.9
Coke and breeze	0.9	0.8	0.8	0.7	0.7	0.6	0.6	0.5	0.5	0.5	0.4	0.3	0.3	0.4	0.5	0.5
Other solid fuel	0.6	0.6	0.5	0.5	0.4	0.4	0.4	0.4	0.4	0.4	0.2	0.2	0.2	0.2	0.2	0.2
Coke oven gas	0.2	0.2	0.2	0.1	0.1	0.1	0.1	0.1	0.1	0.1	0.0	0.1	0.1	0.0	0.1	0.1
Natural gas (direct use)	55.1	57.1	57.8	55.2	56.7	57.1	55.4	52.6	50.0	51.8	46.6	51.9	42.8	47.1	47.4	40.2
Electricity	27.8	28.3	28.6	28.7	28.9	29.1	30.0	29.7	29.4	29.4	27.7	28.3	27.3	27.3	27.3	26.1
Petroleum (direct use)	65.1	66.3	67.1	66.1	66.8	68.6	69.5	69.8	69.5	66.5	63.4	63.2	61.5	61.1	60.8	61.0
Renewables [6]	0.7	0.7	0.7	0.7	0.7	0.7	0.8	1.0	1.2	2.4	2.7	3.3	3.1	3.2	3.8	4.1
Heat	2.5	2.5	2.3	2.1	1.8	1.3	1.3	1.2	1.3	1.5	1.2	1.3	1.2	1.2	1.4	1.3
Final energy consumption by class of consumer																
Agriculture	1.3	1.2	1.3	1.2	0.9	0.9	1.0	0.9	0.9	0.9	0.9	1.0	0.9	1.0	1.0	1.0
Iron and steel industry	3.8	2.2	2.3	2.0	1.9	1.9	1.8	1.9	1.8	1.6	1.2	1.4	1.3	1.2	1.3	1.4
Other industries	30.5	33.3	33.2	31.8	32.1	31.0	30.5	29.6	28.8	27.5	23.2	24.7	23.1	22.7	22.5r	22.4
Railways	1.4	1.4	1.4	1.4	1.4	1.0	1.0	1.0	1.0	1.0	1.0	1.0	1.0	1.0	1.0	1.1
Road transport	41.4	41.1	41.1	41.9	41.8	42.2	42.6	42.7	43.2	41.9	40.7	40.4	39.8	39.5	39.3	40.0
Water transport	1.1	1.0	0.8	0.7	1.2	1.2	1.4	1.8	1.6	1.0	1.0	0.9	0.9	0.8	0.8	0.7
Air transport	11.0	12.0	11.8	11.7	11.9	12.9	13.9	14.0	13.9	13.4	12.8	12.3	12.8	12.4	12.4	12.4
Domestic	46.1	46.9	48.2	47.5	48.3	49.3	47.8	46.6	44.9	46.0	44.6	49.3	39.5	44.5	44.8r	38.2
Public administration	8.2	8.1	8.0	7.0	6.7	7.2	7.1	6.6	6.3	7.0	6.2	6.4	6.1	6.2	6.3	5.6
Commercial and other services	11.8	12.2	12.8	11.3	11.8	12.2	12.7	12.0	11.8	14.1	12.6	13.2	13.0	13.2	13.5r	12.4

Source: Department of Energy and Climate Change

Datasource — **Location**
DUKES 1.1.2 — https://www.gov.uk/government/publications/energy-chapter-1-digest-of-united-kingdom-energy-statistics-dukes
DUKES 1.1.5 — https://www.gov.uk/government/publications/energy-chapter-1-digest-of-united-kingdom-energy-statistics-dukes
DUKES 1.1-1.3 — https://www.gov.uk/government/publications/energy-chapter-1-digest-of-united-kingdom-energy-statistics-dukes
((-Transformation in total column) + industry use + losses) in DUKES 1.1-1.3

18.6 Coal: supply and demand

United Kingdom

Million tonnes

	1999	2000	2001	2002	2003	2004	2005	2006	2007	2008	2009	2010	2011	2012	2013	2014
Supply																
Production of deep-mined coal	20.9	17.2	17.3	16.4	15.6	12.5	9.6	9.4	7.7	8.1	7.5	7.4	7.3	6.2	4.1	3.7
Production of opencast coal	15.3	13.4	14.2	13.1	12.1	12.0	10.4	8.6	8.9	9.5	9.9	10.4	10.6	10.1	8.6	8.0
Total	36.2	30.6	31.5	29.5	27.8	24.5	20.0	18.1	16.5	17.6	17.4	17.8	17.9	16.3	12.7	11.7
Recovered slurry, fines, etc	0.9	0.6	0.4	0.4	0.5	0.6	0.5	0.4	0.5	0.4	0.5	0.5	0.7	0.7	0.1	0.0
Imports	20.3	23.4	35.5	28.7	31.9	36.2	44.0	50.5	43.4	43.9	38.2	26.5	32.5	44.8	49.4	42.2
Total	57.4	54.6	67.5	58.7	60.2	61.2	64.5	69.0	60.4	61.9	56.0	44.9	51.1	61.8	62.2	53.9
Change in stocks at collieries and opencast sites	-0.6	3.5	0.1	-0.9	0.9	0.4	0.1	0.3	0.0	-0.1	-0.6	-0.1	0.6	-0.2	0.6r	-0.1
Total supply	56.8	58.2	67.5	57.8	61.0	61.7	64.6	69.4	60.4	61.8	55.4	44.8	51.7	61.6	62.8r	53.9
Home consumption																
Total home consumption	55.4	59.8	63.5	58.6	62.9	60.6	61.8	67.3	62.9	58.2	48.8	51.4	51.4	64.3	60.3r	48.5
Overseas shipments and bunkers	0.8	0.7	0.5	0.5	0.5	0.6	0.5	0.4	0.5	0.6	0.6	0.7	0.5	0.5	0.6	0.4
Total consumption and shipments	56.2	60.5	64.1	59.2	63.4	61.2	62.3	67.8	63.4	58.8	49.4	52.1	51.9	64.7	60.9r	48.9
Change in distributed stocks	-0.6	2.3	-3.5	1.4	2.4	-0.5	-1.9	-1.9	3.0	-3.0	-6.2	7.3	0.3	3.2	-1.9r	-4.9
Balance	0.0	0.0	0.0	0.0	0.0	0.0	0.3	-0.3	0.0	0.0	-0.2	0.0	0.0	0.1	0.0	0.0
Stocks at end of year																
Distributed	14.8	12.4	15.9	14.5	12.1	12.6	14.5	16.4	13.4	16.4	22.6	15.4	15.1	11.9	13.8r	18.6
At collieries and opencast sites	5.2	1.6	1.6	2.5	1.6	1.2	1.1	0.8	0.7	0.9	1.4	1.5	0.9	1.1	0.5r	0.6
Total stocks	19.9	14.1	17.5	17.0	13.7	13.8	15.6	17.2	14.2	17.2	24.1	16.9	16.0	13.0	14.3	19.3

Source: Department of Energy and Climate Change

18.7 Fuel input and gas output: gas consumption

United Kingdom

Giga-watt hours

	2001	2002	2003	2004	2005	2006	2007	2008	2009	2010	2011	2012	2013	2014
Analysis of gas consumption														
Transformation sector	336,525	351,856	344,410	362,668	354,146	333,431	379,518	402,236	382,061	400,828r	332,012r	241,634r	231,049r	244,423
Electricity generation	312,939	329,847	324,580	340,824	331,658	311,408	355,878	376,810	359,303	377,121r	309,076r	216,543r	206,322r	218,395
Heat generation	23,586	22,009	19,830	21,844	22,488	22,023	23,640	25,426	22,758	23,707	22,936	25,091	24,727r	26,028
Energy industry use total	91,451	91,260	88,907	88,468	87,161	81,859	76,025	72,280	70,597	71,219r	62,905r	56,333r	53,873r	49,379
Oil and gas extraction	78,457	79,364	76,837	77,753	73,372	69,252	64,230	61,292	61,110	61,124	53,163	48,461	46,556	42,494
Petroleum refineries	4,189	3,350	2,773	3,076	5,163	5,161	5,206	4,971	1,601	1,785	1,757	1,619	1,151	1,140
Coal extraction and coke manufacture	220	196	188	150	114	112	91	95	217	260	223	194	158	168
Blast furnaces	375	222	539	728	941	611	719	718	450	641	453	266	363	338
Other	8,210	8,128	8,570	6,761	7,572	6,723	5,779	5,204	7,218	7,409r	7,309r	5,793r	5,645r	5,240
Final consumption total	683,753	653,151	669,457	673,860	652,024	620,035	591,274	599,018	550,142	611,526r	503,762r	553,867r	556,475r	472,401
Iron and steel industry	8,502	8,791	10,327	9,715	8,453	8,391	7,323	6,920	5,346	6,124	5,829	5,091	5,338	5,448
Other industries	171,341	156,375	155,890	144,238	142,988	136,150	126,028	127,013	4,900	5,373	5,155	5,071r	5,178r	5,027
Domestic	379,426	376,372	386,486	396,411	381,879	366,928	352,868	359,554	344,499	389,595	293,400	345,080	342,501r	278,101
Public administration	46,232	42,998	44,362	51,934	50,319	45,803	42,444	45,665	42,372	45,473	42,960	43,243	44,419r	36,969
Commercial	37,098	36,224	39,537	37,595	38,197	34,273	33,098	38,448	53,025	57,320	55,757	57,377	57,791r	48,443
Agriculture	2,329	2,346	2,324	2,355	2,261	2,013	1,998	2,161	1,468	1,619	1,351	1,162	1,096	886
Miscellaneous	27,452	19,265	20,510	21,591	20,014	18,564	17,286	11,052	10,627	10,501r	9,830r	9,711r	12,065r	10,079
Non energy use	11,373	10,780	10,021	10,021	7,913	7,913	10,228	8,206	6,887	8,089	5,949	5,771	5,598	5,430
Total gas consumption	1,111,729	1,096,267	1,102,774	1,124,996	1,093,331	1,035,325	1,046,817	1,073,535	1,013,943	1,096,368r	908,605r	859,725r	848,871r	773,059

Source: Department of Energy and Climate Change

Data source
DUKES 4.2 - Supply and consumption of natural gas and colliery methane

Location
https://www.gov.uk/government/publications/natural-gas-chapter-4-digest-of-united-kingdom-energy-statistics-dukes

18.8 Electricity: generation, supply and consumption

United Kingdom

Gigawatt-hours

	2002	2003	2004	2005	2006	2007	2008	2009	2010	2011	2012	2013	2014
Electricity generated													
Major power producers: total	353,994	362,600	358,313	362,212	361,232	361,317	355,209	342,374	347,846	332,461r	328,270	324,725	300,823
Conventional thermal and other	135,579	147,536	140,576	143,091	160,566	146,706	128,944	106,939	111,127	111,255	147,946	141,114	114,534
Combined cycle gas turbine stations	123,987	121,076	131,182	130,748	117,669	140,011	160,109	151,454	160,518	131,886	85,647	82,533	88,259
Nuclear stations	87,848	88,686	79,999	81,618	75,451	63,028	52,486	69,098	62,140	68,980	70,405	70,607	63,748
Hydro-electric stations:													
Natural flow	3,927	2,568	3,908	3,826	3,693	4,144	4,224	4,294	2,703	4,594	4,169	3,609	4,635
Pumped storage	2,652	2,734	2,649	2,930	3,853	3,859	4,089	3,685	3,150	2,906	2,966	2,904	2,883
Renewables other than hydro	856	1,154	1,471	2,744	2,928	5,910	7,966	9,574	11,893	17,358	23,204	33,243	39,470
Other generators: total	33,252	35,609	35,616	36,148	36,050	35,513	33,663	34,378	33,926	34,960	35,309	34,443	38,104
Conventional thermal and other	15,788	17,244	14,419	13,407	12,354	13,865	19,457	20,218	18,862	20,258	20,065	17,813	19,592
Combined cycle gas turbine stations	10,577	10,879	11,852	11,792	11,561	11,516	11,522	10,790	12,113	10,560	10,074	9,078	7,957
Hydro-electric stations (natural flow)	860	660	936	1,096	900	933	931	947	862	1,086	1,116	1,093	1,250
Renewables other than hydro	6,028	6,825	8,408	9,853	11,235	8,702	8,680	10,428	10,325	11,491	12,635	15,332	19,299
All generating companies: total	387,246	398,209	393,929	398,360	397,282	396,830	388,872	376,753	381,772	367,422r	363,579	359,168	338,927
Conventional thermal and other	151,367	164,780	154,995	156,498	172,920	160,571	148,401	127,157	129,989	131,513	168,011	158,927	134,126
Combined cycle gas turbine stations	134,564	131,955	143,034	142,540	129,230	151,527	171,631	162,244	172,631	142,447	95,721	91,612r	96,217
Nuclear stations	87,848	88,686	79,999	81,618	75,451	63,028	52,486	69,098	62,140	68,980	70,405	70,607	63,748
Hydro-electric stations:													
Natural flow	4,787	3,228	4,844	4,922	4,593	5,077	5,155	5,241	3,565	5,680	5,285	4,702	5,885
Pumped storage	2,652	2,734	2,649	2,930	3,853	3,859	4,089	3,685	3,150	2,906	2,966	2,904	2,883
Renewables other than hydro	6,884	7,979	9,879	12,597	14,164	14,612	16,645	20,002	22,218	28,849	35,839	48,575	58,769
Electricity used on works: Total	17,126	18,136	17,032	17,873	18,503	17,694	16,340	16,571	16,112	16,430	17,967	17,891	16,520
Major generating companies	15,746	16,747	15,582	16,265	17,031	16,090	14,662	14,750	14,403	14,479	15,859	15,669	13,957
Other generators	1,380	1,389	1,451	1,608	1,472	1,605	1,678	1,821	1,710	1,951	2,108	2,222	2,563
Electricity supplied (gross)													
Major power producers: total	338,248	345,854	342,732	345,947	344,201	345,227	340,547	327,624	333,443	317,983	312,411	309,056	286,865
Conventional thermal and other	128,795	140,196	133,607	135,999	151,866	138,793	121,816	101,100	105,142	105,345	139,994	133,330	107,945
Combined cycle gas turbine stations	121,886	118,546	128,983	128,179	115,695	137,657	157,417	148,907	157,818	129,669	84,207	81,145	86,775
Nuclear stations	81,090	81,911	73,682	75,173	69,237	57,249	47,673	62,762	56,442	62,655	63,949	64,133	57,903
Hydro-electric stations:													
Natural flow	3,914	2,559	3,901	3,821	3,680	4,114	4,209	4,279	2,694	4,578	4,168	3,596	4,606
Pumped storage	2,562	2,641	2,559	2,776	3,722	3,846	4,075	3,672	3,139	2,895	2,956	2,894	2,873
Renewables other than hydro	802	1,059	1,367	2,486	2,643	5,675	7,704	9,306	11,523	16,904	22,595	32,311	38,194
Other generators: total	31,873	34,220	34,165	34,539	34,578	33,908	31,985	32,558	32,216	33,009	33,200	32,221	35,541
Conventional thermal and other	19,716	21,942	20,046	19,494	18,598	19,801	18,371	18,952	17,771	18,854	18,480	16,066	17,454
Combined cycle gas turbine stations	10,049	10,336	11,260	11,204	10,859	11,471	10,947	10,251	11,509	10,033	9,571	8,625	7,560
Hydro-electric stations (natural flow)	849	653	919	930	885	918	915	930	847	1,066	1,095	1,071	1,223
Renewables other than hydro	5,764	6,519	8,000	9,380	10,702	8,147	8,000	9,584	9,584	10,502	11,452	13,836	17,481
All generating companies: total	370,121	380,074	376,896	380,486	378,779	379,136	372,532	360,182	365,660	350,992	345,611	341,277	322,407
Conventional thermal and other	148,511	162,138	153,653	155,493	170,464	158,594	140,186	120,052	122,914r	124,200r	158,474	149,396	125,399
Combined cycle gas turbine stations	131,935	128,882	140,243	139,382	126,554	149,127	168,364	159,159	169,327	139,702	93,778	89,771r	94,336
Nuclear stations	81,090	81,911	73,682	75,173	69,237	57,249	47,673	62,762	56,442	62,655	63,949	64,133	57,903
Hydro-electric stations:													
Natural flow	4,763	3,212	4,821	4,750	4,566	5,032	5,124	5,209	3,541	5,643	5,263	4,667	5,829
Pumped storage	2,562	2,641	2,559	2,776	3,722	3,846	4,075	3,672	3,139	2,895	2,956	2,894	2,873
Renewables other than hydro	6,566	7,578	9,367	11,867	13,345	13,822	15,704	18,889	21,107	27,406	34,047	46,147	55,675
Electricity used in pumping													
Major power producers	3,463	3,546	3,497	3,707	4,918	5,071	5,371	4,843	4,212	3,843	3,978	3,930	3,884
Electricity supplied (net): Total	366,657	376,528	373,399	376,780	373,861	374,064	367,161	355,339	361,448	347,149	341,633	337,348	318,522
Major power producers	334,785	342,308	339,235	342,240	339,283	340,156	335,175	322,781	329,231	314,140	308,433	305,127	282,981
Other generators	31,873	34,220	34,165	34,539	34,578	33,908	31,985	32,558	32,216	33,009	33,200	32,221	35,541
Net imports	10,399	8,414	2,160	7,490	8,321	7,517	5,215	11,022	2,860	2,663	6,222	11,871	14,430
Electricity available	375,072	378,687	380,889	385,101	381,378	379,279	378,183	358,200	364,111	353,371	353,504	351,018r	338,326r
Losses in transmission etc	29,980	29,862	30,728	27,674	27,410	28,223	27,852	28,043	27,032	28,128r	28,905r	27,725r	28,562
Electricity consumption: Total	343,608	346,126	347,246	356,685	353,367	350,970	349,648	329,555	337,203	325,620	324,801	323,908r	310,050
Fuel industries	10,206	9,908	8,299	8,010	8,137	9,313	7,825	7,807	8,377	7,793	6,841	7,673	7,182
Final users: total	333,401	336,218	338,948	348,675	345,229	341,656	341,822	321,748	328,825	317,827	317,959	316,235r	302,867r
Industrial sector	110,168	109,278	111,467	116,024	114,896	112,799	114,151	99,738	104,523r	102,361r	98,175r	97,669r	93,373
Domestic sector	120,014	123,001	124,200	125,711	124,704	123,076	119,800	118,541	118,833r	111,591r	114,667r	113,445r	108,881
Other sectors	103,219	103,939	103,280	106,939	105,629	105,781	107,871	103,469	105,470	103,875	105,117	105,863	101,155

Source: Department of Energy and Climate Change

Datasource
Electricity fuel use, generation and supply (DUKES 5.5)
https://www.gov.uk/government/publications/electricity-chapter-5-digest-of-united-kingdom-energy-statistics-dukes
Electricity commodity balances : (DUKES 5.1)
https://www.gov.uk/government/publications/electricity-chapter-5-digest-of-united-kingdom-energy-statistics-dukes
Electricity supply, electricity supplied (net), electricity available, electricity consumption and electricity sales (DUKES 5.4)
https://www.gov.uk/government/publications/electricity-chapter-5-digest-of-united-kingdom-energy-statistics-dukes
DUKES 5.5 and DUKES 5.1.3
https://www.gov.uk/government/publications/electricity-chapter-5-digest-of-united-kingdom-energy-statistics-dukes

18.9 Electricity: plant capacity and demand

United Kingdom
At end of December

Megawatts

	2001	2002	2003	2004	2005	2006	2007	2008	2009	2010	2011	2012	2013	2014
Major power producers														
Total declared net capability	73,382	70,369	71,471	73,293	73,941	74,996	75,979	76,993	77,881	83,438	81,789	81,879	77,169r	75,696
Conventional steam stations	34,835	32,227	31,867	31,982	32,292	33,608	34,134	32,823	32,831	32,839	31,763	28,523	23,141r	21,282
Combined cycle gas turbine stations	20,517	20,260	21,452	23,178	23,678	24,274	24,269	26,203	26,785	31,724	30,183	33,113	32,967	31,994
Nuclear stations	12,486	12,240	11,852	11,852	11,852	10,969	10,979	10,979	10,858	10,865	10,663	9,946	9,906	9,937
Gas turbines and oil engines	1,291	1,432	1,582	1,540	1,541	1,629	1,630	1,641	1,779	1,779	1,706	1,651	1,639r	1,643
Hydro-electric stations:														
Natural flow	1,348	1,304	1,273	1,276	1,273	1,294	1,293	1,392	1,395	1,397	1,397	1,398	1,399	1,400
Pumped storage	2,788	2,788	2,788	2,788	2,788	2,726	2,744	2,744	2,744	2,744	2,744	2,744	2,744	2,744
Renewables other than hydro	117	117	117	117	117	96	929	1,210	1,488	2,090	3,333	4,504	5,373	6,695
Other generators:														
Total capacity of own generating plant	6,296	6,336	6,793	6,829	7,422	7,407	6,763	6,700	6,945	7,035	7,241	7,420	7,430r	7,847
Conventional steam stations	3,464	3,325	3,480	3,275	3,269	3,059	2,924	2,749	2,408	2,475	2,401	2,464	2,089	2,110
Combined cycle gas turbine stations	1,777	1,854	1,927	1,968	2,182	2,106	2,076	1,988	2,267	2,302	2,212	2,244	1,905r	1,813
Hydro-electric stations (natural flow)	160	162	129	132	127	123	126	125	127	129	153	158	163r	169
Renewables other than hydro	895	995	1,257	1,454	1,852	2,118	1,637	1,837	2,144	2,129	2,475	2,553	3,274	3,755
All generating companies: Total capacity	79,678	76,705	78,264	80,122	81,363	82,403	82,742	83,693	84,826	90,473	89,031	89,299	84,598	83,543
Conventional steam stations	38,299	35,552	35,347	35,257	35,561	36,667	37,058	35,572	35,239	35,315	34,164	30,988	25,230r	23,392
Combined cycle gas turbine stations	22,294	22,114	23,379	25,146	25,860	26,380	26,345	28,191	29,051	34,026	32,395	35,357	34,872r	33,807
Nuclear stations	12,486	12,240	11,852	11,852	11,852	10,969	10,979	10,979	10,858	10,865	10,663	9,946	9,906	9,937
Gas turbines and oil engines	1,291	1,432	1,582	1,540	1,541	1,629	1,630	1,641	1,779	1,779	1,706	1,651	1,639r	1,643
Hydro-electric stations:														
Natural flow	1,508	1,466	1,402	1,408	1,400	1,417	1,419	1,517	1,523	1,526	1,550	1,556	1,561	1,569
Pumped storage	2,788	2,788	2,788	2,788	2,788	2,726	2,744	2,744	2,744	2,744	2,744	2,744	2,744	2,744
Renewables other than hydro	1,012	1,112	1,374	1,571	1,969	2,214	2,566	3,048	3,632	4,218	5,808	7,057	8,647	10,451
Major power producers:														
Simultaneous maximum load met	58,589	61,717	60,501	61,013	61,697	59,071	61,527	60,289	60,231	60,893	57,086	57,490	53,420	53,858
System load factor (percentages)	69	65	67	67	66	69	66	68	64	65	67	66	71	67

Source: Department of Energy and Climate Change

Data source
DUKES Table 5.6 - Plant capacity
DUKES Table 5.9 - Plant loads, demand
and efficiency

18.10 Electricity: fuel used in generation

United Kingdom
At end of December

Million tonnes of oil equivalent

	2000	2001	2002	2003	2004	2005	2006	2007	2008	2009	2010	2011	2012	2013	2014
Major power producers: total all fuels	74.4	77.4	75.8	77.5	76.8	78.2	78.7	76.0	74.2	70.2	70.9	68.4	69.7	68.1r	62.0
Coal	27.8	30.6	28.6	31.6	30.4	31.7	35.0	32.0	29.0	23.8	24.8	25.2	33.7	31.3	24.0
Oil	0.8	0.8	0.7	0.7	0.6	0.9	1.0	0.7	1.1	1.0	0.6	0.3	0.4	0.2	0.2
Gas	24.4	23.8	25.0	24.5	26.2	25.4	23.9	27.5	29.6	28.2	29.4	23.9	15.8	15.1	16.3
Nuclear	19.6	20.8	20.1	20.0	18.2	18.4	17.1	14.0	11.9	15.2	13.9	15.6	15.2	15.4	13.9
Hydro (natural flow)	0.4	0.3	0.3	0.2	0.3	0.3	0.3	0.4	0.4	0.4	0.2	0.4	0.4	0.3	0.4
Wind					-	-	-	0.3	0.5	0.6	0.7	1.1	1.5	2.1	2.3
Other renewables	0.2	0.3	0.3	0.4	0.5	0.8	0.7	0.6	0.8	0.7	1.0	1.3	1.8	2.2	3.0
Net imports	1.2	0.9	0.7	0.2	0.6	0.7	0.6	0.4	0.9	0.2	0.2	0.5	1.0	1.2	1.8
Other generators: total all fuels	8.0	7.6	8.0	8.7	8.4	9.2	9.0	8.8	8.3	8.5	8.4	8.7	8.5	7.9r	8.5
Transport under takings															
Gas	0.189	0.192	0.154	0.008	0.002	0.003	0.002	0.002	0.002	0.001	0.002	0.001	0.001	0.001	0.001
Under takings in industrial sector															
Coal	0.9	1.0	1.0	1.0	0.9	0.9	0.9	0.9	1.0	0.9	0.8	0.79	0.66	0.02r	0.01
Oil	0.8	0.6	0.6	0.5	0.5	0.4	0.5	0.5	0.5	0.5	0.5	0.44	0.32	0.35r	0.37
Gas	3.3	2.9	3.2	3.4	3.1	3.1	2.9	3.1	2.8	2.7	2.7	2.71	2.77	2.64r	2.40
Hydro (natural flow)	0.1	0.1	0.1	0.1	0.1	0.1	0.1	0.1	0.1	0.1	0.1	0.09	0.10	0.09	0.11
Wind, wave and solar photovoltaics	0.1	0.1	0.1	0.1	0.2	0.3	0.4	0.1	0.2	0.2	0.2	0.26	0.35	0.55	0.79
Other renewables	1.3	1.6	1.8	2.0	2.2	2.5	2.7	2.8	2.7	3.1	3.3	3.36	3.17	2.81r	3.15
Other fuels	1.4	1.0	1.1	1.5	1.4	1.9	1.6	1.3	1.1	1.0	0.8	1.02	1.11	1.41r	1.63
All generating companies: total fuels	82.4	84.9	83.8	86.2	85.2	87.4	87.7	84.7	82.5	78.7	79.3	77.1	78.2	75.8r	70.3
Coal	28.7	31.6	29.6	32.5	31.3	32.6	35.9	32.9	30.0	24.7	25.6	26.0	34.3	31.3r	24.0
Oil	1.5	1.4	1.3	1.2	1.1	1.3	1.4	1.2	1.6	1.5	1.2	0.8	0.7	0.6	0.6
Gas	27.9	26.9	28.4	27.9	29.3	28.5	26.8	30.6	32.4	30.9	32.1	26.6	18.6	17.7r	18.7
Nuclear	19.6	20.8	20.1	20.0	18.2	18.4	17.1	14.0	11.9	15.2	13.9	15.6	15.2	15.4	13.9
Hydro (natural flow)	0.4	0.3	0.4	0.3	0.4	0.4	0.4	0.4	0.4	0.4	0.3	0.5	0.5	0.4	0.5
Wind, wave and solar photovoltaics	0.1	0.1	0.1	0.1	0.2	0.3	0.4	0.5	0.6	0.8	0.9	1.4	1.8	2.6	3.1
Other renewables	1.6	1.9	2.1	2.4	2.8	3.4	3.5	3.4	3.5	3.9	4.3	4.6	4.9	5.0r	6.1
Other fuels	1.4	1.0	1.1	1.5	1.4	1.9	1.6	1.3	1.1	1.0	0.8	1.0	1.1	1.4r	1.6
Net imports	1.2	0.9	0.7	0.2	0.6	0.7	0.6	0.4	0.9	0.2	0.2	0.5	1.0	1.2	1.8

Source: Department of Energy and Climate Change

Data source
DUKES 5.3 - Fuel used in generation

18.11 Indigenous petroleum production, refinery receipts, imports and exports of oil

Thousand tonnes

	2000	2001	2002	2003	2004	2005	2006	2007	2008	2009	2010	2011	2012	2013	2014
Total indigenous petroleum production	126,245	116,678	115,944	106,073	95,374	84,721	76,578	76,575	71789r	68,199	62,962	51,972	44,561	40,646	39,928
Crude petroleum:															
Refinery receipts total	88,013	83,343	84,784	84,585	89,821	86,134	83,213	81,477	81,034	75,551r	73,543	75,080	71,839r	65,687r	60,823
Foreign trade															
Imports	54,386	53,551	56,968	54,177	62,517	58,885	59,443	57,357	60,335	55,002r	55,064	58,092	60,476r	59,137	53,798
Exports	92,917	86,930	87,144	74,898	64,504	54,099	50,195	50,999	48,235r	45,351r	42 064r	33,625r	30,946r	33,105r	30,946
Net imports	-38,531	-33,378	-30,176	-20,720	-1,987	4,786	9,249	6,357	12,100	9,651	13,000	24,467	29,530	26,032	22,852
Petroleum products															
Foreign trade															
Imports	14,212	17,234	14,900	16,472	18,545	22,481	26,836	25,110	23,741	22,172	23,665	22,656	26,207r	28,769r	29,055
Exports	20,677	19,088	23,444	23,323	30,495	29,722	28,945	29,983	28,803	25,491	26,065	27,800	29,904r	26,910r	22,748
Net imports	-6,464	-1,854	-8,544	-6,851	-11,950	-7,241	-2,109	-4,874	-5,062	-3,319	-2,400	-5,145	-3,697	1,859	6,307
International marine bunkers	2,079	2,274	1,913	1,764	2,085	2,055	2,348	2,371	3,472	3,306	2,807	3,130	2,663	2,540	2,340

Source: Department of Energy and Climate Change

Data source
DUKES 3.1 - Primary oil commodity balances
https://www.gov.uk/government/publications/petroleum-chapter-3-digest-of-united-kingdom-energy-statistics-dukes

DUKES 3.2-3.4 - Petroleum products commodity balances
https://www.gov.uk/government/publications/petroleum-chapter-3-digest-of-united-kingdom-energy-statistics-dukes

18.12 Throughput of crude and process oils and output of refined products from refineries

United Kingdom

Thousand tonnes

	2001	2002	2003	2004	2005	2006	2007	2008	2009	2010	2011	2012	2013	2014
Throughput of crude and process oils	83438	84356	84814	89710	86069	83130	81509	81241	75754	73,543	75,080	71,839r	65,687r	60,823
less: Refinery fuel:	5059	5677	5456	5417	5601	4879	4676	4706	4304	4,378	4,585	4,299	3,759r	3,245
Losses	1233	788	56	-7	371	374	293	470	777	566	373	209r	312r	523
Total output of refined products	77146	77891	79302	84301	80097	77877	76541	76065	70674	68599	70122	67331	61616	57055
Gases:														
Butane and propane	1770	2149	2300	2170	2222	2142	2298	2250	2113	2247	2598	2512	2326	2105
Other petroleum	272	537	715	520	427	661	517	369	449	518	434	285	342r	304
Naphtha and other feedstock	3428	3153	3503	3168	3019	2734	2561	2660r	2507r	2440r	2526r	2328r	2013r	2290
Aviation spirit	101	28	26	31	32	25	0	0	0	0	0	0	0	0
Motor spirit	21455	22944	22627	24589	22604	21443	21313	19,521r	19,184r	19,074r	18,823r	18,650r	17,691r	15,709
Industrial and white spirit	121	121	104	100	136	107	70	55	61	66	65	72	106	165
Kerosene:														
Aviation turbine fuel	5910	5365	5277	5615	5167	6261	6176	6549	6022	5781	6411	5775	4527	4635
Burning oil	3088	3506	3521	3613	3325	3374	2968	3092	2830	2570	2377	2268	2705	2093
DERV					19056	15821	16138	16350	15908	15332	16801	15772	14831	13,726
Gas/diesel oil	26748	28343	27380	28646	9430	10215	10165	10566	9487	9505	8683	8941	8193	8,049
Fuel oil	10179	8507	9495	11308	10155	11280	10433	10483	8043	7004	7432	7158r	6230r	5235
Lubricating oil	656	509	576	1136	936	617	547	514	530	412	430	457	387r	373
Bitumen	1707	1918	1925	2196	1912	1749	1628	1485	1338	1276	1476	1222	777	1,006
Petroleum coke	513	441	612	633	660	606	676	781	847	817	654	640r	528	581
Other products	1140	818	1030	702	1103	964	1058	1182	1204	1557	1412	1252	1017	783

Source: Department of Energy and Climate Change

Data source

DUKES 3.5 - Supply and disposal of petroleum

https://www.gov.uk/government/publications/petroleum-chapter-3-digest-of-united-kingdom-energy-statistics-dukes

DUKES 3.2-3.4 - Petroleum product

https://www.gov.uk/government/publications/petroleum-chapter-3-digest-of-united-kingdom-energy-statistics-dukes

18.13 Deliveries of pertoleum products for inland consumption
United Kingdom

	2002	2003	2004	2005	2006	2007	2008	2009	2010	2011	2012	2013	2014
Total (including refinery fuel)	76233	77154	79066	80736	79812	77424	75160	71252	70,673r	68,829r	67,347r	66,628r	66,100
Total (excluding refinery fuel)	70557	71697	73649	75135	74933	72748	70455	66948	66295r	64244r	63048r	62869r	62855
Butane and propane	2553	3017	3115	3310	3123	2823	3315r	3223r	3026r	3065r	2475r	2603r	2,496
Other Petroleum Gases (includes Ethane)	1953	1885	1737	1838	1714	1563	1459	1344	1199	1003	899	983r	1056
Naphtha	1592	2332	2029	1916	2278	1608	741r	988	1037	1061r	1094r	1012r	802
Aviation spirit	50	46	49	52	46	33	30	22	21	21	17	16	18
Motor spirit													
Retail deliveries													
Lead Replacement Petrol/Super premium unleaded	1107	1044	884	851	737	787	757	745	647	560	446	-	-
Premium unleaded	19167	18291	17795	17221	16615	16322	15250	14300	13435	12870	12357	-	-
Total retail deliveries	20274	19335	18679	18071	17351	17109	16007	15045	14082	13430	12803	-	-
Commercial consumers													
Lead Replacement Petrol/Super premium unleaded (6)	36	41	40	22	21	16	12	12	11	11	2	-	-
Premium unleaded	499	542	765	759	719	624	523	555	509	454	426	-	-
Total commercial consumers	535	583	805	781	739	641	535	567	520	465	428	-	-
Total motor spirit	20808	19918	19484	18852	18091	17615	16542	15613	14602	13895	13231	12574	12326
Industrial and white spirits	157	147	281	284	156	167	145	174	224	143	219	279	126
Kerosene													
Aviation turbine fuel	10519	10765	11637	12497	12641	12574	12142	11533	11116	11574	11221	11242r	11220
Burning oil	3578	3569	3950	3870	4017	3629	3681	3732	4012	3288	3329	3507r	3179
Gas/diesel oil													
DERV fuel													
Retail deliveries	8153	9057	9517	10532	11501	12685	12777	12669	13157	13549	13965	-	-
Commercial consumers	8774	8655	8997	8845	8660	8730	7724	7443	7583	7442	7573	-	-
Total DERV fuel	16926	17712	18514	19377	20161	21038	20501	20112	20740	20991	21538	21926	22675
Other gas/diesel oil (includes MDF)	6099	6326	6023	6719	6525	6116	5632	5034	5,059	4,759	4,990	5,174r	5,241
Fuel oil	3767	3562	3743	3780	3248	3228	2660	2113	1892	1415	1052	911r	728
Lubricating oils	829	868	914	750	713	672	510	510	580	491	412	437r	436
Bitumen	2002	1959	1991	1906	1610	1563	1741	1381	1370	1621	1355	1358	1,410
Petroleum coke	893	880	1146	1042	925	366	738r	447r	607r	399r	461r	444r	475
Miscellaneous products	647	506	526	556	437	338	590	573	671	592	541	361	526

Source: Department for Energy and Climate Change

- Data no longer available

Datasource
Supply and demand of petroleum (DUKES Table 3.5)
https://www.gov.uk/government/publications/petroleum-chapter-3-digest-of-united-kingdom-energy-statistics-dukes
Additional information on inland deliveries of selected products (DUKES 3.6)
https://www.gov.uk/government/publications/petroleum-chapter-3-digest-of-united-kingdom-energy-statistics-dukes
Additional information on inland deliveries for non-energy uses (DUKES 3.8)
https://www.gov.uk/government/publications/petroleum-chapter-3-digest-of-united-kingdom-energy-statistics-dukes
Inland deliveries of petroleum (DUKES 3.1.2)
https://www.gov.uk/government/publications/petroleum-chapter-3-digest-of-united-kingdom-energy-statistics-dukes
Commodity (DUKES 3.2-3.4)
https://www.gov.uk/government/publications/petroleum-chapter-3-digest-of-united-kingdom-energy-statistics-dukes

18.14 Iron and steel:[1] summary of steel supplies, deliveries and stocks
United Kingdom

		2010	2011	2012	2013	2014
Supply, disposal and consumption -(Finished product weight -Thousand tonnes)						
UK producers' home deliveries	**KLTA**	4685	4604	4256	4166	4194
Imports excluding steelworks receipts	**KLTB**	5168	5613	5554	5420	6445
Total deliveries to home market (a)	**KLTC**	9853	10217	9810	9586	10639
Total exports (producers, consumers, merchants)	**KLTD**	5830	5779	6185	8162	8254
Exports by UK producers	**KLTE**	4767	4614	4950	7041	7643
Derived consumers' and merchants' exports (b)	**KLTF**	1063	1165	1235	1121	611
Net home disposals (a)-(b)	**KLTG**	8790	9052	8575	8465	10028
Estimated home consumption	**KLTI**	8790	9052	8575	8465	10028
Stocks -(Finished product weight - Thousand tonnes)						
Producers						
-ingots & semis	**KLTJ**	552	470	564	507	427
-finished steel	**KLTK**	704	632	632	705	653
Estimated home consumption -(Crude steel equivalent -Million tonnes)						
Crude steel production[2]	**KLTN**	9.71	9.48	9.58	11.86	12.03
Producers' stock change	**KLTO**	-0.18	-0.20	0.14	0.01	-0.13
Re-usable material	**KLTP**	0.00	0.00	0.00	0.00	0.00
Total supply from home sources	**KLTQ**	9.89	9.68	9.44	11.85	12.16
Total imports[3]	**KLTR**	6.86	8.03	7.83	6.95	8.14
Total exports[3]	**KLTS**	6.67	6.66	7.02	9.11	9.27
Net home disposals	**KLTT**	10.08	11.05	10.25	9.69	11.03
Estimated home consumption	**KLTV**	10.08	11.05	10.25	9.69	11.03

1 The figures relate to periods of 52 weeks.
2 Includes liquid steel for castings only up to 2003.

Source: International Steel Statistics Bureau (ISSB)

18.15 Iron and steel:[1] iron ore, manganese ore, pig iron and iron and steel scrap

United Kingdom

Thousand tonnes

		2010	2011	2012	2013	2014
Iron ore consumption	KLOF	10572	9735	10511	14034	14353
Manganese ore consumption	KLOG	0	0	0	3	0

Pig iron (and blast furnace ferro-alloys)

		2010	2011	2012	2013	2014
Average number of furnaces in blast during period	KLOH	5	5	5	4	4
Production Steelmaking iron	KLOI	7233	6625	7183	9471	9705
In blast furnaces: total	KLOL	7233	6625	7183	9471	9705
In steel works	KLOM	7233	6625	7183	9471	9705
Consumption of pig iron: total	KLOO	7233	6625	7183	9471	9705

Iron and steel scrap

		2010	2011	2012	2013	2014
Steelworks and steel foundries Circulating scrap	KLOQ	1256	1317	1413	1689	1756
Purchased receipts	KLOR	2507	2517	2384	2456	2379
Consumption	KLOS	3713	3890	3675	4085	4145
Stocks (end of period)	KLOT	179	123	245	306	296

1 The figures relate to periods of 52 weeks.

2 Consumption.

Source: International Steel Statistics Bureau (ISSB)

18.16 Iron and steel:[1] furnaces and production of steel

United Kingdom   Number and thousand tonnes

		2010	2011	2012	2013	2014
Steel furnaces (numbers[2])	**KLPA**					
Oxygen converters	**KLPC**					
Electric	**KLPD**					
Production of crude steel	**KLPF**	9708	9478	9579	11858	12034
by process						
Oxygen converters	**KLPH**	7323	6946	7525	9915	10079
Electric	**KLPI**	2385	2532	2054	1943	1955
by cast method						
Cast to ingot	**KLPK**	153	205	189	158	171
Continuously cast	**KLPL**	9555	9273	9390	11699	11863
Steel for castings	**KLPM**					
by quality						
Non alloy steel	**KLPN**	9201	8835	8992	11303	11418
Stainless and other alloy steel	**KLPO**	508	643	587	555	616

Production of finished steel products (All qualities)

		2010	2011	2012	2013	2014
Rods and bars for reinforcement (in coil and lengths)	**KLPP**	792	637	606	578	553
Wire rods and other rods and bars in coil	**KLPQ**	874	787	728	738	726
Hot rolled bars in lengths	**KLPR**	887	1002	849	809	845
Bright steel bars	**KLPS**	239	225	102	154	175
Light sections other than rails	**KLPT**	129	117	112	125	128
Heavy sections	**KGQZ**	1069	978	883	927	1006
Hot rolled plates, sheets and strip in coil and lengths	**KLPW**	4733	4575	3962	4944	4975
Cold rolled plates and sheets in coil and lengths	**KLPX**	2200	2215	1939	2419	2437
Cold rolled strip	**KLPZ**	81	73	39	45	39
Tinplate	**KLQW**	468	411	411	401	430
Other coated sheet	**KLQX**	1278	1262	1161	1373	1383
Tubes and pipes	**KLQY**	991	842	515	702	666
Forged bars	**KLQZ**	0	0	0	0	16

1. The figures relate to periods of 52 weeks.   Source: International Steel Statistics Bureau (ISSB)
2 Includes steel furnaces at steel foundries, only up to 2003.

18.17 Fertilisers - UK consumption

Years ending 30 June   Thousand tonnes

Nutrient Content		2001	2002	2003	2004	2005	2006	2007	2008	2009	2010	2011	2012	2013	2014
Nitrogen (N):	**XXXX**	1162	1197	1131	1125	1061	1003	1008	1001	948	1016	1022	1000	999	1060
Straight	**KGRM**	714	751	664	662	691	631	656	744	733	771				
Compounds	**KGRN**	448	446	467	463	370	372	352	292	180	245				
Phosphate (P2O5)	**KGRO**	279	283	282	278	259	235	224	215	129	184	192	188	194	201
Potash (K2O)	**KGRP**	369	391	375	375	352	325	317	325	208	251	283	259	267	284
Compounds - total product	**KGRQ**	2,471	2,511	2,558	2,550	2,221	2,134	2,039	1,827	1,116	1,529				

Source: British Survey of Fertiliser Practice (Defra)

Table 18.17 gives the quantity of the fertiliser nutrients nitrogen (N), phosphate (P2O5) and potash (K2O) used by UK farmers during the fertiliser year, which runs from 1st July to 30th June. The year shown in the table is the year in which the harvest takes place, at the end of each fertiliser year.

18.18a United Kingdom production of minerals 2008–2013

Thousand tonnes

Mineral	2008	2009	2010	2011	2012	2013
Coal:						
Deep-mined	8,096	7,520	7,390	7,312	6,153	4,089
Opencast	9,509	9,854	10,426	10,580	10,134	8,584
Other (a)	449	500	540	660	680	95
Natural gas and oil:						
Methane (oil equivalent)						
Colliery	63	62	71	58	52	52
Onshore	92	89	88	27	15	10
Offshore	69,525	59,581	57,036	45,204	38,850	36,460
Crude oil						
Onshore	1,248	1,181	941	678	870	1,003
Offshore	64,249	61,639	57,106	47,893	41,182	37,453
Condensates and other (c)						
Onshore	33	32	17	0	13	20
Offshore	6,135	5,346	4,898	3,401	2,495	2,170
Iron ore	0.1	—	—	—	—	—
Non-ferrous ores (metal content):						
Tin	—	—	—	—	—	—
Lead (h)	0.3	0.4	0.4	0.3	0.1	0.1
Gold (kg)	163	187	177	202	102	42
Silver (kg)	398	514	506	531	230	82
Chalk (e)	5,874	4,047	3,626	3,996	3,473	3,528
Clay and shale (e)	8,459	5,310	5,934	6,154	5,497	6,464
Igneous rock (j) (k)	53,490	44,618	44,876	(l) 44 400	(l) 40 200	(l) 40 500
Limestone (excluding dolomite)	74,145	60,111	56,985	(l) 58 100	(l) 54 800	(l) 56 900
Dolomite (excluding limestone)	5,509	3,164	4,540	4,490	4,896	3,432
Sand and gravel:						
Land	66,640	50,973	47,167	(l) 45 800	(l) 41 800	(l) 43 400
Marine (i)	18,833	15,253	14,533	17,287	14,840	14,577
Sandstone	12,255	12,335	11,556	(l) 12 300	(l) 11 500	(l) 11 500
Slate (g)	1,058	683	695	763	701	885
Ball clay (sales)	1,020	727	(h) 900	(h) 930	(h) 748	(h) 740
Barytes	43	36	34	31	30	30
Chert and flint	1	1	...	...	...	...
China clay (sales) (d)	1,355	1,060	(h) 1 140	(h) 1 290	(h) 1 150	(h) 1 110
China stone	0.5	—	—	—	—	—
Fireclay (e)	180	129	110	162	96	105
Fluorspar (h)	37	19	26	—	—	16
Gypsum (natural) (h)	1,200	1,200	1,200	1,200	1,200	1,200
Lignite	...	...	...	...	...	...
Peat (000 m³)	760	887	1,004	825	568	1,254
Potash (b)	673	(h) 700	(h) 700	(h) 770	(h) 900	(h) 900
Salt	5,565	6,166	6,666	6,060	6,460	6,930
Silica sand	4,777	3,755	4,070	3,969	3,888	3,961
Talc	2	3	3	4	4	3

(a) Slurry etc. recovered from dumps, ponds, rivers etc.
(b) Marketable product (KCl).
(c) Including ethane, propane and butane, in addition to condensates.
(d) Dry weight.
(e) Excluding a small production in Northern Ireland.
(f) BGS estimates based on data from producing companies.
(g) Slate figures include waste used for constructional fill and powder and granules used in industry.
(h) BGS estimate.
(i) Including marine-dredged landings at foreign ports (exports).
(j) Excluding a small production of granite in Northern Ireland.
(k) In addition, the following amounts of igneous rock were produced in Guernsey (thousand tonnes):2007: 160; 2008: 139; 2009: 120; 2010: 116; 2011: 156; 2012: 169; 2014: 117 and Jersey: 2007: 295; 2008: 325; 2009: 249; 2010: 238; 2011: 220; 2012: 239 ; 2013: 176 2013: 149.
(l) Contains an estimate related to Northern Ireland production.

Sources: Office for National Statistics, Department of Business, Innovation and Skills, Dept. of Enterprise, Trade & Investment (NI), Crown Estate Commissioners (marine sand and gravel produced for export), and company data.

18.18b Minerals produced in Northern Ireland, the Isle of Man, Guernsey and Jersey 2009-2013

Thousand tonnes

	2009	2010	2011	2012	2013
Northern Ireland					
Gold (kg)	187	177	202	102	42
Silver (kg)	514	506	531	230	82
Lead (tonnes)	243	251	280	60	36
Limestone	3,972	3,689	...	...	...
Sand and gravel	4,856	2,178	...	...	...
Basalt and igneous rock (a)	5,758	5,438	...	...	...
Sandstone	3,793	2,768	...	...	...
Granite	...	...	...	...	...
Clay and shale	...	...	...	...	...
Others (b)	1,998	2,087	...	...	...
Total	**20,377**	**16,160**	...	...	...
Isle of Man					
Limestone	352	71	82	72	56
Sand and gravel	171	145	141	101	96
Igneous rock	132	109	96	94	110
Slate	45	28	29	23	17
Total	**701**	**353**	**347**	**290**	**279**
Guernsey					
Igneous rock	120	116	156	169	149
Jersey					
Igneous rock (c)	249	238	220	239	176
Sand and gravel	67	57	74	46	44

(a) Excluding granite.
(b) Including rock salt, chalk, dolomite, fireclay and granite.
(c) BGS estimates.

Sources: Department of Enterprise, Trade & Investment (Northern Ireland),
Department of Economic Development (Isle of Man), Company data (Guernsey
and Jersey).

18.19a Building materials and components

Bricks - Production, Deliveries and Stocks

Great Britain   Millions of Bricks

Brick Type	Seasonally Adjusted Deliveries	Production	Deliveries (from)	Stocks*	Production	Deliveries (from)	Stocks*	Production	Deliveries (from)	Stocks*	Production	Deliveries (from)	Stocks*
	All Types		All Types			Commons			Facings			Engineerings	
2010	1,606	1,430	1,606	702	182	194	94	1,124	1,280	570	124	132	39
2011	1,646	1,554	1,646	610	172	185	82	1,230	1,304	494	152	157	34
2012	1,551	1,459	1,551	515	137	166	52	1,172	1,239	425	150	146	38
2013	1,736	1,555	1,736	339	151	169	35	1,244	1,384	288	160	183	16
2014	1,819	1,824	1,812	349	169	173	29	1,489	1,470	306	167	169	15
2013 Q2	482	408	434	339	39	41	35	327	347	288	41	46	16
Q3	449	442	437	343	43	41	38	360	358	290	39	39	15
Q4	438	466	476	336	43	48	32	380	384	289	43	45	15
2014 Q1	449	475	479	330	43	47	26	386	386	289	46	46	15
Q4	453	442	419	349	40	37	29	363	343	306	38	39	15
2015 Q1	439	464	403	415	42	35	36	372	329	354	51	39	25
Q2	435	511	475	452	41	45	33	419	383	391	51	47	28
Q3	410	510	462	502	41	44	31	412	374	430	57	44	41
2013 November	158	149	152	336	13	14	35	120	121	283	16	17	19
December	158	107	108	339	11	10	35	89	88	288	7	10	16
2014 January	171	133	138	334	14	13	35	107	112	283	13	13	15
February	153	144	137	341	14	12	37	119	114	289	11	12	15
March	150	165	162	343	16	15	38	134	132	290	15	14	15
April	151	151	156	341	14	16	36	124	125	291	13	15	14
May	147	160	158	342	14	15	35	130	129	293	16	15	15
June	147	156	162	336	16	18	32	126	130	289	14	15	15
July	145	160	169	325	15	17	28	130	137	282	15	15	15
August	145	151	145	331	13	14	27	123	117	288	16	14	16
September	150	163	164	330	15	16	26	133	132	289	15	17	15
October	151	161	168	323	15	16	25	132	137	285	14	16	13
November	147 p	161	138	343	15	12	28	132	113	301	13	13	14
December	161 p	120	113	349	10	9	29	98	94	306	11	10	15
2015 January	148 p	140	117	373	16	10	35	107	96	317	18	11	21
February	145 p	151	128	400	14	12	37	122	103	340	16	13	23
March	144 p	173	158	415	12	13	36	144	130	354	17	15	25
April	152 p	162	158	420	13	14	35	132	126	360	16	17	24
May	143 p	175	149	446	12	15	33	146	120	386	17	14	27
June	147 p	174	168	452	15	16	33	141	136	391	18	16	28
July	144 p	176	169	461	16	17	33	141	135	398	19	17	30
August	143 p	163	143	481	11	13	31	132	116	414	19	13	37
September	138 p	171	151	502	14	14	31	139	123	430	19	14	41
October	136 p	174	148	529	15	15	30	145	119	456	15	14	42
November p	136	155	130	554	14	12	32	127	105	477	15	12	45

* Refers to stocks at end of period

Source: Department for Business, Innovation and Skills (BIS)

In the March 2015 edition of these tables, entries for clay, sand-lime and concrete bricks were removed. This is because data for these categories of bricks have been confidential since 2009. We will continue to monitor these material types and will reinstate them if they become publishable at a later date.

From March 2015, seasonally adjusted figures for deliveries of bricks have been included in this table. In the production of these figures, brick deliveries data back to January 1983 have been seasonally adjusted. This long run data series is available on request.

p Provisional

18.19b Building and components

Concrete Blocks - Production, Deliveries and Stocks

Great Britain
Thousand square metres

	All Types	All Types			Dense			Lightweight			Aerated		
	Seasonally Adjusted Deliveries	Production	Deliveries (from)	Stocks*	Production	Deliveries (from)	Stocks*	Production	Deliveries (from)	Stocks*	Production	Deliveries (from)	Stocks*
2004	94,854	96,256	94,854	10,088	37,677	37,444	3,690	25,462	25,736	2,271	33,117	31,674	4,127
2005	89,551	89,997	89,551	9,680	36,188	36,473	3,465	25,561	25,673	2,173	28,248	27,405	4,042
2006	87,015	87,510	87,015	:	34,956	34,741	:	25,345	25,222	:	27,209	27,051	:
2007	88,746	89,951	88,746	:	36,686	35,396	:	25,965	25,667	:	27,300	27,682	:
2008	67,136	67,743	67,136	8,920	29,675	29,889	3,498	18,168	18,363	2,149	19,900	18,884	3,273
2009	50,639	50,394	50,639	8,320	22,607	22,748	3,291	13,421	13,989	1,522	14,367	13,903	3,507
2010	51,758	53,629	51,758	10,152	22,393	21,731	3,833	14,415	13,923	2,044	16,822	16,104	4,276
2011	52,901	54,583	52,901	10,810	22,940	22,101	4,486	15,153	14,821	1,728	16,490	15,978	4,596
2012	52,021	51,693	52,021	10,700	21,551	22,323	3,808	14,383	14,103	2,024	15,759	15,595	4,868
2013	57,995	56,031	57,995	4,171	23,599	24,340	1,894	17,055	17,508	1,208	15,377	16,147	1,069
2014	56,660	57,943	56,953	5,413	25,088	24,943	2,147	17,499	17,447	1,402	15,356	14,563	1,864
2010 Q3	13,522	15,172	14,343	9,832	6,477	6,125	3,837	4,208	3,899	2,023	4,487	4,319	3,971
Q4	11,612	10,887	10,590	10,152	4,541	4,534	3,833	2,832	2,822	2,044	3,515	3,234	4,276
2011 Q1	13,284	13,982	12,795	11,516	5,642	5,278	4,197	3,916	3,665	2,301	4,423	3,852	5,017
Q2	13,104	14,761	13,911	12,510	6,217	5,871	4,647	4,008	3,827	2,507	4,537	4,212	5,357
Q3	12,957	14,208	14,076	12,352	6,217	5,931	4,862	3,908	3,970	2,218	4,083	4,175	5,272
Q4	13,555	11,632	12,120	10,810	4,864	5,021	4,486	3,321	3,359	1,728	3,447	3,739	4,596
2012 Q1	13,011	13,323	12,642	11,493	5,374	5,426	4,456	3,559	3,314	1,964	4,389	3,903	5,074
Q2	12,470	13,268	13,235	11,595	5,535	5,824	4,209	3,487	3,437	2,006	4,245	3,973	5,380
Q3	12,919	12,584	13,795	10,471	5,360	5,773	3,773	3,756	3,887	1,904	3,467	4,135	4,794
Q4	13,620	12,519	12,349	10,700	5,281	5,300	3,808	3,580	3,465	2,024	3,658	3,584	4,868
2013 Q1	13,732	12,125	12,713	10,165	5,212	5,430	3,643	3,094	3,389	1,730	3,818	3,893	4,793
Q2	14,979	14,960	16,188	4,401	6,351	6,655	2,190	4,691	4,809	1,303	3,918	4,723	908
Q3	14,790	15,333	16,042	3,683	6,345	6,609	1,875	5,079	5,162	1,210	3,909	4,271	597
Q4	14,494	13,614	13,052	4,171	5,691	5,646	1,894	4,191	4,147	1,208	3,732	3,259	1,069
2014 Q1	13,545	14,021	12,907	5,311	5,918	5,595	2,236	4,164	4,058	1,320	3,939	3,254	1,755
Q2	14,183	14,867	15,095	5,228	6,257	6,627	1,867	4,503	4,710	1,256	4,107	3,758	2,104
Q3	14,431	15,399	16,038	4,610	7,012	7,112	1,784	4,854	4,794	1,322	3,533	4,133	1,504
Q4	14,501	13,656	12,913	5,413	5,902	5,610	2,147	3,977	3,885	1,402	3,777	3,418	1,864
2015 Q1	15,295	15,609	14,238	6,635	6,534	6,137	2,533	4,406	4,199	1,619	4,668	3,902	2,483
Q2	15,669	15,524	16,659	5,433	6,520	6,713	2,243	5,324	5,518	1,456	3,679	4,428	1,734
Q3	16,888	17,194	18,643	5,332	6,797	6,842	2,215	4,882	4,862	1,482	5,514	6,940	1,635
2013 November	4,824	4,989	4,545	:	2,031	1,986	:	1,604	1,481	:	1,354	1,078	:
December	4,798	3,418	3,296	4,171	1,462	1,418	1,894	901	1,032	1,208	1,055	847	1,069
2014 January	4,508	4,376	3,749	:	1,984	1,738	:	1,324	1,104	:	1,068	908	:
February	4,452	4,596	4,093	:	1,856	1,679	:	1,383	1,379	:	1,357	1,036	:
March	4,586	5,049	5,064	5,311	2,078	2,178	2,236	1,457	1,575	1,320	1,514	1,311	1,755
April	4,664	4,960	4,825	:	2,011	2,132	:	1,602	1,625	:	1,346	1,068	:
May	4,622	4,773	5,009	:	2,080	2,258	:	1,396	1,529	:	1,298	1,223	:
June	4,896	5,134	5,261	5,228	2,165	2,237	1,867	1,505	1,556	1,256	1,463	1,467	2,104
July	4,795	5,288	5,692	:	2,444	2,585	:	1,770	1,712	:	1,074	1,395	:
August	4,773	4,728	4,905	:	2,211	2,172	:	1,480	1,478	:	1,036	1,256	:
September	4,864	5,384	5,441	4,610	2,357	2,355	1,784	1,605	1,604	1,322	1,422	1,481	1,504
October	4,510	5,040	4,913	:	2,177	2,167	:	1,540	1,555	:	1,323	1,191	:
November	4,694 p	4,740	4,239	:	1,993	1,823	:	1,392	1,316	:	1,354	1,101	:
December	5,297 p	3,876	3,761	5,413	1,731	1,620	2,147	1,045	1,015	1,402	1,100	1,126	1,864
2015 January	4,933 p	4,569	3,893	6,806	1,563	1,412	2,044	1,181	1,051	1,399	1,824	1,431	3,363
February	5,069 p	5,202	4,572	6,545	2,347	2,154	2,479	1,503	1,381	1,642	1,351	1,038	2,423
March	5,293 p	5,838	5,772	6,635	2,624	2,572	2,533	1,722	1,767	1,619	1,493	1,434	2,483
April	5,249 p	5,032	5,599	6,399	2,245	2,314	2,467	1,780	1,944	1,783	1,007	1,340	2,149
May	5,176 p	5,062	5,333	6,108	2,035	2,092	2,395	1,869	1,826	1,821	1,158	1,415	1,892
June	5,244 p	5,430	5,727	5,433	2,240	2,307	2,243	1,676	1,747	1,456	1,514	1,672	1,734
July	5,509 p	5,908	6,485	6,206	2,369	2,372	2,252	1,911	1,785	1,593	1,628	2,328	2,361
August	5,800 p	5,114	5,946	5,352	2,132	2,225	2,149	1,432	1,463	1,549	1,551	2,257	1,654
September	5,579 p	6,171	6,213	5,332	2,296	2,245	2,215	1,540	1,614	1,482	2,335	2,355	1,635
October	5,866 p	6,392	6,247	5,530	2,402	2,353	2,317	1,653	1,626	1,509	2,337	2,268	1,704
November p	5,535	5,862	5,116	6,276	2,150	2,011	2,456	1,466	1,455	1,520	2,247	1,651	2,299

* Refers to stocks at end of period

Source: Department for Business, Innovation and Skills (BIS)

From March 2015, seasonally adjusted figures for deliveries of concrete blocks have been included in this table. In the production of these figures, blocks deliveries data back to January 1983 have been seasonally adjusted. This long run data series is available on request.

Data from December 2011 to June 2012 has been revised following receipt of corrected data. The period August 2007 to November 2011 may also be affected, but non-availability of a back-series of corrected data means that this period cannot be revised, and should be treated with caution. Full details are available in the 'Summary of revision to monthly statistics of building materials and components publication' document on our website

18.19c Building materials and components

Concrete Roofing Tiles and Ready-Mixed Concrete

		Great Britain		United Kingdom	United Kingdom
		Concrete Roofing Tiles (Th.sq.m. of roof area covered)		**Ready-Mixed Concrete #** (Th.cu.m.)	**Seasonally Adjusted Ready-Mixed Concrete** (Th.cu.m.)
	Production	Deliveries	Stocks *	Deliveries	Deliveries
2004	20,739	19,403	2,850	22,856	22,856
2005	25,719	24,489	4,902	22,432	22,432
2006	23,730	24,118	4,426	23,029	23,029
2007	23,551	23,812	3,646	23,548	23,548
2008	20,084	19,926	3,899	20,051	20,051
2009	14,079	15,612	2,344	14,069	14,069
2010	17,817	17,146	3,023	14,038	14,038
2011	17,712	17,684	3,126	15,121	15,121
2012	17,476	17,578	3,061	13,758	13,758
2013	18,745	19,580	2,214	15,089	15,089
2014	24,086	23,058	3,275	15,348	15,348
2006 Q3	5,448	6,371	4,688	6,047	5,885
Q4	5,489	5,787	4,426	5,542	5,743
2007 Q1	6,618	5,629	5,368	5,554	5,809
Q2	5,775	5,728	5,360	6,103	5,855
Q3	5,129	6,541	3,929	6,205	5,924
Q4	6,028	5,914	3,646	5,686	5,960
2008 Q1	5,708	5,421	3,922	5,193	5,731
Q2	5,815	5,679	4,488	5,773	5,334
Q3	4,657	4,977	3,840	4,902	4,706
Q4	3,903	3,849	3,899	4,183	4,281
2009 Q1	3,664	3,281	4,273	3,583	3,838
Q2	3,055	3,936	3,391	3,637	3,511
Q3	3,580	4,447	2,522	3,628	3,381
Q4	3,779	3,949	2,344	3,221	3,339
2010 Q1	4,129	3,505	2,967	3,328	3,432
Q2	4,961	4,922	3,008	3,819	3,715
Q3	4,783	4,824	2,967	3,831	3,702
Q4	3,945	3,894	3,023	3,060	3,188
2011 Q1	4,820	4,079	3,858	3,827	3,938
Q2	4,565	4,398	4,022	3,907	3,787
Q3	4,210	4,901	3,316	3,908	3,740
Q4	4,116	4,306	3,126	3,479	3,656
2012 Q1	4,673	3,928	3,872	3,463	3,552
Q2	4,236	4,100	4,008	3,399	3,309
Q3	4,095	5,004	3,136	3,556	3,387
Q4	4,471	4,547	3,061	3,340	3,509
2013 Q1	4,514	4,055	3,520	3,325	3,651
Q2	4,209	4,598	3,131	4,108	3,803
Q3	4,550	5,468	2,214	3,972	3,834
Q4	5,471	5,459	2,214	3,684	3,802
2014 Q1	6,151	5,414	2,932	3,475	3,687 r
Q2	6,195	5,491	3,687	3,977	3,875 r
Q3	5,815	6,238	3,261	4,183	3,922 p
Q4	5,925	5,915	3,275	3,713	3,865 p
2015 Q1	6,547	5,400	4,422	4,035	4,194 p
Q2	6,296	5,843	4,875	3,992	3,867 p
Q3	4,560	5,326	3,146	4,225	4,007

Source: Department for Business, Innovation and Skills (BIS)

* Refers to stocks at the end of the period.

In April 2012, the Mineral Products Association (who provide these figures), estimated that data understates UK deliveries by around 20-25%. Previously, they had estimated that figures understate UK deliveries by 14-18%.

Concrete roofing tiles data have included imputation for non-responders in each quarter since 2012 Q1.

From March 2015, seasonally adjusted figures for deliveries of ready-mixed concrete have been included in this table. In the production of these figures, ready-mixed concrete deliveries data back to Q1 1983 have been seasonally adjusted. This long run data series is available on request.

p Provisional

18.19d Building materials and components

Slate - Production, Deliveries and Stocks

Great Britain   Tonnes

	Production			Deliveries			Stocks 1			Deliveries
	Roofing [2]	Cladding, decorative & crude blocks	Powder & Granules	Roofing [2]	Cladding, decorative & crude blocks	Powder & Granules	Roofing [2]	Cladding, decorative & crude blocks	Powder & Granules	Fill & Other Uses
2003	34,471	15,623	29,003	34,700	14,576	29,240	2,477	8,849	3,416	669,818
2004	c	c	c	c	c	c	c	c	c	c
2005	c	c	c	c	c	c	2,824	10,281	5,347	c
2006	c	61,612	22,967	c	64,037	22,719	c	6,454	4,274	860,395
2007	c	65,260	19,141	c	62,646	19,431	2,563	2,521	3,746	c
2008	c	59,644	16,915	c	58,129	18,402	c	2,749	2,253	c
2009	c	33,759	9,150	22,555	34,322	10,637	2,420	2,186	766	615,346
2010	c	28,001	c	c	27,355	c	c	3,063	c	582,111
2011	c	30,665	c	c	30,437	c	c	3,245	c	662,003
2012	c	29,634	c	c	28,083	c	c	1,351	c	607,127
2013	c	32,419	c	c	31,375	c	c	c	665	692,319
2014	19,358	30,900	15,467	18,596	31,268	15,393	2,925	1,076	0	620,887
2007 Q3	c	16,017	4,672	c	15,475	4,929	2,977	6,391	3,754	c
Q4	c	14,879	4,583	c	15,577	4,591	2,563	2,521	3,746	255,249
2008 Q1	c	18,608	4,282	c	18,071	4,414	c	3,059	3,594	246,495
Q2	c	15,465	4,738	c	14,457	4,862	c	3,801	3,484	c
Q3	c	13,811	3,843	c	13,841	5,511	3,851	2,749	1,816	c
Q4	c	11,760	4,052	c	11,760	3,615	c	2,749	2,253	c
2009 Q1	c	7,370	2,128	5,315	7,688	2,724	c	2,431	1,658	148,722
Q2	5,084	9,124	2,046	5,328	9,319	3,385	4,142	2,236	318	169,661
Q3	5,503	8,263	2,046	6,534	8,267	2,163	3,111	2,232	201	154,862
Q4	4,687	9,002	2,930	5,378	9,048	2,365	2,420	2,186	766	142,101
2010 Q1	c	6,772	c	c	6,662	c	c	2,296	c	88,805
Q2	c	7,517	c	c	7,388	c	2,049	3,284	683	175,098
Q3	c	7,335	c	c	7,184	c	1,326	3,332	281	159,574
Q4	4,907	6,377	c	4,909	6,121	c	c	3,063	c	158,634
2011 Q1	4,736	6,516	3,314	4,449	6,504	3,399	c	3,029	c	198,547
Q2	4,677	8,167	3,370	4,630	8,187	3,094	2,012	3,009	472	216,524
Q3	c	9,851	c	c	9,732	c	c	3,128	c	139,359
Q4	c	6,131	c	c	6,014	c	c	3,245	c	107,573
2012 Q1	c	9,247	c	c	8,829	c	c	2,646	c	131,311
Q2	c	8,216	c	c	9,677	c	c	1,154	c	177,748
Q3	c	6,219	c	c	6,167	c	c	1,206	c	146,152
Q4	c	5,952	c	c	3,410	c	c	1,351	c	151,916
2013 Q1	c	6,052	c	c	9,220	c	c	c	802	157,215
Q2	c	9,638	c	c	9,440	c	c	c	736	216,035
Q3	c	10,429	c	c	6,843	c	c	c	537	169,995
Q4	c	6,300	c	c	5,872	c	c	c	665	149,074
2014 Q1	4,670	5,639	4,036	4,337	5,637	4,209	2,721	1,134	492	159,818
Q2	4,693	7,413	3,946	4,299	7,428	3,657	3,085	1,049	781	179,396
Q3	5,141	8,533	3,837	4,996	8,145	4,054	3,034	988	564	152,155
Q4	4,854	9,315	3,648	4,964	10,058	3,473	2,925	1,076	0	129,518
2015 Q1	c	7,488	c	c	7,564	c	c	833	c	156,704
Q2	3,575	8,461	3,421	4,075	8,443 r	3,692	2,143	583 r	0	148,002
Q3	4,115	7,209	3,636	3,940	7,177	3,667	2,318	615	0	130,949

Source: Department for Business, Innovation and Skills (BIS)

Note : 1) We have improved our sampling panel to include some new sites and have removed some non-pure slate sites. In line with the Code of Practice we have revised the data for Q2, Q3 and Q4 2010.

2) From Q1 1995, the coverage of 'powder & granules' has been extended to include non-quarry manufacture

[1]   Refers to stocks at the end of the period.

[2]   Consists of all slate tiles which could be used as roofing tiles.

r   Revised: These figures have been revised due to an error made by a manufacturer in their initial slate deliveries and stocks survey data for 2015Q1

c   confidential

18.19e Building materials and components
Cement & Clinker - Production and Deliveries

Great Britain   Thousand tonnes

	Cement			Imports *(into GB)*		Cementitious Material		Clinker
	Production		Deliveries					Production
	of which .	**Exports**	*(into GB from*	by	by			
		(from GB)	*GB production)*	'Manuf.	Others*	other	total	
2001	11,090	206	10,656	1,182	360	2,063	14,261	10,183
2002	11,089	146	10,762	966	452	2,175	14,355	10,327
2003	11,215	164	11,072	576	646	2,329	14,623	10,146
2004	11,405	141	11,074	609	825	2,443	14,951	10,402
2005	11,216	110	11,004	306	971	2,385	14,666	10,074
2006	11,469	127	11,221	124	1,089	2,648	15,082	10,069
2007	11,887	74	11,638	255	1,121	2,769	15,783	10,227
2008	10,071	61	9,937	283	1,084	2,432	13,660	8,700
2009	7,623	21	7,474	99	1,085	1,680	10,338	6,421
2010	7,883	0	7,767	61	1,153	1,535	10,515	6,598
2011	8,529	0	8,318	86	1,173	1,736	11,312	7,096
2012	7,952	0	7,728	61	1,122	1,605	10,515	6,555
2013	8,203	0	8,204	117	1,322	1,892	11,535	6,712
2014	8,958	3	8,751	227	1,590	1,864	12,433	7,197

Source: Department of Business, Innovation and Skills (BIS)

1. Arrangements for publication of the cementitious data have been revised following discussion and agreement by the Mineral Products Association (MPA) Cement members. Data are now provided on an annual basis. For quarterly and monthly data up to September 2013, please refer to earlier editions of this publication.

2. Where the coverage is for Great Britain, the figures for imports & exports are defined accordingly and have been estimated. Cementitious material covers cement itself, fly ash to EN 450 Part 1 where used as part of the cement in concrete (previously known as pulverised fuel ash (pfa) to BS 3892 Part 1) and ground granulated blast furnace slag (ggbs) to EN 15167 Part 1 (previously BS 6699)

* Estimated

18.19f Building materials and components
Sales of Sand and Gravel in Great Britain

Great Britain   Thousand tonnes

	Seasonally Adjusted Sand & Gravel Total	Sand for Building	for Concreting	Gravel for Concreting & other uses	Sand & Gravel for Coating	Sand, Gravel & Hoggin for Fill	Sand & Gravel Total	of which Marine-Dredged
2004	81,346	11,017	32,366	30,184	1,380	6,399	81,346	12,996
2005	80,513	12,419	30,704	30,648	1,569	5,173	80,513	13,025
2006	77,896	9,499	29,893	31,963	2,346	4,195	77,896	13,974
2007	75,515	8,649	29,803	31,114	1,695	4,254	75,515	13,777
2008	74,651	8,864	28,922	28,297	c	c	74,651	12,582
2009	58,482	7,270	21,582	c	c	c	58,482	9,589
2010	54,530	6,074	19,887	c	c	c	54,530	9,341
2011	57,062	6,041	23,489	c	c	c	57,062	11,169
2012	57,972	6,499	21,994	23,077	c	c	57,972	10,320
2013	52,591	5,722	19,036	18,890	c	c	52,591	10,489
2014	52,552	5,803	19,217	20,356	1,416	5,640	52,430	11,713
2009 Q3	14,310	1,992	5,598	c	c	c	14,878	2,457
Q4	14,415	1,635	5,034	c	c	1,432	13,614	2,106
2010 Q1	14,046	1,539	4,952	c	c	c	13,711	2,131
Q2	13,431	1,585	4,983	c	c	c	13,940	2,444
Q3	13,522	1,584	5,268	c	c	c	14,112	2,592
Q4	13,531	1,366	4,684	c	c	c	12,767	2,174
2011 Q1	14,490	1,572	5,665	c	c	c	14,150	2,746
Q2	14,401	1,579	6,127	5,291	c	c	14,831	2,923
Q3	13,986	1,533	6,085	5,160	c	c	14,684	2,937
Q4	14,185	1,357	5,612	4,719	c	c	13,397	2,563
2012 Q1	14,322	1,481	5,635	5,039	c	c	13,894	2,675
Q2	14,099	1,712	5,608	5,633	c	c	14,474	2,609
Q3	14,301	1,778	5,612	6,259	c	c	15,192	2,749
Q4	15,250	1,528	5,139	6,146	c	c	14,412	2,287
2013 Q1	13,522	1,380	4,854	5,107	c	c	12,957	2,260
Q2	13,289	1,570	4,665	4,908	c	c	13,662	2,681
Q3	13,001	1,545	5,007	4,760	322	2,264	13,898	2,914
Q4	12,778	1,227	4,510	4,115	c	c	12,074	2,634
2014 Q1	12,699	1,379	4,221	4,393	394	1,533	11,919	2,447
Q2	13,036	1,472	4,744	5,627	302	1,379	13,524	3,296
Q3	13,392 p	1,593	5,456	5,511	387	1,388	14,334	3,138
Q4	13,425 p	1,359	4,796	4,825	333	1,340	12,653	2,832
2015 Q1	13,427 p	1,352	4,722	4,643	283	1,598	12,599	2,905
Q2	13,669 p	1,626	5,539	5,170	413	1,617	14,364	3,150
Q3	12,450 p	1,465	5,140	4,841	386	1,464	13,297	3,003

Note :   The figures above are from a quarterly sample inquiry whereas those below are from the Annual Minerals Raised Inquiry, a census. The two inquiries differ because some respondents are only able to provide estimated information for the quarterly inquiry.

From March 2015, seasonally adjusted figures for sales of sand and gravel have been included in this table. In the production of these figures, data back to 1983Q1 have been seasonally adjusted. This long run data series is available on request.

2000		11,758	31,167	31,797	2,461	12,051	89,234	14,356
2001		11,515	31,656	35,135	2,257	7,647	88,210	13,611
2002		11,190	31,224	32,434	2,031	5,842	82,721	12,832
2003		11,851	31,411	30,236	1,766	4,957	80,221	12,131
2004		10,688	32,529	32,346	2,437	8,058	86,057	12,996
2005		11,558	29,848	32,163	2,172	6,651	82,392	13,024
2006		9,907	29,815	31,002	2,648	6,869	80,242	13,974
2007		9,877	30,202	29,350	2,636	6,436	78,501	13,777
2008		8,527	26,885	23,388	2,222	11,106	72,127	12,621
2009		6,296	21,570	19,553	2,270	6,021	55,709	9,592
2010		6,110	20,947	18,540	2,112	6,621	54,330	9,341
2011		6,140	22,591	18,712	1,913	5,659	55,015	11,189
2012		5,474	19,697	18,072	1,817	4,985	50,044	10,291
2013		5,204	20,361	18,175	1,225	6,960	51,925	10,487

Source: Department of Buiness, Innovation and Skills (BIS)

c Confidential
p Provisional

18.20 Volume of construction output in Great Britain. Seasonally adjusted index numbers by sector

2013=100

Period	New Housing			Other New Work Excluding Infrastructure				All New Work	Repair and Maintenance Housing			Non Housing R&M	All Repair and Maintenance	All Work
	Public	Private	Total Housing	Infrastr-ucture	Public	Private Industrial	Private Commercial		Public	Private	Total			
	MV36	MV37	MVL7	MV38	MV39	MV3A	MV3B	MV3C	MV3D	MV3E	MV3F	MV3G	MV3H	MV3I
2010 Q1	101.3	77.0	81.7	102.8	147.1	105.9	104.5	103.0	109.5	93.2	98.5	86.0	92.2	98.9
Q2	105.5	84.7	88.8	107.6	154.2	108.4	107.4	108.1	114.8	101.0	105.4	92.3	98.9	104.5
Q3	117.2	91.2	96.2	101.7	149.5	126.8	113.6	111.4	111.1	107.8	108.8	90.5	99.7	106.9
Q4	114.7	90.7	95.3	91.6	154.9	103.1	107.5	106.8	108.8	106.0	106.9	92.4	99.7	104.0
2011 Q1	119.6	92.5	97.8	104.2	156.6	99.3	106.2	109.7	103.5	102.4	102.7	95.0	98.9	105.5
Q2	114.3	93.3	97.4	114.6	143.3	102.7	110.7	111.4	104.2	101.6	102.4	94.8	98.6	106.5
Q3	109.5	95.5	98.2	109.2	133.7	99.8	112.6	109.8	99.9	101.3	100.9	97.4	99.1	105.7
Q4	104.9	93.3	95.6	109.5	126.4	100.4	114.0	108.5	100.6	106.0	104.3	98.3	101.3	105.7
2012 Q1	100.8	97.1	97.8	98.6	121.0	107.9	104.0	103.5	100.7	102.8	102.1	97.2	99.7	102.0
Q2	89.3	89.3	89.3	91.8	111.4	108.1	103.6	98.1	103.9	98.2	100.1	96.6	98.3	98.2
Q3	93.3	87.8	88.9	99.1	107.3	107.7	95.4	96.3	106.3	96.4	99.6	94.5	97.1	96.6
Q4	91.8	91.4	91.5	101.7	102.7	116.9	96.9	97.9	106.1	93.5	97.6	95.6	96.6	97.4
2013 Q1	91.1	90.9	90.9	99.0	99.5	108.5	97.9	96.7	102.4	96.6	98.4	96.6	97.5	97.0
Q2	95.6	98.8	98.1	98.6	101.1	98.6	97.5	98.5	99.8	98.8	99.1	99.1	99.1	98.7
Q3	101.3	102.2	102.0	98.8	102.8	97.6	103.6	101.8	98.0	101.9	100.6	101.4	101.0	101.5
Q4	112.1	108.2	108.9	103.6	96.6	95.3	101.0	103.1	99.8	102.7	101.8	103.0	102.4	102.8
2014 Q1	122.4	115.9	117.1	95.6	96.1	106.6	105.1	105.7	101.5	108.6	106.3	103.1	104.7	105.3
Q2	130.2	119.9	121.9	91.9	98.6	118.0	105.7	107.5	102.0	107.3	105.6	107.6	106.6	107.1
Q3	138.2	128.6	130.4	95.7	100.3	118.0	105.9	111.2	102.2	109.9	107.4	108.4	107.9	109.9
Q4	132.0	130.1	130.4	102.3	100.6	113.9	107.6	112.8	100.7	107.0	105.0	107.1	106.0	110.2
2015 Q1	123.7	131.8	130.2	122.8	96.2	124.9	106.7	116.6	103.0	106.0	105.1	105.8	105.4	112.3

Source: Office for National Statistics (ONS)

18.21 Value of orders for new construction obtained by main contractors in Great Britain, by sector

£million

		New Housing			Other New Work Excluding Infrastructure						Period on period growths (%)	Period on same period one year ago growths (%)
		Public	Private	All New Housing	Infra-structure	Public	Private Industrial	Private Commercial	All Other Work	All New Work		
2010		3,482	9,953	13,435	9,774	13,430	2,131	13,581	38,916	52,349	3.1	
2011		2,691	10,506	13,196	8,499	9,065	2,145	13,005	32,714	45,911	-12.3	
2012		2,450	10,805	13,255	12,510	8,028	2,659	11,973	35,170	48,423	5.5	
2013		3,990	14,575	18,565	10,819	9,062	3,604	13,563	37,047	55,612	14.8	
2014		2,034	16,627	18,661	9,666	9,841	3,934	16,916	40,357	59,019	6.1	
2010	Q1	1,333	2,294	3,627	3,350	3,712	492	3,348	10,902	14,529	18.8	28.5
	Q2	738	2,182	2,920	2,533	3,465	603	3,586	10,187	13,106	-9.8	-5.3
	Q3	544	2,913	3,457	1,501	2,882	526	3,650	8,559	12,016	-8.3	-10.4
	Q4	867	2,564	3,431	2,390	3,371	510	2,997	9,268	12,698	5.7	3.8
2011	Q1	1,203	2,798	4,001	2,110	2,927	530	3,279	8,846	12,847	1.2	-11.6
	Q2	535	2,594	3,129	1,461	2,141	551	3,225	7,378	10,508	-18.2	-19.8
	Q3	533	2,573	3,105	1,726	2,355	537	3,928	8,546	11,652	10.9	-3.0
	Q4	420	2,541	2,961	3,202	1,642	527	2,573	7,944	10,904	-6.4	-14.1
2012	Q1	736	2,524	3,260	3,347	1,709	778	3,550	9,384	12,643	15.9	-1.6
	Q2	490	2,631	3,121	1,941	2,103	578	2,833	7,455	10,577	-16.3	0.7
	Q3	592	2,644	3,236	2,681	2,128	734	2,716	8,259	11,494	8.7	-1.4
	Q4	632	3,006	3,638	4,541	2,088	569	2,874	10,072	13,709	19.3	25.7
2013	Q1	1,032	3,240	4,272	2,022	2,572	627	3,277	8,498	12,769	-6.9	1.0
	Q2	892	3,811	4,704	2,958	2,210	750	3,498	9,415	14,119	10.6	33.5
	Q3	1,058	3,605	4,663	2,974	2,048	992	3,363	9,378	14,040	-0.6	22.2
	Q4	1,007	3,920	4,927	2,864	2,231	1,236	3,425	9,756	14,683	4.6	7.1
2014	Q1	766	4,264	5,030	1,893	2,531	1,060	3,608	9,092	14,123	-3.8	10.6
	Q2	557	3,954	4,511	2,122	2,747	1,051	4,040	9,960	14,472	2.5	2.5
	Q3	379	4,355	4,735	2,598	2,372	682	5,013	10,665	15,400	6.4	9.7
	Q4	332	4,053	4,385	3,053	2,191	1,141	4,255	10,639	15,024	-2.4	2.3
2015	Q1	433	4,393	4,827	3,175	2,105	1,217	4,185	10,682	15,509	3.2	9.8

Source: Office for National Statistics (ONS)

18.22 Total engineering[1]

Values at current prices

£ million

	Turnover			New Orders		
	Export	Home	Total	Export	Home	Total
	JWO5	JWO6	JWO7	JWO8	JWO9	JWP2
2008	33,929.2	68,053.8	101,983.0	30,512.2	54,571.6	85,084.4
2009	29,994.1	56,556.9	86,550.6	26,189.2	44,661.1	70,850.7
2010	37,532.0	61,679.2	99,211.2	35,537.8	54,997.3	90,535.1
2011	40,021.3	63,718.0	103,739.3	38,364.0	53,445.6	91,809.6
2012	40,458.8	66,938.9	107,397.7	38,569.9	52,650.2	91,220.1
2013	41,248.8	61,547.6	102,796.4	-	-	-
2014	40,394.7	64,246.7	104,641.4	-	-	-
2009 Q1	7,396.6	14,414.2	21,810.7	6,415.1	10,982.5	17,398.1
Q2	7,065.8	13,824.1	20,889.9	6,452.2	10,589.0	17,041.3
Q3	7,094.7	14,005.9	21,100.4	6,328.2	11,271.4	17,599.5
Q4	8,437.0	14,312.7	22,749.6	6,993.7	11,818.2	18,811.8
2010 Q1	8,405.6	14,561.7	22,967.3	8,184.8	13,131.0	21,315.8
Q2	9,268.8	15,326.0	24,594.8	9,293.0	14,418.4	23,711.4
Q3	9,498.2	16,005.1	25,503.3	8,595.8	13,589.2	22,185.0
Q4	10,359.4	15,786.4	26,145.8	9,464.2	13,858.7	23,322.9
2011 Q1	10,003.1	15,286.3	25,289.4	10,198.5	12,874.7	23,073.2
Q2	10,216.5	15,953.7	26,170.2	10,357.6	13,311.0	23,668.6
Q3	9,737.5	16,471.0	26,208.5	8,777.4	13,159.5	21,936.9
Q4	10,064.2	16,007.0	26,071.2	9,030.5	14,100.4	23,130.9
2012 Q1	9784.2	16,486.3	26,270.5	10,167.2	13,636.5	23,803.7
Q2	10224.1	17,159.1	27,383.2	9,528.5	13,034.2	22,562.7
Q3	9862.7	16,861.3	26,724.0	8,794.5	12,945.7	21,740.2
Q4	10587.8	16,432.2	27,020.0	10,079.7	13,033.8	23,113.5
2013 Q1	10,034.20	14,750.6	24,784.8	-	-	-
Q2	10,682.30	15,189.0	25,871.3	-	-	-
Q3	10,154.90	15,767.1	25,922.0	-	-	-
Q4	10,377.40	15,840.9	26,218.3	-	-	-
2014 Q1	9,857.3	15,703.2	25,560.5	-	-	-
Q2	10,127.1	16,002.1	26,129.2	-	-	-
Q3	9,778.6	16,277.0	26,055.6	-	-	-
Q4	10,631.7	16,264.4	26,896.1	-	-	-
2013 Jan	2,907.2	5,056.4	7,963.6	-	-	-
Feb	3,066.0	5,229.0	8,295.0	-	-	-
Mar	4,061.0	6,200.9	10,261.9	-	-	-
Apr	3,604.2	5,165.3	8,769.5	-	-	-
May	3,391.1	5,819.0	9,210.1	-	-	-
June	3,687.0	6,174.8	9,861.8	-	-	-
July	3,539.3	5,913.4	9,452.7	-	-	-
August	3,008.5	5,514.2	8,522.7	-	-	-
September	3,607.1	5,433.7	9,040.8	-	-	-
October	3,428.0	5,847.2	9,275.2	-	-	-
November	3,395.9	5,835.4	9,231.3	-	-	-
December	3,553.5	4,749.6	8,303.1	-	-	-
2014 Jan	3,116.0	4,929.5	8,045.5	-	-	-
Feb	3,017.4	5,003.9	8,021.3	-	-	-
Mar	3,723.9	5,769.8	9,493.7	-	-	-
Apr	3,188.3	5,125.5	8,313.8	-	-	-
May	3,275.8	5,206.0	8,481.8	-	-	-
June	3,663.0	5,670.6	9,333.6	-	-	-
July	3,266.4	5,623.0	8,889.4	-	-	-
August	2,853.5	4,923.6	7,777.1	-	-	-
September	3,658.7	5,730.4	9,389.1	-	-	-
October	3,521.5	5,619.5	9,141.0	-	-	-
November	3,407.3	5,317.2	8,724.5	-	-	-
December	3,702.9	5,327.7	9,030.6	-	-	-

Source: Office for National Statistics : 01633 646659

- As of January 2013, New Orders data is no longer being collected

1 The data for this table is based on SIC 2007 (the Industrial Classification for 2007). The change is a result of the SIC 2003 based MPI survey (which provided figures up to the April edition of the Monthly Digest) becoming part of the SIC 2007 based Monthly Business Survey (MBS). This is part of an ONS wide project to convert all data series to the latest SIC. This means that this table is now Total engineering (SIC 07 25-28) Please note this new table does not include Orders on Hand.

18.23 Manufacture of fabricated metal products and machinery and equipment n.e.c.[1]

Values at current prices

£ million

	Turnover			New Orders		
	Export	Home	Total	Export	Home	Total
	JWM9	JWN2	JWN3	JWN4	JWN5	JWN6
2008	20,022.2	46,615.9	66,638.5	16,445.4	36,125.6	52,571.6
2009	16,407.4	37,694.8	54,102.1	14,092.0	26,752.2	40,844.4
2010	22,257.5	42,731.1	64,988.6	21,727.5	34,866.8	56,594.3
2011	24,209.6	46,149.6	70,359.2	24,884.9	35,766.8	60,651.7
2012	24,794.0	47,704.2	72,498.2	24,489.3	34,234.2	58,723.5
2013	23,644.6	43,936.4	67,581.0	-	-	-
2014	23,079.1	46,767.2	69,846.3	-	-	-
2009 Q1	3,975.4	9,812.2	13,787.6	3,238.9	6,990.6	10,229.9
Q2	3,776.4	9,349.0	13,125.4	3,620.6	6,259.2	9,879.8
Q3	3,866.1	9,359.6	13,225.5	3,398.0	6,789.5	10,187.4
Q4	4,789.5	9,174.0	13,963.6	3,834.5	6,712.9	10,547.3
2010 Q1	4,838.8	9,902.9	14,741.7	4,810.6	8,203.9	13,014.5
Q2	5,567.2	10,577.9	16,145.1	5,852.1	9,155.6	15,007.7
Q3	5,622.2	11,313.3	16,935.5	5,113.6	8,520.7	13,634.3
Q4	6,229.3	10,937.0	17,166.3	5,951.2	8,986.6	14,937.8
2011 Q1	6,033.3	10,736.0	16,769.3	6,554.6	8,407.0	14,961.6
Q2	6,110.9	11,745.8	17,856.7	6,830.3	9,006.5	15,836.8
Q3	5,978.8	12,137.6	18,116.4	5,756.8	8,804.5	14,561.3
Q4	6,086.6	11,530.2	17,616.8	5,743.2	9,548.8	15,292.0
2012 Q1	5,995.6	11,728.6	17,724.2	6,493.8	8,721.4	15,215.2
Q2	6,327.4	12,382.9	18,710.3	6,089.3	8,674.9	14,764.2
Q3	6,095.4	12,006.9	18,102.3	5,459.0	8,355.3	13,814.3
Q4	6,375.6	11,585.8	17,961.4	6,447.2	8,482.6	14,929.8
2013 Q1	10,034.2	14,750.6	24,784.8	-	-	-
Q2	10,682.3	15,189.0	25,871.3	-	-	-
Q3	10,154.9	15,767.1	25,922.0	-	-	-
Q4	10,377.4	15,840.9	26,218.3	-	-	-
2014 Q1	5,836.5	11,255.1	17,091.6	-	-	-
Q2	5,875.0	11,827.6	17,702.6	-	-	-
Q3	5,579.8	12,006.1	17,585.9	-	-	-
Q4	5,787.8	11,678.4	17,466.2	-	-	-
2013 Jan	2,907.2	4,635.9	7,543.1	-	-	-
Feb	3,066.0	4,667.6	7,733.6	-	-	-
Mar	4,061.0	5,447.1	9,508.1	-	-	-
Apr	3,604.2	4,954.2	8,558.4	-	-	-
May	3,391.1	5,006.6	8,397.7	-	-	-
June	3,687.0	5,228.2	8,915.2	-	-	-
July	3,539.3	5,401.1	8,940.4	-	-	-
August	3,008.5	4,975.0	7,983.5	-	-	-
September	3,607.1	5,391.0	8,998.1	-	-	-
October	3,428.0	5,814.0	9,242.0	-	-	-
November	3,395.9	5,313.3	8,709.2	-	-	-
December	3,553.5	4,713.6	8,267.1	-	-	-
2014 Jan	1,848.3	3,549.6	5,397.9	-	-	-
Feb	1,850.1	3,597.0	5,447.1	-	-	-
Mar	2,138.1	4,108.5	6,246.6	-	-	-
Apr	1,875.2	3,736.4	5,611.6	-	-	-
May	1,945.2	3,869.3	5,814.5	-	-	-
June	2,054.6	4,221.9	6,276.5	-	-	-
July	1,958.6	4,180.0	6,138.6	-	-	-
August	1,569.2	3,641.5	5,210.7	-	-	-
September	2,052.0	4,184.6	6,236.6	-	-	-
October	2,017.0	4,119.2	6,136.2	-	-	-
November	1,902.6	3,834.9	5,737.5	-	-	-
December	1,868.2	3,724.3	5,592.5	-	-	-

Source: Office for National Statistics : 01633 646659

- As of Jan 2013, new orders data is no longer collected

1 The data for this table is based on SIC 2007 (the Industrial Classification for 2007). The change is a result of the SIC 2003 based MPI survey (which provided figures up to the April edition of the Monthly Digest) becoming part of the SIC 2007 based Monthly Business Survey (MBS). This is part of an ONS wide project to convert all data series to the latest SIC. Manufacture of fabricated metal products and machinery and equipment n.e.c. (SIC 07 25, 28). Please note this new table does not include Orders on Hand.

18.24 Alcoholic drink

Calendar Year	Spirits					Beer			
	Production (hl of pure alcohol)	Whisky (hl of pure alcohol)	RTD (hl of pure alcohol)	Imported and other (hl of pure alcohol)	Total (hl of pure alcohol)	Production (thousand hl)	Released for home consumption (thousand hl)	Production (thousand hl of pure alcohol)	Clearances (thousand hl of pure alcohol)
2002	4508	321	105	689	1115	56672	59384	2352	2473
2003	4553	318	124	744	1187	58014	60301	2414	2515
2004	4081	319	114	792	1226	57461	59194	2433	2499
2005	4365	301	84	822	1206	56255	57572	2338	2398
2006	4485	283	65	767	1114	53768	55751	2250	2335
2007	5498	286	52	832	1170	51341	53465	2160	2247
2008	6072	289	42	817	1148	49611	51498	2062	2145
2009	5757	258	32	802	1091	45141	46817	1891	1957
2010	5074	267	35	842	1144	44997	45872	1905	1932
2011	5697	257	30	828	1116	45694	42527	1934	1881
2012	6185	258	24	836	1117	42047	42962	1752	1790
2013	8434	245	22	821	1087	41956	42422	1735	1758

Calendar Year	Wine of Fresh Grapes				Made Wine				Cider and Perry
	Fortified (hl)	Still table (hl)	Sparkling (hl)	Total (hl)	Still (hl)	Sparkling (hl)	Coolers (hl)	Total (hl)	Released for home consumption (thousand hl)
2002	325	10319	578	11222	366	2	1606	1974	5939
2003	296	10647	640	11584	338	1	423	762	5876
2004	298	11768	676	12742	351	1	508	859	6139
2005	306	12117	721	13143	334	0	597	931	6377
2006	302	11655	715	12672	316	1	528	844	7523
2007	305	12559	838	13702	343	5	720	1068	8046
2008	324	12402	757	13483	374	7	611	993	8412
2009	219	11729	731	12680	390	2	597	989	9404
2010	220	11870	810	12900	400	5	758	1162	9399
2011	217	11844	800	12860	440	7	828	1275	9280
2012	224	11705	872	12808	424	3	1000	1427	8737
2013	228	11586	925	12739	422	5	1395	1822	8640

Source: Her Majesty's Revenue and Customs
Published in the HMRC Alcohol Bulletin

18.25 Tobacco products: recent receipts

Calendar Year	Cigarettes			Other			Overall Total (thousand kg)
	Home Produced (million sticks)	Imported (million sticks)	Total (million sticks)	Cigars (thousand kg)	HRT (thousand kg)	Other (thousand kg)	
2008	7005	579	7585	86	473	27	8171
2009	7473	578	8051	92	607	29	8779
2010	7590	662	8252	86	683	29	9051
2011	7899	657	8556	87	845	28	9517
2012	7954	637	8591	88	991	29	9699
2013	7723	625	8348	82	1073	27	9530

Source: Her Majesty's Revenue and Customs
Published in the HMRC Tobacco Bulletin

National accounts

Chapter 19

National accounts

The tables are based on those in The Blue Book 2015 Edition. The Blue Book presents the full set of economic accounts for the United Kingdom. The accounts are based on the European System of Accounts 2010 (ESA 2010), a system of national accounts that all European Union members have agreed to use.

The Blue Book contains an introduction which provides an overview of the accounts and an explanation of the underlying framework.

Brief definitions of some national accounting terms used in this chapter are included here. Current prices (or, more precisely, current price estimates) describe values during the period of the observation. Hence, in a time series, they will describe changes to price and to volume. Chain volume measures exclude the effects of price change. Basic prices do not include taxes and subsidies on products, whereas these are included in market prices.

Gross Domestic Product and Gross National Income
(Tables 19.1, 19.2, 19.3)

Table 19.1 shows three of the most important economic aggregates: Gross Domestic Product (GDP), Gross National Income (GNI) and Gross National Disposable Income (GNDI). In all three cases 'gross' denotes that depreciation (or consumption) of fixed capital is ignored. GDP is the total value of the UK's output. GNI is GDP plus primary incomes received from the rest of the world minus primary incomes paid to the rest of the world. Primary income comprises taxes on production and imports, property income and compensation of employees. These measures are given as current price estimates and chained volume measures. GNDI equals GNI plus net current transfers to the rest of the world. Transfers are unrequited payments such as taxes, social benefits and remittances.

There are three different approaches to measuring GDP: output, income and expenditure. Table 19.2 shows the various money flows which are used in these different approaches, and those that are used to measure GNI at current prices. The output approach to measuring GDP takes the gross value added for the entire economy (that is, the value of the UK's output minus the goods and services consumed in the productive process) to give gross value added at basic prices. This figure is then adjusted to include taxes and exclude subsidies on products. This gives gross value added at market prices for the UK, which is equivalent to GDP.

The expenditure approach to GDP shows consumption expenditure by households and government, gross capital formation and expenditure on UK exports. The sum of these items overstates the amount of income generated in the UK by the value of imported goods and services. This item is therefore subtracted to produce GDP at market prices.

The income approach to GDP shows gross operating surplus, mixed income and compensation of employees (previously known as income from employment). Production taxes less subsidies are added to produce the total of the income-based components at market prices.

Table 19.2 also shows the primary incomes received from the rest of the world, which are added to GDP, and primary incomes payable to non-resident units, which are deducted from GDP, to arrive at GNI. Primary income comprises compensation of employees, taxes less subsidies on production, and property and entrepreneurial income. The data in Table 19.2 are in current prices. This means that changes between years will be driven by a combination of price effects and changes in the volume of production. The second of these components is often referred to as 'real growth'.

Table 19.3 shows the expenditure approach to the chained volume measure of GDP, that is to say the effects of price change have been removed. In chained volume series, volume measures for each year are produced in prices of the previous year. These volume measures are then 'chain-linked' together to produce a continuous time series.

Industrial analysis
(Tables 19.4, 19.5)

The analysis of gross value added by industry at current prices shown in Table 19.4 reflects the estimates based on the 2007 Standard Industrial Classification (SIC2007). The table is based on current price data reconciled through the input–output process for 2006 to 2013.

Table 19.5 shows chained volume measures of gross value added by industry. These indices are based on basic price measures. Chained volume measures of gross value added provides a lead economic indicator. The analysis of gross value added is estimated in terms of change and expressed in index number form.

Sector analysis – Distribution of income accounts and capital account
(Tables 19.6 to 19.13)

The National Accounts accounting framework includes the sector accounts which provide, by institutional sector, a description of the different stages of the economic process, from the income generated by production and its distribution and re-distribution to different economic units, and finally, capital accumulation and financing. Tables 19.6 to 19.12 show the 'allocation of primary income account' and the 'secondary distribution of income account' for the non-financial corporations, financial corporations, government and households sectors. Additionally, Table 19.12 shows the 'use of income account' for the households sector and Table 19.13 provides a summary of the capital account. The full sequence of accounts is shown in The Blue Book.

The allocation of primary income account shows the resident units and institutional sectors as recipients rather than producers of primary income. The balancing item of this account is the gross balance of primary income (B.5g) for each sector and, if the gross balance is aggregated across all sectors of the economy, the result is Gross National Income.

The secondary distribution of income account describes how the balance of income for each sector is allocated by redistribution; through transfers such as taxes on income, social contributions and benefits, and other current transfers. The balancing item of this account is Gross Disposable Income (GDI). For the households sector, the chained volume measure of GDI is shown as real household disposable income.

Table 19.12 shows, for the household sector, the use of disposable income where the balancing item is saving (B.8g). For the non-financial corporations sector the balancing item of the secondary distribution of income account, gross disposable income (B.6g), is equal to saving (B.8g).

The summary capital account (Table 19.13) brings together the saving and investment of the sectors of the economy. It shows saving, capital transfers, gross capital formation and net acquisition of non-financial assets for each of these.

Households' and non-profit institutions serving households' consumption expenditure at current market prices and chained volume measures
(Tables 19.14 to 19.17)

Households' and non-profit institutions serving households' (NPISH) final consumption expenditure is a major component of the expenditure measure of GDP. In Table 19.2 this expenditure is given at current market prices, broken down by the type of good or service purchased. Table 19.3 supplies the same breakdown in chain volume measures. Household final consumption expenditure includes the value of income-in-kind and imputed rent of owner-occupied dwellings. It includes expenditure on durable goods (for instance motor cars) which, from the point of view of the individual might more appropriately be treated as capital expenditure. The purchase of land and dwellings (including costs incurred in connection with the transfer of their ownership) and expenditure on major improvements by occupiers are treated as personal capital expenditure. Other goods and services purchased by the household sector (with the exception of goods and services that are to be used in self-employment) are treated as final consumption expenditure. The most detailed figures are published quarterly in Consumer Trends

Change in inventories (previously known as value of physical increase in stocks and work in progress
(Table 19.18)

This table gives a broad analysis by industry of the value of entries less withdrawals and losses of inventories (stocks), and analysis by asset for manufacturing industry.

Gross fixed capital formation
(Table 19.19 to 19.22)

Gross fixed capital formation is the total value of the acquisition less disposal of fixed assets, and improvements to land.

19.1 UK national and domestic product
Main aggregates: Index numbers and values
Current prices and chained volume measures (reference year 2012)

		2001	2002	2003	2004	2005	2006	2007
Indices (2012=100)								
	Values at current prices							
B.1*g Gross domestic product at current market prices ("Money GDP")	YBEU	64.1	67.3	71.5	75.4	79.9	84.5	89.1
B.1g Gross value added at current basic prices	YBEX	64.1	67.5	71.7	75.6	80.3	84.9	89.6
	Chained volume measures							
B.1*g Gross domestic product at market prices	YBEZ	85.0	87.1	90.0	92.3	95.0	97.6	100.1
B.6*g Gross national disposable income at market prices	YBFP	86.5	89.2	92.5	95.0	98.2	99.4	101.7
B.1g Gross value added at basic prices	CGCE	85.1	87.0	90.0	92.1	95.1	97.6	100.1
	Prices							
Implied deflator of GDP at market prices	YBGB	75.4	77.3	79.4	81.7	84.1	86.6	89.0
Values at current prices (£ million)								
Gross measures (before deduction of consumption of fixed capital) at current market prices								
B.1*g Gross domestic product ("Money GDP")	YBHA	1067019	1121067	1190103	1255107	1330418	1406620	1484273
D.1+D.4 Employment, property and entrepreneurial income from rest of the world (receipts less payments)	YBGG	10681	17928	19383	22202	31484	15636	15892
-D.21+D.31 Subsidies (receipts) less taxes (payments) on products from/to rest of the world	QZOZ	3	-449	-680	-687	2261	2329	2412
+D.29-D.39 Other subsidies on production from/to rest of the world	IBJL	-582	-519	-592	-592	-3408	-3221	-2952
B.5*g Gross balance of primary incomes/gross national income (GNI)	ABMX	1078279	1139963	1210758	1278590	1363053	1423148	1500710
D.5,6,7 Current transfers from rest of the world (receipts less payments)	YBGF	6893	9382	10822	11090	12865	12702	13977
B.6*g Gross national disposable income	NQCO	1071386	1130581	1199936	1267500	1350188	1410446	1486733
Adjustment to current basic prices								
B.1*g Gross domestic product (at current market prices)	YBHA	1067019	1121067	1190103	1255107	1330418	1406620	1484273
D.21 Adjustment to current basic prices D.31 (less taxes plus subsidies on products)	NQBU	114204	118297	124390	132101	137631	144779	153153
B.1g Gross value added (at current basic prices)	ABML	952815	1002770	1065713	1123006	1192787	1261841	1331120
P.51c Net measures (after deduction of consumption of fixed capital) at current market prices	NQAE	149966	160717	171254	180028	187535	201722	211450
B.1*n Net domestic product	NHRK	917053	960350	1018849	1075079	1142883	1204898	1272823
B.5*n Net national income	NSRX	928313	979246	1039504	1098560	1175514	1221426	1289255
B.6*n Net national disposable income	NQCP	921420	969864	1028682	1087472	1162653	1208724	1275283
Chained volume measures (reference year 2012, £ million)								
Gross measures (before deduction of consumption of fixed capital) at market prices								
B.1*g Gross domestic product	ABMI	1415605	1450910	1499322	1536631	1582675	1624802	1666821
TGL Terms of trade effect ("trading gain or loss")	YBGJ	966	4233	9006	10845	8648	5310	2225
GDI Real gross domestic income	YBGL	1416571	1455143	1508328	1547476	1591323	1630112	1669046
D.1+D.4 Real employment, property and entrepreneurial income from rest of the world (receipts less payments)	YBGI	14166	23282	24597	27443	37750	18159	17915
-D.21+D.31 Subsidies (receipts) less taxes (payments) on products from/to rest of the world	QZPB	4	-582	-862	-849	2711	2705	2719
+D.29-D.39 Other subsidies on production from/to rest of the world	IBJN	-772	-674	-751	-732	-4086	-3741	-3328
B.5*g Gross balance of primary incomes/gross national income (GNI)	YBGM	1431472	1479657	1534512	1576471	1630393	1649301	1687566
D.5,6,7 Real current transfers from rest of the world (receipts less payments)	YBGP	9143	12185	13734	13709	15426	14753	15759
B.6*g Gross national disposable income	YBGO	1422326	1467466	1520774	1562756	1614964	1634544	1671804
Adjustment to basic prices								
B.1*g Gross domestic product (at market prices)	ABMI	1415605	1450910	1499322	1536631	1582675	1624802	1666821
D.21 Adjustment to basic prices D.31 (less taxes plus subsidies on products)	NTAQ	151050	158206	162656	169615	170414	175480	180364
B.1g Gross value added (at basic prices)	ABMM	1265107	1293255	1337207	1367688	1412732	1449829	1486995
P.51c Net measures (after deduction of consumption of fixed capital) at market prices	CIHA	176535	187677	198657	207383	211728	222251	230330
B.5*n Net national income at market prices	YBET	1254879	1291211	1334598	1367554	1417379	1425306	1455387
B.6*n Net national disposable income at market prices	YBEY	1245836	1279074	1320898	1353883	1401983	1410588	1439661

19.1

UK national and domestic product
Main aggregates: Index numbers and values
Current prices and chained volume measures (reference year 2012)

continued

			2008	2009	2010	2011	2012	2013	2014
	Indices (2012=100)								
	Values at current prices								
B.1*g	Gross domestic product at current market prices ("money GDP")	YBEU	91.3	89.2	93.4	97.3	100.0	104.2	109.1
B.1g	Gross value added at current basic prices	YBEX	92.2	90.8	94.1	97.1	100.0	104.1	108.9
	Chained volume measures								
B.1*g	Gross domestic product at market prices	YBEZ	99.6	95.5	96.9	98.8	100.0	102.2	105.2
B.6*g	Gross national disposable income at market prices	YBFP	99.5	95.7	98.2	99.8	100.0	101.4	103.8
B.1g	Gross value added at basic prices	CGCE	99.9	95.5	97.2	99.0	100.0	102.2	105.1
	Prices								
	Implied deflator of GDP at market prices	YBGB	91.6	93.5	96.4	98.4	100.0	102.0	103.7
	Values at current prices (£ million)								
	Gross measures (before deduction of consumption of fixed capital) at current market prices								
B.1*g	Gross domestic product ("Money GDP")	YBHA	1519597	1485727	1555548	1619480	1665213	1734949	1816439
D.1+D.4	Employment, property and entrepreneurial income from rest of the world (receipts less payments)	YBGG	4919	4604	20079	20254	1371	-16362	-32457
-D.21+D.31	Subsidies (receipts) less taxes (payments) on products from/to rest of the world	QZOZ	2636	2645	2945	2937	2898	2926	2960
+D.29-D.39	Other subsidies on production from/to rest of the world	IBJL	-3051	-3411	-3059	-3166	-2625	-2455	-2309
B.5*g	Gross balance of primary incomes/gross national income (GNI)	ABMX	1524933	1491097	1575742	1639966	1666313	1718118	1783331
D.5,6,7	Current transfers from rest of the world (receipts less payments)	YBGF	14094	15836	20662	21673	21913	26842	25249
B.6*g	Gross national disposable income	NQCO	1510839	1475261	1555080	1618293	1644400	1691276	1758082
	Adjustment to current basic prices								
B.1*g	Gross domestic product (at current market prices)	YBHA	1519597	1485727	1555548	1619480	1665213	1734949	1816439
D.21 D.31	Adjustment to current basic prices (less taxes plus subsidies on products)	NQBU	150092	137220	157804	176199	179437	188035	198093
B.1g	Gross value added (at current basic prices)	ABML	1369505	1348507	1397744	1443281	1485776	1546914	1618346
P.51c	**Net measures (after deduction of consumption of fixed capital) at current market prices**	NQAE	205303	206642	208411	214975	222022	231192	241275
B.1*n	Net domestic product	NHRK	1314294	1279085	1347137	1404505	1443191	1503757	1575164
B.5*n	Net national income	NSRX	1319628	1284455	1367330	1424988	1444289	1486924	1542056
B.6*n	Net national disposable income	NQCP	1305536	1268619	1346669	1403318	1422378	1460084	1516807
	Chained volume measures (reference year 2012, £ million)								
	Gross measures (before deduction of consumption of fixed capital) at market prices								
B.1*g	Gross domestic product	ABMI	1659039	1589493	1613974	1645808	1665213	1701180	1751198
TGL	Terms of trade effect ("trading gain or loss")	YBGJ	-13015	-5213	1190	-3766	–	8706	13251
GDI	Real gross domestic income	YBGL	1646024	1584280	1615164	1642042	1665213	1709886	1764449
D.1+D.4	Real employment, property and entrepreneurial income from rest of the world (receipts less payments)	YBGI	5329	4914	20852	20523	1371	-16120	-31573
-D.21+D.31	Subsidies (receipts) less taxes (payments) on products from/to rest of the world	QZPB	2856	2823	3058	2976	2898	2883	2879
+D.29-D.39	Other subsidies on production from/to rest of the world	IBJN	-3306	-3640	-3177	-3208	-2625	-2419	-2246
B.5*g	Gross balance of primary incomes/gross national income (GNI)	YBGM	1651830	1590038	1636148	1662810	1666311	1693302	1732243
D.5,6,7	Real current transfers from rest of the world (receipts less payments)	YBGP	15270	16900	21456	21959	21913	26445	24560
B.6*g	Gross national disposable income	YBGO	1636556	1573134	1614691	1640851	1644398	1666857	1707683
	Adjustment to basic prices								
B.1*g	Gross domestic product (at market prices)	ABMI	1659039	1589493	1613974	1645808	1665213	1701180	1751198
D.21 D.31	Adjustment to basic prices (less taxes plus subsidies on products)	NTAQ	175776	170569	169860	175032	179437	182712	189185
B.1g	Gross value added (at basic prices)	ABMM	1483607	1419415	1444101	1470835	1485776	1518468	1562013
P.51c	**Net measures (after deduction of consumption of fixed capital) at market prices**	CIHA	215247	210276	214587	217758	222022	226825	235886
B.5*n	Net national income at market prices	YBET	1435250	1378482	1420487	1444105	1444289	1466477	1496356
B.6*n	Net national disposable income at market prices	YBEY	1420013	1361604	1399031	1422146	1422376	1440032	1471796

Source: Office for National Statistics, Blue Book 2015

19.2 UK gross domestic product and national income
Current prices

£ million

			2001	2002	2003	2004	2005	2006	2007
	Gross domestic product								
	Gross domestic product: production								
B.1g	Gross value added, at basic prices	KN26	1898246	1986539	2084696	2198377	2294410	2483425	2642580
P.1	Output of goods and services	KN25	945431	983769	1018983	1075371	1101623	1221584	1311460
P.2	less intermediate consumption								
B.1g	Total gross value added	ABML	952815	1002770	1065713	1123006	1192787	1261841	1331120
D.211	Value added taxes (VAT) on products	QYRC	67100	71066	77343	81544	83425	87758	92025
D.212,4	Other taxes on products	NSUI	53075	54410	55116	58593	59519	63239	67052
D.31	less subsidies on products	NZHC	5971	7179	8069	8036	5313	6218	5924
B.1*g	Gross domestic product at market prices	YBHA	1067019	1121067	1190103	1255107	1330418	1406620	1484273
	Gross domestic product: expenditure								
P.3	Final consumption expenditure								
P.41	Actual individual consumption								
P.3	Household final consumption expenditure	ABPB	665058	695912	731780	772164	813580	851456	898478
P.3	Final consumption expenditure of NPISH[1]	ABNV	27502	30528	32985	36307	39095	41259	43718
P.31	Individual govt. final consumption expenditure	NNAQ	111337	123629	136484	148447	159917	172512	181206
P.41	Total actual individual consumption	NQEO	803897	850069	901249	956918	1012592	1065227	1123402
P.32	Collective govt. final consumption expenditure	NQEP	81826	87872	95711	103458	108906	113347	115940
P.3	Total final consumption expenditure	ABKW	885723	937941	996960	1060376	1121498	1178574	1239342
P.3	Households and NPISH	NSSG	692560	726440	764765	808471	852675	892715	942196
P.3	Central government	NMBJ	115824	127533	139974	150536	159914	171220	176817
P.3	Local government	NMMT	77339	83968	92221	101369	108909	114639	120329
P.5	Gross capital formation								
P.51g	Gross fixed capital formation	NPQX	200475	210653	216419	226030	241658	257875	277764
P.52	Changes in inventories	ABMP	6290	4034	5624	4298	3546	5308	7530
P.53	Acquisitions less disposals of valuables	NPJO	492	1197	1256	-339	102	986	-630
P.5	Total gross capital formation	NQFM	207257	215884	223299	229989	245306	264169	284664
P.6	Exports of goods and services	KTMW	278040	279998	293138	306291	341318	389794	380617
P.7	less imports of goods and services	KTMX	304001	312756	323294	341549	377704	425917	420350
B.11	External balance of goods and services	KTMY	-25961	-32758	-30156	-35258	-36386	-36123	-39733
de	Statistical discrepancy between expenditure components and GDP	RVFD	–	–	–	–	–	–	–
B.1*g	Gross domestic product at market prices	YBHA	1067019	1121067	1190103	1255107	1330418	1406620	1484273
	Gross domestic product: income								
B.2g	Operating surplus, gross								
	Non-financial corporations								
	Public non-financial corporations	NRJT	8348	7883	8725	7937	9692	10696	11344
	Private non-financial corporations	NRJK	196009	211441	224228	233654	249419	261539	268791
	Financial corporations	NQNV	13335	18264	26422	32277	44242	42061	50445
	General government	NMXV	14048	14861	16228	17008	18222	19416	20204
	Households and NPISH	QWLS	64007	67372	71741	77949	81965	86886	95208
B.2g	Total operating surplus, gross	ABNF	295747	319821	347344	368825	403540	420598	445992
B.3g	Mixed income	QWLT	67813	73476	79953	79070	85567	90353	88839
D.1	Compensation of employees	HAEA	573107	592564	621845	658157	689528	736073	780920
D.2	Taxes on production and imports	NZGX	137578	143805	150893	158896	162544	171671	180540
D.3	less subsidies	AAXJ	7226	8599	9932	9841	10761	12075	12018
di	Statistical discrepancy between income components and GDP	RVFC	–	–	–	–	–	–	–
B.1*g	Gross domestic product at market prices	YBHA	1067019	1121067	1190103	1255107	1330418	1406620	1484273
	Gross national income at market prices								
B.1*g	Gross domestic product at market prices	YBHA	1067019	1121067	1190103	1255107	1330418	1406620	1484273
D.1	Compensation of employees								
	Receipts from rest of the world	KTMN	1087	1121	1116	931	974	938	984
	less payments to rest of the world	KTMO	1021	1054	1057	1425	1584	1896	1718
D.1	Total	KTMP	66	67	59	-494	-610	-958	-734
-D.21+D.31	Subsidies (receipts) less taxes (payments) on products from/to rest of the world	QZOZ	3	-449	-680	-687	2261	2329	2412
+D.29-D.39	Other subsidies on production from/to rest of the world	IBJL	-582	-519	-592	-592	-3408	-3221	-2952
D.4	Property and entrepreneurial income								
	from rest of the world	HMBN	139884	124178	124908	140914	193049	249298	307890
	(receipts less payments)	HMBO	129269	106317	105584	118218	160955	232704	291264
D.4	Total	HMBM	10615	17861	19324	22696	32094	16594	16626
B.5*g	Gross balance of primary incomes/gross national income (GNI)	ABMX	1078279	1139963	1210758	1278590	1363053	1423148	1500710

1 Non-profit institutions serving households

19.2 UK gross domestic product and national income
Current prices

continued

£ million

			2008	2009	2010	2011	2012	2013	2014
	Gross domestic product								
	Gross domestic product: production								
B.1g	Gross value added, at basic prices								
P.1	Output of goods and services[2]	KN26	2718493	2677153	2765628	2866919	2939024	3073339	..
P.2	less intermediate consumption[2]	KN25	1348988	1328646	1367884	1423638	1453248	1526425	..
B.1g	Total gross value added	ABML	1369505	1348507	1397744	1443281	1485776	1546914	1618346
D.211	Value added taxes (VAT) on products	QYRC	92002	79900	95865	111437	113892	118296	124260
'D.212,4	Other taxes on products	NSUI	63772	63805	68876	71057	72667	76580	81318
D.31	less subsidies on products	NZHC	5682	6485	6937	6295	7122	6841	7485
B.1*g	Gross domestic product at market prices	YBHA	1519597	1485727	1555548	1619480	1665213	1734949	1816439
	Gross domestic product: expenditure								
P.3	Final consumption expenditure								
P.41	Actual individual consumption								
P.3	Household final consumption expenditure	ABPB	928265	911665	954781	990828	1029378	1073106	1119496
P.3	Final consumption expenditure of NPISH[1]	ABNV	46893	50205	50885	53259	53186	54978	56162
P.31	Individual govt. final consumption expenditure	NNAQ	193847	206296	211690	213214	215696	218531	223842
P.41	Total actual individual consumption	NQEO	1169005	1168166	1217356	1257301	1298260	1346615	1399500
P.32	Collective govt. final consumption expenditure	NQEP	123110	125105	126677	126709	130254	129513	133454
P.3	Total final consumption expenditure	ABKW	1292115	1293271	1344033	1384010	1428514	1476128	1532954
P.3	Households and NPISH	NSSG	975158	961870	1005666	1044087	1082564	1128084	1175658
P.3	Central government	NMBJ	190005	199158	204393	209441	219710	222446	231808
P.3	Local government	NMMT	126952	132243	133974	130482	126240	125598	125488
P.5	Gross capital formation								
P.51g	Gross fixed capital formation	NPQX	273689	239875	249029	258689	268221	280520	306108
P.52	Changes in inventories	ABMP	535	-14441	5458	2686	1533	7175	11837
P.53	Acquisitions less disposals of valuables	NPJO	-312	1733	73	305	828	5359	-93
P.5	Total gross capital formation	NQFM	273912	227167	254560	261680	270582	293054	317852
P.6	Exports of goods and services	KTMW	420822	398614	444372	497079	501734	521039	515191
P.7	less imports of goods and services	KTMX	467252	433325	487417	523289	535617	555272	549723
B.11	External balance of goods and services	KTMY	-46430	-34711	-43045	-26210	-33883	-34233	-34532
de	Statistical discrepancy between expenditure components and GDP	RVFD	–	–	–	–	–	–	165
B.1*g	Gross domestic product at market prices	YBHA	1519597	1485727	1555548	1619480	1665213	1734949	1816439
	Gross domestic product: income								
B.2g	Operating surplus, gross								
	Non-financial corporations								
	Public non-financial corporations	NRJT	9691	9402	9634	9177	10020	10045	9222
	Private non-financial corporations	NRJK	280173	251968	265867	287637	290491	313326	339387
	Financial corporations	NQNV	46670	61623	46120	50260	48584	59032	65298
	General government	NMXV	21612	22667	23850	25266	26500	27387	28268
	Households and NPISH	QWLS	106613	92622	113478	119567	129047	130150	137384
B.2g	Total operating surplus, gross	ABNF	464759	438282	458949	491907	504642	539940	579559
B.3g	Mixed income	QWLT	96464	97483	97042	99814	108747	110469	115859
D.1	Compensation of employees	HAEA	791731	795137	819177	830888	850054	873202	893100
D.2	Taxes on production and imports	NZGX	178756	167873	192677	208052	213510	223053	234236
D.3	less subsidies	AAXJ	12113	13048	12297	11181	11740	11715	12451
di	Statistical discrepancy between income components and GDP	RVFC	–	–	–	–	–	–	6136
B.1*g	Gross domestic product at market prices	YBHA	1519597	1485727	1555548	1619480	1665213	1734949	1816439
	Gross national income at market prices								
B.1*g	Gross domestic product at market prices	YBHA	1519597	1485727	1555548	1619480	1665213	1734949	1816439
D.1	Compensation of employees								
	Receipts from rest of the world	KTMN	1046	1176	1097	1121	1124	1094	1074
	less payments to rest of the world	KTMO	1761	1435	1486	1294	1272	1420	1517
D.1	Total	KTMP	-715	-259	-389	-173	-148	-326	-443
-D.21+D.31	Subsidies (receipts) less taxes (payments) on products from/to rest of the world	QZOZ	2636	2645	2945	2937	2898	2926	2960
+D.29-D.39	Other subsidies on production from/to rest of the world	IBJL	-3051	-3411	-3059	-3166	-2625	-2455	-2309
D.4	Property and entrepreneurial income from rest of the world	HMBN	287868	175117	174003	199995	170406	148507	141067
	(receipts less payments)	HMBO	282234	170254	153535	179568	168887	164543	173081
D.4	Total	HMBM	5634	4863	20468	20427	1519	-16036	-32014
B.5*g	Gross balance of primary incomes/gross national income (GNI)	ABMX	1524933	1491097	1575742	1639966	1666313	1718118	1783331

1 Non-profit institutions serving households
2 These series are not available for the latest year

Source: Office for National Statistics, Blue Book 2015

19.3 UK gross domestic product
Chained volume measures (reference year 2012)

£ million

			2001	2002	2003	2004	2005	2006	2007
	Gross domestic product								
	Gross domestic product: expenditure approach								
P.3	Final consumption expenditure								
P.41	Actual individual consumption								
P.3	Household final consumption expenditure	ABPF	870315	905703	938915	971329	1001781	1021577	1053452
P.3	Final consumption expenditure of NPISH1	ABNU	45403	47279	48141	50234	51066	51182	51131
P.31	Individual government final consumption expenditure	NSZK	169535	174780	180641	185757	190714	194628	197307
P.41	Total actual individual consumption	YBIO	1083626	1126251	1166292	1205842	1242097	1265953	1300299
P.32	Collective government final consumption expenditure	NSZL	108312	113832	119860	124625	126713	129712	130678
P.3	Total final consumption expenditure	ABKX	1191934	1240099	1286209	1330547	1368825	1395707	1430931
P.5	Gross capital formation								
P.51g	Gross fixed capital formation	NPQR	252033	258983	264961	272416	281649	290059	306454
P.52	Changes in inventories	ABMQ	9801	2763	4143	-33	-2773	1814	79
P.53	Acquisitions less disposals of valuables	NPJP	-489	-878	168	-248	-545	-148	210
P.5	Total gross capital formation	NPQU	253631	254726	258639	260912	266433	276540	284370
	Gross domestic final expenditure	YBIK	1450201	1498879	1548491	1594593	1638303	1675858	1719097
P.6	Exports of goods and services	KTMZ	364272	373006	383403	402780	435265	489369	481576
	Gross final expenditure	ABME	1817087	1874545	1934679	2000061	2075314	2164926	2201569
P.7	less imports of goods and services	KTNB	399558	421563	433141	461986	492375	542359	535536
de	Statistical discrepancy between expenditure components and GDP	GIXS	–	–	–	–	–	–	–
B.1*g	Gross domestic product at market prices	ABMI	1415605	1450910	1499322	1536631	1582675	1624802	1666821
B.11	Of which: external balance of goods and services	KTNC	-35286	-48557	-49738	-59206	-57110	-52990	-53960

1 Non-profit institutions serving households

continued

£ million

			2008	2009	2010	2011	2012	2013	2014
	Gross domestic product								
	Gross domestic product: expenditure approach								
P.3	Final consumption expenditure								
P.41	Actual individual consumption								
P.3	Household final consumption expenditure	ABPF	1045809	1009965	1010428	1009521	1029378	1049204	1077393
P.3	Final consumption expenditure of NPISH1	ABNU	51310	52585	51837	53767	53186	53774	54772
P.31	Individual government final consumption expenditure	NSZK	201793	206588	208833	211116	215696	219444	222722
P.41	Total actual individual consumption	YBIO	1297699	1268788	1270901	1274401	1298260	1322422	1354887
P.32	Collective government final consumption expenditure	NSZL	133249	132341	130694	128584	130254	128184	131402
P.3	Total final consumption expenditure	ABKX	1430971	1401199	1401621	1402984	1428514	1450606	1486289
P.5	Gross capital formation								
P.51g	Gross fixed capital formation	NPQR	288263	246741	259170	264251	268221	275083	295764
P.52	Changes in inventories	ABMQ	-8749	-17856	5492	-4247	1533	13632	17539
P.53	Acquisitions less disposals of valuables	NPJP	-852	57	-667	-1391	828	4500	242
P.5	Total gross capital formation	NPQU	265192	224002	258799	264982	270582	293215	313545
	Gross domestic final expenditure	YBIK	1697480	1622225	1660291	1667965	1699096	1743821	1799834
P.6	Exports of goods and services	KTMZ	487809	444874	470511	498017	501734	507798	517018
	Gross final expenditure	ABME	2185112	2068021	2131223	2166031	2200830	2251619	2316852
P.7	less imports of goods and services	KTNB	526226	478062	517521	520372	535617	550439	565812
de	Statistical discrepancy between expenditure components and GDP	GIXS	–	–	–	–	–	–	158
B.1*g	Gross domestic product at market prices	ABMI	1659039	1589493	1613974	1645808	1665213	1701180	1751198
B.11	Of which: external balance of goods and services	KTNC	-38417	-33188	-47010	-22355	-33883	-42641	-48794

1 Non-profit institutions serving households

Source: Office for National Statistics, Blue Book 2015

19.4 Output and capital formation: by industry[1,2]
Gross value added at current basic prices

£ million

			2006	2007	2008	2009	2010	2011	2012	2013
	Agriculture									
	Output									
D.1	Compensation of employees	KLR2	3438	3961	4002	4151	4234	4298	4442	4626
D.29-D.39	Taxes less subsidies on production other than those on products	KLR3	-3052	-2848	-2678	-3515	-2609	-2559	-2158	-2249
B.2g+B.3g	Operating surplus and mixed income, gross	KLR4	7716	7527	8513	7679	8689	8169	7847	8357
B.1g	Gross value added at basic prices	KLR5	8102	8640	9837	8315	10314	9908	10131	10734
P.2	Intermediate consumption at purchasers' prices	KLR6	11463	13361	13671	15665	14872	15947	16132	17459
P.1	Total output at basic prices	KLR7	19565	22001	23508	23980	25186	25855	26263	28193
P.5	Gross capital formation	KLR8	4528	5785	5947	6265	5745	5776	6998	7289
	Production									
	Output									
D.1	Compensation of employees	KLR9	116810	118785	119530	115564	118580	121914	125406	130065
D.29-D.39	Taxes less subsidies on production other than those on products	KLS4	3788	3618	3958	3868	3878	3802	3969	4173
B.2g+B.3g	Operating surplus and mixed income, gross	KLS3	83318	82762	89353	82284	84575	89037	91873	103962
B.1g	Gross value added at basic prices	KLS5	203916	205165	212841	201716	207033	214753	221248	238200
P.2	Intermediate consumption at purchasers' prices	KLS6	350187	364772	379110	358665	387437	415634	428192	443283
P.1	Total output at basic prices	KLS7	554103	569937	591951	560381	594470	630387	649440	681483
P.5	Gross capital formation	KLS8	38681	41513	43915	34410	37670	47782	51600	54881
	Construction									
	Output									
D.1	Compensation of employees	KLS9	41615	47302	46277	44801	45126	46521	47625	48023
D.29-D.39	Taxes less subsidies on production other than those on products	KLT3	747	813	918	962	1009	904	1125	973
B.2g+B.g	Operating surplus and mixed income, gross	KLT2	47482	47802	44203	33903	37244	40441	38462	42034
B.1g	Gross value added at basic prices	KLT4	89844	95917	91398	79666	83379	87866	87212	91030
P.2	Intermediate consumption at purchasers' prices	KLT5	115217	129182	135008	118926	121356	124311	127294	136873
P.1	Total output at basic prices	KLT6	205061	225099	226406	198592	204735	212177	214506	227903
P.5	Gross capital formation	KLT7	16502	21354	20273	13055	18256	19074	19240	19221

1 The contribution of each industry to the gross domestic product before providing for consumption of fixed capital. The industrial composition in this table is consistent with the Supply-Use Tables in Table 2.1, which show data from 2010-2013.
2 Components may not sum to totals due to rounding.

Source: Office for National Statistics, Blue Book 2015

19.4
Output and capital formation: by industry[1,2]
Gross value added at current basic prices

continued

£ million

			2006	2007	2008	2009	2010	2011	2012	2013
	Distribution, transport, hotels and restaurants									
	Output										
D.1	Compensation of employees	KLT8	153243	161759	166840	165134	169403	172852	175093	185684
D.29-D.39	Taxes less subsidies on production other than those on products	KLU2	9311	9267	10300	11422	11493	12022	12548	12996
B.2g+B.3g	Operating surplus and mixed income, gross	KLT9	71664	74156	75091	67149	73748	74301	77494	79393
B.1g	Gross value added at basic prices	KLU3	234218	245182	252231	243705	254644	259175	265135	278073
P.2	Intermediate consumption at purchasers' prices	KLU4	227642	239810	247930	239370	241785	246931	257624	270543
P.1	Total output at basic prices	KLU5	461860	484992	500161	483075	496429	506106	522759	548616
P.5	Gross capital formation	KLU6	33928	37974	36421	26625	40094	34129	32967	37797
	Information and communication									
	Output										
D.1	Compensation of employees	KLU7	47798	51455	52795	50141	51353	54086	57069	58549
D.29-D.39	Taxes less subsidies on production other than those on products	KLU9	968	997	910	742	780	798	695	689
B.2g+B.3g	Operating surplus and mixed income, gross	KLU8	31755	32120	34105	34730	34203	36634	35326	38113
B.1g	Gross value added at basic prices	KLV2	80521	84572	87810	85613	86336	91518	93090	97351
P.2	Intermediate consumption at purchasers' prices	KLV3	61324	63768	64099	63589	68367	68103	69338	73977
P.1	Total output at basic prices	KLV4	141845	148340	151909	149202	154703	159621	162428	171328
P.5	Gross capital formation	KLV5	19601	18884	19403	17614	17509	17464	17613	19033
	Financial and insurance									
	Output										
D.1	Compensation of employees	KLV6	59139	66214	58434	61289	63500	61022	60673	59878
D.29-D.39	Taxes less subsidies on production other than those on products	KLV8	1550	1648	1783	1762	5448	2429	2527	2595
B.2g+B.3g	Operating surplus and mixed income, gross	KLV7	43556	51762	48185	63041	47412	51439	49804	60752
B.1g	Gross value added at basic prices	KLV9	104245	119624	108402	126092	116360	114890	113004	123225
P.2	Intermediate consumption at purchasers' prices	KLW2	118704	141458	133792	122121	116578	129406	127628	132063
P.1	Total output at basic prices	KLW3	222949	261082	242194	248213	232938	244296	240632	255288
P.5	Gross capital formation	KLW4	6617	7485	8144	6486	8336	8068	9895	8138

1 The contribution of each industry to the gross domestic product before providing for consumption of fixed capital. The industrial composition in this table is consistent with the Supply-Use Tables in Table 2.1, which show data from 2010-2013.
2 Components may not sum to totals due to rounding.

Source: Office for National Statistics, Blue Book 2015

19.4
Output and capital formation: by industry[1,2]
Gross value added at current basic prices

continued

£ million

			2006	2007	2008	2009	2010	2011	2012	2013
	Real estate									
	Output									
D.1	Compensation of employees	KLW5	8584	9392	9846	9138	9381	9984	10471	11211
D.29-D.39	Taxes less subsidies on production other than those on products	KLW7	-1250	-1052	-1717	-1088	-811	-314	-335	61
B.2g+B.3g	Operating surplus and mixed income, gross	KLW6	101885	110729	126258	114396	134177	150008	163276	163260
B.1g	Gross value added at basic prices	KLW8	109219	119069	134387	122446	142747	159678	173412	174532
P.2	Intermediate consumption at purchasers' prices	KLW9	41023	43655	36053	62871	66975	64086	60039	66786
P.1	Total output at basic prices	KLX2	150242	162724	170440	185317	209722	223764	233451	241318
P.5	Gross capital formation	KLX3	5488	5960	3906	-1000	-1549	-1825	-1957	-2393
	Professional and support									
	Output									
D.1	Compensation of employees	KLX4	86535	93792	96047	95973	96027	98364	103206	105646
D.29-D.39	Taxes less subsidies on production other than those on products	KLX6	1668	1907	1930	2104	2091	2427	2473	2493
B.2g+B.3g	Operating surplus and mixed income, gross	KLX5	57172	58133	62331	57462	61956	65126	69875	75003
B.1g	Gross value added at basic prices	KLX7	145375	153832	160308	155539	160074	165917	175554	183142
P.2	Intermediate consumption at purchasers' prices	KLX8	102950	112514	120544	115744	119370	123161	127129	134797
P.1	Total output at basic prices	KLX9	248325	266346	280852	271283	279444	289078	302683	317939
P.5	Gross capital formation	KLY2	17421	19622	17480	14832	17167	20239	20119	21503
	Government, health and education									
	Output									
D.1	Compensation of employees	KLY3	194049	201835	210483	220923	228569	228796	231325	232617
D.29-D.39	Taxes less subsidies on production other than those on products	KLY5	340	333	401	367	448	419	496	565
B.2g+B.3g	Operating surplus and mixed income, gross	KLY4	44036	46848	48014	50310	50053	52248	52813	52314
B.1g	Gross value added at basic prices	KLY6	238425	249016	258898	271600	279070	281463	284634	285496
P.2	Intermediate consumption at purchasers' prices	KLY7	161852	171071	186411	200298	201357	203745	206696	214809
P.1	Total output at basic prices	KLY8	400277	420087	445309	471898	480427	485208	491330	500305
P.5	Gross capital formation	KLY9	27529	28550	35084	37697	38027	35711	35428	35859

1 The contribution of each industry to the gross domestic product before providing for consumption of fixed capital. The industrial composition in this table is consistent with the Supply-Use Tables in Table 2.1, which show data from 2010-2013.
2 Components may not sum to totals due to rounding.

Source: Office for National Statistics, Blue Book 2015

19.4 Output and capital formation: by industry[1,2]
Gross value added at current basic prices

continued

£ million

			2006	2007	2008	2009	2010	2011	2012	2013
	Other services									
	Output									
D.1	Compensation of employees	KLZ2	24862	26425	27477	28023	33004	33051	34744	36903
D.29-D.39	Taxes less subsidies on production other than those on products	KLZ4	747	686	746	981	849	744	993	1007
B.2g+B.3g	Operating surplus and mixed income, gross	KLZ3	22367	22992	25170	24811	23934	24318	26619	27221
B.1g	Gross value added at basic prices	KLZ5	47976	50103	53393	53815	57787	58113	62356	65131
P.2	Intermediate consumption at purchasers' prices	KLZ6	31222	31869	32370	31397	29787	32314	33176	35835
P.1	Total output at basic prices	KLZ7	79198	81972	85763	85212	87574	90427	95532	100966
P.5	Gross capital formation	KLZ8	4587	5258	5365	5391	5518	5487	5806	5855
	Not allocated to industries									
P.5	Gross capital formation[3]	KN28	89287	92279	77974	65792	67787	69775	72874	85871
	All industries									
	Output									
D.1	Compensation of employees	HAEA	736073	780920	791731	795137	819177	830888	850054	873202
D.29-D.39	Taxes less subsidies on production other than those on products	KN22	14817	15369	16551	17605	22576	20672	22333	23303
B.2g	Operating surplus, gross	ABNF	420598	445992	464759	438282	458949	491907	504642	539940
B.3g	Mixed income, gross	QWLT	90353	88839	96464	97483	97042	99814	108747	110469
di	Statistical discrepancy between income and GDP	RVFC	–	–	–	–	–	–	–	–
B.1g	Gross value added at basic prices	ABML	1261841	1331120	1369505	1348507	1397744	1443281	1485776	1546914
P.2	Intermediate consumption at purchasers' prices	KN25	1221584	1311460	1348988	1328646	1367884	1423638	1453248	1526425
P.1	Total output at basic prices	KN26	2483425	2642580	2718493	2677153	2765628	2866919	2939024	3073339
	Gross capital formation									
P.51g	Gross fixed capital formation	NPQX	257875	277764	273689	239875	249029	258689	268221	280520
P.52	Changes in inventories	ABMP	5308	7530	535	-14441	5458	2686	1533	7175
P.53	Acquisitions less disposals of valuables	NPJO	986	-630	-312	1733	73	305	828	5359
P.5	Total gross capital formation	NQFM	264169	284664	273912	227167	254560	261680	270582	293054

1 The contribution of each industry to the gross domestic product before providing for consumption of fixed capital. The industrial composition in this table is consistent with the Supply-Use Tables in Table 2.1, which show data from 2010-2013.
2 Components may not sum to totals due to rounding.
3 GFCF of dwellings and costs associated with the transfer of non-produced as and acquisitions less disposals of valuables.

Source: Office for National Statistics, Blue Book 2015

19.5 Gross value added at basic prices: by industry[1,2,3]
Chained volume indices

		Weight per 1000[1]		Indices 2012=100								
		2012		2006	2007	2008	2009	2010	2011	2012	2013	2014
A	Agriculture	6.8	L2KL	101.2	97.4	104.1	97.8	97.2	107.9	100.0	100.7	114.3
B-F	Production and construction											
B-E	Production											
B	Mining and quarrying	20	L2KR	162.6	157.4	148.6	135.3	130.9	112.3	100.0	96.7	96.2
C	Manufacturing											
CA	Food products, beverages and tobacco	16.3	KN3D	96.9	96.7	93.7	92.4	96.3	102.6	100.0	98.3	102.8
CB	Textiles, wearing apparel and leather products	3.4	KN3E	110.4	108.5	109.0	99.1	102.2	103.5	100.0	95.5	92.2
CC	Wood, paper products and printing	7.6	KN3F	124.9	124.4	119.5	111.0	111.8	105.6	100.0	102.2	103.1
CD	Coke and refined petroleum products	2.9	KN3G	123.4	122.4	118.3	111.5	109.7	111.3	100.0	98.1	89.6
CE	Chemicals and chemical products	5.7	KN3H	109.4	111.2	110.6	96.3	95.6	102.0	100.0	98.9	101.6
CF	Basic pharmaceutical products and preparations	9	KN3I	127.2	121.8	124.1	132.0	122.8	106.2	100.0	97.3	92.4
CG	Rubber, plastic and other non-metallic mineral products	8.3	KN3J	128.0	127.2	121.0	104.5	104.5	104.3	100.0	97.2	109.9
CH	Basic metals and metal products	11.6	KN3K	111.4	113.6	108.7	87.8	93.1	97.2	100.0	97.1	99.3
CI	Computer, electronic and optical products	6.4	KN3L	117.3	117.2	109.8	105.2	100.7	99.5	100.0	98.0	101.9
CJ	Electrical equipment	3.1	KN3M	108.6	110.7	108.3	84.1	93.8	90.2	100.0	95.3	92.5
CK	Machinery and equipment n.e.c.	8	KN3N	93.7	96.2	95.6	76.1	91.1	98.9	100.0	88.1	92.2
CL	Transport equipment	11.5	KN3O	81.4	83.5	81.4	71.0	87.1	95.9	100.0	107.6	110.8
CM	Other manufacturing and repair	9.1	KN3P	103.5	105.7	102.0	97.1	101.4	106.8	100.0	104.4	109.7
C	Total manufacturing	102.9	L2KX	107.1	107.8	104.8	95.0	99.3	101.4	100.0	98.9	101.6
D	Electricity, gas, steam and air conditioning supply	13.9	L2MW	102.9	103.7	105.7	103.2	107.5	100.9	100.0	100.4	95.0
E	Water supply, sewerage, waste mgmt and remediation	12.1	L2N2	96.4	100.2	100.4	92.7	94.7	100.1	100.0	104.3	105.1
B - E	Total production	148.9	L2KQ	112.3	112.6	109.7	100.2	103.4	102.8	100.0	99.2	100.5
F	Construction	58.7	L2N8	112.8	115.2	112.2	97.4	105.8	108.2	100.0	101.6	109.8
B - F	Total production and construction	207.6	L2KP	112.4	113.4	110.4	99.4	104.1	104.3	100.0	99.9	103.2

Office for National Statistics, Blue Book 2015

1 The weights shown are in proportion to total gross value added (GVA) in 2012 and are used to combine the industry output indices to calculate the totals. For 2011 and earlier, totals are calculated using the equivalent weights for the previous year (e.g. totals for 2009 use 2008 weights). Weights may not sum to totals due to rounding.

2 As GVA is expressed in index number form, it is inappropriate to show as a statistical adjustment any divergence from the other measures of GDP. Such an adjustment does, however, exist implicitly.

3 Because of the differences in the annual and monthly production inquiries, estimates of current price output and gross value added by industry derived from the current price Input-Output Supply and Use tables are not consistent with the equivalent measures of chained volume measures growth given in 19.5. These differences do not affect GDP totals.

19.5 Gross value added at basic prices: by industry[1,2,3]
Chained volume indices

continued

		Weight per 1000[1] 2012		2006	2007	2008	2009	2010	2011	Indices 2012=100 2012	2013	2014
G-T	**Services**											
G-I	**Distribution, transport, hotels and restaurants**											
G	Wholesale, retail, repair of motor vehicles and m/cycles	108.1	L2NE	100.9	105.1	101.9	96.2	97.3	98.9	100.0	105.6	111.0
H	Transportation and storage	42.9	L2NI	113.1	113.5	112.0	101.5	100.5	101.1	100.0	101.3	107.4
I	Accommodation and food service activities	27.4	L2NQ	95.3	97.9	96.1	91.2	93.2	95.9	100.0	98.3	101.2
G - I	Total distribution, transport, hotels and restaurants	178.4	L2ND	102.8	105.9	103.3	96.7	97.4	99.0	100.0	103.4	108.6
J	**Information and communication**											
JA	Publishing, audiovisual and broadcasting activities	16.5	L2NU	94.3	97.4	96.2	89.7	91.6	96.0	100.0	105.5	101.3
JB	Telecommunications	17.7	L2NZ	80.0	86.5	90.1	93.3	97.5	100.0	100.0	96.4	92.7
JC	IT and other information service activities	28.5	L2O3	82.0	87.8	89.8	84.4	92.8	94.1	100.0	105.1	112.0
J	Total information and communication	62.7	L2NT	84.3	89.6	91.3	88.2	93.7	96.2	100.0	102.7	103.8
K	Financial and insurance	76.1	L2O6	102.5	107.3	109.5	109.5	100.7	99.8	100.0	99.6	99.1
L	Real estate	116.7	L2OC	86.7	88.3	89.7	92.4	94.2	96.8	100.0	102.9	105.8
M-N	**Professional and support**											
M	**Professional, scientific and technical activities**											
MA	Legal, accounting, management, architect, engineering etc	52.6	L2OJ	85.3	95.8	97.9	90.7	91.3	96.0	100.0	108.4	115.3
MB	Scientific research and development	6.2	L2OQ	94.3	96.0	94.6	91.0	102.0	96.8	100.0	108.2	111.8
MC	Other professional, scientific and technical activities	13.4	L2OS	84.5	85.6	84.2	75.2	80.5	94.0	100.0	102.1	108.7
M	Total professional, scientific and technical activities	72.2	L2OI	85.8	93.7	94.7	87.6	90.0	95.7	100.0	107.2	113.8
N	Administrative and support service activities	45.9	L2OX	80.1	87.7	87.9	76.8	85.7	92.2	100.0	106.0	116.2
M - N	Total professional and support	118.2	L2OH	83.4	91.2	91.8	83.1	88.3	94.3	100.0	106.7	114.7
O-Q	**Government, health and education**											
O	Public admin, defence, compulsory social security	53.7	L2P8	104.9	103.6	105.1	106.3	105.0	101.0	100.0	98.7	96.9
P	Education	65	L2PA	99.7	97.7	97.2	96.9	95.7	96.8	100.0	101.4	102.2
Q	**Human health and social work activities**											
QA	Human health activities	54.4	L2PD	81.4	83.3	86.4	90.9	93.1	95.9	100.0	104.1	106.1
QB	Residential care and social work activities	18.5	L2PF	94.7	94.8	91.2	90.3	95.9	98.3	100.0	101.0	101.9
Q	Total human health and social work activities	72.9	L2PC	84.9	86.3	87.6	90.6	93.8	96.5	100.0	103.3	105.1
O - Q	Total government, health and education	191.6	L2P7	95.1	94.7	95.5	96.9	97.5	97.9	100.0	101.4	101.8
R-T	**Other services**											
R	Arts, entertainment and recreation	15.5	L2PJ	103.4	102.7	103.7	93.6	91.7	95.5	100.0	102.2	105.4
S	Other service activities	22.4	L2PP	100.3	94.3	97.4	100.2	97.3	103.8	100.0	101.2	109.9
T	Activities of households as employers, undiff. Goods	4.1	L2PT	97.9	94.9	98.4	89.5	99.2	94.8	100.0	103.1	103.6
R - T	Total other services	42	L2PI	101.0	97.3	99.8	96.6	95.4	99.8	100.0	101.7	107.6
G - T	Total service industries	785.6	L2NC	93.8	96.8	97.2	94.6	95.5	97.6	100.0	102.8	106.1
B.1g	All industries	1000	CGCE	97.6	100.1	99.9	95.5	97.2	99.0	100.0	102.2	105.1

1 The weights shown are in proportion to total gross value added (GVA) in 2012 and are used to combine the industry output indices to calculate the totals. For 2011 and earlier, totals are calculated using the equivalent weights for the previous year (e.g. totals for 2009 use 2008 weights). Weights may not sum to totals due to rounding.

2 As GVA is expressed in index number form, it is inappropriate to show as a statistical adjustment any divergence from the other measures of GDP. Such an adjustment does, however, exist implicitly.

3 Because of the differences in the annual and monthly production inquiries, estimates of current price output and gross value added by industry derived from the current price Input-Output Supply and Use tables are not consistent with the equivalent measures of chained volume measures growth given in 19.5. These differences do not affect GDP totals.

Office for National Statistics, Blue Book 2015

19.6 Non-financial corporations
ESA 2010 sector S.11

£ million

			2006	2007	2008	2009	2010	2011	2012	2013	2014
II.1.2	Allocation of primary income account										
	Resources										
B.2g	Operating surplus, gross	NQBE	272235	280135	289864	261370	275501	296814	300511	323371	348609
D.4	Property income, received										
D.41g	Interest before FISIM[1] allocation	J4WQ	23742	26579	26055	9281	9089	9202	8731	9614	9736
P.119	plus FISIM	IV89	4131	3728	5769	3305	2664	3749	3584	3108	4883
D.41	Interest	EABC	27873	30307	31824	12586	11753	12951	12315	12722	14619
D.42	Distributed income of corporations	EABD	43927	38964	47124	62614	57887	68097	62537	63757	78591
D.43	Reinvested earnings on foreign direct investment	WEYD	36725	50749	37714	12455	26240	27262	11717	-1389	-15293
D.44	Other investment income										
D.441	Attributable to insurance policy holders	L8GM	943	715	972	975	430	297	217	263	231
D.443	Attributable to collective investment fund shareholders										
D.4431	Dividends	L8H9	8	8	6	2	5	3	3	2	4
D.4432	Retained earnings	L8HG	12	16	8	4	8	4	4	4	4
D.443	Total	L8H2	20	24	14	6	13	7	7	6	8
D.44	Total other investment income	FAOF	963	739	986	981	443	304	224	269	239
D.45	Rent	FAOG	124	123	126	132	130	132	132	132	132
D.4	Total	FAKY	109612	120882	117774	88768	96453	108746	86925	75491	78288
Total	Total resources	FBXJ	381847	401017	407638	350138	371954	405560	387436	398862	426897
	Uses										
D.4	Property income, paid										
D.41g	Interest before FISIM allocation	J4WS	56885	68464	74556	50386	38609	36585	37116	34306	37799
P.119	less FISIM	IV88	5917	7672	5588	9081	9521	8466	7967	7988	6353
D.41	Interest	EABG	50968	60792	68968	41305	29088	28119	29149	26318	31446
D.42	Distributed income of corporations	NVCS	108052	108140	113873	119926	122545	141221	145976	153110	161871
D.43	Reinvested earnings on foreign direct investment	HDVB	15452	15049	3656	-4539	156	-5971	-5363	2780	5225
D.45	Rent	FBXO	1265	1273	1259	1285	1281	1287	1302	1429	1423
D.4	Total	FBXK	175737	185254	187756	157977	153070	164656	171064	183637	199965
B.5g	Balance of primary incomes, gross	NQBG	206110	215763	219882	192161	218884	240904	216372	215225	226932
Total	Total uses	FBXJ	381847	401017	407638	350138	371954	405560	387436	398862	426897
P.51c	less consumption of fixed capital	DBGF	102661	105691	109407	112670	111319	114598	116906	119736	122378
B.5n	Balance of primary incomes, net	FBXQ	103449	110072	110475	79491	107565	126306	99466	95489	104554

1 Financial intermediation services indirectly measured

Office for National Statistics, Blue Book 2015

19.7 Non-financial corporations
ESA 2010 sector S.11

£ million

			2006	2007	2008	2009	2010	2011	2012	2013	2014
II.2	Secondary distribution of income account										
	Resources										
B.5g	Balance of primary incomes, gross	NQBG	206110	215763	219882	192161	218884	240904	216372	215225	226932
D.61	Net social contributions										
D.612	Employers' imputed social contributions	L8RD	3272	3391	3742	4181	3136	2926	3408	3047	2897
D.61	Total net social contributions	L8TP	3272	3391	3742	4181	3136	2926	3408	3047	2897
D.7	Current transfers other than taxes, social contributions and benefits										
D.72	Non-life insurance claims	FCBP	5361	5595	5230	5578	5775	3745	3525	6114	5736
D.75	Miscellaneous current transfers	CY8C	–	–	–	–	–	–	724	136	–
D.7	Total	NRJB	5361	5595	5230	5578	5775	3745	4249	6250	5736
Total	Total resources	FCBR	214743	224749	228854	201920	227795	247575	224029	224522	235565
	Uses										
D.5	Current taxes on income, wealth etc.										
D.51	Taxes on income	FCBS	37204	38309	40826	33942	35701	35733	32944	32508	32660
D.62	Social benefits other than social transfers in kind										
D.622	Other social insurance benefits	L8S3	3272	3391	3742	4181	3136	2926	3408	3047	2897
D.62	Total	L8TD	3272	3391	3742	4181	3136	2926	3408	3047	2897
D.7	Current transfers other than taxes, social contributions and benefits										
D.71	Net non-life insurance premiums	FCBY	5361	5595	5230	5578	5775	3745	3525	6114	5736
D.75	Miscellaneous current transfers	CY8B	477	488	488	488	488	488	488	488	488
D.7	Total, other current transfers	FCBX	5838	6083	5718	6066	6263	4233	4013	6602	6224
B.6g	Gross disposable income	NRJD	168429	176966	178568	157731	182695	204683	183664	182365	193784
Total	Total uses	FCBR	214743	224749	228854	201920	227795	247575	224029	224522	235565
P.51c	less consumption of fixed capital	DBGF	102661	105691	109407	112670	111319	114598	116906	119736	122378
B.6n	Disposable income, net	FCCF	65768	71275	69161	45061	71376	90085	66758	62629	71406

Source: Office for National Statistics, Blue Book 2015

19.8 Private non-financial corporations
ESA 2010 sectors S.11002 National controlled and S.11003 Foreign controlled

£ million

			2006	2007	2008	2009	2010	2011	2012	2013	2014
II.1.2	Allocation of primary income account before deduction of fixed capital consumption										
	Resources										
B.2g	Operating surplus, gross	NRJK	261539	268791	280173	251968	265867	287637	290491	313326	339387
D.4	Property income, received										
D.41g	Interest before FISIM[1] allocation	I69R	22879	25840	25221	9004	8793	8965	8511	9440	9580
P.119	plus FISIM	IV87	4105	3727	5765	3313	2662	3745	3573	3095	4853
D.41	Interest	DSZR	26984	29567	30986	12317	11455	12710	12084	12535	14433
D.42	Distributed income of corporations	DSZS	43889	38473	46389	62589	57803	68011	62452	63674	78517
D.43	Reinvested earnings on foreign direct investment	HDVR	36511	50598	37890	12337	26179	27201	11656	-1455	-15357
D.44	Other investment income										
D.441	Attributable to insurance policy holders	KZI4	943	715	972	975	430	297	217	263	231
D.443	Attributable to collective investment fund shares										
D.4431	Dividends	KZI6	8	8	6	2	5	3	3	2	4
D.4432	Retained earnings	KZI7	12	16	8	4	8	4	4	4	4
D.443	Total	L5U6	20	24	14	6	13	7	7	6	8
D.44	Total other investment income	FCFP	963	739	986	981	443	304	224	269	239
D.45	Rent	FAOL	124	123	126	132	130	132	132	132	132
D.4	Total	FACV	108471	119500	116377	88356	96010	108358	86548	75155	77964
Total	Total resources	FCFQ	370010	388291	396550	340324	361877	395995	377039	388481	417351
	Uses										
D.4	Property income, paid										
D.41g	Interest before FISIM allocation	I6A2	55304	66528	72142	48380	37290	35573	36324	33295	36996
P.119	less FISIM	IV86	5877	7600	5518	9023	9483	8424	7943	7975	6345
D.41	Interest	DSZV	49427	58928	66624	39357	27807	27149	28381	25320	30651
D.42	Distributed income of corporations	NVDC	107314	107414	113222	119129	121783	140146	144692	151838	160808
D.421	Of which: dividend payments	NETZ	83624	83811	88073	84637	82534	103728	106074	107975	118944
D.43	Reinvested earnings on foreign direct investment	HDVB	15452	15049	3656	-4539	156	-5971	-5363	2780	5225
D.45	Rent	FCFU	1265	1273	1259	1285	1281	1287	1302	1429	1423
D.4	Total	FCFR	173458	182664	184761	155232	151027	162611	169012	181367	198107
B.5g	Balance of primary incomes, gross	NRJM	196552	205627	211789	185092	210850	233384	208027	207114	219244
Total	Total uses	FCFQ	370010	388291	396550	340324	361877	395995	377039	388481	417351
P.51c	less consumption of fixed capital	NSRK	95096	98020	101455	104523	103320	106550	108865	111383	113884
B.5n	Balance of primary incomes, net	FCFW	101456	107607	110334	80569	107530	126834	99162	95731	105360

1 Financial intermediation services indirectly measured

Source: Office for National Statistics, Blue Book 2015

19.9

Private non-financial corporations

ESA 2010 sectors S.11002 National controlled and S.11003 Foreign controlled

£ million

			2006	2007	2008	2009	2010	2011	2012	2013	2014
II.2	Secondary distribution of income account										
	Resources										
B.5g	Balance of primary incomes, gross	NRJM	196552	205627	211789	185092	210850	233384	208027	207114	219244
D.61	Net social contributions										
D.612	Employers' imputed social contributions	L8RJ	3151	3273	3591	4024	3012	2811	3283	2944	2813
D.61	Total net social contributions	L8TV	3151	3273	3591	4024	3012	2811	3283	2944	2813
D.7	Other current transfers										
D.72	Net non-life insurance claims	FDBA	5361	5595	5230	5578	5775	3745	3525	6114	5736
Total	Total resources	FDBC	205064	214495	220610	194694	219637	239940	214835	216172	227793
	Uses										
D.5	Current taxes on income, wealth etc.										
D.51	Taxes on income	FCCP	36832	38084	40572	33691	35552	35624	32838	32435	32625
D.62	Social security benefits other than social transfers in kind										
D.622	Other social insurance benefits	L8S9	3151	3273	3591	4024	3012	2811	3283	2944	2813
D.62	Total	L8TH	3151	3273	3591	4024	3012	2811	3283	2944	2813
D.7	Current transfers other than taxes, social contributions and benefits										
D.71	Net non-life insurance premiums	FDBH	5361	5595	5230	5578	5775	3745	3525	6114	5736
D.75	Miscellaneous current transfers	CY88	477	488	488	488	488	488	488	488	488
D.7	Total	FCCN	5838	6083	5718	6066	6263	4233	4013	6602	6224
B.6g	Gross disposable income	NRJQ	159243	167055	170729	150913	174810	197272	174701	174191	186131
Total	Total uses	FDBC	205064	214495	220610	194694	219637	239940	214835	216172	227793
P.51c	less consumption of fixed capital	NSRK	95096	98020	101455	104523	103320	106550	108865	111383	113884
B.6n	Disposable income, net	FDBK	64147	69035	69274	46390	71490	90722	65836	62808	72247

Source: Office for National Statistics, Blue Book 2015

19.10

Households and non-profit institutions serving households
ESA 2010 sectors S.14 and S.15

£ million

			2007	2008	2009	2010	2011	2012	2013	2014
II.1.2	Allocation of primary income account before deduction of fixed capital consumption									
	Resources									
B.2g	Operating surplus, gross	QWLS	95208	106613	92622	113478	119567	129047	130150	137384
B.3g	Mixed income, gross	QWLT	88839	96464	97483	97042	99814	108747	110469	115859
D.1	Compensation of employees									
D.11	Wages and salaries	QWLW	647532	661081	662411	671053	681583	694404	711054	732655
D.12	Employers' social contributions	QWLX	132654	129935	132467	147735	149132	155502	161822	160002
D.1	Total	QWLY	780186	791016	794878	818788	830715	849906	872876	892657
D.4	Property income, received									
D.41g	Interest before FISIM[1] allocation	J4WY	44292	43529	20831	20411	22309	23543	21374	17713
P.119	plus FISIM	IV8W	14734	23517	3015	-695	548	216	-629	8367
D.41	Interest	QWLZ	59026	67046	23846	19716	22857	23759	20745	26080
D.42	Distributed income of corporations	QWMA	50509	46411	54392	58179	58223	55344	59855	55362
D.44	Other investment income									
D.441	Attributable to insurance policy holders	L8GL	28802	28990	24219	24936	24480	22141	21112	19430
D.442	Payable on pension entitlements	L8GS	80172	79922	69283	80106	77775	70167	67528	78350
D.443	Attributable to collective investment fund shareholders									
D.4431	Dividends	L8H8	3238	1656	771	1660	766	713	648	1114
D.4432	Retained earnings	L8HF	5065	2588	1203	2596	1195	1117	1016	1744
D.443	Total	L8GZ	8303	4244	1974	4256	1961	1830	1664	2858
D.44	Total other investment income	QWMC	117277	113156	95476	109298	104216	94138	90304	100638
D.45	Rent	QWMD	110	115	115	118	123	127	128	128
D.4	Total	QWME	226922	226728	173829	187311	185419	173368	171032	182208
Total	Total resources	QWMF	1191155	1220821	1158812	1216619	1235515	1261068	1284527	1328108
	Uses									
D.4	Property income, paid									
D.41g	Interest before FISIM allocation	J4WZ	94682	98724	72196	64957	62168	61816	61671	60817
P.119	less FISIM	IV8X	16959	9958	44708	44908	38619	36341	39829	32816
D.41	Interest	QWMG	77723	88766	27488	20049	23549	25475	21842	28001
D.45	Rent	QWMH	225	233	239	239	243	247	248	248
D.4	Total	QWMI	77948	88999	27727	20288	23792	25722	22090	28249
B.5g	Balance of primary incomes, gross	QWMJ	1113207	1131822	1131085	1196331	1211723	1235346	1262437	1299859
Total	Total uses	QWMF	1191155	1220821	1158812	1216619	1235515	1261068	1284527	1328108
P.51c	less consumption of fixed capital	QWLL	79908	68065	64542	66407	67957	71051	76284	82221
B.5n	Balance of primary incomes, net	QWMK	1033299	1063757	1066543	1129924	1143766	1164295	1186153	1217638

1 Financial intermediation services indirectly measured

Office for National Statistics, Blue Book 2015

19.11 Households and non-profit institutions serving households
ESA 2010 sectors S.14 and S.15

£ million

			2007	2008	2009	2010	2011	2012	2013	2014
II.2	Secondary distribution of income account									
	Resources									
B.5g	Balance of primary incomes, gross	QWMJ	1113207	1131822	1131085	1196331	1211723	1235346	1262437	1299859
D.612	Employers' imputed social contributions	L8RF	524	685	754	872	819	908	775	797
D.62	Social benefits other than social transfers in kind									
D.621	Social security benefits in cash	L8QF	69037	73871	80826	82117	83826	89187	91231	93652
D.622	Other social insurance benefits	L8QT	88719	93461	100124	105929	108277	117715	121129	114282
D.623R	Social assistance benefits in cash	MT3B	87411	94147	105596	112739	116117	119423	120144	121270
D.62	Total	QWML	245167	261479	286546	300785	308220	326325	332504	329204
D.7	Other current transfers									
D.72	Non-life insurance claims	QWMM	24141	21674	21975	30811	32085	30112	28701	28379
D.75	Miscellaneous current transfers	QWMN	38650	37899	39502	40728	39451	43381	39264	36612
D.7	Total	QWMO	62791	59573	61477	71539	71536	73493	67965	64991
	Total resources	QWMP	1421689	1453559	1479862	1569527	1592298	1636072	1663681	1694851
	Uses									
D.5	Current taxes on income, wealth, etc									
D.51	Taxes on income	QWMQ	155326	159860	151348	152424	157598	153734	158990	162625
D.59	Other current taxes	NVCO	31579	32909	33752	34578	34924	35354	36534	37284
D.5	Total	QWMS	186905	192769	185100	187002	192522	189088	195524	199909
D.61	Net social contributions									
D.611	Employers' actual social contributions	L8NJ	109483	106047	106770	121198	123083	128345	136091	133489
D.612	Employers' imputed social contributions	M9X2	23172	23887	25694	26536	26050	27157	25737	26513
D.613	Households' actual social contributions	L8PR	59794	60186	57155	58668	60422	63558	65589	68455
D.614	Households' social contribution supplements	L8Q7	80172	79922	69283	80106	77775	70167	67528	78350
D.61SC	Social insurance scheme service charge	L8LT	-12686	-12777	-11101	-12568	-14740	-17045	-18311	-18505
D.61	Total	QWMY	259935	257265	247801	273940	272590	272182	276634	288302
D.62	Social benefits other than social transfers in kind									
D.622	Other social insurance benefits	L8S5	524	685	754	872	819	908	775	797
D.623U	Social assistance benefits in cash	MT3D	496	496	494	486	496	496	496	496
D.62	Total	QWMZ	1020	1181	1248	1358	1315	1404	1271	1293
D.7	Other current transfers									
D.71	Net non-life insurance premiums	QWNA	24141	21674	21975	30811	32085	30112	28701	28379
D.75	Miscellaneous current transfers	QWNB	14247	13616	13939	14113	14387	15378	15898	16483
D.7	Total	QWNC	38388	35290	35914	44924	46472	45490	44599	44862
B.6g	Gross disposable income [1]	QWND	935441	967054	1009799	1062303	1079399	1127908	1145653	1160485
	Total uses	QWMP	1421689	1453559	1479862	1569527	1592298	1636072	1663681	1694851
P.51c	less consumption of fixed capital	QWLL	79908	68065	64542	66407	67957	71051	76284	82221
B.6n	Disposable income, net	QWNE	855533	898989	945257	995896	1011442	1056857	1069369	1078264
	Real households disposable income: (Chained volume measures) £ Million (reference year 2012)	RVGK	1096558	1087897	1115479	1122028	1099265	1127908	1120156	1117553
	Index (2012=100)	OSXR	97.2	96.5	98.9	99.5	97.5	100	99.3	99.1

1 Gross household disposable income revalued by the implied household and NPISH final consumption expenditure deflator is as follows:

Office for National Statistics, Blue Book 2015

19.12 Households and non-profit institutions serving households
ESA 2010 sectors S.14 and S.15

£ million

			2007	2008	2009	2010	2011	2012	2013	2014
II.3	Redistribution of income in kind account									
	Resources									
B.6g	Gross disposable income	QWND	935441	967054	1009799	1062303	1079399	1127908	1145653	1160485
D.63	Social transfers in kind	NSSB	224924	240740	256501	262575	266473	268882	273509	280004
Total	Total resources	NSSC	1160365	1207794	1266300	1324878	1345872	1396790	1419162	1440489
	Uses									
D.63	Social transfers in kind	HAEK	43718	46893	50205	50885	53259	53186	54978	56162
B.7g	Adjusted disposable income, gross	NSSD	1116647	1160901	1216095	1273993	1292613	1343604	1364184	1384327
Total	Total uses	NSSC	1160365	1207794	1266300	1324878	1345872	1396790	1419162	1440489

£ million

			2007	2008	2009	2010	2011	2012	2013	2014
II.4	Use of income account									
II.4.1	Use of disposable income account									
	Resources									
B.6g	Gross disposable income	QWND	935441	967054	1009799	1062303	1079399	1127908	1145653	1160485
D.8	Adjustment for the change in pension entitlements	NSSE	80669	68265	56907	75076	68913	58452	58135	75364
Total	Total resources	NSSF	1016110	1035319	1066706	1137379	1148312	1186360	1203788	1235849
	Uses									
P.3	Final consumption expenditure									
P.31	Individual consumption expenditure	NSSG	942196	975158	961870	1005666	1044087	1082564	1128084	1175658
B.8g	Gross saving	NSSH	73914	60161	104836	131713	104225	103796	75704	60191
Total	Total uses	NSSF	1016110	1035319	1066706	1137379	1148312	1186360	1203788	1235849
P.51c	less consumption of fixed capital	QWLL	79908	68065	64542	66407	67957	71051	76284	82221
B.8n	Saving, net	NSSI	-5994	-7904	40294	65306	36268	32745	-580	-22030
II.4.2	Use of adjusted disposable income account									
	Resources									
B.7g	Adjusted disposable income, gross	NSSD	1116647	1160901	1216095	1273993	1292613	1343604	1364184	1384327
D.8	Adjustment for the change in pension entitlements	NSSE	80669	68265	56907	75076	68913	58452	58135	75364
Total	Total resources	NSSJ	1197316	1229166	1273002	1349069	1361526	1402056	1422319	1459691
	Uses									
P.4	Actual final consumption									
P.41	Actual individual consumption	ABRE	1123402	1169005	1168166	1217356	1257301	1298260	1346615	1399500
B.8g	Gross saving[1]	NSSH	73914	60161	104836	131713	104225	103796	75704	60191
Total	Total uses	NSSJ	1197316	1229166	1273002	1349069	1361526	1402056	1422319	1459691
	Households saving ratio (per cent)	RVGL	7.3	5.8	9.8	11.6	9.1	8.7	6.3	4.9

1 Household saving as a percentage of total available household
resources is as follows:

Office for National Statistics, Blue Book 2015

19.13 The sector accounts: Key economic indicators

£ million

		2006	2007	2008	2009	2010	2011	2012	2013	2014
	Net lending(+)/borrowing(-) by:									
B.9	Non-financial corporations	EABO	34802	28004	40501	59191	55566	71887	42525	27306	26223
B.9	Financial corporations	NHCQ	-10919	-9520	-5770	6233	-22482	-14172	3862	-2960	5383
B.9	General government	NNBK	-40990	-44238	-77088	-160618	-150484	-124907	-138972	-98597	-103123
B.9	Households and NPISH[1]	NSSZ	-16717	-11688	-12611	50421	73890	39415	37722	-4127	-28105
B.9	Rest of the world	NHRB	33824	37447	54970	44773	43511	27780	54865	78380	93651
	Private non-financial corporations										
	Gross trading profits										
	Continental shelf profits	CAGD	27311	26080	28120	21452	25379	29806	25246	23470	17542
	Others	CAED	221830	233748	243200	213104	226295	242479	242125	266645	294040
	Rental of buildings	DTWR	17345	18910	22406	21625	22628	24150	25797	26415	26736
	less holding gains of inventories	DLRA	4947	9947	13553	4213	8435	8798	2677	3204	-1069
B.2g	Gross operating surplus	CAER	261539	268791	280173	251968	265867	287637	290491	313326	339387
	Households and NPISH										
B.6g	Disposable income, gross	QWND	887857	935441	967054	1009799	1062303	1079399	1127908	1145653	1160485
	Implied deflator of households and NPISH										
	Individual consumption expenditure										
	Index (2012=100)[2]	YBFS	83.2	85.3	88.9	90.5	94.7	98.2	100	102.3	103.8
	Real households disposable income:										
	Chained volume measures (reference year 2012)	RVGK	1066768	1096558	1087897	1115479	1122028	1099265	1127908	1120156	1117553
	Index (2012=100)[2]	OSXR	94.6	97.2	96.5	98.9	99.5	97.5	100	99.3	99.1
B.8g	Gross saving	NSSH	63536	73914	60161	104836	131713	104225	103796	75704	60191
	Households total resources	NSSF	956251	1016110	1035319	1066706	1137379	1148312	1186360	1203788	1235849
	Saving ratio (per cent)	RVGL	6.6	7.3	5.8	9.8	11.6	9.1	8.7	6.3	4.9

1 Non-profit institutions serving households
2 Rounded to one decimal place

Source: Office for National Statistics, Blue Book 2015

19.14 Household final consumption expenditure: classified by purpose
At current market prices

£ million

			2007	2008	2009	2010	2011	2012	2013	2014
P.31	Final consumption expenditure of households									
	Durable goods									
05	Furnishings, household equipment and routine maintenance of the house	LLIJ	23311	23099	20420	20607	21572	21487	22304	23150
06	Health	LLIK	2955	3071	3169	2964	2968	3104	3649	3620
07	Transport	LLIL	39315	35515	35079	35225	35978	39094	41639	44961
08	Communication	LLIM	717	803	871	758	757	861	969	1004
09	Recreation and culture	LLIN	22678	24279	23184	23517	22611	23226	22190	24662
12	Miscellaneous goods and services	LLIO	5384	5540	5324	5662	6579	7472	7221	8284
D	Total durable goods	UTIA	94360	92307	88047	88733	90465	95244	97972	105681
	Semi-durable goods									
03	Clothing and footwear	LLJL	46640	48364	48125	49729	53074	54801	57896	61971
05	Furnishings, household equipment and routine maintenance of the house	LLJM	14646	13842	13872	14258	14025	14765	15439	17286
07	Transport	LLJN	3725	4102	4122	3907	3837	4296	4620	4587
09	Recreation and culture	LLJO	29713	30176	27827	27678	26227	26695	24855	26491
12	Miscellaneous goods and services	LLJP	3483	3270	3553	5475	5774	5279	6704	7333
SD	Total semi-durable goods	UTIQ	98207	99754	97499	101047	102937	105836	109514	117668
	Non-durable goods									
01	Food and drink	ABZV	73842	78755	80468	83053	87009	91377	96199	95318
02	Alcoholic beverages, tobacco and narcotics	ADFL	36496	36407	38358	38896	41999	42878	43526	44637
04	Housing, water, electricity, gas and other fuels	LLIX	28735	33772	34178	35494	34584	38168	40575	37546
05	Furnishings, household equipment and routine maintenance of the house	LLIY	3883	3888	4277	4260	4152	4155	4428	4421
05	Health	LLIZ	4974	4914	4658	4792	5047	6397	6995	7514
07	Transport	LLJA	26649	29740	26632	30648	35458	35637	35381	34079
09	Recreation and culture	LLJB	15839	16081	15289	15125	15220	15182	15921	16392
12	Miscellaneous goods and services	LLJC	16099	15886	15996	15999	16884	17402	18569	20156
ND	Total non-durable goods	UTII	206517	219443	219856	228267	240353	251196	261594	260063
	Total goods	UTIE	399084	411504	405402	418047	433755	452276	469080	483412
	Services									
03	Clothing and footwear	LLJD	970	1099	1185	1109	992	1013	1009	1076
04	Housing, water, electricity, gas and other fuels	LLJE	153086	161232	174975	202665	211032	217445	224587	232372
05	Furnishings, household equipment and routine maintenance of the house	LLJF	6057	6470	5967	6723	6604	6758	7129	7497
06	Health	LLJG	6936	6418	7070	7935	8344	8317	8477	9127
07	Transport	LLJH	56796	57328	55878	57613	60989	64447	68484	72203
08	Communication	LLJI	18205	18135	17683	18684	19189	19559	21006	21654
09	Recreation and culture	LLJJ	33414	34694	33813	34514	36621	38856	41387	43671
10	Education	ADIE	12384	13663	14811	14982	15032	15865	17882	19587
11	Restaurants and hotels	ADIF	86516	87687	82087	85737	91897	96399	101277	105916
12	Miscellaneous goods and services	LLJK	110211	112743	98998	93953	95217	97888	103455	114183
S	Total services	UTIM	484575	499469	492467	523915	545917	566547	594693	627286
0	Final consumption expenditure in the UK by resident and non-resident households (domestic concept)	ABQI	883659	910973	897869	941962	979672	1018823	1063773	1110698
P.33	Final consumption expenditure outside the UK by UK resident households	ABTA	34548	37374	33661	34358	33659	34375	36245	37356
P.34	Final consumption expenditure in the UK by households resident in rest of the world	CDFD	-19729	-20082	-19865	-21539	-22503	-23820	-26912	-28558
P.31	Final consumption expenditure by UK resident households in the UK and abroad (national concept)	ABPB	898478	928265	911665	954781	990828	1029378	1073106	1119496

Source: Office for National Statistics, Blue Book 2015

19.15 Household final consumption expenditure: classified by purpose
Chained volume measures (reference year 2012)

£ million

		2007	2008	2009	2010	2011	2012	2013	2014
P.31	Final consumption expenditure of households								
	Durable goods								
05	Furnishings, household equipment and routine maintenance of the house	LLME	26956	26084	22290	21803	22115	21487	22162	22887
06	Health	LLMF	3061	3148	3235	2996	2983	3104	3674	3570
07	Transport	LLMG	42557	39595	39993	36713	36039	39094	42134	44996
08	Communication	LLMH	787	909	980	817	783	861	945	968
09	Recreation and culture	LLMI	14111	17818	18520	19644	20793	23226	23271	26929
12	Miscellaneous goods and services	LLMJ	7365	7176	6551	6527	7051	7472	7062	8117
D	Total durable goods	UTIC	90557	92980	90582	88200	89626	95244	99248	107467
	Semi-durable goods								
03	Clothing and footwear	LLNG	40929	45514	49085	51201	53453	54801	57375	61902
05	Furnishings, household equipment and routine maintenance of the house	LLNH	16715	15845	15613	15637	14438	14765	15409	17080
07	Transport	LLNI	4299	4633	4506	4099	3873	4296	4579	4494
09	Recreation and culture	LLNJ	27517	28653	26825	26778	26107	26695	24655	26034
12	Miscellaneous goods and services	LLNK	3613	3348	3595	5578	5855	5279	6577	7188
SD	Total semi-durable goods	UTIS	92400	97784	99546	103255	103722	105836	108595	116698
	Non-durable goods								
01	Food and drink	ADIP	95380	93299	90424	90397	89709	91377	92780	92156
02	Alcoholic beverages, tobacco and narcotics	ADIS	47565	46130	44272	44403	42583	42878	41019	40923
04	Housing, water, electricity, gas and other fuels	LLMS	40785	41147	39010	41508	37214	38168	38185	34013
05	Furnishings, household equipment and routine maintenance of the house	LLMT	4863	4708	4829	4661	4270	4155	4373	4331
06	Health	LLMU	5329	5221	4871	4935	5133	6397	6918	7277
07	Transport	LLMV	38543	37215	36122	34629	35769	35637	35738	35979
09	Recreation and culture	LLMW	18930	18575	16996	16108	15570	15182	15557	15656
12	Miscellaneous goods and services	LLMX	17828	17307	16969	16562	17027	17402	18614	20444
ND	Total non-durable goods	UTIK	268860	263175	253070	252960	247298	251196	253184	250779
	Total goods	UTIG	448170	452529	442620	443956	440537	452276	461027	474944
	Services								
03	Clothing and footwear	LLMY	1099	1208	1274	1172	1010	1013	994	1036
04	Housing, water, electricity, gas and other fuels	LLMZ	203603	206469	209341	211127	215260	217445	220728	224168
05	Furnishings, household equipment and routine maintenance of the house	LLNA	6794	6946	6289	6941	6701	6758	7026	7199
06	Health	LLNB	8093	7296	7707	8350	8525	8317	8222	8627
07	Transport	LLNC	68318	66197	62618	62851	63050	64447	65079	67912
08	Communication	LLND	20401	20843	20114	20263	20022	19559	20377	20747
09	Recreation and culture	LLNE	40096	40432	37923	37265	37698	38856	40003	40959
10	Education	ADMJ	17904	17696	17806	17102	16319	15865	15248	15157
11	Restaurants and hotels	ADMK	103715	101137	92415	94016	95478	96399	98984	100576
12	Miscellaneous goods and services	LLNF	107974	102065	97928	95625	95427	97888	102996	105354
S	Total services	UTIO	581045	571799	553617	554591	559422	566547	579657	591735
0	Final consumption expenditure in the UK by resident and non-resident households (domestic concept)	ABQJ	1028629	1024171	996186	998504	999929	1018823	1040684	1066679
P.33	Final consumption expenditure outside the UK by UK resident households	ABTC	47873	44076	35490	34981	32842	34375	34549	37645
	Final consumption expenditure in the UK by households resident in rest of the world	CCHX	-22249	-22191	-21797	-23100	-23208	-23820	-26027	-26931
P.3	Final consumption expenditure by UK resident households in the UK and abroad (national concept)	ABPF	1053452	1045809	1009965	1010428	1009521	1029378	1049204	1077393

Source: Office for National Statistics, Blue Book 2015

19.16 Individual consumption expenditure at current market prices
by households, non-profit institutions serving households and general government

Classified by function (COICOP/COPNI/COFOG)[1]

£ million

			2007	2008	2009	2010	2011	2012	2013	2014
P.31	Final consumption expenditure of households									
01	Food and non-alcoholic beverages	ABZV	73842	78755	80468	83053	87009	91377	96199	95318
01.1	Food	ABZW	64881	69683	71131	73417	76409	80441	84957	84247
01.2	Non-alcoholic beverages	ADFK	8961	9072	9337	9636	10600	10936	11242	11071
02	Alcoholic beverages, tobacco and narcotics	ADFL	36496	36407	38358	38896	41999	42878	43526	44637
02.1	Alcoholic beverages	ADFM	14189	14132	14574	15291	16215	16807	17499	18087
02.2	Tobacco	ADFN	15766	15879	16209	17176	18217	18702	18683	19527
02.3	Narcotics	MNC2	6541	6396	7575	6429	7567	7369	7344	7023
03	Clothing and footwear	ADFP	47610	49463	49310	50838	54066	55814	58905	63047
03.1	Clothing	ADFQ	40701	42240	41795	43231	46396	47665	50601	53678
03.2	Footwear	ADFR	6909	7223	7515	7607	7670	8149	8304	9369
04	Housing, water, electricity, gas and other fuels	ADFS	181821	195004	209153	238159	245616	255613	265162	269918
04.1	Actual rentals for housing	ADFT	38414	40826	43409	48921	52631	55157	56799	59403
04.2	Imputed rentals for housing	ADFU	108963	114716	125803	147954	152404	155935	161132	166172
04.3	Maintenance and repair of the dwelling	ADFV	2883	2543	2359	2249	2197	2471	2494	2591
04.4	Water supply and miscellaneous dwelling services	ADFW	7664	8086	8276	8579	8946	9244	9600	9935
04.5	Electricity, gas and other fuels	ADFX	23897	28833	29306	30456	29438	32806	35137	31817
05	Furnishings, household equipment and routine maintenance of the house	ADFY	47897	47299	44536	45848	46353	47165	49300	52354
05.1	Furniture, furnishings, carpets and other floor coverings	ADFZ	18238	17594	15697	15601	16746	16367	16708	17517
05.2	Household textiles	ADGG	5459	5509	5718	6270	4930	5263	5799	6576
05.3	Household appliances	ADGL	6001	6102	5691	6007	6167	6320	6731	6914
05.4	Glassware, tableware and household utensils	ADGM	4561	4375	4224	4102	4721	4865	4905	5254
05.5	Tools and equipment for house and garden	ADGN	4260	3830	3424	3391	3667	4033	4182	4773
05.6	Goods and services for routine household maintenance	ADGO	9378	9889	9782	10477	10122	10317	10975	11320
06	Health	ADGP	14865	14403	14897	15691	16359	17818	19121	20261
06.1	Medical products, appliances and equipment	ADGQ	7929	7985	7827	7756	8015	9501	10644	11134
06.2	Out-patient services	ADGR	4224	3621	3953	4821	5322	5253	5427	5799
06.3	Hospital services	ADGS	2712	2797	3117	3114	3022	3064	3050	3328
07	Transport	ADGT	126485	126685	121711	127393	136262	143474	150124	155830
07.1	Purchase of vehicles	ADGU	39315	35515	35079	35225	35978	39094	41639	44961
07.2	Operation of personal transport equipment	ADGV	52545	56724	53621	58411	63427	64789	65148	64909
07.3	Transport services	ADGW	34625	34446	33011	33757	36857	39591	43337	45960
08	Communication	ADGX	18922	18938	18554	19442	19946	20420	21975	22658
08.1	Postal services	CDEF	1080	1017	1055	961	1062	1245	1345	1373
08.2	Telephone and telefax equipment	ADWO	717	803	871	758	757	861	969	1004
08.3	Telephone and telefax services	ADWP	17125	17118	16628	17723	18127	18314	19661	20281
09	Recreation and culture	ADGY	101644	105230	100113	100834	100679	103959	104353	111216
09.1	Audio-visual, photographic and information processing equipment	ADGZ	21682	22917	20781	20429	19515	19766	16816	17683
09.2	Other major durables for recreation and culture	ADHL	6776	7156	7381	7683	7208	7725	8456	10076
09.3	Other recreational items and equipment; flowers, garden and pets	ADHZ	29512	30524	29184	29880	28726	29257	29066	31091
09.4	Recreational and cultural services	ADIA	30739	32123	31064	31481	33768	35745	38066	40740
09.5	Newspapers, books and stationery	ADIC	12935	12510	11703	11361	11462	11466	11949	11825
09.6	Package holidays[2]	ADID	–	–	–	–	–	–	–	–
10	Education									
10	Education services	ADIE	12384	13663	14811	14982	15032	15865	17882	19587
11	Restaurants and hotels	ADIF	86516	87687	82087	85737	91897	96399	101277	105916
11.1	Catering services	ADIG	73511	74274	70662	73478	78696	80964	84274	87269
11.2	Accommodation services	ADIH	13005	13413	11425	12259	13201	15435	17003	18647
12	Miscellaneous goods and services	ADII	135177	137439	123871	121089	124454	128041	135949	149956
12.1	Personal care	ADIJ	22599	22350	22763	23419	24196	24742	26227	28210
12.2	Prostitution	MNC8	4979	5245	5400	5580	5741	5886	6037	6111
12.3	Personal effects n.e.c.	ADIK	7723	7836	7713	9784	10969	11396	12413	14097
12.4	Social protection	ADIL	12121	12646	12513	13205	12932	13506	14831	16815
12.5	Insurance	ADIM	23862	19238	21449	20117	21312	23878	27167	26591
12.6	Financial services n.e.c.	ADIN	54643	61039	45091	41448	41523	39468	39716	48412
12.7	Other services n.e.c.	ADIO	9250	9085	8942	7536	7781	9165	9558	9720
0	Final consumption expenditure in the UK by resident and non-resident households (domestic concept)	ABQI	883659	910973	897869	941962	979672	1018823	1063773	1110698
P.33	Final consumption expenditure outside the UK by UK resident households	ABTA	34548	37374	33661	34358	33659	34375	36245	37356
P.34	Final consumption expenditure in the UK by households resident in rest of the world	CDFD	-19729	-20082	-19865	-21539	-22503	-23820	-26912	-28558
P.31	Final consumption expenditure by UK resident households in the UK and abroad (national concept)	ABPB	898478	928265	911665	954781	990828	1029378	1073106	1119496

19.16 Individual consumption expenditure at current market prices
by households, non-profit institutions serving households and general government

continued   Classified by function (COICOP/COPNI/COFOG)[1]

£ million

		2007	2008	2009	2010	2011	2012	2013	2014
P.31	Consumption expenditure of UK resident households								
P.31	Final consumption expenditure of UK resident households in the UK and abroad	ABPB	898478	928265	911665	954781	990828	1029378	1073106	1119496
13	Final individual consumption expenditure of NPISH									
P.31	Final individual consumption expenditure of NPISH	ABNV	43718	46893	50205	50885	53259	53186	54978	56162
14	Final individual consumption expenditure of general government									
14.1	Health	IWX5	93652	100875	109076	112387	115316	117162	120096	125949
14.2	Recreation and culture	IWX6	6186	6122	6225	6100	6145	6277	5609	5523
14.3	Education	IWX7	51649	55330	58484	60298	59426	59708	60397	60495
14.4	Social protection	IWX8	29719	31520	32511	32905	32327	32549	32429	31875
P.31	Final individual consumption expenditure of general government	NNAQ	181206	193847	206296	211690	213214	215696	218531	223842
P.31 P.41	Total, individual consumption expenditure/ actual individual consumption	ABRE	1123402	1169005	1168166	1217356	1257301	1298260	1346615	1399500

1 'Purpose' or 'function' classifications are designed to indicate the 'socio-economic objectives' that institutional units aim to achieve through various kinds of outlays. COICOP is the Classification of Individual Consumption by Purpose and applies to households. COPNI is the Classification of the Purposes of Non-profit Institutions Serving Households and COFOG the Classification of the Functions of Government.

2 Package holidays data are dispersed between components (transport etc)

Source: Office for National Statistics, Blue Book 2015

19.17 Individual consumption expenditure by households, NPISH and general government
Chained volume measures (reference year 2012)
Classified by function (COICOP/COPNI/COFOG)[1]

£ million

		2007	2008	2009	2010	2011	2012	2013	2014
P.31	Final consumption expenditure of households								
01	Food and non-alcoholic beverages	ADIP	95380	93299	90424	90397	89709	91377	92780	92156
01.1	Food	ADIQ	83858	81926	79231	79490	78684	80441	81697	81222
01.2	Non-alcoholic beverages	ADIR	11527	11377	11208	10901	11028	10936	11083	10934
02	Alcoholic beverages, tobacco and narcotics	ADIS	47565	46130	44272	44403	42583	42878	41019	40923
02.1	Alcoholic beverages	ADIT	18021	17517	16843	17194	16873	16807	16722	16997
02.2	Tobacco	ADIU	22101	21159	20733	20494	19618	18702	17481	16992
02.3	Narcotics	MNC4	7748	7710	6984	6980	6357	7369	6816	6934
03	Clothing and footwear	ADIW	42011	46706	50346	52367	54463	55814	58369	62938
03.1	Clothing	ADIX	35830	40000	43128	45014	46810	47665	49984	53465
03.2	Footwear	ADIY	6177	6699	7211	7356	7656	8149	8385	9473
04	Housing, water, electricity, gas and other fuels	ADIZ	243971	247205	247825	252187	252499	255613	258913	258181
04.1	Actual rentals for housing	ADJA	48914	50907	51802	51858	54407	55157	55438	56657
04.2	Imputed rentals for housing	ADJB	147850	149142	151332	153044	154601	155935	158902	161158
04.3	Maintenance and repair of the dwelling	ADJC	3382	2843	2559	2360	2219	2471	2504	2601
04.4	Water supply and miscellaneous dwelling services	ADJD	9464	9383	9133	9360	9440	9244	9160	9217
04.5	Electricity, gas and other fuels	ADJE	34666	35273	33506	36008	31808	32806	32909	28548
05	Furnishings, household equipment and routine maintenance of the house	ADJF	55312	53575	48959	49009	47525	47165	48970	51497
05.1	Furniture, furnishings, carpets and other floor coverings	ADJG	21202	19800	17191	16614	17260	16367	16602	17261
05.2	Household textiles	ADJH	5825	6005	6216	6733	5018	5263	5773	6631
05.3	Household appliances	ADJI	6775	6894	6082	6163	6190	6320	6704	6938
05.4	Glassware, tableware and household utensils	ADJJ	5237	4966	4676	4368	4795	4865	4866	5109
05.5	Tools and equipment for house and garden	ADJK	5460	4865	4257	4081	3933	4033	4228	4654
05.6	Goods and services for routine household maintenance	ADJL	11013	11163	10601	11076	10335	10317	10797	10904
06	Health	ADJM	16486	15709	15837	16279	16639	17818	18814	19474
06.1	Medical products, appliances and equipment	ADJN	8390	8372	8116	7936	8120	9501	10592	10847
06.2	Out-patient services	ADJO	4553	3868	4110	4927	5353	5253	5311	5610
06.3	Hospital services	ADJP	3575	3513	3681	3450	3174	3064	2911	3017
07	Transport	ADJQ	153795	147560	143218	138343	138701	143474	147530	153381
07.1	Purchase of vehicles	ADJR	42557	39595	39993	36713	36039	39094	42134	44996
07.2	Operation of personal transport equipment	ADJS	68854	67645	65711	64056	64115	64789	65038	65757
07.3	Transport services	ADJT	42123	40335	37451	37547	38574	39591	40358	42628
08	Communication	ADJU	21186	21751	21095	21079	20805	20420	21322	21715
08.1	Postal services	CCGZ	1727	1526	1452	1247	1259	1245	1212	1187
08.2	Telephone and telefax equipment	ADQF	786	908	979	816	783	861	945	968
08.3	Telephone and telefax services	ADQG	18786	19356	18694	19009	18761	18314	19165	19560
09	Recreation and culture	ADJV	97049	103893	99462	99434	100003	103959	103486	109578
09.1	Audio-visual, photographic and information processing equipment	ADJW	11659	14946	15445	16279	17638	19766	17907	20202
09.2	Other major durables for recreation and culture	ADJX	8045	8331	8304	8253	7448	7725	8361	9748
09.3	Other recreational items and equipment; flowers, gardens and pets	ADJY	29759	30979	29103	29530	28684	29257	28968	30916
09.4	Recreational and cultural services	ADJZ	36820	37429	34857	34011	34789	35745	36757	37964
09.5	Newspapers, books and stationery	ADKM	15078	14026	12708	11864	11610	11466	11493	10748
09.6	Package holidays[2]	ADMI	–	–	–	–	–	–	–	–
10	Education									
10	Education services	ADMJ	17904	17696	17806	17102	16319	15865	15248	15157
11	Restaurants and hotels	ADMK	103715	101137	92415	94016	95478	96399	98984	100576
11.1	Catering services	ADML	89525	86722	80154	81070	81942	80964	82289	82685
11.2	Accommodation services	ADMM	14237	14401	12322	12984	13560	15435	16695	17891
12	Miscellaneous goods and services	ADMN	136972	129985	125142	124362	125369	128041	135249	141103
12.1	Personal care	ADMO	25179	24377	24246	24324	24438	24742	26198	28355
12.2	Prostitution	MND2	5588	5641	5689	5766	5831	5886	5937	5891
12.3	Personal effects n.e.c.	ADMP	9444	9192	8718	10738	11537	11396	12121	13743
12.4	Social protection	ADMQ	14449	14416	13632	13943	13262	13506	14536	16001
12.5	Insurance	ADMR	29255	22756	24232	21406	21480	23878	26680	25300
12.6	Financial services n.e.c.	ADMS	42454	42504	39111	40089	40749	39468	40540	42543
12.7	Other services n.e.c.	ADMT	11085	10184	9814	8042	8012	9165	9237	9270
0	Final consumption expenditure in the UK by resident and non-resident households (domestic concept)	ABQJ	1028629	1024171	996186	998504	999929	1018823	1040684	1066679
P.33	Final consumption expenditure outside the UK by UK resident households	ABTC	47873	44076	35490	34981	32842	34375	34549	37645
P.34	Final consumption expenditure in the UK by households resident in rest of the world	CCHX	-22249	-22191	-21797	-23100	-23208	-23820	-26027	-26931
P.31	Final consumption expenditure by UK resident households in the UK and abroad (national concept)	ABPF	1053452	1045809	1009965	1010428	1009521	1029378	1049204	1077393

19.17
continued

Individual consumption expenditure by households, NPISH and general government
Chained volume measures (reference year 2012)

Classified by function (COICOP/COPNI/COFOG)[1]

£ million

			2007	2008	2009	2010	2011	2012	2013	2014
P.31	Consumption expenditure of UK resident households									
P.31	Final consumption expenditure of UK resident households in the UK and abroad	ABPF	1053452	1045809	1009965	1010428	1009521	1029378	1049204	1077393
13	Final individual consumption expenditure of NPISH									
P.31	Final individual consumption expenditure of NPISH	ABNU	51131	51310	52585	51837	53767	53186	53774	54772
14	Final individual consumption expenditure of general government									
14.1	Health	K4CP	99476	104746	109240	111583	113592	117162	121316	123578
14.2	Recreation and culture	K4CQ	6693	6439	6472	6256	6237	6277	5595	5706
14.3	Education	K4CR	57135	56805	56947	57249	58353	59708	60477	61948
14.4	Social protection	K4CS	34301	33944	34064	33854	32977	32549	32056	31490
P.31	Final individual consumption expenditure of general government	NSZK	197307	201793	206588	208833	211116	215696	219444	222722
P.31 P.41	Total, individual consumption expenditure/ actual individual consumption	YBIO	1300299	1297699	1268788	1270901	1274401	1298260	1322422	1354887

1 'Purpose' or 'function' classifications are designed to indicate the 'socio-economic objectives' that institutional units aim to achieve through various kinds of outlays. COICOP is the Classification of Individual Consumption by Purpose and applies to households. COPNI is the Classification of the Purposes of Non-profit Institutions Serving Households and COFOG the Classification of the Functions of Government.
2 Package holidays data are dispersed between components (transport etc)

Office for National Statistics, Blue Book 2015

675

19.18 Changes in inventories
Chained volume measures[1]

Reference year 2011, £ million

| | Mining and quarrying | Manufacturing industries | | | | Electricity, gas and water supply | Distributive trades | | Other industries | Changes in inventories |
		Materials and fuel	Work in progress	Finished goods	Total		Wholesale[2]	Retail[2]		
Level of inventories held at end-December[3] 2012	1 326	20 094	17 344	19 742	57 193	5 508	36 974	36 039	74 439	212 531
	FAEA	FBNF	FBNG	FBNH	DHBM	FAEB	FAJX	FBYN	DLWX	CAFU
2011	262	1 294	−423	141	1 012	−75	1 546	351	−345	2 751
2012	179	−1 174	743	738	307	−238	1 586	235	1 528	3 597
2013	−197	736	773	−162	1 347	434	5 342	−973	2 812	8 765
2014	1 798	1 368	1 939	2 800	6 107	775	−179	1 711	2 977	13 189
Seasonally adjusted										
2011 Q4	−147	681	−27	−242	412	−95	2 638	981	−3 110	679
2012 Q1	49	−814	328	116	−370	95	760	558	−3 342	−2 250
Q2	2 321	491	279	1 667	2 437	−89	727	876	−5 426	846
Q3	−1 555	−1 104	−53	−85	−1 242	−122	719	−1 104	6 994	3 690
Q4	−636	253	189	−960	−518	−122	−620	−95	3 302	1 311
2013 Q1	−27	45	−11	−402	−368	−575	710	−1 871	398	−1 733
Q2	47	130	288	−357	61	−20	1 636	−392	−1 338	−6
Q3	−212	26	38	−229	−165	520	1 771	479	2 865	5 258
Q4	−5	535	458	826	1 819	509	1 225	811	887	5 246
2014 Q1	201	774	964	165	1 903	539	1 788	261	−1 398	3 294
Q2	4	500	90	650	1 241	593	−400	247	748	2 433
Q3	473	158	371	546	1 074	856	−2 597	616	3 653	4 075
Q4	1 120	−64	514	1 439	1 889	−1 213	1 030	587	−26	3 387
2015 Q1	424	391	71	1 238	1 700	406	−578	2 767	−2 185	2 535

1 Estimates are given to the nearest £ million but cannot be regarded as accurate to this degree.
2 Wholesaling and retailing estimates exclude the motor trades.
3 Note that levels are not expected to sum to totals, because they are constructed from the sum of the change series, and these are not additive prior to the reference year (2011)

Source: Office for National Statistics

19.19 Gross fixed capital formation at current purchasers' prices[1]
Analysis by broad sector and type of asset

Total economy

£ million

		2006	2007	2008	2009	2010	2011	2012	2013	2014
Private sector										
New dwellings, excluding land	L5ZQ	51009	52457	53094	44451	47236	50475	50931	55524	64786
Other buildings and structures	EQBU	30461	37515	38869	30882	29865	35626	39199	43539	46199
Transport equipment	EQBV	11603	10361	10466	9385	12795	8089	9046	7642	9023
ICT equipment and other machinery and equipment, and cultivated biological resources	EQBW	39929	44150	43495	35410	37829	44159	47146	47229	48670
Intellectual property products	EQBX	44464	48131	51909	48260	49987	52607	54710	57690	60513
Costs associated with the transfer of ownership of non-produced assets	L5ZR	37887	40088	20827	11848	12576	11737	13571	16497	19705
P.51g Total	EQBZ	215354	232702	218658	180238	190288	202692	214602	228121	248897
S.11001 Public non-financial corporations										
New dwellings, excluding land	L5YQ	4048	3897	3966	4068	3883	3340	3135	3263	3658
Other buildings and structures	DEES	2440	2246	1736	1836	1890	1646	1547	1559	1767
Transport equipment	DEEP	173	145	274	340	196	156	204	78	101
ICT equipment and other machinery and equipment, and cultivated biological resources	DEEQ	966	1254	1778	1155	903	945	937	964	741
Intellectual property products	DLXJ	2028	2067	2081	2055	2055	2024	2024	2014	2005
Costs associated with the transfer of ownership of non-produced assets	L5ZL	-3589	-3062	-1654	-370	-406	-388	-427	-505	-621
P.51g Total	FCCJ	6066	6547	8181	9084	8521	7723	7420	7373	7651
S.13 General government										
New dwellings, excluding land	L5ZU	9	3	15	1	-5	-8	115	130	188
Other buildings and structures	EQCH	25186	27552	31383	31758	28760	27412	26295	24780	26952
Transport equipment	EQCI	501	483	512	605	702	602	462	435	470
ICT equipment, other machinery and equipment, Cultivated biological resources, weapons	EQCJ	8614	7630	9211	10254	11175	11046	9719	9261	9669
Intellectual property products	EQCK	3209	3321	3691	3874	5159	4908	4885	4817	5423
Costs associated with the transfer of ownership of non-produced assets	L5ZV	-1064	-474	2038	4061	4429	4315	4722	5602	6858
P.51g Total	NNBF	36455	38515	46850	50553	50220	48275	46198	45025	49560
P.51g Total gross fixed capital formation	NPQX	257875	277764	273689	239875	249029	258689	268221	280520	306108

1 Components may not sum to totals due to rounding.

Source: Office for National Statistics, Blue Book 2015

19.20 Gross fixed capital formation at current purchasers' prices[1]
Analysis by type of asset

Total economy

£ million

		2006	2007	2008	2009	2010	2011	2012	2013	2014
Tangible fixed assets										
New dwellings, excluding land	DFDK	55066	56357	57075	48520	51114	53807	54181	58917	68632
Other buildings and structures	DLWS	58087	67313	71988	64476	60515	64684	67041	69878	74918
Transport equipment	DLWZ	12277	10989	11252	10331	13693	8847	9712	8154	9594
ICT equipment, other machinery and equipment, cultivated biological resources, weapons	DLXI	49509	53034	54484	46819	49906	56149	57802	57454	59080
Total	EQCQ	174939	187693	194799	170146	175228	183487	188736	194403	212224
Intellectual property products	DLXP	49701	53520	57681	54188	57201	59539	61618	64521	67941
Costs associated with the transfer of ownership of non-produced assets	DFBH	33235	36552	21211	15539	16600	15663	17865	21595	25942
P.51g Total gross fixed capital formation	NPQX	257875	277764	273689	239875	249029	258689	268221	280520	306108

1 Components may not sum to totals due to rounding.

Source: Office for National Statistics, Blue Book 2015

19.21

Gross fixed capital formation[1,2]
Chained volume measures (reference year 2012)
Total economy: Analysis by broad sector and type of asset

£ million

		2006	2007	2008	2009	2010	2011	2012	2013	2014
Private sector										
New dwellings, excluding land	L62K	62884	61559	58452	47385	50071	52429	50931	53829	60754
Other buildings and structures	EQCU	31634	37045	37340	30244	31009	36954	39199	41932	42837
Transport equipment	EQCV	12586	11217	10856	9620	13141	8025	9046	7703	9635
ICT equipment and other machinery and equipment and cultivated biological resources	EQCW	46571	53152	49955	36408	39414	44651	47146	47360	49574
Intellectual property products	EQCX	48557	51666	54036	50510	51453	52791	54710	56895	59161
Costs associated with the transfer of ownership of non-produced assets	L62L	44709	46291	23259	12542	13107	11956	13571	16392	19424
P.51g Total	EQCZ	244212	258986	232813	186728	198218	206723	214602	224110	241385
S .11001 Public non-financial corporations										
New dwellings, excluding land	L62M	4999	4573	4367	4336	4115	3472	3135	3163	3426
Other buildings and structures	DEEX	2627	2338	1695	1833	1974	1710	1547	1504	1633
Transport equipment	DEEU	187	156	283	347	203	155	204	79	108
ICT equipment and other machinery and equipment and cultivated biological resources	DEEV	1183	1542	2041	1182	943	955	937	959	758
Intellectual property products	EQDE	2495	2456	2372	2251	2198	2096	2024	1924	1907
Costs associated with the transfer of ownership of non-produced assets	L62N	-4234	-3534	-1843	-392	-422	-396	-427	-502	-612
P.51g Total	EQDG	7358	7576	8882	9551	9005	7989	7420	7127	7220
S.13 General government										
New dwellings, excluding land costs	L62O	11	3	17	2	-5	-8	115	126	177
Other buildings and structures	EQDI	25897	27296	29945	30877	29643	28426	26295	23833	24757
Transport equipment	EQDJ	542	520	531	615	724	601	462	437	498
ICT equipment, other machinery and equipment, Cultivated biological resources, weapons	EQDK	10179	9033	10257	10511	11636	11195	9719	9143	9722
Intellectual property services	EQDL	3624	3664	3872	4054	5346	4939	4885	4741	5243
Costs associated with the transfer of ownership of non-produced assets	L62P	-1256	-547	2270	4299	4616	4393	4722	5566	6763
P.51g Total	EQDN	39508	40694	47101	50480	51963	49559	46198	43845	47159
P.51g Total gross fixed capital formation	NPQR	290059	306454	288263	246741	259170	264251	268221	275083	295764

1 For the years before 2012, totals differ from the sum of their components.
2 Components may not sum to totals due to rounding.

Source: Office for National Statistics, Blue Book 2015

19.22

Gross fixed capital formation[1,2]
Chained volume measures (reference year 2012)
Total economy: Analysis by type of asset

£ million

		2006	2007	2008	2009	2010	2011	2012	2013	2014
Tangible fixed assets										
New dwellings, excluding land	DFDV	67893	66137	62837	51720	54181	55893	54181	57118	64356
Other buildings and structures	EQDP	60130	67144	69086	62994	62647	67097	67041	67268	69227
Transport equipment	DLWJ	13315	11893	11671	10581	14067	8780	9712	8218	10241
ICT equipment, other machinery and equipment, cultivated biological resources, weapons	DLWM	57778	63583	62137	48097	51990	56799	57802	57463	60054
Total	EQDS	197128	207506	204479	173545	182915	188495	188736	190067	203878
Intellectual property products	EQDT	54622	57753	60263	56795	58984	59822	61618	63561	66312
Costs associated with the transfer of ownership of non-produced assets	DFDW	39217	42211	23687	16450	17299	15955	17865	21456	25575
P.51g Total gross fixed capital formation	NPQR	290059	306454	288263	246741	259170	264251	268221	275083	295764

1 For the years before 2012, totals differ from the sum of their components.
2 Components may not sum to totals due to rounding.

Source: Office for National Statistics, Blue Book 2015

Education

Chapter 20

Education

Educational establishments in the UK are administered and financed in several ways. Most schools are controlled by local authorities, which are part of the structure of local government, but some are 'assisted', receiving grants direct from central government sources and being controlled by governing bodies who have a substantial degree of autonomy. Completely outside the public sector are non.maintained schools run by individuals, companies or charitable institutions.

For the purposes of UK education statistics, schools fall under the following broad categories:

Mainstream state schools
(In Northern Ireland, grant-aided mainstream schools)

These schools work in partnership with other schools and local authorities and they receive funding from local authorities. Since 1 September 1999, the categories (typically in England) are:

Community – schools formerly known as 'county' plus some former grant-maintained (GM) schools

Foundation – most former GM schools

Voluntary Aided – schools formerly known as 'aided' and some former GM schools

Voluntary Controlled – schools formerly known as 'controlled'

Non-maintained mainstream schools

These consist of:

(a) Independent schools

Schools which charge fees and may also be financed by individuals, companies or charitable institutions. These include Direct Grant schools, where the governing bodies are assisted by departmental grants and a proportion of the pupils attending them do so free or under an arrangement by which local authorities meet tuition fees. City Technology Colleges (CTCs) and Academies (applicable in England only) are also included as independent schools.

(b) Non-maintained schools
Run by voluntary bodies who may receive some grant from central government for capital work and for equipment, but their current expenditure is met primarily from the fees charged to local authorities for pupils placed in schools.

Special schools

Special schools provide education for children with Special Educational Needs (SEN) (in Scotland, Record of Needs or a Coordinated Support Plan), who cannot be educated satisfactorily in an ordinary school. Maintained special schools are run by local authorities, while non-maintained special schools are financed as described at (b) above.

Pupil Referral Units

Pupil Referral Units (PRUs) operate in England and Wales and provide education outside of a mainstream or special school setting, to meet the needs of difficult or disruptive children.

Schools in Scotland are categorised as Education Authority, Grant-aided, Opted-out/Self-governing (these three being grouped together as 'Publicly funded' schools), Independent schools and Partnership schools.

The home government departments dealing with education statistics are:

Department for Education (DfE)
Department for Business, Innovation and Skills (BIS)
Welsh Government (WG)
Scottish Government (SG)
Northern Ireland Department of Education (DENI)
Northern Ireland Department for Employment and Learning (DELNI)

Each of the home education departments in Great Britain, along with the Northern Ireland Department of Education, have overall responsibility for funding the schools sectors in their own country.

Up to March 2001, further education (FE) courses in FE sector colleges in England and in Wales were largely funded through grants from the respective FE funding councils. In April 2001, however, the Learning and Skills Council (LSC) took over the responsibility for funding the FE sector in England, and the National Council for Education and Training for Wales (part of Education and Learning Wales – ELWa) did so for Wales. The Apprenticeships, Skills, Children and Learning Act 2009 received Royal Assent on 12 November 2009 for the dissolution of the Learning and Skills Council by 2010 and the transfer of its functions on 1 April 2010 to local authorities and two new agencies: the Young People's Learning Agency (YPLA) and the Skills Funding Agency. The YPLA champions young people's learning by providing financial support to young learners; by funding academies, general FE and sixth form colleges and other 16 to 19 providers; and supporting local authorities to secure sufficient education and training places for all 16 to 19 year olds in England. The Skills Funding Agency funds further education colleges and training providers in England to deliver adult skills and apprenticeships. In Wales, the National Council – ELWa, funds FE provision made by FE institutions via a third party or sponsored arrangements. The Scottish Further Education Funding Council (SFEFC) funds FE colleges in Scotland, while the Department for Employment and Learning funds FE colleges in Northern Ireland.

From 1 April 2012, funding for the education and training of 3 to 19 year olds in England will become the responsibility of the Education Funding Agency (EFA), which will be a new executive agency of the Department for Education. The EFA will directly fund academies, free schools, university technology colleges, studio schools and 16 to 19 providers. It will distribute funding to local authorities for them to pass on to their maintained schools and it will also be responsible for the distribution of capital funding.

Higher education (HE) courses in higher education establishments are largely publicly funded through block grants from the HE funding councils in England and Scotland, the Higher Education Council – ELWa in Wales, and the Department for Employment and Learning in Northern Ireland. In addition, some designated HE (mainly HND/HNC Diplomas and Certificates of HE) is also funded by these sources. The FE sources mentioned above fund the remainder.

Statistics for the separate systems obtained in England, Wales, Scotland and Northern Ireland are collected and processed separately in accordance with the particular needs of the responsible departments. Since 1994/95 the Higher Education Statistics Agency (HESA) has undertaken the data collection for all higher education institutions (HEIs) in the UK. This includes the former Universities Funding Council (UFC) funded UK universities previously collected by the Universities Statistical Record. There are some structural differences in the information collected for schools, FE and HE in each of the four home countries and in some tables the GB/UK data presented are amalgamations from sources that are not entirely comparable.

Stages of education

There are five stages of education: early years, primary, secondary, FE and HE, and education is compulsory for all children between the ages of 5 (4 in Northern Ireland) and 16. The non-compulsory fourth stage, FE, covers non-advanced education, which can be taken at further (including tertiary) education colleges, HE institutions (HEIs) and increasingly in secondary schools. The fifth stage, HE, is study beyond GCE A levels and their equivalent which, for most full-time students, takes place in universities and other HEIs.

Early years education

Children under 5 attend a variety of settings including state nursery schools, nursery classes within primary schools and, in England and Wales, reception classes within primary schools, as well as s ettings outside the state sector such as voluntary pre-schools or privately run nurseries. In recent years there has been a major expansion of early years education, and the Education Act 2002 extended the National Curriculum for England to include the foundation stage. The foundation stage was introduced in September 2000, and covered children's education from the age of 3 to the end of the reception year, when most are just 5 and some almost 6 years old. The Early Years Foundation Stage (EYFS), came into force in September 2008, and is a single regulatory and quality framework for the provision of learning, development and care for children in all registered early years settings between birth and the academic year in which they turn 5.

Children born in Scotland between March and December are eligible for early years education at the time the Pre-School Education and Day Care Census is carried out. In Scotland, early years education is called ante-pre-school education for those aged 3 to 4 years old, and pre-school education for those aged 4.

Primary education

The primary stage covers three age ranges: nursery (under 5), infant (5 to 7 or 8) and junior (up to 11 or 12) but in Scotland and Northern Ireland there is generally no distinction between infant and junior schools. Most public sector primary schools take both boys and girls in mixed classes. It is usual to transfer straight to secondary school at age 11 (in England, Wales and Northern Ireland) or 12 (in Scotland), but in England some children make the transition via middle schools catering for various age ranges between 8 and 14. Depending on their individual age ranges middle schools are classified as either primary or secondary.

Secondary education

Public provision of secondary education in an area may consist of a combination of different types of school, the pattern reflecting historical circumstance and the policy adopted by the local authority. Comprehensive schools largely admit pupils without reference to ability or aptitude and cater for all the children in a neighbourhood, but in some areas they co.exist with grammar, secondary modern or technical schools. In 2005/06, 88 per cent of secondary pupils in England attended comprehensive schools while all secondary schools in Wales are comprehensive schools.

The majority of education authority secondary schools in Scotland are comprehensive in character and offer six years of secondary education; however, in remote areas there are several two-year and four-year secondary schools.

In Northern Ireland, post-primary education is provided by grammar schools and non-selective secondary schools.

In England, the Specialist Schools Programme helps schools, in partnership with private sector sponsors and supported by additional government funding, to establish distinctive identities through their chosen specialisms and achieve their targets to raise standards. Specialist schools have a special focus on their chosen subject area but must meet the National Curriculum requirements and deliver a broad and balanced education to all pupils. Any maintained secondary school in England can apply to be designated as a specialist school in one of ten specialist areas: arts, business & enterprise, engineering, humanities, languages, mathematics & computing, music, science, sports and technology. Schools can also combine any two specialisms.

Academies, operating in England, are publicly funded independent local schools that provide free education. They are all-ability schools established by sponsors from business, faith or voluntary groups working with partners from the local community.

Academies benefit from greater freedoms to help innovate and raise standards. These include freedom from local authority control, ability to set pay and conditions for staff, freedom from following the National Curriculum and the ability to change the lengths of terms and school days.

The Academies Programme was first introduced in March 2000 with the objective of replacing poorly performing schools. Academies were established and driven by external sponsors, to achieve a transformation in education performance.

The Academies Programme was expanded through legislation in the Academies Act 2010. This enables all maintained primary, secondary and special schools to apply to become an Academy. The early focus is on schools rated outstanding by Ofsted and the first of these new academies opened in September 2010. These schools do not have a sponsor but instead are expected to work with underperforming schools to help raise standards.

Special schools

Special schools (day or boarding) provide education for children who require specialist support to complete their education, for example because they have physical or other difficulties. Many pupils with special educational needs are educated in mainstream schools. All children attending special schools are offered a curriculum designed to overcome their learning difficulties and to enable them to become self-reliant. Since December 2005, special schools have also been able to apply for the Special Educational Needs (SEN) specialism, under the Specialist Schools Programme. They can apply for a curriculum specialism, but not for both the SEN and a curriculum specialism.

Further education

The term further education may be used in a general sense to cover all non.advanced courses taken after the period of compulsory education, but more commonly it excludes those staying on at secondary school and those in higher education, that is, courses in universities and colleges leading to qualifications above GCE A Level, Scottish Certificate of Education (SCE) Higher Grade, GNVQ/NVQ level 3, and their equivalents. Since 1 April 1993, sixth form colleges in England and Wales have been included in the further education sector.

Higher education

Higher education is defined as courses that are of a standard that is higher than GCE A level, the Higher Grade of the SCE/National Qualification, GNVQ/NVQ level 3 or the Edexcel (formerly BTEC) or SQA National Certificate/Diploma. There are three main levels of HE course:

(i) Postgraduate courses leading to higher degrees, diplomas and certificates (including postgraduate certificates of education (PGCE) and professional qualifications) which usually require a first degree as entry qualification.

(ii) Undergraduate courses which include first degrees, first degrees with qualified teacher status, enhanced first degrees, first degrees obtained concurrently with a diploma, and intercalated first degrees (where first degree students, usually in medicine, dentistry or veterinary medicine, interrupt their studies to complete a one-year course of advanced studies in a related topic).

(iii) Other undergraduate courses which include all other higher education courses, for example HNDs and Diplomas in HE.

As a result of the Further and Higher Education Act 1992, former polytechnics and some other HEIs were designated as universities in 1992/93. Students normally attend HE courses at HEIs, but some attend at FE colleges. Some also attend institutions which do not receive public grant (such as the University of Buckingham) and these numbers are excluded from the tables. However, the University of Buckingham is included in Tables 20.6 and 20.7.

20.1: Number of schools by type of school - time series

United Kingdom

	2000/01	2010/11	2011/12	2012/13	2013/14
UNITED KINGDOM					
Public sector mainstream					
Nursery	3,228	3,130	3,095	3,085	3,031
Primary	22,902	21,281	21,165	21,069	21,040
Middle[1]	.	.	.	4	4
Secondary[2]	4,352	4,121	4,072	4,077	4,116
of which Middle deemed secondary	316	225	196	189	176
Non-maintained mainstream	2,397	2,498	2,502	2,497	2,497
Special schools	1,498	1,293	1,281	1,269	1,264
of which state-funded	1,401	1,218	1,209	1,198	1,195
of which non-maintained	97	75	72	71	69
Pupil referral units	338	427	403	400	371
ALL SCHOOLS	34,715	32,750	32,518	32,401	32,323
ENGLAND					
Public sector mainstream					
Maintained nursery	506	423	423	417	414
State-funded primary[3]	18,069	16,884	16,818	16,784	16,788
State-funded secondary[2]	3,496	3,310	3,268	3,281	3,329
of which Middle deemed secondary	316	225	196	189	176
Non-maintained mainstream[4]	2,190	2,417	2,421	2,414	2,412
Special schools	1,175	1,046	1,039	1,032	1,033
of which state-funded[5]	1,113	971	967	961	964
of which non-maintained	62	75	72	71	69
Pupil referral units	308	427	403	400	371
ALL SCHOOLS	25,744	24,507	24,372	24,328	24,347
WALES					
Public sector mainstream					
Nursery	41	23	22	20	17
Primary	1,631	1,435	1,412	1,374	1,357
Middle[1]	.	.	.	4	4
Secondary	229	222	221	216	213
Non-maintained mainstream	54	66	66	68	70
Special (maintained)	45	43	43	42	42
Pupil referral units	30	..	..	..	..
ALL SCHOOLS	2,030	1,789	1,764	1,724	1,703
SCOTLAND					
Public sector mainstream					
Nursery[6]	2,586	2,586	2,553	2,551	2,504
Primary	2,278	2,099	2,081	2,064	2,056
Secondary	389	372	367	365	364
Non-maintained mainstream	127	..	..	..	..
Special schools	230	163	158	155	149
of which maintained	195	163	158	155	149
of which non-maintained	35	..	..	..	..
ALL SCHOOLS	5,610	5,220	5,159	5,135	5,073
NORTHERN IRELAND					
Grant aided mainstream					
Nursery[7]	95	98	97	97	96
Primary	924	863	854	847	839
Secondary	238	217	216	215	210
Non-maintained mainstream	26	15	15	15	15
Special (maintained)	48	41	41	40	40
ALL SCHOOLS	1,331	1,234	1,223	1,214	1,200

Source: Department for Education; Welsh Government; Scottish Government; Northern Ireland Department of Education

1 In Wales, the Middle School for pupils of both primary and secondary school age was introduced in 2012/13.

2 In England, includes secondary sponsor-led academies, secondary converter academies and secondary free schools.

3 In England, includes middle deemed primary schools as well as primary sponsor-led academies, primary convertor academies and primary free schools.

4 In England, includes direct grant nurseries.

5 In England, includes special converter academies. Excludes general hospital schools.

6 In Scotland, there was a change in the timing of the Pre-School Education Census in 2010/11, from January to September. September figures from 2010/11 may not be directly comparable with previously published January figures.

7 In Northern Ireland, excludes voluntary and private pre-school education centres.

20.2: Full-time and part-time pupils by gender[1,2], age and school type, 2014/15

United Kingdom   Thousand

| | Maintained schools[3] | | | | | | | | | Non-maintained[4] | | | |
| | Primary Schools[5,6,7] | | | | | | | | | | | | |
Age	Nursery Schools[8]	Nursery Classes	Other Classes[9]	Total	Middle Schools[10]	Secondary Schools[5,11]	Special schools[12]	Pupil Referral Units[13]	All maintained schools	Special schools	Other Schools[14]	All non-maintained schools	All schools
Age at 31 August 2014[15]													
All													
2-4[16]	146.0	260.8	559.9	1,044.0	0.3	9.7	6.8	-	1,206.8	0.1	64.4	65.2	1,27
5[17]	3.9	-	606.4	741.8	0.2	5.7	5.3	-	757.0	0.1	28.5	28.9	78
6	-	-	616.5	752.0	0.1	5.2	5.8	0.1	763.3	0.1	30.2	30.6	79
7	-	-	588.7	723.4	0.2	4.7	6.2	0.1	734.6	0.1	33.0	33.4	76
8	-	-	569.3	699.3	0.2	4.3	6.6	0.2	710.5	0.1	33.8	34.3	74
9	-	-	545.1	670.4	0.2	17.5	7.1	0.2	695.5	0.2	35.3	35.9	73
10	-	-	532.4	654.3	0.2	19.9	7.5	0.3	682.1	0.2	37.4	38.1	72
11	-	-	53.5	53.8	0.5	593.7	10.2	0.2	658.6	0.3	42.6	43.6	702
12	-	-	4.7	4.9	0.5	620.6	10.5	0.7	637.3	0.3	42.0	43.0	680
13	-	-	-	-	0.5	630.5	11.2	1.5	643.8	0.4	44.4	45.5	68
14	-	-	-	-	0.5	641.9	11.7	3.0	657.2	0.4	47.0	48.2	70
15	-	-	-	-	0.6	651.6	12.2	6.6	671.0	0.5	50.3	51.7	72
16	-	-	-	-	0.2	306.7	6.8	0.2	313.9	0.4	42.6	44.0	357
17	-	-	-	-	0.2	252.3	5.8	0.1	258.5	0.4	40.5	41.9	300
18	-	-	-	-	-	28.9	3.9	-	32.8	0.3	8.1	8.7	4
19 and over	-	-	-	-	-	1.0	0.1	-	1.1	-	3.4	3.5	4
Total[18]	**149.9**	**260.8**	**4,076.6**	**5,344.0**	**4.4**	**3,794.5**	**117.7**	**13.6**	**9,424.0**	**4.0**	**583.5**	**596.5**	**10,020**
of which													
England	41.5	251.7	3,525.5	4,510.3	.	3,184.7	101.2	13.6	7,851.3	4.0	582.9	586.8	8,438
Wales	1.1	..	..	273.4	4.4	182.4	4.4	..	465.7	..	..	9.0	474
Scotland	101.5	.	385.2	385.2	.	284.8	7.0	.	778.4	..	..	..	778
Northern Ireland	5.9	9.2	165.9	175.0	.	142.6	5.1	.	328.5	.	0.6	0.6	329
Males													
2-4[16]	25.2	132.3	286.3	532.5	0.2	4.9	4.7	-	567.4	-	32.0	32.4	599
5[17]	-	-	308.9	378.2	0.1	2.8	3.8	-	385.0	0.1	14.5	14.7	399
6	-	-	314.4	383.8	0.1	2.5	4.3	0.1	390.7	0.1	15.3	15.5	406
7	-	-	300.3	369.1	0.1	2.4	4.6	0.1	376.2	0.1	17.0	17.2	393
8	-	-	290.0	356.4	0.1	2.1	4.8	0.2	363.7	0.1	17.3	17.6	38
9	-	-	277.4	341.3	0.1	9.0	5.2	0.2	355.8	0.1	18.2	18.5	374
10	-	-	271.2	333.5	0.1	10.0	5.5	0.3	349.4	0.1	19.3	19.7	369
11	-	-	27.5	27.6	0.3	302.1	7.4	0.2	337.5	0.2	21.9	22.4	360
12	-	-	3.0	3.1	0.3	314.7	7.7	0.6	326.3	0.2	21.5	22.1	348
13	-	-	-	-	0.3	319.6	8.1	1.1	329.1	0.3	22.8	23.4	352
14	-	-	-	-	0.3	325.7	8.5	2.1	336.5	0.3	24.1	24.8	361
15	-	.	-	-	0.3	330.1	8.7	4.4	343.4	0.4	25.8	26.6	370
16	-	-	-	-	0.1	147.8	4.4	0.1	152.4	0.3	22.0	22.8	175
17	-	-	-	-	-	117.5	3.9	0.1	121.4	0.3	20.5	21.3	142
18	-	-	-	-	-	15.6	2.5	-	18.0	0.2	4.4	4.8	22
19 and over	-	-	-	-	-	0.5	-	-	0.5	-	2.0	2.0	2
Total[18]	**25.2**	**132.3**	**2,079.0**	**2,725.5**	**2.1**	**1,907.4**	**83.9**	**9.6**	**4,753.7**	**2.8**	**298.4**	**305.9**	**5,059**
of which													
England	21.7	127.6	1,797.7	2,299.8	.	1,601.6	72.3	9.6	4,005.0	2.8	298.1	300.9	4,305
Wales	0.6	..	..	139.7	2.1	91.8	3.2	..	237.4	..	..	4.6	242
Scotland	..	.	196.7	196.7	.	143.2	4.9	.	344.8	..	..	..	344
Northern Ireland	3.0	4.6	84.6	89.2	.	70.7	3.5	.	166.5	.	0.3	0.3	166
Females													
2-4[16]	23.2	128.5	273.6	511.5	0.2	4.8	2.1	-	541.7	-	32.3	32.7	574
5[17]	-	-	297.5	363.6	0.1	2.9	1.5	-	368.1	-	14.1	14.2	382
6	-	-	302.1	368.2	0.1	2.7	1.6	-	372.5	-	14.9	15.1	387
7	-	-	288.4	354.3	0.1	2.3	1.7	-	358.4	-	16.0	16.3	374
8	-	-	279.2	342.8	0.1	2.2	1.8	-	346.9	-	16.5	16.8	363
9	-	-	267.7	329.1	0.1	8.5	1.9	-	339.7	-	17.1	17.3	357
10	-	-	261.2	320.7	0.1	9.9	2.0	-	332.8	-	18.1	18.4	35
11	-	-	26.1	26.2	0.2	291.6	2.9	-	321.0	0.1	20.8	21.1	342
12	-	-	1.8	1.9	0.3	305.9	2.9	0.1	311.0	0.1	20.6	21.0	331
13	-	-	-	-	0.3	310.9	3.1	0.4	314.7	0.1	21.6	22.1	336
14	-	-	-	-	0.3	316.3	3.3	0.9	320.7	0.1	22.9	23.4	344
15	-	-	-	-	0.3	321.5	3.5	2.2	327.5	0.1	24.5	25.1	352
16	-	-	-	-	0.1	159.0	2.3	0.1	161.6	0.1	20.6	21.1	182
17	-	-	-	-	0.1	134.9	2.0	0.1	137.0	0.1	20.0	20.6	157
18	-	-	-	-	-	13.3	1.5	-	14.8	0.1	3.7	3.9	18
19 and over	-	-	-	-	-	0.5	-	-	0.6	-	1.4	1.4	2

.2: Full-time and part-time pupils by gender[1,2], age and school type, 2014/15

ted Kingdom

Thousands

| | Maintained schools[3] | | | | | | | | | Non-maintained[4] | | | |
| | Nursery Schools[8] | Primary Schools[5,6,7] | | | Middle Schools[10] | Secondary Schools[5,11] | Special schools[12] | Pupil Referral Units[13] | All maintained schools | Special schools | Other Schools[14] | All non-maintained schools | All schools |
		Nursery Classes	Other Classes[9]	Total									
e at 31 August 2014[15]													
Total[18]	23.2	128.5	1,997.5	2,618.5	2.3	1,887.1	33.9	4.0	4,568.9	1.1	285.1	290.6	4,859.4
of which													
England	19.8	124.0	1,727.8	2,210.5	.	1,583.1	28.9	4.0	3,846.3	1.1	284.8	285.9	4,132.2
Wales	0.5	..	..	133.7	2.3	90.6	1.3	..	228.3	..	..	4.4	232.7
Scotland	..	.	188.5	188.5	.	141.6	2.1	.	332.2	..	..	..	332.2
Northern Ireland	2.9	4.5	81.3	85.8	.	71.8	1.5	.	162.1	.	0.3	0.3	162.4

Sources: Department for Education; Welsh Government; Scottish Government; Northern Ireland Department of Education

In Scotland gender split is not collected by age but has been calculated according to figures collected in September each year. There are a small number of pupils for whom it has not been ssible to assign an age; these pupils are included in the Scotland total but excluded from the age breakdowns.

In Northern Ireland a gender split is not available by age but is available by year group and so this is used as a proxy. For example pupils in Year 1 are counted as age 4, pupils in Year 2 are unted as age 5 etc.

Maintained school figures includes all state-funded schools (Grant-aided schools in Northern Ireland).

In Scotland figures for the Non-maintained sector have not been provided, the collection was discontinued in 2010.

In England includes middle schools as deemed.

In England includes primary converter academies, primary sponsor led academies and primary free schools.

A Primary school breakdown by class type is not available in Wales.

For centres providing early learning and childcare in Scotland (this includes nursery classes within schools); children are counted once for each centre they are registered with. Only the 'All' ures are provided for early learning and childcare registrations in Scotland, as these cannot be split by gender.

Includes reception pupils in primary classes and, in Northern Ireland, pupils in preparatory departments of grammar schools.

In Wales, the Middle School for pupils of both primary and secondary school age was introduced in 2012/13.

Includes City Technology Colleges (CTCs) and Academies in England. Also includes secondary free schools, university technical colleges and studio schools.

Includes general hospital schools. Also includes special converter academies, special sponsored academies and special free schools. Hospital schools not included in Northern Ireland ures.

Only England and Wales have pupil referral units. Data for England includes alternative provision academies and free schools, and sole and dual main registrations. Data are not available for ales.

Includes pupils less than 2 years of age in England.

1 July for Northern Ireland, 28 February for maintained primary and secondary school pupils in Scotland and age at census date in September for pupils in early learning and childcare ovision in Scotland.

Includes the so-called rising five's (i.e. those pupils who became 5 during the autumn term). Also includes under twos for England and Scotland in 2014/15.

In Scotland, includes some 4-year-olds.

Some figures do not equal the sum of the component parts due to rounding.

20.3: Pupil: teacher ratios and pupil: adult ratios within schools by type of school - time series

United Kingdom

Numbers

	Pupil: teacher ratio within schools[1]					Pupil: adult ratio within schools[2]				
	2000/01	2010/11	2011/12	2012/13	2013/14	2000/01	2010/11	2011/12	2012/13	2013/14
United Kingdom										
Public sector mainstream										
Nursery schools[3]	23.1	17.2	17.7	17.5	18.0	..	..	..	..	..
Primary schools[4,5]	22.3	20.4	20.5	20.5	20.5	..	..	..	..	..
Middle[6]	.	.	.	16.2	15.8	.	.	..	..	..
Secondary schools[7]	16.5	15.3	15.3	15.2	15.4	..	..	..	..	..
Non-maintained mainstream schools	9.7	10.6	8.0	8.0	8.1	..	..	..	..	..
Special schools										
Maintained[8]	6.4	6.1	6.0	5.9	5.7	..	..	..	..	..
Non-maintained	..	..	..	..	..	..	..	..	..	..
All schools[9]	17.9	16.3	16.2	16.2	16.3	..	..	..	..	..
England[10]										
Public sector mainstream										
Nursery schools	17.7	16.1	16.7	16.5	17.1	6.8	..	4.9	4.9	4.8
State-funded primary schools[5]	22.9	20.9	21.0	20.9	21.0	15.7	..	11.9	11.5	11.3
State-funded secondary schools[7]	17.1	15.6	15.6	15.5	15.7	14.0	..	10.6	10.5	10.6
Non-maintained mainstream schools	9.7	10.6	8.0	8.0	8.1	..	..	..	..	..
Special schools										
State-funded[8]	6.7	6.4	6.3	6.2	5.9	..	..	..	..	..
Non-maintained	4.8	..	..	..	..	..	..	..	..	..
All schools	18.1	16.4	16.3	16.2	16.3	..	..	..	..	..
Wales										
Public sector mainstream										
Nursery schools	17.3	15.7	15.2	15.1	14.9	..	5.6	5.6	5.4	5.3
Primary schools	21.5	20.5	20.7	20.7	20.8	..	10.5	10.2	9.9	9.8
Middle[6]	.	.	.	16.2	15.8	.	.	.	10.6	10.2
Secondary schools	16.6	16.6	16.7	16.3	16.1	..	12.0	11.9	11.5	11.2
Non-maintained mainstream schools	9.6	8.0	8.1	7.9	7.9	..	..	..	..	..
Special schools (maintained)	6.8	6.4	6.6	6.7	6.5	..	..	..	..	..
All schools	18.4	17.8	17.9	17.8	17.7	..	..	..	..	..
Scotland										
Public sector mainstream										
Nursery schools[3]	28.5	..	..	..	..	..	..	..	..	..
Primary schools[11]	19.0	15.8	16.0	16.3	16.5	..	11.4	11.7	11.8	11.9
Secondary schools	13.0	12.1	12.3	12.2	12.2	..	10.2	9.9	10.3	10.3
Non-maintained mainstream schools	10.1	..	..	..	..	..	..	..	..	..
Special schools										
Maintained	4.2	3.6	3.5	3.4	3.5	..	..	..	..	..
Non-maintained	3.3	..	..	..	..	..	..	..	..	..
All schools	15.4	13.5	13.7	13.8	13.9	..	..	..	..	..
Northern Ireland[12]										
Grant-aided sector mainstream										
Nursery schools	24.4	25.9	26.1	25.6	25.5	..	..	..	..	..
Primary schools[4]	20.1	21.1	21.4	21.1	21.1	..	..	..	..	..
Secondary schools	14.5	15.0	15.2	15.3	15.4	..	..	..	..	..
Non-maintained mainstream schools	9.3	6.6	6.7	6.8	6.8	..	..	..	..	..
Special schools (maintained)	5.9	6.3	6.3	6.0	5.9	..	..	..	..	..
All schools	16.6	17.3	17.5	17.5	17.5	..	..	..	..	..

Source: Department for Education; Welsh Government; Scottish Government; Northern Ireland Department of Education

1 The Pupil:teacher ratio (PTR) within schools is calculated by dividing the total full-time equivalent (FTE) number of pupils on roll in schools by the total FTE number of qualified teachers. It excludes centrally employed teachers regularly employed in schools.

2 The Pupil: adult ratio (PAR) within schools is calculated by dividing the total FTE number of pupils on roll in schools by the total FTE number of all teachers and support staff employed in schools, excluding administrative and clerical staff.

3 Excludes pre-school education figures for Scotland as FTE pupil numbers are not available.

4 Includes figures for preparatory departments attached to grammar schools in Northern Ireland.

5 Figures for England include primary converter academies, primary sponsor-led academies and primary free schools.

6 In Wales, the Middle School for pupils of both primary and secondary school age was introduced in 2012/13.

7 Figures for England include secondary converter academies, secondary sponsor-led academies and secondary free schools.

8 Figures for England include special converter academies. Excludes general hospital schools.

9 The UK PTR excludes pupil referral units and non-maintained special schools.

10 Figures for England from 2010 are derived from the School Workforce Census and are not comparable with figures for earlier years.

11 In Scotland, 2010, 2011 and 2012 pre-school and primary school teacher FTEs and PTRs were revised to remove double counting across these two sectors.

12 Figures for Northern Ireland exclude temporary teachers i.e. teachers filling vacant posts, secondments or career breaks.

20.4 Pupils with statements of Special Educational Needs (SEN) or Education, Health and Care (EHC) plans (1)(2)

As at January each year: 2007-2014
England

	2007	2008	2009	2010	2011	2012	2013	2014
ALL SCHOOLS								
Pupils with statements or EHC plans	232,760	227,315	225,400	223,945	224,210	226,125	229,390	232,190
Pupils on roll	8,167,715	8,121,955	8,092,280	8,098,360	8,123,865	8,178,200	8,249,810	8,331,385
Incidence (%) (3)	2.8	2.8	2.8	2.8	2.8	2.8	2.8	2.8
STATE-FUNDED SCHOOLS								
Maintained nursery								
Pupils with statements or EHC plans	310	265	285	265	250	305	245	265
Pupils on roll	37,640	37,440	37,285	37,575	38,830	39,395	38,820	39,915
Incidence (%) (3)	0.8	0.7	0.8	0.7	0.6	0.8	0.6	0.7
Placement (%) (4)	0	0	0	0.1	0.1	0.1	0.1	0.1
State-funded primary (5)(6)								
Pupils with statements or EHC plans	61,800	59,695	58,505	57,850	57,855	58,535	59,710	60,830
Pupils on roll	4,110,750	4,090,400	4,077,350	4,096,580	4,137,755	4,217,000	4,309,580	4,416,710
Incidence (%) (3)	1.5	1.5	1.4	1.4	1.4	1.4	1.4	1.4
Placement (%) (4)	26.6	26.3	26.0	25.8	25.8	25.9	26.0	26.2
State-funded secondary (5)(7)								
Pupils with statements or EHC plans	71,190	67,875	65,890	64,605	63,720	62,630	61,615	59,700
Pupils on roll	3,325,625	3,294,575	3,278,130	3,278,485	3,262,635	3,234,875	3,210,120	3,181,360
Incidence (%) (3)	2.1	2.1	2.0	2.0	2.0	1.9	1.9	1.9
Placement (%) (4)	30.6	29.9	29.2	28.8	28.4	27.7	26.9	25.7
Maintained special (8)								
Pupils with statements or EHC plans	83,645	83,600	84,295	85,445	86,660	88,230	90,845	94,120
Pupils on roll	87,010	87,135	87,615	88,690	89,860	91,590	94,350	97,395
Incidence (%) (3)	96.1	95.9	96.2	96.3	96.4	96.3	96.3	96.6
Placement (%) (4)	35.9	36.8	37.4	38.2	38.7	39.0	39.6	40.5
Pupil Referral Units (9)								
Pupils with statements or EHC plans	3,425	3,260	3,230	1,910	1,695	1,610	1,630	1,545
Pupils on roll	24,165	25,290	24,760	15,550	14,050	13,495	12,950	12,895
Incidence (%) (3)	14.2	12.9	13.0	12.3	12.1	11.9	12.6	12.0
Placement (%) (4)	1.5	1.4	1.4	0.9	0.8	0.7	0.7	0.7
OTHER SCHOOLS								
Independent (10)								
Pupils with statements or EHC plans	7,760	8,055	8,690	9,470	9,750	10,630	11,265	11,790
Pupils on roll	577,785	582,425	582,490	576,940	576,325	577,515	579,740	579,035
Incidence (%) (3)	1.3	1.4	1.5	1.6	1.7	1.8	1.9	2.0
Placement (%) (4)	3.3	3.5	3.9	4.2	4.3	4.7	4.9	5.1
Non-maintained special								
Pupils with statements or EHC plans	4,630	4,565	4,500	4,400	4,280	4,185	4,085	3,945
Pupils on roll	4,740	4,695	4,655	4,540	4,415	4,325	4,245	4,080
Incidence (%) (3)	97.7	97.3	96.7	97.0	97.0	96.7	96.1	96.7
Placement (%) (4)	2.0	2.0	2.0	2.0	1.9	1.9	1.8	1.7

Source: School Census and School Level Annual School Census

(1) Includes pupils who are sole or dual main registrations.
(2) Education, Health and Care (EHC) plans were introduced from September 2014 as part of a range of SEND reforms.
(3) Incidence of pupils - the number of pupils with statements or EHC plans expressed as a proportion of the number of pupils on roll.
(4) Placement of pupils - the number of pupils with statements or EHC plans expressed as a proportion of the number of pupils with statements in all schools.
(5) Includes middle schools as deemed.
(6) Includes all primary academies, including free schools.
(7) Includes city technology colleges, university technology colleges, studio schools and all secondary academies, including free schools. Includes all-through schools
(8) Includes general hospital schools and special academies, including free schools.
(9) Includes pupils registered with other providers, in alternative provision academies, including free schools and in further education colleges.
Prior to 2010 includes dual subsidiary registered pupils.
(10) Includes direct grant nursery schools.

Totals may not appear to equal the sum of the component parts because numbers have been rounded to the nearest 5.

20.5: GCSE, A level, SCE/NQ[1] and vocational qualifications obtained by pupils and students - time series

United Kingdom   Percentages and thousands

	2000/01	2010/11	2011/12	2012/13
All				
Pupils in their last year of compulsory education[2]				
England, Wales and Northern Ireland [3]				
Percentage achieving GCSE or equivalent				
5 or more grades A*-C[4]	51.0	78.7	81.2	81.5
5 or more grades A*-C incl English and Maths	..	58.5	59.0	58.9
Any Passes	..	99.1	99.4	99.6
Pupils/students in education[5,6]				
England, Wales and Northern Ireland[3]				
Percentage achieving A Levels and equivalent[7]				
2 or more passes	37.4	52.8	54.7	54.8
Population aged 17 (thousands)[8]	717.9	707.4	700.4	709.0
School leavers				
Scotland [9]				
Percentage of school leavers attaining				
1 or more qualifications at SCQF level 4 or better	..	..	95.8	96.3
1 or more qualifications at SCQF level 5 or better	..	..	81.6	82.7
1 or more qualifications at SCQF level 6 or better	..	..	55.8	55.8
Males				
Pupils in their last year of compulsory education[2]				
England, Wales and Northern Ireland [3]				
Percentage achieving GCSE or equivalent				
5 or more grades A*-C[4]	45.7	75.0	77.6	77.7
5 or more grades A*-C incl English and Maths	..	54.8	54.3	53.7
Any Passes	..	98.9	99.1	99.3
Pupils/students in education[5,6]				
England, Wales and Northern Ireland[3]				
Percentage achieving A levels and equivalent[7]				
2 or more passes	33.4	48.0	49.7	50.1
Population aged 17 (thousands)[8]	366.6	364.0	359.9	364.1
School leavers				
Scotland[9]				
Percentage of school leavers attaining				
1 or more qualifications at SCQF level 4 or better	..	..	95.1	95.8
1 or more qualifications at SCQF level 5 or better	..	..	79.8	81.0
1 or more qualifications at SCQF level 6 or better	..	..	50.6	50.6
Females				
Pupils in their last year of compulsory education[2]				
England, Wales and Northern Ireland[3]				
Percentage achieving GCSE or equivalent				
5 or more grades A*-C[4]	56.5	82.6	85.0	85.4
5 or more grades A*-C incl English and Maths	..	62.4	63.9	64.4
Any Passes	..	99.4	99.8	100.0
Pupils/students in education[5,6]				
England, Wales and Northern Ireland[3]				
Percentage achieving A levels and equivalent[7]				
2 or more passes	41.6	57.9	60.1	59.9
Population aged 17 (thousands)[8]	351.3	343.4	340.4	345.0
School leavers				
Scotland[9]				
Percentage of school leavers attaining				
1 or more qualifications at SCQF level 4 or better	..	..	96.5	96.8
1 or more qualifications at SCQF level 5 or better	..	..	83.4	84.5
1 or more qualifications at SCQF level 6 or better	..	..	61.1	61.1

Source: Department for Education; Welsh Government; Scottish Government; Northern Ireland Department of Education

20.5: GCSE, A level, SCE/NQ[1] and vocational qualifications obtained by pupils and students - time series

1   National Qualifications (NQ) include Standard Grades, Intermediate 1 & 2 and Higher Grades.

2   Pupils aged 15 at the start of the academic year in Wales; pupils in Year S4 in Scotland. From 2004/05, pupils at the end of Key Stage 4 in England.

3   Also includes Scotland for 2009/10 and earlier.

4   Standard Grades 1-3/Intermediate 2 A-C/Intermediate 1 A in England for 2009/10 and earlier.

5   The number of pupils in schools and students in further education colleges in England, Wales and Northern Ireland expressed as a percentage of the of the 17-year-old population. Pupils and students are generally aged 16-18 at the start of the academic year in England, and aged 17 at the start of the academic year in Wales. Figures from 2002/03 for Wales and Northern Ireland relate to schools only.

6   Figures, other than for Scotland, include Vocational Certificates of Education (VCE) and, previously, Advanced level GNVQ, which is equivalent to 2 A levels or AS equivalents. From 2006/07, figures included for England cover achievements in all Level 3 qualifications approved under Section 96 of the Learning and Skills Act (2000), therefore UK aggregates are not comparable with previous years.

7   2 AS levels or 2 Highers/1 Advanced Higher or 1 each in Scotland, count as 1 A level pass for 2009/10 and earlier.

8   For 2013/14, based on mid-2013 based population projections. These take into account the 2011 Census. The figures for UK excluding Scotland are derived by the summation of England, Wales and Northern Ireland.

9   Qualifications in Scotland are based on the Scottish Credit and Qualifications Framework (SCQF). There are 12 levels on the framework, SCQF levels 1 to 7 are covered by school education. The new National qualifications, along with Standard Grades and Intermediates make up SCQF levels 3 to 5. Since 2013/14, under Curriculum for Excellence, Standard Grades are being phased out and replaced with National 3, 4 and 5 qualifications, and Intermediates will cease to exist from 2015/16. For most young people in Scotland S4 is the last compulsory year of school, but the majority will choose to stay on and complete S5 and S6. Highers (SCQF level 6) are generally taken in S5/S6; Highers, sometimes along with Advanced Highers (SCQF level 7, usually taken in S6) are the qualifications required for entry to Higher Education. School leaver data looks at a pupil's attainment throughout their school education. The leaver cohort is made up of all pupils who leave during or at the end of that year, so it contains pupils who leave at various stages of their schooling. Although Standard Grades were not available in 2013/14, the 2013/14 school leaver data will include Standard Grade attainment of leavers who sat these qualifications in earlier years of their schooling.

20.6 HE qualifications obtained by sex, subject area** and level of qualification obtained 2010/11 to 2013/14

	2010/11 All levels	2011/12 All levels	2012/13 All levels	2013/14 Postgraduate research	Postgraduate taught	Total postgraduate	First degree	Foundation degree	Other undergraduate	Total undergraduate	All levels
Female											
Medicine & dentistry	10145	10650	10755	1285	3630	4915	5500	0	215	5715	10630
Subjects allied to medicine	67025	68470	70440	1045	13025	14070	33200	1525	18390	53115	67190
Biological sciences	33210	34450	36685	2050	7615	9660	25555	565	2395	28515	38180
Veterinary science	820	875	800	40	110	145	695	0	35	730	880
Agriculture & related subjects	3860	3635	3920	125	665	790	1905	595	510	3005	3800
Physical sciences	10840	11110	11395	1155	2285	3435	7175	245	650	8070	11505
Mathematical sciences	4445	4720	5015	195	865	1060	3630	0	315	3945	5005
Computer science	5860	5750	5455	215	1675	1890	2710	95	395	3195	5085
Engineering & technology	8320	8595	8755	780	3535	4310	3875	160	355	4395	8705
Architecture, building & planning	7270	7340	7125	140	2835	2975	3125	80	540	3745	6720
Total - Science subject areas	151800	155590	160340	7025	36230	43260	87370	3265	23800	114440	157695
Percentage - Science subject areas	35%	35%	36%	61%	27%	29%	37%	28%	50%	39%	35%
Social studies	44980	46255	46720	1140	13495	14635	25970	1545	4255	31770	46400
Law	19080	19585	19590	200	6370	6570	11180	70	1200	12455	19025
Business & administrative studies	64445	69655	69835	450	30115	30565	32060	1255	4330	37645	68210
Mass communications & documentation	11125	11815	11645	100	4340	4435	7085	145	425	7655	12090
Languages	25035	25345	25555	855	4710	5565	17225	10	2630	19860	25425
Historical & philosophical studies	14110	15000	14780	695	3115	3805	9835	215	945	11000	14805
Creative arts & design	35905	37680	38165	345	7260	7605	27705	1480	2310	31490	39090
Education	60425	61430	58815	745	30445	31195	16305	3495	6660	26460	57650
Combined	3870	4100	4025	0	70	70	2770	20	1010	3800	3875
Total - All subject areas	430780	446450	449470	11550	136150	147700	237505	11500	47565	296570	444270
Male											
Medicine & dentistry	7190	7555	7670	1010	2195	3205	4285	0	125	4410	7610
Subjects allied to medicine	16580	17280	17640	690	3940	4630	8245	590	3610	12440	17070
Biological sciences	19795	20970	23460	1355	3440	4795	17020	700	2015	19735	24530
Veterinary science	250	255	260	25	45	70	200	0	5	205	275
Agriculture & related subjects	2370	2255	2380	100	480	585	1045	340	295	1680	2260
Physical sciences	15055	15100	15770	1965	2750	4715	10120	265	1165	11550	16265
Mathematical sciences	6415	6765	7430	390	1320	1705	4975	0	495	5470	7175
Computer science	25265	24765	22880	695	4920	5610	13375	565	2345	16280	21895
Engineering & technology	41245	42085	41585	2365	11310	13675	21990	1500	4310	27800	41475
Architecture, building & planning	15190	14405	13600	215	3855	4070	6310	215	1415	7945	12015
Total - Science subject areas	149360	151440	152675	8810	34250	43060	87565	4175	15775	107515	150575
Percentage - Science subject areas	45%	44%	45%	67%	35%	39%	48%	56%	50%	48%	45%
Social studies	26320	27485	27850	1105	8335	9435	16745	420	1690	18855	28290
Law	13295	13480	13100	245	4905	5150	6700	45	955	7705	12850
Business & administrative studies	66825	70370	68650	680	27990	28665	31940	1405	4705	38055	66720
Mass communications & documentation	7855	8090	7870	75	1785	1860	5265	230	475	5970	7825
Languages	11390	11495	11400	650	1885	2535	6930	10	1755	8695	11235
Historical & philosophical studies	12720	13170	13440	885	2580	3465	8805	135	800	9745	13210
Creative arts & design	22300	23520	23000	370	3805	4175	15935	750	1745	18430	22605
Education	19735	18915	17965	315	11465	11780	2560	245	3000	5810	17590
Combined	2565	2705	2410	5	20	25	1640	15	615	2270	2295
Total - All subject areas	332370	340670	338355	13130	97020	110150	184095	7430	31515	223045	333195
All sexes											
Medicine & dentistry	17335	18200	18425	2295	5825	8120	9780	0	340	10125	18245
Subjects allied to medicine	83605	85750	88085	1740	16965	18705	41450	2115	22000	65560	84265
Biological sciences	53000	55420	60150	3405	11050	14455	42580	1265	4410	48255	62715
Veterinary science	1075	1135	1060	60	155	215	900	0	40	940	1155
Agriculture & related subjects	6235	5885	6300	225	1150	1375	2950	935	805	4685	6060
Physical sciences	25895	26210	27170	3120	5030	8155	17300	510	1815	19620	27775
Mathematical sciences	10860	11485	12445	585	2185	2765	8605	0	810	9415	12180
Computer science	31125	30520	28340	910	6595	7500	16080	660	2740	19480	26980
Engineering & technology	49565	50680	50345	3140	14845	17990	25870	1660	4665	32195	50185
Architecture, building & planning	22460	21745	20730	355	6690	7045	9435	295	1955	11690	18735
Total - Science subject areas	301160	307025	313045	15840	70490	86330	174950	7440	39575	221970	308295
Percentage - Science subject areas	39%	39%	40%	64%	30%	33%	41%	39%	50%	43%	40%
Social studies	71300	73740	74585	2245	21845	24085	42720	1960	5945	50625	74715
Law	32380	33065	32695	445	11280	11720	17885	115	2155	20160	31880
Business & administrative studies	131270	140020	138490	1130	58110	59240	64000	2665	9035	75700	134940
Mass communications & documentation	18980	19905	19515	175	6125	6295	12350	375	900	13625	19920
Languages	36430	36845	36955	1500	6600	8100	24160	15	4385	28560	36660
Historical & philosophical studies	26830	28170	28220	1580	5695	7275	18645	355	1750	20745	28025
Creative arts & design	58205	61200	61175	710	11070	11780	43645	2230	4050	49925	61705
Education	80160	80340	76785	1060	41920	42985	18865	3740	9665	32270	75250
Combined	6435	6810	6435	5	90	95	4415	40	1620	6070	6165
Total - All subject areas*	763150	787120	787900	24690	233220	257905	421635	18930	79085	519650	777555

In this table 0,1, 2 are rounded to 0. All other numbers are rounded up or down

Source: Higher Education Statistics Agency Limited

Percentages are calculated on un-rounded data. Percentages are rounded to the nearest whole number. Percentages calculated on populations which contain fewer than 22.5 individuals are suppressed and represented as "..".

* Students with a sex of 'other' are included in total figures but not in separate breakdowns.

** Analyses of subject information show Full-person equivalent (FPE). These are derived by splitting student instances between the different subjects that make up their course aim.

20.7 HE qualifications obtained by sex, level of qualification obtained, and mode of study, 2010/11 to 2013/14

	2010/11 All modes	2011/12 All modes	2012/13 All modes	2013/14 Full-time	2013/14 Part-time	2013/14 All modes
All UK HE providers						
Female						
Postgraduate research	10440	11190	12035	9305	2240	11550
Postgraduate taught	122965	132015	135990	93125	43025	136150
..of which Postgraduate Certificate in Education	14895	14490	15165	15340	755	16100
First degree	209240	221805	227130	214545	22960	237505
Foundation degree	16370	16390	15030	6070	5430	11500
Other undergraduate	71760	65050	59285	24635	22925	47565
..of which Professional Graduate Certificate in Education	4470	3925	3340	1905	855	2755
Total female	430780	446450	449470	347685	96585	444270
Male						
Postgraduate research	12615	12925	13865	11070	2060	13130
Postgraduate taught	106230	107965	100110	69230	27790	97020
..of which Postgraduate Certificate in Education	6320	5785	5885	5960	295	6255
First degree	160205	169085	176595	168845	15255	184095
Foundation degree	10945	10755	10205	4360	3070	7430
Other undergraduate	42380	39940	37580	18800	12715	31515
..of which Professional Graduate Certificate in Education	2185	1840	1570	880	405	1285
Total male	332370	340670	338355	272305	60890	333195
All sexes						
Postgraduate research	23055	24115	25900	20385	4305	24690
Postgraduate taught	229200	239975	236115	162380	70835	233220
..of which Postgraduate Certificate in Education	21215	20275	21055	21305	1055	22355
First degree	369445	390890	403770	383420	38215	421635
Foundation degree	27315	27145	25240	10435	8500	18930
Other undergraduate	114140	104990	96875	43440	35645	79085
..of which Professional Graduate Certificate in Education	6655	5760	4910	2785	1260	4040
Total all sexes*	763150	787120	787900	620060	157500	777555

Source: Higher Education Statistics Agency Limited

In this table 0,1, 2 are rounded to 0. All other numbers are rounded up or down to the nearest multiple of 5.

Percentages are calculated on un-rounded data. Percentages are rounded to the nearest whole number. Percentages calculated on populations which contain fewer than 22.5 individuals are suppressed and represented as "..".

* Students with a sex of 'other' are included in total figures but not in separate breakdowns.

◊ From 2013/14 European Union domiciled students includes Croatia which joined the European Union on 1 July 2013. In previous years Croatia has been included in non-European Union totals.

20.8 Students[1] in further[2] and higher[3] education - time series
United Kingdom

Thousands

Further education students	2008/09	2009/10	2010/11	2011/12	2012/13	2013/14
All						
England[4]	4,837.1	4,635.5	4,264.9	4,216.6	4,320.3	3,913.5
Wales[5]	218.1	187.3	212.7	211.3	197.5	188.8
Scotland	381.0	353.2	311.0	256.5	235.8	237.3
Northern Ireland	132.2	151.9	144.4	141.7	145.4	130.2
Males						
England[4]	2,141.9	2,089.3	1,941.2	1,940.9	1,985.9	1,793.2
Wales[5]	83.2	79.6	94.0	92.1	86.5	82.9
Scotland	172.0	160.6	144.8	121.0	113.1	115.6
Northern Ireland	64.7	75.0	72.2	71.1	73.9	66.7
Females						
England[4]	2,695.2	2,546.2	2,323.7	2,275.7	2,334.4	2,120.2
Wales[5]	117.8	107.7	118.7	119.3	111.1	105.9
Scotland	209.0	192.6	166.2	135.5	122.7	121.6
Northern Ireland	67.6	76.9	72.3	70.8	71.5	63.6

Higher education students	2008/09		2009/10		2010/11		2011/12		2012/13		2013/14	
	Full-time	Part-time	Full-time	Part-time	Full-time	Part-time	Full-time	Part-time	Full-time	Part-time	Full-time	Part-time
All												
Postgraduate	268.7	273.8	298.9	284.6	310.5	282.5	309.7	261.8	297.0	242.7	305.4	237.0
of which												
PhD & equivalent	58.6	23.1	61.4	23.9	65.5	24.5	69.5	25.5	71.3	25.3	74.4	25.9
Masters and Others	210.1	250.7	237.5	260.8	245.0	257.9	240.2	236.3	225.6	217.3	231.1	211.1
First Degree	1,154.0	214.6	1,215.9	222.7	1,258.0	224.7	1,319.8	241.3	1,319.6	229.8	1,351.8	203.6
Other Undergraduate	174.1	471.3	177.9	458.2	170.5	413.1	151.1	378.5	123.6	301.4	92.5	286.9
Total	1,596.9	959.7	1,692.7	965.5	1,739.0	920.3	1,780.6	881.6	1,740.1	773.8	1,749.7	727.5
Males												
Postgraduate	136.5	113.8	151.5	118.5	155.5	115.9	148.8	108.2	139.3	100.0	142.3	96.9
of which												
PhD & equivalent	32.1	11.6	33.4	11.7	35.7	12.0	38.0	12.4	39.0	12.2	40.7	12.4
Masters and Others	104.4	102.2	118.1	106.8	119.8	103.9	110.8	95.8	100.3	87.8	101.6	84.5
First Degree	524.7	86.5	553.3	91.2	573.9	92.9	601.9	100.0	599.8	95.5	610.5	86.3
Other Undergraduate	68.7	175.3	73.3	168.2	70.7	154.0	63.8	142.3	54.4	114.5	42.2	114.3
Total	729.9	375.5	778.1	378.0	800.1	362.8	814.5	350.5	793.5	310.1	795.0	297.6
Females												
Postgraduate	132.2	160.0	147.3	166.1	155.0	166.5	160.9	153.6	157.6	142.7	163.1	140.1
of which												
PhD & equivalent	26.5	11.5	27.9	12.2	29.8	12.6	31.5	13.1	32.3	13.1	33.7	13.5
Masters and Others	105.7	148.5	119.4	153.9	125.2	154.0	129.4	140.5	125.3	129.6	129.4	126.7
First Degree	629.3	128.1	662.6	131.4	684.0	131.8	717.9	141.3	719.8	134.3	741.3	117.2
Other Undergraduate	105.5	296.1	104.6	289.9	99.8	259.2	87.3	236.2	69.2	186.9	50.3	172.6
Total	867.0	584.2	914.5	587.5	938.9	557.5	966.1	531.1	946.6	463.8	954.7	429.9

Source: Department for Business, Innovation and Skills; Welsh Government; Scottish Funding Council; Northern Ireland Department for Employment and Learning

1. Includes home and overseas students.

2. Figures for Further Education Colleges (FECs) in Wales, Scotland and Northern Ireland are based on whole year enrolments. Figures for FECs in England are based on headcounts. Figures for FECs include apprenticeships. There are further education students in both Higher Education Institutions (HEIs) and FECs, mainly in FECs.

3. Figures for HEIs are based on the HESA 'standard registration' count (enrolments). They include students at The Open University. There are higher education students in both HEIs and FECs, mainly in HEIs.

4. These are figures for FECs in England. They are based on learner participation data from the Individualised Learner Record. They cannot be split by mode of attendance. There are no figures for HEIs in England.

5. From 2010/11, these figures include students undertaking work based learning in FECs in Wales .

6. The data field "gender" has changed to be consistent with the Managing Information across Partners (MIAP) common data definitions coding frame. Students of "indeterminate gender" are included in totals over all students. Indeterminate means unable to be classified as either male or female and is not related in any way to trans-gender.

7. Full-time includes sandwich. Part-time comprises both day and evening, including block release and open/distance learning. For Scotland, full-time covers programmes of at least 640 hours of planned notional hours. Part-time includes short full-time, block/day release, evenings/weekends, assessment of work based learning. For Northern Ireland from 2013/14 sandwich courses or short courses of less than 4 weeks full-time study are considered to be part-time rather than full-time.

9 Students in higher education[1] by level, mode of study[2], gender[3] and subject group, 2013/14

United Kingdom[4,5,6,7]

Home and Overseas Students

Thousands

	Postgraduate level						Undergraduate level						Total higher education students	
	PhD & equivalent[8]		Masters and Others[9]		Total Postgraduate		First degree[10]		Other Undergraduate[11]		Total Undergraduate			
	Full-time	Part-time	Full-time	Part-time	Full-time	Part-time	Full-time	Part-time	Full-time	Part-time	Full-time	Part-time	Full-time	Part-time
Medicine & Dentistry	5.7	2.5	4.1	9.2	9.8	11.7	45.3	0.1	0.5	0.3	45.8	0.4	55.5	12.1
Subjects Allied to Medicine	4.1	2.3	12.6	40.1	16.7	42.5	135.1	20.2	11.7	53.9	146.8	74.1	163.5	116.6
Biological Sciences	10.7	2.3	10.8	9.3	21.5	11.6	142.5	23.5	4.6	9.5	147.1	33.0	168.5	44.6
Vet. Science, Agriculture & related	0.9	0.1	1.4	1.8	2.3	1.9	14.7	0.6	3.0	5.6	17.7	6.2	20.0	8.1
Physical Sciences	10.3	0.7	5.8	2.4	16.2	3.1	64.5	6.6	1.1	2.3	65.7	8.8	81.9	12.0
Mathematical and Computing Sciences	5.9	0.9	10.7	5.1	16.6	6.0	90.1	16.1	6.2	8.9	96.3	25.0	112.8	31.0
Engineering & Technology	11.9	1.4	16.5	9.4	28.5	10.8	94.2	12.4	8.4	22.1	102.6	34.5	131.1	45.3
Architecture, Building & Planning	1.3	0.5	7.1	5.2	8.4	5.7	26.4	5.0	2.4	6.4	28.8	11.4	37.3	17.1
Social Sciences (inc Law)	7.7	3.0	34.8	23.2	42.5	26.2	188.3	28.3	10.7	18.9	199.0	47.2	241.5	73.4
Business & Administrative Studies	4.0	2.4	64.1	38.0	68.1	40.4	186.6	21.9	15.8	48.3	202.4	70.3	270.5	110.7
Mass Communications & Documentation	0.6	0.3	6.6	2.5	7.2	2.8	37.5	1.0	1.6	1.0	39.1	2.0	46.3	4.9
Languages	3.9	1.3	6.9	3.5	10.8	4.8	77.9	11.1	2.3	11.2	80.2	22.3	91.0	27.2
Historical and Philosophical Studies	3.8	2.1	5.5	5.1	9.3	7.2	54.2	13.7	0.5	5.0	54.7	18.7	64.0	25.9
Creative Arts & Design	1.8	1.3	13.1	5.8	14.9	7.0	140.4	5.4	13.8	12.2	154.2	17.5	169.1	24.6
Education[12]	1.6	4.7	30.9	48.5	32.6	53.2	51.0	11.1	6.9	35.3	57.9	46.3	90.4	99.5
Other subjects[13]	-	-	-	2.0	-	2.0	2.9	26.6	3.0	24.5	5.9	51.1	5.9	53.1
Unknown[14]	-	-	-	0.1	-	0.1	0.3	-	-	21.5	0.3	21.5	0.4	21.5
All subjects	74.4	25.9	231.1	211.1	305.4	237.0	1,351.8	203.6	92.5	286.9	1,444.3	490.5	1,749.7	727.5
of which overseas students	37.3	5.5	138.9	22.8	176.2	28.3	204.5	7.3	9.2	34.3	213.7	41.6	389.9	69.9
Males														
Medicine & Dentistry	2.3	1.3	1.4	4.1	3.7	5.4	20.2	-	0.1	0.1	20.3	0.2	24.0	5.6
Subjects Allied to Medicine	1.7	0.8	3.0	9.7	4.7	10.5	27.3	4.2	2.4	8.1	29.7	12.3	34.4	22.7
Biological Sciences	4.1	0.8	3.7	3.0	7.8	3.8	58.2	7.2	2.7	4.6	60.9	11.8	68.7	15.6
Vet. Science, Agriculture & related	0.4	0.1	0.6	0.7	1.0	0.8	4.2	0.2	1.2	2.5	5.4	2.8	6.4	3.5
Physical Sciences	6.7	0.4	3.1	1.4	9.8	1.8	39.2	3.8	0.7	1.4	39.9	5.2	49.7	6.9
Mathematical and Computing Sciences	4.3	0.7	7.6	3.9	11.9	4.6	69.1	12.5	5.4	7.3	74.5	19.7	86.4	24.4
Engineering & Technology	9.0	1.1	12.5	7.6	21.5	8.7	79.9	11.3	7.5	20.5	87.4	31.8	108.9	40.5
Architecture, Building & Planning	0.8	0.3	4.0	3.3	4.8	3.6	17.0	4.0	1.8	5.5	18.7	9.5	23.5	13.1
Social Sciences (inc Law)	3.8	1.4	14.1	8.1	17.9	9.4	73.9	9.1	2.7	4.7	76.6	13.8	94.5	23.2
Business & Administrative Studies	2.3	1.4	31.3	20.0	33.6	21.4	95.8	10.9	7.1	19.9	102.8	30.8	136.5	52.2
Mass Communications & Documentation	0.3	0.2	2.0	0.9	2.2	1.0	16.1	0.5	0.9	0.6	17.0	1.1	19.3	2.1
Languages	1.5	0.5	2.1	1.1	3.6	1.6	22.6	3.1	1.1	4.6	23.7	7.7	27.3	9.3
Historical and Philosophical Studies	2.1	1.1	2.6	2.5	4.8	3.7	25.8	5.7	0.2	1.9	26.0	7.6	30.8	11.3
Creative Arts & Design	0.9	0.6	4.5	2.1	5.4	2.7	52.0	2.1	5.2	5.0	57.1	7.1	62.5	9.7
Education[12]	0.5	1.7	9.0	15.4	9.5	17.1	7.8	1.1	1.6	9.5	9.4	10.6	19.0	27.7
Other subjects[13]	-	-	-	0.8	-	0.8	1.1	10.7	1.8	8.8	2.9	19.4	2.9	20.3
Unknown[14]	-	-	-	-	-	-	0.2	-	-	9.4	0.2	9.4	0.2	9.4
All subjects	40.7	12.4	101.6	84.5	142.3	96.9	610.5	86.3	42.2	114.3	652.7	200.7	795.0	297.6
of which overseas students	21.1	3.0	64.6	12.3	85.7	15.3	99.8	4.1	4.6	15.1	104.5	19.1	190.2	34.4
Females														
Medicine & Dentistry	3.4	1.2	2.6	5.1	6.0	6.3	25.1	0.1	0.4	0.2	25.5	0.2	31.5	6.5
Subjects Allied to Medicine	2.4	1.5	9.6	30.5	12.0	32.0	107.8	15.9	9.3	45.9	117.1	61.8	129.0	93.8
Biological Sciences	6.6	1.5	7.1	6.3	13.7	7.8	84.2	16.3	1.9	4.8	86.1	21.2	99.8	28.9
Vet. Science, Agriculture & related	0.5	0.1	0.8	1.1	1.3	1.2	10.5	0.4	1.8	3.1	12.3	3.4	13.6	4.6
Physical Sciences	3.7	0.3	2.7	1.1	6.4	1.4	25.3	2.8	0.5	0.9	25.8	3.6	32.1	5.0
Mathematical and Computing Sciences	1.6	0.2	3.1	1.2	4.6	1.4	20.9	3.6	0.8	1.6	21.8	5.2	26.4	6.6
Engineering & Technology	2.9	0.3	4.1	1.8	7.0	2.1	14.3	1.1	0.9	1.6	15.2	2.8	22.2	4.8
Architecture, Building & Planning	0.5	0.2	3.2	1.9	3.7	2.1	9.4	1.0	0.7	0.9	10.1	1.9	13.8	4.0
Social Sciences (inc Law)	3.9	1.7	20.7	15.1	24.6	16.7	114.4	19.2	8.0	14.3	122.5	33.4	147.1	50.2
Business & Administrative Studies	1.8	1.0	32.8	18.0	34.5	19.0	90.8	11.0	8.8	28.4	99.6	39.4	134.1	58.4
Mass Communications & Documentation	0.4	0.2	4.6	1.7	5.0	1.8	21.4	0.5	0.7	0.4	22.1	1.0	27.1	2.8
Languages	2.4	0.8	4.8	2.5	7.2	3.2	55.2	8.1	1.2	6.6	56.5	14.6	63.7	17.9

20.9 Students in higher education[1] by level, mode of study[2], gender[3] and subject group, 2013/14

United Kingdom[4,5,6,7]   Home and Overseas Students

Thousand

| | Postgraduate level | | | | | | Undergraduate level | | | | | | Total higher education students | |
| | PhD & equivalent[8] | | Masters and Others[9] | | Total Postgraduate | | First degree[10] | | Other Undergraduate[11] | | Total Undergraduate | | | |
	Full-time	Part-time	Full-time	Part-time	Full-time	Part-time	Full-time	Part-time	Full-time	Part-time	Full-time	Part-time	Full-time	Part-time
Historical and Philosophical Studies	1.7	1.0	2.9	2.6	4.5	3.5	28.4	8.0	0.2	3.1	28.6	11.1	**33.2**	14.
Creative Arts & Design	0.9	0.6	8.6	3.7	9.5	4.4	88.4	3.3	8.6	7.2	97.0	10.5	**106.6**	14.
Education[12]	1.1	2.9	21.9	33.1	23.1	36.1	43.2	10.0	5.3	25.7	48.4	35.8	**71.5**	71.
Other subjects[13]	-	-	-	1.2	-	1.2	1.8	16.0	1.2	15.7	3.0	31.7	**3.0**	32.
Unknown[14]	-	-	-	-	-	-	0.1	-	-	12.1	0.1	12.1	**0.1**	12.
All subjects	33.7	13.5	129.4	126.7	163.1	140.1	741.3	117.2	50.3	172.6	791.6	289.8	**954.7**	429.
of which overseas students	16.2	2.6	74.3	10.5	90.5	13.0	104.7	3.2	4.6	19.2	109.3	22.4	**199.7**	35.

Source: Department for Business, Innovation and Skills; Welsh Government; Scottish Funding Council; Northern Ireland Department for Employment and Learning

1   Figures for Higher Education Institutions (HEIs) are Higher Education Statistics Agency 'standard registration' counts. HEIs include Open University. Figures for Further Education Colleges are whole year enrolments.

2   Full-time mode of study includes sandwich. Part-time comprises both day and evening, including block release and open/distance learning. In Scotland, full-time covers programmes of at least 480 hours of planned notional hours. Part-time includes short full-time, block/day release, evenings/weekends, assessment of work based learning, distance/locally based learning, college based private study, other open learning and flexible learning. In Wales, full-time learners are those with at least 450 guided contact hours in the academic year. In Northern Ireland from 2013/1 sandwich courses or short courses of less than 4 weeks full-time study are considered to be part-time rather than full-time.

3   The data field "gender" has changed to be consistent with the Managing Information across Partners (MIAP) common data definitions coding frame. Students of "indeterminate gender" are included in totals over all students. Indeterminate means unable to be classified as either male or female and is not related in any way to trans-gender.

4   Figures for Further Education Colleges in England count all students on postgraduate level courses as Masters and Others; and, all students on undergraduate other than first degree courses as part-time.

5   Figures for Further Education Colleges in Wales are counts of unique learners. As a learner may pursue more than one course, only one subject per learner has been selected (based on th most recently started course of the learner where applicable). Students have been assigned a level on the basis of learning programme type. For the purpose of this table, HE learners are thos pursuing a (non-WBL) overarching HE learning programme. (It excludes learners pursuing HE level activities within an FE or WBL programme.)

6   Figures for Further Education Colleges in Scotland do not include students with under 25% attendance rate.
7   Figures for Further Education Colleges in Northern Ireland are regulated course enrolments rather than headcounts.
8   Defined as 'Doctorate' in Scotland.
9   For Scotland includes masters (research/taught) and postgraduate diploma/certificate.
10   For Scotland includes first degree honours/ordinary.
11   For Scotland includes 'SVQ or NVQ: Level 4 and Level 5,' 'Diploma (HNC/D level for diploma and degree holders),' and 'HNC/D or equivalent'.
12   Includes Initial Teacher Training (ITT) and In-Service Education and Training (INSET).
13   Includes Combined and general programmes and programmes not otherwise classified.
14   Includes data for Further Education Colleges that cannot be split by subject group.

.10 Qualified teachers by type of school and gender - time series

ited Kingdom

(i) Full-time teachers

Thousands

	2000/01	2011/12	2012/13	2013/14	2014/15 UK	of which: England[9]	Wales	Scotland[10,11]	Northern Ireland[12]
Public sector mainstream									
Nursery[1,2] and Primary[3]	211.2	198.6	205.2	209.6	214.8	175.9	10.7	21.2	6.9
Middle[4]	.	.	0.2	0.2	0.3	.	0.3	.	.
Secondary[5]	225.7	218.8	222.9	220.2	218.6	179.1	10.2	21.1	8.3
Non-maintained mainstream[6]	52.3	55.5	56.9	57.3	59.7	59.7	..	..	0.1
All Special[7]	16.5	14.8	15.4	18.8	19.4	16.4	0.6	1.7	0.7
All schools[8]	**505.7**	**487.7**	**500.6**	**506.1**	**512.8**	**431.1**	**21.8**	**44.0**	**15.9**
les									
Public sector mainstream									
Nursery[1,2] and Primary[3]	32.1	30.2	31.9	33.2	34.6	29.4	2.0	1.9	1.2
Middle[4]	.	.	0.1	0.1	0.1	.	0.1	.	.
Secondary[5]	102.9	89.8	90.8	89.3	88.2	73.1	3.9	8.3	2.9
Non-maintained mainstream[6]	21.3	22.3	22.8	23.0	23.9	23.9	..	..	..
All Special[7]	5.0	4.1	4.2	5.4	5.6	4.8	0.2	0.4	0.1
All schools[8]	**161.3**	**146.4**	**149.8**	**151.0**	**152.4**	**131.3**	**6.2**	**10.6**	**4.3**
males									
Public sector mainstream									
Nursery[1,2] and Primary[3]	179.1	166.8	171.7	175.1	178.4	146.4	8.7	17.5	5.7
Middle[4]	.	.	0.1	0.1	0.2	.	0.2	.	.
Secondary[5]	122.8	128.8	131.8	130.7	130.3	105.9	6.2	12.8	5.3
Non-maintained mainstream[6]	30.9	33.2	34.1	34.4	35.7	35.7	..	..	..
All Special[7]	11.6	10.7	11.2	13.4	13.8	11.6	0.4	1.3	0.5
All schools[8]	**344.4**	**339.5**	**349.0**	**353.7**	**358.4**	**299.7**	**15.5**	**31.6**	**11.6**

(ii) Full-time equivalent (FTE) of part-time teachers

Thousands

	2000/01	2011/12	2012/13	2013/14	2014/15 UK	of which: England[9]	Wales	Scotland[10]	Northern Ireland[12]
Public sector mainstream									
Nursery[1,2] and Primary[3]	21.9	39.5	39.7	41.4	39.5	33.4	1.6	3.7	0.8
Middle[4]	.	.	-	-	-	.	.	.	.
Secondary[5]	16.7	27.3	27.4	28.5	26.9	22.5	1.1	2.5	0.8
Non-maintained mainstream[6]	10.2	13.0	12.7	12.4	12.7	12.7	..	..	-
All Special[7]	1.6	2.6	2.5	3.3	3.1	2.7	0.1	0.3	0.1
All schools[8]	**50.4**	**82.3**	**82.4**	**85.7**	**82.2**	**71.3**	**2.7**	**6.5**	**1.7**

urces: Department for Education; Welsh Government; Scottish Government; Northern Ireland Department of Education

Figures for Scotland from 2015/06 include only centres providing pre-school education as a local authority centre or in partnership with the local authority. Figures are not directly omparable with previous years.

Figures for full-time teachers in pre-school education centres in Scotland from 2005/06 are based on the total full-time equivalent (FTE) of General Teaching Council (GTC) of Scotland gistered staff.

Figures for England include primary converter academies, primary sponsor-led academies and primary free schools from 2010/11.

In Wales, the Middle School for pupils of both primary and secondary school age was introduced in 2012/13.

Figures for England include secondary converter academies, secondary sponsor-led academies and secondary free schools from 2010/11.

Excludes Scotland from 2011/12 because the collection was discontinued in 2010.

Includes PRU figures for England.

Excludes Pupil Referral Units (PRUs).

Figures for England were derived from the School Workforce Census from 2009/10. Prior to 2009/10 figures were derived from the 618g Survey and the Database of Teacher Records.

0 Figures for pre-school education centres for Scotland cannot be split by gender.

1 Nursery figures for Scotland from 2010/11 are not directly comparable with previously published figures, due to a change in the timing of the Pre-school Education Census from January to eptember.

2 Figures for Northern Ireland exclude temporary teachers i.e. teachers filling vacant posts, secondments or career breaks.

this page is intentionally blank

Crime and Justice

Chapter 21

Crime and Justice

There are differences in the legal and judicial systems of England and Wales, Scotland and Northern Ireland which make it impossible to provide tables covering the UK as a whole in this section. These differences concern the classification of offences, the meaning of certain terms used in the statistics, the effects of the several Criminal Justice Acts and recording practices.

Recorded crime statistics
(Table 21.3)

Crimes recorded by the police provide a measure of the amount of crime committed. For a variety of reasons, many offences are either not reported to the police or not recorded by them. The changes in the number of offences recorded do not necessarily provide an accurate reflection of changes in the amount of crime committed.

The recorded crime statistics include all indictable and triable-either-way offences together with a few summary offences which are closely linked to these offences. The revised rules changed the emphasis of measurement more towards one crime per victim, and also increased the coverage of offences.

In order to further improve the consistency of recorded crime statistics and to take a more victim-oriented approach to crime recording, the National Crime Recording Standard (NCRS) was introduced across all forces in England, Wales and Northern Ireland from 1 April 2002. Some police forces implemented the principles of NCRS in advance of its introduction across all forces. The NCRS had the effect of increasing the number of offences recorded by the police and data before and after 2002/03 are not directly comparable.

For a variety of reasons many offences are either not reported to the police or not recorded by them. The changes in the number of offences recorded do not necessarily provide an accurate reflection of changes in the amount of crime committed.

Similarly, the Scottish Crime Recording Standard (SCRS) was introduced by the eight Scottish police forces with effect from 1 April 2004. This means that no corroborative evidence is required initially to record a crime-related incident as a crime if the victim perceived it as a crime. Again, the introduction of this new recording standard was expected to increase the numbers of minor crimes recorded by the police, such as minor crimes of vandalism and minor thefts and offences of petty assault and breach of the peace. However, it was expected that the SCRS would not have much impact on the figures for the more serious crimes such as serious assault, sexual assault, robbery or housebreaking.

The Sexual Offences Act 2003 introduced in May 2004 altered the definition and coverage of sexual offences. In particular, it redefined indecent exposure as a sexual offence, which is likely to account for much of the increase in sexual offences.

The Sexual Offences (Scotland) Act 2009 introduced in 1 December 2010 repealed a number of common law crimes including rape, clandestine injury to women and sodomy and replaced them with new statutory sexual offences. The Act created a number of new "protective" offences, which criminalise sexual activity with children and mentally disordered persons. Protective offences are placed into categories concerning young children (under 13) and older (13-15 years). The new legislation may result in some increases in Group 2 crimes. For example, the offences of voyeurism or indecent communication towards an adult would previously have been classified as breach of the peace. It is likely that the effect will be to change the distribution of these crimes among the sub classifications. For example, some crimes previously categorised as lewd and libidinous practices will now be classified as sexual assault. The standard breakdown provided in response to information requests on sexual offences has had to be revised to accommodate these changes.

Offences committed before 1 December 2010:

Rape & attempted rape includes:

- Rape
- Assault with intent to rape

Indecent assault includes:

- Indecent assault

Lewd and indecent behaviour includes:

- Public indecency

'Other' includes:

- Incest
- Unnatural crimes
- Prostitution
- Procuration and other sexual offences

Offences committed on or after 1 December 2010:

Rape & attempted rape includes:

- Rape
- Attempted rape

Sexual assault includes:

- Contact sexual assault (13-15 years old or adult 16+)

- other sexually coercive conduction (adult 16+)

- Sexual offences against children under 13

- Sexual activity with children aged 13-15

- Other sexual offences involving children aged 13-15

- Lewd and libidinous practices

Prostitution

- Offences relating to prostitution

'Other' includes:

- Incest
- Unnatural crimes
- Public indecency
- Sexual exposure
- Procuration and other sexual offences

Further information is available from Crime in England and Wales.

Court proceedings and police cautions
(Tables 21.4 to 21.8, 21.12 to 21.16, 21.19 to 21.20

The statistical basis of the tables of court proceedings is broadly similar in England and Wales, Scotland and Northern Ireland; the tables show the number of persons found guilty, recording a person under the heading of the principal offence of which they were found guilty, excluding additional findings of guilt at the same proceedings. A person found guilty at a number of separate court proceedings is included more than once.

The statistics on offenders cautioned in England and Wales cover only those who, on admission of guilt, were given a formal caution by, or on the instructions of, a senior police officer as an alternative to prosecution. Written warnings by the police for motor offences and persons paying fixed penalties for certain motoring offences are excluded. Formal cautions are not issued in Scotland. There are no statistics on cautioning available for Northern Ireland.

The Crime and Disorder Act 1998 created provisions in relation to reprimands and final warnings, new offences and orders which have been implemented nationally since 1 June 2000. They replace the system of cautioning for offenders aged under 18. Reprimands can be given to first-time offenders for minor offences. Any further offending results in either a final warning or a charge.

For persons proceeded against in Scotland, the statistics relate to the High Court of Justiciary, the sheriff courts and the district courts. The High Court deals with serious solemn (that is, jury) cases and has unlimited sentencing power. Sheriff courts are limited to imprisonment of 3 years for solemn cases, or 3 months (6 months when specified in legislation for second or subsequent offences and 12 months for certain statutory offences) for summary (that is, non-jury) cases. District courts deal only with summary cases and are limited to 60 days imprisonment and level 4 fines. Stipendiary magistrates sit in Glasgow District Court and have the summary sentencing powers of a sheriff.

In England and Wales, indictable offences are offences which are:

• triable only on indictment. These offences are the most serious breaches of the criminal law and must be tried at the Crown Court. 'Indictable-only' offences include murder, manslaughter, rape and robbery
• triable either way. These offences may be tried at the Crown Court or a magistrates' court

The Criminal Justice Act 1991 led to the following main changes in the sentences available to the courts in England and Wales:

• introduction of combination orders
• introduction of the 'unit fine scheme' at magistrates' courts
• abolishing the sentence of detention in a young offender institution for 14-year-old boys and changing the minimum and maximum sentence lengths for 15 to 17-year-olds to 10 and 12 months respectively, and
• abolishing partly suspended sentences of imprisonment and restricting the use of a fully suspended sentence

(The Criminal Justice Act 1993 abolished the 'unit fine scheme' in magistrates' courts, which had been introduced under the Criminal Justice Act 1991.

A charging standard for assault was introduced in England and Wales on 31 August 1994 with the aim of promoting consistency between the police and prosecution on the appropriate level of charge to be brought.

The Criminal Justice and Public Order Act 1994 created several new offences in England and Wales, mainly in the area of public order, but also including male rape (there is no statutory offence of male rape in Scotland, although such a crime may be charged as serious assault). The Act also:

• extended the provisions of section 53 of the Children and Young Persons Act 1993 for 10 to 13-year-olds
• increased the maximum sentence length for 15 to 17-year-olds to 2 years
• increased the upper limit from £2,000 to £5,000 for offences of criminal damage proceeded against as if triable only summarily
• introduced provisions for the reduction of sentences for early guilty pleas, and
• increased the maximum sentence length for certain firearm offences

Provisions within the Crime (Sentences) Act 1997 (as amended by the Powers of Criminal Courts Sentencing Act 2000) in England and Wales, and the Crime and Punishment (Scotland) Act 1997 in Scotland, included:

• an automatic life sentence for a second serious violent or sexual offence unless there are exceptional circumstances (this provision has not been enacted in Scotland)
• a minimum sentence of 7 years for an offender convicted for a third time of a class A drug trafficking offence unless the court considers this to be unjust in all the circumstances, and
• in England and Wales, the new section 38A of the Magistrates' Courts' Act 1980 extending the circumstances in which a magistrates' court may commit a person convicted of an offence triable-either-way to the Crown Court for sentence – it was implemented in conjunction with section 49 of the Criminal Procedure and Investigations Act 1996, which involves the magistrates' courts in asking defendants to indicate a plea before the mode of trial decision is taken and compels the court to sentence, or commit for sentence, any defendant who indicates a guilty plea.

Under the Criminal Justice and Court Service Act 2000 new terms were introduced for certain orders. Community rehabilitation order is the new name for a probation order. A community service order is now known as a community punishment order. Finally, the new term for a combination order is community punishment and rehabilitation order. In April 2000 the secure training order was replaced by the detention and training order. Section 53 of the Children and Young Persons Act 1993 was repealed on 25 August 2000 and its provisions were transferred to sections 90 to 92 of the Powers of Criminal Courts (Sentencing) Act 2000. Reparation and action plan orders were implemented nationally from 1 June 2000. The drug treatment and testing order was introduced in England, Scotland and Wales from October 2000. The referral order was introduced in England, Scotland and Wales from April 2000. Youth rehabilitation orders came into effect in November 2009 as part of the Criminal Justice and Immigration Act 2008. These changes are now reflected in Table 21.8.

Following the introduction of the Libra case management system during 2008, offenders at magistrates' courts can now be recorded as sex 'Not Stated'. In 2008 one per cent of offenders sentenced were recorded as sex 'Not Stated' as well as 'Male', 'Female', or 'Other'. Amendments to the data tables have been made to accommodate this new category.

The system of magistrates' courts and Crown courts in Northern Ireland operates in a similar way to that in England and Wales. A particularly significant statutory development, however, has been the Criminal Justice (NI) Order 1996 which introduced a new sentencing regime into Northern Ireland, largely replicating that which was introduced into England and Wales by the Criminal Justice Acts of 1991 and 1993. The order makes many changes to both community and custodial sentences, while introducing new orders such as the combination order, the custody probation order, and orders for release on licence of sexual offenders.

Abbreviations
(Tables 21.4a, 21.6a-c, 21.6d-f)

Every effort is made to ensure that the figures presented are accurate and complete. However, it is important to note that these data have been extracted from large administrative data systems generated by the police forces and cour

As a consequence, care should be taken to ensure data collection processes and their inevitable limitations are taken into account when those data are used.

Abbreviation	Description
Total Proc Against	Total Proceeded Against
Proc Disc	Proceedings Discontinued
Proc Disc	Discharge Section 6 Magistrates' Courts Act 1980
Charge Wdrn	Charge Withdrawn
Charge Dism	Charge Dismissed
Comm For Trial	Committed for Trial
Comm For Sent	Committed for Sentence
Total For Sent	Total for Sentence
Abslt Disch	Absolute Discharge
Condl Disch	Conditional Discharge
CRO	Community Rehabilitation Order
YRO	Youth Rehabilitation Order
SO	Supervision Order
CPO	Community Punishment Order
ACO	Attendance Centre Order
CP & RO	Community Punishment Order and Rehabilitation Order
Curf Order	Curfew Order
Rep Order	Reparation Order
APO	Action Plan Order
DTTO	Drug Treatment and Test Order
Ref Order	Referral Order
Comm Order	Community Order
YRO	Youth Rehabilitation Order
SS	Suspended Sentence
DTO	Detention and Training Order
YOI	Young Offender Institution
Unsus Sent Impri	Unsuspended sentence of imprisonment
Imm Cust	Immediate Custody
ODW	Otherwise dealt with

21.1a Police officers in England and Wales, by police force area, as at 31 March 2015

England and Wales

Police force	All officers (full-time equivalent)[1]			Officers available for duty[2] (full-time equivalent)		
	Male	Female	Total	Male	Female	Total
Avon & Somerset	1,962	745	2,707	1,919	678	2,598
Bedfordshire	740	333	1,073	733	306	1,040
Cambridgeshire	974	388	1,362	961	359	1,320
Cheshire	1,398	554	1,952	1,369	523	1,892
Cleveland[22]	1,006	320	1,326	908	269	1,177
Cumbria	738	405	1,143	729	372	1,101
Derbyshire	1,336	527	1,863	1,310	504	1,813
Devon & Cornwall	2,198	870	3,068	2,166	823	2,990
Dorset	938	334	1,272	919	311	1,230
Durham	841	328	1,169	823	309	1,131
Essex	2,172	897	3,069	2,121	823	2,943
Gloucestershire	803	362	1,165	789	333	1,123
Greater Manchester	4,807	1,895	6,703	4,669	1,709	6,378
Hampshire	2,130	934	3,064	2,045	824	2,869
Hertfordshire	1,306	605	1,911	1,278	542	1,820
Humberside	1,135	478	1,614	1,111	436	1,548
Kent	2,300	889	3,188	2,252	829	3,081
Lancashire	2,062	857	2,919	1,998	764	2,763
Leicestershire	1,457	498	1,955	1,423	454	1,877
Lincolnshire	792	308	1,100	750	273	1,023
London, City of	573	166	739	564	154	718
Merseyside	2,770	1,024	3,794	2,712	948	3,660
Metropolitan Police	23,719	8,158	31,877	23,214	7,449	30,663
Norfolk	1,149	420	1,569	1,132	391	1,522
Northamptonshire	860	370	1,229	850	352	1,202
Northumbria	2,514	1,000	3,514	2,462	920	3,382
North Yorkshire	984	411	1,395	964	378	1,341
Nottinghamshire	1,509	593	2,102	1,431	532	1,963
South Yorkshire	1,818	769	2,587	1,772	716	2,488
Staffordshire	1,257	456	1,714	1,242	434	1,676
Suffolk	837	310	1,147	828	292	1,120
Surrey	1,245	618	1,863	1,218	556	1,774
Sussex	1,950	860	2,810	1,914	794	2,708
Thames Valley	3,022	1,343	4,365	2,973	1,220	4,193
Warwickshire	587	240	828	566	211	777
West Mercia	1,416	599	2,014	1,350	527	1,876
West Midlands	4,999	2,134	7,133	4,883	1,955	6,838
West Yorkshire	3,302	1,445	4,748	3,235	1,326	4,561
Wiltshire	681	334	1,015	660	306	966
Dyfed-Powys	836	339	1,176	821	320	1,141
Gwent	861	368	1,229	830	335	1,165
North Wales	1,033	454	1,487	1,022	430	1,451
South Wales	2,064	800	2,864	2,041	758	2,799
Total 43 forces[22]	**91,081**	**35,738**	**126,818**	**88,958**	**32,744**	**121,702**
Central service secondments	243	49	292	243	49	292
British Transport Police	2,381	496	2,877	2,292	465	2,757
Total [22]	**93,705**	**36,282**	**129,987**	**91,493**	**33,258**	**124,751**

Source: Home Office

1. Full-time equivalent figures. There may appear to be small discrepancies between the totals and the sums of the constituent items as the figures are presented to the nearest whole number but are actually provided unrounded.

2. Officers available for duty is the number of officers in post excluding long-term absentees. In previous publications, these figures were provided on a headcount basis.

22. Police officer available for duty figures were updated on 28 January 2016 following a large revision to Cleveland's long-term sickness absence data.

21.1b Special constables, by police force area and gender, as at 31 March 2015

England and Wales

Headcount[5]

	Total			Minority Ethnic			Joiners			Leavers		
	Male	Female	Total	Male	Female	Total	Male	Female	Total	Male	Female	Total
Avon & Somerset	320	133	453	14	1	15	33	15	48	52	41	93
Bedfordshire	159	68	227	14	2	16	77	24	101	49	22	71
Cambridgeshire	193	84	277	7	2	9	55	18	73	49	16	65
Cheshire	264	126	390	9	3	12	85	45	130	55	35	90
Cleveland	59	34	93	0	1	1	11	10	21	7	1	8
Cumbria	84	35	119	2	1	3	21	10	31	20	18	38
Derbyshire	152	60	212	12	2	14	22	9	31	44	23	67
Devon & Cornwall	439	234	673	1	1	2	135	72	207	58	43	101
Dorset	155	72	227	1	1	2	56	37	93	51	28	79
Durham	74	36	110	0	0	0	28	18	46	15	6	21
Essex	269	97	366	11	4	15	54	29	83	81	36	117
Gloucestershire	85	30	115	3	0	3	15	8	23	17	13	30
Greater Manchester	508	195	703	64	17	81	158	82	240	179	88	267
Hampshire	332	124	456	6	5	11	41	23	64	139	50	189
Hertfordshire	234	69	303	19	3	22	43	12	55	118	39	157
Humberside	262	154	416	3	5	8	81	37	118	49	38	87
Kent	207	41	248	6	1	7	45	13	58	75	17	92
Lancashire	262	114	376	23	8	31	68	40	108	137	72	209
Leicestershire	184	70	254	25	5	30	28	15	43	48	26	74
Lincolnshire	147	82	229	0	1	1	37	26	63	48	33	81
London, City of	46	15	61	4	1	5	3	0	3	10	6	16
Merseyside	215	94	309	9	5	14	62	28	90	122	79	201
Metropolitan Police	2,496	1,163	3,659	807	309	1,116	333	181	514	830	396	1,226
Norfolk	183	74	257	2	1	3	48	29	77	46	14	60
Northamptonshire	296	116	412	6	5	11	112	52	164	48	14	62
Northumbria	191	57	248	2	0	2	43	10	53	75	38	113
North Yorkshire	116	68	184	3	0	3	40	30	70	23	17	40
Nottinghamshire	164	88	252	9	2	11	27	21	48	78	34	112
South Yorkshire	264	179	443	12	14	26	90	68	158	58	45	103
Staffordshire	231	87	318	10	2	12	64	31	95	60	54	114
Suffolk	159	75	234	5	0	5	26	24	50	32	17	49
Surrey	98	24	122	3	2	5	6	2	8	38	18	56
Sussex	271	122	393	7	4	11	122	52	174	95	46	141
Thames Valley	396	166	562	26	7	33	118	57	175	203	77	280
Warwickshire	180	77	257	14	6	20	32	15	47	42	19	61
West Mercia	207	92	299	4	4	8	68	40	108	62	42	104
West Midlands	289	85	374	58	19	77	19	6	25	56	26	82
West Yorkshire	521	303	824	51	27	78	298	224	522	108	60	168
Wiltshire	124	52	176	3	0	3	20	6	26	25	13	38
Dyfed-Powys	103	44	147	0	0	0	11	3	14	36	23	59
Gwent	81	43	124	1	1	2	8	8	16	25	6	31
North Wales	77	54	131	0	0	0	21	16	37	14	16	30
South Wales	55	13	68	55	13	68	11	6	17	22	6	28
Total all 43 forces	**11,152**	**4,949**	**16,101**	**1,311**	**485**	**1,796**	**2,675**	**1,452**	**4,127**	**3,399**	**1,711**	**5,110**
British Transport Police	197	33	230	24	0	24	36	2	38	69	12	81
Total	11,349	4,982	16,331	1,335	485	1,820	2,711	1,454	4,165	5,619	9,784	15,403

Source: Home Office

5. Excludes the British Transport Police.

Special constable figures are provided on a headcount basis.

21.1c Police forces strength:[1] by country and sex

As at 31 March

Numbers

		2002	2003	2004	2005	2006	2007	2008	2009	2010	2011	2012	2013	2014	2015
Northern Ireland															
Regular police[2,3]															
Strength:															
Men	**KERU**	6,057	6,171	6,108	6,016	5,992	5,949	5,761	5,669	5,548	5,371	5238	5085	4988	4988
Women	**KERV**	1,080	1,266	1,418	1,547	1,534	1,600	1,653	1,735	1,837	1,922	1907	1877	1882	1882
Reserve[4]															
Strength:															
Men	**KERW**	2,223	1,983	1,824	1,431	1,424	1,212	1,119	930	774	597	333	313	278	278
Women	**KERX**	510	453	485	410	402	400	382	345	311	283	247	222	184	184

Source: Police Service of Northern Ireland

1. All figures are full-time equivalent strength figures that have been rounded to the nearest whole

2 Does not include officers on secondment.

3 Also includes student officers.

4 As at 31/03/12 No longer any FTR in PSNI, As at 31/03/12 Reserve figures only include Con PT (Formerly known as PTR)

21.1d Number of Police Officers (Full-time Equivalent) in Scotland[1,2], and by Local Policing Divisions, as at 31 March 2015

as at 31 March	Scotland
2015	17,295

Police Officer Distribution

The chart below outlines the distribution of officers across each of the 14 local policing divisions together with the available regional and national resources.

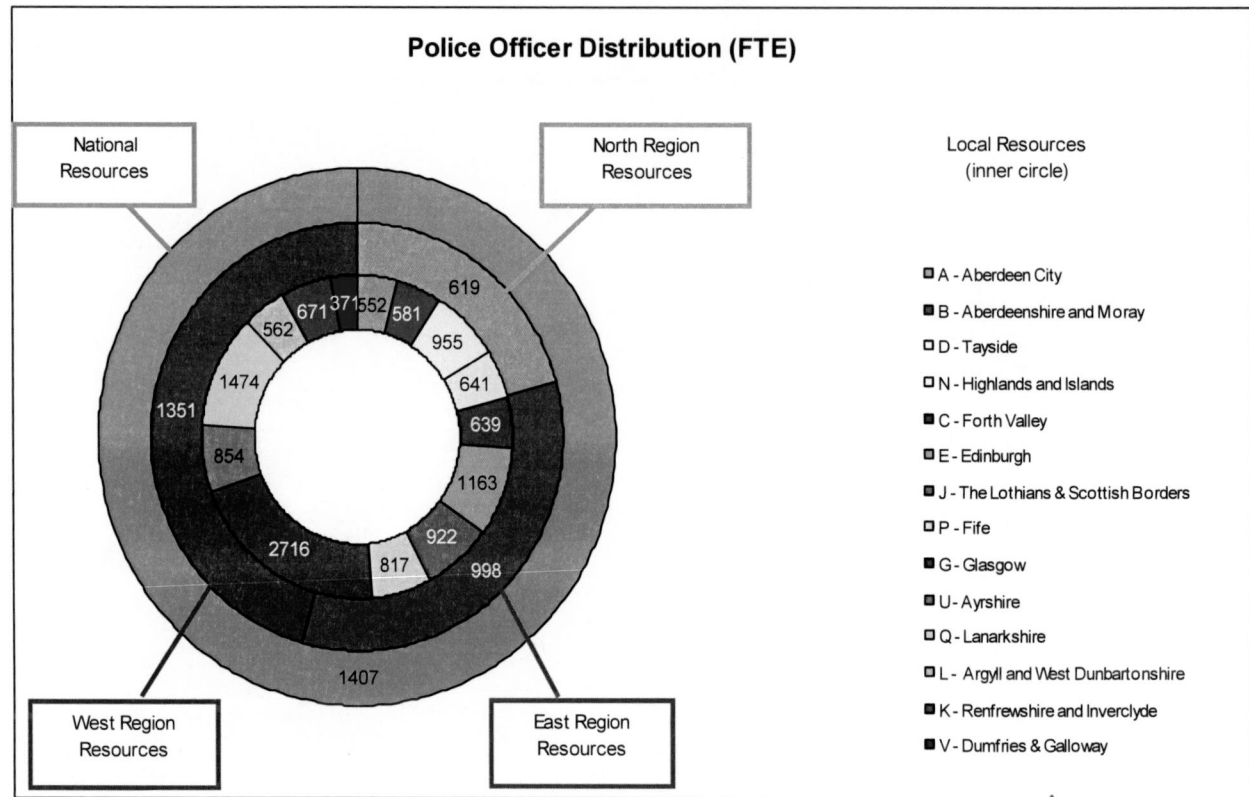

Police Officer Distribution (FTE)

National Resources

North Region Resources

Local Resources (inner circle)

- A - Aberdeen City
- B - Aberdeenshire and Moray
- D - Tayside
- N - Highlands and Islands
- C - Forth Valley
- E - Edinburgh
- J - The Lothians & Scottish Borders
- P - Fife
- G - Glasgow
- U - Ayrshire
- Q - Lanarkshire
- L - Argyll and West Dunbartonshire
- K - Renfrewshire and Inverclyde
- V - Dumfries & Galloway

West Region Resources

East Region Resources

1. All figures are expressed in terms of full-time equivalent (FTE) police officers, rounded to the nearest whole number.

2. Police Officers in Scotland - includes all officers deployed with the 14 local policing divisions, specialist and operational support, central functions, officers undertaking Scottish Police College training, long-term sick leave and maternity/adoption leave, officers at ports and airports paid either wholly or partially by the port/airport authority, and additional officers either wholly or partially funded by the local authority or an external body, and all officers otherwise seconded to Scottish Government, Her Majesty's Inspectorate of Constabulary for Scotland (HMICS), Scottish Police Authority and elsewhere.

Sources: Scottish Government Justice Analytical Services;
Police Scotland

21.2 Prison Population International Comparisons with other EU Countries

	Prison population total (no in penal institutions incl. Pre-trial detainees/remand prisoners)	Date	Estimated national population	Prison population rate (per 100,000 of national population)	Source of Prison Population Total
Northern Europe					
Denmark	3,314	at 1.1.2016	5.71M	58	C of E
Estonia	2,868	at 26.9.2016	1.32M	217	NPA
Finland	3,002	at 1.1.2016	5.49M	55	NPA
Iceland	147	at 1.1.2014	325,700	45	NPA
Ireland	3,688	at 31.8.2016	4.66M	79	NPA
Latvia	4,409	at 31.12 2015	1.97M	224	NPA
Lithuania	7,355	at 1.1.2016	2.9M	254	C of E
Norway	3,679	at 1.1.2016	5.22M	70	NPA
Sweden	5,245	at 1.1.2016	9.85M	53	NPA
United Kingdom					
- England & Wales	85,639	at 30.9.2016	58.48M	146	Ministry of Justice
- Northern Ireland	1,478	at 23.9.2016	1.87M	79	NI Prison Administration
- Scotland	7,672	at 23.9.2016	5.4M	142	Scottish Prison Administration
Faeroe Islands (Denmark)	10	average for 2015	48,935	19	Danish NPA
Guernsey (UK)	83	at 2.10.2015	65,450	127	Guernsey Prison Administration
Isle of Man (UK)	80	at 26.10.2015	87,000	92	Isle of Man Prison Administration
Jersey (UK)	154	at 21.10.2015	101,500	152	Jersey Prison Administration
Southern Europe					
Albania	5,826	at June 2016	2.88M	202	NPA
Andorra	41	at 1.1.2016	78,000	53	C of E
Bosnia & Hertzegovina					
- Federation	1,722	at 31.12.2014	2.35M	73	Government Report to Human Rights Council
- Republika Srpska	877	at 31.12.2015	1.3M	67	Rep.Srpska Prison Administration
Croatia	3,341	at 1.1.2016	4.19M	80	NPA
Cyprus	681	at 1.9.2014	850,700	80	C of E Annual Penal Statistics
Greece	9,621	at 1.9.2016	10.75M	89	Ministry of Justice
Italy	54,195	at 31.8.2016	60.82M	89	Ministry of Justice
Kosovo/Kosova	1,816	at 1.10.2014	1.81M	100	U.S. State Dept. human rights report
Macedonia (FYR)	3,427	at 1.1.2016	2.07M	166	NPA
Malta	569	at 31.12.2015	433,300	131	Home Affairs Minister
Montenegro	1,131	at 31.12.2015	622,700	182	NPA
Portugal	14,061	at 1.9.2016	10.29M	137	NPA
San Marino	2 *	1.1.2016	33,700	-	C of E Annual Penal Statistics

* most prisoners serve their sentences in Italian prisons and are not included in prison population for San Marino

Serbia	10,067	at 1.1.2016	7.07M	142	NPA
Slovenia	1,308	at 1.9.2016	2.07M	63	NPA
Spain	60,799	at 26.8.2016	46.32M	131	NPA
Gibraltar (UK)	52	at November 2014	32,900	158	C of E
Western Europe					
Austria	8,177	at 1.6.2016	8.75M	93	NPA
Belgium	11,071	at 5.1.2016	11.29M	98	C of E
France	69,375*	at 1.7.2016	67.4M	103	NPA

* including French overseas departments and territories; excluding 11,530 persons not detained in penal institutions (écrouées non détenues)

Germany	64,397	at 1.3.2016	82.5M	78	German Federal Statistical Office
Liechtenstein	10*	at 1.1.2016	37,600	27	C of E

* additional prisoners, serving more than two years (11 at November 2013), are held in Austrian & Swiss prisons in accordance with treaty agreements

Luxembourg	705	at 1.9.2016	585,000	121	NPA
Monaco	28	at 1.1.2015	37,800	74	C of E
Netherlands	11,603	at 30.9.2014	16.88M	69	NPA
Switzerland	6,884	at 2.9.2015	8.3M	83	Swiss Federal Statistical Office
Europe/Asia					
Armenia	4,873	1.1.2016	3M	162	C of E
Azerbaijan	22,526	at 2014	9.54M	236	Ministry of Justice
Georgia	9,765	at 31.7.2016	3.72M	263	National Statistical Office
Russian Federation	645,350	at 01.9.2016	144.4M	447	NPA
Turkey	187,609	at 1.4.2016	78.98M	238	NPA
Central and Eastern Europe					
Belarus	29,000	at 1.10.2014	9.47M	306	U.S. State Dept. Human Rights Report
Bulgaria	9,028	at October 2014	7.21M	125	U.S. State Dept. Human Rights Report
Czech Republic	22,334	at 31.8.2016	10.58M	211	NPA
Hungary	17,976	at 8.3.2016	9.82M	183	NPA
Moldova	7,881	at 1.4.2016	3.55M	222	NPA
Poland	70,951	at 31.8.2016	37.94M	187	NPA
Romania	27,774	at 6.9.2016	19.69M	141	NPA
Slovakia	10,181	at 1.9.2016	5.43M	187	NPA
Ukraine	60,771*	at 1.9.2016	36.3M	167	NPA

* not including prisoners in Crimea, Sebastopol and those Donetsk & Luhansk areas that are not under the control of the Ukrainian authorities

Source: Institute for Criminal Policy Research, World Prison Brief

C of E - Council of Europe
NPA - National Prison Administration

21.3 Police recorded crime by offence, year ending March 2005 to year ending December 2015 and percentage change between year ending December 2014 and year ending December 2015

England and Wales

Offence	Apr '04 to Mar '05	Apr '05 to Mar '06	Apr '06 to Mar '07	Apr '07 to Mar '08	Apr '08 to Mar '09	Apr '09 to Mar '10	Apr '10 to Mar '11	Apr '11 to Mar '12	Apr '12 to Mar '13	Apr '13 to Mar '14	Apr '14 to Mar '15	Jan '14 to Dec '14	Jan '15 to Dec '15	% change between years
VICTIM BASED CRIME	5,022,946	4,910,238	4,788,218	4,338,484	4,091,230	3,760,387	3,598,145	3,454,955	3,150,551	3,107,866	3,176,113	3,142,656	3,388,070	8
1 Murder														
4.1 Manslaughter														
4.10 Corporate manslaughter														
4.2 Infanticide														
Homicide [3,4]	868	764	758	775	664	620	639	553	558	533	537	517	573	11
2 Attempted murder [4]	740	920	633	621	574	591	523	483	412	501	570	524	689	31
4.3 Intentional destruction of viable unborn child	4	5	5	4	2	3	3	3	1	4	8	7	9	
4.4 Causing death or serious injury by dangerous driving [5]					373	296	213	200	174	290	394	358	409	14
4.6 Causing death by careless driving when under the influence of drink or drugs					29	36	25	24	14	23	11	13	22	
4.8 Causing death by careless or inconsiderate driving					35	188	172	179	139	136	147	154	120	-22
4.4/6/8 Causing death by dangerous or careless driving	441	432	459	422										
5 More serious wounding or other act endangering life [6]	19,612													
5A Wounding [6,7]		18,825	17,276	15,118										
5B Use of substance or object to endanger life [6,7]					462	416	371	315						
5C Possession of items to endanger life [6,7]					266	331	329	298						
5D Assault with intent to cause serious harm [7]					22,663	22,795	19,489	17,777	17,006	17,929	20,566	19,984	22,346	12
5E Endangering life [7]	718	646	484	402	320	231	257	214	778	801	994	953	1,209	27
6 Endangering railway passengers [7]														
7 Endangering life at sea [7]	3	13	5	10	8	6	4	6						
8F Inflicting grievous bodily harm (GBH) without intent [8,9]					17,159	16,482	15,112	14,409						
8H Racially or religiously aggravated inflicting GBH without intent [8,9]					384	224	188	169						
37.1 Causing death by aggravated vehicle taking	40	24	18	18										
4.7 Causing or allowing death or serious physical harm of child or vulnerable person [10]														
4.9 Causing death by driving: unlicensed or disqualified or uninsured drivers														
8A Other wounding [8]	488,135	516,523	481,822	430,818	374,255	355,962	328,463	301,223						
8G Actual bodily harm (ABH) and other injury [8,9]														
8D Racially or religiously aggravated other wounding [8]	5,426	6,107	5,620	4,830	3,921	3,521	2,985	2,688						
8J Racially or religiously aggravated ABH or other injury [8,9]					163	138	118	118						
8K Poisoning or female genital mutilation [8,9]														
8N Assault with injury [9]									290,956	300,653	348,733	338,281	390,519	15
8P Racially or religiously aggravated assault with injury [9]									2,579	2,452	2,730	2,605	2,893	11
Violence with injury	515,119	543,500	506,325	452,247	420,643	401,244	368,277	338,125	312,085	322,820	374,179	362,898	418,261	15
3 Threat or conspiracy to murder [11]	23,758	18,683	12,822	9,966										
3A Conspiracy to murder [11]					56	45	36	36	28	30	39	42	45	
3B Threats to kill [11]					9,448	9,523	9,480	7,643	7,347	8,471	12,928	11,671	16,569	42
8L Harassment [12,13,14]	49,815	54,644	55,493	52,107	48,363	52,959	51,173	48,141	54,532	61,211	81,745	75,062	132,640	77
8M Racially or religiously aggravated harassment [12,13]	2,302	2,548	2,657	2,424	2,395	2,370	1,971	1,625	1,500	1,445	1,876	1,742	1,917	10
8Q Stalking [12]											2,880	2,189	3,776	
11 Cruelty to and neglect of children [15]	5,724	5,045	4,917	5,287	6,204	6,611	6,087	6,081	6,370					
11A Cruelty to children/young persons [15]										8,000	8,934	8,443	11,168	32
12 Abandoning a child under the age of two years [15]	49	49	23	19	23	9	6	12	5	6	7	5	12	
13 Child abduction	1,035	919	696	595	567	560	548	532	513	565	821	753	1,039	38
14 Procuring illegal abortion	7	6	6	6	5	3	5	3	5	6	7	5	12	
36 Kidnapping	2,814	2,799	2,367	1,991	2,035	1,860	1,717	1,516	1,388	1,728	2,194	2,061	2,788	35
104 Assault without injury on a constable	23,604	22,217	21,749	20,384	17,384	15,781	15,510	15,873	14,527	14,456	14,402	14,396	15,132	5
105A Assault without injury	216,712	183,555	202,701	198,653	197,035	203,098	205,975	202,509	198,390	211,257	273,440	256,439	329,573	29
105B Racially or religiously aggravated assault without injury	3,866	3,945	4,351	4,325	4,186	4,328	4,062	4,071	3,898	4,103	4,928	4,642	5,524	19
106 Modern Slavery [16]													501	
Violence without injury	329,686	294,410	307,782	295,757	287,701	297,147	296,570	288,042	288,498	311,272	404,194	377,445	520,684	38
TOTAL VIOLENCE AGAINST THE PERSON	845,673	838,674	814,865	748,779	709,008	699,011	665,486	626,720	601,141	634,625	778,910	740,860	939,518	27

21.3 Police recorded crime by offence, year ending March 2005 to year ending December 2015 and percentage change between year ending December 2014 and year ending December 2015

England and Wales

Offence		Apr '04 to Mar '05	Apr '05 to Mar '06	Apr '06 to Mar '07	Apr '07 to Mar '08	Apr '08 to Mar '09	Apr '09 to Mar '10	Apr '10 to Mar '11	Apr '11 to Mar '12	Apr '12 to Mar '13	Apr '13 to Mar '14	Apr '14 to Mar '15	Jan '14 to Dec '14	Jan '15 to Dec '15	% change between years
19A	Rape of a female [17,18]	693	61	25	145	170	..	..	..	..	..	..	..	..	..
19C	Rape of a female aged 16 or over [17]	8,192	8,725	8,222	7,610	7,768	9,027	9,469	9,773	9,646	12,307	18,263	16,614	21,729	31
19D	Rape of a female child under 16 [17]	3,014	3,153	2,853	2,422	2,537	2,908	2,877	2,777	2,803	3,407	4,448	3,993	5,295	33
19E	Rape of a female child under 13 [17]	970	1,388	1,524	1,487	1,658	1,967	2,243	2,212	2,372	2,835	3,475	3,262	4,108	26
19B	Rape of a male [17,18]	81	22	18	10	22	..	..	..	..	..	..	..	..	..
19F	Rape of a male aged 16 or over [17]	444	438	413	332	317	368	387	387	413	661	1,015	946	1,241	31
19G	Rape of a male child under 16 [17]	322	292	261	237	216	241	246	288	352	416	661	581	689	19
19H	Rape of a male child under 13 [17]	297	364	458	430	408	563	670	601	788	1,125	1,364	1,287	1,679	30
	Rape [17,18]	14,013	14,443	13,774	12,673	13,096	15,074	15,892	16,038	16,374	20,751	29,226	26,683	34,741	30
16	Buggery [17,18]	73	39	35	49	36	..	..	..	..	..	..	..	..	..
17	Indecent assault on a male [17,18]	1,003	347	76	209	158	..	..	..	..	..	..	..	..	..
17A	Sexual assault on a male aged 13 and over [17]	1,316	1,428	1,450	1,323	1,161	1,208	1,285	1,261	1,400	1,957	2,929	2,618	3,425	31
17B	Sexual assault on a male child under 13 [17]	1,227	1,394	1,237	1,121	1,004	1,054	1,126	1,011	1,270	1,652	2,390	2,120	2,644	25
18	Gross indecency between males [17,18]	49	20	12	17	14	..	..	..	..	..	..	..	..	..
20	Indecent assault on a female [17,18]	5,152	1,215	267	768	575	..	..	..	..	..	..	..	..	..
20A	Sexual assault on a female aged 13 and over [17]	15,087	17,158	16,883	15,793	15,500	15,693	16,346	15,794	15,518	17,377	23,122	21,487	27,061	26
20B	Sexual assault on a female child under 13 [17]	4,391	4,647	4,245	3,984	3,665	4,148	4,298	3,991	4,177	5,129	6,274	5,802	7,366	27
21	Unlawful sexual intercourse with a girl under 13 [17]	1,510	1,950	1,936	1,836	1,650	1,817	1,769	1,808	2,173	2,892	4,683	3,857	5,798	50
21	Sexual activity involving a child under 13 [17]	436	138	67	33	51	..	..	..	..	..	..	..	..	..
22	Unlawful sexual intercourse with a girl under 16 [17,18]	2,546	3,283	3,208	3,123	3,318	3,992	4,039	3,971	4,468	5,881	8,582	7,413	10,790	46
22B	Sexual activity involving a child under 16 [17]	239	744	224	217	151	130	167	203	191	274	484	424	579	37
22A	Causing sexual activity without consent [17,19]	713	966	1,344	1,125	1,041	1,111	803	637	509	491	624	570	746	31
23	Incest or familial sexual offences [17]	86	36	21	4	4	124	130	101	115	134	212	186	241	30
25	Abduction of female [17,18]	104	139	163	127	131	..	..	..	..	..	..	..	..	..
70	Sexual activity with a person with a mental disorder [17]	99	124	101	108	116	134	153	159	176	289	362	319	562	76
71	Abuse of children through sexual exploitation [17,20]	21	33	43	57	52	58	66	59	70	123	192	131	100	-24
72	Trafficking for sexual exploitation [16,17]	682	463	361	328	195	185	146	176	192	194	210	216	235	9
73	Abuse of position of trust of a sexual nature [17]	398	120	64	149	121	..	..	..	..	..	..	..	..	..
74	Gross indecency with a child [17,18]	11,593	11,363	10,209	8,848	..	..	..	..	..	..	..	..	..	..
88A	Sexual grooming [17]	186	237	322	274	313	393	309	371	370	459	683	598	985	65
88B	Other miscellaneous sexual offences [17,21,22]	..	..	..	..	298	354	198	163	160	200	221	212	252	19
88C	Other miscellaneous sexual offences [17,22]	..	..	..	..	5	15	12	11	16	18	19	17	27	-
88D	Unnatural sexual offences [17,22]	..	..	..	..	..	..	..	..	..	..	..	..	..	..
88E	Exposure and voyeurism [17,22]	..	..	..	..	7,530	7,516	7,201	7,006	6,420	6,411	7,869	7,612	8,062	6
	Other sexual offences [17]	46,911	45,844	42,268	39,493	37,089	37,932	38,048	36,722	37,225	43,481	58,856	53,582	68,873	29
	TOTAL SEXUAL OFFENCES [17]	60,924	60,287	56,042	52,166	50,185	53,006	53,940	52,760	53,599	64,232	88,082	80,265	103,614	29
34A	Robbery of business property	7,934	8,760	9,454	9,173	9,350	8,182	7,729	6,770	6,120	5,789	5,406	5,519	5,463	-1
34B	Robbery of personal property	83,076	89,438	91,922	75,600	70,780	66,923	68,460	67,918	59,035	52,039	44,833	46,081	45,309	-2
	TOTAL ROBBERY	91,010	98,198	101,376	84,773	80,130	75,105	76,189	74,688	65,155	57,828	50,239	51,600	50,772	-2
28	Burglary in a dwelling	318,969	298,355	290,454	279,125	282,977	..	..	..	..	..	..	..	..	..
28A	Burglary in a dwelling	..	..	..	..	..	214,889	208,484	198,853	185,147	171,416	157,271	160,830	153,580	-5
28B	Attempted burglary in a dwelling	..	..	..	..	..	44,706	42,298	40,287	37,386	36,361	35,122	35,342	35,445	0
28C	Distraction burglary in a dwelling	..	..	..	..	..	6,936	5,480	4,467	3,305	2,847	3,086	3,084	2,935	-5
28D	Attempted distraction burglary in a dwelling	..	..	..	..	..	722	543	368	257	189	239	212	289	36
29	Aggravated burglary in a dwelling	2,538	2,162	1,806	1,571	1,454	1,353	1,360	1,337	1,181	1,175	1,283	1,257	1,602	27
	Domestic burglary	321,507	300,517	292,260	280,696	284,431	268,606	258,165	245,312	227,276	211,988	197,001	200,725	193,851	-3
	of which: distraction burglary	13,258	11,552	12,750	10,058	9,092	7,658	6,023	4,835	3,562	3,036	3,325	3,296	3,224	-2

21.3 Police recorded crime by offence, year ending March 2005 to year ending December 2015 and percentage change between year ending December 2014 and year ending December 2015

England and Wales

Offence		Apr '04 to Mar '05	Apr '05 to Mar '06	Apr '06 to Mar '07	Apr '07 to Mar '08	Apr '08 to Mar '09	Apr '09 to Mar '10	Apr '10 to Mar '11	Apr '11 to Mar '12	Apr '12 to Mar '13	Apr '13 to Mar '14	Apr '14 to Mar '15	Jan '14 to Dec '14	Jan '15 to Dec '15	% change between years
30	Burglary in a building other than a dwelling	358,398	344,195	329,473	302,799	296,970									
30A	Burglary in a building other than a dwelling						236,019	230,868	223,153	202,440	200,570	185,533	189,345	179,025	-5
30B	Attempted burglary in a building other than a dwelling						35,868	33,515	32,473	29,959	30,549	28,721	29,098	28,661	-2
31	Aggravated burglary in a building other than a dwelling	453	356	279	215	183	152	135	110	120	105	167	157	181	15
	Non-domestic burglary	358,851	344,551	329,752	303,014	297,153	272,039	264,518	255,736	232,519	231,224	214,421	218,600	207,867	-5
	Burglary	680,358	645,068	622,012	583,710	581,584	540,645	522,683	501,048	459,795	443,212	411,422	419,325	401,718	-4
37.2	Aggravated vehicle taking[23]	11,409	10,943	10,920	10,334	9,730	8,000	6,954	6,253	5,662	5,255	5,400	5,444	5,502	1
45	Theft from a vehicle	500,360	507,239	502,651	432,412	396,976	339,170	313,467	300,377	285,047	276,366	237,402	245,857	239,336	-3
48	Theft or unauthorised taking of a motor vehicle	231,323	203,239	182,464	159,704	137,508	109,684	99,208	85,803	74,168	70,053	70,390	69,518	75,656	9
126	Vehicle interference[24]	77,004	71,400	68,980	54,003	47,639	38,019	29,987	25,009	22,492	20,367	38,246	32,482	43,974	35
	Vehicle offences	820,096	792,821	765,015	656,453	591,853	494,873	449,616	417,442	387,359	372,041	351,438	353,301	364,468	3
39.3	Theft from the person	122,081	123,867	114,852	101,660	89,652	92,247	92,902	100,588	109,757	98,282	78,803	80,710	82,384	2
	Theft from the person	122,081	123,867	114,852	101,660	89,652	92,247	92,902	100,588	109,757	98,282	78,803	80,710	82,384	2
44	Theft or unauthorised taking of a pedal cycle	105,953	113,192	110,526	104,000	104,169	109,847	108,962	115,902	97,286	97,686	93,447	94,270	87,895	-7
	Bicycle theft	105,953	113,192	110,526	104,000	104,169	109,847	108,962	115,902	97,286	97,686	93,447	94,270	87,895	-7
46	Shoplifting	281,127	295,999	294,282	290,653	320,739	307,823	305,896	308,326	300,623	321,065	326,468	325,541	333,671	2
	Shoplifting	281,127	295,999	294,282	290,653	320,739	307,823	305,896	308,326	300,623	321,065	326,468	325,541	333,671	2
35	Blackmail[25]	1,465	1,645	2,481	1,201	1,363	1,450	1,491	1,369	1,497	2,134	3,519	3,163	5,118	62
40	Theft in a dwelling other than from an automatic machine or meter	57,713	54,757	54,471	51,336	51,220	53,338	54,798	54,518	52,384	50,513	50,901	51,245	51,156	0
41	Theft by an employee	17,251	17,048	16,323	15,864	15,467	13,169	12,141	11,589	10,446	10,320	10,776	10,667	10,904	2
42	Theft of mail	22,509	9,351	4,740	3,051	3,724	3,098	2,792	2,447	2,878	2,163	2,011	2,033	2,356	16
43	Dishonest use of electricity	1,296	1,299	1,497	2,024	1,785	1,736	1,860	1,948	2,007	2,229	2,551	2,358	2,773	18
47	Theft from automatic machine or meter[26]	35,918	42,049	33,721	11,932	7,651	7,753	6,215	6,692	6,394	4,950	4,220	4,207	4,086	-3
49	Other theft	589,189	554,368	536,603	526,949	472,325	436,244	481,585	491,559	419,685	389,024	359,952	364,571	351,972	-3
49A	Making off without payment[27]	102,906	87,767	82,261	73,895	80,048	70,397	66,505	61,351	50,833	51,550	59,586	58,709	63,972	9
	All other theft offences	828,247	768,284	732,097	686,252	633,583	587,185	627,387	631,473	546,124	512,883	493,516	496,953	492,337	-1
	TOTAL THEFT OFFENCES	2,837,862	2,739,231	2,638,784	2,422,728	2,321,580	2,132,620	2,107,446	2,074,779	1,900,944	1,845,169	1,755,094	1,770,100	1,762,473	0
56	Arson[28]	48,368	45,731	43,100	39,327										
56A	Arson endangering life[28]					3,629	3,623	3,325	3,100	2,588	2,574	2,812	2,658	3,253	22
56B	Arson not endangering life[28]					31,198	28,957	25,791	24,119	16,717	16,008	16,782	16,279	18,651	15
	Arson	48,368	45,731	43,100	39,327	34,827	32,580	29,116	27,219	19,305	18,582	19,594	18,937	21,904	16
58A	Criminal damage to a dwelling	308,973	297,579	288,285	256,804	235,424	198,623	172,916	155,982	131,157	121,525	118,074	116,698	124,081	6
58B	Criminal damage to a building other than a dwelling	174,489	161,436	160,207	131,146	109,440	88,687	75,677	67,329	57,631	52,599	50,619	50,552	51,699	2
58C	Criminal damage to a vehicle	461,346	468,143	483,237	425,632	389,719	336,927	289,045	259,871	222,770	217,994	214,985	215,798	223,988	4
58D	Other criminal damage	188,842	195,069	197,036	173,127	157,109	140,575	125,751	113,478	97,008	93,438	98,681	96,061	108,017	12
58E	Racially or religiously aggravated criminal damage to a dwelling[29]	1,845	1,742	1,543	1,150	999	849	639	499						
58F	Racially or religiously aggravated criminal damage to a building other than a dwelling[29]	1,137	1,274	1,079	833	778	663	534	431						
58G	Racially or religiously aggravated criminal damage to a vehicle[29]	1,640	1,899	1,711	1,338	1,304	1,135	869	788						
58H	Racially or religiously aggravated other criminal damage[29]	837	975	953	681	727	606	537	411						
58J	Racially or religiously aggravated criminal damage[29]									1,841	1,874	1,835	1,785	2,004	12
	Criminal damage	1,139,109	1,128,117	1,134,051	990,711	895,500	768,065	665,968	598,789	510,407	487,430	484,194	480,894	509,789	6
	TOTAL CRIMINAL DAMAGE AND ARSON	1,187,477	1,173,848	1,177,151	1,030,038	930,327	800,645	695,084	626,008	529,712	506,012	503,788	499,831	531,693	6

21.3 Police recorded crime by offence, year ending March 2005 to year ending December 2015 and percentage change between year ending December 2014 and year ending December 2015

England and Wales

Offence	Apr '04 to Mar '05	Apr '05 to Mar '06	Apr '06 to Mar '07	Apr '07 to Mar '08	Apr '08 to Mar '09	Apr '09 to Mar '10	Apr '10 to Mar '11	Apr '11 to Mar '12	Apr '12 to Mar '13	Apr '13 to Mar '14	Apr '14 to Mar '15	Jan '14 to Dec '14	Jan '15 to Dec '15	% change between years
OTHER CRIMES AGAINST SOCIETY	453,825	515,453	534,159	542,656	539,153	504,649	480,330	448,626	402,617	398,679	403,536	401,513	429,759	7
92A Trafficking in controlled drugs	24,190	25,276	26,550	28,323	29,885	33,223	32,336	31,316	29,746	29,348	26,931	28,025	26,257	-6
Trafficking of drugs	24,190	25,276	26,550	28,323	29,885	33,223	32,336	31,316	29,746	29,348	26,931	28,025	26,257	-6
92B Possession of controlled drugs [30]	781	601	680	817	1,123	1,122	1,142	1,127	1,034	1,198	769	867	603	-30
92C Other drug offences	32,603	32,685	36,608	42,519	44,578	38,439	38,711	36,453	34,596	34,066	31,857	32,499	29,409	-10
92D Possession of controlled drugs (excluding cannabis) [30]	88,263	119,917	130,395	158,254	167,950	162,800	160,733	160,203	142,627	133,604	110,200	117,454	94,511	-20
92E Possession of cannabis [30]	..	..	..	..	..	..	..	..	..	..	..	..	..	
Possession of drugs	121,647	153,203	167,683	201,590	213,651	202,361	200,586	197,783	178,257	168,868	142,826	150,820	124,523	-17
TOTAL DRUG OFFENCES	145,837	178,479	194,233	229,913	243,536	235,584	232,922	229,099	208,003	198,216	169,757	178,845	150,780	-16
8B Possession of weapons [31]	36,374	35,590	34,689	32,513	..	..	..	..	..	..	..	..	..	
10A Possession of firearms with intent [31]	..	..	..	..	1,973	1,587	1,385	1,151	998	1,077	1,276	1,149	1,508	31
10B Possession of firearms offences [32]	..	..	..	..	4,460	4,070	3,650	3,402	3,052	2,929	3,011	3,061	3,038	-1
10C Possession of other weapons [31]	..	..	..	..	14,944	11,950	10,564	9,138	7,274	7,328	7,470	7,346	8,585	17
10D Possession of article with blade or point [31]	..	..	..	..	13,985	10,885	10,474	9,762	8,425	9,050	9,952	9,650	11,227	16
81 Other firearms offences [33]	4,210	4,106	4,239	4,560	293	253	254	229	160	237	193	196	259	32
90 Other knives offences	21	15	9	6	7	13	0	6	1	2	1	1	4	
TOTAL POSSESSION OF WEAPONS OFFENCES	40,605	39,711	38,937	37,079	35,662	28,758	26,327	23,688	19,910	20,623	21,903	21,403	24,621	15
9A Public fear, alarm or distress [12,13]	147,801	164,061	173,152	158,045	142,246	126,597	114,781	97,085	81,139	79,601	96,177	89,864	124,770	39
9B Racially or religiously aggravated public fear, alarm or distress [12,13]	21,061	24,057	25,828	24,086	23,355	23,226	20,967	20,188	20,420	21,685	26,355	24,992	29,009	16
62 Treason [34]	0	0	0	0	0	0	0	0	..	..	..	..	..	
62A Violent disorder [34]	..	..	..	..	..	..	..	..	656	640	766	754	947	26
63 Treason felony [34]	0	0	0	0	0	0	0	0	..	..	..	..	..	
64 Riot [34]	4	7	4	2	3	0	2	3	..	..	..	..	..	
65 Violent disorder [34]	2,636	2,457	1,742	1,180	1,022	859	751	696	..	..	..	..	..	
66 Other offences against the State or public order	20,370	31,999	35,935	35,067	37,663	37,572	36,580	32,886	29,990	32,474	36,180	35,490	38,584	9
TOTAL PUBLIC ORDER OFFENCES	191,872	222,581	236,661	218,380	204,289	188,254	173,081	150,858	132,205	134,400	159,478	151,100	193,310	28
15 Concealing an infant death close to birth	6	8	4	8	8	6	9	5	2	2	5	5	3	
24 Exploitation of prostitution [17]	117	153	190	184	173	148	153	110	120	124	152	130	184	42
26 Bigamy	104	101	61	74	64	60	44	31	39	40	47	49	67	
27 Soliciting for prostitution [17]	1,821	1,640	1,290	1,216	1,071	1,190	826	797	883	750	868	786	656	-17
33 Going equipped for stealing, etc.	4,567	4,382	4,253	3,781	3,791	3,647	4,129	3,765	3,473	3,472	3,046	3,173	2,757	-13
33A Making, supplying or possessing articles for use in fraud [35]	..	..	..	..	..	..	..	..	..	2,927	2,467	2,620	2,706	3
38 Profiting from or concealing proceeds of crime [35]	438	1,548	1,961	2,382	2,505	2,609	2,344	1,779	1,427	1,485	1,455	1,509	1,535	2
53H Making or supplying articles for use in fraud [36]	..	..	..	183	611	862	975	1,301	1,384	..	..	..	..	
53J Possession of articles for use in fraud [36]	..	..	..	1,108	1,466	1,564	1,559	1,366	1,287	..	..	..	..	
54 Handling stolen goods	14,157	12,714	11,826	11,335	10,766	9,448	9,184	9,769	8,134	8,526	6,539	7,075	5,566	-21
59 Threat etc. to commit criminal damage	10,066	10,501	7,889	6,318	6,034	5,996	5,916	5,214	4,950	5,790	9,010	7,989	12,077	51
60 Forgery or use of drug prescription	747	693	593	440	446	343	298	361	379	416	418	432	378	-13
61 Other forgery	10,249	10,627	8,479	4,211	4,241	2,526	1,632	2,124	2,984	2,864	2,270	2,316	2,430	5
61A Possession of false documents	..	..	..	2,301	2,646	2,263	1,770	1,378	962	934	973	1,084	1,030	-5
67 Perjury	265	245	197	193	177	184	339	151	134	96	89	88	120	36
68 Libel	0	1	1	0	1	4	..	..	..	..	..	..	..	
69 Offender Management Act offences [37]	..	..	..	..	1	533	518	583	1,024	1,113	1,531	1,418	2,329	64
75 Betting, gaming and lotteries [37]	12	6	13	11	22	21	14	12	11	11	20	18	31	
76 Aiding suicide	6	11	13	9	7	17	7	10	..	..	..	..	..	
78 Immigration offences [37]	550	935	792	661	573	411	445	344	..	..	..	..	..	
79 Perverting the course of justice	11,567	12,712	11,114	9,131	8,396	7,997	6,890	5,698	4,947	5,368	6,295	6,094	6,407	5
80 Absconding from lawful custody	1,362	1,272	979	828	651	557	499	414	482	370	439	459	459	0

21.3 Police recorded crime by offence, year ending March 2005 to year ending December 2015 and percentage change between year ending December 2014 and year ending December 2015

England and Wales

Offence		Apr '04 to Mar '05	Apr '05 to Mar '06	Apr '06 to Mar '07	Apr '07 to Mar '08	Apr '08 to Mar '09	Apr '09 to Mar '10	Apr '10 to Mar '11	Apr '11 to Mar '12	Apr '12 to Mar '13	Apr '13 to Mar '14	Apr '14 to Mar '15	Jan '14 to Dec '14	Jan '15 to Dec '15	% change between years
82	Customs and Revenue offences [37]	30	49	27	10	13	10	3	5	:	:	:	:	:	:
83	Bail offences	202	177	83	25	3	4	6	3	2	3	6	5	37	-
84	Trade descriptions, etc [37]	1,344	1,360	1,353	1,321	1,143	809	486	263	:	:	:	:	:	:
85	Health and Safety offences [37]	15	8	9	8	15	6	2	8	:	:	:	:	:	:
86	Obscene publications, etc and protected sexual material [37]	2,861	2,592	2,378	2,672	2,775	3,215	3,342	3,335	3,506	4,618	7,917	6,395	11,716	83
87	Protection from eviction [37]	70	75	69	81	71	81	73	68	:	:	:	:	:	:
89	Adulteration of food [37]	29	45	32	44	13	4	9	0	:	:	:	:	:	:
91	Public health offences [37,38]	112	128	50	44	115	488	398	289	:	:	:	:	:	:
94	Planning laws [37]	4	5	0	0	1	0	1	1	:	:	:	:	:	:
95	Disclosure, obstruction, false or misleading statements etc	144	368	266	425	506	426	348	363	294	359	322	346	263	-24
96	Wildlife crime [39]	:	:	:	:	:	:	:	:	:	:	29	27	65	:
99	Other indictable or triable-either-way offences [37,40]	2,577	2,197	1,915	1,391	1,735	1,629	1,569	1,589	2,510	2,575	4,865	4,545	6,013	32
802	Dangerous driving	6,669	5,923	5,353	4,725	4,240	3,941	3,475	3,239	3,092	3,152	3,253	3,213	3,773	17
814	Fraud, forgery associated with vehicle driver records	5,420	4,206	3,138	2,164	1,387	1,058	733	606	473	445	382	389	446	15
	TOTAL MISCELLANEOUS CRIMES AGAINST SOCIETY	75,511	74,682	64,328	57,284	55,666	52,053	48,000	44,981	42,499	45,440	52,398	50,165	61,048	22
	TOTAL RECORDED CRIME - ALL OFFENCES EXCLUDING FRAUD [41,42,43]	5,476,771	5,425,691	5,322,377	4,881,140	4,630,383	4,265,036	4,078,475	3,903,581	3,553,168	3,506,545	3,579,649	3,544,169	3,817,829	8
	FRAUD OFFENCES [44]														
51	Fraud by company director [45]	51	626	101	162	815	85	207	45	103	:	:	:	:	:
52	False accounting	541	487	462	251	146	155	108	75	59	:	:	:	:	:
53A	Cheque and credit card fraud (pre Fraud Act 2006) [36]	121,376	87,860	59,011	:	:	:	:	:	:	:	:	:	:	:
53B	Preserved other fraud and repealed fraud offences (pre-Fraud Act 2006) [27,36]	38,761	40,415	45,593	9,984	3,494	3,666	3,342	3,799	3,027	:	:	:	:	:
53C	Fraud by false representation: cheque, plastic card and online bank accounts [26,36]	:	:	:	23,345	26,578	27,148	24,942	22,703	17,873	1	:	:	:	:
53D	Fraud by false representation: other frauds [36]	:	:	:	34,544	38,884	39,626	42,460	44,719	40,325	5	:	-2	-1	:
53E	Fraud by failing to disclose information [36]	:	:	:	265	304	364	339	246	163	:	:	:	:	:
53F	Fraud by abuse of position [36]	:	:	:	675	926	1,160	1,033	1,170	927	1	:	:	:	:
53G	Obtaining services dishonestly [36]	:	:	:	1,880	1,152	1,042	:	:	:	:	:	:	:	:
55	Bankruptcy and insolvency offences	11	93	14	31	15	13	10	11	12	:	:	:	:	:
	TOTAL FRAUD OFFENCES RECORDED BY THE POLICE [36,44]	160,740	129,481	105,181	71,137	72,314	73,259	72,441	72,768	62,489	7	:	-2	-1	:
	FRAUD OFFENCES RECORDED BY ACTION FRAUD [44,46]	:	:	:	:	:	:	:	46,658	117,402	211,221	230,373	224,685	224,683	0
	Fraud offences referred to NFIB by Cifas [46,47,48]	:	:	:	:	:	:	:	235,499	217,369	214,156	257,762	254,843	295,525	16
	Fraud offences referred to NFIB by Financial Fraud Action UK [46,48,49,50]	:	:	:	:	:	:	:	121,478	113,143	96,534	104,982	115,243	97,411	-15
	TOTAL FRAUD OFFENCES	160,740	129,481	105,181	71,137	72,314	73,259	72,441	476,403	510,403	521,918	593,117	594,769	617,618	4
	TOTAL RECORDED CRIME – ALL OFFENCES INCLUDING FRAUD [41]	5,637,511	5,555,172	5,427,558	4,952,277	4,702,697	4,338,295	4,150,916	4,379,984	4,063,571	4,028,463	4,172,766	4,138,938	4,435,447	7

Source: Police recorded crime, Home Office

Police recorded crime data are not designated as National Statistics.

NOTES TO ACCOMPANY TABLE 21.3

1. The National Crime Recording Standard (NCRS) was introduced in April 2002, although some forces adopted NCRS practices before the standard was formally introduced. Figures before and after that date are not directly comparable. The introduction of NCRS led to a rise in recording in year ending March 2003 and, particularly for violent crime, in the following years as forces continued to improve compliance with the new standard.

2. Includes the British Transport Police from year ending March 2003 onwards.

3. The homicide figure for year ending March 2003 includes 172 homicides attributed to Harold Shipman in previous years but coming to light in the official inquiry in 2002.

4. The homicide figure in year ending March 2006 of 764 includes 52 homicide victims of the 7 July London bombings, which also accounted for approximately one-quarter of the total of 920 attempted murders.

5. New offence of 'causing serious injury by dangerous driving' was added to this category in April 2013

6. Offence classifications 5A, 5B and 5C were introduced from 1 April 2008 and replaced classification 5. Classification 5A was influenced by a clarification in recording rules that had the effect of significantly increasing levels of recording in some forces. Classification 5A also included some other offences of endangering life as well as GBH with intent, though GBH with intent was the major part of this category.

7. Offence classifications 5D and 5E were introduced from 1 April 2012 and replaced classification 5A offences. Offence classification 5E was also introduced and replaced the remaining classification 5A offences, 5B, 5C, 6 and 7.

8. Offence classifications 8F, 8G, 8H, 8J and 8K were introduced from 1 April 2008 and had previously been recorded as part of classifications 8A or 8D.

9. Offence classification 8N was introduced from 1 April 2012 and replaced classifications 8F, 8G and 8K. Offence classification 8P was also introduced and replaced classifications 8H and 8J.

10. New offence of 'cause or allow a child or vulnerable adult to suffer serious physical harm' was added to this category in April 2013

11. Offence classifications 3A and 3B were introduced from 1 April 2008 and had previously been recorded as classification 3.

12. Prior to year ending March 2009, the police sent combined figures for harassment (8L, 8M) and public fear, alarm and distress (9A, 9B) offences. For the years ending March 2003 to March 2008, figures for these offence groups are estimated based upon the proportionate split between the offences in year ending March 2009. Stalking (8Q) was introduced as a separate crime classification in April 2014, following the introduction of the Protection of Freedoms Act 2012 section 111. Before this, stalking offences were included within harassment offences (8L).

13. Prior to year ending March 2009, the police sent combined figures for harassment (8L, 8M) and public fear, alarm and distress (9A, 9B) offences. For the years ending March 2003 to March 2008, figures for these offence groups are estimated based upon the proportionate split between the offences in year ending March 2009.

14. Changes in the Home Office Counting Rules (HOCR), implemented in April 2015, have resulted in the recording of two additional harassment offences (Disclosure of private sexual photographs and flims with the intent to cause distress or anxiety' and 'Sending letters with intent to cause distress or anxiety'; the latter includes any form of electronic communication), not previously counted as notifiable offences under the headline category of violence without injury. There is no available back-series for these additional notifiable offences.

15. Offence classification 11A was introduced from 1 April 2012 and replaced classifications 11 and 12.

16. Modern Slavery (106) was introduced as a separate crime classification in April 2015. During April-July 2015 this classification included all of the offences that were previously recorded under category 72 (Trafficking for sexual exploitation).

17. The Sexual Offences Act 2003, introduced in May 2004, altered the definition and coverage of sexual offences.

18. Prior to year ending March 2010, a small number of offences continued to be recorded relating to offences repealed by the Sexual Offences Act 2003. While these may have been legitimately recorded for offences committed prior to May 2004 it is also possible that some may have been recorded in these old categories in error, so any changes based on small numbers should be interpreted with caution.

19. The increase in year ending March 2006 was accounted for by a large number of offences that were dealt with by the Norfolk Constabulary.

20. In April 2015 offence classification 71 was renamed 'Abuse of children through sexual exploitation'. This offence classification was previously named 'Abuse of children through prostitution and pornography'

21. This offence consists solely of the former offence of 'Indecent Exposure' for years prior to year ending March 2005. This became the offence of 'Exposure' and was included within 'Other miscellaneous sexual offences' from May 2004.

22. Offence classification 88B was split into 88C–E with effect from year ending March 2009. Since that time offences of exposure have been recorded as classification 88E.

23. Due to an issue with Home Office database mapping, data on 'aggravated vehicle offences' (code 37.2) were not collected from Derbyshire and West Mercia police forces from April 2015 onwards. Therefore the 'aggravated vehicle offences' shown for these forces were those recorded during January to March 2015 only, meaning that the total number of vehicle offences recorded by these forces in the year ending December 2015 is around 1% too low. This is expected to be resolved by the next crime statistics publication. The impact at national level is very small.

24. Includes tampering with a motor vehicle.

25. The large increase in year ending March 2007 was due to the recording of threats made against shareholders of GlaxoSmithKline by animal rights activists.

26. Following a change in the implementation of the Fraud Act 2006, offences involving theft from an automatic machine using a plastic card are now regarded as false representation and recorded under classification 53C.

27. Offence classification 49A was introduced as a separate theft classification in year ending March 2014. Before this, it was recorded under the fraud offence classification 53B. Data for 49A are provided for all years following a special request to forces. In some cases, these have been estimated where forces were unable to provide data.

28. Offence classifications 56A and 56B were introduced from 1 April 2008 and had previously been recorded as classification 56.

29. Offence classifications 58E-58H were amalgamated on 1 April 2012 to form classification 58J.

30. Possession of controlled drugs offences were split with effect from April 2004 into possession of cannabis and possession of drugs other than cannabis.

NOTES TO ACCOMPANY TABLE 21.3

31. Offence classifications 10A, 10C and 10D were introduced from 1 April 2008 and had previously been recorded as classification 8B.

32. Offence classification 10B was introduced from 1 April 2008. Possession of firearms offences are those offences where the weapon has not been used during the commission of another offence.

33. These are offences under the Firearms Act 1968 and other Firearms Acts connected with licensing and certification of firearms. Such offences are not included in the firearms offences statistics.

34. Offence classifications 62-65 were amalgamated on 1 April 2012 to form classification 62A.

35. These offences were added to the series from 1 April 2003.

36. New offences were introduced under the Fraud Act 2006, which came into force on 15 January 2007.

37. Offence classifications 68, 75, 78, 82, 84, 85, 87, 89, 91 and 94 were included with classification 99 with effect from 1 April 2012.

38. The large increase in this offence from year ending March 2009 is mainly due to the recording of fly-tipping by some forces following advice that this offence is notifiable.

39. Wildlife crime (96) was introduced as a separate crime classification in April 2014. This saw a number of offences that were previously recorded under "Other notifiable offences" (99) brought together.

40. Due to the introduction of fly-tipping as an offence under "Other notifiable offences" (99) in April 2014, percentage changes may appear high in certain publications.

41. Some forces have revised their data and totals may therefore not agree with those previously published.

42. Following a system change at Norfolk constabulary in October 2015 a range of data reliability issues have been identified. At a national level the impact of this is small. The constabulary is expected to resolve these issues and revise data for the next quarterly publication.

43. Following a system change at Suffolk constabulary in October 2015 a range of data reliability issues have been identified, including the fact that some of the data submitted by the force is known to be duplicated. For instance, around 3% of offences submitted by Suffolk for October to December are estimated to be duplicates. In particular, 20% of sexual offences recorded between October to December 2015 are estimated to be duplicates. At a national level the impact of this is small. The constabulary is expected to resolve these issues and provide revised data during 2016/17.

44. Action Fraud have taken over the recording of fraud offences on behalf of individual police forces. This process began in April 2011 and was rolled out to all police forces by March 2013. Due to this change caution should be applied when comparing data over this transitional period and with earlier years. There were 7 cases in year ending March 2014 where police forces recorded a fraud offence after the transfer of responsibility to Action Fraud. These cases may be revised in future quarters. See the User Guide for more details including information on transfer date to Action Fraud for each force.

45. The large increase in this offence in year ending March 2006 was due to one large-scale fraud recorded by the Cambridgeshire Constabulary. The increase in year ending March 2008 was due to a fraud recorded by North Yorkshire Police. The large increase in year ending March 2009 was due to large-scale frauds recorded by Gwent Police, Leicestershire Constabulary and the Metropolitan Police. The increase in year ending March 2011 was due to a large-scale fraud recorded by North Yorkshire Police.

46. It is possible that there may be some double or triple counting between Action Fraud, Cifas and FFA UK. Experts believe this duplication to be so small as to have an insignificant effect on crime trends, but there is currently no simple cross-referencing method within NFIB to detect the scale of it. Section 5.4 of the User Guide provides more information.

47. Cifas is a UK-wide fraud prevention service representing around 350 organisations from the public and private sectors. These organisations mainly share data on confirmed cases of fraud, particularly application, identity and first party frauds, via the Cifas National Fraud Database. Data supplied by Cifas to the National Fraud Intelligence Bureau (NFIB) are recorded in line with the Home Office Counting Rules (HOCR) for recorded crime.

48. Both sets of industry data from Cifas and FFA UK relate only to fraud affecting those organisations that are part of the respective membership networks. While membership of Cifas and FFA UK has remained fairly stable over the last few years, it is possible that coverage could change as new members join or previous members withdraw, which could impact on overall figures for fraud reported. Prior to year ending March 2012, fraud cases for these organisations were not sent to the NFIB.

49. Financial Fraud Action UK (FFA UK) is responsible for coordinating activities on fraud prevention in the UK payments industry. FFA UK collates information relating to cheque, plastic card and online bank accounts via its Fraud Intelligence Sharing System (FISS) database, and this is in turn provided to NFIB. FISS is an intelligence tool rather than a fraud reporting tool, and its main purpose is to share actionable intelligence about the criminals or entities relating to fraud offences rather than count the numbers of victims of fraud. As a result, the number of cases presented in Table A4 is considerably less than the total number reported to FFA UK by its members. Comprehensive statistics on these fraud types are published twice yearly by FFA UK.

50. In July 2015 the company that was contracted to provide the Action Fraud call centre service went into administration. This led to an immediate downscaling of the call centre operation which is likely to have had had an effect on the volume of frauds recorded by Action Fraud during July, August and September 2015.

- Indicates that data are not reported because the base number of offences is less than 50.

21.4 Persons[1] sentenced at all courts, by type of sentence and offence group, 2005 to 2014[2][3]

England and Wales

Number of persons sentenced and ACSL

Year ending and type of sentence	Violence against the person	Sexual offences	Robbery	Theft Offences	Criminal damage and arson	Drug offences	Possession of weapons	Public order offences	Miscellaneous crimes against society	Fraud offences	All indictable offences	Summary non-motoring	Summary motoring	All summary offences	All offences
2005 All sentenced	**28,873**	**4,719**	**7,139**	**119,877**	**41,817**	**38,898**	**14,685**	**8,814**	**61,221**	**13,019**	**339,062**	**473,591**	**660,622**	**1,134,213**	**1,473,275**
Immediate custody	10,996	2,689	4,407	28,527	2,102	7,783	2,654	2,697	13,154	2,643	77,652	10,714	12,870	23,584	101,236
Suspended sentence	1,078	115	60	1,765	186	516	356	270	876	499	5,721	1,405	2,540	3,945	9,666
Community sentence	13,057	1,438	2,539	48,754	15,480	9,693	6,990	4,562	14,961	5,980	123,454	46,299	34,494	80,793	204,247
Fine[5]	1,114	178	21	16,180	7,866	13,539	2,149	609	21,000	1,466	64,122	367,677	584,409	952,086	1,016,208
Absolute discharge	79	11	7	679	558	370	110	34	909	31	2,788	3,429	6,779	10,208	12,996
Conditional discharge	1,330	196	17	20,923	11,895	6,400	2,217	494	4,657	2,212	50,341	33,898	8,431	42,329	92,670
Compensation	488	10	12	1,138	3,014	7		35	73	103	4,885	2,048	3,477	5,525	10,410
Otherwise dealt with[6]	731	82	76	1,911	716	590	204	113	5,591	85	10,099	8,121	7,622	15,743	25,842
Average custodial sentence (months)[7]	20.8	41.6	35.0	8.5	9.4	35.8	11.7	10.6	6.9	11.2	15.5	2.9	3.4	3.2	12.6
2006 All sentenced	**29,798**	**4,880**	**8,169**	**116,224**	**42,015**	**39,478**	**14,639**	**8,761**	**57,153**	**13,016**	**334,133**	**461,149**	**617,564**	**1,078,713**	**1,412,846**
Immediate custody	10,479	2,787	4,802	27,502	2,312	7,532	2,667	2,322	12,354	2,260	75,017	11,082	9,914	20,996	96,013
Suspended sentence	4,449	290	264	6,744	699	1,848	1,333	1,207	3,043	1,376	21,253	5,586	6,669	12,255	33,508
Community sentence	11,198	1,332	2,957	44,640	16,194	9,127	6,866	4,178	13,101	5,332	114,925	47,612	28,281	75,893	190,818
Fine[5]	999	164	13	13,565	6,961	13,271	1,590	478	18,005	1,411	56,457	349,087	548,556	897,643	954,100
Absolute discharge	53	17	7	736	590	334	88	20	838	32	2,715	3,176	5,858	9,034	11,749
Conditional discharge	1,229	139	26	19,065	11,369	6,532	1,851	390	4,297	2,349	47,247	32,764	7,340	40,104	87,351
Compensation	593	14	23	1,331	2,922	4	4	59	68	122	5,140	2,561	3,922	6,483	11,623
Otherwise dealt with[6]	798	137	77	2,641	968	830	240	107	5,447	134	11,379	9,281	7,024	16,305	27,684
Average custodial sentence (months)[7]	19.5	41.1	32.3	8.4	7.5	33.8	11.2	10.3	7.2	11.9	15.0	2.9	3.4	3.1	12.4
2007 All Sentenced	**30,161**	**4,986**	**8,495**	**124,143**	**43,720**	**44,500**	**14,659**	**9,112**	**52,083**	**13,820**	**346,046**	**455,027**	**605,715**	**1,060,742**	**1,406,788**
Immediate custody	10,615	2,777	5,095	27,657	2,335	8,186	2,758	2,357	12,120	1,998	75,575	11,739	7,892	19,631	95,206
Suspended sentence	5,928	423	444	8,483	878	2,678	1,509	1,816	3,662	1,993	27,822	6,698	6,168	12,866	40,688
Community sentence	10,127	1,359	2,832	48,091	17,151	10,296	6,884	3,839	12,045	5,384	118,646	51,684	26,094	77,778	196,424
Fine[5]	1,004	130	6	14,143	6,769	14,190	1,330	458	14,794	1,485	54,336	336,127	543,354	879,481	933,817
Absolute discharge	58	11	2	826	560	379	81	31	738	28	2,716	3,109	5,161	8,270	10,986
Conditional discharge	1,145	157	23	21,065	11,866	7,825	1,826	389	4,627	2,625	51,555	36,285	6,171	42,456	94,011
Compensation	480	20	13	1,506	3,444	7	6	54	94	119	5,756	2,367	3,965	6,332	12,088
Otherwise dealt with[6]	804	109	75	2,372	717	939	265	168	4,003	188	9,640	7,018	6,910	13,928	23,568
Average custodial sentence (months)[7]	19.7	43.2	31.3	8.0	7.3	31.9	11.9	10.5	7.4	11.4	14.9	2.8	3.3	3.0	12.4
2008[4] All sentenced	**29,147**	**5,049**	**8,862**	**129,829**	**42,163**	**52,909**	**14,997**	**8,588**	**46,301**	**13,416**	**350,894**	**456,498**	**546,545**	**1,003,043**	**1,353,937**
Immediate custody	10,897	2,952	4,772	29,675	2,315	9,488	3,406	2,382	12,307	2,178	80,695	12,452	6,378	18,830	99,525
Suspended sentence	5,943	406	452	8,539	832	2,958	1,843	1,908	3,951	2,249	29,073	7,078	5,000	12,078	41,151
Community sentence	9,553	1,360	3,470	48,739	16,349	12,273	6,891	3,452	10,725	4,801	116,975	51,495	21,702	73,197	190,172
Fine[5]	832	89	33	14,273	6,749	17,674	1,131	403	11,942	1,571	54,670	336,911	490,923	827,834	882,504
Absolute discharge	54	7	4	727	499	382	76	19	538	20	2,324	2,850	4,505	7,355	9,679
Conditional discharge	881	125	30	21,481	11,211	8,099	1,318	281	3,872	2,242	49,533	33,562	4,553	38,115	87,648
Compensation	337	7	26	1,229	3,070	2	2	19	81	109	4,869	1,798	3,232	5,030	9,899
Otherwise dealt with[6]	650	103	75	5,166	1,138	2,033	330	124	2,885	246	12,755	10,352	10,252	20,604	33,359
Average custodial sentence (months)[7]	20.6	44.5	32.5	8.2	7.6	32.7	13.3	11.2	7.8	13.2	15.7	2.8	3.2	2.9	13.3
2009 All sentenced	**30,493**	**5,028**	**8,664**	**130,559**	**40,409**	**56,656**	**15,368**	**16,921**	**43,746**	**14,686**	**362,530**	**477,383**	**558,365**	**1,035,748**	**1,398,278**
Immediate custody	11,530	2,940	5,155	28,795	2,258	9,426	3,479	5,147	10,583	2,654	81,967	12,996	5,268	18,264	100,231
Suspended sentence	6,385	402	476	8,854	854	3,119	2,479	2,586	4,083	2,586	31,824	8,277	5,056	13,333	45,157
Community sentence	9,937	1,388	2,915	49,969	16,788	13,657	6,943	5,984	10,244	5,522	123,347	52,468	20,162	72,630	195,977
Fine[5]	909	84	8	15,753	6,799	20,993	1,089	1,715	12,396	1,663	61,409	362,385	513,963	876,348	937,757
Absolute discharge	39	8	5	389	389	353	56	134	421	31	1,992	2,615	4,292	6,907	8,899
Conditional discharge	839	86	15	22,644	10,456	7,207	956	802	3,169	2,053	48,227	32,027	3,630	35,657	83,884
Compensation	280	6	9	1,099	2,317	-	-	18	50	97	3,876	1,399	2,313	3,712	7,588
Otherwise dealt with[6]	574	114	81	2,889	548	1,901	366	535	2,800	80	9,888	5,216	3,681	8,897	18,785
Average custodial sentence (months)[7]	21.0	49.3	33.6	8.9	8.9	32.1	12.7	7.2	8.2	12.2	16.1	2.7	3.1	2.8	13.7
2010 All sentenced	**32,522**	**5,720**	**8,514**	**140,177**	**39,509**	**61,435**	**13,259**	**19,303**	**46,313**	**15,481**	**382,233**	**457,534**	**517,833**	**975,367**	**1,357,600**
Immediate custody	11,743	3,259	4,946	31,360	2,341	9,693	2,974	5,470	10,225	2,657	84,668	12,905	3,940	16,845	101,513
Suspended sentence	7,073	450	505	9,910	882	3,820	2,078	3,012	4,301	2,814	34,845	8,891	4,382	13,273	48,118
Community sentence	10,460	1,641	2,768	49,976	14,862	13,418	5,897	6,494	10,296	6,031	121,843	51,387	16,103	67,490	189,333

21.4 Persons[1] sentenced at all courts, by type of sentence and offence group, 2005 to 2014[2][3]

England and Wales

Number of persons sentenced and ACSL

Year ending and type of sentence	Violence against the person	Sexual offences	Robbery	Theft Offences	Criminal damage and arson	Drug offences	Possession of weapons	Public order offences	Miscellaneous crimes against society	Fraud offences	All indictable offences	Summary non-motoring	Summary motoring	All summary offences	All offences
Fine[5]	952	106	4	16,912	6,320	23,354	1,066	2,166	12,434	1,807	65,121	337,966	483,234	821,200	886,321
Absolute discharge	41	7	4	591	436	425	53	179	465	21	2,222	2,522	4,068	6,590	8,812
Conditional discharge	1,023	127	13	24,650	10,883	8,526	903	976	3,400	1,917	52,418	34,982	3,033	38,015	90,433
Compensation	562	8	196	1,834	2,810	3	2	58	69	100	5,642	2,121	192	2,313	7,955
Otherwise dealt with[6]	668	122	78	4,944	975	2,196	286	948	5,123	134	15,474	6,760	2,881	9,641	25,115
Average custodial sentence (months)[7]	20.8	49.0	34.5	8.6	8.5	30.7	13.2	7.1	8.2	13.4	15.9	2.6	3.1	2.7	13.7
2011 All sentenced	**30,564**	**5,928**	**9,334**	**141,556**	**36,586**	**61,094**	**12,600**	**17,885**	**43,792**	**14,944**	**374,283**	**460,771**	**470,616**	**931,387**	**1,305,670**
Immediate custody	12,135	3,413	5,585	34,157	2,487	9,788	3,212	5,498	10,112	2,948	89,335	13,384	3,451	16,835	106,170
Suspended sentence	6,415	503	541	10,497	933	4,205	2,088	2,634	4,322	3,001	35,139	8,795	4,219	13,014	48,153
Community sentence	8,814	1,646	2,937	48,833	13,692	12,724	5,246	5,592	9,734	5,457	114,675	48,373	14,555	62,928	177,603
Fine[5]	1,140	120	1	17,069	5,990	23,317	956	2,154	11,361	1,617	63,725	346,435	439,676	786,111	849,836
Absolute discharge	42	8	1	574	335	428	48	157	487	18	2,098	2,430	3,624	6,054	8,152
Conditional discharge	990	89	12	24,197	9,854	8,345	778	893	3,160	1,689	50,007	33,570	2,722	36,292	86,299
Compensation	415	10	173	1,692	2,383	1	5	54	72	91	4,896	1,729	155	1,884	6,780
Otherwise dealt with[6]	613	139	84	4,537	912	2,286	267	903	4,544	123	14,408	6,055	2,214	8,269	22,677
Average custodial sentence (months)[7]	21.8	53.5	35.4	9.0	9.0	30.7	13.0	7.3	8.8	14.9	16.5	2.6	3.1	2.7	14.3
2012 All sentenced	**26,325**	**5,715**	**8,342**	**128,100**	**32,109**	**57,601**	**10,309**	**16,190**	**37,878**	**12,284**	**334,853**	**440,659**	**447,720**	**888,379**	**1,223,232**
Immediate custody	11,341	3,397	5,002	32,802	2,156	9,011	2,663	5,001	8,640	2,629	82,642	12,390	3,012	15,402	98,044
Suspended sentence	5,582	477	555	9,863	785	4,215	1,798	2,299	4,114	2,843	32,531	8,361	3,751	12,112	44,643
Community sentence	6,434	1,512	2,583	40,541	11,079	11,513	4,150	4,761	8,133	4,136	94,842	43,523	12,818	56,341	151,183
Fine[5]	1,305	101	1	15,976	5,746	21,344	816	2,244	10,183	1,218	58,934	337,263	420,629	757,892	816,826
Absolute discharge	59	8	2	533	300	407	36	157	336	23	1,861	2,334	3,301	5,635	7,496
Conditional discharge	929	92	17	22,297	9,119	8,816	590	850	2,793	1,216	46,719	30,802	2,344	33,146	79,865
Compensation	203	18	74	2,490	2,220	4	3	42	65	122	5,241	1,727	173	1,900	7,141
Otherwise dealt with[6]	472	110	108	3,598	704	2,291	253	836	3,614	97	12,083	4,259	1,692	5,951	18,034
Average custodial sentence (months)[7]	23.1	54.5	35.8	9.1	10.3	28.7	12.9	7.4	9.1	14.6	16.7	2.7	3.1	2.8	14.5
2013 All sentenced	**24,279**	**5,634**	**6,768**	**123,114**	**29,296**	**56,323**	**10,045**	**16,240**	**34,527**	**12,140**	**318,366**	**408,523**	**443,796**	**852,319**	**1,170,685**
Immediate custody	10,384	3,360	4,298	31,995	1,905	9,024	2,631	4,772	8,525	2,535	79,429	10,848	2,689	13,537	92,966
Suspended sentence	5,582	581	499	11,293	875	5,173	2,116	2,537	4,527	3,094	36,277	8,810	3,678	12,488	48,765
Community sentence	5,312	1,354	1,838	32,879	9,130	9,388	3,612	4,309	6,685	3,971	78,478	37,388	10,669	48,057	126,535
Fine[5]	1,376	125	29	16,550	5,663	20,712	846	2,828	9,269	1,199	58,597	315,132	419,672	734,804	793,401
Absolute discharge	60	5	1	582	235	346	33	116	355	13	1,746	2,147	3,107	5,254	7,000
Conditional discharge	874	91	19	21,675	8,441	9,396	500	973	2,380	1,092	45,441	28,468	1,934	30,402	75,843
Compensation	194	19	8	3,987	2,436	4	2	95	73	141	6,959	2,236	127	2,363	9,322
Otherwise dealt with[6]	497	99	76	4,153	611	2,280	305	610	2,713	95	11,439	3,494	1,920	5,414	16,853
Average custodial sentence (months)[7]	24.6	59.1	39.6	9.1	10.9	31.2	13.3	7.5	9.6	14.9	17.7	2.8	3.1	2.8	15.5
2014 All sentenced	**26,257**	**6,233**	**5,579**	**117,627**	**27,796**	**51,297**	**10,085**	**17,070**	**31,922**	**13,388**	**307,254**	**430,582**	**471,366**	**901,948**	**1,209,202**
Immediate custody	11,130	3,687	3,684	30,315	1,894	8,756	2,659	4,820	8,056	2,298	77,299	11,407	2,607	14,014	91,313
Suspended sentence	6,480	721	440	12,122	913	5,525	2,327	3,037	4,839	3,357	39,761	9,550	3,668	13,218	52,979
Community sentence	5,245	1,497	1,319	26,291	8,098	7,154	3,353	4,024	5,765	4,443	67,189	35,774	9,675	45,449	112,638
Fine[5]	1,561	119	2	17,717	5,779	19,632	860	3,081	8,449	1,526	58,726	338,312	449,902	788,214	846,940
Absolute discharge	68	7	3	523	257	321	37	110	293	20	1,639	1,684	2,439	4,123	5,762
Conditional discharge	907	87	13	21,272	7,884	8,223	493	1,060	1,825	1,463	43,227	27,774	1,431	29,205	72,432
Compensation	130	5	7	2,505	2,052	-	-	44	48	93	4,884	1,269	76	1,345	6,229
Otherwise dealt with[6]	736	110	111	6,882	919	1,686	356	894	2,647	188	14,529	4,812	1,568	6,380	20,909
Average custodial sentence (months)[7]	23.4	62.0	40.8	9.0	8.9	32.1	12.8	6.7	10.2	15.9	18.0	2.7	3.0	2.7	15.6

(1) Excludes companies.
(2) Data relate to persons for whom these offences were the principal offences for which they were dealt with. When a defendant has been found guilty of two or more offences it is the offence for which the heaviest penalty is imposed. Where the same disposal is imposed for two or more offences, the offence selected is the offence for which the statutory maximum penalty is the most severe.
(3) Data are given on a principal disposal basis - i.e. reporting the most severe sentence for the principal offence.
(4) Excludes data for Cardiff magistrates' court for April, July and August 2008.
(5) Due to limitations in data supply, fine data from magistrates' courts has been omitted from our data since 2009 of values between £10,000 and £99,999.
(6) Including restriction orders, hospital orders, guardianship orders, police cells, and other disposals.
(7) Excludes life and indeterminate sentences

Source: Ministry of Justice

21.5 Persons cautioned for summary offences (excluding motoring) by offence, sex and age, 2014

	Ages					
Offence	10-11	12-14	15-17	18-20	21+	Total
104 Assaulting, resisting or obstructing a constable or designated officer in execution of duty	**10**	**79**	**344**	**572**	**1,840**	**2,845**
Female	5	42	150	191	759	1,147
Male	5	37	194	381	1,081	1,698
Unstated	0	0	0	0	0	0
105 Common assault and battery	**194**	**1,202**	**2,109**	**4,007**	**29,409**	**36,921**
Female	42	411	709	1,144	7,338	9,644
Male	152	791	1,400	2,863	22,071	27,277
Unstated	0	0	0	0	0	0
106 Betting or Gaming Offence	**0**	**0**	**0**	**8**	**39**	**47**
Female	0	0	0	0	2	2
Male	0	0	0	8	37	45
Unstated	0	0	0	0	0	0
107 Brothel Keeping	**0**	**0**	**0**	**5**	**13**	**18**
Female	0	0	0	3	11	14
Male	0	0	0	2	2	4
108 Cruelty to Animal	**0**	**0**	**0**	**0**	**23**	**23**
Female	0	0	0	0	6	6
Male	0	0	0	0	17	17
Other	0	0	0	0	0	0
Unstated	0	0	0	0	0	0
111A Offences under Dangerous Dogs Acts - summary	**0**	**0**	**0**	**1**	**36**	**37**
Female	0	0	0	0	16	16
Male	0	0	0	1	20	21
Unstated	0	0	0	0	0	0
111B Other offences relating to dogs	**0**	**0**	**0**	**0**	**1**	**1**
Female	0	0	0	0	1	1
Male	0	0	0	0	0	0
Unstated	0	0	0	0	0	0
112A Education Acts - Truancy	**0**	**0**	**0**	**0**	**0**	**0**
Female	0	0	0	0	0	0
Male	0	0	0	0	0	0
Unstated	0	0	0	0	0	0
112B Education Acts - Other	**0**	**2**	**2**	**0**	**1**	**5**
Female	0	0	0	0	0	0
Male	0	2	2	0	1	5
Unstated	0	0	0	0	0	0
115 Firearms Acts - summary offences	**1**	**11**	**13**	**46**	**138**	**209**
Female	0	1	0	0	2	3
Male	1	10	13	46	136	206
Unstated	0	0	0	0	0	0
118 Night Poaching	**0**	**0**	**0**	**0**	**5**	**5**
Male	0	0	0	0	5	5
119 Day Poaching	**0**	**3**	**3**	**1**	**4**	**11**
Male	0	3	3	1	4	11
121B Other offences related to Game Law	**0**	**0**	**0**	**0**	**2**	**2**
Male	0	0	0	0	2	2
122 Obstruction (of highways, etc, other than by vehicle	**0**	**0**	**0**	**1**	**0**	**1**
Female	0	0	0	0	0	0
Male	0	0	0	1	0	1
Other	0	0	0	0	0	0
Unstated	0	0	0	0	0	0
123 Nuisance (other than by vehicle)	**0**	**1**	**0**	**0**	**1**	**2**
Male	0	1	0	0	1	2
Other	0	0	0	0	0	0
Unstated	0	0	0	0	0	0
125A Causing intentional harassment, alarm or distress - summary	**6**	**42**	**117**	**136**	**816**	**1,117**
Female	0	8	22	28	177	235
Male	6	34	95	108	639	882
Unstated	0	0	0	0	0	0
125B Causing fear or provocation of violence - summary	**11**	**38**	**206**	**670**	**2,557**	**3,482**
Female	3	6	39	81	408	537
Male	8	32	167	589	2,149	2,945
Unstated	0	0	0	0	0	0

21.5 Persons cautioned for summary offences (excluding motoring) by offence, sex and age, 2014

Offence	Ages					Total
	10-11	12-14	15-17	18-20	21+	
125C Causing harassment, alarm or distress - summary	9	98	399	414	1,840	2,760
Female	1	31	95	66	423	616
Male	8	67	304	348	1,417	2,144
Unstated	0	0	0	0	0	0
125D Racially or religiously aggravated harassment, alarm or distress - summary	0	2	9	7	63	81
Female	0	0	4	3	18	25
Male	0	2	5	4	45	56
Unstated	0	0	0	0	0	0
125E Public Order Act 1986 - other offences	0	2	18	25	67	112
Female	0	0	1	1	4	6
Male	0	2	17	24	63	106
Other	0	0	0	0	0	0
Unstated	0	0	0	0	0	0
126 Interference with Motor Vehicles	0	9	29	17	47	102
Female	0	0	1	3	4	8
Male	0	9	28	14	43	94
Unstated	0	0	0	0	0	0
130 Theft of a motor vehicle (excl. aggravated vehicle taking) - summary (MOT)	9	64	271	186	265	795
Female	2	7	28	20	34	91
Male	7	57	243	166	231	704
Unstated	0	0	0	0	0	0
137 Pedal cycle - Careless driving	0	0	0	0	0	0
Female	0	0	0	0	0	0
Male	0	0	0	0	0	0
Unstated	0	0	0	0	0	0
137 Pedal cycle - Neglect of traffic directions	0	0	0	0	1	1
Female	0	0	0	0	0	0
Male	0	0	0	0	0	0
Unstated	0	0	0	0	1	1
137 Pedal cycle - Other offences	1	3	17	11	15	47
Female	0	0	2	0	0	2
Male	1	3	15	11	15	45
Unstated	0	0	0	0	0	0
137 Pedal cycle - Reckless and dangerous driving	0	0	0	0	0	0
Male	0	0	0	0	0	0
137 Pedal cycle - Riding on footpath	0	0	2	0	0	2
Female	0	0	0	0	0	0
Male	0	0	2	0	0	2
Unstated	0	0	0	0	0	0
138 Offences involving impersonation, giving false or misleading information, failing to supply information, etc	0	0	1	2	5	8
Female	0	0	0	1	1	2
Male	0	0	1	1	4	6
Unstated	0	0	0	0	0	0
140 Drunkenness, simple	0	0	6	9	140	155
Female	0	0	0	0	20	20
Male	0	0	6	9	120	135
Unstated	0	0	0	0	0	0
141 Drunkenness, with aggravation - disorderly in a public place	12	17	402	570	2,661	3,662
Female	3	8	106	129	567	813
Male	9	9	296	441	2,094	2,849
Unstated	0	0	0	0	0	0
141 Drunkenness, with aggravation - other	1	0	0	3	204	208
Female	0	0	0	3	148	151
Male	1	0	0	0	56	57
Unstated	0	0	0	0	0	0
142 Other offences by licenced persons	0	0	0	0	0	0
Male	0	0	0	0	0	0
Other	0	0	0	0	0	0
Unstated	0	0	0	0	0	0

21.5 Persons cautioned for summary offences (excluding motoring) by offence, sex and age, 2014

Offence	Ages					Total
	10-11	12-14	15-17	18-20	21+	
142A Responsible person allowing individual aged under 18 to sell or supply alcohol	**0**	**0**	**0**	**0**	**1**	**1**
Male	0	0	0	0	1	1
142B Remain on / enter premises in contravention of a closure notice or similar direction	**0**	**0**	**0**	**0**	**0**	**0**
Female	0	0	0	0	0	0
Male	0	0	0	0	0	0
Unstated	0	0	0	0	0	0
143A Sale of alcohol to a person aged under 18	**0**	**0**	**0**	**2**	**19**	**21**
Female	0	0	0	1	6	7
Male	0	0	0	1	13	14
Other	0	0	0	0	0	0
Unstated	0	0	0	0	0	0
143B Buying, attempting to buy or delivering alcohol to persons aged under 18	**0**	**0**	**0**	**3**	**3**	**6**
Male	0	0	0	3	3	6
143C Purchase of alcohol by a person aged under 18	**0**	**0**	**0**	**0**	**0**	**0**
Male	0	0	0	0	0	0
143D Sale of alcohol to, or obtaining alcohol for a person who is drunk	**0**	**0**	**0**	**0**	**1**	**1**
Female	0	0	0	0	0	0
Male	0	0	0	0	1	1
143E Other offences related to the sale of alcohol and licensed premises	**0**	**0**	**2**	**31**	**136**	**169**
Female	0	0	0	0	16	16
Male	0	0	2	31	120	153
Other	0	0	0	0	0	0
Unstated	0	0	0	0	0	0
149 Summary Criminal or Malicious Damage Offence	**146**	**855**	**1,561**	**2,268**	**9,763**	**14,593**
Female	38	155	270	311	1,759	2,533
Male	108	700	1,291	1,957	8,004	12,060
Unstated	0	0	0	0	0	0
151 Benefit fraud offences - summary	**0**	**0**	**1**	**2**	**5**	**8**
Female	0	0	0	1	4	5
Male	0	0	1	1	1	3
Other	0	0	0	0	0	0
Unstated	0	0	0	0	0	0
153-155 Offences against Military Law - Army, Navy and Air Force	**0**	**0**	**2**	**1**	**3**	**6**
Female	0	0	0	0	0	0
Male	0	0	2	1	3	6
Other	0	0	0	0	0	0
Unstated	0	0	0	0	0	0
160 Pedlars Act - Acting without certificate, refusal to produce certificate, etc	**0**	**0**	**0**	**2**	**9**	**11**
Female	0	0	0	0	2	2
Male	0	0	0	2	7	9
Unstated	0	0	0	0	0	0
162 Disorderly Behaviour	**0**	**2**	**2**	**2**	**9**	**15**
Female	0	0	2	0	4	6
Male	0	2	0	2	5	9
Other	0	0	0	0	0	0
Unstated	0	0	0	0	0	0
166 Offence by Prostitute	**0**	**0**	**0**	**13**	**60**	**73**
Female	0	0	0	13	51	64
Male	0	0	0	0	9	9
167 Aiding, etc. Offence by Prostitute	**1**	**3**	**1**	**26**	**436**	**467**
Female	0	1	0	0	1	2
Male	1	2	1	26	435	465
Unstated	0	0	0	0	0	0
168 Public Health Offence	**0**	**0**	**0**	**1**	**3**	**4**
Female	0	0	0	0	0	0
Male	0	0	0	1	3	4
Other	0	0	0	0	0	0
Unstated	0	0	0	0	0	0

21.5 Persons cautioned for summary offences (excluding motoring) by offence, sex and age, 2014

Offence	Ages					
	10-11	12-14	15-17	18-20	21+	Total
169A Travelling by railway without paying correct fare, failing to show ticket, failing to give name and address, etc	0	8	63	236	589	896
Female	0	3	10	35	57	105
Male	0	5	53	201	532	791
Unstated	0	0	0	0	0	0
169B Other railway offences	1	7	12	13	81	114
Female	0	0	1	5	12	18
Male	1	7	11	8	69	96
Other	0	0	0	0	0	0
Unstated	0	0	0	0	0	0
173 Stage Carriage or Public Service Vehicle Offence	0	0	1	2	313	316
Female	0	0	0	0	0	0
Male	0	0	1	2	313	316
Other	0	0	0	0	0	0
Unstated	0	0	0	0	0	0
175 Sexual Offences- Miscellaneous	0	0	0	1	16	17
Male	0	0	0	1	16	17
182 Begging	0	0	1	24	306	331
Female	0	0	0	11	82	93
Male	0	0	1	13	224	238
Unstated	0	0	0	0	0	0
183 Sleeping Out	0	0	0	1	0	1
Female	0	0	0	0	0	0
Male	0	0	0	1	0	1
185 Being on enclosed premises for an unlawful purpose	2	10	17	17	48	94
Female	1	1	1	0	3	6
Male	1	9	16	17	45	88
193 Drug offences - summary	0	1	1	2	11	15
Female	0	0	0	0	2	2
Male	0	1	1	2	9	13
Unstated	0	0	0	0	0	0
194 Immigration Offence	0	0	0	0	8	8
Female	0	0	0	0	1	1
Male	0	0	0	0	7	7
Unstated	0	0	0	0	0	0
Other summary non-motoring offences	0	6	9	11	118	144
Female	0	1	0	3	15	19
Male	0	5	9	8	103	125
Other	0	0	0	0	0	0
Unstated	0	0	0	0	0	0

Source: Ministry of Juctice

CJS Outcomes by Offence 2004 to 2014: Pivot Table Analytical Tool for England and Wales

21.6a Offenders[1] found guilty at all courts by offence group, sex and age group, 12 months ending September 2014

England and Wales   Number of offenders (thousands)

Offence group	All offenders[1]	Males			Females			Other offenders[2]
		All ages	Aged 10-17	Aged 18 & over	All ages	Aged 10-17	Aged 18 & over	
Indictable offences								
Violence against the person	25.1	22.2	1.2	21.0	2.7	0.2	2.5	0.1
Sexual offences	6.0	5.9	0.4	5.5	0.1	0.0	0.1	0.0
Robbery	5.8	5.3	1.6	3.7	0.4	0.2	0.3	0.0
Theft Offences	113.3	90.1	6.0	84.1	22.5	1.0	21.4	0.7
Criminal damage and arson	2.6	2.2	0.3	1.9	0.4	0.0	0.3	0.0
Drug offences	51.9	48.0	2.6	45.4	3.7	0.1	3.6	0.2
Possession of weapons	9.5	8.8	1.2	7.6	0.7	0.1	0.6	0.0
Public order offences	16.7	15.1	0.9	14.2	1.5	0.1	1.4	0.1
Miscellaneous crimes against society	31.9	26.5	1.2	25.3	3.9	0.1	3.8	1.5
Fraud Offences	12.8	7.5	0.1	7.4	4.4	0.0	4.3	0.9
Total indictable	275.5	231.6	15.5	216.1	40.3	1.9	38.4	3.6
Summary offences								
Offences (excluding motoring offences)	419.4	236.0	9.2	226.9	157.2	2.2	155.0	26.1
Motoring offences	455.7	338.9	1.9	337.0	88.3	0.1	88.1	28.6
Total summary	875.1	574.9	11.1	563.8	245.5	2.3	243.2	54.7
All offences	**1,150.6**	**806.5**	**26.6**	**779.9**	**285.8**	**4.2**	**281.5**	**58.3**

Source: Ministry of Justice

(1) Includes males, females, persons where sex "Not Stated" and other offenders, ie companies, public bodies, etc.

(2) Includes sex 'not stated' and other offenders, i.e. companies, public bodies, etc.

21.6b Persons found guilty at all courts or cautioned[1] for indictable offences and number per 100,000 population in the age group by sex and age, 2004 to 2014

England and Wales — Number of persons

Year	All persons [2] All ages	Males All ages	Aged 10-11	Aged 12-14	Aged 15-17	Aged 18-20	Aged 21 & over	Females All ages	Aged 10-11	Aged 12-14	Aged 15-17	Aged 18-20	Aged 21 & over
					Number of persons cautioned (thousands)								
2004	156.3	110.0	2.6	16.1	25.9	16.7	48.7	46.3	0.8	9.8	10.6	5.2	19.9
2005	182.9	129.9	3.0	18.1	28.0	19.8	61.1	53.0	0.9	11.3	12.2	5.8	22.8
2006	203.8	147.6	2.9	18.7	30.2	22.9	72.8	56.2	0.9	11.6	12.7	6.2	24.7
2007	205.1	148.5	2.7	17.0	30.0	23.7	75.1	56.6	0.9	11.7	13.0	6.3	24.8
2008[3]	181.2	133.4	2.1	12.5	24.5	21.7	72.5	47.8	0.6	8.4	10.2	5.6	23.1
2009	159.5	114.9	1.4	9.5	20.2	19.2	64.6	44.7	0.5	7.6	9.3	5.3	22.0
2010	133.5	98.6	0.8	6.2	15.5	16.9	59.2	35.0	0.2	4.0	5.8	4.5	20.6
2011	123.9	94.0	0.5	5.3	13.8	15.9	58.5	29.5	0.1	2.2	4.0	3.8	19.3
2012	105.6	80.8	0.4	3.8	10.6	13.0	52.9	24.5	0.1	1.4	2.8	3.0	17.1
2013	94.1	71.7	0.3	3.1	9.3	11.1	48.1	21.9	0.1	1.0	2.2	2.5	16.0
2014	75.9	58.1	0.3	2.4	7.3	8.6	39.5	17.7	0.1	0.6	1.7	2.0	13.3
					Number of persons found guilty (thousands)								
2004	317.8	268.4	0.4	8.0	31.9	39.9	188.2	48.4	0.1	1.6	5.0	5.7	35.9
2005	308.5	261.3	0.4	8.1	32.0	38.5	182.2	46.1	0.0	1.7	5.5	5.3	33.6
2006	303.1	258.4	0.4	7.9	32.5	39.0	178.6	43.7	0.0	1.6	5.1	4.8	32.1
2007	313.3	266.7	0.4	8.1	35.0	40.5	182.7	45.3	0.0	1.7	5.5	4.6	33.4
2008[3]	316.9	267.7	0.3	7.3	31.9	38.3	189.8	46.4	0.0	1.6	4.9	4.7	35.3
2009	329.2	277.6	0.2	6.3	30.9	39.8	200.4	49.0	0.0	1.4	5.0	5.0	37.6
2010	350.6	296.8	0.1	5.4	30.3	41.5	219.5	51.1	0.0	1.1	4.4	5.1	40.5
2011	344.5	292.8	0.1	4.8	27.3	38.5	222.0	48.5	0.0	0.8	3.6	4.4	39.8
2012	308.9	262.9	0.1	3.7	20.8	31.4	206.9	42.7	0.0	0.6	2.7	3.5	35.9
2013	294.6	249.8	0.0	2.5	16.0	26.3	205.0	41.1	0.0	0.4	2.0	2.8	35.9
2014	283.1	237.2	0.0	2.3	13.2	24.1	197.6	42.1	0.0	0.3	1.5	2.6	37.7
					Number of persons found guilty or cautioned (thousands)								
2004	474.1	378.4	3.0	24.2	57.8	56.5	236.8	94.6	0.8	11.4	15.7	10.9	55.8
2005	491.4	391.2	3.4	26.2	60.1	58.3	243.3	99.1	0.9	13.0	17.7	11.1	56.4
2006	506.9	406.0	3.3	26.7	62.7	61.9	251.4	99.9	1.0	13.2	17.8	11.0	56.8
2007	518.4	415.2	3.1	25.1	65.0	64.2	257.8	101.9	0.9	13.4	18.5	10.9	58.2
2008[3]	498.0	401.1	2.4	19.8	56.4	60.1	262.3	94.2	0.6	9.9	15.0	10.3	58.4
2009	488.7	392.5	1.6	15.7	51.1	59.0	265.0	93.7	0.5	9.0	14.3	10.3	59.6
2010	484.2	395.3	0.9	11.6	45.8	58.4	278.6	86.1	0.2	5.0	10.2	9.5	61.1
2011	468.4	386.8	0.7	10.1	41.1	54.4	280.5	78.0	0.1	3.0	7.6	8.2	59.0
2012	414.6	343.6	0.5	7.5	31.4	44.4	259.8	67.1	0.1	2.0	5.5	6.5	53.0
2013	388.6	321.6	0.3	5.6	25.2	37.4	253.1	63.0	0.1	1.4	4.2	5.3	52.0
2014	358.9	295.3	0.3	4.6	20.6	32.7	237.0	59.8	0.1	1.0	3.2	4.6	51.0
					Number of persons found guilty or cautioned per 100,000 population								
2004	1,011	1,660	441	2,260	5,549	5,432	1,249	393	126	1,123	1,551	1,097	274
2005	1,039	1,699	497	2,461	5,690	5,568	1,269	408	147	1,278	1,735	1,085	274
2006	1,064	1,749	483	2,541	5,840	5,862	1,299	409	152	1,320	1,744	1,063	274
2007	1,079	1,772	454	2,421	5,992	6,006	1,318	414	138	1,358	1,793	1,040	278
2008[3]	1,028	1,696	360	1,920	5,225	5,529	1,327	380	97	1,012	1,449	967	277
2009	1,002	1,648	243	1,525	4,776	5,339	1,329	375	80	917	1,388	963	280
2010	985	1,646	137	1,127	4,311	5,186	1,383	343	38	515	1,007	879	285
2011	946	1,597	106	990	3,869	4,816	1,377	309	20	312	758	752	273
2012	833	1,411	82	751	2,979	3,992	1,264	264	14	212	552	608	244
2013	777	1,313	49	568	2,408	3,416	1,221	247	10	154	421	511	237
2014	718	1,206	48	473	1,964	2,992	1,143	234	15	102	322	440	232

Source: Ministry of Justice

(1) Motoring offences may attract written warnings, which are excluded from this table.
(2) Includes sex 'not stated'.
(3) Excludes convictions data for Cardiff Magistrates' court for April, July and August 2008.
Note: Some figures may not sum due to rounding.

21.7a Proceedings at the magistrates and trials at the Crown Court by result, 2004 to 2014 [1]

All Defendants (thousands)

Offence Group	2004	2005	2006	2007	2008[8]	2009	2010	2011	2012	2013	2014
Indictable Only											
Number of offenders proceeded against at MC	33.6	33.4	33.3	35.0	34.7	36.9	36.7	35.1	31.0	30.7	29.1
Committed for trial at CC	27.2	27.5	26.9	28.2	29.5	31.8	31.5	29.7	26.5	27.3	26.5
Proceedings terminated early[2]	1.8	1.4	1.4	1.3	1.2	0.4	0.4	0.5	0.3	0.2	0.2
Tried at MC	4.7	4.5	4.9	5.4	4.0	4.8	4.8	4.9	4.2	3.2	2.4
Discharged at committal proceedings[3]	1.6	1.0	0.6	0.5	0.3	1.2	1.3	1.2	1.0	0.8	0.6
Dismissed (found not guilty after summary trial	0.5	0.6	0.7	0.7	0.3	0.3	0.3	0.3	0.3	0.2	0.2
Found guilty at MC	2.6	2.8	3.6	4.2	3.3	3.3	3.2	3.5	2.9	2.2	1.6
Magistrates' court conviction trial rate	54.9%	63.5%	72.5%	78.0%	83.7%	68.7%	67.0%	70.1%	69.6%	68.5%	68.1%
For trial at CC[4]	19.8	18.8	19.8	22.0	22.8	22.8	22.9	22.1	20.6	18.8	18.6
Not Tried	0.4	0.3	0.3	0.3	0.3	0.3	0.4	0.3	0.2	0.2	0.2
Tried at CC	19.4	18.5	19.5	21.6	22.5	22.5	22.6	21.8	20.3	18.6	18.4
Acquitted	5.8	5.5	5.4	5.4	5.1	5.6	6.1	5.6	5.3	4.8	5.3
Found guilty at CC	13.6	13.0	14.1	16.2	17.3	16.9	16.5	16.2	15.0	13.8	13.1
Crown court conviction trial rate[5]	70.1%	70.4%	72.4%	75.0%	77.1%	75.3%	73.2%	74.3%	74.0%	74.0%	71.3%
All convictions	16.2	15.9	17.7	20.4	20.7	20.2	19.7	19.7	18.0	15.9	14.7
Conviction Ratio[6]	48.1	47.5	53.3	58.4	59.6	54.7	53.7	55.9	57.9	51.9	50.6
Either Way Offences[7]											
Number of offenders proceeded against at MC	419.7	390.0	372.8	369.9	362.8	378.7	401.3	388.9	345.9	339.9	325.9
Committed for trial at CC	50.5	52.4	51.8	55.2	59.1	70.5	74.9	70.3	59.4	69.9	71.7
Proceedings terminated early[2]	90.6	69.4	62.1	54.4	48.2	47.7	50.7	48.5	41.8	37.4	34.8
Tried at MC	278.6	268.2	259.0	260.3	255.5	260.6	275.7	270.1	244.8	232.6	219.3
Discharged at committal proceedings[3]	13.0	10.0	7.0	5.7	4.2	3.8	3.3	2.6	2.2	0.8	0.0
Dismissed (found not guilty after summary trial	8.0	8.1	8.0	7.0	5.0	4.2	4.5	4.1	4.3	4.2	4.9
Found guilty at MC	257.6	250.0	244.0	247.6	246.3	252.5	268.0	263.4	238.3	227.6	214.4
Magistrates' court conviction trial rate	92.5%	93.2%	94.2%	95.1%	96.4%	96.9%	97.2%	97.5%	97.3%	97.9%	97.8%
For trial at CC[4]	57.0	54.6	53.9	57.8	62.2	70.2	78.7	75.8	64.8	61.6	65.0
Not Tried	1.0	0.8	0.7	0.8	0.8	0.8	1.0	0.8	0.6	0.6	0.6
Tried at CC	56.0	53.8	53.2	56.9	61.4	69.4	77.7	75.0	64.1	61.0	64.4
Acquitted	11.9	11.2	11.7	11.7	11.5	12.9	14.8	13.5	11.5	10.0	10.5
Found guilty at CC	44.1	42.6	41.4	45.2	49.9	56.5	62.9	61.4	52.7	51.0	53.9
Crown court conviction trial rate[5]	78.7%	79.2%	77.9%	79.5%	81.2%	81.4%	81.0%	82.0%	82.1%	83.6%	83.8%
All convictions	301.7	292.6	285.4	292.9	296.2	309.0	330.9	324.9	291.0	278.7	268.4
Conviction Ratio[6]	71.9	75.0	76.6	79.2	81.7	81.6	82.5	83.5	84.1	82.0	82.4

21.7a Proceedings at the magistrates and trials at the Crown Court by result, 2004 to 2014 [1]

All Defendants (thousands)

Offence Group	2004	2005	2006	2007	2008[8]	2009	2010	2011	2012	2013	2014
Summary non-motoring offences											
Number of offenders proceeded against at MC	665.3	637.0	612.0	599.3	593.3	619.2	607.1	606.5	581.9	546.1	566.2
Committed for trial at CC	0.5	0.7	0.6	0.8	0.7	0.7	0.5	0.5	0.3	0.7	0.6
Proceedings terminated early[2]	132.3	115.8	104.2	96.6	90.9	97.2	107.0	106.3	104.9	102.2	99.4
Tried at MC	532.5	520.5	507.1	502.0	501.7	521.2	499.5	499.7	476.6	443.2	466.2
Discharged at committal proceedings[3]	0.0	0.0	0.0	0.1	0.0	.	.	.	.	.	.
Dismissed (found not guilty after summary trial	12.1	13.8	14.0	13.1	10.5	9.9	10.3	9.2	9.3	9.5	10.6
Found guilty at MC	520.4	506.6	493.2	488.7	491.2	511.3	489.2	490.5	467.2	433.7	455.6
Magistrates' court conviction trial rate	97.7%	97.3%	97.2%	97.4%	97.9%	98.1%	97.9%	98.2%	98.0%	97.9%	97.7%
For trial at CC[4]	2.4	2.3	2.6	2.9	3.0	3.5	4.4	3.7	2.9	2.8	2.9
Not Tried	0.0	0.0	0.0	0.0	0.0	0.0	0.0	0.0	0.0	0.0	0.0
Tried at CC	2.4	2.3	2.6	2.9	3.0	3.5	4.4	3.7	2.9	2.7	2.9
Acquitted	0.0	0.1	0.1	0.1	0.1	0.1	0.2	0.2	0.1	0.1	0.1
Found guilty at CC	2.3	2.2	2.5	2.8	2.9	3.4	4.2	3.5	2.8	2.6	2.8
Crown court conviction trial rate[5]	98.3%	97.2%	96.8%	97.0%	97.0%	95.8%	96.1%	95.5%	95.9%	96.5%	95.4%
All convictions	522.8	508.9	495.7	491.5	494.2	514.7	493.5	494.0	470.1	436.3	458.4
Conviction Ratio[6]	78.6	79.9	81.0	82.0	83.3	83.1	81.3	81.5	80.8	79.9	81.0
Summary motoring offences											
Number of offenders proceeded against at MC	904.0	834.7	761.1	728.4	649.2	659.6	608.1	549.6	525.8	524.7	546.7
Committed for trial at CC	0.2	0.2	0.2	0.2	0.1	0.1	0.1	0.0	0.0	0.1	0.1
Proceedings terminated early[2]	183.7	155.5	129.2	108.6	89.0	87.3	76.9	67.0	66.6	69.1	64.1
Tried at MC	720.0	679.0	631.8	619.5	560.1	572.3	531.2	482.5	459.2	455.4	482.6
Discharged at committal proceedings[3]	0.0	0.0	0.0	0.1	0.0	0.0	0.0	0.0	0.0	0.0	.
Dismissed (found not guilty after summary trial	12.6	12.3	9.6	8.9	8.4	8.2	8.3	7.3	6.9	7.2	6.6
Found guilty at MC	707.4	666.6	622.1	610.5	551.7	564.1	522.9	475.2	452.3	448.3	476.0
Magistrates' court conviction trial rate	98.2%	98.2%	98.5%	98.5%	98.5%	98.6%	98.4%	98.5%	98.5%	98.4%	98.6%
For trial at CC[4]	0.5	0.5	0.4	0.6	0.5	0.5	0.5	0.4	0.3	0.3	0.3
Not Tried	.	.	.	.	0.0	.	0.0	.	.	0.0	.
Tried at CC	0.5	0.5	0.4	0.6	0.5	0.5	0.5	0.4	0.3	0.3	0.3
Acquitted	0.0	0.0	0.0	0.0	0.0	0.0	0.0	0.0	0.0	0.0	0.0
Found guilty at CC	0.5	0.4	0.4	0.6	0.5	0.4	0.5	0.4	0.3	0.3	0.2
Crown court conviction trial rate[5]	97.6%	96.7%	97.7%	97.7%	98.3%	97.4%	97.8%	97.2%	97.1%	97.8%	96.5%
All convictions	707.9	667.1	622.5	611.1	552.2	564.6	523.4	475.6	452.6	448.5	476.2
Conviction Ratio[6]	78.3	79.9	81.8	83.9	85.1	85.6	86.1	86.5	86.1	85.5	87.1

21.7a Proceedings at the magistrates and trials at the Crown Court by result, 2004 to 2014 [1]

All Defendants (thousands)

Offence Group	2004	2005	2006	2007	2008[8]	2009	2010	2011	2012	2013	2014
All Offences											
Number of offenders proceeded against at MC	2,022.6	1,895.0	1,779.2	1,732.5	1,640.0	1,694.4	1,653.2	1,580.0	1,484.6	1,441.3	1,467.8
Committed for trial at CC	78.4	80.9	79.5	84.4	89.5	103.1	107.0	100.5	86.3	98.0	99.0
Proceedings terminated early[2]	408.3	342.0	296.9	260.9	229.3	232.5	235.0	222.2	213.6	208.9	198.5
Tried at MC	1,535.9	1,472.1	1,402.8	1,387.2	1,321.2	1,358.9	1,311.2	1,257.3	1,184.8	1,134.4	1,170.4
Discharged at committal proceedings[3]	14.7	11.1	7.7	6.5	4.6	5.1	4.6	3.8	3.2	1.6	0.6
Dismissed (found not guilty after summary trial)	33.2	34.8	32.3	29.7	24.1	22.6	23.3	20.9	20.8	21.1	22.3
Found guilty at MC	1,488.0	1,426.1	1,362.8	1,351.1	1,292.5	1,331.2	1,283.3	1,232.6	1,160.8	1,111.7	1,147.6
Magistrates' court conviction trial rate	96.9%	96.9%	97.1%	97.4%	97.8%	98.0%	97.9%	98.0%	98.0%	98.0%	98.1%
For trial at CC[4]	79.6	76.2	76.8	83.2	88.5	97.0	106.6	102.0	88.6	83.5	86.8
Not Tried	1.4	1.1	1.1	1.2	1.1	1.1	1.4	1.2	0.9	0.9	0.8
Tried at CC	78.2	75.0	75.7	82.0	87.4	95.8	105.1	100.8	87.7	82.6	85.9
Acquitted	17.8	16.8	17.2	17.2	16.8	18.6	21.0	19.3	16.9	14.9	15.9
Found guilty at CC	60.5	58.3	58.5	64.8	70.7	77.2	84.1	81.5	70.8	67.7	70.1
Crown court conviction trial rate[5]	77.3%	77.7%	77.3%	79.0%	80.8%	80.6%	80.0%	80.9%	80.7%	81.9%	81.5%
All convictions	1,548.5	1,484.4	1,421.3	1,415.9	1,363.2	1,408.4	1,367.5	1,314.2	1,231.6	1,179.4	1,217.7
Conviction Ratio[6]	76.6	78.3	79.9	81.7	83.1	83.1	82.7	83.2	83.0	81.8	83.0

Source: Ministry of Justice

(1) Youth Courts are included within magistrates' courts figures.

(2) Includes proceedings discontinued under s.23(3) of the Prosecution of Offences Act 1985, charge withdrawn and cases "written off" (eg bench warrant unexecuted, adjourned sine die, defendant cannot be traced etc.).

(3) Sec. 6 of Magistrates' Court Act 1980

A magistrates' court inquiring into an offence as examining justices shall on consideration of the evidence -

  a) commit the accused for trial if it is of opinion that there is sufficient evidence to put him on trial by jury for any indictable offence;

  b) discharge him if it is not of that opinion and he is in custody for no other cause than the offence under inquiry;

Comparison with Crown Prosecution Service data suggests that these figures are overstated.

(4) Includes offenders that were sent for trial and committed for sentence from the Magistrates' court

(5) The conviction trial rate for each court is calculated as the number of convictions as a proportion of the number tried

(6) Conviction ratio is calculated as the number of convictions as a proportion of the number of proceedings.

(7) Figures for Either way offences may include instances where an offence has been downgraded.

(8) Excludes data for Cardiff magistrates' court for April, July, and August 2008.

21.7b Defendants proceeded against at magistrates' courts[1] by offence group, 2004 to 2014

England and Wales | | | | | | | | | | Defendants (thousands)

	Magistrates' courts										
Offence group	2004	2005	2006	2007	2008[1]	2009	2010	2011	2012	2013	2014
Indictable											
Violence against the person	56.0	53.1	49.5	46.2	45.1	49.2	50.4	44.4	36.7	36.6	38.9
Sexual offences	9.6	9.7	9.0	8.6	8.4	9.3	10.5	10.1	9.4	10.9	11.9
Robbery	12.4	12.5	13.2	14.0	13.1	13.7	13.7	14.4	12.3	10.9	9.0
Theft Offences	156.9	143.8	136.9	143.1	146.3	147.9	158.4	159.6	145.0	142.0	135.4
Criminal damage and arson	16.4	15.1	16.2	15.6	11.3	9.0	8.9	8.0	7.0	5.6	3.6
Drug offences	44.1	43.4	44.0	48.9	57.0	61.7	67.8	67.7	63.6	63.8	57.6
Possession of weapons	19.1	18.5	18.4	18.0	18.0	19.5	17.4	16.4	13.7	13.7	13.7
Public order offences	16.5	13.6	12.1	11.2	10.5	18.5	21.1	18.7	16.5	17.5	18.3
Miscellaneous crimes against society	105.2	97.5	90.8	81.9	71.7	68.2	70.2	66.1	56.9	53.1	49.4
Fraud Offences	17.1	16.2	16.1	17.3	16.3	18.8	19.7	18.7	15.9	16.5	17.3
Total indictable offences	453.3	423.4	406.1	404.9	397.5	415.6	438.0	424.0	377.0	370.6	354.9
Summary											
Summary non-motoring	665.3	637.0	612.0	599.3	593.3	619.2	607.1	606.5	581.9	546.1	566.2
Summary motoring	904.0	834.7	761.1	728.4	649.2	659.6	608.1	549.6	525.8	524.7	546.7
All summary defendants	1,569.3	1,471.6	1,373.1	1,327.7	1,242.6	1,278.8	1,215.2	1,156.0	1,107.6	1,070.7	1,112.9
Total defendants	**2,022.6**	**1,895.0**	**1,779.2**	**1,732.5**	**1,640.0**	**1,694.4**	**1,653.2**	**1,580.0**	**1,484.6**	**1,441.3**	**1,467.8**

Source: Ministry of Justice

(1) Excludes data for Cardiff magistrates' court for April, July, and August 2008.

Note: Some figures may not sum due to rounding.

21.7c Offenders[1] found guilty at all courts by offence group, 2004 to 2014

England and Wales | | | | | | | | | | Offenders (thousands)

Offence group	2004	2005	2006	2007	2008[2]	2009	2010	2011	2012	2013	2014
Indictable offences											
Violence against the person	27.3	29.0	29.7	30.0	29.2	30.7	32.6	30.7	26.4	24.4	26.4
Sexual offences	4.8	4.8	4.9	5.0	5.0	5.0	5.7	6.0	5.7	5.7	6.3
Robbery	7.5	7.1	8.1	8.8	8.5	8.6	8.5	9.3	8.3	6.8	5.6
Theft Offences	125.6	118.6	114.7	122.5	128.2	128.7	138.8	140.0	127.2	122.6	116.8
Criminal damage and arson	11.1	11.0	12.0	11.9	9.0	7.3	7.1	6.5	5.4	4.1	2.5
Drug offences	39.2	39.1	39.6	44.6	52.9	56.8	62.0	61.7	58.1	57.0	51.8
Possession of weapons	13.9	14.1	14.2	14.1	14.6	15.1	13.1	12.5	10.3	10.0	10.1
Public order offences	9.1	8.8	8.7	9.0	8.5	17.3	19.6	18.1	16.3	16.4	17.5
Miscellaneous crimes against society	66.2	63.2	58.4	53.6	47.6	44.8	47.4	44.9	38.7	35.3	32.6
Fraud Offences	13.3	13.0	12.9	13.9	13.3	14.8	15.7	15.0	12.4	12.3	13.5
Total indictable	317.8	308.5	303.1	313.3	316.9	329.2	350.6	344.5	308.9	294.6	283.1
Summary offences											
Summary Non-Motoring	522.8	508.9	495.7	491.5	494.2	514.7	493.5	494.0	470.1	436.3	458.4
Summary motoring	707.9	667.1	622.495	611.1	552.2	564.6	523.4	475.6	452.6	448.5	476.2
Total summary	1,230.7	1,175.9	1,118.2	1,102.6	1,046.3	1,079.3	1,016.8	969.7	922.6	884.8	934.6
All offences [2]	**1,548.5**	**1,484.4**	**1,421.3**	**1,415.9**	**1,363.2**	**1,408.4**	**1,367.5**	**1,314.2**	**1,231.6**	**1,179.4**	**1,217.7**

Source: Ministry of Justice

(1) Includes males, females, persons where sex "Not Stated" and other offenders, ie companies, public bodies, etc.

(2) Excludes convictions data for Cardiff magistrates' court for April, July, and August 2008.

Note: Some figures may not sum due to rounding.

21.8 Persons sentenced to immediate custody at all courts by length of sentence and average custodial sentence length, 2004 to 2014

England and Wales

Number of persons

All Offences	2004	2005	2006	2007	2008[1]	2009	2010	2011	2012	2013	2014
Up to and including 3 months	39,688	37,100	34,711	34,427	35,738	36,071	38,316	39,419	36,442	34,821	35,578
Over 3 months and up to and including 6 months	28,491	26,756	24,421	23,109	22,338	21,321	20,181	20,269	19,332	18,236	17,176
Over 6 months and less than 12 months	5,678	5,851	5,728	6,154	6,920	7,177	7,052	7,891	6,787	6,431	5,996
12 months	5,244	5,414	5,245	5,479	5,652	5,837	5,618	5,947	4,788	4,380	4,155
Over 12 months and up to and including 18 months	6,366	6,258	6,232	6,271	6,751	7,289	7,343	8,022	7,343	6,375	5,810
Over 18 months and up to and including 3 years	10,695	10,385	10,372	10,470	11,516	12,077	12,358	13,138	12,621	12,225	11,829
Over 3 years and less than 4 years	2,082	1,745	1,533	1,458	1,629	1,811	1,937	1,990	1,973	2,092	2,120
4 years	2,146	1,745	1,607	1,603	1,903	1,977	1,934	2,094	1,787	1,704	1,639
Over 4 years and up to and including 5 years	2,161	1,920	1,670	1,611	1,998	1,980	2,061	2,208	1,913	1,945	1,932
Over 5 years and up to and including 10 years	2,772	2,658	2,190	2,109	2,614	2,784	2,796	3,307	3,238	3,417	3,653
Over 10 years and less than life	409	353	309	316	405	485	514	671	661	936	983
Indeterminate sentence[2]	-	426	1,445	1,707	1,538	1,001	1,019	819	747	9	-
Life	590	625	550	492	523	421	384	395	412	395	442
Number given immediate custody	**106,322**	**101,236**	**96,013**	**95,206**	**99,525**	**100,231**	**101,513**	**106,170**	**98,044**	**92,966**	**91,313**
Average custodial sentence length (months)[3]	12.9	12.6	12.4	12.4	13.3	13.7	13.7	14.3	14.5	15.5	15.6

Indictable Offences	2004	2005	2006	2007	2008[1]	2009	2010	2011	2012	2013	2014
Up to and including 3 months	25,417	23,808	22,378	22,421	23,533	23,692	26,290	27,245	25,676	25,437	25,550
Over 3 months and up to and including 6 months	16,380	15,109	14,284	13,952	14,083	13,768	13,684	13,900	13,146	12,619	11,664
Over 6 months and less than 12 months	5,677	5,848	5,725	6,150	6,916	7,158	7,023	7,824	6,778	6,427	5,994
12 months	5,243	5,412	5,241	5,477	5,650	5,828	5,607	5,947	4,786	4,378	4,154
Over 12 months and up to and including 18 months	6,366	6,257	6,230	6,271	6,750	7,284	7,337	8,020	7,341	6,375	5,810
Over 18 months and up to and including 3 years	10,695	10,385	10,369	10,470	11,516	12,076	12,353	13,138	12,621	12,225	11,829
Over 3 years and less than 4 years	2,082	1,745	1,532	1,458	1,629	1,811	1,937	1,990	1,973	2,092	2,120
4 years	2,146	1,745	1,607	1,603	1,903	1,977	1,934	2,094	1,787	1,704	1,639
Over 4 years and up to and including 5 years	2,161	1,920	1,670	1,611	1,998	1,980	2,061	2,208	1,913	1,945	1,932
Over 5 years and up to and including 10 years	2,772	2,658	2,189	2,109	2,614	2,784	2,796	3,307	3,238	3,417	3,653
Over 10 years and less than life	409	353	309	316	405	485	514	671	661	936	983
Indeterminate sentence[2]	-	426	1,444	1,707	1,538	1,001	1,019	819	747	9	-
Life	590	625	550	492	523	421	384	395	412	395	442
Number given immediate custody	**79,938**	**76,291**	**73,528**	**74,037**	**79,058**	**80,265**	**82,939**	**87,558**	**81,079**	**77,959**	**75,770**
Average custodial sentence length (months)[3]	16.1	15.8	15.3	15.2	16.0	16.5	16.2	16.8	17.0	18.0	18.3

Source: Ministry of Justice

(1) Excludes data for Cardiff magistrates' court for April, July and August 2008.
(2) Sentences of imprisonment for public protection introduced by the Criminal Justice Act 2003 on 4 April 2005.
(3) Excludes life and indeterminate sentences.

21.9a Persons sentenced to life imprisonment by sex and age, 2005 to 2014

England and Wales   Number of persons

Sex and age	2005	2006	2007	2008	2009	2010	2011	2012	2013	2014
Males										
Aged 10-17	27	19	23	24	22	17	13	13	13	21
Aged 18-20	50	46	70	54	57	39	30	47	33	41
Aged 21 and over	517	469	378	417	322	308	328	320	320	360
All ages	594	534	471	495	401	364	371	380	366	422
Females										
Aged 10-17	1	0	3	1	1	2	2	1	0	0
Aged 18-20	4	2	3	2	1	2	5	1	0	1
Aged 21 and over	26	14	15	25	18	16	17	30	29	19
All ages	31	16	21	28	20	20	24	32	29	20
All persons										
Aged 10-17	28	19	26	25	23	19	15	14	13	21
Aged 18-20	54	48	73	56	58	41	35	48	33	42
Aged 21 and over	543	483	393	442	340	324	345	350	349	379
All ages	625	550	492	523	421	384	395	412	395	442

Source: Ministry of Justice

21.9b persons sentenced to determinate an indeterminate custodial sentences by age group, sex and type of sentence, 2009 to 2014

Sex and age	Year	Determinate Sentence	Extended sentence of imprisonment - EPP	Imprisonment for public protection - IPP	Life sentence	Total Immediate Custody
Male						
Aged Under 18	2009	4,485	17	25	22	4,549
	2010	3,877	10	41	17	3,945
	2011	3,864	26	28	13	3,931
	2012	2,819	6	30	13	2,868
	2013	2,196	0	0	13	2,209
	2014	1,716	0	0	21	1,737
Aged 18-20	2009	12,978	59	120	57	13,214
	2010	12,296	58	107	39	12,500
	2011	11,555	94	70	30	11,749
	2012	9,262	34	76	47	9,419
	2013	7,591	6	0	33	7,630
	2014	7,445	0	0	41	7,486
Aged 21 and over	2009	72,957	346	835	322	74,460
	2010	75,491	370	845	308	77,014
	2011	80,817	502	703	328	82,350
	2012	76,628	280	620	320	77,848
	2013	75,159	24	9	320	75,512
	2014	73,760	0	0	360	74,120
Female						
Aged Under 18	2009	378	0	2	1	381
	2010	256	0	0	2	258
	2011	266	1	1	2	270
	2012	181	0	0	1	182
	2013	117	0	0	0	117
	2014	106	0	0	0	106
Aged 18 - 20	2009	803	2	2	1	808
	2010	734	0	3	2	739
	2011	582	3	0	5	590
	2012	509	0	2	1	512
	2013	329	0	0	0	329
	2014	389	0	0	1	390
Aged 21 and over	2009	6,878	10	17	18	6,923
	2010	7,160	15	23	16	7,214
	2011	7,528	22	17	17	7,584
	2012	6,966	12	19	30	7,027
	2013	6,663	1	0	29	6,693
	2014	7,010	0	0	19	7,029
Sex not Stated						
Aged under 18	2009	27	0	0	0	27
	2010	26	0	0	0	26
	2011	31	0	0	0	31
	2012	41	0	0	0	41
	2013	27	0	0	0	27
	2014	17	0	0	0	17
Aged 18-20	2009	56	0	0	0	56
	2010	43	0	0	0	43
	2011	38	0	0	0	38
	2012	62	0	0	0	62
	2013	45	0	0	0	45
	2014	33	0	0	0	33

21.9b persons sentenced to determinate an indeterminate custodial sentences by age group, sex and type of sentence, 2009 to 2014

Sex and age	Year	Determinate Sentence	Extended sentence of imprisonment - EPP	Imprisonment for public protection - IPP	Life sentence	Total Immediate Custody
Aged 21 and over	2009	247	0	0	0	247
	2010	227	0	0	0	227
	2011	275	0	0	0	275
	2012	417	0	0	0	417
	2013	435	0	0	0	435
	2014	395	0	0	0	395
All Persons						
Aged Under 18	2009	4,890	17	27	23	4,957
	2010	4,159	10	41	19	4,229
	2011	4,161	27	29	15	4,232
	2012	3,041	6	30	14	3,091
	2013	2,340	0	0	13	2,353
	2014	1,839	0	0	21	1,860
Aged 18 - 20	2009	13,837	61	122	58	14,078
	2010	13,073	58	110	41	13,282
	2011	12,175	97	70	35	12,377
	2012	9,833	34	78	48	9,993
	2013	7,965	6	0	33	8,004
	2014	7,867	0	0	42	7,909
Aged 21 and over	2009	80,082	356	852	340	81,630
	2010	82,878	385	868	324	84,455
	2011	88,620	524	720	345	90,209
	2012	84,011	292	639	350	85,292
	2013	82,257	25	9	349	82,640
	2014	81,165	0	0	379	81,544
All Ages	2009	98,809	434	1,001	421	100,665
	2010	100,110	453	1,019	384	101,966
	2011	104,956	648	819	395	106,818
	2012	96,885	332	747	412	98,376
	2013	92,562	31	9	395	92,997
	2014	90,871	0	0	442	91,313

Source: Ministry of Justice

Criminal Justice System Statistics publication: Sentencing: Pivot Table Analytical Tool for England and Wales

a) The figures given relate to persons for whom these offences were the principal offences for which they were dealt with. When a defendant has been found guilty of two or more offences it is the offence for which the heaviest penalty is imposed. Where the same disposal is imposed for two or more offences, the offence selected is the offence for which the statutory maximum penalty is the most severe.

b) Every effort is made to ensure that the figures presented are accurate and complete. However, it is important to note that these data have been extracted from large administrative data systems generated by the courts. As a consequence, care should be taken to ensure data collection processes and their inevitable limitations are taken into account when those data are used.

21.10 Prison receptions and population in custody
England and Wales

Numbers[1]

		2004	2005	2006	2007	2008	2009	2010*	2011	2012	2013	2014
Receptions												
Type of inmate:												
Untried	**KEDA**	54,556	55,455	55,809	55,305	57,417	55,207	-	54,837	**50,227**	**48,875**	**48,330**
Convicted, unsentenced	**KEDB**	50,115	49,104	47,995	43,566	44,773	37,003	-	39,391	**36,646**	**33,692**	**32,011**
Sentenced	**KEDE**	95,161	92,452	90,038	91,736	100,348	94,964	-	90,955	**86,479**	**82,305**	**78,488**
Immediate custodial sentence	**KEDF**	93,326	90,414	88,134	90,261	98,820	93,621	-	89,822	**85,364**	**81,442**	**77,728**
ADULTS												
Remand - untried		**41,684**	**42,692**	**42,772**	**42,546**	**44,953**	**43,505**	..	**44,681**	**41,955**	**42,203**	**42,637**
Remand - convicted unsentenced		**40,088**	**39,333**	**38,312**	**34,656**	**35,832**	**30,012**	..	**32,213**	**30,771**	**29,039**	**28,155**
Prisoners under sentence		**76,742**	**74,471**	**71,935**	**72,622**	**80,758**	**77,146**	..	**75,170**	**73,243**	**71,798**	**69,873**
Fine defaulter		1,680	1,876	1,786	1,383	1,427	1,270	..	1,079	1,070	827	740
Less than or equal to 6 months		43,927	42,288	39,474	39,949	44,954	41,345	..	37,048	34,811	33,208	31,860
Greater than 6 months to less than 12 months		5,887	5,902	6,294	6,757	7,377	7,195	..	7,224	7,452	7,531	7,099
12 months to less than 4 years		17,988	17,397	16,970	17,233	19,061	19,804	..	21,855	21,692	21,603	21,215
4 years or more (excluding Indeterminate)		6,754	6,130	5,613	5,472	6,394	6,426	..	7,252	7,589	8,308	8,675
Indeterminate sentences		506	878	1,798	1,828	1,545	1,107	..	712	629	321	328
18-20 YEAR OLDS												
Remand - untried		**8,517**	**8,405**	**8,499**	**8,299**	**8,413**	**8,205**	..	**7,255**	**6,269**	**5,610**	**4,783**
Remand - convicted unsentenced		**7,598**	**7,391**	**7,239**	**6,706**	**6,782**	**5,566**	..	**5,794**	**4,917**	**4,117**	**3,425**
Prisoners under sentence		**13,247**	**12,806**	**12,812**	**13,758**	**14,300**	**13,804**	..	**12,788**	**10,941**	**8,879**	**7,308**
Fine defaulter		155	162	118	92	101	73	..	54	45	35	20
Less than or equal to 6 months		7,275	6,892	6,857	7,442	7,816	7,202	..	6,092	4,859	3,720	2,918
Greater than 6 months to less than 12 months		1,239	1,227	1,212	1,295	1,381	1,323	..	1,273	1,137	884	744
12 months to less than 4 years		3,764	3,726	3,691	3,939	3,988	4,226	..	4,406	3,965	3,433	2,909
4 years or more (excluding Indeterminate)		756	671	639	629	778	818	..	890	866	780	680
Indeterminate sentences		58	128	295	361	236	162	..	73	69	27	37
15-17 YEAR OLDS												
Remand - untried		**4,355**	**4,358**	**4,538**	**4,460**	**4,051**	**3,497**	..	**2,901**	**2,003**	**1,062**	**910**
Remand - convicted unsentenced		**2,429**	**2,380**	**2,444**	**2,204**	**2,159**	**1,425**	..	**1,384**	**958**	**536**	**430**
Prisoners under sentence		**5,172**	**5,175**	**5,291**	**5,356**	**5,290**	**4,014**	..	**2,997**	**2,295**	**1,628**	**1,307**
Fine defaulter		0	0	0	0	0	0	..	0	0	1	0
Less than or equal to 6 months		2,474	2,637	2,593	2,669	2,563	1,895	..	1,242	913	599	544
Greater than 6 months to less than 12 months		867	854	864	889	894	677	..	538	409	266	201
12 months to less than 4 years		1,662	1,517	1,626	1,591	1,585	1,249	..	1,056	851	650	467
4 years or more (excluding Indeterminate)		151	126	143	117	177	147	..	134	102	102	80
Indeterminate sentences		18	41	65	90	71	46	..	27	20	10	15
Non-criminal prisoners	**KEDM**	3,669	3,668	4,734	3,888	3,836	4,282	-	2,565	2,495	2,766	2,199
Immigration Act 1971	**KEDN**	3,041	3,093	4,073	3,347	3,466	-	-	2,304	2,238	2,521	2,022
Others	**KEDO**	628	575	661	541	370	-	-	261	257	245	177

21.10 Prison receptions and population in custody
England and Wales

Numbers[1]

Population (30 June)		2004	2005	2006	2007	2008	2009	2010*	2011	2012	2013	2014
Total in prison service establishments	KFBQ	74,488	76,190	77,982	79,734	83,193	83,454	85,002	85,374	86,048	83,842	85,509
Untried	KEDQ	7,716	8,084	8,064	8,387	8,750	8,933	8,487	8,299	7,671	7,743	8,618
Convicted, unsentenced	KEDR	4,779	4,780	5,003	4,457	4,690	4,523	4,517	4,165	3,653	3,228	3,579
Total sentenced	KEDU	60,976	62,257	63,493	65,601	68,233	68,488	71,000	71,964	73,562	70,913	71,481
Total Immediate custodial sentence	KFBR	60,924	62,179	63,404	65,533	68,123	68,375	70,871	71,835	73,435	70,781	71,361
Young offenders	KFBS	7,644	7,700	7,852	8,518	8,689	8,405	7,808	7,305	6,846	5,557	6,442
Determinate sentence	I7IJ	7,498	7,541	7,533	7,936	7,984	7,781	6,877	6,442	6,125	5,022	5,981
Indeterminate sentence	I7IL	146	159	319	582	705	624	454	358	300	226	170
Recalls		0	0	0	0	0	0	477	505	421	309	291
Adults	KFCO	53,280	54,479	55,552	57,015	59,434	59,970	63,063	64,530	66,589	65,224	79,067
Determinate sentence	I7IK	47,832	48,756	48,596	48,116	48,757	48,073	45,510	46,103	48,139	47,469	61,681
Indeterminate sentence	I7IM	5,448	5,723	6,956	8,899	10,677	11,897	12,680	13,286	13,454	12,956	12,417
Recalls		0	0	0	0	0	0	4,873	5,141	4,996	4,799	4,969
Committed in default of payment of a fine	KFCS	52	78	89	68	110	113	129	129	127	132	120
Young offenders	KFEW	5	3	5	4	6	5	5	6	4	3	1
Adults	KFEX	47	75	84	64	104	108	124	123	123	129	119
Non-criminal prisoners	KEEB	1,017	1,069	1,422	1,289	1,520	1,510	998	946	1,162	1,958	1,831

Source: Ministry of Justice

1 Due to the introduction of a new prison IT system the 2010 prison population data is now taken from a different source and recalls are shown separately (they were previously included in the relevant sentence length band). See OMCS 2010 for more details.

* Data for 2010 is unavailable due to problems in the supply of data for statistical purposes

21.11 Prison population under an immediate custodial sentence by offence group, age group and sex, 2006 to 2014, England and Wales

	30-Jun-06	30-Jun-07	30-Jun-08	30-Jun-09	30-Jun-09[1]	30-Jun-10	30-Jun-11	30-Jun-12	30-Jun-13	30-Jun-14
Males and females	**63,404**	**65,533**	**68,124**	**68,375**	**68,461**	**70,871**	**71,835**	**73,435**	**70,781**	**71,361**
Violence against the person	16,215	17,616	18,930	19,946	19,762	20,247	20,431	20,437	19,473	19,596
Sexual offences	6,598	7,336	7,616	7,972	8,176	9,304	9,850	10,473	10,540	11,192
Robbery	8,415	8,747	8,733	9,049	8,738	8,834	9,141	9,279	8,873	8,507
Burglary	7,791	7,920	7,935	7,884	7,403	6,857	7,102	7,345	7,073	7,141
Theft and handling	4,125	3,706	3,836	3,382	3,134	3,850	4,198	4,646	4,500	4,377
Fraud and forgery	1,692	1,738	2,020	1,875	1,923	1,544	1,376	1,454	1,320	1,352
Drug offences	10,647	10,613	10,982	10,696	10,420	11,064	10,621	10,682	10,175	10,306
Motoring offences	1,920	1,484	1,377	1,149	1,050	931	841	798	723	820
Other offences	5,594	5,991	6,439	6,117	6,186	7,353	7,755	7,826	7,625	7,644
Offence not recorded	408	383	256	304	1,669	887	520	495	479	426
Adults	**55,552**	**57,015**	**59,435**	**59,970**	**60,186**	**63,063**	**64,530**	**66,589**	**65,224**	**66,472**
Violence against the person	14,187	15,323	16,483	17,515	17,433	17,997	18,496	18,686	18,010	18,348
Sexual offences	6,314	6,986	7,242	7,597	7,822	8,841	9,396	10,044	10,187	10,867
Robbery	6,450	6,627	6,688	6,942	6,780	7,055	7,398	7,545	7,460	7,358
Burglary	6,790	6,808	6,770	6,711	6,329	5,808	6,052	6,379	6,316	6,527
Theft and handling	3,500	3,100	3,308	2,949	2,738	3,454	3,797	4,216	4,168	4,111
Fraud and forgery	1,634	1,688	1,973	1,828	1,881	1,513	1,352	1,425	1,298	1,337
Drug offences	10,021	9,951	10,144	9,926	9,695	10,382	10,002	10,124	9,670	9,699
Motoring offences	1,633	1,288	1,210	1,029	943	842	766	743	672	762
Other offences	4,676	4,931	5,404	5,215	5,221	6,403	6,813	6,984	7,011	7,062
Offence not recorded	347	313	212	258	1,344	768	458	443	432	401
18-20 year olds	**5,987**	**6,634**	**6,757**	**6,846**	**6,669**	**6,623**	**6,155**	**5,851**	**4,876**	**4,336**
Violence against the person	1,638	1,871	1,942	2,050	1,947	1,934	1,696	1,526	1,298	1,128
Sexual offences	216	277	300	298	281	406	406	382	326	291
Robbery	1,461	1,611	1,561	1,656	1,521	1,491	1,450	1,431	1,190	968
Burglary	719	828	846	922	816	848	846	815	676	556
Theft and handling	434	415	375	306	268	318	315	358	288	233
Fraud and forgery	47	40	43	46	41	28	22	29	21	13
Drug offences	554	588	727	685	641	618	560	524	471	575
Motoring offences	218	152	141	107	93	84	67	53	50	57
Other offences	652	800	788	734	760	784	745	690	518	491
Offence not recorded	48	51	35	42	301	112	48	43	38	24
15-17 year olds	**1,865**	**1,883**	**1,932**	**1,559**	**1,606**	**1,185**	**1,150**	**995**	**681**	**553**
Violence against the person	391	422	505	381	382	316	239	225	165	120
Sexual offences	68	73	74	77	73	57	48	47	27	34
Robbery	503	509	485	451	437	288	293	303	223	181
Burglary	282	283	319	251	258	201	204	151	81	58
Theft and handling	192	191	153	127	128	78	86	72	44	33
Fraud and forgery	11	10	4	1	1	3	2	0	1	2
Drug offences	71	74	111	86	84	64	59	34	34	32
Motoring offences	69	44	26	13	14	5	8	2	1	1
Other offences	265	259	247	168	205	166	197	152	96	91
Offence not recorded	13	19	9	4	24	7	14	9	9	1

1) Due to the introduction of a new prison IT system the 2010 prison population data is now taken from a different source. The 2009 figures from both the old and new systems have been presented to aid comparison.

	30-Jun-06	30-Jun-07	30-Jun-08	30-Jun-09	30-Jun-09[1]	30-Jun-10	30-Jun-11	30-Jun-12	30-Jun-13	30-Jun-14
Males	**59,898**	**62,188**	**64,600**	**64,993**	**65,047**	**67,450**	**68,424**	**69,976**	**67,587**	**68,163**
Violence against the person	15,537	16,929	18,159	19,108	18,913	19,349	19,520	19,488	18,568	18,694
Sexual offences	6,561	7,287	7,569	7,918	8,116	9,221	9,767	10,390	10,463	11,100
Robbery	8,100	8,437	8,437	8,715	8,406	8,562	8,840	8,951	8,551	8,210
Burglary	7,563	7,723	7,733	7,678	7,202	6,706	6,931	7,137	6,874	6,926
Theft and handling	3,691	3,332	3,373	2,963	2,741	3,412	3,747	4,141	4,034	3,852
Fraud and forgery	1,456	1,512	1,725	1,628	1,669	1,359	1,202	1,249	1,166	1,189
Drug offences	9,484	9,569	9,992	9,803	9,561	10,235	9,899	10,108	9,704	9,866
Motoring offences	1,887	1,453	1,356	1,130	1,034	910	824	778	701	794
Other offences	5,242	5,598	6,024	5,758	5,797	6,895	7,219	7,284	7,090	7,142
Offence not recorded	378	348	232	291	1,608	801	475	450	436	390
Adults	**52,368**	**54,007**	**56,270**	**56,882**	**57,088**	**59,951**	**61,394**	**63,374**	**62,181**	**63,397**
Violence against the person	13,594	14,755	15,830	16,792	16,707	17,223	17,673	17,832	17,162	17,493
Sexual offences	6,281	6,939	7,195	7,546	7,765	8,765	9,321	9,967	10,112	10,775
Robbery	6,200	6,383	6,448	6,663	6,507	6,828	7,143	7,254	7,165	7,081
Burglary	6,581	6,625	6,587	6,520	6,144	5,667	5,887	6,187	6,125	6,317
Theft and handling	3,090	2,754	2,880	2,559	2,371	3,039	3,365	3,734	3,719	3,598
Fraud and forgery	1,406	1,469	1,688	1,583	1,628	1,329	1,180	1,222	1,146	1,174
Drug offences	8,925	8,951	9,214	9,078	8,882	9,593	9,315	9,570	9,209	9,266
Motoring offences	1,602	1,259	1,191	1,010	927	822	749	723	651	738
Other offences	4,366	4,590	5,047	4,886	4,871	5,987	6,341	6,482	6,500	6,589
Offence not recorded	323	280	190	245	1,286	698	420	403	392	366
18-20 year olds	**5,716**	**6,354**	**6,454**	**6,593**	**6,398**	**6,337**	**5,896**	**5,623**	**4,733**	**4,213**
Violence against the person	1,563	1,772	1,843	1,949	1,840	1,820	1,615	1,439	1,244	1,081
Sexual offences	213	276	300	295	279	399	399	376	324	291

21.11 Prison population under an immediate custodial sentence by offence group, age group and sex, 2006 to 2014, England and Wales

	30-Jun-06	30-Jun-07	30-Jun-08	30-Jun-09	30-Jun-09[1]	30-Jun-10	30-Jun-11	30-Jun-12	30-Jun-13	30-Jun-14
Robbery	1,413	1,558	1,517	1,611	1,473	1,451	1,408	1,396	1,165	948
Burglary	707	817	831	909	803	838	840	800	669	551
Theft and handling	412	392	346	281	245	296	296	335	271	221
Fraud and forgery	39	34	33	45	40	27	21	27	19	13
Drug offences	491	546	672	643	598	579	525	506	461	568
Motoring offences	216	150	139	107	93	83	67	53	49	55
Other offences	619	758	739	711	729	746	684	652	495	462
Offence not recorded	43	51	34	42	298	98	41	39	36	23
15-17 year olds	**1,814**	**1,827**	**1,876**	**1,517**	**1,561**	**1,162**	**1,134**	**979**	**673**	**553**
Violence against the person	381	402	486	366	366	306	232	217	162	120
Sexual offences	67	73	74	77	72	57	47	47	27	34
Robbery	486	495	472	440	426	283	289	301	221	181
Burglary	275	281	315	248	255	201	204	150	80	58
Theft and handling	189	185	147	124	125	77	86	72	44	33
Fraud and forgery	11	9	4	1	1	3	1	0	1	2
Drug offences	68	71	106	82	81	63	59	32	34	32
Motoring offences	69	44	26	13	14	5	8	2	1	1
Other offences	258	250	238	161	197	162	194	150	95	91
Offence not recorded	12	17	8	4	24	5	14	8	8	1

1) Due to the introduction of a new prison IT system the 2010 prison population data is now taken from a different source. The 2009 figures from both the old and new systems have been presented to aid comparison.

	30-Jun-06	30-Jun-07	30-Jun-08	30-Jun-09	30-Jun-09[1]	30-Jun-10	30-Jun-11	30-Jun-12	30-Jun-13	30-Jun-14
Females	**3,506**	**3,345**	**3,524**	**3,382**	**3,414**	**3,421**	**3,411**	**3,459**	**3,194**	**3,198**
Violence against the person	678	687	771	839	849	898	911	949	905	902
Sexual offences	37	48	47	54	60	83	83	83	77	92
Robbery	315	310	295	334	332	272	301	328	322	297
Burglary	228	197	203	207	201	151	171	208	199	215
Theft and handling	435	374	462	418	393	438	451	505	466	525
Fraud and forgery	236	227	295	246	254	185	174	205	154	163
Drug offences	1,163	1,044	990	893	859	829	722	574	471	440
Motoring offences	33	31	22	19	16	21	17	20	22	26
Other offences	352	392	416	359	389	458	536	542	535	502
Offence not recorded	30	35	24	13	61	86	45	45	43	36
Adults	**3,185**	**3,009**	**3,164**	**3,088**	**3,098**	**3,112**	**3,136**	**3,215**	**3,043**	**3,075**
Violence against the person	593	568	653	723	726	774	823	854	848	855
Sexual offences	33	47	47	51	57	76	75	77	75	92
Robbery	250	244	239	279	273	227	255	291	295	277
Burglary	209	183	183	191	185	141	165	192	191	210
Theft and handling	410	346	428	391	367	415	432	482	449	513
Fraud and forgery	227	219	285	245	253	184	172	203	152	163
Drug offences	1,097	999	930	847	813	789	687	554	461	433
Motoring offences	31	29	20	19	16	20	17	20	21	24
Other offences	310	341	358	329	350	416	472	502	511	473
Offence not recorded	24	33	22	13	58	70	38	40	40	35
18-20 year olds	**271**	**280**	**303**	**253**	**271**	**286**	**259**	**228**	**143**	**123**
Violence against the person	75	99	99	101	107	114	81	87	54	47
Sexual offences	3	1	0	3	2	7	7	6	2	0
Robbery	48	54	43	45	48	40	42	35	25	20
Burglary	13	11	15	13	13	10	6	15	7	5
Theft and handling	22	23	29	25	23	22	19	23	17	12
Fraud and forgery	8	6	9	1	1	1	1	2	2	0
Drug offences	62	42	56	42	43	39	35	18	10	7
Motoring offences	2	2	2	0	0	1	0	0	1	2
Other offences	34	43	49	23	31	38	61	38	23	29
Offence not recorded	5	0	1	0	3	14	7	4	2	1
15-17 year olds	**50**	**56**	**57**	**42**	**45**	**23**	**16**	**16**	**8**	**0**
Violence against the person	11	20	19	15	16	10	7	8	3	0
Sexual offences	1	0	0	0	1	0	1	0	0	0
Robbery	17	13	13	10	11	5	4	2	2	0
Burglary	7	2	5	3	3	0	0	1	1	0
Theft and handling	3	6	6	3	3	1	0	0	0	0
Fraud and forgery	0	1	0	0	0	0	1	0	0	0
Drug offences	4	3	5	4	3	1	0	2	0	0
Motoring offences	0	0	0	0	0	0	0	0	0	0
Other offences	7	9	9	7	8	4	3	2	1	0
Offence not recorded	1	2	1	0	0	2	0	1	1	0

Source: Ministry of Justice

1) Due to the introduction of a new prison IT system the 2010 prison population data is now taken from a different source. The 2009 figures from both the old and new systems have been presented to aid comparison.

21.12 Crimes recorded by the police, Scotland, 2005-06 to 2014-15

Number & Percentage

Crime group	2005-06	2006-07	2007-08	2008-09	2009-10	2010-11	2011-12	2012-13	2013-14	2014-15	% change 13-14 to 14-15
Total Crimes	417,785	419,257	385,509	377,433	338,124	323,247	314,188	273,053	270,397	256,350	-5
Non-sexual crimes of violence	13,726	14,099	12,874	12,612	11,228	11,438	9,533	7,530	6,785	6,357	-6
Homicide etc.[3] (incl. causing death by driving)	121	159	142	134	106	122	121	91	106	105	-1
Attempted murder & serious assault[4]	7,030	7,345	6,711	6,472	5,621	5,493	4,693	3,643	3,268	3,166	-3
Robbery	3,553	3,578	3,064	2,963	2,496	2,557	2,244	1,832	1,499	1,497	0
Other	3,022	3,017	2,957	3,043	3,005	3,266	2,475	1,964	1,912	1,589	-17
Sexual crimes[5]	6,558	6,726	6,552	6,331	6,527	6,696	7,361	7,693	8,604	9,557	11
Rape & attempted rape	1,161	1,123	1,053	963	996	1,131	1,274	1,462	1,808	1,901	5
Sexual assault	3,392	3,452	3,502	3,297	3,412	3,220	2,908	3,008	3,405	3,727	9
Crimes associated with prostitution	730	779	682	765	661	576	567	534	490	374	-24
Other sexual crimes	1,275	1,372	1,315	1,306	1,458	1,769	2,612	2,689	2,901	3,555	23
Crimes of dishonesty	187,798	183,760	166,718	167,812	153,256	155,870	154,337	135,899	137,324	126,857	-8
Housebreaking[6]	31,319	30,580	25,443	25,496	23,774	25,017	24,222	21,515	22,272	20,607	-7
Theft by opening a lockfast place (OLP)	8,263	7,422	6,378	6,952	5,074	4,059	3,529	3,239	3,218	2,879	-11
Theft from a motor vehicle by OLP	16,453	16,060	15,217	13,649	10,173	9,495	8,988	6,159	6,189	5,816	-6
Theft of a motor vehicle	14,041	15,000	12,105	11,551	9,304	8,716	7,060	5,731	5,976	5,423	-9
Shoplifting	28,247	28,750	29,186	32,048	30,332	29,660	29,758	26,449	27,693	27,364	-1
Other theft	72,128	70,241	64,645	64,384	61,008	64,680	66,681	58,704	58,794	53,539	-9
Fraud	11,074	9,332	8,409	8,316	8,283	8,983	8,892	8,898	8,088	6,913	-15
Other dishonesty	6,273	6,375	5,335	5,416	5,308	5,260	5,207	5,204	5,094	4,316	-15
Fire-raising, vandalism etc.	127,889	129,734	118,025	109,430	93,443	82,020	75,201	59,479	54,418	52,091	-4
Fire-raising	4,856	4,976	4,635	4,651	4,244	3,966	3,755	3,066	2,549	2,351	-8
Vandalism etc.	123,033	124,758	113,390	104,779	89,199	78,054	71,446	56,413	51,869	49,740	-4
Other crimes	81,814	84,938	81,340	81,248	73,670	67,223	67,756	62,452	63,266	61,488	-3
Crimes against public justice	27,668	32,052	31,353	29,493	26,885	26,294	26,635	23,401	23,610	21,100	-11
Handling offensive weapons	9,628	10,110	8,989	8,980	7,042	6,283	5,631	4,015	3,795	3,289	-13
Drugs	44,247	42,422	40,746	42,509	39,408	34,347	35,157	34,688	35,616	36,836	3
Other	271	354	252	266	335	299	333	348	245	263	7

Source: Recorded Crime in Scotland, Scottish Government

Notes:

3. Includes Murder, and Culpable homicide (common law), which includes Causing death by dangerous driving, Causing death by careless driving while under the influence of drink or drugs, Causing death by careless driving, Illegal driver involved in fatal accident and Corporate homicide.

4. For the definition of Serious assault and the distinction between Serious assault and Common assault please see Paragraph 6.9 within Annex 1 of Recorded Crime in Scotland.

5. Implementation of the Sexual Offences (Scotland) Act on 1 December 2010 affected the comparability of the breakdown of Sexual crimes over time. For further information please see the 'Data Considerations' section under Sexual crimes within Chapter 3 of Recorded Crime in Scotland

6. Includes dwellings, non-dwellings and other premises. For a more detailed definition see Paragraph 6.11 within Annex 1 of Recorded Crime in Scotland

21.13 People with a charge proved by main crime/offence, 2005-06 to 2014-15, Scotland

Main crime or offence	2005-06	2006-07	2007-08	2008-09	2009-10	2010-11	2011-12	2012-13	2013-14	2014-15[1]	% change 2013-14 to 2014-15	All offences proved, 2014-15 [2]
All crimes and offences	**128,204**	**134,413**	**133,607**	**125,892**	**121,041**	**115,575**	**108,388**	**101,015**	**105,626**	**106,507**	**1**	**141,381**
All crimes	**44,891**	**48,807**	**48,641**	**46,798**	**43,551**	**42,283**	**40,640**	**36,975**	**36,165**	**36,455**	**1**	**48,960**
Non-sexual crimes of violence	**2,459**	**2,461**	**2,749**	**2,658**	**2,462**	**2,539**	**2,438**	**2,138**	**1,781**	**1,718**	**-4**	**1,961**
Homicide etc	111	121	136	116	118	117	111	114	91	80	-12	87
Attempted murder and serious assault	1,561	1,496	1,731	1,709	1,511	1,418	1,352	1,283	1,026	1,037	1	1,125
Robbery	512	529	548	562	532	526	596	518	442	377	-15	448
Other non-sexual crimes of violence	275	315	334	271	301	478	379	223	222	224	1	301
Sexual crimes	**865**	**855**	**727**	**914**	**832**	**756**	**784**	**865**	**1,057**	**1,145**	**8**	**1,999**
Rape and attempted rape	61	60	49	42	57	36	49	77	89	125	40	283
Sexual assault	186	184	145	182	159	160	151	204	236	273	16	619
Crimes associated with prostitution	292	306	254	334	250	245	200	142	169	145	-14	151
Other sexual crimes	326	305	279	356	366	315	384	442	563	602	7	946
Crimes of dishonesty	**17,997**	**18,381**	**17,728**	**17,429**	**15,951**	**15,613**	**14,772**	**13,250**	**12,575**	**12,512**	**-1**	**16,814**
Housebreaking	2,074	2,025	1,867	1,860	1,604	1,540	1,498	1,365	1,037	980	-5	1,355
Theft by opening lockfast places	366	398	389	349	312	284	291	247	217	211	-3	344
Theft from a motor vehicle	489	408	447	387	297	270	250	200	143	112	-22	168
Theft of a motor vehicle	847	851	776	733	572	483	450	373	270	318	18	656
Shoplifting	8,162	8,548	8,457	8,287	8,098	7,853	7,267	6,500	6,530	6,940	6	8,663
Other theft	3,289	3,430	3,260	3,113	2,768	2,871	2,961	2,720	2,578	2,336	-9	3,119
Fraud	1,457	1,355	1,337	1,438	1,142	1,065	811	624	681	601	-12	1,180
Other dishonesty	1,313	1,366	1,195	1,262	1,158	1,247	1,244	1,221	1,119	1,014	-9	1,329
Fire-raising, vandalism, etc.	**5,000**	**5,438**	**5,392**	**4,375**	**3,836**	**3,362**	**3,016**	**2,584**	**2,502**	**2,439**	**-3**	**2,992**
Fire-raising	192	251	224	244	190	159	146	134	129	133	3	162
Vandalism etc.	4,808	5,187	5,168	4,131	3,646	3,203	2,870	2,450	2,373	2,306	-3	2,830
Other crimes	**18,570**	**21,672**	**22,045**	**21,422**	**20,470**	**20,013**	**19,630**	**18,138**	**18,250**	**18,641**	**2**	**25,194**
Crimes against public justice	7,347	9,018	9,825	10,350	9,744	9,822	10,170	9,767	9,669	10,036	4	14,169
Handling offensive weapons	3,500	3,547	3,405	3,516	2,838	2,445	2,265	1,710	1,685	1,580	-6	1,934
Drugs	7,614	8,904	8,547	7,318	7,699	7,527	6,982	6,449	6,717	6,857	2	8,892
Other crime	109	203	268	238	189	219	213	212	179	168	-6	199
All offences	**83,313**	**85,606**	**84,966**	**79,094**	**77,490**	**73,292**	**67,748**	**64,040**	**69,461**	**70,052**	**1**	**92,421**
Miscellaneous offences	**38,074**	**40,492**	**39,610**	**34,165**	**31,509**	**29,186**	**29,465**	**28,587**	**29,174**	**31,107**	**7**	**43,740**
Common assault	12,918	13,717	13,834	13,647	12,967	12,600	12,757	11,649	11,218	11,758	5	15,955
Breach of the peace etc.	16,894	18,104	17,494	16,003	14,077	12,113	12,544	12,961	13,731	15,580	13	22,281
Drunkenness and other disorderly conduct	293	261	235	129	146	160	124	102	85	115	35	228
Urinating etc.	345	473	514	81	47	43	20	32	41	43	5	94
Other miscellaneous	7,624	7,937	7,533	4,305	4,272	4,270	4,020	3,843	4,099	3,611	-12	5,182
Motor vehicle offences	**45,239**	**45,114**	**45,356**	**44,929**	**45,981**	**44,106**	**38,283**	**35,453**	**40,287**	**38,945**	**-3**	**48,681**
Dangerous and careless driving	3,620	3,774	3,967	3,696	3,405	3,167	2,858	2,811	3,576	3,412	-5	3,934
Driving under the influence	7,970	8,066	7,820	7,222	6,232	5,351	5,287	4,735	4,091	3,676	-10	4,183
Speeding	12,252	13,395	14,156	13,589	14,357	12,955	12,381	12,034	14,125	14,001	-1	14,283
Unlawful use of motor vehicle	14,703	13,450	13,609	12,740	12,175	11,052	9,001	7,855	8,515	8,303	-2	13,604
Vehicle defect offences	1,652	1,707	1,414	1,483	1,662	1,723	1,504	1,243	1,611	1,580	-2	2,678
Seat belt offences	1,234	1,211	1,010	1,257	2,199	2,673	1,982	2,052	2,539	2,172	-14	2,359
Mobile phone offences	631	814	1,197	2,265	2,856	3,603	2,641	2,663	3,096	3,160	2	3,354
Other motor vehicle offences	3,177	2,697	2,183	2,677	3,095	3,582	2,629	2,060	2,734	2,641	-3	4,286

Source: Scottish Government

1. Figures for some categories dealt with by the high court - including homicide, rape and major drug cases - may be underestimated due to late recording of disposals
2. Number of individual offences relating to people with a charge proved, whether or not the main crime/offence involved.

21.14 People with a charge proved by type of court, 2005-06 to 2014-15, Scotland

Number

Type of court	2005-06	2006-07	2007-08	2008-09	2009-10	2010-11	2011-12	2012-13	2013-14	2014-15
All court types	128,204	134,413	133,607	125,892	121,041	115,575	108,388	101,015	105,626	106,507
High court [1,2]	885	908	861	810	770	702	732	705	673	567
Sheriff solemn	3,969	4,682	5,195	4,532	4,222	4,020	4,138	4,304	4,234	4,773
Sheriff summary [3]	82,611	87,087	85,703	78,329	69,773	65,360	64,264	60,045	59,146	59,788
Justice of the Peace court [4]	40,739	41,736	41,848	42,221	46,276	45,493	39,254	35,961	41,573	41,379

Per cent

Type of court	2005-06	2006-07	2007-08	2008-09	2009-10	2010-11	2011-12	2012-13	2013-14	2014-15
All court types	100	100	100	100	100	100	100	100	100	100
High court [1,2]	1	1	1	1	1	1	1	1	1	1
Sheriff solemn	3	3	4	4	3	3	4	4	4	4
Sheriff summary [3]	64	65	64	62	58	57	59	59	56	56
Justice of the Peace court [4]	32	31	31	34	38	39	36	36	39	39

Index: 2005-06=100

Type of court	2005-06	2006-07	2007-08	2008-09	2009-10	2010-11	2011-12	2012-13	2013-14	2014-15
All court types	100	105	104	98	94	90	85	79	82	83
High court [1,2]	100	103	97	92	87	79	83	80	76	64
Sheriff solemn	100	118	131	114	106	101	104	108	107	120
Sheriff summary [3]	100	105	104	95	84	79	78	73	72	72
Justice of the Peace court [4]	100	102	103	104	114	112	96	88	102	102

Source: Scottish Government

1. Includes cases remitted to the High court from the Sheriff court.

2. The figures for 2014-15, and to an extent earlier years, may be underestimated due to late recording of disposals.

3. Includes the stipendiary magistrates court in Glasgow. Revision in 2014-15 bulletin has corrected some records for stipendiary court proceedings that were incorrectly coded as sheriff summary cases.

4. Includes District courts up to 2009-10.

21.15 People with a charge proved by main penalty, 2005-06 to 2014-15, Scotland

Number

Main penalty	2005-06[1]	2006-07	2007-08	2008-09	2009-10	2010-11	2011-12	2012-13	2013-14	2014-15	% change 2013-14 to 2014-15
Total	128,204	134,413	133,607	125,892	121,041	115,575	108,388	101,015	105,626	106,507	1
Custody	15,081	16,758	16,761	16,944	15,800	15,313	15,921	14,785	14,142	13,977	-1
Prison	12,154	13,489	13,593	13,905	13,016	13,120	13,703	13,068	12,808	12,736	-1
Young offenders institution	2,903	3,245	3,142	3,017	2,753	2,168	2,202	1,690	1,312	1,217	-7
Order for life-long restriction	-	-	-	1	9	13	10	17	17	20	18
Other custody	24	24	26	21	22	12	6	10	5	4	-20
Community sentence	15,974	16,077	16,709	17,922	16,350	15,616	16,934	17,264	18,273	18,519	1
Community payback order	-	-	-	-	-	461	10,380	14,940	16,375	16,693	2
Community service order	5,183	5,286	5,601	5,784	5,471	5,307	2,642	479	141	68	-52
Probation	8,786	8,614	9,002	9,912	8,893	7,935	2,305	293	82	48	-41
Restriction of liberty order	1,136	1,179	1,155	1,143	931	831	845	919	1,078	1,172	9
Drug treatment & testing order	758	865	822	885	808	806	642	608	590	538	-9
Other community sentences[2]	111	133	129	198	247	276	120	25	7	-	-100
Financial penalty	82,194	84,820	83,344	73,991	72,491	67,576	59,320	53,429	57,795	56,843	-2
Fine	80,723	83,445	82,019	72,838	71,452	66,492	58,395	52,661	56,921	56,003	-2
Compensation order	1,471	1,375	1,325	1,153	1,039	1,084	925	768	874	840	-4
Other sentence[1]	14,951	16,758	16,793	17,035	16,400	17,070	16,213	15,537	15,416	17,168	11
Admonition[3]	14,175	15,967	16,084	16,398	15,687	16,421	15,577	15,011	14,839	16,418	11
Absolute discharge, no order made	401	413	430	412	523	460	472	361	462	658	42
Remit to children's hearing	260	313	259	209	175	170	140	133	94	67	-29
Insanity, hospital, guardianship order	115	65	20	16	15	19	24	32	21	25	19
Average amount of penalty											
Custody (days)[4]	229	232	248	262	281	277	286	284	293	285	
Fine[5,6] (£)	150	150	175	200	180	180	200	200	180	200	
Compensation order [6,7](£)	101	150	150	180	180	190	200	200	200	200	

1. Includes a small number of sentences unknown for the years 2005-06.
2. Includes supervised attendance orders, community reparation orders and anti-social behaviour orders.
3. Includes a small number of court cautions and dog-related disposals.
4. Figures for 2014-15 may be underestimated due to delayed reporting of high court records..
5. Excludes company fines.
6. Excludes a small number of large fines and calculated as the median.
7. As main or secondary penalty.

Percentage

Main penalty	2005-06	2006-07	2007-08	2008-09	2009-10	2010-11	2011-12	2012-13	2013-14	2014-15
Total										
Custody	12	12	13	13	13	13	15	15	13	13
Prison	9	10	10	11	11	11	13	13	12	12
Young offenders institution	2	2	2	2	2	2	2	2	1	1
Order for life-long restriction	-	-	-	*	*	*	*	*	*	*
Other custody	*	*	*	*	*	*	*	*	*	*
Community sentence	12	12	13	14	14	14	16	17	17	17
Community payback order	-	-	-	-	-	*	10	15	16	16
Community service order	4	4	4	5	5	5	2	*	*	*
Probation	7	6	7	8	7	7	2	*	*	*
Restriction of liberty order	1	1	1	1	1	1	1	1	1	1
Drug treatment & testing order	1	1	1	1	1	1	1	1	1	1
Supervised attendance order	*	*	*	*	*	*	*	*	*	-
Financial penalty	64	63	62	59	60	58	55	53	55	53
Fine	63	62	61	58	59	58	54	52	54	53
Compensation order	1	1	1	1	1	1	1	1	1	1
Other sentence	12	12	13	14	14	15	15	15	15	16
Admonition	11	12	12	13	13	14	14	15	14	15
Absolute discharge	*	*	*	*	*	*	*	*	*	1
Remit to children's hearing	*	*	*	*	*	*	*	*	*	*
Insanity, hospital, guardianship order	*	*	*	*	*	*	*	*	*	*

Source: Scottish Government

21.16 People with a charge proved by main penalty, sex and age, 2005-06 to 2014-15, Scotland

		2005-06	2006-07	2007-08	2008-09	2009-10	2010-11	2011-12	2012-13	2013-14	2014-15	% change 13-14 to 14-15
Total[1]		128,204	134,413	133,607	125,892	121,041	115,575	108,388	101,015	105,626	106,507	1
Males[2]	Total	107,802	113,510	112,787	106,299	101,613	97,036	90,866	84,344	87,948	88,593	1
	Under 21	24,185	25,639	24,525	20,535	17,328	15,145	13,130	10,358	9,184	8,624	-6
	21-30	38,079	40,404	41,222	38,899	37,315	35,176	32,742	30,338	30,690	30,138	-2
	Over 30	45,538	47,467	47,040	46,865	46,970	46,715	44,994	43,648	48,074	49,831	4
Females[2]	Total	20,039	20,600	20,565	19,581	19,424	18,530	17,437	16,556	17,590	17,908	2
	Under 21	2,937	3,264	3,306	2,830	2,511	2,228	1,952	1,616	1,429	1,448	1
	21-30	7,387	7,401	7,387	7,314	7,010	6,573	5,989	5,872	5,656	5,513	-3
	Over 30	9,715	9,935	9,872	9,437	9,903	9,729	9,496	9,068	10,505	10,947	4
Custody[1]		15,081	16,758	16,761	16,944	15,800	15,313	15,921	14,785	14,142	13,977	-1
Males[2]	Total	13,938	15,583	15,486	15,591	14,520	14,011	14,553	13,496	12,930	12,689	-2
	Under 21	2,803	3,070	2,986	2,856	2,601	2,014	2,049	1,588	1,235	1,137	-8
	21-30	6,029	6,684	6,864	6,718	6,154	6,073	6,043	5,487	5,008	4,956	-1
	Over 30	5,106	5,829	5,636	6,017	5,765	5,924	6,461	6,421	6,687	6,596	-1
Females[2]	Total	1,143	1,175	1,275	1,353	1,280	1,302	1,368	1,289	1,212	1,288	6
	Under 21	125	200	182	182	175	168	160	116	83	84	1
	21-30	563	592	615	682	581	588	620	598	491	482	-2
	Over 30	455	383	478	489	524	546	588	575	638	722	13
Community sentence[1]		15,974	16,077	16,709	17,922	16,350	15,616	16,934	17,264	18,273	18,519	1
Males[2]	Total	13,356	13,566	13,886	14,955	13,484	12,978	14,087	14,396	15,244	15,450	1
	Under 21	4,158	4,486	4,471	4,608	3,640	3,446	3,292	2,743	2,635	2,509	-5
	21-30	4,921	4,878	4,935	5,303	5,037	4,696	5,246	5,590	5,674	5,752	1
	Over 30	4,277	4,202	4,480	5,044	4,807	4,836	5,549	6,063	6,935	7,189	4
Females[2]	Total	2,618	2,511	2,823	2,967	2,866	2,638	2,847	2,868	3,028	3,069	1
	Under 21	532	633	667	593	559	453	433	428	340	378	11
	21-30	1,126	926	1,092	1,177	1,013	1,020	1,014	1,063	1,030	1,008	-2
	Over 30	960	952	1,064	1,197	1,294	1,165	1,400	1,377	1,658	1,683	2
Monetary[1]		82,194	84,820	83,344	73,991	72,491	67,576	59,320	53,429	57,795	56,843	-2
Males2	Total	69,503	72,050	71,057	63,240	61,480	57,359	50,260	45,144	48,433	47,795	-1
	Under 21	14,029	14,646	13,597	9,886	8,462	7,071	5,365	4,061	3,697	3,352	-9
	21-30	23,884	25,214	25,791	23,102	22,258	20,360	17,798	15,812	16,478	15,576	-5
	Over 30	31,590	32,190	31,669	30,252	30,760	29,928	27,097	25,271	28,258	28,867	2
Females[2]	Total	12,357	12,488	12,047	10,739	11,007	10,209	8,983	8,174	9,282	9,043	-3
	Under 21	1,507	1,572	1,569	1,206	1,061	909	746	530	519	533	3
	21-30	4,254	4,253	4,140	3,754	3,818	3,382	2,907	2,705	2,772	2,610	-6
	Over 30	6,596	6,663	6,338	5,779	6,128	5,918	5,330	4,939	5,991	5,900	-2
Other sentence[1]		14,951	16,758	16,793	17,035	16,400	17,070	16,213	15,537	15,416	17,168	11
Males[2]	Total	11,005	12,311	12,358	12,513	12,129	12,688	11,966	11,308	11,341	12,659	12
	Under 21	3,195	3,437	3,471	3,185	2,625	2,614	2,424	1,966	1,617	1,626	1
	21-30	3,245	3,628	3,632	3,776	3,866	4,047	3,655	3,449	3,530	3,854	9
	Over 30	4,565	5,246	5,255	5,552	5,638	6,027	5,887	5,893	6,194	7,179	16
Females[2]	Total	3,921	4,426	4,420	4,522	4,271	4,381	4,239	4,225	4,068	4,508	11
	Under 21	773	859	888	849	716	698	613	542	487	453	-7
	21-30	1,444	1,630	1,540	1,701	1,598	1,583	1,448	1,506	1,363	1,413	4
	Over 30	1,704	1,937	1,992	1,972	1,957	2,100	2,178	2,177	2,218	2,642	19

1. Includes a small number of cases for companies and where age and gender are unknown.
2. Gender totals exclude companies and where age and gender are unknown. The sum of gender totals may not equal disposal totals.

Source: Scottish Government

21.17a Average daily population in penal establishments by type of custody: 2004-05 to 2013-14

	2004-05	2005-06	2006-07	2007-08	2008-09	2009-10	2010-11	2011-12	2012-13	2013-14	% change over past year
Total	**6,776**	**6,856**	**7,187**	**7,376**	**7,827**	**7,964**	**7,854**	**8,179**	**8,057**	**7,894**	-2
Remand	1,223	1,250	1,572	1,561	1,679	1,522	1,474	1,601	1,469	1,474	*
Untried	1,036	1,032	1,329	1,306	1,415	1,170	1,112	1,238	1,155	1,163	1
Convicted awaiting sentence	188	218	243	255	264	352	362	363	314	311	-1
Young persons	261	285	361	355	334	305	262	258	198	167	-16
Adults	962	965	1,211	1,206	1,344	1,217	1,212	1,342	1,271	1,307	3
Sentenced	5,553	5,606	5,615	5,815	6,148	6,442	6,380	6,578	6,588	6,420	-3
Young persons (direct sentence)	545	607	621	658	658	690	576	533	473	383	-19
Adults (direct sentence)	4,599	4,553	4,433	4,516	4,879	5,120	5,111	5,332	5,392	5,334	-1
Fine defaulters	51	47	46	28	11	9	9	8	9	9	1
Recalls from supervision/licence	351	397	515	611	600	622	682	702	713	693	-3
Others	5	1	*	*	-	-	-	-	-	-	-
Sentenced by court martial	1	-	-	*	1	-	1	1	1	*	-
Civil prisoners	1	1	1	1	*	1	*	1	*	1	-
Men	**6,444**	**6,521**	**6,833**	**7,004**	**7,413**	**7,538**	**7,418**	**7,710**	**7,598**	**7,462**	-2
Remand	1,138	1,166	1,471	1,444	1,545	1,417	1,369	1,493	1,362	1,368	*
Untried	980	975	1,257	1,232	1,330	1,107	1,044	1,171	1,086	1,093	1
Convicted awaiting sentence	159	191	213	213	215	311	325	322	276	275	-1
Sentenced	5,305	5,355	5,362	5,560	5,868	6,121	6,049	6,217	6,236	6,094	-2
Young persons (direct sentence)	515	583	591	634	632	662	545	506	452	365	-19
Adults (direct sentence)	4,386	4,332	4,217	4,294	4,632	4,835	4,825	5,012	5,072	5,037	-1
Fine defaulters	47	44	43	26	10	8	9	8	9	9	*
Recalls from supervision/licence	350	395	511	604	593	615	670	690	702	683	-3
Others	5	1	*	*	-	-	-	-	-	-	-
Sentenced by court martial	1	-	-	*	1	-	1	1	1	*	-
Civil prisoners	1	*	*	1	*	1	*	*	*	*	-
Women	**332**	**335**	**354**	**372**	**414**	**426**	**436**	**469**	**459**	**432**	-6
Remand	85	84	101	117	133	105	105	108	107	106	-1
Untried	56	57	72	75	85	63	68	67	69	70	2
Convicted awaiting sentence	29	27	29	42	49	41	38	41	38	36	-5
Sentenced	247	251	253	256	280	321	331	361	353	326	-8
Young persons (direct sentence)	30	24	30	24	26	28	32	28	21	17	-18
Adults (direct sentence)	212	221	216	223	247	286	286	320	319	297	7
Fine defaulters	4	4	3	2	1	1	*	*	1	1	-
Recalls from supervision/licence	1	2	4	7	7	6	13	13	11	10	-
Others	*	*	-	-	-	-	-	-	-	-	-
Sentenced by court martial	-	-	-	-	-	-	-	-	*	*	-
Civil prisoners	*	*	*	*	*	*	*	*	*	*	-

- Nil
* Less than 0.5

Source: Scottish Government: Prison Statistics and Population Projections Scotland 2013-14

21.17b Average daily sentenced prison population by sentence length: 2004-05 to 2013-14

	2004-05	2005-06	2006-07	2007-08	2008-09	2009-10	2010-11	2011-12	2012-13	2013-14	% change over past year
Total	**5,551**	**5,605**	**5,614**	**5,814**	**6,147**	**6,441**	**6,378**	**6,576**	**6,587**	**6,419**	**-3**
Fine default	51	47	46	28	11	9	9	8	9	9	1
Less than 3 months	81	101	124	116	98	89	78	50	54	55	2
3 months - less than 6 months	450	442	444	426	402	350	347	383	355	364	3
6 months - less than 2 years	1,161	1,214	1,160	1,226	1,568	1,768	1,683	1,822	1,771	1,715	-3
2 years - less than 4 years	884	913	959	1,058	1,099	1,211	1,183	1,172	1,192	1,077	-10
4 years or over (excluding life)	1,957	1,841	1,701	1,653	1,642	1,630	1,596	1,599	1,619	1,597	-1
Life/Section 205/206 sentences	612	650	666	696	726	763	800	838	875	908	4
Persons recalled from supervision/licence	351	397	515	611	600	622	682	702	713	693	-3
Others	5	1	*	*	-	-	-	-	-	-	-
Young persons	**559**	**624**	**644**	**685**	**687**	**719**	**604**	**555**	**492**	**399**	**-19**
Fine default	5	5	4	2	1	1	1	1	1	1	-
Less than 3 months	9	14	13	13	11	8	6	3	3	3	2
3 months - less than 6 months	55	57	58	58	50	45	37	34	26	27	5
6 months - less than 2 years	212	241	241	244	268	307	242	246	200	170	-15
2 years - less than 4 years	118	142	136	175	165	182	164	137	129	91	-29
4 years or over (excluding life)	131	127	143	136	134	126	103	94	95	73	-23
Life/Section 205/206 sentences	19	26	30	31	30	22	23	19	21	18	-11
Persons recalled from supervision/licence	8	11	19	25	28	28	26	22	18	15	-16
Others	1	*	-	-	-	-	-	-	-	-	-
Adults	**4,992**	**4,981**	**4,970**	**5,129**	**5,460**	**5,722**	**5,775**	**6,021**	**6,096**	**6,021**	**-1**
Fine default	46	43	41	26	10	8	8	8	9	9	*
Less than 3 months	71	87	111	102	88	81	72	47	50	51	2
3 months - less than 6 months	395	386	386	367	352	305	310	349	329	337	2
6 months - less than 2 years	949	972	918	982	1,300	1,461	1,441	1,577	1,571	1,545	-2
2 years - less than 4 years	766	771	823	883	935	1,029	1,019	1,035	1,063	986	-7
4 years or over (excluding life)	1,826	1,713	1,558	1,517	1,509	1,504	1,492	1,506	1,524	1,524	*
Life/Section 205/206 sentences	592	623	637	664	696	741	776	819	854	890	4
Persons recalled from supervision/licence	343	385	496	586	572	594	656	681	695	678	-2
Others	4	1	*	*	-	-	-	-	-	-	-
Men	**5,304**	**5,355**	**5,362**	**5,558**	**5,867**	**6,120**	**6,048**	**6,215**	**6,235**	**6,094**	**-2**
Fine default	47	44	43	26	10	8	9	8	9	9	*
Less than 3 months	75	94	116	108	91	83	73	45	49	50	3
3 months - less than 6 months	421	415	419	402	375	324	319	352	331	339	2
6 months - less than 2 years	1,075	1,120	1,070	1,133	1,464	1,644	1,554	1,689	1,628	1,580	-3
2 years - less than 4 years	831	862	903	1,002	1,035	1,128	1,114	1,096	1,128	1,022	-9
4 years or over (excluding life)	1,905	1,791	1,651	1,605	1,593	1,580	1,537	1,528	1,548	1,538	-1
Life/Section 205/206 sentences	595	633	649	678	707	739	773	807	841	872	4
Persons recalled from supervision/licence	350	395	511	604	593	615	670	690	702	683	-3
Others	5	1	*	*	-	-	-	-	-	-	-
Women	**247**	**250**	**253**	**255**	**280**	**321**	**331**	**361**	**352**	**325**	**-8**
Fine default	4	4	3	2	1	1	*	*	1	1	-
Less than 3 months	6	7	8	8	7	7	5	5	5	4	-15
3 months - less than 6 months	30	27	25	24	28	26	28	31	24	25	3
6 months - less than 2 years	86	94	90	93	104	124	130	133	143	135	-5
2 years - less than 4 years	52	51	56	56	64	83	70	76	64	55	-14
4 years or over (excluding life)	52	49	49	48	49	50	59	71	71	59	-17
Life/Section 205/206 sentences	16	17	18	18	19	24	26	31	34	36	5
Persons recalled from supervision/licence	1	2	4	7	7	6	13	13	11	10	-6
Others	*	*	-	-	-	-	-	-	-	-	-

Note: Civil prisoners are excluded from this table.

Source: Scottish Government Prison Statistics and Population Projections Scotland

21.17c Receptions to penal establishments by type of custody: 2004-05 to 2013-14

	2004-05	2005-06	2006-07	2007-08	2008-09	2009-10	2010-11	2011-12	2012-13	2013-14	% change over past year
Total	**38,348**	**38,747**	**43,504**	**40,448**	**38,986**	**36,518**	**35,990**	**37,003**	**33,837**	**33,626**	*-1*
Remand	18,539	19,105	22,811	22,136	22,303	20,637	21,022	21,658	19,171	19,323	*1*
Unruly certificate [1]	20	24	29	15	10	5	-				
Sentenced	19,653	19,489	20,429	18,227	16,566	15,821	14,942	15,333	14,652	14,294	*-2*
Young persons	2,673	2,935	2,982	2,762	2,447	2,324	1,862	1,804	1,411	1,191	*-16*
Direct sentenced	1,947	2,164	2,285	2,359	2,262	2,144	1,709	1,687	1,325	1,091	*-18*
Fine defaulters	726	771	697	403	185	180	153	117	86	100	*16*
Adults	16,710	16,207	16,980	15,053	13,698	13,057	12,560	13,038	12,788	12,631	*-1*
Direct sentenced	10,629	10,757	11,707	11,842	12,376	11,904	11,461	11,992	11,764	11,570	*-2*
Fine defaulters	6,081	5,450	5,273	3,211	1,322	1,153	1,099	1,046	1,024	1,061	*4*
Recalls from supervision/licence	270	347	467	412	421	440	520	491	453	472	*4*
Sentenced by court martial	6	-	-	2	1	-	2	-	1	-	*n/a*
Civil prisoners	6	4	4	11	4	12	22	12	13	9	*-31*
Legalised police cells [2]	124	125	231	57	102	43	2				
Men	**35,201**	**35,687**	**40,087**	**37,053**	**35,603**	**33,543**	**32,980**	**33,905**	**30,972**	**30,791**	*-1*
Remand	16,787	17,370	20,809	19,965	20,057	18,792	19,129	19,681	17,359	17,518	*1*
Unruly certificate [1]	19	24	26	14	10	5	-				
Sentenced	18,265	18,170	19,041	17,008	15,433	14,697	13,827	14,212	13,600	13,264	*-2*
Young persons	2,519	2,820	2,808	2,630	2,319	2,193	1,725	1,696	1,327	1,119	*-16*
Direct sentenced	1,826	2,076	2,155	2,245	2,143	2,019	1,576	1,587	1,250	1,024	*-18*
Fine defaulters	693	744	653	385	176	174	149	109	77	95	*23*
Adults	15,480	15,008	15,778	13,976	12,703	12,077	11,592	12,035	11,826	11,687	*-1*
Direct sentenced	9,898	10,011	10,904	11,012	11,470	11,008	10,568	11,048	10,873	10,689	*-2*
Fine defaulters	5,582	4,997	4,874	2,964	1,233	1,069	1,024	987	953	998	*5*
Recalls from supervision/licence	266	342	455	402	411	427	510	481	447	458	*2*
Sentenced by court martial	6	-	-	2	1	-	2	-	-	-	*n/a*
Civil prisoners	6	4	3	10	3	11	20	12	13	9	*-31*
Legalised police cells [2]	118	119	208	54	99	38	2				
Women	**3,147**	**3,060**	**3,417**	**3,395**	**3,383**	**2,975**	**3,010**	**3,098**	**2,865**	**2,835**	*-1*
Remand	1,752	1,735	2,002	2,171	2,246	1,845	1,893	1,977	1,812	1,805	*
Unruly certificate [1]	1	-	3	1	-	-	-				
Sentenced	1,388	1,319	1,388	1,219	1,133	1,124	1,115	1,121	1,052	1,030	*-2*
Young persons	154	115	174	132	128	131	137	108	84	72	*-14*
Direct sentenced	121	88	130	114	119	125	133	100	75	67	*-11*
Fine defaulters	33	27	44	18	9	6	4	8	9	5	*-44*
Adults	1,230	1,199	1,202	1,077	995	980	968	1,003	962	944	*-2*
Direct sentenced	731	746	803	830	906	896	893	944	891	881	*-1*
Fine defaulters	499	453	399	247	89	84	75	59	71	63	*-11*
Recalls from supervision/licence	4	5	12	10	10	13	10	10	6	14	*133*
Sentenced by court martial	-	-	-	-	-	-	-	-	1	-	*n/a*
Civil prisoners	-	-	1	1	1	1	2	-	-	-	*n/a*
Legalised police cells [2]	6	6	23	3	3	5					

Source: Scottish Government Prison Statistics and Population Projections Scotland

Notes: Receptions do not equate to persons received since someone receiving a custodial sentence after a period on remand, or several custodial sentences at different times or from different courts, will be counted more than once.

1. The legislation under which children may be remanded in custody on an unruly certificate was repealed in 2010.
2. Reporting on legalised police cells was discontinued in 2010-11 due to closures and very low volumes of usage of these facilities.

21.18 Scottish Prison Service Statement of Comprehensive Net Expenditure for the year ended 31 March 2014

	2013-14 £000	2012-13 £000
Income		
Income from all sources	**(7,518)**	(7,493)
Expenditure		
Staff costs	**150,176**	144,221
Running costs	**78,235**	176,593
Other current expenditure	**31,932**	28,280
Total expenditure	**260,343**	349,094
Operating cost	**252,825**	341,601
Interest payable and similar charges	**11,302**	11,455
Net operating cost	**264,127**	353,056

Other Comprehensive Net Expenditure

	Note	2013-14 £000	2012-13 £000
Items that will not be reclassified to net operating costs:			
Net (gain)/loss on revaluation of property, plant and equipment		**(56,831)**	7,715
Total comprehensive net expenditure		**207,296**	360,771

Source: Scottish Prison Service Annual Report & Accounts 2013-14

21.19 Number of recorded crimes in the 12 months to February 2016 compared with the previous 12 months - Northern Ireland

Offence group	Number and percentage changes			
	Recorded crime			
	12 months to February 2015	12 months to February 2016[1,2]	change between years	% change between years[3]
VICTIM-BASED CRIME				
VIOLENCE AGAINST THE PERSON	34,425	35,414	989	2.9
Homicide	*25*	*22*	*-3*	*-*
Violence with injury	*14,562*	*14,907*	*345*	*2.4*
Violence without injury	*19,838*	*20,485*	*647*	*3.3*
SEXUAL OFFENCES	2,664	2,997	333	12.5
Rape	*715*	*773*	*58*	*8.1*
Other sexual offences	*1,949*	*2,224*	*275*	*14.1*
ROBBERY	893	756	-137	-15.3
Robbery of personal property	*646*	*562*	*-84*	*-13.0*
Robbery of business property	*247*	*194*	*-53*	*-21.5*
THEFT OFFENCES	35,530	34,739	-791	-2.2
Burglary	*8,930*	*8,977*	*47*	*0.5*
Domestic burglary	*5,839*	*5,988*	*149*	*2.6*
Non-domestic burglary	*3,091*	*2,989*	*-102*	*-3.3*
Theft from the person	*522*	*557*	*35*	*6.7*
Vehicle offences	*5,223*	*4,954*	*-269*	*-5.2*
Bicycle theft	*982*	*735*	*-247*	*-25.2*
Shoplifting	*6,484*	*6,827*	*343*	*5.3*
All other theft offences	*13,389*	*12,689*	*-700*	*-5.2*
CRIMINAL DAMAGE	19,783	20,595	812	4.1
OTHER CRIMES AGAINST SOCIETY				
DRUG OFFENCES	5,079	5,478	399	7.9
Trafficking of drugs	*895*	*870*	*-25*	*-2.8*
Possession of drugs	*4,184*	*4,608*	*424*	*10.1*
POSSESSION OF WEAPONS OFFENCES	780	894	114	14.6
PUBLIC ORDER OFFENCES	1,465	1,423	-42	-2.9
MISCELLANEOUS CRIMES AGAINST SOCIETY	2,716	2,823	107	3.9
TOTAL RECORDED CRIME – ALL OFFENCES (excluding fraud)	**103,335**	**105,289**	**1,954**	**1.9**

Source: Police Service Northern Irel

1. Figures for the 12 months to 29th February 2016 are provisional and will be subject to change.
2. Individual crime types may not add to Total Recorded Crime – All Offences as there will be some crimes yet to complete the validation process and be allocated to a crime classification.
3 '-' indicates that for offences recorded a percentage change is not reported because the base number of offences is less than 50.

21.20 Northern Ireland Prison Receptions by Prisoner Type, Gender and Establishment

		2012	2013	2014
Remand	Maghaberry	2,688	2,236	2,194
	Hydebank Wood YOC Males	544	420	350
	Hydebank Wood Females	208	209	192
	Total	3,440	2,865	2,736
Immediate Custody	Maghaberry	1,689	1,783	1,710
	Hydebank Wood YOC Males	276	258	195
	Hydebank Wood Females	107	132	118
	Total	2,072	2,173	2,023
Fine Defaulter	Maghaberry	1,936	244	121
	Hydebank Wood YOC Males	276	33	11
	Hydebank Wood Females	261	27	7
	Total	2,473	304	139
Non Criminal	Maghaberry	17	17	18
	Hydebank Wood YOC Males	0	1	1
	Hydebank Wood Females	2	1	0
	Total	19	19	19
Males		7,426	4,992	4,600
Females		578	369	317
Establishment	Maghaberry	6,330	4,280	4,043
	Hydebank Wood YOC Males	1,096	712	557
	Hydebank Wood Females	578	369	317
	Total	8,004	5,361	4,917

Source: Northern Ireland Population 2014

this page is intentionally blank

Transport and
communications

Chapter 22

Transport and communication

Road data (Tables 22.4 & 22.5)

The Department for Transport has undertaken significant development work over the last few years to improve its traffic estimates and measurement of traffic flow on particular stretches of the road network. This work has previously been outlined in a number of publications (Road Traffic Statistics: 2001 SB(02)23, Traffic in Great Britain Q4 2002 Data SB(03)5 and Traffic in Great Britain Q1 2003 SB(03)6).

The main point to note is that figures for 1993 onwards have been calculated on a different basis from years prior to 1993. Therefore, figures prior to 1993 are not directly comparable with estimates for later years. Estimates on the new basis for 1993 and subsequent years were first published by the Department on 8 May 2003 in Traffic in Great Britain Q1 2003 SB(03)6. A summary of the main methodological changes to take place over the last couple of years appears below.

Traffic estimates are now disaggregated for roads in urban and rural areas rather than between built-up and non built-up roads. Built-up roads were defined as those with a speed limit of 40 mph or lower. This created difficulties in producing meaningful disaggregated traffic estimates because an increasing number of clearly rural roads were subject to a 40 mph speed limit for safety reasons. The urban/rural split of roads is largely determined by whether roads lie within the boundaries of urban areas with a population of 10,000 or more with adjustments in some cases for major roads at the boundary.

Traffic estimates are based on the results of many 12-hour manual counts in every year, which are grossed up to estimates of annual average daily flows using expansion factors based on data from automatic traffic counters on similar roads. These averages are needed so that traffic in off-peak times, at weekends and in the summer and winter months (when only special counts are undertaken) can be taken into account when assessing the traffic at each site. For this purpose roads are now sorted into 22 groupings (previously there were only seven) and this allows a better match of manual count sites with our automatic count sites. These groupings are based on a detailed analysis of the results from all the individual automatic count sites and take into account regional groupings, road category (that is, both the urban/rural classification of the road and the road class) and traffic flow levels. The groupings range from lightly trafficked, rural minor roads in holiday areas such as Cornwall and Devon, to major roads in central London.

With the increasing interest in sub-regional statistics, we have undertaken a detailed study of traffic counts on minor roads carried out in the last ten years. This has been done in conjunction with a Geographic Information System to enable us to establish general patterns of minor road traffic in each local authority. As a result of this, we have been able to produce more reliable estimate of traffic levels in each authority in our base year of 1999. This in turn has enabled us to produce better estimates of traffic levels back to 1993, as well as more reliable estimates for 1999 onwards.

The Department created a database for major roads based on a Geographic Information System and Ordnance Survey data. This was checked by local authorities and discussed with government regional offices and the Highways Agency to ensure that good local knowledge supplemented the available technical data.

Urban major and minor roads, from 1993 onwards, are defined as being within an urban area with a population of more than 10,000 people, based on the 2001 urban settlements. The definition for urban settlement can be found on the CLG web site at:
 www.communities.gov.uk/planningandbuilding/planningbuilding/planningstatistics/urbanrural.

Rural major and minor roads, from 1993 onwards, are defined as being outside an urban settlement.

New vehicle registrations (Table 22.8)

Special concession group
Various revisions to the vehicle taxation system were introduced on 1 July 1995 and on 29 November 1995. Separate taxation classes for farmers' goods vehicles were abolished on 1 July 1995; after this date new vehicles of this type were registered as Heavy Goods Vehicles (HGVs). The total includes 5,900 vehicles registered between 1 January and 30 June in the (now abolished) agricultural and special machines group in classes which were not eligible to register in the special concession group. The old agricultural and special machines taxation group was abolished at end June 1995. The group includes agricultural and mowing machines, snow ploughs and gritting vehicles. Electric vehicles are also included in this group and are no longer exempt from Vehicle Excise Duty (VED). Steam propelled vehicles were added to this group from November 1995.

Other licensed vehicles
Includes three wheelers, pedestrian controlled vehicles, general haulage and showmen's tractors and recovery vehicles. Recovery vehicle tax class introduced January 1988.

Special vehicles group
The special vehicles group was created on 1 July 1995 and consists of various vehicle types over 3.5 tonnes gross weight but not required to pay VED as heavy goods vehicles. The group includes mobile cranes, work trucks, digging machines, road rollers and vehicles previously taxed as showman's goods and haulage. The figure shown for 1995 covers the period from 1 July to 31 December only.

National Travel Survey data (Tables 22.1 & 22.11)
The National Travel Survey (NTS) is designed to provide a databank of personal travel information for Great Britain. It has been conducted as a continuous survey since July 1988, following ad hoc surveys since the mid-1960s. The survey is designed to identify long-term trends and is not suitable for monitoring short-term trends.

In 2006, a weighting strategy was introduced to the NTS and applied retrospectively to data back to 1995. The weighting methodology adjusts for non-response bias and also adjusts for the drop-off in the number of trips recorded by respondents during the course of the travel week. All results now published for 1995 onwards are based on weighted data, and direct comparisons cannot be made to earlier years or previous publications.

During 2008, over 8,000 households provided details of their personal travel by filling in travel diaries over the course of a week. The drawn sample size from 2002 was nearly trebled compared with previous years following recommendations in a National Statistics Review of the NTS. This enables most results to be presented on a single year basis from 2002.

Travel included in the NTS covers all trips by British residents within Great Britain for personal reasons, including travel in the course of work.

A trip is defined as a one-way course of travel having a single main purpose. It is the basic unit of personal travel defined in the survey.

A round trip is split into two trips, with the first ending at a convenient point about half-way round as a notional stopping point for the outward destination and return origin.

A stage is that portion of a trip defined by the use of a specific method of transport or of a specific ticket (a new stage being defined if either the mode or ticket changes). The main mode of a trip is that used for the longest stage of the trip. With stages of equal length, the mode of the latest stage is used. Walks of less than 50 yards are excluded.

Travel details provided by respondents include trip purpose, method of travel, time of day and trip length. The households also provided personal information, such as their age, sex, working status, driving licence holding, and details of the cars available for their use.

Because estimates made from a sample survey depend on the particular sample chosen, they generally differ from the true values of the population. This is not usually a problem when considering large samples (such as all car trips in Great Britain), but it may give misleading information when considering data from small samples even after weighting.

The most recent editions of all NTS publications are available on the DfT website at: www.dft.gov.uk/transtat/personaltravel. Bulletins of key results are published annually. The most recent bulletin is National Travel Survey: 2014.

Households with regular use of cars (Table 22.11)

The mid-year estimates of the percentage of households with regular use of a car or van are based on combined data from the NTS, the Expenditure and Food Survey (previously the Family Expenditure Survey) and the General Household Survey. The method for calculating these figures was changed slightly in 2006, to incorporate weighted data from the NTS and the GHS. Figures since have also been revised to incorporate weighted data. Results by area type are based on weighted data from the NTS only.

Continuing Survey of Road Goods Transport (Tables 22.2, 22.17 & 22.18)

The estimates are derived from the Continuing Survey of Road Goods Transport (CSRGT). The samples are drawn from the computerised vehicle licence records held by the Driver and Vehicle Licensing Agency. Questionnaires are sent to the registered keepers of the sampled vehicles asking for a description of the vehicle and its activity during the survey week. The estimates are grossed to the vehicle population,, and at the overall national level have a 2 per cent margin of error (at 95 per cent confidence level). Further details and results are published in Road Freight Statistics, and previously in Transport of Goods by Road in Great Britain.

Methodological changes

A key component of National Statistics outputs is a programme of quality reviews carried out at least every five years to ensure that such statistics are fit for purpose and that their quality and value continue to improve. A quality review of the Department for Transport's road freight surveys, including the CSRGT, was carried out in 2003. A copy of the report can be accessed at: www.statistics.gov.uk/nsbase/methods_quality/quality_review/downloads/NSQR30FinalReport.doc

The quality review made a number of recommendations about the CSRGT. The main methodological recommendation was that, to improve the accuracy of survey estimates, the sample strata should be amended to reflect current trends in vehicle type, weight and legislative groups. These new strata are described more fully in Appendix C of the survey report. For practical and administrative reasons, changes were also made to the sample selection methodology (see Appendix B of the report). These changes have resulted in figures from 2004 not being fully comparable with those for 2003 and earlier years. Detailed comparisons should therefore be made with caution.

Railways: permanent way and rolling stock (Table 22.21)

1) Locomotives - locos owned by Northern Ireland Railways (NIR), does not include those from the Republic of Ireland Railway System.

2) Diesel electric etc rail motor vehicles - powered passenger carrying vehicles, includes diesel electric (DE) power cars and all Construcciones y Auxiliar de Ferocarriles (CAF) vehicles. (Note: only 16 of the CAF sets were delivered to NIR at the time.)

3) Loco hauled coaches - NIR owned De Dietrich plus Gatwick but not including gen van.

4) Rail car trailers - 80 class and 450 class trailers. Not CAF, they are all powered.

5) Rolling stock for maintenance and repair - a 'standalone' figure - may or may not be included in the above totals. Anything listed as 'repair' or 'workshop' in the motive power sheets is included. Also, those CAF vehicles not yet delivered at the time.

6) The information is a 'snapshot' taken from the motive power sheets at end of March, together with any other known information.

22.23 - 22.26

All data from Airline Statistics, Civil Aviation Authority

22.1 Average number of trips (trip rates) by purpose and main mode: England, 2014

Purpose					Trips per person per year					
	Walk	Bicycle	Car / van driver	Car / van passenger	Motorcycle	Other private transport[1]	Local bus	Rail[2]	Other public transport[3]	All modes
Commuting	15	6	81	14	2	1	11	15	2	147
Business	2	1	23	2	-	-	1	3	-	32
Education / escort education	42	2	26	27	-	2	11	2	1	113
Shopping	38	2	78	36	-	1	15	2	2	174
Other escort	9	-	48	25	-	-	2	-	-	85
Personal business	20	1	39	22	-	1	7	2	2	93
Leisure[4]	36	6	89	80	1	2	12	8	6	239
Other including just walk	39	0	-	-	0	0	0	0	-	39
All purposes	200	18	384	206	3	6	59	31	14	921
Unweighted sample size: trips ('000s)	63	5	116	64	1	2	18	8	4	280

Source: National Travel Survey
Telephone: 020 7944 3097
Email: national.travelsurvey@dft.gsi.gov.uk

1 Mostly private hire bus (including school buses).
2 Surface rail and London Underground.
3 Non-local bus, taxi / minicab and other public transport (air, ferries, light rail).
4 Visit friends at home and elsewhere, entertainment, sport, holiday and day trip.

The figures in this table are National Statistics

Note:
The results presented in this table are weighted. The base (unweighted sample size) is shown in the table for information.
Weights are applied to adjust for non-response to ensure the characteristics of the achieved sample match the population of Great Britain (1995-2012) or England (2013 onwards) and for the drop off in trip recording in diary data.
The survey results are subject to sampling error.

22.2 Domestic freight transport[1]: by mode: 2000-2013

	2000	2001	2002	2003	2004	2005	2006	2007	2008	2009	2010	2011[2]	2012[2]	2013[2]
(a) Goods moved												Billion tonne kilometres/percentage		
Petroleum products														
Road [3]	6.4	5.8	5.2	5.5|	5.7	5.5	5.5	5.0	6.2	4.5	6.0	..	..	..
Rail [4]	1.4	1.2	1.2	1.2	1.2	1.2	1.5	1.6	1.5	1.4	1.3	1.2	1.2	1.3
Water	52.7	43.5	51.7	46.9	46.9	47.2	37.8	36.4	36.4	36.4	28.3	29.6	22.1	16.1
ow: coastwise	26.0	23.1	24.2	23.3	26.6	30.3	22.8	25.1	26.5	27.1	20.6	22.6	15.6	11.6
Pipeline	11.4	11.5	10.9	10.5	10.7	10.8	10.4	10.2	10.2	10.2	10.3	10.1	..	..
All modes	**71.9**	**62.0**	**69.0**	**64.1**|	**64.5**	**64.7**	**55.2**	**53.2**	**54.3**	**52.5**	**45.9**	..	..	..
Coal and coke														
Road [3]	1.5	2.1	1.5	1.5|	1.2	1.5	1.3	1.5	1.0	0.9	1.4	..	..	..
Rail [4]	4.8	6.2	5.7	5.8	6.7	8.3	8.6	7.7	7.9	6.2	5.5	6.4	7.5	8.1
Water	0.2	0.5	0.3	0.5	0.3	0.4	0.5	0.5	0.5	0.3	1.0	0.4	0.3	0.4
All modes	**6.5**	**8.8**	**7.5**	**7.9**|	**8.2**	**10.2**	**10.4**	**9.7**	**9.4**	**7.5**	**7.9**	..	..	..
Other freight														
Road [3]	151.5	150.6	152.7	154.7|	155.6	156.4	156.6	162.3	150.2	131.3	143.1	..	..	..
Rail [4]	11.9	12.0	11.7	11.9	12.5	12.2	11.8	11.9	11.2	11.4	12.5	13.4	14.0	14.6
Water	14.6	14.8	15.2	13.5	12.2	13.3	13.5	13.9	12.7	11.9	12.6	13.1	12.6	12.0
All modes	**178.1**	**177.4**	**179.6**	**180.0**|	**180.3**	**181.9**	**182.0**	**188.1**	**174.1**	**154.6**	**168.2**	..	..	..
All traffic														
Road [3]	159.4	158.5	159.4	161.7|	162.5	163.4	163.4	168.8	157.4	136.8	150.5	..	..	..
Rail [4]	18.1	19.4	18.5	18.9	20.3	21.7	21.9	21.2	20.6	19.1	19.2	21.1	21.5	22.7
Water	67.4	58.8	67.2	60.9	59.4	60.9	51.8	50.8	49.7	48.6	41.9	43.0	35.0	28.5
Pipeline	11.4	11.5	10.9	10.5	10.7	10.8	10.4	10.2	10.2	10.2	10.3	10.1	..	..
All modes	**256.3**	**248.2**	**256.0**	**252.0**|	**253.0**	**256.8**	**247.6**	**251.0**	**237.8**	**214.6**	**221.9**	..	..	..
Percentage of all traffic														
Road [3]	62	64	62	64	64	64	66	67	66	64	68	..	..	..
Rail [4]	7	8	7	7	8	8	9	8	9	9	9	..	..	..
Water	26	24	26	24	24	24	21	20	21	23	19	..	..	..
Pipeline	4	5	4	4	4	4	4	4	4	5	5	..	..	..
All modes	100	100	100	100	100	100	100	100	100	100	100	..	..	..
(b) Goods lifted												Million tonnes/percentage		
Petroleum products														
Road [3]	75	74	59	64|	67	70	66	69	76	57	67	..	..	..
Rail [4]	..	..	..	..|	..|	..	..|	..	..	..	..	..	..	..
Water	72	60	67	64	63	66	57	56	58	55	46	46	41	35
ow: coastwise	40	34	36	35	38	42	34	35	36	35	28	28	23	19
Pipeline	151	151	146	141	158	168	159	146	147	148	149	151	..	..
All modes	**298**	**285**	**272**	**269**|	**288**|	**304**	**282**|	**272**	**281**	**259**	**263**	..	..	..
Coal and coke														
Road [3]	22	21	17	22|	14	21	16	23	14	10	11	..	..	..
Rail [4]	35	39	34	35|	44|	48	49|	43	47	38	39	44	52	52
Water	3	3	2	2	1	2	2	2	2	1	2	1	1	1
All modes	**60**	**63**	**53**	**59**|	**59**|	**71**	**68**|	**68**	**63**	**49**	**52**	..	..	..
Other freight														
Road [3]	1,596	1,587	1,658	1,667|	1,782	1,777	1,819	1,861	1,709	1,422	1,543	..	..	..
Rail [4]	60	54	53	54|	57|	58	59|	59	56	49	51	57	61	65
Water [3]	62	68	70	67	63	65	66	68	63	54	57	57	54	55
All modes	**1,718**	**1,709**	**1,781**	**1,788**|	**1,902**|	**1,900**	**1,945**|	**1,988**	**1,828**	**1,525**	**1,651**	..	..	..
All traffic														
Road [3]	1,693	1,682	1,734	1,753|	1,863	1,868	1,901	1,953	1,800	1,488	1,621	..	..	..
Rail [4]	96	94	87	89|	101|	105	108|	102	103	87	90	102	113	117
Water	137	131	139	133	127	133	126	126	123	110	106	104	96	91
Pipeline	151	151	146	141	158	168	159	146	147	148	149	151		
All modes	**2,077**	**2,058**	**2,106**	**2,116**|	**2,249**|	**2,275**	**2,294**|	**2,328**	**2,173**	**1,833**	**1,966**	..	..	..
Percentage of all traffic														
Road [3]	82	82	82	83	83	82	83	84	83	81	82	..	..	..
Rail [4]	5	5	4	4	4	5	5	4	5	5	5	..	..	..
Water	7	6	7	6	6	6	6	5	6	6	5	..	..	..
Pipeline	7	7	7	7	7	7	7	6	7	8	8	..	..	..
All modes	100	100	100	100	100	100	100	100	100	100	100	..	..	..

Sources: Road and water - DfT; Rail - ORR; Pipeline - DECC

1. Discontinuities in the series (denoted by lines) are described in detail in the Notes and Definitions.
2. Road freight data are not currently available.
3. Statistics for all goods vehicles, including those 3.5 tonnes gross vehicle weight or less.
4. Figures for rail are for financial years (e.g. 2013 will be 2013/14).

Telephone:
Rail: 020 7944 2419
Road: 020 7944 3180
Pipeline: 020 7215 2718

22.3 Passenger transport: by mode, annual from 2001

Billion passenger kilometres/*percentage*

Year	Buses & coaches	%	Cars, vans & taxis	%	Motor cycles	%	Pedal cycles	%	All Road	%	Rail[1]	%	Air (UK)[2]	%	All modes [3]	%
2001	47	6	651	85	5	1	4	1	707	93	48	6	8	1.0	763	100
2002	41	5	673	86	5	1	4	1	723	93	48	6	8	1.1	780	100
2003	45	6	669	86	5	1	4	1	723	92	50	6	9	1.2	782	100
2004	41	5	673	86	6	1	4	1	724	92	50	6	10	1.2	784	100
2005	43	5	667	85	5	1	4	1	719	92	52	7	10	1.3	781	100
2006	41	5	672	85	6	1	5	1	723	92	55	7	10	1.3	788	100
2007	41	5	674	85	5	1	4	1	724	91	59	7	10	1.2	792	100
2008	43	5	666	84	6	1	5	1	720	91	61	8	9	1.1	789	100
2009	44	6	661	84	5	1	5	1	716	91	61	8	8	1.1	785	100
2010	45	6	644	83	5	1	5	1	699	91	65	8	8	1.0	771	100
2011	43	6	642	83	5	1	5	1	694	90	68	9	8	1.1	770	100
2012	42	5	645	83	5	1	5	1	697	90	70	9	8	1.1	776	100
2013	40	5	641	83	5	1	5	1	691	90	72	9	8	1.1	771	100
2014 P	40	5	654	83	5	1	5	1	704	89	75	10	8	1.1	788	100

Sources: Road - DfT Traffic Estimates, National Travel Survey; Rail - ORR; Air - CAA

1. Financial years. National Rail (franchised operators only to 2008, franchised and non-franchised operators from 2009), urban metros and modern trams.
2. UK airlines, domestic passengers uplifted on scheduled and non-scheduled flights.
3. Excluding travel by water.
See Notes and Definitions for details of discontinuity in road passengers figures from 1993 and 1996 onwards.

Telephone:
Road: 020 7944 3097
Rail: 020 7944 2419
Air: 020 7944 3088
Email: publicationgeneral.enq@dft.gsi.gov.uk
The Rail and Air figures in this table are outside the scope of National Statistics

22.4 Motor vehicle traffic (vehicle kilometres) by road class in Great Britain, annual from 2001

Billion vehicle kilometres

		Major roads 'A' roads				Minor roads			
	Motorway [1]	Rural	Urban [2]	All 'A' roads	All major roads	Rural	Urban [2]	All minor roads	All roads
2001	90.8	133.3	81.8	215.1	305.9	61.2	105.5	166.7	**472.6**
2002	92.6	136.4	82.2	218.6	311.2	63.9	108.6	172.5	**483.7**
2003	93.0	139.3	81.8	221.0	314.0	63.6	109.0	172.6	**486.7**
2004	96.6	141.3	82.8	224.1	320.7	64.9	108.3	173.3	**493.9**
2005	97.0	141.4	81.8	223.1	320.2	65.6	108.1	173.7	**493.9**
2006	99.5	143.6	82.5	226.1	325.5	67.9	107.6	175.5	**501.1**
2007	100.6	143.5	81.3	224.9	325.4	70.3	109.7	180.0	**505.4**
2008	100.1	142.8	80.1	222.8	323.0	70.3	107.3	177.6	**500.6**
2009	99.5	142.0	80.4	222.4	321.9	68.3	105.7	174.0	**495.8**
2010	98.2	139.8	79.7	219.5	317.7	68.1	102.1	170.2	**487.9**
2011	99.5	141.2	79.3	220.4	319.9	66.3	102.7	169.0	**488.9**
2012	100.4	140.4	78.1	218.5	319.0	64.6	103.5	168.1	**487.1**
2013	101.9	140.5	78.1	218.6	320.5	66.4	101.9	168.3	**488.8**
2014 R	104.3	143.5	79.4	222.9	327.2	70.1	104.2	174.4	**501.5**

1 Includes trunk motorways and principal motorways
2 Urban roads: Major and minor roads within an urban area with a population of 10,000 or more. These are based on the 2001 urban settlements. The definition for 'urban settlement' is in 'Urban and rural area definitions: a user guide' which can be found on the Notes & definitions web page www.gov.uk/transport-statistics-notes-and-guidance-road-traffic
R 2014 traffic estimates were revised as part of the production of 2015 traffic statistics

Source: DfT National Road Traffic Survey
Telephone: 020 7944 3095
Email: roadtraff.stats@dft.gsi.gov.uk

The figures in this table are National Statistics.

22.5 Road lengths (kilometres) by road type in Great Britain, 2001-2014

Kilometres

Year	Motorways			'A' roads			All major roads	Minor roads					All roads
	Trunk	Principal	Total	Trunk	Principal	Total		'B' road	'C' road	'U' road	'C' and 'U' roads	All minor roads	
2001 [1]	3,431	45	3,476	11,369	35,285	46,654	50,130	30,196	84,742	225,901	310,643	340,838	390,968
2002	3,433	45	3,478	10,679	35,995	46,674	50,152	30,192	84,858	226,462	311,320	341,512	391,664
2003	3,432	46	3,478	9,615	37,038	46,653	50,131	30,188	84,976	227,048	312,024	342,212	392,343
2004 [2]	3,478	46	3,523	9,147	37,521	46,669	50,192	30,178	84,223	223,082	307,304	337,482	387,673
2005	3,471	48	3,518	8,708	38,019	46,727	50,246	30,189	84,459	223,183	307,642	337,830	388,076
2006 [2]	3,508	48	3,555	8,706	38,030	46,735	50,291	30,018	84,469	229,605	314,074	344,092	394,383
2007	3,518	41	3,559	8,670	38,073	46,743	50,302	30,265	84,423	229,889	314,312	344,577	394,879
2008	3,518	41	3,559	8,634	38,057	46,691	50,249	30,161	84,574	229,482	314,056	344,217	394,467
2009	3,519	41	3,560	8,596	38,173	46,770	50,329	30,141	84,813	229,145	313,958	344,099	394,428
2010	3,517	41	3,558	8,489	38,218	46,707	50,265	30,192	84,827	228,970	313,797	343,989	394,253
2011	3,529	41	3,570	8,508	38,225	46,734	50,304	30,208	84,831	228,953	313,784	343,992	394,296
2012	3,576	41	3,617	8,507	38,235	46,742	50,359	30,214	84,903	229,414	314,317	344,531	394,890
2013 [3]	3,600	41	3,641	8,505	38,245	46,749	50,391	30,217	:	:	314,853	345,070	395,461
2014 [3]	3,603	41	3,645	8,485	38,301	46,785	50,430	30,207	:	:	314,983	345,190	395,620

Source: Department for Transport
Telephone: 020 7944 5032
Email: road.length@dft.gsi.gov.uk

Values may not sum to totals due to rounding

1. Figures for trunk and principal 'A' roads in England, from 2001 onwards, are affected by the detrunking programme.

2. New information from 2004 and from 2006 enabled better estimates of road lengths to be made - see Notes and definitions.

3. Minor roads figures in 2013 and 2014 have been derived differently, with 'C' and 'U' roads combined, as no R199b road length consultation took place.

Symbols

: Value not available

. Not applicable

The figures in this table are National Statistics

22.6 Road traffic (vehicle kilometres) by vehicle type in Great Britain, annual from 2001

Billion vehicle kilometres

	Cars and taxis	Light vans [1]	Goods vehicles [2]	Other Vehicles			All motor vehicles
				Motorcycles	Buses & Coaches	Total [3]	
2001	381.2	53.4	28.0	4.8	5.1	9.9	472.6
2002	390.6	54.7	28.3	5.0	5.2	10.2	483.7
2003	390.0	57.4	28.4	5.6	5.3	10.9	486.7
2004	394.2	60.2	29.3	5.1	5.1	10.2	493.9
2005	392.7	61.8	28.9	5.3	5.1	10.4	493.9
2006	397.4	64.3	29.0	5.1	5.3	10.4	501.1
2007	397.9	67.4	29.3	5.5	5.4	10.9	505.4
2008	395.0	66.9	28.6	5.0	5.0	10.1	500.6
2009	394.0	65.5	26.2	5.1	5.0	10.1	495.8
2010	385.9	66.1	26.3	4.6	5.0	9.6	487.9
2011	387.4	66.6	25.6	4.6	4.7	9.3	488.9
2012	386.7	66.4	25.0	4.6	4.4	8.9	487.1
2013	386.2	68.5	25.2	4.3	4.5	8.8	488.8
2014 [R]	394.2	72.4	25.9	4.5	4.5	9.0	501.5

Source: DfT National Road Traffic Survey
Telephone: 020 7944 3095
Email: roadtraff.stats@dft.gsi.gov.uk

1 Not exceeding 3,500 kgs gross vehicle weight, post 1982

2 Over 3,500 kgs gross vehicle weight, post 1982

3 Total of all other vehicles (i.e. motorcycles, buses, and coaches)

R 2014 traffic estimates were revised as part of the production of 2015 statistics

The figures in this table are National Statistics.

22.7 Cars licensed by propulsion / fuel type, Great Britain, from 1994 to 2013

Great Britain   Thousands/*Percentages*

Year	Petrol	Diesel	Hybrid Electric	Gas[1]	Electric	Other[2]	Total
Total number of cars							
1994	19,620.9	1,576.2	0.0	1.8	0.1	0.2	21,199.2
1995	19,499.8	1,891.3	0.0	2.9	0.1	0.1	21,394.1
1996	20,051.6	2,181.6	0.0	4.1	0.1	0.1	22,237.5
1997	20,384.7	2,440.5	0.0	6.2	0.1	0.1	22,831.7
1998	20,590.5	2,692.9	0.0	9.6	0.2	0.1	23,293.3
1999	21,031.0	2,929.9	0.0	13.8	0.2	0.1	23,974.9
2000	21,232.6	3,152.7	-	20.0	0.2	-	24,405.5
2001	21,641.1	3,459.5	0.6	24.4	0.3	0.1	25,125.9
2002	21,839.5	3,912.4	0.9	28.8	0.3	0.1	25,781.9
2003	21,805.5	4,399.6	1.2	33.7	0.3	0.1	26,240.4
2004	21,976.6	5,010.6	2.8	37.6	0.4	0.1	27,028.1
2005	21,876.0	5,596.1	8.1	39.5	0.6	0.1	27,520.4
2006	21,465.8	6,083.3	16.6	42.4	0.8	0.2	27,609.2
2007	21,264.4	6,657.4	31.8	45.1	1.2	0.3	28,000.3
2008	20,899.1	7,163.5	46.7	49.6	1.3	0.4	28,160.7
2009	20,491.2	7,641.4	61.1	50.9	1.5	0.4	28,246.5
2010	20,083.1	8,202.7	82.1	51.0	1.5	0.5	28,420.9
2011	19,548.5	8,763.5	102.3	50.0	2.6	0.4	28,467.3
2012	19,158.8	9,385.1	125.3	48.7	4.1	0.4	28,722.5
2013	18,870.3	10,064.2	153.6	46.3	6.3	0.4	29,140.9
Percentage of cars							
1994	92.6	7.4	0.0	-	-	-	100.0
1995	91.1	8.8	0.0	-	-	-	100.0
1996	90.2	9.8	0.0	-	-	-	100.0
1997	89.3	10.7	0.0	-	-	-	100.0
1998	88.4	11.6	0.0	-	-	-	100.0
1999	87.7	12.2	0.0	0.1	-	-	100.0
2000	87.0	12.9	-	0.1	-	-	100.0
2001	86.1	13.8	-	0.1	-	-	100.0
2002	84.7	15.2	-	0.1	-	-	100.0
2003	83.1	16.8	-	0.1	-	-	100.0
2004	81.3	18.5	-	0.1	-	-	100.0
2005	79.5	20.3	-	0.1	-	-	100.0
2006	77.7	22.0	0.1	0.2	-	-	100.0
2007	75.9	23.8	0.1	0.2	-	-	100.0
2008	74.2	25.4	0.2	0.2	-	-	100.0
2009	72.5	27.1	0.2	0.2	-	-	100.0
2010	70.7	28.9	0.3	0.2	-	-	100.0
2011	68.7	30.8	0.4	0.2	-	-	100.0
2012	66.7	32.7	0.4	0.2	-	-	100.0
2013	64.8	34.5	0.5	0.2	-	-	100.0

Source: DVLA/DfT
Telephone: 020 7944 3077

1. Includes gas, gas bi-fuel, petrol/gas and gas-diesel
2. Includes new fuel technologies, fuel cells and steam.

Email : vehicles.stats@dft.gsi.gov.uk

22.8 Motor vehicles registered for the first time by tax class: Great Britain annually 2000 to 2013

Great Britain
Thousands

	Private and light goods[1]							
Year	Private cars[1]	Other vehicles[1]	Goods vehicles	Motor cycles, scooters and mopeds	Buses[2]	Special machines etc[5]	Other vehicles [3,4,5]	Total
2000	2,430.0		50.0	183.0	8.0	24.0	176.0	2,871.0
2001	2,431.8	277.9	48.6	177.1	6.8	26.8	168.8	3,137.7
2002	2,528.8	286.8	44.9	162.2	7.8	.	199.0	3,229.0
2003	2,497.1	323.5	48.4	157.3	8.4	.	197.1	3,231.9
2004	2,437.4	347.3	48.0	133.7	8.3	.	210.7	3,185.4
2005	2,266.3	337.2	51.2	132.3	8.9	.	225.5	3,021.4
2006	2,160.7	338.4	47.9	131.9	7.6	.	227.1	2,913.6
2007	2,191.5	347.8	41.1	143.0	9.0	.	264.6	2,996.9
2008	1,891.9	296.4	47.0	138.4	8.3	.	290.2	2,672.2
2009	1,765.5	193.5	27.0	111.5	7.2	.	266.3	2,371.2
2010	1,765.3	229.3	27.0	97.1	6.4	.	292.7	2,417.8
2011	1,663.8	264.8	36.9	96.2	5.8	.	314.0	2,381.5
2012	1,784.1	244.4	38.0	96.6	7.8	.	299.0	2,469.8
2013	1,988.1	276.0	48.1	94.2	7.6	.	302.1	2,716.1

Source: DVLA/DfT

1. From 1980 onwards figures refer to the October 1990 taxation classes. Figures for 1969 and 1980 are given twice, once for the tax regime before and once for the tax regime afterwards.
2. Prior to 1995 this tax class was called 'Public Transport' and taxis and Hackney Carriages were included. Prior to 1969, tram cars were also included.
3. Includes crown and exempt vehicles, three wheelers, pedestrian controlled vehicles and showmen's goods vehicles.
4. Excludes vehicles officially registered by the armed forces.
5. Special Machines became part of the 'Crown and Exempt' taxation class with effect from January 2002.

Telephone: 020 7944 3077
Email : vehicles.stats@dft.gsi.gov.uk
Notes & definitions (https://www.gov.uk/government/publications/vehicles-statistics-guidance)

22.9a Practical car test[1] pass rates by gender, Great Britain: 2007/08 to 2014/15

Numbers / *Per cent*

	Male tests			Female tests			Total tests[2]		
	Conducted	Passes	Pass rate (%)	Conducted	Passes	Pass rate (%)	Conducted	Passes	Pass rate (%)
Annually (financial years)									
2007/08	865,427	409,222	*47.3*	896,314	369,795	*41.3*	1,762,148	779,207	*44.2*
2008/09	849,757	413,014	*48.6*	888,917	374,466	*42.1*	1,738,992	787,618	*45.3*
2009/10	753,618	370,049	*49.1*	780,007	333,770	*42.8*	1,533,738	703,859	*45.9*
2010/11	772,551	383,417	*49.6*	833,040	360,639	*43.3*	1,605,599	744,058	*46.3*
2011/12	744,487	374,472	*50.3*	824,572	361,685	*43.9*	1,569,069	736,158	*46.9*
2012/13	682,699	345,599	*50.6*	753,774	331,653	*44.0*	1,436,481	677,255	*47.1*
2013/14	706,757	358,143	*50.7*	770,823	337,436	*43.8*	1,477,585	695,580	*47.1*
2014/15	733,161	370,343	*50.5*	799,341	348,367	*43.6*	1,532,504	718,711	*46.9*

Source: DVSA/DfT

1 Includes test categories B and B1

2 Gender details about licence holders from other countries (such as Northern Ireland) are reliant upon information being captured accurately at the time of booking a test. In some cases, gender will not have been captured.
Where gender has not been captured these candidates will only be recorded in total tests conducted. There will therefore be small anomalies where the gender totals do not match overall totals.
Please note that all statistics are provisional until information for the whole financial year is published. Until that point, data for months / quarters from within the current financial year can be revised.
Telephone: 020 7944 3077
Email : vehicles.stats@dft.gsi.gov.uk
Notes & definitions (https://www.gov.uk/government/organisations/department-for-transport/series/driving-tests-and-instructors-statistics)

22.9b Practical motorcycle test[1] (Module 1) pass rates by gender, Great Britain, 2009/10 to 2014/15

Numbers / *Per cent*

	Male tests			Female tests			Total tests		
	Conducted	Passes	Pass rate (%)	Conducted	Passes	Pass rate (%)	Conducted	Passes	Pass rate (%)
Annually (financial years)									
2009/10[1]	44,165	28,123	63.7	6,655	2,765	41.5	50,823	30,891	60.8
2010/11	50,046	33,735	67.4	7,665	3,498	45.6	57,711	37,233	64.5
2011/12	52,726	38,325	72.7	6,868	3,706	54.0	59,594	42,031	70.5
2012/13	58,280	42,490	72.9	7,770	4,092	52.7	66,050	46,582	70.5
2013/14	41,299	29,366	71.1	4,964	2,458	49.5	46,263	31,824	68.8
2014/15	46,361	33,398	72.0	5,644	2,863	50.7	52,005	36,261	69.7

Source: DVSA/DfT

1 All test data excludes mopeds.

2 The two-part modular motorcycle test was introduced on 27 April 2009. The figures for April 2009 only includes tests conducted between 27 and 30 April 2009. Please note that all statistics are provisional until information for the whole financial year is published. Until that point, data for months / quarters from within the current financial year can be revised.

Telephone: 020 7944 3077

Email : vehicles.stats@dft.gsi.gov.uk

Notes & definitions (https://www.gov.uk/government/organisations/department-for-transport/series/driving-tests-and-instructors-statistics)

22.9c Practical motorcycle test[1] (Module 2) pass rates by gender, Great Britain 2009/10 to 2014/15

Numbers / *Per cent*

	Male tests			Female tests			Total tests		
	Conducted	Passes	Pass rate (%)	Conducted	Passes	Pass rate (%)	Conducted	Passes	Pass rate (%)
Annually (financial years)									
2009/10[1]	34,550	24,122	69.8	3,363	2,352	69.9	37,914	26,474	69.8
2010/11	44,991	31,236	69.4	4,654	3,249	69.8	49,645	34,485	69.5
2011/12	52,619	36,367	69.1	5,292	3,559	67.3	57,911	39,926	68.9
2012/13	59,237	40,871	69.0	5,891	4,018	68.2	65,128	44,889	68.9
2013/14	40,052	28,110	70.2	3,423	2,343	68.4	43,475	30,453	70.0
2014/15	45,211	31,847	70.4	3,983	2,709	68.0	49,194	34,556	70.2

Source: DVSA/DfT

1 All test data excludes mopeds.

2 The two-part modular motorcycle test was introduced on 27 April 2009. The figures for April 2009 only includes tests conducted between 27 and 30 April 2009. Please note that all statistics are provisional until information for the whole financial year is published. Until that point, data for months / quarters from within the current financial year can be revised.

Telephone: 020 7944 3077

Email : vehicles.stats@dft.gsi.gov.uk

Notes & definitions (https://www.gov.uk/government/organisations/department-for-transport/series/driving-tests-and-instructors-statistics)

22.9d Practical large goods vehicle (LGV) test[1] rates by gender, Great Britain: 2007/08 to 2014/15

Numbers / *Per cent*

	Male tests			Female tests			Total tests		
	Conducted	Passes	Pass rate (%)	Conducted	Passes	Pass rate (%)	Conducted	Passes	Pass rate (%)
Annually (financial years)									
2007/08	66,445	30,693	46.2	4,305	2,077	48.2	70,766	32,779	46.3
2008/09	61,950	30,258	48.8	3,892	2,035	52.3	65,852	32,298	49.0
2009/10	43,119	22,058	51.2	3,305	1,816	54.9	46,426	23,876	51.4
2010/11	41,011	21,122	51.5	2,883	1,542	53.5	43,894	22,664	51.6
2011/12	43,525	22,762	52.3	3,024	1,639	54.2	46,549	24,401	52.4
2012/13	42,937	22,736	53.0	3,309	1,762	53.2	46,246	24,498	53.0
2013/14	44,993	24,296	54.0	3,290	1,928	58.6	48,283	26,224	54.3
2014/15	51,314	28,310	55.2	3,847	2,264	58.9	55,161	30,574	55.4

Source: DVSA/DfT

1 Includes test categories C, C1, C+E, C1+E

Please note that all statistics are provisional until information for the whole financial year is published. Until that point, data for months / quarters from within the current financial year can be revised.

Telephone: 020 7944 3077
Email : vehicles.stats@dft.gsi.gov.uk
Notes & definitions (https://www.gov.uk/government/organisations/department-for-transport/series/driving-tests-and-instructors-statistics)

22.9e Practical passenger carrying vehicle (PCV) CPC test[1] rates by gender, Great Britain: 2008/09 to 2014/15

Numbers / *Per cent*

	Male tests			Female tests			Total tests		
	Conducted	Passes	Pass rate (%)	Conducted	Passes	Pass rate (%)	Conducted	Passes	Pass rate (%)
Annually (financial years)									
2008/09	1,089	763	70.1	123	92	74.8	1,212	855	70.5
2009/10	2,436	1,881	77.2	273	225	82.4	2,709	2,106	77.7
2010/11	2,280	1,892	83.0	265	230	86.8	2,545	2,122	83.4
2011/12	2,177	1,852	85.1	296	263	88.9	2,474	2,116	85.5
2012/13	2,626	2,254	85.8	309	259	83.8	2,935	2,513	85.6
2013/14	3,179	2,760	86.8	372	330	88.7	3,551	3,090	87.0
2014/15	2,720	2,364	86.9	325	291	89.5	3,046	2,656	87.2

Source: DVSA/DfT

1 Includes all PCV CPC mod 4 tests

Please note that all statistics are provisional until information for the whole financial year is published. Until that point, data for months / quarters from within the current financial year can be revised.

Telephone: 020 7944 3077
Email : vehicles.stats@dft.gsi.gov.uk
Notes & definitions (https://www.gov.uk/government/organisations/department-for-transport/series/driving-tests-and-instructors-statistics)

22.10 Full car driving licence holders by age and gender: England, 1975/76 to 2014

	All aged 17+	Percentage							Estimated licence holders (millions)	Unweighted sample size (individuals aged 17+)
		17-20	21-29	30-39	40-49	50-59	60-69	70+		
All adults:										
1975/76	48	28	59	67	60	50	35	15	19.4	17,064
1985/86	57	33	63	74	71	60	47	27	24.3	19,835
1989/91[1]	64	44	74	78	79	68	55	32	24.1	17,466
1992/94	67	48	75	82	80	74	59	33	25.4	16,401
1995/97[2]	69	44	74	82	82	76	64	39	26.3	16,716
1998/00	71	41	75	85	83	78	68	40	27.3	16,529
2002	71	32	67	83	83	81	70	45	27.6	13,836
2003	71	29	67	82	84	81	72	44	27.8	14,556
2004	70	27	65	82	83	81	73	46	27.8	14,228
2005	72	31	65	82	84	83	75	52	28.8	15,063
2006	72	35	67	82	84	82	76	51	29.3	14,815
2007	72	38	66	81	84	82	76	53	29.5	14,693
2008	73	36	64	83	84	83	78	53	30.0	14,290
2009	73	36	64	80	84	83	80	55	30.2	14,791
2010	73	33	63	81	85	83	80	57	30.6	14,118
2011	72	31	64	78	84	83	80	59	30.7	13,723
2012	73	36	64	78	85	82	80	59	31.1	14,578
2013	74	31	66	80	85	84	82	62	31.9	14,694
2014	73	29	63	79	85	83	81	62	31.8	13,964
Males:										
1975/76	69	36	78	85	83	75	58	32	13.4	8,113
1985/86	74	37	73	86	87	81	72	51	15.1	9,367
1989/91[1]	80	54	83	88	90	86	79	58	14.5	8,306
1992/94	82	55	83	90	89	88	82	59	14.8	7,652
1995/97[2]	82	51	81	90	89	89	83	65	14.9	7,934
1998/00	82	44	81	90	91	89	83	66	15.2	7,857
2002	80	34	72	89	89	89	85	68	15.2	6,586
2003	81	34	72	87	91	91	88	69	15.4	6,950
2004	80	29	69	87	89	90	87	72	15.3	6,723
2005	81	36	68	86	90	91	88	74	15.7	7,159
2006	81	37	71	87	88	90	90	77	15.9	7,078
2007	81	41	69	86	90	90	88	77	16.0	6,978
2008	81	36	67	88	90	91	90	75	16.2	6,818
2009	80	38	67	85	89	91	91	77	16.3	7,021
2010	80	34	66	86	90	89	90	78	16.4	6,769
2011	80	31	68	81	89	90	90	79	16.4	6,521
2012	80	40	67	81	88	89	90	80	16.6	6,981
2013	81	30	67	83	90	90	91	82	16.9	7,048
2014	80	34	66	82	91	89	90	80	17.0	6,630
Females:										
1975/76	29	20	43	48	37	24	15	4	6.0	8,951
1985/86	41	29	54	62	56	41	24	11	9.2	10,468
1989/91[1]	50	35	65	68	67	50	33	15	9.7	9,160
1992/94	55	42	69	74	71	59	38	16	10.8	8,749
1995/97[2]	58	36	68	74	74	63	46	22	11.4	8,781
1998/00	61	38	70	79	75	67	54	22	12.1	8,672
2002	61	30	62	77	77	74	55	28	12.5	7,250
2003	61	24	62	77	77	71	58	26	12.4	7,606
2004	61	24	61	77	77	71	60	28	12.5	7,505
2005	64	26	61	77	79	75	62	36	13.2	7,904
2006	64	32	62	78	80	74	64	32	13.4	7,737
2007	64	35	63	76	78	74	64	36	13.4	7,715
2008	65	35	61	78	80	76	67	37	13.8	7,472
2009	65	33	62	76	79	75	69	38	13.9	7,770
2010	66	32	60	77	80	77	70	41	14.2	7,349
2011	66	30	59	74	79	76	71	44	14.3	7,202
2012	66	31	62	75	81	75	71	43	14.5	7,597
2013	68	31	64	77	80	77	73	47	14.9	7,646
2014	67	25	61	75	80	78	73	47	14.8	7,334

Source: National Travel Survey
Telephone: 020 7944 3097
Email: national.travelsurvey@dft.gsi.gov.uk

1 Figures prior to 1989 for Great Britain, rather than England only.

2 Figures prior to 1995 are based on unweighted data.

Notes and Definitions: https://www.gov.uk/government/collections/national-travel-survey-statistics

The figures in this table are National Statistics

The results presented in this table are weighted. The base (unweighted sample size) is shown in the table for information.

Weights are applied to adjust for non-response to ensure the characteristics of the achieved sample match the population of Great Britain (1995-2012) or England (2013 onwards) and for the drop off in trip recording in diary data.

The survey results are subject to sampling error.

22.11a Household car availability: England, 2002 to 2014

Year	Percentage				Cars / vans per household	Cars / vans per adult (aged 17+)	Unweighted sample size (households)
	No car / van	One car / van	Two or more cars / vans	All households			
2002	26	44	30	100	1.09	0.59	7,535
2003	26	42	31	100	1.11	0.60	7,853
2004	25	44	30	100	1.11	0.59	7,692
2005	25	43	33	100	1.16	0.61	8,065
2006	24	44	32	100	1.16	0.61	7,884
2007	25	43	33	100	1.16	0.61	7,879
2008	25	43	33	100	1.15	0.61	7,665
2009	25	43	32	100	1.15	0.60	7,858
2010	25	42	33	100	1.17	0.61	7,534
2011	25	43	32	100	1.15	0.60	7,289
2012	25	44	31	100	1.14	0.60	7,724
2013	25	43	32	100	1.15	0.60	7,820
2014	24	43	32	100	1.16	0.61	7,436

Source: National Travel Survey
Telephone: 020 7944 3097
Email: national.travelsurvey@dft.gsi.gov.uk

The results presented in this table are weighted. The base (unweighted sample size) is shown in the table for information.

Weights are applied to adjust for non-response to ensure the characteristics of the achieved sample match the population of Great Britain (1995-2012) or England (2013 onwards) and for the drop off in trip recording in diary data.
The survey results are subject to sampling error.
Notes & definitions: https://www.gov.uk/government/publications/national-travel-survey-2013

The figures in this table are National Statistics

GB data no longer available. Since 2013, the National Travel Survey has covered residents of England only

22.11b Household car ownership by region and Rural-Urban Classification: England, 2002/03 and 2013/14[1b]

	Percentage						Cars / vans per household		Unweighted sample size (households)	
	No car / van		One car / van		Two or more cars / vans					
	2002/03	2013/14	2002/03	2013/14	2002/03	2013/14	2002/03	2013/14	2002/03	2013/14
Region of residence:										
North East	37	30	44	44	20	26	0.86	1.00	847	855
North West	27	24	44	44	28	32	1.05	1.16	2,164	2,035
Yorkshire and The Humber	30	26	45	42	25	33	0.99	1.13	1,605	1,587
East Midlands	20	21	45	43	34	36	1.20	1.23	1,321	1,306
West Midlands	26	22	40	43	34	35	1.15	1.24	1,593	1,574
East of England	20	18	42	44	38	38	1.26	1.29	1,637	1,670
London	41	43	40	40	19	17	0.82	0.78	2,228	2,204
South East	18	18	43	45	39	37	1.30	1.30	2,332	2,498
South West	19	18	47	45	34	38	1.24	1.29	1,661	1,527
England excluding London	24	21	44	44	33	35	1.16	1.22	13,160	13,052
England	26	25	43	43	31	32	1.10	1.16	15,388	15,256
Rural-Urban Classification[2] of residence:										
Urban Conurbation	35	34	41	42	24	25	0.93	0.96	5,882	5,767
Urban City and Town	24	22	46	45	31	33	1.13	1.18	6,842	6,681
Rural Town and Fringe	17	15	42	44	41	41	1.32	1.37	1,440	1,419
Rural Village, Hamlet and Isolated Dwelling	7	6	39	35	53	59	1.63	1.74	1,224	1,389
All areas	26	25	43	43	31	32	1.10	1.16	15,388	15,256

Source: National Travel Survey
Telephone: 020 7944 3097
Email: national.travelsurvey@dft.gsi.gov.uk

1 Two survey years combined, e.g. 2013 and 2014. A survey year runs from mid-January to mid-January.
2 For more information on Rural-Urban Classifications see:
https://www.gov.uk/government/collections/rural-urban-definition

The figures in this table are National Statistics

The results presented in this table are weighted. The base (unweighted sample size) is shown in the table for information.

Weights are applied to adjust for non-response to ensure the characteristics of the achieved sample match the population of Great Britain (1995-2012) or England (2013 onwards) and for the drop off in trip recording in diary data.
The survey results are subject to sampling error.

GB data no longer available. Since 2013, the National Travel Survey has covered residents of England only

22.12 Vehicles licensed by taxation group: Northern Ireland, 2010-2014

Number at 31 December

Taxation Group (Taxation Classes)	2010		2011		2012		2013		2014	
	Number	%	Number	%	Number	%	Number	%	Number	%
Private Light Goods (11, 36, 39, 48, 49, 59, 91, 92)	877,034	83.5	879,787	83.5	885,976	83.6	901,357	84.5	916,598	84.7
Motorcycles, Scooters & Mopeds (17, 18, 93)	26,771	2.5	25,196	2.4	23,560	2.2	22,745	2.1	22,151	2.0
General (HGV) Goods (1, 2, 10, 23, 45, 46, 53)	23,863	2.3	23,084	2.2	22,114	2.1	22,052	2.1	21,868	2.0
Bus (34, 38)	3,035	0.3	3,015	0.3	3,094	0.3	3,315	0.3	3,262	0.3
Agricultural/Tractors (40 & 44)	17,059	1.6	18,555	1.8	19,775	1.9	20,784	1.9	21,963	2.0
Other (14-16, 19, 37, 47, 50, 55-58, 79, 81, 82)	2,180	0.2	2,159	0.2	2,154	0.2	2,200	0.2	2,426	0.2
Crown (60)	7,488	0.7	7,646	0.7	7,862	0.7	1,936	0.2	1,855	0.2
Exempt (>60 except 79, 81, 82, 91, 92, 93)	93,051	8.9	93,896	8.9	95,793	9.0	92,115	8.6	91,604	8.5
All Vehicles	1,050,481	100.0	1,053,338	100.0	1,060,328	100.0	1,066,504	100.0	1,081,727	100.0

Source: Driver and Vehicle Agency (DVA)

22.13 Motor vehicles registered for the first time in NI by vehicle type: 2010-2014 [1]

Number

Vehicle Type	2010	2011	2012	2013	2014
Private Cars					
New cars	54,443	47,766	47,990	52,951	59,232
Used cars	30,450	30,129	31,601	34,814	21,448
All Private Cars	**84,893**	**77,895**	**79,591**	**87,765**	**80,680**
Buses	**486**	**319**	**411**	**584**	**594**
Light Goods	**8,058**	**8,984**	**8,609**	**9,573**	**9,079**
Heavy Goods	**2,606**	**2,509**	**2,531**	**2,973**	**2,232**
Agricultural Vehicles[2]	**1,963**	**1,985**	**2,099**	**2,022**	**2,021**
Motorcycles[3]	**2,648**	**2,198**	**2,011**	**2,048**	**2,080**
Other Vehicles[4]	**25**	**23**	**15**	**21**	**207**
All Vehicles	**100,679**	**93,913**	**95,267**	**104,986**	**96,893**

Source: DVA

1 Prior to July 2014, any vehicle registered in NI for the first time, even if previously registered in GB, would have been counted as a first registration in NI. Since July 2014, only vehicles that have not previously been registered anywhere else in the UK are now classed as NI first registrations, in line with the UK definition (See User Information section on page 10).

2 This category of vehicle body type has been changed to reflect the full coverage of agricultural vehicles (including tractors).

3 This category of vehicle body type also includes mopeds and scooters.

4 Prior to July 2014, this category of vehicle body type was classified as 'General Haulage and Special Types'. From July 2014 it is titled 'Other Vehicles' which brings the classification into line with the category presentation used by DfT. The category now includes special purpose vehicles, taxis, tricycles, not recorded and others.

22.14 Vehicle kilometres on local bus services by metropolitan area status and country: Great Britain,2000/01 to 2014/15

Million

Year	Estimation method[1]	London	English metropolitan areas	English non-metropolitan areas	England	Scotland	Wales	Great Britain	England outside London
2000/01		371	654	1,134	2,158	369	126	2,653	1,788
2001/02		381	646	1,102	2,129	368	126	2,622	1,748
2002/03		404	630	1,088	2,122	374	123	2,619	1,718
2003/04		444	596	1,069	2,109	369	113	2,590	1,665
2004/05	Old	:	575	1,077	2,122	357	116	2,594	1,652
2004/05 [r]	New	470	592	1,061	2,122	359	130	2,611	1,652
2005/06 [r]		461	588	1,071	2,121	374	128	2,622	1,660
2006/07 [r]		465	591	1,066	2,122	384	124	2,630	1,657
2007/08 [r]		465	597	1,067	2,129	397	124	2,650	1,664
2008/09 [r]		474	589	1,076	2,139	386	126	2,651	1,665
2009/10 [r]		479	569	1,071	2,119	377	125	2,620	1,640
2010/11 [r]		481	567	1,072	2,120	346	125	2,591	1,639
2011/12 [r]		485	563	1,054	2,103	338	117	2,558	1,617
2012/13 [r]		486	554	1,050	2,091	327	116	2,534	1,605
2013/14 [r]		486	548	1,048	2,082	332	113	2,527	1,596
2014/15		485	538	1,047	2,070	330	107	2,507	1,585

Source: DfT Public Service Vehicle Survey, Transport for London
Telephone: 020 7944 3094
Email: bus.statistics@dft.gsi.gov.uk

[1] Break in the local bus series (outside London) due to changes in the estimation methodology from 2004/05
[2] Deregulation of the bus market took place in October 1986. For more information see the technical information (link below).
[r] Previously published figures have been revised. For details of the revisions (which include planned updates) please see the technical information (link below).

Notes & Definitions https://www.gov.uk/government/statistics/buses-statistics-guidance
The figures in this table are National Statistics

22.15 Local bus fares index (at current prices[2]) by metropolitan area status and country: Great Britain, annual from 2000

Index: March 2005=100

		Local bus fares index							
Year[1]	All items Retail Prices Index[3]	London	English metropolitan areas	English non-metropolitan areas	England	Scotland	Wales	Great Britain	England outside London
2000	88.4	83.2	79.1	78.4	79.6	89.6	80.3	80.9	78.7
2001	90.4	83.9	83.3	82.7	82.9	92.2	84.7	84.1	82.9
2002	91.6	81.5	87.3	86.6	85.3	93.5	88.6	86.4	86.9
2003	94.4	81.8	90.3	90.8	88.0	96.1	91.6	89.2	90.6
2004	96.9	86.9	94.7	95.3	92.7	97.1	95.8	93.4	95.1
2005	100.0	100.0	100.0	100.0	100.0	100.0	100.0	100.0	100.0
2006	102.4	105.7	111.9	107.8	108.3	105.1	105.0	107.9	109.6
2007	107.3	116.6	113.6	102.0	110.2	111.4	111.5	110.4	106.9
2008	111.3	111.2	121.6	106.7	112.8	116.7	117.5	113.4	113.0
2009	110.9	120.0	136.5	113.9	122.5	126.5	125.3	123.1	123.2
2010	115.9	135.2	137.6	115.6	128.8	129.5	128.7	129.0	124.7
2011	122.0	144.5	146.4	119.4	135.7	132.2	130.1	135.2	130.3
2012	126.4	152.3	156.2	127.0	144.0	139.1	137.8	143.4	138.9
2013	130.6	159.4	161.3	134.3	150.8	145.1	147.2	150.1	145.4
2014	133.8	164.3	165.3	138.9	155.5	149.8	149.5	154.7	149.8
2015	135.0	168.8	171.4	143.9	160.6	153.2	155.8	159.7	155.3

[1] Index as at March.
[2] Not adjusted for inflation.
[3] These figures are not National Statistics.

Source: DfT Fares Survey, Office for National Statistics
Telephone: 020 7944 3094
Email: bus.statistics@dft.gsi.gov.uk

Notes & Definitions: https://www.gov.uk/government/statistics/buses-statistics-guidance
The figures in this table are National Statistics except where indicated

22.16 Reported road accident casualties by road user type and severity, Great Britain, 2004 - 2014

Number of casualties

	2004	2005	2006	2007	2008	2009	2010	2011	2012	2013	2014
Pedestrians											
Killed	671	671	675	646	572	500	405	453	420	398	446
KSI[1]	7,478	7,129	7,051	6,924	6,642	6,045	5,605	5,907	5,979	5,396	5,509
All severities	34,881	33,281	30,982	30,191	28,482	26,887	25,845	26,198	25,218	24,033	24,748
of which, children[2]											
Killed	77	63	71	57	57	37	26	33	20	26	29
KSI	2,339	2,134	2,025	1,899	1,784	1,660	1,646	1,602	1,545	1,358	1,379
All severities	12,234	11,250	10,131	9,527	8,648	7,983	7,929	7,807	6,999	6,396	6,481
Pedal cyclists											
Killed	134	148	146	136	115	104	111	107	118	109	113
KSI	2,308	2,360	2,442	2,564	2,565	2,710	2,771	3,192	3,340	3,252	3,514
All severities	16,648	16,561	16,196	16,195	16,297	17,064	17,185	19,215	19,091	19,438	21,287
of which, children											
Killed	25	20	31	13	12	14	7	6	13	6	6
KSI	577	527	503	522	417	458	398	398	324	282	279
All severities	4,682	4,286	3,765	3,633	3,306	3,204	2,828	2,881	2,198	1,958	2,005
Motorcyclists users[3]											
Killed	83	569	599	588	493	472	403	362	328	331	339
KSI	2,301	6,508	6,484	6,737	6,049	5,822	5,183	5,609	5,328	5,197	5,628
All severities	11,885	24,824	23,326	23,459	21,550	20,703	18,686	20,150	19,310	18,752	20,366
Car occupants											
Killed	8	1,675	1,612	1,432	1,257	1,059	835	883	801	785	797
KSI	99	14,617	14,254	12,967	11,968	11,112	9,749	9,225	9,033	8,426	8,832
All severities	1,001	178,302	171,000	161,433	149,188	143,412	133,205	124,924	119,708	109,787	115,530
Bus and coach occupants											
Killed	20	9	19	12	6	14	9	7	11	10	7
KSI	488	363	426	455	432	370	401	332	323	342	300
All severities	8,820	7,920	7,253	7,079	6,929	6,317	6,268	6,177	5,234	4,873	5,198
Van occupants											
Killed	62	54	52	58	43	36	34	34	33	37	33
KSI	631	587	564	494	445	417	359	340	363	371	400
All severities	6,166	6,048	5,914	5,340	4,913	4,743	4,494	4,499	4,533	4,426	4,915
HGV occupants											
Killed	47	55	39	52	23	14	28	28	29	21	14
KSI	406	395	383	363	240	189	212	195	198	168	176
All severities	2,883	2,843	2,530	2,476	1,930	1,519	1,578	1,415	1,339	1,296	1,353
All road users[4]											
Killed	3,221	3,201	3,172	2,946	2,538	2,222	1,850	1,901	1,754	1,713	1,775
KSI	34,351	32,155	31,845	30,720	28,572	26,912	24,510	25,023	24,793	23,370	24,582
All severities	280,840	271,017	258,404	247,780	230,905	222,146	208,648	203,950	195,723	183,670	194,477

1. Killed and seriously injured.
2. Casualties aged 0 -15.
3. Includes mopeds and scooters.
4. Includes other motor or non-motor vehicle users, and unknown road user type and casualty age

Source: DfT STATS19
Telephone: 020 7944 6595
Email: roadacc.stats@dft.gsi.gov.uk

Notes & Definitions: https://www.gov.uk/government/uploads/system/uploads/attachment_data/file/48822/reported-road-casualties-gb-notes-definitions.pdf
The figures in this table are National Statistics

22.17a Goods lifted and goods moved by mode of working: by GB HGVs in the UK

UK activity of GB registered heavy goods vehicles

Year	Tonnes lifted (millions)					Tonne kilometres (billions)				
	Mainly public haulage	% of total	Mainly own account	% of total	All modes	Mainly public haulage	% of total	Mainly own account	% of total	All modes
2000	1,038	65	556	35	1,593	113	75	37	25	150
2001	1,052	67	529	33	1,581	115	77	35	23	149
2002	1,019	63	608	37	1,627	111	74	39	26	150
2003	1,053	64	590	36	1,643	114	75	37	25	152
2004	1,101	63	643	37	1,744	111	73	41	27	152
2005	1,079	62	667	38	1,746	110	72	43	28	153
2006	1,104	62	671	38	1,776	110	72	43	28	152
2007	1,116	61	706	39	1,822	113	72	45	28	157
2008	948	57	720	43	1,668	99	68	47	32	146
2009	690	51	666	49	1,356	77	62	48	38	125
2010	800	54	689	46	1,489	89	64	50	36	139
2011	789	51	770	49	1,559	86	60	59	40	145
2012	858	54	729	46	1,587	97	65	53	35	150
2013	810	55	665	45	1,475	92	66	48	34	139

Source: Continuing Survey of Road Goods Transport (Great Britain)
Telephone: 020 7944 3903
Email: roadfreight.stats@dft.gsi.gov.uk

Note: discontinuities in the series (denoted by lines) are described in detail within the methodology note; comparisons across years where methodological changes have occurred should be treated with caution.

Methodology note: https://www.gov.uk/government/collections/road-freight-domestic-and-international-statistics
Notes & definitions: https://www.gov.uk/government/collections/road-freight-domestic-and-international-statistics

22.17b Goods moved by type and weight of vehicle, by GB HGVs in the UK

UK activity of GB registered heavy goods vehicles

Billion tonne kilometres

Year	Rigids					Articulated vehicles			All vehicles
	Over 3.5t to 7.5t	Over 7.5t to 17t	Over 17t to 25t	Over 25t	All Rigids	Over 3.5t to 33t	Over 33t	All artics	
1999	5	13	4	15	37	14	98	112	149
2000	5	11	5	15	36	14	100	114	150
2001	5	9	6	16	34	13	102	115	149
2002	5	7	6	17	36	10	104	114	150
2003	4	6	7	18	35	9	108	116	152
2004	4	5	7	19	36	7	109	116	152
2005	4	5	8	21	37	6	110	116	153
2006	4	3	8	20	36	6	111	117	152
2007	3	3	9	22	37	6	115	120	157
2008	3	2	8	20	33	5	108	113	146
2009	3	2	7	17	30	5	91	96	125
2010	3	2	7	18	31	4	104	108	139
2011	3	2	8	23	36	5	105	109	145
2012	3	2	8	22	35	4	111	115	150
2013	2	1	7	20	31	4	104	108	139

Source: Continuing Survey of Road Goods Transport (Great Britain)
Telephone: 020 7944 3903
Email: roadfreight.stats@dft.gsi.gov.uk

Note: discontinuities in the series (denoted by lines) are described in detail within the methodology note; comparisons across years where methodological changes have occurred should be treated with caution.

Methodology note: https://www.gov.uk/government/collections/road-freight-domestic-and-international-statistics
Notes & definitions: https://www.gov.uk/government/collections/road-freight-domestic-and-international-statistics

22.17c Goods moved by commodity
UK activity of GB registered heavy goods vehicles

Billion tonne kilometres

Commodity	2004	2005	2006	2007	2008	2009	2010	2011	2012	2013[1]
Products of agriculture, forestry, raw materials										
Agricultural products	12.8	11.9	11.5	12.3	11.7	10.1	10.7	11.8	13.1	11.5
Coal and lignite	1.2	1.5	1.4	1.5	1.7	1.2	1.5	0.7	1.0	1.0
Metal ore and other mining and quarrying	15.1	16.3	16.3	16.8	14.4	11.5	13.6	10.9	12.5	10.6
Subtotal	**29.1**	**29.6**	**29.2**	**30.6**	**27.9**	**22.8**	**25.8**	**23.5**	**26.6**	**23.0**
Food products, includ. beverages and tobacco										
Food products	30.3	29.9	30.7	32.8	31.2	32.2	34.3	33.7	38.2	35.8
Textile, leather and wood products										
Textiles and textile products; leather and leather products	2.0	1.9	2.2	2.2	1.6	2.0	2.0	1.5	1.4	2.4
Wood products	13.4	12.6	12.8	11.8	10.6	9.0	10.3	9.3	7.9	8.1
Subtotal	**15.4**	**14.5**	**15.0**	**14.0**	**12.3**	**11.0**	**12.3**	**10.8**	**9.3**	**10.5**
Metal, mineral and chemical products										
Coke and refined petroleum products	5.7	5.5	5.4	5.0	5.5	4.3	5.9	5.8	7.1	5.3
Chemical products	7.0	8.8	7.1	7.7	6.9	6.1	5.9	7.8	7.7	5.7
Glass, cement and other non-metallic mineral products	12.2	11.0	11.5	11.5	10.8	8.2	9.1	9.8	8.1	8.9
Metal products	7.3	7.3	6.7	8.2	5.7	4.9	5.0	5.1	7.2	4.5
Subtotal	**32.2**	**32.5**	**30.7**	**32.4**	**28.9**	**23.6**	**25.9**	**28.4**	**30.0**	**24.4**
Machinery and equipment, consumer durables										
Machinery and equipment	4.2	4.5	4.5	4.8	4.1	3.6	3.7	4.1	3.4	3.0
Transport equipment	4.7	4.7	4.7	4.5	4.4	3.3	3.8	3.7	4.3	2.5
Furniture	6.5	5.9	5.8	5.8	4.3	3.4	2.9	2.5	2.4	1.6
Subtotal	**15.4**	**15.2**	**15.1**	**15.1**	**12.8**	**10.3**	**10.4**	**10.2**	**10.2**	**7.1**
Other products										
Waste related products	5.5	6.4	6.4	7.4	6.3	4.6	5.6	9.3	9.0	8.9
Mail, parcels	4.3	4.1	4.2	3.6	3.8	3.0	3.9	5.8	4.3	3.1
Empty containers, pallets and other packaging	3.6	3.4	3.4	3.5	3.7	3.7	3.9	3.9	4.4	3.0
Household and office removals	0.1	0.2	0.2	0.1	0.1	0.0	0.1	1.0	1.6	2.4
Grouped goods	16.1	16.7	17.6	17.8	18.9	13.9	16.7	16.8	15.5	16.1
Unidentifiable goods	0.1	0.1	:	:	:	:	:	1.8	1.2	4.9
Other goods	:	:	:	:	:	:	:	:	0.0	0.0
Subtotal	**29.7**	**30.9**	**31.8**	**32.4**	**32.8**	**25.3**	**30.2**	**38.6**	**36.0**	**38.4**
All commodities	**152.1**	**152.6**	**152.4**	**157.3**	**145.8**	**125.2**	**138.9**	**145.2**	**150.1**	**139.2**

':' = none recorded in the sample or not available due to small sample size
'~' = rounds to zero but different from a real zero

Source: Continuing Survey of Road Goods Transport (Great Britain)
Telephone: 020 7944 3903
Email: roadfreight.stats@dft.gsi.gov.uk

1. Commodity data from 2013 have been coded using a different coding frame, with classifications being retrospectively applied to earlier years. See the notes and definitions for more information.

Note: discontinuities in the series (denoted by lines) are described in detail within the methodology note; comparisons across years where methodological changes have occurred should be treated with caution.
Methodology note: https://www.gov.uk/government/collections/road-freight-domestic-and-international-statistics
Notes & definitions: https://www.gov.uk/government/collections/road-freight-domestic-and-international-statistics

22.18a Goods lifted by type and weight of vehicle: by GB HGVs in the UK
UK activity of GB registered heavy goods vehicles

Million tonnes

| Year | Rigids | | | | | Articulated vehicles | | | |
	Over 3.5t to 7.5t	Over 7.5t to 17t	Over 17t to 25t	Over 25t	All Rigids	Over 3.5t to 33t	Over 33t	All artics	All vehicles
2000	77	152	87	424	741	107	746	852	1,593
2001	80	123	86	443	733	97	751	848	1,581
2002	77	111	90	491	768	81	778	859	1,627
2003	70	89	100	506	765	69	809	878	1,643
2004	77	87	108	540	812	59	873	932	1,744
2005	70	70	110	562	812	51	883	934	1,746
2006	64	64	118	585	831	49	896	945	1,776
2007	54	52	127	614	848	49	926	975	1,822
2008	56	44	118	513	731	44	892	937	1,668
2009	56	37	102	377	572	38	746	785	1,356
2010	54	37	103	414	607	33	848	881	1,489
2011	55	36	108	479	677	39	844	883	1,559
2012	50	29	112	454	645	37	905	942	1,587
2013	44	25	97	448	614	37	824	861	1,475

Source: Continuing Survey of Road Goods Transport (Great Britain)
Telephone: 020 7944 3903
Email: roadfreight.stats@dft.gsi.gov.uk

Note: discontinuities in the series (denoted by lines) are described in detail within the methodology note; comparisons across years where methodological changes have occurred should be treated with caution.
Methodology note: https://www.gov.uk/government/collections/road-freight-domestic-and-international-statistics
Notes & definitions: https://www.gov.uk/government/collections/road-freight-domestic-and-international-statistics

22.18b Goods lifted by commodity
UK activity of GB registered heavy goods vehicles

Million tonnes

Commodity	2004	2005	2006	2007	2008	2009	2010	2011	2012	2013[1]
Products of agriculture, forestry, raw materials										
Agricultural products	117	112	103	107	102	100	106	111	119	107
Coal and lignite	12	20	17	23	21	13	12	9	10	9
Metal ore and other mining and quarrying	381	394	390	398	335	234	270	232	236	234
Subtotal	**510**	**526**	**510**	**529**	**458**	**347**	**389**	**352**	**365**	**349**
Food products, includ. beverages and tobacco										
Food products	245	236	257	266	261	259	285	295	311	299
Textile, leather and wood products										
Textiles and textile products; leather and leather products	15	14	15	13	11	15	15	12	11	18
Wood products	103	95	89	92	89	71	74	67	59	58
Subtotal	**118**	**109**	**104**	**104**	**100**	**85**	**89**	**78**	**70**	**76**
Metal, mineral and chemical products										
Coke and refined petroleum products	68	69	66	69	69	53	67	66	82	59
Chemical products	53	64	55	56	53	46	44	63	57	41
Glass, cement and other non-metallic mineral products	187	170	177	173	173	121	140	136	121	119
Metal products	62	61	61	65	51	44	46	41	58	39
Subtotal	**369**	**364**	**360**	**363**	**346**	**264**	**296**	**306**	**318**	**257**
Machinery and equipment, consumer durables										
Machinery and equipment	38	44	46	48	40	39	39	40	32	24
Transport equipment	31	32	32	34	33	26	29	30	33	22
Furniture	43	40	41	40	29	26	22	16	16	12
Subtotal	**112**	**116**	**119**	**122**	**101**	**90**	**90**	**86**	**82**	**59**
Other products										
Waste related products	169	195	220	239	178	131	140	196	194	175
Mail, parcels	36	32	31	29	29	22	33	38	34	25
Empty containers, pallets and other packaging	41	39	37	41	40	36	37	40	39	29
Household and office removals	2	2	1	1	1	1	1	14	21	34
Grouped goods	140	128	135	129	152	121	128	143	145	136
Unidentifiable goods	2	1	:	:	:	:	:	12	8	36
Other goods	:	:	:	:	:	:	:	:	~	~
Subtotal	**389**	**396**	**426**	**439**	**401**	**310**	**340**	**442**	**441**	**434**
All commodities	**1,744**	**1,746**	**1,776**	**1,822**	**1,668**	**1,356**	**1,489**	**1,559**	**1,587**	**1,475**

':' = none recorded in the sample or not available due to small sample size
'~' = rounds to zero but different from a real zero

Source: Continuing Survey of Road Goods Transport (Great Britain)
Telephone: 020 7944 3903
Email: roadfreight.stats@dft.gsi.gov.uk

1. Commodity data from 2013 have been coded using a different coding frame, with classifications being retrospectively applied to earlier years. See the notes and definitions for more information.

Note: discontinuities in the series (denoted by lines) are described in detail within the methodology note; comparisons across years where methodological changes have occurred should be treated with caution.
Methodology note: https://www.gov.uk/government/collections/road-freight-domestic-and-international-statistics
Notes & definitions: https://www.gov.uk/government/collections/road-freight-domestic-and-international-statistics

22.19a Passenger journeys by sector - Great Britain

Great Britain annual data from 2002-03, Number of passenger journeys made (millions)

Financial year	Franchised long distance operators	Franchised London and South East operators	Franchised regional operators	Total franchised passenger journeys	Non franchised
2002-03	77.2	679.1	219.2	975.5	:
2003-04	81.5	690.0	240.2	1011.7	:
2004-05	83.7	704.5	251.3	1039.5	:
2005-06	89.5	719.7	267.3	1076.5	:
2006-07	99.0	769.5	276.5	1145.0	:
2007-08	103.9	828.4	285.8	1218.1	:
2008-09	109.4	854.3	302.8	1266.5	:
2009-10	111.6	842.2	304.0	1257.9	1.4
2010-11	117.9	917.6	318.2	1353.8	1.8
2011-12	125.3	993.8	340.9	1460.0	1.5
2012-13	127.7	1,032.4	340.9	1500.9	1.7
2013-14	129.0	1,106.9	350.5	1586.5	1.9

Source: Office of Rail and Road; LENNON ticketing and revenue database and Train Operating Companies (TOCs)

Symbols: (:) Data not available   (r) Data revised   (p)   Data are provisional

1.   Data does not include Heathrow Express, Eurostar or light rail (inc. underground) services.
2.   Data are provisional until the end of the financial year as train operators may revise data submitted to ORR.

More details on methodology can be found in the quality report relating to this dataset:
http://orr.gov.uk/statistics/published-stats/statistical-releases

For the latest information on data revisions, please see the revisions log:
http://orr.gov.uk/statistics/code-of-practice/revisions-log

Passenger journeys on light rail and trams by system[1]: England

Million

Financial year	Docklands Light Railway	London Tramlink	Nottingham Express Transit	Midland Metro	Sheffield Supertram	Tyne and Wear Metro	Manchester Metrolink[2]	Blackpool Tramway	England
1999/00	31.3	:	:	4.8	10.9	32.7	14.2	4.3	98.2
2000/01	38.4	15.0	:	5.4	11.1	32.5	17.2	4.1	123.6
2001/02	41.3	18.2	:	4.8	11.4	33.4	18.2	4.9	132.2
2002/03	45.7	18.7	:	4.9	11.5	36.6	18.8	4.5	140.7
2003/04	48.5	19.8	0.4	5.1	12.3	37.9	18.9	3.7	146.5
2004/05	50.1	22.0	8.5	5.0	12.8	36.8	19.7	3.9	158.7
2005/06	53.5	22.5	9.8	5.1	13.1	35.8	19.9	3.6	163.4
2006/07	63.9	24.6	10.1	4.9	14.0	37.9	19.8	3.4	178.6
2007/08	66.6	27.2	10.2	4.8	14.8	39.8	20.0	2.9	186.2
2008/09	67.8	27.2	9.8	4.7	15.0	40.6	21.1	2.3	188.6
2009/10	69.4	25.8	9.0	4.7	14.7	40.8	19.6	2.2	186.2
2010/11	78.3	27.9	9.7	4.8	15.0	39.9	19.2	1.6	196.5
2011/12	86.1	28.6	9.0	4.9	15.0	37.9	22.3	1.1	204.8
2012/13	100.0	30.1	7.4	4.8	14.4	37.0	25.0	3.7	222.5
2013/14	101.6	31.2	7.9	4.7	12.6	35.7	29.2	4.3	227.1
2014/15	110.2	30.7	8.1	4.4	11.5	38.1	31.2	4.1	238.2

Source: DfT Light Rail and Tram Survey
Telephone: 020 7944 3094
Email: bus.statistics@dft.gsi.gov.uk

[1] For further information on these systems including network and infrastructure changes that may affect the figures, please refer to the technical information.
[2] Manchester Metrolink have revised their method for calculation of passenger boardings so the figures from 2010/11 are not directly comparable with previous years.

Notes and Definitions: https://www.gov.uk/government/publications/light-rail-and-tram-statistics-guidance

The figures in this table are National Statistics

22.19b Passenger revenue by sector

Great Britain annual data from 2003-04 - passenger revenue by sector (£ millions)

Financial year	Franchised long distance operators	Franchised London and South East operators	Franchised regional operators	Total franchised passenger revenue	Non franchised
2003-04	1,384	1,932	585	3,901	:
2004-05	1,465	2,059	634	4,158	:
2005-06	1,609	2,197	687	4,493	:
2006-07	1,842	2,437	733	5,012	:
2007-08	2,036	2,717	801	5,555	:
2008-09	2,168	2,963	872	6,004	:
2009-10	2,216	3,046	916	6,179	36.7
2010-11	2,366	3,264	990	6,620	45.5
2011-12	2,533	3,602	1,094	7,229	43.9
2012-13	2,652	3,888	1,167	7,707	49.9
2013-14	2,779	4,180	1,244	8,203	54.4

Source: Office for Rail and Road; LENNON database and train operating companies

Data can be subject to revisions indicated by (R). For the latest information on data revisions, please see the revisions log:
http://orr.gov.uk/statistics/code-of-practice/revisions-logs

The quality report relating to this dataset can be found at http://orr.gov.uk/statistics/published-stats/statistical-releases.

The quality report pulls together the key qualitative information on relevance, accuracy and reliability, timeliness and punctuality, accessibility and clarity and coherence and comparability. It also includes information on some additional quality principles on user needs and perceptions, confidentiality, transparency and security of data.

Passenger revenue at current prices[1] on light rail and trams by system[2]: England

£ million

Financial year	Docklands Light Railway	Croydon Tramlink	Nottingham Express Transit	Midland Metro	Sheffield Supertram	Tyne and Wear Metro	Manchester Metrolink	Blackpool Tramway	England
1999/00	21.0	:	:	2.5	6.8	23.3	17.0	4.3	**74.8**
2000/01	28.8	12.2	:	3.1	7.1	24.1	18.1	4.3	**97.7**
2001/02	32.2	12.9	:	3.9	7.6	25.0	20.1	4.7	**106.5**
2002/03	35.6	15.0	:	5.0	10.2	28.7	21.0	4.6	**120.0**
2003/04	37.2	16.1	:	5.2	9.2	31.4	20.9	3.9	**124.0**
2004/05	40.4	18.0	5.9	5.4	11.1	32.6	22.1	4.3	**139.7**
2005/06	46.1	18.8	7.3	5.9	10.4	34.4	22.6	4.4	**150.0**
2006/07	53.9	19.0	7.5	6.3	12.4	35.2	23.6	4.5	**162.3**
2007/08	63.1	20.9	7.9	6.3	13.7	37.3	22.4	4.0	**175.5**
2008/09	64.0	18.1	8.6	6.6	15.2	41.3	22.5	3.5	**179.7**
2009/10	74.9	16.2	7.9	6.5	15.0	40.8	23.4	3.0	**187.7**
2010/11	88.8	19.1	9.0	7.0	15.3	41.6	27.4	2.5	**210.6**
2011/12	105.3	21.2	8.4	7.4	15.4	42.2	33.7	1.7	**235.3**
2012/13	124.9	22.5	8.5	7.8	14.4	43.6	42.0	5.0	**268.7**
2013/14	133.1	23.5	8.3	7.9	13.9	45.2	51.8	6.1	**289.8**

Source: DfT Light Rail and Tram Survey
Telephone: 020 7944 3094
Email: bus.statistics@dft.gsi.gov.uk

[1] These figures are not adjusted for inflation.

[2] For further information on these systems including infrastructure changes that may affect the figures, please refer to the technical information.

Notes and Definitions: https://www.gov.uk/government/publications/light-rail-and-tram-statistics-guidance

The figures in this table are National Statistics

22.19c Passenger kilometres by sector

Great Britain annual from 2002-03 - number of passenger kilometres travelled (billions)

Financial year	Franchised long distance operators	Franchised London and South East operators	Franchised regional operators	Total franchised passenger kilometres	Non franchised
2002-03	12.9	19.8	6.9	39.7	:
2003-04	13.3	20.1	7.5	40.9	:
2004-05	13.4	20.5	7.8	41.7	:
2005-06	14.2	20.7	8.2	43.1	:
2006-07	15.6	22.2	8.4	46.2	:
2007-08	16.5	23.5	8.9	48.9	:
2008-09	17.0	24.2	9.4	50.6	:
2009-10	17.6	23.8	9.7	51.1	0.3
2010-11	18.6	25.0	10.4	54.1	0.4
2011-12	19.2	26.4	11.1	56.7	0.4
2012-13	19.5	27.3	11.0	57.8	0.4
2013-14	19.7	28.6	11.4	59.7	0.5

Source: Office for Road and Rail; LENNON database and train operating companies

Data can be subject to revisions indicated by (R). For the latest information on data revisions, please see the revisions log:
http://orr.gov.uk/statistics/code-of-practice/revisions-logs
Data are provisional (P) as train operating companies can revise their data.

This dataset is used in the passenger rail usage statistical release. To view or download the statistical release: http://orr.gov.uk/statistics/published-stats/statistical-releases

The quality report relating to this dataset can be found at http://orr.gov.uk/statistics/published-stats/statistical-releases

The quality report pulls together the key qualitative information on relevance, accuracy and reliability, timeliness and punctuality, accessibility and clarity and coherence and comparability. It also includes information on some additional quality principles on user needs and perceptions, confidentiality, transparency and security of data.

Passenger miles on light rail and trams by system[1]: England

Million

Financial year	Docklands Light Railway	London Tramlink	Nottingham Express Transit	Midland Metro	Sheffield Supertram	Tyne and Wear Metro	Manchester Metrolink[2]	Blackpool Tramway[3]	England
1999/00	106.9	:	:	31.0	47.3	142.9	78.3	8.1	414.6
2000/01	124.3	59.7	:	34.7	48.1	142.4	94.6	7.8	511.6
2001/02	128.5	61.5	:	31.1	49.7	148.1	100.2	9.3	528.5
2002/03	144.2	62.1	:	31.1	50.0	170.8	103.5	8.5	570.3
2003/04	146.3	65.2	1.2	33.3	53.5	176.4	105.0	7.0	588.0
2004/05	152.5	69.7	23.0	32.5	55.7	176.0	126.8	7.4	643.7
2005/06	160.0	72.7	25.9	33.5	57.0	173.4	128.0	6.9	657.4
2006/07	186.8	79.5	26.9	31.9	60.9	183.2	129.0	6.5	704.7
2007/08	202.8	87.9	27.3	31.4	64.4	194.4	130.5	5.4	744.1
2008/09	197.5	89.2	26.1	31.0	65.2	198.5	137.1	4.4	749.0
2009/10	226.5	83.5	23.6	30.8	64.0	203.2	128.1	4.1	763.8
2010/11	257.2	90.0	25.7	31.3	60.5	195.8	124.8	3.1	788.4
2011/12	283.0	92.2	24.9	31.7	60.3	188.8	141.9	2.1	824.9
2012/13	316.8	97.2	20.5	31.3	58.0	186.0	162.6	9.9	882.2
2013/14	333.6	100.9	22.2	30.5	50.7	183.5	188.3	12.7	922.4

Source: DfT Light Rail and Tram Survey

Telephone: 020 7944 3094

Email: bus.statistics@dft.gsi.gov.uk

[1] For further information on these systems including infrastructure changes that may affect the figures, please refer to the technical information.
[2] Manchester Metrolink have revised their approach calculation of passenger boardings so the figure for 2010-11 is not directly comparable with previous years.
[3] 1983/84 to 1998/99 Blackpool Tramway data are imputed. The figures use passenger journeys data and an assumed average distance.

Notes and Definitions: https://www.gov.uk/government/publications/light-rail-and-tram-statistics-guidance

The figures in this table are National Statistics

22.19d Infrastructure on the railways
Great Britain

Year	Route open for traffic	Of which electrified	Route Open for Passenger & Freight Traffic	Route Open for Freight Traffic Only	Passenger Stations
1987-88	16,633	4,207	14,302	2,331	2,426
1988-89	16,599	4,376	14,309	2,290	2,470
1989-90	16,587	4,546	14,318	2,269	2,471
1990-91	16,584	4,912	14,317	2,267	2,488
1991-92	16,588	4,886	14,291	2,267	2,468
1992-93	16,528	4,910	14,317	2,211	2,468
1993-94	16,536	4,968	14,357	2,179	2,493
1994-95	16,542	4,970	14,359	2,183	2,489
1995-96	16,666	5,163	15,002	1,664	2,497
1996-97	16,666	5,176	15,034	1,632	2,498
1997-98	16,656	5,166	15,024	1,632	2,495
1998-99	16,659	5,166	15,038	1,621	2,499
1999-00	16,649	5,167	15,038	1,610	2,503
2000-01	16,652	5,167	15,042	1,610	2,508
2001-02	16,652	5,167	15,042	1,610	2,508
2002-03	16,670	5,167	15,042	1,610	2,508
2003-04	16,493	5,200	14,883	1,610	2,507
2004-05	16,116	5,200	14,328	1,788	2,508
2005-06	15,810	5,205	14,356	1,454	2,510
2006-07	15,795	5,250	14,353	1,442	2,520
2007-08	15,814	5,250	14,484	1,330	2,516
2008-09	15,814	5,250	14,494	1,320	2,516
2009-10	15,753	5,239	14,482	1,271	2,516
2010-11	15,777	5,262	14,506	1,271	2,532
2011-12	15,742	5,261	14,506	1,236	2,535
2012-13	15,753	5,265	14,504	1,249	2,532
2013-14	15,753	5,268	14,504	1,249	2,550

Source: Network Rail

Data can be subject to revisions indicated by (R). For the latest information on data revisions, please see the revisions log: http://www.rail-reg.gov.uk/upload/xls/stats-revisions-log.xls

This dataset is used in the rail infrastructure, assets, and environment statistical release. To view or download the statistical release: http://www.rail-reg.gov.uk/server/show/nav.3016

The quality report relating to this dataset can be found at http://www.rail-reg.gov.uk/server/show/nav.3016.

The quality report pulls together the key qualitative information on relevance, accuracy and reliability, timeliness and punctuality, accessibility and clarity and coherence and comparability. It also includes information on some additional quality principles on user needs and perceptions, confidentiality, transparency and security of data.

22.19d Vehicle miles on light rail and trams by system[1]: England

Million

Financial year	Docklands Light Railway	London Tramlink	Nottingham Express Transit	Midland Metro	Sheffield Supertram	Tyne and Wear Metro	Manchester Metrolink	Blackpool Tramway	England
2000/01	1.8	1.3	:	1.2	1.5	2.9	2.7	0.8	**12.2**
2001/02	1.8	1.5	:	1.0	1.5	2.9	2.8	0.8	**12.4**
2002/03	2.0	1.5	:	1.1	1.6	3.9	2.9	0.7	**13.7**
2003/04	2.1	1.6	0.0	1.0	1.5	3.6	2.8	0.6	**13.2**
2004/05	2.0	1.5	0.6	1.0	1.5	3.5	2.8	0.5	**13.5**
2005/06	2.1	1.5	0.7	1.0	1.5	3.4	2.8	0.5	**13.5**
2006/07	2.7	1.6	0.7	1.0	1.5	3.6	2.3	0.6	**14.1**
2007/08	2.8	1.4	0.7	1.0	1.5	3.8	2.5	0.5	**14.1**
2008/09	2.5	1.4	0.7	1.0	1.5	3.5	2.4	0.5	**13.5**
2009/10	2.8	1.6	0.7	1.0	1.5	3.5	2.1	0.4	**13.6**
2010/11	2.9	1.6	0.7	1.0	1.5	3.5	2.3	0.3	**13.9**
2011/12	3.1	1.7	0.7	1.0	1.5	3.5	2.9	0.1	**14.5**
2012/13	3.6	1.8	0.7	1.0	1.5	3.4	3.6	0.5	**16.1**
2013/14	3.6	1.9	0.7	1.0	1.4	3.4	5.2	0.6	**17.8**

Source: DfT Light Rail and Tram Survey
Telephone: 020 7944 3094
Email: bus.statistics@dft.gsi.gov.uk

[1] For further information on these systems including infrastructure changes that may affect the figures, please refer to the technical information.

[2] Figures for Manchester Metrolink represent total mileage of each tram 'set'. Where two sets are joined to form one train, the vehicle miles run will therefore be counted twice. Based on information supplied by the operator, this affects approximately 7% of services to 2012, around 12% in 12/13 and 20% in 13/14, meaning that figures for later years are not directly comparable with earlier ones (or with other systems). We estimate that the increasing use of double sets to form trains contributes around a third of the overall increase in vehicle mileage shown for this system since 2011/12.

Notes and Definitions: https://www.gov.uk/government/publications/light-rail-and-tram-statistics-guidance

The figures in this table are National Statistics

22.19e Number of stations or stops on light rail and trams by system[1]: England

Financial year	Docklands Light Railway	Croydon Tramlink	Nottingham Express Transit	Midland Metro	Sheffield Supertram	Tyne and Wear Metro	Manchester Metrolink	Blackpool Tramway[2,3]	England
1995/96	28	:	:	:	45	46	26	62	**207**
1996/97	28	:	:	:	45	46	26	62	**207**
1997/98	29	:	:	:	46	46	26	62	**209**
1998/99	29	:	:	:	47	46	26	62	**210**
1999/00	34	:	:	23	47	46	36	62	**248**
2000/01	34	38	:	23	47	46	36	62	**286**
2001/02	34	38	:	23	48	58	36	62	**299**
2002/03	34	38	:	23	48	58	37	62	**300**
2003/04	34	38	23	23	48	58	37	62	**323**
2004/05	34	38	23	23	48	58	37	62	**323**
2005/06	38	39	23	23	48	59	37	62	**329**
2006/07	34	39	23	23	48	59	37	61	**324**
2007/08	39	38	23	23	48	60	37	61	**329**
2008/09	40	39	23	23	48	60	37	61	**331**
2009/10	40	39	23	23	48	60	37	59	**329**
2010/11	40	39	23	23	48	60	38	59	**330**
2011/12	45	39	23	23	48	60	42	31	**311**
2012/13	45	39	23	23	48	60	65	37	**340**
2013/14	45	39	23	23	48	60	77	37	**352**

Source: DfT Light Rail and Tram Survey
Telephone: 020 7944 3094
Email: bus.statistics@dft.gsi.gov.uk

[1] For further information on these systems including infrastructure changes that may affect the figures, please refer to the technical information.

[2] The number of stops has been shown for one direction of the route (as is the case with the other systems). In publications prior to 2011/12 the figures shown covered both directions.

[3] In 2012/13, Blackpool Tramway had 37 stops on the outward journey and 36 stops on the inward journey, as Fleetwood Ferry only had one platform.

Notes and Definitions: https://www.gov.uk/government/publications/light-rail-and-tram-statistics-guidance

The figures in this table are National Statistics

22.19f London Underground statistics, annual

	Passenger Journeys (millions)								Receipts (£ million)					
	Ordinary[1]	Season ticket	All journeys	Passenger miles (millions)	Loaded train miles (millions)	Stations	Rail carriages	Route miles	Ordinary[1]	Season ticket	Traffic receipts	Traffic receipts at 2015/16 prices[2]	Receipts per journey (£)	Receipts per journey at 2015/16 prices[2]
2000/01	486	484	**970**	4,642	40	40	274	3,954	254	610	519	**1,129**	1,574	1.16	1.62
2001/02	491	462	**953**	4,630	40	40	274	3,954	254	636	515	**1,151**	1,583	1.21	1.66
2002/03	495	446	**942**	4,578	41	274	3,954	254	628	510	**1,138**	1,525	1.21	1.62
2003/04	491	457	**948**	4,561	43	274	3,959	254	625	536	**1,161**	1,516	1.22	1.60
2004/05	486	490	**976**	4,726	43	274	3,959	254	663	578	**1,241**	1,572	1.27	1.61
2005/06	460	510	**970**	4,714	43	274	4,070	254	678	630	**1,308**	1,610	1.35	1.66
2006/07	519	521	**1,040**	4,938	43	273	4,070	254	782	635	**1,417**	1,694	1.36	1.63
2007/08	581	515	**1,096**	5,190	43	268	4,070	254	880	645	**1,525**	1,772	1.39	1.62
2008/09	616	473	**1,089**	5,372	44	270	4,070	254	962	654	**1,615**	1,828	1.48	1.68
2009/10	634	425	**1,059**	5,255	43	270	4,078	249	840	612	**1,635**	1,808	1.54	1.71
2010/11	660	447	**1,107**	5,515	43	270	4,134	249	1,087	672	**1,759**	1,889	1.59	1.71
2011/12	685	486	**1,171**	5,915	45	270	4,127	249	1,208	774	**1,982**	2,096	1.69	1.79
2012/13	723	506	**1,229**	6,275	47	270	4,180	249	1,293	833	**2,125**	2,207	1.73	1.80
2013/14	717	548	**1,265**	6,476	47	270	4,283	249	1,372	915	**2,287**	2,326	1.81	1.84

Source: Transport for London
Telephone: 020 7944 3094
Email: bus.statistics@dft.gsi.gov.uk

[1] Ordinary journeys include daily travelcards and those where concessionary fares apply
[2] Adjustment to values using the HM Treasury GDP Deflator (as at 31 March 2016). 'Other' income no longer available on the same basis as previously published.

The figures in this table are outside the scope of National Statistics

22.19g Glasgow Underground statistics, annual

Financial year	Passenger journeys (millions)	Passenger miles (millions)	Loaded train or tram miles [also referred to as vehicle miles] (millions)[1,r]	Stations or stops served	Passenger carriages or tramcars	Route miles open for passenger traffic	Passenger revenue at current prices (£ million)	Passenger revenue at 2015/16 prices (£ millions)
1999/00	14.7	29.2	0.7	15	41	6.8	10.0	14.2
2000/01	14.4	28.6	0.7	15	41	6.8	10.0	13.9
2001/02	13.8	27.4	0.7	15	41	6.8	10.1	13.9
2002/03	13.4	26.6	0.7	15	41	6.8	10.2	13.6
2003/04	13.3	26.5	0.6	15	41	6.8	10.3	13.5
2004/05	13.3	26.5	0.6	15	41	6.8	10.9	13.9
2005/06	13.2	26.2	0.6	15	41	6.5	11.2	13.8
2006/07	13.5	26.8	0.6	15	41	6.5	12.4	14.8
2007/08	14.5	28.8	0.6	15	41	6.5	12.9	15.0
2008/09	14.1	28.1	0.7	15	41	6.5	14.7	16.6
2009/10	13.1	26.0	0.6	15	41	6.5	14.1	15.6
2010/11	13.0	25.9	0.6	15	41	6.5	14.2	15.2
2011/12	12.9	25.6	0.7	15	41	6.5	14.3	15.1
2012/13	12.6	25.0	0.7	15	41	6.5	14.5	15.1
2013/14	12.7	25.3	0.7	15	41	6.5	16.0	16.2

Source: DfT Light Rail and Tram Survey
Telephone: 020 7944 3094
Email: bus.statistics@dft.gsi.gov.uk

: data not available at time of release. These figures will be updated as soon as the data is available.

[1] Loaded tram kilometers are only available as rolling stock totals, to calculate vehicle kilometres the figure provided by Glasgow is divided by 3, as all trams run with three carriages.

[r] Figures for 1982/83 to 2012/13 have been revised due to changes in the calculation, as advised by the operator.

Notes & Definitions: https://www.gov.uk/government/statistics/buses-statistics-guidance

The figures in this table are outside the scope of National Statistics

22.20a Freight moved

Great Britain annual data from 2003-04 - amount of freight moved on the rail network (billion net tonne kilometres)

Financial year	Coal	Metals	Construction	Oil and petroleum	International	Domestic intermodal	Other	Total (1)	Infrastructure (2)
2003-04	5.82	2.41	2.68	1.19	0.48	3.53	2.77	18.87	1.23
2004-05	6.66	2.59	2.86	1.22	0.54	3.96	2.53	20.35	1.29
2005-06	8.26	2.22	2.91	1.22	0.46	4.33	2.29	21.70	1.38
2006-07	8.56	2.04	2.70	1.53	0.44	4.72	1.89	21.88	1.36
2007-08	7.73	1.83	2.79	1.58	0.37	5.15	1.73	21.18	1.70
2008-09	7.91	1.53	2.70	1.52	0.42	5.17	1.38	20.63	1.55
2009-10	6.23	1.64	2.78	1.45	0.44	5.51	1.01	19.06	1.43
2010-11	5.46	2.23	3.19	1.32	0.42	5.68	0.94	19.23	1.54
2011-12	6.41	2.24	3.45	1.20	0.45	6.31	0.99	21.06	1.86
2012-13	7.50	1.81	3.05	1.21	0.43	6.30	1.16	21.46	1.73
2013-14	8.07	1.77	3.56	1.27	0.47	6.19	1.36	22.71	1.72

Source: Network Rail

(1) Infrastructure data are not included in the total.
(2) This series excludes some possession trains used during engineering works.
Annual and quarterly data up to and including 1998-99 are only available to one decimal place so any discrepancies in the totals is due to rounding.

Data can be subject to revisions indicated by (R). For the latest information on data revisions, please see the revisions log: http://orr.gov.uk/statistics/code-of-practice/revisions-log
This dataset is used in the freight rail usage statistical release. To view or download the statistical release please see: http://orr.gov.uk/statistics/published-stats/statistical-releases

The quality report relating to this dataset can be found at http://orr.gov.uk/statistics/published-stats/statistical-releases

The quality report pulls together the key qualitative information on relevance, accuracy and reliability, timeliness and punctuality, accessibility and clarity and coherence and comparability. It also includes information on some additional quality principles on user needs and perceptions, confidentiality, transparency and security of data.

22.20b Freight lifted

Great Britain annual data from 2000-01 - mass of freight goods carried on the rail network (million tonnes)

Financial year	Coal	Other	Total
2000-01	35.3	60.3	95.6
2001-02	39.5	54.5	93.9
2002-03	34.0	53.0	87.0
2003-04	35.2	53.7	88.9
2004-05	44.1	56.8	100.9
2005-06	47.6	57.7	105.3
2006-07	48.7	59.5	108.2
2007-08	43.3	59.1	102.4
2008-09	46.6	56.1	102.7
2009-10	37.9	49.3	87.2
2010-11	38.8	51.1	89.9
2011-12	44.4	57.3	101.7
2012-13	52.0	61.1	113.1
2013-14	51.5	65.1	116.6

Source: Freight operating companies

Annual and quarterly data up to and including 1998-99 are only available to one decimal place so any discrepancies in the totals is due to rounding.

Data can be subject to revisions indicated by (R). For the latest information on data revisions, please see the revisions log: http://orr.gov.uk/statistics/code-of-practice/revisions-log

This dataset is used in the freight rail usage statistical release. To view or download the statistical release please see: http://orr.gov.uk/statistics/published-stats/statistical-releases

The quality report relating to this dataset can be found at http://orr.gov.uk/statistics/published-stats/statistical-releases

The quality report pulls together the key qualitative information on relevance, accuracy and reliability, timeliness and punctuality, accessibility and clarity and coherence and comparability. It also includes information on some additional quality principles on user needs and perceptions, confidentiality, transparency and security of data.

22.21 Railways: permanent way and rolling stock

Northern Ireland

At end of year

Numbers

		2000	2001	2002	2003	2004	2005	2006	2007	2008	2009/10	2010/11	2011/12	2012/13	2013/14
Length of road open for traffic[1] (Km)	KNRA	356	334	334	334	299	299	299	299	299	299	299	299	299	299
Length of track open for traffic (Km)															
Total	KNRB	547	480	480	480	445	445	445	445	445	445	445	445	445	445
Running lines	KNRC	505	464	464	464	427	427	427	427	427	427	427	427	427	427
Sidings (as single track)	KNRD	42	16	16	16	18	18	18	18	18	18	18	18	18	18
Locomotives															
Diesel-electrics	KNRE	6	6	6	5	6	5	5	5	5	5				5
Passenger carrying vehicles															
Total	KNRF	105	106	100	100	102	124	125	128	130	130	130	130	156	150
Rail motor vehicles:															
Diesel-electric,etc	KNRG	30	29	28	28	28	70	85	84	84	84	84	84	110	134
Trailer carriages:															
Total locomotive hauled	KNRH	21	25	22	22	22	22	22	22	22	22	22	22	22	16
Ordinary coaches	KNRI	19	23	20	20	20	20	20	20	20	20	20	20	20	14
Restaurant cars	KNRJ	2	2	2	2	2	2	2	2	2	2				2
Rail car trailers	KNRK	54	52	50	50	52	32	18	22	24	24	24	24	10	0
Rolling stock for maintenance and repair	KNRT	18	18	18	39	46	48	48	48	48	48	48	48	50	47

1 The total length of railroad open for traffic irrespective of the number of tracks comprising the road.

Sources: Department for Regional Development;
Northern Ireland: 02890 540981

22.22 Operating statistics of railways
Northern Ireland

		Unit	2002	2003	2004	2005 /06	2006 /07	2007 /08	2008 /09	2009 /10	2010 /11	2011 /12	2012 /13	2013 /14	2014 /15
Maintenance of way and works															
Material used:															
Ballast	KNSA	Thousand m^2	40.0	130.0	70.0	90.0	30.0	15.0	10.0	35.0	10.0	16.2	46.2	10.0	5.0
Rails	KNSB	Thousand tonnes	1.0	4.5	1.0	3.2	1.0	1.0	0.1	1.4	1.2	3.4	0.2	0.1	0.6
Sleepers	KNSC	Thousands	5.0	40.0	28.0	45.0	2.0	5.0	2.0	2.0	2.0	27.7	2.7	0.3	10.0
Track renewed	KNSD	Km	5.0	25.8	2.0	29.0	1.0	-	..	6.0	1.0	0.5	21.6	0.0	0.0
New Track laid	KPGD	Km	-	-	-	-	-	-	..	−	0.0	-	-	-	-
Engine kilometres															
Total[1]	KNSE	Thousand Km	4,056	4,170	4,110	4,618	4,677	5,108	5,047	4,899	5,088	5,082	5,258	5,760	5,904
Train kilometres:															
Total	KNSF	"	3,626	3,704	4,110	4,618	4,677	5,108	5,047	4,899	5,088	5,082	5,258	5,760	5,904
Coaching	KNSG	"	3,622	3,700	4,110	4,618	4,677	5,108	5,047	4,899	5,088	5,082	5,258	5,760	5,904
Freight	KNSH	"	4	4	-	-	-	-	-	-	-	-	-	-	-

1 Including shunting, assisting, light, departmental, maintenance and repair.

Sources: Department for Regional Development;
Northern Ireland: 02890 540981

22.23 Main Outputs of UK Airlines 1994 - 2014 in Tonne-kilometres Available and Used (a)

	Available Tonne-Kilometres						Tonne-Kilometres Used					
	Total (000 000)	Percentage growth on previous year	Scheduled services (000 000)	Percentage growth on previous year	Non-scheduled services (000 000)	Percentage growth on previous year	Total (000 000)	Percentage growth on previous year	Scheduled services (000 000)	Percentage growth on previous year	Non-scheduled services (000 000)	Percentage growth on previous year
1994	27 713	10.5	20 359	9.5	7 354	13.2	19 350	11.4	13 314	11.3	6 035	11.6
1995	29 901	7.9	22 016	8.1	7 885	7.2	21 306	10.1	14 890	11.8	6 416	6.3
1996	32 214	7.7	23 795	8.1	8 419	6.8	23 001	8.0	16 198	8.8	6 803	6.0
1997	35 571	10.4	26 507	11.4	9 064	7.7	25 091	9.1	17 914	10.6	7 176	5.5
1998	40 022	12.5	29 762	12.3	10 261	13.2	27 552	9.8	19 598	9.4	7 954	10.8
1999	41 911	4.7	31 856	7.0	10 055	-2.0	28 530	3.5	20 596	5.1	7 934	-0.3
2000	43 393	3.5	32 950	3.4	10 443	3.9	29 989	5.1	21 846	6.1	8 143	2.6
2001	42 374	-2.3	31 864	-3.3	10 510	0.6	28 118	-6.2	19 907	-8.9	8 211	0.8
2002	40 550	-4.3	30 433	-4.5	10 117	-3.7	27 913	-0.7	20 032	0.6	7 881	-4.0
2003	42 784	5.5	31 513	3.6	11 271	11.4	29 325	5.1	20 671	3.2	8 654	9.8
2004	43 904	2.6	32 442	2.9	11 462	1.7	29 923	2.0	20 963	1.4	8 960	3.5
2005	48 294	10.0	36 937	13.9	11 357	-0.9	29 494	-1.4	21 133	0.8	8 362	-6.7
2006	50 396	4.4	38 590	4.5	11 806	4.0	30 932	4.9	22 404	6.0	8 528	2.0
2007	54 190	7.5	40 979	6.2	13 211	11.9	32 863	6.2	23 557	5.1	9 306	9.1
2008	53 392	-1.5	41 316	0.8	12 076	-8.6	32 509	-1.1	24 107	2.3	8 402	-9.7
2009	49 150	-7.9	39 207	-5.1	9 944	-17.7	30 411	-6.5	23 427	-2.8	6 984	-16.9
2010	47 168	-4.0	38 059	-2.9	9 109	-8.4	29 915	-1.6	23 263	-0.7	6 651	-4.8
2011	50 120	6.3	41 043	7.8	9 078	-0.3	31 405	5.0	24 796	6.6	6 609	-0.6
2012	50 348	0.5	41 694	1.6	8 653	-4.7	31 621	0.7	25 251	1.8	6 370	-3.6
2013	50 111	-0.5	42 098	1.0	8 014	-7.4	31 704	0.3	25 684	1.7	6 019	-5.5
2014	50 543	0.9	43 737	3.9	6 806	-15.1	31 928	0.7	27 061	5.4	4 867	-19.2

Source: Civil Aviation Authority

(a) Excludes some charter operations performed by aircraft below 15 MTOM
(b) Excludes Small Airlines Public Transport Operations
(c) Excludes Air Europe Operations

22.24a Air Transport Movements(a) by Type and Nationality of Operator 2014

	Total	Scheduled Services			Charter Flights		
		UK Operators	Other EU Operators	Other Overseas Operators	UK Operators	Other EU Operators	Other Overseas Operators
London Area Airports							
GATWICK	254 540	175 237	23 012	33 957	19 245	1 830	1 259
HEATHROW	470 708	261 023	98 858	108 565	755	1 456	51
LONDON CITY	70 133	32 726	29 351	8 054	-	2	-
LUTON	75 616	37 413	30 842	1 587	3 737	1 932	105
SOUTHEND	11 541	7 978	3 346	163	2	51	1
STANSTED	143 230	22 853	105 168	3 808	6 137	672	4 592
Total London Area Airports	1 025 768	537 230	290 577	156 134	29 876	5 943	6 008
Other UK Airports							
ABERDEEN	106 143	41 053	11 382	3 035	50 032	474	167
BARRA	882	882	-	-	-	-	-
BELFAST CITY (GEORGE BEST)	36 052	28 688	7 233	-	44	87	-
BELFAST INTERNATIONAL	34 795	28 609	16	562	3 327	2 203	78
BENBECULA	1 681	1 681	-	-	-	-	-
BIGGIN HILL	34	-	-	-	7	25	2
BIRMINGHAM	89 056	44 204	30 602	5 760	7 695	699	96
BLACKPOOL	8 231	1 355	1 655	-	5 216	5	-
BOURNEMOUTH	6 714	226	3 236	9	3 193	43	7
BRISTOL	52 574	30 517	16 410	227	5 002	325	93
CAMBRIDGE	1 479	-	1 053	349	36	6	35
CAMPBELTOWN	1 035	1 035	-	-	-	-	-
CARDIFF WALES	14 228	3 438	7 388	2	3 023	338	39
CITY OF DERRY (EGLINTON)	2 537	-	2 503	-	2	32	-
COVENTRY	539	-	-	-	539	-	-
DONCASTER SHEFFIELD	5 118	714	2 070	2	2 170	79	83
DUNDEE	1 204	859	293	-	43	9	-
DURHAM TEES VALLEY	4 047	2 003	1 981	-	6	56	1
EAST MIDLANDS INTERNATIONAL	57 197	18 220	12 773	-	12 338	11 633	2 233
EDINBURGH	101 407	65 405	25 256	4 076	4 631	1 964	75
EXETER	12 469	10 060	1	-	2 110	260	38
GLASGOW	74 036	54 408	10 499	3 346	4 644	533	606
GLOUCESTERSHIRE	1 227	-	1 227	-	-	-	-
HUMBERSIDE	11 970	2 098	2 157	29	7 090	556	40
INVERNESS	9 624	9 582	-	-	30	12	-
ISLAY	1 540	1 540	-	-	-	-	-
ISLES OF SCILLY (ST.MARYS)	9 483	9 483	-	-	-	-	-
KIRKWALL	10 747	10 630	-	-	117	-	-
LANDS END (ST JUST)	5 530	5 530	-	-	-	-	-
LEEDS BRADFORD	29 873	20 569	8 419	76	622	186	1
LERWICK (TINGWALL)	1 043	1 041	-	-	2	-	-
LIVERPOOL (JOHN LENNON)	29 777	17 631	11 902	50	111	77	6
LYDD	113	96	-	-	7	7	3
MANCHESTER	162 919	79 923	47 178	16 424	17 135	1 273	986
MANSTON (KENT INT)	621	2	387	-	2	95	135
NEWCASTLE	42 873	25 352	9 611	1 142	5 881	270	617
NEWQUAY	5 938	5 871	55	-	-	10	2
NORWICH	23 117	5 644	2 494	-	8 574	1 067	5 338
OXFORD (KIDLINGTON)	55	36	-	-	1	11	7
PRESTWICK	6 615	9	6 475	-	10	32	89
SCATSTA	12 381	-	-	-	12 381	-	-
SHOREHAM	382	-	-	-	382	-	-
SOUTHAMPTON	35 710	35 532	45	-	80	53	-
STORNOWAY	6 296	6 278	-	-	14	4	-
SUMBURGH	10 227	6 999	-	-	3 114	73	41
TIREE	1 018	1 018	-	-	-	-	-
WICK JOHN O GROATS	2 364	1 919	-	-	221	222	2
Total Other UK Airports	1 032 901	580 140	224 301	35 089	159 832	22 719	10 820
Total All Reporting UK Airports	2 058 669	1 117 370	514 878	191 223	189 708	28 662	16 828
Non UK Reporting Airports							
ALDERNEY	6 183	6 183	-	-	-	-	-
GUERNSEY	25 766	23 948	80	-	1 702	35	1
ISLE OF MAN	17 332	10 459	6 287	-	572	14	-
JERSEY	28 396	25 597	851	16	1 711	212	9
Total Non UK Reporting Airports	77 677	66 187	7 218	16	3 985	261	10

Note
(a) Excludes Air Taxi operations

Source: Civil Aviation Authority

22.24b Air Passengers by Type and Nationality of Operator 2014

	Total Terminal and Transit Passengers	Scheduled Services — UK Operators Terminal	Scheduled — UK Operators Transit	Scheduled — Other EU Operators Terminal	Scheduled — Other EU Operators Transit	Scheduled — Other Overseas Operators Terminal	Scheduled — Other Overseas Operators Transit	Charter Flights — UK Operators Terminal	Charter — UK Operators Transit	Charter — Other EU Operators Terminal	Charter — Other EU Operators Transit	Charter — Other Overseas Operators Terminal	Charter — Other Overseas Operators Transit
London Area Airports													
GATWICK	38 103 667	25 318 121	3 127	2 962 372	509	5 338 727	1 314	3 997 628	3 836	260 410	511	216 672	440
HEATHROW	73 405 330	39 319 348	357	11 773 190	347	22 163 101	33 530	108 938	-	3 834	-	2 685	-
LONDON CITY	3 647 824	1 786 564	-	1 342 248	-	518 905	-	-	-	107	-	-	-
LUTON	10 484 938	5 214 798	1 963	4 658 752	1 213	167 633	7	422 017	183	16 658	71	1 643	-
SOUTHEND	1 102 358	981 464	98	113 708	-	1 932	-	76	-	5 080	-	-	-
STANSTED	19 965 093	2 903 435	3 476	16 090 851	1 012	363 302	1 089	563 113	527	11 849	160	25 497	782
Total London Area Airports	146 709 210	75 523 730	9 021	36 941 121	3 081	28 553 600	35 940	5 091 772	4 546	297 938	742	246 497	1 222
Other UK Airports													
ABERDEEN	3 723 662	1 931 730	84	783 789	31	109 135	-	819 535	29	55 196	-	24 026	107
BARRA	10 521	10 521	-	-	-	-	-	-	-	-	-	-	-
BELFAST CITY (GEORGE BEST)	2 555 145	1 944 474	-	595 136	34	-	-	4 981	-	10 520	-	-	-
BELFAST INTERNATIONAL	4 033 954	3 677 605	237	1 881	-	82 958	-	226 169	1 117	33 239	915	9 833	-
BENBECULA	31 213	31 190	23	-	-	-	-	-	-	-	-	-	-
BIGGIN HILL	497	-	-	-	-	-	-	-	-	-	-	14	-
BIRMINGHAM	9 705 955	3 814 513	3 148	3 202 674	1 172	1 087 544	708	1 507 851	992	74 351	358	11 555	1 089
BLACKPOOL	223 998	175 107	-	28 542	-	920	-	20 257	-	92	-	-	-
BOURNEMOUTH	661 584	25 461	718	451 394	116	-	179	176 398	197	5 351	-	850	-
BRISTOL	6 339 805	3 732 162	472	1 796 089	231	10 736	-	738 078	4 661	43 959	338	12 034	1 045
CAMBRIDGE	20 663	-	-	13 805	-	4 054	-	1 531	-	220	-	1 053	-
CAMPBELTOWN	9 365	9 331	34	-	-	-	-	-	-	-	-	-	-
CARDIFF WALES	1 023 932	111 356	3 059	382 045	-	99	-	479 431	754	39 957	574	6 657	-
CITY OF DERRY (EGLINTON)	350 257	-	-	344 317	-	-	-	96	-	5 844	-	-	-
DONCASTER SHEFFIELD	724 885	10 800	-	312 728	247	-	-	379 597	386	9 211	-	11 916	-
DUNDEE	22 069	15 726	-	4 568	-	-	-	1 583	-	192	-	-	-
DURHAM TEES VALLEY	142 379	37 418	105	101 883	-	-	-	411	-	2 562	-	-	-
EAST MIDLANDS INTERNATIONAL	4 510 544	1 712 062	2 222	1 975 298	229	-	-	796 200	554	15 278	788	7 953	155
EDINBURGH	10 160 004	6 492 518	592	2 831 418	-	563 162	122	214 210	279	46 180	190	11 418	-
EXETER	767 404	533 300	363	10	-	-	-	197 060	-	30 054	-	6 148	-
GLASGOW	7 715 988	5 159 595	1 741	830 885	40	719 668	1 969	911 435	530	57 855	1 303	29 429	1 538
GLOUCESTERSHIRE	15 172	-	-	15 141	31	-	-	-	-	-	-	-	-
HUMBERSIDE	239 173	41 286	765	120 536	205	4 399	-	53 387	-	11 819	610	5 902	264
INVERNESS	612 725	608 769	1 575	-	-	-	-	854	-	1 527	-	-	-
ISLAY	27 659	27 412	247	-	-	-	-	-	-	-	-	-	-
ISLES OF SCILLY (ST MARYS)	90 944	90 944	-	-	-	-	-	-	-	-	-	-	-
KIRKWALL	161 347	150 601	10 012	-	-	-	-	276	458	-	-	-	-
LANDS END (ST JUST)	44 475	44 284	191	-	-	-	-	-	-	-	-	-	-
LEEDS BRADFORD	3 274 474	2 081 349	10 090	1 049 714	152	13 530	172	106 103	10	12 549	803	2	-
LERWICK (TINGWALL)	3 739	3 588	148	-	-	-	-	3	-	-	-	-	-
LIVERPOOL (JOHN LENNON)	3 986 654	2 227 334	791	1 736 040	1 418	4 639	-	7 372	375	8 235	47	403	-
LYDD	1 227	513	-	-	-	-	-	35	-	672	-	7	-
MANCHESTER	21 989 682	9 304 625	4 430	5 584 744	962	3 181 427	26 136	3 693 074	6 270	139 112	757	47 241	904
MANSTON (KENT INT)	12 508	-	123	12 344	-	-	-	26	-	15	-	-	-
NEWCASTLE	4 516 739	2 607 898	2 206	744 625	32	232 183	-	875 995	192	29 756	1 145	22 519	188
NEWQUAY	221 047	214 066	1 794	3 599	-	-	-	-	-	1 254	86	248	-
NORWICH	458 968	119 195	17	137 071	-	-	-	78 739	20	75 888	-	48 038	-

22.24b Air Passengers by Type and Nationality of Operator 2014

| | Scheduled Services | | | | | | Charter Flights | | | | | |
| | UK Operators | | Other EU Operators | | Other Overseas Operators | | UK Operators | | Other EU Operators | | Other Overseas Operators | |
Total Terminal and Transit Passengers	Terminal	Transit	Terminal	Transit	Terminal	Transit	Terminal	Transit	Terminal	Transit	Terminal	Transit
Other UK Airports(Continued)												
OXFORD (KIDLINGTON) 1 194	1 099	-	-	-	-	-	1	-	34	-	60	-
PRESTWICK 913 685	178	352	910 867	125	-	-	472	446	761	165	121	198
SCATSTA 279 799	-	-	-	-	-	-	279 799	-	-	-	-	-
SHOREHAM 452	-	-	-	-	-	-	452	-	-	-	-	-
SOUTHAMPTON 1 831 700	1 814 745	2 125	5 393	-	-	-	6 656	-	2 781	-	-	-
STORNOWAY 129 481	126 716	2 244	-	-	-	-	510	-	11	-	-	-
SUMBURGH 264 521	176 754	236	-	-	-	-	83 123	1 659	2 491	-	258	-
TIREE 9 322	9 026	296	-	-	-	-	-	-	-	-	-	-
WICK JOHN O GROATS 28 145	23 396	49	-	-	-	-	1 989	361	2 248	-	-	102
Total Other UK Airports 91 848 656	49 098 647	50 736	23 976 536	4 967	6 014 454	29 286	11 663 828	19 290	719 558	8 079	257 685	5 590
Total All Reporting UK Airports 238 557 866	124 622 377	59 757	60 917 657	8 048	34 568 054	65 226	16 755 600	23 836	1 017 496	8 821	504 182	6 812
Non UK Reporting Airports												
ALDERNEY 61 317	61 317	-	-	-	-	-	-	-	-	-	-	-
GUERNSEY 894 602	856 894	33 874	2 872	512	-	-	309	3	135	-	3	-
ISLE OF MAN 729 703	629 432	38	95 285	1 074	-	-	2 914	-	960	-	-	-
JERSEY 1 495 707	1 407 030	20 945	38 822	159	1 100	-	8 564	323	18 160	1	603	-
Total Non UK Reporting Airports 3 181 329	2 954 673	54 857	136 979	1 745	1 100	-	11 787	326	19 255	1	606	-

Source: Civil Aviation Authority

22.23 Scheduled and Non-Scheduled Services: All Services 2014 (a)

	Aircraft -Km (000)	Stage Flights	A/C Hours	(b) Number of Passengers Uplifted	Seat-Km Available (000)	Seat-Km Used (000)	As % of Avail	(b) Cargo Uplifted Tonnes	Tonne-Km Available (000)	Tonne-Kilometres Used Total (000)	Mail (000)	Freight (000)	Passenger (000)	As % of Avail
Passenger Services														
ACROPOLIS AVIATION LTD	410	136	586	929	7 769	3 174	40.9	-	4 905	292	-	-	292	6.0
AIRTANKER SERVICES LTD	2 660	426	3 421	55 889	771 995	356 451	46.2	3 695	108 622	57 584	-	23 728	33 856	53.0
ARAVCO LTD	534	245	751	921	7 662	1 718	22.4	-	1 045	194	-	-	194	18.6
AURIGNY AIR SERVICES	2 949	15 487	12 519	518 923	200 333	135 789	67.8	289	19 178	10 179	11	36	10 132	53.1
BA CITYFLYER LTD	21 766	29 326	43 897	1 710 920	1 921 034	1 364 777	71.0	2	192 976	113 728	-	1	113 727	58.9
BAE SYSTEMS (CORP AIR TVL) LTD	117	117	190	3 328	7 507	3 143	41.9	-	992	264	-	-	264	26.6
BLUE ISLANDS LIMITED	2 385	11 627	8 895	336 414	109 528	65 613	59.9	273	9 857	6 009	-	106	5 903	61.0
BMI REGIONAL	13 334	19 240	27 294	406 699	616 618	331 201	53.7	9	70 249	28 155	-	3	28 152	40.1
BRITISH AIRWAYS (BA) LTD	5 649	1 521	8 003	23 868	180 974	133 088	73.5	-	18 198	6 637	-	-	6 637	36.5
BRITISH AIRWAYS PLC	695 367	284 516	1 027 581	39 643 245	167 823 904	136 130 710	81.1	596 202	24 329 984	13 829 503	121 029	3 931 131	9 777 343	56.8
CELLO AVIATION LTD	603	783	1 269	5 885	43 213	29 442	68.1	-	5 049	2 902	-	-	2 902	57.5
EASTERN AIRWAYS	11 032	28 749	29 088	509 525	433 623	236 958	54.6	-	38 574	17 576	-	-	17 576	45.6
EASYJET AIRLINE COMPANY LTD	430 244	381 788	747 686	54 137 361	70 938 651	62 999 097	88.8	-	6 029 785	4 999 332	-	-	4 999 332	82.9
EXECUTIVE JET CHARTER LTD	118	72	163	232	1 556	450	28.9	-	118	40	-	-	40	33.9
FLYBE LTD	59 130	128 247	155 682	7 178 111	5 028 361	3 670 169	73.0	596	543 065	311 973	-	138	311 835	57.4
GAMA AVIATION (UK) LTD	381	249	522	862	5 338	1 748	32.7	-	440	162	-	-	162	36.8
HANGAR 8 AOC LTD	184	103	281	446	2 269	818	36.1	-	350	78	-	-	78	22.3
ISLES OF SCILLY SKYBUS	784	8 490	3 421	89 189	13 322	8 877	66.6	-	1 066	661	-	-	661	62.0
JET2.COM LTD	76 542	39 362	121 281	6 007 549	13 776 273	12 255 212	89.0	-	1 341 751	1 041 803	-	-	1 041 803	77.6
JOTA AVIATION LTD	12	11	24	433	1 112	403	36.2	759	108	34	-	-	34	31.5
LOGANAIR	8 865	37 211	31 354	642 578	295 965	194 429	65.7	1 757	27 886	16 565	12	147	16 406	59.4
MONARCH AIRLINES	92 048	42 343	136 665	7 027 580	19 357 049	15 704 512	81.1	1 757	1 931 108	1 252 664	-	5 314	1 247 350	64.9
ORYX JET LTD	220	84	312	222	2 208	517	23.4	-	243	50	-	-	50	20.6
TAG AVIATION (UK) LTD	2 800	1 911	3 601	7 863	33 583	11 714	34.9	-	9 380	1 026	-	-	1 026	10.9
THOMAS COOK AIRLINES LTD	89 802	28 858	127 001	6 043 480	22 644 075	20 695 693	91.4	3 608	2 475 749	1 785 215	-	25 840	1 759 375	72.1
THOMSON AIRWAYS LTD	154 840	54 257	220 335	10 366 959	34 018 220	31 651 763	93.0	6 930	3 127 552	2 417 143	-	47 736	2 369 407	77.3
TITAN AIRWAYS LTD	4 900	2 854	7 865	119 600	975 583	704 758	72.2	-	83 002	59 907	-	-	59 907	72.2
TRIAIR (BERMUDA) LTD	227	67	298	267	2 757	1 038	37.6	-	504	113	-	-	113	22.4
TWINJET AIRCRAFT	112	41	167	591	3 793	1 521	40.1	-	1 238	139	-	-	139	11.2
VIRGIN ATLANTIC AIRWAYS LTD	149 991	29 710	198 382	5 965 993	48 771 527	37 664 254	77.2	206 266	8 118 714	4 580 122	-	1 502 441	3 077 681	56.4
Total Passenger Services	1 828 006	1 147 831	2 918 531	140 805 862	387 995 802	324 359 037	83.6	820 386	48 491 688	30 540 050	121 052	5 536 621	24 882 377	63.0
Cargo Services														
AIRTANKER SERVICES LTD	9	9	18	-	-	-	..	13	378	12	-	12	-	3.2
ATLANTIC AIRLINES LTD	4 075	10 471	12 293	-	-	-	..	35 861	43 427	19 761	5 986	13 775	-	45.5
BRITISH AIRWAYS PLC	7 313	3 200	11 681	-	-	-	..	70 027	551 268	393 785	-	393 785	-	71.4
DHL AIR LTD	26 509	18 855	42 896	-	-	-	..	118 334	1 051 155	693 919	-	693 919	-	66.0
GLOBAL SUPPLY SYSTEMS LTD	2 795	638	3 771	-	-	-	..	25 668	365 320	266 651	-	266 651	-	73.0
ISLES OF SCILLY SKYBUS	56	895	280	-	-	-	..	245	45	17	13	4	-	37.8
JET2.COM LTD	1 911	4 619	4 851	-	-	-	..	2	2	-	-	-	-	..
LOGANAIR	-	1	1	-	-	-	..	-	30 602	10 446	10 446	-	-	34.1
TITAN AIRWAYS LTD	565	1 317	1 359	-	-	-	..	7 688	8 940	3 293	3 068	225	-	36.8
Total Cargo Services	43 233	40 005	77 149	-	-	-	..	257 835	2 051 137	1 387 884	19 513	1 368 371	-	67.7
Grand Total	1 871 239	1 187 836	2 995 681	140 805 862	387 995 802	324 359 037	83.6	1 078 221	50 542 825	31 927 934	140 565	6 904 992	24 882 377	63.2

Source: Civil Aviation Authority

(a) Excludes small airlines' public transport operations

(b) Excludes passengers and cargo uplifted on sub-charter operations

22.26a Aircraft Movements 2014

| | Total | Commercial Movements | | | | | | Non-Commercial Movements | | | | |
		Air Transport	Of Which Air Taxi	Positioning Flights	Local Movements	Test and Training	Other Flights by Air Transport Operators	Aero Club	Private	Official	Military	Business Aviation
London Area Airports												
GATWICK	259 962	254 591	51	3 533	11	126	123	-	77	9	7	1 485
HEATHROW	472 802	470 851	143	1 092	4	92	95	-	47	241	48	332
LONDON CITY	76 260	75 057	4 924	597	-	360	1	-			-	245
LUTON	101 950	79 757	4 141	5 724	10	143	392	-	615	48	4	15 257
SOUTHEND	30 514	12 588	1 047	796	315	1 353	153	9 755	4 385	230	99	840
STANSTED	157 117	144 873	1 772	5 030	5	138	481	-	4	87	56	6 443
Total London Area Airports	1 098 605	1 037 717	12 078	16 772	345	2 212	1 245	9 755	5 128	615	214	24 602
METRO LONDON HELIPORT	8 925	1 976	1 976	2 013	961	-	1 003	-	2 522	20	132	298
Other UK Airports												
ABERDEEN	124 282	112 537	6 394	4 604	-	3 726	140	2 899	178	-	112	86
BARRA	988	888	6	4	-	4	-	-	90	-	2	-
BELFAST CITY (GEORGE BEST)	37 112	36 672	620	120	7	32	13	-	216	25	13	14
BELFAST INTERNATIONAL	50 973	36 513	1 718	1 231	4 039	152	2	1 087	1 523	-	6 185	241
BENBECULA	3 504	3 013	1 332	346	14	5	-	-	84	-	42	-
BIGGIN HILL	45 477	6 833	6 799	22	-	10	23	26 120	8 222	-	138	4 132
BIRMINGHAM	97 346	89 599	543	2 677	2 364	104	23	-	1 392	-	86	1 101
BLACKPOOL	32 776	9 326	1 095	424	100	2 090	5	15 707	3 589	18	391	1 126
BOURNEMOUTH	43 122	7 096	382	1 295	7	16 346	7 719	2 318	5 567	-	790	1 984
BRISTOL	64 230	54 244	1 670	728	4	-	17	3 129	5 917	4	187	-
CAMBRIDGE	20 036	1 537	58	35	2 021	337	-	9 874	3 104	9	376	2 743
CAMPBELTOWN	1 628	1 150	115	110	-	2	-	-	136	-	230	-
CARDIFF WALES	25 864	14 252	24	885	-	147	4	4 465	5 908	2	200	1
CARLISLE	16 427	464	464	143	142	62	-	11 019	3 366	-	756	475
CITY OF DERRY (EGLINTON)	5 764	2 595	58	23	26	940	7	1 022	1 000	3	58	90
COVENTRY	42 928	1 672	1 133	876	-	30 581	9	2 519	7 258	2	11	-
DONCASTER SHEFFIELD	11 697	5 430	312	327	156	2 179	-	1 665	1 026	2	942	126
DUNDEE	35 730	1 407	203	205	-	784	113	31 762	731	3	23	546
DURHAM TEES VALLEY	17 940	4 786	738	107	1 666	230	5	4 059	6 400	2	685	-
EAST MIDLANDS INTERNATIONAL	76 726	61 579	4 382	3 074	5	922	5 263	-	857	1	114	4 911
EDINBURGH	109 545	103 388	1 981	1 739	14	66	38	331	572	110	164	3 123
EXETER	32 852	13 238	769	532	1 911	1 871	404	7 420	5 424	7	373	1 672
GLASGOW	84 000	77 447	3 411	1 662	2	137	40	4 015	229	16	144	308
GLOUCESTERSHIRE	73 687	1 430	203	321	1 129	10 045	491	43 696	14 930	6	285	1 354
HAWARDEN	13 533	-	-	8	2 114	206	2 147	4 173	2 229	18	802	1 836
HUMBERSIDE	27 647	13 557	1 587	3 791	6	4 746	1 197	-	3 890	4	121	335
INVERNESS	28 495	13 886	4 262	1 496	25	1 894	122	8 840	1 503	-	57	672
ISLAY	2 610	1 730	190	180	-	3	-	-	529	-	160	8
ISLES OF SCILLY (ST.MARYS)	10 965	9 674	191	36	-	111	-	-	977	2	165	-
KIRKWALL	14 420	12 935	2 188	783	22	225	19	5	410	-	6	15
LANDS END (ST JUST)	7 088	5 853	323	85	107	623	15	26	357	6	16	-
LEEDS BRADFORD	42 989	30 663	790	1 626	89	3 029	34	5 015	2 384	21	72	56
LERWICK (TINGWALL)	2 169	1 583	540	381	44	31	14	-	111	-	-	5
LIVERPOOL (JOHN LENNON)	52 249	30 552	775	237	-	96	20	18 108	1 456	10	348	1 422
LYDD	19 808	665	552	179	146	1 030		5 489	13 068	52	418	70

22.26a Aircraft Movements 2014

| | Total | Commercial Movements | | | | Non-Commercial Movements | | | | | | |
		Air Transport	Of Which Air Taxi	Positioning Flights	Local Movements	Other Flights Test and Training	Other Flights by Air Transport Operators	Aero Club	Private	Official	Military	Business Aviation
Other UK Airports (Continued)												
MANSTON (KENT INT)	6 494	778	157	332	20	1 102	-	2 183	1 994	-	81	4
NEWCASTLE	59 114	43 191	318	1 384	786	314	81	-	10 377	2 301	614	66
NEWQUAY	9 261	6 110	172	353	-	602	-	-	643	-	1 531	22
NORWICH	37 391	25 372	2 255	5 639	158	1 937	245	2 447	1 564	4	25	-
OXFORD (KIDLINGTON)	42 456	559	504	4 790	149	27 181	486	628	6 583	-	52	2 028
PRESTWICK	25 643	6 659	44	270	-	4 352	-	7 893	2 416	-	4 053	-
SCATSTA	13 778	12 503	122	1 053	-	212	10	-	-	-	-	-
SHOREHAM	54 344	382	-	87	1 448	600	38	40 009	11 517	37	226	2 082
SOUTHAMPTON	40 374	36 263	551	1 335	2	71	53	-	484	2	82	5
STORNOWAY	10 909	8 358	2 062	368	302	1 418	-	-	390	-	68	-
SUMBURGH	18 171	14 677	4 450	1 429	365	1 566	-	-	95	-	39	-
SWANSEA	14 100	34	34	38	602	20	-	9 013	3 642	2	490	259
TIREE	1 295	1 138	120	16	-	2	-	-	127	-	12	-
WICK JOHN O GROATS	5 711	2 885	521	1 098	4	812	-	4	860	-	38	10
Total Other UK Airports	1 786 287	1 090 207	57 303	51 652	20 039	122 947	18 892	276 940	144 443	2 672	21 559	36 936
Total All Reporting UK Airports	2 893 817	2 129 900	71 357	70 437	21 345	125 159	21 140	286 695	152 093	3 307	21 905	61 836
Non UK Reporting Airports												
ALDERNEY	10 754	6 641	458	217	943	66	26	699	2 158	4	-	-
GUERNSEY	43 189	27 556	1 790	1 886	4 302	206	202	5 209	3 758	28	38	4
ISLE OF MAN	27 645	19 123	1 791	844	-	124	7	3 336	2 603	-	120	1 488
JERSEY	49 912	30 280	1 884	1 211	-	210	642	4 532	12 691	35	275	36
Total Non UK Reporting Airports	131 500	83 600	5 923	4 158	5 245	606	877	13 776	21 210	67	433	1 528

Source: Civil Aviation Authority

Note
Business Aviation was collected under a category in its own right with effect from June 2001 data. However, currently it is not possible for all airports to report using this category

22.26b Terminal and Transit Passengers 2014 Comparison with the Previous Year

	Terminal and Transit Passengers			Terminal Passengers			Transit Passengers		
	2014	2013	Percentage Change	2014	2013	Percentage Change	2014	2013	Percentage Change
London Area Airports									
GATWICK	38 103 667	35 444 206	8	38 093 930	35 428 548	8	9 737	15 658	-38
HEATHROW	73 405 330	72 367 054	1	73 371 096	72 331 690	1	34 234	35 364	-3
LONDON CITY	3 647 824	3 379 753	8	3 647 824	3 379 753	8	-	-	-
LUTON	10 484 938	9 697 944	8	10 481 501	9 693 487	8	3 437	4 457	-23
SOUTHEND	1 102 358	969 912	14	1 102 260	969 912	14	98	-	-
STANSTED	19 965 093	17 852 393	12	19 958 047	17 848 871	12	7 046	3 522	100
Total London Area Airports	146 709 210	139 711 262	5	146 654 658	139 652 261	5	54 552	59 001	-8
Other UK Airports									
ABERDEEN	3 723 662	3 440 617	8	3 723 411	3 440 177	8	251	440	-43
BARRA	10 521	9 410	12	10 521	9 410	12	-	-	-
BELFAST CITY (GEORGE BEST)	2 555 145	2 541 740	1	2 555 111	2 541 703	1	34	37	-8
BELFAST INTERNATIONAL	4 033 954	4 023 336	0	4 031 685	4 022 469	0	2 269	867	162
BENBECULA	31 213	30 738	2	31 190	30 612	2	23	126	-82
BIGGIN HILL	497	326	52	497	326	52	-	-	-
BIRMINGHAM	9 705 955	9 120 201	6	9 698 488	9 114 226	6	7 467	5 975	25
BLACKPOOL	223 998	262 630	-15	223 998	262 630	-15	-	-	-
BOURNEMOUTH	661 584	660 272	0	660 374	659 021	0	1 210	1 251	-3
BRISTOL	6 339 805	6 131 896	3	6 333 058	6 125 149	3	6 747	6 747	-
CAMBRIDGE	20 663	9 307	122	20 663	9 249	123	-	58	-
CAMPBELTOWN	9 365	9 550	-2	9 331	9 427	-1	34	123	-72
CARDIFF WALES	1 023 932	1 072 062	-4	1 019 545	1 057 073	-4	4 387	14 989	-71
CITY OF DERRY (EGLINTON)	350 257	384 973	-9	350 257	384 973	-9	-	-	-
DONCASTER SHEFFIELD	724 885	690 351	5	724 252	689 761	5	633	590	7
DUNDEE	22 069	27 595	-20	22 069	27 560	-20	-	35	-
DURHAM TEES VALLEY	142 379	161 092	-12	142 274	159 311	-11	105	1 781	-94
EAST MIDLANDS INTERNATIONAL	4 510 544	4 334 117	4	4 506 791	4 327 556	4	3 753	6 561	-43
EDINBURGH	10 160 004	9 775 443	4	10 158 906	9 775 026	4	1 098	417	163
EXETER	767 404	741 465	3	766 572	737 919	4	832	3 546	-77
GLASGOW	7 715 988	7 363 764	5	7 708 867	7 358 099	5	7 121	5 665	26
GLOUCESTERSHIRE	15 172	14 168	7	15 141	14 129	7	31	39	-21
HUMBERSIDE	239 173	236 083	1	237 329	234 641	1	1 844	1 442	28
INVERNESS	612 725	608 184	1	611 150	606 722	1	1 575	1 462	8
ISLAY	27 659	26 085	6	27 412	25 721	7	247	364	-32
ISLES OF SCILLY (ST.MARYS)	90 944	89 170	2	90 944	89 170	2	-	-	-
KIRKWALL	161 347	159 325	1	150 877	149 574	1	10 470	9 751	7
LANDS END (ST JUST)	44 475	46 626	-5	44 284	46 299	-4	191	327	-42
LEEDS BRADFORD	3 274 474	3 318 358	-1	3 263 247	3 314 395	-2	11 227	3 963	183
LERWICK (TINGWALL)	3 739	3 784	-1	3 591	3 784	-5	148	-	-
LIVERPOOL (JOHN LENNON)	3 986 654	4 187 493	-5	3 984 023	4 185 757	-5	2 631	1 736	52
LYDD	1 227	670	83	1 227	670	83	-	-	-
MANCHESTER	21 989 682	20 751 581	6	21 950 223	20 680 467	6	39 459	71 114	-45
MANSTON (KENT INT)	12 508	40 391	-69	12 385	40 143	-69	123	248	-50
NEWCASTLE	4 516 739	4 420 839	2	4 512 976	4 415 262	2	3 763	5 577	-33
NEWQUAY	221 047	174 891	26	219 167	174 632	26	1 880	259	626
NORWICH	458 968	463 401	-1	458 931	463 029	-1	37	372	-90

22.26b Terminal and Transit Passengers 2014 Comparison with the Previous Year

	Terminal and Transit Passengers			Terminal Passengers			Transit Passengers		
	2014	2013	Percentage Change	2014	2013	Percentage Change	2014	2013	Percentage Change
Other UK Airports(Continued)									
OXFORD (KIDLINGTON)	1 194	6 847	-83	1 194	6 840	-83	-	7	..
PRESTWICK	913 685	1 145 836	-20	912 399	1 144 568	-20	1 286	1 268	1
SCATSTA	279 799	298 308	-6	279 799	298 308	-6	-	-	..
SHOREHAM	452	732	-38	452	732	-38			
SOUTHAMPTON	1 831 700	1 722 730	6	1 829 575	1 722 443	6	2 125	287	640
STORNOWAY	129 481	122 410	6	127 237	119 904	6	2 244	2 506	-10
SUMBURGH	264 521	212 233	25	262 626	209 747	25	1 895	2 486	-24
TIREE	9 322	8 560	9	9 026	8 270	9	296	290	2
WICK JOHN O GROATS	28 145	33 639	-16	27 633	33 091	-16	512	548	-7
Total Other UK Airports	91 848 656	88 883 229	3	91 730 708	88 729 975	3	117 948	153 254	-23
Total All Reporting UK Airports	238 557 866	228 594 491	4	238 385 366	228 382 236	4	172 500	212 255	-19
Non UK Reporting Airports									
ALDERNEY	61 317	62 855	-2	61 317	62 855	-2	-	-	..
GUERNSEY	894 602	886 396	1	860 213	856 731	0	34 389	29 665	16
ISLE OF MAN	729 703	739 683	-1	728 591	738 522	-1	1 112	1 161	-4
JERSEY	1 495 707	1 453 863	3	1 474 279	1 429 378	3	21 428	24 485	-12
Total Non UK Reporting Airports	3 181 329	3 142 797	1	3 124 400	3 087 486	1	56 929	55 311	3

Source: Civil Aviation Authority

22.26c Freight by Type and Nationality of Operator 2014 - Tonnes

| | Total | Scheduled Services | | | | | | Charter Flights | | | | | |
| | | UK Operators | | Other EU Operators | | Other Overseas Operators | | UK Operators | | Other EU Operators | | Other Overseas Operators | |
		Set Down	Picked Up	Set Down	Picked Up	Set Down	Picked Up	Set Down	Picked Up	Set Down	Picked Up	Set Down	Picked Up
London Area Airports													
GATWICK	88 508	20 229	27 051	1 306	459	18 886	15 183	3 353	2 161	24	43	1	11
HEATHROW	1 498 906	348 988	341 202	10 360	9 051	388 934	365 537	56	15	17 696	15 600	743	725
LONDON CITY	28	1	1	3	13	7	3	-	-	-	-	-	-
LUTON	27 414	56	118	8	22	3 370	1 329	985	1 180	14 695	5 636	4	12
SOUTHEND	6	-	-	-	-	-	-	-	-	2	-	4	-
STANSTED	204 725	11 874	3 130	4 777	391	9 102	7 961	36	84	18 133	1 791	87 783	59 664
Total London Area Airports	1 819 587	381 148	371 502	16 454	9 935	420 098	390 013	4 430	3 440	50 550	23 070	88 535	60 411
Other UK Airports													
ABERDEEN	6 278	132	201	290	320	91	115	2 305	2 780	6	7	19	11
BARRA	20	20	-	-	-	-	-	-	-	-	-	-	-
BELFAST CITY (GEORGE BEST)	491	126	230	61	75	-	-	-	-	-	-	-	-
BELFAST INTERNATIONAL	30 073	1	13	-	-	28	2	25	35	18 718	11 161	88	4
BENBECULA	6	1	5	-	-	-	-	-	-	-	-	-	-
BIRMINGHAM	5 119	11	21	64	58	1 997	2 915	26	26	-	-	-	-
BOURNEMOUTH	1 888	-	-	-	-	-	-	-	1 873	15	-	-	-
CARDIFF WALES	36	-	-	-	-	-	-	30	-	2	4	-	-
COVENTRY	2 303	-	-	-	-	-	-	1 226	1 077	-	-	-	-
DONCASTER SHEFFIELD	858	-	-	-	205	-	190	4	4	2	285	6	162
DURHAM TEES VALLEY	2	-	-	-	-	-	-	-	-	-	-	2	-
EAST MIDLANDS INTERNATIONAL	277 413	-	8	3	63	1	14	19 492	19 203	95 814	93 438	27 886	21 571
EDINBURGH	19 369	125	-	-	-	-	-	114	73	10 668	8 307	-	-
GLASGOW	15 411	342	282	47	35	3 206	10 684	14	13	1	6	412	370
HUMBERSIDE	129	-	20	-	-	-	-	30	74	-	3	-	3
ISLAY	218	104	115	-	-	-	-	-	-	-	-	-	-
ISLES OF SCILLY (ST MARYS)	81	68	12	-	-	-	-	-	-	-	-	-	-
KIRKWALL	36	10	26	-	-	-	-	-	-	-	-	-	-
LANDS END (ST JUST)	57	7	50	-	-	-	-	-	-	-	-	-	-
LEEDS BRADFORD	68	1	7	1	-	49	8	-	-	1	-	-	-
LIVERPOOL (JOHN LENNON)	236	38	104	-	94	-	-	-	-	-	-	-	-
MANCHESTER	93 466	2 883	3 789	1 058	616	39 690	33 297	2 020	1 394	2 185	2 616	1 322	2 594
MANSTON (KENT INT)	12 696	-	-	-	-	-	-	-	-	5 686	370	5 713	927
NEWCASTLE	4 450	3	3	7	4	1 234	2 430	-	-	-	12	249	508
NEWQUAY	12	3	9	-	-	-	-	-	-	-	-	-	-
NORWICH	247	-	-	-	-	-	-	78	169	-	-	-	-
OXFORD (KIDLINGTON)	16	-	-	-	-	-	-	-	-	-	-	16	-
PRESTWICK	12 540	-	-	6 764	4 217	-	-	-	-	-	105	427	953
SCATSTA	788	-	-	-	-	-	-	358	430	-	-	-	-
SOUTHAMPTON	133	-	130	-	-	-	-	-	-	-	-	-	-
STORNOWAY	114	98	16	-	-	-	-	-	-	-	-	-	-
SUMBURGH	335	277	18	-	-	-	-	26	13	-	-	-	-
TIREE	11	11	1	-	-	-	-	-	-	-	-	-	-
Total Other UK Airports	484 898	4 259	5 060	8 296	5 688	46 296	49 655	25 749	27 166	133 184	116 304	36 140	27 100

22.26c Freight by Type and Nationality of Operator 2014 - Tonnes

| | Total | Scheduled Services | | | | | | Charter Flights | | | | | |
| | | UK Operators | | Other EU Operators | | Other Overseas Operators | | UK Operators | | Other EU Operators | | Other Overseas Operators | |
		Set Down	Picked Up	Set Down	Picked Up	Set Down	Picked Up	Set Down	Picked Up	Set Down	Picked Up	Set Down	Picked Up
Other UK Airports (Continued)													
Total All Reporting UK Airports	2 304 486	385 408	376 562	24 750	15 623	466 394	439 668	30 179	30 606	183 734	139 374	124 675	87 511
Non UK Reporting Airports													
ALDERNEY	119	77	42	-	-	-	-	-	-	-	-	-	-
GUERNSEY	2 027	216	118	-	-	-	-	1 502	175	16	1	-	-
ISLE OF MAN	358	139	62	3	-	-	-	148	-	7	-	-	-
JERSEY	2 876	167	80	-	-	-	-	2 305	312	8	4	-	-
Total Non UK Reporting Airports	5 380	599	301	3	-	-	-	3 954	486	32	5	-	-

Source:: Civil Aviation Authority

22.26d Mail by Type and Nationality of Operator 2014 - Tonnes

	Total	Scheduled Services — UK Operators Set Down	Scheduled UK Picked Up	Scheduled Other EU Set Down	Scheduled Other EU Picked Up	Scheduled Other Overseas Set Down	Scheduled Other Overseas Picked Up	Charter Flights — UK Operators Set Down	Charter UK Picked Up	Charter Other EU Set Down	Charter Other EU Picked Up	Charter Other Overseas Set Down	Charter Other Overseas Picked Up
London Area Airports													
GATWICK	5 301	212	1 104	578	2 153	372	849	1	31	-	-	1	-
HEATHROW	89 570	8 948	14 259	6 101	6 090	21 729	32 424	2	-	-	-	5	12
LONDON CITY	2 035	-	1 010	1	99	438	1 498	-	-	-	-	-	-
STANSTED	20 922	669	-	1	19	1	2	7 635	11 585	-	-	-	-
Total London Area Airports	117 828	9 830	16 372	6 681	8 361	22 540	34 772	7 638	11 616	-	-	6	12
Other UK Airports													
ABERDEEN	1 450	-	3	-	1	-	2	1 041	403	-	-	-	-
BELFAST INTERNATIONAL	15 985	6	-	-	-	2	7	9 425	6 514	30	-	-	-
BIRMINGHAM	24	-	-	8	17	-	-	-	-	-	-	-	-
BOURNEMOUTH	7 821	-	-	-	-	-	-	3 570	4 252	-	-	-	-
CARDIFF WALES	1 234	-	-	-	-	-	-	1 234	-	-	-	-	-
EAST MIDLANDS INTERNATIONAL	30 344	8	275	-	-	-	-	12 951	17 101	-	9	-	-
EDINBURGH	17 761	145	3	-	2	-	-	9 824	7 652	43	91	-	-
EXETER	5 407	-	-	-	-	-	-	2 953	2 453	-	-	-	-
GLASGOW	109	33	69	-	-	-	5	-	-	-	-	-	2
INVERNESS	15	-	-	-	-	-	-	15	-	-	-	-	-
ISLAY	67	41	26	-	-	-	-	-	-	-	-	-	-
ISLES OF SCILLY (ST MARYS)	166	98	68	-	-	-	-	-	-	-	-	-	-
KIRKWALL	27	8	19	-	-	-	-	-	-	-	-	-	-
LANDS END (ST JUST)	119	42	77	-	-	-	-	-	-	-	-	-	-
LEEDS BRADFORD	1	-	-	-	-	-	-	-	-	-	-	-	-
MANCHESTER	457	6	4	1	8	35	391	11	1	-	-	-	-
NEWCASTLE	4 738	-	-	-	-	-	-	2 568	2 163	3	-	1	3
NEWQUAY	18	10	9	-	-	-	-	-	-	-	-	-	-
SUMBURGH	1	1	-	-	-	-	-	-	-	-	-	-	-
TIREE	33	28	5	-	-	-	-	-	-	-	-	-	-
Total Other UK Airports	85 778	427	559	9	28	38	405	43 593	40 539	75	100	1	5
Total All Reporting UK Airports	203 606	10 256	16 931	6 690	8 389	22 578	35 177	51 231	52 155	75	100	8	17
Non UK Reporting Airports													
ALDERNEY	82	51	31	-	-	-	-	-	-	-	-	-	-
GUERNSEY	2 744	32	48	-	-	-	-	1 424	1 239	-	-	-	-
ISLE OF MAN	2 521	-	-	-	-	-	-	1 469	1 052	-	-	-	-
JERSEY	1 728	-	-	-	-	-	-	1 266	462	-	-	-	-
Total Non UK Reporting Airports	7 076	84	80	-	-	-	-	4 159	2 754	-	-	-	-

Source: Civil Aviation Authority

Government finance

Chapter 23

Government Finance

Public sector (Tables 23.1 to 23.3 and 23.6)

In Table 23.1 the term public sector describes the consolidation of central government, local government and public corporations. General government is the consolidated total of central government and local government. The table shows details of the key public sector finances' indicators, consistent with the European System of Accounts 2010 (ESA10), by sub-sector.

The concepts in Table 23.1 are consistent with the format for public finances in the Economic and Fiscal Strategy Report (EFSR), published by HM Treasury on 11 June 1998, and the Budget. The public sector current budget is equivalent to net saving in national accounts plus capital tax receipts. Net investment is gross capital formation, plus payments less receipts of investment grants, less depreciation. Net borrowing is net investment less current budget. Net borrowing differs from the net cash requirement (see below) in that it is measured on an accruals basis whereas the net cash requirement is mainly a cash measure which includes some financial transactions.

Table 23.2 shows the public sector key fiscal balances. The table shows the component detail of the public sector key fiscal balance by economic category. The tables are consistent with the Budget.

Table 23.3 shows public sector net debt. Public sector net debt consists of the public sector's financial liabilities at face value, minus its liquid assets – mainly foreign currency exchange reserves and bank deposits. General government gross debt (consolidated) in Table 23.3 is consistent with the definition of general government gross debt reported to the European Commission under the requirements of the Maastricht Treaty.

More information on the concepts in Table 23.1, 23.2 and 23.3 can be found in a guide to monthly public sector finance statistics, GSS Methodology Series No 12, the ONS First Releases Public Sector Finances and Financial Statistics Explanatory Handbook.

Table 23.6 shows the taxes and National Insurance contributions paid to central government, local government, and to the institutions of the European Union. The table is the same as Table 11.1 of the National Accounts Blue Book. More information on the data and concepts in the table can be found in Chapter 11 of the Blue Book.

Consolidated Fund and National Loans Fund (Tables 23.4, 23.5 and 23.7)

The central government embraces all bodies for whose activities a Minister of the Crown, or other responsible person, is accountable to Parliament. It includes, in addition to the ordinary government departments, a number of bodies administering public policy, but without the substantial degree of financial independence which characterises the public corporations. It also includes certain extra-budgetary funds and accounts controlled by departments.

The government's financial transactions are handled through a number of statutory funds or accounts. The most important of these is the Consolidated Fund, which is the government's main account with the Bank of England. Up to 31 March 1968 the Consolidated Fund was virtually synonymous with the term 'Exchequer', which was then the government's central cash account. From 1 April 1968 the National Loans Fund, with a separate account at the Bank of England, was set up by the National Loans Act 1968. The general effect of this Act was to remove from the Consolidated Fund most of the government's domestic lending and the whole of the government's borrowing transactions, and to provide for them to be brought to account in the National Loans Fund.

Revenue from taxation and miscellaneous receipts, including interest and dividends on loans made from votes, continue to be paid into the Consolidated Fund.

After meeting the ordinary expenditure on Supply Services and the Consolidated Fund Standing Services, the surplus or deficit of the Consolidated Fund (Table 23.4), is payable into or met by the National Loans Fund. Table 23.4 also provides a summary of the transactions of the National Loans Fund. The service of the National Debt, previously borne by the Consolidated Fund, is now met from the National Loans Fund which receives:

• interest payable on loans to the nationalised industries, local authorities and other bodies, whether the loans were made before or after 1 April 1968 and

• the profits of the Issue Department of the Bank of England, mainly derived from interest on government securities, which were formerly paid into the Exchange Equalisation Account.

The net cost of servicing the National Debt after applying these interest receipts and similar items is a charge on the Consolidated Fund as part of the standing services. Details of National Loans Fund loans outstanding are shown in Table 23.5. Details of borrowing and repayments of debt, other than loans from the National Loans Fund, are shown in Table 23.7.

Income tax (Table 23.10, 23.11)

Following the introduction of Independent Taxation from 1990/91, the Married Couple's Allowance was introduced. It is payable in addition to the Personal Allowance and between 1990/91 and 1992/93 went to the husband unless the transfer condition was met. The condition was that the husband was unable to make full use of the allowance himself and, in that case, he could transfer only part or all of the Married Couple's Allowance to his wife. In 1993/94 all or half of the allowance could be transferred to the wife if the couple had agreed beforehand. The wife has the right to claim half the allowance. The Married Couple's Allowance, and allowances linked to it, were restricted to 20 per cent in 1994/95 and to 15 per cent from 1995/96. From 2000/01 only people born before 6 April 1935 are entitled to Married Couple's Allowance.

The age allowance replaces the single allowance, provided the taxpayer's income is below the limits shown in the table. From 1989/90, for incomes in excess of the limits, the allowance is reduced by £1 for each additional £2 of income until the ordinary limit is reached (before it was £2 for each £3 of additional income). The relief is due where the taxpayer is aged 65 or over in the year of assessment.

The additional Personal Allowance could be claimed by a single parent (or by a married man if his wife was totally incapacitated) who maintained a resident child at his or her own expense. Widow's Bereavement Allowance was due to a widow in the year of her husband's death and in the following year provided the widow had not remarried before the beginning of that year. Both the additional Personal Allowance and the Widow's Bereavement Allowance were abolished from April 2000.

The Blind Person's Allowance may be claimed by blind persons (in England and Wales, registered as blind by a local authority) and surplus Blind Person's Allowance may be transferred to a husband or wife. Relief on life assurance premiums is given by deduction from the premium payable. From 1984/85, it is confined to policies made before 14 March 1984.

From 1993/94 until 1998/99 a number of taxpayers with taxable income in excess of the lower rate limit only paid tax at the lower rate. This was because it was only their dividend income and (from 1996/97) their savings income which took their taxable income above the lower rate limit but below the basic rate limit, and such income was chargeable to tax at the lower rate and not the basic rate.

In 1999/2000 the 10 per cent starting rate replaced the lower rate and taxpayers with savings or dividend income at the basic rate of tax are taxed at 20 per cent and 10 per cent respectively. Before 1999/2000 these people would have been classified as lower rate taxpayers.

Rateable values (Table 23.12)

Major changes to local government finance in England and Wales took effect from 1 April 1990. These included the abolition of domestic rating (replaced by the Community Charge, then replaced in 1993 by the Council Tax), the revaluation of all non-domestic properties, and the introduction of the Uniform Business Rate. Also in 1990, a new classification scheme was introduced which has resulted in differences in coverage. Further differences are caused by legislative changes which have changed the treatment of certain types of property. There was little change in the total rateable value of non-domestic properties when all these properties were re-valued in April 1995. Rateable values for offices fell and there was a rise for all other property types shown in the table.

With effect from 1 April 2000, all non-domestic properties were re-valued. Overall there was an increase in rateable values of over 25 per cent compared with the last year of the 1995 list. The largest proportionate increase was for offices and cinemas, with all property types given in the table showing rises.

The latest revaluation affecting all non-domestic properties took effect from 1 April 2010. In this revaluation the overall increase in rateable values between 1 April of the first year of the new list and the same day on the last year of the 2005 list was 21 per cent. The largest proportionate increase was for offices and educational properties, with all property types in the table showing rises.

Local authority capital expenditure and receipts (Table 23.16)

Authorities finance capital spending in a number of ways, including use of their own revenue funds, borrowing or grants and contributions from elsewhere. Until 31 March 2004, the capital finance system laid down in Part 4 of the Local Government and Housing Act 1989 (the '1989 Act') provided the framework within which authorities were permitted to finance capital spending from sources other than revenue - that is by the use of borrowing, long-term credit or capital receipts.

Until 31 March 2004, capital spending could be financed by:

• revenue resources – either the General Fund Revenue Account, the Housing Revenue Account (HRA) or the Major Repairs Reserve – but an authority could not charge council tenants for spending on general services, or spending on council houses to local taxpayers

• borrowing or long-term credit as authorised by the credit approvals issued by central government. Credit approvals were normally accompanied by an element of Revenue Support Grant (RSG) covering most of the costs of borrowing

• grants received from central government

• contributions or grants from elsewhere – including the National Lottery and non-departmental public bodies (NDPBs) such as Sport England, English Heritage and Natural England, as well as private sector partners, capital receipts (that is, proceeds from the sale of land, buildings or other fixed assets) and sums set aside as Provision for Credit Liabilities (PCL). This required the use of a credit approval, unless the authority was debt-free

From 1 April 2004, capital spending can be financed in the same ways, except that central government no longer issues credit approvals to allow authorities to finance capital spending by borrowing. However, it continues to provide financial support in the usual way, via RSG or HRA subsidy, towards some capital spending financed by borrowing that is Supported Capital Expenditure (Revenue). Authorities are now free to finance capital spending by self-financed borrowing within limits of affordability set, having regard to the 2003 Act and the CIPFA Prudential Code. The concept of PCL has not been carried forward into the new system, although authorities that were debt-free and had a negative credit ceiling at the end of the old system could still spend amounts of PCL built up under the old rules.

Local authority financing for capital expenditure (Table 23.16, 23.17)

Capital spending by local authorities is mainly for buying, constructing or improving physical assets such as:
• buildings – schools, houses, libraries and museums, police and fire stations
• land – for development, roads, playing fields
• vehicles, plant and machinery – including street lighting and road signs

It also includes grants and advances made to the private sector or the rest of the public sector for capital purposes, such as advances to Registered Social Landlords Local authority capital expenditure more than doubled between 2001/02 and 2007/08.

The underlying trend in capital expenditure shows an increase of 8 per cent from 2008/09 to 2009/10. The exceptional event was the payment by the Greater London Authority (Transport for London) of £1.7 billion to Metronet in 2007/08.

New construction, conversion and renovation forms the major part of capital spending. The largest increases in capital expenditure in 2008/09 were in police (44 per cent), and education (22 per cent). Capital expenditure on transport increased by 14 per cent, allowing for the Greater London Authority's grant payment via TfL in respect of Metronet in 2007/08. Between 2004/05 and 2008/09 capital expenditure on transport had risen from 20 per cent to 24 per cent of the total, while capital expenditure on housing has fallen from 28 per cent to 25 per cent of the total.

The largest percentage increase in capital expenditure in 2009/10 was in transport (24 per cent). Capital expenditure on housing and police fell by 8 per cent and 11 per cent respectively. Between 2005/06 and 2009/10 capital expenditure on transport has risen from 21 per cent to 28 per cent of the total, while capital expenditure on housing has fallen from 27 per cent to 21 per cent of the total.

23.1

Sector analysis of key fiscal balances[1]
United Kingdom
Not seasonally adjusted

£ million[2]

		2008 /09	2009 /10	2010 /11	2011 /12	2012 /13	2013 /14	2014 /15
Surplus on current budget[3]								
Central Government	ANLV	−46 129	−100 728	−96 321	−85 935	−85 094	−68 665	−53 447
Local government	NMMX	−7 676	−8 489	−5 877	−4 975	−4 760	−5 034	−6 113
General Government	ANLW	−53 805	−109 217	−102 198	−90 910	−89 854	−73 699	−59 560
Public corporations	IL6M	13 123	16 597	19 246	19 626	13 800	10 002	9 157
Public sector	ANMU	−39 905	−86 135	−74 978	−62 317	−72 638	−63 233	−48 655
Net investment[4]								
Central government	-ANNS	48 073	55 263	42 653	27 241	39 669	33 819	35 357
Local government	-ANNT	−598	−2 329	−1 572	5 815	−3 002	−3 561	−4 200
General Government	-ANNV	47 475	52 934	41 081	33 056	36 667	30 258	31 157
Public corporations	-JSH6	−5 855	−6 350	2 159	1 524	1 892	1 641	3 443
Public sector	-ANNW	41 622	46 581	43 245	34 589	38 584	31 910	34 623
Net borrowing[5]								
Central government	-NMFJ	94 202	155 991	138 974	113 176	124 763	102 484	88 804
Local government	-NMOE	7 078	6 160	4 305	10 790	1 758	1 473	1 913
General Government	-NNBK	101 280	162 151	143 279	123 966	126 521	103 957	90 717
Public corporations	-IL6E	−18 977	−22 945	−17 087	−18 102	−11 908	−8 361	−5 714
Public sector	-ANNX	81 528	132 718	118 223	96 906	111 222	95 143	83 278
Net cash requirement								
Central government[6]	RUUX	163 909	197 488	132 069	108 644	94 596	79 811	83 659
Local government	ABEG	4 401	4 958	773	8 816	1 815	−3 207	271
General Government	RUUS	166 914	202 673	138 454	126 325	..	..	..
Public corporations	IL6F	17 466	−103 496	−117 821	−160 869	−102 959	−63 630	−5 372
Public sector	RURQ	184 887	94 665	7 641	−54 661	−19 128	288	66 295
Public sector debt								
Public sector net debt	BKQK	2 177 693	2 293 106	2 310 550	2 236 659	2 265 491	2 032 132	1 849 595
Public sector net debt (£ billion)	RUTN	2 177.7	2 293.1	2 310.6	2 236.7	2 265.5	2 032.1	1 849.6
Public sector net debt as a percentage of GDP	RUTO	143.1	147.1	143.0	134.8	131.5	112.6	99.5
Excluding financial interventions								
Net debt	HF6W	769.9	1 004.3	1 149.9	1 242.6	1 352.7	1 459.0	1 546.3
Net debt as a % GDP	HF6X	50.6	64.4	71.2	74.9	78.5	80.9	83.2

1 Consistent with the latest Public Sector Finances data, compliant with the European System of Accounts 2010 (ESA10).
2 Unless otherwise stated.
3 Net saving *plus* capital taxes.
4 Gross capital formation *plus* payments *less* receipts of investment grants *less* depreciation.

5 Net investment *less* surplus on current budget. A version of General government net borrowing is reported to the European Commision under the requirements of the Maastricht Treaty.
6 Central government net cash requirement (own account).

Source: Office for National Statistics: 020 7014 2124

23.2 Public sector transactions and fiscal balances[1]
United Kingdom

£ million

		2008 /09	2009 /10	2010 /11	2011 /12	2012 /13	2013 /14	2014 /15
Current receipts								
Taxes on income and wealth	ANSO	211 350	188 883	201 886	202 328	198 674	201 943	211 323
Taxes on production	NMYE	170 275	172 397	194 293	207 193	211 838	223 913	232 161
Other current taxes[2]	MJBC	33 257	33 943	34 618	36 936	37 208	39 179	40 422
Taxes on capital	NMGI	26 552	2 431	2 722	2 955	3 150	4 417	3 879
Social contributions	ANBO	96 613	96 638	97 747	101 597	104 483	107 306	110 260
Gross operating surplus	ANBP	44 142	46 387	51 016	51 181	49 321	51 307	56 880
Interest and dividends from private sector and Rest of World	ANBQ	46 914	51 184	45 732	49 519	44 214	34 077	13 734
Rent and other current transfers[3]	ANBS	950	1 811	−136	−951	1 184	1 005	1 948
Total current receipts	ANBT	606 432	593 674	627 878	650 758	650 072	663 147	670 607
Current expenditure								
Current expenditure on goods and services[4]	GZSN	321 220	334 501	341 069	341 261	345 350	353 042	358 528
Subsidies	NMRL	8 404	10 083	8 512	7 878	9 143	9 374	10 501
Social benefits	ANLY	177 793	194 293	201 982	210 608	220 564	222 914	228 694
Net current grants abroad[5]	GZSI	−1 394	999	3 166	2 555	2 728	3 509	2 068
Other current grants	NNAI	25 548	28 711	27 345	25 981	23 490	22 094	20 769
Interest and dividends paid to private sector and Rest of World	ANLO	73 918	68 869	75 031	77 822	73 070	65 091	47 687
Total current expenditure	ANLT	616 516	649 173	670 420	679 510	689 095	692 056	684 798
Saving, gross plus capital taxes	ANSP	−10 084	−55 499	−42 542	−28 752	−39 023	−28 909	−14 191
Depreciation	-ANNZ	−31 010	−32 887	−34 354	−35 812	−36 764	−37 886	−38 287
Surplus on current budget	ANMU	−39 905	−86 135	−74 978	−62 317	−72 638	−63 233	−48 655
Net investment								
Gross fixed capital formation[6]	ANSQ	56 561	60 847	59 480	54 497	52 467	55 691	54 945
Less depreciation	-ANNZ	−31 010	−32 887	−34 354	−35 812	−36 764	−37 886	−38 287
Increase in inventories and valuables	ANSR	345	34	55	−38	5	159	61
Capital grants to private sector and Rest of World	ANSS	39 757	16 768	14 462	12 239	20 080	11 078	12 677
Capital grants from private sector and Rest of World	-ANST	−27 013	−1 206	−827	−1 033	−1 451	−2 441	−2 135
Total net investment	-ANNW	41 622	46 581	43 245	34 589	38 584	31 910	34 623
Net borrowing[7]	-ANNX	81 528	132 718	118 223	96 906	111 222	95 143	83 278
Financial transactions determining net cash requirement								
Net lending to private sector and Rest of World	ANSU	−9 557	−33 782	−56 144	−29 189	−48 936	−8 480	−567
Net acquisition of UK company securities	ANSV	54 024	53 259	−28 571	−67 232	−53 510	−66 251	−14 271
Accounts receivable/payable	ANSW	−2 060	23 412	−628	−772	1 591	−642	9 082
Adjustment for interest on gilts	ANSX	−4 885	1 817	−7 819	−2 291	−5 126	1 761	−1 396
Other financial transcations[8]	ANSY	65 838	−82 760	−17 421	−52 083	−24 368	−21 243	−9 831
Public sector net cash requirement	RURQ	184 887	94 665	7 641	−54 661	−19 128	288	66 295

1 See chapter text.
2 Includes domestic rates, council tax, community charge, motor vehicle duty paid by household and some licence fees.
3 ESA10 transactions D44, D45, D74, D75 and D72-D71: includes rent of land, oil royalties, other property income and fines.
4 Includes non-trading capital consumption.
5 Net of current grants received from abroad.
6 Including net acquisition of land.
7 Net investment *less* surplus on current budget.
8 Includes statistical discrepancy, finance leasing and similar borrowing, insurance technical reserves and some other minor adjustments.

Source: Office for National Statistics: 020 7014 2124

23.3 Public sector net debt[1]
United Kingdom

£ million

		2008 /09	2009 /10	2010 /11	2011 /12	2012 /13	2013 /14	2014 /15
Central government sterling gross debt:								
British government stock								
Conventional gilts	BKPK	426 107	608 511	697 968	788 568	..	..	..
Index linked gilts	BKPL	154 038	178 170	220 631	253 779	..	..	..
Total	BKPM	580 145	786 681	918 599	1 042 347	1 142 442	1 244 355	1 300 401
Sterling Treasury bills	BKPJ	43 748	62 866	63 174	69 933	56 370	56 453	65 011
National savings	ACUA	97 231	98 804	98 886	102 903	102 238	105 663	123 801
Tax instruments	ACRV	1 121	819	679	638	633	880	1 158
Other sterling debt[2]	BKSK	64 612	39 934	34 068	42 506	34 260	35 251	38 141
Central government sterling gross debt total	BKSL	786 857	989 104	1 115 406	1 258 327	1 335 943	1 442 602	1 528 712
Central government foreign currency gross debt:								
US$ bonds	BKPG	–	–	–	–	–	–	–
ECU bonds	EYSJ	–	–	–	–	..	..	..
ECU/Euro Treasury notes	EYSV	–	–	–	–	..	..	..
Other foreign currency debt	BKPH	–	–	–	–	..	..	..
Central government foreign currency gross debt total	BKPI	–	–	–	–	–	–	–
Central government gross debt total	BKPW	809 649	1 059 345	1 196 643	1 329 736	1 403 764	1 505 264	1 584 140
Local government gross debt total	EYKP	67 568	68 798	71 496	82 101	84 586	85 235	86 566
less								
Central government holdings of local government debt	-EYKZ	−50 508	−50 889	−52 848	−61 641	..	..	..
Local government holdings of central government debt	-EYLA	−2 960	−2 689	−2 076	−3 415	..	..	..
General government gross debt (consolidated)	BKPX	823 529	1 074 005	1 212 630	1 345 699	1 420 755	1 521 377	1 601 697
Public corporations gross debt	EYYD	62 580	63 166	63 708	68 055	71 411	72 778	77 098
less:								
Central government holdings of public corporations debt	-EYXY	−4 879	−5 617	−5 604	−5 839	..	..	..
Local government holdings of public corporations debt	-EYXZ	−107	−153	−155	−152	..	..	..
Public corporations holdings of central government debt	-BKPZ	−3 947	−3 352	−3 301	−4 383	..	..	..
Public corporations holdings of local government debt	-EYXV	−33	−63	−150	−110	..	..	..
Public sector gross debt (consolidated)	BKQA	2 854 230	2 920 886	2 940 728	2 926 703	2 859 892	2 510 829	2 244 061
Public sector liquid assets:								
Official reserves	AIPD	31 527	44 652	52 969	..	..	..	..
Central government deposits[3]	BKSM	5 242	4 351	5 783	6 672	6 034	8 280	7 274
Other central government	BKSN	39 075	48 143	21 204	45 634	31 813	45 572	27 344
Local government deposits[3]	BKSO	21 781	18 177	19 145	18 123	21 110	23 170	23 683
Other local government short term assets	BKQG	2 072	1 780	3 227	4 733	4 119	4 722	6 263
Public corporations deposits[3]	BKSP	3 831	5 011	4 470	5 712	6 809	6 960	7 093
Other public corporations short term assets	BKSQ	2 166	2 284	2 170	2 296	2 280	2 169	2 229
Public sector liquid assets total	BKQJ	676 013	640 232	634 808	684 580	616 744	520 460	436 308
Public sector net debt	BKQK	2 177 693	2 293 106	2 310 550	2 236 659	2 265 491	2 032 132	1 849 595
as percentage of GDP[4]	RUTO	*143.1*	*147.1*	*143.0*	*134.8*	*131.5*	*112.6*	*99.5*

1 See chapter text.
2 Including overdraft with Bank of England.
3 Bank and building society deposits.
4 Gross domestic product at market prices from 12 months centred on the end
of the month.

Source: Office for National Statistics: 020 7014 2124

23.4a Central government surplus on current budget and net borrowing

£ million

	Current receipts										
	Taxes on production	of which	Taxes on income and wealth					Interest	Asset	Other	
				Income and capital		Other		and	Purchase		
	Total	VAT	Total	gains tax[1]	Other[2]	taxes	NICs[3]	dividends	Facility	receipts[4]	Total
	NMBY	NZGF	NMCU	LIBR	LIBP	LIQR	AIIH	LIQP	L6BD	LIQQ	ANBV
2003	148,853	77,343	147,034	116,509	30,525	10,118	71,540	7,700	0	12,910	398,155
2004	156,727	81,544	158,434	125,032	33,402	10,862	79,224	7,426	0	13,202	425,875
2005	160,321	83,425	176,676	135,867	40,809	11,481	84,459	7,125	0	13,931	453,993
2006	169,375	87,758	196,494	145,608	50,886	12,262	89,550	6,747	0	14,397	488,825
2007	178,107	92,025	203,716	157,087	46,629	13,213	93,210	7,970	0	14,781	510,997
2008	176,102	91,997	212,358	161,631	50,727	12,939	98,319	9,772	0	15,907	525,397
2009	165,260	79,862	190,532	152,553	37,979	12,295	94,445	9,079	0	16,755	488,366
2010	189,699	95,865	197,652	153,507	44,145	12,881	97,346	7,915	0	17,426	522,919
2011	205,025	111,437	204,706	159,070	45,636	14,798	101,441	8,070	0	18,263	552,303
2012	210,639	113,859	198,737	155,278	43,459	15,308	104,319	11,867	0	19,876	560,746
2013	220,033	118,234	203,077	160,697	42,380	17,148	106,085	26,743	18,609	21,116	594,202
2014	231,528	124,211	206,879	164,156	42,723	17,178	109,120	16,755	8,682	22,715	604,175
2003/04	151,986	79,207	149,400	119,146	30,254	10,309	75,148	7,663	0	12,447	406,953
2004/05	157,160	81,864	164,727	128,714	36,013	10,950	80,923	7,054	0	13,496	434,310
2005/06	162,236	83,507	184,158	139,116	45,042	11,760	85,559	7,048	0	14,042	464,803
2006/07	172,169	90,008	198,045	150,325	47,720	12,520	90,916	6,779	0	14,466	494,895
2007/08	179,015	92,467	211,791	162,360	49,431	13,264	95,437	8,683	0	14,954	523,144
2008/09	170,316	87,791	205,982	158,691	47,291	12,717	96,613	9,707	0	16,232	511,567
2009/10	172,384	84,798	187,834	149,640	38,194	12,389	96,638	8,574	0	16,910	494,729
2010/11	194,076	99,523	202,000	156,851	45,149	12,882	97,747	8,006	0	17,656	532,367
2011/12	206,970	112,057	202,847	157,043	45,804	15,355	101,597	9,601	0	18,520	554,890
2012/13	211,614	114,428	199,068	156,222	42,846	15,441	104,483	16,662	6,428	20,236	567,504
2008 Q1	43,876	23,010	72,018	58,197	13,821	3,311	27,222	2,653	0	3,841	152,921
2008 Q2	45,708	24,681	40,689	31,515	9,174	3,315	23,784	2,144	0	3,936	119,576
2008 Q3	43,947	22,938	54,467	40,021	14,446	3,293	23,597	2,422	0	4,073	131,799
2008 Q4	42,571	21,368	45,184	31,898	13,286	3,020	23,716	2,553	0	4,057	121,101
2009 Q1	38,090	18,804	65,642	55,257	10,385	3,089	25,516	2,588	0	4,166	139,091
2009 Q2	40,450	19,070	37,265	30,160	7,105	3,040	22,990	2,659	0	4,104	110,508
2009 Q3	42,652	20,649	45,250	36,786	8,464	3,243	22,535	1,773	0	4,204	119,657
2009 Q4	44,068	21,339	42,375	30,350	12,025	2,923	23,404	2,059	0	4,281	119,110
2010 Q1	45,214	23,740	62,944	52,344	10,600	3,183	27,709	2,083	0	4,321	145,454
2010 Q2	49,705	23,810	38,661	30,987	7,674	3,202	23,115	1,591	0	4,289	120,563
2010 Q3	47,014	24,090	50,770	38,451	12,319	3,391	22,983	2,251	0	4,374	130,783
2010 Q4	47,766	24,225	45,277	31,725	13,552	3,105	23,539	1,990	0	4,442	126,119
2011 Q1	49,591	27,398	67,292	55,688	11,604	3,184	28,110	2,174	0	4,551	154,902
2011 Q2	50,123	27,363	40,089	32,055	8,034	3,394	24,484	1,909	0	4,510	124,509
2011 Q3	52,780	28,427	51,358	38,637	12,721	4,494	24,326	2,124	0	4,580	139,662
2011 Q4	52,531	28,249	45,967	32,690	13,277	3,726	24,521	1,863	0	4,622	133,230
2012 Q1	51,536	28,018	65,433	53,661	11,772	3,741	28,266	3,705	0	4,808	157,489
2012 Q2	51,115	28,135	39,492	31,481	8,011	3,704	25,631	4,252	0	4,965	129,159
2012 Q3	53,085	28,030	49,297	38,314	10,983	4,066	25,201	1,950	0	5,031	138,630
2012 Q4	54,903	29,676	44,515	31,822	12,693	3,797	25,221	1,960	0	5,072	135,468
2013 Q1	52,511	28,587	65,764	54,605	11,159	3,874	28,430	8,500	6,428	5,168	164,247
2013 Q2	53,544	29,091	41,894	34,028	7,866	4,951	26,556	13,701	11,655	5,193	145,839
2013 Q3	56,546	30,064	49,933	38,765	11,168	4,256	25,239	2,749	526	5,238	143,961
2013 Q4	57,432	30,492	45,486	33,299	12,187	4,067	25,860	1,793	0	5,517	140,155
2014 Q1	56,296	30,520	66,320	55,438	10,882	4,183	29,651	2,135	0	5,428	164,013
2014 Q2	56,701	30,567	41,698	32,940	8,758	4,259	26,432	5,975	4,107	5,277	140,342
2014 Q3	58,240	30,592	51,475	40,891	10,584	4,574	26,279	2,729	525	5,535	148,832
2014 Q4	60,291	32,532	47,386	34,887	12,499	4,162	26,758	5,916	4,050	6,475	150,988
2015 Q1	57,004	31,155	72,172	60,463	11,709	4,262	30,791	4,547	2,057	5,379	174,155

Source: Office for National Statistics; HM Treasury

1. Includes capital gains tax paid by households. Includes income tax and capital gains tax paid by corporations.
2. Mainly comprises corporation tax and petroleum revenue tax.
3. Formerly titled compulsory social contributions.
4. Consists largely of gross operating surplus, equates to depreciation for government. Also includes rent receipts.

23.4a Central government surplus on current budget and net borrowing

£ million

	Current expenditure				Saving, gross plus capital		Current budget	Net	Net
	Interest	Net Social Benefits	Other	Total	taxes	Depreciation	deficit	investment	borrowing
	NMFX	GZSJ	LIQS	ANLP	ANPM	NSRN	-ANLV	-ANNS	-NMFJ
2003	21,840	117,683	263,104	402,627	-4,472	11,102	15,574	23,973	39,547
2004	23,420	126,449	281,059	430,928	-5,053	11,450	16,503	23,534	40,037
2005	26,256	130,527	300,452	457,235	-3,242	12,125	15,367	25,405	40,772
2006	27,413	134,482	322,700	484,595	4,230	12,730	8,500	30,165	38,665
2007	31,520	143,582	332,417	507,519	3,478	13,150	9,672	31,206	40,878
2008	32,831	154,145	349,602	536,578	-11,181	14,155	25,336	45,222	70,558
2009	27,698	170,873	369,058	567,629	-79,263	14,804	94,067	57,126	151,193
2010	44,756	178,158	387,158	610,072	-87,153	15,515	102,668	44,485	147,153
2011	51,160	183,643	383,119	617,922	-65,619	16,417	82,036	37,300	119,336
2012	47,828	193,223	396,719	637,770	-77,024	17,135	94,159	35,341	129,500
2013	49,071	195,678	394,678	639,427	-45,225	17,497	62,722	30,884	93,606
2014	48,342	200,377	403,996	652,715	-48,540	17,843	66,383	35,578	101,961
2003/04	22,028	120,876	267,128	410,032	-3,079	10,795	13,874	23,002	36,876
2004/05	24,570	126,997	287,817	439,384	-5,074	11,707	16,781	25,327	42,108
2005/06	26,289	131,741	305,696	463,726	1,077	12,247	11,170	25,170	36,340
2006/07	28,580	135,745	322,796	487,121	7,774	12,804	5,030	31,638	36,668
2007/08	31,220	145,283	339,623	516,126	7,018	13,355	6,337	36,612	42,949
2008/09	31,520	159,241	352,516	543,277	-31,710	14,419	46,129	48,073	94,202
2009/10	31,566	172,792	376,215	580,573	-85,844	14,884	100,728	55,263	155,991
2010/11	46,609	178,825	387,447	612,881	-80,514	15,807	96,321	42,653	138,974
2011/12	49,704	186,180	388,270	624,154	-69,264	16,671	85,935	27,241	113,176
2012/13	48,856	194,768	391,845	635,469	-67,965	17,129	85,094	39,669	124,763
2013/14	48,668	196,336	400,046	645,050	-51,082	17,583	68,665	33,819	102,484
2014/15	45,241	201,677	402,894	649,812	-35,495	17,952	53,447	35,357	88,804
2008 Q1	7,100	34,851	87,757	129,708	23,213	3,441	-19,772	16,415	-3,357
2008 Q2	8,869	38,220	89,208	136,297	-16,721	3,515	20,236	7,494	27,730
2008 Q3	7,716	39,340	85,652	132,708	-909	3,579	4,488	9,813	14,301
2008 Q4	9,146	41,734	86,985	137,865	-16,764	3,620	20,384	11,500	31,884
2009 Q1	5,789	39,947	90,671	136,407	2,684	3,705	1,021	19,266	20,287
2009 Q2	7,886	42,077	95,350	145,313	-34,805	3,648	38,453	12,475	50,928
2009 Q3	4,348	43,141	91,312	138,801	-19,144	3,698	22,842	10,092	32,934
2009 Q4	9,675	45,708	91,725	147,108	-27,998	3,753	31,751	15,293	47,044
2010 Q1	9,657	41,866	97,828	149,351	-3,897	3,785	7,682	17,403	25,085
2010 Q2	12,259	43,631	98,129	154,019	-33,456	3,842	37,298	7,562	44,860
2010 Q3	10,092	44,979	94,564	149,635	-18,852	3,911	22,763	9,661	32,424
2010 Q4	12,748	47,682	96,637	157,067	-30,948	3,977	34,925	9,859	44,784
2011 Q1	11,510	42,533	98,117	152,160	2,742	4,077	1,335	15,571	16,906
2011 Q2	14,081	45,523	99,503	159,107	-34,598	4,065	38,663	5,887	44,550
2011 Q3	11,147	47,206	92,935	151,288	-11,626	4,118	15,744	7,336	23,080
2011 Q4	14,422	48,381	92,564	155,367	-22,137	4,157	26,294	8,506	34,800
2012 Q1	10,054	45,070	103,268	158,392	-903	4,331	5,234	5,512	10,746
2012 Q2	14,219	48,459	98,277	160,955	-31,796	4,226	36,022	16,143	52,165
2012 Q3	9,600	49,047	96,363	155,010	-16,380	4,270	20,650	6,291	26,941
2012 Q4	13,955	50,647	98,811	163,413	-27,945	4,308	32,253	7,395	39,648
2013 Q1	11,082	46,615	98,394	156,091	8,156	4,325	-3,831	9,840	6,009
2013 Q2	14,427	48,596	105,554	168,577	-22,738	4,363	27,101	5,472	32,573
2013 Q3	10,229	49,610	93,695	153,534	-9,573	4,400	13,973	7,256	21,229
2013 Q4	13,333	50,857	97,035	161,225	-21,070	4,409	25,479	8,316	33,795
2014 Q1	10,679	47,273	103,762	161,714	2,299	4,411	2,112	12,775	14,887
2014 Q2	13,908	49,750	104,586	168,244	-27,902	4,443	32,345	6,678	39,023
2014 Q3	10,978	50,958	96,643	158,579	-9,747	4,481	14,228	7,070	21,298
2014 Q4	12,777	52,396	99,005	164,178	-13,190	4,508	17,698	9,055	26,753
2015 Q1	7,578	48,573	102,660	158,811	15,344	4,520	-10,824	12,554	1,730

Source: Office for National Statistics; HM Treasury

1. Includes capital gains tax paid by households. Includes income tax and capital gains tax paid by corporations.
2. Mainly comprises corporation tax and petroleum revenue tax.
3. Formerly titled compulsory social contributions.
4. Consists largely of gross operating surplus, equates to depreciation for government. Also includes rent receipts.

23.4b Central government surplus on current budget and net borrowing - monthly

£ million

	Taxes on production	of which	Taxes on income and wealth			Other taxes	NICs[3]	Interest and dividends	Asset Purchase Facility	Other receipts[4]	Total
			Income and capital gains								
	Total	VAT	Total	capital gains tax[1]	Other[2]						
	NMBY	NZGF	NMCU	LIBR	LIBP	LIQR	AIIH	LIQP	L6BD	LIQQ	ANBV
2013 Jan	17,010	9,617	34,495	26,458	8,037	1,216	8,716	4,274	3,757	1,720	67,431
2013 Feb	16,897	9,282	16,382	14,781	1,601	1,235	8,995	3,121	2,671	1,743	48,373
2013 Mar	18,604	9,688	14,887	13,366	1,521	1,423	10,719	1,105	0	1,705	48,443
2013 Apr	17,310	9,606	17,044	12,124	4,920	1,282	9,175	4,660	3,885	1,753	51,224
2013 May	17,922	9,634	12,096	10,627	1,469	2,305	8,503	4,531	3,885	1,691	47,048
2013 Jun	18,312	9,851	12,754	11,277	1,477	1,364	8,878	4,510	3,885	1,749	47,567
2013 Jul	19,102	10,112	23,850	16,820	7,030	1,451	8,332	1,156	526	1,746	55,637
2013 Aug	18,610	9,883	12,747	11,229	1,518	1,453	8,350	566	0	1,746	43,472
2013 Sep	18,834	10,069	13,336	10,716	2,620	1,352	8,557	1,027	0	1,746	44,852
2013 Oct	18,926	9,783	18,036	10,623	7,413	1,483	8,231	520	0	1,915	49,111
2013 Nov	18,843	10,133	11,963	10,495	1,468	1,272	8,400	678	0	1,865	43,021
2013 Dec	19,663	10,576	15,487	12,181	3,306	1,312	9,229	595	0	1,737	48,023
2014 Jan	18,536	10,355	32,692	25,163	7,529	1,370	8,969	544	0	1,821	63,932
2014 Feb	18,221	9,919	17,124	15,462	1,662	1,379	9,490	495	0	1,782	48,491
2014 Mar	19,539	10,246	16,504	14,813	1,691	1,434	11,192	1,096	0	1,825	51,590
2014 Apr	18,585	10,226	16,792	11,470	5,322	1,329	8,853	4,697	4,107	1,759	52,015
2014 May	18,978	10,134	11,934	10,222	1,712	1,513	8,511	624	0	1,762	43,322
2014 Jun	19,138	10,207	12,972	11,248	1,724	1,417	9,068	654	0	1,756	45,005
2014 Jul	19,562	10,189	24,175	17,586	6,589	1,455	8,753	1,264	525	1,808	57,017
2014 Aug	19,075	10,058	13,970	12,341	1,629	1,582	8,774	707	0	1,885	45,993
2014 Sep	19,603	10,345	13,330	10,964	2,366	1,537	8,752	758	0	1,842	45,822
2014 Oct	20,218	10,789	18,604	11,121	7,483	1,463	8,534	4,930	4,050	1,788	55,537
2014 Nov	19,792	10,770	12,592	11,140	1,452	1,358	8,761	478	0	2,906	45,887
2014 Dec	20,281	10,973	16,190	12,626	3,564	1,341	9,463	508	0	1,781	49,564
2015 Jan	18,906	10,684	36,639	28,458	8,181	1,374	9,214	2,606	2,057	1,778	70,517
2015 Feb	18,774	10,305	18,297	16,558	1,739	1,412	9,982	612	0	1,786	50,863
2015 Mar	19,324	10,166	17,236	15,447	1,789	1,476	11,595	1,329	0	1,815	52,775
2015 Apr	19,267	10,601	18,038	11,776	6,262	1,401	9,148	4,596	3,904	1,856	54,306
2015 May	19,399	10,452	12,966	11,384	1,582	1,553	9,309	678	0	2,023	45,928
2015 Jun	19,889	10,656	13,318	11,525	1,793	1,634	9,392	650	0	2,189	47,072

	Current expenditure				Saving, gross plus capital taxes	Depreciation	Current budget deficit	Net investment	Net borrowing
	Interest	Net Social Benefits	Other	Total					
	NMFX	GZSJ	LIQS	ANLP	ANPM	NSRN	-ANLV	-ANNS	-NMFJ
2013 Jan	3,816	16,161	32,457	52,434	14,997	1,465	-13,532	3,850	-9,682
2013 Feb	4,669	14,490	31,250	50,409	-2,036	1,464	3,500	971	4,471
2013 Mar	2,597	15,964	34,687	53,248	-4,805	1,396	6,201	5,019	11,220
2013 Apr	5,211	16,145	42,742	64,098	-12,874	1,478	14,352	2,322	16,674
2013 May	4,691	16,680	30,783	52,154	-5,106	1,432	6,538	1,426	7,964
2013 Jun	4,525	15,771	32,029	52,325	-4,758	1,453	6,211	1,724	7,935
2013 Jul	3,707	16,902	31,333	51,942	3,695	1,467	-2,228	3,207	979
2013 Aug	3,454	16,371	30,618	50,443	-6,971	1,467	8,438	1,784	10,222
2013 Sep	3,068	16,337	31,744	51,149	-6,297	1,466	7,763	2,265	10,028
2013 Oct	5,131	16,484	31,387	53,002	-3,891	1,471	5,362	2,779	8,141
2013 Nov	4,630	17,565	31,345	53,540	-10,519	1,469	11,988	2,226	14,214
2013 Dec	3,572	16,808	34,303	54,683	-6,660	1,469	8,129	3,311	11,440
2014 Jan	3,691	16,402	32,461	52,554	11,378	1,491	-9,887	3,494	-6,393
2014 Feb	4,388	14,829	35,994	55,211	-6,720	1,491	8,211	3,779	11,990
2014 Mar	2,600	16,042	35,307	53,949	-2,359	1,429	3,788	5,502	9,290
2014 Apr	5,367	16,867	40,627	62,861	-10,846	1,481	12,327	2,504	14,831
2014 May	4,226	16,842	30,825	51,893	-8,571	1,481	10,052	2,070	12,122
2014 Jun	4,315	16,041	33,134	53,490	-8,485	1,481	9,966	2,104	12,070
2014 Jul	3,710	17,239	32,456	53,405	3,612	1,494	-2,118	2,865	747
2014 Aug	4,253	16,716	31,603	52,572	-6,579	1,494	8,073	1,803	9,876
2014 Sep	3,015	17,003	32,584	52,602	-6,780	1,493	8,273	2,402	10,675
2014 Oct	4,873	17,029	32,460	54,362	1,175	1,503	328	2,986	3,314
2014 Nov	4,191	18,063	31,769	54,023	-8,136	1,503	9,639	2,328	11,967
2014 Dec	3,713	17,304	34,776	55,793	-6,229	1,502	7,731	3,741	11,472
2015 Jan	2,864	16,661	32,552	52,077	18,440	1,507	-16,933	3,226	-13,707
2015 Feb	3,824	15,298	35,239	54,361	-3,498	1,507	5,005	3,058	8,063
2015 Mar	890	16,614	34,869	52,373	402	1,506	1,104	6,270	7,374
2015 Apr	4,989	17,041	37,980	60,010	-5,704	1,518	7,222	2,448	9,670
2015 May	3,939	16,809	31,902	52,650	-6,722	1,518	8,240	2,095	10,335
2015 Jun	4,456	16,701	33,990	55,147	-8,075	1,518	9,593	2,591	12,184

Source: Office for National Statistics; HM Treasury

1. Includes capital gains tax paid by households. Includes income tax and capital gains tax paid by corporations.
2. Mainly comprises corporation tax and petroleum revenue tax.
3. Formerly titled compulsory social contributions.
4. Consists largely of gross operating surplus, equates to depreciation for government. Also includes rent receipts.

23.5 National Loans Fund: assets and liabilities

United Kingdom as at 31 March 2015

	At 31 March 2015 £m	At 31 March 2014 £m
Assets		
Advances	**232,899**	217,820
Loans	**2,652**	2,542
Other assets	**89,203**	67,412
IMF Quota Subscription & Lending	**11,775**	12,186
Total assets	**336,529**	299,960
Liabilities		
Gilt-edged stock	**1,479,177**	1,408,776
National Savings and Investments products	**123,889**	105,663
Liabilities to the IMF	**8,839**	7,554
Other debt:		
FLS Treasury Bills	**77,885**	61,707
Other	**51,269**	44,496
Total liabilities	**1,741,059**	1,628,196
Net liabilities	**1,404,530**	1,328,236
Liability of the Consolidated Fund to the National Loans Fund	**1,404,530**	1,328,236

Nick Macpherson
Accounting Officer
HM Treasury

13 July 2015

Source: HM Treasury

23.6a
Taxes paid by UK residents
to general government and the European Union
Total economy sector S.1

£ million

		2006	2007	2008	2009	2010	2011	2012	2013	2014
	Generation of income									
	Uses									
D.2	Taxes on production and imports									
D.21	Taxes on products and imports									
D.211	Value added tax (VAT)									
	Paid to central government	NZGF	87758	92025	92002	79900	95865	111437	113892	118296	124260
D.211	Total	QYRC	87758	92025	92002	79900	95865	111437	113892	118296	124260
D.212	Taxes and duties on imports excluding VAT									
D.2121	Paid to central government: import duties [1]	NMXZ	–	–	–	–	–	–	–	–	–
D.2121	Paid to EU: import duties	FJWE	2329	2412	2636	2645	2933	2925	2885	2914	2949
D.212	Total	QYRB	2329	2412	2636	2645	2933	2925	2885	2914	2949
D.214	Taxes on products excluding VAT and import duties									
	Paid to central government									
	Customs and excise revenue									
	Beer	GTAM	3065	3042	3140	3189	3278	3429	3425	3337	3337
	Wines, cider, perry and spirits	GTAN	4779	5008	5533	5728	6075	6439	6775	7063	7246
	Tobacco	GTAO	8072	7862	8203	9056	9076	9361	9897	9479	9436
	Hydrocarbon oils	GTAP	23448	24512	24790	25894	27013	26923	26703	26698	27095
	Car tax	GTAT	–	–	–	–	–	–	–	–	–
	Betting, gaming and lottery	CJQY	958	959	989	1013	1092	1206	1207	1538	1708
	Air passenger duty	CWAA	961	1883	1876	1800	2094	2605	2766	2960	3154
	Insurance premium tax	CWAD	2314	2306	2281	2259	2401	2942	3022	3018	2964
	Landfill tax	BKOF	804	877	954	842	1065	1090	1094	1191	1143
	Other	ACDN	–	–	–	–	–	–	–	–	–
	Fossil fuel levy	CIQY	–	–	–	–	–	–	–	–	–
	Gas levy	GTAZ	–	–	–	–	–	–	–	–	–
	Stamp duties	GTBC	13074	14634	9499	7141	9098	8831	8918	11542	14069
	Levies on exports (third country trade)	CUDF	–	–	–	–	–	–	–	–	–
	Camelot payments to national lottery									
	Distribution fund	LIYH	1440	1310	1405	1553	1625	1793	1832	1644	1721
	Purchase tax	EBDB	–	–	–	–	–	–	–	–	–
	Hydro-benefit	LITN	–	–	–	–	–	–	–	–	–
	Aggregates levy	MDUQ	321	339	334	275	290	290	264	282	342
	Milk super levy	DFT3	1	–	–	–	–	–	–	–	–
	Climate change levy	LSNT	711	690	717	693	666	675	624	1098	1506
	Channel 4 funding formula	EG9G	–	–	–	–	–	–	–	–	–
	Renewable energy obligations	EP89	700	833	996	1099	1243	1423	1842	2391	2931
	Rail franchise premia	LITT	125	244	285	496	792	993	1275	1275	1554
	Other taxes and levies	GCSP	–	–	–	–	–	–	–	–	–
	Vehicle registration tax	MVPC	137	141	134	122	123	120	125	138	152
	Total paid to central government	NMYB	60910	64640	61136	61160	65931	68120	69769	73654	78358
	Paid to the european union									
	Sugar levy	GTBA	–	–	–	–	12	12	13	12	11
	European coal and steel community levy	GTBB	–	–	–	–	–	–	–	–	–
	Total paid to the european union	FJWG	–	–	–	–	12	12	13	12	11
D.214	Total taxes on products excluding VAT and import duties	QYRA	60910	64640	61136	61160	65943	68132	69782	73666	78369
D.21	Total taxes on products and imports	NZGW	150997	159077	155774	143705	164741	182494	186559	194876	205578
D.29	Production taxes other than on products									
	Paid to central government									
	Consumer credit act fees	CUDB	223	281	328	435	480	480	480	480	480
	National non-domestic rates	CUKY	18762	19344	20607	21361	21509	22444	23535	24364	24837
	Northern Ireland non-domestic rates	NSEZ	318	353	328	325	361	368	366	373	378
	Levies paid to central government levy-funded bodies	LITK	232	261	459	746	569	576	600	585	630
	London regional transport levy	GTBE	–	–	–	–	–	–	–	–	–
	IBA levy	GTAL	–	–	–	–	–	–	–	–	–
	Motor vehicle duties paid by businesses	EKED	865	878	885	908	937	931	940	977	958
	Regulator fees	GCSQ	72	76	70	72	90	78	81	84	93
	Northern Ireland driver vehicle agency	IY9N	–	3	4	4	4	4	4	4	4
	Bank payroll tax: accrued receipts	JT2Q	–	–	–	–	3413	–	–	–	–
	Emissions trading scheme	M98G	–	–	–	–	244	341	257	356	356
	Carbon reduction commitment	L8UA	–	–	–	–	–	–	344	604	569
	Total	NMBX	20472	21196	22681	23851	27607	25222	26607	27827	28305
	Paid to local government									
	Non-domestic rates [2]	NMYH	202	267	301	317	329	336	344	350	353
D.29	Total production taxes other than on products	NMYD	20674	21463	22982	24168	27936	25558	26951	28177	28658
D.2	Total taxes on production and imports, paid									
	Paid to central government	NMBY	169140	177861	175819	164911	189403	204779	210268	219777	230923
	Paid to local government	NMYH	202	267	301	317	329	336	344	350	353
	Paid to the European Union	FJWB	2329	2412	2636	2645	2945	2937	2898	2926	2960
D.2	Total	NZGX	171671	180540	178756	167873	192677	208052	213510	223053	234236

1 These taxes existed before the UK's entry into the EEC in 1973.
2 From 1990/1991 onwards these series only contain rates paid in Northern Ireland.

Source: Office for National Statistics, The Blue Book 2015

23.6b Taxes paid by UK residents to general government and the European Union

Total economy sector S.1

£ million

		2006	2007	2008	2009	2010	2011	2012	2013	2014
	Secondary distribution of income									
	Uses									
D.5	Current taxes on income, wealth etc.									
D.51	Taxes on income									
	Paid to central government									
	Households income taxes	DRWH	141053	151749	154833	143640	150056	154074	149466	155214	158876
	Corporation tax	ACCD	47108	43912	46487	35402	41253	42267	39710	39367	40619
	Petroleum revenue tax	DBHA	2546	1387	2663	1047	1349	1775	2106	1296	568
	Windfall tax	EYNK	–	–	–	–	–	–	–	–	–
	Other taxes on income	BMNX	5787	6601	8190	10387	5041	6594	7308	7129	6749
D.51	Total	NMCU	196494	203649	212173	190476	197699	204710	198590	203006	206812
D.59	Other current taxes									
	Paid to central government									
	Motor vehicle duty paid by households	CDDZ	4145	4506	4639	4722	4903	4889	4933	5124	5029
	Northern Ireland domestic rates	NSFA	244	265	329	355	335	391	416	409	404
	Boat licences	NSNP	–	–	–	–	–	–	–	–	–
	Fishing licences	NRQB	20	20	20	20	20	23	21	21	21
	National non-domestic rates paid by										
	Non-market sectors[1]	BMNY	1260	1304	1354	1423	1481	1637	1688	1714	1740
	Passport fees	E8A6	322	377	376	351	400	368	362	343	386
	Television licence fee	DH7A	2696	2862	2949	3009	3088	3088	3117	3082	3124
	Northern Ireland driver vehicle agency	IY9O	–	12	15	14	12	12	12	12	12
	Bank levy	KIH3	–	–	–	–	–	1454	1609	2171	2693
	Total	NMCV	8687	9346	9682	9894	10239	11862	12158	12876	13409
	Paid to local government									
	Domestic rates[2]	NMHK	155	127	122	131	146	157	164	170	176
	Community charge	NMHL	–	–	–	–	–	–	–	–	–
	Council tax	NMHM	22057	23217	24252	24916	25429	25715	26030	27048	27781
	Total	NMIS	22212	23344	24374	25047	25575	25872	26194	27218	27957
D.59	Total	NVCM	30899	32690	34056	34941	35814	37734	38352	40094	41366
D.5	Total current taxes on income, wealth etc									
	Paid to central government	NMCP	205181	212995	221855	200370	207938	216572	210748	215882	220221
	Paid to local government	NMIS	22212	23344	24374	25047	25575	25872	26194	27218	27957
D.5	Total	NMZL	227393	236339	246229	225417	233513	242444	236942	243100	248178
D.61	Social contributions									
	Actual social contributions									
	Paid to central government									
	(National insurance contributions)									
	Employers' compulsory contributions	CEAN	49568	53765	57080	54411	55887	58174	60638	61912	63746
	Employees' compulsory contributions	GCSE	37052	36585	38186	37184	38703	40626	41118	41587	42702
	Self- and non-employed persons' Compulsory contributions	NMDE	2930	2860	3053	2850	2756	2641	2563	2586	2672
	Total	AIIH	89550	93210	98319	94445	97346	101441	104319	106085	109120
Part	Capital account									
	Changes in liabilities and net worth									
D.91	Other capital taxes									
	Paid to central government									
	Inheritance tax	GILF	3471	3764	3130	2305	2592	2856	3041	3293	3698
	Tax on other capital transfers	GILG	50	50	50	50	50	50	50	50	50
	Tax on swiss bank accounts[3]	KW69	–	–	–	–	–	–	–	876	–
	Development land tax and other	GCSV	–	–	–	–	–	–	–	–	–
	Tax paid on local government equal pay settlements	C625	54	53	77	46	–	30	38	36	134
	FSCS levies on private sector[4]	HZQ4	–	–	21816	1805	–	–	–	–	–
D.91	Total	NMGI	3575	3867	25073	4206	2642	2936	3129	4255	3882
	Total taxes and Compulsory social contributions									
	Paid to central government	GCSS	467446	487933	521066	463932	497329	525728	528464	545999	564146
	Paid to local government	GCST	22414	23611	24675	25364	25904	26208	26538	27568	28310
	Paid to the European Union	FJWB	2329	2412	2636	2645	2945	2937	2898	2926	2960
	Total	GCSU	492189	513956	548377	491941	526178	554873	557900	576493	595416

1 Up until 1995/96 these payments are included in national non-domestic rates under production taxes other than on products
2 From 1990/1991 onwards these series only contain rates paid in Northern Ireland
3 Tax liable from banking deposits of UK residents held in Swiss banks.
4 Financial Services Compensation Scheme.

Source: Office for National Statistics, The Blue Book 2015

23.7 Central government
ESA 2010 sector S.1311

£ million

		2006	2007	2008	2009	2010	2011	2012	2013	2014
III.2 Financial account										
F.A Net acquisition of financial assets										
F.1 Monetary gold and special drawing rights										
F.11 Monetary gold	NARO	-4	–	–	–	–	–	–	–	–
F.12 Special drawing rights	NARP	51	-50	-24	8522	18	333	111	43	-14
F.1 Total	NWXM	47	-50	-24	8522	18	333	111	43	-14
F.2 Currency and deposits										
F.22 Transferable deposits	NART	2116	2486	17989	7554	-5318	4798	5222	-3186	2544
F.22N1 With UK monetary financial institutions	NARV	289	456	-1208	-782	28	1737	-271	901	-1117
F.22N12 Of which: foreign currency deposits with UK MFIs[1]	NARX	-671	-579	2913	540	423	140	935	142	463
F.22N9 With rest of the world monetary financial institutions										
F.29 Other deposits	RYWO	161	3761	11021	7075	-9754	7583	-898	9862	4152
F.2 Total	NARQ	1606	5668	31923	15169	-14649	12521	5259	6818	7159
F.3 Debt securities										
F.31 Short-term										
F.31N5 Issued by UK monetary financial institutions	NSUN	1768	-2038	1974	-2144	-400	–	–	–	–
Money market instruments										
F.31N6 Issued by other UK residents	NSRI	1192	-1142	–	882	1349	3336	-3404	1459	-1137
F.31N9 Issued by rest of the world	NASM	1363	2125	-1029	471	466	315	-967	-2314	363
F.32 Long-term										
Issued by UK monetary financial institutions										
F.32N5-6 and other UK residents	NASV	-601	-21	4978	-5236	–	–	1152	-327	–
F.32N9 Issued by rest of the world	NASW	-854	2155	-1085	-820	5439	4099	5182	-2863	5566
F.3 Total	NARZ	2868	1079	4838	-6847	6854	7750	1963	-4045	4792
F.4 Loans										
F.42 Long-term										
F.422 Secured on dwellings	NATM	–	–	–	–	-6616	-9162	-6649	-6500	-9030
F.424N1 Other loans by UK residents	NATR	3445	5527	6445	3751	8707	5513	16889	6140	11666
F.424N9 Other loans by rest of the world	NATS	–	–	–	–	–	–	–	–	–
F.4 Total	NATB	3445	5527	6445	3751	2091	-3649	10240	-360	2636
F.5 Equity and investment fund shares/units										
F.51 Equity										
F.511N1 Listed UK shares	NATY	-755	-727	11546	40574	-903	-1242	1832	-9222	-5559
F.512N1 Unlisted UK shares	NATZ	–	-2102	-1545	-277	–	–	7	-21957	-2375
F.519 Other equity										
F.519N6 Other UK equity	NAUA	-1356	-2416	–	-4421	–	–	–	-10	-40
F.519N7 UK shares and bonds issued by other UK residents	NSOX	–	–	–	–	–	–	–	–	–
F.519N9 Shares and other equity issued by rest of the world	NAUD	324	233	179	300	77	337	178	1497	285
F.5 Total	NATT	-1787	-5012	10180	36176	-826	-905	2017	-29692	-7689
F.7 Financial derivatives and employee stock options	MN5T	-648	37	1151	619	-317	-123	557	-37	-889
F.71 Of which: financial derivatives	CFZG	-648	37	1151	619	-317	-123	557	-37	-889
F.8 Other accounts receivable	NAUN	2218	-2009	18956	119	3269	362	2116	5174	3216
F.A Total net acquisition of financial assets	NARM	7749	5240	73469	57509	-3560	16289	22263	-22099	9211

1 Monetary financial institutions

Source: Office for National Statistics, The Blue Book 2015

23.7 Central government
ESA 2010 sector S.1311
continued

£ million

			2006	2007	2008	2009	2010	2011	2012	2013	2014
III.2	Financial account										
F.L	Net acquisition of financial liabilities										
F.12	Special drawing rights	M98C	–	–	–	8654	–	–	–	–	–
F.2	Currency and deposits										
F.21	Currency	NAUV	129	57	95	48	82	30	158	30	271
F.29	Other deposits	NAVC	5219	7971	21013	8236	-7118	9209	-2348	-7959	17439
F.2	Total	NAUU	5348	8028	21108	8284	-7036	9239	-2190	-7929	17710
F.3	Debt securities										
F.31	Short-term										
F.31N1	Issued by UK central government	NAVF	-3336	-2767	13179	25975	-2077	14454	-18706	-14315	25809
F.32	Long-term										
F.32N11	UK central government securities	NAVT	40970	39095	95850	195725	170951	121587	129373	103137	64398
F.32N12	Other UK central government bonds	NAVU	2155	2675	3454	-1459	900	3239	4590	2999	199
F.32N5-6	Bonds issued by UK MFIs[1] and other UK residents	MNR7	–	–	–	–	-5416	-10967	-5296	-11682	-3738
F.3	Total	NAVD	39789	39003	112483	220241	164358	128313	109961	80139	86668
F.4	Loans										
F.41	Short-term										
F.41N1	By UK monetary financial institutions	NAWH	-3277	-554	7815	-28068	-1794	238	-601	848	-1423
F.41N9	By rest of the world	NAWL	451	-217	504	-1731	-44	-208	911	-825	1228
F.42	Long-term										
F.423	Finance leasing	NAWU	299	410	86	50	145	–	–	–	–
F.424N1	Other loans by UK residents	NAWV	-7	-6	-7	-18	-9	-9	193	194	-296
F.424N9	Other loans by rest of the world	NAWW	164	16	-59	-21	-561	-2055	-453	86	751
F.4	Total	NAWF	-2370	-351	8339	-29788	-2263	-2034	50	303	260
F.8	Other accounts payable	NAXR	4025	-1165	3028	3056	-11128	-265	45975	1094	7263
F.L	Total net acquisition of financial liabilities	NAUQ	46792	45515	144958	210447	143931	135253	153796	73607	111901
B.9	Net lending(+) / net borrowing(-)										
F.A	Total net acquisition of financial assets	NARM	7749	5240	73469	57509	-3560	16289	22263	-22099	9211
F.L	less total net acquisition of financial liabilities	NAUQ	46792	45515	144958	210447	143931	135253	153796	73607	111901
B.9f	Net lending(+) / borrowing(-) from the financial account	NZDX	-39043	-40275	-71489	-152938	-147491	-118964	-131533	-95706	-102690
dB.9	Statistical discrepancy between the financial and non-financial accounts	NZDW	295	-865	16	297	93	-991	847	815	493
B.9n	Net lending (+) / borrowing (-) from non-financial accounts	NMFJ	-38748	-41140	-71473	-152641	-147398	-119955	-130686	-94891	-102197

1 Monetary financial institutions

Source: Office for National Statistics, The Blue Book 2015

23.8 Central government net cash requirement on own account (receipts and outlays on a cash basis)

£ million

	Cash receipts								Cash outlays				
	HM Revenue and Customs[8]									Net acquisition	Net depart-		Own
	Total paid over[1]	Income tax[2]	Corporation tax[10]	NICs[3]	V.A.T.[4]	Interest and dividends	Other receipts[5]	Total	Interest payments	of company securities[6]	mental outlays[7]	Total	account NCR[9]
	1	2	3	4	5	6	7	8	9	10	11	12	13
	MIZX	RURC	N445	ABLP	EYOO	RUUL	RUUM	RUUN	RUUO	ABIF	RUUP	RUUQ	M98S
2003	325,138	116,627	28,835	69,360	67,525	7,335	25,329	357,802	20,348	-39	379,418	399,727	41,925
2004	347,514	125,909	31,536	77,026	71,907	6,855	25,137	379,506	21,027	0	400,631	421,658	42,152
2005	372,567	135,213	38,282	83,612	73,012	6,549	26,341	405,457	22,434	0	421,021	443,455	37,998
2006	401,362	144,983	47,616	87,156	76,103	6,640	28,115	436,117	25,834	-347	448,131	473,618	37,501
2007	422,465	154,346	44,528	96,656	80,301	8,251	30,083	460,799	25,537	-2,340	470,169	493,366	32,567
2008	428,380	162,758	47,288	98,504	80,709	9,354	30,556	468,290	26,033	19,714	544,720	590,467	122,177
2009	384,875	153,101	36,236	95,053	68,637	6,666	31,282	422,823	29,304	41,809	548,810	619,923	197,100
2010	411,846	153,237	42,153	95,860	80,865	5,274	34,063	451,183	34,008	0	569,599	603,607	152,424
2011	434,438	157,066	43,236	101,033	95,208	5,757	42,235	482,430	43,923	0	557,494	601,417	118,987
2012	436,196	154,430	40,726	102,232	98,619	9,842	38,399	484,437	39,934	-14,287	565,919	591,566	107,129
2013	451,668	159,730	40,417	106,702	103,726	46,577	36,652	534,897	48,025	-6,584	567,570	609,011	74,114
2014	467,588	164,107	41,576	109,238	109,165	16,854	92,517	576,959	41,777	-5,207	635,158	671,728	94,769
2003 Q1	88,763	36,516	7,252	17,598	15,780	2,324	4,994	96,081	3,801	-39	91,497	95,259	-822
2003 Q2	76,531	25,986	5,966	17,760	16,529	1,547	6,240	84,318	7,053	0	95,376	102,429	18,111
2003 Q3	81,637	29,992	7,359	17,404	17,047	1,728	6,901	90,266	4,167	0	93,496	97,663	7,397
2003 Q4	78,207	24,133	8,258	16,598	18,169	1,736	7,194	87,137	5,327	0	99,049	104,376	17,239
2004 Q1	94,758	40,033	6,881	20,695	17,330	2,161	5,013	101,932	4,704	0	97,198	101,902	-30
2004 Q2	82,029	26,273	7,188	20,601	18,039	1,546	5,791	89,366	5,140	0	98,121	103,261	13,895
2004 Q3	87,673	32,619	8,142	18,585	17,707	1,549	7,474	96,696	5,192	0	98,424	103,616	6,920
2004 Q4	83,054	26,984	9,325	17,145	18,831	1,599	6,859	91,512	5,991	0	106,888	112,879	21,367
2005 Q1	103,161	43,699	9,367	21,767	18,449	1,939	4,950	110,050	5,487	0	99,835	105,322	-4,728
2005 Q2	86,274	30,011	7,887	20,941	17,342	1,469	6,592	94,335	5,568	0	105,729	111,297	16,962
2005 Q3	94,524	33,214	9,885	22,007	18,188	1,611	7,430	103,565	5,836	0	105,215	111,051	7,486
2005 Q4	88,608	28,289	11,143	18,897	19,033	1,530	7,369	97,507	5,543	0	110,242	115,785	18,278
2006 Q1	112,661	46,442	13,394	23,677	18,293	1,783	5,631	120,075	6,174	-347	107,430	113,257	-6,818
2006 Q2	91,224	31,700	8,012	22,211	18,021	1,497	6,459	99,180	5,298	0	117,434	122,732	23,552
2006 Q3	100,664	37,048	13,087	20,798	18,731	1,428	8,403	110,495	8,628	0	108,129	116,757	6,262
2006 Q4	96,813	29,793	13,123	20,470	21,058	1,932	7,622	106,367	5,734	0	115,138	120,872	14,505
2007 Q1	117,636	52,992	10,605	23,795	19,550	1,897	4,875	124,408	6,619	0	110,361	116,980	-7,428
2007 Q2	96,004	30,504	8,177	25,932	20,123	1,864	8,204	106,072	5,959	-2,340	121,026	124,645	18,573
2007 Q3	107,134	38,606	12,627	24,165	19,301	1,986	9,934	119,054	6,486	0	114,418	120,904	1,850
2007 Q4	101,691	32,244	13,119	22,764	21,327	2,504	7,070	111,265	6,473	0	124,364	130,837	19,572
2008 Q1	126,971	55,652	13,108	27,550	19,850	2,646	5,997	135,614	6,472	0	118,768	125,240	-10,374
2008 Q2	97,153	35,630	8,722	23,517	20,087	2,252	8,154	107,559	6,449	0	131,441	137,890	30,331
2008 Q3	108,990	40,772	12,955	24,801	21,235	2,266	9,143	120,399	6,566	-255	150,477	156,788	36,389
2008 Q4	95,266	30,704	12,503	22,636	19,537	2,190	7,262	104,718	6,546	19,969	144,034	170,549	65,831
2009 Q1	115,103	54,185	9,749	25,930	17,580	2,016	3,449	120,568	6,386	12,536	131,608	150,530	29,962
2009 Q2	85,699	32,649	6,569	22,727	16,102	1,892	9,626	97,217	8,534	-2,021	145,058	151,571	54,354
2009 Q3	93,410	37,031	8,256	23,574	16,847	1,357	9,721	104,488	7,577	0	133,158	140,735	36,247
2009 Q4	90,663	29,236	11,662	22,822	18,108	1,401	8,486	100,550	6,807	31,294	138,986	177,087	76,537
2010 Q1	112,559	48,458	10,146	26,393	19,103	1,551	4,493	118,603	9,271	0	139,909	149,180	30,577
2010 Q2	94,699	35,719	7,404	22,870	19,886	1,049	8,868	104,616	6,956	0	147,380	154,336	49,720
2010 Q3	107,569	38,793	11,525	23,950	20,564	1,370	11,557	120,496	10,782	0	136,851	147,633	27,137
2010 Q4	97,019	30,267	13,078	22,647	21,312	1,304	9,145	107,468	6,999	0	145,459	152,458	44,990
2011 Q1	120,293	52,311	11,038	27,081	21,737	1,836	9,019	131,148	11,840	0	135,142	146,982	15,834
2011 Q2	99,487	34,458	7,591	24,283	24,084	1,229	10,614	111,330	7,392	0	145,667	153,059	41,729
2011 Q3	110,502	38,849	11,846	25,861	23,984	1,506	13,346	125,354	17,071	0	137,097	154,168	28,814
2011 Q4	104,156	31,448	12,761	23,808	25,403	1,186	9,256	114,598	7,620	0	139,588	147,208	32,610
2012 Q1	123,458	50,524	10,937	27,665	24,821	3,331	6,142	132,931	12,421	-747	135,613	147,287	14,356
2012 Q2	100,129	34,290	7,529	24,669	24,469	3,583	11,978	115,690	7,542	-11,109	147,487	143,920	28,230
2012 Q3	109,251	38,709	10,099	25,873	24,524	1,462	10,843	121,556	12,622	-1,174	136,553	148,001	26,445
2012 Q4	103,358	30,907	12,161	24,025	24,805	1,466	9,436	114,260	7,349	-1,257	146,266	152,358	38,098
2013 Q1	124,619	52,049	10,693	27,470	26,772	13,219	14,153	151,991	13,618	-733	143,648	156,533	4,542
2013 Q2	105,685	36,960	7,485	27,227	24,915	13,088	7,493	126,266	7,110	-382	148,767	155,495	29,229
2013 Q3	114,459	39,123	10,530	26,916	25,681	14,898	8,414	137,771	20,372	-3,355	135,380	152,397	14,626
2013 Q4	106,905	31,598	11,709	25,089	26,358	5,372	6,592	118,869	6,925	-2,114	139,775	144,586	25,717
2014 Q1	129,451	53,123	10,603	28,459	27,488	4,136	51,055	184,642	13,707	-4,217	186,209	195,699	11,057
2014 Q2	109,055	36,578	8,358	26,589	26,961	5,319	11,695	126,069	7,044	-85	154,377	161,336	35,267
2014 Q3	118,047	41,060	10,416	28,124	26,883	1,725	12,207	131,979	14,039	-518	140,325	153,846	21,867
2014 Q4	111,035	33,346	12,199	26,066	27,833	5,674	17,560	134,269	6,987	-387	154,247	160,847	26,578
2015 Q1	138,508	57,683	12,031	29,629	29,478	4,087	16,646	159,241	13,714	-1,043	154,303	166,974	7,733

Sources: HM Revenue & Customs; Office for National Statistics

Relationships between columns: 1+6+7=8; 9+10+11=12; 12-8=13

1. Comprises payments into the Consolidated Fund and all payovers of NICS excluding those for Northern Ireland.
2. Income tax includes capital gains tax and is gross of any tax credits treated by HM Revenue and Customs as tax deductions.
3. UK receipts net of personal pension rebates; gross of Statutory Maternity Pay and Statutory Sick Pay.
4. Payments into Consolidated Fund.
5. Including some elements of expenditure not separately identified.
6. Mainly comprises privatisation proceeds.
7. Net of certain receipts, and excluding on-lending to local authorities and public corporations.
8. A much more detailed breakdown of tax receipts is available from HM Revenue and Customs at www.hmrc.gov.uk/statistics/receipts.htm.
9. NCR = Net Cash Requirement. Without Northern Rock Asset Management & Bradford and Bingley.
10. Gross of tax credits

23.9 HM Revenue and Customs receipts

Amounts: £ million

Year	Total Paid Over[1]	Total HMRC receipts[2,3,10]	Total Income Tax[4]	Of which: PAYE Income Tax**	Of which: SA Income Tax**	Capital Gains Tax	NICs	VAT	Total Corporation Tax[5]	Of which offshore**[6]	Bank Levy	Bank payroll tax	Petroleum Revenue Tax	Fuel duties	IHT[7]	Shares	Stamp Duty Land Tax	Annual Tax on Enveloped Dwellings	Tobacco duties
	MIZX			BKMR	LISB	BKLO	ABLP	EYOO	N445			JT2R	ACCJ	ACDD	ACCH	BKST	BKSU		ACDE
2003-04	331,133	347,946	117,917	101,389	15,772	2,225	72,457	69,075	28,459	3,057			1,179	22,786	2,504	2,559	4,986		8,091
2004-05	355,917	375,801	127,294	108,699	17,141	2,282	78,098	73,026	34,031	3,831			1,284	23,313	2,922	2,715	6,251		8,100
2005-06	382,067	402,824	134,916	113,894	18,077	3,042	85,522	72,856	42,355	7,307			2,016	23,438	3,259	3,465	7,454		7,959
2006-07	406,337	428,629	147,712	124,799	20,306	3,830	87,274	77,360	44,875	6,709			2,155	23,585	3,545	3,757	9,635		8,149
2007-08	431,800	456,121	151,738	126,760	22,443	5,268	100,410	80,599	47,036	5,728			1,680	24,905	3,824	4,167	9,958		8,094
2008-09	416,512	445,531	153,442	128,470	22,531	7,852	96,882	78,439	43,927	9,826			2,567	24,615	2,839	3,203	4,796		8,219
2009-10	382,331	414,920	144,881	122,584	21,708	2,491	95,517	70,160	36,628	4,998			923	26,197	2,384	3,017	4,886		8,813
2010-11	419,580	453,614	153,491	132,263	22,108	3,601	96,548	83,502	43,040	6,864		3,416	1,458	27,256	2,717	2,971	5,961		9,144
2011-12	437,603	472,315	150,939	132,189	20,334	4,337	101,617	98,292	43,130	8,840	1,612	-2	2,032	26,800	2,903	2,794	6,125		9,551
2012-13	437,357	473,777	152,030	132,433	20,550	3,927	102,037	100,572	40,482	4,412	1,595	0	1,737	26,571	3,105	2,234	6,907		9,681
2013-14	456,500	493,646	156,898	134,686	20,854	3,908	107,690	104,718	40,327	3,556	2,200	0	1,118	26,881	3,402	3,108	9,273	100	9,531
2014-15	476,633	515,348	163,109	139,506	23,645	5,559	110,406	111,363	43,005	2,073	2,748	0	77	27,156	3,804	2,926	10,738	116	9,548
Apr-11	44,593	46,609	13,440	13,709	85	7	9,916	10,608	5,676	-		1	124	2,384	221	267	552		1,492
May-11	29,847	33,117	10,570	10,548	-61	5	7,990	7,999	1,176	-		0	83	2,157	241	244	415		185
Jun-11	25,047	28,267	10,426	10,584	-72	9	6,377	5,474	739	-		0	99	2,269	257	218	377		651
Jul-11	47,037	51,323	17,069	11,238	5,104	6	9,484	9,960	8,658	-	42	0	63	2,254	254	289	573		805
Aug-11	34,904	37,122	12,220	10,803	1,723	6	8,476	8,552	1,345	-		8	70	2,187	277	241	571		808
Sep-11	28,561	31,133	9,545	10,283	86	2	7,901	5,470	1,843	3,272		0	577	2,311	275	252	581		878
Oct-11	42,789	44,940	10,224	10,421	-24	2	8,017	10,560	8,740	-	1,098	-9	114	2,305	234	244	566		935
Nov-11	32,548	36,105	10,671	10,378	-64	6	7,983	9,465	1,153	-		-3	117	2,302	239	201	548		1,037
Dec-11	28,819	32,199	10,540	10,157	441	4	7,808	5,381	2,868	2,787		0	125	2,262	215	233	572		478
Jan-12	56,559	60,606	21,929	11,112	10,184	3,324	9,693	10,343	9,121	-	472	0	67	2,100	222	140	461		855
Feb-12	37,279	38,631	13,112	11,291	2,650	868	9,000	8,796	1,142	-		0	72	2,197	252	208	431		668
Mar-12	29,620	32,261	11,192	11,666	281	97	8,972	5,684	674	2,781		0	521	2,070	218	257	478		760
Apr-12	44,065	46,867	14,148	14,179	19	11	9,798	10,232	4,976	-	287	0	150	2,386	236	204	479		1,818
May-12	30,304	33,410	10,166	10,912	-103	4	8,335	8,363	1,330	-		0	127	2,119	261	75	534		136
Jun-12	25,760	28,927	9,956	10,264	-67	3	6,536	5,873	1,223	-		0	53	2,247	255	213	509		600
Jul-12	46,840	50,799	17,464	11,290	6,146	4	9,699	10,058	6,947	-	526	0	101	2,212	288	189	666		759
Aug-12	33,976	37,053	11,443	10,648	977	4	8,287	9,047	1,293	-		0	108	2,237	335	218	683		1,054
Sep-12	28,435	30,989	9,794	10,318	28	2	7,887	5,420	1,859	1,573		0	533	2,260	235	166	588		680
Oct-12	41,068	44,041	11,030	10,772	-12	9	8,259	10,248	7,890	-	366	0	126	2,220	282	174	624		979
Nov-12	31,877	34,095	9,265	10,301	-67	4	7,890	8,756	1,389	-		0	141	2,324	256	231	611		769
Dec-12	30,413	33,088	10,596	10,204	409	4	7,876	5,803	2,881	1,493		0	107	2,331	237	188	591		622
Jan-13	57,228	62,301	23,578	11,103	10,685	2,971	9,926	11,210	7,903	-	416	0	75	2,008	221	159	623		1,052
Feb-13	36,473	39,227	13,588	11,018	2,347	820	8,751	9,129	1,438	-		0	115	2,155	163	145	502		566
Mar-13	30,918	32,982	11,002	11,426	189	90	8,793	6,434	1,351	1,346		0	101	2,072	337	271	496		648
Apr-13	44,225	47,392	14,785	14,051	52	2	9,916	10,177	4,777	-	334	0	77	2,258	309	222	660	-	1,725
May-13	32,327	35,813	11,858	12,048	-132	3	8,528	8,263	1,322	-		0	91	2,267	293	323	646	-	201
Jun-13	29,133	32,422	10,309	10,405	-79	3	8,783	6,505	1,386	-		0	45	2,319	304	225	560	-	560

23.9 HM Revenue and Customs receipts

Amounts: £ million

Year	Total Paid Over [1]	Total HMRC receipts [2,3,10]	Total Income Tax [4]	Of which: PAYE Income Tax**	Of which: SA Income Tax**	Capital Gains Tax	NICs	VAT	Total Corporation Tax [5]	Of which offshore** [6]	Bank Levy	Bank payroll tax	Petroleum Revenue Tax	Fuel duties	IHT [7]	Shares	Stamp Duty Land Tax	Annual Tax on Enveloped Dwellings	Tobacco duties
	MIZX			BKMR	LISB	BKLO	ABLP	EYOO	N445			JT2R	ACCJ	ACDD	ACCH	BKST	BKSU		ACDE
Jul-13	49,068	53,114	17,840	11,267	6,548	3	10,543	10,230	6,990	-	658	0	-1	2,187	339	304	886	-	724
Aug-13	35,214	36,969	10,947	10,338	862	2	8,254	9,192	1,385	-	-	0	80	2,317	266	207	803	-	880
Sep-13	30,177	33,250	10,329	10,371	12	3	8,119	6,259	2,155	1,306	-	0	410	2,260	251	191	817	2	822
Oct-13	42,906	45,812	10,931	10,537	-77	3	8,495	11,546	7,261	-	624	0	98	2,226	312	312	852	76	964
Nov-13	32,907	35,808	9,982	10,136	-81	2	8,219	9,056	1,324	-	-	0	84	2,347	270	249	781	6	858
Dec-13	31,092	34,243	10,679	10,366	414	2	8,375	5,756	3,124	1,229	-	0	121	2,282	259	256	960	8	530
Jan-14	58,102	61,513	22,539	11,488	10,673	3,006	10,246	11,139	7,478	-	584	0	-1	2,070	263	244	843	1	1,001
Feb-14	39,569	42,179	14,048	11,285	2,427	732	9,157	10,432	1,538	-	-	0	69	2,215	271	276	721	2	625
Mar-14	31,780	35,130	12,650	12,395	235	149	9,056	6,162	1,587	1,021	-	0	45	2,134	264	299	743	5	640
Apr-14	46,696	50,002	15,344	14,822	103	2	10,001	11,192	5,181	-	485	0	83	2,303	362	233	872	40	1,751
May-14	33,140	36,299	10,754	11,463	-128	5	8,212	9,426	1,587	-	-	0	70	2,231	296	363	828	51	229
Jun-14	29,219	32,757	10,467	10,859	-113	6	8,376	6,347	1,590	-	-	0	80	2,317	288	219	898	6	576
Jul-14	50,178	54,263	18,499	11,610	6,666	5	10,630	11,076	6,599	-	734	0	-52	2,245	324	235	1,091	3	667
Aug-14	37,064	39,574	11,903	10,868	1,349	2	8,726	9,975	1,585	-	-	0	-13	2,375	336	256	994	2	933
Sep-14	30,805	33,643	10,647	10,900	48	3	8,768	5,834	2,232	860	783	0	82	2,238	343	151	1,074	2	657
Oct-14	43,878	46,850	11,511	10,865	-50	2	8,750	11,238	7,388	-	-	0	54	2,271	335	319	965	2	940
Nov-14	34,530	37,704	10,521	10,654	-84	4	8,467	9,991	1,349	-	-	0	66	2,374	309	192	893	2	835
Dec-14	32,627	36,656	11,310	10,844	495	-2	8,849	6,601	3,462	657	-	0	85	2,322	338	225	1,016	2	589
Jan-15	62,655	67,005	24,671	11,876	12,213	4,258	10,563	12,155	8,368	-	747	0	-201	2,064	273	247	717	1	994
Feb-15	41,295	42,911	14,170	11,699	2,819	1,101	9,414	10,238	1,685	-	-	0	39	2,297	306	236	666	1	600
Mar-15	34,546	37,684	13,311	13,046	326	172	9,652	7,291	1,978	556	-	0	-216	2,119	292	249	724	4	778
Apr-15 [14]	48,302	51,511	15,237	14,762	-90	2	11,122	10,921	6,117	-	587	0	19	2,300	379	274	792	77	1,453

23.9 HM Revenue and Customs receipts

Amounts: £ million

Year	Spirits duties	Beer duties	Wines duties	Cider duties	Betting & Gaming	Air Passenger Duty	Insurance Premium Tax	Landfill Tax	Climate Change Levy[8]	Aggregates Levy	Swiss Capital Tax	Misc	Customs Duties	Child and Working Tax Credits	Corporation Tax Credits[11]	Child Benefit Payments[9]
	ACDF	ACDG	ACDH	ACDI	ACDJ	ACDP	ACDO	DOLC	LSNS	MDUP			ADET			
2003-04	2,362	3,044	2,006	153	1,347	791	2,294	607	832	339		-8	1,941	13,361	555	9,425
2004-05	2,385	3,101	2,233	157	1,421	864	2,359	672	764	334		0	2,195	15,896	610	9,593
2005-06	2,309	3,076	2,308	168	1,421	905	2,343	733	744	326		1	2,258	17,332	669	9,770
2006-07	2,256	3,072	2,385	200	1,391	971	2,314	804	712	321		1	2,325	18,684	715	10,156
2007-08	2,374	3,067	2,641	220	1,481	1,994	2,306	877	688	339		0	2,456	20,030	918	10,603
2008-09	2,358	3,127	2,741	244	1,474	1,862	2,281	954	716	334		0	2,659	24,099	1,181	11,262
2009-10	2,570	3,182	2,949	311	1,439	1,856	2,259	842	695	275		0	2,646	27,601	1,147	11,824
2010-11	2,675	3,296	3,101	324	1,533	2,155	2,400	1,065	674	288		0	2,998	28,879	1,313	12,160
2011-12	2,889	3,463	3,356	329	1,633	2,607	2,941	1,090	676	290	0	0	2,912	29,830	1,399	12,177
2012-13	2,931	3,426	3,537	326	1,680	2,791	3,021	1,092	635	265	342	0	2,854	29,888	1,471	12,167
2013-14	3,056	3,346	3,713	340	2,098	3,013	3,014	1,189	1,068	285	466	0	2,901	29,710	1,582	11,438
2014-15	3,023	3,310	3,837	320	2,116	3,175	2,965	1,144	1,491	342	66	0	3,007	29,732	2,033	11,582
Apr-11	322	345	314	32	118	182	123	192	26	32		0	236	2,403	n/a	1,075
May-11	128	287	230	28	174	216	531	58	161	22		0	216	2,439	n/a	1,037
Jun-11	180	302	271	31	104	227	1	7	4	15		0	231	2,660	n/a	938
Jul-11	228	293	270	31	156	226	150	188	45	41		0	239	2,667	n/a	1,040
Aug-11	194	290	268	29	186	274	621	102	120	23		0	254	2,599	n/a	1,038
Sep-11	225	317	291	30	109	255	12	12	3	14		0	230	2,390	n/a	991
Oct-11	235	278	278	27	134	233	157	215	40	42		0	272	2,417	n/a	932
Nov-11	310	285	321	28	154	234	605	52	103	21		0	274	2,453	n/a	1,058
Dec-11	402	320	404	29	106	177	3	19	2	13		0	240	2,657	n/a	1,155
Jan-12	231	313	259	23	167	223	149	194	46	39		0	235	2,258	n/a	900
Feb-12	154	193	215	18	122	179	576	34	122	17		0	255	2,409	n/a	973
Mar-12	281	240	236	23	105	180	14	17	3	11		0	230	2,478	n/a	1,040
Apr-12	352	386	381	36	147	213	133	186	54	33	0	0	220	2,378	n/a	943
May-12	115	238	217	22	154	223	574	45	139	18	0	0	216	2,881	n/a	1,180
Jun-12	202	336	284	35	105	231	8	11	2	12	0	0	231	2,401	n/a	949
Jul-12	202	286	259	28	163	246	157	219	55	39	0	0	231	2,766	n/a	1,042
Aug-12	184	287	291	31	188	284	627	57	108	19	0	0	268	2,666	n/a	1,059
Sep-12	228	308	282	31	118	272	16	38	2	12	0	0	261	2,220	n/a	987
Oct-12	222	251	261	23	127	246	189	184	44	37	0	0	252	2,527	n/a	1,009
Nov-12	365	289	355	27	164	260	561	60	82	19	0	0	278	2,418	n/a	996
Dec-12	430	318	427	29	124	195	12	68	2	14	0	0	234	2,532	n/a	1,027
Jan-13	217	293	291	24	147	237	163	153	48	36	342	0	209	2,351	n/a	1,016
Feb-13	151	205	236	20	150	119	562	66	97	16		0	232	2,302	n/a	895
Mar-13	263	230	252	21	95	263	20	6	3	11		0	225	2,446	n/a	1,064
Apr-13	387	283	370	33	161	242	171	198	57	30	0	0	217	2,394	n/a	886
May-13	125	267	229	24	212	217	544	53	117	18	0	0	213	2,655	n/a	1,003
Jun-13	192	310	287	33	112	227	11	13	2	12	0	0	224	2,450	n/a	968

23.9 HM Revenue and Customs receipts

Amounts: £ million

Year	Spirits duties	Beer duties	Wines duties	Cider duties	Betting & Gaming	Air Passenger Duty	Insurance Premium Tax	Landfill Tax	Climate Change Levy[8]	Aggregates Levy	Swiss Capital Tax	Misc	Customs Duties	Child and Working Tax Credits	Corporation Tax Credits[11]	Child Benefit Payments[9]
	ACDF	ACDG	ACDH	ACDI	ACDJ	ACDP	ACDO	DOLC	LSNS	MDUP			ADET			
Jul-13	206	271	276	30	226	289	212	183	185	36	258	0	238	2,932	n/a	989
Aug-13	211	319	323	40	206	302	568	98	135	26	147	0	263	2,412	n/a	1,010
Sep-13	228	285	310	34	125	308	8	43	4	14	0	0	274	2,348	n/a	861
Oct-13	237	255	287	22	198	273	216	168	102	40	35	0	279	2,539	n/a	1,034
Nov-13	391	286	378	28	191	265	532	89	162	21	10	0	278	2,275	n/a	943
Dec-13	419	298	455	30	137	216	21	39	10	14	8	0	246	2,729	n/a	965
Jan-14	224	328	291	23	222	239	158	242	107	40	0	0	225	2,373	n/a	986
Feb-14	161	208	236	22	188	222	545	53	183	20	5	0	251	2,286	n/a	883
Mar-14	276	235	272	22	121	213	28	12	6	13	4	0	194	2,317	n/a	911
Apr-14	271	257	371	28	191	232	184	184	115	35	58	0	228	2,654	n/a	1,023
May-14	178	300	255	28	220	255	512	53	201	21	0	0	224	2,453	n/a	980
Jun-14	218	333	302	33	136	267	30	16	2	16	1	0	234	2,442	n/a	904
Jul-14	241	289	298	29	210	270	209	224	153	47	1	0	237	2,882	n/a	1,006
Aug-14	218	295	324	33	196	301	544	64	241	25	1	0	256	2,286	n/a	1,007
Sep-14	212	271	304	26	137	334	20	21	12	18	1	0	258	2,410	n/a	919
Oct-14	277	259	315	26	242	294	207	222	122	49	0	0	281	2,510	n/a	970
Nov-14	376	287	392	27	217	283	518	67	222	25	0	0	285	2,209	n/a	937
Dec-14	410	298	448	27	121	229	23	17	6	20	4	0	257	2,748	n/a	974
Jan-15	240	305	326	21	153	254	186	200	175	46	0	0	244	2,221	n/a	983
Feb-15	175	186	240	18	213	234	516	63	236	24	0	0	254	2,263	n/a	898
Mar-15	205	230	261	25	82	223	18	14	6	17	0	0	251	2,656	n/a	981
Apr-15[12]	251	279	332	25	174	261	195	166	223	42	28	0	258	2,436	n/a	967

Source: HM Revenue & Customs

[1] Comprises of payments into the Consolidated Fund and all payovers of NICs excluding those of Northern Ireland.

[2] Total HMRC Receipts includes payments into the Consolidated Fund and all payovers of NICs including those of Northern Ireland. Receipts are gross of Tax Credits (Expenditure): this follows the changes generated by revisions to the European System of Accounts (ESA2010) and the Public Sector Finances Review.

[3] Consistent with the OBR definition published in the supplementary fiscal table 2.8 i.e. on a cash basis.

[4] Gross of tax credits and includes other smaller elements of income tax.

[5] Receipts gross of all tax credits. As of November 2014 Bank Levy receipts are shown seperately and no longer included within the CT total.

[6] The majority of UK Oil & Gas companies payments are due in three instalments, (Jul, Oct and Jan): receipts are reported in a similar pattern following each instalment.

[7] Excludes non cash elements which are shown in the table Inheritance Tax: Analysis of Receipts

[8] From April 2013, includes receipts from Carbon Price Floor.

[9] From April 2011, the Child Benefit series has been revised to ensure consistency with HMRC Resource Accounts.

[10] Total of columns D, G to J, and L to AG

[11] Monthly Data unavailable.

[12] 2015-16 figures have been updated in line with the Trust Statement published July 2016.

* Provisional

** Figures in italic are included with the relevant total for either income tax or corporation tax

Archived tables can be found here: https://www.gov.uk/government/collections/hm-revenue-customs-receipts

For any queries regarding this table, please email Karen Mason
Room 2/62, 100 Parliament Street, London, WC1A 2BQ

23.10 INCOME TAX PERSONAL ALLOWANCES AND RELIEFS, 1990-91 TO 2015-16

Financial years	Non-aged allowances						Aged allowances				Income limit (3)
							Personal		Married couple's		
	Personal	Married couple's (1)	Blind person's (2)	Dividend	Savings Basic rate	Savings Higher rate	65-74	75+	65-74	75+	
1990-91	3,005	1,720	1,080	-	-	-	3,670	3,820	2,145	2,185	12,300
1991-92	3,295	1,720	1,080	-	-	-	4,020	4,180	2,355	2,395	13,500
1992-93	3,445	1,720	1,080	-	-	-	4,200	4,370	2,465	2,505	14,200
1993-94	3,445	1,720	1,080	-	-	-	4,200	4,370	2,465	2,505	14,200
1994-95	3,445	1,720 (4)	1,200	-	-	-	4,200	4,370	2,665 (4)	2,705 (4)	14,200
1995-96	3,525	1,720 (5)	1,200	-	-	-	4,630	4,800	2,995 (5)	3,035 (5)	14,600
1996-97	3,765	1,790 (5)	1,250	-	-	-	4,910	5,090	3,115 (5)	3,155 (5)	15,200
1997-98	4,045	1,830 (5)	1,280	-	-	-	5,220	5,400	3,185 (5)	3,225 (5)	15,600
1998-99	4,195	1,900 (5)	1,330	-	-	-	5,410	5,600	3,305 (5)	3,345 (5)	16,200
1999-00	4,335	1,970 (6)	1,380	-	-	-	5,720	5,980	5,125 (6)	5,195 (6)	16,800
2000-01	4,385	-	1,400	-	-	-	5,790	6,050	5,185 (6,7)	5,255 (6,7)	17,000
2001-02	4,535	-	1,450	-	-	-	5,990	6,260	5,365 (6,7)	5,435 (6,7)	17,600
2002-03	4,615	-	1,480	-	-	-	6,100	6,370	5,465 (6,7)	5,535 (6,7)	17,900
2003-04	4,615	-	1,510	-	-	-	6,610	6,720	5,565 (6,7)	5,635 (6,7)	18,300
2004-05	4,745	-	1,560	-	-	-	6,830	6,950	5,725 (6,7)	5,795 (6,7)	18,900
2005-06	4,895	-	1,610	-	-	-	7,090	7,220	5,905 (6,7)	5,975 (6,7)	19,500
2006-07	5,035	-	1,660	-	-	-	7,280	7,420	6,065 (6,7)	6,135 (6,7)	20,100
2007-08	5,225	-	1,730	-	-	-	7,550	7,690	6,285 (6,7)	6,365 (6,7)	20,900
2008-09	6,035	-	1,800	-	-	-	9,030	9,180	6,535 (6,7)	6,625 (6,7)	21,800
2009-10	6,475	-	1,890	-	-	-	9,490	9,640	-	6,965 (6,7)	22,900
2010-11	6,475 (8)	-	1,890	-	-	-	9,490	9,640	-	6,965 (6,7)	22,900
2011-12	7,475 (8)	-	1,980	-	-	-	9,940	10,090	-	7,295 (6,7)	24,000
2012-13	8,105 (8)	-	2,100	-	-	-	10,500	10,660	-	7,705 (6,7)	25,400
2013-14	9,440 (8)	-	2,160	-	-	-	10,500 (9)	10,660 (10)	-	7,915 (6,7)	26,100
2014-15	10,000 (8)	-	2,230	-	-	-	10,500 (9)	10,660 (10)	-	8,165 (6,7)	27,000
2015-16	10,600 (8)	-	2,290	-	-	-	-	10,660 (10)	-	8,355 (6,7)	27,700

Source: HM Revenue & Customs - Table updated April 2016

(1) Given in addition to the personal allowance to married couples. The additional personal allowance and the widow's bereavement allowance have the same value as the married couple's allowance.

(2) Married couples where both spouses are blind get double the single amount.

(3) Where an individual's income exceeds the income limit, their aged personal allowance is reduced by £1 for every £2 above the income limit, potentially down to the non aged allowance level.

(4) Allowance available at a flat rate of 20%.

(5) Allowance available at a flat rate of 15%.

(6) Allowance available at a flat rate of 10%.

(7) At least one of the partners must have been born before 6 April 1935.

(8) The Personal Allowance reduces where an individuals income is above £100,000 - by £1 for every £2 of income above the £100,000 limit. This reduction applies irrespective of age or date of birth.

(9) Available to people born in the period 6 April 1938 to 5 April 1948.

(10) Available to people born on or before 5 April 1938.

(11) The Dividend Allowance, introduced for 2016-17, means that no tax is payable on the first £5,000 of dividend income, irrespective of the total amount of dividend and non-dividend income received.

(12) The Personal Savings Allowance, introduced for 2016-17, provides for an amount of savings income to be received tax-free. The upper bound for the tax-free allowance depends on the top marginal tax rate on an individual's total income; the threshold for higher rate taxpayers is half that for basic rate taxpayers and is set to £0 for additional rate taxpayers. The effect of the Personal Allowance, Starting Rate and Personal Savings Allowance for 2016-17 is that an individual with total taxable income of £17,000 will pay no tax on savings income.

23.11 RATES OF INCOME TAX: 2001-02 TO 2015-16

	2001-02			2002-03			2003-04	
	Bands of taxable income(1) £	Rate of tax %		Bands of taxable income(1) £	Rate of tax %		Bands of taxable income(1) £	Rate of tax %
Starting rate	1-1,880	10		1-1,920	10		1-1,960	10
Basic rate	1,881-29,400	22	(5)	1,921-29,900	22	(5)	1,961-30,500	22 (5)
Higher rate	Over 29,400	40	(6)	Over 29,900	40	(6)	Over 30,500	40 (6)

	2004-05			2005-06			2006-07	
	Bands of taxable income(1) £	Rate of tax %		Bands of taxable income(1) £	Rate of tax %		Bands of taxable income(1) £	Rate of tax %
Starting rate	1-2,020.	10		1-2.090	10		1-2,150	10
Basic rate	2,021-31,400	22	(5)	2,091-32,400	22	(5)	2,151-33,300	22 (5)
Higher rate	Over 31,400	40	(6)	Over 32,400	40	(6)	Over 33,300	40 (6)

	2007-08		2008-09			2009-10	
	Bands of taxable income(1) £	Rate of tax %	Bands of taxable income(1) £	Rate of tax %		Bands of taxable income(1) £	Rate of tax %
Basic rate (7)	1-2,230	10	1-34,800	20	(8)	1-37,400	20 (8)
Higher rate	2,231-34,600	22 (5)	Over 34,800	40	(6)	Over 37,400	40 (6)
Additional Rate	Over 34,600	40 (6)	Not Applicable			Not Applicable	

	2010-11			2011-12			2012-13	
	Bands of taxable income(1) £	Rate of tax %		Bands of taxable income(1) £	Rate of tax %		Bands of taxable income(1) £	Rate of tax %
Basic rate (7)	1-37,400	20	(8)	1-35,000	20	(8)	1-34,370	20 (8)
Higher rate	Over 37,400	40	(6)	Over 35,000	40	(6)	Over 34,370	40 (6)
Additional Rate	Over 150,000	50	(9)	Over 150,000	50	(9)	Over 150,000	50 (9)

	2013-14			2014-15			2015-16	
	Bands of taxable income(1) £	Rate of tax %		Bands of taxable income(1) £	Rate of tax %		Bands of taxable income(1) £	Rate of tax %
Basic rate (7)	1-32,010	20	(8)	1-31,865	20	(8)	1-31,785	20 (8)
Higher rate	Over 32,010	40	(6)	Over 31,865	40	(6)	Over 31,785	40 (6)
Additional Rate	Over 150,000	45	(10)	Over 150,000	45	(10)	Over 150,000	45 (10)

Source: HM Revenue & Customs - Table updated April 2016

(1) Taxable income is defined as gross income for income tax purposes less any allowances and reliefs available at the taxpayer's marginal rate.

(2) Applies to the income of discretionary and accumulation trusts. Prior to 1993-94 trusts paid tax at the basic rate, with an additional rate of 10%.

(3) The basic rate of tax on gross dividend income is 20%.

(4) The basic rate of tax on gross dividends and savings income is 20%.

(5) The basic rate of tax on gross dividends is 10% and savings income is 20%.

(6) The higher rate of tax on gross dividends is 32.5%.

(7) From 2008-09 the starting rate is abolished for all non-savings income (e.g. employment, self-employed trading profits, pensions and property income), which is the first slice of income to be charged to income tax. The starting rate and the starting rate limit for savings is shown in the table below. Where taxable non-savings income does not fully occupy the starting rate limit the remainder of the starting rate limit is available for savings income.

(8) The basic rate of tax on gross dividends is 10%.

(9) The additional rate of tax on gross dividends is 42.5%.

(10) The additional rate of tax on gross dividends is 37.5%.

(11) The basic rate of tax on net dividends is 7.5%.

(12) The higher rate of tax on net dividends is 32.5%.

(13) The additional rate of tax on net dividends is 38.1%.

23.12 Non-domestic rating in England & Wales

Analysis of 2010 rating lists. Number of Rateable Properties[1] and Total Rateable Value[2] by Property Type 1[A] and Country as at 31 March 2015

Properties (Thousands), Value (£millions)

Property Type 1[A]	England		Wales		England & Wales	
	Rateable Properties[1]	Rateable Value[2]	Rateable Properties[1]	Rateable Value[2]	Rateable Properties[1]	Rateable Value[2]
All properties	**1,828**	**57,282**	**110**	**2,437**	**1,938**	**59,719**
Commercial	**1,369**	**41,640**	**79**	**1,534**	**1,449**	**43,175**
Advertising rights	37	66	1	1	38	67
Holiday sites	6	197	1	27	7	224
Garages & petrol stations	38	1,090	3	51	41	1,141
Hotels etc.	53	1,515	6	57	58	1,573
Pubs & wine bars	54	1,586	4	85	58	1,672
Markets	2	37	-	2	2	38
Offices	355	13,420	16	277	371	13,697
Car parks	58	526	2	19	60	545
Restaurants & cafes	39	1,165	2	46	42	1,210
Showroom and premises	8	209	-	7	8	216
Hypermarket and premises	-	90	-	5	-	95
Superstore and premises	2	2,742	-	168	2	2,910
Other Shops	463	10,062	28	409	490	10,470
Shops[3]	472	13,102	28	589	500	13,691
Warehouses & stores[4]	214	8,089	12	353	226	8,442
Other commercial	42	847	3	27	45	874
Educational, training & cultural	**44**	**3,236**	**3**	**143**	**47**	**3,379**
Local authority schools & colleges	22	1,834	2	95	24	1,929
Libraries and museums	4	255	-	9	5	264
Private schools & colleges	3	411	-	4	4	415
Universities	1	453	-	26	1	480
Other educational, training and cultural	13	282	1	9	13	291
Utilities	**10**	**1,085**	**1**	**121**	**11**	**1,205**
Docks	-	64	-	5	-	69
Electricity companies	1	572	-	92	1	664
Bus stations, moorings etc.	2	53	-	1	2	54
Other utilities	7	396	1	22	8	418
Industrial	**235**	**6,082**	**16**	**396**	**251**	**6,478**
Factories, mills & workshops[5]	227	5,153	15	338	242	5,491
Quarries, mines etc.	5	467	-	23	6	489
Other industrial	3	463	-	35	4	498
Leisure	**83**	**1,626**	**5**	**80**	**89**	**1,707**
Community centres & halls	32	604	3	30	35	634
Sports centres & stadia	1	176	-	10	1	186
Sports grounds, golf courses etc	10	246	1	13	11	259
Cinemas, theatres etc.	2	209	-	12	3	221
Other leisure	38	391	1	15	39	406
Miscellaneous	**86**	**3,612**	**6**	**163**	**92**	**3,775**
Cemeteries and crematoria	2	31	-	2	3	33
Medical facilities	26	1,317	2	67	28	1,384
Local government offices[6]	2	187	-	16	2	202
Police stations & courts	2	392	-	19	2	411
Hostels & homes	1	23	-	2	2	25
Other properties	52	1,662	4	57	56	1,719

Source: VOA Administrative Data as at 31 March 2015

Table notes

Counts are rounded to the nearest thousand with counts fewer than 500 but greater than 0 reported as negligible and denoted by '-'.
Total rateable values are rounded to the nearest £1million with amounts smaller than £0.5million but larger than £0 reported as negligible and denoted by '-'.
Totals may not sum due to rounding.

Footnotes

[1] **Rateable Property (also known as Hereditament)**: a unit of property that is, or may become, liable to non-domestic rating and thus appears in a rating list.

[2] **Rateable Value** - The legal term for the notional annual rent of a rateable property assessed by the VOA. Every property has a rateable value that is based broadly on the annual rent that the property could have been let for on the open market at a particular date (this is 1 April 2003 for the 2005 lists and 1 April 2008 for the 2010 lists).

[3] **Shops** - This is the total of showrooms, hypermarket, superstore and premises including "other shops".

[4] **Warehouses & Stores** - In tables CL4, CL5 and CL6 warehouses and stores are labelled as warehouses.

[5] **Factories, mills & workshops** - In tables CL4, CL5 and CL6 factories, mills and workshops are labelled as factories.

[6] **Local government offices** - Local government offices are shown in this table under the 'Miscellaneous' category but are included in the figures for property type 'Offices' in all other tables.

[A] **Property Type 1** - This splits the properties up into 6 broad property types and 35 more detailed property types. These are categorised using Primary Description Codes. There are 119 Primary description Codes and are more generic than SCat Code and show the nature of the use of the rateable property.

23.13 Revenue expenditure of local authorities

£ million

	2013/14 outturn	2014/15 outturn	2015/16 outturn	2016/17 budget
England				
Education services	35,881	34,477	34,976	34,211
Highways and Transport services	4,795	4,537	4,922	4,401
Social care services	21,480	22,587	21,779	22,224
Public Health services	2,508	2,737	3,321	3,496
Housing services (excluding HRA)	2,025	1,852	1,742	1,610
Cultural, environmental and planning services	9,176	8,915	8,695	8,438
of which:				
Cultural services	2,831	2,682	2,496	2,351
Environmental services	4,992	4,945	5,048	5,028
Planning and development services	1,353	1,288	1,151	1,059
Police services	10,920	10,889	10,951	11,094
Fire and rescue services	2,089	2,045	2,080	2,052
Central services	2,845	3,068	3,112	3,055
Other services	91	92	281	342
Total Service Expenditure	**91,809**	**91,199**	**91,859**	**90,923**
plus precepts, levies, trading accounts and adjustments				
Housing Benefits [1]	20,982	21,113	21,103	20,792
Parish Precepts	367	389	409	445
Levies [2]	56	48	56	58
Trading Account Adjustments and other adjustments [3]	-368	-345	-339	-332
Total Net current expenditure	**112,885**	**112,404**	**113,089**	**111,886**
Capital financing [4]	4,468	4,528	4,463	4,193
Capital Expenditure charged to Revenue Account (CERA) [5]	2,778	3,010	1,320	1,265
Bad debt provision	114	131	57	46
Flood defence payments to Environment Agency	34	34	30	32
Private Finance Initiative (PFI) schemes - difference from service charge	33	41	4	-7
Appropriation to(+)/from(-) financial instruments adjustment account [6]	-45	3	-22	-21
Appropriation to(+)/from(-) unequal pay back pay account [7]	28	33	2	2
less interest receipts	839	865	793	889
less Capital receipts used to finance revenue expenditure	-	-	-	83
less specific grants outside AEF [8]	22,805	23,045	22,427	21,966
less Business Rates Supplement	212	221	223	224
less Community Infrastructure Levy (CIL)	47	123	87	122
less Carbon Reduction Commitment	-26	-13	-25	-21
Revenue expenditure	**96,419**	**95,943**	**95,437**	**94,134**
Government Grants	64,578	61,312	56,611	54,008
Local Services Support Grant (LSSG)	77	48	28	26
Revenue Support Grant	15,175	12,675	9,509	7,184
Police grant	7,565	7,784	7,421	7,387
Retained income from Business Rate Retention Scheme	10,719	11,331	11,867	11,555
Appropriations to(-) / from (+) revenue reserves	-2,379	-949	1,834	1,885
Other items [9]	130	284	390	605
Council tax requirement	**23,371**	**23,964**	**24,734**	**26,082**

1. Includes Housing benefits: subsidy limitation transfers from HRA and Contribution to the HRA re items shared by the whole community

2. Includes Integrated Transport Authority Levy, Waste Disposal Authority Levy, London Pensions Fund Authority Levy and Other levies

3. Includes External Trading Accounts, Internal Trading Accounts, Capital items accounted for in External Trading Accounts, Capital items accounted for in Internal Trading Accounts, Adjustments to net current expenditure and Appropriations to/from Accumulated Asbences Account

4. Includes provision for repayment of principal, leasing payments, external interest payments and HRA item 8 interest payments and receipts

5. Includes both Capital expenditure charged to the General Fund Revenue account and for Public Health

6 Adjustments permitted by regulation to the revenue account charges for financial instruments

7. The deferral of revenue account charges for unequal pay back pay as permitted by regulation and the reversal of the deferral in the year that payment of the back pay is due

8. Aggregate External Finance

9 Other items includes 'Inter-authority transfers in respect of reorganisation' and 'Other Items' which is the net collection fund surpluses/deficits from the previous year

23.13 Revenue expenditure of local authorities

	2011/12 outturn	2012/13 outturn	2013/14 outturn	2014/15 outturn	2015/16 budget	2016/17 budget
Scotland						
Net revenue expenditure on general fund	12,696,622	12,799,446	11,674,901	11,898,827	11,877,050	11,723,830
Wales[10]						
Education[11]	2,590.523	2,630.360	2,616.865	2,610.336	2,555.069	2,576.920
Personal social services[11]	1,486.524	1,536.238	1,640.010	1,673.329	1,638.977	1,666.607
Housing[12]	1,058.643	1,109.978	1,149.553	1,151.088	1,141.249	1,128.514
Local environmental services[13]	419.441	431.904	424.872	404.167	377.849	373.310
Roads and transport	317.902	314.686	306.751	278.887	286.537	283.273
Libraries, culture, heritage, sport and recreation	284.186	283.015	269.717	252.720	218.554	207.834
Planning, economic development and community development	147.897	132.313	138.733	115.133	80.649	80.907
Council tax benefit and administration[14]	28.939	29.588	35.583	36.083	36.179	30.239
Debt financing costs: counties	314.067	320.911	323.388	330.077	338.257	320.533
Central administrative and other revenue expenditure: counties[15,16]	275.031	309.677	277.506	288.037	313.317	345.123
Total county and county borough council expenditure	6,923.154	7,098.669	7,182.977	7,139.857	6,986.637	7,013.259
Total police expenditure[16]	655.867	656.182	675.109	701.723	666.871	668.364
Total fire expenditure[16]	145.599	145.842	150.003	146.105	144.757	147.626
Total national park expenditure[16]	15.996	17.844	18.084	15.570	14.545	13.792
Gross revenue expenditure	7,740.616	7,918.538	8,026.172	8,003.256	7,812.810	7,843.042
less specific and special government grants[17]	-2,013.808	-2,112.384	-2,064.187	-2,108.778	1,935.118	1,904.000
Net revenue expenditure	5,726.807	5,806.153	5,961.985	5,894.478	5,877.692	5,939.042
Putting to (+)/drawing from (-) reserves[18]	28.267	32.008	4.088	7.275	84.477	105.063
Council tax reduction scheme[19]			244.703	246.885	255.672	257.706
Budget requirement	5,755.074	5,774.145	6,202.600	6,134.088	6,048.886	6,091.685
Plus discretionary non-domestic rate relief	3.122	3.237	3.470	3.526	3.608	3.515
less revenue support grant	3,382.132	3,257.005	3,488.834	3,363.466	3,303.719	3,261.307
less council tax reduction scheme grant		.	22.000			
less police grant	245.744	228.481	240.091	236.153	221.923	218.140
less re-distributed non-domestic rates income	787.000	911.000	1,032.000	1,041.000	956.000	977.000
Council tax requirement	1,343.321	1,380.896	1,423.145	1,496.995	1,570.852	1,638.753
of which:						
Paid by council tax reduction scheme[19]	242.161	246.720	243.999	246.885	255.672	257.706
Paid directly by council tax payers	1,101.160	1,134.176	1,179.145	1,250.110	1,315.181	1,381.047

Sources: Communities and Local Government: 0303 444 1333
Scottish Government, Statistical Support for Local Government: 0131 245 7034
Welsh Government: 02920 825355

10 Service expenditure is shown excluding that financed by sales, fees and charges, but including that financed by specific and special government grants.

11 In 2013-14, the decrease in education and increase in social services was mainly due to a reclassification of Flying Start expenditure to social services.

12 Includes housing benefit and private sector costs such as provision for the homeless. Includes rent rebates granted to HRA tenants which is 100% grant funded. Excludes council owned housing.

13 Includes cemeteries and crematoria, community safety, environmental health, consumer protection, waste collection/disposal and central services to the public such as birth registration and elections.

14 For years up to 2012-13, Council Tax Benefit Grant was funded from the Department of Work And Pensions, this ended in 2013-14 and was replaced with council tax reduction scheme from the Welsh Government. This was paid via RSG with an additional £22 million top up grant. Because of this, figures are not comparable with previous years.
15 Includes agricultural services, coastal and flood defence and community councils.

16 Includes central administrative costs of corporate management, democratic representation and certain costs, such as those relating to back year or additional pension contributions which should not be allocated to individual services, capital expenditure charged to the revenue account and is net of any interest expected to accrue on balances.

17 Excludes police grant and council tax benefit grant.
18 Includes Council Tax collected in year adjustments and other adjustments.
19 In 2013-14, council tax reduction scheme, funded by the Welsh Government, replaced council tax benefit grant funded from the Department for Work & Pensions.
. Data not applicable.

23.14 Financing of revenue expenditure England and Wales

England and Wales
Years ending 31 March

£ million

		2005 /06	2006 /07	2007 /08	2008 /09	2009 /10	2010 /11	2011 /12	2012 /13	2013 /14	2014 /15[1]	2015 /16[1]
England[2]												
Revenue expenditure[3]												
Cash £m	KRTN	84,422	88,172	92,384	98,107	103,276	104,256	99,278	94,148	96,419	95942	95437
Government grants												
Cash £m	KRTO	45,838	49,093	51,657	53,007	57,755	57,657	56,237	46,765	64,578	61312	56611
Percentage of revenue expenditure	KRTP	54	56	56	54	56	55	57	50	67	64	59
Redistributed business rates[4]												
Cash £m	KRTQ	18,004	17,506	18,506	20,506	19,515	21,517	19,017	23,129	-	-	-
Percentage of revenue expenditure	KRTR	21	20	20	21	19	21	19	25	-	-	-
Retained income from rate retention												
Cash £m		-	-	-	-	-	-	-	-	10,719	11331	11867
Percentage of revenue expenditure		-	-	-	-	-	-	-	-	11	12	12
Council tax												
Cash £m	KRTS	21,315	22,453	23,608	24,759	25,633	26,254	26,451	26,715	23,371	23964	24734
Percentage of revenue expenditure	KRTT	25	25	26	25	25	25	27	28	24	25	26
Wales												
Gross revenue expenditure[5]	ZBXH	6,128	6,472	6,739	7,184	7,523	7,636	7,741	7,919	8026[10]	8,003	7,813
General government grants[6]	ZBXI	2,987	3,169	3,287	3,335	3,428	3,525	3,628	3,485	3751[10]	3,600	3,526
Specific government grants[7]	ZBXG	1,473	1,530	1,630	1,809	1,987	2,020	2,014	2,112	2064[10]	2,109	1,935
Share of redistributed business rates	ZBXJ	672	730	791	868	894	935	787	911	1032[10]	1,041	956
Council tax income[8]	ZBXK	1,012	1,071	1,131	1,188	1,240	1,295	1,343	1,381	1423[10]	1,497	1,571
Other[9]	ZBXL	-16	-27	-99	-16	-26	-139	-31	29	-244[10]	-243	-175

Sources: Communities and Local Government: 0303 444 1333;
Welsh Government 02920 825355

1. Budget estimates.

2 Produced on a non-Financial Reporting Standard 17 (FRS17) basis.

3 The sum of government grants, business rates and local taxes does not normally equal revenue expenditure because of the use of reserves.

4 1993-94 to 2003-04 includes City of London Offset.

5 Gross revenue expenditure is total local authority expenditure on services, plus capital charges, but net of any income from sales, fees, and charges and other non-grant sources. It includes expenditure funded by specific grants. The figures have been adjusted to account for FRS17 pension costs.

6 Includes all unhypothecated grants, namely revenue support grant, police grant, council tax reduction scheme grant, transitional grant and the adjustment to reverse the transfer.

7 Comprises specific and supplementary grants,excluding police grant.

8 This includes community council precepts, and income covered by charge/council tax benefit grant, but excludes council tax reduction scheme (2013-14).

9 Includes use of reserves and discretionary non-domestic rate relief.

10. In 2013-14, the education revenue outturn data collection was changed to be comparable with the revenue budget collection. Overall education expenditure is not comparable with previous years due to the movement of all Flying Start expenditure to Social Services. Gross revenue expenditure and income for Neath Port Talbot are not consistent with previous years due to errors in reporting.

23.15 Financing of capital expenditure

£ million

	2009-10	2010-11	2011-12	2012-13	2013-14	2014-15	2015-16 (P)
Central government grants [g]	7,494	8,063	7,170	8,481	7,483	8,520	9,329 [r]
EU structural funds grants	43	38	77	55	57	132	106
Grants and contributions from private developers and from leaseholders etc	502	634	747	693	750	727	962 [r]
Grants and contributions from NDPBs [a]	602	753	522	442	443	564	426 [r]
National lottery grants	119	104	121	67	49	53	48
Use of capital receipts	1,603	1,409	1,647	1,294	1,516	1,879	2.148 [r]
Revenue financing of capital expenditure	3,532	3,984	4,504	3,167	4,920	5,241	4.367 [r]
of which:							
Housing Revenue Account (CERA)	247	235	324	466	578	686	924 [r]
Major Repairs Reserve	1,377	1,069	1,160	1,259	1,491	1,526	1,683
General Fund (CERA)	1,908	2,680	3,020	1442 [b]	2,851	3,029	1,760 [r]
Capital expenditure financed by borrowing/credit	7,931	8,399	18,818	4,842	4,454	4,422	4.747 [r]
of which:							
SCE(R) Single Capital Pot [c]	2,181	1,581	338	88	70	-	-
SCE(R) Separate Programme Element [c]	748	484	74	30	8	-	-
Other borrowing & credit arrangements not supported by central government [d]	5,002	6,335	18406 [e]	4,724	4,376	4,422	4,747 [r]
Total [i]	**21,826**	**23,385**	**33,606** [e]	**19,042**	**19,671**	**21,539**	**22,133** [r]

Source: Department for Communities and Local Governmentand Local Government

(a)   Non-Departmental Public Bodies, organisations that are not government departments but which have a role in the processes of national government, such as the Sport England, English Heritage and Natural England.

(b)   This reflects reallocation of expenditure by TfL as part of year end process of reconciling funding to its subsidiaries

(c)   Supported capital expenditure (SCE) financed by borrowing that is attracting central government support has been discontinued as of March 31 2011. This may have a bearing on the financing of capital expenditure. A residue of schemes up to 2013-14 w ere financed through this form of borrowing from earlier years.

(d)   The Prudential System, which came into effect on 1 April 2004, allows local authorities to raise finance for capital expenditure - without Government consent - where they can afford to service the debt without extra Government support.

(e)   It is estimated that approximately £13 billion is associated with the financing of the HRA self-financing determination payment.

(f)   Flexibility of Capital Receipts allow s local authorities to use the receipts from the sale of capital assets for efficiency savings projects that would be recorded in the revenue account.

(g)   Central government grants includes grants awarded by the GLA.

(h)   Total provisional capital expenditure may differ from the expenditure total due to rounding error and exclusion of spend by virtue of 16 (2)(b) direction.

(i)   Financing of capital expenditure forecast has not been adjusted. This means total forecast spend is approximately 20% lower than the resource total.

(R) Marked items have been revised due to minor revisions by six authorities

23.16a Capital receipts: all services: England 2013-14: final outturn

£ thousand

	Sales & disposal of tangible fixed assets (10)	Sales of intangible assets (11)	Repayments of grants loans & financial assistance (12)	Total receipts(a) (10+11+12)
Pre-primary & Primary Education	32,030	0	44	32,074
Secondary Education	30,705	0	520	31,225
Special Education	4,694	0	0	4,694
Non-school funding	21,098	0	4,294	25,392
Education	**88,527**	**0**	**4,858**	**93,385**
Roads, Street Lights & Safety	13,991	0	16	14,007
Parking of Vehicles	12,565	0	0	12,565
Public Passenger Transport-Bus	2,491	0	932	3,423
Public Passenger Transport-Rail & Other	4,255	0	0	4,255
Airports	2	0	112	114
Local Authority Ports and Piers	0	0	119	119
Tolled Road bridges, tunnels, ferries, PTC	23	0	0	23
Highways & transport	**33,327**	**0**	**1,179**	**34,506**
Social services	**53,317**	**0**	**255**	**53,572**
Public health	**419**	**0**	**0**	**419**
Housing	**1,178,630**	**3,458**	**21,368**	**1,203,456**
Culture and heritage	12,691	60	385	13,136
Recreation and sport	28,855	0	1,985	30,840
Open spaces	13,074	0	106	13,180
Tourism	380	0	0	380
Library Services	14,779	0	0	14,779
Total Culture and related services	**69,779**	**60**	**2,476**	**72,315**
Cemeteries, cremation and mortuary	884	0	35	919
Coast protection	0	0	0	0
Community safety	88	0	0	88
Community safety (CCTV)	0	0	0	0
Flood defence and land drainage	0	0	42	42
Agriculture and fisheries services	43,508	0	0	43,508
Regulatory services (environmental health)	649	0	28	677
Regulatory services (trading standards)	203	0	0	203
Street cleaning not chargeable to highways	198	0	0	198
Waste collection	3,734	0	1,508	5,242
Waste disposal	5,177	0	2	5,179
Trade waste	12	0	0	12
Recycling	652	0	0	652
Waste minimisation	249	0	0	249
Climate change costs	0	0	51	51
Total environmental and regulatory services	**55,354**	**0**	**1,666**	**57,020**
Planning and development services	**96,112**	**0**	**192,221**	**288,333**
Police	**184,677**	**512**	**736**	**185,925**
Fire and rescue services	**13,826**	**0**	**0**	**13,826**
Central services	**473,118**	**4,216**	**5,243**	**482,577**
Industrial and commercial trading	175,111	0	327	175,438
Other trading	4,016	0	254	4,270
Total Trading	**179,127**	**0**	**581**	**179,708**
Total all services	**2,426,213**	**8,246**	**230,583**	**2,665,042**

Source: Department for Communities and Local Government

(a) Figures in this column do not include disposals of share and loan capital

23.16b Capital expenditure: all services: England 2013-14: final outturn

£ thousand

	Total expenditure on fixed & intangible assets (6) (1+2+3+4+5)	Expenditure on grants (7)	Expenditure on loans & other financial assistance (8)	Total Expenditure[a] (9) (6+7+8)
Pre-primary & Primary Education	1,825,602	170,409	7,957	2,003,968
Secondary Education	1,044,000	216,242	1,772	1,262,014
Special Education	283,854	12,832	149	296,835
Non-school funding	150,026	25,033	4,080	179,139
Education	**3,303,482**	**424,516**	**13,958**	**3,741,956**
Roads, Street Lights & Safety	2,691,781	42,451	6,059	2,740,291
Parking of Vehicles	83,797	334	0	84,131
Public Passenger Transport-Bus	174,397	21,189	3,832	199,418
Public Passenger Transport-Rail & Other	307,867	1,550,629	334,011	2,192,507
Airports	3,509	13	0	3,522
Local Authority Ports and Piers	13,303	293	0	13,596
Tolled Road bridges,tunnels,ferries, PTC	32,245	0	250	32,495
Highways & transport	**3,306,899**	**1,614,909**	**344,152**	**5,265,960**
Social services	**180,630**	**48,032**	**114,378**	**343,040**
Public health	**760**	**3,651**	**0**	**4,411**
Housing	**3,095,935**	**802,243**	**69,222**	**3,967,400**
Culture and heritage	146,029	16,011	7,188	169,228
Recreation and sport	369,180	24,156	4,239	397,575
Open spaces	129,332	8,856	77	138,265
Tourism	14,670	297	300	15,267
Library Services	106,713	2,041	500	109,254
Total Culture and related services	**765,924**	**51,361**	**12,304**	**829,589**
Cemeteries, cremation and mortuary	38,343	335	0	38,678
Coast protection	34,766	447	0	35,213
Community safety	4,012	331	0	4,343
Community safety (CCTV)	8,041	53	0	8,094
Flood defence and land drainage	34,322	8,531	498	43,351
Agriculture and fisheries	8,879	77	0	8,956
Regulatory services (environmental health)	14,863	265	13	15,141
Regulatory services (trading standards)	381	0	0	381
Street cleaning (not chargeable to highways)	23,144	36	0	23,180
Waste collection	153,949	106	0	154,055
Waste disposal	103,251	944	4,996	109,191
Trade waste	1,444	0	0	1,444
Recycling	88,338	288	0	88,626
Waste minimisation	26,164	0	0	26,164
Climate change costs	21,429	1,075	1,145	23,649
Total environmental services	**561,326**	**12,488**	**6,652**	**580,466**
Planning and development services	**741,555**	**331,772**	**53,382**	**1,126,709**
Police	**480,586**	**57**	**0**	**480,643**
Fire and rescue services	**177,914**	**125**	**0**	**178,039**
Central services	**1,221,494**	**26,004**	**73,474**	**1,320,972**
Industrial and commercial trading	341,550	2,258	11,548	355,356
Other trading	103,026	99	3,870	106,995
Total Trading	**444,576**	**2,357**	**15,418**	**462,351**
Total all services	**14,281,081**	**3,317,515**	**702,940**	**18,301,536**

Source: Department for Communities and Local Government

(a) Figures in this column do not include acquisitions of share and loan capital

23.17 Local authority capital expenditure by service

Wales

£ million

	1996-97	2008-09	2009-10	2010-11	2011-12	2012-13	2013-14	2014-15	2014-15 over 2013-14 percentage change
Education	57.4	203.6	215.5	233.3	260.6	267.4	274.0	245.6	-10
Social services	12.4	22.1	21.9	22.3	18.8	22.9	17.7	22.9	30
Transport	113.2	231.4	204.0	210.9	206.9	231.5	175.1	168.1	-4
Housing	271.0	238.2	217.4	210.1	230.1	216.4	223.6	260.3	16
General administration	36.0	61.7	47.4	50.6	42.6	63.4	47.7	41.9	-12
Planning and development	39.3	95.6	56.5	73.9	94.7	109.2	123.7	103.3	-16
Other services	145.3	214.3	126.8	143.3	144.7	143.4	125.1	125.1	-0
Law, order and protective services	18.6	61.6	44.6	53.2	37.9	33.9	53.7	48.0	-10
Total expenditure	693.2	1,128.4	934.1	997.7	1,036.3	1,088.1	1,040.6	1,015.2	-2

Source: Local Authority Revenue and Capital Outturn Expenditure; Welsh Government

23.18 Service Analysis of General Fund Revenue Expenditure and Income, Scotland 2013-14

£ thousands

	Revenue Contributions to Capital	Support Service Costs	All other Expenditure	Adjustment for Inter Account and Inter Authority Transfers	Total Expenditure	Total Income	Net Revenue Expenditure
Education	**21,726**	**177,928**	**4,632,605**	**-27,257**	**4,805,002**	**204,797**	**4,600,205**
Pre-primary education	1,027	11,526	308,379	-776	320,156	13,923	306,233
Primary education	10,830	70,375	1,773,339	-7,900	1,846,644	75,191	1,771,453
Secondary education	7,992	67,320	1,877,091	-7,904	1,944,499	78,050	1,866,449
Special education	692	15,983	515,109	-8,607	523,177	14,079	509,098
Community Learning	645	7,735	125,427	-1,470	132,337	16,318	116,019
Other non-school funding	540	4,989	33,260	-600	38,189	7,236	30,953
Cultural and related services	**6,826**	**39,192**	**694,639**	**-32,620**	**708,037**	**87,265**	**620,772**
Museums and galleries	150	2,559	43,178	-137	45,750	3,951	41,799
Other cultural and heritage services	249	3,498	62,239	-879	65,107	14,827	50,280
Library service	106	8,747	108,636	-598	116,891	4,187	112,704
Tourism	3	662	26,070	-391	26,344	2,595	23,749
Countryside recreation and management	134	1,757	23,679	-249	25,321	3,366	21,955
Sport facilities	3,870	8,001	202,813	-2,323	212,361	34,291	178,070
Community parks and open spaces	1,806	10,491	161,955	-27,000	147,252	12,645	134,607
Other recreation and sport	508	3,477	66,069	-1,043	69,011	11,403	57,608
Social work	**4,995**	**196,501**	**3,690,794**	**-36,421**	**3,855,869**	**819,814**	**3,036,055**
Service Strategy	276	2,463	33,855	-1,579	35,015	1,984	33,031
Children's Panel	0	211	1,478	-102	1,587	426	1,161
Children and families	548	43,710	820,366	-6,206	858,418	21,468	836,950
Older persons	1,721	87,430	1,637,758	-12,061	1,714,848	391,184	1,323,664
Adults with physical or sensory disabilities	1,095	12,022	212,400	-2,149	223,368	29,243	194,125
Adults with learning disabilities	1,267	31,716	662,865	-6,979	688,869	187,356	501,513
Adults with mental health needs	41	7,223	149,994	-921	156,337	63,111	93,226
Adults with other needs	10	3,490	67,825	-2,116	69,209	23,521	45,688
Criminal justice social work services	37	8,236	104,253	-4,308	108,218	101,521	6,697
Roads and transport[2]	**21,535**	**40,085**	**750,020**	**-126,214**	**685,426**	**224,233**	**461,193**
Road construction	1,397	312	22,592	-18,982	5,319	-10,401	15,720
Winter maintenance	75	2,353	59,107	-2,542	58,993	2,641	56,352
Maintenance & repairs	12,405	17,447	248,091	-45,945	231,998	47,773	184,225
Road lighting	749	3,583	74,291	-3,741	74,882	6,238	68,644
School crossing patrols	0	712	13,458	-105	14,065	39	14,026
Other network and traffic management	1,469	8,650	66,997	-10,105	67,011	19,738	47,273
Parking	547	2,070	33,167	-189	35,595	64,141	-28,546
Non-LA PT: Concessionary fares	0	263	9,018	-13	9,268	1,043	8,225
Non-LA PT: Support to operators	0	1,638	94,405	-8,695	87,348	5,473	81,875
Non-LA PT: Co-ordination	4,893	2,269	101,462	-34,874	73,750	79,693	-5,943
Local authority Transport	0	788	27,432	-1,023	27,197	7,855	19,342

Source: Scottish Government, Local Government Finance Statistics

23.18 Service Analysis of General Fund Revenue Expenditure and Income, Scotland 2013-14

£ thousands

	Revenue Contributions to Capital	Support Service Costs	All other Expenditure	Adjustment for Inter Account and Inter Authority Transfers	Total Expenditure	Total Income	Net Revenue Expenditure
Environmental services	**11,891**	**58,517**	**764,178**	**-31,675**	**802,911**	**132,515**	**670,396**
Cemetery, cremation and mortuary services	419	3,775	35,709	-1,177	38,726	30,781	7,945
Coast protection	0	164	1,773	-15	1,922	684	1,238
Flood defence and land drainage	125	620	8,658	-331	9,072	343	8,729
Environmental Health	5	13,087	97,609	-5,264	105,437	15,528	89,909
Trading Standards	202	4,275	29,683	-497	33,663	1,950	31,713
Waste Collection	3,173	15,182	205,324	-6,407	217,272	42,166	175,106
Waste Disposal	7,622	9,398	275,947	-6,720	286,247	37,546	248,701
Other waste management	345	12,016	109,475	-11,264	110,572	3,517	107,055
Planning and Development Services	**5,066**	**44,024**	**423,793**	**-10,131**	**462,752**	**178,392**	**284,360**
Planning: Building control	14	5,197	32,007	-862	36,356	29,462	6,894
Planning: Development control	135	7,513	38,812	-267	46,193	27,079	19,114
Planning: Policy	450	5,739	34,099	-2,813	37,475	6,512	30,963
Planning: Environmental initiatives	1,195	2,814	23,578	-2,720	24,867	8,269	16,598
Economic development	3,272	22,761	295,297	-3,469	317,861	107,070	210,791
Central Services[3]	**32,272**	**174,495**	**742,387**	**-241,945**	**707,209**	**194,694**	**512,515**
Council tax collection	345	24,120	37,958	-185	62,238	28,129	34,109
Council tax reduction administration	1	10,192	25,373	-3,059	32,507	15,636	16,871
Non-domestic rates collection	3	3,362	5,926	-67	9,224	2,620	6,604
Housing benefit administration	868	13,981	30,473	-3,065	42,257	24,815	17,442
Registration of births, deaths and marriages	1	3,924	9,960	-95	13,790	9,074	4,716
Emergency Planning (non Police or Fire)	1	797	4,391	-233	4,956	640	4,316
Licensing	0	4,705	14,533	-262	18,976	21,080	-2,104
Conducting Elections	0	980	2,646	-260	3,366	586	2,780
Registration of electors	56	776	9,611	-427	10,016	865	9,151
Council tax valuation	54	642	10,219	0	10,915	138	10,777
Non-domestic lands valuation	57	1,220	15,777	0	17,054	319	16,735
Local Land Charges	0	1	478	0	479	25	454
Non-road lighting	0	405	10,794	-90	11,109	3,746	7,363
General grants, bequests and donations	0	498	7,347	-2	7,843	82	7,761
Corporate and democratic core costs	212	95,538	75,336	-5,031	166,055	1,486	164,569
Non-distributed costs	167	5,202	115,269	-498	120,140	308	119,832
Other	30,507	8,152	366,296	-228,671	176,284	85,145	91,139
Non-HRA Housing	**2,032**	**26,253**	**2,386,106**	**-25,047**	**2,389,344**	**2,063,651**	**325,693**
Private sector housing renewal	994	3,633	66,317	-1,706	69,238	45,560	23,678
Housing benefits: Rent allowances	0	0	1,142,477	-959	1,141,518	1,106,697	34,821
Housing benefits: Rent rebate	0	0	635,557	-546	635,011	653,417	-18,406
Homelessness	884	7,728	180,164	-3,397	185,379	110,467	74,912
Welfare Services	0	361	9,901	-249	10,013	874	9,139
Administration of housing advances	0	91	68	-16	143	263	-120
Housing Support Services	1	5,461	152,019	-998	156,483	7,096	149,387
Other non-HRA housing (excl admin of Housing Benefits)	153	8,979	199,603	-17,176	191,559	139,277	52,282
Trading Services	**246**	**1,999**	**67,687**	**-1,624**	**68,308**	**69,909**	**-1,601**
Add Ring Fenced Grants Back In	.	.	.	.	**0**	**-8,584**	**8,584**
Interest and investment income	.	.	.	.	**673,808**	**84,505**	**589,303**
Surplus/deficit from Significant Trading Operations	.	.	.	.	**-30,724**	**0**	**-30,724**
Statutory repayment of debt	.	.	.	.	**598,150**		**598,150**
All services	**106,589**	**758,994**	**14,152,209**	**-532,934**	**15,726,092**	**4,051,191**	**11,674,901**

Source: Scottish Government, Local Government Finance Statistics

1. The Police and Fire Reform (Scotland) Act 2012 created Police Scotland and Fire Scotland, which replaced the former Police and Fire Boards. These new bodies are classified as Central Government, rather than Local Government. As it is not possible to remove income and expenditure from all Police/Fire Boards from previous returns, figures for All services and Central Services (due to police and fire board expenditure in this category) from 2013-14 onwards are not strictly comparable with previous years.

2. Regional Transport Partnerships expenditure is apportioned to councils by population (NRS 2013 mid-year population estimates).

3. Expenditure on council tax and non-domestic valuation and registration of electors is apportioned to councils using the amount that the Valuation Joint Boards requisition from them.

23.19a Revenue Income by Source, 2009-10 to 2013-14, Scotland

£ millions

	2009-10	2010-11	2011-12	2012-13	2013-14
General Revenue Grant[1]	7,757	8,149	7,790	7,782	7,225
Council Tax	1,910	1,923	1,926	1,947	1,981
Council Tax Benefit Subsidy	368	375	376	371	
Non Domestic Rates	2,165	2,068	2,182	2,263	2,435
Customer and Client Receipts	2,287	2,179	2,298	2,341	2,327
Other Income	3,400	3,357	3,308	3,246	2,513
Total revenue income	**17,886**	**18,052**	**17,879**	**17,950**	**16,481**

Source: Scottish Local Government Financial Statistics

1. Figures for 2013-14 are not comparable as prior years include income relating to police and fire joint board expenditure.
2. Council Tax Reduction (CTR) was introduced from 1 April 2013 to replace Council Tax Benefit (CTB), which has been abolished by the UK Government as part of its welfare reform programme.
3. Sources: General Revenue Funding (Up to 2010-11) – Finance Circulars; Non-Domestic Rates – Finance Circulars; All Other Data – Local Financial Returns (LFRs)

23.19b – Total Capital Expenditure and Financing, 2009-10 to 2013-14

£ thousands

	2009-10[a]	2010-11	2011-12	2012-13	2013-14[b]
Acquisition of land, leases, existing buildings or works	477,203	98,730	137,332	146,930	90,335
New construction, conversions & enhancement to existing buildings	2,385,906	1,876,692	2,142,293	2,037,385	1,967,310
Vehicles, machinery & equipment	183,013	156,289	194,836	197,022	189,509
Intangible assets	11,197	5,042	6,052	6,638	13,119
Total Gross Capital Expenditure	**3,057,319**	**2,136,753**	**2,480,513**	**2,387,975**	**2,260,273**
Revenue Expenditure funded from Capital Resources	214,040	211,409	181,021	161,349	199,728
Total Expenditure to be met from Capital Resources	**3,271,359**	**2,348,162**	**2,661,534**	**2,549,324**	**2,460,001**
Scottish Government General Capital Grant	462,640	352,652	565,541	450,088	438,163
Scottish Government Specific Capital Grants	268,370	228,865	234,365	217,281	180,549
Grants from Scottish Government Agencies and NDPBs	160,281	115,726	82,764	141,311	150,761
Other Grants and Contributions	104,575	94,486	85,714	124,311	142,077
Borrowing from Loans fund	1,091,548	1,113,929	1,261,468	1,165,387	1,105,526
Capital receipts used from asset sales/disposals	164,746	114,722	94,020	105,937	92,167
Capital Fund applied	28,616	14,916	21,653	36,867	24,798
Capital funded from current revenue	166,141	208,894	209,122	294,087	295,335
Assets acquired under credit arrangements (e.g. finance leases, PPP/PFI)	824,442	103,972	106,888	14,055	30,625
Total Financing		**2,348,162**	**2,661,534**	**2,549,324**	**2,460,001**

Source: Scottish Local Government Financial Statistics

a. Figures for 2009-10 include assets acquired through PPP/PFI for past years. (more information on the changes can be found here - http://www.scotland.gov.uk/Topics/Government/local-government/17999/LACapital/CapExReport200910)
b. Following the Police and Fire Reform (Scotland) Act 2012 figures for 2013-14 may not be comparable with previous years.
c. Source: Capital Returns (CR Final)

23.20 Subjective Analysis of General Fund Revenue Expenditure and Income, 2013-14

£thousands

	Education Services	Culture and Related Services	Social Work Services	Roads and Transport	Environmental Services	Planning and Development Services	Central Services	Housing Services (Non-HRA)	Trading with the Public	Total General Fund Services	HRA Housing Services	Total General Fund Services (inc HRA)
EXPENDITURE												
Employee Costs												
Teachers	2,393,209									2,393,209		2,393,209
All other Employees	878,823	220,726	1,288,141	193,578	294,214	150,861	477,640	105,246	23,014	3,632,243	133,774	3,766,017
Total Employee Costs	3,272,032	220,726	1,288,141	193,578	294,214	150,861	477,640	105,246	23,014	6,025,452	133,774	6,159,226
Operating Costs												
Premises Related Costs	503,773	88,724	67,550	63,923	40,323	36,414	56,181	66,693	5,046	928,627	360,029	1,288,656
Transport Related Expenditure	165,787	22,169	56,906	56,904	92,587	2,783	16,470	1,782	18,294	433,682	5,219	438,901
Supplies and Services	399,224	98,902	135,334	165,329	179,860	62,112	144,830	54,279	16,740	1,256,610	71,525	1,328,135
Third Party Payments	259,740	245,062	2,068,440	263,402	155,707	125,605	52,086	283,947	4,516	3,458,505	24,904	3,483,409
Other local authorities	15,882	10,254	9,800	33,719	837	1,090	430	224	0	72,236	4	72,240
Health authorities	8,193	0	102,360	0	0	372	38	294	0	111,669	0	111,669
All Other Third Party Payments	235,665	234,808	1,956,280	229,271	154,870	124,143	51,618	283,429	4,516	3,274,600	24,900	3,299,500
Total Operating Costs	1,328,524	454,857	2,328,230	549,558	468,477	226,914	269,567	406,701	44,596	6,077,424	461,677	6,539,101
Transfer Payments												
School Children and students	24,166									24,166		24,166
Social Work Clients			50,243							50,243		50,243
Housing benefits								1,778,034		1,778,034		1,778,034
Debits resulting from soft loans to clients etc.	0	0	0	0	0	8	0	0	0	8	0	8
Other Transfer Payments	7,883	18,657	24,180	6,059	1,487	46,010	-933	93,462	77	196,882	4,657	201,539
Total Transfer Payments	32,049	18,657	74,423	6,059	1,487	46,018	-933	1,871,496	77	2,049,333	4,657	2,053,990
Support Services												
Total Support Services	177,928	39,192	196,501	40,085	58,517	44,024	174,495	26,253	1,999	758,994	70,151	829,145
Revenue Contribution to Capital												
Total Revenue Contribution to Capital Expenditure	21,726	6,826	4,995	21,535	11,891	5,066	32,272	2,032	246	106,589	187,153	293,742
Adjustment for Inter Account and Inter Authority Transfers												
Contributions from other local authorities	-9,042	-516	-14,249	-42,869	-1,577	-572	-5,574	-35	-949	-75,383	0	-75,383
Recharges (income from other accounts within the authority)	-18,215	-32,104	-22,172	-83,345	-30,098	-9,559	-236,371	-25,012	-675	-457,551	-26,704	-484,255
Total Adjustment for Inter Account and Inter Authority Transfers	-27,257	-32,620	-36,421	-126,214	-31,675	-10,131	-241,945	-25,047	-1,624	-532,934	-26,704	-559,638
Gross Expenditure	4,805,002	707,638	3,855,869	684,601	802,911	462,752	711,096	2,386,681	68,308	14,484,858	830,708	15,315,566

23.20 Subjective Analysis of General Fund Revenue Expenditure and Income, 2013-14

£thousands

	Education Services	Culture and Related Services	Social Work Services	Roads and Transport	Environmental Services	Planning and Development Services	Central Services	Housing Services (Non-HRA)	Trading with the Public	Total General Fund Services	HRA Housing Services	Total General Fund Services (inc HRA)
INCOME												
Government Grants												
Ring-fenced Revenue Grants	4,357	0	0	0	0	0	0	4,227	0	8,584	3,673	12,257
General Capital Grant used to fund grants to third parties	0	1,038	0	22,468	0	2,844	0	98,962	0	125,312	0	125,312
Other Central Government Grants (excl GRG)	39,480	1,507	94,284	11,363	6,990	23,373	37,389	1,612,393	66	1,826,845	2,299	1,829,144
Total Government Grants	**43,837**	**2,545**	**94,284**	**33,831**	**6,990**	**26,217**	**37,389**	**1,715,582**	**66**	**1,960,741**	**5,972**	**1,966,713**
Other Grants reimbursements and Contributions												
Contributions from Health Authorities			404,068							404,068		404,068
All other grants, reimbursements and contributions	40,397	13,535	45,450	15,184	8,068	31,096	25,595	187,269	0	366,594	3,209	369,803
Total Other Grants reimbursements and Contributions	**40,397**	**13,535**	**449,518**	**15,184**	**8,068**	**31,096**	**25,595**	**187,269**	**0**	**770,662**	**3,209**	**773,871**
Customer and Client Receipts												
Income from charges to service users	46,448	31,927	252,456	87,141	39,237	22,951	29,789	16,272	18,168	544,389	56,272	600,661
Rent Income	1,681	5,786	3,172	13,707	1,136	35,779	12,851	100,481	1,070	175,663	998,237	1,173,900
Other Sales, Fees and Charges	72,434	33,472	20,384	74,370	77,084	62,347	89,069	44,047	50,605	523,812	18,853	542,665
Total Customer and Client Receipts	**120,563**	**71,185**	**276,012**	**175,218**	**117,457**	**121,077**	**131,709**	**160,800**	**69,843**	**1,243,864**	**1,073,362**	**2,317,226**
Credits resulting from soft loans	0	0	0	0	0	2	1	0	0	3	0	3
Total Income	**204,797**	**87,265**	**819,814**	**224,233**	**132,515**	**178,392**	**194,694**	**2,063,651**	**69,909**	**3,975,270**	**1,082,543**	**5,057,813**

Source: Scottish Local Government Financial Statistics

827

23.21 Expenditure of local authorities

Northern Ireland
Years ending 31 March

£ thousand

	1998 /99	1999 /00	2000 /01	2001 /02	2002 /03	2003 /04	2004 /05	2005 /06	2006 /07	2007 /08	2008 /09[1]	2009 /10	2010 /11	2011 /12	2012 /13
Libraries,museums and art galleries	14,571	19,900	23,097	24,181	32,728	30,062	30,481	33,516	28,655	31,557	36,527	35,549	37,163	40,321	48,852
Environmental health services:															
Refuse collection and disposal	56,360	62,226	65,289	73,336	90,148	94,715	102,633	113,768	121,879	136,181	142,071	151,332	155,540	159,518	159,753
Public baths	2,634	1,750	1,724	1,423	..	..	..	..	..	..	..	..	..	..	..
Parks, recreation grounds,etc	118,396	158,304	170,999	184,406	194,224	193,617	205,734	221,298	198,314	213,780	265,720	257,522	278,716	263,211	278,729
Other sanitary services	42,923	44,214	45,552	48,784	52,075	55,349	59,906	66,294	68,641	74,624	86,428	87,000	90,966	91,358	88,817
Housing (grants and small dwellings acquisition)	358	37	28	27	12	21	18	10	15	17	8	15	79	13,474	0
Trading services:															
Cemeteries	5,887	5,973	6,151	6,538	7,208	7,980	8,455	8,520	7,752	8,726	9,125	9,353	10,994	10,274	10,350
Other trading services (including markets, fairs and harbours)	10,779	9,366	7,209	7,769	18,281	17,489	18,776	19,596	15,240	17,498	27,711	21,115	15,610	13,222	14,667
Miscellaneous	161,790	86,649	89,881	98,244	79,645	114,971	105,031	128,304	141,717	160,606	263,230	183,563	107,841	129,889	130,318
Total expenditure	413,698	388,419	409,930	444,708	474,321	490,619	531,034	591,306	582,213	642,991	830,820	745,450	696,909	707,809	731,490
Total loan charges	26,413	..	..	..	..	..	..	..	..	..	..	..	..	..	..

Source: Department of the Environment for Northern Ireland: 028 9025 6086

1. The overall expenditure figure for 2008/2009 is much higher than 2009/2010 substantially due to the Capital Finance Reserve of one particular council.

Department of the Environment for Northern Ireland no longer collates this information

23.21 Local government current expenditure on services in Northern Ireland by function, 2010-11 to 2014-15

£ million

	National Statistics				
	2010-11 outturn	2011-12 outturn	2012-13 outturn	2013-14 outturn	2014-15 plans
Northern Ireland					
Economic affairs	20	20	23	21	21
of which: enterprise and economic development	20	20	23	21	21
Environment protection	173	175	178	180	178
Housing and community amenities	-13	106	91	98	135
Health	52	52	50	52	43
Recreation, culture and religion	218	204	215	221	184
Total Northern Ireland	**449**	**558**	**557**	**571**	**562**

Source: HM Treasury

Agriculture

Chapter 24

Agriculture

Input and Output (Tables 24.1 and 24.2)

For both tables, output is net of VAT collected on the sale of non-edible products. Figures for total output include subsidies on products, that is, payments that have the purpose of influencing production, their prices or remuneration of the factors of production. Unspecified crops include turf, other minor crops and arable area payments for fodder maize. Eggs include the value of duck eggs and exports of eggs for hatching. Landlords' expenses are included within farm maintenance, miscellaneous expenditure and depreciation of buildings and works. Also included within 'Other farming costs' are livestock and crop costs, water costs, insurance premia, bank charges, professional fees, rates, and other farming costs.

Non-subsidy payments

Payments other than subsidies on products from which farmers can benefit as a consequence of engaging in agriculture. This includes:
• environment and countryside management schemes
• organic farming schemes
• support schemes for less favoured areas
• Single Payment Scheme
• animal disease compensation attributable to income
• other payments

Compensation of employees and interest charges

Total compensation of employees excludes the value of work done by farm labour on own account capital formation in buildings and work. 'Interest' relates to interest charges on loans for current farming purposes and buildings, less interest on money held on short-term deposit.

Rent

Rent paid (after deductions) is the rent paid on all tenanted land including 'conacre' land in Northern Ireland, less landlords' expenses and the benefit value of dwellings on that land. Rent received (after deductions) is the rent received by farming landowners from renting of land to other farmers, less landlords' expenses and the benefit value of dwellings on that land. Total net rent is the net rent flowing out of the agricultural sector paid to non-farming landowners, including that part of tenanted land in Northern Ireland.

Agricultural censuses and surveys (Tables 24.3 and 24.5 and 24.12)

Data in thse tables are sourced primarily from the June/July Surveys of Agriculture carried out in the four UK countries each year. The exceptions to this are the holder age data (sourced from the EU Farm Structure Survey) and land use data in Scotland (sourced from Single Application Form (SAF) subsidy data). Also, cattle data are sourced from the Cattle Tracing System (CTS) in England, Wales and Scotland (from 2013) and from the equivalent Animal and Public Health Administration (APHIS) system in Northern Ireland. Prior to 2013 Scottish cattle data was sourced from agricultural surveys.

From 2009 onwards, England data relate to "commercial" holdings only. The term "commercial" covers all English holdings which have more than 5 hectares of agricultural land, 1 hectare of orchards, 0.5 hectares of vegetables or 0.1 hectares of protected crops, or more than 10 cattle, 50 pigs, 20 sheep, 20 goats, or 1,000 poultry. These thresholds are specified in the EU Farm Structure Survey Regulation EC 1166/2008.

Estimated quantity of crops and grass harvested
(Table 24.4)

The estimated yield of sugar beet is obtained from production figures supplied by British Sugar plc in England and Wales. In Great Britain, potato yields are estimated in consultation with the Potato Council Limited.

Forestry
(Table 24.6)

Statistics for state forestry are from Forestry Commission and Forest Service management information systems. For private forestry in Great Britain, statistics on new planting and restocking are based on records of grant aid and estimates of planting undertaken without grant aid, and softwood production is estimated from a survey of the largest timber harvesting companies. Hardwood production is estimated from deliveries of roundwood to primary wood processors and others, based on surveys of the UK timber industry, data provided by trade associations and estimates provided by the Expert Group on Timber and Trade Statistics.

Fisheries
(Table 24.14)
Figures show the number of registered and licensed fishing vessels based on information provided by the Marine Management Organisation.

Estimated average household food consumption – 'Family Food' Expenditure and Food Survey
(Table 24.15)
In 2008 the Expenditure and Food Survey (EFS) was renamed as the Living Costs and Food Survey (LCFS) when it became part of the Integrated Household Survey (IHS). The Expenditure and Food Survey started in April 2001, having been preceded by the National Food Survey (NFS) and the Family Expenditure Survey (FES). Both surveys were brought into one to provide value for money without compromising data quality. The EFS was effectively a continuation of the FES extended to record quantities of purchases. This extension is now known as the Family Food Module of the LCFS. Estimates from the NFS prior to 2000 have been adjusted by aligning estimates for the year 2000 with corresponding estimates from the FES. From 2006 the survey moved onto a calendar year basis (from the previous financial year basis) in preparation for its integration to the Integrated Household Survey from January 2008.

The Living Costs and Food Survey is a voluntary sample survey of private households throughout the UK. The basic unit of the survey is the household which is defined as a group of people living at the same address and sharing common catering arrangements. The survey is continuous, interviews being spread evenly over the year to ensure that seasonal effects are covered. Each household member over the age of seven keeps a diary of all their expenditure over a two-week period. A simplified version of the diary is used by those aged between seven and 15. The diaries record expenditure and quantities of purchases of food and drink rather than consumption of food and drink. Items of food and drink are defined as either household or eating out and are recorded in the form the item was purchased not how it was consumed. 'Household' covers all food that is brought into the household. 'Eating out' covers all food that never enters the household, for example restaurant meals, school meals and snacks eaten away from home.

24.1 Production and income accounts (at current prices) [a] United Kingdom

Contact: Helen Mason, Department for Environment, Food and
Rural Affairs, Room 201, Foss House, Kings Pool, 1-2
Peasholme Green, York, YO1 7PX

Email: farmingaccounts@defra.gsi.gov.uk

£ million   Calendar years

	2003	2004	2005	2006	2007	2008	2009	2010	2011	2012	2013	2014
1 Output of cereals	1 491	1 707	1 434	1 507	1 949	3 180	2 312	2 267	3 230	3 201	3 375	3 470
of which: wheat	1 001	1 232	1 018	1 066	1 325	2 270	1 562	1 680	2 322	2 162	2 073	2 465
barley	446	433	380	384	555	817	675	521	809	920	1 136	900
oats	43	40	34	54	65	90	72	63	94	114	160	99
2 Output of industrial crops	719	683	679	597	702	1 010	913	1 051	1 524	1 356	1 183	1 160
of which: oilseed rape	304	257	261	310	426	631	485	674	1 110	986	744	684
protein crops	93	109	94	72	81	131	136	127	103	98	123	123
sugar beet	283	280	278	178	162	208	246	197	251	227	270	315
3 Output of forage plants	141	142	155	167	132	143	190	189	186	146	217	265
4 Output of vegetables and horticultural products	1 662	1 613	1 682	1 738	1 822	1 909	1 966	2 263	2 337	2 398	2 530	2 382
of which: fresh vegetables	898	834	912	1 001	1 054	1 090	1 088	1 266	1 224	1 255	1 340	1 216
plants and flowers	764	779	770	737	768	819	879	997	1 114	1 142	1 191	1 166
5 Output of potatoes (including seeds)	562	715	535	650	708	793	681	598	711	659	947	677
6 Output of fruit	310	318	390	377	459	535	570	585	604	573	602	622
7 Output of other crop products incl. seeds	203	238	271	252	189	335	383	439	475	644	581	648
Total crop output (sum 1-7)	**5 087**	**5 416**	**5 147**	**5 288**	**5 961**	**7 904**	**7 016**	**7 392**	**9 067**	**8 977**	**9 435**	**9 223**
8 Output of livestock	4 811	4 812	5 090	5 065	5 146	6 372	7 027	7 313	8 167	8 628	9 128	8 964
primarily for meat	4 081	4 154	4 296	4 362	4 430	5 502	5 843	6 106	6 902	7 244	7 738	7 468
of which: cattle	1 227	1 279	1 466	1 561	1 623	2 071	2 131	2 154	2 573	2 794	2 886	2 611
pigs	671	680	677	685	736	866	968	978	1 070	1 132	1 274	1 264
sheep	696	726	686	709	641	798	967	979	1 149	1 027	1 037	1 122
poultry	1 328	1 306	1 300	1 233	1 249	1 579	1 590	1 799	1 904	2 078	2 324	2 250
gross fixed capital formation	730	657	794	703	716	870	1 184	1 208	1 265	1 384	1 390	1 496
of which: cattle	448	337	545	419	410	577	750	714	631	856	917	925
pigs	7	8	6	8	5	6	8	8	8	8	6	5
sheep	146	176	112	146	153	125	238	295	413	317	272	332
poultry	129	136	131	131	149	162	188	191	213	203	195	234
9 Output of livestock products	3 031	3 038	3 010	2 918	3 286	4 019	3 711	3 973	4 387	4 486	5 072	5 369
of which: milk	2 628	2 610	2 592	2 497	2 823	3 447	3 123	3 329	3 738	3 767	4 271	4 594
eggs	336	378	349	362	410	520	531	561	559	662	718	679
Total livestock output (8+9)	**7 842**	**7 849**	**8 100**	**7 983**	**8 432**	**10 391**	**10 738**	**11 286**	**12 554**	**13 113**	**14 200**	**14 333**
10 Other agricultural activities	632	717	638	622	680	790	868	918	1 026	1 015	1 052	1 122
11 Inseparable non-agricultural activities	592	637	678	684	763	813	897	936	1 003	1 041	1 176	1 176
12 Output (at market prices) (sum 1 to 11)	14 154	14 619	14 563	14 577	15 836	19 897	19 519	20 532	23 649	24 146	25 864	25 854
13 Total subsidies (less taxes) on product	1 978	2 172	214	87	62	57	38	29	28	20	21	21
14 Gross output at basic prices (12+13)	**16 131**	**16 791**	**14 777**	**14 664**	**15 898**	**19 955**	**19 557**	**20 561**	**23 677**	**24 166**	**25 885**	**25 875**
Intermediate consumption												
15 Seeds	540	692	723	635	683	790	779	737	761	742	867	769
16 Energy	600	669	779	831	897	1 166	1 101	1 216	1 380	1 429	1 450	1 397
of which: electricity and fuels for heating	204	209	235	258	274	340	344	357	369	386	386	373
motor and machinery fuels	395	460	544	573	623	826	758	859	1 012	1 043	1 065	1 024
17 Fertilisers	746	734	785	791	792	1 455	1 176	1 339	1 589	1 523	1 511	1 466
18 Plant protection products	501	576	547	518	571	656	674	711	772	839	856	943
19 Veterinary expenses	253	279	280	284	302	338	364	405	401	420	447	458

24.1 Production and income accounts (at current prices) [a] United Kingdom

Contact: Helen Mason, Department for Environment, Food and
Rural Affairs, Room 201, Foss House, Kings Pool, 1-2
Peasholme Green, York, YO1 7PX

Email: farmingaccounts@defra.gsi.gov.uk

£ million

Calendar years

	2003	2004	2005	2006	2007	2008	2009	2010	2011	2012	2013	2014
20 Animal feed	2 547	2 716	2 490	2 595	2 983	3 863	3 694	4 087	4 508	4 891	5 563	5 065
of which: compounds	1 348	1 450	1 318	1 426	1 702	2 186	2 088	2 255	2 622	2 876	3 290	2 999
straights	849	883	807	785	879	1 197	1 156	1 387	1 374	1 448	1 574	1 415
feed produced & used on farm or purchased from other farms	350	384	365	384	401	480	450	444	512	566	699	651
21 Total maintenance	967	1 014	993	1 012	1 084	1 204	1 280	1 364	1 444	1 442	1 500	1 544
of which: materials	633	654	644	645	687	734	789	846	900	903	937	961
buildings	334	359	349	367	397	470	491	518	544	539	563	583
22 Agricultural services	592	635	629	621	679	789	868	918	1 025	1 015	1 052	1 122
23 FISIM	86	90	111	115	122	115	71	86	111	106	116	103
24 Other goods and services	2 120	2 361	2 348	2 323	2 387	2 619	2 717	2 807	3 013	3 118	3 140	3 139
25 Total intermediate consumption (sum 15 to 24)	8 952	9 766	9 686	9 723	10 501	12 996	12 725	13 669	15 006	15 526	16 503	16 005
26 Gross value added at market prices (12-25)	5 201	4 853	4 878	4 853	5 334	6 902	6 795	6 863	8 644	8 620	9 361	9 849
27 Gross value added at basic prices (14-25)	7 179	7 025	5 092	4 941	5 397	6 959	6 832	6 891	8 671	8 640	9 382	9 869
28 Total consumption of Fixed Capital	2 813	2 712	2 915	2 962	3 023	3 427	3 521	3 534	3 877	4 008	3 986	4 077
of which: equipment	1 256	1 194	1 207	1 208	1 222	1 280	1 363	1 440	1 535	1 610	1 674	1 719
buildings	806	851	928	956	992	1 055	982	940	980	1 004	979	985
livestock	750	667	779	798	809	1 091	1 176	1 154	1 362	1 394	1 333	1 373
cattle	441	364	490	499	503	743	731	679	791	870	857	876
pigs	8	9	7	7	6	7	8	8	8	8	7	5
sheep	173	167	151	162	157	188	269	291	358	301	267	295
poultry	128	127	132	129	142	153	167	176	205	216	202	197
29 Net value added at market prices (26-28)	2 389	2 142	1 963	1 892	2 312	3 475	3 273	3 329	4 767	4 612	5 376	5 772
30 Net value added at basic prices (27-28)	4 366	4 314	2 177	1 979	2 374	3 532	3 311	3 358	4 795	4 632	5 396	5 793
31 Other taxes on production	- 83	- 95	- 101	- 99	- 101	- 102	- 106	- 112	- 121	- 121	- 118	- 96
32 Other subsidies on production	781	781	2 852	3 042	2 932	3 237	3 616	3 472	3 482	3 262	3 338	2 953
33 Net value added at factor cost (30+31+32)	5 065	5 000	4 928	4 923	5 205	6 667	6 821	6 717	8 155	7 773	8 617	8 650
34 Compensation of employees	1 827	1 894	1 944	1 973	2 004	2 065	2 165	2 226	2 341	2 353	2 403	2 406
35 Rent	403	411	389	395	381	408	420	436	476	491	520	553
36 Interest	340	391	403	372	417	349	220	230	295	308	327	406
37 Total Income from Farming (33-34-35-36)	2 494	2 304	2 193	2 183	2 403	3 844	4 016	3 826	5 043	4 620	5 367	5 285

Table source: Defra

	2003	2004	2005	2006	2007	2008	2009	2010	2011	2012	2013	2014
GDP deflator (a) 2012 = 100 (b)	79.4	81.7	84.1	86.6	89.0	91.6	93.5	96.4	98.4	100.0	102.0	103.9
Total Income from Farming in real terms	*3 270*	*2 936*	*2 714*	*2 624*	*2 811*	*4 369*	*4 471*	*4 131*	*5 336*	*4 810*	*5 478*	*5 295*

Source: Department for Environment, Food and Rural Affairs

(a) Values are expressed in current prices, i.e. based on prices in the year in question. GDP deflator is used to convert current prices into real term prices

(b) GDP deflator is used to convert current prices into real term prices

24.2 Total factor productivity volume indices (2010=100)

Enquiries: David Fernall on +44 (0) 20 8026 6202
email: david.fernall@defra.gsi.gov.uk

	2003	2004	2005	2006	2007	2008	2009	2010	2011	2012	2013	2014
1 Output of cereals	100.2	101.8	96.6	96.3	89.2	116.7	102.4	100.0	105.0	92.6	92.6	118.9
wheat	95.1	100.6	96.7	96.4	86.8	113.7	93.6	100.0	104.2	88.2	75.9	109.9
rye	86.4	86.4	86.4	86.4	86.4	86.4	86.4	100.0	100.0	68.2	90.9	90.9
barley	125.2	113.6	103.6	97.9	100.4	132.4	141.2	100.0	110.7	111.3	154.3	152.9
oats and summer cereal mixtures	110.1	84.9	71.2	106.6	103.0	119.6	109.8	100.0	92.1	93.3	150.6	114.0
other cereals	83.0	79.9	80.8	80.8	67.9	77.5	120.2	100.0	99.5	93.3	106.0	105.3
2 Output of industrial crops	95.0	90.6	96.6	87.7	86.2	93.9	99.5	100.0	118.3	105.8	98.6	111.6
oil seeds	71.3	65.1	78.0	75.9	83.1	86.8	87.0	100.0	122.9	112.9	95.2	108.3
oilseed rape	71.3	65.1	76.8	76.4	85.2	88.5	87.5	100.0	123.7	114.6	95.4	110.3
other oil seeds	81.4	73.5	124.3	70.1	27.3	41.2	75.4	100.0	98.9	58.0	86.4	54.7
protein crops	121.6	119.2	125.9	102.5	71.1	93.0	117.2	100.0	76.0	55.5	68.9	81.8
sugar beet	140.5	138.5	133.1	113.4	103.2	117.1	129.6	100.0	130.3	111.7	129.2	142.6
other industrial crops	109.1	107.0	105.1	105.3	101.8	99.7	98.1	100.0	101.1	101.1	101.1	101.1
3 Output of forage plants	112.2	115.2	114.3	112.2	117.8	104.1	105.3	100.0	107.1	109.0	121.3	121.3
4 Output of vegetables and horticultural products	100.4	103.4	103.4	97.7	96.6	98.5	96.4	100.0	97.7	95.0	97.8	100.1
fresh vegetables	89.7	91.9	95.9	94.3	89.9	92.2	96.4	100.0	98.1	93.4	97.9	102.7
plants and flowers	115.0	119.1	113.6	101.9	106.1	107.2	96.4	100.0	97.2	96.7	97.7	97.3
5 Output of potatoes	132.0	138.5	126.7	119.3	115.7	124.9	126.6	100.0	116.4	90.7	112.8	109.7
6 Output of fruit	58.2	70.0	80.0	78.2	92.5	94.8	99.7	100.0	101.3	93.0	100.1	106.8
7 Output of other crop products	100.7	108.0	97.8	97.7	78.8	98.8	103.5	100.0	114.4	126.9	119.1	132.6
Total crop output (sum 1 - 7)	**97.9**	**100.6**	**99.8**	**95.4**	**93.5**	**105.8**	**101.8**	**100.0**	**105.5**	**95.7**	**98.0**	**110.4**
8 Output of livestock (meat)	97.8	98.4	102.4	99.9	100.6	99.6	96.7	100.0	102.8	102.8	103.0	102.8
cattle	90.6	89.4	101.7	97.5	99.8	98.1	95.4	100.0	102.8	101.9	97.9	96.2
pigs	94.7	95.6	95.0	94.8	99.8	98.7	95.3	100.0	106.4	108.6	111.9	115.8
sheep	106.6	113.3	115.0	115.4	114.8	111.7	108.1	100.0	105.9	101.2	103.3	108.3
poultry	103.2	102.3	101.2	98.0	94.7	95.7	92.7	100.0	99.5	102.2	105.5	102.6
other animals	100.0	100.0	100.0	100.1	100.0	100.0	100.0	100.0	100.0	100.0	100.0	100.0
9 Output of livestock products	104.2	101.7	101.9	100.6	98.3	97.0	96.2	100.0	101.3	98.9	100.2	107.3
milk	107.8	104.5	103.8	102.8	100.9	98.6	97.5	100.0	101.5	99.8	100.5	108.5
eggs	80.2	86.7	88.1	85.0	83.0	88.3	89.2	100.0	99.6	96.5	99.5	100.0
raw wool	129.0	131.0	134.4	121.3	112.5	107.7	99.0	100.0	105.3	110.4	97.4	99.8
other animal products	135.3	81.9	135.1	135.2	107.2	87.8	92.9	100.0	98.7	57.5	84.2	106.8
Total livestock output (8 + 9)	**100.5**	**99.8**	**102.2**	**100.3**	**99.7**	**98.6**	**96.5**	**100.0**	**102.2**	**101.3**	**101.9**	**104.7**
10 Inseparable non-agricultural activities	84.6	87.0	88.8	85.5	90.4	91.0	100.5	100.0	101.5	103.1	115.4	113.7
11 All outputs	**98.3**	**99.1**	**100.3**	**97.3**	**96.6**	**100.9**	**98.7**	**100.0**	**103.4**	**99.2**	**101.0**	**107.1**
12 Seeds	73.4	65.6	78.2	85.3	98.9	94.5	92.7	100.0	97.6	101.6	107.0	106.8
13 Energy	99.7	102.0	95.0	90.0	94.0	89.9	102.5	100.0	96.3	96.3	97.0	97.2
electricity and fuels for heating	116.1	109.5	104.2	94.9	94.0	94.0	100.5	100.0	94.5	93.8	87.4	80.5
motor and machinery fuels	92.8	98.8	91.1	87.8	94.0	88.2	103.4	100.0	96.9	97.2	100.9	104.2
14 Fertilisers	126.8	123.2	115.1	108.4	109.7	97.6	88.4	100.0	103.2	97.9	99.2	100.8
15 Plant protection products	79.0	88.3	81.2	74.9	81.3	91.5	92.3	100.0	108.1	117.9	124.9	130.8
16 Veterinary expenses	76.3	81.6	82.5	78.3	81.9	95.5	102.4	100.0	97.2	100.3	104.1	105.7
17 Animal feed	91.5	93.3	91.6	90.9	88.3	92.5	92.6	100.0	93.0	94.7	99.1	101.3
compounds	90.7	91.7	88.4	92.7	95.5	95.0	93.7	100.0	97.7	103.0	109.3	109.9
straights	93.0	96.2	97.3	87.9	76.3	88.2	90.9	100.0	85.3	81.3	82.5	87.4
18 Total maintenance	97.9	98.0	90.8	87.6	90.1	95.0	98.7	100.0	99.8	99.3	100.5	101.9
materials	106.3	104.2	96.3	91.3	93.7	94.7	97.4	100.0	101.4	100.2	102.2	103.0
buildings	85.0	88.3	82.3	81.9	84.4	95.6	100.8	100.0	97.2	97.8	97.6	100.0
19 FISIM	100.0	100.0	100.0	100.0	100.0	100.0	100.0	100.0	100.0	100.0	100.0	100.0
20 Other goods and services	101.7	108.7	104.3	100.0	101.3	99.7	103.3	100.0	102.7	97.6	98.5	87.5
21 Intermediate consumption (excl Agricultural services)	**95.2**	**97.4**	**94.8**	**92.2**	**94.2**	**94.9**	**96.3**	**100.0**	**98.5**	**98.3**	**101.1**	**100.2**
22 Consumption fixed capital (excluding livestock)	**100.3**	**99.4**	**98.5**	**97.5**	**97.2**	**97.9**	**98.8**	**100.0**	**102.2**	**103.9**	**105.7**	**107.1**
equipment	96.9	95.8	94.8	93.5	93.6	95.5	97.7	100.0	103.9	107.2	110.8	113.7
buildings	105.0	104.3	103.6	102.8	102.0	101.2	100.5	100.0	99.5	98.8	98.0	97.2
23 All Labour	**107.5**	**105.8**	**104.6**	**103.1**	**102.4**	**102.0**	**100.5**	**100.0**	**101.6**	**101.6**	**100.8**	**101.0**
Compensation of employees	108.4	106.9	105.3	102.0	101.2	102.0	100.7	100.0	102.4	102.4	101.7	101.7
Entrepreneurial workers (farm and specialist contractor)	107.0	105.3	104.3	103.7	103.0	102.0	100.3	100.0	101.2	101.2	100.3	100.6
24 Land	**100.2**	**99.9**	**100.0**	**101.6**	**100.7**	**100.5**	**100.5**	**100.0**	**99.6**	**99.7**	**100.1**	**100.0**
25 All Inputs and Entrepreneurial Labour	**100.5**	**100.8**	**99.0**	**97.2**	**97.7**	**98.0**	**98.3**	**100.0**	**100.1**	**100.1**	**101.4**	**101.2**
Total factor productivity (11 divided by26)	**97.8**	**98.3**	**101.3**	**100.2**	**98.8**	**102.9**	**100.3**	**100.0**	**103.4**	**99.0**	**99.5**	**105.8**
Partial factor productivity indicators												
Productivity by intermediate consumption (11 divided by 21)	103.3	101.8	105.8	105.6	102.5	106.3	102.4	100.0	105.0	100.9	99.9	106.8
Productivity by capital consumption (11 divided by 22)	98.0	99.7	101.8	99.9	99.4	103.1	99.8	100.0	101.3	95.5	95.5	100.0
Productivity by labour (11 divided by 23)	91.5	93.6	95.8	94.4	94.3	98.9	98.2	100.0	101.8	97.6	100.2	106.0
Productivity by land (11 divided by 24)	98.2	99.1	100.3	95.8	95.9	100.4	98.1	100.0	103.8	99.4	100.8	107.0

Source: Department for Environment, Food and Rural Affairs

24.3 Agricultural land use (a)

Enquiries: Louise Rawlings on +44 (0) 208 0268948
Email: farming-statistics@defra.gsi.gov.uk

Thousand hectares

At June of each year

	2002	2003	2004	2005	2006	2007	2008	2009	2010	2011	2012	2013	2014
Utilised agricultural area (UAA) (b)	17701	17644	17606	17614	17897	17737	17703	17325	17234	17172	17190	17259	17240
UAA as a proportion of total UK area	72%	72%	72%	72%	73%	73%	73%	71%	71%	70%	70%	71%	71%
Total agricultural area	18507	18465	18431	18486	18770	18692	18697	18297	18282	18263	18349	18449	18456
Common rough grazing	1234	1236	1237	1236	1241	1238	1238	1237	1228	1199	1200	1198	1199
Total area on agricultural holdings	17272	17228	17194	17250	17529	17453	17459	17060	17054	17064	17149	17250	17257
Total croppable area	6460	6395	6423	6313	6197	6215	6070	6092	6015	6106	6258	6310	6278
Total crops	4574	4476	4589	4421	4397	4440	4735	4607	4610	4673	4748	4665	4722
Arable crops (c)	4398	4301	4413	4251	4231	4271	4565	4437	4441	4497	4576	4502	4559
Cereals	3245	3057	3130	2919	2864	2885	3274	3076	3013	3075	3142	3028	3179
Oilseeds (includes linseed and borage)	369	492	528	564	605	687	621	600	686	742	785	752	691
Potatoes	158	145	148	137	140	140	144	144	138	146	149	139	141
Other crops	625	607	607	631	623	559	527	616	604	534	500	582	548
Horticultural crops	176	176	175	170	166	169	170	170	169	175	172	163	164
Uncropped arable land (d)(e)	644	718	589	699	663	599	194	244	174	156	153	255	160
Temporary grass under 5 years old	1243	1200	1246	1193	1137	1176	1141	1241	1232	1278	1357	1390	1396
Total permanent grassland	10006	10013	9946	10065	10458	10284	10395	9996	9980	9858	9725	9742	9755
Grass over 5 years old	5519	5683	5620	5711	5967	5965	6036	5865	5925	5877	5799	5802	5824
Sole right rough grazing (f)	4488	4329	4326	4354	4491	4319	4359	4131	4055	3981	3926	3940	3930
Other land on agricultural holdings	806	821	825	872	874	954	994	972	1059	1100	1166	1198	1224
Woodland	524	544	563	583	606	663	705	726	774	786	827	865	897
Land used for outdoor pigs	..	..	..	..	..	..	..	..	10	9	7	9	8
All other non-agricultural land	282	276	262	289	268	291	289	246	274	305	332	324	318

Source: June Surveys/Census of Agriculture/SAF land data Scotland.

Please note that totals may not add up to the sum of components due to rounding. Totals may not agree across tables for the same reason.

#: The 2011 UK totals for other arable crops and glasshouse crops were revised in May 2012 to account for calculation changes in the Scotland and Northern Ireland figures. As a result some subtotals have also been revised.

(a) Figures for England from 2009 onwards relate to commercial holdings only. More information on commercial holdings can be found in the introduction section of this chapter.

(b) UAA includes all arable and horticultural crops, uncropped arable land, common rough grazing, temporary and permanent grassland and land used for outdoor pigs (it excludes woodland and other non-agricultural land).

(c) Includes crops grown on previous set-aside land for England for 2007.

(d) Includes uncropped set-aside land for 2007.

(e) Includes all arable land not in production, including land managed in Good Agricultural and Environmental Condition (GAEC12), wild bird cover and game cover. In the 2009 form guidance notes for England, bird cover and game strips were for the first time explicitly stated as belonging in this category, so the 2009 figure may have captured more of this land than in previous years.

(f) Also includes mountains, hills, heathland or moorland.

- means 'nil' or 'negligible' (less than half the last digit shown).
.. means 'not available' or 'not applicable'.

© Crown copyright 2016

24.4a Estimated quantity of crops and grass harvested

United Kingdom

Thousand tonnes

		2002	2003	2004	2005	2006	2007	2008	2009	2010	2011	2012	2013	2014
Wheat	BADO	15 973	14 288	15 473	14 863	14 755	13 221	17 227	14 076	14 878	15 257	13 261	11 921	16 606
Barley	BADP	6 128	6 370	5 816	5 495	5 239	5 079	6 144	6 668	5 252	5 494	5 522	7 092	6 911
Oats	BADQ	753	749	627	528	728	712	784	744	685	613	627	964	820
Sugar Beet	BADR	9 557	9 168	9 042	8 687	7 400	6 733	7 641	8 457	6 527	8 504	7 291	8 432	9 310
Potatoes	BADS	6 921	6 058	6 246	5 979	5 727	5 564	6 132	6 396	6 056	6 310	4 658	5 902	5 911

Source: Department for Environment, Food and Rural Affairs

24.4b Fruit: Home Production marketed for the calendar year in the UK

(Thousand tonnes)

CALENDAR YEAR	2002	2003	2004	2005	2006	2007	2008	2009	2010	2011	2012	2013	2014 Provisional
ORCHARD FRUIT													
Dessert Apples -													
Cox's Orange Pippin	41.4	34.5	46.6	60.1	64.0	39.2	50.8	46.5	46.4	45.9	32.0	35.1	37.8
Worcester Pearmain	2.5	2.0	2.6	2.6	2.3	1.8	1.9	2.3	2.1	1.9	1.6	1.9	2.1
Discovery	2.9	2.4	2.2	2.9	3.0	2.9	2.8	2.8	3.0	2.7	2.2	2.7	3.1
Early Season	1.0	0.9	1.7	1.9	2.3	2.2	2.0	2.0	2.2	2.0	1.7	2.1	2.5
Mid Season Desserts	7.1	6.8	7.3	7.8	7.7	7.4	6.7	7.5	7.2	6.8	5.7	6.8	7.9
Late Season Desserts	29.1	22.4	31.7	42.8	50.0	52.7	54.3	60.7	63.9	68.6	73.0	82.3	94.5
Total Dessert Apples :	**84.0**	**69.0**	**92.2**	**118.0**	**129.3**	**106.2**	**118.4**	**121.7**	**124.9**	**127.9**	**116.2**	**130.8**	**147.9**
Culinary Apples -													
Bramley's Seedling	94.0	73.3	76.6	98.5	109.9	135.3	123.0	105.9	109.0	110.8	86.4	84.0	93.4
Other Culinary (a)	1.3	1.6	1.2	1.2	1.1	1.0	1.1	1.2	1.1	1.0	0.9	1.1	1.1
Total Culinary Apples :	**95.3**	**74.9**	**77.8**	**99.7**	**111.0**	**136.3**	**124.1**	**107.1**	**110.1**	**111.8**	**87.2**	**85.0**	**94.5**
Pears -													
Conference	29.6	26.6	20.8	19.6	24.6	17.7	17.2	16.6	27.1	26.9	21.1	18.2	22.0
Williams Bon Chretien	0.1	0.1	n/a	n/a	n/a	n/a	n/a	n/a	n/a	n/a	n/a	n/a	n/a
Comice	3.8	1.6	n/a	n/a	n/a	n/a	n/a	n/a	n/a	n/a	n/a	n/a	n/a
Others (b)	0.7	1.3	1.9	3.8	3.9	2.9	2.5	3.9	4.3	5.3	4.5	3.5	3.9
Total Pears :	**34.2**	**29.6**	**22.7**	**23.4**	**28.4**	**20.6**	**19.8**	**20.5**	**31.4**	**32.2**	**25.6**	**21.7**	**25.9**
Plums -													
Victoria	6.0	7.1	8.1	7.3	6.9	6.8	1.1	6.2	6.1	6.0	2.5	5.5	5.5
Marjorie's Seedling	1.8	2.2	n/a	n/a	n/a	n/a	n/a	n/a	n/a	n/a	n/a	n/a	n/a
Pershore Yellow Egg (c)	n/a	n/a	n/a	n/a	n/a	n/a	n/a	n/a	n/a	n/a	n/a	n/a	n/a
Damsons (d)	0.5	0.7	n/a	n/a	n/a	n/a	n/a	n/a	n/a	n/a	n/a	n/a	n/a
Other Plums (e)	4.2	5.1	5.5	6.2	6.3	6.2	1.4	6.7	7.1	7.0	3.1	6.9	6.1
Total Plums :	**12.6**	**15.1**	**13.6**	**13.5**	**13.2**	**13.0**	**2.5**	**13.0**	**13.2**	**12.9**	**5.6**	**12.4**	**11.7**
Cherries (f):	**1.3**	**1.0**	**1.1**	**1.1**	**1.1**	**1.2**	n/a	n/a	n/a	**1.5**	**1.7**	**3.5**	4.0
Others & Mixed :	**2.3**	**1.9**	**2.9**	**3.3**	**3.8**	**4.8**	**6.1**	**6.7**	**6.4**	**5.7**	**4.7**	**5.9**	7.2
TOTAL ORCHARD FRUIT :	**229.7**	**191.5**	**210.2**	**259.0**	**286.9**	**282.2**	**270.9**	**268.9**	**286.0**	**292.1**	**241.0**	**259.3**	291.1
Soft Fruit													
Strawberries	41.4	47.1	52.5	68.6	67.5	83.1	94.0	98.5	95.7	101.9	94.8	93.9	104.4
Raspberries	7.3	8.5	10.0	12.2	12.2	14.8	15.5	15.6	15.9	15.5	15.6	14.6	17.8
Blackcurrants	13.0	19.1	18.2	19.7	15.6	12.3	13.7	15.8	17.7	11.7	11.9	17.0	12.7
Other Soft Fruit:	5.3	5.2	5.4	5.1	6.0	7.8	7.8	8.9	8.9	7.7	7.5	8.0	8.0
TOTAL SOFT FRUIT (g):	**67.1**	**79.9**	**86.0**	**105.5**	**101.3**	**118.1**	**130.9**	**138.9**	**138.3**	**136.8**	**129.9**	**133.4**	142.9
TOTAL FRUIT :	**296.7**	**271.3**	**296.2**	**364.4**	**388.2**	**400.3**	**401.9**	**407.8**	**424.3**	**428.9**	**370.9**	**392.8**	434.0

Source: Basic Horticultural Statistics, Department for Environment, Food and Rural Affairs

(a) Data for both 'Early' and 'Mid/Late Season Culinary' apples has been combined under 'Total Other Culinary'.
(b) Data for 'other' includes Williams & Comice
(c) Data for 'Pershore Yellow Egg' included in 'Other Plums' from 2000.
(d) Data for 'Damsons' included in Other plums from 2004.
(e) Other plums - Includes other varieties from 2004.
(f) Data for 'Cherries' included in 'Others & Mixed' from 2008
(g) Excludes Glasshouse Fruit.
(h) All Import data for strawberries relates to fresh produce only.
(i) Trade figures, where distinguishable, relate to fresh produce.
(j) Value for 'Cider Apples and Perry Pears' only included in 'total orchard fruit' from 2008.
n/a This crop data is no longer available for the individual category and is now combined with other data.
... Blanks in data indicate that the information is not available.

24.4c Field Vegetables: Home production marketed for the calendar year in the UK

(Thousand Tonnes)

CALENDAR YEAR	2002	2003	2004	2005	2006	2007	2008	2009	2010	2011	2012	2013	2014
Roots and Onions													
Beetroot	56	59	53	51	57	57	55	55	57	59	62	69	72
Carrots	718	602	676	710	712	727	711	695	768	685	674	732	786
Parsnips	102	92	77	72	84	86	90	86	90	87	83	83	93
Turnips and Swedes	104	97	97	103	115	101	106	109	113	102	84	100	106
Onions, Dry Bulb	283	374	341	414	359	304	349	355	364	313	374	355	374
Onions, Spring	11	16	14	24	24	20	15	14	14	15	14	14	14
Total :	1,275	1,239	1,259	1,374	1,351	1,294	1,327	1,314	1,408	1,260	1,291	1,353	1,445
Brassicas													
Brussels Sprouts	43	56	44	46	50	41	43	44	43	47	43	51	52
Cabbage, Spring	22	29	34	32	36	35	30	28	24	24	23	23	26
Cabbage, Summer and Autumn	44	41	44	77	61	56	56	62	61	60	49	56	56
Cabbage, Winter	178	159	143	157	158	126	149	146	162	151	151	141	150
Cauliflower	117	126	168	133	124	122	116	108	109	102	90	91	94
Broccoli	53	62	66	87	72	68	73	78	79	78	65	69	69
Total :	456	473	500	532	500	448	468	465	479	463	421	431	447
Legumes													
Beans, Broad (d)	10	12	10	10	10	10	9	12	12	11	12	15	15
Beans, Runner and Dwarf (a)	19	20	23	21	18	17	16	15	16	15	14	15	15
Peas, Green for Market	7	6	6	6	6	6	6	6	6	6	6	6	6
Peas, Green for Processing (b,d)	169	168	131	130	124	98	153	168	156	178	124	155	159
Peas, Harvested Dry (e)	24	16	30	37	24	33	25	40	49	57	22	44	44
Total :	230	222	199	204	182	163	209	241	239	268	178	235	238
Others													
Asparagus	2	2	2	2	3	3	3	4	4	5	5	5	6
Celery	32	37	41	47	36	47	50	49	51	51	51	51	54
Leeks	38	36	41	51	47	50	42	37	42	41	37	35	35
Lettuce	110	126	143	133	126	108	117	128	127	126	116	117	124
Rhubarb (c)	19	18	21	19	17	16	16	20	21	20	22	24	25
Watercress	2	2	2	2	2	2	2	2	2	2	2	2	2
Others (f)	104	104	110	124	116	113	116	144	141	128	118	123	131
Total :	307	325	360	378	348	339	346	384	388	373	352	356	377
TOTAL FIELD VEGETABLES :	2,268	2,260	2,318	2,488	2,382	2,244	2,349	2,405	2,513	2,362	2,242	2,376	2,509

Source: Basic Horticultural Statistics, Department for Environment, Food and Rural Affairs

(a) Dwarf beans are sometimes called French beans.
(b) Vining peas.
(c) Including forced rhubarb grown in sheds.
(d) Shelled weight.
(e) Dried shelled weight, excluding factory waste; for human consumption only.
(f) Includes all smaller field grown crops.

24.5 Crop areas and livestock numbers (a)

Enquiries: Louise Rawlings on +44 (0) 208 0268948
email: farming-statistics@defra.gsi.gov.uk

At June of each year

	2003	2004	2005	2006	2007	2008	2009	2010	2011	2012	2013	2014
Crop areas (thousand hectares)												
Total area of arable crops (b)	4 301	4 413	4 251	4 231	4 271	4 565	4 437	4 441	4 497	4 576	4 502	4 559
of which: wheat	1 836	1 990	1 867	1 836	1 830	2 080	1 775	1 939	1 969	1 992	1 615	1 936
barley	1 076	1 007	938	881	898	1 032	1 143	921	970	1 002	1 213	1 080
oats	121	108	90	121	129	135	129	124	109	122	177	137
rye, mixed corn and triticale	23	25	24	25	27	27	28	29	27	26	24	26
oilseed rape	460	498	519	568	674	598	570	642	705	756	715	675
linseed	32	29	45	36	13	16	28	44	36	29	34	15
potatoes	145	148	137	140	140	144	144	138	146	149	139	141
sugar beet (not for stockfeeding)	162	154	148	130	125	120	114	118	113	120	117	116
peas for harvesting dry and field beans	235	242	239	231	161	148	228	210	155	120	147	139
maize	119	118	131	137	146	153	163	164	164	158	194	183
Total area of horticultural crops	176	175	170	166	169	170	170	169	175	172	163	164
of which: vegetables grown outdoors	125	125	121	119	121	122	125	121	129	123	116	116
orchard fruit (c)	25	24	23	23	23	24	22	24	24	24	23	23
soft fruit & wine grapes	9	9	9	10	10	10	10	10	10	9	10	9
outdoor plants and flowers	14	15	14	12	13	13	11	12	11	12	12	12
glasshouse crops	2	2	2	2	2	2	2	2	2	3	3	3
Livestock numbers (thousand head)												
Total cattle and calves (d)	10 508	10 588	10 770	10 644	10 370	10 163	10 082	10 170	9 988	9 952	9 844	9 837
of which: cows in the dairy herd (e)	2 191	2 129	1 998	1 963	1 937	1 892	1 838	1 830	1 796	1 796	1 782	1 841
cows in the beef herd (f)	1 698	1 736	1 751	1 745	1 709	1 678	1 633	1 668	1 687	1 666	1 611	1 569
Total sheep and lambs	35 812	35 817	35 416	34 722	33 946	33 131	31 445	31 084	31 634	32 215	32 856	33 743
of which: breeding flock 1 year and over	17 580	17 630	16 935	16 637	16 064	15 616	14 636	14 740	14 868	15 229	15 561	16 026
lambs under one year old	17 322	17 238	17 488	17 058	16 855	16 574	15 892	15 431	15 990	16 229	16 381	16 936
Total pigs	5 046	5 159	4 862	4 933	4 834	4 714	4 540	4 460	4 441	4 481	4 885	4 815
of which: sows in pig and other sows for breeding	442	449	403	401	398	365	379	360	362	357	355	349
gilts in pig	73	66	67	67	57	55	48	67	70	69	66	57
Total poultry	178 800	181 759	173 909	173 081	167 667	166 200	152 753	163 867	162 551	160 061	162 609	169 684
of which: table fowl	116 738	119 888	111 475	110 672	109 794	109 859	98 754	105 309	102 461	102 558	104 576	110 374
laying flock (including pullets)	37 560	37 811	40 472	38 257	36 257	35 253	33 266	37 497	38 357	36 646	35 841	37 146
breeding flock	10 988	10 125	8 561	9 273	11 461	9 068	9 397	9 610	10 253	9 987	11 184	11 258
turkeys, ducks, geese and all other poultry	13 514	13 935	13 400	14 879	10 154	12 019	11 335	11 451	11 481	10 870	11 008	10 907

Source: Department for Environment, Food and Rural Affairs

Please note that totals may not add up to the sum of components due to rounding. Totals may not agree across tables for the same reason.

#: The 2011 UK totals for other arable crops and glasshouse crops were revised in May 2012 to account for calculation changes in the Scotland and Northern Ireland figures. As a result some subtotals have also been revised.
(a) Figures for England from 2009 onwards relate to commercial holdings only.
(b) Includes arable crops grown on set-aside land in 2007 for England only.
(c) Includes non-commercial orchards.
(d) Cattle figures in this table are based on all agricultural holdings. Therefore these figures do not match the totals in table 3.5, which are based on commercial holdings for England.
(e) Dairy cows are defined as female dairy cows over 2 years old with offspring.
(f) Beef cows are defined as female beef cows over 2 years old with offspring.

- means 'nil' or 'negligible' (less than half the last digit shown).
.. means 'not available' or 'not applicable'.

© Crown copyright 2016

24.6 Forestry

United Kingdom

Woodland area - (Thousand hectares)

		2004	2005	2006	2007	2008	2009	2010	2011	2012	2013	2014	2015
United Kingdom	C5OF	2816	2825	2829	2837	2841	2841	3059	3067	3110	3125	3138	3154
England [3]	C5OG	1114	1119	1121	1124	1127	1128	1290	1292	1298	1298	1302	1304
Wales [3]	C5OI	286	286	285	285	285	284	303	304	305	305	306	306
Scotland [3]	C5OH	1330	1334	1337	1341	1342	1341	1378	1383	1403	1411	1419	1432
Northern Ireland [4]	C5OJ	86	85	86	87	87	88	88	88	105	111	111	112
Forestry Commission/Forest Service [1]	C5OK	842	838	832	827	821	814	868	869	874	874	870	871
Private Sector Woodland [2]	C5OL	1974	1987	1997	2010	2020	2027	2191	2199	2236	2252	2268	2283
Conifer	C5OM	1651	1647	1642	1640	1635	1628	1603	1604	1619	1617	1608	1614
Broadleaved [5]	C5ON	1165	1178	1187	1197	1207	1213	1457	1463	1493	1508	1531	1540

		2001 /02	2002 /03	2003 /04	2004 /05	2005 /06	2006 /07	2007 /08	2008 /09	2009 /10	2010 /11	2011 /12	2012 /13	2013 /14	2014 /15
New Planting [7] - (Thousand hectares)															
United Kingdom	C5OO	14.4	13.7	12.4	12.0	8.8	10.8	7.5	6.4	5.4	8.2	12.7	10.8	12.9	10.3
England	C5OP	5.4	5.9	4.6	5.3	3.7	3.2	2.6	2.5	2.3	2.5	2.6	2.6	3.3	2.4
Wales	C5OR	0.3	0.5	0.4	0.6	0.5	0.6	0.2	0.2	0.2	0.3	0.8	0.9	0.9	0.1
Scotland	C5OQ	8.0	6.7	6.8	5.7	4.0	6.6	4.2	3.4	2.7	5.1	9.0	7.0	8.3	7.6
Northern Ireland	C5OS	0.7	0.6	0.5	0.4	0.6	0.5	0.6	0.3	0.2	0.3	0.3	0.3	0.3	0.2
Forestry Commission/Forest Service/Natural Resources Wales [1]	C5OT	0.8	0.9	0.2	0.1	0.3	0.2	0.2	0.9	0.7	0.8	1.3	0.9	0.6	0.4
Private Sector Woodland [6]	C5OU	13.6	12.8	12.1	11.9	8.5	10.6	7.4	5.5	4.7	7.3	11.4	9.9	12.3	9.9
Conifer	C5OV	3.9	3.8	2.9	2.1	1.1	2.1	0.9	1.2	0.5	1.5	3.5	1.9	2.2	2.6
Broadleaved5	C5OW	10.5	9.9	9.4	9.9	7.7	8.7	6.7	5.2	4.9	6.6	9.2	8.9	10.7	7.7
Restocking [8,9] - (Thousand hectares)															
United Kingdom	C5OX	13.9	14.5	14.9	16.1	15.9	19.0	18.9	16.1	15.1	14.0	12.3	13.1	15.8	17.6
England	C5OY	3.4	3.4	3.2	2.8	3.2	2.8	3.5	3.5	2.8	4.0	3.6	4.0	4.5	6.4
Wales	C5P2	1.9	1.9	1.8	1.8	2.8	3.0	2.3	2.2	2.1	2.1	2.0	2.0	2.3	1.9
Scotland	C5OZ	7.8	8.5	8.9	10.4	9.0	12.4	12.6	9.6	9.5	6.9	5.7	6.0	7.9	8.5
Northern Ireland	C5P3	0.9	0.7	1.1	1.0	0.9	0.8	0.5	0.8	0.7	1.0	1.0	1.2	1.2	0.8
Forestry Commission/Forest Service/Natural Resources Wales [1]	C5P4	9.2	9.1	9.9	10.6	10.4	11.0	10.4	9.2	7.1	10.0	8.9	9.3	10.9	11.0
Private Sector Woodland [6]	C5P5	4.7	5.3	5.0	5.5	5.5	8.0	8.5	6.9	8.0	4.1	3.3	3.8	4.9	6.6
Conifer	C5P6	11.5	12.0	12.1	13.0	12.5	15.3	14.8	12.1	11.5	10.3	9.0	9.7	11.6	10.7
Broadleaved [5]	C5P7	2.4	2.4	2.8	3.0	3.4	3.6	4.1	4.0	3.6	3.8	3.3	3.4	4.2	6.9

		2003	2004	2005	2006	2007	2008	2009	2010	2011	2012	2013	2014
Wood Production (volume - Thousand green tonnes)													
United Kingdom	C5P8	8470	8650	8670	8680	9180	8670	8930	9760	10540	10627	11469	11963
Softwood total	C5PA	7910	8140	8080	8240	8740	8240	8390	9220	10000	10095	10940	11431
Forestry Commission/Forest Service/Natural Resources Wales [8]	C5PB	4940	5000	4680	4630	4690	4460	5220	4700	4950	4891	5163	4971
Private Sector [10]	C5PC	3540	3650	3990	4050	4480	4210	3720	5070	5600	5737	6307	6992
Hardwood [11]	C5PD	560	510	590	440	440	430	540	540	540	532	529	532

Source: Forestry Commission, Natural Resources Wales, Forest Service, National Forest Inventory.

1. FC: Forestry Commission (England and Scotland), NRW: Natural Resources Wales, FS: Forest Service (Northern Ireland). NRW estimates only relate to woodland formerly owned/managed by FC Wales

2. Private sector: all other woodland. Includes woodland previously owned/managed by the Countryside Council for Wales and the Environment Agency in Wales, other publicly owned woodland (e.g. owned by local authorities) and privately owned woodland.

3. Figures for England, Wales and Scotland are based on data obtained from the National Forest Inventory (NFI) and adjusted for new planting, but at present no adjustment is made for woodland recently converted to another land use.

4. Figures for Northern Ireland are obtained from the Northern Ireland Woodland Register.

5. Broadleaves include coppice and coppice with standards.

6. Private sector figures are based on areas for which grants were paid during the year. Estimate of areas planted without grant aid are also included (where possible), although private sector non grant-aided planting may be under-represented in the figures. Figures for grant-aided planting under Rural Development Contracts in Scotland relate to calendar years.

7. The planting season lies both sides of 31 March, and the weather can cause planting to be advanced or delayed.

8. Includes natural colonisation and natural regeneration.

9. Restocking by natural regeneration in non-clearfell areas may be under-represented in the above table.

10. Private sector: removals from all other woodland (including some publicly owned woodland).

11. Most hardwood production in the UK comes from private sector woodland; the figures are estimates based on reported deliveries to wood processing industries and others.

24.7 Sales for food of agricultural produce and livestock

			2002	2003	2004 (e)	2005	2006	2007	2008	2009	2010 (e)	2011	2012	2013	2014
Milk:															
Utilised for liquid consumption	KCQO	Million litres	6 825	6 753	6 693	6 652	6 734	6 724	6 678	6 626	6 836	6 892	6 816	6 861	7 028
Utilised for manufacture	KCQP	"	6 883	7 140	6 724	6 490	6 266	6 085	5 840	5 699	6 112	6 260	6 089	6 220	7 018
Total available for domestic use (a)	KCQQ	"	14 100	14 290	13 765	13 478	13 325	13 146	12 816	12 777	13 131	13 292	13 113	13 200	14 310
Hen eggs in shell	KCQR	Million dozens	747	730	773	772	742	720	754	751	826	821	797	829	839
Cattle and calves:															
Cattle	KCQS	Thousands	2 184	2 188	2 290	2 302	2 593	2 616	2 588	2 470	2 698	2 757	2 607	2 534	2 557
Calves (f)	KCQT	"	98	87	103	111	51	46	44	43	62	81	74	91	112
Total	KCQU	"	2 282	2 275	2 393	2 413	2 644	2 661	2 632	2 513	2 760	2 838	2 681	2 625	2 669
Sheep and lambs	KCQV	"	14 993	15 095	15 492	16 284	16 414	15 804	16 697	15 600	14 289	14 477	13 746	14 517	13 900
Pigs:															
Clean pigs	MBGD	"	10 260	9 133	9 150	8 971	8 900	9 274	9 192	8 824	9 411	9 813	10 035	10 050	10227
Sows and boars (d)	KCQZ	"	314	241	240	202	196	210	235	207	c	c	265	252	243
Total (d)	KCRA	"	10 575	9 374	9 390	9 173	9 097	9 484	9 427	9 031	c	c	10 300	10 302	10 470
Poultry (b)	KCRB	Millions	862	882	881	903	886	874	862	868	933	931	952	976	972

Source: Defra statistics, Agriculture in the UK and slaugher statistics: 01904 455096

(a) The totals of liquid consumption and milk used for manufacture may not add up to total available for domestic use because of adjustments for dairy wastage, stock changes and other uses such as famhouse consumption, milk fed to stock and on farm waste.

(b) fowls, turkeys, ducks and geese

(c) provisional data

(d) data marked as "C" are confidential

(e) denotes a 53 week year for slaughter of livestock

Totals of categories may not agree due to rounding

(f) The definition of Calves from May 2014 is "Bovines less than 1 year old". Pre-May 2014, the definition was "Bovines weighing less than 165kg".

(p) Provisional data

24.8 Number of livestock farmed organically

Thousand heads

	2005	2006	2007	2008	2009	2010	2011	2012	2013	2014
United Kingdom										
Cattle	214.3	244.8	250.4	319.6	331.2	350.2	334.8	290.2	283.3	304.4
Sheep (a)	:	:	:	:	884.8	981.2	1,161.7	1,152.1	999.2	958.9
Pigs	30.0	32.9	50.4	71.2	49.4	47.4	52.6	34.6	30.2	28.3
Poultry	3,439.5	4,421.3	4,440.7	4,362.9	3,958.7	3,870.9	2,838.2	2,457.7	2,487.6	2,398.8
Other livestock (b)	2.0	4.9	4.0	4.8	3.4	4.5	5.0	4.2	4.1	5.7
England										
Cattle	152.2	177.1	176.0	214.1	236.5	248.6	233.5	201.7	199.5	215.6
Sheep (a)	:	:	:	:	380.4	431.3	423.6	434.5	400.8	405.0
Pigs	27.1	32.3	49.0	57.1	46.5	42.1	47.9	29.5	26.5	25.8
Poultry	2,240.7	2,820.2	2,674.2	2,293.9	1,969.4	1,931.1	1,746.1	1,681.2	1,687.5	1,495.9
Other livestock (b)	1.6	3.6	2.2	2.7	1.6	2.0	1.3	3.6	3.4	3.1

(a) We are unable to provide full historical data for sheep as there are some inconsistencies in the historical data

(b) "Other livestock" includes goats, farmed deer, horses, camelids and any livestock not recorded elsewhere.

Source: Department for Environment, Food and Rural Affairs

Enquiries : Keith Seabridge

organic-stats@defra.gsi.gov.uk

24.9 Number of organic producers and processor

Number

	2005	2006	2007	2008	2009	2010	2011	2012	2013	2014
United Kingdom	**6 413**	**7 043**	**7 631**	**7 896**	**7 567**	**7 287**	**6 929**	**6 487**	**6072**	**6002**
England	4 554	5 005	5 516	5 474	5 278	5 131	4 897	4 592	4419	4454
Wales	800	835	953	1 230	1 176	1 166	1 119	1 080	913	779
Scotland	792	911	860	889	820	737	679	611	551	576
Northern Ireland	267	292	302	303	293	253	234	204	189	193
North East	129	161	173	179	167	160	152	137	127	130
North West	311	332	367	367	333	315	301	273	253	246
Yorkshire & Humberside	279	319	356	330	308	302	278	262	240	238
East Midlands	416	446	487	449	422	408	383	366	351	346
West Midlands	478	520	556	555	507	494	476	442	426	424
Eastern	508	556	574	551	529	515	481	456	449	445
South East (Inc London)	901	939	1 042	1 041	1 024	984	975	950	957	1020
South West	1 532	1 732	1 961	2 002	1 988	1 953	1 851	1 706	1616	1605

Source: Department for Environment, Food and Rural Affairs

Enquiries : Keith Seabridge

organic-stats@defra.gsi.gov.uk

24.10a Organic and In-Conversion Land

Thousand hectares

	2005	2006	2007	2008	2009	2010	2011	2012	2013	2014
In conversion land area										
North East	6.6	6.9	4.8	9.8	6.5	4.0	2.9	2.7	1.0	0.8
North West	3.2	1.8	3.3	3.8	3.4	2.4	1.4	1.1	0.9	0.6
Yorkshire & Humberside	2.3	3.4	4.1	3.8	2.7	0.9	0.7	0.6	0.5	0.6
East Midlands	2.4	2.1	3.1	3.7	3.1	1.0	0.5	0.6	0.7	0.9
West Midlands	3.2	4.0	5.7	8.2	5.7	2.1	1.8	1.4	0.8	1.2
Eastern	2.6	3.6	5.3	4.8	4.1	1.4	1.0	0.7	0.7	0.5
South East (inc. London)	10.7	13.2	14.6	10.4	7.3	4.3	3.7	3.1	3.0	1.9
South West	22.0	31.6	48.2	46.5	34.7	13.6	13.5	8.9	6.3	6.1
England	**53.2**	**66.5**	**89.0**	**91.1**	**67.6**	**29.8**	**25.4**	**19.2**	**14.0**	**12.5**
Wales	12.8	15.4	30.9	49.5	36.8	4.0	2.4	1.5	1.9	4.1
Scotland	16.7	35.2	34.8	6.2	12.0	12.6	5.1	8.0	8.4	3.0
Northern Ireland	3.2	4.0	3.2	2.3	3.0	4.4	4.0	3.6	0.1	0.2
United Kingdom	**86.0**	**121.1**	**157.9**	**149.1**	**119.4**	**50.8**	**36.9**	**32.2**	**24.4**	**19.7**
Fully organic land area										
North East	29.3	22.6	25.8	25.6	26.8	30.6	28.1	27.3	26.9	26.3
North West	18.9	19.4	20.4	21.2	19.8	20.0	16.4	15.5	14.0	13.6
Yorkshire & Humberside	9.0	9.0	9.6	10.9	11.9	13.8	12.5	9.9	10.2	10.1
East Midlands	13.2	12.5	13.2	12.2	14.4	16.3	15.2	15.5	14.1	13.7
West Midlands	27.0	26.3	28.2	29.7	32.0	35.4	28.9	30.6	30.8	29.3
Eastern	11.8	10.8	12.7	13.2	14.2	17.3	15.8	14.1	14.1	13.8
South East (inc. London)	35.2	35.8	42.5	47.2	51.6	54.1	51.4	46.5	48.1	45.6
South West	94.0	93.4	106.3	123.9	140.4	174.6	157.2	145.5	144.2	143.1
England	**238.4**	**229.9**	**258.7**	**284.0**	**311.2**	**362.0**	**325.6**	**304.8**	**302.4**	**295.7**
Wales	58.0	63.5	65.1	75.1	88.6	118.8	120.4	118.4	100.0	91.6
Scotland	231.2	200.1	193.1	225.1	209.3	176.3	164.8	143.7	140.0	132.9
Northern Ireland	6.3	5.1	7.3	10.1	10.3	10.4	8.3	6.6	9.3	8.8
United Kingdom	**533.9**	**498.6**	**524.3**	**594.4**	**619.3**	**667.6**	**619.1**	**573.4**	**551.7**	**529.0**
Total fully organic and in conversion land area										
North East	35.9	29.5	30.6	35.4	33.3	34.6	31.1	30.0	27.9	27.1
North West	22.1	21.2	23.7	25.0	23.2	22.4	17.8	16.6	14.9	14.2
Yorkshire & Humberside	11.3	12.4	13.7	14.7	14.6	14.6	13.2	10.5	10.7	10.8
East Midlands	15.6	14.5	16.3	16.0	17.6	17.3	15.7	16.1	14.8	14.6
West Midlands	30.2	30.3	33.9	37.9	37.7	37.5	30.7	31.9	31.6	30.5
Eastern	14.4	14.4	18.0	18.0	18.4	18.7	16.7	14.8	14.9	14.3
South East (inc. London)	46.0	49.0	57.1	57.6	58.9	58.4	55.1	49.6	51.1	47.5
South West	116.0	125.0	154.5	170.5	175.1	188.2	170.7	154.4	150.4	149.2
England	**291.6**	**296.4**	**347.8**	**375.1**	**378.8**	**391.8**	**351.0**	**323.9**	**316.4**	**308.1**
Wales	70.8	79.0	96.0	124.6	125.4	122.9	122.7	119.9	101.9	95.7
Scotland	247.9	235.3	227.9	231.3	221.3	188.9	169.9	151.7	148.4	135.8
Northern Ireland	9.5	9.1	10.5	12.5	13.3	14.8	12.3	10.1	9.4	9.0
United Kingdom	**619.9**	**619.8**	**682.2**	**743.5**	**738.7**	**718.3**	**656.0**	**605.7**	**576.0**	**548.6**

Source: Department for Environment, Food and Rural Affairs

Enquiries : Keith Seabridge

organic-stats@defra.gsi.gov.uk

24.10b Fully organic and in conversion land use in England

England	2005	2006	2007	2008	2009	2010	2011	2012	2013	2014
In-conversion area										
Cereals	8.6	8.4	9.0	8.4	5.3	1.6	1.0	1.1	1.1	0.8
Other crops	3.2	2.9	2.9	2.0	1.5	0.5	0.4	0.2	0.2	0.2
Fruit & nuts	0.1	0.2	0.4	0.4	0.3	0.2	0.2	0.1	0.1	0.1
Vegetables (including potatoes)	1.0	1.6	2.0	1.7	1.2	0.4	0.2	0.2	0.1	0.1
Herbaceous & ornamentals	0.2	0.1	0.1	0.5	0.5	0.9	0.4	0.3	0.5	0.0
Temporary pasture	12.9	19.1	28.6	27.8	16.0	6.4	5.2	5.0	3.4	2.7
Permanent pasture (inc rough grazing)	21.3	27.9	37.9	46.0	38.6	16.8	14.1	10.2	7.4	7.3
Woodland	3.3	3.5	4.8	2.2	1.7	1.6	1.6	0.8	0.6	0.9
Unutilised land	2.6	2.7	3.3	2.2	2.4	1.2	2.3	1.3	0.6	0.3
Total	**53.2**	**66.5**	**89.0**	**91.1**	**67.6**	**29.8**	**25.4**	**19.2**	**14.0**	**12.5**
Fully organic area										
Cereals	30.8	28.7	31.1	35.5	41.1	43.6	40.4	36.8	34.1	34.1
Other crops	6.0	5.3	6.0	5.7	6.4	7.2	6.6	5.7	5.4	5.1
Fruit & nuts	1.4	1.5	1.5	1.5	1.8	2.0	1.9	2.0	1.9	2.0
Vegetables (including potatoes)	10.3	10.8	11.4	13.4	13.2	13.2	11.9	9.5	9.0	7.6
Herbaceous & ornamentals	0.6	0.6	0.4	3.7	3.8	3.9	4.6	4.8	5.3	0.2
Temporary pasture	64.7	62.9	72.9	78.5	87.1	96.7	90.9	82.1	77.9	74.6
Permanent pasture (inc rough grazing)	118.8	114.2	127.0	139.0	148.2	182.6	159.0	152.9	155.9	154.4
Woodland	1.8	2.3	4.3	2.1	3.3	4.5	4.6	4.6	4.8	11.2
Unutilised land	3.9	3.7	4.1	4.6	6.3	8.3	5.6	6.3	7.3	6.5
Total	**238.4**	**229.9**	**258.7**	**284.0**	**311.2**	**362.0**	**325.6**	**304.8**	**301.7**	**295.7**
Total fully organic and in conversion land use										
Cereals	39.3	37.1	40.1	44.0	46.4	45.3	41.4	37.9	35.2	34.9
Other crops	9.2	8.2	8.9	7.6	7.9	7.8	7.0	6.0	5.6	5.3
Fruit & nuts	1.6	1.7	1.9	1.8	2.1	2.2	2.1	2.1	2.0	2.1
Vegetables (inc potatoes)	11.3	12.4	13.5	15.2	14.5	13.7	12.2	9.7	9.2	7.7
Herbaceous & ornamentals	0.8	0.7	0.5	4.2	4.3	4.8	5.0	5.1	5.8	0.3
Temporary pasture	77.6	82.0	101.5	106.3	103.1	103.1	96.1	87.1	81.2	77.3
Permanent pasture (inc rough grazing)	140.2	142.1	164.9	184.9	186.8	199.4	173.2	163.1	163.2	161.7
Woodland	5.1	5.8	9.1	4.3	4.9	6.1	6.2	5.4	5.4	12.1
Unutilised land	6.5	6.4	7.5	6.8	8.7	9.5	7.9	7.6	8.0	6.8
Total	**291.6**	**296.4**	**347.8**	**375.1**	**378.8**	**391.8**	**351.0**	**323.9**	**315.6**	**308.1**

Source: Department for Environment, Food and Rural Affairs

Enquiries : Keith Seabridge

organic-stats@defra.gsi.gov.uk

24.11 Wages in Agriculture: Minimum weekly rates of pay

Minimum weekly rates of pay in force in 2014 for workers working <u>standard weekly hours</u>

1 January to 30 September 2014					
Grade 6	Grade 5	Grade 4	Grade 3	Grade 2	Grade 1
£	£	£	£	£	£
366.60	339.30	320.19	298.74	271.44	242.19

Grade 1 - Initial Grade
Grade 2 - Standard Grade
Grade 3 - Lead Worker
Grade 4 - Craft Grade
Grade 5 - Supervisory Grade
Grade 6 - Farm Management Grade

Higher rates apply to Full Time and Part Time Flexible Workers.

Source: Department for Environment, Food and Rural Affairs

24.12 Agricultural labour force on commercial holdings [a]

Thousands

	2003	2004	2005	2006	2007	2008	2009	2010	2011	2012	2013	2014
Total labour force (incl. farmers and spouses)	**491**	**501**	**494**	**491**	**481**	**483**	**464**	**466**	**476**	**481**	**464**	**476**
Farmers, business partners, directors and spouses	**313**	**315**	**311**	**313**	**305**	**302**	**289**	**295**	**299**	**298**	**290**	**294**
Full time	155	151	149	146	141	140	137	134	140	141	138	140
Part time [b]	158	164	162	167	165	161	152	161	159	158	152	155
Salaried managers	**11**	**14**	**15**	**14**	**15**	**14**	**11**	**11**	**11**	**11**	**11**	**11**
Regular and casual workers	**166**	**171**	**169**	**164**	**161**	**167**	**164**	**160**	**166**	**172**	**162**	**170**
Full time regular workers	**69**	**66**	**66**	**63**	**61**	**64**	**63**	**64**	**64**	**65**	**63**	**64**
Male	60	57	56	53	51	54	52	-	-	-	-	-
Female	10	9	10	10	10	11	11	-	-	-	-	-
Part time regular workers [b]	**36**	**38**	**39**	**39**	**43**	**43**	**42**	**39**	**39**	**41**	**39**	**40**
Male	20	22	23	23	27	27	27	-	-	-	-	-
Female	16	16	16	16	16	16	16	-	-	-	-	-
Seasonal, casual or gang labour	**61**	**66**	**64**	**62**	**57**	**60**	**59**	**56**	**62**	**67**	**61**	**66**
Male	44	48	45	43	40	42	42	40	44	48	40	47
Female	17	18	18	19	17	18	17	17	18	19	21	19
Total number of people working on non-commercial holdings	42	46	46	44	45	48	70	-	-	-	-	-
Total number of people working on all agricultural holdings	533	546	541	534	526	531	535	-	-	-	-	-

Source: Department for Environment, Food and Rural Affairs
UK Agriculture departments June Survey/Census of Agriculture

As the results are based on sample surveys, they are subject to a degree of sampling error and do not take into account other sources of survey errors, such as non-response bias or administrative data errors.

- No longer available. Data are only being collected from 2010 onwards on "commercial" holdings only in England so no data is available on the numbers of people on non-commercial agricultural holdings. Data is no longer being collected on the split between male and female regular workers so is not available after 2009.
.. not available

(a) Figures for England relate to commercial holdings only.
(b) Part time is defined as less than 39 hours per week in England and Wales, less than 38 hours per week in Scotland and less than 30 hours per week in Northern Ireland

24.13 Summary of UK fishing industry: 2004 to 2014

£ million (unless otherwise specified)

	2004	2005	2006	2007	2008	2009	2010	2011	2012	2013	2014
Fleet size at end of year [a]											
(no. of vessels)	7,022	6,716	6,752	6,763	6,573	6,500	6,477	6,444	6,406	6,399	6,383
Employment											
(no. of fishermen)	13,453	12,831	12,934	12,871	12,614	12,212	12,703	12,405	12,445	12,235 [R]	11,845
Total landings by UK vessels [b]											
Quantity ('000 tonnes)	653.7	715.7	619.6	613.9	587.2	582.9	605.3	596.0 [R]	628.0 [R]	626.7 [R]	756.0
Value (£ million)	513.0	574.6	614.3	646.3	634.5	679.6	720.3	832.1 [R]	788.3 [R]	741.1 [R]	861.0
Imports											
Quantity ('000 tonnes)	671.3	720.4	753.3	747.9	781.7	720.6	703.8	720.2	754.5	739.4 [R]	720.6
Value (£ million) [c]	1,474.0	1,696.0	1,920.6	1,993.9	2,210.1	2,177.2	2,254.7	2,558.6	2,570.0	2,757.0 [R]	2736.3
Exports											
Quantity ('000 tonnes)	477.8	461.4	415.6	466.9	415.8	479.7	516.7	436.1	465.9	452.1 [R]	499.1
Value (£ million) [c]	886.0	939.0	942.2	982.0	1009.4	1,166.1	1,345.7	1,463.9	1,343.9	1,460.3 [R]	1560.3
Total household consumption											
of fish ('000 tonnes) [d]	480	509	519	515	510	501	483	472	467	481	nd
Population ('000 persons) [j]	58,313	58,473	58,603	59,737	60,816	60,907	61,464	61,528	61,946	63,421	nd
Total consumer expenditure											
on fish (£ million)	3,011	3,179	3,410	3,599	3,650	3,711	3,742	3,866	3,998	4,271	nd
on food (£ million) [e]	70,085	71,833	74,193	77,716	67,635	70,143	72,587	73,744	77,523	81,291	nd
Fish as a % of food [e]	4.3%	4.4%	4.6%	4.6%	5.4%	5.3%	5.2%	5.2%	5.2%	5.3%	nd
Landed Price Index [f]	109.3	123.8	134.4	136.2	141.1	141.7	152.2	163.7	153.9	146.9	142.7
Retail Price Index [g]	101.7	102.3	108.5	115.7	124.0	130.3	138.3	151.0	157.4	163.4	168.2
Consumer Price Index [h]	101.5	103.2	111.4	120.7	126.7	131.4	140.0	152.9	158.4	163.6	167.8
GDP for Fishing [i]											
Current price gross value added at basic prices (KK37)	375 [R]	429 [R]	447 [R]	487 [R]	467 [R]	473 [R]	542 [R]	466 [R]	438 [R]	454 [R]	426
Output index (chain volume measures) (L2KO) (2009=100)	100.5 [R]	100.1 [R]	92.3 [R]	99.1 [R]	94.2 [R]	96.4 [R]	99.6 [R]	100.0 [R]	99.8 [R]	100.3 [R]	105.1
GDP for Agriculture, Forestry and Fishing											
Current price gross value added at basic prices (KKD5)	9,595 [R]	7,402 [R]	7,540 [R]	8,234 [R]	9,083 [R]	7,505 [R]	9,482 [R]	9,224 [R]	9,997 [R]	10,031 [R]	10,305
Output index (chain volume measures) (L2KL) (2010=100)	90.7 [R]	95.7 [R]	92.8 [R]	89.5 [R]	98.9 [R]	92.3 [R]	92.2 [R]	100.0 [R]	95.4 [R]	91.7 [R]	100.0
GDP at Market Prices											
Current price GDP at market prices (KKP5) (£ billion)	1,123 [R]	1,189 [R]	1,259 [R]	1,328 [R]	1,369 [R]	1,345 [R]	1,401 [R]	1,442 [R]	1,476 [R]	1,525 [R]	1,595
Chain volume measures index (YBEZ) (2010=100)	93.2 [R]	95.8 [R]	98.7 [R]	101.2 [R]	100.9 [R]	96.5 [R]	98.4 [R]	100.0 [R]	100.7 [R]	102.3 [R]	105.2
Percentage contribution of GVA from fishing to GVA for agriculture, hunting, forestry and fishing											
Current prices (%)	3.9%	5.8% [R]	5.9% [R]	5.9% [R]	5.1% [R]	6.3% [R]	5.7% [R]	5.1% [R]	4.4% [R]	4.5%	4.1%

Source: Fisheries Administrations in the UK, H.M. Customs and Excise, Expenditure and Food Survey, Office for National Statistics

(a) The number of vessels includes those registered in the Channel Islands and Isle of Man.

(b) The quantity of landed fish is expressed in terms of liveweight. The figures relate to landings both into the UK and abroad.

(c) Imports are valued at cost, including insurance and freight terms whereas exports are valued at free on board terms.

(d) Figures for 2001 to 2005 are based on financial year data.

(e) Including non-alcoholic beverages.

(f) The landed price index has been calculated on an annual basis with 2000 = 100.

(g) The fish component of the RPI which includes canned and processed fish. The index has been re-based such that 2000 = 100.

(h) The fish component of the CPI which includes canned and processed fish. The index has been re-based such that 2000 = 100.

(i) GDP for fishing includes landings abroad, according to the KK37 index.

(j) The population estimate has been updated to be consistent with the Living Costs and Food Survey figures, which provide the basis for the household consumption and consumers expenditure figures given in this table

24.14 UK Fishing Fleet [1]

UK Fleet as of 1st January	2011	2012	2013	2014
By Size				
Total	**6474**	**6428**	**6428**	**6420**
10m and under	5042	5038	5048	5049
10 - 12m	404	407	412	403
12 - 18m	499	486	480	479
18 - 24m	273	250	243	246
24 - 40m	199	190	191	190
40m and over	57	57	54	53
By Segment				
Drift and/or fixed netters	731	717	636	664
Dredgers	283	267	291	301
Demersal trawlers and/or demersal seiners	905	889	855	828
Vessels using pots and/or traps	2105	2011	1991	1994
Vessels using hooks	519	574	565	496
Vessels using polyvalent active gears only	37	39	30	39
Vessels using polyvalent passive gears only	86	77	92	80
Vessels using active and passive gears	7	8	6	9
Purse seiners	40	41	37	
Beam trawlers	83	96	93	83
Pelagic trawlers				37
Inactive during previous year	1678	1709	1832	1889
Total UK Fleet	**6474**	**6428**	**6428**	**6420**

Source: Marine Management Organisation

1 Includes Channel Islands and Isle of Man

2 An inactive vessel is defined as a registered vessel that has not undertaken fishing activity in the reference year

24.15 Estimated household food consumption[1]

Grammes per person per week

		Great Britain					2002 /03	2003 /04	2004 /05	2005 /06
		1998	1999	2000						
Liquid wholemilk[2] (ml)	KPQM	693	634	664	VQEW		555	585	484	460
Fully skimmed (ml)	KZBH	164	167	164	VQEX		166	154	158	159
Semi skimmed (ml)	KZBI	945	958	975	VQEZ		919	926	975	1008
Other milk and cream (ml)	KZBJ	243	248	278	VQFA		350	358	366	385
Cheese	KPQO	104	104	110	VQFB		112	113	110	116
Butter	KPQP	39	37	39	VQFC		37	35	35	38
Margarine	KPQQ	26	20	21	VQFD		13	12	11	20
Low and reduced fat spreads	KZBK	69	71	68	VQFE		70	71	68	55
All other oils and fats (ml for oils)	KPQR	62	58	58	VQFF		70	68	68	70
Eggs (number)	KPQS	2	2	2	VQFG		2	2	2	2
Preserves and honey	KPQT	38	33	33	VQFH		35	33	34	35
Sugar	KPQU	119	107	105	VQFI		111	102	99	94
Beef and veal	KPQV	109	110	124	VQFJ		118	119	123	120
Mutton and lamb	KPQW	59	57	55	VQFK		51	49	50	53
Pork	KPQX	76	69	68	VQFL		61	56	56	52
Bacon and ham, uncooked	KPQY	76	68	71	VQFM		69	70	70	68
Bacon and ham, cooked (including canned)	KPQZ	40	39	41	VQFN		45	47	43	44
Poultry uncooked	JZCH	218	201	214	VQFO		199	200	197	212
Cooked poultry (not purchased in cans)	KYBP	33	35	39	VQFQ		45	48	49	48
Other cooked and canned meats	KPRB	49	48	51	VQFR		58	60	58	56
Offals	KPRC	5	5	5	VQFS		6	7	5	5
Sausages, uncooked	KPRD	60	58	60	VQFT		66	70	67	64
Other meat products	KPRE	216	221	239	VQFU		319	335	330	323
Fish, fresh and processed (including shellfish)	KPRF	70	70	67						
Canned fish	KPRG	29	31	32						
Fish and fish products, frozen	KPRH	46	42	44						
Fish, fresh chilled or frozen					VQAI		48	45	42	45
Other fish and fish products					VQAJ		107	111	115	122
Potatoes (excluding processed)	KPRI	715	673	707	VQFY		617	600	570	587
Fresh green vegetables	KPRJ	246	245	240	VQAK		231	228	225	235
Other fresh vegetables	KPRK	486	500	492	VQAL		505	505	536	567
Frozen potato products	KYBQ	111	113	120						
Other frozen vegetables	KPRL	88	87	80						
Potato products not frozen	JZCF	89	86	82						
Canned beans	KPRM	118	112	114						
Other canned vegetables (excl. potatoes)	KPRN	99	92	97						
Other processed vegetables (excl. potatoes)	LQZH	54	59	54						
All processed vegetables					VQAM		621	611	597	608
Apples	KPRO	181	169	180	VQGN		172	171	173	179
Bananas	KPRP	198	202	206	VQGO		208	211	217	225
Oranges	KPRQ	63	50	54	VQGP		62	64	57	59
All other fresh fruit	KPRR	274	290	304	VQGS		351	343	358	392
Canned fruit	KPRS	37	38	38	VQGT		39	40	38	36
Dried fruit, nuts and fruit and nut products	KPRT	34	30	35	VQGU		41	40	46	51
Fruit juices (ml)	KPRU	304	284	303	VQGX		333	322	280	350
Flour	KPRV	55	56	67	VQGY		61	52	55	60
Bread	KPRW	742	717	720	VQGZ		757	728	695	701
Buns, scones and teacakes	KPRX	41	40	43	VQHA		41	44	47	46
Cakes and pastries	KPRY	88	87	89	VQHB		122	120	117	122
Biscuits	KPRZ	137	132	141	VQHC		174	163	165	165
Breakfast cereals	KPSA	136	134	143	VQHE		132	134	131	135
Oatmeal and oat products	KPSB	11	13	15	VQHF		13	12	14	19
Other cereals and cereal products	JZCG	270	284	291	VQHG		370	360	354	378
Tea	KPSC	35	32	34	VQHK		34	31	31	33
Instant coffee	KPSD	12	11	11	VQHL		12	13	13	13
Canned soups	KPSE	71	67	71	VQHM		80	77	76	82
Pickles and sauces	KPSF	96	91	107	VQHN		123	121	120	125

1 See chapter text.

2 Including also school and welfare milk (pre-2001-02)

24.15 Estimated household food consumption[1]

Grammes per person per week

		2006	2007	2008	2009	2010	2011	2012	2013	2014
Liquid wholemilk[2] (ml)	VQEW	477	420	410	412	352	355	297	285	263
Fully skimmed (ml)	VQEX	163	173	158	165	172	167	158	155	154
Semi skimmed (ml)	VQEZ	974	982	987	991	985	984	1051	996	1045
Other milk and cream (ml)	VQFA	395	397	392	427	389	398	394	410	387
Cheese	VQFB	116	119	111	116	118	118	114	118	111
Butter	VQFC	40	41	40	39	40	40	41	42	40
Margarine	VQFD	18	19	22	24	23	20	24	23	18
Low and reduced fat spreads	VQFE	57	53	51	48	49	46	43	38	39
All other oils and fats (ml for oils)	VQFF	69	68	72	71	71	63	71	67	61
Eggs (number)	VQFG	2	2	2	2	2	2	2	2	2
Preserves and honey	VQFH	34	33	34	35	36	33	32	31	31
Sugar	VQFI	92	92	93	90	90	93	91	91	78
Beef and veal	VQFJ	128	126	111	112	114	112	104	97	101
Mutton and lamb	VQFK	54	55	45	46	44	37	36	35	37
Pork	VQFL	55	54	55	54	53	56	55	51	57
Bacon and ham, uncooked	VQFM	66	64	63	68	70	69	68	64	62
Bacon and ham, cooked (including canned)	VQFN	45	45	45	43	43	43	40	39	40
Poultry uncooked	VQFO	207	208	207	205	201	206	214	203	206
Cooked poultry (not purchased in cans)	VQFQ	48	43	44	41	41	41	37	38	35
Other cooked and canned meats	VQFR	53	50	51	51	48	46	44	43	42
Offals	VQFS	5	5	5	6	5	7	6	5	5
Sausages, uncooked	VQFT	65	65	62	65	66	64	67	61	59
Other meat products	VQFU	315	316	311	309	331	318	317	313	311
Fish, fresh and processed (including shellfish)										
Canned fish										
Fish and fish products, frozen										
Fish, fresh chilled or frozen	VQAI	47	43	43	41	38	34	37	36	39
Other fish and fish products	VQAJ	123	122	118	117	113	113	108	110	105
Potatoes (excluding processed)	VQFY	565	537	535	514	501	496	478	439	431
Fresh green vegetables	VQAK	221	224	203	201	192	189	183	179	181
Other fresh vegetables	VQAL	566	566	557	552	565	550	551	569	564
Frozen potato products										
Other frozen vegetables										
Potato products not frozen										
Canned beans										
Other canned vegetables (excl. potatoes)										
Other processed vegetables (excl. potatoes)										
All processed vegetables	VQAM	601	594	599	597	592	601	597	597	574
Apples	VQGN	180	178	162	163	156	149	135	137	131
Bananas	VQGO	226	230	219	205	204	220	214	219	221
Oranges	VQGP	55	59	49	45	47	48	50	47	48
All other fresh fruit	VQGS	394	389	360	348	348	347	346	340	365
Canned fruit	VQGT	39	35	32	29	30	30	29	26	26
Dried fruit, nuts and fruit and nut products	VQGU	53	51	52	51	52	49	51	56	57
Fruit juices (ml)	VQGX	366	340	325	302	296	307	282	288	247
Flour	VQGY	54	54	63	58	58	71	73	57	52
Bread	VQGZ	692	677	659	656	634	621	615	607	555
Buns, scones and teacakes	VQHA	45	44	43	47	45	46	45	47	48
Cakes and pastries	VQHB	120	115	111	111	108	105	105	103	99
Biscuits	VQHC	165	163	170	169	162	164	160	165	162
Breakfast cereals	VQHE	135	130	130	133	133	132	128	127	126
Oatmeal and oat products	VQHF	17	19	20	21	21	20	22	24	23
Other cereals and cereal products	VQHG	378	387	386	393	402	395	392	398	411
Tea	VQHK	30	30	30	29	28	27	26	25	25
Instant coffee	VQHL	14	13	14	15	15	14	13	14	12
Canned soups	VQHM	79	79	76	78	76	75	85	79	70
Pickles and sauces	VQHN	128	129	130	132	131	131	129	130	128

1 See chapter text.

2 Including also school and welfare milk (pre-2001-02)

Sources: Living Costs and Food Survey; Department for Environment Food and Rural Affairs; Office for National Statistics. Contact: 020802 66129

familyfood@defra.gsi.gov.uk

Sources:

This index of sources gives the titles of official publications or other sources containing statistics allied to those in the tables of this Annual Abstract. These publications provide more detailed analyses than are shown in the Annual Abstract. This index includes publications to which reference should be made for short–term (monthly or quarterly) series.

Table number	Government department or other organisation

Chapter 1: Area

1.1	ONS Geography Codes; Office for National Statistics - Standard Area Measurement for UK Local Authority Districts (SAM 2014)

Chapter 2: Parliamentary elections

2.1	British Electoral Facts 1832-2012; Plymouth University for the Electoral Commission
2.2a	Plymouth University for the Electoral Commission
2.2b	Chronology of British Parliamentary By-elections 1833-1987; British Electoral Facts 1832-2006; House of Commons Library, RP10/50 By-election results 2005-10; SN05833 By-elections since 2010 General Election
2.2c	British Parliamentary Election Results; House of Commons Library By-election results
2.3a	British Electoral Facts 1832-2012; Plymouth University for the Electoral Commission
2.3b	House of Commons Library Briefing Paper CBP7594, National Assembly for Wales Elections: 2016
2.3c	British Electoral Facts 1832-2006; House of Commons Library
2.4a	Electoral Facts 1832-2012; Plymouth University for the Electoral Commission
2.4b	British Electoral Facts 1832-2006; Electoral Office for Northern Ireland

Chapter 3 International Development

3.1	Department for International Development
3.2	Department for International Development
3.3	Department for International Development

Chapter 4 Labour Market

4.1	Labour Force Survey, Office for National Statistics
4.2	Labour Force Survey, Office for National Statistics
4.3	Labour Force Survey, Office for National Statistics
4.4	Labour Force Survey, Office for National Statistics
4.5a	Eurostat, OECD, National Statistical Offices. Labour market statistics
4.5b	Labour Disputes Inquiry, Office for National Statistics
4.6	Annual Civil Service Employment Survey, Office for National Statistics
4.7	Labour Force Survey, Office for National Statistics
4.8	Labour Force Survey, Office for National Statistics
4.9	Office for National Statistics
4.10	Labour Market Statistics,Office for National Statistics; Nomisweb
4.11a	Annual Survey of Hours and Earnings, Office for National Statistics
4.11b	Annual Survey of Hours and Earnings, Office for National Statistics
4.12a	Annual Survey of Hours and Earnings, Office for National Statistics
4.12b	Annual Survey of Hours and Earnings, Office for National Statistics
4.13	Office for National Statistics
4.14a	Monthly Wages & Salaries Survey, Office for National Statistics
4.14b	Monthly Wages & Salaries Survey, Office for National Statistics
4.14c	Monthly Wages & Salaries Survey, Office for National Statistics
4.14d	Monthly Wages & Salaries Survey, Office for National Statistics
4.15a	Annual Survey of Hours and Earnings, Office for National Statistics
4.15b	Annual Survey of Hours and Earnings, Office for National Statistics
4.16	Annual Survey of Hours and Earnings, Office for National Statistics
4.17	Certification Officer Annual Report 2014/15

Chapter 5 Social Protection

5.1	HM Revenue and Customs; Department for Work and Pensions
5.2	HM Revenue and Customs; National Insurance Fund Account Great Britain
5.3	HM Revenue and Customs
5.4	Department for Work and Pensions
5.5	Department for Work and Pensions
5.6	Department for Work and Pensions
5.7	Department for Work and Pensions Work and Pensions Longitudinal Study 100% data
5.8	DWP Information, Governance and Security, Work and Pensions Longitudinal Study
5.9a	HM Revenue and Customs

Chapter 6 External Trade

Chapter 7 Research and development

Chapter 8 Personal income, expendiure & wealth

Chapter 9 Lifestyles

Table number	Government department or other organisation
12.2f	UK Payments Administration Ltd
12.3a	Bank of England
12.3b	Bank of England
12.3c	Bank of England
12.3d	Bank of England
12.3e	Bank of England
12.3f	Bank of England
12.3g	Bank of England
12.3h	Bank of England
12.4a	Bank of England
12.4b	Bank of England
12.4c	Bank of England
12.4d	Bank of England
12.5a	Bank of England
12.5b	Bank of England
12.6a	Bank of England
12.6b	Bank of England
12.7	Bank of England
12.8	Bank of England
12.9	Bank of England
12.10	Bank of England
12.11	Bank of England
12.12	Bank of England
12.13a	Office for National Statistics
12.13b	Office for National Statistics
12.14	Office for National Statistics
12.15a	Office for National Statistics
12.15b	Office for National Statistics
12.16a	Insolvency Service
12.16b	Accountant in Bankruptcy (AiB), Companies House
12.16c	Department for Enterprise, Trade and Investment, Northern Ireland (DETINI)
12.17a	Insolvency Service; Companies House
12.17b	Companies House
12.17c	Department for Enterprise, Trade and Investment Northern Ireland (DETINI); Companies House
12.18a	Bank of England
12.18b	Bank of England
12.18c	Bank of England
12.18d	Bank of England
12.19	Bank of England
12.20	Mergers and Acquisitions Surveys, Office for National Statistics

Chapter 13 Services

13.1a	Annual Business Survey (ABS), Office for National Statistics
13.1b	Annual Business Survey (ABS), Office for National Statistics
13.2	Office for National Statistics
13.3	Annual Business Survey (ABS), Office for National Statistics
13.4	Annual Business Survey (ABS), Office for National Statistics

Chapter 14 Defence

14.1	Defence Economics (Defence Expenditure Analysis) and Defence Resources, Ministry of Defence
14.2	Defence Statistics (Tri-Service), Ministry of Defence
14.3a	Finance & Military Capability, Ministry of Defence
14.3b	Army HQ Plans Directorate, Ministry of Defence
14.3c	Finance & Military Capability, Ministry of Defence
14.3d	Finance & Military Capability, Ministry of Defence
14.4	Defence Statistics (Tri-Service), Ministry of Defence
14.5	Defence Statistics (Tri-Service), Ministry of Defence
14.6a	Defence Statistics (Civilian), Ministry of Defence
14.6b	Defence Statistics (Civilian), Ministry of Defence
14.7a	MOD Defence Infrastructure Organisation, Ministry of Defence
14.7b	MOD Defence Infrastructure Organisation, Ministry of Defence
14.8a	Defence Statistics (Tri-Service), Ministry of Defence
14.8b	Defence Statistics (Tri-Service), Ministry of Defence
14.9a	Defence Statistics (Health), Ministry of Defence
14.9b	Defence Statistics (Health), Ministry of Defence
14.10a	UK Defence Statistics, Ministry of Defence
14.10b	UK Defence Statistics, ARCC Database, Ministry of Defence
14.10c	UK Defence Statistics, ARCC Database, Ministry of Defence
14.10d	HQ Surgeon General